# Looking for ways ... the Web into your ...

ClassZone[SM]

www.mcdougallittell.com

**ClassZone, McDougal Littell's textbook-companion Web site, is the solution! Online teaching support for you and engaging, interactive content for your students!**

**ClassZone** is your online site to **McDougal Littell's *Creating America***:

- Links provide updated connections to relevant websites.
- Quiz checks comprehension with self-scoring assessment.
- Activities offer students a fun and engaging way to study history.
- Current Events checks students' knowledge of the weekly news.
- Teacher Center provides lesson planning support and teaching ideas.

**Log on to ClassZone at www.mcdougallittell.com**

With the purchase of **McDougal Littell's *Creating America,*** you have immediate access to ClassZone.

**Teacher Access Code**

**MCD5UBQ2IQZHI**

Use this code to create your own username and password. Then, access both teacher only and student resources.

**Student Access Code**

**MCD5LPCED6GIB**

Give this code to your class. Each student creates a unique username and password to access resources for students.

www.mcdougallittell.com

ANNOTATED TEACHER'S EDITION

# Creating America

## A History of the United States

McDOUGAL LITTELL

Acknowledgments begin on page R97.

ISBN 0-618-00766-0

Printed in the United States of America
2 3 4 5 6 7 8 9-VJM-05 04 03 02 01 00

## Table of Contents

## Program Overview

*Creating America: A History of the United States* is a highly integrated program that provides teachers with a motivational and engaging approach to teaching United States history and to helping students think critically. The wide range of resources in the program helps teachers address the needs of all their students effectively. (For more information about each component, see pages T6-T28.)

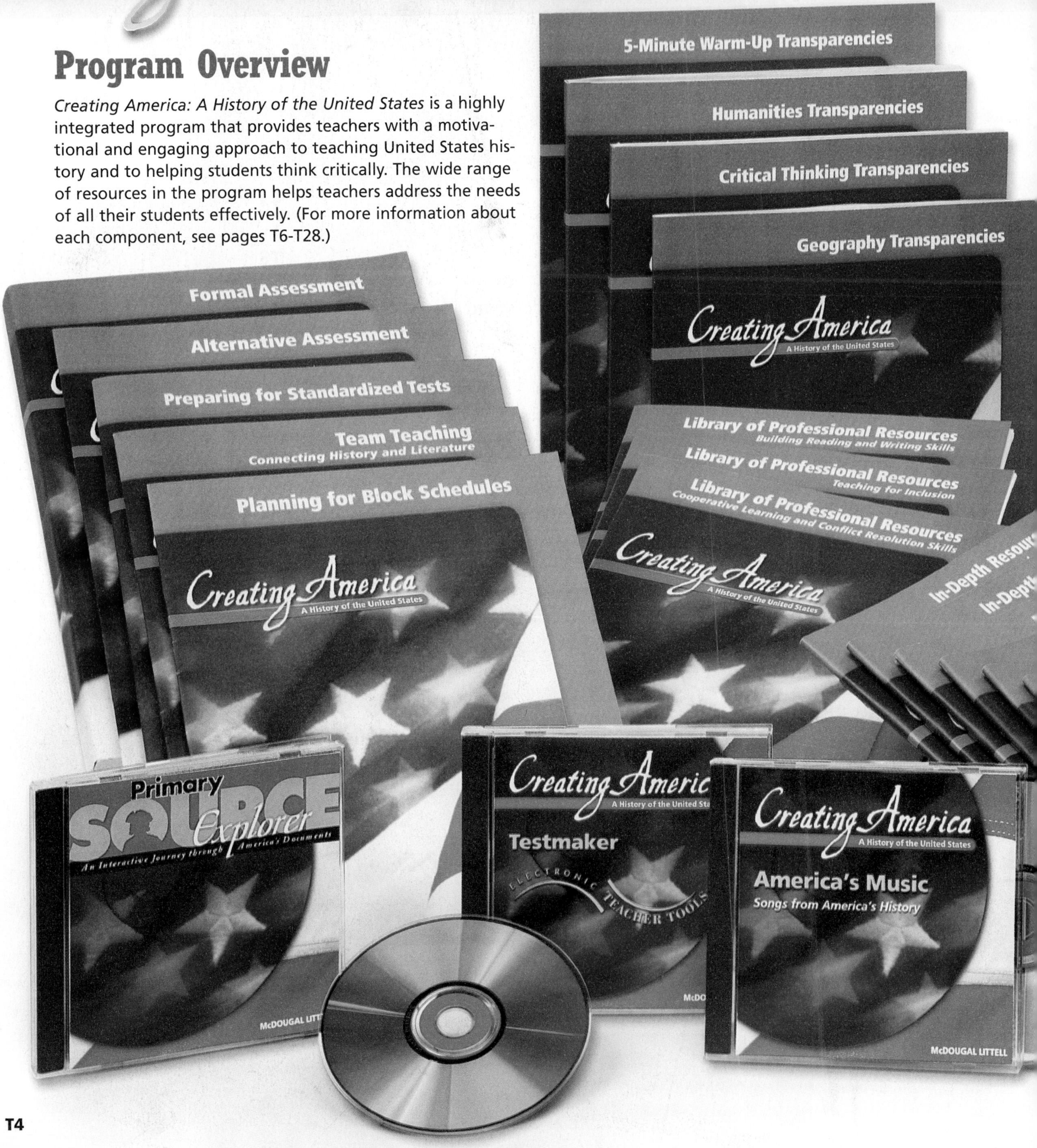
5-Minute Warm-Up Transparencies
Humanities Transparencies
Critical Thinking Transparencies
Geography Transparencies
Creating America
A History of the United States
Formal Assessment
Alternative Assessment
Preparing for Standardized Tests
Team Teaching
Connecting History and Literature
Planning for Block Schedules
Creating America
A History of the United States
Library of Professional Resources
Building Reading and Writing Skills
Library of Professional Resources
Teaching for Inclusion
Library of Professional Resources
Cooperative Learning and Conflict Resolution Skills
Creating America
A History of the United States
Primary Source Explorer
An Interactive Journey through America's Documents
McDOUGAL LITTELL
Creating America
Testmaker
Electronic Teacher Tools
Creating America
A History of the United States
America's Music
Songs from America's History
McDOUGAL LITTELL

Reading Study Guide
*Spanish Translation*

Reading Study Guide

Access for Students Acquiring English
*Spanish Translations*

McDOUGAL LITTELL

INTEGRATED TECHNOLOGY

Creating America
A History of the United States

America's History Makers

American History Plays and Reader's Theater

Citizenship Today

Interdisciplinary Projects

Outline Map Activities

Economics in History

Why It Matters Now

GeoQuest™
An Interactive Geographic Tutorial

In-Depth Resources UNIT 1
Three Worlds Meet

- Setting the Stage
- Tracing Themes
- Guided Reading
- Building Vocabulary
- Skillbuilder Practice
- Geography Applications
- Primary Sources
- Literature Selections
- Reteaching Activities
- Enrichment Activities (for Gifted and Talented Students)
- History Workshop
- Answer Key

McDougal Littell

Creating America
A History of the United States
Chapter Summaries
*In English and Spanish*

Creating America
A History of the United States
Power Presentations
- *Interactive lectures*
- *Fully customizable*
- *Visual summaries, maps, and other graphics*

McDOUGAL LITTELL

# Creating America

## Motivate students to interact with history.

Students are much more motivated to study history when they are actively involved in their learning. *Creating America* provides this motivation by bringing history alive through interactive exercises and hands-on activities. Through these interactive approaches, students will make personal connections to the people, events, and issues that form the panorama of American history.

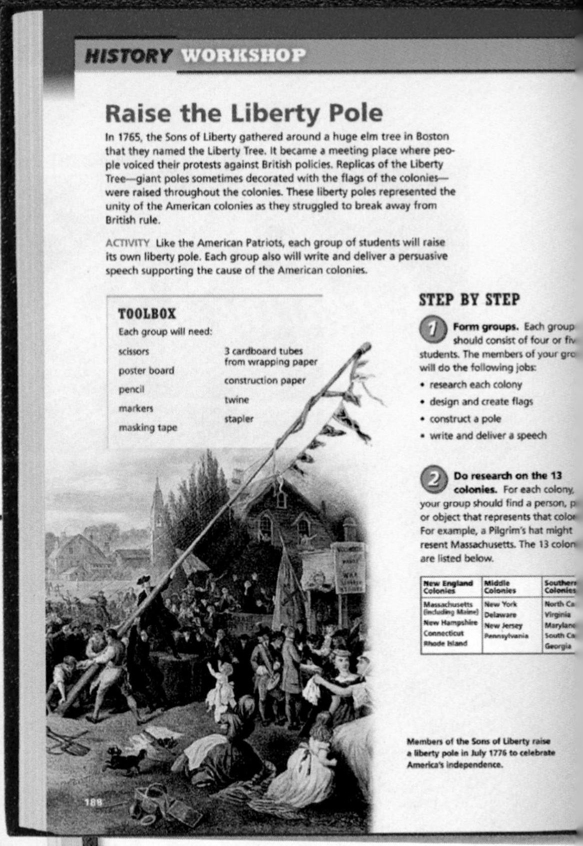
HISTORY WORKSHOP

Raise the Liberty Pole

In 1765, the Sons of Liberty gathered around a huge elm tree in Boston that they named the Liberty Tree. It became a meeting place where people voiced their protests against British policies. Replicas of the Liberty Tree—giant poles sometimes decorated with the flags of the colonies—were raised throughout the colonies. These liberty poles represented the unity of the American colonies as they struggled to break away from British rule.

ACTIVITY Like the American Patriots, each group of students will raise its own liberty pole. Each group also will write and deliver a persuasive speech supporting the cause of the American colonies.

TOOLBOX
Each group will need:
scissors, poster board, pencil, markers, masking tape, 3 cardboard tubes from wrapping paper, construction paper, twine, stapler

STEP BY STEP

1. Form groups.

2. Do research on the 13 colonies.

Members of the Sons of Liberty raise a liberty pole in July 1776 to celebrate America's independence.

188

CHAPTER 6 The Road to Revolution 1763–1776

Section 1 Tighter British Control
Section 2 Colonial Resistance Grows
Section 3 The Road to Lexington and Concord
Section 4 Declaring Independence

Angry colonists watch the arrival of British troops in Boston.

156

Interact with History

The year is 1765. Your neighbors are enraged by Britain's attempt to tax them without their consent. Britain has never done this before. Everyone will be affected by the tax. There are protests in many cities. You have to decide what you would do.

What Do You Think?
- What is the best way to show opposition to policies you consider unjust?
- Is there anything to be gained by protesting? Anything to be lost?
- Does government have the right to tax without consent of the people? Why or why not?

Would you join the protest?



The Road to Revolution 157

## 1 Interact with History

In an interactive situation at the beginning of every chapter, students face the difficult problems and decisions that faced real people in American history. By putting themselves into these actual situations, students learn to analyze issues and make decisions. Also, history becomes more relevant to students.

## 2 History Workshops

In these engaging hands-on activities, students learn about the daily life of the past. In each of the nine Workshops in the textbook, students work in cooperative learning groups to create a historical product and present their product to the class. In creating that product, students explore the social history of the period in a highly interactive way.

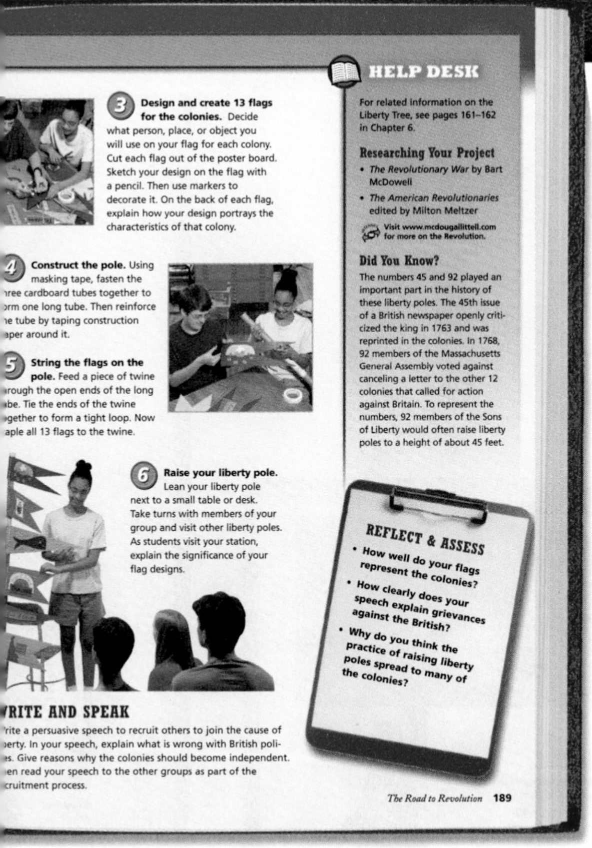

4

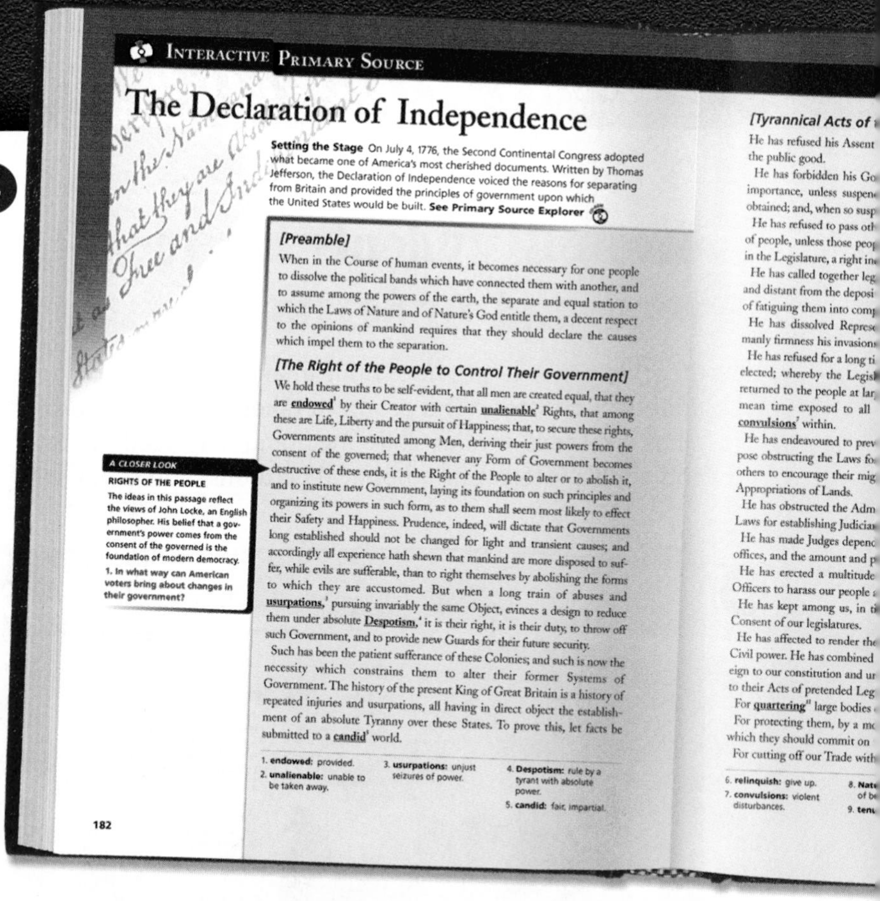

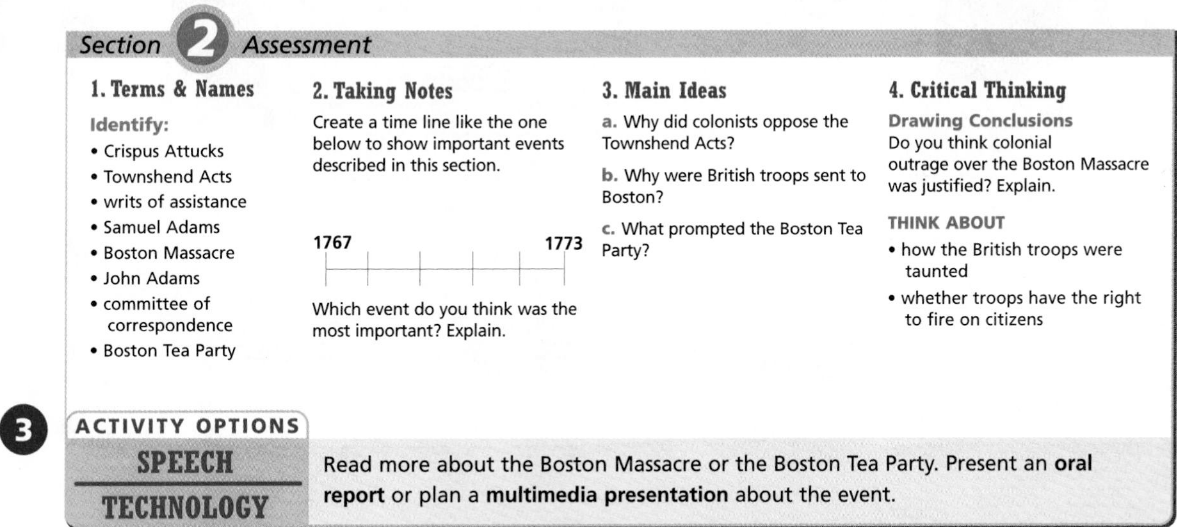
*Section* **2** *Assessment*

**1. Terms & Names**

**Identify:**
- Crispus Attucks
- Townshend Acts
- writs of assistance
- Samuel Adams
- Boston Massacre
- John Adams
- committee of correspondence
- Boston Tea Party

**2. Taking Notes**

Create a time line like the one below to show important events described in this section.

1767 ———————— 1773

Which event do you think was the most important? Explain.

**3. Main Ideas**

**a.** Why did colonists oppose the Townshend Acts?

**b.** Why were British troops sent to Boston?

**c.** What prompted the Boston Tea Party?

**4. Critical Thinking**

**Drawing Conclusions**
Do you think colonial outrage over the Boston Massacre was justified? Explain.

**THINK ABOUT**
- how the British troops were taunted
- whether troops have the right to fire on citizens

3 **ACTIVITY OPTIONS**

**SPEECH**
**TECHNOLOGY**

Read more about the Boston Massacre or the Boston Tea Party. Present an **oral report** or plan a **multimedia presentation** about the event.

## 3 Activity Options

Every **Section Assessment** includes **Activity Options**—short culminating activities for the section. These interdisciplinary activities allow students to demonstrate, in a variety of ways, that they have understood the historical concepts taught in the section.

## 4 Interactive Primary Sources and Primary Source Explorer

*Creating America* features 17 of the key primary source documents of American history. Side notes entitled **A Closer Look** rephrase the important ideas of the document and ask students critical thinking questions. Each document is also featured on the **Primary Source Explorer CD-ROM**. The CD-ROM contains numerous activities—including creating multimedia presentations—that invite students to interact with each of the primary sources.

Creating America

# Give all students the tools to read and understand history.

*Creating America* provides built-in aids to help students read and understand history. The program takes a flexible approach to teaching all of the social studies skills, including map reading, interpreting graphs and charts, interpreting political cartoons, and other skills.

1

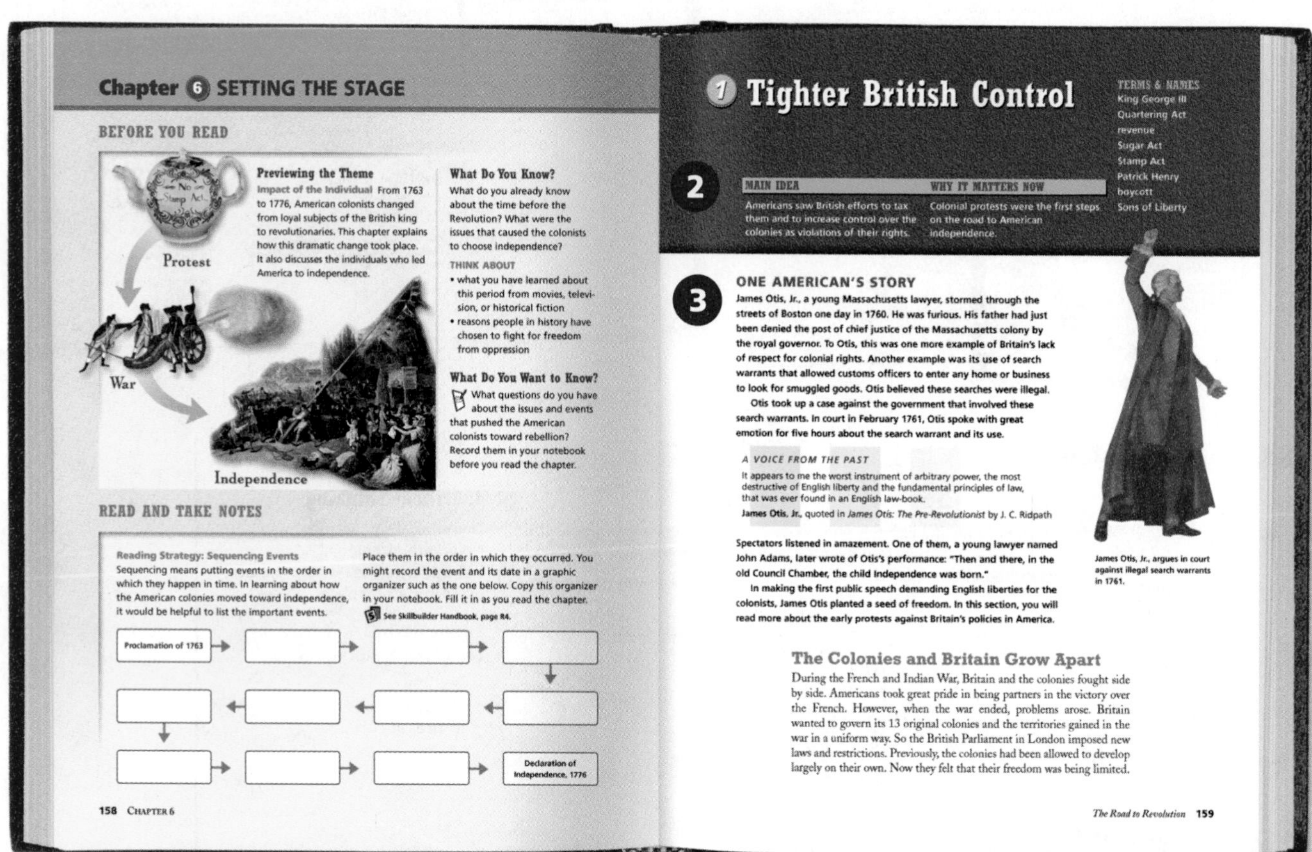

**Chapter 6 SETTING THE STAGE**

**BEFORE YOU READ**

**Previewing the Theme**

Impact of the Individual From 1763 to 1776, American colonists changed from loyal subjects of the British king to revolutionaries. This chapter explains how this dramatic change took place. It also discusses the individuals who led America to independence.



**What Do You Know?**

What do you already know about the time before the Revolution? What were the issues that caused the colonists to choose independence?

THINK ABOUT

- what you have learned about this period from movies, television, or historical fiction
- reasons people in history have chosen to fight for freedom from oppression

**What Do You Want to Know?**

What questions do you have about the issues and events that pushed the American colonists toward rebellion? Record them in your notebook before you read the chapter.

**READ AND TAKE NOTES**

Reading Strategy: Sequencing Events Sequencing means putting events in the order in which they happen in time. In learning about how the American colonies moved toward independence, it would be helpful to list the important events. Place them in the order in which they occurred. You might record the event and its date in a graphic organizer such as the one below. Copy this organizer in your notebook. Fill it in as you read the chapter.

See Skillbuilder Handbook, page R4.



158 CHAPTER 6

**1 Tighter British Control**

2

| MAIN IDEA | WHY IT MATTERS NOW |
| --- | --- |
| Americans saw British efforts to tax them and to increase control over the colonies as violations of their rights. | Colonial protests were the first steps on the road to American independence. |

TERMS & NAMES: King George III, Quartering Act, revenue, Sugar Act, Stamp Act, Patrick Henry, boycott, Sons of Liberty

3

**ONE AMERICAN'S STORY**

James Otis, Jr., a young Massachusetts lawyer, stormed through the streets of Boston one day in 1760. He was furious. His father had just been denied the post of chief justice of the Massachusetts colony by the royal governor. To Otis, this was one more example of Britain's lack of respect for colonial rights. Another example was its use of search warrants that allowed customs officers to enter any home or business to look for smuggled goods. Otis believed these searches were illegal.

Otis took up a case against the government that involved these search warrants. In court in February 1761, Otis spoke with great emotion for five hours about the search warrant and its use.

A VOICE FROM THE PAST

It appears to me the worst instrument of arbitrary power, the most destructive of English liberty and the fundamental principles of law, that was ever found in an English law-book.

James Otis, Jr., quoted in *James Otis: The Pre-Revolutionist* by J. C. Ridpath

Spectators listened in amazement. One of them, a young lawyer named John Adams, later wrote of Otis's performance: "Then and there, in the old Council Chamber, the child Independence was born."

In making the first public speech demanding English liberties for the colonists, James Otis planted a seed of freedom. In this section, you will read more about the early protests against Britain's policies in America.

James Otis, Jr., argues in court against illegal search warrants in 1761.

**The Colonies and Britain Grow Apart**

During the French and Indian War, Britain and the colonies fought side by side. Americans took great pride in being partners in the victory over the French. However, when the war ended, problems arose. Britain wanted to govern its 13 original colonies and the territories gained in the war in a uniform way. So the British Parliament in London imposed new laws and restrictions. Previously, the colonies had been allowed to develop largely on their own. Now they felt that their freedom was being limited.

*The Road to Revolution* 159

The colonial view of the hated stamp tax is shown by the skull and crossbones on this emblem (above); a royal stamp is pictured at right.

160

## 1 Setting the Stage

This page follows Interact with History at the beginning of every chapter. The page features the widely-used K-W-L strategy, asking students what they **know** about the historical period, and **what** they would like to know. The Chapter Assessment asks students what they **learned**. The page also teaches students a reading strategy and provides a graphic organizer to help students take notes.

## 2 Main Idea and Why It Matters Now

By answering the age-old question "Why does it matter now?" students begin to understand that historical events have influenced their own lives. Every section of *Creating America* clearly tells students what the main idea is and why the history of that period matters today.

## 3 One American's Story and A Voice from the Past

*Creating America* tells the varied stories of people who helped to create America through the force of their ideas or the heroism of their actions. **One American's Story** begins every section with a story of one of these people. **A Voice from the Past** incorporates primary source material into the narrative of the textbook, giving American history a human voice.

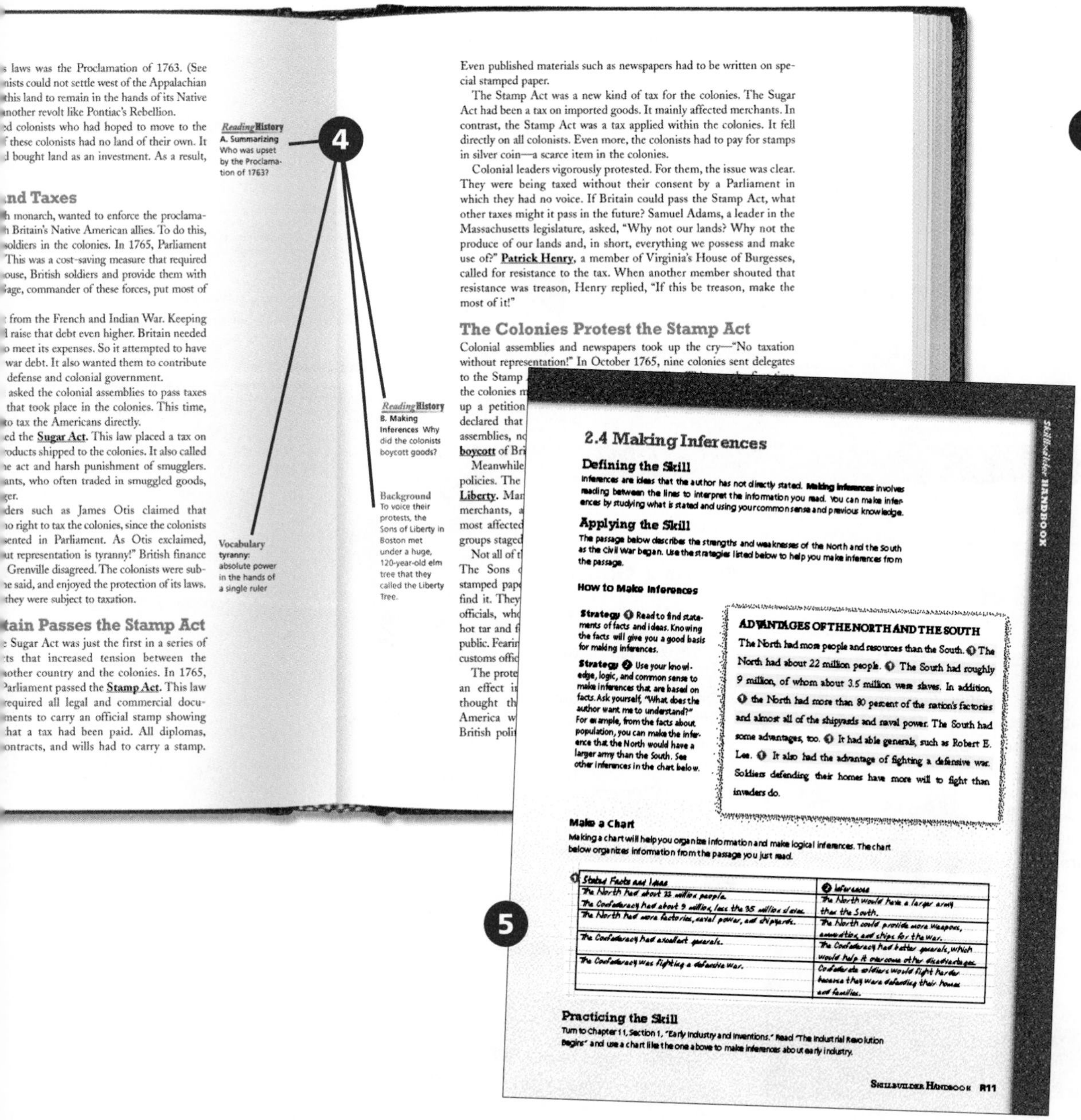

6

**THE SUPREME COURT TODAY**

The principle of judicial review is still a major force in American society. In June 1999, the Supreme Court used this power to restrict the ability of the federal government to enforce its laws in the 50 states.

In one case, *Alden* v. *Maine*, the Court ruled that employees of a state government cannot sue their state even when the state violates federal labor laws—such as those that set guidelines for overtime wages.

## 4 Reading History, Vocabulary, and Background Notes

*Creating America* provides reading support for students as they read. Side-column notes on every page support student comprehension at point of use. **Reading History** notes ask students comprehension and critical thinking questions. **Vocabulary** notes define important vocabulary words at point of use. **Background** notes provide vital historical information that helps to clarify events for students.

## 5 Skillbuilder Handbook

To develop their abilities in critical thinking, reading maps, and other social studies skills, students need access to direct and clear explanations of skills. *Creating America* provides this access in its unique **Skillbuilder Handbook**, found in the reference section of the textbook. The handbook teaches students 30 essential social studies skills. References throughout the textbook suggest when students should access the handbook.

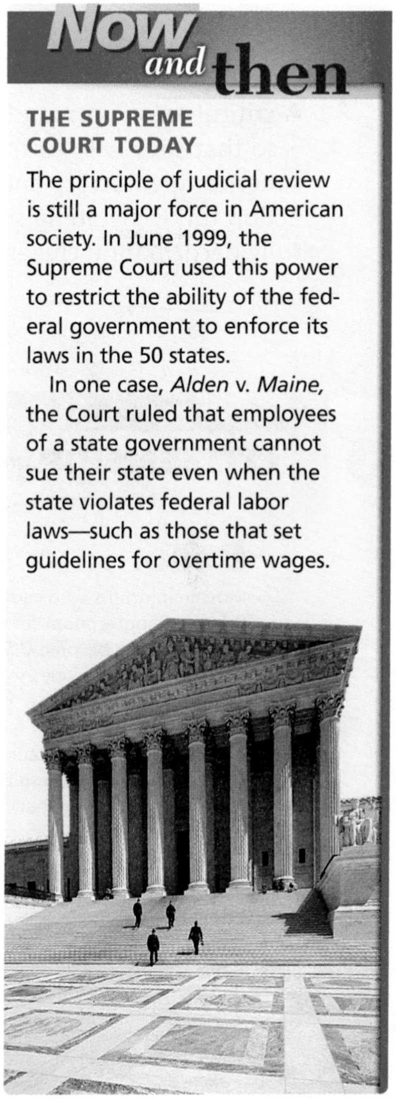

## 6 Now and Then

Students understand history better when they see how it impacts their lives today. **Now and Then** connects past events to contemporary issues and events.

# Creating America

# Inspire students to become active citizens.

A critical reason for students to study American history is so that they will learn about the foundations of American democracy and put the lessons of the past into action today. By doing so, they will take their place as fully participating citizens in our democracy.

2

Citizenship HANDBOOK

## The Role of the Citizen

Citizens of the United States enjoy many basic rights and freedoms. Freedom of speech and religion are examples. These rights are guaranteed by the Constitution, the Bill of Rights, and other amendments to the Constitution. Along with these rights, however, come responsibilities. Obeying rules and laws, voting, and serving on juries are some examples.

Active citizenship is not limited to adults. Younger citizens can help their communities become better places. The following pages will help you to learn about your rights and responsibilities. Knowing them will help you to become an active and involved citizen of your community, state, and nation.

In this book you will find examples of active citizenship by young people like yourself. **Look for the Citizenship Today features.**

President John F. Kennedy urged all Americans to become active citizens and work to improve their communities.

The weather was sunny but cold on January 20, 1961—the day that John F. Kennedy became the 35th president of the United States. In his first speech as president, he urged all Americans to serve their country. Since then, Kennedy's words have inspired millions of Americans to become more active citizens.

*"Ask not what your country can do for you—ask what you can do for your country!"*

—JOHN F. KENNEDY

### What Is a Citizen?

A citizen is a legal member of a nation and pledges loyalty to that nation. A citizen has certain guaranteed rights, protections, and responsibilities. A citizen is a member of a community and wants to make it a good place to live.

Today in the United States there are a number of ways to become a citizen. The most familiar are citizenship by birth and citizenship by naturalization. All citizens have the right to equal protection under the law.

1

CITIZENSHIP TODAY

## Becoming a Citizen

Most immigrants who came to America in the 1800s shared one thing: an appreciation for the nation's values and laws. As a result, many chose to become U.S. citizens.

This trend continues today. In recent decades, more than half a million Vietnamese have immigrated to the United States. Many became citizens of their new country. One of them was Lam Ton, who is a successful restaurant owner in Chicago. Ton viewed U.S. citizenship as both a privilege and a duty. "We have to stick to this country and help it do better," he said.

Each year, immigrants from around the world are sworn in as U.S. citizens on Citizenship Day, September 17. But first they must pass a test on English, the U.S. political system, and the rights and duties of citizenship.

This young immigrant proudly holds up his certificate of citizenship.

### How Does Someone Become a Citizen?

1. In a small group, discuss what questions you would ask those seeking to become U.S. citizens.
2. Create a citizenship test using your questions.
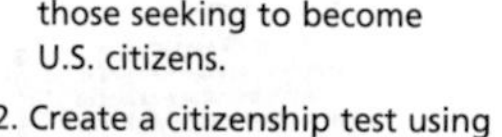
3. Have another group take the test and record their scores.
4. Use the McDougal Littell Internet site to link to the actual U.S. citizenship test. Compare it to your test.

See Citizenship Handbook, page 281.

Visit www.mcdougallittell.com to learn more about becoming a U.S. citizen.

*A New Spirit of Change* 427

### 1 Citizenship Today

This feature focuses on young Americans who have made a difference in their communities. By reading about the community activities of other young people, students learn about positive role models, and they learn important lessons about being American citizens. A community-based activity concludes each Citizenship Today feature.

### 2 Citizenship Handbook

This special section of the textbook teaches students about their responsibilities as citizens, the role that government plays, and the many ways in which students can get involved in helping their own communities.

### 3 Constitution Handbook and The Living Constitution

*Creating America* presents the Constitution in a highly interactive way that is firmly grounded in history yet connects the Constitution to important issues today. The Constitution Handbook begins by explaining the seven principles of the Constitution. The Constitution itself is then presented in a highly interactive format, including side-column notes entitled **A Closer Look**. The Constitution is also featured on the **Primary Source Explorer CD-ROM**, with additional resources and activities.

3

Constitution **HANDBOOK**

## The Living Constitution

The Framers of the Constitution created a flexible plan for governing the United States far into the future. They also described ways to allow changes in the Constitution. For over 200 years, the Constitution has guided the American people. It remains a "living document." The Constitution still thrives, in part, because it echoes the principles the delegates valued. Each generation of Americans renews the meaning of the Constitution's timeless ideas. These two pages show you some ways in which the Constitution has shaped events in American history. **See Primary Source Explorer**

*"In framing a system which we wish to last for ages, we should not lose sight of the changes which ages will produce."*

—JAMES MADISON, CONSTITUTIONAL CONVENTION

**1787**
Delegates in Philadelphia sign the Constitution.

**1965**
Civil rights leaders protest to end the violation of their constitutional rights. Dr. Martin Luther King, Jr., Coretta Scott King, and others march from Selma toward Montgomery, Alabama, to gain voting rights.

4

AMERICA'S HISTORY MAKERS

**ELIZABETH CADY STANTON**

**1815–1902**

Elizabeth Cady Stanton's first memory was the birth of a sister when she was four. So many people said, "What a pity it is she's a girl!" that Stanton felt sorry for the new baby. She later wrote, "I did not understand at that time that girls were considered an inferior order of beings."

When Stanton was 11, her only brother died. Her father said, "Oh, my daughter, I wish you were a boy!" That sealed Stanton's determination to prove that girls were just as important as boys.

**How did Stanton's childhood experiences motivate her to help other people besides herself?**

5

*America's* **HERITAGE**

**THE STAR-SPANGLED BANNER**

The "Star Spangled Banner," inspired by the flag that flew over Fort McHenry (see below), continues to move Americans. On hearing this national anthem, patriotic listeners stand, take off their hats, and put their hands over their hearts. These actions pay respect to the American flag and the song that celebrates it.

Francis Scott Key's song enjoyed widespread popularity for more than 100 years before an act of Congress made it the national anthem in 1931.

## 4 America's History Makers

These features focus on Americans who made an impact on American history through their leadership and decision-making. A question at the end of each feature challenges students to think about the qualities of citizenship and leadership.

## 5 America's Heritage

The United States is rich in traditions and symbols. This feature teaches students about the rich and varied heritage of America. Some inform students about long-standing traditions of the United States, such as the writing of "The Star-Spangled Banner." Others focus on newer traditions, such as the celebration of Cinco de Mayo.

# Creating America

## Make interdisciplinary connections.

Students see history as more relevant when they see how it connects to other subjects they are studying. *Creating America* makes numerous interdisciplinary connections through activities and features that show how history relates to literature, art, science, mathematics, and other subjects.

1

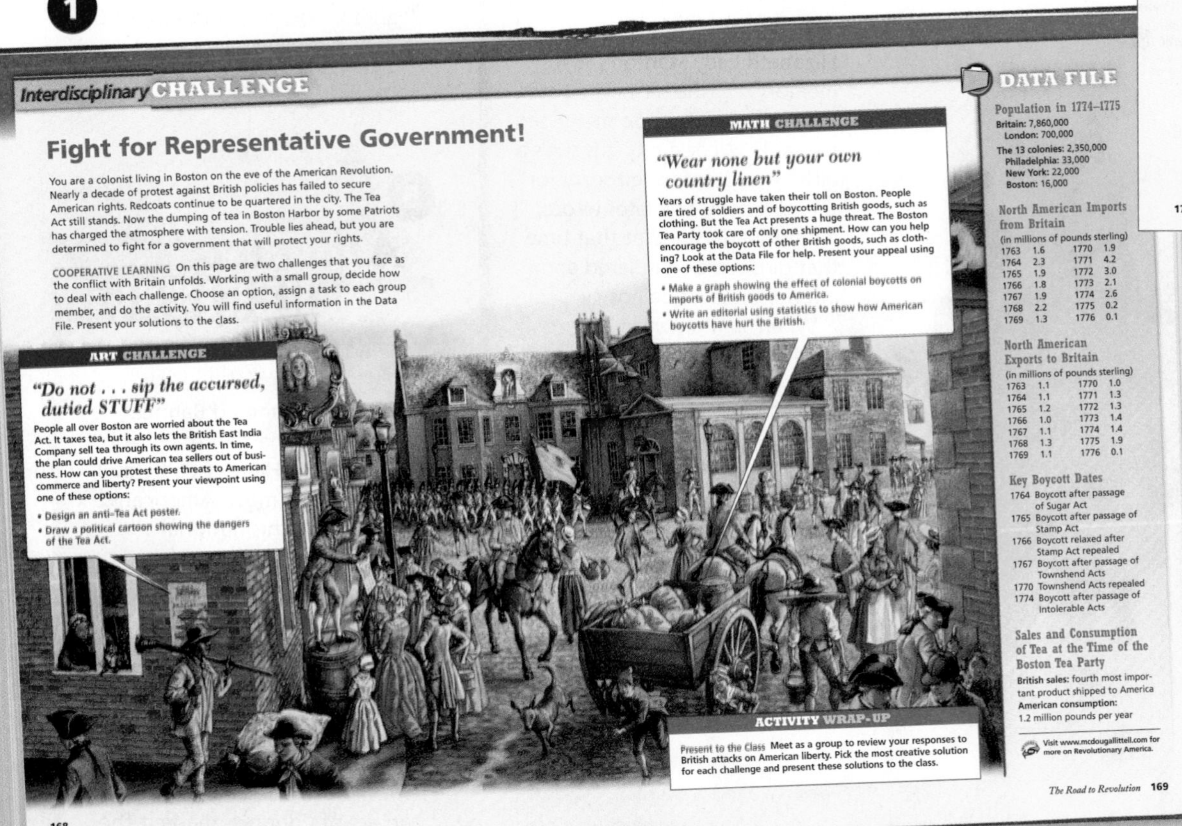

Interdisciplinary CHALLENGE

### Fight for Representative Government!

You are a colonist living in Boston on the eve of the American Revolution. Nearly a decade of protest against British policies has failed to secure American rights. Redcoats continue to be quartered in the city. The Tea Act still stands. Now the dumping of tea in Boston Harbor by some Patriots has charged the atmosphere with tension. Trouble lies ahead, but you are determined to fight for a government that will protect your rights.

COOPERATIVE LEARNING On this page are two challenges that you face as the conflict with Britain unfolds. Working with a small group, decide how to deal with each challenge. Choose an option, assign a task to each group member, and do the activity. You will find useful information in the Data File. Present your solutions to the class.

**ART CHALLENGE**

*"Do not . . . sip the accursed, dutied STUFF"*

People all over Boston are worried about the Tea Act. It taxes tea, but it also lets the British East India Company sell tea through its own agents. In time, the plan could drive American tea sellers out of business. How can you protest these threats to American commerce and liberty? Present your viewpoint using one of these options:

- Design an anti-Tea Act poster.
- Draw a political cartoon showing the dangers of the Tea Act.

**MATH CHALLENGE**

*"Wear none but your own country linen"*

Years of struggle have taken their toll on Boston. People are tired of soldiers and of boycotting British goods, such as clothing. But the Tea Act presents a huge threat. The Boston Tea Party took care of only one shipment. How can you help encourage the boycott of other British goods, such as clothing? Look at the Data File for help. Present your appeal using one of these options:

- Make a graph showing the effect of colonial boycotts on imports of British goods to America.
- Write an editorial using statistics to show how American boycotts have hurt the British.

**ACTIVITY WRAP-UP**

Present to the Class Meet as a group to review your responses to British attacks on American liberty. Pick the most creative solution for each challenge and present these solutions to the class.

**DATA FILE**

**Population in 1774–1775**

Britain: 7,860,000
London: 700,000
The 13 colonies: 2,350,000
Philadelphia: 33,000
New York: 22,000
Boston: 16,000

**North American Imports from Britain**

(in millions of pounds sterling)

| | | | |
|---|---|---|---|
| 1763 | 1.6 | 1770 | 1.9 |
| 1764 | 2.3 | 1771 | 4.2 |
| 1765 | 1.9 | 1772 | 3.0 |
| 1766 | 1.8 | 1773 | 2.1 |
| 1767 | 1.9 | 1774 | 2.6 |
| 1768 | 2.2 | 1775 | 0.2 |
| 1769 | 1.3 | 1776 | 0.1 |

**North American Exports to Britain**

(in millions of pounds sterling)

| | | | |
|---|---|---|---|
| 1763 | 1.1 | 1770 | 1.0 |
| 1764 | 1.1 | 1771 | 1.3 |
| 1765 | 1.2 | 1772 | 1.3 |
| 1766 | 1.0 | 1773 | 1.4 |
| 1767 | 1.1 | 1774 | 1.4 |
| 1768 | 1.3 | 1775 | 1.9 |
| 1769 | 1.1 | 1776 | 0.1 |

**Key Boycott Dates**

1764 Boycott after passage of Sugar Act
1765 Boycott after passage of Stamp Act
1766 Boycott relaxed after Stamp Act repealed
1767 Boycott after passage of Townshend Acts
1770 Townshend Acts repealed
1774 Boycott after passage of Intolerable Acts

**Sales and Consumption of Tea at the Time of the Boston Tea Party**

**British sales:** fourth most important product shipped to America
**American consumption:** 1.2 million pounds per year

Visit www.mcdougallittell.com for more on Revolutionary America.

168

*The Road to Revolution* 169

2

**Literature Connections**

*From*

JOHNNY TREMAIN

*by Esther Forbes*

**In 1775, 16-year-old Johnny Tremain lives in Boston and works as a delivery boy for a newspaper. Because he travels so much around the city, he is able to help the Patriots gather information about what the British are doing.**

**On the night of April 18, Johnny learns that British troops will be leaving on an expedition to seize the gunpowder at Lexington and Concord. He rushes to tell this news to Dr. Joseph Warren, who is a Patriot. Then Johnny goes to bed, wondering if the war has started and worried about his friend Rab, who has gone to join the Minutemen at Lexington.**

So Johnny slept. It was daylight when he woke with Warren's hand upon his shoulder. Outside on Tremont Street he could hear the clumping of army boots. A sergeant was swearing at his men. The soldiers were paraded so close to the house, which stood **flush**[1] with the sidewalkless street, that Johnny at first thought they must be in the room.

Doctor Warren dared speak no louder than a whisper.

"I'm going now."

"Something's happened?"

"Yes." He motioned Johnny to follow him into the kitchen. This room was on the back of the house. They could talk without danger of being overheard by the troops in the street.

Doctor Warren had on the same clothes as the day before. He had not been to bed. But now his hat was on his head. His black bag of instruments and medicines was packed and on the table. Silently he put milk, bread, herrings beside it, and gestured to Johnny to join him.

"Where did it begin?" asked Johnny.

"Lexington."

"Who won?"

"They did. Seven hundred against seventy. It wasn't a battle. It was . . . just target practice . . . for them. Some of our men were killed and the British **huzzaed**[2] and took the road to Concord."

"And did they get our supplies there?"

"I don't know. Paul Revere sent for me just after the firing on Lexington Green."

The young man's usually fresh-colored face was **haggard**.[3] He knew the seriousness of this day for himself and for his country.

"But everywhere the alarm is spreading. Men are grabbing their guns—marching for Concord. Paul Revere did get through in time last night. Billy Dawes a little later. Hundreds—maybe thousands—of Minute Men are on the march. Before the day's over, there'll be real fighting—not target practice. But Gage doesn't know that it's begun. You see, long before Colonel Smith got to Lexington—just as soon as he heard that Revere had warned the country—he sent back for reinforcements. For Earl Percy. You and I, Johnny, are just about the only people in Boston who know that blood has already been shed."

"Were many killed—at Lexington?"

"No, not many. They stood up—just a handful. The British fired on them. It was dawn."

Johnny licked his lips. "Did they tell you the names of those killed?"

1. **flush:** in a line with.
2. **huzzaed:** cheered.
3. **haggard:** tired.

174 CHAPTER 6

### 1 Interdisciplinary Challenge

These interactive features place students into historical situations and challenge them to solve problems by making connections to other disciplines. Every **Interdisciplinary Challenge** includes a **Data File** of historical information that students use in solving the problems.

### 2 Literature Connections

To emphasize the drama and human dimension of history, *Creating America* presents excerpts from important historical literature that shows how history has been presented in fiction. All excerpts are from the **Literature Connections** series of books from McDougal Littell.

### 3 Technology of the Time

Students see the critical role that science and technology have played in American history in this highly visual feature. Each feature concludes with **Connect to History** and **Connect to Today**, providing opportunities for critical thinking and research. Links through McDougal Littell's Web site (www.mcdougallittell.com) give students access to information on the Internet.

**Technology OF THE Time**

## Surface Mining

Gold is found in cracks, called veins, in the earth's rocky crust. As mountains and other outcrops of rock erode, the gold veins come to the surface. The gold breaks apart into nuggets, flakes, and dust. Flood waters then wash it downhill into stream beds. To mine this surface gold, forty-niners had to use tools designed to separate it from the mud and sand around it. American miners learned some technology from Mexicans who came from the mining region of Sonora.

Miners shoveled dirt into the sluice. The rushing water carried lightweight materials along with it. Heavy gold sank to the bottom and was trapped between the ridges.

A sluice was a series of long boxes with ridges on the bottom. Water ran through the sluice, which angled downward.

Although this photograph shows American and Chinese miners working together, in many places Americans chased the Chinese away.

Mexican miners introduced the use of the pan. A miner would fill a pan with dirt and water. Then he would swirl the pan. Water sloshed over the sides, carrying lightweight minerals with it. Gold settled in the bottom.

**CONNECT TO HISTORY**

1. **Drawing Conclusions** Which mining method could be used by an individual miner and which needed a group of miners? Explain your answer.

See Skillbuilder Handbook, page R12.

**CONNECT TO TODAY**

2. **Researching** How is gold mined today?

Visit www.mcdougallittell.com to learn more about the California gold rush.

415

3

4

## HISTORY *through* ART

In 1838, the Cherokees left their homeland by wagon, horse, donkey, and foot, forced to travel hundreds of miles along the Trail of Tears. This painting is by Robert Lindneux, a 20th-century artist.

**How does the artist show the suffering on the Trail of Tears?**

5

## Connections TO LITERATURE

**PHILLIS WHEATLEY**

Phillis Wheatley was America's first important African-American poet. She was born in Africa about 1753 and sold into slavery as a child. She was a household servant for the Wheatley family of Boston but was raised and educated as a family member.

Some of Wheatley's poems were about the Patriot cause. Of George Washington, she wrote:

*Proceed, great chief, with*
*virtue on thy side,*
*Thy ev'ry action let the*
*goddess guide.*
*A crown, a mansion, and*
*a throne that shine,*
*With gold unfading,*
*Washington! be thine.*

In other poems, Wheatley connected America's fight against British oppression with the struggle for freedom for enslaved African Americans.

### 4 History Through Art

Students see how historical events have been portrayed in masterpieces of fine art and in photographs. Each feature asks students to think critically about the image, reinforcing visual literacy.

### 5 Connections Features

The Connections features link history to to other disciplines, including literature, science, mathematics, and the arts—as well as to world history.

# Creating America

## Map a course through history.

The numerous colorful maps in *Creating America* help students build their skills in geography and see its important connection to history.

2

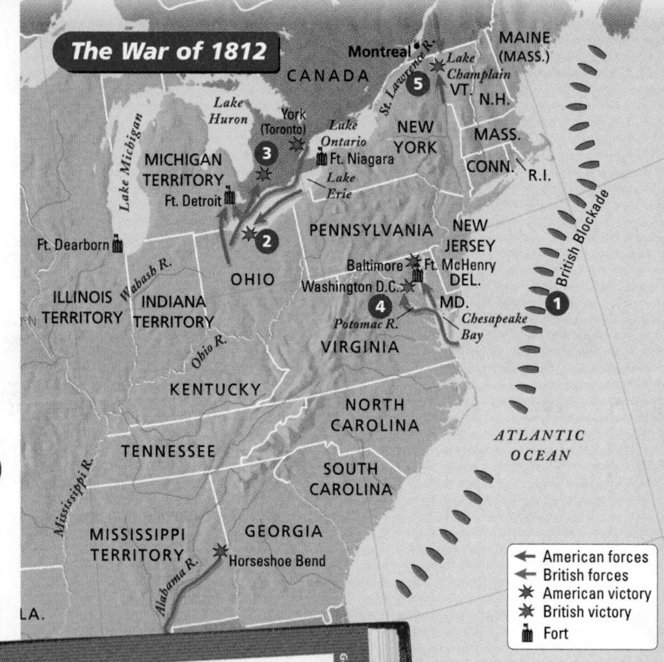


**BATTLES OF THE WAR**

1. **Atlantic Ocean.** British navy blockade American coast, 1813
2. **Lake Erie.** Perry's fleet defeats a British fleet, 1813
3. **Thames River.** Harrison defeats British in Canada, killing Tecumseh, 1813
4. **Washington, D.C.** British burn the capital but later fail to capture nearby Baltimore, 1814
5. **Lake Champlain.** American ships defeat British, who retreat to Canada, 1814
6. **New Orleans.** Jackson's army defeats British in Battle of New Orleans, 1815

**GEOGRAPHY SKILLBUILDER**
**Interpreting Maps**

1. **Location** *Where was Fort McHenry located?*
2. **Movement** *Which battle required American troops to march into Canada?*

1

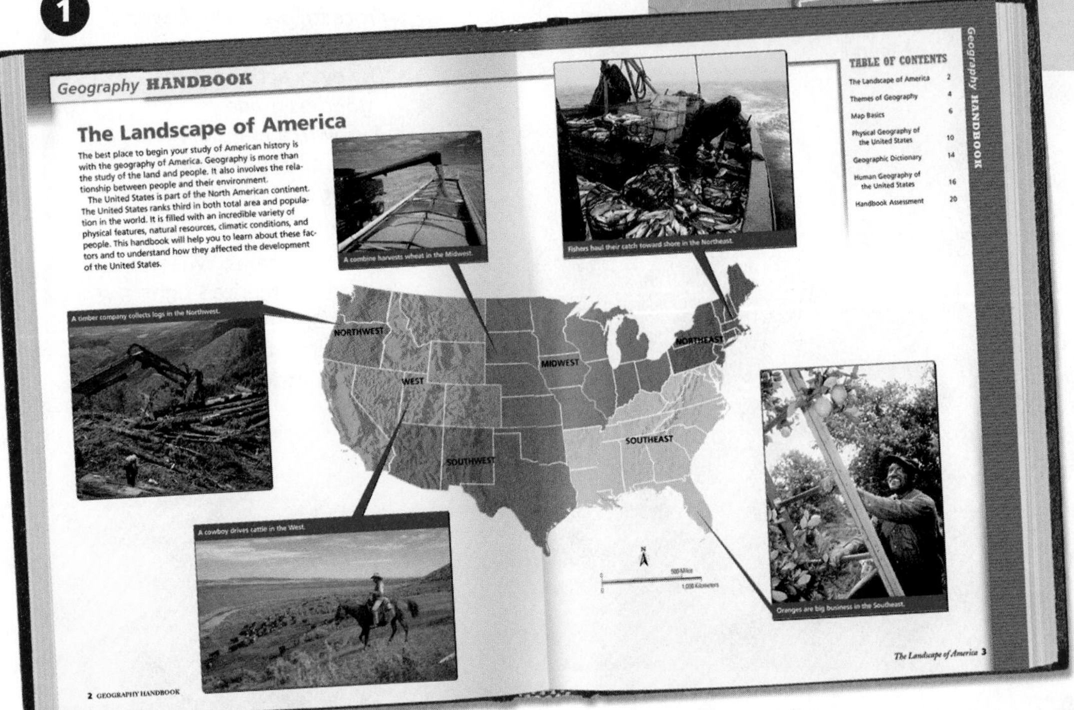

Geography HANDBOOK

The Landscape of America

The best place to begin your study of American history is with the geography of America. Geography is more than the study of the land and people. It also involves the relationship between people and their environment.

The United States is part of the North American continent. The United States ranks third in both total area and population in the world. It is filled with an incredible variety of physical features, natural resources, climatic conditions, and people. This handbook will help you to learn about these factors and to understand how they affected the development of the United States.

A combine harvests wheat in the Midwest.

Fishers haul their catch toward shore in the Northeast.

A timber company collects logs in the Northwest.

A cowboy drives cattle in the West.

Oranges are big business in the Southeast.

NORTHWEST
WEST
MIDWEST
NORTHEAST
SOUTHWEST
SOUTHEAST

TABLE OF CONTENTS



2 GEOGRAPHY HANDBOOK

The Landscape of America 3

### 1 The Geography Handbook

This handbook at the beginning of *Creating America* teaches students the basics of map-reading and gives them an overview of the physical geography and human geography of the United States.

### 2 Layered Maps

Many of the maps in *Creating America* connect geography to history through time lines, charts, graphs, and photographs.

### 3 Geography Skillbuilder

**Geography Skillbuilder** questions challenge students to examine the maps closely and interpret them. Each question is connected to one of the five geographic themes.

5

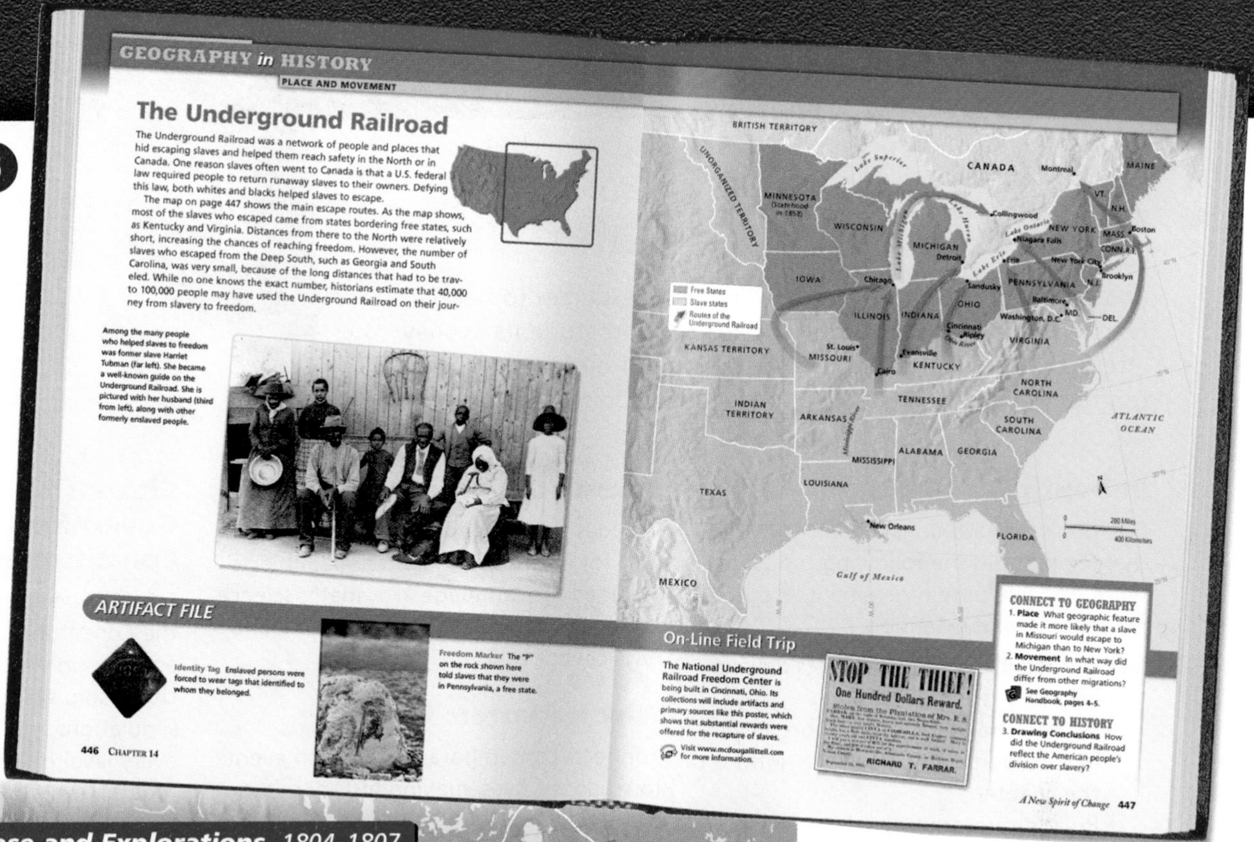

GEOGRAPHY *in* HISTORY

PLACE AND MOVEMENT

## The Underground Railroad

The Underground Railroad was a network of people and places that hid escaping slaves and helped them reach safety in the North or in Canada. One reason slaves often went to Canada is that a U.S. federal law required people to return runaway slaves to their owners. Defying this law, both whites and blacks helped slaves to escape.

The map on page 447 shows the main escape routes. As the map shows, most of the slaves who escaped came from states bordering free states, such as Kentucky and Virginia. Distances from there to the North were relatively short, increasing the chances of reaching freedom. However, the number of slaves who escaped from the Deep South, such as Georgia and South Carolina, was very small, because of the long distances that had to be traveled. While no one knows the exact number, historians estimate that 40,000 to 100,000 people may have used the Underground Railroad on their journey from slavery to freedom.

Among the many people who helped slaves to freedom was former slave Harriet Tubman (far left). She became a well-known guide on the Underground Railroad. She is pictured with her husband (third from left), along with other formerly enslaved people.

ARTIFACT FILE

Identity Tag Enslaved persons were forced to wear tags that identified to whom they belonged.

Freedom Marker The "P" on the rock shown here told slaves that they were in Pennsylvania, a free state.

On-Line Field Trip

The National Underground Railroad Freedom Center is being built in Cincinnati, Ohio. Its collections will include artifacts and primary sources like this poster, which shows that substantial rewards were offered for the recapture of slaves.

Visit www.mcdougallittell.com for more information.

STOP THE THIEF! One Hundred Dollars Reward. ... RICHARD T. FARRAR.

CONNECT TO GEOGRAPHY

1. **Place** What geographic feature made it more likely that a slave in Missouri would escape to Michigan than to New York?
2. **Movement** In what way did the Underground Railroad differ from other migrations?

See Geography Handbook, pages 4–5.

CONNECT TO HISTORY

3. **Drawing Conclusions** How did the Underground Railroad reflect the American people's division over slavery?

446 CHAPTER 14

*A New Spirit of Change* 447

4

## The Louisiana Purchase and Explorations, 1804–1807

The Rocky Mountain summit of Pikes Peak is 14,110 feet high.

**GEOGRAPHY SKILLBUILDER Interpreting Maps**

1. **Location** *What two rivers met at the starting point of the Lewis and Clark expedition?*
2. **Movement** *How were Lewis and Clark's return routes different from each other?*

## 4 Realistic Maps

The maps in *Creating America* have been created with the latest technology, resulting in maps that are three-dimensional and realistic in appearance.

## 5 Geography in History

These features show dramatically how geography has played a major role in key events in American history. Each of these features includes an **Artifact File** with an **On-Line Field Trip** to a local or regional museum.

# Creating America

## Teacher's Resource Materials

*Creating America* offers a wide variety of resources to help teachers manage their classroom and support students as they interact with history. The complete range of options will help teachers meet the needs of all the students in the classroom.

### In-Depth Resources

One book for each unit, organized by chapter, includes the following complete set of options for reinforcement, practice, enrichment, and extension.

- **Guided Reading** worksheets develop essential reading skills.
- **Setting the Stage** graphic organizers give students a way to take notes on the chapter.
- **Building Vocabulary** worksheets develop and enrich students' vocabularies.
- **History Workshop** resources give students information to enrich the History Workshops in the Pupil's Edition.
- **Primary Sources** feature historical documents, diary entries, letters, and much more.
- **Literature Selections** allow your students to experience history through quality works of literature.
- **Geography Application** worksheets provide practice in geography skills.
- **Tracing Themes** activities lead students to examine the theme of each chapter in depth.
- **Reteaching Activities** review and reinforce the important history of each section.
- **Enrichment Activities** challenge gifted and talented students with advanced activities.

### Interdisciplinary Projects

Includes projects and resource information for interdisciplinary teams. Subjects included are language arts, math, science, art, music, home economics, health, and physical education.

### Why It Matters Now

Connects contemporary issues and events to students' lives, making history relevant to them.

### America's History Makers

Provides extended biographies of Americans who made significant contributions to history and overcame obstacles along the way.

### Outline Map Activities

Includes outline maps and copymasters for teaching geography skills.

### Economics in History

Features worksheets that explain economic concepts in depth.

### American History Plays and Reader's Theater

Includes plays based on key historical events and tips on using the textbook for reader's theater.

### Citizenship Today: Government and the Constitution

Extends the Pupil's Edition sections on the Constitution and citizenship with activities in which students apply citizenship skills. The book also includes simulations and information about every level of government, from the federal level to the local level.

### Reading Study Guide

Supports low-level readers with an interactive summary and study guide for each section of the textbook.

### Reading Study Guide (Spanish)

Spanish translation of the Reading Study Guide for students who need reading support in Spanish.

### Access for Students Acquiring English/ESL: Spanish Translations

Provides strategies for teaching ESL students and Spanish translations of Guided Reading, Skillbuilder Practice, and Geography Application worksheets.

## Formal Assessment

Includes the following:

- **Section Quizzes**
- **Chapter Tests**, Forms A and B
- **Additional Test Maker questions**

## Alternative Assessment

Provides explanations and forms for a variety of assessment options, including cooperative learning, group discussion, role-playing, oral presentations, peer assessment, self-assessment, and portfolio assessment.

## Writing Research Reports for Social Studies

Offers support for writing research reports, essays, book reports, interviews, oral histories, and historical narratives.

## Planning for Block Schedules

Includes a pacing guide, chapter teaching models, organization charts, and suggestions for addressing multiple learning styles.

## Library of Professional Resources

Offers teachers strategies for cooperative learning, conflict resolution, reaching students of all learning styles, and teaching reading and writing skills.

## Preparing for Standardized Tests

Helps students prepare to take the common standardized tests.

## Team Teaching: Connecting History and Literature

Provides teachers with options for integrating literature from McDougal Littell's Literature Connections, *The Language of Literature*, and *Literature and Language* into their history lessons.

## Warm-Up Transparencies

5-minute warm-up activities to help introduce each section of every chapter.

## Critical Thinking Transparencies

Builds students' critical thinking skills through graphic organizers, cause-and-effect charts, and visual summaries.

## Geography Transparencies

Includes map transparencies for teaching geography skills.

## Humanities Transparencies

Provides fine art, artifacts, photographs, and political cartoons for enriching the lessons.

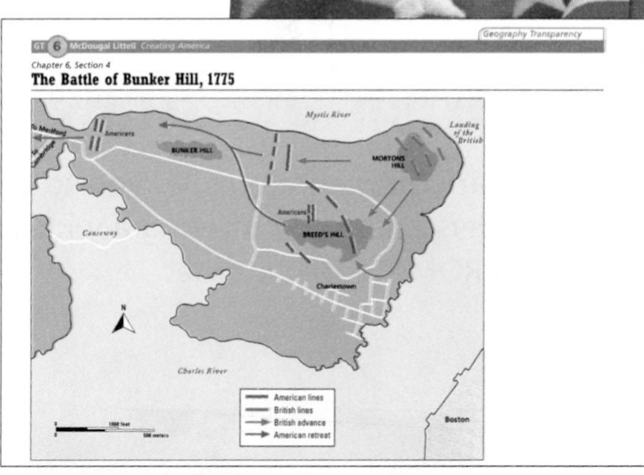


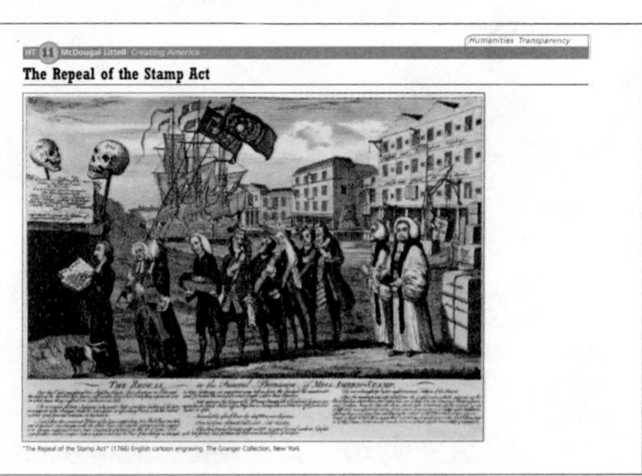


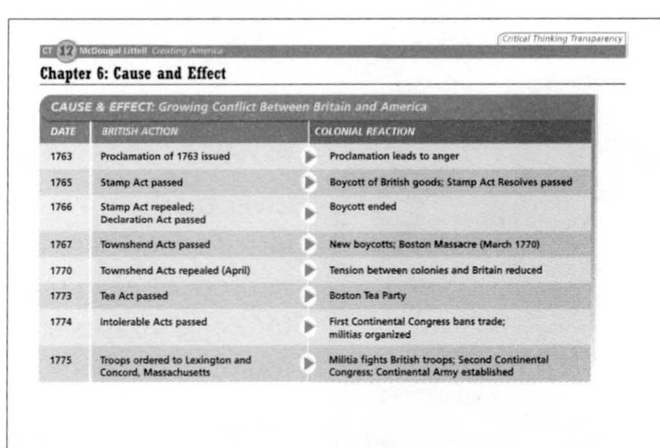
Critical Thinking Transparency

CT 17 McDougal Littell Creating America

**Chapter 6: Cause and Effect**

*CAUSE & EFFECT: Growing Conflict Between Britain and America*

| DATE | BRITISH ACTION | COLONIAL REACTION |
|---|---|---|
| 1763 | Proclamation of 1763 issued | Proclamation leads to anger |
| 1765 | Stamp Act passed | Boycott of British goods; Stamp Act Resolves passed |
| 1766 | Stamp Act repealed; Declaration Act passed | Boycott ended |
| 1767 | Townshend Acts passed | New boycotts; Boston Massacre (March 1770) |
| 1770 | Townshend Acts repealed (April) | Tension between colonies and Britain reduced |
| 1773 | Tea Act passed | Boston Tea Party |
| 1774 | Intolerable Acts passed | First Continental Congress bans trade; militias organized |
| 1775 | Troops ordered to Lexington and Concord, Massachusetts | Militia fights British troops; Second Continental Congress; Continental Army established |

# Creating America

## Integrate technology to enrich the study of history.

*Creating America* enables you to enrich and expand students' understanding by offering a wide array of technology, from CD-ROMs to the Internet.

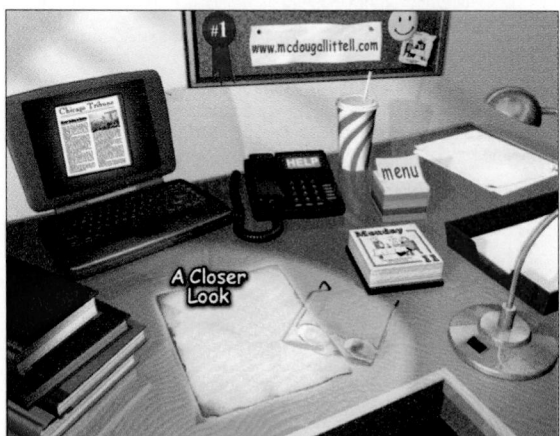

### Primary Source Explorer CD-ROM

Expand students' exploration of America's most important documents with this highly innovative CD-ROM. The **Primary Source Explorer** asks students to think critically about primary sources, learn about the issues of the time period of the documents, and understand their historical impact.

Additionally, the software provides multimedia resources about the historical period of the document, such as photos, art, audio clips, and newspaper articles. Students can draw on all these resources to create their own multimedia presentations, newspapers, research papers, advertisements, and Web pages—using the software on the CD-ROM.

### America's Music CD

Features well-known songs from American history, enhancing students' study of America's cultural heritage.

### Power Presentations CD-ROM

Gives teachers a tool to use in classroom instruction. These presentations contain outlines of each chapter in the book, slides for key concepts and terms, and maps found in the book.

### GeoQuest CD-ROM
### Interactive Maps of American History

This engaging CD-ROM contains 30 interactive maps that illuminate events throughout American history. Each group is accompanied by an introduction, exercises, and essay questions, making GeoQuest an informative and thought-provoking companion for *Creating America*.

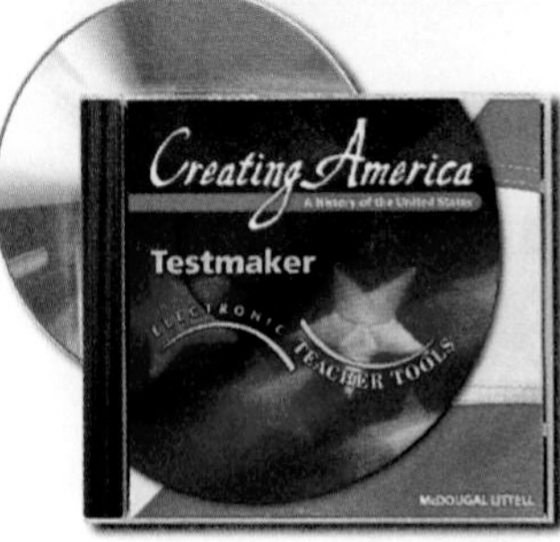


### Electronic Teacher Tools / Test Maker CD-ROM

Contains most of the teacher resources in the print ancillaries on one convenient CD-ROM. View, search, and print the ancillaries, which are organized by resource and chapter.

This same CD contains Test Maker software, which allows teachers to create customized tests. You can use items created by McDougal Littell or create your own test items.

### Chapter Summaries CDs (English and Spanish)

Provides audio versions of chapter summaries on compact disc. Available in English and Spanish.

# Internet Resources at www.mcdougallittell.com

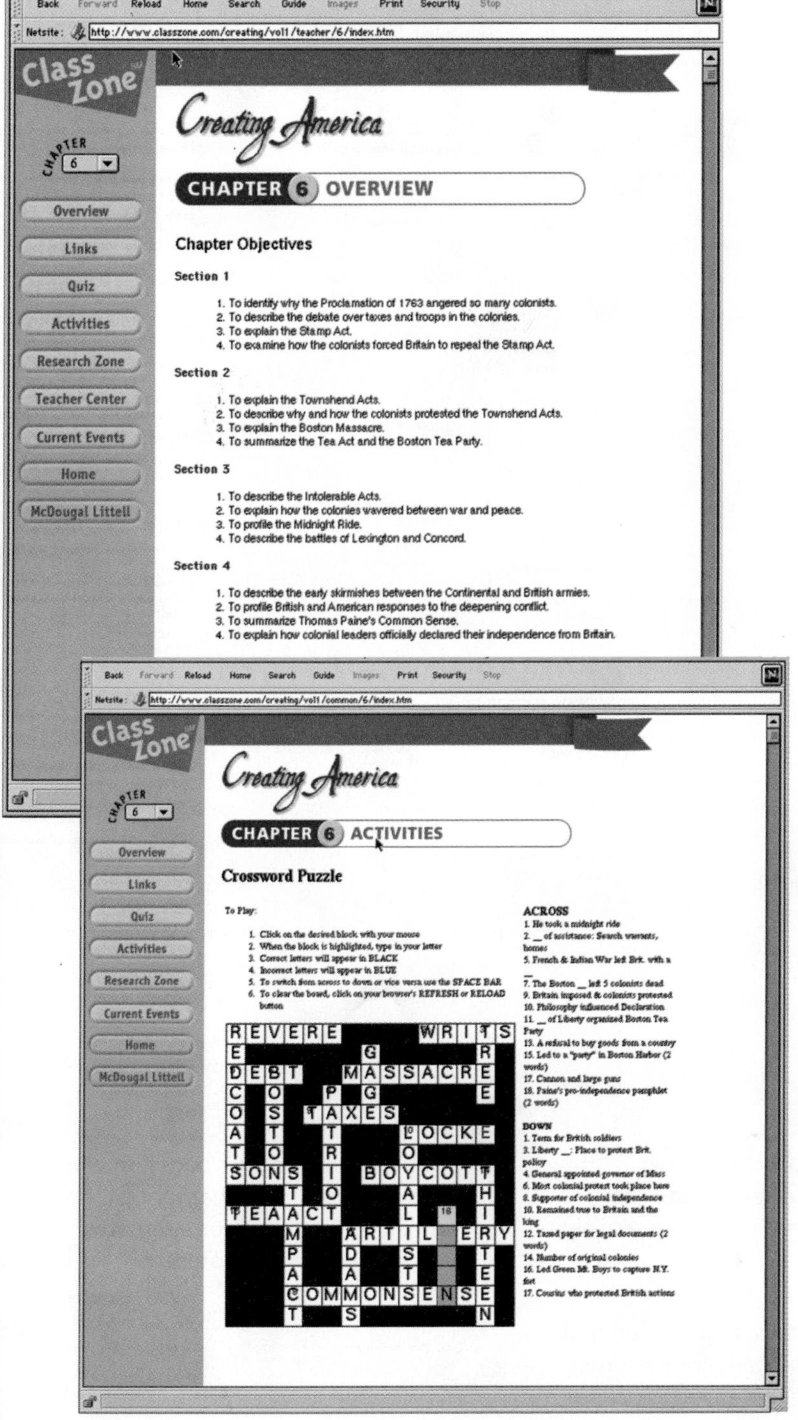


## ClassZone

Offers a wealth of online resources for the student and teacher. This Web site serves as a companion to the textbook and offers the following resources to enrich student learning and classroom teaching. ClassZone is password protected.

- **Section Objectives** for every section of the textbook.
- **Quizzes** of 5 multiple-choice questions about each chapter.
- **Links** to other Web sites for further historical study.
- A **Crossword Puzzle** or **Flipcard Game** for each chapter.
- A **Geography Game** to help your students develop their knowledge of world geography.
- **Current Events Quiz** based on the week's events.
- **Research Zone** tutorial to help students do research on the Internet.
- **Simulation Activity** that presents decision-making and problem-solving activities that are regularly updated.
- **Teacher Center** has answers to the chapter quizzes and current events quizzes.
- **Online Lesson Planner** lets you create customized daily lesson plans that help you use the components of *Creating America* to meet the needs of your students.

## maps101.com

This subscription-based Web site features a variety of easily accessible, up-to-date maps. Maps in the news, historical maps, reference atlases, state-specific maps, lesson plans and activities, and more are available with a few clicks of your mouse. Every map can be downloaded, printe and photocopied for classroom use.

# Creating America

## Chapter Planning Guide

Every chapter of the *Creating America* Teacher's Edition opens with a convenient two-page Planning Guide. By giving an overview of the chapter's key ideas, copymasters, technology, and assessment resources, the Planning Guide can help teachers meet the diverse needs of the classroom.

Name ______________________ Date ______________________

*Economics in History*

*Chapter 6 Section 1, Tighter British Control*

### The Impact of British Taxes

Changes in British taxes—required payments to the government—helped bring about the American Revolution. The British began to increase taxes on American colonists after the French and Indian War (1754–1763). The war proved to be long and costly to Britain. Britain had borrowed huge sums of money to cover the costs of this war, as well as other European wars. In 1754, Britain's national debt was about £72 million. (£ is the symbol for a British pound.) By 1763, the debt nearly doubled to more than £132 million (more than $10 billion today).

After the French and Indian War, Britain stationed 10,000 troops in North America. Maintaining these troops added another heavy expense to the British treasury—about £400,000 a year. To raise money, the British Parliament passed the Sugar Act (1764) and the Stamp Act (1765). The Sugar Act and the Stamp Act marked the beginning of a series of laws that forced colonists to ask this question: Did the benefits of belonging to the British empire outweigh the benefits of becoming an independent nation?

**The Sugar Act** In passing the Sugar Act, Parliament's goal was to collect £100,000 a year. This amount was expected to cover about 20 percent of Britain's military costs in North America. The Sugar Act included a three-pence tax on every gallon of imported molasses from the French West Indies. Molasses was a thick, sugary syrup used in making rum. The act also taxed many other goods, such as indigo, coffee, wine, and silk. From 1766 to 1775, Britain raised about £30,000 a year in revenue.

The Sugar Act struck an economic blow to merchants and ship captains. Many colonists feared Britain was seizing powers, such as the right to tax, from the colonial legislatures.

**The Stamp Act** The Sugar Act did not solve Britain's financial problems. Its national debt kept increasing. In 1765, Parliament took more drastic measures and passed the Stamp Act. The goal was to raise £60,000 to £100,000 a year.

The Stamp Act was the first time that the colonists directly paid a tax on goods and services. The Stamp Act required colonists to buy specially stamped paper for printed materials, such as legal documents, pamphlets, and newspapers.

British tax stamp used in 1765.
The Granger Collection, New York

The tax affected all free men and women, both rich and poor, in the colonies. Churchgoers had to pay a stamp tax on prayer books. Engaged couples had to pay a stamp tax on their marriage licenses. African-American laborers, craft workers, small farmers, southern planters, and northern merchants—all paid the stamp tax.

Especially hard-hit were lawyers and publishers. Lawyers had to pay a 10-pound stamp tax on their law licenses. They also became alarmed about losing clients who had to pay a tax on documents, such as wills, mortgages, and deeds. Many colonial lawyers spoke out against the Stamp Act and embraced the revolutionary cause. Of the 56 men who signed the Declaration of Independence in 1776, 26 were lawyers.

The American Revolution that followed was not fought over the issue of paying taxes. Rather, the Revolution was fought, in part, over Britain's authority to impose taxes.

#### Activity

The British government passed the Sugar Act and the Stamp Act to pay the expense of keeping troops in North America. If you had been in charge of the British government, what would you have done to raise the needed money? Write your ideas on a piece of paper. Then exchange papers with a partner. Each of you should then write how you think the colonists would have reacted to the plan.



6 CHAPTER 6 THE ROAD TO REVOLUTION

References to specific ancillaries help teachers to plan lessons.

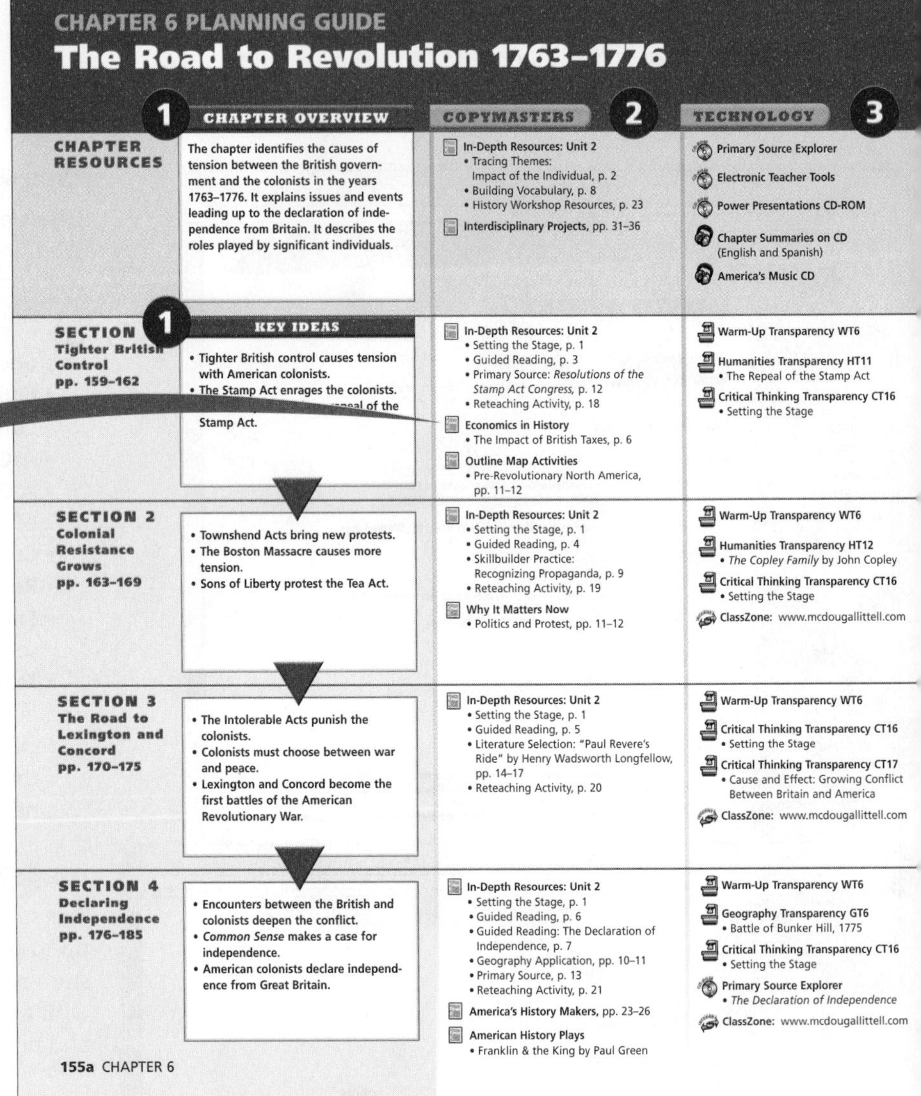

CHAPTER 6 PLANNING GUIDE

### The Road to Revolution 1763–1776

| | 1 CHAPTER OVERVIEW | COPYMASTERS 2 | TECHNOLOGY 3 |
|---|---|---|---|
| **CHAPTER RESOURCES** | The chapter identifies the causes of tension between the British government and the colonists in the years 1763–1776. It explains issues and events leading up to the declaration of independence from Britain. It describes the roles played by significant individuals. | **In-Depth Resources: Unit 2**<br>• Tracing Themes: Impact of the Individual, p. 2<br>• Building Vocabulary, p. 8<br>• History Workshop Resources, p. 23<br>**Interdisciplinary Projects**, pp. 31–36 | **Primary Source Explorer**<br>**Electronic Teacher Tools**<br>**Power Presentations CD-ROM**<br>**Chapter Summaries on CD** (English and Spanish)<br>**America's Music CD** |
| | 1 KEY IDEAS | | |
| **SECTION 1**<br>**Tighter British Control**<br>**pp. 159–162** | • Tighter British control causes tension with American colonists.<br>• The Stamp Act enrages the colonists.<br>• ...peal of the Stamp Act. | **In-Depth Resources: Unit 2**<br>• Setting the Stage, p. 1<br>• Guided Reading, p. 3<br>• Primary Source: *Resolutions of the Stamp Act Congress*, p. 12<br>• Reteaching Activity, p. 18<br>**Economics in History**<br>• The Impact of British Taxes, p. 6<br>**Outline Map Activities**<br>• Pre-Revolutionary North America, pp. 11–12 | **Warm-Up Transparency WT6**<br>**Humanities Transparency HT11**<br>• The Repeal of the Stamp Act<br>**Critical Thinking Transparency CT16**<br>• Setting the Stage |
| **SECTION 2**<br>**Colonial Resistance Grows**<br>**pp. 163–169** | • Townshend Acts bring new protests.<br>• The Boston Massacre causes more tension.<br>• Sons of Liberty protest the Tea Act. | **In-Depth Resources: Unit 2**<br>• Setting the Stage, p. 1<br>• Guided Reading, p. 4<br>• Skillbuilder Practice: Recognizing Propaganda, p. 9<br>• Reteaching Activity, p. 19<br>**Why It Matters Now**<br>• Politics and Protest, pp. 11–12 | **Warm-Up Transparency WT6**<br>**Humanities Transparency HT12**<br>• *The Copley Family* by John Copley<br>**Critical Thinking Transparency CT16**<br>• Setting the Stage<br>**ClassZone:** www.mcdougallittell.com |
| **SECTION 3**<br>**The Road to Lexington and Concord**<br>**pp. 170–175** | • The Intolerable Acts punish the colonists.<br>• Colonists must choose between war and peace.<br>• Lexington and Concord become the first battles of the American Revolutionary War. | **In-Depth Resources: Unit 2**<br>• Setting the Stage, p. 1<br>• Guided Reading, p. 5<br>• Literature Selection: "Paul Revere's Ride" by Henry Wadsworth Longfellow, pp. 14–17<br>• Reteaching Activity, p. 20 | **Warm-Up Transparency WT6**<br>**Critical Thinking Transparency CT16**<br>• Setting the Stage<br>**Critical Thinking Transparency CT17**<br>• Cause and Effect: Growing Conflict Between Britain and America<br>**ClassZone:** www.mcdougallittell.com |
| **SECTION 4**<br>**Declaring Independence**<br>**pp. 176–185** | • Encounters between the British and colonists deepen the conflict.<br>• *Common Sense* makes a case for independence.<br>• American colonists declare independence from Great Britain. | **In-Depth Resources: Unit 2**<br>• Setting the Stage, p. 1<br>• Guided Reading, p. 6<br>• Guided Reading: The Declaration of Independence, p. 7<br>• Geography Application, pp. 10–11<br>• Primary Source, p. 13<br>• Reteaching Activity, p. 21<br>**America's History Makers**, pp. 23–26<br>**American History Plays**<br>• Franklin & the King by Paul Green | **Warm-Up Transparency WT6**<br>**Geography Transparency GT6**<br>• Battle of Bunker Hill, 1775<br>**Critical Thinking Transparency CT16**<br>• Setting the Stage<br>**Primary Source Explorer**<br>• *The Declaration of Independence*<br>**ClassZone:** www.mcdougallittell.com |

155a CHAPTER 6

### 1 Chapter Overview and Key Ideas

An overview summarizes the important events covered in the chapter. A chronological, section-by-section summary then lists the key ideas in the chapter.

### 2 Copymasters

A complete listing of reproducible materials for each section reveals the depth of resource material that is available.

### 3 Technology

Technology is listed for each section and includes a wealth of tranparencies, the Primary Source Explorer CD-ROM, audio resources, and Internet ideas.

### 4 Assessment

This column identifies pages on which section quizzes and chapter tests are available. Resources for alternative assessment are also noted.

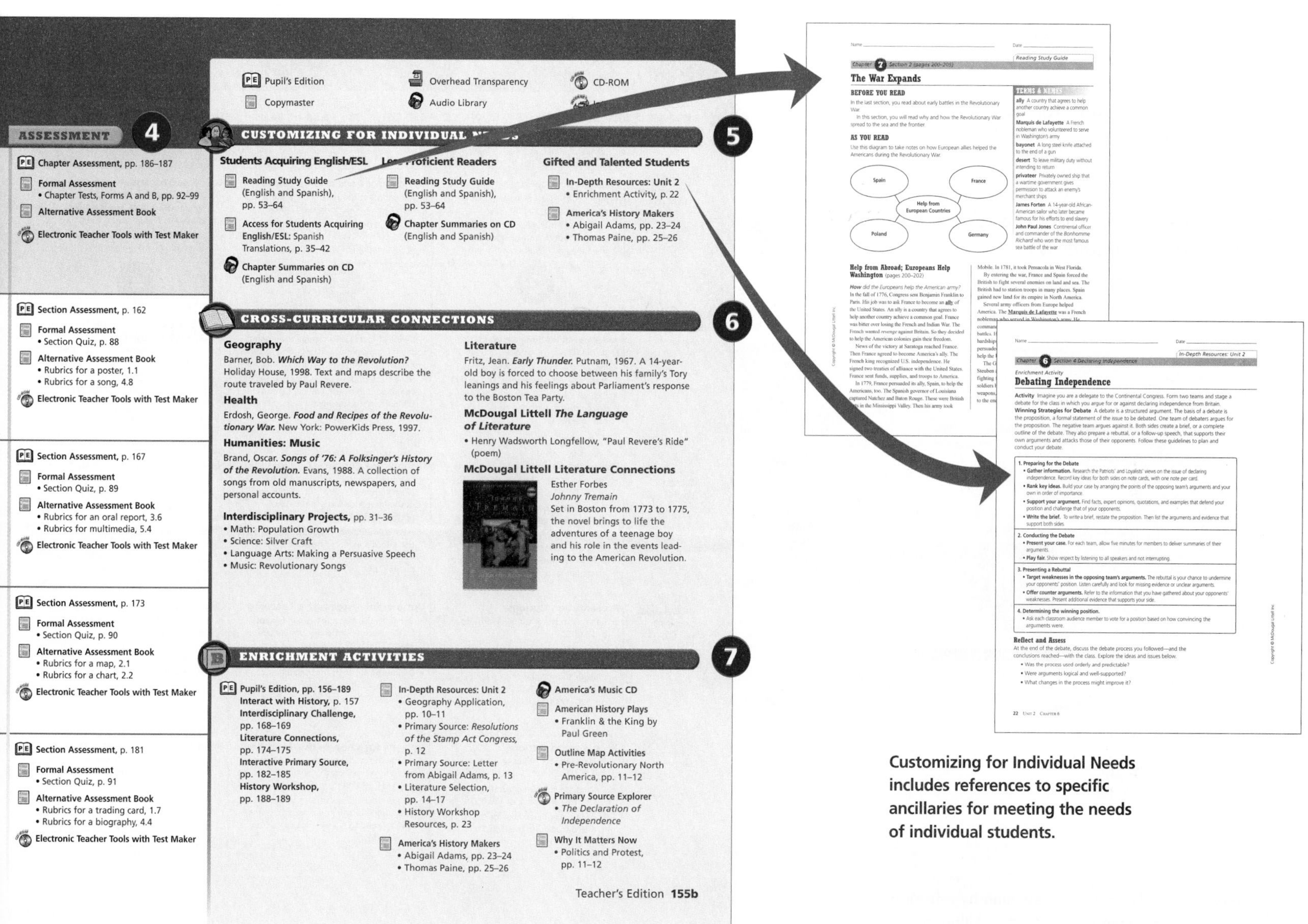

Pupil's Edition
Copymaster
Overhead Transparency
Audio Library
CD-ROM

ASSESSMENT 4

Chapter Assessment, pp. 186–187

Formal Assessment
- Chapter Tests, Forms A and B, pp. 92–99

Alternative Assessment Book

Electronic Teacher Tools with Test Maker

Section Assessment, p. 162

Formal Assessment
- Section Quiz, p. 88

Alternative Assessment Book
- Rubrics for a poster, 1.1
- Rubrics for a song, 4.8

Electronic Teacher Tools with Test Maker

Section Assessment, p. 167

Formal Assessment
- Section Quiz, p. 89

Alternative Assessment Book
- Rubrics for an oral report, 3.6
- Rubrics for multimedia, 5.4

Electronic Teacher Tools with Test Maker

Section Assessment, p. 173

Formal Assessment
- Section Quiz, p. 90

Alternative Assessment Book
- Rubrics for a map, 2.1
- Rubrics for a chart, 2.2

Electronic Teacher Tools with Test Maker

Section Assessment, p. 181

Formal Assessment
- Section Quiz, p. 91

Alternative Assessment Book
- Rubrics for a trading card, 1.7
- Rubrics for a biography, 4.4

Electronic Teacher Tools with Test Maker

CUSTOMIZING FOR INDIVIDUAL NEEDS 5

**Students Acquiring English/ESL**

Reading Study Guide (English and Spanish), pp. 53–64

Access for Students Acquiring English/ESL: Spanish Translations, p. 35–42

Chapter Summaries on CD (English and Spanish)

**Less Proficient Readers**

Reading Study Guide (English and Spanish), pp. 53–64

Chapter Summaries on CD (English and Spanish)

**Gifted and Talented Students**

In-Depth Resources: Unit 2
- Enrichment Activity, p. 22

America's History Makers
- Abigail Adams, pp. 23–24
- Thomas Paine, pp. 25–26

CROSS-CURRICULAR CONNECTIONS 6

**Geography**

Barner, Bob. ***Which Way to the Revolution?*** Holiday House, 1998. Text and maps describe the route traveled by Paul Revere.

**Health**

Erdosh, George. ***Food and Recipes of the Revolutionary War.*** New York: PowerKids Press, 1997.

**Humanities: Music**

Brand, Oscar. ***Songs of '76: A Folksinger's History of the Revolution.*** Evans, 1988. A collection of songs from old manuscripts, newspapers, and personal accounts.

**Interdisciplinary Projects,** pp. 31–36
- Math: Population Growth
- Science: Silver Craft
- Language Arts: Making a Persuasive Speech
- Music: Revolutionary Songs

**Literature**

Fritz, Jean. ***Early Thunder.*** Putnam, 1967. A 14-year-old boy is forced to choose between his family's Tory leanings and his feelings about Parliament's response to the Boston Tea Party.

**McDougal Littell *The Language of Literature***
- Henry Wadsworth Longfellow, "Paul Revere's Ride" (poem)

**McDougal Littell Literature Connections**

Esther Forbes
*Johnny Tremain*
Set in Boston from 1773 to 1775, the novel brings to life the adventures of a teenage boy and his role in the events leading to the American Revolution.

ENRICHMENT ACTIVITIES 7

Pupil's Edition, pp. 156–189
Interact with History, p. 157
Interdisciplinary Challenge, pp. 168–169
Literature Connections, pp. 174–175
Interactive Primary Source, pp. 182–185
History Workshop, pp. 188–189

In-Depth Resources: Unit 2
- Geography Application, pp. 10–11
- Primary Source: *Resolutions of the Stamp Act Congress,* p. 12
- Primary Source: Letter from Abigail Adams, p. 13
- Literature Selection, pp. 14–17
- History Workshop Resources, p. 23

America's History Makers
- Abigail Adams, pp. 23–24
- Thomas Paine, pp. 25–26

America's Music CD

American History Plays
- Franklin & the King by Paul Green

Outline Map Activities
- Pre-Revolutionary North America, pp. 11–12

Primary Source Explorer
- *The Declaration of Independence*

Why It Matters Now
- Politics and Protest, pp. 11–12

Teacher's Edition **155b**

The War Expands

Debating Independence

Customizing for Individual Needs includes references to specific ancillaries for meeting the needs of individual students.

## 5 Customizing for Individual Needs

Here are suggested resources for teaching students acquiring English, less proficient readers, and gifted and talented students. From Spanish-language resources to Enrichment Activities designed specifically for gifted and talented students, *Creating America* offers practical help for the classroom needs of all students.

## 6 Cross-Curricular Connections

This section lists resources for interdisciplinary teaching. There are always references to Interdisciplinary Projects, the component of *Creating America* designed specifically for interdisciplinary teams. In addition, resources are listed for literature, science, geography, and other subjects.

## 7 Enrichment Activities

These are resources in *Creating America* that will help teachers to extend and enrich their teaching of the chapter.

## Chapter Pacing Guide

A two-page Pacing Guide appears immediately after the Planning Guide for every chapter in the *Creating America* Teacher's Edition. This easy-to-use guide is a valuable aid in planning lessons. In addition to the Pacing Guide for traditional 50-minute periods, a special Pacing Guide for block schedules is provided.

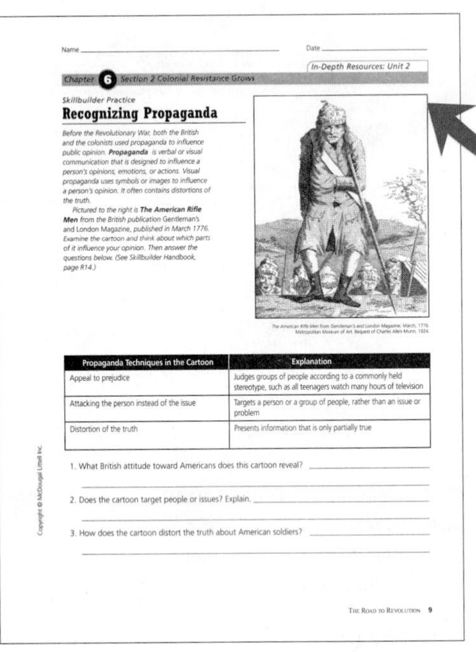

Name ______ Date ______

In-Depth Resources: Unit 2

Chapter 6 Section 2 Colonial Resistance Grows

*Skillbuilder Practice*

**Recognizing Propaganda**

*Before the Revolutionary War, both the British and the colonists used propaganda to influence public opinion.* ***Propaganda*** *is verbal or visual communication that is designed to influence a person's opinions, emotions, or actions. Visual propaganda uses symbols or images to influence a person's opinion. It often contains distortions of the truth.*

*Pictured to the right is* ***The American Rifle Men*** *from the British publication* Gentleman's and London Magazine, *published in March 1776. Examine the cartoon and think about which parts of it influence your opinion. Then answer the questions below. (See Skillbuilder Handbook, page R14.)*

*The American Rifle Men from Gentleman's and London Magazine, March, 1776. Metropolitan Museum of Art. Bequest of Charles Allen Munn, 1924.*

| Propaganda Techniques in the Cartoon | Explanation |
|---|---|
| Appeal to prejudice | Judges groups of people according to a commonly held stereotype, such as all teenagers watch many hours of television |
| Attacking the person instead of the issue | Targets a person or a group of people, rather than an issue or problem |
| Distortion of the truth | Presents information that is only partially true |

1. What British attitude toward Americans does this cartoon reveal? ______
2. Does the cartoon target people or issues? Explain. ______
3. How does the cartoon distort the truth about American soldiers? ______

Copyright © McDougal Littell Inc.

The Road to Revolution 9

**The Pacing Guide helps teachers plan by referring to specific components, such as this Skillbuilder Practice in In-Depth Resources.**

**CHAPTER 6 PACING GUIDE**

**1 LESSON PLAN OPTIONS (50-MINUTE PERIOD)** (TE) = Teacher's Edition (PE) = Pupil's Edition

| | TEACHER-DIRECTED ACTIVITIES<br>Class Time: 15 minutes | STUDENT-CENTERED ACTIVITIES<br>Class Time: 25 minutes | INDIVIDUAL ACTIVITIES<br>Class Time: 10 minutes |
|---|---|---|---|
| **DAY 1**<br>Introduction<br>pp. 156–158 | **Presentation Options**<br>• Begin with a class discussion of the engraving on p. 156 **(PE)**.<br>• Lead a class discussion on the "What Do You Know?" question in Setting the Stage, p. 158. Then introduce the graphic organizer for the chapter **(PE)**.<br>2 | **Options for Cooperative Learning**<br>• Have student groups discuss the Interact with History questions, p. 157 **(PE)**.<br>• Have student groups respond to the "What Do You Want to Know?" question in Setting the Stage, p. 158 **(PE)**.<br>3 | **Head Start on Homework Options**<br>• Have students skim Section 1 Main Idea, Why It Matters Now, Terms & Names, and the main headings, p. 159 **(PE)**.<br>• Have students begin Guided Reading activity and Building Vocabulary sheet.<br>4 |
| **DAY 2**<br>Section 1<br>pp. 159–162 | **Presentation Options**<br>• Begin with the 5-Minute Warm-Up, p. 159 **(TE)**.<br>• Review the Main Idea, Why It Matters Now, and Terms & Names, p. 159 **(PE)**.<br>• Choose 5 key questions for Objectives 1–4 to discuss with the class, pp. 159–161 **(TE)**. | **Options for Cooperative Learning**<br>• Divide students into groups to complete the Interdisciplinary Activity on Protesting the Stamp Act, p. 161 **(TE)**.<br>• Have student pairs work together to complete one of the Activity Options in the Section 1 Assessment, p. 162 **(PE)**. | **Head Start on Homework Options**<br>• Have students begin working on the Section 1 Assessment, p. 162 **(PE)**.<br>• Have students preview Section 2 by skimming the Main Idea, Why It Matters Now, Terms & Names, and the main headings, p. 163 **(PE)**. |
| **DAY 3**<br>Section 2<br>pp. 163–169 | **Presentation Options**<br>• Begin with the 5-Minute Warm-Up, p. 163 **(TE)**.<br>• Choose 5 key questions for Objectives 1–4 to discuss with the class, pp. 163–167 **(TE)**.<br>• Lead the students through the Skillbuilder Mini-Lesson: Recognizing Propaganda, p. 165 **(TE)**. | **Options for Cooperative Learning**<br>• Divide students into groups and have them complete one of the challenges in the Interdisciplinary Challenge, pp. 168–169 **(PE)**.<br>• Have students work together to complete the Interdisciplinary Link, Language Arts: Committees of Correspondence, p. 166 **(TE)**. | **Head Start on Homework Options**<br>• Have students begin working on the Section 2 Assessment, p. 167 **(PE)**.<br>• Have students read Literature Connections, a selection from *Johnny Tremain*, pp. 174–175 **(PE)**. |
| **DAY 4**<br>Section 3<br>pp. 170–175 | **Presentation Options**<br>• Begin with the 5-Minute Warm-Up, p. 170 **(TE)**.<br>• Review the Cause and Effect chart, p. 171 **(PE)**.<br>• Choose 5 Key Questions for Objectives 1–4 to discuss with the class, pp. 170–173 **(TE)**. | **Options for Cooperative Learning**<br>• Divide the students into small groups to complete the Interdisciplinary Link, Math: Effects of the Boycott, p. 171 **(TE)**.<br>• Divide the students into small groups to create a skit based on the *Johnny Tremain* reading, pp. 174–175 **(PE)**. | **Head Start on Homework Options**<br>• Have students complete the History from Visuals extension activity, p. 172 **(TE)**.<br>• Have students complete the History Skills questions in Chapter Assessment, p. 187 **(PE)**. |
| **DAY 5**<br>Section 4<br>pp. 176–185 | **Presentation Options**<br>• Begin with the 5-Minute Warm-Up, p. 176 **(TE)**.<br>• Discuss the follow-up question to Interact with History, p. 186 **(PE)**.<br>• Choose 5 Key Questions for Objectives 1–4 to discuss with the class, pp. 176–179 **(TE)**. | **Options for Cooperative Learning**<br>• Divide the students into small groups and begin work on the History Workshop, pp. 188–189 **(PE)**.<br>• Divide the students into small groups and complete the Interdisciplinary Link, Civics: Creating a New *Common Sense*, p. 179 **(TE)**. | **Head Start on Homework Options**<br>• Have students complete the Setting the Stage graphic organizer for the chapter, p. 158 **(PE)**.<br>• Have students begin working on the Chapter Assessment, pp. 186–187 **(PE)**.<br>• Prepare for Chapter Test<br>**Formal Assessment, pp. 92–99** |

**155c** CHAPTER 6

### 1 Lesson Plan Options for 50-Minute Periods

For each day of instruction, the Pacing Guide provides options for teacher-directed activities, student-directed activities, and individual activities.

### 2 Teacher-Directed Activities

The first column includes at least two options for presenting concepts to the class and leading whole-class instruction and discussion.

### 3 Student-Centered Activities

The second column includes numerous options for student-centered activities, including resources for cooperative learning.

TEACHER-TESTED ACTIVITY | Holly West Brewer, Buena Vista Paideia Magnet School, Nashville, Tennessee

**ILLUSTRATED TIME LINE** 5

**Class Time** Two class periods for preparation and one for presentation

**Task** Creating an illustrated time line of the events leading to the American Revolution

**Purpose** To visualize and sequence events that led to the Revolution

**Supplies Needed**
- reference books and Internet sources on the American Revolution
- markers, colored pencils
- poster paper or rolls of paper

**Activity** Divide the class into small groups. Students should compile at least ten events that led to the Revolution. Each student should be responsible for researching two or three events. In addition, each student chooses one of the following roles: illustrator or recorder.

The illustrators should create original drawings for each event. Each event should be placed on the large time line in chronological order. In addition, the recorders should write a cause-and-effect explanation as a caption for each event. Present the time line to the class.

**BLOCK SCHEDULING — LESSON PLAN OPTIONS (90-MINUTE PERIOD)** 6

**DAY 1**

**Interact with History,** p. 157
**Class Time** 20 minutes
Options for pacing and variety:
- Role-Playing Have students meet in groups of four or five and act as neighbors meeting to discuss the "What Do You Think?" questions and the main questions. **Class Time** 15 minutes

**Setting the Stage,** p. 158
**Class Time** 20 minutes
Options for pacing and variety:
- Time Saver Assign the "What Do You Know?" and "What Do You Want to Know?" questions as homework so that students can get a head start on preparing to read the chapter. **Class Time** 5 minutes

**Section 1,** pp. 159–162
**Class Time** 50 minutes
Options for pacing and variety:
- Time Saver Use the political cartoon transparency, "Repeal of the Stamp Act," as a summary of the section. **Class Time** 10 minutes
- Peer Teaching Have students work in pairs to answer the Reading History questions in the section and Critical Thinking question in the Section 1 assessment. **Class Time** 15 minutes

**DAY 2**

**Section 2,** pp. 163–169
**Class Time** 45 minutes

**Interdisciplinary Challenge,** pp. 168–169
**Class Time** 55 minutes
Options for pacing and variety:
- Team Teaching Invite the math teacher to your class to coach student groups as they solve the Math Challenge or the Interdisciplinary Link (Math) on p. 171 in the Teacher's Edition. **Class Time** 55 minutes.
- Peer Teaching Assign the content under each heading to a small group of students. Each group is responsible for explaining the information to the class. **Class Time** 30 minutes

**Section 3,** pp. 170–175
**Class Time** 45 minutes
Options for pacing and variety:
- Peer Teaching Divide students into small groups. Using the information from the chart on p. 171, create a different way to present the information to the class. **Class Time** 25 minutes
- Internet Extend students' background knowledge of the Battles at Lexington and Concord by having them visit www.mcdougallittell.com **Class Time** 20 minutes

**DAY 3**

**Section 4,** pp. 176–185
**Class Time** 50 minutes
Options for pacing and variety:
- Peer Teaching Divide the class into small groups. Assign one group to become a living time line. Have another group become living b[...] of individuals in this chapter. A third grou[...] the Cooperative Learning Activity on pag[...] **Class Time** 50 minutes
- History on Film Extend students' background on the Revolutionary War by viewing either episode one or two, "The Conflict Ignites" or "1776," of *The American Revolution.* A&E Home Video, 1994. **Class Time** 50 minutes

**History Workshop,** pp. 188–189
**Class Time** 50 minutes
Options for pacing and variety:
- Time Saver Have students work on steps 1–5 in Raise the Liberty Pole. **Class Time** 30 minutes

**Chapter 6 Assessment,** pp. 186–187
**Class Time** 40 minutes
Options for pacing and variety:
- Peer Evaluation Have student pairs work out the answers to the Critical Thinking Questions, p. 186. Then have them exchange papers with another team to evaluate their answers. **Class Time** 20 minutes
- Peer Teaching Divide the class into four groups. Assign each group one section of the Review Questions to complete. Students should exchange answers for the review questions. **Class Time** 20 minutes

Teacher's Edition **155d**

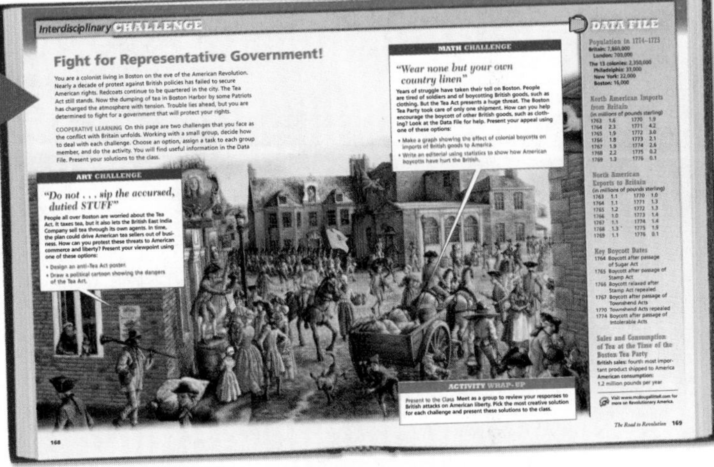


**The Block Scheduling Options refer to ancillaries and features—such as the Interdisciplinary Challenges—that are especially valuable for block schedules.**

## 4 Individual Activities

The third column provides ideas for individual student activities, with specific suggestions for students to start on homework.

## 5 Teacher-Tested Activity

The **Pacing Guide** for every chapter includes an activity written by an actual classroom teacher to teach the content in the chapter.

## 6 Block Scheduling Options

For teachers who teach in blocks, a special **Pacing Guide** is provided. It estimates the time needed for each activity and includes numerous options that help to vary the pacing of the class and the types of activities in which students are engaged.

*Creating America*

# Teacher's Edition Lesson Support

The *Creating America* Teacher's Edition provides you with a wealth of information and practical teaching suggestions at your fingertips. Meet the needs of each student, link history to other subjects, connect the past to the present, and more.

The side columns focus on core instruction. At the bottom of the pages, you will find optional activities and teaching activities—including those for block schedules.

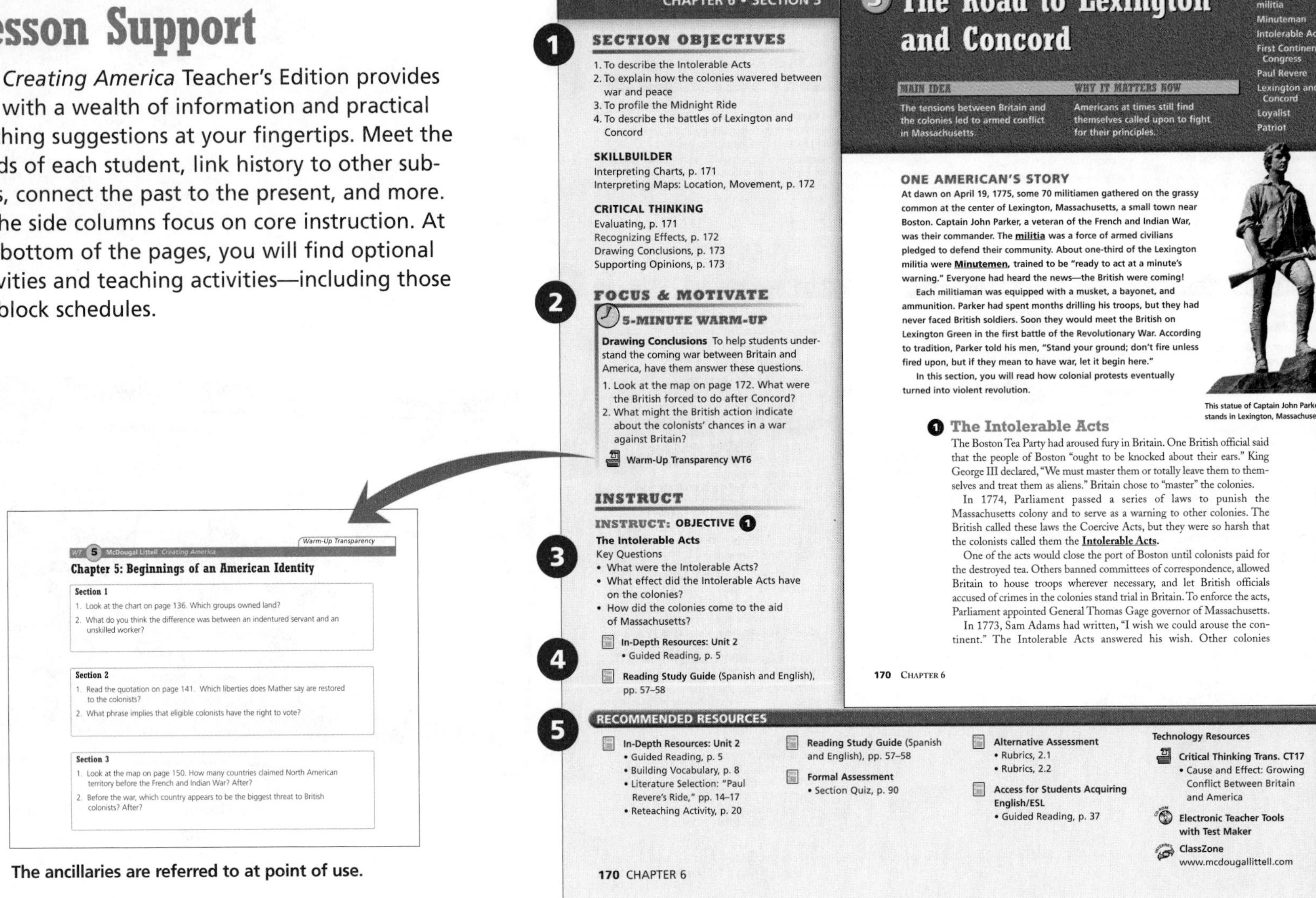

CHAPTER 6 • SECTION 3

**1** **SECTION OBJECTIVES**

1. To describe the Intolerable Acts
2. To explain how the colonies wavered between war and peace
3. To profile the Midnight Ride
4. To describe the battles of Lexington and Concord

**SKILLBUILDER**
Interpreting Charts, p. 171
Interpreting Maps: Location, Movement, p. 172

**CRITICAL THINKING**
Evaluating, p. 171
Recognizing Effects, p. 172
Drawing Conclusions, p. 173
Supporting Opinions, p. 173

**2** **FOCUS & MOTIVATE**

**5-MINUTE WARM-UP**

**Drawing Conclusions** To help students understand the coming war between Britain and America, have them answer these questions.

1. Look at the map on page 172. What were the British forced to do after Concord?
2. What might the British action indicate about the colonists' chances in a war against Britain?

Warm-Up Transparency WT6

**INSTRUCT**

**INSTRUCT: OBJECTIVE 1**

**3** **The Intolerable Acts**
Key Questions
- What were the Intolerable Acts?
- What effect did the Intolerable Acts have on the colonies?
- How did the colonies come to the aid of Massachusetts?

**4** **In-Depth Resources: Unit 2**
- Guided Reading, p. 5

**Reading Study Guide** (Spanish and English), pp. 57–58

**3 The Road to Lexington and Concord**

MAIN IDEA
The tensions between Britain and the colonies led to armed conflict in Massachusetts.

WHY IT MATTERS NOW
Americans at times still find themselves called upon to fight for their principles.

TERMS & NAMES
militia
Minuteman
Intolerable Acts
First Continental Congress
Paul Revere
Lexington and Concord
Loyalist
Patriot

**ONE AMERICAN'S STORY**

At dawn on April 19, 1775, some 70 militiamen gathered on the grassy common at the center of Lexington, Massachusetts, a small town near Boston. Captain John Parker, a veteran of the French and Indian War, was their commander. The **militia** was a force of armed civilians pledged to defend their community. About one-third of the Lexington militia were **Minutemen**, trained to be "ready to act at a minute's warning." Everyone had heard the news—the British were coming!

Each militiaman was equipped with a musket, a bayonet, and ammunition. Parker had spent months drilling his troops, but they had never faced British soldiers. Soon they would meet the British on Lexington Green in the first battle of the Revolutionary War. According to tradition, Parker told his men, "Stand your ground; don't fire unless fired upon, but if they mean to have war, let it begin here."

In this section, you will read how colonial protests eventually turned into violent revolution.

This statue of Captain John Parker stands in Lexington, Massachusetts.

**1 The Intolerable Acts**

The Boston Tea Party had aroused fury in Britain. One British official said that the people of Boston "ought to be knocked about their ears." King George III declared, "We must master them or totally leave them to themselves and treat them as aliens." Britain chose to "master" the colonies.

In 1774, Parliament passed a series of laws to punish the Massachusetts colony and to serve as a warning to other colonies. The British called these laws the Coercive Acts, but they were so harsh that the colonists called them the **Intolerable Acts**.

One of the acts would close the port of Boston until colonists paid for the destroyed tea. Others banned committees of correspondence, allowed Britain to house troops wherever necessary, and let British officials accused of crimes in the colonies stand trial in Britain. To enforce the acts, Parliament appointed General Thomas Gage governor of Massachusetts.

In 1773, Sam Adams had written, "I wish we could arouse the continent." The Intolerable Acts answered his wish. Other colonies

170 CHAPTER 6

**5** **RECOMMENDED RESOURCES**

**In-Depth Resources: Unit 2**
- Guided Reading, p. 5
- Building Vocabulary, p. 8
- Literature Selection: "Paul Revere's Ride," pp. 14–17
- Reteaching Activity, p. 20

**Reading Study Guide** (Spanish and English), pp. 57–58

**Formal Assessment**
- Section Quiz, p. 90

**Alternative Assessment**
- Rubrics, 2.1
- Rubrics, 2.2

**Access for Students Acquiring English/ESL**
- Guided Reading, p. 37

Technology Resources

**Critical Thinking Trans. CT17**
- Cause and Effect: Growing Conflict Between Britain and America

**Electronic Teacher Tools with Test Maker**

**ClassZone**
www.mcdougallittell.com

170 CHAPTER 6

WT 5 McDougal Littell *Creating America* — Warm-Up Transparency

**Chapter 5: Beginnings of an American Identity**

**Section 1**
1. Look at the chart on page 136. Which groups owned land?
2. What do you think the difference was between an indentured servant and an unskilled worker?

**Section 2**
1. Read the quotation on page 141. Which liberties does Mather say are restored to the colonists?
2. What phrase implies that eligible colonists have the right to vote?

**Section 3**
1. Look at the map on page 150. How many countries claimed North American territory before the French and Indian War? After?
2. Before the war, which country appears to be the biggest threat to British colonists? After?

The ancillaries are referred to at point of use.

## 1 Section Objectives

The objectives of the section are clearly spelled out. Each objective is number-coded to help you know when in the lesson you are teaching to that objective. The Skillbuilder skills and critical thinking skills covered in the section are also listed.

## 2 Focus & Motivate/ 5-Minute Warm-Up

A Warm-Up Activity begins every section to help you begin your classes in motivational ways that focus student attention on the lesson. A Warm-Up Transparency supports each Warm-Up Activity.

## 3 Key Questions

These questions help you reinforce students' understanding of what they read.

## 4 References to Resource Materials

These references to specific program resources help you to incorporate the resources at the appropriate point in your lesson.

## 5 Recommended Resources

For your convenience, all of the program resources that are appropriate for teaching the section are listed at the bottom of the first page of that section.

immediately offered Massachusetts their support. They sent food and money to Boston. The committees of correspondence also called for a meeting of colonial delegates to discuss what to do next.

## 2 The First Continental Congress Meets

In September 1774, delegates from all the colonies except Georgia met in Philadelphia. At this meeting, called the **First Continental Congress**, delegates voted to ban all trade with Britain until the Intolerable Acts were repealed. They also called on each colony to begin training troops. Georgia agreed to be a part of the actions of the Congress even though it had voted not to send delegates.

The First Continental Congress marked a key step in American history. Although most delegates were not ready to call for independence, they were determined to uphold colonial rights. This meeting planted the seeds of a future independent government. John Adams called it "a nursery of American statesmen." The delegates agreed to meet in seven months, if necessary. By that time, however, fighting with Britain had begun.

*dingHistory* valuating do you : the First inental gress was rtant?

## Between War and Peace

The colonists hoped that the trade boycott would force a repeal of the Intolerable Acts. After all, past boycotts had led to the repeal of the Stamp Act and the Townshend Acts. This time, however, Parliament stood firm. It even increased restrictions on colonial trade and sent more troops.

By the end of 1774, some colonists were preparing to fight. In Massachusetts, John Hancock headed the Committee of Safety, which had the power to call out the militia. The colonial troops continued to train.

**CAUSE AND EFFECT:** *Growing Conflict Between Britain and America*

| DATE | BRITISH ACTION | COLONIAL REACTION |
|---|---|---|
| 1763 | Proclamation of 1763 issued | Proclamation leads to anger |
| 1765 | Stamp Act passed | Boycott of British goods; Stamp Act Resolves passed |
| 1766 | Stamp Act repealed; Declaration Act passed | Boycott ended |
| 1767 | Townshend Acts passed | New boycotts; Boston Massacre (March 1770) |
| 1770 | Townshend Acts repealed (April) | Tension between colonies and Britain reduced |
| 1773 | Tea Act passed | Boston Tea Party |
| 1774 | Intolerable Acts passed | First Continental Congress bans trade; militias organized |
| 1775 | Troops ordered to Lexington and Concord, Massachusetts | Militia fights British troops; Second Continental Congress; Continental Army established |

SKILLBUILDER **Interpreting Charts**
1. *What British action caused the first violence in the growing conflict between Britain and America?*
2. *How might the Intolerable Acts be seen as a reaction as well as an action?*

*The Road to Revolution* **171**

CHAPTER 6 • SECTION 3

**INSTRUCT: OBJECTIVE 2**

**The First Continental Congress Meets/ Between War and Peace**
Key Questions
- What happened at the First Continental Congress?
- How did the colonists protest the Intolerable Acts? How successful were they?
- What did most colonial leaders think about the prospect of war with Britain?

**MORE ABOUT . . .** 6

**First Continental Congress**
In the first session of the Continental Congress, the delegates rejected, by a vote of six to five, Pennsylvania delegate Joseph Galloway's plan to create a union of the colonies. Galloway's Plan of Union included a Grand Council with delegates from all the colonies that would deal with issues affecting more than one colony. Legislation would be subject to Parliament's approval. The council would also have the right to reject Parliament's legislation.

**HISTORY FROM VISUALS** 7

**Interpreting the Chart** Have students note the span of years on the chart, and explain that the graphic shows how British-American tension built up over time and did not stem from one or two incidents. Ask students how colonial leaders might use this chart to defend their desire to break free from Britain. **Possible Response** Colonial leaders might use the chart to emphasize Britain's pattern of injustice and to show how the colonies have been enduring such injustice for too long.

**Extension** Have students work in pairs to create a different way of showing the same information.

**Critical Thinking Transparency CT17**
- Cause and Effect: Growing Conflict Between Britain and America

**ACTIVITY OPTIONS**

**INTERDISCIPLINARY LINK: MATH** BLOCK SCHEDULING 9

**EFFECTS OF A BOYCOTT**

**Class Time** 30 minutes
**Task** Determining a boycott's economic impact
**Purpose** To understand the effectiveness of boycotting as a form of protest

**Supplies Needed**
- Scratch paper and pencils
- Calculators

**Activity** Divide students into groups representing British colonial businesses (tea, woolens, foodstuffs, tinware, glass and pottery, textiles). Provide each group with a figure that represents the business's average monthly earnings (e.g., $50,000). Have each group determine the economic impact of a six-month boycott against its products by using several different assigned loss percentages (2 percent, 5 percent, 10 percent, etc.). Each group should share its findings with the class and discuss how the losses would affect the political views of the British businessmen.

Teacher's Edition **171**

## Teacher's Edition notes may also include:

- Assessment Suggestions
- Cooperative Learning activities
- Gifted and Talented Students activities
- Less Proficient Readers activities
- Multiple Learning Styles suggestions
- Skillbuilder Mini-Lessons
- Standards for Evaluation
- Students Acquiring English/ESL activities
- Teaching Strategies

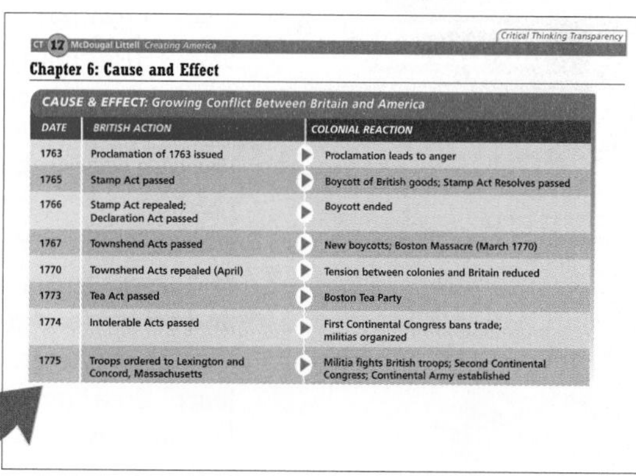

CT 17 McDougal Littell *Creating America* — *Critical Thinking Transparency*

**Chapter 6: Cause and Effect**

**CAUSE & EFFECT:** *Growing Conflict Between Britain and America*

| DATE | BRITISH ACTION | COLONIAL REACTION |
|---|---|---|
| 1763 | Proclamation of 1763 issued | Proclamation leads to anger |
| 1765 | Stamp Act passed | Boycott of British goods; Stamp Act Resolves passed |
| 1766 | Stamp Act repealed; Declaration Act passed | Boycott ended |
| 1767 | Townshend Acts passed | New boycotts; Boston Massacre (March 1770) |
| 1770 | Townshend Acts repealed (April) | Tension between colonies and Britain reduced |
| 1773 | Tea Act passed | Boston Tea Party |
| 1774 | Intolerable Acts passed | First Continental Congress bans trade; militias organized |
| 1775 | Troops ordered to Lexington and Concord, Massachusetts | Militia fights British troops; Second Continental Congress; Continental Army established |

**The ancillaries are referred to at point of use.**

## 6 More About . . .

These terrific nuggets of information occur often to supplement the text.

## 7 History from Visuals

These notes provide a variety of learning strategies and extension activities to help students make the most of maps, charts, graphs, political cartoons, and historical photographs.

## 8 Activity Options/ Interdisciplinary Links

Activity options at the bottom of the Teacher's Edition pages offer a range of choices. Many of these choices are Interdisciplinary Links to math, science, language arts, literature, humanities, civics, economics, and health. The amount of time required for the activity is listed.

## 9 Block Scheduling

The logo labeled Block Scheduling appears wherever an Activity Option is appropriate for block schedules.

# Helping Students Read History

DONNA M. OGLE
*Professor, Reading and Language, National-Louis University, Evanston, Illinois; President, International Reading Association*

The best learners are active and engaged readers. Successful readers connect what they are reading with what they already know. These readers:

- build associations among ideas
- create visual images of what they are reading
- continually revise their interpretations as they gather more information.

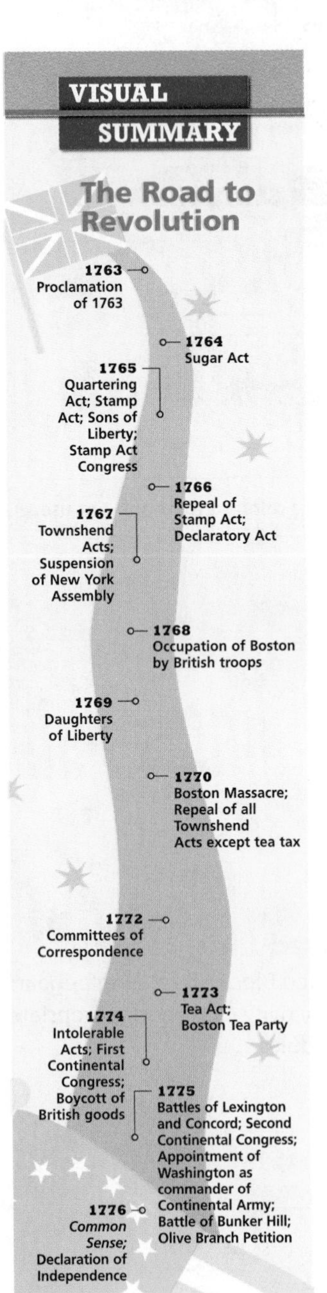

VISUAL
SUMMARY
The Road to Revolution
1763 Proclamation of 1763
1764 Sugar Act
1765 Quartering Act; Stamp Act; Sons of Liberty; Stamp Act Congress
1766 Repeal of Stamp Act; Declaratory Act
1767 Townshend Acts; Suspension of New York Assembly
1768 Occupation of Boston by British troops
1769 Daughters of Liberty
1770 Boston Massacre; Repeal of all Townshend Acts except tea tax
1772 Committees of Correspondence
1773 Tea Act; Boston Tea Party
1774 Intolerable Acts; First Continental Congress; Boycott of British goods
1775 Battles of Lexington and Concord; Second Continental Congress; Appointment of Washington as commander of Continental Army; Battle of Bunker Hill; Olive Branch Petition
1776 Common Sense; Declaration of Independence


## Supporting Readers

*Creating America: A History of the United States* uses many strategies to help students become active and engaged readers.

**Various Learning Styles** We know that readers have different styles of understanding. Some rely heavily on verbal input and discussion, some need visual supports, and some need to make notes and drawings or create graphic organizers as they learn. *Creating America* addresses various learning styles by including a variety of activity options, posing problems, providing graphic organizers to help students take notes, and asking thought-provoking questions for discussion.

**Visual Information** Many readers rely on visual information when reading unfamiliar material. Pictures make abstractions of time and space more real; photos and artifacts create a context for new ideas; maps help readers associate and compare ideas. In addition, charts of ideas and events in each chapter summarize and clarify information. A visual summary at the end of each chapter provides another way for remembering important ideas and events.

**Inner-Column Notes** Inner-column notes in *Creating America* help students read the text. Vocabulary notes explain and define words and phrases. Background notes provide additional information about a person, idea, or event. Reading History questions help students to read critically.

**Personal Connections** Personal stories and human connections can help to bring a subject such as history alive. *Creating America* uses personal voices throughout to support student learning.

> *A VOICE FROM THE PAST*
>
> Gentlemen may cry peace, peace—but there is no peace. The war is actually begun! The next gale that sweeps from the north will bring to our ears the clash of resounding arms! Our brethren are already in the field! Why should we idle here? . . . I know not what course others may take. But as for me, give me liberty or give me death.
>
> **Patrick Henry**, quoted in *Patriots* by A. J. Langguth

**Students Acquiring English** Second-language learners need to have information and ideas presented to them in multiple ways. Being able to "see" history helps make it real for them. *Creating America* uses illustrations and visuals to present information to students in a variety of ways.

## Evolving Forms of Reading

Students today need to be able to read in new ways.

**Nonlinear Materials** Today's students must:

- gather ideas from multiple sources—resource books, magazines, computerized databases, CD-ROMs, the Internet
- find their way through nonlinear materials, such as by deciding which area of a computer screen contains the information they want.

To help students using *Creating America* to develop these skills, the Interactive Primary Sources in the textbook also appear on a separately available CD-ROM entitled **Primary Source Explorer**, along with resources for exploring each primary source in depth.

**Graphic Layouts** Today's readers must deal with informational materials that come in various formats.

- multiple columns of text with many pictures, graphs, and maps
- single-column texts with large marginal areas used for illustrations, highlighted information, and thought-provoking ideas

## Strategies for Teachers

You can help your students become active, engaged, and confident readers. As part of your introduction of the textbook, ask students to read and discuss "Reading to Remember" on pages xxx-1. These four pages give students a number of practical strategies that will help them to read and study the textbook effectively. Here are some additional strategies you might try.

- Ask students to observe how they read.
- Do a "think aloud" as students begin to read a text. Ask them to tell you where they look on the page; when they look at the charts, maps, and pictures; and when they read the headings and titles.
- Introduce the text layout and features, and discuss students' options for reading.
- Have students experiment with reading the graphics first before reading the text on a page.
- Demonstrate how headings and subheadings can help readers find specific information.
- Use graphic organizers and reading guides to help students gain confidence.

Reading and discussing different types of written material and material expressing different points of view will help students learn to think critically about what they read.

1. **Vocabulary**
2. **Background Notes**
3. **Political, Physical, and Historical Maps**
4. **Skillbuilder Questions**
5. **Reading History Questions**
6. **A Voice from the Past**
7. **Pictures of Artifacts**

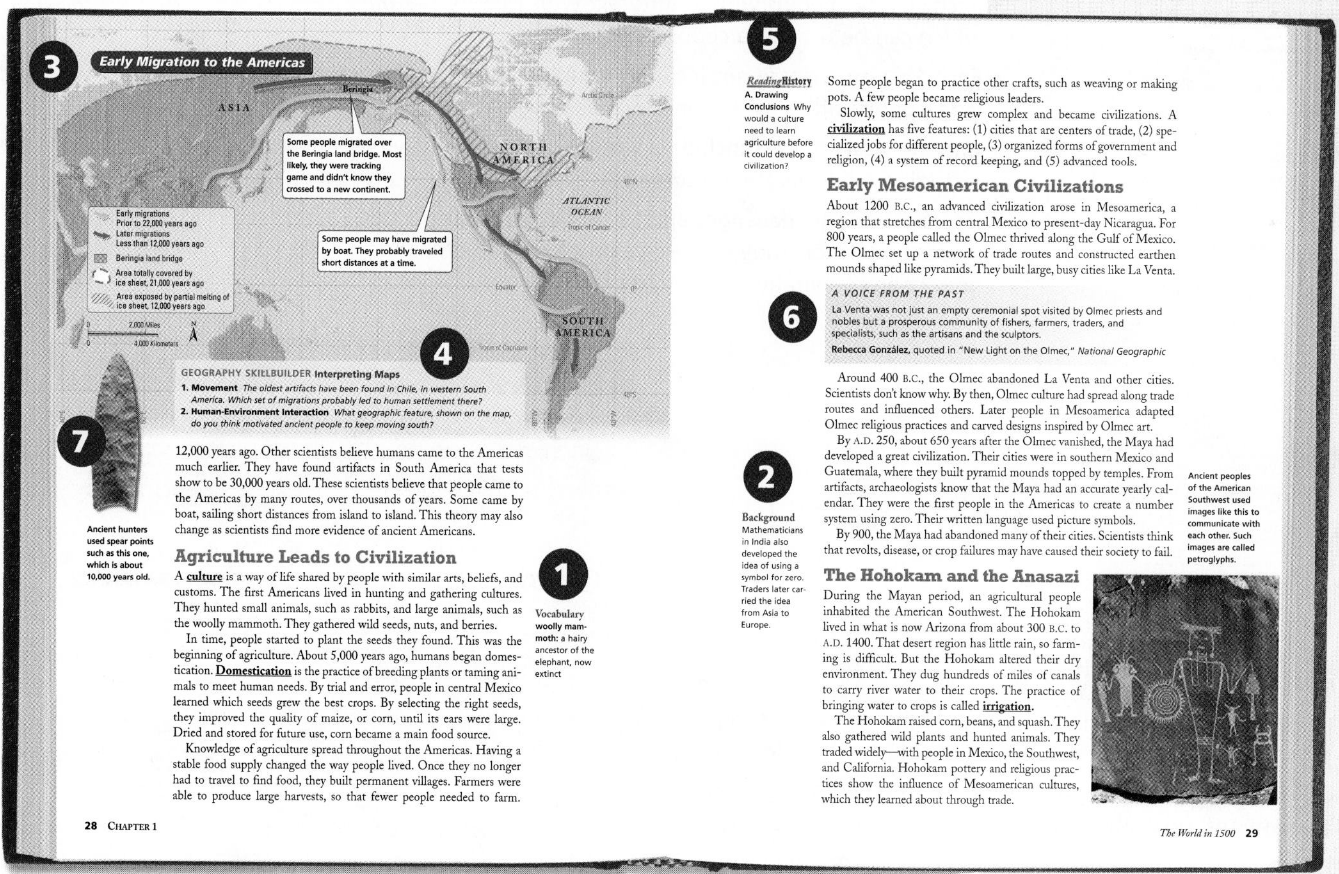


GEOGRAPHY SKILLBUILDER **Interpreting Maps**

1. **Movement** *The oldest artifacts have been found in Chile, in western South America. Which set of migrations probably led to human settlement there?*
2. **Human-Environment Interaction** *What geographic feature, shown on the map, do you think motivated ancient people to keep moving south?*

12,000 years ago. Other scientists believe humans came to the Americas much earlier. They have found artifacts in South America that tests show to be 30,000 years old. These scientists believe that people came to the Americas by many routes, over thousands of years. Some came by boat, sailing short distances from island to island. This theory may also change as scientists find more evidence of ancient Americans.

Ancient hunters used spear points such as this one, which is about 10,000 years old.

### Agriculture Leads to Civilization

A **culture** is a way of life shared by people with similar arts, beliefs, and customs. The first Americans lived in hunting and gathering cultures. They hunted small animals, such as rabbits, and large animals, such as the woolly mammoth. They gathered wild seeds, nuts, and berries.

Vocabulary **woolly mammoth:** a hairy ancestor of the elephant, now extinct

In time, people started to plant the seeds they found. This was the beginning of agriculture. About 5,000 years ago, humans began domestication. **Domestication** is the practice of breeding plants or taming animals to meet human needs. By trial and error, people in central Mexico learned which seeds grew the best crops. By selecting the right seeds, they improved the quality of maize, or corn, until its ears were large. Dried and stored for future use, corn became a main food source.

Knowledge of agriculture spread throughout the Americas. Having a stable food supply changed the way people lived. Once they no longer had to travel to find food, they built permanent villages. Farmers were able to produce large harvests, so that fewer people needed to farm.

28 CHAPTER 1

*Reading* **History** **A. Drawing Conclusions** Why would a culture need to learn agriculture before it could develop a civilization?

Some people began to practice other crafts, such as weaving or making pots. A few people became religious leaders.

Slowly, some cultures grew complex and became civilizations. A **civilization** has five features: (1) cities that are centers of trade, (2) specialized jobs for different people, (3) organized forms of government and religion, (4) a system of record keeping, and (5) advanced tools.

### Early Mesoamerican Civilizations

About 1200 B.C., an advanced civilization arose in Mesoamerica, a region that stretches from central Mexico to present-day Nicaragua. For 800 years, a people called the Olmec thrived along the Gulf of Mexico. The Olmec set up a network of trade routes and constructed earthen mounds shaped like pyramids. They built large, busy cities like La Venta.

*A VOICE FROM THE PAST*

La Venta was not just an empty ceremonial spot visited by Olmec priests and nobles but a prosperous community of fishers, farmers, traders, and specialists, such as the artisans and the sculptors.

**Rebecca González,** quoted in "New Light on the Olmec," *National Geographic*

Around 400 B.C., the Olmec abandoned La Venta and other cities. Scientists don't know why. By then, Olmec culture had spread along trade routes and influenced others. Later people in Mesoamerica adapted Olmec religious practices and carved designs inspired by Olmec art.

By A.D. 250, about 650 years after the Olmec vanished, the Maya had developed a great civilization. Their cities were in southern Mexico and Guatemala, where they built pyramid mounds topped by temples. From artifacts, archaeologists know that the Maya had an accurate yearly calendar. They were the first people in the Americas to create a number system using zero. Their written language used picture symbols.

**Background** Mathematicians in India also developed the idea of using a symbol for zero. Traders later carried the idea from Asia to Europe.

By 900, the Maya had abandoned many of their cities. Scientists think that revolts, disease, or crop failures may have caused their society to fail.

Ancient peoples of the American Southwest used images like this to communicate with each other. Such images are called petroglyphs.

### The Hohokam and the Anasazi

During the Mayan period, an agricultural people inhabited the American Southwest. The Hohokam lived in what is now Arizona from about 300 B.C. to A.D. 1400. That desert region has little rain, so farming is difficult. But the Hohokam altered their dry environment. They dug hundreds of miles of canals to carry river water to their crops. The practice of bringing water to crops is called **irrigation.**

The Hohokam raised corn, beans, and squash. They also gathered wild plants and hunted animals. They traded widely—with people in Mexico, the Southwest, and California. Hohokam pottery and religious practices show the influence of Mesoamerican cultures, which they learned about through trade.

*The World in 1500* 29

# Creating America

## Block Schedules

Today block schedules provide new opportunites and challenges for teachers. *Creating America* offers help for teaching in the block in both the pupil's edition and the teacher's edition. In addition, *Planning for Block Schedules*, found in the teacher's resource materials, includes a wealth of information and strategies.

### Planning For Block Schedules

This resourse has been developed specifically to help teachers in block scheduling situations. The book includes two articles by teachers on teaching in the block, a pacing guide for *Creating America*, and specific teaching strategies for taking advantage of the longer class periods in block schedules

### Team Teaching: Connecting History and Literature

If you are teaching in a block with a literature and language arts teacher, this resource will be useful. It includes ideas and activities for integrating literature from McDougal Littell's *Literature Connections, The Language of Literature,* and *Literature and Language* into history lessons.

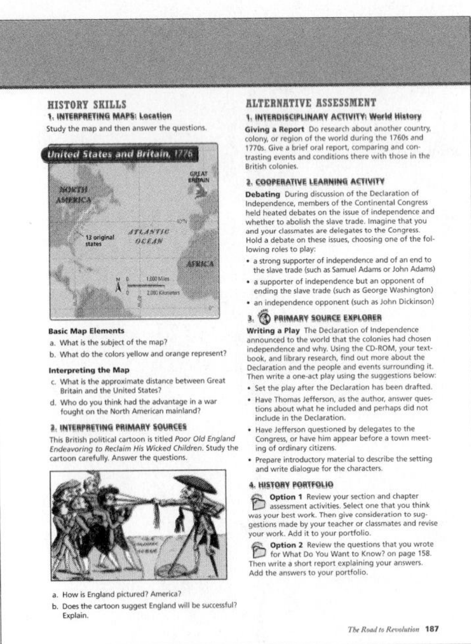

HISTORY SKILLS

1. INTERPRETING MAPS: Location

Study the map and then answer the questions.



**Basic Map Elements**

a. What is the subject of the map?
b. What do the colors yellow and orange represent?

**Interpreting the Map**

c. What is the approximate distance between Great Britain and the United States?
d. Who do you think had the advantage in a war fought on the North American mainland?

2. INTERPRETING PRIMARY SOURCES

This British political cartoon is titled *Poor Old England Endeavoring to Reclaim His Wicked Children*. Study the cartoon carefully. Answer the questions.

a. How is England pictured? America?
b. Does the cartoon suggest England will be successful? Explain.

ALTERNATIVE ASSESSMENT

1. INTERDISCIPLINARY ACTIVITY: World History

**Giving a Report** Do research about another country, colony, or region of the world during the 1760s and 1770s. Give a brief oral report, comparing and contrasting events and conditions there with those in the British colonies.

2. COOPERATIVE LEARNING ACTIVITY

**Debating** During discussion of the Declaration of Independence, members of the Continental Congress held heated debates on the issue of independence and whether to abolish the slave trade. Imagine that you and your classmates are delegates to the Congress. Hold a debate on these issues, choosing one of the following roles to play:

- a strong supporter of independence and of an end to the slave trade (such as Samuel Adams or John Adams)
- a supporter of independence but an opponent of ending the slave trade (such as George Washington)
- an independence opponent (such as John Dickinson)

3. PRIMARY SOURCE EXPLORER

**Writing a Play** The Declaration of Independence announced to the world that the colonies had chosen independence and why. Using the CD-ROM, your textbook, and library research, find out more about the Declaration and the people and events surrounding it. Then write a one-act play using the suggestions below:

- Set the play after the Declaration has been drafted.
- Have Thomas Jefferson, as the author, answer questions about what he included and perhaps did not include in the Declaration.
- Have Jefferson questioned by delegates to the Congress, or have him appear before a town meeting of ordinary citizens.
- Prepare introductory material to describe the setting and write dialogue for the characters.

4. HISTORY PORTFOLIO

**Option 1** Review your section and chapter assessment activities. Select one that you think was your best work. Then give consideration to suggestions made by your teacher or classmates and revise your work. Add it to your portfolio.

**Option 2** Review the questions that you wrote for What Do You Want to Know? on page 158. Then write a short report explaining your answers. Add the answers to your portfolio.

*The Road to Revolution* **187**

### Pupil's Edition

- Each chapter begins with an **Interact with History** feature, which can be used as a cooperative activity.
- Each **Section Assessment** includes **Activity Options,** which provide opportunities for cooperative learning.
- **Chapter Assessments** include a variety of chapter activities, including a Cooperative Learning Activity.
- **Interdisciplinary Challenges** and **History Workshops** provide opportunities for students to solve problems and do hands-on projects in cooperative learning groups.

### Teacher's Edition

- **The Pacing Guide** at the beginning of every chapter provides suggestions for planning instruction and activities for block schedules.
- **Technology Resources** in the Planning Guide at the beginning of every chapter list many resources that are useful for cooperative activities.
- **Activity Options** that are suitable for block schedules are clearly labeled and described throughout the Teacher's Edition. The time of each activity is included.

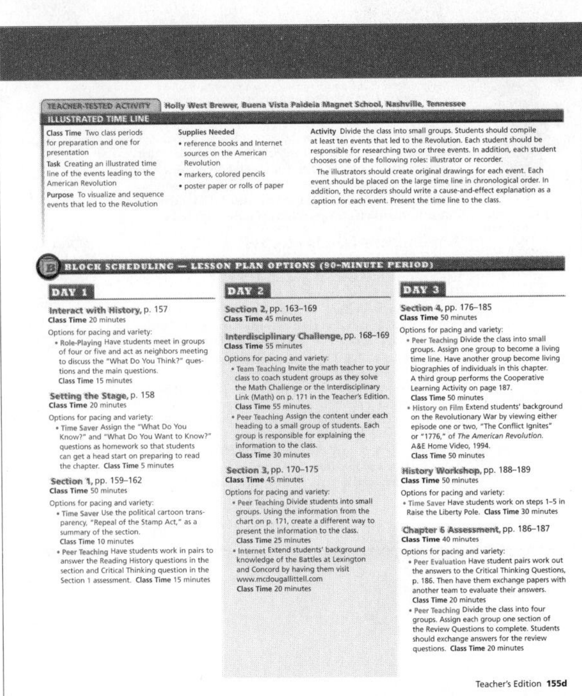

TEACHER-TESTED ACTIVITY Holly West Brewer, Buena Vista Paideia Magnet School, Nashville, Tennessee

ILLUSTRATED TIME LINE

**Class Time** Two class periods for preparation and one for presentation

**Task** Creating an illustrated time line of the events leading to the American Revolution

**Purpose** To visualize and sequence events that led to the Revolution

**Supplies Needed**

- reference books and Internet sources on the American Revolution
- markers, colored pencils
- poster paper or rolls of paper

**Activity** Divide the class into small groups. Students should compile at least ten events that led to the Revolution. Each student should be responsible for researching two or three events. In addition, each student chooses one of the following roles: illustrator or recorder.

The illustrators should create original drawings for each event. Each event should be placed on the large time line in chronological order. In addition, the recorders should write a cause-and-effect explanation as a caption for each event. Present the time line to the class.

BLOCK SCHEDULING — LESSON PLAN OPTIONS (90-MINUTE PERIOD)

DAY 1

**Interact with History,** p. 157
**Class Time** 20 minutes

Options for pacing and variety:

- Role-Playing Have students meet in groups of four or five and act as neighbors meeting to discuss the "What Do You Think?" questions and the main questions. **Class Time** 15 minutes

**Setting the Stage,** p. 158
**Class Time** 20 minutes

Options for pacing and variety:

- Time Saver Assign the "What Do You Know?" and "What Do You Want to Know?" questions as homework so that students can get a head start on preparing to read the chapter. **Class Time** 5 minutes

**Section 1,** pp. 159–162
**Class Time** 50 minutes

Options for pacing and variety:

- Time Saver Use the political cartoon transparency, "Repeal of the Stamp Act," as a summary of the section. **Class Time** 10 minutes
- Peer Teaching Have students work in pairs to answer the Reading History questions in the section and Critical Thinking question in the Section 1 assessment. **Class Time** 15 minutes

DAY 2

**Section 2,** pp. 163–169
**Class Time** 45 minutes

**Interdisciplinary Challenge,** pp. 168–169
**Class Time** 55 minutes

Options for pacing and variety:

- Team Teaching Invite the math teacher to your class to coach student groups as they solve the Math Challenge or the Interdisciplinary Link (Math) on p. 171 in the Teacher's Edition. **Class Time** 55 minutes.
- Peer Teaching Assign the content under each heading to a small group of students. Each group is responsible for explaining the information to the class. **Class Time** 30 minutes

**Section 3,** pp. 170–175
**Class Time** 45 minutes

Options for pacing and variety:

- Peer Teaching Divide students into small groups. Using the information from the chart on p. 171, create a different way to present the information to the class. **Class Time** 25 minutes
- Internet Extend students' background knowledge of the Battles at Lexington and Concord by having them visit www.mcdougallittell.com **Class Time** 20 minutes

DAY 3

**Section 4,** pp. 176–185
**Class Time** 50 minutes

Options for pacing and variety:

- Peer Teaching Divide the class into small groups. Assign one group to become a living time line. Have another group become living biographies of individuals in this chapter. A third group performs the Cooperative Learning Activity on page 187. **Class Time** 50 minutes
- History on Film Extend students' background on the Revolutionary War by viewing either episode one or two, "The Conflict Ignites" or "1776," of *The American Revolution.* A&E Home Video, 1994. **Class Time** 50 minutes

**History Workshop,** pp. 188–189
**Class Time** 50 minutes

Options for pacing and variety:

- Time Saver Have students work on steps 1–5 in Raise the Liberty Pole. **Class Time** 30 minutes

**Chapter 6 Assessment,** pp. 186–187
**Class Time** 40 minutes

Options for pacing and variety:

- Peer Evaluation Have student pairs work out the answers to the Critical Thinking Questions, p. 186. Then have them exchange papers with another team to evaluate their answers. **Class Time** 20 minutes
- Peer Teaching Divide the class into four groups. Assign each group one section of the Review Questions to complete. Students should exchange answers for the review questions. **Class Time** 20 minutes

Teacher's Edition **155d**

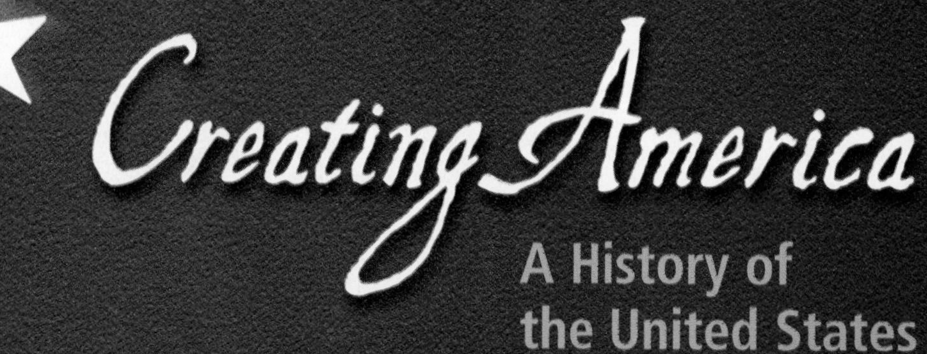


McDOUGAL LITTELL

**Zitkala-Ša**
Native American author

**Benjamin Franklin**
Author, printer, scientist, diplomat

**Abigail Adams**
Supporter of women's rights; married to President John Adams

**Maya Lin**
Designer of the Vietnam Veterans Memorial

**Juan Seguín**
A hero of the Texas Revolution

**Amelia Earhart**
Aviator; first woman to fly solo across the Atlantic Ocean

**Ida B. Wells**
Journalist and reformer who fought against discrimination

**Abraham Lincoln**
Sixteenth president of the United States

**Dr. Martin Luther King, Jr.**
Civil rights leader

**Harry S. Truman**
Thirty-third president of the United States

# Creating America

## A History of the United States

Jesus Garcia

Donna M. Ogle

C. Frederick Risinger

Joyce Stevos

Winthrop D. Jordan

McDougal Littell

Evanston, Illinois • Boston • Dallas

# Senior Consultants

**Jesus Garcia** is Professor of Curriculum and Instruction at the University of Kentucky. A former elementary and secondary social studies teacher, Dr. Garcia has co-authored many books and articles on subjects that range from teaching social studies in elementary school to seeking diversity in education. Dr. Garcia has also worked for both the Chicago and Washington, D.C., public schools as a consultant on social studies standards.

**Donna M. Ogle** is Professor of Reading and Language Arts at National-Louis University in Evanston, Illinois, and is a specialist in reading in the content areas with an interest in social studies. She was recently elected president of the International Reading Association. A former social studies teacher, Dr. Ogle is also Director of a Goals 2000 grant for four Chicago high schools. She developed the K-W-L strategy that is so widely used in schools.

**C. Frederick Risinger** is Associate Director of the Social Studies Development Center at Indiana University. He is a past president of the National Council for the Social Studies. Dr. Risinger also served on the coordinating committee for the National History Standards Project. Dr. Risinger writes a monthly column on technology in the social studies classroom for *Social Education.*

**Joyce Stevos** is the Director of Strategic Planning and Professional Development for the Providence, Rhode Island, Public Schools. She is also an adjunct faculty member at Rhode Island College. Previously, she served 15 years as the social studies area supervisor in Providence, in which position she developed programs on Holocaust studies, the Armenian genocide, character education, voter education, and government and law.

**Winthrop D. Jordan** is the William F. Winter Professor of History and Professor of Afro-American Studies at the University of Mississippi, where he has taught since 1982. Since 1998, he has been the Frederick A. P. Barnard Distinguished Professor at that university. Dr. Jordan holds a Ph.D. from Brown University. He is the author of several books, including the highly acclaimed *White Over Black.* The book won four national awards, one of which was the National Book Award.



Acknowledgments begin on page R97.

ISBN 0-395-92899-0

Printed in the United States of America
1 2 3 4 5 6 7 8 9 – DWO – 06 05 04 03 02 01 00


iv

# Consultants and Reviewers

## Content Consultants

The content consultants reviewed the manuscript for historical depth and accuracy and for clarity of presentation.

**Roger Beck**
Department of History
Eastern Illinois University
Charleston, Illinois

**David Farber**
Department of History
University of New Mexico
Albuquerque, New Mexico

**Cheryl Johnson-Odim**
Department of History
Loyola University
Chicago, Illinois

**Joseph Kett**
Department of History
University of Virginia
Charlottesville, Virginia

**Jack N. Rakove**
Department of History
Stanford University
Stanford, California

**Virginia Stewart**
Department of History
University of North Carolina, Wilmington
Wilmington, North Carolina

**Christopher Waldrep**
Department of History
Eastern Illinois University
Charleston, Illinois

**Nancy Woloch**
Department of History
Barnard College
New York, New York

## Multicultural Advisory Board

The multicultural advisors reviewed the manuscript for appropriate historical content.

**Betty Dean**
Social Studies Consultant
Pearland, Texas

**Tyrone C. Howard**
College of Education
The Ohio State University
Columbus, Ohio

**Jose C. Moya**
Department of History
University of California at Los Angeles
Los Angeles, California

**Pat Payne**
Office of Multicultural Education
Indianapolis Public Schools
Indianapolis, Indiana

**Betto Ramirez**
Former Teacher, La Joya, Texas
Social Studies Consultant
Mission, Texas

**Jon Reyhner**
Department of Education
Northern Arizona University
Flagstaff, Arizona

**Ronald Young**
Department of History
Georgia Southern University
Statesboro, Georgia



v

# Consultants and Reviewers

## Teacher Consultants

The following educators contributed activity options for the Pupil's Edition and teaching ideas and activities for the Teacher's Edition.

**Paul C. Beavers**
J. T. Moore Middle School
Nashville, Tennessee

**Holly West Brewer**
Buena Vista Paideia Magnet School
Nashville, Tennessee

**Ron Campana**
Social Studies Consultant
New York, New York

**Patricia B. Carlson**
Swanson Middle School
Arlington, Virginia

**Ann Cotton**
Ft. Worth Independent School District
Ft. Worth, Texas

**Kelly Ellis**
Hamilton Junior High School
Cypress, Texas

**James Grimes**
Middlesex County Vocational–Technical High School
Woodbridge, New Jersey

**Brent Heath**
De Anza Middle School
Ontario, California

**Suzanne Hidalgo**
Serrano Middle School
Highland, California

**Barbara Kennedy**
Sylvan Middle School
Citrus Heights, California

**Pamela Kniffin**
Navasota Junior High School
Navasoto, Texas

**Tammy Leiber**
Navasota Junior High School
Navasoto, Texas

**Lori Lesslie**
Cedar Bluff Middle School
Knoxville, Tennessee

**Brian McKenzie**
Dr. Charles R. Drew Science Magnet School
Buffalo, New York

**W. W. Bear Mills**
Goddard Junior High School
Midland, Texas

**Lindy Poling**
Millbrook High School
Raleigh, North Carolina

**Jean Price**
T. H. Rogers Middle School
Houston, Texas

**Meg Robbins**
Wilbraham Middle School
Wilbraham, Massachusetts

**Philip Rodriguez**
McNair Middle School
San Antonio, Texas

**Leslie Schubert**
Parkland School
McHenry, Illinois

**Robert Sisko**
Carteret Middle School
Carteret, New Jersey

**Marci Smith**
Hurst-Euless-Bedford Independent School District
Bedford, Texas

**James Sorenson**
Chippewa Middle School
Des Plaines, Illinois

**Nicholas G. Sysock**
Carteret Middle School
Carteret, New Jersey

**Lisa Williams**
Lamberton Middle School
Carlisle, Pennsylvania

**Michael Yell**
Hudson Middle School
Hudson, Wisconsin


vi

## Teacher Panels

The following educators provided ongoing review during the development of prototypes, the table of contents, and key components of the program.

**Bill Albright**
Wilson Southern Junior High School
Sinking Spring, Pennsylvania

**Henry Assetto**
Gordon Middle School
Coatesville, Pennsylvania

**James Berry**
Kennedy Middle School
Grand Prairie, Texas

**Ralph Burnley**
Roosevelt Middle School
Philadelphia, Pennsylvania

**Mary Ann Canamar**
Garner Middle School
San Antonio, Texas

**Zoe Carter**
San Jacinto Junior High School
Midland, Texas

**Stephen Cicero**
Butler Area Junior High School
Butler, Pennsylvania

**Charles Crescenzi**
Dover Intermediate School
Dover, Pennsylvania

**Sharon McDonald**
Cook Junior High School
Houston, Texas

**Phil Mifsud**
Roosevelt Middle School
Erie, Pennsylvania

**Joel Mumma**
Centerville Middle School
Lancaster, Pennsylvania

**September Olson**
Richardson Middle School
El Paso, Texas

**Donald Roberts**
Frick International Studies Academy
Pittsburgh, Pennsylvania

**Mary Rogers**
Brookside Intermediate School
Friendswood, Texas

**Lucy Sanchez**
John F. Kennedy High School
San Antonio, Texas

**Steve Seale**
Hamilton Middle School
Houston, Texas

**Yolanda Villalobos**
Dallas Independent School District
Dallas, Texas

**Diane Williams**
Hill-Freedman Middle School
Philadelphia, Pennsylvania

**Lisa Williams**
Lamberton Middle School
Carlisle, Pennsylvania

## Student Board

The following students reviewed pages for the textbook.

**Adam Backhaus**
Parkland School
McHenry, Illinois

**Ben Barney**
Hamilton Junior High School
Cypress, Texas

**Amanda Berrier**
Lamberton Middle School
Carlisle, Pennsylvania

**Debra Hurwitz**
T. H. Rogers Middle School
Houston, Texas

**Reginald Jones**
Dr. Charles R. Drew Science Magnet School
Buffalo, New York

**Brendon Keinath**
Wilbraham Middle School
Wilbraham, Massachusetts

**Daniel MacDonald**
Carteret Middle School
Carteret, New Jersey

**Cameron Mote**
Serrano Middle School
Highland, California

**Kim Nguyen**
Sylvan Middle School
Citrus Heights, California

**Arianna G. Noriega**
De Anza Middle School
Ontario, California

**Nicholas Tofilon**
Burlington Middle School
Burlington, Wisconsin

**Emmanuel Zepeda**
Haven Middle School
Evanston, Illinois



vii

# UNIT 1 Three Worlds Meet BEGINNINGS TO 1763

viii

Pontiac

ix

# UNIT 2 Creating a New Nation 1763 – 1791



George Washington

# The Early Republic 1789 – 1844

UNIT 3

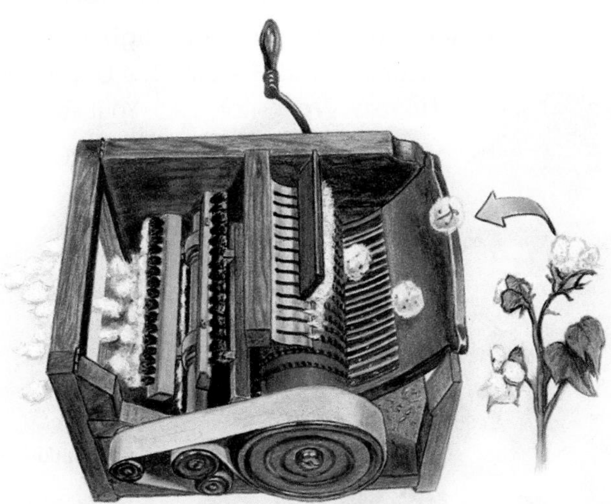



xi

# UNIT 4 A Changing Nation 1810 – 1860



California gold miner

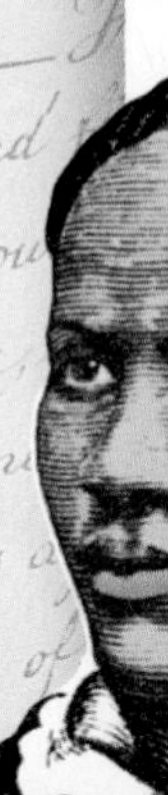

Frances Ellen Watkins Harper


xii

# The Nation Divided and Rebuilt 1846 – 1877

UNIT 5



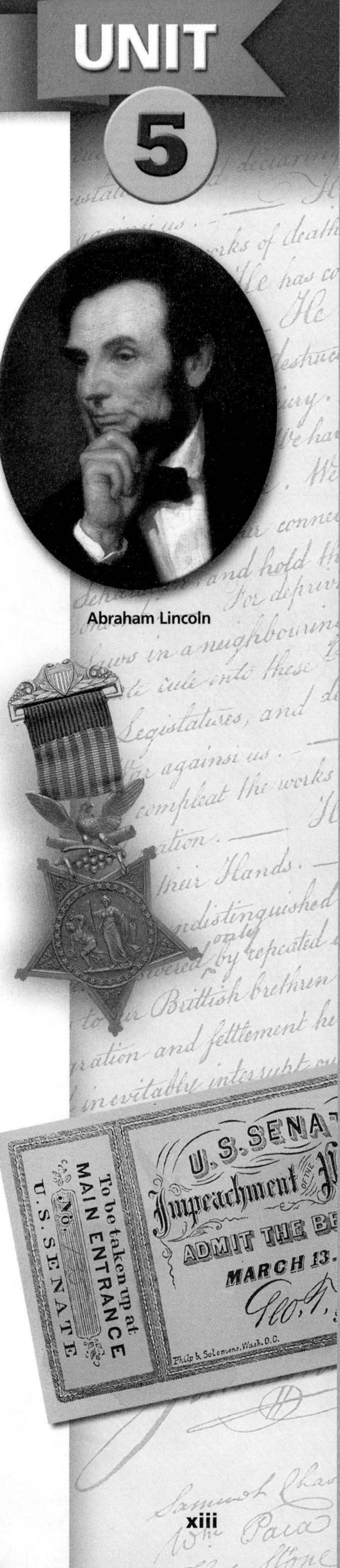


Abraham Lincoln


xiii

# UNIT 6 America Transformed 1860 – 1914

Immigrants approaching Ellis Island


xiv

# Modern America Emerges 1880 – 1920

UNIT 7

Queen Liliuokalani

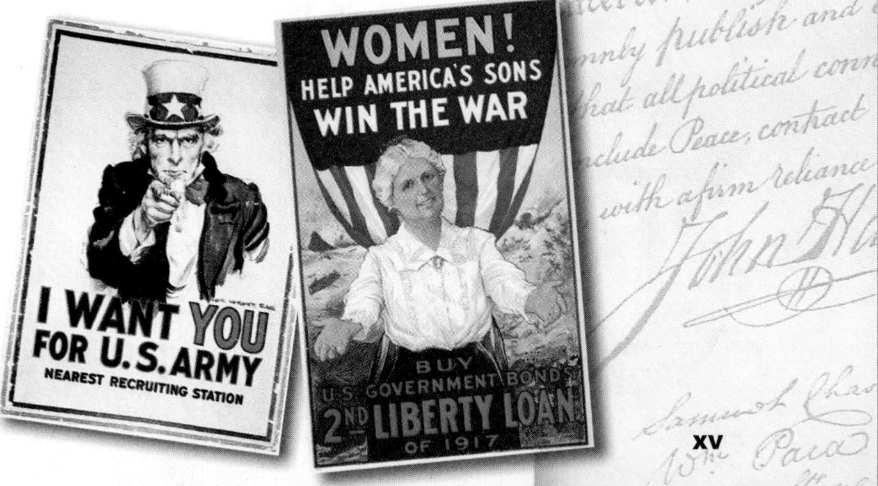

UNIT 8

# Depression, War, and Recovery 1919 – 1960

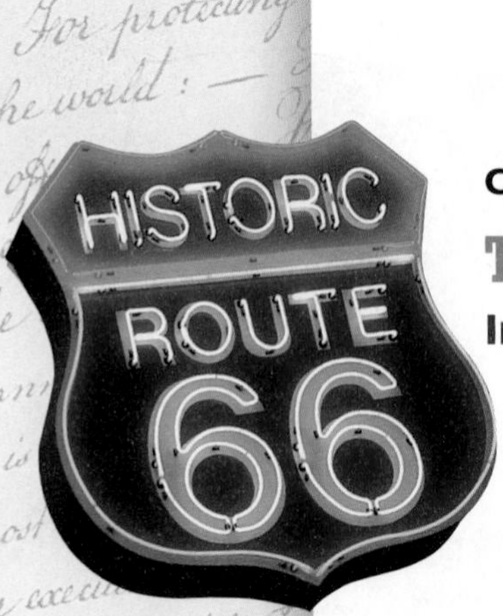

xvi

# Tensions at Home and Abroad 1954 – PRESENT

UNIT 9



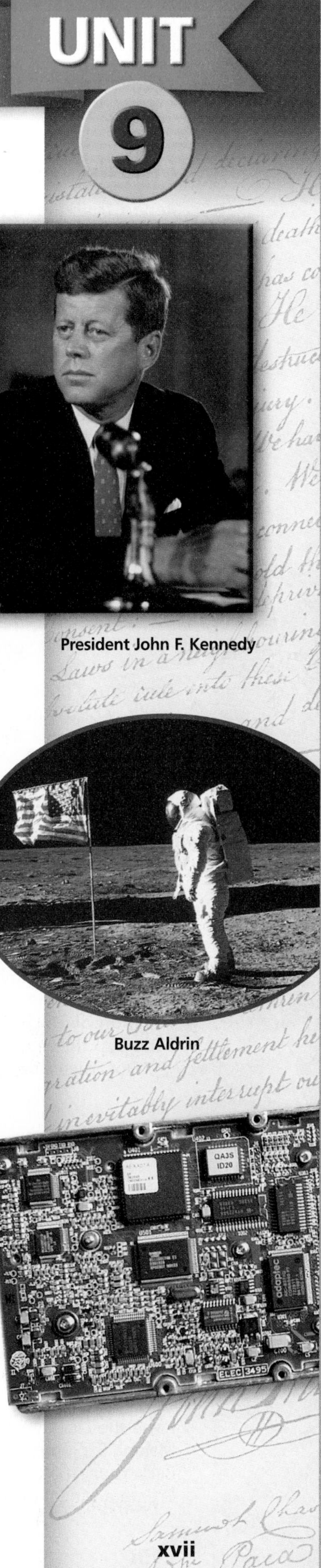

President John F. Kennedy

Buzz Aldrin



xvii

# Features

## *Interdisciplinary* CHALLENGE



## GEOGRAPHY *in* HISTORY



## Technology *OF THE* Time



## INTERACTIVE PRIMARY SOURCES



## Literature *Connections*



## *HISTORY* WORKSHOP




xviii

## CITIZENSHIP TODAY



## Economics in History



## America's HERITAGE



## AMERICA'S HISTORY MAKERS



## daily life





xix

# Features

## HISTORY *through* ART



## Now *and* then



## Connections TO



## STRANGE *but* True

# Voices from the Past



*A VOICE FROM THE PAST*

These, with the pictures, busts [sculptures of the head and shoulders], and prints (of which copies upon copies are spread everywhere), have made your father's face as well known as that of the moon.

**Benjamin Franklin,**
letter to his daughter Sally





xxi

# Voices from the Past



*A VOICE FROM THE PAST*

Eliza made her desperate retreat across the river just in the dusk of twilight. The gray mist of evening, rising slowly from the river, enveloped her as she disappeared up the bank, and the swollen current and floundering masses of ice presented a hopeless barrier between her and her pursuer.

**Harriet Beecher Stowe,**
*Uncle Tom's Cabin*





xxii

*A VOICE FROM THE PAST*

Is it possible . . . that nine millions of men can make effective progress in economic lines if they are deprived of political rights? . . . If history and reason give any distinct answer to these questions, it is an emphatic *No.*

**W. E. B. Du Bois,**
*The Souls of Black Folk*

xxiii

# Voices from the Past



# Visual Primary Sources for Assessment





xxiv

# Historical Maps





xxv

# Charts and Graphs

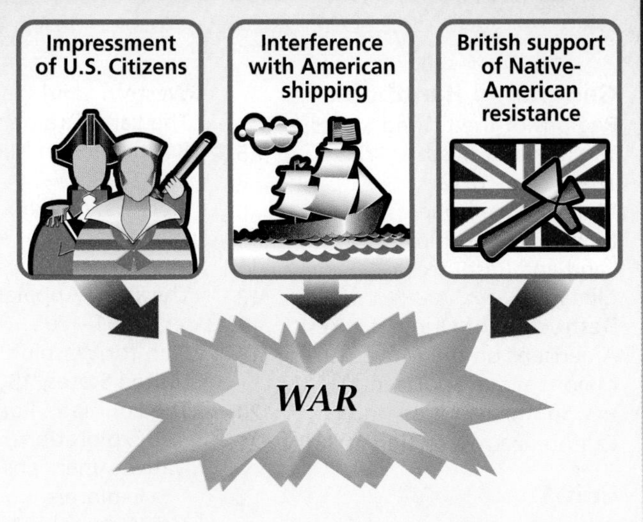
Causes of the War of 1812
Impressment of U.S. Citizens
Interference with American shipping
British support of Native-American resistance
WAR

## Charts

## Graphs

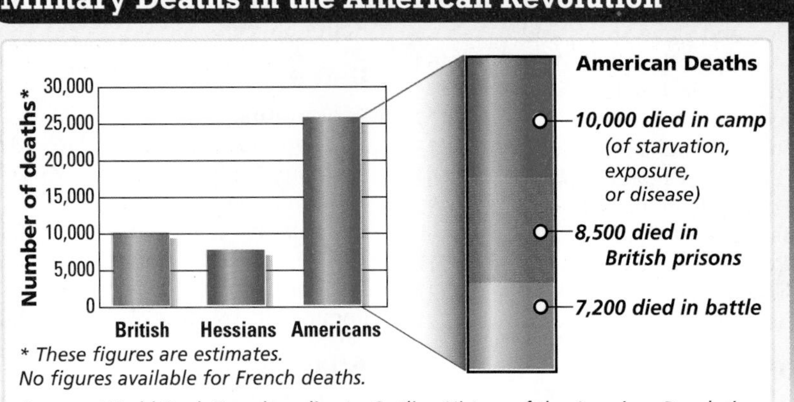
CONNECTIONS TO MATH
Military Deaths in the American Revolution
Number of deaths*
30,000
25,000
20,000
15,000
10,000
5,000
0
British
Hessians
Americans
American Deaths
10,000 died in camp (of starvation, exposure, or disease)
8,500 died in British prisons
7,200 died in battle
* These figures are estimates.
No figures available for French deaths.
Sources: World Book Encyclopedia; An Outline History of the American Revolution

# Time Lines and Infographics

## Time Lines



## Infographics



### The Rise and Decline of Feudalism

In feudalism, nobles offered to protect peasants from invaders. In return, the peasants farmed the nobles' lands.

Feudalism made people feel safe enough to travel. Trade increased and towns grew.

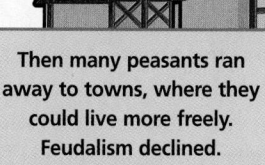

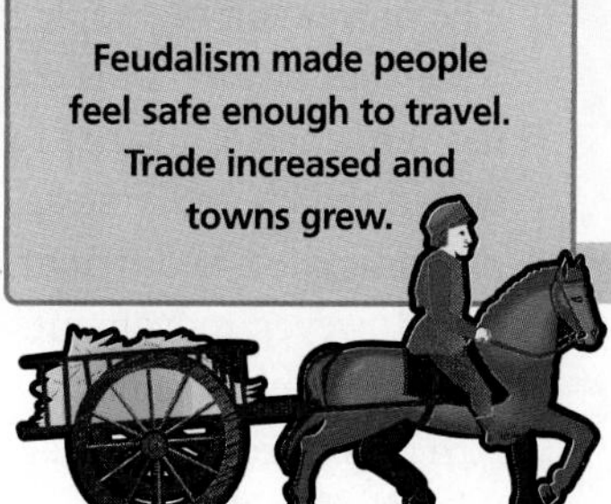

Then many peasants ran away to towns, where they could live more freely. Feudalism declined. Trade continued to grow.



xxvii

# THEMES of AMERICAN HISTORY

Imagine life in Jamestown, America's first permanent English settlement. The nation we inhabit now is a much different place than it was then, more than three centuries ago. Yet there are repeating themes—ideas and issues—in American history that tie the past and present together. This book focuses on nine significant themes in U.S. history. Understanding these themes will help you to make sense of American history.

## Democratic Ideals

From the day they declared themselves citizens of a new nation, Americans have built their society around the principles of democracy. In a democracy, power lies with the people, and every individual enjoys basic rights that cannot be taken away. Throughout the nation's history, however, some Americans—mainly women and minorities—have had to struggle to gain their full rights. Still, the ideals of democracy remain the guiding principles of this land.

***What right or freedom do you consider the most important? Why?***

## Citizenship

The citizens of the United States enjoy rights and freedoms found in very few other places in the world. Yet Americans know that with such freedoms come responsibilities and duties. Whether they stand in line to vote or spend a weekend to clean up a local river, Americans recognize that citizen participation is what keeps a democracy strong.

***How do citizens that you know contribute to your community?***

Dr. Martin Luther King, Jr.

## Impact of the Individual

The history of the United States is the story not only of governments and laws but of individuals. Indeed, individuals have made the United States what it is today through their extraordinary achievements. American history provides a variety of examples of the impact of the individual on society in both the United States and the world.

***Name several individuals who have an impact on American society today. What impact do they have?***

## Diversity and Unity

The United States has been a land of many peoples, cultures, and faiths. Throughout the nation's history, this blend of ethnic, racial, and religious groups has helped to create a rich and uniquely American culture. The nation's many different peoples are united in their belief in American values and ideals.

***What things do you enjoy that came to the United States from other cultures?***

## Immigration and Migration

The movement of people has played a vital role in American history. This country was settled by and has remained a magnet for immigrants. Even within the United States, large numbers of people have migrated to different regions of the country. However, movements to and within the United States have not always been voluntary. Africans were brought against their will to this country. Native Americans were forced from their homelands in order to make room for European settlers.

***Why do you think people continue to immigrate to the United States?***

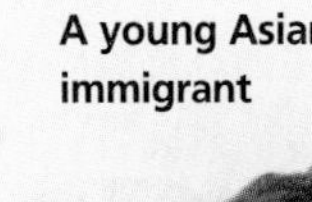

A young Asian immigrant



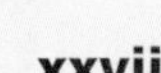

xxviii

## Expansion

When the United States declared its independence from Great Britain, it was only a collection of states along the Atlantic Ocean. But the new country would not remain that way for long. Many Americans shared a sense of curiosity, adventure, and a strong belief that their destiny was to expand all the way to the Pacific Ocean. Driven by this belief, they pushed westward. Americans' efforts to increase the size of their nation is a recurring theme in early U.S. history.

***Where do you predict that the exploration of space—the final frontier—will lead?***

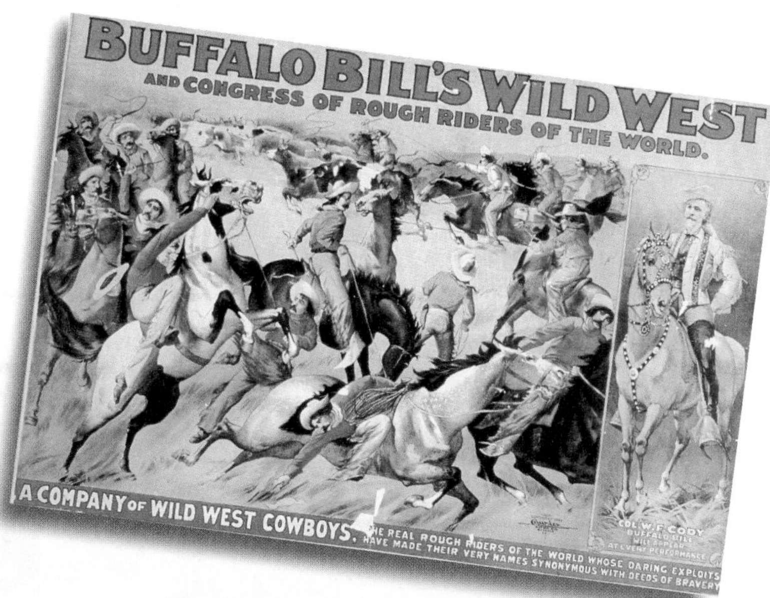


Poster for Buffalo Bill's Wild West show

## America and the World

As the power and prestige of the United States have grown, the nation has played a much more active role in world affairs. Indeed, throughout the 20th century, the United States focused much of its energy on events beyond its borders. The nation fought in two world wars and tried to promote democracy, peace, and economic growth around the globe. As one of the world's political and economic leaders, the United States will continue to be a key player in world affairs throughout the new century.

***What do you think the role of the United States in the world should be today?***

## Science and Technology

Americans have always been quick to embrace inventions and new ways of doing things. After all, this country was settled by people who turned away from old ways and tried new ones. In the past two centuries, new inventions, new technologies, and scientific breakthroughs have transformed the United States—and will continue to do so in the new century.

***What recent inventions or innovations affect your life?***

## Economics in History

Economics has had a powerful impact on the course of U.S. history. For example, the desire for wealth led thousands to join the California Gold Rush in 1849. The nation as a whole has grown wealthy, thanks to its abundant resources and the hard work of its citizens. An important economic issue, however, has been how to make sure that all people have opportunities to share fully in the nation's wealth. This issue will continue to be important in the 21st century.

***What do you think are the most exciting economic opportunities for Americans today?***

Thomas Edison's first light bulb



xxix

# READING to REMEMBER

Reading is a little like playing a sport; you'll improve if you practice and if you learn the right techniques. This book is designed to help you read better and to remember more of what you read. That, in turn, will help you to learn history.

Think about what it's like learning to play a sport, such as basketball. There are certain steps you can follow. You can use those same steps in reading to remember.

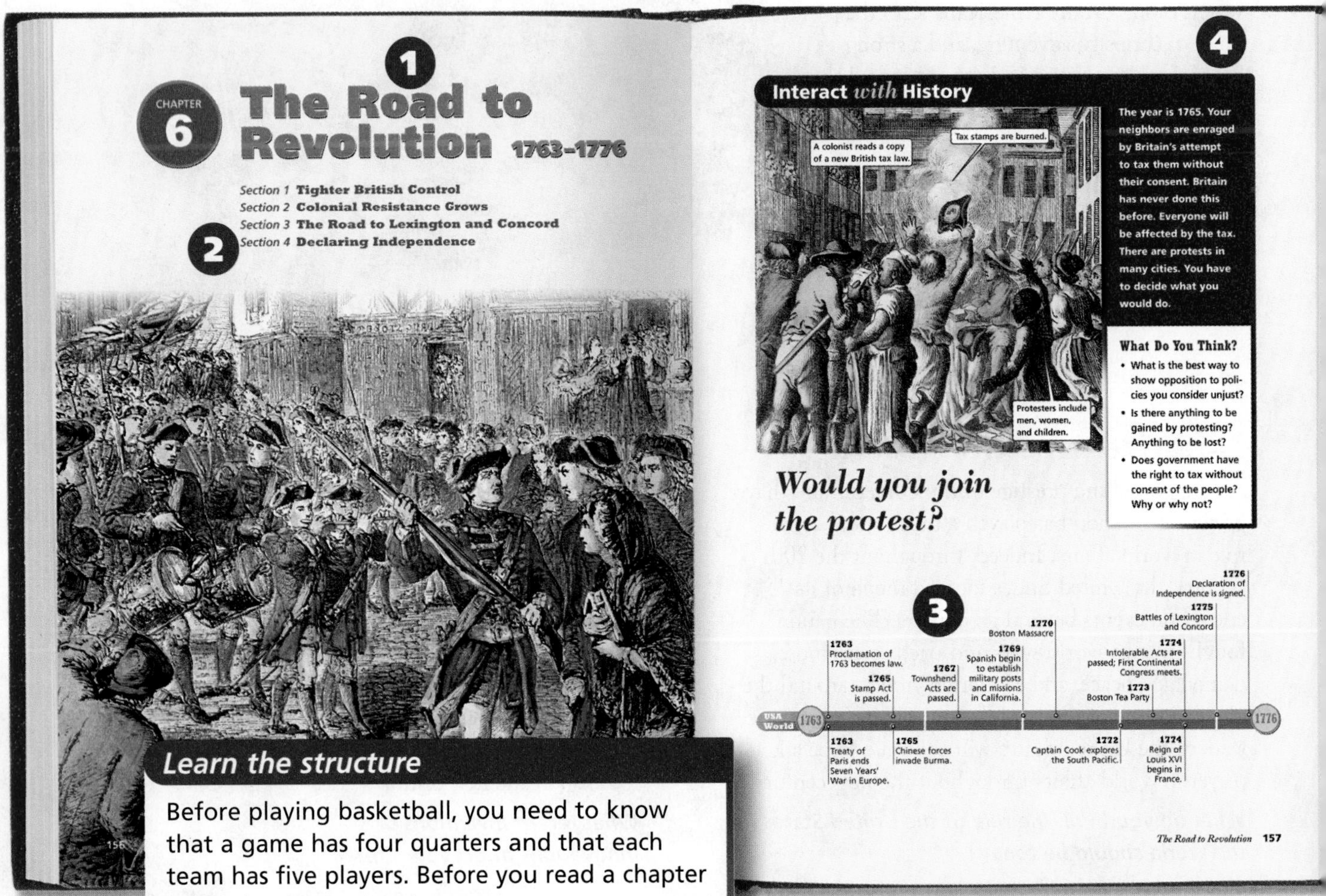

1

CHAPTER 6 **The Road to Revolution** 1763–1776

*Section 1* **Tighter British Control**
*Section 2* **Colonial Resistance Grows**
*Section 3* **The Road to Lexington and Concord**
2 *Section 4* **Declaring Independence**

156

4

**Interact *with* History**

A colonist reads a copy of a new British tax law.
Tax stamps are burned.
Protesters include men, women, and children.

The year is 1765. Your neighbors are enraged by Britain's attempt to tax them without their consent. Britain has never done this before. Everyone will be affected by the tax. There are protests in many cities. You have to decide what you would do.

**What Do You Think?**

- What is the best way to show opposition to policies you consider unjust?
- Is there anything to be gained by protesting? Anything to be lost?
- Does government have the right to tax without consent of the people? Why or why not?

***Would you join the protest?***

3

USA
1763 Proclamation of 1763 becomes law.
1765 Stamp Act is passed.
1767 Townshend Acts are passed.
1769 Spanish begin to establish military posts and missions in California.
1770 Boston Massacre
1773 Boston Tea Party
1774 Intolerable Acts are passed; First Continental Congress meets.
1775 Battles of Lexington and Concord
1776 Declaration of Independence is signed.

World
1763 Treaty of Paris ends Seven Years' War in Europe.
1765 Chinese forces invade Burma.
1772 Captain Cook explores the South Pacific.
1774 Reign of Louis XVI begins in France.

*The Road to Revolution* 157

## *Learn the structure*

Before playing basketball, you need to know that a game has four quarters and that each team has five players. Before you read a chapter in this book, preview its structure.

1. See what clues are in the chapter's title.
2. Notice how many sections there are and the title of each one.
3. Look at the time line on the chapter opener. What years does the chapter cover? What happened during those years?

Scan the chapter and look at the pictures, maps, and graphs. They will give you a hint of what the chapter is about.

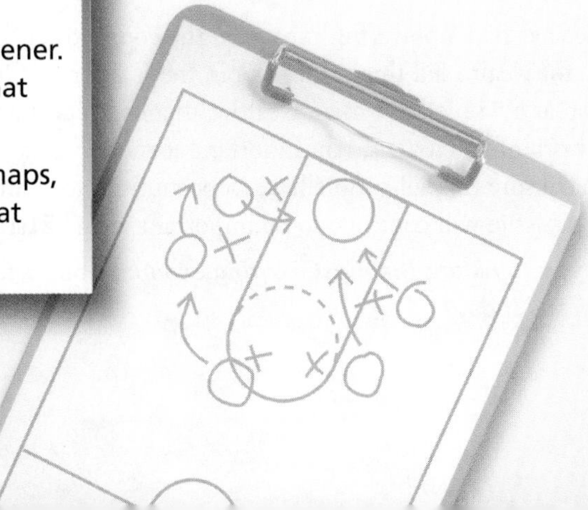

## Do warm-up exercises

Before a game, an athlete does stretching exercises and takes practice shots. This book also has warm-up exercises for each chapter.

4. Interact with History (at left) will help you imagine what it was like to live in the past. Look at the pictures and decide how you would respond to the question.

5. Setting the Stage (below) will help you start thinking about the chapter's theme and time period. It also teaches a reading skill and gives you a graphic organizer to help you take notes.

**Chapter 6 SETTING THE STAGE**

**BEFORE YOU READ**

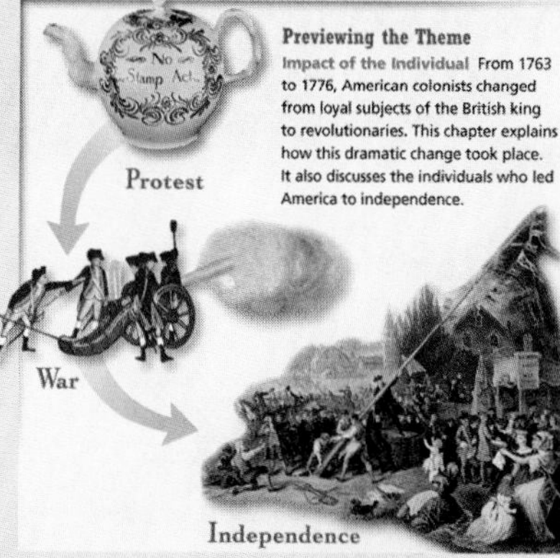


**Previewing the Theme**

Impact of the Individual From 1763 to 1776, American colonists changed from loyal subjects of the British king to revolutionaries. This chapter explains how this dramatic change took place. It also discusses the individuals who led America to independence.

**What Do You Know?**

What do you already know about the time before the Revolution? What were the issues that caused the colonists to choose independence?

THINK ABOUT

- what you have learned about this period from movies, television, or historical fiction
- reasons people in history have chosen to fight for freedom from oppression

**What Do You Want to Know?**

What questions do you have about the issues and events that pushed the American colonists toward rebellion? Record them in your notebook before you read the chapter.

**READ AND TAKE NOTES**

Reading Strategy: Sequencing Events

Sequencing means putting events in the order in which they happen in time. In learning about how the American colonies moved toward independence, it would be helpful to list the important events. Place them in the order in which they occurred. You might record the event and its date in a graphic organizer such as the one below. Copy this organizer in your notebook. Fill it in as you read the chapter.

See Skillbuilder Handbook, page R4.

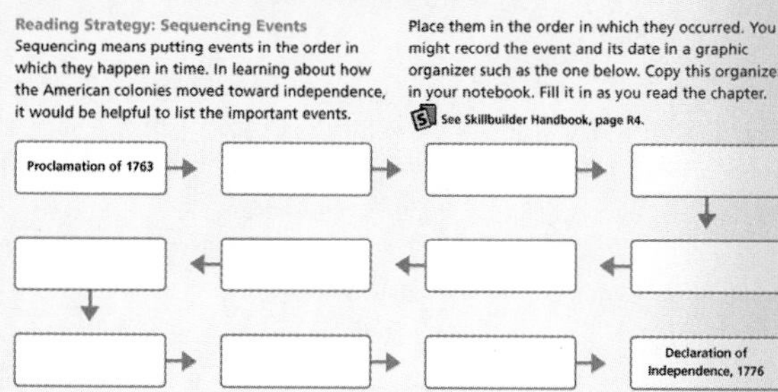


158 CHAPTER 6

# 1 Tighter British Control

**TERMS & NAMES**
King George III
Quartering Act
revenue
Sugar Act
Stamp Act
Patrick Henry
boycott
Sons of Liberty

| MAIN IDEA | WHY IT MATTERS NOW |
|---|---|
| Americans saw British efforts to tax them and to increase control over the colonies as violations of their rights. | Colonial protests were the first steps on the road to American independence. |

**ONE AMERICAN'S STORY**

James Otis, Jr., a young Massachusetts lawyer, stormed through the streets of Boston one day in 1760. He was furious. His father had just been denied the post of chief justice of the Massachusetts colony by the royal governor. To Otis, this was one more example of Britain's lack of respect for colonial rights. Another example was its use of search warrants that allowed customs officers to enter any home or business to look for smuggled goods. Otis believed these searches were illegal.

Otis took up a case against the government that involved these search warrants. In court in February 1761, Otis spoke with great emotion for five hours about the search warrant and its use.

A VOICE FROM THE PAST

It appears to me the worst instrument of arbitrary power, the most destructive of English liberty and the fundamental principles of law, that was ever found in an English law-book.

James Otis, Jr., quoted in *James Otis: The Pre-Revolutionist* by J. C. Ridpath

Spectators listened in amazement. One of them, a young lawyer named John Adams, later wrote of Otis's performance: "Then and there, in the old Council Chamber, the child Independence was born."

In making the first public speech demanding English liberties for the colonists, James Otis planted a seed of freedom. In this section, you will read more about the early protests against Britain's policies in America.

James Otis, Jr., argues in court against illegal search warrants in 1761.

### The Colonies and Britain Grow Apart

During the French and Indian War, Britain and the colonies fought side by side. Americans took great pride in being partners in the victory over the French. However, when the war ended, problems arose. Britain wanted to govern its 13 original colonies and the territories gained in the war in a uniform way. So the British Parliament in London imposed new laws and restrictions. Previously, the colonies had been allowed to develop largely on their own. Now they felt that their freedom was being limited.

*The Road to Revolution* 159



xxxi

# READING to REMEMBER

1

2

## 4 Declaring Independence

**TERMS & NAMES**
Ethan Allen
artillery
Second Continental Congress
Continental Army
Benedict Arnold
Declaration of Independence
Thomas Jefferson

**MAIN IDEA**
Fighting between American and British troops led the colonies to declare their independence.

**WHY IT MATTERS NOW**
The United States of America was founded at this time.

### ONE AMERICAN'S STORY

In May 1775—one month after the battle at Lexington and Concord—Abigail Adams wrote to her husband, John Adams. "The house is a Scene of Confusion," she said. Colonial militiamen were camped outside. Everyone was preparing for war. John Adams was away in Philadelphia at the time, meeting with other Patriot leaders at the Second Continental Congress.

Abigail and John Adams would spend most of the Revolutionary War apart. In his absence, she ran the household and farm in Braintree, Massachusetts, and raised their four children. During their separation, they exchanged many letters. Abigail was a very sharp observer of the political scene. In one letter, she shared her concerns about the future of the American government.

*A VOICE FROM THE PAST*

If we separate from Britain, what Code of Laws will be established? How shall we be governed so as to retain our Liberties? Can any government be free which is not administered by general stated Laws? Who shall frame these Laws? Who will give them force and energy?

**Abigail Adams**, quoted in *Abigail Adams: Witness to a Revolution* by Natalie S. Bober

Abigail Adams was an early advocate of women's rights and one of the great letter writers in history.

These questions would be answered later. First, a war had to be fought and won.

### The Continental Army Is Formed

After the fighting at Lexington and Concord, militiamen from Massachusetts and other colonies began gathering around Boston. Their numbers eventually reached some 20,000. General Gage decided to move his soldiers from the peninsula opposite Boston to the city itself. Boston was nearly surrounded by water. This fact, he thought, made a colonial attack by land almost impossible.

Not long after, on May 10, 1775, Americans attacked Britain's Fort Ticonderoga on the New York side of Lake Champlain. **Ethan Allen** led this band of backwoodsmen known as the Green Mountain Boys. They captured the fort and its large supply of **artillery**—cannon and large guns. These guns would be used later to drive the British from Boston.

Also on May 10, the **Second Continental Congress** began meeting in Philadelphia. Delegates included John and Samuel Adams, John Hancock, Benjamin Franklin, George Washington, and Patrick Henry. They agreed to form the **Continental Army**. Washington, who was from Virginia, was chosen as its commanding general. He had served as a colonial officer with the British during the French and Indian War. Congress also authorized the printing of paper money to pay the troops. It was beginning to act as a government.

3

### The Battle of Bunker Hill

**Background** The battle was called Bunker Hill because the original plan was to fight the battle there.

Meanwhile, tensions were building in Boston in June 1775. Militiamen seized Bunker Hill and Breed's Hill behind Charlestown. They built fortifications on Breed's Hill. Alarmed, the British decided to attack.

*"Don't fire until you see the whites of their eyes!"*
Colonel William Prescott

General William Howe crossed the bay with 2,200 British soldiers. Forming in ranks, they marched up Breed's Hill. On the hilltop, the militia waited. According to the legend, Colonel William Prescott ordered, "Don't fire until you see the whites of their eyes!" When the British got close, the militia unleashed murderous fire. The British fell back and then charged again. Finally, they forced the militia off the hill.

The redcoats had won the battle of Bunker Hill, but at tremendous cost. More than 1,000 were killed or wounded, compared with some 400 militia casualties. "The loss we have sustained is greater than we can bear," wrote General Gage. The inexperienced colonial militia had held its own against the world's most powerful army.

The bloody fighting between militiamen and British troops is shown in *The Death of General Warren at Bunker Hill* by John Trumbull (1786).

176 CHAPTER 6

177

## Start reading

Once the preparation is over, an athlete starts playing the game. After preparation, you'll be ready to read the chapter.

1. Read one section at a time. Each chapter is divided into sections that are only three to six pages long.
2. First, read the Terms & Names in the bar at the top of the first page. Also read the sentences labeled Main Idea and Why It Matters Now. They tell you what's important in the material you're about to read.
3. Notice how the section is divided into smaller chunks, each with a red headline. Read each headline and ask yourself what the section will be about.

Then read the section from beginning to end.

xxxii

## Get helpful tips

This book is designed to offer you help as you read. On the inside margin of every page are three types of help.

4 Reading History questions allow you to stop and make sure you understand what you just read. You can also use them to review for a test.

5 Background notes explain some of the history behind an event.

6 Vocabulary notes give the definition of words that you may not know.

The first of Parliament's laws was the Proclamation of 1763. (See Chapter 5.) It said that colonists could not settle west of the Appalachian Mountains. Britain wanted this land to remain in the hands of its Native American allies to prevent another revolt like Pontiac's Uprising.

The proclamation angered colonists who had hoped to move to the fertile Ohio Valley. Many of these colonists had no land of their own. It also upset colonists who had bought land as an investment. As a result, many ignored the law.

**ReadingHistory** A. Summarizing Who was upset by the Proclamation of 1763?

### British Troops and Taxes

**King George III**, the British monarch, wanted to enforce the proclamation and also keep peace with Britain's Native American allies. To do this, he decided to keep 10,000 soldiers in the colonies. In 1765, Parliament passed the **Quartering Act**. This was a cost-saving measure that required the colonies to quarter, or house, British soldiers and provide them with supplies. General Thomas Gage, commander of these forces, put most of the troops in New York.

Britain owed a large debt from the French and Indian War. Keeping troops in the colonies would raise that debt even higher. Britain needed more **revenue**, or income, to meet its expenses. So it attempted to have the colonies pay part of the war debt. It also wanted them to contribute toward the costs of frontier defense and colonial government.

**Background** Fought between 1754 and 1763, this war was part of a global conflict between Britain and France.

In the past, the king had asked the colonial assemblies to pass taxes to support military actions that took place in the colonies. This time, however, Parliament voted to tax the Americans directly.

In 1764, Parliament passed the **Sugar Act**. This law placed a tax on sugar, molasses, and other products shipped to the colonies. It also called for strict enforcement of the act and harsh punishment of smugglers.

Colonial merchants, who often traded in smuggled goods, reacted with anger.

Colonial leaders such as James Otis claimed that Parliament had no right to tax the colonies, since the colonists were not represented in Parliament. As Otis exclaimed, "Taxation without representation is tyranny!" British finance minister George Grenville disagreed. The colonists were subjects of Britain, he said, and enjoyed the protection of its laws. For that reason, they were subject to taxation.

**Vocabulary** tyranny: absolute power in the hands of a single ruler

The colonial view of the hated stamp tax is shown by the skull and crossbones on this emblem (above); a royal stamp is pictured at right.

### Britain Passes the Stamp Act

The Sugar Act was just the first in a series of acts that increased tension between the mother country and the colonies. In 1765, Parliament passed the **Stamp Act**. This law required all legal and commercial documents to carry an official stamp showing that a tax had been paid. All diplomas, contracts, and wills had to carry a stamp.

160

When the British moved, so did Revere and Dawes. They galloped over the countryside on their "midnight ride," spreading the news. In Lexington, they were joined by Dr. Samuel Prescott. When Revere and Dawes were stopped by a British patrol, Prescott broke away and carried the message to Concord.

7

### Lexington and Concord

At dawn on April 19, some 700 British troops reached Lexington. They found Captain John Parker and about 70 militiamen waiting. The British commander ordered the Americans to drop their muskets. They refused. No one knows who fired first, but within a few minutes eight militiamen lay dead. The British then marched to Concord, where they destroyed military supplies. A battle broke out at a bridge north of town, forcing the British to retrea

Nearly 4,000 Minutemen and militiamen arrive the area. They lined the road from Concord Lexington and peppered the retreating redcoats with musket fire. "It seemed as if men came down from the clouds," one soldier said. Only the arrival of 1,000 more troops saved the British from destruction as they scrambled back to Boston.

**Lexington and Concord** were the first battles of the Revolutionary War. As Ralph Waldo Emerson later wrote, colonial troops had fired the "shot heard 'round the world." Americans would now have to choose sides and back up their political opinions by force of arms. Those who supported the British were called **Loyalists**. Those who sided with the rebels were **Patriots**. The conflict between the two sides divided communities, families, and friends. The war was on!

**Background** British losses totaled 273 soldiers compared to 95 militiamen.

**ReadingHistory** C. Drawing Conclusions Why did Emerson call it the "shot heard 'round the world"?

Now

PATRIOTS
The "shot world" is in Massa Patriots' Day, the third Monday of Ap Concord and nearby towns. modern-day Minutemen like those below reenact the battle that began the Revolution on April 19, 1775. The Boston Marathon is also run on Patriots' Day.

8

9

**Section 3 Assessment**

**1. Terms & Names**
Identify:
- militia
- Minuteman
- Intolerable Acts
- First Continental Congress
- Paul Revere
- Lexington and Concord
- Loyalist
- Patriot

**2. Taking Notes**
Use a diagram like the one below to show events that led to the Revolutionary War.

Revolution

**3. Main Ideas**
a. Why did Britain pass the Intolerable Acts?
b. Who took part in the First Continental Congress?
c. What was the purpose of the "midnight ride"?

**4. Critical Thinking**
Supporting Opinions
Do you think the fighting between Britain and the colonies could have been avoided? Why or why not?
THINK ABOUT
- Britain's attitude toward the colonies
- colonial feelings about Britain

ACTIVITY OPTIONS
GEOGRAPHY
MATH
Research the Battles of Lexington and Concord. Draw a map of key events or create a chart showing statistics from the battles.

*The Road to Revolution* 173

## Review what you read

When you finish reading a section, review and remember what you read. Don't worry if you have to go back and read something a second time. You can also use the following tips to review.

7 Reread the red headlines. Do you remember what was discussed in the paragraphs that follow?

8 Look at the pictures, maps, and graphs. Do you understand how they relate to what you just read?

9 Complete all the parts of the Section Assessment. They will help you review the section.

# GEOGRAPHY HANDBOOK OBJECTIVE

**The student will examine the five themes of geography, explore how they aid geographic observation and analysis, and identify some ways in which the geography of the United States has affected its development.**

## GEOGRAPHY FROM VISUALS

**Interpreting the Photographs** Have students look at the photographs on pages 2 and 3. Point out that each provides information about both the physical and human geography of the region. Have student volunteers describe what each picture suggests about climate, soil, natural resources, terrain, or ways of making a living in these five regions. Ask students to find similarities in the interactions between people and their environment in the pictures. **Possible Response** In all pictures, people are using unique aspects of the environment to make a living.

**Extension** Have students consult an encyclopedia or a world almanac to find out how important each of the economic activities shown in the photographs is to the area in which it occurs.

## MORE ABOUT . . .

**Geography**

The term *geography* was coined more than 2,000 years ago in ancient Greece. It combines *geo,* meaning "earth," with *graphia,* meaning a "way of writing, drawing, or describing."



# The Landscape of America

The best place to begin your study of American history is with the geography of America. Geography is more than the study of the land and people. It also involves the relationship between people and their environment.

The United States is part of the North American continent. The United States ranks third in both total area and population in the world. It is filled with an incredible variety of physical features, natural resources, climatic conditions, and people. This handbook will help you to learn about these factors and to understand how they affected the development of the United States.

A combine harvests wheat in the Midwest.

A timber company collects logs in the Northwest.

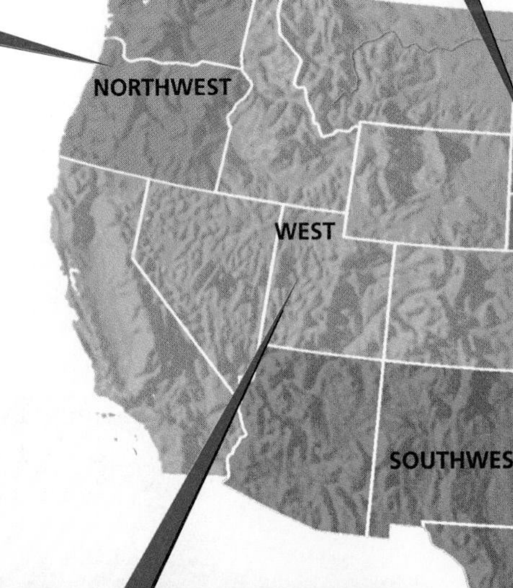


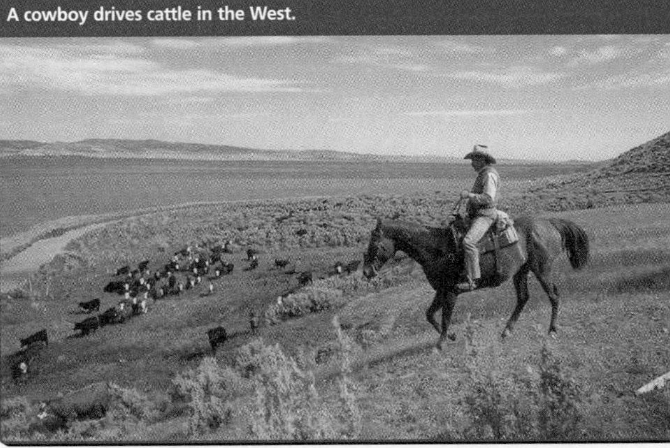

A cowboy drives cattle in the West.



## RECOMMENDED RESOURCES

**BOOKS FOR THE TEACHER**

Birdsall, Stephen. ***Regional Landscapes of the United States and Canada.*** New York: John Wiley & Sons, 1999. Looks at the land and people of Canada and the United States from a geographic perspective.

De Blij, Harm J. and Peter O. Muller. ***Geography: Realms, Regions, and Concepts.*** New York: John Wiley & Sons, 1999. Introduction to world geography by one of the nation's finest geographers.

Monmonier, Mark. ***How to Lie with Maps.*** Chicago: University of Chicago Press, 1996. Examines the use and abuse of maps.

**SOFTWARE**

***Inspirer Collection.*** CD-ROM. Tom Snyder, 1998. Five fast-paced map search games.

**VIDEO**

***Basics of Geography.*** United Learning, 1996. Discusses water, landforms, climate, and resources.

**INTERNET**

For more about the Geographic Learning Site, visit www.mcdougallittell.com

## TABLE OF CONTENTS



Fishers haul their catch toward shore in the Northeast.

NORTHEAST

WEST

SOUTHEAST

N

0 500 Miles

0 1,000 Kilometers

Oranges are big business in the Southeast.



## GEOGRAPHY HANDBOOK

### MORE ABOUT . . .

**Massachusetts Fisheries**

Fishing the offshore banks of the North Atlantic has been an important industry in the Northeast since colonial times. In the 1500s, European fishing crews crossed the Atlantic to catch cod, which could be salted and dried to keep for long periods without spoiling. Today, Massachusetts is a leading commercial fishing state. It supplies cod, ocean perch, flounder, haddock, whiting, and about half of the scallops in the United States. In the early 1990s, overfishing and poor management of cod stocks led to a sharp decline in Atlantic cod. The U.S. and Canadian governments restricted cod fishing to aid in species recovery.

### MORE ABOUT . . .

**Florida Citrus**

Citrus fruits such as oranges, grapefruits, lemons, and limes require a warm climate. They grow best in places with almost no frost or wind. Although citrus trees yield fruit in tropical regions, they produce better fruit in a slightly cooler climate. Much of Florida has a subtropical climate with many months of frost-free weather. Like Arizona, California, and Texas, it is well suited to citrus production. Approximately four out of every five oranges and grapefruits grown in the United States are produced in Florida.

### TEACHING STRATEGY

**Setting the Stage** Have students work in small groups to create a chart like the one here. In the first column, have students list the six regions shown on the map and discuss what they already know about the location, physical features, natural resources, climate, and people of each region. In the third column, have students list at least three questions they have about the people of each region and their environment. Have each group describe a photograph or draw a picture to illustrate the Southwest, and share both the chart and the picture suggestion with the class.

| Region | What I Already Know | What I Want to Know |
|---|---|---|
| | | |
| | | |
| | | |
| | | |

## FOCUS & MOTIVATE

### 5-MINUTE WARM-UP

**Finding Main Ideas** To help students identify the five major themes of geography and how they apply to Boston, Massachusetts, have them answer these questions.

1. Look at the illustrations on pages 4–5. How might Boston's location on the shores of the Atlantic Ocean have affected its economic development?
2. Judging by the illustrations, how would you answer the question, "What is Boston like?"

## INSTRUCT

**Themes of Geography**
Key Questions

- What is the difference between absolute and relative location?
- How might the physical characteristics of a place influence its human characteristics?
- How is technology changing the way ideas and goods move?

### MORE ABOUT . . .

**Place**
Human characteristics of place can also include patterns of livelihood, land use and ownership, town planning, and communication and transportation networks. In earlier times, Boston was known for its outspoken patriots, who helped make it a birthplace of the American Revolution. Later, Boston's writers, thinkers, and religious leaders turned the city into a center of culture and religious thought. Today, it is known for the academic excellence of its numerous colleges, its fine museums, symphony, and variety of cultural activities as well as for its respected medical centers and its scientific and technological resources.

# Themes of Geography

One useful way to think about geography is in terms of major themes or ideas. These pages examine the five major themes of geography and show how they apply to Boston, Massachusetts. Recognizing and understanding these themes will help you to understand all the different aspects of geography.

Boston is located on the shores of the Atlantic Ocean.

## Location

"Where am I?" Your answer to this question is your *location.* One way to answer it is to use *absolute* location. That means you'll use the coordinates of longitude and latitude to give your answer (see page 8). For example, if you're in Boston, its absolute location is approximately 42° north latitude and 71° west longitude.

Like most people, however, you'll probably use *relative* location to answer the question. Relative location describes where a certain area is in relation to another area. For example, Boston lies in the northeast corner of the United States, next to the Atlantic Ocean.

THINKING ABOUT GEOGRAPHY What is the relative location of your school?

## Place

"What is Boston like?" *Place* can help you answer this question. Place refers to the physical and human factors that make one area different from another. Physical characteristics are natural features, such as physical setting, plants, animals, and weather. For example, Boston sits on a hilly peninsula.

Human characteristics include cultural diversity and the things people have made—including language, the arts, and architecture. For instance, Boston includes African Americans, as well as people of Irish, Italian, Chinese, and Hispanic ancestry.

THINKING ABOUT GEOGRAPHY What physical and human characteristics make where you live unique?

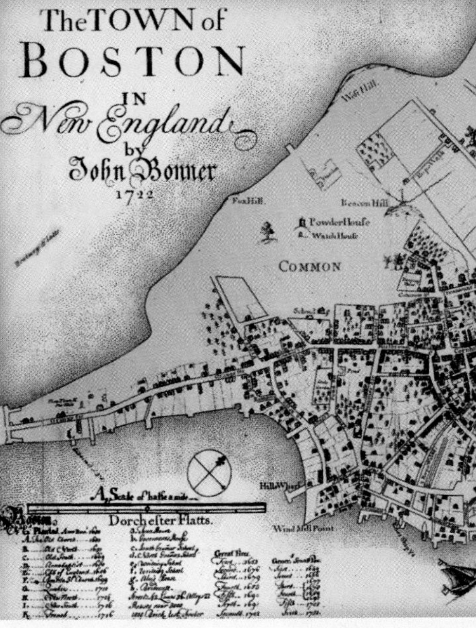


Boston has grown and changed since this 1722 map.

## Region

Geographers can't easily study the whole world at one time. So they break the world into regions. A *region* can be as large as a continent or as small as a neighborhood. A region has certain shared characteristics that set it apart. These characteristics might include political division, climate, language, or religion. Boston is part of the northeast region. It shares a climate—continental temperate—with the cities of New York and Philadelphia.

THINKING ABOUT GEOGRAPHY What characteristics does your city or town share with nearby cities or towns?



### ACTIVITY OPTIONS

**INTERDISCIPLINARY LINK: ART** — BLOCK SCHEDULING

**ILLUSTRATING THE FIVE THEMES OF GEOGRAPHY**

**Class Time** One class period

**Task** Making a poster showing how the five themes of geography apply to a city in the United States

**Purpose** To use the five themes of geography to analyze and organize geographic information

**Supplies Needed**

- Encyclopedias and other reference materials on cities in the United States
- Internet access
- Posterboard
- Art supplies

**Activity** Divide students into groups of five. As a class, select a region of the United States. Within this region, have each group pick a city and create a poster that illustrates how the city chosen reflects each theme of geography. Within groups, one student can be responsible for illustrating each theme. Posters should have both pictures or drawings and captions. After each group has presented its poster to the class, have students identify the regional characteristics the cities share.

Airplanes from Boston's Logan International Airport move people and ideas around the globe.

People shop, eat, and interact at Boston's famous Quincy Market.

## Movement

*Movement* refers to the shifting of people, goods, and ideas from one place to another. People constantly move in search of better places to live, and they trade goods with one another over great distances. Movement also causes ideas to travel from place to place. In recent years, technology has quickened the movement of ideas and goods.

Boston became known as the *Cradle of Liberty* because of the movement of ideas. The concepts of freedom and self-government that developed in Boston spread to the other colonies and helped to start the American Revolution.

**THINKING ABOUT GEOGRAPHY** What are some of the different ways you spread information and ideas?

## Human-Environment Interaction

*Human-environment interaction* refers to ways people interact with their environment, such as building a dam, cutting down a tree, or even sitting in the sun.

In Boston, human-environment interaction occurred when officials filled in swampy areas to make the city larger. In other ways, the environment has forced people to act. For example, people have had to invent ways to protect themselves from extreme weather and natural disasters.

**THINKING ABOUT GEOGRAPHY** What are ways that people in your city or town have changed their environment?

### *Themes of Geography Assessment*

**1. Main Ideas**

a. What is the relative location of your home?

b. What are three characteristics of the region in which you live?

c. What are at least three ways in which you have recently interacted with the environment?

**2. Critical Thinking**

**Forming and Supporting Opinions** Which aspect of geography described in these themes do you think has most affected your life? Explain.

**THINK ABOUT**

- ways that you interact with your environment
- how you travel from place to place



### MORE ABOUT . . .

**Movement Reshapes Boston**

In the 1850s, Boston inaugurated its first horse-drawn trolleys, or horse cars. These forerunners of the electric trolley made it possible for city workers to live farther from their workplaces. The horse-car and trolley lines fueled the movement of people out of the center city and into smaller surrounding towns, such as Roxbury, Dorchester, Brighton, and Charlestown. Between 1855 and 1873, these once independent communities became a part of the larger city.

### MORE ABOUT . . .

**Boston's Human-Environment Interaction**

When Boston was first settled, it covered the Shawmut Peninsula and was almost completely surrounded by water. Its only connection with the mainland was a narrow neck of land to the south. West of the neck was a vast area of mud flats and salt marshes, which were submerged at high tide. Throughout the 1800s, the salt flats in this area, known as the Back Bay, were filled in by cutting down hills and bringing in gravel from neighboring towns. In the 1830s, a public garden was built in the Back Bay. By century's end, the Back Bay was one of the city's best-known residential areas.

## *Assessment: Themes of Geography*

**1. Main Ideas**

**a.** Answers should demonstrate understanding of the term *relative location.* **b.** Answers should demonstrate understanding of the term *region.* **c.** Answers should demonstrate understanding of human-environment interaction.

**2. Critical Thinking**

**Forming and Supporting Opinions** Answers should demonstrate understanding of the themes of geography.

## FOCUS & MOTIVATE

### 5-MINUTE WARM-UP

**Comparing** These questions focus on the tools used by geographers.

1. Look at the illustrations of the tools of geography and read the captions on page 6. List similarities between the tools of the 19th-century surveyor and the contemporary geographer.
2. What are some reasons that might make maps out of date?

## INSTRUCT

**Map Basics**
Key Questions

- How do physical, political, and historical maps differ?
- How are computers used in map making?

### MORE ABOUT . . .

**Global Positioning Systems**
A global positioning system, or GPS, is a navigational system that uses radio signals broadcast by satellites. Airplanes, ships, and other vehicles—as well as people on foot—determine their own location by "reading" the signals through computerized radio receivers. The current GPS has been fully operational since 1995. It has 24 satellites in six orbits at a height of about 12,500 miles. The satellites send back signals to GPS receivers indicating their location and broadcast time. With this information, the GPS receiver can determine the latitude, longitude, and altitude of its location and find its own position in seconds to an accuracy of 165 feet.

# Map Basics

Geographers use many different types of maps, and these maps all have a variety of features. The map on the next page gives you information on a historical event—the War of 1812. But you can use it to learn about different parts of a map, too.

## Types of Maps

**Physical maps** Physical maps show mountains, hills, plains, rivers, lakes, oceans, and other physical features of an area.

**Political maps** Political maps show political units, such as countries, states, provinces, counties, districts, and towns. Each unit is normally shaded a different color, represented by a symbol, or shown with a different typeface.

**Historical maps** Historical maps illustrate such things as economic activity, migrations, battles, and changing national boundaries.

### Tools of Geography

The ancient Greeks developed some of the first ways to study geography. Today, geographers and map makers use advanced technology to study geography.

**GPS**
A Global Positioning System (GPS) is a navigational system that uses at least three satellites to identify a person's absolute location. It is also used to study other aspects of geography.

**Surveyors**
An American surveys the land in the 19th century.

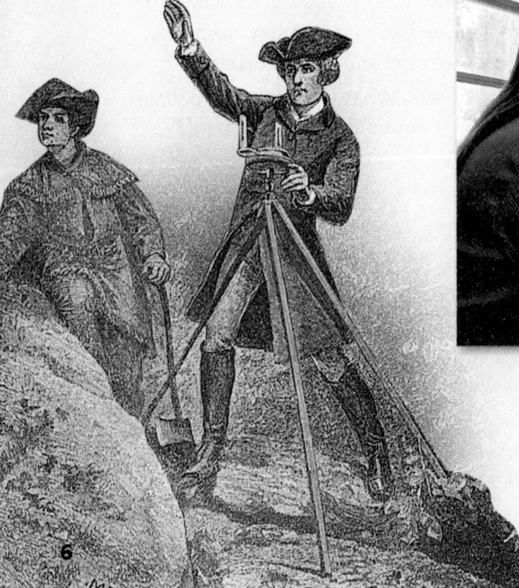

**Computers**
Computers can create electronic maps in which geographers can quickly add or remove features that keep the map current. Computers can also be used to monitor environmental problems such as deforestation and global warming.

6

### TEACHING STRATEGY

**Comparing** Have students skim newspapers, newsmagazines, advertising circulars, travel brochures, and Internet sources for examples of different kinds of maps. Then have students identify as many types of maps as they can, such as the types of maps found in telephone books, national parks, almanacs, amusement parks, state highway visitor's centers, history books, newspapers and newsmagazines, and on television programs.

Have each student present one map to the class and explain what type of map it is, what information it provides, who might use it, and why. Have students suggest alternative ways that information on the map might be presented. After the presentations, put students into groups by the type of map they selected, and have each group list ways its maps are similar.

## Reading a Map

**A** **Lines** Lines indicate political boundaries, roads and highways, human movement, and rivers and other waterways.

**B** **Symbols** Symbols represent such items as capital cities, battle sites, or economic activities.

**C** **Labels** Labels are words or phrases that explain various items or activities on a map.

**D** **Compass Rose** A compass rose shows which way the directions north (N), south (S), east (E), and west (W) point on the map.

**E** **Scale** A scale shows the ratio between a unit of length on the map and a unit of distance on the earth. A typical one-inch scale indicates the number of miles and kilometers that length represents on the map.

**F** **Colors** Colors show a variety of information on a map, such as population density or the physical growth of a country.

**G** **Legend or Key** A legend or key lists and explains the symbols, lines, and colors on a map.

**H** **Lines of Longitude** These are imaginary, north-south lines that run around the globe.
**Lines of Latitude** These are imaginary, east-west lines that run around the globe. Together, latitude and longitude lines form a grid on a map or globe to indicate an area's absolute location.

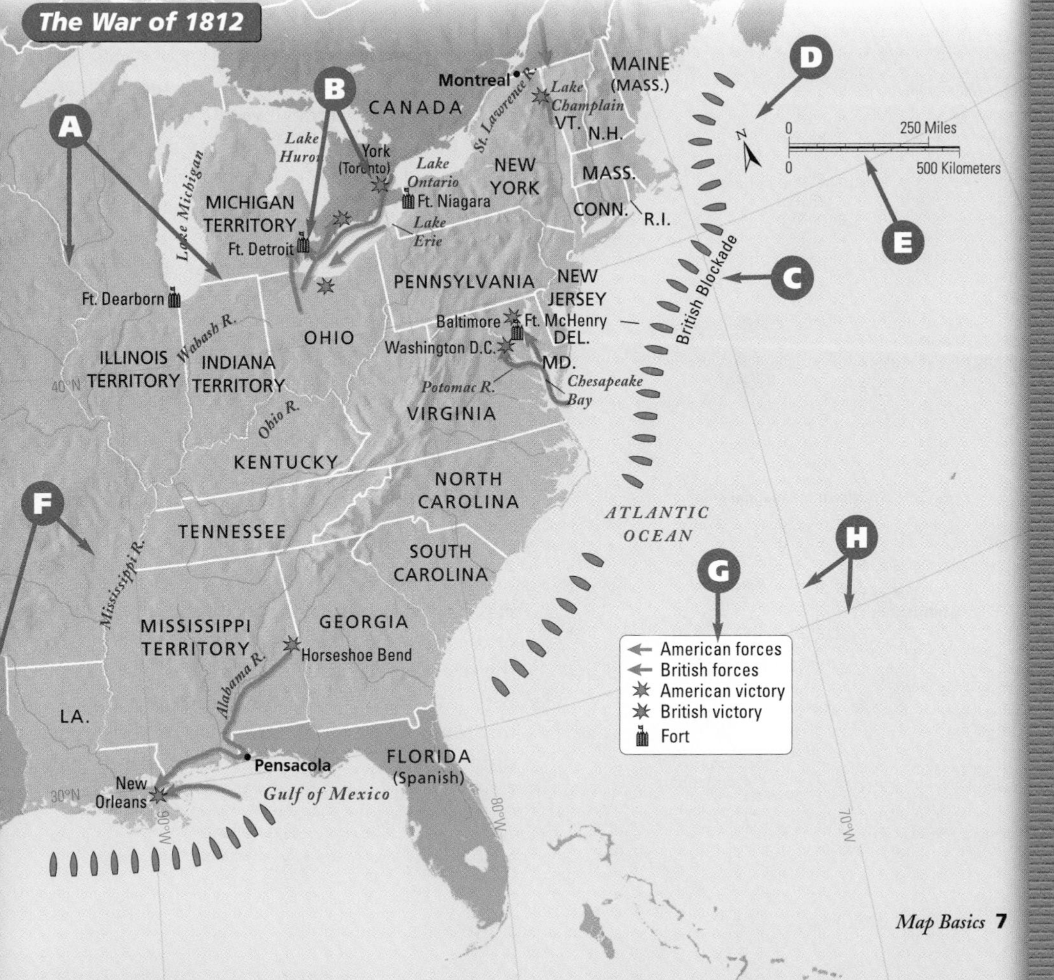




### GEOGRAPHY FROM VISUALS

**Reading the Map** Ask students what the lines/arrows labeled "A" on the map shown stand for. **Answer** rivers, territorial boundaries. What symbols are used to represent British and American victories? **Answer** red and blue stars. What does a red arrow represent? **Answer** the direction in which British forces were moving. What does the orange color on the map indicate? **Answer** land areas that are not a part of the United States

**Extension** Have students look in reference books or history books to find other maps showing the War of 1812. Ask students to work in pairs to identify similarities and differences between maps.

### MORE ABOUT . . .

**Surveying**
During colonial times and into the 1900s, the surveyor worked to determine locations and boundaries of places by measuring angles, distances, and heights with mechanical instruments. In the 20th century, newer technologies like aerial photography, infrared and radar imaging systems that perform remote sensing, global positioning systems, and computerized data systems have transformed the ways maps are made.

### TEACHING STRATEGY

**Comparing Maps with Different Scales** To give students practice in reading and measuring scale on maps, provide small groups with two maps of the same place in two different scales. For example, you might pair a map of a city with one of the city's financial district or of a neighborhood within the city. Pair a highway map of a state with a map of a city in the state. Pair two maps of different scale of the same historical event. Have small groups of students examine paired maps, noting the scale of each, the overall size of each, and describing differences in the details that can be seen on each map. Have groups use the map scale to measure two distances on each map. Check student answers. Then have each group make up three questions about its maps that require measuring distances on the maps. Have groups exchange maps and questions.

**MORE ABOUT . . .**

**Longitude**

Parallels of latitude and meridians of longitude together form a grid that can be used to specify any point on the earth's surface. The space between two meridians is greatest at the equator, about 69 miles, and narrows as the meridians approach the North and South Poles. A degree of longitude at New Orleans is about 60 miles wide. At Winnipeg, Canada, closer to the North Pole, a degree of longitude is less than 45 miles wide.

**MORE ABOUT . . .**

**Latitude**

The Tropic of Cancer and the Tropic of Capricorn mark the farthest points north and south of the equator where the sun's rays fall vertically. The Arctic Circle and the Antarctic Circle mark the farthest points north and south of the equator where the sun appears above the horizon each day of the year. North of the Arctic Circle and south of the Antarctic Circle in the polar regions, the sun remains continuously visible in the sky for 24 hours a day during certain times of the year.

**Longitude Lines (Meridians)**

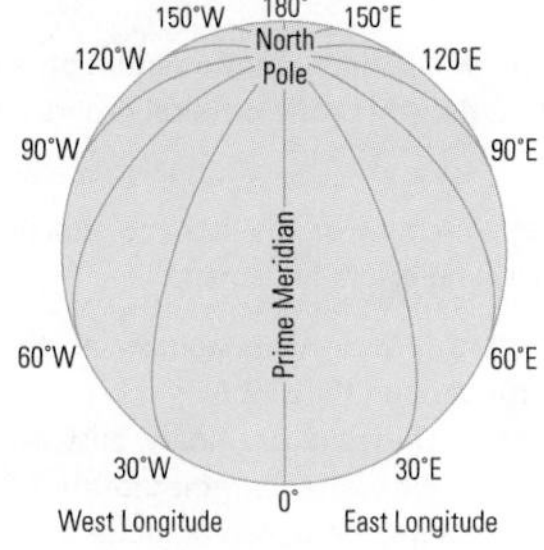


**Latitude Lines (Parallels)**

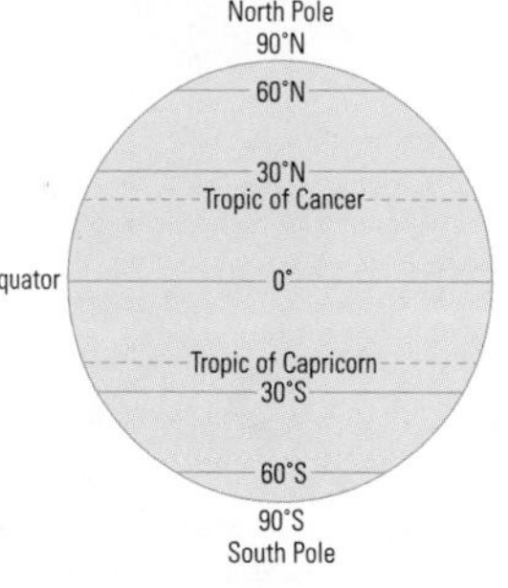


**Northern Hemisphere**

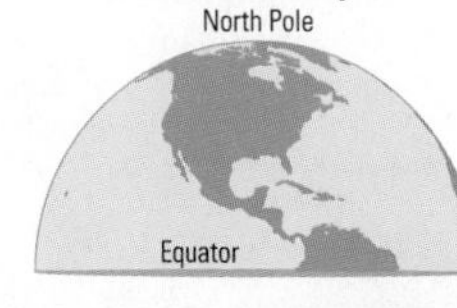


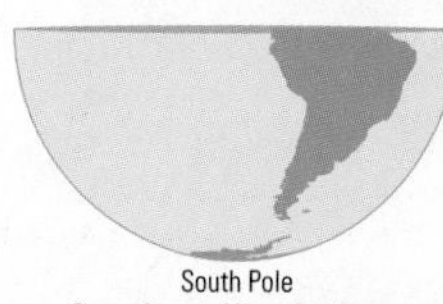


**Southern Hemisphere**

**Western Hemisphere**

**Eastern Hemisphere**

## Longitude lines

- are imaginary lines that run north to south around the globe and are known as meridians
- show the distance in degrees east or west of the prime meridian

The prime meridian is a longitude line that runs from the North Pole to the South Pole. It passes through Greenwich, England, and measures 0° longitude.

## Latitude lines

- are imaginary lines that run east to west around the globe and are known as parallels
- show distance in degrees north or south of the equator

The equator is a latitude line that circles the earth halfway between the North and South poles. It measures 0° latitude.

The tropics of Cancer and Capricorn are parallels that form the boundaries of the Tropics, a region that stays warm all year.

Latitude and longitude lines appear together on a map and allow you to pinpoint the absolute location of cities and other geographic features. You express this location through coordinates of intersecting lines. These are measured in degrees.

## Hemisphere

Hemisphere is a term for half the globe. The globe can be divided into Northern and Southern hemispheres (separated by the equator) or into Eastern and Western hemispheres. The United States is located in the Northern and Western hemispheres.

## Projections

A projection is a way of showing the curved surface of the earth on a flat map. Flat maps cannot show the size, shape, and direction of a globe all at once with total accuracy. As a result, all projections distort some aspect of the earth's surface. Some maps distort distances, while other maps distort angles. On the next page are four projections.



**ACTIVITY OPTIONS**

**MULTIPLE LEARNING STYLES: INTERPERSONAL**

**BLOCK SCHEDULING**

**REVIEWING LATITUDE AND LONGITUDE**

**Class Time** One class period

**Task** Identifying places by longitude and latitude

**Purpose** To review basics of latitude and longitude

**Supplies Needed**
- World atlases

**Activity** Divide students into teams. Have each team pick five cities, use an atlas to find the absolute location of each city, and write a clue in the following form to describe its relative location: My city is in the Eastern and Northern Hemisphere, north of the Tropic of Cancer, south of 40° N latitude, northeast of Kyoto, south of Hokkaido. *(Tokyo, Japan, 35° N, 139° E)* Have teams take turns writing their clues on the board. The first team to identify the city and its absolute location wins the round.

### Mercator Projection

180° 90°W 0° 90°E

The Mercator projection shows most of the continents as they look on a globe. However, the projection stretches out the lands near the North and South poles. The Mercator is used for all kinds of navigation.

### Azimuthal Projection

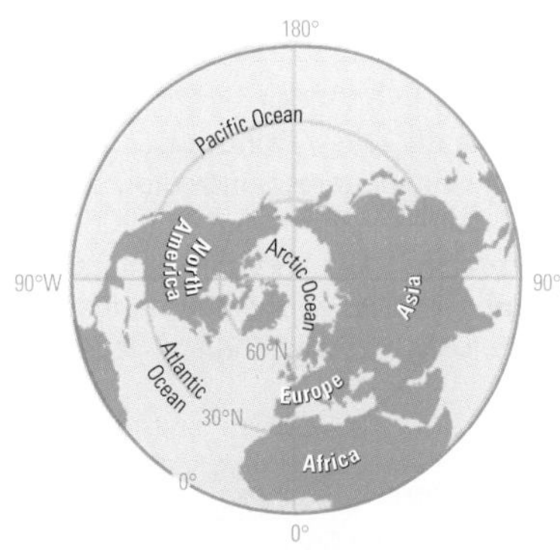
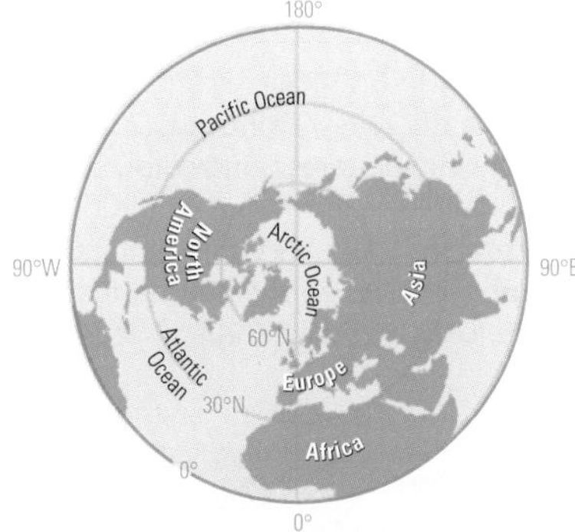


An azimuthal projection shows the earth so that a straight line from the central point to any other point on the map gives the shortest distance between the two points. Size and shape of the continents are also distorted.

### Homolosine Projection

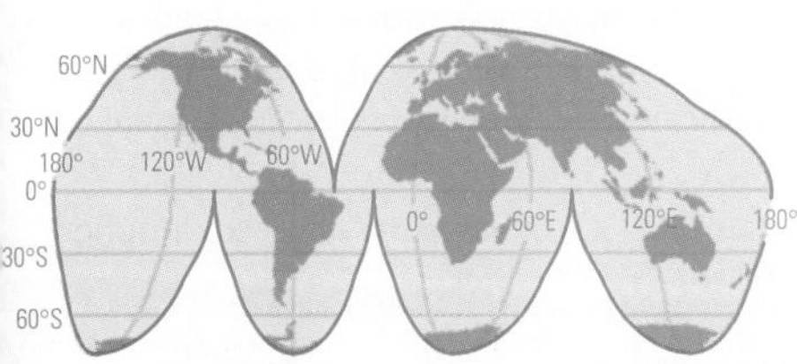


This projection shows the accurate shapes and sizes of the landmasses, but distances on the map are not correct.

### Robinson Projection

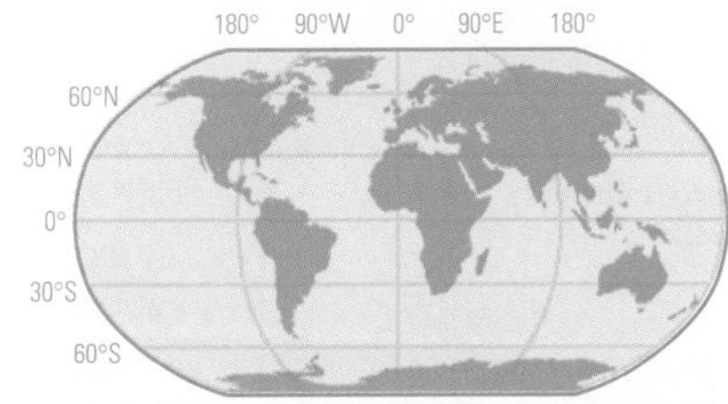


Textbook maps commonly use the Robinson projection. It shows the entire earth with nearly the true sizes and shapes of the continents and oceans. However, the shapes of the landforms near the poles appear flat.

### Map Basics Assessment

**1. Main Ideas**

a. What is the longitude and latitude of your city or town?

b. What information is provided by the legend on the map on page 7?

c. What is a projection? Compare and contrast Antarctica on the Mercator and the Robinson projections.

**2. Critical Thinking**

**Making Inferences** Why do you think latitude and longitude are so important to sailors?

**THINK ABOUT**
- the landmarks you use to find your way around
- the landmarks available to sailors on the ocean



Geography HANDBOOK

## MORE ABOUT . . .

**Azimuthal Projections**

Only a globe can accurately represent the shape of the earth and the relationship among the earth's surface features. An azimuthal projection depicts a part of the earth as a flattened disk viewed from one of several different points. Azimuthal projections can show the earth's surface from a point at the center of the earth, on the opposite side of the earth's surface, or from a point out in space. A polar projection is an azimuthal projection from a point in space over the North or South Pole. In a polar projection, parallels of latitude are concentric circles, while meridians are straight lines.

## MORE ABOUT . . .

**Mercator Projection**

Flemish geographer Gerardus Mercator created the Mercator projection in 1569. It broke new ground in showing the earth on a flat sheet of paper. In a Mercator projection, the parallels of latitude, which on the globe are equal distances apart, are drawn farther and farther apart from each other as their distance from the equator increases. This preserves the shapes of land areas but distorts their size, especially those that are far from the equator. Greenland, for example, is shown with its proper shape but appears much larger than it actually is.

## Assessment: Map Basics

**1. Main Ideas**

**a.** Students may check their answers in a geographical dictionary or atlas. **b.** The legend identifies the symbols used on the map. **c.** A projection is a way of showing the curved surface of the earth on a flat map. Antarctica appears larger than it is on a Mercator projection; a Robinson projection flattens the landforms of Antarctica.

**2. Critical Thinking**

**Possible Response** Latitude and longitude provide absolute location. On the open seas, sailors cannot depend on relative location because they cannot compare one part of the ocean to another.

## FOCUS & MOTIVATE

### 5-MINUTE WARM-UP

**Comparing** These questions focus on the resources of the United States

1. Look at the map on page 11. Where in the country are deposits of iron ore located?
2. In which part of the nation are oil deposits found?

## INSTRUCT

**Physical Geography of the United States**
Key Questions

- What natural features do physical geographers study?
- What natural resources have helped the growth of U.S. industries?
- How do human-environment interactions affect climate?
- What explains regional variations in the types of vegetation found in the United States?

### MORE ABOUT . . .

**Alaska's Resources**
Oil production is Alaska's single most important economic activity. Oil drilled in Alaska is shipped by tanker and Trans-Alaskan pipeline to the lower 48 states. Other valuable minerals and metals found in Alaska are gold, zinc, molybdenum, and tin plus smaller quantities of antimony, chromite, copper, nickel, platinum, silver, and tungsten.

# Physical Geography of the United States

From the heights of Mount McKinley (20,320 feet above sea level) in Alaska to the depths of Death Valley, California (282 feet below sea level), the geography of the United States is incredibly diverse. In between these extremes lie such varied features and conditions as scorching Arizona deserts, lush Oregon forests, freezing Vermont winters, and sunny Florida beaches. Physical geography involves all the natural features on the earth. This includes the land, resources, climate, and vegetation.

Flowers and brush cover the Coral Pink Sand Dunes in southern Utah.

## Land

Separated from much of the world by two oceans, the United States covers 3,717,796 square miles and spans the entire width of North America. To the west, Hawaii stretches the United States into the Pacific Ocean. To the north, Alaska extends the United States to the Arctic Circle. On the U.S. mainland, a huge central plain separates large mountains in the West and low mountains in the East. Plains make up almost half of the country, while mountains and plateaus make up a quarter each.

An abundance of lakes—Alaska alone has three million—and rivers also dot the landscape. Twenty percent of the United States is farmed, providing the country with a steady food supply. Urban areas cover only about two percent of the nation. Refer to the map on the next page for a complete look at the U.S. landscape.

**THINKING ABOUT GEOGRAPHY** What is the land like around your city or state?

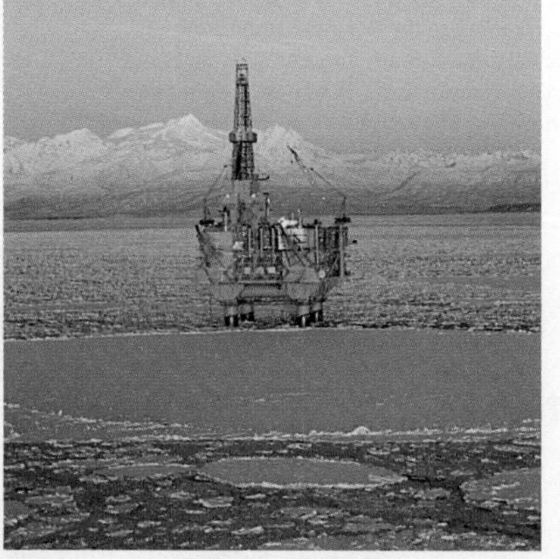

Oil drilled from Alaska helps power the nation's planes, trains, cars, and factories.

## Resources

The United States has a variety of natural resources. Vast amounts of coal, oil, and natural gas lie underneath American soil. Valuable deposits of lead, zinc, uranium, gold, and silver also exist. These resources have helped the United States become the world's leading industrial nation—producing nearly 21 percent of the world's goods and services.

These resources have also helped the United States become both the world's largest producer of energy (natural gas, oil, coal, nuclear power, and electricity) and the world's largest consumer of it. Other natural resources include the Great Lakes, which are shared with Canada. They contain about 20 percent of the world's total supply of fresh surface water. Refer to the map on the next page to examine the nation's natural resources.

**THINKING ABOUT GEOGRAPHY** What are the different natural resources that you and your family use in your daily lives?



### ACTIVITY OPTIONS

**INTERDISCIPLINARY LINK: SCIENCE**

**EXAMINING FOSSIL FUELS**

**Class Time** One class period

**Task** Making a diagram showing how fossil fuels are formed and where reserves are located

**Purpose** To understand how fossil fuels are formed and how they are distributed worldwide

**Supplies Needed**

- Encyclopedias and other reference materials on fossil-fuel formation
- Graph paper
- Art supplies

**Activity** Divide students into groups. Have each group make a diagram that shows how either coal or oil and natural gas are formed. Diagrams should also indicate the time span for formation of these energy resources. Have groups write captions for their diagrams explaining why fossil fuels are called nonrenewable energy sources.

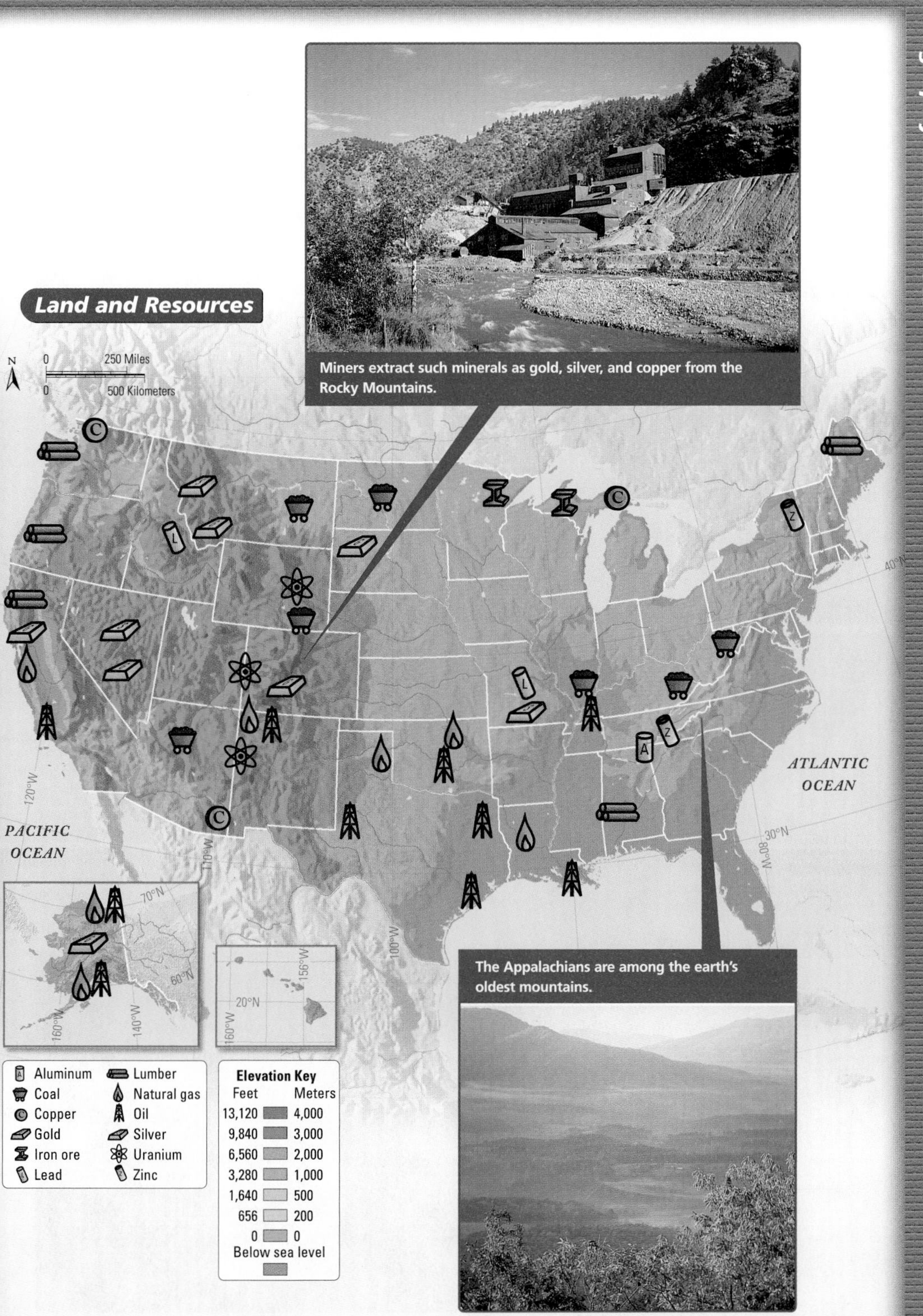


Miners extract such minerals as gold, silver, and copper from the Rocky Mountains.

The Appalachians are among the earth's oldest mountains.



# GEOGRAPHY HANDBOOK

## MORE ABOUT . . .

### Petroleum Resources

The United States has about 22 billion barrels of oil in reserves. Most of these reserves are in Texas, Louisiana, California, Oklahoma, and Alaska. The United States is one of the world's leading producers and refiners of petroleum. Despite its leading role in production, U.S. demand for oil far exceeds domestic production, and the nation imports more than 60 percent of the oil it uses. Petroleum helps fuel the industrial economy, provides jobs for thousands of people, and is one of the nation's largest private employers.

## GEOGRAPHY FROM VISUALS

**Reading the Map** Ask students to look at the map and the map key. Then ask the following questions: What can be learned from the map about the distribution of oil and natural gas? *(The map suggests that natural gas is usually found where oil is found.)* Judging by this map would you say that natural resources are evenly distributed? *(No, the Northeast and Midwest seem to have fewer than other regions.)* What evidence does the map provide to show that the Appalachian Mountains are older than the Rockies? *(The Rockies are higher; the Appalachians have experienced more erosion and are at lower elevations.)*

**Extension** Ask students to research one of the resources on the map to find how it is used in U.S. industries.

## TEACHING STRATEGY

**Applying Geographic Themes** Have students apply the theme of human-environment interaction to the process of extracting oil, minerals, and other natural resources from the earth. The production, transportation, and use of such minerals and fossil fuels has greatly affected the environment. In many places, strip-mining has caused erosion, while offshore drilling for oil and the shipment of petroleum has at times resulted in pollution of the ocean. Have each student pick one state on the map that is rich in natural resources. Tell students to bring to class a newspaper, newsmagazine article, or article from the Internet illustrating a human-environment interaction resulting from the extraction, production, transportation, or consumption process in their chosen state.

## MORE ABOUT . . .

**Climate**

Climates vary for many reasons. Latitude or distance from the equator affects climate, as does altitude. Surface features, such as mountains or deserts, also have an influence on climate. Because water has a moderating influence on climate, distance from oceans and large lakes can affect climate. Finally, wind patterns influence climate by distributing heat and moisture.

## GEOGRAPHY FROM VISUALS

**Reading the Map** Have students use the key to identify climate regions of North America. Ask students to describe the location of each climate region. Then discuss with students how the diversity of climate regions within the United States might affect industry and transportation. **Possible Response** Climate diversity causes demand for different products in different parts of the country. For example, a manufacturer of snow shovels would not find customers in a tropical climate.

**Extension** Ask students to tell what clothes they would pack for a summer trip to southern California and northwestern Montana.

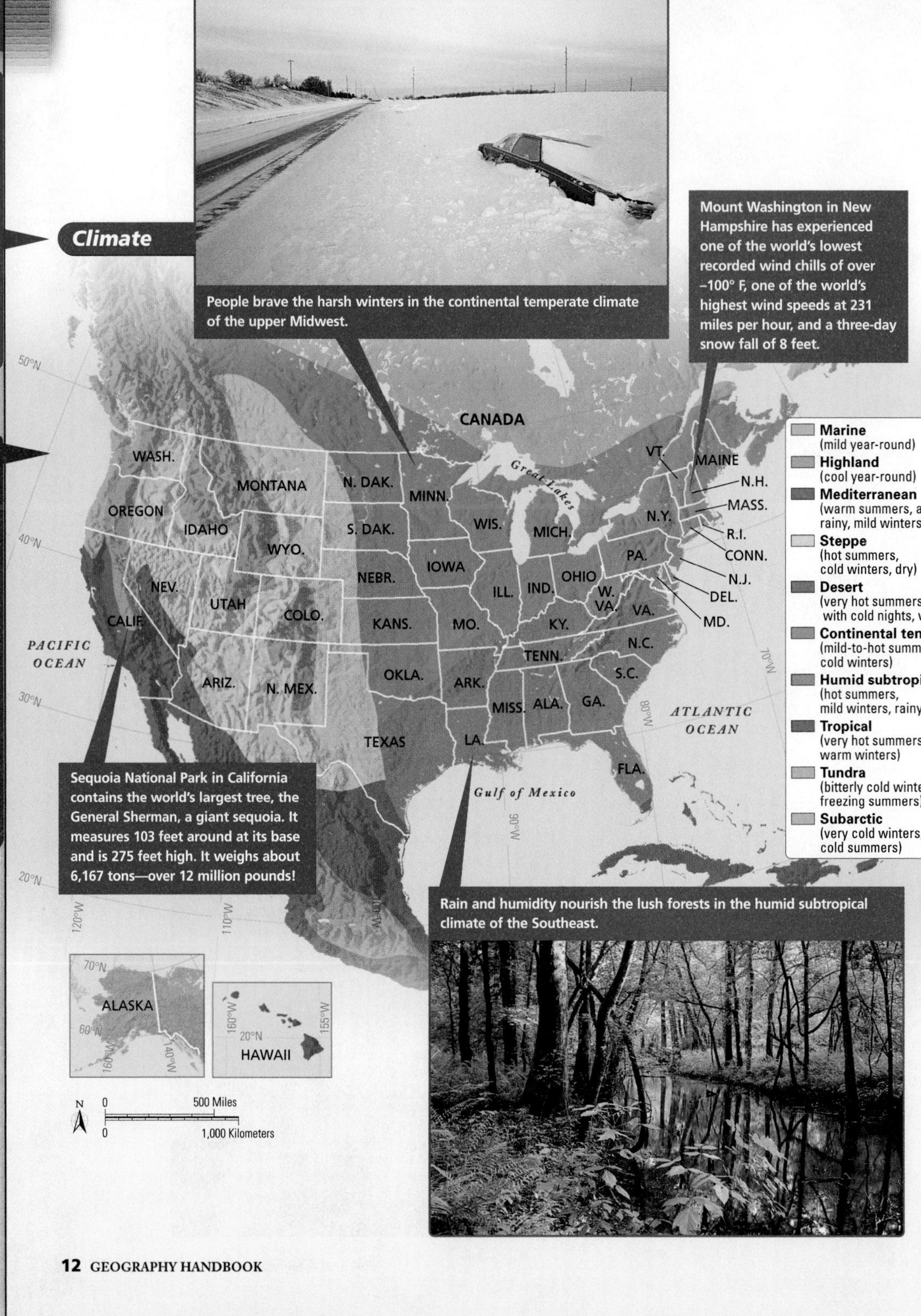


## ACTIVITY OPTIONS

### INTERDISCIPLINARY LINK: GEOGRAPHY

BLOCK SCHEDULING

**MAKING A CLIMATE GRAPH**

**Class Time** One class period

**Task** Making a climate graph

**Purpose** To identify the weather patterns associated with different climate zones

**Supplies Needed**
- Reference materials on United States geography and climate
- Internet access
- Graph paper
- Colored pencils
- Sample climate graphs

**Activity** Have pairs of students pick one of the climate zones shown on the map and identify two major cities within that zone. Have students research climate data for each of their selected cities. Then have student pairs create a climate graph for each city selected. The graphs should show average monthly temperature and precipitation. When graphs are completed, have students decide which graphs most closely match the descriptions of the climate zones listed in the map key on page 12.

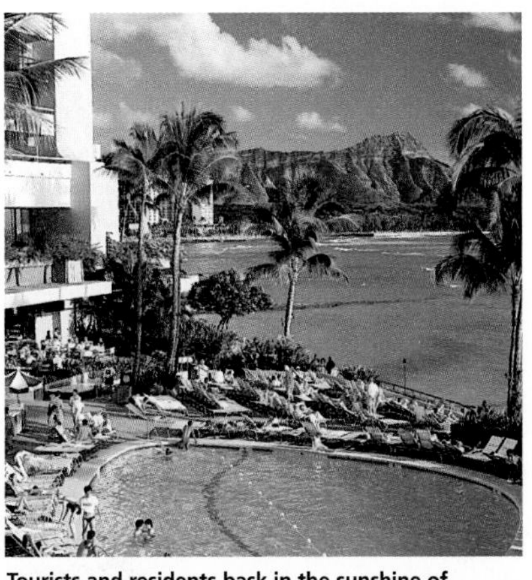

Tourists and residents bask in the sunshine of Waikiki Beach in Hawaii.

## Climate

The United States contains a variety of climates. For example, the mean temperature in January in Miami, Florida, is 67° F, while it is 11° F in Minneapolis, Minnesota. Most of the United States experiences a continental climate, or distinct change of seasons. Some regional climatic differences include hot and humid summers in the Southeast versus hot and dry summers in the Southwest. Harsh winters and heavy snow can blanket parts of the Midwest, the Northeast, and the higher elevations of the West and Northwest. Refer to the map on the previous page to see the nation's climatic regions.

Human activities have affected the climate, too. For example, pollution from cars and factories can affect local weather conditions and may be contributing to a dangerous rise in the earth's temperature.

**THINKING ABOUT GEOGRAPHY** How would you describe the climate where you live?

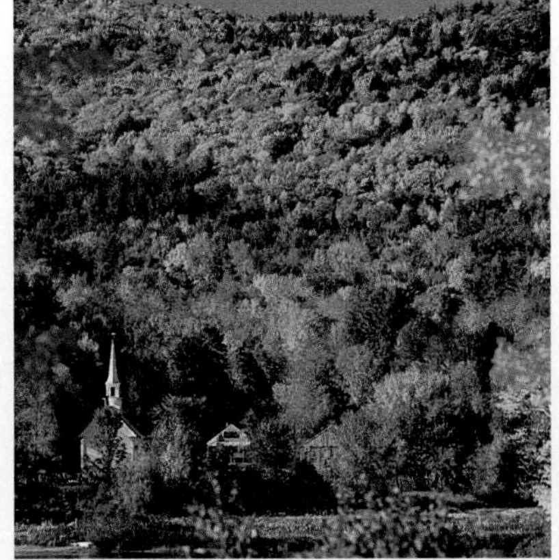

This mountainside burns with the autumn foliage of New Hampshire.

## Vegetation

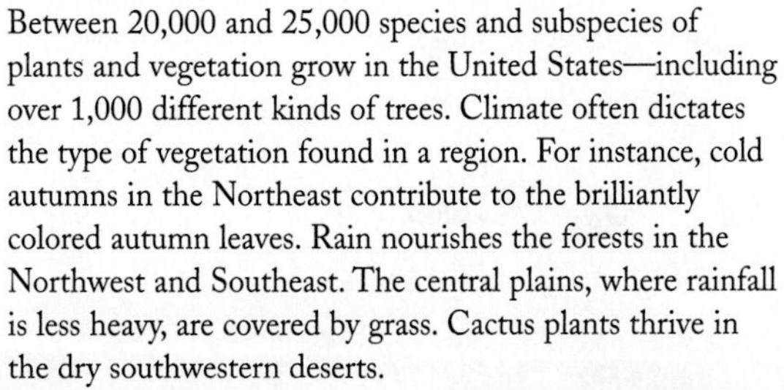

Between 20,000 and 25,000 species and subspecies of plants and vegetation grow in the United States—including over 1,000 different kinds of trees. Climate often dictates the type of vegetation found in a region. For instance, cold autumns in the Northeast contribute to the brilliantly colored autumn leaves. Rain nourishes the forests in the Northwest and Southeast. The central plains, where rainfall is less heavy, are covered by grass. Cactus plants thrive in the dry southwestern deserts.

Along with natural vegetation, climate dictates the nation's variety of planted crops. For example, temperate weather in the Midwest helps wheat to grow, while warm weather nourishes citrus fruit in Florida and California.

**THINKING ABOUT GEOGRAPHY** What kinds of trees or plants grow in your region?

### *Physical Geography Assessment*

**1. Main Ideas**

a. What are the different aspects of physical geography?

b. Which state contains the largest variety of climates?

c. What two states contain most of the country's oil resources?

**2. Critical Thinking**

**Drawing Conclusions** What do you think are the advantages of living in a country with diverse physical geography?

**THINK ABOUT**

- the different resources available in your region
- the variety of recreational activities in your region



### MORE ABOUT . . .

**Global Warming**

Human activity, especially the burning of fossil fuels, such as coal, oil, and natural gas, may be changing the earth's climate. Since the late 1800s, the average temperature of the earth's surface has increased about .5°F to 1.5°F. Certain manufacturing processes and activities, such as driving cars and generating electricity, increase the amount of carbon dioxide gas in the atmosphere. This gas may be causing global warming. Scientists disagree about what effect this warming trend will have, but some fear it could affect rainfall patterns and plant and animal habitats or melt enough polar ice to raise sea levels.

### MORE ABOUT . . .

**Tundra Climate and Vegetation**

Because of its climate, northern Alaska's tundra has no trees. Long, cold winters and short, cool summers prevent their growth. Tundra soil remains permanently frozen to a depth of up to 10 feet. The permafrost, as it is called, keeps water from draining away, so that the soil remains cold and wet even in summer. Tundra vegetation consists of mosses, lichens, grasses, and low shrubs. Although lacking in trees, Alaska's tundra becomes grazing land for caribou, reindeer, and musk oxen in the spring, and a place for wolves to prey on the grazing animals.

### *Assessment: Physical Geography*

**1. Main Ideas**

**a.** land, resources, climate, and vegetation **b.** California **c.** Texas and Alaska

**2. Critical Thinking**

Answers may include diverse resources, good recreational opportunities, and variety.

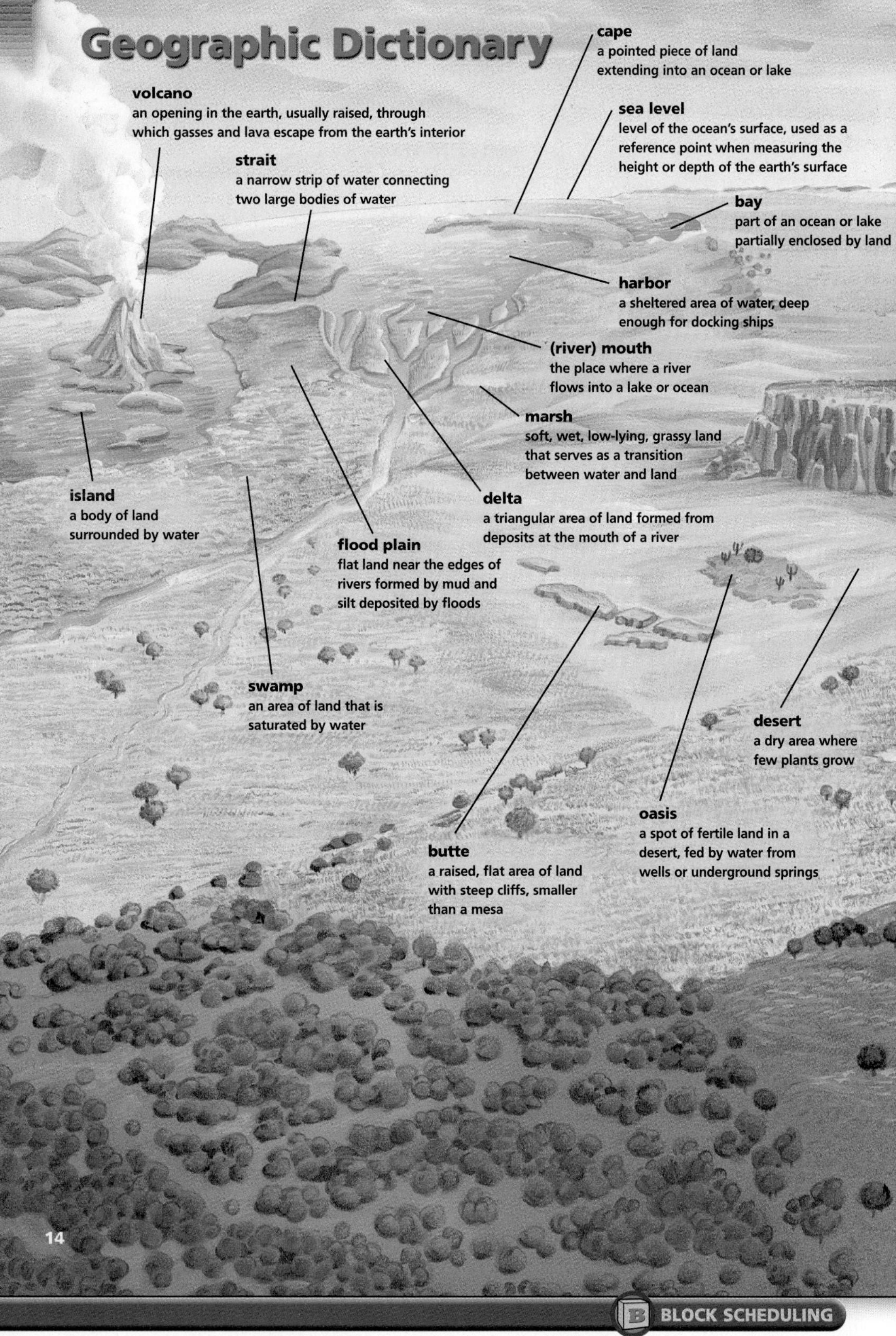
Geographic Dictionary
cape
a pointed piece of land extending into an ocean or lake
volcano
an opening in the earth, usually raised, through which gasses and lava escape from the earth's interior
sea level
level of the ocean's surface, used as a reference point when measuring the height or depth of the earth's surface
strait
a narrow strip of water connecting two large bodies of water
bay
part of an ocean or lake partially enclosed by land
harbor
a sheltered area of water, deep enough for docking ships
(river) mouth
the place where a river flows into a lake or ocean
marsh
soft, wet, low-lying, grassy land that serves as a transition between water and land
island
a body of land surrounded by water
delta
a triangular area of land formed from deposits at the mouth of a river
flood plain
flat land near the edges of rivers formed by mud and silt deposited by floods
swamp
an area of land that is saturated by water
desert
a dry area where few plants grow
oasis
a spot of fertile land in a desert, fed by water from wells or underground springs
butte
a raised, flat area of land with steep cliffs, smaller than a mesa
14

## MORE ABOUT . . .

### Wetlands

Many wetland areas exist throughout the United States. In these areas, water levels remain near or above the surface of the ground most of the year. Marshes and swamps are common in wetland areas. Freshwater marshes develop in the shallow waters of lakes and streams. Salt marshes and mangrove swamps exist in areas where freshwater and saltwater mix. Wetlands are important habitats for plants and animals. They also play a role in flood control by soaking up large amounts of water.

## MORE ABOUT . . .

### Everglades National Park

One of the nation's most distinctive swamps is the 1.5-million-acre Everglades in southern Florida. The northern part of the swamp is a prairie covered by shallow water and saw grass. Near the southern coast, the Everglades turn into salt marshes and mangrove swamps. The Everglades were created about 10,000 years ago, at the end of the Pleistocene Ice Age. Since the 1970s, urban development of the surrounding area and water pollution caused by chemical runoff from sugar plantations and vegetable farms have created environmental problems for the Everglades.

## ACTIVITY OPTIONS

### MULTIPLE LEARNING STYLES: SPATIAL

BLOCK SCHEDULING

#### PLAYING A GEOGRAPHY GAME

**Class Time** One class period

**Task** Identifying landforms and bodies of water visually

**Purpose** To recognize different types of landforms and bodies of water

**Supplies Needed**

- Colored markers
- Stopwatch or timer
- Small pieces of paper
- Jar or basket

**Activity** Write the labels from the Geographic Dictionary on small pieces of paper and put them in a jar or basket. Divide students into pairs to play "Quick-Draw Geography." In this game, pairs of students compete at the chalkboard to see how quickly one partner can name a geographic term drawn on the board by his or her partner. The student who is drawing chooses a term at random from the papers in the jar. There is no talking during this game; all clues are visual. Set a time limit for identifying the term.

prairie
a large, level area of grassland with few or no trees
mountain
natural elevation of the earth's surface with steep sides and greater height than a hill
glacier
a large ice mass that moves slowly down a mountain or over land
steppe
a wide, treeless plain
valley
low land between hills or mountains
mesa
a wide, flat-topped mountain with steep sides, larger than a butte
cataract
a large, powerful waterfall
canyon
a narrow, deep valley with steep sides
cliff
the steep, almost vertical edge of a hill, mountain, or plain
plateau
a broad, flat area of land higher than the surrounding land
15

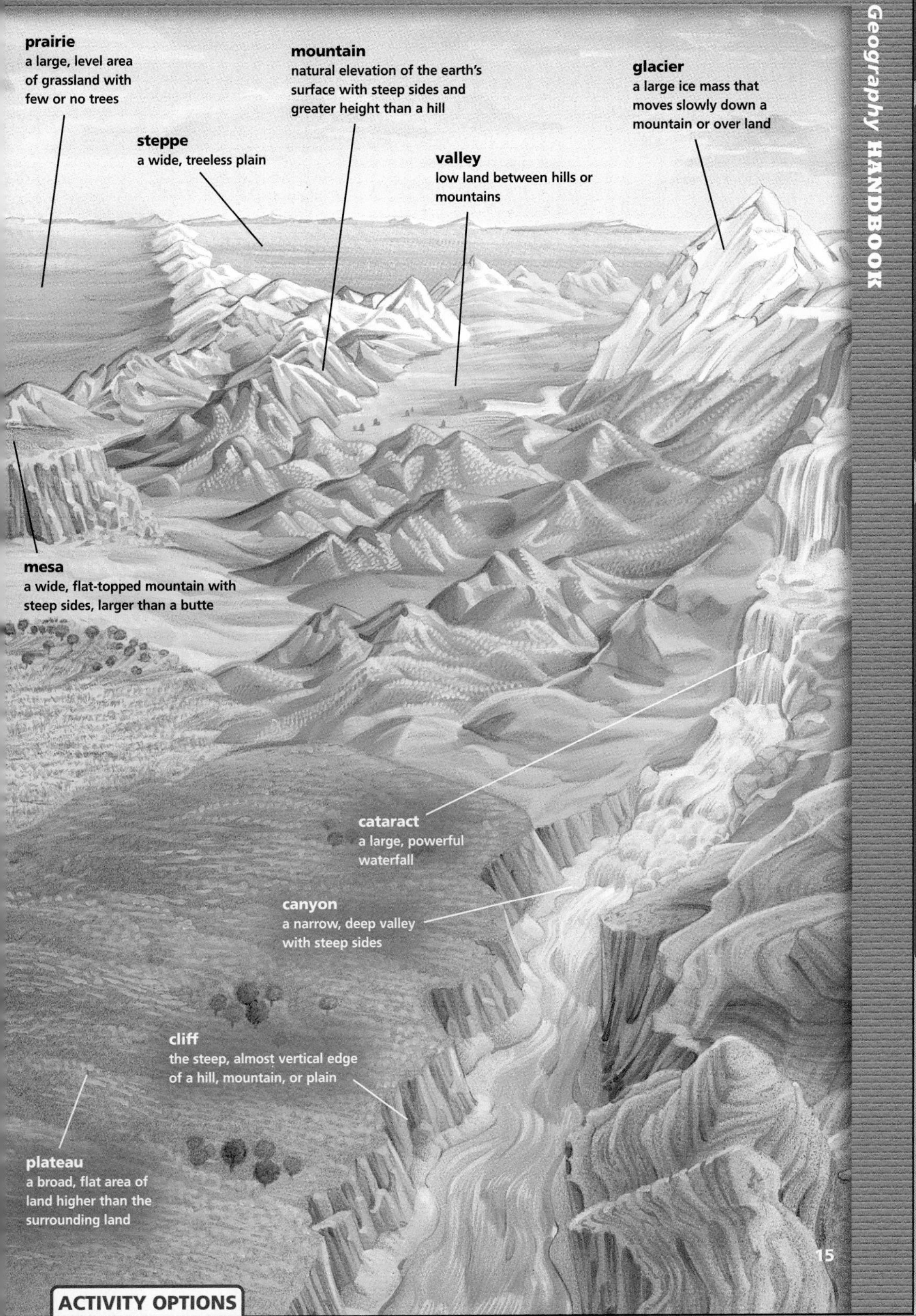

## MORE ABOUT . . .

### Deltas

The name *delta* comes from the Greek letter *delta* because many deltas have a somewhat triangular shape like that of the Greek letter. A delta is a low plain formed by the deposition of clay, sand, gravel, and other sediments at the mouth of a river. The Mississippi Delta is one of the nation's largest. It covers about 13,000 square miles, about one-fourth of Louisiana's total area. Deltas form at the mouths of rivers where the river's speed and ability to carry silt is suddenly reduced. Delta soils are often quite fertile.

## MORE ABOUT . . .

### Deserts

Deserts in the United States include Death Valley in California and Nevada, the Mojave Desert in southern California, the Painted Desert in Arizona, and the Sonoran Desert in Arizona and California. The high heat of the desert results from the fact that deserts absorb more heat from the sun than land in humid climates does. Most deserts average less than 10 inches of rain a year. In North America, many deserts developed in regions separated from the Pacific Ocean by mountains, partly because of the rain shadow effect. Moist winds blowing inland from the ocean cool and lose their moisture as they rise over the mountains. When the winds reach the leeward side, they are warm and dry with scant rainfall.

## ACTIVITY OPTIONS

### INDIVIDUAL NEEDS: GIFTED AND TALENTED

#### ADDING TO THE GEOGRAPHIC DICTIONARY

**Class Time** Two class periods

**Task** Proposing additions to the Geographic Dictionary

**Purpose** To expand students' geographic vocabularies

**Supplies Needed**
- Art supplies
- Clay

**Activity** Have students propose additions to the Geographic Dictionary. Students should work as a group to decide the criteria for new words to be added to the dictionary. Each student should then find one or more geographic terms that meet the criteria, write a definition of each proposed term, and make a visual representation of it, such as a drawing or clay model. Allow students to work as a group to decide where the terms should be placed on pages 14 and 15.

## FOCUS & MOTIVATE

### 5-MINUTE WARM-UP

**Finding Main Ideas** These questions focus on the ways humans have adapted to their environments.

1. Look at the pictures on page 16. How did the builders of the cliff dwellings adapt to a climate of cold winters and hot summers?
2. In what ways does the dam change the environment?

## INSTRUCT

**Human Geography**

Key Questions

- What is the focus of human geography?
- Which of the five themes of geography are most closely related to human geography?

### MORE ABOUT . . .

**The Colorado River and the Hoover Dam**

Changes to the Colorado River system show some of the ways humans have adapted the natural environment to meet their needs. The Colorado River drainage basin provides hydroelectric power and water for irrigation, flood control, and recreational uses for many Western states. Hoover Dam, completed in 1936, was the first major development of the river system. The dam became not only an important energy source but also a major tourist attraction.

# Human Geography of the United States

Human geography focuses on people's relationships with each other and the surrounding environment. It includes two main themes of geography: human-environment interaction and movement. The following pages will help you to better understand the link between people and geography.

## Humans Adapt to Their Surroundings

Humans have always adapted to their environment. For example, in North America, many Native American tribes burned forest patches to create grazing area to attract animals and to clear area for farmland. In addition, Americans have adapted to their environment by building numerous dams, bridges, and tunnels. More recently, scientists and engineers have been developing building materials that will better withstand the earthquakes that occasionally strike California.

**THINKING ABOUT GEOGRAPHY** What are some of the ways in which you interact with your environment on a daily basis?

Early Americans of the Southwest protected themselves from the weather by building cliff dwellings.

The Hoover Dam, located on the Colorado River between Arizona and Nevada, provides electricity for Arizona, Nevada, and Southern California.



### ACTIVITY OPTIONS

**INTERDISCIPLINARY LINK: SCIENCE**

BLOCK SCHEDULING

**RESEARCHING AN ENVIRONMENTAL ISSUE**

**Class Time** One class period

**Task** Writing a position paper on an environmental issue

**Purpose** To analyze and form an opinion on an environmental issue

**Supplies Needed**

- Reference materials on the protection of salmon populations on the Snake River
- Internet access

**Activity** In recent years, scientists and environmentalists in Washington State have debated how best to protect diminishing salmon populations on the Snake and Columbia rivers. Scientists say several human-environment interactions have affected salmon stocks, including overfishing, construction of dams, and destruction of spawning areas. Solutions that have been proposed include breaching dams on the lower Snake River, a moratorium on fishing, or changing water- and land-use policies. Have students research this issue and write a position paper explaining the problem, alternative solutions, and recommendations for action.

An oil spill from the ship *Exxon Valdez* harmed wildlife, such as this bird, in Prince William Sound, Alaska, in 1989.

## Humans Affect the Environment

When humans interact with the environment, sometimes nature suffers. In the United States, for example, major oil leaks or spills occur each year—fouling shorelines and harming wildlife. Building suburbs and strip malls has also destroyed forests, farmland, and valuable wetlands.

**THINKING ABOUT GEOGRAPHY** What are some of the environmental problems in your city or town?

### Destruction of Original Forests

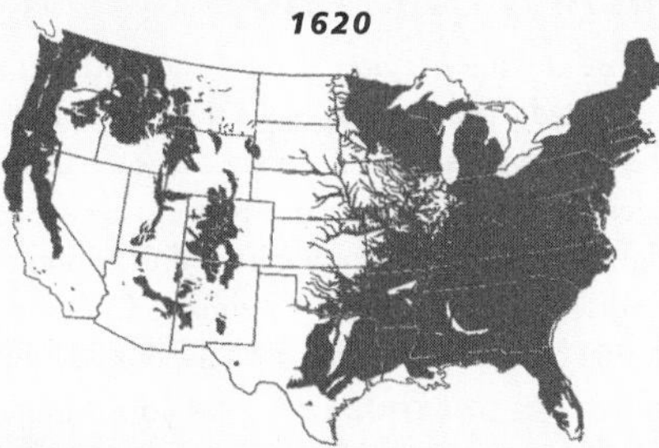


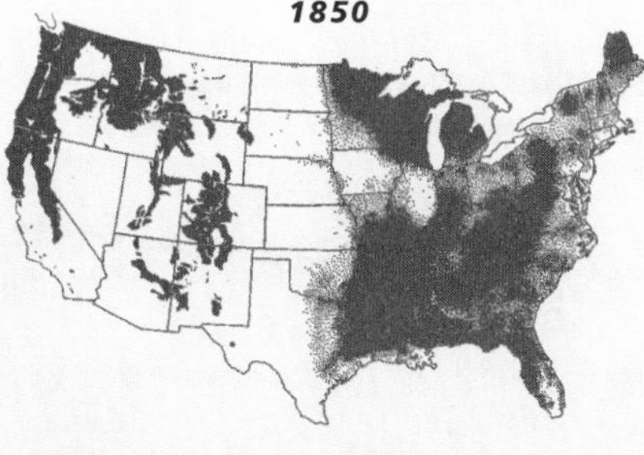


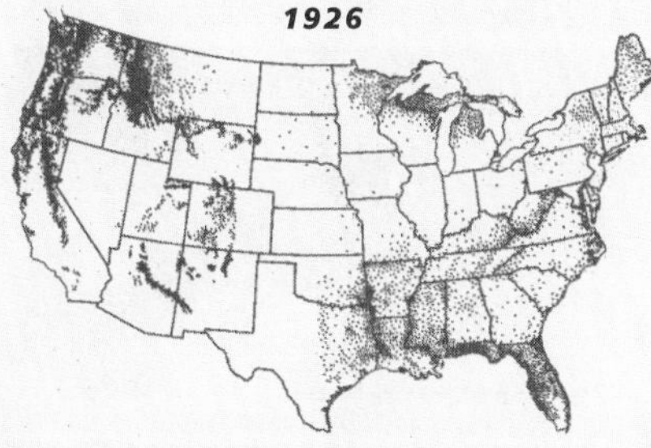


These maps show that, over the years, human beings have nearly cut down all the original forests in the United States. Each dot represents 25,000 acres.

Children plant trees along a Chicago expressway.

## Preserving and Restoring

Americans—as well as people all over the world—have been working hard to balance economic progress with conservation. For example, car companies in the United States and around the world are working to develop pollution-free vehicles. In 1994, the average American family of four recycled around 1,100 pounds of waste. And, in the 1990s, Americans have planted more than two million acres of new trees each year.

**THINKING ABOUT GEOGRAPHY** What are some of the ways in which you help the environment?



## GEOGRAPHY HANDBOOK

### GEOGRAPHY FROM VISUALS

**Reading the Map** Ask students to look carefully at the maps showing the destruction of the original forests. Ask students what parts of the country were covered with original forest in 1620. **Answer** Most of the eastern half, the Northwest Coast, and some parts of the mountain region and Southwest. Ask students to compare the 1620 map to the 1850 map. What does the comparison show about settlement along the Atlantic Coast? **Possible Response** Settlement was very thick; few of the original trees remained by 1850.

**Extension** Ask students to write one or two sentences describing the original forests in their state in 1620, 1850, and 1926.

### MORE ABOUT . . .

***Exxon Valdez***

On March 24, 1989, the oil tanker *Exxon Valdez* ran aground in Alaska's Prince William Sound. Delays in attempts to contain the spill, along with high winds and waves, resulted in a spill of 10.9 million gallons of crude oil. It was the biggest oil spill in U.S. history. Over time, thousands of miles of the Alaskan shoreline were polluted. Despite an intensive clean-up effort, the fragile ecosystem of the sound was damaged.

### ACTIVITY OPTIONS

### INTERDISCIPLINARY LINK: CIVICS

BLOCK SCHEDULING

**IDENTIFYING LOCAL ENVIRONMENTAL ISSUES**

**Class Time** One class period

**Task** Identifying a local environmental issue and expressing an opinion about it

**Purpose** To identify local issues related to human-environment interaction

**Supplies Needed**
- Current local newspapers
- Internet access

**Activity** Have students read local newspapers to identify local environmental issues. Tell students that community concerns often include such issues as waste management and disposal, land use, air and water quality, noise pollution, and treatment of animal populations. As a class, identify five local environmental issues and how humans have affected the environment in each case. Then, working in groups, have students pick one of these issues and create a political cartoon or write a letter to the editor of the school newspaper expressing an opinion on this topic.

## GEOGRAPHY FROM VISUALS

**Reading the Map** Have students look at the map and explain the meaning of the arrows and the letters. Ask the following questions: Judging by this map, which regions have lost population since the 1970s? **Answer** Northeast and Midwest. From which region of the United States did the greatest out-migration take place? **Answer** Northeast. How has the population shift affected Arizona? The Phoenix-Mesa area now has more people than the entire state did in 1980.

**Extension** Have students do research about population trends in their state over the past five years.

## MORE ABOUT . . .

**The Sunbelt**

The growth of the Sunbelt increased not only the population but also the area's economic base. The Sunbelt attracted a variety of new high-tech industries, such as aerospace, plastics, chemicals, and electronics. The space industry brought Northern transplants to Florida, Alabama, and Texas. Scientists and medical researchers also flocked to research and development zones like the Research Triangle Park in North Carolina and other facilities in Florida, Texas, and California. Many factors besides the warmer climate sparked the industrial growth of the Southeast, including land that was cheaper than in the crowded cities of the Northeast and lower labor costs because there were fewer unionized workers.

## Human Movement

In prehistoric times, people roamed the earth in search of food. Today in the United States, people move from place to place for many different reasons. Among them are cost of living, job availability, and climate. Since the 1970s, many Americans—as well as many new immigrants—moved to the Sunbelt. This region runs through the southern United States from Virginia to California. Between 1950 and 1990, that region's population soared from 52 million to 118 million.

**THINKING ABOUT GEOGRAPHY** Has your family ever moved? If so, what were some of the reasons?

This map shows human movement in the 1970s. The information below explains some of the results of this movement in the 1990s.

### Americans on the Move, 1970s

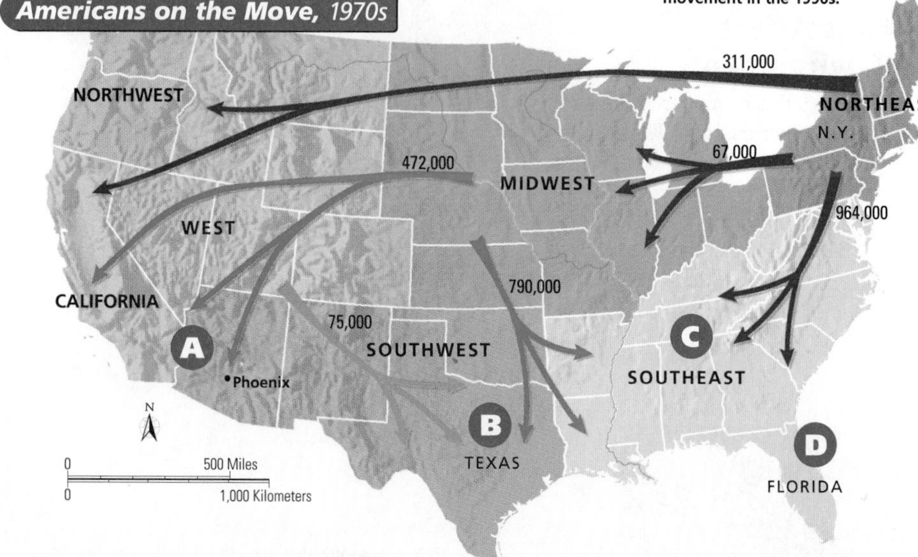


**A** By 1996, the Phoenix-Mesa metropolitan area reached a population of 2.75 million, more than the number of people living in the entire state in 1980.

**B** Between 1990 and 1994, Texas overtook New York as the nation's second most populous state, behind California.

**C** One of the nation's fastest growing areas was the Southeast, where population growth ranged from six to nine percent between 1990 and 1994. Jobs grew in the area by 14 percent.

**D** Florida's population is growing so much that it could become as populous as New York state by around 2020.

New home developments cover the desert in Las Vegas, Nevada.



## ACTIVITY OPTIONS

### INTERDISCIPLINARY LINK: AMERICAN HISTORY

BLOCK SCHEDULING

**AMERICANS ON THE MOVE, 1990s**

**Class Time** One class period

**Task** Making a map showing population change in the United States in the 1990s

**Purpose** To illustrate contemporary population movement

**Supplies Needed**
- World almanacs
- Internet access
- Outline map of the United States

**Activity** Have students use the most recent census data to make a three-column chart. In the first column, tell students to list the states with the greatest increases in population during the decade. In the second, have them list states with moderate to low population gain, and in the third, states with population losses. Have students color-code their chart and use the same colors on a map showing population movement and change during the 1990s.

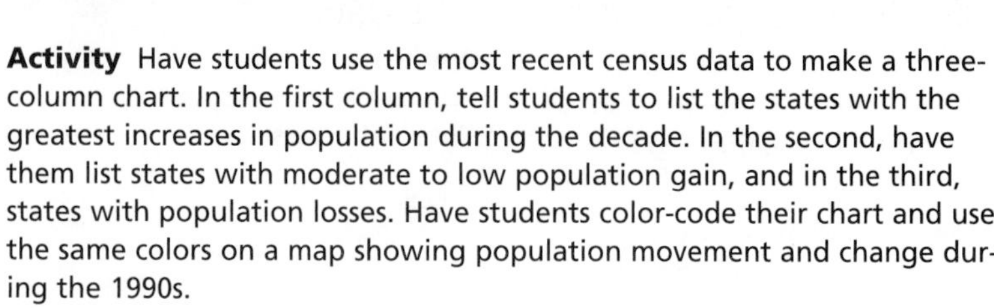

In the late 19th century, millions of immigrants arrived on the shores of the United States.

The Sears Tower overlooks Chinatown in Chicago.

## Humans Spread Ideas and Information

Throughout U.S. history, people from all over the world have come to the United States. They have brought with them food, music, language, technology, and other aspects of their culture. As a result, the United States is one of the most culturally rich and diverse nations in the world. Look around your town or city. You'll probably notice different people, languages, and foods.

Today, the spreading of ideas and customs does not rely solely on human movement. Technology—from the Internet to television to satellites—spreads ideas and information throughout the world faster than ever. This has created an ever-growing, interconnected world. As the 21st century opens, human geography will continue to play a key role in shaping the United States and the world.

**THINKING ABOUT GEOGRAPHY** How have computers and the Internet affected your life?

### *Human Geography Assessment*

**1. Main Ideas**

**a.** What are some of the ways that people have helped to restore the environment?

**b.** What are some of the ways that residents of your region have successfully modified their landscape?

**c.** What are some of the reasons that people move from place to place?

**2. Critical Thinking**

**Recognizing Effects** In what ways has technology helped bring people in the world together?

**THINK ABOUT**
- the different ways in which people communicate today
- the speed in which people today can communicate over long distances





### MORE ABOUT . . .

**Immigration**

Immigration patterns have greatly affected the human geography of many American cities. Patterns of immigration often shape the neighborhoods and cultures that develop in cities. When immigrants first come to a new country, they tend to settle near others with similar cultural backgrounds. As shops, grocery stores, restaurants, and houses of worship spring up to meet the needs of people in these neighborhoods, the neighborhoods themselves develop distinctive identities—as "Chinatowns" or "Little Saigons," for example—that contribute to the diversity and richness of city life.

### MORE ABOUT . . .

**Internet Interaction**

A December 1999 *U.S. News and World Report* poll reported that most American adults used personal computers mainly for writing and sending e-mail, for searching the Internet for information, and for word processing. In the near future, small, wireless handheld devices may replace PCs for Internet use. In Finland, young and old use wireless phones with Internet connections to pay bills, buy airline and concert tickets, and shop for everything from automobiles to zithers. In the future, even grocery shopping may become obsolete, as tiny boxes in the refrigerator automatically dial up an Internet grocer to order milk when the Internet user needs a refill.

### *Assessment: Human Geography*

**1. Main Ideas**

**a.** working to develop pollution-free vehicles, recycling, planting new trees **b.** Answers should demonstrate understanding of the concept of modifying landscapes. **c.** cost of living, job availability, climate

**2. Critical Thinking**

**Recognizing Effects** Advances in technology have brought communication devices to many more people and increased the speed of communication.

## TERMS

1. **physical map,** p. 6
2. **political map,** p. 6
3. **longitude,** p. 8
4. **latitude,** p. 8
5. **hemisphere,** p. 8
6. **projection,** p. 8
7. **flood plain,** p. 14
8. **sea level,** p. 14
9. **human geography,** p. 16
10. **human movement,** p. 18

## REVIEW QUESTIONS

**Answers**

1. Absolute location describes the location of a place using latitude and longitude, while relative location describes where a place is relative to another area.
2. Place refers to what an area looks like in both physical and human terms.
3. Movement refers to the transfer of people, goods, and ideas, while human-environment interaction includes how humans interact with their surroundings.
4. Advanced technology can help scientists and geographers keep track of serious environmental problems, and it can also improve the quality of maps.
5. physical, political, and historical maps
6. Latitude lines are imaginary lines that run east to west around the globe, and longitude lines are imaginary lines that run north to south around the globe.
7. An abundance of natural resources has aided the growth of the U.S. economy because the United States hasn't had to rely on the resources of foreign nations.
8. marine, highland, Mediterranean, steppe, desert, continental temperate, humid subtropical, tropical, tundra, subarctic
9. Human geography focuses on people's relationship with each other and the surrounding environment, while physical geography focuses on the land, natural resources, vegetation, and climate.
10. People move for a variety of reasons, including cost of living, job availability, and climate.

# GEOGRAPHY HANDBOOK ASSESSMENT

## TERMS

Briefly explain and identify each of the following.

1. physical map
2. political map
3. longitude
4. latitude
5. hemisphere
6. projection
7. flood plain
8. sea level
9. human geography
10. human movement

## REVIEW QUESTIONS

**Themes of Geography (pages 4–5)**

1. What is the difference between *absolute* location and *relative* location?
2. What is meant by the theme of place?
3. What are the themes of movement and human-environment interaction?

**Map Basics (pages 6–9)**

4. What do you think are some of the benefits of using technology to study geography?
5. What are the three major kinds of maps?
6. What are latitude and longitude lines?

**Physical Geography (pages 10–13)**

7. How have the natural resources in the United States helped its economic development?
8. What are the different climates within the United States?

**Human Geography (pages 16–19)**

9. How is human geography different from physical geography?
10. What aspects of human geography might cause people to move?

## CRITICAL THINKING

1. **Forming and Supporting Opinions** Which of the five themes of geography do you think has had the most impact on history? Why?
2. **Analyzing Causes** How do the climate and natural resources of an area affect its economy?
3. **Drawing Conclusions** How have computers helped geographers make more accurate maps?
4. **Making Inferences** Why do you think the Mercator projection is used for all types of navigation?
5. **Recognizing Effects** How does a diverse landscape help or hurt the economy of an area?

## GEOGRAPHY SKILLS

**1. INTERPRETING MAPS: Movement**

**Basic Map Elements**

a. What region of the United States is shown?

b. Compare the number of teams on the 1987 map and the 2000 map. How many more teams are on the 2000 map?

**Interpreting the Map**

c. What geographic theme(s) is most responsible for the increase in sports teams in this region?

d. According to the map, which sport enjoyed the biggest surge in popularity in this region?

***Major League Sports in Southeast Cities***

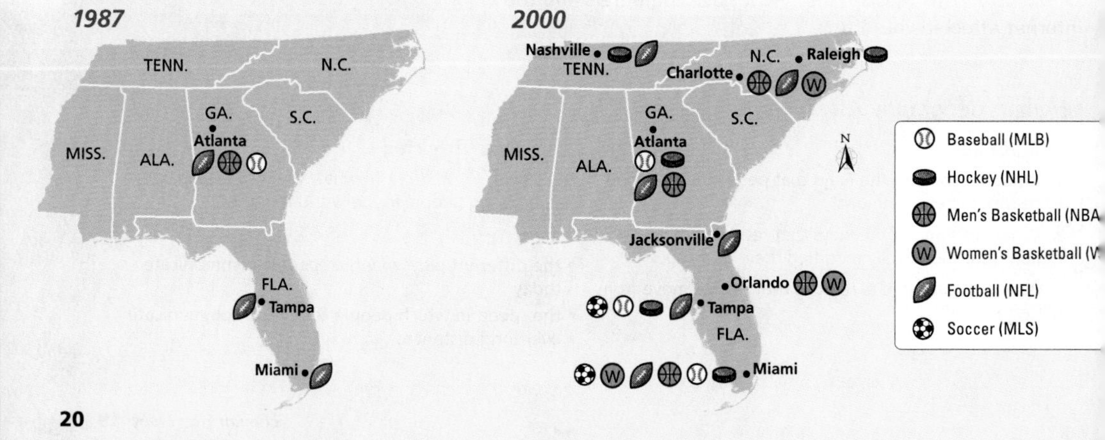


20

## CRITICAL THINKING

**Possible Responses**

1. Some students might say location, because a civilization's location—near steady food and water supplies or surrounded by enemies—often determined whether or not it flourished. Others might say movement, because it was by moving that humans spread so many ideas and goods. Accept other reasonable responses.
2. The natural resources that are available in a region often determine an area's main economic activity. For instance, because coal is an abundant resource in the Appalachian region, coal mining is a main economic activity there. The ability to grow crops—which is determined by climate and land type—also plays a key role in an area's economic activity. Those regions that can grow oranges, for example, have made orange production an integral part of their economy.
3. Computers and satellites enable map makers and geographers to constantly update map information and environmental conditions.
4. It shows clearly all the landmasses as well as the large bodies of water.
5. A diverse landscape can help a region's economy by sustaining a wide variety of economic activities and by providing jobs in many different areas.

## GEOGRAPHY SKILLS

**2. INTERPRETING MAPS: Region**

Study the map and then answer the questions.

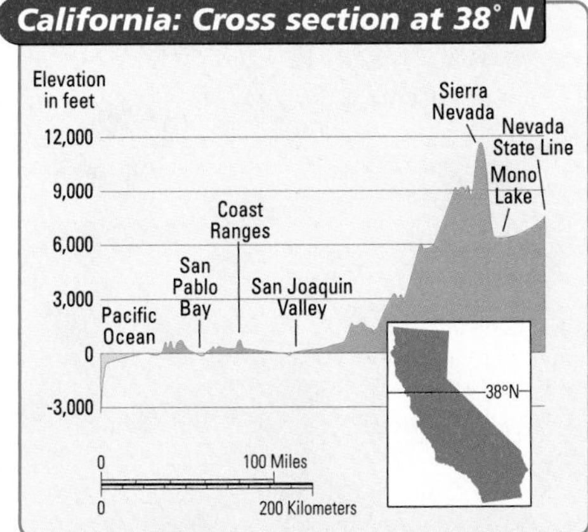


**Basic Map Elements**

a. What are the different landforms on the map?

**Interpreting the Map**

b. What is the level of the San Joaquin Valley? How many miles does it take to get from there to the highest point in California at the 38th parallel?

**3. INTERPRETING PRIMARY SOURCES**

In 1803, President Thomas Jefferson appointed Meriwether Lewis to explore the lands of the Louisiana Purchase. Jefferson gave him these instructions:

> The object of your mission is to explore the Missouri river . . . by its course & communication with the waters of the Pacific Ocean, may offer the most direct & practicable water communication across this continent, for the purposes of commerce. . . .
>
> Other object worthy of notice will be the soil & face of the country, its growth & vegetable productions . . . the mineral productions of every kind. . . . climate as characterized by the thermometer . . . the dates at which particular plants put forth or lose their flowers, or leaf, times of appearance of particular birds, reptiles, or insects.
>
> **Thomas Jefferson,** quoted in *The Journals of Lewis and Clark*

a. What was Jefferson expecting to find in the West?

b. Why might the president want to know about the land's soil and vegetable production?

c. What aspect of human geography might be of interest to the president?

## ALTERNATIVE ASSESSMENT

**1. INTERDISCIPLINARY ACTIVITY: Math**

**Plotting Latitude and Longitude** On a piece of graph paper, sketch a map of the United States. Be sure to draw in state boundaries, too. Then, using an atlas as a reference, draw and mark the latitude and longitude lines that cross the nation at five degree intervals. Plot the estimated longitude and latitude location of your city or town. Determine at which degrees the lines intersect where you live. Repeat this exercise for at least five different places you have visited or would like to visit within the United States.

**2. COOPERATIVE LEARNING ACTIVITY**

**Making a Map** How well do you know the neighborhood around your school? Form groups of three to four students. Then work together to draw a map of the neighborhood around your school. Include:

- streets
- residences
- stores
- geographic features
- important landmarks

The map should be accurate but not too cluttered with unnecessary details. Compare your group's map with those of the other groups in the class.

**3. TECHNOLOGY ACTIVITY**

**Writing Directions** Several Internet sites provide detailed maps of the United States. They also provide driving directions to most places in the country.

- Locate one of these map sites on the Internet.
- Think of a place in the United States that you would like to visit.
- Work with the computer to find the best route for reaching it.

Write out clear directions as well as the total mileage of your trip. Also, note the type of map it is and the features it highlights.

 **Visit www.mcdougallittell.com for important geography sites.**

**4. HISTORY PORTFOLIO**

Review your alternative assessment activities. Select the one that you think was your best work. Choose one of the options below.

 **Option 1** Use comments made by your teacher or classmates to improve your work.

 **Option 2** Depict your work visually, in a graph or chart, for example.

Add your work to your History portfolio.



## ALTERNATIVE ASSESSMENT

1. INTERDISCIPLINARY ACTIVITY: Math

**Maps should**
- be clearly labeled and neatly presented.
- include a legend and title.
- include both latitude and longitude for all locations.

2. COOPERATIVE LEARNING ACTIVITY

**Maps should**
- be clearly labeled and neatly presented.
- include a legend and title.
- include landmarks in the neighborhood of the school.

3.  TECHNOLOGY ACTIVITY

**Directions should**
- accurately deliver instructions to reach the designated location.
- be logically organized.
- include total mileage and identify map type and highlights.
- use standard grammar, spelling, sentence structure, and punctuation.

4. HISTORY PORTFOLIO

 **Option 1 Revised alternative assessment activities should**
- address teacher and peer responses to the selected work.
- solve problems present in the first versions of the work.

 **Option 2 A graph or chart should**
- present information in a style that will aid the viewer's understanding.
- present information accurately.
- use bar, line, or pie styles.
- be presented neatly.

**Formal Assessment**
- Geography Handbook quizzes and tests, pp. 5–16

## GEOGRAPHY SKILLS

1. INTERPRETING MAPS: MOVEMENT

**Basic Map Elements**

**a.** southeast

**b.** 18

**Interpreting the Map**

**c.** movement

**d.** hockey

2. INTERPRETING MAPS: REGION

**Basic Map Elements**

**a.** ocean, bay, valley, lake, mountains

**Interpreting the Map**

**b.** sea level or slightly below; about 120 miles

3. INTERPRETING PRIMARY SOURCES

**a.** a water route to the Pacific Ocean

**b.** to learn whether or not the land would be inhabitable for American settlers

**c.** what types of—and how many—Native Americans live in the area

# UNIT 1

## Three Worlds Meet

### Beginnings to 1763



## BEFORE YOU READ

### Previewing Unit 1

Unit 1 begins with the arrival of the first Americans after the last Ice Age and traces a great sweep of history through settlement by diverse groups of colonists. For the first time, complex societies of Native Americans come into contact with people from Europe and Africa. The result is a cultural mingling full of tension and adaptation for both the Native Americans and the newcomers. British colonies develop, expand, and mature. By 1763, a new American culture and sense of identity has developed.

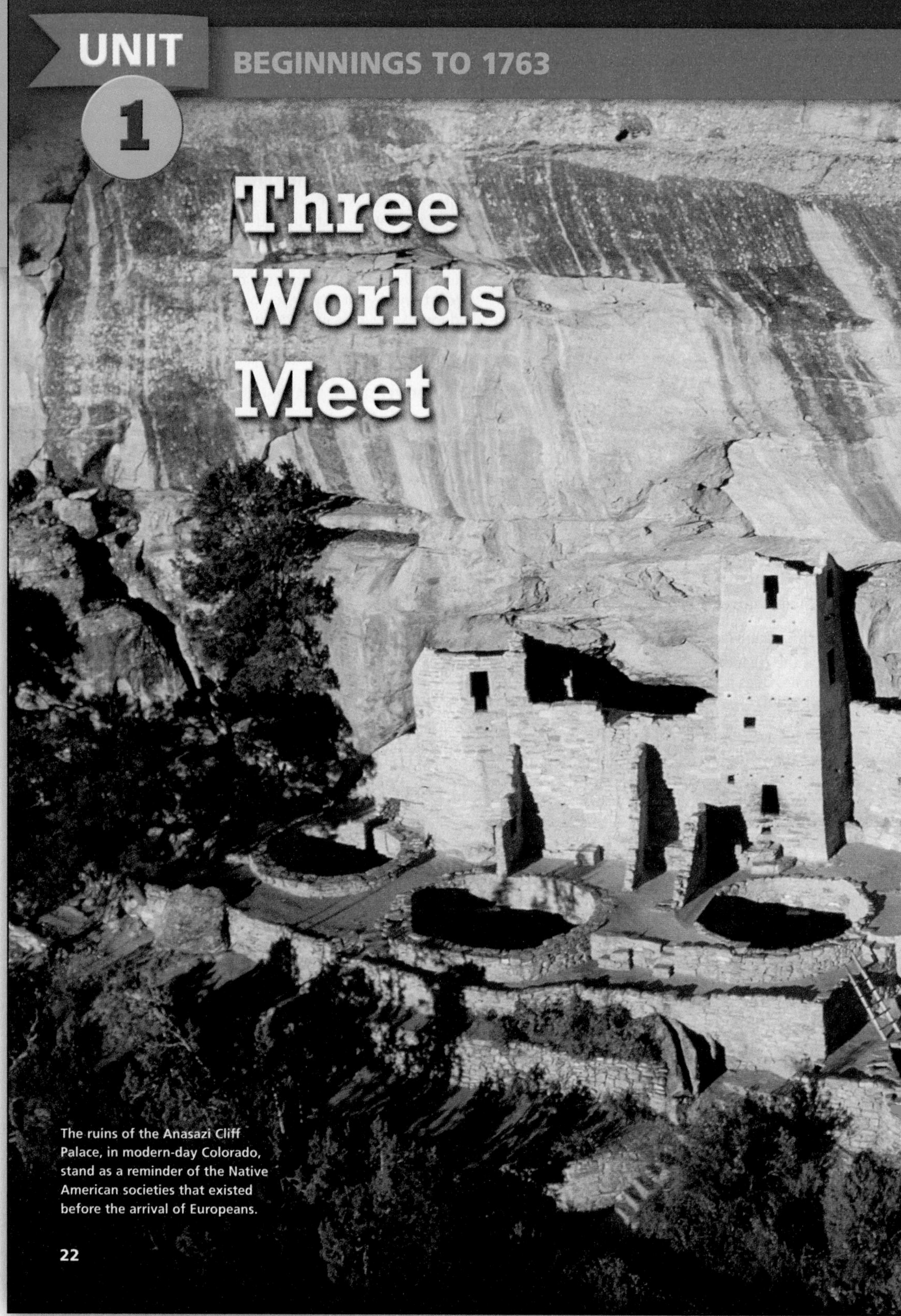


The ruins of the Anasazi Cliff Palace, in modern-day Colorado, stand as a reminder of the Native American societies that existed before the arrival of Europeans.

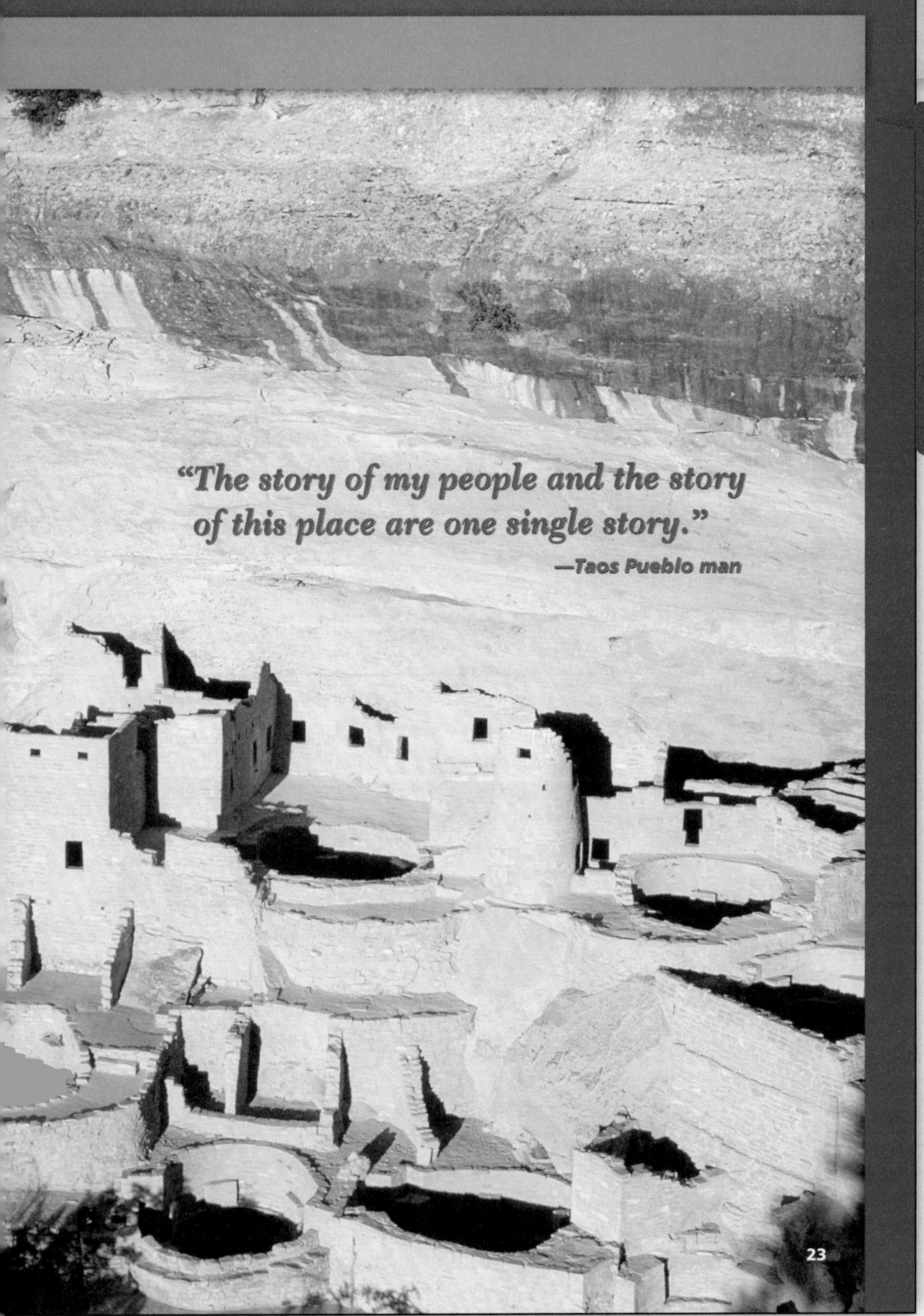

"The story of my people and the story of this place are one single story."
—Taos Pueblo man
23

## HISTORY FROM VISUALS

**Interpreting the Photograph** Ask students to study the photograph and brainstorm ideas about the people who lived in the cliff dwellings. List students' ideas on the chalkboard. Ask students what the buildings suggest about the culture of the people who lived here. **Possible Responses** The people were well organized, understood how to construct buildings with several stories, and most likely had a sophisticated society.

**Extension** Ask students to find out how the Anasazi used the round pit houses, or *kivas.*

# CHAPTER 1 PLANNING GUIDE
# THE WORLD IN 1500 Beginnings–1500

| | CHAPTER OVERVIEW | COPYMASTERS | TECHNOLOGY |
|---|---|---|---|
| **CHAPTER RESOURCES** | The chapter discusses the migration of ancient peoples to the Americas and the development of Native American cultures. It also describes the societies of West Africa and Europe in the 1500s, and explains the motivations behind the European explorations. | **In-Depth Resources: Unit 1**<br>• Tracing Themes: Diversity and Unity, p. 2<br>• Building Vocabulary, p. 8<br>• History Workshop Resources, p. 23<br>**Interdisciplinary Projects,** pp. 1–6 | CD-ROM **Primary Source Explorer**<br>CD-ROM **Electronic Teacher Tools**<br>CD-ROM **Power Presentations CD-ROM**<br>**Chapter Summaries on CD** (English and Spanish) |
| **SECTION 1** **Crossing to the Americas** **pp. 27–31** | **KEY IDEAS**<br>• The first people in the Americas migrate from Asia.<br>• The use of agriculture leads these people to develop civilizations.<br>• Native Americans create complex, communal cultures. | **In-Depth Resources: Unit 1**<br>• Setting the Stage, p. 1<br>• Guided Reading, p. 3<br>• Skillbuilder Practice: Using Secondary Sources, p. 9<br>• Reteaching Activity, p. 17<br>**Outline Map Activities**<br>• Landforms of North America, pp. 1–2 | **Warm-Up Transparency WT1**<br>**Humanities Transparency HT1**<br>• Mississippian Warrior<br>**Critical Thinking Transparency CT1**<br>• Setting the Stage<br>INTERNET **ClassZone:** www.mcdougallittell.com |
| **SECTION 2** **Societies of North America** **pp. 32–38** | • Native American groups are extremely diverse throughout North America.<br>• The Aztecs build a strong empire based on conquests.<br>• The Iroquois League brings peace to the warring tribes. | **In-Depth Resources: Unit 1**<br>• Setting the Stage, p. 1<br>• Guided Reading, p. 4<br>• Literature Selections, pp. 14–16<br>• Reteaching Activity, p. 18<br>**America's History Makers**<br>• Deganawida, pp. 1–2 | **Warm-Up Transparency WT1**<br>**Geography Transparency GT1**<br>• Native American Lifestyles, 1500<br>**Critical Thinking Transparency CT1**<br>• Setting the Stage<br>CD-ROM **Primary Source Explorer**<br>• *The Iroquois Great Law of Peace*<br>INTERNET **ClassZone:** www.mcdougallittell.com |
| **SECTION 3** **Societies of West Africa** **pp. 39–43** | • Africa's coastal ports are central to world trade.<br>• The kingdom of Ghana rises to power influenced by Islamic culture.<br>• Mali replaces Ghana as most prosperous kingdom, only to be replaced by Songhai. | **In-Depth Resources: Unit 1**<br>• Setting the Stage, p. 1<br>• Guided Reading, p. 5<br>• Primary Source, p. 12<br>• Reteaching Activity, p. 19 | **Warm-Up Transparency WT1**<br>**Critical Thinking Transparency CT1**<br>• Setting the Stage<br>INTERNET **ClassZone:** www.mcdougallittell.com |
| **SECTION 4** **Societies of Europe** **pp. 44–48** | • Feudalism dominates Europe in the Middle Ages.<br>• The revival of trade and towns leads to a decline in feudalism.<br>• The Renaissance and Reformation are periods of dramatic social change. | **In-Depth Resources: Unit 1**<br>• Setting the Stage, p. 1<br>• Guided Reading, p. 6<br>• Reteaching Activity, p. 20<br>**Economics in History**<br>• The Benefits of Trade, p. 1 | **Warm-Up Transparency WT1**<br>**Critical Thinking Transparency CT1**<br>• Setting the Stage<br>**Critical Thinking Transparency CT2**<br>• Cause and Effect: Causes of Exploration<br>INTERNET **ClassZone:** www.mcdougallittell.com |
| **SECTION 5** **Early European Explorers** **PP. 49–53** | • Europeans search for new trade routes.<br>• Columbus seeks financial backing from Spain to sail across the Atlantic Ocean.<br>• Columbus reaches islands that he believes to be Asia, but that are really the Americas, thus changing the European worldview. | **In-Depth Resources: Unit 1**<br>• Setting the Stage, p. 1<br>• Guided Reading, p. 7<br>• Primary Source, p. 13<br>• Geography Application, pp. 10–11<br>• Reteaching Activity, p. 21<br>**America's History Makers,** pp. 3–4<br>**Why It Matters Now,** pp. 1–2 | **Warm-Up Transparency WT1**<br>**Humanities Transparency HT2**<br>• Map of the American Southeast, 1606<br>**Critical Thinking Transparency CT3**<br>• Visual Summary<br>INTERNET **ClassZone:** www.mcdougallittell.com |

Pupil's Edition
Copymaster
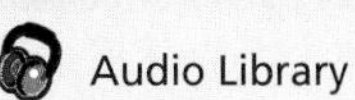
Overhead Transparency
Audio Library
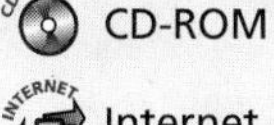
CD-ROM

Internet

## ASSESSMENT

**Chapter Assessment,** pp. 54–55

**Formal Assessment**
- Chapter Tests, Forms A and B, pp. 24–31

**Alternative Assessment Book**

**Electronic Teacher Tools with Test Maker**

---

**Section Assessment,** p. 31

**Formal Assessment**
- Section Quiz, p. 19

**Alternative Assessment Book**
- Rubrics for a diagram, 1.3
- Rubrics for a description, 2.5

**Electronic Teacher Tools with Test Maker**

---

**Section Assessment,** p. 37

**Formal Assessment**
- Section Quiz, p. 20

**Alternative Assessment Book**
- Rubrics for an illustration, 1.3
- Rubrics for verses, 4.8

**Electronic Teacher Tools with Test Maker**

---

**Section Assessment,** p. 43

**Formal Assessment**
- Section Quiz, p. 21

**Alternative Assessment Book**
- Rubrics for an oral history, 3.6
- Rubrics for a map, 2.1

**Electronic Teacher Tools with Test Maker**

---

**Section Assessment,** p. 48

**Formal Assessment**
- Section Quiz, p. 22

**Alternative Assessment Book**
- Rubrics for a Web site, 5.1
- Rubrics for a song, 4.8

**Electronic Teacher Tools with Test Maker**

---

**Section Assessment,** p. 53

**Formal Assessment**
- Section Quiz, p. 23

**Alternative Assessment Book**
- Rubrics for a map, 2.1
- Rubrics for a table, 2.2

**Electronic Teacher Tools with Test Maker**

## CUSTOMIZING FOR INDIVIDUAL NEEDS

### Students Acquiring English/ESL

**Reading Study Guide** (English and Spanish), pp. 5–16

**Access for Students Acquiring English/ESL: Spanish Translations,** pp. 1–8

**Chapter Summaries on CD** (English and Spanish)

### Less Proficient Readers

**Reading Study Guide** (English and Spanish), pp. 5–16

**Chapter Summaries on CD** (English and Spanish)

### Gifted and Talented Students

**In-Depth Resources: Unit 1**
- Enrichment Activity, p. 22

**America's History Makers**
- Deganawida, pp. 1–2
- Christopher Columbus, pp. 3–4

## CROSS-CURRICULAR CONNECTIONS

### World Cultures

Fritz, Jean, Katherine Paterson, Patricia McKissack, and Fredrick McKissack. ***The World in 1492.*** New York: Holt, 1995. A survey of world regions—Europe, Asia, Africa, Oceania, and the Americas—on the eve of the great voyages of discovery.

Koslow, Philip. **Centuries of Greatness. The West African Kingdoms, 750–1900.** New York: Chelsea, 1995. Solid, factual treatment focusing on military, economic, and political developments in more than 1,000 years of African history.

Tanaka, Shelley. ***The Lost Temple of the Aztec: What It Was Like When the Spaniards Invaded Mexico.*** New York: Hyperion, 1998. Aztec society was fully as urban and complex as that of Spain.

**Interdisciplinary Projects,** pp. 1–6
- Math: Time Line—A Number Line with Dates
- Science: Surveying an Archaeological Site
- Language Arts: Oral Literature: Storytelling
- Physical Education: Playing Lacrosse

### Humanities: Art

Cavendish, Marshall. ***The Marshall Cavendish Illustrated History of the North American Indians.*** New York: Marshall Cavendish, 1996. Native Americans developed a rich variety of artistic styles.

### Literature

Eboch, Chris. ***The Well of Sacrifice.*** Boston: Houghton Mifflin, 1999. Incorporates much new scholarship on the Maya in exciting fiction.

Litowinsky, Olga. ***High Voyage: The Final Crossing of Christopher Columbus.*** New York: Delacorte, 1991. Well-researched tale of Columbus's last voyage, through the eyes of his illegitimate son Fernando.

### McDougal Littell *The Language of Literature*

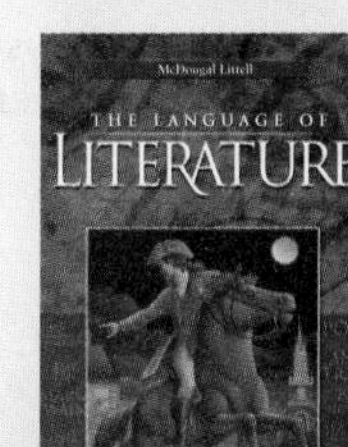


- Joseph Bruchac, "Racing the Great Bear" (Iroquois legend)
- Robert D. San Souci, "Otoomah" (Inuit legend)

## ENRICHMENT ACTIVITIES

**Pupil's Edition, pp. 24–57**
**Interact with History,** p. 25
**Technology of the Time,** p. 30
**Interactive Primary Source,** p. 38
**History Workshop,** pp. 56–57

**In-Depth Resources: Unit 1**
- Geography Application: Ocean Currents, pp. 10–11
- Primary Source, p. 12
- Primary Source, p. 13
- Literature Selections, pp. 14–16
- History Workshop Resources, p. 23

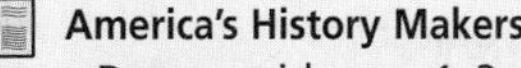
**America's History Makers**
- Deganawida, pp. 1–2
- Christopher Columbus, pp. 3–4

**Outline Map Activities**
- Land Forms of North America, pp. 1–2

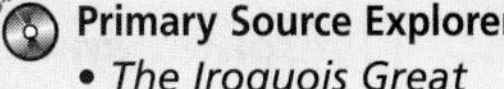
**Primary Source Explorer**
- *The Iroquois Great Law of Peace*

**Why It Matters Now**
- Cultural Diversity, pp. 1–2

# CHAPTER 1 PACING GUIDE

## LESSON PLAN OPTIONS (50-MINUTE PERIOD)

(TE) = Teacher's Edition (PE) = Pupil's Edition

| | TEACHER-DIRECTED ACTIVITIES<br>Class Time: 15 minutes | STUDENT-CENTERED ACTIVITIES<br>Class Time: 25 minutes | INDIVIDUAL ACTIVITIES<br>Class Time: 10 minutes |
|---|---|---|---|
| **DAY 1**<br>Introduction<br>pp. 24–26 | **Presentation Options**<br>• Begin with a class discussion of the painting on p. 24 **(PE)**.<br>• Lead a class discussion on the "What Do You Know?" question in Setting the Stage, p. 26. Then introduce the graphic organizer for the chapter **(PE)**. | **Options for Cooperative Learning**<br>• Have student groups discuss the Interact with History questions, p. 25 **(PE)**.<br>• Have student groups respond to the "What Do You Want to Know?" question in Setting the Stage, p. 26 **(PE)**. | **Head Start on Homework Options**<br>• Have students skim Section 1 Main Idea, Why It Matters Now, Terms & Names, and the main headings, p. 27 **(PE)**.<br>• Have students begin Guided Reading activity and Building Vocabulary sheet. |
| **DAY 2**<br>Section 1<br>pp. 27–31 | **Presentation Options**<br>• Begin with the 5-Minute Warm-Up, p. 27 **(TE)**.<br>• Review the Section 1 Main Idea, Why It Matters Now, p. 27 **(PE)**.<br>• Lead the students through the Skillbuilder Mini-Lesson: Using Secondary Sources, p. 29 **(TE)**. | **Options for Cooperative Learning**<br>• Divide students into groups to answer the questions posed in Technology of the Time, p. 30 **(PE)**.<br>• Have student pairs work together to complete one of the Activity Options in the Section 1 Assessment, p. 31 **(PE)**. | **Head Start on Homework Options**<br>• Have students begin working on Section 1 Assessment, p. 31 **(PE)**.<br>• Have students preview Section 2 Main Idea, Why It Matters Now, Terms & Names, and the main headings, p. 32 **(PE)**. |
| **DAY 3**<br>Section 2<br>pp. 32–38 | **Presentation Options**<br>• Begin with the 5-Minute Warm-Up, p. 32 **(TE)**.<br>• Choose 5 key questions for Objectives 1–4 to discuss with the class, pp. 32–38 **(TE)**.<br>• Lead the students through the Interactive Primary Source Activity, p. 38 **(TE)**. | **Options for Cooperative Learning**<br>• Divide students into groups and have them complete the Interdisciplinary Link, Geography: Interpreting Maps, p. 33 **(TE)**.<br>• Have students construct the chart that is part of the Critical Thinking Activity, p. 35 **(TE)**. | **Head Start on Homework Options**<br>• Have students begin reading the Literature Selection. **In-Depth Resources,** pp. 14–16.<br>• Have students preview Section 3 Main Idea, Why It Matters Now, Terms & Names, and the main headings, p. 39 **(PE)**. |
| **DAY 4**<br>Section 3<br>pp. 39–43 | **Presentation Options**<br>• Begin with the 5-Minute Warm-Up, p. 39 **(TE)**.<br>• Choose 5 key questions for Objectives 1–4 to discuss with the class, pp. 39–42 **(TE)**.<br>• Lead the students through the Geography Skillbuilder, p. 40 **(PE)**. | **Options for Cooperative Learning**<br>• Divide students into groups and have them complete the Interdisciplinary Link, Science/Health: Gold and Salt, p. 40 **(TE)**.<br>• Have student pairs work together to complete one of the Activity Options in the Section 3 Assessment, p. 43 **(PE)**. | **Head Start on Homework Options**<br>• Have students begin reading the Primary Source. **In-Depth Resources,** p. 12.<br>• Have students preview Section 4 Main Idea, Why It Matters Now, Terms & Names, and the main headings, p. 44 **(PE)**. |
| **DAY 5**<br>Section 4<br>pp. 44–48 | **Presentation Options**<br>• Begin with the 5-Minute Warm-Up, p. 44 **(TE)**.<br>• Review the cause-and-effect chart, p. 48 **(PE)**.<br>• Choose 5 key questions for Objectives 1–4 to discuss with the class, pp. 44–46 **(TE)**. | **Options for Cooperative Learning**<br>• Divide students into groups and have them complete the Interdisciplinary Link, World History: Feudalism, p. 45 **(TE)**.<br>• Divide students into groups and have them complete the Interdisciplinary Link, Humanities: Renaissance Art, p. 47 **(TE)**. | **Head Start on Homework Options**<br>• Have students begin working on the Reading History questions for Section 4 **(PE)**.<br>• Have students preview Section 5 Main Idea, Why It Matters Now, Terms & Names, and the main headings, p. 49 **(PE)**. |
| **DAY 6**<br>Section 5<br>pp. 49–53 | **Presentation Options**<br>• Begin with the 5-Minute Warm-Up, p. 49 **(TE)**.<br>• Discuss the follow-up question to Interact with History, p. 54 **(PE)**.<br>• Choose 5 key questions for Objectives 1–4 to discuss with the class, pp. 49–53 **(TE)**. | **Options for Cooperative Learning**<br>• Divide students into small groups and begin work on the History Workshop, pp. 56–57 **(PE)**.<br>• Divide students into groups and have them complete the Interdisciplinary Link, Language Arts: Writing a Dialogue, p. 50 **(TE)**. | **Head Start on Homework Options**<br>• Have students complete the Setting the Stage graphic organizer for the chapter, p. 26 **(PE)**.<br>• Have students begin working on the Chapter Assessment, pp. 54–55 **(PE)**.<br>• Prepare for Chapter Test<br>**Formal Assessment,** pp. 24–31 |

TEACHER-TESTED ACTIVITY | Lisa Williams, Lamberton Middle School, Carlisle, Pennsylvania

## SILENT TRADING OF GHANA

**Class Time** 20 minutes

**Task** Trading items without speaking

**Purpose** To understand the silent system used in the trans-Sahara trade to compensate for the lack of a common language

**Supplies Needed**

- Two different kinds of small items to trade (marbles, jelly beans, paper clips, mints, or such); have enough so that each student can have about ten pieces

**Activity** Divide the class into two groups. Give marbles to one group and jelly beans to the other. Explain that one item represents gold and the other salt. To the people of Ghana, salt was worth its weight in gold.

Set up pairs of students, one from each group. Students with the "salt" begin by silently placing what they are willing to trade on a desk, then retreating a few steps. Then the "gold" traders approach and examine the amount. They leave what they believe to be fair payment, then retreat. The salt traders return. If the payment is acceptable, they take the gold and the transaction is complete. If the trade is unacceptable, they leave the gold and the process repeats.

## BLOCK SCHEDULING — LESSON PLAN OPTIONS (90-MINUTE PERIOD)

### DAY 1

**Interact with History,** p. 25
**Class Time** 20 minutes

Options for pacing and variety:

- Role-Playing Have students meet in groups of four or five and act as Europeans and Native Americans meeting for the first time. Have them discuss the "What Do You Think?" questions. **Class Time** 15 minutes

**Setting the Stage,** p. 26
**Class Time** 20 minutes

Options for pacing and variety:

- Time Saver For a homework assignment, have students make a three-column chart labeled "What I Know," "What I Want to Know," and "What I Learned." Have students complete the first two columns before reading the chapter. The third column can be completed as part of the Chapter Assessment. **Class Time** 10 minutes

**Section 1,** pp. 27–31
**Class Time** 50 minutes

Options for pacing and variety:

- Peer Teaching Have students work in pairs to answer the Reading History questions in the section and the Critical Thinking question in the Section 1 Assessment. **Class Time** 15 minutes
- Internet Extend students' knowledge of the early peoples of America by having them visit www.mcdougallittell.com **Class Time** 20 minutes

### DAY 2

**Section 2,** pp. 32–38
**Class Time** 45 minutes

Options for pacing and variety:

- Time Saver Use the map North America, 1500 as a summary of the section. **Class Time** 10 minutes
- History on Film Extend students' background knowledge of Native American cultures by viewing one or more of the 20 videos in the *Indians of North America* video collection. Library Video, 1993–95 **Class Time** 30 minutes

**Section 3,** pp. 39–43
**Class Time** 45 minutes

Options for pacing and variety:

- Peer Competition Divide the class into small groups. Have each group make up five questions that can be answered with one of the Terms & Names for the section. Have groups take turns asking the class their questions. **Class Time** 20 minutes
- Peer Evaluation Have students pairs answer the Main Ideas and Critical Thinking questions in the Section Assessment. Then have them exchange papers with another team to evaluate their answers. **Class Time** 15 minutes

### DAY 3

**Section 4,** pp. 44–48
**Class Time** 45 minutes

Options for pacing and variety:

- Time Saver Use the chart The Rise and Decline of Feudalism on page 46 and Causes of Exploration on page 48 to summarize the section. **Class Time** 10 minutes

**Section 5,** pp. 49–53
**Class Time** 50 minutes

Options for pacing and variety:

- Peer Evaluation Have student pairs fill in the diagram in the Section 5 Assessment. After they complete it, have them swap diagrams with another pair. Have the pairs provide suggestions and comments about the diagrams to each other. **Class Time** 30 minutes

**History Workshop,** pp. 56–57
**Class Time** 50 minutes

- Time Saver Have students work on steps 1–4 in Create and Decode a Pictograph. **Class Time** 30 minutes
- Peer Evaluation Have students complete the pictograph (steps 5 & 6). **Class Time** 20 minutes

**Chapter 1 Assessment,** pp. 54–55
**Class Time** 40 minutes

Options for pacing and variety:

- Time Saver For a homework assignment, have students complete the What I Learned column of the chart they made prior to starting the chapter on Day 1. Have them share their responses with the class. **Class Time** 20 minutes
- Peer Teaching Divide students into groups of five students each. Have each student in a group prepare answers to the Review Questions for a different section. Within groups students can exchange answers. **Class Time** 20 minutes

## CHAPTER 1 OBJECTIVE

**The student will describe how events on four continents—Europe, Africa, and the Americas—led to the exploration of the Americas and the meeting of peoples from diverse cultures.**

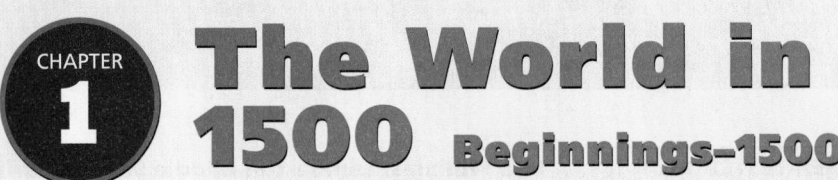

# The World in 1500 Beginnings–1500



### HISTORY FROM VISUALS

**Interpreting the Painting** Ask the students to study the painting of Native Americans looking out at the ship on the far horizon. Have them speculate about what emotions the people in the picture might have felt as they watched the ship approach. **Possible Responses** They might have been curious, frightened, or excited, depending on whether they had seen a ship before. Students could consider how prior experiences or lack of them would affect how Native Americans and Europeans thought about each other.

**Extension** Have the students write three questions that the Native Americans might want to ask the people on the ship and three questions the Europeans might have for the Native Americans.

Imagine how these Native Americans might feel at their first sight of strange ships.

24

### RECOMMENDED RESOURCES

**BOOKS FOR THE TEACHER**

Davidson, Basil. ***African Kingdoms.*** New York: Time, 1966. One of the few complete histories of the subject.

Gies, Frances and Joseph. ***Life in a Medieval Village.*** New York: Harper, 1990. Detailed, vivid, and fascinating account of daily life.

Trigger, Bruce G., and Wilcomb E. Washburn. ***North America.*** New York: Cambridge Univ. Press, 1996. Authoritative reference on the history of native peoples of the Americas.

**VIDEOS**

***Indians of North America.*** January Productions, Inc., 1994. Five-cassette set vividly introduces the many native cultures of North America.

***Roots.*** Wolper Productions, Warner, 1992. Episode 1. African beginning of the much-acclaimed saga of one family.

**INTERNET**

For more about the first Americans or the voyage of 1492, visit www.mcdougallittell.com.

## Interact *with* History

The Europeans will plant this flag and claim the island for Spain.
This picture is an artist's idea of the first meeting between European explorers and Native Americans.
The Native Americans offer a tray of the island's fruit as a welcome gift.
The Native Americans may wonder if this long object is a walking stick or a weapon.

**The year is 1492, and you live on an island in the Caribbean. One day you see a giant boat topped by strange white cloths. Men climb into smaller boats and row toward you. You have never seen men like this. They have pale skin and wear heavy, colorful clothing. You wonder what will happen when they land.**

### What Do You Think?

- What can different societies learn from each other?
- What might they want to gain from each other?
- What positive and negative things might happen when they meet?

# *What happens when different societies meet?*

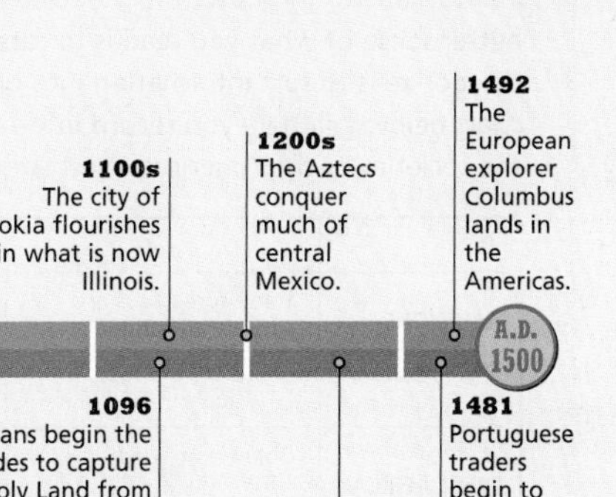

**Americas / World — 100 B.C. to A.D. 1500**

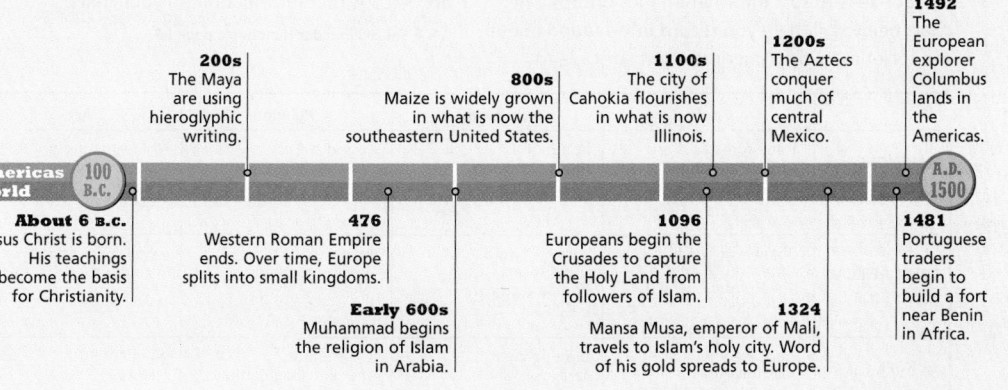

Americas:
- **200s** The Maya are using hieroglyphic writing.
- **800s** Maize is widely grown in what is now the southeastern United States.
- **1100s** The city of Cahokia flourishes in what is now Illinois.
- **1200s** The Aztecs conquer much of central Mexico.
- **1492** The European explorer Columbus lands in the Americas.

World:
- **About 6 B.C.** Jesus Christ is born. His teachings become the basis for Christianity.
- **476** Western Roman Empire ends. Over time, Europe splits into small kingdoms.
- **Early 600s** Muhammad begins the religion of Islam in Arabia.
- **1096** Europeans begin the Crusades to capture the Holy Land from followers of Islam.
- **1324** Mansa Musa, emperor of Mali, travels to Islam's holy city. Word of his gold spreads to Europe.
- **1481** Portuguese traders begin to build a fort near Benin in Africa.

*The World in 1500* **25**

## Interact *with* History

**OBJECTIVES**
- To identify the challenges of interactions among people of different cultures
- To differentiate between the viewpoints of the Native Americans and the European explorers

### What Do You Think?

1. Ask students what these different societies might teach each other.
2. Have students explain why each society might have difficulty understanding the other.
3. Encourage students to consider how the Europeans' motives for exploration might affect the way they viewed the Native Americans they met.

### *What happens when different societies meet?*

Encourage students to think about the ways that differences in beliefs, customs, languages, and other aspects of culture can affect the way people interact with one another and also how they resolve conflicts.

**MAKING PERSONAL CONNECTIONS**

Ask students to recall someone they have met who came from a different country or another part of the United States. What was their initial reaction to meeting that person? Did any misunderstandings arise? How did their impressions change as they got to know the person better?

## TIME LINE DISCUSSION

**Point out that this time line covers a span of 1,600 years. As indicated, events on the red line occurred in the Americas, while those on the blue line occurred in other parts of the world.**

**Remind students that the Americas were populated by many different groups with varying levels of development.**

- Ask students what can be learned from the time line about the cultures of some of the Native American groups living in the Americas prior to contact.
**Possible Response** The Maya had a system of writing; people in the present-day southeastern United States knew how to grow food; people in what is now Illinois built a city; the Aztecs were sufficiently skilled in warfare to conquer others.

- Ask students to find the time period in which Europeans began overseas exploration.
**Answer** late 1400s

## BEFORE YOU READ

### Previewing the Theme: Diversity and Unity

Ask students to think about what these monumental structures suggest about the differences and similarities among the societies that built them. **Possible Responses** Students might note that the building materials, design, and sizes of the structures reflect differences in technology, available resources, religious beliefs, and artistic preferences. All three societies had sufficient resources (time, capital, and labor) and the engineering and organizational skills needed to build such structures. Moreover, all three societies considered it important to create public buildings.

### What Do You Know?

Ask students to think about the organizational skills needed for such massive construction projects. Ask what such projects suggest about the power of the leaders who organized them. Point out that societies typically must meet basic needs for food, shelter, and clothing before devoting time and labor to other activities.

 **In-Depth Resources: Unit 1**
- Tracing Themes: Diversity and Unity, p. 2

## READ AND TAKE NOTES

### Reading Strategy: Categorizing

Tell students that categorizing information will help them identify common characteristics among groups. Organizing that information in a chart will help students develop critical thinking skills such as comparing and contrasting. When the chart is completed, students can use it to compare the societies of the Americas, West Africa, and Europe.

 **In-Depth Resources: Unit 1**
- Setting the Stage, p. 1

 **Critical Thinking Transparency CT1**
- Setting the Stage

# Chapter 1 SETTING THE STAGE

## BEFORE YOU READ

### Previewing the Theme

**Diversity and Unity** Chapter 1 explains that by 1500, diverse societies had developed in North America, West Africa, and Europe. After 1500, economic, political, social, and religious forces brought West Africans and Europeans to North America. Those people and Native Americans helped create the United States.

CENTRAL AMERICA **This pyramid at Chíchen Itzá, in what is now Mexico, was built between the 900s and 1200s.**

AFRICA **This Muslim mosque in Timbuktu, Mali, was built in the 1300s and 1400s.**

EUROPE **St. Peter's Basilica (a Christian church) in Rome, Italy, was built in the 1500s and early 1600s.**

### What Do You Know?

What do you know about the history of North America, West Africa, and Europe? How advanced must a society be to build large structures like the ones at the left?

**THINK ABOUT**
- what you know about other societies, such as Egypt, that built large structures
- what you've read in books

### What Do You Want to Know?

What questions do you have about the past societies of North America, West Africa, and Europe? What do you want to know about how they met? Record those questions in your notebook before you read the chapter.

## READ AND TAKE NOTES

**Reading Strategy: Categorizing** One way to make better sense of what you read is to categorize. To categorize is to sort information into groups. The chart below will help you record information about the societies of the Americas, West Africa, and Europe. As you read, look for information relating to the categories of trade, technology, religion, and art. Record that information on your chart.

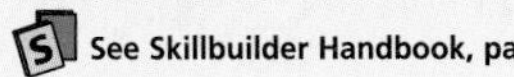
See Skillbuilder Handbook, page R6.

| | Trade | Technology | Religion | Art |
|---|---|---|---|---|
| AMERICAS | Trade spread culture. Groups exchanged regional products. | irrigation<br>mound building<br>seashell and bone tools | sacred places<br>sacred animals and natural forces | rock paintings<br>wooden carvings<br>jewelry<br>baskets |
| WEST AFRICA | Gold was traded for salt. Kingdoms grew rich on trade. | Songhai swords and spears<br>Yoruba cast metal sculpture | traditional African religions<br>Islam | wood, ivory, and metal sculptures |
| EUROPE | Trade declined during Middle Ages. Crusades spurred trade. Italy controlled trade with East. | printing press<br>caravels | Christianity<br>split between Catholics and Protestants | paintings<br>statues |



## TEACHING STRATEGY

### READING THE CHAPTER

This is a thematic chapter focusing on the diverse societies of the Americas, West Africa, and Europe. Encourage students to compare and contrast these societies and the reasons that brought people from each of these societies to North America.

### ALTERNATIVE ASSESSMENT

The Chapter Assessment describes three activities for alternative assessment on page 55. You may wish to have students work on these activities during the course of the chapter and then present them at the end.

# 1 Crossing to the Americas

**TERMS & NAMES**
archaeologist
artifact
migrate
culture
domestication
civilization
irrigation
Mound Builders

**MAIN IDEA**

Ancient peoples came from Asia to the Americas and over time developed complex civilizations.

**WHY IT MATTERS NOW**

Archaeologists and other scientists continue to make new discoveries about these ancient people.

## ONE AMERICAN'S STORY

**To do her work, Solveig Turpin must climb rugged cliffs, step over rattlesnakes, and dodge sharp cactus spines. For more than 20 years, she has searched the caves and cliffs of Texas for paintings that ancient people left on rock walls. Turpin is an archaeologist. That is a scientist who studies the human past by examining the things people left behind. One painting that Turpin found shows a red, 9-foot-long panther. She believes it shows a religious leader who turned himself into an animal.**

Archaeologist Solveig Turpin wears a shirt displaying the rock art of ancient peoples as she discusses her work.

*A VOICE FROM THE PAST*

This is the Shaman [religious leader] who transforms into the largest and most powerful animal here. . . . I like to call [the shamans] supramen because they were over everything.

**Solveig Turpin,** quoted in *In Search of Ancient North America*

**Archaeologists make theories about the past based on what they learn from bones and artifacts. Artifacts are tools and other objects that humans made. They give clues about who ancient people were and how they lived. This section discusses some theories about early Americans.**

## 1 The First People in America

As many societies do, many Native Americans have stories explaining the origin of their people. Some believe the gods created their ancestors. Others believe their ancestors were born of Mother Earth. In contrast, scientists think that the first Americans **migrated**, or moved, here from Asia. But scientists disagree about how and when this move took place.

Some ancient people may have crossed a land bridge that joined Asia and North America during the last Ice Age. The Ice Age was a time of extreme cold that lasted for thousands of years. Glaciers trapped so much water that ocean levels dropped. A bridge of land, now called Beringia, appeared where the Bering Strait is now. (See map, page 28.) When the earth grew warm again, the glaciers melted and flooded Beringia. Some scientists who hold this theory believe the earliest Americans arrived





## SECTION OBJECTIVES

1. To explain how people first migrated to the Americas
2. To analyze the link between the development of agriculture and the rise of civilizations
3. To identify the early peoples of Mesoamerica and the American Southwest
4. To locate the Mound Builders

**SKILLBUILDER**

Interpreting Maps: Movement, Human–Environment Interaction, p. 28

**CRITICAL THINKING**

Drawing Conclusions, pp. 29, 30
Comparing, p. 31

## FOCUS & MOTIVATE

### 5-MINUTE WARM-UP

**Making Inferences** Have students discuss these questions to understand how people first came to the Americas.

1. Look at the map on page 28. Where did the first peoples to reach the Americas come from?
2. What can you conclude about the North American climate 12,000 years ago?
3. What role might the ice sheets have played in the creation of the Beringia land bridge?

 **Warm-Up Transparency WT1**

## INSTRUCT

### INSTRUCT: OBJECTIVE 1

**The First People in America**

Key Questions

- How did the extreme cold of the Ice Age help to create the land bridge?
- Why do scientists think humans may have arrived in the Americas earlier than 12,000 years ago?

**In-Depth Resources: Unit 1**
- Guided Reading, p. 3

**Reading Study Guide** (Spanish and English), pp. 5–6

## RECOMMENDED RESOURCES

**In-Depth Resources: Unit 1**
- Guided Reading, p. 3
- Building Vocabulary, p. 8
- Skillbuilder Practice, p. 9
- Reteaching Activity, p. 17

**Reading Study Guide** (Spanish and English), pp. 5–6

**Outline Map Activities**
- Landforms of North America, pp. 1–2

**Formal Assessment**
- Section Quiz, p. 19

**Alternative Assessment**
- Rubrics, 1.3
- Rubrics, 2.5

**Access for Students Acquiring English/ESL**
- Guided Reading, p. 1
- Skillbuilder Practice, p. 6

Technology Resources

**Humanities Transparency HT1**
- Mississippian Warrior

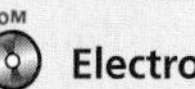

**Electronic Teacher Tools with Test Maker**

**Classzone**
www.mcdougallittell.com

## HISTORY FROM VISUALS

**Reading the Map** Ask students to look at the two migration routes. In what way are they different? **Possible Response** Earlier migrations followed coastlines; later ones went inland. Ask the class to discuss how gradual warming at the end of the last Ice Age affected migration. **Possible Response** Water levels rose and the land bridge disappeared, ending the possibility of migration by foot from Asia.

**Extension** Ask students to use an atlas with a map of South America to find Chile. Ask students what geographic barriers would have prevented earlier migrations from moving inland. Why were people able to move inland in later migrations?

### Early Migration to the Americas

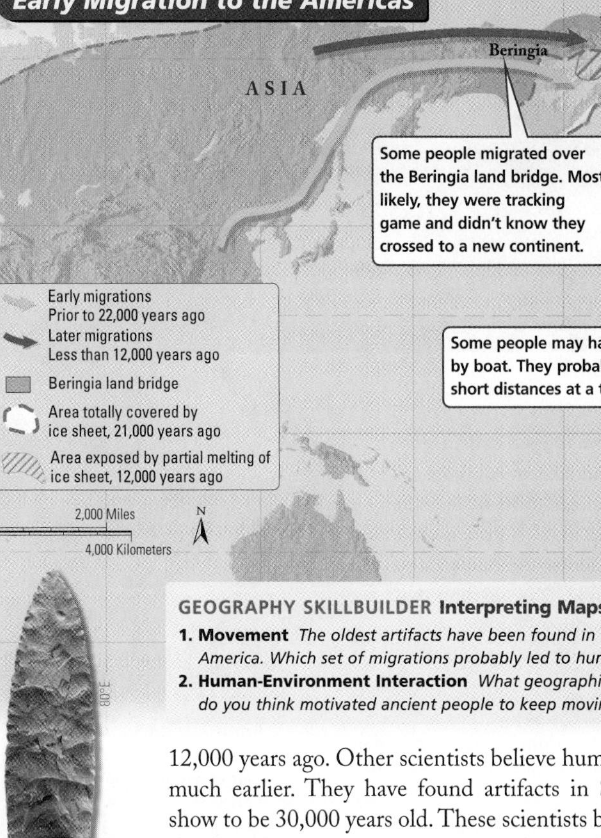


**GEOGRAPHY SKILLBUILDER Interpreting Maps**

1. **Movement** *The oldest artifacts have been found in Chile, in western South America. Which set of migrations probably led to human settlement there?*
2. **Human-Environment Interaction** *What geographic feature, shown on the map, do you think motivated ancient people to keep moving south?*

Ancient hunters used spear points such as this one, which is about 10,000 years old.

12,000 years ago. Other scientists believe humans came to the Americas much earlier. They have found artifacts in South America that tests show to be 30,000 years old. These scientists believe that people came to the Americas by many routes, over thousands of years. Some came by boat, sailing short distances from island to island. This theory may also change as scientists find more evidence of ancient Americans.

Skillbuilder Answers
1. the early migrations by boat, shown by the yellow arrow
2. the ice sheets

## 2 Agriculture Leads to Civilization

A **culture** is a way of life shared by people with similar arts, beliefs, and customs. The first Americans lived in hunting and gathering cultures. They hunted small animals, such as rabbits, and large animals, such as the woolly mammoth. They gathered wild seeds, nuts, and berries.

Vocabulary
**woolly mammoth:** a hairy ancestor of the elephant, now extinct

In time, people started to plant the seeds they found. This was the beginning of agriculture. About 5,000 years ago, humans began domestication. **Domestication** is the practice of breeding plants or taming animals to meet human needs. By trial and error, people in central Mexico learned which seeds grew the best crops. By selecting the right seeds, they improved the quality of maize, or corn, until its ears were large. Dried and stored for future use, corn became a main food source.

Knowledge of agriculture spread throughout the Americas. Having a stable food supply changed the way people lived. Once they no longer had to travel to find food, they built permanent villages. Farmers were able to produce large harvests, so that fewer people needed to farm.



## INSTRUCT: OBJECTIVE 2

**Agriculture Leads to Civilization**

Key Questions
- How did agriculture develop in the Americas?
- How did the way the first Americans lived change as knowledge of agriculture spread?
- What are the five features of a civilization?

**Outline Map Activities**
- Landforms of North America, pp. 1–2

## ACTIVITY OPTIONS
## INDIVIDUAL NEEDS

**LESS PROFICIENT READERS**

**Focusing on Important Details** Some students may have trouble identifying the significant achievements of the civilizations described in this section. As students read, work with them to create a chart that shows the names of these civilizations and significant achievements of each one.

| | |
|---|---|
| **Olmec** | developed trade routes |
| **Maya** | created calendar, number system |
| **Hohokam** | developed irrigation techniques |
| **Anasazi** | built large houses |
| **Mound Builders** | built large earthen structures |

Some people began to practice other crafts, such as weaving or making pots. A few people became religious leaders.

Slowly, some cultures grew complex and became civilizations. A **civilization** has five features: (1) cities that are centers of trade, (2) specialized jobs for different people, (3) organized forms of government and religion, (4) a system of record keeping, and (5) advanced tools.

**Reading History**

**A. Drawing Conclusions** Why would a culture need to learn agriculture before it could develop a civilization?

A. Possible Answer Unless it could produce a food surplus, it could not develop specialized jobs or engage in much trade.

## 3 Early Mesoamerican Civilizations

About 1200 B.C., an advanced civilization arose in Mesoamerica, a region that stretches from central Mexico to present-day Nicaragua. For 800 years, a people called the Olmec thrived along the Gulf of Mexico. The Olmec set up a network of trade routes and constructed earthen mounds shaped like pyramids. They built large, busy cities like La Venta.

*A VOICE FROM THE PAST*

La Venta was not just an empty ceremonial spot visited by Olmec priests and nobles but a prosperous community of fishers, farmers, traders, and specialists, such as the artisans and the sculptors.

**Rebecca González,** quoted in "New Light on the Olmec," *National Geographic*

Around 400 B.C., the Olmec abandoned La Venta and other cities. Scientists don't know why. By then, Olmec culture had spread along trade routes and influenced others. Later people in Mesoamerica adapted Olmec religious practices and carved designs inspired by Olmec art.

By A.D. 250, about 650 years after the Olmec vanished, the Maya had developed a great civilization. Their cities were in southern Mexico and Guatemala, where they built pyramid mounds topped by temples. From artifacts, archaeologists know that the Maya had an accurate yearly calendar. They were the first people in the Americas to create a number system using zero. Their written language used picture symbols.

By 900, the Maya had abandoned many of their cities. Scientists think that revolts, disease, or crop failures may have caused their society to fail.

**Background**

Mathematicians in India also developed the idea of using a symbol for zero. Traders later carried the idea from Asia to Europe.

## 4 The Hohokam and the Anasazi

During the Mayan period, an agricultural people inhabited the American Southwest. The Hohokam lived in what is now Arizona from about 300 B.C. to A.D. 1400. That desert region has little rain, so farming is difficult. But the Hohokam altered their dry environment. They dug hundreds of miles of canals to carry river water to their crops. The practice of bringing water to crops is called **irrigation.**

The Hohokam raised corn, beans, and squash. They also gathered wild plants and hunted animals. They traded widely—with people in Mexico, the Southwest, and California. Hohokam pottery and religious practices show the influence of Mesoamerican cultures, which they learned about through trade.

Ancient peoples of the American Southwest used images like this to communicate with each other. Such images are called petroglyphs.



**INSTRUCT: OBJECTIVE 3**

**Early Mesoamerican Civilizations**

Key Questions

- Where did the earliest advanced civilizations in the Americas develop?
- How did the Olmec influence later cultures?
- What were some of the achievements of the Maya?

**MORE ABOUT . . .**

**The Mayan Calendar**

Mayan astronomers made highly accurate observations of the movements of the sun, moon, and stars. They used that information to create two kinds of calendars. The sacred round calendar recorded the religious year, which had 260 days. Each day had a name associated with one of 20 deities; each day also had a number from 1 to 13. Mayan priests predicted good or bad luck and the proper day for planting, marrying, and other important activities by studying the combinations of gods and numbers on the calendar. The Maya also had a 365-day solar calendar with 18 months of 20 days each. The five days at year's end were considered unlucky.

**INSTRUCT: OBJECTIVE 4**

**The Hohokam and the Anasazi/ The Mound Builders**

Key Questions

- What challenges did the Hohokam face in adapting to their environment?
- What was distinctive about the houses built by the Anasazi?
- What were the features of the Mound Builders' civilization?

**ACTIVITY OPTIONS**

**SKILLBUILDER MINI-LESSON: USING SECONDARY SOURCES** — BLOCK SCHEDULING

**Explaining the Skill** In studying history, students must learn to use both primary and secondary sources. Primary sources are letters, diaries, speeches, and other documents by people who witnessed a historical event. Secondary sources are accounts, usually written later, by people who were not present at the original event. Secondary sources include archaeological reports, history books, and biographies. In evaluating a secondary source, it is important to know what qualifications its author had for writing about the subject.

**Applying the Skill** After students read *A Voice from the Past,* ask:

1. Is this a primary or a secondary source? Explain. *(secondary. The writer is not an eyewitness.)*
2. What primary sources might the author have used to create this secondary source? *(Olmec artifacts)* What secondary sources? *(Maya and other peoples' writings about the Olmec; the works of other archaeologists)*
3. What information would help you assess the writer's qualifications? *(her occupation or expertise on this topic and whether her knowledge of Olmec sites is firsthand or secondhand)*

 **In-Depth Resources: Unit 1**

- Skillbuilder Practice, p. 9

## Technology OF THE Time

**OBJECTIVES**

1. To analyze written information, a site map, and an aerial photograph to learn about the early peoples of North America
2. To explain how the Great Serpent Mound was built

## INSTRUCT

Key Questions

- How was the Great Serpent Mound constructed?
- What do archaeologists think were possible uses for this mound?
- What artifacts and other evidence would help to support their theory?
- What can be learned about the social and political organization of the Mound Builders from looking at this structure?

**MORE ABOUT . . .**

**The Great Serpent Mound**

Every year thousands of visitors come to see the Great Serpent Mound at Serpent Mound State Memorial, a public park near Hillsboro, Ohio. In the late 1800s, archaeologist Fredric Ward Putnam, the director of Harvard University's Peabody Museum, saved the Great Serpent Mound from almost certain destruction when he raised $5,880 from private donors in Boston to purchase the land. In 1900, Harvard University deeded the 60-acre site to the state of Ohio.

Technology OF THE Time

# The Mound Builders

During the 1700s, Europeans discovered several mysterious earthen mounds in what is now the American Southeast and Midwest. They believed a lost civilization had built the mounds. Historians now know that different Native American groups, known as the Mound Builders, built these structures. The builders may have used the mounds for burial tombs, as a tribute to their gods, or for some other religious purpose. One famous mound is the Great Serpent Mound in present-day Ohio. The Adena, Fort Ancient, or Hopewell cultures possibly built it. An aerial photograph of the Great Serpent Mound is shown below.

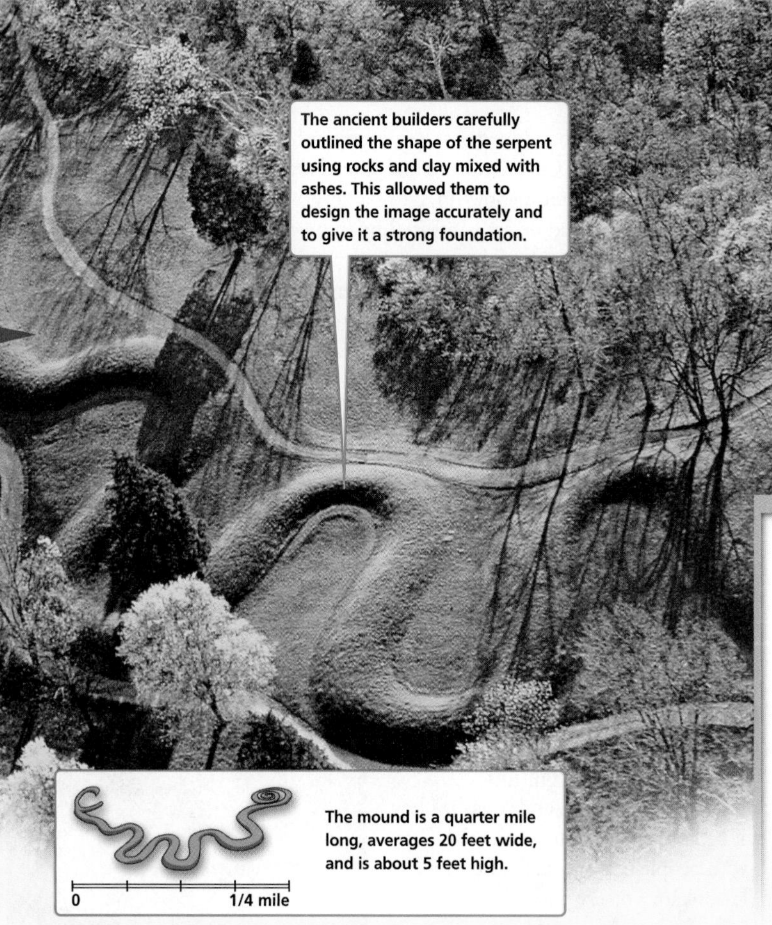

Workers dug with large, flat stones and shoulder-blade bones from deer and elk. They used about 300,000 baskets of soil to build the mound. Construction most likely took between five and ten years and required hundreds of laborers.
The ancient builders carefully outlined the shape of the serpent using rocks and clay mixed with ashes. This allowed them to design the image accurately and to give it a strong foundation.
0
1/4 mile
The mound is a quarter mile long, averages 20 feet wide, and is about 5 feet high.

**CONNECT TO HISTORY**

1. **Drawing Conclusions** Review the five characteristics of a civilization on page 29. Which of these characteristics would a culture need to be able to build something like the Great Serpent Mound?

See Skillbuilder Handbook, page R12.

**CONNECT TO TODAY**

2. **Researching** How do modern monuments to the dead differ from those constructed by the Mound Builders?

Visit www.mcdougallittell.com to learn more about the Mound Builders.

30 CHAPTER 1

**CONNECT TO HISTORY**

1. **Drawing Conclusions** **Possible Response** A society would need an organized form of government to carry out a building project of this size. Possibly the builders had specialized jobs and used advanced tools in the construction of the mound. The builders also had an organized religion and a system of record keeping.

**CONNECT TO TODAY**

2. **Researching** **Possible Response** Students might think about monuments that honor past leaders or veterans. Building materials, design, and construction methods are areas for comparison. Modern monuments are often conceived and executed by one artist, while mounds were communal efforts. Modern monuments are often made of materials that require advanced technology, and they have written inscriptions.

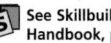

Beginning about A.D. 100, the Anasazi lived in the area where Utah, Arizona, Colorado, and New Mexico now meet. Scientists don't know their origin. Like the Hohokam, the Anasazi were mainly farmers who also traded widely.

The Anasazi built houses with hundreds of rooms and many stories. For protection, they placed some buildings against overhanging canyon walls. The 800-room Pueblo Bonito in Chaco Canyon, New Mexico, housed perhaps 1,000 people. In the 1500s, when Spanish explorers first saw these houses, they called them *pueblos,* meaning villages. Around 1300, drought or warfare caused the Anasazi to leave their homes.

## The Mound Builders

In the eastern part of what is now the United States lived several groups of people called Mound Builders. The **Mound Builders** were early Native Americans who built large earthen structures.

The two oldest Mound Builder societies were the Adena and the Hopewell. Archaeologists know little about the Adena. The Hopewell, located in what is now the Midwest, lived from 400 B.C. to A.D. 400. Like the Hohokam, they grew corn. Artifacts show that they had a large trade network. It stretched from the Atlantic to the Rocky Mountains, and from the Great Lakes to Florida. Hopewell mounds served as burial sites. Their tombs contained jewelry and other gifts for the dead.

B. Answer the Olmec and the Maya

*Reading*History

**B. Comparing** What other ancient American cultures built pyramid-shaped mounds?

The last group of Mound Builders, the Mississippians, lived from A.D. 800 to 1700. They built some of the first cities in North America. For example, Cahokia in Illinois has more than 100 mounds. One of them, Monks Mound, rises 100 feet and covers 16 acres. In some cities, the Mississippians built flat-topped, pyramid-shaped temple mounds.

By the 1700s, most of the Mississippians had died from diseases they caught from Europeans. But many Native American groups continued to thrive throughout the United States, as you will read in Section 2.

### Section 1 Assessment

**1. Terms & Names**

**Identify:**
- archaeologist
- artifact
- migrate
- culture
- domestication
- civilization
- irrigation
- Mound Builders

**2. Taking Notes**

Use a chart like the one below to list ancient cultures of Mesoamerica and North America and their locations.

| Ancient Culture | Location |
|---|---|
| | |

Which of these cultures was closest to where you live?

**3. Main Ideas**

a. By what land bridge did some ancient people migrate to North America, and how was it created?

b. How did the development of farming lead to the growth of civilization?

c. How did trade help to spread culture?

**4. Critical Thinking**

**Comparing** How did the Hohokam and the Anasazi adapt to living in their environment?

THINK ABOUT
- Hohokam agriculture
- Anasazi dwellings

**ACTIVITY OPTIONS**

**SCIENCE**
**LANGUAGE ARTS**

Research the growing of corn. Draw a **diagram** of a corn plant with its parts labeled or write a **description** of how corn grows.





### MORE ABOUT . . .

**Chaco Canyon**

After the descendants of Chaco's builders left the settlement, the "great houses" like Casa Bonito stood abandoned. Not for 500 years did another group dare to settle in the shadows of those massive monuments. Then, in the 1700s, the Navajo moved into the canyon. The Chaco Canyon settlement was designated a national monument in 1907.

Archaeologists have been studying this dramatic site since 1877. Today, experts continue to study the finds from earlier generations of archaeologists, but new excavations at the site are strictly limited. The goal is to preserve Chaco Canyon for future investigators with new, nondestructive techniques.

**Humanities Transparency HT1**
- Mississippian Warrior

## ASSESS & RETEACH

**Setting the Stage** Have students fill in as much as possible in the Americas row on the chapter graphic organizer.

**Formal Assessment**
- Section Quiz, p. 19

**Critical Thinking Transparency CT1**
- Setting the Stage

### RETEACHING ACTIVITY

Have pairs of students turn the five subheads in this section into questions. For example, "Agriculture Leads to Civilization" might become "How did agriculture lead to civilization?" Have pairs trade questions and answer the questions they receive.

**In-Depth Resources: Unit 1**
- Reteaching Activity, p. 17

### Section 1 Assessment

**1. Terms & Names**

**archaeologist,** p. 27
**artifact,** p. 27
**migrate,** p. 27
**culture,** p. 28
**domestication,** p. 28
**civilization,** p. 29
**irrigation,** p. 29
**Mound Builders,** p. 31

**2. Taking Notes**

Olmec—Mesoamerica along the Gulf of Mexico
Maya—southern Mexico and Guatemala
Hohokam—American Southwest
Anasazi—where Utah, Arizona, Colorado, and New Mexico meet
Hopewell—the Midwest
Mississippians—the Midwest

**3. Main Ideas**

**a.** They came across Beringia when glaciers trapped so much water that the ocean level dropped. **b.** Fewer people were needed to grow food, so specialized jobs developed. **c.** Other cultures learned Olmec religion and art; the Hohokam were influenced by Mesoamerica through trade.

**4. Critical Thinking**

The Hohokam built irrigation canals so they could farm in the desert; the Anasazi built their houses against cliffs for protection.

**ACTIVITY OPTIONS**

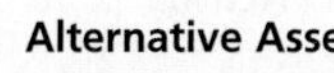

**Alternative Assessment**
- Rubrics for a diagram, 1.3
- Rubrics for a description, 2.5

## SECTION OBJECTIVES

1. To describe Native American diversity
2. To explain how the cultures of the North, the Northwest Coast, and the West adapted to their environments
3. To differentiate among the peoples of Mexico, the Southwest, and the Great Plains
4. To compare the ways of life of the peoples of the Southeast and the Eastern Woodlands

**SKILLBUILDER**
Interpreting Maps: Movement, Location, p. 33

**CRITICAL THINKING**
Making Inferences, p. 34
Drawing Conclusions, pp. 35, 37
Analyzing Causes, p. 36

## FOCUS & MOTIVATE

### 5-MINUTE WARM-UP

**Reading a Map** These questions focus on the diversity of North American societies.

1. Look at the map on page 33. How many different culture areas are shown?
2. Which cultures seem to be less connected to others by trade?

 **Warm-Up Transparency WT1**

## INSTRUCT

### INSTRUCT: OBJECTIVE 1

**Native American Diversity**
Key Questions
- What was one reason for the great diversity of Native American groups?
- How did different environments lead to differences in technology?
- What were Native American beliefs about the natural world?

**In-Depth Resources: Unit 1**
- Guided Reading, p. 4
- Building Vocabulary, p. 8

**Reading Study Guide** (Spanish and English), pp. 7–8

# 2 Societies of North America

**TERMS & NAMES**
technology
tundra
kayak
matrilineal
slash-and-burn agriculture
Deganawida
Iroquois League

| MAIN IDEA | WHY IT MATTERS NOW |
|---|---|
| By 1500, a variety of Native American groups—each with a distinct culture—lived in North America. | Many Americans today claim one or more of these cultures as part of their heritage. |

## ONE AMERICAN'S STORY

**Many Native Americans today work to save their culture, so it won't vanish as some ancient cultures did. Haida artist Bill Reid took part in this effort. When he was a teenager in the 1930s, totem poles and other Haida crafts existed mostly in museums. Few Haida carvers were making new ones. Reid himself did not learn about Haida arts until he was 23 and visited his grandparents' island village off the west coast of Canada. Reid's grandfather showed him the tools of a great Haida artist of the 1800s.**

**Reid began to study Northwest Coast native arts by reading books and visiting museums. After taking a class in jewelry making, he created gold jewelry with Haida designs. He also carved totem poles and sculptures. When Reid died in 1998, his work was praised.**

*A VOICE FROM THE PAST*

Canada has lost one of its greatest artists. A descendant of a lineage of great Haida artists . . . , Bill Reid revived an artistic tradition that had survived only in museum collections.

**Dr. George MacDonald,** at Bill Reid's memorial service, March 24, 1998

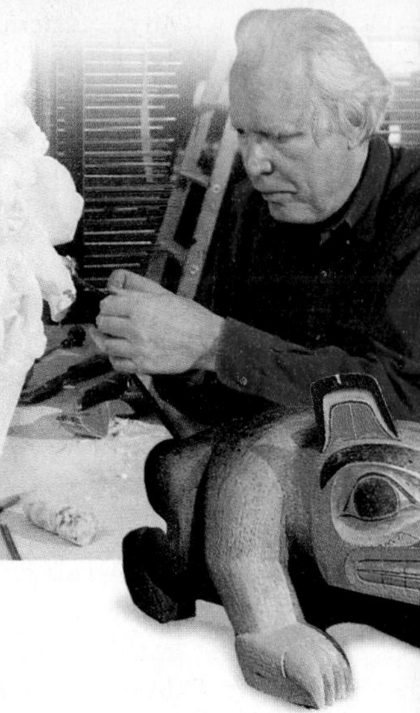

Creating sculptures of traditional designs was one way Bill Reid kept Haida culture alive.

**Written records and people like Reid have preserved knowledge of the cultures that flourished in the Americas when Europeans arrived. This section explains the diversity of Native American groups in 1500.**

## 1 Native American Diversity

By 1500, Native Americans had divided into hundreds of cultural groups, speaking perhaps 2,000 languages. One reason Native Americans were so diverse was that each group adapted to its own environment—whether subzero ice fields, scorching deserts, or dense forests.

Environment shaped each group's economy, technology, and religion. **Technology** is the use of tools and knowledge to meet human needs. In some regions, Native Americans based their economy on farming. In others, they relied on hunting or fishing. Different environments caused technology to vary. In coastal areas, farmers made tools from shells. In



## RECOMMENDED RESOURCES

 **In-Depth Resources: Unit 1**
- Guided Reading, p. 4
- Building Vocabulary, p. 8
- Literature Selections: Coyote Steals Otter's Coat, pp. 14–15; Song of the Sky Loom, p. 16
- Reteaching Activity, p. 18

**America's History Makers**
- Deganawida, pp. 1–2

**Reading Study Guide** (Spanish and English), pp. 7–8

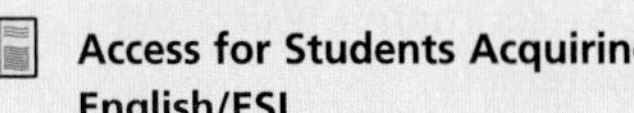

**Formal Assessment**
- Section Quiz, p. 20

**Alternative Assessment**
- Rubrics, 1.3
- Rubrics, 4.8

**Access for Students Acquiring English/ESL**
- Guided Reading, p. 2

Technology Resources

 **Geography Transparency GT1**
- Native American Lifestyles, 1500

 **Electronic Teacher Tools with Test Maker**

 **Classzone**
www.mcdougallittell.com

**North America, 1500**

Native American Cultures
- Subarctic
- Northwest Coast
- California
- Plateau
- Great Basin
- Mesoamerican
- Southwest
- Plains
- Eastern Woodlands
- Southeastern
- Caribbean
- Major trade routes

Haida, Kwakiutl, Blackfoot, Nez Perce, Crow, Mandan, Cree, Ojibwa, Algonquin, Ottawa, Huron, Chinook, Shoshone, Cheyenne, Dakota (Sioux), Sauk, Potawatomi, Iroquois, Wampanoag, Pequot, Iowa, Miami, Pawnee, Arapaho, Delaware, Susquehanna, Pomo, Paiute, Kansas, Shawnee, Powhatan, Kiowa, Osage, Navajo, Hopi, Apache, Chickasaw, Tuscarora, Cherokee, Chumash, Zuni, Pueblo, Pima, Comanche, Choctaw, Creek, Seminole, Huichol, Aztec, Taino

PACIFIC OCEAN · ATLANTIC OCEAN · Gulf of Mexico · Tropic of Cancer · 40°N · 80°W · 120°W · 500 Miles · 1,000 Kilometers

**GEOGRAPHY SKILLBUILDER**
**Interpreting Maps**
1. **Movement** *Which Native American culture was able to trade directly with the Aztecs?*
2. **Location** *Which culture lived around the Great Lakes?*

deserts, they used irrigation. Environment affected religion, too. Native Americans strongly believed that certain places were sacred—and that animals, plants, and natural forces had spiritual importance.

Although Native American groups had many differences, they all felt closely connected to nature, as shown in the following chant.

Skillbuilder Answers
1. the people of the Southwest
2. the people of the Eastern Woodlands

> *A VOICE FROM THE PAST*
>
> Earth's body has become my body
> by means of these I shall live on.
> Earth's mind has become my mind
> by means of these I shall live on.
>
> **Navajo Blessing Way,** quoted in *America in 1492*

In addition, trade linked Native Americans. Trading centers developed across North America, especially at points where two cultures met.

## 2 Peoples of the North and Northwest Coast

**Background**
The Inuit are also called the Eskimo.

The Aleut (uh•LOOT) and the Inuit (IHN•yoo•iht) were peoples of the far North. The Aleut lived on islands off Alaska, and the Inuit lived near the coast on tundra. **Tundra** is a treeless plain that remains frozen under its top layer of soil. Ice and snow cover the ground most of the year.

Because their climate was too cold for farming, the Inuit and Aleut were hunters. They paddled **kayaks**, small boats made of animal skins,





### HISTORY FROM VISUALS

**Reading the Map** Ask students to use the map to identify the major culture groups of Native Americans within North America in 1500. Have students name the culture region with the coldest climate and the regions likely to be hottest and driest. What effects might trade among regions have had on the way people lived? **Possible Response** Besides giving people access to resources that were lacking in their own areas, trade might have led to the exchange of technology and ideas as well as goods. How might trade between peoples of different culture areas have spread ideas? What natural resources might have been most scarce in the Subarctic? In the Southwest?

**Extension** Tell students to pick one of the Native American groups shown on the map and do research to learn if members of this group still live within this region today.

**Geography Transparency GT1**
- Native American Lifestyles, 1500

### INSTRUCT: OBJECTIVE 

**Peoples of the North and Northwest Coast/ Peoples of the West**

Key Questions
- How did climate and environment affect the way of life of the Inuit, Aleut, and peoples of the West?
- How were natural resources different in the North from the Northwest Coast?
- How were the religious beliefs of the peoples of the North, Northwest, and West similar?

### ACTIVITY OPTIONS

**INTERDISCIPLINARY LINK: GEOGRAPHY**

BLOCK SCHEDULING

**INTERPRETING MAPS**

**Class Time** 20 minutes

**Task** Identifying geographic features of Native American culture regions

**Purpose** To draw conclusions about some of the challenges of adapting to various environments

**Supplies Needed**
- Physical, climate, and vegetation maps of North America

**Activity** Divide the class into groups. Let each group pick a culture region on the map and locate this area on physical, climate, and vegetation maps. Ask groups to write one paragraph about the geographic features of the region. Repeat this process using climate and vegetation maps for information on weather, plant life, and natural resources. Write another paragraph describing the challenges of life in this environment. Each group should make three inferences about how Native American groups in this region might have adapted to their environment.

**MORE ABOUT . . .**

**The Potlatch**
From northern California to Alaska, the potlatch was central to the lives of Native American peoples. Among these groups, generosity was the key to high social standing. The community looked with suspicion and disapproval at the person who kept all his wealth to himself. European traders were bewildered by the potlatch. They considered the Indians extravagant, while the Indians considered the Europeans selfish.

**MORE ABOUT . . .**

**The Aztec Calendar**
The Aztec Calendar, or Sun Stone, is more than 13 feet in diameter, making it the largest Aztec sculpture known. The images between the sun god and the day symbols are arranged in four squares. Each square depicts an earlier stage of creation, destroyed long ago. The Aztec believed that human beings appeared only in the current, fifth, world creation.

**INSTRUCT: OBJECTIVE 3**

**Peoples of Mexico/Peoples of the Southwest/ Peoples of the Great Plains**
Key Questions
- How did the peoples of Mexico, the Southwest, and the Great Plains adapt to their environment?
- In what ways did the life of peoples of the Southwest and Great Plains differ from peoples of Mexico?
- Why was the bison valuable to Plains tribes?

into icy seas to spear whales, seals, and walruses. They hunted these mammals for food, and they made seal and walrus skins into clothes. Some Inuit religious ceremonies honored the spirits of the whales and seals they caught. The Inuit also hunted such land animals as caribou. They made arrowheads and spear points from bones and antlers.

Farther south, Northwest Coast people also hunted sea mammals. But they mostly fished for salmon. Living by forests, Northwest Coast people used wood for houses, boats, and carved objects. They traded such coastal products as shells for items from the inland, such as furs.

A. Possible Answer because those items were unavailable in their area

*Reading*History
**A. Making Inferences** Why would inland people trade for seashells?

*"The term [potlatch] comes from Chinook . . . and means 'to give.'"*
Gloria Cranmer Webster, U'mista Cultural Centre

Northwest Coast groups such as the Kwakiutl (KWAH•kee•OOT•uhl) and Haida had a special ceremony—the potlatch. Individuals would give away most or all of their goods as a way to claim status and benefit their community. They held potlatches to mark life events, such as naming a child or mourning the dead.

## Peoples of the West

Unlike the Native Americans of the Northwest Coast, those of the West did not rely mainly on the sea. The peoples of the West included tribes in California, the Columbia Plateau, and the Great Basin. Much of the West is desert or is not suitable for farming. The people who lived there existed mainly by hunting and gathering.

*Reading*History
**B. Reading a Map** On the map on page 33, locate the cultures of California, the Plateau, and the Great Basin. Notice why these three together are called the peoples of the West.

The men hunted deer, elk, antelope, rabbits, and birds. They also fished, especially for salmon that swam up the western rivers. Women gathered such wild foods as nuts, seeds, and berries. Many western groups moved with the seasons to collect food.

**The Aztec Calendar**

This stone is the Aztec calender wheel. In the center is the sun god. Around it are symbols for the 20 days of the Aztec month. Three are enlarged below.

The women of some western tribes became expert weavers. Pomo women wove beautiful baskets that they used to gather and store food. They wove some baskets tightly enough to be watertight.

The peoples of the West had strong spiritual beliefs, often linked to nature. Some held ceremonies to ensure a large food supply. Others held dances to ask for rain, for plant growth, and for good hunting. Still others believed that their religious leaders could contact the spirit world.

## 3 Peoples of Mexico

Far to the south, the Aztecs ruled a great civilization in what is now central Mexico. The origin of the Aztecs is unclear. They may have been hunters and gatherers like the Native Americans of the West. Sometime during the 1100s, they migrated into the Valley of Mexico.

In 1325, they began to build their capital city, Tenochtitlán (teh•NAWCH•tee•TLAHN), on islands in Lake Texcoco. Two things helped the Aztecs become a strong empire. First, they drained swamps and built an

34

**ACTIVITY OPTIONS**

**INDIVIDUAL NEEDS**

**STUDENTS ACQUIRING ENGLISH/ESL**

**Identifying Geographic Regions** Review the four major compass directions, as well as intermediate directions such as northwest and southeast. Have the students draw a compass on a sheet of paper. Include eight directions. Next have the students read the text headings. When a heading includes a direction, stop and read which peoples lived there. Have the students write the names of the groups next to the direction on the compass sheet. Then have them locate the specified areas on the map on page 33 or on another map of the United States. Continue this practice for the entire section. Finally, ask students to use direction words to identify the geographic region in which they live.

irrigation system. This enabled them to grow plenty of food. Second, they were a warlike people who conquered most of their neighbors. The defeated people then had to send the Aztecs food and resources.

The Aztecs had a complex society. Rulers were the highest class. Priests and government workers ranked next. Slaves and servants were at the bottom. The Aztecs had elaborate religious ceremonies linked to their calendar and their study of the sun, moon, and stars. Many of their beliefs came from earlier Mesoamerican cultures.

The Aztecs' most important ritual involved feeding their sun god human blood. To do this, the Aztecs sacrificed prisoners of war by cutting out the person's heart while he was still alive. One reason the Aztecs fought so many wars was to capture prisoners to sacrifice.

## Peoples of the Southwest

North of the Aztec, in what is now the American Southwest, lived the Pueblo people. Their ancestors were the ancient Hohokam and Anasazi. Like their ancestors, the Pueblo used irrigation to alter their desert region for farming. They lived in many-storied houses of adobe—dried mud bricks. These large buildings sometimes held an entire village.

Pueblo Indian farmers raised corn, beans, and squash. For meat, they hunted game and raised turkeys. Men did most of the farming, hunting, weaving, and building. Women ground the corn and cooked the food, repaired the adobe houses, and crafted pottery.

The Navajo and the Apache were nomadic, or wandering, hunter-gatherers who came to the region later than the Pueblo. For food, they relied mainly on game and on cactus, roots, and piñon nuts. Often, they traded these wild products for crops that the Pueblo had grown. Over time, the Navajo adopted farming and other Pueblo practices.

*Reading* **History**

**C. Drawing Conclusions** Why do you think the Navajo adopted farming?

C. Possible Answer because they saw that it gave the Pueblo a stable food supply

## Peoples of the Great Plains

Farther north, the Great Plains is a flat grassland region stretching from the Mississippi River west to the Rocky Mountains. Today, most people think of Plains Indians on horseback, but originally they had no horses. The Spanish first brought horses to the Americas in the 1500s.

**Background**

Horses spread across North America through trade and by escaping from humans and wandering on their own.

Some Plains groups were nomads. Others lived in villages by rivers, where land was easier to farm. In summer, entire villages set out to track bison. Hunting bison on foot was difficult, but Plains tribes used their environment to help them. Working together, the villagers stampeded the herd over a cliff, so the fall would kill or disable the animals. Plains Indians not only ate the bison's meat. They also made its hide into clothes and its bones into tools.

**daily *life***

**KACHINA DANCES**

Every year in summer the Hopi, Zuni, and other Pueblo Indians held a religious celebration. The ceremony called on the kachinas, or spirits of the ancestors. The Pueblo believed the kachinas had the power to bring a plentiful harvest. At the festival, masked dancers played the role of different kachinas. They danced and sang songs to bring rain in the year ahead. Today, the Pueblo also carve kachina dolls, shown below, as well as hold dances.

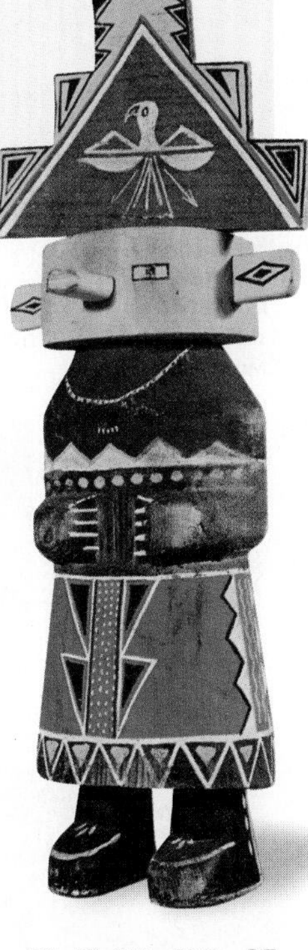



**daily*life***

**Kachina Dances**

According to Pueblo beliefs, the kachinas are spirits who live six months of the year in their own land known as the World Below. For the other six months, from winter to summer solstice, they come to Pueblo villages and inhabit the bodies of men. These men embody the kachinas in religious dances. While acting as a kachina, a dancer is believed to have the power to intercede on behalf of the Pueblos with their gods.

**CRITICAL THINKING ACTIVITY**

**Comparing** Have students construct a chart like the one below to categorize information about the various Native American cultural groups. The information in the completed chart will provide the basis for comparing and contrasting the groups. Categories might include food sources, types of dwellings, customs or beliefs, and political or social organization.

| Cultural Group | Food Sources | Dwellings | Etc. |
|---|---|---|---|
| North/Northwest Coast | | | |
| West | | | |
| Mexico | | | |
| Southwest | | | |
| Great Plains | | | |
| Southeast | | | |
| Eastern Woodlands | | | |

**Class Time** 25 minutes

**ACTIVITY OPTIONS**

**INTERDISCIPLINARY LINK: LITERATURE** — BLOCK SCHEDULING

**NATIVE AMERICAN LEGENDS**

**Class Time** One class period

**Task** Choosing a Native American legend to be retold or dramatized for the class

**Purpose** To understand the diversity and richness of Native American literature

**Supplies Needed**
- Anthologies of Native American literature

**Activity** Divide the class into groups and tell each group to choose a myth or legend and present it to the class. Presentations can take different forms such as a storyteller or a play. Each member of the group should have a task. As groups present their legends or myths, tell students to compare and contrast themes, types of characters, or lessons the stories teach.

 **In-Depth Resources: Unit 1**
- Literature Selection: Coyote Steals Otter's Coat, pp. 14–15; Song of the Sky Loom, p.16

**INSTRUCT: OBJECTIVE 4**

**Peoples of the Southeast/ Peoples of the Eastern Woodlands**

Key Questions

- How did the climate of the Southeast influence the way of life of the southeastern groups?
- How did the Iroquois and the Algonquin use the resources of their forest environment?
- How did creation of the Iroquois League change the way the Iroquois nations lived?

**MORE ABOUT . . .**

**Matrilineal Customs**

In matrilineal societies, both men and women trace their ancestry through the mother's family. When a man marries, he usually moves to his wife's village. Property is passed down from mother to daughter. A woman's brother plays an important part in bringing up her children. Often, it is a boy's maternal uncle—not his father—who teaches the boy hunting, fishing, and other necessary skills.

In winter such northern Plains groups as the Mandans and Pawnee lived in large circular lodges. Wooden beams held up the earthen walls. A hole at the top provided air, light, and an outlet for smoke from the fire. Buried partly underground, the earth lodge protected the people from the extreme cold and wind of the Plains climate.

**Vocabulary**
**lodge:** house

The spiritual beliefs of Plains tribes varied. Some felt a close tie to regional animals such as the bison or plants such as corn. Some honored sacred places, such as the Black Hills of South Dakota and Wyoming. Many Plains tribes held a ceremony called the Sun Dance, which involved making a vow and asking the Creator for aid.

## 4 Peoples of the Southeast

The Southeast, which stretches from east Texas to the Atlantic Ocean, has mild winters and warm summers with plentiful rainfall. The long growing season led the Choctaw (CHAHK•taw), Chickasaw (CHIHK•uh•SAW), and other southeastern groups to become farmers. As many other Native Americans did, they grew corn, beans, squash, and pumpkins.

*Reading* **History**

**D. Analyzing Causes** Why would a long growing season lead people to become farmers?

**D. Possible Answer** because the long season would enable them to produce more crops

Women did most of the farming, while men hunted, fished, and cleared land. The men spent months in the forest tracking deer. In the Southeast, people traced their family ties through the women. Societies in which ancestry is traced through the mother are called **matrilineal.**

In southeastern villages, people gathered at a central square for public meetings and such religious ceremonies as the Green Corn Festival. Held once a year, this festival offered thanks for the corn harvest and also served as a kind of New Year's celebration. People cleaned their houses, threw away old pots, and settled quarrels as a sign of a fresh start for the year.

## Peoples of the Eastern Woodlands

Like the Southeast, the Northeast had plenty of fish, game, and rain. But the climate was colder with snowy winters. Forests covered much of the region, so it is called the Eastern Woodlands. Most of the people living there spoke either an Iroquoian or Algonquian language.

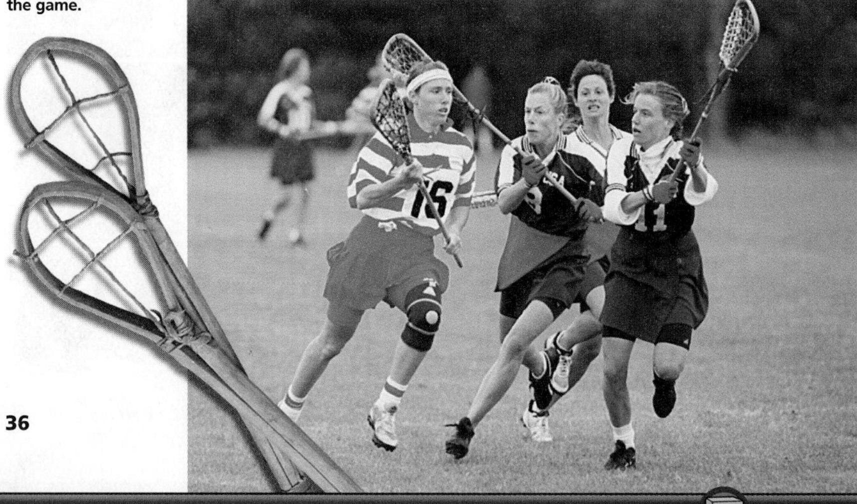

Many Native Americans in the Southeast and Eastern Woodlands played lacrosse using sticks like these. Modern Americans have adopted the game.



**ACTIVITY OPTIONS**

**MULTIPLE LEARNING STYLES: SPATIAL** — BLOCK SCHEDULING

**NATIVE AMERICAN HOUSES**

**Class Time** One class period

**Task** Making models of shelters from different culture areas

**Purpose** To understand how the geography and natural resources of an area influenced the homes Native Americans built

**Supplies Needed**

- Reference materials showing houses of various Native American peoples such as longhouses, tipis, earth lodges
- Modeling clay, cardboard boxes, art supplies

**Activity** Working in small groups, students create models of the houses built by Native Americans in various culture regions of North America. Have groups present their models to the class. Each group can explain why people in this area used particular building materials, how the house's design might be adapted to a hot or cold climate or a nomadic way of life, and whether the house was for an individual family or a group.

Like all Native Americans, the Iroquois learned to live in their environment. They hunted wild game. They adapted the forest for farming by using slash-and-burn agriculture. In **slash-and-burn agriculture,** farmers chopped down and then burned trees on a plot of land. The ashes from the fire enriched the soil. When a field's soil became worn out, the farmer abandoned it and cleared a new field. The Iroquois lived in longhouses, bark-covered shelters as long as 300 feet. One longhouse held eight to ten families.

**Background**
Although it is a quick way to clear fields, slash-and-burn agriculture does cause environmental damage by destroying forests.

The Algonquin lived in wigwams, domelike houses covered with deerskin and slabs of bark. For protection, both the Iroquois and Algonquin surrounded their villages with high fences made of poles. Iroquois villagers often needed protection not only from the enemies of the Iroquois, but from each other. The Iroquois often raided neighboring villages for food and captives.

In the late 1500s, five northern Iroquois nations took the advice of a peace-seeking man named **Deganawida.** They stopped warring with each other and formed an alliance. This alliance of the Cayuga, Mohawk, Oneida, Onondaga, and Seneca was the **Iroquois League.** The League brought a long period of peace to the Iroquois. A council of leaders from each nation governed the League. They followed rules called the Great Law of Peace. The Iroquois were also a matrilineal society. If a leader did something wrong, the women of his clan could vote him out of office.

Across the Atlantic, the peoples of West Africa also adapted to their environment and engaged in trade. West Africa was the region from which most Africans were brought to the Americas. You will read about it in the next section.

### AMERICA'S HISTORY MAKERS

**DEGANAWIDA (THE PEACEMAKER)**

Iroquois tradition honors Deganawida as the Peacemaker. Seeing how destructive warfare was for the Iroquois, Deganawida went from tribe to tribe and described his dream of peace. A poor speaker, he persuaded few warriors. Finally, an Iroquois chief named Hiawatha spoke for him. After long negotiations, the leaders of the warring nations made peace. However, Deganawida's own tribe, the Huron, did not join the League.

**How did both Deganawida and Hiawatha lead the Iroquois toward peace?**

## Section 2 Assessment

### 1. Terms & Names

**Identify:**
- technology
- tundra
- kayak
- matrilineal
- slash-and-burn agriculture
- Deganawida
- Iroquois League

### 2. Taking Notes

Use a cluster diagram to record how Native Americans from each region adapted to their environment.

### 3. Main Ideas

a. What were some of the religious ceremonies of Native Americans?

b. How were the Pueblo like their ancestors, the Hohokam?

c. How did the formation of the Iroquois League benefit its member nations?

### 4. Critical Thinking

**Drawing Conclusions**
How did trade benefit both groups that took part in it?

**THINK ABOUT**
- who the Northwest Coast people traded with and what they exchanged
- what the Pueblo exchanged with nomadic groups

**ACTIVITY OPTIONS**

**ART**
**LANGUAGE ARTS**

Reread the Navajo chant on page 33. Draw an **illustration** to go with the chant or write additional **verses.**





## AMERICA'S HISTORY MAKERS

**Deganawida**

According to legend, around 1570 Deganawida had a vision in which he saw the union of the Five Nations. Thereafter, his message was a simple one: The Iroquois must stop fighting each other and join together under a symbolic Tree of Great Peace. The Iroquois League was almost immediately successful. Within 50 years of its formation, it was the most powerful confederation of Native American peoples on the continent.

**Possible Response:** Deganawida was a visionary who saw the need for a peace alliance. He inspired Hiawatha to use his skills as a speaker and a negotiator to work for peace.

**America's History Makers**
- Deganawida, pp. 1–2

## ASSESS & RETEACH

**Setting the Stage** Tell students to fill in additional information in the Americas row on the chapter graphic organizer.

**Formal Assessment**
- Section Quiz, p. 20

### RETEACHING ACTIVITY

Ask students to make a six-column chart on a sheet of paper. Label the columns *Culture Region, Location, Major Tribes, Natural Resources, Shelter,* and *Adaptations to Environment.* Students can use the map on page 33 and the information in the section to complete the chart.

**In-Depth Resources: Unit 1**
- Reteaching Activity, p. 18

## Section 2 Assessment

### 1. Terms & Names

**technology,** p. 32
**tundra,** p. 33
**kayak,** p. 33
**matrilineal,** p. 36
**slash-and-burn agriculture,** p. 37
**Deganawida,** p. 37
**Iroquois League,** p. 37

### 2. Taking Notes

North—kayaks, sealskin clothes
Northwest Coast—wooden homes
West—hunting and gathering
Mexico—irrigation system
Southwest—dried mud brick houses
Great Plains—hunting buffalo, building lodges
Southeast—farming and hunting
Eastern Woodlands—agriculture

### 3. Main Ideas

**a.** Inuit—to honor seals and whales; Western—to ask for rain; Aztec—human sacrifice; Pueblo—Kachina dances; Plains—sun dances; Southeastern—Green Corn Festival **b.** They used irrigation to farm corn, beans, and squash. **c.** They stopped fighting each other and helped defend each other.

### 4. Critical Thinking

The Northwest Coast people gained furs; the inland people, seashells. The Pueblo gained wild game; the Apache and Navajo, farm produce.

**ACTIVITY OPTIONS**

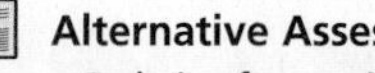
**Alternative Assessment**
- Rubrics for an illustration, 1.3
- Rubrics for verses, 4.8

## INTERACTIVE PRIMARY SOURCE

**OBJECTIVE**

Students will analyze the introduction to the Great Law of Peace and evaluate its importance to the establishment and stability of the Iroquois League.

Primary Source Explorer
- *Iroquois Great Law of Peace*

## FOCUS & MOTIVATE

**Evaluating** Ask students to consider the importance of symbols in any organization. What is the function of team mascots? Of national flags? How do such symbols promote unity? Tell them to identify the symbols of unity for the Iroquois League as they read and to consider why these symbols are powerful.

## INSTRUCT

Key Questions
- How does the tree serve as a symbol for the unity of the Five Nations? What purposes do the roots of a tree serve? What purpose do the branches and leaves serve?
- Why might Deganawida believe that it takes "strength" to be peaceful?

### MORE ABOUT . . .

**The Great Law of Peace**

The Great Law was originally handed down through oral tradition, for which a set of wampum belts served as a record. The Onondaga Nation, who live in central New York State, are the keepers of these wampum, or shell, belts. Eventually, the terms of the Great Law of Peace were recorded in writing.

INTERACTIVE PRIMARY SOURCE

# The Iroquois Great Law of Peace

**Setting the Stage** The five nations of the Iroquois League created a constitution, called the Great Law of Peace, that had 117 laws and customs. These laws governed all aspects of life and war. In this excerpt, Deganawida introduces the Great Law by describing a tree that symbolizes the permanence and stability of the league. **See Primary Source Explorer**

**1** I am Deganawida and with the Five Nations' Confederate **Lords**[1] I plant the Tree of Great Peace. I plant it in your territory, **Adodarhoh,**[2] and the Onondaga Nation, in the territory of you who are Firekeepers.

I name the tree the Tree of the Great Long Leaves. Under the shade of this Tree of the Great Peace we spread the soft white feathery down of the globe thistle as seats for you, Adodarhoh, and your cousin Lords.

We place you upon those seats, spread soft with the feathery down of the globe thistle, there beneath the shade of the spreading branches of the Tree of Peace. There shall you sit and watch the Council Fire of the **Confederacy of the Five Nations,**[3] and all the affairs of the Five Nations shall be transacted at this place before you, Adodarhoh, and your cousin Lords, by the Confederate Lords of the Five Nations.

**2** Roots have spread out from the Tree of the Great Peace, one to the north, one to the east, one to the south, and one to the west. The name of these roots is The Great White Roots and their nature is Peace and Strength.

If any man or any nation outside the Five Nations shall obey the laws of the Great Peace and make known their disposition to the Lords of the Confederacy, they may trace the Roots to the Tree and if their minds are clean and they are obedient and promise to obey the wishes of the Confederate Council, they shall be welcomed to take shelter beneath the Tree of the Long Leaves.

*A CLOSER LOOK*

**THE COUNCIL FIRE**

**The council fire of the Iroquois League was kept burning for about 200 years.**

***1. What do you think it would mean if the council fire were allowed to die?***

*A CLOSER LOOK*

**THE GREAT WHITE ROOTS**

**The roots of a tree help to anchor it in the ground, and they draw water and food from the soil.**

***2. Why might Deganawida say the nature of the roots is "Peace and Strength"?***

1. **Lords:** chiefs.
2. **Adodarhoh:** the name of the office of the Onondaga chief.
3. **Confederacy of the Five Nations:** the Iroquois League.

*Interactive Primary Source Assessment*

**1. Main Ideas**

a. In what territory was the Tree of the Great Peace planted?

b. Where will the affairs of the Five Nations be conducted?

c. Where have the Tree's roots spread?

**2. Critical Thinking**

**Making Inferences** Were outsiders welcome to join the Iroquois League? Explain.

**THINK ABOUT**
- the phrase *they may trace the Roots to the Tree*
- the phrase *take shelter beneath the Tree*



*Interactive Primary Source Assessment*

**1. Main Ideas**

**a.** It was planted in the territory of the Onondaga Nation, whose chief is Adodarhoh.
**b.** They will meet near or in the shade of the Tree of Great Peace. They will meet before the council fire.
**c.** in all four directions

**2. Critical Thinking**

yes, if they obey the League's laws

*A CLOSER LOOK*

1. that the alliances of the Iroquois League had ended
2. He wants the League to be founded on those qualities.

# 3 Societies of West Africa

**TERMS & NAMES**
Ghana
Muslims
Islam
Mali
Songhai
Hausa
Yoruba
Benin

**MAIN IDEA**

The peoples of West Africa developed sophisticated kingdoms, trade networks, and artistic achievements.

**WHY IT MATTERS NOW**

It was from this region that many Africans were brought to the Americas.

## ONE AFRICAN'S STORY

**King Tenkaminen (TEHN•kah•MEE•nehn) of the West African empire of Ghana was a powerful ruler. He grew rich by taxing gold traders who traveled through his land. Travelers who visited Tenkaminen were impressed by his wealth. In 1067, a geographer wrote a description of the royal court.**

*A VOICE FROM THE PAST*

The king adorns himself . . . wearing necklaces round his neck and bracelets on his forearms. . . . Behind the king stand ten pages holding shields and swords decorated with gold and on his right are the sons of the vassal [lower] kings of his country wearing splendid garments and their hair plaited [braided] with gold.

**al-Bakri,** quoted in *The Horizon History of Africa*

**Kumasi, a modern West African chief, wears gold to show his status, just as the ancient king of Ghana did.**

**West Africa had several other kingdoms and empires that grew powerful through trade. It was also the homeland of many of the enslaved Africans who were brought to the Americas after 1500. You will read about West Africa in this section.**

## 1 African Geography and World Trade

Africa is the world's second largest continent after Asia. (See the map on page 40.) Although Africa has a variety of land forms and climates, almost three quarters of it lies within the tropics. The equator runs east-west across the center of Africa. Dense rain forests stretch along the equator in central and western Africa. North and south of the rain forests are broad savannas, which are grassy plains with thorny bushes and scattered trees. Beyond the savanna in the North lies the Sahara, the world's largest desert. Beyond the savanna in the South lies the smaller Kalahari Desert.

By A.D. 1500, coastal ports had linked Africa with the rest of the world for many centuries. Ships from ports on the Mediterranean and the Red Sea carried goods to Arabia and Persia. On Africa's east coast, city-states carried on a brisk trade with ports across the Indian Ocean.





## SECTION OBJECTIVES

1. To describe the geography of Africa and the continent's trade links
2. To explain how Ghana grew wealthy
3. To identify Mali and Songhai
4. To describe other West African kingdoms

**SKILLBUILDER**

Interpreting Maps: Place, Movement, p. 40

**CRITICAL THINKING**

Analyzing Causes, p. 40
Making Inferences, p. 41
Recognizing Effects, p. 42
Analyzing Points of View, p. 43
Identifying Facts and Opinions, p. 43

## FOCUS & MOTIVATE

### 5-MINUTE WARM-UP

**Drawing Conclusions** To examine the importance of trade to West African empires, have students answer these questions.

1. Study the map on page 40. What port cities in northern Africa are linked to West African empires by trade routes?
2. Why would these ports be likely to trade with Europe?

 **Warm-Up Transparency WT1**

## INSTRUCT

**INSTRUCT: OBJECTIVE 1**

**African Geography and World Trade**

Key Questions

- What types of vegetation and landforms are found in Africa?
- To what parts of the world did Africa have trading connections by 1500?

**In-Depth Resources: Unit 1**
- Guided Reading, p. 5

**Reading Study Guide** (Spanish and English), pp. 9–10

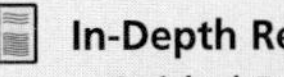

## RECOMMENDED RESOURCES

 **In-Depth Resources: Unit 1**
- Guided Reading, p. 5
- Building Vocabulary, p. 8
- Primary Source: from *Travels in Asia and Africa* by Ibn Battuta, p. 12
- Reteaching Activity, p. 19

**Reading Study Guide** (Spanish and English), pp. 9–10

**Formal Assessment**
- Section Quiz, p. 21

**Alternative Assessment**
- Rubrics, 3.6
- Rubrics, 2.1

 **Access for Students Acquiring English/ESL**
- Guided Reading, p. 3

Technology Resources

 **Electronic Teacher Tools with Test Maker**

 **Classzone**
www.mcdougallittell.com

**INSTRUCT: OBJECTIVE 2**

**Ghana Grows Wealthy/Islam Enters Ghana**

Key Questions

- How did Ghana's location help it grow rich?
- What role did Islam play in Ghana's history?
- What led to Ghana's decline?

Like other parts of Africa, West Africa has rain forest along the equator and savanna to the north. The Niger River arcs across those grasslands and forests and then empties into the Atlantic Ocean. Along its northern edge, West Africa borders the Sahara.

## 2 Ghana Grows Wealthy

On a map, the Sahara appears to be a barrier between West Africa and the ports on the Mediterranean coast. But by A.D. 500, camel caravans led by eager merchants made regular journeys across the great desert. This connected West Africa to the wider world.

**Background** The camel is used in the desert because it can travel up to 10 days without water.

Ghana became the first West African kingdom to grow rich through trade. From the 700s to the mid 1000s, Ghana prospered by controlling the busy trade in gold and salt. Located on the southern edge of the Sahara, Ghana became a marketplace for traders going north and south in search of salt and gold. (Ancient Ghana was northwest of modern Ghana.) Salt was important because it helps the human body retain water in hot weather. Traders carried salt from the Saharan salt mines in the north. In Ghana's markets, they met other traders offering gold from the forests of West Africa.

Ghana's king benefited from this trade. He imposed taxes on all gold and salt passing through his kingdom. The taxes had to be paid in gold. The king also claimed all gold nuggets found in his kingdom. Ghana's king used the resulting wealth to pay for an army and build an empire.

A. Possible Answer so he would grow rich

*Reading* **History**

**A. Analyzing Causes** Why did the king want taxes to be paid in gold and all gold nuggets to be given to him?

Skillbuilder Answers
1. Songhai
2. Possible Response Tunis to Fez to Sijilmasa to Taghaza to Timbuktu

**HISTORY FROM VISUALS**

**Reading the Map** Ghana, Mali, and Songhai are all located on the southern edge of the Sahara. How did their location help them prosper? What evidence suggests that the Sahara was not a barrier to trade? **Possible Response** They were central meeting places for merchants traveling south from ports on the Mediterranean and traders coming north bringing gold from mines or gold fields farther south. The many trade routes across the Sahara indicate that it was not a barrier to trade.

**Extension** Tell students to use an encyclopedia to determine what products are traded in modern West Africa.

***West African Empires, 800–1500***

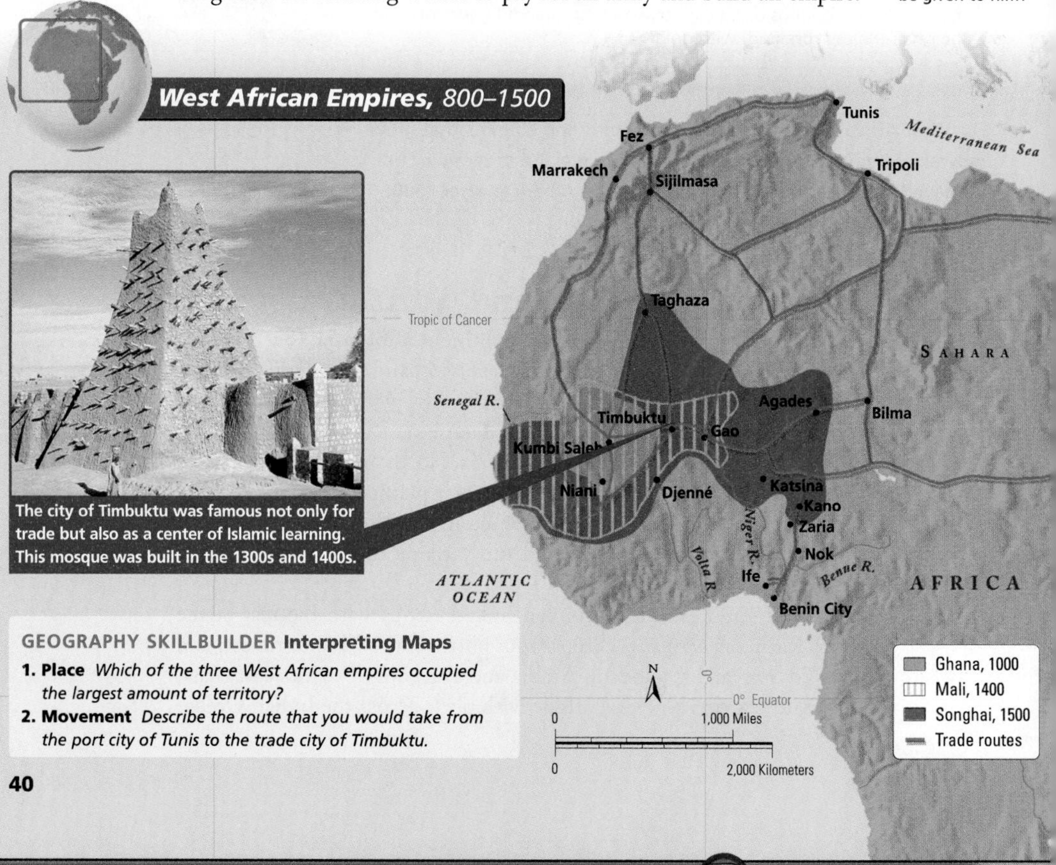

The city of Timbuktu was famous not only for trade but also as a center of Islamic learning. This mosque was built in the 1300s and 1400s.

**GEOGRAPHY SKILLBUILDER Interpreting Maps**

1. **Place** *Which of the three West African empires occupied the largest amount of territory?*
2. **Movement** *Describe the route that you would take from the port city of Tunis to the trade city of Timbuktu.*



**ACTIVITY OPTIONS**

**INTERDISCIPLINARY LINK: SCIENCE/HEALTH**

**BLOCK SCHEDULING**

**GOLD AND SALT**

**Class Time** 20 minutes

**Task** Finding fun facts about gold and salt

**Purpose** To explain why these commodities were valued in the past and to examine their current uses

**Supplies Needed**

- Reference materials on gold and salt
- Index cards

**Activity** Ask a science or health teacher to speak to the class about why the body needs salt. Divide the class in half and distribute index cards. One half will find information about salt and the other half information on gold. Students can search for information on the properties, chemical makeup, and past and current uses of each commodity. Encourage them to consider why each was so highly valued in Africa south of the Sahara. Have students write one fact about salt or gold on their index cards. Collect the cards and share the most interesting facts with the class.

## Islam Enters Ghana

Many of the traders who came to Ghana from North Africa were Muslims. **Muslims** are followers of the religion of Islam. Founded by the prophet Muhammad in the 600s, **Islam** teaches that there is one God, named Allah. Muslims must perform such duties as praying five times a day and making a pilgrimage to the holy city of Mecca in Arabia. Muslim traders crossing the Sahara brought Islam from North Africa to West Africa. Ghana's rulers allowed those Muslims to build mosques, or houses of worship, in Ghana's capital, Kumbi Saleh. In time, Ghana's rulers employed Muslims as advisers.

Vocabulary
**pilgrimage:** a trip to a holy place

The Muslim empires of North Africa wanted to convert Ghana's people to Islam and to control Ghana's gold trade. In 1076, a Muslim army conquered Kumbi Saleh. This lessened Ghana's power. A number of local leaders took advantage of Ghana's weakness. They built up their own small states on the edges of the once mighty empire. Ghana never regained its former strength.

Over the next several centuries, more and more West Africans converted to Islam. In fact, many of the enslaved Africans who were brought to the Americas were Muslims.

### MORE ABOUT . . .

**Ghana and Islam**

Eager to strengthen their ties with Islamic empires in North Africa, Ghana's rulers welcomed the new religion. Although Ghana's kings and court did not at first convert to Islam, by the 11th century Ghana's rulers had Muslim advisers at court helping them run the kingdom. Eventually many of Ghana's rulers and members of the royal court converted to Islam. However, most of the common people retained their traditional beliefs.

## 3 Mali Replaces Ghana

By the 1200s, another West African kingdom had taken over most of Ghana's territory. This kingdom, called **Mali,** became West Africa's most powerful state. Its wealth also came from control of the gold-salt trade. But because it was located farther south than Ghana, Mali was better able to control the trade on the upper Niger River. (Ancient Mali stretched farther west than modern Mali and not as far north.)

A European mapmaker placed this picture of Mansa Musa on a map in 1375. It was drawn from his imagination.

Mali's first great ruler, Sundiata (sun•JAHT•ah), reigned from about 1230 to 1255. He came to power by crushing a cruel, unpopular leader. Sundiata's armies conquered many important trading cities. This made Mali's hold on trade stronger and made Mali more prosperous. Sundiata was a Muslim, but he did not force his people to accept Islam. Most of the people of Mali retained their traditional African beliefs.

Mali's other great leader was Mansa Musa (MAHN•sah moo•SAH), who was a devout Muslim. Mansa Musa came to the throne in 1312. Under his leadership, the empire became one of the largest in the world.

Vocabulary
**devout:** very religious

*Reading*History
**B. Making Inferences** How do you think the Egyptians reacted to Mansa Musa's caravan?
**B. Possible Answer** They were impressed by his wealth.

Mansa Musa is best remembered for making the Muslim pilgrimage to Mecca in 1324 and 1325. On his way to Mecca, he stopped in Cairo, Egypt. According to some stories, Mansa Musa entered the city leading a huge caravan that included 500 servants who waved staffs decorated with gold. Each of the 80 camels in his caravan struggled under the weight of a 300-pound sack of gold. The legend of Mali's wealth spread

### INSTRUCT: OBJECTIVE 3

**Mali Replaces Ghana/The Empire of Songhai**

Key Questions
- What was the source of Mali's wealth and power?
- In what ways did Mansa Musa spread Islamic culture and learning?
- Who were Songhai's two greatest rulers, and how did each contribute to the growth of the empire?

### MORE ABOUT . . .

**Mansa Musa**

In 1324, the Muslim ruler of Mali, Mansa Musa, set out on a pilgrimage to Mecca. He traveled in a caravan with some 60,000 relatives, officials, musicians, cooks, camel drivers, servants, slaves, and hangers-on. According to one report, his treasury included 20,000 pounds (10 tons) of gold. When he arrived in Cairo, Egypt, he spent gold so freely that prices skyrocketed in all the bazaars of the city—a classic example of inflation resulting from a rapid increase in the money supply.



### ACTIVITY OPTIONS

### MULTIPLE LEARNING STYLES: VISUAL

BLOCK SCHEDULING

**MAKING A TRAVEL POSTER**

**Class Time** One class period

**Task** Creating a travel poster for Ghana, Mali, or Songhai

**Purpose** To describe aspects of the history and culture of one of the West African kingdoms

**Supplies Needed**
- Reference materials on Ghana, Mali, and Songhai
- Current travel posters
- Posterboard and art supplies

**Activity** Students choose one of the West African kingdoms from this section and create a travel poster. In designing their posters, students may want to choose a single image or a variety of drawings showing religious sites or cities. Posters can include all or some of the following information: location, economic activities, artifacts, outstanding rulers. Display the completed posters on the bulletin board.

 **In-Depth Resources: Unit 1**
- Primary Source: from *Travels in Asia and Africa* by Ibn Battuta, p. 12

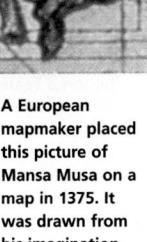

**MORE ABOUT . . .**

**Sunni Ali and His Successors**
Sunni Ali reigned from 1464 to 1492, when the European age of exploration was reaching its height. But Songhai was growing in power as well, achieving its greatest extent in the early 1500s under Askia Muhammad, Sunni Ali's successor. Muslim scholars came from all across northern Africa to study at the empire's intellectual center, the university at Timbuktu.

all the way to Europe. This was one reason that Europeans began to trade with Africa about 150 years later.

On his return to Mali, Mansa Musa brought back many Muslim scholars, artists, and architects. They helped spread Islamic culture and learning throughout the empire. The city of Timbuktu (TIHM•buhk•TOO) in eastern Mali became a leading center of trade and Islamic learning. After Mansa Musa's death in 1337, Mali slowly grew weaker.

## The Empire of Songhai

As Mali's power decreased, the **Songhai** (SAWNG•HY) people living at the Great Bend in the Niger River broke away from its control. In 1464, under the leader Sunni Ali, they began their own empire. Sunni Ali was a Muslim, but he also practiced the traditional Songhai religion.

Under Sunni Ali, the Songhai captured the great city of Timbuktu. Then they put the important trading city of Djenné (jeh•NAY) under siege and captured it after seven years. In addition to conquering territory, Sunni Ali set up an organized system of government.

**Vocabulary**
**siege:** surrounding a castle or city with an army until it surrenders

After Sunni Ali died in 1492, conflicts arose. Some Muslims began a rebellion because they wanted Islam to be the only religion of Songhai. The leader of the revolt was Askia Muhammad, a devoted Muslim.

Askia Muhammad won his fight and became Songhai's second great ruler. For 35 years, he ably governed the empire. He chose capable officials who made the government run smoothly. He also expanded trade and set up an efficient tax system. Askia Muhammad used his wealth to build mosques and support Muslim scholars.

***Reading*History**
**C. Recognizing Effects** How would Askia Muhammad's actions promote Islam in Songhai?
C. Possible Answer by encouraging Islamic worship and study

After Askia Muhammad's reign, several weak rulers succeeded him. Even when a strong ruler took the throne again, the empire faced problems. In spite of Songhai's wealth and learning, it lacked modern weapons. In 1591, a Moroccan fighting force from North Africa invaded Songhai with gunpowder and cannon. They easily defeated Songhai's soldiers, who were defending their empire with swords and spears.

**Now *and* then**

**Kwanzaa**
During this seven-day celebration from December 26 to January 1, families gather each night to light the candles in the *kinara,* a seven-branched candelabra, and to talk about the value honored for that day. On December 31, many families come together for a community feast called the *karamu.*

**Now *and* then**

**AFRICAN HERITAGE**
One way many African Americans show pride in their heritage is by wearing kente cloth. Kente cloth, shown below, is a colorful fabric woven by the Akan and Ewe people of Ghana.

Some African Americans celebrate the holiday of Kwanzaa in December. Based on traditional African harvest festivals, Kwanzaa lasts a week. Each day honors a value held by Africans: unity, self-determination, collective responsibility, cooperative economics, purpose, creativity, and faith.

## 4 Other West African Kingdoms

As empires rose and fell in some parts of West Africa, small city-states arose in other parts of the region. The **Hausa** (HOW•suh) states emerged after A.D. 1000 in what is now northern Nigeria. Hausa city-states, such as Katsina and Kano, thrived on trade. Although the Hausa people shared a language, their city-states were independent of each other.

The **Yoruba** (YAWR•uh•buh) lived in the forests southwest of the Niger River. Ife and Oyo, the largest Yoruba states, had kings



**INSTRUCT: OBJECTIVE 4**

**Other West African Kingdoms**
Key Questions
- How were the Hausa city-states different from the empires of Ghana, Mali, and Songhai?
- For what achievements are the people of the Yoruba states and Benin remembered?
- Why did the Portuguese and other Europeans come to West Africa?

**ACTIVITY OPTIONS**

**INDIVIDUAL NEEDS: GIFTED AND TALENTED**

**REGIONAL DEVELOPMENT FACTORS**

**Class Time** One class period

**Task** Identifying the factors that contributed to the growth of your state or region

**Purpose** To familiarize students with factors that contribute to the development of individual states or regions

**Supplies Needed**
- Maps of your state or region
- Local newspapers

**Activity** After students read about the factors that contributed to the development of the Kingdom of Ghana, ask them to suppose that they are historians in the year 3000. Their assignment is to describe the geographic, political, or economic factors that led to the development of their own state or region up to the year 2000. Students should identify the characteristics that led to the development of their area, such as natural resources, tourism, trade, government, or industry.

who were considered to be partly divine. The Yoruba were mostly farmers, but they also had gifted artists, who carved wood and ivory and cast metal sculptures. Yoruba statues are still considered great art.

Another kingdom famous for its art was Benin. **Benin,** located in the delta of the Niger River, lay on main trade routes and prospered because of that. The capital, Benin City, was large and surrounded by thick, earthen walls. About 1600, a Dutch visitor compared Benin City to his home city of Amsterdam in Europe.

*Reading* **History**

**D. Analyzing Points of View** Do you think Dapper's view of Benin City is positive or negative? Explain.

**D. Possible Answer** Positive, because he compares it favorably to his home town.

*A VOICE FROM THE PAST*

The houses in this town stand in good order, each one close and evenly placed with its neighbor, just as the houses in Holland stand. . . . The king's court is very great. It is built around many square-shaped yards.

**Olfert Dapper,** quoted in *Centuries of Greatness*

Benin artists produced sophisticated bronze statues such as this figure of a horn-blower.

In the late 1400s, Europeans reached Benin. Portuguese ships arrived, and the Portuguese set up a trade center near Benin City. Benin traders sold the Portuguese pepper, ivory, and leopard skins in exchange for copper and guns. In time, the Portuguese and other Europeans also began to trade for enslaved Africans. The Europeans who came to West Africa were not seeking information about its rich history or culture. They wanted a supply of laborers to work on large farms, called plantations. Chapter 2 explains more about plantations and slavery.

Trade was just one reason Europeans were sailing far beyond their lands. Social changes were also spurring them to explore the world. Those changes are discussed in Section 4.

## Section 3 Assessment

**1. Terms & Names**

**Identify:**
- Ghana
- Muslims
- Islam
- Mali
- Songhai
- Hausa
- Yoruba
- Benin

**2. Taking Notes**

Compare the Ghana Empire and the Mali Empire using a Venn diagram like the one shown.

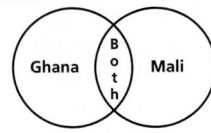

Ghana | Both | Mali

How was the influence of Islam different in each?

**3. Main Ideas**

a. How did Ghana's ruler benefit from controlling the gold-salt trade?

b. How did Islam spread within West Africa?

c. For what artistic achievements are the Yoruba and the people of Benin known?

**4. Critical Thinking**

**Identifying Facts and Opinions** Is the description of Benin City above mainly a statement of fact or opinion?

**THINK ABOUT**
- whether Dapper's statement can be proven by measurement or observation
- whether his statement expresses his own bias

**ACTIVITY OPTIONS**

**SPEECH**
**GEOGRAPHY**

Retell Mansa Musa's famous journey as an **oral history** or create a **map** that shows the route you think he took from Mali to Mecca.





### MORE ABOUT . . .

**Benin Art**

Benin is noted for its brass, bronze, and ivory sculpture. Nailed to the pillars of the palace courtyard, bronze plaques recorded the deeds of the kings of Benin and chronicled the main events of their reigns. The plaques give modern viewers insight into life at the royal court of Benin. They show warriors, court musicians, and dancers. They record the coming of Portuguese soldiers. Such modern artists as Pablo Picasso were influenced by the paintings and sculpture of African artists.

## ASSESS & RETEACH

**Setting the Stage** Have students fill in the West Africa sections on the chapter graphic organizer.

**Formal Assessment**
- Section Quiz, p. 21

**RETEACHING ACTIVITY**

Have students create a spider map like the one below and add additional information about the West African kingdoms.

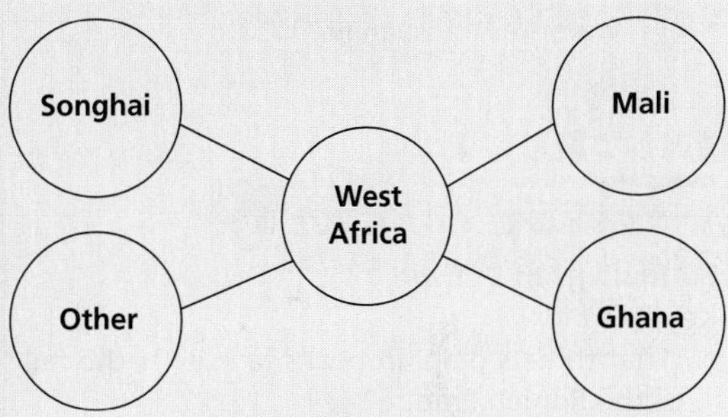

**In-Depth Resources: Unit 1**
- Reteaching Activity, p. 19

## Section 3 Assessment

**1. Terms & Names**

**Ghana,** p. 39
**Muslims,** p. 41
**Islam,** p. 41
**Mali,** p. 41
**Songhai,** p. 42
**Hausa,** p. 42
**Yoruba,** p. 42
**Benin,** p. 43

**2. Taking Notes**

Ghana—lasted from 700s to 1000s, first West African empire
Both—controlled gold-salt trade, Muslim traders and advisers
Mali—began in 1200s, one of largest empires of its time, more influenced by Islam than Ghana

**3. Main Ideas**

**a.** He taxed the trade, which made him wealthy and enabled him to pay for an army and to build an empire. **b.** through the migration of Muslim traders and scholars and the conversion of some rulers **c.** sculpture and art

**4. Critical Thinking**

It is mainly a statement of fact because it would be easy to prove the description given.

**ACTIVITY OPTIONS**

**Alternative Assessment**
- Rubrics for an oral history, 3.6
- Rubrics for a map, 2.1

## SECTION OBJECTIVES

1. To trace the rise of feudalism
2. To explain how trade and towns revived in Europe
3. To analyze the decline of feudalism
4. To describe the changes that occurred during the Renaissance and the Reformation

**SKILLBUILDER**
Interpreting Charts, p. 48

**CRITICAL THINKING**
Identifying Problems, p. 45
Recognizing Effects, p. 45
Analyzing Causes, p. 46
Making Generalizations, p. 48
Contrasting, p. 48

## FOCUS & MOTIVATE

### 5-MINUTE WARM-UP

**Analyzing Causes** Answering these questions will introduce students to feudalism.

1. Study the diagram on page 46. What did peasants and nobles expect from each other?
2. How are feudalism and trade linked?

 **Warm-Up Transparency WT1**

## INSTRUCT

### INSTRUCT: OBJECTIVE 

**Feudalism in Europe**
Key Questions
- What threats did Europeans face after the fall of the Roman Empire?
- What did nobles owe to a king in exchange for grants of land?
- How did the manor system work?
- What new roles did the Church take on?

 **In-Depth Resources: Unit 1**
- Guided Reading, p. 6

**Reading Study Guide** (Spanish and English), pp. 11–12

# 4 Societies of Europe

**TERMS & NAMES**
European Middle Ages
feudalism
manor system
Crusades
Renaissance
printing press
Reformation
profit

| MAIN IDEA | WHY IT MATTERS NOW |
|---|---|
| By 1500, Europe was going through a period of social change that sparked interest in learning and exploration. | The changes taking place in Europe led to the exploration of the Americas. |

### ONE EUROPEAN'S STORY

**After telling her son to watch the baby, Ermentrude left her tiny hut. She gathered up a chicken and five eggs and went to see the steward. He was the man who managed the land where she lived for its owners. Ermentrude and her husband, Bodo, were farmers who worked on a small piece of a large estate owned by someone else.**

**When Ermentrude arrived at the big house on the estate, she gave the chicken and eggs to the steward as part of her rent. For a while, she visited some women. Then she hurried home to tend her grapevines, weave cloth, and cook supper before Bodo came home from plowing.**

**Ermentrude lived in the early 800s, but her life was typical of the way many Europeans lived for centuries. This section explains that way of life and how it had changed by 1500. The changes led Europeans to make voyages of exploration that took them to America.**

The peasants in this 11th-century drawing are probably plowing land owned by someone else. European peasants like Ermentrude hardly ever left the manor where they lived.

##  Feudalism in Europe

Ermentrude lived in the **European Middle Ages,** which lasted from the late 400s, when the Western Roman Empire ended, to about the 1300s. (In some parts of Europe, the Middle Ages lasted to the 1400s.) The Romans used written laws and a mighty army to keep order. But over time, the empire grew weak. Germanic tribes from the east and north invaded the empire and contributed to its fall. The rough, uneducated Germanic tribes destroyed the strong Roman government and trade networks, and the tribes set up small kingdoms. With no trade, people stopped using money. They paid in goods, such as chickens and eggs.

Other groups also disrupted Europe. During the 800s to 1000s, Vikings swept down from the north. From their warships, they carried out lightning raids, looting villages and then racing back out to sea. To survive such difficult times, Europeans turned to feudalism. **Feudalism** is a political system in which a king allows nobles, or lords, to use lands



**RECOMMENDED RESOURCES**

 **In-Depth Resources: Unit 1**
- Guided Reading, p. 6
- Building Vocabulary, p. 8
- Reteaching Activity, p. 20

 **Reading Study Guide** (Spanish and English), pp. 11–12

**Economics in History**
- The Benefits of Trade, p. 1

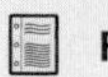 **Formal Assessment**
- Section Quiz, p. 22

 **Alternative Assessment**
- Rubrics, 5.1
- Rubrics, 4.8

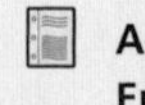 **Access for Students Acquiring English/ESL**
- Guided Reading, p. 4

**Technology Resources**

 **Critical Thinking Transparency CT2**
- Cause and Effect: Causes of Exploration

 **Electronic Teacher Tools with Test Maker**

 **Classzone**
www.mcdougallittell.com

that belong to him. In return, the lords owe the king military service and protection for the people living on the land.

*Reading*History
**A. Identifying Problems** What problems were Europeans trying to solve with feudalism and the manor system?
A. Possible Answer The problems were safety during attack and an adequate labor force for the lords' estates.

Along with feudalism, Europeans developed the **manor system.** In this system, lords divided their lands into manors, or large estates, that were farmed mostly by serfs. Serfs were landless peasants who weren't allowed to leave the manor. In return for the serfs' work, the lord promised to protect them. The lords built heavily walled castles where people could go in times of danger.

The Roman Catholic Church also gained power during these uncertain times. Taking on the roles once filled by government officials, the Church collected taxes, aided the sick, and punished criminals. It became a powerful, unifying force throughout Europe.

## 2 Revival of Trade and Towns

By the 1000s, feudalism had brought more stability to society. As strong lords gained more control over their lands, long periods of peace and security followed. Merchants once again felt safe to travel. New farming methods, such as better ways to plant and plow fields, led to a food surplus. With more to eat, the population increased. More people meant more demand for goods, which spurred trade. Old towns near busy trade routes revived, and new towns grew up near manor houses and churches. Money came back into use.

**Vocabulary**
**craftspeople:** those who work in skilled trades

As the economy grew, many serfs ran away to towns. Some became craftspeople who practiced such trades as shoemaking. Others became merchants who sold the goods that craftspeople made. Merchants and craftspeople formed a new social class, the middle class. They had fewer riches, rights, and privileges than lords, but far more freedom than they had known as serfs.

## Trade with the East

Trade increased, not only within Europe, but also with places outside Europe. Located on the Mediterranean, Italy had an advantage in this trade. Italian cities such as Venice traded with other port cities, such as Constantinople, located in what is now Turkey.

B. Possible Answer It increased trade, because Italy was able to use the ships that carried the Crusaders to bring back Asian trade goods.

*Reading*History
**B. Recognizing Effects** What effect did the Crusades have on Italian trade?

War also spurred trade. Many European Christians were angry that Muslims held the Holy Land, where Jesus had lived. In 1096, European Christians launched the **Crusades,** a series of wars to capture the Holy Land. They ultimately failed to take the Holy Land, but the Crusades changed European life. Italians supplied the ships that carried Crusaders to the Middle East. On the return trip, the ships brought Asian goods to Europe. These goods had traveled across the Indian Ocean and then overland to the Mediterranean.

### STRANGE *but* True

**PEPPER MILLIONAIRES**

Europeans were desperate to get spices, such as pepper and cloves. Before refrigeration, meat often spoiled. Spices helped disguise the taste of rotten meat.

In the 1500s, just one shipload of spices could make a merchant wealthy for life. The average working person would have to work at least 1,000 years to earn as much as a merchant could earn from one load of pepper!

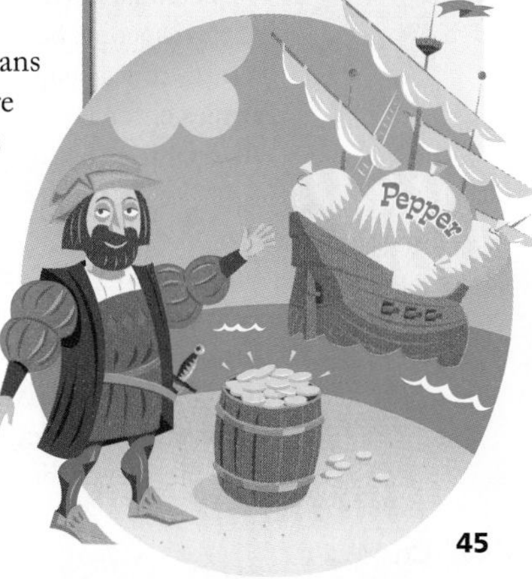




### INSTRUCT: OBJECTIVE 2

**Revival of Trade and Towns/ Trade with the East**

Key Questions

- What caused the revival of trade and the growth of new towns?
- Why did Italian cities take the lead in trade with places outside Europe?
- How did the Crusades increase European trade in Asian goods?

### STRANGE *but* True

**Pepper Millionaires**

Long before the 1500s, merchants had been making a tidy profit on the spice trade. During the Roman Empire, Arab merchants conducted a brisk trade in cinnamon, cardamom, ginger, and turmeric. To keep others from guessing the whereabouts of their suppliers, merchants spread rumors that their spices grew in snake-infested valleys or in shallow lakes guarded by winged monsters. Not everyone was fooled. The Roman writer Pliny the Elder scoffed at such tales. They had been invented, he said, "for the purpose of enhancing the price of these commodities."

**ACTIVITY OPTIONS**

**INTERDISCIPLINARY LINK: WORLD HISTORY** — BLOCK SCHEDULING

**FEUDALISM**

**Class Time** 20 minutes

**Task** Making a diagram to show how the feudal system worked

**Purpose** To understand the obligations and rewards of participating in feudalism and the manor system

**Supplies Needed**

- Reference materials on feudalism

**Activity** Have each student make a diagram that shows what part each level of society played in the feudal system: king, nobles, knights, peasants, serfs. On their diagrams students should indicate the responsibilities each group had to those above and below it and how each benefited from the system. After students have shared their diagrams with the class, have them explain how this system weakened the power of kings, while strengthening the power of the nobility.

**INSTRUCT: OBJECTIVE 3**

**The Decline of Feudalism**

Key Questions

- How did the growth of towns and trade weaken feudalism?
- What effect did the bubonic plague have on feudalism?
- Why did kings become more powerful as feudal lords weakened?

**MORE ABOUT . . .**

**Bubonic Plague**

Between 1347 and 1352, the bubonic plague, known more dramatically as the Black Death, killed about 25 million people in Europe. (It had already killed uncounted millions in Asia.) Spread by fleas, the disease was especially devastating wherever people lived in close quarters, such as in towns or in medieval monasteries. In some Italian cities, as many as nine-tenths of the population died. The eerie cry "Bring out your dead" sounded in the streets as plague carts carried corpses off to mass graves. No other event in recorded history has killed such a large share of the world's population.

**INSTRUCT: OBJECTIVE 4**

**The Renaissance and Reformation/ Changes in Trade**

Key Questions

- What was the Renaissance and where did it begin?
- How did the Reformation affect the Roman Catholic Church?
- Why did Italians gain control of the trade in Asian goods?
- Why did other European countries begin looking for an all-water route to Asia?

**The Rise and Decline of Feudalism**

In feudalism, nobles offered to protect peasants from invaders. In return, the peasants farmed the nobles' lands.

Feudalism made people feel safe enough to travel. Trade increased and towns grew.

Then many peasants ran away to towns, where they could live more freely. Feudalism declined. Trade continued to grow.

After the Crusades, Italians continued to trade with Muslims in other Mediterranean cities.

An Italian merchant named Marco Polo also stirred European curiosity about distant lands. Polo had spent 24 years traveling in China and central Asia. A book written about Polo's travels described China's riches and wonders. It increased European interest in Asia.

## 3 The Decline of Feudalism

The growth of trade and towns weakened feudalism because so many serfs left the manors for town life. The power of the lords shrank because they had fewer people under their control. Beginning in 1347, a deadly disease also weakened feudalism. The bubonic plague swept across Europe, killing about one-fourth of the population and reducing the number of workers. Lords competed for the laborers who survived, so they began to pay wages to peasants, such as John of Cayworth.

*A VOICE FROM THE PAST*

John of Cayworth . . . ought to carry in autumn beans or oats for 2 days with a cart and 3 animals of his own, the value of the work being 12 denarii [about a penny]. And he shall receive from the lord each day 3 meals.

**Contract of John of Cayworth,** from *Readings in European History*

As feudal lords lost power, kings grew stronger. They won the support of townspeople because they could raise large armies to enforce order. In return, townspeople agreed to support their kings by paying taxes. The armies enforced order and imposed the king's authority over lesser lords. As countries became safer, trade flourished even more.

*Reading* **History**

**C. Analyzing Causes** What three causes led to the decline of feudalism?

**C. Answer** the growth of towns and trade, the bubonic plague, and the growing power of kings

## 4 The Renaissance and Reformation

Italy, which was thriving because of trade, became the birthplace of the **Renaissance**—a time of increased interest in art and learning. *Renaissance* is a French term meaning "rebirth." Lasting from the 1300s to 1600, the Renaissance spread from Italy throughout Europe.

Several forces led to this rebirth of learning. As feudalism weakened and the plague brought great suffering, Europeans began to question



**ACTIVITY OPTIONS**

**INDIVIDUAL NEEDS**

**LESS PROFICIENT READERS**

**Cause and Effect** Point out the cause-and-effect chart on page 48. Review how an effect can become a cause that triggers a subsequent effect. Then pair a proficient reader with a less proficient reader. Have the students look at each cause and effect in the chart and identify what steps and information are implied in each combination. For example: After the Crusades, Europeans wanted Asian goods, but they needed to find a way to get goods from Asia to Europe. Italy had already developed a trade network with Asia during the Crusades, so the Italians were the first Europeans able to import goods from Asia.

Ask students to create a three-column graphic organizer. Have them write causes in the left column and effects in the right column. Then ask them to supply the implied information in the center column.

what life meant. In their search for new answers, some people turned to old sources. They read the writings and studied the art of the Greeks and Romans. The classical Greeks and Romans lived from about 750 B.C. to A.D. 476. As a result of these studies, European ideas changed.

**Vocabulary**
**philosophy:** the study of the meaning of life

1. The Greeks had praised human achievement. European scholars began humanism, the study of human worth, ideas, and potential.
2. Classical education stressed such subjects as history, philosophy, and literature. Europeans spent more time studying those subjects.
3. From classical art, European artists learned to make art more realistic. They created some of the world's finest paintings and statues.
4. Muslim scholars had saved classical manuscripts about science. Also, Muslim mathematicians had invented algebra. Contact with Muslim societies influenced European science and mathematics.

**Background**
A printing press uses movable type—blocks of metal or wood that have raised characters. The Chinese invented movable type in about 1045. Gutenberg re-invented it.

A new invention helped spread Renaissance ideas. In about 1455, a German named Johannes Gutenberg invented the **printing press,** a machine that mechanically prints pages. People no longer had to copy books by hand. Printers could make hundreds of copies of a book cheaply and accurately. More people read, and ideas spread quickly.

By the early 1500s, Renaissance ideas and other forces weakened the Catholic Church. Many church leaders were corrupt. Some claimed to grant God's forgiveness for money. Martin Luther, a German monk, publicly posted 95 statements that criticized such practices. This began the **Reformation,** a movement to correct problems in the Church.

The Reformation split the Church into two groups—Catholics and Protestants. In time, Protestants divided into many different churches.

## HISTORY through ART

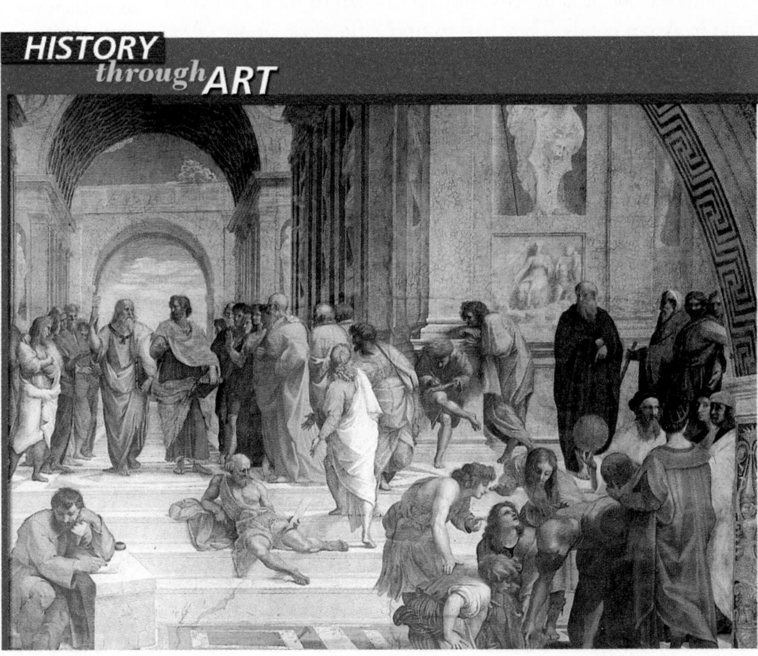

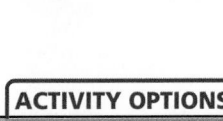

This painting, *School of Athens* by Raphael, shows many aspects of Renaissance art and culture.

- Like much Renaissance art, it looks more realistic than the art of the Middle Ages. (See page 44 for comparison.)
- It honors the Greek thinkers Aristotle and Plato, who are the two men in the center arch.
- It also honors Renaissance artists. Raphael himself is in the group to the right.

**Why might Raphael have wanted to include himself in a painting with famous Greeks?**





### MORE ABOUT . . .

**Gutenberg's Press**
Both the Chinese and Koreans had some form of printing when Gutenberg invented his press. In Europe, printers had developed a method of stamping letters on various surfaces. However, Gutenberg's method of printing from movable type had several unique features. His press most closely resembled those used in making wine or paper. He also created a mold for accurately casting type and developed an oil-based printing ink.

### HISTORY through ART

**Interpreting the Painting** By age 21, Raphael (1483–1520) was already a successful and respected painter. In 1508, Pope Julius II called him to Rome to paint a series of frescoes in the private apartments in the Vatican where the pope lived and worked. The *School of Athens* is one of these frescoes. Charming and handsome as well as talented, Raphael's popularity earned him the nickname "the prince of painters." His works have been called a perfect expression of the "classical spirit—harmonious, beautiful and serene."

**Possible Responses: He wanted to show himself as their student. He is indicating his desire to be as great as they were.**

## ACTIVITY OPTIONS

### INTERDISCIPLINARY LINK: HUMANITIES

**RENAISSANCE ART**

**Class Time** 20 minutes

**Task** Examining prints or pictures of Renaissance art to identify key features

**Purpose** To identify characteristics of Renaissance art and to contrast it with medieval art

**Supplies Needed**
- Slides or illustrated references showing examples of medieval and Italian Renaissance art
- Slide or overhead projector

**Activity** With the class, create a list of characteristics of Renaissance art or ask an art teacher to discuss the topic with the class. Among the features students might identify are the following: people in realistic, three-dimensional forms; use of perspective; religious subject matter; admiration for the Greeks and Romans. Point out that not all these features occur in all works. Begin by showing two or three examples of medieval art. Then have volunteers take turns pointing out what makes each work an example of Renaissance art.

## HISTORY FROM VISUALS

**Interpreting the Chart** Point out that events have both intended and unintended consequences. Ask students to identify the intended and unintended consequences of the Italian domination of Asian trade. **Answer** The intended effect was to make Italy powerful and rich; the unintended effect was to make other European nations wanting power and riches begin exploration.

**Extension** Suggest that students do research to find out which Asian trade goods were most desired by Europeans.

 **Critical Thinking Transparency CT2**
- Cause and Effect: Causes of Exploration

 **Economics in History**
- The Benefits of Trade, p. 1

## ASSESS & RETEACH

**Setting the Stage** Ask students to fill in the Europe sections on the chapter graphic organizer.

 **Formal Assessment**
- Section Quiz, p. 22

### RETEACHING ACTIVITY

Have students write a summary of the section using the Key Terms and Names for the section listed on page 44.

 **In-Depth Resources: Unit 1**
- Reteaching Activity, p. 20

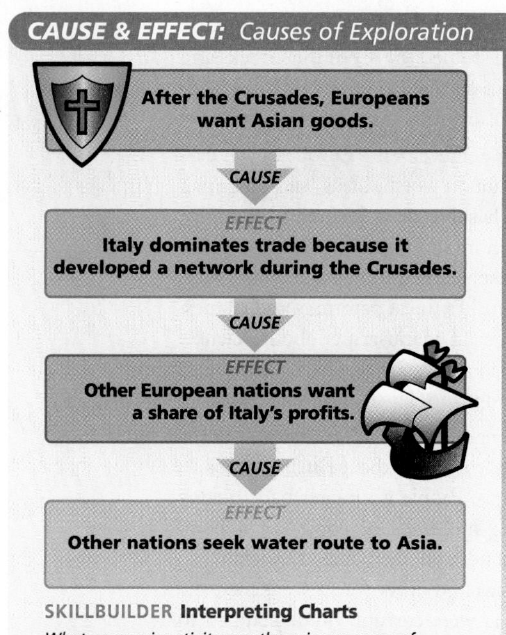

CAUSE & EFFECT: Causes of Exploration
After the Crusades, Europeans want Asian goods.
CAUSE
EFFECT
Italy dominates trade because it developed a network during the Crusades.
CAUSE
EFFECT
Other European nations want a share of Italy's profits.
CAUSE
EFFECT
Other nations seek water route to Asia.


SKILLBUILDER **Interpreting Charts**
*What economic activity was the primary cause of exploration?*

Skillbuilder **Answer** trade

When European colonists came to America, they carried their religious disagreements and hopes for religious freedom with them.

## Changes in Trade

The Renaissance period saw not only changes in learning and religion, but also in trade. As trade grew, Italian merchants needed to improve the way they did business. They began to use more exact ways of keeping track of a business's income and its costs. By subtracting the costs from the income, the merchants determined the **profit**.

Italian merchants made huge profits by trading in Asian goods. Because Italians had done business with Muslims for centuries, they had a special relationship. In addition to that, the Italians used military strength to control the trade on the Mediterranean—and didn't allow other Europeans to take part in it.

Merchants in other European countries envied the profits made by Italian merchants. As a result, other Europeans began to want a share of the rich trade in Asian goods. They had to find different routes to Asia from the ones controlled by the Italians and Muslims. Other European countries began to search for a non-Mediterranean water route to Asia, as you will read in Section 5.

**D. Possible Answer** They will do whatever they can to find a way to undermine the first country's control.

*Reading* **History**
**D. Making Generalizations** If a country tries to completely dominate trade in a certain area, how will other countries respond?

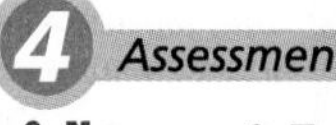

### Section 4 Assessment

**1. Terms & Names**
**Identify:**
- European Middle Ages
- feudalism
- manor system
- Crusades
- Renaissance
- printing press
- Reformation
- profit

**2. Taking Notes**
On a chart like this one, list how the Renaissance changed art and learning.

| Changes to Art and Learning |
|---|
| • |
| • |
| • |
| • |

**3. Main Ideas**
a. What caused feudalism to develop?
b. What led to the revival of trade and towns?
c. How did Italy come to control European trade with Asia?

**4. Critical Thinking**
**Contrasting** How did the Renaissance differ from the European Middle Ages?
**THINK ABOUT**
- the economy
- how power was distributed
- the authority of the church

**ACTIVITY OPTIONS**
**TECHNOLOGY**
**MUSIC**
Design a **Web site** or compose a **song** advertising the great new Renaissance invention—the printing press.

### Section 4 Assessment

**1. Terms & Names**
**European Middle Ages,** p. 44
**feudalism,** p. 44
**manor system,** p. 45
**Crusades,** p. 45
**Renaissance,** p. 46
**printing press,** p. 47
**Reformation,** p. 47
**profit,** p. 48

**2. Taking Notes**
- study of humanism
- increased study of history, philosophy, literature
- more realism in art
- rediscovery of classical science and exposure to algebra
- printing press, which spread learning

**3. Main Ideas**
**a.** The authority of Rome disappeared, and Europe was disrupted by raiders. Feudalism was a system of protection in exchange for work.
**b.** Feudalism made society safer, which led to a revival of towns and trade. **c.** Its location on the Mediterranean gave it an advantage.

**4. Critical Thinking**
Under feudalism, the economy was agricultural; power was divided among kings and nobles. During the Renaissance, trade revived; kings gained power.

**ACTIVITY OPTIONS**
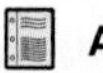 **Alternative Assessment**
- Rubrics for a Web site, 5.1
- Rubrics for a song, 4.8

# 5 Early European Explorers

**TERMS & NAMES**
navigator
caravel
Christopher Columbus

| MAIN IDEA | WHY IT MATTERS NOW |
|---|---|
| As Europeans searched for sea routes to Asia, Christopher Columbus reached the Americas. | Columbus's journey permanently linked the Americas to the rest of the world. |



## SECTION OBJECTIVES

1. To describe the Portuguese water route to Asia
2. To explain why Spain's rulers financed Columbus's voyages of discovery
3. To describe Columbus's first voyage
4. To evaluate the geographic knowledge Columbus brought back from his voyages

**SKILLBUILDER**
Interpreting Maps: Movement, Human–Environment Interaction, p. 51

**CRITICAL THINKING**
Comparing, p. 50
Drawing Conclusions, p. 51
Analyzing Causes, p. 52
Making Inferences, p. 53
Analyzing Points of View, p. 53

**Why It Matters Now**
- Cultural Diversity, pp. 1–2

## FOCUS & MOTIVATE

### 5-MINUTE WARM-UP

**Making Inferences** Have students answer these questions to understand the challenges that early European explorers faced.

1. Study the painting on page 53. How does the man appear to be finding his location?
2. How do the tools that navigators use today differ from those of early explorers?

**Warm-Up Transparency WT1**

## INSTRUCT

**INSTRUCT: OBJECTIVE 1**

**A Water Route to Asia**
Key Questions
- In what way was the caravel an improvement over earlier ships?
- How did Dias's new route to Asia help Portugal?

**In-Depth Resources: Unit 1**
- Guided Reading, p. 7

## ONE EUROPEAN'S STORY

**Sailors seeking a route to Asia depended on the skill of their navigator. A <u>navigator</u> plans the course of a ship by using instruments to find its position. In the 1400s, Portugal had a famous prince called Henry the Navigator. Yet, Henry wasn't a navigator. He never sailed on any of the ships trying to find Asia. So how did he earn his name?**

**Henry lived at Sagres, on the southwestern tip of Portugal. It was a site that overlooked the Atlantic Ocean. He invited astronomers, mathematicians, mapmakers, and navigators to Sagres. There he began a school of navigation.**

**Henry decided to organize and pay for sailing expeditions to explore the Atlantic and the west coast of Africa. He was hoping to find African gold, to learn more about geography, and to spread Christianity. His ships traveled farther down the African coast than Europeans had ever gone. Because Henry sponsored the voyages, the English named him "the navigator." Those voyages began Europe's age of discovery. As you will read in this section, this age of discovery eventually led Europeans to the Americas.**

Henry the Navigator sponsored voyages that helped Portugal find a water route to Asia.

## 1 A Water Route to Asia

Under Prince Henry, the Portuguese developed an improved ship called the **<u>caravel</u>**. The caravel had triangular sails as well as square sails. Square sails carried the ship forward when the wind was at its back. Triangular sails allowed the caravel to sail into the wind. The caravel was better than other European ships of the time at sailing into the wind.

In January 1488, the Portuguese explorer Bartolomeu Dias (DEE•uhs) reached the southern tip of Africa. After sailing around it, he returned to Portugal at the urging of his crew. Portugal's king named the tip the Cape of Good Hope because he hoped they had found a route to Asia.

Ten years later, another Portuguese explorer, Vasco da Gama, followed Dias's route around the cape. He continued north along the eastern coast of Africa. Then he sailed east across the Indian Ocean to India. At last, someone had found an all-water route to Asia.



## RECOMMENDED RESOURCES

**In-Depth Resources: Unit 1**
- Guided Reading, p. 7
- Geography Application: Ocean Currents, pp. 10–11
- Primary Source, p. 13
- Reteaching Activity, p. 21
- Enrichment Activity, p. 22
- History Workshop Resources, p. 23

**America's History Makers**
- Christopher Columbus, pp. 3–4

**Reading Study Guide** (Spanish and English), pp. 13–14

**Why It Matters Now**
- Cultural Diversity, pp. 1–2

**Formal Assessment**
- Section Quiz, p. 23

**Alternative Assessment**
- Rubrics, 2.1
- Rubrics, 2.2

**Access for Students Acquiring English/ESL**
- Guided Reading, p. 5
- Geography Application, pp. 7–8

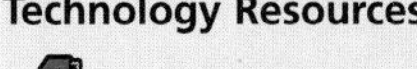
Technology Resources

**Humanities Transparency HT2**
- Map of the American Southeast, 1606

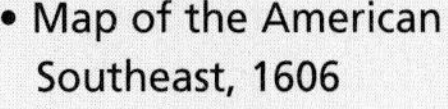

**Electronic Teacher Tools with Test Maker**

**Classzone**
www.mcdougallittell.com

## AMERICA'S HISTORY MAKERS

**Christopher Columbus**

Today historians argue about Columbus's character or judgment, but not his talent as a navigator. With few tools to help him cross an unknown sea, he relied upon dead reckoning, a navigation method used when few visible landmarks exist. Crossing the Atlantic, he measured latitude by the North Star. A quadrant, an instrument for measuring altitude, aided him in guessing his ship's position from the stars but only when seas were calm. He charted the ship's course with a compass, using a chart to estimate distances. A half-hour glass measured time. Estimating speed was guesswork.

**Possible Responses:** He showed courage, persistence, willingness to learn from others, and the ability to apply what he had learned to new situations. He was adventurous and interested in learning about the sea.

 **America's History Makers**
- Christopher Columbus, pp. 3–4

**INSTRUCT: OBJECTIVE 2**

**Columbus's Plan/Help from Spain's Rulers**

Key Questions
- What two mistakes made Columbus think that sailing west to Asia would be a short journey?
- Why did Ferdinand and Isabella support Columbus?

AMERICA'S HISTORY MAKERS

**CHRISTOPHER COLUMBUS**
**1451–1506**

Christopher Columbus's son Ferdinand wrote that his father "took to the sea at the age of 14 and followed it ever after."

Columbus's early voyages nearly cost him his life. When he was 25, pirates off the coast of Portugal sank his ship. Columbus survived by grabbing a floating oar and swimming to shore.

But he also learned a lot from sailing on Portuguese ships. The sailors taught Columbus about Atlantic wind patterns. This knowledge later helped him on his history-making voyage.

**What character traits, shown in Columbus's early life, might have made him a good leader?**

That route meant that the Portuguese could now trade with Asia without dealing with the Muslims or Italians. Portugal took control of the valuable spice trade. The merchants of Lisbon, Portugal's capital, grew rich. Spain and other European rivals wanted to take part in this profitable trade. They began to look for their own water routes to Asia.

**Reading History**
**A. Comparing** Compare what happened after Portugal began to control the spice trade to what happened when Italy controlled it.
**A. Possible Answer** In both cases, rival countries tried to find ways to end that control.

## 2 Columbus's Plan

By the time of da Gama's voyage, an Italian sailor named **Christopher Columbus** thought he knew a faster way to reach Asia. Europeans had known for centuries that the earth is round. Columbus decided that instead of sailing around Africa and then east, he would sail west across the Atlantic. He calculated that it would be a short journey.

But Columbus made several mistakes. First, he relied on the writings of two people—Marco Polo and a geographer named Paolo Toscanelli—who were wrong about the size of Asia. They claimed that Asia stretched farther from west to east than it really did.

**Background**
As you read in Section 4, Marco Polo's book about his travels had increased European interest in Asia.

Second, Columbus underestimated the distance around the globe. He thought the earth was only two thirds as large as it actually is! Because of Polo and Toscanelli, Columbus thought that Asia took up most of that distance. Therefore, he believed that the Atlantic Ocean must be small. And a voyage west to Asia would be short.

In 1483, Columbus asked the king of Portugal to finance a voyage across the Atlantic. The king's advisers opposed the plan. They argued that Columbus had miscalculated the distance to Asia. They also reminded the king of the progress that Portuguese explorers had made sailing down the coast of Africa looking for a route to Asia. The advisers persuaded the king not to finance the voyage. So in 1486, Columbus turned to Portugal's rival, Spain.

## Help from Spain's Rulers

Spain's rulers, King Ferdinand and Queen Isabella, liked Columbus's plan because they wanted a share of the rich Asian trade. As a strong Catholic, the Queen also welcomed a chance to spread Christianity. But there were also reasons not to support Columbus. First, a royal council had doubts about Columbus's calculations and advised Ferdinand and Isabella not to finance him. Second, the Spanish monarchs were in the middle of a costly war to drive the Muslims out of Spain. Third, Columbus was asking a high payment for his services.

**Vocabulary**
**monarch:** a king or queen

The years of waiting had made Columbus determined to profit from his explorations. As a reward for his efforts, he demanded the high title



**ACTIVITY OPTIONS**

**INTERDISCIPLINARY LINK: LANGUAGE ARTS** — BLOCK SCHEDULING

**WRITING A DIALOGUE**

**Class Time** One class period

**Task** Creating a dialogue between Columbus and the Spanish monarchs

**Purpose** To analyze how Columbus might have attempted to persuade the rulers to back his explorations

**Supplies Needed**
- Reference materials on Columbus, Ferdinand, and Isabella

**Activity** Invite the language arts teacher to discuss techniques of persuasive writing with the class. Then as a pre-writing activity, ask students to list some arguments Columbus might have used to convince Spain's rulers to give him money. Next, let them list the possible responses the rulers might have given to each argument. Students can use these lists to help them write their dialogues. When dialogues are completed, have several volunteers read them aloud, taking the part of each speaker.

Admiral of the Ocean Sea and a percentage of any wealth he brought from Asia. He also expected to be made the ruler of the lands he found.

Finally in January of 1492, the Spanish conquered the last Muslim stronghold in Spain. The Spanish monarchs could now afford to finance Columbus but still had doubts about doing so. Columbus left the palace to return home. But after listening to a trusted adviser, the king and queen changed their minds and sent a rider on horseback to bring Columbus back. He and the rulers finally reached an agreement.

*Reading* **History**

**B. Drawing Conclusions** Did this agreement give Columbus what he was asking for? Explain.

**B. Possible Answer** Almost everything. It offers him rewards, the title he wanted, and the position of governor. There is no mention of a specific percentage of wealth.

*A VOICE FROM THE PAST*

Your Highnesses . . . accorded me great rewards and ennobled me so that from that time henceforth I might . . . be high admiral of the Ocean Sea and perpetual Governor of the islands and continent which I should discover.

**Christopher Columbus,** letter to King Ferdinand and Queen Isabella

Preparing to sail, Columbus assembled his ships—the *Niña,* the *Pinta,* and the *Santa María*—at the port of Palos de la Frontera in southern Spain.

## 3 Setting Sail

At first, Columbus had trouble finding a crew. Then a respected local shipowner agreed to sign on as captain of the *Pinta.* Other crew members soon followed. About 90 men loaded the ships with enough food for one year, casks of fresh water, firewood, and other necessities.

Skillbuilder Answers

1. between 4,000 and 5,000
2. Dias was venturing into new territory, while da Gama had the knowledge acquired by Dias to guide him.

***Exploration Leads to New Sea Routes,*** *1487–1504*

Route of Dias, 1487–1488
Route of da Gama, 1497–1498
Routes of Columbus:
1492–1493
1493–1496
1498–1500
1502–1504

EUROPE
NORTH AMERICA
ATLANTIC OCEAN
PORTUGAL
SPAIN
SAN SALVADOR
CUBA
HISPANIOLA
PACIFIC OCEAN
ASIA
AFRICA
SOUTH AMERICA
INDIAN OCEAN
Tropic of Cancer
Tropic of Capricorn
0° Equator
40°N
40°S
40°W
40°E
80°E
0 1,000 Miles
0 2,000 Kilometers

**GEOGRAPHY SKILLBUILDER Interpreting Maps**

1. **Movement** *Approximately how many miles did Columbus sail before he reached San Salvador on his first voyage?*
2. **Human-Environment Interaction** *Why do you suppose that Dias stayed close to the west coast of Africa during his voyage, while da Gama sailed farther out?*

51

# CHAPTER 1 • SECTION 5

### CRITICAL THINKING ACTIVITY

**Making Decisions** The decision to finance Columbus's first voyage was a difficult one for Spain's rulers. The monarchs had to weigh the advice of their counselors and the possible risks to Spain's welfare. Use a decision tree to help students weigh costs and benefits.

**Class Time** 10 minutes

### INSTRUCT: OBJECTIVE 3

**Setting Sail/Reaching the Americas**

Key Questions

- What kinds of problems did the sailors on Columbus's ships face?
- What convinced Columbus that he had reached Asia?

**In-Depth Resources: Unit 1**

- Geography Application: Ocean Currents, pp. 10–11
- Primary Source: from *The Journal of Christopher Columbus*, p. 13

### HISTORY FROM VISUALS

**Reading the Map** Ask the students to look at the four routes of Columbus. Ask how the routes differ. **Possible Response** Each route is slightly different. The later trips explore more areas of the West Indies. One trip goes to the land bridge connecting North and South America.

**Extension** Have the students research the Line of Demarcation (Treaty of Tordesillas) to understand why Portugal did not explore in the western hemisphere during this time.

**Humanities Transparency HT2**

- Map of the American Southeast, 1606

### ACTIVITY OPTIONS

### INDIVIDUAL NEEDS: GIFTED AND TALENTED

**THE COLUMBUS CONTROVERSY**

**Class Time** 30 minutes

**Task** Researching a historical controversy

**Purpose** To summarize the varying interpretations of Columbus as a pivotal figure in history

**Supplies Needed**

- Access to research sources at the library or on the Internet

**Activity** Have students research these topics: Should Columbus's arrival in the Americas be labeled a "discovery"? Should North and South America be called the "New World"? Excellent sources to begin this project are Marvin Lunenfeld, *1492: Discovery, Invasion, Encounter: Sources and Interpretations* (Houghton Mifflin, 1991) and Ronald Wright, *Stolen Continents: The "New World" Through Indian Eyes* (Houghton Mifflin, 1993).

**In-Depth Resources: Unit 1**

- Enrichment Activity, p. 22

**MORE ABOUT . . .**

**The *Pinta,* the *Nina,* and the *Santa Maria***
By modern standards, the three ships that Columbus commanded on his first voyage were tiny indeed. The *Santa Maria* was the largest of the three; at about 100 feet in length, it carried 39 crew members. The *Pinta,* with a crew of 26, and the *Nina,* with 22, were even smaller—each about 70 feet long.

**Now *and* then**

**Native American View of Columbus**
Harjo also had this to say about Columbus: "His story is very complex history in and of itself. Too often this history is posed as romantic myth and the uncomfortable facts . . . are eliminated. Explaining the unpleasant truths . . . does not take away from the fact that he was able to lurch over to these shores in three little boats. In fact, it gives the story of Columbus more dimension."

The tiny fleet of wooden ships glided out of the harbor on August 3, 1492. First they sailed southwest toward the Canary Islands off the northwest coast of Africa. From there, Columbus was relying on trade winds that blew toward the west to speed his ships across the ocean.

Once aboard ship, Columbus kept a log, or daily record of each day's sailing. In fact, he kept two logs. One he showed to his men and one he kept secret. Columbus's secret log recorded the truth about the journey.

*A VOICE FROM THE PAST*

[We] made 15 leagues [this] day and . . . [I] decided to report less than those actually traveled so in case the voyage were long the men would not be frightened and lose courage.

**Christopher Columbus,** quoted in *Columbus and the Age of Discovery*

***Reading* History**
**C. Analyzing Causes** What caused Columbus to decide to keep two logs?
**C. Possible Answer** He was afraid his crew would be frightened if they knew the truth, so he kept a phony log to share with them.

By October 10, the men had lost both courage and confidence in their leader. They had been at sea for almost ten weeks and had not seen land for over a month. Afraid that they would starve if the trip went on longer, they talked of returning home. To avoid mutiny, Columbus and the crew struck a bargain. The men agreed to sail on for three more days, and Columbus promised to turn back if they had not sighted land by then. Two days later in the early morning hours of October 12, a sailor on the *Pinta* called out "Tierra, tierra" [Land, land].

## Reaching the Americas

By noon, the ships had landed on an island in the Caribbean Sea. Columbus believed that he had reached the Indies, islands in Southeast Asia where spices grew. The islanders who greeted Columbus and his men were Taino (TY•noh) people, but Columbus mistakenly called them Indians.

**Background**
Today, the Indies are called the East Indies. The islands of the Caribbean are called the West Indies.

Columbus named the island San Salvador. After unfurling the royal banner and flags, he ordered his crew to "bear witness that I was taking possession of this island for the King and Queen." Eager to reach the rich country of Japan, which he believed was nearby, he left San Salvador. He took six or seven Taino with him as guides. For the next three months, he visited several of the Caribbean islands.

Finally, he reached an island that he named Española, which we call Hispaniola today. (See map on page 51.) On that island, Columbus and his men found some gold and precious objects such as pearls. This convinced Columbus that he had reached Asia. He decided to return home, leaving 39 of his men on Hispaniola. Even before Columbus left, his men had angered the Taino people by stealing from them and committing violence. By the time Columbus returned ten months later, the Taino had killed the men.

**Now *and* then**

**NATIVE AMERICAN VIEW OF COLUMBUS**

In 1992, many Native Americans protested the 500th anniversary of Columbus's voyage. Suzan Shown Harjo, who is Cheyenne and Creek, explained why.

*As Native American peoples in this red quarter of Mother Earth, we have no reason to celebrate an invasion that caused the demise [death] of so many of our people and is still causing destruction today.*

The Spanish enslaved the Taino, who nearly all died from disease and bad treatment. This statue is one of the few Taino artifacts left from the 1500s.



**ACTIVITY OPTIONS**

**MULTIPLE LEARNING STYLES: LINGUISTIC** — BLOCK SCHEDULING

**COLUMBUS'S LOG**

**Class Time** One class period

**Task** Performing dramatic readings

**Purpose** To analyze Columbus's first voyage to the Americas from a reading of his log

**Supplies Needed**
- Selections from Columbus's log
- Audiotapes and tape recorder

**Activity** Instruct students to choose passages from Columbus's log that they find especially interesting and prepare short dramatic readings from the log. Each presentation can begin with two or three sentences telling at what part of the voyage these entries were made. Assign one student to be the sound engineer, who will tape students reading their selections; one student to write an introduction to the tape; and another to write a conclusion. After the class has listened to the tape, ask students how they think an account of this voyage from the perspective of a crew member might be different.

In January 1493, he sailed back to Spain. Firmly believing that he had found a new water route to Asia, he wrote to Ferdinand and Isabella. The Spanish rulers called him to the royal court to report on his voyage. Neither Columbus nor the king and queen suspected that he had landed near continents entirely unknown to Europeans.

## 4 An Expanding Horizon

Columbus made three more voyages to the Americas, but never brought back the treasures he had promised Spain's rulers. He also failed to meet Queen Isabella's other goal. She wanted Christianity brought to new people. When she learned that Columbus had mistreated and enslaved the people of Hispaniola, she became angry.

A French mapmaker uses an instrument to learn his exact position on the globe.

After the fourth voyage, Spain's rulers refused to give Columbus any more help. He died in 1506, still believing he had reached Asia and bitter that he had not received the fame or fortune that he deserved.

In time, the geographic knowledge Columbus brought back changed European views of the world. People soon realized that Columbus had reached continents that had been unknown to them previously. And Europeans were eager to see if these continents could make them rich.

For centuries, Europeans had seen the ocean as a barrier. With one voyage, Columbus changed that. Instead of a barrier, the Atlantic Ocean became a bridge that connected Europe, Africa, and the Americas. As you will learn in Chapter 2, Columbus's explorations began an era of great wealth and power for Spain. As Spain grew rich, England, France, and other European countries also began to send ships to the Americas.

**D. Possible Answer** It was the body people crossed to get from one continent to the other.

*Reading* **History**

**D. Making Inferences** How did the Atlantic become a bridge connecting Europe, Africa, and the Americas?

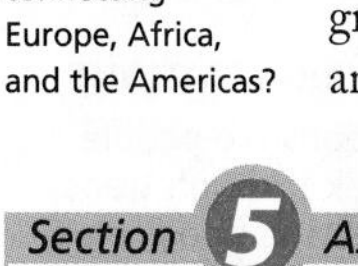

### Section 5 Assessment

**1. Terms & Names**

**Identify:**
- navigator
- caravel
- Christopher Columbus

**2. Taking Notes**

On a diagram like the one shown, list the effects of Columbus's voyages.

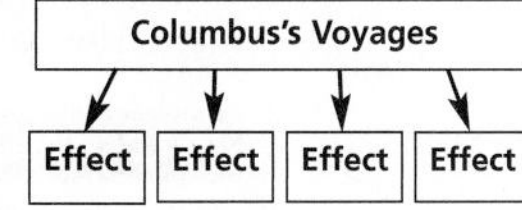


Which effects were negative and which were positive?

**3. Main Ideas**

**a.** Why was Prince Henry eager to find an all-water route to Asia?

**b.** Why did Spain's king and queen decide to support Columbus's first voyage?

**c.** Why was Columbus disappointed by the outcome of his four voyages to the Americas?

**4. Critical Thinking**

**Analyzing Points of View**
Explain how each of the following people might have viewed Columbus's first voyage. Give reasons for their points of view.

**THINK ABOUT**
- Columbus
- Queen Isabella
- a Taino chief

**ACTIVITY OPTIONS**

**GEOGRAPHY**
**MATH**

Use the map on page 31. Create an enlarged **map** of Columbus's first voyage, or measure the distance of each voyage to list on a **table**.





### INSTRUCT: OBJECTIVE 4

**An Expanding Horizon**

Key Questions
- Were Columbus's voyages viewed as successful?
- How did Columbus's voyages change the way Europeans looked at the world?

## ASSESS & RETEACH

**Setting the Stage** Tell students to review all sections on the chapter graphic organizer.

 **Formal Assessment**
- Section Quiz, p. 23

 **Critical Thinking Transparency CT1**
- Setting the Stage

**RETEACHING ACTIVITY**

Tell students to use the information in this section to create a time line of Columbus's life. As a summary, they can write a paragraph explaining how events in Columbus's life changed European history.

 **In-Depth Resources: Unit 1**
- Reteaching Activity, p. 21

### Section 5 Assessment

**1. Terms & Names**

**navigator,** p. 49
**caravel,** p. 49
**Christopher Columbus,** p. 50

**2. Taking Notes**

Effects: conflict with Taino; enslavement and death of Taino; failure to bring back treasures; Europeans realized Americas were a previously unknown land; Spanish colonization; further European explorations

Most students will cite the effect on the Taino as negative. Opinion about the other effects may vary.

**3. Main Ideas**

**a.** He wanted to find African gold, to learn more about geography, and to spread Christianity. **b.** They wanted a share of the Asian trade and to spread Christianity. **c.** The monarchs did not reward him as much as he thought he deserved.

**4. Critical Thinking**

Columbus continued to insist his voyages were a success. Isabella was disappointed that the native peoples were abused. The Taino chief wished that Columbus had never come.

**ACTIVITY OPTIONS**

**Alternative Assessment**
- Rubrics, 2.1, 2.2

## TERMS & NAMES

1. **migrate,** p. 27
2. **civilization,** p. 29
3. **technology,** p. 32
4. **Iroquois League,** p. 37
5. **Islam,** p. 41
6. **feudalism,** p. 44
7. **Crusades,** p. 45
8. **Renaissance,** p. 46
9. **navigator,** p. 49
10. **Christopher Columbus,** p. 50

## REVIEW QUESTIONS

**Possible Responses**

1. that people crossed from Asia on the land bridge Beringia, which was created when the Ice Age caused ocean levels to drop, and that people came from many different places at many different times
2. as burial mounds and temples
3. They drained swamps and built irrigation canals, enabling them to grow a lot of food, and they conquered most of their neighbors and forced them to pay tribute.
4. Deganawida devised a plan for the Five Nations to be at peace and form an alliance, and Hiawatha persuaded the nations.
5. They were able to control and tax the profitable trade in gold and salt.
6. More. Ghana's rulers had Muslim advisers, Mali's rulers actually were Muslim, and many of Songhai's people were Muslim.
7. Lords divided their lands into manors, or large estates, which were farmed by serfs. In return for the serfs' work, the lords offered them protection.
8. The Italian ships that took Crusaders to the Middle East brought back Asian goods, which increased European desire for them.
9. because the Italians controlled the existing trade routes and would not allow others to share in the profitable trade
10. He based his calculations on incorrect sources and assumptions.

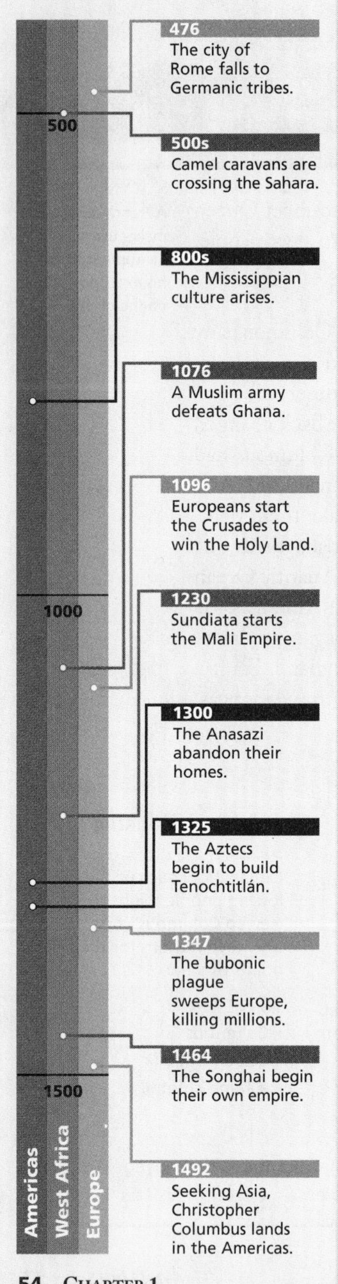
VISUAL SUMMARY
The World in 1500
476
The city of Rome falls to Germanic tribes.
500
500s
Camel caravans are crossing the Sahara.
800s
The Mississippian culture arises.
1076
A Muslim army defeats Ghana.
1096
Europeans start the Crusades to win the Holy Land.
1000
1230
Sundiata starts the Mali Empire.
1300
The Anasazi abandon their homes.
1325
The Aztecs begin to build Tenochtitlán.
1347
The bubonic plague sweeps Europe, killing millions.
1464
The Songhai begin their own empire.
1500
1492
Seeking Asia, Christopher Columbus lands in the Americas.
Americas
West Africa
Europe
54 CHAPTER 1

# Chapter 1 ASSESSMENT

## TERMS & NAMES

Briefly explain the importance of each of the following.

1. migrate
2. civilization
3. technology
4. Iroquois League
5. Islam
6. feudalism
7. Crusades
8. Renaissance
9. navigator
10. Christopher Columbus

## REVIEW QUESTIONS

**Crossing to the Americas (pages 27–31)**

1. What are two theories about migration to the Americas?
2. For what purposes did the Mound Builders construct earthen mounds?

**Societies of North America (pages 32–38)**

3. What enabled the Aztecs to become a strong empire?
4. How did the Iroquois League come about?

**Societies of West Africa (pages 39–43)**

5. What enabled Ghana, Mali, and Songhai all to grow rich?
6. Did Islam become more or less influential in West Africa from the 700s to the 1400s? Explain.

**Societies of Europe (pages 44–48)**

7. How did the manor system work during the Middle Ages?
8. How did the Crusades increase European interest in trade?

**Early European Explorers (pages 49–53)**

9. Why did non-Italian Europeans seek new trade routes to Asia?
10. How did Columbus miscalculate the distance to Asia?

## CRITICAL THINKING

**1. USING YOUR NOTES**

Using your completed chart, answer the questions below.

| | Trade | Technology | Religion | Art |
|---|---|---|---|---|
| AMERICAS (Sections 1 and 2) | | | | |
| WEST AFRICA (Section 3) | | | | |
| EUROPE (Sections 4 and 5) | | | | |

a. What was one instance in which trade spread knowledge?

b. Which of the technologies that you listed are still used today?

c. What religions were practiced in each of the three regions?

**2. ANALYZING LEADERSHIP**

Do you think Columbus was a good leader or a bad one? Use details from the chapter to explain your answer.

**3. THEME: DIVERSITY AND UNITY**

How have Native Americans, Africans, and Europeans all influenced American culture? Give examples from your own experience.

**4. MAKING GENERALIZATIONS**

What types of goods are people most likely to seek through trade? Think about the trade goods mentioned in the chapter and why people wanted them.

**5. APPLYING CITIZENSHIP SKILLS**

Compare the Iroquois League to what you know of the U.S. government. How are they similar?

**Interact *with* History**

Think about the various encounters between societies mentioned in the chapter. What do you think happened when more Europeans came to the Americas and met Native Americans?

## CRITICAL THINKING

**Possible Responses**

1. **USING YOUR NOTES** **a.** Trade in Mesoamerica spread knowledge of Olmec culture. **b.** irrigation, printing press **c.** America—Native American religions; Africa—African religions and Islam; Europe—Christianity
2. **ANALYZING LEADERSHIP** Encourage students to consider his actions in historical context.
3. **THEME: DIVERSITY AND UNITY** Students may cite examples such as food, art, music, religion, and dress.
4. **MAKING GENERALIZATIONS** People tend to seek items that are universally valued, such as gold, or items that will benefit their lives but cannot be found in their environment. Examples of this include West Africans seeking salt and Northwest Coast people seeking furs.
5. **APPLYING CITIZENSHIP SKILLS** Both are representative forms of government, and in both a leader can be voted out of office for wrongdoing.

**Interact *with* History** Most students will predict war and conflict, based on their own knowledge of history.

## HISTORY SKILLS

**1. INTERPRETING MAPS: Human-Environment Interaction**

Study the map. Answer the questions.

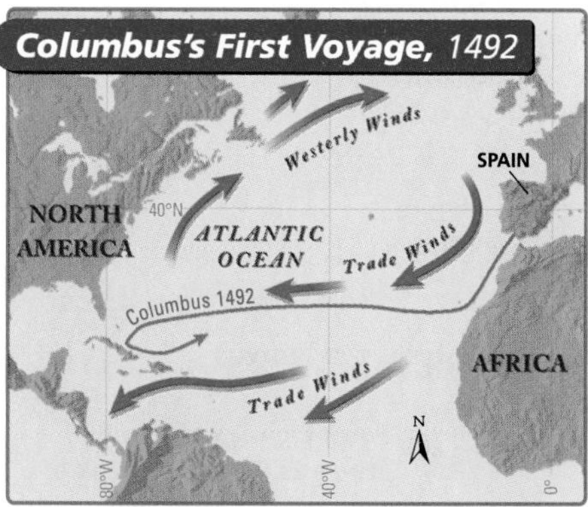


**Basic Map Elements**

a. What is the name of the winds blowing west across the Atlantic? blowing east?

b. In what direction did Columbus sail on his first journey from Europe?

**Interpreting the Map**

c. How did the winds affect Columbus's journey?

d. If Columbus's route had been farther north, would his voyage have taken more or less time? Explain.

**2. INTERPRETING PRIMARY SOURCES**

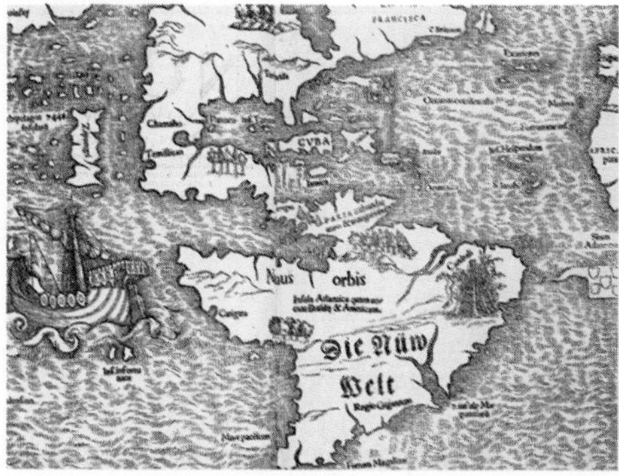

Drawn in 1570, this is the earliest map to show North America and South America as separate continents.

a. What are the names of any places that you recognize on this map?

b. Compare this map to the map of the world on page 51. Which continent on this map do you think looks more accurate? Explain why.

## ALTERNATIVE ASSESSMENT

**1. INTERDISCIPLINARY ACTIVITY: Literature**

**Retelling a Folk Tale** Many North American Indian tales give insight into the relationship between Native Americans and their environment. Select a tale from a collection of Native American literature and retell the tale for the class.

**2. COOPERATIVE LEARNING ACTIVITY**

**Creating a Sound Collage** Columbus's log of his first voyage can be found in many public libraries. Have one or two members of your group select portions of the log for audiotaping. Other members of the group can decide on sound effects to be heard in the background. Consider using some of the following:

- sounds of the ocean or of storms
- shipboard sounds, such as bells, clanking chains, and flapping sails
- shouted commands to the crew
- seafaring songs or other music

You may want to use a sound effects tape, available in many libraries, or create your own sounds.

**3. CD-ROM PRIMARY SOURCE EXPLORER**

**Choosing a Symbol** Countries and alliances often use a symbol to represent who they are. The Iroquois League chose a tree. Think of a group you belong to and choose a symbol to represent it. Before you choose, use the CD-ROM, library, or Internet to find out more about why the Iroquois chose a tree.

- Think about what your group stands for. Write a list of adjectives to describe it.
- Brainstorm animals, plants, or objects that share those qualities. Choose one to be your symbol.
- Write an explanation of your symbol and why you chose it.

**4. HISTORY PORTFOLIO**

**Option 1** Review your section and chapter assessment activities. Select one that you think is your best work. Then use comments made by your teacher or classmates to improve your work and add it to your portfolio.

**Option 2** Review the questions that you wrote for What Do You Want to Know? on page 26. Then write a short report in which you explain the answers to your questions. If any questions were not answered, do research to answer them. Add your answers to your portfolio.



## ALTERNATIVE ASSESSMENT

1. INTERDISCIPLINARY ACTIVITY: **Literature**

**Folk tale presentations should**
- have a clear introduction about the story.
- exhibit an understanding of basic concepts or ideas.
- have adequate delivery and establish rapport with the audience.

2. COOPERATIVE LEARNING ACTIVITY

**Sound collages should**
- clearly demonstrate an understanding of the concepts presented.
- present a concept visually.
- show technical proficiency.

3. CD-ROM PRIMARY SOURCE EXPLORER

**Symbols should**
- present a concept visually.
- clearly demonstrate an understanding of the concepts presented.
- exhibit creativity.
- demonstrate grade-level artistic skill.

4. HISTORY PORTFOLIO

**Option 1 Revised section or chapter assessment activities should**
- address teacher and peer responses to the selected work.
- solve problems present in the first versions of the work.

**Option 2 Short reports should**
- answer questions about the history of peoples in North America, Africa, and Europe.
- use evidence to develop and support ideas.
- cite sources of information.
- use standard grammar, spelling, sentence structure, and punctuation.

**Critical Thinking Transparency CT3**
- Visual Summary

**Formal Assessment**
- Chapter Test, Forms A and B, pp. 24–31

## HISTORY SKILLS

**Possible Responses**

1. INTERPRETING MAPS

**Basic Map Elements**

**a.** the trade winds, the westerly

**b.** southwest

**Interpreting the Map**

**c.** He used the trade winds, which probably made his journey faster.

**d.** It would have been longer, because he would not have had the wind at his back.

2. INTERPRETING PRIMARY SOURCES

**a.** North America, South America, Florida, Gulf of Mexico, Cuba, Atlantic Ocean, Hudson Bay

**b.** Students may choose either continent but should give reasons for their choice.

## *HISTORY* WORKSHOP

**OBJECTIVE**

Students create and decode pictographs, analyzing how the Native Americans of the Southwest used such symbols to communicate.

 **BLOCK SCHEDULING**

## PROCEDURE

Have students assemble the materials listed in the "Toolbox." Divide the class into groups of four or five. Then review the steps for choosing a message to communicate, researching and making a pictograph, and exchanging the pictograph with another pair of students.

 **In-Depth Resources: Unit 1**
- History Workshop Resources, p. 23

### HISTORY FROM VISUALS

**Interpreting the Petroglyph** Ask students who or what the largest image in this petroglyph might represent and what it might be holding. **Possible Responses** The figure could be a chief, a hunter/warrior, or a god. In its hands the figure may be holding a shield and some type of weapon used in hunting; or these objects might have religious significance, with the item in the right hand perhaps representing the sun.

*HISTORY* WORKSHOP

# Create and Decode a Pictograph

Native Americans of the Southwest created thousands of images to communicate with each other. These images, known as pictographs, helped people recall certain events, ideas, or information. Even if the people who created them were no longer present, others could read the messages. Most images were painted or carved on the surfaces of rock. There are three types of pictographs: petroglyphs, petrograms, and geoglyphs. (See HELP DESK on the next page.)

ACTIVITY Create a pictograph that other students will decode, or figure out. Then, acting as an anthropologist, interview students in one other group about their pictograph.

### TOOLBOX

Each group will need:

- drawing paper or poster board
- watercolor paints and brushes (optional)
- markers
- an envelope
- regular and colored pencils

The Fremont culture carved this petroglyph. It is currently located in Dinosaur National Monument—most of which sits in northwestern Colorado.

56

## STEP BY STEP

**1 Form a group of 4 or 5 students.** Together, think of a message to tell someone living in the future. What might you want future generations to know about your culture, or way of life? If you're having trouble coming up with a message, copy the chart below into your notebook. Write information for each category that you think would be interesting to future generations. Then choose one of these categories for your message.

| | |
|---|---|
| **Sports** | |
| **Politics** | |
| **Fashion** | |
| **Music** | |
| **Entertainment** | |
| **Weather** | |
| **Daily Life** | |

**2 Examine reference materials.** In the library or on the Internet, research Native American pictographs. Use the information you find to help start your project. (See HELP DESK on the next page.)

### RECOMMENDED RESOURCES

**BOOKS FOR THE TEACHER**

Patterson-Rudolph, Carol. ***On the Trail of the Spider Woman: Petroglyphs, Pictographs and Myths of the Southwest.*** Santa Fe, NM: Ancient City Press, 1997.

Muench, David, and Polly Schaafsma. ***Images in Stone: Southwest Rock Art.*** San Francisco, CA: Browntrout Publishing, 1995.

**VIDEO**

***The Ancestors.*** Warner Home Video, 1994. This video is part of the series *500 Nations,* which chronicles the history of Native Americans using period art, interviews with contemporary Native Americans, and computer re-creations. This video focuses on the prehistory of the Americas.

**BOOKS FOR THE STUDENTS**

Huck, Bruce. ***Art on the Rocks.*** San Francisco, CA: Sierra Club Books, 1998.

Kopper, Philip. ***The Smithsonian Book of North American Indians: Before the Coming of the Europeans.*** Washington, D.C.: Smithsonian Books, 1997.

For related information see Chapter 1, p. 29.

### Researching Your Project

- *On the Trail of Spider Woman: Petroglyphs, Pictographs, and Myths of the Southwest* by Carol Patterson-Rudolph. Shows variety of actual pictographs.
- *21 Kinds of American Folk Art and How to Make Each One* by Jean and Cle Kinney. Explains process of making pictographs.

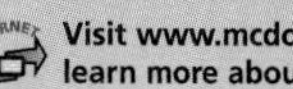

Visit www.mcdougallittell.com to learn more about pictographs.

### Did You Know?

**Petroglyphs** are images carved into a rock using stone tools. **Petrograms** are images painted on a rock. **Geoglyphs** are images formed on the ground by scraping away soil or by arranging stones to form an image.

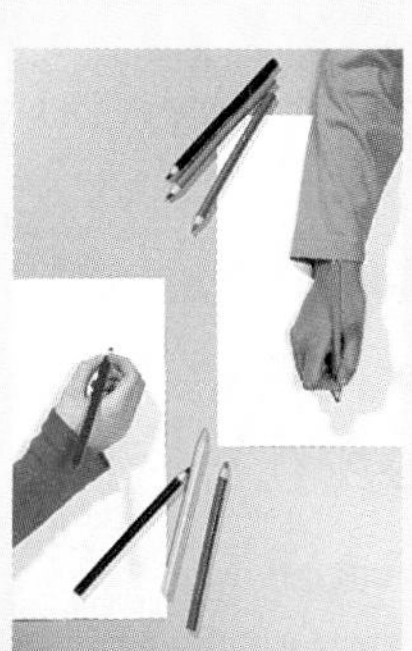

**3 Create your pictograph.** Communicate your message with symbols like the ones that you have researched. Sketch your pictograph on the drawing paper or poster board with a pencil first. Make the pictograph simple so that the decoders will understand your message. Remember to use symbols—not letters.

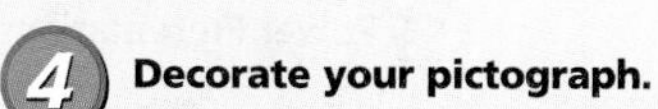

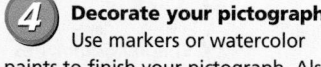

**4 Decorate your pictograph.** Use markers or watercolor paints to finish your pictograph. Also, record the translation of your pictograph in your notebook.

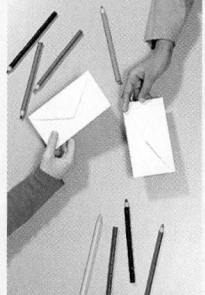

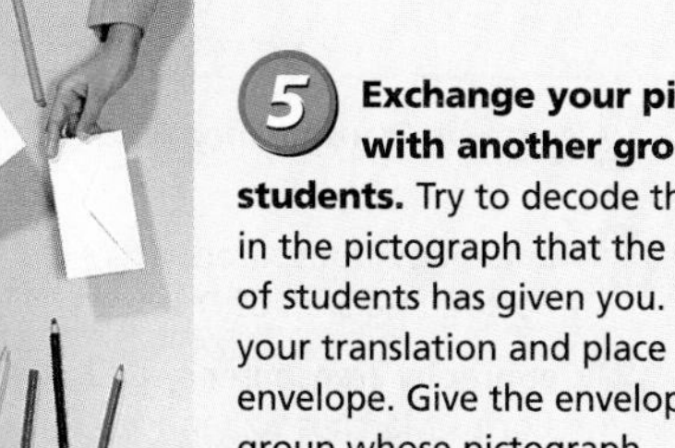

**5 Exchange your pictograph with another group of students.** Try to decode the message in the pictograph that the other group of students has given you. Write your translation and place it in your envelope. Give the envelope to the group whose pictograph you decoded.

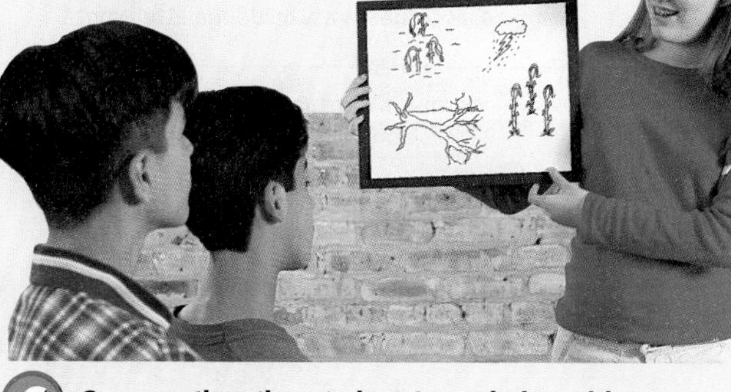

**6 Compare the other students' translation with your actual message.** Did the other students understand your message? Let them know how accurate they were.

## WRITE AND SPEAK

Using the information in the pictograph that you decoded, write a description of the people who created the message. Use the symbols as well as the message itself to help you in your description. Explain to the class how you came to your conclusions.

### REFLECT & ASSESS

- **Which symbols in your pictograph were clear to the decoders? Which were not clear?**
- **What methods did you use to decode the messages of others?**
- **What did you learn about language and communication from doing this pictograph decoding activity?**



### MORE ABOUT . . .

**Ancient Pictographs**

Some of the first people to use pictographs, or picture writing, were the ancient Egyptians. They carved or painted them on tombs and monuments. In the Americas, the Aztecs developed two different kinds of pictographs. One type stood for ideas. The other stood for the sounds of syllables. The Aztecs used their pictographs mainly for tax lists, business records, and historical and religious writings.

### MORE ABOUT . . .

**Modern Pictographs**

Today pictographs are making a comeback as icons on computer screens, automobile dashboards, and all sorts of electronic equipment. Ask students to suggest reasons for the proliferation of icons as replacements for words. What problems does the use of icons solve? What problems does it create?

Icons also appear in the form of logos for companies that make cosmetics, tennis shoes, CDs, soap, clothing, and many other products. Ask students to walk through a shopping mall, noticing the modern-day "pictographs" that advertisers use to attract consumers.

### REFLECT & ASSESS

1. Ask students why certain symbols were difficult to decode. Creators might work with the decoders to design alternate symbols that everyone agrees are clearer.
2. Students may want to review mentally the sequence of steps they used to decode their message and then write these steps down.
3. Have students identify the strengths and limitations of this form of communication. Students might compare this form of communication to a writing system based on an alphabet.

## STANDARDS FOR EVALUATION

### HISTORY WORKSHOP

**Pictographs should**

- contain a message about some aspect of American culture today.
- be based on knowledge of the design and functions of real pictographs.
- use only symbols, not letters.
- be simple, clear, and readable.

### WRITE AND SPEAK

**Descriptions should**

- clearly depict an aspect of the way of life of the people who wrote the message.
- use the symbols on the pictograph to link the message to the way of life of the people who wrote it.
- logically explain how the pictograph symbols led to the conclusions drawn.

CHAPTER 2 PLANNING GUIDE

# European Exploration of the Americas 1492–1700

| | CHAPTER OVERVIEW | COPYMASTERS | TECHNOLOGY |
|---|---|---|---|
| **CHAPTER RESOURCES** | The chapter discusses the competition among European countries for control of the Americas from 1492 to 1700. It also describes the conquest of many Native American groups, the culture of Spanish colonies, and the origins of slavery in the Americas. | **In-Depth Resources: Unit 1**<br>• Tracing Themes: Immigration and Migration, p. 25<br>• Building Vocabulary, p. 30<br>**Interdisciplinary Projects,** pp. 7–12 | **Primary Source Explorer**<br>**Electronic Teacher Tools**<br>**Power Presentations CD-ROM**<br>**Chapter Summaries on CD** (English and Spanish)<br>**America's Music CD** |
| **SECTION 1**<br>**Spain Claims an Empire**<br>**pp. 61–66** | **KEY IDEAS**<br>• Spain and Portugal argue over the Line of Demarcation.<br>• Following mercantile theory, Europe gains wealth through its colonies.<br>• Spain sends conquistadors to conquer the Aztecs and the Incas. | **In-Depth Resources: Unit 1**<br>• Setting the Stage, p. 24<br>• Guided Reading, p. 26<br>• Skillbuilder Practice, p. 31<br>• Literature Selection, pp. 36–38<br>• Reteaching Activity, p. 39<br>**Economics in History,** p. 2<br>**America's History Makers,** pp. 5–10<br>**Outline Map Activities,** pp. 3–4 | **Warm-Up Transparency WT2**<br>**Humanities Transparency HT3**<br>• Portuguese Ship of Discovery<br>**Geography Transparency GT2**<br>• Cortés Marches to Tenochtitlán<br>**Critical Thinking Transparency CT4**<br>• Setting the Stage<br>**ClassZone:** www.mcdougallittell.com |
| **SECTION 2**<br>**European Competition in North America**<br>**pp. 67–70** | • France and England seek out their own claims to North America.<br>• Spain and England clash, and England defeats the Spanish Armada.<br>• France and the Netherlands seek wealth through the fur trade. | **In-Depth Resources: Unit 1**<br>• Setting the Stage, p. 24<br>• Guided Reading, p. 27<br>• Reteaching Activity, p. 40<br>**Why It Matters Now**<br>• The Space Race, pp. 3–4 | **Warm-Up Transparency WT2**<br>**Humanities Transparency HT4**<br>• St. Augustine<br>**Critical Thinking Transparency CT4**<br>• Setting the Stage<br>**ClassZone:** www.mcdougallittell.com |
| **SECTION 3**<br>**The Spanish and Native Americans**<br>**pp. 71–75** | • Spain sets up viceroyalties in its colonies.<br>• The Church and plantations are central features of Spanish colonial society.<br>• The Columbian Exchange takes plants and animals to new regions of the world. | **In-Depth Resources: Unit 1**<br>• Setting the Stage, p. 24<br>• Guided Reading, p. 28<br>• Primary Source, p. 34<br>• Geography Application: Spain's American Empire Expands, pp. 32–33<br>• Reteaching Activity, p. 41 | **Warm-Up Transparency WT2**<br>**Critical Thinking Transparency CT4**<br>• Setting the Stage<br>**Critical Thinking Transparency CT5**<br>• The Columbian Exchange<br>**ClassZone:** www.mcdougallittell.com |
| **SECTION 4**<br>**Beginnings of Slavery in the Americas**<br>**pp. 76–79** | • Slavery arises in the colonies with the increasing demand for workers.<br>• The voyage from Africa to America is known as the middle passage.<br>• Some colonies establish slave codes to prevent rebellion. | **In-Depth Resources: Unit 1**<br>• Setting the Stage, p. 24<br>• Guided Reading, p. 29<br>• Primary Source, p. 35<br>• Reteaching Activity, p. 42 | **Warm-Up Transparency WT2**<br>**Critical Thinking Transparency CT4**<br>• Setting the Stage<br>**Critical Thinking Transparency CT6**<br>• Visual Summary<br>**ClassZone:** www.mcdougallittell.com |

Pupil's Edition
Copymaster

Overhead Transparency
Audio Library

CD-ROM
Internet

## ASSESSMENT

**Chapter Assessment,** pp. 80–81

**Formal Assessment**
- Chapter Tests, Forms A and B, pp. 38–45

**Alternative Assessment Book**

**Electronic Teacher Tools with Test Maker**

**Section Assessment,** p. 66

**Formal Assessment**
- Section Quiz, p. 34

**Alternative Assessment Book**
- Rubrics for a replica, 1.10
- Rubrics for a description, 4.5

**Electronic Teacher Tools with Test Maker**

**Section Assessment,** p. 70

**Formal Assessment**
- Section Quiz, p. 35

**Alternative Assessment Book**
- Rubrics for a song, 4.8
- Rubrics for a Web page, 5.1

**Electronic Teacher Tools with Test Maker**

**Section Assessment,** p. 75

**Formal Assessment**
- Section Quiz, p. 36

**Alternative Assessment Book**
- Rubrics for a collage, 1.8
- Rubrics for a story, 4.6

**Electronic Teacher Tools with Test Maker**

**Section Assessment,** p. 79

**Formal Assessment**
- Section Quiz, p. 37

**Alternative Assessment Book**
- Rubrics for a picture, 1.3
- Rubrics for a graph, 2.3

**Electronic Teacher Tools with Test Maker**

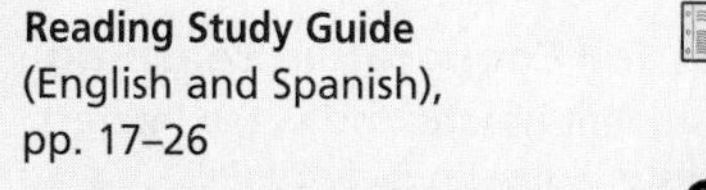

## CUSTOMIZING FOR INDIVIDUAL NEEDS

### Students Acquiring English/ESL

**Reading Study Guide** (English and Spanish), pp. 17–26

**Access for Students Acquiring English/ESL: Spanish Translations,** pp. 9–15

**Chapter Summaries on CD** (English and Spanish)

### Less Proficient Readers

**Reading Study Guide** (English and Spanish), pp. 17–26

**Chapter Summaries on CD** (English and Spanish)

### Gifted and Talented Students

**In-Depth Resources: Unit 1**
- Enrichment Activity, p. 43

**America's History Makers**
- Amerigo Vespucci, pp. 5–6
- Hernando Cortés, pp. 7–8
- Cabeza de Vaca, pp. 9–10

## CROSS-CURRICULAR CONNECTIONS

### Geography

Facts on File, Inc. ***Ancient America.*** New York: Facts on File, 1990. Cultural atlas.

### Science/Math

DK Publishing. ***The Visual Dictionary of Ships and Sailing.*** New York: DK Publishing, 1991. Detailed illustrations and cut-away diagrams.

### Primary Sources

Lester, Julius. ***To Be a Slave.*** New York: Dial, 1968. Easy-to-read primary source accounts assembled by noted scholar.

### Interdisciplinary Projects, pp. 7–12

- Math: Calculating the Value of Wampum
- Science: Gathering and Analyzing Disease Statistics
- Language Arts: Explorer's Logs
- Art: Mexican Pyramids

### Language Arts/Literature

Brown, Virginia. ***Cochula's Journey.*** Mobile: Black Belt Press, 1996. De Soto's expedition through the eyes of the 16-year-old daughter of an Alabama chief.

Fox, Paula. ***The Slave Dancer.*** New York: Bantam Doubleday Dell, 1988. Powerful story of a boy who is kidnapped and forced to play music on the deck of a slave ship.

### McDougal Littell Literature Connections

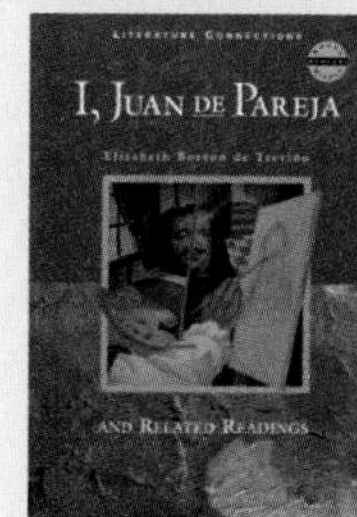


Elizabeth Borton De Trevino

***I, Juan de Pareja***

Born a black slave in Seville, Spain, in the 1600s, Juan goes through many hardships before finding friendship and an outlet for his talents with the great painter Velasquez.

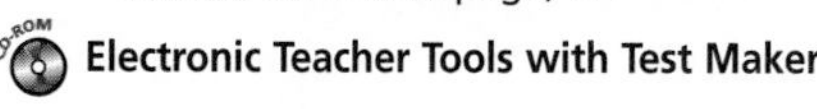

## ENRICHMENT ACTIVITIES

**Pupil's Edition, pp. 58–81**
**Interact with History,** p. 59
**Economics in History,** p. 62

**In-Depth Resources: Unit 1**
- Geography Application: Spain's American Empire Expands, pp. 32–33
- Primary Source: Protesting the Mistreatment of Native Americans, p. 34
- Primary Source: from *The Interesting Narrative of the Life of Olaudah Equiano,* p. 35
- Literature Selection, pp. 36–38

**America's History Makers**
- Amerigo Vespucci, pp. 5–6
- Hernando Cortés, pp. 7–8
- Cabeza de Vaca, pp. 9–10

**America's Music CD**

**Outline Map Activities**
- Spain Explores the Americas, 1500s, pp. 3–4

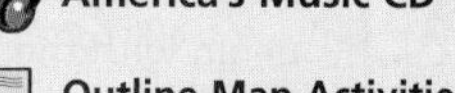

**Why It Matters Now**
- The Space Race, pp. 3–4

# CHAPTER 2 PACING GUIDE

## LESSON PLAN OPTIONS (50-MINUTE PERIOD)

(TE) = Teacher's Edition (PE) = Pupil's Edition

| | TEACHER-DIRECTED ACTIVITIES<br>Class Time: 15 minutes | STUDENT-CENTERED ACTIVITIES<br>Class Time: 25 minutes | INDIVIDUAL ACTIVITIES<br>Class Time: 10 minutes |
|---|---|---|---|
| **DAY 1**<br>Introduction<br>pp. 58–60 | **Presentation Options**<br>• Begin with a class discussion of the illustration on p. 58 **(PE)**.<br>• Lead a class discussion on the "What Do You Know?" question in Setting the Stage, p. 60. Then introduce the graphic organizer for the chapter **(PE)**. | **Options for Cooperative Learning**<br>• Have student groups discuss the Interact with History questions, p. 59 **(PE)**.<br>• Have student groups respond to the "What Do You Want to Know?" question in Setting the Stage, p. 60 **(PE)**. | **Head Start on Homework Options**<br>• Have students skim Section 1 Main Idea, Why It Matters Now, Terms & Names, and the main headings, p. 61 **(PE)**.<br>• Have students begin Guided Reading activity and Building Vocabulary sheet. |
| **DAY 2**<br>Section 1<br>pp. 61–66 | **Presentation Options**<br>• Begin with the 5-Minute Warm-Up, p. 61 **(TE)**.<br>• Lead the students through the Skillbuilder Mini-Lesson: Reading a Map, p. 63 **(TE)**.<br>• Choose 5 key questions for Objectives 1–4 to discuss with the class, pp. 61–66 **(TE)**. | **Options for Cooperative Learning**<br>• Divide students into groups to answer the questions posed in Economics in History, p. 62 **(PE)**.<br>• Have student pairs work together to complete one of the Activity Options in the Section 1 Assessment, p. 66 **(PE)**. | **Head Start on Homework Options**<br>• Have students begin working on Section 1 Assessment, p. 66 **(PE)**.<br>• Have students preview Section 2 Main Idea, Why It Matters Now, Terms & Names, and the main headings, p. 67 **(PE)**. |
| **DAY 3**<br>Section 2<br>pp. 67–70 | **Presentation Options**<br>• Begin with the 5-Minute Warm-Up, p. 67 **(TE)**.<br>• Choose 5 key questions for Objectives 1–4 to discuss with the class, pp. 67–70 **(TE)**. | **Options for Cooperative Learning**<br>• Divide students into groups and have them complete the Interdisciplinary Link, Language Arts: A Celebratory Speech, p. 68 **(TE)**.<br>• Have student pairs work together to complete one of the Activity Options in the Section 2 Assessment, p. 70 **(PE)**. | **Head Start on Homework Options**<br>• Have students begin working on Section 2 Assessment, p. 70 **(PE)**.<br>• Have students preview Section 3 Main Idea, Why It Matters Now, Terms & Names, and the main headings, p. 71 **(PE)**. |
| **DAY 4**<br>Section 3<br>pp. 71–75 | **Presentation Options**<br>• Begin with the 5-Minute Warm-Up, p. 71 **(TE)**.<br>• Review the Columbian Exchange Graphic, p. 74 **(PE)**.<br>• Choose 5 key questions for Objectives 1–4 to discuss with the class, pp. 71–74 **(TE)**. | **Options for Cooperative Learning**<br>• Divide students into groups and have them complete the Interdisciplinary Link, Civics: Petitions, p. 73 **(TE)**.<br>• Have student pairs work together to discuss the History through Art question, p. 73 **(PE)**. | **Head Start on Homework Options**<br>• Have students complete the History from Visuals extension activity, p. 72 **(TE)**.<br>• Have students complete the History Skills questions in Chapter Assessment, p. 81 **(PE)**. |
| **DAY 5**<br>Section 4<br>pp. 76–79 | **Presentation Options**<br>• Begin with the 5-Minute Warm-Up, p. 76 **(TE)**.<br>• Discuss the follow-up question to Interact with History, p. 80 **(PE)**.<br>• Choose 5 key questions for Objectives 1–4 to discuss with the class, pp. 76–79 **(TE)**. | **Options for Cooperative Learning**<br>• Divide students into groups and have them complete the Multiple Learning Styles: Mathematical, p. 77 **(TE)**.<br>• Divide students into groups and have them complete the History from Visuals extension activity, p. 77 **(TE)**. | **Head Start on Homework Options**<br>• Have students complete the Setting the Stage graphic organizer for the chapter, p. 60 **(PE)**.<br>• Have students begin working on the Chapter Assessment, pp. 80–81 **(PE)**.<br>• Prepare for Chapter Test<br>**Formal Assessment**, pp. 38–45 |

TEACHER-TESTED ACTIVITY **Jim Sorenson, Chippewa Middle School, Des Plaines, Illinois**

## EXPEDITION PREPARATION

**Class Time** Two class periods for preparation and one for presentation

**Task** Planning an expedition to the Americas and creating a poster illustrating these plans

**Purpose** To understand the complexities and dangers of undertaking an expedition to the Americas in the 1500s–1600s

**Supplies Needed**

- Reference books and internet sources about explorers to the Americas
- Posterboard
- Construction paper
- Colored pencils or markers

**Activity** Divide students into small groups. Ask each team to select an explorer discussed in Chapter 2 and make plans for an expedition led by that explorer. Each team member can consider one of these topics: skills needed by the crew for the expedition, equipment, food, water, clothing, money to finance the expedition. Teams must plan supplies and crew, based on an actual journey to the Americas made by their explorer. Have each group create a poster showing a picture of their explorer, a map of his expedition, and the supplies they should take for each category from equipment to clothing.

## BLOCK SCHEDULING — LESSON PLAN OPTIONS (90-MINUTE PERIOD)

### DAY 1

**Interact with History,** p. 59
**Class Time** 20 minutes

Options for pacing and variety:

- **Role-Playing** Divide students into pairs, with one student taking the part of a person eager to join an expedition and the other of a parent, sibling, or friend trying to discourage him or her from going. Have them discuss the "What Do You Think?" questions.
**Class Time** 10 minutes

**Setting the Stage,** p. 60
**Class Time** 20 minutes

Options for pacing and variety:

- **Time Saver** Assign the "What Do You Know?" and "What Do You Want To Know?" questions as homework so that students can get a head start on preparing to read the chapter.
**Class Time** 5 minutes

**Section 1,** pp. 61–66
**Class Time** 50 minutes

Options for pacing and variety:

- **Peer Teaching** Have students work in pairs to answer the Connect to History and Connect to Today questions in the Economics in History feature. **Class Time** 20 minutes
- **Internet** Extend students' knowledge of the *conquistadors* by having them visit www.mcdougallittell.com
**Class Time** 20 minutes

### DAY 2

**Section 2,** pp. 67–70
**Class Time** 50 minutes

Options for pacing and variety:

- **History on Film** Extend students' background on the new world by viewing Episode 1 of Ken Burns's *America.* **Class Time** 50 minutes
- **Peer Teaching** Have students work in pairs to complete the song composition activity in the Activity Options in the Section 2 Assessment.
**Class Time** 30 minutes

**Section 3,** pp. 71–75
**Class Time** 40 minutes

Options for pacing and variety:

- **Peer Teaching** Have students work in small groups to create the collage in the Activity Options in the Section 3 Assessment.
**Class Time** 40 minutes
- **Peer Evaluation** Have student pairs fill in the diagram in the Section 3 assessment. After they complete it, have them swap diagrams with another pair. Have the pairs provide suggestions and comments about the diagrams to each other.
**Class Time** 20 minutes

### DAY 3

**Section 4,** pp. 76–79
**Class Time** 50 minutes

Options for pacing and variety:

- **Role-Playing** Divide the class into small groups. Assign each group the content of a small heading. Have each group act out the events in the heading. Have one student from each group narrate the story.
**Class Time** 50 minutes
- **Time Saver** Ask students to complete Interpreting Charts on page 81 of the Chapter Assessment as a homework assignment for this section. Have students share with the class what they have learned about slavery from analyzing this chart.
**Class Time** 10 minutes
- **Internet** Extend students' background knowledge of slavery in the Americas with a look at slave narratives at www.mcdougallittell.com
**Class Time** 30 minutes

**Chapter 2 Assessment,** pp. 80–81
**Class Time** 40 minutes

Options for pacing and variety:

- **Peer Evaluation** Have student pairs work out the answers to the Critical Thinking Questions, p. 80. Then have them exchange papers with another team to evaluate their answers. **Class Time** 20 minutes
- **Peer Teaching** Divide the class into four groups. Assign each group one section of the Review Questions to complete.
**Class Time** 20 minutes

## CHAPTER 2 OBJECTIVE

The student will identify the leading European explorers of North America, explain the effects of European colonization on Native Americans, and describe the origins and development of slavery in the colonies.

### HISTORY FROM VISUALS

**Interpreting the Illustration** The 1592 engraving that opens the chapter shows the harbor of Lisbon, Portugal. Ask students to look at the city that the sailors are leaving. What can students observe about Lisbon at this time? **Possible Responses** The number of ships and piles of casks suggest busy trade. The city is walled, built of stone and brick, with church towers and large, solid buildings. The men are elaborately dressed in woven materials. One man carries a sword.

**Extension** Ask students to find out about the city of Lisbon in the late 1500s. What factors helped Lisbon become such an active trading center? With what parts of the world did Lisbon trade? What did the city's merchants trade for?

### CRITICAL THINKING ACTIVITY

**Making Inferences** Present the following scenario: Scientists have discovered a new planet capable of sustaining human life and on which other life forms exist. Ask students to think of reasons why people might want to make the long, dangerous trip to explore the planet. Ask students what a nation might gain by exploring a new planet. Do students think potential explorers should consider possible harm that explorers might bring to the new planet?

**Class Time** 20 minutes

# CHAPTER 2 European Exploration of the Americas

## 1492–1700

*Section 1* **Spain Claims an Empire**
*Section 2* **European Competition in North America**
*Section 3* **The Spanish and Native Americans**
*Section 4* **Beginnings of Slavery in the Americas**

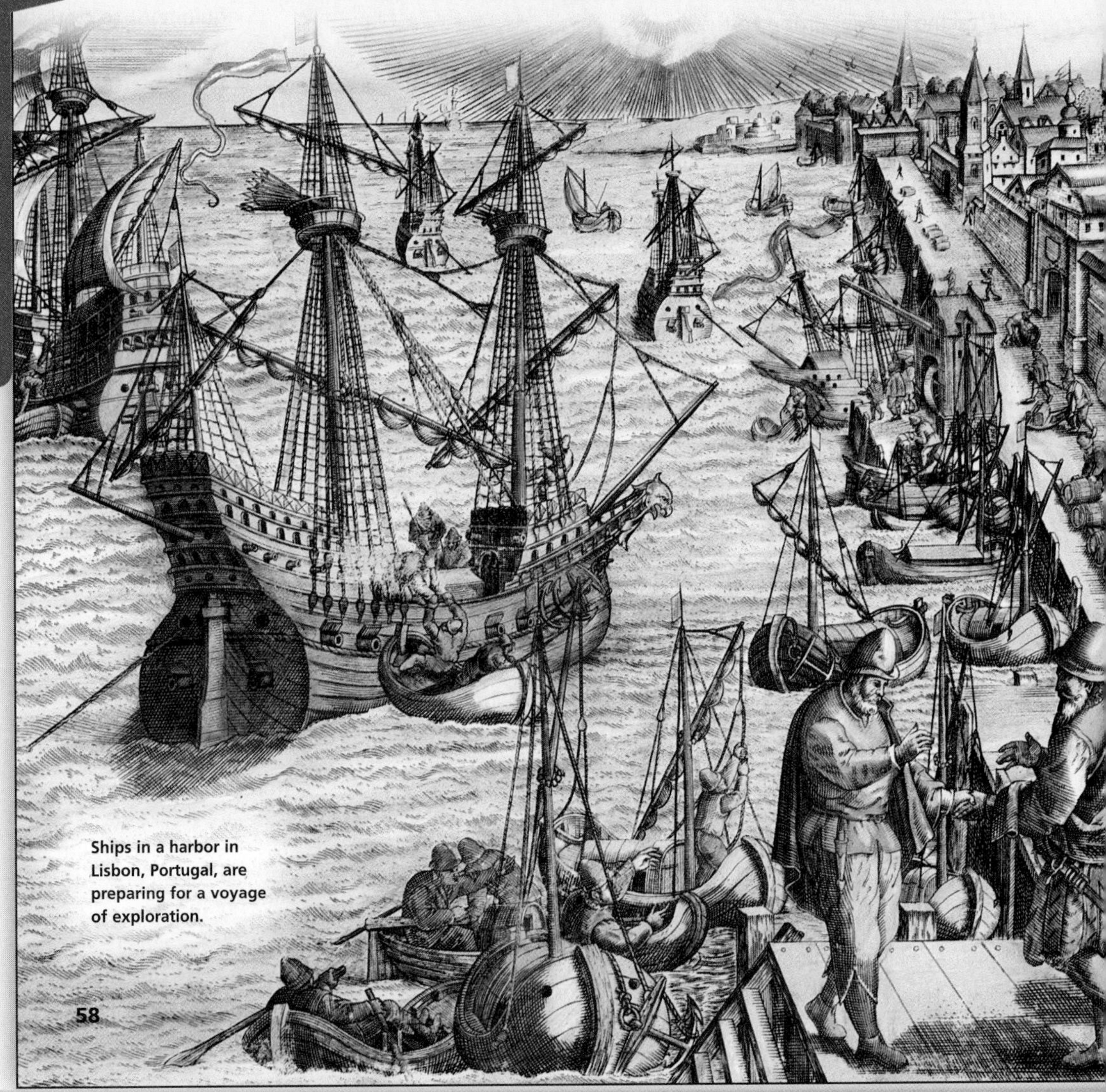

Ships in a harbor in Lisbon, Portugal, are preparing for a voyage of exploration.

58

### RECOMMENDED RESOURCES

**BOOKS FOR THE TEACHER**

Bontemps, Arna. ***Great Slave Narratives.*** New York: Beacon Press, 1969. Classic compilation of first-hand material on slavery.

De la Vega, Garcilaso. ***Royal Commentaries of the Incas and General History of Peru.*** Tr. Harold W. Livermore. Austin: U. of Texas Press, 1987. Primary source written between 1609 and 1617.

Morison, Samuel Eliot. ***The European Discovery of America.*** New York: Oxford University Press, 1971–1974. Lively and readable, though sometimes controversial, history by a U.S. admiral.

**VIDEO**

***America, Episode 1: The New Found Land.*** Midwest Tape. Part 1 of well-made series by Ken Burns.

**INTERNET**

For more about slave narratives or the LaSalle shipwreck, visit www.mcdougallittell.com

## Interact *with* History

Vasco Núñez de Balboa led expeditions to explore the Americas for Spain.
Balboa claimed the Pacific Ocean for Spain.
Balboa crossed Panama to reach the Pacific Ocean.

**The year is 1510. You live in a European port town and have heard exciting tales about mysterious lands across the sea. You decide to join a voyage of exploration in search of fortune.**

### What Do You Think?

- **What do you think led people like Balboa to explore distant lands?**
- **What reasons would make you want to join a voyage of exploration?**
- **What reasons would keep you from joining such a voyage?**

# *Would you join a voyage of exploration?*

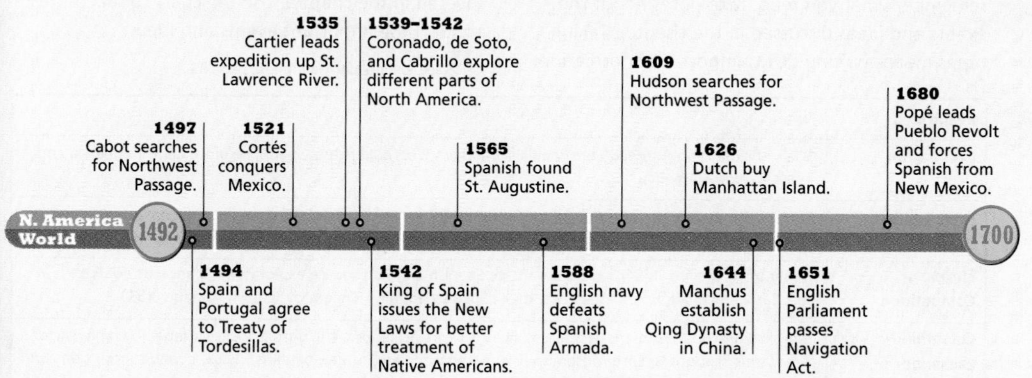




## Interact *with* History

### OBJECTIVES

- To identify European motives for exploring the Americas
- To pose and answer questions about the challenges of exploration

### What Do You Think?

1. What characteristics might explorers need to be successful?
2. Have students suggest what can be gained from learning about new places.
3. Ask students to consider the effects on family members and friends who would be left behind if they went on a long and possibly dangerous trip.

### *Would you join a voyage of exploration?*

Suggest that students weigh the possible dangers and rewards of a voyage of exploration.

### MAKING PERSONAL CONNECTIONS

Ask students whether they or people they know have ever taken a long trip to a place they had never visited before. Why did they go? What kinds of questions and expectations did they have as they prepared for the trip?

### TIME LINE DISCUSSION

**Remind students that "in 1492, Columbus sailed the ocean blue." Point out how quickly other explorers followed him to the Americas. By 1700, European nations claimed much of North and South America.**

- Ask students to identify the first major European conquest in the Americas. How many years after Columbus's voyage did that conquest take place? **Answer** Spanish under Cortés conquered Mexico by 1521, only 29 years after Columbus's voyage.
- Ask students to identify the year in which the English navy defeated the Spanish Armada. **Answer** 1588
- Why might the defeat of the Spanish Armada be important to European exploration?

**Answer** It may have reduced Spain's ability to explore and hold other lands.

## BEFORE YOU READ

### Previewing the Theme: Immigration and Migration

Ask students to speculate about why Europeans and others went to the Americas.

Europeans came to the Americas for a variety of reasons. Some came for religious reasons or for economic opportunities. However, Africans were brought to the Americas by force and served as slaves. Many Native Americans who survived the conquest by Europeans also became slaves. Their civilizations and cultures were either destroyed or greatly altered.

### What Do You Know?

Tell students that by the mid-1400s, strong rulers in Spain and in England had gained much power. Competition among these rulers and others encouraged their efforts to explore and claim new territories.

 **In-Depth Resources: Unit 1**
- Tracing Themes: Immigration and Migration, p. 25

## READ AND TAKE NOTES

### Reading Strategy: Taking Notes

Tell students that taking notes as they read will help them focus on main ideas and supporting details. Point out that recording notes in a chart will help them organize information in a format that is easy to reference. Remind students to note only the most important details and to take notes in a sequential order.

 **In-Depth Resources: Unit 1**
- Setting the Stage, p. 24

 **Critical Thinking Transparency CT4**
- Setting the Stage

# Chapter 2 SETTING THE STAGE

## BEFORE YOU READ

### Previewing the Theme

**Immigration and Migration** From the 15th century to the 18th century, millions of people came to the Americas from other continents. Chapter 2 discusses why people came to the Americas and the effect that these migrations had on the people who already lived there.

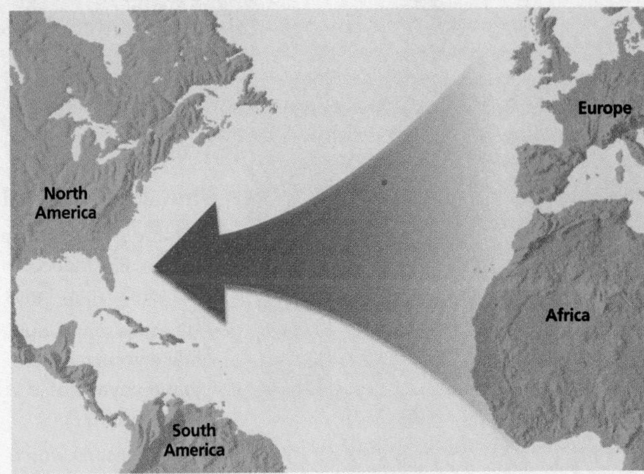


### What Do You Know?

What comes to mind when someone uses the word *explorer*? Why do you think people explored different territories?

**THINK ABOUT**
- what you've learned about explorers from movies, school, or your parents
- reasons that people travel throughout the world today

### What Do You Want to Know?

What questions do you have about exploration or the early colonization of the Americas? Write those questions in your notebook before you read the chapter.

## READ AND TAKE NOTES

**Reading Strategy: Taking Notes** To help you remember what you read, take notes about the events and ideas discussed in the chapter. Taking notes means writing down important information.

The chart below lists the major events and ideas covered in the chapter. Use the chart to take notes about these important events and ideas.

 See Skillbuilder Handbook, page R3.

| Event/Idea | Notes |
|---|---|
| Exploration | Goals of exploration: spread Christianity, expand empires, gain riches. Spanish explore Central America and southern North America. |
| Establishing Colonies | Reasons for Spanish success: disease, weapons, alliances with some Native Americans, brutal oppression of conquered peoples. Life in colonies is organized around *encomiendas, haciendas,* and missions. |
| European Competition | Treaty of Tordesillas (1494) sets boundary for Spanish and Portuguese exploration. Spanish attack French at Fort Caroline (1564). English sea dogs attack Spanish shipping. Defeat of Spanish Armada (1588). |
| Columbian Exchange | Items brought to the Americas: diseases, livestock, grains, onions, citrus fruits, olives, grapes, bananas, sugar cane. Items brought to Eastern Hemisphere: tobacco, squash, turkey, peppers, cocoa, peanuts, potatoes, corn. |
| Origins of Slavery | Modern slavery was established in the Americas to provide labor in mines and plantations. Slave trade grew quickly between Africa and the Americas. |



## TEACHING STRATEGY

### READING THE CHAPTER

This is a thematic chapter focusing on European exploration and conquest, European contact with Native Americans, and the origins of slavery. Encourage students to pause after reading each section to identify the main idea and supporting details of the material before continuing to the next section.

### ALTERNATIVE ASSESSMENT

The Chapter Assessment describes three activities for alternative assessment on page 81. You may wish to have students work on these activities during the course of the chapter and then present them at the end.

# 1 Spain Claims an Empire

**MAIN IDEA**

Spain claimed a large empire in the Americas.

**WHY IT MATTERS NOW**

The influence of Spanish culture remains strong in modern America.

**TERMS & NAMES**

Treaty of Tordesillas
missionary
mercantilism
Amerigo Vespucci
*conquistador*
Hernando Cortés
Montezuma
Francisco Pizarro

### ONE EUROPEAN'S STORY

**Pope Alexander VI had an important decision to make. In 1493, the rulers of Spain and Portugal wanted him to decide who would control the lands that European sailors were exploring. Ferdinand and Isabella of Spain expected Alexander VI to give Spain the rights over many of these lands. But King John II of Portugal claimed territories, too. What would the new pope do?**

**In May 1493, Alexander VI issued his ruling. He drew an imaginary line around the world. It was called the Line of Demarcation. Portugal could claim all non-Christian lands to the east of the line. Spain could claim the non-Christian lands to the west. In this section, you will learn how Spain and Portugal led Europe in the race to gain colonies in the Americas.**

Pope Alexander VI

## 1 Spain and Portugal Compete

King John II was unhappy with the pope's placement of the line. He believed that it favored Spain. So he demanded that the Spanish rulers meet with him to change the pope's decision. In June 1494, the two countries agreed to the **Treaty of Tordesillas** (TAWR•day•SEEL•yahs). This treaty moved the Line of Demarcation more than 800 miles farther west.

The change eventually allowed Portugal to claim much of eastern South America, which later became the Portuguese colony of Brazil. After making this agreement, Spain and Portugal increased their voyages of exploration in search of wealth, power, and glory.

European countries had three main goals during this age of exploration. First, they wanted to spread Christianity beyond Europe. Each expedition included **missionaries,** or people sent to convert the native peoples to Christianity. Second, they wanted to expand their empires. Third, they wanted to become rich.

By increasing their wealth, European countries could gain power and security. An economic system called **mercantilism** describes how





## SECTION OBJECTIVES

1. To explain the competition between Spain and Portugal to claim foreign lands
2. To describe Spain's conquest of Mexico and the Incan Empire
3. To explain the reasons for Spanish victories
4. To identify important Spanish explorers

**SKILLBUILDER**

Interpreting Maps: Movement, Region, p. 63

**CRITICAL THINKING**

Finding Main Ideas, pp. 62, 63
Making Inferences, p. 62
Drawing Conclusions, pp. 65, 66
Comparing, p. 66

## FOCUS & MOTIVATE

### 5-MINUTE WARM-UP

**Making Inferences** These questions focus on the extent of European exploration in the Americas by 1700.

1. Look at the map on page 63. Which European country was the most active in exploring the Americas?
2. Which American empires existed at the time of European exploration?

 **Warm-Up Transparency WT2**

## INSTRUCT

### INSTRUCT: OBJECTIVE 1

**Spain and Portugal Compete/ Europeans Explore Foreign Lands**

Key Questions

- Why did Spain and Portugal want to control territory in the Americas?
- How did the Treaty of Tordesillas affect Portugal?
- Who were some of the important early European explorers?

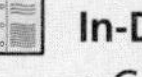 **In-Depth Resources: Unit 1**
- Guided Reading, p. 26
- Literature Selection: from *The High Voyage*, pp. 36–38

### RECOMMENDED RESOURCES

**In-Depth Resources: Unit 1**
- Guided Reading, p. 26
- Building Vocabulary, p. 30
- Skillbuilder Practice, p. 31
- Literature Selection: from *The High Voyage* by Olga Litowinsky, pp. 36–38
- Reteaching Activity, p. 39

**Reading Study Guide** (Spanish and English), pp. 17–18

**Economics in History**
- Mercantilism and Colonies, p. 2

**Outline Map Activities**
- Spain Explores the Americas, 1500s, pp. 3–4

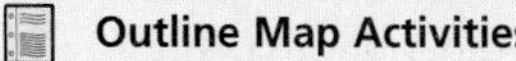
**America's History Makers**
- Amerigo Vespucci, pp. 5–6
- Hernando Cortés, pp. 7–8
- Cabeza de Vaca, pp. 9–10

**Formal Assessment**
- Section Quiz, p. 34

**Alternative Assessment**
- Rubrics, 1.10
- Rubrics, 4.5

**Access for Students Acquiring English/ESL**
- Guided Reading, p. 9
- Skillbuilder Practice, p. 13

Technology Resources

 **Geography Transparency GT2**
- Cortés Marches to Tenochtitlán

 **Humanities Transparency HT3**
- Portuguese Ship of Discovery

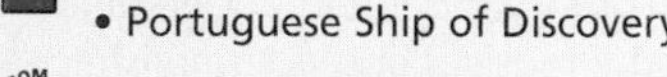
 **Electronic Teacher Tools with Test Maker**

## Economics *in* History

**OBJECTIVE**
Students will summarize the ways mercantilism helped to create wealth.

**Mercantile Governments**
Mercantile governments were very involved in their domestic economies. They tried to ensure—through tariffs and other trade measures—that imports did not exceed exports. Those policies typically favored the economy in the home country over that of the colonies. In the 1700s, Britain tried to ensure that its North American colonies imported more goods from England than they exported.

1. **Finding Main Ideas Possible Responses** A nation needed a favorable balance of trade. Colonies enrich their country by providing precious metals, producing goods that could be traded for precious metals, and by serving as a market.
2. **Making Inferences Possible Responses** In the long run, the family would lose its possessions and its ability to buy on credit, or "charge." Students most likely will say that a nation would experience a similar situation.

**Economics in History**
- Mercantilism and Colonies, p. 2

## MORE ABOUT . . .

**Asian Explorers**
Europeans in the 1400s and 1500s were not the only people curious about lands far from home. In the early 1400s, a Chinese explorer named Cheng Ho led seven voyages to southern Asia and eastern Africa. Cheng Ho's fleets were large; the largest included about 300 ships. The fleet's crew contained interpreters, accountants, and doctors. Unlike European countries, the Chinese did not establish a large trading empire.

## Economics *in* History

# Mercantilism

The main goal of mercantilism was to increase the money in a country's treasury by creating a favorable balance of trade. A country had a favorable balance of trade if it had more exports than imports. Colonies helped a country have the goods to maintain a favorable balance of trade.

For example, say Spain sold $500 in sugar to France, and France sold $300 in cloth to Spain. France would also have to pay Spain $200 worth of precious metals to pay for all the sugar. Spain would then have a favorable balance of trade because the value of its exports (sugar) was greater than the value of its imports (cloth). Spain would become richer because of the precious metals it received from France.

**CONNECT TO HISTORY**
1. **Finding Main Ideas** Under mercantilism, what did a country need to do to become rich? Discuss the way colonies enriched a country according to mercantilism.

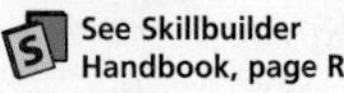
See Skillbuilder Handbook, page R5.

**CONNECT TO TODAY**
2. **Making Inferences** Think about your own family budget. What do you think would happen if your family collected less money than it paid for goods for several years? Do you think this situation would be the same for a nation as it would for a family?

Visit www.mcdougallittell.com to learn more about mercantilism.

Europeans enriched their treasuries. (See *Economics in History*, above.) Colonies helped nations do this in several ways. They provided mines that produced gold and silver. They also produced goods such as crops that could be traded for gold and silver. Finally, they served as a market for the home country. The search for riches spurred European exploration.

**Vocabulary**
**colony:** a region or people that is politically and economically controlled by another country

## Europeans Explore Foreign Lands

After Columbus's first voyage, many explorers went to sea. **Amerigo Vespucci** (vehs•POO•chee) was one of the first. He was an Italian sailor who set out in 1501 to find a sea route to Asia. Vespucci realized that the land he saw on this voyage was not Asia. A German mapmaker was impressed by Vespucci's account of the lands, so he named the continent "America" after him.

Another famous explorer was the Spaniard Vasco Núñez de Balboa. Balboa heard Native American reports of another ocean. In 1513, he led an expedition through the jungles of Panama and reached the Pacific Ocean. Raising his sword, Balboa stepped into the surf and claimed the ocean and all the lands around it for Spain. (See page 59.)

Perhaps no explorer was more capable than the Portuguese sailor Ferdinand Magellan. He proposed to reach Asia by sailing west around South America. The Spanish king agreed to fund Magellan's voyage.

In 1519, Magellan set out from Spain with five ships and about 240



## ACTIVITY OPTIONS

**MULTIPLE LEARNING STYLES: INTERPERSONAL** — BLOCK SCHEDULING

**EXPLORER DIALOGUE**

**Class Time** 45 minutes

**Task** Creating a dialogue among early European explorers

**Purpose** To gain an understanding of the motives and accomplishments of European explorers

**Supplies Needed**
- Reference materials about early European explorers

**Activity** Divide the class into groups of four. Each student in a group should take one of the following roles: Amerigo Vespucci, Vasco Núñez de Balboa, Ferdinand Magellan. Tell students to do some research about their explorer. Then each group should present a dialogue with students taking the roles of the explorers. They should discuss their reasons for exploring, where they went, what they found, and what happened to them after their explorations.

**America's History Makers**
- Amerigo Vespucci, pp. 5–6

men. After a stormy passage around South America, Magellan entered the Pacific Ocean. For several months his crew crossed the Pacific, suffering great hardship. A member of the crew described what they ate.

*A VOICE FROM THE PAST*

We were three months and twenty days without . . . fresh food. We ate biscuit, which was no longer biscuit, but powder of biscuits swarming with worms. . . . We drank . . . water that had been putrid for many days.

**Antonio Pigafetta,** quoted in *The Discoverers*

*Reading* **History**

**A. Finding Main Ideas** What were the main contributions of Vespucci, Balboa, and Magellan as explorers?

A. Answer Vespucci was the first to realize that the Americas were not Asia. Balboa reached the Pacific by crossing Panama. Magellan led an expedition that travelled around the world.

Eventually, Magellan reached the Philippines, where he became involved in a local war and was killed. But his crew traveled on. In 1522, the one remaining ship arrived back in Spain. The sailors in Magellan's crew became the first people to sail around the world.

## 2 The Invasion of Mexico

While Magellan's crew was sailing around the world, the Spanish began their conquest of the Americas. Soldiers called ***conquistadors*** (kahn•KWIHS•tuh•DAWRZ), or conquerors, explored the Americas and claimed them for Spain. **Hernando Cortés** was one of these *conquistadors.* He landed on the Central American coast with 508 men in 1519.

The Spanish arrival shook the Aztec Empire, which dominated most of Mexico. The Aztec emperor **Montezuma** feared that Cortés had been

Skillbuilder Answers
1. Eight
2. North America

### European Exploration of the Americas, 1500–1550

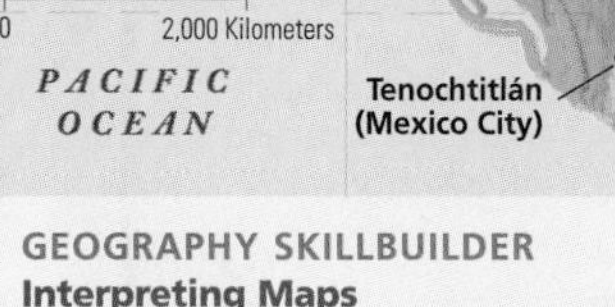


**GEOGRAPHY SKILLBUILDER**
**Interpreting Maps**
1. **Movement** *How many years did it take Cabeza de Vaca to travel from Florida to Central Mexico?*
2. **Region** *Which continent did the English and French explore?*

**Humanities Transparency HT3**
- Portuguese Ship of Discovery

**INSTRUCT: OBJECTIVE 2**
**The Invasion of Mexico/ The Conquest of the Incan Empire**

Key Questions
- Why were the Spanish able to defeat the Aztec and the Inca?
- How did the Aztec and Inca respond to the Spanish invasion?

**Geography Transparency GT2**
- Cortés Marches to Tenochtitlán

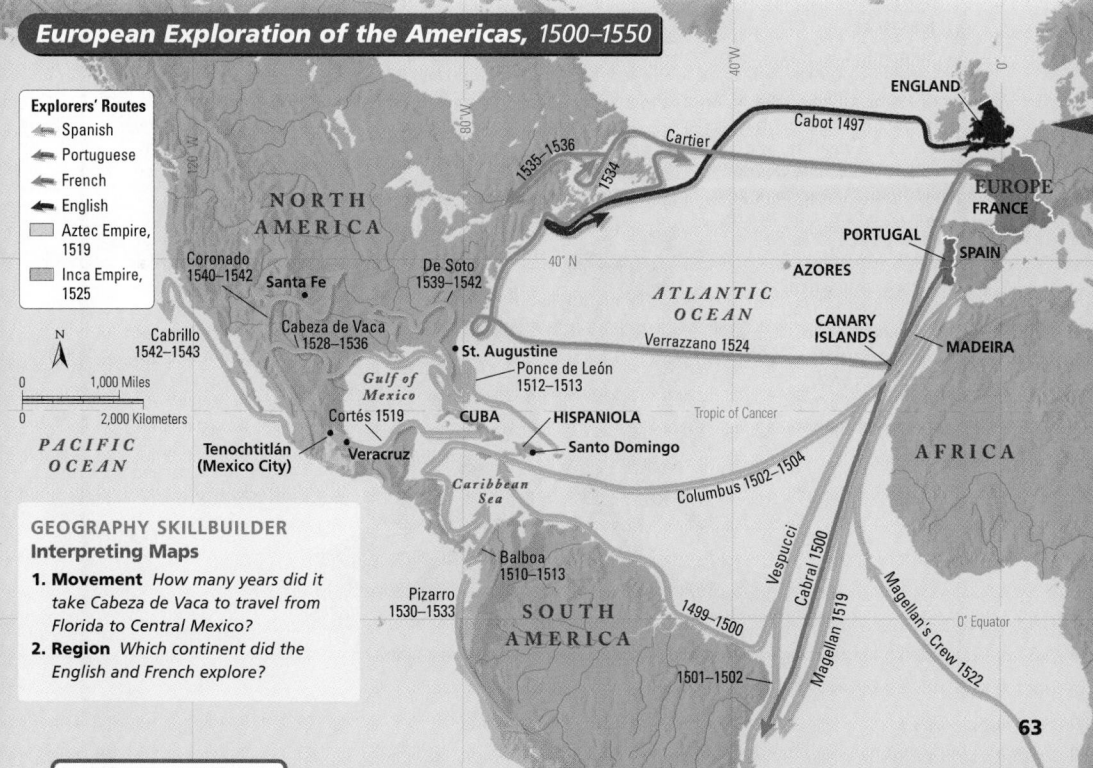

**HISTORY FROM VISUALS**

**Reading the Map** Point out that many of the explorations shown on this map were confined mostly to coastal areas and areas along inland waters, such as rivers. Have students discuss why they think this often was the case. **Possible Responses** Traveling along coasts and waterways was faster and safer than traveling through unfamiliar inland regions. In addition, European explorers at this stage were still trying to determine the sizes and shapes of the new continents they had encountered.

**Extension** Ask students to use an encyclopedia to learn about improvements in ship design and navigation that made possible long voyages out of sight of land.

**ACTIVITY OPTIONS**

**SKILLBUILDER MINI-LESSON: READING A MAP** — BLOCK SCHEDULING

**Explaining the Skill** Maps organize information visually to help users understand concepts. Most maps have common elements, such as a title, and various colors or symbols representing specific information. Many have a compass rose, distance scale, and lines of latitude and longitude. Special colors and symbols are identified in a map legend, sometimes called a map key.

**Applying the Skill** Ask students to identify the map legend and the symbols and colors in the legend. Then ask the following:

1. Which nation explored most extensively along the coasts and interior of the Americas? *(Spain)*
2. When and in which area(s) did England explore the Americas? France? *(England: 1497, northeastern North America; France: 1524, along eastern North America and 1535–1536 in interior North America)*
3. Who explored the region around Santa Fe? When? *(Coronado, 1540–1542)*

**In-Depth Resources: Unit 1**
- Skillbuilder Practice, p. 31

## MORE ABOUT . . .

**Tenochtitlán**

Tell students that Tenochtitlán, the Aztec capital, was a large city with hundreds of temples, government buildings, and other structures. Some scholars have estimated the population of the city and surrounding communities at about 400,000, spread over an area of more than 5 square miles (13 km), in 1519. The heart of the city lay on two islands linked by causeways to the shores of Lake Texcoco. The lake was drained in the early 1600s, and Mexico City was built on its site.

## AMERICA'S HISTORY MAKERS

**Hernando Cortés and Montezuma**

Cortés and Montezuma were wary of each other when they met in 1519. Cortés took advantage of Montezuma's fear that the Spaniard was a legendary Aztec god. Cortés spoke directly to Montezuma: "We have come to your house in Mexico as friends. There is nothing to fear." He destroyed the Aztec Empire within two years.

**Possible Responses: Some students might say Cortés because he conquered the Aztecs. Others might say Montezuma because he was just.**

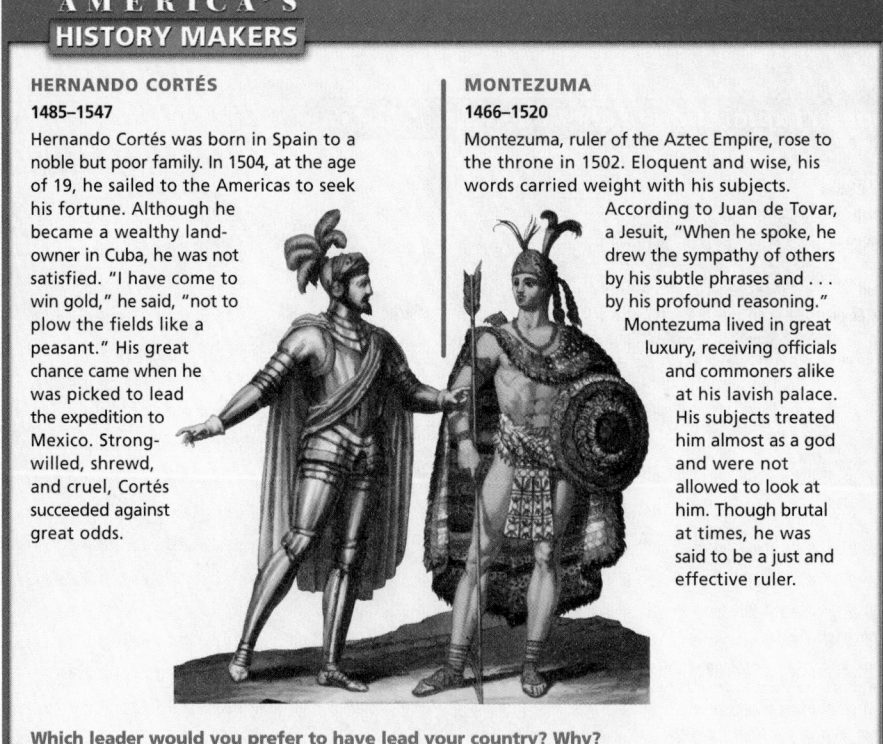

**America's History Makers**
- Hernando Cortés, pp. 7–8

sent by an Aztec god to rule Mexico. Montezuma sent Cortés gifts—including two disks of solid gold and silver—to get him to leave. But the gifts only excited Spanish dreams of riches.

The Spaniards marched inland and formed alliances (agreements with friendly peoples) with the native peoples who hated Aztec rule. After a few months, Cortés reached the Aztec capital, Tenochtitlán (teh•NAWCH•tee•TLAHN). Montezuma received Cortés with great ceremony and housed the *conquistadors* in a magnificent palace. But Cortés took Montezuma captive and tried to rule the Aztec Empire by giving commands through Montezuma. The Aztecs rebelled.

**Background**
One of the people whom Cortés brought into his group was Malintzin. She was the daughter of a local chief and served as an interpreter for Cortés.

The Aztecs surrounded the Spaniards and their allies in their headquarters in Tenochtitlán. On the night of June 30, 1520, the Spaniards tried to sneak out of the city, but the Aztecs discovered them and vicious fighting broke out. About 800 Spaniards and more than 1,000 of their allies were killed that night. The Spaniards later called the event *La Noche Triste* (lah NAW•cheh TREES•teh)—the Sad Night.

Despite this defeat, the Spaniards and their allies regrouped. In May 1521, Cortés led his forces back to Tenochtitlán. At this point, the Spaniards got help from an invisible ally. Many Aztecs fell victim to an outbreak of smallpox, which severely weakened their ranks. The germs

### AMERICA'S HISTORY MAKERS

**HERNANDO CORTÉS**
**1485–1547**

Hernando Cortés was born in Spain to a noble but poor family. In 1504, at the age of 19, he sailed to the Americas to seek his fortune. Although he became a wealthy landowner in Cuba, he was not satisfied. "I have come to win gold," he said, "not to plow the fields like a peasant." His great chance came when he was picked to lead the expedition to Mexico. Strong-willed, shrewd, and cruel, Cortés succeeded against great odds.

**MONTEZUMA**
**1466–1520**

Montezuma, ruler of the Aztec Empire, rose to the throne in 1502. Eloquent and wise, his words carried weight with his subjects. According to Juan de Tovar, a Jesuit, "When he spoke, he drew the sympathy of others by his subtle phrases and . . . by his profound reasoning." Montezuma lived in great luxury, receiving officials and commoners alike at his lavish palace. His subjects treated him almost as a god and were not allowed to look at him. Though brutal at times, he was said to be a just and effective ruler.

**Which leader would you prefer to have lead your country? Why?**



## ACTIVITY OPTIONS
## INDIVIDUAL NEEDS

**STUDENTS ACQUIRING ENGLISH/ESL**

**Expanding Vocabulary** Write the word *ally* on the board and define it as "a partner." Begin a word pyramid with *ally* at the top. Then ask students to reread the third, fourth, and fifth paragraphs under the heading "The Invasion of Mexico." As they read, ask them to identify words that have *ally* as the base word. Write them below *ally* to form a word pyramid. (alliances, allies) Define the words and then ask such questions as the following: Who did the Spanish form alliances with? What was the invisible ally?

| | ally | |
|---|---|---|
| alliance | allies | ally |

that caused this disease had been brought to America by the Europeans.

**Vocabulary**
**siege:** surrounding of a city

Cortés placed Tenochtitlán under siege for three months. When Tenochtitlán finally fell, the Aztec Empire lay in ruins. An Aztec poet described the scene.

> *A VOICE FROM THE PAST*
>
> Broken spears lie in the roads; we have torn our hair in our grief. The houses are roofless now, and their walls are red with blood. . . . We have pounded our hands in despair against the adobe walls, for our inheritance, our city, is lost and dead.
>
> **Aztec poet,** quoted in *Seeds of Change*

On the rubble of the Aztec capital, the Spanish built Mexico City. Over time, the populations and cultures of Spain and Mexico merged and produced a new society, that of the present-day nation of Mexico.

**This Aztec mask represents Quetzalcoatl, the god that Montezuma feared had sent Cortés.**

## The Conquest of the Incan Empire

***Reading*History**
**B. Reading a Map** Use the map on page 63 to find the Incan Empire.

Despite the fall of the Aztecs, a people called the Inca still had a powerful empire centered in the Cuzco Valley in what is now Peru. By 1525, the Inca ruled a 2,000-mile-long territory in the Andes Mountains along the western coast of South America. The Inca also possessed much gold and silver.

Native American stories of Incan wealth reached the Spanish. In 1531, a *conquistador* named **Francisco Pizarro** led an expedition of 180 men into Peru. Like the Aztecs, the Incas feared that the Spanish might be gods. The Incan emperor Atahualpa (AH•tuh•WAHL•puh) ordered his troops not to fight. Then he went to meet the *conquistadors.* The Spanish attacked quickly. They killed thousands of Incas and took Atahualpa captive. In an attempt to free himself, the Incan emperor gave the Spanish a treasure of gold. The Spaniards strangled him anyway.

***Reading*History**
**C. Drawing Conclusions** Why did the Incan Empire fall to the Spanish?
C. Answer The Incas feared that the Spaniards might be gods. The Inca warriors refused to defend themselves because Atahualpa had ordered them not to fight.

With Atahualpa dead, the Incan Empire collapsed. Having been ordered by Atahualpa not to fight, the Incas refused to defend themselves even after his death. Then Pizarro took control of this area for Spain. The Spanish called the area Peru.

## 3 Reasons for Spanish Victories

People have long been amazed that the great Aztec and Incan empires fell to such small groups of Spanish *conquistadors.* But Spanish success can be explained by four major reasons.

1. The spread of European diseases killed millions of Native Americans and weakened their resistance to conquest.
2. The Spanish were excellent soldiers and sailors. They also had superior weapons, such as guns, that helped them defeat much larger Native American armies.





**MORE ABOUT . . .**

**Aztec Arts**

The Aztecs made beautiful mosaics from a variety of materials, such as turquoise and shells as in the mask on this page. Other materials used for mosaics include coral, obsidian, onyx, and jade. Masks were symbolic. They were used with music and dance as part of Aztec worship. Aztec artists also wove beautiful headdresses and clothing of feathers. They especially prized the beautiful green feathers of the quetzal. A headdress said to belong to Montezuma contains the feathers of at least 250 birds. Only Aztec nobles wore clothing of feathers.

**INSTRUCT: OBJECTIVE 3**

**Reasons for Spanish Victories**

Key Questions

- How did disease help the Spanish defeat Native Americans?
- What were Spain's military advantages?
- How did the *conquistadors* rule the Native Americans they conquered?

**ACTIVITY OPTIONS**

**INTERDISCIPLINARY LINK: LANGUAGE ARTS**

**BLOCK SCHEDULING**

**PANEL DISCUSSION**

**Class Time** One class period

**Task** Conducting panel discussions on the Spanish conquests of the Aztec and Incan empires

**Purpose** To synthesize and analyze information and create oral presentations about the Spanish conquests

**Supplies Needed**
- Textbook
- A table, chairs, and a speaker's chair or podium

**Activity** Have students conduct a panel discussion about the Spanish conquest of the Aztec and Incan empires. Each group should select a moderator and representatives from the Spanish government, the Aztec Empire, and the Incan Empire. Instruct the moderator to develop questions about the Spanish conquest. The panelists should answer the questions from the perspective of their characters.

**INSTRUCT: OBJECTIVE 4**

**Other Spanish Explorers**

Key Questions
- What lured Spanish explorers into North America?
- Which Spanish explorers led expeditions through the southwestern United States, California, and Florida?

 **America's History Makers**
- Cabeza de Vaca, pp. 9–10

 **Outline Map Activities**
- Spain Explores the Americas, 1500s, pp. 3–4

## ASSESS & RETEACH

**Setting the Stage** Have students complete the section of the graphic organizer on Exploration and Establishing Colonies.

 **Formal Assessment**
- Section Quiz, p. 34

 **Critical Thinking Transparency CT4**
- Setting the Stage

**RETEACHING ACTIVITY**

Have students work in pairs as reporters for a newspaper covering European exploration in the Americas. Each pair should write newspaper headlines for at least six important events or individuals that helped Spain establish a large empire in the Americas. One headline should correspond to a different event or individual discussed in one of the six subsections in Section 1. As a guided review, invite students to share their headlines with the rest of the class.

 **In-Depth Resources: Unit 1**
- Reteaching Activity, p. 39

Estevanico was a slave who helped the Spanish explore parts of North America. He was killed during Coronado's search for golden cities.

3. Spain made alliances with Native Americans who were enemies of the Aztecs and Incas.
4. The Spanish *conquistadors* acted brutally toward the Native Americans under their control.

Having conquered the major Native American empires in Central and South America, the Spaniards began to explore other parts of North and South America.

*Reading***History**
**D. Drawing Conclusions** What was the most important reason for the Spanish success in conquering territory in the Americas?
**D. Possible Responses** Some students will say disease. Others might say better weapons.

## 4 Other Spanish Explorers

The Spaniards hoped to collect treasures from North America as they had from Mexico and Peru. Rumors of golden cities kept Spanish hopes high. For example, a few men, including the Spaniard Álvar Núñez Cabeza de Vaca and Estevanico, a slave of North African descent, survived a shipwreck off the North American mainland. As the men wandered across the continent, they heard Native American stories about cities of gold. When they reached Mexico, Cabeza de Vaca and Estevanico thrilled the Spaniards with these rumors.

Between 1539 and 1542, three expeditions set out to find these cities. Francisco Vázquez de Coronado traveled through present-day Arizona and New Mexico. Hernando de Soto set out from Florida to explore the southeast. Juan Rodríguez Cabrillo sailed up the California coast. But all three failed to find the fabled cities of gold.

For a while, it seemed that the Spaniards would explore the Americas all by themselves. As you will read in the next section, however, the Spanish would soon face competition from other Europeans.

### Section 1 Assessment

**1. Terms & Names**
**Identify:**
- Treaty of Tordesillas
- missionary
- mercantilism
- Amerigo Vespucci
- *conquistador*
- Hernando Cortés
- Montezuma
- Francisco Pizarro

**2. Taking Notes**
Review the section and find four events to place on a time line that shows how Spain built its empire.

**Spain Builds an Empire**

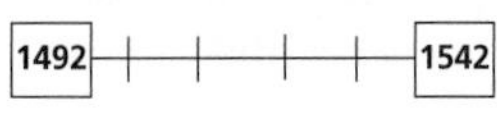


Which event do you think is the most important? Why?

**3. Main Ideas**
a. Why did Europeans explore different territories?
b. Why did Spain succeed in conquering so much of the Americas?
c. What was significant about the Magellan expedition?

**4. Critical Thinking**
**Comparing** What was similar about the conquests of Mexico and Peru?
THINK ABOUT
- the *conquistadors*
- the Incan and Aztec leaders

**ACTIVITY OPTIONS**
**ART** / **LANGUAGE ARTS**
Use the library or the Internet to find a photograph of an Aztec or Incan artifact. Create a **replica** or write a **description** of the object.



### Section 1 Assessment

**1. Terms & Names**
**Treaty of Tordesillas,** p. 61
**missionary,** p. 61
**mercantilism,** p. 61
**Amerigo Vespucci,** p. 62
***conquistador*,** p. 63
**Hernando Cortés,** p. 63
**Montezuma,** p. 63
**Francisco Pizarro,** p. 65

**2. Taking Notes**
1494 Treaty of Tordesillas
1513 Balboa reaches the Pacific.
1521 Cortés conquers Mexico.
1531 Pizarro conquers Peru.

**3. Main Ideas**
**a.** to spread Christianity, expand their empires, and gain riches
**b.** Native Americans fell to disease; the Spanish had better weapons; the Spanish made alliances with some Native Americans; the Spanish acted brutally toward Native Americans. **c.** It was the first to travel around the world.

**4. Critical Thinking**
Students may note that both were led by Spanish leaders who overcame powerful Native American empires against great odds.

**ACTIVITY OPTIONS**

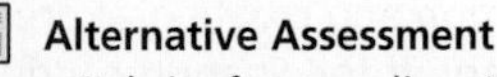 **Alternative Assessment**
- Rubrics for a replica, 1.10
- Rubrics for a description, 4.5

# 2 European Competition in North America

**TERMS & NAMES**
Henry Hudson
John Cabot
Giovanni da Verrazzano
Jacques Cartier
Spanish Armada
Samuel de Champlain
New France



**MAIN IDEA**

Other European countries competed with Spain for control over territory in the Americas.

**WHY IT MATTERS NOW**

European culture has strongly influenced American culture.

## ONE EUROPEAN'S STORY

**In 1609, an Englishman named Henry Hudson set sail from Europe. He sailed under the Dutch flag and hoped to find a route to China. Arriving at the coast of present-day New York, he sailed up the river that now bears his name. In his journal, Hudson described what he saw.**

*A VOICE FROM THE PAST*

The land is the finest for cultivation that I ever in my life set foot upon, and it also abounds in trees of every description. The natives are a very good people; for, when they saw that I would not remain, they supposed that I was afraid of their bows, and taking the arrows, they broke them in pieces and threw them into the fire.

**Henry Hudson,** quoted in *Discoverers of America*

**Hudson did not find a passage to Asia, but he led another expedition in 1610, this time sailing for the English. He made his way through ice-clogged waters in Canada and entered a large bay, today called Hudson Bay. There he sailed for months, but still found no westward passage.**

**After enduring a harsh winter, his crew rebelled. They put Hudson, his young son, and several loyal sailors in a small boat and set them adrift (shown at right). Hudson's party was never heard from again.**

## 1 The Search for the Northwest Passage

Hudson's voyages showed that some European countries hoped to find a westward route to Asia as late as the 1600s. While Spain was taking control of the Americas, other Europeans were sending out expeditions to find the Northwest Passage, a water route through North America to Asia.

One of the first explorers to chart a northern route across the Atlantic in search of Asia was the Italian sailor **John Cabot.** In 1497, Cabot crossed the Atlantic Ocean to explore for the English. He landed in the area of Newfoundland, Canada. He was certain that he had reached Asia and claimed the land for England. The next year he set sail once more,



## SECTION OBJECTIVES

1. To trace the search for a water route through North America to Asia
2. To explain Spanish reaction to competition in North America and to identify effects of the defeat of the Spanish Armada
3. To describe the search for trade by the French and Dutch

**CRITICAL THINKING**

Drawing Conclusions, p. 69
Making Inferences, p. 70

 **Why It Matters Now**
- Space Exploration, pp. 3–4

## FOCUS & MOTIVATE

### 5-MINUTE WARM-UP

**Recognizing Effects** These questions focus on rivalries that developed among European nations.

1. Look at the painting and caption on page 69. Which nations are fighting?
2. Why might the outcome of this battle be important to the history of the Americas?

**Warm-Up Transparency WT2**

## INSTRUCT

### INSTRUCT: OBJECTIVE 1

**The Search for the Northwest Passage**

Key Questions
- What was the Northwest Passage?
- Which European nations actively sought to discover the Northwest Passage?
- Why were European nations interested in finding a Northwest Passage?

 **In-Depth Resources: Unit 1**
- Guided Reading, p. 27
- Building Vocabulary, p. 30

**Reading Study Guide** (Spanish and English), pp. 19–20

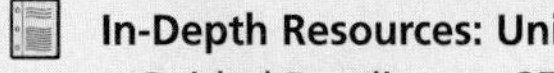

## RECOMMENDED RESOURCES

**In-Depth Resources: Unit 1**
- Guided Reading, p. 27
- Building Vocabulary, p. 30
- Reteaching Activity, p. 40

**Reading Study Guide** (Spanish and English), pp. 19–20

**Why It Matters Now**
- Space Exploration, pp. 3–4

**Formal Assessment**
- Section Quiz, p. 35

**Alternative Assessment**
- Rubrics, 4.8
- Rubrics, 5.1

**Access for Students Acquiring English/ESL**
- Guided Reading, p. 10

**Technology Resources**

 **Humanities Transparency HT4**
- St. Augustine

 **Electronic Teacher Tools with Test Maker**

 **ClassZone**
www.mcdougallittell.com

hoping to reach Japan. He was never seen again. Even so, his voyages were the basis for future English colonies along North America's Atlantic shore.

In 1524, another Italian, **Giovanni da Verrazzano,** set out under the French flag to find the Northwest Passage. He explored the Atlantic coastline of North America, but there was no passage to be found.

France tried again between 1534 and 1536 with the voyages of **Jacques Cartier** (ZHAHK kahr•TYAY). Cartier traveled up the St. Lawrence River to the site of present-day Montreal. At that point, rapids blocked the way and ended his search for the Northwest Passage. It would be almost 75 years before the French would return to colonize the region.

*Reading* **History**
**A. Reading a Map** Use the maps on pages 63 and 67 to see the areas Cabot, Hudson, Verrazzano, and Cartier visited.

**INSTRUCT: OBJECTIVE 2**
**Spain Responds to Competition/ Spain and England Clash/ The Defeat of the Spanish Armada**
Key Questions
- What factors increased the tension among Spain, England, and France?
- What role did sea dogs play in the conflict between Spain and England?
- Identify the effects of the defeat of the Spanish Armada.

## 2 Spain Responds to Competition

French and English claims to North America angered Spain, which had claimed the land under the Treaty of Tordesillas. The tensions between Spain, England, and France stemmed from religious conflicts in Europe, such as the Reformation, which you read about in Chapter 1. These conflicts also led to fighting in the Americas.

Florida was one of the battlegrounds between the Spanish and the French. In 1564, a group of French Protestants, called Huguenots (HYOO•guh•NAHTS), founded a colony called Fort Caroline. Before long, Spanish troops under the command of Pedro Menéndez de Avilés arrived in that area. "This is the armada of the King of Spain," he announced, "who has sent me [here] to burn and hang the Lutheran [Protestant] French." Menéndez built a fort, St. Augustine, a short distance away. Then he brutally massacred the French.

**Vocabulary**
**armada:** a fleet of warships

***America's* HERITAGE**

**St. Augustine**
St. Augustine was named for a Roman Catholic saint. Evidence of Spanish influence in North America can be found in the names of many cities, counties, and states across the United States. Florida, for example, was named in honor of the "Feast of Flowers," the Easter celebration in Spain. Ask students to list other place names in the United States that have Spanish origins.

**Humanities Transparency HT4**
- St. Augustine

***America's* HERITAGE**

**ST. AUGUSTINE**
The thick stone walls of the fort at St. Augustine (shown below) still stand guard over the Florida coast today. Founded in 1565, St. Augustine is the oldest permanent European settlement in the United States. For more than two centuries, St. Augustine was an important outpost of Spain's empire in the Americas. Many Spanish colonial buildings remain at the site. The fort is now a national monument.

## Spain and England Clash

Religious differences and the quest for national power also led to conflict between Spain and England. In 1558, Queen Elizabeth I, a Protestant, came to the English throne. Spain, which was Catholic, plotted to remove the Protestant queen. But Elizabeth fought to defend England and challenge Spain's power at sea.

Although England's navy was not as powerful as Spain's, the English fleet had many speedy ships with skillful sailors. Daring sailors, known as sea dogs, used these ships to attack the bulky Spanish sailing ships—called galleons—that brought gold and silver from the Americas.

Sir Francis Drake became the most famous of the sea dogs because of his bold adventures and attacks against the Spanish. In 1577, Drake began a three-year voyage that took him around the world. During this voyage,

68

**ACTIVITY OPTIONS**
**INTERDISCIPLINARY LINK: LANGUAGE ARTS** | **BLOCK SCHEDULING**

**A CELEBRATORY SPEECH**
**Class Time** 45 minutes
**Task** Planning a television news program
**Purpose** To analyze reasons for the English delight with the exploits of Francis Drake

**Supplies Needed**
- Reference material about Francis Drake
- Video camera and tape (optional)

**Activity** Divide students into groups. Tell students to plan and write copy for a television news segment on the arrival of Francis Drake in England after his trip around the world in 1580. The segment should last two minutes and include the newscaster's narration, a short welcome to Drake by a London resident, and a brief response by Drake. If the students are videotaping their segments, they should divide the tasks involved.

The English navy used its smaller, quicker ships to defeat the larger, slower galleons of the Spanish Armada.

he raided Spanish ports and ships in South America. He stole great amounts of treasure from them. When he arrived home in 1580, he was a national hero. Not only had Drake and his men hounded the Spanish, but they were also the first Englishmen to sail around the world.

## The Defeat of the Spanish Armada

The attacks of Drake and other sea dogs enraged Philip II, the Spanish king. Determined to teach the English a lesson, Philip sent the **Spanish Armada** to conquer England and restore Catholicism to that nation. This fleet, made up of 130 ships, set out for England in the summer of 1588.

The English and Spanish navies met in the English Channel, which separates England from the European continent. In their smaller but faster craft, the English darted among the Spanish warships, firing deadly rounds with their cannons. Confused and crippled, the armada was retreating when it was hit by a severe storm. With half of its ships destroyed, the armada barely made it home.

Spain was still quite strong after the defeat of the armada. It quickly rebuilt its navy and maintained its large colonial possessions. But Spain would never again be as powerful as it was in 1588.

The English victory over Spain had two important effects. First, England remained independent and Protestant. Although England was less powerful than Spain, it had shown that it could defend itself. Second, Spain's image suffered. The world saw that Spain could be beaten. Other nations joined England in challenging Spain.

**B. Possible Response** England remained independent, and Spain was weakened.

*Reading***History**

**B. Drawing Conclusions** Why was the defeat of the Spanish Armada important?



**HISTORY FROM VISUALS**

**Interpreting the Painting** Have students look at the painting on this page and read the caption. Tell students that the most damaging cannon fire typically came from a ship that had moved so that it could fire *broadside* into an enemy ship, meaning that it would fire all its cannons on one side at once. Ask students why smaller ships, such as those of the English fleet, might have an advantage in this type of combat. **Possible Response** Smaller ships could outmaneuver larger ones and get off more broadsides while escaping enemy cannon fire.

**Extension** Have students write a first-person journal entry from the perspective of a sailor on board an English or Spanish ship during the battle.

**MORE ABOUT . . .**

**Queen Elizabeth I**

Queen Elizabeth I was the daughter of Henry VIII. Protestant Elizabeth inherited the throne from her Catholic half-sister Mary, who had been married to Philip II of Spain. For a while, Philip hoped to marry Elizabeth. Gradually, however, it became clear that Elizabeth intended to keep England Protestant and independent of Spain. Elizabeth further angered Philip by supporting Dutch Protestants rebelling against Spanish rule.

**ACTIVITY OPTIONS**

**INDIVIDUAL NEEDS**

**LESS PROFICIENT READERS**

**Defeat of the Spanish Armada** To help students understand the links between cause and effect, have them copy the cause-and-effect diagrams shown here. Have the students read the text on page 69 under the heading "The Defeat of the Spanish Armada." Then have them find the sentences that indicate the effects.

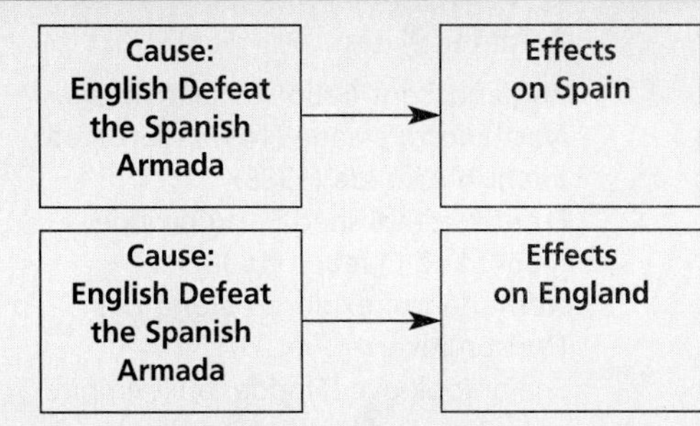

**INSTRUCT: OBJECTIVE 3**

**The French and Dutch Seek Trade**

Key Questions

- Where did the French and Dutch establish their first settlements in North America?
- In what economic activities were the French and Dutch colonies engaged?
- How did the French and Dutch settlements compare to those of the Spanish?

**CRITICAL THINKING ACTIVITY**

**Contrasting** Contrast the actions of the Spanish conquerors toward the Native Americans with those of French and Dutch settlers by using a three-column graphic organizer.

| SPANISH | DUTCH | FRENCH |
|---|---|---|
| | | |

**Class Time** 10 minutes

English adventurers like Drake continued to attack Spanish interests abroad. In addition, England challenged Spanish claims to lands in North America, such as California and Newfoundland. Even so, England took a cautious approach to overseas expansion. The English government refused to provide money to start colonies. Instead, private citizens had to provide the money for colonization. As a result, England did not establish a successful colony in America until after 1600.

## 3 The French and Dutch Seek Trade

France and the Netherlands were also looking for ways to gain wealth through exploration and colonization. At first, their goal in the Americas was to find the Northwest Passage to Asia. When that search failed, they began to focus on North America itself.

The Frenchman **Samuel de Champlain** (sham•PLAYN) explored the St. Lawrence River. In 1608, he founded a fur-trading post at Quebec. This post became the first permanent French settlement in North America. Champlain's activities opened a rich fur trade with local Native Americans. After a couple of decades, **New France**, as the colony was called, began to thrive.

At the same time, the Dutch were building a colony called New Netherland. It was located along the Hudson River in present-day New York. After Hudson's voyage up the river in 1609, the Dutch built Fort Nassau in 1614, near the site of the modern city of Albany.

In 1626, the Dutch bought Manhattan Island from Native Americans. The Dutch then founded the town of New Amsterdam on that site, where New York City is currently located. New Netherland was soon thriving from the fur trade with Native Americans.

These early French and Dutch colonies, however, were small compared to the large empire Spain was building in the Americas. You will read about the growth of Spain's American empire in the next section.

C. Possible **Response** They were not as powerful as Spain. At first, they looked for the Northwest Passage and only set up colonies when they could not find it.

*Reading*History

**C. Making Inferences** Why do you think it took France and the Netherlands so long to set up colonies in the Americas?

### Section 2 Assessment

**1. Terms & Names**

**Identify:**

- Henry Hudson
- John Cabot
- Giovanni da Verrazzano
- Jacques Cartier
- Spanish Armada
- Samuel de Champlain
- New France

**2. Taking Notes**

Use a chart like the one below to show how European nations competed for power.

| England | |
|---|---|
| France | |
| Netherlands | |
| Spain | |

**3. Main Ideas**

a. What were the English, French, and Dutch searching for in their early voyages of exploration?

b. How did England defeat the Spanish Armada?

c. Where did the French and Dutch set up their first American colonies?

**4. Critical Thinking**

**Making Inferences** Why do you think England founded colonies later than Spain did?

THINK ABOUT

- conditions in Spain and England
- the lands each country discovered

**ACTIVITY OPTIONS**

**MUSIC**

**TECHNOLOGY**

Research the life of one of the explorers discussed in this section. Compose a **song** or design a **Web page** about that person.



## ASSESS & RETEACH

**Setting the Stage** Have students complete the section of the graphic organizer on European Competition.

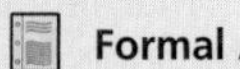

**Formal Assessment**

- Section Quiz, p. 35

**RETEACHING ACTIVITY**

Have students create an annotated time line showing important events discussed in this section. The annotations should include short explanations of Spanish reaction to other European explorations and the effects of the defeat of the Spanish Armada.

**In-Depth Resources: Unit 1**

- Reteaching Activity, p. 40

### Section 2 Assessment

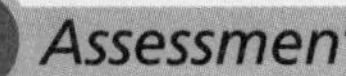

**1. Terms & Names**

**Henry Hudson,** p. 67
**John Cabot,** p. 67
**Giovanni da Verrazzano,** p. 68
**Jacques Cartier,** p. 68
**Spanish Armada,** p. 69
**Samuel de Champlain,** p. 70
**New France,** p. 70

**2. Taking Notes**

England: sent Cabot to search for Northwest Passage (1497); defeated Spanish Armada (1588)
France: established Fort Caroline (1564) and Quebec (1608)
Netherlands: explored along the Hudson River
Spain: took over Florida; built empire in Central and South America

**3. Main Ideas**

**a.** Northwest Passage to Asia and the spice trade **b.** The smaller, faster English ships outmaneuvered the Spanish galleons. **c.** The French set up a colony at Fort Caroline in Florida in 1564. The Dutch built Fort Nassau near modern-day Albany in 1614.

**4. Critical Thinking**

Spain was already much richer and more powerful. England was weaker and less willing to expand into the lands it discovered.

**ACTIVITY OPTIONS**

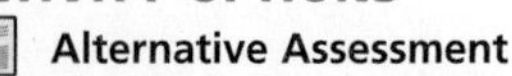

**Alternative Assessment**

- Rubrics for a song, 4.8
- Rubrics for a Web page, 5.1

# 3 The Spanish and Native Americans

**TERMS & NAMES**
viceroyalty
*encomienda*
*hacienda*
mission
Popé
plantation
Bartolomé de Las Casas
Columbian Exchange

**MAIN IDEA**

Spanish rule in the Americas had terrible consequences for Native Americans.

**WHY IT MATTERS NOW**

The destruction of Native American cultures created social problems that continue today.

## ONE AMERICAN'S STORY

**Huamán Poma, a Peruvian Native American, was angry about the abuse the Spanish heaped upon Native Americans. He wrote to King Philip III of Spain to complain about the bad treatment.**

*A VOICE FROM THE PAST*

It is their [the Spanish] practice to collect Indians into groups and send them to forced labor without wages, while they themselves receive the payment for the work. . . . The royal administrators and the other Spaniards lord it over the Indians with absolute power.

**Huamán Poma,** *Letter to a King*

**In his letter, Poma asked the king to help the Native Americans and uphold the rule of law in Peru. If the king actually read the letter, it made no difference. Spanish colonists continued to mistreat Native Americans as the Spanish Empire expanded in the Americas.**

A Spanish priest forces a Native American woman to work at a loom.

## 1 Spanish Colonies in the Americas

The Spanish Empire grew rapidly, despite efforts by other European countries to compete with Spain. By 1700, it controlled much of the Americas. Spain took several steps to establish an effective colonial government. First, it divided its American empire into two provinces called New Spain and Peru. Each province was called a **viceroyalty**. The top official of each viceroyalty was called the viceroy. He ruled in the king's name.

The Spanish also built new roads to transport people and goods across the empire. These roads stretched outward from the capitals at Mexico City and Lima. The roads helped Spain to control the colonies by allowing soldiers to move quickly from place to place. Roads also improved the Spanish economy because materials, such as gold and silver, could be transported efficiently to the coast and then to Spain.





## SECTION OBJECTIVES

1. To analyze the organization of government and society in Spanish colonies
2. To describe economic activities of the Spanish colonies
3. To evaluate Spanish treatment of Native Americans
4. To trace the Columbian Exchange

**SKILLBUILDER**

Interpreting Maps: Location, Region, p. 72

**CRITICAL THINKING**

Summarizing, p. 72
Making Inferences, p. 74
Recognizing Effects, p. 75

## FOCUS & MOTIVATE

### 5-MINUTE WARM-UP

**Reading a Map** Examining this map will help students understand the vast size of Spain's empire in the Americas.

1. Look at the map on page 72. Describe the area included in the Viceroyalty of New Spain and the Viceroyalty of Peru.
2. How do you suppose dividing Spain's vast empire into two units may have made it easier to govern?

 **Warm-Up Transparency WT2**

## INSTRUCT

**INSTRUCT: OBJECTIVE 1**

**Spanish Colonies in the Americas/ Life in Spanish America**

Key Questions

- What steps did Spain take to govern lands in the Americas?
- How did the Spanish manage the economy of the American colonies?
- How was Spanish colonial society organized?

 **In-Depth Resources: Unit 1**
- Guided Reading, p. 28

**Reading Study Guide** (Spanish and English), pp. 21–22

## RECOMMENDED RESOURCES

 **In-Depth Resources: Unit 1**
- Guided Reading, p. 28
- Building Vocabulary, p. 30
- Geography Application: Spain's American Empire Expands, pp. 32–33
- Primary Source: Protesting the Mistreatment of Native Americans, p. 34
- Reteaching Activity, p. 41
- Enrichment Activity, p. 43

 **Reading Study Guide** (Spanish and English), pp. 21–22

 **Formal Assessment**
- Section Quiz, p. 36

 **Alternative Assessment**
- Rubrics, 1.8
- Rubrics, 4.6

 **Access for Students Acquiring English/ESL**
- Guided Reading, p. 11
- Geography Application, pp. 14–15

**Technology Resources**

 **Critical Thinking Trans. CT5**
- Cause and Effect: The Columbian Exchange

 **Electronic Teacher Tools with Test Maker**

 **ClassZone**
www.mcdougallittell.com

## HISTORY FROM VISUALS

**Reading the Map** Point out the large distance between the cities of Mexico City and Lima. Have students suggest the kinds of problems that the distance might cause for administrators in each city. **Possible Responses** Administrators would have difficulty. They could not keep in touch with distant areas, nor could they send troops or supplies quickly.

**Extension** Using an atlas, have the students identify a present-day transportation network between Mexico City and Lima.

## INSTRUCT: OBJECTIVE 2

**The Role of the Church**

Key Questions

- What role did the Catholic Church play in the Spanish colonies?
- Why did many Native Americans grow increasingly unhappy with the Catholic missions?

**In-Depth Resources: Unit 1**

- Geography Application: Spain's American Empire Expands, pp. 32–33

## MORE ABOUT . . .

**Spanish Missions**

Although many Spanish missions in the Americas were destroyed over the centuries, some survived and are popular tourist attractions. The oldest Spanish mission in the United States is Nombre de Díos, built in 1565 in St. Augustine, Florida. One of the most famous missions is San Antonio de Valero, also called the Alamo, in San Antonio, Texas. Between 1769 and 1845, Spanish priests established 21 missions in California. The southernmost mission is San Diego; the most northerly is San Francisco Solona (Sonoma Mission).

**Spain's American Empire, 1700**

NORTH AMERICA
ATLANTIC OCEAN
WEST INDIES
Mexico City
CENTRAL AMERICA
SOUTH AMERICA
Lima
PACIFIC OCEAN
Tropic of Cancer
0° Equator
Tropic of Capricorn
40°N
40°S
120°W
80°W
40°W
0 1,000 Miles
0 2,000 Kilometers
Viceroyalty of New Spain
Viceroyalty of Peru

**GEOGRAPHY SKILLBUILDER Interpreting Maps**

1. **Location** *Which viceroyalty included the West Indies?*
2. **Region** *Which viceroyalty covered more territory?*

Skillbuilder Answers
1. New Spain
2. Peru

## Life in Spanish America

Spanish colonists received *encomiendas* to help them make the colonies productive. An ***encomienda*** was a grant of Native American labor. Hernando Cortés received a grant of more than 100,000 Native Americans to work his estate.

The Spanish rulers also created large estates, called ***haciendas,*** to provide food for the colony. *Haciendas* usually became large farms where Native Americans worked to grow cash crops, such as coffee and cotton. The *encomienda* and *hacienda* systems put much of the power and land in the hands of a few people.

**Background**
The problem of unequal wealth, especially in land, continues to trouble Latin American societies today.

The Spaniards made sure that people with Spanish backgrounds held power in the colonies. Spanish-born colonists such as Cortés made up the top layer of colonial society. Just below the Spanish were the Creoles—people of Spanish descent who were born in the colonies. The next step down the social order were the *mestizos. Mestizos* are people of mixed Spanish and Native American ancestry. The people with the least power and fewest rights were Native Americans and enslaved Africans.

## 2 The Role of the Church

The Catholic Church played an important role in Spanish colonial society. In places like New Mexico and California, the church built **missions,** settlements that included a church, a town, and farmlands. The goal of the missions was to convert Native Americans to Christianity. The missions also increased Spanish control over the land.

Missionaries helped the Native Americans to create a better supply of food. They also offered Native Americans protection against enemies. Many Native Americans learned how to read and write in the missions. Others developed skills such as carpentry and metalworking.

**Reading History**
**A. Summarizing** How did the Spanish missions change the lives of Native Americans?
**A. Answer** They helped Native Americans get better food and protected them from enemies. They also taught many Native Americans to read and learn other skills.

Over time, however, many Native Americans grew increasingly unhappy. The missionaries often worked them as if they were slaves. The missionaries also tried to replace Native American religions and traditions. As a result, some Native Americans ran away, while others rebelled. Some destroyed churches and killed missionaries.

In 1680, a man named **Popé** led the Pueblo Indians in a rebellion against the Spanish. His forces surrounded the Spanish settlement at

72 CHAPTER 2

## ACTIVITY OPTIONS

**INTERDISCIPLINARY LINK: GEOGRAPHY** — BLOCK SCHEDULING

**COUNTRY POSTERS**

**Class Time** One class period

**Task** Creating an informative poster about a country

**Purpose** To explore the geography and present-day economy of a former Spanish colony

**Supplies Needed**
- Poster paper or large sheets of plain paper
- Color pencils and/or markers
- World atlases, almanacs, and other reference books

**Activity** As a class, use atlases or geography textbooks to list the present-day nations of South America that were once Spanish colonies. Assign each student one of these countries. Have students prepare a poster with information about the country, including a small map and information about its population, exports, government, and principal religions. Display the completed posters. Have students identify which present-day conditions in South American countries show the influence of colonial practices.

Santa Fe, in present-day New Mexico, and forced the colonists to flee. Popé ordered the churches and other Spanish buildings to be destroyed. He then tried to revive native customs that had been lost under Spanish rule. But before long, attacks from neighboring tribes weakened Pueblo control. In 1692, the Spanish regained control of Santa Fe.

## 3 Sugar Plantations Develop

The Spanish also forced Native Americans to work on **plantations,** large farms that raised cash crops. These crops were usually exported to Europe. The most important crop was sugar.

Although sugar was in great demand in Europe, there was not much land there to grow it. The resulting demand led to the development of sugar plantations in the Americas. On his second voyage to the Americas, in 1493, Columbus brought sugar cane to Hispaniola, one of the Caribbean islands he had landed on in 1492. He found ideal conditions for sugar production there. Spanish planters soon expanded operations to the nearby islands that Spain colonized.

**Background** Other plantation crops included tobacco, cotton, cochineal (a dye), and cacao.

Sugar plantations required many workers, so the Spanish planters turned to native peoples, such as the Taino. Through *encomiendas,* the Spaniards forced thousands of Taino to work in the fields. The plantations thrived, but many of the Taino suffered and died.

## The Abuse of Native Americans

Most Spaniards treated the Native Americans as little more than beasts of burden. According to Fray Toribio de Benavente, a Catholic missionary, the Spanish "do nothing but command. They are the drones who suck the honey which is made by the poor bees, the Indians."

Not all Spaniards approved of this treatment. One man in particular fought for better treatment of Native

**HISTORY through ART**

Theodore de Bry created this picture, *Sugar: the greatest gift of the Old World to the New,* in the 1600s. It shows workers processing sugar in the Americas. Europeans brought sugar production to the Americas from the Mediterranean.

**How does the picture help explain why the Europeans used slaves to make sugar?**

73



**INSTRUCT: OBJECTIVE**  3

**Sugar Plantations Develop/ The Abuse of Native Americans**

Key Questions
- How did the plantation system affect Native Americans?
- Who was Bartolomé de Las Casas?
- Why did the New Laws of 1542 fail to protect Native Americans?

 **In-Depth Resources: Unit 1**
- Primary Source: Protesting the Mistreatment of Native Americans, p. 34
- Enrichment Activity, p. 43

### HISTORY through ART

**Interpreting the Painting** Flemish engraver Theodore de Bry (1528–1598) never visited the Americas, but he used the accounts of geographers and explorers to produce many scenes of life in the Americas. In this scene, Native Americans carry tall sugar canes. They turn the heavy wheel that crushes the cane. Then they boil the sap down into molasses.

**Answer: The picture shows many people doing hard work to make sugar. The Europeans would have to force people, through slavery, to do such work.**

### MORE ABOUT . . .

**Sugar**

Today, sugar remains an important product in many former Spanish colonies in the Americas. This is especially true in northern South America and in the Caribbean, where sugar cane can be grown year round. The economies of some countries in those regions, such as Cuba, are heavily dependent on the success of each year's sugar cane crop.

### ACTIVITY OPTIONS

### INTERDISCIPLINARY LINK: CIVICS

 BLOCK SCHEDULING

**PETITIONS**

**Class Time** 45 minutes

**Task** Writing a petition about the treatment of Native Americans

**Purpose** To identify and present arguments against the abuse of Native Americans in the Spanish colonies

**Supplies Needed**
- Textbook
- Encyclopedias or reference books about Spanish America
- Writing paper
- Color pencils

**Activity** Direct students to work in pairs. Have them write petitions asking the Spanish king to require colonists to stop abusing Native Americans in the colonies. Petitions should describe the treatment of Native Americans and make a case for requiring better treatment. Students might want to research some of the arguments on the subject made by Bartolomé de Las Casas and others. Students can decorate their petitions, roll them, seal them with wax, and tie them with a ribbon for presentation.

## HISTORY FROM VISUALS

**Interpreting the Illustration** Ask students to study the illustration and identify products that Europeans brought to the Americas to cultivate for trade. Ask students which American products they think will be most valuable in Europe, Africa, and Asia. Ask students to explain the skull and crossbones on the map. **Possible Responses** Sugar cane, bananas, citrus fruits, grains, and livestock. Answers may vary but should include tomatoes, corn, and potatoes. The skull and crossbones symbolizes the danger of diseases spread by Europeans.

**Extension** Have students research the work of the Centers for Disease Control and Prevention in Atlanta, Georgia, in reducing the spread of the listed diseases.

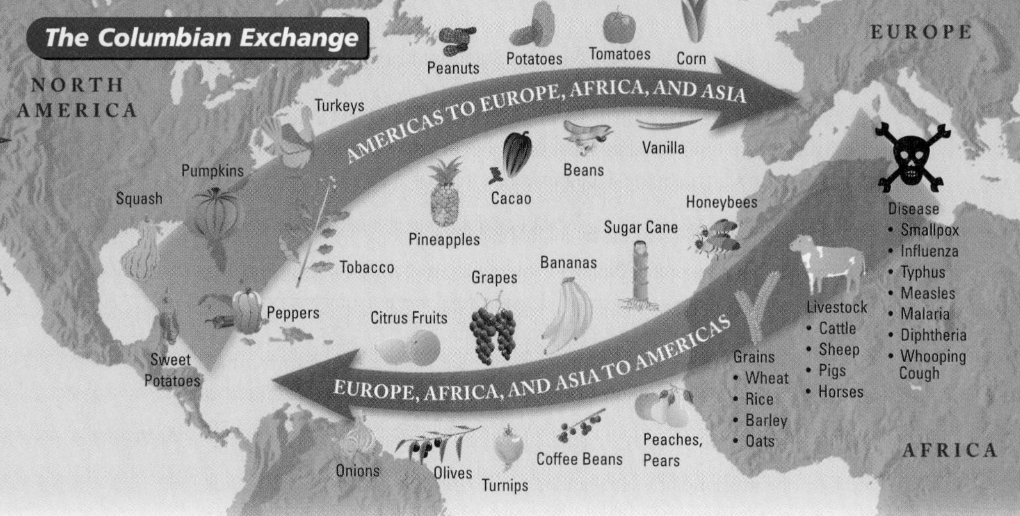


Americans. His name was **Bartolomé de Las Casas.** Las Casas had come to Hispaniola in 1502 and taken part in the conquest of Cuba a decade later. For his part in the conquest, he received an *encomienda.* Las Casas was also a Catholic priest, however, and he soon faced a moral dilemma: How can a person serve God and enslave Native Americans at the same time?

In 1514, Las Casas gave up his claim to the Native Americans who worked for him. For the next 50 years, he fought against the abuse of Native Americans, earning the title "Protector of the Indians."

Because of his efforts, the Spanish king issued the New Laws in 1542. These laws ordered the gradual freeing of all enslaved Native Americans. Holders of *encomiendas* who were found guilty of mistreating Native Americans had their *encomiendas* taken away. However, Spanish colonists strongly protested against the New Laws, and the king eventually reversed many of them.

### INSTRUCT: OBJECTIVE 4

**The Columbian Exchange**

Key Question
- How did the Columbian Exchange contribute to the spread of disease in the Americas?
- What were some of the beneficial effects of the Columbian Exchange?

 **Critical Thinking Trans. CT5**
- Cause and Effect: The Columbian Exchange

## 4 The Columbian Exchange

The arrival of the Spanish in the Americas brought more than a clash of peoples and cultures. It also brought a movement of plants, animals, and diseases between the Eastern and Western hemispheres. This movement of living things between hemispheres is called the **Columbian Exchange.**

One result of the Columbian Exchange was the transfer of germs from Europe to the Americas. When Europeans came to America, they brought with them germs that caused diseases such as smallpox, measles, and influenza. Native Americans had no immunity to them.

Although exact numbers are unknown, historians estimate that diseases brought by Europeans killed more than 20 million Native Americans in Mexico in the first century after conquest. Many scholars agree that the population of Native Americans in Central America decreased by 90 to 95 percent between the years 1519 and 1619. The

*Reading* **History**

**B. Making Inferences** What might have happened if Native Americans had been immune to European diseases?

**B. Answer** They would not have been so easily conquered or dominated.



### ACTIVITY OPTIONS

### INDIVIDUAL NEEDS

**LESS PROFICIENT READERS**

**Recognizing Effects** Review with students the effects of colonization for Native Americans. Have the students create a graphic like the one shown. Have them write the textbook heading in the first box. Then identify actions that were the results of colonization and write them in the second box. Remind the students that effects can be both positive and negative.

| Textbook Heading | Effect for Native Americans |
|---|---|
| Life in Spanish America | Native Americans were forced to work for colonists.<br>Native Americans were lowest level in social order; had fewest rights. |
| The Role of the Church | The Church created better food supplies, offered protection, taught them skills.<br>Missionaries treated Native Americans as slaves; tried to replace their religions and traditions. |

result was similar in Peru and other parts of the Americas. A Spanish missionary in Mexico described the effects of smallpox on the Aztecs.

*A VOICE FROM THE PAST*

There was a great havoc. Very many died of it. They could not walk. . . . They could not move; they could not stir; they could not change position, nor lie on one side; nor face down, nor on their backs. And if they stirred, much did they cry out. Great was its destruction.

**Bernardino de Sahagún,** quoted in *Seeds of Change*

Other effects of the Columbian Exchange were more positive. The Spanish brought many plants and animals to the Americas. European livestock—cattle, pigs, and horses—all thrived in the Americas. Crops from the Eastern Hemisphere, such as grapes, onions, and wheat, also thrived in the Western Hemisphere.

The Columbian Exchange benefited Europe, too. Many American crops became part of the European diet. Two that had a huge impact were potatoes and corn, which are highly nutritious. They helped feed European populations that might otherwise have gone hungry. Potatoes, for example, became an important food in Ireland, Russia, and other parts of northern Europe. Without potatoes, Europe's population might not have grown as rapidly as it did.

**Background**
In Ireland, the population increased from 3.2 million in 1754 to more than 8 million in 1845, largely because of the nutrition of potatoes.

By mixing the products of two hemispheres, the Columbian Exchange brought the world closer together. Of course, people were also moving from one hemisphere to the other, blending their cultures in the process. The next section focuses on one important aspect of the movement of peoples: the forced migration of enslaved Africans to the Americas.

## Now *and* then

**KILLER BEES**

Even today, plant and animal species continue to move from one hemisphere to the other. A recent example of this is the killer bee (shown below).

Killer bees were first brought to Brazil from Africa to help make honey in the 1950s. Killer bees are aggressive, however, and can kill large animals when they swarm. After some of these bees escaped from a Brazilian laboratory in 1957, they began to migrate. In recent years, they have been responsible for the deaths of a number of pets in the American Southwest.

## Section 3 Assessment

**1. Terms & Names**

**Identify:**
- viceroyalty
- *encomienda*
- *hacienda*
- mission
- Popé
- plantation
- Bartolomé de Las Casas
- Columbian Exchange

**2. Taking Notes**

Use a cluster diagram like the one below to show how Spain organized its colonies.

How did these actions help the Spanish control the Americas?

**3. Main Ideas**

a. What were the four levels of Spanish colonial society?

b. What was the main crop grown on colonial plantations?

c. How were Native Americans abused in the colonies?

**4. Critical Thinking**

**Recognizing Effects**
What were the positive and negative effects of the Columbian Exchange?

**THINK ABOUT**
- disease
- food
- livestock

**ACTIVITY OPTIONS**

**ART**
**LANGUAGE ARTS**

Make a **collage** that shows the plants and animals involved in the Columbian Exchange, or write a **story** that tells how Native Americans reacted to the animals.





## Now and then

**Killer Bees**

The Africanized honey bee, or killer bee, was identified in Texas in 1990. Killer bees have also been confirmed in Arizona, New Mexico, Puerto Rico, California, the Virgin Islands, and, most recently, Nevada. When killer bees attack, a person can usually escape, although the bees have caused over 1,000 deaths since the 1950s.

## MORE ABOUT . . .

**Smallpox**

Smallpox—which decimated Native American populations after the arrival of Europeans in the Americas—was one of the most feared diseases in the world for centuries. In 1980, the World Health Assembly declared that the world was free of smallpox, thanks to a worldwide vaccination campaign. However, some countries have stockpiled smallpox germs as part of their arsenals of germ warfare. Scientists worry that if these germs are released, there will not be enough vaccine to prevent a terrible epidemic.

## ASSESS & RETEACH

**Setting the Stage** Have students complete the section of the chart on the Columbian Exchange.

 **Formal Assessment**
- Section Quiz, p. 36

### RETEACHING ACTIVITY

Organize the class into groups of four. Assign one section objective to each group member. Each group member should prepare a short summary of that section's main idea. Members should then share their summaries with the rest of the group.

 **In-Depth Resources: Unit 1**
- Reteaching Activity, p. 41

## Section 3 Assessment

**1. Terms & Names**

**viceroyalty,** p. 71
***encomienda,*** p. 72
***haciendas,*** p. 72
**mission,** p. 72
**Popé,** p. 72
**plantation,** p. 73
**Bartolomé de Las Casas,** p. 74
**Columbian Exchange,** p. 74

**2. Taking Notes**

[first oval] There were two viceroyalties, New Spain and Peru. [second oval] Land and labor were organized into *haciendas* and *encomiendas.* [third oval] The church and missions were important in colonial society. The actions put power and land in the hands of a few Spanish people.

**3. Main Ideas**

**a.** Spanish-born, Creoles, mestizos, Native Americans/African slaves **b.** sugar **c.** They were forced into hard labor and sometimes tortured and killed.

**4. Critical Thinking**

Millions of Native Americans died from European diseases. New foods became available, enriching diets and increasing population.

**ACTIVITY OPTIONS**

 **Alternative Assessment**
- Rubrics for a collage, 1.8
- Rubrics for a story, 4.6

## SECTION OBJECTIVES

1. To analyze the origins of slavery in the Americas
2. To explain the development of the slave trade
3. To describe the middle passage
4. To pose and answer questions about the system of slavery in the Americas

**SKILLBUILDER**
Interpreting Graphs, p. 77

**CRITICAL THINKING**
Drawing Conclusions, p. 77
Making Inferences, p. 78
Analyzing Causes, p. 79
Recognizing Effects, p. 79

## FOCUS & MOTIVATE

### 5-MINUTE WARM-UP

**Drawing Conclusions** To help students understand the human impact of the slave trade, ask the following questions.

1. Look at the illustrations on page 78. What can you infer about the conditions aboard the ships on which Africans were transported to the Americas?
2. What do these conditions suggest about the attitude of the traders toward the Africans?

**Warm-Up Transparency WT2**

## INSTRUCT

### INSTRUCT: OBJECTIVE 1

**The Origins of American Slavery**
Key Questions
- What forms has slavery taken through history?
- How did slavery change with the rise of sugar plantations?
- Why did the Spanish and Portuguese enslave Africans?

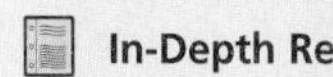

**In-Depth Resources: Unit 1**
- Guided Reading, p. 29

**Reading Study Guide** (Spanish and English), pp. 23–24

# 4 Beginnings of Slavery in the Americas

**TERMS & NAMES**
slavery
African Diaspora
middle passage
slave codes
racism

| MAIN IDEA | WHY IT MATTERS NOW |
|---|---|
| Slavery in the Americas began in order to provide cheap labor for the colonies. | The effects of slavery, including racism, helped shape attitudes and social conditions in the United States. |

### ONE AMERICAN'S STORY

**In 1546, Diego de Campo may have been the most powerful man on the island of Hispaniola. He was the leader of 7,000 maroons, or runaway slaves. By contrast, there were only about 1,000 European men on the island.**

**The Spanish planters greatly feared de Campo. They did not dare to order their slaves around too harshly because the slaves might rebel with the help of the maroons. When the Spanish attacked the maroons, de Campo and his followers defeated the Spanish. Then the maroons burned the Spaniards' sugar mills.**

**Eventually the Spaniards captured de Campo. He pleaded to be spared and offered to lead the fight against the maroons. The Spanish accepted the offer. With de Campo's help, the Spanish brought the maroons under control, and slavery in Hispaniola grew. In this section, you will read how slave labor expanded and threatened the freedom of Native Americans and Africans.**

Colonial troops searched for communities of maroons to destroy them.

### 1 The Origins of American Slavery

By the 1600s, **slavery,** the practice of holding a person in bondage for labor, was firmly established in the Americas. But slavery was not new. Its roots went back to the world's ancient civilizations.

Slavery took many different forms throughout history. In some societies, slaves were mainly domestic servants in wealthy households. Some slaves also labored in mines and fields.

People were often enslaved when they were captured in battle or sold to pay off debts. Some slaves were treated with respect. Some were allowed to marry and own property. The children of many slaves were allowed to go free.

Slavery began to change, however, with the rise of sugar plantations. Europeans had used slaves to grow sugar in the eastern Mediterranean since the 1100s. Then, in the 1400s and 1500s, Portugal and Spain set up sugar plantations on islands in the eastern Atlantic. To work these plantations, they used African slaves bought from traders in Africa.



## RECOMMENDED RESOURCES

**In-Depth Resources: Unit 1**
- Guided Reading, p. 29
- Building Vocabulary, p. 30
- Primary Source: from *The Interesting Narrative of the Life of Olaudah Equiano,* p. 35
- Reteaching Activity, p. 42

**Reading Study Guide** (Spanish and English), pp. 23–24

**Formal Assessment**
- Section Quiz, p. 37

**Alternative Assessment**
- Rubrics, 1.3
- Rubrics, 2.3

**Access for Students Acquiring English/ESL**
- Guided Reading, p. 12

**Technology Resources**

**Electronic Teacher Tools with Test Maker**

**ClassZone**
www.mcdougallittell.com

When the Spanish and Portuguese founded their colonies in the Americas, they brought the plantation system with them. At first they tried to enslave Native Americans to work in the fields and mines. But the Native Americans quickly died from overwork and disease. In some cases, they rebelled with the help of local allies.

The Spaniards then looked to other sources of slave labor, including Spanish slaves, black Christian slaves, and Asian slaves. But there was not enough of any of these groups to meet demand.

*Reading* **History**
**A. Drawing Conclusions** Why did colonists decide that African slaves were more useful than Native American slaves?
A. Answer Africans survived longer and seemed to work better than Native Americans. They also were cut off from their homelands and might be easier to control than Native Americans or Europeans.

Finally, the Spanish and Portuguese enslaved Africans to provide labor. They enslaved Africans for four basic reasons. First, Africans were immune to most European diseases. Second, Africans had no friends or family in the Americas to help them resist or escape enslavement. Third, enslaved Africans provided a permanent source of cheap labor. Even their children could be held in bondage. Fourth, many Africans had worked on farms in their native lands.

## 2 The Slave Trade

The slave trade grew slowly at first. In 1509, the Spanish governor of Hispaniola, Diego Colón—Columbus's son—wrote to King Ferdinand to complain about a labor shortage on the island. In response, the king sent 50 African slaves to Hispaniola. The slave trade increased with the demand for slaves to work in the colonies. Eventually the colonies came to depend on slave labor. As one Spanish official in Peru wrote, "The black slave is the basis of the *hacienda* and the source of all wealth which this realm produces."

European slave traders carried out the shipment of Africans to the Americas. The rulers of West African kingdoms participated in the trade, too. On the coast of Africa, local kings gathered captives from inland. The local kings then traded these captives for European goods, such as textiles, ironware, wine, and guns.

This trade made the coastal kingdoms rich while weakening inland African societies. In 1526, King Afonso, a West African ruler, protested against the slave trade in a letter to Portugal's king. Afonso wrote, "Everyday these [slave] merchants take our people. . . . So great is this corruption and evil that our country is becoming completely depopulated."

**Vocabulary**
**depopulated:** to lose population

CONNECTIONS TO MATH

### Slaves Imported to the Americas, *1493–1810*

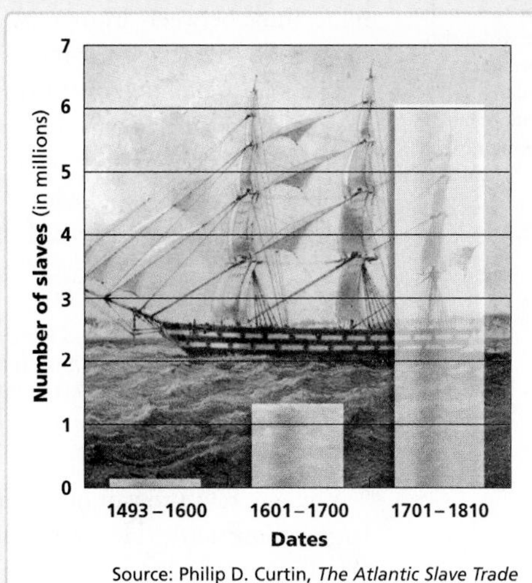


Source: Philip D. Curtin, *The Atlantic Slave Trade*

SKILLBUILDER **Interpreting Graphs**
1. *About how many slaves were imported to the Americas between 1493 and 1810?*
2. *Why do you think the numbers increased?*

Skillbuilder Answers
1. about 7.5 million
2. Possible Response As colonial plantations grew, Europeans needed many people to work on them. So they imported increasing numbers of slaves from Africa.



### MORE ABOUT . . .

**Diseases and History**

Africans and Europeans had developed resistance to many of the same diseases—such as measles, chickenpox, and influenza—because of the long history of contact between Europe and Africa. Native Americans had little resistance or immunity to these diseases.

In addition, Africans had immunities to many diseases that proved deadly to Europeans. For example, while many African adults had some immunity to malaria, European adults exposed to the disease for the first time suffered mortality rates as high as 50 percent.

### INSTRUCT: OBJECTIVE 2

**The Slave Trade**

Key Questions
- Why did the slave trade increase between 1500 and 1800?
- What groups participated in the slave trade?
- How did the slave trade affect African societies?

### HISTORY FROM VISUALS

**Interpreting Graphs** Point out that the number of slaves increased sharply in the 1600s and 1700s. Ask students to make inferences about changes in the Americas that might cause such a huge rise in the number of Africans enslaved in the colonies.

**Possible Response** More Europeans were settling in the Americas, developing more and larger plantations that relied on slave labor.

**Extension** Ask students what problems might confront a historian trying to calculate the number of Africans sent as slaves to the Americas.

### ACTIVITY OPTIONS

### MULTIPLE LEARNING STYLES: LOGICAL-MATHEMATICAL

BLOCK SCHEDULING

**CREATING GRAPHS**

**Class Time** 30 minutes

**Task** Graphing data about the slave trade

**Purpose** To work with data showing the destinations of enslaved Americans

**Supplies Needed** None

**Activity** Write the following on the board: *THE ATLANTIC SLAVE TRADE, 1451–1600.* Brazil: 18% of total imports; Spanish America: 27%; Europe and other: 55%.

Write another heading, *THE ATLANTIC SLAVE TRADE, 1601–1700,* followed by these percentages: Brazil: 41% of total imports; Caribbean: 35%; Spanish America, 22%; Europe: 2%. Ask students to make two pie graphs showing the percentages for the two periods. Ask students to compare the pie graphs and describe two ways the slave trade changed over time. Then ask if they can suggest reasons for the changes.

## MORE ABOUT . . .

**The Middle Passage**

Estimates of death rates among Africans on the slave ships have varied widely. Some recent estimates range from 10 percent to more than 30 percent, often depending on the time of year and the length of voyage. Diseases, which spread rapidly in the squalid cargo holds, killed most. Storms, shipwrecks, and disease also threatened both the Africans and the captains and crews of the slave ships, and many perished at sea. Of course, the Europeans took the risks voluntarily, for the most part, unlike the enslaved Africans.

## INSTRUCT: OBJECTIVE 3

**The Middle Passage**

Key Questions

- How many Africans were enslaved and shipped to the Americas?
- Why was their voyage called the middle passage?
- What conditions prevailed on slave ships?

## MORE ABOUT . . .

**Olaudah Equiano**

Equiano's ship took him to Barbados. There he saw Africans who spoke many languages. He saw his first horse and his first two-story building. Equiano was sent to a plantation in Virginia, where he worked by himself clearing weeds and rocks from the fields. He suffered greatly from loneliness: there was no one with whom he could speak. Soon he was purchased by a sea captain as a present for London cousins. Equiano eventually became a sailor and learned to read and write English. He was able to purchase his own freedom when he was 21 years old. When he was 44, he published his autobiography.

 **In-Depth Resources: Unit 1**

- Primary Source: from *The Interesting Narrative of the Life of Olaudah Equiano*, p. 35

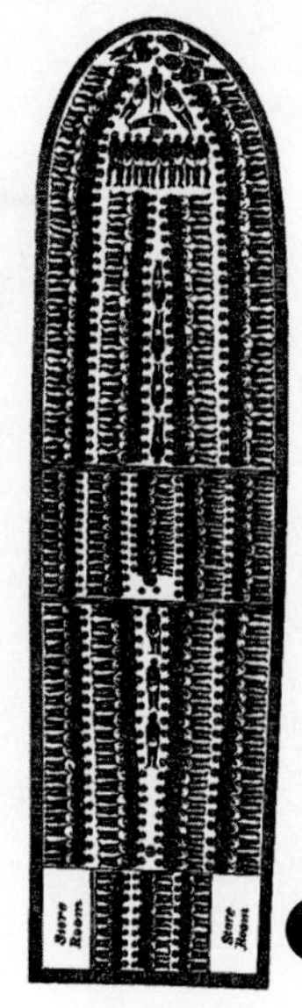

**The diagram above shows how slave traders packed enslaved Africans onto slave ships for the middle passage. A British naval officer painted the picture on the right, which also shows the crowded conditions on slave ships.**

## 3 The Middle Passage

Afonso's protest did not stop the forced removal of people from Africa. This removal has become known as the **African Diaspora.** Before the slave trade ended in the late 1800s, approximately 12 million Africans had been enslaved and shipped to the Western Hemisphere. Of these, perhaps two million died during the voyage.

**Vocabulary**
**diaspora:** the scattering of people outside their homeland

The voyage from Africa to the Americas was called the **middle passage.** The voyage was given this name because it was the middle leg of the triangular trade. The triangular trade refers to the movement of trade ships between Europe, Africa, and the Americas. You will learn more about the triangular trade in Chapter 4.

Olaudah Equiano (oh•LOW•duh EHK•wee•AHN•oh) was one of these kidnapped Africans. He made this journey in the 1700s. He was about 11 years old when he was taken from his home and sold into slavery. Later, after he bought his freedom, he wrote his life story and told what the middle passage was like.

*A VOICE FROM THE PAST*

> The first object which saluted my eyes when I arrived on the coast, was the sea, and a slave ship . . . waiting for its cargo. These filled me with astonishment, which was soon converted into terror, when I was carried on board.
>
> **Olaudah Equiano,** quoted in *Great Slave Narratives*

**B. Possible Response** The slave traders did not care about the captives. Their goal was to sell as many captives as they could to slave owners.

Equiano saw a row of men shackled together in chains. He also saw a large boiling kettle. He feared that he was going to be cooked and eaten "by those white men with horrible looks, red faces, and long hair."

The scene on the slave deck below was even worse. Several hundred slaves were crammed into a space so small that there was not even enough room to stand up. Foul smells and disease, along with the shrieks and groans of the dying, made the middle passage a terrifying experience. The captives who did not die faced new horrors in the Americas.

*Reading* **History**
**B. Making Inferences** Why would slave traders pack so many captives onto slave ships?



## ACTIVITY OPTIONS

### INDIVIDUAL NEEDS: GIFTED AND TALENTED

**AFRICAN DIASPORA**

**Class Time** Two class periods

**Task** Finding primary source accounts of the African Diaspora

**Purpose** To gain an understanding of the African Diaspora from personal accounts

**Supplies Needed**

- Reference materials and primary sources on the African Diaspora
- Internet access for additional information

**Activity** Have students use reference materials and on-line resources to find additional background material about the African Diaspora. Encourage them to find personal accounts of the experience in primary source materials. Students may want to locate a copy of *Great Slave Narratives* and read quotes from other slaves. Then have students read aloud some of the narratives that they found. Have them discuss their similarities.

## 4 Slavery in the Americas

Once the enslaved Africans arrived in the colonies, they were sold at auction. Some were taken to large homes where they worked as servants. Most were forced to do hard labor in *haciendas* or mines. They were also fed and housed poorly.

Many slaves resisted slavery by running away. Across Peru and New Spain, maroons formed communities, often with Native Americans. Sometimes enslaved Africans rebelled. To prevent rebellion, the Spanish government passed **slave codes,** laws to regulate the treatment of slaves. Some of these laws tried to soften the harsh conditions of slavery, but most were designed to punish slaves and keep them in bondage.

*Reading* **History**
**C. Analyzing Causes** What could have caused slave traders to treat other humans with such cruelty?
**C. Possible Response** They saw the slaves as goods that had to be kept alive but little more. Over time, racism played an important role in maintaining this attitude.

Over time, Europeans came to associate slavery with black Africans. To many Europeans, dark skin color became a sign of inferiority. Slavery, which developed to provide a labor force, led to racism. **Racism** is the belief that some people are inferior because of their race.

The slave trade lasted for nearly 400 years, from the early 1500s to the mid-1800s. This contact between Africa and the Americas also formed part of the Columbian Exchange that you read about in Section 3. Africans brought to the Americas a vast knowledge about farming and animals. At the same time, American crops such as sweet potatoes, peanuts, and chilies made their way to Africa.

Enslaved Africans also brought with them a strong artistic heritage of dance, music, and storytelling. The slave trade brought together people from different parts of Africa with different cultural traditions. The experience of slavery helped create a common African-based culture in the Americas. By the 1700s, all the American colonies of European countries had African slaves. As you will read in the next chapter, African culture would be one of the forces that shaped life in the American colonies.

### Section 4 Assessment

**1. Terms & Names**

**Identify:**
- slavery
- African Diaspora
- middle passage
- slave codes
- racism

**2. Taking Notes**

Use a diagram like the one below to compare the experience of Native Americans and Africans under slavery.

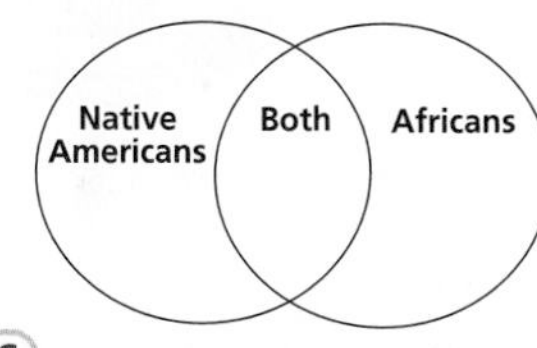


**3. Main Ideas**

a. When did slavery begin?

b. Why did Europeans bring Africans to the Americas?

c. What are three examples of bad conditions faced by enslaved Africans?

**4. Critical Thinking**

**Recognizing Effects** What were the long-term effects of slavery in the Americas?

**THINK ABOUT**
- the economy in the Americas
- the African Diaspora
- cultural diversity in the Americas

**ACTIVITY OPTIONS**

**ART**
**MATH**

Research some aspect of the slave trade, such as the middle passage or the number of people enslaved. Paint a **picture** or draw a **graph** to show what you learned.





### INSTRUCT: OBJECTIVE 

**Slavery in the Americas**

Key Questions
- What happened to enslaved Africans once they arrived in the colonies?
- How did slavery influence racial attitudes among Europeans?
- What part did the slave trade play in the Columbian Exchange, and how did Africans influence culture in the Americas?

### MORE ABOUT . . .

**The Columbian Exchange**

Some foods first grown in the Americas made a roundtrip from the Americas to Africa and back to the Americas. For example, the peanut first grew in South America. It was introduced to Africa by Spanish and Portuguese explorers and traders and then brought to the present-day United States by enslaved Africans. Tomatoes, which first grew in Central America, reached Italy in the 16th century. Most likely, they were a yellow or orange variety. Later, Italians brought red tomatoes to America.

## ASSESS & RETEACH

**Setting the Stage** Have students complete the section of the chart on the Origins of Slavery.

 **Formal Assessment**
- Section Quiz, p. 37

 **Critical Thinking Transparency CT4**
- Setting the Stage

**RETEACHING ACTIVITY**

Have students create an outline of information in the section with the section's Main Idea (on p. 76) as the topic sentence. The outline should include information about the origin and development of slavery in the Americas.

 **In-Depth Resources: Unit 1**
- Reteaching Activity, p. 42

### Section  Assessment

**1. Terms & Names**

**slavery,** p. 76
**African Diaspora,** p. 78
**middle passage,** p. 78
**slave codes,** p. 79
**racism,** p. 79

**2. Taking Notes**

Native Americans—could run away because friends and family were nearby; died of disease, overwork
Both—faced hard work and abuse; became victims of racism; escapees formed maroon communities
Africans—had less opportunity to escape; immune to many European diseases

**3. Main Ideas**

**a.** in ancient times **b.** Europeans needed labor. Enslaved Africans were immune to European diseases and had experience doing the work Europeans wanted done. **c.** The middle passage was a horrific voyage. Work conditions were hard. Slaves were oppressed by owners.

**4. Critical Thinking**

As workers, slaves created great wealth in the Americas. Africans brought parts of their cultures to the Americas.

**ACTIVITY OPTIONS**

 **Alternative Assessment**
- Rubrics for a picture, 1.3
- Rubrics for a graph, 2.3

## TERMS & NAMES

1. **mercantilism,** p. 61
2. **Hernando Cortés,** p. 63
3. **Montezuma,** p. 63
4. **Spanish Armada,** p. 69
5. **New France,** p. 70
6. ***encomienda,*** p. 72
7. **Columbian Exchange,** p. 74
8. **slavery,** p. 76
9. **African Diaspora,** p. 78
10. **middle passage,** p. 78

## REVIEW QUESTIONS

**Possible Responses**

1. to spread Christianity, to increase national power, to win fame and riches for individual explorers
2. Two Spanish conquistadors—Cortés conquered the Aztecs and Pizarro conquered the Incas.
3. Possible responses: Spain had better weapons than Native Americans. Diseases killed millions of Native Americans. Spain made allies with some Native Americans. The Spanish acted brutally toward Native Americans.
4. a northwest route from Europe to Asia that explorers never found
5. to conquer England and return it to Catholicism
6. the fur trade
7. Native Americans died in great numbers from disease and overwork. They were enslaved and badly treated. Some converted to Christianity. Some learned to read.
8. Possible response: It introduced new foods and goods to Europe. It greatly improved European diets, helping to increase European population.
9. They needed workers to make their colonies productive. Slaves provided cheap labor.
10. European traders took goods to the coast of Africa, where African slave traders supplied captives from the African interior. These slaves were taken to the Americas and sold there.

# Chapter 2 ASSESSMENT

## TERMS & NAMES

Briefly explain the importance of each of the following.

1. mercantilism
2. Hernando Cortés
3. Montezuma
4. Spanish Armada
5. New France
6. *encomienda*
7. Columbian Exchange
8. slavery
9. African Diaspora
10. middle passage

## REVIEW QUESTIONS

**Spain Claims an Empire (pages 61–66)**

1. What were three reasons for the European voyages of exploration in the 1400s and 1500s?
2. Who conquered the Aztecs and Incas?
3. What three reasons explain Spain's success in building an empire in the Americas?

**European Competition in North America (pages 67–70)**

4. What was the Northwest Passage?
5. Why did the Spanish Armada attack England?
6. What did the French and Dutch colonists trade?

**The Spanish and Native Americans (pages 71–75)**

7. How did Spanish rule affect Native Americans?
8. How did the Columbian Exchange affect Europe?

**Beginnings of Slavery in the Americas (pages 76–79)**

9. Why did the Spanish and Portuguese use slave labor in their colonies?
10. How did the slave trade work?

## CRITICAL THINKING

**1. USING YOUR NOTES**

| Event/Concept | Notes |
|---|---|
| Exploration | |
| Establishing Colonies | |
| European Competition | |
| Columbian Exchange | |
| Origins of Slavery | |

Using your completed chart, answer the questions below.

a. What causes did European competition and exploration have in common?

b. How did the establishment of colonies in the Americas lead to slavery?

c. Which concept in the chart contributed most to the Columbian Exchange?

**2. ANALYZING LEADERSHIP**

Think about the explorers and *conquistadors* discussed in this chapter. What qualities did they possess that made them successful in their efforts?

**3. THEME: IMMIGRATION AND MIGRATION**

What were the causes and effects of the migration of Europeans and Africans to the Americas?

**4. APPLYING CITIZENSHIP SKILLS**

What kind of values did Bartolomé de Las Casas demonstrate in his actions? How effective was he in improving his society?

**Interact *with* History**

Have your answers about whether or not you would join a voyage of exploration changed after reading the chapter? Explain.

## VISUAL SUMMARY

### European Exploration of the Americas

Causes

National Competition

Desire for Wealth

Spread Christianity

European Exploration of the Americas

Effects

Destruction of Aztec and Incan Empires

The Columbian Exchange

European Colonies in the Americas

Slavery

80 CHAPTER 2

## CRITICAL THINKING

**Possible Responses**

**1. USING YOUR NOTES** **a.** The desire for wealth and power motivated both. **b.** Europeans used slave labor on sugar plantations. **c.** Students should give evidence to support their answer.

**2. ANALYZING LEADERSHIP** strength, determination, ambition; sometimes religious devotion; sometimes brutality

**3. THEME: IMMIGRATION AND MIGRATION** Europeans migrated in search of wealth and power. Most Africans were forcibly brought to the Americas.

**4. APPLYING CITIZENSHIP SKILLS** Las Casas exhibited courage and compassion, but he neglected to help enslaved Africans. He got some laws passed to protect Native Americans, but the laws were not very effective.

**Interact *with* History** Students' decisions will vary but should be supported by evidence.

## HISTORY SKILLS

### 1. INTERPRETING CHARTS

**Slaves Imported to the Americas** *(in thousands)* 1601–1810

| REGION/COUNTRY | 1601–1700 | 1701–1810 |
|---|---|---|
| British N. America | * | 348 |
| British Caribbean | 263.7 | 1,401.3 |
| French Caribbean | 155.8 | 1,348.4 |
| Spanish America | 292.5 | 578.6 |
| Dutch Caribbean | 40 | 460 |
| Danish Caribbean | 4 | 24 |
| Brazil (Portugal) | 560 | 1,891.4 |

*=less than 1,000

Source: Philip D. Curtin, *The Atlantic Slave Trade*

**Basic Chart Elements**

a. What is the subject of the chart?

b. How many years are covered in each column?

**Interpreting the Chart**

c. Which European nation imported the most slaves to the Americas?

d. Which region imported less than 1,000 slaves before 1700?

### 2. INTERPRETING PRIMARY SOURCES

Bernal Díaz del Castillo was a *conquistador* who accompanied Cortés during the conquest of Mexico. Díaz described what he saw when Cortés and Montezuma met. Read the passage. Then answer the questions.

> On our arrival we entered the large court, where the great Montezuma was awaiting our Captain [Cortés]. Taking him by the hand, the prince led him to his apartment in the hall where he was to lodge, which was very richly furnished. . . . Montezuma had ready for him a very rich necklace, made of golden crabs, a marvelous piece of work, which he hung round Cortés's neck. His captains were greatly astonished at this sign of honour.
>
> **Bernal Díaz del Castillo,** from *The Conquest of New Spain*

a. What can you tell about Montezuma from this passage?

b. How would you describe the relationship between Montezuma and Cortés?

## ALTERNATIVE ASSESSMENT

### 1. INTERDISCIPLINARY ACTIVITY: Language Arts

**Writing a News Report** Research an event in the conquest of the Americas, such as *La Noche Triste* or the death of Atahualpa. Write a news report about the event that explains what happened and who was involved. You should also explain when, where, why, and how the event occurred.

### 2. COOPERATIVE LEARNING ACTIVITY

**Creating a Diorama** With a group of classmates, research the communities of Spanish America in the 1600s. Then create a diorama of one of those settlements, including a mission, a *hacienda,* roads, and mines or sugar mills. Use elements such as drawings, maps, and written text to show significant features of life there. Display your diorama and discuss it in class.

### 3. TECHNOLOGY ACTIVITY

**Making a Class Presentation** The Columbian Exchange refers to the movement of plants and animals around the world as a result of exploration. Today, species of plants and animals, such as killer bees, continue to move across the planet. Using the library or the Internet, find diaries and news articles about the effects of this continued movement of plants and animals.

**Visit www.mcdougallittell.com to learn more about the migration of plants and animals.**

Create a class presentation about the movement of plants and animals around the world, using the suggestions below.

- Choose a specific species of plant or animal. Use a map or globe to show where that species has moved in recent years.
- Choose one specific place, and list any species that are new to the area as well as their effects on the ecology.

### 4. HISTORY PORTFOLIO

**Option 1** Review your section and chapter assessment activities. Select one that you think was your best work. Then revise your work based on the comments of your teacher or classmates and add your work to your portfolio.

**Option 2** Review the questions that you wrote for What Do You Want to Know? on page 60. Then write a short report that explains the answers to your questions. If any questions were not answered, do research to answer them. Add your answers to your history portfolio.



## ALTERNATIVE ASSESSMENT

1. INTERDISCIPLINARY ACTIVITY: **Language Arts**
   **News reports should**
   - use a journalistic style.
   - present information in an unbiased way.
   - cover the topic adequately.
   - have a headline and portray the historical events accurately.
   - use correct grammar, spelling, and punctuation.

2. COOPERATIVE LEARNING ACTIVITY
   **Dioramas should**
   - accurately represent the Spanish-American community in 2- or 3-dimensional manner clear to the viewers.
   - exhibit creativity.
   - demonstrate grade-level artistic skill.

3. TECHNOLOGY ACTIVITY
   **Class presentations should**
   - clearly demonstrate an understanding of the concept of movement of plants and animals.
   - have adequate delivery and establish rapport with the audience.
   - show proficiency in the use of technology.

4. HISTORY PORTFOLIO

**Option 1 Revised section or chapter assessment activities should**
- address teacher and peer responses to the selected work.
- solve problems present in the first versions of the work.

**Option 2 Short reports should**
- answer questions about the early exploration and colonization of the Americas.
- use evidence to develop and support ideas.
- cite sources of information.
- use standard grammar, spelling, sentence structure, and punctuation.

**Critical Thinking Transparency CT6**
- Visual Summary

**Formal Assessment**
- Chapter Test, Forms A and B, pp. 38–45

## HISTORY SKILLS

**Possible Responses**

1. INTERPRETING CHARTS
   **Basic Chart Elements**
   **a.** slave imports
   **b.** 100 years in left column, 110 years in right column
   **Interpreting the Chart**
   **c.** Portugal
   **d.** British North America

2. INTERPRETING PRIMARY SOURCES
   **a.** Montezuma was wealthy and powerful. He gave Cortés a valuable gift.
   **b.** Montezuma was trying to get on Cortés's good side.

CHAPTER 3 PLANNING GUIDE

# The English Establish 13 Colonies 1585–1732

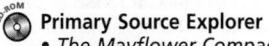

| | CHAPTER OVERVIEW | COPYMASTERS | TECHNOLOGY |
|---|---|---|---|
| **CHAPTER RESOURCES** | The chapter discusses the English colonization of North America and the leading individuals who took part in settling the colonies. It also differentiates among the three major areas of settlement on the eastern seaboard. | **In-Depth Resources: Unit 1**<br>• Tracing Themes: Impact of the Individual, p. 45<br>• Building Vocabulary, p. 49<br>**Interdisciplinary Projects,** pp. 13–18 | **Primary Source Explorer**<br>**Electronic Teacher Tools**<br>**Power Presentations CD-ROM**<br>**Chapter Summaries on CD** (English and Spanish)<br>**America's Music CD** |
| | **KEY IDEAS** | | |
| **SECTION 1**<br>**Early Colonies Have Mixed Success**<br>**pp. 85–91** | • England finances colonies through joint stock companies.<br>• Jamestown, founded in 1607, survives under John Smith's leadership.<br>• Bacon's Rebellion forces England to limit the powers of royal governors. | **In-Depth Resources: Unit 1**<br>• Setting the Stage, p. 44<br>• Guided Reading, p. 46<br>• Geography Application: Roanoke Colony, pp. 51–52<br>• Primary Source, p. 53<br>• Reteaching Activity, p. 58<br>**America's History Makers**<br>• Pocahontas, pp. 11–12 | **Warm-Up Transparency WT3**<br>**Humanities Transparency HT5**<br>• John Smith Takes a Prisoner, 1624<br>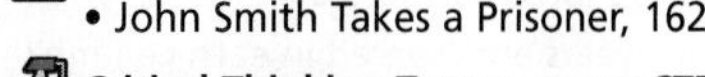<br>**Critical Thinking Transparency CT7**<br>• Setting the Stage<br>**ClassZone:** www.mcdougallittell.com |
| **SECTION 2**<br>**New England Colonies**<br>**pp. 92–99** | • Pilgrims and Puritans found New England colonies.<br>• The New England Way sets standards of godliness and hard work, but also provokes challenges to its strictness.<br>• In King Philip's War, Native Americans resist English expansion in New England. | **In-Depth Resources: Unit 1**<br>• Setting the Stage, p. 44<br>• Guided Reading, p. 47<br>• Skillbuilder Practice, p. 50<br>• Literature Selection, pp. 55–57<br>• Reteaching Activity, p. 59<br>**America's History Makers**<br>• William Bradford, pp. 13–14<br>**Economics in History**<br>• Farming in the English Colonies, p. 3 | **Warm-Up Transparency WT3**<br>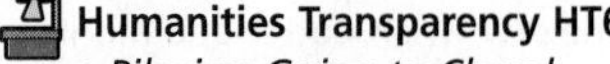<br>**Humanities Transparency HT6**<br>• *Pilgrims Going to Church* by George Henry Boughton<br>**Critical Thinking Transparency CT8**<br>• Cause and Effect: King Philip's War, 1675–1676<br>**Primary Source Explorer**<br>• *The Mayflower Compact*<br>• *The Fundamental Orders of Connecticut* |
| **SECTION 3**<br>**Founding the Middle and Southern Colonies**<br>**pp. 100–103** | • England takes over New York from the Dutch.<br>• William Penn founds Pennsylvania as a colony based on religious freedom and equality.<br>• Southern colonies thrive on economies of warm-weather crops. | **In-Depth Resources: Unit 1**<br>• Setting the Stage, p. 44<br>• Guided Reading, p. 48<br>• Primary Source, p. 54<br>• Reteaching Activity, p. 60<br>**Why It Matters Now**<br>• British Connections Today, pp. 5–6<br>**Outline Map Activities**<br>• The 13 Colonies, pp. 5–6 | **Warm-Up Transparency WT3**<br>**Geography Transparency GT3**<br>• European Colonies, 1650<br>**Critical Thinking Transparency CT9**<br>• Visual Summary<br>**ClassZone:** www.mcdougallittell.com |

Pupil's Edition
Copymaster

Overhead Transparency
Audio Library

CD-ROM

Internet

## ASSESSMENT

**Chapter Assessment,** pp. 104–105

**Formal Assessment**
- Chapter Tests, Forms A and B, pp. 51–58

**Alternative Assessment Book**

**Electronic Teacher Tools with Test Maker**

---

**Section Assessment,** p. 89

**Formal Assessment**
- Section Quiz, p. 48

**Alternative Assessment Book**
- Rubrics for a poster, 1.1
- Rubrics for an advertisement, 4.9

**Electronic Teacher Tools with Test Maker**

---

**Section Assessment,** p. 97

**Formal Assessment**
- Section Quiz, p. 49

**Alternative Assessment Book**
- Rubrics for an article, 4.5
- Rubrics for an oral history, 3.6

**Electronic Teacher Tools with Test Maker**

---

**Section Assessment,** p. 103

**Formal Assessment**
- Section Quiz, p. 50

**Alternative Assessment Book**
- Rubrics for an article, 4.5
- Rubrics for a television report, 5.3

**Electronic Teacher Tools with Test Maker**

## CUSTOMIZING FOR INDIVIDUAL NEEDS

### Students Acquiring English/ESL

**Reading Study Guide** (English and Spanish), pp. 27–34

**Access for Students Acquiring English/ESL: Spanish Translations,** pp. 16–21

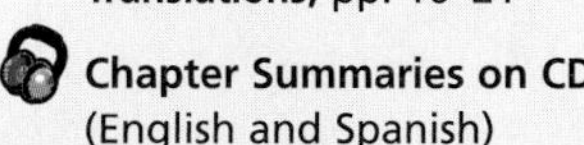
**Chapter Summaries on CD** (English and Spanish)

### Less Proficient Readers

**Reading Study Guide** (English and Spanish), pp. 27–34

**Chapter Summaries on CD** (English and Spanish)

### Gifted and Talented Students

**In-Depth Resources: Unit 1**
- Enrichment Activity, p. 61

**America's History Makers**
- Pocahontas, pp. 11–12
- William Bradford, pp. 13–14

## CROSS-CURRICULAR CONNECTIONS

### Science/Math

Woods, Geraldine. ***Science of the Early Americans.*** New York: Franklin Watts, 1999.

### Popular Culture

Erdosh, George. ***Food and Recipes of the Pilgrims.*** Powerkids Press, 1998.

Hale, Anna W. ***The Mayflower People: Triumphs and Tragedies.*** Niwot, CO: Rinehart, 1995. Colorful coverage of the ocean voyage filled with human detail; useful bibliography as well.

### Interdisciplinary Projects, pp. 13–18

- Math: Dimensions of the *Mayflower*
- Science: Cultivating Plants
- Language Arts: Advertising for Colonists
- Home Economics: Plan a Thanksgiving Menu

### Language Arts/Literature

Harragh, Madge. ***My Brother, My Enemy.*** New York: Simon & Schuster, 1997. When 14-year-old Robert Bradford finds himself caught up in Bacon's Rebellion, his loyalties and beliefs are tested to the limit.

Jacobs, Paul S. ***James Printer: A Novel of King Philip's War.*** New York: Scholastic, 1997. The story of a true-life figure, Nipmuck Indian James Printer, showing the fears, tragedies, and courage of both sides in the war.

### McDougal Littell Literature Connections

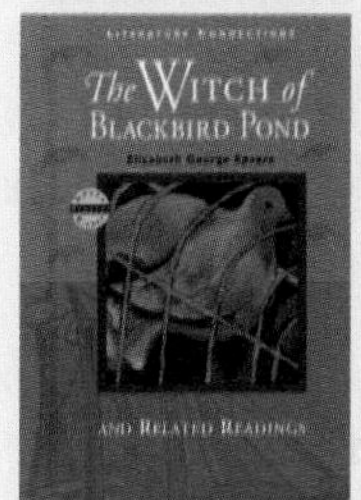


Elizabeth Speare

***The Witch of Blackbird Pond***

Unconventional Kit Tyler does not fit well with the society of Puritan Connecticut and finds herself accused of witchcraft.

## ENRICHMENT ACTIVITIES

**Pupil's Edition, pp. 82–105**
**Interact with History,** p. 83
**Interdisciplinary Challenge,** pp. 90–91
**Interactive Primary Sources,** pp. 98–99

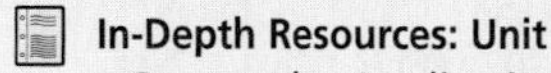
**In-Depth Resources: Unit 1**
- Geography Application: Roanoke Colony, pp. 51–52
- Primary Source, p. 53
- Primary Source, p. 54
- Literature Selection, pp. 55–57

**America's History Makers**
- Pocahontas, pp. 11–12
- William Bradford, pp. 13–14

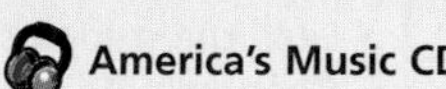
**America's Music CD**

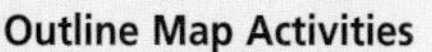
**Outline Map Activities**
- The 13 Colonies, pp. 5–6

**Primary Source Explorer**
- *The Mayflower Compact*
- *The Fundamental Orders of Connecticut*

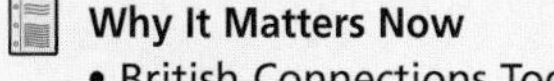
**Why It Matters Now**
- British Connections Today, pp. 5–6

**LESSON PLAN OPTIONS (50-MINUTE PERIOD)** **(TE) = Teacher's Edition (PE) = Pupil's Edition**

| | TEACHER-DIRECTED ACTIVITIES<br>Class Time: 15 minutes | STUDENT-CENTERED ACTIVITIES<br>Class Time: 25 minutes | INDIVIDUAL ACTIVITIES<br>Class Time: 10 minutes |
|---|---|---|---|
| **DAY 1**<br>Introduction<br>pp. 82–84 | **Presentation Options**<br>• Begin with a class discussion of the drawing on p. 82 **(PE)**.<br>• Lead a class discussion on the "What Do You Know?" question in Setting the Stage, p. 84. Then introduce the graphic organizer for the chapter **(PE)**. | **Options for Cooperative Learning**<br>• Have student groups discuss the Interact with History questions, p. 83 **(PE)**.<br>• Have student groups respond to the "What Do You Want to Know?" question in Setting the Stage, p. 84 **(PE)**. | **Head Start on Homework Options**<br>• Have students skim Section 1 Main Idea, Why It Matters Now, Terms & Names, and the main headings, p. 85 **(PE)**.<br>• Have students begin Guided Reading activity and Building Vocabulary sheet. |
| **DAY 2**<br>Section 1<br>pp. 85–91 | **Presentation Options**<br>• Begin with the 5-Minute Warm-Up, p. 85 **(TE)**.<br>• Review the Section 1 Main Idea, Why It Matters Now, and Terms & Names, p. 85 **(PE)**.<br>• Choose 5 key questions for Objectives 1–4 to discuss with the class, pp. 85–88 **(TE)**. | **Options for Cooperative Learning**<br>• Divide students into groups to work on one of the challenges in the Interdisciplinary Challenge, pp. 90–91 **(PE)**.<br>• Have student pairs work together to complete one of the Activity Options in the Section 1 Assessment, p. 89 **(PE)**. | **Head Start on Homework Options**<br>• Have students begin working on Section 1 Assessment, p. 89 **(PE)**.<br>• Have students preview Section 2 Main Idea, Why It Matters Now, Terms & Names, and the main headings, p. 92 **(PE)**. |
| **DAY 3**<br>Section 2<br>pp. 92–99 | **Presentation Options**<br>• Begin with the 5-Minute Warm-Up, p. 92 **(TE)**.<br>• Lead students through Interactive Primary Sources, pp. 98–99 **(TE)**.<br>• Lead the students through the Skillbuilder Mini-Lesson: Using Primary Sources, p. 93 **(TE)**. | **Options for Cooperative Learning**<br>• Divide students into groups and have them complete the Interactive Primary Source A Closer Look questions, pp. 98–99 **(PE)**.<br>• Have student pairs work together to complete one of the Activity Options in the Section 2 Assessment, p. 97 **(PE)**. | **Head Start on Homework Options**<br>• Have students begin working on Section 2 Assessment, p. 97 **(PE)**.<br>• Have students begin working on the Interactive Primary Sources Assessment, p. 99 **(PE)**. |
| **DAY 4**<br>Section 3<br>pp. 100–103 | **Presentation Options**<br>• Begin with the 5-Minute Warm-Up, p. 100 **(TE)**.<br>• Choose 5 key questions for Objectives 1–4 to discuss with the class, pp. 100–103 **(TE)**.<br>• Lead the students through the Geography Skillbuilder, p. 102 **(PE)**. | **Options for Cooperative Learning**<br>• Divide students into groups and have them complete the Interdisciplinary Link, Art/Language Arts, p. 102 **(TE)**.<br>• Have student pairs work together to complete one of the Activity Options in the Section 3 Assessment, p. 103 **(PE)**. | **Head Start on Homework Options**<br>• Have students complete the Setting the Stage graphic organizer for the chapter, p. 84 **(PE)**.<br>• Have students begin working on the Chapter Assessment, pp. 104–105 **(PE)**.<br>• Prepare for Chapter Test<br>**Formal Assessment**, pp. 51–58 |

TEACHER-TESTED ACTIVITY James G. Grimes, Middlesex County Vocational Technical High School, Woodbridge, New Jersey

## WORD BY WORD

**Class Time** One class period

**Task** Writing a short report using assigned names and terms

**Purpose** To demonstrate understanding of key names and terms

**Supplies Needed**
- Dictionary
- Thesaurus

**Activity** Write the following words and names from Section 1 on the chalkboard, or duplicate the list and distribute it to the class: *John Smith, Powhatan, Pocahontas, John Rolfe, John White, Virginia, Jamestown, Sir Walter Raleigh, colony, Native American, persecution, joint stock company, charter, climate, control, "starving time," indentured servant.* Have each student write a short account of the founding of Jamestown using as many of these names and terms as possible. Then assign students to small groups to check the accuracy of their accounts and the correct usage of terms and names.

## BLOCK SCHEDULING — LESSON PLAN OPTIONS (90-MINUTE PERIOD)

### DAY 1

**Interact with History,** p. 83
**Class Time** 20 minutes

Options for pacing and variety:
- **Role-Playing** Have students suppose they are the leaders of the first colonists to arrive at Jamestown. As leaders, they need to write a short speech explaining to the other settlers why they must build a fort. **Class Time** 10 minutes

**Setting the Stage,** p. 84
**Class Time** 20 minutes

Options for pacing and variety:
- **Time Saver** For a homework assignment, have students pick one of the 13 colonies shown on the graphic organizer in Read and Take Notes and make a list of what they already know about this colony and what they would like to know. Have students share their lists with the class. **Class Time** 10 minutes

**Section 1,** pp. 85–91
**Class Time** 50 minutes

Options for pacing and variety:
- **History on Film** Extend students' background knowledge of Jamestown and other early Virginia settlements by viewing *Where America Began: Colonial Williamsburg, Jamestown, Yorktown.* Finley-Holiday. **Class Time** 60 minutes

**Interdisciplinary Challenge,** pp. 90–91
Options for pacing and variety:
- **Peer Evaluation** As each group presents its report to the class on how it solved the civics and economics challenges, have the other students evaluate the presentations using the guidelines in the Activity Wrap-Up. Remind students that criticism should be constructive. **Class Time** 30 minutes

### DAY 2

**Section 2,** pp. 92–99
**Class Time** 45 minutes

Options for pacing and variety:
- **Internet** Extend students' background knowledge of the Pilgrims and the Plymouth Colony by taking a virtual tour of Plimoth Plantation at www.mcdougallittell.com **Class Time** 20 minutes

**Section 3,** pp. 100–103
**Class Time** 45 minutes

Options for pacing and variety:
- **Peer Evaluation** Have student pairs create two Reading History questions for the section and exchange them with another team to be answered. **Class Time** 15 minutes

**Chapter 3 Assessment,** pp. 104–105
**Class Time** 40 minutes

Options for pacing and variety:
- **Time Saver** Use the map "The 13 English Colonies, 1732" on page 102 to summarize the chapter. **Class Time** 10 minutes
- **Peer Competition** Divide the class into small groups. Have each group write three short "Who Am I?" paragraphs describing colony founders listed on the chart on page 104. Have teams compete to see which can provide the founder's name first. Teams can vary the game by writing "Where Am I?" descriptions. **Class Time** 30 minutes

## CHAPTER 3 OBJECTIVE

The student will understand how the first English colonies survived and began to grow, while colonists both learned from and experienced conflict with Native Americans.

# CHAPTER 3 The English Establish 13 Colonies 1585–1732



### HISTORY FROM VISUALS

**Interpreting the Illustration** Ask the students to study the woodcut. Point out the lean-to shelter where the settlers live while building their houses. Also note the location along a river. Have students name any tools they see in the woodcut. Ask students how they can tell that members of several families are helping to build this house. Ask students who these people might be. **Possible Responses** Tools include axes, plane, sledgehammer. The people are newly arrived settlers who are clearing the land. The many adult males in this drawing suggest that this is a community effort.

**Extension** Have the students write one piece of advice they would give the settlers.

Early settlers build the fort at Jamestown.

82

### RECOMMENDED RESOURCES

**BOOKS FOR THE TEACHER**

Hulton, Paul, ed. ***America in Fifteen Eighty-Five: The Complete Drawings of John White.*** Chapel Hill: U. of N.C. Press, 1984. A visual record of Native American life in the early contact period.

Johnson, Thomas, ed. ***Puritans: A Sourcebook.*** New York: Harper, 1965. Many primary sources, some familiar, others surprising.

Noël Hume, Ivor. ***Martin's Hundred.*** New York: Knopf, 1979. Firsthand account of an archaeological dig at the site of an early-17th-century plantation in Virginia.

**SOFTWARE**

***PilgrimQuest & PilgrimQuest II.*** Decision Devel. Corp. Complex simulation of Pilgrim experience from 1620 to 1626. A school version contains lessons and resources.

**VIDEO**

***Colonial Williamsburg.*** Ed. Record Ctr., Inc. Life in colonial Virginia was a considerable contrast to that in colonial Massachusetts.

**INTERNET**

For more about Plimoth Plantation, visit www.mcdougallittell.com

## Interact *with* History

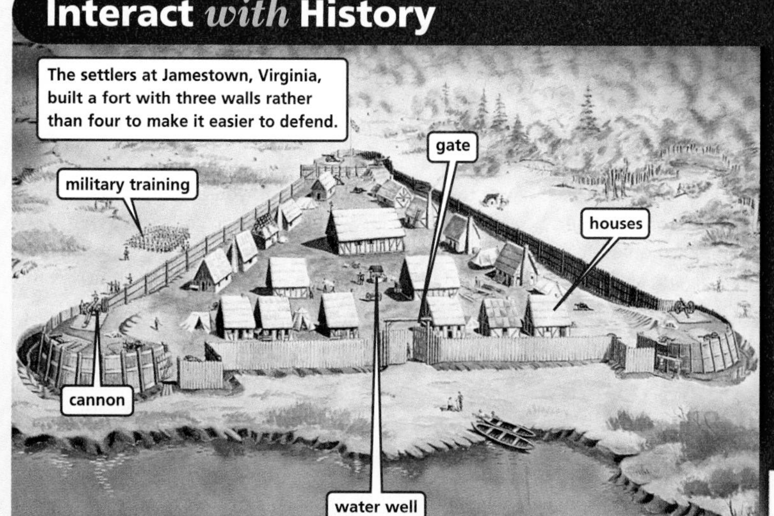

The settlers at Jamestown, Virginia, built a fort with three walls rather than four to make it easier to defend.
gate
military training
houses
cannon
water well

**The year is 1607. You have just sailed across the ocean and arrived in a strange land. Your family has traveled to the eastern coast of North America in search of freedom and prosperity. Your first task in the new land is to decide what you need to do to survive.**

### What Do You Think?

- **What do you need to survive in the wilderness?**
- **This settlement is actually a fort, with an armed force and high fences. What reasons might there be for building a fort?**
- **What kind of settlement would you build?**

# *What dangers would you face as a settler?*

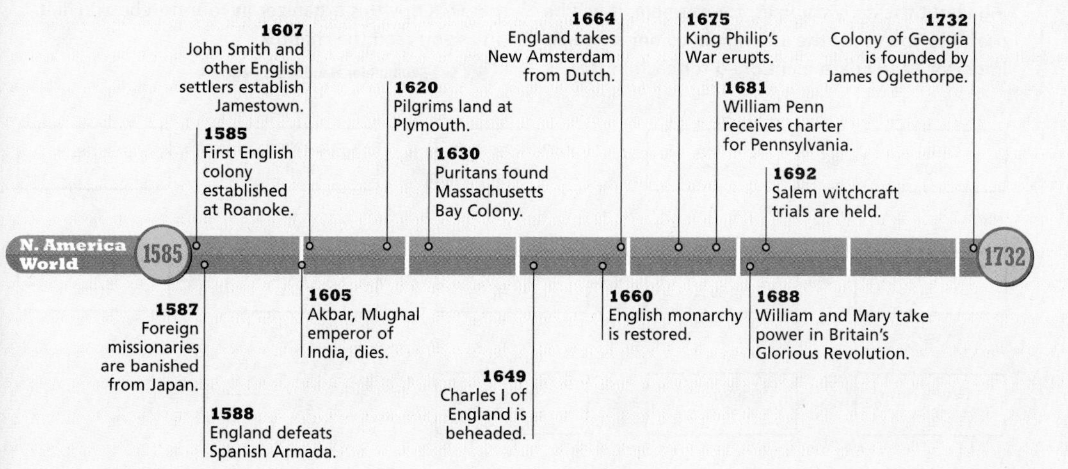




## Interact *with* History

### OBJECTIVES

- To help students identify the first colonists' basic survival needs
- To help students connect with the people and events they will study in this chapter

### What Do You Think?

1. Ask students to list the basic needs of survival: food, clothing, shelter, protection from wild animals and enemies.
2. Have students think about the security needs of the settlers: protection, supplies, weapons, tools, and defense of their families and land against both Native Americans and hostile European nations.
3. Ask students to think about the natural resources they can use to construct and repair their settlement, how they plan to use the surrounding land, and the climate of the area where they will build their settlement.

### *What dangers would you face as a settler?*

Encourage students to think not only about the most obvious challenges of protecting themselves from attacks from animals and other humans but also the dangers of severe weather; of failing to get crops planted, harvested, and preserved; and of illnesses or injuries that cannot be treated with simple remedies. Conflict among settlers and failure to cooperate are also potential dangers.

### MAKING PERSONAL CONNECTIONS

Ask students to think about any experiences they have had while camping or walking in forests or wilderness areas. Have students think about how their attitudes toward the wilderness might differ from those of settlers who planned to live there permanently.

### TIME LINE DISCUSSION

**Point out to students that during the period of English settlement in North America much political activity was occurring in England.**

- Ask the students why settlement activities in North America don't seem to be affected by European activities. **Possible Answers** The events were too far away to impact the colonists, news traveled slowly, and colonists knew little about the events.
- Ask students what event shows that Spain's power in Europe was declining. **Answer** England's defeat of Spanish Armada
- Ask students to name another European group that claimed land in North America in the 1600s. **Answer** the Dutch
- Ask students how many years elapsed between the settlement of the first English colony and the founding of Georgia, the 13th colony. **Answer** 112 years

## BEFORE YOU READ

### Previewing the Theme: Impact of the Individual

Remind students that both new colonies and Native American groups had some good leaders. Ask students to describe traits and skills that help a leader maintain order and get others to cooperate. Have students explain why each of these skills would be important to successful leadership.

Good leaders are often people who are fair but firm, have strong decision-making and planning skills, remain calm under pressure, and can motivate others to cooperate and work hard to reach shared goals.

### What Do You Know?

Most students will be familiar with the Pilgrims, and some may also have visited re-creations of colonial settlements such as Jamestown or Plimoth Plantation. The names of colonial figures such as John Smith, Pocahontas, Peter Stuyvesant, and William Penn may also be familiar. Explore students' associations with these names.

 **In-Depth Resources: Unit 1**
- Tracing Themes: Impact of the Individual, p. 45

## READ AND TAKE NOTES

### Reading Strategy: Sequencing Events

Explain to students that sequencing events, or putting them in the order in which they occurred, will make them easier to remember. Sequencing also makes it easier to understand the relationships among events. Using a sequence chart such as the one provided will allow students to see at a glance when each of the original colonies was formed.

 **In-Depth Resources: Unit 1**
- Setting the Stage, p. 44

 **Critical Thinking Transparency CT7**
- Setting the Stage

# Chapter 3 SETTING THE STAGE

## BEFORE YOU READ

### Previewing the Theme Impact of the Individual

Beginning in 1585, English settlers started colonies along the eastern coast of North America. This chapter explains how the determination of a few leaders led to new colonies. It also explains how the colonies survived, gained more diverse settlers, and began to drive Native Americans (shown in the map below) off the land.

### What Do You Know?

What do you already know about the American colonies? What sort of person might choose to leave his or her native country and cross the ocean to settle in a new land?

**THINK ABOUT**
- what you've learned about American settlers from movies, television, historical fiction, or science fiction about space travel
- opportunities and challenges offered in a new land

### What Do You Want to Know?

What questions do you have about the Europeans who settled in North America? about those who were already here? Record your questions in your notebook before you read this chapter.

## READ AND TAKE NOTES

**Reading Strategy: Sequencing Events**
Sequencing means putting events in order. In learning about the early colonies, for example, it will be useful to you to list the 13 original colonies and an important early date mentioned for each in the chapter. You might record the name and a date for each colony in a graphic organizer such as the one below. Copy this organizer in your notebook. Fill it in as you read the chapter.

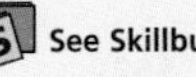 See Skillbuilder Handbook, page R4.

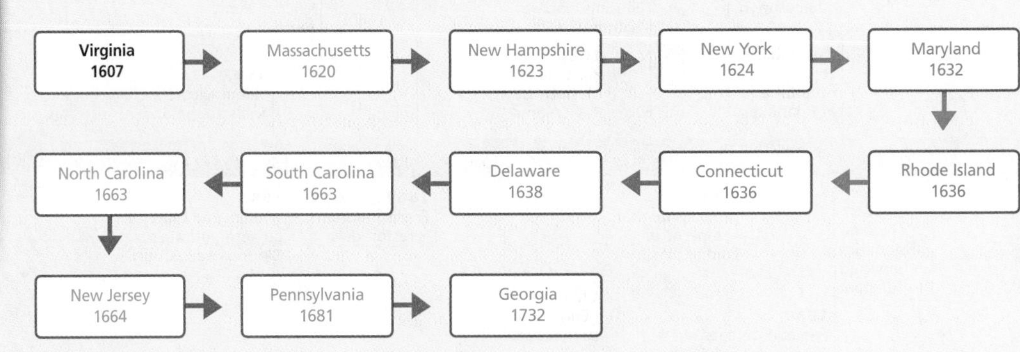


84 CHAPTER 3

## TEACHING STRATEGY

### READING THE CHAPTER

This is a chronological chapter focusing on the successes and failures of the early colonies. Ask students to look for reasons why some colonies failed while others survived and grew. Encourage them to note the influence of religious groups such as the Pilgrims, the Puritans, and the Quakers on colonial development.

### ALTERNATIVE ASSESSMENT

The Chapter Assessment describes three activities for alternative assessment on page 105. You may wish to have students work on these activities during the course of the chapter and then present them at the end.

# 1 Early Colonies Have Mixed Success

**TERMS & NAMES**
joint-stock company
charter
Jamestown
John Smith
indentured servant
House of Burgesses
Bacon's Rebellion

**MAIN IDEA**

Two early English colonies failed, but Jamestown survived—partly through individual effort and hard work.

**WHY IT MATTERS NOW**

Jamestown's survival led to more English colonies and a lasting English influence in the United States.



## SECTION OBJECTIVES

1. To describe early English attempts at colonizing
2. To explain English financing of a colony
3. To summarize how Jamestown was founded and grew
4. To analyze the conflicts of the Jamestown colonists both with Native Americans and among the colonists themselves

**SKILLBUILDER**

Interpreting Maps: Location, Human-Environment Interaction, p. 87

**CRITICAL THINKING**

Summarizing, p. 86
Solving Problems, p. 87
Analyzing Causes, p. 88
Finding Main Ideas, p. 88
Drawing Conclusions, p. 89

## FOCUS & MOTIVATE

### 5-MINUTE WARM-UP

**Making Inferences** These questions focus on the difficulties of founding a colony.

1. Look at the map on page 87. When and where was the first English settlement?
2. Judging by the dates on the map, how long did the settlement last?

**Warm-Up Transparency WT3**

## INSTRUCT

### INSTRUCT: OBJECTIVE 1

**The English Plan Colonies**
Key Questions
- Why did Hakluyt favor founding English colonies in the Americas?
- Why did the English want to go to America?

**In-Depth Resources: Unit 1**
- Guided Reading, p. 46

**Reading Study Guide** (Spanish and English), pp. 27–28

## ONE AMERICAN'S STORY

**John White was a talented artist. He traveled with the first English expedition to Roanoke, an island off North Carolina, in 1585. While there, he painted scenes of Native American villages. White sailed back to England in 1586 and then returned to Roanoke as governor the next year, bringing with him more than 100 settlers. White's daughter Elinor gave birth to a baby girl, Virginia Dare, during their stay. John White described the event.**

*A VOICE FROM THE PAST*

On August 18 a daughter was born to Elinor, . . . wife of Ananias Dare. . . . The child was christened on the following Sunday and was named Virginia because she was the first Christian born in Virginia.

**John White,** *The New World*

Drawing by John White of an old man of the Pomeiock tribe.

**In 1587, White was forced to sail back to England a second time to get needed supplies. He left the colonists, including his granddaughter, Virginia, in Roanoke. Delayed by the Spanish Armada (a fleet of ships that attempted to invade England in 1588), White did not return to Roanoke until 1590.**

**To his shock and grief, he found no trace of the colonists or his granddaughter, all of whom had disappeared. The only clues to their whereabouts were the letters *CRO* carved in a tree and the word *Croatoan* carved in a doorpost. White never discovered the fate of his family and the other colonists. In this section, you will learn why English settlers such as White came to America despite such hardships. You'll also learn how they lived and what they believed.**

## 1 The English Plan Colonies

As you read in Chapter 2, religious and political rivalries increased between England and Spain in the late 1500s. Spain had many colonies in the Americas, but England had none. England began directing its resources toward establishing colonies after its defeat of the Spanish Armada in 1588.



## RECOMMENDED RESOURCES

**In-Depth Resources: Unit 1**
- Guided Reading, p. 46
- Building Vocabulary, p. 49
- Geography Application: Roanoke Colony, pp. 51–52
- Primary Source: from *Generall Historie of Virginia* by John Smith, p. 53
- Reteaching Activity, p. 58
- Enrichment Activity, p. 61

**Reading Study Guide** (Spanish and English), pp. 27–28

**America's History Makers**
- Pocahontas, pp. 11–12

**Formal Assessment**
- Section Quiz, p. 48

**Alternative Assessment**
- Rubrics, 1.1
- Rubrics, 4.9

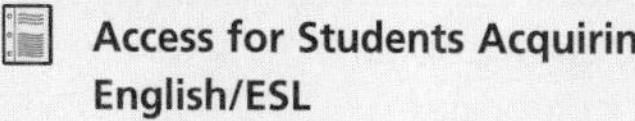
**Access for Students Acquiring English/ESL**
- Guided Reading, p. 16
- Geography Application, pp. 20–21

**Technology Resources**

**Humanities Transparency HT5**
- *John Smith Takes a Prisoner,* 1624

**Electronic Teacher Tools with Test Maker**

**ClassZone**
www.mcdougallittell.com

Richard Hakluyt (HAK•LOOT), an English geographer, urged England to start a colony. Hakluyt thought that colonies would provide a market for English exports. They also would serve as a source of raw materials. By having colonies, England hoped to increase its trade and build up its gold supply. This is the economic theory of mercantilism (see page 62). In mercantilism, the state controls trade and attempts to transfer wealth from colonies to the parent country. Hakluyt also thought that English colonies would help to plant the Protestant faith in the Americas.

The earliest English colonists had many reasons for going to America. The lack of economic opportunity in England forced many to seek their fortunes abroad. Stories of gold mines lured some to leave England. Others left to escape religious persecution.

*Reading* **History**
**A. Summarizing** Why did English colonists settle in America?
**A. Answer** They were looking for economic opportunity and religious freedom.

## 2 Two Early Colonies Fail

Sir Walter Raleigh was a soldier, statesman, and adventurer who served under Queen Elizabeth I of England. She gave him permission to sponsor the colony at Roanoke. He named England's first colony Virginia after the unmarried, or virgin, queen. Financed by Raleigh, the colony began in 1585 on Roanoke Island. The colonists relied on the Native Americans for food. But when the Native Americans realized that the settlers wanted their land, they cut off the colonists' food supply. Those who survived returned to England in 1586.

**Vocabulary**
**financed:** paid for; raised funds for

In 1587, artist John White convinced Raleigh to try again to establish the Roanoke colony, with the disastrous results described in One American's Story (page 85). To this day, no one knows for sure what happened. Some historians think that the colonists mingled with the neighboring Native Americans. Others believe that they moved to Chesapeake Bay and were killed by Native Americans defending their land.

In 1607, the Plymouth Company sponsored the Sagadahoc colony at the mouth of the Kennebec River in Maine. Some of the settlers were English convicts. One colonist wrote of George Popham, the governor, "He stocked or planted [the colony] out of all the jails of England." Within the first year, arguments among colonists, a harsh winter, fights with Native Americans, and food shortages forced most of the colonists to return to England.

**Now and then**

**THE LUMBEE AND THE LOST COLONISTS**

The Lumbee tribe lives mainly in North Carolina. Some of the Lumbee believe they are descendants of the lost colonists of Roanoke. Among the evidence cited is the fact that 41 of the 95 last names of the Lumbee were last names of the colonists.

Other Lumbee don't believe that they are descended from English ancestors. The Lumbee are trying to win federal recognition as a Native American tribe. English ancestry might weaken their claim for federal financial support.

## Financing a Colony

Raleigh had financed the colony at Roanoke. When the colony failed, he lost his investment. The English learned from Raleigh's financial loss at Roanoke that one person could not finance a colony. To raise money, they turned to the **joint-stock company.** Joint-stock companies were backed by investors, people who put money into a project to earn profits. Each investor received pieces of ownership of the company called



**INSTRUCT: OBJECTIVE 2**

**Two Early Colonies Fail/Financing a Colony**
Key Questions
- What part did Sir Walter Raleigh play in the first English settlements?
- Why did the Roanoke colony fail?
- What did a joint-stock company have to do with colonial settlement?

 **In-Depth Resources: Unit 1**
- Geography Application: Roanoke Colony, pp. 51–52

**Now and then**

**The Lumbee and the Lost Colonists**
Other evidence cited for Lumbee descent from the lost colonists comes from the writings of European travelers in the later 1600s. One traveler recorded meeting Native Americans familiar with European customs in what is now Robeson County in south-central North Carolina. Another told of traveling in this same area and being captured by Native Americans who spoke English. Two centuries later, in 1891, historian Stephen Weeks published a scholarly paper claiming that the distinctive dialect spoken by the Lumbee was very similar to English as it was spoken in England at the time of Queen Elizabeth. Other theories suggest that the Lumbee are descendants of the Cherokee, the Eastern Siouan, or the Iroquois-speaking Tuscarora people.

**ACTIVITY OPTIONS**

**INTERDISCIPLINARY LINK: ECONOMICS** — BLOCK SCHEDULING

**FORMING A JOINT-STOCK COMPANY**

**Class Time** One class period

**Task** Simulating the workings of a joint-stock company

**Purpose** To understand the way a joint-stock company obtained funds and to understand the risks taken by investors

**Supplies Needed**
- Ten pennies for each student
- "Stock certificates," handwritten or photocopied
- A box or hat
- An "annual report," a card for each student indicating that his/her investment has tripled, been lost completely, or not changed

**Activity** Give each student ten pennies. Tell the class that you are forming a joint-stock company to fund a colony beneath the Atlantic Ocean. Ask for investors. Tell the class that each penny will represent five thousand dollars. Discuss the risks and possible rewards of such an investment. Collect the students' "investments" and give each "investor" a stock certificate for each five thousand dollars invested. Then ask students to draw an annual report card from a hat or box. Discuss the results of their investments.

shares of stock. In this way, the investors split any profits and divided any losses.

Merchants organized the Virginia Company of London and the Virginia Company of Plymouth. King James I of England granted charters to both companies in 1606. A **charter** was a written contract, issued by a government, giving the holder the right to establish a colony.

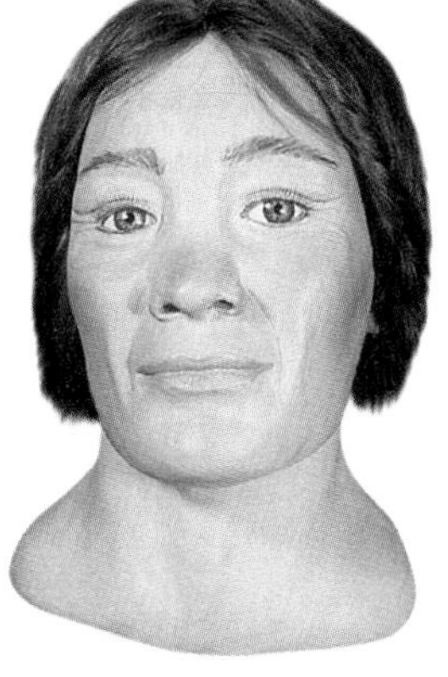

This is a computer reconstruction of the face of Mistress Forrest, believed to be the first woman to come to Jamestown.

## 3 Jamestown Is Founded in 1607

In 1607, the Virginia Company of London financed an expedition to Chesapeake Bay that included more than 100 colonists. They sailed up the James River until they found a spot to settle. They named the first permanent English settlement **Jamestown** in honor of King James.

**Background** Historians used to believe that the colony's original site had been flooded by the James River. Recent archaeological digs, however, have discovered the site on higher ground.

From the start, the Jamestown colonists endured terrible hardships. The site of the colony was swampy and full of malaria-carrying mosquitoes. This disease made the colonists sick with fever. Many also became ill from drinking the river water. To make matters worse, the London Company had incorrectly told the settlers that the colony would be rich in gold. They spent their days searching for gold rather than building houses and growing food.

The climate was also a hardship. The colonists soon learned that the summers were hot and humid and the winters bitter cold. As one colonist recalled, "There were never Englishmen left in a foreign country in such misery as we were in this newly discovered Virginia."

## Jamestown Grows

By January 1608, only 38 colonists remained alive. Later that year, **John Smith,** a soldier and adventurer, took control. To make sure the colonists worked, Smith announced, "He that will not work shall not eat." Smith's methods worked. He ordered an existing wall extended around Jamestown. He also persuaded the Powhatan tribe to trade their corn to the colonists. In 1609, Smith was injured in a gunpowder explosion and returned to England. That same year, 800 more English settlers arrived in Jamestown.

B. Answer Physical punishment, banishment, and a system of penalties or fines might have worked.

*Reading* **History**
**B. Solving Problems** If you had been John Smith, how would you have forced the colonists to work?

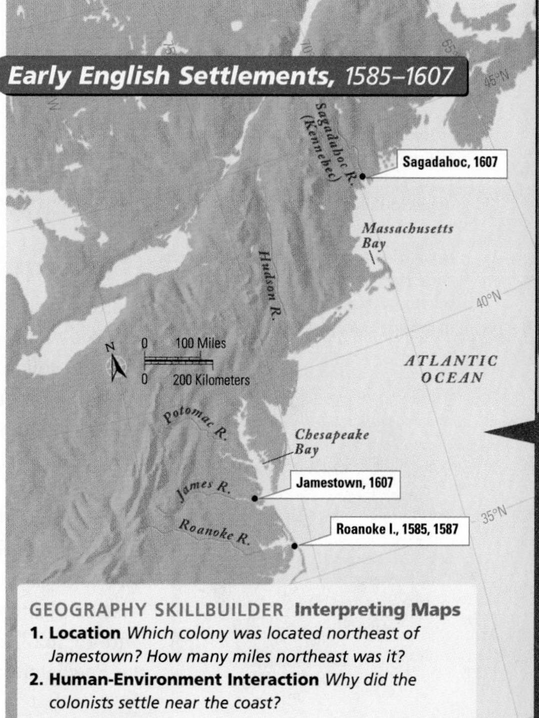


GEOGRAPHY SKILLBUILDER **Interpreting Maps**
1. **Location** *Which colony was located northeast of Jamestown? How many miles northeast was it?*
2. **Human-Environment Interaction** *Why did the colonists settle near the coast?*

Skillbuilder Answers
1. Sagadahoc. Approximately 500 miles.
2. The ocean provided a source of food and a means of transportation.

87

**INSTRUCT: OBJECTIVE 3**

**Jamestown Is Founded in 1607/ Jamestown Grows**

Key Questions
- When and where was the first permanent English colony founded?
- What hardships did the colonists face in the early years of settlement?
- How did the colonists' decision to grow tobacco change Jamestown?

 **Humanities Transparency HT5**
- John Smith Takes a Prisoner, 1624

 **In-Depth Resources: Unit 1**
- Primary Source, p. 53

**MORE ABOUT . . .**

**Dining at Jamestown**

Jamestown colonists faced the "starving time" in the winter of 1609 in part because their main sources of food were seasonal. In a garbage pit from before 1610, archaeologists have found the bones of the animals that the colonists ate. From May to September, when the sturgeon were running, these huge fish (up to 800 pounds) kept the colony well supplied. The settlers also ate a quantity of land tortoises. In addition, they consumed oysters, birds, and raccoons. But with the cold weather, many of these fish and animals migrated to warmer areas or hibernated.

**HISTORY FROM VISUALS**

**Reading the Map** Ask students what barriers they see on the map that would make travel difficult for settlers. **Possible Responses** Mountains might create barriers to travel westward. The rivers flow toward the sea. Travel up river might be difficult.

**Extension** Have students locate this segment of the coast on a map of the United States and name the states that this area covers today.

**ACTIVITY OPTIONS**

**INDIVIDUAL NEEDS**

**LESS PROFICIENT READERS**

**Taking Notes** Some students may have difficulty understanding the importance of the historical figures discussed in the section. To help them focus on the key figures and their roles, have them create a concept web for Sir Walter Raleigh, John Smith, John Rolfe, the Powhatan, and Nathaniel Bacon. You might provide a web such as the one shown as a model.

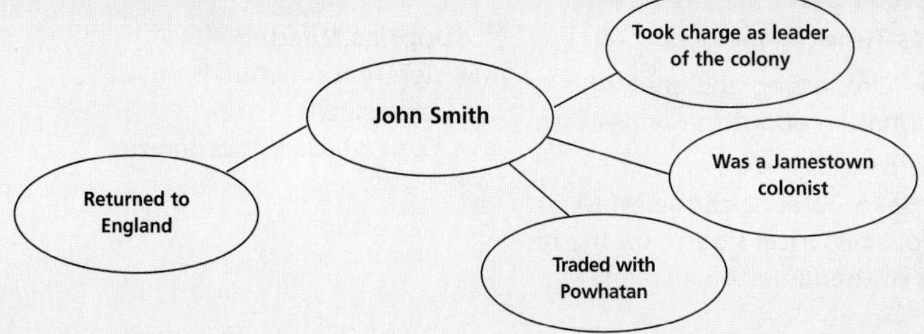

## MORE ABOUT . . .

**Tobacco**

Not everyone in England was thrilled by the successes of the tobacco trade. King James called smoking "a custome lothsome to the eye, hatefull to the Nose, harmefull to the braine, [and] dangerous to the Lungs." He tried to prevent its spread.

## AMERICA'S HISTORY MAKERS

**Pocahontas**

Pocahontas was famous in London long before she arrived there. Many English people had read John Smith's account of how she had saved his life. She was presented to Queen Anne and King James I at the royal court. She attended elegant parties and met famous people such as Sir Walter Raleigh. She succeeded so well in making the Virginia Company the talk of the town that the company's managers gave her a salary.

**Possible Responses: Pocahontas managed to bridge the two cultures of English and Native American, as shown in her marriage to John Rolfe and her trip to England to raise money for the Jamestown colony.**

**America's History Makers**
- Pocahontas, pp. 11–12

**In-Depth Resources: Unit 1**
- Enrichment Activities, p. 61

## INSTRUCT: OBJECTIVE 

**Conflicts with the Powhatan/ Bacon's Rebellion in 1676**

Key Questions
- What were the causes of conflict between English colonists and the Powhatan?
- Why did the colonists create the House of Burgesses?
- What were the causes of Bacon's Rebellion?

Because of growing tensions between the settlers and Native Americans, the Powhatan stopped trading food and attacked the settlers. The settlers did not dare leave the fort. During the "starving time," the colonists ate rats, mice, and snakes. Only 60 of the colonists were still alive when two ships arrived in 1610. Lord De La Warr, the new governor, imposed discipline, and the "starving time" ended.

In 1612, John Rolfe developed a high-grade tobacco that the colonists learned to grow. It quickly became very popular in England. The success of tobacco growing changed Jamestown in many ways. The Virginia Company thought of the colonists as employees. The colonists, however, wanted a share of the profits.

The company responded by letting settlers own land. Settlers worked harder when the land was their own. The company offered a 50-acre land grant for each man, woman, or child who could pay his or her way to the colony. In 1619, the first African Americans arrived in Jamestown. The population of Virginia jumped from about 600 in 1619 to more than 2,000 in 1621.

Even more laborers were needed. Those who could not afford passage to America were encouraged to become **indentured servants**. These men and women sold their labor to the person who paid their passage to the colony. After working for a number of years, they were free to farm or take up a trade of their own.

The colonists soon became annoyed at the strict rule of the governor, who represented the Virginia Company's interests back in London. To provide for more local control, the company decided that burgesses, or elected representatives, of the colonists would meet once a year in an assembly. The **House of Burgesses**, created in 1619, became the first representative assembly in the American colonies.

### AMERICA'S HISTORY MAKERS

**POCAHONTAS**
**1595?–1617**

Pocahontas met John Smith when she was about 12 years old. Smith taught her English and admired her spirit. She admired Smith's bravery and saved his life twice. After Smith returned to England, she married the colonist John Rolfe in 1614. Shown below is a portrait of Pocahontas, done in 1616.

Two years later, the Rolfes went to England to raise money for the Jamestown colony. While getting ready to sail home, Pocahontas died of smallpox.

**How did Pocahontas show that Native Americans and white settlers might live in peace?**

*Reading History*
**C. Analyzing Causes** What was the main reason for the various arrangements the Virginia Company came up with to bring people to America?

C. Answer The company needed people to help grow tobacco.

## 4 Conflicts with the Powhatan

Cultural differences put the Powhatan and the English on a collision course. At first, the Powhatan traded food with the colonists. Then, as more colonists arrived and wanted land, relations grew worse. In an effort to improve relations between the English colonists and the Powhatan, John Rolfe married Chief Powhatan's daughter, Pocahontas, in 1614.

For a time, there was an uneasy peace. The colonists learned from the Powhatan how to grow corn, catch fish, and capture wild fowl. However, the expanding tobacco plantations took over more and more Powhatan land. In 1622, in response to land grabs by the colonists, the Powhatan killed hundreds of Jamestown's residents.

D. Answer Both groups wanted the same land.

*Reading History*
**D. Finding Main Ideas** What was the central dispute between the Powhatan and the settlers?



## ACTIVITY OPTIONS

**MULTIPLE LEARNING STYLES: LOGICAL-MATHEMATICAL** | BLOCK SCHEDULING

**JAMESTOWN SURVIVES**

**Class Time** 20 minutes

**Task** Organizing and analyzing information about the Jamestown colony

**Purpose** To analyze the effect of various historical figures on the history of the Jamestown colony

**Supplies Needed**
- Reference materials on Jamestown
- Copy of graphic organizer

**Activity** Draw a graphic organizer like the one below on the chalkboard. Have students complete the organizer.

| Person | Effect on Jamestown |
|---|---|
| John Smith | |
| Pocahontas | |
| Lord De La Warr | |
| John Rolfe | |
| Chief Powhatan | |

## Bacon's Rebellion in 1676

As you have seen, many of the English colonists who came to Virginia during the 1600s fought with the Native Americans. They also battled one another. By the 1670s, one-fourth of the free white men were former indentured servants. These colonists, who did not own land, resented the wealthy eastern landowners. The poor settlers lived mostly on Virginia's western frontier, where they battled the Native Americans for land.

Nathaniel Bacon and a group of landless frontier settlers opposed Governor William Berkeley. They complained about high taxes and Governor Berkeley's favoritism toward large plantation owners. Bacon demanded that Berkeley approve a war against the Native Americans to seize their land for tobacco plantations. Governor Berkeley's refusal of Nathaniel Bacon's demand sparked **Bacon's Rebellion** in 1676.

Nathaniel Bacon (right) confronts Virginia governor William Berkeley at Jamestown in 1676.

Bacon marched into Jamestown, took control of the House of Burgesses, and burned Jamestown to the ground. Bacon's sudden illness and death ended the rebellion. Berkeley hanged Bacon's followers. Angered by Berkeley's actions, King Charles II recalled the governor to England. After that incident, the House of Burgesses passed laws to prevent a royal governor from assuming such power again. The burgesses had taken an important step against tyranny. In the next section, you will read about the New England colonies and their steps toward independence.

**Vocabulary**
**tyranny:** a government in which a single ruler has absolute power

### Section 1 Assessment

**1. Terms & Names**

**Identify:**
- joint-stock company
- charter
- Jamestown
- John Smith
- indentured servant
- House of Burgesses
- Bacon's Rebellion

**2. Taking Notes**

Use a series-of-events chain to review events that led to the founding of Jamestown.

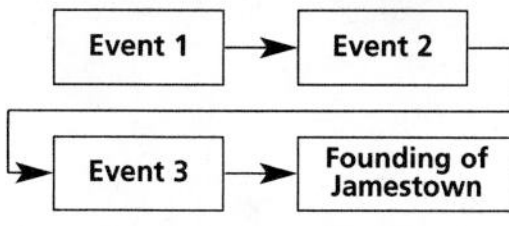


What were reasons England wanted colonies in America?

**3. Main Ideas**

a. Why did the first English settlement at Roanoke fail?

b. How did the English finance their colonies after 1606?

c. What was the outcome of Bacon's Rebellion?

**4. Critical Thinking**

**Drawing Conclusions**
What were the main reasons that Jamestown survived and prospered?

**THINK ABOUT**
- how, after the "starving time," Lord De La Warr took control
- John Rolfe's development of a high-grade tobacco plant

**ACTIVITY OPTIONS**
ART
LANGUAGE ARTS

You need indentured servants to work on your plantation. Draw a **poster** or write an **advertisement** that will attract people to your plantation.



### MORE ABOUT . . .

**Bacon's Rebellion**

Robert Beverley was a plantation owner and an ally of Governor Berkeley. The following is his description of Nathaniel Bacon:

"This gentleman had been brought up at one of the Inns of court in England, and had a moderate fortune. He was young, bold, active, of an inviting aspect, and powerful elocution. In a word, he was every way qualified to head a giddy and unthinking multitude."

### ASSESS & RETEACH

**Setting the Stage** Have students complete sequencing boxes for colonies discussed in this section.

 **Formal Assessment**
- Section Quiz, p. 48

 **Critical Thinking Transparency CT7**
- Setting the Stage

**RETEACHING ACTIVITY**

Divide the class into pairs to make time lines for the settlement of the Jamestown colony. Have students pick three events from the colony's early history and write a paragraph explaining how these actions helped ensure Jamestown's survival.

**In-Depth Resources: Unit 1**
- Reteaching Activity, p. 58

### Section 1 Assessment

**1. Terms & Names**

**joint-stock company,** p. 86
**charter,** p. 87
**Jamestown,** p. 87
**John Smith,** p. 87
**indentured servant,** p. 88
**House of Burgesses,** p. 88
**Bacon's Rebellion,** p. 89

**2. Taking Notes**

**Event 1.** England and Spain were political rivals.
**Event 2.** Spanish Armada defeated.
**Event 3.** England wanted colonies to increase trade.

England wanted colonies for religious purposes, as a market, and as a source of raw materials.

**3. Main Ideas**

**a.** It was poorly planned, it ran out of supplies, and the Spanish Armada delayed the return of the supply ships. **b.** by forming joint-stock companies **c.** The King appointed a new governor. House of Burgesses passed laws to prevent a royal governor from assuming too much power—a step toward self-government.

**4. Critical Thinking**

John Smith instilled discipline and made everyone work. Growing tobacco attracted new colonists and strengthened the colony.

**ACTIVITY OPTIONS**

 **Alternative Assessment**
- Rubrics for a poster, 1.1
- Rubrics for an ad, 4.9

## *Interdisciplinary* CHALLENGE

**OBJECTIVE**
Students will work cooperatively to meet some of the social, geographic, and economic challenges faced by colonists in adapting to their new environment in America.

**BLOCK SCHEDULING**

## PROCEDURE

Gather supplies that students might need, such as poster boards, colored markers, pencils, and paper. For each challenge, have students form groups of three or four. Ask group members to divide the work among themselves. Then have them choose an option for presenting their solution.

### CIVICS CHALLENGE

**Class Time** 50 minutes

Use the following suggestions to help students figure out how to get the colonists to do the work necessary for survival.

- Make a list of the tasks to be done.
- Make at least one work rule for each task and list a punishment for not following the rule.
- Pick ten rules and punishments that everyone agrees on.

**POSSIBLE SOLUTIONS**
Here are the ways colonial leaders got colonists to work:

- denying food to nonworkers
- forcing those who did not follow the rules to leave the community

*Interdisciplinary* CHALLENGE

# Report from the New World

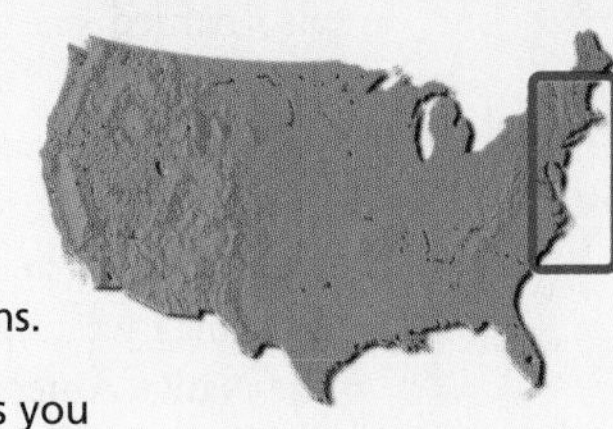

You are a settler who has landed on the wild eastern shore of North America. You and your 93 fellow colonists survived a frightening nine-week Atlantic voyage. Now you are struggling to build a new home in the wilderness. There are no roads, inns, or towns in this land. The game, berries, and fish here taste strange, sometimes unpleasant. Your only neighbors are small groups of Native Americans.

COOPERATIVE LEARNING On these pages are challenges you face as you put down roots in America. Working with a small group, decide how to deal with each challenge. Choose an option, assign a task to each group member, and do the activity. You will find useful information in the Data File. Be prepared to present your solutions to the class as part of a report to your sponsors back in England.

### CIVICS CHALLENGE

*"They had little or no care of any other thing, but to pamper their bellies."*

**As your colony takes root, most members work hard to farm, cook, wash, mend, trade, and defend the colony. But a few colonists think only of their own comfort. You call a meeting to set some rules about work. Present your solution to this problem using one of these options:**

- **Make a poster for the meeting hall that states the new work rules and punishments.**
- **Write a report describing the problem and how the colony solved it.**

90

## STANDARDS FOR EVALUATION

### CIVICS CHALLENGE

**Option 1** Poster of rules and punishments should
- clearly state each rule.
- list a punishment for not obeying each rule.

**Option 2** Written reports should
- state the problem clearly.
- explain how the problem arose.
- include reasons that justify rules and punishments.

### ECONOMICS CHALLENGE

**Option 1** Role-plays of meeting should
- present different views on how to open trade.
- result in an action plan.

**Option 2** Written instructions should
- logically and clearly state the duties of each team member.
- include a set of steps for the process.
- indicate the desired outcome.

### GEOGRAPHY CHALLENGE

**Option 1** Diagrams should
- show the placement of windows, doors, fireplace, and furniture through symbols.
- include labels to clarify the diagram.

**Option 2** Written accounts should
- describe, inform, and engage.
- give details to make the account more vivid.
- have a chronological or thematic order.

## ECONOMICS CHALLENGE

### *"A bright tin dish most pleased him."*

**By the time spring arrives, your stores of English foods are running low. You and your friends decide to try trading with the neighboring Native Americans. They could provide a steady supply of meat, fish, and vegetables until your harvest comes in. Develop a plan for opening trade. Present your plan using one of these options:**

- As a group, role-play the meeting in which you create your trading plan.
- Write instructions for the team of colonists who will open trade with the Native Americans.

## ACTIVITY WRAP-UP

Present to the class **As a group, review your solution to each challenge. Consider the following:**

- How well each solution meets its particular challenge
- Which solution shows the most creativity

**Once you have made your decision, present your solutions to the class. Each group member should take part in the presentation.**

## DATA FILE

### The Journey

**Distance:** more than 5,000 nautical miles from Europe to the east coast of North America

**Length:** 6–14 weeks

**Dangers:** storms, scurvy, dysentery, malnutrition, seasickness, overcrowding

### Food and Livestock Taken

barrels of salted beef, oatmeal, dried grains, cheese, oil, vinegar, and salt; seeds for peas, barley, herbs, and other crops; cows, horses, goats, pigs, sheep, and chickens

### Equipment Taken

axes, hoes, nails, hooks for doors, hammers, chisels, hatchets, spades, pickaxes, iron pots, copper kettles, skillets, platters, dishes, wooden spoons, rugs

### Weapons Taken

swords, muskets, daggers, gunpowder, light armor, cannon

### Clothes Taken

shirts, several pairs of shoes, leather for mending, waistcoats, caps, skirts, jackets, trousers

### Dangers in America

**Biggest killers:** typhoid, dysentery, famine

**Other dangers:** pneumonia, malaria, and other diseases; exposure to harsh weather; fire; wild animals; attacks by Native Americans

### Benefits in America

religious and political freedom; opportunity to own land; abundant timber for shelters, forts, heat, ships, and trade; rich food resources

**Visit www.mcdougallittell.com for more on the American colonies.**



## ACTIVITY WRAP-UP

Presentations should
- provide a clear, concise statement of the problem.
- give a workable solution.
- evaluate the effectiveness of the solution.
- assess the creativity of the solution.

## ECONOMICS CHALLENGE

**Class Time** 50 minutes

Tell students that each person in the group should choose a part for the role play and formulate an opinion about trading with the Native Americans. Each student should then present that opinion in the role play. Each group member should speak and present ideas in the role play. Tell students to list the items they want to buy and what goods they have to trade in return. Remind them to consider the consequences of trading guns.

**POSSIBLE SOLUTIONS**

Typically goods were exchanged by barter. Native Americans were interested in the colonists' metal tools, utensils, and guns. Because clearing the land, planting, and harvesting took at least a year, the colonists' most pressing need was food.

**ALTERNATIVE ACTIVITY**

## GEOGRAPHY CHALLENGE

### *"A . . . desolate wilderness"*

**Your ship reached the shores of America in raw December weather. Your leader called your new home "a hideous and desolate wilderness, full of wild beasts and wild men." You built shelters for protection. Now you are preparing a report on your first months in a new land. Present your report using one of these options:**

- **Make a diagram that shows your first shelter.**
- **Write a personal account that explains how your family survived the winter in America.**

## SECTION OBJECTIVES

1. To explain why the Pilgrims established Plymouth Colony
2. To explain why the Puritans set up the Massachusetts Bay Colony
3. To identify the New England Way and to evaluate challenges to Puritan leadership
4. To summarize the causes and effects of King Philip's War and the Salem witchcraft trials

**SKILLBUILDER**
Interpreting Maps: Location, Place, p. 95
Interpreting Charts, p. 96

**CRITICAL THINKING**
Making Inferences, pp. 93, 94
Summarizing, p. 95
Forming Opinions, p. 96
Recognizing Effects, p. 97

## FOCUS & MOTIVATE

### 5-MINUTE WARM-UP

**Drawing Conclusions** These questions focus on the diversity of North American societies.

1. Read the quote about Squanto on page 92. Why might the colonists need help?
2. Why might the Native Americans want to help the colonists?

 Warm-Up Transparency WT3

## INSTRUCT

### INSTRUCT: OBJECTIVE 

**The Voyage of the *Mayflower*/ The Pilgrims Found Plymouth**
Key Questions
- Why did the Separatists decide to leave Europe for America?
- What did the first Thanksgiving symbolize for the Pilgrims?

 **In-Depth Resources: Unit 1**
- Guided Reading, p. 47
- Building Vocabulary, p. 49

 **America's History Makers**
- William Bradford, pp. 13–14

# 2 New England Colonies

**TERMS & NAMES**
Pilgrims
Mayflower Compact
Puritans
Great Migration
Fundamental Orders of Connecticut
Roger Williams
Anne Hutchinson
King Philip's War

**MAIN IDEA**
Religion influenced the settlement and government of the New England colonies.

**WHY IT MATTERS NOW**
The Puritan work ethic and religious beliefs influence American culture today.

### ONE AMERICAN'S STORY

**In 1605, English fishermen captured and enslaved a Native American named Squanto and took him to England. While there, he learned to speak English. After a series of misadventures, including serving as a slave in Spain, Squanto returned to America in 1619. There he discovered that his Pawtuxet tribe had been wiped out by disease in the years 1616–1618. In 1621, Squanto set about helping the English plant corn, beans, and pumpkins on tribal lands. Colonist William Bradford made the following comment about Squanto.**

*A VOICE FROM THE PAST*

Squanto . . . was a special instrument sent of God for their [the colonists'] good beyond their expectation. . . . He directed them how to set their corn, where to take fish, and to procure other commodities, and was also their pilot to bring them to unknown places.

**William Bradford,** quoted in *The Pilgrim Reader*

**Thanks to Squanto, the first settlers in New England prospered and lived in peace with the Native Americans. In this section, you will learn about the Pilgrims and Puritans, their relations with the Native Americans, and their settlement of the New England colonies.**

Squanto teaches the Pilgrims how to grow corn.

### 1 The Voyage of the *Mayflower*

In the early 1500s, King Henry VIII of England broke that country's ties with the Catholic Church and established the Church of England, an official state church under his control. In the early 1600s, a religious group called the Separatists called for a total break with the Church of England. They thought it was too much like the Catholic Church.

The **Pilgrims** were a Separatist group. King James attacked them for rejecting England's official church. To escape this harsh treatment, the Pilgrims fled to Holland, a country known for its acceptance of different opinions. Eventually, the Pilgrims became dissatisfied with life in Holland. They approached the Virginia Company and asked if they could settle in America "as a distinct body by themselves." The Virginia



## RECOMMENDED RESOURCES

 **In-Depth Resources: Unit 1**
- Guided Reading, p. 47
- Building Vocabulary, p. 49
- Skillbuilder Practice, p. 50
- Literature Selection, pp. 55–57
- Reteaching Activity, p. 59

 **Reading Study Guide** (Spanish and English), pp. 29–30

**Economics in History,** p. 3

 **America's History Makers**
- William Bradford, pp. 13–14

   **Formal Assessment**
- Section Quiz, p. 49

 **Alternative Assessment**
- Rubrics, 4.5
- Rubrics, 3.6

 **Access for Students Acquiring English/ESL**
- Guided Reading, p. 17
- Skillbuilder Practice, p. 19

**Technology Resources**

 **Humanities Transparency HT6**
- *Pilgrims Going to Church* by George Henry Boughton

 **Critical Thinking Trans. CT8**
- Cause and Effect: King Philip's War, 1675–1676

 **Electronic Teacher Tools with Test Maker**

 **ClassZone**
www.mcdougallittell.com

The *Mayflower* brings the Pilgrims to Plymouth in 1620.

Company arranged for them to settle on land within its boundaries on the eastern coast of North America.

On a cold, raw November day in 1620, a ship called the *Mayflower* arrived off Cape Cod on the Massachusetts coast. Blown north of its course, the *Mayflower* landed in an area that John Smith had mapped and called New England. They landed at a site that had been named Plymouth.

Because the Pilgrims landed outside the limits of the Virginia Company, their charter did not apply. For the sake of order, the men aboard the *Mayflower* signed an agreement called the **Mayflower Compact.** In it, they vowed to obey laws agreed upon for the good of the colony. The Mayflower Compact helped establish the idea of self-government and majority rule. (See Interactive Primary Sources, page 98.)

## The Pilgrims Found Plymouth

Like the early settlers at Jamestown, the Pilgrims at Plymouth endured a starving time. That first winter, disease and death struck with such fury that "the living were scarce able to bury the dead." Half the group had died by spring.

However, energy, hope, and help returned. One day a Native American walked up to a group of colonists. To their astonishment, he called out, "Welcome, Englishmen." This was Samoset, a Pemaquid who had learned to speak English from European fishermen. Samoset introduced the settlers to another Native American named Squanto, a Pawtuxet, who also spoke English.

> "Welcome, Englishmen."
> Samoset

The Pilgrims had angered the Native Americans by taking their corn. Squanto acted as an interpreter between the Pilgrims and Chief Massasoit. He helped them to negotiate a peace treaty and showed them how to plant, hunt, and fish. While their crops grew, the colonists began trading with the Native Americans for furs and preparing lumber to ship back to England in order to make a profit.

Sometime in the fall—no one knows exactly when—the Plymouth settlement celebrated the blessings of a good harvest by holding a three-day feast. It was the first Thanksgiving. This Thanksgiving came to represent the peace that existed at that time between the Native Americans and Pilgrims.

A. Possible Answer Perhaps because his tribe had died out, Squanto wished to make himself useful to others. He may have wanted to see peaceful relations between the Native Americans and settlers.

*Reading* **History**
**A. Making Inferences** Why do you think Squanto was so helpful to the Pilgrims?



### MORE ABOUT . . .

**Passengers on the *Mayflower***
Three pregnant women were among the 102 passengers who sailed on the *Mayflower.* Elizabeth Hopkins gave birth at sea to a son named Oceanus because of the circumstances of his birth. While the Pilgrims were in Provincetown Harbor, Susan White gave birth to a boy. His parents named him Peregrine, meaning "one who journeys to foreign lands." The third baby was stillborn on the *Mayflower* while the Pilgrims were building their houses at Plymouth.

 **Economics in History**
- Farming in the English Colonies, p. 3

### MORE ABOUT . . .

**Native Americans**
Among the Native American peoples who came into contact with the Pilgrims were the Wampanoag, a people whose name means "People of the First Light" or "Eastern People." In 1620, about 30 Wampanoag villages existed in New England. Today the Wampanoag still live in parts of southeastern Massachusetts and eastern Rhode Island. Among the best known Wampanoag groups are those living in Mashpee on Cape Cod and Gay Head on Martha's Vineyard in Massachusetts. The Gay Head Wampanoag are recognized by the federal government and are governed by the Tribal Council of Gay Head. This recognition created a government-to-government relationship between the federal government and the tribal council.

### ACTIVITY OPTIONS

### SKILLBUILDER MINI-LESSON: USING PRIMARY SOURCES

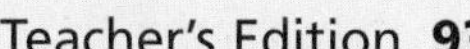

**Explaining the Skill** Primary sources are materials that present an eyewitness account of events in the past. Visual primary sources include paintings, photographs, and video footage. Written primary sources include letters, diaries, speeches, autobiographies, and other documents produced by people who observed or participated in a historical event. Historical documents such as charters, treaties, and laws are also primary sources. In evaluating a primary source, it is important to know who wrote the piece in order to evaluate his or her qualifications for writing about this subject.

**Applying the Skill** Have students read the *Mayflower Compact* on page 98. Ask:

1. Is this a primary or a secondary source? Explain. (*Primary; it was written by colonists aboard the* Mayflower *in 1620.)*
2. Why is this source useful for learning about the Pilgrims? (*It provides insight into their political beliefs and their government and social organization.*)

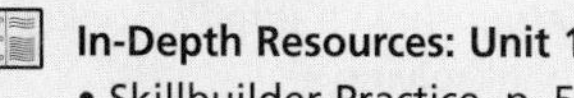

**In-Depth Resources: Unit 1**
- Skillbuilder Practice, p. 50

## *America's* HERITAGE

**The First Thanksgiving**

The Thanksgiving holiday as we know it today was made official by President Abraham Lincoln in 1863. Thanks for Thanksgiving goes to Sarah Josepha Hale, editor of *Godey's Lady's Book.* Beginning in 1846, this determined writer used her position at this popular periodical to lobby for creation of an official Thanksgiving holiday. Every November, Hale wrote editorials calling for recognition of the holiday. In the summer she kept the heat on with letters to the governors of every state. Almost 20 years after she started, Hale's one-woman campaign succeeded.

### INSTRUCT: OBJECTIVE 2

**The Puritans Come to Massachusetts Bay/ The New England Way**

Key Questions

- Why did the Puritans decide to leave England in the 1630s?
- How was the Puritans' colonial experience different from that of the Jamestown settlers?
- What is a commonwealth?
- What was the New England Way?

 **Humanities Transparency HT6**

- *Pilgrims Going to Church* by George Henry Boughton

### CRITICAL THINKING ACTIVITY

**Contrasting** Have students use a Venn diagram to examine the differences and similarities between the Pilgrims and Puritans. Look at their attitudes toward the Church of England; their reasons for coming to New England; and their early experiences as colonial settlements.

**Class Time** 10 minutes

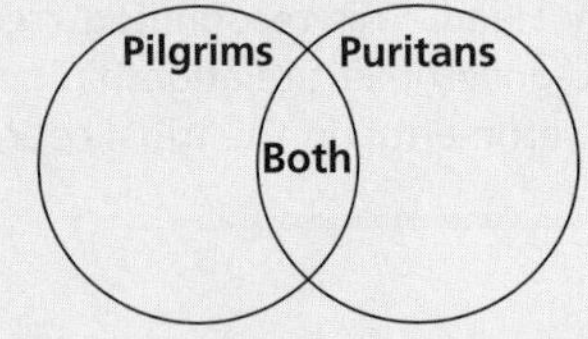


Thanks to the help of Squanto and other Native Americans, the Pilgrims learned to survive in their new environment. Soon more people would sail to New England seeking religious freedom.

> *America's* HERITAGE
>
> **THE FIRST THANKSGIVING**
>
> It is hard to believe, but turkey was not on the menu at the first Thanksgiving. The Pilgrims and Native Americans ate venison (deer), roast duck, roast goose, clams and other shellfish, and eel (shown below). Other treats were white bread and corn bread, leeks, watercress, and salad herbs. The guests topped off their meal with wild plums and dried berries for dessert.

## 2 The Puritans Come to Massachusetts Bay

Between about 1630 and 1640, a religious group called the **Puritans** left England to escape bad treatment by King James I. Unlike the Separatists, who wanted to break away from the Church of England, the Puritans wanted to reform, or "purify," its practices. By the thousands, Puritan families left for the Americas. Their leaving is known as the **Great Migration.** Many thousands of Puritans left their homeland to found new settlements around the world. Of these settlers, about 20,000 crossed the Atlantic Ocean to New England.

**Background** During the Great Migration, the Puritans also went to Ireland, the Netherlands, the Rhineland, and the West Indies.

Many Puritan merchants had invested in the Massachusetts Bay Company. In 1629, the company received a royal charter to settle land in New England. In 1630, 11 well-supplied ships carried about 1,000 passengers to the Massachusetts Bay Colony. Unlike earlier colonists, the Puritans were well prepared and did not suffer through a starving time. John Winthrop was the colony's Puritan governor. He stated that the new colony would be a commonwealth, a community in which people work together for the good of the whole.

***Reading*History**

**B. Making Inferences** After Winthrop, politicians sometimes spoke of America as "a city upon a hill." What does this phrase suggest about America's role in the world?

**B. Possible Answer** The phrase suggests that America will set an example for the rest of the world.

> ***A VOICE FROM THE PAST***
>
> So shall we keep the unity of the spirit, in the bond of peace. . . . Ten of us will be able to resist a thousand of our enemies. . . . For we must consider that we shall be as a City upon a Hill, the eyes of all people are on us.
>
> **John Winthrop,** *"Model of Christian Charity"*

## The New England Way

The basic unit of the commonwealth was the congregation—a group of people who belong to the same church. Each Puritan congregation set up its own town. The meetinghouse was the most important building in each town. There people gathered for town meetings, a form of self-government in which people made laws and other decisions for the community. In the Massachusetts Bay Colony, only male church members could vote or hold office. They elected representatives to a lawmaking body called the General Court, which in turn chose the governor.

By law, everyone in town had to attend church services held in the meetinghouse. The sermon, the most important part of the church service, provided instruction in the "New England Way." This was a term



### ACTIVITY OPTIONS

**INTERDISCIPLINARY LINK: POPULAR CULTURE** — BLOCK SCHEDULING

**THE FIRST THANKSGIVING**

**Class Time** One class period

**Task** Comparing the first Thanksgiving with the way this event is portrayed in children's books today

**Purpose** To analyze the treatment of the first Thanksgiving in contemporary books for children

**Supplies Needed**

- Reference materials on Pilgrims; on the Wampanoag, Pequot, and Narragansett Indians; and on accounts by Pilgrims of the first Thanksgiving
- Contemporary children's books on Thanksgiving

**Activity** Have students read illustrated children's books about Thanksgiving to analyze the treatment of the first Thanksgiving. Ask students to compare these accounts with the actual historical event. Areas for comparison might include the implied or stated purpose of the celebration, the relationships between Pilgrims and Native Americans, the types of food eaten, and the dress and customs of the Native Americans shown participating in the celebration. Have students choose a book that accurately depicts the first Thanksgiving or a book that has historical inaccuracies and report on it to the class.

used by the Puritans to describe both their beliefs and their society, which emphasized duty, godliness, hard work, and honesty. The Puritans thought that amusements such as dancing and playing games would lead to laziness. They believed that God required them to work long and hard at their vocation.

Vocabulary
**godliness:** piety, reverence

The Puritan work ethic helped contribute to the rapid growth and success of the New England colonies. The New England Way also depended on education. Because the Puritans wanted everyone to be able to read the Bible, laws required that all children learn to read.

*Reading***History**
**C. Summarizing** What were some important elements of the New England Way?
C. Answer
Town meetings, church attendance, strong work ethic

Some Puritan congregations set up new colonies. In 1636, Thomas Hooker moved his congregation to the Connecticut Valley. There they wrote and adopted the **Fundamental Orders of Connecticut** in 1639 (see page 98). In effect, these laws were a constitution. The Fundamental Orders extended voting rights to nonchurch members and limited the power of the governor. They expanded the idea of representative government.

The first European settlement in New Hampshire was a village near Portsmouth in 1623. In 1638, John Wheelwright established the town of Exeter. The town's founders drew up the Exeter Compact, which was based on the Mayflower Compact.

***New England Settlements,*** *1620-1636*

Settlements shown in modern state boundaries.
NEW HAMPSHIRE
Portsmouth (1623)
ATLANTIC OCEAN
Connecticut River
MASSACHUSETTS
Massachusetts Bay
Plymouth (1620)
Providence (1636)
Hartford (1636)
Hudson River
CONNECTICUT
RHODE ISLAND
70°W
N
0 50 Miles
0 100 Kilometers

**GEOGRAPHY SKILLBUILDER Interpreting Maps**
1. **Location** *Which of these early colonies does the Connecticut River not flow through or touch?*
2. **Place** *What was the earliest major English settlement in the New England colonies?*

Skillbuilder Answers
1. Rhode Island
2. Plymouth, in 1620

## 3 Challenges to Puritan Leaders

Not everyone agreed with the New England Way. **Roger Williams** was a minister in Salem, Massachusetts, who founded the first Baptist church in America. He opposed forced attendance at church. He also opposed the English colonists' taking of Native American lands by force. Because of his beliefs, the General Court forced Williams to leave the colony. In 1636, he fled southward and founded the colony of Rhode Island, which guaranteed religious freedom and the separation of church and state.

**Anne Hutchinson** believed that a person could worship God without the help of a church, minister, or Bible. She conducted discussions in her home that challenged church authority. Hutchinson was brought to trial and forced to leave Massachusetts. In 1638, she fled to Rhode Island.

**Anne Hutchinson preaches in her home in Boston.**





### HISTORY FROM VISUALS

**Reading the Map** Have students name the four settlements shown on the map. Ask students to identify two routes from Hartford to Providence.
**Possible Response** One route is by water down the Connecticut River to the Atlantic Ocean. The other is over land.

**Extension** Have students use an encyclopedia to find out what economic activities are associated with these communities today.

### CRITICAL THINKING ACTIVITY

**Drawing Conclusions** Have students read the Mayflower Compact on page 98. Then ask: What did the Pilgrims fear might happen if they did not have a charter? If the Pilgrims had landed in the place assigned by the Virginia Company, who would have governed the colony? Discuss the importance of self-government and majority rule in a democratic government.

**Class Time** 10 minutes

### INSTRUCT: OBJECTIVE 3

**Challenges to Puritan Leaders**
Key Questions
- Why did some individuals and groups challenge Puritan leaders?
- How did Rhode Island differ from the Massachusetts Bay Colony?
- What beliefs and practices set the Quakers apart from the Puritans?

**In-Depth Resources: Unit 1**
- Literature Selection: Poems by Anne Bradstreet, pp. 55–57

### ACTIVITY OPTIONS

**INTERDISCIPLINARY LINK: CIVICS** BLOCK SCHEDULING

**CHALLENGES TO PURITAN LEADERS**

**Class Time** 20 minutes

**Task** Writing a statement describing challenges to Puritan authority or responding to such a statement

**Purpose** To analyze the conflict between the Puritan leaders of Massachusetts and Roger Williams or Anne Hutchinson

**Supplies Needed**
- Reference materials on Roger Williams, Anne Hutchinson, and the Puritans

**Activity** Discuss the options open to a government in dealing with citizens who disagree with its policies. Then divide the class into pairs. Direct each pair to research the conflicts that arose between the Puritan leaders of Massachusetts and Roger Williams or Anne Hutchinson. Have one member of each pair write a speech stating the reasons Puritan leaders might have given for banishing Williams or Hutchinson. The second member of the pair should write a reply that the person banished might have given.

## INSTRUCT: OBJECTIVE 

**King Philip's War/**
**The Salem Witchcraft Trials**

Key Questions

- How did Native Americans and Europeans differ in their views of land ownership?
- What was the outcome of King Philip's War?
- What role did the clergy play in the Salem witchcraft trials?
- What were the results of the witchcraft trials?

## MORE ABOUT . . .

**King Philip's War**

Although the Wampanoag torched towns from Connecticut to the outskirts of Boston, they spared Rhode Island out of respect for Roger Williams and the Quakers. After the war ended, hundreds of Wampanoag, including many who had been promised protection if they surrendered, were sold as slaves to buyers from the West Indies or Spain.

## HISTORY FROM VISUALS

**Interpreting the Chart** Have students study the chart to identify the causes of the conflict. How did each of these causes lead to tensions between Native Americans and Europeans? **Possible Responses** Native Americans believed land was shared and could not be owned by individuals. Europeans believed they could claim the land for themselves. Puritans did not understand or respect the beliefs of the Native Americans. An increase in European population put pressure on Europeans to take more land used by Native Americans and claim it for themselves.

**Extension** Have students research the fate of the Wampanoag after the war ended, and have them make a new cause-and-effect chart on the topic of the Native American defeat.

 **Critical Thinking Transparency CT8**

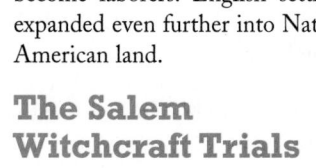

- Cause and Effect: King Philip's War, 1675–1676

Another religious group was the Quakers. Their name came from an early leader's statement that they should "tremble [quake] at the word of the Lord." Opponents coined the name as an insult. Quakers challenged the Massachusetts commonwealth. They believed that each person could know God directly through "an inner light." Neither ministers nor the Bible were needed. Quakers also believed in treating Native Americans fairly, which set them apart from other colonists. For such beliefs, Quakers were whipped, imprisoned, and hanged. Many left for Rhode Island.

*Reading***History**
**D. Forming Opinions** Why is it odd that the Puritans persecuted certain individuals and groups for their religious beliefs?
**D. Answer** The Puritans had themselves been persecuted in England for their beliefs.

## 4 King Philip's War

The growing population of colonists began to force the Native Americans from their land. Europeans and Native Americans defined land ownership differently. To Europeans, land could be owned by individuals. To Native Americans, land belonged to everyone. Conflict over land resulted in warfare.

In 1675–1676, the Puritan colonies fought a brutal war with the Native Americans. This was known as **King Philip's War.** "King Philip" was the English name of Metacom, leader of the Wampanoag. To help fight the war, Metacom organized an alliance of tribes. The Wampanoag lost the war. Many were killed, while others were sold into slavery in the West Indies. Those who remained lost their land and were forced to become laborers. English settlers expanded even further into Native American land.

**Background**
Metacom was the son of Massasoit, friend of the Pilgrims.

**CAUSE & EFFECT:** *King Philip's War, 1675–1676*

*Reasons for Conflict*
- Land ownership
- Religion
- Increased population of Europeans

*KING PHILIP'S WAR*

*Native American Losses*
- Approximately 3,000 killed
- King Philip (Metacom) killed
- About 500 Native Americans enslaved

*European Losses*
- About 600 settlers killed
- More than 45 villages attacked
- About 12 villages destroyed

SKILLBUILDER **Interpreting Charts**

1. *Was there a greater loss of life among the settlers or the Native Americans?*
2. *How might the growing population of Europeans have created more conflict with the Native Americans?*

## The Salem Witchcraft Trials

Puritan New England was originally a society centered on the church. By the late 1600s, however, this had begun to change. The younger generations did not share the strict religious views of their parents. Several Salem village girls were told frightening stories about witches by Tituba, a slave from the West Indies. Pretending to be bewitched, the girls falsely accused others of witchcraft. The witch-hunts began in 1692. The clergy viewed the Salem witch-hunts and trials as a sign from God for the village to return to a strict Puritan lifestyle.

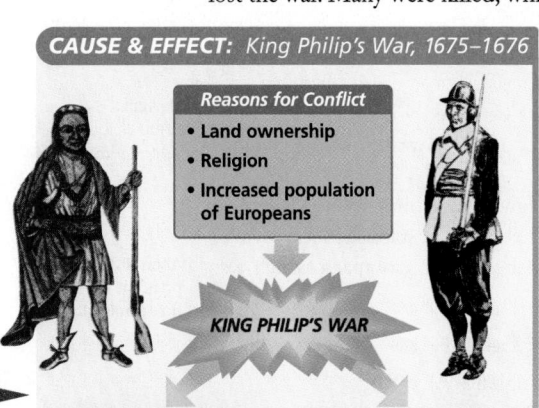

Skillbuilder Answers
1. Many more Native Americans died.
2. More settlers needed more land for their crops and livestock.



## ACTIVITY OPTIONS

## INDIVIDUAL NEEDS: GIFTED AND TALENTED

### A BIOGRAPHY OF KING PHILIP

**Class Time** Two class periods

**Task** Writing a biography of King Philip, or Metacom, for younger students

**Purpose** To encourage students to use research skills and to deepen their understanding of a historical figure

**Supplies Needed**
- Reference materials on King Philip
- Art supplies or computer access

**Activity** Tell students to prepare an illustrated biography of King Philip suitable for fifth-grade students. The biography should include information about King Philip's family, his leadership of the Wampanoag, and his attempts to unite many groups of Native Americans. Tell students that many stories exist about King Philip that have not been documented by historians. Students should be sure to differentiate between fact and legend. Biographies should include a bibliography.

## HISTORY through ART

This mid-nineteenth-century oil painting, *The Trial of George Jacobs, August 5, 1692,* was painted by T. H. Matteson in 1855. It captures the horrors of the Salem witch trials. As the young women cry out, the accused tries to defend himself against charges that he bewitched them.

Jacobs's own granddaughter testified against him. He was tried and convicted on August 5, 1692, and executed two weeks later along with four neighbors.

**How accurately do you think the painting shows the strong emotions in the courtroom?**

Hysteria spread through Salem. Those accused were forced to name others as witches. More than 100 people were arrested and tried. Of those, 20 were found guilty and put to death. Nineteen persons were hanged, and another was pressed to death by heavy stones when he refused to enter a plea in response to the charge of witchcraft. The panic was short-lived, and Salem came to its senses. The experience showed, however, how a society can create scapegoats for its problems.

Vocabulary
**scapegoat:** one that is made to bear the blame of others

In the next section, you will read about the Middle and Southern colonies, how they were founded, and how they provided the new settlers with economic opportunities.

### Section 2 Assessment

**1. Terms & Names**

**Identify:**
- Pilgrims
- Mayflower Compact
- Puritans
- Great Migration
- Fundamental Orders of Connecticut
- Roger Williams
- Anne Hutchinson
- King Philip's War

**2. Taking Notes**

Use a cluster diagram to review details about the New England Way.

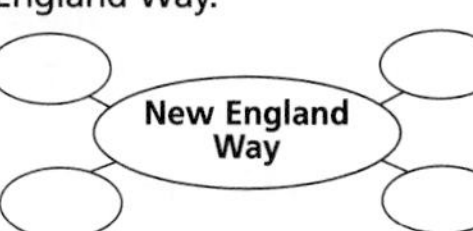


Which parts would you find easy to accept? Which difficult?

**3. Main Ideas**

a. What is the Mayflower Compact?

b. What is the meaning of the term the "Great Migration"?

c. What were some of the causes of King Philip's War?

**4. Critical Thinking**

**Recognizing Effects** What impact did the arrival of the English in New England have on the Native Americans?

THINK ABOUT
- Squanto
- Chief Massasoit
- King Philip's War

**ACTIVITY OPTIONS**

**LANGUAGE ARTS**
**SPEECH**

Choose one of the Puritan dissenters from this section and retell his or her story. Either write a **newspaper article** about the person or give an **oral history.**



### HISTORY through ART

**Interpreting the Illustration** At the time of the Salem trials, belief in witchcraft was widespread in both Europe and America. The noted English jurist Lord Coke defined a witch as a "person who hath conference with the devil, to consult him and/or to do his bidding." Under British law, which was the basis for the Massachusetts Bay Colony's legal system, those who were accused of working with the devil were considered felons. Their crime was punishable by hanging.

**Possible Responses: The scene is chaotic. People are fainting, pointing their fingers at the accused, or being restrained by guards or soldiers. The judge is standing, as if to demand order or show his concern.**

## ASSESS & RETEACH

**Setting the Stage** Have students complete sequencing boxes for colonies founded in this section.

**Formal Assessment**
- Section Quiz, p. 49

### RETEACHING ACTIVITY

Have students work in pairs to make up five "Who am I?" questions about the New England settlements that follow this form: "My name is _____. I guaranteed separation of church and state in the Rhode Island colony I founded. Who am I?" Have groups exchange statements, complete them, and return them to their authors for checking.

**In-Depth Resources: Unit 1**
- Reteaching Activity, p. 59

### Section 2 Assessment

**1. Terms & Names**

**Pilgrims,** p. 92
**Mayflower Compact,** p. 93
**Puritans,** p. 94
**Great Migration,** p. 94
**Fundamental Orders of Connecticut,** p. 95
**Roger Williams,** p. 95
**Anne Hutchinson,** p. 95
**King Philip's War,** p. 96

**2. Taking Notes**

Items for cluster diagram:
- Everyone attended church services.
- Amusements were frowned upon.
- Education was emphasized.
- They had a strong work ethic.

Answers will vary as to which would be easy or difficult to accept.

**3. Main Ideas**

**a.** a document written by the men aboard the *Mayflower* saying that they would obey any laws agreed upon for the good of the colony **b.** a term used to describe the departure of thousands of Puritans for the Americas **c.** land ownership, religion, increase in European population

**4. Critical Thinking**

It forced the Native Americans from their land and led to King Philip's War, with heavy Native American casualties.

**ACTIVITY OPTIONS**

**Alternative Assessment**
- Rubrics for an article, 4.5
- Rubrics for an oral history, 3.6

## INTERACTIVE PRIMARY SOURCES

**OBJECTIVE**
Students will analyze rules of settlement—the Mayflower Compact and the Fundamental Orders of Connecticut—to understand how they provided for self-government and laid a foundation for the republican government of the United States.

Primary Source Explorer
- *The Mayflower Compact*
- *The Fundamental Orders of Connecticut*

The Explorer will help students select and produce their own presentations.

Specific information about the document can be found in **A Closer Look.** To learn more about key people and events of the time, students should click on **Life in These Times. What Happened Next** will show students the impact of the document both at home and abroad, and tie the document to today.

## FOCUS & MOTIVATE

**Evaluating** Tell students that the Pilgrims and Puritans wrote and signed these documents far from any official government. Ask students why the colonists might have felt it necessary to write down this plan. Then ask students to look in the documents for evidence about what the colonists considered important for their settlements.

### MORE ABOUT . . .

**Ancestors on the *Mayflower***
Some Americans proudly trace their ancestry back to passengers on the *Mayflower.* The General Society of Mayflower Descendants, which requires new members to produce strongly documented genealogies, has about 24,500 members. However, the Society estimates that about 35 million Mayflower descendants are alive today.

INTERACTIVE PRIMARY SOURCES

# The Mayflower Compact

**Setting the Stage** In 1620, 41 of the colonists aboard the *Mayflower* drew up the Mayflower Compact. This document refers to the area where they landed as "Virginia" because the land grants of the Virginia Company extended into New England. The colonists provided for self-government under majority rule of the male voters. **See Primary Source Explorer**

*A CLOSER LOOK*

**REASONS FOR VOYAGE**

**The three reasons the colonists give for their voyage to the eastern seaboard of North America are the glory of God, the advancement of Christianity, and the honor of the king.**

**1. Might there have been other, more practical reasons for the voyage?**

*A CLOSER LOOK*

**GUIDING PURPOSE**

The general good of the colony is the guiding purpose of the colonists in signing the compact.

**2. What does this suggest about the relationship between the individual and the community?**

We, whose names are underwritten, . . . having undertaken for the glory of God, and advancement of the Christian faith, and the honor of our King and country, a voyage to plant the first colony in the northern parts of Virginia, do by these presents, solemnly and mutually in the presence of God and one another **covenant**[1] and combine ourselves together into a civil **body politic,**[2] for our better ordering and preservation; and furtherance of the ends aforesaid . . . do enact, constitute, and frame such just and equal laws, ordinances, acts, constitutions, and offices from time to time as shall be thought most [proper] and convenient for the general good of the colony unto which we promise all due submission and obedience. In witness whereof we have hereunto subscribed our names at Cape Cod the eleventh of November, in the year of our **sovereign**[3] lord King James of England . . . Anno Domini 1620.

From B. P. Poore, ed., *The Federal and State Constitutions,* Part I, p. 931.

1. **covenant:** promise in a binding agreement.
2. **body politic:** the people of a politically organized group.
3. **sovereign:** supreme.

# The Fundamental Orders of Connecticut

**Setting the Stage** In January 1639, male citizens of three townships in Connecticut (Hartford, Windsor, and Wethersfield) assembled and drew up the Fundamental Orders of Connecticut. This document is often called the first written constitution in America. It contains a preamble, or introduction, and a set of laws. **See Primary Source Explorer**

### *Preamble*

Forasmuch as it has pleased the Almighty God by the wise disposition of His Divine Providence so to order and dispose of things that we, the inhabitants and residents of Windsor, Hartford, and Wethersfield are now cohabiting



### TEACHING STRATEGY

**Understanding the Document** Practice reading the selections with expression and then read them aloud to the class. As you read a phrase, ask for volunteers to translate the phrase into modern English. When you have read both documents to the class, ask students to compare the reasons given in both documents for their writing and signing. Ask students to copy the graphic shown to summarize their answers.

| | The Mayflower Compact | The Fundamental Orders of Connecticut |
|---|---|---|
| **Reasons for Writing this Document** | for better order and for the preservation of the new colony and to further the ends for which the settlers made their voyage, the glory of God and the advancement of the Christian faith | to maintain peace and union among the settlers |

and dwelling in and upon the river of Conectecotte [Connecticut] and the lands thereunto adjoining; and well knowing where a people are gathered together the Word of God requires that, to maintain the peace and union of such a people, there should be an orderly and decent government established according to God, to order and dispose of the affairs of the people at all seasons as occasion shall require; do therefore associate and **conjoin**[1] ourselves to be as one public state or commonwealth. . . . As also in our civil affairs to be guided and governed according to such laws, rules, orders, and decrees as shall be made, ordered and decreed, as follows:

## *Laws, Rules, and Orders*

**1.** It is ordered, sentenced, and decreed that there shall be yearly two general assemblies or courts. . . . The first shall be called the Court of Election, wherein shall be yearly chosen . . . so many magistrates and other public officers as shall be found **requisite.**[2] . . .

**4.** It is ordered . . . that no person be chosen governor above once in two years, and that the governor be always a member of some approved congregation. . . .

**5.** It is ordered . . . that to the aforesaid Court of Election the several towns shall send their deputies. . . . Also, the other General Court in September shall be for making of laws, and any other public occasion which concerns the good of the Commonwealth. . . .

**7.** It is ordered . . . that after there are warrants given out for any of the said General Courts, the constable or constables of each town shall forthwith give notice distinctly to the inhabitants of the same . . . that at a place and time . . . they meet and assemble themselves together to elect and choose certain deputies to be at the General Court then following to [manage] the affairs of the Commonwealth. . . .

1. **conjoin:** unite.
2. **requisite:** required.

***A CLOSER LOOK***

**GOOD GOVERNMENT**

**Good government is pleasing to God in the eyes of the colonists. An orderly and decent government helps to maintain peace and order within a community and between people.**

**3. How would you define good government today?**

***A CLOSER LOOK***

**THE GOVERNOR'S ROLE**

**The person serving as governor can serve only once every two years and must be a member of an approved congregation.**

**4. Why might the colonists have wished to limit the power of the chief executive?**

***A CLOSER LOOK***

**THE COURTS**

**The Court of Election chooses officials to serve; the General Court makes laws.**

**5. Why might it be a good idea to separate these two functions?**

### *Interactive Primary Sources Assessment*

**1. Main Ideas**

a. Whose rights did the Mayflower Compact protect?

b. Why are written documents useful in setting up a government?

c. How were the Fundamental Orders based on religion?

**2. Critical Thinking**

**Comparing**

In what way are these two documents alike?

**THINK ABOUT**

- self-government
- majority rule

99

### *Interactive Primary Sources Assessment*

**1. Main Ideas**

**a.** It protected the rights of the Plymouth colonists.
**b.** They can provide a concrete statement of the roles and powers of the government.
**c.** It suggests that good government is divinely sanctioned.

**2. Critical Thinking**

Both assert the colonists will set aside individual interests to work for the good of the colony as a whole. Both also indicate that the purpose of government is based on consent of the governed.

## INSTRUCT

Key Questions

- What was the major purpose of the Mayflower Compact and the Fundamental Orders of Connecticut?
- Describe how the Fundamental Orders of Connecticut provides for a legislature, an executive, and a system of courts.
- How do the Mayflower Compact and the Fundamental Orders of Connecticut set up governments by the people?

### MAKING PERSONAL CONNECTIONS

If students were going to create a perfect community, what sort of government would it have? What laws would it have?

### MORE ABOUT . . .

**The Charter Oak**

The Fundamental Orders of Connecticut lasted until 1662, when Charles II issued a royal charter for the Connecticut colony. In 1687, James II wanted to revoke the charter. He sent Sir James Andros and an armed delegation to take the charter back, by force if necessary. Legend has it that as king's representatives and the colony's leaders debated with the charter on a table between them, suddenly all the candles went out. When someone lit the candles again, the charter had vanished. The story continues that Joseph Wadsworth, a colonial leader, seized the charter and hid it in a hole in a large oak tree at a nearby estate. The "charter oak" remains a revered symbol of Connecticut freedom to this day.

### *A CLOSER LOOK*

1. The colonists were looking for a better life, including economic prosperity, for themselves and their children.
2. The colonists were probably willing to put their own individual interests and opinions aside in favor of the common good of the group. The individual was expected to obey the rules of the community.
3. Most students will mention that a government should be representative, responsive, and fair.
4. They probably wished to avoid one person acquiring enough power to make him a despot or petty tyrant who could limit the freedom of the colonists.
5. By separating functions, the colonists separated the making of laws from the contest for power.

## SECTION OBJECTIVES

1. To compare the founding of the four Middle Colonies
2. To trace the growth of the Middle Colonies
3. To explain how economics influenced the development of the Southern Colonies
4. To identify unique reasons for the founding of Georgia and Maryland

**SKILLBUILDER**

Interpreting Maps: Region, Location, p. 102

**CRITICAL THINKING**

Forming Opinions, p. 101
Comparing and Contrasting, p. 102
Analyzing Causes, p. 103

**Why It Matters Now**
- British Connections Today, pp. 5–6

## FOCUS & MOTIVATE

### 5-MINUTE WARM-UP

**Reading a Map** These questions focus on how the English colonies grew.

1. Compare the map on page 102 with the one on page 87. How did the English colonies change in number and location?
2. In which set of colonies is the oldest settlement found?

 **Warm-Up Transparency WT3**

## INSTRUCT

### INSTRUCT: OBJECTIVE 

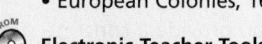

**The Middle Colonies**

Key Questions

- What attracted Catholics, Quakers, and Jews to these colonies?
- What economic activities were important in the Middle Colonies?

**In-Depth Resources: Unit 1**
- Guided Reading, p. 48

**Reading Study Guide** (Spanish and English), pp. 31–32

# 3 Founding the Middle and Southern Colonies

**TERMS & NAMES**
Peter Stuyvesant
patroon
Duke of York
proprietary colony
William Penn
Quaker
royal colony
James Oglethorpe

**MAIN IDEA**

The founding of the Middle and Southern colonies provided settlers with many economic opportunities.

**WHY IT MATTERS NOW**

America is still a place where immigrants seek freedom and economic opportunity.

## ONE AMERICAN'S STORY

**The Dutch had founded the colony of New Netherland (later New York) on the eastern coast of North America in 1624. Peter Stuyvesant, the new governor, arrived in the city of New Amsterdam in May 1647. Because of his harsh personality and rough manner, he soon lost the support of the Dutch colonists. In 1664, a British fleet ordered the city of New Amsterdam to surrender itself to British control. Stuyvesant was unable to gain the support of the Dutch colonists against the British. He surrendered and then defended his decision to his superiors back in the Netherlands.**

*A VOICE FROM THE PAST*

Powder and provisions failing, and no relief or reinforcements being expected, we were necessitated [forced] to come to terms with the enemy, not through neglect of duty or cowardice . . . but in consequence of an absolute impossibility to defend the fort, much less the city of New Amsterdam, and still less the country.

**Peter Stuyvesant**, quoted in *Peter Stuyvesant and His New York*

Peter Stuyvesant, governor of the Dutch colony of New Netherland, lost his leg in 1644 during a military action against the island of St. Martin in the Caribbean.

**After the surrender, Stuyvesant retired to his farm. This land later became part of New York City. In this section, you will read about the founding of the Middle Colonies (such as New York) and the Southern Colonies. You will learn who settled there and why they came.**

## 1 The Middle Colonies

The Middle Colonies were New York, New Jersey, Pennsylvania, and Delaware. They were located between New England to the north and the Chesapeake region to the south. (See the map on page 102.) Swedes, Dutch, English, Germans, and Africans were among the groups who came to these colonies.

Religious freedom attracted many groups, including Protestants, Catholics, Quakers, and Jews. The Hudson and Delaware rivers supported shipping and commerce. The river valleys had rich soil and mild winters. These conditions were favorable for farming and raising livestock.



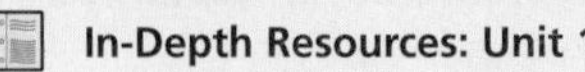

## RECOMMENDED RESOURCES

**In-Depth Resources: Unit 1**
- Guided Reading, p. 48
- Building Vocabulary, p. 49
- Primary Source: from Letter of Judith Giton Manigault, p. 54
- Reteaching Activity, p. 60

**Reading Study Guide** (Spanish and English), pp. 31–32

**Outline Map Activities**
- The 13 Colonies, pp. 5–6

**Why It Matters Now**
- British Connections Today, pp. 5–6

**Formal Assessment**
- Section Quiz, p. 50

**Alternative Assessment**
- Rubrics, 4.5
- Rubrics, 5.3

**Access for Students Acquiring English/ESL**
- Guided Reading, p. 18

**Technology Resources**

 **Geography Transparency GT3**
- European Colonies, 1650

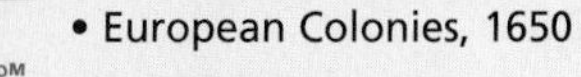

 **Electronic Teacher Tools with Test Maker**

 **ClassZone**
www.mcdougallittell.com

## ❷ New Netherland Becomes New York

In 1624, Dutch settlers financed by the Dutch West India Company founded the colony of New Netherland. New Netherland included the Hudson River valley, Long Island, and the land along the Delaware River.

To attract more settlers, the Dutch West India Company employed the patroon system. A **patroon** was a person who brought 50 settlers to New Netherland. As a reward, a patroon received a large land grant. He also received special privileges in hunting, fishing, and fur trading on his land.

In the early years, many different kinds of people settled in New Netherland. Twenty-three Jewish settlers arrived in 1654, and others soon followed. Later, Africans were brought to the colony as slaves and indentured servants. Many Puritans also came.

Peter Stuyvesant, the colony's governor, wanted to add land to New Netherland. He attacked the nearby charter colony of New Sweden in 1655. This colony was located along the Delaware River. The main settlement was Fort Christina (later named Wilmington, Delaware). It had been settled by Swedes in 1638. After an attack by the Dutch, the Swedes surrendered Fort Christina.

### America's HERITAGE

**THE LOG CABIN**

Swedish colonists living in Delaware built the first log cabin in America in 1638. The log cabin was the perfect house to build where there were many trees. Settlers needed few tools to build such cabins, which were made of round logs with curved notches at the ends. After the ends were placed in the notches, the logs were secured. After 1780, the log cabin became the typical frontier home.

**Background**
The Duke of York became King James II in 1685.

England's King Charles II decided that his brother, the **Duke of York,** should drive the Dutch out of New Netherland. The Dutch colony was a threat to England because of its trade. It was also a threat because of its expanding settlements and its location. There were English colonies in New England to the north and Virginia to the south. As you have seen, when the duke's ships appeared off New Amsterdam in August 1664, the colony surrendered. New Netherland became the **proprietary colony** of New York. The Duke of York was now the proprietor, or owner, of the colony.

**ReadingHistory**
**A. Forming Opinions** Why might the promise of religious freedom encourage a diverse population in a colony?
A. Answer
Different sorts of people with different beliefs would be drawn to a colony that promised religious freedom.

## New Jersey, Pennsylvania, and Delaware

The Duke of York had become the largest single landowner in America. He gave part of his claim, the province of New Jersey, to his friends Sir George Carteret and Lord John Berkeley in 1664. They encouraged settlers to come by promising freedom of religion. They also promised large grants of land and a representative assembly.

**William Penn** became another large landowner in America. Born into a wealthy English family, Penn joined the **Quakers,** to his father's disapproval. The young Penn was attacked for his Quaker beliefs. King Charles II owed the Penn family money. In repayment, in 1681 he gave Penn a large piece of land in America that came to be called Pennsylvania. The name means "Penn's woods."





### INSTRUCT: OBJECTIVE ❷

**New Netherland Becomes New York/ New Jersey, Pennsylvania, and Delaware**

Key Questions
- How did the patroon system help attract settlers to New Netherland?
- How did the English acquire New Netherland?
- How did the owners of the New Jersey colony attract settlers?
- How did Penn's religious beliefs affect the way he governed Pennsylvania?

**Geography Transparency GT3**
- European Colonies, 1650

### America's HERITAGE

**The Log Cabin**

The log cabin was the perfect shelter for the new colonists. It could be built easily using only an axe. After notching the logs at each end and stacking them, colonists filled in the spaces between the logs with moss, mud, or dried manure, a process known as chinking. With logs tightly fitted and cracks sealed with mud, houses were warm and snug.

### MORE ABOUT . . .

**William Penn**

Penn's Quaker beliefs included a belief that all people are equal. He was determined to treat the Native Americans of Pennsylvania fairly. Penn purchased land from the Lenapes, also called the Delawares, the largest Native American group in the area. Penn visited Lenape villages and learned the Lenape language. Penn also set up strict rules for colonists trading with Native Americans. He made it illegal to sell alcohol to Native Americans.

### ACTIVITY OPTIONS

#### INDIVIDUAL NEEDS

**STUDENTS ACQUIRING ENGLISH/ESL**

**Using Proper Nouns** To help students expand their use of proper nouns in relation to country of origin, pair proficient English speakers with students who are acquiring English. Invite student pairs to create charts with the headings "Country/Continent of Origin" and "Name of Group." Have students complete the chart for the groups who settled in the Middle Colonies. They can then expand the chart to include groups who have since settled in the United States.

| Country/Continent of Origin | Name of Group |
|---|---|
| Sweden | Swedes |
| Netherlands | Dutch |
| England | English |
| Germany | Germans |
| Africa | Africans |

## HISTORY FROM VISUALS

**Reading the Map** Point out to students the dates of the settlements on the map. Ask students what all the settlements shown on the map except Hartford have in common. **Answer** They are all located on or near the Atlantic coast. Have students suggest reasons for this. **Possible Responses** Initial settlements were along the coast. Ports often developed into cities as they became centers of shipping and the export-import trade.

**Extension** Have students use a current atlas or almanac to find out which of these cities rank as major population centers in their states today.

**Outline Map Activities**
- The 13 Colonies, pp. 5–6

## INSTRUCT: OBJECTIVE 

**The Southern Colonies/ Maryland and the Carolinas**

Key Questions
- Why did Lord Baltimore establish Maryland?
- How did slavery begin in the Carolinas?
- In what way did Carolina change after it became a royal colony?

 **In-Depth Resources: Unit 1**
- Primary Source, p. 54

## MORE ABOUT . . .

**Lord Baltimore**

Charles I gave Lord Baltimore a large slice of land from the Virginia colony. The boundary for the new colony was designated as the "further bank" of the Potomac River. This meant that the new colony had been granted the entire river, including fishing rights! The ensuing "oyster war" between Maryland and Virginia crab and oyster fishermen lasted for many years. In 1785 a powerful group of Virginians including Thomas Jefferson, James Madison, and George Washington helped negotiate rights for Virginians to fish the waters of the Potomac River.

### The 13 English Colonies, 1732



**GEOGRAPHY SKILLBUILDER**
**Interpreting Maps**
1. **Region** *What geological feature formed a logical western boundary for the colonies?*
2. **Location** *For approximately how many miles did the colonies extend along the eastern coast of North America?*

Skillbuilder Answers
1. Appalachian Mountains
2. About 1,200 miles

Penn used this land to create a colony where Quakers could live according to their beliefs. Among other things, the Quakers believed that all people should live in peace and harmony. They welcomed different religions and ethnic groups. In Pennsylvania, Penn extended religious freedom and equality to all. He especially wanted the Native Americans to be treated fairly. In a letter to them in 1681, Penn said, "May [we] always live together as neighbors and friends."

*Reading* **History**
**B. Comparing and Contrasting** How did Penn's policies toward Native Americans compare with those of other colonies you have read about?
B. Answer Penn's policies were more enlightened and tolerant than those in other colonies.

Penn's policies helped make Pennsylvania one of the wealthiest of the American colonies. Many settlers came to Pennsylvania seeking religious freedom and a better life. In 1704, Penn granted the three lower counties of Delaware their own assembly. The counties later broke away to form the colony of Delaware.

## 3 The Southern Colonies

The new Southern Colonies were Maryland, the Carolinas, and Georgia. The Appalachian Mountains bordered parts of these colonies in the west. In the east, the colonies bordered the Atlantic Ocean. The soil and climate of this region were suitable for warm-weather crops such as tobacco, rice, and indigo.

### Maryland and the Carolinas

Lord Baltimore established Maryland in 1632 for Roman Catholics fleeing persecution in England. To attract other settlers besides Catholics, Lord Baltimore promised religious freedom. In 1649, Maryland passed the Toleration Act.

Maryland based its economy on tobacco, which required backbreaking work. Every three or four years, the tobacco crop used up the soil, and workers had to clear new land. Most laborers came as either servants or slaves. Maryland attracted few women as settlers.

In 1663, Carolina was founded as a colony. English settlers from Barbados built Charles Town, later called Charleston, in 1670. They



## ACTIVITY OPTIONS

**INTERDISCIPLINARY LINK: ART/LANGUAGE ARTS** 

### ADVERTISING THE COLONIES

**Class Time** One class period

**Task** Creating an advertising brochure

**Purpose** To summarize attractions of the Southern and Middle Colonies for new settlers

**Supplies Needed**
- Reference materials on the Middle and Southern Colonies
- Construction paper
- Art supplies

**Activity** Assign each student a Middle or Southern Colony. Have students create advertising brochures to attract new settlers to the colony. The brochures may highlight geographic features such as climate and soil, economic opportunities, or incentives such as land grants or freedom of religion. Tell students to identify their target audience, their message, and the action they want their readers to take before beginning to work on their brochures. Have them draw or photocopy pictures and maps for their brochures.

busied themselves cutting timber, raising cattle, and trading with the Native Americans. After 1685, Charleston became a refuge for Huguenots, French Protestants seeking religious freedom.

**Vocabulary**
**Carolina:** The name of the colony is based on a Latin form of "Charles," in honor of King Charles II.

Carolina's colonists needed laborers to grow rice and indigo. The English settlers encouraged the use of enslaved Africans. They also sold local Native Americans into slavery. As a result, wars broke out between the settlers and the Tuscarora and Yamasee tribes. The settlers' taking of tribal lands also fueled the wars.

Carolina's proprietors, or owners, refused to send help to stop a threatened Spanish attack on Charleston. Because of this, the colonists overthrew the colony's proprietary rule in 1719. In 1729, Carolina became a **royal colony.** Then it was ruled by governors appointed by the king. The colony was divided into North Carolina and South Carolina.

## 4 Georgia

In 1732, **James Oglethorpe** founded Georgia as a refuge for debtors. The English government wanted to use the colony as a military outpost against Spanish Florida to the south and French Louisiana to the west. In 1739, during a war between England and Spain, the Spanish tried to force the English colonists out of Georgia but were unsuccessful. English, German, Swiss, and Scottish colonists settled in Georgia. All religions were welcome. As the colony's leader, Oglethorpe set strict rules that upset the colonists. The king, in response to unrest, made Georgia a royal colony in 1752.

***Reading*History**
**C. Reading a Map** Use the map on page 102 to check the location of Georgia in relation to the Spanish territory of Florida.

By the early 1700s, there were 13 English colonies along the eastern coast of North America. In the next chapter, you will read about how these colonies developed.

James Oglethorpe was the founder of Georgia.

### Section 3 Assessment

**1. Terms & Names**
**Identify:**
- Peter Stuyvesant
- patroon
- Duke of York
- proprietary colony
- William Penn
- Quaker
- royal colony
- James Oglethorpe

**2. Taking Notes**
Identify an effect for each cause listed in the chart below.

| Cause | Effect |
|---|---|
| New Netherland threat to English | |
| English attacked Quakers | |
| Laborers needed in Carolinas | |
| Oglethorpe too strict in Georgia | |

**3. Main Ideas**
a. What were the goals of the patroon system?
b. What three Middle Colonies offered religious freedom?
c. What were three crops grown in the Southern Colonies?

**4. Critical Thinking**
**Analyzing Causes** Why did colonists in Maryland and the Carolinas enslave Native Americans and use African slaves?
**THINK ABOUT**
- the crops being grown
- the nature of farm work

**ACTIVITY OPTIONS**
**LANGUAGE ARTS**
**SCIENCE**
What are the health effects of tobacco? Write a **news article** or give a **television report** for a science show about the effects of tobacco on the body.





**INSTRUCT: OBJECTIVE 4**

**Georgia**
Key Questions
- Why did James Oglethorpe found Georgia?
- How did the English government intend to use the Georgia colony?

**MORE ABOUT . . .**

**James Oglethorpe**
Before coming to the Americas, James Oglethorpe was educated at Oxford University. In 1722, he entered Parliament where he headed a committee on prison reforms. His committee work led him to think about founding a colony where people who were poor and had been imprisoned for debt could start over. Oglethorpe came to Georgia in 1733 with the first settlers. During the war between England and Spain, Oglethorpe led the defense of the territory.

## ASSESS & RETEACH

**Setting the Stage** Have students complete sequencing boxes for colonies in this section.

**Formal Assessment**
- Section Quiz, p. 50

**Critical Thinking Transparency CT7**
- Setting the Stage

**RETEACHING ACTIVITY**
Have the students read the introductory paragraph on the Middle Colonies. Then have students write one main idea and find two supporting statements about the Middle Colonies. Repeat for the Southern Colonies.

**In-Depth Resources: Unit 1**
- Reteaching Activity, p. 60

### Section 3 Assessment

**1. Terms & Names**
**Peter Stuyvesant,** p. 100
**patroon,** p. 101
**Duke of York,** p. 101
**proprietary colony,** p. 101
**William Penn,** p. 101
**Quaker,** p. 101
**royal colony,** p. 103
**James Oglethorpe,** p. 103

**2. Taking Notes**
Items for effects column:
- English attacked New Netherland.
- Penn founded Pennsylvania.
- African slaves were used.
- Georgia became a royal colony.

**3. Main Ideas**
**a.** to attract settlers and encourage farming in New Netherland **b.** Pennsylvania, New Jersey, New York **c.** rice, indigo, tobacco

**4. Critical Thinking**
These colonies grew labor-intensive crops cultivated on large tracts of land and requiring many laborers.

**ACTIVITY OPTIONS**

**Alternative Assessment**
- Rubrics for an article, 4.5
- Rubrics for a television report, 5.3

## TERMS & NAMES

1. **joint-stock company,** p. 86
2. **Jamestown,** p. 87
3. **John Smith,** p. 87
4. **House of Burgesses,** p. 88
5. **Pilgrims,** p. 92
6. **Mayflower Compact,** p. 93
7. **Great Migration,** p. 94
8. **Fundamental Orders of Connecticut,** p. 95
9. **proprietary colony,** p. 101
10. **William Penn,** p. 101

## REVIEW QUESTIONS

**Possible Responses**

1. to provide a market for English exports, to serve as a source of raw materials, to plant the Protestant faith in America
2. to split profits and divide losses
3. He developed a high-grade tobacco, which became a basic crop.
4. He saw it as a commonwealth that would serve as a model for other people and communities.
5. Each congregation set up its own town. People gathered for town meetings in the meetinghouse. Only church members could vote or hold office. They elected the members of the General Court, which chose the governor.
6. Many settlers and Native Americans were killed, many villages were attacked and destroyed, and many Native Americans were enslaved.
7. The Dutch colony was a threat to England because of its expanding settlements, location, and trade.
8. The relations between the Native Americans and settlers in Pennsylvania were better than in any other colony.
9. This was an act passed in the colony of Maryland that promised religious freedom to attract settlers.
10. tobacco, rice, and indigo

# Chapter 3 ASSESSMENT

## TERMS & NAMES

Briefly explain the importance of each of the following.

1. joint-stock company
2. Jamestown
3. John Smith
4. House of Burgesses
5. Pilgrims
6. Mayflower Compact
7. Great Migration
8. Fundamental Orders of Connecticut
9. proprietary colony
10. William Penn

## REVIEW QUESTIONS

**Early Colonies Have Mixed Success (pages 85–91)**

1. What were the reasons given by Richard Hakluyt that England should start a colony?
2. Why were Jamestown and Plymouth financed by joint-stock companies?
3. How did John Rolfe change the Virginia colony?

**New England Colonies (pages 92–99)**

4. What was John Winthrop's vision for Massachusetts Bay?
5. What was the system of government in the Massachusetts Bay Colony?
6. What were some of the effects of King Philip's War?

**Founding the Middle and Southern Colonies (pages 100–103)**

7. Why did Charles II want New Netherland?
8. What were relations like between Native Americans and settlers in Pennsylvania?
9. What was the Toleration Act of 1649?
10. What sorts of crops were particularly well suited to the soil and climate in the Southern colonies?

## CRITICAL THINKING

**1. USING YOUR NOTES**

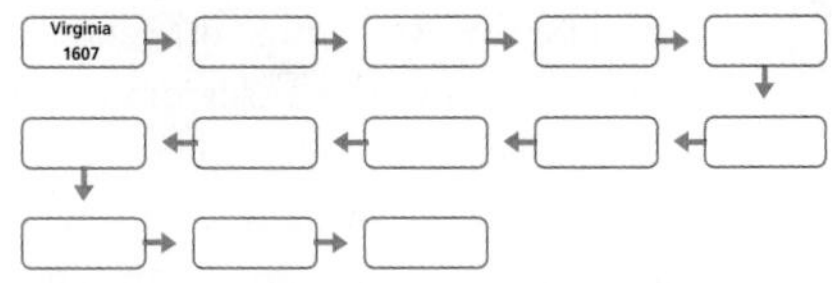


Using your completed chart, answer these questions:

a. Which was the earliest successful settlement in Virginia?

b. Which colony was founded last?

**2. ANALYZING LEADERSHIP**

Why do you think William Penn was a more successful leader than Peter Stuyvesant?

**3. APPLYING CITIZENSHIP SKILLS**

What were some of the common ideals that link the Mayflower Compact, the establishment of the House of Burgesses, and town meetings?

**4. THEME: IMPACT OF THE INDIVIDUAL**

How did individual effort help ensure the success of England's colonies in America?

**5. ANALYZING CAUSES**

Why might the Puritans have been intolerant of religious dissenters?

**Interact *with* History**

How do the dangers you discussed before you read this chapter compare with the dangers people actually faced?

## VISUAL SUMMARY

### The 13 Colonies

| | Colony | Important Early Dates | Founder(s) |
|---|---|---|---|
| New England Colonies | Massachusetts | Plymouth,1620; Mass. Bay, 1630 | Pilgrims; Puritans |
| | New Hampshire | Portsmouth, 1623 | Proprietors |
| | Rhode Island | Providence, 1636 | Roger Williams |
| | Connecticut | Hartford, 1636 | Thomas Hooker |
| Middle Colonies | New York (New Netherland) | Dutch settlers arrive, 1624 | Dutch West India Company |
| | Delaware | Fort Christina, 1638 | Swedes |
| | New Jersey | Duke of York establishes, 1664 | George Carteret, John Berkeley |
| | Pennsylvania | Charles II bestows land, 1681 | William Penn |
| Southern Colonies | Virginia | Jamestown, 1607 | Virginia Company of London |
| | Maryland | Founded as religious haven, 1632 | Lord Baltimore |
| | North Carolina | Founded, 1663 | Proprietors |
| | South Carolina | Founded, 1663 | Proprietors |
| | Georgia | Founded as debtors' refuge, 1732 | James Oglethorpe |

104

## CRITICAL THINKING

**Possible Responses**

1. **USING YOUR NOTES** **a.** Jamestown in 1607 **b.** Georgia in 1732
2. **ANALYZING LEADERSHIP** Penn promised freedom of religion and equality to all settlers. He wanted to treat Native Americans fairly.
3. **APPLYING CITIZENSHIP SKILLS** All are based on the ideals of self-government and majority rule.
4. **THEME: IMPACT OF THE INDIVIDUAL** Some of the earliest individuals saved the Virginia colony through discipline, bravery, and hard work. The Pilgrims and Puritans structured communities around strict religious ideals, self-government, and hard work.
5. **ANALYZING CAUSES** The Puritans believed that they had a covenant with God to build a holy society. They believed that anybody who broke the laws of the commonwealth went against the will of God.

**Interact *with* History** Answers will vary, but most discussions will probably center on the dangers of starvation, bad weather, shipwreck, and hostile Native Americans.

## HISTORY SKILLS

### 1. INTERPRETING GRAPHS

Study the graph and then answer the questions.

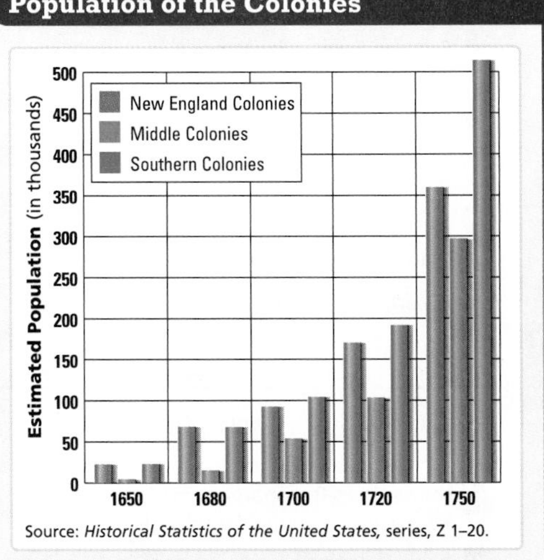


a. How much did the population of the Southern colonies increase between 1720 and 1750?

b. What was the increase in the population of the New England colonies between 1700 and 1720?

c. Which region had the largest population over the years, and which region had the smallest?

### 2. INTERPRETING PRIMARY SOURCES

The early colonists used a surveyor's compass (below) to divide up the land they had come to settle.

a. What attitudes about ownership of the land are revealed by the use of a surveyor's compass?

b. How might the use of a surveyor's compass reflect differences in attitudes toward the land between European settlers and Native Americans?

## ALTERNATIVE ASSESSMENT

### 1. INTERDISCIPLINARY ACTIVITY: Geography

**Drawing a Map** Draw a map of the New England, Middle, and Southern colonies. Place on the map the major cities and rivers of each colony. Explain how each region's geographic location contributed to the colonies' economic activities. Share your map with the class.

### 2. COOPERATIVE LEARNING ACTIVITY

**Performing a Scene from a Play** The "lost colonists" of Roanoke disappeared sometime between 1588 and 1590. Write and perform a play depicting a meeting of the colonists in which they try to decide what to do. John White has not returned with the supplies he promised to bring. How are the colonists to deal with food shortages, illness, and relations with the Native Americans?

Take the roles of Elinor Dare and her husband, Ananias; their child, Virginia; and other colonists. Come up with different solutions to their problems. Then vote on your preferred course of action.

### 3. PRIMARY SOURCE EXPLORER

**Planning a Government** As with any group of people living in a community, some sort of government was needed in Plymouth. The Pilgrims devised the Mayflower Compact. Using the CD-ROM, library, and Internet, find out more about the Mayflower Compact.

Create your own plan for a government using the following suggestions:

- Draw up a plan for a government that will apply to your class.
- Adapt ideas from the Mayflower Compact that you think will work for the class.
- Decide what rules are needed in your government. Decide who will hold office, how they will be appointed or selected, and how long they will serve.
- Decide whether there should be limits on majority rule in your government.

### 4. HISTORY PORTFOLIO

**Option 1** Review your section and chapter assessment activities. Select the one that you think is your best work. Then use comments made by your teacher or classmates to improve your work, and add it to your portfolio.

**Option 2** Review the questions that you wrote for What Do You Want to Know? on page 84. Then write a short report in which you explain the answers to your questions. Add your answers to your portfolio.



## ALTERNATIVE ASSESSMENT

**1. INTERDISCIPLINARY ACTIVITY: Geography**
**Map should**
- contain major rivers and cities.
- explain the connection between location and economics.
- include clear, informative labels and captions.

**2. COOPERATIVE LEARNING ACTIVITY**
**Scenes from plays should**
- include stage directions that describe the setting, cast of characters, and props.
- contain authentic-sounding dialogue.
- dramatize moments from the meeting of the colonists.

**3. PRIMARY SOURCE EXPLORER**
**Plans for a government should**
- apply to the specific situation of the class.
- adapt some ideas from the Mayflower Compact.
- present detailed rules and ideas for choosing officers.
- address the problem of majority rule and minority rights.

**4. HISTORY PORTFOLIO**

**Option 1 Revised section or chapter assessment activities should**
- address teacher and peer responses to the selected work.
- solve problems present in the first versions of the work.

**Option 2 Short reports should**
- answer questions about the Europeans who settled in North America.
- use evidence to develop and support ideas.
- cite sources of information.
- use standard grammar, spelling, sentence structure, and punctuation.

**Critical Thinking Transparency CT9**
- Visual Summary

**Formal Assessment**
- Chapter Test, Forms A and B, pp. 51–58

## HISTORY SKILLS

**Possible Responses**

**1. INTERPRETING GRAPHS**

**a.** The population increased by more than 322,000.

**b.** The population increased by more than 78,000.

**c.** The Southern Colonies had the largest population, and the Middle Colonies had the smallest.

**2. INTERPRETING PRIMARY SOURCES**

**a.** The surveyor's compass suggests that the land can be divided up and owned by individuals.

**b.** Native Americans did not believe that individuals could own the land.

## CHAPTER 4 PLANNING GUIDE

# The Colonies Develop 1700–1753

## CHAPTER RESOURCES

**CHAPTER OVERVIEW**

The chapter examines the development of the English colonies into four distinct regions: New England, the Middle Colonies, the Southern Colonies, and the Backcountry. The chapter also discusses the influence of religion on the early colonies and the increasing economic dependence on slavery in the South.

**COPYMASTERS**

**In-Depth Resources: Unit 1**
- Tracing Themes: Economics in History, p. 63
- Building Vocabulary, p. 68

**Interdisciplinary Projects,** pp. 19–24

**TECHNOLOGY**

**Primary Source Explorer**

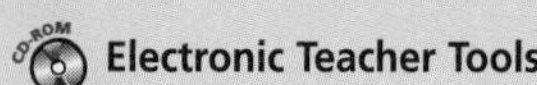
**Electronic Teacher Tools**

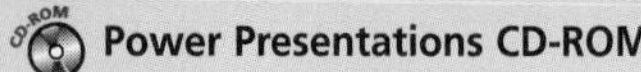
**Power Presentations CD-ROM**

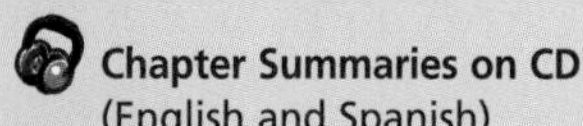
**Chapter Summaries on CD** (English and Spanish)

**America's Music CD**

## SECTION 1 New England: Commerce and Religion pp. 109–113

**KEY IDEAS**

- New England colonists depend on subsistence farming, fishing, and timber.
- Trade is also a major factor in the New England economy.
- Puritanism declines as a result of increasing religious diversity and the drive for economic success.

**COPYMASTERS**

**In-Depth Resources: Unit 1**
- Setting the Stage, p. 62
- Guided Reading, p. 64
- Reteaching Activity, p. 77

**Citizenship Today,** pp. 42–45

**TECHNOLOGY**

**Warm-Up Transparency WT4**

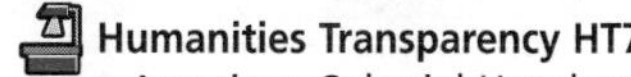
**Humanities Transparency HT7**
- American Colonial Hornbook

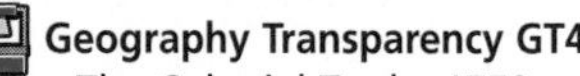
**Geography Transparency GT4**
- The Colonial Trade, 1750

**Critical Thinking Transparency CT10**
- Setting the Stage

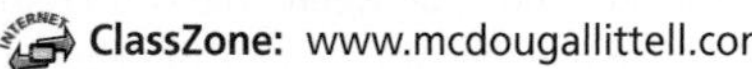
**ClassZone:** www.mcdougallittell.com

## SECTION 2 The Middle Colonies: Farms and Cities pp. 114–118

- The Middle Colonies prosper based on a wealth of resources and cash crops.
- Cities thrive as trading centers in the Middle Colonies.
- The Middle Colonies foster diversity of culture and religious tolerance.

**COPYMASTERS**

**In-Depth Resources: Unit 1**
- Setting the Stage, p. 62
- Guided Reading, p. 65
- Skillbuilder Practice: Creating a Map, p. 69
- Geography Application: Colonial Immigrant Groups, 1750, pp. 70–71
- Reteaching Activity, p. 78

**TECHNOLOGY**

**Warm-Up Transparency WT4**

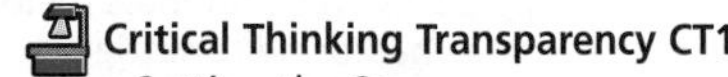
**Critical Thinking Transparency CT10**
- Setting the Stage

**ClassZone:** www.mcdougallittell.com

## SECTION 3 The Southern Colonies: Plantations and Slavery pp. 119–125

- The Southern Colonies develop plantations that depend on slave labor.
- The planter class dominates the Southern economy, while small landowners move west.
- African Americans resist slavery, and slaveholders respond with harsh slave codes.

**COPYMASTERS**

**In-Depth Resources: Unit 1**
- Setting the Stage, p. 62
- Guided Reading, p. 66
- Literature Selection, pp. 74–76
- Reteaching Activity, p. 79

**America's History Makers**
- Eliza Lucas Pinckney, pp. 15–16

**Outline Map Activities**
- Colonial Products, pp. 7–8

**TECHNOLOGY**

**Warm-Up Transparency WT4**

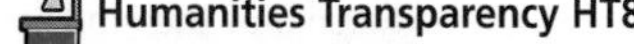
**Humanities Transparency HT8**
- Maryland Plantation, 18th Century

**Critical Thinking Transparency CT10**
- Setting the Stage

**Critical Thinking Transparency CT11**
- Cause and Effect: The Slave Trade

**ClassZone:** www.mcdougallittell.com

## SECTION 4 The Backcountry pp. 126–129

- The Backcountry, along the Appalachian Mountains, is a region of small farms and log cabins.
- Backcountry farms are isolated, forcing settlers to be self-sufficient.
- Backcountry settlers come into conflict with the area's Spanish, French, and Native American residents.

**COPYMASTERS**

**In-Depth Resources: Unit 1**
- Setting the Stage, p. 62
- Guided Reading, p. 67
- Primary Source, pp. 72–73
- Reteaching Activity, p. 80

**America's History Makers**
- Alexander Spotswood, pp. 17–18

**Economics in History**
- Native American Economies, p. 4

**Why It Matters Now**
- Regional Differences, pp. 7–8

**TECHNOLOGY**

**Warm-Up Transparency WT4**

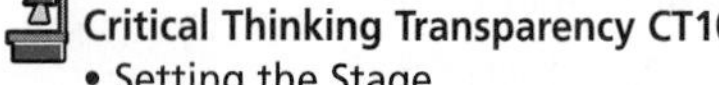
**Critical Thinking Transparency CT10**
- Setting the Stage

**Critical Thinking Transparency CT12**
- Visual Summary

**ClassZone:** www.mcdougallittell.com

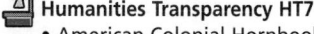

PE Pupil's Edition
Copymaster
Overhead Transparency
Audio Library
 CD-ROM
 Internet

## ASSESSMENT

**PE** **Chapter Assessment,** pp. 130–131

**Formal Assessment**
- Chapter Tests, Forms A and B, pp. 65–72

**Alternative Assessment Book**

**Electronic Teacher Tools with Test Maker**

---

**PE** **Section Assessment,** p. 113

**Formal Assessment**
- Section Quiz, p. 61

**Alternative Assessment Book**
- Rubrics for a mobile, 1.9
- Rubrics for multimedia, 5.4

**Electronic Teacher Tools with Test Maker**

---

**PE** **Section Assessment,** p. 118

**Formal Assessment**
- Section Quiz, p. 62

**Alternative Assessment Book**
- Rubrics for a database, 2.6
- Rubrics for a map, 2.1

**Electronic Teacher Tools with Test Maker**

---

**PE** **Section Assessment,** p. 123

**Formal Assessment**
- Section Quiz, p. 63

**Alternative Assessment Book**
- Rubrics for a diagram, 1.3
- Rubrics for a report, 2.5

**Electronic Teacher Tools with Test Maker**

---

**PE** **Section Assessment,** p. 129

**Formal Assessment**
- Section Quiz, p. 64

**Alternative Assessment Book**
- Rubrics for a newspaper, 4.5
- Rubrics for a cartoon, 1.3

**Electronic Teacher Tools with Test Maker**

## CUSTOMIZING FOR INDIVIDUAL NEEDS

### Students Acquiring English/ESL

**Reading Study Guide** (English and Spanish), pp. 35–44

**Access for Students Acquiring English/ESL: Spanish Translations,** pp. 22–28

**Chapter Summaries on CD** (English and Spanish)

### Less Proficient Readers

**Reading Study Guide** (English and Spanish), pp. 35–44

**Chapter Summaries on CD** (English and Spanish)

### Gifted and Talented Students

**In-Depth Resources: Unit 1**
- Enrichment Activity, p. 81

**America's History Makers**
- Eliza Lucas Pinckney, pp. 15–16
- Alexander Spotswood, pp. 17–18

## CROSS-CURRICULAR CONNECTIONS

### Science/Technology

Murphy, Jim. ***Gone A-Whaling: The Lure of the Sea and the Hunt for the Great Whale.*** Boston: Houghton Mifflin, 1998.

### Popular Culture

Kamensky, Jane. ***The Colonial Mosaic: American Women 1600–1760.*** The Young Oxford History of Women in the United States. New York: Oxford University Press, 1995.

Wood, Peter H. ***Strange New Land: Africans in Colonial America, 1516–1776.*** The Young Oxford History of African Americans. New York: Oxford University Press, 1996.

### Interdisciplinary Projects, pp. 19–24

- Math: People of North America
- Science: Vibration and Sound
- Language Arts: American English
- Art: Dyeing Colonial Fabrics

### Language Arts/Literature

Cwiklik, Robert. ***King Philip.*** New York: Silver Burdett, 1989. Novel of the life of Metacom and his 1675–1676 rebellion.

Pyle, Howard. ***Tales of Pirates and Buccaneers.*** New York: Random House, reissued 1994. Classic adventure stories based on historical pirates.

Richter, Conrad. ***The Light in the Forest.*** New York: Bantam, (1953) 1984. Acclaimed novel based on the true story of John Butler, who was captured by the Delaware Indians in 1765 and chose to stay with his captors rather than return home.

### McDougal Littell Literature Connections

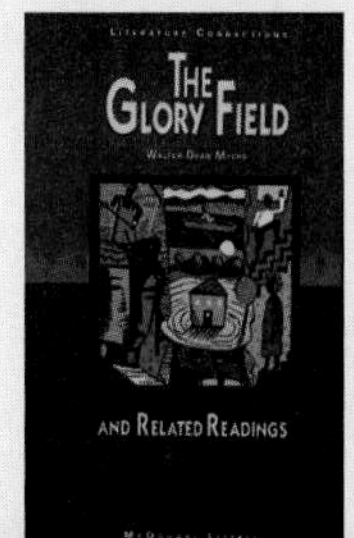


Walter Dean Myers

***The Glory Field***

Beginning with a voyage on a slave ship, this novel chronicles the saga of an African-American family from the 1700s to the present.

## ENRICHMENT ACTIVITIES

**PE** **Pupil's Edition, pp. 106–131**
**Interact with History,** p. 107
**Geography in History,** pp. 124–125

**In-Depth Resources: Unit 1**
- Geography Application: Colonial Immigrant Groups, 1750, pp. 70–71
- Primary Source: Culture Clash in the Colonies, pp. 72–73
- Literature Selection: from *Roots* by Alex Haley, pp. 74–76

**America's History Makers**
- Eliza Lucas Pinckney, pp. 15–16
- Alexander Spotswood, pp. 17–18

**Outline Map Activities**
- Colonial Products, pp. 7–8

**Why It Matters Now**
- Regional Differences, pp. 7–8

# CHAPTER 4 PACING GUIDE

**LESSON PLAN OPTIONS (50-MINUTE PERIOD)** (TE) = Teacher's Edition (PE) = Pupil's Edition

| | TEACHER-DIRECTED ACTIVITIES<br>Class Time: 15 minutes | STUDENT-CENTERED ACTIVITIES<br>Class Time: 25 minutes | INDIVIDUAL ACTIVITIES<br>Class Time: 10 minutes |
|---|---|---|---|
| **DAY 1**<br>Introduction<br>pp. 106–108 | **Presentation Options**<br>• Begin with a class discussion of the painting on p. 106 **(PE)**.<br>• Lead a class discussion on the "What Do You Know?" question in Setting the Stage, p. 108. Then introduce the graphic organizer for the chapter **(PE)**. | **Options for Cooperative Learning**<br>• Have student groups discuss the Interact with History questions, p. 107 **(PE)**.<br>• Have student groups respond to the "What Do You Want to Know?" question in Setting the Stage, p. 108 **(PE)**. | **Head Start on Homework Options**<br>• Have students skim Section 1 Main Idea, Why It Matters Now, Terms & Names, and the main headings, p. 109 **(PE)**.<br>• Have students begin Guided Reading activity and Building Vocabulary sheet. |
| **DAY 2**<br>Section 1<br>pp. 109–113 | **Presentation Options**<br>• Begin with the 5-Minute Warm-Up, p. 109 **(TE)**.<br>• Review the Section 1 Main Idea, Why It Matters Now, and Terms & Names, p. 109 **(PE)**.<br>• Choose 5 key questions for Objectives 1–4 to discuss with the class, pp. 109–113 **(PE)**. | **Options for Cooperative Learning**<br>• Divide students into groups to answer the questions posed in Geography Skillbuilder and do the History from Visuals Extension, p. 110 **(PE) (TE)**.<br>• Have student pairs work together to complete one of the Activity Options in the Section 1 Assessment, p. 113 **(PE)**. | **Head Start on Homework Options**<br>• Have students begin working on Section 1 Assessment, p. 113 **(PE)**.<br>• Have students preview Section 2 Main Idea, Why It Matters Now, Terms & Names, and the main headings, p. 114 **(PE)**. |
| **DAY 3**<br>Section 2<br>pp. 114–118 | **Presentation Options**<br>• Begin with the 5-Minute Warm-Up, p. 114 **(TE)**.<br>• Choose 5 key questions for Objectives 1–4 to discuss with the class, pp. 114–118 **(TE)**.<br>• Lead the students through the Skillbuilder Mini-Lesson: Creating a Map, p. 115 **(TE)**. | **Options for Cooperative Learning**<br>• Divide students into groups and have them complete the Interdisciplinary Link, Math: Calculating Diversity, p. 117 **(TE)**.<br>• Have student pairs work together to complete one of the Activity Options in the Section 2 Assessment, p. 118 **(PE)**. | **Head Start on Homework Options**<br>• Have students begin working on Section 2 Assessment, p. 118 **(PE)**.<br>• Have students complete Skillbuilder Practice. **In-Depth Resources,** p. 69. |
| **DAY 4**<br>Section 3<br>pp. 119–125 | **Presentation Options**<br>• Begin with the 5-Minute Warm-Up, p. 119 **(TE)**.<br>• Choose 5 key questions for Objectives 1–4 to discuss with the class, pp. 119–122 **(TE)**.<br>• Lead the students through the Geography Skillbuilder, p. 120 **(PE)**. | **Options for Cooperative Learning**<br>• Divide students into groups and have them complete the Geography in History questions, pp. 124–125 **(PE)**.<br>• Have student pairs work together to complete the answers to the Reading History questions for the section **(PE)**. | **Head Start on Homework Options**<br>• Have students read the Literature Selection. **In-Depth Resources,** pp. 74–76.<br>• Have students preview Section 4 Main Idea, Why It Matters Now, Terms & Names, and the main headings, p. 126 **(PE)**. |
| **DAY 5**<br>Section 4<br>pp. 126–129 | **Presentation Options**<br>• Begin with the 5-Minute Warm-Up, p. 126 **(TE)**.<br>• Choose 5 key questions for Objectives 1–4 to discuss with the class, pp. 126–128 **(TE)**.<br>• Lead the students through Geography in History, pp. 124–125 **(PE)**. | **Options for Cooperative Learning**<br>• Divide students into groups and have them complete the Interdisciplinary Link, The Arts: American Quilts, p. 127 **(TE)**.<br>• Divide students into groups and have them complete the Geography Skillbuilder, p. 127 **(PE)**. | **Head Start on Homework Options**<br>• Have students complete the Setting the Stage graphic organizer for the chapter, p. 108 **(PE)**.<br>• Have students begin working on the Chapter Assessment, pp. 130–131 **(PE)**.<br>• Prepare for Chapter Test<br>**Formal Assessment,** pp. 65–72 |

**TEACHER-TESTED ACTIVITY** **Robert Sisko, Carteret Middle School, Carteret, New Jersey**

## THE FOUR COLONIAL REGIONS

**Class Time** Two class periods

**Task** Reporting historical events as an oral presentation

**Purpose** To identify and describe key events of the colonial period

**Supplies Needed**

- Reference books and Internet sources on New England, the Middle and Southern Colonies, and the Backcountry

**Activity** Divide the class into small groups. Assign each group one of the four colonial regions. Tell students that they are news teams at the scene of an event that occurred in their region. Their assignment is to give a two-minute oral presentation about this event. The report should focus on the key aspects of a news story—Who, What, Where, When, Why, and How. After each group chooses its event and decides how to report it, students can select their reporter and give him or her a "pen name" by combining his or her first name with the last name of a colonial historical figure.

## BLOCK SCHEDULING — LESSON PLAN OPTIONS (90-MINUTE PERIOD)

### DAY 1

**Interact with History,** p. 107
**Class Time** 20 minutes

Options for pacing and variety:

- **Role Playing** Have students make up identities for themselves as immigrants arriving in a port city of the 1700s. Have students write short descriptions of themselves telling where they came from, how they made a living in their homeland, and whether they hope to settle on a farm or in a town and why. **Class Time** 20 minutes

**Setting the Stage,** p. 108
**Class Time** 20 minutes

Options for pacing and variety:

- **Time Saver** For a homework assignment, have students create the Read and Take Notes graphic organizer. Remind students to complete the organizer as they read the chapter. **Class Time** 5 minutes
- **Peer Teaching** From their study of Chapter 3, students already have some knowledge of three of the colonial regions. Have them work in pairs to share their knowledge with each other and then make a list of four questions they would like to have answered. **Class Time** 15 minutes

**Section 1,** pp. 109–113
**Class Time** 50 minutes

Options for pacing and variety:

- **Internet** Extend students' background knowledge of colonial life in New England with a visit to Old Sturbridge Village at www.mcdougallittell.com **Class Time** 20 minutes

### DAY 2

**Section 2,** pp. 114–118
**Class Time** 45 minutes

Options for pacing and variety:

- **Time Saver** Use the map The Middle Colonies, 1750 on page 115 and the chart by the same name on page 117 as graphic summaries of the section. **Class Time** 10 minutes

**Section 3,** pp. 119–125
**Class Time** 45 minutes

Options for pacing and variety:

- **Time Saver** For a homework assignment after the completion of this section, have students answer the Analyzing Leadership Critical Thinking question on page 130. Have volunteers share responses with the class. **Class Time** 20 minutes
- **History on Film** Extend students' background knowledge of the Southern Colonies by viewing *Colonial Life in the South.* Coronet. **Class Time** 20 minutes

### DAY 3

**Section 4,** pp. 126–129
**Class Time** 45 minutes

Options for pacing and variety:

- **Time Saver** As a homework assignment have students complete the Read and Take Notes chart shown on page 108. Ask them to write three or four sentences telling how the Backcountry differed from other regions in resources and people. **Class Time** 10 minutes

**Chapter 4 Assessment,** pp. 130–131
**Class Time** 40 minutes

Options for pacing and variety:

- **Role Playing** Have students review the Interact with History questions on page 130 and write a response for the immigrant they role-played before they read the chapter. **Class Time** 15 minutes
- **Peer Evaluation** Have students work in groups of four to answer the Economics in History Critical Thinking question on page 130. Ask each student to answer the question for a different colonial region and let other members of the group evaluate his or her response. **Class Time** 20 minutes

## CHAPTER 4 OBJECTIVE

The student will analyze the economic and social development of the American colonies during the first half of the 18th century.

# The Colonies Develop 1700–1753



### HISTORY FROM VISUALS

**Interpreting the Painting** Ask the students to study the painting of Philadelphia harbor or the Delaware River in 1702. Ask them to make inferences about the effect of the city's location on its economy and on its physical and social development. **Possible Responses** The city had access to a large harbor; the presence of sailing ships in the painting emphasizes the importance of trade during this period. The location probably affected its physical development because houses can be seen near the port area in the painting. Wealthy merchants and tradespeople probably built their homes close to their businesses.

**Extension** Have students name five occupations of citizens living in 18th-century colonial Philadelphia.

### CRITICAL THINKING ACTIVITY

**Making Inferences** Have students make inferences about the kinds of goods that citizens of colonial Philadelphia would have imported and exported. Ask them to organize their answers on two web diagrams.

**Class Time** 15 minutes

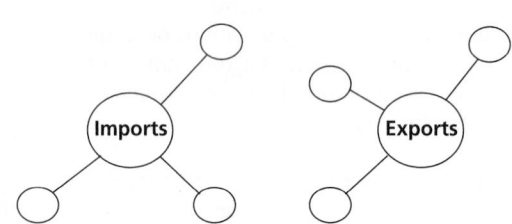

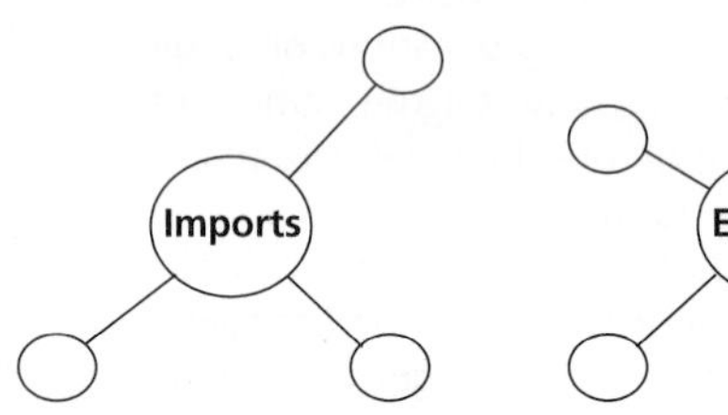


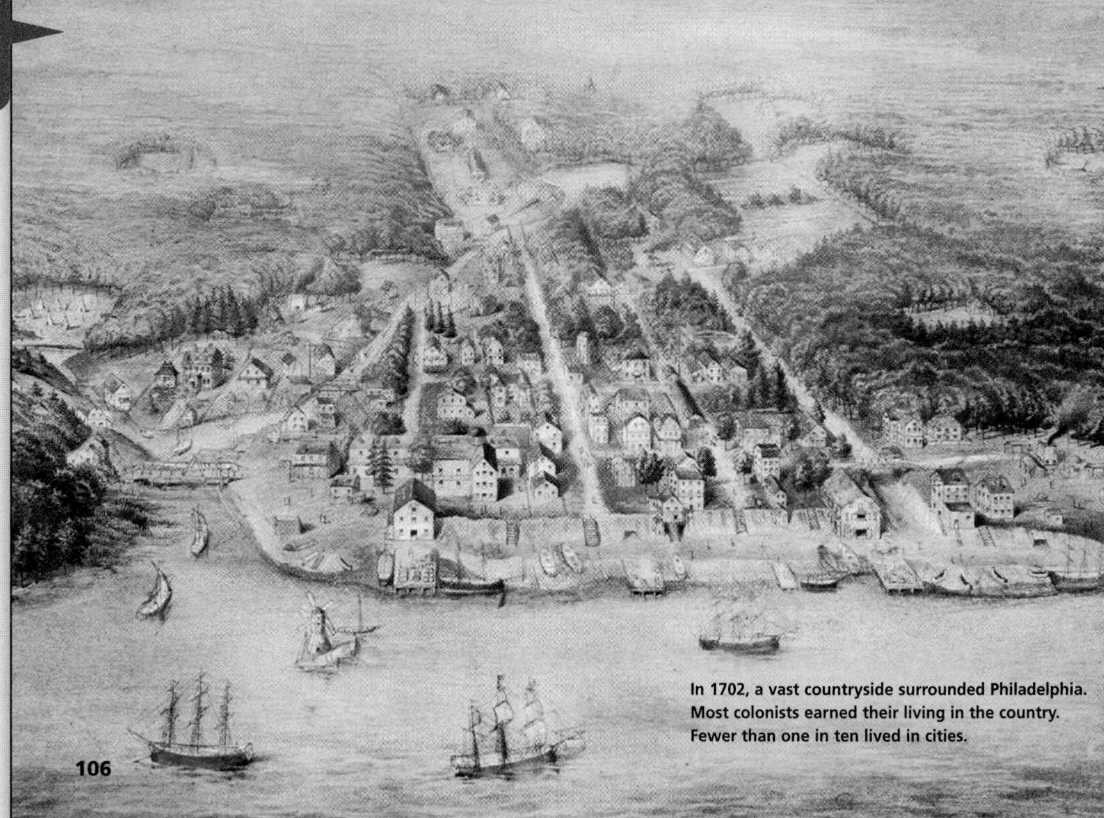

In 1702, a vast countryside surrounded Philadelphia. Most colonists earned their living in the country. Fewer than one in ten lived in cities.



### RECOMMENDED RESOURCES

**BOOKS FOR THE TEACHER**

Leach, Douglas. ***Flintlock and Tomahawk: New England in King Philip's War.*** New York: Parnassus, 1992.

Merrell, James H. ***Into the American Woods.*** New York: Norton, 1999. Life on the Pennsylvania frontier.

Woodmason, Charles. ***The Carolina Backcountry on the Eve of the Revolution.*** Ed. Richard J. Hooker. Chapel Hill, NC: U. of N.C. Press, 1953. Classic account of frontier life from the journal of an itinerant minister.

**SOFTWARE**

***Colonization.*** Diskette. Tom Snyder Productions/Software. Interesting presentation of colonizing process.

**VIDEO**

***Silversmith of Williamsburg.*** U. Press of Va., n.d. Together with similar titles on a gunsmith and a hammerman, a useful look at the practice of some colonial crafts.

**INTERNET**

For more about Old Sturbridge Village, visit www.mcdougallittell.com

## Interact *with* History

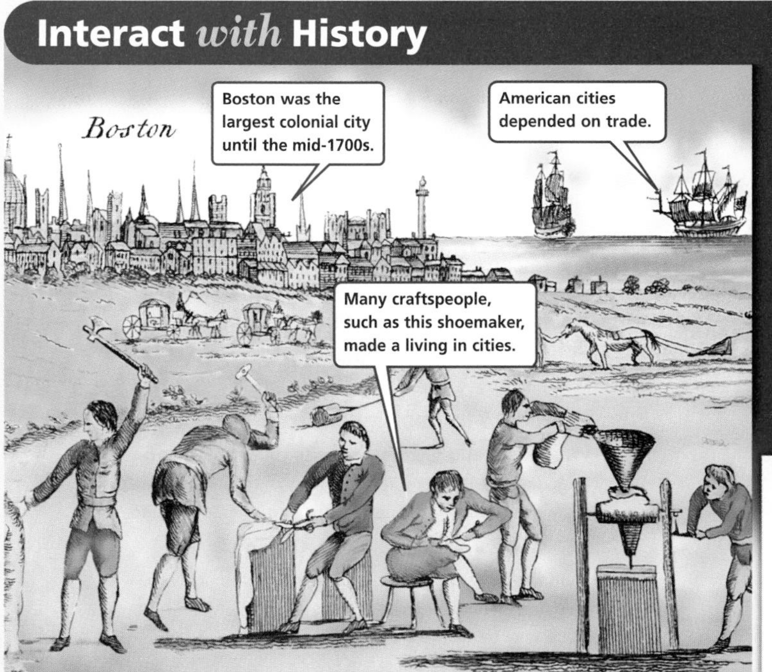
Boston
Boston was the largest colonial city until the mid-1700s.
American cities depended on trade.
Many craftspeople, such as this shoemaker, made a living in cities.

**It is the early 1700s when you arrive in one of America's larger port cities. After nearly a month of ocean travel, you are thrilled to see land. As you leave the ship, you wonder where you will live and how you will earn a living.**

### What Do You Think?

- **Will you choose to live where other people from your homeland live? Or will you try somewhere new?**
- **How did you make a living in your old country? Will this influence your choice?**

# *Would you settle on a farm or in a town?*

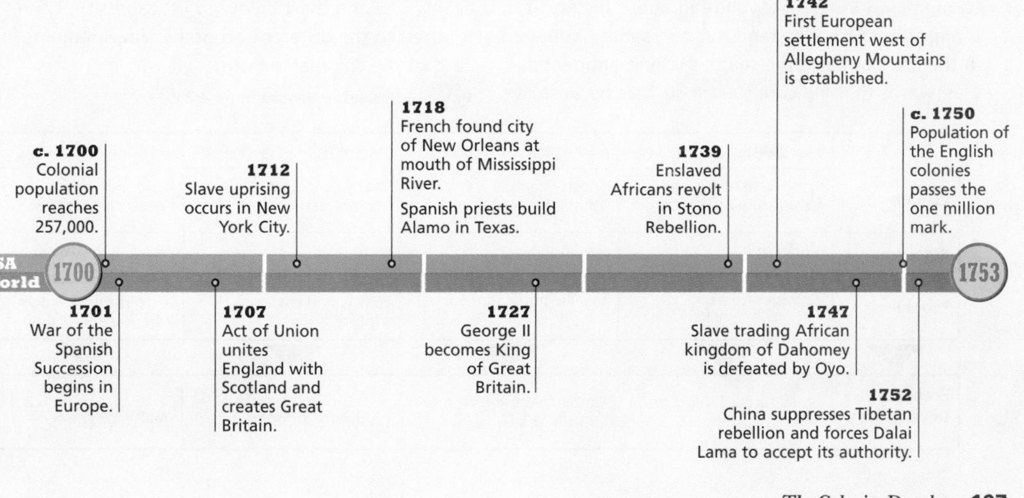
c. 1700
Colonial population reaches 257,000.
1712
Slave uprising occurs in New York City.
1718
French found city of New Orleans at mouth of Mississippi River.
Spanish priests build Alamo in Texas.
1739
Enslaved Africans revolt in Stono Rebellion.
1742
First European settlement west of Allegheny Mountains is established.
c. 1750
Population of the English colonies passes the one million mark.
USA
World
1700
1753
1701
War of the Spanish Succession begins in Europe.
1707
Act of Union unites England with Scotland and creates Great Britain.
1727
George II becomes King of Great Britain.
1747
Slave trading African kingdom of Dahomey is defeated by Oyo.
1752
China suppresses Tibetan rebellion and forces Dalai Lama to accept its authority.

## Interact *with* History

### OBJECTIVES

- To help students understand the economic and social problems facing immigrants to colonial America
- To help students connect with the people and events they will study in this chapter

### What Do You Think?

1. Ask students why living near others from your homeland might be important.
2. Have students explain how the occupations of newcomers to America might affect where they would settle.

### *Would you settle on a farm or in a town?*

Encourage students to think about the factors (social connections, occupations, finances) that would influence their decisions to live in a rural or an urban area.

### MAKING PERSONAL CONNECTIONS

Ask students to think about experiences they might have had moving to a new country, city, or neighborhood. How would their experiences compare and contrast to those of newcomers to colonial America? What might have influenced their families' choice of a new home? Would their reasons for choosing a community be similar to or different from the reasons that influenced American colonists?

### TIME LINE DISCUSSION

**Remind students that the English established 13 colonies along the Atlantic Coast of North America from 1607 to 1732. Colonists were not content to remain on the seaboard. They continued to push into the continent to establish new settlements. Land and economic activity drew many immigrants, both voluntary and involuntary.**

- Ask students to identify how the population of the English colonies changed between 1700 and 1750. **Answer** The population more than quadrupled from 257,000 to more than 1 million people.
- Ask students in what areas of North America settlements were being developed. **Answer** New Orleans, Texas, west of the Allegheny Mountains

## BEFORE YOU READ

### Previewing the Theme:
**Economics in History**

Ask the students to think of ways that the climate, geography, and resources of a particular area affected the work of the colonists.

Point out that the climate and geography of the land along the Atlantic coast differed widely and affected the length of the growing season, the size of the farms, and the economic focus of each area. While the types of farming might differ in the four regions, nearly all the European immigrants expected to farm the land.

### What Do You Know?

Point out to students that the differences in the climate influenced the economy and the way of life that developed in each region. In the North, for example, while farming remained important, industry, including manufacturing and trade, became increasingly important.

 **In-Depth Resources: Unit 1**
- Tracing Themes: Economics in History, p. 63

## READ AND TAKE NOTES

### Reading Strategy: Analyzing Causes and Recognizing Effects

Tell students that analyzing causes and recognizing their effects will help them understand how and why New England and the Middle and Southern Colonies developed in unique and specific ways. Explain that factors such as climate and resources affected how people worked and survived. Point out to students that recording causes and effects in a chart will help them compare and contrast colonial development in the three regions.

 **In-Depth Resources: Unit 1**
- Setting the Stage, p. 62

 **Critical Thinking Transparency CT10**
- Setting the Stage

# Chapter 4 SETTING THE STAGE

## BEFORE YOU READ

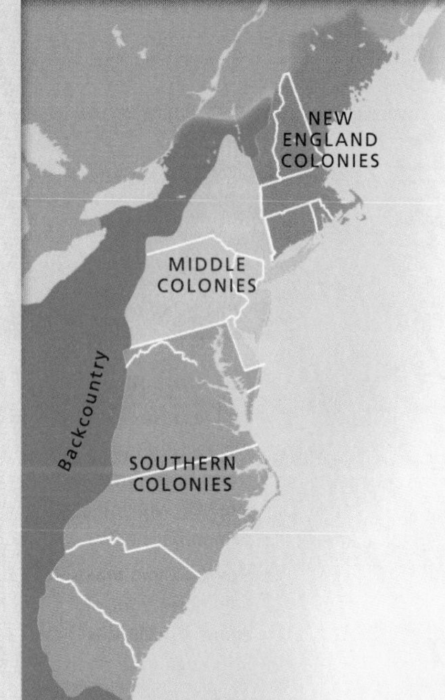


### Previewing the Theme

**Economics in History** When immigrants came to the Americas, they settled in places with different climates and resources. These conditions affected the economic choices made by colonists. As Chapter 4 explains, those choices contributed to the formation of four different colonial regions.

### What Do You Know?

What ideas and pictures come to mind when you hear people talk about "the South" or "the North"? Why do you think these distinct regions developed?

**THINK ABOUT**
- what you have learned about these regions from books or movies
- the way geography affects people's choices

### What Do You Want to Know?

What questions do you have about how the four colonial regions developed? Record these questions in your notebook before you read the chapter.

## READ AND TAKE NOTES

**Reading Strategy: Analyzing Causes and Recognizing Effects** As you read about history, it is important to understand not only what happened in the past, but also the reasons why it happened. Clue words that indicate cause—such as *because* and *since*—can help you look for causes of historical events. Use the chart below to list causes that contributed to the different economic developments in each of the colonial regions.

 See Skillbuilder Handbook, page R10.

| | | NEW ENGLAND COLONIES | MIDDLE COLONIES | SOUTHERN COLONIES | BACKCOUNTRY |
|---|---|---|---|---|---|
| CAUSES | Climate | Long, cold winters and a short growing season | Shorter winters and a longer growing season | Nearly year-round growing season | Varied with latitude |
| CAUSES | Resources | Rocky soil | Fertile soil | Fertile soil | Woods and streams |
| CAUSES | People | English settlers | Diverse population | English and enslaved Africans | Scots-Irish and Native Americans |
| EFFECT | Economic Development | Small farms, fishing, and trade | Larger farms and cash crops of grain | Plantation economy | Small farms |



## TEACHING STRATEGY

### READING THE CHAPTER

This is a thematic chapter that focuses on development of the New England, Middle, and Southern Colonies. Encourage students to use the maps in each section to help them understand each region's growth and development. Ask students to summarize each section, and then note the similarities and differences in the development of each.

### ALTERNATIVE ASSESSMENT

The Chapter Assessment describes three activities for alternative assessment on page 131. You may wish to have students work on these activities during the course of the chapter and then present them at the end.

# 1 New England: Commerce and Religion

**TERMS & NAMES**
Backcountry
subsistence farming
triangular trade
Navigation Acts
smuggling

| MAIN IDEA | WHY IT MATTERS NOW |
|---|---|
| Fishing and trade contributed to the growth and prosperity of the New England Colonies. | Coastal cities in New England continue to engage in trade. |

## ONE AMERICAN'S STORY

**Peleg Folger, a New England sailor, was only 18 years old when he began whaling. Folger kept a journal that describes what whaling was like in the 1750s. In one journal entry, Folger explained what happened after whales were sighted and small boats were launched to pursue them.**

*A VOICE FROM THE PAST*

So we row'd about a mile and a Half from the [ship], and then a whale come up under us, & [smashed in] our boat . . . and threw us every man overboard [except] one. And we all came up and Got Hold of the Boat & Held to her until the other boat (which was a mile and half off) came up and took us in, all Safe, and not one man Hurt, which was remarkable, the boat being threshed to pieces very much.

**Peleg Folger,** quoted in *The Sea-Hunters*

**Whales hunted by New Englanders, such as Peleg Folger, might weigh as much as 50 tons and be over 60 feet in length.**

**When Folger and his mates did manage to kill a whale, they cut a hole in its head. Then "a man got in up to his armpits and Dipt out [barrels] of clear oil." When the ship returned to port, this oil was sold to colonists, who used it as fuel in their lamps.**

**Many settlers in the New England Colonies—Massachusetts, New Hampshire, Connecticut, and Rhode Island—turned to the Atlantic Ocean to make a living. The majority of New Englanders, however, were farmers.**

## 1 Distinct Colonial Regions Develop

Between 1700 and 1750, the population of England's colonies in North America doubled and then doubled again. At the start of the century, the colonial population stood at about 257,000. By 1750, more than 1,170,000 settlers called the English colonies home.

By the 1700s, the colonies formed three distinct regions: the New England Colonies, the Middle Colonies, and the Southern Colonies. Another area was the **Backcountry.** It ran along the Appalachian Mountains through the far western part of the other regions.





## SECTION OBJECTIVES

1. To explain how distinct regions developed during the colonial period
2. To describe life in the New England farms and towns
3. To describe the three types of Atlantic trade
4. To identify the reasons for changes in Puritan society

### SKILLBUILDER

Interpreting Maps: Location, Region, p. 110

### CRITICAL THINKING

Recognizing Effects, p. 111
Analyzing Causes, p. 112
Making Inferences, p. 113

## FOCUS & MOTIVATE

### 5-MINUTE WARM-UP

**Drawing Conclusions** These questions focus on the impact of the environment on the New England Colonies.

1. Look at the map on page 110. How did New Englanders make their living from the sea?
2. What reasons might there be for no grain products shown?

 **Warm-Up Transparency WT4**

## INSTRUCT

### INSTRUCT: OBJECTIVE 

**Distinct Colonial Regions Develop**

Key Questions

- What major regions developed in the colonies by the 1700s?
- What were the key factors that made the colonies regions different from one another?
- What influenced the type of agriculture that developed in each region?

**In-Depth Resources: Unit 1**
- Guided Reading, p. 64

**Reading Study Guide** (Spanish and English), pp. 35–36

## RECOMMENDED RESOURCES

 **In-Depth Resources: Unit 1**
- Guided Reading, p. 64
- Building Vocabulary, p. 68
- Reteaching Activity, p. 77

 **Reading Study Guide** (Spanish and English), pp. 35–36

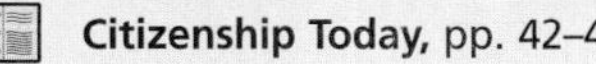 **Citizenship Today,** pp. 42–45

 **Formal Assessment**
- Section Quiz, p. 61

 **Alternative Assessment**
- Rubrics, 1.9
- Rubrics, 5.4

 **Access for Students Acquiring English/ESL**
- Guided Reading, p. 22

**Technology Resources**

 **Humanities Transparency HT7**
- Puritan Hornbook

 **Geography Transparency GT4**
- The Colonial Trade, 1750

 **Electronic Teacher Tools with Test Maker**

 **ClassZone**
www.mcdougallittell.com

Several factors made each colonial region distinct. Some of the most important were each region's climate, resources, and people.

1. New England had long winters and rocky soil. English settlers made up the largest group in the region's population.
2. The Middle Colonies had shorter winters and fertile soil. The region attracted immigrants from all over Europe.
3. The Southern Colonies had a warm climate and good soil. There, some settlers used enslaved Africans to work their plantations.
4. The Backcountry's climate and resources varied, depending on the latitude. Many Scots-Irish immigrants settled there.

**Vocabulary**
**latitude:** the distance north or south of the equator, measured in degrees

During the colonial era, the majority of people made their living by farming. However, the type of agriculture they practiced depended on the climate and resources in the region where they settled.

## 2 The Farms and Towns of New England

Life in New England was not easy. The growing season was short, and the soil was rocky. Most farmers practiced **subsistence farming.** That is, they produced just enough food for themselves and sometimes a little extra to trade in town.

Most New England farmers lived near a town. This was because colonial officials usually did not sell scattered plots of land to individual

**Skillbuilder Answers**
1. Hudson River
2. ships, fish, and whales

### INSTRUCT: OBJECTIVE 2

**The Farms and Towns of New England/ Harvesting the Sea**

Key Questions

- How did the geography of New England affect the kind of farming practiced there?
- Describe the settlement patterns in New England.
- What role did fishing play in the economy of colonial New England?

**Citizenship Today,** pp. 42–45

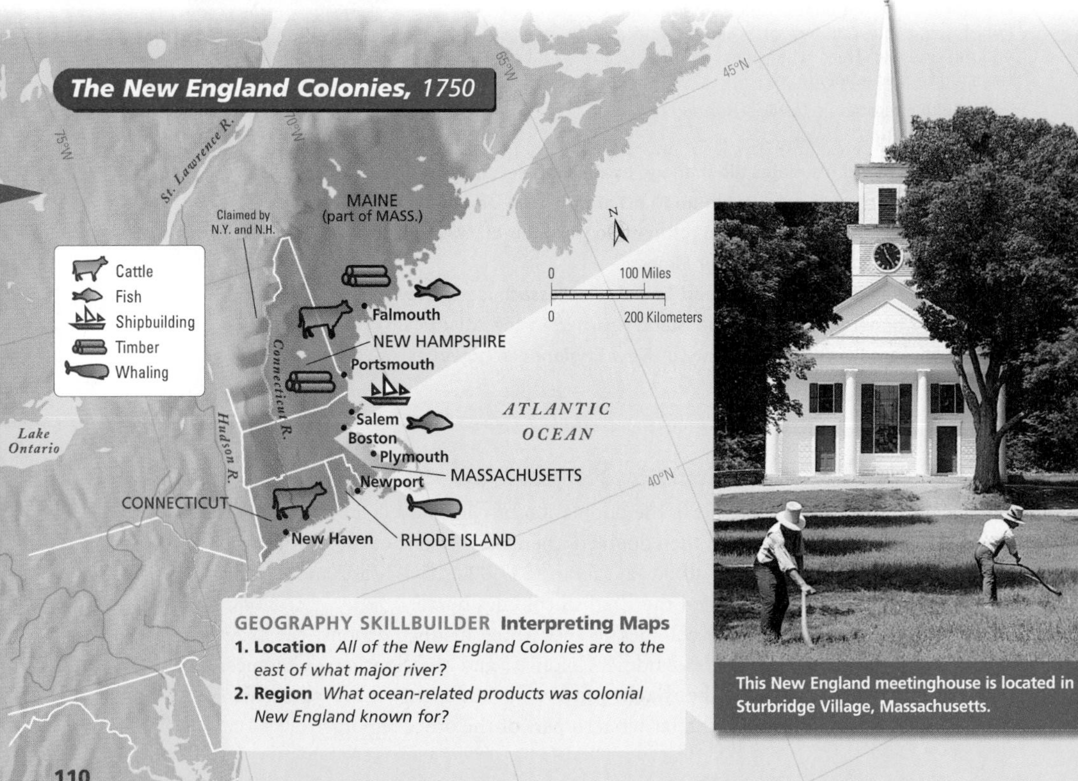


**GEOGRAPHY SKILLBUILDER Interpreting Maps**
1. **Location** *All of the New England Colonies are to the east of what major river?*
2. **Region** *What ocean-related products was colonial New England known for?*

This New England meetinghouse is located in Sturbridge Village, Massachusetts.

### HISTORY FROM VISUALS

**Reading the Map** Point out the symbols for the various economic products produced in colonial New England. Ask students why there were so many nonagricultural products produced in colonial New England. Have the students identify relationships between the kinds of products. **Possible Responses** Nonagricultural products dominated the economy because the region had direct access to the sea and because farming was difficult. Fishing and whaling were both important and depended on shipbuilding, which required timber that was abundant in the region.

**Extension** Have students choose one New England state and find out its chief products today. Direct students to resources such as almanacs, encyclopedias, and state pages on the Internet.

110

### ACTIVITY OPTIONS

### MULTIPLE LEARNING STYLES: SPATIAL

BLOCK SCHEDULING

**TOWN PLANNING**

**Class Time** One class period

**Task** Researching the layout of a colonial New England town

**Purpose** To gain understanding of how the plan of a New England town reflected its economy

**Supplies Needed**
- Art supplies, including rulers
- Encyclopedias, Internet access

**Activity** Divide the class into small groups and assign each group one of the New England towns shown on the map on this page. Tell groups to consult encyclopedias or on-line references to find information about the town's colonial history. Have students draw a diagram showing how the town was planned. Town plans should include the green, church, school, surrounding houses, shops, and farm fields.

farmers. Instead, they sold larger plots of land to groups of people—often to the congregation of a Puritan church. A congregation then settled the town and divided the land among the members of its church.

*Reading* **History**
**A. Recognizing Effects** How did the way land was sold in New England affect the way people lived?
A. Possible Response Because colonial officials sold large plots of land to groups, many New Englanders lived together in towns.

This pattern of settlement led New England towns to develop in a unique way. Usually, a cluster of farmhouses surrounded a green—a central square where a meetinghouse was located and where public activities took place. Because people lived together in small towns, shopkeepers had enough customers to make a living. Also, if the townspeople needed a blacksmith or a carpenter, they could pool their money and hire one.

## Harvesting the Sea

New England's rocky soil made farming difficult. In contrast, the Atlantic Ocean offered many economic opportunities. In one story, a group of settlers was standing on a hill overlooking the Atlantic. One of them pointed out to sea and exclaimed, "There is a great pasture where our children's grandchildren will go for bread!"

The settler's prediction came true. Not far off New England's coast were some of the world's best fishing grounds. The Atlantic was filled with mackerel, halibut, cod, and many other types of fish.

New England's forests provided everything needed to harvest these great "pastures" of fish. The wood cut from iron-hard oak trees made excellent ship hulls. Hundred-foot-tall white pines were ideal for masts. Shipbuilders used about 2,500 trees to produce just one ship!

New England's fish and timber were among its most valuable articles of trade. Coastal cities like Boston, Salem, New Haven, and Newport grew rich as a result of shipbuilding, fishing, and trade.

**Background**
In 1742, over 16,000 people lived in Boston.

## 3 Atlantic Trade

New England settlers engaged in three types of trade. First was the trade with other colonies. Second was the direct exchange of goods with Europe. The third type was the triangular trade.

**Triangular trade** was the name given to a trading route with three stops. For example, a ship might leave New England with a cargo of rum

### Triangular Trade, *1750*

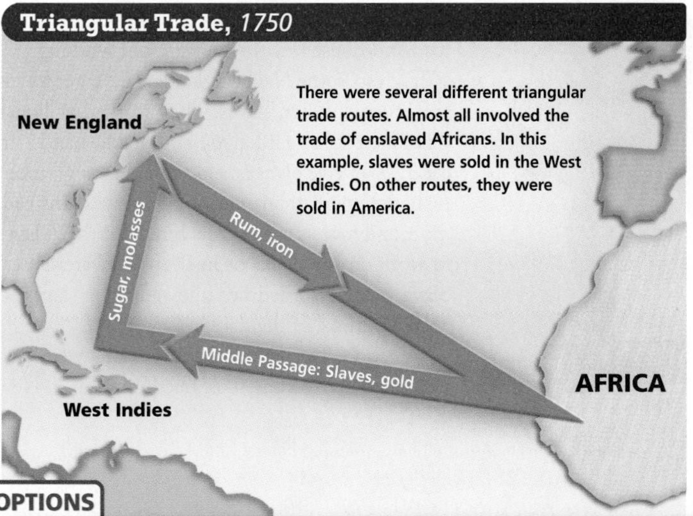

New England
There were several different triangular trade routes. Almost all involved the trade of enslaved Africans. In this example, slaves were sold in the West Indies. On other routes, they were sold in America.
Rum, iron
Sugar, molasses
Middle Passage: Slaves, gold
AFRICA
West Indies

### MORE ABOUT . . .

**Harvesting the Sea**
New England fishing vessels usually headed for the Grand Banks, one of the world's richest fishing areas. The Grand Banks are a series of raised underwater plateaus off the southeast coast of the island of Labrador. Many kinds of plants and fish flourish in the shallow water of the Grand Banks. In the 1960s and 1970s, however, fish stocks were declining. In 1977, Canada declared its exclusive fishing rights to most of the Grand Banks. Strict conservation measures are working to restore the populations of cod, flounder, turbot, ocean perch, haddock, and other species.

### INSTRUCT: OBJECTIVE 3

**Atlantic Trade/**
**African Americans in New England**
Key Questions
- What kinds of trade did New England colonists engage in?
- What is an example of triangular trade?
- What was the purpose of the Navigation Acts?

 **Geography Transparency GT4**
- The Colonial Trade, 1750

### HISTORY FROM VISUALS

**Reading the Map** Point out the relative distances of the segments of the triangular trade route pictured on the map. Ask students to discuss what happened to slaves during the Middle Passage. **Possible Response** Because of the length of the journey and the horrible conditions on board the ships, many people probably died on the trip.

**Extension** Have students do research on the experiences of enslaved Africans during the Middle Passage. Ask students to produce a monologue, journal entry, or essay about the Middle Passage.

### ACTIVITY OPTIONS
### INDIVIDUAL NEEDS

**STUDENTS ACQUIRING ENGLISH/ESL**

**Understanding Prefixes** Ask students to look at the map *Triangular Trade, 1750* on this page. Point out the three arrows that form a triangle. Review that a triangle is a three-sided figure and that the prefix *tri-* means "three." Discuss other words with the prefix *tri-*, and write them on the board. *(tripod, tricycle, triceps, triceratops)*

Explain that the three sides of the triangle represent three sides of a trade relationship. Help students to see the benefits of a trade arrangement with three locations. You might ask questions such as the following to prompt discussion:
- What products did Africa want from the New England Colonies?
- What products did New England colonists want from the West Indies?

## STRANGE *but* True

**Blackbeard the Pirate**

Blackbeard's real name was Edward Teach. His nickname came from his thick, black beard. Beginning his career as a pirate around 1716, Blackbeard operated along the Virginia and Carolina coasts. By 1718, Blackbeard had established a base in a North Carolina inlet from which he collected tolls from ships passing through Pamlico Sound. He even had an agreement to share his booty with Charles Eden, governor of the North Carolina colony. Through the years, many people have searched for the treasure supposedly buried by Teach. It probably never existed.

## MORE ABOUT . . .

**African Americans in Whaling**

African Americans played an important part in the whaling industry of New England. Many Quaker whaling captains from New Bedford or on the island of Nantucket welcomed free blacks and runaway slaves as crew members. In addition, sailors of color from the Cape Verde Islands and the Caribbean often joined New England whaling crews. Crispus Attucks, the African American killed during the Boston Massacre, spent many years as a whaler. There even were a few whalers with all African-American crews.

and iron. In Africa, the captain would trade his cargo for slaves. Slaves then endured the horrible Middle Passage to the West Indies, where they were exchanged for sugar and molasses. Traders then took the sugar and molasses back to New England. There, colonists used the molasses to make rum, and the pattern started over.

**Background**
See Olaudah Equiano's descriptions of the Middle Passage on page 78.

### STRANGE *but* True

**BLACKBEARD THE PIRATE**

Of all the pirates who attacked colonial ships, Blackbeard (shown below) was the most famous. He was a fearsome man known to stick matches in his hair to light up his face during battle.

Blackbeard's pirate career finally came to an end in 1718, when Virginia's governor sent an expedition against him. Nearly half the expedition's men died in the key battle. Blackbeard himself did not fall until he had suffered nearly 25 wounds. Before sailing back to port, sailors cut off his head and put it on the front of their ship.

New England won enormous profits from trade. England wanted to make sure that it received part of those profits. So the English government began to pass the **Navigation Acts** in 1651. The Navigation Acts had four major provisions designed to ensure that England made money from its colonies' trade.

1. All shipping had to be done in English ships or ships made in the English colonies.
2. Products such as tobacco, wood, and sugar could be sold only to England or its colonies.
3. European imports to the colonies had to pass through English ports.
4. English officials were to tax any colonial goods not shipped to England.

But even after the passage of the Navigation Acts, England had trouble controlling colonial shipping. Merchants ignored the acts whenever possible. **Smuggling**—importing or exporting goods illegally—was common. England also had great difficulty preventing pirates—like the legendary Blackbeard—from interfering with colonial shipping.

### African Americans in New England

There were few slaves in New England. Slavery simply was not economical in this region of small farms. Also, because the growing season was short, there was little work for slaves during the long winter months. Farmers could not afford to feed and house slaves who were not working.

*Reading* **History**
**B. Analyzing Causes** Why were there relatively few enslaved workers in New England?
**B. Possible Response** Because of the small size of farms and the short growing season, slavery was not economical.

Even so, some New Englanders in larger towns and cities did own slaves. They worked as house servants, cooks, gardeners, and stable-hands. In the 1700s, slave owners seldom had enough room to house more than one or two slaves. Instead, more and more slave owners hired out their slaves to work on the docks or in shops or warehouses. Slave owners sometimes allowed their slaves to keep a portion of their wages.

Occasionally, some enslaved persons were able to save enough to buy their freedom. In fact, New



## ACTIVITY OPTIONS

**INTERDISCIPLINARY LINK: LANGUAGE ARTS** — BLOCK SCHEDULING

**WRITING EDITORIALS**

**Class Time** 20 minutes

**Task** Writing a newspaper editorial

**Purpose** To form and express an opinion about the Navigation Acts

**Supplies Needed**
- Examples of editorials from school or community newspapers

**Activity** Have students read examples of editorials from school or community newspapers. Briefly discuss with students the characteristics of a good editorial, including the presentation of a point of view about an issue. Ask students to write editorials for an 18th-century colonial or British newspaper, either supporting or opposing the Navigation Acts. Their editorials should include reasons that support their opinions. Ask volunteers to read their editorials aloud to the group.

England was home to more free blacks than any other region. A free black man might become a merchant, sailor, printer, carpenter, or landowner. Still, white colonists did not treat free blacks as equals.

## 4 Changes in Puritan Society

> "[Boston] is so conveniently Situated for Trade."
> An observer in 1713

The early 1700s saw many changes in New England society. One of the most important was the gradual decline of the Puritan religion. There were a number of reasons for this decline.

**Reading History**
**C. Making Inferences** Why might an interest in material things compete with the Puritan religion?
**C. Possible Response** Many religions, including Puritanism, teach that too much concern with material things is wrong.

One reason was that the drive for economic success competed with Puritan ideas. Many colonists, especially those who lived along the coast, seemed to care as much about business and material things as they did about religion. One observer had this complaint.

**A VOICE FROM THE PAST**

[Boston] is so conveniently Situated for Trade and the Genius of the people are so inclined to merchandise, that they seek no other Education for their children than writing and Arithmetick.

**An observer in 1713,** quoted in *A History of American Life*

Another reason for the decline of the Puritan religion was the increasing competition from other religious groups. Baptists and Anglicans established churches in Massachusetts and Connecticut, where Puritans had once been the most powerful group.

Political changes also weakened the Puritan community. In 1691, a new royal charter for Massachusetts guaranteed religious freedom for all Protestants, not just Puritans. The new charter also granted the vote based on property ownership instead of church membership. This change put an end to the Puritan churches' ability to control elections.

To the south of New England were the Middle Colonies, which developed in quite different ways—as the next section shows.

### Section 1 Assessment

**1. Terms & Names**
Identify:
- Backcountry
- subsistence farming
- triangular trade
- Navigation Acts
- smuggling

**2. Taking Notes**
Use a chart like the one shown to record how New Englanders prospered from the Atlantic Ocean.

| Economic Activity | Benefits to Colonists |
|---|---|
| | |

How did some profit illegally from the ocean?

**3. Main Ideas**
a. How did most people in New England earn a living?
b. Why did England pass the Navigation Acts?
c. What factors led to the decline of the Puritan religion in New England?

**4. Critical Thinking**
**Making Inferences** What advantages might there be in living near other people in small towns, such as those in New England?
THINK ABOUT
- the transportation options available to colonists
- why shopkeepers chose to open businesses in towns

**ACTIVITY OPTIONS**

ART / TECHNOLOGY
Read more about whaling. Make a **mobile** that shows different kinds of whales or plan a **multimedia presentation** on whaling today.





**INSTRUCT: OBJECTIVE 4** 

**Changes in Puritan Society**
Key Questions
- How did economic success compete with Puritan ideas?
- What religious groups competed with the Puritans?
- How did the new royal charter for Massachusetts affect the Puritan community?

**Humanities Transparency HT7**
- American Colonial Hornbook

**MORE ABOUT . . .**

**Puritan Practices**
Leaders of Puritan churches assigned seating according to social status. The most wealthy and respected church members sat in the first rows in pews they owned themselves. Their wives sat with them, but not their children. The rest of the congregation was divided by gender—men on one side, women on the other.

## ASSESS & RETEACH

**Setting the Stage** Have students fill in information about the New England Colonies on the chapter graphic organizer.

**Formal Assessment**
- Section Quiz, p. 61

**Critical Thinking Transparency CT10**
- Setting the Stage

**RETEACHING ACTIVITY**
Divide the class into four teams, representing each of the objectives for this section. Each team should create a graphic organizer that identifies the main ideas about its objective. After the teams have completed their assignments, display the graphic organizers in the classroom. Review the information on each one with the class.

**In-Depth Resources: Unit 1**
- Reteaching Activity, p. 77

### Section 1 Assessment

**1. Terms & Names**
**Backcountry,** p. 109
**subsistence farming,** p. 110
**triangular trade,** p. 111
**Navigation Acts,** p. 112
**smuggling,** p. 112

**2. Taking Notes**
**Fishing**—Fish could be sold for consumption or export.
**Whaling**—Whale oil provided oil for lamps or for export.
**Trading**—Colonists made money from three types of Atlantic trade.
**Smuggling**—Smuggling was widespread, though illegal.

**3. Main Ideas**
**a.** farming **b.** England wanted to make sure that it, too, profited from its colonies' trade. **c.** People were more interested in making money; other religions began to compete; a new charter decreased the political power of the Puritan churches.

**4. Critical Thinking**
People could walk to the nearby locations to take care of business. Shopkeepers would have enough customers to make a living.

**ACTIVITY OPTIONS**

**Alternative Assessment**
- Rubrics for a mobile, 1.9
- Rubrics for multimedia, 5.4

## SECTION OBJECTIVES

1. To identify the resources of the Middle Colonies
2. To describe the prosperity of the cities
3. To evaluate the diversity of the region
4. To analyze the treatment of African Americans

**SKILLBUILDER**
Interpreting Maps: Place, Movement, p. 115
Interpreting Graphs, p. 117

**CRITICAL THINKING**
Summarizing, p. 117
Forming Opinions, p. 118
Analyzing Causes, p. 118

## FOCUS & MOTIVATE

### 5-MINUTE WARM-UP

**Drawing Conclusions** These questions focus on the economic diversity of the Middle Colonies.

1. Look at the pictures on page 116. How many occupations can you identify?
2. What can you conclude about the economy of the region from the variety of occupations represented?

 **Warm-Up Transparency WT4**

## INSTRUCT

**INSTRUCT: OBJECTIVE** 

**A Wealth of Resources/ The Importance of Mills**
Key Questions
- What resources were available in the Middle Colonies?
- Why were the Middle Colonies called the "breadbasket" colonies?
- What did the immigrants contribute to the economy?

 **In-Depth Resources: Unit 1**
- Guided Reading, p. 65
- Building Vocabulary, p. 68

# 2 The Middle Colonies: Farms and Cities

**TERMS & NAMES**
cash crop
gristmill
diversity
artisan
Conestoga wagon

| MAIN IDEA | WHY IT MATTERS NOW |
|---|---|
| The people who settled in the Middle Colonies made a society of great diversity. | States in this region still boast some of the most diverse communities in the world. |

### ONE AMERICAN'S STORY

**Elizabeth Ashbridge was only 19 years old when she arrived in America from England in the 1730s. Even though she was young, she had already been married and widowed. And although she was an indentured servant, she hoped to earn her freedom and find a way to express her strong religious feelings.**

**After several years, Elizabeth did gain freedom. She started to search for a religion that she could devote her life to. Finally, in the colony of Pennsylvania, she found what she was looking for—the Society of Friends, or Quakers. The new Quaker longed to share her beliefs openly.**

*A VOICE FROM THE PAST*

I was permitted to see that all I had gone through was to prepare me for this day; and that the time was near, when it would be required of me, to go and declare to others what the God of mercy had done for my soul.

**Elizabeth Ashbridge,** *Some Account . . . of the Life of Elizabeth Ashbridge*

A woman speaks out at a Quaker meeting. The Society of Friends allowed women a more active role than other religions.

**The Quakers believed that people of different beliefs could live together in harmony. They helped to create a climate of tolerance and acceptance in the Middle Colonies of New York, New Jersey, Pennsylvania, and Delaware. These colonies began to attract a wide variety of immigrants, as you will read in this section.**

## 1 A Wealth of Resources

The Middle Colonies had much to offer in addition to a climate of tolerance. A Frenchman named Michel Guillaume Jean de Crèvecoeur (krehv•KUR) praised the region's "fair cities, substantial villages, extensive fields . . . decent houses, good roads, orchards, meadows, and bridges, where an hundred years ago all was wild, woody, and uncultivated."

The prosperity that Crèvecoeur described was typical of the Middle Colonies. Immigrants from all over Europe came to take advantage of this region's productive land. Their settlements soon crowded out Native Americans, who had lived in the region for thousands of years.



## RECOMMENDED RESOURCES

 **In-Depth Resources: Unit 1**
- Guided Reading, p. 65
- Skillbuilder Practice, p. 69
- Geography Application: Colonial Immigrant Groups, 1750, pp. 70–71
- Reteaching Activity, p. 78
- Enrichment Activity, p. 81

 **Reading Study Guide** (Spanish and English), pp. 37–38

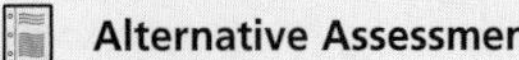 **Formal Assessment**
- Section Quiz, p. 62

**Alternative Assessment**
- Rubrics, 2.6
- Rubrics, 2.1

 **Access for Students Acquiring English/ESL**
- Guided Reading, p. 23
- Skillbuilder Practice, p. 26
- Geography Application, pp. 27–28

**Technology Resources**

 **Electronic Teacher Tools with Test Maker**

 **ClassZone**
www.mcdougallittell.com

Among the immigrants who came to the Middle Colonies were Dutch and German farmers. They brought the advanced agricultural methods of their countries with them. Their skills, knowledge, and hard work would soon result in an abundance of foods.

The Middle Colonies boasted a longer growing season than New England and a soil rich enough to grow **cash crops.** These were crops raised to be sold for money. Common cash crops included fruits, vegetables, and, above all, grain. The Middle Colonies produced so much grain that people began calling them the "breadbasket" colonies.

## The Importance of Mills

**Vocabulary**
**grist:** another name for grain, the one-seeded fruit of cereal grasses like wheat and rye

After harvesting their crops of corn, wheat, rye, or other grains, farmers took them to a **gristmill.** There, millers crushed the grain between heavy stones to produce flour or meal. Human or animal power fueled some of these mills. But water wheels built along the region's plentiful rivers powered most of the mills.

The bread that colonists baked with these products was crucial to their diet. Colonists ate about a pound of grain in some form each day—nearly three times more than Americans eat today. Even though colonists ate a great deal of grain, they had plenty left over to send to the region's coastal markets for sale.

**Skillbuilder Answers**
1. Hudson, Susquehanna, and Delaware rivers
2. The rivers would enable nearby farmers to send their crops to market easily.

### MORE ABOUT . . .

**Mills**
Building and running a mill required a large investment and many skills. The miller had to import the grinding stones from Europe, and they had to be assembled by an expert. Millers charged a fee on every bushel of grain they milled. Fees might be as high as 15 percent. However, farmers could not grind enough grain by hand to sell, so the miller became one of the most important people in a community.

***The Middle Colonies,* 1750**

Cattle
Fish
Furs
Iron
Pigs
Sheep
Timber
Wheat

Claimed by N.Y. and N.H.
Lake Ontario
Lake Erie
Albany
NEW YORK
Hudson R.
Connecticut R.
Susquehanna R.
Delaware R.
New York
PENNSYLVANIA
NEW JERSEY
Philadelphia
Wilmington
Dover
DELAWARE
ATLANTIC OCEAN
75°W
80°W
40°N
35°N
0 100 Miles
0 200 Kilometers

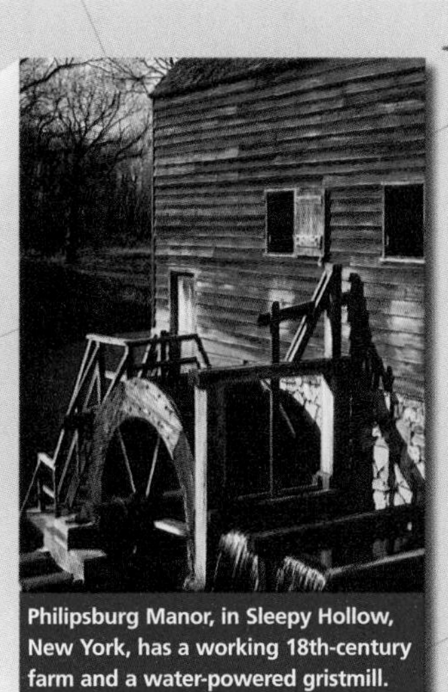

Philipsburg Manor, in Sleepy Hollow, New York, has a working 18th-century farm and a water-powered gristmill.

**GEOGRAPHY SKILLBUILDER Interpreting Maps**
1. **Place** *What are the three major rivers in the Middle Colonies?*
2. **Movement** *Why might the Middle Colonies' rivers that empty into the ocean be important for farmers?*

### HISTORY FROM VISUALS

**Reading the Map** Ask students to name the Middle Colonies. Then have them name some categories of information presented on the map. **Possible Responses** products, cities, bodies of water, latitude and longitude, scale, topography

**Extension** Ask students to write a paragraph describing the characteristics of the Middle Colonies that made them good places to settle.



### ACTIVITY OPTIONS

### SKILLBUILDER MINI-LESSON: CREATING A MAP

BLOCK SCHEDULING

**Explaining the Skill** Maps are visual representations of information. Maps can show physical, political, or other information such as economic activities, battles, or population density. Creating a map helps students to understand information and also helps them to understand how maps are put together.

**Applying the Skill** Ask students to look at the maps in this chapter on pages 110, 115, and 120. Tell them to draw a map that combines the economic information from all three maps. Ask the following questions to help students prepare their maps:

1. What would you call a map that combines the three maps of colonial regions? *(The Economy of the 13 Colonies)*
2. How many items would you include in the legend if you combined the three maps? *(16)*
3. What items must you add to the legend if you show the three colonial regions in different colors? *(a color block and label identifying each color)*

 **In-Depth Resources: Unit 1**
- Skillbuilder Practice, p. 69

## INSTRUCT: OBJECTIVE 2

**The Cities Prosper**
Key Questions
- How did the geography of the Middle Colonies contribute to the growth of cities?
- Why did Philadelphia grow so quickly?

### daily*life*

**Names and Occupations**
While links between some last names and occupations are obvious (Barber, Plumber), other "occupational" last names are misleading. For example, a "Farmer" was not an agricultural worker; he collected taxes. Similarly, "Banker" is not connected with finances at all. It means "dweller on a hillside."

### MORE ABOUT . . .

**Philadelphia**
William Penn called the capital of his new colony *Philadelphia,* a Greek word meaning "brotherly love." The city benefited from the numerous contributions of its most famous citizen, Benjamin Franklin. Franklin founded a subscription library, a fire company, a hospital, a militia, and a philosophical society and was instrumental in the founding of the University of Pennsylvania.

## INSTRUCT: OBJECTIVE 3

**A Diverse Region/A Climate of Tolerance**
Key Questions
- Why did so many German immigrants come to this region?
- How did their cultural diversity affect the Middle Colonies?
- What are three principles of Quaker life?

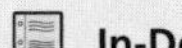
**In-Depth Resources: Unit 1**
- Geography Application: Colonial Immigrant Groups, 1750, pp. 70–71

## 2 The Cities Prosper

The excellent harbors along the coasts of the Middle Colonies were ideal sites for cities. New York City grew up at the mouth of the Hudson River, and Philadelphia was founded on the Delaware River. The merchants who lived in these growing port cities exported cash crops, especially grain, and imported manufactured goods.

*Reading*History
**A. Reading a Map** Locate New York and Philadelphia on the map on page 115. Note the rivers next to which they were built.

Because of its enormous trade, Philadelphia was the fastest growing city in the colonies. The city owed its expansion to a thriving trade in wheat and other cash crops. By 1720, it was home to a dozen large shipyards—places where ships are built or repaired.

The city's wealth also brought many public improvements. Large and graceful buildings, such as Philadelphia's statehouse—which was later renamed Independence Hall—graced the city's streets. Streetlights showed the way along paved roads. In 1748, a Swedish visitor named Peter Kalm exclaimed that Philadelphia had grown up overnight.

### daily*life*

**NAMES AND OCCUPATIONS**
Many English colonists had names like Miller and Smith—names that reflected how their families had made a living in England. For example, a colonist named Miller probably had an ancestor who had operated a mill. Similarly, Smith probably had an ancestor who had been a blacksmith.

Sometimes colonists continued in the same occupations as their ancestors. But as time went on, colonists turned to other occupations, and their names no longer reflected how they earned a living. Yet names like Smith and Miller remain common in the United States, reflecting the country's past as English colonies.

*A VOICE FROM THE PAST*

And yet its natural advantages, trade, riches and power, are by no means inferior to any, even of the most ancient towns in Europe.

**Peter Kalm,** quoted in *America at 1750*

New York could also thank trade for its rapid growth. This bustling port handled flour, bread, furs, and whale oil. At midcentury, an English naval officer admired the city's elegant brick houses, paved streets, and roomy warehouses. "Such is this city," he said, "that very few in England can rival it in its show."

**Background**
In 1742, New York City's population was about 11,000, and nearly 13,000 people lived in Philadelphia.

## 3 A Diverse Region

Many different immigrant groups arrived in the port cities of the Middle Colonies. Soon, the region's population showed a remarkable

### ACTIVITY OPTIONS
### INDIVIDUAL NEEDS

**LESS PROFICIENT READERS**

**Finding Main Ideas/Details** To help students focus on the most important information in the section, suggest that they create a concept web for the main ideas and details. In the center circle have students write the label *Middle Colonies,* and in the surrounding circles have them write the main ideas *Resources, Cities, Diverse Populations,* and *Quakers.* Encourage students to add important details to each part of the web.

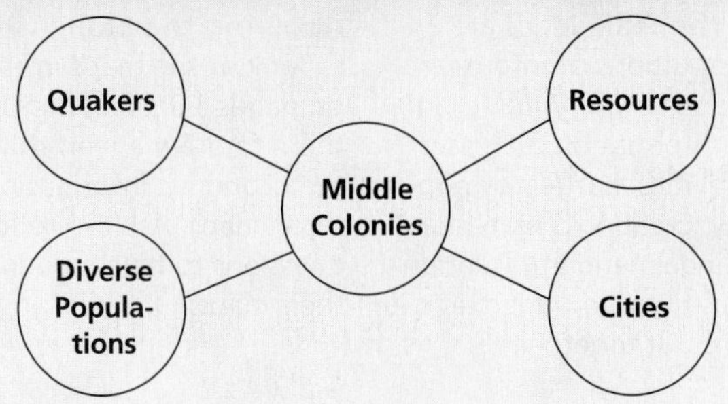

**diversity**, or variety, in its people. One of the largest immigrant groups in the region, after the English, was the Germans.

Many of the Germans arrived between 1710 and 1740. Most came as indentured servants fleeing religious intolerance. Known for their skillful farming, these immigrants soon made a mark on the Middle Colonies. "German communities," wrote one historian, "could be identified by the huge barns, the sleek cattle, and the stout workhorses."

**Background**
By the second half of the 1700s, more than one in three colonists in Pennsylvania claimed German ancestry.

**The Middle Colonies,** *1750*

**Population Diversity**

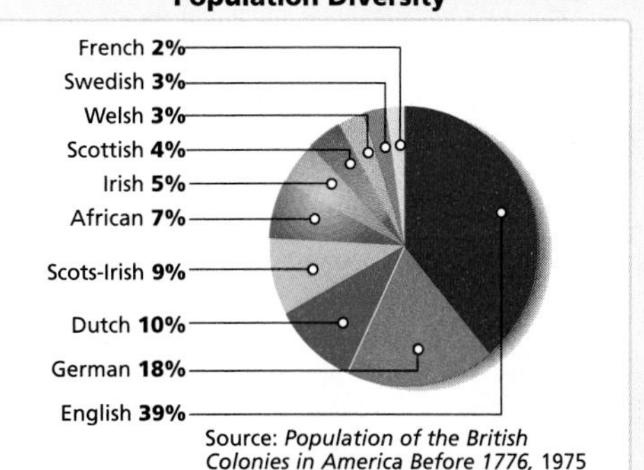


Source: *Population of the British Colonies in America Before 1776,* 1975

SKILLBUILDER **Interpreting Graphs**

1. *What group made up nearly one-fifth of the population in the Middle Colonies?*
2. *What were the two main languages spoken in the Middle Colonies?*

Skillbuilder Answers
1. Germans
2. English and German

Germans also brought a strong tradition of craftsmanship to the Middle Colonies. For example, German gunsmiths first developed the long rifle. Other German **artisans,** or craftspeople, became ironworkers and makers of glass, furniture, and kitchenware.

Germans built **Conestoga wagons** to carry their produce to town. These wagons used wide wheels suitable for dirt roads, and the wagons' curved beds prevented spilling when climbing up and down hills. The wagons' canvas covers offered protection from rain. Conestoga wagons would later be important in settling the West.

The Middle Colonies became home to many people besides the Germans. There were also the English, Dutch, Scots-Irish, African, Irish, Scottish, Welsh, Swedish, and French. Because of the diversity in the Middle Colonies, different groups had to learn to accept, or at least tolerate, one another.

*Reading***History**
**B. Summarizing** How would you describe the population of the Middle Colonies?
B. Possible Response The large variety of immigrant groups made it a diverse region.

## A Climate of Tolerance

While the English Puritans shaped life in the New England Colonies, many different groups contributed to the culture of the Middle Colonies. Because of the greater number of different groups, it was difficult for any single group to dominate the others. Thus, the region's diversity helped to create a climate of tolerance. Some of the region's religious groups also helped to promote tolerance.

The Middle Colonies' earliest settlers, the Dutch in New York and the Quakers in Pennsylvania, both practiced religious tolerance. That is, they honored the right of religious groups to follow their own beliefs without interference. Quakers also insisted on the equality of men and women. As a result, Quaker women served as preachers, and female missionaries traveled the world spreading the Quaker message.



### HISTORY FROM VISUALS

**Interpreting the Graph** Point out the various ethnic groups represented on this graph. Have the students discuss which area of the world most of the immigrants to the Middle Colonies came from. **Possible Responses** northern and western Europe and the British Isles, Africa

**Extension** Have students study a map of the Middle Colonies to see if they can find names of cities that are similar to names found in the countries the immigrants came from.

### MORE ABOUT . . .

**A Climate of Tolerance**
Some historians think that religious toleration in the Middle Colonies was caused by the indifference of many immigrants to organized religion. Many German and Scots-Irish immigrants, for example, did not have ministers and were slow to form churches. Because they lived among so many different sects, they could join any church of their choice or none at all. Probably fewer than one in 15 became church members.

**In-Depth Resources: Unit 1**
- Enrichment Activity, p. 81

**ACTIVITY OPTIONS**

### INTERDISCIPLINARY LINK: MATH

BLOCK SCHEDULING

**CALCULATING DIVERSITY**

**Class Time** 20 minutes

**Task** Making calculations using information from a graph

**Purpose** To use math skills to find out the total numbers of people from various ethnic groups living in the Middle Colonies

**Supplies Needed**
- Calculators or paper and pencil
- Graph paper

**Activity** Tell students that the total population of the Middle Colonies in 1750 was 296,459. Ask students to calculate the total number of people in each of the ethnic groups shown on the graph. Ask students to display their results in a bar graph or pictograph. **Answers** Africans (free and slave)—20,736; English—115,186; Welsh—9,983; Scots-Irish—28,017; Scottish—12,704; Irish—14,454; German—53,631; Dutch—28,183; French—6,048; Swedish—7,506

**INSTRUCT: OBJECTIVE** 

**African Americans in the Middle Colonies**

Key Questions

- What percentage of the population of the Middle Colonies was made up of enslaved persons?
- How was the work of African Americans in the Middle Colonies different from that in New England?
- What happened in the 1712 race riot in New York City?

**CRITICAL THINKING ACTIVITY**

**Comparing and Contrasting** Have students compare and contrast the treatment of African Americans in the Middle Colonies and the New England Colonies. Was slavery practiced in both regions? Which area had more slaves? Were there free African Americans living in the regions?

**Class Time** 10 minutes

## ASSESS & RETEACH

**Setting the Stage** Have students fill in the chart with information about the Middle Colonies.

 **Formal Assessment**
- Section Quiz, p. 62

**RETEACHING ACTIVITY**

Have pairs of students create two questions related to the main ideas in each section of the chapter. Students should write the questions and answers on the front and back of a 3 x 5 card. Ask two pairs of students to quiz each other by using the questions as flashcards.

 **In-Depth Resources: Unit 1**
- Reteaching Activity, p. 78

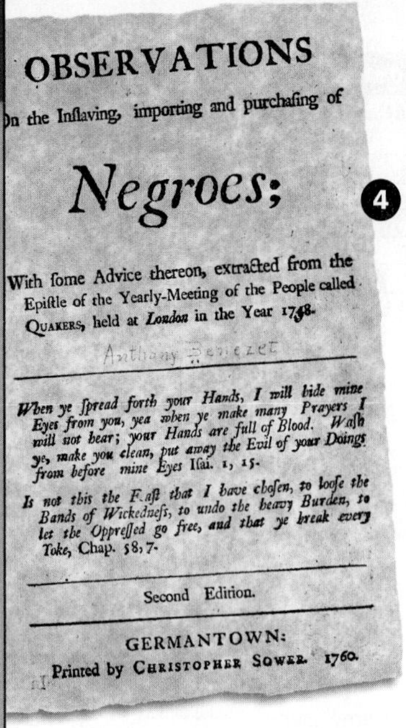

OBSERVATIONS

On the Inslaving, importing and purchasing of

*Negroes;*

With some Advice thereon, extracted from the Epistle of the Yearly-Meeting of the People called QUAKERS, held at *London* in the Year 1748.

*When ye spread forth your Hands, I will hide mine Eyes from you, yea when ye make many Prayers I will not hear; your Hands are full of Blood. Wash ye, make you clean, put away the Evil of your Doings from before mine Eyes* Isai. 1, 15.

*Is not this the Fast that I have chosen, to loose the Bands of Wickedness, to undo the heavy Burden, to let the Oppressed go free, and that ye break every Yoke,* Chap. 58, 7.

Second Edition.

GERMANTOWN:
Printed by CHRISTOPHER SOWER. 1760.

**Most Quakers were opposed to slavery. Shown here is a Quaker antislavery pamphlet printed in the Middle Colonies.**

Quakers were also the first to raise their voices against slavery. Quaker ideals influenced immigrants in the Middle Colonies—and eventually the whole nation.

## 4 African Americans in the Middle Colonies

The tolerant attitude of many settlers in the Middle Colonies did not prevent slavery in the region. In 1750, about 7 percent of the Middle Colonies' population was enslaved. As in New England, many people of African descent lived and worked in cities.

New York City had a larger number of people of African descent than any other city in the Northern colonies. In New York City, enslaved persons worked as manual laborers, servants, drivers, and as assistants to artisans and craftspeople. Free African-American men and women also made their way to the city, where they worked as laborers, servants, or sailors.

*Reading***History**

**C. Forming Opinions** Why do you think that force was needed to keep Africans enslaved?

C. Possible **Response** Because enslaved Africans wanted their freedom and were ready to fight for it.

Tensions existed between the races in New York City, sometimes leading to violence. In 1712, for example, about 24 rebellious slaves set fire to a building. They then killed nine whites and wounded several others who came to put out the fire. Armed colonists caught the suspects, who were punished horribly. Such punishments showed that whites would resort to force and violence to control slaves. Even so, the use of violence did little to prevent the outbreak of other slave rebellions.

Force would also be used in the South, which had far more enslaved Africans than the North. In the next section, you will learn how the South's plantation economy came to depend on the labor of enslaved Africans.

### Section 2 Assessment

**1. Terms & Names**

**Identify:**
- cash crop
- gristmill
- diversity
- artisan
- Conestoga wagon

**2. Taking Notes**

Use a cluster diagram like the one shown to indicate where different immigrants in the Middle Colonies came from.

What was the third largest group in the region?

**3. Main Ideas**

**a.** What attracted settlers to the Middle Colonies?

**b.** What service was performed at gristmills?

**c.** Why might enslaved Africans be able to join in rebellion more easily in the city than the country?

**4. Critical Thinking**

**Analyzing Causes** What factors allowed large coastal cities to develop in the Middle Colonies?

THINK ABOUT
- geography
- people
- trade

**ACTIVITY OPTIONS**

**MATH**

**GEOGRAPHY**

Read more about Philadelphia. Create a **database** of the city's population growth in the 1700s or draw a **map** that shows its physical growth.



### Section 2 Assessment

**1. Terms & Names**

**cash crop,** p. 115
**gristmill,** p. 115
**diversity,** p. 117
**artisan,** p. 117
**Conestoga wagon,** p. 117

**2. Taking Notes**

Answers should include four of the following: England, Germany, Holland, Scotland, Africa, Ireland. The third largest group was the Dutch.

**3. Main Ideas**

**a.** the long growing season; fertile soil and wealth of resources; the climate of tolerance; excellent harbors **b.** grinding grain into flour and meal **c.** Communication was easier; they might not be recognized as easily as in the smaller communities.

**4. Critical Thinking**

excellent harbors along the coast; immigration; the profitable trade of cash crops

**ACTIVITY OPTIONS**

 **Alternative Assessment**
- Rubrics for a database, 2.6
- Rubrics for a map, 2.1

# 3 The Southern Colonies: Plantations and Slavery

**TERMS & NAMES**
indigo
Eliza Lucas
William Byrd II
overseer
Stono Rebellion

**MAIN IDEA**

The economy of the Southern Colonies relied heavily on slave labor.

**WHY IT MATTERS NOW**

The existence of slavery deeply affected the South and the nation.

## ONE AMERICAN'S STORY

**George Mason was born to a wealthy Virginia family in 1725. Mason—who later described the slave trade as "disgraceful to mankind"—wrote about the contributions of enslaved persons on his family's plantation.**

*A VOICE FROM THE PAST*

My father had among his slaves carpenters, coopers [barrel makers], sawyers, blacksmiths, tanners, curriers, shoemakers, spinners, weavers and knitters, and even a distiller. . . . His woods furnished timber and plank for the carpenters and coopers, and charcoal for the blacksmith; his cattle killed for his own consumption and for sale supplied skins for the tanners, curriers, and shoemakers, and his sheep gave wool and his fields produced cotton and flax for the weavers and spinners, and his orchards fruit for the distiller.

**George Mason,** quoted in *Common Landscape of America*

George Mason was active in local affairs in Virginia. He would later play a role in the drafting of the United States Constitution.

**Because the Masons and other wealthy landowners produced all that they needed on their own plantations, they appeared to be independent. But their independence usually depended on the labor of enslaved Africans. Although planters were only a small part of the Southern population, the plantation economy and slavery shaped life in the Southern Colonies: Maryland, Virginia, the Carolinas, and Georgia.**

## 1 The Plantation Economy

The South's soil and almost year-round growing season were ideal for plantation crops like rice and tobacco. These valuable plants required much labor to produce, but with enough workers they could be grown as cash crops. Planters had no trouble transporting their crops because the region's many waterways made it easy for oceangoing ships to tie up at plantation docks.

Like George Mason's boyhood home, most plantations were largely self-sufficient. That is, nearly everything that planters, their families, and their workers needed was produced on the plantation. Because plantations were so self-sufficient, large cities like those in the North were rare





## SECTION OBJECTIVES

1. To analyze the plantation economy and the use of slaves
2. To describe plantation life
3. To understand life under slavery
4. To describe resistance to slavery

**SKILLBUILDER**

Interpreting Maps: Location, Place, p. 120

**CRITICAL THINKING**

Drawing Conclusions, p. 120
Analyzing Causes, p. 121
Recognizing Effects, p. 121
Finding Main Ideas, p. 122
Contrasting, p. 123

## FOCUS & MOTIVATE

### 5-MINUTE WARM-UP

**Making Inferences** These questions will help students examine plantation life in the United States.

1. What can you infer about the people who lived in the plantation mansion shown on page 120?
2. Why did planters who lived in mansions such as this one require many workers?

 **Warm-Up Transparency WT4**

## INSTRUCT

### INSTRUCT: OBJECTIVE 

**The Plantation Economy/ The Turn to Slavery**

Key Questions

- What geographic factors made plantation crops profitable?
- Why did planters begin to use enslaved Africans for labor?
- How did the use of slaves change the population of the Southern Colonies?

 **In-Depth Resources: Unit 1**
- Guided Reading, p. 66

## RECOMMENDED RESOURCES

 **In-Depth Resources: Unit 1**
- Guided Reading, p. 66
- Building Vocabulary, p. 68
- Literature Selection, pp. 74–76
- Reteaching Activity, p. 79
- Enrichment Activity, p. 81

  **Reading Study Guide** (Spanish and English), pp. 39–40

 **Outline Map Activities**
- Colonial Products, pp. 7–8

 **America's History Makers**
- Eliza Lucas Pinckney, pp. 15–16

 **Formal Assessment**
- Section Quiz, p. 63

 **Alternative Assessment**
- Rubrics, 1.3
- Rubrics, 2.5

 **Access for Students Acquiring English/ESL**
- Guided Reading, p. 24

**Technology Resources**

 **Critical Thinking Trans. CT11**
- Cause and Effect: The Rise of Slave Labor

 **Humanities Transparency HT8**
- Maryland Plantation, 18th Century

 **Electronic Teacher Tools with Test Maker**

## HISTORY FROM VISUALS

**Reading the Map** Point out the map legend, then discuss the symbols and their placement on the map. Have students talk about the kinds of products provided in the Southern Colonies, and explain to them how these goods would have been transported to other colonies as well as to European nations. **Possible Responses** The products were primarily agricultural. These goods would have been transported by ship up the coast or across the Atlantic Ocean.

**Extension** Have students research plantations that are open to the public and report about the architecture and decoration of one of the plantation houses.

**Outline Map Activities**
- Colonial Products, pp. 7–8

## HISTORY FROM VISUALS

**Understanding the Graph** Point out the differences in the U.S. slave population in the North and South between 1600 and 1750. Ask students to write a sentence describing the percentage of the population that were slaves in the North and the South in 1660. Then ask them to revise their sentences to reflect the data for 1750. **Possible Responses** In 1660, the percentage of the population in slavery in the Northern and Southern Colonies was about equal, at around 9 percent of the population. In 1750, slaves made up about 40 percent of the population of the Southern Colonies and only about 3 percent of the Northern Colonies.

**Extension** Have students do research to find out how much tobacco was shipped from the colonies in 1650 and in 1750.

**Critical Thinking Transparency CT11**
- Cause and Effect: The Rise of Slave Labor

### The Southern Colonies, 1750

Corn
Indigo
Naval stores
Pigs
Rice
Tobacco

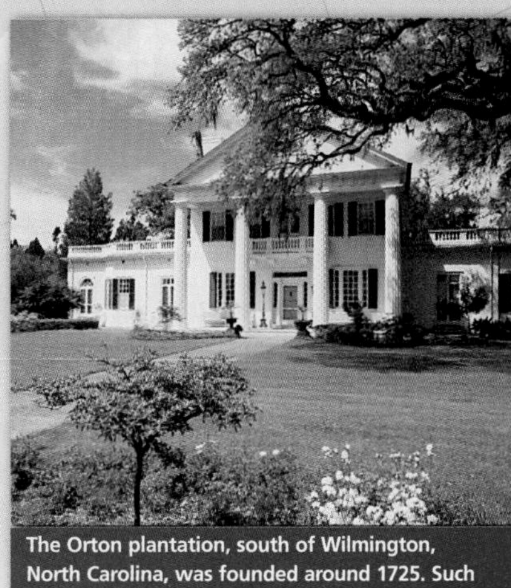

The Orton plantation, south of Wilmington, North Carolina, was founded around 1725. Such plantations were representative of the economic and political power held by Southern planters.

**GEOGRAPHY SKILLBUILDER Interpreting Maps**
1. **Location** *The Southern Colonies were south of what latitude?*
2. **Place** *Which Southern Colonies grew crops of both rice and indigo?*

Skillbuilder Answers
1. 40° North
2. South Carolina and Georgia

in the Southern Colonies. The port city of Charles Town (later called Charleston) in South Carolina was an early exception.

**Background**
In 1742, Charles Town's population was 6,800.

As the plantation economy continued to grow, planters began to have difficulty finding enough laborers to work their plantations. Toward the end of the 1600s, the planters began to turn to enslaved Africans for labor.

## The Turn to Slavery

For the first half of the 1600s, there were few Africans in Virginia, whether enslaved or free. In 1665, fewer than 500 Africans had been brought into the colony. At that time, African and European indentured servants worked in the fields together.

**U.S. Slave Population**

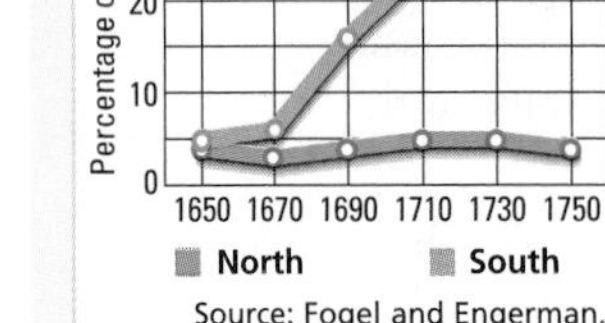


Source: Fogel and Engerman, *Time on the Cross,* 1974

Starting in the 1660s, the labor system began to change as indentured white servants started to leave the plantations. One reason they left was the large amount of land available in the Americas. It was fairly easy for white men to save enough money to buy land and start their own farms. White servants could not be kept on the plantations permanently. As Bacon's rebellion showed, it was also politically dangerous for planters to try to keep them there (see page 89). As a result, the landowners had to find another source of labor.

A. Possible Response
Because many could buy land and start their own farms.

*Reading* **History**
**A. Drawing Conclusions** Why did white workers choose not to remain on the plantations as laborers?



## ACTIVITY OPTIONS

### INTERDISCIPLINARY LINK: THE ARTS

BLOCK SCHEDULING

**CREATE A POSTER**

**Class Time** 30 minutes

**Task** Making a poster advertising land to former indentured servants in the Southern Colonies

**Purpose** To gain an understanding of reasons servants wanted to own land

**Supplies Needed**
- Drawing paper
- Art supplies

**Activity** Briefly discuss with the class the elements of an advertising poster: a slogan, information clearly and concisely expressed, and an interesting visual. Brainstorm with the class some reasons indentured servants wanted to own land. Tell students that posters should address those reasons.

After the students have completed their projects, display the posters in the classroom. Discuss different posters with the class.

Planters tried to force Native Americans to work for them. But European diseases caused many Native Americans to die. Those who survived usually knew the country well enough to run away.

*Reading* **History**
**B. Analyzing Causes** What factors led to the importation of enslaved Africans into the South?
**B. Possible Responses** The shortage of labor, the unsuitability of whites and Native Americans as laborers.

To meet their labor needs, the planters turned to enslaved Africans. As a result, the population of people of African descent began to grow rapidly. By 1750, there were over 235,000 enslaved Africans in America. About 85 percent lived in the Southern Colonies. Enslaved Africans made up about 40 percent of the South's population.

## 2 Plantations Expand

The growth of slavery allowed plantation farming to expand in South Carolina and Georgia. Without slave labor, there probably would have been no rice plantations in the region's swampy lowlands.

Enslaved workers drained swamps, raked fields, burned stubble, and broke ground before planting. They also had to flood, drain, dry, hoe, and weed the same fields several times before the harvest.

The cultivation of rice required not only back-breaking labor but also considerable skill. Because West Africans had these skills, planters sought out slaves who came from Africa's rice-growing regions.

On higher ground, planters grew **indigo,** a plant that yields a deep blue dye. A young woman named **Eliza Lucas** had introduced indigo as a successful plantation crop after her father sent her to supervise his South Carolina plantations when she was 17.

## The Planter Class

Slave labor allowed planters, such as the Byrd family of Virginia, to become even wealthier. These families formed an elite planter class. They had money or credit to buy the most slaves. And because they had more slaves, they could grow more tobacco, rice, or indigo to sell.

**C. Possible Response** The economic power of planters with large numbers of slaves allowed them to assume political power, too.

*Reading* **History**
**C. Recognizing Effects** How did the growth of slavery affect political power in the South?

Small landowners with just one or two slaves simply could not compete. Many gave up their land and moved westward. As a result, the powerful planter class gained control of the rich land along the coast. The planter class was relatively small compared to the rest of the population. However, this upper class soon took control of political and economic power in the South. A foreign traveler in the South commented that the planters "think and act precisely as do the nobility in other countries."

Some planters, following the traditions of nobility, did feel responsible for the welfare of their enslaved

**AMERICA'S HISTORY MAKERS**

**WILLIAM BYRD II**
**1674–1744**

William Byrd II was one of the best known of the Southern planters. His family owned a large estate in Virginia. After his father died, Byrd took on his father's responsibilities, including membership in the House of Burgesses.

But Byrd is best remembered for his writing. His most famous work is *History of the Dividing Line betwixt Virginia and North Carolina.* In it, Byrd celebrates the land and climate of the South. At times, however, he is critical of its people. Even today, the book creates a vivid picture of life in the Southern Colonies.

**How did William Byrd II demonstrate his leadership abilities?**





**INSTRUCT: OBJECTIVE 2**

**Plantations Expand/The Planter Class**

Key Questions

- How did the growth of slavery affect farming in South Carolina and Georgia?
- How did the planter class become so powerful?
- How did the planter class treat its enslaved workers?

**Humanities Transparency HT8**
- Maryland Plantation, 18th Century

### AMERICA'S HISTORY MAKERS

**William Byrd II**

William Byrd II was an avid writer throughout his life, producing letters, diaries, travel journals, and poems. In 1709, he began a secret diary that he wrote in code. When the code was finally broken in the 1940s, Byrd's secret diaries were published. They contain richly detailed information about Byrd's life, including what he ate, what he drank, how often he quarreled with his wife, even how often he forgot his prayers.

**Possible Response: by becoming a member of the House of Burgesses**

### MORE ABOUT . . .

**Indigo and Eliza Lucas**

In the early 1740s, Eliza Lucas was managing her father's South Carolina plantations. Lucas was born on the Caribbean island of Antigua, where indigo was an important crop. She began to experiment with cultivating indigo and extracting its dye. Lucas was helped by white and black people from the West Indies. Her procedures for growing the plant and for processing the dye spread throughout the colony of South Carolina. Later in life, Eliza Lucas married Charles Pinckney. Their sons were important figures in the American Revolution.

**America's History Makers**
- Eliza Lucas Pinckney, pp. 15–16

### ACTIVITY OPTIONS

### INDIVIDUAL NEEDS: GIFTED AND TALENTED

**LEARNING ABOUT GULLAH**

**Class Time** One class period

**Task** Researching topics about Gullah

**Purpose** To encourage students to explore Gullah, the language of enslaved persons on the Sea Islands of Georgia and South Carolina

**Supplies Needed**
- Reference sources, including encyclopedias and Internet access

**Activity** Invite students to research Gullah, the speech of enslaved Africans and their descendants on the Sea Islands and coastal regions of South Carolina and Georgia. Ask students to prepare a report on one of these topics: origins of Gullah and Gullah words that have become part of the English language; aspects of Gullah culture; efforts to learn about and preserve Gullah.

## HISTORY through ART

**Interpreting the Painting** Benjamin Henry Latrobe (1764–1820) was a famous architect and landscape and topographical painter of the colonial period. Born in England, he was educated in Germany and later studied engineering and architecture in London. He moved to Virginia in 1796. Latrobe was later the chief architect of public buildings in the country's capital.

**Possible Response: Students may note the lounging, insolent posture of the overseer, his tobacco, and the frightened looks of the enslaved workers. From these clues they will probably decide that Latrobe opposed slavery.**

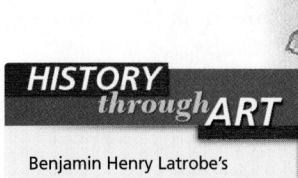

### INSTRUCT: OBJECTIVE 

**Life Under Slavery**

Key Questions

- How did overseers treat the enslaved Africans?
- How did the enslaved people live?
- What was the effect of the plantation system on the culture of the enslaved people?

 **In-Depth Resources: Unit 1**
- Literature Selection, pp. 74–76

### INSTRUCT: OBJECTIVE 

**Resistance to Slavery**

Key Questions

- How did enslaved Africans fight against their enslavement?
- What is the significance of the Stono Rebellion?
- In what ways did slave codes change?

**HISTORY through ART**

Benjamin Henry Latrobe's watercolor sketch, *An Overseer Doing His Duty,* shows enslaved African women on a Virginia plantation. An overseer looks on as the two women work to remove tree stumps.

**What opinion do you think Latrobe had of the conditions on plantations?**

workers. Power, they believed, brought with it the responsibility to do good. Many planters, though, were tyrants. They held complete authority over everyone in their households. Planters frequently used violence against slaves to enforce their will.

Vocabulary
**tyrant:** harsh ruler

## 3 Life Under Slavery

On large Southern plantations, slaves toiled in groups of about 20 to 25 under the supervision of **overseers.** Overseers were men hired by planters to watch over and direct the work of slaves. Enslaved persons performed strenuous and exhausting work, often for 15 hours a day at the peak of the harvest season. If slaves did not appear to be doing their full share of work, they were often whipped by the overseer.

Enslaved people usually lived in small, one-room cabins that were furnished only with sleeping cots. For a week's food, a slave might receive only around a quarter bushel of corn and a pound of pork. Some planters allowed their slaves to add to this meager ration by letting them raise their own potatoes, greens, fruit, or chicken.

In spite of the brutal living conditions, Africans preserved many customs and beliefs from their homelands. These included music, dances, stories, and, for a time, African religions—including Islam. African kinship customs became the basis of African-American family culture. A network of kin was a source of strength even when families were separated.

*Reading* **History**

**D. Finding Main Ideas** What customs and beliefs from their homelands provided strength for enslaved Africans?

D. Possible Responses Music, dances, stories, Islam, and kinship customs.

## 4 Resistance to Slavery

At the same time that enslaved Africans struggled to maintain their own culture, they fought against their enslavement. They sometimes worked



**ACTIVITY OPTIONS**

**INTERDISCIPLINARY LINK: LANGUAGE ARTS**

**DIARY ENTRIES**

**Class Time** 30 minutes

**Task** Creating diary entries for an enslaved African and a planter family member on a Southern plantation

**Purpose** To compare the experiences of Southern colonists of different groups

**Supplies Needed**
- Reference materials about plantation life in the colonial South

**Activity** Ask the language arts teacher to discuss writing diary entries. Then have students read accounts of plantation life in the colonial South.

Have students write a diary entry from the point of view of an enslaved African or from that of a member of a planter family. When the students are finished, have them read their entries aloud to a group.

slowly, damaged goods, or purposely carried out orders the wrong way. A British traveler in 1746 noted that many slaves pretended not to understand tasks they often had performed as farmers in West Africa.

*A VOICE FROM THE PAST*

You would really be surpriz'd at their Perseverance; let an hundred Men shew him how to hoe, or drive a wheelbarrow, he'll still take the one by the Bottom, and the other by the Wheel; and they often die before they can be conquer'd.

**Edward Kimber,** quoted in *White over Black*

At times, slaves became so angry and frustrated by their loss of freedom that they rose up in rebellion. One of the most famous incidents was the **Stono Rebellion.** In September 1739, about 20 slaves gathered at the Stono River just south of Charles Town. Wielding guns and other weapons, they killed several planter families and marched south, beating drums and loudly inviting other slaves to join them in their plan to seek freedom in Spanish-held Florida. By late that afternoon, however, a white militia had surrounded the group of escaping slaves. The two sides clashed, and many slaves died in the fighting. Those captured were executed.

**Background**
Slave codes were laws designed to control slaves and keep them in bondage.

Stono and similar revolts led planters to make slave codes even stricter. Slaves were now forbidden from leaving plantations without permission. The laws also made it illegal for slaves to meet with free blacks. Such laws made the conditions of slavery even more inhumane.

The Southern Colonies' plantation economy and widespread use of slaves set the region on a very different path from that of the New England and Middle Colonies. In the next section, you will learn how settlers used the unique resources of the Backcountry to create settlements there.

## Section 3 Assessment

**1. Terms & Names**

**Identify:**
- indigo
- Eliza Lucas
- William Byrd II
- overseer
- Stono Rebellion

**2. Taking Notes**

Use a diagram like the one shown to review the factors that led to the use of slaves in the South.

| Causes | Effect |
|---|---|
| | |
| | |

Why didn't planters use Native American workers?

**3. Main Ideas**

a. What percentage of the South's population was enslaved in 1750?

b. What crops did plantations in Georgia and South Carolina grow?

c. How did enslaved persons resist their slavery?

**4. Critical Thinking**

**Contrasting** How did geographic differences between the Southern Colonies and the New England Colonies affect their labor systems?

**THINK ABOUT**
- the climate of the regions
- the nature of the soil

**ACTIVITY OPTIONS**

**ART**
**SCIENCE**

Do more research on rice plantations. Draw a **diagram** of a typical plantation or write a **report** on how rice is cultivated today.





## MORE ABOUT . . .

**Daily Life Under Slavery**

In the 1600s, the living conditions of enslaved Africans was about the same as that of their owners. However, by the 1800s, most colonists lived in houses made of brick or wood, while their slaves continued to live in rough shacks. To save money, owners gave their slaves the cheapest cloth—called Negro cloth—for their clothes. Slaves ate corn, rice, beans, salt pork, and molasses. Enslaved Africans used these ingredients to make foods that resembled foods they had known in Africa. Hoe cakes, mush, and spoon bread are foods made by slaves that entered the white Southern diet.

## ASSESS & RETEACH

**Setting the Stage** Have students complete the chart with information about the Southern Colonies.

**Formal Assessment**
- Section Quiz, p. 63

### RETEACHING ACTIVITY

Have students copy the graphic below and fill it in with details about life in the Southern Colonies for members of the planter class and for slaves.

| Group | Details |
|---|---|
| Planter Class | |
| Slaves | |

**In-Depth Resources: Unit 1**
- Reteaching Activity, p. 79

## Section 3 Assessment

**1. Terms & Names**

**indigo,** p. 121
**Eliza Lucas,** p. 121
**William Byrd II,** p. 121
**overseer,** p. 122
**Stono Rebellion,** p. 123

**2. Taking Notes**

Causes: Labor-intensive cash crops required lots of workers; availability of land made it difficult to keep white laborers.
Effect: Planters turned to enslaved Africans for labor.

They were susceptible to European diseases and knew the country well enough to run away.

**3. Main Ideas**

**a.** almost 40 percent **b.** rice; indigo **c.** They worked slowly, damaged goods, and participated in violent rebellions.

**4. Critical Thinking**

Southern Colonies had a long growing season and fertile soil good for cash crops. New England had a short growing season and poor soil.

### ACTIVITY OPTIONS

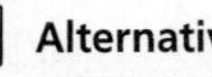
**Alternative Assessment**
- Rubrics for a diagram, 1.3
- Rubrics for a report, 2.5

## GEOGRAPHY in HISTORY

### OBJECTIVE

Students will analyze and interpret information from a map to understand the relationship between the climate and natural resources of New England and the Middle and Southern Colonies.

 **BLOCK SCHEDULING**

### MORE ABOUT . . .

**Rice and Indigo**

Rice and indigo were compatible crops because rice required great labor in the winter, when the fields had to be prepared. The dams, dikes, and ditches used to flood the fields had to be repaired. In early spring, workers set out the new rice plants in the flooded fields. Indigo needed little work in the winter, but for the rest of the year, it took massive labor. Rice was grown in the lowest-lying fields. Indigo, on the other hand, was grown on higher ground.

### INSTRUCT

Key Questions

- Why is the physical geography of a region important to its economy?
- How does a region's growing season affect its economy?
- How does soil quality affect a region's economy?

**MAP SKILL QUESTIONS**

Which map would tell you what parts of the country had the coldest and the warmest temperatures?

Use the maps to determine what physical factors enabled the Southern Colonies to prosper.

Which region produced no grain for export?

## GEOGRAPHY in HISTORY

REGION AND HUMAN-ENVIRONMENT INTERACTION

# Differences Among the Colonies

Many factors shape a region's economy and the way its settlers make a living. One of the most important is its physical geography—the climate, soil, and natural resources of the region. The geography of the American colonies varied from one colony to another. For example, in some areas, farmers could dig into rich, fertile soil. In others, they could not stick their shovels in the ground without hitting rocks.

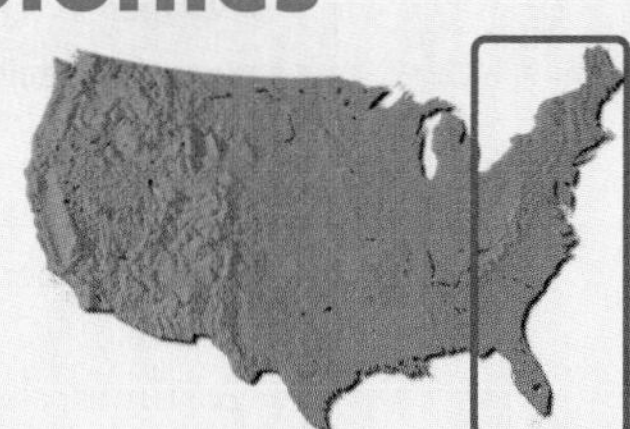

### Major Regional Exports (by export value*)

***NEW ENGLAND COLONIES***

**New England had a short growing season and rocky soil. Colonists took advantage of other opportunities in the region, especially fishing and whaling.**

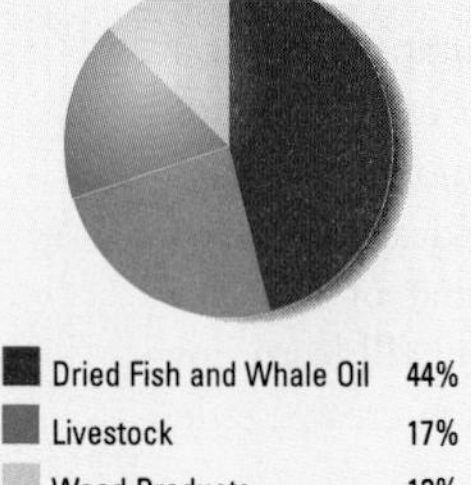

| | |
|---|---|
| Dried Fish and Whale Oil | 44% |
| Livestock | 17% |
| Wood Products | 13% |
| Other | 26% |

***MIDDLE COLONIES***

**The longer growing season of the Middle Colonies—the "breadbasket colonies"—allowed farmers to grow cash crops of grain.**

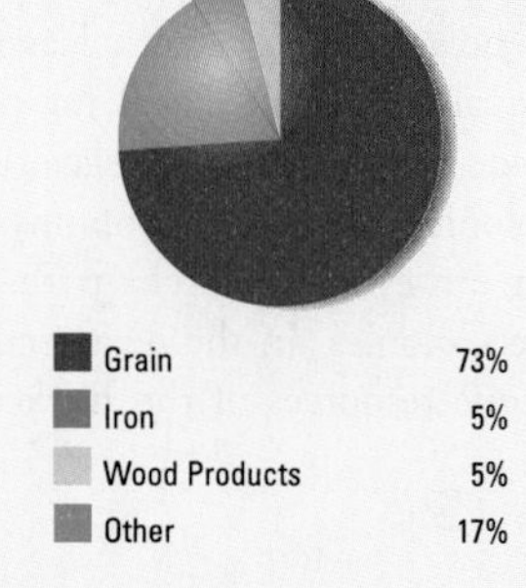

| | |
|---|---|
| Grain | 73% |
| Iron | 5% |
| Wood Products | 5% |
| Other | 17% |

***SOUTHERN COLONIES***

**The South had a nearly year-round growing season. The use of enslaved Africans allowed Southern planters to produce cash crops of tobacco and rice.**

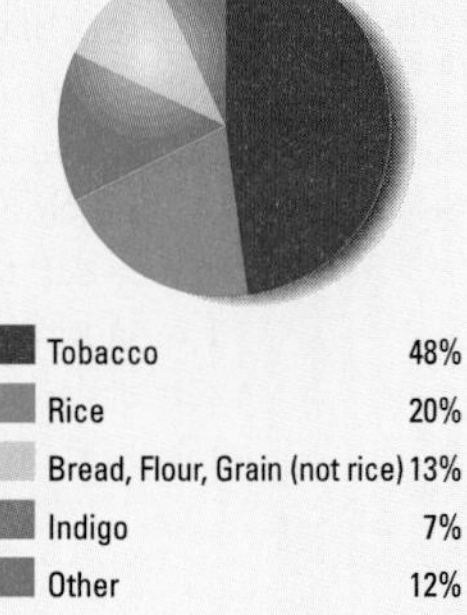

| | |
|---|---|
| Tobacco | 48% |
| Rice | 20% |
| Bread, Flour, Grain (not rice) | 13% |
| Indigo | 7% |
| Other | 12% |

*Export Value in Pounds Sterling (Five-Year Average, 1768–1772)

Source: James F. Shepherd and Gary M. Walton, *Shipping, Maritime Trade, and the Economic Development of Colonial North America* (Cambridge: Cambridge University Press, 1972.)

## ARTIFACT FILE

**Farmer's Plow** Middle colonists relied on the heavy blades of plows to cut seed rows into the region's fertile soil.

**Indigo** On some plantations in the South, planters grew crops of indigo plants—like the one pictured here—to produce the rich blue dyes used to color this yarn.



### MUSEUM CONNECTIONS

The New Bedford Whaling Museum is the country's largest museum dedicated to the whaling industry and the port of New Bedford, the greatest of the whaling ports. The museum brings to life the history of American whaling and the age of the sailing ship through displays and exhibits. The museum houses art, artifacts, and manuscripts.

The museum's Web site provides links to many whaling sites and to detailed discussions of topics such as Yankee Seafaring and Merchant Trade, New Bedford and Its People, and African Americans in New Bedford. For the Web site address, visit www.mcdougallittell.com

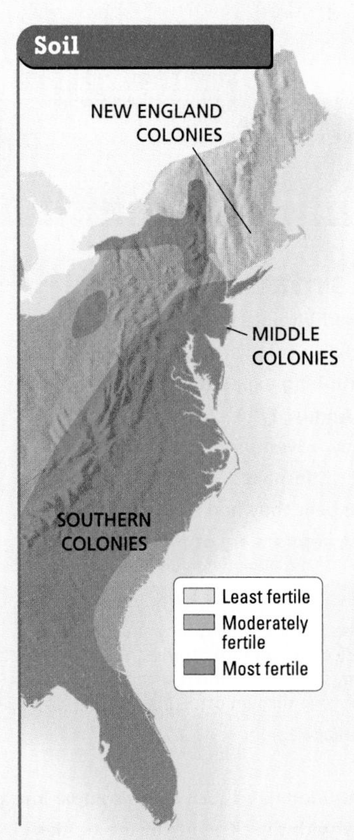


**Growing Season**

NEW ENGLAND COLONIES

MIDDLE COLONIES

SOUTHERN COLONIES

3 to 5 months
5 to 7 months
7 to 9 months
9 to 12 months

**Physical Geography** The maps above show the different types of land forms, soil, and growing seasons that were found in the different colonial regions. These factors helped to shape the economies of each of the regions, which were quite different, as the pie graphs show on the previous page.

## On-Line Field Trip

**The New Bedford Whaling Museum** in Massachusetts has many objects related to whaling, including bone or ivory objects called scrimshaws. A sailor carved this whale's tooth with a jackknife or sail needle and colored the design with ink.

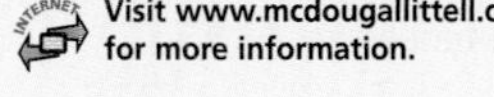

Visit www.mcdougallittell.com for more information.

### CONNECT TO GEOGRAPHY

1. **Region** How long was the growing season in most of the Southern Colonies?
2. **Human-Environment Interaction** How might the soil quality in the Middle Colonies have influenced the region's population?

See Geography Handbook, pages 10–13.

### CONNECT TO HISTORY

3. **Analyzing Causes** Why did the land forms and soil of New England cause many to turn to the Atlantic Ocean for a living?



### CRITICAL THINKING ACTIVITY

**Recognizing Important Details** Have students make a graphic like the one below. Then have them study the map and pie graphs and list the geographical features, natural resources, and exports of each of these colonial regions.

| New England Colonies | Middle Colonies | Southern Colonies |
|---|---|---|
| | | |
| | | |
| | | |
| | | |

**Class Time** 20 minutes

### MORE ABOUT . . .

**The Appalachian Mountains**

*Appalachia* is the name for the area covered by the Appalachian Mountains. The Appalachians reach for approximately 1,500 miles from Alabama to the province of Quebec. The Appalachians include a number of smaller mountain ranges, such as the Alleghenies, the Blue Ridge, the Great Smoky Mountains, and the Catskills.

### CONNECT TO GEOGRAPHY

1. **Region** They had a short growing season, from seven to nine months.
2. **Human-Environment Interaction** Settlers used the Middle Colonies' fertile soil to form the region into a rich farming landscape.

### CONNECT TO HISTORY

3. **Analyzing Causes** The rocky hills and poor soil of New England made farming difficult so people turned to skilled trade and coastal occupations.

## SECTION OBJECTIVES

1. To describe the geography of the Backcountry
2. To identify Backcountry settlers and to understand Backcountry life
3. To identify other peoples in North America and explain their conflict with the English colonists

**SKILLBUILDER**

Interpreting Maps: Region, p. 127

**CRITICAL THINKING**

Analyzing Points of View, p. 127
Making Inferences, p. 128
Summarizing, p. 128
Identifying Problems, p. 129

**Why It Matters Now**
- Regional Differences, pp. 7–8

## FOCUS & MOTIVATE

### 5-MINUTE WARM-UP

**Making Inferences** These questions focus on the interaction between settlers and Native Americans.

1. Look at the picture on page 126. What can you infer about the relationship between these Native Americans and settlers?
2. As more settlers came to the Backcountry, how do you think their relationship with the Native Americans changed?

**Warm-Up Transparency WT4**

## INSTRUCT

### INSTRUCT: OBJECTIVE 1

**Geography of the Backcountry**

Key Questions
- What are the geographical boundaries of the Backcountry?
- What attracted settlers to the Backcountry?

**In-Depth Resources: Unit 1**
- Guided Reading, p. 67

**America's History Makers**
- Alexander Spotswood, pp. 17–18

# 4 The Backcountry

**TERMS & NAMES**
Appalachian Mountains
fall line
piedmont
clan

| MAIN IDEA | WHY IT MATTERS NOW |
|---|---|
| Settlers moved to the Backcountry because land was cheap and plentiful. | Backcountry settlers established a rural way of life that still exists in certain parts of the country. |

### ONE AMERICAN'S STORY

**Alexander Spotswood governed Virginia from 1710 to 1722. He believed that the future of English colonists lay to the west. To prove his point, he led a month-long expedition over the crest of the Blue Ridge Mountains in August 1716.**

**During the 400-mile journey, adventurers braved dense thickets, muddy streams, and rattlesnakes. At night, they feasted on the deer, wild turkeys, and bear they had shot. John Fontaine, who accompanied Spotswood, kept a diary of the trip.**

*A VOICE FROM THE PAST*

We had a rugged way; we passed over a great many small runs of water, some of which were very deep, and others very miry. Several of our company were dismounted, some were down with their horses, others under their horses, and some thrown off.

**John Fontaine,** quoted in *Colonial Virginia*

Alexander Spotswood meets Native Americans in the Blue Ridge Mountains—a segment of the Appalachians Mountains.

**After the expedition, Spotswood gave each of his companions a golden horseshoe. His journey with the "Knights of the Golden Horseshoe" is considered a symbol of Virginia's westward expansion.**

## 1 Geography of the Backcountry

Just as Spotswood predicted, settlers soon began to move into the Backcountry. This was a region of dense forests and rushing streams in or near the **Appalachian Mountains**. The Appalachians stretch from eastern Canada south to Alabama.

In the South, the Backcountry began at the **fall line**. The fall line is where waterfalls prevent large boats from moving farther upriver. Beyond the fall line is the **piedmont**. Piedmont means "foot of the mountains." It is the broad plateau that leads to the Blue Ridge Mountains of the Appalachian range.

The Backcountry's resources made it relatively easy for a family to start a small farm. The region's many springs and streams provided water, and forests furnished wood that settlers could use for log cabins and fences.



## RECOMMENDED RESOURCES

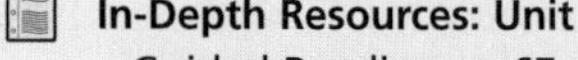

**In-Depth Resources: Unit 1**
- Guided Reading, p. 67
- Building Vocabulary, p. 68
- Primary Source: Culture Clash in the Colonies, pp. 72–73
- Reteaching Activity, p. 80

**Reading Study Guide** (Spanish and English), pp. 41–42

**Economics in History**
- Native American Economies, p. 4

**America's History Makers**
- Alexander Spotswood, pp. 17–18

**Why It Matters Now**
- Regional Differences, pp. 7–8

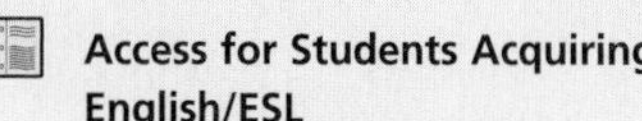

**Formal Assessment**
- Section Quiz, p. 64

**Alternative Assessment**
- Rubrics, 4.5
- Rubrics, 1.3

**Access for Students Acquiring English/ESL**
- Guided Reading, p. 25

**Technology Resources**

**Electronic Teacher Tools with Test Maker**

**ClassZone**
www.mcdougallittell.com

## 2 Backcountry Settlers

The first Europeans in the Backcountry made a living by trading with the Native Americans. Backcountry settlers paid for goods with deerskins. A unit of value was one buckskin or, for short, a "buck."

Vocabulary
**buck:** an adult male deer; the adult female is called a *doe*

Farmers soon followed the traders into the region, but they had to be cautious. As the number of settlements grew, the farmers often clashed with the Native Americans whose land they were taking.

Farmers sheltered their families in log cabins. They filled holes between the logs with mud, moss, and clay. Then they sawed out doors and windows. Lacking glass, settlers used paper smeared with animal fat to cover their windows.

*Reading* **History**
**A. Analyzing Points of View** What was William Byrd's attitude toward Backcountry settlers?
**A. Possible Response** Byrd's membership in the planter class may have made him prejudiced against the lifestyle of Backcountry settlers.

William Byrd—on his expedition to establish the southern border of Virginia—described a long night that he spent in one such cabin. He complained that he and at least ten other people were "forct to pig together in a Room . . . troubled with the Squalling of peevish, dirty children into the Bargain."

Backcountry life may have been harsh, but by the late 1600s many families had chosen to move there. Some of them went to escape the plantation system, which had crowded out many small farmers closer to the seacoast. Then, in the 1700s, a new group of emigrants—the Scots-Irish—began to move into the Backcountry.

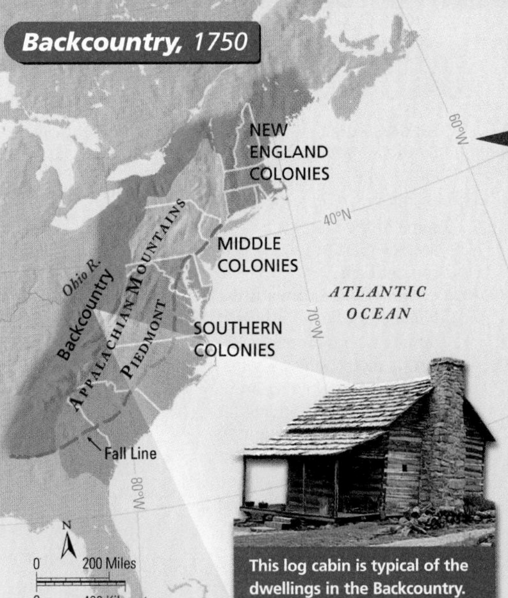


This log cabin is typical of the dwellings in the Backcountry.

**GEOGRAPHY SKILLBUILDER Interpreting Maps**
**Region** *What geographical feature did the northern and southern areas of the Backcountry have in common?*

Skillbuilder Answer
They were in or near the Appalachian Mountains.

## The Scots-Irish

The Scots-Irish came from the borderland between Scotland and England. Most of them had lived for a time in northern Ireland. In 1707, England and Scotland merged and formed Great Britain. The merger caused many hardships for the Scots-Irish. Poverty and crop failures made this bad situation even worse.

As a result, Scots-Irish headed to America by the thousands. After they arrived, they quickly moved into the Backcountry. The Scots-Irish brought their clan system with them to the Backcountry. **Clans** are large groups of families—sometimes in the thousands—that claim a common ancestor. Clan members were suspicious of outsiders and banded together when danger threatened. These clans helped families to deal with the dangers and problems of the Backcountry.

Vocabulary
**clan:** comes from an Old Irish word that means offspring, or descendants



### HISTORY FROM VISUALS

**Reading the Map** The Backcountry region bordered most of the American colonies. Ask the students which groups of colonies most Backcountry settlers probably came from and why. **Possible Response** The majority probably came from the Middle or Southern Colonies, since these colonies bordered most of the Backcountry. It would have been easier for colonists from these regions to resettle in the Backcountry.

**Extension** Have students use an atlas to identify present-day cities and towns in the Backcountry.

### INSTRUCT: OBJECTIVE 2

**Backcountry Settlers/**
**The Scots-Irish/Backcountry Life**

Key Questions

- How did the relationship between the settlers and the Native Americans change?
- Why did the Scots-Irish come to the Backcountry?
- How did life in the Backcountry differ from life along the seaboard?

### MORE ABOUT . . .

**Log Cabins**

The first log cabins in the New World were built by Swedes and Finns, beginning in the mid-1600s near the Delaware River. Other groups of colonists, including English, Scots-Irish, Welsh, and Dutch settlers, adapted this easily constructed dwelling. Various types of log cabins were also built by Russians in Alaska, French in Quebec, Spaniards and Mexicans in areas of New Mexico, and French fur traders in western North America. Five American presidents claimed to have been born in log cabins: Andrew Jackson, James Polk, James Buchanan, Abraham Lincoln, and James Garfield.

### ACTIVITY OPTIONS

**INTERDISCIPLINARY LINK: THE ARTS**

BLOCK SCHEDULING

**AMERICAN QUILTS**

**Class Time** One class period

**Task** Planning a quilt pattern

**Purpose** To research and draw a pattern for a quilt

**Supplies Needed**

- Reference materials about American quilts
- Art supplies, including drawing paper, pencils, ruler, colored pencils, paints

**Activity** Have students find reference materials about American quilts. Tell students to choose a traditional American quilt pattern and reproduce it in the colors of their choice on a large piece of drawing paper. Ask students to display their completed designs in class and discuss what they know about the design and history of their quilts.

## *Now and* then

**Backcountry Sports Today**
Many Americans enjoy competing in and watching Scottish, or Highland, games. Some events in these games are very similar to those of colonial days in the Backcountry. In one event, the caber toss, competitors run with a wood pole weighing as much as 130 pounds. Then they toss the pole end over end. The toss is judged on distance and accuracy. Another event, the Farmer's Walk, requires strength and endurance. Competitors pick up and carry two 150-pound weights and then walk around pylons. The winner is the athlete who walks the farthest.

## INSTRUCT: OBJECTIVE 3

**Other Peoples in North America**
Key Questions
- How did contact with the Spanish colonists affect Native American culture?
- What caused conflict between colonists and Native Americans?
- What other groups of people were establishing claims in North America?

## MORE ABOUT . . .

**Native Americans and Horses**
The coming of horses to the Great Plains changed the culture of the Native Americans of the Plains. Young men of Plains tribes acquired status by capturing wild horses. A family's rank was determined by the number of horses it owned. Because horses could carry heavy loads, peoples of the Plains could make taller and wider tepees.

 **Economics in History**
- Native American Economies, p. 4

### *Now and* then

**BACKCOUNTRY SPORTS TODAY**

Three centuries ago, crowds in the Backcountry were thrilled by some of the same games that are now part of track and field competitions.

One of these games is the hammer throw. In this event, an athlete swings around a 16-pound metal ball on a wire-rope handle. After whirling around several times, the athlete lets go of the hammer, hoping it will travel the farthest distance.

The Scots-Irish brought other games to America, including the shotput, high jump, and long jump.

## Backcountry Life

Life in the Backcountry was very different from life along the seaboard. Settlers along the coast carried on a lively trade with England. But in the Backcountry, rough roads and rivers made it almost impossible to move goods.

As a result, Backcountry farmers learned quickly to depend on themselves. They built log cabins and furnished them with cornhusk mattresses and homemade benches and tables. They fed their families with the hogs and cattle they raised and with the fish and game they killed. They grew yellow corn to feed their livestock and white corn to eat. Popcorn was probably their only snack food. To protect their precious corn from pests, daytime patrols of women, children, and the elderly served as human scarecrows.

*Reading***History**
**B. Making Inferences** How would you describe the way people in the Backcountry lived?
B. Possible Response Because of the rough conditions in the Backcountry, settlers developed a rugged lifestyle.

Women in the Backcountry worked in the cabin and fields, but they also learned to use guns and axes. An explorer who traveled in the region described one of these hardy Backcountry women.

***A VOICE FROM THE PAST***

She is a very civil woman and shows nothing of ruggedness or Immodesty in her carriage, yett she will carry a gunn in the woods and kill deer, turkeys, etc., shoot doun wild cattle, catch and tye hoggs, knock down [cattle] with an ax and perform the most manfull Exercises.

**A visitor to the Backcountry,** quoted in *A History of American Life*

Settlers in the Backcountry often acted as if there were no other people in the region, but this was not so. In the woods and meadows that surrounded their cabins, settlers often encountered Native Americans and other groups that had made America their home.

## 3 Other Peoples in North America

The Backcountry settlers started a westward movement that would play a critical role in American history. Most settlers' motivation to move west was simple—the desire for land.

*Reading***History**
**C. Summarizing** As England's colonies expanded westward, what groups did they encounter?
C. Possible Responses Native Americans, Spanish, and French.

Yet the push to the west brought settlers into contact with other peoples of North America. Native Americans had made their homes there for thousands of years. In addition, France and Spain claimed considerable territory in North America.

Sometimes this contact led to changes in people's cultures. For instance, North America had no horses until the Spanish colonists brought them into Mexico in the 1500s. Horses migrated north, and Native Americans caught them and made them an important part of their culture.



## ACTIVITY OPTIONS

### INDIVIDUAL NEEDS

**LESS PROFICIENT READERS**

**Supporting Details** To help students understand the isolated geographic position and lifestyle of the settlers in the Backcountry, write this sentence from page 128 on the board: "As a result, Backcountry farmers learned quickly to depend on themselves." After students read the sentence, ask them to find details in the text to support it. Write their responses on the board in a Main Idea/Details chart such as the one shown.

As a result, Backcountry farmers learned quickly to depend on themselves.

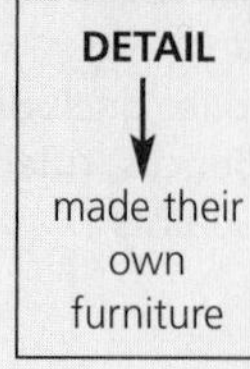


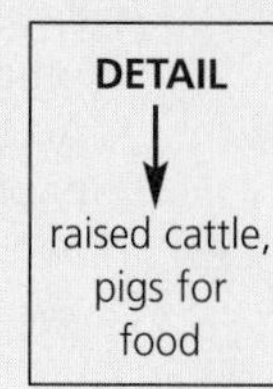

Contact also led to conflict. As English settlers pushed into the Backcountry, they put pressure on Native American tribes. Some tribes reacted by raiding isolated homesteads and small settlements. White settlers struck back, leading to more bloodshed.

This painting shows Native Americans catching wild horses. Many would later use the horses to hunt buffalo on the Great Plains.

The English colonists also came into conflict with the French. The French had colonized eastern Canada and had moved into the territories, rich with fur, along the Mississippi River. French fur traders wanted to prevent English settlers from moving west and taking away part of the trade. One Native American told an Englishman, "You and the French are like two edges of a pair of shears, and we are the cloth that is cut to pieces between them."

**Vocabulary**
**shears:** scissors

Spain also controlled large areas of North America—including territories that today form part or all of the states of Arizona, California, Colorado, Florida, Nevada, New Mexico, Texas, Utah, and Wyoming. Spanish settlers were farmers, ranchers, and priests. Priests, who established missions to convert Native Americans, built forts near the missions for protection. In 1718, Spaniards built Fort San Antonio de Bexar to guard the mission of San Antonio de Valero, later renamed the Alamo.

These different groups continued to compete—and sometimes fight—with one another. Frequently, England's colonies had to unite against these other groups. As a result, a common American identity began to take shape, as you will read in Chapter 5.

## Section 4 Assessment

### 1. Terms & Names

**Identify:**
- Appalachian Mountains
- fall line
- piedmont
- clan

### 2. Taking Notes

Use a chart like the one shown to list some of the geographic characteristics of the Backcountry.

| Backcountry Geography |
|---|
| 1. |
| 2. |
| 3. |
| 4. |

### 3. Main Ideas

**a.** Which settlers migrated to the Backcountry?

**b.** How did clans help the Scots-Irish survive?

**c.** What economic activities did women carry out in the region?

### 4. Critical Thinking

**Identifying Problems** As England's colonies expanded farther west, what problems would they face?

**THINK ABOUT**
- other inhabitants of the Americas
- the resources desired by the colonists

**ACTIVITY OPTIONS**

**LANGUAGE ARTS / ART** Read an account of the Backcountry written in the 1700s. Write a **newspaper article** or draw a series of **cartoons** that describe what you have read.



## MORE ABOUT . . .

### Diversity on the Frontier

The frontier was not so much a boundary as a zone of contact where many people encountered one another. According to one study of a northern Ohio town in the late 1700s, the population included Shawnee, Iroquois, Miami, Delaware, Cherokee, British, French, Americans, and African Americans. The residents celebrated Mardi Gras, St. Patrick's Day, Indian holidays, and the birthday of the British monarch, not to mention Christmas, New Year's Day, and—after American independence—the Fourth of July.

## ASSESS & RETEACH

**Setting the Stage** Have students fill in the chart with the information about the Backcountry.

 **Formal Assessment**
- Section Quiz, p. 64

 **Critical Thinking Transparency CT10**
- Setting the Stage

### RETEACHING ACTIVITY

Divide the class into four groups, assigning each group one section objective. Ask each group to produce a chart that includes the objective and three to four bulleted key ideas. Have the group illustrate the chart with a visual that supports the main objective. Display the completed graphics in class.

 **In-Depth Resources: Unit 1**
- Reteaching Activity, p. 80

## Section 4 Assessment

### 1. Terms & Names

**Appalachian Mountains,** p. 126
**fall line,** p. 126
**piedmont,** p. 126
**clan,** p. 127

### 2. Taking Notes

1. dense forests
2. rushing streams
3. near or in Appalachian Mountains
4. climate varied with latitude

### 3. Main Ideas

**a.** small farmers who couldn't compete with wealthy plantation owners; Scots-Irish **b.** Large groups of families banded together to deal with dangers and problems. **c.** worked in the fields and in the cabin; used guns and axes

### 4. Critical Thinking

They would run into other inhabitants of the continent and compete with them for land, furs, and other resources.

**ACTIVITY OPTIONS**

 **Alternative Assessment**
- Rubrics for a newspaper, 4.5
- Rubrics for a cartoon, 1.3

## TERMS & NAMES

1. **Backcountry,** p. 109
2. **subsistence farming,** p. 110
3. **triangular trade,** p. 111
4. **Navigation Acts,** p. 112
5. **cash crop,** p. 115
6. **gristmill,** p. 115
7. **Conestoga wagon,** p. 117
8. **overseer,** p. 122
9. **Stono Rebellion,** p. 123
10. **Appalachian Mountains,** p. 126

## REVIEW QUESTIONS

**Possible Responses**

1. They often lived near towns and practiced subsistence farming. Because of the short growing season and rocky soil, farming was challenging.
2. They became shipbuilders, traders, whalers, and fishermen.
3. A compact plot of land was often sold to a congregation, which then divided the land between members.
4. These farms often produced large cash crops.
5. The population was remarkably diverse.
6. Southern planters were self-sufficient, producing most of what they needed with the resources on their plantations. When necessary, they used nearby rivers to transport their crops.
7. Native Americans and white Europeans were unreliable sources of labor.
8. They worked slowly, damaged goods, purposely carried out orders incorrectly, and rebelled.
9. It was in or near the Appalachian Mountains in the far western part of most of the colonies.
10. Because of the Backcountry's distance from the coast, settlers there developed an independent and rugged lifestyle.



## VISUAL SUMMARY

### The Colonies Develop

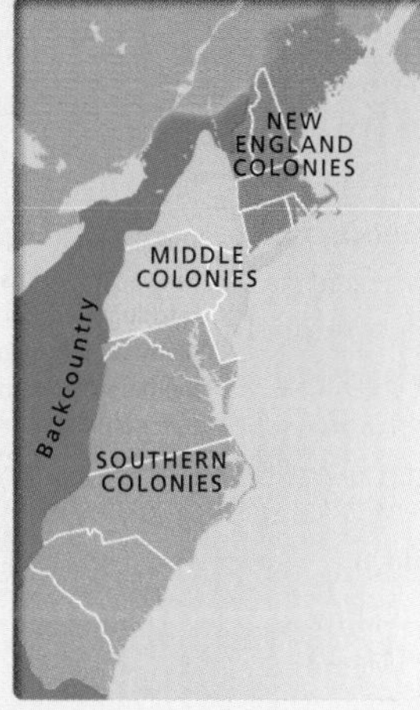


**New England: Commerce and Religion**

New England was distinguished by its small farming towns and profitable fishing and trade.

**The Middle Colonies: Farms and Cities**

Middle Colony farms produced large cash crops that fueled trade in its coastal cities.

**The Southern Colonies: Plantations and Slavery**

The South's plantation economy and large number of enslaved Africans made it different from the other regions.

**The Backcountry**

The Backcountry was distant from the denser coastal populations, so settlers there developed an independent and rugged way of life.



## TERMS & NAMES

Briefly explain the importance of the following.

1. Backcountry
2. subsistence farming
3. triangular trade
4. Navigation Acts
5. cash crop
6. gristmill
7. Conestoga wagon
8. overseer
9. Stono Rebellion
10. Appalachian Mountains

## REVIEW QUESTIONS

**New England: Commerce and Religion (pages 109–113)**

1. How would you describe the life of a New England farmer?
2. In what ways did settlers in the region take advantage of the Atlantic Ocean?
3. How were New England towns settled?

**The Middle Colonies: Farms and Cities (pages 114–118)**

4. How were farms in the Middle Colonies different than those in New England?
5. What characterized the population of the Middle Colonies?

**The Southern Colonies: Plantations and Slavery (pages 119–125)**

6. Why did Southern planters infrequently travel to towns to sell their crops or to buy food and supplies?
7. Why did planters turn to enslaved Africans for labor?
8. In what ways did slaves resist?

**The Backcountry (pages 126–129)**

9. Where was the Backcountry located in the 1700s?
10. How was life in the Backcountry different from that along the coast?

## CRITICAL THINKING

**1. USING YOUR NOTES**

Using your completed chart, answer the questions below.

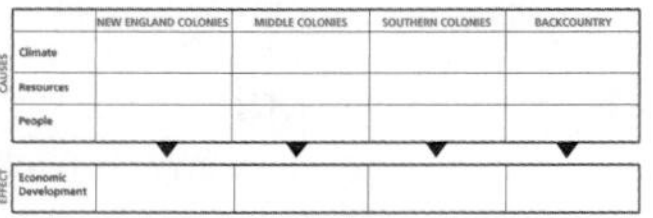


a. How was the Middle Colonies' climate different from the Backcountry's?
b. How did the South's labor system differ from the North's?
c. How did the resources of New England affect its economy?

**2. ANALYZING LEADERSHIP**

How did the South's plantation economy influence who became leaders in the region?

**3. THEME: ECONOMICS IN HISTORY**

What factors influenced the economic development of each of the four colonial regions?

**4. APPLYING CITIZENSHIP SKILLS**

How did the Quaker influence in the Middle Colonies contribute to the behavior of citizens of the region?

**5. SEQUENCING EVENTS**

What changes took place in the population and treatment of African Americans between 1650 and 1750?

**Interact *with* History**

How would the choice that you made at the beginning of the chapter have varied according to the region in which you lived? Would you still make the same choice?

## CRITICAL THINKING

**Possible Response**

1. **USING YOUR NOTES** **a.** The shorter winters meant a longer growing season and more productive farms. **b.** The South relied much more heavily on enslaved Africans for labor than the North. **c.** The poor soil and small farms led people to economic opportunities offered by the Atlantic Ocean.
2. **ANALYZING LEADERSHIP** Because planters held all the wealth, this small class also assumed political leadership in the South.
3. **THEME: ECONOMICS IN HISTORY** climate, resources, and people
4. **APPLYING CITIZENSHIP SKILLS** Quaker religious tolerance, belief in the equality of men and women, and belief that slavery was wrong all positively influenced civic behavior.
5. **SEQUENCING EVENTS** Between 1650 and 1750, the African-American population went from 5 percent to 40 percent. By 1750, there were 235,000 enslaved Africans in America—about 85 percent lived in the South. The treatment of the enslaved African Americans worsened.

**Interact *with* History** Answers should acknowledge the characteristics of the region and explain reasons for their choice.

## HISTORY SKILLS

### 1. INTERPRETING MAPS: Human-Environment Interaction

Study the map. Answer the questions.

**Claims in North America, 1750**

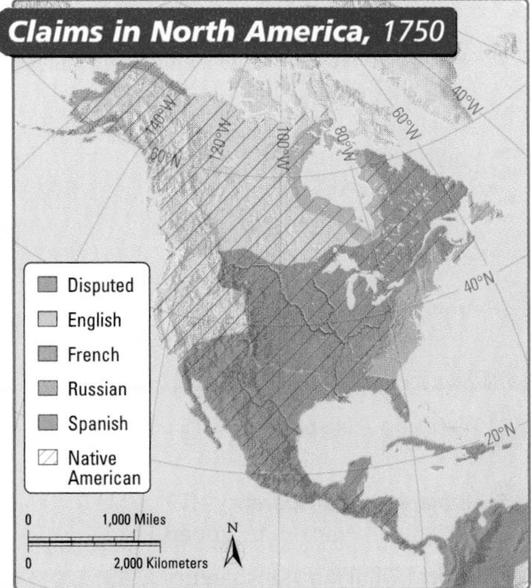


**Basic Map Elements**

a. What is the subject of the map?

**Interpreting the Map**

b. Which of the groups shown inhabited the largest area of North America?

c. Which groups claimed the northernmost territory?

### 2. INTERPRETING PRIMARY SOURCES

In the backwoods of North Carolina, William Byrd met a family he suspected of being escaped slaves. Read the selection below and answer the questions.

> [They] called themselves free, though by the shyness of the master of the house, who took care to keep least in sight, their freedom seemed a little doubtful. . . . Many slaves [hide] in this obscure part of the world, nor will any of their righteous neighbors discover them. On the contrary, [their neighbors profit by] settling such fugitives on some out-of-the-way corner of their land to raise stocks for a mean and inconsiderable share, well knowing their condition makes it necessary for them to [accept any pay they are offered].
>
> **William Byrd,** from *Secret History of the Dividing Line*

a. Why does Byrd suspect the family members are escaped slaves?

b. Why don't their neighbors turn them in?

## ALTERNATIVE ASSESSMENT

### 1. INTERDISCIPLINARY ACTIVITY: Geography

**Making a Map** Using the library or the Internet, read more about the history of the slave trade in the 1700s. Create a map of Africa that shows countries that were major sources of enslaved persons.

 **Visit www.mcdougallittell.com to learn more about the history of Africa.**

### 2. COOPERATIVE LEARNING ACTIVITY

**Building a Log Cabin** Do some more research on the Backcountry and the history of log cabins. Work with others to record details about the location where you will build your cabin. Then design and construct a model of a log cabin that could be compared to the cabins in which Backcountry settlers lived. Be sure to build a setting for your cabin that shows the landscape where you chose to make your home.

### 3. TECHNOLOGY ACTIVITY

**Making a Class Presentation** Life on a farm in colonial New England was a real challenge. Using the library or the Internet, find accounts of how New England farmers and their families lived. Then design a multimedia presentation that focuses on a typical New England farmer and his family.

 **Visit www.mcdougallittell.com to learn more about the way people lived during colonial times.**

- Create a map of the town in which the farmer and his family lived.
- Dress up like a farmer to discuss the challenges of New England agriculture.
- Create a chart that lists the differences between your family's lifestyle and the colonial family's.

### 4. HISTORY PORTFOLIO

**Option 1** Review your section and chapter assessment activities. Select one that you think is your best work. Then use comments made by your teacher or classmates to improve your work and add it to your portfolio.

**Option 2** Review the questions that you wrote for What Do You Want to Know? on page 108. Then write a short report in which you explain the answers to your questions. If any questions were not answered, do research to answer them. Add your answers to your portfolio.



## ALTERNATIVE ASSESSMENT

1. INTERDISCIPLINARY ACTIVITY: **Geography**

**A map should**
- include a legend and title.
- include either or both physical and political locations.
- be clearly labeled and neatly presented.
- clearly demonstrate an understanding of the sources of enslaved persons.

2. COOPERATIVE LEARNING ACTIVITY

**A log cabin should**
- represent the cabin in a three-dimensional manner clear to viewers.
- exhibit creativity.
- demonstrate grade-level artistic skill.

3.  TECHNOLOGY ACTIVITY

**Class presentations should**
- utilize two or more media.
- clearly demonstrate an understanding of life on a colonial New England farm.
- engage or educate the audience about the topic.
- show technical proficiency.
- use correct grammar, spelling, and punctuation.

4. HISTORY PORTFOLIO

 **Option 1 Revised section or chapter assessment activities should**
- address teacher and peer responses to the selected work.
- solve problems present in the first versions of the work.

**Option 2 Short reports should**
- answer questions about the four colonial regions.
- use evidence to develop and support ideas.
- cite sources of information.
- use standard grammar, spelling, sentence structure, and punctuation.

 **Critical Thinking Transparency CT12**
- Visual Summary

 **Formal Assessment**
- Chapter Test, Forms A and B, pp. 65–72

## HISTORY SKILLS

**Possible Responses**

1. INTERPRETING MAPS

**Basic Map Elements**

**a.** claims in North America in 1750

**Interpreting the Map**

**b.** Native Americans

**c.** Russians

2. INTERPRETING PRIMARY SOURCES

**a.** because they are shy and the master stayed out of sight

**b.** because they know that the slaves' fear of being turned in will make them work for little pay

CHAPTER 5 PLANNING GUIDE

# Beginnings of an American Identity 1689–1763

| | CHAPTER OVERVIEW | COPYMASTERS | TECHNOLOGY |
|---|---|---|---|
| **CHAPTER RESOURCES** | The chapter explores the social and economic classes developing in the colonies as well as the new religious and philosophical movements. It also describes the major war that occurred between Britain and France over the settlement of western lands. | **In-Depth Resources: Unit 1**<br>• Tracing Themes: Democratic Ideals, p. 83<br>• Building Vocabulary, p. 87<br>**Interdisciplinary Projects,** pp. 25–30 | **Primary Source Explorer**<br>**Electronic Teacher Tools**<br>**Power Presentations CD-ROM**<br>**Chapter Summaries on CD** (English and Spanish)<br>**America's Music CD** |
| **SECTION 1**<br>**Early American Culture**<br>**pp. 135–140** | **KEY IDEAS**<br>• Land ownership determines social position in the colonies.<br>• The work of women and children is essential to the colonial economy.<br>• Schooling, literacy, the Great Awakening, and the Enlightenment influence the intellectual life of the colonies. | **In-Depth Resources: Unit 1**<br>• Setting the Stage, p. 82<br>• Guided Reading, p. 84<br>• Skillbuilder Practice, p. 88<br>• Primary Source, p. 91<br>• Reteaching Activity, p. 96<br>**America's History Makers,** pp. 19–22<br>**Economics in History,** p. 5<br>**Why It Matters Now,** pp. 9–10 | **Warm-Up Transparency WT5**<br>**Humanities Transparency HT9**<br>• *Benjamin Franklin* by Robert Feke<br>**Critical Thinking Transparency CT13**<br>• Setting the Stage<br>**ClassZone:** www.mcdougallittell.com |
| **SECTION 2**<br>**Roots of Representative Government**<br>**pp. 141–145** | • Colonial governments follow the English parliamentary model.<br>• Royal governors threaten the colonies' representative governments.<br>• England's Glorious Revolution made political liberties more secure in both England and the colonies. | **In-Depth Resources: Unit 1**<br>• Setting the Stage, p. 82<br>• Guided Reading, p. 85<br>• Reteaching Activity, p. 97<br>**Citizenship Today,** pp. 1–2<br>**American History Plays**<br>• *The Trial of Peter Zenger* by Paul T. Nolan | **Warm-Up Transparency WT5**<br>**Critical Thinking Transparency CT13**<br>• Setting the Stage<br>**ClassZone:** www.mcdougallittell.com |
| **SECTION 3**<br>**The French and Indian War**<br>**pp. 146–151** | • France and Britain go to war over western lands and trade.<br>• Native Americans ally with France and fight against both British troops and colonists.<br>• Britain's victory gives it control of Canada and French lands east of the Mississippi River. | **In-Depth Resources: Unit 1**<br>• Setting the Stage, p. 82<br>• Guided Reading, p. 86<br>• Geography Application, pp. 89–90<br>• Primary Source, p. 92<br>• Literature Selection, pp. 93–95<br>• Reteaching Activity, p. 98<br>**Outline Map Activities**<br>• Mississippi River Drainage Basin, pp. 9–10 | **Warm-Up Transparency WT5**<br>**Humanities Transparency HT10**<br>• George Washington, 1755<br>**Geography Transparency GT5**<br>• Proclamation of 1763<br>**Critical Thinking Transparency CT14**<br>• Cause and Effect: The French and Indian War |

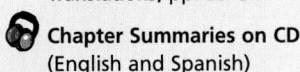

PE Pupil's Edition
Copymaster
Overhead Transparency
Audio Library
CD-ROM
Internet

## ASSESSMENT

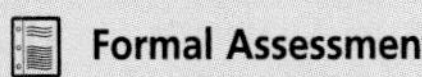

PE **Chapter Assessment,** pp. 152–153

**Formal Assessment**
- Chapter Tests, Forms A and B, pp. 78–85

**Alternative Assessment Book**

**Electronic Teacher Tools with Test Maker**

PE **Section Assessment,** p. 140

**Formal Assessment**
- Section Quiz, p. 75

**Alternative Assessment Book**
- Rubrics for a saying, 4.9
- Rubrics for an illustration, 1.3

**Electronic Teacher Tools with Test Maker**

PE **Section Assessment,** p. 145

**Formal Assessment**
- Section Quiz, p. 76

**Alternative Assessment Book**
- Rubrics for an argument, 3.6
- Rubrics for a leaflet, 1.13

**Electronic Teacher Tools with Test Maker**

PE **Section Assessment,** p. 151

**Formal Assessment**
- Section Quiz, p. 77

**Alternative Assessment Book**
- Rubrics for a model, 1.10
- Rubrics for a song, 4.8

**Electronic Teacher Tools with Test Maker**

## CUSTOMIZING FOR INDIVIDUAL NEEDS

### Students Acquiring English/ESL

**Reading Study Guide** (English and Spanish), pp. 45–52

**Access for Students Acquiring English/ESL: Spanish Translations,** pp. 29–34

**Chapter Summaries on CD** (English and Spanish)

### Less Proficient Readers

**Reading Study Guide** (English and Spanish), pp. 45–52

**Chapter Summaries on CD** (English and Spanish)

### Gifted and Talented Students

**In-Depth Resources: Unit 1**
- Enrichment Activity, p. 99

**America's History Makers**
- Benjamin Franklin, pp. 19–20
- Sarah Kemble Knight, pp. 21–22

## CROSS-CURRICULAR CONNECTIONS

### Popular Culture

Kalman, Bobbie. ***Early Artisans.*** Early Settler Life Series. New York: Crabtree, 1983. Looks at the crafts of bookbinders, printers, co-opers, and glassblowers, among others.

### Primary Sources

Smith, Carter, ed. ***The Explorers and Settlers: A Sourcebook on Colonial America*** (American Albums from the Library of Congress). Brookfield, CT: Millbrook Press, 1994.

### Interdisciplinary Projects, pp. 25–30

- Math: Early Colonial Industries
- Science: Franklin's Experiments with Lightning
- Language Arts: *The New England Primer*
- Art: Colonial Furnishings

### Health

Terkel, Susan N. ***Colonial American Medicine.*** New York: Franklin Watts, 1993. From the Colonial America series, this book looks at the "cures"—from herbs to leeches—with which doctors in the 1600s and 1700s treated the diseases and epidemics of their day.

### Language Arts/Literature

Dorris, Michael. ***Guests.*** New York: Hyperion, 1994. Story of a young Algonquian named Moss, his quest for manhood, and his relationship with a girl named Trouble.

Durrant, Lynda. ***The Beaded Moccasins: The Story of Mary Campbell.*** New York: Clarion Books, 1998. Based on a historical incident, the story of a girl kidnapped from her Pennsylvania farm by Delaware Indians in 1759.

Longfellow, Henry W. ***Evangeline.*** LaVergne, TN: Ingram, 1999. Narrative poem relating the adventures of the Acadians and their emigration to Louisiana.

## ENRICHMENT ACTIVITIES

PE **Pupil's Edition, pp. 132–153**
**Interact with History,** p. 133
**Citizenship Today,** p. 142

**In-Depth Resources: Unit 1**
- Geography Application: Native American Confederacies, pp. 89–90
- Primary Source, p. 91
- Primary Source, p. 92
- Literature Selection, pp. 93–95

**America's History Makers**
- Benjamin Franklin, pp. 19–20
- Sarah Kemble Knight, pp. 21–22

**America's Music CD**

**American History Plays**
- *The Trial of Peter Zenger* by Paul T. Nolan

**Outline Map Activities**
- Mississippi River Drainage Basin, pp. 9–10

**Why It Matters Now**
- American Identity Today, pp. 9–10

# CHAPTER 5 PACING GUIDE

**LESSON PLAN OPTIONS (50-MINUTE PERIOD)** **(TE) = Teacher's Edition (PE) = Pupil's Edition**

| | TEACHER-DIRECTED ACTIVITIES<br>Class Time: 15 minutes | STUDENT-CENTERED ACTIVITIES<br>Class Time: 25 minutes | INDIVIDUAL ACTIVITIES<br>Class Time: 10 minutes |
|---|---|---|---|
| **DAY 1**<br>Introduction<br>pp. 132–134 | **Presentation Options**<br>• Begin with a class discussion of the drawing on p. 132 **(PE)**.<br>• Lead a class discussion on the "What Do You Know?" question in Setting the Stage, p. 134. Then introduce the graphic organizer for the chapter **(PE)**. | **Options for Cooperative Learning**<br>• Have student groups discuss the Interact with History questions, p. 133 **(PE)**.<br>• Have student groups respond to the "What Do You Want to Know?" question in Setting the Stage, p. 134 **(PE)**. | **Head Start on Homework Options**<br>• Have students skim Section 1 Main Idea, Why It Matters Now, Terms & Names, and the main headings, p. 135 **(PE)**.<br>• Have students begin Guided Reading activity and Building Vocabulary sheet. |
| **DAY 2**<br>Section 1<br>pp. 135–140 | **Presentation Options**<br>• Begin with the 5-Minute Warm-Up, p. 135 **(TE)**.<br>• Review the Section 1 Main Idea, Why It Matters Now, and Terms & Names, p. 135 **(PE)**.<br>• Choose 5 key questions for Objectives 1–4 to discuss with the class, pp. 135–139 **(TE)**. | **Options for Cooperative Learning**<br>• Divide students into groups to work on the Skillbuilder Mini-Lesson: Finding Main Ideas, p. 136 **(TE)**.<br>• Have student pairs work together to complete one of the Activity Options in the Section 1 Assessment, p. 140 **(PE)**. | **Head Start on Homework Options**<br>• Have students begin working on Section 1 Assessment, p. 140 **(PE)**.<br>• Have students preview Section 2 Main Idea, Why It Matters Now, Terms & Names, and the main headings, p. 141 **(PE)**. |
| **DAY 3**<br>Section 2<br>pp. 141–145 | **Presentation Options**<br>• Begin with the 5-Minute Warm-Up, p. 141 **(TE)**.<br>• Choose 5 key questions for Objectives 1–4 to discuss with the class, pp. 141–144 **(TE)**.<br>• Lead the students through the Citizenship Today Critical Thinking Activity, p. 142 **(TE)**. | **Options for Cooperative Learning**<br>• Divide students into groups and have them complete the Citizenship Today questions, p. 142 **(PE)**.<br>• Have students do a readers' theater of *The Trial of Peter Zenger* in American History Plays. | **Head Start on Homework Options**<br>• Have students read the Primary Source. **In-Depth Resources,** p. 92.<br>• Have students preview Section 3 Main Idea, Why It Matters Now, Terms & Names, and the main headings, p. 146 **(PE)**. |
| **DAY 4**<br>Section 3<br>pp. 146–151 | **Presentation Options**<br>• Begin with the 5-Minute Warm-Up, p. 146 **(TE)**.<br>• Choose 5 key questions for Objectives 1–4 to discuss with the class, pp. 146–150 **(TE)**.<br>• Lead the students through the Geography Skillbuilder, p. 148 **(PE)**. | **Options for Cooperative Learning**<br>• Divide students into groups and have them complete the Interdisciplinary Link, Music: Cajun Music and Zydeco, p. 149 **(TE)**.<br>• Have student pairs work together to complete the History from Visuals Extension Activity, p. 148 **(TE)**. | **Head Start on Homework Options**<br>• Have students complete the Setting the Stage graphic organizer for the chapter, p. 134 **(PE)**.<br>• Have students begin working on the Chapter Assessment, pp. 152–153 **(PE)**.<br>• Prepare for Chapter Test<br>**Formal Assessment,** pp. 78–85 |

TEACHER-TESTED ACTIVITY **Leslie Schubert, Parkland School, McHenry, Illinois**

## ILLUSTRATED TIME LINE

**Class Time** Two class periods for preparation and one for presentation

**Task** Creating an illustrated time line of events that occurred during the French and Indian War

**Purpose** To identify and understand significant events of the French and Indian War

**Supplies Needed**
- Reference materials and Internet sources on the French and Indian War
- Markers, colored pencils
- A roll of heavy white paper

**Activity** Working in small groups, students can create time lines of eight to ten events that occurred during or as a result of the French and Indian War. The time lines should include one paragraph for each event explaining its importance to the outcome of the war. The group as a whole can decide which events to include on the time line, how each should be illustrated, and why each was significant. Then some students can be illustrators and others writers. During their class presentations, groups should identify the event they felt was most important to the future of the European settlers in North America and why.

## BLOCK SCHEDULING — LESSON PLAN OPTIONS (90-MINUTE PERIOD)

### DAY 1

**Interact with History,** p. 133
**Class Time** 20 minutes

Options for pacing and variety:
- **Role-Playing** Have each student pick a colony and answer the "What Do You Think?" questions from the perspective of a person living in that colony. **Class Time** 15 minutes

**Setting the Stage,** p. 134
**Class Time** 20 minutes

Options for pacing and variety:
- **Time Saver** Ask students to come to class with a list of beliefs they consider to be "American." **Class Time** 10 minutes

**Section 1,** pp. 135–140
**Class Time** 50 minutes

Options for pacing and variety:
- **Peer Competition** Ask each student to make up one true and one false statement about the colonial economy, colonial education, and publishing and religion. Put the statements on the board and have students take turns identifying the true statements. **Class Time** 30 minutes

### DAY 2

**Section 2,** pp. 141–145
**Class Time** 45 minutes

Options for pacing and variety:
- **History on Film** Extend students' knowledge of the Magna Carta with two 16-minute films—*Rise of the English Monarchy* and *Revolt of the Nobles and the Signing of the Charter.* Encyclopaedia Britannica. **Class Time** 35 minutes
- **Time Saver** Use the chart on page 144 to describe the key features of colonial government to students. **Class Time** 10 minutes

**Section 3,** pp. 146–151
**Class Time:** 45 minutes

Options for pacing and variety:
- **Internet** Extend students' background knowledge of the French and Indian War by learning about the battle that took place at Louisbourg at www.mcdougallittell.com **Class Time** 20 minutes

**Chapter 5 Assessment,** pp. 152–153
**Class Time** 40 minutes

Options for pacing and variety:
- **Peer Teaching** Working in six-member groups, students can answer the Critical Thinking questions by a round robin. Students should seat themselves in a circle. Give one person a legal-size notepad and have that person answer Question 1, then pass the paper to the next person, who adds his or her responses. When the notepad returns to the person who began it, the response is complete. Continue until all questions have been answered. **Class Time** 40 minutes

**CHAPTER 5 OBJECTIVE**
**The student will identify the political, social, and economic values shared by British colonists and learn how these values and historical events led to the growth of a representative government and a new "American" identity.**

# Beginnings of an American Identity 1689–1763

*Section 1* **Early American Culture**
*Section 2* **Roots of Representative Government**
*Section 3* **The French and Indian War**

## HISTORY FROM VISUALS

**Interpreting the Painting** Ask students to study the painting and caption. Have the students describe the expressions on the faces of the audience. Ask them what Patrick Henry might be saying. **Possible Responses** Some listeners are very intent, others look puzzled. Patrick Henry may be criticizing the king.

**Extension** Ask students to write a short story describing the scene portrayed in the painting.

Conflicts with the British government helped shape a separate identity for British colonists. Here, Patrick Henry argues against the king in 1763.

132

## CRITICAL THINKING ACTIVITY

**Analyzing Causes** What experiences might have made American colonists think they were different from the British in England? **Possible Responses** They had experiences with Native Americans, the frontier, a different style of economy, and different types of government.

**Class Time** 5 minutes

## RECOMMENDED RESOURCES

### BOOKS FOR THE TEACHER

Demos, John. ***The Unredeemed Captive: A Family Story from Early America.*** New York: Knopf, 1994. Highly readable story of the Williams family, captured during a raid on Deerfield, Massachusetts.

Knight, Sarah K. ***The Journal of Madam Knight.*** Washington: Scholarly Pr., 1991. The entire story of this amusing and difficult journey.

Lambert, Frank. ***Inventing the Great Awakening.*** Princeton: Princeton U. Press, 1999. A new look at historiography.

### SOFTWARE

***Landmark Documents in American History, 2.0.*** Facts on File, 1998. Award-winning resource including over 20,000 pages.

### VIDEO

***Benjamin Franklin: Citizen of the World.*** A&E Biography. Lively life of America's first Renaissance man—inventor, writer, diplomat.

### INTERNET

For more about the Fortress of Louisbourg, visit www.mcdougallittell.com

## Interact *with* History

Conflicts with Native Americans and French colonists also helped shape the identity of British colonists. In response to attacks on the Pennsylvania frontier, Benjamin Franklin published this cartoon in 1754 urging the colonies to unite for defense.

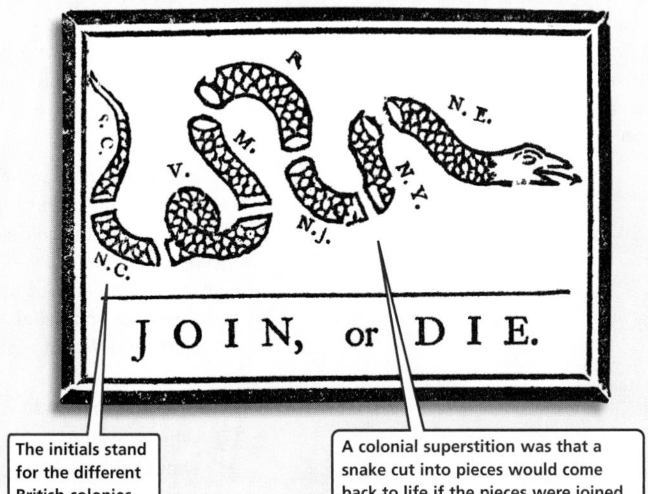


The initials stand for the different British colonies.

A colonial superstition was that a snake cut into pieces would come back to life if the pieces were joined.

**You have seen this cartoon in the *Pennsylvania Gazette*. You are outraged by the attacks on British traders and settlers. You wonder whether it is wise to join with other colonies, though. Will it mean that Virginians or New Englanders will be able to make laws for Pennsylvania?**

### What Do You Think?

- What are some good reasons to join with the other British colonies?
- How great are the differences between the British colonies?
- What separates British colonists from French colonists?

# *What do you have in common with other British colonists?*

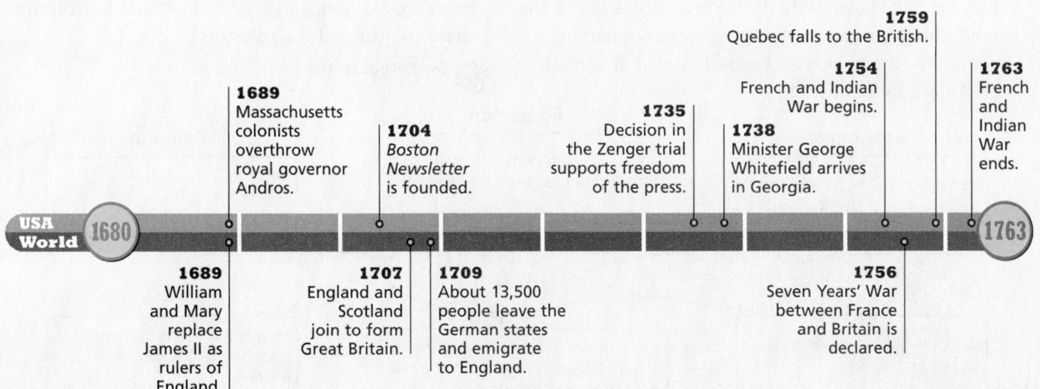

USA
World
1680
1763
1689 Massachusetts colonists overthrow royal governor Andros.
1704 Boston Newsletter is founded.
1735 Decision in the Zenger trial supports freedom of the press.
1738 Minister George Whitefield arrives in Georgia.
1754 French and Indian War begins.
1759 Quebec falls to the British.
1763 French and Indian War ends.
1689 William and Mary replace James II as rulers of England.
1707 England and Scotland join to form Great Britain.
1709 About 13,500 people leave the German states and emigrate to England.
1756 Seven Years' War between France and Britain is declared.

## Interact *with* History

### OBJECTIVES

- To identify political loyalties of the colonists
- To analyze how colonial leaders hoped to unify the colonists' loyalties

### What Do You Think?

1. Ask students to study Franklin's political cartoon. What did Franklin believe would be the result if the colonies refused to fight together?
2. Ask students whether they identify themselves as citizens of their colony, as citizens of England, or as Americans.
3. Why might French colonists' experiences be different from those of British colonists?

### *What do you have in common with other British colonists?*

Ask students to list as many connections as they can that were shared by all British colonists. **Possible Responses** English language and customs, British government, connections to family and friends, trade with Great Britain

### MAKING PERSONAL CONNECTIONS

Ask students to think about what things they have in common with students in other parts of the United States. Then ask how these experiences may be different from those of young people in other nations of the world.

### TIME LINE DISCUSSION

**Explain to students that the time line presents years during which a national spirit and demands for democratic government gathered force and power in the colonies. Point out that during the 1700s, the colonists began to think of themselves as American, not British.**

- Ask students which world events shown on the time line might affect the colonies. Ask for reasons for their choices. **Possible Responses** succession of William and Mary, because a change in British rulers could mean a change in British colonial policy; war between Britain and France, because both countries had colonies in the Americas
- Ask students which events on the USA time line might have helped build the feeling that American colonists were different from other British colonies.

**Possible Responses** 1689—overthrowing the royal governor; 1735—Zenger trial

## BEFORE YOU READ

### Previewing the Theme: Democratic Ideals

Ask students to name some of the rights to which they feel entitled because they are Americans. Ask if they have any particular rights as citizens of their state.

The British people enjoyed a 500-year heritage of slowly accumulated individual rights. Colonists expected to enjoy those rights equally with other Britons.

### What Do You Know?

Most eighth-grade students have a keen awareness of what they consider personal rights. As they volunteer answers, caution them to separate their personal desires from rights to which they are entitled by their democratic government.

 **In-Depth Resources: Unit 1**
- Tracing Themes: Democratic Ideals, p. 83

## READ AND TAKE NOTES

### Reading Strategy: Finding Main Ideas

Explain to students that finding main ideas means noting the most important points in a chapter. Remind them that each section has a Main Idea statement to help them find the bigger ideas. Suggest that students use the details they find in the chapter to reinforce main ideas. Using a web diagram will help them record important details as they read.

 **In-Depth Resources: Unit 1**
- Setting the Stage, p. 82

 **Critical Thinking Transparency CT13**
- Setting the Stage

# Chapter 5 SETTING THE STAGE

## BEFORE YOU READ

### Previewing the Theme

**Democratic Ideals** In the 1700s and even earlier, American colonists demanded protection of their "rights as Englishmen." Among these was the right to elect representatives to government. Chapter 5 explains how a heritage of English rights was one of many forces drawing the different British colonies together.

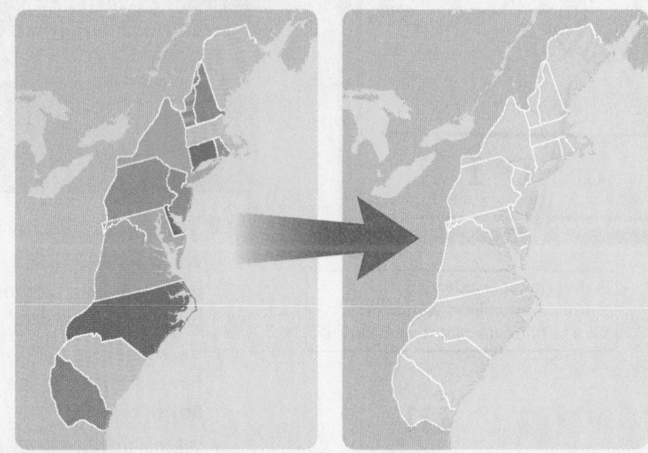

### What Do You Know?

What beliefs do you consider American? How do you think people in Britain's American colonies saw themselves?

**THINK ABOUT**
- your own beliefs as an American
- what you know about the regions where the colonies were established
- what you know about the backgrounds and beliefs of colonists in different regions

### What Do You Want to Know?

What questions do you have about colonial America in the early and middle 1700s? Write them down in your notebook before you read this chapter.

## READ AND TAKE NOTES

**Reading Strategy: Finding Main Ideas** To recognize a main idea, you must notice how smaller details are connected. In your notebook, copy a web like the one shown here. Write brief notes about the main things people in the British colonies had in common—the beliefs and experiences that formed an American identity.

- Read and remember the Main Idea at the beginning of each section.
- At the end of each group of paragraphs under a heading, ask yourself, "Have I learned about something that united the colonists?"

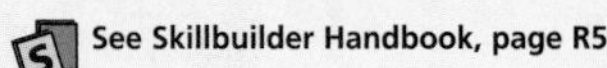
See Skillbuilder Handbook, page R5.

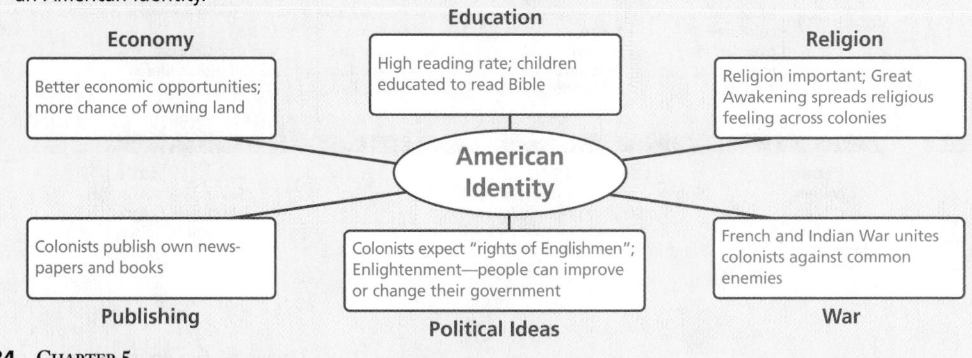




## TEACHING STRATEGY

### READING THE CHAPTER

This is a thematic chapter focusing on the basis for an American identity. For each section have students write summary sentences identifying distinctive American ideals, values, or behaviors. Encourage them to think about and discuss how these values have prevailed over the years.

### ALTERNATIVE ASSESSMENT

The Chapter Assessment describes three activities for alternative assessment on page 153. You may wish to have students work on these activities during the course of the chapter and then present them at the end.

# 1 Early American Culture

**TERMS & NAMES**
apprentice
Great Awakening
Jonathan Edwards
George Whitefield
Enlightenment
Benjamin Franklin
John Locke

**MAIN IDEA**

The British colonies were shaped by prosperity, literacy, and new movements in religion and thought.

**WHY IT MATTERS NOW**

These forces began to create an American identity that is still developing today.

### ONE AMERICAN'S STORY

**On October 2, 1704, Sarah Kemble Knight set out on horseback from her home in Boston. She was riding all the way to New Haven, Connecticut. Today the ride is two hours by car, but then it took five days.**

**In her journal, Madam Knight described her travel hardships and commented on people she met—country girls, tobacco-chewing farmers, and rude housewives.**

*A VOICE FROM THE PAST*

We hoped to reach the french town and Lodg there that night, but unhapily lost our way about four miles short. . . . A surly old shee Creature, not worthy the name of woman, . . . would hardly let us go into her Door, though the weather was so stormy none but shee would have turnd out a Dogg.

**Sarah Kemble Knight,** *The Journal of Madam Knight*

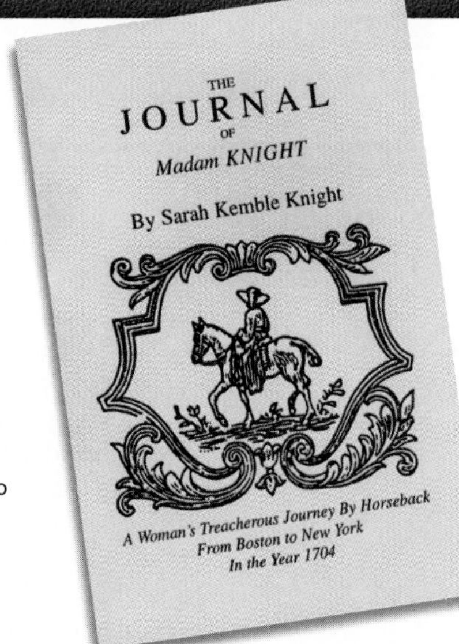

THE
JOURNAL
OF
Madam KNIGHT
By Sarah Kemble Knight
A Woman's Treacherous Journey By Horseback
From Boston to New York
In the Year 1704


This reprint of *The Journal of Madam Knight* is a 1920 edition.

**Her attitude toward people from other colonies was typical. In the early 1700s, people of the different British colonies did not think of themselves as living in one country. They were separated by distance and customs. In this section, you will learn what began to draw the colonies together.**

## 1 Land, Rights, and Wealth

At the time of Madam Knight's journey, the colonies were thriving. Cheap farmland and plentiful natural resources gave colonists a chance to prosper. They would have had less opportunity in Europe. In England, fewer than 5 percent of the people owned land. In fact, land rarely went up for sale. By contrast, in the colonies, land was plentiful—once Native American groups were forced to give up their claims. Colonists who owned land were free to use or sell whatever it produced.

Land ownership gave colonists political rights as well as prosperity. Generally, only white male landowners or property owners could vote. There were some exceptions. City dwellers could vote by paying a fee.





## SECTION OBJECTIVES

1. To analyze colonial values
2. To identify roles of colonial women and children
3. To evaluate the results of a high literacy rate in the colonies
4. To identify the effects of the Great Awakening and the Enlightenment

### CRITICAL THINKING

Finding Main Ideas, p. 136
Contrasting, pp. 137, 138, 140
Categorizing, p. 138
Recognizing Effects, p. 140

**Why It Matters Now**
- American Identity Today, pp. 9–10

## FOCUS & MOTIVATE

### 5-MINUTE WARM-UP

**Recognizing Effects** These questions focus on colonial culture.

1. Look at the chart on page 136. Which groups owned land?
2. What do you think the difference was between an indentured servant and an unskilled worker?

**Warm-Up Transparency WT5**

## INSTRUCT

### INSTRUCT: OBJECTIVE 1

**Land, Rights, and Wealth**
Key Questions
- What special rights did landowners enjoy?
- How did land ownership affect a colonist's place in society?

**In-Depth Resources: Unit 1**
- Guided Reading, p. 84
- Building Vocabulary, p. 87

**America's History Makers**
- Sarah Kemble Knight, pp. 21–22

**Reading Study Guide** (Spanish and English), pp. 45–46

## RECOMMENDED RESOURCES

**In-Depth Resources: Unit 1**
- Guided Reading, p. 84
- Building Vocabulary, p. 87
- Skillbuilder Practice, p. 88
- Primary Source: An Indentured Servant's Plea, p. 91
- Reteaching Activity, p. 96

**Reading Study Guide** (Spanish and English), pp. 45–46

**Economics in History**
- Growth of Colonial Economies, p. 5

**America's History Makers**
- Benjamin Franklin, pp. 19–20
- Sarah Kemble Knight, pp. 21–22

**Why It Matters Now**
- American Identity Today, pp. 9–10

**Formal Assessment**
- Section Quiz, p. 75

**Alternative Assessment**
- Rubrics, 4.9
- Rubrics, 1.3

**Access for Students Acquiring English/ESL**
- Guided Reading, p. 29
- Skillbuilder Practice, p. 32

Technology Resources

**Humanities Transparency HT9**
- *Benjamin Franklin* by Robert Feke

**Electronic Teacher Tools with Test Maker**

**ClassZone**
www.mcdougallittell.com

## HISTORY FROM VISUALS

**Interpreting the Chart** Remind students that owning land was very important in colonial society. Ask them what other kinds of property or occupation entitled a man to rank in the middle and upper classes. Also have them note which groups made up the lowest rank of the middle class. **Answers** merchants, officials in church and government, tradespeople, renters, and unskilled workers

**Extension** Ask students to write a story about an indentured servant who moves upward in social status, becoming a small farmer, a merchant, or a wealthy landowner. Tell students to describe what helped their character rise in society.

## INSTRUCT: OBJECTIVE 

**Women and the Economy/ Young People at Work**

Key Questions
- What work did colonial women and young people do?
- What rights were denied women?

 **Economics in History**
- Growth of Colonial Economies, p. 5

## MORE ABOUT . . .

**Women's Work**

Studies of colonial life have shown that in early colonial days, wives and husbands worked together to plant and harvest crops and to tend the animals. During these times, women had great authority and power within their families. As life in the colonies became more settled, women became more confined to their traditional roles and lost some of the power they had once held.

**Colonial Social Ranks**

| |
|---|
| **HIGH** |
| • large landowners |
| • church officials |
| • government officials |
| • wealthy merchants |
| **UPPER MIDDLE** |
| • small farmers |
| • tradespeople |
| **LOWER MIDDLE** |
| • renters |
| • unskilled workers |
| **LOW** |
| • indentured servants |
| • slaves |

Land ownership also helped determine colonists' social position. Unlike England, America had no class of nobles whose titles passed from parent to child. But people were still divided into high, middle, and low ranks, as they were in England. Large landholders were high in rank. Small farmers who owned their land were in the middle rank. Most colonists fit this category. People who did not own land, such as servants, slaves, or hired workers, were low in rank. Colonial women held the same rank as their husbands or fathers.

*Reading* **History**
**A. Finding Main Ideas** What did colonists gain by owning land?
A. Answer Prosperity, political rights, and a higher social position.

Colonists showed respect to their "betters" by curtsying or tipping a hat, for example. Seats in church were assigned by rank, with wealthy families in the front pews and poor people in the back. Despite such divisions, the wealthy were expected to aid the poor.

## 2 Women and the Economy

Although women were not landholders, their work was essential to the colonial economy. As you learned in Chapter 4, enslaved African women helped raise cash crops such as tobacco and indigo. Most white women were farm wives who performed tasks and made products their families needed. They cooked, churned butter, made soap and candles, spun fibers, wove cloth, sewed and knitted clothes, and did many other chores. They usually tended a garden and looked after farm animals. At harvest time, they often worked in the fields alongside men and older children.

Because cash was scarce, farm wives bartered, or traded, with their neighbors for goods and services. For example, a woman who nursed a sick neighbor or helped deliver a baby might be paid in sugar or cloth.

Women in towns and cities usually did the same types of housework that rural women did. In addition, some urban women ran inns or other businesses. Madam Knight, whose journey was described in One American's Story on page 135, sold writing paper, taught handwriting, and rented rooms to guests. A few women, usually the wives or widows of tradesmen, practiced trades themselves.

*Reading* **History**
**B. Finding Main Ideas** In what ways was women's work essential to the economy?
B. Answer Women did tasks and made products necessary for their families and neighbors. They also ran some businesses.

Although women contributed to the colonial economy, they did not have many rights. Women could not vote. In most churches, they could not preach or hold office. (Quakers meetings were an exception.) A married woman could not own property without her husband's permission. By law, even the money a woman earned belonged to her husband.

## Young People at Work

Children's work also supported the colonial economy. Families were large. New England families, for example, had an average of six to eight children. More children meant more workers. Children as young as three or four were expected to be useful. They might help look after farm animals, gather berries, and watch younger children.



## ACTIVITY OPTIONS

### SKILLBUILDER MINI-LESSON: FINDING MAIN IDEAS

BLOCK SCHEDULING

**Explaining the Skill** The main idea of a paragraph or section is the most important point of the writer. Finding the main idea helps the student understand the focus of a paragraph or section. The heading of every section in the textbook tells the topic of that section; the main ideas about the topic are presented in the paragraphs that follow the heads.

**Applying the Skill** Ask the students to find the heading "Women and the Economy." Tell students to read the section or ask for volunteers to read it aloud.

1. Ask students to summarize the section in their own words. Then ask them to identify the sentence that contains the main idea. *(the first sentence of the section)*
2. Direct students to the next section, "Young People at Work." Challenge them to find the sentence that states the main idea. *(the first sentence of the section)*

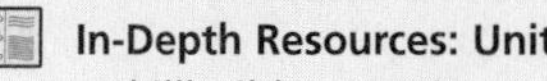

**In-Depth Resources: Unit 1**
- Skillbuilder Practice, p. 88

Around age six, boys were "breeched." This meant that they no longer wore the skirts or smocks of all young children but were given a pair of pants. They then began to help their fathers at work. Sons of farmers worked all day clearing land and learning to farm. Sons of craftsmen tended their fathers' shops and learned their fathers' trades.

Around age 11, many boys left their fathers to become apprentices. An **apprentice** learned a trade from an experienced craftsman. The apprentice received food, clothing, lodging, and a general education, as well as training in the specific craft or business. He worked for free, usually for four to seven years, until his contract was fulfilled. Then he could work for wages or start his own business.

Girls rarely were apprenticed. They learned sewing and other household skills from their mothers. In New England, girls of 13 or 14 often were sent away to other households to learn specialized skills such as weaving or cheese making. Orphaned girls and boys worked as servants for families who housed and fed them until adulthood.

*Reading* **History**

**C. Contrasting** How did the training of boys and girls differ?

**C. Answer** Boys learned from their fathers or were apprenticed to craftsmen. Girls learned from their mothers or neighbors.

## 3 Colonial Schooling

If land, wealth, and hard work were valued across the colonies, so was education. Most children were taught to read so that they could understand the Bible. Only children from wealthy families went beyond reading to learn writing and arithmetic. These children learned either from private tutors or in private schools. Poorer children sometimes learned to read from their mothers.

**HISTORY *through* ART**

This drawing shows the inside of an 18th-century one-room schoolhouse.

**What does the picture suggest to you about colonial schooling?**

**MORE ABOUT . . .**

**Apprentices**

If orphan children had no relatives or neighbors willing to take them in, they were "bound out" as apprentices. In Pennsylvania and in the Southern Colonies, these orphan apprentices were treated in the same manner as indentured servants.

***HISTORY through ART***

**Interpreting the Drawing** Tell the students the schoolroom scene pictured here was not a common one in all colonies. Although most colonists had a great respect for education, and many were eager to establish and support free grammar schools, they often did not have resources of time and money.

**Possible Response: It suggests that schoolrooms were crowded but orderly and that children of different ages learned together.**

**INSTRUCT: OBJECTIVE 3**

**Colonial Schooling/Newspapers and Books**

Key Questions

- Why were most colonial children taught to read?
- What were some common colonial attitudes about the importance of education?
- What types of books did colonists read?

**ACTIVITY OPTIONS**

**MULTIPLE LEARNING STYLES: KINESTHETIC**

**BLOCK SCHEDULING**

**ROLE PLAY**

**Class Time** 30 minutes

**Task** Dramatizing differences between colonial and contemporary youth

**Purpose** To describe the daily lives of colonial children

**Supplies Needed**
- Textbook pages 136–137
- Props or costumes (optional)

**Activity** Divide the class into groups of six. In each group, designate three students as colonial young people and three students as contemporary young people. Have each group present a conversation between colonials and contemporaries. Students can discuss differences in clothing, pastimes, manners, chores, or a typical day in their lives. Students should be able to support their conversations as colonial youngsters with evidence from the painting on page 137 or from the text.

## daily*life*

**The School of Manners**

During the 17th century, nearly all the textbooks used in the colonies were imported from England. The earliest "textbooks" printed in the colonies appeared in the late 1600s and were actually reprints of English books. Well into the 1700s, books remained scarce in the colonies, and costly.

## MORE ABOUT . . .

**Newspapers and Books**

In 1671, royal appointee Governor William Berkeley of Virginia proudly told the king: ". . . there are no free schools nor printing and I hope we shall not have these . . . for learning has brought disobedience, and heresy, and sects into the world, and printing has divulged them, and libels against the best government. God keep us from both!"

Governor Berkeley's hope was not realized: By the mid-1700s, most colonies had established weekly newspapers. And, just as Berkeley had feared, the political discussions in the newspapers were highly influential in breaking down relations with the Crown—and preparing the colonists for revolution.

### daily *life*

**THE SCHOOL OF MANNERS**

Colonial children learned proper behavior from *The School of Manners,* a book published in 1701. Here are examples of rules and an illustration from the book.

"Spit not in the Room, but in a corner, and rub it out with thy Foot, or rather go out and do it abroad."

"If thou meetest the scholars of any other School jeer not nor affront them, but show them love and respect and quietly let them pass along."

Or they attended "dame schools," where women taught the alphabet and used the Bible to teach reading. Most children finished their formal education at age seven.

Children's textbooks emphasized religion. The widely used *New England Primer* paired the letter *A* with the verse "In *Adam's* fall / We Sinned all." Beside the letter *B* was a picture of the Bible. The primer contained the Lord's Prayer and *The Shorter Catechism,* more than 100 questions and answers about religion.

Colonial America had a high literacy rate, as measured by the number of people who could sign their names. In New England, 85 percent of white men were literate, compared with 60 percent of men in England. In the Middle Colonies, 65 percent of white men were literate, and in the South, about 50 percent were. In each region of the colonies, roughly half as many white women as men were literate. Most colonists thought schooling was more important for males. Educated African Americans were rare. If they were enslaved, teaching them to read was illegal. If they were free, they were often kept out of schools.

*Reading*History

**D. Contrasting** How was colonial education different from education today?

**D. Answer** Education today lasts longer, covers more subjects, is less religious, and is available to more people.

## Newspapers and Books

Colonial readers supported a publishing industry that also drew the colonies together. In the early 1700s, the colonies had only one local newspaper, the *Boston News-letter.* But over the next 70 years, almost 80 different newspapers appeared in America. Many were published for decades.

Most books in the colonies were imported from England, but colonists slowly began to publish their own books. Almanacs were very popular. A typical almanac included a calendar, weather predictions, star charts, farming advice, home remedies, recipes, jokes, and proverbs. In 1732, Benjamin Franklin began to publish *Poor Richard's Almanack.* It contained sayings that are still repeated today, such as "Haste makes waste."

Colonists also published poetry, regional histories, and autobiographies. Most personal stories told of struggles to maintain religious faith during hard times. A form of literature unique to the Americas was the captivity narrative. In it, a colonist captured by Native Americans described living among them.

*Reading*History

**E. Categorizing** What were some types of colonial literature?

**E. Answer** Newspapers, almanacs, poetry, histories, autobiographies, captivity narratives.

Mary Rowlandson's 1682 captivity narrative, *The Sovereignty and Goodness of God,* was one of the first colonial bestsellers. Native Americans attacked Rowlandson's Massachusetts village in 1676, during King Philip's War. They held her hostage for 11 weeks. During that time, she was a servant to a Narragansett chieftain, knitting stockings and making shirts for his family and others. "I told them it was Sabbath day," she recalled, "and desired them to let me rest, and told them I



## ACTIVITY OPTIONS

### INDIVIDUAL NEEDS: GIFTED AND TALENTED

**FRANKLIN'S PROVERBS**

**Class Time** 20 minutes

**Task** Writing explanations or contemporary versions of proverbs from *Poor Richard's Almanac*

**Purpose** To familiarize students with the literary form of the proverb and with Franklin's writings

**Supplies Needed**
- Copies of *Poor Richard's Almanac* or books of quotations including proverbs by Benjamin Franklin
- Paper

**Activity** Direct students to read some of Franklin's proverbs or read several aloud to the class. Tell students to choose one proverb and rewrite it in contemporary terms, or write a brief explanation of the proverb's meaning. Ask students to share their work. Some students may wish to make illustrated posters presenting their proverb for display.

Vocabulary
**ransom:** to pay for a captive's release

would do as much more tomorrow. To which they answered me, they would break my face." After townspeople raised money to ransom Rowlandson, she was released. Although she mourned a young daughter who had died in captivity, she praised God for returning her safely.

## 4 The Great Awakening

Mary Rowlandson's religious faith was central to her life. But in the early 1700s, many colonists feared they had lost the religious passion that had driven their ancestors to found the colonies. Religion seemed dry, dull, and distant, even to regular churchgoers.

In the 1730s and 1740s, a religious movement called the **Great Awakening** swept through the colonies. The traveling ministers of this movement preached that inner religious emotion was more important than outward religious behavior. Their sermons appealed to the heart and drew large crowds. **Jonathan Edwards,** one of the best-known preachers, terrified listeners with images of God's anger but promised they could be saved.

Background
Religious meetings with large, intensely emotional crowds remain part of American religious tradition.

*A VOICE FROM THE PAST*

And now you have an extraordinary opportunity, a day wherein Christ has thrown the door of mercy wide open, and stands in calling and crying with a loud voice to poor sinners. . . . How awful it is to be left behind at such a day!

**Jonathan Edwards,** "Sinners in the Hands of an Angry God"

The Great Awakening lasted for years and changed colonial culture. Congregations argued over religious practices and often split apart. People left their old churches and joined other Protestant groups such as Baptists. Some of these groups welcomed women, African Americans, and Native Americans. Overall, churches gained 20,000 to 50,000 new members. To train ministers, religious groups founded colleges such as Princeton and Brown.

The Great Awakening inspired colonists to help others. **George Whitefield** (HWIT•feeld) drew thousands of people with his sermons and raised funds to start a home for orphans. Other ministers taught religion and reading to Native Americans and African Americans. The Great

George Whitefield preaching to a crowd



## CHAPTER 5 • SECTION 1

**INSTRUCT: OBJECTIVE 4**

**The Great Awakening/The Enlightenment**

Key Questions

- What was the Great Awakening? How did it change colonial culture?
- How did the Enlightenment affect the colonies?
- In what ways were the Great Awakening and the Enlightenment similar? How were they different?

**MORE ABOUT . . .**

**The Great Awakening**

The preachers of the Great Awakening challenged the regular clerics of the colonies. While these clerics at first welcomed the visiting preachers, they soon found that the teachings of the traveling ministers contradicted their own. Many congregations split into two factions: "Old Lights," adherents of traditional religious teaching, and "New Lights," followers of evangelistic preachers such as George Whitefield. New Lights affected the colonial way of thinking, bringing greater tolerance for independent thinking. Far more than traditional clerics, New Lights were willing to challenge authority, including political and social authority.

**ACTIVITY OPTIONS**

**INTERDISCIPLINARY LINK: SCIENCE**

**BLOCK SCHEDULING**

**USING *THE OLD FARMER'S ALMANAC***

**Class Time** 15 minutes

**Task** Using *The Old Farmer's Almanac* as a reference source

**Purpose** To allow students to explore an almanac as a reference source

**Supplies Needed**

- Copies of *The Old Farmer's Almanac* or Internet access: see www.mcdougallittell.com

**Activity** Remind students that almanacs were among the first books published by the colonists. Point out that almanacs such as *The Old Farmer's Almanac* are still widely used today.

Encourage students to skim the almanac and locate information for the current year about such topics as the calendar, weather predictions, star charts, or farming advice. Ask students why this information would have been important to colonists. Ask students to identify other resources where colonists might have found this kind of information.

## AMERICA'S HISTORY MAKERS

**Benjamin Franklin**

Benjamin Franklin was a self-made, self-educated man who directed his life by using his intelligence, talents, and freedom. Franklin gained wealth and fame through his own hard work and moved upward in social class. He became the symbolic American for many Europeans of his time. He deliberately contributed to his own "frontier" image in Europe by often wearing a fur cap and always speaking in plain, direct language.

**Answer: by inventing useful products, founding institutions, and promoting independence**

 **America's History Makers**
- Benjamin Franklin, pp. 19–20

 **Humanities Transparency HT9**
- *Benjamin Franklin* by Robert Feke

## ASSESS & RETEACH

**Setting the Stage** Have students fill in the Economy, Publishing, Education, and Religion sections on the chapter graphic organizer.

 **Formal Assessment**
- Section Quiz, p. 75

 **Critical Thinking Transparency CT13**
- Setting the Stage

### RETEACHING ACTIVITY

Divide students into three teams. Assign each team one of the following viewpoints: that of a colonial woman, a colonial child, or a colonial minister. Have each team work together to write a description of colonial life based on the point of view assigned them. Allow time for groups to share and discuss descriptions.

 **In-Depth Resources: Unit 1**
- Reteaching Activity, p. 96

### AMERICA'S HISTORY MAKERS

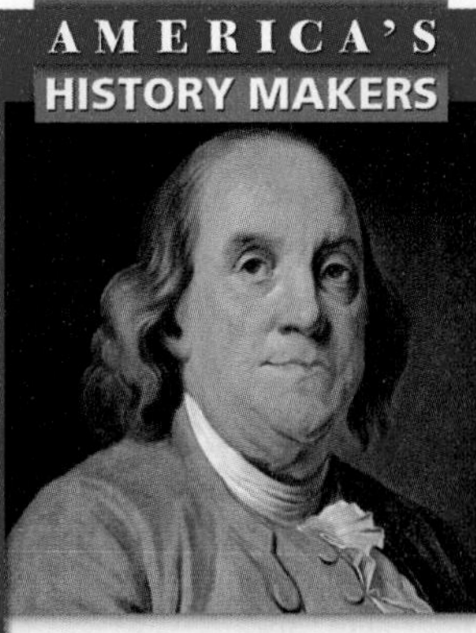

**BENJAMIN FRANKLIN**
**1706–1790**

As an Enlightenment thinker, Benjamin Franklin used reason to improve society. At 42, he retired from business to devote his life to science and public service. He proved that lightning was a form of electricity. Then he invented the lightning rod to protect buildings. The Franklin stove and bifocal eyeglasses were also his inventions. He organized a fire department, a lending library, and a society to discuss philosophy. Later he helped draft the Declaration of Independence.

**How did Franklin help improve colonial society?**

Awakening encouraged ideas of individual worth, equality, and the right to challenge authority. In this way, the movement helped prepare colonists to declare independence from England years later.

*Reading***History**

**F. Recognizing Effects** What were five effects of the Great Awakening?

**F. Answer** It encouraged religious debate, church membership, new colleges, charitable projects, and ideas of equality and independence.

## The Enlightenment

Unlike the Great Awakening, which stressed religious emotion, the **Enlightenment** emphasized reason and science as the paths to knowledge. **Benjamin Franklin** was a famous American Enlightenment figure. This intellectual movement appealed mostly to wealthy, educated men. But it, too, had far-reaching effects on the colonies.

The Enlightenment began in Europe, as scientists discovered natural laws governing the universe. Isaac Newton, for example, explained the law of gravity.

Other Enlightenment thinkers applied the idea of natural law to human societies. The English philosopher **John Locke** argued that people have natural rights. These are rights to life, liberty, and property. People create governments to protect their natural rights, he claimed. If a government fails in this duty, people have the right to change it. Locke challenged the belief that kings had a God-given right to rule.

Enlightenment ideas of natural rights and government by agreement influenced leaders across Europe and the colonies. As you will see in Section 2, colonists began to wonder whether the British government protected their rights and freedoms. Eventually, they would rebel and form a new government.

### Section 1 Assessment

**1. Terms & Names**

**Identify:**
- apprentice
- Great Awakening
- Jonathan Edwards
- George Whitefield
- Enlightenment
- Benjamin Franklin
- John Locke

**2. Taking Notes**

Describe the parts of colonial culture in a chart.

| Economy | |
|---|---|
| Education | |
| Publishing | |
| Religion | |

Why was each important in colonial culture?

**3. Main Ideas**

a. Why was land ownership so important to the colonists?

b. How did women and young people contribute to the colonial economy?

c. How did the Great Awakening affect the colonies?

**4. Critical Thinking**

**Contrasting** How were the Great Awakening and the Enlightenment different?

**THINK ABOUT**
- the ideas each movement promoted
- the people to whom each movement appealed

**ACTIVITY OPTIONS**

**LANGUAGE ARTS**
**ART**

Make up a **saying** that reflects some part of colonial culture, or draw an **illustration** of a saying from colonial times.

### Section 1 Assessment

**1. Terms & Names**

**apprentice,** p. 137
**Great Awakening,** p. 139
**Jonathan Edwards,** p. 139
**George Whitefield,** p. 139
**Enlightenment,** p. 140
**Benjamin Franklin,** p. 140
**John Locke,** p. 140

**2. Taking Notes**

Econ—small farming
Edu—emphasis on religion; many colonists semi-literate
Pub—80 different newspapers
Rel—Great Awakening

Each part helped to create a new American cultural identity for the colonists.

**3. Main Ideas**

**a.** It allowed them to gain wealth and political rights. **b.** Enslaved women raised cash crops; free women ran businesses; young people learned trades. **c.** It encouraged deep religious feelings and led congregations to debate, split apart, and gain new members.

**4. Critical Thinking**

The Great Awakening was a religious movement that appealed to emotion. The Enlightenment was an intellectual movement that emphasized reason and science.

**ACTIVITY OPTIONS**

 **Alternative Assessment**
- Rubrics for a saying, 4.9
- Rubrics for an illustration, 1.3

# 2 Roots of Representative Government

**TERMS & NAMES**
Magna Carta
Parliament
Edmund Andros
Glorious Revolution
English Bill of Rights
salutary neglect
John Peter Zenger

| MAIN IDEA | WHY IT MATTERS NOW |
| --- | --- |
| Colonists expected their government to preserve their basic rights as English subjects. | U.S. citizens expect these same rights, such as the right to a trial by jury. |

## ONE AMERICAN'S STORY

**On April 7, 1688, the famous Puritan minister Increase Mather set sail for England. He was to speak to King James II to get relief for the Massachusetts colony. The English government had canceled the charter of Massachusetts and sent a royal governor to rule.**

**The colonists thought that the governor trampled their rights as English subjects. Mather stayed in England for four years. During this time, he saw the king driven out and replaced by new rulers. In the end, he came home with a new charter that he hoped would satisfy the New England colonists.**

*A VOICE FROM THE PAST*

For all English liberties are restored to them: No Persons shall have a Penny of their Estates taken from them; nor any Laws imposed on them, without their own Consent by Representatives chosen by themselves.

**Increase Mather,** quoted in *The Last American Puritan*

This is a detail of *Increase Mather* by Jan van der Spriett.

**Mather called the new charter "a Magna Carta for New England." In this section, you will learn about the rights of English people set forth in the Magna Carta and later documents. These rights are the basis for the rights Americans enjoy today, such as the right not to be jailed without cause and the right to a jury trial.**

### 1 The Rights of Englishmen

English colonists expected certain rights that came from living under an English government. These "rights of Englishmen" had developed over centuries.

The first step toward guaranteeing these rights came in 1215. That year, a group of English noblemen forced King John to accept the **Magna Carta** (Great Charter). The king needed the nobles' money to finance a war. This document guaranteed important rights to noblemen and freemen—those not bound to a master. They could not have their property seized by the king or his officials. They could not be taxed, in most





## SECTION OBJECTIVES

1. To identify the rights that colonists expected as English subjects
2. To explain why colonies challenged the rule of Governor Edmund Andros
3. To evaluate how England's Glorious Revolution affected the colonies
4. To explain the importance of the Zenger trial verdict

**SKILLBUILDER**
Interpreting Charts, p. 144

**CRITICAL THINKING**
Comparing, p. 142
Making Inferences, p. 143
Recognizing Effects, p. 143
Drawing Conclusions, p. 145
Supporting Opinions, p. 145

## FOCUS & MOTIVATE

### 5-MINUTE WARM-UP

**Analyzing Causes** These questions focus on the colonial expectation of representative government.

1. Read the quotation on page 141. Which liberties does Mather say are restored to the colonists?
2. What phrase implies that eligible colonists have the right to vote?

 **Warm-Up Transparency WT5**

## INSTRUCT

**INSTRUCT: OBJECTIVE** 

**The Rights of Englishmen/ Parliament and Colonial Government**
Key Questions
- What rights does the Magna Carta guarantee?
- What was the purpose of the colonial assemblies?
- How could the king limit the power of the colonial assemblies?

**In-Depth Resources: Unit 1**
- Guided Reading, p. 85

## RECOMMENDED RESOURCES

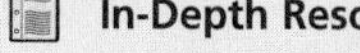

**In-Depth Resources: Unit 1**
- Guided Reading, p. 85
- Building Vocabulary, p. 87
- Reteaching Activity, p. 97
- Enrichment Activity, p. 99

**Reading Study Guide** (Spanish and English), pp. 47–48

**Citizenship Today,** pp. 1–2

**American History Plays**
- *The Trial of Peter Zenger* by Paul T. Nolan

**Formal Assessment**
- Section Quiz, p. 76

**Alternative Assessment**
- Rubrics, 3.6
- Rubrics, 1.13

**Access for Students Acquiring English/ESL**
- Guided Reading, p. 30

**Technology Resources**

 **Electronic Teacher Tools with Test Maker**

 **ClassZone**
www.mcdougallittell.com

### CRITICAL THINKING ACTIVITY

**Contrasting** Copy the following graphic onto the chalkboard. Ask students to read the paragraphs under the heading "Parliament and Colonial Government." Then have the students compare the colonists' expectation of representative government to the reality of government by the British.

| Right to Representative Government | |
|---|---|
| **Colonists' Expectations** | **British Authority** |
| To elect representatives to government | Colonists did not send representatives to Parliament, but Parliament made laws that affected the colonies. |

**Class Time** 10 minutes

cases, unless a council of prominent men agreed. They could not be put to trial based only on an official's word, without witnesses. They could be punished only by a jury of their peers, people of the same social rank.

> *A VOICE FROM THE PAST*
>
> No freeman shall be seized, imprisoned, dispossessed, outlawed, or exiled, . . . nor will we proceed against or prosecute him except by the lawful judgment of his peers, or by the law of the land.
>
> **Magna Carta,** translated in *A Documentary History of England*

*Reading* **History**

**A. Comparing** What rights from the Magna Carta remain rights in America today?

**A. Answer** Trial by jury, protection from arbitrary taxation and seizure of property

The Magna Carta limited the powers of the king. Over time, the rights it listed were granted to all English people, not just noblemen and freemen.

## Parliament and Colonial Government

One of the most important English rights was the right to elect representatives to government. **Parliament,** England's chief lawmaking body, was the colonists' model for representative government. Parliament was made up of two houses. Members of the House of Commons were elected by the people. Members of the House of Lords were nonelected nobles, judges, and church officials.

The king and Parliament were too far away to manage every detail of the colonies. Also, like the citizens of England, English colonists in America wanted to have a say in the laws governing them. So they formed

### CITIZENSHIP TODAY

### OBJECTIVE

Students will be able to explain the value of trial by jury and the importance of serving as a juror.

**Serving on Juries**

Jurors are selected from sources such as tax rolls, voting lists, and telephone directories. The Constitution states that jurors in a criminal trial (one that determines the guilt or innocence of a person accused of a crime) must be neutral regarding the case. In addition, a juror must be selected from the community where the crime is supposed to have happened. Every juror is questioned by both defense and prosecuting lawyers, and either lawyer may reject a juror if he/she feels the juror would not serve fairly.

 **Citizenship Today,** pp. 1–2

### CITIZENSHIP TODAY

## The Importance of Juries

The right to a trial by jury, established in the Magna Carta, is an important legal right. When you become an adult, you will likely be asked to serve on a jury.

Many young people in Knox County, Illinois, have already served as jurors on a teen court (shown below, with an advisor). They decide the best punishment for other teenagers who have admitted breaking a law. For example, shoplifters might be sentenced to write an apology to the store. Knox County is one of more than 500 U.S. communities that have teen courts.

Knox County Teen Court volunteers

142

### How Can You Serve on a Teen Court?

1. Search the library or Internet to learn more about teen courts.
2. Ask the police department whether your town has a teen court. If it does, volunteer.
3. If you want to start a teen court, seek advice from a community that has one.
4. Invite a lawyer to your class to talk about a juror's role.
5. Find a group to sponsor your court, and get support from youth officers and judges.

**See the Citizenship Handbook, page 280.**

**Visit www.mcdougallittell.com to learn more about courts and juries.**

### STANDARDS FOR EVALUATION

**Each student should**

- engage in productive research.

**Student groups should**

- contact the police department and communities that have teen courts.
- prepare an invitation to a lawyer that includes an explanation of the topic for discussion.
- explore community support for a teen court by contacting youth officers and judges.

their own elected assemblies, similar to the House of Commons. Virginia's House of Burgesses was the first of these. In Pennsylvania, William Penn allowed colonists to have their own General Assembly. These Virginia and Pennsylvania assemblies imposed taxes and managed the colonies.

Although the colonists governed themselves in some ways, England still had authority over them. The king appointed royal governors to rule some colonies on his behalf. Parliament had no representatives from the colonies. Even so, it passed laws that affected the colonies. The colonists disliked these laws, and they began to clash with royal governors over how much power England should have in America. These conflicts became more intense in the late 1600s.

*Reading* **History**
**B. Making Inferences** Why did the colonists dislike laws passed by Parliament?
B. Answer They had no say in making those laws.

## 2 A Royal Governor's Rule

*"You have no more privileges left you."*
a Boston court official

The reign of James II threatened the colonies' tradition of self-government. James became king in 1685. He wanted to rule England and its colonies with total authority. One of his first orders changed the way the Northern colonies were governed. These colonies, especially Massachusetts, had been smuggling goods and ignoring the Navigation Acts (see Chapter 4). When challenged, the people of Massachusetts had claimed that England had no right to make laws for them. The previous king, Charles II, had then canceled their charter.

King James combined Massachusetts and the other Northern colonies into one Dominion of New England, ruled by royal governor **Edmund Andros.** Andros angered the colonists by ending their representative assemblies and allowing town meetings to be held only once a year.

*Reading* **History**
**C. Recognizing Effects** How did James II weaken self-government in the colonies?
C. Answers He put the New England colonies under one royal governor, abolished their assemblies, and limited town meetings.

With their assemblies outlawed, some colonists refused to pay taxes. They said that being taxed without having a voice in government violated their rights. Andros jailed the loudest complainers. At their trial, they were told, "You have no more privileges left you than not to be Sould [sold] for Slaves."

The colonists hated Governor Andros.

The colonists sent Increase Mather to England to plead with King James (see One American's Story on page 141). However, a revolution in England swept King James and Governor Andros from power.

**Background**
England had become Protestant in the 16th century. Catholics were kept out of high office.

## 3 England's Glorious Revolution

The English Parliament had decided to overthrow King James for not respecting its rights. Events came to a head in 1688. King James, a Catholic, had been trying to pack his next Parliament with officials who would overturn anti-Catholic laws. He had dismissed the last Parliament in 1685. The Protestant leaders of Parliament were outraged. They offered



### INSTRUCT: OBJECTIVE 2

**A Royal Governor's Rule**
Key Questions
- Who was Edmund Andros?
- Why did he anger the residents of Massachusetts?
- What rights did Andros deny to the colonists?

### MORE ABOUT . . .

**Edmund Andros**
Andros arrived in New England with a troop of English soldiers and a naval frigate—a clear sign of his intentions for the colonies. Andros violated colonial rights in several ways. He placed the militia under his direct control. He dispensed with juries for those accused of breaking trade laws. He also decreed that juries could be appointed by sheriffs, who were themselves appointed by royal decree. Other unpopular actions by the royal governor included converting Boston's Old South Meeting House into an Anglican church.

### INSTRUCT: OBJECTIVE 3

**England's Glorious Revolution**
Key Questions
- What happened in England during the Glorious Revolution?
- What rights were guaranteed in the English Bill of Rights?
- How did colonists react to the Glorious Revolution and the new English Bill of Rights?

### ACTIVITY OPTIONS

**INTERDISCIPLINARY LINK: GOVERNMENT/CIVICS** — BLOCK SCHEDULING

**GOVERNOR ANDROS ON TRIAL**

**Class Time** 20 minutes

**Task** Holding a mock trial of Governor Andros

**Purpose** To understand colonial displeasure with Governor Andros and to engage in a trial-like simulation

**Supplies Needed**
- Textbook

**Activity** Form students into two groups: One group (royal supporters) will defend Edmund Andros and the other (colonists) will prosecute him. Alternating from group to group, have colonists present an accusation against Andros, then ask royal supporters to respond to the accusation. When students have exhausted their accusations, call time and ask students to write on a piece of paper whether they find Andros guilty of grossly violating colonists' rights or whether they find him innocent.

the throne to James's Protestant daughter, Mary, and her husband, William of Orange. William was the ruler of the Netherlands. Having little support from the people, James fled the country at the end of 1688. Parliament named William and Mary the new monarchs of England. This change in leadership was called England's **Glorious Revolution.**

After accepting the throne, William and Mary agreed to uphold the **English Bill of Rights.** This was an agreement to respect the rights of English citizens and of Parliament. Under it, the king or queen could not cancel laws or impose taxes unless Parliament agreed. Free elections and frequent meetings of Parliament must be held. Excessive fines and cruel punishments were forbidden. People had the right to complain to the king or queen in Parliament without being arrested.

**Background**
The English Bill of Rights was the model for the Bill of Rights in the U.S. Constitution.

The English Bill of Rights established an important principle: the government was to be based on laws made by Parliament, not on the desires of a ruler. The rights of English people were strengthened.

The American colonists were quick to claim these rights. When the people of Boston heard of King James's fall, they jailed Governor Andros and asked Parliament to restore their old government.

**Skillbuilder Answers**
1. Governor and council were appointed; assembly was elected.
2. Assembly made laws, but governor approved the laws.

## 4 Shared Power in the Colonies

After the Glorious Revolution, the Massachusetts colonists regained some self-government. They could again elect representatives to an assembly. However, they still had a governor appointed by the crown.

**Background**
Massachusetts colonists also gained more religious freedom. They no longer had to be church members to vote.

The diagram on this page shows how most colonial governments were organized by 1700. Note how the royal governor, his council, and the colonial assembly shared power. The governor could strike down laws passed by the assembly, but the assembly was responsible for the governor's salary. If he blocked the assembly, the assembly might refuse to pay him.

During the first half of the 1700s, England interfered very little in colonial affairs. This hands-off policy was called **salutary neglect.** Parliament passed many laws regulating trade, the use of money, and even apprenticeships in the colonies. But governors rarely enforced these laws. The colonists got used to acting on their own.

**Vocabulary**
salutary: healthful or beneficial

### Colonial Government

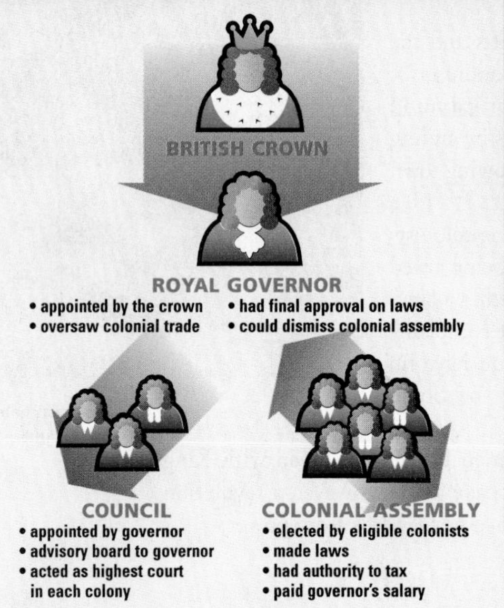

**SKILLBUILDER Interpreting Charts**
1. *Which officials were appointed, and which were elected?*
2. *How were lawmaking powers shared?*



**INSTRUCT: OBJECTIVE 4**

**Shared Power in the Colonies/ The Zenger Trial**

Key Questions
- How were most colonial governments organized after the Glorious Revolution?
- What was Parliament's policy toward the colonies after the Glorious Revolution?
- What right was at stake in the Zenger trial?

American History Plays
- *The Trial of Peter Zenger* by Paul T. Nolan

### HISTORY FROM VISUALS

**Reading the Chart** Have students study the directional arrows, noting that only one suggests interaction. Ask students which kind of official would be most responsive to the people: one appointed by the monarch or one elected by the people. **Possible Response** Students may note that an elected official is always aware of his or her standing with the voters.

**Extension** Ask students to identify which parts of colonial government made laws, enforced the laws, and administered justice through the courts.

### ACTIVITY OPTIONS
### INDIVIDUAL NEEDS

**STUDENTS ACQUIRING ENGLISH/ESL**

**Understanding Political Terms** Write the words *appointed* and *elected* on the board. Discuss the differences between being appointed to an office and being chosen by the voting process.

Refer students to the chart *Colonial Government* on this page. Point out the appointed and the elected officials. Explain that some government officials are appointed today while others are elected by citizens. Create a chart such as the one shown in which you list current appointed and elected officials.

| Appointed | Elected |
|---|---|
| Judges | President |
| Ambassadors | Governor |
| Members of Cabinet | Senator |
| Postmaster General | Member of Congress |
| | Mayor |

Government officials burn the *New-York Weekly Journal.*

## The Zenger Trial

Colonists moved toward gaining a new right, freedom of the press, in 1735. That year, **John Peter Zenger,** publisher of the *New-York Weekly Journal,* stood trial for printing criticism of New York's governor. The governor had removed a judge and tried to fix an election.

D. Answer The jury would not punish Zenger for criticizing the government.

*Reading* **History**
**D. Drawing Conclusions** Why was the Zenger trial a step toward freedom of the press?

*A VOICE FROM THE PAST*

A Governor turns rogue [criminal], does a thousand things for which a small rogue would have deserved a halter [hanging], and because it is difficult . . . to obtain relief against him, . . . it is prudent [wise] to . . . join in the roguery.

***New-York Weekly Journal,*** quoted in *Colonial America, 1607–1763*

At that time, it was illegal to criticize the government in print. Andrew Hamilton defended Zenger at his trial, claiming that people had the right to speak the truth. The jury agreed, and Zenger was released.

English rights were part of the heritage uniting people in the British colonies. In the next section, you will read about another unifying force—a war against the French and their Indian allies.

### Section 2 Assessment

**1. Terms & Names**

Identify:
- Magna Carta
- Parliament
- Edmund Andros
- Glorious Revolution
- English Bill of Rights
- salutary neglect
- John Peter Zenger

**2. Taking Notes**

In the boxes, show how the rights of English people developed in the three years mentioned.

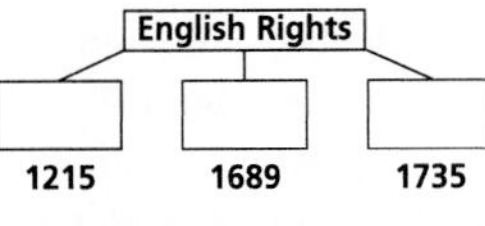


Which right is most important to you?

**3. Main Ideas**

a. What were three of the traditional rights expected by English colonists?

b. In what ways did the English government anger the colonists in the late 1600s?

c. How did England's policies toward the colonies change after the Glorious Revolution?

**4. Critical Thinking**

**Supporting Opinions** In your opinion, who had the most power—the royal governor, the council, or the assemblies? Defend your opinion.

THINK ABOUT
- their roles in making laws
- their roles in raising money
- who had final approval in matters

ACTIVITY OPTIONS

SPEECH / ART

Deliver **closing arguments** or create a **leaflet** defending John Peter Zenger and freedom of the press.





### MORE ABOUT . . .

**John Peter Zenger**

John Peter Zenger emigrated to New York in 1710 from Germany. A group of powerful men opposed to the actions of Governor William Cosby hired Zenger to print and publish articles critical of the governor, until Cosby had him arrested. Zenger was held in jail for ten months. Zenger expressed his view of freedom of the press in these words: "No nation ancient or modern ever lost the liberty of freely speaking, writing, or publishing their sentiments but forthwith lost their liberty in general and became slaves."

 **In-Depth Resources: Unit 1**
- Enrichment Activity, p. 99

## ASSESS & RETEACH

**Setting the Stage** Have students fill in the Political Ideas section on the chapter graphic organizer.

 **Formal Assessment**
- Section Quiz, p. 76

**RETEACHING ACTIVITY**

Copy the graphic onto the chalkboard. Ask students to fill it with the reasons the effects came about.

| Problems | Reasons | Effects |
|---|---|---|
| Colonists disliked laws passed by Parliament that affected them. | | Colonists began to clash with royal governors. |
| From about 1700 to 1750, the British government interfered very little in colonial affairs. | | The colonists became accustomed to acting on their own. |
| John Peter Zenger was placed on trial for his criticism of the governor of New York. | | The colonists moved toward freedom of the press. |

 **In-Depth Resources: Unit 1**
- Reteaching Activity, p. 97

### Section 2 Assessment

**1. Terms & Names**

**Magna Carta,** p. 141
**Parliament,** p. 142
**Edmund Andros,** p. 143
**Glorious Revolution,** p. 144
**English Bill of Rights,** p. 144
**salutary neglect,** p. 144
**John Peter Zenger,** p. 145

**2. Taking Notes**

1215—King John signed the Magna Carta.
1689—English Bill of Rights established Parliament's supremacy over the Crown in making laws.
1735—Zenger trial helped establish freedom of the press.

Responses will vary.

**3. Main Ideas**

**a.** property could not be seized without reason; taxes could not be levied without representation; trial by jury; the power to elect representatives **b.** placing royal governors in charge of the colonies and outlawing assemblies **c.** England instituted a policy of salutary neglect.

**4. Critical Thinking**

Student answers may vary. Be sure the defense of their choice is accurate.

**ACTIVITY OPTIONS**

 **Alternative Assessment**
- Rubrics for an argument, 3.6
- Rubrics for a leaflet, 1.13

## SECTION OBJECTIVES

1. To identify French colonial claims
2. To trace the French and Indian War
3. To explain how the British won the French and Indian War
4. To evaluate the results of the war

**SKILLBUILDER**

Interpreting Maps: Place, p. 148
Interpreting Maps: Region, p. 150

**CRITICAL THINKING**

Recognizing Effects, p. 147
Making Inferences, p. 147
Drawing Conclusions, p. 149
Finding Main Ideas, p. 150
Analyzing Points of View, p. 151

## FOCUS & MOTIVATE

### 5-MINUTE WARM-UP

**Reading a Map** These questions focus on the French and Indian War.

1. Look at the map on page 150. How many countries claimed North American territory before the French and Indian War? After?
2. Before the war, which country appears to be the biggest threat to British colonists? After?

 **Warm-Up Transparency WT5**

## INSTRUCT

**INSTRUCT: OBJECTIVE 1**

**France Claims Western Lands/ Native American Alliances**

Key Questions

- What parts of North America were claimed by France?
- Why did Native Americans form alliances with colonists?
- In what ways did France and England clash between 1689 and 1763?

 **In-Depth Resources: Unit 1**
- Guided Reading, p. 86

# 3 The French and Indian War

**MAIN IDEA**

Britain's victory in the French and Indian War forced France to give up its North American colonies.

**WHY IT MATTERS NOW**

British influence spread over North America, though French populations and place names still exist here.

**TERMS & NAMES**

French and Indian War
Albany Plan of Union
Battle of Quebec
Treaty of Paris
Pontiac's Rebellion
Proclamation of 1763

### ONE AMERICAN'S STORY

**Charles de Langlade, born in 1729, was the son of a French fur trader and his Ottawa wife. His family controlled the fur trade around what is now Green Bay, Wisconsin.**

**In 1752, Charles commanded 250 Ottawa and Chippewa warriors in an attack on the village of Pickawillany, in present-day Ohio. His reason: the Miami people who lived there had stopped trading with the French and were now trading with the British. Charles and his men destroyed the village's British trading post and killed the Miami chief. This attack helped lead to the French and Indian War.**

**This section describes the war, in which French forces fought British forces in North America. Each side had Native American allies. Charles de Langlade led several successful attacks against the British. But in the end, he saw the British drive French armies from the continent.**

This 1903 painting by Edward Deming shows Charles de Langlade attacking British forces in 1755.

## 1 France Claims Western Lands

As you learned in Chapters 2 and 4, the French were exploring the North American interior while English colonists were settling the eastern coast. By the late 1600s, French explorers had claimed the Ohio River valley, the Mississippi River valley, and the entire Great Lakes region. The French territory of Louisiana, claimed by the explorer La Salle in 1682, stretched from the Appalachian Mountains to the Rocky Mountains.

The French built their main settlements, Quebec and Montreal, along the St. Lawrence River in Canada. (See the map on page 148.) They also built forts along the Great Lakes and along rivers draining into the Mississippi. By 1760, the French colony, New France, had a European population of about 80,000. By contrast, the British colonies had more than a million settlers.

Some Europeans in New France were Jesuit priests. They wanted to convert Native Americans to Christianity. Other Europeans in New France worked as fur traders. Native Americans brought furs to French forts and

### RECOMMENDED RESOURCES

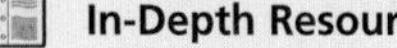

**In-Depth Resources: Unit 1**
- Guided Reading, p. 86
- Building Vocabulary, p. 87
- Geography Application, pp. 89–90
- Primary Source, p. 92
- Literature Selection, pp. 93–95
- Reteaching Activity, p. 98

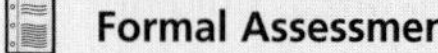

**Reading Study Guide** (Spanish and English), pp. 49–50

**Formal Assessment**
- Section Quiz, p. 77

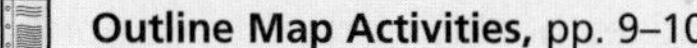

**Outline Map Activities**, pp. 9–10

**Alternative Assessment**
- Rubrics, 1.10
- Rubrics, 4.8

**Access for Students Acquiring English/ESL**
- Guided Reading, p. 31
- Geography Application, pp. 33–34

**Technology Resources**

**Humanities Transparency HT10**
- George Washington, 1755

**Critical Thinking Trans. CT14**
- Cause and Effect: The French and Indian War

**Geography Transparency GT5**
- Proclamation of 1763

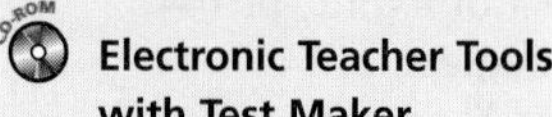

**Electronic Teacher Tools with Test Maker**

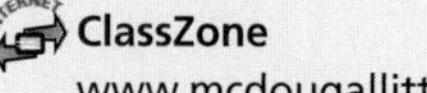

**ClassZone**
www.mcdougallittell.com

**Background** Often French traders lived among and married Native Americans.

exchanged them for goods such as iron pots and steel knives. Many French traders carried goods by canoe into remote parts of New France.

## Native American Alliances

**Background** The Iroquois were a union of six nations.

The English competed with the French for furs. Also, different Native American groups competed to supply furs to the Europeans. The fur trade created economic and military alliances between the Europeans and their Native American trading partners. The Huron and Algonquin peoples of the Great Lakes region were allied with the French. The Iroquois of upper New York often were allied with the Dutch and, later, the English.

Alliances between Europeans and Native Americans led to their involvement in each other's wars. For example, by the mid-1600s, the Iroquois had trapped all the beavers in their own lands. To get more furs, they made war on their Huron and Algonquin neighbors, driving them west. Eventually the Iroquois controlled an area ranging from Maine west to the Ohio Valley and north to Lake Michigan. Iroquois expansion threatened the French fur trade. In response, the French armed the Huron and Algonquin peoples to fight the Iroquois. The Iroquois were armed by the English.

***Reading* History**
**A. Recognizing Effects** How did the fur trade lead to wars?
**A. Answer** Native American groups competed for furs, and through their alliances with European trading partners, they obtained weapons and became involved in European conflicts.

When France and England declared war on each other in Europe in 1689, French and English colonists in America also began to fight. With their Native American allies, they attacked each other's settlements and forts. During the 1700s, two more wars between France and England fueled wars in their colonies. Neither side won a clear victory in these wars. A final war, the **French and Indian War** (1754–1763), decided which nation would control the northern and eastern parts of North America.

A French trader visits a Native American family.

### MORE ABOUT . . .

**Native American Alliances**

A majority of Native American groups allied with the French, although neither side totally trusted the other. All the non-Iroquois groups—Delaware, Shawnee, Abnaki, Ojibwa, Ottawa, Potawatomi—wanted protection, not only from the British, whom they viewed as arrogant and dishonest, but also from the Iroquois. The extremely powerful Iroquois Confederation hoped to dominate all other tribes, as well as play the French against English, to the destruction of both.

 **In-Depth Resources: Unit 1**
- Geography Application: Native American Confederacies, pp. 89–90

## 2 Conflict in the Ohio River Valley

**B. Answer** To the French, it linked Canada and Louisiana and was a source of furs. To the British, it was also a source of furs and a place for new settlement.

***Reading* History**
**B. Making Inferences** Why was the Ohio River Valley important to the French and British governments?

The seeds for the French and Indian War were planted when British fur traders began moving into the Ohio River valley in the 1750s. British land companies were also planning to settle colonists there. The French and their Native American allies became alarmed. To keep the British out of the valley, Charles de Langlade destroyed the village of Pickawillany and its British trading post (see One American's Story on page 146).

The British traders left, and the French built forts to protect the region linking their Canadian and Louisiana settlements. This upset the Virginia colony, which claimed title to the land. In 1753, the lieutenant governor of Virginia sent a small group of soldiers to tell the French to

### INSTRUCT: OBJECTIVE 2

**Conflict in the Ohio River Valley/ War Begins and Spreads**

Key Questions
- How did the French attempt to keep the English out of the Ohio Valley?
- Who are the sides in the French and Indian War?
- Why was the Albany Plan of Union significant?

 **Outline Map Activities**
- Mississippi Drainage Basin, pp. 9–10



**ACTIVITY OPTIONS**

**INDIVIDUAL NEEDS**

**LESS PROFICIENT READERS**

**Sequencing Events** To help students understand the events that led up to the French and Indian War and the results of the war, work with them to create a sequence chart of events as they read. Ask students to identify key dates and events and record them on the board.

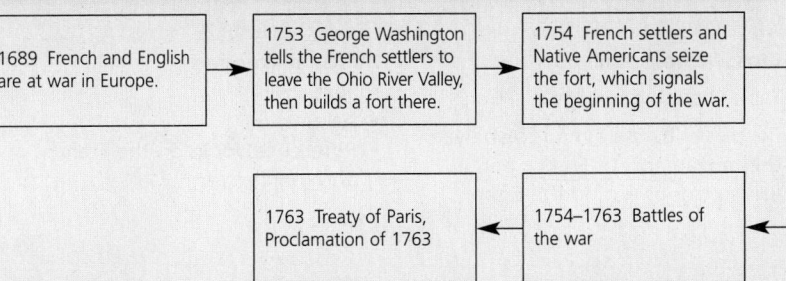

1689 French and English are at war in Europe. → 1753 George Washington tells the French settlers to leave the Ohio River Valley, then builds a fort there. → 1754 French settlers and Native Americans seize the fort, which signals the beginning of the war. → 1754–1763 Battles of the war → 1763 Treaty of Paris, Proclamation of 1763 leave. Their leader was a 21-year-old major named George Washington. Washington reported the French commander's reply.

*A VOICE FROM THE PAST*

He told me the Country belong'd to them, that no English Man had a right to trade upon them Waters; & that he had Orders to make every Person Prisoner that attempted it on the Ohio or the Waters of it.

**George Washington,** *"Journey to the French Commandant"*

Virginia's lieutenant governor sent about 40 men to build a fort at the head of the Ohio River, where Pittsburgh stands today. French and Native American troops seized the partially built fort in April 1754 and completed it themselves. The French named it Fort Duquesne (du•KAYN).

## War Begins and Spreads

George Washington was on his way to defend Fort Duquesne when he learned of its surrender. He and his men pushed on and built another small fort, Fort Necessity. Following Washington's surprise attack on a French force, the French and their allies attacked Fort Necessity on July 3, 1754. After Washington surrendered, the French let him march back to Virginia. The French and Indian War had begun. This war became part of the Seven Years' War (1756–1763), a worldwide struggle for empire between France and Great Britain.

**Background**
The Seven Years' War was fought not only in North America but also in the Caribbean, throughout Europe, and in India and Africa.

**Skillbuilder Answers**
1. France
2. Niagara, Frontenac, Ticonderoga, Quebec, Beauséjour, Louisbourg

**MORE ABOUT . . .**

**The French and Indian War**
The French and Indian War, at first a colonial conflict between France and Great Britain, became linked to a global war that began in 1756. This first true world war eventually involved all of Europe, India, and the Americas. France, Austria, Sweden, many small German states, and Spain were allied against Great Britain and Prussia. Europeans called it The Great War for the Empire, but the English called it the Seven Years' War. By the war's end, Great Britain was the dominant force both in Europe and in North America.

**Critical Thinking Transparency CT14**
- Cause and Effect: The French and Indian War

**HISTORY FROM VISUALS**

**Reading the Map** Point out that many of the war's battle sites were fought in hilly or rough terrain. Ask students to list some obstacles such terrain may have presented, as well as to suggest how the terrain might have prolonged the war. Also note that several battles were fought on the edge of the colonies. Ask students how those colonists living on the coast might have felt about this war. **Possible Responses** Students may note the difficulty of moving troops and supplies over rugged terrain. They may also note that colonists living in New York City or Boston would not have known about battles on the frontier until many days later.

**Extension** Have students create a time line for the places and dates shown on the map.

***French and Indian War,*** *1754–1763*

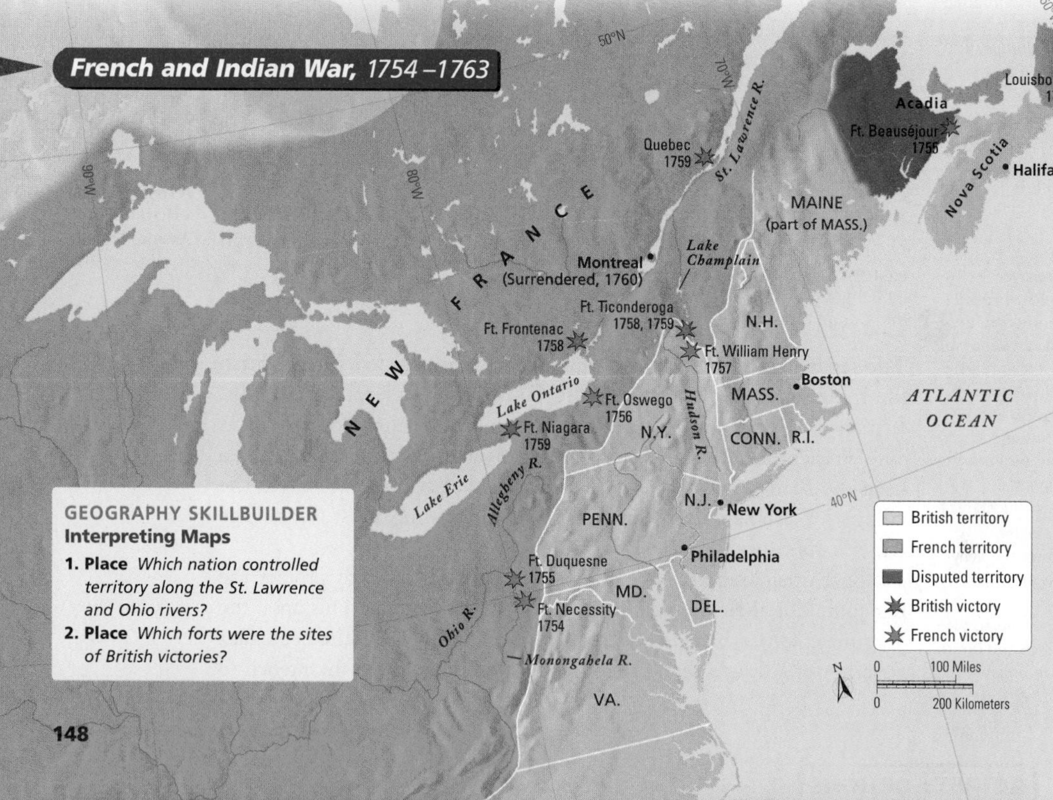


**GEOGRAPHY SKILLBUILDER**
**Interpreting Maps**
1. **Place** *Which nation controlled territory along the St. Lawrence and Ohio rivers?*
2. **Place** *Which forts were the sites of British victories?*

148

**ACTIVITY OPTIONS**

**INTERDISCIPLINARY LINK: GEOGRAPHY**

**BLOCK SCHEDULING**

**KEY BATTLE SITES OF THE FRENCH AND INDIAN WAR**

**Class Time** 15 minutes

**Task** Planning a route

**Purpose** To use a map to analyze the movements of French and British troops during the war

**Supplies Needed**
- Textbook
- Atlases
- Reference books on the French and Indian War

**Activity** Have students use the map on this page to plan two different tours of the battle sites of the French and Indian War. Students should plan one tour in chronological order: The first stop on the tour will be the site of the first battle, the second stop will be the site of the second battle, and so on. The second tour should be planned by geographical location, beginning with the southernmost battle site. After students have determined the stops on each tour, have them estimate which tour would take longer and why.

While Washington was surrendering Fort Necessity, representatives from the British colonies and the Iroquois nations were meeting at Albany, New York. The colonists wanted the Iroquois to fight with them against the French. The Iroquois would not commit to this alliance.

Benjamin Franklin, who admired the union of the six Iroquois nations, suggested that the colonies band together for defense. His **Albany Plan of Union** was the first formal proposal to unite the colonies. The plan called for each colony to send representatives to a Grand Council. This council would be able to collect taxes, raise armies, make treaties, and start new settlements. The leaders in Albany supported Franklin's plan, but the colonial legislatures later defeated it because they did not want to give up control of their own affairs.

## 3 Braddock's Defeat

Britain realized that to win the war, it could not rely solely on the colonists for funding or for troops. Therefore, the British sent General Edward Braddock and two regiments to Virginia. In 1755, Braddock marched toward the French at Fort Duquesne. George Washington was at his side. Their red-coated army of 2,100 moved slowly over the mountains, weighed down by a huge cannon.

On July 9, on a narrow trail eight miles from Fort Duquesne, fewer than 900 French and Indian troops surprised Braddock's forces. Washington suggested that his men break formation and fight from behind the trees, but Braddock would not listen. The general held his position and had four horses shot out from under him. Washington lost two horses. Four bullets went through Washington's coat, but, miraculously, none hit him. In the end, nearly 1,000 men were killed or wounded. General Braddock died from his wounds. American colonists were stunned by Braddock's defeat and by many other British losses over the next two years.

**Reading History**
**C. Drawing Conclusions** Why was Braddock defeated by a smaller enemy force?
C. Answer Braddock's force was unprotected and easy to see.

## The British Take Quebec

In 1757, Britain had a new secretary of state, William Pitt, who was determined to win the war in the colonies. He sent the nation's best generals to America and borrowed money to pay colonial troops for fighting. The British controlled six French forts by August 1759, including Fort Duquesne (rebuilt as Fort Pitt). In late summer, the British began to attack New France at its capital, Quebec.

**Background**
Because the British seemed likely to win the war, some Iroquois had joined them as allies.

**America's HERITAGE**

**ACADIANS TO CAJUNS**

Braddock's defeat and other early losses in the war increased British concern about the loyalty of the French people in Acadia (now Nova Scotia). The British had won Acadia from France in 1713.

In 1755, British officers forced out 6,000 Acadians who would not take a loyalty oath. The British burned Acadian villages and spread the people to various British colonies, as shown. Eventually, some Acadians made their way to the French territory of Louisiana. There they became known as Cajuns.

149



**INSTRUCT: OBJECTIVE 3**

**Braddock's Defeat/The British Take Quebec**

Key Questions
- Why did Britain send money and men to fight in the colonies?
- What course did the war take from Braddock's defeat in 1755 to 1757?
- How did the British take Quebec?

 **Humanities Transparency HT10**
- George Washington, 1755

**America's HERITAGE**

**Acadians to Cajuns**

The Acadians' journey to Louisiana was not easy. The English shipped some of the French Acadians to New England; others went to the West Indies. However, the Acadians found a welcome in Louisiana. They settled along the Mississippi River, Bayou Teche, Bayou Lafourche, and other streams in the southern part of the state. Many Cajuns settled in the swamplands where they became trappers and fishers. In 1971, the state of Louisiana officially recognized Acadiana: the 22-parish homeland of Cajun and Acadian culture. (Louisiana uses the French division of parish instead of county.) Tourism has become important in Acadiana. Visitors enjoy the distinctive Cajun dialect, cooking style, and music.

**ACTIVITY OPTIONS**

**INTERDISCIPLINARY LINK: MUSIC**

 **BLOCK SCHEDULING**

**CAJUN MUSIC AND ZYDECO**

**Class Time** 30 minutes

**Task** Exploring Cajun music and Zydeco, a related musical form

**Purpose** To introduce students to one aspect of a unique American culture

**Supplies Needed**
- CDs or tapes of Cajun and Zydeco music

**Activity** Play selected Cajun songs for the class. Ask students to identify the language of the songs and the instruments being played. Then play some Zydeco music for the class. Explain that Zydeco is accordion-based Creole music of people of color and shares some similarities with Cajun music. (Creoles are people descended from French and Spanish settlers.) Ask students to compare and contrast Cajun music and Zydeco.

## MORE ABOUT . . .

**James Wolfe**

Ambitious, brilliant, and dedicated to the art of war, Wolfe was just 31 years old at the Battle of Quebec. He wrote to Jeffrey Amherst, his commander in chief, that "An offensive, daring kind of war will awe the Indians and ruin the French. Block-houses and a trembling defense will encourage the meanest scoundrels to attack us."

Quebec sat on cliffs 300 feet above the St. Lawrence River. Cannon and thousands of soldiers guarded its thick walls. British general James Wolfe sailed around the fort for two months, unable to capture it. Then, in September, a scout found a steep, unguarded path up the cliffs to the plains just west of Quebec. At night, Wolfe and 4,000 of his men floated to the path and secretly climbed the cliffs.

When the French awoke, the British were lined up on the plains, ready to attack. In the short, fierce battle that followed, Wolfe was killed. The French commander, Montcalm, died of his wounds the next day. Quebec surrendered to the British. The **Battle of Quebec** was the turning point of the war. When Montreal fell the next year, all of Canada was in British hands.

D. Answer They surprised the French by climbing an unguarded path up to the city.

*Reading* **History**

**D. Finding Main Ideas** How were the British able to capture Quebec?

## INSTRUCT: OBJECTIVE 4

**The Treaty of Paris (1763)/ Pontiac's Rebellion**

Key Questions

- What were the results of the Treaty of Paris?
- Why did the British government issue the Proclamation of 1763? How did the colonists react?
- What brutal plan was used to squelch Native American uprisings?

**Geography Transparency GT5**
- Proclamation of 1763

**In-Depth Resources: Unit 1**
- Primary Source: from *Alexander Henry's Travels and Adventures*, p. 92
- Literature Selection: from *The Light in the Forest* by Conrad Richter, pp. 93–95

## 4 The Treaty of Paris

Britain and France battled in other parts of the world for almost three more years. Spain made a pact in 1761 to aid France, but its help came too late. When the Seven Years' War ended in 1763, Britain had won.

By the **Treaty of Paris,** Britain claimed all of North America east of the Mississippi River. To reward Spain for its help, France gave it New Orleans and Louisiana, the French territory west of the Mississippi. Britain, which had seized Cuba and the Philippines from Spain, gave them back in exchange for Florida. The treaty ended French power in North America.

**Background**
France kept only a few islands near Newfoundland and in the West Indies.

Skillbuilder Answers
1. France, Spain
2. Britain, Spain

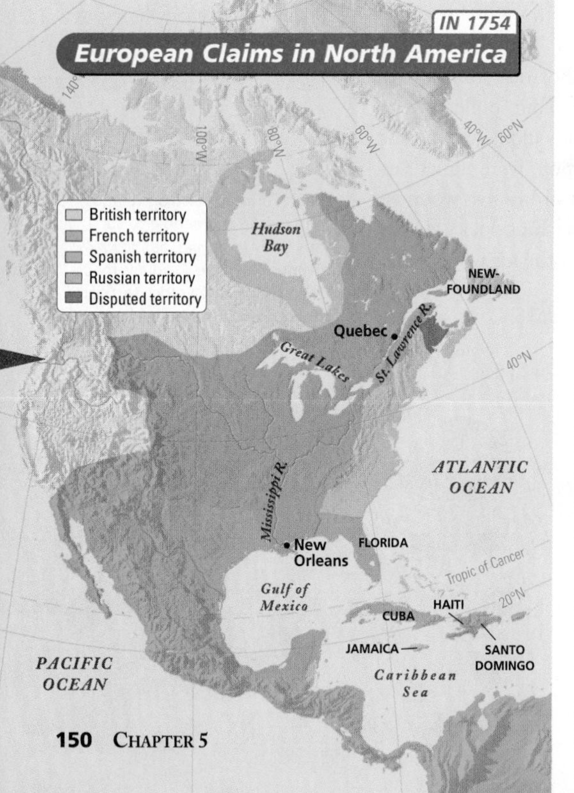


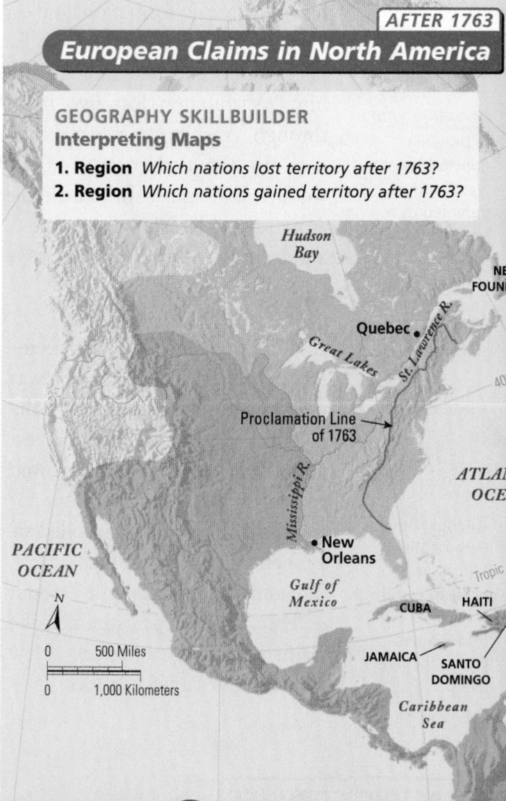




## HISTORY FROM VISUALS

**Reading the Map** Ask students to study the maps and answer the following questions. Which country acquired valuable fur-trapping land along the Great Lakes? Which country gained control of New Orleans? **Answers** Britain, Spain

**Extension** Ask students to use atlas maps of North America to find names of geographical features or cities and towns that show the influence of the nation that claimed that territory in 1754.

## ACTIVITY OPTIONS

**INTERDISCIPLINARY LINK: GEOGRAPHY/MATH** — BLOCK SCHEDULING

### FIGURING AREA

**Class Time** 15 minutes

**Task** Measuring distances/areas on a map

**Purpose** To compare approximate amounts of territory that changed hands after the French and Indian War

**Supplies Needed**
- Rulers

**Activity** Ask students to measure the scale on the map on page 150 (1/2 in. = 500 miles). Challenge them to use that measurement to determine the amounts of territory in North America that each country claimed before and after the French and Indian War. Remind students that area equals length multiplied by width (Area = length x width). Discuss various ways to make these measurements, such as picturing the territory to be measured as a rough geometric shape. Ask students to explain why their results can only be estimates, at best.

## Pontiac's Rebellion

After French forces withdrew, the British took over their forts. They refused to give supplies to the Native Americans, as the French had. British settlers also moved across the mountains onto Native American land. In the spring and summer of 1763, Native American groups responded by attacking settlers and destroying almost every British fort west of the Appalachians. They surrounded the three remaining forts. This revolt was called **Pontiac's Rebellion,** although the Ottawa war leader Pontiac was only one of many organizers.

*Reading* **History**
**E. Analyzing Points of View** Why did the Native Americans attack the British?
E. Answer Settlers claimed their land, and soldiers treated them harshly.

British settlers reacted with equal viciousness, killing even Indians who had not attacked them. British officers came up with a brutal plan to end the Delaware siege at Fort Pitt.

Pontiac

*A VOICE FROM THE PAST*

Could it not be contrived to send the Small Pox among those disaffected [angry] tribes of Indians? We must on this occasion use every stratagem in our power to reduce them.

**Major General Jeffrey Amherst,** quoted in *The Conspiracy of Pontiac*

The officers invited Delaware war leaders in to talk and then gave them smallpox-infected blankets as gifts. This started a deadly outbreak.

By the fall, the Native Americans had retreated. Even so, the uprising made the British government see that defending Western lands would be costly. Therefore, they issued the **Proclamation of 1763,** which forbade colonists to settle west of the Appalachians.

*Reading* **History**
**F. Reading a Map** Find the Proclamation Line of 1763 on the map on page 150.

The colonists were angry. They thought they had won the right to settle the Ohio River Valley. The British government was angry at the colonists, who did not want to pay for their own defense. This hostility helped cause the war for American independence, as you will read.

### MORE ABOUT . . .

**Pontiac**

Pontiac believed that the French would support an Indian revolt against the British and hoped to return the region to French control. When his attack on Fort Detroit failed, Pontiac moved with a small group of followers through Illinois country. In 1769, Pontiac was clubbed to death on the streets of the French village of Cahokia by a member of the Peoria tribe. The British commander of Fort De Chartres ordered that Pontiac's body should be buried in Cahokia. Stories persist that Pontiac was buried by the French in St. Louis. Another reputed burial site is in Oakland County, Michigan.

## Section 3 Assessment

**1. Terms & Names**

**Identify:**
- French and Indian War
- Albany Plan of Union
- Battle of Quebec
- Treaty of Paris
- Pontiac's Rebellion
- Proclamation of 1763

**2. Taking Notes**

Write the month and year each battle occurred. Classify each as a French or British victory.

| Date | Incident | Victor |
|---|---|---|
| | Seizure of Fort Duquesne | |
| | Surrender of Fort Necessity | |
| | Braddock's defeat | |
| | Battle of Quebec | |

Which was most important?

**3. Main Ideas**

a. How did the fur trade contribute to the French and Indian War?

b. Why did the British begin to win the war after 1758?

c. What were some causes and effects of Pontiac's Rebellion?

**4. Critical Thinking**

**Analyzing Points of View** Why did the French, British, and Native Americans fight over the Ohio River Valley?

THINK ABOUT
- how the British viewed the valley
- how the French viewed it
- how the Native Americans viewed it

**ACTIVITY OPTIONS**

**GEOGRAPHY**
**MUSIC**

Learn more about the Battle of Quebec and its setting. Make a three-dimensional **model** of the battle or write a **song** about it.



## ASSESS & RETEACH

**Setting the Stage** Have students fill in the War section on the chapter graphic organizer.

**Formal Assessment**
- Section Quiz, p. 77

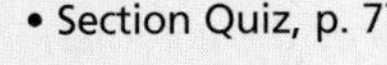

**Critical Thinking Transparency CT13**
- Setting the Stage

### RETEACHING ACTIVITY

Have students compose ten True-False statements that cover the most important points of the section. Separate them into groups of four to share their statements and discuss answers.

**In-Depth Resources: Unit 1**
- Reteaching Activity, p. 98

## Section 3 Assessment

**1. Terms & Names**

**French and Indian War,** p. 147
**Albany Plan of Union,** p. 149
**Battle of Quebec,** p. 150
**Treaty of Paris,** p. 150
**Pontiac's Rebellion,** p. 151
**Proclamation of 1763,** p. 151

**2. Taking Notes**

April 1754, French
July 1754, French
July 1755, French
September 1759, British

Student opinions may vary. Be sure they give reasons to support their opinions.

**3. Main Ideas**

**a.** British fur trade threatened French fur trade. **b.** because they sent their best generals to America and began to pay colonial troops for fighting **c.** causes—harsh treatment by British soldiers; land claims by British settlers; effects—attacks on Native Americans; the Proclamation of 1763

**4. Critical Thinking**

French: because it connected their settlements; British: wanted to trade and settle there; Native Americans: lived there

### ACTIVITY OPTIONS

**Alternative Assessment**
- Rubrics for a model, 1.10
- Rubrics for a song, 4.8

### TERMS & NAMES

1. **Great Awakening,** p. 139
2. **Enlightenment,** p. 140
3. **Magna Carta,** p. 141
4. **Parliament,** p. 142
5. **Edmund Andros,** p. 143
6. **Glorious Revolution,** p. 144
7. **John Peter Zenger,** p. 145
8. **French and Indian War,** p. 147
9. **Treaty of Paris,** p. 150
10. **Proclamation of 1763,** p. 151

### REVIEW QUESTIONS

**Possible Responses**

1. to gain wealth and political rights
2. to help raise cash crops; to provide needed products and services for their families; to run some businesses
3. debate and splits within congregations; founding of colleges to train ministers; spreading of Christianity to Native Americans and African Americans
4. The king and Parliament were too far away to manage every detail of the colonies, and they wanted a voice in the making of their laws.
5. the right to a jury trial; the right not to be taxed or have property seized arbitrarily
6. The trial upheld the notion that people have the right to speak the truth.
7. William and Mary, who took the English throne during the Glorious Revolution, agreed to uphold the English Bill of Rights.
8. He told the French to leave the Ohio Valley, his surrender of Fort Necessity was one of the first battles of the war, and he behaved heroically at Braddock's defeat.
9. the former French territories of Canada and Louisiana east of the Mississippi River; Florida from Spain
10. British soldiers treated Native Americans harshly; British settlers moved onto Native American land.

## VISUAL SUMMARY

## Beginnings of an American Identity

### Early American Culture

English colonists shared certain values, such as land ownership and hard work. The Great Awakening and the Enlightenment also drew colonists together.

### Roots of Representative Government

English colonists expected the right to elect representatives to government and other political rights that had developed in England over centuries.

### The French and Indian War

English colonists were also drawn together as they fought against common enemies—the French and their Native American allies.

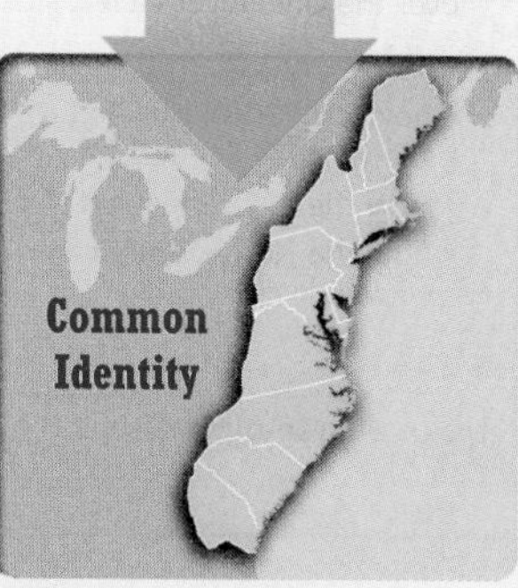




## Chapter 5 ASSESSMENT

### TERMS & NAMES

Briefly explain the importance of each of the following.

1. Great Awakening
2. Enlightenment
3. John Peter Zenger
4. Magna Carta
5. Parliament
6. Glorious Revolution
7. Edmund Andros
8. French and Indian War
9. Treaty of Paris
10. Proclamation of 1763

### REVIEW QUESTIONS

**Early American Culture (pages 135–140)**

1. Why did colonists want to own land?
2. What was women's role in the colonial economy?
3. What were three effects of the Great Awakening on colonial culture?

**Roots of Representative Government (pages 141–145)**

4. Why did colonies have representative assemblies?
5. What was one important right granted in the Magna Carta?
6. How did the Zenger trial help lead to freedom of the press?
7. How was the English Bill of Rights related to the Glorious Revolution?

**The French and Indian War (pages 146–151)**

8. What was George Washington's role in the French and Indian War?
9. What did England gain as a result of the French and Indian War?
10. What was one reason for Pontiac's Rebellion?

### CRITICAL THINKING

**1. USING YOUR NOTES**

Using your completed chart, answer the questions below.

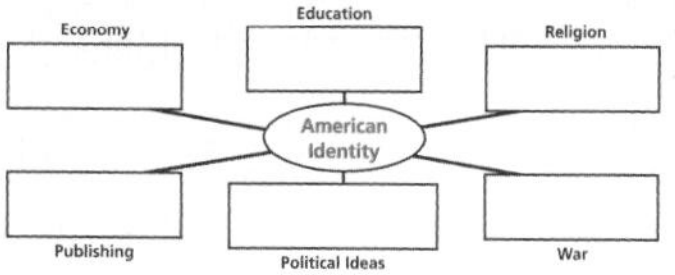


a. What were some political ideas shared by people in the American colonies?

b. How was religion important to American identity?

c. How did publishing help build an American identity?

**2. THEME: DEMOCRATIC IDEALS**

What democratic ideals did Americans inherit from England?

**3. APPLYING CITIZENSHIP SKILLS**

Why is jury duty an example of responsible citizenship?

**4. CONTRASTING**

How did colonial government differ from present-day government in the United States?

**5. ANALYZING CAUSES**

What do you think was the most important cause of the French and Indian War?

**6. ANALYZING LEADERSHIP**

Give an example of bad military or political leadership from the chapter. What mistake was made?

**Interact *with* History**

Now that you have read the chapter, what would you say British colonists in America had in common?

### CRITICAL THINKING

**Possible Responses**

1. USING YOUR NOTES **a.** the right to elect representatives; people could change their government **b.** The Great Awakening paved the way for independence from England. **c.** Colonists stopped relying on British publications and published their own.
2. THEME: DEMOCRATIC IDEALS representative government; trial by jury; limits on the power of government; respect for individual rights
3. APPLYING CITIZENSHIP SKILLS Jurors are responsible for the fate of an accused person.
4. CONTRASTING The colonies were part of the English government, which had no colonial representatives. States are part of the federal government and have representatives.
5. ANALYZING CAUSES English desire for more land; France and Britain's struggle for supremacy
6. ANALYZING LEADERSHIP General Braddock's refusal to take cover. He was stubborn and overconfident.

**Interact *with* History** language; government; customs; religion

## HISTORY SKILLS

**1. INTERPRETING MAPS: Movement**

Study the map. Answer the questions.

**French Explorers on the Mississippi**

L. Superior
St. Lawrence R.
Quebec
Montreal
L. Ontario
L. Huron
L. Michigan
Fox R.
Wisconsin R.
L. Erie
Ft. Detroit
Illinois R.
Mississippi R.
Ohio R.
APPALACHIAN MTS.
ATLANTIC OCEAN
Arkansas R.
New Orleans
Gulf of Mexico
90°W
80°W
70°W
40°N
30°N
N
0 300 Miles
0 600 Kilometers
Marquette and Joliet, 1673
La Salle 1679–1682
Present-day state boundary

**Basic Map Elements**

a. What do the colors indicate?

**Interpreting the Map**

b. Who traveled earlier?

c. Who reached the Gulf of Mexico?

d. Along whose route were Fort Detroit and New Orleans later founded?

**2. INTERPRETING PRIMARY SOURCES**

An unnamed Frenchman who knew Pontiac quotes a speech Pontiac gave to support an attack on British soldiers. Read the quote carefully. Answer the questions.

> When I go to see the English commander and say to him that some of our comrades are dead, instead of bewailing their death, as our French brothers do, he laughs at me and at you. If I ask anything for our sick, he refuses with the reply that he has no use for us. From all this you can well see that they are seeking our ruin. Therefore, my brothers, we must all swear their destruction and wait no longer.
>
> **Journal of Pontiac's Conspiracy,** 1763

a. Why does Pontiac want to attack the English?

b. What is Pontiac's attitude toward the French?

## ALTERNATIVE ASSESSMENT

**1. INTERDISCIPLINARY ACTIVITY: Language Arts**

**Making a Speech** Do research to learn more about freedom of the press. Then make a speech to convince people that it is important.

**2. COOPERATIVE LEARNING ACTIVITY**

**Holding a Diplomatic Council** Working in a small group, review the causes of the French and Indian War, and do further research. Then hold a diplomatic council to try to prevent the war. Role-play representatives from the following groups.

- officials of the English government
- officials of the French government
- English settlers
- French fur traders
- English-allied Iroquois
- French-allied Huron or Algonquin

**3. TECHNOLOGY ACTIVITY**

**Making a Class Presentation** Colonial American culture was not like modern American culture. Using the library or the Internet, find images, literature, and informative articles that tell you about daily life in the early and middle 1700s.

**Visit www.mcdougallittell.com to learn more about colonial America.**

Create a class presentation about colonial culture using the suggestions below.

- Stage a fashion show that illustrates what people of different ranks and ethnic backgrounds wore.
- Act out an interview with an interesting figure from the chapter, such as Madam Sarah Knight, Benjamin Franklin, or Pontiac.
- Illustrate sayings from *Poor Richard's Almanack.*
- Give an oral book report on a colonial captivity narrative. For example, find out what happened to Mary Rowlandson among the Narragansett.

**4. HISTORY PORTFOLIO**

**Option 1** Review your section and chapter assessment activities. Select one that you think is your best work. Then use comments made by your teacher or classmates to improve your work and add it to your portfolio.

**Option 2** Review the questions that you wrote for What Do You Want to Know? on page 134. Then write a short report in which you explain the answers to your questions. If any questions were not answered, do research to answer them. Add your answers to your portfolio.



## ALTERNATIVE ASSESSMENT

1. INTERDISCIPLINARY ACTIVITY: **Language Arts**

**A speech should**
- reflect the student's understanding of the principles of freedom of speech.
- have a clear introduction and conclusion.
- have adequate delivery and establish rapport with the audience.

2. COOPERATIVE LEARNING ACTIVITY

**A diplomatic council should**
- focus on resolving the problem.
- have students support their own positions with evidence or logic.
- have students appropriately respond to each other's statements.
- have students exhibit understanding of the role they are playing.

3. TECHNOLOGY ACTIVITY

**Class presentations should**
- clearly demonstrate an understanding of colonial culture.
- utilize several sources of information.
- have adequate delivery and establish rapport with the audience.
- show proficiency in the use of technology.

4. HISTORY PORTFOLIO

**Option 1 Revised section or chapter assessment activities should**
- address teacher and peer responses to the selected work.
- solve problems present in the first versions of the work.

**Option 2 Short reports should**
- answer questions about colonial America in the early 1700s.
- use evidence to develop and support ideas.
- cite sources of information.
- use standard grammar, spelling, sentence structure, and punctuation.

**Critical Thinking Transparency CT15**
- Visual Summary

**Formal Assessment**
- Chapter Test, Forms A and B, pp. 78–85

## HISTORY SKILLS

**Possible Responses**

1. INTERPRETING MAPS

**Basic Map Elements**

**a.** the voyages of LaSalle and Marquette and Joliet

**Interpreting the Map**

**b.** Marquette and Joliet

**c.** La Salle

**d.** La Salle's

2. INTERPRETING PRIMARARY SOURCES

**a.** because he believes the English are trying to ruin his people

**b.** He seems to like the French, calling them "brothers."

# UNIT 2

## Creating a New Nation

1763–1791



## BEFORE YOU READ

### Previewing Unit 2

Unit 2 traces the increasing dissatisfaction of American colonists with their position in Great Britain's empire. The fires of revolution grow from the first sparks struck by Patriots who challenge the rule of a Parliament and a monarch across the Atlantic Ocean. The 13 colonies unite to declare themselves independent and confirm their stand by defeating Britain on the battlefield in the American Revolution. After the war, the newly independent states create a new republican government for themselves, first under the Articles of Confederation and then under the United States Constitution.

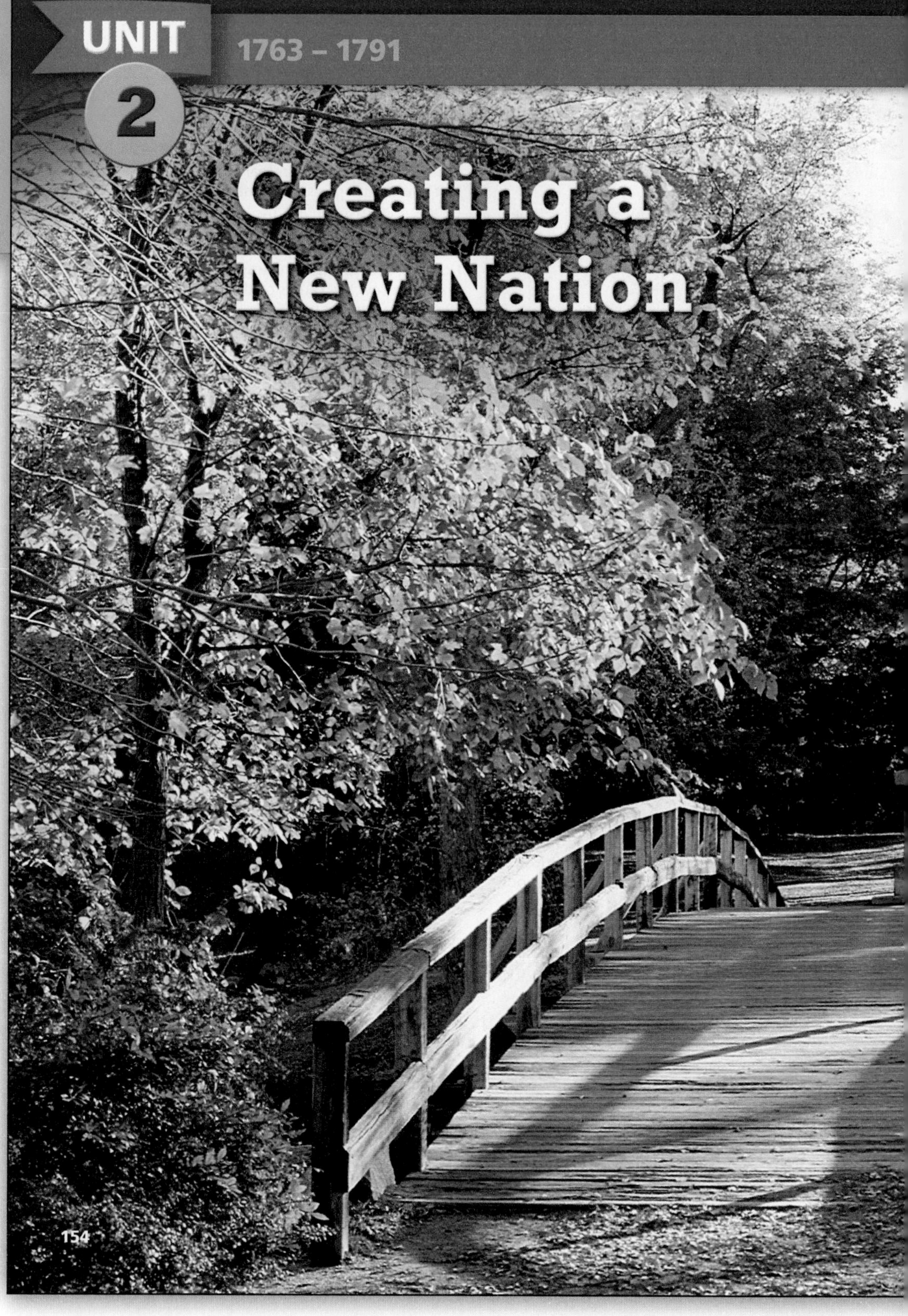

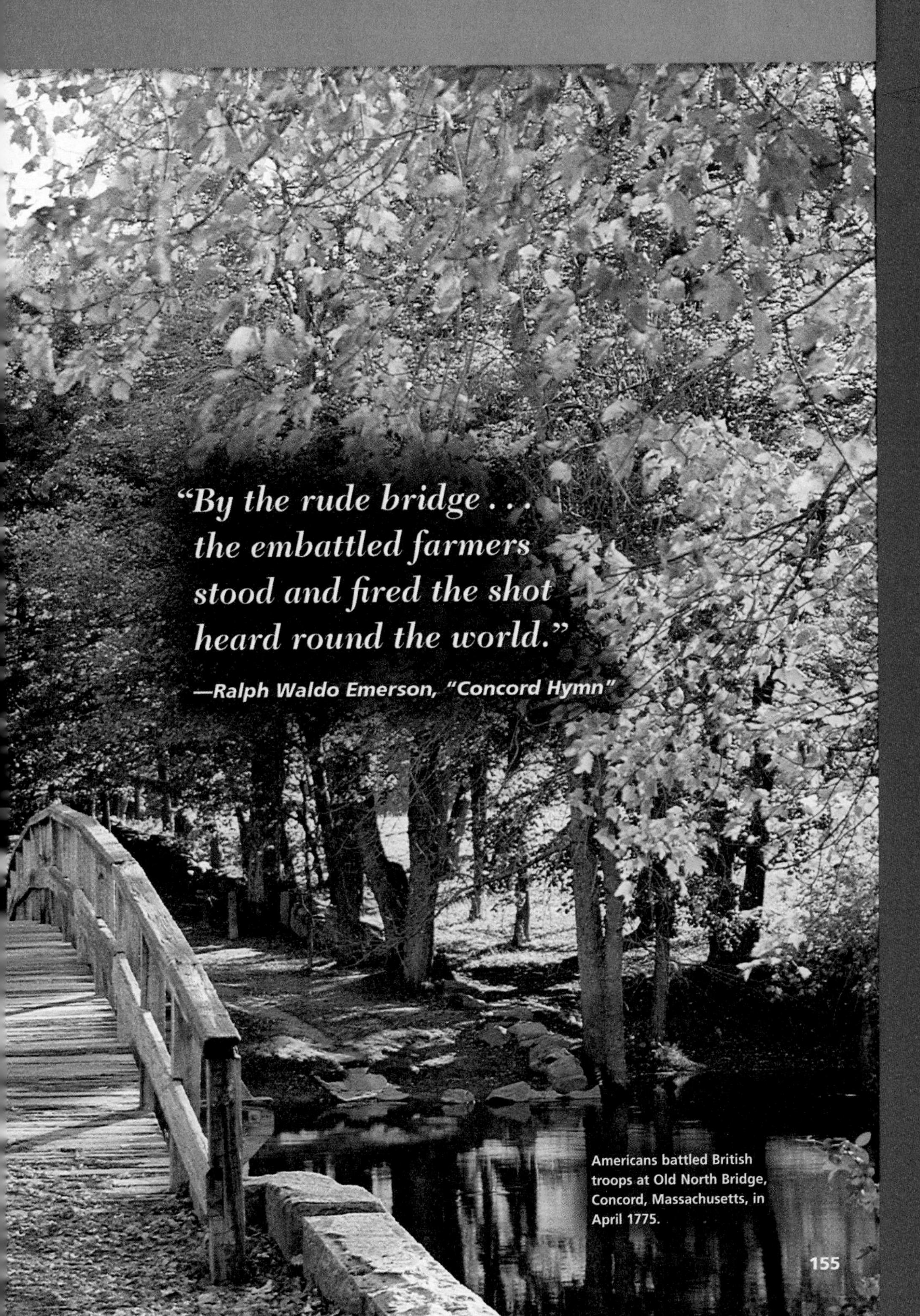
"By the rude bridge . . .
the embattled farmers
stood and fired the shot
heard round the world."
—Ralph Waldo Emerson, "Concord Hymn"

Americans battled British troops at Old North Bridge, Concord, Massachusetts, in April 1775.

155

## HISTORY FROM VISUALS

**Interpreting the Photograph** Ask students to study the photograph and read the lines from the "Concord Hymn" by Ralph Waldo Emerson. Ask students to define *rude* and *embattled* in this context. Then ask them to why the shots fired here by the American farmers were important in other parts of the world. **Possible Responses** The American Revolution inspired democratic revolutions in other countries. The formation of the United States has affected the rest of the world in countless ways.

**Extension** Ask students to find the complete "Concord Hymn" and select portions to read aloud to the class.

## CHAPTER 6 PLANNING GUIDE

# The Road to Revolution 1763–1776

### CHAPTER RESOURCES

**CHAPTER OVERVIEW**

The chapter identifies the causes of tension between the British government and the colonists in the years 1763–1776. It explains issues and events leading up to the declaration of independence from Britain. It describes the roles played by significant individuals.

**COPYMASTERS**

**In-Depth Resources: Unit 2**
- Tracing Themes: Impact of the Individual, p. 2
- Building Vocabulary, p. 8
- History Workshop Resources, p. 23

**Interdisciplinary Projects,** pp. 31–36

**TECHNOLOGY**

**Primary Source Explorer**

**Electronic Teacher Tools**

**Power Presentations CD-ROM**

**Chapter Summaries on CD** (English and Spanish)

**America's Music CD**

### SECTION 1 Tighter British Control pp. 159–162

**KEY IDEAS**

- Tighter British control causes tension with American colonists.
- The Stamp Act enrages the colonists.
- American protests force repeal of the Stamp Act.

**In-Depth Resources: Unit 2**
- Setting the Stage, p. 1
- Guided Reading, p. 3
- Primary Source: Resolutions of the Stamp Act Congress, p. 12
- Reteaching Activity, p. 18

**Economics in History**
- The Impact of British Taxes, p. 6

**Outline Map Activities**
- Pre-Revolutionary North America, pp. 11–12

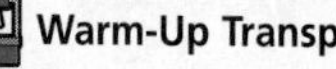

**Warm-Up Transparency WT6**

**Humanities Transparency HT11**
- The Repeal of the Stamp Act

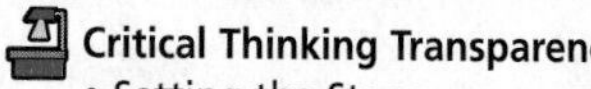

**Critical Thinking Transparency CT16**
- Setting the Stage

### SECTION 2 Colonial Resistance Grows pp. 163–169

- Townshend Acts bring new protests.
- The Boston Massacre causes more tension.
- Sons of Liberty protest the Tea Act.

**In-Depth Resources: Unit 2**
- Setting the Stage, p. 1
- Guided Reading, p. 4
- Skillbuilder Practice: Recognizing Propaganda, p. 9
- Reteaching Activity, p. 19

**Why It Matters Now**
- Politics and Protest, pp. 11–12

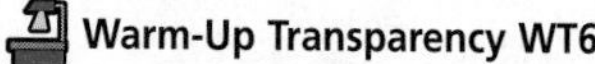

**Warm-Up Transparency WT6**

**Humanities Transparency HT12**
- *The Copley Family* by John Copley

**Critical Thinking Transparency CT16**
- Setting the Stage

**ClassZone:** www.mcdougallittell.com

### SECTION 3 The Road to Lexington and Concord pp. 170–175

- The Intolerable Acts punish the colonists.
- Colonists must choose between war and peace.
- Lexington and Concord become the first battles of the American Revolutionary War.

**In-Depth Resources: Unit 2**
- Setting the Stage, p. 1
- Guided Reading, p. 5
- Literature Selection: "Paul Revere's Ride" by Henry Wadsworth Longfellow, pp. 14–17
- Reteaching Activity, p. 20

**Warm-Up Transparency WT6**

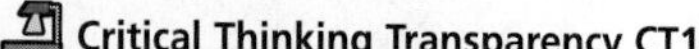

**Critical Thinking Transparency CT16**
- Setting the Stage

**Critical Thinking Transparency CT17**
- Cause and Effect: Growing Conflict Between Britain and America

**ClassZone:** www.mcdougallittell.com

### SECTION 4 Declaring Independence pp. 176–185

- Encounters between the British and colonists deepen the conflict.
- *Common Sense* makes a case for independence.
- American colonists declare independence from Great Britain.

**In-Depth Resources: Unit 2**
- Setting the Stage, p. 1
- Guided Reading, p. 6
- Guided Reading: The Declaration of Independence, p. 7
- Geography Application, pp. 10–11
- Primary Source, p. 13
- Reteaching Activity, p. 21

**America's History Makers,** pp. 23–26

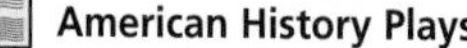

**American History Plays**
- *Franklin & the King* by Paul Green

**Warm-Up Transparency WT6**

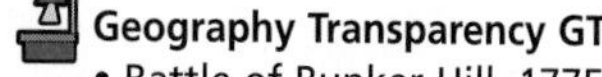

**Geography Transparency GT6**
- Battle of Bunker Hill, 1775

**Critical Thinking Transparency CT16**
- Setting the Stage

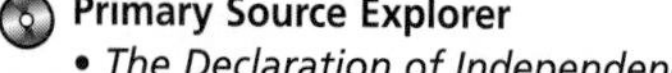

**Primary Source Explorer**
- *The Declaration of Independence*

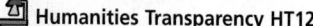

**ClassZone:** www.mcdougallittell.com

PE Pupil's Edition
Copymaster
Overhead Transparency
Audio Library
CD-ROM
Internet

## ASSESSMENT

**Chapter Assessment,** pp. 186–187

**Formal Assessment**
- Chapter Tests, Forms A and B, pp. 92–99

**Alternative Assessment Book**

**Electronic Teacher Tools with Test Maker**

---

**Section Assessment,** p. 162

**Formal Assessment**
- Section Quiz, p. 88

**Alternative Assessment Book**
- Rubrics for a poster, 1.1
- Rubrics for a song, 4.8

**Electronic Teacher Tools with Test Maker**

---

**Section Assessment,** p. 167

**Formal Assessment**
- Section Quiz, p. 89

**Alternative Assessment Book**
- Rubrics for an oral report, 3.6
- Rubrics for multimedia, 5.4

**Electronic Teacher Tools with Test Maker**

---

**Section Assessment,** p. 173

**Formal Assessment**
- Section Quiz, p. 90

**Alternative Assessment Book**
- Rubrics for a map, 2.1
- Rubrics for a chart, 2.2

**Electronic Teacher Tools with Test Maker**

---

**Section Assessment,** p. 181

**Formal Assessment**
- Section Quiz, p. 91

**Alternative Assessment Book**
- Rubrics for a trading card, 1.7
- Rubrics for a biography, 4.4

**Electronic Teacher Tools with Test Maker**

## CUSTOMIZING FOR INDIVIDUAL NEEDS

### Students Acquiring English/ESL

**Reading Study Guide** (English and Spanish), pp. 53–64

**Access for Students Acquiring English/ESL:** Spanish Translations, p. 35–42

**Chapter Summaries on CD** (English and Spanish)

### Less Proficient Readers

**Reading Study Guide** (English and Spanish), pp. 53–64

**Chapter Summaries on CD** (English and Spanish)

### Gifted and Talented Students

**In-Depth Resources: Unit 2**
- Enrichment Activity, p. 22

**America's History Makers**
- Abigail Adams, pp. 23–24
- Thomas Paine, pp. 25–26

## CROSS-CURRICULAR CONNECTIONS

### Geography

Barner, Bob. ***Which Way to the Revolution?*** Holiday House, 1998. Text and maps describe the route traveled by Paul Revere.

### Health

Erdosh, George. ***Food and Recipes of the Revolutionary War.*** New York: PowerKids Press, 1997.

### Humanities: Music

Brand, Oscar. ***Songs of '76: A Folksinger's History of the Revolution.*** Evans, 1988. A collection of songs from old manuscripts, newspapers, and personal accounts.

**Interdisciplinary Projects,** pp. 31–36
- Math: Population Growth
- Science: Silver Craft
- Language Arts: Making a Persuasive Speech
- Music: Revolutionary Songs

### Literature

Fritz, Jean. ***Early Thunder.*** Putnam, 1967. A 14-year-old boy is forced to choose between his family's Tory leanings and his feelings about Parliament's response to the Boston Tea Party.

### McDougal Littell *The Language of Literature*

- Henry Wadsworth Longfellow, "Paul Revere's Ride" (poem)

### McDougal Littell Literature Connections

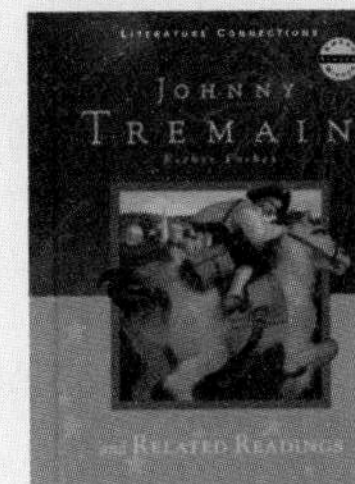


Esther Forbes
*Johnny Tremain*
Set in Boston from 1773 to 1775, the novel brings to life the adventures of a teenage boy and his role in the events leading to the American Revolution.

## ENRICHMENT ACTIVITIES

**Pupil's Edition, pp. 156–189**
**Interact with History,** p. 157
**Interdisciplinary Challenge,** pp. 168–169
**Literature Connections,** pp. 174–175
**Interactive Primary Source,** pp. 182–185
**History Workshop,** pp. 188–189

**In-Depth Resources: Unit 2**
- Geography Application, pp. 10–11
- Primary Source: Resolutions of the Stamp Act Congress, p. 12
- Primary Source: Letter from Abigail Adams, p. 13
- Literature Selection, pp. 14–17
- History Workshop Resources, p. 23

**America's History Makers**
- Abigail Adams, pp. 23–24
- Thomas Paine, pp. 25–26

**America's Music CD**

**American History Plays**
- *Franklin & the King* by Paul Green

**Outline Map Activities**
- Pre-Revolutionary North America, pp. 11–12

**Primary Source Explorer**
- *The Declaration of Independence*

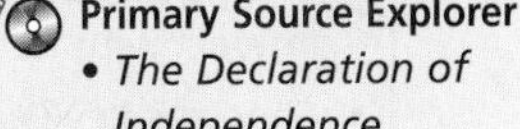

**Why It Matters Now**
- Politics and Protest, pp. 11–12

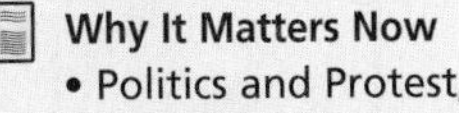

# CHAPTER 6 PACING GUIDE

**LESSON PLAN OPTIONS (50-MINUTE PERIOD)** (TE) = Teacher's Edition (PE) = Pupil's Edition

| | TEACHER-DIRECTED ACTIVITIES<br>Class Time: 15 minutes | STUDENT-CENTERED ACTIVITIES<br>Class Time: 25 minutes | INDIVIDUAL ACTIVITIES<br>Class Time: 10 minutes |
|---|---|---|---|
| **DAY 1**<br>Introduction<br>pp. 156–158 | **Presentation Options**<br>• Begin with a class discussion of the engraving on p. 156 **(PE)**.<br>• Lead a class discussion on the "What Do You Know?" question in Setting the Stage, p. 158. Then introduce the graphic organizer for the chapter **(PE)**. | **Options for Cooperative Learning**<br>• Have student groups discuss the Interact with History questions, p. 157 **(PE)**.<br>• Have student groups respond to the "What Do You Want to Know?" question in Setting the Stage, p. 158 **(PE)**. | **Head Start on Homework Options**<br>• Have students skim Section 1 Main Idea, Why It Matters Now, Terms & Names, and the main headings, p. 159 **(PE)**.<br>• Have students begin Guided Reading activity and Building Vocabulary sheet. |
| **DAY 2**<br>Section 1<br>pp. 159–162 | **Presentation Options**<br>• Begin with the 5-Minute Warm-Up, p. 159 **(TE)**.<br>• Review the Main Idea, Why It Matters Now, and Terms & Names, p. 159 **(PE)**.<br>• Choose 5 key questions for Objectives 1–4 to discuss with the class, pp. 159–161 **(TE)**. | **Options for Cooperative Learning**<br>• Divide students into groups to complete the Interdisciplinary Activity on Protesting the Stamp Act, p. 161 **(TE)**.<br>• Have student pairs work together to complete one of the Activity Options in the Section 1 Assessment, p. 162 **(PE)**. | **Head Start on Homework Options**<br>• Have students begin working on the Section 1 Assessment, p. 162 **(PE)**.<br>• Have students preview Section 2 by skimming the Main Idea, Why It Matters Now, Terms & Names, and the main headings, p. 163 **(PE)**. |
| **DAY 3**<br>Section 2<br>pp. 163–169 | **Presentation Options**<br>• Begin with the 5-Minute Warm-Up, p. 163 **(TE)**.<br>• Choose 5 key questions for Objectives 1–4 to discuss with the class, pp. 163–167 **(TE)**.<br>• Lead the students through the Skillbuilder Mini-Lesson: Recognizing Propaganda, p. 165 **(TE)**. | **Options for Cooperative Learning**<br>• Divide students into groups and have them complete one of the challenges in the Interdisciplinary Challenge, pp. 168–169 **(PE)**.<br>• Have students work together to complete the Interdisciplinary Link, Language Arts: Committees of Correspondence, p. 166 **(TE)**. | **Head Start on Homework Options**<br>• Have students begin working on the Section 2 Assessment, p. 167 **(PE)**.<br>• Have students read Literature Connections, a selection from *Johnny Tremain,* pp. 174–175 **(PE)**. |
| **DAY 4**<br>Section 3<br>pp. 170–175 | **Presentation Options**<br>• Begin with the 5-Minute Warm-Up, p. 170 **(TE)**.<br>• Review the Cause and Effect chart, p. 171 **(PE)**.<br>• Choose 5 Key Questions for Objectives 1–4 to discuss with the class, pp. 170–173 **(TE)**. | **Options for Cooperative Learning**<br>• Divide the students into small groups to complete the Interdisciplinary Link, Math: Effects of the Boycott, p. 171 **(TE)**.<br>• Divide the students into small groups to create a skit based on the *Johnny Tremain* reading, pp. 174–175 **(PE)**. | **Head Start on Homework Options**<br>• Have students complete the History from Visuals extension activity, p. 172 **(TE)**.<br>• Have students complete the History Skills questions in Chapter Assessment, p. 187 **(PE)**. |
| **DAY 5**<br>Section 4<br>pp. 176–185 | **Presentation Options**<br>• Begin with the 5-Minute Warm-Up, p. 176 **(TE)**.<br>• Discuss the follow-up question to Interact with History, p. 186 **(PE)**.<br>• Choose 5 Key Questions for Objectives 1–4 to discuss with the class, pp. 176–179 **(TE)**. | **Options for Cooperative Learning**<br>• Divide the students into small groups and begin work on the History Workshop, pp. 188–189 **(PE)**.<br>• Divide the students into small groups and complete the Interdisciplinary Link, Civics: Creating a New *Common Sense,* p. 179 **(TE)**. | **Head Start on Homework Options**<br>• Have students complete the Setting the Stage graphic organizer for the chapter, p. 158 **(PE)**.<br>• Have students begin working on the Chapter Assessment, pp. 186–187 **(PE)**.<br>• Prepare for Chapter Test<br>**Formal Assessment,** pp. 92–99 |

TEACHER-TESTED ACTIVITY Holly West Brewer, Buena Vista Paideia Magnet School, Nashville, Tennessee

## ILLUSTRATED TIME LINE

**Class Time** Two class periods for preparation and one for presentation

**Task** Creating an illustrated time line of the events leading to the American Revolution

**Purpose** To visualize and sequence events that led to the Revolution

**Supplies Needed**
- reference books and Internet sources on the American Revolution
- markers, colored pencils
- poster paper or rolls of paper

**Activity** Divide the class into small groups. Students should compile at least ten events that led to the Revolution. Each student should be responsible for researching two or three events. In addition, each student chooses one of the following roles: illustrator or recorder.

The illustrators should create original drawings for each event. Each event should be placed on the large time line in chronological order. In addition, the recorders should write a cause-and-effect explanation as a caption for each event. Present the time line to the class.

## BLOCK SCHEDULING — LESSON PLAN OPTIONS (90-MINUTE PERIOD)

### DAY 1

**Interact with History,** p. 157
**Class Time** 20 minutes

Options for pacing and variety:
- Role-Playing Have students meet in groups of four or five and act as neighbors meeting to discuss the "What Do You Think?" questions and the main questions.
  **Class Time** 15 minutes

**Setting the Stage,** p. 158
**Class Time** 20 minutes

Options for pacing and variety:
- Time Saver Assign the "What Do You Know?" and "What Do You Want to Know?" questions as homework so that students can get a head start on preparing to read the chapter. **Class Time** 5 minutes

**Section 1,** pp. 159–162
**Class Time** 50 minutes

Options for pacing and variety:
- Time Saver Use the political cartoon transparency, "Repeal of the Stamp Act," as a summary of the section.
  **Class Time** 10 minutes
- Peer Teaching Have students work in pairs to answer the Reading History questions in the section and Critical Thinking question in the Section 1 assessment. **Class Time** 15 minutes

### DAY 2

**Section 2,** pp. 163–169
**Class Time** 45 minutes

**Interdisciplinary Challenge,** pp. 168–169
**Class Time** 55 minutes

Options for pacing and variety:
- Team Teaching Invite the math teacher to your class to coach student groups as they solve the Math Challenge or the Interdisciplinary Link (Math) on p. 171 in the Teacher's Edition.
  **Class Time** 55 minutes.
- Peer Teaching Assign the content under each heading to a small group of students. Each group is responsible for explaining the information to the class.
  **Class Time** 30 minutes

**Section 3,** pp. 170–175
**Class Time** 45 minutes

Options for pacing and variety:
- Peer Teaching Divide students into small groups. Using the information from the chart on p. 171, create a different way to present the information to the class.
  **Class Time** 25 minutes
- Internet Extend students' background knowledge of the Battles at Lexington and Concord by having them visit www.mcdougallittell.com
  **Class Time** 20 minutes

### DAY 3

**Section 4,** pp. 176–185
**Class Time** 50 minutes

Options for pacing and variety:
- Peer Teaching Divide the class into small groups. Assign one group to become a living time line. Have another group become living biographies of individuals in this chapter. A third group performs the Cooperative Learning Activity on page 187.
  **Class Time** 50 minutes
- History on Film Extend students' background on the Revolutionary War by viewing either episode one or two, "The Conflict Ignites" or "1776," of *The American Revolution.* A&E Home Video, 1994.
  **Class Time** 50 minutes

**History Workshop,** pp. 188–189
**Class Time** 50 minutes

Options for pacing and variety:
- Time Saver Have students work on steps 1–5 in Raise the Liberty Pole. **Class Time** 30 minutes

**Chapter 6 Assessment,** pp. 186–187
**Class Time** 40 minutes

Options for pacing and variety:
- Peer Evaluation Have student pairs work out the answers to the Critical Thinking Questions, p. 186. Then have them exchange papers with another team to evaluate their answers.
  **Class Time** 20 minutes
- Peer Teaching Divide the class into four groups. Assign each group one section of the Review Questions to complete. Students should exchange answers for the review questions. **Class Time** 20 minutes

**CHAPTER 6 OBJECTIVE**

The student will understand the events that pushed Great Britain and the American colonies apart and ultimately led to the signing of the Declaration of Independence.

# The Road to Revolution 1763–1776



## HISTORY FROM VISUALS

**Interpreting the Illustration** Ask students to study the engraving of British troops arriving in the colonies. Have them draw conclusions about the mood of the colonists and explain why they might feel that way. **Possible Responses** The colonists were angry because they saw the influx of British troops as a sign of Britain's attempt to restrict their freedom. The colonists felt nervous and uneasy about living among so many armed British troops.

**Extension** Have students write a descriptive paragraph about the scene in this painting.

### CRITICAL THINKING ACTIVITY

**Making Inferences** Have the students look at the titles of the sections in this chapter. Ask them how the images on these opening pages illustrate the ideas found in the section titles. Then ask them what images they would expect to see illustrate the rest of the chapter.

**Class Time** 10 minutes

Angry colonists watch the arrival of British troops in Boston.

156

## RECOMMENDED RESOURCES

### BOOKS FOR THE TEACHER

Maier, Pauline. ***American Scripture: Making the Declaration of Independence.*** New York: A. A. Knopf, 1997. A closer look at the creation of the nation's cornerstone document.

Miller, John C. ***Origins of the American Revolution.*** Stanford: SU Press, 1943. An examination of events that led to the Revolutionary War.

Morgan, Edmund S. and Helen M. ***The Stamp Act Crisis: Prologue to Revolution.*** Chapel Hill: The UNC Press, 1953. A look at one of the pivotal events leading up to the war.

Zobel, Hiller B. ***The Boston Massacre.*** New York: W. W. Norton, 1970. An examination of the famous pre-war shooting incident.

### VIDEOS

***Liberty! The American Revolution.*** PBS Video, 1997. See episode one, "The Reluctant Revolutionaries."

***The American Revolution.*** A&E Home Video, 1994. See episodes one and two, "The Conflict Ignites" and "1776."

### INTERNET

For more about the American Revolution, visit www.mcdougallittell.com

## Interact *with* History

A colonist reads a copy of a new British tax law.
Tax stamps are burned.
Protesters include men, women, and children.

**The year is 1765. Your neighbors are enraged by Britain's attempt to tax them without their consent. Britain has never done this before. Everyone will be affected by the tax. There are protests in many cities. You have to decide what you would do.**

### What Do You Think?

- **What is the best way to show opposition to policies you consider unjust?**
- **Is there anything to be gained by protesting? Anything to be lost?**
- **Does government have the right to tax without consent of the people? Why or why not?**

# *Would you join the protest?*

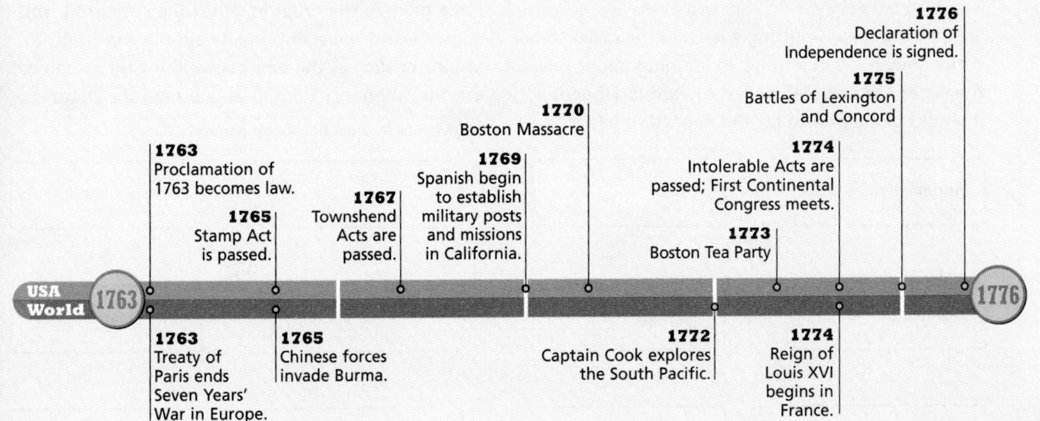




## Interact *with* History

### OBJECTIVES

- To help students identify one reason for the growing tension between Britain and the colonies
- To help students better understand the mood of the American colonists in the years before the Revolutionary War

### What Do You Think?

1. Ask students how they would react if politicians collected taxes from them but ignored their views and needs.
2. Have students consider why a large public rally is an effective way to protest an unpopular policy.
3. Ask students to think about the different ways the British could react to the colonists' protest.

### *Would you join the protest?*

Encourage students to think about the best- and worst-case scenarios facing the protesters. Possible scenarios: best—Britain repeals the tax; worst—British troops jail or beat the protesters.

### MAKING PERSONAL CONNECTIONS

Ask students to think about policies either in their homes or community that they considered unjust. What did they do to protest? Did their protest achieve anything? Why or why not?

### TIME LINE DISCUSSION

**Explain to students that after the Seven Years' War, Great Britain was the most powerful nation in Europe. Its colonial empire included North America, holdings in the Caribbean, and India. In light of Britain's strength, the American colonists' declaration of independence seemed all the more bold and daring.**

- Ask students how many years it was between Britain's passage of the Stamp Act and the Intolerable Acts. **Answer** Eight years.
- Ask students to hypothesize what colonists thought about these acts based on the events shown between 1774 and 1776.

**Possible Response** The colonists opposed these acts, for what followed them were fighting and a declaration of independence from British rule.

- Have students look at the time line and determine which world event and U.S. event are linked. **Possible Response** The two events in 1763 are linked. The end of the Seven Years' War set up the need for the proclamation.

## BEFORE YOU READ

### Previewing the Theme:

**Impact of the Individual**

Ask students why strong and popular leaders would be so important to the colonists' attempts to gain independence from Great Britain. **Possible Response** Strong and dynamic leaders are vital to such an effort because they inspire citizens and help them to maintain their courage and determination.

### What Do You Know?

Students may know that Britain and the colonists clashed over the issue of taxes. Tell them that increased taxation was just one example of Britain's attempt to achieve greater control over the colonies after the French and Indian War. Remind them that Britain had long allowed the colonies to develop with a notable degree of independence. As Britain sought to reverse this policy, however, tensions grew.

**In-Depth Resources: Unit 2**
- Tracing Themes: Impact of the Individual, p. 2

## READ AND TAKE NOTES

**Reading Strategy: Sequencing Events**

Tell students that sequencing events, or arranging them in chronological order, will help them to better understand the relationship among those events. Knowing which event followed another may help students accomplish such critical-thinking tasks as analyzing causes and recognizing effects. The effect, or consequence, of one event often becomes the cause of another. By sequencing events in a chart such as the one shown here, students can more clearly see the cause-and-effect relationship among historical events.

**In-Depth Resources: Unit 2**
- Setting the Stage, p. 1

**Critical Thinking Transparency CT16**
- Setting the Stage

# Chapter 6 SETTING THE STAGE

## BEFORE YOU READ

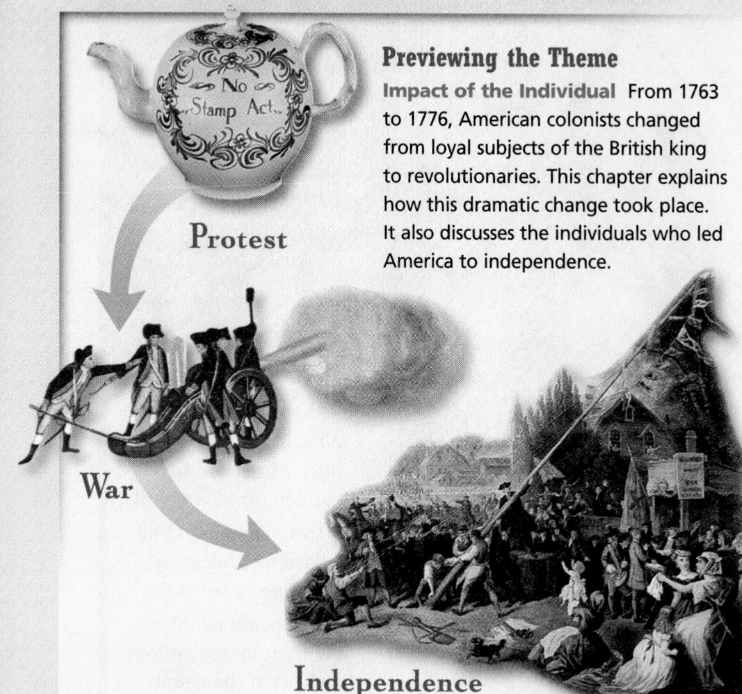



### Previewing the Theme

**Impact of the Individual** From 1763 to 1776, American colonists changed from loyal subjects of the British king to revolutionaries. This chapter explains how this dramatic change took place. It also discusses the individuals who led America to independence.

### What Do You Know?

What do you already know about the time before the Revolution? What were the issues that caused the colonists to choose independence?

**THINK ABOUT**
- what you have learned about this period from movies, television, or historical fiction
- reasons people in history have chosen to fight for freedom from oppression

### What Do You Want to Know?

What questions do you have about the issues and events that pushed the American colonists toward rebellion? Record them in your notebook before you read the chapter.

## READ AND TAKE NOTES

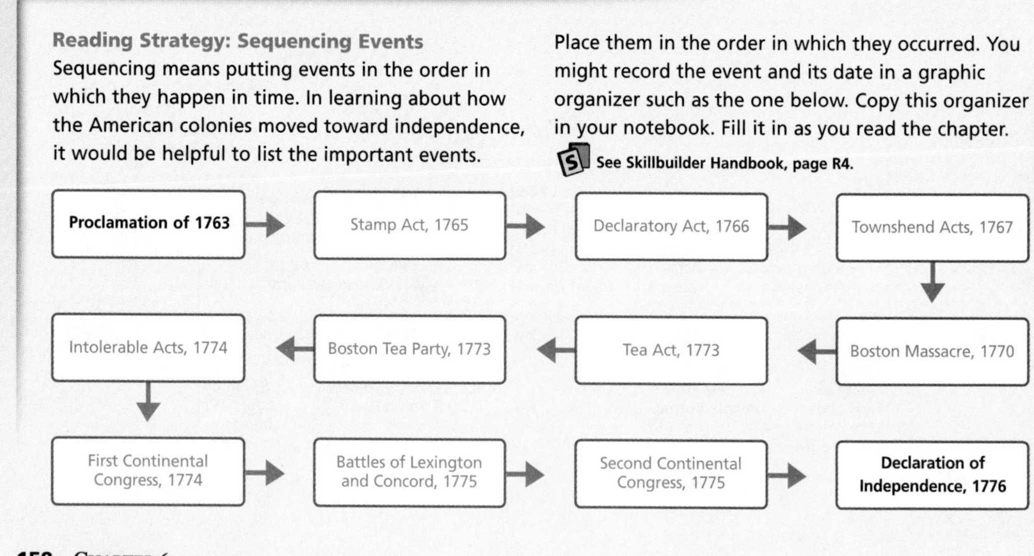

**Reading Strategy: Sequencing Events** Sequencing means putting events in the order in which they happen in time. In learning about how the American colonies moved toward independence, it would be helpful to list the important events. Place them in the order in which they occurred. You might record the event and its date in a graphic organizer such as the one below. Copy this organizer in your notebook. Fill it in as you read the chapter.

See Skillbuilder Handbook, page R4.





## TEACHING STRATEGY

### READING THE CHAPTER

This is a chronological chapter focusing on the chain of events that led to the colonists' declaring their independence from Great Britain. Encourage students to look for the causes and effects of each event. Have them also consider how each event increased tensions between Britain and the colonies. Pause after each section to summarize the causes and effects of the main events described in the section.

### ALTERNATIVE ASSESSMENT

The Chapter Assessment describes three activities for alternative assessment on page 187. You may wish to have students work on these activities during the course of the chapter and then present them at the end.

# 1 Tighter British Control

**TERMS & NAMES**
King George III
Quartering Act
revenue
Sugar Act
Stamp Act
Patrick Henry
boycott
Sons of Liberty

| MAIN IDEA | WHY IT MATTERS NOW |
| --- | --- |
| Americans saw British efforts to tax them and to increase control over the colonies as violations of their rights. | Colonial protests were the first steps on the road to American independence. |

## ONE AMERICAN'S STORY

**James Otis, Jr., a young Massachusetts lawyer, stormed through the streets of Boston one day in 1760. He was furious. His father had just been denied the post of chief justice of the Massachusetts colony by the royal governor. To Otis, this was one more example of Britain's lack of respect for colonial rights. Another example was its use of search warrants that allowed customs officers to enter any home or business to look for smuggled goods. Otis believed these searches were illegal.**

**Otis took up a case against the government that involved these search warrants. In court in February 1761, Otis spoke with great emotion for five hours about the search warrant and its use.**

*A VOICE FROM THE PAST*

It appears to me the worst instrument of arbitrary power, the most destructive of English liberty and the fundamental principles of law, that was ever found in an English law-book.

**James Otis, Jr.,** quoted in *James Otis: The Pre-Revolutionist* by J. C. Ridpath

**Spectators listened in amazement. One of them, a young lawyer named John Adams, later wrote of Otis's performance: "Then and there, in the old Council Chamber, the child Independence was born."**

**In making the first public speech demanding English liberties for the colonists, James Otis planted a seed of freedom. In this section, you will read more about the early protests against Britain's policies in America.**

**James Otis, Jr., argues in court against illegal search warrants in 1761.**

## 1 The Colonies and Britain Grow Apart

During the French and Indian War, Britain and the colonies fought side by side. Americans took great pride in being partners in the victory over the French. However, when the war ended, problems arose. Britain wanted to govern its 13 original colonies and the territories gained in the war in a uniform way. So the British Parliament in London imposed new laws and restrictions. Previously, the colonies had been allowed to develop largely on their own. Now they felt that their freedom was being limited.





## SECTION OBJECTIVES

1. To identify why the Proclamation of 1763 angered so many colonists
2. To describe the debate over taxes and troops in the colonies
3. To explain the Stamp Act
4. To examine how the colonists forced Britain to repeal the Stamp Act

**CRITICAL THINKING**

Summarizing, p. 160
Making Inferences, p. 161
Drawing Conclusions, p. 162
Analyzing Points of View, p. 162

## FOCUS & MOTIVATE

### 5-MINUTE WARM-UP

**Drawing Conclusions** These questions focus on the issue of taxation and the relationship between Britain and the colonies.

1. Look at the images on pages 160 and 162. How do the colonists feel about being taxed, according to these images?
2. Why might Great Britain feel justified in imposing taxes on its colonies?

 **Warm-Up Transparency WT6**

## INSTRUCT

### INSTRUCT: OBJECTIVE 1

**The Colonies and Britain Grow Apart**

Key Questions

- How did Britain's policy toward its American colonies change after the French and Indian War?
- Why did the Proclamation of 1763 anger many colonists?
- What did many colonists choose to do about the proclamation?

**In-Depth Resources: Unit 2**
- Guided Reading, p. 3

**Reading Study Guide** (Spanish and English), pp. 53–54

## RECOMMENDED RESOURCES

 **In-Depth Resources: Unit 2**
- Guided Reading, p. 3
- Building Vocabulary, p. 8
- Primary Source: Resolutions of the Stamp Act Congress, p. 12
- Reteaching Activity, p. 18

 **Reading Study Guide** (Spanish and English), pp. 53–54

 **Economics in History**
- The Impact of British Taxes, p. 6

 **Outline Map Activities**
- Pre-Revolutionary North America, pp. 11–12

 **Formal Assessment**
- Section Quiz, p. 88

 **Alternative Assessment**
- Rubrics, 1.1
- Rubrics, 4.8

 **Access for Students Acquiring English/ESL**
- Guided Reading, p. 35

**Technology Resources**

 **Humanities Transparency HT11**
- The Repeal of the Stamp Act

 **Electronic Teacher Tools with Test Maker**

 **ClassZone**
www.mcdougallittell.com

The first of Parliament's laws was the Proclamation of 1763. (See Chapter 5.) It said that colonists could not settle west of the Appalachian Mountains. Britain wanted this land to remain in the hands of its Native American allies to prevent another revolt like Pontiac's Rebellion.

The proclamation angered colonists who had hoped to move to the fertile Ohio Valley. Many of these colonists had no land of their own. It also upset colonists who had bought land as an investment. As a result, many ignored the law.

*Reading*History
**A. Summarizing** Who was upset by the Proclamation of 1763?
A. Answer colonists who wanted land of their own and those who had bought land as investments

## 2 British Troops and Taxes

**King George III**, the British monarch, wanted to enforce the proclamation and also keep peace with Britain's Native American allies. To do this, he decided to keep 10,000 soldiers in the colonies. In 1765, Parliament passed the **Quartering Act.** This was a cost-saving measure that required the colonies to quarter, or house, British soldiers and provide them with supplies. General Thomas Gage, commander of these forces, put most of the troops in New York.

Britain owed a large debt from the French and Indian War. Keeping troops in the colonies would raise that debt even higher. Britain needed more **revenue,** or income, to meet its expenses. So it attempted to have the colonies pay part of the war debt. It also wanted them to contribute toward the costs of frontier defense and colonial government.

In the past, the king had asked the colonial assemblies to pass taxes to support military actions that took place in the colonies. This time, however, Parliament voted to tax the Americans directly.

In 1764, Parliament passed the **Sugar Act.** This law placed a tax on sugar, molasses, and other products shipped to the colonies. It also called for strict enforcement of the act and harsh punishment of smugglers. Colonial merchants, who often traded in smuggled goods, reacted with anger.

Colonial leaders such as James Otis claimed that Parliament had no right to tax the colonies, since the colonists were not represented in Parliament. As Otis exclaimed, "Taxation without representation is tyranny!" British finance minister George Grenville disagreed. The colonists were subjects of Britain, he said, and enjoyed the protection of its laws. For that reason, they were subject to taxation.

**Vocabulary**
**tyranny:** absolute power in the hands of a single ruler



The colonial view of the hated stamp tax is shown by the skull and crossbones on this emblem (above); a royal stamp is pictured at right.

## 3 Britain Passes the Stamp Act

The Sugar Act was just the first in a series of acts that increased tension between the mother country and the colonies. In 1765, Parliament passed the **Stamp Act.** This law required all legal and commercial documents to carry an official stamp showing that a tax had been paid. All diplomas, contracts, and wills had to carry a stamp.

160

**INSTRUCT: OBJECTIVE 2**

**British Troops and Taxes**

Key Questions
- What was the Quartering Act?
- Why did Parliament seek to impose greater taxes on the colonies?
- Why did the colonists oppose the Sugar Act?

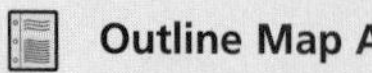

**Outline Map Activities**
- Pre-Revolutionary North America, pp. 11–12

**MORE ABOUT . . .**

**George Grenville**

The colonists would have been hard pressed to find a person more unsympathetic to their plight than George Grenville. Grenville was obsessed with remedying Britain's financial difficulties after the French and Indian War. Such concerns led him to develop an intense hatred for colonial smuggling—which denied England vital tax revenues. He told an aide that smugglers should be "prosecuted and punished as severely as the law will allow." As he imposed his unpopular policies on the colonists, he showed little worry about their growing anger. Americans, he once declared, "could not hope to get any good by a controversy with the Mother Country."

**INSTRUCT: OBJECTIVE 3**

**Britain Passes the Stamp Act**

Key Questions
- What was the Stamp Act?
- How did the Stamp Act differ from previous taxes imposed on the colonies?
- What objection did colonial leaders voice about the Stamp Act?

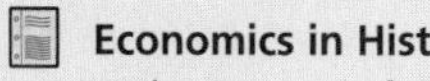

**Economics in History**
- The Impact of British Taxes, p. 6

**ACTIVITY OPTIONS**

**INDIVIDUAL NEEDS**

**LESS PROFICIENT READERS**

**Summarizing** To help less proficient readers better understand the reasons for the growing tension between Britain and the colonies, have them chart the events of this section in a graphic organizer like the one shown here. Students should copy the chart and write a brief explanation of how the colonists reacted in each case. Then have the students share their answers with a more proficient reader.

| Event | Colonial Response |
|---|---|
| Proclamation of 1763 | |
| Sugar Act | |
| Stamp Act | |

Even published materials such as newspapers had to be written on special stamped paper.

The Stamp Act was a new kind of tax for the colonies. The Sugar Act had been a tax on imported goods. It mainly affected merchants. In contrast, the Stamp Act was a tax applied within the colonies. It fell directly on all colonists. Even more, the colonists had to pay for stamps in silver coin—a scarce item in the colonies.

Colonial leaders vigorously protested. For them, the issue was clear. They were being taxed without their consent by a Parliament in which they had no voice. If Britain could pass the Stamp Act, what other taxes might it pass in the future? Samuel Adams, a leader in the Massachusetts legislature, asked, "Why not our lands? Why not the produce of our lands and, in short, everything we possess and make use of?" **Patrick Henry,** a member of Virginia's House of Burgesses, called for resistance to the tax. When another member shouted that resistance was treason, Henry replied, "If this be treason, make the most of it!"

## 4 The Colonies Protest the Stamp Act

Colonial assemblies and newspapers took up the cry—"No taxation without representation!" In October 1765, nine colonies sent delegates to the Stamp Act Congress in New York City. This was the first time the colonies met to consider acting together in protest. Delegates drew up a petition to the king protesting the Stamp Act. The petition declared that the right to tax the colonies belonged to the colonial assemblies, not to Parliament. Later, colonial merchants organized a **boycott** of British goods. A boycott is a refusal to buy.

B. Answer They thought Britain would fear losing trade and repeal the law.

*Reading*History

**B. Making Inferences** Why did the colonists boycott goods?

Meanwhile, some colonists formed secret societies to oppose British policies. The most famous of these groups was the **Sons of Liberty.** Many Sons of Liberty were lawyers, merchants, and craftspeople—the colonists most affected by the Stamp Act. These groups staged protests against the act.

**Background**
To voice their protests, the Sons of Liberty in Boston met under a huge, 120-year-old elm tree that they called the Liberty Tree.

Not all of their protests were peaceful. The Sons of Liberty burned the stamped paper whenever they could find it. They also attacked customs officials, whom they covered with hot tar and feathers and paraded in public. Fearing for their safety, many customs officials quit their jobs.

The protests in the colonies had an effect in Britain. Merchants thought that their trade with America would be hurt. Some British political leaders, including

Colonists protest the Stamp Act.





### CONNECT TO TODAY

**Tax Resistance**
Point out to students that the tradition of resisting the payment of taxes began in this era and continues today. Many groups in the United States have organized to resist paying taxes for a variety of reasons. For example, the Libertarian political party has as one of its platform positions resistance to the payment of taxes. Have students do research to see if there are tax resistance groups in their own community.

### INSTRUCT: OBJECTIVE 

**The Colonies Protest the Stamp Act**
Key Questions
- In what ways did the colonists challenge the Stamp Act?
- Who were the Sons of Liberty?
- What eventually became of the Stamp Act?

 **In-Depth Resources: Unit 2**
- Primary Source: Resolutions of the Stamp Act Congress, p. 12

### MORE ABOUT . . .

**The Sons of Liberty**
Although we hear often about the Boston Sons of Liberty, the secret organizations were found in many colonies. In New York, the "Sons" were led by wealthy, high-born men. These men were not reluctant to use violence to resist the Stamp Act. The New York Sons of Liberty are believed to be the first in New York to die for independence. On January 18, 1775, the Sons of Liberty had an encounter with British soldiers. Several "Sons" were wounded, and one was killed.

 **Humanities Transparency HT11**
- The Repeal of the Stamp Act

### ACTIVITY OPTIONS

### INTERDISCIPLINARY LINK: HUMANITIES

 BLOCK SCHEDULING

**PROTESTING THE STAMP ACT**

**Class Time** 30 minutes

**Task** Creating protest material regarding the Stamp Act

**Purpose** To examine the different ways to sway public opinion

**Supplies Needed**
- Markers and drawing paper

**Activity** Break students into small groups and have them protest the Stamp Act in one of three ways: draw a poster or cartoon, create a slogan or jingle, or make a commercial. Students may focus on any aspect of the tax but should make their point clear and easy to understand. Groups that choose to draw a poster or cartoon should pick the student who is the best artist to draw the work. Have the groups display their work to the class. Groups that made a commercial should act it out, while those that created a slogan or jingle should recite it.

## MORE ABOUT . . .

### Tarring and Feathering

Ironically, the colonists adopted the practice of tarring and feathering from their mother country. This form of punishment reportedly began among English naval officers under the reign of King Richard the Lionhearted. English mobs occasionally performed this procedure on tax collectors and other unpopular figures. While recipients of this punishment certainly came away humiliated, they also could end up in a great deal of pain. The hot tar was known to cause third-degree burns, from which it took weeks to recover.

## ASSESS & RETEACH

**Setting the Stage** Have students fill in the first three boxes on the graphic organizer.

**Formal Assessment**
- Section Quiz, p. 88

**Critical Thinking Transparency CT16**
- Setting the Stage

### RETEACHING ACTIVITY

Have students work in pairs to perform an imaginary interview on the rising tensions between Britain and the colonies. One student should play a colonist, the other a local newspaper reporter. Have the reporter ask the colonist his or her views on the various acts and proclamations passed by the British. The reporter should write down the colonist's answers in outline form and hand them in.

**In-Depth Resources: Unit 2**
- Reteaching Activity, p. 18

### Bostonians Paying the Taxman

**In this British political cartoon, Americans are depicted as barbarians who would tar and feather a customs official, or tax collector, and pour hot tea down his throat.**

**A** Liberty Tree as a gallows

**B** Stamp Act posted upside down

**C** Protesters in Boston

**D** Customs official tarred and feathered

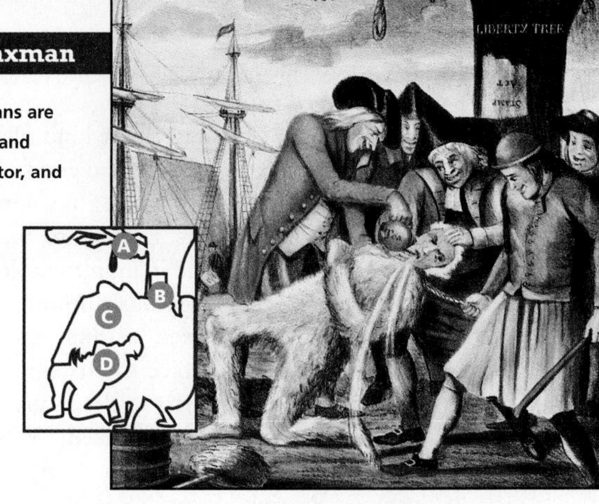


the popular parliamentary leader William Pitt, agreed with American thinking about taxing the colonies. Pitt spoke out against the Stamp Act.

*A VOICE FROM THE PAST*

> The Americans have not acted in all things with prudence and [good] temper. They have been driven to madness by injustice. Will you punish them for the madness you have [caused]? . . . My opinion . . . is that the Stamp Act be repealed absolutely, totally and immediately.
>
> **William Pitt,** quoted in *Patriots* by A. J. Langguth

**C. Possible Answer** It showed the colonists that even though they had won repeal of the Stamp Act, Parliament was still the supreme authority.

*Reading* **History**

**C. Drawing Conclusions** Why was it important for Parliament to pass the Declaratory Act?

Parliament finally saw that the Stamp Act was a mistake and repealed it in 1766. But at the same time, Parliament passed another law—the Declaratory Act. This law said that Parliament had supreme authority to govern the colonies. The Americans celebrated the repeal of the Stamp Act and tried to ignore the Declaratory Act. A great tug of war between Parliament and the colonies had begun. The central issue was control of the colonies, as you will learn in the next section.

## Section 1 Assessment

### 1. Terms & Names

**Identify:**
- King George III
- Quartering Act
- revenue
- Sugar Act
- Stamp Act
- Patrick Henry
- boycott
- Sons of Liberty

### 2. Taking Notes

Use a cluster diagram like the one below to review points of conflict between Britain and the colonies.

Which do you think was the most serious? Explain.

### 3. Main Ideas

**a.** Why did the Proclamation of 1763 anger colonists?

**b.** How did colonists react to the Stamp Act?

**c.** What was the goal of secret societies such as the Sons of Liberty?

### 4. Critical Thinking

**Analyzing Points of View** What were the two sides in the debate over British taxation of the colonies?

**THINK ABOUT**
- how Parliament viewed the colonies
- what concerned the colonists about taxes

**ACTIVITY OPTIONS**

**ART** / **MUSIC**

Imagine that you are a colonial leader who wants to get your fellow colonists to protest British policy. Design a **poster** or write a **song of protest.**



## Section 1 Assessment

### 1. Terms & Names

**King George III,** p. 160
**Quartering Act,** p. 160
**revenue,** p. 160
**Sugar Act,** p. 160
**Stamp Act,** p. 160
**Patrick Henry,** p. 161
**boycott,** p. 161
**Sons of Liberty,** p. 161

### 2. Taking Notes

Sugar Act (tax on sugar and other goods); Stamp Act (direct tax); trial without jury; Proclamation of 1763 (prevented colonists from settling in the Ohio Valley); Quartering Act (forced colonists to house soldiers). Answers will vary but should include support from the chapter.

### 3. Main Ideas

**a.** It tried to prevent them from moving west in search of land. **b.** They protested, sometimes violently, and called for its repeal. **c.** to oppose British policies and organize protests

### 4. Critical Thinking

The British felt the colonies should pay taxes to cover colonial expenses. The colonists said no taxes without consent and feared, once begun, taxation might never stop.

### ACTIVITY OPTIONS

**Alternative Assessment**
- Rubrics for a poster, 1.1
- Rubrics for a song, 4.8

# 2 Colonial Resistance Grows

**TERMS & NAMES**
Crispus Attucks
Townshend Acts
writs of assistance
Samuel Adams
Boston Massacre
John Adams
committee of correspondence
Boston Tea Party

**MAIN IDEA**
Many Americans began to organize to oppose British policies.

**WHY IT MATTERS NOW**
Americans continue to protest what they view as wrongs and injustices.

### ONE AMERICAN'S STORY

**Crispus Attucks knew about the struggle for freedom. The son of an African-American father and a Native American mother, Attucks was born into slavery in Framingham, Massachusetts, around 1723. As a young man, Attucks escaped by running away to sea. He spent the next 20 years as a sailor, working on whaling boats. To avoid recapture, he used a false name, calling himself Michael Johnson.**

**In March 1770, Attucks found himself in Boston, where feelings against British rule were reaching a fever pitch. The words *freedom* and *liberty* seemed to be on everyone's lips. One night Attucks heard about a disturbance involving colonists and British troops and decided to investigate. He had no idea that he was about to play a key role in American history—losing his life to a British bullet in a protest that came to be known as the Boston Massacre. In this section, you will read how the tension between Britain and its colonies led to violence.**

Crispus Attucks, a sailor of African-American and Native American ancestry, was an early hero of America's struggle for freedom.

## 1 The Townshend Acts Are Passed

After the uproar over the Stamp Act, Britain hoped to avoid further conflict. Even so, it still needed to raise money to pay for troops and other expenses in America. The Quartering Act was not working. Most of the British army was in New York, and New York saw that as an unfair burden. Its assembly refused to pay to house the troops.

The king's finance minister, Charles Townshend, told Parliament that he had a way to raise revenue in the colonies. So in 1767, Parliament passed his plan, known as the **Townshend Acts.**

The first of the Townshend Acts suspended New York's assembly until New Yorkers agreed to provide housing for the troops. The other acts placed duties, or import taxes, on various goods brought into the colonies, such as glass, paper, paint, lead, and tea. Townshend thought that duties, which were collected before the goods entered the colonies, would anger the colonists less than the direct taxes of the Stamp Act. The money raised would be used to pay the salaries of British governors and other officials in the colonies. To enforce the acts, British officers





## SECTION OBJECTIVES

1. To explain the Townshend Acts
2. To describe why and how the colonists protested the Townshend Acts
3. To explain the Boston Massacre
4. To summarize the Tea Act and the Boston Tea Party

### CRITICAL THINKING

Making Inferences, p. 164
Recognizing Propaganda, p. 165
Drawing Conclusions, pp. 166, 167
Recognizing Effects, p. 167

**Why It Matters Now**
- Politics and Protest, pp. 11–12

## FOCUS & MOTIVATE

### 5-MINUTE WARM-UP

**Evaluating** Answering these questions will help students understand how colonial resentment toward the British grew.

1. Look at the engraving on page 165. Based on this picture, who appears to be at fault for the Boston Massacre?
2. Why might colonial leaders interested in independence want to blame the massacre on the British?

**Warm-Up Transparency WT6**

## INSTRUCT

### INSTRUCT: OBJECTIVE 1

**The Townshend Acts Are Passed**

Key Questions
- What were the Townshend Acts?
- Why did the British think the acts would anger the colonists less than the Stamp Act did?
- How did the British attempt to enforce the Townshend Acts?

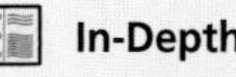

**In-Depth Resources: Unit 2**
- Guided Reading, p. 4
- Building Vocabulary, p. 8

## RECOMMENDED RESOURCES

**In-Depth Resources: Unit 2**
- Guided Reading, p. 4
- Building Vocabulary, p. 8
- Skillbuilder Practice, p. 9
- Reteaching Activity, p. 19

**Reading Study Guide** (Spanish and English), pp. 55–56

**Why It Matters Now**
- Politics and Protest, pp. 11–12

**Formal Assessment**
- Section Quiz, p. 89

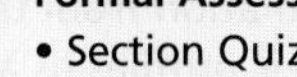

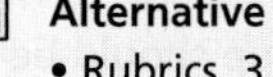

**Alternative Assessment**
- Rubrics, 3.6
- Rubrics, 5.4

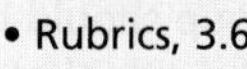

**Access for Students Acquiring English/ESL**
- Guided Reading, p. 36
- Skillbuilder Practice, p. 40

**Technology Resources**

**Humanities Transparency HT12**
- *The Copley Family*

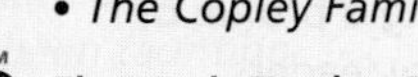

**Electronic Teacher Tools with Test Maker**

**ClassZone**
www.mcdougallittell.com

## AMERICA'S HISTORY MAKERS

**John and Samuel Adams**

Though different in ages and personalities—John was cautious and reasonable, Samuel was fiery and boisterous—the two cousins got along rather well. However, the two men's relationship collapsed over the issue of politics. In 1796, John ran for president as a member of the Federalist Party—a party Samuel considered elitist and an enemy of the common people. Samuel accused John of betraying "the principles of '75," and he campaigned vigorously against his cousin. Nonetheless, John Adams and the Federalists won the election. Disgusted, Samuel retired from political life. He died in 1803.

**Answer: Samuel used fiery speeches and propaganda, while John believed in moderate but steady resistance.**

## INSTRUCT: OBJECTIVE 4

**The Tea Act/The Boston Tea Party**

Key Questions

- For what reason did the British repeal the Townshend Acts?
- Why did the Tea Act upset the colonists?
- What was the Boston Tea Party?

## AMERICA'S HISTORY MAKERS

**SAMUEL ADAMS**
**1722–1803**

Samuel Adams was a Harvard graduate. But unlike his cousin John, also a Harvard graduate, he showed little skill for the law. Later, when he took control of the family business, he lost his father's fortune. Yet he succeeded in one important undertaking—moving America toward independence.

Adams's true talent lay in rousing people to action in support of a cause. A fiery orator and a master of propaganda, he used words as a weapon. One British official said that "every dip of his pen stings."

**JOHN ADAMS**
**1735–1826**

John Adams, unlike Samuel, was considered a moderate in the struggle against Britain. He was an important voice of reason and at first opposed resisting by force.

Adams believed in the rule of law. He called his defense of the soldiers in the Boston Massacre "one of the best pieces of service I ever rendered my country."

Eventually, Adams became convinced that only outright resistance would gain liberty for America. He said, "Britain has at last driven America, to the last Step, a compleat Seperation from her."

**How did the cousins John and Samuel Adams differ in the way they protested British actions?**

the colonial cause but wanted to show that the colonists followed the rule of law. Adams argued that the soldiers had acted in self-defense. The jury agreed. To many colonists, however, the Boston Massacre would stand as a symbol of British tyranny.

## 4 The Tea Act

The colonists were unaware that on the day of the Boston Massacre, Parliament proposed the repeal of the Townshend Acts. One month later, all the acts except the tax on tea were repealed. The colonial boycott had been effective—British trade had been hurt. But Parliament kept the tea tax to show that it still had the right to tax the colonists. For most Americans, the crisis was over.

Samuel Adams, however, wanted to make sure people did not forget the cause of liberty. He started a drive to form **committees of correspondence** in various towns in Massachusetts. These groups exchanged letters on colonial affairs. Before long, committees throughout Massachusetts were corresponding with one another and with committees in other colonies.

Then, in 1773, Parliament opened up old wounds when it passed the Tea Act. Tea was very popular in the colonies, but much of it was smuggled in from Holland. The Tea Act gave the British East India Company control over the American tea trade. The tea would arrive in the colonies only in the trading company's ships and be sold there by its merchants. Colonists who had not been paying any tax on smuggled tea would now have to pay a tax on this regulated tea. This enraged colonial shippers and merchants. The colonists wondered what Parliament would do next.

*Reading* **History**

**C. Drawing Conclusions** Why did Samuel Adams think that the colonists might forget the cause of liberty?

**C. Possible Answer** Adams may have thought that since there was no crisis, the colonists would just go back to being involved in their daily lives.



**ACTIVITY OPTIONS**

**INTERDISCIPLINARY LINK: LANGUAGE ARTS**

**BLOCK SCHEDULING**

**COMMITTEES OF CORRESPONDENCE**

**Class Time** One class period

**Task** Writing a letter from a committee of correspondence

**Purpose** To identify and explain the issues that concerned the colonists

**Supplies Needed**

- Reference materials on colonial objections to British policies
- Internet access for additional resources

**Activity** Have students break into small groups, each representing a committee of correspondence from a particular colony. Have each group draft a letter to another colony's committee discussing the issues of the day. Letters should display the committee's feelings as well as suggest a possible course of action. Tell students to use whatever style of writing they wish to most effectively convey their message. Have a member from each group read the group's letter before the class.

# 2 Colonial Resistance Grows

**MAIN IDEA**

Many Americans began to organize to oppose British policies.

**WHY IT MATTERS NOW**

Americans continue to protest what they view as wrongs and injustices.

**TERMS & NAMES**

Crispus Attucks
Townshend Acts
writs of assistance
Samuel Adams
Boston Massacre
John Adams
committee of correspondence
Boston Tea Party

## ONE AMERICAN'S STORY

**Crispus Attucks** knew about the struggle for freedom. The son of an African-American father and a Native American mother, Attucks was born into slavery in Framingham, Massachusetts, around 1723. As a young man, Attucks escaped by running away to sea. He spent the next 20 years as a sailor, working on whaling boats. To avoid recapture, he used a false name, calling himself Michael Johnson.

In March 1770, Attucks found himself in Boston, where feelings against British rule were reaching a fever pitch. The words *freedom* and *liberty* seemed to be on everyone's lips. One night Attucks heard about a disturbance involving colonists and British troops and decided to investigate. He had no idea that he was about to play a key role in American history—losing his life to a British bullet in a protest that came to be known as the Boston Massacre. In this section, you will read how the tension between Britain and its colonies led to violence.

Crispus Attucks, a sailor of African-American and Native American ancestry, was an early hero of America's struggle for freedom.

## 1 The Townshend Acts Are Passed

After the uproar over the Stamp Act, Britain hoped to avoid further conflict. Even so, it still needed to raise money to pay for troops and other expenses in America. The Quartering Act was not working. Most of the British army was in New York, and New York saw that as an unfair burden. Its assembly refused to pay to house the troops.

The king's finance minister, Charles Townshend, told Parliament that he had a way to raise revenue in the colonies. So in 1767, Parliament passed his plan, known as the **Townshend Acts**.

The first of the Townshend Acts suspended New York's assembly until New Yorkers agreed to provide housing for the troops. The other acts placed duties, or import taxes, on various goods brought into the colonies, such as glass, paper, paint, lead, and tea. Townshend thought that duties, which were collected before the goods entered the colonies, would anger the colonists less than the direct taxes of the Stamp Act. The money raised would be used to pay the salaries of British governors and other officials in the colonies. To enforce the acts, British officers



## SECTION OBJECTIVES

1. To explain the Townshend Acts
2. To describe why and how the colonists protested the Townshend Acts
3. To explain the Boston Massacre
4. To summarize the Tea Act and the Boston Tea Party

**CRITICAL THINKING**

Making Inferences, p. 164
Recognizing Propaganda, p. 165
Drawing Conclusions, pp. 166, 167
Recognizing Effects, p. 167

 **Why It Matters Now**
- Politics and Protest, pp. 11–12

## FOCUS & MOTIVATE

### 5-MINUTE WARM-UP

**Evaluating** Answering these questions will help students understand how colonial resentment toward the British grew.

1. Look at the engraving on page 165. Based on this picture, who appears to be at fault for the Boston Massacre?
2. Why might colonial leaders interested in independence want to blame the massacre on the British?

 **Warm-Up Transparency WT6**

## INSTRUCT

**INSTRUCT: OBJECTIVE 1**

**The Townshend Acts Are Passed**

Key Questions
- What were the Townshend Acts?
- Why did the British think the acts would anger the colonists less than the Stamp Act did?
- How did the British attempt to enforce the Townshend Acts?

 **In-Depth Resources: Unit 2**
- Guided Reading, p. 4
- Building Vocabulary, p. 8

## RECOMMENDED RESOURCES

 **In-Depth Resources: Unit 2**
- Guided Reading, p. 4
- Building Vocabulary, p. 8
- Skillbuilder Practice, p. 9
- Reteaching Activity, p. 19

 **Reading Study Guide** (Spanish and English), pp. 55–56

**Why It Matters Now**
- Politics and Protest, pp. 11–12

 **Formal Assessment**
- Section Quiz, p. 89

 **Alternative Assessment**
- Rubrics, 3.6
- Rubrics, 5.4

 **Access for Students Acquiring English/ESL**
- Guided Reading, p. 36
- Skillbuilder Practice, p. 40

Technology Resources

 **Humanities Transparency HT12**
- *The Copley Family*

 **Electronic Teacher Tools with Test Maker**

 **ClassZone**
www.mcdougallittell.com

**INSTRUCT: OBJECTIVE 2**

**The Reasons for Protest/Tools of Protest**

Key Questions

- Why did the writs of assistance anger the colonists?
- What methods did the colonists use to protest the Townshend Acts?

**dailylife**

**Women and Protest**

Colonial women took very seriously their boycott of British items such as tea. On one occasion, for example, a young woman named Susan Boudinot was offered a cup of tea while visiting the home of New Jersey governor William Franklin. She politely accepted the drink and then threw it out of the window.

Some women even put their commitment to the struggle above their social relationships. In Mecklenburg, North Carolina, a group of women signed a pledge to allow only men who had signed up for military service to court them.

**Humanities Transparency HT12**
- *The Copley Family*

would use **writs of assistance,** or search warrants, to enter homes or businesses to search for smuggled goods.

## 2 The Reasons for Protest

Protests immediately broke out at news of the Townshend Acts. New Yorkers were angry that their elected assembly had been suspended. People throughout the colonies were upset that Britain was placing new taxes on them. "The issue," said John Dickinson, an important Pennsylvania lawyer, was "whether Parliament can legally take money out of our pockets without our consent." He explained his opposition to the Townshend Acts in essays called *Letters from a Farmer in Pennsylvania,* published in 1767.

A. Answer
He says that happiness depends on freedom, which depends on security of property. Taxes imposed without consent take away that security and should be opposed.

*Reading***History**

**A. Making Inferences** Why does Dickinson believe that taxes interfere with happiness?

**daily life**

**WOMEN AND PROTEST**

Women were not allowed to participate in political life in the colonies. So their role in protesting British actions was not as prominent as that of men. However, women made their beliefs known by taking part in demonstrations.

Also, some women formed the Daughters of Liberty. This was a patriotic organization that joined in the boycott of British tea and other goods. The refusal of these colonial women to use British imports caused them personal hardship. They were forced to make many of the boycotted items, such as clothing, themselves.

*A VOICE FROM THE PAST*

Let these truths be . . . impressed on our minds—that we cannot be happy without being free—that we cannot be free without being secure in our property—that we cannot be secure in our property if without our consent others may . . . take it away—that taxes imposed on us by Parliament do thus take it away—that duties laid for the sole purpose of raising money are taxes—that attempts to lay such duties should be instantly and firmly opposed.

**John Dickinson,** quoted in *A New Age Now Begins* by Page Smith

The colonists were also angry about the writs of assistance. Many believed, as James Otis had argued (see page 159), that the writs went against their natural rights. These rights had been described by English philosopher John Locke during the Enlightenment. The law of nature, said Locke, teaches that "no one ought to harm another in his life, health, liberty, or possessions." The colonists felt that the Townshend Acts were a serious threat to their rights and freedoms.

### Tools of Protest

To protest the Townshend Acts, colonists in Boston announced another boycott of British goods in October 1767. The driving force behind this protest was **Samuel Adams,** a leader of the Boston Sons of Liberty. Adams urged colonists to continue to resist British controls.

The boycott spread throughout the colonies. The Sons of Liberty pressured shopkeepers not to sell imported goods. The Daughters of Liberty called on colonists to weave their own cloth and use American products. As a result, trade with Britain fell sharply.

Colonial leaders asked for peaceful protests. Articles in the *Boston Gazette* asked the people to remain calm—



**ACTIVITY OPTIONS**

**INDIVIDUAL NEEDS: GIFTED AND TALENTED**

**IMPACT OF THE INDIVIDUAL**

**Class Time** One class period

**Task** Creating a profile of Revolutionary leaders

**Purpose** To describe the personal characteristics and leadership qualities of Revolutionary leaders

**Supplies Needed**
- Reference materials on patriots of the Revolutionary War
- Internet access for additional resources

**Activity** Have small groups of students select at least three of the individuals named in this section. They should prepare a profile of each individual by using the information from the text and outside references. Then they should present their profiles as a "Who Am I?" challenge, without revealing the name of the person to the class. After the correct answer has been given, the small group should be prepared to tell the class how that individual influenced the colonists' move toward independence.

This engraving, *The Bloody Massacre Perpetrated in King Street* by Boston silversmith Paul Revere, appeared in the *Boston Gazette.*

"no mobs. . . . Constitutional methods are best." However, tempers were running high. When customs officers in Boston tried to seize the American merchant ship *Liberty,* which was carrying smuggled wine, a riot broke out. The rioters forced the customs officers to flee.

Fearing a loss of control, officials called for more British troops. A defiant Samuel Adams replied, "We will destroy every soldier that dares put his foot on shore. . . . I look upon them as foreign enemies."

## 3 The Boston Massacre

In the fall of 1768, 1,000 British soldiers (known as redcoats for their bright red jackets) arrived in Boston under the command of General Thomas Gage. With their arrival, tension filled the streets of Boston.

Since the soldiers were poorly paid, they hired themselves out as workers, usually at rates lower than those of American workers. Resentment against the redcoats grew. Soldiers and street youths often yelled insults at each other. "Lobsters for sale!" the youths would yell, referring to the soldiers' red coats. "Yankees!" the soldiers jeered. *Yankee* was supposed to be an insult, but the colonists soon took pride in the name.

On March 5, 1770, tensions finally exploded into violence. A group of youths and dockworkers—among them Crispus Attucks—started trading insults in front of the Custom House. A fight broke out, and the soldiers began firing. Attucks and four laborers were killed.

*Reading* **History**

**B. Recognizing Propaganda** How did the use of the word *massacre* show an anti-British view?

B. Answer
A massacre is a mass killing, often planned; this was not a massacre.

The Sons of Liberty called the shooting the **Boston Massacre.** They said that Attucks and the four others had given their lives for freedom. The incident became a tool for anti-British propaganda in newspaper articles, pamphlets, and posters. The people of Boston were outraged.

Meanwhile, the redcoats who had fired the shots were arrested for murder. **John Adams,** a lawyer and cousin of Samuel Adams, defended them in court. Adams was criticized for taking the case. He replied that the law should be "deaf . . . to the clamors of the populace." He supported



### MORE ABOUT . . .

**The Boston Massacre**

Much about Paul Revere's famous Boston Massacre engraving is less than accurate. The work depicts only seven British musket men, while eight were charged in the incident. Furthermore, Crispus Attucks, reportedly the first man killed in the shootings, does not appear in the engraving.

Even Revere's claim as the artist of the engraving is a bit misleading. Revere borrowed heavily from a piece done by Henry Pelham. He rushed his work to the public ahead of Pelham's. By the time Pelham could protest, Revere's now-famous work was going up on walls throughout Boston.

### INSTRUCT: OBJECTIVE 3

**The Boston Massacre**

Key Questions

- Why did colonists in Boston resent the presence of so many British soldiers?
- How did the Boston Massacre begin? What was the outcome?
- Why was the massacre an important event in the cause for independence?

### ACTIVITY OPTIONS

### SKILLBUILDER MINI-LESSON: RECOGNIZING PROPAGANDA

**Explaining the Skill** Propaganda is verbal or visual communication that aims to influence people's opinions, emotions, or actions. Visual propaganda often employs symbols or images to grab attention. Wartime propaganda often seeks to portray the home country as especially good.

**Applying the Skill** The Boston Massacre—especially as it was portrayed in articles and paintings—was considered an effective tool of anti-British propaganda. Examine the image of the massacre, as well as the text describing it on page 165, and answer the following questions.

1. Why might this engraving have stirred anti-British feeling among colonists? *(It shows British soldiers shooting colonists.)*
2. Based on the text, what aspect of the incident does the engraving leave out? *(the fact that the colonists had been taunting and fighting with the soldiers before the shooting began)*
3. How might an engraving of the massacre have differed? *(It might have shown the soldiers shooting in self-defense.)*

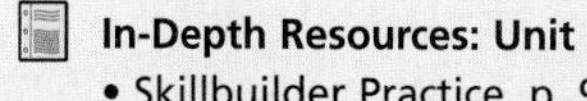

**In-Depth Resources: Unit 2**
- Skillbuilder Practice, p. 9

## AMERICA'S HISTORY MAKERS

**John and Samuel Adams**

Though different in ages and personalities—John was cautious and reasonable, Samuel was fiery and boisterous—the two cousins got along rather well. However, the two men's relationship collapsed over the issue of politics. In 1796, John ran for president as a member of the Federalist Party—a party Samuel considered elitist and an enemy of the common people. Samuel accused John of betraying "the principles of '75," and he campaigned vigorously against his cousin. Nonetheless, John Adams and the Federalists won the election. Disgusted, Samuel retired from political life. He died in 1803.

Answer: Samuel used fiery speeches and propaganda, while John believed in moderate but steady resistance.

### INSTRUCT: OBJECTIVE 4

**The Tea Act/The Boston Tea Party**

Key Questions

- For what reason did the British repeal the Townshend Acts?
- Why did the Tea Act upset the colonists?
- What was the Boston Tea Party?

## AMERICA'S HISTORY MAKERS

**SAMUEL ADAMS**
**1722–1803**

Samuel Adams was a Harvard graduate. But unlike his cousin John, also a Harvard graduate, he showed little skill for the law. Later, when he took control of the family business, he lost his father's fortune. Yet he succeeded in one important undertaking—moving America toward independence.

Adams's true talent lay in rousing people to action in support of a cause. A fiery orator and a master of propaganda, he used words as a weapon. One British official said that "every dip of his pen stings."

**JOHN ADAMS**
**1735–1826**

John Adams, unlike Samuel, was considered a moderate in the struggle against Britain. He was an important voice of reason and at first opposed resisting by force.

Adams believed in the rule of law. He called his defense of the soldiers in the Boston Massacre "one of the best pieces of service I ever rendered my country."

Eventually, Adams became convinced that only outright resistance would gain liberty for America. He said, "Britain has at last driven America, to the last Step, a compleat Seperation from her."

**How did the cousins John and Samuel Adams differ in the way they protested British actions?**

the colonial cause but wanted to show that the colonists followed the rule of law. Adams argued that the soldiers had acted in self-defense. The jury agreed. To many colonists, however, the Boston Massacre would stand as a symbol of British tyranny.

## 4 The Tea Act

The colonists were unaware that on the day of the Boston Massacre, Parliament proposed the repeal of the Townshend Acts. One month later, all the acts except the tax on tea were repealed. The colonial boycott had been effective—British trade had been hurt. But Parliament kept the tea tax to show that it still had the right to tax the colonists. For most Americans, the crisis was over.

Samuel Adams, however, wanted to make sure people did not forget the cause of liberty. He started a drive to form **committees of correspondence** in various towns in Massachusetts. These groups exchanged letters on colonial affairs. Before long, committees throughout Massachusetts were corresponding with one another and with committees in other colonies.

Then, in 1773, Parliament opened up old wounds when it passed the Tea Act. Tea was very popular in the colonies, but much of it was smuggled in from Holland. The Tea Act gave the British East India Company control over the American tea trade. The tea would arrive in the colonies only in the trading company's ships and be sold there by its merchants. Colonists who had not been paying any tax on smuggled tea would now have to pay a tax on this regulated tea. This enraged colonial shippers and merchants. The colonists wondered what Parliament would do next.

*Reading* **History**

**C. Drawing Conclusions** Why did Samuel Adams think that the colonists might forget the cause of liberty?

C. Possible Answer Adams may have thought that since there was no crisis, the colonists would just go back to being involved in their daily lives.



**ACTIVITY OPTIONS**

**INTERDISCIPLINARY LINK: LANGUAGE ARTS**

BLOCK SCHEDULING

**COMMITTEES OF CORRESPONDENCE**

**Class Time** One class period

**Task** Writing a letter from a committee of correspondence

**Purpose** To identify and explain the issues that concerned the colonists

**Supplies Needed**

- Reference materials on colonial objections to British policies
- Internet access for additional resources

**Activity** Have students break into small groups, each representing a committee of correspondence from a particular colony. Have each group draft a letter to another colony's committee discussing the issues of the day. Letters should display the committee's feelings as well as suggest a possible course of action. Tell students to use whatever style of writing they wish to most effectively convey their message. Have a member from each group read the group's letter before the class.

## The Boston Tea Party

Protests against the Tea Act took place all over the colonies. In Charleston, South Carolina, colonists unloaded tea and let it rot on the docks. In New York City and Philadelphia, colonists blocked tea ships from landing. In Boston, the Sons of Liberty organized what came to be known as the **Boston Tea Party.**

*Reading* **History**
**D. Reading a Map** Find Boston Harbor on the map on page 172.

On the evening of December 16, 1773, a group of men disguised as Native Americans boarded three tea ships docked in Boston Harbor. One of the men, George Hewes, a Boston shoemaker, later recalled the events.

Colonists dumped hundreds of chests of tea into Boston Harbor in 1773 to protest the Tea Act.

*A VOICE FROM THE PAST*

We then were ordered by our commander to open the hatches and take out all the chests of tea and throw them overboard. . . . In about three hours from the time we went on board, we had thus broken and thrown overboard every tea chest to be found on the ship, while those in the other ships were disposing of the tea in the same way, at the same time.

**George Hewes,** quoted in *A Retrospect of the Boston Tea-Party*

E. Possible Answer Britain wanted repayment for the destroyed tea and wanted those involved brought to trial.

*Reading* **History**
**E. Recognizing Effects** How did Britain react to the Tea Party?

That night, Hewes and the others destroyed 342 chests of tea. Many colonists rejoiced at the news. They believed that Britain would now see how strongly colonists opposed taxation without representation.

Others doubted that destroying property was the best way to settle the tax debate. Some colonial leaders offered to pay for the tea if Parliament would repeal the Tea Act. Britain rejected the offer. It not only wanted repayment, but it also wanted the men who destroyed the tea to be brought to trial. The British reaction to the Boston Tea Party would fan the flames of rebellion in the 13 colonies, as you will read in the next section.

### Section 2 Assessment

**1. Terms & Names**

**Identify:**
- Crispus Attucks
- Townshend Acts
- writs of assistance
- Samuel Adams
- Boston Massacre
- John Adams
- committee of correspondence
- Boston Tea Party

**2. Taking Notes**

Create a time line like the one below to show important events described in this section.

1767 — 1773

Which event do you think was the most important? Explain.

**3. Main Ideas**

a. Why did colonists oppose the Townshend Acts?

b. Why were British troops sent to Boston?

c. What prompted the Boston Tea Party?

**4. Critical Thinking**

**Drawing Conclusions** Do you think colonial outrage over the Boston Massacre was justified? Explain.

**THINK ABOUT**
- how the British troops were taunted
- whether troops have the right to fire on citizens

**ACTIVITY OPTIONS**

**SPEECH** / **TECHNOLOGY**

Read more about the Boston Massacre or the Boston Tea Party. Present an **oral report** or plan a **multimedia presentation** about the event.





### MORE ABOUT . . .

**The Boston Tea Party**

The day after the Tea Party, news of the incident spread. It stirred both outrage and admiration. John Adams praised his fellow colonists' actions. "There is a dignity, a majesty, a sublimity, in this last effort of the patriots that I greatly admire," he wrote. However, Benjamin Franklin condemned the act and suggested that Boston repay the ship owners for their lost tea. The fiery Samuel Adams curtly dismissed Franklin's words. "Franklin may be a good philosopher," Adams said, "but he is a bungling politician."

## ASSESS & RETEACH

**Setting the Stage** Have students fill in the next four boxes on the chapter graphic organizer.

**Formal Assessment**
- Section Quiz, p. 89

### RETEACHING ACTIVITY

Help students focus on the cause and effect relationships in this section. Students should copy the graphic below and fill it in with Townshend Acts, Tea Act, Boston Massacre, and Boston Tea Party. When they finish, have them write a paragraph describing the connections between the acts and the events.

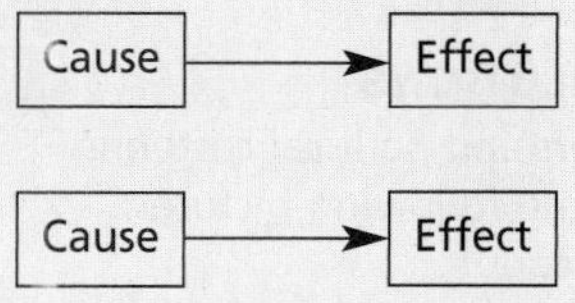

**In-Depth Resources: Unit 2**
- Reteaching Activity, p. 19

### Section 2 Assessment

**1. Terms & Names**

**Crispus Attucks,** p. 163
**Townshend Acts,** p. 163
**writs of assistance,** p. 164
**Samuel Adams,** p. 164
**Boston Massacre,** p. 165
**John Adams,** p. 165
**committee of correspondence,** p. 166
**Boston Tea Party,** p. 167

**2. Taking Notes**

1767: Townshend Acts passed; October 1767: Boston boycotts British goods; March 1770: Boston Massacre; 1773: Tea Act passed; Dec. 1773: Boston Tea Party

Students' responses will vary but should include support from the chapter.

**3. Main Ideas**

**a.** because the acts suspended the New York assembly, imposed new taxes, and called for the use of writs of assistance **b.** to keep order after the riot over the merchant ship *Liberty* **c.** the Tea Act of 1773

**4. Critical Thinking**

Opinions will vary. Justified: soldiers have no right to fire on unarmed citizens; Not Justified: the soldiers were acting in self-defense.

**ACTIVITY OPTIONS**

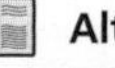
**Alternative Assessment**
- Rubric for an oral report, 3.6
- Rubric for a presentation, 5.4

## Interdisciplinary CHALLENGE

### OBJECTIVE

Students work cooperatively to express persuasive ideas through artwork, words, and statistics that justify the American colonists' goal of independence.

 **BLOCK SCHEDULING**

## PROCEDURE

Gather supplies that students might need, such as posterboard, colored markers, and graph paper. For each challenge, have students form groups of three or four. Ask group members to divide the work among themselves. Then have them choose an option for presenting their solution.

### ART CHALLENGE

**Class Time** 50 minutes

To help students present their viewpoints visually, suggest they consider using these kinds of pictures in their posters or political cartoons:

- *symbols*—images that represent concepts or issues
- *caricatures*—drawings that exaggerate or distort characters to convey a message

### POSSIBLE SOLUTIONS

Students' posters and political cartoons might feature the following pictures:

- a shattered teapot
- a scene from the Boston Tea Party
- caricatures of penniless American tea sellers, unpopular tax collectors, or tyrannical Parliament members

*Interdisciplinary* CHALLENGE

# Fight for Representative Government!

You are a colonist living in Boston on the eve of the American Revolution. Nearly a decade of protest against British policies has failed to secure American rights. Redcoats continue to be quartered in the city. The Tea Act still stands. Now the dumping of tea in Boston Harbor by some Patriots has charged the atmosphere with tension. Trouble lies ahead, but you are determined to fight for a government that will protect your rights.

COOPERATIVE LEARNING On this page are two challenges that you face as the conflict with Britain unfolds. Working with a small group, decide how to deal with each challenge. Choose an option, assign a task to each group member, and do the activity. You will find useful information in the Data File. Present your solutions to the class.

### ART CHALLENGE

***"Do not . . . sip the accursed, dutied STUFF"***

**People all over Boston are worried about the Tea Act. It taxes tea, but it also lets the British East India Company sell tea through its own agents. In time, the plan could drive American tea sellers out of business. How can you protest these threats to American commerce and liberty? Present your viewpoint using one of these options:**

- **Design an anti–Tea Act poster.**
- **Draw a political cartoon showing the dangers of the Tea Act.**

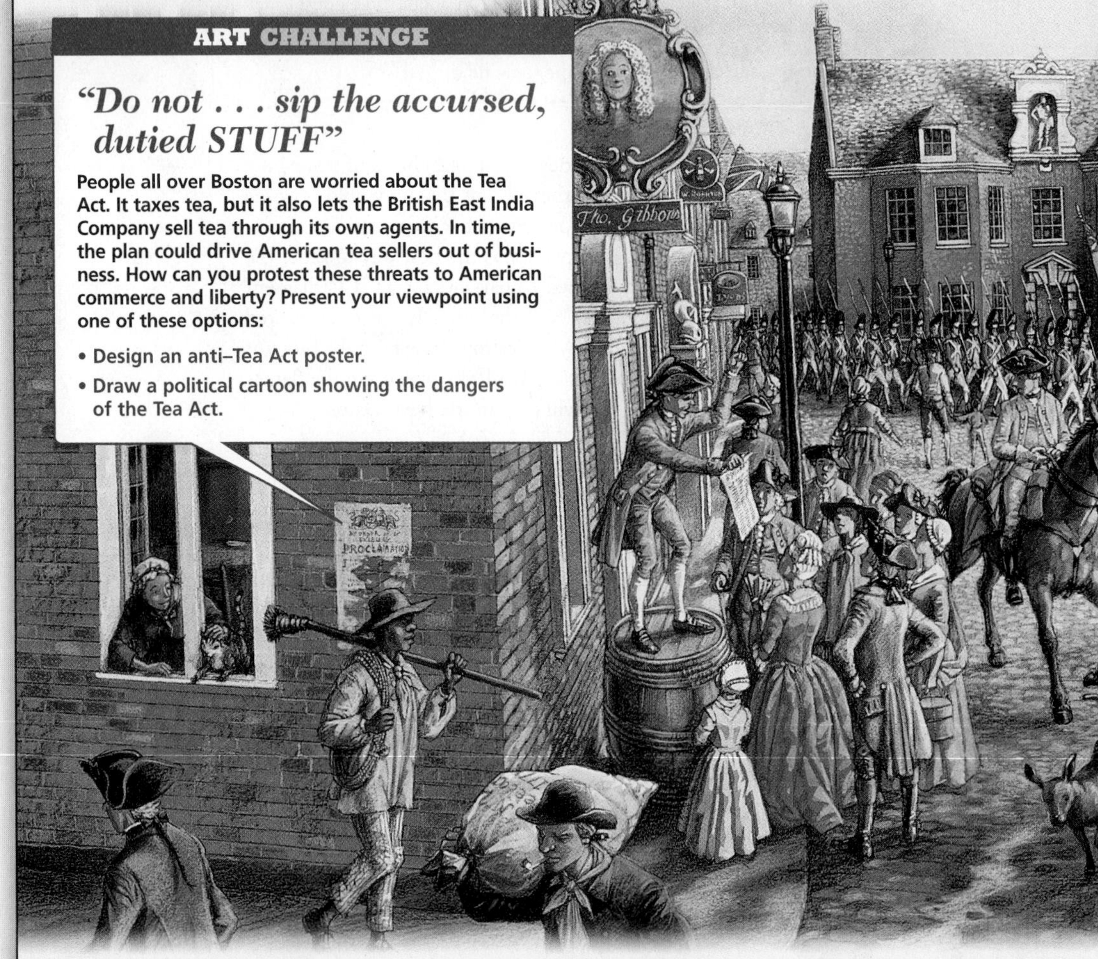




## STANDARDS FOR EVALUATION

### ART CHALLENGE

**Option 1** Posters should
- depict the injustices of the Tea Act.
- convince colonists to take action.

**Option 2** Political cartoons should
- portray historical figures, events, or objects related to the Tea Act.
- include a descriptive caption.

### MATH CHALLENGE

**Option 1** Graphs (bar or line) should
- have clearly labeled axes.
- show the correlation between boycotts and British exports.

**Option 2** Editorials should
- state the viewpoint clearly.
- use supporting facts and evidence.

### CIVICS CHALLENGE

**Option 1** Debate should
- include reasons for or against the tactics.
- include supporting evidence.
- rebut the opposing arguments.

**Option 2** Proposal should
- be specific and concrete.
- provide a clear guide to citizen action.

## MATH CHALLENGE

### "Wear none but your own country linen"

**Years of struggle have taken their toll on Boston. People are tired of soldiers and of boycotting British goods, such as clothing. But the Tea Act presents a huge threat. The Boston Tea Party took care of only one shipment. How can you help encourage the boycott of other British goods, such as clothing? Look at the Data File for help. Present your appeal using one of these options:**

- **Make a graph showing the effect of colonial boycotts on imports of British goods to America.**
- **Write an editorial using statistics to show how American boycotts have hurt the British.**

## ACTIVITY WRAP-UP

Present to the Class **Meet as a group to review your responses to British attacks on American liberty. Pick the most creative solution for each challenge and present these solutions to the class.**

## DATA FILE

### Population in 1774–1775

**Britain:** 7,860,000
**London:** 700,000
**The 13 colonies:** 2,350,000
**Philadelphia:** 33,000
**New York:** 22,000
**Boston:** 16,000

### North American Imports from Britain

(in millions of pounds sterling)

| Year | Amount | Year | Amount |
|---|---|---|---|
| 1763 | 1.6 | 1770 | 1.9 |
| 1764 | 2.3 | 1771 | 4.2 |
| 1765 | 1.9 | 1772 | 3.0 |
| 1766 | 1.8 | 1773 | 2.1 |
| 1767 | 1.9 | 1774 | 2.6 |
| 1768 | 2.2 | 1775 | 0.2 |
| 1769 | 1.3 | 1776 | 0.1 |

### North American Exports to Britain

(in millions of pounds sterling)

| Year | Amount | Year | Amount |
|---|---|---|---|
| 1763 | 1.1 | 1770 | 1.0 |
| 1764 | 1.1 | 1771 | 1.3 |
| 1765 | 1.2 | 1772 | 1.3 |
| 1766 | 1.0 | 1773 | 1.4 |
| 1767 | 1.1 | 1774 | 1.4 |
| 1768 | 1.3 | 1775 | 1.9 |
| 1769 | 1.1 | 1776 | 0.1 |

### Key Boycott Dates

1764 Boycott after passage of Sugar Act
1765 Boycott after passage of Stamp Act
1766 Boycott relaxed after Stamp Act repealed
1767 Boycott after passage of Townshend Acts
1770 Townshend Acts repealed
1774 Boycott after passage of Intolerable Acts

### Sales and Consumption of Tea at the Time of the Boston Tea Party

**British sales:** fourth most important product shipped to America
**American consumption:** 1.2 million pounds per year

Visit www.mcdougallittell.com for more on Revolutionary America.



## MATH CHALLENGE

**Class Time** 50 minutes

Suggest that students look at current newspaper editorials and graphs to use as models. Ask them to consider how statistics can make ideas more meaningful and paint a clearer picture of an event.

### POSSIBLE SOLUTION

Students might convert facts and figures from the Data File into a line graph organized as follows:

- Vertical axis scale ranges from 0 to 4.5 (in millions of pounds sterling) to indicate British Exports to North America.
- Dates on the horizontal axis range from 1763 to 1776. Callouts identify the years that correspond to Key Policy Dates listed in the Data File.
- Points plotted on the line graph correspond to the numbers listed by year in the Data File.

### ALTERNATIVE CHALLENGE

## CIVICS CHALLENGE

### "The destruction of the Tea"

**After the Boston Tea Party, John Adams writes in his diary, "The destruction of the Tea is so bold and it must have so important Consequences." You and other colonists wonder if this protest by the Sons of Liberty was too bold. Was the Boston Tea Party an act of patriotism or terrorism? Present your position using one of these options:**

- **Stage a debate in which you argue for or against the tactics used by the Sons of Liberty.**
- **Write a proposal explaining what citizens should do about unjust laws.**

## ACTIVITY WRAP-UP

To help student groups evaluate the creativity of their challenge solutions, ask them to make a grid with criteria like the one shown. Then have them rate each solution on a scale from 1 to 5.

| | | | | | |
|---|---|---|---|---|---|
| Originality | 1 | 2 | 3 | 4 | 5 |
| Persuasive appeal | 1 | 2 | 3 | 4 | 5 |
| Audience impact | 1 | 2 | 3 | 4 | 5 |
| Overall effectiveness | 1 | 2 | 3 | 4 | 5 |

## SECTION OBJECTIVES

1. To describe the Intolerable Acts
2. To explain how the colonies wavered between war and peace
3. To profile the Midnight Ride
4. To describe the battles of Lexington and Concord

**SKILLBUILDER**
Interpreting Charts, p. 171
Interpreting Maps: Location, Movement, p. 172

**CRITICAL THINKING**
Evaluating, p. 171
Recognizing Effects, p. 172
Drawing Conclusions, p. 173
Supporting Opinions, p. 173

## FOCUS & MOTIVATE

### 5-MINUTE WARM-UP

**Drawing Conclusions** To help students understand the coming war between Britain and America, have them answer these questions.

1. Look at the map on page 172. What were the British forced to do after Concord?
2. What might the British action indicate about the colonists' chances in a war against Britain?

 **Warm-Up Transparency WT6**

## INSTRUCT

### INSTRUCT: OBJECTIVE 

**The Intolerable Acts**
Key Questions
- What were the Intolerable Acts?
- What effect did the Intolerable Acts have on the colonies?
- How did the colonies come to the aid of Massachusetts?

 **In-Depth Resources: Unit 2**
- Guided Reading, p. 5

 **Reading Study Guide** (Spanish and English), pp. 57–58

# 3 The Road to Lexington and Concord

**TERMS & NAMES**
militia
Minuteman
Intolerable Acts
First Continental Congress
Paul Revere
Lexington and Concord
Loyalist
Patriot

| MAIN IDEA | WHY IT MATTERS NOW |
|---|---|
| The tensions between Britain and the colonies led to armed conflict in Massachusetts. | Americans at times still find themselves called upon to fight for their principles. |

### ONE AMERICAN'S STORY

**At dawn on April 19, 1775, some 70 militiamen gathered on the grassy common at the center of Lexington, Massachusetts, a small town near Boston. Captain John Parker, a veteran of the French and Indian War, was their commander. The militia was a force of armed civilians pledged to defend their community. About one-third of the Lexington militia were Minutemen, trained to be "ready to act at a minute's warning." Everyone had heard the news—the British were coming!**

**Each militiaman was equipped with a musket, a bayonet, and ammunition. Parker had spent months drilling his troops, but they had never faced British soldiers. Soon they would meet the British on Lexington Green in the first battle of the Revolutionary War. According to tradition, Parker told his men, "Stand your ground; don't fire unless fired upon, but if they mean to have war, let it begin here."**

**In this section, you will read how colonial protests eventually turned into violent revolution.**

This statue of Captain John Parker stands in Lexington, Massachusetts.

## 1 The Intolerable Acts

The Boston Tea Party had aroused fury in Britain. One British official said that the people of Boston "ought to be knocked about their ears." King George III declared, "We must master them or totally leave them to themselves and treat them as aliens." Britain chose to "master" the colonies.

In 1774, Parliament passed a series of laws to punish the Massachusetts colony and to serve as a warning to other colonies. The British called these laws the Coercive Acts, but they were so harsh that the colonists called them the **Intolerable Acts.**

One of the acts would close the port of Boston until colonists paid for the destroyed tea. Others banned committees of correspondence, allowed Britain to house troops wherever necessary, and let British officials accused of crimes in the colonies stand trial in Britain. To enforce the acts, Parliament appointed General Thomas Gage governor of Massachusetts.

In 1773, Sam Adams had written, "I wish we could arouse the continent." The Intolerable Acts answered his wish. Other colonies



### RECOMMENDED RESOURCES

 **In-Depth Resources: Unit 2**
- Guided Reading, p. 5
- Building Vocabulary, p. 8
- Literature Selection: "Paul Revere's Ride," pp. 14–17
- Reteaching Activity, p. 20

 **Reading Study Guide** (Spanish and English), pp. 57–58

 **Formal Assessment**
- Section Quiz, p. 90

**Alternative Assessment**
- Rubrics, 2.1
- Rubrics, 2.2

 **Access for Students Acquiring English/ESL**
- Guided Reading, p. 37

Technology Resources

 **Critical Thinking Trans. CT17**
- Cause and Effect: Growing Conflict Between Britain and America

 **Electronic Teacher Tools with Test Maker**

 **ClassZone**
www.mcdougallittell.com

immediately offered Massachusetts their support. They sent food and money to Boston. The committees of correspondence also called for a meeting of colonial delegates to discuss what to do next.

## 2 The First Continental Congress Meets

In September 1774, delegates from all the colonies except Georgia met in Philadelphia. At this meeting, called the **First Continental Congress,** delegates voted to ban all trade with Britain until the Intolerable Acts were repealed. They also called on each colony to begin training troops. Georgia agreed to be a part of the actions of the Congress even though it had voted not to send delegates.

The First Continental Congress marked a key step in American history. Although most delegates were not ready to call for independence, they were determined to uphold colonial rights. This meeting planted the seeds of a future independent government. John Adams called it "a nursery of American statesmen." The delegates agreed to meet in seven months, if necessary. By that time, however, fighting with Britain had begun.

*Reading*History
**A. Evaluating** Why do you think the First Continental Congress was important?
A. Possible Answer It was important because it showed that colonists were determined to uphold colonial rights.

## Between War and Peace

The colonists hoped that the trade boycott would force a repeal of the Intolerable Acts. After all, past boycotts had led to the repeal of the Stamp Act and the Townshend Acts. This time, however, Parliament stood firm. It even increased restrictions on colonial trade and sent more troops.

By the end of 1774, some colonists were preparing to fight. In Massachusetts, John Hancock headed the Committee of Safety, which had the power to call out the militia. The colonial troops continued to train.

**CAUSE AND EFFECT:** *Growing Conflict Between Britain and America*

| DATE | BRITISH ACTION | COLONIAL REACTION |
|---|---|---|
| 1763 | Proclamation of 1763 issued | Proclamation leads to anger |
| 1765 | Stamp Act passed | Boycott of British goods; Stamp Act Resolves passed |
| 1766 | Stamp Act repealed; Declaration Act passed | Boycott ended |
| 1767 | Townshend Acts passed | New boycotts; Boston Massacre (March 1770) |
| 1770 | Townshend Acts repealed (April) | Tension between colonies and Britain reduced |
| 1773 | Tea Act passed | Boston Tea Party |
| 1774 | Intolerable Acts passed | First Continental Congress bans trade; militias organized |
| 1775 | Troops ordered to Lexington and Concord, Massachusetts | Militia fights British troops; Second Continental Congress; Continental Army established |

SKILLBUILDER **Interpreting Charts**

1. *What British action caused the first violence in the growing conflict between Britain and America?*
2. *How might the Intolerable Acts be seen as a reaction as well as an action?*

Skillbuilder Answers
1. The Townshend Acts led to the Boston Massacre.
2. The Intolerable Acts were passed as a result of the Boston Tea Party, and they caused the calling of the First Continental Congress.





### INSTRUCT: OBJECTIVE 

**The First Continental Congress Meets/ Between War and Peace**

Key Questions

- What happened at the First Continental Congress?
- How did the colonists protest the Intolerable Acts? How successful were they?
- What did most colonial leaders think about the prospect of war with Britain?

### MORE ABOUT . . .

**First Continental Congress**

In the first session of the Continental Congress, the delegates rejected, by a vote of six to five, Pennsylvania delegate Joseph Galloway's plan to create a union of the colonies. Galloway's Plan of Union included a Grand Council with delegates from all the colonies that would deal with issues affecting more than one colony. Legislation would be subject to Parliament's approval. The council would also have the right to reject Parliament's legislation.

### HISTORY FROM VISUALS

**Interpreting the Chart** Have students note the span of years on the chart, and explain that the graphic shows how British-American tension built up over time and did not stem from one or two incidents. Ask students how colonial leaders might use this chart to defend their desire to break free from Britain. **Possible Response** Colonial leaders might use the chart to emphasize Britain's pattern of injustice and to show how the colonies have been enduring such injustice for too long.

**Extension** Have students work in pairs to create a different way of showing the same information.

 **Critical Thinking Transparency CT17**
- Cause and Effect: Growing Conflict Between Britain and America

### ACTIVITY OPTIONS

**INTERDISCIPLINARY LINK: MATH** 

**EFFECTS OF A BOYCOTT**

**Class Time** 30 minutes

**Task** Determining a boycott's economic impact

**Purpose** To understand the effectiveness of boycotting as a form of protest

**Supplies Needed**
- Scratch paper and pencils
- Calculators

**Activity** Divide students into groups representing British colonial businesses (tea, woolens, foodstuffs, tinware, glass and pottery, textiles). Provide each group with a figure that represents the business's average monthly earnings (e.g., $50,000). Have each group determine the economic impact of a six-month boycott against its products by using several different assigned loss percentages (2 percent, 5 percent, 10 percent, etc.). Each group should share its findings with the class and discuss how the losses would affect the political views of the British businessmen.

**INSTRUCT: OBJECTIVE 3**

**The Midnight Ride**

Key Questions

- What was the role of spies in the pre-revolutionary period?
- Why did Britain's General Gage send troops to Lexington and Concord?
- What was the mission of the midnight riders?

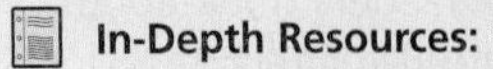

**In-Depth Resources: Unit 2**

- Literature Selection: "Paul Revere's Ride," pp. 14–17

## MORE ABOUT . . .

**A Revolutionary Spy**

One of the most shocking spy cases of the Revolutionary period involved Dr. Benjamin Church, the colonial army's Surgeon General. Church was a member of the inner circle of patriot leaders—and a British agent. Church's spying days ended after a coded message ended up in the hands of colonial leaders. This particular memo described the strength and movement of colonial troops. After serving several months in prison, Church was released in the spring of 1776 due to ill health and allowed to sail to the West Indies. His ship sank during the trip, and he was lost at sea.

## HISTORY FROM VISUALS

**Reading the Map** Point out to students the number of riders, as well as the routes each one took. Ask them who appeared to take the longest route to Lexington. **Answer** William Dawes

**Extension** Have students imagine they are a midnight rider, and ask them to write a brief diary entry about their ride.

Most colonial leaders believed that any fight with Britain would be short. They thought that a show of force would make Britain change its policies. Few expected a war. One who did was Patrick Henry.

*A VOICE FROM THE PAST*

Gentlemen may cry peace, peace—but there is no peace. The war is actually begun! The next gale that sweeps from the north will bring to our ears the clash of resounding arms! Our brethren are already in the field! Why should we idle here? . . . I know not what course others may take. But as for me, give me liberty or give me death.

**Patrick Henry,** quoted in *Patriots* by A. J. Langguth

Henry delivered what became his most famous speech in the Virginia House of Burgesses in March 1775.

## 3 The Midnight Ride

Meanwhile, spies were busy on both sides. Sam Adams had built a spy network to keep watch over British activities. The British had their spies too. They were Americans who were loyal to Britain. From them, General Gage learned that the Massachusetts militia was storing arms and ammunition in Concord, about 20 miles northwest of Boston. He also heard that Sam Adams and John Hancock were in Lexington. On the night of April 18, 1775, Gage ordered his troops to arrest Adams and Hancock in Lexington and to destroy the supplies in Concord.

The Sons of Liberty had prepared for this moment. **Paul Revere,** a Boston silversmith, and a second messenger, William Dawes, were charged with spreading the news about British troop movements. Revere had arranged a system of signals to alert colonists in Charlestown, on the shore opposite Boston. If one lantern burned in the North Church steeple, the British troops were coming by land; if two, they were coming by water. Revere would go across the water from Boston to Charlestown and ride to Lexington and Concord from there. Dawes would take the land route.

*Reading* **History**

**B. Recognizing Effects** What effect might spying have had on the people of Boston?

B. Possible Answer It might have turned them against one another.

**Background**

The signals were a backup system in case Revere was captured.

Skillbuilder Answers

1. Lexington and Concord
2. About six miles

**The Revolution Begins, 1775**

Concord R.
North Bridge
Concord
Revere captured.
Prescott joins Dawes and Revere.
Lexington
Prescott goes forward.
Dawes escapes and turns back.
Sudbury R.
0 2 Miles
0 4 Kilometers
MASS.
Boston
Mystic River
Old North Church
Charlestown
Cambridge
Charles River
Boston
Boston Harbor

- Revere's route
- Dawes' route
- Prescott's route
- British advance
- British retreat
- Battle

**GEOGRAPHY SKILLBUILDER**

**Interpreting Maps**

1. **Location** *Where were battles fought?*
2. **Movement** *What was the distance between Lexington and Concord?*

172

## ACTIVITY OPTIONS

## INDIVIDUAL NEEDS

**STUDENTS ACQUIRING ENGLISH/ESL**

**Social Studies Vocabulary** To help students understand the many social studies concept vocabulary words in this section, have the students add the following list to their personal dictionaries: *militia, musket, intolerable, committees, correspondence, continental, congress, delegate, boycott, repeal.*

Next have students look up the words in a dictionary. Help them understand each word by discussing its meaning and use. Then have them write a definition of the term in their own words in their personal dictionaries.

Have the students find the words in a sentence in the text. (The words listed are in order according to appearance.) Ask them to read the sentence aloud and explain what the sentence means. Finally, have the students write a sentence using the term.

When the British moved, so did Revere and Dawes. They galloped over the countryside on their "midnight ride," spreading the news. In Lexington, they were joined by Dr. Samuel Prescott. When Revere and Dawes were stopped by a British patrol, Prescott broke away and carried the message to Concord.

## 4 Lexington and Concord

At dawn on April 19, some 700 British troops reached Lexington. They found Captain John Parker and about 70 militiamen waiting. The British commander ordered the Americans to drop their muskets. They refused. No one knows who fired first, but within a few minutes eight militiamen lay dead. The British then marched to Concord, where they destroyed military supplies. A battle broke out at a bridge north of town, forcing the British to retreat.

C. Possible Answer The American revolt stunned the world.

Nearly 4,000 Minutemen and militiamen arrived in the area. They lined the road from Concord to Lexington and peppered the retreating redcoats with musket fire. "It seemed as if men came down from the clouds," one soldier said. Only the arrival of 1,000 more troops saved the British from destruction as they scrambled back to Boston.

**Background** British losses totaled 273 soldiers compared to 95 militiamen.

**Lexington and Concord** were the first battles of the Revolutionary War. As Ralph Waldo Emerson later wrote, colonial troops had fired the "shot heard 'round the world." Americans would now have to choose sides and back up their political opinions by force of arms. Those who supported the British were called **Loyalists.** Those who sided with the rebels were **Patriots.** The conflict between the two sides divided communities, families, and friends. The war was on!

*Reading History* **C. Drawing Conclusions** Why did Emerson call it the "shot heard 'round the world"?

### Now and then

**PATRIOTS' DAY**

The "shot heard 'round the world" is celebrated every year in Massachusetts and Maine. Patriots' Day, as it is called, is the third Monday of April. In Concord and nearby towns, modern-day Minutemen like those below reenact the battle that began the Revolution on April 19, 1775. The Boston Marathon is also run on Patriots' Day.

### Section 3 Assessment

**1. Terms & Names**
Identify:
- militia
- Minuteman
- Intolerable Acts
- First Continental Congress
- Paul Revere
- Lexington and Concord
- Loyalist
- Patriot

**2. Taking Notes**
Use a diagram like the one below to show events that led to the Revolutionary War.

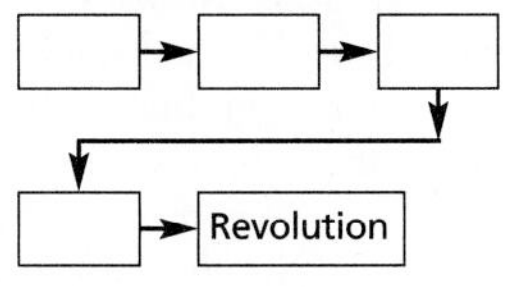


**3. Main Ideas**
a. Why did Britain pass the Intolerable Acts?
b. Who took part in the First Continental Congress?
c. What was the purpose of the "midnight ride"?

**4. Critical Thinking**
Supporting Opinions
Do you think the fighting between Britain and the colonies could have been avoided? Why or why not?

THINK ABOUT
- Britain's attitude toward the colonies
- colonial feelings about Britain

**ACTIVITY OPTIONS**
GEOGRAPHY
MATH
Research the Battles of Lexington and Concord. Draw a **map** of key events or create a **chart** showing statistics from the battles.





**INSTRUCT: OBJECTIVE 4**

**Lexington and Concord**
Key Questions
- What happened at the battles of Lexington and Concord?
- Who were the Loyalists and Patriots?

**MORE ABOUT . . .**

**Lexington and Concord**
The last person said to die in the battles of Lexington and Concord was not a Minuteman or redcoat—but a teenage boy. As the British fought their way back from Concord to Boston, they passed through Charlestown, home of 14-year-old Edward Barber. Barber rushed to his window to watch the fighting. By this time, British troops had endured numerous hit-and-run attacks from colonists. As a result, they considered anyone moving in a house to be a possible sniper. A British soldier aimed his musket at the Barber home and killed young Edward with one shot.

## ASSESS & RETEACH

**Setting the Stage** Have students fill in the next three boxes on the chapter graphic organizer.

**Formal Assessment**
- Section Quiz, p. 90

**RETEACHING ACTIVITY**
Divide students into groups of five. Have each group create a section review, with each member of the group writing a one- or two-sentence summary of a subsection. Have each member read the summary sentence to the rest of the group.

**In-Depth Resources: Unit 2**
- Reteaching Activity, p. 20

### Section 3 Assessment

**1. Terms & Names**
**militia,** p. 170
**Minuteman,** p. 170
**Intolerable Acts,** p. 170
**First Continental Congress,** p. 171
**Paul Revere,** p. 172
**Lexington and Concord,** p. 173
**Loyalist,** p. 173
**Patriot,** p. 173

**2. Taking Notes**
Intolerable Acts; First Continental Congress; troop training; Battles of Lexington and Concord

**3. Main Ideas**
**a.** to punish Massachusetts for the Boston Tea Party **b.** delegates from all the colonies except Georgia **c.** to warn Lexington and Concord that British troops were coming

**4. Critical Thinking**
Students might say the fighting was inevitable; there was little room for compromise; tensions had been building; each side believed it was right.

**ACTIVITY OPTIONS**
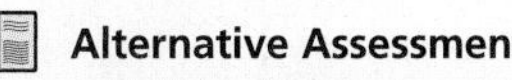
**Alternative Assessment**
- Rubrics for a map, 2.1
- Rubrics for a chart, 2.2

## Literature *Connections*

**OBJECTIVE**

Students analyze a passage from historical fiction that imaginatively depicts issues about the battles of Lexington and Concord during the American Revolution.

 **BLOCK SCHEDULING**

## FOCUS & MOTIVATE

**Making Inferences** To help the students picture the events of *Johnny Tremain,* have them study the image on page 175 and answer the following questions.

1. What information can you gather about the event shown in the picture?
2. How do you think news of this event will reach those who were not present?

### MORE ABOUT . . .

***Johnny Tremain***

Set in Boston from 1773 to 1775, *Johnny Tremain* tells the story of a young silversmith apprentice and his role in events, such as the Boston Tea Party and the battles of Lexington and Concord, that lead to the Revolutionary War. The fictional characters in the novel become involved with actual historical figures, including Paul Revere, William Dawes, General Thomas Gage, John Hancock, and Samuel Adams.

## Literature *Connections*

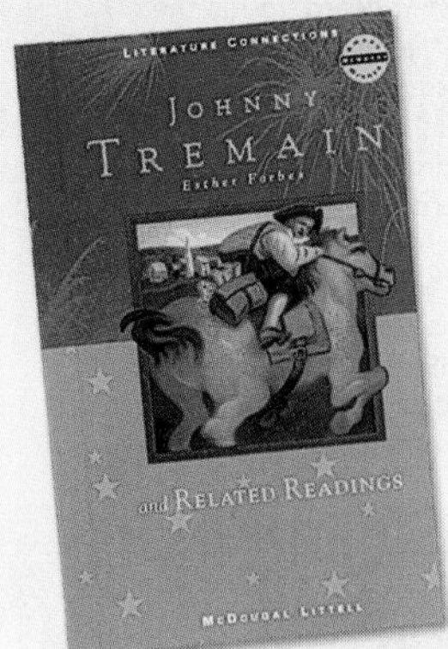


*From*

# Johnny Tremain

*by Esther Forbes*

**In 1775, 16-year-old Johnny Tremain lives in Boston and works as a delivery boy for a newspaper. Because he travels so much around the city, he is able to help the Patriots gather information about what the British are doing.**

**On the night of April 18, Johnny learns that British troops will be leaving on an expedition to seize the gunpowder at Lexington and Concord. He rushes to tell this news to Dr. Joseph Warren, who is a Patriot. Then Johnny goes to bed, wondering if the war has started and worried about his friend Rab, who has gone to join the Minutemen at Lexington.**

So Johnny slept. It was daylight when he woke with Warren's hand upon his shoulder. Outside on Tremont Street he could hear the clumping of army boots. A sergeant was swearing at his men. The soldiers were paraded so close to the house, which stood **flush**[1] with the sidewalkless street, that Johnny at first thought they must be in the room.

Doctor Warren dared speak no louder than a whisper.

"I'm going now."

"Something's happened?"

"Yes." He motioned Johnny to follow him into the kitchen. This room was on the back of the house. They could talk without danger of being overheard by the troops in the street.

Doctor Warren had on the same clothes as the day before. He had not been to bed. But now his hat was on his head. His black bag of instruments and medicines was packed and on the table. Silently he put milk, bread, herrings beside it, and gestured to Johnny to join him.

"Where did it begin?" asked Johnny.

"Lexington."

"Who won?"

"They did. Seven hundred against seventy. It wasn't a battle. It was . . . just target practice . . . for them. Some of our men were killed and the British **huzzaed**[2] and took the road to Concord."

"And did they get our supplies there?"

"I don't know. Paul Revere sent for me just after the firing on Lexington Green."

The young man's usually fresh-colored face was **haggard**[3]. He knew the seriousness of this day for himself and for his country.

"But everywhere the alarm is spreading. Men are grabbing their guns—marching for Concord. Paul Revere did get through in time last night. Billy Dawes a little later. Hundreds—maybe thousands—of Minute Men are on the march. Before the day's over, there'll be real fighting—not target practice. But Gage doesn't know that it's begun. You see, long before Colonel Smith got to Lexington—just as soon as he heard that Revere had warned the country—he sent back for reinforcements. For Earl Percy. You and I, Johnny, are just about the only people in Boston who know that blood has already been shed."

"Were many killed—at Lexington?"

"No, not many. They stood up—just a handful. The British fired on them. It was dawn."

Johnny licked his lips. "Did they tell you the names of those killed?"

1. **flush:** in a line with.
2. **huzzaed:** cheered.
3. **haggard:** tired.



### ACTIVITY OPTIONS

### INDIVIDUAL NEEDS

#### LESS PROFICIENT READERS

**Building Language Skills** Call on some fluent readers to perform an oral reading of the passage from *Johnny Tremain* for small groups of less proficient readers. In each group, have two students read aloud the dialogue between Johnny and Doctor Warren. Coach the readers to express the emotions conveyed in the characters' spoken words.

After the oral reading, have the less proficient readers in each group dramatize moments from the scene they have just listened to. Assuming the role of either Johnny or Doctor Warren, they can take turns retelling parts of the conversation. As an alternative, student groups can create a comic strip version of the passage, using speech balloons to retell the discussion between Johnny and Doctor Warren.

"No. Did Rab get out in time?"

"Yes. Last Sunday."

The Doctor's clear blue eyes darkened. He knew what was in Johnny's mind. He picked up his bag. "I've got to get to them. They'll need surgeons. Then, too, I'd rather die fighting than on a gallows. Gage won't be so **lenient**[4] now—soon as he learns war has begun."

"Wait until I get my shoes on."

"No, Johnny, you are to stay here today. Pick up for me any information. For instance, out of my bedroom window I can see soldiers standing the length of the street 'way over to the Common. You find out what regiments are being sent—and all that. And today go about and listen to what folk are saying. And the names of any the British arrest. We know Gage expects to move his men back here tonight. If so, there'll be a lot of confusion getting them into town. You watch your chance and slip out to me."

"Where'll I find you?"

" . . . Ask about."

"I will do so."

"They've begun it. We'll end it, but this war . . . it may last quite a long time."

They shook hands silently. Johnny knew that Warren was always conscious of the fact that he had a crippled hand. Everybody else had accepted and forgotten it. The back door closed softly. Warren was gone.

Johnny went to the **surgery**,[5] put on his boots and jacket. The wall clock said eight o'clock. It was time to be about. There was no leaving by the front door. The soldiers were leaning against it. Through the curtains of the windows he could see the muskets. He noticed the facings on their uniforms. The Twenty-Third Regiment. The narrow course of Tremont Street was filled to the brim and overflowing with the waiting scarlet-coated men. Like a river of blood. He left by the kitchen.

4. **lenient:** not strict.
5. **surgery:** operating room.

### CONNECT TO HISTORY

1. **Recognizing Effects** What was Johnny's reaction to the news about Lexington? Discuss what roles Johnny and Dr. Warren were to play in the early days of the Revolutionary War.

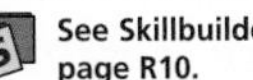
See Skillbuilder Handbook, page R10.

### CONNECT TO TODAY

2. **Researching** Where are there revolutions in the world today?

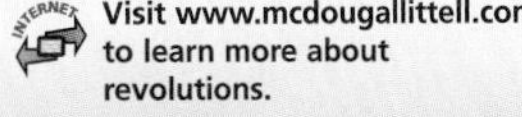
Visit www.mcdougallittell.com to learn more about revolutions.

British troops fire on the Lexington militia on April 19, 1775. The war begins here!

175

## INSTRUCT

Key Questions
- What issues about the battles of Lexington and Concord do Johnny and Doctor Warren discuss?
- How are the British portrayed in this reading selection? Do you think the account is one-sided? Explain.
- What do you predict will happen next in the story?

### MAKING PERSONAL CONNECTIONS

Ask students to think about ways in which young people can contribute to political causes today. What roles might they play to promote America's ideals of freedom? What individual rights would they consider defending?

### VOCABULARY ACTIVITY

Ask students to tell or write a sentence of their own, using each of the words defined on the bottom of pages 174 and 175.

### HISTORY FROM VISUALS

**Interpreting the Painting** Have students cite details from the painting that illustrate Doctor Warren's account of the battle of Lexington on page 174. **Possible Responses** British troops won a quick victory because they appeared well-organized and better prepared to fight. They outnumbered the Minutemen, who are pictured as easy targets.

### CONNECT TO HISTORY

1. **Recognizing Effects Possible Responses** Johnny shows deep personal concern and recognizes the political consequences of the battle at Lexington. Johnny will continue to report and gather information about the British, while Doctor Warren will treat Patriot soldiers wounded in battle.

### CONNECT TO TODAY

2. **Researching** Using the Internet or a current encyclopedia, students should find out about independence movements today. Examples include the Basques in Spain, groups in Wales and Scotland, people in Corsica, the people in Kosovo, and the Tamil people of Sri Lanka. Have students create an annotated map that identifies both the location and the goals of various modern independence movements.

## SECTION OBJECTIVES

1. To describe the early skirmishes between the Continental and British armies
2. To profile British and American responses to the deepening conflict
3. To summarize Thomas Paine's *Common Sense*
4. To explain how colonial leaders officially declared their independence from Britain

### CRITICAL THINKING

Analyzing Points of View, p. 178
Forming Opinions, p. 179
Summarizing, p. 181
Drawing Conclusions, p. 181

## FOCUS & MOTIVATE

### 5-MINUTE WARM-UP

**Interpreting a Painting** These questions will help students see art as a source of information.

1. Look at the picture on page 177. Based on the artist's view, who do you think won the Battle of Bunker Hill?
2. What information about both armies can you learn from studying the painting?

 **Warm-Up Transparency WT6**

## INSTRUCT

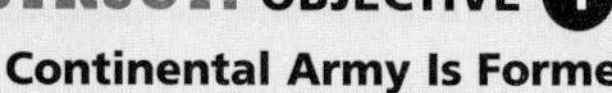

### INSTRUCT: OBJECTIVE 1

**The Continental Army Is Formed/ The Battle of Bunker Hill**

Key Questions

- For what reasons did General Gage move his troops to Boston after the battles at Lexington and Concord?
- What did the Second Continental Congress accomplish?
- Why was the Battle of Bunker Hill considered an important one for the colonists?

 **In-Depth Resources: Unit 2**
- Guided Reading, p. 6
- Primary Source: Letter from Abigail Adams, p. 13

 **America's History Makers**
- Abigail Adams, pp. 23–24

# 4 Declaring Independence

**TERMS & NAMES**
Ethan Allen
artillery
Second Continental Congress
Continental Army
Benedict Arnold
Declaration of Independence
Thomas Jefferson

| MAIN IDEA | WHY IT MATTERS NOW |
|---|---|
| Fighting between American and British troops led the colonies to declare their independence. | The United States of America was founded at this time. |

### ONE AMERICAN'S STORY

**In May 1775—one month after the battle at Lexington and Concord—Abigail Adams wrote to her husband, John Adams. "The house is a Scene of Confusion," she said. Colonial militiamen were camped outside. Everyone was preparing for war. John Adams was away in Philadelphia at the time, meeting with other Patriot leaders at the Second Continental Congress.**

**Abigail and John Adams would spend most of the Revolutionary War apart. In his absence, she ran the household and farm in Braintree, Massachusetts, and raised their four children. During their separation, they exchanged many letters. Abigail was a very sharp observer of the political scene. In one letter, she shared her concerns about the future of the American government.**

Abigail Adams was an early advocate of women's rights and one of the great letter writers in history.

*A VOICE FROM THE PAST*

If we separate from Britain, what Code of Laws will be established? How shall we be governed so as to retain our Liberties? Can any government be free which is not administered by general stated Laws? Who shall frame these Laws? Who will give them force and energy?

**Abigail Adams,** quoted in *Abigail Adams: Witness to a Revolution* by Natalie S. Bober

**These questions would be answered later. First, a war had to be fought and won.**

## 1 The Continental Army Is Formed

After the fighting at Lexington and Concord, militiamen from Massachusetts and other colonies began gathering around Boston. Their numbers eventually reached some 20,000. General Gage decided to move his soldiers from the peninsula opposite Boston to the city itself. Boston was nearly surrounded by water. This fact, he thought, made a colonial attack by land almost impossible.

Not long after, on May 10, 1775, Americans attacked Britain's Fort Ticonderoga on the New York side of Lake Champlain. **Ethan Allen** led



## RECOMMENDED RESOURCES

 **In-Depth Resources: Unit 2**
- Geography Application, pp. 10–11
- Primary Source: Letter from Abigail Adams, p. 13
- Reteaching Activity, p. 21
- Enrichment Activity, p. 22
- History Workshop Resources, p. 23

 **America's History Makers**
- Abigail Adams, pp. 23–24
- Thomas Paine, pp. 25–26

**Reading Study Guide** (Spanish and English), pp. 59–60

 **Formal Assessment**
- Section Quiz, p. 91

 **Alternative Assessment**
- Rubrics, 1.7
- Rubrics, 4.3

 **Access for Students Acquiring English/ESL**
- Guided Reading, p. 38
- Geography Application, pp. 41–42

**Technology Resources**

 **Geography Transparency GT6**
- Battle of Bunker Hill, 1775

 **Electronic Teacher Tools with Test Maker**

 **ClassZone**
www.mcdougallittell.com

this band of backwoodsmen known as the Green Mountain Boys. They captured the fort and its large supply of **artillery**—cannon and large guns. These guns would be used later to drive the British from Boston.

Also on May 10, the **Second Continental Congress** began meeting in Philadelphia. Delegates included John and Samuel Adams, John Hancock, Benjamin Franklin, George Washington, and Patrick Henry. They agreed to form the **Continental Army**. Washington, who was from Virginia, was chosen as its commanding general. He had served as a colonial officer with the British during the French and Indian War. Congress also authorized the printing of paper money to pay the troops. It was beginning to act as a government.

## The Battle of Bunker Hill

**Background**
The battle was called Bunker Hill because the original plan was to fight the battle there.

Meanwhile, tensions were building in Boston in June 1775. Militiamen seized Bunker Hill and Breed's Hill behind Charlestown. They built fortifications on Breed's Hill. Alarmed, the British decided to attack.

General William Howe crossed the bay with 2,200 British soldiers. Forming in ranks, they marched up Breed's Hill. On the hilltop, the militia waited. According to the legend, Colonel William Prescott ordered, "Don't fire until you see the whites of their eyes!" When the British got close, the militia unleashed murderous fire. The British fell back and then charged again. Finally, they forced the militia off the hill.

*"Don't fire until you see the whites of their eyes!"*
Colonel William Prescott

The redcoats had won the battle of Bunker Hill, but at tremendous cost. More than 1,000 were killed or wounded, compared with some 400 militia casualties. "The loss we have sustained is greater than we can bear," wrote General Gage. The inexperienced colonial militia had held its own against the world's most powerful army.

The bloody fighting between militiamen and British troops is shown in *The Death of General Warren at Bunker Hill* by John Trumbull (1786).

177

### MORE ABOUT . . .

**General Washington**
George Washington did not become commander of the Continental Army without some reservations. Colonial leaders from New England, for example, voiced concerns about handing the army over to a Southerner—Washington was from Virginia.

Washington himself questioned his own abilities. He ultimately accepted the post, but declared, "I feel great distress from a consciousness that my abilities and military experience may not be equal to the extensive and important trust."

### MORE ABOUT . . .

**The Battle of Bunker Hill**
Questionable tactics and overconfidence may have played a role in Britain's difficulty in taking Breed's Hill. British troops moved in tight formation, wearing roughly 125 pounds of gear each. Positioned so close together and slowed by their added weight, the redcoats made easy targets for the colonials shooting at them from above. When the bloody battle had ended, a British officer stated, "From an absurd and destructive confidence, carelessness, or ignorance, we have lost a thousand of our best men and officers."

 **Geography Transparency GT6**
• Battle of Bunker Hill, 1775

### ACTIVITY OPTIONS
### INDIVIDUAL NEEDS

**LESS PROFICIENT READERS**

**Creating a Time Line** To help less proficient readers keep track of events leading up to the adoption of the Declaration of Independence, have them create a time line such as the one to the right and mark the key events of the section. Students should begin with the formation of the Second Continental Congress and end with the signing of the Declaration. After students have completed their time lines, have them discuss which event they think played the greatest role in prompting the colonists to declare their independence from Britain.

**INSTRUCT: OBJECTIVE** 

**A Last Attempt at Peace/**
**The British Retreat from Boston**

Key Questions

- What was the purpose and outcome of the Olive Branch Petition?
- What was the purpose and outcome of the colonial attack on Quebec? on Boston?
- Why did so many Loyalists flee Boston with the British?

 **In-Depth Resources: Unit 2**

- Geography Application: Historic Boston—1775 and Today, pp. 10–11

## Connections TO *LITERATURE*

**Phillis Wheatley**

From a very early age, Wheatley showed herself to have an extraordinary gift for words. With no formal schooling, she mastered the English language just 16 months after arriving from Africa. She wrote her first poem at the age of 14 and soon gained international acclaim for her work. The French writer and philosopher Voltaire commented about Wheatley, "There is right now a Negress who writes excellent verse in English." Wheatley's poetry often dealt with the colonists' struggle against Britain.

## Connections TO *LITERATURE*

**PHILLIS WHEATLEY**

Phillis Wheatley was America's first important African-American poet. She was born in Africa about 1753 and sold into slavery as a child. She was a household servant for the Wheatley family of Boston but was raised and educated as a family member.

Some of Wheatley's poems were about the Patriot cause. Of George Washington, she wrote:

*Proceed, great chief, with*
*virtue on thy side,*
*Thy ev'ry action let the*
*goddess guide.*
*A crown, a mansion, and*
*a throne that shine,*
*With gold unfading,*
*Washington! be thine.*

In other poems, Wheatley connected America's fight against British oppression with the struggle for freedom for enslaved African Americans.

## A Last Attempt at Peace

Despite this deepening conflict, most colonists still hoped for peace. Even some Patriot leaders considered themselves loyal subjects of the king. They blamed Parliament for the terrible events taking place.

In July 1775, moderates in Congress drafted the Olive Branch Petition and sent it to London. This document asked the king to restore harmony between Britain and the colonies. Some members opposed the petition but signed it anyway as a last hope.

**Background**
The olive branch is considered a symbol of peace.

The king rejected the petition, however, and announced new measures to punish the colonies. He would use the British navy to block American ships from leaving their ports. He also would send thousands of hired German soldiers, called Hessians, to fight in America. "When once these rebels have felt a smart blow, they will submit," he declared.

***Reading*History**
**A. Analyzing Points of View** Why did King George reject the petition?
**A. Possible Answer** He was not used to having his authority questioned. He felt that he had a right to demand obedience.

The colonial forces were not going to back down, though. They thought they were equal to the British troops. George Washington knew otherwise. The British soldiers were professionals, while the colonial troops had little training and were poorly equipped. The Massachusetts militia barely had enough gunpowder to fight one battle.

During the summer of 1775, Washington arrived at the militia camp near Boston. He immediately began to gather supplies and train the army. In the fall, Washington approved a bold plan. Continental Army troops would invade Quebec, in eastern Canada. They hoped to defeat British forces there and draw Canadians into the Patriot camp. One of the leaders of this expedition was **Benedict Arnold.** He was an officer who had played a role in the victory at Fort Ticonderoga.

After a grueling march across Maine, Arnold arrived at Quebec in November 1775. By that time, however, winter had set in. Under harsh conditions, the Americans launched their attack but failed. After several months, they limped home in defeat.

## The British Retreat from Boston

In Massachusetts, the Continental Army had surrounded British forces in Boston. Neither side was able or willing to break the standoff. However, help for Washington was on the way. Cannons were being hauled from Fort Ticonderoga. This was a rough job, since there were no roads across the snow-covered mountains. It took soldiers two months to drag the 59 heavy weapons to Boston, where they arrived in January 1776.



**ACTIVITY OPTIONS**

**MULTIPLE LEARNING STYLES: LINGUISTIC**

 **BLOCK SCHEDULING**

**WRITING A REVOLUTIONARY POEM**

**Class Time** 30 minutes

**Task** Writing a poem

**Purpose** To create a poem illustrating an understanding of an event or person of the Revolutionary War period

**Supplies Needed** None

**Activity** Remind students that poetry attempts to re-create emotions and experiences. Students should select a person or event about which to write. Have them brainstorm adjectives describing the event or person. Remind them that they also may rely more on the sounds of words and less on fixed rhythms and rhyme schemes. Tell students they may write their poems in any style they wish. They also may work with a partner. When they are finished, have a poetry reading, and have the group discuss the meaning of each work.

Armed with these cannons, Washington moved his troops to Dorchester Heights, overlooking Boston. The Americans threatened to bombard the city. General Howe, who was now in charge of the British forces, decided to withdraw his troops. On March 17, about 9,000 British soldiers departed Boston in more than 100 ships. Boston Patriots joyfully reclaimed their city. Although the British had damaged homes and destroyed possessions, Boston was still standing.

More than 1,000 Loyalist supporters left along with the British troops. Anti-British feeling in Boston was so strong that the Loyalists feared for their safety. Some Patriots even called for Loyalists to be hanged as traitors. This did not happen, but Loyalists' homes and property were seized.

**ReadingHistory**
**B. Forming Opinions** Did the Loyalists deserve punishment? Explain.
B. Possible Answer Some students may say punishment was fair because the Loyalists were traitors; others may say they should have been allowed to express their opinions and keep their possessions.

## 3 *Common Sense* Is Published

In early 1776, most Americans still wanted to avoid a final break with Britain. However, the publication of a pamphlet titled *Common Sense* helped convince many Americans that a complete break with Britain was necessary. Written by Thomas Paine, a recent immigrant from England, this pamphlet made a strong case for American independence.

Paine ridiculed the idea that kings ruled by the will of God. Calling George III "the Royal Brute," Paine argued that all monarchies were corrupt. He also disagreed with the economic arguments for remaining with Britain. "Our corn," he said, "will fetch its price in any market in Europe." He believed that America should follow its own destiny.

This is the front page of *Common Sense* by Thomas Paine (above). It was one of the most influential political documents in history.

**A VOICE FROM THE PAST**

> Everything that is right or natural pleads for separation. The blood of the slain, the weeping voice of nature cries, "'Tis time to part." Even the distance at which the Almighty has placed England and America is a strong and natural proof that the authority of the one over the other was never the design of heaven.
>
> **Thomas Paine,** *Common Sense*

*Common Sense* was an instant success. Published in January, it sold more than 100,000 copies in three months. The call for independence had become a roar.

## 4 A Time of Decision

The Continental Congress remained undecided. A majority of the delegates still did not support independence. Even so, in May 1776, Congress adopted a resolution authorizing each of the 13 colonies to establish its own government.

On June 7, Richard Henry Lee of Virginia introduced a key resolution. It called the colonies "free and independent states" and declared





### INSTRUCT: OBJECTIVE 

**Common Sense Is Published**

Key Questions
- What points does Thomas Paine make in *Common Sense?*
- What impact did Paine's pamphlet have on the colonies?

 **America's History Makers**
- Thomas Paine, pp. 25–26

### MORE ABOUT . . .

***Common Sense***

Some historians credit *Common Sense,* more than any other document, with generating popular support of the Declaration of Independence. About *Common Sense* Benjamin Rush said, "It was read by public men, repeated in clubs, spouted in schools." However, not everyone found the arguments satisfactory. None other than John Adams attacked the ideas about government in the document as either "honest ignorance or knavish hypocrisy." In response to Paine's pamphlet, Adams wrote a response entitled *Thoughts on Government.*

### INSTRUCT: OBJECTIVE 

**A Time of Decision/ The Declaration Is Adopted**

Key Questions
- Why did colonial leaders choose Thomas Jefferson to write the Declaration of Independence?
- What is the core idea of the Declaration of Independence?
- Which parts of the population does the Declaration neglect?

**ACTIVITY OPTIONS**

**INTERDISCIPLINARY LINK: CIVICS**  BLOCK SCHEDULING

**CREATING A NEW *COMMON SENSE***

**Class Time** 30 minutes

**Task** Creating a political pamphlet

**Purpose** To understand the colonists' feelings about the war

**Supplies Needed**
- Drawing paper, markers
- Word processors, if available

**Activity** Divide the class into small groups. Have each group produce a pamphlet designed to persuade the colonists to accept the Patriot or Loyalist position. Tell students that the pamphlet should use persuasive language to express the Loyalist or Patriot point of view. It also should express the views of the day and end with some kind of call to action. Suggest that students include an eye-catching front page, with hand-drawn illustrations or other art forms. Have the groups share their work with the class.

## HISTORY *through* ART

**Interpreting the Painting** The artist John Trumbull produced more than 200 works about the American Revolution. One of his most famous paintings, shown here, is entitled *The Declaration of Independence.*

In 1786, Thomas Jefferson urged Trumbull to depict the famous event to help ensure that it lived on in the nation's memory. Jefferson even supplied Trumbull with a rough sketch of the scene from which the artist could work.

Trumbull took eight years to complete the work, painstakingly painting 36 of the Congress members from life portraits.

**Possible Response: By presenting a dark scene with somber-looking men, the artist conveys the gravity and seriousness of declaring independence from a ruling country.**

## MORE ABOUT . . .

**A New Home for Old Documents**

Known as the Charters of Freedom, the Declaration of Independence, the U.S. Constitution, and the Bill of Rights are on display at the National Archives in Washington, D.C.

The documents are moved to a bombproof vault every day at closing time. Over time, the outside elements have invaded the glass cases that contain them. As a result, the documents are beginning to show slight signs of decay.

A team of scientists, engineers, designers, and archivists is working to create an advanced, airtight encasement for the documents by 2003.

**HISTORY *through* ART**

The Declaration of Independence is presented for adoption to the Continental Congress by John Adams, Roger Sherman, Robert Livingston, Thomas Jefferson, and Benjamin Franklin (left to right). John Trumbull painted this work many years after the adoption of the Declaration on July 4, 1776.

**What is the artist trying to show about the mood of the American leaders as they declare independence?**

that "all political connection between them and the state of Great Britain is . . . totally dissolved."

Congress debated the resolution, but not all the delegates were ready to vote on it. They did, however, appoint a committee to draft a **Declaration of Independence**. The committee included Benjamin Franklin, John Adams, Roger Sherman, Robert Livingston, and **Thomas Jefferson.**

The group chose Jefferson to compose the Declaration. Two reasons for selecting Jefferson were that he was an excellent writer and that he came from Virginia. The members knew that no independence movement could succeed without Virginia's support. Jefferson immediately went to work. In two weeks, he had prepared most of the Declaration. (See pages 182–185.) On July 2, 1776, Congress considered Lee's resolution again. Despite some strong opposition, the measure passed. From this point forward, the colonies considered themselves independent.

**The Liberty Bell was rung to announce the first public reading of the Declaration of Independence, in Philadelphia on July 8, 1776.**

## The Declaration Is Adopted

Two days later, on July 4, 1776, Congress adopted the document that proclaimed independence—the Declaration of Independence. John Hancock, the president of the Congress, was the first to sign the Declaration. According to tradition, he wrote in large letters and commented, "There, I guess King George will be able to read that." The core idea of the Declaration is based on the philosophy of John Locke. This idea is that people have unalienable rights, or rights that government



## ACTIVITY OPTIONS

### INDIVIDUAL NEEDS: GIFTED AND TALENTED

**DEBATING INDEPENDENCE**

**Class Time** 30 minutes

**Task** Re-creating the debate over the Declaration of Independence

**Purpose** To understand the different views on severing ties with Great Britain

**Supplies Needed**
- Resource materials on the views of Patriots and Loyalists concerning independence from Great Britain

**Activity** Have students act as congressional delegates debating independence. Those favoring independence should note the core ideas of the Declaration of Independence, as well as the events and acts of the chapter that support their stance. Those opposing independence should focus on the consequences of severing ties with Britain (such as a war), as well as what difficulties the colonists might face in trying to create a new country (no government, no currency, etc.).

**In-Depth Resources: Unit 2**
- Enrichment Activity, p. 22

cannot take away. Jefferson stated this belief in what was to become the Declaration's best-known passage.

*A VOICE FROM THE PAST*

We hold these truths to be self-evident, that all men are created equal, that they are endowed by their Creator with certain unalienable Rights, that among these are Life, Liberty and the pursuit of Happiness.

**Thomas Jefferson,** The Declaration of Independence

*Reading* **History**
**C. Summarizing** When does the Declaration say it is right to overthrow an established government?
C. Possible Answer People can abolish a government when it disregards their rights.

If a government disregards these rights, Jefferson explained, it loses its right to govern. The people then have the right to abolish that government, by force if necessary. They can form a new government that will protect their rights. When Jefferson spoke of "the people," however, he meant only free white men. Women and enslaved persons were left out of the Declaration.

The Declaration also explained the reasons for breaking with Britain. It then declared the colonies to be free and independent states. This was a very serious action—treason from the British point of view—and the delegates knew it. John Hancock urged the delegates to stand together in mutual defense. Each realized that if the war were to be lost, they would most likely be hanged.

The Declaration closed with this pledge: "And for the support of this Declaration, with a firm reliance on the protection of divine Providence, we mutually pledge to each other our Lives, our Fortunes, and our sacred Honor."

Americans had declared independence. Now they had to win their freedom on the battlefield.

AMERICA'S HISTORY MAKERS

**THOMAS JEFFERSON**
**1743–1826**

Jefferson was just 33 when chosen to write the Declaration of Independence. He was already a brilliant thinker and writer and a highly respected political leader. Jefferson came from a wealthy Virginia family. As a child, he was interested in everything, and he became an inventor, scientist, and architect, among other things. In 1769, he began his political career in the House of Burgesses.

Jefferson felt that writing the Declaration was a major achievement of his life. He had that fact carved on his tombstone.

**Why do you think Jefferson felt the Declaration was one of his greatest achievements?**

## Section 4 Assessment

**1. Terms & Names**

**Identify:**
- Ethan Allen
- artillery
- Second Continental Congress
- Continental Army
- Benedict Arnold
- Declaration of Independence
- Thomas Jefferson

**2. Taking Notes**

Use the chart below to explain colonial views for and against independence.

**Views About Independence**

| For | |
|---|---|
| Against | |

What is the strongest reason for independence? against independence?

**3. Main Ideas**

a. What challenges did George Washington face in forming the army?

b. What forced the British to leave Boston?

c. What is *Common Sense*?

**4. Critical Thinking**

**Drawing Conclusions** Why did it take colonists so long to declare independence?

THINK ABOUT
- the colonists' British traditions
- the risk of revolution

**ACTIVITY OPTIONS**

**ART**
**LANGUAGE ARTS**

Find out more about a person discussed in this section. Create a **trading card** or write a **biography** of that person.





## AMERICA'S HISTORY MAKERS

**Thomas Jefferson**

Jefferson was a "silent member" of the Continental Congress. He had great difficulty speaking in public. In fact, during the entire session of the Second Continental Congress he never gave a speech. Jefferson, of course, let his writing speak for him. In insisting that Jefferson craft the Declaration of Independence, John Adams pointed to his fellow delegate's "peculiar felicity of expression" when it came to the written word.

**Possible Response: The Declaration inspired Americans to work for and, ultimately, to win their freedom.**

## ASSESS & RETEACH

**Setting the Stage** Have students fill in the next three boxes on the graphic organizer.

**Formal Assessment**
- Section Quiz, p. 91

**Critical Thinking Transparency CT16**
- Setting the Stage

### RETEACHING ACTIVITY

Have students pretend they are reporters for a colonial newspaper, and have them write an article chronicling one of three events: the Battle of Bunker Hill; the publishing of *Common Sense;* the signing of the Declaration of Independence.

**In-Depth Resources: Unit 2**
- Reteaching Activity, p. 21

## Section 4 Assessment

**1. Terms & Names**

**Ethan Allen,** p. 176
**artillery,** p. 177
**Second Continental Congress,** p. 177
**Continental Army,** p. 177
**Benedict Arnold,** p. 178
**Declaration of Independence,** p. 180
**Thomas Jefferson,** p. 180

**2. Taking Notes**

For: blood had been spilled; wanted new kind of government
Against: still felt British; loyal to king

Student answers may vary but should include support from the chapter.

**3. Main Ideas**

**a.** creating a trained force and getting enough supplies **b.** colonial artillery fire from Dorchester Heights **c.** a pamphlet written by Thomas Paine that gave arguments for independence

**4. Critical Thinking**

The colonists were used to British rule, had a habit of loyalty, and knew that revolution would be bloody and they might lose.

**ACTIVITY OPTIONS**

**Alternative Assessment**
- Rubrics for a trading card, 1.7
- Rubrics for a biography, 4.3

## INTERACTIVE PRIMARY SOURCE

**OBJECTIVE**

Student will be able to identify colonial grievances against the British and explain why independence was declared.

Primary Source Explorer
- *The Declaration of Independence*

The Explorer will help students select and produce their own presentations.

Specific information about the document can be found in **A Closer Look.** To learn more about key people and events of the time, students should click on **Life in These Times. What Happened Next** will show the student the impact of the document both at home and abroad, and tie the document to today.

## FOCUS & MOTIVATE

**Finding Main Ideas** To help students understand the main ideas of the Declaration, write the blue headings on the board. Then ask the students what kind of information they would expect to find in each section. Write that information under each heading. After reading, check to see how accurate the predictions were.

**In-Depth Resources: Unit 2**
- Guided Reading, p. 7

**Access for Students Acquiring English/ESL**
- Guided Reading, p. 39

### MORE ABOUT . . .

**The Declaration of Independence**

The Declaration is divided into five parts: a preamble that announces the reason for the document; a section that explains the political principles underlying the rights of the people; a list of the unfair acts of the British king; a list of actions the colonials took to redress the problems; and the actual declaration of independence from Britain.

Note: The headings shown in the document are to aid student learning and do not appear in the original document.

INTERACTIVE PRIMARY SOURCE

# The Declaration of Independence

**Setting the Stage** On July 4, 1776, the Second Continental Congress adopted what became one of America's most cherished documents. Written by Thomas Jefferson, the Declaration of Independence voiced the reasons for separating from Britain and provided the principles of government upon which the United States would be built. **See Primary Source Explorer**

### *[Preamble]*

When in the Course of human events, it becomes necessary for one people to dissolve the political bands which have connected them with another, and to assume among the powers of the earth, the separate and equal station to which the Laws of Nature and of Nature's God entitle them, a decent respect to the opinions of mankind requires that they should declare the causes which impel them to the separation.

### *[The Right of the People to Control Their Government]*

We hold these truths to be self-evident, that all men are created equal, that they are **endowed**[1] by their Creator with certain **unalienable**[2] Rights, that among these are Life, Liberty and the pursuit of Happiness; that, to secure these rights, Governments are instituted among Men, deriving their just powers from the consent of the governed; that whenever any Form of Government becomes destructive of these ends, it is the Right of the People to alter or to abolish it, and to institute new Government, laying its foundation on such principles and organizing its powers in such form, as to them shall seem most likely to effect their Safety and Happiness. Prudence, indeed, will dictate that Governments long established should not be changed for light and transient causes; and accordingly all experience hath shewn that mankind are more disposed to suffer, while evils are sufferable, than to right themselves by abolishing the forms to which they are accustomed. But when a long train of abuses and **usurpations**,[3] pursuing invariably the same Object, evinces a design to reduce them under absolute **Despotism**,[4] it is their right, it is their duty, to throw off such Government, and to provide new Guards for their future security.

Such has been the patient sufferance of these Colonies; and such is now the necessity which constrains them to alter their former Systems of Government. The history of the present King of Great Britain is a history of repeated injuries and usurpations, all having in direct object the establishment of an absolute Tyranny over these States. To prove this, let facts be submitted to a **candid**[5] world.

***A CLOSER LOOK***

**RIGHTS OF THE PEOPLE**

**The ideas in this passage reflect the views of John Locke, an English philosopher. His belief that a government's power comes from the consent of the governed is the foundation of modern democracy.**

**1. In what way can American voters bring about changes in their government?**

1. **endowed:** provided.
2. **unalienable:** unable to be taken away.
3. **usurpations:** unjust seizures of power.
4. **Despotism:** rule by a tyrant with absolute power.
5. **candid:** fair, impartial.

182

### TEACHING STRATEGY

**Analyzing Causes** To help students understand the events and causes that led to the demand for independence, have them copy the graphic shown. Use the information in the *Efforts of the Colonies* section (p. 184) to identify actions taken by the colonists and the responses by the British.

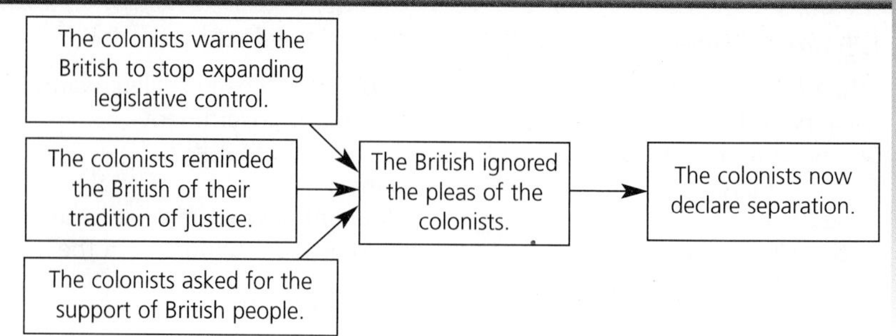

The colonists warned the British to stop expanding legislative control.
The colonists reminded the British of their tradition of justice.
The colonists asked for the support of British people.
The British ignored the pleas of the colonists.
The colonists now declare separation.

## [Tyrannical Acts of the British King]

He has refused his Assent to Laws, the most wholesome and necessary for the public good.

He has forbidden his Governors to pass Laws of immediate and pressing importance, unless suspended in their operation till his assent should be obtained; and, when so suspended, he has utterly neglected to attend to them.

He has refused to pass other Laws for the accommodation of large districts of people, unless those people would **relinquish**[6] the right of Representation in the Legislature, a right inestimable to them, and formidable to tyrants only.

He has called together legislative bodies at places unusual, uncomfortable, and distant from the depository of their public Records, for the sole purpose of fatiguing them into compliance with his measures.

He has dissolved Representative Houses repeatedly, for opposing with manly firmness his invasions on the rights of the people.

He has refused for a long time, after such dissolutions, to cause others to be elected; whereby the Legislative powers, incapable of Annihilation, have returned to the people at large for their exercise; the State remaining in the mean time exposed to all the dangers of invasions from without, and **convulsions**[7] within.

He has endeavoured to prevent the population of these States; for that purpose obstructing the Laws for **Naturalization**[8] of Foreigners; refusing to pass others to encourage their migration hither, and raising the conditions of new Appropriations of Lands.

He has obstructed the Administration of Justice, by refusing his Assent to Laws for establishing Judiciary powers.

He has made Judges dependent on his Will alone, for the **tenure**[9] of their offices, and the amount and payment of their salaries.

He has erected a multitude of New Offices, and sent hither swarms of Officers to harass our people and **eat out their substance.**[10]

He has kept among us, in times of peace, Standing Armies, without the Consent of our legislatures.

He has affected to render the Military independent of and superior to the Civil power. He has combined with others to subject us to a jurisdiction foreign to our constitution and unacknowledged by our laws; giving his Assent to their Acts of pretended Legislation:

For **quartering**[11] large bodies of armed troops among us;

For protecting them, by a mock Trial, from punishment for any Murders which they should commit on the Inhabitants of these States;

For cutting off our Trade with all parts of the world;

6. **relinquish:** give up.
7. **convulsions:** violent disturbances.
8. **Naturalization:** process of becoming a citizen.
9. **tenure:** term.
10. **eat out their substance:** drain their resources.
11. **quartering:** housing or giving lodging to.

**A CLOSER LOOK**

**GRIEVANCES AGAINST BRITAIN**

The list contains 27 offenses by the British king and others against the colonies. It helps explain why it became necessary to seek independence.

**2. Which offense do you think was the worst? Why?**

**A CLOSER LOOK**

**LOSS OF REPRESENTATIVE GOVERNMENT**

One of the Intolerable Acts of 1774 stripped the Massachusetts Legislature of many powers and gave them to the colony's British governor.

**3. Why was this action so "intolerable"?**

**A CLOSER LOOK**

**QUARTERING TROOPS WITHOUT CONSENT**

The Quartering Act of 1765 required colonists to provide housing and supplies for British troops in America.

**4. Why did colonists object to this act?**

183

## INSTRUCT

Key Questions
- Why do you think the colonists believed they had to explain their actions?
- According to the Declaration of Independence, when is it right to overthrow a government?
- In what ways did the acts of the king prove he was becoming a despot?
- Which acts are related to actions of the military, and why do you think they are cited by the colonists as problems?

## MORE ABOUT . . .

**Tyrannical Acts of the British King**

The Declaration picked up on Thomas Paine's ideas in *Common Sense.* Before Paine's publication, colonists' anger had been focused against the Parliament. Appeals to the king to intercede were made to no avail. In fact, the king favored the use of force to bring the colonies back into line.

The Declaration cleared the air for many colonists. Joseph Barton of Delaware wrote on July 9, 1776, "I could hardly own the King and fight against him at the same time, but now these matters are cleared up Heart and hand shall move together."

## VOCABULARY ACTIVITY

Have students substitute the definitions for the highlighted words in the sentences in which they are found. Have them read the sentence aloud to see if it makes the sentence meaning more clear. Then have them rewrite each sentence in their own words.

## TEACHING STRATEGY

**Recognizing Tone** To help students understand the tone of accusation of the document, have volunteers read aloud from the list of grievances using the beginning word *he.* Have the students read only the first three words of each grievance, for example: *He has refused; He has forbidden; He has dissolved.* Also point out how the parallel sentence structure reinforces the tone of the document.

Review the strong verbs used by the writer of the Declaration. Ask students how this language helps the reader understand the tone of the message. Discuss how substituting the weaker verbs would change the impact of the document. For example: "He has refused to pass other laws" reads differently from "He failed to pass other laws."

## INSTRUCT

Key Questions

- Why did the actions listed on this page cause increased tension between Britain and the colonists?
- Do you believe that the actions of the colonists were reasonable? Support your opinion.
- Why do you think the British government took the actions it did?

### MORE ABOUT . . .

**Further Grievances Against the King**

In this section of the grievances against the king, the Declaration refers to actions by the British military against colonists. Falmouth (now Portland), Maine, was burned in 1775, and the coast of Virginia was attacked in the same year. These actions reinforced the colonists' belief that Britain would not resolve differences with the colonies.

Furthermore, Virginia's Governor Dunmore was inciting Ohio Valley Indians on the frontiers of Virginia. Rumors were flying about the hiring of mercenaries to attack the colonies.

*A CLOSER LOOK*

**TAXATION WITHOUT REPRESENTATION**

The colonists believed in the long-standing British tradition that Parliament could tax only those citizens it represented—and the colonists claimed to have no representation in Parliament.

**5. How do persons today give consent to taxation?**

For imposing Taxes on us without our Consent;

For depriving us, in many cases, of the benefits of Trial by Jury;

For transporting us beyond Seas to be tried for pretended offenses;

For abolishing the free System of English Laws in a neighboring Province, establishing therein an **Arbitrary**[12] government, and enlarging its Boundaries so as to render it at once an example and fit instrument for introducing the same absolute rule into these Colonies;

For taking away our Charters, abolishing our most valuable laws, and altering fundamentally the Forms of our Governments;

For suspending our own Legislatures, and declaring themselves invested with power to legislate for us in all cases whatsoever.

He has **abdicated**[13] Government here, by declaring us out of his Protection and waging War against us.

He has plundered our seas, ravaged our Coasts, burnt our towns, and destroyed the lives of our people.

He is at this time transporting large Armies of **foreign Mercenaries**[14] to compleat the works of death, desolation, and tyranny, already begun with circumstances of Cruelty & **perfidy**[15] scarcely paralleled in the most barbarous ages, and totally unworthy the Head of a civilized nation.

He has constrained our fellow Citizens, taken Captive on the high Seas, to bear Arms against their Country, to become the executioners of their friends and Brethren, or to fall themselves by their Hands.

He has excited **domestic insurrections**[16] amongst us, and has endeavoured to bring on the inhabitants of our frontiers the merciless Indian Savages, whose known rule of warfare is an undistinguished destruction of all ages, sexes and conditions.

*A CLOSER LOOK*

**PETITIONING THE KING**

The colonists sent many petitions to King George III. In the Olive Branch Petition of 1775, the colonists expressed their desire to achieve "a happy and permanent reconciliation." The king rejected the petition.

**6. Why did the colonists at first attempt to solve the dispute and remain loyal?**

### *[Efforts of the Colonies to Avoid Separation]*

In every stage of these Oppressions We have **Petitioned for Redress**[17] in the most humble terms; Our repeated Petitions have been answered only by repeated injury. A Prince, whose character is thus marked by every act which may define a Tyrant, is unfit to be the ruler of a free people.

Nor have We been wanting in attentions to our British brethren. We have warned them from time to time of attempts by their legislature to extend an unwarrantable jurisdiction over us. We have reminded them of the circumstances of our emigration and settlement here. We have appealed to their native justice and **magnanimity,**[18] and we have conjured them by the ties of our common kindred, to disavow these usurpations, which would inevitably interrupt our connections and correspondence. They too have been deaf to

12. **Arbitrary:** not limited by law.
13. **abdicated:** given up.
14. **foreign Mercenaries:** professional soldiers hired to serve in a foreign army.
15. **perfidy:** dishonesty, disloyalty.
16. **domestic insurrections:** rebellions at home.
17. **Petitioned for Redress:** asked for the correction of wrongs.
18. **magnanimity:** generosity, forgiveness.



### TEACHING STRATEGY

**The Colonists' Responses** Remind the students that the tension between the colonies and Britain was caused by the actions of both. Use the graphic to help students review the responses of the colonists to the actions of the king. For example: imposing taxes without consent was met by the Stamp Act Congress and the boycott and protests by the colonists. Ask the students to think of other action-reaction situations.

| British Action | Colonial Response |
|---|---|
| Imposing taxes without consent | Stamp Act Congress; boycotts; protest |
| | |

the voice of justice and of **consanguinity**.[19] We must, therefore, **acquiesce**[20] in the necessity, which denounces our Separation, and hold them, as we hold the rest of mankind, Enemies in War, in Peace Friends.

### [The Colonies Are Declared Free and Independent]

We, therefore, the Representatives of the United States of America, in General Congress, Assembled, appealing to the Supreme Judge of the world for the **rectitude**[21] of our intentions, do, in the name, and by the Authority of the good People of these Colonies solemnly publish and declare, That these United Colonies are, and of Right ought to be, Free and Independent States; that they are Absolved from all Allegiance to the British Crown, and that all political connection between them and the State of Great Britain is, and ought to be, totally dissolved; and that as Free and Independent States, they have full Power to levy War, conclude Peace, contract Alliances, establish Commerce, and do all other Acts and Things which Independent States may of right do.

And for the support of this Declaration, with a firm reliance on the protection of divine Providence, we mutually pledge to each other our Lives, our Fortunes, and our sacred Honor. [Signed by]

John Hancock *President, from Massachusetts*
**[Georgia]** Button Gwinnett; Lyman Hall; George Walton
**[Rhode Island]** Stephen Hopkins; William Ellery
**[Connecticut]** Roger Sherman; Samuel Huntington; William Williams; Oliver Wolcott
**[North Carolina]** William Hooper; Joseph Hewes; John Penn
**[South Carolina]** Edward Rutledge; Thomas Heyward, Jr.; Thomas Lynch, Jr.; Arthur Middleton
**[Maryland]** Samuel Chase; William Paca; Thomas Stone; Charles Carroll
**[Virginia]** George Wythe; Richard Henry Lee; Thomas Jefferson; Benjamin Harrison; Thomas Nelson, Jr.; Francis Lightfoot Lee; Carter Braxton
**[Pennsylvania]** Robert Morris; Benjamin Rush; Benjamin Franklin; John Morton; George Clymer; James Smith; George Taylor; James Wilson; George Ross
**[Delaware]** Caesar Rodney; George Read; Thomas McKean
**[New York]** William Floyd; Philip Livingston; Francis Lewis; Lewis Morris
**[New Jersey]** Richard Stockton; John Witherspoon; Francis Hopkinson; John Hart; Abraham Clark
**[New Hampshire]** Josiah Bartlett; William Whipple; Matthew Thornton
**[Massachusetts]** Samuel Adams; John Adams; Robert Treat Paine; Elbridge Gerry

19. **consanguinity:** relationship by a common ancestor; close connection.
20. **acquiesce:** accept without protest.
21. **rectitude:** moral uprightness.

**A CLOSER LOOK**

**POWERS OF AN INDEPENDENT GOVERNMENT**

The colonists identified the ability to wage war and agree to peace; to make alliances with other nations; and to set up an economic system as powers of a free and independent government.

**7. What other powers are held by an independent government?**

**A CLOSER LOOK**

**DECLARATION SIGNERS**

The Declaration was signed by 56 representatives from the 13 original states.

**8. Which signers do you recognize? Write one line about each of those signers.**

*Interactive Primary Source Assessment*

**1. Main Ideas**

a. What is the purpose of the Declaration of Independence as stated in the Preamble?

b. What are the five main parts of the Declaration?

c. What are three rights that all people have?

**2. Critical Thinking**

**Drawing Conclusions** Why did the colonies feel that they had to declare their independence?

THINK ABOUT
- colonial grievances against Britain
- Britain's response to these grievances

185

## INSTRUCT

Key Questions
- By whose authority is independence declared? Why would that group be chosen?
- Why do you think the signers pledged everything they had in support of the Declaration?
- How do you think this document was viewed by the British king and Parliament?

### MAKING PERSONAL CONNECTIONS

Have the entire class read aloud the final paragraph of the Declaration. Ask them to discuss what the pledge means. Then ask them if there are any causes that they feel so strongly about that they would make a similar pledge. If the answer is no, ask them why they would not take this kind of a pledge.

### MORE ABOUT . . .

**Lesser-Known Signers**

Elbridge Gerry served as vice-president under James Madison. Richard Stockton was captured by the British and treated so harshly he became an invalid. Thomas Lynch, Jr., signed the Declaration but did little else in the Revolution. He disappeared at sea with his wife. Button Gwinett was killed in a duel during the Revolutionary War. Charles Carroll was the only Roman Catholic to sign the Declaration and the last signer to die, living until 1832.

*Interactive Primary Source Assessment*

**1. Main Ideas**

a. to explain why the colonists declared independence
b. Preamble, The Right of the People to Control Their Government, Tyrannical Acts of the British King, Efforts of the Colonies to Avoid Separation, The Colonies are Declared Free and Independent
c. life, liberty, and the pursuit of happiness

**2. Critical Thinking**

The colonists believed that the British government had abused its powers by taking away their rights, and it had ignored their pleas to settle grievances.

### A CLOSER LOOK

1. The people can vote elected officials out of office by casting their ballots for other candidates.
2. Answers will vary, but each answer should include an explanation.
3. The people of Massachusetts found this action intolerable because it took away their only representation in government.
4. The people believed that this act violated their freedom.
5. Citizens elect representatives to the legislative bodies that enact taxes.
6. Many colonists viewed themselves as British citizens and thus had difficulty separating from Great Britain.
7. the ability to make laws and to seek membership in world organizations
8. Student responses will vary.

## TERMS & NAMES

1. **Stamp Act,** p. 160
2. **Sons of Liberty,** p. 161
3. **writs of assistance,** p. 164
4. **Samuel Adams,** p. 164
5. **Boston Tea Party,** p. 167
6. **militia,** p. 170
7. **Lexington and Concord,** p. 173
8. **Loyalist,** p. 173
9. **Declaration of Independence,** p. 180
10. **Thomas Jefferson,** p. 180

## REVIEW QUESTIONS

**Possible Responses**

1. They worsened as Britain tried to impose controls on the colonies.
2. to earn revenue to pay debts carried over from the French and Indian War and to pay for housing troops in the colonies
3. because they felt they should not be taxed without representation in Parliament
4. They organized a boycott of British goods and held peaceful protests. Sometimes they reacted violently.
5. The Sons of Liberty exaggerated the incident to raise anti-British feelings.
6. Groups of leaders in various towns and colonies exchanged letters and shared information.
7. to plan a response to the Intolerable Acts
8. the ride of Paul Revere, William Dawes, and Samuel Prescott to warn Lexington and Concord that British troops were coming to seize Patriot war supplies
9. It was a battle on the hills above Charlestown, across the bay from Boston, in which the British defeated the militia but suffered high casualties in their victory.
10. the idea of natural rights: that people have basic rights that governments cannot and should not take away

## VISUAL SUMMARY

### The Road to Revolution

**1763** Proclamation of 1763

**1764** Sugar Act

**1765** Quartering Act; Stamp Act; Sons of Liberty; Stamp Act Congress

**1766** Repeal of Stamp Act; Declaratory Act

**1767** Townshend Acts; Suspension of New York Assembly

**1768** Occupation of Boston by British troops

**1769** Daughters of Liberty

**1770** Boston Massacre; Repeal of all Townshend Acts except tea tax

**1772** Committees of Correspondence

**1773** Tea Act; Boston Tea Party

**1774** Intolerable Acts; First Continental Congress; Boycott of British goods

**1775** Battles of Lexington and Concord; Second Continental Congress; Appointment of Washington as commander of Continental Army; Battle of Bunker Hill; Olive Branch Petition

**1776** *Common Sense;* Declaration of Independence

186

# Chapter 6 ASSESSMENT

## TERMS & NAMES

Briefly explain the importance of each of the following.

1. Stamp Act
2. Sons of Liberty
3. writs of assistance
4. Samuel Adams
5. Boston Tea Party
6. militia
7. Lexington and Concord
8. Loyalist
9. Declaration of Independence
10. Thomas Jefferson

## REVIEW QUESTIONS

**Tighter British Control (pages 159–162)**

1. How did relations between Britain and the colonies change after the Seven Years' War?
2. Why did Britain try to tax the colonies?
3. Why did the colonists cry, "No taxation without representation"?

**Colonial Resistance Grows (pages 163–169)**

4. How did the colonists protest the Townshend Acts?
5. How was the Boston Massacre used for propaganda purposes?
6. How did the committees of correspondence help keep people informed?

**The Road to Lexington and Concord (pages 170–175)**

7. Why was the First Continental Congress held?
8. What was the Midnight Ride?

**Declaring Independence (pages 176–185)**

9. What was the Battle of Bunker Hill?
10. What was the core idea of the Declaration of Independence?

## CRITICAL THINKING

**1. USING YOUR NOTES**

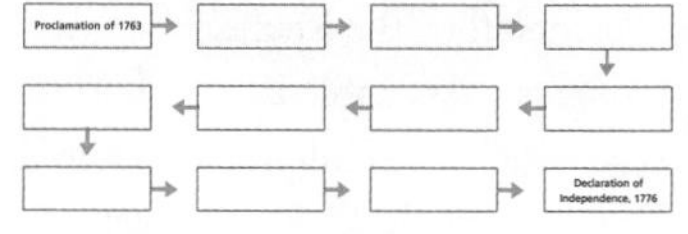


Using your completed chart, answer the questions below.

a. What city was the site of early protest activity?

b. What event happened after the Tea Act?

**2. ANALYZING LEADERSHIP**

How did colonial leaders differ in their methods of defending and securing basic rights for the colonies?

**3. APPLYING CITIZENSHIP SKILLS**

Did colonial leaders have a responsibility to include women, African Americans, and other groups in the Declaration of Independence? Explain.

**4. THEME: IMPACT OF THE INDIVIDUAL**

How did John Adams's role as lawyer for the British soldiers involved in the Boston Massacre help set a tone for the Revolutionary cause?

**5. DRAWING CONCLUSIONS**

What factors and events led the colonies to seek independence?

**6. SUPPORTING OPINIONS**

Do you think the American Revolution would have occurred if Britain had not taxed the colonies? Why or why not?

### Interact *with* History

Now that you have read about the road to revolution, do you consider your decision made at the beginning of the chapter to join or not join the protest a wise choice or a poor choice? Explain.

## CRITICAL THINKING

**Possible Responses**

**1. USING YOUR NOTES a.** Boston **b.** Boston Tea Party

**2. ANALYZING LEADERSHIP** Some leaders were quite radical, even violent. Others were very moderate, not wishing to offend Britain.

**3. APPLYING CITIZENSHIP SKILLS** Students may say leaving them out denied them full rights, or that including them might have jeopardized approval of the Declaration.

**4. THEME: IMPACT OF THE INDIVIDUAL** He showed that colonists could seek their rights and oppose British policy in a lawful, nondestructive way.

**5. DRAWING CONCLUSIONS** Taxes and other restrictive policies. Their protests brought even more controls from Britain and led to armed conflict.

**6. SUPPORTING OPINIONS** It might have been delayed, but eventually the colonists would probably have found other reasons to resist British rule.

**Interact *with* History** Answers will vary depending on whether students chose to join the protest or not. In their responses, they should show understanding of the events in the chapter.

## HISTORY SKILLS

**1. INTERPRETING MAPS: Location**

Study the map and then answer the questions.

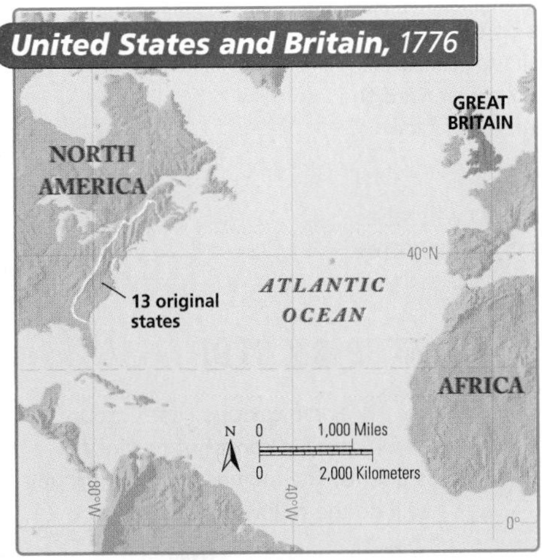


**Basic Map Elements**

a. What is the subject of the map?

b. What do the colors yellow and orange represent?

**Interpreting the Map**

c. What is the approximate distance between Great Britain and the United States?

d. Who do you think had the advantage in a war fought on the North American mainland?

**2. INTERPRETING PRIMARY SOURCES**

This British political cartoon is titled *Poor Old England Endeavoring to Reclaim His Wicked Children*. Study the cartoon carefully. Answer the questions.

a. How is England pictured? America?

b. Does the cartoon suggest England will be successful? Explain.

## ALTERNATIVE ASSESSMENT

**1. INTERDISCIPLINARY ACTIVITY: World History**

**Giving a Report** Do research about another country, colony, or region of the world during the 1760s and 1770s. Give a brief oral report, comparing and contrasting events and conditions there with those in the British colonies.

**2. COOPERATIVE LEARNING ACTIVITY**

**Debating** During discussion of the Declaration of Independence, members of the Continental Congress held heated debates on the issue of independence and whether to abolish the slave trade. Imagine that you and your classmates are delegates to the Congress. Hold a debate on these issues, choosing one of the following roles to play:

- a strong supporter of independence and of an end to the slave trade (such as Samuel Adams or John Adams)
- a supporter of independence but an opponent of ending the slave trade (such as George Washington)
- an independence opponent (such as John Dickinson)

**3. PRIMARY SOURCE EXPLORER**

**Writing a Play** The Declaration of Independence announced to the world that the colonies had chosen independence and why. Using the CD-ROM, your textbook, and library research, find out more about the Declaration and the people and events surrounding it. Then write a one-act play using the suggestions below:

- Set the play after the Declaration has been drafted.
- Have Thomas Jefferson, as the author, answer questions about what he included and perhaps did not include in the Declaration.
- Have Jefferson questioned by delegates to the Congress, or have him appear before a town meeting of ordinary citizens.
- Prepare introductory material to describe the setting and write dialogue for the characters.

**4. HISTORY PORTFOLIO**

**Option 1** Review your section and chapter assessment activities. Select one that you think was your best work. Then give consideration to suggestions made by your teacher or classmates and revise your work. Add it to your portfolio.

**Option 2** Review the questions that you wrote for What Do You Want to Know? on page 158. Then write a short report explaining your answers. Add the answers to your portfolio.



## ALTERNATIVE ASSESSMENT

1. INTERDISCIPLINARY ACTIVITY: **World History**

**Each student's report should**
- be well organized and clearly stated.
- provide evidence and factual support.
- present the information in a lively and interesting style.

2. COOPERATIVE LEARNING ACTIVITY

**Debate should**
- clearly state a position.
- present and support main points.
- refute the ideas of the opposition.

3. PRIMARY SOURCE EXPLORER

**A play should**
- accurately portray the event.
- exhibit creativity in creating the scene.
- clearly portray all sides of the issue.

4. HISTORY PORTFOLIO

**Option 1 Revised section or chapter assessment activities should**
- address teacher and peer responses to the selected work.
- solve problems present in the first versions of the work.

**Option 2 Short reports should**
- answer questions about the American Revolution.
- use evidence to develop and support ideas.
- cite sources of information.
- use standard grammar, spelling, sentence structure, and punctuation.

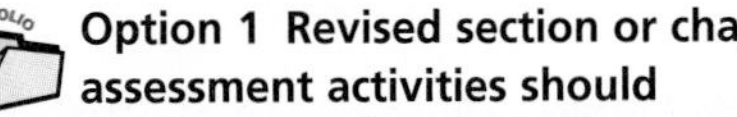

**Critical Thinking Transparency CT18**
- Visual Summary

**Formal Assessment**
- Chapter Test, Forms A and B, pp. 92–99

## HISTORY SKILLS

**Possible Responses**

1. INTERPRETING MAPS

**Basic Map Elements**

**a.** the United States and Britain in 1776

**b.** yellow for 13 original states, orange for Great Britain, and green for all other areas

**Interpreting the Map**

**c.** about 3,000 miles

**d.** the United States, because the war was being fought on its own territory whereas Britain had to bring soldiers and supplies from 3,000 miles away

2. INTERPRETING PRIMARY SOURCES

**a.** England is an old man trying to get his wicked children back; America is pictured as his children pulling away.

**b.** No, England is too weak to get America back.

## *HISTORY* WORKSHOP

**OBJECTIVE**

Students role-play activities, re-create cultural artifacts, and present issues related to the declaring of independence during the American Revolution.

 **BLOCK SCHEDULING**

## PROCEDURE

Gather the materials listed in the "Toolbox." Divide the class into groups of four or five. Then review the steps for raising the liberty pole and for preparing a persuasive speech.

 **In-Depth Resources: Unit 2**

- History Workshop Resources, p. 23

### MORE ABOUT . . .

**The Liberty Tree**

The Sons of Liberty met at the Liberty Tree in Boston to sing songs, condemn the British government, and stage imaginary hangings of hated officials. In 1775, British soldiers cut the tree down and turned it into firewood.

Each of the 13 colonies had its own Liberty Tree. The last surviving Liberty Tree, a 400-year-old tulip poplar in Maryland, had to be cut down after it suffered great damage in a 1999 hurricane.

### HISTORY FROM VISUALS

**Interpreting the Painting** Have students point out images from the painting that convey the country's patriotic spirit in July 1776. **Possible Responses** the liberty pole; the recruiting station and recruiting sign; the drummer with the red sash; the gestures of the men, women, and children



# Raise the Liberty Pole

In 1765, the Sons of Liberty gathered around a huge elm tree in Boston that they named the Liberty Tree. It became a meeting place where people voiced their protests against British policies. Replicas of the Liberty Tree—giant poles sometimes decorated with the flags of the colonies—were raised throughout the colonies. These liberty poles represented the unity of the American colonies as they struggled to break away from British rule.

ACTIVITY Like the American Patriots, each group of students will raise its own liberty pole. Each group also will write and deliver a persuasive speech supporting the cause of the American colonies.

### TOOLBOX

Each group will need:

- scissors
- poster board
- pencil
- markers
- masking tape
- 3 cardboard tubes from wrapping paper
- construction paper
- twine
- stapler

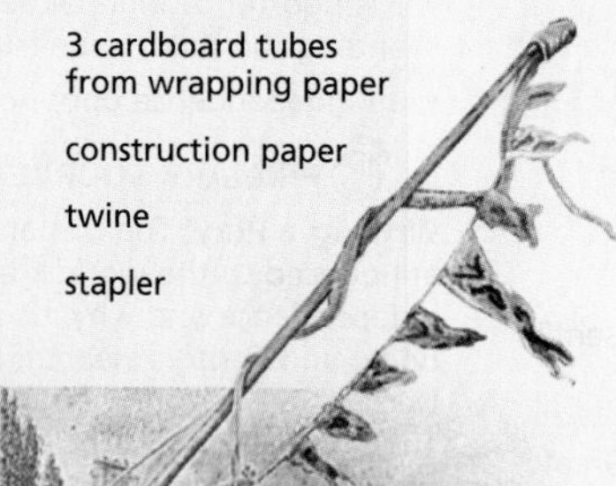

Members of the Sons of Liberty raise a liberty pole in July 1776 to celebrate America's independence.

### STEP BY STEP

**1 Form groups.** Each group should consist of four or five students. The members of your group will do the following jobs:

- research each colony
- design and create flags
- construct a pole
- write and deliver a speech

**2 Do research on the 13 colonies.** For each colony, your group should find a person, place, or object that represents that colony. For example, a Pilgrim's hat might represent Massachusetts. The 13 colonies are listed below.

| New England Colonies | Middle Colonies | Southern Colonies |
|---|---|---|
| Massachusetts (including Maine)<br>New Hampshire<br>Connecticut<br>Rhode Island | New York<br>Delaware<br>New Jersey<br>Pennsylvania | North Carolina<br>Virginia<br>Maryland<br>South Carolina<br>Georgia |



### RECOMMENDED RESOURCES

**JOURNALS AND BOOKS FOR THE TEACHER**

Kreamer, Todd Alan. "Sons of Liberty: Patriots or Terrorists?" ***The Early America Review. A Journal of People, Issues, and Events in 18th Century America.*** Washington: DEV Communications, Inc., Fall 1996.

Shearer, Benjamin F. and Barbara S. Shearer. ***State Names, Seals, Flags, and Symbols.*** Greenwood Publishing Group, 1994.

**VIDEOS**

***LIBERTY! The American Revolution.*** PBS Home Video. 1997. Three-part documentary covering the years 1763–1791.

***To Keep Our Liberty.*** National Park Service. Dramatic portrayal of the early revolutionary period, 1763–1775.

**BOOKS FOR THE STUDENTS**

Bloss, Janet Adele. ***State Flags.*** Willowisp Press, 1996.

Langguth, A. J. ***Patriots: The Men Who Started the American Revolution.*** Touchstone, 1989.

**3 Design and create 13 flags for the colonies.** Decide what person, place, or object you will use on your flag for each colony. Cut each flag out of the poster board. Sketch your design on the flag with a pencil. Then use markers to decorate it. On the back of each flag, explain how your design portrays the characteristics of that colony.

**4 Construct the pole.** Using masking tape, fasten the three cardboard tubes together to form one long tube. Then reinforce the tube by taping construction paper around it.

**5 String the flags on the pole.** Feed a piece of twine through the open ends of the long tube. Tie the ends of the twine together to form a tight loop. Now staple all 13 flags to the twine.

**6 Raise your liberty pole.** Lean your liberty pole next to a small table or desk. Take turns with members of your group and visit other liberty poles. As students visit your station, explain the significance of your flag designs.

## WRITE AND SPEAK

Write a persuasive speech to recruit others to join the cause of liberty. In your speech, explain what is wrong with British policies. Give reasons why the colonies should become independent. Then read your speech to the other groups as part of the recruitment process.

## HELP DESK

For related information on the Liberty Tree, see pages 161–162 in Chapter 6.

### Researching Your Project

- *The Revolutionary War* by Bart McDowell
- *The American Revolutionaries* edited by Milton Meltzer

**Visit www.mcdougallittell.com for more on the Revolution.**

### Did You Know?

The numbers 45 and 92 played an important part in the history of these liberty poles. The 45th issue of a British newspaper openly criticized the king in 1763 and was reprinted in the colonies. In 1768, 92 members of the Massachusetts General Assembly voted against canceling a letter to the other 12 colonies that called for action against Britain. To represent the numbers, 92 members of the Sons of Liberty would often raise liberty poles to a height of about 45 feet.

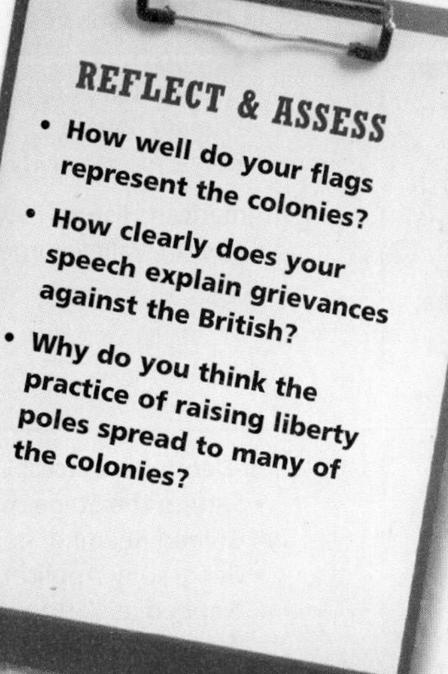

REFLECT & ASSESS
• How well do your flags represent the colonies?
• How clearly does your speech explain grievances against the British?
• Why do you think the practice of raising liberty poles spread to many of the colonies?




## MORE ABOUT . . .

**Protest Symbols Today**

Many people still rely on images and artworks as expressions of protest. For example, a blue ribbon symbolizes freedom of speech, while raised fists, featured in many outdoor murals, often represent the fight against social injustices. Have the class brainstorm visual symbols of protest they have observed, such as graffiti, bumper stickers, hairstyles, compact disc covers, and so on.

## REFLECT & ASSESS

1. Ask students to defend their choices of symbols by referring to the written explanations on the back of each flag.
2. Have students work with a peer editor who comments on the clarity of the grievances.
3. Have students imagine members of the Sons of Liberty from different colonies writing letters to one another.

## STANDARDS FOR EVALUATION

### HISTORY WORKSHOP

**Liberty poles should**

- appear well-constructed and realistic.
- include flags that are symbolic of the 13 colonies.
- show evidence of research.

### WRITE AND SPEAK

**Persuasive speeches should**

- state opinions clearly.
- include historical details about unfair British policies.
- present convincing reasons for supporting the colonies' goal of independence.

CHAPTER 7 PLANNING GUIDE

# The American Revolution 1776–1783

| | CHAPTER OVERVIEW | COPYMASTERS | TECHNOLOGY |
|---|---|---|---|
| **CHAPTER RESOURCES** | The chapter describes the battles, people, strategies, and hardships involved in fighting the American Revolution. It also discusses the aftermath of the war and how the newly independent United States will govern itself. | **In-Depth Resources: Unit 2**<br>• Tracing Themes: Citizenship, p. 25<br>• Building Vocabulary, p. 30<br>**Interdisciplinary Projects,** pp. 37–42 | **Primary Source Explorer**<br>**Electronic Teacher Tools**<br>**Power Presentations CD-ROM**<br>**Chapter Summaries on CD** (English and Spanish) |
| **SECTION 1 The Early Years of the War pp. 193–199** | **KEY IDEAS**<br>• Americans are divided on the question of independence, making it difficult for Washington to raise an army.<br>• Britain seeks to control the Middle Colonies and Hudson River Valley.<br>• The Battles of Saratoga turn the tide of the war. | **In-Depth Resources: Unit 2**<br>• Setting the Stage, p. 24<br>• Guided Reading, p. 26<br>• Skillbuilder Practice, p. 31<br>• Literature Selection, pp. 36–38<br>• Reteaching Activity, p. 39<br>**America's History Makers**<br>• George Washington, pp. 27–28<br>• Haym Salomon, pp. 29–30<br>**Citizenship Today,** pp. 3–4 | **Humanities Transparency HT13**<br>• *Battle of Saratoga*<br>**Humanities Transparency HT14**<br>• *The Spirit of '76*<br>**Geography Transparency GT7**<br>• Final Battle of Saratoga, 1777<br>**Critical Thinking Transparency CT20**<br>• Cause and Effect: The American Revolution<br>**ClassZone:** www.mcdougallittell.com |
| **SECTION 2 The War Expands pp. 200–205** | • France enters the war on the American side, preventing the British from concentrating their strength.<br>• The Continental Army endures a harsh winter at Valley Forge, but Americans win key victories on the frontier.<br>• American privateers wage war at sea, disrupting British trade. | **In-Depth Resources: Unit 2**<br>• Setting the Stage, p. 24<br>• Guided Reading, p. 27<br>• Primary Source, p. 34<br>• Reteaching Activity, p. 40<br>**American History Plays**<br>• *Fires at Valley Forge* by Barret H. Clark | **Warm-Up Transparency WT7**<br>**Critical Thinking Transparency CT19**<br>• Setting the Stage<br>**ClassZone:** www.mcdougallittell.com |
| **SECTION 3 The Path to Victory pp. 206–210** | • Britain moves the war to the Southern colonies, seeking Loyalist support.<br>• After several British victories, Americans turn to guerrilla warfare.<br>• The American army and French fleet surround the British at Yorktown, Virginia, forcing British leader, Cornwallis, to surrender. | **In-Depth Resources: Unit 2**<br>• Setting the Stage, p. 24<br>• Guided Reading, p. 28<br>• Geography Application: Cornwallis Is Trapped at Yorktown, 1781, pp. 32–33<br>• Reteaching Activity, p. 41 | **Warm-Up Transparency WT7**<br>**Critical Thinking Transparency CT19**<br>• Setting the Stage<br>**ClassZone:** www.mcdougallittell.com |
| **SECTION 4 The Legacy of the War pp. 211–215** | • Factors in the American victory are better leadership, aid from abroad, knowledge of the land, and motivation.<br>• The Treaty of Paris acknowledges American independence, boundaries, and defines the terms of peace.<br>• The United States institutes a republican form of government. | **In-Depth Resources: Unit 2**<br>• Setting the Stage, p. 24<br>• Guided Reading, p. 29<br>• Primary Source, p. 35<br>• Reteaching Activity, p. 42<br>**Economics in History**<br>• Independence and Free Enterprise, p. 7<br>**Why It Matters Now**<br>• Democracy in South Africa, pp. 13–14<br>**Outline Map Activities**<br>• North America, 1783, pp. 13–14 | **Warm-Up Transparency WT7**<br>**Critical Thinking Transparency CT19**<br>• Setting the Stage<br>**ClassZone:** www.mcdougallittell.com<br>**Critical Thinking Transparency CT21**<br>• Visual Summary |

PE Pupil's Edition
Copymaster
Overhead Transparency
Audio Library
CD-ROM
Internet

## ASSESSMENT

PE **Chapter Assessment,** pp. 216–217

**Formal Assessment**
- Chapter Tests, Forms A and B, pp. 106–113

**Alternative Assessment Book**

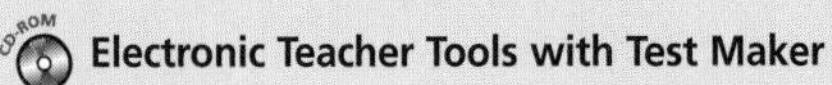

**Electronic Teacher Tools with Test Maker**

---

PE **Section Assessment,** p. 199

**Formal Assessment**
- Section Quiz, p. 102

**Alternative Assessment Book**
- Rubrics for a biography, 4.4
- Rubrics for a trading card, 1.7

**Electronic Teacher Tools with Test Maker**

---

PE **Section Assessment,** p. 205

**Formal Assessment**
- Section Quiz, p. 103

**Alternative Assessment Book**
- Rubrics for a comic strip, 1.3
- Rubrics for a talk, 3.4

**Electronic Teacher Tools with Test Maker**

---

PE **Section Assessment,** p. 210

**Formal Assessment**
- Section Quiz, p. 104

**Alternative Assessment Book**
- Rubrics for a Web page, 5.1
- Rubrics for a song, 4.8

**Electronic Teacher Tools with Test Maker**

---

PE **Section Assessment,** p. 215

**Formal Assessment**
- Section Quiz, p. 105

**Alternative Assessment Book**
- Rubrics for a speech, 3.6
- Rubrics for a pie graph, 2.3

**Electronic Teacher Tools with Test Maker**

## CUSTOMIZING FOR INDIVIDUAL NEEDS

### Students Acquiring English/ESL

**Reading Study Guide** (English and Spanish), pp. 65–74

**Access for Students Acquiring English/ESL:** Spanish Translations, pp. 43–49

**Chapter Summaries on CD** (English and Spanish)

### Less Proficient Readers

**Reading Study Guide** (English and Spanish), pp. 65–74

**Chapter Summaries on CD** (English and Spanish)

### Gifted and Talented Students

**In-Depth Resources: Unit 2**
- Enrichment Activity, p. 43

**America's History Makers**
- George Washington, pp. 27–28
- Haym Salomon, pp. 29–30

## CROSS-CURRICULAR CONNECTIONS

### Culture

Cox, Clinton. ***Come All You Brave Soldiers: Blacks in the Revolutionary War.*** New York: Cartwheel Books. A factual, easy-to-read account of African-American contributions to the Revolution.

### Geography

King, David C. ***Saratoga.*** Battlefields across America series. Fairfield, IA: Twenty-First Century, 1998. Information on this battle is well presented in maps, text, and historic images.

### Interdisciplinary Projects, pp. 37–42

- Math: Calculating the Value of Currency
- Science: Chemical Reactions
- Language Arts: Broadsides
- Health: Health and Nutrition in the Army

### Primary Sources

Meltzer, Milton, ed. ***The American Revolution: A History in Their Own Words 1750-1800.*** New York: Harper Trophy, 1993. Chronological collection of first-person accounts.

### Humanities: Music

McNeil, Rusty. ***Colonial & Revolution Songs.*** WEM, 1989. Two audio cassettes and a songbook.

### Literature

Collier, James. ***My Brother Sam Is Dead.*** New York: S&S, 1984. Prize-winning, fact-based story of one family's wrenching experience in the Revolution.

O'Dell Scott. ***Sarah Bishop.*** A girl's father and brother take opposite sides in the Revolution.

Yates, Elizabeth. ***Amos Fortune: Free Man.*** New York: Dutton, 1967. The life of an 18th-century prince who is captured by slavers and lives in Massachusetts as a slave during the Revolution.

## ENRICHMENT ACTIVITIES

PE **Pupil's Edition, pp. 190–217**
**Interact with History,** p. 191
**Citizenship Today,** p. 198
**Technology of the Time,** p. 208
**Economics in History,** p. 214

**In-Depth Resources: Unit 2**
- Geography Application: Cornwallis Is Trapped at Yorktown, 1781, pp. 32–33
- Primary Source: from *Private Yankee Doodle,* p. 34
- Primary Source: An African-American Petition for Freedom, p. 35
- Literature Selection: from *Citizen Tom Paine,* pp. 36–38

**America's History Makers**
- George Washington, pp. 27–28
- Haym Salomon, pp. 29–30

**Outline Map Activities**
- North America, 1783, pp. 13–14

**Why It Matters Now**
- Democracy in South Africa, pp. 13–14

**LESSON PLAN OPTIONS (50-MINUTE PERIOD)** (TE) = Teacher's Edition (PE) = Pupil's Edition

| | TEACHER-DIRECTED ACTIVITIES<br>Class Time: 15 minutes | STUDENT-CENTERED ACTIVITIES<br>Class Time: 25 minutes | INDIVIDUAL ACTIVITIES<br>Class Time: 10 minutes |
|---|---|---|---|
| **DAY 1**<br>Introduction<br>pp. 190–192 | **Presentation Options**<br>• Begin with a class discussion of the painting on p. 190 **(PE)**.<br>• Lead a class discussion on the "What Do You Know?" question in Setting the Stage, p. 192. Then introduce the graphic organizer for the chapter **(PE)**. | **Options for Cooperative Learning**<br>• Have student groups discuss the Interact with History questions, p. 191 **(PE)**.<br>• Have student groups respond to the "What Do You Want to Know?" question in Setting the Stage, p. 192 **(PE)**. | **Head Start on Homework Options**<br>• Have students skim Section 1 Main Idea, Why It Matters Now, Terms & Names, and the main headings, p. 193 **(PE)**.<br>• Have students begin Guided Reading activity and Building Vocabulary sheet. |
| **DAY 2**<br>Section 1<br>pp. 193–199 | **Presentation Options**<br>• Begin with the 5-minute Warm-Up, p. 193 **(TE)**.<br>• Review the Section 1 Main Idea, Why It Matters Now, and Terms & Names, p. 193 **(PE)**.<br>• Lead the students through the Skillbuilder Mini-Lesson: Creating a Multimedia Presentation, p. 194 **(TE)**. | **Options for Cooperative Learning**<br>• Divide students into groups to answer the questions posed in Citizenship Today, p. 198 **(PE)**.<br>• Have student pairs work together to complete one of the Activity Options in the Section 1 Assessment, p. 199 **(PE)**. | **Head Start on Homework Options**<br>• Have students begin working on Section 1 Assessment, p. 199 **(PE)**.<br>• Have students preview Section 2 Main Idea, Why It Matters Now, Terms & Names, and the main headings, p. 200 **(PE)**. |
| **DAY 3**<br>Section 2<br>pp. 200–205 | **Presentation Options**<br>• Begin with the 5-Minute Warm-Up, p. 200 **(TE)**.<br>• Choose 5 key questions for Objectives 1–4 to discuss with the class, pp. 200–204 **(TE)**.<br>• Lead a discussion on daily life in army camps using p. 202 **(PE, TE)**. | **Options for Cooperative Learning**<br>• Divide students into groups and have them complete the Interdisciplinary Link, Humanities: The Revolution in Art, p. 203 **(TE)**.<br>• Have student pairs work together to complete one of the Activity Options in the Section 2 Assessment, p. 205 **(PE)**. | **Head Start on Homework Options**<br>• Have students begin working on Section 2 Assessment, p. 205 **(PE)**.<br>• Have students complete the History Skills questions in the Chapter Assessment, p. 217 **(PE)**. |
| **DAY 4**<br>Section 3<br>pp. 206–210 | **Presentation Options**<br>• Begin with the 5-Minute Warm-Up, p. 206 **(TE)**.<br>• Choose 5 key questions for Objectives 1–4 to discuss with the class, pp. 206–210 **(TE)**.<br>• Lead the students through the Geography Skillbuilder, p. 209 **(PE)**. | **Options for Cooperative Learning**<br>• Divide students into groups and have them complete the Technology of the Time questions, p. 208 **(PE)**.<br>• Have students do the Geography Skillbuilder and Extension, p. 209 **(TE)**. | **Head Start on Homework Options**<br>• Have students begin working on Section 3 Assessment, p. 210 **(PE)**.<br>• Have students complete the Reading History questions in Section 4, pp. 211–215 **(PE)**. |
| **DAY 5**<br>Section 4<br>pp. 211–215 | **Presentation Options**<br>• Begin with the 5-Minute Warm-Up, p. 211 **(TE)**.<br>• Choose 5 key questions for Objectives 1–4 to discuss with the class, pp. 211–214 **(TE)**.<br>• Lead students through the Critical Thinking Activity, p. 215 **(TE)**. | **Options for Cooperative Learning**<br>• Divide students into groups and have them complete the Economics in History questions, p. 214 **(PE)**.<br>• Have student pairs work together to complete one of the Activity Options in the Section 4 Assessment, p. 215 **(PE)**. | **Head Start on Homework Options**<br>• Have students complete the Setting the Stage graphic organizer for the chapter, p. 192 **(PE)**.<br>• Have students begin working on the Chapter Assessment, pp. 216–217 **(PE)**.<br>• Prepare for Chapter Test<br>**Formal Assessment**, pp. 106–113 |

TEACHER-TESTED ACTIVITY **Barbara Kennedy, Sylvan Middle School, Citrus Heights, California**

## MEDIA INTERVIEW SKITS

**Class Time** Two class periods for preparation and two for presentation

**Task** Creating a videotape to present arguments for and against war with Britain

**Purpose** To understand the beliefs of Americans on both sides of the debate over the Revolution

**Supplies Needed**
- Reference materials and Internet resources on the American Revolution
- Costumes supplied by students
- Video camera and tapes

**Activity** Divide the class into small groups. Within groups, students should choose roles such as camera person, producer, interviewer, pro-Revolution and anti-Revolution colonists, Native Americans, enslaved African Americans, or free black colonists. Have each group write a script for the "person-on-the-street" interview, making sure that interviews capture multiple points of view. Students may use cue cards to help them with their presentations while filming. Have them practice their skits before taping them.

## BLOCK SCHEDULING — LESSON PLAN OPTIONS (90-MINUTE PERIOD)

### DAY 1

**Interact with History,** p. 191
**Class Time** 20 Minutes

Options for pacing and variety:
- Role-Playing Have students assume the role of Mrs. Schuyler and write a letter from Mrs. Schuyler to her husband explaining why she set fire to the fields and how she felt as the British approached. **Class Time** 20 minutes

**Setting the Stage,** p. 192
**Class Time** 20 minutes

Options for pacing and variety:
- Time Saver For a homework assignment, have students preview the section, looking at subsection heads and illustrations. Then students can make a list of "What Do You Want to Know?" questions for the section. **Class Time** 5 minutes

**Section 1,** pp. 193–199
**Class Time** 50 minutes

Options for pacing and variety:
- History on Film Extend students' background knowledge of the American Revolution by viewing *The American Revolution.* Schlesinger, 1996. **Class Time** 35 minutes
- Team Teaching Invite a music teacher to talk to the class about the instruments used in Revolutionary War bands and to play some popular music of the war years. **Class Time** 30 minutes

### DAY 2

**Section 2,** pp. 200–205
**Class Time** 45 minutes

Options for pacing and variety:
- Internet Extend students' background knowledge of the American Revolution by visiting www.mcdougallittell.com **Class Time** 20 minutes
- Time Saver For a homework assignment, have students answer the Reading History questions. **Class Time** 5 minutes

**Section 3,** pp. 206–210
**Class Time:** 45 minutes

Options for pacing and variety:
- Peer Teaching Have pairs of students choose two events in this chapter and write news headlines for them. Then have student pairs exchange headlines and write short news articles to go with the ones they receive. **Class Time** 40 minutes
- Peer Evaluation Have small groups of students work together to answer the Section Assessment Critical Thinking question and create a cause-and-effect graphic organizer to show their conclusions. **Class Time** 20 minutes

### DAY 3

**Section 4,** pp. 211–215
**Class Time** 45 minutes

Options for pacing and variety:
- Peer Evaluation Have students work in pairs to answer the Connect to History and Connect to Today questions in the Economics in History feature on page 214. **Class Time** 20 minutes
- Time Saver As a homework assignment after completing the Economics in History feature, have students answer Critical Thinking question 3 in the chapter assessment on page 217. **Class Time** 10 minutes

**Chapter 7 Assessment,** pp. 216–217
**Class Time** 40 minutes

Options for pacing and variety:
- Peer Evaluation Have students prepare a summary of the chapter using the words in the Terms & Names in the Chapter Assessment. Have them exchange papers and evaluate each other's summaries. **Class Time** 20 minutes
- Peer Teaching Have pairs of students make up five questions based on the Visual Summary on page 216. **Class Time** 20 minutes

**CHAPTER 7 OBJECTIVE**
The student will organize events of the American Revolution in chronological sequence and analyze the causes that led to an American victory.

# The American Revolution 1776–1783

*Section 1* **The Early Years of the War**
*Section 2* **The War Expands**
*Section 3* **The Path to Victory**
*Section 4* **The Legacy of the War**

This painting shows General Washington and his ragged troops traveling to their winter camp at Valley Forge.

190

## HISTORY FROM VISUALS

**Interpreting the Painting** Ask students to read the caption on page 190, then to study the painting of the Patriot troops at Valley Forge. Ask them to describe the weather and the men's clothing and physical condition. **Possible Responses** The weather appears cold and snowy. The mounted men are heavily cloaked, but the men on foot are less warmly dressed. They have no cloaks, hats, or gloves. One soldier is wounded and is being helped by another. The soldier in front is acknowledging Washington. The soldier standing at the horse's head appears to be talking with the officers on horseback.

**Extension** Ask students to write three things the soldier in the coat may be reporting to General Washington and his aides.

## CRITICAL THINKING ACTIVITY

**Making Inferences** Ask students to make inferences about the physical and mental condition of both the troops and the officers. Encourage them to discuss the relationship between morale and physical conditions such as being cold, hungry, tired, or injured. Ask them to explain the adage, attributed to Napoleon not long after the American Revolution, "An army marches on its stomach." How might physical hardship affect a soldier's loyalty as well as his ability to fight?

**Class Time** 10 minutes

## RECOMMENDED RESOURCES

### BOOKS FOR THE TEACHER

Bobrick, Benson. ***Angel in the Whirlwind: The Triumph of the American Revolution.*** New York: Simon and Schuster, 1997. Packed with human drama.

Flexner, James T. ***Washington: The Indispensable Man.*** New York: Little, Brown, 1974. Shorter version of the authoritative biography.

Franklin, Benjamin. ***Autobiography & Other Writings.*** Ormond Seavey, ed. New York: Oxford, 1999. Observations from America's scientist, sage, and diplomat.

### SOFTWARE

***American Leaders Series.*** Decision Development Corp. Sortable, searchable, and highly graphic biographies.

### VIDEO

***The American Revolution: Two Views.*** Queue, 1994. Unusual presentation of both sides in the war.

### INTERNET

For more about the Revolutionary War, visit www.mcdougallittell.com

## Interact *with* History

The British army is on the other side of this hill and coming fast.
These are the family and servants of the American general Philip Schuyler.
Mrs. Schuyler sets fire to her harvest to prevent the British from taking it.

**It is 1777. Your brother is an American soldier. In his last letter to you, he wrote that the army has no shoes or bullets and little food. But he plans to keep fighting.**

**Now, a British army is coming toward your farm. You hear that they are stealing crops to feed themselves and their horses.**

### What Do You Think?

- **What sacrifices do civilians like Mrs. Schuyler make during wartime?**
- **What sacrifices do soldiers make?**
- **Is it worth such sacrifices to win independence for your country? Why or why not?**

# *What would you sacrifice to win freedom?*

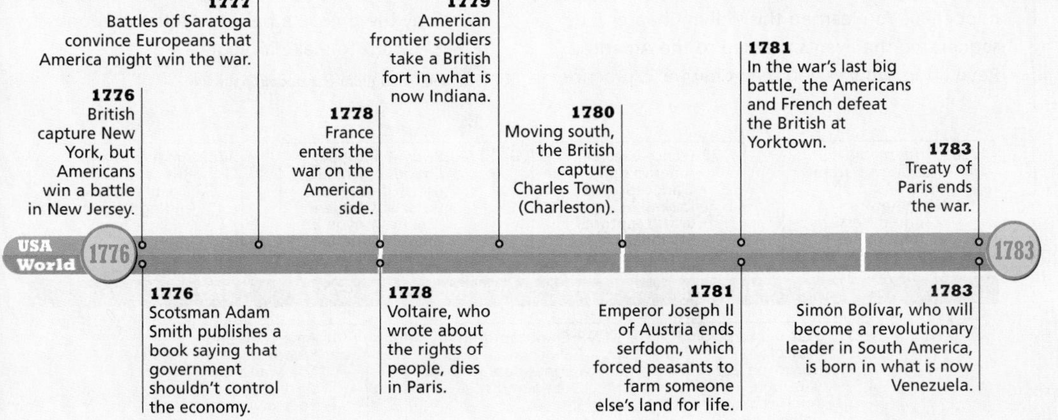

USA
World
1776
1783
1776 British capture New York, but Americans win a battle in New Jersey.
1777 Battles of Saratoga convince Europeans that America might win the war.
1778 France enters the war on the American side.
1779 American frontier soldiers take a British fort in what is now Indiana.
1780 Moving south, the British capture Charles Town (Charleston).
1781 In the war's last big battle, the Americans and French defeat the British at Yorktown.
1783 Treaty of Paris ends the war.
1776 Scotsman Adam Smith publishes a book saying that government shouldn't control the economy.
1778 Voltaire, who wrote about the rights of people, dies in Paris.
1781 Emperor Joseph II of Austria ends serfdom, which forced peasants to farm someone else's land for life.
1783 Simón Bolívar, who will become a revolutionary leader in South America, is born in what is now Venezuela.

## Interact *with* History

### OBJECTIVES

- To describe the harsh conditions that many soldiers and civilians faced during the Revolution
- To identify physical hardships and material sacrifices that students might endure for the sake of freedom

### What Do You Think?

1. Ask students to think about the role of civilians in wartime. Discuss how war affects civilians, whether or not they are near the battlefield.
2. Besides the obvious risk of death, suggest that students also think about the hardships of a soldier's daily life.
3. Discuss the various meanings that independence might have had in the 1770s for the members of the Schuyler household. Remind students that independence did not bring the same political rights for women and African Americans that it did for white men. Still, everyone in the picture will share in the hardships of the war.

### *What would you sacrifice to win freedom?*

Ask students to predict the consequences of Mrs. Schulyer's action for herself and her family, as well as what she hopes to accomplish with her act.

### MAKING PERSONAL CONNECTIONS

Have students think about the meaning of freedom in their own lives. Ask them to consider which of their personal possessions they would be willing to sacrifice to preserve their freedom. Ask them to consider recent events in the news that relate to the issue of political independence, and ask which event they found most gripping or personally touching.

### TIME LINE DISCUSSION

**Remind students that the battles of Lexington and Concord and the signing of the Declaration of Independence took place in 1776. Thus this chapter begins in the same year that the previous chapter ended.**

- Ask students how many years are represented on the time line. **Answer** Eight, 1776–1783 inclusive. Have them compare the period covered by this time line to several from earlier chapters. Ask why this time line might show such a short period.

**Possible Response** These are very important years in U.S. history, and crucial events during these years should be studied very closely.

- Ask students what reaction American Patriots might have had to Adam Smith's book.

**Possible Response** Given that much of the conflict between Britain and the colonies arose over trade regulation, colonial Patriots would probably have agreed with Smith.

## BEFORE YOU READ

### Previewing the Theme: Citizenship

Ask students to think about why the Patriots persisted in declaring independence, even though they knew it would lead to a war they might not win.

### What Do You Know?

Students often forget that Washington and other Patriots could not be certain that the colonists would win the war. In the event of capture or defeat, American leaders faced execution as traitors to the British Crown. Understanding that it was as difficult to predict the outcome of events in 1776 as it is today is one of the most important historical lessons that students can learn.

 **In-Depth Resources: Unit 2**
- Tracing Themes: Citizenship, p. 25

## READ AND TAKE NOTES

### Reading Strategy: Sequencing Events

Tell students that sequencing events in the chapter will help them relate events to one another. Viewing events on a time line will help students develop such critical thinking skills as recognizing cause and effect. When the time line is completed, students should be able to use it to identify key events in the early years of the war in chronological order.

 **In-Depth Resources: Unit 2**
- Setting the Stage, p. 24

 **Critical Thinking Transparency CT19**
- Setting the Stage

# Chapter 7 SETTING THE STAGE

## BEFORE YOU READ

This Patriot has climbed a flagpole to tear down the British flag and replace it with an American one.

### Previewing the Theme

**Citizenship** During the Revolution, many Americans saw themselves as citizens of a new country—the United States. They made great sacrifices and risked their lives and fortunes to win independence. This chapter explains how those Patriots overcame enormous odds to defeat the powerful British Empire.

### What Do You Know?

What stories do you know about the people or events of the Revolution? How do people display courage and self-sacrifice during wartime?

**THINK ABOUT**
- what you've learned about the American Revolution from books, movies, and other classes
- news stories you've heard about revolutions or civil wars in other countries today

### What Do You Want to Know?

What would you like to learn about the steps that people took to win the American Revolution? In your notebook, record what you hope to learn from this chapter.

## READ AND TAKE NOTES

**Reading Strategy: Sequencing Events** To sequence is to put events in the order in which they happened. You learned this skill in Chapter 6 by sequencing the events that led to the American Revolution. Now as you read Chapter 7, practice sequencing again. Put the major battles and events of the war in order by recording them on a time line. Copy the time line below in your notebook. You may want to make it bigger.

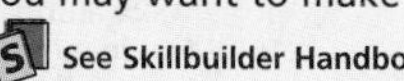
See Skillbuilder Handbook, page R4.

| | |
|---|---|
| 1776 | British forced Washington from New York. Washington surprised Hessians at Trenton. |
| 1777 | Washington won at Princeton. Burgoyne lost at Saratoga. Americans suffer at Valley Forge. |
| 1778 | France became America's ally. Clark captured Kaskaskia. British captured Savannah. |
| 1779 | Clark captured Vincennes. Jones defeated the *Serapis*. |
| 1780 | British captured Charles Town. British defeated Gates at Camden. Americans won at Kings Mountain. |
| 1781 | Americans and French forced Cornwallis to surrender at Yorktown. |
| 1782 | |
| 1783 | Americans and British signed the Treaty of Paris ending the war. |



## TEACHING STRATEGY

### READING THE CHAPTER

This is a chronological chapter focusing on the events in the early years of the American Revolution. Encourage students to relate the events to one another and look for events that led to the war. Encourage them also to look for causes and effects of these events. Pause after each section to review the chronology of the key events described.

### ALTERNATIVE ASSESSMENT

The Chapter Assessment describes three activities for alternative assessment on page 217. You may wish to have students work on these activities during the course of the chapter and then present them at the end.

# 1 The Early Years of the War

**TERMS & NAMES**
George Washington
mercenary
strategy
rendezvous
Battles of Saratoga

**MAIN IDEA**

The American desire to gain rights and liberties led them to fight for independence from Britain.

**WHY IT MATTERS NOW**

Today those same rights and liberties are protected by the U.S. Constitution.

Haym Salomon sacrificed his health and his fortune to help his new country.

### ONE AMERICAN'S STORY

**In search of liberty, Haym Salomon moved from eastern Europe to America sometime between 1764 and 1775. He was a Jew from Poland. Arriving in New York City, Salomon soon became a successful merchant and banker. After the war broke out, Salomon supported the Patriot cause.**

**When the British captured New York in 1776, many Patriots fled but Salomon stayed. The British arrested him as a spy. Salomon spoke many languages. The British thought he could help their supply officers deal with foreign merchants, so they let him out of prison. Salomon used this opportunity to help other prisoners escape.**

**In 1778, the British wanted to arrest Salomon again, so he fled to Philadelphia. His earlier time in the cold, damp prison had permanently damaged his health. Even so, he continued to aid the Patriots. He loaned the new government more than $600,000, which was never repaid.**

**Like Salomon, many people made hard choices about which side to support during the Revolutionary War. This section discusses those choices and the obstacles Americans faced in the war's early years.**

## 1 Americans Divided

The issue of separating from Great Britain divided American society. Opinion polls did not exist in the 1700s, so we don't know exactly how many people were on each side. But historians estimate that roughly 20 to 30 percent of Americans were Loyalists, roughly 40 to 45 percent were Patriots, and the rest remained neutral. Most Americans did not support the Revolution.

Both Patriots and Loyalists came from all walks of life and all parts of America. In general, New England and Virginia had high numbers of Patriots. Loyalists were numerous in cities, in New York State, and in the

**Choosing Sides**

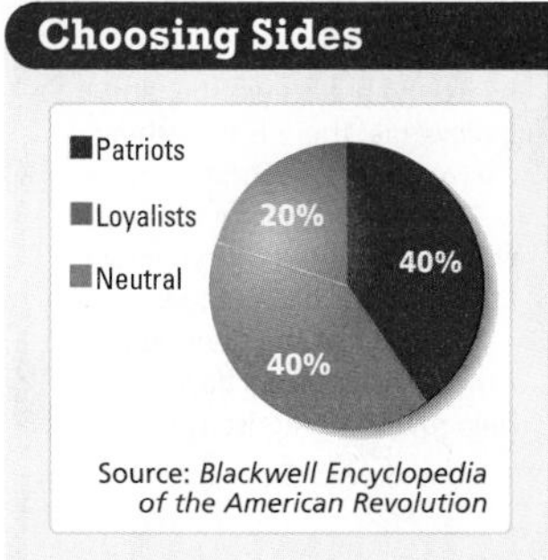


Source: *Blackwell Encyclopedia of the American Revolution*





## SECTION OBJECTIVES

1. To describe colonial opinions on American independence
2. To explain the importance of the mid-Atlantic coastal cities
3. To analyze early British strategy
4. To summarize the causes and effects of the Battles of Saratoga

**SKILLBUILDERS**

Interpreting Maps: Place, Movement, pp. 195, 197

**CRITICAL THINKING**

Analyzing Causes, p. 194
Solving Problems, p. 195
Recognizing Propaganda, p. 196
Evaluating, p. 197
Forming and Supporting Opinions, p. 199
Contrasting, p. 199

## FOCUS & MOTIVATE

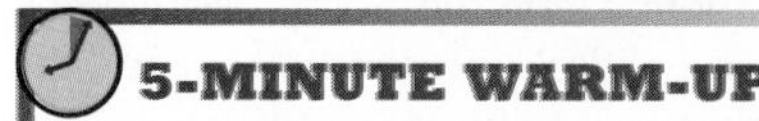

**5-MINUTE WARM-UP**

**Making Inferences** The questions will help students understand important early battles.

1. Look at the map on page 195. Where are the earliest battles of the Revolution?
2. What major city did the British win?

 **Warm-Up Transparency WT7**

## INSTRUCT

**INSTRUCT: OBJECTIVE** 

**Americans Divided/Creating an Army**

Key Questions

- What were the major positions among colonists concerning independence?
- How did the issue of revolution affect Native Americans and African Americans?
- What problems challenged Washington in raising an army?

**In-Depth Resources: Unit 2**
- Guided Reading, p. 26

**America's History Makers**
- Haym Salomon, pp. 29–30

## RECOMMENDED RESOURCES

**In-Depth Resources: Unit 2**
- Guided Reading, p. 26
- Building Vocabulary, p. 30
- Skillbuilder Practice, p. 31
- Literature Selection, pp. 36–38
- Reteaching Activity, p. 39

**Reading Study Guide** (Spanish and English), pp. 65–66

**America's History Makers**
- George Washington, pp. 27–28
- Haym Salomon, pp. 29–30

**Citizenship Today,** pp. 3–4

**Formal Assessment**
- Section Quiz, p. 102

**Alternative Assessment**
- Rubrics, 4.4
- Rubrics, 1.7

**Access for Students Acquiring English/ESL**
- Guided Reading, p. 43
- Skillbuilder Practice, p. 47

**Technology Resources**

**Humanities Trans. HT13, HT14**
- *Battle of Saratoga*
- *The Spirit of '76*

 **Geography Transparency GT7**
- Final Battle of Saratoga, 1777

 **Critical Thinking Trans. CT20**
- Cause and Effect: The American Revolution

## HISTORY FROM VISUALS

**Reading the Chart** (p. 193) Point out that fewer than half the colonists supported the Revolution. Ask students how the large number of people who were neutral might have affected the independence movement. **Possible Response** Patriots might not get as many volunteers as they needed for soldiers or enough supplies to support the army.

**Extension** Have students make inferences as to what kinds of practical support Loyalists might have given to Great Britain.

 **Critical Thinking Transparency CT20**
- Cause and Effect: The American Revolution

## AMERICA'S HISTORY MAKERS

**George Washington**

According to Thomas Jefferson, George Washington rarely spoke in political discussion except to "the main point which was to decide the question." Yet Washington's actions spoke volumes. As tensions mounted between the Crown and the colonies, Washington took to wearing his uniform from the French and Indian War. Scholars think he wore it on purpose—to indicate his opinion that it was time for military action and to remind Congress of his soldiering experience.

**Possible Responses: He learned to handle hardship and live outdoors. He learned to fight and discovered his own bravery. He led soldiers.**

 **America's History Makers**
- George Washington, pp. 27–28

South. Many Loyalists worked for the British government or were clergy in the Church of England. Some Quakers were Loyalists, although many wanted peace. (Their faith taught that war was wrong.)

The war divided Native Americans, too. For instance, some Iroquois nations fought with the British and others with the Americans. Those Native Americans who joined the British feared that if the Americans won, they would take Native American land. Some Native Americans who lived near colonists and interacted with them sided with the Americans.

**Background**
The Iroquois League had generally kept peace among the Iroquois nations for about 200 years—until the American Revolution.

African Americans also fought on both sides. At first, slave owners feared that African Americans who had guns might lead slave revolts. Therefore, few states allowed African Americans to enlist, or sign up with the army. Then a British governor offered freedom to any enslaved person who joined the British army. Many slaves ran away to fight for the British. In response, most states began to accept African-American soldiers. In all, about 5,000 African Americans served in the Continental Army. Many African Americans who did so hoped that American independence would bring greater equality.

Differences over the war split families, too. For example, Benjamin Franklin's son William took Britain's side. The father and son stopped speaking.

**AMERICA'S HISTORY MAKERS**

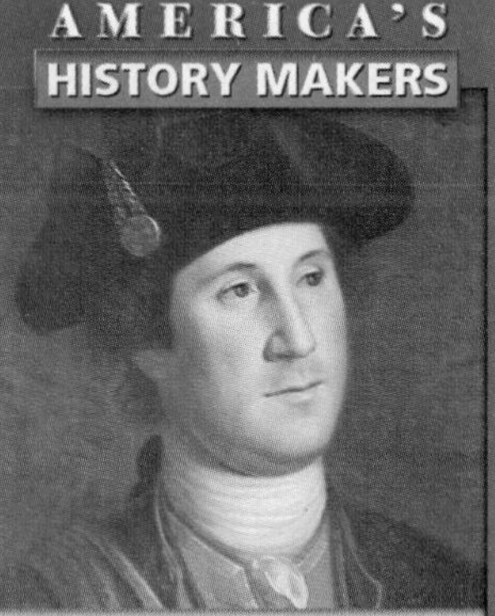

**GEORGE WASHINGTON**
**1732–1799**

At the age of 16, George Washington worked as a surveyor, setting land boundaries in the wilderness. He learned to handle hardship by hunting for food and sleeping outdoors.

In the French and Indian War, Washington had many brushes with death. Yet he wrote, "I heard the bullets whistle, and, believe me, there is something charming in the sound."

That war made him the most famous American officer. People loved him for his courage. As commander of the Continental Army, Washington's popularity helped unite Americans.

**How did Washington's early life prepare him to lead the army?**

## Creating an Army

Because not everyone supported the war, raising an army was difficult. The army also faced other problems. In June 1775, **George Washington** became the commander of the Continental Army. At first, this new national army was formed from state militias, made up of untrained and undisciplined volunteers.

*Reading***History**
**A. Analyzing Causes** Why would the lack of agreement about the war make it hard to raise an army?
**A. Possible Responses** Only Patriots would join the army, and they were a minority. Some Patriots might hesitate to join if most of their neighbors were Loyalists.

After Congress created the Continental Army, men began to enlist, but most of them didn't stay long. At the start of the war, Congress asked men to enlist only for one year. Later Congress did lengthen the term of service. When the soldiers' time was up, they went home. As a result, Washington's army never numbered more than 17,000 men.

Congress's inability to supply the army also frustrated Washington. The soldiers needed everything—blankets, shoes, food, and even guns and ammunition. Angrily, Washington wrote, "Could I have foreseen what I have, and am likely to experience, no consideration upon earth should have induced [persuaded] me to accept this command."

Many women tried to help the army. Martha Washington and other wives followed their husbands to army camps. The women cooked, did laundry, and



**ACTIVITY OPTIONS**

## SKILLBUILDER MINI-LESSON: CREATING A MULTIMEDIA PRESENTATION

BLOCK SCHEDULING

**Explaining the Skill** Explain to students that a multimedia presentation involves using a variety of media that could include any of the following: primary source materials; visual material such as photographs, paintings, charts, maps; electronic materials such as quick time clips, film clips, music or other recordings, or videotaped presentations.

**Applying the Skill** With the class, identify and list on the board several topics that seem suitable for a presentation that combines several media. Possibilities include public opinion, forming an army, or Washington's role.

Then discuss possible formats—a radio interview, a videotaped news report, a press conference, and so on. Be sure that students understand that they will need to incorporate a variety of components to make the presentation multimedia. Encourage students to work together in small groups to choose a topic and plan their presentation. Remind students that further research may be necessary to make their presentations effective.

 **In-Depth Resources: Unit 2**
- Skillbuilder Practice, p. 31

nursed sick or wounded soldiers. A few women even helped fight. Mary Hays earned the nickname "Molly Pitcher" by carrying water to tired soldiers during a battle. Deborah Sampson dressed as a man, enlisted, and fought in several engagements.

*Reading* **History**

**B. Solving Problems** How did Washington try to solve the problem of leading a small, inexperienced force against a large professional army?

**B. Answer** He decided the important thing was to survive, even if he didn't win any big battles. He was buying time until he could build a better army.

Building an army was crucial to Washington's plan. To the British, the Americans were disorganized, inexperienced rebels. The British thought that if they won a decisive battle, the Americans would give up. By contrast, Washington's main goal was to survive. To do so, he needed to keep an army in the field, win some battles—no matter how small—and avoid a crushing defeat. He knew he could not hope to win a major battle until he had a large, well-equipped army.

**These Hessian boots weighed about 12 pounds a pair.**

## 2 Struggle for the Middle States

As Chapter 6 explains, Washington had forced the British to retreat from Boston in March 1776. He then hurried his army to New York City, where he expected the British to go next. One British goal was to occupy coastal cities so that their navy could land troops and supplies in those cities. From there, they could launch their military campaigns.

Washington's hunch was correct. In July 1776, Britain's General William Howe arrived in New York with a large army. Then in August, more soldiers arrived, including about 9,000 Hessian mercenaries. A **mercenary** is a professional soldier hired to fight for a foreign country. British soldiers usually signed up for life—which discouraged enlistment. So Britain needed mercenaries, whom it hired from the German states.

**Background**

The British-hired mercenaries came from a part of Germany called Hesse, which is the origin of the term *Hessian.*

For several months, the British and American armies fought for New York State. Finally, the British forced Washington to retreat through New Jersey. By December, when the American army crossed the Delaware River into Pennsylvania, it was in terrible condition. Charles Willson Peale, a Philadelphia painter who watched the crossing, saw one muddy soldier who "had lost all his clothes. He was in an old, dirty blanket jacket, his beard long, and his face so full of sores he could not clean it." To Peale's shock, the soldier called his name. He was Peale's brother!

Political writer Thomas Paine also witnessed the hard conditions and the soldiers' low spirits on the retreat. To

**Skillbuilder Answers**

1. New Jersey
2. He sailed from New York, down the coast, and then up Chesapeake Bay.

***War in the Middle States,*** *1776–1777*

American forces
British forces
American victory
British victory

**GEOGRAPHY SKILLBUILDER Interpreting Maps**

1. **Place** *In what state did the American victories take place?*
2. **Movement** *How did the British general Howe travel from New York to Brandywine?*

195

## CHAPTER 7 • SECTION 1

**INSTRUCT: OBJECTIVE 2**

**Struggle for the Middle States**

Key Questions

- Why did the British want to occupy the coastal cities of the Middle Atlantic states?
- What course did the war take between July and December 1776?
- What significant gains did the colonial troops make at Trenton?

**MORE ABOUT . . .**

**Howe and Washington**

The case of the American army was so desperate at the end of 1776 that Washington is reported to have told his brother, "I think the game is pretty nearly up." If Howe had followed the Americans across the Delaware River and attacked, the British might have won the war within a few weeks. Instead, Howe followed the European military custom of not fighting during winters. He settled down comfortably in New York City and was taken completely by surprise when Washington attacked.

**HISTORY FROM VISUALS**

**Reading the Map** Point out that this map shows the location of the battlefront in the first year of the war. Ask students to identify which troops traveled on foot and which by boat. **Answer** American forces traveled on foot; British forces went by boat. Ask how travel by sea might have benefited the British and why American troops did not use the same method. **Possible Responses** British troops could rest aboard ship; they did not have to worry about ambush or attack. The Americans could not travel by sea because of the powerful British navy.

**Extension** Ask students to speculate how each method of travel might affect the speed of moving men and supplies.

**ACTIVITY OPTIONS**

**INTERDISCIPLINARY LINK: GEOGRAPHY**

BLOCK SCHEDULING

**TIME AND TRAVEL**

**Class Time** 10–15 minutes

**Task** Plotting the course of British ships across the Atlantic to the colonies

**Purpose** To understand the strategic necessity of controlling the coastal cities

**Supplies Needed**

- Globe, or map of the Atlantic, showing both North America and Europe
- Atlas map of winds and ocean currents

**Activity** Ask students to locate cities in England and the colonies. In the atlas, they can see wind patterns (the westerlies and trade winds). Have them trace routes between cities and estimate the distances across the ocean. Explain that the trip from London to Boston usually took about four weeks, more if weather was bad. Discuss the problems this might pose for British generals. Why was it essential for the British to hold the port cities? **Possible Response** They relied on troops and supplies that arrived by sea.

## MORE ABOUT . . .

***Washington Crossing the Delaware***

Painted in Düsseldorf, Germany, by artist Emanuel Leutze, this work was first exhibited in the United States in September 1851, at the American Art Union in New York. Historians have pointed out the painting's many historical inaccuracies; among other things, Washington probably did *not* stand during the crossing. Nor was he as remote and unapproachable as he appears here. Portraitists John Trumbull and Charles Wilson Peale both served with Washington, and their portraits show him as much more human and approachable.

## MORE ABOUT . . .

**The Battle of Trenton**

The Germans' celebration had consisted of heavy drinking and card playing. They had gone to sleep only a couple of hours before Washington reached Trenton—about 6:30 A.M. The German commander barely had time to dress himself and order his troops into battle. But the Americans had already taken over a number of houses in Trenton, dried their rifles, and positioned themselves at windows in those homes. The German commander fell mortally wounded, the Germans surrendered, and fighting was over by 9:30.

## INSTRUCT: OBJECTIVE 3

**Britain's Strategy/ Battles Along the Mohawk**

Key Questions

- What was the British strategy in 1777?
- How did Howe and St. Leger fail to follow through with the planned strategy?
- How did Howe's and St. Leger's actions affect Burgoyne?

**This famous painting of Washington crossing the Delaware River is inaccurate. Instead of the boats shown here, Washington used flat-bottomed boats that were 40- to 60-feet long.**

urge them to keep fighting, Paine published the first in a series of pamphlets called *The American Crisis.*

*A VOICE FROM THE PAST*

These are the times that try men's souls. The summer soldier and the sunshine patriot will, in this crisis, shrink from the service of their country; but he that stands it *now,* deserves the love and thanks of man and woman.

**Thomas Paine,** *The American Crisis*

*Reading* **History**

**C. Recognizing Propaganda** How does this passage promote the American cause?

**C. Possible Response** It says that those who endure hardships deserve to be honored.

Washington hoped a victory would encourage his weary men. He also knew that he must attack the British quickly because most of his soldiers would leave once their enlistments ended on December 31.

Late on December 25, 1776, Washington's troops rowed across the icy Delaware River to New Jersey. From there, they marched in bitter, early-morning cold to Trenton to surprise the Hessians, some of whom were sleeping after their Christmas celebration. The Americans captured or killed more than 900 Hessians and gained needed supplies. Washington's army won another victory at Princeton eight days later. These victories proved that the American general was better than the British had thought. The American army began to attract new recruits.

## 3 Britain's Strategy

Meanwhile, the British were pursuing a **strategy**—an overall plan of action—to seize the Hudson River Valley. If successful, they would cut off New England from the other states. The strategy called for three armies to meet at Albany, New York. General John Burgoyne would lead a force south from Canada. Lieutenant Colonel Barry St. Leger would lead his army from Lake Ontario down the Mohawk Valley. Burgoyne expected General Howe to follow the Hudson north from New York City.



## ACTIVITY OPTIONS

## INDIVIDUAL NEEDS

### LESS PROFICIENT READERS

**Sequencing Events** Show students how to construct a chart with the following headings: *Date, Battle, American Leader, British Leader.* Then have students review pages 194–196 and fill in appropriate material. They can continue to fill in the chart as they finish reading the section. Encourage them to use the chart as they work with their sequencing organizer; suggest that they keep the chart current as they continue through the chapter.

| Date | Battle | American Leader | British Leader |
|---|---|---|---|
| Dec. 26, 1776 | Trenton | Washington | Howe |
| | | | |
| | | | |
| | | | |

Burgoyne left Canada in June 1777 with an army that included British, Hessians, and Iroquois. In July, they captured Fort Ticonderoga.

Called "Gentleman Johnny" by his soldiers, Burgoyne enjoyed traveling slowly and throwing parties to celebrate victories. After Ticonderoga, his delays gave the Americans time to cut down trees to block his route. They also burned crops and drove off cattle, leaving the countryside bare of supplies for the British troops.

Things grew rougher during the last 25 miles of Burgoyne's march to Albany. On a map, the route looked easy, but it really crossed a swampy wilderness. The army had to build bridges and roads. Burgoyne took four weeks to reach the Hudson. Still confident, he looked forward to the **rendezvous,** or meeting, with St. Leger and Howe in Albany.

On August 4, Burgoyne received a message from Howe. He would not be coming north, Howe wrote, because he had decided to invade Pennsylvania to try to capture General Washington and Philadelphia—where the Continental Congress met. "Success be ever with you," wrote Howe. Yet Burgoyne needed Howe's soldiers, not his good wishes.

Howe did invade Pennsylvania. In September 1777, he defeated but did not capture Washington at the Battle of Brandywine. Howe then occupied Philadelphia. In October, Washington attacked Howe at Germantown. Washington lost the battle, however, and retreated.

*Reading History*
**D. Evaluating** Review Howe's two goals for his invasion of Pennsylvania. Was he successful?
**D. Answer** No. He captured Philadelphia but did not capture Washington.

**War in the North, 1777**

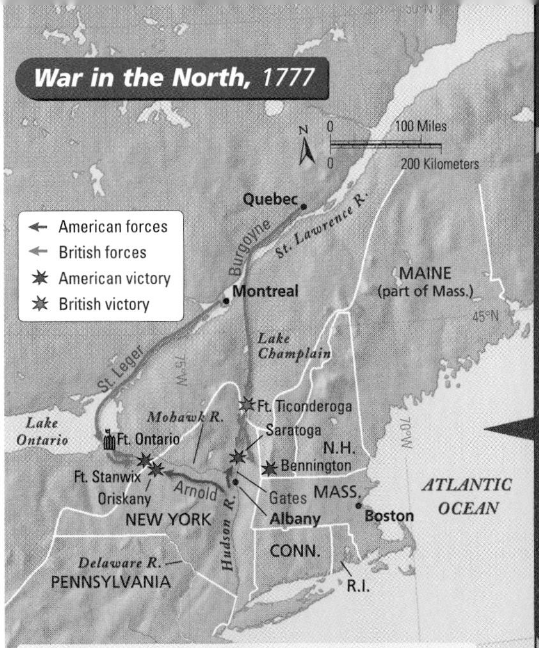

**GEOGRAPHY SKILLBUILDER Interpreting Maps**
1. **Place** *From which two cities did the British invade the United States?*
2. **Movement** *What did St. Leger want to capture by taking the longer route by way of Lake Ontario?*

Skillbuilder Answers
1. Quebec, Montreal
2. Fort Ontario, Fort Stanwix

## Battles Along the Mohawk

As Burgoyne received Howe's message, St. Leger faced his own obstacle in reaching Albany. In the summer of 1777, he was trying to defeat a small American force at Fort Stanwix in the Mohawk River valley of New York. St. Leger's forces included Iroquois led by Mohawk chief Joseph Brant, also called Thayendanegea (THĪ•ehn•DAHG•ee).

Brant and his sister, Molly, had strong ties to the British. Molly was a British official's wife, and Joseph was a convert to the Church of England. Both Joseph and Molly tried to convince the Iroquois to fight for the British, who upheld Iroquois rights to their land.

Vocabulary
**convert:** a person who changes religions

During August 1777, American general Benedict Arnold led a small army up the Mohawk River. He wanted to chase the British away from

**The Iroquois chief Joseph Brant was a British ally.**





### HISTORY FROM VISUALS

**Reading the Map** Point out that the British strategy shifted the battle front from the coastal cities to the inland frontier. Ask students to tell what other geographical obstacles the troops might encounter, in addition to the "swampy wilderness" mentioned in the text. **Possible Responses** The area was rough and mountainous, and probably much of the region was heavily forested.

**Extension** Have students do research to determine the following: How might conditions in Europe differ from those on the colonial frontier? Ask students how unfamiliarity with the territory might affect an army's success.

### MORE ABOUT . . .

**Burgoyne's March**

To "take to the field as a gentleman should," Burgoyne traveled with more than 30 wagons full of his personal belongings, wines, and the wardrobe of his lady friend. He also insisted on bringing overland about 140 artillery pieces. To cross 25 miles of swampy New York wilderness with this wagon train, Burgoyne's men laid log roads. Progress was slow—between a half-mile and a mile a day. Patriot general Philip Schuyler sent his woodsmen to harass the British troops, who also suffered from the heat, humidity, and biting swarms of mosquitoes and black flies.

### ACTIVITY OPTIONS

**MULTIPLE LEARNING STYLES: SPATIAL** — BLOCK SCHEDULING

**MAKING A BOARD GAME**

**Class Time** One class period

**Task** Making a board game to show important battles

**Purpose** To arrange events in the American Revolution in chronological sequence

**Supplies Needed**
- Posterboard
- Markers, rulers, pens

**Activity** Students can work in pairs to list the battles in order and then incorporate that information into a board game such as the one shown here. Have students write rules for the game.

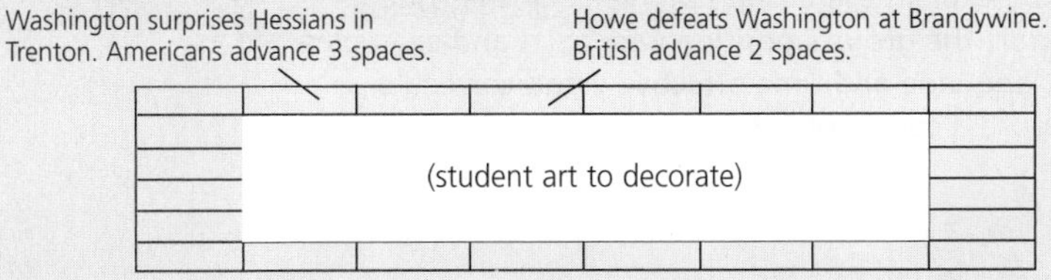

Washington surprises Hessians in Trenton. Americans advance 3 spaces.

Howe defeats Washington at Brandywine. British advance 2 spaces.

(student art to decorate)

**INSTRUCT: OBJECTIVE** 

**Saratoga: A Turning Point**

Key Questions

- Why did Burgoyne send troops into Vermont?
- What were the two most important results of the colonial victories at the Battles of Saratoga?

 **Humanities Transparency HT13, HT14**
- *Battle of Saratoga*
- *The Spirit of '76*

 **Geography Transparency GT7**
- Final Battle of Saratoga, 1777

Fort Stanwix. Arnold sent a captured Loyalist and some Iroquois who were American allies to spread the rumor that he had a large army.

The trick worked. St. Leger's troops were afraid they were about to be outnumbered. The army retreated so fast that it left behind tents, cannon, and supplies. Because of St. Leger's flight and Howe's refusal to follow the strategy, no one was left to rendezvous with Burgoyne.

## 4 Saratoga: A Turning Point

By this time, Burgoyne's army was running out of supplies, and it needed horses. The general sent a raiding party into Vermont to see what it could find. The raiding party encountered New England troops, who badly defeated it at the Battle of Bennington on August 16, 1777.

Despite this setback, Burgoyne's army headed slowly toward Albany. On the way, it met a powerful Continental Army force led by General Horatio Gates. They were waiting on a ridge called Bemis Heights, near Saratoga, New York. There the Americans had created fortifications, or built-up earthen walls, behind which to fight. The Polish engineer Tadeusz Kosciuszko (TAH•deh•oosh KAWSH•choosh•kaw) had helped the Americans do this.

*Reading* **History**

**E. Reading a Map** Find Saratoga on the map on page 197. Notice how close it is to Burgoyne's goal of Albany.

Burgoyne would have to break through the fortifications to proceed to Albany. On September 19, he attacked. While Gates commanded the Americans on the ridge, Benedict Arnold led an attack on nearby

**CITIZENSHIP TODAY**

**OBJECTIVE**

Students will explain the importance of free speech in both historic and modern American life.

***The American Crisis* Supports Independence**

*The American Crisis* includes 16 pamphlets written between 1776 and 1783. The first article appeared in the *Pennsylvania Journal* on December 19, 1776, at a time when the Continental Army had just suffered defeat in New York. The article so impressed George Washington that he ordered it read to all his troops with the hope of inspiring them.

 **Citizenship Today,** pp. 3–4

 **In-Depth Resources: Unit 2**
- Literature Selection: from *Citizen Tom Paine* by Howard Fast, pp. 36–38

**CITIZENSHIP TODAY**

# Exercising Free Speech

The British could have charged Thomas Paine with a crime for writing *The American Crisis.* The crime was sedition, or stirring up rebellion. By saying what he thought, Paine risked going to prison. Today U.S. citizens have the right to speak freely without fear of jail.

Like Thomas Paine, some students have used free speech to urge people to take action. For example, the Sidney Lanier Middle School in Houston, Texas, has published its school newspaper on the Internet. In October 1996, one writer urged other students to get involved in that year's election, saying, "Even though you will not be able to vote yet, you can still influence your parents to do so."

These students are working together to produce a school newspaper.

### How Do You Exercise Free Speech?

1. Working in a small group, choose an issue that you care about. Look through newsmagazines for ideas.
2. Use a cluster diagram to record your feelings and opinions about the issue.
3. As a group, decide what action you think people should take on the issue.
4. Write an article expressing the group's opinion. Each member should read the article and suggest changes. Revise the article.
5. Send the revised article to the editorial page of your school or local newspaper.

 **See Citizenship Handbook, page 282.**

 **Visit www.mcdougallittell.com to learn more about free speech.**

198

**STANDARDS FOR EVALUATION: CITIZENSHIP TODAY**

**Each article should**
- focus on a subject that the students care about.
- be directed to an appropriate audience.
- clearly explain the group's opinions on the issue.
- support the group's position with facts and examples.
- use language and tone effectively and correctly.
- propose a course of action.

Freeman's Farm. His men repeatedly charged the British and inflicted heavy casualties. Still, the British held their position.

On October 7, another battle broke out. Again Arnold led daring charges against the British. Although hundreds of muskets were firing at him, he galloped through the battlefield "like a madman," a sergeant later said. Frightened, Burgoyne's Hessian mercenaries began to fall back. Eventually, a bullet tore into Arnold's leg and stopped him. Even so, the Americans forced Burgoyne to retreat.

Burgoyne's army moved slowly through heavy rain to a former army camp at Saratoga. By the time they arrived, the men were exhausted. Some fell in the mud and slept in their wet uniforms. The Continental Army then surrounded Burgoyne's army and fired on it day and night without stopping. Burgoyne decided to surrender. The series of conflicts that led to this surrender is known as the **Battles of Saratoga**.

The Battles of Saratoga had two very different consequences. As Benedict Arnold was recovering from his wound, he married a woman who was a Loyalist. Over time, Arnold came to feel that Congress had not rewarded him enough for his heroic actions at Saratoga and other battles. Influenced by his bitterness and his wife, he betrayed his army. In 1780, he agreed to turn over an American fort to the British. Although his plot was discovered before he could carry it out, he escaped. Even today, the name *Benedict Arnold* is used to mean traitor.

On the positive side, the victory at Saratoga was a turning point in the Revolution. It caused European nations to think that the Americans might win their war for independence. As you will read in Section 2, several European nations decided to help America in its struggle.

**F. Possible Response** European help for the United States, because that made up for American weaknesses

***Reading*History**

**F. Forming and Supporting Opinions** Which of the two consequences of the Battles of Saratoga was more significant? Why?

## America's HERITAGE

**THE FIRST FLAG**

June 14 is Flag Day in the United States. On June 14, 1777, the Continental Congress adopted the stars and stripes design for the U.S. flag. According to legend, a Philadelphia seamstress named Betsy Ross designed the first flag, illustrated below. Historians have found no evidence to support this legend. However, Ross did make flags for the Pennsylvania navy.

## America's HERITAGE

**The First Flag**

The Continental Congress offered this explanation of the design and color choices for the new flag: "That the flag of the 13 United States be 13 stripes, alternate red and white; that the union be 13 stars, white in a blue field, representing a new constellation. . . . White signifies Purity and Innocence; Red, Hardiness and Valor; Blue signifies Vigilance, Perseverance and Justice."

## ASSESS & RETEACH

**Setting the Stage** Have students complete a sequence of events for 1776 and 1777.

**Formal Assessment**
- Section Quiz, p. 102

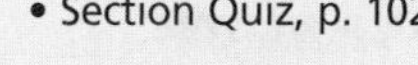

**Critical Thinking Transparency CT19**
- Setting the Stage

**RETEACHING ACTIVITY**

Divide students into six teams and furnish each team with a felt-tip marker, a sheet of 11 x 17 paper, and a pair of scissors. Assign one part of the section to each team and tell them to compose three cause-and-effect statements on their paper. Have teams cut their statements apart, separating causes from effects, and give both sets to you. Redistribute the effects slips to teams. Then read each cause aloud, letting students identify the correct effect. As each cause is paired with its effect, pin the statement on a bulletin board.

**In-Depth Resources: Unit 2**
- Reteaching Activity, p. 39

## Section 1 Assessment

**1. Terms & Names**

**Identify:**
- George Washington
- mercenary
- strategy
- rendezvous
- Battles of Saratoga

**2. Taking Notes**

Use a cluster diagram like the one shown to list the difficulties Americans faced in the early years of the war.

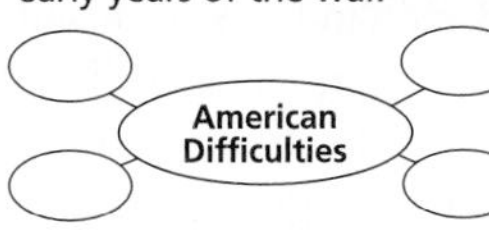


Which difficulty do you think was hardest to overcome?

**3. Main Ideas**

a. How were Americans divided over the issue of separating from Great Britain?

b. Why was it difficult for George Washington to form and keep a large army?

c. How did the Battles of Saratoga mark a turning point in the war?

**4. Critical Thinking**

**Contrasting** How did the British and American strategies differ during the early years of the war?

**THINK ABOUT**
- what the British expected from the Americans
- Washington's main goals for the American army
- why Burgoyne invaded from Canada

**ACTIVITY OPTIONS**

**LANGUAGE ARTS / ART**

Learn more about a Revolutionary War leader. Write a brief **biography** or create a **trading card** with a picture on one side and important facts on the other.



## Section 1 Assessment

**1. Terms & Names**

**George Washington,** p. 194
**mercenary,** p. 195
**strategy,** p. 196
**rendezvous,** p. 197
**Battles of Saratoga,** p. 199

**2. Taking Notes**

divisions in society about the war; short enlistments robbed the army of men; lack of supplies and military experience; brutal conditions

Responses will vary. Make sure the students give reasons why they chose a particular difficulty.

**3. Main Ideas**

**a.** Patriots and Neutrals were about equal; Loyalists made up only a small percentage. **b.** recruiting difficulties; short enlistment terms; lack of supplies **c.** It kept the British from isolating New England; it gave the Europeans more confidence to aid America.

**4. Critical Thinking**

The British tried to split the colonies in two to weaken them. Washington tried to survive by winning and retreating.

**ACTIVITY OPTIONS**

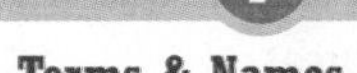

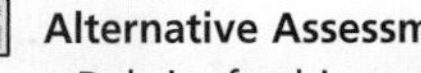

**Alternative Assessment**
- Rubrics for biographies, 4.4
- Rubrics for trading cards, 1.7

## SECTION OBJECTIVES

1. To explain why and how Europeans helped the United States
2. To gain insight into the hardships and sacrifices of the revolutionary forces
3. To describe the war on the frontier
4. To summarize important battles at sea

**SKILLBUILDER**

Interpreting Maps: Movement, Region, p. 203

**CRITICAL THINKING**

Recognizing Effects, p. 201
Identifying Facts and Opinions, p. 202
Analyzing Points of View, pp. 203, 205
Making Decisions, p. 204

## FOCUS & MOTIVATE

### 5-MINUTE WARM-UP

**Making Inferences** To help students understand how the war effort expanded, have them answer the following questions.

1. Read the headings on pages 200–201. Who becomes involved in the Americans' revolt? Why might other countries aid the Patriots?
2. Now read the headings on pages 203–204. Where does the fighting move? When?

 Warm-Up Transparency WT7

## INSTRUCT

### INSTRUCT: OBJECTIVE 

**Help from Abroad/ Europeans Help Washington**

Key Questions

- Why did France and Spain ally themselves with the United States?
- What were Lafayette's early contributions?
- How did Barons de Kalb and von Steuben help General Washington?

**In-Depth Resources: Unit 2**
- Guided Reading, p. 27
- Building Vocabulary, p. 30

**Reading Study Guide** (Spanish and English), pp. 67–68

# 2 The War Expands

**TERMS & NAMES**
ally
Marquis de Lafayette
bayonet
desert
privateer
James Forten
John Paul Jones

| MAIN IDEA | WHY IT MATTERS NOW |
|---|---|
| Some Europeans decided to help America. As the war continued, it spread to the sea and the frontier. | This was the beginning of the United States' formal relationships with other nations. |

## ONE AMERICAN'S STORY

**To defeat the mighty British Empire, the United States needed a foreign ally. An ally is a country that agrees to help another country achieve a common goal. The ideal ally would share America's goal of defeating Britain. It also had to be able to provide money, troops, and ships. So the United States turned to France—Britain's long-time enemy.**

**In the fall of 1776, Congress sent Benjamin Franklin to the French capital, Paris. His job was to persuade France to be the ally of the United States. Franklin was already famous for his experiments with electricity. When he reached Paris, he became a celebrity. He wrote to his daughter, saying that medallions with his likeness were popular there.**

**Franklin's simple Quaker coat and fur hat amused the French. The clothes fit the image they had of him—a wise, noble man from a wild country.**

*A VOICE FROM THE PAST*

These, with the pictures, busts [sculptures of the head and shoulders], and prints (of which copies upon copies are spread everywhere), have made your father's face as well known as that of the moon.

**Benjamin Franklin,** letter to his daughter Sally

**In spite of his popularity, Franklin couldn't convince the French to become America's formal ally until after the victory at Saratoga. Then the French agreed to an alliance. This section explains how the war expanded after foreign allies joined the American side.**

### 1 Help from Abroad

France was still bitter over its defeat by Britain in the French and Indian War, in which France lost its North American colonies. The French hoped to take revenge on the British by helping Britain's American colonies break free. In 1776, France began to give secret aid to the Americans. However, the French didn't want to lose to Britain a second time. That is why they didn't publicly ally themselves with the United States until after the Americans had proved they could win battles.

After hearing of the American victory at Saratoga, King Louis XVI of France recognized U.S. independence. In 1778, France signed two treaties of alliance with the United States. By doing so, France went to



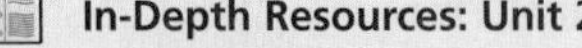

**RECOMMENDED RESOURCES**

**In-Depth Resources: Unit 2**
- Guided Reading, p. 27
- Building Vocabulary, p. 30
- Primary Source, p. 34
- Reteaching Activity, p. 40
- Enrichment Activity p. 43

**Reading Study Guide** (Spanish and English), pp. 67–68

**American History Plays**
- *Fires at Valley Forge* by Barret H. Clark

**Formal Assessment**
- Section Quiz, p. 103

**Alternative Assessment**
- Rubrics, 1.3
- Rubrics, 3.6

**Access for Students Acquiring English/ESL**
- Guided Reading, p. 44

**Technology Resources**

 **Electronic Teacher Tools with Test Maker**

 **ClassZone** www.mcdougallittell.com

war with Britain. As part of its new alliance, France sent badly needed funds, supplies, and troops to America.

In 1779, France persuaded its ally Spain to help the Americans. Spain was also Britain's rival. The Spanish governor of Louisiana, General Bernardo de Gálvez, acted quickly. He captured the British strongholds of Natchez and Baton Rouge in the lower Mississippi Valley.

**Background**
Galveston, Texas, is named for Gálvez.

From there, his small army went on to take Mobile, and in 1781 Pensacola in West Florida. These victories prevented the British from attacking the United States from the southwest. In addition, Britain had to keep thousands of troops fighting Gálvez—instead of fighting the Americans. However, like France, Spain's motives were not simply to help the United States. Gálvez's victories helped extend Spain's empire in North America.

A. Answer They forced Britain to spread its troops over many fronts, such as the West Indies.

*Reading*History
**A. Recognizing Effects** How did America's allies prevent Britain from focusing all its might on the Americans?

By entering the war on America's side, France and Spain forced the British to fight a number of enemies on land and sea. The British had to spread their military resources over many fronts. For example, they were afraid they might have to fight the French in the West Indies, so they sent troops there. This prevented the British from concentrating their strength to defeat the inexperienced Americans.

## Europeans Help Washington

The Americans gained some of the military experience they needed from Europe. Several European military officers came to Washington's aid, including men from France, Poland, and the German states.

**Background**
Many of these European officers were professional soldiers looking for an army that would hire them. Some, like Lafayette, also believed in the American cause.

The **Marquis de Lafayette** (LAF•ee•EHT) was a 19-year-old French nobleman who volunteered to serve in Washington's army. He wanted a military career, and he believed in the American cause. He quickly gained Washington's confidence and was given the command of an army division. Lafayette won respect and love from his men by sharing their hardships. Called "the soldier's friend," he used his own money to buy warm clothing for his ragged troops. Washington regarded him almost as a son.

Lafayette fought in many battles and also persuaded the French king to send a 6,000-man army to America. He became a hero in both France and the United States. Later he took part in France's own revolution.

Along with Lafayette came the Baron de Kalb, a German officer who had served in the French army. He became one of Washington's generals and earned a reputation for bravery. In 1780, he received 11 wounds in the Battle of Camden and died.

Another German, Baron von Steuben, helped turn the inexperienced Americans

Lafayette stands with the slave James Armistead, whose owner allowed him to spy for Lafayette. After the war, the state of Virginia set Armistead free. Armistead then took Lafayette's last name as his own.

201

### MORE ABOUT . . .

**Help from France**
Secretly, the French and Spanish had been aiding the Americans since May 1776. French Foreign Minister Vergennes, along with the Bourbons of Spain, had set up a "dummy" firm, Rodrigue Hortalez et Cie. Cash, credit, and supplies such as bedding, uniforms, muskets, and high-quality gunpowder came to the Patriots through this fictitious business.

On February 6, 1778, France formally recognized the independence of the United States. Along with supplies, France now offered its powerful fleet, second in size only to Great Britain's. The French also opened their ports to American warships. From these bases the American seamen, especially one Captain John Paul Jones, took great pride in harassing British ships and shipping in the English Channel.

### MORE ABOUT . . .

**Frederick von Steuben**
Washington put 47-year-old Steuben in charge of training the Americans at Valley Forge in February 1778. Steuben's rigorous military training included only ten command words; the shorter and fewer the commands, the faster the men could obey. Steuben also instilled professional pride in the demoralized troops. He taught them to conduct themselves as if their ragged clothing were full dress uniform. By late March, Washington could write that "our prospects begin to brighten." By the end of the difficult winter, the Continental Army was a cohesive, disciplined fighting force.

### ACTIVITY OPTIONS

### INDIVIDUAL NEEDS

**LESS PROFICIENT READERS**

**Finding Main Ideas and Details** As a way of previewing the section with students, have them read the headings aloud. On the board, write each heading inside a circle. As students read the paragraphs under each heading, ask them to suggest important words and phrases. Write these in smaller circles around each heading to create concept webs. Point out to students that they are supplying details about the main idea inside each circle.

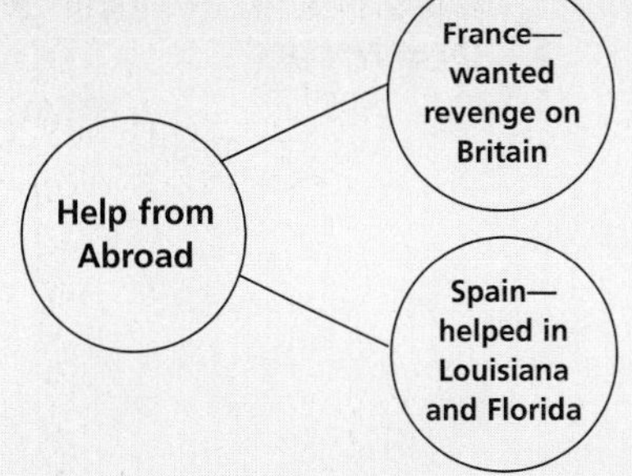

## MORE ABOUT . . .

**Musket Balls**

Along with almost all other supplies, the revolutionaries were often short of musket balls (bullets) and the lead from which to make them. At the very beginning of the war, Patriots had a "leaden windfall": in New York City, a crowd toppled the 4,000-pound lead statue of King George III. After breaking it up, they sent the pieces to munitions makers in Connecticut, who produced 42,000 bullets from the former monument to royalty.

## INSTRUCT: OBJECTIVE 2

**Winter at Valley Forge**

Key Questions

- What kinds of help did the Americans need from their European allies?
- What hardships did American troops endure during the winter at Valley Forge?
- How did private citizens help the revolutionary cause?

## daily*life*

**Camp Life in Winter**

Congress had selected Valley Forge as a winter retreat during the summer of 1777. Supplies had been hidden there—thousands of barrels of flour, horseshoes, tools, and other necessities. But British troops under General Howe had come foraging in the autumn. They had found and removed these provisions.

Nearly everything was lacking at Valley Forge—even water. The nearest source of good drinking water was two miles away. Each day, those men who were healthy enough to work had to carry supplies of water back to camp.

When Steuben first saw the troops he was to train, he said, "No European army could have held together in such circumstances."

 **In-Depth Resources: Unit 2**

- Primary Source, p. 34
- Enrichment Activity, p. 43

into a skilled fighting force. Washington asked him to train the army. In 1778, Steuben began by forming a model company of 100 men. Then he taught them how to move in lines and columns and how to handle weapons properly. Under Steuben's direction, the soldiers practiced making charges with **bayonets**—long steel knives attached to the ends of guns. Within a month, the troops were executing drills with speed and precision. Once the model company succeeded, the rest of the army adopted Steuben's methods.

## 2 Winter at Valley Forge

Help from Europeans came at a time when the Americans desperately needed it. In late 1777, Britain's General Howe forced Washington to retreat from Philadelphia. Beginning in the winter of 1777–1778, Washington and his army camped at Valley Forge in southeast Pennsylvania.

On the march to Valley Forge, Washington's army was so short on supplies that many soldiers had only blankets to cover themselves. They also lacked shoes. The barefoot men left tracks of blood on the frozen ground as they marched. The soldiers' condition did not improve at camp. The Marquis de Lafayette described what he saw.

**A VOICE FROM THE PAST**

> The unfortunate soldiers were in want of everything; they had neither coats, nor hats, nor shirts, nor shoes; their feet and their legs froze till they grew black and it was often necessary to amputate them. . . . The Army frequently passed whole days without food.
>
> **Marquis de Lafayette,** quoted in *Valley Forge: Pinnacle of Courage*

**B. Possible Response** He is recounting facts, such as lack of coats, hats, and so on. However, the phrase *unfortunate soldiers* is an opinion.

*Reading***History**

**B. Identifying Facts and Opinions** Is Lafayette mainly recounting facts or expressing opinions? Explain.

Because of this, the name *Valley Forge* came to stand for the great hardships that Americans endured in the Revolutionary War. Over the winter, the soldiers at Valley Forge grew weak from not having enough food or warm clothing. Roughly a quarter of them died from malnutrition, exposure to the cold, or diseases such as smallpox and typhoid fever.

**daily *life***

**CAMP LIFE IN WINTER**

At Valley Forge, soldiers slept in small huts, 12 men to a hut. They slept in shifts so they could take turns using the scarce blankets. The men also shared clothing. If one went on guard duty, the others lent him their clothes and stayed by the fire in the hut until he came back. Guards had to stand in old hats to keep their shoeless feet warm.

The soldiers cooked on hot stones, in iron kettles, or on portable iron braziers. Often the only food they had was fire cakes—a bread made of flour and water paste.

These iron kettles were so heavy that soldiers often threw them away on a march.

This surgeon's kit includes a saw, used to perform amputations.

Soldiers would place burning coals in braziers like this. Braziers were used to cook food and heat huts.



**ACTIVITY OPTIONS**

**INTERDISCIPLINARY LINK: MATH** — BLOCK SCHEDULING

**FEEDING THE ARMY**

**Class Time** 15–25 minutes

**Task** Figuring the daily cost of feeding one soldier

**Purpose** To gain insight into the supply shortage of the Continental Army

**Supplies Needed**

- Paper, pencil
- Calculators (optional)

**Activity** By March 1778, when supplies were more available, each soldier was theoretically entitled to a daily ration of a pound and a half of flour or bread; a pound of beef or fish, or three-fourths pound of pork; half a pint of peas or beans (dried); and a gill (4 ounces) of spirits. Have students work in pairs or small groups to determine how much food Washington would have needed each week, at this rate, to supply the approximately 8,000 soldiers who had survived the winter.

Washington appealed to Congress to send the soldiers supplies, but it was slow in responding. Luckily, private citizens sometimes came to the soldiers' aid. According to one story, on New Year's Day 1778, a group of Philadelphia women drove ten teams of oxen into camp. The oxen were pulling wagons loaded with supplies and 2,000 shirts. The women had the oxen killed to provide food for the men.

C. Possible Response love of country; love of General Washington

**ReadingHistory**
**C. Analyzing Points of View** What are two different explanations for why American soldiers did not desert?

Despite the hardships, Washington and his soldiers showed amazing endurance. Under such circumstances, soldiers often **desert,** or leave military duty without intending to return. Some soldiers did desert, but Lieutenant Colonel John Brooks wrote that the army stayed together because of "Love of our Country." The men also stayed because of Washington. Private Samuel Downing declared that the soldiers "loved him. They'd sell their lives for him."

*"If a country is not worth protecting, it is not worth claiming."*
George Rogers Clark

## 3 War on the Frontier

Elsewhere, other Americans also took on difficult challenges. In 1777, a 24-year-old frontiersman named George Rogers Clark walked into the office of Virginia's governor, Patrick Henry. Clark said he had come to take part in defending the Western frontier. He lived in Kentucky, which was claimed by Virginia. Clark wanted Virginia to defend that region against British soldiers and their Native American allies in what is now Indiana and Illinois. "If a country is not worth protecting," he said, "it is not worth claiming."

**Background**
In the late 1700s, the Western frontier was the region between the Appalachian Mountains and the Mississippi River.

Skillbuilder Answers
1. Fort Detroit
2. the Ohio and the Mississippi

Clark was difficult to ignore. He stood six feet tall, had red hair, and displayed a dramatic personality. He persuaded Governor Henry that he was right. The governor told Clark to raise an army to capture British posts on the Western frontier.

In May of 1778, Clark and a group of frontiersmen began to travel down the Ohio River. He recruited others on the way, until he had a force of 175 to 200. They went by boat and later on foot to Kaskaskia, a British post on the Mississippi River. They captured Kaskaskia without a fight.

Then they moved east to take Fort Sackville at Vincennes, in present-day Indiana. Earlier, a small force sent by Clark had taken Vincennes, but British forces under Henry Hamilton had recaptured it. Settlers called Hamilton the "Hair Buyer" because he supposedly paid rewards for American scalps.

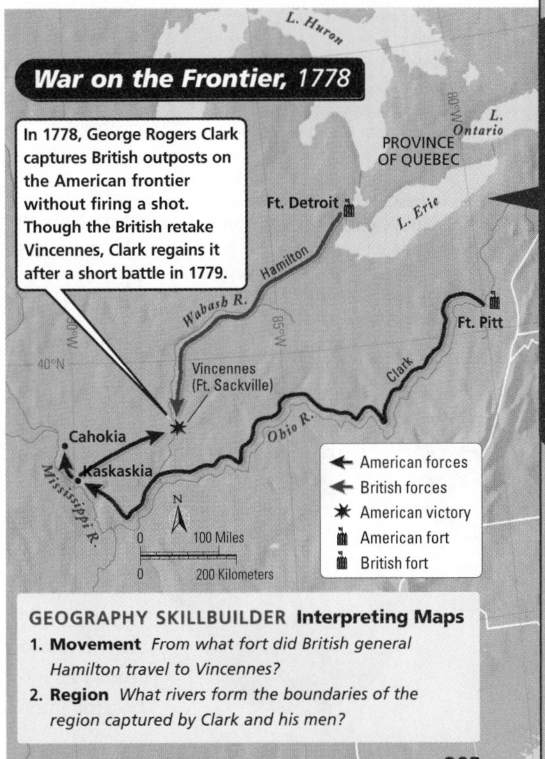
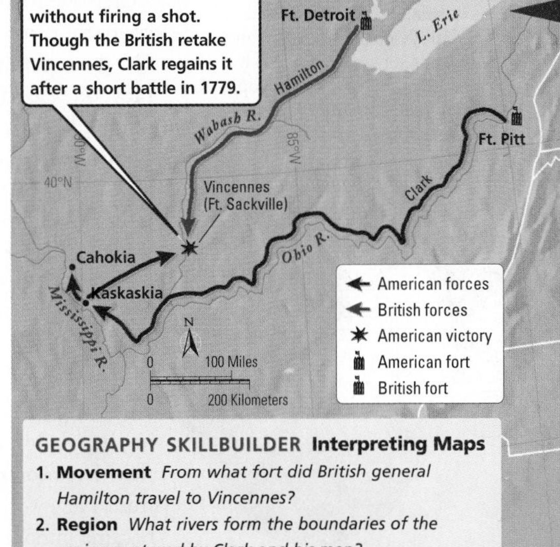


**GEOGRAPHY SKILLBUILDER Interpreting Maps**
1. **Movement** *From what fort did British general Hamilton travel to Vincennes?*
2. **Region** *What rivers form the boundaries of the region captured by Clark and his men?*

203

**MORE ABOUT . . .**

**Desertions**
Soldiers of the militia wanted to stay close to their homes. They were likely to disappear during spring planting or fall harvesting, a source of complaint for Washington and other American officers. However, time and again, the local militia seemed to appear when they were needed in their own region.

**INSTRUCT: OBJECTIVE 3**

**War on the Frontier**
Key Questions
- How did Clark justify his request for a command?
- Why was Clark's victory at Vincennes important to the revolutionary cause?

**HISTORY FROM VISUALS**

**Reading the Map** Have students study the map to gain clues about broad strategic objectives. Why was the sparsely settled frontier region around Kaskaskia, Cahokia, and Vincennes important to both sides? **Possible Response** The confluence of rivers made this area the key to controlling the entire region drained by the Mississippi, Wabash, and Ohio rivers.

**Extension** Have the students use an atlas to find out which states are now in the area labeled *frontier* in 1778.

**ACTIVITY OPTIONS**

**INTERDISCIPLINARY LINK: HUMANITIES** — BLOCK SCHEDULING

**THE REVOLUTION IN ART**

**Class Time** One class period

**Task** Using paintings as historical documents

**Purpose** To make inferences about history from art

**Supplies Needed**
- Sources for paintings on Revolutionary War events (books, museum postcards, Internet sites)
- Construction paper
- Pens and markers

**Activity** Encourage students to find paintings of events from the Revolutionary War. They can print out material from Web sites or photocopy paintings from books. Tell them to remove and save all captions, numbering them to indicate which painting they go with. Have them mount the pictures on construction paper and display them around the room. Let students see how many battles, events, and leaders they can identify without referring to the captions. What inferences can they make from this art?

**MORE ABOUT . . .**

**George Rogers Clark and the Frontier**

Called the "Washington of the West," Clark was one of the intensely patriotic frontiersmen who offered help to fellow soldiers "back east" at the Revolution's start. By capturing British strongholds on the western frontier, Clark not only provided the Americans with a claim to that territory but also opened another front that the British would have to guard—thus forcing them to split their forces and attention.

**INSTRUCT: OBJECTIVE 4**

**War at Sea/A Naval Hero**

Key Questions

- Why did the colonists need to challenge Britain's control of the seas?
- What did privateers contribute to the war effort?
- What effects did the victory of John Paul Jones have?

**STRANGE *but* True**

**The First Combat Submarine**

Earlier in the war, David Bushnell, designer of the *Turtle,* had tried to blow up British ships by setting afloat kegs filled with explosives. No ships were destroyed, but the attack so alarmed the British that they began shooting at anything that floated. The events inspired Philadelphia politician Francis Hopkinson to write a poem, "The Battle of the Kegs," which became quite popular among Patriots.

Determined to retake Fort Sackville, Clark and his men set out for Vincennes from Kaskaskia in February 1779. Hamilton wasn't expecting an attack because the rivers were overflowing their banks and the woods were flooded. Clark's men slogged through miles of icy swamps and waded through chest-deep water. They caught the British at Vincennes by surprise.

When Hamilton and his troops tried to remain in the fort, Clark pretended to have a larger force than he really had. He also found a way to frighten the British into leaving. Clark and his men had captured several Native Americans, who were allies of the British and had American scalps on their belts. Clark executed some of them in plain view of the fort. He promised to do the same to Hamilton and his men if they didn't surrender immediately. The British gave up.

Clark's victory gave the Americans a hold on the vast region between the Great Lakes and the Ohio River. This area was more than half the total size of the original 13 states. However, Fort Detroit on Lake Erie remained in the hands of the British.

**D. Possible Response** They had American scalps; it was the only way he could frighten the larger British force into surrendering.

***Reading*History**

**D. Making Decisions** What factors do you think influenced Clark's decision to execute his prisoners?

**THE FIRST COMBAT SUBMARINE**

During the Revolution, the Americans built the first combat submarine—the *Turtle,* shown below. It held only a pilot, who steered with one hand and cranked a propeller with the other. To submerge, the pilot used a foot pump to let in water.

In 1776, the *Turtle* failed on its mission to attach a bomb to a British warship in New York harbor. It reached the ship but couldn't drill through its copper-clad hull. The *Turtle* failed at later missions, too.

## 4 War at Sea

The war expanded not only to the frontier but also to the sea. By 1777, Britain had about 100 warships off the American coast. This allowed Britain to control the Atlantic trade routes. There was no way the Americans could defeat the powerful British navy.

But American privateers attacked British merchant ships. A **privateer** is a privately owned ship that a wartime government gives permission to attack an enemy's merchant ships. After capturing a British merchant ship, the crew of a privateer sold its cargo and shared the money. As a result, a desire for profit as well as patriotism motivated privateers. The states and Congress commissioned more than 1,000 privateers to prey on the British. During the war, they captured hundreds of British ships. This disrupted trade, causing British merchants to call for the war to end.

**Vocabulary**

**merchant ship:** a ship used in trade

Many men answered the privateers' call for volunteers. Among them was 14-year-old **James Forten,** who was the son of a free African-American sail maker. In 1780, Forten signed up to sail on the *Royal Louis* to earn money for his family after his father died. When a British ship captured the *Royal Louis* in 1781, the British offered Forten a free trip to England. Reportedly, Forten refused, saying he would never betray his country. Released from a British prison after the war, Forten walked barefoot from New York to his home in Philadelphia. He later became famous for his efforts to end slavery.



**ACTIVITY OPTIONS**

**MULTIPLE LEARNING STYLES: INTRAPERSONAL**

**BLOCK SCHEDULING**

**LETTERS FROM A CAPTIVE**

**Class Time** 15 minutes

**Task** Writing a letter to express the thoughts of James Forten

**Purpose** To analyze the major decisions that some young people faced during the Revolution

**Supplies Needed**

- Paper and pencils

**Activity** Ask students to consider the hopes and fears that James Forten must have experienced as a powderboy on the *Royal Louis* and as a prisoner of war. Have each student write a letter telling of these events from one of the following points of view: (1) Forten as a war captive, not knowing whether the British will keep him prisoner or sell him as a slave in the West Indies; (2) Forten writing from New York to his family after his release from the British prison; (3) Forten as an old man, looking back on events of his boyhood.

## A Naval Hero

Though outnumbered, the Continental Navy scored several victories against the British. An officer named **John Paul Jones** won the most famous sea battle.

In 1779, Jones became the commander of a ship named *Bonhomme Richard.* With four other ships, he patrolled the English coast. In September, Jones's vessels approached a convoy in which two British warships were guarding a number of supply ships.

**Vocabulary**
**convoy:** a group of ships traveling together for safety

Jones closed in on the *Serapis,* the larger of the two warships. At one point, the *Bonhomme Richard* rammed the better-armed British vessel. As the two ships locked together, the confident British captain demanded that Jones surrender. In words that have become a famous U.S. Navy slogan, Jones replied, "I have not yet begun to fight!"

The two warships were so close together that the muzzles of their guns almost touched. They blasted away, each seriously damaging the other. On the shore, crowds of Britons gathered under a full moon to watch the fighting. After a fierce three-and-a-half-hour battle, the main mast of the *Serapis* cracked and fell. The ship's captain then surrendered. The *Bonhomme Richard* was so full of holes that it eventually sank, so Jones and his crew had to sail away in the *Serapis*!

Jones's success against the best navy in the world angered the British and inspired the Americans. Even so, the Americans knew that the war had to be won on land. The next section discusses the major land battles in the closing years of the war.

### AMERICA'S HISTORY MAKERS

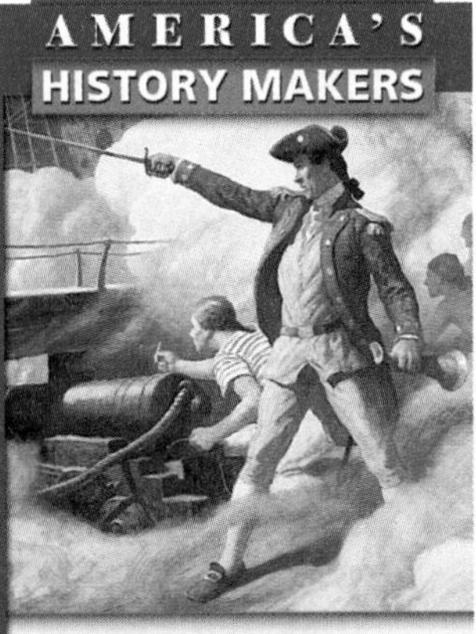

**JOHN PAUL JONES**
**1747–1792**

The most famous naval officer of the Revolution is known by a fake name. He was born John Paul in Scotland and first went to sea as a 12-year-old. By age 21, he had command of a merchant ship.

In 1773, Paul killed the leader of a mutiny on his ship. To avoid a murder trial, he fled to America and added Jones to his name.

Bold and daring, Jones scored many victories against the British. But his battle with the *Serapis* is what earned his place in history.

**What are the two words that you think best describe Jones's character? Explain.**

### AMERICA'S HISTORY MAKERS

**John Paul Jones**

Under a commission from Ben Franklin, Jones commanded three small warships and an old armed French brigantine (*Bonhomme Richard,* to honor Poor Richard, Franklin's famed almanac character). Jones's raids on the merchant ships in the Channel and on towns along the coastline spread panic and brought the war in the colonies much closer to home than the British people liked. In addition to the *Serapis* incident, Jones's career is notable for a "first" and a "last"—his ship was the first to fly the American colors; and his attack on Whitehaven, a port town in western England, was the last invasion of the British mainland.

**Possible Responses: famous, daring, violent, bold, impulsive**

## ASSESS & RETEACH

**Setting the Stage** Have students complete the sequence of events for the years 1778 and 1779.

 **Formal Assessment**
- Section Quiz, p. 103

### RETEACHING ACTIVITY

Assign pairs of students to review various parts of this section and write three- to five-sentence summaries. (More than one pair will be working with any given part.) When students have completed their summaries, have all pairs assigned to the same section division get together to share and discuss their summaries. Have these larger groups compose a revised, edited summary based on their discussion. Post summaries on the bulletin board.

 **In-Depth Resources: Unit 2**
- Reteaching Activity, p. 40

### Section 2 Assessment

**1. Terms & Names**

**Identify:**
- ally
- Marquis de Lafayette
- bayonet
- desert
- privateer
- James Forten
- John Paul Jones

**2. Taking Notes**

Use this diagram to list the effects of the entry of France and Spain into the war.

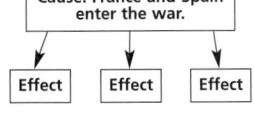

Cause: France and Spain enter the war.
→ Effect | Effect | Effect

**3. Main Ideas**

a. What role did Benjamin Franklin play in helping America win the Revolution?

b. How did European officers such as Lafayette aid America in the Revolutionary War?

c. What was John Paul Jones's major contribution during the war, and why was it important?

**4. Critical Thinking**

**Analyzing Points of View**
Why do you think George Rogers Clark thought the frontier was important to defend?

**THINK ABOUT**
- why General Hamilton was called "Hair Buyer"
- why America might have wanted the frontier region after the war

**ACTIVITY OPTIONS**

**ART** / **SPEECH**

Imagine yourself at Valley Forge in the winter of 1777–1778. Create a **comic strip** or give a **talk** describing your response to the harsh conditions.



### Section 2 Assessment

**1. Terms & Names**

**ally,** p. 200
**Marquis de Lafayette,** p. 201
**bayonet,** p. 202
**desert,** p. 203
**privateer,** p. 204
**James Forten,** p. 204
**John Paul Jones,** p. 205

**2. Taking Notes**

Effects: France sends troops, funds, and supplies; Spain fights the British in the Mississippi Valley and Florida; Britain sends troops to the West Indies to defend against France.

**3. Main Ideas**

**a.** He persuaded France to be America's ally. **b.** They trained special troops; led troops into battle; fought and died; helped attain more foreign aid. **c.** He defeated the British warship *Serapis,* which raised American spirits.

**4. Critical Thinking**

because more Americans would want to move into that region after the war ended

**ACTIVITY OPTIONS**

 **Alternative Assessment**
- Rubrics for comic strip, 1.3
- Rubrics for speeches, 3.6

## SECTION OBJECTIVES

1. To explain why the war shifted to the South
2. To analyze fighting methods and their effects
3. To summarize events that led to the war's end

**SKILLBUILDER**
Interpreting Maps: Place, Movement, p. 209

**CRITICAL THINKING**
Drawing Conclusions, p. 207
Evaluating, p. 207
Contrasting, p. 209
Analyzing Causes, p. 210

## FOCUS & MOTIVATE

### 5-MINUTE WARM-UP

**Making Inferences** These questions will help the student understand fighting methods in the war.

1. Look at the picture on page 206. What does the picture suggest about the involvement of civilians in the war?
2. Look at the heading on page 207. What does the word *guerrilla* mean? Given the picture and this word, what changes in the way the war was fought will this section describe?

 Warm-Up Transparency WT7

## INSTRUCT

**INSTRUCT: OBJECTIVE 1**

**Savannah and Charles Town**
Key Questions
- Why did their victories in the North bring the British no closer to winning the war?
- What considerations led the British to shift their forces to the South?
- Why was the defeat at Charles Town the worst American disaster of the war?

**In-Depth Resources: Unit 2**
- Guided Reading, p. 28

**Reading Study Guide** (Spanish and English), pp. 69–70

# 3 The Path to Victory

**TERMS & NAMES**
Lord Cornwallis
guerrillas
pacifist
Battle of Yorktown

| MAIN IDEA | WHY IT MATTERS NOW |
|---|---|
| Seeking Loyalist support, the British invaded the South—but ultimately lost the war there. | For more than two centuries, the American Revolution has inspired other people to fight tyranny. |

### ONE AMERICAN'S STORY

**Patriot Nancy Hart glared at the five armed Loyalists who burst into her Georgia cabin. Tradition says that the men had shot her last turkey and ordered her to cook it for them. Raids like this were common in the South, where feuding neighbors used the war as an excuse to fight each other. Both Patriots and Loyalists took part in the raids. Many women and children had moved out of Georgia, but the six-foot-tall, freckled Hart chose to stay and fight. She could shoot a gun as accurately as any man.**

**As she prepared the food, Hart planned her attack. When dinner was ready, the men sat down to eat. Seizing one of their muskets, Hart quickly shot and killed one man and wounded another. She kept the gun aimed on the others as her daughter ran for help. A group of nearby Patriots arrived and hanged the Loyalists.**

The state of Georgia named a county after Nancy Hart, who is shown here holding Loyalists prisoner.

**As Nancy Hart's story demonstrates, the fighting between Patriots and Loyalists in the South was vicious. In this section, you will learn why the British war effort shifted to the South and why it failed.**

## 1 Savannah and Charles Town

The British believed that most Southerners were Loyalists. Because of this, in 1778 the British decided to move the war to the South. After three years of fighting in the North, the British were no closer to victory. Although they had captured Northern cities, they couldn't control the countryside because they did not have enough troops to occupy it. The British believed that if they gained territory in the South, Southern Loyalists would hold it for them.

The British also expected large numbers of Southern slaves to join them because they had promised to grant the slaves freedom. Although thousands of African Americans did run away to join the British, not all of them were set free. Instead, some British officers sold African Americans into slavery in the West Indies.

206 CHAPTER 7

### RECOMMENDED RESOURCES

**In-Depth Resources: Unit 2**
- Guided Reading, p. 28
- Building Vocabulary, p. 30
- Geography Application: Cornwallis Is Trapped at Yorktown, 1781, pp. 32–33
- Reteaching Activity, p. 41

**Reading Study Guide** (Spanish and English), pp. 69–70

**Formal Assessment**
- Section Quiz, p. 104

**Alternative Assessment**
- Rubrics, 5.1
- Rubrics, 4.8

**Access for Students Acquiring English/ESL**
- Guided Reading, p. 45
- Geography Application, pp. 48–49

**Technology Resources**

**Electronic Teacher Tools with Test Maker**

**ClassZone**
www.mcdougallittell.com

**ReadingHistory**
**A. Drawing Conclusions** Why was it an advantage to be able to move troops between the West Indies and the South?
A. Answer They could cover both areas with a smaller number of troops by shifting them as needed.

Britain's West Indian colonies were a third reason the British invaded the South. Southern seaports were closer to the West Indies, where British troops were stationed. If the British captured Southern ports, they could move troops back and forth between the two regions.

In December 1778, the British captured the port of Savannah, Georgia. Using Savannah as a base, they then conquered most of Georgia. In 1780, a British army led by General Henry Clinton landed in South Carolina. They trapped American forces in Charles Town (now Charleston), which was the largest Southern city. When the city's 5,000 defenders surrendered, the Americans lost almost their entire Southern army. It was the worst American defeat of the war.

## 2 The Swamp Fox and Guerrilla Fighting

After that loss, Congress assigned General Horatio Gates—the victor at Saratoga—to form a new Southern army. Continental soldiers led by Baron de Kalb formed the army's core. Gates added about 2,000 new and untrained militia. He then headed for Camden, South Carolina, to challenge the army led by the British general **Lord Cornwallis.**

On the way, a band of Patriots from South Carolina approached Gates. "Their number did not exceed 20 men and boys, some white, some black, and all mounted, but most of them miserably equipped," wrote an officer. Their leader was Francis Marion, called the "Swamp Fox." He provided Gates with helpful knowledge of South Carolina's coastal swamplands. Gates sent Marion to destroy boats on the Santee River behind Camden. (See the map on page 209.) This would cut off British communications with Charles Town.

In August 1780, Gates's army ran into British troops outside Camden. The Americans were in no condition to fight. They were out of supplies and half-starved. Even worse, Gates put the inexperienced militia along part of the frontline instead of behind the veterans. When the British attacked, the militia panicked and ran. Gates also fled, but Kalb remained with his soldiers and received fatal wounds. This second defeat in the South ended Gates's term as head of an army and caused American spirits to fall to a new low.

**ReadingHistory**
**B. Evaluating** What do you think was most responsible for the American loss at Camden?
B. Possible Response Gates's poor decision-making in fighting with weak soldiers and not placing his troops properly

After Camden, a small British force set out for Charles Town with a column of American prisoners. Marion's band overwhelmed the British and freed the prisoners. Fighting from a base in the swamps, Marion's men cut the British supply line that led inland and north from Charles Town. Marion used the methods of a guerrilla. **Guerrillas** are small bands of fighters who weaken the enemy with surprise raids and hit-and-run attacks. Both Patriots and Loyalists formed guerrilla bands in the South. They carried out vicious raids.

### Now and then

**BATTLE TACTICS**

A difference in battle tactics affected future warfare. British soldiers marched shoulder to shoulder in three rows. When they neared the enemy, the first row knelt, the second crouched, and the third remained standing. They all fired without aiming.

The Americans were better shots. They often marched in rows, but sometimes they hid in woods or behind walls to take aim. Guerrillas attacked swiftly, then fled into the countryside. Those tactics succeeded and are still used today. This photograph shows modern U.S. soldiers learning guerrilla tactics.

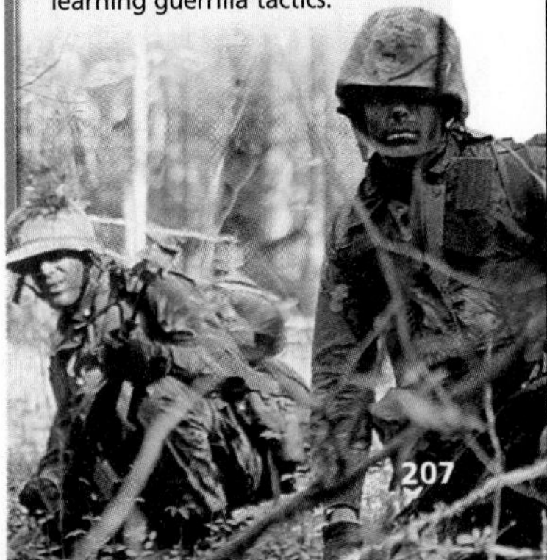

207

### MORE ABOUT . . .

**Loyalist Support**

Ever since the beginning of the war, the British had hoped for help from those loyal to the Crown. When Clinton and Cornwallis raised the King's Standard at Savannah, about 2,000 Tories (Loyalists) did indeed enlist. However, such support was rare. Even the stunning British victories at Savannah and Charles Town did not bring Tories flocking to the British cause. Cornwallis, who needed Loyalist enlistment to help him to victory in the South, was finally forced to observe that the Tories' "friendship was only passive."

### INSTRUCT: OBJECTIVE 2

**The Swamp Fox and Guerrilla Fighting**

Key Questions

- What objective did General Gates and Baron de Kalb have?
- Why was the battle at Camden important?
- What contributions did Francis Marion make to the war effort in the South?

### Now and then

**Battle Tactics**

Some scholars have compared the Revolutionary War to the anticolonial wars of the late 20th century. Consider the following parallels. In the Revolution, the world's most powerful nation—Britain—was bogged down in a war against a small guerrilla army—the Patriots. The superpower had to supply its forces from thousands of miles away; the war was unpopular with the British people; and the rebels received aid from the superpower's chief military and political enemy—France.

### ACTIVITY OPTIONS

**INTERDISCIPLINARY LINK: GOVERNMENT/CIVICS**

BLOCK SCHEDULING

**GOVERNMENT AND GUERRILLAS**

**Class Time** 15 minutes

**Task** Differentiating between guerrilla and regular tactics

**Purpose** To understand the governmental difficulties created by guerrilla warfare

**Supplies Needed**

- Current newspapers
- Internet access for additional resources

**Activity** Have students scan current news sources for world situations where guerrilla fighting has escaped from governmental control. Have the class create a chart identifying the locations of the warfare and damage caused by guerrillas. Review the story of Nancy Hart and ask: What problems do civilians face in such circumstances?

## Technology OF THE Time

**OBJECTIVES**

1. To describe the technology used by fighting forces in the Revolutionary War
2. To use illustrations and captions to explain historical details about weaponry in the Revolution

## INSTRUCT

Key Questions

- What additional supplies did artillery require armies to carry with them?
- How might the presence of artillery have affected the troops' traveling pace?
- What phrases tell you that fires were part of the necessary equipment in using cannons? What additional supplies would troops have had to collect for the fires?
- How long do you estimate the entire process of loading and firing a cannon might take? Explain.



# Artillery of the Revolution

Artillery—large guns and cannon—played a key role in the American Revolution. The ability of these guns to kill and destroy from a distance made them essential in war. One witness of a battle described the destruction: "Many men were badly injured and mortally wounded by the fragments of bombs, . . . their arms and legs severed or themselves struck dead." Most cannon used in the Revolution were made of cast bronze. During the 1700s, artillery design did not change significantly. However, artillery became more mobile (more easily moved).

After each shot, a soldier sponged the inside of the barrel. This put out sparks and cleaned away any dirt left from the last shot.

A soldier loaded the cannon with gunpowder and a cannonball. He did so by ramming them down the barrel.

Soldiers aimed the gun by turning the entire carriage. An instrument called a quadrant told them how high to raise the barrel to reach their target.

Cannon were classified by the weight of the iron ball they fired. American artillery ranged from 3-pounders to 32-pounders.

Soldiers lit the cannon by applying a red-hot wire or a tube of burning powder to a touchhole drilled through the back of the barrel, where the gunpowder lay. The gunpowder exploded, forcing the projectile out of the open end of the barrel.

In the 1700s, most cannon were accurate at ranges of up to 1,000 yards. That is the length of ten football fields laid end to end.



### CONNECT TO HISTORY

1. **Recognizing Effects** Why would it be an advantage to an army to have mobile artillery?

See Skillbuilder Handbook, page R10.

### CONNECT TO TODAY

2. **Researching** Find information about modern artillery in an encyclopedia or on the Internet. How has artillery changed in the 20th century?

Visit www.mcdougallittell.com to learn more about artillery.

### CONNECT TO HISTORY

1. **Recognizing Effects** **Possible Response** The army could move its guns where they were most needed. This would be especially important when using a gun that had short range, because they would need to move close to their target.

### CONNECT TO TODAY

2. **Researching** **Possible Response** According to the *World Book Encyclopedia,* big guns have become less important, artillery has become more mobile, and artillery can now fire atomic shells.

## 3 The Tide Turns

Even battles in the South sometimes turned vicious. One example was the Battle of Kings Mountain, fought on the border of North and South Carolina in October 1780. After surrounding a force of about 1,000 Loyalist militia and British soldiers, the Americans slaughtered most of them. James P. Collins, a 16-year-old American, described the scene.

> *A VOICE FROM THE PAST*
>
> The dead lay in heaps on all sides, while the groans of the wounded were heard in every direction. I could not help turning away from the scene before me with horror and, though exulting in victory, could not refrain from shedding tears.
>
> **James P. Collins,** quoted in *The Spirit of Seventy-Six*

Many of the dead had been shot or hanged after they surrendered. The Americans killed them in revenge for Loyalist raids and an earlier incident in which the British had butchered Americans. Kings Mountain was one of Britain's first losses in the South. It soon suffered more.

After Gates's defeat at Camden, Washington put a new general, Nathanael Greene, in charge of the Southern army. Greene was one of Washington's most able officers. He had been a Quaker, but his church had cast him out because of his belief in the armed struggle against the British. Most Quakers are **pacifist,** or opposed to war.

Under Greene's command, the American army avoided full-scale battles, in which the British had the edge because of superior firepower. So the American forces let the British chase them around the countryside and wear themselves out. When the Americans did fight, they did their best to make sure the British suffered heavy losses.

As the fighting dragged on into its sixth year, opposition to the war grew in Britain. As a result, some British leaders began to think that American independence would not be so bad.

*Reading* **History**

**C. Contrasting** How did Greene's strategy as a general differ from that of Gates at Camden?

C. Possible Response Greene would not risk his army in a large battle like Camden. He tried to hurt the British with as little harm to his army as possible.

## 4 The End of the War

In 1781, most of the fighting took place in Virginia. In July of that year, the British general Cornwallis set up his base at Yorktown, located on a peninsula in Chesapeake Bay. From there, his army could receive supplies by ship from New York.

Skillbuilder Answers
1. Charles Town, Savannah
2. Wilmington—Cornwallis; New York—Washington and Rochambeau

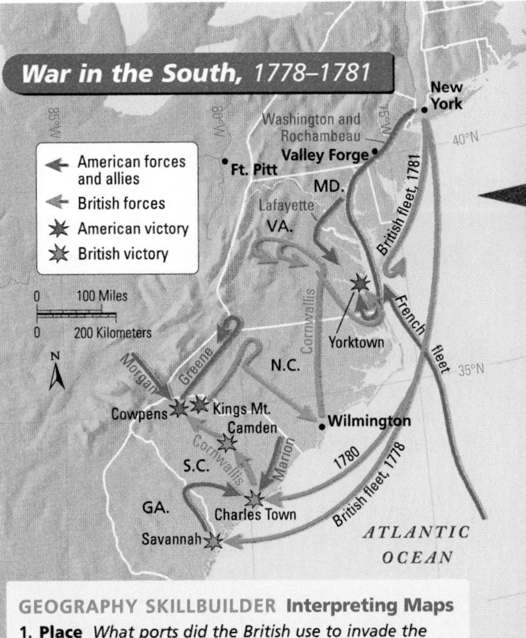


**GEOGRAPHY SKILLBUILDER Interpreting Maps**

1. **Place** *What ports did the British use to invade the South?*
2. **Movement** *Who traveled from Wilmington to Yorktown, and who traveled from New York?*

209

### INSTRUCT: OBJECTIVE 3

**The Tide Turns**

Key Questions

- What factors led Washington to name a new commander in the South?
- Why did Greene avoid full-scale battles with the British?
- How did the course of the war affect public opinion in Britain?

### HISTORY FROM VISUALS

**Reading the Map** Have students read the map carefully, finding text on the page that explains the troop movements. What direction did the French fleet come from? Where did it arrive at the coast? Which side did it support? **Answers** The fleet came from the southeast. It arrived near the Virginia coast. It supported the Americans.

**Extension** Have students use an atlas to identify some French ports from which the French fleet may have sailed, as well as various routes they might have taken. What danger did the French fleet face as it sailed for the United States?

### INSTRUCT: OBJECTIVE 4

**The End of the War**

Key Questions

- Why did Cornwallis establish his base of operations at Chesapeake Bay?
- How did the French and the Americans cooperate militarily to defeat Cornwallis?

**In-Depth Resources: Unit 2**
- Geography Application: Cornwallis Is Trapped at Yorktown, 1781, pp. 32–33

### ACTIVITY OPTIONS

### INDIVIDUAL NEEDS

**STUDENTS ACQUIRING ENGLISH/ESL**

**Figures of Speech** Point out the following figures of speech to students: "the tide turns" (page 209); "wear themselves out" (page 209); and "a golden opportunity" (page 210). Explain what each phrase means, and give students the opportunity to discuss them by asking such questions as:

- What sport or work might you do that would "wear you out"?
- What would you consider a "golden opportunity" in life?

Then ask questions like the following to assess students' comprehension of the section:

- In what way did "the tide turn" for the American army under Nathanael Greene's command?
- How did Cornwallis's decision to set up a base at Yorktown become "a golden opportunity" for Washington?

## HISTORY FROM VISUALS

**Interpreting the Painting** This huge oil painting (12 feet by 18 feet) by John Trumbull hangs in the Capitol Rotunda in Washington, D.C. Although its title is *The Surrender of Cornwallis,* Cornwallis could not bring himself to attend the ceremony in person. He claimed to be sick and sent his aide, General Charles O'Hara, shown on the white horse in the center. O'Hara led the British troops between the two victorious armies—French and American—as British bands played "The World Turned Upside Down."

Ask students what impression the painting creates. What might be the artistic purpose of the dramatic contrasts in the sky? **Possible Responses** The overall impression is one of dignity and formality. The artist may have wanted to highlight George Washington and the American flag.

### CRITICAL THINKING ACTIVITY

**Evaluating** Ask students to define the term *peninsula.* Let a volunteer sketch a peninsula on the board. Discuss the military advantages and disadvantages to such a location. Is it easy to defend against an attack by land? by sea? What are its vulnerabilities? Apply the students' conclusions to Cornwallis's situation.

**Class Time** 10 minutes

## ASSESS & RETEACH

**Setting the Stage** Have students complete the sequence of events for 1780 and 1781.

 **Formal Assessment**
- Section Quiz, p. 104

### RETEACHING ACTIVITY

Have students do mock interviews with Washington, Cornwallis, and a French sea captain to identify the strategies each used.

 **In-Depth Resources: Unit 2**
- Reteaching Activity, p. 41

**The victorious American forces accept the British surrender at Yorktown. George Washington is to the left of the American flag.**

Washington saw Cornwallis's decision as a golden opportunity. In August 1781, a large French fleet arrived from the West Indies and blocked Chesapeake Bay. These ships prevented the British from receiving supplies—and from escaping. They also allowed Washington to come from the North and trap Cornwallis on the peninsula. Washington had enough men to do this because a large French force led by General Jean Rochambeau had joined his army.

Washington and Rochambeau moved south. When British ships tried to reach Cornwallis, French ships drove them back. In the **Battle of Yorktown,** the American and French troops bombarded Yorktown with cannon fire, turning its buildings to rubble. Cornwallis had no way out. On October 19, 1781, he surrendered his force of about 8,000.

Vocabulary
**bombard:** to attack with artillery

Although some fighting continued, Yorktown was the last major battle of the war. When the British prime minister, Lord North, heard the news, he gasped, "It is all over!" Indeed, he and other British leaders were soon forced to resign. Britain's new leaders began to negotiate a peace treaty, which is discussed in the next section.

### *Section 3 Assessment*

**1. Terms & Names**

**Identify:**
- Lord Cornwallis
- guerrillas
- pacifist
- Battle of Yorktown

**2. Taking Notes**

Use a chart like the one below to list the geographic factors that made the British move their war effort to the South.

| Physical factors, such as location | Human factors, such as who lived there |
| --- | --- |
| | |

Were the human factors as helpful as the British hoped?

**3. Main Ideas**

a. Why did the fighting between Patriots and Loyalists in the South turn vicious?

b. What type of warfare did Francis Marion and his men employ?

c. How did Gates's errors in leadership contribute to the American loss at Camden?

**4. Critical Thinking**

**Analyzing Causes** How did each of the following help bring about the British defeat at Yorktown?

THINK ABOUT
- the location chosen by Cornwallis
- the French fleet
- the French troops under Rochambeau
- Washington's planning

**ACTIVITY OPTIONS**

**TECHNOLOGY / MUSIC** Imagine that Congress has asked you to commemorate the Battle of Yorktown. Design a **Web page** or write a **song** celebrating the U.S. victory.



### *Section*  *Assessment*

**1. Terms & Names**

**Lord Cornwallis,** p. 207
**guerrilla,** p. 207
**pacifist,** p. 209
**Battle of Yorktown,** p. 210

**2. Taking Notes**

Physical factors: nearness to the West Indies; valuable sea ports
Human factors: Loyalist Southerners; enslaved African Americans
No, because the South was more divided in its loyalties than the British thought.

**3. Main Ideas**

**a.** Both used the war as an excuse for feuding neighbors to raid each other. **b.** guerrilla warfare **c.** He relied on troops weak with hunger, and he put inexperienced troops on the frontline.

**4. Critical Thinking**

Student answers should be organized in four parts to cover each point.

**ACTIVITY OPTIONS**

 **Alternative Assessment**
- Rubrics for a Web page, 5.1
- Rubrics for songs, 4.8

# The Legacy of the War

**TERMS & NAMES**
Treaty of Paris of 1783
republicanism
Elizabeth Freeman
Richard Allen



**MAIN IDEA**

After the war, the new nation faced issues such as a high national debt and calls for equality.

**WHY IT MATTERS NOW**

To promote liberty, some states passed laws outlawing slavery and protecting religious freedom.

## ONE AMERICAN'S STORY

**In 1776, 15-year-old Joseph Plumb Martin of Connecticut signed up to fight for the Americans. He stayed with the army until the war ended and rose in rank from private to sergeant. Among his experiences were the terrible winter at Valley Forge and the winning battle at Yorktown.**

**One of the hardest things Martin faced was leaving the army after the war was over. Many years later, he wrote about that day.**

*A VOICE FROM THE PAST*

There was as much sorrow as joy. . . . We had lived together as a family of brothers for several years, setting aside some little family squabbles, like most other families, had shared with each other the hardships, dangers, and sufferings incident to a soldier's life; had sympathized with each other in trouble and sickness; had assisted in bearing each other's burdens. . . . And now we were to be . . . parted forever.

**Joseph Plumb Martin,** quoted in *The Revolutionaries*

**At war's end, Martin and his country faced an uncertain future. How would the United States recover from the war? What issues would confront the new nation? Section 4 discusses those questions.**

**Although this painting is not of Joseph Plumb Martin himself, he may have dressed like this American soldier.**

## 1 Why the Americans Won

In November 1783, the last British ships and troops left New York City, and American troops marched in. As Washington said good-bye to his officers in a New York tavern, he hugged each one. Tears ran down his face. He became so upset that he had to leave the room.

Earlier in the fall, Washington had written a farewell letter to his armies. In it, he praised them by saying that their endurance "through almost every possible suffering and discouragement for the space of eight long years, was little short of a standing miracle."

By their persistence, the Americans won independence even though they faced many obstacles. As you have read, they lacked training and experience. They were often short of supplies and weapons. By contrast, the British forces ranked among the best trained in the world. They were



## SECTION OBJECTIVES

1. To evaluate the strengths of the American army in comparison with the British army
2. To summarize the 1783 Treaty of Paris
3. To analyze the costs of the Revolution
4. To identify challenges that the new United States faced after the war

**SKILLBUILDERS**

Interpreting Charts, p. 213

**CRITICAL THINKING**

Evaluating, p. 212
Analyzing Causes, p. 213
Solving Problems, p. 215
Recognizing Effects, p. 215

**Why It Matters Now**
- Democracy in South Africa, pp. 13–14

## FOCUS & MOTIVATE

### 5-MINUTE WARM-UP

**Making Generalizations** These questions will help students understand the soldiers' life.

1. Read "A Voice from the Past" on page 211. How does Joseph Plumb Martin react to the end of the war? Do you think other soldiers felt as he did?
2. Give an example from your own experience of ties forged through shared difficulties.

**Warm-Up Transparency WT7**

## INSTRUCT

### INSTRUCT: OBJECTIVE 1

**Why the Americans Won**

Key Questions
- What drawbacks did the Americans have to overcome?
- What factors aided the Americans?

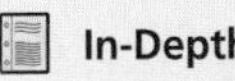

**In-Depth Resources: Unit 2**
- Guided Reading, p. 29

## RECOMMENDED RESOURCES

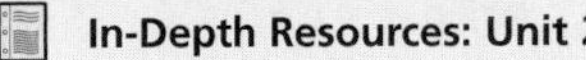

**In-Depth Resources: Unit 2**
- Guided Reading, p. 29
- Building Vocabulary, p. 30
- Primary Source, p. 35
- Reteaching Activity, p. 42

**Reading Study Guide** (Spanish and English), pp. 71–72

**Economics in History**
- Independence and Free Enterprise, p. 7

**Outline Map Activities**
- North America, 1783, pp. 13–14

**Why It Matters Now**
- Democracy in South Africa, pp. 13–14

**Formal Assessment**
- Section Quiz, p. 105

**Alternative Assessment**
- Rubrics, 3.6
- Rubrics, 2.3

**Access for Students Acquiring English/ESL**
- Guided Reading, p. 46

**Technology Resources**

**Electronic Teacher Tools with Test Maker**

**ClassZone**
www.mcdougallittell.com

**INSTRUCT: OBJECTIVE 2**

**The Treaty of Paris**

Key Questions

- What was the most important condition of the Treaty of Paris?
- What provisions benefited the British? the Americans? the Loyalists?

**Outline Map Activities**

- North America, 1783, pp. 13–14

**MORE ABOUT . . .**

**The Treaty of Paris**

Concluding the peace treaty took almost two years—and a lot of talking. At one point, Franklin told the British representatives a tale from ancient Rome. A small state, defeated by the mighty Romans, asked the Roman senate for peace. "How long will the peace last?" the senators asked in response. The country's ambassador replied that the duration of the peace would depend on the conditions Rome set: "If they are reasonable, the peace will be lasting; if not, the peace will be short."

experienced and well-supplied professional soldiers. Yet the Americans had certain advantages that enabled them to win.

1. **Better leadership.** British generals were overconfident and made poor decisions. By contrast, Washington learned from his mistakes. After early defeats, he developed the strategy of dragging out the war to wear down the British. Despite difficulties, he never gave up.
2. **Foreign aid.** Britain's rivals, especially France, helped America. Foreign loans and military aid were essential to America's victory.
3. **Knowledge of the land.** The Americans knew the land where the war took place and used that knowledge well. The British could control coastal cities but could not extend their control to the interior.
4. **Motivation.** The Americans had more reason to fight. At stake were not only their lives but also their property and their dream of liberty.

*Reading* **History**

**A. Evaluating** What do you think was Washington's best characteristic as a leader?

**A. Possible Responses** His courage, his strategy of wearing down the British, his perseverance, his willingness to suffer for his cause, his ability to inspire his men

## 2 The Treaty of Paris

As the winners, the Americans won favorable terms in the **Treaty of Paris of 1783,** which ended the Revolutionary War. The treaty included the following six conditions:

1. The United States was independent.
2. Its boundaries would be the Mississippi River on the west, Canada on the north, and Spanish Florida on the south.
3. The United States would receive the right to fish off Canada's Atlantic Coast, near Newfoundland and Nova Scotia.
4. Each side would repay debts it owed the other.
5. The British would return any enslaved persons they had captured.
6. Congress would recommend that the states return any property they had seized from Loyalists.

Neither Britain nor the United States fully lived up to the treaty's terms. Americans did not repay the prewar debts they owed British merchants or return Loyalist property. For their part, the British did not return

**HISTORY through ART**

**Interpreting the Painting** The British did not take losing gracefully. Cornwallis refused to attend the formal surrender ceremony; he pleaded sick and sent his subordinate, Brigadier General Charles O'Hara, to hand over his sword. King George stubbornly refused to believe that the loss at Yorktown meant the loss of his "American farms."

**Possible Response: Perhaps the British did not want to appear in a painting that showed American "upstarts" as their equals; the British did not want to be portrayed as defeated. The British were bitter and resentful.**

**HISTORY through ART**

The American painter Benjamin West began a portrait of the men who negotiated the Treaty of Paris. But the British officials refused to pose, so West never finished the painting. From left to right are the American officials John Jay, John Adams, Benjamin Franklin, and two others.

**What does this painting reveal about the British response to losing the war?**

**ACTIVITY OPTIONS**

**INTERDISCIPLINARY LINK: LANGUAGE ARTS** — BLOCK SCHEDULING

**COSTS AND BENEFITS OF WAR**

**Class Time** 15–20 minutes

**Task** Debating the costs and benefits of the Revolutionary War

**Purpose** To form opinions and provide supporting evidence

**Supplies Needed**

- Reference materials about the American Revolution

**Activity** On the board, write the following quotation from a letter by Benjamin Franklin to Josiah Quincy: "There never was a good war or a bad peace." Allow students several moments to think about the quote's meaning. Then ask them to apply it to the Revolutionary War. Divide the class into two teams. Assign one team to argue the affirmative (in support of the statement) and the other to argue the negative. Each team should support its argument with evidence from the text.

runaway slaves. They also refused to give up military outposts in the Great Lakes area, such as Fort Detroit.

**Background** Even after George Rogers Clark's Western victories, the British stayed at Fort Detroit.

## 3 Costs of the War

No one knows exactly how many people died in the war, but eight years of fighting took a terrible toll. An estimated 25,700 Americans died in the war, and 1,400 remained missing. About 8,200 Americans were wounded. Some were left with permanent disabilities, such as amputated limbs. The British suffered about 10,000 military deaths.

Many soldiers who survived the war left the army with no money. They had received little or no pay for their service. Instead of back pay, the government gave some soldiers certificates for land in the West. Many men sold that land to get money for food and other basic needs.

Both the Congress and the states had borrowed money to finance the conflict. The war left the nation with a debt of about $27 million—a debt that would prove difficult to pay off.

The losers of the war also suffered. Thousands of Loyalists lost their property. Between 60,000 and 100,000 Loyalists left the United States during and after the war. Among them were several thousand African Americans and Native Americans, including Joseph Brant. Most of the Loyalists went to Canada. There they settled new towns and provinces. They also brought English traditions to areas that the French had settled. Even today, Canada has both French and English as official languages.

**B. Possible Responses** They were afraid of reprisals; they wanted to remain under British rule.

*Reading History*

**B. Analyzing Causes** Why do you think the Loyalists left the United States?

**Postwar Boundaries, 1783**



CONNECTIONS TO MATH

**Military Deaths in the American Revolution**



* These figures are estimates. No figures available for French deaths.

Sources: *World Book Encyclopedia; An Outline History of the American Revolution*

**SKILLBUILDER Interpreting Charts**

1. *How many more deaths did the Americans suffer than the British?*
2. *What percentage of American deaths occurred in battle?*

Skillbuilder Answers
1. about 15,700
2. about 28 percent



**INSTRUCT: OBJECTIVE 3**

**Costs of the War**

Key Questions

- What were some of the human costs of the war?
- What financial problems did the war leave for the new nation?
- How did the Loyalists change Canada?

**HISTORY FROM VISUALS**

**Reading the Map** Guide students in using the map to summarize the changes in North American territorial claims after the Revolutionary War. Ask: About what fraction of North America theoretically belonged to the United States in 1783? On which border did the British still threaten the United States? What country controlled the largest share of the continent? **Answers** about one-fourth or less; the northern boundary; Spain

**Extension** Ask students to make inferences about how these territorial arrangements might have affected international relationships. Which countries might the United States have regarded with suspicion?

**HISTORY FROM VISUALS**

**Interpreting the Chart** Which category would include the American soldiers who died at Valley Forge? **Answer** died in camp

Remind students that the British and Hessians also lost soldiers from the same causes as the Americans—disease, poor camp conditions, American prisons, and battle.

**Extension** Have the students illustrate the statistics in the chart in another way, such as a pie chart or table.

**ACTIVITY OPTIONS**

**INDIVIDUAL NEEDS: GIFTED AND TALENTED**

**THE NATIONAL DEBT**

**Class Time** One class period

**Task** Preparing and presenting a news broadcast about the U.S. national debt

**Purpose** To familiarize students with the concept of national debt and its causes

**Supplies Needed**
- Reference materials such as encyclopedias and almanacs
- Internet access for additional resources

**Activity** Divide students into groups. Their task is to prepare a newscast segment of 1–3 minutes on the concept of the national debt. Encourage students to use a variety of references to research the U.S. national debt. They should determine when and how much the national debt was and is, and what the causes of national debt are.

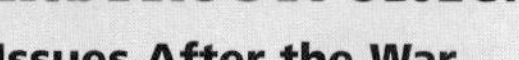

**INSTRUCT: OBJECTIVE 4**

**Issues After the War**

Key Questions

- Explain the idea of republicanism.
- How did the citizenship obligations of men and women differ?
- How did the new principles of government affect other aspects of American life?

## 4 Issues After the War

The American Revolution was not just a war, but a change in ideas about government. Before the war, Americans had demanded their rights as English citizens. But after declaring their independence, they replaced that goal with the idea of **republicanism.** This idea stated that instead of a king, the people would rule. The government would obtain its authority from the citizens and be responsible to them.

For this system to work, individuals would have to place the good of the country above their own interests. At first, only men were allowed to take part in governing by voting or holding public office—and not even all men. However, women could help the nation by teaching their children the virtues that benefited public life. Such virtues included honesty, duty, and the willingness to make sacrifices.

### Economics *in* History

**OBJECTIVE**

Students will be able to explain the elements of free enterprise and how the loosening of British economic controls during the war allowed U.S. free enterprise to begin.

**The Development of Free Enterprise**

Scottish economist Adam Smith outlined his ideas of free enterprise in his book *The Wealth of Nations,* first published in 1776. Smith argued that the world would be a more orderly and progressive place if people were allowed to follow their own interests. He reasoned that sellers made money only by producing things that people wanted to buy. Free enterprise, Smith claimed, would lead to social harmony "as if by an invisible hand." Smith criticized Britain's mercantilist policies and said that a government was necessary only to preserve law and order, defend the country, and provide for a few needs that could not be met by the market.

Economics in History

- Independence and Free Enterprise, p. 7

### Economics *in* History

## Free Enterprise

One cause of the Revolution was the colonists' resentment of British mercantilism. Parliament passed laws to discourage the colonists from developing their own manufacturing and to force them to buy British goods. During the war, British economic control weakened. British exports of woolens to the colonies dropped from £645,900 in 1774 to only £2,540 in 1776. As a result, the colonists were able to make more economic choices—for example, they could choose to manufacture wool clothing.

The end of Britain's mercantilist control allowed free enterprise to begin to develop in the United States. In a free-enterprise system, business can be conducted freely based on the choices of individuals. The government does not control the system, but only protects and regulates it.

**CONNECT TO HISTORY**

1. **Analyzing Causes** Why do you think the colonists were able to manufacture their own wool clothing during the war?

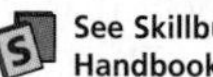

See Skillbuilder Handbook, page R10.

**CONNECT TO TODAY**

2. **Comparing** Think about a mall where you shop. Name examples of businesses that compete with each other. Compare the methods they use to attract customers.

Visit www.mcdougallittell.com to learn more about free enterprise.

- **A** Competition encourages businesses to improve goods and services and to keep prices down.
- **B** Property is owned by individuals and businesses.
- **C** The desire to make a profit motivates businesspeople.
- **D** Individuals, not the government, decide what to buy and what to manufacture and sell.
- **E** The government protects private property and makes sure businesses operate fairly.

**CONNECT TO HISTORY**

1. **Analyzing Causes** **Possible Response** Britain had to direct all its energy to fighting the war and was not able to enforce the mercantilist laws that prevented colonial manufacturing.

**CONNECT TO TODAY**

2. **Comparing** Students should examine the following areas:
   - attractiveness of the store, including cleanliness and store design
   - organization of the products
   - variety of products
   - service
   - prices
   - promotional ideas and advertising

As part of their liberty, Americans called for more religious freedom. Before the war, some laws discriminated against certain religions. Some states had not allowed Jews or Catholics to hold public office. After the war, states began to abolish those laws. They also ended the practice of using tax money to support churches.

**Background**
Only Northern states ended slavery after the war. In the North, slavery was not as important a part of the economy as in the South.

Many people began to see a conflict between slavery and the ideal of liberty. Vermont outlawed slavery, and Pennsylvania passed a law to free slaves gradually. Individual African Americans also tried to end slavery. For example, **Elizabeth Freeman** sued for her freedom in a Massachusetts court and won. Her victory in 1781 and other similar cases ended slavery in that state. Freeman later described her desire for freedom.

*A VOICE FROM THE PAST*

Anytime while I was a slave, if one minute's freedom had been offered to me, and I had been told I must die at the end of that minute, I would have taken it—just to stand one minute on God's earth a free woman.

**Elizabeth Freeman,** quoted in *Notable Black American Women*

Elizabeth Freeman fought a court case that helped end slavery in Massachusetts.

***Reading*History**
**C. Solving Problems** How did free African Americans take on the responsibility of trying to improve their lives?
C. Possible Response They began self-help organizations and African-American churches.

With freedom, African Americans began to form their own institutions. For example, the preacher **Richard Allen** helped start the Free African Society. That society encouraged African Americans to help each other. Allen also founded the African Methodist Episcopal Church, the first African-American church in the United States.

Perhaps the main issue facing Americans after the war was how to shape their national government. American anger over British taxes, violation of rights, and control of trade had caused the war. Now the United States needed a government that would protect citizens' rights and economic freedom. In Chapter 8, you will read how U.S. leaders worked to create such a government.

## Section 4 Assessment

### 1. Terms & Names

**Identify:**
- Treaty of Paris of 1783
- republicanism
- Elizabeth Freeman
- Richard Allen

### 2. Taking Notes

Use a chart like the one below to classify the terms of the Treaty of Paris according to which side they favored. (Do not list terms that don't favor either side.)

| Terms of the Treaty of Paris | |
|---|---|
| Favorable to America | Favorable to Britain |
| | |

### 3. Main Ideas

a. What advantages helped the Americans win the Revolutionary War?

b. How did the end of the war affect Loyalists?

c. What were the economic costs of the war to individuals and to the government?

### 4. Critical Thinking

Recognizing Effects How did republicanism shape the United States after the war?

THINK ABOUT
- American ideas about government
- the roles men and women could play in public life
- religious freedom
- the antislavery movement

**ACTIVITY OPTIONS**

**SPEECH**
**MATH**

Look up the U.S. population in 1780. Calculate what percentage of American people died in the war. Report your findings in a **speech** or a **pie graph**.





### CRITICAL THINKING ACTIVITY

**Analyzing Causes** Ask students what American statements and ideals from the Revolutionary era conflicted with the institution of slavery. Encourage them to locate specific examples from the documents and quotations in this chapter and the preceding one.

**Class Time** 15 minutes

 **In-Depth Resources: Unit 2**
- Primary Source: An African-American Petition for Freedom, p. 35

## ASSESS & RETEACH

**Setting the Stage** Have students complete the section of the time line for 1783.

 **Formal Assessment**
- Section Quiz, p. 105

 **Critical Thinking Transparency CT19**
- Setting the Stage

### RETEACHING ACTIVITY

Divide the students into four groups and assign a portion of each section to each group. Have each group compose three sentences explaining the connection between their assigned portion and the section's title and main idea. Allow time for sharing, discussing, and editing of students' sentences.

 **In-Depth Resources: Unit 2**
- Reteaching Activity, p. 42

## Section 4 Assessment

### 1. Terms & Names

**Treaty of Paris of 1783,** p. 212
**republicanism,** p. 214
**Elizabeth Freeman,** p. 215
**Richard Allen,** p. 215

### 2. Taking Notes

Favorable to America: The United States was independent; its boundaries were the Mississippi River, Canada, and Spanish Florida. Favorable to Britain: The states were to return Loyalist property.

### 3. Main Ideas

**a.** better leadership; foreign aid; knowledge of the land; motivation
**b.** Many lost property; 80,000 to 100,000 left the United States.
**c.** Many soldiers received no pay and were in debt after the war; the government was $27 million in debt.

### 4. Critical Thinking

It led Americans to want a government in which authority came from the people, and that fostered personal and economic freedoms.

### ACTIVITY OPTIONS

 **Alternative Assessment**
- Rubrics for speeches, 3.6
- Rubrics for graphs, 2.3

## TERMS & NAMES

1. **George Washington,** p. 194
2. **mercenary,** p. 195
3. **Battles of Saratoga,** p. 199
4. **ally,** p. 200
5. **Marquis de Lafayette,** p. 201
6. **John Paul Jones,** p. 205
7. **Lord Cornwallis,** p. 207
8. **Battle of Yorktown,** p. 210
9. **Treaty of Paris of 1783,** p. 212
10. **republicanism,** p. 214

## REVIEW QUESTIONS

**Possible Responses**

1. The British promised to free them; the Americans because they hoped that independence would bring greater equality
2. They cooked, sewed, and nursed soldiers. They took supplies to Valley Forge. Some even fought in battle.
3. Arnold forced St. Leger to retreat and miss the rendezvous with Burgoyne. Howe refused to rendezvous with Burgoyne. Burgoyne traveled too slowly, ran out of supplies, and was surrounded by the Americans.
4. France sent troops, money, and supplies. Spain fought the British in the Mississippi Valley and Florida.
5. The weather was cold and harsh. The troops did not have enough food, clothing, or supplies. Many died of starvation, exposure, and disease.
6. Savannah and Charles Town
7. The French fleet prevented British ships from assisting Cornwallis. French troops increased the size of Washington's army.
8. for their endurance during suffering
9. all the land between Canada and Spanish Florida, west to the Mississippi
10. Vermont, Pennsylvania, and Massachusetts

# Chapter 7 ASSESSMENT

## TERMS & NAMES

Briefly explain the importance of each of the following.

1. George Washington
2. mercenary
3. Battles of Saratoga
4. ally
5. Marquis de Lafayette
6. John Paul Jones
7. Lord Cornwallis
8. Battle of Yorktown
9. Treaty of Paris of 1783
10. republicanism

## REVIEW QUESTIONS

**The Early Years of the War (pages 193–199)**

1. What motives led African Americans to fight for the British? The Americans?
2. How did women help the American war effort?
3. What events led to the British defeat at Saratoga?

**The War Expands (pages 200–205)**

4. What foreign countries helped America? How?
5. What were conditions like at Valley Forge?

**The Path to Victory (pages 206–210)**

6. What two Southern ports did the British capture?
7. How did America's ally France contribute to the victory at Yorktown?

**The Legacy of the War (pages 211–215)**

8. For what did Washington praise his army in his farewell letter?
9. What land did the United States acquire from Britain as a result of the Treaty of Paris?
10. What three states outlawed slavery after the war?

## CRITICAL THINKING

**1. USING YOUR NOTES**

Using your completed time line, answer the questions below.

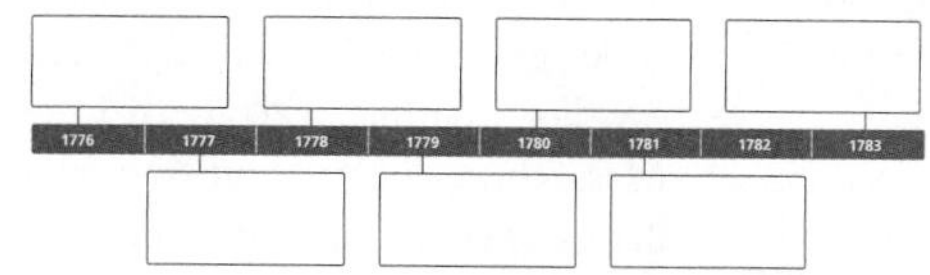


a. What were the main events of 1776 and 1777?

b. While George Rogers Clark was capturing Kaskaskia, what was happening in the South?

**2. ANALYZING LEADERSHIP**

George Washington was the most beloved American leader of his time. What qualities do you think made him such a respected leader?

**3. THEME: CITIZENSHIP**

What Revolutionary leaders displayed civic virtue by putting the good of the nation ahead of their own interests? Explain your answer.

**4. RECOGNIZING EFFECTS**

How did Britain's loss in the war allow free enterprise to develop in the United States?

**5. APPLYING CITIZENSHIP SKILLS**

How was the writing of *The American Crisis* an example of good U.S. citizenship?

**Interact *with* History**

How did the sacrifices you discussed before you read the chapter compare with what Patriots really did?

## VISUAL SUMMARY

### The American Revolution

**People and Events of the Revolution**

| Military | | Civilian | |
|---|---|---|---|
| George Washington | commanded the Continental Army. | Haym Salomon | helped finance the war for America. |
| Marquis de Lafayette | fought for the Americans. | Molly Pitcher | aided soldiers by bringing them water in battle. |
| John Burgoyne | surrendered to the Americans at Saratoga. | Thomas Paine | wrote *The American Crisis* to inspire Americans. |
| John Paul Jones | won a major naval victory for America. | Benjamin Franklin | was a diplomat to France and Britain. |
| George Rogers Clark | helped hold the Western frontier for America. | James Forten | was captured by the British but would not betray America. |
| Lord Cornwallis | surrendered at Yorktown, ending the war. | Nancy Hart | defended her Georgia home against Loyalist raiders. |



## CRITICAL THINKING

**Possible Responses**

1. **USING YOUR NOTES a.** 1776—Washington forced British from Boston; Washington surprised Hessians at Trenton. 1777—Washington won at Princeton; Gates and Arnold defeated Burgoyne at Saratoga. **b.** The British were capturing Savannah.
2. **ANALYZING LEADERSHIP** He suffered with his men, showed caution and courage, and never gave up.
3. **THEME: CITIZENSHIP** Washington gave up running his plantation to fight the war; Salomon and Clark went into debt to help the war effort.
4. **RECOGNIZING EFFECTS** After Britain lost the war, it could no longer impose mercantilist controls on the economy, so Americans were free to make their own economic choices.
5. **APPLYING CITIZENSHIP SKILLS** Paine used that pamphlet to urge people to fight for their country's freedom and not to abandon it just because times were difficult.

**Interact *with* History** Answers will vary but should include information learned in the chapter.

## HISTORY SKILLS

**1. INTERPRETING MAPS: Movement**

Study the map, then answer the questions.

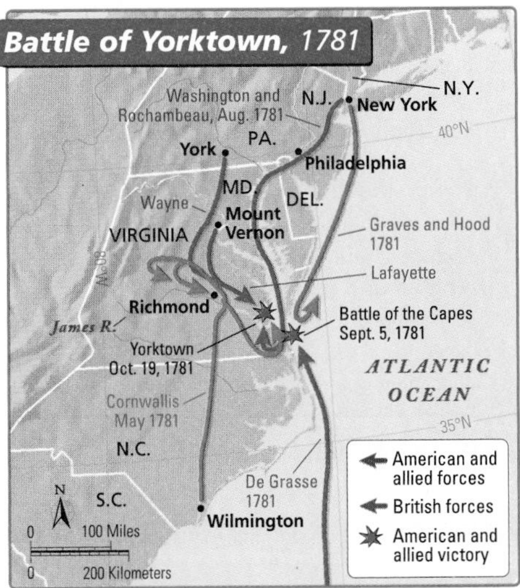


**Basic Map Elements**

a. In what state was the Battle of Yorktown fought?

b. In what battle did De Grasse's fleet defeat the British fleet led by Graves and Hood?

**Interpreting the Map**

c. Describe the route Washington took to reach Yorktown.

d. What British force tried to come to Cornwallis's aid?

**2. INTERPRETING PRIMARY SOURCES**

Read the passage below, which is a longer version of the quotation you read on page 196.

> These are the times that try men's souls. The summer soldier and the sunshine patriot will, in this crisis, shrink from the service of their country; but he that stands it *now,* deserves the love and thanks of man and woman. Tyranny, like hell, is not easily conquered; yet we have this consolation with us, that the harder the conflict, the more glorious the triumph. What we obtain too cheap, we esteem too lightly: it is dearness only that gives everything its value.
>
> **Thomas Paine,** *The American Crisis*

a. In your own words, explain who "the summer soldier and the sunshine patriot" are.

b. What does Paine promise will be the reward of a hard conflict?

## ALTERNATIVE ASSESSMENT

**1. INTERDISCIPLINARY ACTIVITY: Science**

**Creating a Poster** Two of the diseases that killed American soldiers in camp were typhoid fever and smallpox. Do research to learn the following about one of these diseases: its cause, its symptoms, its treatment, and how common it is today. Use the information to create a public health poster to inform people about the disease.

**2. COOPERATIVE LEARNING ACTIVITY**

**Performing a Talk Show** In a small group, prepare to hold a talk show in which the guests discuss which side to take in the Revolutionary War. One member of your group should be the talk show host. The others should play the roles of various Americans. Each person should explain the reasons for his or her position. Perform the talk show before the class. Students might choose from the following roles:

a. the wife of an American soldier

b. an enslaved African American

c. an Iroquois chief

d. a Quaker minister

e. an employee of the British government

**3. TECHNOLOGY ACTIVITY**

**Creating a Multimedia Presentation** Use the Internet, books, and other reference materials to create a multimedia presentation on one of the major battles of the Revolution. Consider including the following:

- paintings of the conflict and photographs of artifacts
- quotations from participants and witnesses
- music of the time period
- recorded sound effects
- graphs showing battle statistics

Show your presentation to the class.

**Visit www.mcdougallittell.com to learn more about Revolutionary battles.**

**4. HISTORY PORTFOLIO**

**Option 1** Review your section and chapter assessment activities. Select one that you think is your best work. Then use comments made by your teacher or classmates to improve your work. Add the completed work to your portfolio.

**Option 2** Review the questions that you wrote for What Do You Want to Know? on page 192. Then write a short report in which you explain the answers to your questions. If any questions were not answered, do research to answer them. Add your report to your portfolio.



## ALTERNATIVE ASSESSMENT

**1. INTERDISCIPLINARY ACTIVITY: Science**

**Posters should**
- convey a concept through effective visuals.
- use persuasive language in slogans or memorable sentences.
- target a specific audience.
- be presented neatly.

**2. COOPERATIVE LEARNING ACTIVITY**

**Talk shows should**
- have questions that reflect the focus on positions in the Revolutionary War.
- have answers that accurately reflect the thoughts and experiences of the subject's life.
- show evidence of involvement of each person in the group.

3.  **TECHNOLOGY ACTIVITY**

**Presentations should**
- utilize two or more media.
- clearly present accurate information about a battle.
- present information about both sides in the battle.
- show technical proficiency.

**4. HISTORY PORTFOLIO**

**Option 1 Revised section or chapter assessment activities should**
- address teacher and peer responses to the selected work.
- solve problems present in the first versions of the work.

**Option 2 Short reports should**
- answer questions about the American Revolution.
- use evidence to develop and support ideas.
- cite sources of information.
- use standard grammar, spelling, sentence structure, and punctuation.

**Critical Thinking Transparency CT21**
- Visual Summary

**Formal Assessment**
- Chapter Test, Forms A and B, pp. 106–113

## HISTORY SKILLS

**Possible Responses**

1. INTERPRETING MAPS

**Basic Map Elements**

**a.** Virginia

**b.** Battle of the Capes

**Interpreting the Map**

**c.** He moved south over land until he reached a bay, then traveled by water to Yorktown.

**d.** the fleet led by Graves and Hood

2. INTERPRETING PRIMARY SOURCES

**a.** They are Americans who will cease to support the war because it is going badly.

**b.** a glorious triumph

# CHAPTER 8 PLANNING GUIDE

# Confederation to Constitution 1776–1791

## CHAPTER RESOURCES

**CHAPTER OVERVIEW**

The chapter describes the development of the United States government from the Articles of Confederation to the Constitution. It focuses on the debate between the Federalists and the Antifederalists over ratification and a Bill of Rights.

**COPYMASTERS**

**In-Depth Resources: Unit 2**
- Tracing Themes: Democratic Ideals, p. 45
- Building Vocabulary, p. 49

**Interdisciplinary Projects,** pp. 43–48

**TECHNOLOGY**

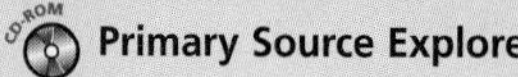
**Primary Source Explorer**

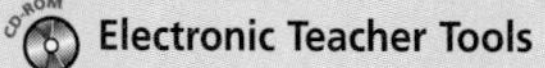
**Electronic Teacher Tools**

**Power Presentations CD-ROM**

**Chapter Summaries on CD** (English and Spanish)

## SECTION 1 The Confederation Era pp. 221–227

**KEY IDEAS**

- The new United States sets up a republic.
- The Land Ordinance of 1785 and the Northwest Ordinance set policy for organizing the new western lands.
- Poor economic conditions in the 1780s lead to Shays's Rebellion.

**COPYMASTERS**

**In-Depth Resources: Unit 2**
- Setting the Stage, p. 44
- Guided Reading, p. 46
- Primary Source, p. 53
- Reteaching Activity, p. 58

**America's History Makers**
- Daniel Boone, pp. 31–32

**Economics in History**
- The Value of Land, p. 8

**TECHNOLOGY**

**Warm-Up Transparency WT8**

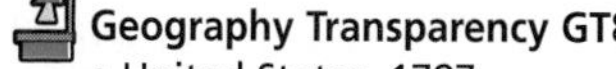
**Geography Transparency GT8**
- United States, 1787

**Critical Thinking Transparency CT22**
- Setting the Stage

**ClassZone:** www.mcdougallittell.com

## SECTION 2 Creating the Constitution pp. 228–233

- James Madison proposes a new plan of government.
- The Great Compromise resolves conflicts among the states over representation.
- Debates over slavery conclude with the Three-Fifths Compromise and the temporary extension of the slave trade.

**COPYMASTERS**

**In-Depth Resources: Unit 2**
- Setting the Stage, p. 44
- Guided Reading, p. 47
- Primary Source, p. 54
- Literature Selection, pp. 55–57
- Reteaching Activity, p. 59

**America's History Makers**
- James Madison, pp. 33–34

**Citizenship Today,** p. 68

**TECHNOLOGY**

**Humanities Transparency HT15**
- George Washington at the Constitutional Convention

**Critical Thinking Transparency CT23**
- Cause and Effect: The Constitutional Convention

**Primary Source Explorer**
- *The Federalist,* Number 51
- *Objections to the Constitution*

**ClassZone:** www.mcdougallittell.com

## SECTION 3 Ratifying the Constitution pp. 234–239

- Federalists support ratification of the Constitution, while Antifederalists oppose it.
- *The Federalist* Papers—essays by Madison, Hamilton, and Jay—win public support for ratification.
- The Constitution is ratified, and a Bill of Rights is added to it.

**COPYMASTERS**

**In-Depth Resources: Unit 2**
- Setting the Stage, p. 44
- Guided Reading, p. 48
- Skillbuilder Practice, p. 50
- Geography Application: Ratifying the Constitution, pp. 51–52
- Reteaching Activity, p. 60

**Why It Matters Now**
- The Living Constitution, pp. 15–16

**Outline Map Activities**
- The Original 13 States, 1790, pp. 15–16

**TECHNOLOGY**

**Warm-Up Transparency WT8**

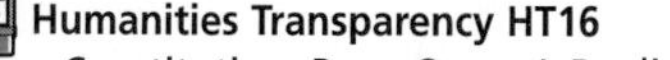
**Humanities Transparency HT16**
- Constitution, Page One—A Replica

**Critical Thinking Transparency CT22**
- Setting the Stage

**ClassZone:** www.mcdougallittell.com

PE Pupil's Edition
Copymaster
Overhead Transparency
Audio Library
CD-ROM
Internet

## ASSESSMENT

**Chapter Assessment,** pp. 240–241

**Formal Assessment**
- Chapter Tests, Forms A and B, pp. 119–126

**Alternative Assessment Book**

**Electronic Teacher Tools with Test Maker**

**Section Assessment,** p. 225

**Formal Assessment**
- Section Quiz, p. 116

**Alternative Assessment Book**
- Rubrics for an opinion, 4.1
- Rubrics for a map, 2.1

**Electronic Teacher Tools with Test Maker**

**Section Assessment,** p. 233

**Formal Assessment**
- Section Quiz, p. 117

**Alternative Assessment Book**
- Rubrics for an audio recording, 5.3
- Rubrics for a political cartoon, 1.2

**Electronic Teacher Tools with Test Maker**

**Section Assessment,** p. 237

**Formal Assessment**
- Section Quiz, p. 118

**Alternative Assessment Book**
- Rubrics for a press conference, 3.3
- Rubrics for a news report, 4.5

**Electronic Teacher Tools with Test Maker**

## CUSTOMIZING FOR INDIVIDUAL NEEDS

### Students Acquiring English/ESL

**Reading Study Guide** (English and Spanish), pp. 75–82

**Access for Students Acquiring English/ESL: Spanish Translations,** pp. 50–55

**Chapter Summaries on CD** (English and Spanish)

### Less Proficient Readers

**Reading Study Guide** (English and Spanish), pp. 75–82

**Chapter Summaries on CD** (English and Spanish)

### Gifted and Talented Students

**In-Depth Resources: Unit 2**
- Enrichment Activity, p. 61

**America's History Makers**
- Daniel Boone, pp. 31–32
- James Madison, pp. 33–34

## CROSS-CURRICULAR CONNECTIONS

### Geography

Aylesworth, Thomas G., and Virginia L. Aylesworth. ***Eastern Great Lakes: Indiana, Michigan, Ohio.*** New York: Chelsea House Publishers, 1988. The geography and culture of these states that were carved from the Northwest Territory.

### Government

Jaffe, Steven H. ***Who Were the Founding Fathers? Two Hundred Years of Reinventing American History.*** New York: Holt, 1996. A lively look at changing views of historic figures, as seen in contemporary and modern journalism, cartoons, and art.

### Interdisciplinary Projects, pp. 43–48

- Math: Finding the Area
- Science: Preserving Important Documents
- Language Arts: Formal English: The Bill of Rights
- Art: Designing the First U.S. Flag

### Primary Sources

Viola, Herman J. ***The National Archives of the United States.*** New York: Abrams, 1984. A beautifully illustrated account of the preservation of American records and documents such as the Constitution.

### Literature

Irving, Washington. ***The Legend of Sleepy Hollow.*** New York: Tor Books, 1990. The much-loved American classic of life in post-Revolutionary New York State.

Willis, Patricia. ***Danger Along the Ohio.*** Boston: Houghton, 1997. Adventures of the three Dunn children as they struggle to return to their father after being cast ashore on the wild banks of the Ohio River in 1793.

## ENRICHMENT ACTIVITIES

**Pupil's Edition, pp. 218–241**
**Interact with History,** p. 219
**Geography in History,** pp. 226–227
**Interactive Primary Sources,** pp. 238–239

**In-Depth Resources: Unit 2**
- Geography Application: Ratifying the Constitution, pp. 51–52
- Primary Source: A Letter from Benjamin Lincoln, p. 53
- Primary Source: from *Debates on the Adoption of the Federal Constitution,* p. 54
- Literature Selection: from *Our Independence and the Constitution,* pp. 55–57

**America's History Makers**
- Daniel Boone, pp. 31–32
- James Madison, pp. 33–34

**Outline Map Activities**
- The Original 13 States, 1790, pp. 15–16

**Primary Source Explorer**
- *The Federalist,* Number 51
- *Objections to the Constitution*

**Why It Matters Now**
- The Living Constitution, pp. 15–16

**LESSON PLAN OPTIONS (50-MINUTE PERIOD)** **(TE) = Teacher's Edition (PE) = Pupil's Edition**

| | TEACHER-DIRECTED ACTIVITIES<br>Class Time: 15 minutes | STUDENT-CENTERED ACTIVITIES<br>Class Time: 25 minutes | INDIVIDUAL ACTIVITIES<br>Class Time: 10 minutes |
|---|---|---|---|
| **DAY 1**<br>Introduction<br>pp. 218–220 | **Presentation Options**<br>• Begin with a class discussion of the drawing on p. 218 **(PE)**.<br>• Lead a class discussion on the "What Do You Know?" question in Setting the Stage, p. 220. Then introduce the graphic organizer for the chapter **(PE)**. | **Options for Cooperative Learning**<br>• Have student groups discuss the Interact with History questions, p. 219 **(PE)**.<br>• Have student groups respond to the "What Do You Want to Know?" question in Setting the Stage, p. 220 **(PE)**. | **Head Start on Homework Options**<br>• Have students skim Section 1 Main Idea, Why It Matters Now, Terms & Names, and the main headings, p. 221 **(PE)**.<br>• Have students begin Guided Reading activity and Building Vocabulary sheet. |
| **DAY 2**<br>Section 1<br>pp. 221–227 | **Presentation Options**<br>• Begin with the 5-Minute Warm-Up, p. 221 **(TE)**.<br>• Review the Section 1 Main Idea, Why It Matters Now, and Terms & Names, p. 221 **(PE)**.<br>• Choose 5 key questions for Objectives 1–4 to discuss with the class, pp. 221–224 **(TE)**. | **Options for Cooperative Learning**<br>• Divide students into groups to work on the Geography in History questions, pp. 226–227 **(PE)**.<br>• Have student pairs work together to complete one of the Activity Options in the Section 1 Assessment, p. 225 **(PE)**. | **Head Start on Homework Options**<br>• Have students begin working on Section 1 Assessment, p. 225 **(PE)**.<br>• Have students preview Section 2 Main Idea, Why It Matters Now, Terms & Names, and the main headings, p. 228 **(PE)**. |
| **DAY 3**<br>Section 2<br>pp. 228–233 | **Presentation Options**<br>• Begin with the 5-Minute Warm-Up, p. 228 **(TE)**.<br>• Choose 5 key questions for Objectives 1–4 to discuss with the class, pp. 228–232 **(TE)**.<br>• Lead the class through the Critical Thinking Activity, p. 231 **(TE)**. | **Options for Cooperative Learning**<br>• Divide students into groups and have them complete the Interdisciplinary Link, Humanities: Great Compromise Play, p. 231 **(TE)**.<br>• Have student pairs work together to complete one of the Activity Options in the Section 2 Assessment, p. 233 **(PE)**. | **Head Start on Homework Options**<br>• Have students begin working on Section 2 Assessment, p. 233 **(PE)**.<br>• Have students complete the Skillbuilder questions and Extension on p. 235 **(PE, TE)**. |
| **DAY 4**<br>Section 3<br>pp. 234–239 | **Presentation Options**<br>• Begin with the 5-Minute Warm-Up, p. 234 **(TE)**.<br>• Choose 5 key questions for Objectives 1–4 to discuss with the class, pp. 234–237 **(TE)**.<br>• Lead the class through the Interactive Primary Sources, pp. 238–239 **(TE)**. | **Options for Cooperative Learning**<br>• Divide students into groups and have them complete the Skillbuilder Mini-Lesson: Analyzing Points of View, p. 235 **(TE)**.<br>• Have student pairs work together to complete the Primary Source A Closer Look questions, pp. 238–239 **(PE)**. | **Head Start on Homework Options**<br>• Have students complete the Setting the Stage graphic organizer for the chapter, p. 220 **(PE)**.<br>• Have students begin working on the Chapter Assessment, pp. 240–241 **(PE)**.<br>• Prepare for Chapter Test<br>**Formal Assessment,** pp. 119–126 |

TEACHER-TESTED ACTIVITY Paul Beavers, J. T. Moore Middle School, Nashville, Tennessee

## NORTH VS. SOUTH

**Class Time** Two class periods

**Task** Solving conflicts that arose between Northern and Southern delegates at the Constitutional Convention

**Purpose** To recognize the difficulties that delegates faced in finding compromises on difficult issues

**Supplies Needed**

- Reference books and Internet sources on the Constitutional Convention

**Activity** Divide the class into groups of five or six students. Within each group, some students should represent the North and others the South. Have each group make a list of what they hope to achieve at the convention and identify issues on which they are willing to compromise. With this list as a starting point, have each group create a framework for government that addresses the issues of slavery and protective tariffs. Have each group explain its plan to the class and defend it. Then allow time for other class members to suggest changes in the plan.

## BLOCK SCHEDULING — LESSON PLAN OPTIONS (90-MINUTE PERIOD)

### DAY 1

**Interact with History,** p. 219
**Class Time** 20 Minutes

Options for pacing and variety:

- **Role-Playing** Have students role-play a dialogue between a newspaper reporter and a delegate to the Constitutional Convention. The reporter can ask the delegate why he or she is there, how decisions will be made, and what the important issues are. After 10 minutes, have students switch roles and resume the conversation. **Class Time** 20 minutes

**Setting the Stage,** p. 220
**Class Time** 20 minutes

Options for pacing and variety:

- **Time Saver** For a homework assignment, have students answer the questions "Why do nations have governments?" and "What does the U.S. government do?" **Class Time** 5 minutes

**Section 1,** pp. 221–227
**Class Time** 50 minutes

Options for pacing and variety:

- **History on Film** Extend students' background knowledge of trailblazer Daniel Boone by viewing *Daniel Boone and the First American Pioneers,* SVE, 1996. **Class Time** 30 minutes
- **Peer Teaching** Have pairs of students use the graph on page 224 to write a summary of the Continental Congress, describing its successes and failures. **Class Time** 20 minutes

### DAY 2

**Section 2,** pp. 228–233
**Class Time** 45 minutes

Options for pacing and variety:

- **Peer Teaching** Using the chart The Great Compromise on page 232 as a model, have pairs of students create a chart showing how a compromise was reached on the issue of slavery. Have pairs exchange their charts and evaluate each other's graphics. **Class Time** 10 minutes
- **Internet** Extend students' background knowledge of the creation of the Constitution by having them visit www.mcdougallittell.com **Class Time** 20 minutes

**Section 3,** pp. 234–239
**Class Time** 45 minutes

Options for pacing and variety:

- **Time Saver** Use the chart on page 235 to summarize the differences between the Federalists and the Antifederalists for the class. **Class Time** 10 minutes
- **Role-Playing** Have two students role-play a conversation between a person who favors ratifying the Constitution and one who opposes it. Ask the class to decide which speaker's arguments are more convincing. **Class Time** 10 minutes

**Chapter 8 Assessment,** pp. 240–241
**Class Time** 40 minutes

Options for pacing and variety:

- **Peer Evaluation** Have student pairs answer the Critical Thinking questions from the Chapter Assessment. Then have them make up one additional Critical Thinking question to pose to the class. **Class Time** 20 minutes
- **Peer Teaching** Within small groups, have students share their completed Reading Strategy charts from page 220 with the class, explaining the problems and solutions they identified. **Class Time** 30 minutes

## CHAPTER 8 OBJECTIVE

The student will analyze the Articles of Confederation, major issues faced by delegates to the Constitutional Convention of 1787, and the debate over ratifying the Constitution.

### HISTORY FROM VISUALS

**Interpreting the Painting** Ask students to study the scene outside the Pennsylvania State House during the Constitutional Convention of 1787. Ask them to make inferences about what the people in the painting may have been talking about. **Possible Responses** the likelihood of a new form of government, the effects such a government might have on their lives, and the issues involved in establishing that government

**Extension** Ask students how Americans learn about government activities today.

### CRITICAL THINKING ACTIVITY

**Identifying and Solving Problems** Draw a problem-solution outline on the board for the following problem: "The existing form of government does not meet the needs of the people." Ask students to suggest ways a country can solve this problem. **Possible Responses** A convention of representatives revamps the government, an election changes the government, or a revolution overthrows the government.

**Class Time** 25 minutes

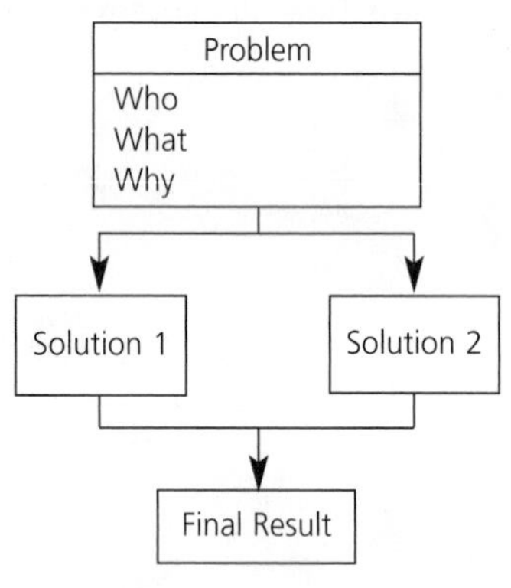


# CHAPTER 8 Confederation to Constitution

## 1776–1791

Delegates to the Constitutional Convention in 1787 gathered in Philadelphia. They held their meetings in the Pennsylvania State House, now known as Independence Hall.

218

### RECOMMENDED RESOURCES

**BOOKS FOR THE TEACHER**

Boone, Daniel and Francis Lister Hawks. ***His Own Story & The Adventures of Daniel Boone: The Kentucky Rifleman.*** Bedford, MA: Applewood Books, 1995. Two volumes—one by Boone himself and one by an early biographer.

Bowen, Catherine Drinker. ***Miracle at Philadelphia: The Story of the Constitutional Convention.*** Boston: Little, Brown, 1986. Highly readable story of the Convention.

Duncan, Christopher M. ***The Anti-Federalists and Early American Political Thought.*** De Kalb: N. Ill. Univ. Pr., 1995. An argument in favor of the Antifederalists.

**SOFTWARE**

***Decisions, Decisions: The Constitution.*** Tom Snyder Prod'ns. 1999. Part of an award-winning set of 15 CDs.

**VIDEO**

***Daniel Boone.*** A&E Biography Series. Moonbeam Pubs.

**INTERNET**

For more about creating a constitution, visit www.mcdougallittell.com

## Interact *with* History

Delegates kept the windows closed during meetings so that the proceedings would be secret.
Some of the most respected men in the nation served as delegates, including Alexander Hamilton and Benjamin Franklin.
The delegates chose George Washington, hero of the Revolutionary War, to be president of the convention.

**The year is 1787, and your young country needs to reform its government. Now everyone is wondering what the new government will be like. You have been called to a convention to decide how the new government should be organized.**

### What Do You Think?

- What will be your main goal in creating a new government?
- How will you get the people at the convention to agree on important issues?

# *How do you form a government?*

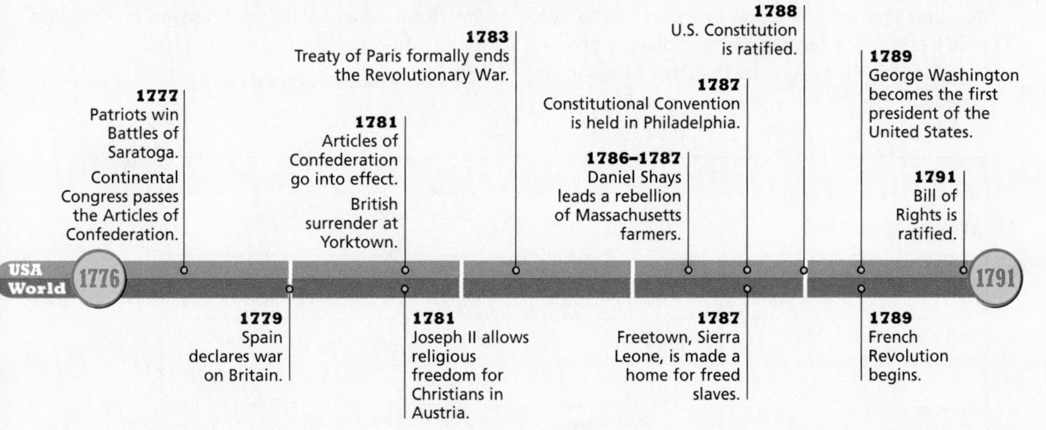




## Interact *with* History

### OBJECTIVES

- To help students evaluate the importance of the Constitutional Convention
- To help students make connections with individuals who participated in the Convention

### What Do You Think?

1. Ask students to explain how they identified their main goal.
2. Have students explain how they and friends or family members make decisions.

### *How do you form a government?*

Ask students to consider the services a government provides and the services they think it should provide.

### MAKING PERSONAL CONNECTIONS

Ask students to think about meetings in which they have participated or that they attended in person. Examples might include student government or special club meetings. Ask: How were those meetings conducted? Did everyone agree on decisions made at the meeting? How did those who presided over the meeting make sure everyone had a chance to express his or her own views on a topic?

### TIME LINE DISCUSSION

**Remind students that in the 1780s, large areas of the world were still dominated by colonial powers such as Great Britain, Spain, and France. The young United States faced threats from outside powers and tensions at home over difficult issues like slavery and the role of government.**

- Ask: How long after independence did the United States experience an internal rebellion? **Answer** Shays's Rebellion occurred in 1786, three years after the Treaty of Paris.
- Ask students to identify an event that occurred in the same year as the Constitutional Convention. **Answer** Freetown, Sierra Leone, becomes a home for freed slaves.
- Ask students to identify an event in Europe after the Constitutional Convention that greatly interested Americans. **Answer** the French Revolution, because France had been a U.S. ally during the American Revolution

## BEFORE YOU READ

### Previewing the Theme: Democratic Ideals

Ask students why they think the states wanted to form any national government at all. Why didn't the states simply remain 13 independent nations?

**Possible Response** Much of the world in the late 1700s was dominated by powerful empires. Many Americans feared that each state would be too weak on its own to defend itself against foreign domination. Together, the states could more successfully defend themselves from foreign military or economic threats. However, they struggled to determine what form their national government should take and how powerful it should be.

### What Do You Know?

Point out to students that state and local governments are not part of our national government. State and local governments have their own powers and responsibilities in the United States. In this chapter they will learn why this is so.

 **In-Depth Resources: Unit 2**
- Tracing Themes: Democratic Ideals, p. 45

## READ AND TAKE NOTES

**Reading Strategy: Solving Problems**
Explain to students that as they study history, they will read about various kinds of problems faced by Americans and about the ways they tried to solve these problems. Point out that if more than one problem is presented in a chapter, it is a good idea to use a chart to keep track of the problems and their solutions. Ask students to look at the chart on page 220 and identify the four problems listed.

 **In-Depth Resources: Unit 2**
- Setting the Stage, p. 44

 **Critical Thinking Transparency CT22**
- Setting the Stage

# Chapter 8 SETTING THE STAGE

## BEFORE YOU READ

### Previewing the Theme

**Democratic Ideals** Between 1776 and 1791, the United States struggled to set up a national government. The Articles of Confederation established the first federal government. Chapter 8 explains how the weaknesses of the Articles led Americans to write a new constitution for the United States.

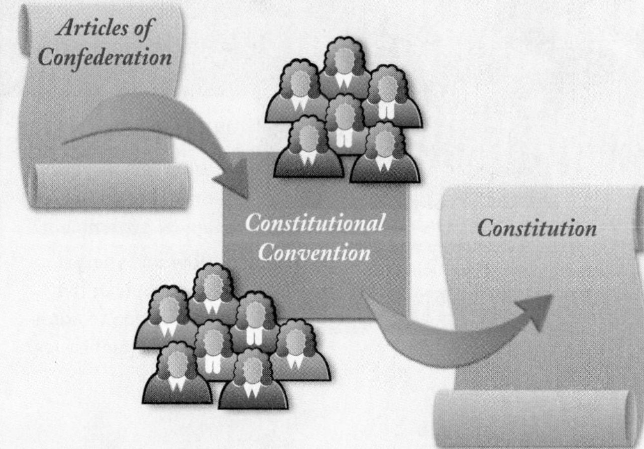


### What Do You Know?

What do you think of when people talk about the U.S. government? Why do nations have governments? What does the U.S. government do?

**THINK ABOUT**
- what you've learned about the U.S. government from the news or your teachers
- what the purpose of a government is
- how the government affects your everyday life

### What Do You Want to Know?

What questions do you have about the creation of the U.S. Constitution? Write those questions in your notebook before you read the chapter.

## READ AND TAKE NOTES

**Reading Strategy: Solving Problems** When you read history, look for how people solved problems they faced in the past. Copy the chart below in your notebook. Use it to identify the methods that Americans used to solve the problems faced by the nation after declaring its independence.

 See Skillbuilder Handbook, page R17.

| Problems | Solutions |
|---|---|
| Western lands | States give up Western claims. Congress passes laws to organize the territories. |
| Postwar depression | Annapolis Convention is called to discuss problems of commerce. |
| Representation in the new government | Philadelphia convention is held. Delegates agree to Great Compromise to settle issue of state representation. |
| Slavery | Three-Fifths Compromise addresses issue of slavery and representation. Congress delays discussion of banning the slave trade. |



## TEACHING STRATEGY

### READING THE CHAPTER

This is a chronological chapter focusing on the origins of government in the new nation. Encourage students to identify problems leading to the creation of the Articles of Confederation, the Constitution, and the Bill of Rights. Have students identify events in this period that illustrate political problems and the solutions people devised. Pause at the end of each section to review the events and their relationships.

### ALTERNATIVE ASSESSMENT

The Chapter Assessment describes three activities for alternative assessment on page 241. You may wish to have students work on these activities during the course of the chapter and then present them at the end.

# 1 The Confederation Era

**TERMS & NAMES**
Wilderness Road
republic
Articles of Confederation
Land Ordinance of 1785
Northwest Territory
Northwest Ordinance
Shays's Rebellion

**MAIN IDEA**

The Articles of Confederation were too weak to govern the nation after the war ended.

**WHY IT MATTERS NOW**

The weakness of the Articles of Confederation led to the writing of the U.S. Constitution.

## ONE AMERICAN'S STORY

**In 1775, Daniel Boone and 30 woodsmen cut a road over the Appalachian Mountains into Kentucky. They hacked through brush, chopped down trees, and bridged creeks. They labored like this for about 250 miles. Eventually, they arrived in a grassy meadow along the banks of the Kentucky River. Felix Walker, a member of Boone's party, described what they saw.**

*A VOICE FROM THE PAST*

On entering the plain we were permitted to view a very interesting and romantic sight. A number of buffaloes . . . supposed to be between two and three hundred, made off . . . in every direction. . . . Such a sight some of us never saw before, nor perhaps ever may again.

**Felix Walker,** quoted in *The Life and Adventures of Daniel Boone*

Early travel to Kentucky is shown in this detail of *Daniel Boone Escorting Settlers Through the Cumberland Gap* (1851–1852) by George Caleb Bingham.

**Boone was one of the earliest American settlers in Kentucky. In the late 1700s, most Americans thought of Kentucky as the wild frontier. Some, like Boone, looked at the frontier and saw a world of opportunity. Exploring and governing these lands was only one of the many challenges that faced the new government of the United States.**

## 1 Moving West

The trail into Kentucky that Daniel Boone helped build was called the **Wilderness Road**. This road was not easy to travel. It was too narrow for carts or wagons, but it became the main road into Kentucky. The settlers came on foot or on horseback. Settlers were drawn to Kentucky's rich river valleys, where few Native Americans lived. But some Native Americans, such as the Shawnee, did live, hunt, and fish in the area.

Tensions between Native Americans and settlers led to violent confrontations. But the settlers did not stop coming. By the early 1790s, about 100,000 Americans lived there. While settlers headed into the Western territories, the people in the East began to create new state governments.





## SECTION OBJECTIVES

1. To describe the expansion of the nation and the development of state governments
2. To analyze the strengths and weaknesses of the Articles of Confederation
3. To evaluate the importance of the Northwest Ordinance
4. To identify the causes and effects of Shays's Rebellion

**SKILLBUILDER**

Interpreting Maps: Location, p. 223
Interpreting Charts, p. 224

**CRITICAL THINKING**

Finding Main Ideas, p. 223
Analyzing Causes, p. 224
Forming and Supporting Opinions, p. 225

## FOCUS & MOTIVATE

### 5-MINUTE WARM-UP

**Making Inferences** The questions below focus on the challenges faced by the new nation.

1. Look at the map on page 223. What kinds of problems do you think might be caused by conflicting state claims to new territories?
2. How do you think those conflicting claims could be resolved?

 **Warm-Up Transparency WT8**

## INSTRUCT

### INSTRUCT: OBJECTIVE  1

**Moving West/New State Governments**

Key Questions

- Into which areas did American settlement expand in the late 1700s?
- What kind of governments did the new states create for themselves?
- What is a republic? Why is the United States a republic?

 **In-Depth Resources: Unit 2**
- Guided Reading, p. 46

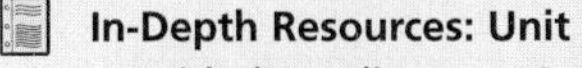

## RECOMMENDED RESOURCES

**In-Depth Resources: Unit 2**
- Guided Reading, p. 46
- Building Vocabulary, p. 49
- Primary Source, p. 53
- Reteaching Activity, p. 58

**Reading Study Guide** (Spanish and English), pp. 75–76

**Economics in History**
- The Value of Land, p. 8

**America's History Makers**
- Daniel Boone, pp. 31–32

**Formal Assessment**
- Section Quiz, p. 116

**Alternative Assessment**
- Rubrics, 4.1
- Rubrics, 2.1

**Access for Students Acquiring English/ESL**
- Guided Reading, p. 50

Technology Resources

 **Geography Transparency GT8**
- United States, 1787

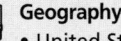

 **Electronic Teacher Tools with Test Maker**

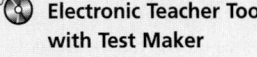

 **ClassZone**
www.mcdougallittell.com

**MORE ABOUT . . .**

**The English Bill of Rights**

The English Bill of Rights limited the power of the English monarch. Among other things, it prevented the monarch from suspending the law, levying taxes, and maintaining an army in peacetime without consent of Parliament. It also guaranteed free elections and free speech for members of Parliament (but not for other people).

**INSTRUCT: OBJECTIVE 2**

**The Articles of Confederation**

Key Questions

- What issues divided the Continental Congress as it developed a plan for a national government?
- What were the structure and powers of the national government under the Articles of Confederation?
- How did state claims to western lands affect the acceptance of the Articles of Confederation?

**CRITICAL THINKING ACTIVITY**

**Analyzing Points of View** Divide the class into pairs of students. Tell one student in each pair to list arguments supporting the views of the large states while the other member of each pair should list the views of the small states, about western land claims and representation in Congress. Tell students to record their lists on a chart like the one below. Allow pairs to use their charts as the basis for a short debate.

| Large States | Small States |
|---|---|
| | |

**Class Time** 25 minutes

## New State Governments

Once the American colonies declared independence, each of the states set out to create its own government. The framers, or creators, of the state constitutions did not want to destroy the political systems that they had had as colonies. They simply wanted to make those systems more democratic. Some states experimented with creating separate branches of government, giving different powers to different branches. By creating separate branches, Americans hoped to prevent the government from becoming too powerful.

**Background** Two states, Connecticut and Rhode Island, kept their old colonial charters as their constitutions. The other 11 states wrote new constitutions.

Some states included a bill of rights in their constitutions as a way to keep the government under control. The idea of a bill of rights came from the English Bill of Rights of 1689. This was a list of rights that the government guaranteed to English citizens.

Although not all the states had a bill of rights, all of them did have a republican form of government. In a **republic,** the people choose representatives to govern them.

## 2 The Articles of Confederation

While the states were setting up their governments, Americans also discussed the form of their national government. During the Revolutionary War, Americans realized that they needed to unite to win the war against Britain. As Silas Deane, a diplomat from Connecticut, wrote, "United we stand, divided we fall."

*"United we stand, divided we fall."*
Silas Deane

In 1776, the Continental Congress began to develop a plan for a national government. Congress agreed that the government should be a republic. But the delegates disagreed about whether each state should have one vote or voting should be based on population. They also disagreed about whether the national government or the individual states should control the lands west of the Appalachians.

The Continental Congress eventually arrived at a final plan, called the **Articles of Confederation.** In the Articles, the national government had few powers, because many Americans were afraid that a strong government would lead to tyranny, or oppressive rule. The national government was run by a Confederation Congress. Each state had only one vote in the Congress. The national government had the power to wage war, make peace, sign treaties, and issue money.

**Reading History** **A. Reading a Map** Look at the map on page 223 to see which states claimed territories in the West.

But the Articles left most important powers to the states. These powers included the authority to set taxes and enforce national laws. The Articles proposed to leave the states in control of the lands west of the Appalachian Mountains.



**ACTIVITY OPTIONS**

**INDIVIDUAL NEEDS**

**LESS PROFICIENT READERS**

**Categorizing** To help students understand the purpose and provisions of the Articles of Confederation, create a two-column chart on the board. Add the headings *States* and *National Government* to the chart. Ask students to list the powers of the states and of the central government under the Articles of Confederation. Add student responses to the appropriate column. You may want students to copy and save the chart for future discussion on the weaknesses of the Articles of Confederation.

| States | National Government |
|---|---|
| Set taxes | Wage war |
| Enforce laws | Make peace |
| Control western lands | Sign treaties |
| Have one vote in Congress | Issue money |

The Continental Congress passed the Articles of Confederation in November 1777. It then sent the Articles to the states for ratification, or approval. By July 1778, eight states had ratified the Articles. But some of the small states that did not have Western land claims refused to sign.

These states felt that unless the Western lands were placed under the control of the national government, they would be at a disadvantage. The states with Western lands could sell them to pay off debts left from the Revolution. But states without lands would have difficulty paying off the high war debts.

Over the next three years, all the states gave up their claims to Western lands. This led the small states to ratify the Articles. In 1781, Maryland became the 13th state to accept the Articles. As a result, the United States finally had an official government.

*Reading* **History**

**B. Finding Main Ideas** Why did the states without Western land claims want the other states to give up their claims?

**B. Answer** The states without claims feared that the states with claims would be richer and stronger than them.

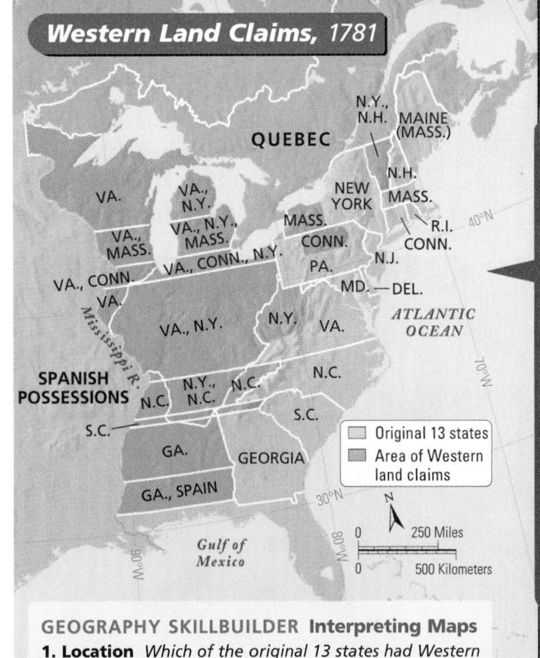


**GEOGRAPHY SKILLBUILDER Interpreting Maps**

1. **Location** *Which of the original 13 states had Western land claims?*
2. **Location** *To what geographic feature did the Western land claims extend?*

Skillbuilder Answers
1. Virginia, New York, Massachusetts, Connecticut, North Carolina, South Carolina, Georgia, and New Hampshire
2. Mississippi River

## ❸ The Northwest Ordinance

One of the most important questions that the Confederation Congress faced was what to do with the Western lands that it now controlled. Congress passed important laws on how to divide and govern these lands—the Land Ordinance of 1785 and the Northwest Ordinance (1787). (See Geography in History on pages 226–227.)

The **Land Ordinance of 1785** called for surveyors to stake out six-mile-square plots, called townships, in the Western lands. These lands later became known as the **Northwest Territory.** The Northwest Territory included land that formed the states of Ohio, Indiana, Michigan, Illinois, and Wisconsin and part of Minnesota.

The **Northwest Ordinance** (1787) described how the Northwest Territory was to be governed. As the territory grew in population, it would gain rights to self-government. When there were 5,000 free males in an area, men who owned at least 50 acres of land could elect an assembly. When there were 60,000 people, they could apply to become a new state.

**Background**

According to the Northwest Ordinance, Native Americans were to be treated fairly, and their lands were not to be taken from them.

The Northwest Ordinance also set conditions for settlement in the Northwest Territory and outlined the settlers' rights. Slavery was outlawed, and the rivers were to be open to navigation by all. Freedom of religion and trial by jury were guaranteed.

The Northwest Ordinance was important because it set a pattern for the orderly growth of the United States. As the nation grew, it followed this pattern in territories added after the Northwest Territory.





### HISTORY FROM VISUALS

**Reading the Map** The western lands of the new United States were vast. Have students list some of the challenges of governing such a large territory.

**Possible Answers** setting up government divisions, keeping order, defending territories from foreign threats

**Extension** Have students create a map of what they think the United States would look like today if the original states had not given up their claims to western lands.

**Geography Transparency GT8**
- United States, 1787

### INSTRUCT: OBJECTIVE ❸

**The Northwest Ordinance**

Key Questions
- How did the Land Ordinance of 1785 state that the western lands should be divided?
- How were the western territories governed under the Northwest Ordinance?
- Why was the Northwest Ordinance important to the growth of the United States?

**Economics in History**
- The Value of Land, p. 8

### MORE ABOUT . . .

**Western Land Claims**

Western land claims originated in vaguely worded colonial charters that gave some colonies control of territory reaching from the Atlantic to the Pacific Oceans. After the Revolution, new states scrambled to claim as much territory as they could.

**ACTIVITY OPTIONS**

**INTERDISCIPLINARY LINK: GOVERNMENT**

BLOCK SCHEDULING

**BECOMING A STATE**

**Class Time** 30 minutes

**Task** Making a time line showing the steps toward statehood

**Purpose** To identify the procedure for territories becoming states

**Supplies Needed**
- Textbook
- Encyclopedias and other reference books on state history
- Paper and art supplies

**Activity** Assign each student one of the following states formed (totally or partially) from the Northwest Territory: Wisconsin, Illinois, Indiana, Michigan, Ohio, Minnesota. Direct students to find out when the first settlers arrived in the territory, when it first applied for statehood, and when it became a state. Make a class time line showing these dates for all states.

**INSTRUCT: OBJECTIVE** 

**Weaknesses of the Articles/ Shays's Rebellion**

Key Questions

- Why was debt a critical problem for the national government under the Articles of Confederation?
- Why did the national government get little financial support from the states?
- How did Shays's Rebellion point out the weaknesses of government under the Articles of Confederation?

**HISTORY FROM VISUALS**

**Interpreting the Chart** Point out to students that the Continental Congress had deliberately created a very weak central government. Ask students why they think the states feared a strong central government. **Possible Answers** The states had resented the power of the British monarch over their affairs. They did not want to replace one form of tyranny with what they believed might be another in the form of a strong national government.

**Extension** Ask students to identify the one duty they believe is most important for a national government. Tell them to explain their choice.

**MORE ABOUT . . .**

**Shays's Rebellion**

Thomas Jefferson, author of the Declaration of Independence, was not alarmed by Shays's Rebellion. "I hold it that a little rebellion now and then is a good thing," he said. He added: "The tree of liberty must be refreshed from time to time with the blood of patriots and tyrants. It is its natural manure."

Skillbuilder Answers
1. Possible Responses Governing the nation during the Revolutionary War, because if the war was lost, there would be no nation.

## 4 Weaknesses of the Articles

Aside from its handling of land issues, however, the Confederation Congress had few successes. By the end of the Revolutionary War, the United States faced serious problems, and the Confederation Congress did not have enough power to solve them.

**U.S. Government, 1776–1787**

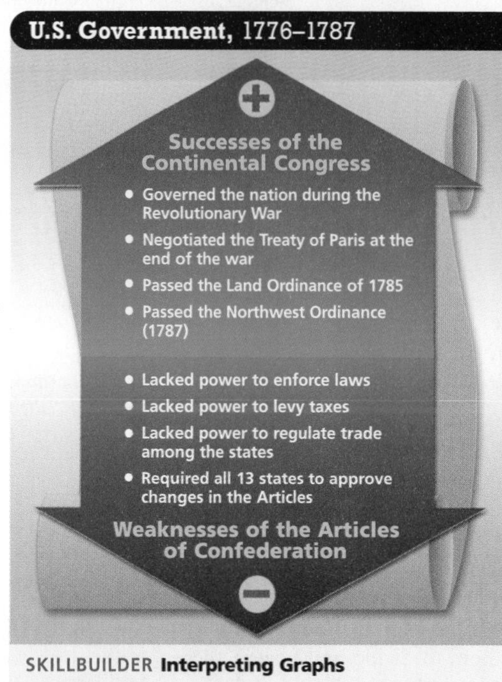

Successes of the Continental Congress
• Governed the nation during the Revolutionary War
• Negotiated the Treaty of Paris at the end of the war
• Passed the Land Ordinance of 1785
• Passed the Northwest Ordinance (1787)
• Lacked power to enforce laws
• Lacked power to levy taxes
• Lacked power to regulate trade among the states
• Required all 13 states to approve changes in the Articles
Weaknesses of the Articles of Confederation


SKILLBUILDER **Interpreting Graphs**

1. *What do you think was the greatest success of the Continental Congress?*
2. *What do you think was the greatest weakness of the Articles of Confederation?*

2. Possible Responses Some students might say the lack of the power to tax, because it meant the government could not pay for what it wanted to do. Others might say the requirement for all 13 states to agree, because it could paralyze Congress.

Debt was a critical problem for the government. Congress had borrowed large sums to pay for the Revolutionary War. Much of that money was owed to soldiers of its own army. Upset at not being paid, several hundred soldiers surrounded the Pennsylvania State House where Congress was meeting in June 1783. The soldiers threatened the legislators, thrusting their bayonets through the windows. The delegates were forced to flee the city. The event was a clear sign of Congress's weakness.

*Reading* **History**
**C. Analyzing Causes** How did debt cause problems for the U.S. government under the Articles of Confederation?
**C. Answer** Congress could not raise money to pay its debts, even to the soldiers who had fought the war.

Even if Congress wanted to pay the soldiers, it did not have the power to levy taxes. The national government depended on the states to send money to Congress. But the states sent very little money.

Congress was not alone in facing economic crises. People throughout the nation faced hard times. In Massachusetts, the economy was so bad that people rose up in arms against the government.

## Shays's Rebellion

In the mid-1780s, Massachusetts faced economic problems, as did other states. People had little money, but the state continued to levy high taxes. The average family owed $200 in taxes per year—more money than most farmers made. Many Massachusetts farmers fell deeply into debt. Debt laws at the time were strict. Anyone who could not repay his debts would have his property auctioned off. If the auction didn't raise enough money to settle the debts, the debtor could be put in jail. In western Massachusetts, many jails were packed with debtors.

Farmers asked the Massachusetts legislature to provide debt relief. But the legislature refused—and the farmers rebelled. One of the leaders of the rebellion was a Revolutionary War veteran named Daniel Shays. He commanded a group of about 1,500 men.



**ACTIVITY OPTIONS**

**INTERDISCIPLINARY LINK: ART**

**DRAWING AN EDITORIAL CARTOON**

**Class Time** One class period

**Task** Drawing an editorial cartoon about the Articles of Confederation

**Purpose** To understand the concerns over the weaknesses of the Articles of Confederation

**Supplies Needed**
- Textbook
- Drawing paper

**Activity** Explain that editorial cartoons express ideas in pictures. Provide some examples of editorial cartoons from local or national newspapers. Then have students draw cartoons about the problems of the United States under the Articles of Confederation. When they have finished their cartoons, invite volunteers to share them with the rest of the class.

Shays's rebels take over a Massachusetts courthouse. A stone marker rests on the spot of the rebellion.

In January 1787, Shays and his men marched on a federal arsenal, a place to store weapons. The arsenal was defended by 900 soldiers from the state militia. The militia quickly defeated Shays's men. But even though the militia put down **Shays's Rebellion,** as the uprising came to be known, the farmers won the sympathy of many people. America's leaders realized that an armed uprising of common farmers spelled danger for the nation.

**Background**
In 1788, Daniel Shays was pardoned for his actions.

Some leaders hoped that the nation's ills could be solved by strengthening the national government. In the next section, you'll read how Americans held a convention to change the Articles of Confederation.

## Section 1 Assessment

### 1. Terms & Names

**Identify:**
- Wilderness Road
- republic
- Articles of Confederation
- Land Ordinance of 1785
- Northwest Territory
- Northwest Ordinance
- Shays's Rebellion

### 2. Taking Notes

Use a diagram like the one below to list some of the challenges Americans faced in shaping a new government.

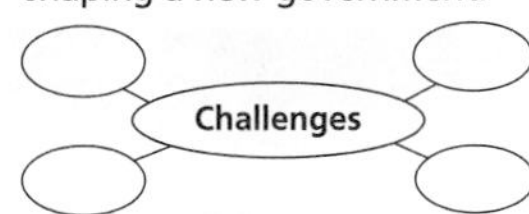


Which challenge do you think was the toughest? Why?

### 3. Main Ideas

**a.** What issues affected the Western territories between 1775 and 1787?

**b.** What were three successes of the Continental Congress?

**c.** What were three weaknesses of the Articles of Confederation?

### 4. Critical Thinking

**Forming and Supporting Opinions** Which side would you have supported during Shays's Rebellion—the farmers or the officials who called out the militia? Why?

**THINK ABOUT**
- the farmers' problems
- the farmers' march on the arsenal
- the job of the government

**ACTIVITY OPTIONS**

**CIVICS**
**GEOGRAPHY**

Write an **opinion article** about how the United States should govern the Western territories or draw a **map** showing how you would have divided the lands.



## MORE ABOUT . . .

**Punishing the Rebels**

The sentences of Shays and his captured followers stirred up great controversy. After 12 of the rebels were sentenced to death, the high sheriff of Pittsfield found a note at his door with this message about the sentences: "I pray have a care that you assist not in the execution of so horrid a crime, for by all that is above, he that condemns and he that executes shall share alike." Two of the rebels were hanged for looting, but all the others, including Shays himself, were pardoned.

**In-Depth Resources: Unit 2**
- Primary Source: A Letter from Benjamin Lincoln, p. 53

## ASSESS & RETEACH

**Setting the Stage** Have students complete the first row on the graphic organizer on page 220.

**Formal Assessment**
- Section Quiz, p. 116

**Critical Thinking Transparency CT22**
- Setting the Stage

### RETEACHING ACTIVITY

Organize the class into groups of four. Each group member should be responsible for answering the Key Questions for one section objective. (See pages 221, 222, 223, and 224 for Key Questions.) Then have group members make copies of their Key Questions and answers and distribute their copies to others in the group.

**In-Depth Resources: Unit 2**
- Reteaching Activity, p. 58

## Section 1 Assessment

### 1. Terms & Names

**Wilderness Road,** p. 221
**republic,** p. 222
**Articles of Confederation,** p. 222
**Land Ordinance of 1785,** p. 223
**Northwest Territory,** p. 223
**Northwest Ordinance,** p. 223
**Shays's Rebellion,** p. 225

### 2. Taking Notes

Challenges: postwar depression; debt; weakness of the Articles of Confederation; all 13 states required to approve changes to the Articles. Answers will vary. Be sure students give support for their opinions.

### 3. Main Ideas

**a.** who would control the territories; how to divide and govern these lands **b.** created the Articles; settled western land claims; passed the Land Ordinances **c.** It lacked the power to enforce laws, to levy taxes, and to regulate trade.

### 4. Critical Thinking

Responses will vary. Be sure students include support for the side they choose.

**ACTIVITY OPTIONS**

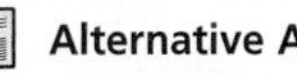

**Alternative Assessment**
- Rubrics for an opinion article, 4.1
- Rubrics for drawing a map, 2.1

## GEOGRAPHY *in* HISTORY

**OBJECTIVE**

Students will analyze the government's division of the Northwest Territory and the interaction between settlers and the environment in the region.

**BLOCK SCHEDULING**

### MORE ABOUT . . .

**Surveying**

A clear and easy-to-understand grid system for dividing land reduced confusion and court cases. New England towns used a grid to divide property before settlers arrived. In New Jersey and other colonies, however, farmers hired private surveyors who drew complicated boundaries to encompass the best farm land. Americans adopted the British system of measuring land, including the furlong (660 feet), the square furlong of 10 acres, and the square mile of 640 acres.

## INSTRUCT

Key Questions

- How did the Land Ordinance show a commitment to formal education in the territory?
- What do you suppose life must have been like for early settlers in the Northwest Territory?
- What do you think Native Americans thought about the increasing numbers of American settlers moving westward?

**MAP SKILL QUESTIONS**

What water routes in the Northwest Territory likely were important for the movement of people and goods?

Into what states was the region eventually divided?

How was land within the territory divided?

## GEOGRAPHY *in* HISTORY

**REGION AND HUMAN-ENVIRONMENT INTERACTION**

# The Northwest Territory

The Northwest Territory was officially known as "the Territory Northwest of the River Ohio." In the mid-1780s, Congress decided to sell the land in the territory to settlers. The sale of land solved two problems. First, it provided cash for the government. Second, it increased American control over the land.

The Land Ordinance of 1785 outlined how the land in the Northwest Territory would be divided. Congress split the land into grids with clearly defined boundaries. It created townships that could be divided into sections, as shown on the map below. Each township was six miles by six miles. This was an improvement over earlier methods of setting boundaries. Previously, people had used rocks, trees, or other landmarks to set boundaries. There had been constant fights over disputed claims.

### The Land Ordinance of 1785

(MINNESOTA)
Lake Superior
QUEBEC
45°N
(WISCONSIN)
Lake Michigan
Lake Huron
(MICHIGAN)
Mississippi River
Lake Erie
SPANISH POSSESSIONS
NORTHWEST TERRITORY
(ILLINOIS) (INDIANA) (OHIO)
40°N
Ohio River
Future state boundaries shown.
0 250 Miles
0 500 Kilometers
90°W 85°W 80°W 75°W
(OHIO)
36 Miles
PA.
WEST VIRGINIA

### TOWNSHIP, 178

| | | | | |
|---|---|---|---|---|
| 36 | 30 | 24 | 18 | 12 |
| 35 | 29 | 23 | 17 | 11 |
| 34 | 28 | 22 | 16 | 10 |
| 33 | 27 | 21 | 15 | 9 |
| 32 | 26 | 20 | 14 | 8 |
| 31 | 25 | 19 | 13 | 7 |

Each township containe sections. Each section w one square mile.

### ARTIFACT FILE

**The Theodolite** The theodolite is a surveying tool. It consists of a telescope that can be moved from side to side and up and down. A theodolite measures angles and determines alignment. These functions are necessary for land surveyors to establish accurate boundaries for land claims.

**Township Map** Congress reserved several plots (outlined on map) for special purposes. A few were set aside for later sale to raise money for the government. One plot was reserved to support a local school.



### MUSEUM CONNECTIONS

The Shelby County Historical Society Web site offers interesting insights into town life at various times, including an interview with a woman who moved to the area in 1831. Her father cleared the land, and her family watched as other families settled in the area.

The Web site for the Sidney, Ohio, Historical Society provides a state-by-state listing of historical societies and other museums of interest to a student of history.

Campus Martius: The Museum of the Northwest Territory in Marietta, Ohio, is located on the site of the original fort designed to protect the first organized American settlement in the Northwest Territories. Marietta, Ohio, was organized in 1788.

The Web site for this museum provides more information about life in the Northwest Territory.

1 The first things settlers needed were food and shelter. Cutting trees provided fields for crops and wood for log cabins. The first crop most farmers planted was corn. Even if the land was not fully cleared of trees, farmers planted corn between the stumps.

2 A shortage of labor meant that a farmer working alone was doing well if he cleared several acres a year. As a result, few farms were completely fenced in, and forest covered most of the property. Hogs were allowed to find food in the woods. Farmers collected apples from trees and used sap to make syrup.

3 Over time, families planted fruits and vegetables. Cattle raising also became more common. Beef cattle supplied families with meat. Dairy cattle provided milk. Families could sell extra fruits, vegetables, and dairy products, such as butter and cheese.

### CONNECT TO GEOGRAPHY

1. **Region** What was the land in the Northwest Territory like before Americans settled there?
2. **Human-Environment Interaction** How did American settlers affect the landscape in the territory?

See Geography Handbook, pages 4–5.

### CONNECT TO HISTORY

3. **Making Inferences** Why did so many people buy land in the new territory?

## On-Line Field Trip

**The Shelby County Historical Society** is located in Sidney, Ohio. Its collections include documents on the early settlement of Ohio, such as this picture of settlers clearing land.

Visit www.mcdougallittell.com for more information.

### CRITICAL THINKING ACTIVITY

**Questioning** Tell students to look at the inset map on page 226. Ask them to think about a family selecting a plot of land for their farm. Tell students to write as many questions as they can that such a family might have asked before selecting a plot of land. When all the questions are complete, work with the class to create headings for classifying them. **Possible Responses** Students may pose questions about the land itself, including the fertility of the soil, the presence of water, and the kind of trees. Other questions may concern the location of the plot within the township, the neighbors, and other township settlers.

**Class Time** 20 minutes

### MORE ABOUT . . .

**Settlers' Rights**

The Land Ordinance of 1785 included a Bill of Rights that guaranteed settlers freedom of religion and trial by jury, among other rights. The Ordinance also forbade slavery in the territories and stated that "The utmost good faith shall always be observed towards the Indians." The Ordinance states why education is important to the nation in these words: "Religion, morality, and knowledge, being necessary to good government and the happiness of mankind, schools and the means of education shall forever be encouraged."

### CONNECT TO GEOGRAPHY

1. **Region** It was mostly wooded. The land was good, so there were many plants in addition to trees. Many things could grow there.
2. **Human-Environment Interaction Possible Response** Since the land was divided up by the government, things were more orderly. The land was identified as farmland, so most of the settlers were people interested in putting down roots. Farmers faced problems clearing the land and carving farms out of the land.

### CONNECT TO HISTORY

3. **Making Inferences Possible Response** Land in the East was more expensive, and the best farmland was already claimed. Western lands were not only cheaper but the land was very fertile. Also, many people saw the land as an opportunity for prosperity and independence.

## SECTION OBJECTIVES

1. To identify key events leading to the Constitutional Convention and to identify key delegates
2. To describe the delegates' expectations
3. To analyze the major issues and compromises of the Constitutional Convention
4. To explain the compromises made regarding slavery and trade in the Constitution

**SKILLBUILDER**
Interpreting Charts, p. 232

**CRITICAL THINKING**
Evaluating, p. 229
Making Decisions, p. 230
Summarizing, p. 231
Forming and Supporting Opinions, p. 233
Analyzing Points of View, p. 233

## FOCUS & MOTIVATE

### 5-MINUTE WARM-UP

**Making Inferences** These questions focus on the challenges facing the Constitutional Convention.

1. Read the quotation on page 228. What grave danger did Randolph believe the nation faced?
2. What conflicts had already occurred to make Randolph's worries seem justified?

 **Warm-Up Transparency WT8**

## INSTRUCT

### INSTRUCT: OBJECTIVE 

**A Constitutional Convention Is Called/ The Convention's Delegates**
Key Questions

- What events encouraged leaders to call a Constitutional Convention?
- Who were some of the key delegates?
- What groups of Americans were not represented at the Convention?

 **In-Depth Resources: Unit 2**
- Guided Reading, p. 47
- Literature Selection: from *Our Independence and the Constitution* by Dorothy Canfield Fisher, pp. 55–57

# 2 Creating the Constitution

**TERMS & NAMES**
Constitutional Convention
James Madison
Virginia Plan
New Jersey Plan
Great Compromise
Three-Fifths Compromise

**MAIN IDEA**
The states sent delegates to a convention to solve the problems of the Articles of Confederation.

**WHY IT MATTERS NOW**
The Constitutional Convention formed the plan of government that the United States still has today.

### ONE AMERICAN'S STORY

**On the afternoon of May 15, 1787, Edmund Randolph, the young governor of Virginia, arrived in Philadelphia for the Constitutional Convention. The young nation faced violence and lawlessness, as Shays's Rebellion had shown. And now delegates from throughout the states were coming to Philadelphia to discuss reforming the government.**

**Randolph knew the serious task he and the other delegates were about to undertake. Early in the convention, Randolph rose to speak. He looked squarely at the delegates and reminded them of their grave responsibility.**

*A VOICE FROM THE PAST*

Let us not be afraid to view with a steady eye the [dangers] with which we are surrounded. . . . Are we not on the eve of [a civil] war, which is only to be prevented by the hopes from this convention?

**Edmund Randolph,** quoted in *Edmund Randolph: A Biography*

Edmund Randolph (left) and the other delegates gathered in the Pennsylvania State House (above) to discuss creating a new government for the United States.

**Over the next four months, the delegates debated how best to keep the United States from falling apart. In this section, you will read about the Convention of 1787 and the creation of the U.S. Constitution.**

## 1 A Constitutional Convention Is Called

In 1786, a series of events began that would eventually lead to a new form of government for the United States. In September of that year, delegates from five states met in Annapolis, Maryland, to discuss ways to promote trade among their states. At the time, most states placed high taxes on goods from other states. The delegates believed that creating national trade laws would help the economies of all the states.

Making such changes required amending the Articles of Confederation, because the national government had been granted no power to regulate trade among the states. The Annapolis delegates, led by Alexander Hamilton of New York, called for the states to send representatives to



## RECOMMENDED RESOURCES

 **In-Depth Resources: Unit 2**
- Guided Reading, p. 47
- Building Vocabulary, p. 49
- Primary Source, p. 54
- Literature Selection, pp. 55–57
- Reteaching Activity, p. 59

**Reading Study Guide** (Spanish and English), pp. 77–78

**America's History Makers**
- James Madison, pp. 33–34

**Formal Assessment**
- Section Quiz, p. 117

**Citizenship Today,** p. 68

**Alternative Assessment**
- Rubrics, 5.3
- Rubrics, 1.2

**Access for Students Acquiring English/ESL**
- Guided Reading, p. 51

**Technology Resources**

**Critical Thinking Trans. CT23**
- Cause and Effect: The Constitutional Convention

 **Humanities Transparency HT15**
- George Washington at the Constitutional Convention

 **Electronic Teacher Tools with Test Maker**

 **ClassZone**
www.mcdougallittell.com

Philadelphia the following May to discuss such changes.

At first, many Americans doubted that the national government needed strengthening. But news of Shays's Rebellion in late 1786 and early 1787 quickly changed many people's minds. Fearing that rebellion might spread, 12 states sent delegates to the meeting in Philadelphia in the summer of 1787. Only Rhode Island refused to participate.

**Background**
Rhode Island did not send delegates because it feared that a strong national government would force people to repay the war debts on difficult terms.

## The Convention's Delegates

The 55 delegates to the **Constitutional Convention,** as the Philadelphia meeting became known, were a very impressive group. About half were lawyers. Others were planters, merchants, and doctors. Three-fourths of them had been representatives in the Continental Congress. Many had been members of their state legislatures and had helped write their state constitutions. Along with other leaders of the time, these delegates are called the Founders, or Founding Fathers, of the United States.

America's most famous men were at the Constitutional Convention. George Washington, the hero of the Revolution, came out of retirement for the meeting. Benjamin Franklin, the famous scientist and statesman, lent his wit and wisdom to the convention. One of the ablest delegates was **James Madison.** Madison had read more than a hundred books on government in preparation for the meeting. When Thomas Jefferson, serving as ambassador to France, read the list of delegates, he wrote, "It is really an assembly of demigods [highly honored people]."

***Reading* History**
**A. Evaluating** How well do the characteristics of the Founders serve as models of civic virtue?
A. Possible Response
They provide an excellent model of civic virtue because they were educated, well-informed, and actively participated in government.

### America's HERITAGE

**INDEPENDENCE HALL**

The Pennsylvania State House, where the Constitutional Convention took place, is now called Independence Hall. It is protected as part of a national park in Philadelphia.

The State House itself was the site where George Washington received his commission to lead the Continental Army and where the Declaration of Independence was signed. The Liberty Bell is nearby. Many visitors come to Philadelphia to stand in the building where much of America's early history as a nation was made.

Not everyone was at the Constitutional Convention. Thomas Jefferson and John Adams were overseas at their diplomatic posts. But they wrote home to encourage the delegates. Others had a less positive outlook on the convention. For example, Patrick Henry, who had been elected as a delegate from Virginia, refused to attend. He said he "smelled a rat in Philadelphia, tending toward monarchy."

Also, the convention did not reflect the diverse U.S. population of the 1780s. There were no Native Americans, African Americans, or women among the delegates. The nation's early leaders did not consider these groups of people to be citizens and did not invite any of them to attend. However, the framework of government the Founders established is the very one that would eventually provide full rights and responsibilities to all Americans.

## 2 The Delegates Assemble

Most of the delegates arrived at the Constitutional Convention without a clear idea of what to expect. Some thought they would only draft





### America's HERITAGE

**Independence Hall**
Independence Hall is considered a world cultural treasure. It is a World Heritage site, indicating that it has been judged to have "outstanding universal value" by an international group administered by UNESCO. World Heritage sites include the Acropolis in Greece, Stonehenge in England, and the Taj Mahal in India. There are a total of 22 World Heritage sites in the United States.

### MORE ABOUT . . .

**Delegates to the Constitution**
Most of the delegates to the Constitutional Convention owned property and were men of means, and most had been born in America. They represented a number of occupations, including doctors, merchants, and generals, and 23 were lawyers. More than half of the delegates had attended college. The average age of the delegates was 44. Benjamin Franklin was the oldest delegate, at 81 years. The youngest member of the Convention was 26.

### INSTRUCT: OBJECTIVE 2

**The Delegates Assemble/ The Convention Begins**
Key Questions
- What challenge faced the delegates at the Convention?
- Why did the delegates select George Washington as president of the Convention?
- Why did the delegates vote to make discussions at the Convention secret?

**Humanities Transparency HT15**
- George Washington at the Constitutional Convention

**Critical Thinking Trans. CT23**
- Cause and Effect: The Constitutional Convention

**ACTIVITY OPTIONS**

**MULTIPLE LEARNING STYLES: INTERPERSONAL**

BLOCK SCHEDULING

**CONVENTION CROSSWORD**

**Class Time** 30–45 minutes

**Task** Creating a crossword puzzle

**Purpose** To help students work together to identify important people discussed in this section

**Supplies Needed**
- Textbook
- Paper
- Sample crossword puzzle

**Activity** Have students work in pairs to create a crossword puzzle using the names of people mentioned in this section. Show students a sample crossword puzzle if necessary. Tell partners to list the names of people discussed in the chapter and divide the list in half. Each partner should write clues for half the list. Then the partners should work together to mold their clues into the "Across" and "Down" clues of a good puzzle. Allow pairs to exchange puzzles with one another.

## AMERICA'S HISTORY MAKERS

**James Madison**

Madison himself wrote to an admirer that he could not take credit as "Father of the Constitution." Modestly, Madison said that the Constitution "ought to be regarded as the work of many heads and hands." Although Edmund Randolph presented the Virginia Plan, James Madison had worked it out before the Convention began.

Answer: He kept a record of and was a valuable participant in the proceedings.

 **America's History Makers**
- James Madison, pp. 33–34

## MORE ABOUT . . .

**Private Sessions**

Although today most congressional hearings are open to the public, Congress does have the right to hold sessions in private. One reason for a private session is a threat to national security. At other times, members of Congress, like their predecessors at the Constitutional Convention, hope to reduce political pressure by debating highly controversial issues in private.

## INSTRUCT: OBJECTIVE 3

**The Virginia Plan/The Great Compromise**

Key Questions
- How did the Virginia Plan and New Jersey Plan differ?
- Why did the issue of representation in Congress divide the large states from the smaller states?
- How did the Great Compromise satisfy the concerns of the large and the smaller states?

 **Citizenship Today,** p. 72

AMERICA'S HISTORY MAKERS

**JAMES MADISON**
**1751–1836**

James Madison was a short, soft-spoken man, but he may have made the greatest contribution of any of the Founders at the Constitutional Convention. He took thorough notes of the convention's proceedings. His notes are the most detailed picture we have of the debates and drama of the convention.

But Madison did not just observe the convention. He was perhaps the most important participant. One of the other delegates called him "the best informed Man of any point in debate." Madison was so important that he earned the title "Father of the Constitution."

**How did Madison contribute to the Constitutional Convention?**

amendments to the Articles of Confederation. Others thought they would design an entirely new plan for the government. But they all agreed that the government should protect people's rights.

Back in 1776, many Americans thought that government was the main threat to people's rights. But by 1787, many realized that the people often came into conflict and needed a government that could maintain order. As a result, the government had to be strong enough to protect people's rights but not too strong to be controlled. Madison later wrote about this problem.

B. Possible Responses The problem is in framing a government that can control itself as well as the governed.

*Reading* **History**
**B. Using Primary Sources** According to Madison, what is the central problem in framing a government?

*A VOICE FROM THE PAST*

If men were angels, no government would be necessary. If angels were to govern men, neither external nor internal controls on government would be necessary. In framing a government which is to be administered by men over men, the great difficulty lies in this: you must first enable the government to control the governed; and in the next place oblige it [the government] to control itself.

**James Madison,** *The Federalist* "Number 51"

This was the challenge that faced the delegates: how to set up a strong but limited federal government. By May 25, 1787, at least two delegates from each of seven states had arrived in Philadelphia. With 29 delegates in attendance, the convention was officially under way.

C. Possible Responses Some students might agree because the delegates might not have felt free to have an honest debate without secrecy. Others might disagree because they believe people should have had the right to know what the delegates were doing.

*Reading* **History**
**C. Making Decisions** Do you agree with the Founders' decision to keep the convention secret? Why or why not?

## The Convention Begins

The first order of business was to elect a president for the convention. Robert Morris of Pennsylvania nominated George Washington. No American was more respected or admired than Washington. Every delegate voted for him. Washington's quiet and dignified leadership set a solemn and serious tone for the convention.

At their next meeting, the delegates decided on the rules for the convention. They wanted to be able to consider all ideas and to be able to change sides in any debate. They did not want to be pressured by the politics of the day. For these reasons, they decided that their discussions would remain secret. To ensure privacy, the windows in their meeting room were kept shut even though it was summer. Guards were posted outside the door. Whenever the door was opened, the delegates stopped talking. With the secrecy rule approved, they got down to business.

## 3 The Virginia Plan

On May 29, the delegates began the real work of designing a new national government. Presiding over the convention, George Washington



## ACTIVITY OPTIONS
## INDIVIDUAL NEEDS

**STUDENTS ACQUIRING ENGLISH/ESL**

**Understanding Key Concepts** Write the word *compromise* on the board and define it as "an agreement reached by bargaining, with both sides giving up some part of their demands." Discuss examples of compromises reached by students with their friends or family members. Ask students to use a Venn diagram to illustrate one compromise. Then point out *The Great Compromise* chart on page 232. Discuss the terms of each plan agreed upon in the Constitutional Convention. Ask students to tell why they think the delegates at the Convention considered the compromise fair.

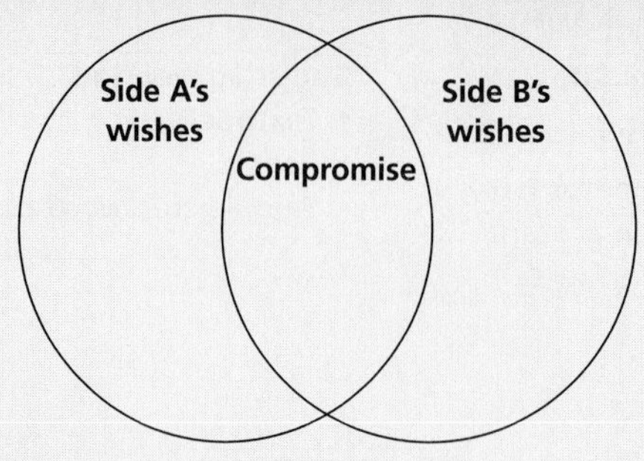

The delegates at the Constitutional Convention debated the Constitution intensely.

recognized Edmund Randolph as the first speaker. Randolph offered a plan for a whole new government. The plan became known as the **Virginia Plan.** Madison, Randolph, and the other Virginia delegates had drawn up the plan while they waited for the convention to open.

The Virginia Plan proposed a government that would have three branches. The first branch of government was the legislature, which made the laws. The second branch was the executive, which enforced the laws. The third branch was the judiciary, which interpreted the laws.

> ***"If men were angels, no government would be necessary."***
> James Madison

The Virginia Plan proposed a legislature with two houses. In both houses, the number of representatives from each state would be based on the state's population or its wealth. The legislature would have the power to levy taxes, regulate commerce, and make laws "in all cases where the separate states are incompetent [unable]."

*Reading* **History**
**D. Summarizing** What was the Virginia Plan?
**D. Answer** It was the plan for the legislature offered by the Virginia delegates to the convention. It proposed a legislature with two houses with representation based on population or wealth.

The Virginia Plan led to weeks of debate. Because they had larger populations, larger states supported the plan. It would give them greater representation in the legislature. The smaller states opposed this plan. They worried that the larger states would end up ruling the others. Delaware delegate John Dickinson voiced the concerns of the small states.

*A VOICE FROM THE PAST*

Some of the members from the small states wish for two branches in the general legislature and are friends to a good [strong] national government; but we would sooner submit [give in] to a foreign power than submit to be deprived, in both branches of the legislature, of an equal suffrage [vote], and thereby be thrown under the domination of the larger states.

**John Dickinson,** quoted in *Mr. Madison's Constitution*

## The Great Compromise

In response to the Virginia Plan, New Jersey delegate William Paterson presented an alternative on June 15. The **New Jersey Plan** called for a legislature with only one house. In it, each state would have one vote. In providing equal representation to each state, the New Jersey Plan was similar to the Articles of Confederation.

Even though the New Jersey Plan gave the legislature the power to regulate trade and to raise money by taxing foreign goods, it did not offer the broad powers proposed by the Virginia Plan. The delegates



### CRITICAL THINKING ACTIVITY

**Analyzing Points of View** After students read the material for Objective 3, have them draw a graphic like the one below. Then have the students fill in the views of large and small states.

| | Large States | Small States |
|---|---|---|
| Legislative Houses | | |
| Representation in Legislature | | |
| Legislative Powers | | |

**Class Time** 25 minutes

### MORE ABOUT . . .

**Large States and Small States**

The most populous states represented at the Constitutional Convention were Virginia, Pennsylvania, North Carolina, and Massachusetts. South Carolina and Georgia tended to side with the large states because their own populations were growing at a rapid pace. The small states were Connecticut, New Jersey, Delaware, and Maryland. New York was somewhere in the middle and tended to side with the smaller states. New Hampshire's delegation arrived too late to take part in debate over the most important issues. Rhode Island refused to participate at all.

**In-Depth Resources: Unit 2**
- Primary Source: from *Debates on the Adoption of the Federal Constitution*, p. 54

### ACTIVITY OPTIONS

**INTERDISCIPLINARY LINK: HUMANITIES** — BLOCK SCHEDULING

**GREAT COMPROMISE PLAY**

**Class Time** One class period to prepare; one class period to present

**Task** Producing a short play about the Great Compromise

**Purpose** To demonstrate knowledge of the Virginia Plan, the New Jersey Plan, and the Great Compromise by producing a short drama summarizing the arguments on all sides

**Supplies Needed**
- Textbook
- Reference books on the Constitutional Convention

**Activity** Have groups of students write and produce short plays about the debate in the Constitutional Convention over representation in Congress. Each group should do research on the Convention and assign one or more actors to represent actual delegates who supported the Virginia Plan, the New Jersey Plan, and the Great Compromise. Plays should clearly explain the reasons for supporting each plan. Allow groups to rehearse their plays, and then allow each group to present its work to the class.

## HISTORY FROM VISUALS

**Interpreting the Chart** Point out that in a *compromise* each side gives up some things so that both sides can agree. Ask: What did each side give up in the Great Compromise? **Answer** Supporters of the Virginia Plan conceded that representation in one house of Congress would be equal for all states; supporters of the New Jersey Plan conceded their demand for a one-house legislature and their demand that each state would have equal representation in Congress by allowing representation based on population in one house.

**Extension** Ask students to draw a chart or sketch showing what representation in Congress today would be under the Virginia Plan or the New Jersey Plan.

## MORE ABOUT . . .

**Slavery and the Constitution**
You might wish to point out to students that some scholars argue that most delegates—from Southern as well as Northern states—believed slavery would eventually fade away. The debate, however, occurred before cotton production and its extensive labor needs became king in the South.

## INSTRUCT: OBJECTIVE 4

**Slavery and the Constitution/ Regulating Trade**
Key Questions
- How did the states resolve the debate over representation for enslaved Americans?
- How did the states compromise over the issue of slave trade?
- What did Southern states give up in debates over trade issues?

### The Great Compromise

**VIRGINIA PLAN**
- The legislative branch would have two houses.
- Both houses in the legislature would assign representatives according to state population or wealth.

**NEW JERSEY PLAN**
- The legislature would have one house.
- Each state would have one vote in the legislature.

**THE GREAT COMPROMISE**
- The Senate would give each state equal representation.

The legislature would have two houses.

- The House of Representatives would have representation according to state population.

**SKILLBUILDER Interpreting Charts**
1. *Which plan appealed more to the small states?*
2. *Did the Great Compromise include more of what the large states wanted or more of what the small states wanted?*

**Skillbuilder Answers**
1. the New Jersey Plan
2. **Possible Response** It included more of what the large states wanted because there were two houses in the legislature, one of which had representation by population.

voted on these two plans on June 19. The Virginia Plan won and became the framework for drafting the Constitution.

During the rest of June, the delegates argued over representation in the legislature. Emotions ran high as the delegates struggled for a solution. In desperation, the delegates selected a committee to work out a compromise in early July. The committee offered the **Great Compromise**. (Some people also refer to it as the Connecticut Compromise.)

To satisfy the smaller states, each state would have an equal number of votes in the Senate. To satisfy the larger states, the committee set representation in the House of Representatives according to state populations. More than a week of arguing followed the introduction of the plan, but on July 16, 1787, the convention passed it.

## 4 Slavery and the Constitution

Because representation in the House of Representatives would be based on the population of each state, the delegates had to decide who would be counted in that population. The Southern states had many more slaves than the Northern states. Southerners wanted the slaves to be counted as part of the general population for representation but not for taxation. Northerners argued that slaves were not citizens and should not be counted for representation but should be counted for taxation.

On this issue, the delegates reached another compromise, known as the **Three-Fifths Compromise**. Under this compromise, three-fifths of the slave population would be counted when setting direct taxes on the states. This three-fifths ratio also would be used to determine representation in the legislature.

The delegates had another heated debate about the slave trade. Slavery had already been outlawed in several Northern states. All of the Northern states and several of the Southern states had banned the

**ACTIVITY OPTIONS**

**MULTIPLE LEARNING STYLES: SPATIAL**

**BLOCK SCHEDULING**

### MUSEUM EXHIBIT

**Class Time** One class period

**Task** Planning a museum exhibit that summarizes important compromises of the Constitutional Convention

**Purpose** To analyze key conflicts of the Constitutional Convention and to illustrate how they were resolved by compromise

**Supplies Needed**
- Art supplies (optional)
- Video camera (optional)

**Activity** Tell students to plan a museum exhibit that illustrates and explains one major conflict of the Constitutional Convention and its resolution through compromise. Students may choose from different media for their exhibit: a poster, a video presentation, or manipulatives. You may want students to continue working on the display during other class periods and display completed projects.

*Reading***History**

**E. Forming and Supporting Opinions** Did the delegates do the right thing in agreeing to the Three-Fifths Compromise? Explain.

**E. Possible Responses** Some might say no, because the Founders should have abolished slavery. Others might say yes, because otherwise the Southern states might not have ratified the Constitution.

importation of slaves. Many Northerners wanted to see this ban extended to the rest of the nation. But Southern slaveholders strongly disagreed. The delegates from South Carolina and Georgia stated that they would never accept any plan "unless their right to import slaves be untouched." Again, the delegates settled on a compromise. On August 29, they agreed that Congress could not ban the slave trade until 1808.

## Regulating Trade

In the compromise over slavery, the North gave in to the South by delaying the end of the African slave trade until 1808. But the South gave in to the North on a few issues as well. For example, the South agreed to a tax on the slave trade.

Southerners also agreed to allow the national government to pass laws on how goods could be exported. Since the Southern economy was based on exports, such laws would affect them greatly. The delegates from most states, however, were glad to grant the national government the power to regulate trade. After all, this was one of the issues that had led to the Annapolis Convention the previous year.

The Constitutional Convention continued to meet into September. On Saturday, September 15, 1787, the delegates voted their support for the Constitution in its final form. On Sunday, it was written out on four sheets of thick parchment. On Monday, all but three delegates signed the Constitution. It was then sent, with a letter signed by George Washington, to the Confederation Congress, which sent it to the states for ratification, or approval. In the next section, you will read about the debate over ratification.

### Now and then

**PRESERVING THE CONSTITUTION**

The National Archives is responsible for preserving the 200-year-old sheets of parchment on which the original Constitution was first written.

The Archives stores the document in an airtight glass case enclosed in a 55-ton vault of steel and concrete. Every few years, scientists examine the pages with the latest technology. For the last examination in 1995, they used fiber-optic light sources and computer-guided electronic cameras designed for space exploration.

### Section 2 Assessment

**1. Terms & Names**

- Constitutional Convention
- James Madison
- Virginia Plan
- New Jersey Plan
- Great Compromise
- Three-Fifths Compromise

**2. Taking Notes**

Use a chart like the one below to take notes on the contributions made by the leading delegates at the Constitutional Convention.

| Delegate | Contribution |
|---|---|
| | |
| | |
| | |
| | |

**3. Main Ideas**

a. What was the relationship between the Annapolis Convention and the Constitutional Convention?

b. What were the delegates to the Constitutional Convention like as a group?

c. How did the Constitutional Convention address the issue of slavery?

**4. Critical Thinking**

**Analyzing Points of View** How did the delegates at the convention differ on the issue of representation in the new government?

**THINK ABOUT**

- the large states and the small states
- the Virginia Plan
- the New Jersey Plan
- the Great Compromise

**ACTIVITY OPTIONS**

Think about the Three-Fifths Compromise. Make an **audio recording** of a speech or draw a **political cartoon** that expresses your views on the issue.



### Now *and* then

**Preserving the Constitution**

Congress established the National Archives in 1934 as the repository for all federal papers and records of permanent value. However, the National Archives hold much more, from patent drawings to maps, from letters to military service records. The Archives hold more than 325 billion documents, more than 5 million photographs, and more than 81 million feet of motion picture film.

**CRITICAL THINKING ACTIVITY**

**Forming and Supporting Opinions** To help students understand the dilemmas that faced the delegates, ask students to discuss whether they believe reaching agreement on the Constitution was worth the compromises made on slavery. Point out that without the compromises, the nation may have broken apart. On the other hand, as they will learn later, deep divisions over slavery later pushed the nation into civil war.

**Class Time** 20 minutes

## ASSESS & RETEACH

**Setting the Stage** Have students complete the second, third, and fourth rows on the graphic organizer on page 220.

**Formal Assessment**

- Section Quiz, p. 117

**RETEACHING ACTIVITY**

Give each student five index cards. Tell students to write one of five different key terms or names from the section (including those listed on page 228) on each of the cards. Then have students exchange cards and write the definitions or significance of each term or name on the back of the card. Students may then use their flash cards to quiz each other about the section.

**In-Depth Resources: Unit 2**

- Reteaching Activity, p. 59

### Section 2 Assessment

**1. Terms & Names**

**Constitutional Convention,** p. 229
**James Madison,** p. 229
**Virginia Plan,** p. 231
**New Jersey Plan,** p. 231
**Great Compromise,** p. 232
**Three-Fifths Compromise,** p. 232

**2. Taking Notes**

James Madison—Took notes on the Convention; earned the nickname "Father of the Constitution"
George Washington—Presided over the Convention
Edmund Randolph—Offered the Virginia Plan
William Paterson—Offered the New Jersey Plan

**3. Main Ideas**

a. No conclusion could be drawn at Annapolis, so the delegates agreed to meet the next year; that meeting created the new Constitution.
b. wealthy; well educated; had strong careers as lawyers, politicians, and businessmen **c.** It did not outlaw slavery, and decided no law could be made until 1808.

**4. Critical Thinking**

Large states wanted representation by population; small states wanted each state to have one vote.

**ACTIVITY OPTIONS**

**Alternative Assessment**

- Rubrics for a recording, 5.3
- Rubrics for a cartoon, 1.2

## SECTION OBJECTIVES

1. To identify positions of the Federalists and Antifederalists
2. To explain the role of *The Federalist* papers in the ratification process
3. To describe the battle for ratification
4. To summarize efforts to pass and ratify the Bill of Rights

**SKILLBUILDER**
Interpreting Charts, p. 235

**CRITICAL THINKING**
Making Inferences, p. 235
Drawing Conclusions, p. 236
Recognizing Propaganda, p. 237

**Why It Matters Now**
- The Living Constitution, pp. 15–16

## FOCUS & MOTIVATE

### 5-MINUTE WARM-UP

**Interpreting Pictures** These questions focus on the debate over ratification of the Constitution.

1. Look at the quotation from Hamilton and the illustration on pages 235 and 236. Did Hamilton support or oppose the Constitution?
2. Why does Hamilton think adoption is a good option?

**Warm-Up Transparency WT8**

## INSTRUCT

### INSTRUCT: OBJECTIVE 1

**Federalists and Antifederalists**
Key Questions
- What was the goal of the Federalists?
- Why did Antifederalists oppose the Constitution?
- How did Antifederalists work against ratification?

**In-Depth Resources: Unit 2**
- Guided Reading, p. 48

**Humanities Transparency HT16**
- Constitution, Page One—A Replica

# 3 Ratifying the Constitution

**TERMS & NAMES**
federalism
Federalists
Antifederalists
*The Federalist* papers
George Mason
Bill of Rights

| MAIN IDEA | WHY IT MATTERS NOW |
|---|---|
| Americans across the nation debated whether the Constitution would produce the best government. | American liberties today are protected by the U.S. Constitution, including the Bill of Rights. |

### ONE AMERICAN'S STORY

**For a week in early January 1788, a church in Hartford, Connecticut, was filled to capacity. Inside, 168 delegates were meeting to decide whether their state should ratify the U.S. Constitution. Samuel Huntington, Connecticut's governor, addressed the assembly.**

*A VOICE FROM THE PAST*

This is a new event in the history of mankind. Heretofore, most governments have been formed by tyrants and imposed on mankind by force. Never before did a people, in time of peace and tranquillity, meet together by their representatives and, with calm deliberation, frame for themselves a system of government.

**Samuel Huntington,** quoted in *Original Meanings*

**The governor supported the new Constitution and wanted to see it ratified. Not everyone agreed with him. In this section, you will learn about the debates that led to the ratification of the Constitution.**

Samuel Huntington

## 1 Federalists and Antifederalists

By the time the convention in Connecticut opened, Americans had already been debating the new Constitution for months. The document had been printed in newspapers and handed out in pamphlets across the United States. The framers of the Constitution knew that the document would cause controversy. They immediately began to campaign for ratification, or approval, of the Constitution.

The framers suspected that people might be afraid the Constitution would take too much power away from the states. To address this fear, the framers explained that the Constitution was based on federalism. **Federalism** is a system of government in which power is shared between the central (or federal) government and the states. Linking themselves to the idea of federalism, the people who supported the Constitution took the name **Federalists.**

People who opposed the Constitution were called **Antifederalists.** They thought the Constitution took too much power away from the



## RECOMMENDED RESOURCES

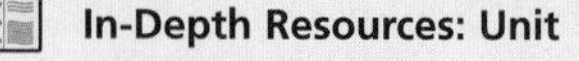

**In-Depth Resources: Unit 2**
- Guided Reading, p. 48
- Building Vocabulary, p. 49
- Skillbuilder Practice, p. 50
- Geography Application: Ratifying the Constitution, pp. 51–52
- Reteaching Activity, p. 60
- Enrichment Activity, p. 61

**Reading Study Guide** (Spanish and English), pp. 79–80

**Outline Map Activities**
- The Original 13 States, 1790, pp. 15–16

**Why It Matters Now**
- The Living Constitution, pp. 15–16

**Formal Assessment**
- Section Quiz, p. 118

**Alternative Assessment**
- Rubrics, 3.3
- Rubrics, 4.5

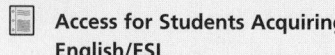

**Access for Students Acquiring English/ESL**
- Guided Reading, p. 52
- Skillbuilder Practice, p. 53
- Geography Application, pp. 54–55

**Technology Resources**

**Humanities Transparency HT16**
- Constitution, Page One—A Replica

**Vocabulary**
**aristocracy:** a group or class considered superior to others

states and did not guarantee rights for the people. Some were afraid that a strong president might be declared king. Others thought the Senate might turn into a powerful aristocracy. In either case, the liberties won at great cost during the Revolution might be lost.

Antifederalists published their views about the Constitution in newspapers and pamphlets. They used logical arguments to convince people to oppose the Constitution. But they also tried to stir people's emotions by charging that it would destroy American liberties. As one Antifederalist wrote, "After so recent a triumph over British despots [oppressive rulers], . . . it is truly astonishing that a set of men among ourselves should have had the effrontery [nerve] to attempt the destruction of our liberties."

## 2 *The Federalist* Papers

The Federalists did not sit still while the Antifederalists attacked the Constitution. They wrote essays to answer the Antifederalists' attacks. The best known of the Federalist essays are ***The Federalist* papers.** These essays first appeared as letters in New York newspapers. They were later published together in a book called *The Federalist.*

Three well-known politicians wrote *The Federalist* papers—James Madison, Alexander Hamilton, and John Jay, the secretary of foreign affairs for the Confederation Congress. Like the Antifederalists, the Federalists appealed to reason and emotion. In *The Federalist* papers, Hamilton described why people should support ratification.

**A. Possible Response** He believes failure to ratify the Constitution will put Americans' liberty, dignity, and happiness at risk.

***Reading*History**
**A. Making Inferences** What does Hamilton think will happen if the Constitution is not ratified?

*A VOICE FROM THE PAST*

Yes, my countrymen, . . . I am clearly of opinion it is in your interest to adopt it [the Constitution]. I am convinced that this is the safest course for your liberty, your dignity, and your happiness.

**Alexander Hamilton,** *The Federalist* "Number 1"

**Federalists and Antifederalists**

| FEDERALISTS | ANTIFEDERALISTS |
|---|---|
| • Supported removing some powers from the states and giving more powers to the national government | • Wanted important political powers to remain with the states |
| • Favored dividing powers among different branches of government | • Wanted the legislative branch to have more power than the executive |
| • Proposed a single person to lead the executive branch | • Feared that a strong executive might become a king or tyrant |
| | • Believed a bill of rights needed to be added to the Constitution to protect people's rights |

**SKILLBUILDER Interpreting Charts**
1. *Which group wanted a stronger central government?*
2. *If you had been alive in 1787, would you have been a Federalist or an Antifederalist?*

John Jay

George Mason

Skillbuilder Answers
1. Federalists
2. Possible Responses Some students may say Federalist because they favor the Constitution. Others may say Antifederalist because they favor individual rights.



### MORE ABOUT . . .

**Antifederalists**
The author of the quote was Samuel Bryan, who often wrote under the name "Centinel" when he wanted to make controversial statements. Mercy Otis Warren was the only prominent woman to speak out against the Constitution. She believed that the Federalists were destroying the American liberties won by the Revolution. Both Bryan and Warren subscribed to the Antifederalist slogan, "Grant Power Cautiously."

### INSTRUCT: OBJECTIVE 2

***The Federalist* Papers**
Key Questions
- What were *The Federalist* papers?
- Who wrote *The Federalist* papers?
- In which states was there strong opposition to the Constitution?

### HISTORY FROM VISUALS

**Interpreting the Chart** Divide the class into two groups. Tell one group to read aloud the bulleted points summarizing the positions of the Federalists. Alternate with the other group reading aloud the positions of the Antifederalists. Ask students to identify a position of the Antifederalists that was likely to be accepted by Federalists. **Answer** adding a Bill of Rights

**Extension** Have students write a letter to the editor expressing their opinion of the Constitution from the point of view of a strong Federalist or a strong Antifederalist.

### ACTIVITY OPTIONS

### SKILLBUILDER MINI-LESSON: ANALYZING POINTS OF VIEW

BLOCK SCHEDULING

**Explaining the Skill** Analyzing points of view means closely studying the opinions people have on a particular issue. It also means examining the methods and arguments people use to support their particular points of view.

**Applying the Skill** Have students consider the points of view of the Federalists and the Antifederalists. Remind them that the main issue dividing the two sides was ratification of the Constitution. Ask the following questions:

1. What were four criticisms raised by Antifederalists against the Constitution? *(It took too much power from the states; didn't guarantee citizens' rights; gave too much power to the executive branch and the chief executive.)*
2. How did Federalists address fears about the Constitution? *(They pointed out that power is shared between the central government and the states. They also suggested that a bill of rights could be added later.)*
3. What kinds of arguments did both sides use in the debate? *(They appealed to logic, or reason, as well as to emotions.)*

**In-Depth Resources: Unit 2**
- Skillbuilder Practice, p. 50

## *HISTORY through ART*

**Interpreting the Illustration** The debate over ratification of the Constitution gripped the entire nation. Both the Federalists and the Antifederalists poured out newspaper articles and pamphlets stating the arguments for their side and took the streets with parades. Ask students what media politicians use today to gain support for their positions.

**Possible Response: It implies that the Constitution was very important to people because thousands attended the parade.**

**HISTORY *through* ART**

Supporters of the Constitution turned out in parades like this one in New York in 1788. The "Ship of State" float has Alexander Hamilton's name on it to celebrate his role in creating the Constitution.

**What does the picture indicate about the importance of the Constitution in people's lives?**

The Federalists had an important advantage over the Antifederalists. Most of the newspapers supported the Constitution, giving the Federalists more publicity than the Antifederalists. Even so, there was strong opposition to ratification in Massachusetts, North Carolina, Rhode Island, New York, and Virginia. If some of these states failed to ratify the Constitution, the United States might not survive.

## 3 The Battle for Ratification

The first four state conventions to ratify the Constitution were held in December 1787. It was a good month for the Federalists. Delaware, New Jersey, and Pennsylvania voted for ratification. In January 1788, Georgia and Connecticut ratified the Constitution. Massachusetts joined these states in early February.

By late June, nine states had voted to ratify the Constitution. That meant that the document was now officially ratified. But New York and Virginia had not yet cast their votes. There were many powerful Antifederalists in both of those states. Without Virginia, the new government would lack the support of the largest state. Without New York, the nation would be separated into two parts geographically.

Virginia's convention opened the first week in June. The patriot Patrick Henry fought against ratification. **George Mason,** perhaps the most influential Virginian aside from Washington, also was opposed to it. Mason had been a delegate to the Constitutional Convention in Philadelphia, but he had refused to sign the final document. Both Henry and Mason would not consider voting for the Constitution until a bill of rights was added. A bill of rights is a set of rules that defines people's rights.

James Madison was also at Virginia's convention. He suggested that Virginia follow Massachusetts's lead and ratify the Constitution, and he recommended the addition of a bill of rights. With the addition of a bill of rights likely, Virginia ratified the Constitution at the end of June.

**B. Answer** Several states refused to ratify the Constitution unless a bill of rights was added.

***Reading*History**

**B. Drawing Conclusions** How did the lack of a bill of rights endanger the Constitution?



**INSTRUCT: OBJECTIVE 3**

**The Battle for Ratification**

Key Questions
- When did the first nine states ratify the Constitution?
- What slowed ratification in Virginia and New York?
- What helped to win ratification in New York?

**In-Depth Resources: Unit 2**
- Geography Application: Ratifying the Constitution, pp. 51–52

**ACTIVITY OPTIONS**

**INDIVIDUAL NEEDS: GIFTED AND TALENTED**

**BILL OF RIGHTS**

**Class Time** One class period

**Task** Reading and interpreting the Bill of Rights

**Purpose** To familiarize students with the Bill of Rights; to analyze the amendments from a historical perspective and to consider which are most applicable today

**Supplies Needed**
- Textbook

**Activity** Have students read the Bill of Rights on pages 266–268. Remind students that the Bill of Rights was intended to preserve and protect the rights of individuals. Then ask them to discuss why they think each specific amendment was included. You might prompt discussion with the following questions:
- Which amendment would you have proposed if you were a delegate at the Convention?
- Which amendment do you think is most important today?
- Which amendment, if any, do you think is not necessary today?

**In-Depth Resources: Unit 2**
- Enrichment Activity, p. 61

The news of Virginia's vote arrived while the New York convention was in debate. The Antifederalists had outnumbered the Federalists when the convention had begun. But with the news of Virginia's ratification, New Yorkers decided to join the Union. New York also called for a bill of rights.

It was another year before North Carolina ratified the Constitution. In 1790, Rhode Island became the last state to ratify it. By then, the new Congress had already written a bill of rights and submitted it to the states for approval.

## 4 The Bill of Rights

**Background**
The seven states that asked for a bill of rights were Massachusetts, South Carolina, New Hampshire, Virginia, New York, North Carolina, and Rhode Island.

At the same time that seven of the states ratified the Constitution, they asked that it be amended to include a bill of rights. Supporters of a bill of rights hoped that it would set forth the rights of all Americans. They believed it was needed to protect people against the power of the national government.

Madison, who was elected to the new Congress in the winter of 1789, took up the cause. He proposed a set of changes to the Constitution. Congress edited Madison's list and proposed placing the amendments at the end of the Constitution in a separate section.

The amendments went to the states for ratification. As with the Constitution, three-quarters of the states had to ratify the amendments for them to take effect. With Virginia's vote in 1791, ten of the amendments were ratified and became law. These ten amendments to the U.S. Constitution became known as the **Bill of Rights**. (See the Constitution Handbook, page 242.)

The passage of the Bill of Rights was one of the first acts of the new government. In the next chapter, you will read about other issues that faced the new government.

### America's HERITAGE

**RELIGIOUS FREEDOM**

Freedom of religion was an important part of the First Amendment. Jefferson and Madison believed that government enforcement of religious laws was the source of much social conflict. They supported freedom of religion as a way to prevent such conflict.

Even before Madison wrote the Bill of Rights, he worked to ensure religious liberty in Virginia. In 1786, he helped pass the Virginia Statute for Religious Freedom, originally written by Jefferson in 1777.

### Section 3 Assessment

**1. Terms & Names**
- federalism
- Federalists
- Antifederalists
- *The Federalist* papers
- George Mason
- Bill of Rights

**2. Taking Notes**
Use a diagram like the one below to compare and contrast the Federalists and the Antifederalists.

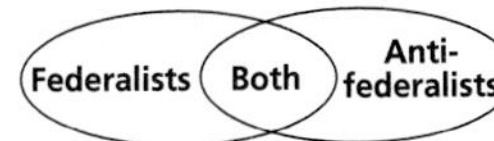


Which group do you think made the stronger argument about ratification? Why?

**3. Main Ideas**
a. How was the Constitution ratified?
b. How did the Federalists and the Antifederalists try to convince people to take their sides in the debate over the Constitution?
c. What was the significance of the Bill of Rights?

**4. Critical Thinking**
**Recognizing Propaganda**
Reread the quotation by Hamilton on page 235. Is it an example of propaganda? Why or why not?

THINK ABOUT
- Hamilton's use of the word *countrymen*
- Hamilton's reference to liberty, dignity, and happiness

**ACTIVITY OPTIONS**
**SPEECH**
**LANGUAGE ARTS**
Review the political fight over ratification of the Constitution. Hold a **press conference** or write a **news report** on the ratification debate.





### INSTRUCT: OBJECTIVE 4
**The Bill of Rights**
Key Questions
- What was the purpose of the Bill of Rights?
- What role did James Madison play in adding the Bill of Rights to the Constitution?
- When did the Bill of Rights become part of the Constitution?

**Outline Map Activities**
- The Original 13 States, 1790, pp. 15–16

### America's HERITAGE
**Religious Freedom**
During colonial times, the Anglican Church was the established religion of the colony. A portion of the taxes paid by the colonists went to support the church. After the Revolution, some Virginians wanted state tax money to support all recognized churches. Madison and Jefferson opposed government support of any religion. They thought that religion was a matter of individual choice and that church and state should be separate.

### ASSESS & RETEACH
**Setting the Stage** Have students create a problem-solution chart such as the one on page 220 for the problems faced by the Federalists in getting the Constitution ratified.

**Formal Assessment**
- Section Quiz, p. 118

**Critical Thinking Transparency CT22**
- Setting the Stage

**RETEACHING ACTIVITY**
Organize a "Meet the Press" discussion about the ratification of the Constitution. Ask for volunteers to represent the Federalists and the Antifederalists. Other class members act as reporters, asking questions about the debates.

**In-Depth Resources: Unit 2**
- Reteaching Activity, p. 60

### Section 3 Assessment

**1. Terms & Names**
**federalism,** p. 234
**Federalists,** p. 234
**Antifederalists,** p. 234
***The Federalist* papers,** p. 235
**George Mason,** p. 236
**Bill of Rights,** p. 237

**2. Taking Notes**
Federalists: stronger national government; one person to head the executive branch. Both: different branches of the government; supported a bill of rights. Antifederalists: stronger state government; feared a strong executive

Responses will vary.

**3. Main Ideas**
**a.** It was sent to the states. The states held their own conventions to debate and ratify it. **b.** Both sides wrote pamphlets, gave speeches outlining their views, and appealed to reason and emotion. **c.** It was key to getting enough support to ensure ratification of the Constitution.

**4. Critical Thinking**
yes, because his tone and words will stir the emotions of Americans

**ACTIVITY OPTIONS**

**Alternative Assessment**
- Rubrics for a press conference, 3.3
- Rubrics for a news report, 4.5

## INTERACTIVE PRIMARY SOURCES

**OBJECTIVE**

Students will compare and evaluate the arguments of two prominent figures, James Madison and George Mason, in the debate over ratification of the Constitution.

**Primary Source Explorer**

- *The Federalist,* "Number 51"
- *Objections to the Constitution*

The Explorer will help students select and produce their own presentations.

Specific information about the document can be found in **A Closer Look.** To learn more about key people and events of the time, students should click on **Life in These Times. What Happened Next** will show the student the impact of the document and tie it to today.

## FOCUS & MOTIVATE

**Finding Main Ideas** To help students understand the conflicting views of Madison and Mason, direct them to the "A Closer Look" callouts on each page. Read these callouts before the students read the documents themselves. The callouts will provide an overview of the main issues in the documents.

### MORE ABOUT . . .

**Madison's Opinions**

Madison thought that a large republic had a second advantage over a small one. He argued that citizens of a large republic would elect qualified and capable leaders to office, not the poorly qualified and self-interested politicians who often won local elections. Madison believed that petty politicians would not have the broad appeal needed for election from a large constituency.

INTERACTIVE PRIMARY SOURCES

# *The Federalist* "Number 51"

**Setting the Stage** James Madison wrote 29 essays in *The Federalist* papers to argue in favor of ratifying the Constitution. In *The Federalist* "Number 51," Madison explains how the government set up by the Constitution will protect the rights of the people by weakening the power of any interest, or group, to dominate the government. **See Primary Source Explorer**

It is of great importance in a republic not only to guard the society against the oppression of its rulers, but to guard one part of the society against the injustice of the other part. Different interests necessarily exist in different classes of citizens. If a majority be united by a common interest, the rights of the minority will be insecure. There are but two methods of providing against this evil: the one by creating a will in the community independent of the majority—that is, of the society itself; the other, by **comprehending**[1] in the society so many separate descriptions of citizens as will render an unjust combination of a majority of the whole very improbable, if not **impracticable.**[2] . . .

**Whilst**[3] all authority in it will be derived from and dependent on the society, the society itself will be broken into so many parts, interests and classes of citizens, that the rights of individuals, or of the minority, will be in little danger from interested combinations of the majority. In a free government the security for civil rights must be the same as that for religious rights. It consists in the one case in the multiplicity of interests, and in the other in the **multiplicity of sects.**[4] . . .

In the extended republic of the United States, and among the great variety of interests, parties, and sects which it embraces, a **coalition**[5] of a majority of the whole society could seldom take place on any other principles than those of justice and the general good. . . .

It is no less certain than it is important . . . that the larger the society, provided it lie within a practicable sphere, the more duly capable it will be of self-government. And happily for the republican cause, the practicable sphere may be carried to a very great extent by a **judicious modification**[6] and mixture of the *federal principle.*

—*James Madison*

**A CLOSER LOOK**

**MINORITY RIGHTS**

In the 1700s, people feared that democratic majorities could turn into mobs that would violate other people's rights. Madison had to explain how the Constitution would prevent this.

1. What two methods does Madison suggest a society can use to protect minority rights?

**A CLOSER LOOK**

**REPUBLICS IN LARGE SOCIETIES**

For centuries, people believed that only small societies could be republics. But Madison argues that large societies are more likely to remain republics.

2. Why does Madison believe that a large republic is likely to protect justice?

1. **comprehending:** understanding.
2. **impracticable:** not practical or realistic.
3. **whilst:** while.
4. **multiplicity of sects:** large number of groups.
5. **coalition:** alliance of groups.
6. **judicious modification:** careful change.

238

### TEACHING STRATEGY

**Comparing** Guide students through the two documents by drawing two spider maps on the board, one for the Madison document and one for the Mason document. Label the central circle for the Madison document "Protections for the Rights of Citizens." Label the central circle for the Mason document "Worries About the Constitution." Then read the documents as a class. As you read, ask students to add topics and subtopics to the maps.

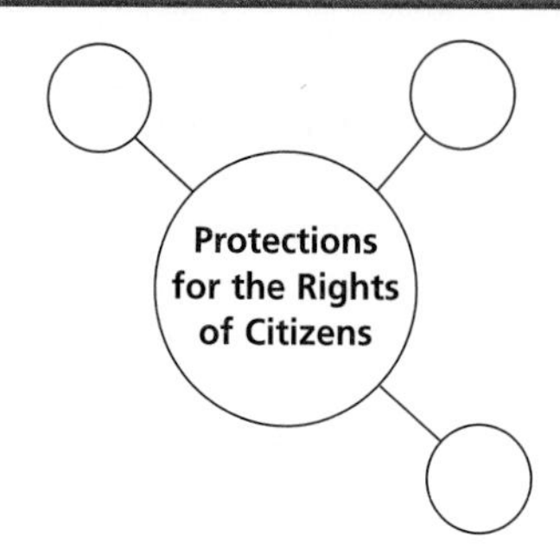


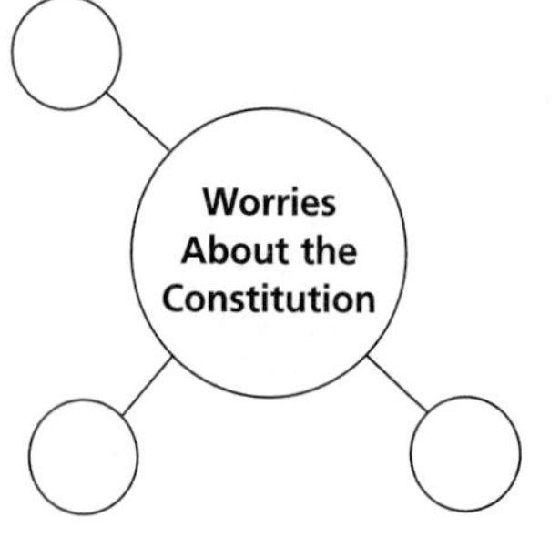

# Objections to the Constitution

**Setting the Stage** George Mason was one of the leading Antifederalists. In "Objections to the Constitution of Government Formed by the Convention," he listed his reasons for opposing ratification. Above all, he feared that the Constitution created a government that would destroy democracy in the young nation. **See Primary Source Explorer** CD-ROM

There is no Declaration of Rights; and the Laws of the general Government being **paramount**[1] to the Laws and Constitutions of several States, the Declaration of Rights in the separate States are no Security. Nor are the people secured even in the Enjoyment of the Benefits of the common-Law; can never produce proper Information in the Legislature, or inspire Confidence in the People; the Laws will therefore be generally made by Men little concern'd in, and **unacquainted**[2] with their Effects and Consequences.

The Senate have the Power of altering all Money-Bills, and of originating Appropriations of Money and the **Sallerys**[3] of the Officers of their own Appointment in **Conjunction**[4] with the President of the United States; altho' they are not the Representatives of the People, or **amenable**[5] to them. . . .

The President of the United States has the unrestrained Power of granting Pardon for Treason; which may be sometimes exercised to screen from Punishment those whom he had secretly **instigated**[6] to commit the Crime, and thereby prevent a Discovery of his own Guilt.

This Government will **commence**[7] in a moderate **Aristocracy;**[8] it is at present impossible to foresee whether it will, in it's Operation, produce a **Monarchy,**[9] or a corrupt oppressive Aristocracy; it will most probably vibrate some Years between the two, and then terminate in the one or the other.

*—George Mason*

**A CLOSER LOOK**

**DECLARATION OF RIGHTS**

At the time of the ratification debate, Americans across the nation complained that the Constitution did not include a bill of rights.

**3. What arguments does Mason make about the lack of a Declaration of Rights?**

**A CLOSER LOOK**

**ABUSE OF POWER**

Mason believed that presidents might abuse the power to grant pardons for treason in order to protect the guilty.

**4. Can you think of any presidents who have granted pardons?**

1. **paramount:** most important.
2. **unacquainted:** unfamiliar.
3. **sallerys:** salaries.
4. **conjunction:** joining.
5. **amenable:** agreeable.
6. **instigated:** caused.
7. **commence:** begin.
8. **aristocracy:** rule by a few, usually nobles.
9. **monarchy:** rule by one, usually a king.

*Interactive Primary Sources Assessment*

**1. Main Ideas**

**a.** Why does Madison believe that a society broken into many parts will not endanger minority rights?

**b.** What does Mason argue might happen if the president had the power to pardon people?

**c.** For each writer, what is one example of a fact and one example of an opinion?

**2. Critical Thinking**

**Drawing Conclusions** Who do you think makes the stronger argument? Explain your reasons.

**THINK ABOUT**

- what you know about the history of the United States
- the evidence used by each writer



## INSTRUCT

Key Questions

- Why was a Declaration of Rights important to Mason?
- Does Madison think that most people work for the common good or for their own interests? Do you agree with his view?
- Why did Madison believe that the government created under the Constitution would not be dominated by an oppressive majority?
- Why did Madison think that a large society could govern itself as a republic?

**MORE ABOUT . . .**

**Mason and the Constitution**

Although he himself owned slaves, Mason hated the institution of slavery and hoped that it would be abolished quickly. Mason objected strongly when the Constitutional Convention accepted the compromise that allowed continuation of the slave trade for 20 years.

*Interactive Primary Sources Assessment*

**1. Main Ideas**

**a.** because no group will be strong enough to oppress the others

**b.** The president could pardon people who had broken the law at his suggestion, hiding his own guilt.

**c.** All of Madison's statements are opinions. Mason's first sentence is a fact. His last paragraph is an opinion.

**2. Critical Thinking**

Some students might say Madison because his argument about multiplicity of sects is plausible. Others might say Mason because he discusses specific aspects of the Constitution.

***A CLOSER LOOK***

1. by creating a will in the community that is not dependent on the majority, and by creating so many different types of citizens to make it impossible for any to create a majority
2. Because there are so many sects, none will be able to oppress the others.
3. There will be no way to protect citizens' rights. The state declarations will lack the power to protect them against the federal government.
4. Some students may know that President Gerald Ford pardoned President Richard Nixon after Watergate.

## TERMS & NAMES

1. **republic,** p. 222
2. **Articles of Confederation,** p. 222
3. **Northwest Ordinance,** p. 223
4. **Shays's Rebellion,** p. 225
5. **Constitutional Convention,** p. 229
6. **James Madison,** p. 229
7. **Great Compromise,** p. 232
8. **Federalists,** p. 234
9. **George Mason,** p. 236
10. **Bill of Rights,** p. 237

## REVIEW QUESTIONS

**Possible Responses**

1. It is a road Daniel Boone and his men made. It led into Kentucky from the east.
2. the problems of winning independence and handling the Western territories
3. the power to wage war; make peace; sign treaties; issue money
4. It convinced many people that a new national government, with stronger powers, was needed.
5. Native Americans; African Americans; women
6. The new government should be a republic; it needed to protect people's rights.
7. the Great Compromise and the Three-Fifths Compromise
8. Federalism is a form of government in which power is divided between the central government and the states.
9. because they were large states in the geographic center of the nation
10. because otherwise a tyrannical government might abuse individual liberties

VISUAL SUMMARY

## Confederation to Constitution

★ **1777** Continental Congress passes the Articles of Confederation.

★ **1777–1781** States debate ratification of the Articles of Confederation.

★ **1781** Articles of Confederation go into effect.

★ **1786** Annapolis Convention is held.

★ **1786–1787** Shays's Rebellion occurs.

★ **1787** Constitutional Convention is held in Philadelphia.

★ **1788** U.S. Constitution is ratified.

★ **1789** Government created by the new Constitution takes power.

★ **1791** Bill of Rights is added to the Constitution.

# Chapter 8 ASSESSMENT

## TERMS & NAMES

Briefly explain the importance of each of the following.

1. republic
2. Articles of Confederation
3. Northwest Ordinance
4. Shays's Rebellion
5. Constitutional Convention
6. James Madison
7. Great Compromise
8. Federalists
9. George Mason
10. Bill of Rights

## REVIEW QUESTIONS

**The Confederation Era (pages 221–227)**

1. What is the Wilderness Road, and where did it lead?
2. What problems did the Continental Congress successfully address?
3. What powers did the government have under the Articles of Confederation?
4. How did Shays's Rebellion affect people's views on the Articles of Confederation?

**Creating the Constitution (pages 228–233)**

5. What groups of people were not represented at the Constitutional Convention?
6. What were some things the delegates agreed on at the convention?
7. What compromises did the delegates make during the convention?

**Ratifying the Constitution (pages 234–239)**

8. What is federalism?
9. Why were Virginia and New York important in the battle for ratification of the Constitution?
10. Why did some states think that it was necessary to add a bill of rights to the Constitution?

## CRITICAL THINKING

**1. USING YOUR NOTES**

| Problems | Solutions |
|---|---|
| Western lands | |
| Postwar depression | |
| Representation in the new government | |
| Slavery | |

Using your completed chart, answer the questions below.

a. What do you think was the most serious problem the young nation faced?

b. Was the nation able to solve this problem? How?

**2. ANALYZING LEADERSHIP**

Think about the leaders discussed in this chapter. Based on their actions, which leader do you think made the greatest contribution to the Constitutional Convention? Why?

**3. THEME: DEMOCRATIC IDEALS**

How do the Articles of Confederation and the Constitution each carry out democratic ideals?

**4. APPLYING CITIZENSHIP SKILLS**

Do you think the Founders were right to make the compromises they did in the Constitution on the issues of representation and slavery? What might have happened if they had not compromised?

**5. RECOGNIZING EFFECTS**

How might U.S. history be different if Virginia had refused to ratify the Constitution? If New York had refused? If both had refused?

**Interact *with* History**

How did your ideas about how you would form a government change after reading this chapter?

## CRITICAL THINKING

**Possible Responses**

1. **USING YOUR NOTES a.** Answers will vary. **b.** All problems in the chart were solved with the exception of slavery.
2. **ANALYZING LEADERSHIP** Students may choose Daniel Boone, James Madison, Daniel Shays, George Mason, or John Jay. Be sure that they discuss contributions made and reasons behind their choice.
3. **THEME: DEMOCRATIC IDEALS** Both documents deal with the national government and worked toward the creation of a republic.
4. **APPLYING CITIZENSHIP SKILLS** Students should discuss the Virginia Plan, the New Jersey Plan, the Great Compromise, and the Three-Fifths Compromise, and how things would have been different without them.
5. **RECOGNIZING EFFECTS** Student responses should include the largeness of these states, their influence over the rest of the country, and their geographic importance. Answers will vary.

**Interact *with* History.** Students should include the idea of considering many different viewpoints and needs of citizens.

## HISTORY SKILLS

**1. INTERPRETING MAPS: Region**

Study the map and then answer the questions.

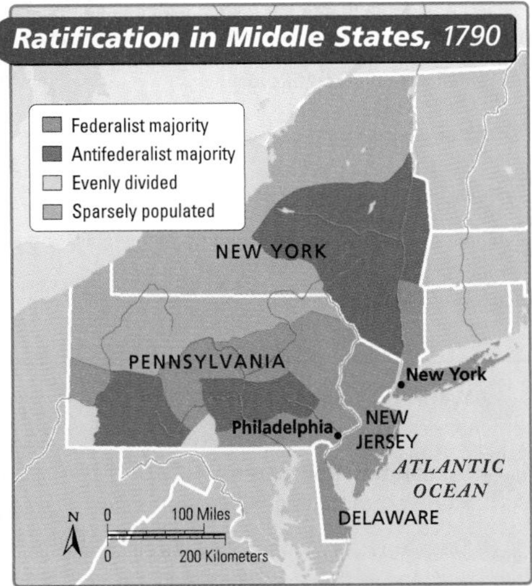


Source: *American Heritage Pictorial Atlas of United States History*

**Basic Map Elements**

a. Which states are identified on the map?

b. In which states did the Federalists have statewide majorities?

**Interpreting the Map**

c. Why do you think the two cities on the map were strong Federalist supporters?

**2. INTERPRETING PRIMARY SOURCES**

The following law was put into effect in Virginia in 1786. Read the law and answer the questions.

> *Be it enacted by the General Assembly,* That no man shall be compelled to frequent or support any religious worship, place, or ministry, whatsoever . . . but that all men shall be free to profess, and by argument maintain, their opinion in matters of religion, and that the same shall in no way diminish, enlarge, or affect their civil capacities.
>
> *The Statute of Virginia for Religious Freedom, 1786*

a. How would you summarize this law?

b. Which right in the Bill of Rights was based on this law?

c. Based on what you know about colonial history, how had American society changed between the early 1600s and the late 1700s?

## ALTERNATIVE ASSESSMENT

**1. INTERDISCIPLINARY ACTIVITY: Government**

**Making a Chart** Do research to learn how the U.S. Constitution has been used as a model by other nations. Make a chart to summarize the information you find about one specific nation. Include the country, the date the country's constitution was ratified, and two ways in which that nation's constitution is similar to and different from the U.S. Constitution.

**2. COOPERATIVE LEARNING ACTIVITY**

**Staging a Debate** Stage a debate between a Federalist and an Antifederalist. Work in small groups to read some of the different arguments each side used. Look for discussions of one or more of the issues listed below. Pick one of the issues and stage a debate, using the strongest arguments from each side. Let the class determine who won the debate and why.

a. the representation of people in Congress

b. the strength of the president and Senate

c. the need for a bill of rights

**3. PRIMARY SOURCE EXPLORER**

**Creating a Museum Exhibit** The creation of the U.S. Constitution was one of the most important events in the nation's history. There is a great amount of information about the Constitution. Using the Primary Source Explorer CD-ROM and your local library, collect information on different topics relating to the Constitution.

Create a museum exhibit about the Constitution using the suggestions below.

- Include information on the historical background of the Constitutional Convention, such as Shays's Rebellion and Enlightenment ideas about government.
- Find biographies about the delegates to the convention, including portraits.
- Collect important primary sources, such as Madison's notes and *The Federalist* papers.
- Include photographs or facsimiles of the documents.
- Draw a diagram that shows a layout for the exhibit.

**4. HISTORY PORTFOLIO**

**Option 1** Review your section and chapter assessment activities. Select one that you think shows your best work. Then use comments made by your teacher or classmates to improve your work and add it to your portfolio.

**Option 2** Review the questions that you wrote for What Do You Want to Know? on page 220. Then write a report that explains the answers to your questions. If any questions were not answered, do research to answer them. Add your answers to your portfolio.



## ALTERNATIVE ASSESSMENT

1. INTERDISCIPLINARY ACTIVITY: **Government**

**Charts should**
- present information accurately.
- present information in a style that will aid the viewer in understanding the information.
- be presented neatly.

2. COOPERATIVE LEARNING ACTIVITY

**Debates should**
- have a central question or proposition.
- support their own positions and refute their opponent's position with evidence.
- appropriately respond to each other's statements.

3.  PRIMARY SOURCE EXPLORER

**Exhibits should**
- have a complete introductory overview.
- contain accurate and well-described textual information.
- use a variety of media.

4. HISTORY PORTFOLIO

 **Option 1 Revised section or chapter assessment activities should**
- address teacher and peer responses to the selected work.
- solve problems present in the first versions of the work.

**Option 2 Short reports should**
- answer questions about the creation of the Constitution.
- use evidence to develop and support ideas.
- cite sources of information.
- use standard grammar, spelling, sentence structure, and punctuation.

 **Critical Thinking Transparency CT24**
- Visual Summary

 **Formal Assessment**
- Chapter Test, Forms A and B, pp. 119–126

## HISTORY SKILLS

**Possible Responses**

1. INTERPRETING MAPS

**Basic Map Elements**

**a.** New York, Pennsylvania, New Jersey, and Delaware

**b.** New Jersey and Delaware

**Interpreting the Map**

**c.** Cities had a great deal of commerce. New York and Philadelphia would have supported the Constitution because it would have solved some of the commerce problems of the Articles of Confederation.

2. INTERPRETING PRIMARY SOURCES

**a.** The law says that people shall have freedom of religion.

**b.** the freedom of religion clause in the First Amendment

**c.** In the early 1600s, some of the colonies were based on religious beliefs. In the late 1700s, some colonists supported freedom of religion.

HANDBOOKS PLANNING GUIDE

# The Constitution and Citizenship Handbook

| | HANDBOOK OVERVIEW | COPYMASTERS | TECHNOLOGY |
|---|---|---|---|
| **RESOURCES** | The Constitution Handbook discusses the underlying principles of the United States Constitution. It also presents the full text of the document for study. The Citizenship Handbook explains who citizens are, lists their rights and responsibilities, and gives examples of ways to become a model citizen. | **In-Depth Resources: Unit 2**<br>• Guided Readings on the Constitution, pp. 62–65 | CD-ROM **Primary Source Explorer**<br>CD-ROM **Electronic Teacher Tools**<br>CD-ROM **Power Presentations CD-ROM**<br>**Chapter Summaries on CD** (English and Spanish) |
| **SECTION 1**<br>**The Seven Principles, Preamble, and Article 1**<br>**pp. 242–255** | **KEY IDEAS**<br>• The Constitution is a living document, based on seven fundamental principles.<br>• The Preamble sets forth the purposes for which the Constitution was written.<br>• Congress makes laws for the nation. | **In-Depth Resources: Unit 2**<br>• Guided Reading, p. 62<br>**Citizenship Today:**<br>• Simulation 1: Senate Debate of a Bill, pp. 19–28<br>• Federalism and the Distribution of Power, p. 73<br>• Separation of Powers and Inefficiency, p. 81 | **Warm-Up Transparency WTCON**<br>**Humanities Transparency HT16**<br>• Constitution, Page One—A Replica<br>INTERNET **ClassZone:** www.mcdougallittell.com |
| **SECTION 2**<br>**Articles 2 and 3**<br>**pp. 256–261** | • The president enforces the laws and commands the military.<br>• The Constitution creates the Supreme Court, which interprets the laws.<br>• The Constitution also gives Congress the power to create lower-ranking federal courts. | **In-Depth Resources: Unit 2**<br>• Guided Reading, p. 63<br>**Citizenship Today:**<br>• Simulation 2: Presidential Press Conference, p. 29<br>• Simulation 3: Mock Trial, pp. 30–41<br>• Organization of the Executive Branch, p. 54<br>• Organization of the Judicial Branch, pp. 58–61 | **Humanities Transparency HT16**<br>• Constitution, Page One—A Replica<br>CD-ROM **Primary Source Explorer**<br>• *The Constitution*<br>INTERNET **ClassZone:** www.mcdougallittell.com |
| **SECTION 3**<br>**Articles 4–7**<br>**pp. 262–265** | • States must honor one another's laws, records, and court rulings.<br>• The Constitution is the supreme law of the land, but it can be changed through amendments.<br>• The Constitution is ratified by 9 of the 13 original states. | **In-Depth Resources: Unit 2**<br>• Guided Reading, p. 64 | **Humanities Transparency HT16**<br>• Constitution, Page One—A Replica<br>CD-ROM **Primary Source Explorer**<br>• *The Constitution*<br>INTERNET **ClassZone:** www.mcdougallittell.com |
| **SECTION 4**<br>**The Bill of Rights and Amendments**<br>**pp. 266–277** | • The first ten amendments, known as the Bill of Rights, protect such basic liberties as freedom of religion and free speech.<br>• Later amendments help the Constitution adapt to social changes and historical trends. | **In-Depth Resources: Unit 2**<br>• Guided Reading, p. 65<br>**Citizenship Today:**<br>• Balancing Liberty and National Security, p. 75<br>• Suspects' Rights versus Public Protection, p. 76<br>• Equality: Its Meaning and Application, p. 77<br>• Minority Rights, p. 79 | **Warm-Up Transparency WTCON**<br>**Humanities Transparency HT16**<br>• Constitution, Page One—A Replica<br>CD-ROM **Primary Source Explorer**<br>• *The Constitution*<br>INTERNET **ClassZone:** www.mcdougallittell.com |
| **SECTION 5**<br>**Citizenship Handbook**<br>**pp. 280–287** | • A person can become a U.S. citizen by birth or by naturalization.<br>• Citizenship includes many rights and responsibilities.<br>• Being a good citizen involves staying informed, making wise decisions, and participating in the community. | **Citizenship Today:**<br>• The Importance of Juries, pp. 1–2<br>• Obeying Rules and Laws, pp. 5–6<br>• Becoming a Citizen, pp. 9–10<br>• Debating Points of View, pp. 11–12<br>• Community Service, pp. 13–14<br>• Detecting Bias in the Media, pp. 15–16<br>• Writing Government Officials, pp. 17–18<br>• Simulation 4: Town Meeting, pp. 42–45 | **Warm-Up Transparency WTCON**<br>INTERNET **ClassZone:** www.mcdougallittell.com |

Pupil's Edition · Copymaster · Overhead Transparency · Audio Library · CD-ROM · Internet

## ASSESSMENT

**Constitution Assessment,** pp. 278–279

**Formal Assessment**
- Chapter Tests, Forms A and B, pp. 136–143

**Alternative Assessment Book**

**Electronic Teacher Tools with Test Maker**

---

**Section Assessment,** pp. 247, 255

**Formal Assessment**
- Section Quiz, pp. 129–130

**Alternative Assessment**

**Electronic Teacher Tools with Test Maker**

---

**Section Assessment,** pp. 259, 261

**Formal Assessment**
- Section Quiz, pp. 131–132

**Alternative Assessment**

**Electronic Teacher Tools with Test Maker**

---

**Section Assessment,** p. 265

**Formal Assessment**
- Section Quiz, p. 133

**Alternative Assessment**

**Electronic Teacher Tools with Test Maker**

---

**Section Assessment,** pp. 268, 277

**Formal Assessment**
- Section Quiz, pp. 134–135

**Alternative Assessment**

**Electronic Teacher Tools with Test Maker**

---

**Alternative Assessment**

**Electronic Teacher Tools with Test Maker**

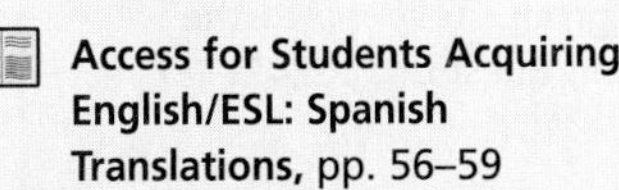

## CUSTOMIZING FOR INDIVIDUAL NEEDS

### Students Acquiring English/ESL

**Reading Study Guide** (English and Spanish), pp. 83–92

**Access for Students Acquiring English/ESL: Spanish Translations,** pp. 56–59

**Handbook Summaries on CD** (English and Spanish)

### Less Proficient Readers

**Reading Study Guide** (English and Spanish), pp. 83–92

**Handbook Summaries on CD** (English and Spanish)

### Gifted and Talented Students

**America's History Makers**
- George Washington, pp. 27–28
- James Madison, pp. 33–34
- Alexander Hamilton, pp. 35–36
- Thomas Jefferson, pp. 39–40

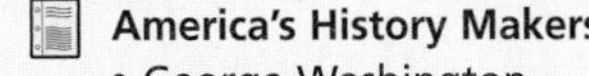

## CROSS-CURRICULAR CONNECTIONS

### Civics

Hjelmeland, Andy. ***Kids in Jail.*** Minneapolis: Lerner, 1992. Gives students a vivid picture of how the justice system works by following a repeat offender from arrest through his time in jail, court appearance, and time spent in a correctional facility.

Lewis, Barbara A. ***The Kids Guide to Social Action.*** Minneapolis: Free Spirit Pub., 1991. A resource guide for young people learning political action skills.

### Geography

Stein, R. Conrad. ***The United States of America (Enchantment of the World).*** Chicago: Children's Press, 1994. Overview of physical and cultural geography of the United States.

### Government

Kent, Deborah. ***The Disability Rights Movement.*** New York: Children's Press, 1996. The story of how one group of Americans worked for greater rights and access.

Whitney, Sharon. ***The Equal Rights Amendment: The History and the Movement.*** New York: F. Watts, 1984. An examination of the ERA movement, its criticisms, and defeat.

### Mathematics

Ashabranner, Melissa, and Brent Ashabranner. ***Counting America: The Story of the United States Census.*** New York: Putnam, 1989. The story of the decennial census required by the Constitution.

### Literature

Rennert, Rick, ed. ***Civil Rights Leaders.*** New York: Chelsea House Pub., 1992. Brief biographies of eight civil rights leaders including James Weldon Johnson; Martin Luther King, Jr.; Jesse Jackson; and Thurgood Marshall.

## ENRICHMENT ACTIVITIES

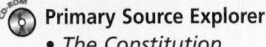

**Pupil's Edition**
**Constitution Handbook,** pp. 242–279
**Citizenship Handbook,** pp. 280–287

**Citizenship Today**
- Constitution Handbook, pp. 19–28, 30–41, 50, 54–63, 64–67, 69, 70–76, 81–83, 85
- Citizenship Handbook, pp. 1–2, 5–6, 9, 11–18, 42–45

**America's History Makers**
- George Washington, pp. 27–28
- James Madison, pp. 33–34
- Alexander Hamilton, pp. 35–36
- Thomas Jefferson, pp. 39–40

**Primary Source Explorer**
- *The Constitution*

## LESSON PLAN OPTIONS (50-MINUTE PERIOD)

(TE) = Teacher's Edition (PE) = Pupil's Edition

| | TEACHER-DIRECTED ACTIVITIES | STUDENT-CENTERED ACTIVITIES | INDIVIDUAL ACTIVITIES |
|---|---|---|---|
| | Class Time: 15 minutes | Class Time: 25 minutes | Class Time: 10 minutes |
| **DAY 1**<br>The Seven Principles, Preamble, and Article 1<br>pp. 242–255 | **Presentation Options**<br>• Begin with a class discussion of the photographs on pp. 242–243 **(PE)**.<br>• Use the 5-Minute Warm-Up on the seven principles, p. 244 **(TE)**.<br>• Lead a class discussion on the terms on the graphic on p. 244 **(TE)**. | **Options for Cooperative Learning**<br>• Have student groups complete the Interdisciplinary Link, Drama, p. 246 **(TE)**.<br>• Have student groups respond to the Critical Thinking question, p. 247 **(PE)**. | **Head Start on Homework Options**<br>• Have students begin the assessment questions on pp. 247, 255 **(PE)**.<br>• Have students begin Guided Reading Activity for Articles 2, 3. |
| **DAY 2**<br>Articles 2 and 3<br>pp. 256–261 | **Presentation Options**<br>• Begin with the History from Visuals, p. 258 **(TE)**.<br>• Choose 3 key questions for Articles 2 and 3 to discuss with the class, pp. 256, 260 **(TE)**. | **Options for Cooperative Learning**<br>• Divide students into groups to prepare for Simulation 3: A Mock Trial, pp. 30–41, **Citizenship Today**.<br>• Have student pairs work together to complete the Interdisciplinary Link, Math, p. 256 **(TE)**. | **Head Start on Homework Options**<br>• Have students begin working on Articles 1–3 Assessments, pp. 255, 259, 261 **(PE)**.<br>• Have students preview the headings and graphics on pp. 262–265 **(PE)**. |
| **DAY 3**<br>Articles 4–7<br>pp. 262–265 | **Presentation Options**<br>• Begin with the graphic on federalism, p. 262 **(PE)**.<br>• Discuss the Critical Thinking Activity with the class, p. 263 **(TE)**. | **Options for Cooperative Learning**<br>• Divide students into groups and have them complete the Interdisciplinary Link, Geography, p. 262 **(TE)**.<br>• Have student pairs work together to complete the History from Visuals and Extension Activity, p. 263 **(TE)**. | **Head Start on Homework Options**<br>• Have students begin working on Articles 4–7 Assessment, p. 265 **(PE)**.<br>• Have students preview the Bill of Rights and Amendments, pp. 266–277 **(PE)**. |
| **DAY 4**<br>The Bill of Rights and Amendments<br>pp. 266–277 | **Presentation Options**<br>• Begin with the 5-Minute Warm-Up, p. 266 **(TE)**.<br>• Choose 3 key questions on the amendments to discuss with the class, pp. 266, 269 **(TE)**.<br>• Lead the students through the Teaching Strategy, p. 266 **(TE)**. | **Options for Cooperative Learning**<br>• Divide students into groups and have them complete the Interdisciplinary Link, Art, p. 270 **(TE)**.<br>• Have class teams organize to complete the Interdisciplinary Link, Language Arts, p. 274 **(TE)**. | **Head Start on Homework Options**<br>• Have students begin working on the Constitution Assessment, pp. 278–279 **(PE)**.<br>• Have students preview the Citizenship Handbook headings and boldfaced terms, pp. 280–287 **(PE)**. |
| **DAY 5**<br>Citizenship Handbook<br>pp. 280–287 | **Presentation Options**<br>• Begin with the 5-Minute Warm-Up, p. 280 **(TE)**.<br>• Guide students through the Critical Thinking Activity, p. 282 **(TE)**.<br>• Choose 5 key questions from the Handbook to discuss, pp. 280–287 **(TE)**. | **Options for Cooperative Learning**<br>• Divide students into groups and have them complete the Interdisciplinary Link, Civics, p. 285 **(TE)**.<br>• Divide students into groups and have them complete one of the Citizenship Activities, pp. 286–287 **(PE)**. | **Head Start on Homework Options**<br>• Have students plan interview questions for the Interdisciplinary Link, Language Arts, p. 281 **(PE)**. |

TEACHER-TESTED ACTIVITY Paul Beavers, J. T. Moore Middle School, Nashville, Tennessee

## FEDERALISM AND POWER SHARING

**Class Time** One class period

**Task** Debating the division of power between the states and the national government

**Purpose** To understand the debates that took place following the Constitutional Convention between the Federalists and the Anti-Federalists

**Supplies Needed**

- Reference materials and Internet sources on the opinions of the Federalists and the Anti-Federalists

**Activity** Review the definition of federalism on page 245. Have students give examples of shared powers, powers delegated to the national government, and powers reserved to the states. Write the following debate topic on the chalkboard: *The states should give up as little power as possible to the central government.* Divide students into small groups. Have half the groups research the Federalists' stand on this topic, while the other half looks at the Anti-Federalists' position. Pick a panel of three from each side to debate the topic.

## BLOCK SCHEDULING — LESSON PLAN OPTIONS (90-MINUTE PERIOD)

### DAY 1

**History from Visuals,** pp. 242–243
**Class Time** 20 minutes

Options for pacing and variety:
- Peer Teaching Divide students into small groups. Have each group discuss the five events shown on these pages and explain how each event is linked to constitutional decision making. **Class Time** 10 minutes

**Principles of the Constitution,** pp. 244–248
**Class Time** 45 minutes

Options for pacing and variety:
- Peer Teaching Have students complete the Interdisciplinary Activity, Art: Presenting the Principles Visually, p. 245 **(TE)**. **Class Time** 30 minutes

**Article 1,** pp. 249–255
**Class Time** 50 minutes

Options for pacing and variety:
- Time Saver Use the chart on pages 252–253 to summarize for students Article 1, Section 7, How a Bill Becomes a Law. **Class Time** 10 minutes
- Peer Evaluation Have student pairs provide written answers to A Closer Look questions 6–10 and share their responses with the class. **Class Time** 20 minutes

### DAY 2

**Article 2,** pp. 256–259
**Class Time** 45 minutes
- Time Saver Use the chart of the electoral college on page 256 to help students understand how the electoral college works. **Class Time** 15 minutes
- Peer Teaching Have students work together to complete the Main Ideas and Critical Thinking questions for the Article 2 Assessment on page 259. **Class Time** 15 minutes

**Article 3,** pp. 260–261
**Class Time** 30 minutes

Options for pacing and variety:
- Time Saver Use the chart on Checks and Balances on page 261 to help students understand the relationship of the judiciary to the executive and legislative branches of government. Assign the Skillbuilder: Interpreting Charts questions for homework. **Class Time** 10 minutes

**Articles 4–7,** pp. 262–265
**Class Time** 30 minutes

Options for pacing and variety:
- Peer Teaching For a homework assignment have students review the chart on page 262 and bring to class newspaper or newsmagazine articles showing an example of a national power, a shared power, and a state power. Have each student pick one article to summarize for the class. Then create a Constitution database using all students' articles. **Class Time** 25 minutes
- Peer Evaluation Have student pairs answer the Applying Citizenship, Critical Thinking question on page 279 of the Constitution Assessment. **Class Time** 10 minutes

### DAY 3

**Bill of Rights and Amendments 11–27,** pp. 266–277
**Class Time** 45 minutes

Options for pacing and variety:
- History on Film Extend students' background knowledge of the amendments to the Constitution by showing some of the seven short films in the series *The Amendments to the Constitution.* Cambridge, 1998. **Class Time** 35 minutes

**Constitution Assessment,** pp. 278–279
**Class Time** 40 minutes

Options for pacing and variety:
- Peer Evaluation To reinforce students, understanding of the principles of the Constitution, have seven-member groups complete the Seven Principles chart on page 278 of the Constitution Assessment. Within groups, have each student complete a different row of the chart. **Class Time** 15 minutes

**Citizenship Handbook,** pp. 280–287
**Class Time** 40 minutes

Options for pacing and variety:
- Peer Teaching Divide students into four groups. Assign each group the information in one of the charts or the diagram on pages 282–283. Have each group create a different way to present this information to the class. **Class Time** 30 minutes
- Peer Evaluation Divide students into three groups. Assign each group one of the three Practicing Citizenship Skills activities on page 287. Work with each group to establish a time line for completion of the group's project and develop a list of criteria for evaluating the project. **Class Time** 25 minutes

## CONSTITUTION HANDBOOK OBJECTIVE

The student will understand the seven principles of government that helped to shape the Constitution.

### HISTORY FROM VISUALS

**Interpreting the Photographs and Painting** Ask students to compare the people shown in the photographs with those in the painting. What groups of people took part in the Constitutional Convention of 1787? What groups were not present? **Possible Responses** The painting shows only white men; they represented various states. In contrast, the photographs show several ethnic groups, women, and young people; members of these groups were not present at the Constitutional Convention. However, over the years, they have won rights as citizens under the Constitution.

**Extension** Have students write five questions they would ask one or more people in the photographs or painting.

### MORE ABOUT . . .

**The Delegates at Philadelphia**
Of the 55 men at the Constitutional Convention, nearly all were substantial property owners. A large majority (39 delegates) had already served in the Continental Congress. More than half were college-educated, and nearly half were lawyers. They ranged in age from 26 to 81, averaging in the early forties. (Ben Franklin was the oldest.) They represented all the states except Rhode Island.



# The Living Constitution

The Framers of the Constitution created a flexible plan for governing the United States far into the future. They also described ways to allow changes in the Constitution. For over 200 years, the Constitution has guided the American people. It remains a "living document." The Constitution still thrives, in part, because it echoes the principles the delegates valued. Each generation of Americans renews the meaning of the Constitution's timeless ideas. These two pages show you some ways in which the Constitution has shaped events in American history. **See Primary Source Explorer** CD-ROM

***"In framing a system which we wish to last for ages, we should not lose sight of the changes which ages will produce."***

—JAMES MADISON, CONSTITUTIONAL CONVENTION

**1787**
Delegates in Philadelphia sign the Constitution.

**1965**
Civil rights leaders protest to end the violation of their constitutional rights. Dr. Martin Luther King, Jr., Coretta Scott King, and others march from Selma toward Montgomery, Alabama, to gain voting rights.



### RECOMMENDED RESOURCES

**BOOKS FOR THE TEACHER**

Frost, Elizabeth, and Kathryn Cullen-Dupont. ***Women's Suffrage in America.*** New York: Facts on File, 1992. Primary sources in the struggle for suffrage.

Garraty, John, ed. ***Quarrels That Have Shaped the Constitution.*** New York: Harper, 1988. Landmark cases.

Lusane, Clarence. ***No Easy Victories.*** Danbury, CT: Franklin Watts, 1996. The African-American struggle for the vote.

St. John, Jeffrey. ***Forge of Union, Anvil of Liberty.*** Ottawa, IL: Jameson, 1992. Story of the Bill of Rights and the first election.

**VIDEOS**

***The Congress: The History and Promise of Representative Government.*** PBS Video, 1988. Part of a series by Ken Burns.

***Mr. Smith Goes to Washington.*** Columbia, 1939. The classic Jimmy Stewart film provides a look at Congress in theory and practice.

**SOFTWARE**

***How a Bill Becomes a Law.*** Word Associates, 3226 Robincrest Drive, Northbrook, IL 60062.

For a tutorial and tests about the Constitution, visit www.mcdougallittell.com

## 1971

The 26th Amendment to the Constitution gives young people "18 years of age or older" the right to vote.

## 1981

A Supreme Court decision rules that Congress can exclude women from the draft. Still, many women who have joined the armed forces have served in combat.

The New York Times

SATURDAY, FEBRUARY 13, 1999

CLINTON ACQUITTED DECISIVELY: NO MAJORITY FOR EITHER CHARGE

President Says He Is Sorry And Seeks Reconciliation

CENSURE IS BARRED

But Rebuke From Both Sides of Aisle Dilutes President's Victory

The Fallout Of the Trial

Effects on the Office Are Far From Certain

'Senators, How Say You?'

## 1999

The Senate tries President Bill Clinton for the impeachment charges brought against him by the House of Representatives. As required by the Constitution, the Senate needs a two-thirds majority vote to convict him. This rule saves his presidency.

## TABLE OF CONTENTS



## HOW TO READ THE CONSTITUTION

**The complete text of the Constitution of the United States begins on page 248. The main column has the actual text. Some of the spellings and punctuation have been updated for easier reading. Headings and subheadings have been added to the Constitution to help you find specific topics. Those parts of the Constitution that are no longer in use have been crossed out. "A Closer Look" notes and charts will help you understand issues related to the Constitution.**





## MORE ABOUT . . .

### The 26th Amendment

Until 1970, the right to vote was limited to citizens aged 21 and over. The Vietnam War created pressure to grant 18-year-olds the right to vote. People questioned the fairness of sending a young soldier to fight and possibly die when he had no voice in setting national policy.

The Voting Rights Act of 1970 extended the right to vote in national elections to citizens 18 and older. However, many states still kept 21 as the voting age in state and local elections. To avoid the problem of maintaining two sets of voter registration books, Congress passed the 26th Amendment, which took priority over state laws on voting age. The states ratified the new amendment in about four months.

## MORE ABOUT . . .

### Women in Combat

During World War II, more than 250,000 women joined the military, participating in every type of work except actual combat. By the Gulf War in 1990–1991, more than 35,000 servicewomen served in such combat-related jobs as air traffic controller, reconnaissance aircraft pilot, and equipment mechanic. Two women were taken prisoners of war, and 15 women were killed in the conflict. As more military missions involve peacekeeping or police actions, the distinction between combat and noncombat positions has become less clear.

## TEACHING STRATEGY

**Comparing** Remind the students that the Framers of the Constitution intended it to be flexible enough to deal with unanticipated problems in the new nation. Have them read the quotation from James Madison on page 242 and discuss the meaning of the statement.

Tell the students to study the photographs and captions. Ask: What political changes would Madison notice if he could compare these photographs to the United States of his own time? **Possible Responses** free African Americans demanding voting rights, young people voting, women in the military

Ask the students which of the pictures shows a situation that the Framers of the Constitution anticipated might happen. **Answer** the impeachment of a president

## FOCUS & MOTIVATE

### 5-MINUTE WARM-UP

**Finding Main Ideas** These questions help students to see that the seven principles of government all relate to questions of power.

1. Read the questions under headings 1–7 on pages 244–247. What important word occurs in five of the questions? Does this word also relate to the other two headings?
2. What events before the Revolution raised questions about the power of government?

 **Warm-Up Transparency WTCON**

## INSTRUCT

**Seven Principles of the Constitution**
Key Questions

- Why do you think the Framers of the Constitution worried about the question of power in government?
- Which of the seven principles of the Constitution deal with governmental power?
- Which principles deal with the rights of the people?

### MORE ABOUT . . .

**Popular Sovereignty**
Popular sovereignty is the idea that the government's authority comes from the people and reflects their will. This philosophy had its roots in classical antiquity but was newly expressed during the Enlightenment by such political writers as John Locke (1632–1704) and Jean-Jacques Rousseau (1712–1778). The Framers were deeply influenced by these ideas.

**Constitution Connections**
The following are parts of the Constitution that embody the principle of popular sovereignty:

- Preamble
- Article 1, Section 2
- Amendments 10, 14, 15, 19, 26

# Seven Principles of the Constitution

The Framers of the Constitution constructed a new system of government. Seven principles supported their efforts. To picture how these principles work, imagine seven building blocks. Together they form the foundation of the United States Constitution. In the pages that follow, you will find the definitions and main ideas of the principles shown in the graphic below.

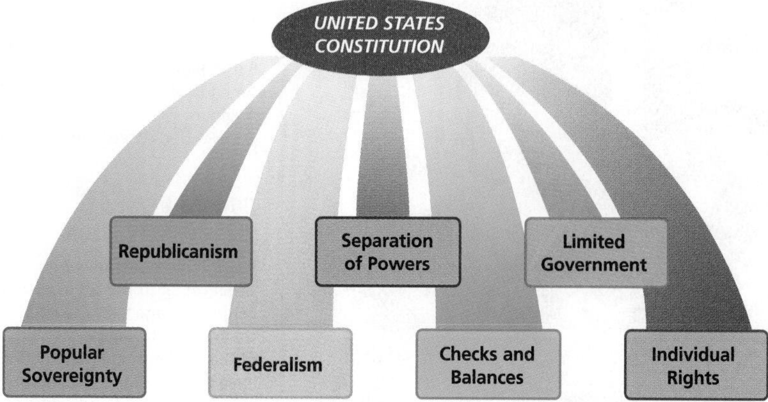


## 1 Popular Sovereignty
### *Who Gives the Government Its Power?*

"We the people of the United States . . . establish this Constitution for the United States of America." These words from the Preamble, or introduction, to the Constitution clearly spell out the source of the government's power. The Constitution rests on the idea of **popular sovereignty**—a government in which the people rule. As the nation changed and grew, popular sovereignty took on new meaning. A broader range of Americans shared in the power to govern themselves.

**In 1987, Americans gathered in Washington, D.C., to celebrate the 200th anniversary of the Constitution. The banner proudly displays that the power to govern belongs to the people.**



### TEACHING STRATEGY

**Using Visual Elements** The concepts behind the seven principles are very complex. To help the students build an understanding of the principles, direct the students' attention to the pictures, graphics, and questions shown with each principle. Ask them to look at the picture or graphic and to read the question. Then discuss how the visual element helps to answer the question.

The concepts of federalism, separation of powers, and checks and balances are especially challenging. The graphic organizers should help the students see the differences among these concepts.

In a republican government, voting citizens make their voices heard at the polls. The power of the ballot prompts candidates to listen to people's concerns.

## 2 Republicanism
### *How Are People's Views Represented in Government?*

The Framers of the Constitution wanted the people to have a voice in government. Yet the Framers also feared that public opinion might stand in the way of sound decision making. To solve this problem, they looked to republicanism as a model of government.

**Republicanism** is based on this belief: The people exercise their power by voting for their political representatives. According to the Framers, these lawmakers played the key role in making a republican government work. Article 4, Section 4, of the Constitution also calls for every state to have a "republican form of government."

## 3 Federalism
### *How Is Power Shared?*

The Framers wanted the states and the nation to become partners in governing. To build cooperation, the Framers turned to federalism. **Federalism** is a system of government in which the states and national government share powers.

The Framers used federalism to structure the Constitution. The Constitution assigns certain powers to the national government. These are *delegated powers*. Powers kept by the states are *reserved powers*. Powers shared or exercised by national and state governments are known as *concurrent powers*.

**Federalism**

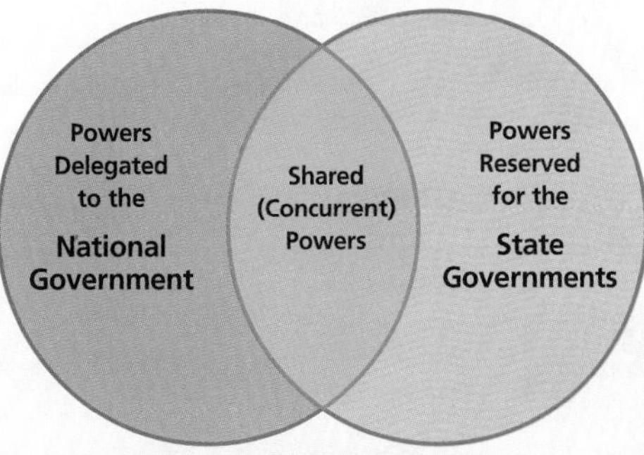


The overlapping spheres of power bind the American people together.





## CONSTITUTION HANDBOOK

### MORE ABOUT . . .

**Republicanism**

Students frequently confuse this term with the American political party. To clarify the term, explain that republicanism is usually defined as *representative democracy.* That is, the people elect representatives to make laws and exercise the powers of government. (When the people themselves make laws, as in town meetings, the process is called *direct democracy.*)

At the time of the Revolution, many people considered republican government to be a very radical idea. The Framers of the Constitution, however, believed that voters were capable of making good choices in selecting the leaders who would govern the nation. Procedures for the election of representatives are a part of the Constitution.

**Constitution Connections**

The following are parts of the Constitution that embody the principle of republicanism:

- Article 1, Section 4
- Article 4, Section 4
- Amendments 12, 20

### MORE ABOUT . . .

**Federalism**

To succeed, federalism requires both a strong central government and vigorous local governments. The idea of federalism is reflected in the motto of the United States, *E pluribus, unum* (From many, one).

**Constitution Connections**

The following are parts of the Constitution that embody the principle of federalism:

- Article 4
- Article 5
- Article 6
- Amendments 10, 11

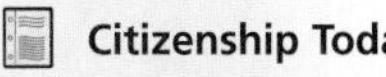

**Citizenship Today**


- Federalism and the Distribution of Power, p. 69
- State Governments, pp. 58–63
- Local Governments, pp. 64–67

**ACTIVITY OPTIONS**

**INTERDISCIPLINARY LINK: ART** — BLOCK SCHEDULING

**PRESENTING THE PRINCIPLES VISUALLY**

**Class Time** 30 minutes

**Task** Making a visual representation of the seven principles explained on pages 244–247

**Purpose** To transform verbal information into a visual representation

**Supplies Needed**

- Textbook
- Art supplies, including markers, posterboard, and construction paper
- Material suitable for three-dimensional work, such as small boxes, string or yarn, and labels

**Activity** Divide the class into seven groups and assign each group one of the seven principles. Each group should carefully study the description of its principle in the textbook. Then the group should decide on a two- or three-dimensional way to illustrate the principle. The group should decide who will create the art and who will explain it to the class. Have students present the principles to the class and combine all the illustrations into a single display.

MORE ABOUT . . .

**Separation of Powers**

The Framers of the Constitution deliberately pitted the branches of government against one another. Although this arrangement lessened the efficiency of government, it also guarded against abuse. James Madison wrote in *Federalist* No. 47, "The accumulation of all powers, legislative, executive, and judiciary, in the same hands, whether one, a few or many . . . may justly be pronounced the very definition of tyranny."

**Constitution Connections**

The following are parts of the Constitution that embody the principle of separation of powers:

- Article 1
- Article 2
- Article 3

**Citizenship Today**

- Separation of Powers and Inefficiency, p. 81

## 4 Separation of Powers
### *How Is Power Divided?*

The Framers were concerned that too much power might fall into the hands of a single group. To avoid this problem, they built the idea of **separation of powers** into the Constitution. This principle means the division of basic government roles into branches. No one branch is given all the power. Articles 1, 2, and 3 of the Constitution detail how powers are split among the three branches.

**Separation of Powers**

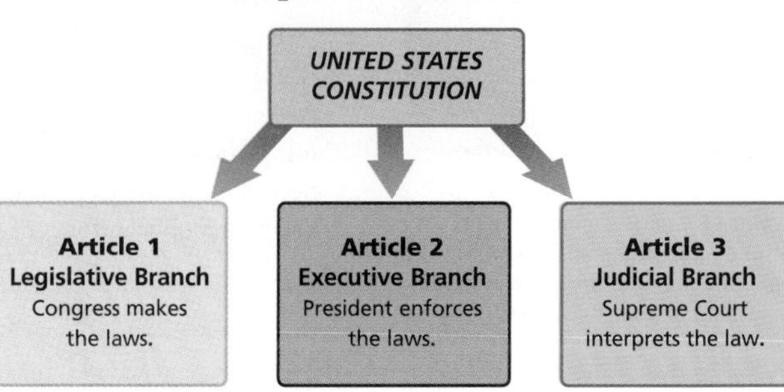


MORE ABOUT . . .

**Checks and Balances**

Like separation of powers, the principle of checks and balances is a way of limiting the power of government. In *Federalist* No. 51, Madison described this principle as a method of "keeping each other [the three branches] in their proper places."

**Constitution Connections**

The following are parts of the Constitution that embody the principle of checks and balances:

- Article 1
- Article 2
- Article 3

## 5 Checks and Balances
### *How Is Power Evenly Distributed?*

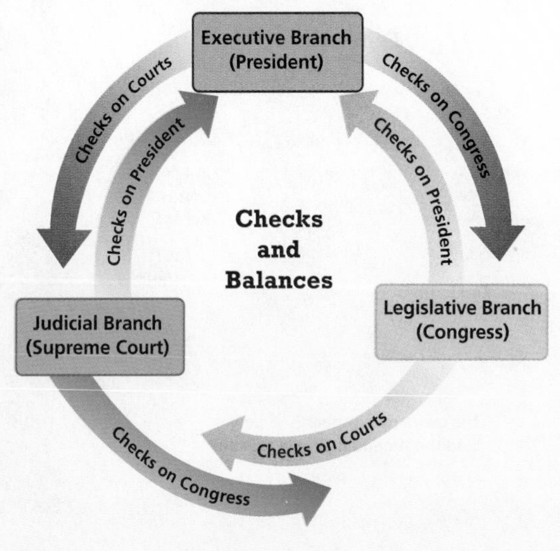


Baron de Montesquieu, an 18th-century French thinker, wrote, "Power should be a check to power." His comment refers to the principle of **checks and balances.** Each branch of government can exercise checks, or controls, over the other branches. Though the branches of government are separate, they rely on one another to perform the work of government.

The Framers included a system of checks and balances in the Constitution to help make sure that the branches work together fairly. For example, only Congress can pass laws. Yet the president can check this power by refusing to sign a law into action. In turn, the Supreme Court can declare that a law, passed by Congress and signed by the president, violates the Constitution.



ACTIVITY OPTIONS

INTERDISCIPLINARY LINK: DRAMA

BLOCK SCHEDULING

**CHECKS AND BALANCES**

**Class Time** 30 minutes

**Task** Dramatizing the concept of checks and balances

**Purpose** To more clearly understand the ability of each branch to check the powers of the others

**Supplies Needed**

- Index cards, each labeled with one of the bulleted items in the chart on page 261; cards may be color-coded according to branch of government

**Activity** Divide the class into three groups. Assign each group one branch of government. Each group should study the powers of its branch in the chart on page 261.

Set up a "power arena" in the room. Have a student draw an index card listing one of the checks on power. Each branch that is affected by this power must then send a representative to the arena to explain how that check limits or enhances its power and influences its relations with the other branches of government. Continue until all the checks have been pulled.

## 6 Limited Government
### *How Is Abuse of Power Prevented?*

The Framers restricted the power of government. Article 1, Section 9, of the Constitution lists the powers denied to the Congress. Article 1, Section 10, forbids the states to take certain actions.

The principle of **limited government** is also closely related to the "rule of law": In the American government everyone, citizens and powerful leaders alike, must obey the law. Individuals or groups cannot twist or bypass the law to serve their own interests.

In this political cartoon, President Richard Nixon shakes his fist as he defies the "rule of law." Faced with charges of violating the Constitution, Nixon resigned as president in 1974.

Students exercise their right to protest. They urge the community to protect the environment.

## 7 Individual Rights
### *How Are Personal Freedoms Protected?*

The first ten amendments to the Constitution shield people from an overly powerful government. These amendments are called the Bill of Rights. The Bill of Rights guarantees certain **individual rights,** or personal liberties and privileges. For example, government cannot control what people write or say. People also have the right to meet peacefully and to ask the government to correct a problem. Later amendments to the Constitution also advanced the cause of individual rights.

*Assessment: Principles of the Constitution*

**1. Main Ideas**

a. What are the seven principles of government?

b. How does the Constitution reflect the principle of separation of powers?

c. Why did the Framers include a system of checks and balances in the Constitution?

**2. Critical Thinking**

**Recognizing Effects** What might happen to the U.S. republic if most Americans did not exercise their right to vote?

THINK ABOUT
- the rights and responsibilities of citizens
- the views of elected representatives





**MORE ABOUT . . .**

**Limited Government**

Having just won a war against the British monarchy, many Americans in 1787 were concerned that a powerful president might make himself a king. In later years, political opponents accused both John Adams and Andrew Jackson of acting like kings.

In the 20th century, the power of the presidency increased sharply, provoking frequent controversy. Theodore Roosevelt, Woodrow Wilson, Franklin Roosevelt, Lyndon Johnson, Richard Nixon, Ronald Reagan, and Bill Clinton were all accused at times of abusing their power.

**Constitution Connections**

The following are parts of the Constitution that embody the principle of limited government:
- Article 1
- Article 2
- Article 3

**MORE ABOUT . . .**

**Individual Rights**

The principle of individual rights includes both civil liberties and civil rights. While these terms are often used interchangeably, their meanings are slightly different.

Usually, *civil liberties* refers to freedoms protected by limits on government. For example, the First Amendment prohibits government from interfering with freedom of speech and of religion.

*Civil rights* usually refers to positive acts by government to protect citizens against injustice. An example is the 14th Amendment's promise of "equal protection of the laws."

**Constitution Connections**

The following are parts of the Constitution that embody the principle of individual rights:
- Article 1, Sections 9, 10
- Article 6, Section 3
- Bill of Rights Amendments 1–10
- Amendments 13, 14, 15, 19, 26

**Formal Assessment**
- Section Quiz, p. 129

*Assessment: Principles of the Constitution*

**1. Main Ideas**

a. popular sovereignty, republicanism, federalism, separation of powers, checks and balances, limited government, individual rights **b.** Articles 1–3 divide roles of government into three branches—legislative, executive, and judicial. **c.** to prevent any one branch from abusing its power

**2. Critical Thinking**

**Possible Response** The republic might fall under the control of a select group, rather than the majority of the people. Popular sovereignty and true representative government might slowly die if elected officials reflected the will of only a small number of voters.

## INTERACTIVE PRIMARY SOURCE

**OBJECTIVE**
Students will be able to identify the basic plan for the structure of the United States government as set forth in the Constitution.

 **Primary Source Explorer**
- *The Constitution*

The Explorer will help students select and produce their own presentations.

Specific information about the document can be found in **A Closer Look.** To learn more about key people and events of the time, students should click on **Life in These Times. What Happened Next** will show the student the impact of the document, both at home and abroad, and tie it to today.

## FOCUS & MOTIVATE

### 5-MINUTE WARM-UP

**Finding Main Ideas** Have students read aloud the Preamble and study the chart on page 248. Ask the following questions:

1. What other examples can you think of for each of the goals in the Preamble?
2. Why is it important to know what the goals of the Framers were?

 **Warm-Up Transparency WTCON**

### MORE ABOUT . . .

**Barbara Jordan**
In 1974, Jordan was a first-term member of Congress on the House Judiciary Committee, which was investigating the Watergate scandal. In a televised speech on the issue of impeachment, Jordan told the nation, "My faith in the Constitution is whole, it is complete, it is total. I am not going to sit here and be an idle spectator to the diminution, the subversion, the destruction of the Constitution."

INTERACTIVE PRIMARY SOURCE

# The Constitution of the United States

See Primary Source Explorer 

*"In 1787, I was not included in that 'We, the people.' . . . But through the process of amendment, interpretation, and court decision, I have finally been included in 'We, the people.'"*

—BARBARA JORDAN, 1974
The first African-American congresswoman from the deep South (Texas)

### Preamble. *Purpose of the Constitution*

We the people of the United States, in order to form a more perfect Union, establish justice, insure domestic tranquility, provide for the common defense, promote the general welfare, and secure the blessings of liberty to ourselves and our posterity, do ordain and establish this Constitution for the United States of America.

**A CLOSER LOOK Goals of the Preamble**

| PREAMBLE | EXPLANATION | EXAMPLES |
|---|---|---|
| "Form a more perfect Union" | Create a nation in which states work together | • Interstate road network<br>• U.S. coins, paper money |
| "Establish justice" | Make laws and set up courts that are fair | • Court system<br>• Jury system |
| "Insure domestic tranquility" | Keep peace within the country | • National Guard<br>• Federal marshals |
| "Provide for the common defense" | Safeguard the country against attack | • Army<br>• Navy |
| "Promote the general welfare" | Contribute to the happiness and well-being of all the people | • Safety in the workplace<br>• Aid to the poor |
| "Secure the blessings of liberty to ourselves and our posterity" | Make sure future citizens remain free | • Commission on Civil Rights<br>• Federal Election Commission |

**SKILLBUILDER Interpreting Charts**
1. *Which goal of the Preamble do you think is most important? Why?*
2. *How does the Preamble reflect the principle of popular sovereignty?*

SKILLBUILDER Possible Responses
1. Students should choose one of the six goals listed and support their choice with convincing reasons.
2. "We the people" expresses that the people are the source of the government's power.



ACTIVITY OPTIONS

**INTERDISCIPLINARY LINK: CURRENT EVENTS** BLOCK SCHEDULING

### WHAT DOES CONGRESS DO?

**Class Time** One class period

**Task** Categorizing congressional activities

**Purpose** To understand the variety of matters that come before Congress

**Supplies Needed**
- Newspapers and magazines
- File folders or shoe boxes
- Markers

**Activity** Label boxes or folders with various areas of congressional responsibility (elections, lawmaking, taxation, commerce, etc.) as outlined on pages 249–254. (Select the headings that pertain to current topics.) Be sure to include a file for the elastic clause. Have students collect news items about current activities in Congress. Tell them to decide which category of congressional responsibility each item falls within and file the article in the appropriate folder. Ask: What activities are hard to categorize? What activities take most of Congress's time?

## Article 1. *The Legislature*

**MAIN IDEA** **The main role of Congress, the legislative branch, is to make laws. Congress is made up of two houses—the Senate and the House of Representatives. Candidates for each house must meet certain requirements. Congress performs specific duties, also called delegated powers.**

**WHY IT MATTERS NOW** **Representatives in Congress still voice the views and concerns of the people.**

**Section 1. Congress** All legislative powers herein granted shall be vested in a Congress of the United States, which shall consist of a Senate and House of Representatives.

### Section 2. The House of Representatives

**1. Elections** The House of Representatives shall be composed of members chosen every second year by the people of the several states, and the **electors** in each state shall have the qualifications requisite for electors of the most numerous branch of the state legislature.

**2. Qualifications** No person shall be a Representative who shall not have attained to the age of twenty-five years, and been seven years a citizen of the United States, and who shall not, when elected, be an inhabitant of that state in which he shall be chosen.

**3. Number of Representatives** Representatives ~~and direct taxes~~ shall be apportioned among the several states which may be included within this Union, according to their respective numbers, ~~which shall be determined by adding to the whole number of free persons, including those bound to service for a term of years, and excluding Indians not taxed, three-fifths of all other Persons.~~ The actual **enumeration** shall be made within three years after the first meeting of the Congress of the United States, and within every subsequent term of ten years, in such manner as they shall by law direct. The number of Representatives shall not exceed one for every thirty thousand, but each state shall have at least one Representative; ~~and until such enumeration shall be made, the state of New Hampshire shall be entitled to choose three, Massachusetts eight, Rhode Island and Providence Plantations one, Connecticut five, New York six, New Jersey four, Pennsylvania eight, Delaware one, Maryland six, Virginia ten, North Carolina five, South Carolina five, and Georgia three.~~

**4. Vacancies** When vacancies happen in the representation from any state, the executive authority thereof shall issue writs of election to fill such vacancies.

**5. Officers and Impeachment** The House of Representatives shall choose their Speaker and other officers; and shall have the sole power of **impeachment.**

***VOCABULARY***

**electors** voters

**enumeration** an official count, such as a census

**impeachment** the process of accusing a public official of wrongdoing

***A CLOSER LOOK***

**ELECTIONS**

**Representatives are elected every two years. There are no limits on the number of terms a person can serve.**

**1. What do you think are the advantages of holding frequent elections of representatives?**

***A CLOSER LOOK***

**REPRESENTATION**

**The 435 members of the House are divided according to state population as determined by a census every ten years.**

**2. How many representatives does your state have?**



## INSTRUCT

**Article 1: The Legislature**
Key Questions

- Why do you think the Framers were careful to give different duties to the House and to the Senate?
- Why do you think the Framers required revenue bills to start in the House of Representatives?
- What powers does the Constitution deny to Congress? to the states?

**In-Depth Resources: Unit 2**
- Guided Reading, p. 62

**Reading Study Guide** (Spanish and English), pp. 83–84

**Access for Students Acquiring English/ESL**
- Guided Reading, p. 56

**Citizenship Today**
- Simulation 1: Senate Debate of a Bill, pp. 19–28

### CRITICAL THINKING ACTIVITY

**Comparing** If your school has an active student government, you may want to discuss how the form of student government is indirectly influenced by the Constitution. Examples could include such things as qualifications for representatives, majority rule, and regular elections. Ask students to list the kinds of decisions that their student government makes. What powers does it have? What are the limits on its powers? How does it interact with other groups within the school, such as clubs, faculty, and administration?

**Class Time** 10 minutes

### *A CLOSER LOOK*

1. Frequent elections keep representatives more accountable to voters; they make it easier to vote ineffective representatives out of office.
2. Have students find their state on the electoral college map on page 256. To figure out the number of representatives, have them subtract two (the number of senators) from the number of electoral votes.

## MORE ABOUT . . .

**From Senator to Vice-President**

The Senate has long been a steppingstone to the vice-presidency. Since World War II, eight senators have served as vice-presidents—Harry Truman, Alben Barkley, Richard Nixon, Lyndon Johnson, Hubert Humphrey, Walter Mondale, Dan Quayle, and Al Gore. Several of these men went on to become president. Although the vice-president is only a heartbeat from the presidency, most of these men agreed that they had more real power as senators than as vice-presidents.

*VOCABULARY*

**pro tempore** for the time being

**indictment** a written statement issued by a grand jury charging a person with a crime

**quorum** the minimum number of members that must be present for official business to take place

## Section 3. The Senate

**1. Numbers** The Senate of the United States shall be composed of two Senators from each state, ~~chosen by the legislature thereof~~, for six years; and each Senator shall have one vote.

**2. Classifying Terms** Immediately after they shall be assembled in consequence of the first election, they shall be divided as equally as may be into three classes. The seats of the Senators of the first class shall be vacated at the expiration of the second year, of the second class at the expiration of the fourth year, and of the third class at the expiration of the sixth year, so that one-third may be chosen every second year; ~~and if vacancies happen by resignation, or otherwise, during the recess of the legislature of any state, the executive thereof may make temporary appointments until the next meeting of the legislature, which shall then fill such vacancies.~~

**3. Qualifications** No person shall be a Senator who shall not have attained to the age of thirty years, and been nine years a citizen of the United States, and who shall not, when elected, be an inhabitant of that state for which he shall be chosen.

SKILLBUILDER Possible Responses
6-year terms give senators more time and political power to carry out legislative programs and make Congress more stable than the House. Higher qualifications allow for older, more experienced people to serve in the Senate.

*A CLOSER LOOK* **Federal Office Terms and Requirements**

| POSITION | TERM | MINIMUM AGE | RESIDENCY | CITIZENSHIP |
|---|---|---|---|---|
| Representative | 2 years | 25 | state in which elected | 7 years |
| Senator | 6 years | 30 | state in which elected | 9 years |
| President | 4 years | 35 | 14 years in the U.S. | natural-born |
| Supreme Court Justice | unlimited | none | none | none |

SKILLBUILDER **Interpreting Charts**
*Why do you think the term and qualifications for a senator are more demanding than for a representative?*

**4. Role of Vice-President** The Vice-President of the United States shall be President of the Senate, but shall have no vote, unless they be equally divided.

**5. Officers** The Senate shall choose their other officers, and also a President **pro tempore**, in the absence of the Vice-President, or when he shall exercise the office of President of the United States.

**6. Impeachment Trials** The Senate shall have the sole power to try all impeachments. When sitting for that purpose, they shall be on oath or affirmation. When the President of the United States is tried, the Chief Justice shall preside: and no person shall be convicted without the concurrence of two-thirds of the members present.

**7. Punishment for Impeachment** Judgment in cases of impeachment shall not extend further than to removal from office, and disqualification to hold and enjoy any office of honor, trust or profit under the United States; but the party convicted shall nevertheless be liable and subject to **indictment**, trial, judgment and punishment, according to law.

*A CLOSER LOOK*

**IMPEACHMENT**

**The House brings charges against the president. The Senate acts as the jury. The Chief Justice of the Supreme Court presides over the hearings.**

**3. How many presidents have been impeached?**

## MORE ABOUT . . .

**Impeachment**

Impeachment is a formal accusation of wrongdoing by a public official. It is a legal process that can be used not only against the president of the United States but also against other officials such as federal judges or cabinet officers. To date, 16 federal officials have been impeached by the House of Representatives, of whom seven have then been convicted by the Senate. All of those convicted were federal judges. Two presidents, Andrew Johnson and Bill Clinton, were impeached, but neither was convicted.



## TEACHING STRATEGY

**Vocabulary Activities** To help students understand the vocabulary words on this page, have them read the words and pronounce them correctly.

Next, discuss the definitions. For the word *indictment,* be sure to explain that a grand jury is not the same as a trial jury. The purpose of a grand jury is to seek information and decide if a crime has been committed. If it concludes that there has been a crime and that there is reason to suspect a particular person, the grand jury can issue an indictment against that person.

Explain to the students that, generally speaking, a *quorum* consists of half the total number of the group, plus one. Thus the Senate, which has 100 members, has a quorum when 51 senators are present.

Finally, have the students find the vocabulary words in the document and read them in context.

## Section 4. Congressional Elections

**1. Regulations** The times, places and manner of holding elections for Senators and Representatives shall be prescribed in each state by the legislature thereof; but the Congress may at any time by law make or alter such regulations, except as to the places of choosing Senators.

**2. Sessions** The Congress shall assemble at least once in every year, ~~and such meeting shall be on the first Monday in December, unless they shall by law appoint a different day.~~

## Section 5. Rules and Procedures

**1. Quorum** Each house shall be the judge of the elections, returns and qualifications of its own members, and a majority of each shall constitute a **quorum** to do business; but a smaller number may adjourn from day to day, and may be authorized to compel the attendance of absent members, in such manner, and under such penalties as each house may provide.

**2. Rules and Conduct** Each house may determine the rules of its proceedings, punish its members for disorderly behavior, and, with the concurrence of two-thirds, expel a member.

**3. Congressional Records** Each house shall keep a journal of its proceedings, and from time to time publish the same, excepting such parts as may in their judgment require secrecy; and the yeas and nays of the members of either house on any question shall, at the desire of one-fifth of those present, be entered on the journal.

**4. Adjournment** Neither house, during the session of Congress, shall, without the consent of the other, adjourn for more than three days, nor to any other place than that in which the two houses shall be sitting.

## Section 6. Payment and Privileges

**1. Salary** The Senators and Representatives shall receive a compensation for their services, to be ascertained by law, and paid out of the treasury of the United States. They shall in all cases, except treason, felony and breach of the peace, be privileged from arrest during their attendance at the session of their respective houses, and in going to and returning from the same; and for any speech or debate in either house, they shall not be questioned in any other place.

**2. Restrictions** No Senator or Representative shall, during the time for which he was elected, be appointed to any civil office under the authority of the United States, which shall have been created, or the emoluments whereof shall have been increased during such time; and no person holding any office under the United States, shall be a member of either house during his continuance in office.

### *A CLOSER LOOK*

**SENATE RULES**

**Senate rules allow for debate on the floor. Using a tactic called filibustering, senators give long speeches to block the passage of a bill. Senator Strom Thurmond holds the filibustering record—24 hours, 18 minutes.**

**4. Why might a senator choose filibustering as a tactic to block a bill?**

### *A CLOSER LOOK*

**SALARIES**

**Senators and representatives are paid $136,700 a year. The Speaker of the House is paid $175,400—the same as the vice-president.**

**5. How do the salaries of members of Congress compare to those of adults you know?**



### MORE ABOUT . . .

**Congressional Meetings**

One of the complaints that the colonists voiced against King George III in the Declaration of Independence was that he refused to allow colonial legislatures to meet regularly. The Framers wanted to ensure that the Congress met on a regular basis, so they specified in Section 4 that meetings were to be held every year. The 20th Amendment changed the meeting day for Congress from the beginning of December to January 3.

### MORE ABOUT . . .

**Congressional Salaries**

In 1790, senators and representatives earned six dollars a day. By 1950, they earned a little over $10,000 per year. By 1978, their salaries had risen to about $60,000 per year. In the late 1990s, the salary reached almost $137,000. In the same period, by comparison, salaries and compensation for business leaders rose even more rapidly; hourly wages rose much less sharply.

### *A CLOSER LOOK*

**3.** two presidents—Andrew Johnson and Bill Clinton

**4.** to prevent a vote on a bill that the majority supports but the filibustering senator strongly opposes

**5.** Some students may say that congressional members earn much more than teachers but considerably less than sports superstars. For additional comparisons, suggest that students find the salaries for various occupations published by the U.S. Department of Labor.

## MORE ABOUT . . .

**Presidential Veto**

Often Congress passes a flurry of bills toward the end of a session. The president faces the task of signing or vetoing many bills. One way to block a bill is called a "pocket veto." A pocket veto occurs when the president does not act on a bill within ten days and Congress adjourns during that time. The bill then "dies" even though it has passed both houses. To revive the bill, the House and the Senate must pass it again when Congress reconvenes.

## MORE ABOUT . . .

**Overriding a Veto**

When the president vetoes a bill, Congress has three choices. One is to give up on the bill and let the veto stand. The second is to make changes in the bill so that it is more acceptable to the president and send it back. The third is to try to override the veto. Historically, Congress has found it hard to round up enough votes for an override. Of the 1,470 bills that were vetoed up to mid-1998, Congress succeeded in overriding only 105. But the percentage of successful overrides has risen sharply in recent years, from about 6 percent before 1969 to about 18 percent since then.

*VOCABULARY*

**revenue** income a government collects to cover expenses

**naturalization** a way to give full citizenship to a person of foreign birth

**tribunals** courts

**felonies** serious crimes

**appropriation** public funds set aside for a specific purpose

## Section 7. How a Bill Becomes a Law

**1. Tax Bills** All bills for raising **revenue** shall originate in the House of Representatives; but the Senate may propose or concur with amendments as on other Bills.

**2. Lawmaking Process** Every bill which shall have passed the House of Representatives and the Senate, shall, before it become a law, be presented to the President of the United States; if he approves he shall sign it, but if not he shall return it, with his objections to that house in which it shall have originated, who shall enter the objections at large on their journal, and proceed to reconsider it. If after such reconsideration two-thirds of that house shall agree to pass the bill, it shall be sent, together with the objections, to the other house, by which it shall likewise be reconsidered, and if approved by two-thirds of that house, it shall become a law. But in all such cases the votes of both houses shall be determined by yeas and nays, and the names of the persons voting for and against the bill shall be entered on the journal of each house respectively. If any bill shall not be returned by the President within ten days (Sundays excepted) after it shall have been presented to him, the same shall be a law, in like manner as if he had signed it, unless the Congress by their adjournment prevent its return, in which case it shall not be a law.

**3. Role of the President** Every order, resolution, or vote to which the concurrence of the Senate and House of Representatives may be necessary (except on a question of adjournment) shall be presented to the President of the United States; and before the same shall take effect, shall be approved by him, or being disapproved by him, shall be repassed by two-thirds of the Senate and House of Representatives, according to the rules and limitations prescribed in the case of a bill.

SKILLBUILDER Possible Responses
1. By vetoing the bill.
2. President can check Congress's lawmaking power by vetoing a bill; Congress can check president's power by overriding the veto with a two-thirds majority vote. The bill then becomes a law without the president's signature.

### *A CLOSER LOOK* How a Bill Becomes a Law

Introduction
Committee Action
Floor Action
The House introduces a bill and refers it to a committee.
The House committee may approve, rewrite, or kill the bill.
The House debates and votes on its version of the bill.
House and Senate committee members work out the differences between the two versions.
1
2
3
4
The Senate introduces a bill and refers it to a committee.
The Senate committee may approve, rewrite, or kill the bill.
The Senate debates and votes on its version of the bill.

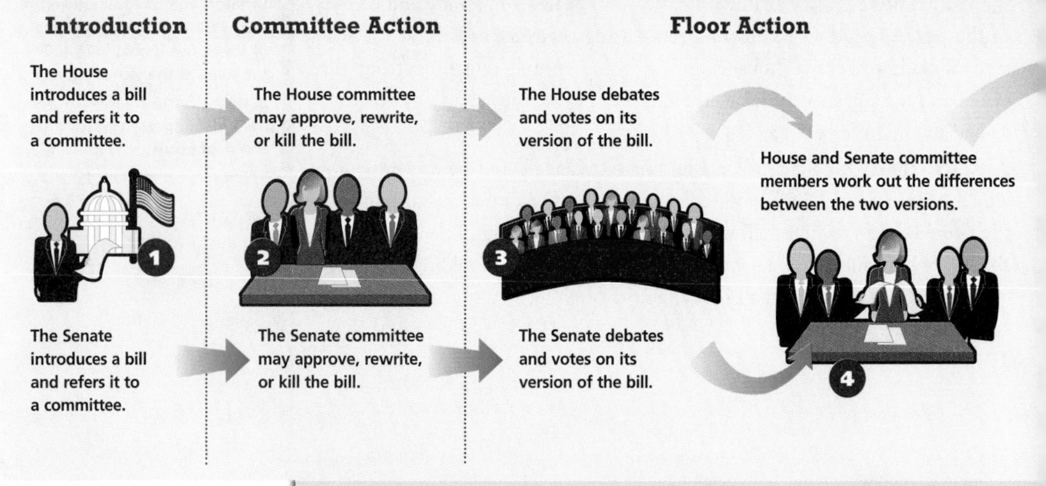

**ACTIVITY OPTIONS**

**MULTIPLE LEARNING STYLES: BODILY-KINESTHETIC** — BLOCK SCHEDULING

**CREATING A PLAY**

**Class Time** One class period

**Task** Creating a dramatic presentation on lawmaking

**Purpose** To illustrate an understanding of the process by which a bill becomes a law

**Supplies Needed**
- Art supplies
- Costumes (optional)

**Activity** Divide the students into groups. The groups should carefully study the diagram on pages 252–253. Then each group should create a presentation to show an audience of younger students how a bill becomes a law. The group will need to assign the tasks of actor, illustrator, narrator, and scriptwriter. After developing a script, the groups should gather props and rehearse their presentations. Finally, let them present the dramas to a class of younger students.

## Section 8. Powers Granted to Congress

**1. Taxation** The Congress shall have power to lay and collect taxes, duties, imposts and excises, to pay the debts and provide for the common defense and general welfare of the United States; but all duties, imposts and excises shall be uniform throughout the United States;

**2. Credit** To borrow money on the credit of the United States;

**3. Commerce** To regulate commerce with foreign nations, and among the several states, and with the Indian tribes;

**4. Naturalization, Bankruptcy** To establish a uniform rule of **naturalization,** and uniform laws on the subject of bankruptcies throughout the United States;

**5. Money** To coin money, regulate the value thereof, and of foreign coin, and fix the standard of weights and measures;

**6. Counterfeiting** To provide for the punishment of counterfeiting the securities and current coin of the United States;

**7. Post Office** To establish post offices and post roads;

**8. Patents, Copyrights** To promote the progress of science and useful arts, by securing for limited times to authors and inventors the exclusive right to their respective writings and discoveries;

**9. Federal Courts** To constitute **tribunals** inferior to the Supreme Court;

**10. International Law** To define and punish piracies and **felonies** committed on the high seas, and offenses against the law of nations;

**11. War** To declare war, grant letters of marque and reprisal, and make rules concerning captures on land and water;

**12. Army** To raise and support armies, but no **appropriation** of money to that use shall be for a longer term than two years;

**13. Navy** To provide and maintain a navy;

***A CLOSER LOOK***

**REGULATING COMMERCE**

Commerce can also apply to travelers crossing state lines. Congress's power to regulate the movement of people from state to state paved the way for the Civil Rights Act of 1964. This act included fair treatment of interstate travelers. People of all races can use public places, such as hotels and bus stations.

**6. To what other areas might the commerce clause apply?**

***A CLOSER LOOK***

**DECLARING WAR**

Only Congress can declare war. Yet in the following "undeclared" wars, Congress bowed to the president's power to take military action and send troops overseas: Korean War (1950–1953), Vietnam War (1957–1975), Persian Gulf War (1991), and Kosovo crisis (1999).

**7. Why do you think the Constitution sets limits on the president's war-making powers?**

Final Approval
Enactment
Both houses of Congress pass the revised bill.
5
President signs the bill.
OR
President vetoes the bill.
6
7
Two-thirds majority vote of Congress is needed to approve a vetoed bill.
Bill Becomes Law.
8
LAW

SKILLBUILDER **Interpreting Charts**

1. *How can a president block a bill?*
2. *What examples of checks and balances are shown in the chart?*

### MORE ABOUT . . .

**Market Economy and the Constitution**

The Framers of the Constitution included many provisions to support and encourage a market economy. In addition to the commerce clause, Section 8 includes clauses on taxation, bankruptcy, money, and patents and copyrights, as well as the elastic clause. Other parts of the Constitution that support a market economy include Article 1, Sections 9 and 10, and Amendments 4, 5, 9, 10, and 14. Of course, the major purpose of the Constitution is political stability, which is an important precondition for economic growth.

### MORE ABOUT . . .

**Sacagawea—The New Dollar Coin**

In the year 2000, a new coin honoring a Native American woman, Sacagawea, replaced the Susan B. Anthony dollar coin. The design was described as "Liberty . . . inspired by Sacagawea."

Sacagawea was a young Shoshone woman who traveled with the Lewis and Clark expedition and is credited with saving Captain Clark's journals when a boat capsized. She also acted as translator for the expedition and saved the expedition from hostile Native Americans.

The new coin is an alloy of manganese, brass, and copper. It will glitter like a gold coin.

### *A CLOSER LOOK*

6. Commerce can apply to all things that cross state lines, such as goods, modes of transportation (buses, trains, and airplanes), and communications (radio, TV, and the Internet).
7. to provide a check on the president's military power; to prevent the president from becoming a military dictator

***VOCABULARY***

**militia** an emergency military force, such as the National Guard, that is not part of the regular army

**bill of attainder** a law that condemns a person without a trial in court

**ex post facto law** a law that would make an act a criminal offense after it was committed

**tender** money

**14. Regulation of Armed Forces** To make rules for the government and regulation of the land and naval forces;

**15. Militia** To provide for calling forth the **militia** to execute the laws of the Union, suppress insurrections and repel invasions;

**16. Regulations for Militia** To provide for organizing, arming, and disciplining the militia, and for governing such part of them as may be employed in the service of the United States, reserving to the states respectively the appointment of the officers, and the authority of training the militia according to the discipline prescribed by Congress;

**17. District of Columbia** To exercise exclusive legislation in all cases whatsoever, over such district (not exceeding ten miles square) as may, by cession of particular states, and the acceptance of Congress, become the seat of the government of the United States, and to exercise like authority over all places purchased by the consent of the legislature of the state in which the same shall be, for the erection of forts, magazines, arsenals, dockyards, and other needful buildings;—and

**18. Elastic Clause** To make all laws which shall be necessary and proper for carrying into execution the foregoing powers, and all other powers vested by this Constitution in the government of the United States, or in any department or officer thereof.

**MORE ABOUT . . .**

**The Elastic Clause**

Also known as the "necessary and proper" clause, the elastic clause has proven to be one of the most farsighted measures in the Constitution. Broadly interpreted, that clause gave Congress authority to do much more than the simple list of duties in clauses 1–17 of Section 8. And, in the 1819 Court case *McCulloch* v. *Maryland,* Chief Justice John Marshall supported the broad interpretation. (See (Chapter 11, Section 3.) Marshall ruled that Congress could use "all means which are appropriate, . . . which are not prohibited" to fulfill legitimate ends.

**Citizenship Today**

- *McCulloch* v. *Maryland,* p. 87

***A CLOSER LOOK* The Elastic Clause**

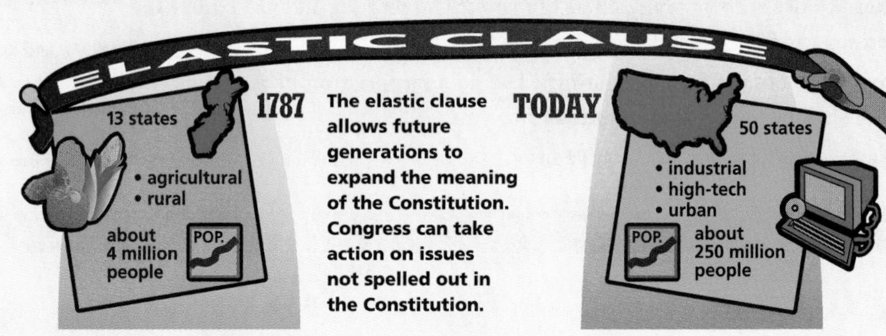


## Section 9. Powers Denied Congress

~~**1. Slave Trade** The migration or importation of such persons as any of the states now existing shall think proper to admit, shall not be prohibited by the Congress prior to the year one thousand eight hundred and eight, but a tax or duty may be imposed on such importation, not exceeding ten dollars for each person.~~

**2. Habeas Corpus** The privilege of the writ of habeas corpus shall not be suspended, unless when in cases of rebellion or invasion the public safety may require it.

***A CLOSER LOOK***

**HABEAS CORPUS**

**A writ of habeas corpus is a legal order. It protects people from being held in prison or jail without formal charges of a crime. In 1992, the Supreme Court recognized that "habeas corpus is the [basic] instrument for safeguarding individual freedom."**

**8. How does habeas corpus help ensure fairness and justice?**

**MORE ABOUT . . .**

**Habeas Corpus**

*Habeas corpus* is a Latin phrase meaning, "You have the body [of the prisoner in question]." The writ orders a sheriff or other official to present the prisoner before a judge to be charged with a specific crime or to be released. Habeas corpus has been considered part of the bedrock of English liberty since Parliament passed the law in 1679.



***A CLOSER LOOK***

**8.** People cannot be held in jail indefinitely without a trial. People who are arrested can demand to be charged with a specific crime or else set free.

**9.** People are concerned about the amount of taxes and the way government uses tax money. People often object to taxes on personal income that reduce their spending money, but they also expect government to provide the services (enumerated in the Preamble) that taxes support.

**10.** Senator (and the person's last name); Congressman or Congresswoman (and the person's last name); Mr. President (or Madame President if a woman is elected)

**3. Illegal Punishment** No **bill of attainder** or **ex post facto law** shall be passed.

**4. Direct Taxes** No capitation, ~~or other direct,~~ tax shall be laid, ~~unless in proportion to the census or enumeration herein before directed to be taken.~~

**5. Export Taxes** No tax or duty shall be laid on articles exported from any state.

**6. No Favorites** No preference shall be given by any regulation of commerce or revenue to the ports of one state over those of another: nor shall vessels bound to, or from, one state be obliged to enter, clear, or pay duties in another.

**7. Public Money** No money shall be drawn from the treasury, but in consequence of appropriations made by law; and a regular statement and account of the receipts and expenditures of all public money shall be published from time to time.

**8. Titles of Nobility** No title of nobility shall be granted by the United States: and no person holding any office of profit or trust under them shall, without the consent of the Congress, accept of any present, emolument, office, or title, of any kind whatever, from any king, prince, or foreign state.

### Section 10. Powers Denied the States

**1. Restrictions** No state shall enter into any treaty, alliance, or confederation; grant letters of marque and reprisal; coin money; emit bills of credit; make anything but gold and silver coin a **tender** in payment of debts; pass any bill of attainder, ex post facto law, or law impairing the obligation of contracts, or grant any title of nobility.

**2. Import and Export Taxes** No state shall, without the consent of the Congress, lay any imposts or duties on imports or exports, except what may be absolutely necessary for executing its inspection laws; and the net produce of all duties and imposts, laid by any state on imports or exports, shall be for the use of the treasury of the United States; and all such laws shall be subject to the revision and control of the Congress.

**3. Peacetime and War Restraints** No state shall, without the consent of Congress, lay any duty of tonnage, keep troops or ships of war in time of peace, enter into any agreement or compact with another state, or with a foreign power, or engage in war, unless actually invaded, or in such imminent danger as will not admit of delay.

*A CLOSER LOOK*

**DIRECT TAX**

In 1913, the 16th Amendment allowed Congress to collect an income tax—a direct tax on the amount of money a person earns. Americans today pay much more in taxes than their ancestors would have imagined.

**9. Why do you think the issue of taxes is so important to people?**

*A CLOSER LOOK*

**TITLES OF NOBILITY**

The Framers disapproved of titles of nobility. The Declaration of Independence, signed in 1776, listed King George III's abuses of power. One symbol of this abuse was English titles of nobility, such as "king," "queen," and "duke." The Framers said clearly that there would be no such titles in the new republic.

**10. How do TV news reporters address members of Congress and the president?**

*Article 1 Assessment*

**1. Main Ideas**

a. What is the main job of the legislative branch?

b. What role does the vice-president of the United States play in the Senate?

c. Why are there more members in the House of Representatives than the Senate?

d. What is one of the powers denied to Congress?

**2. Critical Thinking**

**Drawing Conclusions** How does Article 1 show that the Constitution is a clearly defined yet flexible document?

**THINK ABOUT**

- the powers of Congress
- the "elastic clause"



## MORE ABOUT . . .

**Bill of Attainder**

The individual rights protected by the bill of attainder clause are among the few cited in the Constitution before the Bill of Rights (Amendments 1–10). The question of attainder has cropped up in some unlikely places. The issue was first tested in court after the Civil War. Southerners who wanted to practice law were required to take an oath that they had not participated in the Confederate rebellion. But the courts struck down that requirement as being a bill of attainder; the would-be lawyers were being deprived of their livelihood without having been convicted of any crime. In 1965, on the same basis, the Supreme Court struck down a law barring a member of the Communist Party from holding office in a labor union.

### CRITICAL THINKING ACTIVITY

**Identifying Problems** Have students study Section 10. Ask them to think about the kinds of problems that would occur if states had the powers listed as "Powers Denied the States."

**Class Time** 15 minutes

**Formal Assessment**

- Section Quiz, p. 130

## *Assessment: Article 1*

**1. Main Ideas**

a. to make laws **b.** acts as president of the Senate **c.** The Framers intended the Senate to be a more select group—older, fewer, serving longer, and presumably wiser. **d.** Under Section 9, Congress cannot suspend habeas corpus, pass bills of attainder and ex post facto laws, favor one state over another, tax any state's exports to another, take public money without appropriation, or grant titles of nobility.

**2. Critical Thinking**

**Possible Responses** It is clearly defined in that it specifically explains the organization and procedures of the House and Senate and spells out Congress's powers. It is flexible in its broad application of the commerce clause and especially in the elastic clause.

**OBJECTIVE**

Students will be able to identify the duties and powers of the executive branch of the United States government.

## INSTRUCT

**Article 2: The Executive**

Key Questions

- What colonial experiences might have influenced the Framers' ideas of duties for the executive branch?
- How is enforcing the laws different from making the laws?
- Who will help the chief executive enforce the laws?

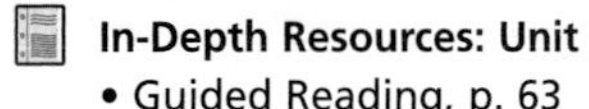

**In-Depth Resources: Unit 2**
- Guided Reading, p. 63

**Reading Study Guide** (Spanish and English), pp. 85–86

**Access for Students Acquiring English/ESL**
- Guided Reading, p. 57

### MORE ABOUT . . .

**The Electoral College**

The Framers set up the electoral college as a way to get informed votes on the presidency. The Framers assumed that state electors would know which candidate could best serve the people of their state.

By the 20th century, many people had come to believe that the electoral system was outdated and unfair. The principle of "winner takes all" means that a candidate gets 100 percent of a state's electoral votes, even if he or she gets only 50.1 percent of the popular vote. It is quite possible for a person to win the popular vote and lose the presidential election. In fact, that happened in 1824, 1876, and 1888. However, the electoral college has the advantage of being a known process and also of providing a quick, definitive result.

*VOCABULARY*

**natural-born citizen** a citizen born in the United States or a U.S. commonwealth, or to parents who are U.S. citizens living outside the country

**affirmation** a statement declaring that something is true

## Article 2. *The Executive*

**MAIN IDEA The president and vice-president are the leaders of the executive branch. Their main role is to enforce the laws. The president commands the military and makes foreign treaties with the Senate's approval.**

**WHY IT MATTERS NOW As the United States has become a world power, the authority of the president has also expanded.**

### Section 1. The Presidency

**1. Terms of Office** The executive power shall be vested in a President of the United States of America. He shall hold his office during the term of four years, and, together with the Vice-President, chosen for the same term, be elected, as follows:

**2. Electoral College** Each state shall appoint, in such manner as the Legislature thereof may direct, a number of electors, equal to the whole number of Senators and Representatives to which the State may be entitled in the Congress; but no Senator or Representative, or person holding an office of trust or profit under the United States, shall be appointed an elector.

***A CLOSER LOOK* Electoral College** *(1990 Census)*

American voters do not choose their president directly. Members of a group called the electoral college actually elect the president. Each state has electors. Together they form the electoral college. In most states, the winner takes all. Except for Maine and Nebraska, all the electoral votes of a state go to one set of candidates.

**number of electors for each state = total number of its senators and representatives**

WA 11, OR 7, CA 54, ID 4, NV 4, MT 3, WY 3, UT 5, AZ 8, CO 8, NM 5, ND 3, SD 3, NE 5, KS 6, OK 8, TX 32, MN 10, IA 7, MO 11, AR 6, LA 9, WI 11, IL 22, MS 7, MI 18, IN 12, KY 8, TN 11, AL 9, OH 21, GA 13, FL 25, SC 8, NC 14, VA 13, WV 5, PA 23, NY 33, VT 3, NH 4, ME 4, MA 12, RI 4, CT 8, NJ 15, DE 3, DC 3, MD 10, HI 4, AK 3

**SKILLBUILDER Interpreting Maps**

1. *How many electoral votes does your state have?*
2. *In which states would a presidential candidate campaign most heavily? Why?*

SKILLBUILDER Possible Responses

1. Students should locate their state on the map and identify the correct number of electoral votes.
2. California, New York, Texas, Florida Pennsylvania, Illinois, and Ohio—states in the West, East, South, and Midwest with the most electoral votes.

~~**3. Former Method of Electing President** The electors shall meet in their respective states, and vote by ballot for two persons, of whom one at least shall not be an inhabitant of the same state with themselves. And they shall make a list of all the persons voted for, and of the number of votes for each; which list they shall sign and certify, and transmit sealed to the seat of the government of the United States, directed to the President of the Senate. The President of the Senate shall, in the presence of the Senate and House of Representatives, open all the certificates, and the votes shall then be counted. The person having the greatest number of votes shall be the~~



**ACTIVITY OPTIONS**

**INTERDISCIPLINARY LINK: MATH**

BLOCK SCHEDULING

**THE ELECTORAL COLLEGE**

**Class Time** 30 minutes

**Task** Creating a table to illustrate the link between popular and electoral votes

**Purpose** To help students understand the problems with the electoral college

**Supplies Needed**
- Calculators or pencils and paper
- Voting figures, state by state, from a recent election
- Map with electoral votes (page 256)

**Activity** Ask students to calculate the number of electoral votes necessary to win the presidency. In pairs or small groups, have students compute the total popular vote and electoral vote for each candidate. Ask students to scan the list for states where the popular vote was close. How many votes would it have taken to change the result in those states? Would such a change have altered the outcome of the national election? Could a candidate have lost the popular vote but won the election?

~~President, if such number be a majority of the whole number of electors appointed; and if there be more than one who have such majority, and have an equal number of votes, then the House of Representatives shall immediately choose by ballot one of them for President; and if no person have a majority, then from the five highest on the list the said House shall in like manner choose the President. But in choosing the President, the votes shall be taken by States, the representation from each state having one vote; a quorum for this purpose shall consist of a member or members from two-thirds of the states, and a majority of all the states shall be necessary to a choice. In every case, after the choice of the President, the person having the greatest number of votes of the electors shall be the Vice-President. But if there should remain two or more who have equal votes, the Senate shall choose from them by ballot the Vice-President.~~

***A CLOSER LOOK***

**Vice-President Lyndon Johnson, next in line of succession, takes the oath of office after the assassination of President John F. Kennedy in 1963. Johnson, like every U.S. president, promises to uphold the Constitution. The 25th Amendment sets up clearer procedures for presidential succession.**

**4. Election Day** The Congress may determine the time of choosing the electors, and the day on which they shall give their votes, which day shall be the same throughout the United States.

**5. Qualifications** No person except a **natural-born citizen,** ~~or a citizen of the United States at the time of the adoption of this Constitution,~~ shall be eligible to the office of President; neither shall any person be eligible to that office who shall not have attained to the age of thirty-five years, and been fourteen years a resident within the United States.

**6. Succession** In case of the removal of the President from office, or of his death, resignation, or inability to discharge the powers and duties of the said office, the same shall devolve on the Vice-President, and the Congress may by law provide for the case of removal, death, resignation or inability, both of the President and Vice-President, declaring what officer shall then act as President, and such officer shall act accordingly, until the disability be removed, or a President shall be elected.

**7. Salary** The President shall, at stated times, receive for his services, a compensation, which shall neither be increased nor diminished during the period for which he shall have been elected, and he shall not receive within that period any other emolument from the United States, or any of them.

**8. Oath of Office** Before he enter on the execution of his office, he shall take the following oath or **affirmation:**—"I do solemnly swear (or affirm) that I will faithfully execute the office of President of the United States, and will to the best of my ability, preserve, protect and defend the Constitution of the United States."

***A CLOSER LOOK***

**PRESIDENT'S SALARY**

**The president's yearly salary is $200,000. The president also gets special allowances, such as $100,000 for travel expenses. Here are some other benefits:**

- **living in a mansion, the White House**
- **vacationing at Camp David, an estate in Maryland**
- **using *Air Force One*, a personal jet plane**

**11. Why do you think the president needs to have a plane and a vacation spot?**





## HISTORY FROM VISUALS

**Interpreting the Photograph** Ask the class to study the photograph of Lyndon Johnson taking the oath of office. Ask if they can figure out the location of the ceremony and suggest why it is taking place there. **Possible Response** The ceremony is taking place on an airplane (Air Force One), because it was necessary for the security of the country that the office of the presidency should be filled immediately.

**Extension** Have the students find out which other vice-presidents have come to power as a result of the assassination of a president.

## MORE ABOUT . . .

**Presidential Assassinations**

John F. Kennedy was the fourth U.S. president to be assassinated. Abraham Lincoln, James A. Garfield, and William McKinley also died at the hands of assassins. Five presidents survived assassination attempts—Theodore Roosevelt, Franklin Roosevelt, Harry Truman, Gerald Ford, and Ronald Reagan.

### *A CLOSER LOOK*

**11.** Plane—The president's job requires extensive travel, often on short notice.
Vacation spot—The president may need a restful place; Camp David is also used for meetings with foreign heads of state. Presidential security is also a factor in the need for these benefits.

## HISTORY FROM VISUALS

**Interpreting the Photographs** Ask the students to study the photographs of the various roles the president plays. Then ask them to read the sections of the Constitution on page 259 and find the section that pertains to each role. **Possible Responses** commander in chief—2.1; chief executive—2.1; chief diplomat and chief of state—2.2, 2.3; legislative leader—2.3, 3; head of political party, not mentioned

**Extension** Have the students read the newspaper and find articles about the president filling some of the roles shown on page 258. Cut out the articles and mount them on the bulletin board. Ask students to write a sentence for each article, describing the role the president is filling.

## MORE ABOUT . . .

**Power of the President**

Most scholars agree that the power of the presidency increased dramatically during the Civil War, when Abraham Lincoln took extraordinary measures during the crisis. However, the greatest expansion of presidential powers occurred during the presidency of Franklin D. Roosevelt. Confronted with both the Great Depression and World War II, Roosevelt took unprecedented steps to save the country. Many of these steps strengthened the executive branch of the government. Since World War II, the emergence of the United States as a world power also increased the power of the American president as a foreign-policy leader.

## *A CLOSER LOOK* Roles of the President

### Commander in Chief

As a military leader, President Abraham Lincoln meets with his generals during the Civil War.

### Chief Executive

Like a business executive, the president solves problems and makes key decisions. President John F. Kennedy is shown in the oval office in 1962.

### Chief Diplomat and Chief of State

As a foreign policy maker, President Richard M. Nixon visits the People's Republic of China in 1972.

### Legislative Leader

President Lyndon Johnson signs the Civil Rights Act of 1964. All modern presidents have legislative programs they want Congress to pass.

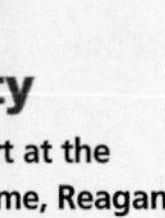

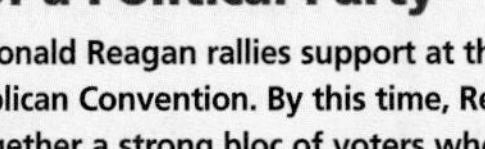

### Head of a Political Party

President Ronald Reagan rallies support at the 1984 Republican Convention. By this time, Reagan had put together a strong bloc of voters who supported the Republican Party's policies. During his presidency (1981–1989), Reagan helped build new unity among party members.



## *A CLOSER LOOK*

12. A candidate often shares the president's basic political views, values, and ideas. Usually the candidate is widely respected in the legal community, with previous judicial experience. The candidate must also be one who can win Senate confirmation.
13. To lead the nation, presidents need widespread support. Effective presidents skillfully use persuasion to "sell" their programs, policies, and decisions to a broad range of people.

## Section 2. Powers of the President

**1. Military Powers** The President shall be commander in chief of the Army and Navy of the United States, and of the militia of the several states, when called into the actual service of the United States; he may require the opinion, in writing, of the principal officer in each of the executive departments, upon any subject relating to the duties of their respective offices, and he shall have power to grant **reprieves** and pardons for offenses against the United States, except in cases of impeachment.

**2. Treaties, Appointments** He shall have power, by and with the advice and consent of the Senate, to make treaties, provided two-thirds of the Senators present concur; and he shall nominate, and by and with the advice and consent of the Senate, shall appoint ambassadors, other public ministers and consuls, judges of the Supreme Court, and all other officers of the United States, whose appointments are not herein otherwise provided for, and which shall be established by law; but the Congress may by law vest the appointment of such inferior officers, as they think proper, in the President alone, in the courts of law, or in the heads of departments.

**3. Vacancies** The President shall have power to fill up all vacancies that may happen during the recess of the Senate, by granting commissions which shall expire at the end of their next session.

**Section 3. Presidential Duties** He shall from time to time give to the Congress information of the State of the Union, and recommend to their consideration such measures as he shall judge necessary and expedient; he may, on extraordinary occasions, **convene** both houses, or either of them, and in case of disagreement between them, with respect to the time of adjournment, he may adjourn them to such time as he shall think proper; he shall receive ambassadors and other public ministers; he shall take care that the laws be faithfully executed, and shall commission all the officers of the United States.

**Section 4. Impeachment** The President, Vice-President and all civil officers of the United States shall be removed from office on impeachment for, and conviction of, treason, bribery, or other high crimes and **misdemeanors**.

*VOCABULARY*

**reprieves** delays or cancellations of punishment

**convene** call together

**misdemeanors** violations of the law

*A CLOSER LOOK*

**SUPREME COURT APPOINTMENTS**

Recent presidents have used their power of appointment to add minorities and women to the Supreme Court. In 1967, President Lyndon Johnson appointed the first African-American justice, Thurgood Marshall. In 1981, President Ronald Reagan appointed the first woman, Sandra Day O'Connor.

**12. What do you think influences a president's choice for a Supreme Court justice?**

*A CLOSER LOOK*

**STATE OF THE UNION**

Major TV networks broadcast the State of the Union address to the whole nation. In this yearly message, the president urges Congress to achieve certain lawmaking goals. The president's speech also must gain the attention of TV viewers.

**13. Why is the president's power to persuade an important political skill?**

### *Article 2 Assessment*

**1. Main Ideas**

a. What is the chief purpose of the executive branch?

b. What are the requirements for becoming president?

c. How does the Constitution limit the president's power to make appointments and treaties?

**2. Critical Thinking**

**Analyzing Issues** Why do you think the Constitution states that the president must seek approval from the Senate for most political appointments and treaties?

**THINK ABOUT**

- the abuse of power
- the will of the voters





## MORE ABOUT . . .

**Military Powers of the President**

The president is the commander in chief of the military, but the president cannot declare war—only Congress can. However, the president can order troops into action without congressional approval.

After Richard Nixon openly defied a request from Congress to be informed about troop deployment, Congress passed the War Powers Resolution. The resolution requires the president to report any combat involvement to the Congress and to end it within 60 or 90 days unless Congress approves a longer time period. Several presidents in the late 20th century have ignored the resolution.

## MORE ABOUT . . .

**The President's Cabinet**

The Constitution does not specifically call for a cabinet of presidential advisers. But it does mention executive departments. The heads of the executive departments become part of the president's advisory board—the cabinet.

George Washington's cabinet consisted of four members—Secretaries of State, Treasury, and War, and the Attorney General. Today's cabinet has the heads of 14 departments. The president may also give cabinet rank to other high-ranking officials whose advice on issues would be valuable.

**Citizenship Today**

• Organization of the Executive Branch, p. 50

**Formal Assessment**

• Section Quiz, p. 131

### *Assessment: Article 2*

**1. Main Ideas**

**a.** to enforce laws **b.** being a natural-born citizen, at least 35 years old, who has been a resident of the United States for 14 years or more

**c.** Many presidential appointments and all treaties with foreign powers require the Senate's approval.

**2. Critical Thinking**

**Possible Responses** This requirement is one of the checks and balances within the Constitution. It limits the power of the president in making foreign policy and appointing important government officials.

## OBJECTIVE

Students will be able to explain the organization and duties of the federal courts.

## INSTRUCT

### Article 3: The Judiciary

Key Questions

- How is interpreting the laws different from enforcing the laws?
- How do the courts shape government policies?
- How do the courts interact with the other branches of government?

**Citizenship Today**

- Simulation 3: Mock Trial, pp. 30–41

## MORE ABOUT . . .

### Federal Courts

The Constitution actually creates only one court—the Supreme Court. It gives Congress the ability to set up "inferior" courts. Today the federal court system consists of three tiers.

At the lowest level are 94 U.S. District Courts. These are the courts where federal trials take place. The second level in the court system includes 12 U.S. Courts of Appeal. These courts hear cases "on appeal." At the third level is the highest court of appeal, the Supreme Court.

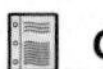

**Citizenship Today**

- Organization of the Judicial Branch, pp. 54–57

## MORE ABOUT . . .

### Judicial Review

The Constitution does not spell out the power of judicial review. This power emerged primarily from a case called *Marbury* v. *Madison.* That was the first case in which the Supreme Court ruled that an act of Congress was unconstitutional. Chief Justice John Marshall wrote, "It is emphatically the province and duty of the judicial department to say what the law is."

**Citizenship Today**

- *Marbury* v. *Madison,* p. 83

---

**VOCABULARY**

**inferior courts** courts with less authority than the Supreme Court

**appellate** having power to review court decisions

**A CLOSER LOOK**

**ORGANIZING FEDERAL COURTS**

**The Judiciary Act of 1789, passed by the First Congress, included establishing a Supreme Court with a chief justice and five associate justices and other lower federal courts.**

**14. How many Supreme Court justices are there today?**

**A CLOSER LOOK**

**JUDICIAL POWER**

**Judicial power gives the Supreme Court and other federal courts the authority to hear certain kinds of cases. These courts have the power to rule in cases involving the Constitution, national laws, treaties, and states' conflicts.**

**15. What federal cases have you seen reported on TV?**

# Article 3. *The Judiciary*

**MAIN IDEA** **The judicial branch interprets the laws. This branch includes the Supreme Court, the highest court in the nation, and other federal courts.**

**WHY IT MATTERS NOW** **Supreme Court rulings can shape government policies on hotly debated issues.**

**Section 1. Federal Courts and Judges** The judicial power of the United States shall be vested in one Supreme Court, and in such **inferior courts** as the Congress may from time to time ordain and establish. The judges, both of the Supreme and inferior courts, shall hold their offices during good behavior, and shall, at stated times, receive for their services a compensation, which shall not be diminished during their continuance in office.

## Section 2. The Courts' Authority

**1. General Authority** The judicial power shall extend to all cases, in law and equity, arising under this Constitution, the laws of the United States, and treaties made, or which shall be made, under their authority;—to all cases affecting ambassadors, other public ministers and consuls;—to all cases of admiralty and maritime jurisdiction;—to controversies to which the United States shall be a party;—to controversies between two or more states;—~~between a state and citizens of another state;~~—between citizens of different states;—between citizens of the same state claiming lands under grants of different states, ~~and between a state, or the citizens thereof, and foreign states, citizens or subjects.~~

**A CLOSER LOOK Judicial Review**

**Judicial review allows the Supreme Court and other federal courts to play a key role in lawmaking. The judges examine a law or government activity. They then decide whether it violates the Constitution. The Supreme Court established this important right in the case of *Marbury* v. *Madison* (1803). (See Chapter 10.)**

**2. Supreme Court** In all cases affecting ambassadors, other public ministers and consuls, and those in which a state shall be party, the Supreme Court shall have original jurisdiction. In all the other cases before mentioned, the Supreme Court shall have **appellate** jurisdiction, both as to law and fact, with such exceptions, and under such regulations, as the Congress shall make.



---

## A CLOSER LOOK

**14.** nine

**15.** Examples of federal cases include those involving states' rights; acts of terrorism within the United States; protection of constitutional rights, such as freedom of speech and religion; and protection of civil liberties. Be sure students understand that ordinary criminal cases—even those involving major crimes such as murder—fall under the jurisdiction of state courts.

## A CLOSER LOOK Checks and Balances

CHECKS ON COURTS
• Appoints federal judges
• Can grant reprieves and pardons for federal crimes
Executive Branch
(President)
CHECKS ON CONGRESS
• Can veto acts of Congress
• Can call special sessions of Congress
• Can suggest laws and send messages to Congress
CHECKS ON PRESIDENT
• Can impeach and remove the president
• Can override veto
• Controls spending of money
• Senate can refuse to confirm presidential appointments and to ratify treaties
Legislative Branch
(Congress)
CHECKS ON COURT
• Can impeach and remove federal judges
• Establishes lower federal courts
• Can refuse to confirm judicial appointments
CHECKS ON PRESIDENT
• Can declare executive acts unconstitutional
• Judges, appointed for life, are free from executive control
Judicial Branch
(Supreme Court)
CHECKS ON CONGRESS
• Judicial review—Can declare acts of Congress unconstitutional

**SKILLBUILDER Interpreting Charts**

1. *Why is judicial review an important action of the Supreme Court?*
2. *Which check do you think is most powerful? Why?*

**3. Trial by Jury** The trial of all crimes, except in cases of impeachment, shall be by jury; and such trial shall be held in the state where the said crimes shall have been committed; but when not committed within any state, the trial shall be at such place or places as the Congress may by law have directed.

### Section 3. Treason

**1. Definition** Treason against the United States shall consist only in levying war against them, or in adhering to their enemies, giving them aid and comfort. No person shall be convicted of treason unless on the testimony of two witnesses to the same overt act, or on confession in open court.

**2. Punishment** The Congress shall have power to declare the punishment of treason, but no attainder of treason shall work corruption of blood, or forfeiture except during the life of the person attained.

**SKILLBUILDER Possible Responses**

1. Checks the lawmaking powers of Congress; makes sure that laws and government actions do not violate the Constitution.
2. Students should choose one of the checks shown on the chart and support their choice with convincing reasons.

### *Article 3 Assessment*

**1. Main Ideas**

a. What is the main purpose of the judicial branch?

b. What is judicial review?

c. What are two kinds of cases that can begin in the Supreme Court?

**2. Critical Thinking**

**Drawing Conclusions** Why might the Supreme Court feel less political pressure than Congress in making judgments about the Constitution?

**THINK ABOUT**

- the appointment of Supreme Court justices
- Congress members' obligation to voters

## HISTORY FROM VISUALS

**Interpreting the Chart** Ask students to choose two branches and find the ways they check and balance each other. Remind them that sometimes the powers are clearly stated and other times the answer must be inferred. Continue to compare until all possible pairings have been completed. Help students rephrase in their own words the limitations explained in the chart.

**Extension** Have students devise a way to present the information in the chart in skit form.

 **Citizenship Today**

- The Role of the Judicial Branch, p. 71

## MORE ABOUT . . .

**Treason**

The Constitution sets a high standard of proof for treason. The Framers knew, from examples in English history, that charges of treason were often politically motivated. Thus, the Constitution requires open acts of treason—not merely disloyal thoughts or words—before a person can be convicted.

The first person to be tried for treason under this law was Aaron Burr, a former vice-president, in 1807. Burr was suspected of trying to found a western empire, taking over part of the United States. But the evidence against him did not meet the high constitutional standard, and he was acquitted.

 **Formal Assessment**

- Section Quiz, p. 132

### *Assessment: Article 3*

**1. Main Ideas**

**a.** to interpret laws **b.** the power to examine a law and decide whether or not it violates the Constitution **c.** cases involving the Constitution, national laws, treaties, and state conflicts

**2. Critical Thinking**

**Possible Responses** Supreme Court justices are not elected; they are appointed for life. Therefore, they do not need to be concerned with winning voter support for their decisions about the Constitution.

## HISTORY FROM VISUALS

**Interpreting Graphics** Have the students study the national and state powers. Ask students if they think any of the state powers could be handled by the federal government. Then ask why they think those powers were assigned to the states. **Possible Responses** The federal government might set up schools or regulate state commerce, marriages, and corporations. These are areas that do not involve other states or foreign nations, so there is little reason for national involvement. The states wish to maintain local control.

**Extension** Have the students llustrate a chart showing the national, shared, and state powers.

### OBJECTIVES

1. Students will be able to summarize the processes for adding states and for amending the Constitution.
2. Students will be able to describe the nature of the supremacy of the national government.

## INSTRUCT

**Articles 4–7: States, Amendments, Supremacy, and Ratification**

Key Questions

- In what ways should the "united states" cooperate?
- How can the Constitution be changed?
- What does the "supremacy clause" mean?

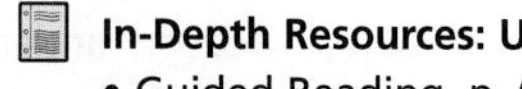

**In-Depth Resources: Unit 2**
- Guided Reading, p. 64

**Reading Study Guide** (Spanish and English), pp. 87–88

**Access for Students Acquiring English/ESL**
- Guided Reading, p. 58

**VOCABULARY**

**immunities** legal protections
**suffrage** right to vote

**A CLOSER LOOK Federalism**

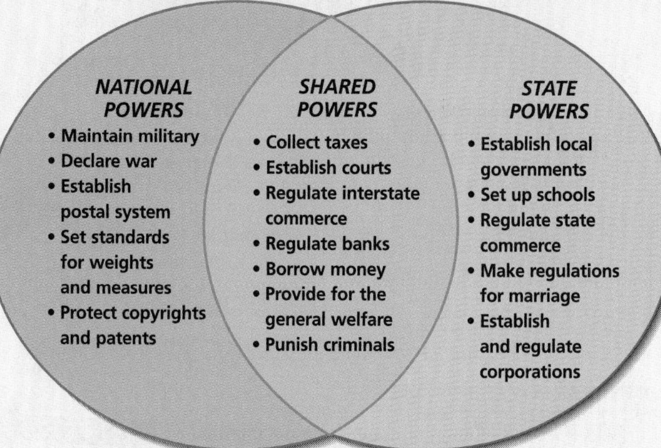


**SKILLBUILDER Interpreting Charts**
*What do you think is the purpose of dividing the powers between national and state governments?*

SKILLBUILDER Possible Responses Makes national and state governments partners in governing; builds cooperation between national and state governments; gives states local control, while allowing national government to direct issues that affect the whole country.

## Article 4. *Relations Among States*

**MAIN IDEA** States must honor one another's laws, records, and court rulings.
**WHY IT MATTERS NOW** Article 4 promotes cooperation, equality, and fair treatment of citizens from all the states.

**Section 1. State Acts and Records** Full faith and credit shall be given in each state to the public acts, records, and judicial proceedings of every other state. And the Congress may by general laws prescribe the manner in which such acts, records and proceedings shall be proved, and the effect thereof.

### Section 2. Rights of Citizens

**1. Citizenship** The citizens of each state shall be entitled to all privileges and **immunities** of citizens in the several states.

**2. Extradition** A person charged in any state with treason, felony, or other crime, who shall flee from justice, and be found in another state, shall on demand of the executive authority of the state from which he fled, be delivered up, to be removed to the state having jurisdiction of the crime. ~~**3. Fugitive Slaves** No person held to service or labor in one state, under the laws thereof, escaping into another, shall, in consequence of any law or regulation therein, be discharged from such service or labor, but shall be delivered up on claim of the party to whom such service or labor may be due.~~

**A CLOSER LOOK**

**EXTRADITION**

**Persons charged with serious crimes cannot escape punishment by fleeing to another state. They must be returned to the first state and stand trial there.**

**16. Why do you think the Framers included the power of extradition?**



## ACTIVITY OPTIONS

**INTERDISCIPLINARY LINK: GEOGRAPHY** — BLOCK SCHEDULING

### CREATING NEW STATES

**Class Time** 30 minutes

**Task** Creating a map of the United States with new states

**Purpose** To understand the constitutional procedure for admitting new states

**Supplies Needed**
- Blank maps of the United States
- Atlas with physical and political maps of the United States
- Tracing paper
- Markers or colored pencils

**Activity** Divide the class into small groups and give each group a blank map of the United States. Tell them to create a new set of states. They may wish to consult the atlas to consider geographical features. Using tracing paper, draw a map with the current state boundaries. Place the tracing paper over the new states so that students can compare their new states with the old ones. Look at Article 4, Section 3.1. How would the new states have to be admitted?

### Section 3. New States

**1. Admission** New states may be admitted by the Congress into this Union; but no new state shall be formed or erected within the jurisdiction of any other state; nor any state be formed by the junction of two or more states, or parts of states, without the consent of the legislatures of the states concerned as well as of the Congress.

**2. Congressional Authority** The Congress shall have power to dispose of and make all needful rules and regulations respecting the territory or other property belonging to the United States; and nothing in this Constitution shall be so construed as to prejudice any claims of the United States, or of any particular state.

### Section 4. Guarantees to the States

The United States shall guarantee to every state in this Union a republican form of government, and shall protect each of them against invasion; and on application of the legislature, or of the executive (when the legislature cannot be convened) against domestic violence.

***A CLOSER LOOK***

**ADMISSION TO STATEHOOD**

**In 1998, Puerto Ricans voted against their island becoming the 51st state. A lawyer in Puerto Rico summed up a main reason: "Puerto Ricans want to have ties to the U. S., but they want to protect their language and culture." Also, as a U.S. commonwealth, Puerto Rico makes its own laws and handles its own finances.**

**17. Do you think Puerto Rico should become a state? Why or why not?**

## Article 5. *Amending the Constitution*

**MAIN IDEA** **The Constitution can be amended, or formally changed.**

**WHY IT MATTERS NOW** **The amendment process allows the Constitution to adapt to modern times.**

The Congress, whenever two-thirds of both houses shall deem it necessary, shall propose amendments to this Constitution, or, on the application of the legislatures of two-thirds of the several states, shall call a convention for proposing amendments, which, in either case, shall be valid to all intents and purposes, as part of this Constitution, when ratified by the legislatures of three-fourths of the several states, or by conventions in three-fourths thereof, as the one or the other mode of ratification may be proposed by the Congress; ~~provided that no amendment which may be made prior to the year one thousand eight hundred and eight shall in any manner affect the first and fourth clauses in the ninth section of the first article~~; and that no state, without its consent, shall be deprived of its equal **suffrage** in the Senate.

***A CLOSER LOOK*** **Process for Amending the Constitution**

| Proposing Amendments | | Ratifying Amendments | |
|---|---|---|---|
| 2/3 vote of both houses of Congress | 2/3 state legislatures' call for a national convention | 3/4 approval of state legislatures | 3/4 approval at a state convention |

SKILLBUILDER **Interpreting Charts**

*Why do you think more votes are needed to ratify an amendment than to propose one?*

SKILLBUILDER **Possible Responses**
Framers wanted ideas for constitutional changes to be considered but not too easily accepted and approved.



### CRITICAL THINKING ACTIVITY

**Analyzing** Ask students to consider the sentence that begins "Full faith and credit" in Article 4, Section 1. Ask why this is an important statement for relations among the states. In Section 2, why is it important that states grant one another's citizens the same "privileges and immunities"?

**Class Time** 10 minutes

### MORE ABOUT . . .

**Unratified Amendments**

Twenty-seven amendments have been added to the Constitution since it was ratified in 1789. Other proposed amendments didn't make it. Among the rejected amendments were proposals involving numbers for representation in Congress, slavery, titles of nobility, and child labor. The most widely publicized amendment that failed in recent years was the Equal Rights Amendment, which would have made equality for men and women a part of the Constitution.

### HISTORY FROM VISUALS

**Interpreting a Chart** Have students study the chart and focus on the ways to change the Constitution. Ask students to identify two ways that a new amendment can begin. **Answers** (1) by a two-thirds vote of both houses of Congress; (2) if two-thirds of state legislatures call for a convention

**Extension** Have students do research to find out which of the above methods has been used most frequently.

### *A CLOSER LOOK*

**16.** The states involved must negotiate with one another. The state where the suspects are in custody usually has first claim. However, if one crime was much more serious than the others, public pressure might force the other states to turn the suspects over for trial where the most serious crime occurred.

**17.** Yes—Puerto Rico should take advantage of the economic and political benefits of becoming a state. No—Puerto Rico should maintain its independence and preserve its cultural identity.

## MORE ABOUT . . .

**Integrating Central High School, 1957**

Ordered to allow African Americans to attend Central High School, Arkansas Governor Orville Faubus, a segregationist, refused to maintain law and order. He allowed angry mobs to threaten the nine African-American teenagers at the school. Even after federal troops arrived, the nine students and their families endured death threats, midnight phone calls, and shots through their home windows. Several times, lynch mobs chased and nearly caught the students. At school, for a full year, the students were shoved, pushed down staircases, slapped, spat upon, and cursed. Their bravery in the face of constant danger, day after day, made the nine teenagers heroes in the struggle for civil rights.

## HISTORY FROM VISUALS

**Interpreting the Photograph** Ask the students to examine the photograph and determine what the soldiers are doing. Then ask why they think the soldiers are present. **Possible Responses** The soldiers are protecting the students, watching for danger; they are ordered to be there to prevent violence.

**Extension** Have the students find out more about the nine students who integrated Central High School in Little Rock, Arkansas.

***VOCABULARY***

**ratification** official approval

**unanimous consent** complete agreement

***A CLOSER LOOK***

**PAYING DEBTS**

**The U.S. government agreed to pay all debts held under the Articles of Confederation. For example, the United States still owed money from the costs of the Revolutionary War.**

**18. What problems might arise in a country that has a huge national debt?**

## Article 6. *Supremacy of the National Government*

**MAIN IDEA** **The Constitution, national laws, and treaties are the supreme, or highest, law of the land. All government officials must promise to support the Constitution.**

**WHY IT MATTERS NOW** **The authority of federal laws over state laws helps keep the nation unified.**

**Section 1. Valid Debts** All debts contracted and engagements entered into, before the adoption of this Constitution, shall be as valid against the United States under this Constitution, as under the Confederation.

**Section 2. Supreme Law** This Constitution, and the laws of the United States which shall be made in pursuance thereof; and all treaties made, or which shall be made, under the authority of the United States, shall be the supreme law of the land; and the judges in every state shall be bound thereby, anything in the constitution or laws of any state to the contrary notwithstanding.

***A CLOSER LOOK***

**In 1957, the "supreme law of the land" was put to a test. The governor of Arkansas defied a Supreme Court order. The Court ruled that African-American students could go to all-white public schools. President Dwight D. Eisenhower then sent federal troops to protect the first African-American students to enroll in Central High School in Little Rock, Arkansas.**

**Section 3. Loyalty to Constitution** The Senators and Representatives before mentioned, and the members of the several state legislatures, and all executive and judicial officers, both of the United States and of the several states, shall be bound by oath or affirmation to support this Constitution; but no religious test shall ever be required as a qualification to any office or public trust under the United States.



### *A CLOSER LOOK*

**18.** damage to nation's economy; lack of economic growth; cuts in federal programs; loss of people's confidence in government; fear of national bankruptcy

**19.** Slavery was not outlawed; slaves were considered three-fifths of a person for the purposes of taxation and representation in Congress; women were denied the right to vote in most places.

The CENTINEL Vol. IX

REDEUNT SATURNIA REGNA.

On the erection of the Eleventh PILLAR of the great National DOME, we beg leave most sincerely to felicitate "OUR DEAR COUNTRY."

Rise it will.

The foundation good—it may yet be SAVED.

DEL. PEN. N. JERSEY GEOR. CON. MASSA. MARY. S. CARO. N. HAMP. VIRG. N. YORK N. CARO. R. ISLAND

The FEDERAL EDIFICE.

**A CLOSER LOOK**

This political cartoon shows that New York was the 11th state to ratify the Constitution. Each of the 13 states is represented by a pillar.

## Article 7. *Ratification*

**MAIN IDEA** Nine of the 13 states had to ratify, or approve, the Constitution before it could go into effect.

**WHY IT MATTERS NOW** The approval of the Constitution launched a new plan of government still followed today.

The **ratification** of the conventions of nine states shall be sufficient for the establishment of this Constitution between the states so ratifying the same. Done in convention by the **unanimous consent** of the states present, the seventeenth day of September in the year of our Lord one thousand seven hundred and eighty-seven and of the independence of the United States of America the twelfth. In witness whereof we have hereunto subscribed our names.

*George Washington—President and deputy from Virginia*

New Hampshire: *John Langdon, Nicholas Gilman*

Massachusetts: *Nathaniel Gorham, Rufus King*

Connecticut: *William Samuel Johnson, Roger Sherman*

New York: *Alexander Hamilton*

New Jersey: *William Livingston, David Brearley, William Paterson, Jonathan Dayton*

Pennsylvania: *Benjamin Franklin, Thomas Mifflin, Robert Morris, George Clymer, Thomas FitzSimons, Jared Ingersoll, James Wilson, Gouverneur Morris*

Delaware: *George Read, Gunning Bedford, Jr., John Dickinson, Richard Bassett, Jacob Broom*

Maryland: *James McHenry, Dan of St. Thomas Jenifer, Daniel Carroll*

Virginia: *John Blair, James Madison, Jr.*

North Carolina: *William Blount, Richard Dobbs Spaight, Hugh Williamson*

South Carolina: *John Rutledge, Charles Cotesworth Pinckney, Charles Pinckney, Pierce Butler*

Georgia: *William Few, Abraham Baldwin*

**A CLOSER LOOK**

**THE SIGNERS**

The 39 men who signed the Constitution were wealthy and well-educated. About half of them were trained in law. Others were doctors, merchants, bankers, and slaveholding planters. Missing from the list of signatures are the names of African Americans, Native Americans, and women. These groups reflected the varied population of the United States in the 1780s.

**19. How do you think the absence of these groups affected the decisions made in creating the Constitution?**

### *Articles 4–7 Assessment*

**1. Main Ideas**

**a.** What rights does Article 4 guarantee to citizens if they go to other states in the nation?

**b.** What are two ways of proposing an amendment to the Constitution?

**c.** What makes up "the supreme law of the land"?

**2. Critical Thinking**

**Forming and Supporting Opinions** Should the Framers of the Constitution have allowed the people to vote directly for ratification of the Constitution? Why or why not?

**THINK ABOUT**

- the idea that the government belongs to the people
- the general public's ability to make sound political decisions



### HISTORY FROM VISUALS

**Interpreting a Political Cartoon** Ask the students to describe the pillars for North Carolina and Rhode Island. What is the cartoonist suggesting about those states? **Possible Response** Those pillars are broken or collapsing. Ratification efforts in those states were apparently not succeeding when the cartoon was drawn.

**Extension** Have the students find the number of states necessary to ratify the Constitution, as listed in Article 7. Then, using the cartoon, determine which state was the final one needed for the Constitution to go into effect.

### MORE ABOUT . . .

**The Signers of the Constitution**

Of the signers, only one—Roger Sherman—signed all four of the most important documents in the history of the new nation. He signed the Articles of Association (1774), the Declaration of Independence (1776), the Articles of Confederation (1781), and the Constitution (1787).

Many of the signers went on to become senators or representatives; several served in the Supreme Court; and two—Washington and Madison—were elected president.

**Formal Assessment**

- Section Quiz, p. 133

### *Assessment: Articles 4–7*

**1. Main Ideas**

**a.** the privileges and immunities (rights) of the citizens in those states **b.** a two-thirds vote of both houses of Congress; call by two-thirds of state legislatures for national conventions **c.** Constitution, national laws, and treaties

**2. Critical Thinking**

**Possible Responses** Yes—People should have had a more direct say because they, in turn, were directly affected by the Constitution. The Preamble states that "We the people . . . establish the Constitution of the United States"; therefore, the people should have been allowed to vote directly on ratification.

No—Too many people lacked the necessary political knowledge, and communication was too slow for a widespread popular vote in 1787–1790.

**OBJECTIVES**

1. To summarize changes made in the original Constitution
2. To identify rights protected in the Bill of Rights
3. To trace the expansion of rights for all citizens as evidenced in the Constitution

## FOCUS & MOTIVATE

### 5-MINUTE WARM-UP

**Recognizing Effects** To help students understand how the Bill of Rights has an impact on their lives, have them answer these questions.

1. Look at the chart on page 266. Which of the freedoms shown have you exercised?
2. What do you think would happen if any of those five freedoms were lost or taken away?

 **Warm-Up Transparency WTCON**

## INSTRUCT

**The Bill of Rights**

Key Questions

- What is the Bill of Rights?
- What specific rights does it protect?
- Why do some individual rights need special protection in the Constitution?

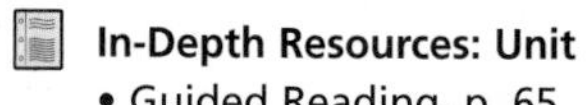

**In-Depth Resources: Unit 2**
- Guided Reading, p. 65

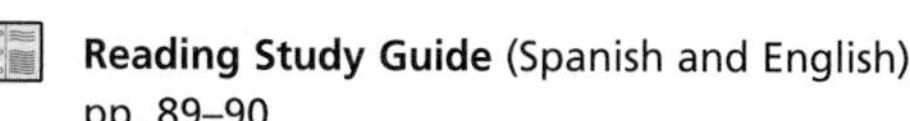

**Reading Study Guide** (Spanish and English), pp. 89–90

**Access for Students Acquiring English/ESL**
- Guided Reading, p. 59

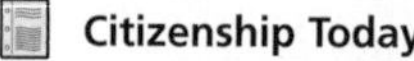

**Citizenship Today**
- Balancing Liberty and National Security, p. 72

# The Bill of Rights and Amendments 11–27

In 1787, Thomas Jefferson sent James Madison a letter about the Constitution. Jefferson wrote, "I will now add what I do not like . . . [there is no] bill of rights." He explained his reasons: "A bill of rights is what the people are entitled to against every government on earth . . . and what no just government should refuse." Jefferson's disapproval is not surprising. In writing the Declaration of Independence, he spelled out basic individual rights that cannot be taken way. These are "life, liberty, and the pursuit of happiness." The Declaration states that governments are formed to protect these rights.

Several states approved the Constitution only if a list of guaranteed freedoms was added. While serving in the nation's first Congress, James Madison helped draft the Bill of Rights. In 1791, these first ten amendments became part of the Constitution.

SKILLBUILDER

Possible Responses

1. Preserves democracy by allowing citizens to voice their ideas and views.
2. Diverse American culture of many religious beliefs; greater acceptance of different religions and sometimes mistrust; opportunities for immigrants who come to the U.S. to escape religious persecution.

## AMENDMENTS 1–10. *The Bill of Rights*

MAIN IDEA **The Bill of Rights protects citizens from government interference.**

WHY IT MATTERS NOW **Issues related to the Bill of Rights are still being applied, tested, and interpreted.**

### AMENDMENT 1. Religious and Political Freedom (1791)

Congress shall make no law respecting an establishment of religion, or prohibiting the free exercise thereof; or **abridging** the freedom of speech, or of the press; or the right of the people peaceably to assemble, and to petition the Government for a redress of grievances.

**A CLOSER LOOK The Five Freedoms**

**Freedom of Religion**
Right to worship

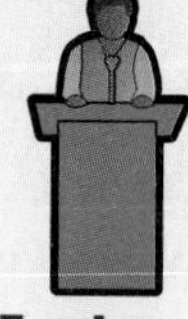

**Freedom of Speech**
Right to state ideas

**Freedom of the Press**
Right to publish ideas

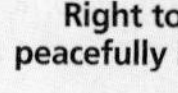

**Freedom of Assembly**
Right to meet peacefully in groups

**Freedom to Petition**
Right to protest the government

PETITION

SKILLBUILDER **Interpreting Charts**

1. *Why is freedom of speech and the press important in a democratic society?*
2. *What impact has religious freedom had on the American way of life?*



**TEACHING STRATEGY**

**Restating the Bill of Rights** To help students understand the rights and impact of the Bill of Rights on their lives, they need to understand the language of the Constitution. As you cover each of the amendments, have them write out the amendment in their own words. Then have them list one or more ways the amendment affects people's lives today.

You may want to have students keep a scrapbook of print media articles or a log of television reports that relate to the freedoms protected by the Bill of Rights.

**AMENDMENT 2. Right to Bear Arms (1791)** A well-regulated militia, being necessary to the security of a free state, the right of the people to keep and bear arms, shall not be infringed.

**AMENDMENT 3. Quartering Troops (1791)** No soldier shall, in time of peace be **quartered** in any house, without the consent of the owner, nor in time of war, but in a manner to be prescribed by law.

**AMENDMENT 4. Search and Seizure (1791)** The right of the people to be secure in their persons, houses, papers, and effects, against unreasonable searches and seizures, shall not be violated, and no warrants shall issue, but upon probable cause, supported by oath or affirmation, and particularly describing the place to be searched, and the persons or things to be seized.

**AMENDMENT 5. Rights of Accused Persons (1791)** No person shall be held to answer for a capital, or otherwise infamous crime, unless on a presentment or indictment of a Grand Jury, except in cases arising in the land or naval forces, or in the militia, when in actual service in time of war or public danger; nor shall any person be subject for the same offense to be twice put in jeopardy of life or limb; nor shall be compelled in any criminal case to be a witness against himself, nor be deprived of life, liberty, or property, without **due process of law**; nor shall private property be taken for public use, without just compensation.

**AMENDMENT 6. Right to a Speedy, Public Trial (1791)** In all criminal prosecutions, the accused shall enjoy the right to a speedy and public trial, by an impartial jury of the State and district wherein the crime shall have been committed, which district shall have been previously ascertained by law, and to be informed of the nature and cause of the accusation; to be confronted with the witnesses against him; to have **compulsory process** for obtaining witnesses in his favor, and to have the assistance of **counsel** for his defense.

***VOCABULARY***

**abridging** reducing

**quartered** given a place to stay

**due process of law** fair treatment under the law

**compulsory process** required procedure

**counsel** a lawyer

***A CLOSER LOOK***

**SEARCHES**

**Metal detectors at airports search passengers. Airline workers search all carry-on luggage. Do these actions violate the 4th Amendment? The courts say no. They have cited many situations that allow for searches without a warrant, or written order. A person's right to privacy is balanced against the government's need to prevent crime.**

**20. What does the right to privacy mean to you at home and at school?**

***A CLOSER LOOK***

**In 1966, the Supreme Court made a decision based on the 5th and 6th Amendments. The warnings outlined in this ruling are often called "Miranda rights." Miranda rights protect suspects from giving forced confessions. Police must read these rights to a suspect they are questioning. For example:**

- **"You have the right to remain silent."**
- **"Anything that you say can and will be used against you in a court of law."**
- **"You have the right to an attorney."**



## CONSTITUTION HANDBOOK

### MORE ABOUT . . .

**Locker Searches**

Throughout the nation, school officials claim the authority to search student lockers, usually for drugs or weapons. Students often assert that such searches violate their rights under the 4th Amendment.

Most courts have ruled that lockers are the property of the school district; therefore, school officials may legally search lockers. In 1998, the Pennsylvania State Supreme Court ruled that "a school district's interests outweigh a student's privacy rights." Searches, however, cannot be conducted without reasonable grounds. That is, school officials must have reason to believe that there is contraband in the locker.

### MORE ABOUT . . .

**Miranda Rights**

The statement "You have the right to remain silent," often heard in television police programs, is part of the well-known list called "Miranda Rights." Ernesto Miranda was charged with kidnapping and rape. After being questioned by police, he confessed and signed a written statement. However, he had never been told that he had the right to say nothing or to have a lawyer. A jury convicted him, based on his written confession. But in 1966, the Supreme Court ruled that the police had violated Miranda's rights under the 5th and 6th Amendments. Now police must inform suspects of their rights before questioning them.

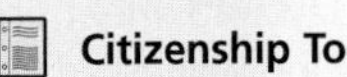

**Citizenship Today**
- Suspects' Rights versus Public Protection, p. 73

**Citizenship Today**
- *Miranda* v. *Arizona,* pp. 81–82

***A CLOSER LOOK***

**20.** at home—private phone conversations; at school—no locker searches without good reason

## HISTORY FROM VISUALS

**Interpreting the Photographs** Have the students examine the photographs. Ask them which side of the death penalty controversy they think the pictured people support. Have the students identify the arguments the placards present. **Possible Responses** The young woman at the left represents the anti-death-penalty group; the group of people at the right supports the death penalty. Their arguments include victim rights, political correctness, equality for victims and guilty parties.

**Extension** Ask students to find the phrase in the 8th Amendment that relates to the debate on the death penalty. **Answer** "cruel and unusual punishments." Have students gather additional information about both sides of the argument and conduct a debate in class.

## MORE ABOUT . . .

**"Cruel and Unusual"?**

Cases involving the death penalty and the 8th Amendment began to arise in the 1970s. In 1972, the Supreme Court ruled that the death penalty itself was not "cruel and unusual" punishment. However, the Court said that the way the death penalty was then administered did violate the Constitution because death sentences were arbitrary and unpredictable. "People live or die," one justice wrote, "dependent on the whim" of a judge or jury.

States quickly revised their laws to meet the Court's objections. In 1976, the Court allowed the death penalty under one of the new laws. Since then, the Court has continued to debate the issue, almost always upholding the death penalty.

**Formal Assessment**
- Section Quiz, p. 134

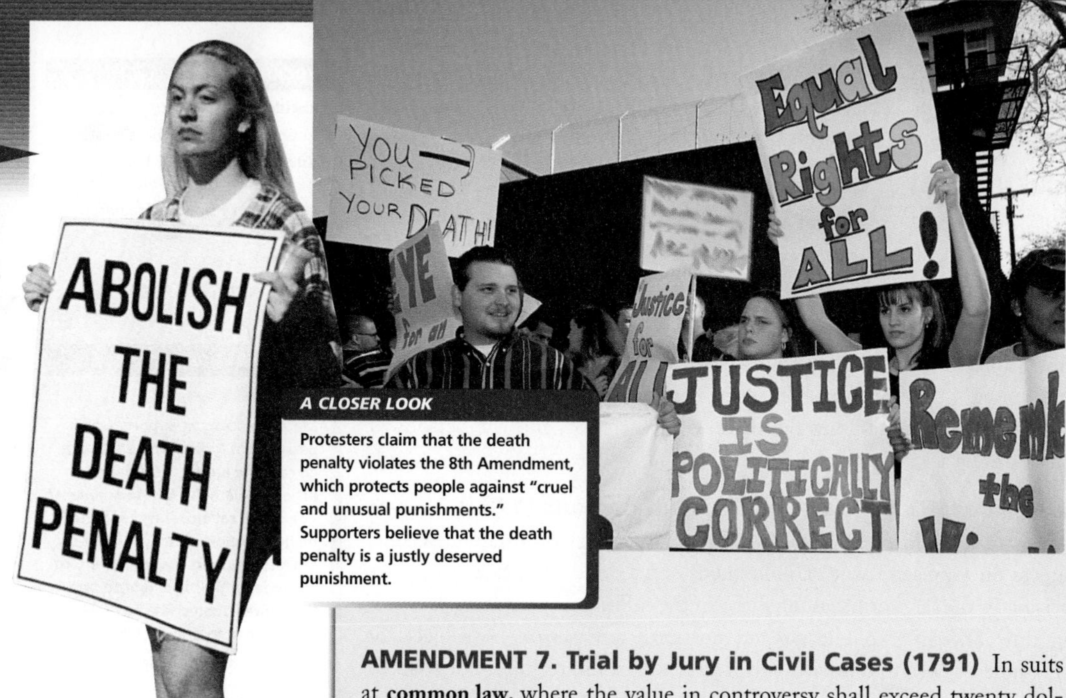


***A CLOSER LOOK***

Protesters claim that the death penalty violates the 8th Amendment, which protects people against "cruel and unusual punishments." Supporters believe that the death penalty is a justly deserved punishment.

**AMENDMENT 7. Trial by Jury in Civil Cases (1791)** In suits at **common law,** where the value in controversy shall exceed twenty dollars, the right of trial by jury shall be preserved, and no fact tried by a jury, shall be otherwise reexamined in any court of the United States, than according to the rules of the common law.

**AMENDMENT 8. Limits of Fines and Punishments (1791)** Excessive **bail** shall not be required, nor excessive fines imposed, nor cruel and unusual punishments inflicted.

**AMENDMENT 9. Rights of People (1791)** The enumeration in the Constitution of certain rights shall not be construed to deny or disparage others retained by the people.

**AMENDMENT 10. Powers of States and People (1791)** The powers not delegated to the United States by the Constitution, nor prohibited by it to the States, are reserved to the States respectively, or to the people.

***A CLOSER LOOK***

**STATES' POWERS**

The 10th Amendment gives the states reserved powers. Any powers not clearly given to the national government by the U.S. Constitution belong to the states. State constitutions sometimes assume authority in unexpected areas. For example, California's constitution sets rules for governing the use of fishing nets.

**21. What are some common areas in which states have authority?**

### *Bill of Rights Assessment*

**1. Main Ideas**

a. Which amendment protects your privacy?

b. Which amendments guarantee fair legal treatment?

c. Which amendment prevents the federal government from taking powers away from the states and the people?

**2. Critical Thinking**

**Forming and Supporting Opinions** The 4th, 5th, 6th, 7th, and 8th Amendments protect innocent people accused of crimes. Do you think these five amendments also favor the rights of actual criminals? Explain.

**THINK ABOUT**
- criminals who go free if valuable evidence is found after their trials
- criminals released on bail



## *Assessment: Bill of Rights*

**1. Main Ideas**

**a.** 3rd and 4th Amendments **b.** 4th, 5th, 6th, 7th, and 8th Amendments
**c.** 9th and 10th Amendments

**2. Critical Thinking**

**Possible Responses** Yes—It's too easy for criminals to skirt the law using these amendments. The police need to be able to gather evidence more freely. No—Police have routinely violated the rights of accused persons. These amendments are necessary to protect all people.

## Amendments 11–27

**MAIN IDEA** The Constitution has adapted to social changes and historical trends.
**WHY IT MATTERS NOW** Amendments 11–27 show that the Constitution is a living document.

### AMENDMENT 11. Lawsuits Against States (1798)

**Passed by Congress March 4, 1794. Ratified February 7, 1795. Proclaimed 1798.**
**Note: Article 3, Section 2, of the Constitution was modified by Amendment 11.**

The Judicial power of the United States shall not be construed to extend to any suit in law or **equity**, commenced or prosecuted against one of the United States by citizens of another state, or by citizens or subjects of any foreign state.

### AMENDMENT 12. Election of Executives (1804)

**Passed by Congress December 9, 1803. Ratified June 15, 1804.**
**Note: Part of Article 2, Section 1, of the Constitution was replaced by the 12th Amendment.**

The electors shall meet in their respective states and vote by ballot for President and Vice-President, one of whom, at least, shall not be an inhabitant of the same state with themselves; they shall name in their ballots the person voted for as President, and in distinct ballots the person voted for as Vice-President, and they shall make distinct lists of all persons voted for as President, and of all persons voted for as Vice-President, and of the number of votes for each, which lists they shall sign and certify, and transmit sealed to the seat of the government of the United States, directed to the President of the Senate;—the President of the Senate shall, in the presence of the Senate and House of Representatives, open all the certificates and the votes shall then be counted;—the person having the greatest number of votes for President, shall be the President, if such number be a majority of the whole number of electors appointed; and if no person have such majority, then from the persons having the highest numbers not exceeding three on the list of those voted for as President, the House of Representatives shall choose immediately, by ballot, the President. But in choosing the President, the votes shall be taken by states, the representation from each state having one vote; a quorum for this purpose shall consist of a member or members from two-thirds of the states, and a majority of all the states shall be necessary to a choice. And if the House of Representatives shall not choose a President whenever the right of choice shall devolve upon them, ~~before the fourth day of March next following~~, then the Vice-President shall act as President, as in the case of the death or other constitutional disability of the President. The person having the greatest number of votes as Vice-President, shall be the Vice-President, if such number be a majority of the whole number of Electors appointed, and if no person have a majority, then from the two highest numbers on the list, the Senate shall choose the Vice-President; a quorum for the purpose shall consist of two-thirds of the whole number of Senators, and a majority of the whole number shall be necessary to a choice. But no person constitutionally ineligible to the office of President shall be eligible to that of Vice-President of the United States.

**VOCABULARY**

**common law** a system of law developed in England, based on customs and previous court decisions

**bail** money paid by arrested persons to guarantee they will return for trial

**equity** a system of justice not covered under common law

**A CLOSER LOOK**

**SEPARATE BALLOTS**

**The presidential election of 1800 ended in a tie between Thomas Jefferson and Aaron Burr. At this time, the candidate with the most votes became president. The runner-up became vice-president. The 12th Amendment calls for separate ballots for the president and vice-president. The vice-president is specifically elected to the office, rather than being the presidential candidate with the second-most votes.**

**22. Why do you think it's important for a presidential election to result in a clear-cut winner?**





**OBJECTIVES**

1. To trace the expansion of voting rights
2. To explain amendments leading to social changes
3. To identify amendments that overturned Supreme Court decisions
4. To summarize changes in election procedures and conditions of office

## FOCUS & MOTIVATE

### 5-MINUTE WARM-UP

**Making Generalizations** To help students categorize Amendments 11–27, have them answer these questions.

1. Look at the graphic on pages 276–277. Which type of amendment has been the most numerous?
2. Which amendments do you think have had the greatest impact on today's citizens?

 **Warm-Up Transparency WTCON**

## INSTRUCT

**Amendments 11–27**
Key Questions
- How have voting rights expanded?
- Why have few amendments been about social change?
- Why have election procedures and conditions of office needed change?
- How have checks and balances played into constitutional changes?

***A CLOSER LOOK***

**21.** Students may list some of the state powers shown in the federalism diagram on page 262.
**22.** Lack of a clear-cut winner could result in recounts, court cases, and long delays in determining the outcome of an election; this situation could leave the country leaderless in a crisis. Doubts about an election might make citizens mistrustful of the government and insecure about the leadership.

## MORE ABOUT . . .

### Slavery and the Constitution

The Constitutional Convention struggled with the issue of slavery. Many of the Framers were uneasy about referring openly to slavery in this document, given the ideals of human equality expressed in the Declaration of Independence. So they avoided the word *slave* by using such phrases as "other persons" or "person held to service."

Three places in the body of the Constitution dealt with slavery. Article 1, Section 2, Paragraph 3 established that a slave would count as three-fifths of a person in determining a state's representation in Congress. Article 1, Section 9, Paragraph 1 stated that Congress could not ban the importation of slaves until 1808. And Article 4, Section 2, Paragraph 3 required the return of runaway slaves to their owners. The 13th Amendment overturned all these provisions.

## MORE ABOUT . . .

### Equality in Sports

Like the Americans with Disabilities Act, the Education Amendments Act of 1972 is based on the 14th Amendment. One of the provisions of the Education Act required schools to provide equal resources for girls and boys in athletics. Known as Title IX, the provision opened up athletics for girls and permanently changed American sports.

Title IX has led to a dramatic increase in the number of girls who participate in high school sports. In 1972, only 1 girl in 27 played sports. By 1999, 1 girl in 3 participated. Many people have said that the U.S. women's victory in the 1999 World Cup Soccer Championship was a direct result of Title IX sports programs.

**Citizenship Today**
- Equality: Its Meaning and Application, p. 74

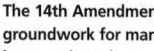

**VOCABULARY**

**servitude** being under the authority of an owner or master

**naturalized** granted nationality

**insurrection** revolt against authority

**bounties** rewards

## AMENDMENT 13. Slavery Abolished (1865)

**Passed by Congress January 31, 1865. Ratified December 6, 1865.**

**Note: A portion of Article 4, Section 2, of the Constitution was superseded by the 13th Amendment.**

**Section 1.** Neither slavery nor involuntary **servitude,** except as a punishment for crime whereof the party shall have been duly convicted, shall exist within the United States, or any place subject to their jurisdiction.

**Section 2.** Congress shall have power to enforce this article by appropriate legislation.

## AMENDMENT 14. Civil Rights (1868)

**Passed by Congress June 13, 1866. Ratified July 9, 1868.**

**Note: Article 1, Section 2, of the Constitution was modified by Section 2 of the 14th Amendment.**

**Section 1.** All persons born or **naturalized** in the United States, and subject to the jurisdiction thereof, are citizens of the United States and of the state wherein they reside. No state shall make or enforce any law which shall abridge the privileges or immunities of citizens of the United States; nor shall any state deprive any person of life, liberty, or property, without due process of law; nor deny to any person within its jurisdiction the equal protection of the laws.

**Section 2.** Representatives shall be apportioned among the several states according to their respective numbers, counting the whole number of persons in each state, excluding Indians not taxed. But when the right to vote at any election for the choice of electors for President and Vice-President of the United States, Representatives in Congress, the executive and judicial officers of a state, or the members of the legislature thereof, is denied to any of the male inhabitants of such state, being twenty-one years of age, and citizens of the United States, or in any way abridged, except for participation in rebellion, or other crime, the basis of representation therein shall be reduced in the proportion which the number of such male citizens shall bear to the whole number of male citizens twenty-one years of age in such state.

**A CLOSER LOOK**

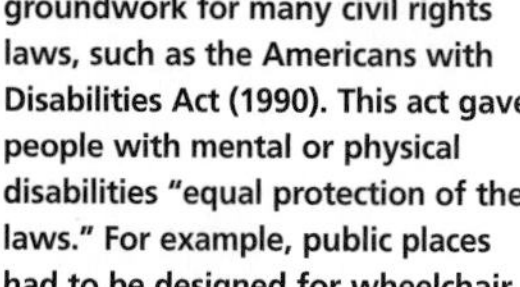

**The 14th Amendment laid the groundwork for many civil rights laws, such as the Americans with Disabilities Act (1990). This act gave people with mental or physical disabilities "equal protection of the laws." For example, public places had to be designed for wheelchair use. Wider doors and ramps allow disabled people to go in and out of buildings.**

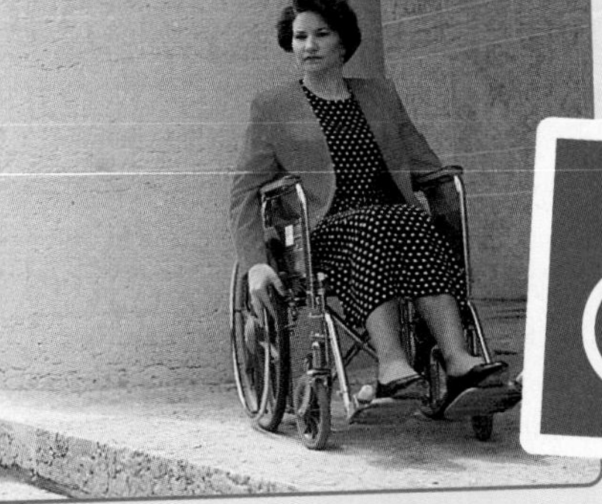



**ACTIVITY OPTIONS**

**INTERDISCIPLINARY LINK: ART**

**BLOCK SCHEDULING**

### CREATING A MURAL

**Class Time** One class period

**Task** Creating a design for a mural

**Purpose** To identify the impact on American society of the 13th, 14th, and 15th Amendments

**Supplies Needed**
- Drawing paper or graph paper
- Art supplies
- Research materials on the 13th, 14th, and 15th Amendments

**Activity** Divide the class into small groups and have each group design an outdoor mural to show how the 13th, 14th, and 15th Amendments changed life in the United States even in the 20th century. Then post all the designs and either select one design or create a new design with a combination of ideas from all the plans. The class may wish to paint the design on a large roll of paper.

**Section 3.** No person shall be a Senator or Representative in Congress, or elector of President and Vice-President, or hold any office, civil or military, under the United States, or under any state, who, having previously taken an oath, as a member of Congress, or as an officer of the United States, or as a member of any state legislature, or as an executive or judicial officer of any state, to support the Constitution of the United States, shall have engaged in **insurrection** or rebellion against the same, or given aid or comfort to the enemies thereof. But Congress may, by a vote of two-thirds of each house, remove such disability.

**Section 4.** The validity of the public debt of the United States, authorized by law, including debts incurred for payment of pensions and **bounties** for services in suppressing insurrection or rebellion, shall not be questioned. But neither the United States nor any state shall assume or pay any debt or obligation incurred in aid of insurrection or rebellion against the United States, or any claim for the loss or emancipation of any slave; but all such debts, obligations and claims shall be held illegal and void.

**Section 5.** The Congress shall have power to enforce, by appropriate legislation, the provisions of this article.

## AMENDMENT 15. Right to Vote (1870)

**Passed by Congress February 26, 1869. Ratified February 3, 1870.**

**Section 1.** The right of citizens of the United States to vote shall not be denied or abridged by the United States or by any state on account of race, color, or previous condition of servitude.

**Section 2.** The Congress shall have power to enforce this article by appropriate legislation.

### *A CLOSER LOOK*

**VOTING RIGHTS**

**The Voting Rights Act of 1965 extended the 15th Amendment. To qualify as voters, African Americans were no longer required to take tests proving that they could read and write. Also, federal examiners could help register voters. As a result, the number of African-American voters rose sharply.**

**23. What effect do you think the Voting Rights Act had on candidates running for office?**

### *A CLOSER LOOK* Reconstruction Amendments

**The 13th, 14th, and 15th Amendments are often called the Reconstruction Amendments. They were passed after the Civil War during the government's attempt to rebuild the Union and to grant rights to recently freed African Americans.**

**Amendment 13**

**1865**

- Ended slavery in the United States

**Amendment 14**

**1868**

- Defined national and state citizenship
- Protected citizens' rights
- Promised "equal protection of the laws"

**Amendment 15**

**1870**

- Designed to protect African Americans' voting rights

SKILLBUILDER **Interpreting Charts**
*What problems did these amendments try to solve?*

SKILLBUILDER Possible Responses
Corrected unjust treatment of African Americans before the Civil War—enslavement; inequality; denial of citizenship, civil rights, and voting rights.





### CRITICAL THINKING ACTIVITY

**Recognizing Effects** Explain to the class that the 15th Amendment was rarely enforced in the South between 1877 and 1965. Then, in 1965, Congress passed the Voting Rights Act, which provided federal enforcement for African Americans' right to vote.

Write the following statistics on the board or, if possible, on an outline map of the United States. They show the percentage increase in African-American voter registration between 1960 and 1966: Texas, 76.2; Louisiana, 52.8; Mississippi, 695.4; Alabama, 278.8; Georgia, 66.7; Florida, 65.6; Arkansas, 57.5; Tennessee, 21.6; South Carolina, 229.3; North Carolina, 34.3; Virginia, 105.0.

Ask which states had the greatest increase in registration. Then ask students to suggest possible reasons for the greater increases in those states. Finally, ask what other political changes the increase in registered African Americans may have brought about.

**Class Time** 10 minutes

### HISTORY FROM VISUALS

**Interpreting the Chart** Ask the students to place a sheet of paper over the captions under the three symbols on the chart. Ask them to determine what each of the amendments is about by looking only at the symbols. Then have them read the captions for additional information. **Possible Responses** 13th—freedom; 14th—equality and justice; 15th—voting.

**Extension** Have the students suggest a way to commemorate the 150th anniversary of these amendments, which will occur in their lifetimes.

 **Citizenship Today**
- Minority Rights, p. 75

### *A CLOSER LOOK*

**23.** Candidates had to consider the views of increasing numbers of African-American voters; more African-American candidates ran for office.

## MORE ABOUT . . .

### Income Tax

The Constitution gave the federal government the power to tax, a power it had lacked under the Articles of Confederation. But the Constitution denied the federal government the power to levy a direct tax—that is, a tax paid directly to the government by the taxpayer. For many years, the government received most of its money from tariffs on imported goods. During the Civil War, Congress briefly enacted an income tax to pay war expenses. Then, in 1894, Congress passed a permanent income tax, but the Supreme Court struck it down. The 16th Amendment made it possible for the government to levy a direct tax. By 1917, when the United States entered World War I, the income tax was the largest source of government revenue. It remains so today.

**A CLOSER LOOK**

**INCOME TAX**

**People below the poverty level, as defined by the federal government, do not have to pay income tax. In 1997, the poverty level for a family of four was $16,400 per year. About 13.3 percent of all Americans were considered poor in 1997.**

**24. Why do you think people below the poverty level do not pay any income tax?**

## AMENDMENT 16. Income Tax (1913)

**Passed by Congress July 12, 1909. Ratified February 3, 1913.**

**Note: Article 1, Section 9, of the Constitution was modified by the 16th Amendment.**

The Congress shall have power to lay and collect taxes on incomes, from whatever source derived, without apportionment among the several states, and without regard to any census or enumeration.

## AMENDMENT 17. Direct Election of Senators (1913)

**Passed by Congress May 13, 1912. Ratified April 8, 1913.**

**Note: Article 1, Section 3, of the Constitution was modified by the 17th Amendment.**

**Section 1.** The Senate of the United States shall be composed of two Senators from each state, elected by the people thereof, for six years; and each Senator shall have one vote. The electors in each state shall have the qualifications requisite for electors of the most numerous branch of the state legislatures.

**Section 2.** When vacancies happen in the representation of any state in the Senate, the executive authority of such state shall issue writs of election to fill such vacancies: Provided, that the legislature of any state may empower the executive thereof to make temporary appointments until the people fill the vacancies by election as the legislature may direct.

**Section 3.** This amendment shall not be so construed as to affect the election or term of any Senator chosen before it becomes valid as part of the Constitution.

## MORE ABOUT . . .

### Prohibition and Bootlegging

One of the effects of the Prohibition Amendment was to create an illegal trade in alcohol. That trade was run by "bootleggers." The term comes from the practice of hiding flasks of liquor in a boot top. Bootleggers developed an entire chain of distribution from distillers or brewers to bars. Those bars were often called "speakeasies," because of the need to speak quietly to avoid attracting police attention. Prohibition was repealed in 1933 by the 21st Amendment.

**A CLOSER LOOK**

**Under Prohibition, people broke the law if they made, sold, or shipped alcoholic beverages. Powerful crime gangs turned selling illegal liquor into a big business. This photo shows federal agents getting ready to smash containers of illegal whiskey. The 21st Amendment ended Prohibition.**

## AMENDMENT 18. Prohibition (1919)

**Passed by Congress December 18, 1917. Ratified January 16, 1919. Repealed by the 21st Amendment.**

~~**Section 1.** After one year from the ratification of this article the manufacture, sale, or transportation of intoxicating liquors within, the importation thereof into, or the exportation thereof from the United States and all territory subject to the jurisdiction thereof for beverage purposes is hereby prohibited.~~

~~**Section 2.** The Congress and the several states shall have concurrent power to enforce this article by appropriate legislation.~~

~~**Section 3.** This article shall be inoperative unless it shall have been ratified as an amendment to the Constitution by the legislatures of the several states, as provided in the Constitution, within seven years from the date of the submission hereof to the states by the Congress.~~

**ACTIVITY OPTIONS**

**INTERDISCIPLINARY LINK: WORLD HISTORY** — **BLOCK SCHEDULING**

### RESEARCHING SUFFRAGE MOVEMENTS

**Class Time** One class period

**Task** Tracing women's suffrage movements in other parts of the world

**Purpose** To identify the links between the American suffrage movement and similar movements in other countries

**Supplies Needed**
- Research materials on woman suffrage in the United States and in other nations
- Large sheets of paper
- Markers

**Activity** Divide students into small groups. They should do research into suffrage movements both in the United States and in other countries. Tell them to look for connections or comparisons among the various movements.

Next, each group should create a graphic to illustrate the information they have found. The graphic could be a time line, a world map, a sequence chart, or another visual method of showing the information.

**A CLOSER LOOK**

At left, marchers campaign for the 19th Amendment—woman suffrage. Since winning the right to vote in 1920, women have slowly gained political power. Pictured below are Congress members who belong to the Congressional Caucus for Women's Issues.

## AMENDMENT 19. Woman Suffrage (1920)

**Passed by Congress June 4, 1919. Ratified August 18, 1920.**

**Section 1.** The right of citizens of the United States to vote shall not be denied or abridged by the United States or by any state on account of sex.

**Section 2.** Congress shall have power to enforce this article by appropriate legislation.

## AMENDMENT 20. "Lame Duck" Sessions (1933)

**Passed by Congress March 2, 1932. Ratified January 23, 1933.**

**Note: Article 1, Section 4, of the Constitution was modified by Section 2 of this amendment. In addition, a portion of the 12th Amendment was superseded by Section 3.**

**Section 1.** The terms of the President and Vice-President shall end at noon on the 20th day of January, and the terms of Senators and Representatives at noon on the 3rd day of January, of the years in which such terms would have ended if this article had not been ratified; and the terms of their successors shall then begin.

**Section 2.** The Congress shall assemble at least once in every year, and such meeting shall begin at noon on the 3rd day of January, unless they shall by law appoint a different day.

**Section 3.** If, at the time fixed for the beginning of the term of the President, the President elect shall have died, the Vice-President elect shall become President. If a President shall not have been chosen before the time fixed for the beginning of his term, or if the President elect shall have failed to qualify, then the Vice-President elect shall act as President until a President shall have qualified; and the Congress may by law provide for the case wherein neither a President elect nor a Vice-President elect shall have

**A CLOSER LOOK**

**LAME DUCKS**

Before the 20th Amendment, an official defeated in a November election stayed in office until March. These politicians were compared to "lame ducks" whose wings were clipped. The 20th Amendment shortens the time that a newly elected president, vice-president, or Congress member must wait to take office.

**25. What are the benefits of having a shorter "lame duck" period?**



### MORE ABOUT . . .

**Woman Suffrage**

More than a century before the 19th Amendment, a few women in the United States were already voting. After the Revolution, New Jersey granted the vote to all citizens who owned the required amount of property—and some of those property owners were women. But in 1807, New Jersey limited suffrage to white males.

Not until 1890 did another state grant women the right to vote. In that year, Wyoming became the first state to enact a constitution that allowed woman suffrage. By 1918, women could vote in 15 states, mostly in the West.

**Citizenship Today**
• The Rights of Women, p. 80

### MORE ABOUT . . .

**Women in Congress**

Jeanette Rankin was the first woman elected to Congress. A Republican representative from Montana, she served from 1917 to 1919 and again from 1941 to 1943. Best known for her pacifist stands against both World Wars I and II, she was also a vigorous supporter of social and electoral reforms.

The number of women in Congress increased gradually. By the end of the 1990s, there were 58 women among the 435 representatives in the House and 9 women among the 100 senators. Reflecting the increased participation of women in politics, the Congressional Caucus for Women's Issues informs other members of Congress about such matters as economic equity, education, domestic violence, and family concerns.

### A CLOSER LOOK

**24.** The government recognizes that poor people need to use all their earnings to pay for basic needs—food, clothing, and shelter.

**25.** Transferring power quickly to newly elected officials supports democratic ideals by following the will of the people.

## MORE ABOUT . . .

**The Repeal of Prohibition**

It proved virtually impossible to enforce the Volstead Act (Prohibition). There were only 1,550 federal agents to police the entire country. Although the consumption of alcohol did decline significantly, many people broke the law and patronized speakeasies. Some public officials got rich by taking part in the bootlegging industry they were supposed to prosecute. Organized crime grew by enormous proportions. This widespread disregard for the law led many influential individuals to support repeal. In 1932, the Democratic Party included a call for repeal in its platform.

## MORE ABOUT . . .

**Roosevelt's Four Terms**

When Franklin Roosevelt accepted the nomination for a third term, even some of his strongest supporters objected. His previous vice-president, John Nance Garner, was among those who disagreed. With war raging in Europe and economic depression still a threat in the United States, Roosevelt ran in 1940 on the idea that the country shouldn't "switch horses in the middle of the stream." In 1944, as World War II continued, Roosevelt won a fourth term.

Fearing an "imperial presidency," Congress moved to institutionalize the custom of a two-term presidency. The 22nd Amendment guaranteed that no future president would equal FDR's record.

**VOCABULARY**

**inoperative** no longer in force

**primary** an election in which registered members of a political party nominate candidates for office

qualified, declaring who shall then act as President, or the manner in which one who is to act shall be selected, and such person shall act accordingly until a President or Vice-President shall have qualified.

**Section 4.** The Congress may by law provide for the case of the death of any of the persons from whom the House of Representatives may choose a President whenever the right of choice shall have devolved upon them, and for the case of the death of any of the persons from whom the Senate may choose a Vice-President whenever the right of choice shall have devolved upon them.

**Section 5.** Sections 1 and 2 shall take effect on the 15th day of October following the ratification of this article.

**Section 6.** This article shall be **inoperative** unless it shall have been ratified as an amendment to the Constitution by the legislatures of three-fourths of the several states within seven years from the date of its submission.

### AMENDMENT 21. Repeal of Prohibition (1933)

**Passed by Congress February 20, 1933. Ratified December 5, 1933.**

**Section 1.** The eighteenth article of amendment to the Constitution of the United States is hereby repealed.

**Section 2.** The transportation or importation into any state, territory, or possession of the United States for delivery or use therein of intoxicating liquors, in violation of the laws thereof, is hereby prohibited.

**Section 3.** This article shall be inoperative unless it shall have been ratified as an amendment to the Constitution by conventions in the several states, as provided in the Constitution, within seven years from the date of the submission hereof to the states by the Congress.

### AMENDMENT 22. Limit on Presidential Terms (1951)

**Passed by Congress March 21, 1947. Ratified February 27, 1951.**

**Section 1.** No person shall be elected to the office of the President more than twice, and no person who has held the office of President, or acted as President, for more than two years of a term to which some other person was elected President shall be elected to the office of the President more than once. ~~But this article shall not apply to any person holding the office of President when this article was proposed by the Congress, and shall not prevent any person who may be holding the office of President, or acting as President, during the term within which this article becomes operative from holding the office of President or acting as President during the remainder of such term.~~

**Section 2.** This article shall be inoperative unless it shall have been ratified as an amendment to the Constitution by the legislatures of three-fourths of the several states within seven years from the date of its submission to the states by the Congress.

**A CLOSER LOOK**

**George Washington set the tradition of limiting the presidency to two terms. Franklin Roosevelt broke this custom when he was elected president four terms in a row—1932, 1936, 1940, and 1944. His record-long presidency led to the 22nd Amendment. A two-term limit, written into the Constitution, checks the president's power.**

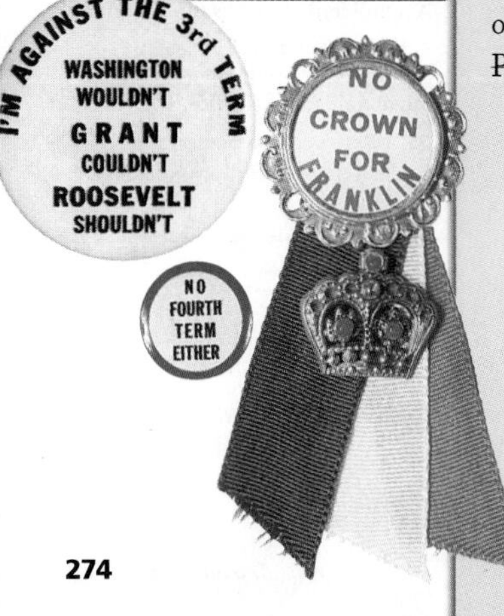


274

**ACTIVITY OPTIONS**

**INTERDISCIPLINARY LINK: LANGUAGE ARTS**

BLOCK SCHEDULING

**DEBATING TERM LIMITS**

**Class Time** Two class periods

**Task** Debating the idea of term limits

**Purpose** To pose and answer questions about the proposal to limit the number of terms a person can serve in Congress

**Supplies Needed**
- Research materials on term limits

**Activity** Divide the class into two parts. Assign one group to present arguments in favor of term limits and the other, arguments against limits. Have students research their side and write out a minimum of three questions and answers supporting their position.

Next, divide the class into sets of four—two students from the pro side with two students from the con side. Let the students conduct their debates within these small-group settings, using the questions and answers that they generated.

## AMENDMENT 23. Voting in District of Columbia (1961)

**Passed by Congress June 17, 1960. Ratified March 29, 1961.**

**Section 1.** The district constituting the seat of government of the United States shall appoint in such manner as Congress may direct: a number of electors of President and Vice-President equal to the whole number of Senators and Representatives in Congress to which the district would be entitled if it were a state, but in no event more than the least populous state; they shall be in addition to those appointed by the states, but they shall be considered, for the purposes of the election of President and Vice-President, to be electors appointed by a state; and they shall meet in the district and perform such duties as provided by the twelfth article of amendment.

**Section 2.** The Congress shall have power to enforce this article by appropriate legislation.

## AMENDMENT 24. Abolition of Poll Taxes (1964)

**Passed by Congress August 27, 1962. Ratified January 23, 1964.**

**Section 1.** The right of citizens of the United States to vote in any **primary** or other election for President or Vice-President, for electors for President or Vice-President, or for Senator or Representative in Congress, shall not be denied or abridged by the United States or any state by reason of failure to pay any poll tax or other tax.

**Section 2.** The Congress shall have power to enforce this article by appropriate legislation.

## AMENDMENT 25. Presidential Disability, Succession (1967)

**Passed by Congress July 6, 1965. Ratified February 10, 1967.**

**Note: Article 2, Section 1, of the Constitution was affected by the 25th Amendment.**

**Section 1.** In case of the removal of the President from office or of his death or resignation, the Vice-President shall become President.

**Section 2.** Whenever there is a vacancy in the office of the Vice-President, the President shall nominate a Vice-President who shall take office upon confirmation by a majority vote of both houses of Congress.

**Section 3.** Whenever the President transmits to the President pro tempore of the Senate and the Speaker of the House of Representatives his written declaration that he is unable to discharge the powers and duties of his office, and until he transmits to them a written declaration to the contrary, such powers and duties shall be discharged by the Vice-President as Acting President.

***A CLOSER LOOK***

**POLL TAX**

**The poll tax was aimed at preventing African Americans from exercising their rights. Many could not afford to pay this fee required for voting.**

**26. How do you think the 24th Amendment affected elections?**

***A CLOSER LOOK***

**PRESIDENTIAL DISABILITY**

**President John F. Kennedy's death in 1963 signaled the need for the 25th Amendment. The Constitution did not explain what to do in the case of a disabled president. James Reston, a writer for *The New York Times,* summed up the problem: Suppose Kennedy was "strong enough to survive [the bullet wounds], but too weak to govern." The 25th Amendment provides for an orderly transfer of power.**

**27. What do you think can happen in a country where the rules for succession are not clear?**



### MORE ABOUT . . .

**Barriers to Voting**

Article 1, Section 4 of the Constitution gives the states the right to establish voter qualifications. The poll tax was one of a number of methods that some states used to prevent certain individuals—usually African Americans—from voting. Other barriers to voting included property ownership, literacy tests, residency requirements, and "grandfather" clauses. Grandfather clauses guaranteed the vote to people whose ancestors had voted before 1867—nearly all of whom were white—even if they could not pay the poll tax or pass the literacy test that was required of African Americans.

In addition to the 24th Amendment, the Voting Rights Act of 1965 and two extensions of the act in 1970 and 1975 removed some of the barriers. Supreme Court decisions during the 1960s removed other barriers to voting.

### MORE ABOUT . . .

**Presidential Succession**

Earlier questions about presidential succession arose when Woodrow Wilson had a severe stroke in 1919. Dwight Eisenhower's heart attack brought the issue back into discussion in 1957. What would happen if a president was too ill or badly injured to govern? Finally, John F. Kennedy's death presented the additional problem of how to replace a vice-president. When Lyndon Johnson became president, there was no longer a vice-president to succeed him if he were to die or become unable to govern. The presidency would have passed to the Speaker of the House. The only solution lay in a constitutional amendment.

### *A CLOSER LOOK*

**26.** More African Americans voted and were elected to office.

**27.** Political disorder might follow as groups and individuals compete to take over the top leadership position.

## MORE ABOUT . . .

**A Vice-Presidential Successor**

Amendment 25, Section 2 provides a way to replace a vice-president who leaves office before completing the term. The president nominates a new vice-president, who must win confirmation by a majority vote of each house of Congress.

In 1973, Gerald Ford became vice-president in this way after Spiro Agnew resigned. The following year, when Ford became president after Nixon resigned, Nelson Rockefeller became vice-president through the same procedure.

## HISTORY FROM VISUALS

**Interpreting the Time Line** Ask the students to study the time line. Tell them to find the ten-year period in which the greatest number of amendments were passed. Then ask if they can infer reasons why so many amendments were enacted in that decade. **Possible Response** Four amendments were enacted between 1913 and 1923, and four more between 1961 and 1971. Both were periods of great political turbulence and social change.

**Extension** Have the students create an illustrated time line showing all 27 amendments in a logo form.

***A CLOSER LOOK***

**SUCCESSION**

**Who takes over if a president dies in office or is unable to serve? The top five in the line of succession follow:**

- **vice-president**
- **speaker of the house**
- **president pro tempore of the Senate**
- **secretary of state**
- **secretary of the treasury**

**28. Why should voters know the views of the vice-president?**

**Section 4.** Whenever the Vice-President and a majority of either the principal officers of the executive departments or of such other body as Congress may by law provide, transmit to the President pro tempore of the Senate and the Speaker of the House of Representatives their written declaration that the President is unable to discharge the powers and duties of his office, the Vice-President shall immediately assume the powers and duties of the office as Acting President. Thereafter, when the President transmits to the President pro tempore of the Senate and the Speaker of the House of Representatives his written declaration that no inability exists, he shall resume the powers and duties of his office unless the Vice-President and a majority of either the principal officers of the executive department[s] or of such other body as Congress may by law provide, transmit within four days to the President pro tempore of the Senate and the Speaker of the House of Representatives their written declaration that the President is unable to discharge the powers and duties of his office. Thereupon Congress shall decide the issue, assembling within forty-eight hours for that purpose if not in session. If the Congress, within twenty-one days after receipt of the latter written declaration, or, if Congress is not in session, within twenty-one days after Congress is required to assemble, determines by two thirds vote of both houses that the President is unable to discharge the powers and duties of his office, the Vice-President shall continue to discharge the same as Acting President; otherwise, the President shall resume the powers and duties of his office.

***A CLOSER LOOK*** **Amendments Time Line** *1791–1992*

**Use the key below to help you categorize the amendments.**

- **Voting Rights**
- **Social Changes**
- **Overturned Supreme Court Decisions**
- **Election Procedures and Conditions of Office**

1790

**Bill of Rights Amendments 1–10 1791**

**Amendment 11 1798** Protects state from lawsuits filed by citizens of other states or countries.

**Amendment 12 1804** Requires separate electoral ballots for president and vice-president.

**Amendment 13 1865** Bans slavery.

**Amendment 14 1868** Defines American citizenship and citizens' rights.

**Amendment 15 1870** Stops national and state governments from denying the vote based on race.



***A CLOSER LOOK***

**28.** If the president dies or is unable to serve, the vice-president will become president.

## AMENDMENT 26. 18-year-old Vote (1971)

**Passed by Congress March 23, 1971. Ratified July 1, 1971.**

**Note: Amendment 14, Section 2, of the Constitution was modified by Section 1 of the 26th Amendment.**

**Section 1.** The right of citizens of the United States, who are eighteen years of age or older, to vote shall not be denied or abridged by the United States or by any state on account of age.

**Section 2.** The Congress shall have power to enforce this article by appropriate legislation.

## AMENDMENT 27. Congressional Pay (1992)

**Passed by Congress September 25, 1991. Ratified May 7, 1992.**

No law, varying the compensation for the services of the Senators and Representatives, shall take effect, until an election of Representatives shall have intervened.

ROCK
THE
VOTE

***A CLOSER LOOK***

**Members of the recording industry founded Rock the Vote. They urge young people to vote in elections.**

### MORE ABOUT . . .

**Rock the Vote**

Founded in 1990, Rock the Vote has worked to increase the number of young people participating in the political life of their communities. At the end of the 1990s, only about 38 percent of people between the ages of 18 and 29 turned out to vote.

The organization provides information on local issues and elections, as well as tracking voter turnout. It is exploring such ideas as expanding elections to more than one day and using technology to increase the participation and education of voters.

### *Amendments 11–27 Assessment*

**1. Main Ideas**

a. Which amendments affected the office of president?

b. Which pair of amendments shows the failure of laws to solve a social problem?

c. Which amendments corrected unfair treatment toward African Americans and women?

**2. Critical Thinking**

**Supporting Opinions** Which of the amendments has had the greatest effect on you?

**THINK ABOUT**

- your rights as a citizen
- your responsibilities as a citizen
- your role in government

### MORE ABOUT . . .

**The 27th Amendment**

The 27th Amendment is the newest—and oldest—amendment in the Constitution. It was actually proposed on September 25, 1789, one day earlier than the Bill of Rights. But it lay dormant until the 1980s, when an aide to a Texas legislator discovered it and began a campaign to get the amendment adopted. The 27th Amendment was finally ratified more than 200 years after it was introduced.

**Citizenship Today**

- Constitutional Change and Flexibility, p. 77

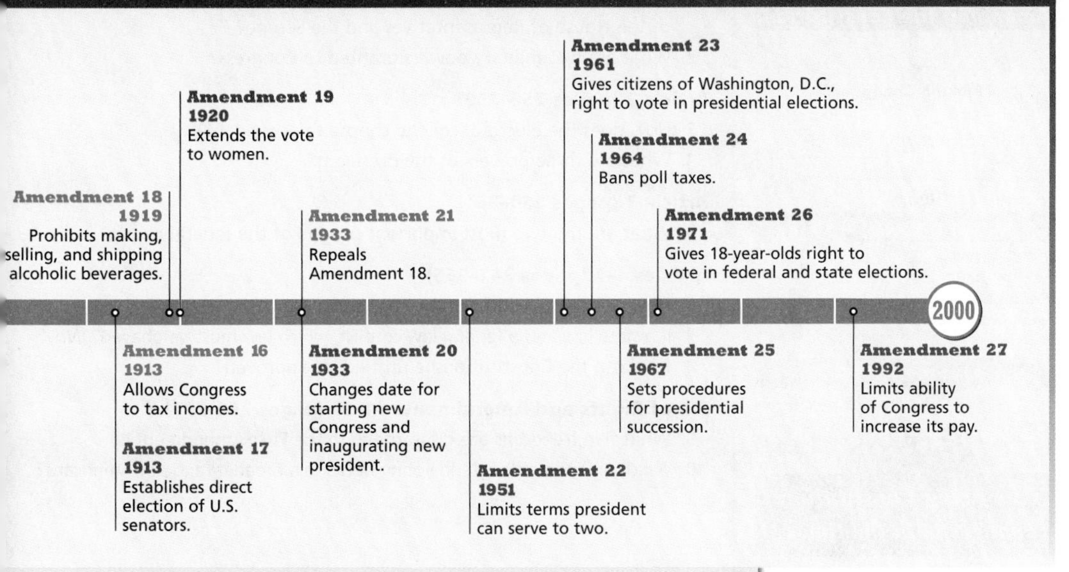
Amendment 16
1913
Allows Congress to tax incomes.
Amendment 17
1913
Establishes direct election of U.S. senators.
Amendment 18
1919
Prohibits making, selling, and shipping alcoholic beverages.
Amendment 19
1920
Extends the vote to women.
Amendment 20
1933
Changes date for starting new Congress and inaugurating new president.
Amendment 21
1933
Repeals Amendment 18.
Amendment 22
1951
Limits terms president can serve to two.
Amendment 23
1961
Gives citizens of Washington, D.C., right to vote in presidential elections.
Amendment 24
1964
Bans poll taxes.
Amendment 25
1967
Sets procedures for presidential succession.
Amendment 26
1971
Gives 18-year-olds right to vote in federal and state elections.
Amendment 27
1992
Limits ability of Congress to increase its pay.
2000

**Formal Assessment**

- Section Quiz, p. 135

### *Assessment: Amendments 11–27*

**1. Main Ideas**

**a.** 12th, 20th, 22nd, and 25th Amendments **b.** 18th and 21st Amendments **c.** African Americans—13th, 14th, 15th, and 24th Amendments; women—14th and 19th Amendments

**2. Critical Thinking**

Responses will vary. Students should choose one of the amendments and support their choice with convincing reasons.

## VOCABULARY

1. **electors,** p. 249
2. **impeachment,** p. 249
3. **naturalization,** p. 252
4. **felonies,** p. 252
5. **bill of attainder,** p. 254
6. **ex post facto law,** p. 254
7. **suffrage,** p. 262
8. **due process of law,** p. 267
9. **servitude,** p. 270
10. **primary,** p. 274

## SEVEN PRINCIPLES OF THE CONSTITUTION

**Possible Responses**

1. government in which the people rule—Preamble ("We the people . . .")
2. people exercise their power by voting for their political representatives—Article 1 (popular election of representatives)
3. states and national government share powers—10th Amendment (powers reserved to the states)
4. division of government roles into branches—Articles 1, 2, 3 (legislative, executive, and judicial branches)
5. each branch of government exercises controls over the other branches—Article 1 (impeachment)
6. restrictions of government powers—Article 1, Section 9 (powers denied Congress)
7. personal liberties and privileges—Bill of Rights

## REVIEW QUESTIONS

**Possible Responses**

1. House—at least age 25; resident of state in which elected; citizen for 7 years

   Senate—at least age 30; resident of state in which elected; citizen for 9 years
2. declare war; raise armies; provide a navy; organize the National Guard (militia)
3. In a presidential election, the "winner takes all"; all the electoral votes of a state (except Maine and Nebraska) go to one set of candidates.

## VISUAL SUMMARY

### The Constitution of the United States

Preamble

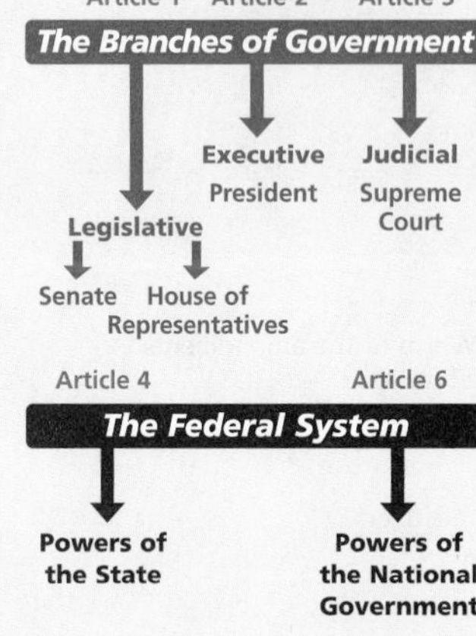


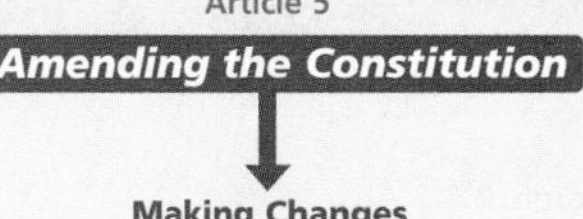


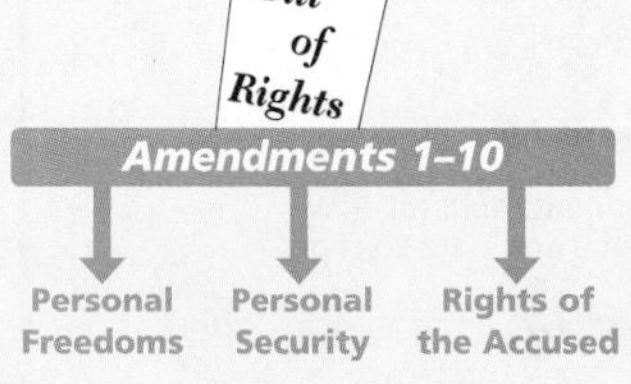


Amendments 11–27

*The living Constitution changes with the times.*



# Constitution ASSESSMENT

## VOCABULARY

Briefly explain the importance of each of the following.

1. electors
2. impeachment
3. naturalization
4. felonies
5. bill of attainder
6. ex post facto law
7. suffrage
8. due process of law
9. servitude
10. primary

## SEVEN PRINCIPLES OF THE CONSTITUTION

Make a chart like the one shown. Then fill it in with a definition of each principle and an example from the Constitution.

| Principle | Definition | Example |
|---|---|---|
| 1. popular sovereignty | | |
| 2. republicanism | | |
| 3. federalism | | |
| 4. separation of powers | | |
| 5. checks and balances | | |
| 6. limited government | | |
| 7. individual rights | | |

## REVIEW QUESTIONS

**Article 1 (pages 249–255)**

1. What are the requirements for becoming a member of the House of Representatives and the Senate?
2. What are two military powers granted to Congress?

**Article 2 (pages 256–259)**

3. How does the electoral college choose the president?
4. What are three powers of the president?

**Article 3 (pages 260–261)**

5. What are the two most important powers of the federal courts?

**Articles 4–7 (pages 262–265)**

6. How can the Constitution be changed?
7. If a state law and a federal law conflict, which law must be obeyed? Why?
8. How can the Constitution be ratified, or approved?

**Bill of Rights and Amendments 11–27 (pages 266–277)**

9. What five freedoms are guaranteed in the First Amendment?
10. Which amendments extend voting rights to a broader range of Americans?

## CRITICAL THINKING

**Possible Responses**

1. **DRAWING CONCLUSIONS** Proposing—two-thirds of both houses of Congress approve or two-thirds of state legislatures call for national convention. Ratifying—three-fourths of state legislatures approve or three-fourths of state conventions approve. **a.** pressuring senators and representatives to propose amendments **b.** to make sure the Constitution keeps pace with the times; to address unsolved problems (such as slavery) present in the original document
2. **MAKING INFERENCES** The elastic clause suggests that Congress has the power to deal with matters not specifically mentioned in the Constitution.
3. **ANALYZING LEADERSHIP** problem solver; decision maker; effective planner and manager; strong communicator; powerful persuader

## CRITICAL THINKING

**1. DRAWING CONCLUSIONS**

In a two-column chart, summarize the processes for changing the Constitution. Then use your completed chart to answer the questions below.

| Proposing Amendments | Ratifying Amendments |
|---|---|
| 1. | 1. |
| 2. | 2. |

a. What role can citizens play in proposing amendments?
b. What do you think are the main reasons for changing the Constitution?

**2. MAKING INFERENCES**

Explain how the "elastic clause" in Article 1 gives Congress the authority to take action on other issues unknown to the Framers of the Constitution.

**3. ANALYZING LEADERSHIP**

Think about the president's roles described in the Constitution. What qualities does a president need to succeed as a leader in so many different areas?

**4. RECOGNIZING EFFECTS**

How would you describe the impact of the 14th, 15th, and 16th Amendments on life in the United States?

**5. APPLYING CITIZENSHIP**

Suppose you and your family go on a road trip across several states. According to Article 4 of the Constitution, what citizens' rights do you have in the states you are visiting?

## HISTORY SKILLS

**INTERPRETING PRIMARY SOURCES**

In 1937, President Franklin D. Roosevelt gave a speech over the radio. He used interesting comparisons to explain how the government works.

> I described the American form of government as a three-horse team provided by the Constitution to the American people so that their field might be plowed. The three horses are, of course, the three branches of government—the Congress, the Executive, and the Courts. . . . It is the American people themselves who are in the driver's seat. It is the American people themselves who want the furrow plowed.
>
> **Franklin D. Roosevelt,** Radio Address

- How does Roosevelt describe the separation of powers?
- How does Roosevelt explain popular sovereignty?

## ALTERNATIVE ASSESSMENT

**1. INTERDISCIPLINARY ACTIVITY: Math**

**Creating a Data Display** Do research on methods that political candidates use to raise money for their campaigns. Examples include public money, political action committees, direct mail, and so on. Summarize your findings in a graph or chart.

**2. COOPERATIVE LEARNING ACTIVITY**

**Drafting a Constitution** Imagine you are asked to write a constitution for a newly formed country. Working with a group, make an outline like the one shown to help you organize your draft.

I. Purpose of the Constitution (Preamble)
II. Making Laws (Legislative Branch)
III. Carrying Out the Laws (Executive Branch)
IV. Making Laws Fair (Judicial Branch)
V. Choosing Leaders
VI. Citizens' Rights (Bill of Rights)

**3. CD-ROM PRIMARY SOURCE EXPLORER**

**Making a Learning Center** Creating the U.S. Constitution was one of the most important events in the nation's history. Use the CD-ROM and the library to collect information on different topics related to the Constitution.

Create a learning center featuring the suggestions below.

- Find biographies and portraits of the Framers.
- Collect important primary sources such as James Madison's notes and *The Federalist* papers.
- Gather recent pictures and news articles about the Congress, the president, the Supreme Court, and the Bill of Rights.

**4. HISTORY PORTFOLIO**

Review your draft of the constitution you wrote for the assessment activity. Choose one of these options below.

**Option 1** Use comments made by your teacher or classmates to improve your work.

**Option 2** Illustrate your constitution. Add your work to your history portfolio.



4. acts as commander in chief of the military; makes treaties and appointments; approves bills passed by Congress
5. interpret laws and judicial review
6. through the amendment process
7. federal law, under the supremacy clause
8. Nine of 13 states had to ratify.
9. religion, speech, press, assembly, petition
10. 15th, 19th, and 26th Amendments

## ALTERNATIVE ASSESSMENT

**Standards for Evaluation**

**1. INTERDISCIPLINARY ACTIVITY: Math**
**Each data display (chart or graph) should**
- be clear and easy to read.
- include back-up documentation.

**2. COOPERATIVE LEARNING ACTIVITY**
**Each constitution should**
- have a clear statement of its goals.
- reflect an understanding of the functions of various parts of government.
- follow the rules of spelling, punctuation, and grammar.

**3. CD-ROM PRIMARY SOURCE EXPLORER**
**Learning centers should**
- have a clear focus and logical organization.
- use interesting images or audio elements to make points.
- give appropriate background and research information.

**4. HISTORY PORTFOLIO**

**Option 1 Revised assessment activities should**
- address teacher and peer response to the selected work.
- solve problems present in the first versions of the work.

**Option 2 Illustrated constitutions should**
- be creative and neatly presented.
- present information to aid the viewer in understanding the material.
- demonstrate an understanding of methods of governing.

**Formal Assessment**
- Chapter Test, Forms A and B, pp. 136–143

4. **RECOGNIZING EFFECTS** African Americans slowly gained civil rights and political power. Their example inspired other minorities to demand fair treatment.
5. **APPLYING CITIZENSHIP** the same rights and privileges that citizens of those states have

## HISTORY SKILLS

**Possible Responses**

Roosevelt describes the separation of powers as a "three-horse team provided by the Constitution." The three horses are the three branches of government. He explains popular sovereignty as the "American people . . . in the driver's seat," directing the three-horse team.

## CITIZENSHIP HANDBOOK OBJECTIVE

The student will be able to define citizenship and to explain a citizen's rights and responsibilities.

## FOCUS & MOTIVATE

### 5-MINUTE WARM-UP

**Categorizing** Answering this question will help students to understand that being a citizen has specific requirements.

1. Read the Kennedy quote on page 280. Why do you think he wanted all persons to be active citizens?
2. How is a citizen different from a person who lives in a country but is not a citizen?

 Warm-Up Transparency WTCON

## INSTRUCT

**What Is a Citizen?**
Key Questions

- Why does a country have rules about who is considered a citizen?
- What are two ways to become a United States citizen?
- Why might a person want to change citizenship from one country to another?

# The Role of the Citizen

Citizens of the United States enjoy many basic rights and freedoms. Freedom of speech and religion are examples. These rights are guaranteed by the Constitution, the Bill of Rights, and other amendments to the Constitution. Along with these rights, however, come responsibilities. Obeying rules and laws, voting, and serving on juries are some examples.

Active citizenship is not limited to adults. Younger citizens can help their communities become better places. The following pages will help you to learn about your rights and responsibilities. Knowing them will help you to become an active and involved citizen of your community, state, and nation.

In this book you will find examples of active citizenship by young people like yourself. **Look for the Citizenship Today features.**

Citizen → KNOW YOUR RIGHTS → BE RESPONSIBLE → STAY INFORMED → MAKE GOOD DECISIONS → PARTICIPATE IN YOUR COMMUNITY → Model Citizen

President John F. Kennedy urged all Americans to become active citizens and work to improve their communities.

The weather was sunny but cold on January 20, 1961—the day that John F. Kennedy became the 35th president of the United States. In his first speech as president, he urged all Americans to serve their country. Since then, Kennedy's words have inspired millions of Americans to become more active citizens.

> *"Ask not what your country can do for you—ask what you can do for your country!"*
>
> —JOHN F. KENNEDY

## What Is a Citizen?

A citizen is a legal member of a nation and pledges loyalty to that nation. A citizen has certain guaranteed rights, protections, and responsibilities. A citizen is a member of a community and wants to make it a good place to live.

Today in the United States there are a number of ways to become a citizen. The most familiar are citizenship by birth and citizenship by naturalization. All citizens have the right to equal protection under the law.



### TEACHING STRATEGY

**CITIZENS**

The term *citizen* is often used in a very broad sense to mean a resident of a community. However, the term can also describe a specific legal status. Some students may not easily identify with their legal status as citizens. To help students think about citizenship and its importance for preserving democracy, discuss the meaning of the following quotation: "Whether in private or in public the good citizen does something to support democratic habits and the constitutional order." (Judith Shklar, 1991) Prompt students by asking how the quotation combines the two meanings of *citizen.*

Next, have students look at the graphic on page 280. Ask them how it illustrates the ideas in the quotation. Guide the discussion so that they understand that the information in the graphic exemplifies the "democratic habits" needed to fulfill the role of a citizen in a democracy.

**CITIZENSHIP BY BIRTH** A child born in the United States is a citizen by birth. Children born to U.S. citizens traveling or living outside the country, such as military personnel, are citizens. Even children born in the United States to parents who are not citizens of the United States are considered U.S. citizens. These children have dual citizenship. This means they are citizens of two countries—both the United States and the country of their parents' citizenship. At the age of 18, the child may choose one of the countries for permanent citizenship.

**CITIZENSHIP BY NATURALIZATION** A person who is not a citizen of the United States may become one through a process called naturalization. The steps in this process are shown below. To become a naturalized citizen, a person must meet certain requirements.

- Be at least 18 years old. Children under the age of 18 automatically become naturalized citizens when their parents do.
- Enter the United States legally.
- Live in the United States for at least five years immediately prior to application.
- Read, write, and speak English.
- Show knowledge of American history and government.

**See Citizenship Today: Becoming a Citizen, p. 467**

***Steps in the Naturalization Process***

1. **File an application.**
2. **Take an examination.**
3. **File a legal petition for naturalization.**
4. **Appear at a court hearing.**
5. **Take an oath of allegiance.**

**Hundreds of people become new citizens at a single ceremony in San Antonio, Texas.**



## CITIZENSHIP HANDBOOK

### MORE ABOUT . . .

**Naturalization**

Naturalization can occur individually, as described in this handbook, or collectively. In collective naturalization, an entire group of people are naturalized at the same time. This process takes place through treaties, a Joint Resolution of Congress, an act of Congress to acquire new territory, or a constitutional amendment. For example, when the United States passed an act of Congress to acquire the new territory of Puerto Rico in 1917, all of the people of Puerto Rico became naturalized citizens of the United States.

### MORE ABOUT . . .

**Ethnic Restrictions**

For much of the 20th century, the U.S. government used ethnicity to determine the number of people allowed to immigrate to the United States. In 1924, Congress passed the Johnson-Reed Act to preserve the "racial composition" of the country. This act set quotas for immigrants, based on their country of origin. These quotas favored Northern Europeans over Southern and Eastern Europeans. Not until 1965 were ethnic quotas removed from immigration laws. The new law limits each country, regardless of ethnicity, to an annual quota of 20,000 people.

### MORE ABOUT . . .

**Citizenship Test**

The U.S. government's Immigration and Naturalization Service Web site has sample questions for the naturalization test. Have students visit www.mcdougallittell.com for more information.

You may also want students to review the INS site for eligibility standards for immigrants to become citizens.

**Citizenship Today**
- Becoming a Citizen, p. 9

### ACTIVITY OPTIONS

**INTERDISCIPLINARY LINK: LANGUAGE ARTS** — BLOCK SCHEDULING

**INTERVIEW**

**Class Time** 10 minutes for explanation

**Task** Interviewing adults about citizenship

**Purpose** To identify the public's view of citizenship

**Supplies Needed**
- Log book
- Audio or video recording equipment (optional)

**Activity** Have each student interview five adults. Discuss with students some of the people they may choose to interview. Explain that techniques of a good interviewer include listening carefully, asking open-ended questions, and taking good notes. Have them ask the following questions:
- What does it mean to be a citizen?
- What rights does a citizen have?
- What responsibilities does a citizen have?

Students should write a summary answer to each question that incorporates all their findings and report their findings to the class.

## INSTRUCT

**What Are Your Rights?/ What Are Your Responsibilities?**

Key Questions

- What are the three categories of rights?
- What are the two categories of responsibilities?
- How are rights and responsibilities linked?

### MORE ABOUT . . .

**Freedom of Speech**

No right is absolute or unlimited. The Supreme Court has struggled, for example, with the issue of free speech. Ruling in *Schenck* v. *United States,* Justice Oliver Wendell Holmes, Jr., created what became known as the "clear and present danger" rule. He stated, "Words can be weapons. . . . The question in every case is whether the words . . . create a clear and present danger that they will bring about the substantive evils that Congress has the right to prevent."

### CRITICAL THINKING ACTIVITY

**Analyzing** Explain that rights are valuable, yet can cause conflict and create debate within society. Have students choose two rights, one from the basic freedoms box and the other from the personal protections box. Then have them create a chart for each right that lists why that right is valuable and how that right can cause debate. After they have completed the charts, have a class discussion about their answers.

**Class Time** 20 minutes

| Why is this right valuable? | How does this right create debate? |
|---|---|
| | |

# What Are Your Rights?

Citizens of the United States are guaranteed rights by the U.S. Constitution, state constitutions, and state and federal laws. All citizens have three kinds of rights: basic freedoms, protection from unfair government actions, and equal treatment under the law.

Citizens' basic rights and freedoms are sometimes called **civil rights**. Some of these rights are personal, and others are political.

The U.S. Constitution grants these five basic freedoms.

**BASIC FREEDOMS**

- Freedom of religion
- Freedom of speech
- Freedom of the press
- Freedom of peaceful assembly
- Freedom to petition the government for change

The second category of rights is intended to protect citizens from unfair government actions.

**PERSONAL PROTECTIONS**

- The right to bear arms
- Freedom from being forced to house soldiers
- Protection from unreasonable search and seizure
- The right to a speedy public trial by an impartial jury
- No excessive bail or fines
- Protection from cruel and unusual punishment

Other parts of the Bill of Rights grant these rights.

The third category is the right to equal treatment under the law. The government cannot treat one individual or group differently from another.

Rights of citizenship have expanded over the years.

**EQUAL PROTECTION UNDER THE LAW**

- No slavery
- The right to vote to all male citizens over 21 years old
- The right to vote to women
- The right to vote to 18 year olds
- The Civil Rights Acts of 1964 protects voting rights and prevents discrimination.
- The Americans with Disabilities Act of 1990 protects the rights of disabled citizens.

**LIMITS TO RIGHTS** The rights guaranteed to citizens have sensible limits. For example, the right to free speech does not allow a person to falsely shout, "Fire!" at a crowded concert. The government may place limits on certain rights to protect national security or to provide equal opportunities for all citizens. And rights come with responsibilities.



### ACTIVITY OPTIONS

**MULTIPLE LEARNING STYLES: VISUAL** — BLOCK SCHEDULING

**CITIZENS' RIGHTS**

**Class Time** 30 minutes

**Task** Creating a visual representation of citizens' rights

**Purpose** To explain citizens' rights in an alternative format

**Supplies Needed**

- Art supplies
- Software to create graphics (optional)

**Activity** Have students create a visual representation of the information on page 282. Tell them that their representations should be geared toward younger children or people who do not read English. Some ideas may include a poster, a sculpture, or a mobile. If software is available, students can create computer artwork. Then have students present their visual representation to the class.

## What Are Your Responsibilities?

For American democracy to work, citizens must carry out important responsibilities. There are two kinds of responsibilities—personal and civic. Personal responsibilities include taking care of yourself, helping your family, knowing right from wrong, and behaving in a respectful way.

Civic responsibilities are those that involve your government and community. They include obeying rules and laws, serving on juries, paying taxes, and defending your country when called upon. One of the most important responsibilities is voting. When you turn 18, you will have that right.

As a young person, you can be a good citizen in a number of ways. You might work with other people in your community to make it a fair and just place to live. Working for a political party or writing to your elected officials about issues that concern you are some other examples.

The chart below shows how responsibilities change with a citizen's age. Notice that all citizens share the responsibility to obey the laws of their communities.

**See Citizenship Today: Obeying Rules and Laws, p. 300**

***Responsibilities of a Citizen***

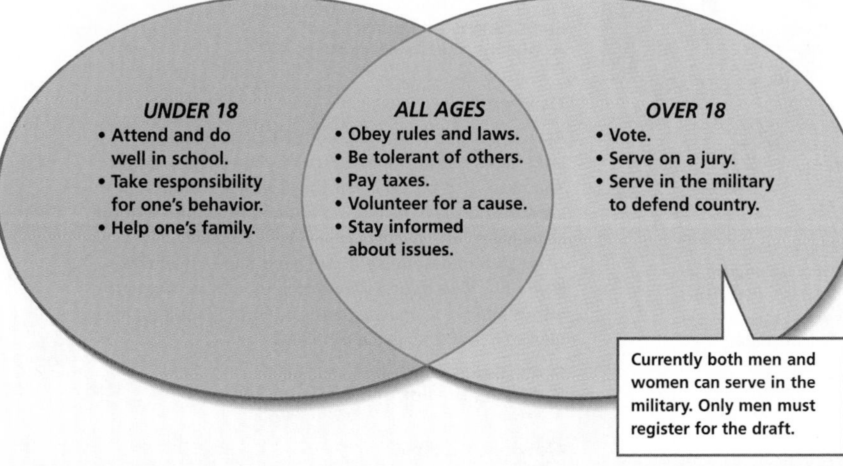

UNDER 18
• Attend and do well in school.
• Take responsibility for one's behavior.
• Help one's family.
ALL AGES
• Obey rules and laws.
• Be tolerant of others.
• Pay taxes.
• Volunteer for a cause.
• Stay informed about issues.
OVER 18
• Vote.
• Serve on a jury.
• Serve in the military to defend country.
Currently both men and women can serve in the military. Only men must register for the draft.

### CITIZENSHIP ACTIVITIES

1. Interview a recently naturalized citizen. Ask about the test he or she took to become a U.S. citizen. Write a report of your findings.
2. Using newspapers or magazines, find examples of citizens using their unalienable rights or practicing responsible citizenship. Cut out five articles to illustrate the points. Mount them and write a one-sentence explanation of each article.





### CRITICAL THINKING ACTIVITY

**Making Inferences** Tell the class that in the presidential election of 1996, less than a third of voters aged 18 and 19 (32.4%) voted versus almost three-fourths of voters aged 65 to 74 (72.6%).

Ask the students why they think the voter turnout is low among young people. How does their not voting affect the law-making process? Discuss the reasons given and consider ways to improve voter turnout among young people.

**Class Time** 20 minutes

**Citizenship Today**
- Obeying Rules and Laws, pp. 5–6

### MORE ABOUT . . .

**Juries**

Any citizen over 18 and under 70 can be called to serve on a jury. People are chosen from a list created by jury commissioners. When a person is called, he or she receives a writ of *venire facias,* which means "you must come." Then he or she must go to the designated courthouse to be assigned to a case. Typically, 12 people are selected from a large pool of potential jurors to serve on each trial jury. The chosen juror must sit in the court for the entire length of the trial, which can last from one day to several months, depending on the trial's complexity. A juror's obligation is to hear the evidence and to deliver a verdict.

**Citizenship Today**
- The Importance of Juries, pp. 1–2

### INDIVIDUAL NEEDS: CITIZENSHIP ACTIVITIES

**An interview report should**
- fully and accurately record the answers to the questions.
- evaluate the information.
- follow the rules of spelling, punctuation, and grammar.

**A scrapbook should**
- be neatly presented.
- provide a clear summary of the selected article.
- follow the rules of spelling, punctuation, and grammar.

## INSTRUCT

**How Do You Stay Informed?/**
**How Do You Make Wise Decisions?/**
**How Do You Participate in Your Community?**

Key Questions

- Why is it important to stay informed about community issues?
- What are some steps involved in making important decisions?
- How can you contribute to your community?

 **Citizenship Today**

- Debating Points of View, pp. 11–12
- Detecting Bias in the Media, pp. 15–16
- Writing Government Officials, pp. 17–18

### CRITICAL THINKING ACTIVITY

**Identifying Facts and Opinions** Find a brief article on a local issue. Reproduce it for each member of the class. Remind the class that a *fact* is a piece of information that can be checked for accuracy, whereas an *opinion* expresses the beliefs, attitudes, or feelings of an individual. Have each student read the article, underlining any facts and circling any opinions. Then divide the class into pairs. Have students compare their answers with those of their partner. Then have a class discussion about how the facts and opinions in the article shaped their understanding of the issue.

**Class Time** 25 minutes

# Building Citizenship Skills

Good citizenship skills include **staying informed, solving problems** or **making decisions,** and **taking action.** Every citizen can find ways to build citizenship skills. By showing respect for the law and for the rights of others in your daily life, you promote democracy. You can also work to change conditions in your community to make sure all citizens experience freedom and justice.

## How Do You Stay Informed?

Americans can sometimes feel that they have access to too much information. It may seem overwhelming. Even so, you should stay informed on issues that affect your life. Staying informed gives you the information you need to make wise decisions and helps you find ways to solve problems.

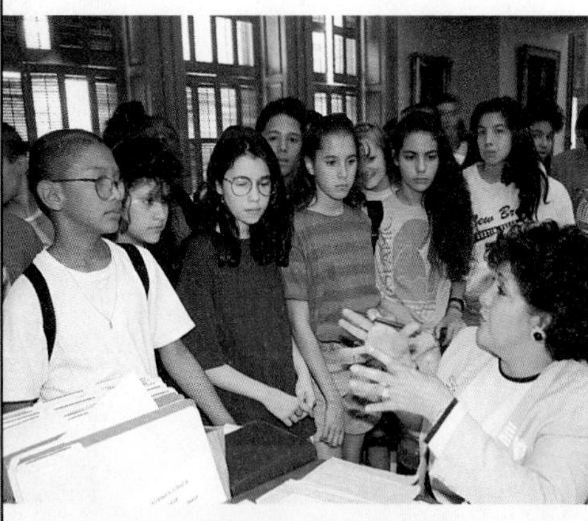

These Texas middle school students are staying informed by talking to their Texas State Representative. Many public officials enjoy having students visit and ask them questions about their jobs, and about issues students think are important.

### Watch, Listen, and Read

**The first step in practicing good citizenship is to know how to find information that you need.**

**Sources of information include broadcast and print media and the Internet. Public officials and civic organizations are also good sources for additional information. Remember as you are reading to evaluate your sources.**

**See Citizenship Today: Analyzing Points of View, p. 467**

### Evaluate

**As you become informed, you will need to make judgments about the accuracy of your news sources. You must also be aware of those sources' points of view and biases. (A bias is a judgment formed without knowing all of the facts.)**

**You should determine if you need more information. If you do, then decide where to find it. After gathering information, you may be ready to form an opinion or a plan of action to solve a problem.**

**See Citizenship Today: Detecting Bias in the Media, p. 661**

### Communicate

**To bring about change in their communities, active citizens may need to contact public officials. In today's world, making contact is easy.**

**You can reach most public officials by telephone, voice mail, fax, or letter. Many public officials also have Internet pages or e-mail that encourage input from the public.**

**See Citizenship Today: Writing Government Officials, p. 774**



### ACTIVITY OPTIONS

### INDIVIDUAL NEEDS

#### STUDENTS ACQUIRING ENGLISH/ESL

This activity provides an opportunity for students who speak a language other than English to develop a brochure in their own language that informs community members of important information.

Pair an English-speaking student with a student acquiring English. Have the pairs identify community services or information they think would benefit members of the community. Then they should plan a brochure by determining a written or visual way to present the information that is appealing and informative. One brochure should be produced in the language of the ESL student as well as one in English. Once the brochures are completed, have the pairs pass them around the class.

## How Do You Make Wise Decisions?

Civic life involves making important decisions. As a voter, whom should you vote for? As a juror, should you find the defendant guilty or not guilty? As an informed citizen, should you support or oppose a proposed government action? Unlike decisions about which video to rent, civic decisions cannot be made by a process as easy as tossing a coin. Instead, you should use a problem-solving approach like the one shown in the chart below. Decision-making won't always proceed directly from step to step. Sometimes it's necessary to backtrack a little. For example, you may get to the "Analyze Information" step and realize that you don't have enough information to analyze. Then you can go back a step and gather more information.

### Problem-Solving and Decision-Making Process

Problem-solving and decision-making involves many steps. This diagram shows you how to take those steps. Notice that you may have to repeat some steps depending on the information you gather.

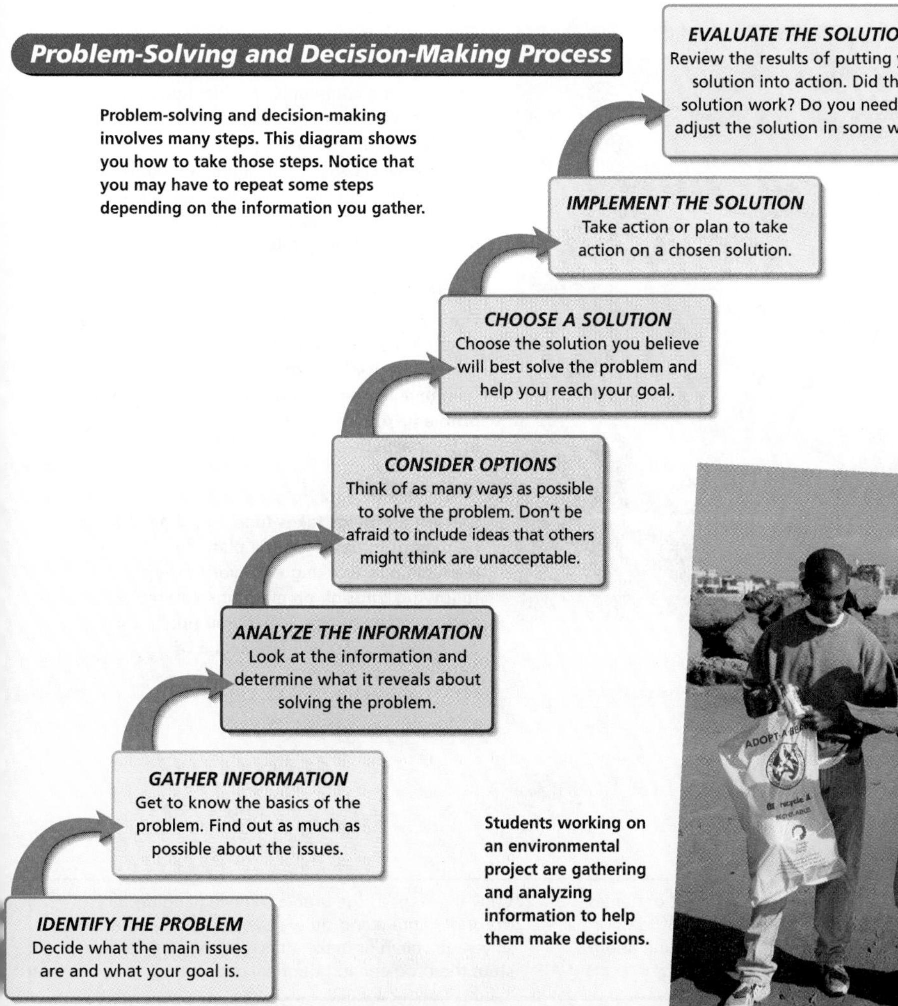

***IDENTIFY THE PROBLEM*** Decide what the main issues are and what your goal is.

***GATHER INFORMATION*** Get to know the basics of the problem. Find out as much as possible about the issues.

***ANALYZE THE INFORMATION*** Look at the information and determine what it reveals about solving the problem.

***CONSIDER OPTIONS*** Think of as many ways as possible to solve the problem. Don't be afraid to include ideas that others might think are unacceptable.

***CHOOSE A SOLUTION*** Choose the solution you believe will best solve the problem and help you reach your goal.

***IMPLEMENT THE SOLUTION*** Take action or plan to take action on a chosen solution.

***EVALUATE THE SOLUTION*** Review the results of putting your solution into action. Did the solution work? Do you need to adjust the solution in some way?

Students working on an environmental project are gathering and analyzing information to help them make decisions.





### MORE ABOUT . . .

**Decision Making**

Problem solving and decision making are both public and private processes. Both processes are used in every branch and at every level of government. Some key decisions of the 20th century that have shaped the lives of American citizens include the following:

- Entering World Wars I and II, the Korean War, and the Vietnam War
- Dropping the atomic bombs on Hiroshima and Nagasaki
- Desegregation of all schools
- Financing a space program

### CRITICAL THINKING ACTIVITY

**Evaluating** Have students study each of the steps in the diagram. Then ask them to think about which steps are most often ignored in the decision-making process. Discuss why eliminating steps in the process may lead to poor decisions.

**Class Time** 10 minutes

### ACTIVITY OPTIONS

### INTERDISCIPLINARY LINK: CIVICS

**PROBLEM-SOLVING PROCESS**

**Class Time** One class period

**Task** Using the decision-making model to solve a problem

**Purpose** To identify a school need and formulate a plan to meet that need

**Supplies Needed** None

**Activity** Have the class brainstorm about needs they think the school may have (for example, a recycling program, more choices for lunch, a new playground). Write those ideas on the board. Once students agree on a need, divide them into groups. Using the problem-solving model on page 285, each group should follow the steps necessary to meet that need. When the students feel their solution is sound, have them present it to the principal or another school official to help implement the solution.

**MORE ABOUT . . .**

**Suitcases for Kids**

Aubyn Burnside collected 300 suitcases within a few months after she started her project. As of 1999, she had over 10,000 suitcases dropped off at her house. American Airlines and TWA encourage flight attendants to donate their used luggage. Boys and Girls Clubs of America and trucking firms have helped out. Her project has spread to 45 states.

Hoping to inspire other young people to volunteer, Aubyn said, "Age is not a limit. . . . Listen to people when they ask for help. Just try to do stuff, because if you don't try, you're not gonna get anywhere."

**Citizenship Today**
- Community Service, pp. 13–14
- Simulation 4: Town Meeting, pp. 42–45

**CRITICAL THINKING ACTIVITY**

**Making Inferences** Have students look at the picture on this page. Ask them to infer why these students organized the rally. Then ask how this rally reflects the problem-solving model on the previous page.

**Class Time** 10 minutes

## How Do You Participate in Your Community?

Across the country many young people have come up with ways to make their communities better places to live. Thirteen-year-old Aubyn Burnside of Hickory, North Carolina, is just one example. Aubyn felt sorry for foster children she saw moving their belongings in plastic trash bags. She founded Suitcases for Kids. This program provides used luggage for foster children who are moving from one home to another. Her program has been adopted by other young people in several states. Below are some ways in which you can participate in your community.

**See Citizenship Today: Community Service, p. 610**

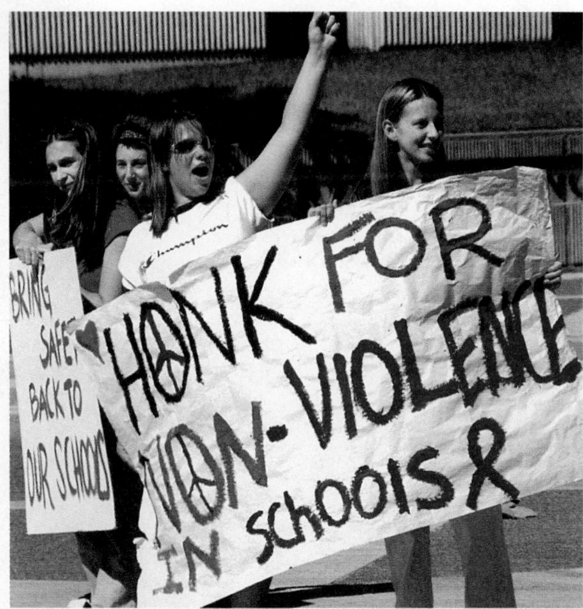


Students participate in a rally to promote safety in their school.

### Find a Cause

How can you become involved in your community? First, select a community problem or issue that interests you. Some ideas from other young people include starting a support group for children with cancer, publishing a neighborhood newspaper with children's stories and art, and putting on performances to entertain people in shelters and hospitals.

### Develop Solutions

Once you have found a cause on which you want to work, develop a plan for solving the problem. Use the decision-making or problem-solving skills you have learned to find ways to approach the problem. You may want to involve other people in your activities.

### Follow Through

Solving problems takes time. You'll need to be patient in developing a plan. You can show leadership in working with your group by following through on meetings you set up and plans you make. When you finally solve the problem, you will feel proud of your accomplishments.

**CITIZENSHIP ACTIVITIES**

1. Use the telephone directory to make a list of names, addresses, and phone numbers of public officials or organizations that could provide information about solving problems in your community.
2. Copy the steps in the problem-solving and decision-making diagram and show how you followed them to solve a problem or make a decision. Be sure to clearly state the problem and the final decision.



**INDIVIDUAL NEEDS: CITIZENSHIP ACTIVITIES**

**The list should**
- include information from various levels of government.
- include information from private or nonprofit organizations.
- contain accurate and up-to-date phone numbers and addresses.

**The problem-solving report should**
- accurately copy the steps of the model.
- clearly state the problem and steps taken to solve it.
- identify the solution.

# Practicing Citizenship Skills

You have learned that good citizenship involves three skills: staying informed, solving problems, and taking action. Below are some activities to help you improve your citizenship skills. By practicing these skills you can work to make a difference in your own life and in the lives of those in your community.

## CITIZENSHIP ACTIVITIES

### Stay Informed

**CREATE A PAMPHLET OR RECRUITING COMMERCIAL**

Ask your school counselors or write to your state department of education to get information on state-run colleges, universities, or technical schools. Use this information to create a brochure or recruiting commercial showing these schools and the different programs and degrees they offer.

**KEEP IN MIND**

**What's there for me?** It may help you think about what areas students are interested in and may want to pursue in later life.

**Where is it?** You may want to have a map showing where the schools are located in your state.

**How can I afford it?** Students might want to know if financial aid is available to attend the schools you have featured.

### Make Wise Decisions

**CREATE A GAME BOARD OR SKIT**

Study the decision-making diagram on page 285. With a small group, develop a skit that explains the steps in problem solving. Present your skit to younger students in your school. As an alternative, create a game board that would help younger students understand the steps in making a decision.

**KEEP IN MIND**

**What do children this age understand?** Be sure to create a skit or game at an age-appropriate level.

**What kinds of decisions do younger students make?** Think about the kinds of decisions that the viewers of your skit or players of the game might make.

**How can I make it interesting?** Use visual aids to help students understand the steps in decision making.

### Take Action

**CREATE A BULLETIN BOARD FOR YOUR CLASS**

Do some research on the Internet or consult the yellow pages under "Social Services" to find the names of organizations that have volunteer opportunities for young people. Call or write for more information. Then create a bulletin board for your class showing groups that would like volunteer help.

**KEEP IN MIND**

**What kinds of jobs are they?** You may want to list the types of skills or jobs volunteer groups are looking for.

**How old do I have to be?** Some groups may be looking for younger volunteers; others may need older persons.

**How do I get there?** How easy is it to get to the volunteer group's location?







### CRITICAL THINKING ACTIVITY

**Forming and Supporting Opinions** After looking at the diagram, ask students to describe what they think the characteristics of a model citizen are. Make sure the students support their opinions about the characteristics. Then ask if they think young people can be model citizens. They should support this opinion as well.

**Class Time** 10 minutes

## ASSESS & RETEACH

### RETEACHING ACTIVITY

Have students copy the graphic on page 280. Working in small groups or pairs, students should write specific information they have learned about each element shown in the ovals. For example, under Know Your Rights, the students should be able to list rights guaranteed to an American citizen.

## INDIVIDUAL NEEDS: CITIZENSHIP ACTIVITIES

**Stay Informed**

**The pamphlet or commercial should**

- clearly present all information.
- use art that aids the viewer in understanding the information.
- be neatly presented and creative.

**Make Wise Decisions**

**The game should**

- have a clear focus and logical organization throughout.
- use pictures, words, and symbols to explain each step in a process.

**The skit should**

- capture the audience's attention.
- clearly present the concepts.

**Take Action**

**The bulletin board should**

- accurately and factually present all information.
- capture the audience's attention with an interesting layout.
- reflect opportunities appropriate for middle-school volunteers.

# UNIT 3
## The Early Republic
### 1789–1844



### BEFORE YOU READ

#### Previewing Unit 3

Unit 3 details the struggles of the new nation to meet challenges, both those from within and those from abroad. Political parties develop, and the United States faces another war with Great Britain. The nation almost doubles in size with the purchase of the Louisiana Territory, and the Lewis and Clark expedition brings back exciting information about the vast lands between the Mississippi River and the Pacific Ocean. As the nation's economy develops, sectional divisions also emerge.

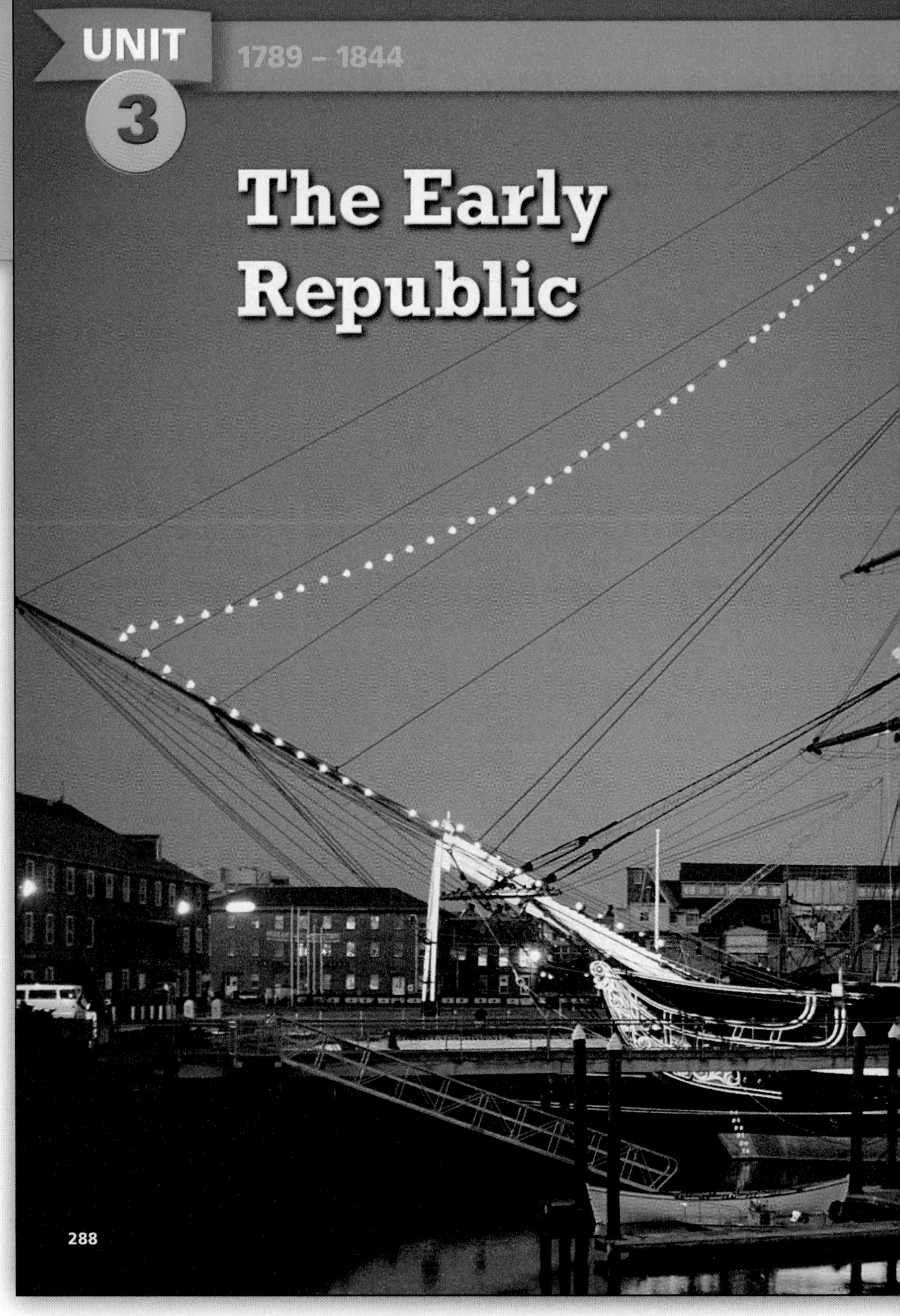

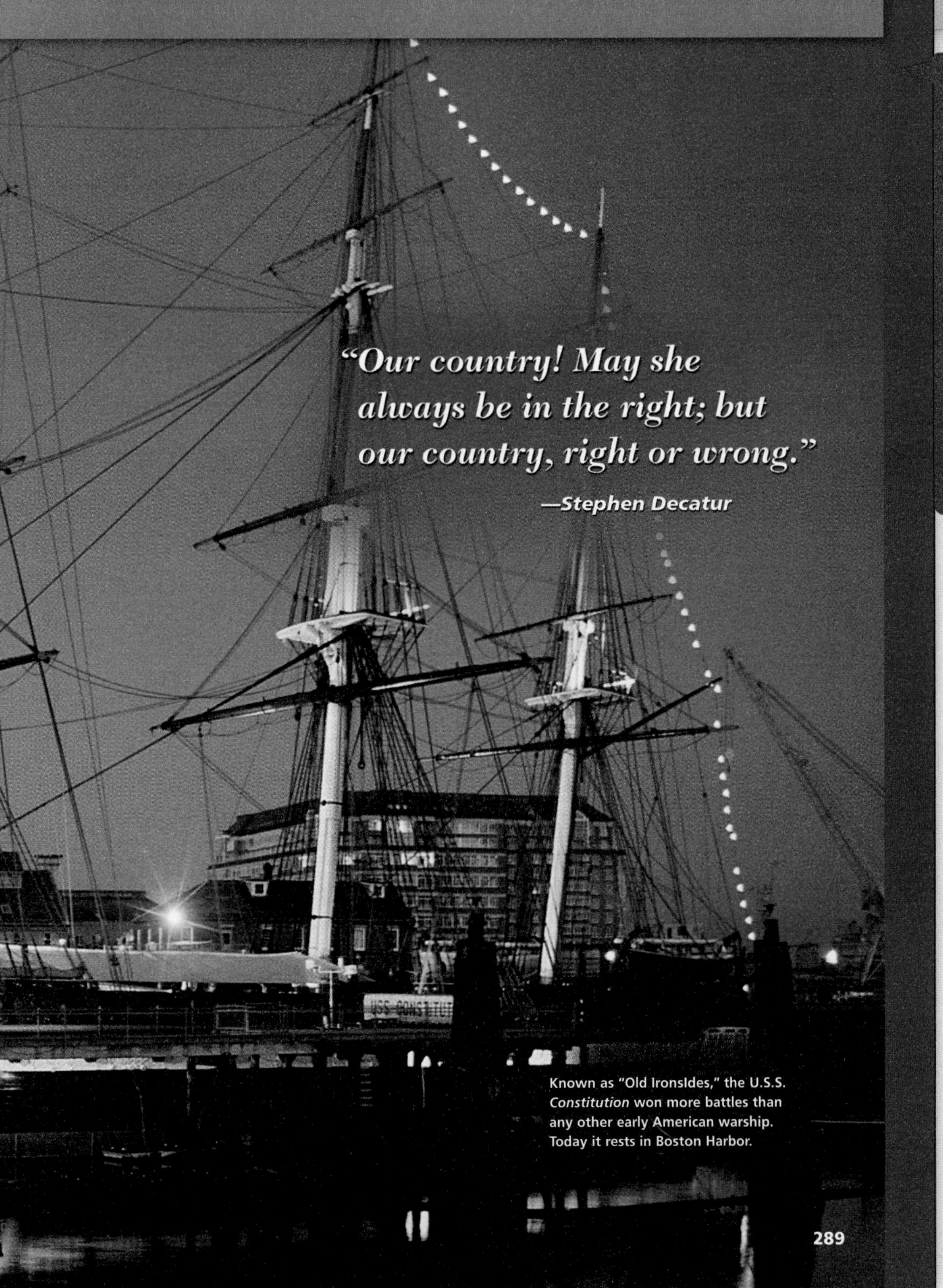

"Our country! May she always be in the right; but our country, right or wrong."
—Stephen Decatur
USS CONSTITU


Known as "Old Ironsides," the U.S.S. *Constitution* won more battles than any other early American warship. Today it rests in Boston Harbor.

289

## HISTORY FROM VISUALS

**Interpreting the Photograph** Ask the class to discuss how the quotation from Stephen Decatur reflects a feeling of nationalism. Then ask students what they think might have inspired Decatur's words. **Possible Response** Perhaps someone had said something to Decatur implying that the United States was at fault for some action or policy. Then ask why a picture of this particular ship was chosen to represent the Early Republic. **Possible Response** The name U.S.S. *Constitution* may point to the way the early republic began.

**Extension** Ask students to find out when the U.S.S. *Constitution* was built, how it earned its nickname, and how it has been preserved as a national treasure.

## CHAPTER 9 PLANNING GUIDE

# Launching a New Republic 1789–1800

### CHAPTER RESOURCES

**CHAPTER OVERVIEW**

The chapter discusses Washington's presidency and the difficulties of interpreting the Constitution. It also describes expansion into the Northwest Territory, problems in foreign policy, and the development of political parties during the Adams administration.

**COPYMASTERS**

**In-Depth Resources: Unit 3**
- Tracing Themes: Democratic Ideals, p. 2
- Building Vocabulary, p. 6

**Interdisciplinary Projects,** pp. 49–54

**TECHNOLOGY**

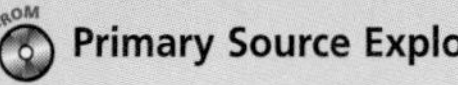
**Primary Source Explorer**

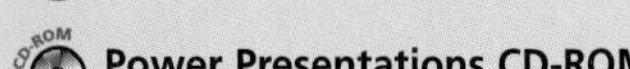
**Electronic Teacher Tools**

**Power Presentations CD-ROM**

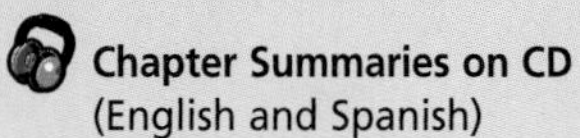
**Chapter Summaries on CD** (English and Spanish)

### SECTION 1 Washington's Presidency pp. 293–297

**KEY IDEAS**

- George Washington takes office and appoints his Cabinet; Congress sets up a federal court system.
- Hamilton develops a financial plan to improve the U.S. economy.
- Jefferson and Hamilton clash over how to interpret the Constitution.

**In-Depth Resources: Unit 3**
- Setting the Stage, p. 1
- Guided Reading, p. 3
- Primary Source, p. 10
- Reteaching Activity, p. 15

**America's History Makers**
- Alexander Hamilton, pp. 35–36

**Economics in History**
- Personal Banking, p. 9

**Why It Matters Now**
- The Importance of Leadership, pp. 17–18

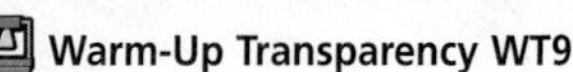
**Warm-Up Transparency WT9**

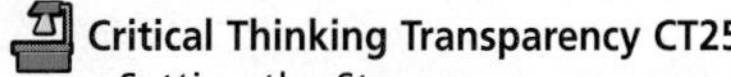
**Critical Thinking Transparency CT25**
- Setting the Stage

**ClassZone:** www.mcdougallittell.com

### SECTION 2 Challenges to the New Government pp. 298–302

- U.S. troops defeat Native Americans at the Battle of Fallen Timbers in the Northwest Territory.
- Washington asserts federal authority by using troops to put down the Whiskey Rebellion.
- The United States remains neutral in European conflicts.

**In-Depth Resources: Unit 3**
- Setting the Stage, p. 1
- Guided Reading, p. 4
- Skillbuilder Practice: Making Inferences, p. 7
- Literature Selection, pp. 12–14
- Reteaching Activity, p. 16

**Citizenship Today,** pp. 5–6

**Warm-Up Transparency WT9**

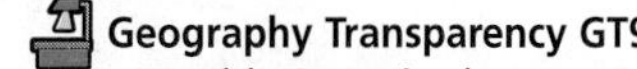
**Geography Transparency GT9**
- Trouble Spots in the New Republic 1790–1794

**Critical Thinking Transparency CT25**
- Setting the Stage

**ClassZone:** www.mcdougallittell.com

### SECTION 3 The Federalists in Charge pp. 303–307

- After Washington retires, two parties dominate national politics.
- During John Adams's presidency, the French Revolution increased political division within the United States.
- The Federalists pass the Alien and Sedition Acts, clamping down on freedom of speech and of the press.

**In-Depth Resources: Unit 3**
- Setting the Stage, p. 1
- Guided Reading, p. 5
- Geography Application: The Nation's Capital, pp. 8–9
- Primary Source, p. 11
- Reteaching Activity, p. 17

**America's History Makers**
- Benjamin Banneker, pp. 37–38

**Outline Map Activities**
- The 13 States Become 16, pp. 17–18

**Warm-Up Transparency WT9**

**Humanities Transparencies HT17, HT18**
- *Abigail Adams* by Gordon Phillips
- Engraving of Washington, D.C.

**Critical Thinking Transparency CT26**
- Cause and Effect: Growth of Political Parties

**Critical Thinking Transparency CT27**
- Visual Summary

Pupil's Edition | Overhead Transparency | CD-ROM
Copymaster | Audio Library | Internet

## ASSESSMENT

**Chapter Assessment,** pp. 308–309

**Formal Assessment**
- Chapter Tests, Forms A and B, pp. 149–156

**Alternative Assessment Book**

**Electronic Teacher Tools with Test Maker**

**Section Assessment,** p. 297

**Formal Assessment**
- Section Quiz, p. 146

**Alternative Assessment Book**
- Rubrics for an article, 4.1
- Rubrics for a cartoon, 1.2

**Electronic Teacher Tools with Test Maker**

**Section Assessment,** p. 302

**Formal Assessment**
- Section Quiz, p. 147

**Alternative Assessment Book**
- Rubrics for a map, 2.1
- Rubrics for a scene, 1.3

**Electronic Teacher Tools with Test Maker**

**Section Assessment,** p. 307

**Formal Assessment**
- Section Quiz, p. 148

**Alternative Assessment Book**
- Rubrics for a video, 5.3
- Rubrics for a reading, 3.1

**Electronic Teacher Tools with Test Maker**

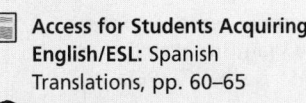

## CUSTOMIZING FOR INDIVIDUAL NEEDS

### Students Acquiring English/ESL

**Reading Study Guide** (English and Spanish), pp. 93–100

**Access for Students Acquiring English/ESL:** Spanish Translations, pp. 60–65

**Chapter Summaries on CD** (English and Spanish)

### Less Proficient Readers

**Reading Study Guide** (English and Spanish), pp. 93–100

**Chapter Summaries on CD** (English and Spanish)

### Gifted and Talented Students

**In-Depth Resources: Unit 3**
- Enrichment Activity, p. 18

**America's History Makers**
- Alexander Hamilton, pp. 35–36
- Benjamin Banneker, pp. 37–38

## CROSS-CURRICULAR CONNECTIONS

### Geography

McCall, Edith. ***Biography of a River: The Mississippi.*** New York: Walker, 1990. Entertainingly describes the Mississippi as both a natural system and a human highway.

### Economics

Whitelaw, Nancy. ***More Perfect Union: The Story of Alexander Hamilton.*** Greensboro, NC: Morgan Reynolds, 1997. Story of the first secretary of the treasury.

### Science

Litwin, Laura Baskes. ***Benjamin Banneker: Astronomer and Mathematician.*** Berkeley Heights, NJ: Enslow, 1999. Illustrated biography uses contemporary documents.

### Interdisciplinary Projects, pp. 49–54

- Math: Mathematical Puzzles
- Science: Preserving Food
- Language Arts: Newspaper Editorials
- Art: Neoclassical Architecture of Washington, D.C.

### Literature

Benet, Stephen Vincent. ***A Book of Americans.*** New York: Holt, 1995. Short, memorable, and sometimes amusing poems about Americans from Thomas Jefferson to Captain Kidd.

Collier, James Lincoln and Christopher Collier. ***Jump Ship to Freedom.*** New York: Yearling Books, 1987. A young boy headed for a life of slavery in the West Indies escapes to post-Revolutionary New York.

Rinaldi, Ann. ***The Second Bend in the River.*** New York: Scholastic, 1997. Romance between Tecumseh and an Ohio girl. An appended note explains what's factual.

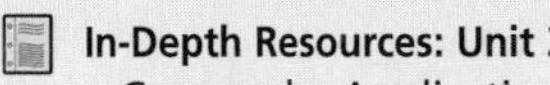

## ENRICHMENT ACTIVITIES

**Pupil's Edition, pp. 290–309**
**Interact with History,** p. 291
**Economics in History,** p. 296
**Citizenship Today,** p. 300

**In-Depth Resources: Unit 3**
- Geography Application: The Nation's Capital, pp. 8–9
- Primary Source: from *Journal* by William Maclay, p. 10
- Primary Source: "Hail Columbia" by Joseph Hopkinson, p. 11
- Literature Selection: from *Davy Crockett, Tennessee Settler,* pp. 12–14

**America's History Makers**
- Alexander Hamilton, pp. 35–36
- Benjamin Banneker, pp. 37–38

**Outline Map Activities**
- The 13 States Become 16, pp. 17–18

**Why It Matters Now**
- The Importance of Leadership, pp. 17–18

# CHAPTER 9 PACING GUIDE

## LESSON PLAN OPTIONS (50-MINUTE PERIOD)

(TE) = Teacher's Edition (PE) = Pupil's Edition

| | TEACHER-DIRECTED ACTIVITIES<br>Class Time: 15 minutes | STUDENT-CENTERED ACTIVITIES<br>Class Time: 25 minutes | INDIVIDUAL ACTIVITIES<br>Class Time: 10 minutes |
|---|---|---|---|
| **DAY 1**<br>Introduction<br>pp. 290–292 | **Presentation Options**<br>• Begin with a class discussion of the drawing on p. 290 **(PE)**.<br>• Lead a class discussion on the "What Do You Know?" question in Setting the Stage, p. 292. Then introduce the graphic organizer for the chapter **(PE)**. | **Options for Cooperative Learning**<br>• Have student groups discuss the Interact with History questions, p. 291 **(PE)**.<br>• Have student groups respond to the "What Do You Want to Know?" question in Setting the Stage, p. 292 **(PE)**. | **Head Start on Homework Options**<br>• Have students skim Section 1 Main Idea, Why It Matters Now, Terms & Names, and the main headings, p. 293 **(PE)**.<br>• Have students begin Guided Reading activity and Building Vocabulary sheet. |
| **DAY 2**<br>Section 1<br>pp. 293–297 | **Presentation Options**<br>• Begin with the 5-Minute Warm-Up, p. 293 **(TE)**.<br>• Review the Section 1 Main Idea, Why It Matters Now, and Terms & Names, p. 293 **(PE)**.<br>• Choose 5 key questions for Objectives 1–4 to discuss with the class, pp. 293–295 **(TE)**. | **Options for Cooperative Learning**<br>• Divide students into groups to work on the Economics in History questions, p. 296 **(PE)**.<br>• Have student pairs work together to complete one of the Activity Options in the Section 1 Assessment, p. 297 **(PE)**. | **Head Start on Homework Options**<br>• Have students begin working on Section 1 Assessment, p. 297 **(PE)**.<br>• Have students preview Section 2 Main Idea, Why It Matters Now, Terms & Names, and the main headings, p. 298 **(PE)**. |
| **DAY 3**<br>Section 2<br>pp. 298–302 | **Presentation Options**<br>• Begin with the 5-Minute Warm-Up, p. 298 **(TE)**.<br>• Choose 5 key questions for Objectives 1–4 to discuss with the class, pp. 298–301 **(TE)**.<br>• Lead the students through the Citizenship Today Critical Thinking Activity, p. 300 **(TE)**. | **Options for Cooperative Learning**<br>• Divide students into groups to work on the Skillbuilder Mini-Lesson: Making Inferences, p. 299 **(TE)**.<br>• Divide students into groups and have them complete the Citizenship Today questions, p. 300 **(PE)**. | **Head Start on Homework Options**<br>• Have students begin working on Section 2 Assessment, p. 302 **(PE)**.<br>• Have students do the Reading History questions and chart Skillbuilder for Section 3 **(PE)**. |
| **DAY 4**<br>Section 3<br>pp. 303–307 | **Presentation Options**<br>• Begin with the 5-Minute Warm-Up, p. 303 **(TE)**.<br>• Choose 5 key questions for Objectives 1–4 to discuss with the class, pp. 303–307 **(TE)**.<br>• Lead a discussion using the Cause and Effect Transparency CT26 on the growth of political parties. | **Options for Cooperative Learning**<br>• Divide students into groups and have them complete the Interdisciplinary Link, Language Arts: Expressing an Opinion, p. 306 **(TE)**.<br>• Have student pairs work together to complete one of the Activity Options in the Section 3 Assessment, p. 307 **(PE)**. | **Head Start on Homework Options**<br>• Have students complete the Setting the Stage graphic organizer for the chapter, p. 292 **(PE)**.<br>• Have students begin working on the Chapter Assessment, pp. 308–309 **(PE)**.<br>• Prepare for Chapter Test<br>**Formal Assessment,** pp. 149–156 |

TEACHER-TESTED ACTIVITY **Brent Heath, De Anza Middle School, Ontario, California**

## GEORGE WASHINGTON'S FAREWELL

**Class Time** Two class periods

**Task** Analyzing George Washington's Farewell Address

**Purpose** To understand this important speech and its impact on U.S. history

**Supplies Needed**
- Reference materials and Internet resources on George Washington
- Copies of Washington's Farewell Address

**Activity** Have each student read through the Farewell Address at his or her own pace, highlighting key ideas, words, or phrases on a copy of the document. Divide students into trios and have them read aloud their marked copies to their group, stopping at each highlighted idea or phrase to discuss with other group members what it means. Then have groups choose three ideas, words, or phrases that they all consider important. Have groups share their choices with the class, explaining why they think these ideas, words, or phrases are important and how these concepts might influence the nation's future history.

## BLOCK SCHEDULING — LESSON PLAN OPTIONS (90-MINUTE PERIOD)

### DAY 1

**Interact with History,** p. 291
**Class Time** 20 Minutes

Options for pacing and variety:
- **Role-Playing** Divide students into groups of five students each. Have each group member assume the role of one of the people shown in the Interact with History painting. Have each tell the others why his experience makes him well suited to his job in the new government.
**Class Time** 20 minutes

**Setting the Stage,** p. 292
**Class Time** 20 minutes

Options for pacing and variety:
- **Time Saver** For a homework assignment, have students create their own definitions of *democracy* and *republic* and make a list of three questions they have about the roles of Washington, Jefferson, Hamilton, Randolph, or Knox in the new government.
**Class Time** 5 minutes

**Section 1,** pp. 293–297
**Class Time** 50 minutes

Options for pacing and variety:
- **Peer Teaching** Ask a pair of students to review the Economics in History lesson on page 296 as well as the information at www.mcdougallittell.com on banking. Tell them to create a poster to explain to the class how banks work. **Class Time** 20 minutes
- **Time Saver** Assign the Taking Notes and Critical Thinking questions in the Section Assessment as homework.
**Class Time** 35 minutes

### DAY 2

**Section 2,** pp. 298–302
**Class Time** 45 minutes

Options for pacing and variety:
- **Internet** Extend students' background knowledge of George Washington and his Mount Vernon home by visiting www.mcdougallittell.com
**Class Time** 20 minutes
- **Peer Teaching** After reading Citizenship Today on page 300, ask a panel of four students to debate the question: Should American communities have curfew laws? Have the rest of the class act as debate judges, deciding which speakers make the most convincing arguments.
**Class Time** 25 minutes

**Section 3,** pp. 303–307
**Class Time** 45 minutes

Options for pacing and variety:
- **Time Saver** Use the chart on page 304 to summarize the differences between the Federalists and the Democratic-Republicans.
**Class Time** 5 minutes
- **History on Film** Extend students' background knowledge of the Alien and Sedition Acts and many other events in this chapter by viewing *A New Nation.* Schlessinger, 1996.
**Class Time** 35 minutes

**Chapter 9 Assessment,** pp. 308–309
**Class Time** 40 minutes

Options for pacing and variety:
- **Peer Evaluation** Divide students into pairs. Using the information in the Visual Summary on page 308, have students identify two events in each president's term that they consider most important and explain why.
**Class Time** 20 minutes
- **Peer Teaching** Assign different groups of students each of the four Critical Thinking questions and the Interact with History question on page 308. Have groups answer the question assigned and share their responses with the class.
**Class Time** 10 minutes

## CHAPTER 9 OBJECTIVE

The student will explain how the leaders of the new nation met the challenges of establishing a sound economy and a stable, democratic government.

### HISTORY FROM VISUALS

**Interpreting the Painting** Have students note the expressions on the faces of the people on the shore and Washington's sober, steady gaze. Ask students how the artist suggests the patriotic nature of the event and the seriousness and significance of the occasion. **Possible Responses** *Patriotic:* Students may note the two American flags and the eagle. *Seriousness:* Students may note the expressions on the faces of those on the boat and on the shore and the restrained way in which Washington greets the crowd and the crowd watches Washington.

**Extension** Have the students pick one of the people waiting on the shore and write a diary entry for April 23, 1789, explaining what he or she hoped the new government would do.

# CHAPTER 9 Launching a New Republic 1789–1800

George Washington arrives by boat in New York on April 23, 1789, for his presidential inauguration.

290

### RECOMMENDED RESOURCES

**BOOKS FOR THE TEACHER**

Levy, L. W. ***Emergence of a Free Press.*** New York: Oxford Univ. Press, 1985. A noted authority takes a fresh look at the topic.

McCoy, Drew R. ***The Elusive Republic: Political Economy in Jeffersonian America.*** Chapel Hill, NC: Univ. of North Carolina Press, 1980. A look at underlying trends and stresses in the period.

Stinchcombe, William. ***The XYZ Affair.*** Westport, CT: Greenwood, 1980. Scholarly but engrossing account of this early cloak-and-dagger episode.

**VIDEO**

***Abigail Adams.*** American Women of Achievement Video Collection. Schlessinger Media, 1995. Life and times of the second First Lady.

**INTERNET**

For more about virtual tours of Mt. Vernon or Monticello, visit www.mcdougallittell.com

Interact with History

Alexander Hamilton, brilliant lawyer and economist, becomes secretary of the treasury.
Thomas Jefferson, farmer, diplomat, and principal author of the Declaration of Independence, becomes secretary of state.
Edmund Randolph, attorney general of Virginia, becomes attorney general of the federal government.
Henry Knox, a general of artillery during the Revolution, becomes secretary of war.
George Washington, general and Revolutionary War hero, is president.

**The year is 1789, and George Washington has been inaugurated as the first president of the United States. It quickly becomes obvious to you and to others that the president will need help. He chooses people with different talents and experience to help him govern.**

### What Do You Think?

- Why might you want people with different viewpoints in your government?
- How would you go about setting up a government?
- What do you think your biggest challenges would be?

# *What kind of person would you choose to help you govern?*

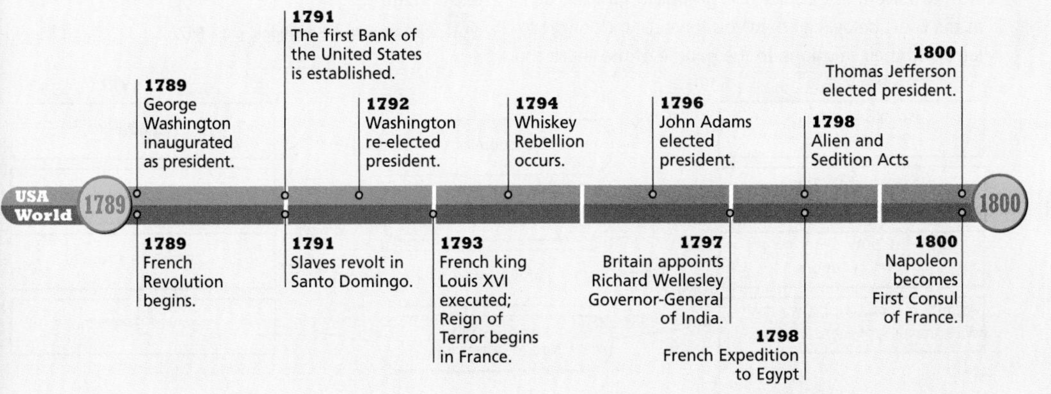
USA
World
1789
1800
1789 George Washington inaugurated as president.
1791 The first Bank of the United States is established.
1792 Washington re-elected president.
1794 Whiskey Rebellion occurs.
1796 John Adams elected president.
1798 Alien and Sedition Acts
1800 Thomas Jefferson elected president.
1789 French Revolution begins.
1791 Slaves revolt in Santo Domingo.
1793 French king Louis XVI executed; Reign of Terror begins in France.
1797 Britain appoints Richard Wellesley Governor-General of India.
1798 French Expedition to Egypt
1800 Napoleon becomes First Consul of France.

## Interact *with* History

### OBJECTIVES

- To understand the reasons that Washington needed a cabinet
- To speculate on the responsibilities of each cabinet member

### What Do You Think?

1. Note that the men shown with Washington formed the first cabinet, which was made up of the attorney general and the secretaries (heads) of the three departments. They advised the president on various issues. Ask why Washington might have felt he needed advisers.
2. Ask students to name some of the responsibilities that they would expect each man to have.
3. Have students list some of the national issues government leaders will have to address: security, finance, domestic and foreign trade, relations with other countries and with Native Americans, law and order, expansion of white settlement.

### *What kind of person would you choose to help you govern?*

Encourage students to think not only about the responsibilities of government but also about the temperament and character of the people they would choose to have as leaders.

### MAKING PERSONAL CONNECTIONS

Ask students to think about any groups that they have worked in, perhaps to complete a group project for a class or a club committee. How easy and enjoyable do students find working in a group? What sort of qualities make a good group member?

### TIME LINE DISCUSSION

**Point out to students that in the 11-year period shown on this time line, the United States was establishing a stable government. Meanwhile, in Europe, there was great upheaval.**

- Ask students which events show the United States government was stable. **Answer** the election of three presidents and the establishment of a U.S. bank
- Ask students which events suggest that France experienced great political instability during this time. **Answer** 1789 revolution; 1793 execution of monarch, Reign of Terror; 1800 Napoleon heads new government
- Ask students what differences existed in the ways the French and the Americans chose leaders during this period. **Answer** Americans chose leaders peacefully through the electoral process; French leaders rose and fell through revolution and violent conflict.

## BEFORE YOU READ

### Previewing the Theme: Democratic Ideals

Have students make a list of what they consider "democratic ideals," or basic beliefs about how the democratic system should function. Have students explain why each ideal is important.

Tell students that Washington and other leaders of the new nation knew how important it was that they make the new government work to solve the nation's problems.

### What Do You Know?

Remind students that the Constitution provided only an outline for the government of the nation. It remained for the newly elected officials to put the Constitution to work.

 **In-Depth Resources: Unit 3**
- Tracing Themes: Democratic Ideals, p. 2

## READ AND TAKE NOTES

### Reading Strategy: Identifying and Solving Problems

Note that identifying problems faced and solutions found will help students gain historical perspective. Point out that the chart on page 292 alerts readers to problems and solutions regarding the major issues of economics, politics, foreign affairs, and relations with Native Americans. Encourage students to identify these problems and solutions as they read the chapter.

 **In-Depth Resources: Unit 3**
- Setting the Stage, p. 1

 **Critical Thinking Transparency CT25**
- Setting the Stage

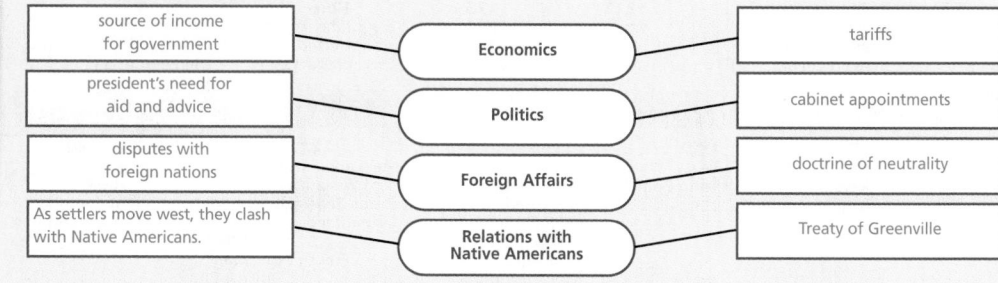

# Chapter 9 SETTING THE STAGE

## BEFORE YOU READ

Inaugural coat buttons, 1789, proclaim the beginning of the Washington presidency.

### Previewing the Theme

**Democratic Ideals** During the Federalist era (1789–1801), the leaders of the United States faced many challenges and difficulties. In this chapter, you will see how the way in which they responded to those obstacles and opportunities established a democratic foundation.

### What Do You Know?

What do you think of when you hear the words *democracy* and *republic?* Why do you think the citizens and leaders of the new country wanted to establish a republic governed by laws?

**THINK ABOUT**
- the experience of the colonists under British rule
- the effect of the Revolutionary War and the period immediately after the war

### What Do You Want to Know?

What questions do you have about the people who created the U.S. government? Record your questions in your notebook before you read the chapter.

## READ AND TAKE NOTES

**Reading Strategy: Identifying and Solving Problems** As you read history, try to identify problems in past times and the solutions that people came up with to solve their problems. A graphic organizer such as the chart below can help you to keep track of problems and their solutions. In the middle of the chart, four headings categorize the major issues faced by the young nation. Copy the chart into your notebook and then record problems and the proposed solutions in each category.

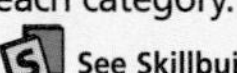 See Skillbuilder Handbook, page R17.

| PROBLEMS | | SOLUTIONS |
|---|---|---|
| source of income for government | Economics | tariffs |
| president's need for aid and advice | Politics | cabinet appointments |
| disputes with foreign nations | Foreign Affairs | doctrine of neutrality |
| As settlers move west, they clash with Native Americans. | Relations with Native Americans | Treaty of Greenville |



## TEACHING STRATEGY

### READING THE CHAPTER

This is a thematic chapter focusing on the work of the government in implementing the Constitution and in dealing with domestic rebellion, relations with Native Americans and foreign nations, and issues of national security. Encourage students to note the obstacles leaders faced and how they attempted to solve those difficulties. You may want to review the problem-solving model found on page 285 in the Citizenship Handbook to compare the steps taken by the leaders to solve problems.

### ALTERNATIVE ASSESSMENT

The Chapter Assessment describes three activities for alternative assessment on page 309. You may wish to have students work on these activities during the course of the chapter and then present them at the end.

# 1 Washington's Presidency

**TERMS & NAMES**
inaugurate
Federal Judiciary Act
cabinet
tariff

**MAIN IDEA**
The president and the Congress began to set up the new government.

**WHY IT MATTERS NOW**
The strength of the U.S. today is due to the decisions of the Founders about how to organize the government.

### ONE AMERICAN'S STORY

Charles Thomson had known George Washington for many years. Thomson had served as secretary of the Continental Congress when delegates from the colonies first met in Philadelphia in 1774.

Now, 15 years later, on April 14, 1789, he had a very different job to do. He had come to Mount Vernon in Virginia with a letter for George Washington. Washington knew the reason for the visit. Thomson's letter was to tell him that he had been elected the nation's first president. Before giving Washington the letter, Thomson made a short speech.

Charles Thomson delivers the letter to Washington announcing his election as president.

*A VOICE FROM THE PAST*

I have now Sir to inform you that . . . your patriotism and your readiness to sacrifice . . . private enjoyments to preserve the liberty and promote the happiness of your Country [convinced the Congress that you would accept] this important Office to which you are called not only by the unanimous votes of the Electors but by the voice of America.

**Charles Thomson,** quoted in Washington's Papers, Library of Congress

As you will read in this section, Washington accepted the honor and the burden of his new office. He guided the nation through its early years.

## 1 Washington Takes Office

Washington had been elected only a few months before. Each member of the electoral college had written down two names. The top vote-getter, Washington, became president. The runner-up, John Adams, became vice-president. Washington left Mount Vernon on April 16, 1789. He traveled north through Baltimore and Philadelphia to New York City, the nation's capital. On April 30 at Federal Hall, Washington was **inaugurated,** or sworn in, as president. John Adams of Massachusetts was his vice-president.





## SECTION OBJECTIVES

1. To explain how the nation's court system was established
2. To describe the first cabinet
3. To analyze Hamilton's financial plans
4. To identify interpretations of the Constitution and explain how they influenced attitudes toward the national bank

### CRITICAL THINKING

Making Inferences, pp. 294, 295
Contrasting, p. 297

 **Why It Matters Now**
- The Importance of Leadership, pp. 17–18

## FOCUS & MOTIVATE

### 5-MINUTE WARM-UP

**Making Inferences** These questions focus on Washington's choice as the first president.

1. Read "A Voice from the Past" on page 293. According to Thomson, why was Washington chosen as president?
2. What does Thomson mean by the "voice of America"?

 **Warm-Up Transparency WT9**

## INSTRUCT

### INSTRUCT: OBJECTIVE 1

**Washington Takes Office/ Setting Up the Courts**

Key Questions
- What does the phrase "Washington would set a precedent" mean?
- What decisions about the nation's court system did the Constitution leave to Congress to decide?
- What was the purpose of the Federal Judiciary Act of 1789?

 **In-Depth Resources: Unit 3**
- Guided Reading, p. 3

**Reading Study Guide** (Spanish and English), pp. 93–94

## RECOMMENDED RESOURCES

 **In-Depth Resources: Unit 3**
- Guided Reading, p. 3
- Building Vocabulary, p. 6
- Primary Source: from *Journal*, p. 10
- Reteaching Activity, p. 15

 **Reading Study Guide** (Spanish and English), pp. 93–94

 **Economics in History**
- Personal Banking, p. 9

 **America's History Makers**
- Alexander Hamilton, pp. 35–36

 **Why It Matters Now**
- The Importance of Leadership, pp. 17–18

 **Formal Assessment**
- Section Quiz, p. 146

 **Alternative Assessment**
- Rubrics, 4.1
- Rubrics, 1.2

 **Access for Students Acquiring English/ESL**
- Guided Reading, p. 60

**Technology Resources**

 **Electronic Teacher Tools with Test Maker**

 **ClassZone**
www.mcdougallittell.com

As the nation's first president, Washington faced a difficult task. He knew that all eyes would be on him. His every action as president would set a precedent—an example that would become standard practice. People argued over what to call him. Some, including John Adams, suggested "His Excellency" or "His Highness." Others argued that such titles would suggest that he was a king. The debate tied up Congress for a month. Finally, "Mr. President" was agreed upon. Congress had to settle other differences about how the new government should be run.

*Reading***History**

**A. Making Inferences** Why were people so concerned about how to address the president?

A. Answer They probably believed that the way the president was addressed might affect how the office was perceived—as a monarchy or a democracy.

## Setting Up the Courts

The writers of the Constitution had left many matters to be decided by Congress. For example, the Constitution created a Supreme Court but left it to Congress to decide the number of justices. Leaders also argued about how much power the Supreme Court should have. One reason for disagreement was that the states already had their own courts. How would authority be divided between the state and federal courts?

To create a court system, Congress passed the **Federal Judiciary Act** of 1789. This act gave the Supreme Court six members: a chief justice, or judge, and five associate justices. Over time, that number has grown to nine. The act also provided for other lower, less powerful federal courts. Washington appointed John Jay, the prominent New York lawyer and diplomat, as chief justice.

**Vocabulary**

**judiciary:** system of courts and judges

**Now *and* then**

**THE PRESIDENT'S CABINET**

The president's cabinet has more than tripled in size since it began with the secretaries of state, war, and treasury, and the attorney general. As the nation has faced new challenges, the government has added new departments. In 1977, concerns about oil shortages led to the creation of the Department of Energy. The Department of Veterans' Affairs was added in 1989. Today the cabinet (shown below) includes the heads of 14 departments.

## 2 Washington's Cabinet

The Constitution also gave Congress the task of creating departments to help the president lead the nation. The president had the power to appoint the heads of these departments, who were to assist the president with the many issues and problems he had to face. These heads of departments became his **cabinet.**

The Congress created three departments. In his first major task as president, Washington chose talented people to run them. For secretary of war, he picked Henry Knox, a trusted general during the Revolution. It was Knox's job to oversee the nation's defenses. For secretary of state, Washington chose Thomas Jefferson. He had been serving as U.S. minister to France. The State Department oversaw relations between the United States and other countries. Washington turned to the brilliant Alexander Hamilton to be the secretary of the treasury. Hamilton had to manage the government's money. The secretary's ties to the president began during the war when he had served as one of Washington's aides. To advise the

**INSTRUCT: OBJECTIVE 2**

**Washington's Cabinet/Economic Problems**

Key Questions

- How did the cabinet help the president govern the nation?
- What financial problems did the nation face? How did Hamilton propose to solve them?
- What beliefs influenced Hamilton's financial plans for the nation?

**Now *and* then**

**The President's Cabinet**

Each president uses his cabinet differently. Andrew Jackson called his cabinet together only 16 times in 8 years. FDR was the first president to appoint a woman to the cabinet when he made Frances Perkins secretary of labor. Robert Weaver, Lyndon Johnson's secretary of housing and urban development, was the first African American to join a presidential cabinet. President Ronald Reagan set up small groups within his cabinet to deal with specific issues.

**ACTIVITY OPTIONS**

**INTERDISCIPLINARY LINK: CIVICS**

**BLOCK SCHEDULING**

**FORMING A CABINET**

**Class Time** One class period

**Task** Writing job descriptions for cabinet members of a new government

**Purpose** To understand the challenges of forming a new government and the functions of the executive branch

**Supplies Needed**

- Civics and/or government textbooks and other reference materials on the executive branch
- Large note cards

**Activity** Divide the class into groups and have them list the departments they would create if they were in charge of a new government. Have group members write job descriptions for the heads of these departments. Descriptions should include the name and mission of the department, the tasks the head must perform, the qualifications and experience needed, and any benefits or perks of the job. Post finished descriptions on a bulletin board. Have students pick a post they would like and write a letter telling why they would like the job.

government on legal matters, Washington picked Edmund Randolph as attorney general.

These department heads and the attorney general made up Washington's cabinet. The Constitution made no mention of a cabinet. However, Washington began the practice of calling his department heads together to advise him.

## Economic Problems

As secretary of the treasury, Alexander Hamilton faced the task of straightening out the nation's finances. First of all, the new government needed to pay its war debts. During the Revolution, the United States had borrowed millions of dollars from France, the Netherlands, and Spain. Within the United States, merchants and other private citizens had loaned money to the government. State governments also had wartime debts to pay back. By 1789, the national debt totaled more than $52 million.

Most government leaders agreed that the nation must repay its debts to win the respect of both foreign nations and its own citizens. Hamilton saw that the new nation must assure other countries that it was responsible about money. These nations would do business with the United States if they saw that the country would pay its debts. If the nation failed to do so, no country would lend it money in the future.

Hamilton came up with a financial plan that reflected his belief in a strong central government. He thought the power of the national government should be stronger than that of the state governments. Hamilton also believed that government should encourage business and industry. He sought the support of the nation's wealthy merchants and manufacturers. He thought that the nation's prosperity depended on them. The government owed money to many of these rich men. By paying them back, Hamilton hoped to win their support for the new government.

### AMERICA'S HISTORY MAKERS

**ALEXANDER HAMILTON**
**1755?–1804**

Alexander Hamilton was born into poverty in the British West Indies. When he was ten years old, the young Alexander went to work as a clerk. He so impressed his employers that they helped to send him to school at King's College (now Columbia University) in New York.

During the Revolutionary War, he became an aide to General Washington. Hamilton moved up quickly in the army and later in political life. Although of humble origins, Hamilton had little faith in the common people and put his trust in the wealthy and educated to govern.

**Why is it odd that Hamilton distrusted the common people to govern?**

*Reading* **History**

**B. Making Inferences** Why might merchants and manufacturers support a strong central government?

B. Answer Because a strong central government could encourage the development of business and make it easier to do business and collect debts.

## 3 Hamilton's Financial Plan

In 1790, Hamilton presented his plan to Congress. He proposed three steps to improve the nation's finances.

1. paying off all war debts
2. raising government revenues
3. creating a national bank

Hamilton wanted the federal government to pay off the war debts of the states. However, sectional differences arose over repayment of state debts. Virginia, Georgia, and many other Southern states had already repaid their debts and did not like being asked to help Northern states pay theirs.





### AMERICA'S HISTORY MAKERS

**Alexander Hamilton**

Hamilton was the son of a Scottish merchant, James Hamilton. His mother, Rachel Lavine, was a French Huguenot woman who was separated from her husband when she met James Hamilton on the island of St. Croix. In 1765, after living with Lavine for some years, he abandoned the family. Desperately poor with two children, Lavine sent young Alexander to work as a clerk in a countinghouse. Three years later his mother died, and he became the ward of her relatives. In 1772, Hamilton's abilities and engaging manner so impressed friends that they paid for him to go to New Jersey for further schooling. He then attended King's College in New York.

**Possible Response: Hamilton himself was born in poverty. He came from the common people. He worked hard to become part of the elite.**

**America's History Makers**
- Alexander Hamilton, pp. 35–36

### INSTRUCT: OBJECTIVE 3

**Hamilton's Financial Plan**

Key Questions
- What were the three steps in Hamilton's financial plan?
- Why did many Southern states object to helping the country pay off its war debts?
- Why did Hamilton favor imposing high tariffs on foreign goods and creating a national bank?

### ACTIVITY OPTIONS

### INDIVIDUAL NEEDS

**LESS PROFICIENT READERS**

**Creating an Outline** Show students how to create an outline using topic sentences from the text as main ideas. After writing the main ideas on the board, ask students to reread the text and identify details to complete the outline. Sample details are given for the first topic sentence below.

I. Hamilton wanted the federal government to pay war debts.
   A. Many Southern states had paid debts.
   B. They did not want to help Northern states repay debts.
   C. In exchange for Southern states helping Northern states repay debts, the capital would be placed in the South.
II. Hamilton favored tariffs.
III. Hamilton called for the creation of a national bank.

### CRITICAL THINKING ACTIVITY

**Analyzing Points of View** Tell students that while tariffs raised revenue and encouraged the purchase of American-made goods, they had other consequences as well. Ask students which businesses were likely to be helped by raising tariffs. Which business owners or consumers might be hurt by tariffs? Use a two column chart to help students examine these questions.

**Class Time** 10 minutes

## Economics *in* History

### OBJECTIVE

Students will be able to explain how a bank could help the economy of the new nation. They will be able to describe how a commercial bank operates and how a commercial bank can help the general economy.

**The Federal Reserve System**

The Federal Reserve System is the present-day "national bank." In 1913, Congress passed laws creating the Federal Reserve System, the central banking system of the United States. The system consists of 12 Federal Reserve banks, each of which is owned by the member banks in its district. The 12 banks are regulated by a central board based in the nation's capital and appointed by the president. The board manages the country's money supply, controlling the lending rate to member banks. It tightens lending rates to fight inflation or lowers rates to spur business growth through lending during economic downturns.

**Economics in History**
- Personal Banking, p. 9

Hamilton asked Thomas Jefferson of Virginia to help him gain Southern support. They reached a compromise. In exchange for Southern support of the plan, Northerners agreed to place the new nation's capital in the South. The location chosen was on the Potomac River between Virginia and Maryland.

The secretary of the treasury favored tariffs. A **tariff** is a tax on imported goods. It serves two purposes: raising money for the government and encouraging the growth of American industry. The government placed the highest tariffs on foreign goods—such as shoes and textiles—that Americans bought in great quantities. This ensured a steady flow of income to the government. In addition, since tariffs made foreign goods more expensive, they encouraged people to buy American goods.

Hamilton also called for the creation of a national bank. Such a bank would meet many needs. It would give the government a safe place to keep

## Economics *in* History

# How Banks Work

Why did Hamilton want to create a national bank? He believed that such a bank could help the economy of the new nation. It would create a partnership between the federal government and American business.

Let's say you deposited money into a bank account. Then you went back another day to withdraw some of the money. What happened in the meantime? Did the money just sit in the bank until you wanted it back? No—the bank used your money, and in doing so, helped fuel economic growth. In this way, money flows in a circular path from people like you into the general economy and back to you again. In the process, money can create goods and services, jobs, and profits, as the diagram explains.

### CONNECT TO HISTORY

1. **Analyzing Points of View** Do you think that the people who feared a strong central government supported Hamilton's idea of a national bank? Why or why not?

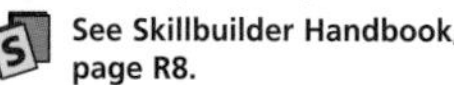
See Skillbuilder Handbook, page R8.

### CONNECT TO TODAY

2. **Making Inferences** How do banks make money?

Visit www.mcdougallittell.com to learn more about banking.

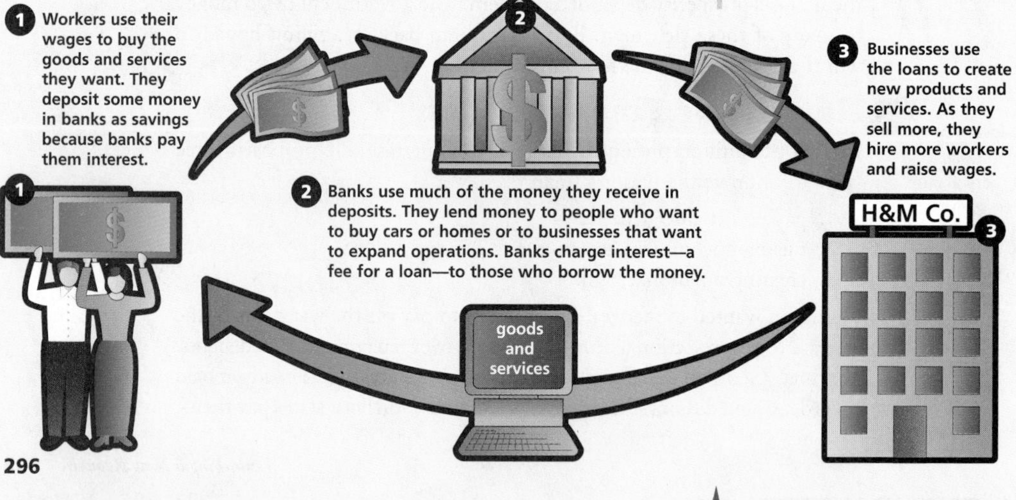

1 Workers use their wages to buy the goods and services they want. They deposit some money in banks as savings because banks pay them interest.
2 Banks use much of the money they receive in deposits. They lend money to people who want to buy cars or homes or to businesses that want to expand operations. Banks charge interest—a fee for a loan—to those who borrow the money.
3 Businesses use the loans to create new products and services. As they sell more, they hire more workers and raise wages.
H&M Co.
goods
and
services

### CONNECT TO HISTORY

1. **Analyzing Points of View** They probably did not favor Hamilton's idea of a national bank because it extended the role of government into the economic sector, increasing the power and influence of the federal government on U.S. businesses.

### CONNECT TO TODAY

2. **Making Inferences** Banks make money by charging interest on the loans they make to individuals and businesses.

**Vocabulary**
**currency:** money

money. It would also make loans to businesses and government. Most important, it would issue bank notes—paper money that could be used as currency. Overall, Hamilton's plan would strengthen the central government. However, this worried Jefferson and Madison.

Two of the first U.S. coins, 1792

##  Interpreting the Constitution

Jefferson and Madison believed that the Constitution discouraged the concentration of power in the federal government. The Constitution's writers had tried to make the document general enough so that it would be flexible. As a result, disagreements sometimes arose over the document's meaning.

The debate over Hamilton's plan for a national bank exposed differences about how to interpret the Constitution. Madison and Jefferson argued that the Constitution did not give the government the power to set up a bank. They believed in the strict construction—narrow or strict interpretation—of the Constitution. They stated that the government has only those powers that the Constitution clearly says it has. Therefore, since the Constitution does not mention a national bank, the government cannot create one.

**C. Answer** Strict construction favors a narrow interpretation of the Constitution, while loose construction favors a broad interpretation.

***Reading*History**
**C. Contrasting** What is the main difference between strict and loose interpretations of the Constitution?

Hamilton disagreed. He favored a loose construction—broad or flexible interpretation—of the Constitution. Pointing to the elastic clause in the document, he argued that the bank was "necessary and proper" to carry out the government's duties. (See The Living Constitution, page 254.) According to this view, when the Constitution grants a power to Congress, it also grants Congress the "necessary and proper" means to carry out that power. Jefferson and Hamilton argued their positions to Washington. Hamilton won, and the Bank of the United States was set up in 1791. The president, meanwhile, was dealing with other challenges at home and abroad, which you will read about in Section 2.

### Section 1 Assessment

**1. Terms & Names**

**Identify:**
- inaugurate
- Federal Judiciary Act
- cabinet
- tariff

**2. Taking Notes**

In a chart, list members of Washington's cabinet and their responsibilities.

| Cabinet member | Responsibilities |
| --- | --- |
| | |

Which cabinet member had the greatest responsibilities? Explain.

**3. Main Ideas**

**a.** What was the purpose of Washington's cabinet?

**b.** What economic problems did the new government face?

**c.** How did Hamilton's financial plan attempt to solve the nation's economic problems?

**4. Critical Thinking**

**Contrasting** How did Hamilton and Jefferson differ in their interpretation of the Constitution?

**THINK ABOUT**
- views on the national bank
- views on the role of government

**ACTIVITY OPTIONS**

**LANGUAGE ARTS**
**ART**

Imagine you oppose or support Hamilton's plan for the nation's finances. Write a **letter to the editor** or draw a **political cartoon** expressing your opinion.





**INSTRUCT: OBJECTIVE 4**

**Interpreting the Constitution**

Key Questions
- What are the two major ways of interpreting the Constitution, and how do they differ?
- Why did Madison and Jefferson oppose the creation of a national bank?
- How was the argument over the bank settled?

## ASSESS & RETEACH

**Setting the Stage** Have students fill in the sections on the chapter graphic organizer.

 **Formal Assessment**
- Section Quiz, p. 146

 **Critical Thinking Transparency CT25**
- Setting the Stage

**RETEACHING ACTIVITY**

Divide the class into groups of three. Have each group member answer one of the review questions for Section 1 in the Chapter Assessment on page 308. Have students share their answers with the group.

 **In-Depth Resources: Unit 3**
- Reteaching Activity, p. 15

### Section  Assessment

**1. Terms & Names**

**inaugurate,** p. 293
**Federal Judiciary Act,** p. 294
**cabinet,** p. 294
**tariff,** p. 296

**2. Taking Notes**

Hamilton—treasury; managed the nation's money
Jefferson—state; oversaw foreign relations
Knox—war; managed defenses
Randolph—attorney general; advised on legal affairs

Accept reasonable answers supported with evidence.

**3. Main Ideas**

**a.** to assist and advise the president on the nation's issues **b.** paying off war debts, creating a financial plan to handle debt agreed to by Congress **c.** He arranged for the government to pay off the state's war debts, argued to raise revenues through tariffs, and supported a national bank.

**4. Critical Thinking**

Jefferson was a strict constructionist. Hamilton was a loose constructionist.

**ACTIVITY OPTIONS**

 **Alternative Assessment**
- Rubrics for writing an opinion article, 4.1
- Rubrics for drawing a cartoon, 1.2

## SECTION OBJECTIVES

1. To explain why Washington wanted to secure the Trans-Appalachian West
2. To analyze the causes and outcome of the Battle of Fallen Timbers
3. To identify the reasons for the Whiskey Rebellion
4. To explain how Washington maintained U.S. neutrality

**SKILLBUILDER**

Interpreting Maps: Region, Location, p. 299

**CRITICAL THINKING**

Making Inferences, p. 299
Drawing Conclusions, p. 302
Evaluating, p. 302

## FOCUS & MOTIVATE

### 5-MINUTE WARM-UP

**Reading a Map** These questions focus on the reasons for conflict in the Trans-Appalachian West.

1. Look at the map on page 299. Which states and territory were part of the Trans-Appalachian West?
2. Which natural feature formed the western boundary of the Trans-Appalachian West?

 **Warm-Up Transparency WT9**

## INSTRUCT

### INSTRUCT: OBJECTIVE 

**Securing the Northwest Territory**

Key Questions

- Why was there conflict over the West?
- How did the Battle of Fallen Timbers affect Native American claims to land?
- Why was Washington's treatment of the Whiskey Rebellion important?

 **In-Depth Resources: Unit 3**
- Guided Reading, p. 4
- Building Vocabulary, p. 6

# 2 Challenges to the New Government

**TERMS & NAMES**
Battle of Fallen Timbers
Treaty of Greenville
Whiskey Rebellion
French Revolution
neutral
Jay's Treaty
Pinckney's Treaty

**MAIN IDEA**

Washington established central authority at home and avoided war with European powers.

**WHY IT MATTERS NOW**

Washington's policies at home and abroad set an example for later presidents.

### ONE AMERICAN'S STORY

**Pioneers had been moving west since before the Revolution. However, the settlers met fierce resistance from Native Americans. One of their most respected military leaders was Chief Little Turtle of the Miami tribe of Ohio. In 1790 and 1791, he had won decisive victories against U.S. troops.**

**Now, two years later, the Miami and their allies again faced attack by American forces. At a council meeting, Little Turtle gave a warning to his people about the troops led by General Anthony Wayne.**

General Anthony Wayne negotiates with a Miami war chief.

*A VOICE FROM THE PAST*

We have beaten the enemy twice under different commanders. . . . The Americans are now led by a chief [Wayne] who never sleeps. . . . During all the time he has been marching on our villages . . . we have not been able to surprise him. Think well of it. . . . It would be prudent [wise] to listen to his offers of peace.

**Little Turtle,** quoted in *The Life and Times of Little Turtle*

**While the council members weighed Little Turtle's warning, President Washington was making plans to secure—guard or protect—the western borders of the new nation.**

### 1 Securing the Northwest Territory

As a general, Washington had skillfully waged war. As the nation's president, however, he saw that the country needed peace in order to prosper. But in spite of his desire for peace, he considered military action as trouble brewed in the Trans-Appalachian West, the land between the Appalachian Mountains and the Mississippi River. The 1783 Treaty of Paris had attempted to resolve the claims. The source of the trouble was competing claims for these lands. Some years later, however, Spain, Britain, the United States, and Native Americans claimed parts of the area as their own.

Spain held much of North America west of the Mississippi. It also claimed Florida and the port of New Orleans at the mouth of the



## RECOMMENDED RESOURCES

 **In-Depth Resources: Unit 3**
- Guided Reading, p. 4
- Building Vocabulary, p. 6
- Skillbuilder Practice, p. 7
- Literature Selection: from "Davy Crockett, Tennessee Settler," pp. 12–14
- Reteaching Activity, p. 16

**Reading Study Guide** (Spanish and English), pp. 95–96

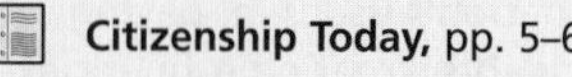

**Citizenship Today,** pp. 5–6

**Formal Assessment**
- Section Quiz, p. 147

**Alternative Assessment**
- Rubrics, 2.1
- Rubrics, 1.3

**Access for Students Acquiring English/ESL**
- Guided Reading, p. 61
- Skillbuilder Practice, p. 63

**Technology Resources**

 **Geography Transparency GT9**
- Trouble Spots in the New Republic, 1790–1794

 **Electronic Teacher Tools with Test Maker**

 **ClassZone**
www.mcdougallittell.com

Mississippi. For American settlers in the West, this port was key to trade. They carried their goods to market by flatboat down the Mississippi to New Orleans. They took Spanish threats to close the port very seriously. The Spanish also stirred up trouble between the white settlers and the Creeks, Choctaws, and other Native American groups in the Southeast.

The strongest resistance to white settlement came from Native Americans in the Northwest Territory. This territory was bordered by the Ohio River to the south and Canada to the north. Native Americans in that territory hoped to join together to form an independent Native American nation. In violation of the Treaty of Paris, the British still held forts north of the Ohio River. The British supported Native Americans in order to maintain their access to fur in these territories. Eventually, Native Americans and white settlers clashed over the Northwest Territory.

*Reading* **History**

**A. Making Inferences** What expectations might the Native Americans have had of the British as the tribes came into conflict with white settlers?

**A. Answer** Native Americans probably expected the British to support them in their conflicts with American settlers since both were clashing with American settlers.

## 2 Battle of Fallen Timbers

Believing the Northwest Territory was critical to the security and growth of the new nation, Washington sent troops to the Ohio Valley. As you read in One American's Story, this first federal army took a beating from warriors led by Little Turtle in 1790. The chief's force came from many tribes, including the Shawnee, Ottawa, and Chippewa, who joined in a confederation to defeat the federal army.

After a second defeat in 1791 of an army headed by General Arthur St. Clair, Washington ordered another army west. This time Anthony Wayne, known as "Mad Anthony" for his reckless courage, was at its head.

The other chiefs ignored Little Turtle's advice to negotiate. They replaced him with a less able leader. Expecting British help, Native American warriors gathered at British-held Fort Miami. On August 20, 1794, a fighting force of around 2,000 Native Americans clashed with Wayne's troops. The site was covered with trees that had been struck down by a storm. The Native Americans were defeated in what became known as the **Battle of Fallen Timbers.**

**Skillbuilder Answers**

1. Land surrendered by Native Americans in Treaty of Greenville
2. Rivers and lakes provided an easy way to move troops and supplies.

The Battle of Fallen Timbers memorial sculpture below shows two American soldiers and a Native American.

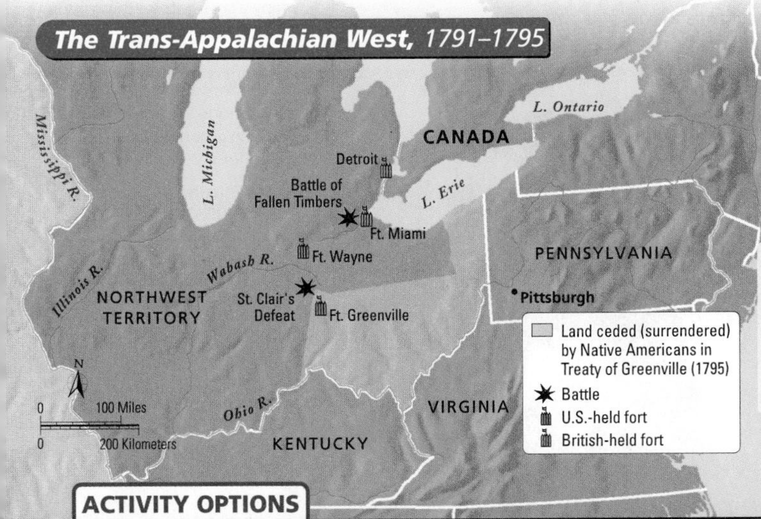

***The Trans-Appalachian West,* 1791–1795**



**GEOGRAPHY SKILLBUILDER**
**Interpreting Maps**

1. **Region** *What does the yellow area of the map represent?*
2. **Location** *Why might the British forts be located near water?*

299

**INSTRUCT: OBJECTIVE 2**

**Battle of Fallen Timbers**

Key Questions

- Why did Washington decide to send troops to the Ohio Valley to fight the force led by Little Turtle?
- What were the results of the Battle of Fallen Timbers for the Native Americans? for the United States?
- Why did the British refuse to help the Native Americans?

**MORE ABOUT . . .**

**Little Turtle**

Little Turtle had good reason to think the British would aid his people at the Battle of Fallen Timbers. During the Revolution, the Miami leader had fought alongside the British against the colonists.

**HISTORY FROM VISUALS**

**Reading the Map** Have the students draw conclusions about what is happening to Native Americans in the time period from 1791 to 1795. Ask them what they think will happen to the Native Americans after 1795. **Possible Response** The Native Americans are being squeezed out of the area by settlement on both sides of the Appalachians. They will probably move West.

**Extension** Have students use a current political map to determine which states or parts of states were created from the area turned over to the United States by Native Americans in 1795.

**ACTIVITY OPTIONS**

**SKILLBUILDER MINI-LESSON: MAKING INFERENCES**

**BLOCK SCHEDULING**

**Explaining the Skill** An *inference* is a conclusion drawn from interpretation of facts, data, and other information contained in a reading. Making an inference often requires the reader to derive information from what is implied as well as what is directly stated. It is important to read carefully to understand both the facts and the implications. Forming questions may also help the reader.

**Applying the Skill** Direct students' attention to the Reading History question on this page. Have them answer this question and questions 1 and 2, which follow.

1. How did the British react to Native American efforts to resist settlement by Americans in the Northwest Territory? Why? *(The British supported Native Americans to maintain the fur trade.)*
2. Given these facts, what can you infer about how Native Americans would expect the British to respond to the conflict with Wayne's troops at Fallen Timbers? *(Native Americans would expect help from the British.)*

**In-Depth Resources: Unit 3**
- Skillbuilder Practice, p. 7

**INSTRUCT: OBJECTIVE 3**

**The Whiskey Rebellion**

Key Questions

- Why were farmers angry about the whiskey tax?
- Why did Washington decide to crush the rebellion and enforce the tax?
- What other options, if any, might Washington have chosen? The farmers?

**Geography Transparency GT9**
- Trouble Spots in the New Republic, 1790–1794

The Native Americans retreated to Fort Miami. The British, not wanting war with the United States, refused to help them. The Battle of Fallen Timbers crushed Native American hopes of keeping their land in the Northwest Territory. Twelve tribes signed the **Treaty of Greenville** in 1795. They agreed to cede, or surrender, much of present-day Ohio and Indiana to the U.S. government.

*Reading* **History**

**B. Reading a Map** Use the map on page 299 to see which two states to the south bordered the land ceded by Native Americans.

## 3 The Whiskey Rebellion

Not long after the Battle of Fallen Timbers, Washington put another army into the field. The conflict arose over the government's tax on whiskey, part of Hamilton's financial plan. From Pennsylvania to Georgia, outraged farmers resisted the tax. For them, whiskey—and the grain it was made from—were important products.

Because of poor roads, backcountry farmers had trouble getting their grain to market. Crops such as wheat and rye were more easily carried to market in liquid form, so farmers made their grain into whiskey. A farmer's horse could haul only two bushels of rye but could carry two barrels of rye whiskey. This was an amount equal to 24 bushels of the grain. In addition, their customers paid more for whiskey than grain. With little cash to buy goods, let alone pay the tax, farmers often traded whiskey for salt, sugar, and other goods. The farmers used whiskey as money to get whatever supplies they needed.

**CITIZENSHIP TODAY**

**OBJECTIVE**

Students will be able to explain some of the issues involved in making and enforcing laws by national and local governments.

**Whiskey Rebellion and the Law**

The Whiskey Rebellion marked the first major challenge to the authority of the federal government. The revolt was fairly widespread, affecting more than 20 counties in Pennsylvania, Maryland, Virginia, Kentucky, Ohio, and North Carolina. When the armed rebels gathered in Pittsburgh in 1794, they were not only angry about the whiskey tax but about their under-representation in state legislatures. Many Backcountry farmers felt the new federal government did not represent or understand their interests any better than had the British Parliament prior to independence.

**Citizenship Today,** pp. 5–6

**CITIZENSHIP TODAY**

# Obeying Rules and Laws

As the Whiskey Rebellion shows, since the earliest days of the republic our government has made laws and punished those who broke them. These laws affect not only adult citizens, but young people as well.

Today, for example, communities across the country are trying to control the problem of juvenile crime by imposing curfews on young people. These laws require minors to be off the streets after a certain time, often ten or eleven at night. Penalties can be harsh. In certain communities, minors who break curfew laws can be detained, and their parents can be fined.

People who favor curfews believe such laws cut crime. Those who oppose curfews think such limits are the responsibility of parents and not the government.

**Why Should You Obey Rules and Laws?**

1. What are some arguments in favor of curfew laws? What are arguments against them? Make a list of each.
2. Poll your classmates to see how many agree with each position.
3. Write an essay expressing your opinion on this issue.
4. Brainstorm changes or adaptations to curfew laws that you think would make them more flexible.

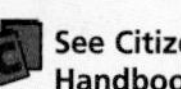

**See Citizenship Handbook, page 283.**

**Visit www.mcdougallittell.com to learn more about young people and the law.**



**STANDARDS FOR EVALUATION**

**CONDUCTING A POLL**

**Each poll should**
- clearly state each position.
- be tabulated correctly.

**WRITING AN ESSAY**

**Each essay should**
- concisely state arguments for and against curfews.
- clearly explain the writer's position on this issue.
- provide facts, examples, or reasoned arguments to support the writer's position.
- demonstrate a balanced understanding of the issue.

In the summer of 1794, a group of farmers in western Pennsylvania staged the **Whiskey Rebellion** against the tax. One armed group beat up a tax collector, coated him with tar and feathers, and stole his horse. Others threatened an armed attack on Pittsburgh.

Washington, urged on by Hamilton, was prepared to enforce the tax and crush the Whiskey Rebellion. They feared that not to act might undermine the new government and weaken its authority. Hamilton condemned the rebels for resisting the law.

*"Such a resistance is treason."*
**Alexander Hamilton**

*A VOICE FROM THE PAST*

Such a resistance is treason against society, against liberty, against everything that ought to be dear to a free, enlightened, and prudent people. To tolerate it were to abandon your most precious interests. Not to subdue it were to tolerate it.

**Alexander Hamilton,** *The Works of Alexander Hamilton*

In October 1794, General Henry Lee, with Hamilton at his side, led an army of 13,000 soldiers into western Pennsylvania to put down the uprising. As news of the army's approach spread, the rebels fled. After much effort, federal troops rounded up 20 barefoot, ragged prisoners. Washington had proved his point. He had shown that the government had the power and the will to enforce its laws. Meanwhile, events in Europe gave Washington a different kind of challenge.

## 4 The French Revolution

In 1789, the French launched a revolution for liberty and equality. At first, the **French Revolution** won strong support from the United States. However, by 1793 the revolution had turned violent. The king of France, Louis XVI, was beheaded, along with thousands of French citizens accused of being enemies of the state. In the same year, France declared war on Britain, Spain, and Holland. The monarchs of these nations had long feared that the revolution would put their own thrones at risk. Britain led the fight to defeat revolutionary France.

The war between France and Britain put the United States in an awkward position. France had been America's ally in the Revolution against the British. A 1778 treaty still bound

### Connections TO WORLD HISTORY

**EYEWITNESS TO REVOLUTION**

In 1789, an American citizen with a strange first name, Gouverneur Morris, went to Paris as a private business agent. Three years later, President Washington appointed him U.S. minister to France. An eyewitness to the French Revolution, Morris kept a detailed record of what he saw, including the execution of the king and queen by guillotine, as shown below.

Here is part of a letter he wrote on October 18, 1793:

"Terror is the order of the Day. . . . The Queen was executed the Day before yesterday. Insulted during her Trial and reviled in her last Moments, she behav'd with Dignity throughout."

301

### Connections TO WORLD HISTORY

**Marie Antoinette**

History has judged Marie Antoinette harshly. Describing her as "frivolous, imprudent, and prodigal," historians have blamed her shallowness and scheming for helping to bring down the French monarchy. Her lavish spending at a time of great financial crisis in France earned her the hatred of the common people. An anecdote of the time tells of the queen asking an official why the poor were protesting. When the official answered that it was because the poor had no bread, the queen callously replied, "Then let them eat cake." Although the story was not true, it was readily believed by Parisians.

### INSTRUCT: OBJECTIVE 4

**The French Revolution/ Remaining Neutral**

Key Questions

- Why did war between France and Britain put the United States in a difficult position?
- How did Jefferson, Hamilton, and Washington think the United States should react to the war?
- What problems did Jay's Treaty and Pinckney's Treaty solve for the United States?

### ACTIVITY OPTIONS

### INDIVIDUAL NEEDS

**STUDENTS ACQUIRING ENGLISH/ESL**

**Building Vocabulary** Point out the word *rebellion* in the heading "The Whiskey Rebellion." Explain that the base word of *rebellion* is *rebel*, which means "to oppose or take arms against a government or ruler," and that a rebellion is armed opposition to authority. Then ask students to read the paragraphs under the heading to identify related words (verb—*rebelled;* noun—*rebels*). Discuss the meanings of those words and ask students to use full sentences to answer questions such as the following:

- In the summer of 1794, who *rebelled* against the tax on whiskey?
- Who condemned the *rebels* for resisting the law?

Then point out the next heading, "The French Revolution." Explain that a *revolution* is a rebellion that results in the overthrow of a government.

## MORE ABOUT . . .

**Jay's Treaty**

The Senate narrowly approved the treaty negotiated by Chief Justice John Jay. The treaty encountered much opposition not only because the British refused to agree to free trade in the British West Indies, but also because the British rejected Jay's proposals that they compensate Americans for slaves abducted during the Revolution. Still, the treaty led to peaceful relations with Britain. It would be 18 years before the United States and Britain were at war again.

## ASSESS & RETEACH

**Setting the Stage** Have students fill in the "Foreign Affairs" and "Relations with Native Americans" sections on the chapter graphic organizer.

 **Formal Assessment**
- Section Quiz, p. 147

### RETEACHING ACTIVITY

On the chalkboard create a web diagram like the one below. Ask students to list ways that actions of the United States government affected two groups of Americans.

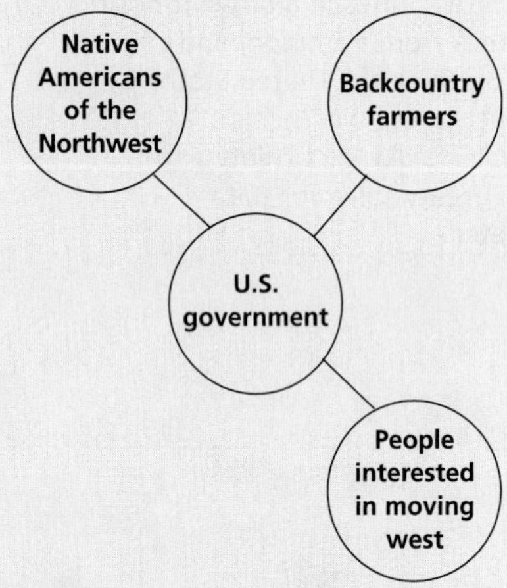

 **In-Depth Resources: Unit 3**
- Reteaching Activity, p. 16

the two nations together. In addition, many saw France's revolution as proof that the American cause had been just. Jefferson felt that a move to crush the French Revolution was an attack on liberty everywhere. Hamilton, though, pointed out that Britain was the United States' most important trading partner, and British trade was too important to risk war.

In April 1793, Washington declared that the United States would remain **neutral,** not siding with one country or the other. He stated that the nation would be "friendly and impartial" to both sides. Congress then passed a law forbidding the United States to help either side.

*Reading* **History**
**C. Drawing Conclusions** What sort of U.S. obligation to France did the wartime alliance and treaty of 1778 create?
C. Answer Since France supported the U.S. in its Revolution, many people thought the U.S. should support France.

## Remaining Neutral

Britain made it hard for the United States to remain neutral. Late in 1792, the British began seizing the cargoes of American ships carrying goods from the French West Indies.

Washington sent Chief Justice John Jay to England for talks about the seizure of U.S. ships. Jay also hoped to persuade the British to give up their forts on the Northwest frontier. During the talks in 1794, news came of the U.S. victory at the Battle of Fallen Timbers. Fearing another entanglement, the British agreed to leave the Ohio Valley by 1796. In **Jay's Treaty,** the British also agreed to pay damages for U.S. vessels they had seized. Jay failed, however, to open up the profitable British West Indies trade to Americans. Because of this, Jay's Treaty was unpopular.

Like Jay, Thomas Pinckney helped the United States reduce tensions along the frontier. In 1795, **Pinckney's Treaty** with Spain gave Americans the right to travel freely on the Mississippi River. It also gave them the right to store goods at the port of New Orleans without paying customs duties. In addition, Spain accepted the 31st parallel as the northern boundary of Florida and the southern boundary of the United States.

Meanwhile, more American settlers moved west. As you will read in the next section, change was coming back east as Washington stepped down.

D. Answer By remaining neutral, the new nation did not make enemies, did not lose a trading partner, did not become involved in a war.

*Reading* **History**
**D. Evaluating** What were some of the advantages to the new nation of remaining neutral?

### Section 2 Assessment

**1. Terms & Names**
**Identify:**
- Battle of Fallen Timbers
- Treaty of Greenville
- Whiskey Rebellion
- French Revolution
- neutral
- Jay's Treaty
- Pinckney's Treaty

**2. Taking Notes**
Use a chart to record U.S. responses to various challenges.

| Challenge | Response |
|---|---|
| From Spain | |
| From Britain | |
| From France | |

Which challenge seemed greatest? Why?

**3. Main Ideas**
a. What military and other actions secured the West for the United States?
b. Why did Washington consider it important to put down the Whiskey Rebellion?
c. How did the French Revolution create problems for the United States?

**4. Critical Thinking**
**Drawing Conclusions** Why was neutrality a difficult policy for the United States to maintain?
THINK ABOUT
- ties with France
- ties with Britain
- restrictions on trade

**ACTIVITY OPTIONS**
**GEOGRAPHY** / **ART**
Make a **map** that describes the Battle of Fallen Timbers, or draw a **scene** from that battle.



### Section 2 Assessment

**1. Terms & Names**
**Battle of Fallen Timbers,** p. 299
**Treaty of Greenville,** p. 300
**Whiskey Rebellion,** p. 301
**French Revolution,** p. 301
**neutral,** p. 302
**Jay's Treaty,** p. 302
**Pinckney's Treaty,** p. 302

**2. Taking Notes**
From Spain—Pinckney's Treaty
From Britain—Jay's Treaty
From France—policy of neutrality

Accept answers that are supported with evidence.

**3. Main Ideas**
**a.** Battle of Fallen Timbers; Treaty of Greenville **b.** to uphold the authority of the federal government **c.** The United States became caught in the middle between France and Great Britain.

**4. Critical Thinking**
because both sides ignored America's policy of neutrality in an attempt to force the new nation to join the conflict

**ACTIVITY OPTIONS**
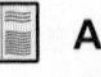 **Alternative Assessment**
- Rubrics for a map, 2.1
- Rubrics for drawing a scene, 1.3

# 3 The Federalists in Charge

**TERMS & NAMES**
foreign policy
political party
XYZ Affair
Alien and Sedition Acts
states' rights

| MAIN IDEA | WHY IT MATTERS NOW |
|---|---|
| The split between Hamilton and Jefferson led to the growth of political parties. | The two-party system is still a major feature of politics in the United States. |

## ONE AMERICAN'S STORY

**In 1796, President George Washington decided that two terms in office was enough. The president was fed up with political quarreling. He wanted to return to Mount Vernon, his estate in Virginia. But as he left office, he feared the development of political parties would split the nation into enemy camps. With Hamilton's help, in 1796 he wrote a final address to the nation.**

This painting portrays Mount Vernon in 1792.

*A VOICE FROM THE PAST*

Let me now . . . warn you . . . against the [harmful] effects of the spirit of party. . . . This spirit, unfortunately . . . exists in different shapes in all governments . . . but in those of the popular form, it is seen in its greatest rankness and is truly their worst enemy.

**George Washington,** Farewell Address

**In his address, Washington warned of the dangers of political division, or what he termed "the spirit of party." As you will see in this section, few people took his advice.**

### 1 Washington Retires

Washington had come to the presidency greatly admired by the American people. Throughout his eight years in office (1789–1797), he had tried to serve as a symbol of national unity. In large part, he succeeded. During his second term, however, opponents of Jay's Treaty led attacks on the president. Thomas Paine called Washington "treacherous in private friendship . . . and a hypocrite in public life" because he failed to support the French Revolution.

Washington saw such attacks as the outcome of political disagreements. In his farewell address, he warned that such differences could weaken the nation. Despite his advice, political parties became a part of American politics.



## SECTION OBJECTIVES

1. To explain how political parties developed
2. To identify the problems President John Adams faced with France
3. To describe and evaluate the Alien and Sedition Acts and responses to them
4. To explain how Adams made peace with France

**SKILLBUILDER**

Interpreting Charts, p. 304

**CRITICAL THINKING**

Summarizing, p. 304
Drawing Conclusions, p. 306
Making Inferences, p. 307
Evaluating, p. 307

## FOCUS & MOTIVATE

### 5-MINUTE WARM-UP

**Drawing Conclusions** These questions focus on Washington's opposition to political parties.

1. Read the quote from Washington's Farewell Address on page 303. What did he mean by the "baneful effects of the spirit of party"?
2. Why might Washington's advice to avoid political parties be hard to follow?

 **Warm-Up Transparency WT9**

## INSTRUCT

**INSTRUCT: OBJECTIVE 1**

**Washington Retires/ Growth of Political Parties**

Key Questions

- What advice did Washington give the nation on foreign affairs?
- Over what issues did political parties develop?
- Who were the leaders and the major groups that supported each party?

**In-Depth Resources: Unit 3**
- Guided Reading, p. 5

**Reading Study Guide** (Spanish and English), pp. 97–98

## RECOMMENDED RESOURCES

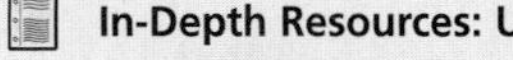

**In-Depth Resources: Unit 3**
- Guided Reading, p. 5
- Building Vocabulary, p. 6
- Geography Application, pp. 8–9
- Primary Source, p. 11
- Reteaching Activity, p. 17
- Enrichment Activity, p. 18

**Reading Study Guide** (Spanish and English), pp. 97–98

**Outline Map Activities**
- The 13 States Become 16, pp. 17–18

**America's History Makers**
- Benjamin Banneker, pp. 37–38

**Formal Assessment**
- Section Quiz, p. 148

**Alternative Assessment**
- Rubrics, 5.3
- Rubrics, 3.1

**Access for Students Acquiring English/ESL**
- Guided Reading, p. 62
- Geography Application, pp. 64–65

**Technology Resources**

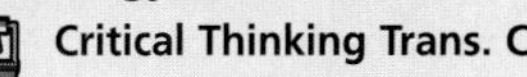

**Critical Thinking Trans. CT26**
- Cause and Effect: Growth of Political Parties

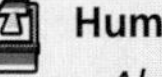

**Humanities Trans. HT17**
- *Abigail Adams* by Gordon Philips

**Humanities Trans. HT18**
- Engraving of Washington, D.C.

## MORE ABOUT . . .

**Democratic-Republicans**

The Democratic-Republicans chose the name *Republicans* to stress their commitment to states' rights and to suggest that their party's concern for individual liberties had a link to the ideals of the ancient Roman republic.

## HISTORY FROM VISUALS

**Interpreting Charts** Have students study the chart to identify the differences between the Federalists and the Democratic-Republicans. Each had beliefs about the role of the national government in American life. How were those beliefs reflected in their stands on the issues of constitutional interpretation and the national bank? **Possible Response** The Federalists, who favored a strong national government, supported a national bank and a loose construction of the Constitution, giving the government more power to act on its own. The Democratic-Republicans, who favored limited government, opposed the bank. They were strict constructionists who favored limiting the policy-making power of the government.

**Extension** Have students research the early history of the two parties to find other differences between them.

 **Critical Thinking Transparency CT26**
- Cause and Effect: Growth of Political Parties

Americans listened more closely to Washington's parting advice on **foreign policy**—relations with the governments of other countries. He urged the nation's leaders to remain neutral and "steer clear of permanent alliances with any portion of the foreign world." He warned that agreements with foreign nations might work against U.S. interests. His advice served to guide U.S. foreign policy into the twentieth century.

## Growth of Political Parties

Despite Washington's warning against political parties, Americans were deeply divided over how the nation should be run. During Washington's first term (1789–1792), Hamilton and Jefferson had hotly debated the direction the new nation should take. Then Jefferson returned to Virginia in 1793. During Washington's second term, Madison took Jefferson's place in the debates with Hamilton.

Both sides disagreed on how to interpret the Constitution and on economic policy. Hamilton favored the British government and opposed the French Revolution. Jefferson and Madison were the opposite. Hamilton fought for a strong central government. Jefferson and Madison feared such a government might lead to tyranny. They had different visions of what the nation should become. Hamilton wanted a United States in which trade, manufacturing, and cities grew. Jefferson and Madison pictured a rural nation of planters and farmers.

These differences on foreign and domestic policy led to the nation's first political parties. A **political party** is a group of people that tries to promote its ideas and influence government. It also backs candidates for office. Together, Jefferson and Madison founded the Democratic-Republican Party. The party name reflected their strong belief in democracy and the republican system. Their ideas drew farmers and workers to the new party. Hamilton and his friends formed the Federalist Party. Many Northern merchants and manufacturers became Federalists.

**A. Answer** The Federalists believed in a strong national government, a national bank, and a loose interpretation of the Constitution. Democratic-Republicans believed in a limited government, an economy based on farming, and a strict interpretation of the Constitution.

*Reading* **History**
**A. Summarizing** What were the major beliefs of each party?

### The First Political Parties

| FEDERALISTS | DEMOCRATIC-REPUBLICANS |
|---|---|
| Strong national government | Limited national government |
| Fear of mob rule | Fear of rule by one person or a powerful few |
| Loose construction (interpretation) of the Constitution | Strict construction (interpretation) of the Constitution |
| Favored national bank | Opposed national bank |
| Economy based on manufacturing and shipping | Economy based on farming |
| Supporters: lawyers, merchants, manufacturers, clergy | Supporters: farmers, tradespeople |

SKILLBUILDER **Interpreting Charts**
1. *Which economic interests were served by the Federalists?*
2. *Which party favored a ruling elite? Which put more trust in the common people?*

Skillbuilder Answers
1. Federalists served the economic interests of business and manufacturing; the propertied classes.
2. Federalists favored a ruling elite; Democratic-Republicans put more trust in the common people.



## ACTIVITY OPTIONS

**MULTIPLE LEARNING STYLES: KINESTHETIC** | BLOCK SCHEDULING

### POLITICAL PARTIES

**Class Time** One hour

**Task** Conducting a press conference for the election of 1796

**Purpose** To compare and contrast the beliefs and ideas of the first two American political parties

**Supplies Needed**
- Reference materials on Jefferson, John Adams, the Federalists, the Democratic-Republicans, and the election of 1796

**Activity** Pick two students to play the roles of John Adams and Thomas Jefferson in the election of 1796. Have the remainder of the class act as members of the press. Allow 15 minutes for candidates to prepare for their roles and for reporters to write questions to ask each candidate. Then hold a forum at which the candidates explain why they think they should be elected. Follow up with questions from reporters about each candidate's stand on such issues as the national bank, relations with France and Britain, the French Revolution, and economic policies.

## America's HERITAGE

**WASHINGTON, D.C., AND BENJAMIN BANNEKER**

Benjamin Banneker was a free African-American farmer. He was a self-taught mathematician and astronomer. He also wrote an almanac (see below). He was named to the survey commission appointed to lay out the boundaries of the nation's new capital. Working with chief planner Pierre L'Enfant, Banneker helped to decide where the White House and Capitol would be located. Their final design is shown at the left.

## 2 John Adams Takes Office

In 1796, the United States held its first elections in which political parties competed. The Federalists picked Washington's vice-president, John Adams, as their candidate for president. An experienced public servant, Adams had been a leader during the Revolution and at the Continental Congress. He had also been a diplomat in France, the Netherlands, and Britain before serving with Washington. The Democratic-Republicans chose Jefferson.

In the electoral college, Adams received 71 votes and Jefferson 68. The Constitution stated that the runner-up should become vice-president. Therefore, the country had a Federalist president and a Democratic-Republican vice-president. Adams became president in 1797. His chief rival, Jefferson, entered office as his vice-president. In 1800, Adams became the first president to govern from the nation's new capital city, Washington, D.C.

## Problems with France

When Washington left office in 1797, relations between France and the United States were tense. With Britain and France still at war, the French began seizing U.S. ships to prevent them from trading with the British. Within the year, the French had looted more than 300 U.S. ships.

Although some Federalists called for war with France, Adams hoped talks would restore calm. To this end, he sent Charles Pinckney, Elbridge Gerry, and John Marshall to Paris. Arriving there, they requested a meeting with the French minister of foreign affairs. For weeks, they were





### America's HERITAGE

**Washington, D.C., and Benjamin Banneker**

L'Enfant was dismissed from his position as chief architect of the new capital of Washington, D.C. The explosive planner left abruptly and took all the plans for the new city with him. Banneker was able to recreate the plans from memory in only two days.

Although Banneker had little formal education and was self-taught in astronomy, he accurately predicted the solar eclipse of 1789. For five years beginning in 1791, he made all the astronomical and tide computations and weather predictions for a yearly almanac.

 **America's History Makers**
- Benjamin Banneker, pp. 37–38

### INSTRUCT: OBJECTIVE 2

**John Adams Takes Office/ Problems with France**

Key Questions
- Why was the election of 1796 different from the previous election?
- How did Thomas Jefferson, Adams's rival for president, become his vice-president?
- What caused the XYZ Affair? How did it affect U.S. relations with France?

 **In-Depth Resources: Unit 3**
- Geography Application: The Nation's Capital, pp. 8–9

 **Outline Map Activities**
- The 13 States Become 16, pp. 17–18

### CRITICAL THINKING ACTIVITY

**Evaluating** Have students explain how John Adams became president in 1796 while his chief rival became his vice-president. What problems might a president face having his political rival as his vice-president? Would there be any advantages?

**Class Time** 5–10 minutes

### ACTIVITY OPTIONS

### INDIVIDUAL NEEDS: GIFTED AND TALENTED

**GEORGE WASHINGTON**

**Class Time** One class period

**Task** Planning a televised biography of George Washington

**Purpose** To familiarize students with the highlights of Washington's life and presidency

**Supplies Needed**
- Reference materials about George Washington
- Posterboard

**Activity** Have students plan a 30-minute television program about the life of Washington. Tell students to find visuals and primary source material to include. Tell them to write an outline and then create a storyboard. A storyboard combines small drawings for each image in the program with a short description.

| [voice over] "First in war, first in peace, first in the hearts of his countrymen." | ➤ | | ➤ | |
|---|---|---|---|---|

 **In-Depth Resources: Unit 3**
- Enrichment Activity, p. 18

## HISTORY *through* ART

**Interpreting the Cartoon** After President Adams learned of the French agents' bribery attempt, he stated publicly that he had lost hope in the talks with France. Congress demanded to see the correspondence from Pinckney, Gerry, and Marshall. Secretary of State Thomas Pickering agreed to give them to Congress, but before he did so, he replaced the names of the French agents with the letters *X, Y,* and *Z.* When American newspapers got hold of the correspondence, they gave the episode the name *XYZ Affair.*

**Answer: The cartoonist is critical of France, as is shown by the depiction of the group ruling France as a monster.**

### CRITICAL THINKING ACTIVITY

**Making Inferences** Outrage over the XYZ Affair temporarily improved the fortunes of the Federalist party. In the 1798 elections, they gained control of both houses of Congress. Ask students why they think the Federalists became more popular with the public during the conflict with France. Have students consider recent foreign conflicts. Why does the president and the party in power often gain support during times of foreign conflict?

**Class Time** 5 minutes

### INSTRUCT: OBJECTIVE 3

**The Alien and Sedition Acts**

Key Questions

- Why did Congress pass the Alien and Sedition Acts?
- How were immigrants and members of the press affected by these acts?
- How did the Democratic-Republicans use the theory of states' rights to fight the Alien and Sedition Acts?
- How did Kentucky and Virginia support the Democratic-Republicans' position?

## HISTORY *through* ART

American newspapers fueled public anger over the XYZ Affair by publishing editorials and cartoons like this one. Here the five-man group ruling France demands money at dagger point from the three Americans. The American diplomats respond, "Cease bawling, monster! We will not give you sixpence!"

**What attitude does the cartoonist have toward France's role in this affair? How can you tell?**

ignored. Then three French agents—later referred to as X, Y, and Z—took the Americans aside to tell them the minister would hold talks. However, the talks would occur only if the Americans agreed to loan France $10 million and to pay the minister a bribe of $250,000. The Americans refused. "No, no, not a sixpence," Pinckney shot back.

Adams received a full report of what became known as the **XYZ Affair.** After Congress and an outraged public learned of it, the press turned Pinckney's words into a popular slogan: "Millions for defense, not one cent for tribute!" In 1798, Congress canceled its treaties with France and allowed U.S. ships to seize French vessels. Congress also set aside money to expand the navy and the army.

*Reading* **History**
**B. Drawing Conclusions** How did the XYZ Affair show the young nation's growing confidence?
B. Answer The nation was willing to defy French power and to build up its strength.

## 3 The Alien and Sedition Acts

The conflict with France made Adams and the Federalists popular with the public. Many Democratic-Republicans, however, were sympathetic to France. One Democratic-Republican newspaper called Adams "the blasted tyrant of America." In turn, Federalists labeled Democratic-Republicans "democrats, mobcrats, and other kinds of rats."

Angered by criticism in a time of crisis, Adams blamed the Democratic-Republican newspapers and new immigrants. Many of the immigrants were Democratic-Republicans. To silence their critics, the Federalist Congress passed the **Alien and Sedition Acts** in 1798. These acts targeted aliens—immigrants who were not yet citizens. One act increased the waiting period for becoming a U.S. citizen from 5 to 14 years. Other acts gave the president the power to arrest disloyal aliens or order them out of the country during wartime. A fourth act outlawed sedition, saying or writing anything false or harmful about the government.

With these acts, the Federalists clamped down on freedom of speech and the press. About 25 Democratic-Republican newspaper editors were



### ACTIVITY OPTIONS

**INTERDISCIPLINARY LINK: LANGUAGE ARTS** — BLOCK SCHEDULING

### EXPRESSING AN OPINION

**Class Time** 20 minutes

**Task** Writing an editorial about the Alien and Sedition Acts

**Purpose** To express an opinion about the constitutionality of and the need for the Alien and Sedition Acts

**Supplies Needed**

- Reference materials on the Alien and Sedition Acts
- Editorials from local or national newspapers

**Activity** Discuss with the class the techniques of persuasive writing or ask the language arts teacher to do so. Have students examine newspaper editorials to find examples of various ways writers argue and support their positions. Then ask each student to write an editorial about the passage of the Alien and Sedition Acts and/or the arrests of Democratic-Republican newspaper editors. Students may write their editorials from the perspective of a Federalist, a Democratic-Republican, or a present-day constitutional scholar.

charged under this act, and 10 were convicted of expressing opinions damaging to the government. A Vermont congressman, Matthew Lyon, was also locked up for saying that the president should be sent "to a mad house." The voters re-elected Lyon while he was in jail.

*Reading* **History**

**C. Making Inferences** How might the theory of states' rights undermine the federal government?

C. Answer Because the states could decide which laws of the federal government they chose to obey.

The Democratic-Republicans, led by Jefferson and Madison, searched for a way to fight the Alien and Sedition Acts. They found it in a theory called **states' rights**. According to this theory, states had the right to judge when the federal government had passed an unconstitutional law.

Jefferson and Madison wrote resolutions (or statements) passed by the Kentucky and Virginia legislatures in 1798 and 1799. These Kentucky and Virginia Resolutions declared that the Alien and Sedition Acts violated the Constitution. No other states supported Kentucky and Virginia. However, within two years the Democratic-Republicans won control of Congress, and they either repealed the Alien and Sedition Acts or let them expire between 1800 and 1802.

## 4 Peace with France

While Federalists and Democratic-Republicans continued to battle at home, the United States made peace with France. Although war fever was high at home, Adams reopened talks with France. This time the two sides quickly signed an agreement to stop all naval attacks. Called the Convention of 1800, this treaty cleared the way for U.S. and French ships to sail the ocean in peace.

Adams's actions made him enemies among the Federalists. Despite this, he spoke proudly of having saved the nation from bloodshed. "I desire no other inscription over my gravestone than: 'Here lies John Adams, who took upon himself the responsibility of the peace with France in the year 1800.'"

Adams lost the presidential election of 1800 to Thomas Jefferson. You will read more about Jefferson in the next chapter.

### Section 3 Assessment

**1. Terms & Names**

**Identify:**
- foreign policy
- political party
- XYZ Affair
- Alien and Sedition Acts
- states' rights

**2. Taking Notes**

Use a cluster diagram to review details about the Alien and Sedition Acts.

What was the worst effect of the Alien and Sedition Acts? Why?

**3. Main Ideas**

**a.** What two pieces of advice did Washington give in his Farewell Address?

**b.** What led to the rise of political parties?

**c.** Why did Congress pass the Alien and Sedition Acts? How did Kentucky and Virginia respond?

**4. Critical Thinking**

**Evaluating** Do you think Washington's warning about political parties was good advice? Explain.

**THINK ABOUT**
- roles of political parties
- advantages of parties
- disadvantages of parties

**ACTIVITY OPTIONS**

**TECHNOLOGY**
**SPEECH**

Read more about Benjamin Banneker. Plan part of a **video presentation** on him or present **dramatic readings** of excerpts from the almanac he wrote.





**INSTRUCT: OBJECTIVE** 

**Peace with France**

Key Questions
- How did Adams settle the conflict between the United States and France?

## ASSESS & RETEACH

**Setting the Stage** Have students add to the Politics and Foreign Affairs sections on the chapter graphic organizer.

 **Formal Assessment**
- Section Quiz, p. 148

 **Critical Thinking Transparency CT25**
- Setting the Stage

**RETEACHING ACTIVITY**

Use the chart on page 304 to reinforce the differences between the Federalists and the Democratic-Republicans. Have students identify the political party of John Adams (Federalist) and Thomas Jefferson (Democratic-Republican).

 **In-Depth Resources: Unit 3**
- Reteaching Activity, p. 17

### Section 3 Assessment

**1. Terms & Names**

**foreign policy,** p. 304
**political party,** p. 304
**XYZ Affair,** p. 306
**Alien and Sedition Acts,** p. 306
**states' rights,** p. 307

**2. Taking Notes**

targeted aliens; increased waiting period for becoming U.S. citizen; president can arrest disloyal aliens; clamped down on freedom of speech; aliens could be ordered out of country during war

Accept all reasonable responses that are supported by evidence.

**3. Main Ideas**

**a.** He warned against political parties and divisions and urged the country to remain neutral.
**b.** disagreements over running the nation; economic policy; Constitutional interpretation
**c.** to silence critics; passed resolutions that declared that the acts violated the Constitution

**4. Critical Thinking**

Students may answer that the state of politics today indicates that Washington was right.

**ACTIVITY OPTIONS**

 **Alternative Assessment**
- Rubrics for a video presentation, 5.3
- Rubrics for a reading, 3.1

## TERMS & NAMES

1. **inaugurate,** p. 293
2. **cabinet,** p. 294
3. **tariff,** p. 296
4. **Battle of Fallen Timbers,** p. 299
5. **Whiskey Rebellion,** p. 301
6. **neutral,** p. 302
7. **foreign policy,** p. 304
8. **political party,** p. 304
9. **Alien and Sedition Acts,** p. 306
10. **states' rights,** p. 307

## REVIEW QUESTIONS

**Possible Responses**

1. the number of justices on Supreme Court; how much power the Court should have; at first the Supreme Court had six members, which has grown to nine
2. war debts; lack of revenues; lack of central financial authority
3. Jefferson believed in a strict and narrow interpretation of the Constitution; Hamilton believed in a broad and loose interpretation.
4. He sent troops to the area.
5. to uphold the authority of the new federal government
6. He believed the nation would grow stronger and more prosperous if it avoided foreign entanglements.
7. Jay's Treaty addressed problems between Britain and the United States caused by U.S. neutrality; Pinckney's Treaty addressed problems with Spain about trade on the Mississippi and boundaries between Spanish territory to the south and the new nation.
8. He thought political parties led to political divisions, conflict, and divisiveness.
9. an attempt by French officials to extort a bribe from U.S. ministers in Paris
10. to silence their Democratic-Republican critics; defied the acts and passed Kentucky and Virginia Resolutions

# Chapter 9 ASSESSMENT

## TERMS & NAMES

Briefly explain the importance of each of the following.

1. inaugurate
2. cabinet
3. tariff
4. Battle of Fallen Timbers
5. Whiskey Rebellion
6. neutral
7. foreign policy
8. political party
9. Alien and Sedition Acts
10. states' rights

## REVIEW QUESTIONS

**Washington's Presidency (pages 293–297)**

1. What questions about the judiciary were left open by the Constitution? How were they answered?
2. What financial problems did the new nation face?
3. How did Hamilton and Jefferson interpret the Constitution differently?

**Challenges to the New Government (pages 298–302)**

4. What did Washington do to secure the West?
5. Why did Washington send troops to put down the Whiskey Rebellion?
6. Why did Washington favor neutrality in the conflict between France and Britain?
7. What problems did the Jay and Pinckney treaties address?

**The Federalists in Charge (pages 303–307)**

8. Why did Washington oppose political parties?
9. What was the XYZ Affair?
10. Why did Federalists pass the Alien and Sedition Acts? How did Republicans respond?

## CRITICAL THINKING

**1. USING YOUR NOTES**

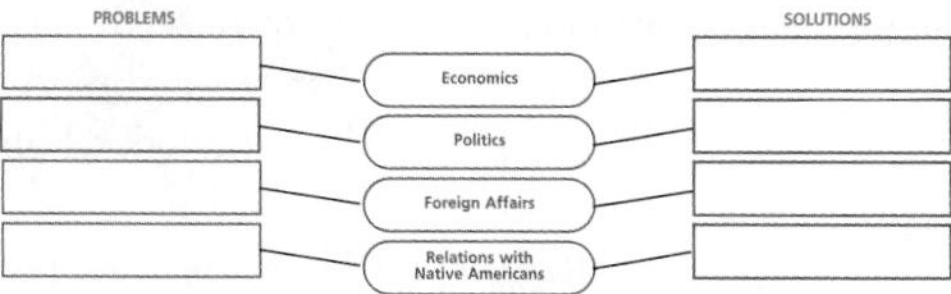


Using your completed chart, answer the questions.

a. Which of the problems listed on the chart were solved peacefully?

b. How might an economic problem require a political solution?

**2. ANALYZING LEADERSHIP**

How did Washington's efforts to serve as a symbol of national unity help the new nation?

**3. APPLYING CITIZENSHIP SKILLS**

How might the farmers in the Whiskey Rebellion have expressed their disapproval of the whiskey tax while staying within the law?

**4. THEME: DEMOCRATIC IDEALS**

Did the formation of political parties make the nation more or less democratic?

**Interact *with* History**

How did the challenges of setting up a government that you discussed before you read the chapter compare with the actual challenges you read about?

## VISUAL SUMMARY

### The First Presidents

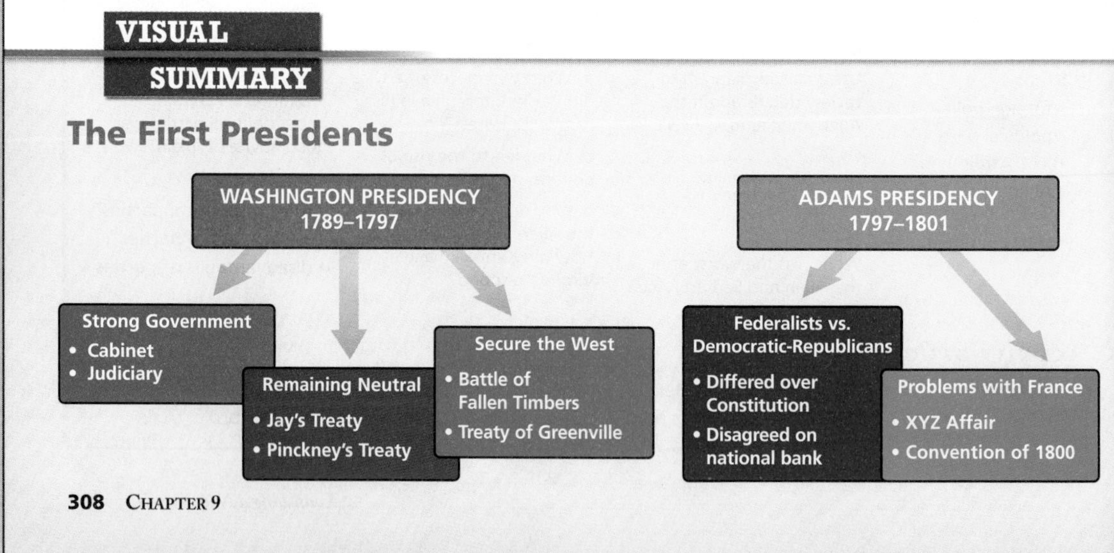




## CRITICAL THINKING

**Possible Responses**

1. **USING YOUR NOTES** **a.** economics and politics; foreign affairs were solved peacefully with the exception of some seizure of American shipping **b.** Laws involving solutions to economic problems involve the political process. For example, Hamilton needed to gain political support in order to institute his financial plan.
2. **ANALYZING LEADERSHIP** Washington acted wisely and modestly. He helped to establish a democratic government by setting a good example of how a president should behave.
3. **APPLYING CITIZENSHIP SKILLS** They could have sent a delegation to the federal government to express their point of view, written a petition, voted their preferences in the next election, or taken their case to the newspapers.
4. **THEME: DEMOCRATIC IDEALS** probably more democratic, since political parties provided an outlet for different points of view

**Interact *with* History** Answers will vary, but students should probably note the extreme difficulties involved in setting up a government.

## HISTORY SKILLS

### 1. INTERPRETING CHARTS

The following chart shows the money problems of the new nation between 1789 and 1791. The numbers have been rounded off. Study the chart and then answer the questions.

**Financial Problems,** *1789–1791*

| DEBTS | EXPENSES | INCOME |
|---|---|---|
| $77,230,000 = total public debt | $4,270,000 budget to run government | $4,400,000 from duties or taxes imposed on imported and exported goods |

Source: *Historical Statistics of the United States*

a. What was the government's total income in these years?

b. How much money did the government owe in these same years?

c. How might the government try to raise more money?

### 2. INTERPRETING PRIMARY SOURCES

In a letter to her sister, John Adams's wife, Abigail, had the following to say about President Washington. Read the quotation and answer the questions.

> He is polite with dignity, affable without familiarity, distant without haughtiness, . . . modest, wise, and good.
>
> **Abigail Adams,** letter of January 5, 1790

a. What qualities seemed to set Washington apart from other political leaders?

b. Is Mrs. Adams's overall impression of Washington positive or negative? Explain your answer.

c. What qualities or characteristics did the people of Washington's time seem to expect in a leader?

## ALTERNATIVE ASSESSMENT

### 1. INTERDISCIPLINARY ACTIVITY: World History

**Writing a Letter** Imagine that you are a U.S. citizen during the French Revolution. Write a letter to the secretary of state recommending a policy you think the U.S. government should follow.

### 2. COOPERATIVE LEARNING ACTIVITY

**Holding a Debate** The controversy over the Alien and Sedition Acts deeply divided Federalists and Democratic-Republicans. Were the acts constitutional or an abuse of basic rights? Should criticism of the government be allowed in a time of near war?

Working in three groups, do research on the Alien and Sedition Acts and the positions taken by both political parties on these acts. Then have Federalist and Democratic-Republican groups pick representatives to debate the questions posed above, while the remaining group acts as audience and judge for the debate.

### 3. TECHNOLOGY ACTIVITY

**Creating a Television Commercial** People of the eighteenth century had different expectations of their political leaders than do people today. The quotation from Abigail Adams on this page is an example of the different perspective people held in Washington's time. Using the library or the Internet, find pictures of, and quotations about, political leaders of the time.

**Visit www.mcdougallittell.com to learn more about the first presidents.**

Create a 30-second television commercial that advertises an American history theme park, using the suggestions below.

- Try to find quotations that suggest the most important qualities of leaders such as Washington, Adams, Hamilton, and Jefferson.
- Try to find more than one image of each leader; find images that suggest different qualities in the person.
- Use quotations from and images of leaders as part of your commercial for a theme park.
- Show your commercial to the class.

### 4. HISTORY PORTFOLIO

**Option 1** Review your section and chapter assessment activities. Select one that you think is your best work. Then use comments made by your teacher or classmates to improve your work and add it to your portfolio.

**Option 2** Review the questions that you wrote for What Do You Want to Know? on page 292. Then write a short report in which you explain the answers to your questions. If any questions were not answered, do research to answer them. Add your answers to your portfolio.



## ALTERNATIVE ASSESSMENT

1. INTERDISCIPLINARY ACTIVITY: World History
   **Letters should**
   - clearly state a position about the issue.
   - present supporting reasons for the position.
   - clearly rebut other viewpoints.
   - use correct grammar, spelling, and punctuation.

2. COOPERATIVE LEARNING ACTIVITY
   **Debates should**
   - have a central question or proposition.
   - support a position and refute their opponent's position with evidence.
   - respond appropriately to each other's statements.

3. TECHNOLOGY ACTIVITY
   **Commercials should**
   - clearly present persuasive reasons for visiting the theme park.
   - utilize a variety of information.
   - use correct grammar in the script or print materials.
   - show technical proficiency.

4. HISTORY PORTFOLIO

**Option 1 Revised section or chapter assessment activities should**
- address teacher and peer responses to the selected work.
- solve problems present in the first versions of the work.

**Option 2 Short reports should**
- answer questions about the people who created the United States government.
- use evidence to develop and support ideas.
- cite sources of information.
- use standard grammar, spelling, sentence structure, and punctuation.

**Critical Thinking Transparency CT27**
- Visual Summary

**Formal Assessment**
- Chapter Test, Forms A and B, pp. 149–156

## HISTORY SKILLS

**Possible Responses**

1. INTERPRETING CHARTS
   **a.** $4,400,000
   **b.** $77,230,000
   **c.** by increasing tariffs and taxes

2. INTERPRETING PRIMARY SOURCES
   **a.** wisdom, seriousness, virtue
   **b.** Her impression is very positive; she sees him as a model of virtue.
   **c.** They do not seem to expect their leader to be too much like them; he is to be polite and friendly without being too familiar. Mainly he is expected to fulfill his public role and function with virtue and dignity.

## CHAPTER 10 PLANNING GUIDE

# The Jefferson Era 1800–1816

| | CHAPTER OVERVIEW | COPYMASTERS | TECHNOLOGY |
|---|---|---|---|
| **CHAPTER RESOURCES** | The chapter describes Thomas Jefferson's presidency, his philosophy of government, and the Louisiana Purchase. It also describes problems in foreign affairs and the War of 1812. | **In-Depth Resources: Unit 3**<br>• Tracing Themes: Expansion, p. 20<br>• Building Vocabulary, p. 25<br>• History Workshop Resources, p. 39<br>**Interdisciplinary Projects,** pp. 55–60 | 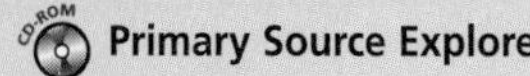<br>**Primary Source Explorer**<br>**Electronic Teacher Tools**<br>**Power Presentations CD-ROM**<br>**Chapter Summaries on CD** (English and Spanish) |
| **SECTION 1**<br>**Jefferson Takes Office**<br>**pp. 313–317** | **KEY IDEAS**<br>• Thomas Jefferson becomes president in 1801.<br>• Jefferson believes the United States should be a nation of small, independent farmers.<br>• Chief Justice John Marshall establishes the principle of judicial review in *Marbury* v. *Madison.* | **In-Depth Resources: Unit 3**<br>• Setting the Stage, p. 19<br>• Guided Reading, p. 21<br>• Geography Application, pp. 27–28<br>• Reteaching Activity, p. 34<br>**America's History Makers**<br>• Thomas Jefferson, pp. 39–40<br>**Citizenship Today,** pp. 83–84<br>**Why It Matters Now**<br>• Peaceful Transfers of Power, pp. 19–20 | **Warm-Up Transparency WT10**<br>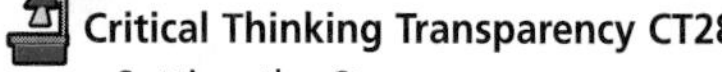<br>**Critical Thinking Transparency CT28**<br>• Setting the Stage<br>**ClassZone:** www.mcdougallittell.com |
| **SECTION 2**<br>**The Louisiana Purchase and Exploration**<br>**pp. 318–325** | • Jefferson buys the Louisiana Purchase from France at a bargain price.<br>• Lewis and Clark explore the new territory from the Mississippi River to the Pacific Ocean.<br>• Western exploration leads to better maps and greater knowledge of the continent. | **In-Depth Resources: Unit 3**<br>• Setting the Stage, p. 19<br>• Guided Reading, p. 22<br>• Literature Selection, pp. 31–33<br>• Reteaching Activity, p. 35<br>**America's History Makers**<br>• Sacagawea, pp. 41–42<br>**American History Plays**<br>• *Land of the Unknown*<br>**Outline Map Activities**<br>• The Louisiana Purchase, pp. 19–20 | **Warm-Up Transparency WT10**<br>**Humanities Transparency HT19**<br>• *Lewis and Clark*<br>**Geography Transparency GT10**<br>• United States, 1803<br>**Critical Thinking Transparency CT28**<br>• Setting the Stage<br>**ClassZone:** www.mcdougallittell.com |
| **SECTION 3**<br>**Problems with Foreign Powers**<br>**pp. 326–329** | • Conflicts with Britain and France disrupt American trade.<br>• Despite Tecumseh's efforts to unite the tribes, Native Americans lose more land through treaties and battles.<br>• A group of congressmen known as War Hawks demand war against Britain. | **In-Depth Resources: Unit 3**<br>• Setting the Stage, p. 19<br>• Guided Reading, p. 23<br>• Skillbuilder Practice: Analyzing Causes, p. 26<br>• Primary Source, p. 29<br>• Reteaching Activity, p. 36 | **Warm-Up Transparency WT10**<br>**Critical Thinking Transparency CT28**<br>• Setting the Stage<br>**ClassZone:** www.mcdougallittell.com |
| **SECTION 4**<br>**The War of 1812**<br>**pp. 330–333** | • The U.S. Navy wins important victories early in the War of 1812.<br>• The Treaty of Ghent ends the war, and Andrew Jackson defeats the British at New Orleans.<br>• The war increases patriotism, bolsters American confidence, and encourages the growth of industry. | **In-Depth Resources: Unit 3**<br>• Setting the Stage, p. 19<br>• Guided Reading, p. 24<br>• Primary Source, p. 30<br>• Reteaching Activity, p. 37<br>**Economics in History**<br>• The Economic Impact of the War of 1812, p. 10 | **Warm-Up Transparency WT10**<br>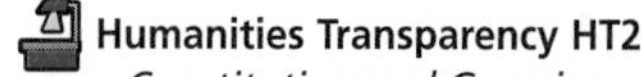<br>**Humanities Transparency HT20**<br>• *Constitution and Guerriere*<br>**Critical Thinking Transparency CT29**<br>• Cause and Effect: The War of 1812<br>**Critical Thinking Transparency CT30**<br>• Visual Summary<br>**ClassZone:** www.mcdougallittell.com |

PE Pupil's Edition
Copymaster
Overhead Transparency
Audio Library
CD-ROM
Internet

## ASSESSMENT

**Chapter Assessment,** pp. 334–335

**Formal Assessment**
- Chapter Tests, Forms A and B, pp. 163–170

**Alternative Assessment Book**

**Electronic Teacher Tools with Test Maker**

**Section Assessment,** p. 317

**Formal Assessment**
- Section Quiz, p. 159

**Alternative Assessment Book**
- Rubrics for a Web page, 5.1
- Rubrics for a model, 1.10

**Electronic Teacher Tools with Test Maker**

**Section Assessment,** p. 323

**Formal Assessment**
- Section Quiz, p. 160

**Alternative Assessment Book**
- Rubrics for a time line, 2.4
- Rubrics for a map, 2.1

**Electronic Teacher Tools with Test Maker**

**Section Assessment,** p. 329

**Formal Assessment**
- Section Quiz, p. 161

**Alternative Assessment Book**
- Rubrics for a comic strip, 1.3
- Rubrics for a press conference, 3.3

**Electronic Teacher Tools with Test Maker**

**Section Assessment,** p. 333

**Formal Assessment**
- Section Quiz, p. 162

**Alternative Assessment Book**
- Rubrics for a poem, 4.8
- Rubrics for a model, 1.10

**Electronic Teacher Tools with Test Maker**

## CUSTOMIZING FOR INDIVIDUAL NEEDS

### Students Acquiring English/ESL

**Reading Study Guide** (English and Spanish), pp. 101–110

**Access for Students Acquiring English/ESL:** Spanish Translations, pp. 66–72

**Chapter Summaries on CD** (English and Spanish)

### Less Proficient Readers

**Reading Study Guide** (English and Spanish), pp. 101–110

**Chapter Summaries on CD** (English and Spanish)

### Gifted and Talented Students

**In-Depth Resources: Unit 3**
- Enrichment Activity, p. 38

**America's History Makers**
- Thomas Jefferson, pp. 39–40
- Sacagawea, pp. 41–42

## CROSS-CURRICULAR CONNECTIONS

### Culture

Hilton, Suzanne. ***A Capital Capital City, 1790–1814.*** New York: Atheneum, 1992. An engaging account of the first 25 years of Washington, D.C.

### Geography

Lourie, Peter. ***In the Path of Lewis and Clark: Traveling the Missouri.*** Englewood Cliffs, NJ: Silver Burdett Press, Inc., 1997. Travel-writers Lourie and William Least Heat-Moon retrace the steps of the explorers of the Louisiana Purchase.

### Science

Weitzman, David. ***Old Ironsides: Americans Build a Fighting Ship.*** Boston: Houghton Mifflin, 1997. Illustrated with detailed charts and drawings.

### Interdisciplinary Projects, pp. 55–60

- Math: Lines of Symmetry
- Science: Taxonomy
- Language Arts: The Poetry of the National Anthem
- Music: Backcountry Folk Music

### Literature

Bohner, Charles. ***Bold Journey: West with Lewis and Clark.*** Boston: Houghton Mifflin, 1990. Private Hugh McNeal tells of his travels with Lewis and Clark.

Sans Souci, Robert D. ***Cut from the Same Cloth: American Women of Myth, Legend, and Tall Tale.*** New York: Putnam, 1992. Folk tales of 15 brave and sometimes outrageous women.

### McDougal Littell *The Language of Literature*

Stephen E. Ambrose, from ***Undaunted Courage*** (nonfiction)

### McDougall Littell Literature Connections

Avi

***The True Confessions of Charlotte Doyle***

Much-acclaimed story of young Charlotte Doyle's voyage from England to America in the early 19th century.

## ENRICHMENT ACTIVITIES

**Pupil's Edition, pp. 310–337**
**Interact with History,** p. 311
**Geography in History,** pp. 324–325
**History Workshop,** pp. 336–337

**In-Depth Resources: Unit 3**
- Geography Application: Election of 1800, pp. 27–28
- Primary Source: A Plea for Native American Unity, p. 29
- Primary Source: from *Memoirs and Letters of Dolley Madison,* p. 30
- Literature Selection, pp. 31–33
- History Workshop Resources, p. 39

**America's History Makers**
- Thomas Jefferson, pp. 39–40
- Sacagawea, pp. 41–42

**American History Plays**
- *Land of the Unknown*

**Outline Map Activities**
- The Louisiana Purchase, pp. 19–20

**Why It Matters Now**
- Peaceful Transfers of Power, pp. 19–20

# CHAPTER 10 PACING GUIDE

**LESSON PLAN OPTIONS (50-MINUTE PERIOD)** (TE) = Teacher's Edition (PE) = Pupil's Edition

| | TEACHER-DIRECTED ACTIVITIES<br>Class Time: 15 minutes | STUDENT-CENTERED ACTIVITIES<br>Class Time: 25 minutes | INDIVIDUAL ACTIVITIES<br>Class Time: 10 minutes |
|---|---|---|---|
| **DAY 1**<br>Introduction<br>pp. 310–312 | **Presentation Options**<br>• Begin with a class discussion of the painting on p. 310 **(PE)**.<br>• Lead a class discussion on the "What Do You Know?" question in Setting the Stage, p. 312. Then introduce the graphic organizer for the chapter **(PE)**. | **Options for Cooperative Learning**<br>• Have student groups discuss the Interact with History questions, p. 311 **(PE)**.<br>• Have student groups respond to the "What Do You Want to Know?" question in Setting the Stage, p. 312 **(PE)**. | **Head Start on Homework Options**<br>• Have students skim Section 1 Main Idea, Why It Matters Now, Terms & Names, and the main headings, p. 313 **(PE)**.<br>• Have students begin Guided Reading activity and Building Vocabulary sheet. |
| **DAY 2**<br>Section 1<br>pp. 313–317 | **Presentation Options**<br>• Begin with the 5-Minute Warm-Up, p. 313 **(TE)**.<br>• Review the Section 1 Main Idea, Why It Matters Now, and Terms & Names, p. 313 **(PE)**.<br>• Choose 5 key questions for Objectives 1–4 to discuss with the class, pp. 313–317 **(TE)**. | **Options for Cooperative Learning**<br>• Divide students into groups to complete the Interdisciplinary Link, Language Arts/Civics: Marshall and the Judiciary, p. 316 **(TE)**.<br>• Have student pairs work together to complete one of the Activity Options in the Section 1 Assessment, p. 317 **(PE)**. | **Head Start on Homework Options**<br>• Have students begin working on Section 1 Assessment, p. 317 **(PE)**.<br>• Have students preview Section 2 Main Idea, Why It Matters Now, Terms & Names, and the main headings, p. 318 **(PE)**. |
| **DAY 3**<br>Section 2<br>pp. 318–325 | **Presentation Options**<br>• Begin with the 5-Minute Warm-Up, p. 318 **(TE)**.<br>• Choose 5 key questions for Objectives 1–4 to discuss with the class, pp. 318–322 **(TE)**.<br>• Lead students through the Geography in History activity pp. 324–325 **(TE)**. | **Options for Cooperative Learning**<br>• Divide students into groups and have them complete the Geography in History questions, pp. 324–325 **(PE)**.<br>• Have student pairs work together to complete one of the Activity Options in the Section 2 Assessment, p. 323 **(PE)**. | **Head Start on Homework Options**<br>• Have students begin working on Section 2 Assessment, p. 323 **(PE)**.<br>• Have students answer the Reading History questions in Section 3, pp. 326–329 **(PE)**. |
| **DAY 4**<br>Section 3<br>pp. 326–329 | **Presentation Options**<br>• Begin with the 5-Minute Warm-Up, p. 226 **(TE)**.<br>• Choose 5 key questions for Objectives 1–4 to discuss with the class, pp. 326–329 **(TE)**.<br>• Lead the students through the Skillbuilder Mini-Lesson: Analyzing Causes, p. 328 **(TE)**. | **Options for Cooperative Learning**<br>• Divide students into groups and have them complete the Skillbuilder Interpreting Charts, p. 329 **(PE)**.<br>• Have student pairs work together to complete one of the Activity Options in the Section 3 Assessment, p. 329 **(PE)**. | **Head Start on Homework Options**<br>• Have students begin working on Section 3 Assessment, p. 329 **(PE)**.<br>• Have students preview Section 4 Main Idea, Why It Matters Now, Terms & Names, and the main headings, p. 330 **(PE)**. |
| **DAY 5**<br>Section 4<br>pp. 330–333 | **Presentation Options**<br>• Begin with the 5-Minute Warm-Up, p. 330 **(TE)**.<br>• Choose 5 key questions for Objectives 1–4 to discuss with the class, pp. 330–333 **(TE)**. | **Options for Cooperative Learning**<br>• Divide students into groups and have them complete the History Workshop, pp. 336–337 **(PE)**.<br>• Have student pairs work together to complete one of the Activity Options in the Section 4 Assessment, p. 333 **(PE)**. | **Head Start on Homework Options**<br>• Have students complete the Setting the Stage graphic organizer for the chapter, p. 312 **(PE)**.<br>• Have students begin working on the Chapter Assessment, pp. 334–335 **(PE)**.<br>• Prepare for Chapter Test<br>**Formal Assessment,** pp. 163–170 |

TEACHER-TESTED ACTIVITY **Meg Robbins, Wilbraham Middle School, Wilbraham, Massachusetts**

## LOUISIANA PURCHASE

**Class Time** One class period

**Task** Making a map

**Purpose** To analyze the physical and economic impact on the United States of the Louisiana Purchase

**Supplies Needed**
- Reference materials and Internet sources on the Louisiana Purchase
- Political map of the United States about 1800
- Current political map of the United States
- Posterboard
- Markers or colored pencils

**Activity** Working in pairs, students should create a map showing how the United States would look today if President Jefferson had not purchased the Louisiana Territory from France. Maps should include only the states that already existed or were territories in 1800 and the nations that bordered the United States at that time. Have each pair display its map along with a short essay hypothesizing on the ways in which the United States would be different today if it had not acquired the Louisiana Purchase.

## BLOCK SCHEDULING — LESSON PLAN OPTIONS (90-MINUTE PERIOD)

### DAY 1

**Interact with History,** p. 311
**Class Time** 20 Minutes

Options for pacing and variety:
- **Role-Playing** Have students work in pairs to create a dialogue between two of the explorers after encountering the bear. The explorers should discuss how to describe the encounter for their expedition's report. **Class Time** 15 minutes

**Setting the Stage,** p. 312
**Class Time** 20 minutes

Options for pacing and variety:
- **Time Saver** For a homework assignment, ask students to list the issues a president might consider before making a major land purchase. **Class Time** 10 minutes

**Section 1,** pp. 313–317
**Class Time** 50 minutes

Options for pacing and variety:
- **Internet** Extend students' background knowledge of the decisions facing Thomas Jefferson as president and how he made them by visiting www.mcdougallittell.com **Class Time** 20 minutes
- **Peer Teaching** Working in pairs, students should make a graphic organizer showing how the opinions of Jefferson and Hamilton differed on the public debt. **Class Time** 30 minutes

### DAY 2

**Section 2,** pp. 318–325
**Class Time** 45 minutes

Options for pacing and variety:
- **History on Film** Extend students' knowledge of the Lewis and Clark expedition with the film *We Proceeded On . . : The Expedition of Lewis and Clark,* Kaw Valley Films. **Class Time** 35 minutes
- **Time Saver** Use the chart on page 323 to summarize the effects of the Lewis and Clark and Pike expeditions. **Class Time** 10 minutes

**Section 3,** pp. 326–329
**Class Time** 45 minutes

Options for pacing and variety:
- **Peer Teaching** Have pairs of students review the Main Idea for the section on page 326 and find three details to support it. Then have each pair list two additional important ideas and trade lists with another group to find details. **Class Time** 10 minutes
- **Time Saver** Use the cartoon on page 335 of the Chapter Assessment to introduce the causes of the War of 1812. **Class Time** 10 minutes

### DAY 3

**Section 4,** pp. 330–333
**Class Time** 45 minutes

Options for pacing and variety:
- **Peer Teaching** Divide students into small groups. Have each group create a cause-and-effect chart for the War of 1812. Then compare their chart to CT29. Discuss the differences. **Class Time** 10 minutes
- **Peer Evaluation** Have students work in groups to answer the Reading History questions. **Class Time** 25 minutes

**Chapter 10 Assessment,** pp. 334–335
**Class Time** 40 minutes

Options for pacing and variety:
- **Peer Teaching** Divide students into groups of four. Have each student in a group answer the Review Questions for one of the four sections. Have students share answers within groups. **Class Time** 20 minutes

**History Workshop,** pp. 336–337
Options for pacing and variety
- **Team Teaching** Invite a science teacher to visit the class to explain to students how botanists and other scientists make and use field notes. **Class Time** 20 minutes

**CHAPTER 10 OBJECTIVE**

The student will understand how the election and presidency of Thomas Jefferson shaped the American system of government and how the Louisiana Purchase and the War of 1812 affected the nation.

## HISTORY FROM VISUALS

**Interpreting the Painting** Ask students to study the painting. Have them describe the various ways Bierstadt emphasizes not only the beauty of the West but its grandeur. Ask students whether they notice the people or the landscape first. To which does Bierstadt give greater importance? Why? **Possible Responses** The artist emphasizes the monumental grandeur of the landscape by making the snowcapped mountains and waterfall focal points of the painting, while the people in the foreground seem small and insignificant by comparison.

**Extension** Have the students make a list of five adjectives that they would use to describe Bierstadt's painting and write a paragraph using their list to describe the scene.

CHAPTER 10

# The Jefferson Era 1800–1816

Albert Bierstadt's painting, *The Rocky Mountains* (1863), celebrates the beauty of the American West.

310

## RECOMMENDED RESOURCES

**BOOKS FOR THE TEACHER**

Kessler, Donna J. ***The Making of Sacajawea: A Native American Legend.*** Tuscaloosa: U. of Alabama Press, 1998. Separates the facts from the legend about this extraordinary person.

Larkin, Jack. ***The Reshaping of Everyday Life, 1790–1840.*** New York: HarperCollins, 1988. Readable account of changes in daily life.

Smith, Jean Edward. ***John Marshall: Definer of a Nation.*** New York: Holt, 1998. Acclaimed as an authoritative biography.

Sugden, John. ***Tecumseh: A Life.*** New York: St. Martin's, 1995. A recent biography that looks at both Tecumseh the man and his effort to unite Native Americans in a coherent resistance movement.

**SOFTWARE**

***Critical Decisions of Thomas Jefferson.*** K–12 MicroMedia, 1996. Allows students to follow historical records day by day.

**VIDEO**

***Lewis & Clark: The Journey of the Corps of Discovery.*** 2 cassettes. Dir. Ken Burns. PBS Home Video, 1997. Acclaimed, gripping, and filled with magnificent scenery.

**INTERNET**

For more about the War of 1812, visit www.mcdougallittell.com

## Interact *with* History

This painting gives a more realistic view of the West than that shown at the left.

Explorers often chose to travel by water.

In the early 1800s, it took about 20 seconds to load and fire a gun.

Adult grizzly bears might weigh as much as 900 pounds and run 30 miles per hour.

**You have been chosen to participate in an expedition to the West in the early 1800s. You are excited and curious, but also a little scared. You know that you will see and experience many new things. But you know there are risks involved, too.**

### What Do You Think?

- **Notice the land features in these scenes. What problems might they hold for an explorer?**
- **What other people might you meet on the expedition?**
- **How will you find food during the long winter?**

# *What dangers will you face on an expedition west?*

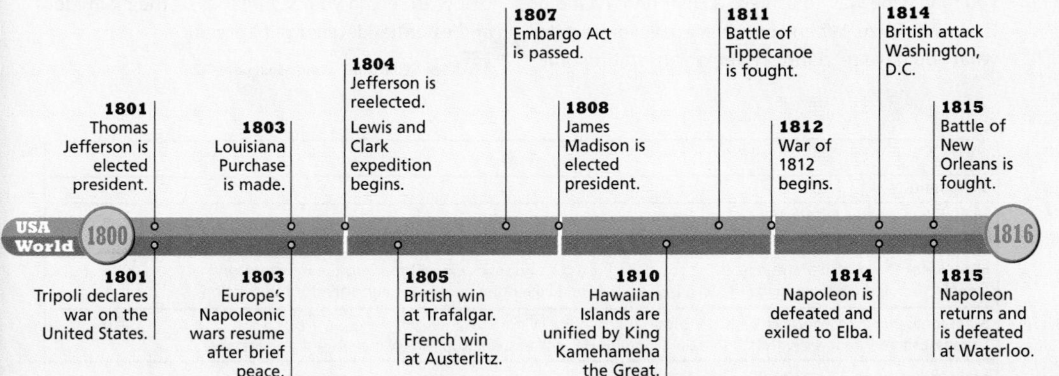
USA
World
1800
1801 Thomas Jefferson is elected president.
1803 Louisiana Purchase is made.
1804 Jefferson is reelected.
Lewis and Clark expedition begins.
1807 Embargo Act is passed.
1808 James Madison is elected president.
1811 Battle of Tippecanoe is fought.
1812 War of 1812 begins.
1814 British attack Washington, D.C.
1815 Battle of New Orleans is fought.
1816
1801 Tripoli declares war on the United States.
1803 Europe's Napoleonic wars resume after brief peace.
1805 British win at Trafalgar.
French win at Austerlitz.
1810 Hawaiian Islands are unified by King Kamehameha the Great.
1814 Napoleon is defeated and exiled to Elba.
1815 Napoleon returns and is defeated at Waterloo.

## Interact *with* History

### OBJECTIVES

- To help students identify the challenges faced by the early explorers of the West
- To help students connect with the people and events they will study in this chapter

### What Do You Think?

1. Students can consider the difficulties of hiking and hauling supplies and boats up and down rugged high-mountain terrain.
2. Students might think about the people living in the West at this time, both Native Americans and people from other nations. Remind students that fur trapping and trading had been important economic activities for both the French and the British.
3. Students might consider that explorers could not carry enough food to stockpile for the winter. They might also consider what wildlife might be available as a source for food.

### *What dangers will you face on an expedition west?*

Encourage students to think about how an expedition to the West in the early 1800s would be different from such a journey today. In addition to facing wild animals, potentially hostile people, and the difficulties of the terrain and the weather, explorers faced challenges in traveling with few or no reliable maps, no personal knowledge of the area, and no way to contact anyone for rescue.

### MAKING PERSONAL CONNECTIONS

Ask students to think about how they might prepare for a camping trip to an area they have never visited. Have students list various sources of information they could use to learn more about the place prior to the trip. Then have them cross off their lists any sources of information that did not exist in 1800.

### TIME LINE DISCUSSION

**Tell students that during this time period European nations were involved in the Napoleonic Wars. Two of the major events on the USA line were related to activities in Europe.**

- Ask students to choose the most important event on this time line during Jefferson's first term as president and the most important event during Madison's presidency. **Answer** Louisiana Purchase, War of 1812
- Ask students what event suggests that Americans were already engaged in conflict before the War of 1812 began. **Answer** Battle of Tippecanoe
- Have students determine with what country the Americans were at war. **Answer** Britain

## BEFORE YOU READ

### Previewing the Theme: Expansion

Have students examine the map and notice how the size of the United States changed between 1800 and 1816. Have students make inferences about how the nation acquired this additional territory and from what nation the territory might have been acquired. Students might also discuss how they think doubling the size of the United States might affect the wealth and power of the nation.

### What Do You Know?

Have students think about the nations and groups that had competed for possession of the Northwest Territory. Which of these groups might have claimed parts of what is now the continental United States? What natural resources of the territory west of the Mississippi did Americans already know about? Have students describe what information they would want to have before purchasing a large parcel of land west of the Mississippi if they had been president in the early 1800s.

 **In-Depth Resources: Unit 3**
- Tracing Themes: Expansion, p. 20

## READ AND TAKE NOTES

### Reading Strategy: Summarizing

Tell students that summarizing material is a useful way to study. Explain that the process of summarizing helps them pick out the most important parts of what they read. They can use their own summaries for review. Point out that the Reading Strategy chart gives them a format for summarizing.

 **In-Depth Resources: Unit 3**
- Setting the Stage, p. 19

 **Critical Thinking Transparency CT28**
- Setting the Stage

# Chapter 10 SETTING THE STAGE

## BEFORE YOU READ

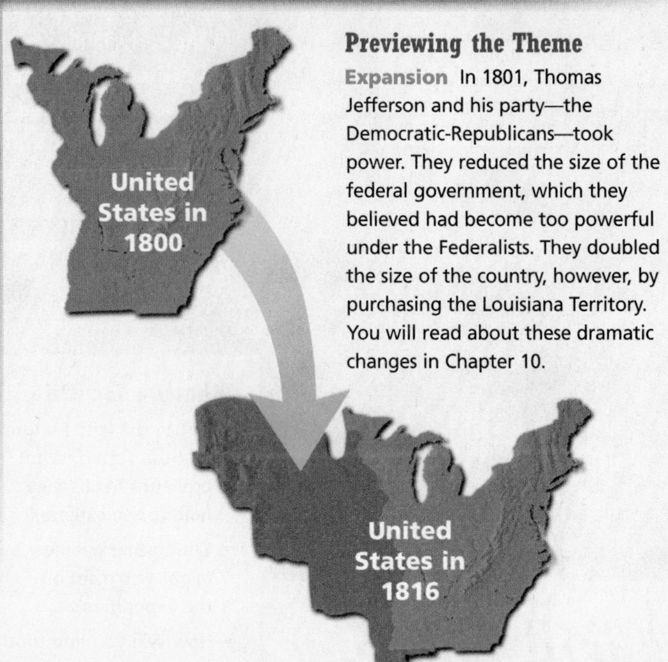


### Previewing the Theme

**Expansion** In 1801, Thomas Jefferson and his party—the Democratic-Republicans—took power. They reduced the size of the federal government, which they believed had become too powerful under the Federalists. They doubled the size of the country, however, by purchasing the Louisiana Territory. You will read about these dramatic changes in Chapter 10.

### What Do You Know?

What parts of the United States today were not part of the country in 1800? What should leaders consider before they buy land for their countries?

**THINK ABOUT**
- where the money for the purchase will come from
- what should be done if people already live on the land

### What Do You Want to Know?

What details do you need to help you understand the nation's expansion in the early 1800s? Make a list of information you need in your notebook before you read the chapter.

## READ AND TAKE NOTES

**Reading Strategy: Summarizing** When you study history, it is important to clearly understand what you read. One way to achieve a clear understanding is to summarize. When you summarize, you restate what you have read into fewer words, stating only the main ideas and essential details. It is important to use your own words in a summary. Use the chart below to record your summaries of the main ideas and essential details in Chapter 10.

 **See Skillbuilder Handbook, page R2.**

| The Jefferson Era |
|---|
| Summaries |
| **Main Idea:** Thomas Jefferson is elected president.<br>**Details:** Jefferson replaces Federalist policies with his own but has problems with the judiciary. |
| **Main Idea:** The United States makes the Louisiana Purchase and sends expeditions into the new territory.<br>**Details:** Napoleon sells Louisiana in 1803; Lewis, Clark, and Pike bring back maps and scientific information. |
| **Main Idea:** British interference with U.S. affairs leads to the War of 1812.<br>**Details:** Britain interferes with U.S. shipping, kidnaps U.S. citizens, and supports Native American resistance. |
| **Main Idea:** The United States wins the War of 1812.<br>**Details:** The war has two phases; U.S. victory weakens Native American resistance and increases patriotism and manufacturing. |



## TEACHING STRATEGY

### READING THE CHAPTER

This is a chronological chapter focusing on the expansion of the nation, conflict among different political parties, and conflict with foreign countries. Encourage students to note differing views on foreign policy and the causes and results of the War of 1812. Remind students to think about how expansion of the nation affects its policies.

### ALTERNATIVE ASSESSMENT

The Chapter Assessment describes three activities for alternative assessment on page 335. You may wish to have students work on these activities during the course of the chapter and then present them at the end.

# 1 Jefferson Takes Office

**TERMS & NAMES**
radical
Judiciary Act of 1801
John Marshall
*Marbury v. Madison*
unconstitutional
judicial review

**MAIN IDEA**
When Jefferson became president in 1801, his party replaced Federalist programs with its own.

**WHY IT MATTERS NOW**
Today's Democratic party traces its roots to the party of Jefferson, the Democratic-Republicans.

## ONE AMERICAN'S STORY

**Supporters of John Adams and Thomas Jefferson—competitors in the presidential election of 1800—fought for their candidates with nasty personal attacks. Scottish immigrant James Callender, a Jefferson supporter, wrote some of the harshest criticisms. During the campaign, he warned voters not to reelect President John Adams.**

*A VOICE FROM THE PAST*

In the fall of 1796 . . . the country fell into a more dangerous juncture than almost any the old confederation ever endured. The tardiness and timidity of Mr. Washington were succeeded by the rancour [bitterness] and insolence [arrogance] of Mr. Adams. . . . Think what you have been, what you are, and what, under [Adams], you are likely to become.

**James Callender,** quoted in *American Aurora*

In the presidential election of 1800, Thomas Jefferson was the candidate of the Democratic-Republican party. John Adams represented the Federalists.

**Adams's defenders were just as vicious. One went so far as to claim that if Jefferson won, "the soil will be soaked with blood, and the nation black with crimes." In spite of the campaign's nastiness, the election ended with a peaceful transfer of power from one party to another. The 1800 election was more than a personal battle, though. It was a contest between two parties with different ideas about the role of government.**

## 1 The Election of 1800

The two parties contesting the election of 1800 were the Federalists, led by President John Adams, and the Democratic-Republicans, represented by Thomas Jefferson. Each party believed that the other was endangering the Constitution and the American republic.

The Democratic-Republicans thought they were saving the nation from monarchy and oppression. They argued, again and again, that the Alien and Sedition Acts supported by the Federalists violated the Bill of Rights. (See pages 306–307.) The Federalists thought that the nation was about to be ruined by **radicals**—people who take extreme political positions. They remembered the violence of the French Revolution, in which radicals executed thousands in the name of liberty.





## SECTION OBJECTIVES

1. To describe the election of 1800 and explain the role of political parties
2. To identify Jefferson's achievements
3. To analyze Jefferson's philosophy of government
4. To analyze the significance of *Marbury* v. *Madison*

**CRITICAL THINKING**

Analyzing Points of View, p. 314
Summarizing, p. 315
Analyzing Causes, p. 316
Making Generalizations, p. 317

 **Why It Matters Now**
- Peaceful Transfers of Power, pp. 19–20

## FOCUS & MOTIVATE

### 5-MINUTE WARM-UP

**Making Inferences** The questions focus on Jefferson's view of politics.

1. Read "A Voice from the Past" on page 315. What does Jefferson urge Americans to do?
2. What might George Washington have said in reply to Jefferson's advice?

 **Warm-Up Transparency WT10**

## INSTRUCT

### INSTRUCT: OBJECTIVE 1

**The Election of 1800/Breaking the Tie**

Key Questions
- How did the political positions of the Federalists and Democratic-Republicans differ?
- What was unusual about the 1800 election?
- Why did Hamilton encourage Federalists to vote for Jefferson instead of Burr?

**In-Depth Resources: Unit 3**
- Guided Reading, p. 21
- Geography Application: Election of 1800, pp. 27–28

**Reading Study Guide** (Spanish and English), pp. 101–102

## RECOMMENDED RESOURCES

**In-Depth Resources: Unit 3**
- Guided Reading, p. 21
- Building Vocabulary, p. 25
- Geography Application: Election of 1800, pp. 27–28
- Reteaching Activity, p. 34

**Reading Study Guide** (Spanish and English), pp. 101–102

**America's History Makers**
- Thomas Jefferson, pp. 39–40

**Why It Matters Now**
- Peaceful Transfers of Power, pp. 19–20

**Citizenship Today,** pp. 87–88

**Formal Assessment**
- Section Quiz, p. 159

**Alternative Assessment**
- Rubrics, 5.1
- Rubrics, 1.10

**Access for Students Acquiring English/ESL**
- Guided Reading, p. 66
- Geography Application, pp. 71–72

**Technology Resources**

 **Electronic Teacher Tools with Test Maker**

 **ClassZone**
www.mcdougallittell.com

### STRANGE *but* True

**Hamilton-Burr Duel**

Although duels were not uncommon in the early 1800s, they were illegal in New York. Burr was vice-president at the time of his duel with Hamilton, which took place in New Jersey. Immediately after the announcement of Hamilton's death, the public turned against Burr. He was indicted for murder in New York and New Jersey. However, public reaction eventually calmed, and Burr returned to Washington to resume his official duties. He completed his term in 1805, but the duel had ended his chances of any further public career.

When election day came, the Democratic-Republicans won the presidency. Jefferson received 73 votes in the electoral college, and Adams earned 65. But there was a problem. Aaron Burr, whom the Democratic-Republicans wanted as vice president, also received 73 votes.

**Background**
In 1804, the Twelfth Amendment solved this problem by creating separate ballots for president and vice president.

### STRANGE *but* True

**HAMILTON-BURR DUEL**

In 1804, the Democratic-Republicans replaced Aaron Burr as their candidate for vice president. Burr then decided to run for governor of New York.

Alexander Hamilton questioned Burr's fitness for public office. He wrote that Burr was a "dangerous man . . . who ought not to be trusted with the reins of government."

Burr lost the election. Furious, he challenged Hamilton to a duel. Hamilton went to the duel but resolved not to fire. Burr, however, shot Hamilton, who died the next day.

## Breaking the Tie

According to the Constitution, the House of Representatives had to choose between Burr and Jefferson. The Democratic-Republicans clearly intended for Jefferson to be president. However, the new House of Representatives, dominated by Jefferson's party, would not take office for some months. Federalists still held a majority in the House, and their votes would decide the winner.

The Federalists were divided. Some feared Jefferson so much that they decided to back Burr. Others, such as Alexander Hamilton, considered Burr an unreliable man and urged the election of Jefferson. Hamilton did not like Jefferson, but he believed that Jefferson would do more for the good of the nation than Burr. "If there be a man in the world I ought to hate," he said, "it is Jefferson. . . . But the public good must be [more important than] every private consideration."

***Reading*History**
**A. Analyzing Points of View** Why did Hamilton think that Jefferson was the better choice for president?
**A. Possible Response** He believed that Jefferson would do more for the public good than Burr.

Over a period of seven days, the House voted 35 times without determining a winner. Finally, two weeks before the inauguration, Alexander Hamilton's friend James A. Bayard persuaded several Federalists not to vote for Burr. On the thirty-sixth ballot, Jefferson was elected president. Aaron Burr, who became vice president, would never forget Hamilton's insults.

People were overjoyed by Jefferson's election. A Philadelphia newspaper reported that bells rang, guns fired, dogs barked, cats meowed, and children cried over the news of Jefferson's victory.

## 2 The Talented Jefferson

In over 200 years, the United States has had more than 40 presidents. Many of them were great leaders. But no president has ever matched Thomas Jefferson in the variety of his achievements.

Jefferson's talents went beyond politics. He was still a young lawyer when he became interested in the architecture of classical Greece and Rome. The look of our nation's capital today reflects that interest. When Washington, D.C., was being built during the 1790s, Jefferson advised its architects and designers.

Jefferson's passion for classical styles can also be seen in his plan of Monticello, his Virginia home. For this elegant mansion, Jefferson designed storm windows, a seven-day clock, and a dumbwaiter—a small elevator that brought bottles of wine from the cellar.



### INSTRUCT: OBJECTIVE 2

**The Talented Jefferson/ Jefferson's Philosophy**

Key Questions

- In what areas did Jefferson excel besides politics?
- How did Jefferson plan to unite Americans?

 **America's History Makers**
- Thomas Jefferson, pp. 39–40

### ACTIVITY OPTIONS

**INDIVIDUAL NEEDS: GIFTED AND TALENTED**

**JEFFERSON EXHIBIT**

**Class Time** One class period

**Task** Planning an exhibit

**Purpose** To create an exhibit that illustrates Jefferson's life and achievements

**Supplies Needed**
- Reference materials about Jefferson, Internet access

**Activity** Tell students to plan an exhibit about Thomas Jefferson suitable for display in elementary schools. The exhibit may contain paintings, artifacts, and large posters containing quotations from Jefferson and others. Have students do research to find the items and quotes they would like to use. Tell them to photocopy pictures of the items or write short descriptions of them. Students should present their final plans with items for the exhibit numbered in order as they would be displayed.

Jefferson was a skilled violinist, horseman, amateur scientist, and a devoted reader, too. His book collection later became the core of the Library of Congress. After his election, Jefferson applied his many talents and ideas to the government of the United States.

## Jefferson's Philosophy

The new president had strong opinions about what kind of country the United States ought to be. But his first order of business was to calm the nation's political quarrels.

*A VOICE FROM THE PAST*

Let us, then, fellow-citizens, unite with one heart and one mind. . . . Every difference of opinion is not a difference of principle. . . . We are all Republicans, we are all Federalists.

**Thomas Jefferson,** First Inaugural Address

*Reading* **History**
**B. Summarizing** How did Thomas Jefferson try to unite the nation after he was elected?
B. Possible Response He promoted a common way of life based on a nation of small independent farmers.

One way Jefferson tried to unite Americans was by promoting a common way of life. He wanted the United States to remain a nation of small independent farmers. Such a nation, he believed, would uphold the strong morals and democratic values that he associated with country living. He hoped that the enormous amount of available land would prevent Americans from crowding into cities, as people had in Europe.

As president, Jefferson behaved more like a gentleman farmer than a privileged politician. Instead of riding in a fancy carriage to his inauguration, Jefferson walked the two blocks from his boarding house to the Capitol. Though his chef served elegant meals, the president's guests ate at round tables so that no one could sit at the head of the table.

To the end, Jefferson refused to elevate himself because of his office. For his tombstone, he chose this simple epitaph: "Here was buried

**The Talented Jefferson**

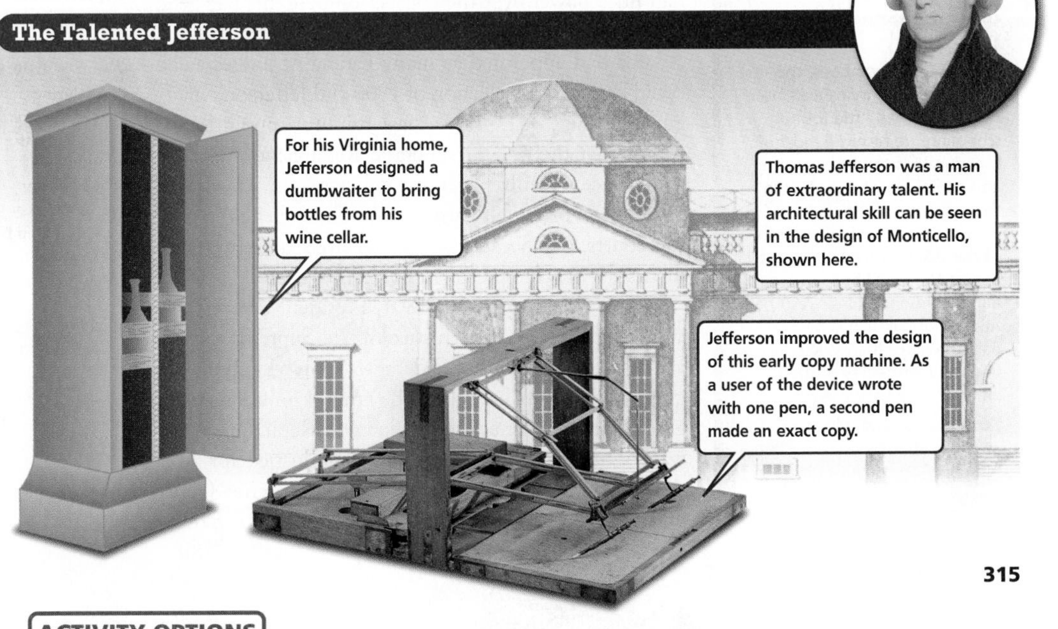

For his Virginia home, Jefferson designed a dumbwaiter to bring bottles from his wine cellar.
Thomas Jefferson was a man of extraordinary talent. His architectural skill can be seen in the design of Monticello, shown here.
Jefferson improved the design of this early copy machine. As a user of the device wrote with one pen, a second pen made an exact copy.

### MORE ABOUT . . .

**Jefferson and JFK**

At a White House dinner for Nobel Prize winners, President John F. Kennedy recalled Jefferson's versatility and brilliance with the following remark. He called his dinner guests "the most extraordinary collection of talents . . . that has ever been gathered at the White House, with the possible exception of when Thomas Jefferson dined alone." Among Jefferson's many interests were farming, architecture, law, geography, botany, natural history, and fine food and wine. His personal library contained almost 6,500 books. These volumes helped to form the initial collection of the Library of Congress in 1815.

### MORE ABOUT . . .

**Thomas Jefferson**

Jefferson brought a studied informality to the office of president. One morning he shocked a British minister by receiving him while wearing slippers. Jefferson held no formal receptions, and when he entertained guests at meals, he did not seat them according to any system of rank—he would not even single out a guest of honor.

### ACTIVITY OPTIONS

### MULTIPLE LEARNING STYLES: VISUAL

**JEFFERSON POSTAGE STAMPS**

**Class Time** One class period

**Task** Creating a postage stamp that commemorates one of Thomas Jefferson's talents, interests, or achievements

**Purpose** To identify Thomas Jefferson's talents and achievements

**Supplies Needed**
- Biographies and other reference materials on Jefferson's life and inventions and on Monticello
- Posterboard
- Art supplies
- Envelopes with canceled postage stamps or pictures of stamps

**Activity** Tell students to design a set of stamps that honor Jefferson's many talents and interests. Divide students into groups. Encourage students to examine some real stamps before beginning so that their stamps will look like actual postage stamps. Remind students that stamps should show at a glance who or what the subject is. Have each group pick one of Jefferson's achievements as the subject of their stamp and prepare a poster-sized rendition of their design. Display the completed stamps.

**INSTRUCT: OBJECTIVE** 

**Undoing Federalist Programs**

Key Questions

- What did Jefferson believe about the role of government?
- How did Jefferson reduce the size and power of government?
- How did Hamilton and Jefferson differ in their views on public debt?

**AMERICA'S HISTORY MAKERS**

**John Marshall**

Before Marshall led the Supreme Court, justices had followed the English custom of having each judge deliver an opinion in a major case. Justices sometimes disagreed, so these presentations added little to the authority of the high court. The Marshall Court changed to the present practice, in which the Supreme Court issues only one opinion on a case. Because Marshall wrote many opinions and his opinions were clear, persuasive, and well reasoned, this practice helped the Supreme Court to gain respect and authority.

**Possible Response: He had to make many difficult decisions and explain them in written opinions. He wrote 519 out of the 1,000 decisions he participated in.**

**INSTRUCT: OBJECTIVE** 

**Marshall and the Judiciary/ *Marbury* v. *Madison***

Key Questions

- How did John Marshall influence the federal court system?
- How did the case of *Marbury* v. *Madison* establish the principle of judicial review?
- How did Marshall help create a balance of power among the three branches of government?

**Citizenship Today,** pp. 85–86

Thomas Jefferson, author of the Declaration of American Independence, of the statute of Virginia for religious freedom, and father of the University of Virginia." Jefferson chose not to list his presidency. His belief in a modest role for the central government is reflected in the changes he made during his presidency.

**Background** In addition to founding the University of Virginia in 1819, Jefferson designed its buildings and supervised their construction.

## 3 Undoing Federalist Programs

Jefferson believed that the federal government should have less power than it had had under the Federalists. During his term of office, he sought to end many Federalist programs.

At the president's urging, Congress—now controlled by Democratic-Republicans—allowed the Alien and Sedition Acts to end. Jefferson then released prisoners convicted under the acts—among them, James Callender. Congress also ended many taxes, including the unpopular whiskey tax. Because the loss of tax revenue lowered the government's income, Jefferson reduced the number of federal employees to cut costs. He also reduced the size of the military.

**JOHN MARSHALL**
**1755–1835**

John Marshall was born, the first of 15 children, in Virginia's backcountry. He had little formal schooling. He received most of his education from his parents and a minister who lived with the family one year.

Even so, the lasting strength of the U.S. Constitution is partly due to Marshall's brilliant legal mind. In his long tenure as Chief Justice, John Marshall participated in more than 1,000 decisions and wrote 519 of them himself.

**How does Marshall's record as Chief Justice demonstrate his decision-making abilities?**

Jefferson next made changes to the Federalists' financial policies. Alexander Hamilton had created a system that depended on a certain amount of public debt. He believed that people who were owed money by their government would make sure the government was run properly. But Jefferson opposed public debt. He used revenues from tariffs and land sales to reduce the amount of money owed by the government.

## 4 Marshall and the Judiciary

Though Jefferson ended many Federalist programs, he had little power over the courts. John Adams had seen to that with the **Judiciary Act of 1801**. Under this act, Adams had appointed as many Federalist judges as he could between the election of 1800 and Jefferson's inauguration in 1801. These last-minute appointments meant that the new Democratic-Republican president would face a firmly Federalist judiciary.

*Reading* **History** **C. Analyzing Causes** Why did the Federalists retain a great deal of power even after they were defeated by the Democratic-Republicans? C. Possible Response They kept firm control of the judiciary.

Jefferson often felt frustrated by Federalist control of the courts. Yet because judges received their appointments for life, the president could do little.

Before he left office in 1801, President Adams also appointed a new Chief Justice of the Supreme Court. He chose a 45-year-old Federalist, **John Marshall**. He guessed that Marshall would be around for a long time to check the power of the Democratic-Republicans. He was right. Marshall served as Chief Justice for over three decades. Under Marshall, the Supreme Court upheld federal authority and strengthened federal



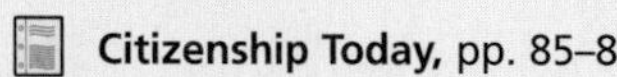

**ACTIVITY OPTIONS**

**INTERDISCIPLINARY LINK: LANGUAGE ARTS/CIVICS**

BLOCK SCHEDULING

**MARSHALL AND THE JUDICIARY**

**Class Time** 30 minutes

**Task** Writing a eulogy for John Marshall

**Purpose** To evaluate the impact of John Marshall and the Marshall Court on the federal judicial system

**Supplies Needed**

- Civics and/or government textbooks and other reference materials on Marshall

**Activity** Explain to students that a eulogy is a speech or written remarks that praise an individual for his or her character and/or achievements. Often speakers give eulogies at funerals or memorial services. Have students review the reference materials on John Marshall and then prepare a five-minute speech on Marshall's life and accomplishments. When students have completed their eulogies, choose several examples for students to read aloud to the class.

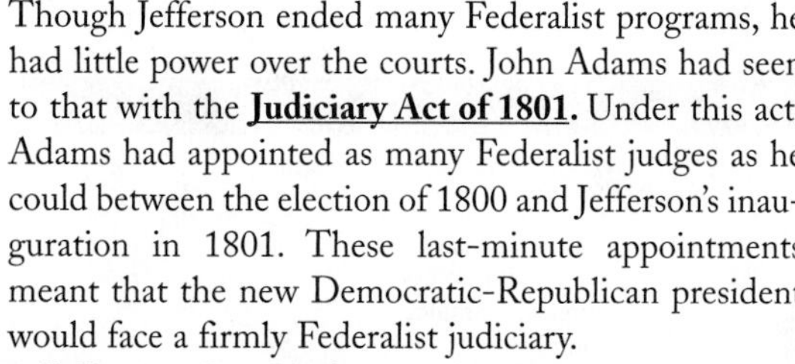

courts. One of the most important decisions of the Marshall Court was ***Marbury* v. *Madison*** (1803).

## *Marbury* v. *Madison*

Vocabulary
**justice of the peace:** a low-level official with limited authority, including the power to perform marriages

William Marbury was one of Adams's last-minute appointments. Adams had named him as a justice of the peace for the District of Columbia.

Marbury was supposed to be installed in his position by Secretary of State James Madison. When Madison refused to give him the job, Marbury sued. The case went to the Supreme Court, which ruled that the law under which Marbury sued was **unconstitutional**—that is, it contradicted the law of the Constitution.

Although the Court denied Marbury's claim, it did establish the principle of **judicial review**. This principle states that the Supreme Court has the final say in interpreting the Constitution. In his decision, Marshall declared, "It is emphatically the province and duty of the Judicial Department to say what the law is." If the Supreme Court decides that a law violates the Constitution, then that law cannot be put into effect.

Jefferson and Madison were angry when Marshall seized this new power for the Supreme Court, but they could hardly fight his decision. After all, he had decided *Marbury* v. *Madison* in their favor.

By establishing judicial review, Marshall helped to create a lasting balance among the three branches of government. The strength of this balance would be tested as the United States grew. In the next section, you will read about a period of great national growth.

### Now and then

**THE SUPREME COURT TODAY**

The principle of judicial review is still a major force in American society. In June 1999, the Supreme Court used this power to restrict the ability of the federal government to enforce its laws in the 50 states.

In one case, *Alden* v. *Maine*, the Court ruled that employees of a state government cannot sue their state even when the state violates federal labor laws—such as those that set guidelines for overtime wages.

### Section 1 Assessment

**1. Terms & Names**

Identify:
- radical
- Judiciary Act of 1801
- John Marshall
- *Marbury* v. *Madison*
- unconstitutional
- judicial review

**2. Taking Notes**

Use a chart like the one below to list some of the changes made by Jefferson and his party.

| Changes made by Democratic-Republicans |
| --- |
| 1. |

What branch of government gave Jefferson trouble?

**3. Main Ideas**

a. How was the tie between Jefferson and Burr settled after the election of 1800?

b. In what ways did Jefferson's talents reach beyond politics?

c. How did the opinions of Jefferson and Hamilton regarding the public debt differ?

**4. Critical Thinking**

**Making Generalizations** How was Thomas Jefferson's philosophy reflected in his personal life?

THINK ABOUT
- how he behaved after being elected
- how he felt about his presidency later in life

**ACTIVITY OPTIONS**

TECHNOLOGY / ART — Read more about Thomas Jefferson. Design Jefferson's **Internet home page** showing his inventions or create a **model** of a building he designed.





### Now and then

**The Supreme Court Today**
*Alden* v. *Maine* (1999) shows how the Supreme Court continues to wrestle with federalism and with questions about how power should be divided between the states and the federal government. In this case, a group of probation officers employed by the state sued Maine under the federal Fair Labor Standards Act. They charged that the state had violated the overtime pay provisions of this act. The state insisted that it could not be sued under federal law even in state court. The Supreme Court agreed with the state, in a narrow decision: five justices voted in favor of the state's view, four against.

## ASSESS & RETEACH

**Setting the Stage** Have students fill in the first section on the chapter graphic organizer.

**Formal Assessment**
- Section Quiz, p. 159

**Critical Thinking Transparency CT28**
- Setting the Stage

**RETEACHING ACTIVITY**

Working in pairs, have students create outlines of the section. Have students use their outline to write a summary of the chapter.

**In-Depth Resources: Unit 3**
- Reteaching Activity, p. 34

### Section 1 Assessment

**1. Terms & Names**

**radical,** p. 313
**Judiciary Act of 1801,** p. 316
**John Marshall,** p. 316
***Marbury* v. *Madison*,** p. 317
**unconstitutional,** p. 317
**judicial review,** p. 317

**2. Taking Notes**

He repealed unpopular taxes; reduced the number of federal employees; reduced the size of the military; and replaced Hamilton's financial system.

the judicial branch

**3. Main Ideas**

**a.** The House of Representatives broke it. **b.** He was an architect, inventor, violinist, and amateur scientist. **c.** Hamilton thought some public debt gave citizens an interest in good government. Jefferson opposed all public debt.

**4. Critical Thinking**

He reflected a gentleman-farmer philosophy, and refused to elevate himself because of his office.

**ACTIVITY OPTIONS**

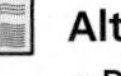
**Alternative Assessment**
- Rubrics for a Web page, 5.1
- Rubrics for a model, 1.10

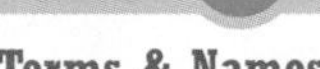

## SECTION OBJECTIVES

1. To explain why Jefferson offered to buy New Orleans from France
2. To analyze why Napoleon sold the Louisiana Territory to the United States
3. To summarize the experiences of the Lewis and Clark expedition
4. To evaluate the results of Pike's expedition

**SKILLBUILDER**

Interpreting Maps: Location, Movement, p. 320
Interpreting Charts, p. 323

**CRITICAL THINKING**

Making Inferences, pp. 319, 321
Finding Main Ideas, p. 322
Recognizing Effects, p. 323

## FOCUS & MOTIVATE

### 5-MINUTE WARM-UP

**Reading a Map** These questions focus on the Lewis and Clark expedition.

1. Look at the map on page 320. What might be forms of transportation used by the expedition? How can you tell?
2. What were some problems of travel by foot or on horseback?

 **Warm-Up Transparency WT10**

## INSTRUCT

### INSTRUCT: OBJECTIVE 1

**The West in 1800/ Napoleon and New Orleans**

Key Questions

- What four nations claimed parts of the area between the Mississippi and the Pacific?
- How did Jefferson attempt to settle the nation's dispute with France?

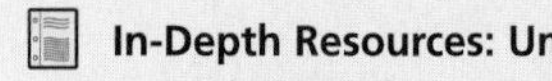

**In-Depth Resources: Unit 3**
- Guided Reading, p. 22
- Building Vocabulary, p. 25

**Reading Study Guide** (Spanish and English), pp. 103–104

# 2 The Louisiana Purchase and Exploration

**TERMS & NAMES**
Louisiana Purchase
Meriwether Lewis
William Clark
Lewis and Clark expedition
Sacagawea
Zebulon Pike

| MAIN IDEA | WHY IT MATTERS NOW |
|---|---|
| Jefferson purchased the Louisiana Territory in 1803 and doubled the size of the United States. | Thirteen more states were eventually organized on the land acquired by the Louisiana Purchase. |

### ONE AMERICAN'S STORY

**In 1790, Captain Robert Gray became the first American to sail around the world. Two years later, Gray explored a harbor in what is now Washington state. This harbor was later named Gray's Harbor, and Washington's largest river was named after Gray's ship, the *Columbia*.**

**New England merchants like Captain Gray had to sail all the way around South America to reach the profitable trading regions of the Oregon Country. (See the map on page 320.) In spite of the long trip, merchants from Boston soon began to appear there frequently. They appeared so often that the Native Americans they traded with began calling all white people "Bostons."**

**Gray's explorations helped to establish U.S. claims to the Pacific Northwest. In this section, you will learn how a lucky land purchase and a daring expedition further hastened westward expansion.**

Robert Gray sailed his ship *Columbia* on trading voyages to the Northwest and China.

## 1 The West in 1800

In 1800, when Americans talked about the "West," they meant the area between the Appalachian Mountains and the Mississippi River. Thousands of settlers were moving westward across the Appalachians to settle in this region. Many moved onto land long-inhabited by Native Americans. Even so, several U.S. territories soon declared statehood. Kentucky and Tennessee had become states by 1800, and Ohio entered the union in 1803.

Although the Mississippi River was the western border of the United States, there was a great deal of activity further west. In 1800, France and Spain were negotiating for ownership of the Louisiana Territory—the vast region between the Mississippi River and the Rocky Mountains.

The Pacific coast region and the Oregon Country, as you read in One American's Story, also attracted increasing attention. In California, Spain had a chain of 21 missions stretching from San Diego to San Francisco. Starting just north of San Francisco, Russian settlements dotted the Pacific coast all the way to Alaska. Great Britain also claimed land in the region.



## RECOMMENDED RESOURCES

**In-Depth Resources: Unit 3**
- Guided Reading, p. 22
- Building Vocabulary, p. 25
- Literature Selection: from *Streams to the River, River to the Sea*, pp. 31–33
- Reteaching Activity, p. 35
- Enrichment Activity, p. 38

**Reading Study Guide** (Spanish and English), pp. 103–104

**Outline Map Activities**
- The Louisiana Purchase, pp. 19–20

**America's History Makers**
- Sacagawea, pp. 41–42

**American History Plays**
- *Land of the Unknown*

**Formal Assessment**
- Section Quiz, p. 160

**Alternative Assessment**
- Rubrics, 2.4
- Rubrics, 2.1

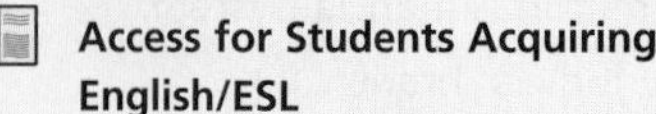

**Access for Students Acquiring English/ESL**
- Guided Reading, p. 67

**Technology Resources**

 **Geography Transparency GT10**
- United States, 1803

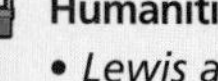

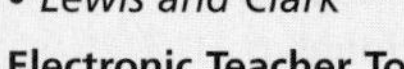 **Humanities Transparency HT19**
- *Lewis and Clark*

 **Electronic Teacher Tools with Test Maker**

 **ClassZone**
www.mcdougallittell.com

**Reading History**

**A. Reading a Map** Use the map on page 320 to find the location of New Orleans.

As the number of westerners grew, so did their political influence. A vital issue for many settlers was the use of the Mississippi River. Farmers and merchants used the river to move their products to the port of New Orleans, and from there to east coast markets. Threats to the free navigation of the Mississippi and the use of the port at New Orleans brought America to the brink of war.

## Napoleon and New Orleans

"There is on the globe one single spot the possessor of which is our natural and habitual enemy," President Jefferson wrote. That spot was New Orleans. This strategic port was originally claimed by France. After losing the French and Indian War, France turned over the Louisiana Territory—including New Orleans—to Spain. But in a secret treaty in 1800, Spain returned Louisiana and the port to France's powerful leader, Napoleon. Now Napoleon planned to colonize the American territory.

**Background**

In 1799, Napoleon was made the top official of the French Republic. In 1804, he became emperor.

In 1802, these developments nearly resulted in war. Just before turning Louisiana over to France, Spain closed New Orleans to American shipping. Angry westerners called for war against both Spain and France. To avoid hostilities, Jefferson offered to buy New Orleans from France. He received a surprising offer back. The French asked if the United States wanted to buy all of the Louisiana Territory—a tract of land even larger than the United States at that time.

## 2 The Louisiana Purchase

A number of factors may have led Napoleon to make his surprising offer. He was probably alarmed by America's fierce determination to keep the port of New Orleans open. Also, his enthusiasm for a colony in America may have been lessened by events in a French colony in the West Indies. There, a revolt led by Toussaint L'Ouverture (too•SAN loo•vehr•TOOR) had resulted in disastrous losses for the French. Another factor was France's costly war against Britain. America's money may have been more valuable to Napoleon than its land.

**B. Possible Response** He believed that acquiring land for a republic of small farmers was important.

**Reading History**

**B. Making Inferences** Why did Jefferson purchase Louisiana even though the Constitution said nothing about the president's right to buy land?

Jefferson was thrilled by Napoleon's offer. However, the Constitution said nothing about the president's right to buy land. This troubled Jefferson, who believed in the strict interpretation of the Constitution. But he also believed in a republic of small farmers, and that required land. So, on April 30, 1803, the **Louisiana Purchase** was approved for $15 million—about three cents per acre. The purchase doubled the size of the United States. At the time, Americans knew little about the territory. But that would soon change.

### Connections TO WORLD HISTORY

**TOUSSAINT L'OUVERTURE**

Toussaint L'Ouverture was born in Hispaniola, an island in the West Indies once colonized by both France and Spain. In 1791, L'Ouverture helped to lead a slave revolt against the French-controlled part of Hispaniola. A natural leader, L'Ouverture won admiration when he preached harmony between former slaves and planters.

In 1801, L'Ouverture overran the Spanish part of the island. He then freed all the slaves and put himself in charge of the entire island.

Hoping to regain their territory, the French invaded in 1802. They arrested L'Ouverture but failed to end the rebellion.

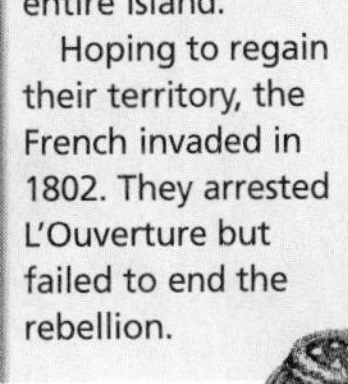

**INSTRUCT: OBJECTIVE 2**

**The Louisiana Purchase/ Lewis and Clark Explore**

Key Questions

- What caused Jefferson to hesitate before agreeing to purchase the Louisiana Territory?
- How did the Louisiana Purchase change the size of the United States?
- What was the purpose of the Lewis and Clark expedition?

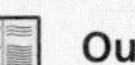

**Outline Map Activities**

- The Louisiana Purchase, pp. 19–20

### Connections TO WORLD HISTORY

**Toussaint L'Ouverture**

In May 1802, L'Ouverture was forced to surrender after a French invasion overwhelmed his small force. He agreed to lay down his weapons in exchange for a French promise not to restore slavery in Haiti. At first, L'Ouverture was allowed to live peacefully on a plantation in Haiti, but he was later seized by the French and sent to France, where he was imprisoned in a dungeon, interrogated, and died in 1803.

**CRITICAL THINKING ACTIVITY**

**Evaluating** Have students review Jefferson's philosophy of government. Did the Louisiana Purchase contradict that philosophy? Why or why not?

**Class Time** 10 minutes

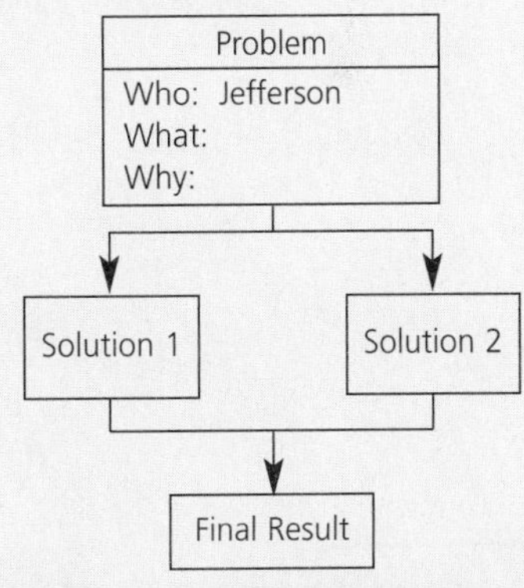


**ACTIVITY OPTIONS**

**INTERDISCIPLINARY LINK: MATHEMATICS**

**BLOCK SCHEDULING**

**LOUISIANA PURCHASE WORD PROBLEMS**

**Class Time** 20 minutes

**Task** Solving math problems using information about the Louisiana Purchase

**Purpose** To analyze the value of the Louisiana Purchase

**Supplies Needed**
- Calculator

**Activity** Put the following information on the chalkboard:
- Louisiana Purchase: approximately 828,000 square miles
- Size of the United States in 1800: 891,000 square miles
- Size of the United States today: 3,781,000 square miles

Have students calculate the following: a) the price per square mile of the Louisiana Territory based on a purchase price of $15 million; b) the percentage of the total land area of the United States today that the Louisiana Purchase represents. Then have students make up one more problem based on these data.

## MORE ABOUT . . .

**The Lewis and Clark Expedition**

The Lewis and Clark expedition consisted of about 40 men in their late twenties or early thirties who were physically fit, experienced outdoorsmen. Expedition members contributed knowledge about many topics to the group, including botany, weather forecasting, zoology, and navigation by the moon and stars. Other members knew some Native American sign language or were skilled at carpentry, gun repair, or piloting boats.

**In-Depth Resources: Unit 3**
- Enrichment Activity, p. 38

## HISTORY FROM VISUALS

**Reading the Map** Ask students what made St. Louis a good starting point for exploring the West. **Possible Response** It could be reached by the Mississippi River and was located on the Missouri River, providing access to the interior of the Louisiana Territory. Then ask why Pike might have chosen to go south in the Louisiana Territory. **Possible Response** to get information different from that of Lewis and Clark

**Extension** Have students use a current political map to determine what states or parts of states were created from the Louisiana Purchase.

**Geography Transparency GT10**
- United States, 1803

## Lewis and Clark Explore

Since 1802, Thomas Jefferson had planned an expedition to explore the Louisiana country. Now that the Louisiana Purchase had been made, learning about the territory became even more important.

Jefferson chose a young officer, Captain **Meriwether Lewis,** to lead the expedition. In Jefferson's map-lined study, the two men eagerly planned the trip. Lewis turned to his old friend, Lieutenant **William Clark,** to select and oversee a volunteer force, which they called the Corps of Discovery. Clark was a skilled mapmaker and outdoorsman and proved to be a natural leader. The Corps of Discovery soon became known as the **Lewis and Clark expedition.**

**Vocabulary**
**corps** (kor): a number of people acting together for a similar purpose

Clark was accompanied by York, his African-American slave. York's hunting skills won him many admirers among the Native Americans met by the explorers. The first black man that many Indians had ever seen, York became something of a celebrity among them.

Lewis and Clark set out in the summer of 1803. By winter, they reached St. Louis. Located on the western bank of the Mississippi River, St. Louis would soon become the gateway to the West. But in 1803, the city was a sleepy town with just 180 houses. Lewis and Clark spent the winter at St. Louis and waited for the ceremony that would mark the transfer of Louisiana to the United States. In March 1804, the American flag flew over St. Louis for the first time.

**Skillbuilder Answers**
1. Missouri and Mississippi rivers
2. For part of the trip, Clark took a southerly route along the Yellowstone River.

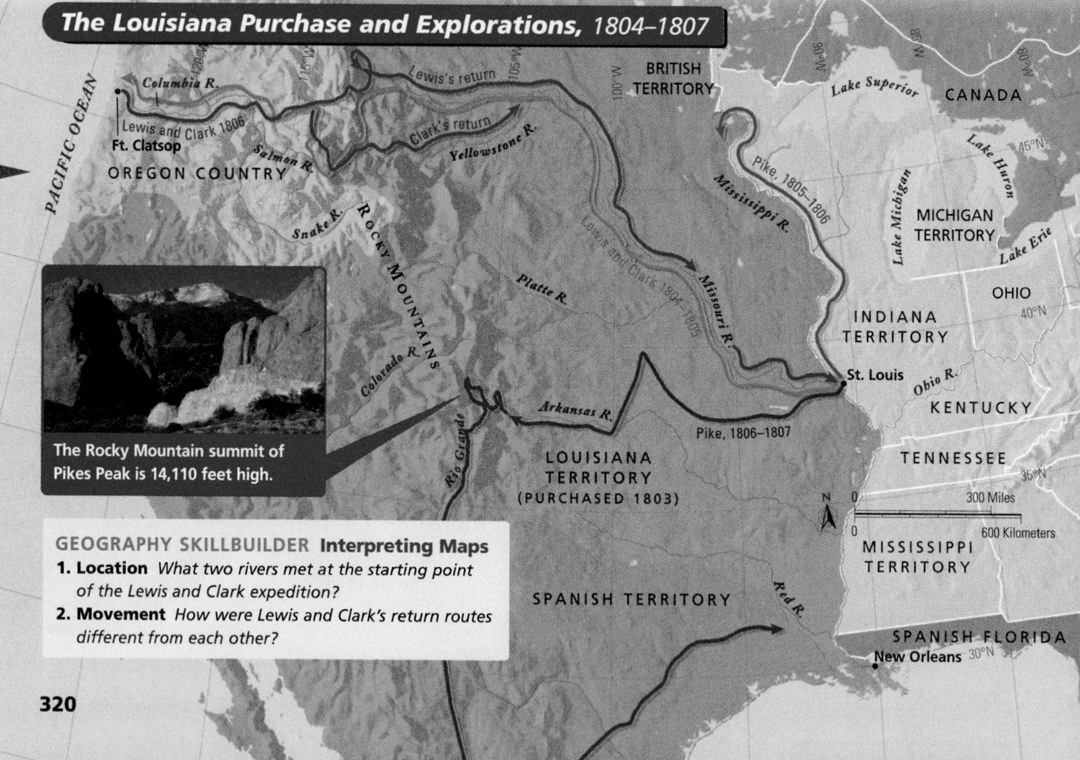

The Rocky Mountain summit of Pikes Peak is 14,110 feet high.

**GEOGRAPHY SKILLBUILDER Interpreting Maps**
1. **Location** *What two rivers met at the starting point of the Lewis and Clark expedition?*
2. **Movement** *How were Lewis and Clark's return routes different from each other?*

320

## ACTIVITY OPTIONS

## INDIVIDUAL NEEDS

### LESS PROFICIENT READERS

**Sequencing Events** To help students follow the sequence of events and understand the importance of the Lewis and Clark expedition, work with them to create a sequence chart. As students read the sections "Lewis and Clark Explore," "Up the Missouri River," and "On to the Pacific Ocean," pause and ask students to identify each new event and its corresponding date. Write students' responses on the board in a chart.

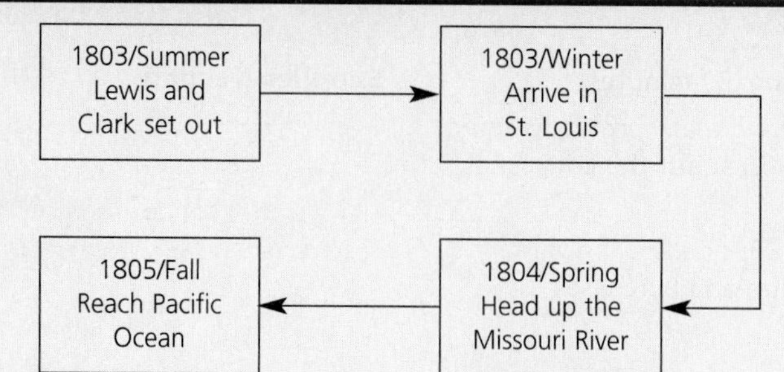

## AMERICA'S HISTORY MAKERS

**MERIWETHER LEWIS**
**1774–1809**

Meriwether Lewis was well qualified for the first overland expedition to the Pacific Northwest. In Virginia, he had become an expert hunter. From 1801 to 1803, he worked for President Jefferson, who had him trained in geography, mineralogy, and astronomy.

The journals Lewis kept tell what the West was like in the early 1800s and are still exciting to read. In one entry, dated September 17, 1804, Lewis describes the "immense herds of Buffaloe, deer Elk and Antelopes which we saw in every direction feeding on the hills and plains."

**WILLIAM CLARK**
**1770–1838**

William Clark was an army friend of Meriwether Lewis. Lewis personally chose him to be co-captain of the Corps of Discovery.

Clark's experience in his state militia and the U.S. Army had taught him how to build forts, draw maps, and lead expeditions through enemy territory.

He had less formal training than Lewis, but with his six feet of height and muscular build, he was a more rugged explorer.

Clark's leadership skills smoothed disputes. Also, his artistic skills made the expedition's maps and drawings both accurate and beautiful.

**What were the different skills of Lewis and Clark that qualified them as co-leaders of the expedition?**

## 3 Up the Missouri River

The explorers, who numbered about 40, set out from St. Louis in May of 1804. They headed up the Missouri River in one shallow-bottomed riverboat and two pirogues—canoes made from hollowed-out tree trunks. They had instructions from President Jefferson to explore the river and hoped to find a water route across the continent. Lewis and Clark were also told to establish good relations with Native Americans and describe the landscape, plants, and animals they saw.

*Reading*History
**C. Making Inferences** Why did Lewis and Clark travel on the Missouri River?
C. Possible Response They were instructed to explore the river and find a water route across the continent.

The explorers inched up the Missouri. The first afternoon, they traveled only about three miles. Sometimes the men had to pull, rather than row or sail, their boats against the current. In late October, they reached the Mandan Indian villages in what is now North Dakota.

The explorers built a small fort and spent the winter with the friendly Mandan. There, they also met British and French-Canadian trappers and traders. They were not happy to see the Americans. They suspected that the Americans would soon compete with them for the rich trade in beaver furs—and they were right.

In the spring of 1805, the expedition set out again. A French trapper, his 17-year-old-wife, **Sacagawea** (SAK•uh•juh•WEE•uh), and their baby went with them. Sacagawea was a Shoshone woman whose language skills and knowledge of geography would be of great value to Lewis and Clark—especially when they reached the area where she was born.



### AMERICA'S HISTORY MAKERS

**Meriwether Lewis**
Thomas Jefferson said of Lewis that he possessed "a firmness & perseverance of purpose which nothing but impossibilities could divert from its direction." Lewis was Jefferson's private secretary when the president began unofficially training him to lead an expedition to chart the Louisiana Territory. After the expedition, in 1807 Lewis became governor of the Louisiana Territory. Two years later he died in an inn on the Natchez Trace. Historians still debate whether the cause of his death was suicide or murder.

**William Clark**
After the expedition, Clark became governor of the Missouri Territory. He held this office until his death in 1838 and also served as governor of the Missouri Territory and surveyor general for Illinois, Missouri, and Arkansas. Both Lewis and Clark received 1,600 acres of public land for leading the successful expedition.

**Possible Responses: Lewis had training in geography, minerology, and astronomy. Clark had extensive experience in the military and was a skilled artist.**

**Humanities Transparency HT19**
- *Lewis and Clark*

### INSTRUCT: OBJECTIVE 

**Up the Missouri River/ On to the Pacific Ocean**
Key Questions
- What goals did Jefferson have for the Lewis and Clark expedition?
- How did the Mandan and Sacagawea help the expedition?
- What did the Lewis and Clark expedition accomplish?

**In-Depth Resources: Unit 3**
- Literature Selection: from *Streams to the River, River to the Sea,* pp. 31–33

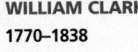

**ACTIVITY OPTIONS**

**INTERDISCIPLINARY LINK: GEOGRAPHY** — BLOCK SCHEDULING

**MAPPING THE LEWIS AND CLARK EXPEDITION**

**Class Time** One class period

**Task** Making a map showing the route of the Lewis and Clark expedition

**Purpose** To apply map skills and to study parts of the western United States

**Supplies Needed**
- Atlas map of the western United States
- Reference materials about the Lewis and Clark expedition
- Art supplies

**Activity** Have students draw their own maps of the Lewis and Clark expedition, using the map on page 320 as a model. Tell students to add present-day state boundaries, state capitals, and other large cities and towns. Tell them to choose one of the following categories to include on their map: state and national parks, mountain ranges and rivers, and Indian groups at the time of the expedition. Motivated students may add some of the Lewis and Clark expedition's stopping places and camps.

MORE ABOUT . . .

**Records of the Expedition**

Patrick Gass came to the Lewis and Clark expedition from the army in Illinois. Gass kept a journal that coincides in most details with the journals of Lewis and Clark. Gass paints a poignant picture of the expedition's Christmas celebration on December 24 and 25, 1804. The men feasted on special items including flour, dried apples, and pepper. Captain Clark presented each man a glass of brandy, and later the men danced.

MORE ABOUT . . .

**Sacagawea**

When the Lewis and Clark expedition reached the area known as the Three Forks of the Missouri in western Montana, Sacagawea recognized her surroundings. Born in what is today Idaho, she was about 12 years old when she was kidnapped by the Hidatsa Sioux and taken from her Shoshone home to a Hidatsa-Mandan village near what is today Bismarck, North Dakota. Later she was bought by Charbonneau, who claimed her as his wife. Sacagawea knew sign language and spoke many Native American dialects. When Sacagawea was reunited with her brother Cameahwait, the Shoshone chief, she and her husband left the expedition.

**America's History Makers**
- Sacagawea, pp. 41–42

**INSTRUCT: OBJECTIVE 4**

**Pike's Expedition/The Effects of Exploration**

Key Questions
- What area of the Louisiana Purchase did Pike explore?
- What did Pike hope to achieve?
- What were the effects of the explorations of Lewis and Clark and Pike?

Lewis and Clark kept beautiful journals that provided priceless information about the West.

## On to the Pacific Ocean

On their way west, the expedition had to stop at the Great Falls of the Missouri. Lewis called this ten-mile-long series of waterfalls "the grandest sight I ever beheld." He described his approach to the falls.

*A VOICE FROM THE PAST*

I had proceeded on this course about two miles . . . whin my ears were saluted with the agreeable sound of a fall of water and advancing a little further I saw the spray arrise above the plain like a collumn of smoke. . . . (It) soon began to make a roaring too tremendious to be mistaken for any cause short of the great falls of the Missouri.

**Meriwether Lewis,** quoted in *Undaunted Courage*

To get around the Great Falls, the explorers had to carry their boats and heavy supplies for 18 miles. They built wheels from cottonwood trees to move the boats. Even with wheels, the trek took nearly two weeks. Rattlesnakes, bears, and even a hailstorm slowed their steps.

As they approached the Rocky Mountains, Sacagawea excitedly pointed out Shoshone lands. Eager to make contact with the tribe, Lewis and a small party made their way overland. Lewis soon found the Shoshone, whose chief recognized Sacagawea as his sister. The chief traded horses to Lewis and Clark, and the Shoshone helped them cross the Rocky Mountains.

The explorers then journeyed to the mighty Columbia River, which leads to the Pacific Ocean. In November 1805, Clark wrote in his journal, "Ocian in view! O! The joy." They soon arrived at the Pacific Coast. There, they spent a rain-soaked winter before returning to St. Louis the following year.

The Lewis and Clark expedition brought back a wealth of scientific and geographic information. Though they learned that an all-water route across the continent did not exist, Americans received an exciting report of what lay to the west.

**D. Possible Response** The explorers brought back important scientific and geographic information about the west.

*Reading* **History**
**D. Finding Main Ideas** Why was the Lewis and Clark expedition valuable?

## 4 Pike's Expedition

Lewis and Clark explored the northern part of the Louisiana Purchase. In 1806, an expedition led by **Zebulon Pike** left St. Louis on a southerly route. (Refer to the map on page 320.) Pike's mission was to find the sources of the Arkansas and Red rivers. The Red River formed a boundary between Spanish territory and Louisiana.

Pike's party of two dozen men headed westward across the Great Plains. When they reached the Arkansas River, they followed it toward the Rocky Mountains. From 150 miles away, Pike spied the Rocky Mountain peak that would later bear his name—Pikes Peak. However, he failed in his attempt to climb it. Then they turned south, hoping that they would eventually run into the Red River. Instead, they ran into the

**Background** The previous year, Pike had led a 5,000-mile expedition to search for the source of the Mississippi River.



ACTIVITY OPTIONS

**INTERDISCIPLINARY LINK: GEOGRAPHY**

BLOCK SCHEDULING

**HISTORICAL MARKERS FOR THE PIKE EXPEDITION**

**Class Time** One class period

**Task** Creating a set of three historical markers for Zebulon Pike's expedition

**Purpose** To locate and describe the route taken by Zebulon Pike

**Supplies Needed**
- Reference materials on the Pike expedition
- Detailed map of the route taken by Pike
- Physical and current political maps of the United States
- Posterboard and markers

**Activity** As a class, compare the map of the route taken by the Pike expedition with a physical map of the United States. Then explain what a historical marker is and give examples of local markers. Have students use the reference materials and map of Pike's route to identify two or three places on the route where they would like to place a marker. The marker should tell when the expedition passed this point and describe anything of interest that took place there. Have each group indicate where on a present-day map of the United States it would be placed.

**EFFECTS:** *Exploration of the West, 1804–1807*

1. **Accurate maps**
   Lewis and Clark and Pike produced the first good maps of the Louisiana Territory. Later travelers would use these maps to make their way west.
2. **Growth of fur trade**
   Exploration boosted interest in the fur trade. Hunters and trappers would add to the knowledge of the West.
3. **Mistaken view of Great Plains**
   Pike inaccurately described the treeless Great Plains as a desert. This led many Americans to believe that the Plains were useless for farming.

SKILLBUILDER **Interpreting Charts**
*Why might Pike's description of the Great Plains have led to the idea that Native Americans east of the Mississippi should be moved there?*

**Compass used by Lewis and Clark**

Skillbuilder Answer
The land of the Great Plains was believed to be less valuable than that of the East.

**Vocabulary**
**Rio Grande:** Spanish for *big river*

Rio Grande, which was in Spanish territory. There, they were arrested by Spanish troops.

The explorers returned to the United States after being released by Spanish officials in 1807. Though Pike and his men never explored the Red River, they did bring back valuable descriptions of the Great Plains and the Rio Grande River Valley.

## The Effects of Exploration

The first American explorers of the West brought back tales of adventure as well as scientific and geographical information. As the chart above shows, this information would have long-lasting effects.

Early in Jefferson's presidency, events at home occupied much of the new president's time. In the next section, you will learn about foreign affairs during the same time period.

### *Section 2 Assessment*

**1. Terms & Names**
**Identify:**
- Louisiana Purchase
- Meriwether Lewis
- William Clark
- Lewis and Clark expedition
- Sacagawea
- Zebulon Pike

**2. Taking Notes**
Use a chart like the one below to record the factors that might have led Napoleon to sell the Louisiana Territory.

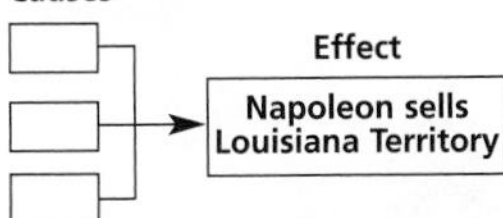


**3. Main Ideas**
**a.** What groups might dispute European land claims in the West?
**b.** Why was New Orleans important to Americans?
**c.** How did Sacagewea help Lewis and Clark?

**4. Critical Thinking**
**Recognizing Effects** What were some of the effects of the explorations of the West in the 1800s?
**THINK ABOUT**
- how other people might use the information brought back by the explorers
- the economic effects of the expedition

**ACTIVITY OPTIONS**
**WORLD HISTORY**
**GEOGRAPHY**
Read more about New Orleans. Make an illustrated **time line** of the French, Spanish, and U.S. ownership of the city or create a **map** of its port.





## HISTORY FROM VISUALS

**Interpreting Charts** Have students explore how these effects of early explorations both spurred and deterred westward settlement by whites. Ask students what was likely to be the impact of Lewis and Clark's and Pike's explorations on Native American groups living in the Louisiana Purchase.
**Possible Response** Since accurate maps and the growth of the fur trade would encourage trade and travel by whites, a long-term effect was likely to be white settlement of the area, leading to conflict between Native Americans and whites.

**Extension** Have students use reference materials to find out why Pike concluded that the Great Plains were useless for farming.

## ASSESS & RETEACH

**Setting the Stage** Have students fill in the second section on the chapter graphic organizer.

 **Formal Assessment**
- Section Quiz, p. 160

### RETEACHING ACTIVITY

Have students make a diagram showing three causes of the sale of the Louisiana Territory to the United States and three or more effects of this sale on the history of the United States.

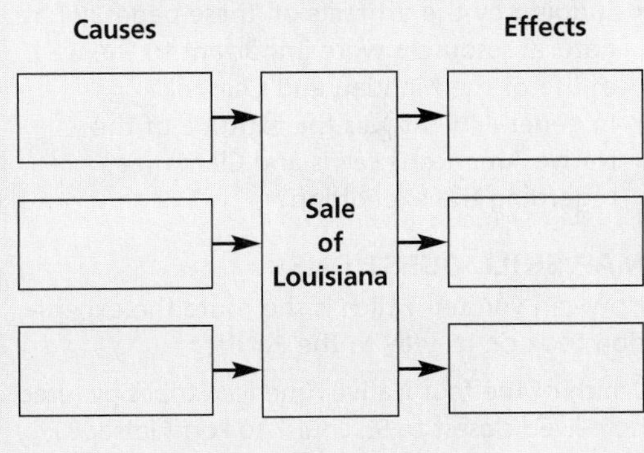


**In-Depth Resources: Unit 3**
- Reteaching Activity, p. 35

### *Section 2 Assessment*

**1. Terms & Names**
**Louisiana Purchase,** p. 319
**Meriwether Lewis,** p. 320
**William Clark,** p. 320
**Lewis and Clark expedition,** p. 320
**Sacajawea,** p. 321
**Zebulon Pike,** p. 322

**2. Taking Notes**
Causes: determination of Americans to use port at New Orleans; losses suffered by France in Caribbean colonies; costly wars in Europe

**3. Main Ideas**
**a.** Native Americans **b.** It was an important port for farmers and merchants. **c.** with her knowledge of geography and language skills

**4. Critical Thinking**
created more detailed maps; boosted interest in the fur trade; led to the mistaken view of the region as useless for farming

**ACTIVITY OPTIONS**
 **Alternative Assessment**
- Rubrics for a time line, 2.4
- Rubrics for a map, 2.1

## GEOGRAPHY in HISTORY

**OBJECTIVE**
Students will analyze and interpret information from a map and paintings to identify Native American groups that Lewis and Clark met along their route. They will note how some of these groups assisted the explorers.

 **BLOCK SCHEDULING**

### MORE ABOUT . . .

**The Shoshone**
The Shoshone lived in a resource-poor area of deserts and salt flats known as the Great Basin, bordered on the east by the Wasatch Mountain Range and on the west by the Sierra Nevada. A nomadic people, they survived by moving from place to place with the seasons, hunting rabbits, and less often, antelope, deer, or sheep. They spent much of their time searching for seeds, berries, nuts, roots, and bulbs. Their diet also consisted of lizards, rats, rabbits, and insects. As hunters and gatherers, they typically traveled in small family bands. They made much of their clothing from rabbit skins.

## INSTRUCT

Key Questions
- Judging by the artifacts on these pages, what natural resources were important to the way of life of the Mandan and Chinook?
- In general, what was the attitude of the Native Americans Lewis and Clark met regarding the expedition?

**MAP SKILL QUESTIONS**
How can you tell which is the route the expedition took on its way to the Pacific?

Which of the four Native American tribes pictured here lived closest to St. Louis? to Fort Clatsop?

Which of the two explorers was more likely to have met the Atsina on his return trip?

## GEOGRAPHY in HISTORY
**PLACE AND LOCATION**

# Native Americans on the Explorers' Route

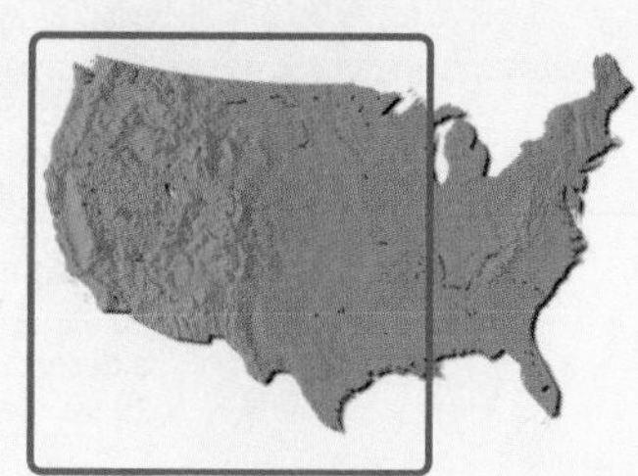

When Thomas Jefferson bought the Louisiana Territory, Native Americans had already been living in that area for thousands of years. Before Lewis and Clark began their trip, Jefferson instructed them to deal with Native Americans in a peaceful manner and to make it clear that the United States wished to be "friendly and useful to them." On their journey, Lewis and Clark met almost 50 different tribes.

**Sacagawea**
In 1805, the explorers arrived in Shoshone territory near the Rocky Mountains. A Shoshone chief, Cameahwait, confirmed that there was no all-water route to the Pacific. Later, when Cameahwait recognized Sacagawea as his sister, he agreed to sell the explorers the horses they needed to cross the mountains.

**1 Oto**
In 1804, Lewis and Clark met the Oto, a buffalo-hunting people. This was the first formal meeting of U.S. representatives with western Native Americans. Lewis told the Oto that they were "children" of a new great "father"—President Thomas Jefferson.

### ARTIFACT FILE

**Buffalo Robe** Pictured to the right is a section of a Mandan buffalo robe. On it, a Mandan painted a battle scene between the Mandan and the Sioux.

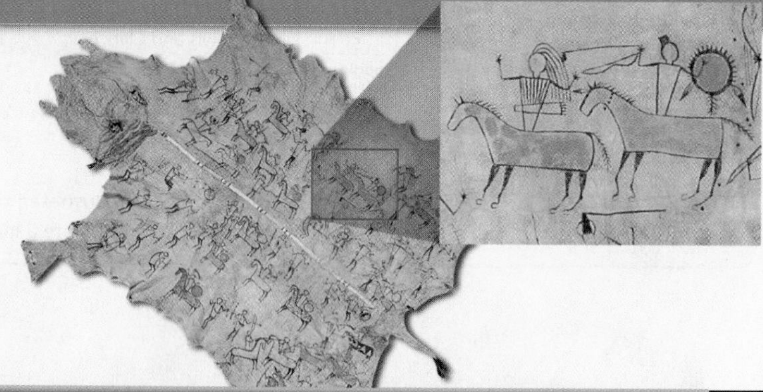



### MUSEUM CONNECTIONS

Among the on-line exhibits at the Web site of the Peabody Museum of Archaeology and Ethnology is a fascinating look at objects relating to Native Americans collected by Lewis and Clark during their expedition. The exhibit is called "The Ethnology of Lewis and Clark: Native American Objects and the American Quest for Commerce and Science." For more on the Peabody Museum, visit www.mcdougallittell.com

The Museum of Westward Expansion is part of the Jefferson National Expansion Memorial in St. Louis, Missouri. Located underneath the soaring Gateway Arch, a memorial to the nation's pioneers, the museum includes an overview of the Lewis and Clark expedition. For an on-line tour of the museum, including an audio presentation of the words of Thomas Jefferson and William Clark, see www.mcdougallittell.com

**2 Mandan**
Neighboring tribes as well as exploring Europeans relied on the mainstay of Mandan culture—corn. The Mandan also crafted beautiful leatherwork and pottery. Lewis and Clark spent an entire winter with the Mandan.

**3 Teton Sioux**
Upon meeting the Teton Sioux, Lewis and Clark showed off an air gun. Known for their aggressiveness, the Teton already viewed the Americans as competitors for trade in this region. As a result, confrontation marked Lewis and Clark's visit.

## On-Line Field Trip

**The Peabody Museum** in Cambridge, Massachusetts, holds an important collection of Native American artifacts. This rain hat was worn by Chinook whalers of the Northwest. The Chinook made these water-repellent hats out of cedar bark and bear grass.

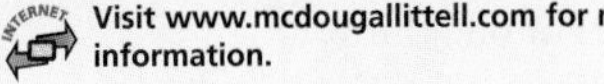
Visit www.mcdougallittell.com for more information.

### CONNECT TO GEOGRAPHY

1. **Place** What fort was built where the Columbia River empties into the Pacific Ocean?
2. **Location** In what mountain range did the Shoshone tribe live?

See Geography Handbook, page 4.

### CONNECT TO HISTORY

3. **Forming Opinions** What do you think the Native Americans that Lewis and Clark met thought about the explorers?





### CRITICAL THINKING ACTIVITY

**Forming and Supporting Opinions** Ask students to make a graphic like the one below. Then have them read the information about the Shoshone, Oto, Mandan, and Teton Sioux and complete the chart. Have students use the information on the chart to decide how important they think Native Americans were to the success of the Lewis and Clark expedition. Have students give reasons for their opinions.

| Native Americans | Response to Lewis and Clark Expedition |
|---|---|
| Shoshone | |
| Oto | |
| Mandan | |
| Teton Sioux | |

**Class Time** 15 minutes

### MORE ABOUT . . .

**The Mandan**
Lewis and Clark met the Mandan when the expedition crossed the Great Plains in 1804. The Mandan made their home in large, fenced-in villages of earthen lodges along the upper Missouri River. They were one of the first Plains tribes to come into frequent contact with whites. French trappers had visited and traded with them as early as the mid-1700s. In the 1830s, American artist George Catlin and Swiss painter Karl Bodmer made paintings of these early farmers of the Plains, recording their vibrant culture and way of life shortly before they were almost completely wiped out by smallpox.

### CONNECT TO GEOGRAPHY

1. **Place** Fort Clatstop
2. **Location** the Rocky Mountains

### CONNECT TO HISTORY

3. **Forming Opinions** They had different reactions. Some tribes, like the Mandan, were friendly. Others, like the Teton Sioux, were hostile.

## SECTION OBJECTIVES

1. To describe foreign policy challenges that Jefferson faced
2. To describe how Tecumseh attempted to unify Native American peoples
3. To explain why many Americans were War Hawks

**SKILLBUILDER**
Interpreting Charts, p. 329

**CRITICAL THINKING**
Analyzing Causes, p. 327
Recognizing Effects, p. 328
Forming Opinions, p. 328
Analyzing Points of View, p. 329

## FOCUS & MOTIVATE

### 5-MINUTE WARM-UP

**Drawing Conclusions** These questions focus on problems with Britain in the early 1800s.

1. Study the picture on page 327 and read the caption. Where is this kidnapping taking place? Who are the kidnappers?
2. How might Jefferson respond to this hostile action?

 Warm-Up Transparency WT10

## INSTRUCT

### INSTRUCT: OBJECTIVE 1

**Jefferson's Foreign Policy**
Key Questions
- Why did Jefferson advise against "entangling alliances"?
- Why was the United States likely to have conflicts with other nations?

 **In-Depth Resources: Unit 3**
- Guided Reading, p. 23

 **Reading Study Guide** (Spanish and English), pp. 105–106

# 3 Problems with Foreign Powers

**TERMS & NAMES**
impressment
Embargo Act of 1807
Tecumseh
War Hawk

| MAIN IDEA | WHY IT MATTERS NOW |
|---|---|
| Jefferson tried to avoid involvement in the problems of other nations. | British interference with the affairs of the United States led to the War of 1812. |

## ONE AMERICAN'S STORY

In 1804, U.S. Navy Lieutenant Stephen Decatur was on a daring mission overseas. The United States was at war with Tripoli, a state on the North African coast. The war, which began in 1801, was the result of repeated attacks on American merchant ships by African pirates. Decatur's mission was to destroy the U.S. warship *Philadelphia*—which had been captured by Tripoli—so that it could not be used by the enemy.

Decatur bravely sailed into Tripoli's harbor and set fire to the *Philadelphia.* He then managed to escape under enemy fire with only one man wounded. Decatur later issued this rallying cry for all Americans.

*A VOICE FROM THE PAST*

Our country! In her [relationships] with foreign nations may she always be in the right; but our country, right or wrong.

**Stephen Decatur,** 1816

Stephen Decatur struggles in hand-to-hand combat with African pirates.

Decatur's attack was one of the most celebrated events of the war, which ended in 1805. The conflict showed how hard it was for the United States to stay out of foreign affairs while its citizens participated so heavily in overseas trade. In this section, you will learn how President Jefferson handled problems with other nations.

## 1 Jefferson's Foreign Policy

When Thomas Jefferson took office in 1801, he expected to concentrate on domestic concerns. In his inaugural address, he happily noted that America was "kindly separated by nature and a wide ocean from the exterminating havoc [wars] of one quarter of the globe." Jefferson advised the United States to seek the friendship of all nations, but to enter into "entangling alliances with none."

However, the president's desire to keep the United States separated from other nations and their problems was doomed to fail. For one thing, American merchants were busily engaged in trade all over the world. For



## RECOMMENDED RESOURCES

 **In-Depth Resources: Unit 3**
- Guided Reading, p. 23
- Building Vocabulary, p. 25
- Skillbuilder Practice, p. 26
- Primary Source: A Plea for Native American Unity, p. 29
- Reteaching Activity, p. 36

 **Reading Study Guide** (Spanish and English), pp. 105–106

 **Formal Assessment**
- Section Quiz, p. 161

 **Alternative Assessment**
- Rubrics, 1.3
- Rubrics, 3.3

 **Access for Students Acquiring English/ESL**
- Guided Reading, p. 68
- Skillbuilder Practice, p. 70

**Technology Resources**

**Electronic Teacher Tools with Test Maker**

**ClassZone**
www.mcdougallittell.com

another, the Louisiana Purchase and the Lewis and Clark expedition were about to open the country to westward expansion. Expansion would bring Americans into closer contact with people from other nations who had already established settlements in the West.

Finally, the United States had little control over the actions of foreign nations—as North African interference with U.S. shipping had shown. Staying out of the ongoing conflict between France and England would be just as difficult.

*Reading*History
**A. Analyzing Causes** Why was it hard for the United States to avoid other nations' problems?
A. Possible Responses because of the overseas involvement of U.S. merchants, westward expansion, and lack of control over the actions of foreign nations

## 2 Problems with France and England

For a long time, the United States managed not to get involved in the European wars that followed the French Revolution. At times, the nation even benefited from the conflict. Busy with affairs in Europe, France sold the Louisiana Territory to the United States. And American shippers eagerly took over the trade interrupted by the war.

By 1805, however, the British began to clamp down on U.S. shipping. They did not want Americans to provide their enemies with food and supplies. After the United States threatened to take action, the British decided to set up a partial blockade. This would only allow some American ships to bring provisions to Europe.

This partial blockade angered France, which enacted its own laws to control foreign shipping. These changes put American merchants in a difficult position. If they obeyed the British rules, their ships could be seized by the French. If they obeyed the French rules, their ships could be seized by the British.

Britain also interfered with U.S. trade by the **impressment,** or kidnapping, of American sailors to work on British ships. Between 1803 and 1812, the British impressed about 6,000 American sailors.

One of the most famous incidents occurred in 1807. The British ship *Leopard* attacked an American naval ship, the *Chesapeake,* off the coast of Virginia. Three Americans lost their lives in the battle. The attack aroused widespread anger. Had Congress been in session, America might have declared war. But Jefferson, who had been re-elected in 1804, decided against it. One critic, furious at the president's caution, called Jefferson a "dish of skim milk curdling at the head of our nation."

British officers seize an American sailor at gunpoint.

## Trade as a Weapon

Vocabulary
**coercion:** the practice of forcing someone to act in a certain way by use of pressure or threats

Instead of declaring war, Jefferson asked Congress to pass legislation that would stop all foreign trade. "Peaceable coercion," as the president described his policy, would prevent further bloodshed.

327

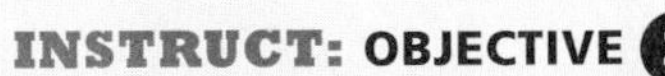

**Problems with France and England/ Trade as a Weapon**

Key Questions

- What caused conflict between the United States and Britain and France?
- Why did Americans call for war against Britain?
- How did both Jefferson and Madison try to use trade as a weapon against Britain and France? Were they successful?

### MORE ABOUT . . .

**Impressment**

When Britain impressed sailors from American ships, it claimed to take only British subjects, ignoring the fact that many native-born Britons had become naturalized American citizens. Britain adopted its policy of impressment to fill its great need for sailors in the Royal Navy, the largest navy in the world. Few men chose to enlist in the Royal Navy, and many that did enlist deserted. Many British subjects, including some deserters, preferred to work on American merchant ships, rather than on ships of the Royal Navy. Conditions on American vessels were much better than on British ships.

### ACTIVITY OPTIONS

### INDIVIDUAL NEEDS

**STUDENTS ACQUIRING ENGLISH/ESL**

**Understanding Key Concepts** To help students understand the concept of *foreign policy,* write the word *foreign* on the board and define it as "of, from, or having to do with other countries." Then write the phrases *foreign nations* and *foreign policy* on the board. Explain that foreign nations are countries other than one's own, and that foreign policy is the way a government deals with other nations or countries. Ask students to name some of the foreign nations the U.S. government had contact with and some of the problems that resulted.

Extend the discussion by comparing *foreign policy* to *domestic policy.* Point out the statement on page 326, "When Thomas Jefferson took office in 1801, he expected to concentrate on domestic concerns." Help students to see that domestic concerns are those of one's own country. Encourage a discussion about current foreign policies and domestic issues.

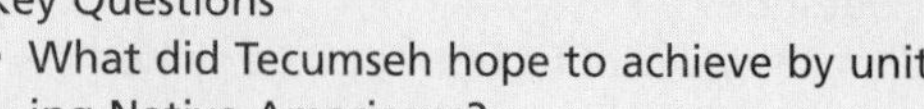

**INSTRUCT: OBJECTIVE**

**Tecumseh and Native American Unity** 3

Key Questions

- What did Tecumseh hope to achieve by uniting Native Americans?
- What was Tecumseh's response to the Treaty of Fort Wayne?
- How did the Battle of Tippecanoe affect Tecumseh's hopes for unity?

**MORE ABOUT . . .**

**Tecumseh**

Tecumseh continues to be one of the most honored Native American leaders. He is revered not only for his gifts as a statesman and a fighter but also for his oratory, his patriotism, and love of his people. In a letter to Sir Isaac Brock, dated August 14, 1812, Tecumseh reflected bitterly on the white man's treatment of his people: "We gave them forest-clad mountains and valleys full of game, and in return what did they give our warriors and our women? Rum and trinkets and a grave."

 **In-Depth Resources: Unit 3**

- Primary Source: A Plea for Native American Unity by Tecumseh, p. 29

**CRITICAL THINKING ACTIVITY**

**Drawing Conclusions** Have students examine Tecumseh's actions. What did he hope to achieve? Why did defeat at Tippecanoe make it more difficult to unite groups of Native Americans? If Native Americans had united, could they have stopped the loss of land? Why or why not?

**Class Time** 10 minutes

In December, Congress passed the **Embargo Act of 1807**. Now American ships were no longer allowed to sail to foreign ports. The act also closed American ports to British ships.

Jefferson's policy was a disaster. It was more harmful to the United States than to the British and French. American farmers and merchants were especially hard hit. Southern and Western farmers, for example, lost important markets for their grain, cotton, and tobacco. Shippers lost income, and many chose to violate the embargo by making false claims about where they were going. One New Englander said the embargo was like "cutting one's throat to cure the nosebleed."

*Reading***History**

**B. Recognizing Effects** What were the results of the Embargo Act?

**B. Possible Response** It was damaging to U.S. trade because farmers and merchants lost important markets.

The embargo became a major issue in the election of 1808. Jefferson's old friend James Madison won the election. By the time he took office, Congress had already repealed the embargo.

Madison's solution to the problem was a law that allowed merchants to trade with any country except France and Britain. Trade with these countries would start again when they agreed to respect U.S. ships. But this law proved no more effective than the embargo.

## Tecumseh and Native American Unity

British interference with American shipping and impressment of U.S. citizens made Americans furious. They also were angered by Britain's actions in the Northwest. Many settlers believed that the British were stirring up Native American resistance to frontier settlements.

The Shawnee chief Tecumseh 3 Native American resistance to white rule in the Ohio River Valley.

Since the Battle of Fallen Timbers in 1794 (see page 299), Native Americans continued to lose their land. Thousands of white settlers had swarmed into Ohio and then into Indiana.

**Tecumseh**, a Shawnee chief, vowed to stop the loss of Native American land. He believed that the reason Native Americans continued to lose their land was because they were separated into many different tribes. He concluded that Native Americans had to do what white Americans had done: unite. Events in 1809 proved him right.

That September, William Henry Harrison, governor of the Indiana Territory, signed the Treaty of Fort Wayne with chiefs of the Miami, Delaware, and Potawatomi tribes. They agreed to sell over three million acres of land. But Tecumseh declared the treaty meaningless.

**C. Possible Response** He believed that land could be sold only when all, not just some, Native Americans gave permission.

*Reading***History**

**C. Forming Opinions** Why did Tecumseh declare the Treaty of Fort Wayne meaningless?

*A VOICE FROM THE PAST*

[Whites] have taken upon themselves to say this [land] belongs to the Miamis, this to the Delawares and so on. But the Great Spirit intended [Native American land] to be the common property of all the tribes, [and it cannot] be sold without the consent of all.

**Tecumseh,** quoted in *Tecumseh and the Quest for Indian Leadership*

After the Treaty of Fort Wayne, many Native Americans began to answer Tecumseh's call for unity. But his efforts ultimately failed. In November 1811, while Tecumseh was away recruiting tribes for his alliance, the Shawnee were defeated by Harrison's forces at the Battle of



**ACTIVITY OPTIONS**

**SKILLBUILDER MINI-LESSON: ANALYZING CAUSES** — BLOCK SCHEDULING

**Explaining the Skill** When historians analyze events, they not only consider when, where, and how an event happened but they also think about why it occurred. In analyzing causes, it is important to look for the reasons behind an event. Words or phrases such as *because, due to, since,* and *therefore* often indicate cause.

**Applying the Skill** Direct students to the subsection "War Hawks" on page 329. Ask these questions:

1. How did Americans react to the British decision to aid Tecumseh? *(This aid fueled anti-British feelings.)*
2. What cause of the war does this reaction suggest? *(American anger over British support of Native Americans)*
3. What clue word in paragraph 3 suggests other causes of the war? *(because)* What causes does it suggest? *(British violations of American rights at sea)*

 **In-Depth Resources: Unit 3**

- Skillbuilder Practice, p. 26

Tippecanoe. It was a severe setback for Tecumseh's movement.

## 4 War Hawks

After the battle of Tippecanoe, Tecumseh and his warriors found a warm welcome with the British in Canada. At that point, the Native Americans and the British became allies. Tecumseh's welcome in Canada raised even higher the anti-British feelings in the West.

Leaders such as Congressman Henry Clay of Kentucky angrily demanded war against Britain. Westerners who called for war were known as **War Hawks.** They wanted British aid to Native Americans stopped, and they wanted the British out of Canada. Conquering Canada would open up a vast new empire for Americans.

**Vocabulary**
**hawk:** a person who favors the use of military force to carry out foreign policy

**Causes of the War of 1812**

Impressment of U.S. Citizens

Interference with American shipping

British support of Native-American resistance

WAR

SKILLBUILDER **Interpreting Charts**
*Which cause of the War of 1812 was not related to activities on the sea?*

Skillbuilder Answer
British support of Native American resistance

Other Americans sought war because of the British violations of American rights at sea. Future president Andrew Jackson said hostilities were necessary "for the protection of our maritime citizens impressed on board British ships of war," and to "open a market for the productions of our soil."

Urged on by Jackson and the War Hawks, Congress declared war on Britain on June 18, 1812. In the next section, you will read about the second—and final—war between the United States and Great Britain.

### Section 3 Assessment

**1. Terms & Names**

Identify:
- impressment
- Embargo Act of 1807
- Tecumseh
- War Hawk

**2. Taking Notes**

Use a chart like the one below to record the effects of Jefferson's Embargo Act.

Causes: Embargo Act
Effects: [ ] [ ]

Why didn't the act work?

**3. Main Ideas**

a. How did the British and French interfere with American shipping?

b. How did Jefferson respond to the interference?

c. Why did the War Hawks favor war?

**4. Critical Thinking**

Analyzing Points of View
Why did Tecumseh think it was important for Native Americans to unite?

THINK ABOUT
- what he learned about white men
- what Native Americans would lose if they did not act together

ACTIVITY OPTIONS

ART
SPEECH

Do research on the Battle of Tippecanoe. Draw a **comic strip story** of the battle or hold a **press conference** to describe the battle's outcome.





**INSTRUCT: OBJECTIVE 4**

**War Hawks**
Key Questions
- Why did War Hawks favor war?
- What were other reasons for war against Britain?
- When did Congress declare war on Britain?

**HISTORY FROM VISUALS**

**Interpreting the Chart** Ask students why they think trade issues and interference with American shipping were so important to the United States at this time. Which cause of war had American leaders tried to resolve peacefully? **Answer** Foreign trade was an important part of the American economy. The Embargo Act was Jefferson's attempt at a peaceful solution to the problems of impressment and interference with American shipping.

**Extension** Have students research the reasons why the War of 1812 is sometimes called the Second War for American Independence.

## ASSESS & RETEACH

**Setting the Stage** Have students fill in the third section on the chapter graphic organizer.

**Formal Assessment**
- Section Quiz, p. 161

**RETEACHING ACTIVITY**

Have students write one or two questions for each of the main topics in the section. Ask pairs of students to take turns answering each other's questions and then work together to verify the answers.

**In-Depth Resources: Unit 3**
- Reteaching Activity, p. 36

### Section 3 Assessment

**1. Terms & Names**

**impressment,** p. 327
**Embargo Act of 1807,** p. 328
**Tecumseh,** p. 328
**War Hawk,** p. 329

**2. Taking Notes**

Effects: Lost markets hurt farmers; merchants lost sources of income.

The act hurt the economy of the United States more than the European economies that it targeted.

**3. Main Ideas**

**a.** They blockaded and seized U.S. ships and kidnapped American sailors. **b.** He got Congress to pass the Embargo Act of 1807, which stopped all foreign trade. **c.** War was the best way to stop British interference with U.S. shipping and support of Native American resistance.

**4. Critical Thinking**

because without joining together, they would not be able to prevent the loss of their land

**ACTIVITY OPTIONS**

**Alternative Assessment**
- Rubrics for a comic strip, 1.3
- Rubrics for a press conference, 3.3

## SECTION OBJECTIVES

1. To analyze the beginning of the War of 1812
2. To describe the battles of the first phase of the war
3. To describe the fighting in the second phase of the war
4. To evaluate the effects of the war and its legacy

**SKILLBUILDER**
Interpreting Maps: Location, Movement, p. 331
Interpreting Charts, p. 333

**CRITICAL THINKING**
Drawing Conclusions, p. 332
Making Inferences, p. 333
Recognizing Effects, p. 333

## FOCUS & MOTIVATE

### 5-MINUTE WARM-UP

**Reading a Map** These questions focus on battles of the War of 1812.

1. Study the map on page 331. Which battles were fought on water?
2. Which bodies of water were blockaded by the British? How could a successful blockade hurt the American war effort?

 **Warm-Up Transparency WT10**

## INSTRUCT

### INSTRUCT: OBJECTIVE 

**The War Begins**
Key Questions
- Why did Britain try to avoid war? What steps did it take to avoid war?
- What were the two main phases of the war?

 **In-Depth Resources: Unit 3**
- Guided Reading, p. 24
- Primary Source, p. 30

 **Reading Study Guide** (Spanish and English), pp. 107–108

# 4 The War of 1812

**TERMS & NAMES**
Oliver Hazard Perry
Battle of the Thames
Francis Scott Key
Treaty of Ghent

| MAIN IDEA | WHY IT MATTERS NOW |
| --- | --- |
| Angered by Britain's interference in the nation's affairs, the United States went to war. | The War of 1812 showed that the United States was willing and able to protect its national interests. |

## ONE AMERICAN'S STORY

**The war between the United States and Britain had begun in 1812. Two years later, British troops were marching toward Washington, D.C. Dolley Madison, the president's wife, stayed behind until the last minute. With bombs bursting in the distance, she hurried to save important historical objects from the White House.**

*A VOICE FROM THE PAST*

I have had [a wagon] filled with . . . the most valuable portable articles belonging to the house. . . . I insist on waiting until the large picture of General Washington is secured . . . It is done! and the precious portrait placed in the hands of two gentlemen of New York, for safe keeping.

**Dolley Madison,** from a letter sent to her sister

Before British troops set fire to the president's mansion, Dolley Madison saved priceless historical objects.

**When the British troops arrived in the city, they set fire to many public buildings, including the White House and the Capitol. The next day, a violent storm caused even more damage. Fortunately, the heavy rains that accompanied the storm helped put out the fires. You will learn about other events of the War of 1812 in this section.**

###  The War Begins

Britain did not really want a war with the United States because it was already involved in another war with France. To try to avoid war, the British announced that they would no longer interfere with American shipping. But the slow mails of the day prevented this news from reaching the United States until weeks after June 18th, when Congress approved Madison's request for a declaration of war.

The War of 1812 had two main phases. From 1812 to 1814, Britain concentrated on its war against France. It devoted little energy to the conflict in North America, although it did send ships to blockade the American coast. The second phase of the war began after the British defeated France in April 1814. With their European war nearly at an end, the British could turn their complete attention to the United States.



## RECOMMENDED RESOURCES

 **In-Depth Resources: Unit 3**
- Guided Reading, p. 24
- Building Vocabulary, p. 25
- Primary Source: from *Memoirs and Letters of Dolley Madison,* p. 30
- Reteaching Activity, p. 37
- History Workshop Resources, p. 39

 **Reading Study Guide** (Spanish and English), pp. 107–108

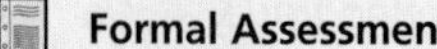 **Economics in History**
- The Economic Impact of the War of 1812, p. 10

**Formal Assessment**
- Section Quiz, p. 162

 **Alternative Assessment**
- Rubrics, 1.10
- Rubrics, 4.8

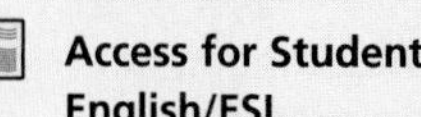 **Access for Students Acquiring English/ESL**
- Guided Reading, p. 69

**Technology Resources**

 **Critical Thinking Trans. CT29**
- Cause and Effect: The War of 1812

 **Humanities Transparency HT20**
- *Constitution and Guerriere*

 **Electronic Teacher Tools with Test Maker**

 **ClassZone**
www.mcdougallittell.com

The United States military was weak when the war was declared. Democratic-Republicans had reduced the size of the armed forces. When the war began, the Navy had only about 16 ships. The army had fewer than 7,000 men. These men were poorly trained and equipped, and were often led by inexperienced officers. A young Virginia army officer complained that the older officers were victims of "sloth, ignorance, or habits of [excessive] drinking."

## 2 The First Phase of the War

In spite of its small size, the United States Navy rose to the challenge. Its warships were the fastest afloat. American naval officers had gained valuable experience fighting pirates in the Mediterranean Sea. Early in the war, before the British blockaded the coast, ships such as the *Constitution* and the *United States* won stirring victories. These victories on the high seas boosted American confidence.

The most important U.S. naval victory took place on Lake Erie. In the winter of 1812-1813, the Americans had begun to build a fleet on the shores of Lake Erie. **Oliver Hazard Perry,** an experienced officer, took charge of this infant fleet. In September 1813, the small British force on the lake set out to attack the American ships. Commodore Perry, who had predicted that this would be "the most important day of my life," sailed out to meet the enemy. Perry's ship, the *Lawrence,* flew a banner declaring, "Don't give up the ship."

Skillbuilder Answers
1. in Baltimore, Maryland; near the Chesapeake Bay
2. the Battle of the Thames River

### The War of 1812



BATTLES OF THE WAR

1. **Atlantic Ocean.** British navy blockades American coast, 1813
2. **Lake Erie.** Perry's fleet defeats a British fleet, 1813
3. **Thames River.** Harrison defeats British in Canada, killing Tecumseh, 1813
4. **Washington, D.C.** British burn the capital but later fail to capture nearby Baltimore, 1814
5. **Lake Champlain.** American ships defeat British, who retreat to Canada, 1814
6. **New Orleans.** Jackson's army defeats British in Battle of New Orleans, 1815

GEOGRAPHY SKILLBUILDER
**Interpreting Maps**
1. **Location** *Where was Fort McHenry located?*
2. **Movement** *Which battle required American troops to march into Canada?*

331



**INSTRUCT: OBJECTIVE 2**

**The First Phase of the War**
Key Questions
- What were the strengths of the U.S. Navy?
- Where did the most important U.S. naval victory take place?
- What were two results of the victory on the Thames River?

**MORE ABOUT . . .**

**Oliver Hazard Perry**
Perry continued his message to Harrison with the details of his victory: "We have met the enemy and they are ours—two ships, two brigs, one schooner, and one sloop." He was only 28 years old at the time. Perry came from a family with a strong naval heritage on both sides. He became a midshipman at the age of 13 and sailed under his father's command to the Caribbean. His career was cut short when he died from yellow fever at the age of 34.

**HISTORY FROM VISUALS**

**Reading the Map** After the students have studied the map, ask if they can think of reasons why so many battles took place along the U.S. border. **Possible Response** Canada was controlled by the British, who wanted to keep Americans out of Canada. Then ask students why they think the British wanted to capture New Orleans. **Answer** It was a major port for the United States and would enable the British to control shipping on the Mississippi.

**Extension** Have students choose one of the battles listed on the map and research the reasons for victory by either the Americans or the British.

**ACTIVITY OPTIONS**

**INDIVIDUAL NEEDS**

LESS PROFICIENT READERS

**Previewing** As a way to preview the section "The War of 1812" and to provide students with a strategy for reading, ask them to read the headings and turn each heading into a question. For example, students may formulate questions such as:
- Why did the war begin? When did the war begin?
- What happened in the first phase of the war? Who was successful in the first phase of the war?
- What happened in the second phase of the war?
- What was the legacy of the war? What were the effects of the war in the United States?

Encourage students to look for answers to their questions as they read each section.

**INSTRUCT: OBJECTIVE** 

**The Second Phase of the War**

Key Questions

- What inspired Francis Scott Key to write "The Star-Spangled Banner"?
- What was the outcome of the Battle of Lake Champlain?
- Why was the Battle of New Orleans unnecessary?

**Humanities Transparency HT20**
- *Constitution and Guerriere.*

## *America's* HERITAGE

**The Star-Spangled Banner**

The national anthem was first published anonymously as a poem with the title "Defence of Fort M'Henry" in the *Baltimore Patriot.* It was soon set to the tune of an English drinking song and quickly gained widespread popularity. The army and navy used it as the national anthem before Congress officially adopted it in 1931. Composer and bandmaster John Philip Sousa prepared the official arrangement of the song. Since Americans and the British have become friends and allies, the second and third verses of the anthem are not usually sung.

**CRITICAL THINKING ACTIVITY**

**Making Inferences** Have students make inferences about how the personal fortunes of Andrew Jackson and the history of the United States might have been different if the Battle of New Orleans had not been fought.

**Class Time** 10 minutes

For two hours, the British and Americans exchanged cannon shots. Perry's ship was demolished and the guns put out of action. He grabbed his ship's banner and leaped into a rowboat. Under British fire, he and four companions rowed to another ship. In command of the second ship, Perry destroyed two of the enemy's ships and soon forced the British to surrender. After the battle, Perry sent a message to General Harrison: "We have met the enemy and they are ours."

> ***"Don't give up the ship."***
>
> Banner on Perry's ship, the *Lawrence*

When General Harrison received Perry's note, he set out to attack the British. But when Harrison transported his army across Lake Erie to Detroit, he discovered that the British had retreated into Canada. Harrison pursued the British forces and defeated them at the **Battle of the Thames** in October. This victory put an end to the British threat to the Northwest—and also claimed the life of Tecumseh, who died in the battle fighting for the British.

*Reading* **History**

**A. Drawing Conclusions** What was the overall result of the Battle of the Thames?

A. Possible Response The victory put an end to the British threat from the Northwest.

## 3 The Second Phase of the War

After defeating Napoleon in April 1814, Britain turned its full attention to the United States. As you read in One American's Story, British forces burned the Capitol building and the president's mansion in August. The British then attacked Fort McHenry at Baltimore.

The commander of Fort McHenry had earlier requested a flag "so large that the British will have no difficulty in seeing it." Detained on a British ship, a Washington lawyer named **Francis Scott Key** watched the all-night battle. At dawn, Key discovered that the flag was still flying. He expressed his pride in what became the U.S. national anthem.

**A VOICE FROM THE PAST**

> Oh say can you see by the dawn's early light
> What so proudly we hail'd at the twilight's last gleaming,
> Whose broad stripes and bright stars through the perilous fight
> O'er the ramparts we watch'd were so gallantly streaming?
> And the rockets' red glare, the bombs bursting in air,
> Gave proof through the night that our flag was still there.
> Oh, say does that star-spangled banner yet wave
> O'er the land of the free and the home of the brave?
>
> **Francis Scott Key**

### *America's* HERITAGE

**THE STAR-SPANGLED BANNER**

The "Star Spangled Banner," inspired by the flag that flew over Fort McHenry (see below), continues to move Americans. On hearing this national anthem, patriotic listeners stand, take off their hats, and put their hands over their hearts. These actions pay respect to the American flag and the song that celebrates it.

Francis Scott Key's song enjoyed widespread popularity for more than 100 years before an act of Congress made it the national anthem in 1931.

Meanwhile, in the north, the British sent a force from Canada across Lake Champlain. Its goal was to push south and cut off New England. The plan failed when the American fleet defeated the British in the Battle of Lake Champlain in September 1814.

In the south, the British moved against the strategic port of New Orleans. In December 1814, dozens of ships carrying 7,500 British troops approached Louisiana. To fight them, the Americans patched together an army under the command of General Andrew Jackson.

*Reading* **History**

**B. Reading a Map** Locate the battles of the second phase of the war on the map on page 331. Note how far apart the sites were.



**ACTIVITY OPTIONS**

**INTERDISCIPLINARY LINK: HUMANITIES**

**BLOCK SCHEDULING**

**NATIONAL ANTHEMS**

**Class Time** 30 minutes

**Task** Analyzing primary sources

**Purpose** To compare and contrast two patriotic songs

**Supplies Needed**
- Lyrics of "The Star-Spangled Banner" and "America the Beautiful"
- Recordings of both songs

**Activity** Make copies of the lyrics for both "The Star-Spangled Banner" and "America the Beautiful" and distribute them to the class. Play each song as students read the lyrics. Ask students what they think is the purpose of a national anthem. Then ask what makes each song patriotic. Tell students that "America the Beautiful" has often been proposed as a substitute for "The Star-Spangled Banner" as the national anthem. Have volunteers tell which song they prefer and why. Then have the class vote on which song they would rather have as their national anthem.

**ReadingHistory**

**C. Making Inferences** Why did Jackson fight the British at New Orleans after a peace treaty was signed?

C. Possible Response because slow mails delayed news of the treaty

The British attacked Jackson's forces on January 8, 1815. Protected by earthworks, American riflemen mowed down the advancing redcoats. It was a great victory for Jackson. American casualties totaled 71, compared to Britain's 2,000. Though the Battle of New Orleans made Jackson a hero, it was unnecessary. Slow mails from Europe had delayed news of the **Treaty of Ghent,** which ended the War of 1812. It had been signed two weeks earlier, on December 24, 1814.

## 4 The Legacy of the War

The treaty showed that the war had no clear winner. No territory changed hands, and trade disputes were left unresolved. Still, the war had important consequences. First, the heroic exploits of men such as Andrew Jackson and Oliver Perry increased American patriotism. Second, the war broke the strength of Native Americans, who had sided with the British. Finally, when war interrupted trade, the Americans were forced to make many of the goods they had previously imported. This encouraged the growth of U.S. manufactures.

The United States had also proved that it could defend itself against the mightiest military power of the era. For perhaps the first time, Americans believed that the young nation would survive and prosper. You will learn about the country's growing prosperity in Chapter 11.

Skillbuilder Answer U.S. manufacturing grew.

**The Effects of the War**

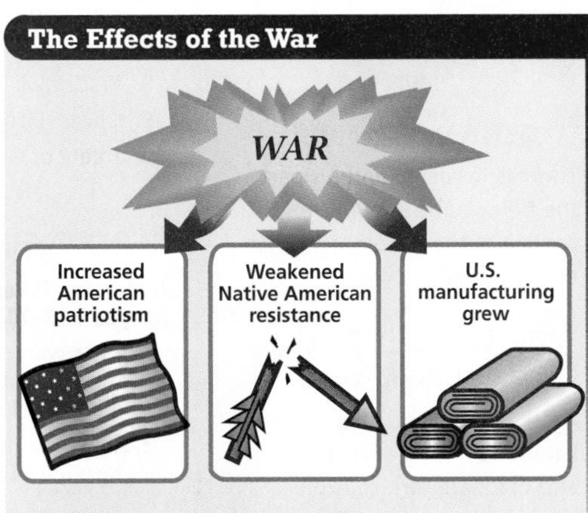


**SKILLBUILDER Interpreting Charts**
*Which effect do you think resulted from the war's interruption of U.S. trade?*

### Section 4 Assessment

**1. Terms & Names**

**Identify:**
- Oliver Hazard Perry
- Battle of the Thames
- Francis Scott Key
- Treaty of Ghent

**2. Taking Notes**

Use a chart like the one shown to record military events of the War of 1812.

| First Phase of War | Second Phase of War |
|---|---|
| 1. | 2. |

Why was the war divided into two phases?

**3. Main Ideas**

a. What was the state of the U.S. military when the war began?

b. What were the results of General Harrison's victory at the Battle of the Thames?

c. Where did the British focus their attacks during the second phase of the war?

**4. Critical Thinking**

**Recognizing Effects** What was the legacy of the War of 1812?

**THINK ABOUT**
- Americans' feelings toward their country
- U.S. relations with Native Americans
- possible economic effects

**ACTIVITY OPTIONS**

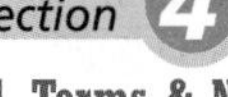

**LANGUAGE ARTS** / **ART** Research the U.S.S. *Constitution.* Write a **poem** to commemorate one of its victories or design a **model** to show its parts.

**INSTRUCT: OBJECTIVE** 

**The Legacy of the War**

Key Questions
- How did the Treaty of Ghent show that the war had no clear winner?
- What were three consequences of the war?
- How did the American victory increase optimism abut the future of the nation?

 **Economics in History**
- The Economic Impact of the War of 1812, p.10

**HISTORY FROM VISUALS**

**Interpreting the Chart** Have students identify specific causes for each of these effects. How did the war increase American patriotism? Why did it weaken Native American resistance? How did it help U.S. manufacturing grow? **Answers** Americans felt more pride in their country and its leaders. It made Tecumseh's drive to unite Native Americans more difficult. It forced Americans to buy homemade goods instead of imports.

**Extension** Have students find out which U.S. industries were helped by the war.

 **Critical Thinking Transparency CT29**
- Cause and Effect: The War of 1812

**ASSESS & RETEACH**

**Setting the Stage** Have students fill in the last section on the chapter graphic organizer.

 **Formal Assessment**
- Section Quiz, p. 162

 **Critical Thinking Transparency CT28**
- Setting the Stage

**RETEACHING ACTIVITY**

Have students create a time line for the years 1812–1815, showing major events of the war and its aftermath. Have students write two or three sentences explaining their effects.

 **In-Depth Resources: Unit 3**
- Reteaching Activity, p. 37

### Section 4 Assessment

**1. Terms & Names**

**Oliver Hazard Perry,** p. 331
**Battle of the Thames,** p. 332
**Francis Scott Key,** p. 332
**Treaty of Ghent,** p. 333

**2. Taking Notes**

First Phase: American victories on high seas; Perry defeats British fleet on Lake Erie; Second Phase: British fail to capture Baltimore; American fleet defeats British fleet on Lake Champlain; because the British were also involved in a war with France

**3. Main Ideas**

**a.** Poor; the navy had only 16 ships, and the army was small, poorly trained, and led by inexperienced officers. **b.** The victory ended the British threat to the Northwest. Tecumseh was killed. **c.** in the Chesapeake Bay area; near Lake Champlain; and in New Orleans

**4. Critical Thinking**

It increased American patriotism, weakened Native American resistance, and encouraged the growth of American manufactures.

**ACTIVITY OPTIONS**

 **Alternative Assessment**
- Rubrics for writing a poem, 4.8
- Rubrics for a model, 1.10

## TERMS & NAMES

1. ***Marbury* v. *Madison*,** p. 317
2. **judicial review,** p. 317
3. **Louisiana Purchase,** p. 319
4. **Lewis and Clark expedition,** p. 320
5. **impressment,** p. 327
6. **Embargo Act of 1807,** p. 328
7. **Tecumseh,** p. 328
8. **War Hawk,** p. 329
9. **Oliver Hazard Perry,** p. 331
10. **Treaty of Ghent,** p. 333

## REVIEW QUESTIONS

**Possible Responses**

1. The Federalists thought the nation was about to be ruined by radicals, and the Democratic-Republicans believed they were saving the country from monarchy and oppression.
2. He believed that the United States should be a democracy of small independent farmers.
3. from the East coast to the territory between the Mississippi River and the Rocky Mountains
4. traveling against strong currents in the Missouri River; stopping for the winter; going around the Great Falls; crossing the Rocky Mountains.
5. He and his men strayed into Spanish territory and were arrested.
6. global activity of American merchants; westward expansion; actions of foreign nations were unpredictable
7. by unifying Native Americans
8. impressment of U.S. citizens; interference with U.S. shipping; British support of Native American resistance
9. Battle of the Thames
10. the British defeat of France in April 1814

# Chapter 10 ASSESSMENT

## VISUAL SUMMARY

### The Jefferson Era

**Jefferson Takes Office**

Thomas Jefferson and his party, the Democratic-Republicans, win control of the government from the Federalists.

**The Louisiana Purchase and Exploration**

After Jefferson purchases Louisiana from France, Lewis and Clark are sent to explore the new American territory.

**Problems With Foreign Powers**

Other countries' interference makes it difficult for Jefferson to stay out of foreign affairs.

**The War of 1812**

When Britain continues to interfere in American affairs, the two nations battle in the War of 1812.

## TERMS & NAMES

Briefly explain the importance of each of the following:

1. *Marbury* v. *Madison*
2. judicial review
3. Louisiana Purchase
4. Lewis and Clark expedition
5. impressment
6. Embargo Act of 1807
7. Tecumseh
8. War Hawk
9. Oliver Hazard Perry
10. Treaty of Ghent

## REVIEW QUESTIONS

**Jefferson Takes Office (pages 313–317)**

1. What were the main parties in the election of 1800, and how did their views differ?
2. How did Jefferson envision the future of America?

**The Louisiana Purchase and Exploration (pages 318–325)**

3. What was the extent of U.S. territory after the Louisiana Purchase?
4. What difficulties did Lewis and Clark face on their expedition?
5. What troubles did Zebulon Pike have on his 1806-1807 trip?

**Problems With Foreign Powers (pages 326–329)**

6. Why did Jefferson have difficulty staying out of foreign affairs?
7. How did Tecumseh intend to prevent the loss of Native American land?
8. What were some of the causes of the War of 1812?

**The War of 1812 (pages 330–333)**

9. Which battle ended the British threat to the U.S. Northwest?
10. What event preceded the second phase of the war?

## CRITICAL THINKING

**1. USING YOUR NOTES**

Using your completed chart, answer the questions below.

| The Jefferson Era |
|---|
| Summaries |
| **Main Idea:** Thomas Jefferson is elected president.<br>**Details:** Jefferson replaces Federalist policies with his own but has problems with the judiciary. |
| **Main Idea:**<br>**Details:** |
| **Main Idea:**<br>**Details:** |
| **Main Idea:**<br>**Details:** |

a. What were the threats to U.S. trade and sailors?

b. How did Jefferson respond to foreign interference with U.S. trade?

**2. ANALYZING LEADERSHIP**

How do you think Thomas Jefferson's behavior as president might have affected the way future presidents viewed the office?

**3. THEME: EXPANSION**

How did the expansion of the United States affect its foreign policy?

**4. RECOGNIZING PROPAGANDA**

Before elections, supporters of different candidates sometimes make outrageous claims. How was the election of 1800 an example of this?

**5. APPLYING CITIZENSHIP SKILLS**

In what ways did Jefferson's behavior as president reflect his idea of good citizenship?

**Interact *with* History**

How did the dangers you predicted before you read the chapter compare to those experienced by people on expeditions west?

## CRITICAL THINKING

**Possible Responses**

1. **USING YOUR NOTES** **a.** foreign nations interfered with U.S. shipping; Britain impressed American sailors **b.** He restricted trade with the Embargo Act of 1807.
2. **ANALYZING LEADERSHIP** Responses should include Jefferson's refusal to elevate himself because of his office and how this idea became a model for leaders of democracies.
3. **THEME: EXPANSION** Expansion brought America into closer contact with other nations who already had establishments in parts of the West.
4. **RECOGNIZING PROPAGANDA** The campaign of 1800 was fought with nasty personal attacks. One individual said a Jefferson victory would result in a "nation black with crimes."
5. **APPLYING CITIZENSHIP SKILLS** Jefferson behaved more like a gentleman farmer than a "privileged politician." He refused to elevate himself above other people because of his office.

**Interact *with* History** Answers will vary, but students should recall the dangers of the expeditions that are shown throughout the chapter.

## HISTORY SKILLS

### 1. INTERPRETING GRAPHS

Study the graph. Answer the questions.

**Foreign Trade,** *1800–1812*

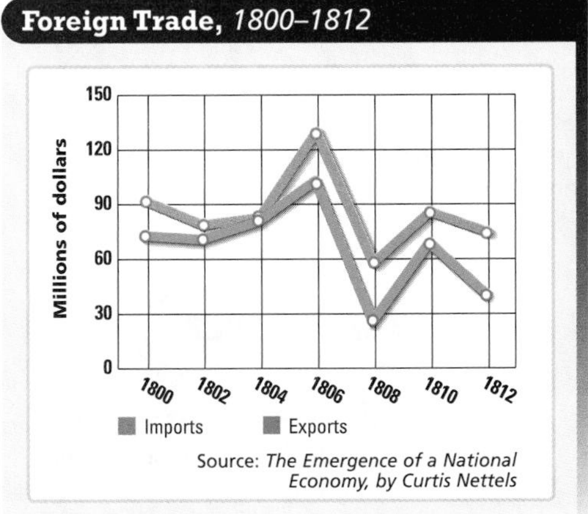


Source: *The Emergence of a National Economy, by Curtis Nettels*

**Basic Graph Elements**

a. What do the numbers on the left side of the chart indicate?

**Interpreting the Graph**

b. In what years did the value of U.S. trade decrease dramatically?

c. What was the value of exports in 1806? In 1808?

### 2. INTERPRETING PRIMARY SOURCES

Examine the cartoon below, which comments on the United States trade policies you read about in Section 3.

a. What does *Ograbme* spell when written backwards?

b. What other clues tell you that this cartoon is about the embargo against Great Britain?

## ALTERNATIVE ASSESSMENT

### 1. INTERDISCIPLINARY ACTIVITY: World History

**Making a Time Line** The history of the Jefferson Era is closely related to events in Europe that were occurring at the same time. Do research to learn about the Napoleonic Wars. Then make a time line with events from U.S. history on one side and events from the Napoleonic Wars on the other.

### 2. COOPERATIVE LEARNING ACTIVITY

**Designing a Plan for Economic Action** Form a group that will develop a plan to end British interference with U.S. shipping. Select a leader for your group. Then pick one member of your group to represent farmers, another to represent shippers, and another to speak for those who are demanding war. Discuss the interests of all these groups and then write down your policy and present it to the class. Be sure to consider:

- the superior power of the British Navy
- where the farmers will sell their products
- how the shippers will earn their money

### 3. TECHNOLOGY ACTIVITY

**Creating a Multimedia Presentation** Use the Internet, books, and other reference materials to create a multimedia presentation on one of the major battles of the War of 1812. Consider including the following:

- paintings or written descriptions of the battle
- pictures of the weapons that were used
- music from the time period
- recorded sound effects
- graphs showing battle statistics

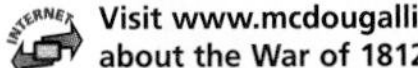

**Visit www.mcdougallittell.com to learn more about the War of 1812.**

### 4. HISTORY PORTFOLIO

**Option 1** Review your section and chapter assessment activities. Select one that you think is your best work. Then use comments made by your teacher or classmates to improve your work and add it to your portfolio.

**Option 2** Review the questions that you wrote for What Do You Want to Know? on page 312. Then write a short report in which you explain the answers to your questions. If any questions were not answered, do research to answer them. Add your answers to your portfolio.



## ALTERNATIVE ASSESSMENT

**1. INTERDISCIPLINARY ACTIVITY: World History**

**Time lines should**

- be organized chronologically.
- have one side for Napoleonic Wars events and one for United States events.
- clearly describe events and illustrations.
- be presented neatly.

**2. COOPERATIVE LEARNING ACTIVITY**

**Plans should**

- support positions with evidence or logic.
- respond to each other's statements.
- be acceptable to at least two of the parties.

**3. TECHNOLOGY ACTIVITY**

**Presentations should**

- utilize two or more media.
- clearly present accurate information about a battle.
- present information about both sides in the battle.
- show technical proficiency.

**4. HISTORY PORTFOLIO**

**Option 1 Revised section or chapter assessment activities should**

- address teacher and peer responses to the selected work.
- solve problems present in the first versions of the work.

**Option 2 Short reports should**

- answer questions about the expansion of the United States in the early 1800s.
- use evidence to develop and support ideas.
- cite sources of information.
- use standard grammar, spelling, sentence structure, and punctuation.

**Critical Thinking Transparency CT30**

- Visual Summary

**Formal Assessment**

- Chapter Test, Forms A and B, pp. 163–170

## HISTORY SKILLS

**Possible Responses**

**1. INTERPRETING GRAPHS**

**Basic Graph Elements**

**a.** the value of imports and exports in millions of dollars

**Interpreting the Graph**

**b.** 1806–1808

**c.** about $100 million; about $30 million

**2. INTERPRETING PRIMARY SOURCES**

**a.** embargo

**b.** The man is taking his goods to a British ship anchored in the distance.

## HISTORY WORKSHOP

**OBJECTIVE**
Students create a journal of field notes and then write a paragraph comparing their field notes with those of Lewis and Clark.

 **BLOCK SCHEDULING**

## PROCEDURE

Have students assemble the materials listed in the "Toolbox." Divide the class into groups of three or four. Then review the steps for assigning tasks within the group, making a journal, and putting the journal together. Have students make notes in their journal as they explore the neighborhood, using the Lewis and Clark journal as a model. Make sure students include a map of their neighborhood walk in their journal.

 **In-Depth Resources: Unit 3**
- History Workshop Resources, p. 39

### MORE ABOUT . . .

**Instructions from Jefferson**
President Jefferson gave Lewis explicit directions about his observations. He told Lewis "Your observations are to be taken with great pains and accuracy, to be entered distinctly and intelligibly for others as well as yourself to comprehend . . ."

### HISTORY FROM VISUALS

**Interpreting the Field Notes of Lewis and Clark**
Ask students why they think the authors of these notes drew such detailed pictures and took so many notes. **Possible Responses** Lewis and Clark knew that they were acting as the "eyes" of many scientists and scholars. They knew that the information they recorded would be of immeasurable assistance to the explorers, scientists, and settlers who would follow them.

## HISTORY WORKSHOP

# Making Explorers' Field Notes

On their expedition in the early 1800s, Lewis and Clark filled their journals with field notes—detailed observations and scientific illustrations of the land, plants, and wildlife they saw. Lewis made drawings of plants and animals. Clark drew detailed maps. For many years, their journals were the main source of information about the West.

ACTIVITY Create a journal of field notes that includes illustrations of plants, animals, and terrain found in your neighborhood. Then write a comparison article between your field notes and those of Lewis and Clark.

### TOOLBOX

Each group will need:

- drawing paper
- poster board for covers
- pencil and pen
- scissors
- ruler
- string
- hole punch and hole reinforcers

### STEP BY STEP

**1** **Form groups.** Each group should consist of 3 to 4 students. The members of your group will do the following tasks:

- design and create a handmade journal
- take a walk in your neighborhood and record observations as field notes
- compare the field notes you have created with those of Lewis and Clark

**2** **Make your journal.** Your group will need a journal to make field notes on the nature walk. Each page of the journal should be six inches wide and roughly eight inches long, approximately the size of the one used by Lewis and Clark. Cut 10–15 sheets of that size out of the drawing paper. Create a front and back cover for the journal using the poster board.

**The scientific and artistic skills of Lewis and Clark made their journals both accurate and beautiful.**



## RECOMMENDED RESOURCES

**JOURNALS AND BOOKS FOR THE TEACHER**

Duncan, Dayton and Ken Burns. ***Lewis & Clark.*** New York: Knopf, 1997.

Fisher, Ron. "Lewis and Clark" ***National Geographic.*** Washington: National Geographic Society, October 1998.

**VIDEO**

***Gone West: The Growth of a Nation.*** United Learning, 1998. Looks at the Lewis and Clark expedition and the Louisiana Purchase through the use of animated maps and period art.

**INTERNET**

For more about Lewis and Clark, visit www.mcdougallittell.com

**BOOKS FOR THE STUDENTS**

Freedman, Russell. ***An Indian Winter.*** New York: Holiday House, 1992.

Calvert, Patricia. ***Great Lives: The American Frontier.*** New York: Atheneum, 1997.

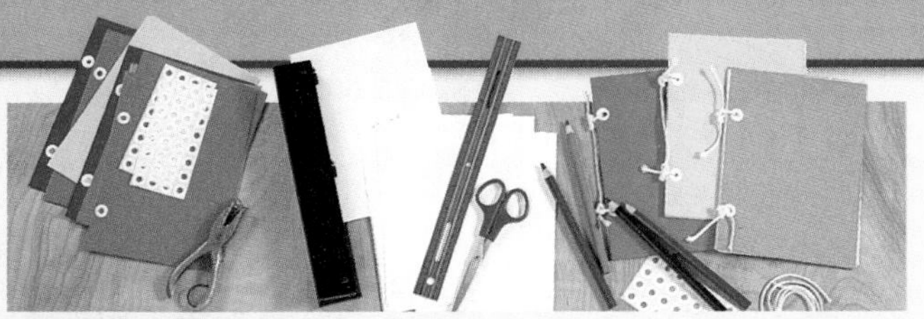

**3** **Put your journal together.** Punch three holes in the left side of the pages, including the covers. Place hole reinforcers around the holes to ensure that the pages won't tear. Bind the pages and the covers together with string.

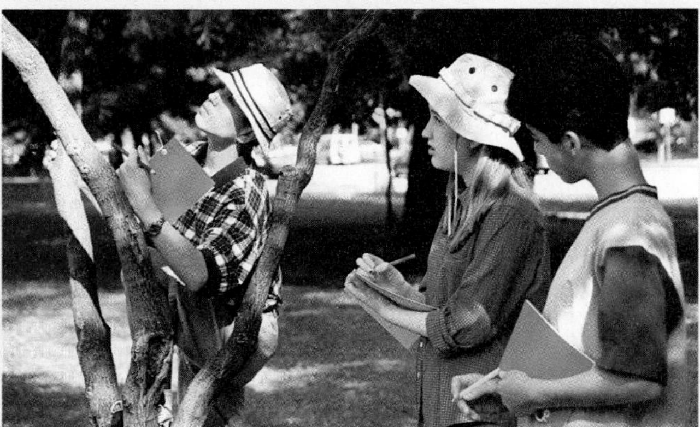

**4** **Explore your neighborhood.** Take a walk in your neighborhood, in the area around your school, or in a nearby woods. You might want to divide the tasks of observing, drawing, describing, and mapping among the members of the group.

**5** **Model your field notes on those of Lewis and Clark.** In their journals, Lewis and Clark included drawings of animals and plants, as well as detailed observations about them. Remember to draw the plants, insects, and animals as if you have never seen them before.

**6** **Make a map of your route.** In addition to the drawings, create a map of your walk. Include any interesting landmarks as well as a detailed description of the terrain. Remember to sketch the route as if it's unexplored territory.

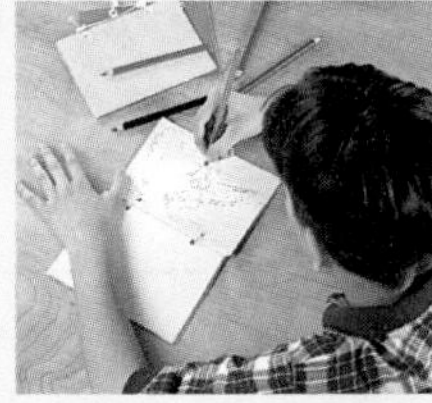

## WRITE AND SPEAK

Write and present a paper that compares and contrasts Lewis and Clark's journal with the one your group has completed. Also, explain how your journal might help someone who has just moved to your school or neighborhood.

## HELP DESK

For related information, see pages 320–325 in Chapter 10.

### Researching Your Project

- You can find copies of Lewis and Clark's journals in many libraries.
- *Undaunted Courage* by Stephen Ambrose gives a fascinating account of the expedition.

Visit www.mcdougallittell.com to learn more about Lewis and Clark.

### Did You Know?

- The Corps of Discovery sent Jefferson six live specimens of animals, including a prairie dog.
- At one point, the men on the expedition consumed nine pounds of buffalo meat a day.
- Swarms of mosquitoes plagued the expedition. The explorers often found it impossible to eat without inhaling some of the pesky insects.
- Clark estimated that the expedition traveled 4,162 miles. His guess was only 40 miles off the actual distance.

### REFLECT & ASSESS

- **What process did your group use to observe, draw, and describe your route?**
- **How did you decide what information to include in your journal?**
- **How important are the illustrations to understanding the area in which your group took its walk?**



### MORE ABOUT . . .

**Myths About the West**

The field notes of Lewis and Clark and the journals of the Corps of Discovery helped dispel many myths about the West. The most widely held myth was the belief that there was a northwest passage, or all-water route, to the Pacific.

### MORE ABOUT . . .

**Exploration Today**

Today scientists, mapmakers, and explorers have not only still cameras, tape recorders, and video cameras but also computers, global positioning satellites, and many other high-tech tools to help them make accurate field notes.

### REFLECT & ASSESS

1. Students can make a diagram showing the sequence of steps in the process of observing, drawing, and describing or recording information about their route.
2. Students can explain what they considered to be the goals of the journal writing and what types of information helped them meet these goals.
3. Students may want to pick out one of their illustrations and talk specifically about what it added to their knowledge of the area.

## STANDARDS FOR EVALUATION

### HISTORY WORKSHOP

**Field Notes should**

- demonstrate an attempt at careful observation.
- contain a detailed drawing of the plants, animals, or objects identified.
- use the written description that accompanies each drawing to add information about the drawing.
- be simple, clear, and readable.

### WRITE AND SPEAK

**Comparison should**

- clearly state the purpose of the comparison.
- describe the ways the journals are alike and different.

# National And Regional Growth 1800–1844

| | CHAPTER OVERVIEW | COPYMASTERS | TECHNOLOGY |
|---|---|---|---|
| **CHAPTER RESOURCES** | The chapter describes the early years of the Industrial Revolution in the North and the cotton boom and spread of slavery in the South. It also discusses the increase in sectionalism and efforts to resolve conflict over slavery with the Missouri Compromise. | **In-Depth Resources: Unit 3**<br>• Tracing Themes: Science and Technology, p. 41<br>• Building Vocabulary, p. 45<br>**Interdisciplinary Projects,** pp. 61–66 | **Primary Source Explorer**<br>**Electronic Teacher Tools**<br>**Power Presentations CD-ROM**<br>**Chapter Summaries on CD** (English and Spanish)<br>**America's Music CD** |
| **SECTION 1**<br>**Early Industry and Inventions**<br>**pp. 341–347** | **KEY IDEAS**<br>• The Industrial Revolution begins in New England using water-powered factories.<br>• The new factories employ men, women, and often children as well.<br>• Technological breakthroughs improve manufacturing, travel, communication, and agriculture. | **In-Depth Resources: Unit 3**<br>• Setting the Stage, p. 40<br>• Guided Reading, p. 42<br>• Primary Source, p. 49<br>• Literature Selection, pp. 51–53<br>• Reteaching Activity, p. 54 | **Warm-Up Transparency WT11**<br>**Humanities Transparency HT21**<br>• New England Textile Mill<br>**Critical Thinking Transparency CT31**<br>• Setting the Stage<br>**Critical Thinking Transparency CT32**<br>• Cause and Effect: Industrial Revolution<br>**ClassZone:** www.mcdougallittell.com |
| **SECTION 2**<br>**Plantation and Slavery Spread**<br>**pp. 348–353** | • The invention of the cotton gin makes cotton "king" of the Southern economy.<br>• The spread of cotton farming leads to an expansion of slavery.<br>• Enslaved African Americans find strength in family life and religion, and they continue to resist enslavement. | **In-Depth Resources: Unit 3**<br>• Setting the Stage, p. 40<br>• Guided Reading, p. 43<br>• Geography Application, pp. 47–48<br>• Primary Source, p. 50<br>• Reteaching Activity, p. 55<br>**America's History Makers**<br>• Eli Whitney, pp. 43–44<br>• Frederick Douglass, pp. 45–46<br>**Economics in History,** p. 11 | **Warm-Up Transparency WT11**<br>**Humanities Transparency HT22**<br>• A Cotton Plantation<br>**Critical Thinking Transparency CT31**<br>• Setting the Stage<br>**ClassZone:** www.mcdougallittell.com |
| **SECTION 3**<br>**Nationalism and Sectionalism**<br>**pp. 354–361** | • The American System, new transportation links, and several Supreme Court decisions promote national unity.<br>• The Missouri Compromise preserves the balance of power.<br>• The Monroe Doctrine announces that the Americas are closed to further European colonization. | **In-Depth Resources: Unit 3**<br>• Setting the Stage, p. 40<br>• Guided Reading, p. 44<br>• Skillbuilder Practice, p. 46<br>• Reteaching Activity, p. 56<br>**Citizenship Today,** pp. 87–88<br>**Why It Matters Now**<br>• Expanding Economies, pp. 21–22<br>**Outline Map Activities**<br>• Economic Expansion, 1841, pp. 21–22 | **Warm-Up Transparency WT11**<br>**Geography Transparency GT11**<br>• Railroads Extend Westward, 1850–1860<br>**Critical Thinking Transparency CT33**<br>• Visual Summary<br>**Primary Source Explorer**<br>• *The Monroe Doctrine*<br>**ClassZone:** www.mcdougallittell.com |

PE Pupil's Edition
Copymaster
Overhead Transparency
Audio Library
CD-ROM
Internet

## ASSESSMENT

**Chapter Assessment,** pp. 362–363

**Formal Assessment**
- Chapter Tests, Forms A and B, pp. 176–183

**Alternative Assessment Book**

**Electronic Teacher Tools with Test Maker**

**Section Assessment,** p. 345

**Formal Assessment**
- Section Quiz, p. 173

**Alternative Assessment Book**
- Rubrics for an oral report, 3.6
- Rubrics for a diagram, 2.3

**Electronic Teacher Tools with Test Maker**

**Section Assessment,** p. 353

**Formal Assessment**
- Section Quiz, p. 174

**Alternative Assessment Book**
- Rubrics for a book report, 4.7
- Rubrics for an oral interpretation, 3.6

**Electronic Teacher Tools with Test Maker**

**Section Assessment,** p. 359

**Formal Assessment**
- Section Quiz, p. 175

**Alternative Assessment Book**
- Rubrics for an editorial, 4.1
- Rubrics for a political cartoon, 1.2

**Electronic Teacher Tools with Test Maker**

## CUSTOMIZING FOR INDIVIDUAL NEEDS

### Students Acquiring English/ESL

**Reading Study Guide** (English and Spanish), pp. 111–118

**Access for Students Acquiring English/ESL:** Spanish Translations, pp. 73–78

**Chapter Summaries on CD** (English and Spanish)

### Less Proficient Readers

**Reading Study Guide** (English and Spanish), pp. 111–118

**Chapter Summaries on CD** (English and Spanish)

### Gifted and Talented Students

**In-Depth Resources: Unit 3**
- Enrichment Activity, p. 57

**America's History Makers**
- Eli Whitney, pp. 43–44
- Frederick Douglass, pp. 45–46

## CROSS-CURRICULAR CONNECTIONS

### Economics

Macaulay, David. ***Mill.*** Boston: Houghton Mifflin, 1983. Detailed drawings illustrate the story of the growth of a Massachusetts mill.

### Primary Sources

Deitch, JoAnne W. ***The Lowell Mill Girls: Life in the Factory.*** Carlisle, MA: Discovery Enterprises, 1998. Plentiful primary sources give this account a fine ring of authenticity.

### Science

Spangenburg, Robert and Diane K. Moser. ***The Story of America's Canals.*** New York: Facts on File, 1992. Part of the series called Connecting a Continent, informative, illustrated and packed with time lines and charts.

### Interdisciplinary Projects, pp. 61–66

- Math: Encoding and Decoding Messages
- Science: Scientific Inquiry
- Language Arts: Describing a Place
- Music: Spirituals

### Literature

Aiken, Joan. ***Midnight Is a Place.*** New York: Viking, 1974. A brilliant novel about child labor in the Industrial Revolution, set in England.

Defelice, Cynthia. ***The Apprenticeship of Lucas Whitaker.*** New York: Avon, 1998. Engrossing and sometimes gruesome story about the scourge of tuberculosis in the mid nineteenth century.

Paterson, Katherine. ***Lyddie.*** New York: Lodestar, 1991. Three years in the life of a Vermont farm girl who goes to work in Lowell.

### McDougal Littell Literature Connections

Scott O'Dell
***Island of the Blue Dolphins***
In this classic novel set in the early 1800s, Karana, a Native American girl, survives 18 years alone on an island off the coast of southern California.

## ENRICHMENT ACTIVITIES

**Pupil's Edition, pp. 338–363**
**Interact with History,** p. 339
**Interdisciplinary Challenge,** pp. 346–347
**Interactive Primary Source,** pp. 360–361

**In-Depth Resources: Unit 3**
- Geography Application: The Internal Slave Movement After 1810, pp. 47–48
- Primary Source: from *Loom and Spindle,* p. 49
- Primary Source: Wes Brady Describes His Life Under Slavery, p. 50
- Literature Selection: from *The Clock,* pp. 51–53

**America's History Makers**
- Eli Whitney, pp. 43–44
- Frederick Douglass, pp. 45–46

**America's Music CD**

**Outline Map Activities**
- Economic Expansion, 1841, pp. 21–22

**Primary Source Explorer**
- *The Monroe Doctrine*

**Why It Matters Now**
- Expanding Economies, pp. 21–22

**LESSON PLAN OPTIONS (50-MINUTE PERIOD)** (TE) = Teacher's Edition (PE) = Pupil's Edition

| | TEACHER-DIRECTED ACTIVITIES<br>Class Time: 15 minutes | STUDENT-CENTERED ACTIVITIES<br>Class Time: 25 minutes | INDIVIDUAL ACTIVITIES<br>Class Time: 10 minutes |
|---|---|---|---|
| **DAY 1**<br>Introduction<br>pp. 338–340 | **Presentation Options**<br>• Begin with a class discussion of the drawing on p. 338 **(PE)**.<br>• Lead a class discussion on the "What Do You Know?" question in Setting the Stage, p. 340. Then introduce the graphic organizer for the chapter **(PE)**. | **Options for Cooperative Learning**<br>• Have student groups discuss the Interact with History questions, p. 339 **(PE)**.<br>• Have student groups respond to the "What Do You Want to Know?" question in Setting the Stage, p. 340 **(PE)**. | **Head Start on Homework Options**<br>• Have students skim Section 1 Main Idea, Why It Matters Now, Terms & Names, and the main headings, p. 341 **(PE)**.<br>• Have students begin Guided Reading activity and Building Vocabulary sheet. |
| **DAY 2**<br>Section 1<br>pp. 341–347 | **Presentation Options**<br>• Begin with the 5-Minute Warm-Up, p. 341 **(TE)**.<br>• Review the way a factory works using the illustration, p. 343 **(PE)**.<br>• Choose 5 key questions for Objectives 1–4 to discuss with the class, pp. 341–345 **(TE)**. | **Options for Cooperative Learning**<br>• Divide students into groups to work on the Interdisciplinary Challenge, pp. 346–347 **(PE)**.<br>• Have student pairs work together to complete one of the Activity Options in the Section 1 Assessment, p. 345 **(PE)**. | **Head Start on Homework Options**<br>• Have students begin working on Section 1 Assessment, p. 345 **(PE)**.<br>• Have students preview Section 2 Main Idea, Why It Matters Now, Terms & Names, and the main headings, p. 348 **(PE)**. |
| **DAY 3**<br>Section 2<br>pp. 348–353 | **Presentation Options**<br>• Begin with the 5-Minute Warm-Up, p. 348 **(TE)**.<br>• Choose 5 key questions for Objectives 1–4 to discuss with the class, pp. 348–353 **(TE)**.<br>• Lead students through the Geography Skillbuilder p. 350 **(PE, TE)**. | **Options for Cooperative Learning**<br>• Divide students into groups to work on the Interdisciplinary Link, Math: Circle Graphs, p. 350 **(TE)**.<br>• Divide students into groups to work on the Interdisciplinary Link, Humanities: Spirituals, p. 352 **(TE)**. | **Head Start on Homework Options**<br>• Have students begin working on Section 2 Assessment, p. 353 **(PE)**.<br>• Have students complete the Taking Notes Question in Section 3 Assessment, p. 359 **(PE)**. |
| **DAY 4**<br>Section 3<br>pp. 354–361 | **Presentation Options**<br>• Begin with the 5-Minute Warm-Up, p. 354 **(TE)**.<br>• Choose 5 key questions for Objectives 1–4 to discuss with the class, pp. 354–359 **(TE)**.<br>• Lead the students through the Skillbuilder Mini-Lesson: Comparing and Contrasting, p. 358 **(TE)**. | **Options for Cooperative Learning**<br>• Divide students into groups and have them complete the Primary Source A Closer Look questions, pp. 360–361 **(PE)**.<br>• Have student pairs work together to complete one of the Activity Options in the Section 3 Assessment, p. 359 **(PE)**. | **Head Start on Homework Options**<br>• Have students complete the Setting the Stage graphic organizer for the chapter, p. 340 **(PE)**.<br>• Have students begin working on the Chapter Assessment, pp. 362–363 **(PE)**.<br>• Prepare for Chapter Test<br>**Formal Assessment,** pp. 176–183 |

TEACHER-TESTED ACTIVITY Kelly Ellis, Hamilton Junior High School, Cypress, Texas

## ERIE CANAL POSTCARDS

**Class Time** 30 minutes

**Task** Creating a postcard featuring the Erie Canal

**Purpose** To summarize information about the Erie Canal

**Supplies Needed**

- Illustrated reference materials and Internet sources on the Erie Canal
- Markers or colored pencils
- Posterboard cut into 6" X 8" rectangles

**Activity** Have each student create a two-sided postcard of the Erie Canal. On the front side, they should draw a picture or diagram of the canal. On the back, they can compose a caption explaining the picture. Then have them use the card to write a message to a friend or relative describing cities along the canal, how the canal operates, types of boats and goods that travel on the canal, or its economic impact on the region. Remind students to include a place for an address and a stamp.

## BLOCK SCHEDULING — LESSON PLAN OPTIONS (90-MINUTE PERIOD)

### DAY 1

**Interact with History,** p. 339
**Class Time** 20 Minutes

Options for pacing and variety:

- **Peer Teaching** Divide the class into small groups. Have students speculate on how each of the four inventions shown in the Interact with History illustration are likely to change how Americans live. Have groups share their opinions with the class. **Class Time** 15 minutes

**Setting the Stage,** p. 340
**Class Time** 20 minutes

Options for pacing and variety:

- **Time Saver** Ask students to come to class with a list of questions to ask people from different regions about their lives in preparation for discussion of "What Do You Want to Know?" **Class Time** 5 minutes

**Section 1,** pp. 341–347
**Class Time** 50 minutes

Options for pacing and variety:

- **Peer Teaching** Have students work in small groups to make up three questions: one about an invention, one about an inventor, and one about the effects of an invention. Collect the questions, group them by category, and have a "Jeopardy" quiz bowl. **Class Time** 30 minutes

### DAY 2

**Interdisciplinary Challenge,** pp. 346–347
**Class Time** 55 minutes

Options for pacing and variety:

- **Team Teaching** Invite a math teacher to your class to coach student groups as they solve the Math Challenge on page 347. **Class Time** 55 minutes

**Section 2,** pp. 348–353
**Class Time** 45 minutes

Options for pacing and variety:

- **History on Film** Extend students' knowledge of slavery by viewing *Slavery: America's Peculiar Institution.* The film describes the family life, education, and living conditions of slaves in the South. Zenger Media **Class Time** 30 minutes
- **Time Saver** For a homework assignment, have students complete the Taking Notes and Critical Thinking exercises in the Section Assessment. **Class Time** 15 minutes

**Section 3,** pp. 354–361
**Class Time** 50 minutes

**Chapter 11 Assessment,** pp. 362–363
**Class Time** 40 minutes

Options for pacing and variety:

- **Peer Evaluation** Have students work in groups to discuss the Interact with History and Critical Thinking questions, page 362. Have groups pick the question they found most interesting and share their response with the class. **Class Time** 20 minutes
- **Peer Teaching** Divide students into small groups. Tell them to study the chart on page 362 and create a different way to present the information to the class. **Class Time** 30 minutes

**CHAPTER 11 OBJECTIVE**
The student will analyze the ways in which new machines changed American society, encouraged the expansion of slavery, and contributed to both nationalism and sectionalism in the first half of the 1800s.

# National and Regional Growth

## 1800–1844

*Section 1* **Early Industry and Inventions**
*Section 2* **Plantations and Slavery Spread**
*Section 3* **Nationalism and Sectionalism**

## HISTORY FROM VISUALS

**Interpreting the Painting** Have students study the painting, which shows a barge on the Erie Canal. Students may not realize that the canal boat is propelled by mule power. Point out the mules at the lower left. A rope connects them to the boat.

Ask students what they observe about the land and activity along the canal. **Possible Responses** The canal cuts a path through farmland. Crops grow in nearby fields, and farmers tend livestock.

Ask students to keep this scene in mind as they read about the changes that canals and other innovations helped bring about in the United States during the early 1800s.

**Extension** Ask students to identify major transportation routes and centers (water, air, or land) in their state and explain how they are important to local people and businesses.

The Erie Canal, which opened in 1825, increased western trade and migration.

338

### CRITICAL THINKING ACTIVITY

**Making Inferences** Ask students why canals were preferred routes for transporting farm produce and manufactured goods in the early 1800s. What other ways might goods have been transported to markets in those days? If students do not understand the advantages of water transportation, explain that two or three mules could not move such a heavy load overland; moving heavy goods by water takes much less power.

**Class Time** 10 minutes

## RECOMMENDED RESOURCES

### BOOKS FOR THE TEACHER

Cunningham, Noble E., Jr. ***The Presidency of James Monroe.*** Lawrence, KA: Univ. Press of Kansas, 1996. A balanced view of a diligent and influential, but rather uncharismatic, president.

Eisler, Benita. ***The Lowell Offering: Writings by New England Mill Women (1840–1845).*** New York: Norton, 1997. Extraordinary collection of women's writings on laundry, love, food, hope, and work.

Tucker, Barbara M. ***Samuel Slater and the Origins of the American Textile Industry, 1790–1860.*** Ithaca, NY: Cornell Univ. Press, 1984. How an early case of industrial espionage jump-started the U.S. textile industry.

### VIDEO

***Indians of North America: The Seminole.*** GPN, 1994. History, culture, and the modern situation.

### INTERNET

For more about the Lowell Mills or inventions made by women, visit www.mcdougallittell.com

## Interact *with* History

rotary printing press
steamboat
steam locomotive
telegraph

This Currier and Ives print, *Progress of the Century,* shows some inventions of the 1800s.

**From 1790 to 1840, you have seen an explosion of new inventions. These include the cotton gin, the steamboat, the steel plow, and the telegraph. You have also seen neighbors leave their farms to run machines in new factories. You sense that the country is changing.**

### What Do You Think?

- **What would it mean to be able to grow more grain and cotton?**
- **What would it mean to communicate and travel more quickly?**
- **How might it feel to do factory work instead of farm work?**

# *How will new inventions change your country?*

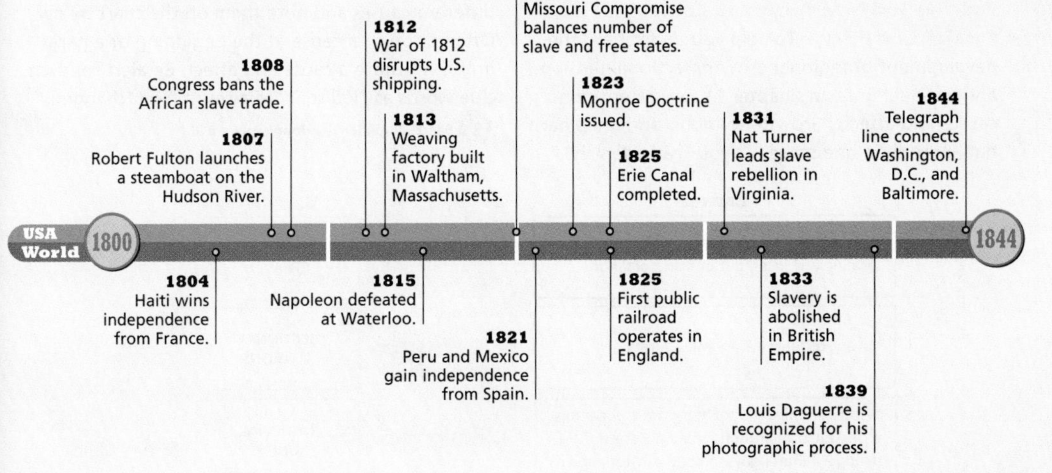
USA
World
1800
1807
Robert Fulton launches a steamboat on the Hudson River.
1808
Congress bans the African slave trade.
1812
War of 1812 disrupts U.S. shipping.
1813
Weaving factory built in Waltham, Massachusetts.
1820
Missouri Compromise balances number of slave and free states.
1823
Monroe Doctrine issued.
1825
Erie Canal completed.
1831
Nat Turner leads slave rebellion in Virginia.
1844
Telegraph line connects Washington, D.C., and Baltimore.
1844
1804
Haiti wins independence from France.
1815
Napoleon defeated at Waterloo.
1821
Peru and Mexico gain independence from Spain.
1825
First public railroad operates in England.
1833
Slavery is abolished in British Empire.
1839
Louis Daguerre is recognized for his photographic process.

## Interact *with* History

### OBJECTIVES

- To identify some important inventions from the period between 1790 and 1840
- To describe how such inventions affected people's lives and businesses

### What Do You Think?

1. Ask students to identify the uses of grain and cotton.
2. Ask students how long they think it would take to travel to a nearby town by horseback or wagon. How often might people make such a trip?
3. Have students describe the kinds of things they think farmers and factory workers do during a typical workday. Ask them to consider which kind of work changes more from week to week and which worker has more independence.

### *How will new inventions change your country?*

Suggest that students consider how modern technologies, such as computers and the Internet, are changing life in the United States today.

### MAKING PERSONAL CONNECTIONS

Ask students to consider how they might be affected if travel to places far from home were slow or dangerous or if communication with friends and family members who live far away were difficult.

### TIME LINE DISCUSSION

**In this chapter, issues such as new links between various regions of the nation, challenges to slavery, and relationships with other nations are changing American society.**

- Ask students to identify events that probably made it easier to communicate and travel over long distances. **Answer** 1807, Fulton's steamboat; 1825, Erie Canal and first public railroad; 1844, telegraph line
- Ask students to identify events involving slavery. **Answer** 1808, Congress banned African slave trade; 1820, Missouri Compromise; 1831, Turner's rebellion; 1833, slavery abolished in British Empire
- Identify which events occurring in the world might worry Americans and why. **Answer** 1821, independence in Mexico because United States shared a border; 1833, slavery abolished in British Empire because American slaves might want freedom too

## BEFORE YOU READ

### Previewing the Theme:
**Science and Technology**
Ask students to explain the links between these inventions and economic growth. Students may note that inventions allowed faster travel or communication and led to increased production.

### What Do You Know?
Students may note that today—because of television and other forms of mass communication, national chains of restaurants and stores, and urbanization—fewer differences exist among regions in the United States. However, in the 1800s, regional differences were much more pronounced. People identified themselves more in terms of region than nation. Point out that differing perspectives and personal experiences often influence people's opinions on an issue.

 **In-Depth Resources: Unit 3**
- Tracing Themes: Science and Technology, p. 41

## READ AND TAKE NOTES

**Reading Strategy: Analyzing Causes and Recognizing Effects**
Tell students that analyzing causes and effects in the chapter will help them relate events to one another. Point out the chart on page 340. Help students understand that their purpose for reading this chapter is to identify the causes that brought about regional growth, sectional tensions, and national unity.

 **In-Depth Resources: Unit 3**
- Setting the Stage, p. 40

 **Critical Thinking Transparency CT31**
- Setting the Stage

# Chapter 11 SETTING THE STAGE

## BEFORE YOU READ

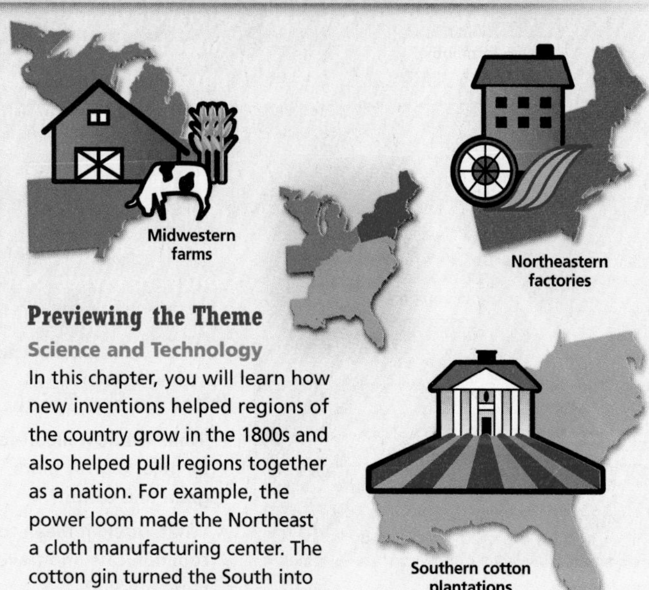


### Previewing the Theme
**Science and Technology**
In this chapter, you will learn how new inventions helped regions of the country grow in the 1800s and also helped pull regions together as a nation. For example, the power loom made the Northeast a cloth manufacturing center. The cotton gin turned the South into a Cotton Kingdom. The telegraph let people communicate instantly across regions.

### What Do You Know?
What connects you to someone who lives in the same region? When have you felt a bond with someone from a different region?

**THINK ABOUT**
- the activities of people in different regions
- the things that unite people as a nation

### What Do You Want to Know?
What would you ask people from different regions—a factory worker, wheat farmer, plantation owner, or field slave—about their lives in the 1800s? Write these questions in your notebook. Read to see if they are answered in Chapter 11.

## READ AND TAKE NOTES

**Reading Strategy: Analyzing Causes and Recognizing Effects** To help you understand the development of regional growth, sectional tensions, and national unity in Chapter 11, pay attention to causes and effects. Growth, tensions, and unity each had more than one cause. As you read, identify different causes and note them on the chart below. Often a topic sentence at the beginning of a paragraph will state a cause and effect. Be alert for such clue words as "led to," "as a result," or "changed."

 See Skillbuilder Handbook, page R10.

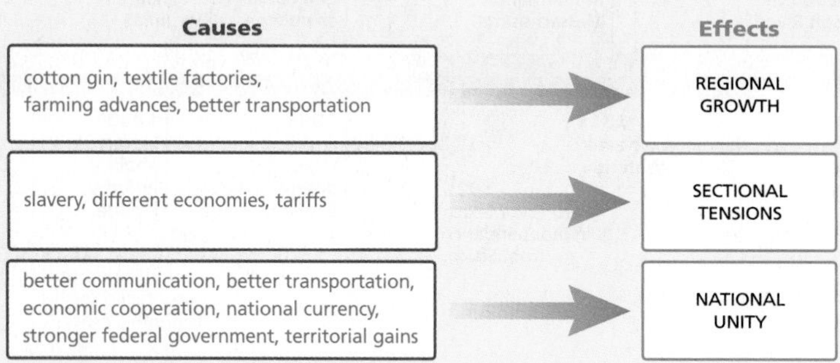

| Causes | Effects |
|---|---|
| cotton gin, textile factories, farming advances, better transportation | REGIONAL GROWTH |
| slavery, different economies, tariffs | SECTIONAL TENSIONS |
| better communication, better transportation, economic cooperation, national currency, stronger federal government, territorial gains | NATIONAL UNITY |



## TEACHING STRATEGY

### READING THE CHAPTER
This is a thematic chapter focusing on early industries and inventions that led to national and regional growth. Encourage students to look for cause-and-effect relationships as they read the chapter. Pause after each section to review key events and their impact on the nation or on a particular region.

### ALTERNATIVE ASSESSMENT
The Chapter Assessment describes three activities for alternative assessment on page 363. You may wish to have students work on these activities during the course of the chapter and then present them at the end.

# 1 Early Industry and Inventions

**TERMS & NAMES**
Samuel Slater
Industrial Revolution
factory system
Lowell mills
interchangeable parts
Robert Fulton
Samuel F. B. Morse

**MAIN IDEA**

New machines and factories changed the way people lived and worked in the late 1700s and early 1800s.

**WHY IT MATTERS NOW**

The industrial development that began more than 200 years ago continues today.

## ONE AMERICAN'S STORY

**In 1789, the Englishman Samuel Slater sailed to the United States under a false name. It was illegal for textile workers like him to leave the country. Britain wanted no other nation to copy its new machines for making thread and cloth. But Slater was going to bring the secret to America. When he got to New York, he wrote a letter to Rhode Island investor Moses Brown.**

*A VOICE FROM THE PAST*

A few days ago I was informed that you wanted a manager of *cotton spinning* . . . in which business I flatter myself that I can give the greatest satisfaction, in making machinery, making good yarn, either for *stockings* or *twist,* as any that is made in England.

**Samuel Slater,** quoted in *Samuel Slater: Father of American Manufactures*

Samuel Slater's mill was located in Pawtucket, Rhode Island.

**With Brown's backing, Slater built the first successful water-powered textile mill in America. You will learn in Section 1 how the development of industries changed the ways Americans lived and worked.**

## 1 The Industrial Revolution Begins

The War of 1812 brought great economic changes to the United States. It sowed the seeds for an Industrial Revolution like the one begun in Britain during the late 18th century. During the **Industrial Revolution,** factory machines replaced hand tools, and large-scale manufacturing replaced farming as the main form of work. For example, before the Industrial Revolution, women spun thread and wove cloth at home using spinning wheels and hand looms. The invention of such machines as the spinning jenny and the power loom made it possible for unskilled workers to produce cloth. These workers, who were often children, could produce more cloth, more quickly.

The **factory system** brought many workers and machines together under one roof. Most factories were built near a source of water to power the machines. People left their farms and crowded into cities where the





## SECTION OBJECTIVES

1. To explain how the Industrial Revolution began
2. To describe the role of the factory system and interchangeable parts
3. To identify inventions that improved transportation and communication
4. To explain increased farm production

**CRITICAL THINKING**

Recognizing Effects, pp. 342, 344, 345
Contrasting, p. 343
Making Judgments, p. 345

## FOCUS & MOTIVATE

### 5-MINUTE WARM-UP

**Making Generalizations** Answering these questions will help students understand the way new machines changed textile production.

1. Look at the illustration on page 343. Why would operating this factory require the efforts of many workers?
2. How do you think this factory could pay for itself over time?

 **Warm-Up Transparency WT11**

## INSTRUCT

**INSTRUCT: OBJECTIVE 1**

**The Industrial Revolution Begins/ Factories Come to New England**

Key Questions

- How did the Industrial Revolution change the way people worked?
- Why was New England a good place to set up factories?

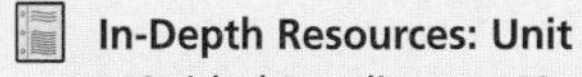
**In-Depth Resources: Unit 3**
- Guided Reading, p. 42

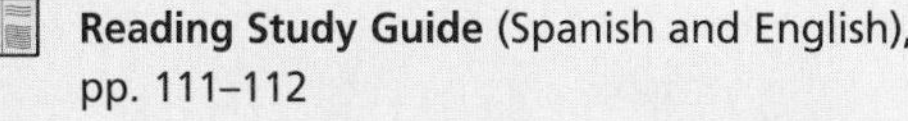
**Reading Study Guide** (Spanish and English), pp. 111–112

**Critical Thinking Transparency CT32**
- Cause and Effect: Industrial Revolution

## RECOMMENDED RESOURCES

 **In-Depth Resources: Unit 3**
- Guided Reading, p. 42
- Building Vocabulary, p. 45
- Primary Source: from *Loom and Spindle,* p. 49
- Literature Selection, pp. 51–53
- Reteaching Activity, p. 54

 **Reading Study Guide** (Spanish and English), pp. 111–112

**Formal Assessment**
- Section Quiz, p. 173

**Alternative Assessment**
- Rubrics, 3.6
- Rubrics, 2.3

**Access for Students Acquiring English/ESL**
- Guided Reading, p. 73

**Technology Resources**

**Humanities Transparency HT21**
- New England Textile Mill

 **Critical Thinking Trans. CT32**
- Cause and Effect: Industrial Revolution

 **Electronic Teacher Tools with Test Maker**

 **ClassZone**
www.mcdougallittell.com

### CRITICAL THINKING ACTIVITY

**Comparing and Contrasting** Have students use a two-column chart to contrast Samuel Slater's mill system with Francis Cabot Lowell's mill system. The charts should note the origins of the machinery designs as well as the work performed and source of employees at the different mills.

**Class Time** 20 minutes

| Slater's Mills | Lowell's Mills |
|---|---|
| children or families as workers | young women as workers |
| machinery copied from English | power looms copied from English |
| spinning mill | cotton to yarn wove cloth |

**Humanities Transparency HT21**
- New England Textile Mill

### INSTRUCT: OBJECTIVE 

**The Lowell Mills Hire Women/ A New Way to Manufacture**

Key Questions
- How did the Lowell mills change the textile industry in the United States?
- How did interchangeable parts change industry and management?

**In-Depth Resources: Unit 3**
- Literature Selection: from *The Clock* by James Lincoln Collier and Christopher Collier, pp. 51–53

factories were. They worked for wages, on a set schedule. Their way of life changed, and not always for the better.

Many Americans, such as Thomas Jefferson, did not want the United States to industrialize. But the War of 1812 led the country in that direction. Because the British naval blockade kept imported goods from reaching U.S. shores, Americans had to start manufacturing their own goods. The blockade also stopped investors from spending money on shipping and trade. Instead, they invested in new American industries. Taking advantage of the country's free enterprise system, American businessmen built their own factories, starting in New England. These businessmen and their region grew wealthier.

**Vocabulary**
**industrialize:** to develop factories

**Reading History**
**A. Recognizing Effects** How did the War of 1812 cause economic changes in America?
**A. Answer** It blocked shipping, forcing Americans to manufacture their own goods and to invest in businesses other than shipping.

## Factories Come to New England

New England was a good place to set up factories for several reasons. Factories needed water power, and New England had many fast-moving rivers. For transportation, it also had ships and access to the ocean. In addition, New England had a willing labor force. The area's first factory workers were families who were tired of scraping a living from their stony fields.

Samuel Slater built his first spinning mill in Pawtucket, Rhode Island, in 1790. He hired eight children between the ages of 7 and 12, paying them a low wage. Later, he built a larger mill and employed whole families. As Slater influenced others to start mills, his family system of employment spread through Rhode Island, Connecticut, and southern Massachusetts.

##  The Lowell Mills Hire Women

In 1813, the American textile industry leaped forward when Francis Cabot Lowell built a factory in Waltham, in eastern Massachusetts. This factory not only spun raw cotton into yarn, but wove it into cloth on power looms. Lowell had seen power looms in English mills and had figured out how to build them. Like Samuel Slater, he had brought secrets to America.

Lowell girls published a literary magazine.

The Waltham factory was so successful that Lowell and his partners built a new factory town, Lowell, near the Merrimack and Concord rivers. The **Lowell mills,** textile mills in the village, employed farm girls who lived in company-owned boardinghouses. "Lowell girls" worked 12½-hour days in deafening noise.

**Background**
Founded in 1826, the town was named for Lowell, who died in 1817.

*A VOICE FROM THE PAST*

At first the hours seemed very long . . . and when I went out at night the sound of the mill was in my ears . . . . You know that people learn to sleep with the thunder of Niagara [falls] in their ears, and a cotton mill is no worse, though you wonder that we do not have to hold our breath in such a noise.

**"Letters from Susan,"** quoted in the *Lowell Offering*



### ACTIVITY OPTIONS
### INDIVIDUAL NEEDS

**STUDENTS ACQUIRING ENGLISH/ESL**

**Building Vocabulary** Help students become more familiar with the specialized vocabulary in this section by having them build a word wall. Write each section heading on a sheet of paper and attach it to a wall or bulletin board. As students read the paragraphs under the headings, have them identify words that are new to them. Write these words on index cards and write out the definition. Then place the cards under the appropriate heading. Encourage students to refer to the wall and use the words frequently in speaking and writing activities.

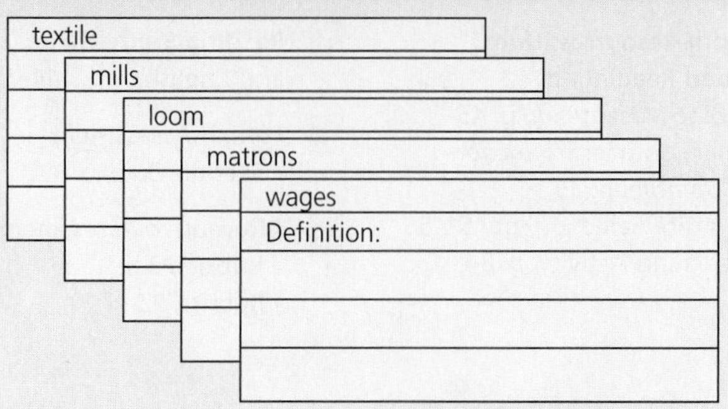

New England Textile Mill
1 Moving water turns a wheel, which powers the machines through a system of gears and belts.
2 Carding and drawing machines straighten raw cotton fibers and twist them loosely.
3 Spinning machines spin the fibers into yarn, or thread.
4 Power looms weave yarn into cloth.

In 1835, Lowell had 22 mills. In 1855, it had 52 mills employing more than 13,000 workers and producing 2.25 million yards of cotton cloth a week.

## HISTORY FROM VISUALS

**Reading the Diagram** Point out that each step in the textile-production process in this mill was done on a separate floor. Ask students to make inferences about what kinds of workers were necessary to keep such a large mill running. **Possible Responses** maintenance workers to keep machinery operating properly; workers to accept raw materials for production, to operate the machines, to transport finished products from one floor to another; managers to supervise work on each floor; accountants to keep track of expenses and income; shippers to send products to markets

**Extension** Have students do research to find out how factories are organized today. Help them make connections between a typical modern factory and the textile mill shown here.

Young women came to Lowell in spite of the noise. In the early years, wages were high—between two and four dollars a week. Older women supervised the girls, making them follow strict rules and attend church. Girls read books, went to lectures, and even published a literary magazine—the *Lowell Offering*. Usually they worked for only a few years, until they married. By the 1830s, however, falling profits meant that wages dropped and working conditions worsened for the Lowell girls.

*Reading* **History**
**B. Contrasting** How did the Lowell mills differ from Slater's mill?
B. Answer Lowell mills wove cloth, employed young women, and were larger than Slater's mill, which only spun thread and employed children and families.

The Lowell mills and other early factories ran on water power. Factories built after the 1830s were run by more powerful steam engines. Because steam engines used coal and wood, not fast-moving water, factories could be built away from rivers and beyond New England.

## A New Way to Manufacture

New manufacturing methods changed the style of work in other industries besides the textile industry. In 1797, the U.S. government hired the inventor Eli Whitney to make 10,000 muskets for the army. He was to have the guns ready in two years. Before this time, guns were made one at a time by gunsmiths, from start to finish. Each gun differed slightly. If a part broke, a new part had to be created to match the broken one.

Whitney sought a better way to make guns. In 1801, he went to Washington with a box containing piles of musket parts. He took a part from each pile and assembled a musket in seconds. He had just demonstrated the use of **interchangeable parts,** parts that are exactly alike.

## MORE ABOUT . . .

**Mill Girls on Strike**
The textile industry saw the first strikes by women factory workers in the United States. Following wage cuts, women workers at the Boston Manufacturing Company in Waltham went on strike in 1821. The strike shut down factory production for two days. Textile workers later formed the Factory Girls' Association. The organization joined others in pushing for a 10-hour workday.

**In-Depth Resources: Unit 3**
- Primary Source: from *Loom and Spindle* by Harriet Hanson Robinson, p. 49

## ACTIVITY OPTIONS

**INTERDISCIPLINARY LINK: ECONOMICS** — BLOCK SCHEDULING

### A BUSINESS PLAN

**Class Time** One class period
**Task** Creating a business plan
**Purpose** To apply the ideas of industrialism to a new enterprise

**Supplies Needed**
- Paper and pencils

**Activity** Have small groups of students create a business plan for a company that sells tools or other manufactured products. On the board, write a sample business plan outline: company name, product, likely customers, methods of production, and employees needed. Discuss whether the product will require interchangeable parts and whether they are suitable for mass production with the factory system. Some students may wish to make a prototype of their group's product.

**MORE ABOUT . . .**

**The *Clermont***

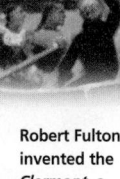

The *Clermont* was 150 feet long with a single-cylinder engine. Its paddle wheels had diameters of 15 feet. When Fulton began using the *Clermont* commercially, other boats would ram the open paddle wheels, hoping to damage their new rival.

**Robert Fulton invented the *Clermont,* a steamboat.**

Machines that produced exactly matching parts soon became standard in industries. Interchangeable parts speeded up production, made repairs easy, and allowed the use of lower-paid, less-skilled workers. But the new system also required a new style of management, with inspectors to make sure each piece was uniform. Workers who were used to more independence disliked such close supervision.

*Reading* **History**

**C. Recognizing Effects** What were the effects of using interchangeable parts?

**C. Answer** They made production faster and repairs easier. They allowed the use of less-skilled workers but required the workers to be closely supervised.

## 3 Moving People, Goods, and Messages

New inventions increased factory production. They also improved transportation and communication. Steamboats carried people and goods farther and faster and led to the growth of cities like New Orleans and St. Louis. **Robert Fulton** invented a steamboat that could move against the current or a strong wind. He launched the *Clermont* on the Hudson River in 1807. Its steam engine turned two side paddle wheels, which pulled the boat through the water.

The *Clermont* was dubbed "Fulton's Folly" and described as "looking precisely like a backwoods saw-mill mounted on a scow [boat] and set on fire." But it made the 300-mile trip from New York to Albany and back in a record 62 hours. Even Fulton had not expected to travel so quickly.

*A VOICE FROM THE PAST*

I overtook many sloops and schooners, beating to the windward, and parted with them as if they had been at anchor. The power of propelling boats by steam is now fully proved.

**Robert Fulton,** quoted in *Robert Fulton and the "Clermont"*

In 1811, the first steamship traveled down the Mississippi and Ohio rivers. But its engine was not powerful enough to return upriver, against the current. Henry Miller Shreve, a trader on the Mississippi, designed



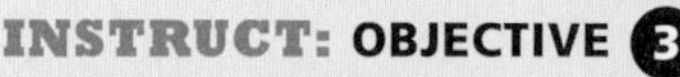

**INSTRUCT: OBJECTIVE 3**

**Moving People, Goods, and Messages**

Key Questions

- Why was the steamboat an improvement over earlier forms of river transportation?
- How did the telegraph revolutionize long-distance communication?

**MORE ABOUT . . .**

**Robert Fulton**

Robert Fulton also contributed to the future of naval warfare. In 1800, he constructed a novel weapon called a submarine, which had been designed by the French for use in their war against the British. The plan was for the crew of the *Nautilus* to place explosives under the hulls of British ships. The *Nautilus* did not succeed in sinking an enemy ship, but the submarine became an especially destructive weapon in naval warfare during World Wars I and II.

**ACTIVITY OPTIONS**

**MULTIPLE LEARNING STYLES: KINESTHETIC** — BLOCK SCHEDULING

**STEAMSHIP MODELS**

**Class Time** One class period

**Task** Creating models

**Purpose** To evaluate the importance of the steamship for river navigation

**Supplies Needed**

- Illustrated encyclopedias or books on steamships
- Light cardboard or heavy construction paper
- Glue or clear tape
- Fine-tip markers

**Activity** Students should research the basic designs of the vessels and construct models on a design of their choice. The models need not be intricate or show interior machinery. Students may describe the functions of different parts, such as the smokestack and paddle wheel, by writing small captions on them. Have students write the name of their ship on the bow. Discuss the importance of a boat that could travel upstream on a major waterway such as the Mississippi.

a more powerful engine. He installed it on a double-decker boat with a paddle wheel in the back. In 1816, he sailed this boat up the Mississippi and launched a new era of trade and transportation on the river.

In 1837, **Samuel F. B. Morse** first demonstrated his telegraph. This machine sent long and short pulses of electricity along a wire. These pulses could be translated into letters of a message. With the telegraph, it took only seconds to communicate with someone in another city. In 1844, the first long-distance telegraph line carried news from Baltimore to Washington, D.C., about who had been nominated for president. Telegraph lines spanned the country by 1861, bringing people closer as a nation. Both the telegraph and the steamboat brought more national unity.

*Reading* **History**
**D. Recognizing Effects** What made the steamboat and telegraph such important inventions?
**D. Answer** They increased commerce and communication between regions of the country.

## 4 Technology Improves Farming

Other new inventions increased farm production. In 1836, the blacksmith John Deere invented a lightweight plow with a steel cutting edge. Older cast-iron plows were designed for the light, sandy soil of New England. But rich, heavy Midwestern soil clung to the bottom of these plows and slowed farmers down. Deere's new plow made preparing ground much less work. As a result, more farmers began to move to the Midwest.

The mechanical reaper and the threshing machine were other inventions that improved agriculture. Cyrus McCormick's reaper, patented in 1834, cut ripe grain. The threshing machine separated kernels of wheat from husks.

**Vocabulary**
**patented:** protected by a patent, which gives an inventor the sole right to make, use, or sell an invention

John Deere invented the steel plow.

New technologies linked regions and contributed to national unity. With new farm equipment, Midwestern farmers grew food to feed Northeastern factory workers. In turn, Midwestern farmers became a market for Northeastern manufactured goods. The growth of Northeastern textile mills increased demand for Southern cotton. This led to the expansion of slavery in the South, as you will learn in Section 2.

### Section 1 Assessment

**1. Terms & Names**
**Identify:**
- Samuel Slater
- Industrial Revolution
- factory system
- Lowell mills
- interchangeable parts
- Robert Fulton
- Samuel F. B. Morse

**2. Taking Notes**
On a chart like the one below, note new inventions, their dates, and their effects on the United States.

| Invention | Date | Effects |
|---|---|---|
| | | |
| | | |

Which inventions did most to link the nation? Explain.

**3. Main Ideas**
a. Why was New England a good place to build early factories?
b. What were working conditions like in Lowell mills?
c. How were different U.S. regions linked economically?

**4. Critical Thinking**
**Evaluating** How would you judge Samuel Slater and Francis Lowell, who brought secrets to the United States illegally?
**THINK ABOUT**
- what they gained
- how they affected the United States and England
- what you believe about keeping technology secret

**ACTIVITY OPTIONS**
**SCIENCE**
**SPEECH**
Explain how an invention from this chapter works, either in an **oral report** or a **labeled diagram.**





### INSTRUCT: OBJECTIVE 4

**Technology Improves Farming**
Key Questions
- Why was John Deere's new plow an important development?
- What other inventions improved agriculture?
- How did new technologies link regions more closely together?

**CRITICAL THINKING ACTIVITY**
**Analyzing Causes and Recognizing Effects**
Have students use an organizer to illustrate how new technologies linked regions of the United States. See example below.

Discuss how the links might have an effect on the balance of power among the regions. **Possible Response** The Northeast had ties to both the South and the Midwest. The Northeast could come to dominate the other regions economically.

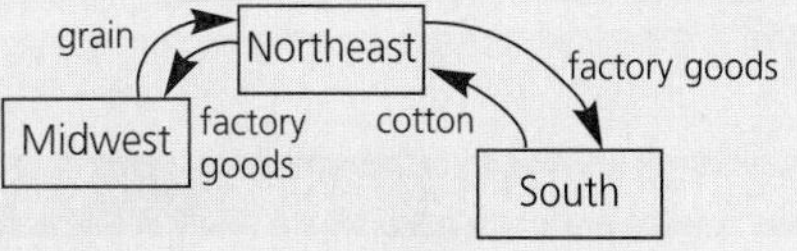


**Class Time** 10 minutes

### ASSESS & RETEACH

**Setting the Stage** Have students place information about the industrial revolution in the first and third cause-and-effect boxes on the graphic.

**Formal Assessment**
- Section Quiz, p. 173

**Critical Thinking Transparency CT31**
- Setting the Stage

**RETEACHING ACTIVITY**
Have students work with partners to create a poster illustrating important inventions or innovations that spurred growth in the United States. Students should write short captions noting the significance of each item.

**In-Depth Resources: Unit 3**
- Reteaching Activity, p. 54

### Section 1 Assessment

**1. Terms & Names**
**Samuel Slater,** p. 341
**Industrial Revolution,** p. 341
**factory system,** p. 341
**Lowell mills,** p. 342
**interchangeable parts,** p. 343
**Robert Fulton,** p. 344
**Samuel F. B. Morse,** p. 345

**2. Taking Notes**
interchangeable parts: 1801, standardized goods; steamboat: 1807, improved river transportation; telegraph: 1837, improved communication; steel plow: 1836, increased food production. The steamboat or telegraph promoted national unity.

**3. Main Ideas**
**a.** available water power; good transportation; a willing labor force **b.** noisy; long hours; many women workers **c.** The Midwest and Northeast exchanged food and manufactured goods. The South provided cotton for Northeast textile mills.

**4. Critical Thinking**
Students may either admire them for enabling America to compete with England or fault them for stealing national secrets for profit.

**ACTIVITY OPTIONS**
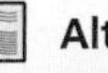
**Alternative Assessment**
- Rubrics for an oral report, 3.6
- Rubrics for a diagram, 2.3

## Interdisciplinary CHALLENGE

**OBJECTIVE**

Students work cooperatively to analyze and solve technological, economic, and occupational-safety problems in running a New England textile mill.

 **BLOCK SCHEDULING**

## PROCEDURE

Assemble the supplies that students may need, such as books about waterwheels, drawing paper, posterboard, markers, pencils, and perhaps calculators. Have students form groups of four or five to complete each challenge. Group members should choose an option and divide the work among themselves.

### HEALTH CHALLENGE

Suggest that students ask the human resources department of a local manufacturing plant for a copy of the company safety manual for employees and copies of safety signs posted in the plant. Other sources of information about occupational safety, such as federal rules, can be found at the library.

**POSSIBLE SOLUTION**

Some Boston mill employers vaccinated employees against smallpox, a disease that could easily spread in a crowded factory. However, many mill owners argued that the health of workers was generally no worse than that of people who did not work at the mills. Accidents were considered the worker's fault. Mill owners had no obligation to compensate workers injured on the job, so there was little financial incentive to improve safety except for the slight cost of training a new worker to replace the injured person.



# Run a Mill Town

You are the owner of a new water-powered textile mill that will soon open in New England. Mills have been around for more than 20 years, and you have studied their operations closely. Even so, you face many problems as you start your business. Machinery failures, labor problems, demanding investors—all will be part of your life from now on.

COOPERATIVE LEARNING On this page are two challenges you face as the owner of a textile mill. Working with a small group, decide how to deal with each challenge. Choose an option, assign a task to each group member, and do the activity. You will find useful information in the Data File. Be prepared to present your solutions to the class.

### HEALTH CHALLENGE

*"Anna Tripp lost three fingers today."*

**A neighboring mill owner has just left after sharing some bad news. Today 12-year-old Anna Tripp lost three fingers in one of his machines. Last week, one of his workers was hit and nearly killed by the flying end of a broken belt. Several girls went home because they had trouble breathing. They blamed the closed, damp machine rooms with lint-filled air. How will you reduce the number of costly health problems like these in your mill? Present your plan using one of these options:**

- Write a speech to workers outlining the company's safety measures.
- Design a sign for each floor of the mill stating the company's safety rules.



## STANDARDS FOR EVALUATION

### HEALTH CHALLENGE

**Option 1** Speeches should
- identify potential health and safety problems.
- provide clear instructions to promote health and safety.

**Option 2** Signs should
- clearly state safety rules.
- explain reasons for the rules.

### MATH CHALLENGE

**Option 1** Reports should
- explain hiring decisions.
- summarize payroll information.

**Option 2** Posters should
- clearly identify the kinds of workers desired.
- include information about wages and open positions.

### SCIENCE CHALLENGE

**Option 1** Diagrams should
- show how the waterwheel works.
- include labels that clearly explain why that particular wheel is the best choice.

**Option 2** Instructions should
- include clear, easy-to-follow directions.
- show how the wheel works.

## MATH CHALLENGE

### *"So many applicants for employment"*

**To make a profit, you must operate at top capacity for the lowest cost. Your mill generates 2 mill power. This dictates how many spinners you can hire. You need about two-and-a-half times that many weavers. What will be your weekly payroll for spinners and weavers? How many men will you hire? Women? Look at the Data File for help. Present your hiring plan for spinners and weavers using one of these options:**

- **Write a report telling investors whom you plan to hire.**
- **Design want-ad posters aimed at the workers you are looking for.**

## DATA FILE

### Water Power

**Potential energy:** energy released when water falls from a height.

**Kinetic energy:** energy provided by fast-moving water.

**1 mill power:** power produced by 25 cubic feet of water per second dropping over a 30-foot fall; about 60 horsepower.

**1 mill power:** runs 3,584 spindles.

### Waterwheels

Overshot

Undershot

Mid-wheel

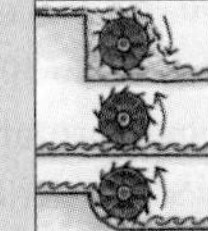

### Wage Rates

**Men:** $.85–$2.09 per day, depending on skill

**Women:** $.52–$.78 per day, depending on skill

### Positions

**Pickers:** clean raw cotton.

**Carders:** feed cotton into machine that makes a thick strand of fibers.

**Spinners:** operate a machine that twists thick fibers into yarn and winds it on bobbins fastened to moving spindles. One worker operates 128 spindles.

**Dressers:** treat finished yarn with a starch paste.

**Drawing-in hands:** attach dressed yarn to the mechanical loom for weavers.

**Weavers:** weave dressed yarn into finished cloth. One worker operates two looms.

### Work Hours

12 hours per day, 6 days per week, 309 days per year with holidays on Fast Day (spring), the Fourth of July, and Thanksgiving

**Visit www.mcdougallittell.com to learn more about textile mills.**

## ACTIVITY WRAP-UP

**Present to the Class** **Meet as a group to review your responses to running a mill town. Pick the most creative solution for each challenge and present these solutions to the class.**

347

## ACTIVITY WRAP-UP

Presentations should
- clearly identify the problems in each challenge.
- provide clear, effective solutions to each problem.
- evaluate and explain the effectiveness of the solutions.
- explain the originality of the solutions.

## MATH CHALLENGE

**Class Time** 50 minutes

Students should use information in the Data File to calculate the number of spinners and weavers needed.

**POSSIBLE SOLUTION**

56 spinners, 140 weavers. Payroll for spinners and weavers will vary depending on whom students employ in those positions. Point out that the most physically demanding jobs were picking and carding.

In general, men held all supervisory jobs. Men also were hired as machinists and for physically demanding jobs that mill owners considered too difficult for women. Women held machine-tending jobs after carding, such as spinning and weaving. Although the great majority of workers were women, men held all the highest-paying jobs.

**ALTERNATIVE CHALLENGE**

## SCIENCE CHALLENGE

### *"Water power . . . invited the enterprise of manufacturers"*

**Like other manufacturers, you buy land for your mill along a deep, fast-moving river. The water cascades over a 10-foot falls. You know that the right waterwheel can harness 60 percent of the energy in this falling water. Which kind of wheel will you choose? Look at the Data File for help and do more research on waterwheels. Present your choice using one of these options:**

- **Draw a labeled diagram of your waterwheel that explains why it is the most efficient choice.**
- **Create illustrated instructions for your carpenters explaining how the wheel works.**

## SECTION OBJECTIVES

1. To explain the relationship between the cotton boom and slavery
2. To analyze the important divisions within Southern society
3. To describe African-American culture and family life under slavery
4. To summarize information about slave rebellions

### SKILLBUILDERS

Interpreting Maps: Human-Environment Interaction, p. 350

### CRITICAL THINKING

Recognizing Effects, pp. 349, 352, 353
Analyzing Points of View, p. 350
Contrasting, p. 351
Making Inferences, p. 351
Drawing Conclusions, p. 353

## FOCUS & MOTIVATE

### 5-MINUTE WARM-UP

**Making Generalizations** These questions focus on the expansion of slavery.

1. Look at the graph on page 350. By how much did cotton growing expand from 1800 to 1860?
2. How does the information on the graph and map support the title of this section?

 **Warm-Up Transparency WT11**

## INSTRUCT

### INSTRUCT: OBJECTIVE 

**The Cotton Boom/Slavery Expands**

Key Questions

- How did the invention of the cotton gin change Southern life?
- How did the rise in cotton production affect slavery?

 **In-Depth Resources: Unit 3**
- Guided Reading, p. 43
- Building Vocabulary, p. 45

# 2 Plantations and Slavery Spread

**TERMS & NAMES**
Eli Whitney
cotton gin
spirituals
Nat Turner

**MAIN IDEA**
The invention of the cotton gin and the demand for cotton caused slavery to spread in the South.

**WHY IT MATTERS NOW**
The spread of slavery created lasting racial and sectional tensions.

### ONE AMERICAN'S STORY

**Catherine Beale was born into slavery in 1838. At the age of 91, in 1929, she recalled her childhood on a Virginia plantation. When asked what games she had played, Catherine replied that enslaved children never played games—they were too busy with chores. Among the tasks were picking and cleaning cotton.**

*A VOICE FROM THE PAST*

We had to work in the field in the day and at night we had to pick out the seed before we went to bed. And we had to clean the wool, we had to pick the burrs and sticks out so it would be clean and could be carded and spun and wove.

**Catherine Beale,** quoted in *Slave Testimony*

Enslaved workers labor in the cotton fields.

**Catherine had to clean cotton by hand because the plantation didn't have a cotton gin. This machine made it easier for enslaved workers to clean cotton. But it also made cotton growing and slave owning more profitable. In this section, you will learn how slavery expanded in the South and how it affected the lives of people living under it.**

## 1 The Cotton Boom

**Eli Whitney** invented a machine for cleaning cotton in 1793, after visiting the Georgia plantation of Catherine Greene, the widow of a Revolutionary War general. Mrs. Greene was struggling to make her plantation profitable. English textile mills had created a huge demand for cotton, but the short-fibered cotton that grew in most parts of the South was hard to clean by hand. A worker could clean just one pound of this cotton in a day.

Whitney's **cotton gin** (short for "engine") made the cotton-cleaning process far more efficient. With the new machine, one worker could now clean as much as 50 pounds of cotton a day. The cotton gin helped set the South on a different course of development from the North. It made



### RECOMMENDED RESOURCES

 **In-Depth Resources: Unit 3**
- Guided Reading, p. 43
- Building Vocabulary, p. 45
- Geography Application: The Internal Slave Movement After 1810, pp. 47–48
- Primary Source: Wes Brady Describes His Life Under Slavery, p. 50
- Reteaching Activity, p. 55
- Enrichment Activity, p. 57

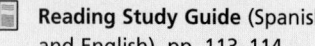

**Reading Study Guide** (Spanish and English), pp. 113–114

**Economics in History**
- The Economics of Slavery, p. 11

 **America's History Makers**
- Eli Whitney, pp. 43–44
- Frederick Douglass, pp. 45–46

 **Formal Assessment**
- Section Quiz, p. 174

**Alternative Assessment**
- Rubrics, 4.7
- Rubrics, 3.6

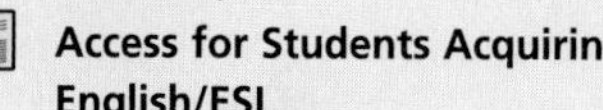 **Access for Students Acquiring English/ESL**
- Guided Reading, p. 74
- Geography Application, pp. 77–78

**Technology Resources**

 **Humanities Transparency HT22**
- A Cotton Plantation

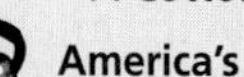 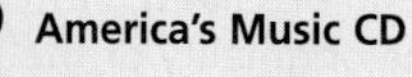 **America's Music CD**

 **Electronic Teacher Tools with Test Maker**

 **ClassZone**
www.mcdougallittell.com

## The Cotton Gin

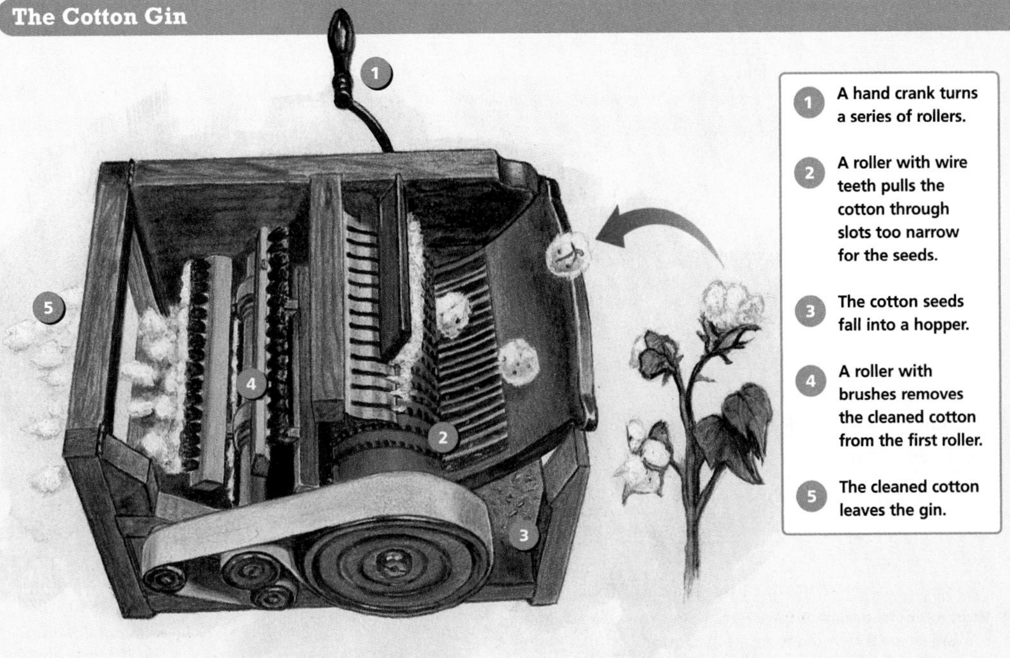
1
2
3
4
5

1. A hand crank turns a series of rollers.
2. A roller with wire teeth pulls the cotton through slots too narrow for the seeds.
3. The cotton seeds fall into a hopper.
4. A roller with brushes removes the cleaned cotton from the first roller.
5. The cleaned cotton leaves the gin.

short-fibered cotton a commercial product and changed Southern life in four important ways.

1. It triggered a vast move westward. Cotton farming moved beyond the Atlantic coastal states, where long-fibered, easy-to-clean cotton grew. Cotton plantations began to spread into northern Florida, Alabama, and Mississippi. Then they crossed into Louisiana and Arkansas. After 1840, they reached Texas.
2. Because cotton was so valuable, planters put most of their efforts into growing it rather than other crops. To Southerners, cotton was king.
3. More Native American groups were driven off Southern land as it was taken over for cotton plantations.
4. Growing cotton required a large work force, and slavery continued to be important as a source of labor. Many slaves from the east were sold south and west to new cotton plantations.

*Reading History*
**A. Reading a Map** Use the map on page 350 to find cotton-growing areas in 1840.

*Reading History*
**B. Recognizing Effects** What impact did the cotton gin have on the South?
**B. Answer** It allowed cotton farming to move west, made cotton more important than other crops, led to the seizure of more Native American land, and kept slavery important as a labor source.

## Slavery Expands

From 1790 to 1860, cotton production rose greatly. So did the number of enslaved people in the South. Using slave labor, the South raised millions of bales of cotton each year for the textile mills of England and the American Northeast. (See the graph on page 350.) In 1820, the South earned $22 million from cotton exports. By the late 1830s, earnings from cotton exports were nearly ten times greater, close to $200 million.

As cotton earnings rose, so did the price of slaves. A male field hand sold for $300 in the 1790s. By the late 1830s, the price had jumped to

### MORE ABOUT . . .

**The Cotton Gin**

Gins in use before Whitney invented his machine were similar to clothes wringers on old washing machines. Friction from the grooved rollers on those gins could remove seeds from long-staple cotton but not from the shorter fibers of the cotton best suited to the South's climate and soil.

**America's History Makers**
• Eli Whitney, pp. 43–44

### HISTORY FROM VISUALS

**Reading the Illustration** Point out the hand crank shown at the top of the illustration. Tell students that gins varied in size from hand-operated ones like this to larger ones turned by horse power or water power. Ask students how this machine helped determine how labor was distributed in cotton production. **Possible Response** Instead of having many slaves spending time cleaning cotton, cotton producers could use most of their slaves for picking cotton. Only a few workers would be needed to run the machine.

**Extension** Have students suggest labor-saving machines that are used today. Ask them to speculate about how those machines save time or change work patterns.

**Economics in History**
• The Economics of Slavery, p. 11

### ACTIVITY OPTIONS

### INDIVIDUAL NEEDS

**LESS PROFICIENT READERS**

**Analyzing Causes and Recognizing Effects** To help students understand the effect of the cotton gin on the South, draw a cause-and-effect chart like the one begun here. Work with students to complete the chart, beginning with Eli Whitney's invention of the cotton gin. Continue with expansion of slavery and new plantations. Point out that an effect can often become a cause that triggers a subsequent event.

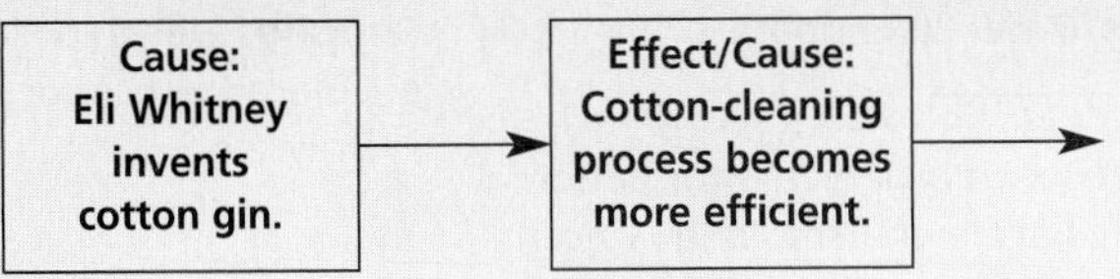
Cause:
Eli Whitney invents cotton gin.
Effect/Cause:
Cotton-cleaning process becomes more efficient.

## HISTORY FROM VISUALS

**Reading the Map** Point out that growing and harvesting cotton was very labor-intensive: the more slaves a landowner had, the more land he could farm and the larger his cotton crop. Based on the map information about cotton production, ask students which states probably had the largest concentrations of enslaved African Americans. **Answers** States of the lower South—Louisiana, Mississippi, Alabama, Georgia, and South Carolina

Based on the graph information, ask the students how they think the map would look in 1860. **Possible Response** More areas of the country would be shown growing cotton.

**Extension** Have students use almanacs and other classroom and library resources to identify states that are major cotton producers today.

 **Humanities Transparency HT22**
- A Cotton Plantation

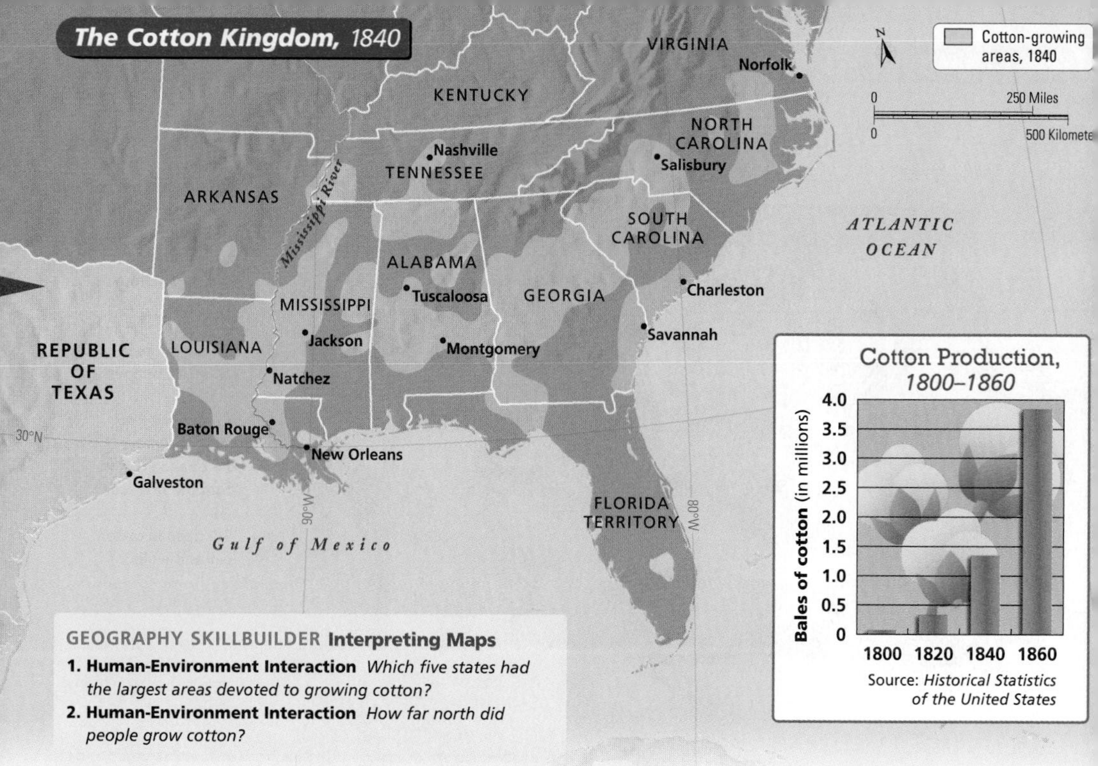


**GEOGRAPHY SKILLBUILDER Interpreting Maps**
1. **Human-Environment Interaction** *Which five states had the largest areas devoted to growing cotton?*
2. **Human-Environment Interaction** *How far north did people grow cotton?*

Skillbuilder Answers
1. South Carolina, Georgia, Alabama, Mississippi, and Louisiana
2. southern Virginia

$1,000. After 1808, when it became illegal to import Africans for use as slaves, the trading of slaves already in the country increased.

The expansion of slavery had a major impact on the South's economy. But its effect on the people living there was even greater.

## INSTRUCT: OBJECTIVE 2

**Slavery Divides the South/ African Americans in the South**

Key Questions
- How widespread was slaveholding in the South?
- What kinds of work did enslaved African Americans do?
- What was life like for free African Americans in the South?

 **In-Depth Resources: Unit 3**
- Geography Application: The Internal Slave Movement After 1810, pp. 47–48

## 2 Slavery Divides the South

Slavery divided white Southerners into those who held slaves and those who did not. Slaveholders with large plantations were the wealthiest and most powerful people in the South, but they were relatively few in number. Only about one-third of white families owned slaves in 1840. Of these slave-owning families, only about one-tenth had large plantations with 20 or more slaves.

Most white Southern farmers owned few or no slaves. Still, many supported slavery anyway. They worked their small farms themselves and hoped to buy slaves someday, which would allow them to raise more cotton and earn more money. For both small farmers and large planters, slavery had become necessary for increasing profits.

*Reading* **History**
**C. Analyzing Points of View** Why did many white farmers without slaves still support slavery?
C. Answer They hoped to own slaves in the future.

## African Americans in the South

Slavery also divided black Southerners into those who were enslaved and those who were free. Enslaved African Americans formed about one-third of the South's population in 1840. About half of them



**ACTIVITY OPTIONS**

**INTERDISCIPLINARY LINK: MATH** — **BLOCK SCHEDULING**

**CIRCLE GRAPHS**

**Class Time** 20 minutes

**Task** Creating graphs

**Purpose** To organize information about slave ownership and African Americans in the South

**Supplies Needed**
- Colored pencils or markers
- Drawing paper

**Activity** Have students create a circle graph titled *White Southern Families in 1840.* Explain that one-third of all white Southern families owned slaves in 1840, so they should make a wedge that takes up about a third of the circle. This wedge should be labeled *Slaveholders.* Students may also create graphs for the proportion of slaveholding families with more than 20 slaves and for the proportion of free African Americans in the South. Students should keep the charts for use as study guides.

worked on large plantations with white overseers. A former slave described the routine.

*A VOICE FROM THE PAST*

The overseer was 'straddle his big horse at three o'clock in the mornin', roustin' the hands off to the field. . . . The rows was a mile long and no matter how much grass [weeds] was in them, if you [left] one sprig on your row they [beat] you nearly to death.

**Wes Brady,** quoted in *Remembering Slavery*

*Reading*History
**D. Contrasting** How was plantation slavery different from slavery in cities?
D. Answer In cities, slaves had more variety in work and were sometimes allowed to keep part of their earnings.

Not all slaves faced the back-breaking conditions of plantations. In cities, enslaved persons worked as domestic servants, skilled craftsmen, factory hands, and day laborers. Sometimes they were hired out and allowed to keep part of their earnings. Frederick Douglass, an African-American speaker and publisher, once commented, "A city slave is almost a freeman, compared with a slave on the plantation." But they were still enslaved.

In 1840, about 8 percent of African Americans in the South were free. They had either been born free, been freed by an owner, or bought their own freedom. Many free African Americans in the South lived in cities such as Baltimore and Washington, D.C.

Though not enslaved, free blacks faced many problems. Some states made them leave once they gained their freedom. Most states did not permit them to vote or receive an education. Many employers refused to hire them. But their biggest threat was the possibility of being captured and sold into slavery.

**daily*life***

**SPIRITUALS**

Singing spirituals offered comfort for pain, bound people together at religious meetings, and eased the boredom of daily tasks. This verse came from a spiritual sung by slaves in Missouri.

*Dear Lord, dear lord,*
*when slavery'll cease*
*Then we poor souls*
*will have our peace;—*
*There's a better day a coming,*
*Will you go along with me?*
*There's a better day a coming,*
*Go sound the jubilee!*

## 3 Finding Strength in Religion

An African-American culture had emerged on plantations by the early 1800s. Slaves relied on that culture—with its strong religious convictions, close personal bonds, and abundance of music—to help them endure the brutal conditions of plantation life.

*Reading*History
**E. Making Inferences** Why would enslaved African Americans be inspired by the biblical story of Moses?
E. Answer Because they hoped for freedom, and Moses led enslaved people to freedom.

Some slaveholders tried to use religion to make slaves accept their treatment. White ministers stressed such Bible passages as "Servants, obey your masters." But enslaved people took their own messages from the Bible. They were particularly inspired by the story of Moses leading the Hebrews out of bondage in Egypt.

Enslaved people expressed their religious beliefs in **spirituals,** religious folk songs. Spirituals often contained coded messages about a planned escape or an owner's unexpected return. African-American spirituals later influenced blues, jazz, and other forms of American music.

Detail of *Plantation Burial,* (1860), John Antrobus.





**MORE ABOUT . . .**

**African-American Craftsmen**
Enslaved African-American craftsmen formed guilds in some large Southern cities, such as Richmond, Virginia, and Charleston, South Carolina. However, white craftsmen then successfully lobbied state and local governments to pass laws restricting the ability of slaves to hire out for work in skilled crafts.

**In-Depth Resources: Unit 3**
- Primary Source, p. 50

**daily*life***

**Spirituals**
Many spirituals concerned the desire for freedom from slavery. Often this desire was expressed in symbolic words and phrases, the real meanings of which were known only to the singers and other slaves. For example, Frederick Douglass (to whom students will be introduced on page 352) recalled a spiritual he and other slaves sang as they prepared to escape to the North:

*O Canaan, sweet Canaan,*
*I am bound for the land of Canaan.*

**In-Depth Resources: Unit 3**
- Enrichment Activity, p. 57

**INSTRUCT: OBJECTIVE 3**

**Finding Strength in Religion/ Families Under Slavery**

Key Questions
- What role did religion play in the system of slavery?
- What was family life like for enslaved people?
- What forms did resistance to slavery take?

**ACTIVITY OPTIONS**

**INTERDISCIPLINARY LINK: LANGUAGE ARTS**

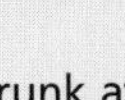 **BLOCK SCHEDULING**

**JOURNAL ENTRY**

**Class Time** One class period

**Task** Creating a journal entry from a historical perspective

**Purpose** To describe the experiences of free African Americans before the Civil War

**Supplies Needed**
- Writing materials

**Activity** Pose the following scenario: In an old trunk at a flea market, students have found the journal of a free African American from a large Southern city in 1840. Ask them to consider the thoughts and feelings free African Americans might have had at the time: their daily lives, expectations, dreams, and fears. Then have students write entries that such a journal might have contained, telling about a day in their lives. Use the entries to frame a discussion about free African Americans in the pre–Civil War South.

## Families Under Slavery

Perhaps the cruelest part of slavery was the sale of family members away from one another. Although some slaveholders would not part mothers from children, many did, causing unforgettable grief. When enslaved people ran away, it was often to escape separation or to see family again.

When slave families could manage to be together, they took comfort in their family life. They married, though their marriages were not legally recognized. They tried to raise children, despite interference from owners. Most slave children lived with their mothers, who tried to protect them from punishment. Parents who lived on other plantations often stole away to visit their children, even at the cost of a whipping. Frederick Douglass recalled visits from his mother, who lived 12 miles away.

*Reading* **History**

**F. Recognizing Effects** How did slavery harm family life?

**F. Answer** It separated families, did not recognize marriages, and took away parents' authority over their children.

*A VOICE FROM THE PAST*

I do not recollect of [remember] ever seeing my mother by the light of day. She was with me in the night. She would lie down with me, and get me to sleep, but long before I waked she was gone.

**Frederick Douglass,** *Narrative of the Life of Frederick Douglass*

Douglass's mother resisted slavery by the simple act of visiting her child. Douglass later rebelled by escaping to the North. Other enslaved people rebelled in more violent ways.

A slave auction threatens to split a family apart.



### MORE ABOUT . . .

**Children Without Parents**

Some students might be particularly concerned about the fate of enslaved children separated from their parents. In such cases, West African traditions of large, extended families proved important. Typically, separated children were raised by other relatives. If that was not possible, other adults in the slave community took the responsibility of caring for the children, serving as surrogate grandparents, uncles, and aunts.

 **America's History Makers**
- Frederick Douglass, pp. 45–46

### MORE ABOUT . . .

**The Slave Trade**

Slave owners rarely blamed themselves or the slave system for the breakup of African-American families; instead they blamed the economy or the slave traders who ran auctions, such as the one shown here. Southerners expressed contempt for slave traders and considered them social inferiors. But such attitudes did not stop slaveholders from doing business with the traders.

Slave auctions were part of what is called the domestic slave trade—the buying and selling of slaves within the United States. Federal law ended the foreign slave trade in 1808, but slave traders continued to smuggle enslaved people from Africa and the West Indies into the United States as late as the 1850s.

### ACTIVITY OPTIONS

**INTERDISCIPLINARY LINK: HUMANITIES** — BLOCK SCHEDULING

**SPIRITUALS**

**Class Time** One class period

**Task** Analyzing a traditional spiritual

**Purpose** To understand the ideas expressed in the music of enslaved African Americans

**Supplies Needed**
- Book of spirituals, such as *Go Down Moses: A Celebration of the African American Spiritual* by Richard Newman
- Recordings of spirituals
- Writing paper
- Drawing materials

**Activity** Have students, working in pairs, choose a spiritual and then explain the emotions expressed in the lyrics. Ask students to make inferences about the meanings of words or phrases: Were they symbols for something that could not be openly expressed, such as a desire for escape and freedom? Invite singers and musicians in your class to sing their spiritual for the other students. Encourage students to draw a sketch or paint a picture illustrating their spiritual. Display the artwork in the classroom.

 **America's Music CD**

## 4 Slave Rebellions

Armed rebellion was an extreme form of resistance to slavery. Gabriel Prosser planned an attack on Richmond, Virginia, in 1800. In 1822, Denmark Vesey planned a revolt in Charleston, South Carolina. Both plots were betrayed, and the leaders were hanged.

The most famous rebellion was led by **Nat Turner** in Virginia in 1831. On August 21, Turner and 70 followers killed 55 white men, women, and children. Later, witnesses claimed that he spoke these words.

*A VOICE FROM THE PAST*

We do not go forth for the sake of blood and carnage; . . . Remember that ours is not a war for robbery, . . . it is a struggle for freedom.

**Nat Turner,** quoted in *Nat Turner,* by Terry Bisson

G. Answer It made them fearful and vengeful. They killed African Americans and passed new laws to control them.

*Reading* **History**

**G. Recognizing Effects** How did Nat Turner's rebellion affect white Southerners?

Most of Turner's men were captured when their ammunition ran out, and 16 were killed. When Turner was caught, he was tried and hanged.

Turner's rebellion spread fear in the South. Whites killed more than 200 African Americans in revenge. State legislatures passed harsh laws that kept free blacks and slaves from having weapons or buying liquor. Slaves could not hold religious services unless whites were present. Postmasters stopped delivering antislavery publications.

After Turner's rebellion, the grip of slavery grew even tighter in the South. Tension over slavery increased between the South and the North, as you will see in the next section.

AMERICA'S HISTORY MAKERS

**NAT TURNER**

**1800–1831**

Nat Turner was born on a plantation in Virginia. As a child, Turner learned to read and write. He became an enthusiastic reader of the Bible. Slaves gathered in forest clearings to listen to his powerful sermons. Turner believed that God wanted him to free the slaves, even if by armed rebellion. He defended the justice of his cause in what came to be known as *Confessions of Nat Turner,* which he dictated to a white lawyer before his execution.

**How did Turner justify his rebellion?**

### Section 2 Assessment

**1. Terms & Names**

**Identify:**
- Eli Whitney
- cotton gin
- spirituals
- Nat Turner

**2. Taking Notes**

In a chart like the one below, note facts about each group of Southerners.

| Group | Facts |
|---|---|
| slaveholding whites | |
| nonslaveholding whites | |
| enslaved blacks | |
| free blacks | |

Why do you think many free blacks lived in cities?

**3. Main Ideas**

a. How did the cotton gin lead to the spread of slavery?

b. How was life different for plantation slaves, city slaves, and free blacks in the South?

c. What were three ways that enslaved people resisted slavery?

**4. Critical Thinking**

**Drawing Conclusions** Why do you think Southern whites reacted as they did to Nat Turner's rebellion?

THINK ABOUT
- Turner's trial and hanging
- the killings that followed the rebellion
- the new laws that were passed

ACTIVITY OPTIONS

LANGUAGE ARTS / SPEECH

Write a **book report** on a slave narrative, or perform an **oral interpretation** of a passage from one.



## AMERICA'S HISTORY MAKERS

**Nat Turner**

It is not known for certain how Nat Turner learned to read. Turner claimed that the ability to read came to him in a vision. Some historians have speculated that older slaves, perhaps his grandmother, taught the young Turner how to read. Others have argued that a son of one of Turner's masters did so, despite laws prohibiting this practice.

Answer: Turner led an armed rebellion with other enslaved African Americans because he believed God wanted him to free the slaves.

### INSTRUCT: OBJECTIVE 4

**Slave Rebellions**

Key Questions
- Who was Nat Turner?
- What were the effects of Turner's rebellion?

### ASSESS & RETEACH

**Setting the Stage** Have students place information about slavery in the second cause-and-effect box on the graphic.

**Formal Assessment**
- Section Quiz, p. 174

**RETEACHING ACTIVITY**

Organize the class into small groups. Assign one of the section's illustrations to each group member. Ask each student to write a paragraph about the significance of the subject of that illustration to the section's Main Idea. Have group members compile their paragraphs into a booklet. Make photocopies of the booklets and distribute them to students.

**In-Depth Resources: Unit 3**
- Reteaching Activity, p. 55

### Section 2 Assessment

**1. Terms & Names**

**Eli Whitney,** p. 348
**cotton gin,** p. 348
**spirituals,** p. 351
**Nat Turner,** p. 353

**2. Taking Notes**

slaveholding whites: one-third of population, wealthy, powerful; nonslaveholding whites: small farms, supported slavery; enslaved blacks: one-third of the Southern population, variety of jobs; free blacks: 8 percent of population in the South; most lived in cities, where more work was available

**3. Main Ideas**

**a.** more efficient production, larger area to work, need for slaves increased **b.** Plantation slaves were field workers, city slaves held a variety of jobs, free blacks lived in cities. **c.** secret visits, escape, rebellions, antislavery religious beliefs

**4. Critical Thinking**

They feared that rebellions would spread across the South.

**ACTIVITY OPTIONS**

**Alternative Assessment**
- Rubrics for a book report, 4.7
- Rubrics for oral interpretation, 3.6

## SECTION OBJECTIVES

1. To describe efforts to make the United States self-sufficient and to improve transportation
2. To explain the growth of national unity and the settling of boundaries
3. To analyze sectional tensions and the compromises that lessened them
4. To explain the Monroe Doctrine

**SKILLBUILDER**

Interpreting Maps: Movement, Region, p. 355
Interpreting Maps: Location, Region, pp. 357, 358

**CRITICAL THINKING**

Recognizing Effects, pp. 355, 359
Finding Main Ideas, p. 356
Analyzing Causes, p. 357
Analyzing Points of View, p. 358

 **Why It Matters Now**
- Expanding Economies, pp. 21–22

## FOCUS & MOTIVATE

### 5-MINUTE WARM-UP

**Making Inferences** These questions focus on nationalism and sectionalism.

1. Look at "A Voice from the Past" on page 354. What do you think Henry Clay is suggesting?
2. How does Clay think independence is achieved?

 **Warm-Up Transparency WT11**

## INSTRUCT

### INSTRUCT: OBJECTIVE 

**Nationalism Unites the Country/ Roads and Canals Link Cities**

Key Questions
- What was the American System?
- How was transportation improved?

**In-Depth Resources: Unit 3**
- Guided Reading, p. 44

**Reading Study Guide** (Spanish and English), pp. 115–116

# 3 Nationalism and Sectionalism

**TERMS & NAMES**
nationalism
Henry Clay
American System
Erie Canal
James Monroe
sectionalism
Missouri Compromise
Monroe Doctrine

| MAIN IDEA | WHY IT MATTERS NOW |
|---|---|
| Patriotic pride united the states, but tension between the North and South emerged. | The tension led to the Civil War, and regional differences can still be found in the United States today. |

## ONE AMERICAN'S STORY

**In the early 1800s, as you have read, the North began to industrialize and the South relied more heavily on growing cotton. At the same time, a rising sense of nationalism pulled people from different regions together. Nationalism is a feeling of pride, loyalty, and protectiveness toward your country. The War of 1812 sent a wave of nationalist feeling through the United States.**

**Representative Henry Clay, from Kentucky, was a strong nationalist. After the war, President James Madison supported Clay's plan to strengthen the country and unify its different regions.**

*A VOICE FROM THE PAST*

Every nation should anxiously endeavor to establish its absolute independence, and consequently be able to feed and clothe and defend itself. If it rely upon a foreign supply that may be cut off . . . it cannot be independent.

**Henry Clay**, quoted in *The Annals of America*

Henry Clay

**In this section, you will learn how nationalism affected U.S. economic growth and foreign policy. You'll also see how Americans were beginning to be torn between the interests of their own regions and those of the country as a whole.**

## 1 Nationalism Unites the Country

In 1815, President Madison presented a plan to Congress for making the United States economically self-sufficient. In other words, the country would prosper and grow by itself, without foreign products or foreign markets.

The plan—which Henry Clay promoted as the **American System**—included three main actions.

1. **Establish a protective tariff,** a tax on imported goods that protects a nation's businesses from foreign competition. Congress passed a tariff in 1816. It made European goods more expensive and encouraged Americans to buy cheaper American-made products.

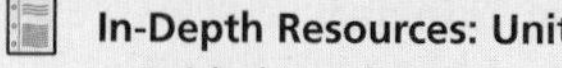

### RECOMMENDED RESOURCES

**In-Depth Resources: Unit 3**
- Guided Reading, p. 44
- Building Vocabulary, p. 45
- Skillbuilder Practice, p. 46
- Reteaching Activity, p. 56

**Reading Study Guide** (Spanish and English), pp. 115–116

**Outline Map Activities**
- Economic Expansion, 1841, pp. 21–22

**Why It Matters Now**
- Expanding Economies, pp. 21–22

**Citizenship Today,** pp. 89–90

**Formal Assessment**
- Section Quiz, p. 175

**Alternative Assessment**
- Rubrics, 4.1
- Rubrics, 1.2

**Access for Students Acquiring English/ESL**
- Guided Reading, p. 75
- Skillbuilder Practice, p. 76

Technology Resources

 **Geography Transparency GT11**
- Railroads Extend Westward, 1850–1860

 **Electronic Teacher Tools with Test Maker**

 **ClassZone**
www.mcdougallittell.com

*Reading*History

**A. Recognizing Effects** How would the three parts of the American System help to make the country self-sufficient?

A. Answer A tariff would protect businesses; a national bank and improved transportation would make internal trade easier.

2. **Establish a national bank** that would promote a single currency, making trade easier. (Most regional banks issued their own money.) In 1816, Congress set up the second Bank of the United States.
3. **Improve the country's transportation systems,** which were important for a strong economy. Poor roads made transportation slow and costly.

## Roads and Canals Link Cities

Representative John C. Calhoun of South Carolina also called for better transportation systems. "Let us bind the Republic together with a perfect system of roads and canals," he declared in 1817. Earlier, in 1806, Congress had funded a road from Cumberland, Maryland, to Wheeling, Virginia. By 1841, the National Road, designed as the country's main east-west route, had been extended to Vandalia, Illinois.

Water transportation improved, too, with the building of canals. In fact, the period from 1825 to 1850 is often called the Age of Canals. Completed in 1825, the massive **Erie Canal** created a water route between New York City and Buffalo, New York. The canal opened the upper Ohio Valley and the Great Lakes region to settlement and trade. It also fueled nationalism by unifying these two sections of the country.

The Erie Canal allowed farm products from the Great Lakes region to flow east and people and manufactured goods from the East to flow

Skillbuilder Answers
1. a route including Lake Erie, the Erie Canal, and the Hudson River
2. the North

### MORE ABOUT . . .

**The Erie Canal**

Building the Erie Canal took more than eight years. The canal's route crossed 363 miles of wilderness and hilly terrain. Engineers had to construct more than 80 locks to raise and lower ships where elevation changed along the route. When the canal opened, freight rates between Albany and Buffalo dropped from $100 per ton to a mere $9 per ton.

For passengers, traveling by canal boat was more comfortable than traveling by coach over bumpy roads—but not by much. Several times an hour, everyone on the boat had to flop down flat on the deck as they passed under one of the many bridges that crossed the canal. As the folk song about the canal puts it:

*Low bridge—everybody down!*
*Low bridge—'cause we're comin' to a town.*

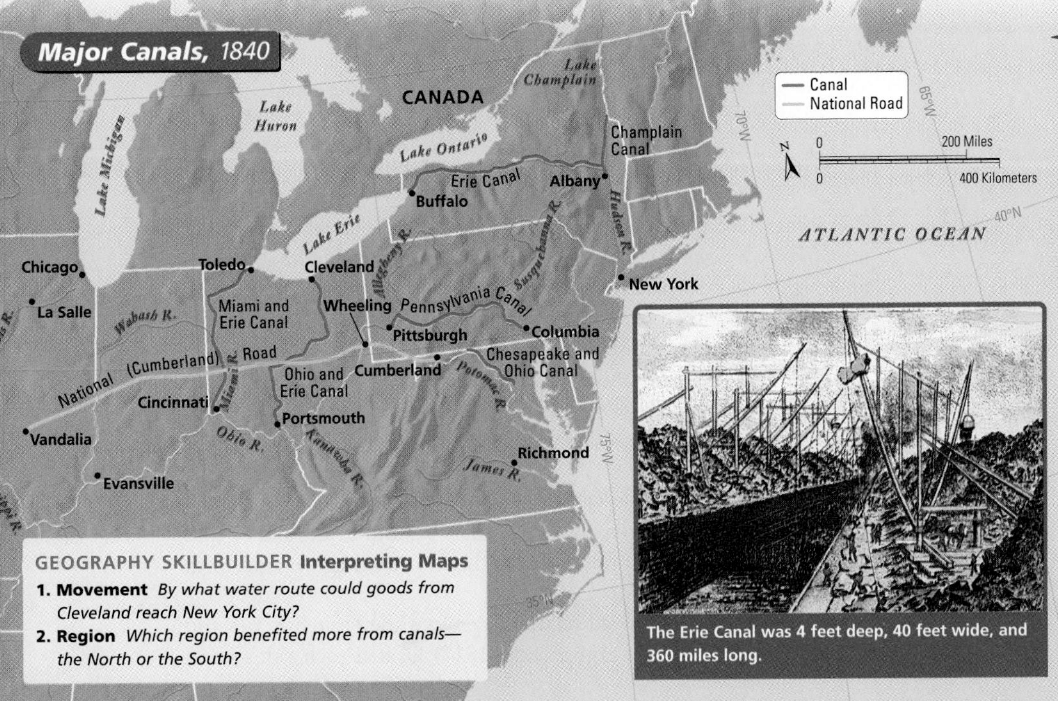


GEOGRAPHY SKILLBUILDER **Interpreting Maps**
1. **Movement** *By what water route could goods from Cleveland reach New York City?*
2. **Region** *Which region benefited more from canals—the North or the South?*

The Erie Canal was 4 feet deep, 40 feet wide, and 360 miles long.

355

### HISTORY FROM VISUALS

**Reading the Map** Ask students to identify cities that likely developed because of the canal system. **Possible Responses** Buffalo, Cleveland, Toledo, Chicago, Albany, Syracuse, Pittsburgh, Columbia, Portsmouth, Cincinnati, Evansville, La Salle, Richmond. Then ask what impact transportation systems have on the development of cities.

**Extension** Ask students to compare the interstate highway system built since the 1950s to the canal boom in its effects.

**Outline Map Activities**
• Economic Expansion, 1841, pp. 21–22

**Geography Transparency GT11**
• Railroads Extend Westward, 1850–1860

### ACTIVITY OPTIONS

### INTERDISCIPLINARY LINK: GEOGRAPHY

BLOCK SCHEDULING

**TRANSPORTATION MAP**

**Class Time** One class period

**Task** Creating a state transportation map

**Purpose** To help students explore the importance of efficient transportation networks to unite large areas

**Supplies Needed**
- Topographic and political maps of your state
- An outline map of your state
- Drawing paper
- Colored pencils or markers

**Activity** Ask students to suppose that they are planning a transportation network for their state in 1840. Their state is only sparsely settled and has no important roads, canals, and railroads yet. Have students use a topographic map to identify major rivers and other important physical features. Then have them use that information to complete a map showing efficient routes for roads, canals, and railroads. Where might towns develop? Use these maps in discussing how transportation helped unite the young United States.

**INSTRUCT: OBJECTIVE 2**

**The Era of Good Feelings/ Settling National Boundaries**

Key Questions

- Why was Monroe's administration called the Era of Good Feelings?
- How did Supreme Court decisions promote national unity?
- How did the United States settle disputes with Britain and Spain in the early 1800s?

**MORE ABOUT . . .**

**John Marshall**

John Marshall is a towering figure in the history of the judicial branch of the government. He served as chief justice (1801–1835) longer than any other man. He helped to make the Supreme Court as important as Congress and the presidency. In cases such as *Marbury* v. *Madison* (1803) and *McCulloch* v. *Maryland* (1819), Marshall helped define the power of the Court to determine whether acts of Congress or the president violated the Constitution. It was while tolling for Marshall's funeral in 1835 that the Liberty Bell cracked.

 **Citizenship Today,** pp. 85–86

**MORE ABOUT . . .**

***Gibbons* v. *Ogden***

You may wish to point out that in *Gibbons* v. *Ogden*, the Supreme Court was guided by the Commerce Clause (Article I, Section 8) of the Constitution. That clause specifically gives the federal government the power to regulate interstate commerce. Congress also used the Commerce Clause to justify the passage of the Civil Rights Act of 1964. That law banned racial discrimination in hotels, restaurants, theaters, and other public places.

west. Trade stimulated by the canal helped New York City become the nation's largest city. Between 1820 and 1830, its population swelled from less than 125,000 to more than 200,000.

Around the 1830s, the nation began to use steam-powered trains for transportation. In 1830, only about 30 miles of track existed in the United States. But by 1850, the number had climbed to 9,000 miles. Improvements in rail travel led to a decline in the use of canals.

## 2 The Era of Good Feelings

James Monroe

As nationalist feelings spread, people slowly shifted their loyalty away from state governments and more toward the federal government. Democratic-Republican **James Monroe** won the presidency in 1816 with a large majority of electoral votes. The Federalist Party provided little opposition to Monroe and soon disappeared. Political differences gave way to what one Boston newspaper called the Era of Good Feelings.

During the Monroe administration, several landmark Supreme Court decisions promoted national unity by strengthening the federal government. For example, in *McCulloch* v. *Maryland* (1819), the state of Maryland wanted to tax its branch of the national bank. If this tax were allowed, the states could claim to have power over the federal government. The Court upheld federal authority by ruling that a state could not tax a national bank.

**Background** Maryland also argued that Congress had no power to create the bank, but the court ruled that it did have such power.

*A VOICE FROM THE PAST*

The States have no power, by taxation or otherwise, to retard, impede, burden, or in any manner control the operations of the constitutional laws enacted by Congress.

**Chief Justice John Marshall,** *McCulloch* v. *Maryland* (1819)

Another Court decision that strengthened the federal government was *Gibbons* v. *Ogden* (1824). Two steamship operators fought over shipping rights on the Hudson River in New York and New Jersey. The Court ruled that interstate commerce could be regulated only by the federal government, not the state governments.

The Supreme Court under John Marshall clearly stated important powers of the federal government. A stronger federal government reflected a growing nationalist spirit.

***Reading*History**
**B. Finding Main Ideas** How did the Supreme Court strengthen the federal government?
**B. Answer** By ruling that states could not interfere with federal laws and that only the federal government could regulate interstate commerce.

## Settling National Boundaries

This nationalist spirit also made U.S. leaders want to define and expand the country's borders. To do this, they had to reach agreements with Britain and Spain.

Two agreements improved relations between the United States and Britain. The Rush-Bagot Agreement (1817) limited each side's naval



**ACTIVITY OPTIONS**

**INTERDISCIPLINARY LINK: GOVERNMENT** — BLOCK SCHEDULING

**BROCHURES**

**Class Time** 20 minutes

**Task** Creating a brochure

**Purpose** To show how the actions of all three branches of the federal government contributed to nationalism and a stronger central government

**Supplies Needed**

- Drawing paper
- Colored pencils or markers

**Activity** Have pairs of students create a brochure titled "Uniting the Country." In the brochure, students should list and illustrate actions taken by the legislative, executive, and judicial branches that helped unite the nation and strengthen the federal government during the early 1800s.

**Answers** Legislative: protective tariff, national bank, transportation network. Executive: negotiated foreign agreements that settled national boundaries. Judicial: Supreme Court decisions, such as *McCulloch* v. *Maryland* (1819) and *Gibbons* v. *Ogden* (1824)

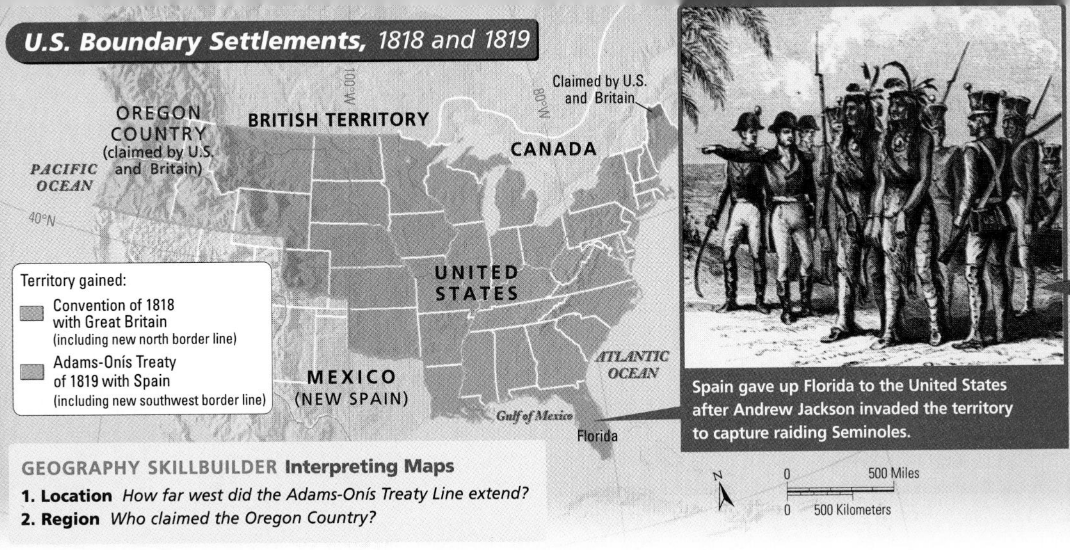


Spain gave up Florida to the United States after Andrew Jackson invaded the territory to capture raiding Seminoles.

**GEOGRAPHY SKILLBUILDER Interpreting Maps**

**1. Location** *How far west did the Adams-Onís Treaty Line extend?*

**2. Region** *Who claimed the Oregon Country?*

forces on the Great Lakes. In the Convention of 1818, the two countries set the 49th parallel as the U.S.-Canadian border as far west as the Rocky Mountains.

But U.S. relations with Spain were tense. The two nations disagreed on the boundaries of the Louisiana Purchase and the ownership of West Florida. Meanwhile, pirates and runaway slaves used Spanish-held East Florida as a refuge. In addition, the Seminoles of East Florida raided white settlements in Georgia to reclaim lost lands.

In 1817, President Monroe ordered General Andrew Jackson to stop the Seminole raids, but not to confront the Spanish. Jackson followed the Seminoles into Spanish territory and then claimed the Floridas for the United States.

Monroe ordered Jackson to withdraw but gave Spain a choice. It could either police the Floridas or turn them over to the United States. In the Adams-Onís Treaty of 1819, Spain handed Florida to the United States and gave up claims to the Oregon Country. The map above shows boundaries drawn and territories gained in 1818 and 1819.

Skillbuilder Answers
1. to the Pacific Ocean
2. both the United States and Great Britain

*Reading* **History**
**C. Analyzing Causes** Why did Andrew Jackson invade East Florida?
C. Answer President Monroe ordered him to stop the Seminole raids.

## ❸ Sectional Tensions Increase

At the same time nationalism was unifying the country, sectionalism was threatening to drive it apart. **Sectionalism** is loyalty to the interests of your own region or section of the country, rather than to the nation as a whole. Economic changes had created some divisions within the United States. As you have seen, white Southerners were relying more on cotton and slavery. In the Northeast, wealth was based on manufacturing and trade. In the West, settlers wanted cheap land and good transportation. The interests of these sections were often in conflict.

Sectionalism became a major issue when Missouri applied for statehood in 1817. People living in Missouri wanted to allow slavery in their state. At the time, the United States consisted of 11 slave states and 11



### HISTORY FROM VISUALS

**Reading the Map** Point out that the United States was bounded on three sides by British and Spanish possessions. Ask students why establishing firm boundaries with these powers was important. **Possible Responses** Firm boundaries would limit disputes that might lead to war. They also would make previous U.S. territorial expansion more secure.

**Extension** Ask students to find state boundaries that, like the U.S.–Canada border, follow parallels of latitude. What is another common way of determining boundaries? **Answer** rivers

### INSTRUCT: OBJECTIVE ❸

**Sectional Tensions Increase/ The Missouri Compromise**

Key Questions
- How did economic changes contribute to growing sectionalism?
- Why did the question of admitting Missouri to the Union divide the nation?
- How did the Missouri Compromise address the issue of slavery in U.S. territories and future states?

### ACTIVITY OPTIONS

**INDIVIDUAL NEEDS: GIFTED AND TALENTED**

**NATIONALISM/SECTIONALISM**

**Class Time** One class period

**Task** Creating a political advertisement that expresses a point of view

**Purpose** To identify and summarize opinions of nationalists and sectionalists

**Supplies Needed**
- Audio recorder and tapes (optional)
- Video recorder and tapes (optional)

**Activity** Have individual students adopt the viewpoint of a citizen who supports nationalism (the concept of loyalty to one's nation as a whole) or the viewpoint of a citizen who supports sectionalism (loyalty to one's region or section of the country). Ask students to write radio or TV ads of no longer than 30 seconds that express their points of view. Remind them to include facts and information that could persuade listeners to adopt their viewpoint. Record or videotape their ads so students can listen to themselves.

## HISTORY FROM VISUALS

**Reading the Map** Ask the students how much of the unorganized U.S. territory west of Missouri and Illinois was open to slavery. **Answer** None north of Missouri Compromise line. South of the line was blocked by New Spain. Ask students how those facts might contribute to increasing tensions between slave and free states. **Possible Responses** People in slave states might fear that free states would soon outnumber slave states.

**Extension** Have students research the history of slavery in Mexico to find when it began and ended. **Answer** Slavery in New Spain dated back to the first decades of the Spanish conquest. However, by the early 1800s, slavery (and Spanish power) was fading in much of Latin America. Mexico abolished slavery in 1829.

## MORE ABOUT . . .

**The Missouri Compromise**
Thomas Jefferson, for one, realized that the Missouri Compromise was a temporary solution to a serious problem. He called it "a fire bell in the night" that filled him with terror. The dispute between North and South, he said, was "a speck on our horizon" that might eventually "burst on us as a tornado." John Quincy Adams called the Missouri Compromise "a mere preamble—a title-page to a great, tragic volume."

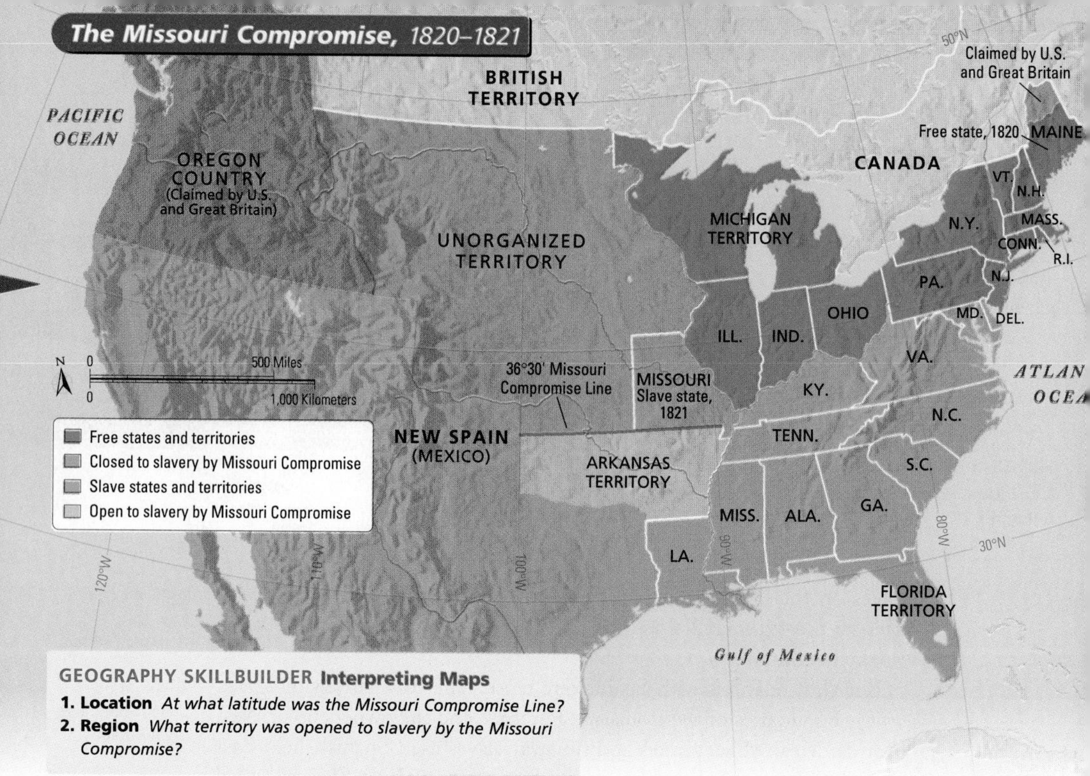


**GEOGRAPHY SKILLBUILDER Interpreting Maps**
1. **Location** *At what latitude was the Missouri Compromise Line?*
2. **Region** *What territory was opened to slavery by the Missouri Compromise?*

Skillbuilder Answers
1. 36° 30′ N
2. Arkansas Territory

free states. Adding Missouri as a slave state would upset the balance of power in Congress. The question of Missouri soon divided the nation.

## The Missouri Compromise

For months, the nation argued over admitting Missouri as a slave state or a free state. Debate raged in Congress over a proposal made by James Tallmadge of New York to ban slavery in Missouri. Angry Southerners claimed that the Constitution did not give Congress the power to ban slavery. They worried that free states could form a majority in Congress and ban slavery altogether. Representative Thomas Cobb of Georgia expressed the Southerners' point of view when he responded to Tallmadge.

*ReadingHistory*
**D. Analyzing Points of View** Why was it so important to Southerners to admit Missouri as a slave state?
**D. Answer** They feared that having more free states than slave states would enable Congress to ban slavery and overturn the South's economic system.

*A VOICE FROM THE PAST*

If you persist, the Union will be dissolved. You have kindled a fire which all the waters of the ocean cannot put out, which seas of blood can only extinguish.

**Thomas Cobb,** quoted in *Henry Clay: Statesman for the Union*

Meanwhile, Maine, which had been part of Massachusetts, also wanted statehood. Henry Clay, the Speaker of the House, saw a chance for compromise. He suggested that Missouri be admitted as a slave state and Maine as a free state. Congress passed Clay's plan, known as the **Missouri Compromise,** in 1820. It kept the balance of power in the Senate



## ACTIVITY OPTIONS

### SKILLBUILDER MINI-LESSON: COMPARING AND CONTRASTING

BLOCK SCHEDULING

**Explaining the Skill** Historians compare and contrast events, people, ideas, and other things in order to understand them well. Comparing involves finding similarities and differences between things. Contrasting means examining only the differences between them.

**Applying the Skill** Ask students to review what they have learned about the North and the South. Then ask the following questions.

1. Contrast the economies of the North and the South. *(North: wealth based on manufacturing and trade; South: relied on cotton and slavery)*
2. Compare the two regions' boundary disputes with foreign powers. *(Similarity: Both had unsettled boundaries with European powers. Difference: The North's dispute was with Britain; the South's, with Spain.)*

 **In-Depth Resources: Unit 3**
- Skillbuilder Practice, p. 46

between the slave states and free states. It also called for slavery to be banned from the Louisiana Territory north of the parallel 36° 30', Missouri's southern border.

> "If you persist, the Union will be dissolved."
>
> Thomas Cobb

Thomas Jefferson, nearing 80 years old and living quietly in Virginia, was troubled by the Missouri Compromise. Worried that sectionalism would destroy the country, Jefferson wrote: "In the gloomiest moment of the Revolutionary War I never had any apprehension equal to what I feel from this source."

## 4 The Monroe Doctrine

**Background** *Latin America* refers to the nations of the Western Hemisphere south of the United States.

The nation felt threatened not only by sectionalism, but by events elsewhere in the Americas. In Latin America, several countries had successfully fought for their independence from Spain and Portugal. Some European monarchies planned to help Spain and Portugal regain their colonies, hoping to keep the urge to revolt from reaching Europe. U.S. leaders feared that if this happened, their own government would be in danger.

Russian colonies in the Pacific Northwest also concerned Americans. The Russians entered Alaska in 1784. By 1812, their trading posts reached almost to San Francisco.

In December 1823, President Monroe issued a statement that became known as the **Monroe Doctrine.** (See Interactive Primary Source, page 360.) Monroe said that the Americas were closed to further colonization. He also warned that European efforts to reestablish colonies would be considered "dangerous to our peace and safety." Finally, he promised that the United States would stay out of European affairs. The Monroe Doctrine showed that the United States saw itself as a world power and protector of Latin America.

In Chapter 12, you will learn how a new democratic spirit grew—and how Native Americans suffered—during Andrew Jackson's presidency.

### Section 3 Assessment

**1. Terms & Names**

**Identify:**
- nationalism
- Henry Clay
- American System
- Erie Canal
- James Monroe
- sectionalism
- Missouri Compromise
- Monroe Doctrine

**2. Taking Notes**

On a diagram like the one below, name things that contributed to national unity in the early 1800s.

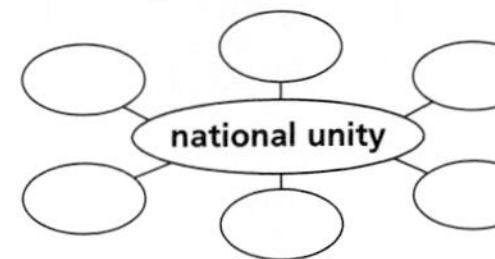


Which of these are still important for national unity?

**3. Main Ideas**

a. How did the Erie Canal help the nation grow?

b. How did the Missouri Compromise resolve a conflict between the North and South?

c. What was the main message of the Monroe Doctrine, and who was it directed toward?

**4. Critical Thinking**

**Recognizing Effects** If the Supreme Court had decided differently in *Gibbons* v. *Ogden* or *McCulloch* v. *Maryland,* what might be one result today?

**THINK ABOUT**
- if states could interfere with federal laws
- if states controlled interstate commerce

**ACTIVITY OPTIONS**

**LANGUAGE ARTS / ART** In an **editorial** or a **political cartoon,** give your opinion of either the Missouri Compromise or the Monroe Doctrine.





**INSTRUCT: OBJECTIVE** 

**The Monroe Doctrine**

Key Questions
- Why did events in the early 1800s in Latin America concern the United States?
- What was the purpose of the Monroe Doctrine?

**MORE ABOUT . . .**

**The Monroe Doctrine**

The Monroe Doctrine has been an important basis for American foreign policy since 1823. At that time, the United States was not in a position to enforce the Monroe Doctrine, as it came to be known some years later. However, in the 1840s, President Polk invoked the doctrine when he warned Britain and Spain not to make settlements in Oregon, California, or in Mexico. President Theodore Roosevelt expanded the Monroe Doctrine in 1904 with the addition of the "Roosevelt Corollary," which states that European nations may not use force to collect debts from Latin American nations.

## ASSESS & RETEACH

**Setting the Stage** Have students place information about slavery and foreign relations in the appropriate box on the graphic organizer.

 **Formal Assessment**
- Section Quiz, p. 175

 **Critical Thinking Transparency CT31**
- Setting the Stage

**RETEACHING ACTIVITY**

Have students write a summary paragraph that uses the section's Main Idea as the topic sentence. The paragraph should identify the things that contributed to a feeling of nationalism and the tensions that over time contributed to sectionalism.

 **In-Depth Resources: Unit 3**
- Reteaching Activity, p. 56

### Section 3 Assessment

**1. Terms & Names**

**nationalism,** p. 354
**Henry Clay,** p. 354
**American System,** p. 354
**Erie Canal,** p. 355
**James Monroe,** p. 356
**sectionalism,** p. 357
**Missouri Compromise,** p. 358
**Monroe Doctrine,** p. 359

**2. Taking Notes**

protective tariffs, national bank, road and canal systems, strong federal government, settled national boundaries

transportation and strong federal government

**3. Main Ideas**

**a.** It opened the upper Ohio Valley and Great Lakes regions to settlement and trade. **b.** It kept the balance of slave and free states in the Senate. **c.** Europe should not colonize the Americas; directed toward Europeans

**4. Critical Thinking**

The federal government would be much weaker, and there would be greater state rivalries.

**ACTIVITY OPTIONS**

 **Alternative Assessment**
- Rubrics for an editorial, 4.1
- Rubrics for a political cartoon, 1.2

## INTERACTIVE PRIMARY SOURCE

**OBJECTIVE**
Students will understand that the Monroe Doctrine declares that the United States will not interfere with the internal affairs or wars of European countries nor with existing European colonies in the Americas, and that the Western Hemisphere was not open to further colonization.

Primary Source Explorer
• *The Monroe Doctrine*

The Explorer will help students select and produce their own presentations.

Specific information about the document can be found in **A Closer Look.** To learn more about key people and events of the time, students should click on **Life in These Times. What Happened Next** will show the student the impact of the document and tie it to today.

## FOCUS & MOTIVATE

**Identifying and Solving Problems** Ask students to recall the nations that have claims to lands in the Americas. Ask why the United States might view those nations as a threat in 1823. **Possible Answer** Britain, Spain, France, Portugal and Russia. They were powerful nations and earlier had been fighting each other. Now they were not fighting and wanted land claims in the Americas.

### MORE ABOUT . . .

**Reasons for Monroe's Statements**
Great Britain had sent a proposal to the United States suggesting that the two nations join in issuing a statement condemning European efforts to regain control of former colonies in the Western Hemisphere. John Quincy Adams, secretary of state to Monroe, said, "It would be more candid, as well as more dignified, to avow our principles explicitly to Russia and France than to come as a cock-boat [row boat] in the wake of the British man-of-war."

## INTERACTIVE PRIMARY SOURCE

# The Monroe Doctrine

**Setting the Stage** On December 6, 1823, President James Monroe gave a State of the Union address. Part of the speech became known as the Monroe Doctrine. The "allied powers" Monroe refers to are Russia, Prussia, Austria, and France. Earlier in the year, these European monarchies had crushed a revolution in Spain and restored the Spanish king to his throne. They were threatening to help Spain regain its Latin American colonies. See **Primary Source Explorer**

**A CLOSER LOOK**

**NO FUTURE COLONIES**

Monroe declares that European countries may not start any new colonies in the Americas.

**1. Why might it threaten the United States to have new European colonies near them?**

**A CLOSER LOOK**

**NEUTRALITY TOWARD EUROPE**

Monroe says that the United States will not take sides in European wars.

**2. Why might the United States want to remain neutral toward conflicts in Europe?**

[T]he occasion has been judged proper for asserting, as a principle in which the rights and interests of the United States are involved, that the American continents, by the free and independent condition which they have assumed and maintain, are henceforth not to be considered as subjects for future colonization by any European powers. . . .

It was stated at the commencement of the last session that great effort was then making in Spain and Portugal to improve the condition of the people of those countries and that it appeared to be conducted with extraordinary moderation. It need scarcely be remarked that the result has been so far very different from what was then anticipated. . . . The citizens of the United States cherish sentiments the most friendly in favor of the liberty and happiness of their fellowmen on that side of the Atlantic. In the wars of the European powers in matters relating to themselves we have never taken any part, nor does it **comport**[1] with our policy so to do. It is only when our rights are invaded or seriously **menaced**[2] that we resent injuries or make preparation for our defense.

With the movements in this hemisphere we are of necessity more immediately connected, and by causes which must be obvious to all enlightened and impartial observers. The political system of the allied powers is essentially different in this respect from that of America. This difference proceeds from that which exists in their respective governments; and to the defense of our own, which has been achieved by the loss of so much blood and treasure, and matured by the wisdom of their most enlightened citizens, and under which we have enjoyed **unexampled felicity**,[3] this whole nation is devoted. We owe it, therefore, to **candor**[4] and to the **amicable**[5] relations existing between the

1. **comport:** agree with.
2. **menaced:** threatened.
3. **unexampled felicity:** the greatest happiness.
4. **candor:** honesty.
5. **amicable:** friendly.



### TEACHING STRATEGY

**Analyzing** Tell students that President Monroe addressed the threat of European nations helping Spain regain its former colonies in South America. Americans strongly supported the new Latin American republics. In addition, Britain seemed interested in taking over Cuba. Read the selection to the class. Pause after every sentence and ask students to explain the sentence in their own words. When you have worked through the document with the class, ask students to identify where in the document Monroe addresses the European threats and American hopes for Latin America. Then complete the cause-and-effect graphic on the right.

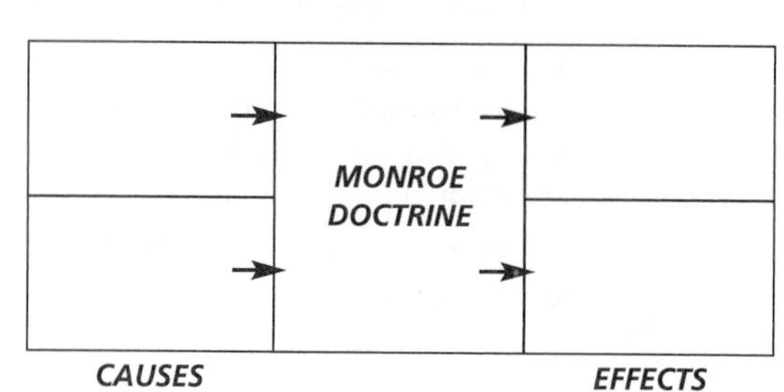

United States and those powers to declare that we should consider any attempt on their part to extend their system to any portion of this hemisphere as dangerous to our peace and safety.

With the existing colonies or dependencies of any European power we have not interfered and shall not interfere. But with the governments who have declared their independence and maintained it, and whose independence we have, on great consideration and on just principles, acknowledged, we could not view any **interposition**[6] for the purpose of oppressing them, or controlling in any other manner their destiny, by any European power in any other light than as the manifestation of an unfriendly disposition toward the United States. In the war between those new governments and Spain we declared our neutrality at the time of their recognition, and to this we have adhered and shall continue to adhere, provided no change shall occur which, in the judgment of the competent authorities of this government, shall make a corresponding change on the part of the United States indispensable to their security.

The late events in Spain and Portugal show that Europe is still unsettled. Of this important fact no stronger proof can be adduced than that the allied powers should have thought it proper, on any principle satisfactory to themselves, to have interposed by force in the internal concerns of Spain. To what extent such interposition may be carried, on the same principle, is a question in which all independent powers whose governments differ from theirs are interested, even those most remote, and surely none more so than the United States.

—*James Monroe*

6. **interposition:** interference.

***A CLOSER LOOK***

**A DIFFERENT SYSTEM**

Monroe states that the United States will defend its republican form of government and would be threatened if Europeans set up monarchies in the Americas.

**3. Why would U.S. citizens want their government to be a republic and not an absolute monarchy?**

***A CLOSER LOOK***

**NO INTERFERENCE**

Monroe warns that if Europeans invade the newly independent republics in Latin America, this would be considered hostile to the United States as well.

**4. What would the United States have to fear if these republics were overthrown?**

*Interactive Primary Source Assessment*

**1. Main Ideas**

a. Why might the United States want no more European colonies in the Americas, particularly in Latin America?

b. How would staying neutral in European wars protect the United States?

c. How might the U.S. system of government be threatened if Europeans regained control of former colonies in the Americas?

**2. Critical Thinking**

**Making Inferences** For decades, the United States lacked the military power to enforce the Monroe Doctrine and depended on the British navy to keep other European powers out of Latin America. Why, then, did the United States proclaim the Monroe Doctrine?

**THINK ABOUT**

- what the doctrine shows about the values and wishes of the United States
- what it shows about how the country saw itself or wanted to be seen

361

## INSTRUCT

Key Questions

- What was the major purpose of Monroe's statements?
- What position does Monroe say that the United States will maintain in European wars?
- What reason does Monroe give for United States concern over events in Latin America?
- How does Monroe say that the United States would view any interference by European nations with the governments of Latin America?

### MAKING PERSONAL CONNECTIONS

Ask students whether they are more interested in national or local news. Discuss why events in their own neighborhood are important to them. Use a map to show the Western Hemisphere and reminds students that the nations of the Americas are "neighbors" of the United States.

### MORE ABOUT . . .

**Invoking the Monroe Doctrine**

The United States cited the Monroe Doctrine when it opposed European interest in building a canal across Central America. In 1895, the United States invoked the Monroe Doctrine when it forced Great Britain and Venezuela to arbitrate a dispute about the boundary between Venezuela and British Guiana. The doctrine was also invoked when the United States sent troops to Nicaragua, Haiti, Guatemala, Cuba, the Dominican Republic, Grenada, and Panama to prevent feared Communist takeovers and civil wars.

### *Interactive Primary Source Assessment*

**1. Main Ideas**

a. The United States might fear colonies in Latin America because of the closeness of borders and because new European colonies might threaten trade or wage war involving the United States.

b. protection from one-sided attack and from committing troops to aid an ally

c. European powers might be tempted to try to take control of the United States.

**2. Critical Thinking**

The United States wanted respect from other nations, hoped the doctrine would help it negotiate settlements, and wanted to uphold the principles of freedom and independence on which it was founded.

### *A CLOSER LOOK*

1. New colonies might have boundary conflicts with the United States, interfere with trade, be on land that the United States wants to acquire, or be battlegrounds in future European wars.
2. It might remain neutral to avoid being attacked, to avoid having to commit troops or funds, to be able to trade with both sides, or to better concentrate on its own affairs.
3. because people want to act in their own interest by electing representatives to make decisions for them instead of having decisions made by a hereditary ruler acting in his or her own interest
4. fear that European nations would invade the United States and return it to colonial status, or that European rulers might outlaw U.S. trade with their colonies or have their military forces blockade U.S. ports

## TERMS & NAMES

1. **Samuel Slater,** p. 341
2. **Industrial Revolution,** p. 341
3. **Robert Fulton,** p. 344
4. **Eli Whitney,** p. 348
5. **cotton gin,** p. 348
6. **Nat Turner,** p. 353
7. **nationalism,** p. 354
8. **sectionalism,** p.357
9. **Missouri Compromise,** p. 358
10. **Monroe Doctrine,** p. 359

## REVIEW QUESTIONS

**Possible Responses**

1. The British blockade forced Americans to develop their own industries.
2. They provided power for factories and transportation for raw materials and finished goods.
3. expanded trade; transportation; national unity
4. sped up production; made repairs easy; allowed use of low-paid, unskilled labor
5. The cotton gin made it easier to raise short-fibered cotton, which grew in many parts of the South. Slavery provided the large work force needed on the plantations.
6. difficult work; severe punishment; separation from family
7. They had faith that God would end slavery. They sang religious spirituals for comfort.
8. It limited state powers by ruling that no state could tax a national bank.
9. Spain gave it to the United States in 1819 with the Adams-Onís Treaty.
10. Maine entered as a free state while Missouri entered as a slave state, and slavery was banned above the 36°30′ parallel.

## VISUAL SUMMARY

### Early Industry and Inventions

New machines allowed the Northeast to industrialize and the Midwest to increase farm production.

### Plantations and Slavery Spread

The cotton gin led to the expansion of plantations and slavery in the South.

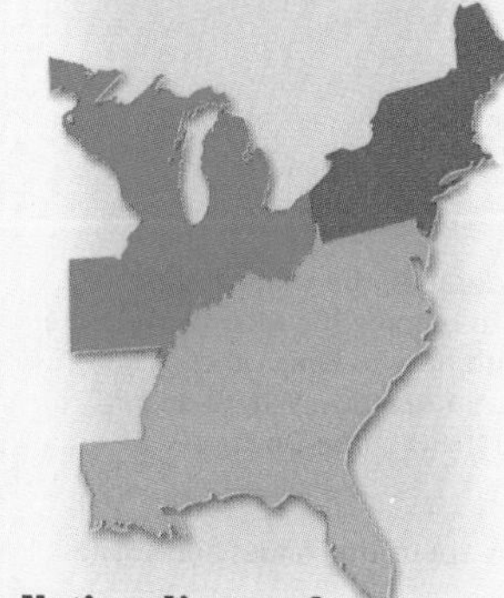

### Nationalism and Sectionalism

Nationalism drew regions together. At the same time, economic differences created tension between regions.



# Chapter 11 ASSESSMENT

## TERMS & NAMES

Briefly explain the importance of each of the following.

1. Samuel Slater
2. Industrial Revolution
3. Robert Fulton
4. Eli Whitney
5. cotton gin
6. Nat Turner
7. nationalism
8. sectionalism
9. Missouri Compromise
10. Monroe Doctrine

## REVIEW QUESTIONS

**Early Industry and Inventions (pages 341–347)**

1. How did the War of 1812 push the United States to build factories?
2. Why did its many rivers make the Northeast a good place to build early factories?
3. What was one effect of the steamboat?
4. How did interchangeable parts transform the manufacturing process?

**Plantations and Slavery Spread (pages 348–353)**

5. Why did slavery spread in the South?
6. What were three hardships faced by enslaved people on plantations?
7. How did religion help people endure or resist slavery?

**Nationalism and Sectionalism (pages 354–361)**

8. How did the Supreme Court's ruling in *McCulloch v. Maryland* strengthen the federal government?
9. How did the United States gain the territory of Florida?
10. What were the terms of the Missouri Compromise?

## CRITICAL THINKING

**1. USING YOUR NOTES**

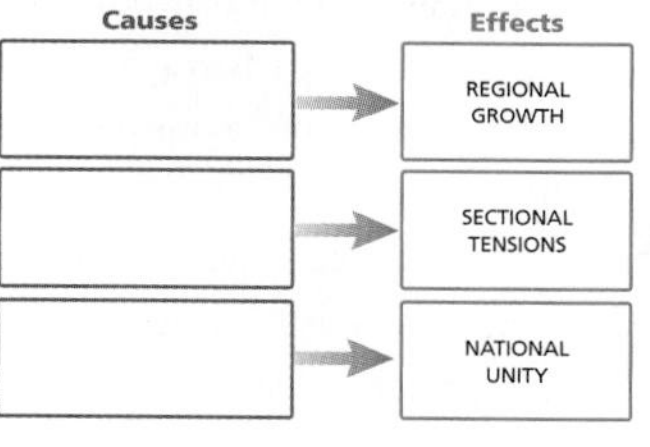


Using your completed chart, answer the questions.

a. What were three causes leading to national unity?
b. What was one cause of sectional tension?

**2. THEME: SCIENCE AND TECHNOLOGY**

Of all the new inventions mentioned in the chapter, which do you think was most important and why?

**3. ANALYZING CAUSES**

How did geographic differences between regions lead to economic differences between them?

**4. APPLYING CITIZENSHIP SKILLS**

Do you think the Missouri Compromise was a wise decision? Consider what might have happened without it, and also why it made Jefferson so uneasy.

**5. ANALYZING LEADERSHIP**

Think about the Monroe Doctrine and the boundary settlements achieved during the Monroe administration. How would you judge Monroe's foreign policy?

**Interact *with* History**

Did you predict the ways that new inventions would change the country? What surprised you?

## CRITICAL THINKING

**Possible Responses**

1. USING YOUR NOTES **a.** better communications; better transportation; economic cooperation **b.** slavery
2. THEME: SCIENCE AND TECHNOLOGY Students may choose the cotton gin because it led to the expansion of slavery in the South, or the steamboat and the telegraph because both linked people in different cities.
3. ANALYZING CAUSES Water power from rivers helped build Northeast factories; good soils built the South and West agricultural economies.
4. APPLYING CITIZENSHIP SKILLS Without it, the country might have engaged in civil war sooner. However, it simply prolonged the debate over slavery. Jefferson worried that this type of sectionalism would destroy the nation.
5. ANALYZING LEADERSHIP Students may see Monroe's policy as bold and nationalistic, or aggressive and arrogant.

**Interact *with* History** Answers will vary based on the student's predictions.

## HISTORY SKILLS

**1. INTERPRETING MAPS: Region**

Study the map. Answer the questions.

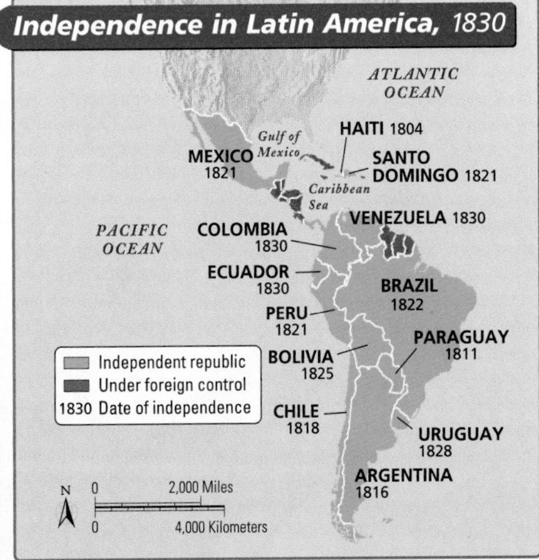


**Basic Map Elements**

a. What region is the subject of the map?

b. What do the dates on the map mean?

**Interpreting the Map**

c. What countries were independent by 1823, when the Monroe Doctrine was issued?

d. When did Mexico become independent?

**2. INTERPRETING PRIMARY SOURCES**

The following verse is from a well-known folk song. Read the verse and answer the questions.

**Low Bridge, Everybody Down**

I've got a mule and her name is Sal,
Fifteen miles on the Erie Canal.
She's a good old worker and a good old pal,
Fifteen miles on the Erie Canal.
We've hauled some barges in our day,
Filled with lumber, coal, and hay,
And we know every inch of the way
From Albany to Buffalo.

a. In the song, how is the Erie Canal used?

b. What feeling does the song give you about working on the Erie Canal?

## ALTERNATIVE ASSESSMENT

**1. INTERDISCIPLINARY ACTIVITY: Science**

**Making a Presentation** Do research to learn how inventions of the early 1800s have been improved upon today. For example, learn what kind of engine powers modern boats, and why it works better than a steam engine. Or find out what modern farmers use instead of the McCormick reaper. Share your findings in an oral presentation with visual aids.

**2. COOPERATIVE LEARNING ACTIVITY**

**Planning an Exhibit** As a class, plan a museum exhibit to show what slavery was like on cotton plantations. Break into small groups to research different topics—for example, what enslaved people wore, what their houses were like, what rules they lived under, and what stories they told. Bring back your research and decide how you can best share what you learned with an audience. Part of your exhibit might be a model of a plantation or dramatic readings from slave narratives.

**3. PRIMARY SOURCE EXPLORER**

**Planning Foreign Policy** The Monroe Doctrine was President Monroe's outline for U.S. foreign policy early in the 19th century. Using the Primary Source Explorer CD-ROM, library, and Internet, find out more about the Monroe Doctrine.

Imagine that you are president of the United States. Come up with four main principles of foreign policy that this country should follow in the 21st century.

- With classmates, talk about broad principles from the Monroe Doctrine. Keeping out of European conflicts would be one example. Protecting free republics would be another.
- Decide whether you agree or disagree with these principles. Think of current U.S. policies that follow or reject them.
- As president, decide how you will communicate U.S. foreign policy for the 21st century to the public. If you make a televised speech, what facts and visual aids would be most persuasive?

**4. HISTORY PORTFOLIO**

**Option 1** Review your section and chapter assessment activities. Choose one that you think is your best work. Try to improve your work, using suggestions from your teacher or classmates. Add the new version to your portfolio.

**Option 2** Review the questions you listed for What Do You Want to Know? on page 340. In a brief report, write what you learned about the lives of people from different regions in the early 1800s.



## ALTERNATIVE ASSESSMENT

1. INTERDISCIPLINARY ACTIVITY: **Science**

**Presentations should**

- present information that reflects the student's research on inventions and improvements.
- use visual aids to support information.
- have a clear introduction and conclusion.
- have adequate delivery and establish rapport with the audience.

2. COOPERATIVE LEARNING ACTIVITY

**Exhibits should**

- have a complete introductory overview.
- contain accurate and well-described textual information.
- use a variety of media.
- be accompanied by well-informed and lively student presenters.

3. PRIMARY SOURCE EXPLORER

**Presentations should**

- clearly state four main principles.
- present supporting reasons for each position.
- clearly rebut other viewpoints.
- include visual aids.
- use standard grammar, spelling, sentence structure, and punctuation.

4. HISTORY PORTFOLIO

**Option 1 Revised section or chapter assessment activities should**

- address teacher and peer responses to the selected work.
- solve problems present in the first versions of the work.

**Option 2 Short reports should**

- answer questions about the differences in the regions of the United States in the first half of the 1800s.
- cite sources of information.
- use standard grammar, spelling, sentence structure, and punctuation.

**Critical Thinking Transparency CT33**

- Visual Summary

**Formal Assessment**

- Chapter Test, Forms A and B, pp. 176–183

## HISTORY SKILLS

**Possible Responses**

1. INTERPRETING MAPS

**Basic Map Elements**

**a.** Latin America

**b.** date of independence

**Interpreting the Map**

**c.** Mexico, Haiti, Santo Domingo, Brazil, Paraguay, Argentina, Chile, Peru

**d.** 1821

2. INTERPRETING PRIMARY SOURCES

**a.** to transport trade goods such as lumber, coal, and hay between Albany and Buffalo

**b.** Work was done with a mule and seems to be repetitive.

# UNIT 4

## A Changing Nation

## 1810–1860



### BEFORE YOU READ

#### Previewing Unit 4

Unit 4 examines the many ways the United States grows and changes from the 1820s to the late 1840s. During these years, a new spirit of democracy and a great interest in politics spread through the nation. Many Americans believe strongly in their country's manifest destiny—to expand across the continent. The United States goes to war with Mexico and claims California and much of the Southwest as a result. But national expansion comes at the expense of the lives and cultures of Native Americans and Hispanics. Reformers of the day work to improve American society, while women and African Americans work toward the goal of equality under the law.

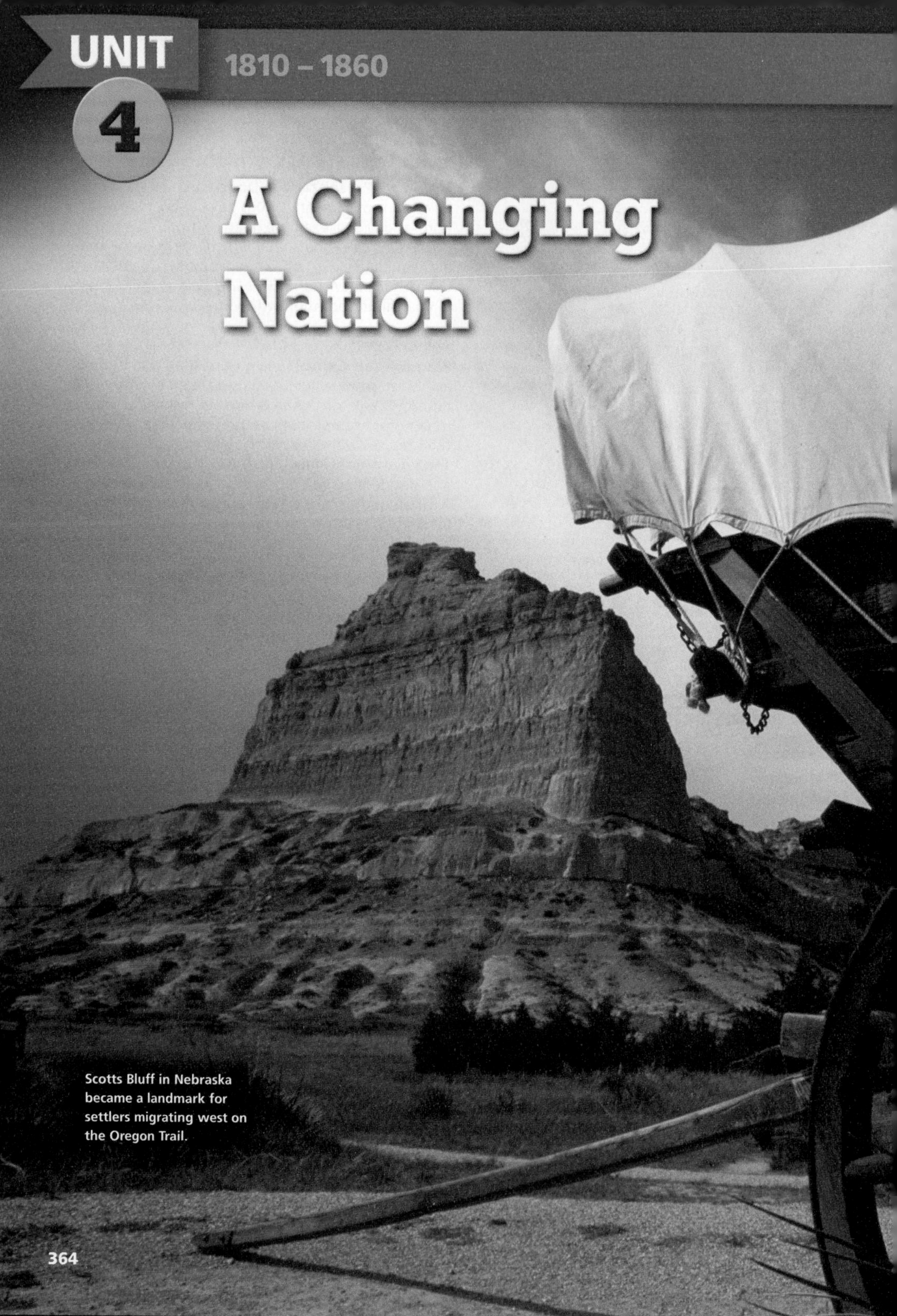


Scotts Bluff in Nebraska became a landmark for settlers migrating west on the Oregon Trail.

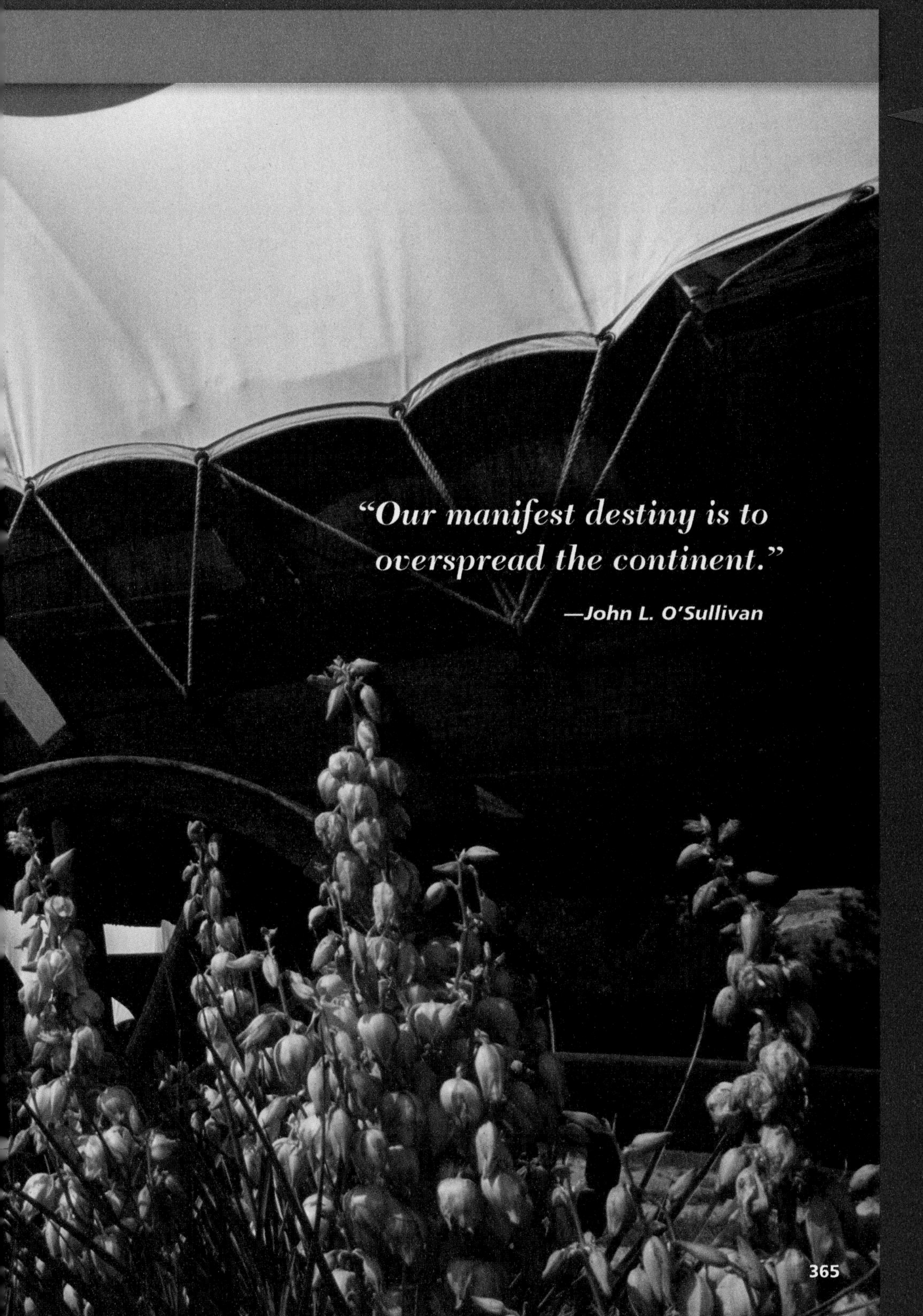

"Our manifest destiny is to overspread the continent."
—John L. O'Sullivan
365


## HISTORY FROM VISUALS

**Interpreting the Photograph** Ask students to think about long trips they have taken by car or bus. Have students brainstorm a list of words and phrases to describe such trips. Write the positive words and phrases in one column on the board and put the negative words and phrases in a second column. Then ask students to make a list of words describing travel in a covered wagon such as the one shown here. Tell students to classify their list into two columns headed *positive aspects* and *negative aspects.* Combine responses on the chalkboard to make a class list.

**Extension** Ask students to write a short story about a family traveling in a covered wagon along the Oregon Trail. Tell students to use Scotts Bluff as the setting of their story.

CHAPTER 12 PLANNING GUIDE

# The Age of Jackson 1824–1840

| | CHAPTER OVERVIEW | COPYMASTERS | TECHNOLOGY |
|---|---|---|---|
| **CHAPTER RESOURCES** | This chapter describes the presidency of Andrew Jackson and the concept of Jacksonian democracy. It also discusses Jackson's policies on Native Americans, the national bank, and states' rights. | **In-Depth Resources: Unit 4**<br>• Tracing Themes: Economic in History, p. 2<br>• Building Vocabulary, p. 7<br>**Interdisciplinary Projects,** pp. 67–72 | **Primary Source Explorer**<br>**Electronic Teacher Tools**<br>**Power Presentations CD-ROM**<br>**Chapter Summaries on CD** (English and Spanish) |
| **SECTION 1 Politics of the People pp. 369–373** | **KEY IDEAS**<br>• Andrew Jackson wins the election of 1828, his popularity based on his humble origins and his military record.<br>• Voting rights expand to include most white men, regardless of economic level.<br>• Jackson gives government jobs to his political backers, a process called the spoils system. | **In-Depth Resources: Unit 4**<br>• Setting the Stage, p. 1<br>• Guided Reading, p. 3<br>• Geography Application, pp. 9–10<br>• Literature Selection, pp. 13–15<br>• Reteaching Activity, p. 16<br>**America's History Makers**<br>• Andrew Jackson, pp. 47–48<br>**Citizenship Today,** pp. 7–8<br>**Why It Matters Now,** pp. 23–24 | **Warm-Up Transparency WT12**<br>**Geography Transparency GT12**<br>• State Voting Qualifications, 1828<br>**Critical Thinking Transparency CT34**<br>• Setting the Stage<br>**ClassZone:** www.mcdougallittell.com |
| **SECTION 2 Jackson's Policy Toward Native Americans pp. 374–378** | • Native Americans who adopt white ways of life hold much land in the Southeast.<br>• Jackson supports the Indian Removal Act, which forces tribes to move west.<br>• Many Native Americans resist removal, but eventually lose their lands. | **In-Depth Resources: Unit 4**<br>• Setting the Stage, p.1<br>• Guided Reading, p. 4<br>• Primary Source, p. 11<br>• Reteaching Activity, p. 17<br>**America's History Makers**<br>• Sequoya, pp. 49–50<br>**Outline Map Activities**<br>• Native American Movement, 1830–1842, pp. 23–24 | **Warm-Up Transparency WT12**<br>**Humanities Transparency HT23**<br>• Political Cartoon: Andrew Jackson and Native Americans<br>**Critical Thinking Transparency CT34**<br>• Setting the Stage<br>**Critical Thinking Transparency CT35**<br>• Cause and Effect: Native American Removal<br>**ClassZone:** www.mcdougallittell.com |
| **SECTION 3 Conflicts Over States' Rights pp. 379–383** | • The country argues over the sale of public lands, tariffs, and internal improvements.<br>• Southerner John C. Calhoun proposes the doctrine of nullification, allowing a state to overrule a federal law.<br>• Jackson insists that federal laws will be enforced, and compromise averts the crisis. | **In-Depth Resources: Unit 4**<br>• Setting the Stage, p. 1<br>• Guided Reading, p. 5<br>• Primary Source, p. 12<br>• Reteaching Activity, p. 18<br>**Economics in History**<br>• Westerners and High Tariffs, p. 12 | **Warm-Up Transparency WT12**<br>**Critical Thinking Transparency CT34**<br>• Setting the Stage<br>**ClassZone:** www.mcdougallittell.com |
| **SECTION 4 Prosperity and Panic pp. 384–387** | • Jackson vetoes the charter of the national bank.<br>• Jackson's economic policies lead to inflation, and an economic depression begins in 1837.<br>• A new political party, the Whig Party, arises and wins the election of 1840. | **In-Depth Resources: Unit 4**<br>• Setting the Stage, p. 1<br>• Guided Reading, p. 6<br>• Skillbuilder Practice: Interpreting Political Cartoons, p. 8<br>• Reteaching Activity, p. 19 | **Warm-Up Transparency WT12**<br>**Humanities Transparency HT24**<br>• Whig Rolling Ball, 1840<br>**Critical Thinking Transparency CT34**<br>• Setting the Stage<br>**Critical Thinking Transparency CT36**<br>• Visual Summary<br>**ClassZone:** www.mcdougallittell.com |

PE Pupil's Edition
Copymaster
Overhead Transparency
Audio Library
CD-ROM
Internet

## ASSESSMENT

**Chapter Assessment,** pp. 388–389

**Formal Assessment**
- Chapter Tests, Forms A and B, pp. 190–197

**Alternative Assessment Book**

**Electronic Teacher Tools with Test Maker**

---

**Section Assessment,** p. 373

**Formal Assessment**
- Section Quiz, p. 186

**Alternative Assessment Book**
- Rubrics for a map, 2.1
- Rubrics for a chart, 2.2

**Electronic Teacher Tools with Test Maker**

---

**Section Assessment,** p. 378

**Formal Assessment**
- Section Quiz, p. 187

**Alternative Assessment Book**
- Rubrics for a map, 2.1
- Rubrics for a chart, 2.2

**Electronic Teacher Tools with Test Maker**

---

**Section Assessment,** p. 383

**Formal Assessment**
- Section Quiz, p. 188

**Alternative Assessment Book**
- Rubrics for a speech, 3.6
- Rubrics for a audiocassette, 5.3

**Electronic Teacher Tools with Test Maker**

---

**Section Assessment,** p. 387

**Formal Assessment**
- Section Quiz, p. 189

**Alternative Assessment Book**
- Rubrics for a slogan, 4.1
- Rubrics for a banner, 1.1

**Electronic Teacher Tools with Test Maker**

## CUSTOMIZING FOR INDIVIDUAL NEEDS

### Students Acquiring English/ESL

**Reading Study Guide** (English and Spanish), pp. 119–128

**Access for Students Acquiring English/ESL:** Spanish Translations, pp. 79–85

**Chapter Summaries on CD** (English and Spanish)

### Less Proficient Readers

**Reading Study Guide** (English and Spanish), pp. 119–128

**Chapter Summaries on CD** (English and Spanish)

### Gifted and Talented Students

**In-Depth Resources: Unit 4**
- Enrichment Activity, p. 20

**America's History Makers**
- Andrew Jackson, pp. 47–48
- Sequoya, pp. 49–50

## CROSS-CURRICULAR CONNECTIONS

### Culture

Tunis, Edwin. ***Frontier Living.*** New York: Harper/Collins, 1976. Award-winning presentation of daily life and work on the frontier, with details about everything from clothing to tools to transportation to social life.

### Economics

Otfinoksi, Steve. ***Kid's Guide to Money.*** New York: Scholastic, 1996. Explains the uses of banks, along with information about how to earn money, save it, and spend it wisely.

### Government

Collier, Christopher. ***Andrew Jackson's America, 1824–1850.*** Tarrytown, NY: Benchmark Books, 1999. Examines politics and government in a turbulent time.

### Interdisciplinary Projects, pp. 67–72

- Math: Calculating Voter Turnouts
- Science: Veterinary Medicine
- Language Arts: Campaign Literature of 1828
- Art: Political Cartoons

### Literature

Cheatham, K. Follis. ***Bring Home the Ghost.*** New York: Harcourt, 1980. A young man and his personal slave return from fighting in the Seminole war to find their home destroyed in an Indian raid. They strike out for the frontier, where the enslaved Jason learns what freedom really means.

Harrell, Beatrice Orcutt and Tony Meers. ***Longwalker's Journey: A Novel of the Choctaw Trail of Tears.*** New York: Dial, 1999. Minko and his family are forced to relocate from Mississippi to Oklahoma.

Holmes, Jean. ***Mornin' Star Risin'.*** Nampa, ID: Pacific Press Publishing Association, 1992. First volume in the highly successful, multi-generational saga of the black and white families whose lives intertwine at the Weldon Oaks Plantation on the Sea Islands of Georgia.

## ENRICHMENT ACTIVITIES

**Pupil's Edition, pp. 366–389**
**Interact with History,** p. 367
**Citizenship Today,** p. 372
**Economics in History,** p. 380

**In-Depth Resources: Unit 4**
- Geography Application: Election of 1828, pp. 9–10
- Primary Source: A Petition by Cherokee Women, p. 11
- Primary Source: from *Reminiscences and Anecdotes of Daniel Webster*, p. 12
- Literature Selection: from *Jackson* by Max Byrd, pp. 13–15

**America's History Makers**
- Andrew Jackson, pp. 47–48
- Sequoya, pp. 49–50

**Outline Map Activities**
- Native American Movement, 1830–1842, pp. 23–24

**Why It Matters Now**
- Expanding Democracy, pp. 23–24

# CHAPTER 12 PACING GUIDE

**LESSON PLAN OPTIONS (50-MINUTE PERIOD)** (TE) = Teacher's Edition (PE) = Pupil's Edition

| | TEACHER-DIRECTED ACTIVITIES<br>Class Time: 15 minutes | STUDENT-CENTERED ACTIVITIES<br>Class Time: 25 minutes | INDIVIDUAL ACTIVITIES<br>Class Time: 10 minutes |
|---|---|---|---|
| **DAY 1**<br>Introduction<br>pp. 366–368 | **Presentation Options**<br>• Begin with a class discussion of the painting on p. 366 **(PE)**.<br>• Lead a class discussion on the "What Do You Know?" question in Setting the Stage, p. 368. Then introduce the graphic organizer for the chapter **(PE)**. | **Options for Cooperative Learning**<br>• Have student groups discuss the Interact with History questions, p. 367 **(PE)**.<br>• Have student groups respond to the "What Do You Want to Know?" question in Setting the Stage, p. 368 **(PE)**. | **Head Start on Homework Options**<br>• Have students skim Section 1 Main Idea, Why It Matters Now, Terms & Names, and the main headings, p. 369 **(PE)**.<br>• Have students begin Guided Reading activity and Building Vocabulary sheet. |
| **DAY 2**<br>Section 1<br>pp. 369–373 | **Presentation Options**<br>• Begin with the 5-Minute Warm-Up, p. 369 **(TE)**.<br>• Review the Section 1 Main Idea, Why It Matters Now, and Terms & Names, p. 369 **(PE)**.<br>• Choose 5 key questions for Objectives 1–4 to discuss with the class, pp. 369–373 **(TE)**. | **Options for Cooperative Learning**<br>• Divide students into groups to begin the Citizenship Today activities, p. 372 **(PE)**.<br>• Have student pairs work together to complete one of the Activity Options in the Section 1 Assessment, p. 373 **(PE)**. | **Head Start on Homework Options**<br>• Have students begin working on Section 1 Assessment, p. 373 **(PE)**.<br>• Have students preview Section 2 Main Idea, Why It Matters Now, Terms & Names, and the main headings, p. 374 **(PE)**. |
| **DAY 3**<br>Section 2<br>pp. 374–378 | **Presentation Options**<br>• Begin with the 5-Minute Warm-Up, p. 374 **(TE)**.<br>• Choose 5 key questions for Objectives 1–4 to discuss with the class, pp. 374–378 **(TE)**.<br>• Lead students through Geography Skillbuilder questions and History from Visuals, p. 376 **(PE, TE)**. | **Options for Cooperative Learning**<br>• Divide students into groups and have them complete the Interdisciplinary Link, Language Arts/Writing: A Letter to the President, p. 375 **(TE)**.<br>• Have student pairs work together to complete one of the Activity Options in the Section 2 Assessment, p. 378 **(PE)**. | **Head Start on Homework Options**<br>• Have students begin working on Section 2 Assessment, p. 378 **(PE)**.<br>• Have students complete the questions for Economics in History, p. 380 **(PE)**. |
| **DAY 4**<br>Section 3<br>pp. 379–383 | **Presentation Options**<br>• Begin with the 5-Minute Warm-Up, p. 379 **(TE)**.<br>• Choose 5 key questions for Objectives 1–4 to discuss with the class, pp. 379–383 **(TE)**.<br>• Lead students in a discussion on tariffs using Economics in History, p. 380 **(PE, TE)**. | **Options for Cooperative Learning**<br>• Have students begin working on a nullification debate in the Interdisciplinary Link, Government, p. 382 **(TE)**.<br>• Have student pairs work together to complete one of the Activity Options in the Section 3 Assessment, p. 383 **(PE)**. | **Head Start on Homework Options**<br>• Have students begin working on Section 3 Assessment, p. 383 **(PE)**.<br>• Have students complete the Reading History questions for Section 4, pp. 379–383 **(PE)**. |
| **DAY 5**<br>Section 4<br>pp. 384–387 | **Presentation Options**<br>• Begin with the 5-Minute Warm-Up, p. 384 **(TE)**.<br>• Choose 5 key questions for Objectives 1–4 to discuss with the class, pp. 384–386 **(TE)**.<br>• Lead the students through the Skillbuilder Mini-Lesson: Interpreting Political Cartoons, p. 385 **(TE)**. | **Options for Cooperative Learning**<br>• Divide students into groups and have them complete the Critical Thinking Activity, p. 387 **(TE)**.<br>• Have student pairs work together to complete one of the Activity Options in the Section 4 Assessment, p. 387 **(PE)**. | **Head Start on Homework Options**<br>• Have students complete the Setting the Stage graphic organizer for the chapter, p. 368 **(PE)**.<br>• Have students begin working on the Chapter Assessment, pp. 388–389 **(PE)**.<br>• Prepare for Chapter Test<br>**Formal Assessment,** pp. 190–197 |

TEACHER-TESTED ACTIVITY **Brent Heath, De Anza Middle School, Ontario, California**

## THE DOCTRINE OF NULLIFICATION

**Class Time** Two class periods

**Task** Presenting a "Face the Nation" talk show on the doctrine of nullification

**Purpose** To identify and summarize conflicting positions in the states' rights debate on the doctrine of nullification

**Supplies Needed**

- Reference books and Internet sources on Daniel Webster, John C. Calhoun, and the nullification controversy

**Activity** Divide students into six-member groups. Within groups, have students assume the following roles: Daniel Webster, John C. Calhoun, host/moderator, newspaper reporters. One member of the group can be the show's producer. Review the positions of Webster and Calhoun on nullification. Then have groups prepare background material for the roles they will play. The host can prepare a short speech introducing each guest, and reporters can make up questions to ask the show's guests. Calhoun and Webster can make short statements about their positions on the issues before questioning by reporters begins.

## BLOCK SCHEDULING — LESSON PLAN OPTIONS (90-MINUTE PERIOD)

### DAY 1

**Interact with History,** p. 367
**Class Time** 20 Minutes

Options for pacing and variety:

- **Role-Play** Have groups of three students assume the roles of new voters in the election of 1828. Students can take turns explaining to their partners what qualities make a strong leader and identifying earlier presidents they consider strong leaders. Have groups report their conclusions to the class. **Class Time** 20 minutes

**Setting the Stage,** p. 368
**Class Time** 20 minutes

Options for pacing and variety:

- **Time Saver** Ask students to come to class with two lists. One list should describe what they already know about Andrew Jackson and a second list should contain questions they would like answered about his presidency. **Class Time** 5 minutes

**Section 1,** pp. 369–373
**Class Time** 50 minutes

Options for pacing and variety:

- **Peer Teaching** Working in groups, have students prepare media reports on the outcome of the election of 1824 and share them with the class. **Class Time** 20 minutes
- **Time Saver** Use the chart on page 373 to summarize the section. **Class Time** 10 minutes

### DAY 2

**Section 2,** pp. 374–378
**Class Time** 45 minutes

Options for pacing and variety:

- **Time Saver** As a homework assignment, have students answer Critical Thinking question 5 in the Chapter Assessment on page 388. Discuss responses in class. **Class Time** 10 minutes
- **Internet** Extend students' background knowledge of the Cherokee by learning about Native American languages at www.mcdougallittell.com **Class Time** 20 minutes

**Section 3,** pp. 379–383
**Class Time** 45 minutes

Options for pacing and variety:

- **Peer Teaching** Ask two volunteers to review Economics in History on page 380 and explain to the class how a protective tariff works. To check student comprehension, the peer teachers can have students give oral answers to the Connect to History and Connect to Today questions for the feature. **Class Time** 15 minutes
- **Time Saver** For a homework assignment, have students complete the Main Ideas and Critical Thinking questions in the section assessment. **Class Time** 5 minutes

### DAY 3

**Section 4,** pp. 384–387
**Class Time** 45 minutes

Options for pacing and variety:

- **Time Saver** Use the cartoon "Jackson Fights the Second Bank" on page 385 to summarize the section. **Class Time** 10 minutes
- **History on Film** Extend students' background knowledge of Andrew Jackson's presidency by viewing "The Jackson Years: Toward Civil War." Learning Corporation of America. **Class Time** 30 minutes

**Chapter 12 Assessment,** pp. 388–389
**Class Time** 40 minutes

Options for pacing and variety:

- **Peer Evaluation** Working in groups, students should review the Visual Summary on page 388 and explain why each of the topics mentioned became a major issue of Jackson's presidency. Students can also discuss whether they agree with the actions Jackson took in each case. **Class Time** 15 minutes
- **Peer Teaching** Ask one student to assume the role of a supporter of Jackson and the other a critic. Pair critics and supporters and have each explain to the other how he or she feels about the cartoon "King Andrew the First" in the Chapter Assessment. **Class Time** 10 minutes

## CHAPTER 12 OBJECTIVE

The student will understand the far-reaching consequences of the political and economic decisions made by Andrew Jackson during his two terms as president.

# CHAPTER 12 The Age of Jackson 1824–1840

*Section 1* **Politics of the People**
*Section 2* **Jackson's Policy Toward Native Americans**
*Section 3* **Conflicts over States' Rights**
*Section 4* **Prosperity and Panic**

The people came by the thousands to the White House on Inauguration Day to see their president—Andrew Jackson.

366

## HISTORY FROM VISUALS

**Interpreting the Illustration** This 1829 print by Robert Cruikshank was originally titled "The President's levee, or all Creation going to the White House." Read students the following pairs of adjectives and ask which word in each pair better describes the crowd in the picture: quiet or noisy; festive or angry; dignified or rowdy.

In supporting their choices, students may notice details like the kicking horse, the boy falling out of the coach, and the brightly colored clothing. Some students may also point out the contrast between the stark, formal White House and the excited, energetic spectators.

**Extension** Have the students write a dialogue about the presidential inauguration that might be taking place between two people in the crowd.

### CRITICAL THINKING ACTIVITY

**Making Inferences** Point out that Jackson is shown on horseback on both pages 367 and 368. Students may also be familiar with equestrian statues that honor noteworthy leaders from their own region. Discuss the implications of military leadership, social rank, and power that such images present.

**Class Time** 10 minutes

## RECOMMENDED RESOURCES

**BOOKS FOR THE TEACHER**

Marszalek, John F. ***The Petticoat Affair: Manners, Sex, & Mutiny in Andrew Jackson's White House.*** New York: Free Press, 1997. Lively account of "the Eaton Affair," in which gossip about a cabinet wife exposed stresses within the administration.

Wallace, Anthony F. C. ***The Long, Bitter Trail: Andrew Jackson and the Indians.*** New York: Hill & Wang, 1993. A succinct account of the politics, ethnic friction, and just plain double-dealing that led to this tragic episode.

Watson, Harry L. ***Andrew Jackson vs. Henry Clay: Democracy and Development in Antebellum America.*** New York: St. Martin's, 1998. Dual biography of these clashing leaders.

**VIDEO**

***Andrew Jackson: A Man for the People.*** A&E (Moonbeam Pubs.), 1995. Life story of one of our most colorful presidents.

**INTERNET**

For more about Native American languages, visit www.mcdougallittell.com

## Interact *with* History

General Andrew Jackson commands his troops in battle.

**The year is 1828. You will vote for president for the first time. Important economic, social, and political issues face the country. The favored candidate is Andrew Jackson, a military hero. Before you vote, you should decide what qualities make a strong leader.**

### What Do You Think?

- **What qualities are suggested by this image?**
- **Which earlier presidents would you consider strong leaders and which not?**
- **Would qualities that make a military leader also make a good president? Why or why not?**

# *What qualities do you think make a strong leader?*

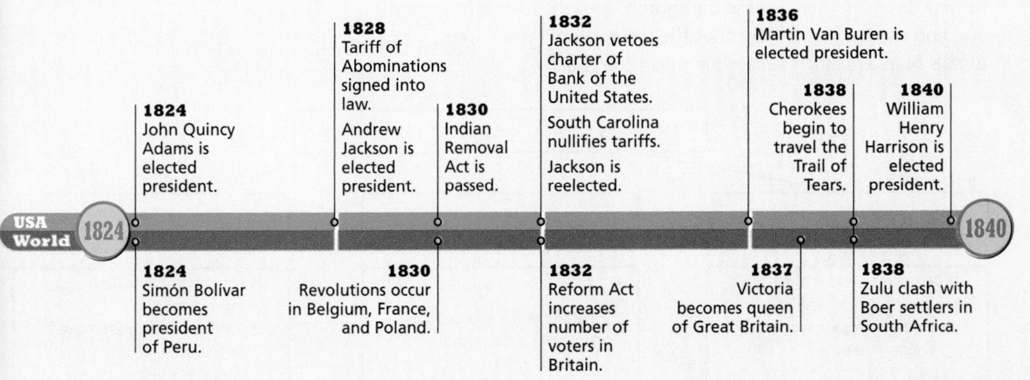

USA
World
1824
1840
1824 John Quincy Adams is elected president.
1828 Tariff of Abominations signed into law. Andrew Jackson is elected president.
1830 Indian Removal Act is passed.
1832 Jackson vetoes charter of Bank of the United States. South Carolina nullifies tariffs. Jackson is reelected.
1836 Martin Van Buren is elected president.
1838 Cherokees begin to travel the Trail of Tears.
1840 William Henry Harrison is elected president.
1824 Simón Bolívar becomes president of Peru.
1830 Revolutions occur in Belgium, France, and Poland.
1832 Reform Act increases number of voters in Britain.
1837 Victoria becomes queen of Great Britain.
1838 Zulu clash with Boer settlers in South Africa.

## Interact *with* History

### OBJECTIVES

- To help students identify the qualities that make a strong leader
- To help students understand the strong feelings—both pro and con—that Jackson aroused

### What Do You Think?

1. Students might begin by listing the presidents who preceded Jackson and reviewing how each responded to the challenges he faced.
2. Students can consider both historic and current figures in framing their definitions of leadership.
3. Students can begin to answer this question by looking at the trait suggested in the illustration of Jackson on this page.

### *What qualities do you think make a strong leader?*

Point out that strong leaders have the ability to make others eager to follow them; the word *charisma* refers to this quality. Encourage students to think about decision-making skills as well as personal qualities.

### MAKING PERSONAL CONNECTIONS

Ask students to think about adults or peers that they have known through school, camp, youth groups, or other activities that they consider to be strong leaders. What traits made them especially effective?

### TIME LINE DISCUSSION

**Tell students that during this time period, many people believed democracy was expanding, both in the United States and in other parts of the world.**

- Ask students what events in western Europe during this time suggest that democracy was expanding. **Answer** universal male suffrage in Switzerland; Reform Act in Britain
- What events on the time line suggest that not everyone was a part of expanding democracy? **Answer** Indian Removal Act; revolutions in Belgium, France, and Poland; Zulu clash with Boer settlers; Cherokee Trail of Tears

## BEFORE YOU READ

### Previewing the Theme: Economics in History

Have students examine the poster and notice the building in the background. Ask what the building is supposed to be. Next ask what impression the poster gives of Jackson. **Possible Response** The White House. The poster suggests that Jackson is a man of action who will act energetically and that he will bring change.

### What Do You Know?

Have students describe causes of earlier conflicts between Native Americans and white settlers. Students might also consider the issues of industrialization, trade, sectionalism, western expansion, and political parties. Encourage them to consider how these matters might develop during the Age of Jackson.

 **In-Depth Resources: Unit 4**
- Tracing Themes: Economics in History, p. 2

## READ AND TAKE NOTES

### Reading Strategy: Finding Main Ideas

Explain to students that they can organize the main ideas in this chapter into three broad topics. Point out the three categories on the chart—*political, economic,* and *social*—and review these concepts with students. Encourage them to take notes by listing main ideas under these headings as they read the section.

 **In-Depth Resources: Unit 4**
- Setting the Stage, p. 1

 **Critical Thinking Transparency CT34**
- Setting the Stage



## BEFORE YOU READ

### Previewing the Theme

**Economics in History** Americans elected Andrew Jackson president in 1828. Many believed that he would bring sweeping changes to the government. This chapter explains how President Jackson made decisions that had far-reaching effects on the American economy and on political life. In fact, because he so dominated the life of the nation, his time in office has been called the Age of Jackson.

### What Do You Know?

What do you already know about the issues that faced the nation in the first half of the 19th century? How did presidents before Jackson deal with problems?

**THINK ABOUT**
- what you have learned about Andrew Jackson from books and movies
- how American life is affected by the actions of a president, by conflicts among different parts of the country, and by the will of the people

### What Do You Want to Know?

What questions do you have about Jackson and his presidency? Record them in your notebook before reading the chapter.

## READ AND TAKE NOTES

**Reading Strategy: Finding Main Ideas** To make it easier for you to understand what you read, learn to find the main idea of each paragraph, topic heading, and section. Remember that the supporting details help explain the main ideas. On the chart below, write down the main ideas about the political, economic, and social changes during Jackson's presidency.

 See Skillbuilder Handbook, page R5.

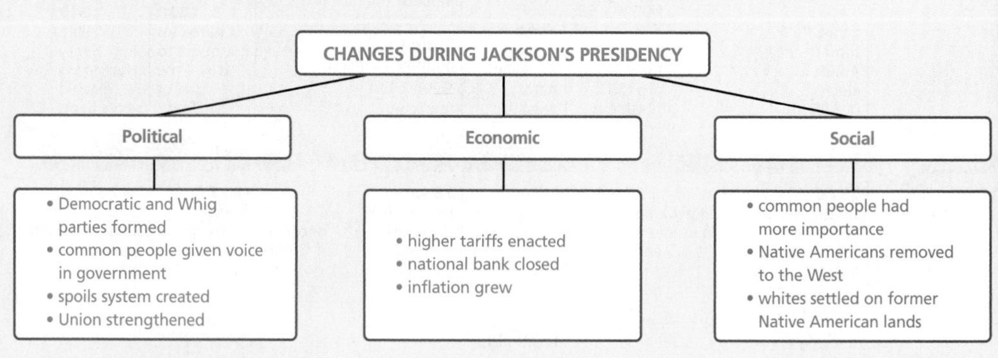

CHANGES DURING JACKSON'S PRESIDENCY
Political
• Democratic and Whig parties formed
• common people given voice in government
• spoils system created
• Union strengthened
Economic
• higher tariffs enacted
• national bank closed
• inflation grew
Social
• common people had more importance
• Native Americans removed to the West
• whites settled on former Native American lands




## TEACHING STRATEGY

### READING THE CHAPTER

This is a thematic chapter focusing on Jackson's presidency and the political, economic, and social changes that took place while he was in office. Encourage students to compare Jackson's policies to those of former presidents John Quincy Adams and Thomas Jefferson. Ask them to note the specific changes Jackson brought to the presidency.

### ALTERNATIVE ASSESSMENT

The Chapter Assessment describes three activities for alternative assessment on page 389. You may wish to have students work on these activities during the course of the chapter and then present them at the end.

# 1 Politics of the People

**TERMS & NAMES**
John Quincy Adams
Andrew Jackson
Jacksonian democracy
spoils system

| MAIN IDEA | WHY IT MATTERS NOW |
|---|---|
| Andrew Jackson's election to the presidency in 1828 brought a new era of popular democracy. | Jackson's use of presidential powers laid the foundation of the modern presidency. |

### ONE AMERICAN'S STORY

**Margaret Bayard Smith was 22 years old when she married and moved to Washington, D.C., in 1800. For the next 40 years, she and her husband, a government official, were central figures in the political and social life of Washington. They entertained presidents from Jefferson to Jackson.**

**Smith wrote magazine articles and numerous letters describing life in Washington. In 1824, she described how John Quincy Adams reacted to his election as president.**

*A VOICE FROM THE PAST*

When the news of his election was communicated to Mr. Adams by the Committee . . . the sweat rolled down his face—he shook from head to foot and was so agitated that he could scarcely stand or speak.

**Margaret Bayard Smith,** *The First Forty Years of Washington Society*

Margaret Bayard Smith wrote about life in the nation's capital in the first half of the 19th century.

**Adams had reason to be shaken by his election. It had been hotly contested, and he knew that he would face much opposition as he tried to govern. In this section, you will learn how Adams defeated Andrew Jackson in 1824, only to lose to him four years later.**

## 1 The Election of 1824

In 1824, regional differences led to a fierce fight over the presidency. The Democratic-Republican Party split apart, with four men hoping to replace James Monroe as president. **John Quincy Adams,** Monroe's secretary of state, was New England's choice. The South backed William Crawford of Georgia. Westerners supported Henry Clay, the "Great Compromiser," and **Andrew Jackson,** a former military hero from Tennessee.

Jackson won the most popular votes. But he did not receive a majority of electoral votes. According to the Constitution, if no person wins a majority of electoral votes, the House of Representatives must choose the president. The selection was made from the top three vote getters.

Clay had come in fourth and was out of the running. In the House vote, he threw his support to Adams, who then won. Because Adams





## SECTION OBJECTIVES

1. To explain the importance of the 1824 election
2. To analyze Jacksonian democracy and the expansion of voting rights
3. To explain why Jackson was known as "the people's president"
4. To evaluate Jackson's use of the spoils system to begin a new political era

**SKILLBUILDER**
Interpreting Charts, p. 373

**CRITICAL THINKING**
Analyzing Causes, p. 370
Recognizing Effects, p. 371
Drawing Conclusions, p. 372
Analyzing Points of View, p. 373

**Why It Matters Now**
- Expanding Democracy, pp. 23–24

## FOCUS & MOTIVATE

### 5-MINUTE WARM-UP

**Comparing** These questions will help students compare and contrast Jefferson and Jackson.

1. Look at the chart on page 373. What beliefs did the two leaders share?
2. How might government for the people be different from government by the people?

**Warm-Up Transparency WT12**

## INSTRUCT

**INSTRUCT: OBJECTIVE 1**

**The Election of 1824**
Key Questions
- Why was the election of 1824 decided by the House of Representatives?
- How did Clay help Adams win the election?

**In-Depth Resources: Unit 4**
- Guided Reading, p. 3

**Reading Study Guide** (Spanish and English), pp. 119–120

## RECOMMENDED RESOURCES

**In-Depth Resources: Unit 4**
- Guided Reading, p. 3
- Building Vocabulary, p. 7
- Geography Application: Election of 1828, pp. 9–10
- Literature Selection: from *Jackson,* pp. 13–15
- Reteaching Activity, p. 16

**Reading Study Guide** (Spanish and English), pp. 119–120

**America's History Makers**
- Andrew Jackson, pp. 47–48

**Why It Matters Now**
- Expanding Democracy, pp. 23–24

**Citizenship Today,** pp. 7–8

**Formal Assessment**
- Section Quiz, p. 186

**Alternative Assessment**
- Rubrics, 2.1
- Rubrics, 2.2

**Access for Students Acquiring English/ESL**
- Guided Reading, p. 79
- Geography Application, pp. 84–85

Technology Resources

**Geography Transparency GT12**
- State Voting Qualifications, 1828

**Electronic Teacher Tools with Test Maker**

**ClassZone**
www.mcdougallittell.com

## AMERICA'S HISTORY MAKERS

**John Quincy Adams**

During his campaign for reelection, Adams refused to defend himself against slurs by Jackson and his followers because he thought it was beneath the dignity of the presidency to take part in political mudslinging.

After his defeat, Massachusetts voters elected Adams to the House of Representatives, a position he held for 17 years. On winning election to the House, he said, "My election as President of the United States was not half so gratifying."

**Andrew Jackson**

Before becoming president, Jackson's fiery temper involved him in several duels. In an 1806 duel he killed Charles Dickinson, a lawyer who had accused Jackson of being a "worthless scoundrel, a poltroon, and a coward" and had also made insulting remarks about his wife, Rachel.

**Possible Answer: Adams was vain, wealthy, and aloof. He came from a privileged background and was unwilling to compromise. Jackson was a war hero with a reputation for toughness. Jackson appealed to common voters because he was a self-made man who had overcome poverty and personal tragedy.**

**America's History Makers**
- Andrew Jackson, pp. 47–48

## INSTRUCT: OBJECTIVE 2

**Jacksonian Democracy**

Key Questions
- How did Jackson portray himself and Adams in the campaign of 1828?
- What does the phrase "Jacksonian democracy" mean?
- How were voting rights still limited?

**Geography Transparency GT12**
- State Voting Qualifications, 1828

## AMERICA'S HISTORY MAKERS

**JOHN QUINCY ADAMS**
**1767–1848**

John Quincy Adams was born into wealth and social position. He was the son of President John Adams. Like his father, he had a sharp mind, spoke eloquently, worked tirelessly in public service, and had high principles. But he was sometimes vain, and unwilling to compromise. This made him unpopular with many people and often ineffective. After his presidency, he served with distinction in Congress.

**ANDREW JACKSON**
**1767–1845**

Andrew Jackson was the son of a poor farm couple from South Carolina. Orphaned by age 14, he was a wild and reckless youth.

Jackson moved on to become a successful lawyer and plantation owner in Tennessee. But his quick temper still got him into brawls and duels. Bullets in his body from two duels frequently caused him pain.

Jackson's humble background and reputation for toughness endeared him to voters. They considered him one of their own.

**Why do you think Jackson was popular but Adams was not?**

later named Clay as his secretary of state, Jackson's supporters claimed that Adams gained the presidency by making a deal with Clay. Charges of a "corrupt bargain" followed Adams throughout his term.

Adams had many plans for his presidency. He wanted to build roads and canals, aid education and science, and regulate the use of natural resources. But Congress, led by Jackson supporters, defeated his proposals.

*Reading* **History**
**A. Analyzing Causes** What was the main reason John Quincy Adams was not effective as president?
A. Possible Answer His proposals faced opposition from Jackson supporters in Congress, and he was unwilling to bargain.

## 2 Jacksonian Democracy

Jackson felt that the 1824 election had been stolen from him—that the will of the people had been ignored. Jackson and his supporters were outraged. He immediately set to work to gain the presidency in 1828.

For the next four years, the split in the Democratic-Republican Party between the supporters of Jackson and of Adams grew wider. Jackson claimed to represent the "common man." He said Adams represented a group of privileged, wealthy Easterners. This division eventually created two parties. The Democrats came from among the Jackson supporters, while the National Republicans grew out of the Adams camp.

The election of 1828 again matched Jackson against Adams. It was a bitter campaign—both sides made vicious personal attacks. Even Jackson's wife, Rachel, became a target. During the campaign, Jackson crusaded against control of the government by the wealthy. He promised to look out for the interests of common people. He also promoted the concept of majority rule. The idea of spreading political power to all the people and ensuring majority rule became known as **Jacksonian democracy**.

Actually, the process of spreading political power had begun before Jackson ran for office. When Jefferson was president in the early 1800s,



**ACTIVITY OPTIONS**

**INDIVIDUAL NEEDS**

**LESS PROFICIENT READERS**

**Setting a Purpose** To help students set a purpose for reading the section and understand how Jackson's policies changed the presidency, prepare a series of questions for students to use as a guide. Write the questions on the board and read them with students. Have students jot down answers to the questions as they read the section. When they have finished reading and answering the questions, encourage students to review and discuss their answers.

You might want to ask questions such as the following:
- What group of people did Jackson represent?
- What is "Jacksonian democracy"?
- How did the expansion of voting rights help Jackson win the election in 1828?
- What experiences in Jackson's life helped prepare him for the presidency?
- What was Jackson's first change to the government?

additional people had gained the right to vote as states reduced restrictions on who could vote. Before, for example, only those who owned property or paid taxes could vote in many states. This easing of voting restrictions increased the number of voters. But voting was still limited to adult white males.

The expansion of voting rights helped Jackson achieve an overwhelming win in the 1828 presidential election. Jackson's triumph was hailed as a victory for common people. Large numbers of Western farmers as well as workers in the nation's cities supported him. Their vote put an end to the idea that the government should be controlled by an educated elite. Now, the common people would be governed by one of their own. (See chart "Changes in Ideas About Democracy," page 373.)

*Reading* **History**
**B. Recognizing Effects** What factor made Jackson's appeal to the "common man" especially important in the election of 1828?
**B. Answer** More people had gained the right to vote, including people without property or much money.

**STRANGE *but* True**

**ADAMS AND JEFFERSON**

John Adams and Thomas Jefferson died on the same day—the Fourth of July, 1826, the 50th anniversary of the adoption of the Declaration of Independence.

Both Adams and Jefferson were founders of the nation, signers of the Declaration, and presidents. They were also political enemies who had become friends late in life.

Adams was 90; Jefferson, 83. Adams's last words were "Jefferson still survives." He was unaware that Jefferson had died hours earlier.

## The People's President ❸

Jackson's humble background, and his reputation as a war hero, helped make him president. Many saw his rise above hardship as a real American success story. He was the first president not from an aristocratic Massachusetts or Virginia family, and the first from the West.

Jackson indeed had had a hard life. His father died shortly before his birth, and Jackson grew up on a frontier farm in South Carolina. At 13, he joined the militia with his older brother to fight in the Revolutionary War. In 1781, they were taken prisoner by the British. While captive, he allegedly refused when commanded to shine an officer's boots. The officer struck Jackson with a sword, leaving scars on his hand and head. Later, Jackson's mother obtained her sons' release from a military prison, where they had become ill with smallpox. Jackson's brother died, but his mother nursed Jackson back to health. A short time later, she also died. Jackson's experiences during the Revolution left him with a lifelong hatred of the British.

After the war, Jackson moved to the Tennessee frontier. In 1784, he began to study law. He built a successful legal practice and also bought and sold land. Jackson then purchased a plantation near Nashville and ran successfully for Congress. After the War of 1812 broke out, he was appointed a general in the army. At the Battle of New Orleans in 1815, Jackson soundly defeated the British even though his troops were greatly outnumbered. He became a national war hero. He earned the nickname "Old Hickory," after a soldier claimed that he was "tough as hickory."

## Jackson Takes Office

Jackson's success in the presidential election of 1828 came at a high price. Shortly after he won, his wife, Rachel, died of a heart attack. Jackson believed that the campaign attacks on her reputation had killed her. She was a private woman who preferred a quiet life. In fact, she had

Jackson usually wore this miniature oil portrait of his beloved wife, Rachel, around his neck.



**STRANGE *but* True**

**Adams and Jefferson**

Adams and Jefferson met in 1775 and worked together to create the Declaration of Independence. Their friendship cooled sharply after 1790, when they disagreed on how the United States should respond to the French Revolution. As heads of the nation's first political parties, they became bitter rivals. Political differences soured the friendship until a mutual friend brought the two together in 1811. They began a correspondence that lasted the rest of their lives.

### INSTRUCT: OBJECTIVE ❸

**The People's President/ Jackson Takes Office**

Key Questions
- What events in Jackson's past had increased his popularity and made him nationally known?
- How did Jackson's supporters celebrate his inauguration?

**In-Depth Resources: Unit 4**
- Geography Application: Election of 1828, pp. 9–10
- Literature Selection: from *Jackson* by Max Byrd, pp. 13–15

**ACTIVITY OPTIONS**

**INTERDISCIPLINARY LINK: CIVICS**

**BLOCK SCHEDULING**

**JACKSON FOR PRESIDENT**

**Class Time** One class period

**Task** Planning a political advertisement for Andrew Jackson's 1828 campaign

**Purpose** To analyze how political ads affect voters' impressions of a candidate

**Supplies Needed**
- Biographies and other reference materials on Jackson
- Video camera and tapes (optional)

**Activity** Divide the class into groups. Tell students they are political consultants hired by the Jackson campaign to create three-minute TV ads. The ads should tell viewers about Jackson's political beliefs and his stands on issues. An ad might also include information about his life. Each group should assign members to write, direct, narrate, and act in the video. They might also find music or create slogans. You may want to take other class periods to actually produce the ads. Let groups show their ads to the class. Conclude by discussing whether ads are a good way for voters to learn about candidates.

### CRITICAL THINKING ACTIVITY

**Forming and Supporting Opinions** Many voters supported Andrew Jackson in the election of 1828 because he came from a humble background, had risen above poverty and hardship, and was a war hero. Ask students whether they think these are sound reasons for supporting a candidate for president. Why or why not?

**Class Time** 10 minutes

said that she would "rather be a doorkeeper in the house of God than . . . live in that palace at Washington." Margaret Bayard Smith described Rachel's importance to Jackson, saying she "not only made him a happier, but a better man."

Jackson looked thin, pale, and sad at his inauguration on March 4, 1829. But the capital was full of joy and excitement. Thousands of people were there. Senator Daniel Webster wrote about the inauguration.

*A VOICE FROM THE PAST*

I have never seen such a crowd before. Persons have come five hundred miles to see General Jackson, and they really seem to think that the country has been rescued from some dreadful danger.

**Daniel Webster,** *Correspondence*

**C. Possible Answer** The common people felt one of their own was now president.

***Reading*History**

**C. Drawing Conclusions** Why did Jackson's supporters react with such enthusiasm at his inauguration?

At the inauguration ceremony, the crowd shouted, waved, applauded, and saluted its hero. He bowed low to the people in turn. A throng followed Jackson to the White House reception. One person described the crowd as containing "all sorts of people, from the highest and most polished, down to the most vulgar and gross in the nation."

The crowd grew rowdy. People broke china and glasses as they grabbed for the food and drinks. The pushing and shoving finally drove the new president to flee the White House. As Supreme Court Justice Joseph Story observed, "The reign of King Mob seemed triumphant."

### CITIZENSHIP TODAY

**OBJECTIVE**

Students will be able to explain the value of mock elections in increasing future voters' political awareness and involvement.

**Exercising the Vote**

Groups and events such as Kid's Voting, Rock the Vote, and the National Student/Parent Mock Election have an urgent mission to interest young people in voting. The reason for their efforts is the sharp decline in voter turnout that has occurred since the 1960s, particularly among younger voters. In 1960, during the Kennedy-Nixon contest, 62.8 percent of the voting-age population went to the polls. By 1996, when Bill Clinton battled Bob Dole and Ross Perot for the presidency, only 49 percent of possible voters cast their ballots.

**Citizenship Today,** pp. 7–8

## CITIZENSHIP TODAY

# Exercising the Vote

During the Age of Jackson, rules on who could vote were eased. This increased the number of voters. But voting was still limited to adult white males. Over the years, other groups gained the right to vote, including African Americans, women, and Native Americans. Today's elections are open to all citizens aged 18 and over.

Future voters can practice casting their votes in mock, or pretend, elections. The National Student/Parent Mock Election teaches students to be informed voters. Mock presidential elections attract coverage by the media. Television stations may even broadcast live from schools, interviewing student voters.

Students register to vote in a mock election.

One high school student, Charlie Tran from San Jose, California, said, "Students seem to catch the important political events surrounding them. Some students are taking their views . . . to a new level by campaigning for the candidate they support."

### How Do You Set Up a Mock Election?

1. Choose issues and candidates and then set up a mock election in your classroom. (You could focus on the national, state, or local level.)
2. Create the materials of an election, such as the polling place, ballots, and posters.
3. Campaign for the candidates or the issues you support.
4. Conduct the voting.
5. Prepare mock media reports on the election's outcome. You may want to interview voters.

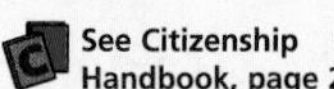

**See Citizenship Handbook, page 283.**

**Visit www.mcdougallittell.com to learn more about citizenship and voting.**



### STANDARDS FOR EVALUATION: CITIZENSHIP TODAY

**Each report should**

- use simple, easy-to-understand language.
- clearly identify the candidates or summarize the issues to be decided.
- offer a balanced treatment.
- give specific numbers for election results.
- analyze the election results and suggest reasons for the outcome.

## Changes in Ideas About Democracy

| JEFFERSONIAN DEMOCRACY | JACKSONIAN DEMOCRACY |
|---|---|
| government for the people by capable, well-educated leaders | government by the people |
| democracy in political life | democracy in social, economic, and political life |
| championed the cause of the farmer in a mainly agricultural society | championed the cause of the farmer and the laborer in an agricultural and industrial society |
| limited government | limited government, but with a strong president |

SKILLBUILDER **Interpreting Charts**

1. *What do you think was the most important change in democracy?*
2. *Did Jefferson or Jackson exercise more power?*

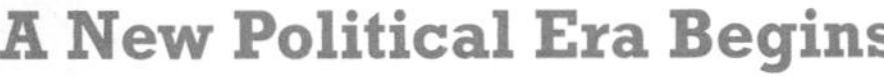

## 4 A New Political Era Begins

Jackson's inauguration began a new political era. In his campaign, he had promised to reform government. He started by replacing many government officials with his supporters. This practice of giving government jobs to political backers became known as the **spoils system**. The name comes from a statement that "to the victor belong the spoils [possessions] of the enemy." Jackson's opponents charged that the practice was corrupt. But he defended it, noting that it broke up one group's hold on government.

As president, Jackson would face three major issues—the status of Native Americans, the rights of the states, and the role of the Bank of the United States. In the next section, you will learn how Jackson's policies affected Native Americans.

Skillbuilder Answers

1. Some students may say government by the people; others might choose the spread of democracy to social and economic life.
2. Jackson exercised more power because he believed in a strong presidency.

### Section 1 Assessment

**1. Terms & Names**

**Identify:**
- John Quincy Adams
- Andrew Jackson
- Jacksonian democracy
- spoils system

**2. Taking Notes**

Use a chart to identify important biographical information about Andrew Jackson.

| Life of Andrew Jackson | |
|---|---|
| Youthful life | |
| Road to Congress | |
| War hero | |
| Appeal to voters | |

**3. Main Ideas**

a. How did Andrew Jackson react to the election of 1824? Why?

b. What factors helped Jackson win the presidency in 1828?

c. What was the effect of expanding voting rights?

**4. Critical Thinking**

**Analyzing Points of View** What are reasons for and against the spoils system?

THINK ABOUT
- the effects of giving government workers lifetime jobs
- the effects of rewarding political supporters

ACTIVITY OPTIONS

GEOGRAPHY

MATH

Find out which states Jackson and Adams won in the 1828 election. Show the results on a **map** or **chart** that includes vote totals and percentages.





### HISTORY FROM VISUALS

**Interpreting Charts** Have students examine the differences between Jefferson and Jackson. Then ask students how Jackson's concept of democracy differed from Jefferson's. How were they similar?
**Possible Response** Jackson had a broader definition of democracy. Jefferson sought to make political life democratic, but was less concerned about expanding economic and social opportunities for ordinary people. Both believed common people were capable of being informed voters and choosing good leaders.

**Extension** Have students use the information on the chart to write a paper comparing and contrasting Jeffersonian and Jacksonian Democracy.

### INSTRUCT: OBJECTIVE  4

**A New Political Era Begins**

Key Questions
- What was the spoils system, and why was it controversial?
- What important issues did Jackson face as president?

### ASSESS & RETEACH

**Setting the Stage** Have students classify information in this section according to the categories presented on the graphic organizer on page 368.

 **Formal Assessment**
- Section Quiz, p. 186

 **Critical Thinking Transparency CT34**
- Setting the Stage

**RETEACHING ACTIVITY**

Working in groups of four, students should write two questions about each of the words or phrases in "Terms & Names" on page 369. Have groups exchange questions, answer each other's questions, and return the answers for checking.

 **In-Depth Resources: Unit 4**
- Reteaching Activity, p. 16

### Section  1 Assessment

**1. Terms & Names**

**John Quincy Adams,** p. 369
**Andrew Jackson,** p. 369
**Jacksonian democracy,** p. 370
**spoils system,** p. 373

**2. Taking Notes**

Youthful life: frontier farm, prisoner in Revolutionary War, wild and reckless; Road to Congress: lawyer in Tennessee, bought a plantation, elected to Congress; War hero: defeated British in Battle of New Orleans; Appeal to voters: poor background; military hero; defender of common people

**3. Main Ideas**

**a.** outraged because he felt the presidency was stolen from him **b.** his background; his appeal to common people; the expansion of voting rights **c.** the election of a president who was a champion of the common people

**4. Critical Thinking**

For: it broke up one group's hold on government jobs; Against: it was just a way to reward political supporters

**ACTIVITY OPTIONS**

 **Alternative Assessment**
- Rubrics for a map, 2.1
- Rubrics for a chart, 2.2

## SECTION OBJECTIVES

1. To explain the conflict between whites and Native Americans in the Southeast
2. To evaluate Jackson's removal policy
3. To describe the hardships of the Trail of Tears
4. To explain how Native American groups in the East resisted removal

**SKILLBUILDER**
Interpreting Maps: Movement, Location, p. 376

**CRITICAL THINKING**
Drawing Conclusions, p. 376
Recognizing Effects, pp. 377, 378

## FOCUS & MOTIVATE

### 5-MINUTE WARM-UP

**Reading a Map** These questions focus on Jackson's Indian removal policy.

1. Look at the map on page 376. What Southeastern tribes were affected by Jackson's Indian policy?
2. Judging by the map, what was the purpose of this policy?

 **Warm-Up Transparency WT12**

## INSTRUCT

### INSTRUCT: OBJECTIVE 

**Native Americans in the Southeast/ The Cherokee Nation**

Key Questions

- What were the conflicts between whites and Native Americans in the Eastern states?
- How had the Cherokee adapted to living among white settlers?
- Why did whites pressure the government to force the Cherokee out of Georgia?

 **In-Depth Resources: Unit 4**
- Guided Reading, p. 4
- Building Vocabulary, p. 7

# 2 Jackson's Policy Toward Native Americans

**TERMS & NAMES**
Sequoya
Indian Removal Act
Indian Territory
Trail of Tears
Osceola

| MAIN IDEA | WHY IT MATTERS NOW |
| --- | --- |
| During Jackson's presidency, Native Americans were forced to move west of the Mississippi River. | This forced removal forever changed the lives of Native Americans in the United States. |

## ONE AMERICAN'S STORY

**For 12 years, a brilliant Cherokee named <u>Sequoya</u> (sih KWOY uh) tried to find a way to "teach the Cherokees to talk on paper like the white man." In 1821, he reached his goal. Sequoya invented a writing system for the Cherokee language without ever having learned to read or write in any other language. Helped by his young daughter, he identified all the sounds in Cherokee and created 86 characters to stand for syllables.**

**Using this simple system, the Cherokees soon learned to read and write. They even published a newspaper and books in their own language. A traveler in 1828 marveled at how many Cherokees had learned to read and write without schools or even paper and pens.**

Sequoya invented a writing system of 86 characters, shown here, for the Cherokee language.

*A VOICE FROM THE PAST*

I frequently saw as I rode from place to place, Cherokee letters painted or cut on the trees by the roadside, on fences, houses, and often on pieces of bark or board, lying about the houses.

**Anonymous traveler,** quoted in the *Advocate*

**Sequoya hoped that by gaining literacy—the ability to read and write—his people could share the power of whites and keep their independence. But even Sequoya's invention could not save the Cherokees from the upheaval to come. In this section, you will learn about President Jackson's policy toward Native Americans and its effects.**

## 1 Native Americans in the Southeast

Since the 1600s, white settlers had pushed Native Americans westward as they took more and more of their land. However, there were still many Native Americans in the East in the early 1800s. Some whites hoped that the Native Americans could adapt to the white people's way of life. Others wanted the Native Americans to move. They believed this was the only way to avoid conflict over land. Also, many whites felt that Native Americans were "uncivilized" and did not want to live near them.

By the 1820s, about 100,000 Native Americans remained east of the Mississippi River. The majority were in the Southeast. The major tribes



## RECOMMENDED RESOURCES

 **In-Depth Resources: Unit 4**
- Guided Reading, p. 4
- Building Vocabulary, p. 7
- Primary Source: A Petition by Cherokee Women, p. 11
- Reteaching Activity, p. 17
- Enrichment Activity, p. 20

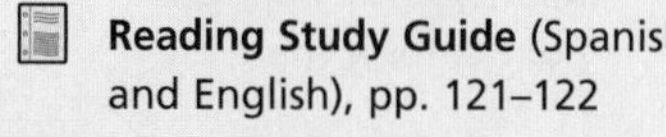 **Reading Study Guide** (Spanish and English), pp. 121–122

**Outline Map Activities**
- Native American Movement, 1830–1842, pp. 23–24

 **America's History Makers**
- Sequoya, pp. 49–50

**Formal Assessment**
- Section Quiz, p. 187

**Alternative Assessment**
- Rubrics, 2.1, 2.2

**Access for Students Acquiring English/ESL**
- Guided Reading, p. 80

**Technology Resources**

 **Critical Thinking Trans. CT35**
- Cause and Effect: Native American Removal

 **Humanities Transparency HT23**
- Political Cartoon: Andrew Jackson and Native Americans

 **Electronic Teacher Tools with Test Maker**

 **ClassZone**
www.mcdougallittell.com

*Reading***History**

**A. Reading a Map** Use the map on page 376 to locate Native American lands in the Southeast.

were the Cherokee, Chickasaw, Choctaw, Creek, and Seminole. Whites called them the Five Civilized Tribes because they had adopted many aspects of white culture. They held large areas of land in Georgia, the Carolinas, Alabama, Mississippi, and Tennessee.

## The Cherokee Nation

More than any other Southeastern tribe, the Cherokee had adopted white customs, including their way of dressing. Cherokees owned prosperous farms and cattle ranches. Some even had slaves. From Sequoya, they acquired a written language, and they published their own newspaper, the *Cherokee Phoenix*. Some of their children attended missionary schools. In 1827, the Cherokees drew up a constitution based on the U.S. Constitution and founded the Cherokee Nation.

A year after the Cherokees adopted their constitution, gold was discovered on their land in Georgia. Now, not only settlers but also miners wanted these lands. The discovery of gold increased demands by whites to move the Cherokees. The federal government responded with a plan to remove all Native Americans from the Southeast.

## 2 Jackson's Removal Policy

Andrew Jackson had long supported a policy of moving Native Americans west of the Mississippi. He first dealt with the Southeastern tribes after the War of 1812. The federal government ordered Jackson, then acting as Indian treaty commissioner, to make treaties with the Native Americans of the region. Through these treaties forced on the tribes, the government gained large tracts of land.

Jackson believed that the government had the right to regulate where Native Americans could live. He viewed them as conquered subjects who lived within the borders of the United States. He thought that Native Americans had one of two choices. They could adopt white culture and become citizens of the United States. Or they could move into the Western territories. They could not, however, have their own governments within the nation's borders.

After the discovery of gold, whites began to move onto Cherokee land. Georgia and other Southern states passed laws that gave them the right to take over Native American lands. When the Cherokee and other tribes protested, Jackson supported the states.

To solve the problem, Jackson asked Congress to pass a law that would require Native Americans to either move west or submit to state laws. Many Americans objected to Jackson's proposal. Massachusetts congressman Edward Everett opposed removing Native Americans against their will to a distant land. There, he said, they would face "the

### Now and then

**CHEROKEE PEOPLE TODAY**

Today, there are more than 300,000 Cherokees. They are part of three main groups—the Cherokee Nation of Oklahoma, the United Keetoowah Band in Oklahoma, and the Eastern Band of Cherokee Indians of North Carolina.

Wilma Mankiller, shown below, was the first woman elected principal chief of the Cherokee Nation of Oklahoma. She has said that the "Cherokee people possess an extraordinary ability to face down adversity and continue moving forward. We are able to do that because our culture, though certainly diminished, has sustained us since time immemorial."

### Now *and* then

**Cherokee People Today**

Wilma Mankiller was elected principal chief of the Cherokee Nation of Oklahoma in 1985. During her years as chief, she has worked for improved health care, better education, and more efficient tribal government. She says that although the Cherokee have many challenges, she is optimistic about the future. "We've had daunting problems in many critical areas," she says, "but I believe in the old Cherokee injunction to be of a good mind. Today it's called positive thinking." Mankiller's last name is a term of respect for warriors who protected villages.

 **America's History Makers**
- Sequoya, pp. 49–50

### INSTRUCT: OBJECTIVE 2

**Jackson's Removal Policy**

Key Questions
- Why did Jackson believe the government had the right to decide where Native Americans could live?
- How did Jackson propose to solve the problem of Native American protests?
- How did the Indian Removal Act affect Native Americans in the Southeast?

 **Outline Map Activities**
- Native American Movement, 1830–1842, pp. 23–24

### CRITICAL THINKING ACTIVITY

**Analyzing Points of View** Ask students why whites called the Cherokee, Chickasaw, Choctaw, Creek, and Seminole the Five Civilized Tribes. What does this name suggest about how most whites at that time viewed Native American cultures? Which of Jackson's criteria for remaining on their land had the Cherokee met? Which had they failed to meet? If the Cherokee had chosen another course of action, would it have changed the outcome?

**Class Time** 10 minutes

### ACTIVITY OPTIONS

**INTERDISCIPLINARY LINK: LANGUAGE ARTS/WRITING**

 BLOCK SCHEDULING

**A LETTER TO THE PRESIDENT**

**Class Time** One class period

**Task** Writing a letter on a public issue

**Purpose** To evaluate the Indian removal policy from different perspectives

**Supplies Needed**
- Reference materials on the Indian Removal Act and on the Native American groups affected
- Writing materials

**Activity** Explain to students that the Indian Removal Act affected peaceful Native American groups that had been considered sovereign nations and that held their lands by treaty with the United States. Then ask students to assume the viewpoints of members of Southeastern tribes and write letters to Jackson expressing their views on the act and describing how it will affect them. Remind them that their purpose is to influence the president, not to antagonize him.

## HISTORY FROM VISUALS

**Reading the Map** Have students identify the Southeastern tribe that was forced to leave Florida. Ask them which group had the largest number of people forced to relocate. **Answers** Seminole; Creeks, over 14,000. Ask students what reason might have been cited to move Native Americans from Wisconsin and Michigan. Ask them why the federal government might have chosen parts of what are now Oklahoma and Kansas for the relocation of Native Americans. **Possible Response** More white settlers were moving into those territories. The area was not considered valuable by white settlers.

**Extension** Have students pick one of the Southeastern peoples shown on the chart and do research to learn its current size, status, and location.

### Removal of Native Americans, 1820–1840

Removal Routes: Cherokee, Chickasaw, Choctaw, Creek, Seminole, Other tribes

0 — 300 Miles; 0 — 600 Kilometers

**Southeastern People Relocated**

Cherokees, Chickasaws, Choctaws, Creeks, Seminoles

0 2 4 6 8 10 12 14 16 (in thousands)

= 2,000 Native Americans

**GEOGRAPHY SKILLBUILDER Interpreting Maps**
1. **Movement** *How long was the Trail of Tears?*
2. **Location** *What states bordered Indian Territory?*

**Skillbuilder Answers**
1. about 700 miles
2. Missouri and Arkansas

perils and hardships of a wilderness." Religious groups such as the Quakers also opposed forced removal of Native Americans. After heated debate, Congress passed the **Indian Removal Act** in 1830. The act called for the government to negotiate treaties that would require Native Americans to relocate west.

Jackson immediately set out to enforce the law. He thought his policy was "just and liberal" and would allow Native Americans to keep their way of life. Instead, his policy caused much hardship and forever changed relations between whites and Native Americans.

**Reading History**
**B. Drawing Conclusions** What were reasons for and against the Indian Removal Act?
**B. Possible Answers** Reasons for: White settlers wanted Native American land. Relocation would prevent tribes from being wiped out. Reasons against: Native Americans did not want to move, and they had treaties protecting their lands.

## 3 The Trail of Tears

As whites invaded their homelands, many Native Americans saw no other choice but to sign treaties exchanging their land for land in the West. Under the treaties, Native Americans would be moved to an area that covered what is now Oklahoma and parts of Kansas and Nebraska. This area came to be called **Indian Territory.**

Beginning in the fall of 1831, the Choctaw and other Southeast tribes were removed from their lands and relocated to Indian Territory. The Cherokees, however, first appealed to the U.S. Supreme Court to protect their land from being seized by Georgia. In 1832, the court, led by Chief Justice John Marshall, ruled that only the federal government, not the states, could make laws governing the Cherokees. This ruling meant that



## INSTRUCT: OBJECTIVE 3

**The Trail of Tears**
Key Questions
- How did the Cherokee fight the takeover of their lands in Georgia?
- How did the Supreme Court rule on the Cherokee case, and why was Jackson able to ignore this ruling?
- Why is the journey of the Cherokee to Indian Territory known as the Trail of Tears?

 **In-Depth Resources: Unit 4**
- Primary Source: A Petition by Cherokee Women, p. 11

 **Critical Thinking Transparency CT35**
- Cause and Effect: Native American Removal

## ACTIVITY OPTIONS

**MULTIPLE LEARNING STYLES: SPATIAL**

### TRAIL OF TEARS MEMORIAL

**Class Time** One class period

**Task** Designing a model for a memorial commemorating the Trail of Tears

**Purpose** To express the hardships of Indian removal for the Cherokee

**Supplies Needed**
- Reference materials on the Trail of Tears
- Photographs of various public monuments and memorials
- Modeling clay and poster paper

**Activity** Using the photographs, encourage the class to discuss what makes a monument effective. Then have students work in groups of three to read more about the Trail of Tears and to create a design for a memorial. Have each group use clay to make a model of its monument or use paper to make a drawing. Designs should include an inscription explaining the monument's purpose. Groups can share their models or drawings with the class or post photos on a class Web site.

the Georgia laws did not apply to the Cherokee Nation. However, both Georgia and President Jackson ignored the Supreme Court. Jackson said, "John Marshall has made his decision. . . . Now let him enforce it."

A small group of Cherokees gave up and signed a treaty to move west. But the majority of the Cherokees, led by John Ross, opposed the treaty. Jackson refused to negotiate with these Cherokees.

In 1838, federal troops commanded by General Winfield Scott rounded up about 16,000 Cherokees and forced them into camps. Soldiers took people from their homes with nothing but the clothes on their backs. Over the fall and winter of 1838–1839, these Cherokees set out on the long journey west. Forced to march in the cold, rain, and snow without adequate clothing, many grew weak and ill. One-fourth died. The dead included John Ross's wife. One soldier never forgot what he witnessed on the trail.

*Reading* **History**
**C. Recognizing Effects** What happened to the Cherokees as a result of the Indian Removal Act?
C. Possible Answers They lost their land, property, and homes. One-fourth of them died on the long journey west. They had to resettle in a strange land.

*A VOICE FROM THE PAST*

Murder is murder and somebody must answer, somebody must explain the streams of blood that flowed in the Indian country in . . . 1838. Somebody must explain the four-thousand silent graves that mark the trail of the Cherokees to their exile. I wish I could forget it all, but the picture of six-hundred and forty-five wagons lumbering over the frozen ground with their Cargo of suffering humanity still lingers in my memory.

**John G. Burnett**, quoted in *The Native Americans*, edited by Betty and Ian Ballantine

This harsh journey of the Cherokee from their homeland to Indian Territory became known as the **Trail of Tears.**

**HISTORY through ART**

In 1838, the Cherokees left their homeland by wagon, horse, donkey, and foot, forced to travel hundreds of miles along the Trail of Tears. This painting is by Robert Lindneux, a 20th-century artist.

**How does the artist show the suffering on the Trail of Tears?**

377

## MORE ABOUT . . .

**Jackson and Native Americans**

Andrew Jackson's complex and contradictory nature was seldom better illustrated than in his attitudes toward Native Americans. He almost always spoke of them in hostile, contemptuous terms. Yet his troops at the Battle of Horseshoe Bend included Indian allies. And after a battle in 1813, he took under his protection a three-year-old Indian boy whose parents had been killed by Jackson's troops. Jackson, who had been orphaned himself, said he felt "an unusual bond of sympathy" for the child, whom he sent home to Rachel to raise with their other adopted son.

**Humanities Transparency HT23**
- Political Cartoon: Andrew Jackson and Native Americans

## HISTORY through ART

**Interpreting the Painting** About 4,000 Cherokee died on the 116-day march, largely of exposure and starvation. The soldiers that led them refused to slow down or stop so that people could recover from exhaustion or illness before continuing the long journey.

**Possible Answer: The artist shows the Native Americans under army guard. Many are forced to walk. They also look cold, tired, and sad.**

**In-Depth Resources: Unit 4**
- Enrichment Activity, p. 20

## ACTIVITY OPTIONS

### INDIVIDUAL NEEDS: GIFTED AND TALENTED

**WRITING HISTORICAL FICTION**

**Class Time** Two class periods

**Task** Writing an outline for a work of historical fiction

**Purpose** To familiarize students with the suffering endured by Native Americans as they journeyed west

**Supplies Needed**
- Reference materials, including primary sources
- For more about Cherokee history, visit www.mcdougallittell.com

**Activity** First, have students use encyclopedias, textbooks, and primary sources to familiarize themselves with the Trail of Tears. Encourage them to focus their research on the length of the journey, the means of travel available, the weather and road conditions, the role of troops, and everyday details. Then have them create outlines for fictional stories based on this historical event. Discuss with the class the advantages and drawbacks of using fiction in history.

## INSTRUCT: OBJECTIVE 4

**Native American Resistance**

Key Questions

- How did some Native American groups in the Southeast resist removal?
- What were the causes and the outcome of the Second Seminole War, and what part did Osceola play in Seminole resistance?
- Besides the Southeastern tribes, what other groups were forced to move to Indian Territory?

### MORE ABOUT . . .

**The Second Seminole War**

The Second Seminole War (1835–1842) was the longest and costliest Indian war in American history. It led to the death of 1,500 American soldiers. The number of Native Americans killed in this war is unknown. By 1842, about 3,000 Seminoles had been forced to move to Indian Territory. Another thousand hid in the Florida swamps and Everglades. Today the descendants of the Seminoles who remained in Florida hold three reservations and in 1957 created the Seminole Tribe of Florida, whose members number around 1,200.

## ASSESS & RETEACH

**Setting the Stage** Have students use information in this section to fill in the appropriate sections on the chapter graphic organizer.

**Formal Assessment**

- Section Quiz, p. 187

### RETEACHING ACTIVITY

Have students create a cause-and-effect chart showing the events that were set in motion when gold was discovered in Georgia and white settlers sought control of Native American lands in the Southeast.

**In-Depth Resources: Unit 4**

- Reteaching Activity, p. 17

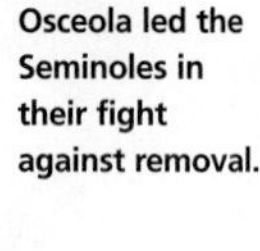

**Osceola led the Seminoles in their fight against removal.**

## 4 Native American Resistance

Not all the Cherokees moved west in 1838. That fall, soldiers had rounded up an old Cherokee farmer named Tsali and his family, including his grown sons. On the way to the stockade, they fought the soldiers. A soldier was killed before Tsali fled with his family to the Great Smoky Mountains in North Carolina. There they found other Cherokees. The U.S. Army sent a message to Tsali. If he and his sons would give themselves up, the others could remain. They surrendered, and all except the youngest son were shot. Their sacrifice allowed some Cherokees to stay in their homeland.

Other Southeast tribes also resisted relocation. In 1835, the Seminoles refused to leave Florida. This refusal led to the Second Seminole War. One elderly Seminole explained why he could not leave: "If suddenly we tear our hearts from the homes around which they are twined [wrapped around], our heart strings will snap."

**Background** The Seminoles fought three wars against the U.S. government between 1817 and 1858, when their resistance ended.

One of the most important leaders in the war was **Osceola** (AHS ee OH luh). Hiding in the Everglades, Osceola and his band used surprise attacks to defeat the U.S. Army in many battles. In 1837, Osceola was tricked into capture when he came to peace talks during a truce. He later died in prison. But the Seminoles continued to fight. Some went deeper into the Everglades, where their descendants live today. Others moved west. The Second Seminole War ended in 1842.

Some tribes north of the Ohio River also resisted relocation. The Shawnee, Ottawa, Potawatomi, Sauk, and Fox were removed to Indian Territory. But in 1832, a Sauk chief named Black Hawk led a band of Sauk and Fox back to their lands in Illinois. In the Black Hawk War, the Illinois militia and the U.S. Army crushed the uprising.

In the next section, you will learn about other issues Jackson faced, especially increasing tensions between various sections of the country.

### Section 2 Assessment

**1. Terms & Names**

**Identify:**

- Sequoya
- Indian Removal Act
- Indian Territory
- Trail of Tears
- Osceola

**2. Taking Notes**

Use a chart to list the reasons for Jackson's Native American removal policy.

| Reasons Native Americans Were Forced West | | |
|---|---|---|
| Economic | Political | Social |
| | | |

What do you think was the main reason?

**3. Main Ideas**

a. How did President Jackson justify the Indian Removal Act?

b. In what ways did Native Americans resist the Indian Removal Act?

c. What were the consequences of the Indian Removal Act?

**4. Critical Thinking**

**Recognizing Effects** What were some economic effects of the Indian Removal Act on Native Americans? On whites?

**THINK ABOUT**

- what the Native Americans lost
- what the white settlers gained

**ACTIVITY OPTIONS**

**GEOGRAPHY / MATH** Use the map on page 376 to estimate the distance traveled by each of the five Southeastern tribes. Show your calculation on a **map** or **chart.**



### Section 2 Assessment

**1. Terms & Names**

**Sequoya,** p. 374
**Indian Removal Act,** p. 376
**Indian Territory,** p. 376
**Trail of Tears,** p. 377
**Osceola,** p. 378

**2. Taking Notes**

Economic: white settlers and miners wanted their land; Political: Native Americans could not maintain independent governments in the United States; Social: many whites considered them uncivilized

Answers will vary but should be supported with information from the chapter.

**3. Main Ideas**

**a.** He said Native Americans could either adopt white culture or move out of the United States. **b.** took up arms; fought against relocation; went into hiding; used the courts for help **c.** Native Americans lost land, property, and homes; many died.

**4. Critical Thinking**

Native Americans became impoverished because they lost all their land and had to move. Whites became richer because they gained land and mined gold.

**ACTIVITY OPTIONS**

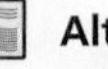

**Alternative Assessment**

- Rubrics for a map, 2.1
- Rubrics for a chart, 2.2

# 3 Conflicts Over States' Rights

**TERMS & NAMES**
John C. Calhoun
Tariff of Abominations
doctrine of nullification
Webster-Hayne debate
Daniel Webster
secession

**MAIN IDEA**

Jackson struggled to keep Southern states from breaking away from the Union over the issue of tariffs.

**WHY IT MATTERS NOW**

Disputes about states' rights and federal power remain important in national politics.

## ONE AMERICAN'S STORY

**Early in his political career, John C. Calhoun was hailed as "one of the master-spirits who stamp their name upon the age in which they live." This was praise indeed for someone from the backwoods of South Carolina who had little formal education before age 18. Elected to the U.S. Congress at 28, Calhoun soon was one of its leaders. He supported the need for a strong central government and became something of a hero to the nation's young people. He spoke out against sectionalism.**

*A VOICE FROM THE PAST*

What is necessary for the common good may apparently be opposed to the interest of particular sections. It must be submitted to [accepted] as the condition of our [nation's] greatness.

**John C. Calhoun,** quoted in *John C. Calhoun: American Portrait* by Margaret L. Coit

**But Calhoun's concern for the economic and political well-being of his home state of South Carolina, and the South in general, later caused him to change his beliefs. He became the foremost champion of states' rights, rigid in his views and increasingly bitter.**

**In this section, you will learn how two strong-willed men—Calhoun and Jackson—came in conflict over the issue of states' rights.**

The bitter debate over state's rights took a physical toll on John C. Calhoun. He is shown here in about 1825 and in 1849.

## 1 Rising Sectional Differences

Andrew Jackson had taken office in 1829. At the time, the country was being pulled apart by conflicts among its three main sections—the Northeast, the South, and the West. Legislators from these regions were arguing over three major economic issues: the sale of public lands, internal improvements, and tariffs.

The federal government had acquired vast areas of land through conquests, treaties, and purchases. It raised money partly by selling these public lands. However, Northeasterners did not want public lands in the West to be sold at low prices. The cheap land would attract workers who were needed in the factories of the Northeast. But Westerners wanted





## SECTION OBJECTIVES

1. To identify the issues that led to rising sectional differences
2. To explain how the "Tariff of Abominations" led to a crisis over nullification
3. To analyze the issues in the debate over states' rights
4. To describe how South Carolina's threat to secede was resolved

**CRITICAL THINKING**

Analyzing Causes, p. 381
Summarizing, p. 381
Analyzing Points of View, p. 383
Recognizing Effects, p. 383

## FOCUS & MOTIVATE

### 5-MINUTE WARM-UP

**Drawing Conclusions** These questions focus on some of the causes of sectionalism.

1. Read the quotation from Calhoun on page 379. What did Calhoun mean by "common good," and what was his advice about sectionalism?
2. Why might sectionalism undermine a nation's "greatness"?

 **Warm-Up Transparency WT12**

## INSTRUCT

**INSTRUCT: OBJECTIVE** 

**Rising Sectional Differences**

Key Questions

- Why did Northerners and Westerners disagree over the sale of public land?
- What were the differences among the sections on internal improvements and tariffs?

**In-Depth Resources: Unit 4**
- Guided Reading, p. 5

**Reading Study Guide** (Spanish and English), pp. 123–124

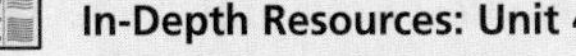

**RECOMMENDED RESOURCES**

**In-Depth Resources: Unit 4**
- Guided Reading, p. 5
- Building Vocabulary, p. 7
- Primary Source: from *Reminiscences and Anecdotes of Daniel Webster,* p. 12
- Reteaching Activity, p. 18

**Reading Study Guide** (Spanish and English), pp. 123–124

**Economics in History**
- Westerners and High Tariffs, p. 12

**Formal Assessment**
- Section Quiz, p. 188

**Alternative Assessment**
- Rubrics, 3.6
- Rubrics, 5.3

**Access for Students Acquiring English/ESL**
- Guided Reading, p. 81

**Technology Resources**

 **Electronic Teacher Tools with Test Maker**

 **ClassZone**
www.mcdougallittell.com

## MORE ABOUT . . .

**Internal Improvements**

Among the most important internal improvements were better roads. Most roads at the time were unpaved paths where wagon wheels sank hub-deep in mud in wet weather and lurched over holes and ruts in dry weather. The new roads, built with both private and public money, were wider, better graded, and better surfaced.

low land prices to encourage settlement. The more people who moved West, the more political power the section would have.

The issue of internal improvements also pulled the sections apart. Business leaders in the Northeast and West backed government spending on internal improvements, such as new roads and canals. Good transportation would help bring food and raw materials to the Northeast and take manufactured goods to Western markets. Southerners opposed more federal spending on internal improvements because the government financed these projects through tariffs, which were taxes on imported goods. The South did not want any increase in tariffs.

Since 1816, tariffs had risen steadily. They had become the government's main source of income. Northerners supported high tariffs because they made imported goods more expensive than American-made goods. The Northeast had most of the nation's manufacturing. Tariffs helped

**Background**
During the Jackson era, the West included states that are now considered part of the Midwest.

## Economics *in* History

**OBJECTIVE**
Students will be able to distinguish between revenue tariffs and protective tariffs and explain how protective tariffs work.

**How Tariffs Work**
Throughout much of American history, protective tariffs have sparked political debate. Most manufacturers and their workers, particularly in the North, have favored such tariffs. Farmers and Southern planters, who relied on foreign markets for the sale of their farm products, usually opposed tariffs. As American industries grew stronger, however, support for tariffs weakened. Since 1948, the United States has worked with other nations to lower tariffs on industrial goods. Once highly controversial, by the 1990s, free trade had become the official political position of both Democrats and Republicans.

**Economics in History**
- Westerners and High Tariffs, p.12

## Economics *in* History

# How Tariffs Work

Tariffs are taxes added to the cost of goods imported from another country. There are two kinds of tariffs—revenue tariffs and protective tariffs. **Revenue tariffs** are used to raise money, like the sales taxes that states add to purchases today. These tariffs tend to be fairly low. **Protective tariffs** usually are much higher. They have another goal: to persuade consumers to buy goods made in their own country instead of purchasing foreign-made products. Congress passed a protective tariff in 1828 to help American companies.

The illustration shows how a protective tariff works. A British-made teapot sells for $3.50, and a similar teapot made in the United States sells for $4.00. Most shoppers will buy the British teapot and save 50 cents. But when the government adds a 40 percent tariff to British goods, the price of the British teapot soars to $4.90. The result: consumers buy the now-cheaper American teapots.

**CONNECT TO HISTORY**

1. **Recognizing Effects** Do consumers benefit from high tariffs? Why or why not?

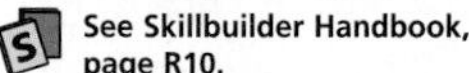
See Skillbuilder Handbook, page R10.

**CONNECT TO TODAY**

2. **Making Inferences** Today, many leaders around the world promote the idea of "free trade." What do you think "free trade" means?

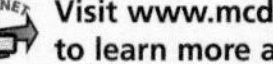
Visit www.mcdougallittell.com to learn more about tariffs.

**CONNECT TO HISTORY**

1. **Recognizing Effects** **Possible Response** Consumers do not usually benefit because they have to pay higher prices.

**CONNECT TO TODAY**

2. **Making Inferences** **Possible Response** Free trade means goods are traded between countries without any tariffs.

American manufacturers sell their products at a lower price than imported goods.

The South opposed rising tariffs because its economy depended on foreign trade. Southern planters sold most of their cotton to foreign buyers. They were not paid in money but were given credit. They then used the credit to buy foreign manufactured goods. Because of higher tariffs, these foreign goods cost more. Eventually, the tariff issue would lead to conflict between North and South.

*Reading* **History**
**A. Analyzing Causes** Why did the three sections of the country differ on the sale of public lands, internal improvements, and tariffs?
**A. Possible Answer** The economy of each section was affected differently by these issues.

## Tariff of Abominations 2

In 1828, in the last months of John Quincy Adams's presidency, Congress passed a bill that significantly raised the tariffs on raw materials and manufactured goods. Southerners were outraged. They had to sell their cotton at low prices to be competitive. Yet tariffs forced them to pay high prices for manufactured goods. Southerners felt that the economic interests of the Northeast were determining national policy. They hated the tariff and called it the **Tariff of Abominations** (an abomination is a hateful thing).

Differences over the tariff helped Jackson win the election of 1828. Southerners blamed Adams for the tariff, since it was passed during his administration. So they voted against him.

**A South Carolina woman sews a palmetto emblem (inset) to her hat to show her support for nullification. The palmetto is a South Carolina symbol.**

## Crisis over Nullification

The Tariff of Abominations hit South Carolinians especially hard because their economy was in a slump. Some leaders in the state even spoke of leaving the Union over the issue of tariffs. John C. Calhoun, then Jackson's vice-president, understood the problems of South Carolina's farmers because he was one himself. But he wanted to find a way to keep South Carolina from leaving the Union. The answer he arrived at was the **doctrine of nullification**. A state, Calhoun said, had the right to nullify, or reject, a federal law that it considers unconstitutional.

*Reading* **History**
**B. Summarizing** How did the issue of tariffs threaten to tear the Union apart?
**B. Possible Answers** The South resented the Northeast for pushing higher tariffs without regard for the effect on the South's economy. South Carolina threatened to secede over the issue.

Calhoun was not the first person to propose the doctrine of nullification. It had been stated earlier by Thomas Jefferson. Jefferson argued that the Union was a league of sovereign, or self-governing, states that had the right to limit the federal government. Calhoun developed the doctrine further. He said that any state could nullify, or refuse to recognize, a federal law within its borders. He believed that Congress had no right to impose a tariff that favored one section of the country. Therefore, South Carolina had the right to nullify the tariff. Calhoun's doctrine was an extreme form of states' rights—the theory that states have the right to judge whether a law of Congress is unconstitutional.

In the summer of 1828, Calhoun wrote a document called the "South Carolina Exposition and Protest." It stated his theory. Calhoun allowed the document to be published, but he did not sign his name. He knew his ideas would cause controversy.

**Vocabulary**
**controversy:** a public dispute

### INSTRUCT: OBJECTIVE 2

**Tariff of Abominations/ Crisis over Nullification**

Key Questions

- Why did the tariff of 1828 anger Southerners?
- What was the doctrine of nullification?
- How did Calhoun apply that doctrine to the "Tariff of Abominations"?

### MORE ABOUT . . .

**Calhoun and Nullification**

In the first half of his public career, Calhoun was a strong nationalist who fought for the Second Bank of the United States, a permanent road system, and a standing army. He supported the protective tariff of 1816. Yet by 1828, he led the fight for states' rights. Calhoun favored nullification in part because he feared that the Northern majority in Congress might one day act against the South on the issue of slavery. Calhoun wrote that the tariff was of "vastly inferior importance to the great question to which it has given rise . . . the right of a state to . . . [stop] an unconstitutional act of the General Government."

### ACTIVITY OPTIONS

### INDIVIDUAL NEEDS

**LESS PROFICIENT READERS**

**Rereading** If students have difficulty completing the "Taking Notes" chart on page 383, you might want to provide a strategy for rereading to review and clarify this complex material. Have students reread pages 379–381 and identify the position taken by each region of the United States on each issue. Then work with students to extend the chart to explain why each region held the position it did. You can create a chart on the board similar to the one pictured, with additional categories for internal improvements and high tariffs.

| | North | West | South |
|---|---|---|---|
| High prices for public lands | Yes | No | No position shown |
| Why? | Would lose workers | Would gain political power | |
| Tariffs | | | |

## MORE ABOUT . . .

**Daniel Webster**

During his lifetime, Daniel Webster was famed for his skill as an orator. Even years after his death, students memorized lines from his speeches. He was best known for the final line of a speech he delivered in the Senate in 1830. "Liberty and Union," he said, "now and forever, one and inseparable." These words became a rallying cry for Union soldiers during the Civil War.

**In-Depth Resources: Unit 4**

- Primary Source: from *Reminiscences and Anecdotes of Daniel Webster,* p. 12

## INSTRUCT: OBJECTIVE 3

**The States' Rights Debate**

Key Questions

- Why did the theory of nullification develop into a national debate?
- What was the importance of the Webster-Hayne debate in Congress?
- How did the nullification issue make Jackson and Calhoun political enemies?

## MORE ABOUT . . .

**Robert Hayne**

Although John C. Calhoun was the leading advocate of states' rights, he was also vice-president and therefore could not take part in Senate debates. So Robert Hayne spoke for him. Like Calhoun, Hayne was from South Carolina. Born on Pon Pon plantation in 1791, he had studied law and served in the War of 1812. He was elected to the Senate in 1823, where he served until 1832. Then he resigned to become governor of South Carolina and thereafter, mayor of Charleston. He died in 1839.

Daniel Webster (standing) and Robert Y. Hayne (seated, with hands extended) debated nullification in the U.S. Senate in 1830.

## 3 The States' Rights Debate

Calhoun was right. His ideas added fuel to the debate over the nature of the federal union. This debate had been going on since independence from Britain. More and more people took sides. Some supported a strong federal government. Others defended the rights of the states. This question would be a major political issue from this time until the Civil War was fought to resolve it some 30 years later.

One of the great debates in American history took place in the U.S. Senate over the doctrine of nullification—the **Webster-Hayne debate** of 1830. On one side was **Daniel Webster,** a senator from Massachusetts and the most powerful speaker of his time. On the other was Robert Y. Hayne, a senator from South Carolina. Hayne defended nullification. He argued that it gave the states a lawful way to protest and to maintain their freedom. He also said that the real enemies of the Union were those "who are constantly stealing power from the States, and adding strength to the Federal Government."

Webster argued that it was the people and not the states that made the Union. In words that were printed and spread across the country, Webster declared that freedom and the Union go together.

*A VOICE FROM THE PAST*

When my eyes shall be turned to behold for the last time the sun in heaven, may I not see him shining on the broken and dishonored fragments of a once glorious Union. . . . Liberty and Union, now and forever, one and inseparable!

**Daniel Webster,** a speech in the U.S. Senate, January 26, 1830

Jackson had not yet stated his position on the issue of states' rights, even though Calhoun was his vice-president. He got his chance in April at a dinner in honor of the birthday of Thomas Jefferson. Calhoun and other



## ACTIVITY OPTIONS

**INTERDISCIPLINARY LINK: GOVERNMENT/CIVICS**

BLOCK SCHEDULING

**DEBATING STATES' RIGHTS**

**Class Time** One class period

**Task** Holding a debate on the following statement: *Resolved: Allowing the states to nullify a federal law would destroy the national government's ability to govern.*

**Purpose** To analyze the effects of the doctrine of nullification

**Supplies Needed**

- Reference materials on the doctrine of nullification and the Webster-Hayne debate

**Activity** Divide students into two groups, one to support nullification and another to oppose it. Before the debate begins, members of each group should develop a list of arguments in support of their side's position on the issue. Allow practice time for each group to brainstorm counterarguments for every argument their opponents might present. Agree on rules for the debate.

supporters of nullification planned to use the event to win support for their position. Jackson learned of their plans and went to the dinner prepared.

After dinner, Jackson was invited to make a toast. He stood up, looked directly at Calhoun, and stated bluntly, "Our Federal Union—it must be preserved." As Calhoun raised his glass, his hand trembled. Called on to make the next toast, Calhoun stood slowly and said, "The Union—next to our liberty, the most dear; may we all remember that it can only be preserved by respecting the rights of the states and distributing equally the benefits and burdens of the Union." From that time, the two men were political enemies.

*Reading* **History**

**C. Analyzing Points of View** What do you think Calhoun meant by "the benefits and burdens of the Union" should be equally distributed?

C. Possible Answer One section should not benefit at the expense of another.

## 4 South Carolina Threatens to Secede

Even though Jackson made it clear that he opposed the doctrine of nullification, he did not want to drive the South out of the Union. He asked Congress to reduce the tariff, and Congress did so in 1832. But Southerners thought the reduced rates were still too high. South Carolina nullified the tariff acts of 1828 and 1832 and voted to build its own army. South Carolina's leaders threatened **secession**, or withdrawal from the Union, if the federal government tried to collect tariffs.

Jackson was enraged. He told a South Carolina congressman that if the state's leaders defied federal laws, he would "hang the first man of them I can get my hands on." Jackson ran for reelection in 1832, this time without Calhoun as his running mate. After he won, he made it clear that he would use force to see that federal laws were obeyed and the Union preserved.

In the Senate, Henry Clay came forward with a compromise tariff in 1833. He hoped that it would settle the issue and prevent bloodshed. Congress quickly passed the bill, and the crisis ended. South Carolina stayed in the Union. In the next section, you will read about another issue of Jackson's presidency—his war on the national bank.

### Section 3 Assessment

**1. Terms & Names**

Identify:
- John C. Calhoun
- Tariff of Abominations
- doctrine of nullification
- Webster-Hayne debate
- Daniel Webster
- secession

**2. Taking Notes**

Use a chart to indicate how each section stood on these issues.

| | North-east | West | South |
|---|---|---|---|
| Sale of public lands | | | |
| Internal improvements | | | |
| High tariffs | | | |

**3. Main Ideas**

a. Why did the South oppose high tariffs?

b. What were Calhoun's reasons for proposing the doctrine of nullification?

c. Why did South Carolina threaten secession, and how was the crisis resolved?

**4. Critical Thinking**

**Recognizing Effects** In what ways would the doctrine of nullification have made it difficult for the federal government to operate?

THINK ABOUT
- its effect on the enforcement of laws
- its effect on the power of the federal government

**ACTIVITY OPTIONS**

**SPEECH** / **TECHNOLOGY** — Research Daniel Webster's speech; a part of it appears on page 382. Deliver a **speech** for or against nullification to the class, or record it on an **audiocassette**.





**INSTRUCT: OBJECTIVE 4**

**South Carolina Threatens to Secede**

Key Questions
- How did Southerners protest the tariffs?
- What was Jackson's response to South Carolina's threat to secede?
- How was the tariff controversy settled?

**MORE ABOUT . . .**

**Henry Clay**

Henry Clay, senator from Kentucky, first gained national attention as a War Hawk urging President Madison to declare war on Britain in 1812. Some years later, however, his sponsorship of a compromise tariff that ended the crisis over the tariff act of 1828 and his efforts to end sectional conflicts earned him the nickname the "Great Compromiser" or the "Great Pacificator." He ran unsuccessfully for president in 1824, 1832, and 1844 and is often remembered for his assertion that he would "rather be right than be president."

## ASSESS & RETEACH

**Setting the Stage** Have students organize the information in this section in the appropriate category on the graphic organizer.

**Formal Assessment**
- Section Quiz, p. 188

**RETEACHING ACTIVITY**

Have students make a cluster diagram showing three causes of sectional conflict and the positions each section took on each issue.

**In-Depth Resources: Unit 4**
- Reteaching Activity, p. 18

### Section 3 Assessment

**1. Terms & Names**

**John C. Calhoun,** p. 379
**Tariff of Abominations,** p. 381
**doctrine of nullification,** p. 381
**Webster-Hayne debate,** p. 382
**Daniel Webster,** p. 382
**secession,** p. 383

**2. Taking Notes**

Sale of public lands: Northeast for, West against, South no opinion; Internal improvements: Northeast and West for, South against; High tariffs: Northeast for, South against, West no opinion

**3. Main Ideas**

**a.** They hurt the economy of the South. **b.** He saw it as a way for the South to avoid paying tariffs and still stay in the Union. **c.** to keep the federal government from collecting the tariffs; resolved by Clay's compromise tariff

**4. Critical Thinking**

The government could not enforce laws across the nation, making the states more powerful than the federal government.

**ACTIVITY OPTIONS**

**Alternative Assessment**
- Rubrics for a speech, 3.6
- Rubrics for audiocassette, 5.3

## SECTION OBJECTIVES

1. To explain why conflict erupted over the Second Bank of the United States
2. To describe how Jackson destroyed the bank
3. To analyze how economic prosperity turned into depression
4. To explain how the Whig Party won the election of 1840

**CRITICAL THINKING**

Analyzing Points of View, p. 385
Recognizing Effects, p. 386
Making Inferences, p. 387
Comparing, p. 387

## FOCUS & MOTIVATE

**5-MINUTE WARM-UP**

**Making Inferences** These questions focus on economic concepts.

1. Look at the list of terms at the top of page 384. Which terms suggest that this section deals with economic problems?
2. What do you think might occur in an economic panic?

 Warm-Up Transparency WT12

## INSTRUCT

**INSTRUCT: OBJECTIVE 1**

**Mr. Biddle's Bank**

Key Questions

- Why was the Second Bank of the United States important, and what was Nicholas Biddle's role in it?
- Why did Jackson oppose the bank?

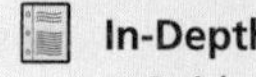 **In-Depth Resources: Unit 4**
- Guided Reading, p. 6

 **Reading Study Guide** (Spanish and English), pp. 125–126

# 4 Prosperity and Panic

**TERMS & NAMES**
inflation
Martin Van Buren
Panic of 1837
depression
Whig Party
William Henry Harrison
John Tyler

**MAIN IDEA**

Jackson's policies caused the economy to collapse after he left office and affected the next election.

**WHY IT MATTERS NOW**

The condition of the economy continues to affect the outcomes of presidential elections.

### ONE AMERICAN'S STORY

**Nicholas Biddle was the kind of person that Andrew Jackson neither liked nor trusted. Biddle was wealthy, well educated, and came from a socially prominent Philadelphia family. He was also the influential president of the powerful Second Bank of the United States—the bank that Jackson believed to be a monster of corruption. Jackson declared war on Biddle and the bank during his 1832 reelection campaign. But Biddle felt sure of his political power.**

*A VOICE FROM THE PAST*

I have always deplored making the Bank a [political] question, but since the President will have it so, he must pay the penalty of his own rashness. . . . [m]y hope is that it will contribute to relieve the country of the domination of these miserable [Jackson] people.

**Nicholas Biddle,** from a letter to Henry Clay dated August 1, 1832

**For his part, Jackson vowed to "kill" the bank. In this section, you will read about his war on the bank and its effect on the economy.**

Nicholas Biddle was the president of the powerful Second Bank of the United States, located in Philadelphia.

## Mr. Biddle's Bank

The Second Bank of the United States was the most powerful bank in the country. It held government funds and issued money. As its president, Nicholas Biddle set policies that controlled the nation's money supply.

Although the bank was run efficiently, Jackson had many reasons to dislike it. For one thing, he had come to distrust banks after losing money in financial deals early in his career. He also thought the bank had too much power. The bank made loans to members of Congress, and Biddle openly boasted that he could influence Congress. In addition, Jackson felt the bank's lending policies favored wealthy clients and hurt the average person.

To operate, the bank had to have a charter, or a written grant, from the federal government. In 1832, Biddle asked Congress to renew the bank's charter, even though it would not expire until 1836. Because 1832 was an election year, he thought Jackson would agree to renewal rather than risk angering its supporters. But Jackson took the risk.



## RECOMMENDED RESOURCES

 **In-Depth Resources: Unit 4**
- Guided Reading, p. 6
- Building Vocabulary, p. 7
- Skillbuilder Practice, p. 8
- Reteaching Activity, p. 19

 **Reading Study Guide** (Spanish and English), pp. 125–126

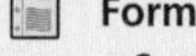 **Formal Assessment**
- Section Quiz, p. 189

 **Alternative Assessment**
- Rubrics, 4.1
- Rubrics, 1.1

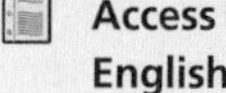 **Access for Students Acquiring English/ESL**
- Guided Reading, p. 82
- Skillbuilder Practice, p. 83

**Technology Resources**

 **Humanities Transparency HT24**
- Whig Rolling Ball, 1840

 **Electronic Teacher Tools with Test Maker**

 **ClassZone**
www.mcdougallittell.com

## 2 Jackson's War on the Bank

Vocabulary
**monopoly:** a company or group with complete control over a product or service

When Congress voted to renew the bank's charter, Jackson vetoed the renewal. In a strongly worded message to Congress, Jackson claimed the bank was unconstitutional. He said the bank was a monopoly that favored the few at the expense of the many. The Supreme Court earlier had ruled that the bank was constitutional. But Jackson claimed elected officials had to judge the constitutionality of a law for themselves. They did not need to rely on the Supreme Court. His veto message also contained this attack on the bank.

*A VOICE FROM THE PAST*

It is to be regretted that the rich and powerful too often bend the acts of government to their selfish purposes. . . . Distinctions in society will always exist under every just government. . . . [B]ut when the laws undertake to . . . make the rich richer and the potent more powerful, the humble members of society . . . have a right to complain of the injustice of their Government.

**Andrew Jackson,** veto message, July 10, 1832

*Reading* **History**
**A. Analyzing Points of View** What reasons did Jackson have for wanting to destroy the Second Bank of the United States?
**A. Possible Answer** Jackson thought that the bank was too powerful and that its lending policies favored the wealthy and hurt the average person.

Jackson's war on the bank became the main issue in the presidential campaign of 1832. The National Republican Party and its candidate, Henry Clay, called Jackson a tyrant. They said he wanted too much power as president. The Democrats portrayed Jackson as a defender of the people. When he won reelection, Jackson took it as a sign that the public approved his war on the bank.

In his second term, Jackson set out to destroy the bank before its charter ended in 1836. He had government funds deposited in state banks, which opponents called Jackson's "pet banks." Biddle fought back by making it harder for people to borrow money. He hoped the resulting economic troubles would force Jackson to return government deposits to the bank. Instead, the people rallied to Jackson's position. Eventually, the bank went out of business. Jackson had won the war, but the economy would be a victim.

### Jackson Fights the Second Bank

In this political cartoon, Jackson fights the many-headed monster—the Second Bank of the United States and its branches—with a cane labeled "VETO."

A President Jackson
B Cane labeled "VETO"
C Nicholas Biddle
D Vice-President Van Buren

**INSTRUCT: OBJECTIVE** 

**Jackson's War on the Bank**
Key Questions
- How did Jackson justify his veto of the bank charter?
- How did the bank issue affect the presidential campaign of 1832?
- How did Jackson drive the national bank out of business?

**CRITICAL THINKING ACTIVITY**

**Analyzing** Ask students to consider Jackson's claim that elected officials should judge a law's constitutionality for themselves. How would such a claim affect the separation of powers? Remind students of Jackson's remark, "John Marshall has made his decision. . . . Now let him enforce it" (page 377). Ask: Which branch is supposed to enforce the laws? **Answer** executive branch

Encourage students to compare Jackson's views on Supreme Court rulings with Calhoun's views on federal laws (nullification). Which branches or levels of government gain power under each man's theory? Which lose power?

**Class Time** 15 minutes

**HISTORY FROM VISUALS**

**Interpreting Political Cartoons** Ask students to look at the cartoon of Jackson fighting the bank. Ask: Why is Nicholas Biddle shown where he is? **Answer** He is the head of the bank. Next, ask: What is Vice-President Van Buren doing? **Possible Response** He seems to be helping Jackson by holding the heads for Jackson to strike.

**ACTIVITY OPTIONS**

**SKILLBUILDER MINI-LESSON: INTERPRETING POLITICAL CARTOONS** — BLOCK SCHEDULING

**Explaining the Skill** A political cartoon presents a point of view on a major issue or a political personality. Political cartoons can be valuable historic sources. They provide visual and written clues to public opinion in their time.

Use these steps to analyze a cartoon: (1) Identify the subject of the cartoon. (2) Pick out key symbols and details that help you interpret the cartoon's message. (3) Analyze the cartoonist's point of view on the subject.

**Applying the Skill** Examine the cartoon on page 385, using these questions to analyze it.

1. What is the cartoon's subject? *(Jackson's war on the bank)*
2. What symbol represents the bank? What does Jackson's cane represent? *(The many-headed monster stands for the bank; the cane, Jackson's veto.)*
3. What is the cartoon's message? *(The bank is a monster that Jackson is struggling to kill with his veto.)*
4. What does the artist think of the bank? *(He opposes it.)*

**INSTRUCT: OBJECTIVE 3**

**Prosperity Becomes Panic**

Key Questions

- How did Jackson's use of "pet banks" cause inflation?
- How did the Panic of 1837 lead to a nationwide depression?
- What were the economic consequences of the depression?

***America's* HERITAGE**

**Political Parties**

The log cabin proved to be such a successful symbol for the Whigs in the 1840 campaign that they built cabins for party rallies, put them on wheels and pulled them in parades, and put them up in every city, town, and village they could find. Whigs distributed log-cabin newspapers and songbooks and sang such ditties as this one, reminding voters that Harrison fought at Tippecanoe:

*Farewell, dear Van*
*You're not our man;*
*To guide the ship,*
*We'll try old Tip.*

**INSTRUCT: OBJECTIVE 4**

**The Rise of the Whig Party/ The Election of 1840**

Key Questions

- How did Clay's and Webster's ideas about the economy differ from Van Buren's?
- What did the Whig Party stand for, and why did Whigs choose Harrison as their candidate?
- How did the Whigs try to win the votes of the common people in 1840?

**Humanities Transparency HT24**
- Whig Rolling Ball, 1840

## 3 Prosperity Becomes Panic

Most of the nation prospered during Jackson's last years in office. Because it was easier to borrow money, people took out loans to buy public lands, and the economy boomed. But the "pet banks" issued too much paper money. The rise in the money supply made each dollar worth less. As a result, prices rose. **Inflation,** which is an increase in prices and decrease in the value of money, was the outcome. To fight inflation, Jackson issued an order that required people to pay in gold or silver for public lands.

Jackson left office proud of the nation's prosperity. But it was a puffed-up prosperity. Like a balloon, it had little substance. Because of Jackson's popularity, his vice-president, **Martin Van Buren,** was elected president in 1836. Within a few months after Van Buren took office, a panic—a widespread fear about the state of the economy—spread throughout the country. It became known as the **Panic of 1837.**

People took their paper money to the banks and demanded gold or silver in exchange. The banks quickly ran out of gold and silver. When the government tried to get its money from the state banks, the banks could not pay. The banks defaulted, or went out of business. A **depression,** or severe economic slump, followed.

The depression caused much hardship. Because people had little money, manufacturers no longer had customers for their goods. Almost 90 percent of factories in the East closed in 1837. Jobless workers had no way of buying food or paying rent. People went hungry. They lived in shelters or on the streets, where many froze in the winter. Every section of the country suffered, but the depression hit hardest in the cities. Farmers were hurt less because they could at least grow their own food. The depression affected politics, too.

***America's* HERITAGE**

**POLITICAL PARTIES**

Today's Democratic and Republican parties were born more than a century ago. Andrew Jackson's supporters first called themselves Democratic-Republicans. But in the 1830s, they became known simply as Democrats. They stood for states' rights and saw themselves as defenders of the common people. The modern Republican Party was formed in 1854 as the successor to the Whig Party, founded in 1834.

In the Jackson era, political parties campaigned for their candidates by staging parades and rallies. Participants often carried banners like the one below with a log cabin, the symbol for the campaign of William H. Harrison in 1840.

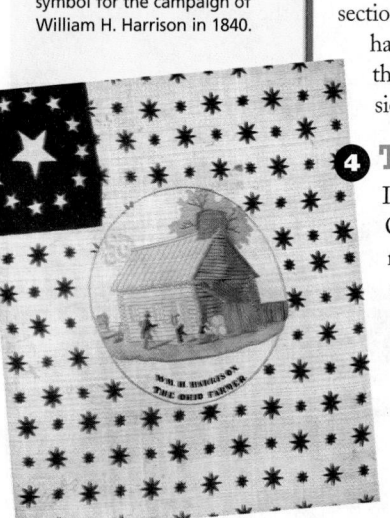


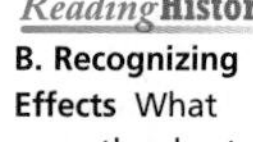
*Reading* **History**

**B. Recognizing Effects** What were the short-term and long-term effects of Jackson's war on the bank?

**B. Possible Answer** In the short run, the economy boomed as credit became easy to get and people borrowed to buy public lands. In the long run, the easy credit and overprinting of money caused inflation and eventually a depression.

## 4 The Rise of the Whig Party

In the depths of the depression, Senators Henry Clay and Daniel Webster argued that the government needed to help the economy. Van Buren disagreed. He believed that the economy would improve if left alone. He argued that "the less government interferes with private pursuits the better for the general prosperity." Many Americans blamed Van Buren for the Panic, though he had taken office only weeks before it started. The continuing depression made it almost impossible for him to win reelection in 1840.



**ACTIVITY OPTIONS**

**INDIVIDUAL NEEDS**

**STUDENTS ACQUIRING ENGLISH/ESL**

**Understanding Specialized Vocabulary** To help students understand how Jackson's policies caused the economy to collapse, you might want to point out some of the specialized vocabulary in the section to students before they begin to read. Write some or all of the following words on the board:

| | | | |
|---|---|---|---|
| *economy* | *funds* | *deposit* | *loans* |
| *prosperity* | *credit* | *borrow* | *lending policies* |

Discuss the words with students to see which ones they already understand and which need clarification. In some cases the words may be familiar, but the concepts may still be challenging. Define words as necessary.

After students read the section, ask them questions based on the section content. Encourage them to use the specialized vocabulary in their responses to the questions.

Van Buren faced a new political party in that election. During Jackson's war on the national bank, Clay, Webster, and other Jackson opponents had formed the **Whig Party.** It was named after a British party that opposed royal power. The Whigs opposed the concentration of power in the chief executive—whom they mockingly called "King Andrew" Jackson. In 1840, the Whigs chose **William Henry Harrison** of Ohio to run for president and **John Tyler** of Virginia to run for vice-president.

*Reading* **History**
**C. Making Inferences** Why did the Whigs want to nominate a candidate like Harrison, who did not have strong political views?
**C. Possible Answer** A candidate without strong political views would be less likely to lose votes by taking stands on the issues.

The Whigs nominated Harrison largely because of his military record and his lack of strong political views. Harrison had led the army that defeated the Shawnees in 1811 at the Battle of Tippecanoe. He also had been a hero during the War of 1812. The Whigs made the most of Harrison's military record and his nickname, "Old Tippecanoe." The phrase "Tippecanoe and Tyler too" became the Whig election slogan.

## The Election of 1840

During the 1840 election campaign, the Whigs emphasized personalities more than issues. They tried to appeal to the common people, as Andrew Jackson had done. Harrison was the son of a Virginia plantation owner. However, because he had settled on a farm in Ohio, the Whigs said Harrison was a true Westerner. They used symbols of the frontier, such as a log cabin, to represent Harrison. The Whigs contrasted Harrison with the wealthy Van Buren. Harrison won in a close election.

At his inauguration, the 68-year-old president spoke for nearly two hours in cold March weather with no hat or coat. Later, he was caught in the rain. He came down with a cold that developed into pneumonia. On April 4, 1841, one month after being inaugurated, Harrison died—the first president to die in office. Vice-President Tyler became president.

The election of 1840 showed the importance of the West in American politics. In the next chapter, you'll learn more about the lure of the West and the westward expansion of the United States.

### Section 4 Assessment

**1. Terms & Names**

**Identify:**
- inflation
- Martin Van Buren
- Panic of 1837
- depression
- Whig Party
- William Henry Harrison
- John Tyler

**2. Taking Notes**

Use a diagram to list the events that led to the closing of the Second Bank of the United States.

Event 1 → Event 2 → Event 3 → Event 4 → Event 5 → Bank closes

What was the most significant event?

**3. Main Ideas**

a. Why did Jackson declare war on the Second Bank of the United States?

b. How did Jackson kill the bank?

c. What role did Jackson's popularity play in the elections of 1836 and 1840?

**4. Critical Thinking**

**Comparing** What strategy did the Whig Party use in the 1840 election?

**THINK ABOUT**
- how Harrison was portrayed
- what group of voters it was trying to attract

**ACTIVITY OPTIONS**

**LANGUAGE ARTS / ART** Imagine yourself as a presidential candidate in 1840. Focusing on the economy as an issue, write a campaign **slogan** or create a **banner** to rally support.





### CRITICAL THINKING ACTIVITY

**Evaluating** Have students evaluate the presidency of Andrew Jackson, focusing on his political ideas, his economic policies, his treatment of Native Americans, his attitude toward the Supreme Court, and his handling of states' rights issues. Was Jackson a great president? Have students give reasons for their opinion. Use the chart to help students make their own assessments of his years in office.

| | Achievements | Failures |
|---|---|---|
| Political Ideas | | |
| National Bank | | |
| Native Americans | | |
| States' Rights | | |
| Supreme Court | | |

**Class Time** 15 minutes

## ASSESS & RETEACH

**Setting the Stage** Have students complete the graphic organizer categorizing changes during the Age of Jackson.

**Formal Assessment**
- Section Quiz, p. 189

**Critical Thinking Transparency CT34**
- Setting the Stage

### RETEACHING ACTIVITY

Give students the following three topics: Jackson's war on the bank; the Panic of 1837; the election of 1840. Ask them to write one sentence about each event, showing how it connects to one of the others.

**In-Depth Resources: Unit 4**
- Reteaching Activity, p. 19

### Section 4 Assessment

**1. Terms & Names**

**inflation,** p. 386
**Martin Van Buren,** p. 386
**Panic of 1837,** p. 386
**depression,** p. 386
**Whig Party,** p. 387
**William Henry Harrison,** p. 387
**John Tyler,** p. 387

**2. Taking Notes**

Event 1: Biddle asks Congress to renew charter in 1832; Event 2: Congress renews charter; Event 3: Jackson vetoes charter; Event 4: Jackson reelected; Event 5: Jackson deposits federal funds in pet banks. Answers will vary, but should include support from information in the chapter.

**3. Main Ideas**

**a.** He considered it too powerful and corrupt; he thought it favored wealthy people. **b.** He vetoed the renewal of the bank's charter, withdrew all federal money, and set up state banks. **c.** His vice-president, Van Buren, won election in 1836; Harrison won the 1840 election by running as a Jackson-like candidate.

**4. Critical Thinking**

They represented Harrison as a man like Jackson; his campaign involved personal attacks on the opposition and avoided real issues.

**ACTIVITY OPTIONS**

**Alternative Assessment**
- Rubrics for a slogan, 4.1
- Rubrics for a banner, 1.1

## TERMS & NAMES

1. **John Quincy Adams,** p. 369
2. **Jacksonian democracy,** p. 370
3. **spoils system,** p. 373
4. **Sequoya,** p. 374
5. **Indian Removal Act,** p. 376
6. **Trail of Tears,** p. 377
7. **secession,** p. 383
8. **inflation,** p. 386
9. **depression,** p. 386
10. **Whig Party,** p. 387

## REVIEW QUESTIONS

**Possible Responses**

1. He was not from the East and did not come from an aristocratic family.
2. He portrayed himself as a common person who had worked his way up, a Westerner, a war hero, and a champion of the common people.
3. to settle and mine
4. He considered Native Americans to have no rights to establish an independent government within the borders of the United States and promoted the idea of relocation.
5. They lost everything they owned and suffered a long, harsh journey to a new land; many lost their lives.
6. The North and South had differing opinions. Each region wanted high or low tariffs based on how the tariff would affect the economy of that region.
7. South Carolina threatened to secede; Jackson vowed to use force to see that federal laws were obeyed.
8. Henry Clay proposed a compromise tariff, Congress passed it, and South Carolina stayed in the Union.
9. because he had lost money in financial deals involving banks; he thought the bank was too powerful, corrupt, and favored wealthy people
10. Credit became easy, people borrowed heavily to buy public land, the banks printed too much money, and money began to lose value.

# Chapter 12 ASSESSMENT

## TERMS & NAMES

Briefly explain the importance of each of the following.

1. John Quincy Adams
2. Jacksonian democracy
3. spoils system
4. Sequoya
5. Indian Removal Act
6. Trail of Tears
7. secession
8. inflation
9. depression
10. Whig Party

## REVIEW QUESTIONS

**Politics of the People (pages 369–373)**

1. How was Jackson different from earlier presidents?
2. How did Jackson appeal to voters in his election campaign of 1828?

**Jackson's Policy Toward Native Americans (pages 374–378)**

3. Why did white settlers want Native American land?
4. What was Jackson's position on Native Americans in the United States?
5. How did the Indian Removal Act affect Native Americans?

**Conflicts over States' Rights (pages 379–383)**

6. How did the issue of tariffs divide the country?
7. Why did nullification threaten the nation?
8. How was the nullification crisis resolved?

**Prosperity and Panic (pages 384–387)**

9. Why did Jackson oppose the Second Bank of the United States?
10. What were the effects of Jackson's war on the bank?

## CRITICAL THINKING

**1. USING YOUR NOTES**

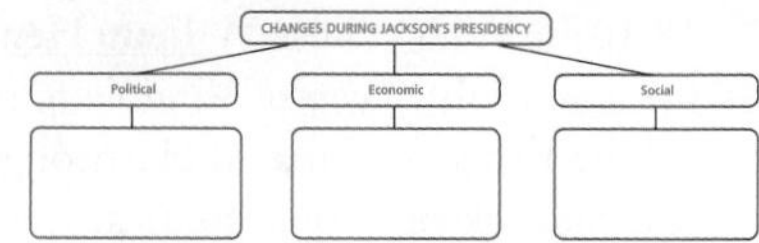


Use your completed chart to answer the questions.

a. What do you think was the most positive change of the Jackson era? Explain.
b. What was the most negative change? Explain.
c. Which change had the most far-reaching effects? Give evidence to support your answer.

**2. ANALYZING LEADERSHIP**

What was the basis of Andrew Jackson's power as president?

**3. APPLYING CITIZENSHIP SKILLS**

How did the majority of voters in the presidential elections of 1828 and 1840 exercise their vote in a similar way?

**4. THEME: ECONOMICS IN HISTORY**

Based on its economic effects, was Jackson's decision to end the national bank a good one? Explain.

**5. RECOGNIZING BIAS**

In what ways did Andrew Jackson's policy toward Native Americans reflect bias?

**Interact *with* History**

Now that you have read the chapter, do you think the qualities that made Jackson a strong military leader made him a good president? Explain your answer.

## VISUAL SUMMARY

### Major Issues of Jackson's Presidency

| POLICY TOWARD NATIVE AMERICANS | CONFLICT OVER STATES' RIGHTS | WAR ON BANK OF THE UNITED STATES |
|---|---|---|
| White settlers wanted Native American lands. | Sectional differences developed. | Second Bank of the United States had economic and political power. |
| Jackson proposed Indian Removal Act of 1830. | Jackson supported strong central government. | Jackson opposed bank and vetoed renewal of its charter. |
| Thousands of Native Americans removed to Indian Territory. | South Carolina threatened to secede over tariff issue, but compromise reached. | Bank driven out of business, but Jackson's policies eventually led to inflation and depression. |

388 CHAPTER 12

## CRITICAL THINKING

**Possible Responses**

1. **USING YOUR NOTES a.** Students might cite the focus on common people gaining a voice in the government because it broadened the base of our democracy. **b.** Students might cite the relocation of Native Americans because it caused so much suffering. **c.** Students might cite the rise of Jacksonian democracy.
2. **ANALYZING LEADERSHIP** his great popularity and public support; the support of the Democratic Party; his lack of fear of using the veto
3. **APPLYING CITIZENSHIP SKILLS** They defeated a president seeking reelection.
4. **THEME: ECONOMICS IN HISTORY** The decision was a poor one because the long-term effects were disastrous for the nation's economy.
5. **RECOGNIZING BIAS** Previous treaties gave the Native Americans the right to their land, but Jackson denied that they had this right. He singled them out as a group and denied their rights.

**Interact *with* History** Students' responses will vary but should include elements discussed in the chapter.

## HISTORY SKILLS

**1. INTERPRETING GRAPHS**

Study the graph. Answer the questions.

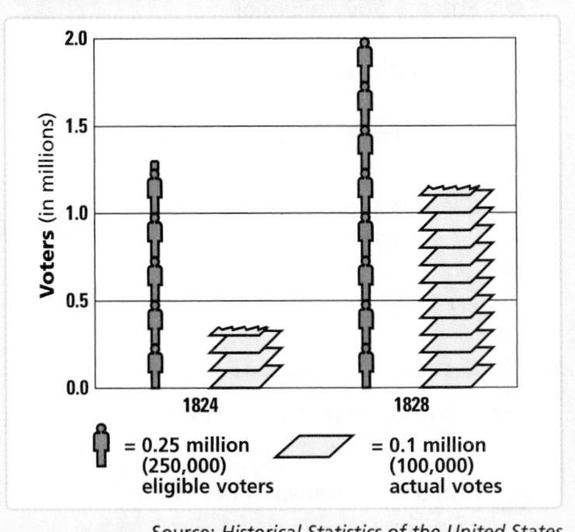


Source: *Historical Statistics of the United States*

**Basic Graph Elements**

a. What is the subject of the graph?

b. What do the symbols represent?

**Interpreting the Graph**

c. How many more eligible voters were there in 1828 than in 1824?

d. What percentage of eligible voters cast their ballots in 1824? in 1828?

**2. INTERPRETING PRIMARY SOURCES**

This is a political cartoon from the 1832 election campaign. It is entitled "King Andrew the First."

a. Is the comparison of Jackson to a king meant as praise or criticism? Explain.

b. What does it mean that he is standing on torn papers entitled "U.S. Constitution" and "U.S. Bank"?

## ALTERNATIVE ASSESSMENT

**1. INTERDISCIPLINARY ACTIVITY: Speech**

**Presenting a Debate** Working with a partner, take sides on the doctrine of nullification and prepare a debate for the class.

**2. COOPERATIVE LEARNING ACTIVITY**

**Preparing a Problem-Solving Proposal** Plan and write a proposal outlining a solution to the problems between white settlers and Native Americans in the Southeast in the early 1800s. Working in a small group, first brainstorm ideas and make a list. Then identify the positives and negatives of each idea. Agree on an outline for a final plan. Then write, revise, and make a final copy of your proposal. Present your proposal to the class and defend it.

**3. TECHNOLOGY ACTIVITY**

**Designing a Political Campaign Web Site** Andrew Jackson was one of the more colorful figures in American history. His election as president brought significant changes to the nation. Plan a Web site for candidate Jackson for the 1828 presidential campaign. Use the Internet or search the library for information on Jackson's life before the presidency and on the 1828 election.

 **Visit www.mcdougallittell.com to learn more about Andrew Jackson.**

Design the Web site using the suggestions below.

- Include biographical facts.
- Select images that tell Jackson's story.
- Present his views on the major issues of the day using quotations from speeches and other documents.
- Locate appropriate links for visitors to your Web site.

**4. HISTORY PORTFOLIO**

**Option 1** Review your section and chapter assessment activities. Select one that you think was your best work. Then use comments made by your teacher or classmates to improve your work and add it to your portfolio.

**Option 2** Review the questions that you wrote for What Do You Want to Know? on page 368. Then write a short report in which you explain the answers to your questions. Add your work to your history portfolio.



## ALTERNATIVE ASSESSMENT

1. INTERDISCIPLINARY ACTIVITY: **Speech**

**Debates should**
- have a central question or proposition.
- support a position and refute opponent's position with evidence.
- respond appropriately to each other's statements.

2. COOPERATIVE LEARNING ACTIVITY

**Proposals should**
- reflect the use of a problem-solving technique.
- focus on resolving the problem.
- support positions with evidence or logic.
- reflect the student's research in the presentation.

3.  TECHNOLOGY ACTIVITY

**Web sites should**
- contain at least three links.
- make effective use of pictures and icons.
- contain written summaries that will encourage browsers to visit other Web sites.
- show technical proficiency.

4. HISTORY PORTFOLIO

 **Option 1 Revised section or chapter assessment activities should**
- address teacher and peer responses to the selected work.
- solve problems present in the first versions of the work.

 **Option 2 Short reports should**
- answer questions about the presidency of Andrew Jackson.
- use evidence to develop and support ideas.
- cite sources of information.
- use standard grammar, spelling, sentence structure, and punctuation.

 **Critical Thinking Transparency CT36**
- Visual Summary

**Formal Assessment**
- Chapter Test, Forms A and B, pp. 190–197

## HISTORY SKILLS

**Possible Responses**

1. INTERPRETING GRAPHS

**Basic Graph Elements**

**a.** voter participation in the 1824 and 1828 elections

**b.** eligible voters and actual votes

**Interpreting the Graph**

**c.** about .7 million, or 700,000

**d.** about 30 percent in 1824, more than 55 percent in 1828

2. INTERPRETING PRIMARY SOURCES

**a.** Criticism—because a king is not elected, a king is not a democratic ruler.

**b.** It shows that he was harming the Constitution and the bank.

# CHAPTER 13 PLANNING GUIDE
# Manifest Destiny 1810–1853

| | CHAPTER OVERVIEW | COPYMASTERS | TECHNOLOGY |
|---|---|---|---|
| **CHAPTER RESOURCES** | This chapter discusses the westward migration of the American people and the national belief in Manifest Destiny. It also describes the Texas Revolution, the War with Mexico, and the California gold rush. | **In-Depth Resources: Unit 4**<br>• Tracing Themes: Expansion, p. 22<br>• Building Vocabulary, p. 27<br>**Interdisciplinary Projects,** pp. 73–78 | **Primary Source Explorer**<br>**Electronic Teacher Tools**<br>**Power Presentations CD-ROM**<br>**Chapter Summaries on CD** (English and Spanish) |
| | **KEY IDEAS** | | |
| **SECTION 1**<br>**Trails West**<br>**pp. 393–399** | • Mountain men open the Far West, and their reports lure others.<br>• Traders and settlers go west on the Oregon and Santa Fe Trails.<br>• The Mormons go to Utah in search of religious freedom. | **In-Depth Resources: Unit 4**<br>• Setting the Stage, p. 21<br>• Guided Reading, p. 23<br>• Primary Source, p. 31<br>• Reteaching Activity, p. 36<br>**America's History Makers**<br>• Narcissa Whitman, pp. 51–52<br>**Outline Map Activities**<br>• The Opening of the West, 1850, pp. 25–26 | **Warm-Up Transparency WT13**<br>**Humanities Transparency HT25**<br>• Cowboy<br>**Humanities Transparency HT26**<br>• *On the Trail*<br>**Critical Thinking Transparency CT37**<br>• Setting the Stage<br>**ClassZone:** www.mcdougallittell.com |
| **SECTION 2**<br>**The Texas Revolution**<br>**pp. 400–405** | • Stephen Austin starts an American colony under Mexican rule in Texas.<br>• Rising tensions eventually lead Texans to revolt against Mexico.<br>• Texans win the Battle of San Jacinto and declare their independence as a republic. | **In-Depth Resources: Unit 4**<br>• Setting the Stage, p. 21<br>• Guided Reading, p. 24<br>• Primary Source, p. 32<br>• Reteaching Activity, p. 37<br>**America's History Makers**<br>• Juan Séguin, pp. 53–54<br>**American History Plays**<br>• *Live from the Alamo* | **Warm-Up Transparency WT13**<br>**Geography Transparency GT13**<br>• The Battle of the Alamo, 1836<br>**Critical Thinking Transparency CT37**<br>• Setting the Stage<br>**ClassZone:** www.mcdougallittell.com |
| **SECTION 3**<br>**The War with Mexico**<br>**pp. 406–411** | • Many Americans support the idea of Manifest Destiny.<br>• The United States declares war on Mexico, provoking debate over expansion and slavery.<br>• The U.S. victory leads to the acquisition of Texas, California, and a vast area in the Southwest. | **In-Depth Resources: Unit 4**<br>• Setting the Stage, p. 21<br>• Guided Reading, p. 25<br>• Skillbuilder Practice, p. 28<br>• Geography Application, pp. 29–30<br>• Reteaching Activity, p. 38<br>**Why It Matters Now**<br>• The Influence of the West, pp. 25–26 | **Warm-Up Transparency WT13**<br>**Critical Thinking Transparency CT37**<br>• Setting the Stage<br>**ClassZone:** www.mcdougallittell.com |
| **SECTION 4**<br>**The California Gold Rush**<br>**pp. 412–417** | • Before 1849, California is home to Native Americans, *Californios*, and some American settlers.<br>• The discovery of gold in California leads to the gold rush of 1849.<br>• The influx of American settlers harms Native Americans and *Californios* but leads to California's statehood. | **In-Depth Resources: Unit 4**<br>• Setting the Stage, p. 21<br>• Guided Reading, p. 26<br>• Literature Selection, pp. 33–35<br>• Reteaching Activity, p. 39<br>**Economics in History**<br>• Gold Rush Entrepreneurs, p. 13 | **Warm-Up Transparency WT13**<br>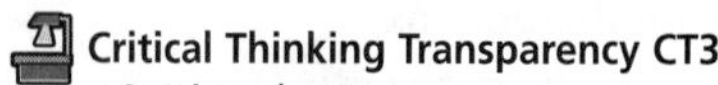<br>**Critical Thinking Transparency CT37**<br>• Setting the Stage<br>**Critical Thinking Transparency CT38**<br>• Cause and Effect: U.S. Expansion, 1846–1853<br>**Critical Thinking Transparency CT39**<br>• Visual Summary<br>**ClassZone:** www.mcdougallittell.com |

Pupil's Edition
Copymaster
Overhead Transparency
Audio Library
CD-ROM
Internet

## ASSESSMENT

**Chapter Assessment,** pp. 418–419

**Formal Assessment**
- Chapter Tests, Forms A and B, pp. 204–211

**Alternative Assessment Book**

**Electronic Teacher Tools with Test Maker**

**Section Assessment,** p. 397

**Formal Assessment**
- Section Quiz, p. 200

**Alternative Assessment Book**
- Rubrics for a letter, 4.3
- Rubrics for an oral history, 3.6

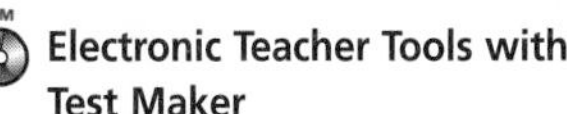
**Electronic Teacher Tools with Test Maker**

**Section Assessment,** p. 405

**Formal Assessment**
- Section Quiz, p. 201

**Alternative Assessment Book**
- Rubrics for a trading card, 1.7
- Rubrics for a biography, 4.4

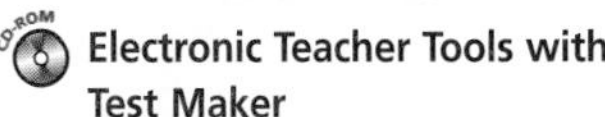
**Electronic Teacher Tools with Test Maker**

**Section Assessment,** p. 411

**Formal Assessment**
- Section Quiz, p. 202

**Alternative Assessment Book**
- Rubrics for graphs, 2.3
- Rubrics for maps, 2.1

**Electronic Teacher Tools with Test Maker**

**Section Assessment,** p. 417

**Formal Assessment**
- Section Quiz, p. 203

**Alternative Assessment Book**
- Rubrics for a news article, 4.5
- Rubrics for maps, 2.1

**Electronic Teacher Tools with Test Maker**

## CUSTOMIZING FOR INDIVIDUAL NEEDS

### Students Acquiring English/ESL

**Reading Study Guide** (English and Spanish), pp. 129–138

**Access for Students Acquiring English/ESL:** Spanish Translations, pp. 86–92

**Chapter Summaries on CD** (English and Spanish)

### Less Proficient Readers

**Reading Study Guide** (English and Spanish), pp. 129–138

**Chapter Summaries on CD** (English and Spanish)

### Gifted and Talented Students

**In-Depth Resources: Unit 4**
- Enrichment Activity, p. 40

**America's History Makers**
- Narcissa Whitman, pp. 51–52
- Juan Séguin, pp. 53–54

## CROSS-CURRICULAR CONNECTIONS

### Culture

Hoyt, Edwin P. ***The Alamo: An Illustrated History.*** Dallas, TX: Taylor Publishing Company, 1999. Beautiful account of the historic mission.

### Geography

Cobb, Hubbard and Stanley Schuler. ***American Battlefields: A Complete Guide to the Historic Conflicts in Words, Maps, and Photos.*** Foster City, CA: IDG Books Worldwide, 1996. A chronologically organized guide to battles fought in the United States, including the Mexican War.

### Humanities: Art

Driesbach, Janice Tolhurst and Harvey Jones and Katherine Church Holland. ***Art of the Gold Rush.*** Los Angeles, CA: Univ. of California Press, 1998. Drawings and paintings of the gold rush era.

### Interdisciplinary Projects, pp. 73–78

- Math: The Geometry of Quilts
- Science: Ecosysmtems Along the Santa Fe Trail
- Language Arts: Tall Tales
- Home Economics: Pioneer Clothing

### Literature

Cushman, Karen. ***The Ballad of Lucy Whipple.*** New York: Harpercollins, 1998. Young Lucy writes from the mining frontier to her grandmother in the East in this well-researched novel.

Karr, Kathleen. ***The Great Turkey Walk.*** New York: Farrar, 1998. Based on a true story, the story of a 15-year-old boy who tries to herd a flock of 1,000 turkeys from Missouri to Colorado.

Mayfield, Thomas Jefferson. ***Adopted by Indians: A True Story.*** ed. by Malcolm Margolin. Berkeley, CA: Heyday Books, 1997. After his mother's death in 1850, young Mayfield lived with the Choinumne Indians. This account of his life and the traditional ways of the Choinumne was edited for children.

### McDougall Littell Literature Connections

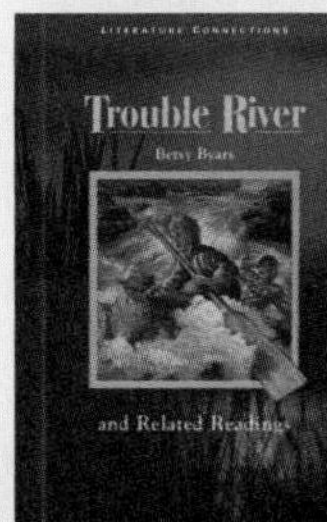


Betsy Byars

***Trouble River***

Dewey Martin, a 12-year-old boy in the 1800s, is left behind to tend the family farm while his parents go to Hunter City. Fearing an Indian raid, Dewey, his grandmother, and their dog Charlie set off on a small raft on Trouble River.

## ENRICHMENT ACTIVITIES

**Pupil's Edition, pp. 390–419**
**Interact With History,** p. 398
**Interdisciplinary Challenge,** pp. 389–399
**Technology of the Time,** p. 415

**In-Depth Resources: Unit 4**
- Geography Application: The United States Gains Land from Mexico, pp. 29–30
- Primary Source: from *Luzena Stanley Wilson, '49er,* p. 31
- Primary Source: A Mexican Account of the Battle of the Alamo, p. 32
- Literature Selection: from *Roughing It* by Mark Twain, pp. 33–35

**America's History Makers**
- Narcissa Whitman, pp. 51–52
- Juan Séguin, pp. 53–54

**Outline Map Activities**
- The Opening of the West, 1850, pp. 25–26

**Why It Matters Now**
- The Influence of the West, pp. 25–26

# CHAPTER 13 PACING GUIDE

**LESSON PLAN OPTIONS (50-MINUTE PERIOD)** (TE) = Teacher's Edition (PE) = Pupil's Edition

| | TEACHER-DIRECTED ACTIVITIES<br>Class Time: 15 minutes | STUDENT-CENTERED ACTIVITIES<br>Class Time: 25 minutes | INDIVIDUAL ACTIVITIES<br>Class Time: 10 minutes |
|---|---|---|---|
| **DAY 1**<br>Introduction<br>pp. 390–392 | **Presentation Options**<br>• Begin with a class discussion of the photograph on p. 390 **(PE)**.<br>• Lead a class discussion on the "What Do You Know?" question in Setting the Stage, p. 392. Then introduce the graphic organizer for the chapter **(PE)**. | **Options for Cooperative Learning**<br>• Have student groups discuss the Interact with History questions, p. 391 **(PE)**.<br>• Have student groups respond to the "What Do You Want to Know?" question in Setting the Stage, p. 392 **(PE)**. | **Head Start on Homework Options**<br>• Have students skim Section 1 Main Idea, Why It Matters Now, Terms & Names, and the main headings, p. 393 **(PE)**.<br>• Have students begin Guided Reading activity and Building Vocabulary sheet. |
| **DAY 2**<br>Section 1<br>pp. 393–399 | **Presentation Options**<br>• Begin with the 5-Minute Warm-Up, p. 393 **(TE)**.<br>• Review the Section 1 Main Idea, Why It Matters Now, and Terms & Names, p. 393 **(PE)**.<br>• Choose 5 key questions for Objectives 1–5 to discuss with the class, pp. 393–397 **(TE)**. | **Options for Cooperative Learning**<br>• Have student work in pairs to complete the Geography Skillbuilders and History from Visuals activities, p. 395 **(PE, TE)**.<br>• Divide students into groups to complete the Interdisciplinary Challenge, pp. 398–399 **(PE)**.<br>• Have student pairs work together to complete one of the Activity Options in the Section 1 Assessment, p. 397 **(PE)**. | **Head Start on Homework Options**<br>• Have students begin working on Section 1 Assessment, p. 397 **(PE)**.<br>• Have students complete the Reading History questions for Section 2, pp. 400–405 **(PE)**. |
| **DAY 3**<br>Section 2<br>pp. 400–405 | **Presentation Options**<br>• Begin with the 5-Minute Warm-Up, p. 400 **(TE)**.<br>• Choose 5 key questions for Objectives 1–4 to discuss with the class, pp. 400–404 **(TE)**.<br>• Lead a discussion on the Texas Revolution using the map on page 405 **(PE)**. | **Options for Cooperative Learning**<br>• Divide students into groups and have them complete the Interdisciplinary Link, Civics: Problem Solving, p. 401 **(TE)**.<br>• Have student pairs work together to complete one of the Activity Options in the Section 2 Assessment, p. 405 **(PE)**. | **Head Start on Homework Options**<br>• Have students begin working on Section 2 Assessment, p. 405 **(PE)**.<br>• Have students preview Section 3 Main Idea, Why It Matters Now, Terms & Names, and the main headings, pp. 406 **(PE)**. |
| **DAY 4**<br>Section 3<br>pp. 406–411 | **Presentation Options**<br>• Begin with the 5-Minute Warm-Up, p. 406 **(TE)**.<br>• Choose 5 key questions for Objectives 1–4 to discuss with the class, pp. 406–410 **(TE)**.<br>• Lead the students through the Skillbuilder Mini-Lesson: Reading A Special Purpose Map, p. 408 **(TE)**. | **Options for Cooperative Learning**<br>• Divide students into groups and have them complete the Interdisciplinary Link, Language Arts: Diary of a Cadet of Chapultepec, p. 410 **(TE)**.<br>• Have student pairs work together to complete one of the Activity Options in the Section 3 Assessment, p. 411 **(PE)**. | **Head Start on Homework Options**<br>• Have students begin working on Section 3 Assessment, p. 411 **(PE)**.<br>• Have students preview Section 4 Main Idea, Why It Matters Now, Terms & Names, and the main headings, p. 412 **(PE)**. |
| **DAY 5**<br>Section 4<br>pp. 412–417 | **Presentation Options**<br>• Begin with the 5-Minute Warm-Up, p. 412 **(TE)**.<br>• Choose 5 key questions for Objectives 1–4 to discuss with the class, pp. 412–416 **(TE)**.<br>• Use the Cause and Effect chart to summarize the chapter, p. 416 **(PE)**. | **Options for Cooperative Learning**<br>• Divide students into groups and have them complete the Technology of the Time questions, p. 415 **(PE)**.<br>• Have student pairs work together to complete one of the Activity Options in the Section 4 Assessment, p. 417 **(PE)**. | **Head Start on Homework Options**<br>• Have students complete the Setting the Stage graphic organizer for the chapter, p. 392 **(PE)**.<br>• Have students begin working on the Chapter Assessment, pp. 418–419 **(PE)**.<br>• Prepare for Chapter Test<br>**Formal Assessment,** pp. 204–211 |

TEACHER-TESTED ACTIVITY | Lisa Williams, Lamberton Middle School, Carlisle, Pennsylvania

## COME TO CALIFORNIA!

**Class Time** One class period

**Task** Creating an advertising poster

**Purpose** To understand the motives that drew people to California and the methods of transportation they used

**Supplies Needed**
- Research materials on the California Gold Rush and on transportation
- Construction paper or posterboard
- Colored markers or crayons

**Activity** Each student should create an advertisement that urges people to join the Gold Rush to California. The ad should focus on a way of getting to the gold fields and present its advantages. Students should be aware that many people reached California by sailing "around the Horn" or by crossing the Isthmus of Panama. Posters should be persuasive and attractive.

## BLOCK SCHEDULING — LESSON PLAN OPTIONS (90-MINUTE PERIOD)

### DAY 1

**Interact with History,** p. 391
**Class Time** 20 Minutes

Options for pacing and variety:
- **Role-Playing** In small groups have students assume the roles of a pioneer family going west. Two can be parents, others can be grandparents, unmarried aunts and uncles, or teenagers. Have each tell what they expect to gain and what they fear they might lose by going west. **Class Time** 20 minutes

**Setting the Stage,** p. 392
**Class Time** 20 minutes

Options for pacing and variety:
- **Time Saver** For a homework assignment, have students bring to class the names of movies, books, or television shows that have influenced their views of the West.
  **Class Time** 5 minutes

**Section 1,** pp. 393–399
**Class Time** 50 minutes

Options for pacing and variety:
- **History on Film** Extend students' background knowledge of the westward journey by viewing "The Story of the Oregon Trail." Boettcher/Trinklein. 1992
  **Class Time** 60 minutes
- **Time Saver** Use the map of western trails in 1850 on page 395 to summarize the section.
  **Class Time** 20 minutes

### DAY 2

**Interdisciplinary Challenge,** pp. 398–399
**Class Time** 45 minutes

Options for pacing and variety:
- **Team Teaching** Invite the science or physics teacher to coach student groups as they solve the Science Challenge on page 398.
  **Class Time** 30 minutes
- **Peer Evaluation** Write the Standards for Evaluation for the Civics Challenge found on page 398 of the Teacher's Edition on the chalkboard. Have students use these criteria to evaluate one another's role plays or written recommendations.
  **Class Time** 30 minutes

**Section 2,** pp. 400–405
**Class Time** 45 minutes

**Section 3,** pp. 406–411
**Class Time** 45 minutes

Options for pacing and variety:
- **Peer Teaching** Assign the content under each heading to a small group of students. Each group is responsible for explaining the information to the class. **Class Time** 30 minutes
- **Peer Evaluation** Have groups of students perform the Cooperative Learning Activity on page 419. **Class Time** 45 minutes

### DAY 3

**Section 4,** pp. 412-417
**Class Time** 45 minutes

Options for pacing and variety:
- **Time Saver** Using Critical Thinking Transparency CT39, ask student volunteers to summarize the chapter.
  **Class Time** 10 minutes
- **Internet** Extend students' background knowledge of the California gold rush by visiting the Library of Congress American Memory collection at www.mcdougallittell.com
  **Class Time** 20 minutes

**Chapter 13 Assessment,** pp. 418-419
**Class Time** 40 minutes

Options for pacing and variety:
- **Peer Teaching** Have students prepare a summary of the chapter using the words in the Terms & Names in the Chapter Assessment. Have students exchange papers and evaluate one another's summaries.
  **Class Time** 20 minutes
- **Peer Evaluation** Have students find partners and compare their Using Your Notes charts, checking each other's charts for completeness and accuracy. **Class Time** 20 minutes

## CHAPTER 13 OBJECTIVE

The student will understand westward expansion and its political, economic, and social effects on the development of the nation.

# CHAPTER 13 Manifest Destiny 1810–1853



### HISTORY FROM VISUALS

**Interpreting the Photograph** Ask the students to study the photograph of pioneers resting beside their wagons. Ask them to draw conclusions about the lives of the adults and children on the trip west. **Possible Responses** The trip west was not an easy one. The people appear tired and dirty. The wagons look too small to carry both people and equipment. Most pioneers probably walked.

**Extension** Have the students write five questions to ask the people in the photograph.

Weary from their trip west, this pioneer family stops for a rest.



### CRITICAL THINKING ACTIVITY

**Making Inferences** Using masking tape, have student teams mark out a 4' x 10' space on the classroom floor. Do as many of these as your classroom will accommodate. Then have students make inferences about how much and what kinds of supplies and personal belongings could fit into the space, which is approximately the size of the floor of a wagon. They may also discuss who would ride and who would walk.

**Class Time** 15 minutes

### RECOMMENDED RESOURCES

**BOOKS FOR THE TEACHER**

Ghent, William J. ***The Road to Oregon.*** London: Longmans, 1929. A noted chronicle of the Oregon Trail.

Lavender, David. ***The Great West.*** New York: Am. Heritage, 1965. A single volume covering exploration and settlement of the West from 1763.

Parkman, Francis. ***The Oregon Trail.*** New York: Viking, 1989. A reprint of Parkman's 1849 chronicle of his journeys in the West.

**SOFTWARE**

***Oregon Trail I and II.*** MECC, 1993. Award-winning simulation of a covered-wagon journey on the Oregon Trail.

***Wagon Train 1848.*** MECC. Puts users in the shoes of pioneers traveling the Oregon Trail.

**VIDEO**

***The West.*** PBS Video, 1996. Ken Burns's nine-part look at the American West. See episode two, "Empire upon the Trails."

**INTERNET**

For more about the West, visit www.mcdougallittell.com

## Interact *with* History

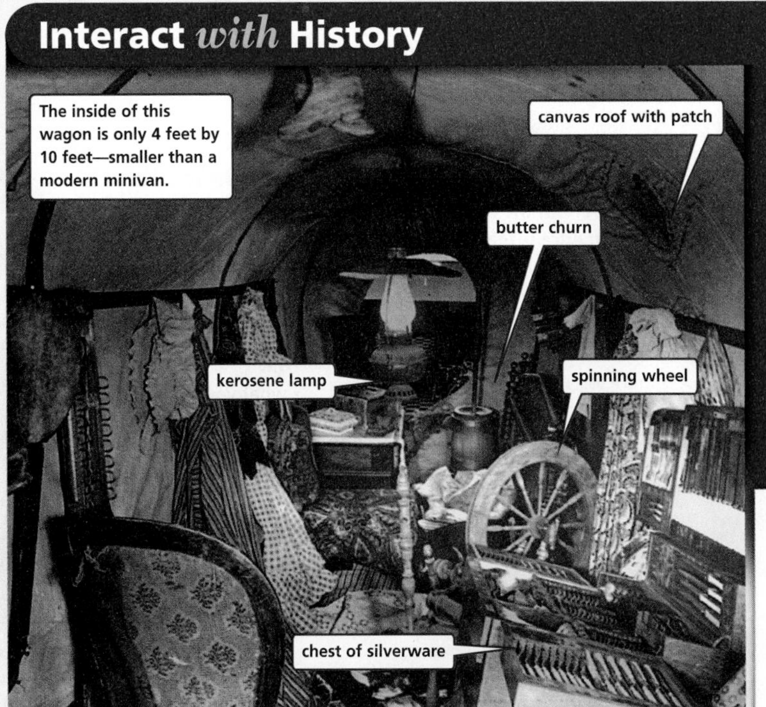
The inside of this wagon is only 4 feet by 10 feet—smaller than a modern minivan.
canvas roof with patch
butter churn
kerosene lamp
spinning wheel
chest of silverware

**The year is 1844, and you live on a small rocky farm in Massachusetts. Your family has decided to move to Oregon to gain cheap, fertile land. Your father says this move will make your family better off—and give you a brighter future.**

### What Do You Think?

- **What do you think daily life on the trail west might be like?**
- **What might be the greatest obstacles that you face?**
- **Notice the necessities packed in this crowded wagon. What might have been left behind?**

# *What might you gain and lose by going west?*

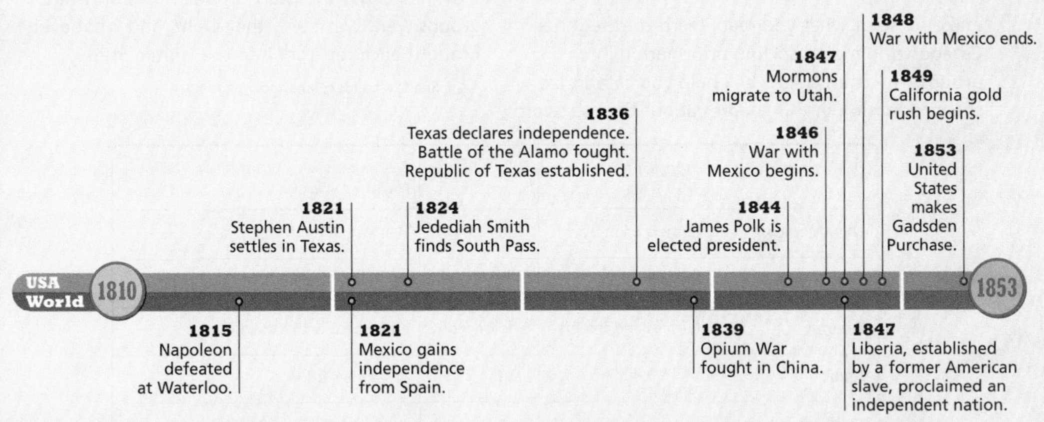
USA
World
1810
1853
1821 Stephen Austin settles in Texas.
1824 Jedediah Smith finds South Pass.
1836 Texas declares independence. Battle of the Alamo fought. Republic of Texas established.
1844 James Polk is elected president.
1846 War with Mexico begins.
1847 Mormons migrate to Utah.
1848 War with Mexico ends.
1849 California gold rush begins.
1853 United States makes Gadsden Purchase.
1815 Napoleon defeated at Waterloo.
1821 Mexico gains independence from Spain.
1839 Opium War fought in China.
1847 Liberia, established by a former American slave, proclaimed an independent nation.

## Interact *with* History

### OBJECTIVES

- To help students understand the difficulty of moving west
- To help students connect with the people and the events they will study in this chapter

### What Do You Think?

1. Ask students why the items they identified would be left behind.
2. Have students think about their daily activities and how those activities would be accomplished on the trail.
3. Ask students to think about the effect of land features, weather, transportation, and other people on the trip.

### *What might you gain and lose by going west?*

Encourage students to think about the jobs, possessions, and people left behind and the challenges of a new life.

### MAKING PERSONAL CONNECTIONS

Ask students to think about moves they have made. How would their move compare or contrast to the trip made by these pioneers? Would the reasons for moving be similar or different?

### TIME LINE DISCUSSION

**Remind the students that in 1803, the United States bought the Louisiana Territory. In this time period (1810–1853), large acquisitions of land would give the United States control of an area of North America that stretched from sea to sea.**

- Ask students to identify which decade seems to be filled with the most historical events. **Answer** 1840–1850. Follow up by asking them to hypothesize about why so many events took place between 1840 and 1850. **Possible Response** There was a great demand for land during that time period.
- Have the students look at the time line and find an event in the world that may have had a direct impact on the United States. **Answer** Mexican independence, because Mexico is so near the United States

## BEFORE YOU READ

### Previewing the Theme: Expansion

Ask the students to think of reasons why the people of the United States might have believed they should take over the entire continent. **Possible Response** Motives for expanding the nation from "sea to sea" ranged from the conviction that the continent needed to become an area of freedom and democracy separate from the dangers of monarchies to support for extending slavery. Still others looked to the lands of the West and the Pacific Coast as areas ready to be developed for agriculture and trade.

### What Do You Know?

To avoid confusion, remind students that this movement westward was not the same as the westward movement that occurred after the Homestead Act of 1862 and the Civil War. Many movies about the West took place during that later time.

 **In-Depth Resources: Unit 4**
- Tracing Themes: Expansion, p. 22

## READ AND TAKE NOTES

### Reading Strategy: Categorizing

Tell students that categorizing information will help them see common characteristics among groups. Knowing that information may help the student accomplish such critical-thinking skills as comparing and contrasting information. For example, by the time the chart is finished, the students should be able to compare the reasons for westward migration.

 **In-Depth Resources: Unit 4**
- Setting the Stage, p. 21

 **Critical Thinking Transparency CT37**
- Setting the Stage

# Chapter 13 SETTING THE STAGE

## BEFORE YOU READ

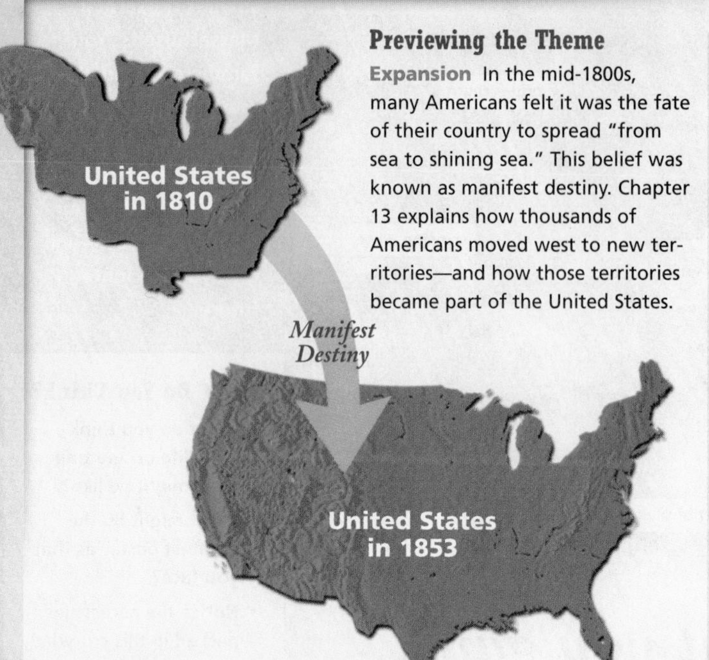


### Previewing the Theme

**Expansion** In the mid-1800s, many Americans felt it was the fate of their country to spread "from sea to shining sea." This belief was known as manifest destiny. Chapter 13 explains how thousands of Americans moved west to new territories—and how those territories became part of the United States.

### What Do You Know?

What do you think of when you hear the phrase "the West"? Who do you think moved west in the early 1800s? What do you think drew them to the West?

**THINK ABOUT**
- what you've learned about the West from movies or travel
- reasons that people move to new places today

### What Do You Want to Know?

What questions do you have about the westward movement of the 1800s? Record those questions in your notebook before you read the chapter.

## READ AND TAKE NOTES

**Reading Strategy: Categorizing** To help you make sense of what you read, learn to categorize. Categorizing means sorting information into groups. The chart below will help you categorize the information in this chapter about the westward movement. Use the chart to take notes on what groups went west, why they went, and what events brought each territory into the United States.

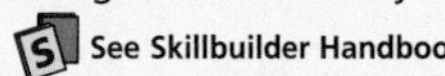
See Skillbuilder Handbook, page R6.

| | Types of people who traveled there | Why they went there | Key events that brought the territory into the United States |
|---|---|---|---|
| **New Mexico** | farmers and traders | land or profit | War with Mexico |
| **Utah** | Mormons | religious freedom | War with Mexico |
| **Oregon** | farmers and traders | land or profit | agreement with Britain |
| **Texas** | farmers and ranchers | land | Texas Revolution |
| **California** | miners and traders | land or profit | War with Mexico |



## TEACHING STRATEGY

### READING THE CHAPTER

This is a thematic chapter focusing on westward movement of both people and a nation. Encourage students to look for the causes and effects of movement during this time period. Have them think about what is happening in the country that encourages this movement. Pause after each section to review the ideas of cause and effect as illustrated in the section.

### ALTERNATIVE ASSESSMENT

The Chapter Assessment describes three activities for alternative assessment on page 419. You may wish to have students work on these activities during the course of the chapter and then present them at the end.

# 1 Trails West

**TERMS & NAMES**
Jedediah Smith
mountain man
Jim Beckwourth
land speculator
Santa Fe Trail
Oregon Trail
Mormon
Brigham Young

| MAIN IDEA | WHY IT MATTERS NOW |
|---|---|
| Thousands of settlers followed trails through the West to gain land and a chance to make a fortune. | This migration brought Americans to the territories that became New Mexico, Oregon, and Utah. |



## SECTION OBJECTIVES

1. To explain the role of mountain men in the exploration and expansion of the West
2. To identify reasons people went west
3. To describe the opening of the Santa Fe Trail
4. To describe the impact of "Oregon Fever" on westward expansion
5. To profile the Mormons' westward journey

**SKILLBUILDER**

Interpreting Maps: Place, Human-Environment Interaction, p. 395

**CRITICAL THINKING**

Making Inferences, p. 395
Finding Main Ideas, p. 397
Analyzing Causes, p. 397
Drawing Conclusions, p. 397

### ONE AMERICAN'S STORY

**The mountain man Jedediah Smith was leading an expedition to find a route through the Rocky Mountains when a grizzly bear attacked. The bear seized Smith's head in its mouth, shredded his face, and partially tore off one ear. Smith's men chased the bear away. Jim Clyman recalled the scene.**

*A VOICE FROM THE PAST*

I asked [Smith] what was best. He said, "One or two go for water and if you have a needle and thread get it out and sew up my wounds around my head." . . . I told him I could do nothing for his ear. "Oh, you must try to stitch it up some way or other," said he. Then I put in my needle and stitched it through and through.

**Jim Clyman,** quoted in *The West,* by Geoffrey C. Ward

This likeness of Jedediah Smith shows the ruggedness and spirit of the mountain man.

**Ten days after this attack, Smith was ready to continue exploring. The following spring, he found what he was looking for—a pass through the Rocky Mountains.**

**Jedediah Smith was one of the daring fur trappers and explorers known as mountain men. The mountain men opened up the West by discovering the best trails through the Rockies. Later, thousands of pioneers followed these trails. In this section, you will learn about the trails—and why people followed them west.**

### 1 Mountain Men and the Rendezvous

Mountain men survived by being tough and resourceful. They spent most of the year alone, trapping small animals such as beavers. Easterners wanted beaver furs to make the men's hats that were in fashion at the time. To obtain furs, mountain men roamed the Great Plains and the Far West, the regions between the Mississippi River and the Pacific Ocean, and set traps in icy mountain streams.

Because of their adventures, mountain men such as Jedediah Smith and **Jim Beckwourth** became famous as rugged loners. However, they were not as independent as the legends have portrayed them. Instead, they were connected economically to the businessmen who bought their furs.



## FOCUS & MOTIVATE

### 5-MINUTE WARM-UP

**Making Inferences** Answering these questions will help students understand the impact the settlers had on the lands and people of the West.

1. Look at the map on page 395. What effects might movement of people on the trails have on the land and people living there?
2. Why did Americans going west think the land was largely empty?

**Warm-Up Transparency WT13**

## INSTRUCT

**INSTRUCT: OBJECTIVE 1**

**Mountain Men and the Rendezvous/ Mountain Men Open the West**

Key Questions

- What motivated mountain men?
- What information helped mountain men open the West?
- How did their exploration lead to expansion of the West?

**In-Depth Resources: Unit 4**
- Guided Reading, p. 23

**Reading Study Guide** (Spanish and English), pp. 129–130

## RECOMMENDED RESOURCES

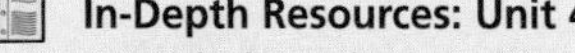

**In-Depth Resources: Unit 4**
- Guided Reading, p. 23
- Building Vocabulary, p. 27
- Primary Source: from *Luzena Stanley Wilson,* '49er, p. 31
- Reteaching Activity, p. 36

**Reading Study Guide** (Spanish and English), pp. 129–130

**Outline Map Activities**
- The Opening of the West, 1850, pp. 25–26

**America's History Makers**
- Narcissa Whitman, pp. 51–52

**Formal Assessment**
- Section Quiz, p. 200

**Alternative Assessment**
- Rubrics, 4.3
- Rubrics, 1.3

**Access for Students Acquiring English/ESL**
- Guided Reading, p. 86

Technology Resources

**Humanities Transparency HT25**
- Cowboy

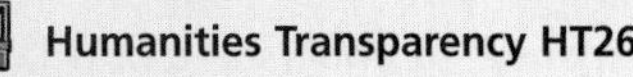

**Humanities Transparency HT26**
- *On the Trail*

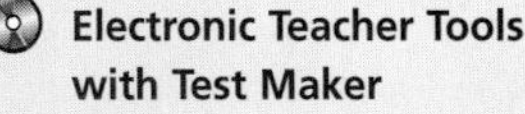

**Electronic Teacher Tools with Test Maker**

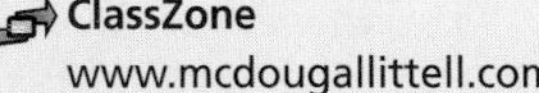

**ClassZone**
www.mcdougallittell.com

## AMERICA'S HISTORY MAKERS

**Jim Beckwourth**

Jim Beckwourth was adopted and taken into a Crow tribe when an old woman claimed he was her long lost son. Named "Morning Star," he quickly became a leader of Crow braves. His prowess as a warrior led to a name change—"Bloody Arm."

Beckwourth left the Crow in 1833. Later, he served as a guide and interpreter for the United States in the wars with Native Americans. Beckwourth's death in 1864 has been attributed to poisoning. Some accounts say it was food poisoning. However, others claim an angry former wife or disgruntled Crow leaders may have poisoned him.

**Answer: He discovered a mountain pass into what is now northern California.**

AMERICA'S HISTORY MAKERS

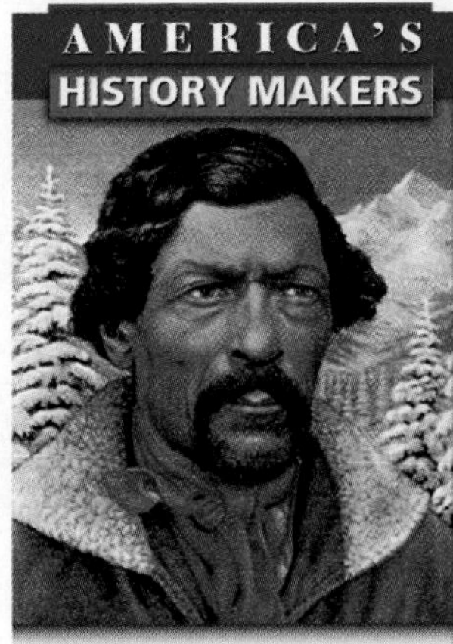

**JIM BECKWOURTH**
**1798–1867**

Jim Beckwourth was born in slavery and set free by his owner. At the age of 25, Beckwourth joined a group of fur traders going west and in time became a daring mountain man.

For several years, Beckwourth lived with a Crow tribe. Later, he worked as an army scout and gold prospector. In 1850, he discovered a mountain pass that became the route into present-day northern California. This pass is still called Beckwourth Pass.

**What was Beckwourth's most important contribution to the westward movement?**

One businessman, William Henry Ashley, created a trading arrangement called the rendezvous system. Under this system, individual trappers came to a prearranged site for a rendezvous with traders from the east. The trappers bought supplies from those traders and paid them in furs. The rendezvous took place every summer from 1825 to 1840. In that year, silk hats replaced beaver hats as the fashion, and the fur trade died out.

**Vocabulary**
**rendezvous** (RAHN•day•voo): meeting; from a French word meaning "present yourselves"

## Mountain Men Open the West

During the height of the fur trade, mountain men worked some streams so heavily that they killed off the animals. This forced the trappers to search for new streams where beaver lived. The mountain men's explorations provided Americans with some of the earliest firsthand knowledge of the Far West. This knowledge, and the trails the mountain men blazed, made it possible for later pioneers to move west.

For example, thousands of pioneers used South Pass, the wide valley through the Rockies that Jedediah Smith had publicized. Smith learned of this pass, in present-day Wyoming, from Native Americans. Unlike the high northern passes used by Lewis and Clark, South Pass was low, so snow did not block it as often as it blocked higher passes. Also, because South Pass was wide and less steep, wagon trails could run through it.

***Reading*** **History**
**A. Reading a Map** Find South Pass on the map on page 395. Notice which two trails used that pass.

Smith wrote to his brother that he wanted to help people in need: "It is for this that I go for days without eating, and am pretty well satisfied if I can gather a few roots, a few snails, . . . a piece of horseflesh, or a fine roasted dog."

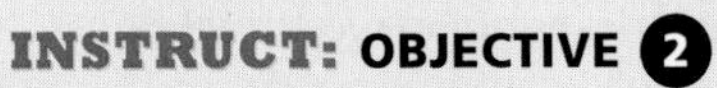

**INSTRUCT: OBJECTIVE 2**

**The Lure of the West**

Key Questions
- How did some people profit during the westward expansion?
- For what reasons did Americans go west?

 **Humanities Transparency HT25**
- Cowboy

## 2 The Lure of the West

Few of the people who went west shared Smith's noble motive. To many, the West with its vast stretches of land offered a golden chance to make money. The Louisiana Purchase had doubled the size of the United States, and some Americans wanted to take the land away from Native Americans who inhabited this territory.

People called **land speculators** bought huge areas of land. To speculate means to buy something in the hope that it will increase in value. If land value did go up, speculators divided their land holdings into smaller sections. They made great profits by selling those sections to the thousands of settlers who dreamed of owning their own farms.

Manufacturers and merchants soon followed the settlers west. They hoped to earn money by making and selling items that farmers needed. Other people made the trip to find jobs or to escape people to whom they owed money.



**ACTIVITY OPTIONS**

**INTERDISCIPLINARY LINK: ECONOMICS** — BLOCK SCHEDULING

**LAND SPECULATION**

**Class Time** 20 minutes

**Task** Determining land values

**Purpose** To understand how land speculators make money

**Supplies Needed**
- Envelopes with varying amounts of play money
- Diagram of a large rectangle with river running through it at an angle, and divided into eight plots; each plot is equal to 80 acres

**Activity** Give each student an envelope with money. Begin an auction for the land plots. Record the price paid for each plot. After the eight plots are sold, discuss the reasons why the plots sold for different prices. Run a second auction for the land. Suggest that the new owners may want to divide their land holdings. After the auction, look at how much profit the owners made from the land sale. Have the students write a paragraph explaining the basic concept of land sales and speculation.

## Trails West, 1850

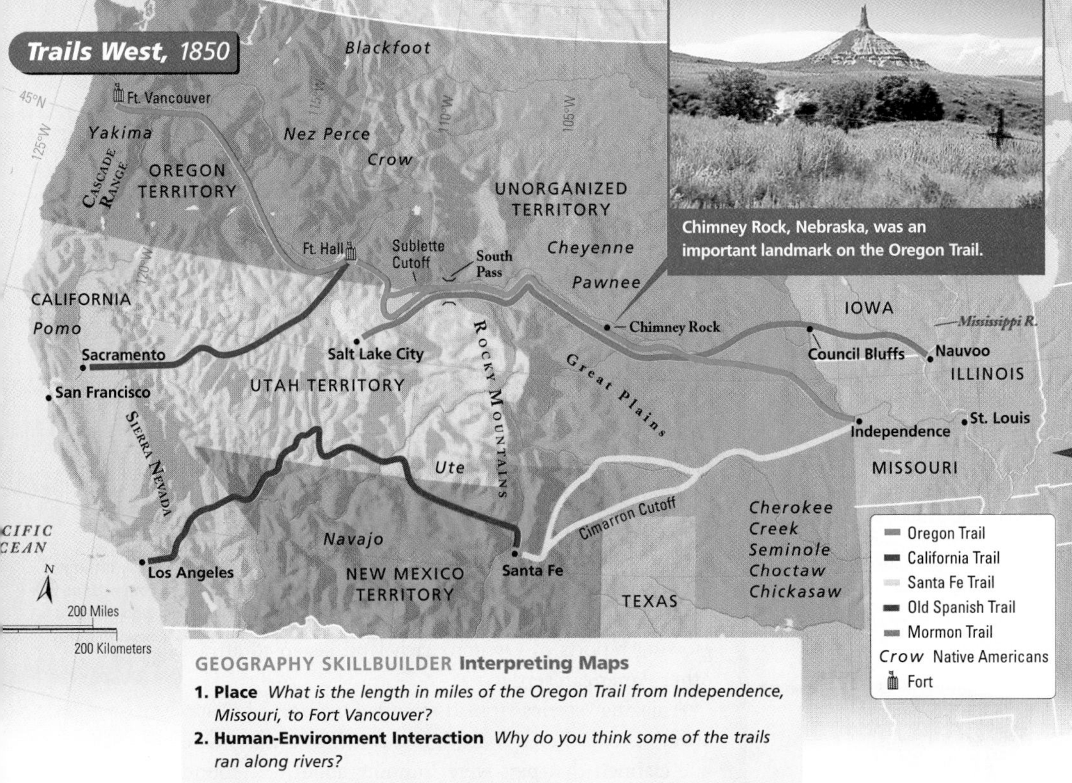


Chimney Rock, Nebraska, was an important landmark on the Oregon Trail.

**GEOGRAPHY SKILLBUILDER Interpreting Maps**

1. **Place** *What is the length in miles of the Oregon Trail from Independence, Missouri, to Fort Vancouver?*
2. **Human-Environment Interaction** *Why do you think some of the trails ran along rivers?*

Skillbuilder Answers
1. about 1,600 miles
2. Rivers provided water, food, and often ran along valleys, allowing travelers to avoid rugged terrain.

## 3 The Trail to Santa Fe

Traders also traveled west in search of markets. After Mexico gained independence from Spain in 1821, it opened its borders to American traders, whom Spain had kept out. In response, the Missouri trader William Becknell set out with hardware, cloth, and china for Santa Fe, capital of the Mexican province of New Mexico. By doing so, he opened the **Santa Fe Trail,** which led from Missouri to Santa Fe. Once in Santa Fe, he made a large profit because the New Mexicans were eager for new merchandise.

When Becknell returned to Missouri weeks later, a curious crowd met him. One man picked up one of Becknell's bags and slit it open with a knife. As gold and silver coins spilled onto the street, the onlookers gasped. The news spread that New Mexico was a place where traders could become rich.

*Reading* **History**
**B. Making Inferences** What do you think other Missourians might decide to do after seeing Becknell's wealth?
B. Possible Answer They might decide to go to Santa Fe to trade and become rich.

The following spring, Becknell headed to Santa Fe again. This time he loaded his trade goods into covered wagons, which Westerners called prairie schooners. Their billowing white canvas tops made them look like schooners, or sailing ships.

Becknell could not haul wagons over the mountain pass he had used on his first trip to Santa Fe. Instead, he found a cutoff, a shortcut that avoided steep slopes but passed through a deadly desert to the south. As his traders crossed the burning sands, they ran out of water. Crazed by



### HISTORY FROM VISUALS

**Reading the Map** Point out different landforms on the map. Have the students discuss how the landforms would affect the progress of the settlers. **Possible Response** Much of the journey passed through mountains, making travel difficult and slow.

**Extension** Have students use an atlas to determine if any major highways follow the routes of the trails shown on the map.

**Outline Map Activities**
- The Opening of the West, 1850, pp. 25–26

### INSTRUCT: OBJECTIVE 3

**The Trail to Santa Fe**

Key Questions
- How did Mexican independence open the New Mexico territory to American traders?
- Who opened the Santa Fe Trail to New Mexico?
- What was important about the Cimarron cutoff?

### MORE ABOUT . . .

**Traveling the Santa Fe Trail**

Council Grove, in present-day Kansas, was the last rendezvous point for joining a caravan to Santa Fe. The complete journey from Missouri to New Mexico took two to three months and covered approximately 800 miles. However, the return trip might take half as long because of the lighter load. The high point of the trip was the arrival in Santa Fe. The whole town turned out to greet the wagoneers, who were dressed in their best clothes in honor of the occasion.

### ACTIVITY OPTIONS

### INDIVIDUAL NEEDS

**STUDENTS ACQUIRING ENGLISH/ESL**

**Asking Questions** To help students focus before they read, have them preview the section and write questions based on the heads in the section. The questions should ask: Who? What? Where? When? Why? or How? Some sample questions follow, but students should be encouraged to write their own questions.

***Who were the mountain men?***
***What was a rendezvous?***
***Why was the Santa Fe Trail important?***

After students have read the section, they should go back and write answers to the questions they have written. As an alternative, have students work in pairs to write the questions and then discuss their answers with each other.

## daily*life*

**Dinner on the Trail**

One historian has estimated that between 1840 and 1860, 133,316,550 meals were eaten on the way to the West. The basic diet was bread, bacon, and coffee. The semi-arid Plains provided little additional food; however, some wild game, fish, berries, and roots were available. The Plains did furnish the principle fuel for fires—buffalo chips. The dried dung of buffalo was picked up along the way. The chips also served another purpose. Children threw them for fun, in a sort of ancestor to the frisbee of today.

 **Humanities Transparency HT26**
- *On the Trail*

### INSTRUCT: OBJECTIVE 4

**Oregon Fever/One Family Heads West**

Key Questions
- What group was among the earliest travelers to the Oregon Territory?
- What kinds of stories encouraged people to make the journey to Oregon?
- What was the journey to Oregon like?

 **America's History Makers**
- Narcissa Whitman, pp. 51–52

 **In-Depth Resources: Unit 4**
- Primary Source, p. 31

### MORE ABOUT . . .

**The Oregon Trail**

Wagons going west had the 19th-century equivalent of bumper stickers. Wagons had signs that identified their destinations and old hometowns or made political statements. Other signs affectionately named the wagons, much as some people name their cars today. Some examples include Prairie Bird, Albatross, Old Settlers of Keokuk [Iowa], T. F. Royal for Oregon, Oregon 54° 40°—all or none!

## daily*life*

**DINNER ON THE TRAIL**

To add to their limited supplies, pioneers on the trail gathered berries and wild onions. They also hunted buffalo and small game. Below is a recipe that many might have used.

**Fricasseed Squirrel**

1 squirrel, skinned
3 slices of bacon, chopped
1 tablespoon chopped onions
2 teaspoons lemon juice
⅓ cup water
salt, pepper, & flour

Cut squirrel in pieces. Rub pieces with salt, pepper, and flour. Fry with bacon for 30 minutes. Add onion, lemon juice, and water. Cover tightly. Cook for 1½ hours.

*Nebraska Centennial First Ladies Cookbook*

thirst, they lopped off mules' ears and killed their dogs to drink the animals' blood. Finally, the men found a stream. The water saved them from death, and they reached Santa Fe.

Becknell returned home with another huge profit. Before long, hundreds of traders and prairie schooners braved the cutoff to make the 800-mile journey from Missouri to New Mexico each year.

## 4 Oregon Fever

Hundreds of settlers also began migrating west on the **Oregon Trail,** which ran from Independence, Missouri, to the Oregon Territory. The first whites to cross the continent to Oregon were missionaries, such as Marcus and Narcissa Whitman in 1836. At that time, the United States and Britain were locked in an argument about which country owned Oregon. To the Whitmans' great disappointment, they made few converts among the Native Americans. However, their glowing reports of Oregon's rich land began to attract other American settlers.

**Vocabulary**
**converts:** people who accept a new religious belief

Amazing stories spread about Oregon. The sun always shone there. Wheat grew as tall as a man. One tale claimed that pigs were "running about, . . . round and fat, and already cooked, with knives and forks sticking in them so you can cut off a slice whenever you are hungry."

Such stories tempted many people to make the 2,000-mile journey to Oregon. In 1843, nearly 1,000 people traveled from Missouri to Oregon. The next year, twice as many came. "The Oregon Fever has broken out," observed a Boston newspaper, "and is now raging."

## One Family Heads West

The experiences of the Sager family show how difficult the trail could be. In 1844, Henry Sager, his wife, and six children left Missouri to find cheap, fertile land in Oregon. They had already moved four times in the past four years. Henry's daughter Catherine explained her family's moves.

*A VOICE FROM THE PAST*

Father was one of those restless men who are not content to remain in one place long at a time. . . . [He] had been talking of going to Texas. But mother, hearing much said about the healthfulness of Oregon, preferred to go there.

**Catherine Sager,** quoted in *The West,* by Geoffrey C. Ward

The Oregon Trail was dangerous, so pioneers joined wagon trains. They knew their survival would depend on cooperation. Before setting out, the wagon train members agreed on rules and elected leaders to enforce them.

Even so, life on the trail was full of hardship. The Sagers had barely begun the trip when Mrs. Sager gave birth to her seventh child. Two

### ACTIVITY OPTIONS

### MULTIPLE LEARNING STYLES: MUSICAL — BLOCK SCHEDULING

**PIONEER SONGS**

**Class Time** 20 minutes

**Task** Analyzing primary sources

**Purpose** To gain an understanding of the trip west or reasons people took the journey by studying song lyrics

**Supplies Needed**
- Songbooks such as *American Ballads and Folk Songs* by Alan Lomax and *The Ballad of America* by John Anthony Scott
- Recordings of ballads or folk songs

**Activity** Suggest that students research songs sung by the people going west. They may want to consult with a music teacher. Have students study the lyrics to understand the reasons pioneers went west and what their journey was like. The song "Sweet Betsy from Pike" is a good one to start with. Students should provide an explanation of the lyrics to the class and, if possible, perform the songs or find recordings and play them.

months later, nine-year-old Catherine fell under a moving wagon, which crushed her left leg. Later, "camp fever" killed both of the Sager parents.

Even though the Sager parents had died, the other families in the train cooperated to help the Sager orphans make it to Oregon. There, the Whitmans agreed to adopt them. When Narcissa met them, Catherine recalled, "We thought as we shyly looked at her that she was the prettiest woman we had ever seen."

*Reading* **History**
**C. Finding Main Ideas** What difficulties did families like the Sagers face?
C. Answer Many faced illness and injury due to harsh conditions.

## 5 The Mormon Trail

While most pioneers went west in search of wealth, one group migrated for religious reasons. The **Mormons,** who settled Utah, were members of the Church of Jesus Christ of Latter-Day Saints. Joseph Smith had founded this church in upstate New York in 1830. The Mormons lived in close communities, worked hard, shared their goods, and prospered.

The Mormons, though, also made enemies. Some people reacted angrily to the Mormons' teachings. They saw the Mormon practice of polygamy—allowing a man to have more than one wife at a time—as immoral. Others objected to their holding property in common.

*Reading* **History**
**D. Analyzing Causes** Why did Brigham Young lead the Mormons to Utah?
D. Answer so that he and his followers could practice their religion in peace

In 1844, an anti-Mormon mob in Illinois killed Smith. **Brigham Young,** the next Mormon leader, moved his people out of the United States. His destination was Utah, then part of Mexico. In this desolate region, he hoped his people would be left to follow their faith in peace.

In 1847, about 1,600 Mormons followed part of the Oregon Trail to Utah. There they built a new settlement by the Great Salt Lake. Because Utah has little rainfall, the Mormons had to work together to build dams and canals. These structures captured water in the hills and carried it to the farms in the valleys below. Through teamwork, they made their desert homeland bloom.

In the meantime, changes were taking place in Texas. As you will read in Section 2, Americans had been moving into that Mexican territory, too.

### Section 1 Assessment

**1. Terms & Names**

Identify:
- Jedediah Smith
- mountain man
- Jim Beckwourth
- land speculator
- Santa Fe Trail
- Oregon Trail
- Mormon
- Brigham Young

**2. Taking Notes**

Use a cluster diagram like the one shown to review details about the trails west.

Which trail would you have wanted to travel? Why?

**3. Main Ideas**

**a.** How did the mountain men open up the West for later settlement?

**b.** What are two examples of pioneer groups who used cooperation to overcome hardship?

**c.** What were the different motives that drew people west?

**4. Critical Thinking**

**Drawing Conclusions** Of all the hardships faced by people who went west, what do you think was the worst? Explain.

THINK ABOUT
- the mountain men
- William Becknell
- the Sagers
- the Mormons

**ACTIVITY OPTIONS**

**LANGUAGE ARTS / ART**

Research a pioneer from this section and either write a **letter** from his or her point of view to a friend or illustrate a **journal entry** with sights from your journey.





**INSTRUCT: OBJECTIVE 5**

**The Mormon Trail**

Key Questions
- Why did some people oppose the Mormons?
- Why did the Mormons move west?
- Where did the Mormons settle?

## ASSESS & RETEACH

**Setting the Stage** Have students fill in the first two columns for New Mexico, Utah, and Oregon on the chapter graphic organizer.

**Formal Assessment**
- Section Quiz, p. 200

**Critical Thinking Transparency CT37**
- Setting the Stage

### RETEACHING ACTIVITY

Divide the class into three teams, each representing one of the three trails discussed in this chapter. Each team should create a set of six flash cards that identify key ideas about that trail. Tape the cards to a string and pin the string across the chalkboard or classroom.

**In-Depth Resources: Unit 4**
- Reteaching Activity, p. 36

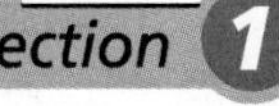

### Section 1 Assessment

**1. Terms & Names**

**Jedediah Smith,** p. 393
**mountain men,** p. 393
**Jim Beckwourth,** p. 393
**land speculators,** p. 394
**Santa Fe Trail,** p. 395
**Oregon Trail,** p. 396
**Mormons,** p. 397
**Brigham Young,** p. 397

**2. Taking Notes**

Mormon Trail—followed Oregon Trail to Utah, taken by Mormons; Oregon Trail—from Missouri to Oregon Territory, people went for land; Santa Fe Trail—from Missouri to Santa Fe, New Mexico, attracted many traders. Answers will vary.

**3. Main Ideas**

**a.** Mountain men had knowledge of trails and passes in the western lands. **b.** travelers on the Oregon Trail; the Mormons **c.** to get rich; to get farm land; to trade; to avoid religious persecution; to start a new life

**4. Critical Thinking**

the dangerous, difficult trip; disease; death; bad food and water

**ACTIVITY OPTIONS**

**Alternative Assessment**
- Rubrics for a letter, 4.3
- Rubrics for an illustration, 1.3

## Interdisciplinary CHALLENGE

**OBJECTIVE**

Students work cooperatively to solve technological, social, and nutritional problems pioneers faced in adapting to their environment.

 **BLOCK SCHEDULING**

## PROCEDURE

For each challenge, have students form groups of four or five. Ask group members to divide the work among themselves. Then have them choose an option for presenting their solution.

### SCIENCE CHALLENGE

**Class Time** 50 minutes

Use the following suggestions to help students figure out how to slow the descent of the wagon.

- Draw a sketch of a wagon on the down slope.
- Test ways of slowing down the speed of a toy car or skateboard going down a ramp.

**POSSIBLE SOLUTIONS**

Here are ways that pioneers used to slow down a wagon:

- chains wrapped around wagon wheels
- logs jammed under the wagon wheels
- a makeshift windlass, or winch (hauling machine)

*Interdisciplinary* **CHALLENGE**

# Survive the Oregon Trail!

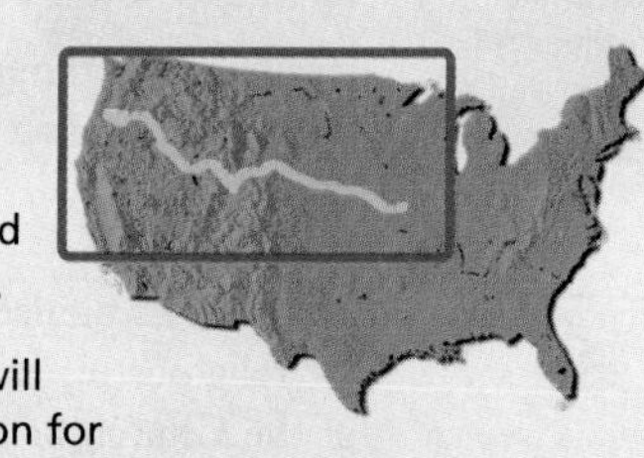

You are part of a wagon train heading west on the Oregon Trail. During your journey, you will cross endless flat prairies and mountains that climb more steeply than a staircase. You will suffer through blazing heat and icy snowstorms. Food is scarce in the land you travel through—and human settlements are even more scarce.

**COOPERATIVE LEARNING** On this page are three challenges you will face on your journey. Working with a small group, create a solution for each challenge. To help your group work together, assign a task to each group member. You will find helpful information in the Data File. Be prepared to present your solutions to the class.

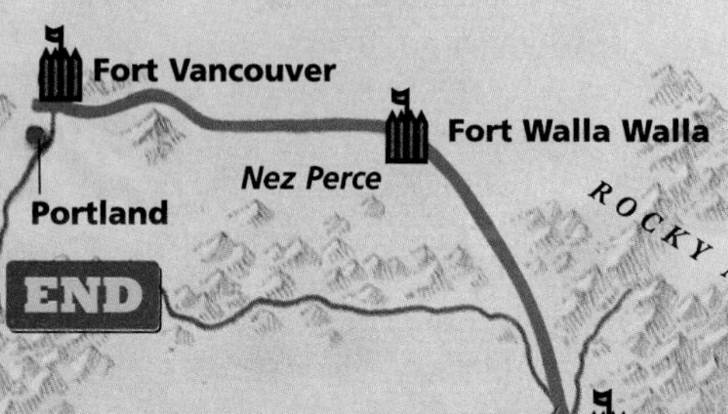


### SCIENCE CHALLENGE

#### *"The most terrible mountains"*

**One pioneer called the Rockies "the most terrible mountains for steepness." Your oxen have struggled for hours to pull your wagon up a steep slope. Now you have to go down the other side without crashing—and wagon wheels have no brakes. How will you slow your descent? Use the Data File for help. Present your ideas using one of these options:**

- Write instructions for climbing and descending the mountain.
- Illustrate your solution in a how-to diagram.

### CIVICS CHALLENGE

#### *"A thieving scoundrel"*

**You wake one morning to the sound of shouting. One of the men in the wagon train has been caught stealing another family's ox—to replace an ox that died from drinking bad water. The wagon train leader asks you to help decide how to punish the thief. Present your decision using one of these options:**

- As a group, role-play a discussion of what the punishment should be.
- Write an explanation of a punishment to the wagon train leader.



## STANDARDS FOR EVALUATION

### SCIENCE CHALLENGE

**Option 1** Written instructions should
- include clear, easy-to-follow directions.
- present the steps in logical order.

**Option 2** How-to diagrams should
- explain a process through the use of arrows, boxes, and other visuals.
- include labels to clarify the sequence of steps.

### CIVICS CHALLENGE

**Option 1** Role-plays of discussions should
- present different views on the issue.
- include realistic comments.
- reflect sound decision making.

**Option 2** Written recommendations should
- describe details of the theft.
- include reasons that justify the punishment.
- reach a logical conclusion.

### HEALTH CHALLENGE

**Option 1** Food illustrations should
- create a realistic image of a pioneer dish.
- include captions that describe the dish.

**Option 2** Recipes should
- list all necessary ingredients.
- describe the preparation in chronological order.

## DATA FILE

### The Journey
**Distance:** 2,000 miles
**Length:** 4–6 months
**Average daily distance:** 12–15 miles
**Best time to travel:** April–September

### The Wagon
**Size of box:** 4 x 10 feet
**Load:** 1,600–2,500 pounds
**Oxen needed per wagon:** 4–8

### Animals Taken
oxen, horses, dairy cows, cattle, chickens, mules, pigs, dogs, cats

### Food Supplies
flour, corn meal, salt, baking soda, sugar, crackers, dried beans, rice, dried fruit, bacon, coffee, vinegar

### Cooking Equipment
Dutch oven, large kettle, frying pan, bread pan, coffee grinder, rolling pin, tin cups and plates, water kegs, knives, spoons

### Other Equipment
bedding, spare wagon parts, tar, rope, chains, pulleys, tools, fishing poles, guns, ammunition, matches, soap, medicines

### Trail Hazards
**Worst discomforts:** heat, cold, wind, rain, dust, mud, mosquitoes, hunger, thirst
**Biggest killer:** disease
**Most common accidents:** shooting, drowning, crushing by wagon wheels, injuries from animals

Visit www.mcdougallittell.com for more information on the Oregon Trail.

### HEALTH CHALLENGE

## "A grand blow-out"

On July 4, your wagon train stops near Independence Rock for "a grand blow-out" to celebrate your progress. Each family will bring a dish to the party. What will you cook that is tasty and nutritious? You might use supplies from your wagon and berries or animals from the area. Look at the Data File for help. Present your choice using one of these options:

- Draw a picture of your dish and describe it.
- Write an original recipe.

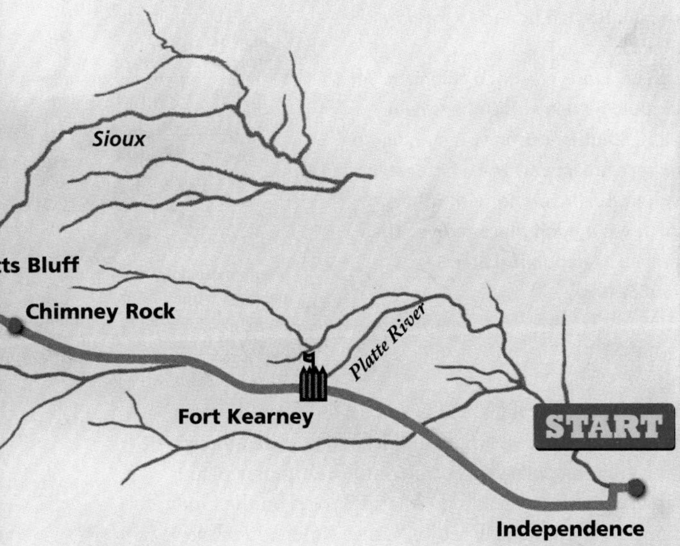


### ACTIVITY WRAP-UP

**Present to the class** As a group, review your responses to the challenges of the Oregon Trail. Choose the most creative solution for each challenge and present these solutions to the class.

*Manifest Destiny* **399**

### CIVICS CHALLENGE

**Class Time** 50 minutes

Suggest that students copy the decision-making chart in the Citizenship Handbook, p. 285, and fill it in to help guide them in choosing a punishment. Ask them to consider a punishment that serves the best interests of the people who belong to the wagon train.

**POSSIBLE SOLUTION**

A man named "Buckskin Rose" described the punishment administered to horse thieves on his wagon train—they were kicked out. In many wagon trains, justice was swift and the punishment unfair.

### HEALTH CHALLENGE

**Class Time** 50 minutes

Have students look at illustrated cookbooks to use as models for drawing pictures of food or writing a recipe.

**POSSIBLE SOLUTION**

Pioneers' food choices would not have met today's standards for a well-balanced diet. Bacon, bread, and coffee were generally part of the daily menu.

### ACTIVITY WRAP-UP

Presentations should
- provide a clear, concise statement of the problem.
- give a workable solution.
- evaluate the effectiveness of the solution.
- explain the originality of the solution.

## SECTION OBJECTIVES

1. To profile Texas under Spanish rule
2. To explain the tension between Texans and *Tejanos*
3. To summarize the war between Texas and Mexico
4. To explain that Texas became its own country

**SKILLBUILDER**

Interpreting Maps: Movement, p. 405

**CRITICAL THINKING**

Analyzing Causes, pp. 401, 402, 405
Summarizing, p. 402
Making Inferences, p. 403
Recognizing Effects, p. 405

## FOCUS & MOTIVATE

### 5-MINUTE WARM-UP

**Making Inferences** These questions focus on how Americans got involved in the Texas Revolution.

1. Study the poster on page 401. What is being offered to settlers coming to Texas?
2. Why do you think this offer is being made?

 **Warm-Up Transparency WT13**

## INSTRUCT

### INSTRUCT: OBJECTIVE 1

**Spanish Texas**

Key Questions

- What made Texas's land so desirable?
- Who are *Tejanos?*
- Why did the Spanish government want to attract settlers to Texas?

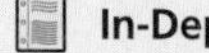

**In-Depth Resources: Unit 4**
- Guided Reading, p. 24
- Building Vocabulary, p. 27

**Reading Study Guide** (Spanish and English), pp. 131–132

# 2 The Texas Revolution

**TERMS & NAMES**
Stephen Austin
*Tejano*
Antonio López de Santa Anna
Sam Houston
William Travis
Juan Seguín
Battle of the Alamo
Lone Star Republic

| MAIN IDEA | WHY IT MATTERS NOW |
|---|---|
| American and *Tejano* citizens led Texas to independence from Mexico. | The diverse culture of Texas has developed from the contributions of many different groups. |

### ONE AMERICAN'S STORY

Son of a bankrupt Missouri mine owner, **Stephen Austin** read his mother's letter, written in 1821, in stunned silence. His father, Moses Austin, was dead. In his last moments, she told her son, "He called me to his bedside, . . . he begged me to tell you to take his place . . . to go on . . . in the same way he would have done."

Stephen knew what that meant. Moses Austin had spent the last years of his life chasing a crazy dream. He had hoped to found a colony for Americans in Spanish Texas.

Stephen's dream, though, was to be a lawyer—not a colonizer. Yet as a loving and obedient son, how could he deny his father's dying wish? A week after his father's death, Stephen Austin was standing on Texas soil. From that day on, his father's dream was to be his destiny.

This section explains how Stephen Austin, along with others, worked hard to make the lands of Texas a good place to live. Their spirit would create an independent Texas Republic. Later, Texas would become a state in the United States.

Stephen Austin, shown in this painting, helped fulfill his father's dream by establishing an American colony in Texas.

## 1 Spanish Texas

The Spanish land called *Tejas* (Tay•HAHS) bordered the United States territory called Louisiana. The land was rich and desirable. It had forests in the east, rich soil for growing corn and cotton, and great grassy plains for grazing animals. It also had rivers leading to natural ports on the Gulf of Mexico. It was home to Plains and Pueblo Native Americans. Even though *Tejas* was a state in the Spanish colony of New Spain, it had few Spanish settlers. Around 1819, Spanish soldiers drove off Americans trying to claim those lands as a part of the Louisiana Purchase.

In 1821, only about 4,000 *Tejanos* (Tay•HAH•nohs) lived in Texas. ***Tejanos*** are people of Spanish heritage who consider Texas their home. The Comanche, Apache, and other tribes fought fiercely against Spanish settlement of Texas. The Spanish officials wanted many more settlers to move to Texas. They hoped that new colonists would help to defend against Native Americans and Americans who illegally sneaked into Texas.



## RECOMMENDED RESOURCES

**In-Depth Resources: Unit 4**
- Guided Reading, p. 24
- Building Vocabulary, p. 27
- Primary Source: A Mexican Account of the Battle of the Alamo, p. 32
- Reteaching Activity, p. 37

**Reading Study Guide** (Spanish and English), pp. 131–132

**America's History Makers**
- Juan Seguín, pp. 53–54

**American History Plays**
- *Live from the Alamo*

**Formal Assessment**
- Section Quiz, p. 201

**Alternative Assessment**
- Rubrics, 1.7
- Rubrics, 5.1

**Access for Students Acquiring English/ESL**
- Guided Reading, p. 87

**Technology Resources**

 **Geography Transparency GT13**
- The Battle of the Alamo, 1836

 **Electronic Teacher Tools with Test Maker**

 **ClassZone**
www.mcdougallittell.com

**Vocabulary**
***empresarios:*** individuals who agreed to recruit settlers for the land

To attract more people to Texas, the Spanish government offered huge tracts of land to *empresarios.* But they were unable to attract Spanish settlers. So, when Moses Austin asked for permission to start a colony in Texas, Spain agreed. Austin was promised a large section of land. He had to agree that settlers on his land had to follow Spanish laws.

**TEXAS!!**

**Emigrants who are desirous of assisting Texas at this important crisis of her affairs may have a free passage and equipments, by applying at the NEW-YORK and PHILADELPHIA HOTEL, On the Old Levee, near the Blue Stores.**

**Now is the time to ensure a fortune in Land:** To all who remain in Texas during the War will be allowed 1280 Acres.
To all who remain Six Months, 640 Acres.
To all who remain Three Months, 320 Acres.
And as Colonists, 4600 Acres for a family and 1470 Acres for a Single Man.
New Orleans, April 23d, 1836.

## 2 Mexican Independence Changes Texas

Shortly after Stephen Austin arrived in Texas in 1821, Mexico successfully gained its independence from Spain. *Tejas* was now a part of Mexico. With the change in government, the Spanish land grant given to Austin's father was worthless. Stephen Austin traveled to Mexico City to persuade the new Mexican government to let him start his colony. It took him almost a year to get permission. And the Mexican government would consent only if the new settlers agreed to become Mexican citizens and members of the Roman Catholic Church.

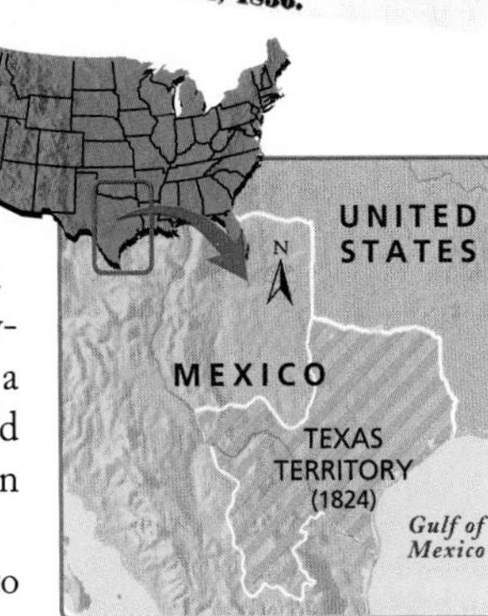


Posters such as the one above encouraged Americans from the East to settle in Texas. Some people scrawled G.T.T. on their doors to indicate they had "gone to Texas."

Between 1821 and 1827, Austin attracted 297 families to his new settlement. These original Texas settler families are known as the "Old Three Hundred." He demanded evidence that each family head was moral, worked hard, and did not drink. So law-abiding were his colonists that Austin could write to a new settler, "You will be astonished to see all our houses with no other fastening than a wooden pin or door latch."

The success of Austin's colony attracted more land speculators and settlers to Texas from the United States. Some were looking for a new life, some were escaping from the law, and others were looking for a chance to grow rich. By 1830, the population had swelled to about 30,000, with Americans outnumbering the *Tejanos* six to one.

A. Answer
Americans had problems adapting to Mexican laws, speaking Spanish, and they wanted slavery to continue.

*Reading* **History**
**A. Analyzing Causes** Why was there growing tension between Americans and *Tejanos?*

## Rising Tensions in Texas

As more and more Americans settled in Texas, tensions between them and the *Tejanos* increased. Used to governing themselves, Americans resented following Mexican laws. Since few Americans spoke Spanish, they were unhappy that all official documents had to be in that language. Slave owners were especially upset when Mexico outlawed slavery in 1829. They wanted to maintain slavery so they could grow cotton. Austin persuaded the government to allow slave owners to keep their slaves.

On the other hand, the *Tejanos* found the Americans difficult to live with, too. *Tejanos* thought that the Americans believed they were superior and deserved special privileges. The Americans seemed unwilling to adapt to Mexican laws.



**INSTRUCT: OBJECTIVE 2**

**Mexican Independence Changes Texas/ Rising Tensions in Texas**

Key Questions
- How successful was Austin in creating a colony in Texas?
- What was a source of tension between American settlers and *Tejanos?*
- How did the Mexican government respond to the problems between these two groups?

**MORE ABOUT . . .**

**Crossing the Border**
In the early 1830s, when Texas was part of Mexico, Mexicans wanted to keep American immigrants out of Texas. Today, the U.S. government patrols the Mexican-American border to keep illegal Mexican immigrants from coming into the United States. In the 1830s, Americans went to Texas for land (economics), while today Mexicans come to the United States for the same reason—greater economic opportunity.

**ACTIVITY OPTIONS**

**INTERDISCIPLINARY LINK: CIVICS**

**BLOCK SCHEDULING**

**PROBLEM SOLVING**

**Class Time** 20 minutes

**Task** Resolving problems between *Tejanos* and Americans

**Purpose** To use problem-solving skills to find ways that *Tejanos* and Americans could have cooperated in Texas

**Supplies Needed**
- Textbook
- Copy of problem-solving steps or the transparency of problem-solving steps

**Activity** Have students work in groups of four. Two students will represent *Tejanos* and the others will be Americans. Hand out a copy of the steps for solving problems or use the overhead transparency. Students should determine the answer to Reading History A. Using those answers as the problems to be solved, the two pairs should use the problem-solving steps to find possible ways the issues could have been solved. Each group should present to the class a solution to one of the problems. The class should discuss which solutions seem most likely to be successful.

**INSTRUCT: OBJECTIVE 3**

**Texans Revolt Against Mexico/ The Fight for the Alamo**

Key Questions

- How did Santa Anna react to the letter given to him by Stephen Austin?
- What happened at the Battle of the Alamo?

 **Geography Transparency GT13**
- The Battle of the Alamo, 1836

### *America's* HERITAGE

**Remember the Alamo!**

Some steps have been taken to combat the moisture problem at the Alamo. Shrubs and grass were removed and replaced with moisture-absorbing gravel and sand. In addition, metal plates were installed underground to block seeping water. One major factor, however, has not been addressed—the breath of the estimated three million tourists that visit the Alamo every year. The tourists' breath brings moisture inside the structure.

 **In-Depth Resources: Unit 4**
- Primary Source: A Mexican Account of the Battle of the Alamo, p. 32

The Mexican government sent an official to Texas to investigate the tensions. He was not happy with what he found. In 1829, he reported to his government, "I am warning you to take timely measures . . . Texas could throw this whole nation into revolution." His advice turned out to be right.

Responding to the warnings, the Mexican government cracked down on Texas. First, it closed the state to further American immigration. Next, it required Texans to pay taxes for the first time. Finally, to enforce these new laws, the government sent more Mexican troops to Texas.

*Reading*History
**B. Summarizing** What three actions did the Mexican government take to control Texas?
**B. Answer** The Mexican government stopped American immigration, levied taxes, and sent troops to Texas.

## 3 Texans Revolt Against Mexico

These actions caused angry protests. Some Texans even talked of breaking away from Mexico. Most, however, listened to Austin, who remained loyal to Mexico. In 1833, Austin set off for Mexico City with a petition. This document listed reforms supported by both Americans and *Tejanos*. The most important request was that Texas become a self-governing state within Mexico.

### *America's* HERITAGE

**REMEMBER THE ALAMO!**

Today the Alamo, shown below, is again under siege. Moisture seeps into the limestone walls and causes them to crumble. Many people view the mission as a memorial to Americans' willingness to fight for freedom, so a Texas group has begun attempts to preserve the Alamo from further damage. The Alamo looks quite different from the battle site of 1836. The famous bell-shaped front was added in the 1850s.

In Mexico City, Austin met General **Antonio López de Santa Anna,** the Mexican president. At first, the general agreed to most of the reforms in Austin's petition. But then Santa Anna learned of a letter Austin had written. The letter said that if the changes weren't approved Austin would support breaking away from Mexican rule. This was rebellion! The general had Austin jailed for an entire year. The Texans were furious and ready to rebel.

Santa Anna's answer to talk of rebellion was to send more troops to Texas. In late September 1835, Mexican soldiers marched to the town of Gonzales. They had orders to seize a cannon used by the Texans for protection against Native Americans. Texas volunteers had hung a flag on the big gun that said, "Come and Take It."

The Mexican troops failed to capture the cannon. Two months later, Texans drove Mexican troops out of an old mission in San Antonio that was used as a fortress. It was called the Alamo. Among the Texas volunteers were free African Americans such as Hendrick Arnold and Greenbury Logan. Angered by these insults, Santa Anna and 6,000 troops headed for Texas.

*Reading*History
**C. Analyzing Causes** What Texan actions moved Santa Anna to head toward Texas?
**C. Answer** American resistance at Gonzales and at San Antonio

## The Fight for the Alamo

On March 1–2, 1836, Texans met at a settlement called Washington-on-the-Brazos to decide what to do about Santa Anna's troops. They believed they could do only one thing: to declare Texas a free and independent republic. **Sam Houston,** the only man at the meeting with military experience, was placed in command of the Texas army.



**ACTIVITY OPTIONS**

**INDIVIDUAL NEEDS**

**LESS PROFICIENT READERS**

**Sequencing Events** Some students may have trouble piecing together the events of the Texas Revolution. To help students understand and remember the events that led to the Texas-Mexican War, have them make a sequence chart like the one at the right.

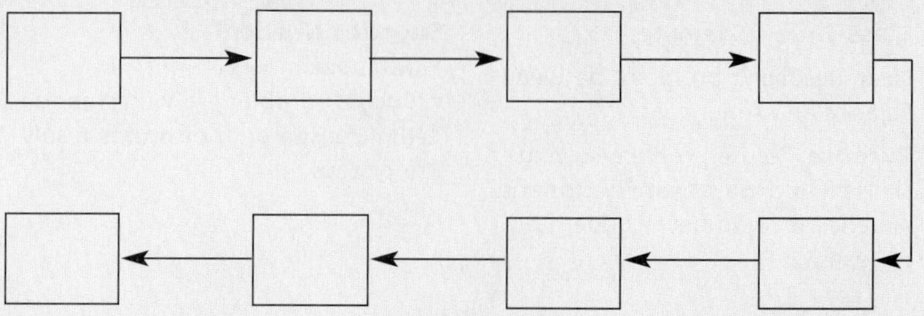

The Texas army hardly existed. At that moment, there were two small forces ready to stand up to Santa Anna's army. One was a company of 420 men, led by James Fannin, stationed at Goliad, a fort in southeast Texas. The second was a company of 183 volunteers at the Alamo. Headed by **William Travis,** this small force included such famous frontiersmen as Davy Crockett and Jim Bowie. In addition, **Juan Seguín** (wahn seh•GEEN) led a band of 25 *Tejanos* in support of revolt.

*"Remember the Alamo!"*
a Texan soldier

On February 23, 1836, Santa Anna's troops surrounded San Antonio. The next day, Mexicans began their siege of the Alamo. Two nights later, Travis scrawled a message to the world.

*Reading* **History**

**D. Making Inferences** Why would William Travis address his message to all Americans?
D. Possible Response Travis wanted to rally support for Texas from all Americans.

*A VOICE FROM THE PAST*

The enemy has demanded a surrender. . . . I have answered the demand with a cannon shot, and our flag still waves proudly from the walls. I shall never surrender or retreat.

**William Travis,** "To the People of Texas and all the Americans in the World."

Because Juan Seguín spoke Spanish, he was chosen to carry the plea through enemy lines. Seguín got the message through to other Texas defenders. But when he returned, he saw the Alamo in flames.

The Alamo's defenders held off the Mexican attack for 12 violent days. Travis and the defenders stubbornly refused to surrender. On the 13th day, Santa Anna ordered more than 1,800 men to storm the fortress. The Texans met the attackers with a hailstorm of cannon and gun fire. Then suddenly it became strangely quiet. The Texans had run out of ammunition. At day's end, all but five Texans were dead. The **Battle of the Alamo** was over.

**HISTORY *through* ART**

The Battle of the Alamo was so intense that Davy Crockett did not have time to reload his gun, which he called "Betsy." He used it as a club. This print is by a 20th-century illustrator, Frederick Yohn.

**What does the print reveal about the battle?**

403



## MORE ABOUT . . .

**William Travis**

When Santa Anna arrived in San Antonio with several thousand Mexican troops, he demanded the surrender of the Alamo. As commander, Travis answered Santa Anna with a cannon shot. Inside the Alamo, Travis drew a line in the sand and asked those who wanted to stay and fight to cross the line and join him. All but one person joined him. Some historians dispute this story, but it was related in three separate eyewitness accounts.

## *HISTORY through ART*

**Interpreting the Painting** The action in the painting is centered on Davy Crockett, and the artist is able to capture the intensity of the hand-to-hand fighting. The Mexican troops are closing in, and the Texans appear to be making their last stand.

**Possible Responses: Davy Crockett was courageous, and the battle was very intense.**

## ACTIVITY OPTIONS

**MULTIPLE LEARNING STYLES: KINESTHETIC**

BLOCK SCHEDULING

### KEY BATTLES OF TEXAS REVOLUTION

**Class Time** One class period

**Task** Reenacting key battles of the Texas-Mexican War

**Purpose** To analyze information and create oral presentations about the Texas Revolution

**Supplies Needed**

- Reference materials on the Texas Revolution
- Drawing paper or posterboard
- Art supplies

**Activity** Have students form three groups. Ask each group to reenact a different battle—the Alamo, Goliad, or San Jacinto. Each group should do research on the action in each of the battles. Then they should make props or a map showing the action in the selected battle. Students should focus on showing movement and location during the battle. Have groups present the battles in chronological order. After each presentation, ask the following questions: Which side had more soldiers? What strategies were used? What was the outcome of the battle? What happened as a result of the battle?

## AMERICA'S HISTORY MAKERS

**Juan Seguín**

Because of his goal of a Texas free from Mexico, Juan Seguín got along well with American settlers in Texas. However, he wanted Texas to remain independent and not become part of the United States. He was elected to the Texas Senate in 1838 and was mayor of San Antonio twice. However, Seguín was often betrayed and harassed by Americans. Finally he was forced to leave. Ten years later, Seguín found himself fighting against Americans in the Mexican War.

 **America's History Makers**
- Juan Seguín, pp. 53–54

**Sam Houston**

As commander of the Texan forces, Sam Houston developed an unpopular war strategy. To lure the Mexican army deep into Texas, Houston ordered his army to retreat through Texas. Then when he thought the Mexicans were overextended he would attack. Houston's officers doubted he would seek battle. The new president of Texas, David Burnet, said, "the Enemy are laughing at you to scorn . . . You must retreat no farther." However, Houston's win at the Battle of San Jacinto proved his strategy was correct.

**Possible Responses: Sequín was a Tejano who fought with Texans. Houston was an American who commanded Texas forces.**

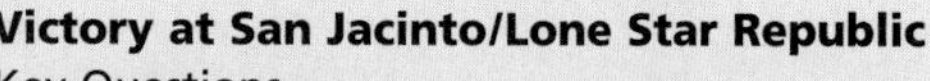

## INSTRUCT: OBJECTIVE 4

**Victory at San Jacinto/Lone Star Republic**

Key Questions
- How did the Texans win the Battle of San Jacinto?
- After independence, what did most Texans want from the United States?
- Why did some groups in the United States oppose annexing Texas?

## AMERICA'S HISTORY MAKERS

**JUAN SEGUÍN**
**1806–1890**

Juan Seguín was a *Tejano* hero of the Texas Revolution. It was Seguín who dashed through enemy lines at the Alamo with a last desperate attempt for aid.

And after the war, it was Seguín who arranged for the remains of the Alamo defenders to be buried with full military honors.

Newcomers to Texas who disliked all *Tejanos* falsely accused Sequín of planning rebellion. Fearing for his life, he fled to Mexico in 1842, there "to seek a refuge amongst my enemies."

**SAM HOUSTON**
**1793–1863**

Raised by a widowed mother, Sam Houston grew up in Tennessee. He lived with the Cherokee for about three years. Later, he served in the U.S. Army, in Congress, and as the governor of Tennessee.

"I was a General without an army," wrote Houston, after taking command of the Texas forces in 1836. Yet by the time the war was over, he and his troops had defeated Santa Anna's larger army.

Houston was elected the first president of the Republic of Texas. When Texas became a state, he served as a U.S. senator.

**In what ways did the experiences of Seguín and Houston differ?**

Those men who had not died in the fighting were executed at Santa Anna's command. A total of 183 Alamo defenders died. A few women and children were not killed. Susanna Dickinson, one of the survivors, was ordered by Santa Anna to tell the story of the Alamo to other Texans. He hoped the story would discourage more rebellion. The slaughter at the Alamo shocked Texans—and showed them how hard they would have to fight for their freedom from Mexico.

### 4 Victory at San Jacinto

With Santa Anna on the attack, Texans—both soldiers and settlers—fled eastward. Houston sent a message to the men at Goliad, ordering them to retreat. They were captured by Mexican forces, who executed more than 300. The Texans would not soon forget the massacre at Goliad. But even in retreat and defeat, Houston's army doubled. Now it was a fighting force of 800 angry men. It included *Tejanos,* American settlers, volunteers from the United States, and many free and enslaved African Americans.

*Reading*History
**E. Reading a Map** Use the map on page 405 to see where battles were taking place.

In late April, Santa Anna caught up with Houston near the San Jacinto (san juh•SIN•toh) River. Late in the afternoon of April 21, 1836, the Texans advanced on the Mexican army "with the stillness of death." When close to Santa Anna's camp, they raced forward, rifles ready, screaming "Remember the Alamo!" "Remember Goliad!"

In just 18 minutes, the Texans killed more than half of the Mexican army. Santa Anna was forced to sign a treaty giving Texas its freedom. With the Battle of San Jacinto, Texas was now independent.



**ACTIVITY OPTIONS**

**INTERDISCIPLINARY LINK: LANGUAGE ARTS** | BLOCK SCHEDULING

**POETRY**

**Class Time** One class period

**Task** Creating a poem

**Purpose** To use a poem to describe an individual or a battle from the Texas Revolution

**Supplies Needed**
- Reference material on the Texas Revolution

**Activity** Have each student select a person or a battle from the Texas Revolution. Each student should do some research on the topic selected. Ask the language arts teacher to help students understand how to create a poem about an event or person. The poem could be a cinquain, haiku, acrostic, or other form. When students have completed their poems, they may share them with the class.

Skillbuilder Answers
1. about 500 miles
2. The Texans probably had the advantage. Mexican forces traveled much further, which probably caused supply and communication problems.

## Lone Star Republic

In September 1836, Texans raised a flag with a single star. They adopted a nickname—**Lone Star Republic**—and proclaimed Texas an independent nation. The new nation set up its own army and navy. Sam Houston was elected president of the Lone Star Republic by a landslide.

Many Texans did not want Texas to remain independent for long. They considered themselves Americans and wanted to be a part of the United States. In 1836, the Texas government asked Congress to annex Texas to the Union.

**Vocabulary**
**annex:** to join territory to an existing country

Many Northerners objected. They argued that Texas would become a slave state, and they opposed any expansion of slavery. If Texas joined the Union, slave states would outnumber free states and have a voting advantage in Congress. Other people feared that annexing Texas would lead to war with Mexico.

F. Answer Some worried about the slavery issue and others about a war with Mexico.

In response, Congress voted against annexation. Texas remained an independent republic for almost ten years. In the next section, you will learn that the question of annexing Texas did lead to a war between the United States and Mexico.

*Reading* **History**
**F. Analyzing Causes** Why didn't Congress annex Texas?

**The Texas Revolution, 1836**

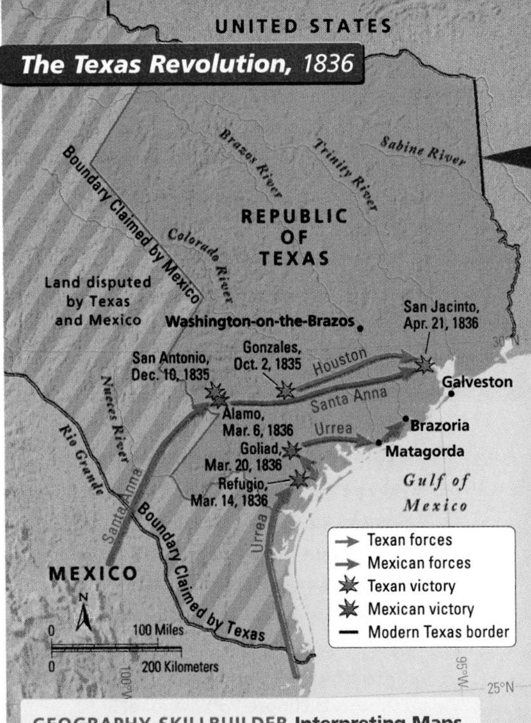


**GEOGRAPHY SKILLBUILDER Interpreting Maps**
1. **Movement** *About how many total miles did Santa Anna travel from Mexico to San Jacinto?*
2. **Movement** *Look at the distances traveled by Mexican forces and those traveled by the Texans. Which side do you think had an advantage? Explain.*

### Section 2 Assessment

**1. Terms & Names**
**Identify:**
- Stephen Austin
- *Tejano*
- Antonio López de Santa Anna
- Sam Houston
- William Travis
- Juan Seguín
- Battle of the Alamo
- Lone Star Republic

**2. Taking Notes**
Use a diagram like the one shown to review events that led to Texan independence and put them in order.

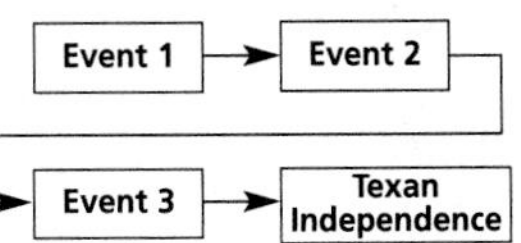


**3. Main Ideas**
a. Why did Americans want to move to Texas?
b. How did the Mexican government respond to the Texas rebellion?
c. Why did Congress refuse to annex Texas?

**4. Critical Thinking**
**Recognizing Effects** How did losing the Battle of the Alamo help the Texans win their independence?

**THINK ABOUT**
- the Texans' and Americans' shock over the loss of the battle to the Mexicans
- the need to recruit more forces to fight with the Texas army

**ACTIVITY OPTIONS**
**ART**
**TECHNOLOGY**
Research a figure from the Texas Revolution. Create a **trading card** or design that person's **Web page** for the Internet.



### HISTORY FROM VISUALS

**Interpreting the Map** The Texas Revolution ended with the defeat of Santa Anna at the Battle of San Jacinto. Ask the students in what way the map suggests that tensions between Texas and Mexico continued after the war. **Possible Responses** Texas and Mexico disagreed over the western and southern boundaries of Texas.

**Extension** Using the scale, have students calculate how much farther Santa Anna traveled. Have students speculate on how that increased distance may have affected the performance of either army.

## ASSESS & RETEACH

**Setting the Stage** Have students fill in the Texas section on the chapter graphic organizer.

**Formal Assessment**
- Section Quiz, p. 201

**RETEACHING ACTIVITY**
Have the students create an annotated time line of the events leading to the creation of the Republic of Texas. The line should begin with Mexican independence in 1821 and have up to ten dates. The annotations should show how each event led toward independence.

**In-Depth Resources: Unit 4**
- Reteaching Activity, p. 37

### Section 2 Assessment

**1. Terms & Names**
**Stephen Austin,** p. 400
***Tejano,*** p. 400
**Antonio López de Santa Anna,** p. 402
**Sam Houston,** p. 402
**William Travis,** p. 403
**Juan Seguín,** p. 403
**Battle of the Alamo,** p. 403
**Lone Star Republic,** p. 405

**2. Taking Notes**
Event 1: changes in Mexican policy toward Americans; Event 2: imprisonment of Austin; Event 3: Battle at Gonzales, Battle of the Alamo, or Battle of San Jacinto

**3. Main Ideas**
**a.** Land was available for farming or ranching. **b.** They sent troops to Texas and finally signed a treaty giving Texas freedom. **c.** There were questions about slavery and fears of war with Mexico.

**4. Critical Thinking**
Texans would have to fight hard to win independence, and more than just Americans living in Texas would be required.

**ACTIVITY OPTIONS**

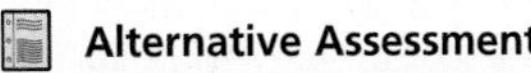

**Alternative Assessment**
- Rubrics for a trading card, 1.7
- Rubrics for a Web page, 5.1

## SECTION OBJECTIVES

1. To explain the origins of manifest destiny
2. To describe how the Mexican War began
3. To describe American actions in California, New Mexico, and Mexico
4. To detail the peace agreement with Mexico and territory gained by the United States

**SKILLBUILDER**

Interpreting Maps: Movement, Location, p. 408
Interpreting Maps: Region, p. 410

**CRITICAL THINKING**

Drawing Conclusions, p. 407
Analyzing Causes, p. 408
Making Inferences, pp. 409, 411
Finding Main Ideas, p. 411
Comparing, p. 411

**Why It Matters Now**
- The Influence of the West, pp. 25–26

## FOCUS & MOTIVATE

### 5-MINUTE WARM-UP

**Reading a Map** These questions focus on the impact of the Mexican War.

1. Study the map on page 410. About how much larger does the United States become as a result of adding Texas and the Mexican Cession?
2. What present-day states were formed from these areas?

Warm-Up Transparency WT13

## INSTRUCT

**INSTRUCT: OBJECTIVE** 

**Americans Support Manifest Destiny**

Key Questions
- Why did Americans want to settle the lands in the West?
- What is meant by *manifest destiny?*
- How was the Oregon Territory acquired?

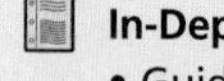

**In-Depth Resources: Unit 4**
- Guided Reading, p. 25

**Reading Study Guide** (Spanish and English), pp. 133–134

# 3 The War with Mexico

**TERMS & NAMES**
James K. Polk
manifest destiny
Zachary Taylor
Bear Flag Revolt
Winfield Scott
Treaty of Guadalupe Hidalgo
Mexican Cession

**MAIN IDEA**

The United States expanded its territory westward to stretch from the Atlantic to the Pacific coast.

**WHY IT MATTERS NOW**

Today, one-third of all Americans live in the areas added to the United States in 1848.

### ONE AMERICAN'S STORY

James Polk's presidential campaign emphasized expansion of the United States.

Henry Clay sneered, "Who is James K. Polk?" Clay had just learned the name of the man nominated by Democrats to run against him for president in 1844. "A mistake!" answered Washington insiders.

News of Polk's nomination was flashed to the capital by the newly invented telegraph machine. People were convinced that the machine didn't work. How could the Democrats choose Polk? A joke!

Polk was America's first "dark horse," a candidate who received unexpected support. The Democrats had nominated this little-known man only when they could not agree on anyone else.

Still, Polk wasn't a complete nobody. He had been governor of Tennessee and served seven terms in Congress. Polk was committed to national expansion. He vowed to annex Texas and take over Oregon. Americans listened and voted.

When those votes were counted, Clay had his answer. James Knox Polk was the eleventh president of the United States.

During his campaign, Polk's ideas about expanding the country captured the attention of Americans. As you will read in this section, after his election Polk looked for ways to expand the nation.

## 1 Americans Support Manifest Destiny

The abundance of land in the West seemed to hold great promise for Americans. Although populated with Native Americans and Mexicans, those lands were viewed by white settlers as unoccupied. Many Americans wanted to settle those lands themselves, and they worried about competition from other nations. Mexico occupied the southwest lands, and Britain shared the northwest Oregon Territory with the United States. Many Americans believed that the United States was

**RECOMMENDED RESOURCES**

**In-Depth Resources: Unit 4**
- Guided Reading, p. 25
- Building Vocabulary, p. 27
- Skillbuilder Practice, p. 28
- Geography Application: The United States Gains Land from Mexico, 1845–1853, pp. 29–30
- Reteaching Activity, p. 38

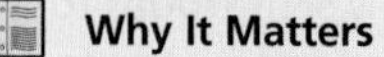

**Reading Study Guide** (Spanish and English), pp. 133–134

**Why It Matters Now**
- The Influence of the West, pp. 25–26

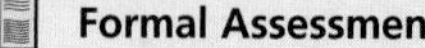

**Formal Assessment**
- Section Quiz, p. 202

**Alternative Assessment**
- Rubrics, 2.3
- Rubrics, 2.1

**Access for Students Acquiring English/ESL**
- Guided Reading, p. 88
- Skillbuilder Practice, p. 90
- Geography Application, pp. 91–92

**Technology Resources**

Electronic Teacher Tools with Test Maker

ClassZone
www.mcdougallittell.com

destined to stretch across the continent from the Atlantic Ocean to the Pacific Ocean. In 1845, a newspaper editor named John O'Sullivan gave a name to that belief.

*A VOICE FROM THE PAST*

Our manifest destiny [is] to overspread and possess the whole of the continent which Providence [God] has given us for the development of the great experiment of liberty and . . . self-government.

**John O'Sullivan,** *United States Magazine and Democratic Review*

*Reading* **History**
**A. Drawing Conclusions** What were the positives and negatives of the idea of manifest destiny?
**A. Possible Responses** Positives include the expansion of democracy on the continent. The negatives include pushing Mexicans and Native Americans out of the territory.

John O'Sullivan used the word *manifest* to mean clear or obvious. The word *destiny* means events sure to happen. Therefore, **manifest destiny** suggested that expansion was not only good but bound to happen—even if it meant pushing Mexicans and Native Americans out of the way. After Polk's election in 1844, manifest destiny became government policy.

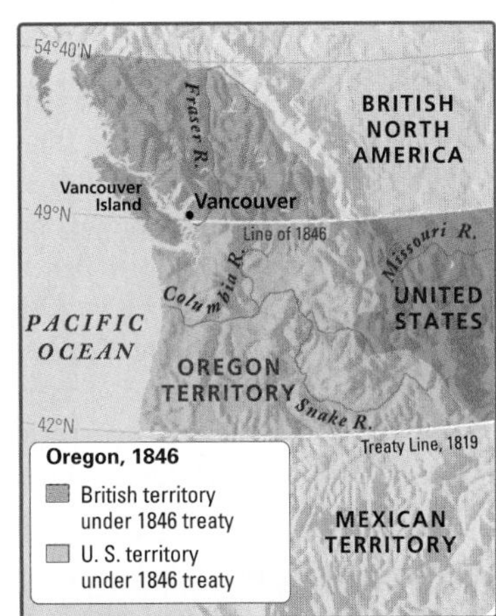


The term "manifest destiny" was new, but the idea was not. By the 1840s, thousands of Americans had moved into the Oregon Territory. Since 1818, Oregon had been occupied jointly by the United States and Britain. In his campaign, Polk had talked of taking over all of Oregon. "Fifty-four forty or fight!" screamed one of his slogans. The parallel of 54° 40' N latitude was the northern boundary of the shared Oregon Territory.

Rather than fight for all of Oregon, however, Polk settled for half. In 1846, the United States and Great Britain agreed to divide Oregon at the 49th parallel. This agreement extended the boundary line already drawn between Canada and the United States. Today this line still serves as the border between much of the United States and Canada.

***"Our manifest destiny [is] to . . . possess the whole of the continent."***
John O'Sullivan

## 2 Troubles with Mexico

Polk had good reason for avoiding war with Britain over Oregon. By 1846, he had much bigger troubles brewing with Mexico over Texas.

*Reading* **History**
**B. Reading a Map** Use the map on page 408 to find the locations of the disputed border between Texas and Mexico.

In 1845, Congress admitted Texas as a slave state, in spite of Northern objections to the spread of slavery. However, Mexico still claimed Texas as its own. Mexico angrily viewed this annexation as an act of war. To make matters worse, Texas and Mexico could not agree on the official border between them. Texas claimed the Rio Grande, a river south of San Antonio, as its southern boundary. Mexico insisted on the Nueces (noo•AY•sis) River as the border of Texas. The difference in the distance between the two rivers was more than 100 miles at some points. Many thousands of miles of territory were at stake.

Mexico said it would fight to defend its claim. Hoping to settle the dispute peacefully, Polk sent John Slidell, a Spanish-speaking





### CRITICAL THINKING ACTIVITY

**Analyzing Causes** Have students examine the attitude of Americans at this time toward Native Americans, Mexicans, the British, and the Spanish. How did the concept of manifest destiny and these attitudes help bring about American expansion? Use the spider map to help students understand the relationships.

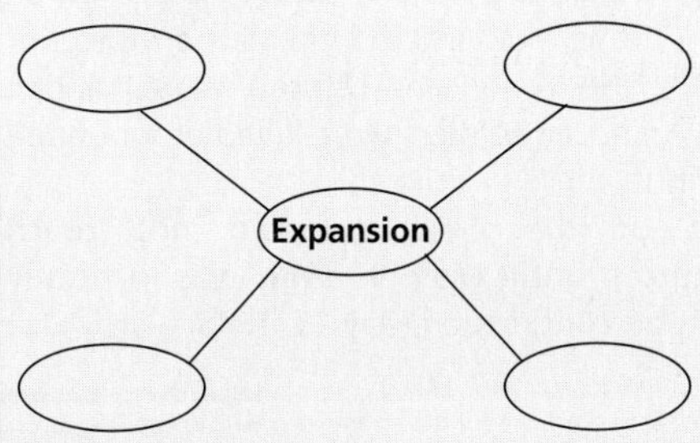


**Class Time** 10 minutes

### INSTRUCT: OBJECTIVE 2

**Troubles with Mexico**

Key Questions

- How did the annexation of Texas affect U.S.–Mexico relations?
- What did Polk do to avoid war?
- How did the War with Mexico begin?
- How did the American public react to the War with Mexico?

**ACTIVITY OPTIONS**

**INDIVIDUAL NEEDS: GIFTED AND TALENTED**

### MANIFEST DESTINY

**Class Time** One class period

**Task** Analyzing the impact of the doctrine of manifest destiny

**Purpose** To familiarize the students with an important doctrine that governed American expansionist ideas in the 19th century and determine if it still influences American foreign policy today

**Supplies Needed**

- Reference materials/primary sources on the idea of manifest destiny
- Newsmagazines or newspapers from recent weeks
- Internet access for additional resources
- Large sheets of paper and markers

**Activity** Students should begin by familiarizing themselves with the basic concepts of manifest destiny. On a large sheet of paper they should create a list of the basic ideas of the doctrine. Next, students should study current news information to determine if any reasons for U.S. involvement in world events today reflect the reasons listed for manifest destiny. Each article that illustrates this point should be highlighted and saved for the final report.

ambassador, to offer Mexico $25 million for Texas, California, and New Mexico. But Slidell's diplomacy failed.

Believing that the American people supported his expansion plans, Polk wanted to force the issue with Mexico. He purposely ordered General **Zachary Taylor** to station troops on the northern bank of the Rio Grande. This river bank was part of the disputed territory. Viewing this as an act of war, Mexico moved an army into place on the southern bank. On April 25, 1846, a Mexican cavalry unit crossed the Rio Grande. They ambushed an American patrol and killed or wounded 16 American soldiers.

When news of the attack reached Washington, Polk sent a rousing war message to Congress, saying, "Mexico has invaded our territory and shed American blood upon American soil." Two days later, Congress declared war. The War with Mexico had begun. Thousands of volunteers, mostly from western states, rushed to enlist in the army. Santa Anna, who was president of Mexico, built up the Mexican army.

However, Americans had mixed reactions to Polk's call for war. Illinois representative Abraham Lincoln questioned the truthfulness of the president's message and the need to declare war. Northeasterners questioned the justice of men dying in such a war. Slavery became an issue in the debates over the war. Southerners saw expansion into Texas as an opportunity to extend slavery and to increase their power in Congress. To

*Reading***History**

**C. Analyzing Causes** How did the War with Mexico start?

**C. Answer** a clash between Mexican and American troops near the Rio Grande

**Skillbuilder Answers**

**1.** about 1,500 miles

**2.** Texas has only one coast to defend, while Mexico has two.

## MORE ABOUT . . .

**The War with Mexico**

The skirmish that started the war happened on April 25, 1846. On that day, a cavalry detachment of Mexicans crossed the Rio Grande about 30 miles up river from the Americans' location. General Taylor sent a 63-man patrol to investigate the reported activities of the Mexican forces. When the Americans encountered the larger force of Mexicans, the Americans refused to surrender. Sixteen American soldiers were killed or wounded in the fight.

News of the encounter did not reach Washington until May 9. War was officially declared by Congress on May 13, 1846.

## *The War with Mexico, 1846–1847*

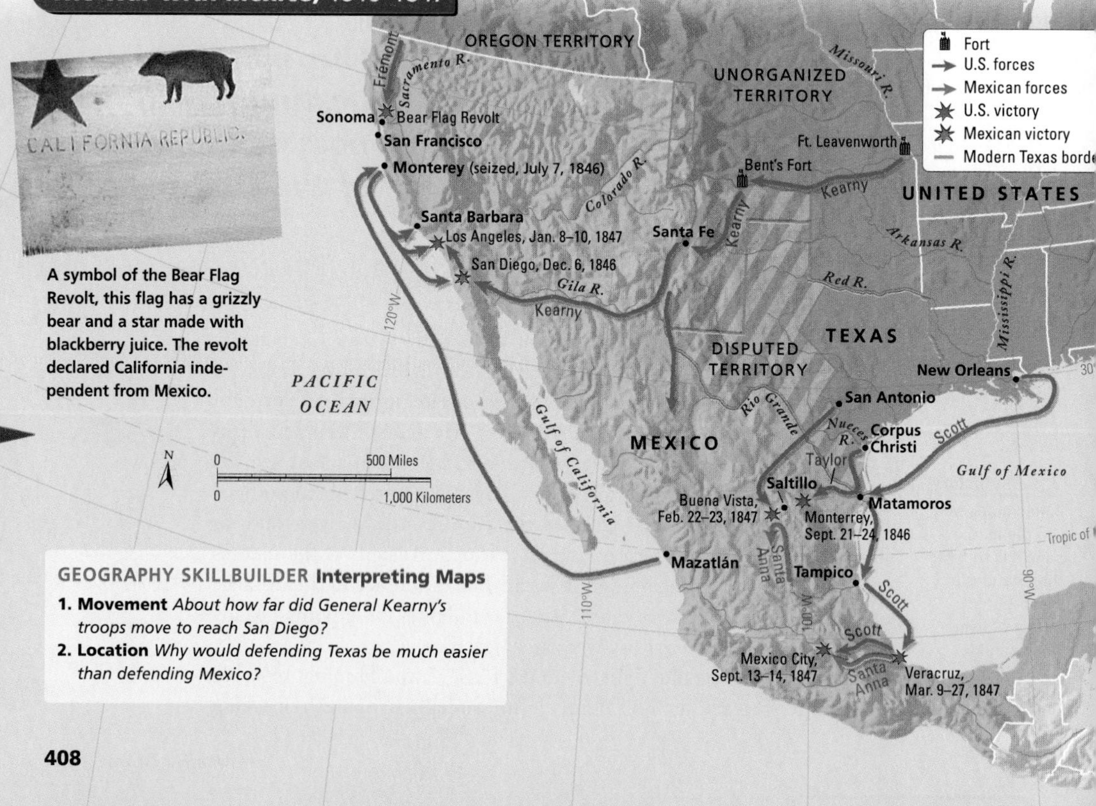


**A symbol of the Bear Flag Revolt, this flag has a grizzly bear and a star made with blackberry juice. The revolt declared California independent from Mexico.**

**GEOGRAPHY SKILLBUILDER Interpreting Maps**

1. **Movement** *About how far did General Kearny's troops move to reach San Diego?*
2. **Location** *Why would defending Texas be much easier than defending Mexico?*

408

## HISTORY FROM VISUALS

**Interpreting the Map** Have the students study the map to gain clues about the strategies of war used by the Americans. What tactics did the Americans use to defeat the Mexicans? **Possible Response** The American forces were divided into groups, one moving to California, another moving toward Mexico by water, and one moving toward Mexico by land.

**Extension** Have students do research to find out why the symbols shown on the flag were chosen.

## ACTIVITY OPTIONS

## SKILLBUILDER MINI-LESSON: READING A SPECIAL PURPOSE MAP

**BLOCK SCHEDULING**

**Explaining the Skill** Special purpose maps are created to help the student understand a concept or idea. The map may use traditional political or physical features or may use colors, symbols, or even map distortions to make a point. The title and legend of this type of map need to be examined carefully to gather information that can help in understanding the concept.

**Applying the Skill** Ask students what the title of the map is and what legend symbols are shown. Then ask the following:

1. On which bodies of water did American forces move? Why do you think they attacked the coastlines? *(Gulf of Mexico and Pacific Ocean; to prevent movement of troops inland to attack American forces)*
2. Which commander's forces divided at Santa Fe, and why do you think that happened? *(Kearny. Forces moved to attack Mexicans and to take California.)*
3. Describe the movements of Santa Anna's troops. *(He moved from Buena Vista south to defend Veracruz in March and Mexico City in September.)*

**In-Depth Resources: Unit 4**
- Skillbuilder Practice, p. 28

prevent this from happening, antislavery representatives introduced a bill to prohibit slavery in any lands taken from Mexico. Frederick Douglass, the abolitionist, summarized the arguments.

*A VOICE FROM THE PAST*

The determination of our slaveholding President to prosecute the war, and the probability of his success in wringing from the people men and money to carry it on, is made evident, . . . None seem willing to take their stand for peace at all risks; and all seem willing that the war should be carried on in some form or other.

**Frederick Douglass** in *The North Star,* January 21, 1848

Despite opposition, the United States plunged into war. In May 1846, General Taylor led troops into Mexico. Many Americans thought it would be easy to defeat the Mexicans, and the war would end quickly.

## 3 Capturing New Mexico and California

Not long after the war began, General Stephen Kearny (KAHR•nee)—a U.S. army officer—and his men left Fort Leavenworth, Kansas, with orders to occupy New Mexico. Then they were to continue west to California. As his troops marched along the Santa Fe Trail, they sang songs like this one.

*Reading*History
**D. Making Inferences** How does this song support the idea of manifest destiny?
D. Possible Response
It suggests that America's land should stretch to the Pacific Ocean.

*A VOICE FROM THE PAST*

Old Colonel Kearny, you can bet,
Will keep the boys in motion,
Till Yankee Land includes the sand
On the Pacific Ocean.

Six weeks and 650 hot and rugged miles later, Kearny's army entered New Mexico. Using persuasion instead of force, he convinced the Mexican troops that he meant to withdraw. This allowed him to take New Mexico without firing a shot. Then Kearny and a small force of soldiers marched on toward California, which had only 6,000 Mexican residents. The remainder of the force moved south toward Mexico.

In California, Americans led by the explorer John C. Frémont rebelled against Mexican rule in the **Bear Flag Revolt**. They arrested the Mexican commander of Northern California and raised a crude flag showing a grizzly bear sketched in blackberry juice. The rebels declared California independent of Mexico and named it the Republic of California. In the fall, U.S. troops reached California and joined forces with the rebels. Within weeks, Americans controlled all of California.

### STRANGE *but* True

**SANTA ANNA'S LOST LEG**

Santa Anna lost his left leg in a battle with the French. In 1842, he held a funeral for his severed limb. On that day, church and political officials followed the dictator's leg through the streets of Mexico City to its final resting place—an urn placed on a column.

Two years later, an angry mob broke the urn and threw the leg away. The leg was rescued by a loyal soldier who took it home and hid it.

Thirty years later, that soldier visited Santa Anna and returned the bones of his long-lost leg.

## The Invasion of Mexico

The defeat of Mexico proved far more difficult. The Mexican army was much larger, but the U.S. troops





**INSTRUCT: OBJECTIVE 3**

**Capturing New Mexico and California/ The Invasion of Mexico**

Key Questions

- How did Stephen Kearny take New Mexico?
- What happened during the Bear Flag Revolt?
- How did the United States defeat Mexico?

**MORE ABOUT . . .**

**The Bear Flag Revolt**

In 1846, tensions were running high in California between the 500 Americans and the 8,000 to 12,000 Mexicans living there. With the approval of U.S. military leader John C. Frémont, some Americans captured horses that supposedly were being driven to the Mexican militia for use in a possible war against the United States.

Days later, these same men captured Sonoma and declared California the Bear Flag Republic. On July 7, 1846, American naval officer John Sloat bloodlessly captured Monterey and officially raised the American flag over California, ending California's existence as an independent state.

**STRANGE *but* True**

**Santa Anna's Lost Leg**

Santa Anna injured his leg when a French cannon shot his horse from under him. The doctors who attended Santa Anna did a poor job, and the bone of the remaining portion of the leg extended two inches beyond the flesh. From that time forward, Santa Anna would use a plain wooden leg for most activities but would replace it with a nice one fitted with a boot for more formal gatherings.

**ACTIVITY OPTIONS**

**INTERDISCIPLINARY LINK: WORLD HISTORY** | BLOCK SCHEDULING

**VIEWPOINTS ON THE WAR WITH MEXICO**

**Class Time** One class period

**Task** Exploring viewpoints about the War with Mexico

**Purpose** To help students understand the viewpoints of various groups involved in the conflict

**Supplies Needed**

- Research materials on the points of view of the groups or persons listed below
- Writing materials or word-processing equipment

**Activity** Divide the class into groups. Each group should be assigned one of the following roles:

- President Polk and his supporters
- Abraham Lincoln, Frederick Douglass, and the Northeasterners
- Santa Anna and the Mexican government
- the Mexican people living in present-day California and New Mexico

Groups should do research to support their arguments. They should divide tasks of writing, researching, and speaking. Each group should convince the class of its position in an oral presentation.

**INSTRUCT: OBJECTIVE 4**

**The Mexican Cession/ "From Sea to Shining Sea"**

Key Questions

- What were the terms of the Treaty of Guadalupe Hidalgo?
- What present-day territory did the United States gain in the Mexican Cession?
- What problems were faced by Mexicans living in the United States after the war?
- What was the last bit of land added after the Mexican War?

**In-Depth Resources: Unit 4**

- Geography Application: The United States Gains Land from Mexico, 1845–1853, pp. 29–30

**HISTORY FROM VISUALS**

**Interpreting the Map** Have the students construct a time line of the expansion of the United States using the dates found on the map. Ask them in which decade the United States acquired the greatest share of land. **Answer** the 1840s

**Extension** Using an almanac, have students determine how many people currently live in the states carved out of the lands added in the decade identified above.

were led by well-trained officers. American forces invaded Mexico from two directions.

General Taylor battled his way south from Texas toward the city of Monterrey in northern Mexico. On February 22, 1847, his 4,800 troops met General Santa Anna's 15,000 Mexican soldiers near a ranch called Buena Vista. After the first day of fighting, Santa Anna sent Taylor a note offering him a chance to surrender. Taylor declined. At the end of the second bloody day of fighting, Santa Anna reported that "both armies have been cut to pieces." However, it was Santa Anna who retreated after the Battle of Buena Vista. The war in the north of Mexico was over.

In southern Mexico, fighting continued. A second force led by General **Winfield Scott** landed at Veracruz on the Gulf of Mexico and battled inland toward Mexico City. Outside the capital, Scott met fierce resistance at the castle of Chapultepec (chuh•POOL•tuh•pek). About 1,000 soldiers and 100 young military cadets bravely defended the fortress. Despite their determined resistance, Mexico City fell to Scott in September 1847. As he watched, a Mexican officer sighed and said, "God is a Yankee."

**Background**
General Winfield Scott had become a national hero during the War of 1812.

**Skillbuilder Answers**
1. all or part of 14 states
2. Louisiana Purchase

## 4 The Mexican Cession

On February 2, 1848, the war officially ended with the **Treaty of Guadalupe Hidalgo** (gwah•duh•LOOP•ay hih•DAHL•go). In this treaty, Mexico recognized that Texas was part of the United States, and the

**Growth of the United States, 1783–1853**

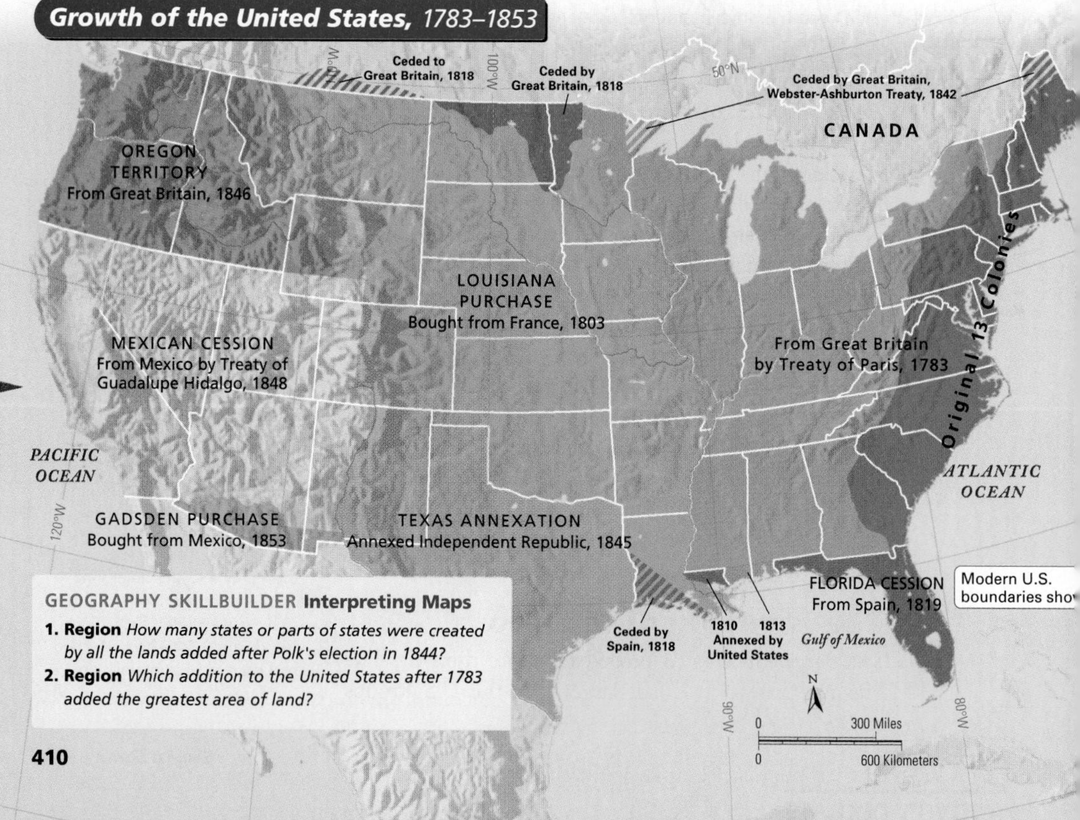


**GEOGRAPHY SKILLBUILDER Interpreting Maps**

1. **Region** *How many states or parts of states were created by all the lands added after Polk's election in 1844?*
2. **Region** *Which addition to the United States after 1783 added the greatest area of land?*

410

**ACTIVITY OPTIONS**

**INTERDISCIPLINARY LINK: LANGUAGE ARTS** — **BLOCK SCHEDULING**

**DIARY OF A CADET OF CHAPULTEPEC**

**Class Time** One class period

**Task** Writing a diary entry of a cadet at the Battle of Chapultepec

**Purpose** To describe the experiences of a Mexican soldier in the War with Mexico

**Supplies Needed**

- Reference material on the actions of the cadets of Chapultepec
- Writing materials or word-processing equipment

**Activity** Ask the language arts teacher to discuss writing diary entries. Then read to or have students read accounts of the attack at Chapultepec and the brave actions of the cadets. Have students write a diary entry of a cadet shortly before the final attack on the castle at Chapultepec. When the students are finished, have them share their entries with one another or bind all of them together as a memory book.

*Reading History*

**E. Finding Main Ideas** What were the three main parts of the Treaty of Guadalupe Hidalgo?

E. Answer United States would pay $15 million to Mexico, pay $3.25 million in U.S. citizen claims against Mexico, and protect Mexicans in Texas and the Mexican Cession.

Rio Grande was the border between the nations. Mexico also ceded, or gave up, a vast region known as the **Mexican Cession.** This area included the present-day states of California, Nevada, Utah, most of Arizona, and parts of New Mexico, Colorado, and Wyoming. Together with Texas, this land amounted to almost one-half of Mexico. The loss was a bitter defeat for Mexico, particularly because many Mexicans felt that the United States had provoked the war in the hope of gaining Mexican territory.

In return, the United States agreed to pay Mexico $15 million. The United States would also pay the $3.25 million of claims U.S. citizens had against Mexico. Finally, it also promised to protect the 80,000 Mexicans living in Texas and the Mexican Cession.

Mexicans living in the United States saw the conquest of their land differently. Suddenly they were a minority in a nation with a strange language, culture, and legal system. At the same time, they would make important contributions to their new country. They taught new settlers how to develop the land for farming, ranching, and mining. A rich new culture resulted from the blend of many cultures in the Mexican Cession.

*Reading History*

**F. Making Inferences** Why did the United States pay a large price for the Gadsden Purchase?

F. Answer The land was needed for a transcontinental railroad.

## "From Sea to Shining Sea"

The last bit of territory added to the continental United States was a strip of land across what is now southern New Mexico and Arizona. The government wanted the land as a location for a southern transcontinental railroad. In 1853, Mexico sold the land—called the Gadsden Purchase—to the United States for $10 million.

On July 4, 1848, in Washington, President Polk laid the cornerstone of a monument to honor George Washington. In Washington's day, the western border of the United States was the Mississippi River. The United States in 1848 now stretched "from sea to shining sea." In August, Polk learned that gold had been found in California. In the next section, you will read about the California gold rush.

### MORE ABOUT . . .

**Treatment of Mexicans After the War**

Though Mexicans living in the United States after the Mexican Cession were supposed to "enjoy all the rights of citizens of the United States," the reality was much different. As Americans became more dominant, many unfair laws were enacted. For example, the antivagrancy act targeted people with Spanish blood, and the foreign miners' tax of $20 per month was aimed at Mexican miners. Ironically, it was in Mexico that the techniques for extracting gold had been developed.

### Section 3 Assessment

**1. Terms & Names**

**Identify:**
- James K. Polk
- manifest destiny
- Zachary Taylor
- Bear Flag Revolt
- Winfield Scott
- Treaty of Guadalupe Hidalgo
- Mexican Cession

**2. Taking Notes**

Review the chapter and find five key events to place on a time line as shown.

**War with Mexico**

1846 — event — event — event — event — event — 1848

**3. Main Ideas**

a. How did the acquisitions of Oregon and the Mexican Cession relate to the idea of manifest destiny?

b. Why were some people opposed to the War with Mexico?

c. What does the phrase "sea to shining sea" mean?

**4. Critical Thinking**

**Comparing** Compare the different ways land was acquired by the United States in the period of manifest destiny from 1844 to 1853.

THINK ABOUT
- the acquisition of the Oregon Territory
- lands in the Southwest

**ACTIVITY OPTIONS**

**MATH / GEOGRAPHY** In an almanac, find the current population of the states formed from the Mexican Cession. Create a **graph** or a **map** to display the information.



### ASSESS & RETEACH

**Setting the Stage** Have students fill in the Key Events column for Oregon, New Mexico, and Utah.

 **Formal Assessment**
- Section Quiz, p. 202

### RETEACHING ACTIVITY

Have the students look at the Main Idea on page 406. Have them write a summary paragraph that uses the Main Idea as the topic sentence. The paragraph should identify all lands added to the United States and explain how they were acquired.

 **In-Depth Resources: Unit 4**
- Reteaching Activity, p. 38

### Section 3 Assessment

**1. Terms & Names**

**James K. Polk,** p. 406
**manifest destiny,** p. 407
**Zachary Taylor,** p. 408
**Bear Flag Revolt,** p. 409
**Winfield Scott,** p. 410
**Treaty of Guadalupe Hidalgo,** p. 410
**Mexican Cession,** p. 411

**2. Taking Notes**

Events could include: attack at the Rio Grande; the fall of New Mexico; the Bear Flag Revolt; the Battle of Buena Vista; the Battle of Veracruz; the Battle of Chapultepec

**3. Main Ideas**

**a.** The lands were viewed as a part of the future lands of the United States. **b.** Some questioned the truthfulness of the president, others disliked war, and still others were concerned about slavery in Texas. **c.** the occupation of land from the Atlantic Ocean to the Pacific Ocean

**4. Critical Thinking**

by treaty (Oregon); by annexation (Texas); by war (Mexican Cession); by purchase (Gadsden Purchase)

**ACTIVITY OPTIONS**

 **Alternative Assessment**
- Rubrics for graphs, 2.3
- Rubrics for maps, 2.1

## SECTION OBJECTIVES

1. To describe California before the gold rush
2. To summarize the activities occurring during the gold rush
3. To describe life in the mining camps
4. To analyze the impact of the gold rush on California

**SKILLBUILDER**
Interpreting Charts, p. 416

**CRITICAL THINKING**
Categorizing, p. 413
Making Inferences, p. 414
Analyzing Causes, pp. 414, 416
Recognizing Effects, p. 417

## FOCUS & MOTIVATE

### 5-MINUTE WARM-UP

**Recognizing Effects** Answering these questions will help students understand the effect the discovery of gold in California had on Americans.

1. Read the James Marshall quote on page 413. What will happen as soon as news of the discovery of gold gets out?
2. What routes might gold seekers take to get to California from the eastern part of the United States? from other countries?

 Warm-Up Transparency WT13

## INSTRUCT

### INSTRUCT: OBJECTIVE 

**California Before the Rush**
Key Questions
- Who was living in California before the gold rush?
- What is a *Californio?*
- What role did Marshall and Sutter have in the gold rush?

 **In-Depth Resources: Unit 4**
- Guided Reading, p. 26

# 4 The California Gold Rush

**TERMS & NAMES**
forty-niner
*Californio*
Mariano Vallejo
John Sutter
James Marshall
California gold rush

**MAIN IDEA**
Gold was found in California, and thousands rushed to that territory. California quickly became a state.

**WHY IT MATTERS NOW**
The gold rush made California grow rapidly and helped bring about California's cultural diversity.

## ONE AMERICAN'S STORY

Luzena Wilson said of the year 1849, "The gold excitement spread like wildfire." The year before, James Marshall had discovered gold in California. Luzena's husband decided to become a **forty-niner**—someone who went to California to find gold, starting in 1849.

Most forty-niners left their families behind, but Luzena traveled to California with her husband. She later said, "I thought where he could go I could, and where I went I could take my two little toddling babies."

Luzena discovered that women—and their homemaking skills—were rare in California. Shortly after she arrived, a miner offered her five dollars for the biscuits she was baking. Shocked, she just stared at him. He quickly doubled his offer and paid in gold. Luzena realized she could make money by feeding miners, so she opened a hotel.

This woman is carrying food to miners, just as Luzena Wilson did.

Like the Wilsons, thousands of people from around the world became forty-niners. In this section, you will read about the forty-niners and what their mining experiences were like. You will learn how the rapid growth of California's population caused problems for the people who lived there before 1849. You will also discover how the gold rush boosted California's economy and changed the nation's history.

## 1 California Before the Rush

Before the forty-niners came, California was populated by as many as 150,000 Native Americans and 6,000 ***Californios***—settlers of Spanish or Mexican descent. Most *Californios* lived on huge cattle ranches. They had acquired their estates when the Mexican government took away the land that once belonged to the California missions.

One important *Californio* was **Mariano Vallejo** (mah•RYAH•noh vah•YEH•hoh). A member of one of the oldest Spanish families in America, he owned 250,000 acres of land. Proudly describing the accomplishments of the *Californios*, Vallejo wrote, "We were the pioneers of the Pacific coast . . . while General Washington was carrying on the war of the Revolution." Vallejo himself had been the commander of Northern California when it belonged to Mexico.



## RECOMMENDED RESOURCES

 **In-Depth Resources: Unit 4**
- Guided Reading, p. 26
- Building Vocabulary, p. 27
- Literature Selection: from *Roughing It*, pp. 33–35
- Reteaching Activity, p. 39
- Enrichment Activity, p. 40

**Reading Study Guide** (Spanish and English), pp. 135–136

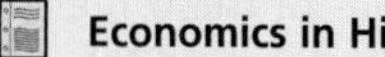

**Economics in History**
- Gold Rush Entrepreneurs, p. 13

**Formal Assessment**
- Section Quiz, p. 203

 **Alternative Assessment**
- Rubrics, 1.5
- Rubrics, 5.4

**Access for Students Acquiring English/ESL**
- Guided Reading, p. 89

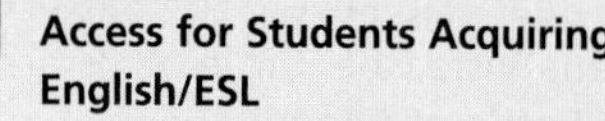

**Technology Resources**

 **Critical Thinking Trans. CT38**
- Cause and Effect: U.S. Expansion, 1846–1853

 **Electronic Teacher Tools with Test Maker**

 **ClassZone**
www.mcdougallittell.com

**Vocabulary**
**immigration:** the movement of people into a country or region where they were not born

When Mexico owned California, its government feared American immigration and rarely gave land to foreigners. But **John Sutter,** a Swiss immigrant, was one exception. Dressed in a secondhand French army uniform, Sutter had visited the Mexican governor in 1839. A charming man, Sutter persuaded the governor to grant him 50,000 acres in the unsettled Sacramento Valley. Sutter built a fort on his land and dreamed of creating his own personal empire based on agriculture.

In 1848, Sutter sent a carpenter named **James Marshall** to build a sawmill on the nearby American River. One day Marshall inspected the canal that brought water to Sutter's Mill. He later said, "My eye was caught by a glimpse of something shining. . . . I reached my hand down and picked it up; it made my heart thump for I felt certain it was gold."

## 2 Rush for Gold

News of Marshall's thrilling discovery spread rapidly. From all over California, people raced to the American River—starting the **California gold rush.** A gold rush occurs when large numbers of people move to a site where gold has been found. Throughout history, people have valued gold because it is scarce, beautiful, easy to shape, and resistant to tarnish.

Miners soon found gold in other streams flowing out of the Sierra Nevada Mountains. Colonel R. B. Mason, the military governor of California, estimated that the region held enough gold to "pay the cost of the present war with Mexico a hundred times over." He sent this news to Washington with a box of gold dust as proof.

The following year thousands of gold seekers set out to make their fortunes. A forty-niner who wished to reach California from the East had a choice of three routes, all of them dangerous:

1. Sail 18,000 miles around South America and up the Pacific coast—suffering from storms, seasickness, and spoiled food.
2. Sail to the narrow Isthmus of Panama, cross overland (and risk catching a deadly tropical disease), and then sail to California.
3. Travel the trails across North America—braving rivers, prairies, mountains, and all the hardships of the trail.

Because the adventure was so difficult, most gold seekers were young men. "A gray beard is almost as rare as a petticoat," observed one miner. Luzena Wilson said that during the six months she lived in the mining city of Sacramento, she saw only two other women.

*Reading*History
**A. Categorizing** What were the three different types of transportation that people took to get to California?
A. Answer People used ships, horses, riverboats, covered wagons, and they also walked.

### HISTORY *through* ART

Clipper ship companies used advertising cards such as this one to convince Easterners that their line provided the fastest, most pleasant voyages.

**How has the artist tried to project a positive image for sailing west?**

### MORE ABOUT . . .

**John Sutter**
Although Sutter had extensive land holdings and other investments in the gold fields, he did not make a profit from the gold rush. In fact, by 1852 he was broke. Squatters took over his lands, killed his cattle, and destroyed his crops. He unsuccessfully petitioned the U.S. Congress for compensation. In June 1880, it appeared Sutter might be successful in getting his money. However, when a senator stopped by to tell him of the news, he found John Sutter dead.

### INSTRUCT: OBJECTIVE 2

**Rush for Gold**
Key Questions
- What is a gold rush?
- How did gold seekers get to the gold fields?
- How difficult was the trip to California?

**Economics in History**
- Gold Rush Entrepreneurs, p. 13

### HISTORY *through* ART

**Interpreting the Advertisement** Clipper ships provided a faster way to reach California if they didn't get caught in storms or become becalmed. Seasickness, bad food, and endless days of boredom plagued the travelers.

**Possible Answer: the use of swallows makes the trip look easy—like flying**

### ACTIVITY OPTIONS

**INTERDISCIPLINARY LINK: GEOGRAPHY**

BLOCK SCHEDULING

**ROUTES TO CALIFORNIA**

**Class Time** 30 minutes

**Task** Analyzing routes to California

**Purpose** To compare the physical geography and hardships of the routes to California

**Supplies Needed**
- World atlases with physical geography maps
- Copies of a blank map of the western hemisphere

**Activity** Give each student a blank map. Students may work in pairs. Students should reread the description of the routes to California on page 413, then consult the text map on page 395 and an atlas. The next task is to draw one line on the map for each of the three routes to California. Then have the students label physical features found on the route. Next, using a graphic organizer, they should list physical features for each route and identify the hardships they may have caused. Finally, they should write annotations about the hardships and place them along each of the routes.

## *Now and* then

**Levi's Blue Jeans**

The term for Levi's pants—*jeans*—comes from the French word for the Italian port of Genoa—Gênes. Working men there wore heavy cotton pants that were a precursor of jeans. The word *denim* also comes from the French. In this case, the phrase *de Nimes,* meaning "from Nimes," was used to identify the tough cotton fabric produced in the French city.

## INSTRUCT: OBJECTIVE 

**Life in the Mining Camps/ Miners from Around the World/ Conflicts Among Miners**

Key Questions

- What was life like in the mining camps?
- Which countries did non-American miners come from?
- How were foreign miners treated?

 **In-Depth Resources: Unit 4**

- Literature Selection: from *Roughing It* by Mark Twain, pp. 33–35
- Enrichment Activity, p. 40

## MORE ABOUT . . .

**Foreign Miners**

Gold fever reached across the Atlantic. Excitement over the prospect of becoming rich was so great that in France lotteries were held with the winning ticket a guaranteed trip to California. French miners stuck together in the gold fields because they were not able to speak English. Other miners sometimes called them "Keskydees"—a nickname derived from the French expression *"Qu'est-ce qu'il dit?"* or "What is he saying?"

### *Now and* then

**LEVI'S BLUE JEANS**

Nearly everyone in the United States owns at least one pair of faded, comfortable blue jeans. The first jeans were invented for California miners.

In 1873, a man named Levi Strauss wanted to sell sturdy pants to miners. Strauss made his pants out of the strongest fabric he could buy—cotton denim. He reinforced the pockets with copper rivets so that they could hold heavy tools without ripping.

For more than 125 years, jeans have remained popular. Levi Strauss's pants have proved to be durable in more ways than one.

## 3 Life in the Mining Camps

The mining camps had colorful names like Mad Mule Gulch, Hangtown, and Coyote Diggings. They began as rows of tents along the streams flowing out of the Sierra Nevada. Gradually, the tents gave way to rough wooden buildings that housed stores and saloons.

Mining camps could be dangerous. One woman who lived in the region wrote about camp violence.

> *A VOICE FROM THE PAST*
>
> In the short space of twenty-four days, we have had murders, fearful accidents, bloody deaths, a mob, whippings, a hanging, . . . and a fatal duel.
>
> **Louise Clappe,** quoted in *Frontier Women*

The mining life was hard for other reasons. Camp gossip told of miners who grew rich overnight by finding eight-pound nuggets, but in reality, such easy pickings were rare. Miners spent their days standing knee-deep in icy streams, where they sifted through tons of mud and sand to find small amounts of gold. Exhaustion, poor food, and disease all damaged the miners' health.

Not only was acquiring gold brutally difficult, but the miners had to pay outrageously high prices for basic supplies. In addition, gamblers and con artists swarmed into the camps to swindle the miners of their money. As a result, few miners grew rich.

*Reading*History

**B. Making Inferences** Why do you think life in the mining camps was so rough?

B. Possible Responses Mining was dirty and dangerous. It attracted dishonest people.

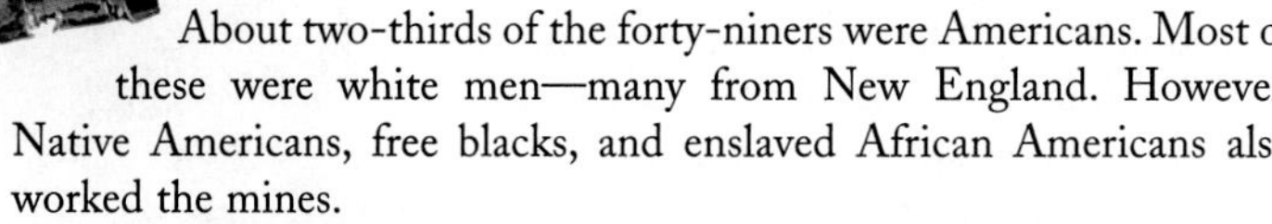

## Miners from Around the World

About two-thirds of the forty-niners were Americans. Most of these were white men—many from New England. However, Native Americans, free blacks, and enslaved African Americans also worked the mines.

Thousands of experienced miners came from Sonora in Mexico. Other foreign miners came from Europe, South America, Australia, and China. Most of the Chinese miners were peasant farmers who fled from a region that had suffered several crop failures. By the end of 1851, one of every ten immigrants was Chinese.

Used to backbreaking labor in their homeland, the Chinese proved to be patient miners. They would take over sites that American miners had abandoned because the easy gold was gone. Through steady, hard work, the Chinese made these "played-out" sites yield profits. American miners resented the success of the Chinese and were suspicious of their different foods, dress, and customs. As the numbers of Chinese miners grew, American anger toward them also increased.

C. Possible Response Americans were unhappy about Chinese success and suspicious of their different customs.

*Reading*History

**C. Analyzing Causes** Why did some Americans resent Chinese miners?



## ACTIVITY OPTIONS

## INDIVIDUAL NEEDS

### LESS PROFICIENT READERS

**Summarizing** For Objective 3, pair a less proficient reader with a good reader. Have them read each of the three subheadings under Objective 3 and formulate a question based on the heading. Then they should read to each other. After each of the three subheadings, they should stop to see if the question they created was answered and summarize the information in the paragraphs.

For example:

1. What was life like in the mining camps?
2. Where did miners come from?
3. What kinds of problems were there among miners?

# Surface Mining

Gold is found in cracks, called veins, in the earth's rocky crust. As mountains and other outcrops of rock erode, the gold veins come to the surface. The gold breaks apart into nuggets, flakes, and dust. Flood waters then wash it downhill into stream beds. To mine this surface gold, forty-niners had to use tools designed to separate it from the mud and sand around it. American miners learned some technology from Mexicans who came from the mining region of Sonora.

Miners shoveled dirt into the sluice. The rushing water carried lightweight materials along with it. Heavy gold sank to the bottom and was trapped between the ridges.

A sluice was a series of long boxes with ridges on the bottom. Water ran through the sluice, which angled downward.

Although this photograph shows American and Chinese miners working together, in many places Americans chased the Chinese away.

Mexican miners introduced the use of the pan. A miner would fill a pan with dirt and water. Then he would swirl the pan. Water sloshed over the sides, carrying lightweight minerals with it. Gold settled in the bottom.

### CONNECT TO HISTORY

1. **Drawing Conclusions** Which mining method could be used by an individual miner and which needed a group of miners? Explain your answer.

See Skillbuilder Handbook, page R12.

### CONNECT TO TODAY

2. **Researching** How is gold mined today?

Visit www.mcdougallittell.com to learn more about the California gold rush.





## Technology OF THE Time

**OBJECTIVES**

1. To use cultural artifacts, such as historical photographs, to acquire information about the United States
2. To explain the technology involved in the process of mining gold in 19th-century America

## INSTRUCT

Key Questions

- What precious metals and stones do people mine?
- What kinds of tools are the miners using?
- If you were a forty-niner, which method of surface mining would you prefer—panning for gold or using a sluice? Why?
- What does the photograph show about the relationship among miners from different cultures?

### MORE ABOUT . . .

**Mexican Miners**

Mexican miners skillfully used a *batea,* a pan made out of wood. Besides sharing this method of sifting gravel for gold, Mexican miners also taught American miners Spanish technical terms related to the process. Here are two examples:

- *bonanza,* meaning "valuable ore, or mineral"
- *placer*, meaning "a deposit containing specks of gold"

### CONNECT TO HISTORY

1. **Drawing Conclusions** **Possible Answers** Using a pan was a simple manual activity, requiring only one miner. The sluice was a more intricate process of mining for gold and needed the efforts of an entire group, who had to keep shoveling dirt into the row of boxes.

### CONNECT TO TODAY

2. **Researching** Students can use an encyclopedia or the Internet to learn about modern gold-mining methods. Suggest that students use a flow chart to summarize their findings. Here is one example.

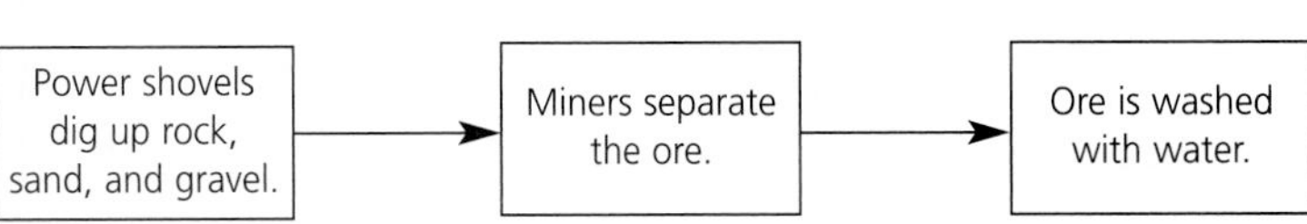

Power shovels dig up rock, sand, and gravel.
Miners separate the ore.
Ore is washed with water.

## MORE ABOUT . . .

**Miners and Discrimination**

The 1850 Foreigner Miner Tax was aimed primarily at Mexican miners. It was repealed in 1852. Its replacement in 1852 was aimed at Chinese miners. It required a three-dollar-per-month payment from every miner who did not want to become a citizen. Chinese people could not become citizens in the United States because that privilege was only for "white" people. The 1852 law remained in effect until 1870, when it was canceled by the Civil Rights Act.

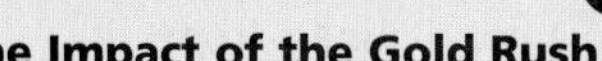

## INSTRUCT: OBJECTIVE 4

**The Impact of the Gold Rush**

Key Questions

- What impact did the gold rush have on the economy of California?
- How were the people already living in California affected by the gold rush?
- What impact did the statehood of California have on the slavery issue in the United States?

## HISTORY FROM VISUALS

**Interpreting the Chart** Remind students that there might have been more than one cause, although the chart shows a single cause for an effect. Ask them what impact the idea of manifest destiny had on each one of the causes.

**Extension** Have the student refer to the time line at the beginning of the chapter and put the effect events in chronological order.

**Critical Thinking Transparency CT38**
- Cause and Effect: U.S. Expansion, 1846–1853

# Conflicts Among Miners

A mixture of greed, anger, and prejudice caused some miners to cheat others. For example, I. B. Gilman promised to free an enslaved African American named Tom if he saved enough gold. For more than a year, Tom mined for himself after each day's work was done. When he finally had $1,000, Gilman gave him a paper saying he was free. The next day, the paper suspiciously disappeared. Even though Tom was certain he had been robbed, he couldn't prove it. He had to work for another year before Gilman would free him.

Once the easy-to-find gold was gone, American miners began to force Native Americans and foreigners such as Mexicans and Chinese out of the gold fields to reduce competition. This practice increased after California became a state in 1850. One of the first acts of the California state legislature was to pass the Foreign Miners Tax, which imposed a tax of $20 a month on miners from other countries. That was more than most could afford to pay. As the tax collectors arrived in the camps, most foreigners left.

D. Answer It passed the Foreign Miners Tax in 1850.

*Reading* **History**

**D. Analyzing Causes** How did the state government make mining harder for foreigners?

Driven from the mines, the Chinese opened shops, restaurants, and laundries. So many Chinese owned businesses in San Francisco that their neighborhood was called Chinatown, a name it still goes by today.

# 4 The Impact of the Gold Rush

By 1852, the gold rush was over. While it lasted, about 250,000 people flooded into California. This huge migration caused economic growth that changed California permanently. The port city of San Francisco grew to become a center of banking, manufacturing, shipping, and trade. Its population exploded from around 400 in 1845 to 35,000 in 1850. Sacramento became the center of a productive farming region.

However, the gold rush ruined many *Californios.* The newcomers did not respect *Californios,* their customs, or their legal rights. In many cases,

***CAUSE AND EFFECT:*** *U.S. Expansion, 1846–1853*

| CAUSE | | EFFECT |
|---|---|---|
| Westward trails move thousands to new territories. | ▶ | Oregon Territory acquired by the United States. |
| Austin and others colonize Texas. | ▶ | Texas Revolution |
| United States annexes Texas. | ▶ | War with Mexico |
| Mexican Cession acquired by the United States. | ▶ | United States expands "sea to sea." |
| Transcontinental railroad route needed. | ▶ | Gadsden Purchase |
| Thousands of gold seekers rush to California. | ▶ | California becomes a state. |

**SKILLBUILDER Interpreting Charts**

1. *Which two causes are related to transportation?*
2. *Which cause fulfilled the nation's "manifest destiny"?*

Skillbuilder Answers
1. westward trails and transcontinental railroad route
2. Transcontinental railroad route needed.



## ACTIVITY OPTIONS

## INDIVIDUAL NEEDS

**STUDENTS ACQUIRING ENGLISH/ESL**

**Cause and Effect** Pair a proficient student with one learning English. Have the students look at each cause and effect and determine what steps and information are implied in each combination. For example: Oregon was a new territory, thousands move there, the U.S. wants the Oregon Territory, the U.S. makes an agreement with Great Britain over the territory.

Have the students create a three-column, six-row graphic organizer. Place the cause in the left column, the effect in the right column. Use the center column to write out the missing information and steps.

| Cause | | Effect |
|---|---|---|
| | | |
| | | |
| | | |
| | | |
| | | |
| | | |

**Reading History**

**E. Recognizing Effects** What impact did the gold rush have on the people who lived in California before the forty-niners came?

E. Possible Responses *Californios* lost land, and many Native Americans were killed.

Americans seized their property. For example, Mariano Vallejo lost all but 300 acres of his huge estate. Even so, their Spanish heritage became an important part of California culture.

Native Americans suffered even more. Thousands of them died from diseases brought by the newcomers. The miners hunted down and killed thousands more. The reason was the Anglo-American belief that Native Americans stood in the way of progress. By 1870, California's Native American population had fallen from 150,000 to only about 58,000.

A final effect of the gold rush was that by 1849 California had enough people to apply for statehood. Skipping the territorial stage, California applied to Congress for admission to the Union and was admitted as a free state in 1850. Although its constitution outlawed slavery, it did not grant African Americans the vote.

For some people, California's statehood proved to be the opportunity of a lifetime. The enslaved woman Nancy Gooch gained her freedom because of the law against slavery. She then worked as a cook and washerwoman until she saved enough money to buy the freedom of her son and daughter-in-law in Missouri. Nancy Gooch's family moved to California to join her. Eventually, they became so prosperous that they bought Sutter's sawmill, where the gold rush first started.

On a national level, California's statehood created turmoil. Before 1850, there was an equal number of free states and slave states. Southerners feared that because the statehood of California made free states outnumber slave states, Northerners might use their majority to abolish slavery. As Chapter 18 explains, conflict over this issue threatened the survival of the Union.

**Mariano Vallejo, unhappy that *Californio* culture was ignored in the new American California, named his home "Tear of the Mountain."**

## Section 4 Assessment

**1. Terms & Names**

Identify:
- forty-niner
- *Californio*
- Mariano Vallejo
- John Sutter
- James Marshall
- California gold rush

**2. Taking Notes**

Use a chart like the one shown to review and record hardships faced by the forty-niners.

| HARDSHIPS | |
|---|---|
| In the camps | |
| At work mining | |

Which hardships would you have found most difficult?

**3. Main Ideas**

a. How did the California gold rush get started?

b. Why didn't many forty-niners become rich?

c. How did California's statehood affect the nation?

**4. Critical Thinking**

Recognizing Effects What were some of the effects of the California gold rush?

THINK ABOUT
- changes in San Francisco
- California's bid for statehood

**ACTIVITY OPTIONS**

**SCIENCE**
**TECHNOLOGY**

Research the hazards of mining gold and either plan a **science exhibit** or give an **electronic presentation.**





**MORE ABOUT . . .**

**California's Growing Population**

California's spectacular growth during the gold rush foreshadowed its growth in the latter half of the 20th century. Between 1980 and 1990, the state grew by more than 25 percent. Currently, California is the most populous state in the nation. Its population is expected to reach 37.3 million by the year 2010. After the turn of the century, the population of Hispanic, Asian, and other minority citizens will pass 50 percent.

## ASSESS & RETEACH

**Setting the Stage** Have students fill in the California section on the chapter graphic organizer.

 **Formal Assessment**
- Section Quiz, p. 203

 **Critical Thinking Transparency CT37**
- Setting the Stage

### RETEACHING ACTIVITY

Create as many groups of four as possible. Each student within the group should be assigned one of the four objectives in the section. Have all the students in one specific objective meet together. Each objective group should write a three- to five-sentence summary of their part of the section. Then the students should return to their original groups and share their section summaries with other students.

 **In-Depth Resources: Unit 4**
- Reteaching Activity, p. 39

## Section 4 Assessment

**1. Terms & Names**

**forty-niner,** p. 412
***Californio,*** p. 412
**Mariano Vallejo,** p. 412
**John Sutter,** p. 413
**James Marshall,** p. 413
**California gold rush,** p. 413

**2. Taking Notes**

In the camps: poor food, disease, swindlers and crooks
At work mining: cold streams, accidents, exhaustion
Answers will vary.

**3. Main Ideas**

**a.** Gold was discovered at Sutter's Mill. **b.** Mining was difficult; prices for basic supplies were high; there was a lot of disease. **c.** As a free state, it upset the balance of slave to free states.

**4. Critical Thinking**

California became a state, and San Francisco became a business center.

**ACTIVITY OPTIONS**

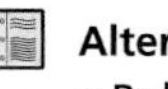 **Alternative Assessment**
- Rubrics for exhibit, 1.5
- Rubrics for electronic presentation, 5.4

## TERMS & NAMES

1. **mountain men,** p. 393
2. **Oregon Trail,** p. 396
3. **Stephen Austin,** p. 400
4. ***Tejano,*** p. 400
5. **Antonio López de Santa Anna,** p. 402
6. **manifest destiny,** p. 407
7. **Bear Flag Revolt,** p. 409
8. **Mexican Cession,** p. 411
9. **forty-niner,** p. 412
10. **California gold rush,** p. 413

## REVIEW QUESTIONS

**Possible Responses**

1. to make money speculating land; to own new farms; to find new jobs; to profit from making and selling goods to farmers; to avoid paying debts; to have greater religious freedom
2. Santa Fe Trail, Oregon Trail, and Mormon Trail
3. They built dams and canals to bring water from the hills to their farms below.
4. Texans resented Spanish as the official language and laws against slavery.
5. Battle of the Alamo—raised Texans' awareness of effort needed to win independence; Battle of San Jacinto—marked Mexicans' defeat and Texan Independence
6. Oregon territory, Texas, and the Mexican Cession
7. Americans in California overthrew the Mexicans and secured the land for the United States.
8. Mexican Cession, or the present-day states of California, Nevada, Utah, most of Arizona, and parts of New Mexico, Colorado, and Wyoming
9. white American men; free African Americans; enslaved African Americans; Native Americans; Mexicans; the Chinese
10. economic growth of San Francisco; agricultural development of Sacramento; California statehood; many immigrants settled in California

# Chapter 13 ASSESSMENT

## VISUAL SUMMARY

### Manifest Destiny

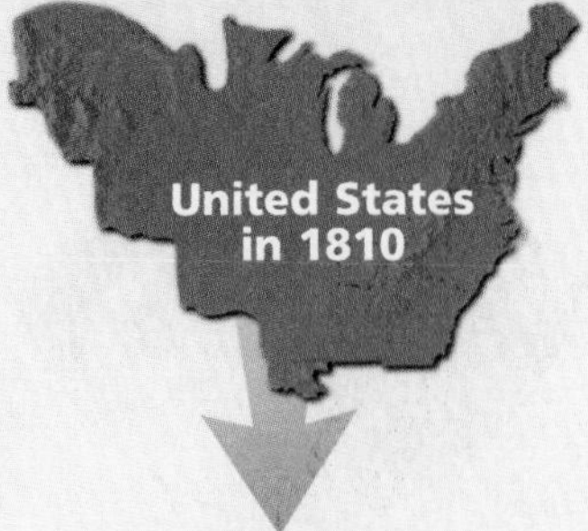


#### Trails West

Mountain men and traders opened trails in the Far West. Pioneers then went west to gain land, wealth, or religious freedom.

#### The Texas Revolution

Americans moved into the Mexican territory of Texas. Conflicts led those Americans to revolt, and Texas gained independence.

#### The War with Mexico

President Polk wanted to expand the nation. He negotiated to gain Oregon. The United States fought Mexico to gain much of the Southwest.

#### The California Gold Rush

The discovery of gold lured thousands of people to California. California's economy and population grew, resulting in statehood.

## TERMS & NAMES

Briefly explain the importance of each of the following.

1. mountain man
2. Oregon Trail
3. Stephen Austin
4. *Tejano*
5. Antonio López de Santa Anna
6. manifest destiny
7. Bear Flag Revolt
8. Mexican Cession
9. forty-niner
10. California gold rush

## REVIEW QUESTIONS

**Trails West (pages 393–399)**

1. What were three reasons why people moved west?
2. What were the three main trails that led to the West?
3. How did the Mormons make the land in Utah productive?

**The Texas Revolution (pages 400–405)**

4. Why were Texans unhappy with Mexican rule?
5. Why were the battles of the Alamo and San Jacinto important to the Texas Revolution?

**The War with Mexico (pages 406–411)**

6. What areas did the United States gain as a result of Americans' belief in manifest destiny?
7. How is the Bear Flag Revolt related to the War with Mexico?
8. What lands did the United States acquire as a result of the Treaty of Guadalupe Hidalgo?

**The California Gold Rush (pages 412–417)**

9. Who were four groups of people who became forty-niners?
10. What were three ways California changed because of the gold rush?

## CRITICAL THINKING

**1. USING YOUR NOTES**

| | Types of people who traveled there | Why they went there | Key events that allowed the U.S. to take ownership of the territory |
|---|---|---|---|
| New Mexico | | | |
| Utah | | | |
| Oregon | | | |
| Texas | | | |
| California | | | |

Using your completed chart, answer the questions below.

a. In what ways were the reasons people went west similar?
b. Which of the five regions listed on your chart entered the United States peacefully?
c. Which event added the most territory to the United States?

**2. ANALYZING LEADERSHIP**

Think about the leaders discussed in this chapter. What characteristics did they have that made them good leaders?

**3. THEME: EXPANSION**

How did the idea of manifest destiny help bring about the expansion of the United States?

**4. DRAWING CONCLUSIONS**

How did the War with Mexico and the California gold rush contribute to the cultural diversity of the United States?

**5. APPLYING CITIZENSHIP SKILLS**

What were the different viewpoints that people held about the War with Mexico?

**Interact *with* History**

Based on this chapter, what do you think you would have gained or lost by going west?

## CRITICAL THINKING

**Possible Responses**

1. **USING YOUR NOTES a.** All centered around pursuing a better life. **b.** Oregon **c.** War with Mexico
2. **ANALYZING LEADERSHIP** ability to gain people's respect and confidence; excellent military skills; courage and bravery
3. **THEME: EXPANSION** Under Polk, manifest destiny became government policy; by the 1840s, thousands of Americans had moved westward to the Oregon Territory.
4. **DRAWING CONCLUSIONS** The war with Mexico added lands that were part of Mexico, bringing the customs of those people into the United States. People from all over the world came to California for the gold rush.
5. **APPLYING CITIZENSHIP SKILLS** President Polk and his supporters viewed the War with Mexico as an attempt to extend U.S. lands. Southerners thought it was an opportunity to extend slavery. Northerners thought the war was unnecessary and unjust.

**Interact *with* History** Answers will vary. Students might say they would have become wealthy, lost relatives, escaped debt, or gained farmland.

## HISTORY SKILLS

**1. INTERPRETING MAPS: Movement**
Study the map. Answer the questions.

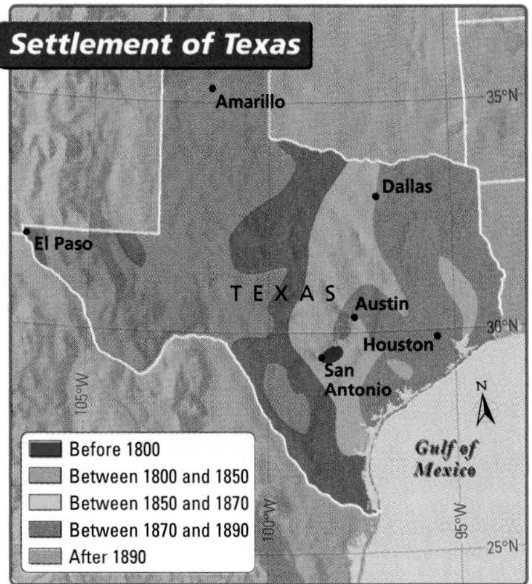


**Basic Map Elements**

a. What is the subject of the map?
b. What years are covered by the map?
c. What do the colors indicate?

**Interpreting the Map**

d. Which area of Texas was settled first?
e. In what general direction was Texas settled?

**2. INTERPRETING PRIMARY SOURCES**
This photograph was taken of a man who planned to go to California to find gold. Study the photo carefully. Answer the questions.

a. What does the photo reveal about the man's expectations of danger?
b. What does the photo suggest about how successful he hopes to be?

## ALTERNATIVE ASSESSMENT

**1. INTERDISCIPLINARY ACTIVITY: Science**
**Creating a Diagram** Do research to learn how gold is deposited into veins in the earth and how erosion later exposes the gold. Draw diagrams showing the processes of gold vein formation and erosion. Share your diagram with the class.

**2. COOPERATIVE LEARNING ACTIVITY**
**Creating a News Magazine Show** With the support of President Polk, Congress declared war on Mexico in 1846. Though many Americans supported the decision, some groups felt that war with Mexico was unnecessary and unjust. Working with a small group, create a news magazine show that explores the different viewpoints surrounding the Mexican War. Research these opinions. Then write and perform the news magazine for the class. One student should be the moderator, while the other students in the group should choose one of the following groups to represent.

a. President Polk and his supporters
b. Northerners, including Abraham Lincoln and Frederick Douglass
c. Southerners

**3. TECHNOLOGY ACTIVITY**
**Making a Class Presentation** Life in the mining camps was not like life "back east." Information about the camps comes from primary sources, like diaries and newspaper articles. Using the Internet and library, find sources about life in the mining camps.

 **Visit www.mcdougallittell.com to learn more about gold mining.**

Your sources might include:

- images of mines, miners, or miners' shacks
- images of items that the general store sold to miners
- tales of the gold fields
- information about the diversity of cultures in the camps

**4. HISTORY PORTFOLIO**
**Option 1** Review your section and chapter assessment activities. Select one that you think is your best work. Then use comments made by your teacher or classmates to improve your work and add it to your portfolio.

**Option 2** Review the questions that you wrote for What Do You Want to Know? on page 392. Then write a short report in which you explain the answers to your questions. If any questions were not answered, do research to answer them. Add your answers to your portfolio.



## ALTERNATIVE ASSESSMENT

**Standards for Evaluation**

**1. INTERDISCIPLINARY ACTIVITY: Science**
**Science diagrams should**
- contain graphic representations of gold vein formation and erosion.
- depict the sequence of scientific processes.
- include clear, informative labels and captions.

**2. COOPERATIVE LEARNING ACTIVITY**
**Shows should**
- include stage directions that describe the setting, cast of characters, and props.
- contain authentic-sounding dialogue.
- dramatize the different viewpoints surrounding the war.

**3. TECHNOLOGY ACTIVITY**
**Class presentations should**
- create oral, visual, or written explanations of social studies material about mining-camp life.
- reflect the use of primary and secondary sources to acquire information.

**4. HISTORY PORTFOLIO**

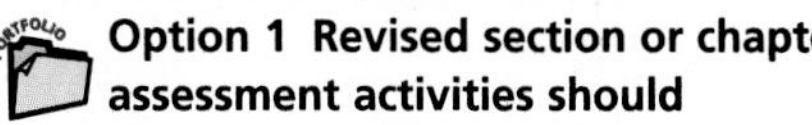
**Option 1 Revised section or chapter assessment activities should**
- address teacher and peer responses to the selected work.
- solve problems present in the first versions of the work.

**Option 2 Short reports should**
- answer questions about the westward movement.
- use evidence to develop and support ideas.
- cite sources of information.
- use standard grammar, spelling, sentence structure, and punctuation.

 **Critical Thinking Transparency CT39**
- Visual Summary

 **Formal Assessment**
- Chapter Test, Forms A and B, pp. 204–211

## HISTORY SKILLS

**Possible Responses**

1. INTERPRETING MAPS
**Basic Map Elements**
**a.** the growth of settled areas of Texas during the 1800s
**b.** 1800–1890
**c.** time spans corresponding to colored regions on the map
**Interpreting the Map**
**d.** the area around San Antonio
**e.** north and east

2. INTERPRETING PRIMARY SOURCES
**a.** Carrying two pistols shows that the man fears for his safety.
**b.** The sack of gold shows that the man believes his dreams for wealth will come true.

CHAPTER 14 PLANNING GUIDE

# A New Spirit of Change 1820–1860

## CHAPTER RESOURCES

**CHAPTER OVERVIEW**

This chapter discusses the surge of immigration to the United States before 1860 and its effects on the population and the culture. It also describes new trends in art and literature as well as a variety of reform movements, including abolitionism and women's rights.

**COPYMASTERS**

- **In-Depth Resources: Unit 4**
  - Tracing Themes: Impact of the Individual, p. 42
  - Building Vocabulary, p. 47
  - History Workshop Resources, p. 61
- **Interdisciplinary Projects**, pp. 79–84

**TECHNOLOGY**

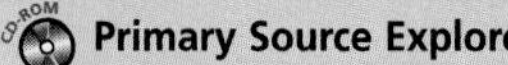

- **Primary Source Explorer**

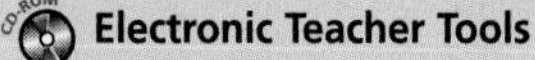

- **Electronic Teacher Tools**
- **Power Presentations CD-ROM**
- **Chapter Summaries on CD** (English and Spanish)
- **America's Music CD**

## SECTION 1 The Hopes of Immigrants pp. 423–428

**KEY IDEAS**

- Economic, political, and religious factors motivate thousands of people to leave Europe and come to the United States.
- Scandinavians, Germans, and Irish are among the most numerous immigrants.
- The influx of immigrants leads to urban overcrowding and nativist opposition.

**COPYMASTERS**

- **In-Depth Resources: Unit 4**
  - Setting the Stage, p. 41
  - Guided Reading, p. 43
  - Skillbuilder Practice, p. 48
  - Reteaching Activity, p. 56
- **Citizenship Today**, pp. 9–10
- **Economics in History**
  - Irish Immigration, p. 14
- **Outline Map Activities**
  - Immigration, Mid-1800s, pp. 27–28

**TECHNOLOGY**

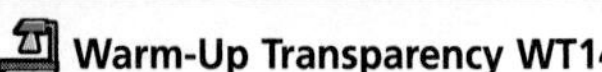

- **Warm-Up Transparency WT14**
- **Geography Transparency GT14**
  - Settlement of Germans and Irish, 1860
- **Critical Thinking Transparency CT40**
  - Setting the Stage
- **ClassZone:** www.mcdougallittell.com

## SECTION 2 American Literature and Art pp. 429–432

- American writers and artists celebrate romanticism, the beauties of nature, and their national past.
- Transcendentalists such as Emerson, Thoreau, and Fuller argue for the importance of the individual's conscience.
- American literature begins to develop its own voice, distinct from Europe's.

**COPYMASTERS**

- **In-Depth Resources: Unit 4**
  - Setting the Stage, p. 41
  - Guided Reading, p. 44
  - Reteaching Activity, p. 57

**TECHNOLOGY**

- **Warm-Up Transparency WT14**

- **Humanities Transparency HT27**
  - Bird of Washington

- **Critical Thinking Transparency CT40**
  - Setting the Stage
- **ClassZone:** www.mcdougallittell.com

## SECTION 3 Reforming American Society pp. 433–439

- The Second Great Awakening brings religious revival and social reform.
- Reform movements promote temperance, better working conditions, public education, and care for the needy.
- Newspapers and magazines spread new ideas, while some groups start utopian communities.

**COPYMASTERS**

- **In-Depth Resources: Unit 4**
  - Setting the Stage, p. 41
  - Guided Reading, p. 45
  - Reteaching Activity, p. 58

**TECHNOLOGY**

- **Warm-Up Transparency WT14**

- **Critical Thinking Transparency CT40**
  - Setting the Stage
- **Critical Thinking Transparency CT41**
  - Cause and Effect: The Reform Movement

- **Primary Source Explorer**
  - *Report to the Massachusetts Legislature*

## SECTION 4 Abolition and Women's Rights pp. 440–447

- Abolitionists demand an end to slavery.
- Eyewitness accounts publicize the evils of slavery, and the Underground Railroad aids those escaping slavery.
- Women reformers seek the right to speak in public, the right to own property, the right to vote, and other aspects of legal equality with men.

**COPYMASTERS**

- **In-Depth Resources: Unit 4**
  - Setting the Stage, p. 41
  - Guided Reading, p. 46
  - Geography Application, pp. 49–50
  - Primary Sources, pp. 51–52
  - Literature Selection, pp. 53–55
  - Reteaching Activity, p. 59
- **America's History Makers**, pp. 55–58
- **American History Plays**
  - *Lucy Stone, Champion of Women's Rights* by Claire Boyco
- **Why It Matters Now**, pp. 27–28

**TECHNOLOGY**

- **Warm-Up Transparency WT14**

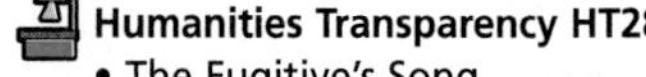

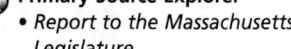

- **Humanities Transparency HT28**
  - The Fugitive's Song
- **Critical Thinking Transparency CT40**
  - Setting the Stage
- **Critical Thinking Transparency CT42**
  - Visual Summary
- **ClassZone:** www.mcdougallittell.com

Pupil's Edition
Copymaster
Overhead Transparency
Audio Library
CD-ROM
Internet

## ASSESSMENT

**Chapter Assessment,** pp. 448–449

**Formal Assessment**
- Chapter Tests, Forms A and B, pp. 218–225

**Alternative Assessment Book**

**Electronic Teacher Tools with Test Maker**

**Section Assessment,** p. 428

**Formal Assessment**
- Section Quiz, p. 214

**Alternative Assessment Book**
- Rubrics for multimedia, 5.4
- Rubrics for a Web page, 5.1

**Electronic Teacher Tools with Test Maker**

**Section Assessment,** p. 432

**Formal Assessment**
- Section Quiz, p. 215

**Alternative Assessment Book**
- Rubrics for a puzzle, 1.3
- Rubrics for an audio recording, 5.3

**Electronic Teacher Tools with Test Maker**

**Section Assessment,** p. 437

**Formal Assessment**
- Section Quiz, p. 216

**Alternative Assessment Book**
- Rubrics for a speech, 3.6
- Rubrics for a letter, 4.3

**Electronic Teacher Tools with Test Maker**

**Section Assessment,** p. 445

**Formal Assessment**
- Section Quiz, p. 217

**Alternative Assessment Book**
- Rubrics for a videotape, 5.3
- Rubrics for a performance, 3.1

**Electronic Teacher Tools with Test Maker**

## CUSTOMIZING FOR INDIVIDUAL NEEDS

### Students Acquiring English/ESL

**Reading Study Guide** (English and Spanish), pp. 139–148

**Access for Students Acquiring English/ESL: Spanish Translations,** pp. 93–99

**Chapter Summaries on CD** (English and Spanish)

### Less Proficient Readers

**Reading Study Guide** (English and Spanish), pp. 139–148

**Chapter Summaries on CD** (English and Spanish)

### Gifted and Talented Students

**In-Depth Resources: Unit 4**
- Enrichment Activity, p. 60

**America's History Makers**
- Elizabeth Cady Stanton, pp. 55–56
- Harriet Tubman, pp. 57–58

## CROSS-CURRICULAR CONNECTIONS

### Culture

Williams, Jean K. ***The Shakers.*** New York: Watts, 1996. A clear and readable history of the Shakers.

### Humanities: Art

Driscoll, John. ***All That Is Glorious Around Us: Paintings from the Hudson River School.*** Ithaca, NY: Cornell U. Press, 1997. Examples of the first school of American landscape painting; for advanced students.

### Interdisciplinary Projects, pp. 79–84

- Math: Graphing Population Data
- Science: Observations in Space
- Language Arts: Nature Writing
- Art: Audubon's Scientific Illustrations

### McDougal Littell *The Language of Literature*

- Emily Dickinson, "Plank to Plank" (poem), Grade 8, Unit 2, Part 2
- Frederick Douglass, "Letter to Harriet Tubman" (letter), Grade 8, Unit 5, Part 1
- Edgar Allan Poe, "The Tell Tale Heart" (story), Grade 8, Unit 4, Part 2
- Henry Wadsworth Longfellow, "The Ride of Paul Revere" (poem), Grade 8, Unit 5, Part 1
- Ann Petrie from *Harriet Tubman: Conductor on the Underground Railroad* (biography), Grade 8, Unit 5, Part 1

### McDougal Littell Literature Connections

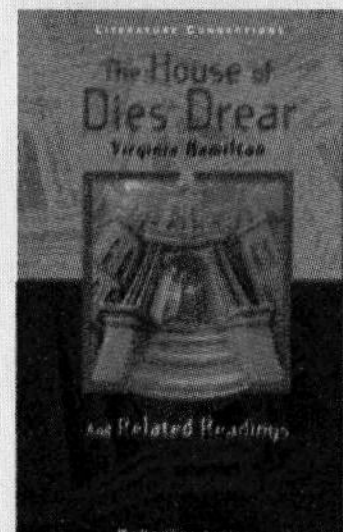


Virginia Hamilton
***The House of Dies Drear***
Acclaimed tale in which a 13-year-old delves into the mysteries of an Ohio house that once formed a part of the Underground Railroad.

## ENRICHMENT ACTIVITIES

**Pupil's Edition, pp. 420–451**
**Interact with History,** p. 421
**Citizenship Today,** p. 427
**Interactive Primary Source,** pp. 438–439
**Geography in History,** p. 446–447

**In-Depth Resources: Unit 4**
- Geography Application: King Cotton, pp. 49–50
- Primary Source: from the *Liberator,* p. 51
- Primary Source: The Seneca Falls Declaration and Resolutions, p. 52
- Literature Selection: from *Narrative of the Life of Frederick Douglass,* pp. 53–55
- History Workshop Resources, p. 61

**America's History Makers**
- Elizabeth Cady Stanton, pp. 55–56
- Harriet Tubman, pp. 57–58

**America's Music CD**

**American History Plays**
- *Lucy Stone, Champion of Women's Rights* by Claire Boyco

**Outline Map Activities**
- Immigration, Mid-1800s, pp. 27–28

**Primary Source Explorer**
- *Report to the Massachusetts Legislature*

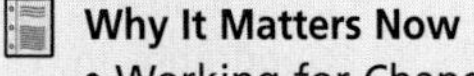
**Why It Matters Now**
- Working for Change, pp. 27–28

**LESSON PLAN OPTIONS (50-MINUTE PERIOD)** (TE) = Teacher's Edition (PE) = Pupil's Edition

| | TEACHER-DIRECTED ACTIVITIES<br>Class Time: 15 minutes | STUDENT-CENTERED ACTIVITIES<br>Class Time: 25 minutes | INDIVIDUAL ACTIVITIES<br>Class Time: 10 minutes |
|---|---|---|---|
| **DAY 1**<br>Introduction<br>pp. 420–422 | **Presentation Options**<br>• Begin with a class discussion of the photograph on p. 420 **(PE)**.<br>• Lead a class discussion on the "What Do You Know?" question in Setting the Stage, p. 422. Then introduce the graphic organizer for the chapter **(PE)**. | **Options for Cooperative Learning**<br>• Have student groups discuss the Interact with History questions, p. 421 **(PE)**.<br>• Have student groups respond to the "What Do You Want to Know?" question in Setting the Stage, p. 422 **(PE)**. | **Head Start on Homework Options**<br>• Have students skim Section 1 Main Idea, Why It Matters Now, Terms & Names, and the main headings, p. 423 **(PE)**.<br>• Have students begin Guided Reading activity and Building Vocabulary sheet. |
| **DAY 2**<br>Section 1<br>pp. 423–428 | **Presentation Options**<br>• Begin with the 5-Minute Warm-Up, p. 423 **(TE)**.<br>• Review the Selection 1 Main Idea, Why It Matters Now, and Terms & Names, p. 423 **(PE)**.<br>• Lead the students through the Skillbuilder Mini-Lesson: Interpreting Graphs, p. 425 **(TE)**. | **Options for Cooperative Learning**<br>• Divide students into groups to complete the Citizenship Today questions, p. 427 **(PE)**.<br>• Have student pairs work together to complete one of the Activity Options in the Section 1 Assessment, p. 428 **(PE)**. | **Head Start on Homework Options**<br>• Have students begin working on Section 1 Assessment, p. 428 **(PE)**.<br>• Have students preview Section 2 Main Idea, Why It Matters Now, Terms & Names, and the main headings, p. 429 **(PE)**. |
| **DAY 3**<br>Section 2<br>pp. 429–432 | **Presentation Options**<br>• Begin with the 5-Minute Warm-Up, p. 429 **(TE)**.<br>• Choose 5 key questions for Objectives 1–4 to discuss with the class, pp. 429–432 **(TE)**.<br>• Lead a discussion about the impact of Thoreau's essay on leaders of the 20th century, p. 431 **(PE)**. | **Options for Cooperative Learning**<br>• Divide students into groups and have them complete the Interdisciplinary Link, Art: Creating Posters, p. 431 **(TE)**.<br>• Have student pairs work together to complete one of the Activity Options in the Section 2 Assessment, p. 432 **(PE)**. | **Head Start on Homework Options**<br>• Have students begin working on Section 2 Assessment, p. 432 **(PE)**.<br>• Have students preview the History Workshop and select a challenge to work on for the next class period, pp. 450–451 **(PE)**. |
| **DAY 4**<br>Section 3<br>pp. 433–439 | **Presentation Options**<br>• Begin with the 5-Minute Warm-Up, p. 433 **(TE)**.<br>• Choose 5 key questions for Objectives 1–4 to discuss with the class, pp. 433–436 **(TE)**.<br>• Lead students through the Interactive Primary Source, pp. 438–439 **(TE)**. | **Options for Cooperative Learning**<br>• Divide students into groups and have them complete the Interactive Primary Source A Closer Look questions, pp. 438–439 **(PE)**.<br>• Divide students into groups to have them complete the History Workshop, pp. 450–451 **(PE)**. | **Head Start on Homework Options**<br>• Have students begin working on Section 3 Assessment, p. 437 **(PE)**.<br>• Have students complete the Connect to Geography questions in the Geography in History Feature, pp. 446–447 **(PE)**. |
| **DAY 5**<br>Section 4<br>pp. 440–447 | **Presentation Options**<br>• Begin with the 5-Minute Warm-Up, p. 440 **(TE)**.<br>• Choose 5 key questions for Objectives 1–4 to discuss with the class, pp. 440–444 **(TE)**.<br>• Lead students in a discussion of the Geography in History feature, pp. 446–447 **(TE)**. | **Options for Cooperative Learning**<br>• Divide students into groups and have them complete the Multiple Learning Styles Activity, pp. 443 **(TE)**.<br>• Have student pairs work together to complete one of the Activity Options in the Section 4 Assessment, p. 445 **(PE)**. | **Head Start on Homework Options**<br>• Have students complete the Setting the Stage graphic organizer for the chapter, p. 422 **(PE)**.<br>• Have students begin working on the Chapter Assessment, pp. 448–449 **(PE)**.<br>• Prepare for Chapter Test<br>**Formal Assessment,** pp. 218–225 |

TEACHER-TESTED ACTIVITY Jean Price, T. H. Rogers School, Houston, Texas

## REFORM RALLY

**Class Time** Two class periods for preparation and one for presentation

**Task** Participating in a rally to promote reform in American society

**Purpose** To identify and examine goals of the reformers

**Supplies Needed**

- Reference materials and Internet sources on reformers
- Markers
- Posterboard
- Patriotic music (optional)

**Activity** Divide the class into groups of four to six students. Assign each group a different reform movement: women's suffrage, temperance, education, treatment of the mentally ill, abolition. Students should design a banner or signs and prepare a slogan for their movement to be used at the rally. Ask each group to prepare a two-minute speech outlining the goals of its movement. On rally day, all groups take part in a short demonstration with slogans, signs, and placards. Following the demonstration, each group gives its speech. After all speakers have finished, ask the class to rank the movements in importance and to justify the rankings.

## BLOCK SCHEDULING — LESSON PLAN OPTIONS (90-MINUTE PERIOD)

### DAY 1

**Interact with History,** p. 421
**Class Time** 20 Minutes

Options for pacing and variety:

- **Role-Playing** Ask students to suppose that they are newspaper reporters who have been assigned to interview the immigrants in this picture. Have each student make a list of questions to ask about the immigrants' lives. **Class Time** 15 minutes

**Setting the Stage,** p. 422
**Class Time** 20 minutes

Options for pacing and variety:

- **Time Saver** Ask students to come to class with a two-column chart. In the first column, have students list what they think were the worst social problems in the United States in the mid-1800s, and in the second column, their ideas about how people at that time might have tried to solve each of these problems. **Class Time** 5 minutes

**Section 1,** pp. 423–428
**Class Time** 50 minutes

Options for pacing and variety:

- **Peer Teaching** After students read Citizenship Today on page 427, divide them into small groups to create the citizenship test suggested for the activity. After administering the test to another group, have students discuss within groups their perceptions of the fairness of the test they took and the one they created. **Class Time** 40 minutes
- **Time Saver** For a homework assignment, have students complete the Taking Notes diagram and answer the Critical Thinking question in the Section Assessment. **Class Time** 5 minutes

### DAY 2

**Section 2,** pp. 429–432
**Class Time** 45 minutes

Options for pacing and variety:

- **Team Teaching** Invite the language arts teacher to your class to talk to your students about James Fenimore Cooper, Henry Wadsworth Longfellow, Ralph Waldo Emerson, and other American writers of this period. **Class Time** 35 minutes
- **Time Saver** As a homework assignment, ask a group of students to prepare the Interdisciplinary Activity on page 449. Have students present their poems to the class. **Class Time** 10 minutes

**Section 3,** pp. 433–439
**Class Time** 45 minutes

Options for pacing and variety:

- **History on Film** Extend students' knowledge of the Second Great Awakening, temperance, and other reform movements with *Democracy and Reform.* Schlesinger, 1996. **Class Time** 35 minutes
- **Time Saver** For a homework assignment, have students answer the Reading History questions for the section and then create one Reading History question of their own to share with the class. **Class Time** 10 minutes

### DAY 3

**Section 4,** pp. 440–447
**Class Time** 45 minutes

Options for pacing and variety:

- **Role-Play** Ask pairs of students to prepare the Section Assessment Activity Option on page 445 and present their dialogue to the class. **Class Time** 40 minutes
- **Internet** Extend students' background knowledge of the Underground Railroad by visiting www.mcdougallittell.com **Class Time** 20 minutes

**Chapter 14 Assessment,** pp. 448–449
**Class Time** 40 minutes

Options for pacing and variety:

- **Peer Evaluation** Working in small groups, students can use the Terms & Names in the Chapter Assessment to write a summary of the chapter. **Class Time** 40 minutes
- **Peer Competition** Assign each student one of the writers, reformers, abolitionists, or women's rights activists discussed in this chapter. Then have the class play a game of "Twenty Questions," guessing the identity of the historical figure each student has been assigned. **Class Time** 40 minutes

## CHAPTER 14 OBJECTIVE

The student will study the era from 1820 to 1860 to identify groups of immigrants who settled in the United States, describe developments in American literature and art, and evaluate the impact of reform movements.

# CHAPTER 14 A New Spirit of Change 1820–1860

*Section 1* **The Hopes of Immigrants**
*Section 2* **American Literature and Art**
*Section 3* **Reforming American Society**
*Section 4* **Abolition and Women's Rights**

### HISTORY FROM VISUALS

**Interpreting the Photograph** The photograph shows a poor neighborhood of New York City in 1860. The photographer, Mathew Brady, is one of the most famous American photographers, known for his work on the battlefields of the Civil War. Ask students to examine the photograph, note the living conditions in the neighborhood, and make inferences about what life may have been like for the people who lived there. **Possible Responses** Students should note the lack of open spaces, the poor condition of the streets and buildings, and the crowded, dirty living conditions.

**Extension** Ask students to identify organizations that work on behalf of the needy in their community. Point out that a number of people and organizations in the early and mid-1800s worked to help the needy in this country.

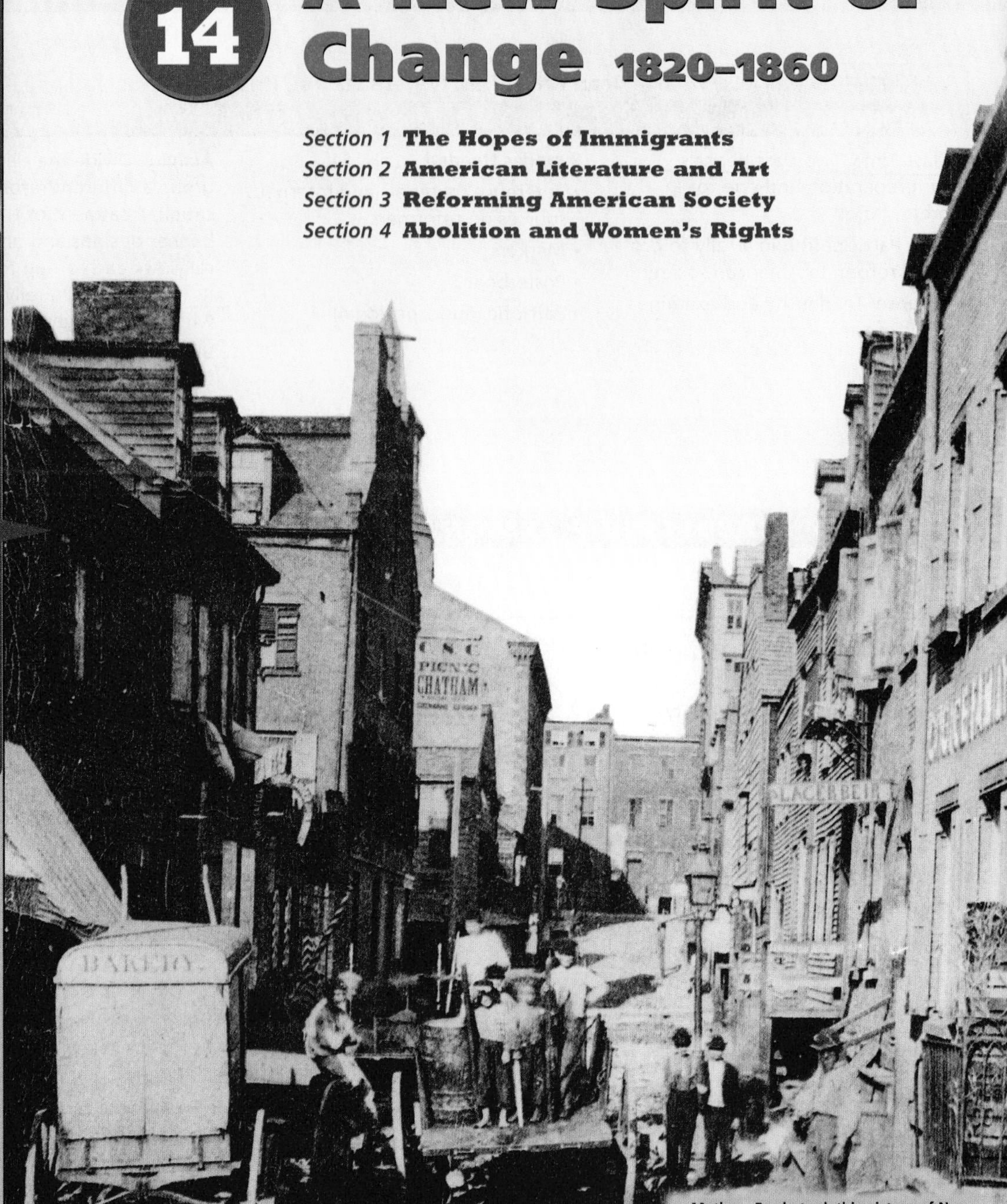


Mathew Brady took this picture of New York City in 1860. It is one of the earliest photographs of a poor city neighborhood.

420

### CRITICAL THINKING ACTIVITY

**Comparing and Contrasting** Ask students to compare the neighborhood in the photograph to two different neighborhoods in their community today. What are some of the similarities and differences? Copy the chart below on the board to record responses.

| Neighborhood in Photo | Neighborhood A | Neighborhood B |
|---|---|---|
| | | |
| | | |

**Class Time** 15 minutes

## RECOMMENDED RESOURCES

### BOOKS FOR THE TEACHER

Daniels, Roger. ***Coming to America: A History of Immigration and Ethnicity in American Life.*** New York: HarperPerennial Library, 1991. Account of the immigrant experience in the United States.

Franklin, John Hope and Loren Schweninger. ***Runaway Slaves: Rebels on the Plantation.*** New York: Oxford University Press, 1999. New analysis of resistance and escape attempts by enslaved Americans.

Gollaher, David L. ***Voice for the Mad: The Life of Dorothea Dix.*** New York: Free Press, 1995. Comprehensive biography of a complicated and sometimes difficult woman.

### SOFTWARE

***Decisions, Decisions: Immigration.*** Tom Snyder Productions, 1996. Encourages students to make their own decisions about immigration policy.

### VIDEO

***Underground Railroad.*** History Channel, 1998. Tells the exciting story of the movement to liberate enslaved persons.

### INTERNET

For more about the Underground Railroad, visit www.mcdougallittell.com

## Interact *with* History

These immigrants live in New York. This one room is their whole apartment.
Women and children have few legal rights. For example, a married woman's earnings are controlled by her husband.
Many people want to outlaw the sale of alcohol. They believe drinking causes poverty.
Many children do not go to school.

You are a writer who moves to New York in the mid-1800s. A newspaper hires you to write about reform. One day, you hear a speaker call for the end of slavery. Another day you talk to a factory worker whose pay has been cut. In the city, you see great poverty and suffering.

### What Do You Think?

- How might you persuade Americans to change life in the city?
- What are the problems that you see in these two pictures?
- Should reform come about through new laws or through individual actions?

# *What reforms do you think will most benefit American society?*

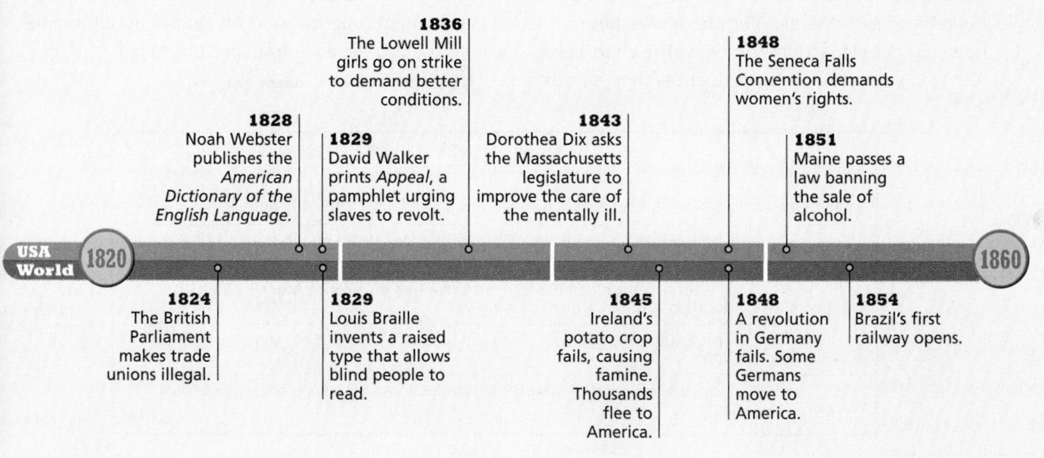

USA
World
1820
1860
1828 Noah Webster publishes the *American Dictionary of the English Language.*
1829 David Walker prints *Appeal*, a pamphlet urging slaves to revolt.
1836 The Lowell Mill girls go on strike to demand better conditions.
1843 Dorothea Dix asks the Massachusetts legislature to improve the care of the mentally ill.
1848 The Seneca Falls Convention demands women's rights.
1851 Maine passes a law banning the sale of alcohol.
1824 The British Parliament makes trade unions illegal.
1829 Louis Braille invents a raised type that allows blind people to read.
1845 Ireland's potato crop fails, causing famine. Thousands flee to America.
1848 A revolution in Germany fails. Some Germans move to America.
1854 Brazil's first railway opens.

## Interact *with* History

### OBJECTIVES

- To help students understand some of the problems affecting poor people in the mid-1800s
- To help students understand why Americans worked to reform their society

### What Do You Think?

1. Encourage the students to identify not only the highlighted problems but also those that can be inferred, such as unhealthy living conditions.
2. Ask students why laws do not always solve social problems.
3. Ask students why they think it sometimes is difficult for government to pass laws designed to address difficult social problems.

### *What reforms do you think will most benefit American society?*

Encourage students to think about how life could be improved for the family in the visual.

### MAKING PERSONAL CONNECTIONS

Ask students whether they, their friends, or family members have ever volunteered to work for an organization that helps needy people. Then ask students what role they think government should have in helping to solve social problems and in meeting the needs that community organizations address.

### TIME LINE DISCUSSION

**Remind students that the United States was expanding westward in the early and mid-1800s. This territorial expansion was accompanied by growth in immigration and total population. Social and political changes also were sweeping much of Europe.**

- Have students identify two events affecting women in the United States. **Answer** Lowell strike in 1836; Seneca Falls Convention in 1848
- Ask students to identify additional events that mark social change. **Possible Response** David Walker's pamphlet; Dorothea Dix's appeal; Maine bans alcohol
- Ask students to identify events in Ireland and Germany that may have encouraged immigration. **Possible Response** the potato famine in Ireland; the revolution in Germany

## BEFORE YOU READ

### Previewing the Theme: Impact of the Individual

Ask students to think of ways in which immigrants, artists, and reformers might have shaped American culture in the 1800s. **Possible Response** The many European immigrants who came to the United States helped the nation's cities to grow. They provided labor for new businesses. They brought their religions and customs to their new home. Writers and artists used their talents to explore ideas and communicate them to their audiences. Reformers worked to solve some of the nation's problems.

### What Do You Know?

Point out that increasing immigration caused overcrowding in cities and prompted hostility from some native-born Americans. Ask students to speculate about the kinds of problems that may be caused by or worsened by crowded living conditions and by hostility from others in society.

 **In-Depth Resources: Unit 4**
- Tracing Themes: Impact of the Individual, p. 42

## READ AND TAKE NOTES

### Reading Strategy: Comparing

Tell students that comparing means looking at the similarities among people, actions, or ideas. Explain that examining relationships in this way helps readers build critical-thinking skills as they gain a deeper understanding of the material they read. When the chart is completed, students should be able to use it to compare the influence of groups and individuals on America in the mid-1800s.

 **In-Depth Resources: Unit 4**
- Setting the Stage, p. 41

 **Critical Thinking Transparency CT40**
- Setting the Stage

# Chapter 14 SETTING THE STAGE

## BEFORE YOU READ

### Previewing the Theme

**Impact of the Individual** In the mid-1800s, millions of Europeans moved to the United States and changed its culture. Writers and artists also shaped American culture. In addition, many individuals worked to reform society in such areas as education and the antislavery movement. Chapter 14 describes how individuals changed America.

This engraving shows a woman teaching a young slave to read, even though it was illegal to do so. The boy grew up, escaped, and became a great reformer—Frederick Douglass.

### What Do You Know?

What do you think were the worst problems in the United States in the mid-1800s? How do you think people tried to solve them?

**THINK ABOUT**
- stories or films that are set in this period
- problems that exist now
- the actions people take to solve today's problems

### What Do You Want to Know?

What would you like to learn about the way individuals changed the United States in the mid-1800s? Record your questions in your notebook before you read the chapter.

## READ AND TAKE NOTES

**Reading Strategy: Comparing** To understand the many influences on U.S. culture, learn to compare. Comparing means examining the similarities between people, actions, or ideas. The chart below will help you compare the influences that various people had upon America in the middle of the 19th century. Use the chart to take notes about how people changed America. Also take notes about people who tried to have an influence but failed.

 See Skillbuilder Handbook, page R8.

| | How People Influenced America in the Mid-1800s |
|---|---|
| Immigrants | Germans—kindergarten, gymnasiums, some foods; Irish—city politics |
| Writers | Thoreau—civil disobedience; Whitman and Dickinson—modern poetry; Poe—horror and detective fiction |
| Reformers | revivalists—reform; temperance workers—ban on alcohol; Mann—public education; Dix—treatment of mentally ill |
| Abolitionists | Walker, Garrison, Douglass, Truth, Grimkés—convinced many that slavery was wrong |
| Women | Stanton, Mott, Truth, Anthony—persuaded some that women deserved equal rights |



## TEACHING STRATEGY

### READING THE CHAPTER

This is a thematic chapter focusing on the European immigrants, writers, reformers, abolitionists, and women who shaped the culture of the United States in the mid-1800s. As students read, have them consider the impact of each of these groups. Pause after each section to review the main idea of the section.

### ALTERNATIVE ASSESSMENT

The Chapter Assessment describes three activities for alternative assessment on page 449. You may wish to have students work on these activities during the course of the chapter and then present them at the end.

# 1 The Hopes of Immigrants

**TERMS & NAMES**
emigrant
immigrant
steerage
push-pull factor
famine
prejudice
nativist

**MAIN IDEA**
In the mid-1800s, millions of Europeans came to the United States hoping to build a better life.

**WHY IT MATTERS NOW**
These Germans, Irish, and Scandinavians had a strong influence on American culture.

## ONE AMERICAN'S STORY

**In June 1831, Gjert Hovland (YEHRT HAHV•LIHND) and his family left Norway for America. After a few years, Hovland wrote to a friend in Norway. He boasted that in the United States a poor man's vote counted as much as a rich man's vote. Americans could travel and work freely. The United States had so much opportunity that Hovland wondered why anyone would choose to stay hungry in Norway.**

*A VOICE FROM THE PAST*

It would greatly please me to learn that all of you who are in need and have little chance of supporting yourselves and your families have decided to leave Norway and come to America; for, even if many more come, there will still be room here for all. Those who are willing to work will not lack employment or business here.

**Gjert Hovland,** letter to Torjuls Maeland, April 22, 1835

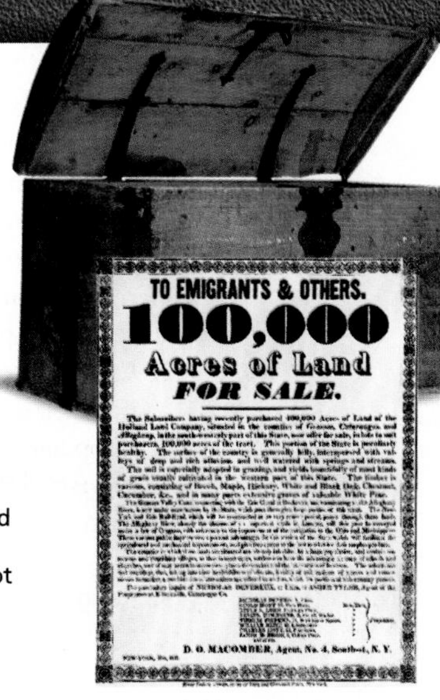

**Advertisements for land attracted immigrants, who came to the United States with only what could fit in trunks like the one shown above.**

**Millions of people like Hovland decided to become emigrants, or people who leave a country. Arriving in the United States, they became immigrants, or people who settle in a new country. This section explains how immigrants enriched the United States with their work and their cultures.**

## 1 Why People Migrated

Most immigrants endured hardships to come to America. Although some, like Hovland, brought their families, many immigrant men came alone and suffered loneliness. Nearly all immigrants made the ocean voyage in **steerage,** the cheapest deck on a ship. In steerage, hundreds of people lived jammed together for ten days to a month. Conditions were filthy. Many passengers became ill or died on the journey.

Despite the hard passage, immigrants flocked to the United States during the mid-1800s. They came from Britain, Ireland, Germany, Scandinavia (Sweden, Denmark, and Norway), and China. Most came from Europe. What made them come to America? Historians talk about



## SECTION OBJECTIVES

1. To identify push-pull factors of immigration
2. To summarize reasons for Scandinavian and German immigration and to identify areas where these immigrants settled
3. To describe the experiences of Irish immigrants in the United States
4. To analyze the effects of immigration on U.S. cities and on public opinion

**SKILLBUILDER**
Interpreting Maps: Place, Region, p. 425

**CRITICAL THINKING**
Solving Problems, p. 424
Making Inferences, p. 425
Drawing Conclusions, p. 426
Identifying Problems, p. 427
Analyzing Causes, p. 428

## FOCUS & MOTIVATE

### 5-MINUTE WARM-UP

**Making Inferences** These questions focus on the reasons for immigration.

1. Look at the poster on page 423. What opportunity was being advertised?
2. Why do you suppose such appeals were attractive?

**Warm-Up Transparency WT14**

## INSTRUCT

**INSTRUCT: OBJECTIVE** 

**Why People Migrated**
Key Questions
- What factors pushed emigrants out of their native lands?
- What factors pulled immigrants to the United States?

**In-Depth Resources: Unit 4**
- Guided Reading, p. 43

**Reading Study Guide** (Spanish and English), pp. 139–140

## RECOMMENDED RESOURCES

**In-Depth Resources: Unit 4**
- Guided Reading, p. 43
- Building Vocabulary, p. 47
- Skillbuilder Practice, p. 48
- Reteaching Activity, p. 56

**Reading Study Guide** (Spanish and English), pp. 139–140

**Economics in History**
- Irish Immigration, p. 14

**Outline Map Activities**
- Immigration, Mid-1800s, pp. 27–28

**Citizenship Today,** pp. 9–10

**Formal Assessment**
- Section Quiz, p. 214

**Alternative Assessment**
- Rubrics, 5.4
- Rubrics, 5.1

**Access for Students Acquiring English/ESL**
- Guided Reading, p. 93
- Skillbuilder Practice, p. 97

**Technology Resources**

**Geography Transparency GT14**
- Settlement of Germans and Irish, 1860

**Electronic Teacher Tools with Test Maker**

**ClassZone**
www.mcdougallittell.com

## HISTORY FROM VISUALS

**Reading Charts** Help students visualize the concept of push-pull factors by demonstrating how an object, such as your desk or desk chair, can be moved across the floor by pushing, pulling, or by both. The combination creates the strongest force. Ask students whether they think many immigrants would have come to the United States if there had been few "push" factors in their home countries.
**Possible Response** It is possible that many would-be emigrants might have found leaving families, friends, and familiar lands and customs more difficult if they had not felt "pushed" to leave by other factors.

**Extension** Ask students which "pull" factors of the 1800s still draw new immigrants today. Have them identify new "pull" factors at work in today's society.

## MORE ABOUT . . .

**Population Growth**
Europe's population nearly doubled between 1750 and 1850, from about 140 million to 265 million people. The growth rate in North America was even faster—from 5 million in 1750 to 39 million by 1850.

## INSTRUCT: OBJECTIVE 2

**Scandinavians Seek Land/ Germans Pursue Economic Opportunity**
Key Questions
- Which of the push-pull factors had the greatest influence on Scandinavians and Germans?
- Where did many Scandinavians and Germans settle in this country?
- How did German immigrants influence American culture?

 **Geography Transparency GT14**
- Settlement of Germans and Irish, 1860

### Push–Pull Factors of Immigration

1. Freedom
2. Economic opportunity
3. Abundant land

1. Population growth
2. Agricultural changes
3. Crop failures
4. Industrial Revolution
5. Religious and political turmoil

**push-pull factors.** These forces push people out of their native lands and pull them toward a new place. **Push factors** included the following:

1. **Population growth.** Better food and sanitation caused Europe's population to boom after 1750, and the land became overcrowded.
2. **Agricultural changes.** As Europe's population grew, so did cities. Landowners wanted to make money selling food to those cities. New methods made it more efficient to farm large areas of land than to rent small plots to tenants. So landlords forced tenants off the land.
3. **Crop failures.** Poor harvests made it difficult for small farmers to pay their debts. Some of these farmers chose to start over in America. Crop failures also led to hunger, causing people to emigrate.
4. **Industrial Revolution.** Goods produced in factories became cheaper than goods produced by artisans. Suddenly out of work, some artisans took factory jobs. Others emigrated.
5. **Religious and political turmoil.** To escape religious persecution, Quakers fled Norway and Jews left Germany. Also, many Germans came to America after a revolution in Germany failed in 1848.

**Vocabulary**
**tenant:** renter

**Vocabulary**
**artisan:** skilled worker

Immigrants chose the United States because of three main **pull factors**:

1. **Freedom.** As Gjert Hovland wrote, "Everyone has the freedom to practice the teaching and religion he prefers."
2. **Economic opportunity.** Immigrants sought a land where they could support their families and have a better future. Immigration often rose during times of U.S. prosperity and fell during hard times.
3. **Abundant land.** The acquisition of the Louisiana Purchase and the Mexican Cession gave the United States millions more acres of land. To land-starved Europeans, America was a land of opportunity.

***Reading* History**
**A. Solving Problems** Many of the push factors were problems. Which pull factors were solutions to which problems?
A. Possible Responses Freedom—religious and political turmoil; economic opportunity—Industrial Revolution; abundant land—population growth, crop failures, and agricultural changes.

## 2 Scandinavians Seek Land

Public land in America was sold for $1.25 an acre, which lured thousands of Scandinavians. At first, their governments tried to keep them at home. A Swedish law of 1768 restricted the right to emigrate. But growing poverty in Scandinavia caused officials to cancel this law in 1840.

Scandinavian clergymen also tried to halt the emigration. At first, they warned their church members against leaving the homeland. Eventually, though, the preachers realized their words had little effect. Some of them even went to America themselves.



## ACTIVITY OPTIONS
## INTERDISCIPLINARY LINK: GEOGRAPHY

BLOCK SCHEDULING

### CREATING AN IMMIGRATION MAP

**Class Time** 30 minutes

**Task** Creating a map showing European immigration to the United States in the early and mid-1800s

**Purpose** To analyze and synthesize information about European immigration to the United States

**Supplies Needed**
- Textbook
- Art supplies
- Outline maps showing North America and Europe (optional)
- Research materials such as a historical statistical abstract (optional)

**Activity** Divide students into groups. Each group should create a map showing immigration from Scandinavia, Germany, or Ireland to the United States in the early and mid-1800s. The map may be an outline or hand-drawn map. Groups should identify areas from which immigrants came and areas where immigrants settled. The students may want to use arrows to show movement, concentration of immigrants, years, or a combination of information about immigration.

*Reading* **History**
**B. Making Inferences** Why do you think Scandinavians moved to places that felt familiar?
B. Possible Responses They knew how to farm in those climates; they thought they would be less homesick there.

In the United States, Scandinavians chose regions that felt familiar. Many settled in the Midwest, especially Minnesota and Wisconsin. These states had lakes, forests, and cold winters like their homelands. A high proportion of Scandinavian immigrants became farmers.

## Germans Pursue Economic Opportunity

Like the Scandinavians, many Germans moved to the Midwest. Germans especially liked Wisconsin because the climate allowed them to grow their traditional crop of oats. Some moved to Milwaukee, Wisconsin, because the Catholic bishop there was German. (In the 1800s, German Christian immigrants included both Catholics and Protestants.)

Germans also settled in Texas. In New Braunfels, a group of German nobles bought land and sold it in parcels to German immigrants. The town had to survive poor harvests and conflicts with Native Americans, but it eventually prospered. Germans also founded Fredericksburg, Texas, which still retains its German culture today.

Immigrants from Germany settled in cities as well as on farms or the frontier. German artisans opened businesses as bakers, butchers, carpenters, printers, shoemakers, and tailors. Many German immigrants achieved great success. For instance, in 1853 John Jacob Bausch and Henry Lomb started a firm to make eyeglasses and other lenses. Their company became the world's largest lens maker.

Skillbuilder Answers
1. Massachusetts, Minnesota, New York, Rhode Island, Wisconsin
2. The South already had a cheap labor supply in slaves, so there might be fewer jobs for immigrants.

### MORE ABOUT . . .

**Scandinavian Immigrants**
One of the best-known literary works about Scandinavian immigrants in the United States is *The Emigrants*, a four-volume epic published between 1949 and 1959 by Swedish author Vilhelm Moberg (1898–1973). The author weaves a story about the experiences of 16 Swedish emigrants who left their small community in Sweden, eventually settling in Minnesota in 1850. *Giants in the Earth* is a famous novel about Norwegian immigrants in the Dakota Territory by O. E. Rölvaag. Rölvaag was himself an emigrant from Norway, and he wrote his novel in Norwegian.

### HISTORY FROM VISUALS

**Reading the Map** Point out that New York and Massachusetts had the highest percentage of immigrants of states on the East Coast. Ask the students which cities in those states would be ports of entry. Then ask why many immigrants might have settled there. **Possible Response** New York City and Boston; Immigrants lacked money to move farther west.

**Extension** Have students use almanacs and other classroom and library resources to identify other major points of entry for immigrants.

**Reading the Graphs** Copy the bar graph on the board. Place a dot at the top right corner of each bar. Then draw a line connecting the dots. Ask students what the line tells us about the trend in immigration during the period. **Answer** Immigration increased throughout the period but was fastest over the period from 1841 to 1850.

**Extension** Have students research immigration figures over the past 40 years. Have them note the trend and create pie graphs showing the sources of immigration over this most recent period.

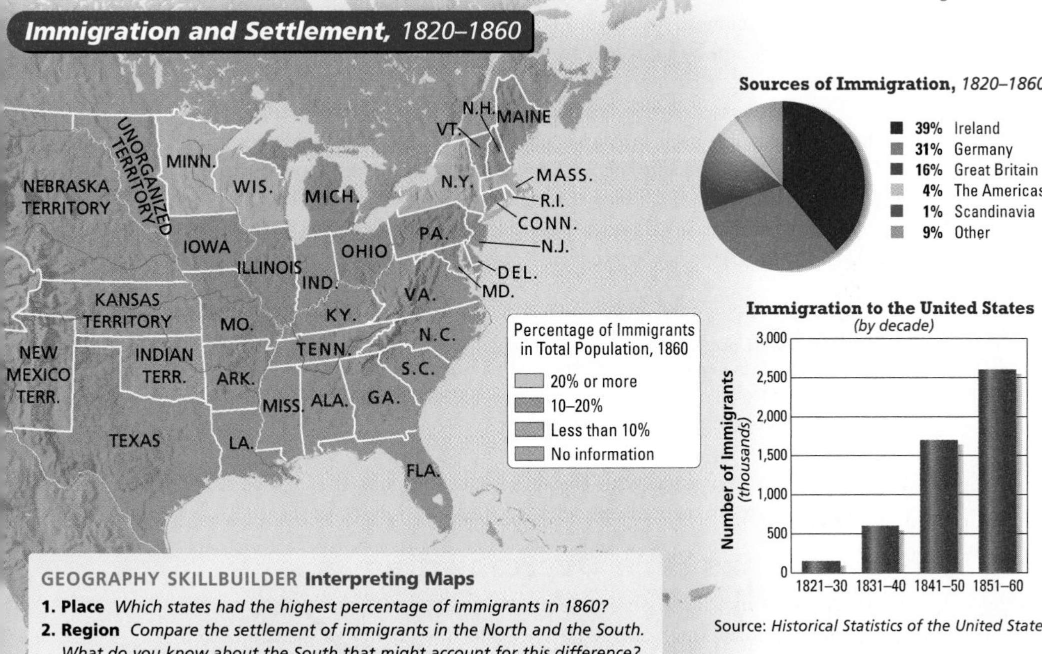


Source: *Historical Statistics of the United States*

GEOGRAPHY SKILLBUILDER **Interpreting Maps**
1. **Place** *Which states had the highest percentage of immigrants in 1860?*
2. **Region** *Compare the settlement of immigrants in the North and the South. What do you know about the South that might account for this difference?*



### ACTIVITY OPTIONS

### SKILLBUILDER MINI-LESSON: INTERPRETING GRAPHS

BLOCK SCHEDULING

**Explaining the Skill** Graphs show statistical information visually. Pie graphs are useful to show relative sizes or proportions of related numbers. The circle represents a whole. The "pie slices" represent parts of the whole. Bar graphs compare numbers. They also can show changes over time.

**Applying the Skill** Ask students to identify the titles of the graphs. Then ask the following questions:

1. Which nation sent the highest percentage of immigrants to the United States from 1820 to 1860? *(Ireland)*
2. What percentage of immigrants did not come from Ireland, Germany, Great Britain, or Scandinavia? *(13 percent)*
3. In which decade did immigration to the United States increase the most? How much did it increase over the previous decade? *(1841–1850; more than 1 million)*

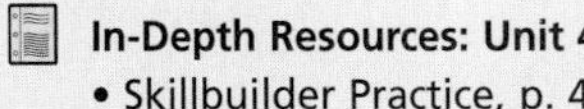

**In-Depth Resources: Unit 4**
• Skillbuilder Practice, p. 48

**daily*life***

**Immigrant Culture**
One cultural import that the Irish brought to the United States is the celebration of St. Patrick's Day on March 17. People throughout the United States observe the feast day of Ireland's patron saint, but the parades and other celebrations are largest in cities with significant Irish-American populations. Irish immigrants began the custom of parades on St. Patrick's Day as part of their fight for equal rights to jobs and fair wages. In Ireland, St. Patrick's Day is observed more quietly as a holy day of the Catholic religion. In the past 20 years, however, the day has become increasingly more festive.

**INSTRUCT: OBJECTIVE 3**

**The Irish Flee Hunger**
Key Questions
- What factors encouraged Irish immigration to the United States?
- Why did the Irish settle primarily in cities?
- What kinds of work did Irish immigrants find?

 **Economics in History**
- Irish Immigration, p. 14

**INSTRUCT: OBJECTIVE 4**

**U.S. Cities Face Overcrowding/ Some Americans Oppose Immigration**
Key Questions
- What were some results of overcrowding in U.S. cities in the early and mid-1800s?
- Why did some native-born Americans oppose immigration?
- What role did the Know-Nothings play in the debate over immigration?

 **Outline Map Activities**
- Immigration, Mid-1800s, pp. 27–28

**daily *life***

**IMMIGRANT CULTURE**
To maintain their culture, immigrants continued many of their traditional activities in the United States. For example, German culture is rich in music. German immigrants put together marching bands, symphony orchestras, and choruses.

In Ireland, many of the Irish had poured their energy into defying the British. This gave them experience with political organization. As a result, Irish immigrants became active in U.S. politics, especially in the cities.

Some German immigrants were Jews. Many of them worked as traveling salespeople. They brought pins, needles, pots—and news—to frontier homes and mining camps. In time, some opened their own general stores. Other Jews settled in cities, where many found success. For example, Alexander Rothschild worked as a grocer upon arriving in Hartford, Connecticut, in the 1840s. By 1851, he ran a popular hotel.

The Germans were the largest immigrant group of the 1800s and strongly influenced American culture. Many things we think of as originating in America came from Germany—the Christmas tree, gymnasiums, kindergartens, and the hamburger and frankfurter.

**Background**
The hamburger and frankfurter are named after the German cities Hamburg and Frankfurt am Main.

## 3 The Irish Flee Hunger

Most Irish immigrants were Catholic. Protestant Britain had ruled Ireland for centuries—and controlled the Catholic majority by denying them rights. Irish Catholics could not vote, hold office, own land, or go to school. Because of the poverty produced by Britain's rule, some Irish came to America in the early 1800s.

Then, in 1845, a disease attacked Ireland's main food crop, the potato, causing a severe food shortage called a **famine.** The Irish Potato Famine killed 1 million people and forced many to emigrate. By 1854, between 1.5 and 2 million Irish had fled their homeland.

In America, Irish farmers became city-dwellers. Arriving with little or no savings, many of these immigrants had to settle in the port cities where their ships had docked. By 1850, the Irish made up one-fourth of the population of Boston, New York, Philadelphia, and Baltimore.

The uneducated Irish immigrants arrived with few skills and had to take low-paying, back-breaking jobs. Irish women took in washing or worked as servants. The men built canals and railroads across America. So many Irishmen died doing this dangerous work that people said there was "an Irishman buried under every [railroad] tie." In 1841, British novelist Charles Dickens observed the huts in which railroad workers lived.

***Reading*History**
**C. Drawing Conclusions** How did the effects of British rule make it hard for Irish immigrants to America to find good jobs?
C. Possible Response
Because the British made it illegal for the Irish to go to school, they had few skills when they came to America.

*A VOICE FROM THE PAST*

The best were poor protection from the weather; the worst let in the wind and rain through the wide breaches in the roofs of sodden grass and in the walls of mud; some had neither door nor window; some had nearly fallen down.

**Charles Dickens,** quoted in *To Seek America*

The Irish competed with free blacks for the jobs that nobody else wanted. Both groups had few other choices in America in the 1800s.

## 4 U.S. Cities Face Overcrowding

Immigrants like the Irish and Germans flocked to American cities. So did native-born Americans, who hoped for the chance to make a better



**ACTIVITY OPTIONS**

**INDIVIDUAL NEEDS: GIFTED AND TALENTED**

**COMMUNITY-LEVEL IMMIGRATION**

**Class Time** Three class periods

**Task** Creating a series of pie graphs showing sources of immigration to your community since 1820

**Purpose** To use a variety of sources to research immigration data

**Supplies Needed**
- Reference sources such as almanacs, encyclopedias, and specialized local library holdings
- Internet access

**Activity** Have students do research about the origins of immigrants to your community since 1820. Direct students to print resources such as encyclopedias, almanacs, the Internet, and specialized references in the local library. If your community has a historical society, suggest that students inquire there for information. Tell students to prepare a series of pie graphs showing the major countries of origin for immigrants to your community for the periods 1820–1860, 1860–1900, 1900–1940, 1940–1980, 1980–present.

living. Between 1800 and 1830, New York's population jumped from 60,489 to 202,589. St. Louis doubled its population every nine years. Cincinnati grew even faster, doubling every seven years.

Rapid urban growth brought problems. Not enough housing existed for all the newcomers. Greedy landlords profited from the housing shortage by squeezing large apartment buildings onto small lots. Using every inch of space for rooms, these cramped living quarters lacked sunlight and fresh air. Their outdoor toilets overflowed, spreading disease. In such depressing urban neighborhoods, crime flourished.

American cities were unprepared to tackle these problems. In fact, before 1845, New York City had no public police force. Until the 1860s, it had only a volunteer fire department. And in 1857, the rapidly growing city had only 138 miles of sewers for 500 miles of streets.

Most immigrant groups set up aid societies to help newcomers from their country. Many city politicians also offered to assist immigrants in exchange for votes. The politicians set up organizations to help new arrivals find housing and work.

**D. Possible Responses** the problem of immigrants finding housing and work, and the problem of getting themselves (the politicians) elected

*Reading*History
**D. Identifying Problems** What problems were politicians trying to solve by offering to help new immigrants?

## Some Americans Oppose Immigration

Some native-born Americans feared that immigrants were too foreign to learn American ways. Others feared that immigrants might come to outnumber natives. As a result, immigrants faced anger and prejudice. **Prejudice** is a negative opinion that is not based on facts. For example,

### CITIZENSHIP TODAY

## Becoming a Citizen

Most immigrants who came to America in the 1800s shared one thing: an appreciation for the nation's values and laws. As a result, many chose to become U.S. citizens.

This trend continues today. In recent decades, more than half a million Vietnamese have immigrated to the United States. Many became citizens of their new country. One of them was Lam Ton, who is a successful restaurant owner in Chicago. Ton viewed U.S. citizenship as both a privilege and a duty. "We have to stick to this country and help it do better," he said.

Each year, immigrants from around the world are sworn in as U.S. citizens on Citizenship Day, September 17. But first they must pass a test on English, the U.S. political system, and the rights and duties of citizenship.

This young immigrant proudly holds up his certificate of citizenship.

### How Does Someone Become a Citizen?

1. In a small group, discuss what questions you would ask those seeking to become U.S. citizens.
2. Create a citizenship test using your questions.
3. Have another group take the test and record their scores.
4. Use the McDougal Littell Internet site to link to the actual U.S. citizenship test. Compare it to your test.

**See Citizenship Handbook, page 281.**

**Visit www.mcdougallittell.com to learn more about becoming a U.S. citizen.**



### CRITICAL THINKING ACTIVITY

**Comparing and Contrasting** Have students use a chart such as the one below to compare and contrast the experiences of Scandinavian, German, and Irish immigrants in the early and mid-1800s.

| Immigrant Groups | Reasons for Emigrating | Where They Settled | Kind of Work |
|---|---|---|---|
| Scandinavian | | | |
| German | | | |
| Irish | | | |

**Class Time** 30–45 minutes

### CITIZENSHIP TODAY

**OBJECTIVE**

Students will be able to explain why it is important that immigrants learn and understand this nation's values and laws before becoming citizens.

**Becoming a Citizen**

As more and more businesses operate internationally, the number of people who have dual citizenship has increased. For example, a baby born to American parents while they are living in another country is an American citizen. But the baby may also be a citizen of the country where he or she was born.

The Supreme Court has ruled that a person cannot be stripped of his or her U.S. citizenship—even for deserting in wartime. The Court's decision means that almost the only way to lose citizenship is to renounce it voluntarily.

**Citizenship Today,** pp. 9–10

### STANDARDS FOR EVALUATION: CITIZENSHIP TODAY

**Each citizenship test should**

- allow the test taker to demonstrate understanding of the U.S. political system and the rights and duties of citizenship.
- include clear, focused questions.
- include a key to the correct answers for test questions.
- use correct grammar, usage, capitalization, punctuation, and spelling.

In 1844, a riot took place between Catholics and non-Catholics in Philadelphia. Several people were killed.

some Protestants in the 1800s believed that Catholics threatened democracy. Those Protestants feared that the Pope, the head of the Roman Catholic Church, was plotting to overthrow democracy in America.

Native-born Americans who wanted to eliminate foreign influence called themselves **nativists.** Some nativists refused to hire immigrants and put up signs like "No Irish need apply." In cities like New York and Boston, nativists formed a secret society. Members promised not to vote for any Catholics or immigrants running for political office. If asked about their secret group, they said, "I know nothing about it."

**Background** Protestants feared the Pope because in many European countries, the Catholic Church worked closely with the ruling monarchs.

In the 1850s, nativists started a political party. Because of the members' answers to questions about their party, it was called the Know-Nothing Party. It wanted to ban Catholics and the foreign-born from holding office. It also called for a cut in immigration and a 21-year wait to become an American citizen. The Know-Nothings did elect six governors. But they disappeared quickly as a national party. Their northern and southern branches couldn't agree on the issue of slavery.

In spite of such barriers as prejudice, the immigrants of the 1800s had a strong impact on American culture. Writers and artists of the 1800s also shaped American culture. Section 2 discusses their influence.

## Section 1 Assessment

**1. Terms & Names**

**Identify:**
- emigrant
- immigrant
- steerage
- push-pull factor
- famine
- prejudice
- nativist

**2. Taking Notes**

Use a cluster diagram like the one below to record details about immigration, such as which groups came, where they settled, and how they influenced America.

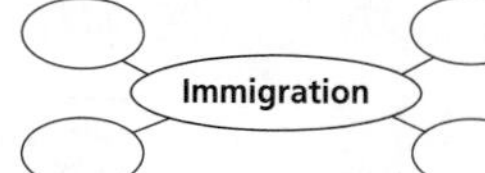


**3. Main Ideas**

a. What were the push-pull factors that led to immigration?

b. How did the arrival of so many immigrants affect U.S. cities?

c. What was the Know-Nothing Party, and what was its point of view about immigration?

**4. Critical Thinking**

**Analyzing Causes** How did the rapid increase in immigration cause conflict?

THINK ABOUT
- why Irish immigrants and free blacks competed for jobs
- the growth of cities and the problems it created
- the prejudices of nativists
- religious differences

**ACTIVITY OPTIONS**

**TECHNOLOGY**
**ART**

Plan a **multimedia presentation** or design a **Web page** that shows immigrants the advantages of settling in the United States.



## MORE ABOUT . . .

**The Know-Nothing Party**

Also called the American Party, the Know-Nothing Party reached its height of national power in 1855, when it had 43 members in Congress. In 1856, the American Party nominated Millard Fillmore for president. As the American Party's nominee, Fillmore carried only one state, Maryland.

## ASSESS & RETEACH

**Setting the Stage** Have students fill in the first row on the graphic organizer.

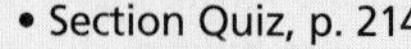

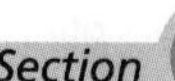

**Formal Assessment**
- Section Quiz, p. 214

**Critical Thinking Transparency CT40**
- Setting the Stage

### RETEACHING ACTIVITY

Have students write a summary paragraph that uses the section's Main Idea as the topic sentence: "In the mid-1800s, millions of Europeans came to the United States hoping to build a better life." Student paragraphs should identify the origin of immigrants, briefly explain why they came, and note the effects of their immigration on this country's cities and on public opinion.

**In-Depth Resources: Unit 4**
- Reteaching Activity, p. 56

## Section 1 Assessment

**1. Terms & Names**

**emigrant,** p. 423
**immigrant,** p. 423
**steerage,** p. 423
**push-pull factors,** p. 424
**famine,** p. 426
**prejudice,** p. 427
**nativist,** p. 428

**2. Taking Notes**

Scandinavians, Germans, Irish; Scandinavians settled on farms, in the northern Midwest; Germans settled in cities and farms on the frontier; Irish settled in port cities. Influences include German kindergartens, gymnasiums, musical groups, and food; Irish labor and political activity.

**3. Main Ideas**

**a.** pull factors: desire for freedom, economic opportunity, land; push factors: population growth, crop failures, religious and political turmoil **b.** Cities grew rapidly, leading to overcrowding, disease, and crime. **c.** a political party; cut immigration to reduce the influence of foreigners

**4. Critical Thinking**

Irish competed with blacks for jobs; overcrowding of neighborhoods increased crime; discrimination led to riots.

### ACTIVITY OPTIONS

**Alternative Assessment**
- Rubrics for multimedia, 5.4
- Rubrics for a Web page, 5.1

# 2 American Literature and Art

**TERMS & NAMES**
romanticism
Hudson River school
transcendentalism
civil disobedience

**MAIN IDEA**

Inspired by nature and democratic ideals, writers and artists produced some of America's greatest works.

**WHY IT MATTERS NOW**

Nineteenth-century writers such as Hawthorne and Thoreau laid the foundation for American literature.

### ONE AMERICAN'S STORY

**As a young man, Washington Irving published articles that made fun of society in the early 1800s. Although he studied to be a lawyer, he eventually made writing his full-time career.**

**Irving wrote some of the first stories to describe America. For example, "Rip Van Winkle" tells of a man in New York State. Rip wakes up after a 20-year nap to find everything changed. He goes to the inn, which once had a picture of King George on its sign.**

*A VOICE FROM THE PAST*

The red coat was changed for one of blue and buff, a sword was held in the hand instead of a sceptre [staff of authority], the head was decorated with a cocked hat, and underneath was painted in large characters, GENERAL WASHINGTON.

**Washington Irving,** "Rip Van Winkle"

**While Rip slept, the Americans had fought and won their revolution!**

**Irving's work helped to win European respect for American writing for the first time. This section discusses other individuals of the 1800s who created uniquely American literature and art.**

In another Irving tale, "The Legend of Sleepy Hollow," a spooky creature—perhaps a ghost from the Revolution—chases a teacher.

## 1 Writing About America

Irving and other writers were influenced by a style of European art called **romanticism.** It stressed the individual, imagination, creativity, and emotion. It drew inspiration from nature. American writers turned their interest in nature into a celebration of the American wilderness.

Many books featured the wilderness. James Fenimore Cooper wrote five novels about the dramatic adventures of wilderness scout Natty Bumppo. One that remains popular is *The Last of the Mohicans.* Francis Parkman wrote a travel book, *The Oregon Trail,* about the frontier trail.





## SECTION OBJECTIVES

1. To analyze how writers and artists celebrated the American wilderness
2. To explain the influence of transcendentalism on American writing
3. To analyze how writers shaped American literature

**CRITICAL THINKING**

Making Inferences, p. 431
Recognizing Effects, p. 432
Evaluating, p. 432

## FOCUS & MOTIVATE

### 5-MINUTE WARM-UP

**Making Inferences** These questions explore the influence of this country's natural environment on American artists.

1. Look at the painting on page 430. What is the focus of the painting?
2. What can you learn about the artist from the painting?

 **Warm-Up Transparency WT14**

## INSTRUCT

### INSTRUCT: OBJECTIVE 1

**Writing About America/ Creating American Art**

Key Questions

- How did romanticism influence the creation of an American style in literature and art?
- How did Noah Webster contribute to a developing American style of writing?
- How did enslaved African Americans contribute to American art?

**In-Depth Resources: Unit 4**
- Guided Reading, p. 44
- Building Vocabulary, p. 47

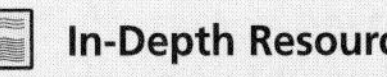

**Reading Study Guide** (Spanish and English), pp. 141–142

## RECOMMENDED RESOURCES

**In-Depth Resources: Unit 4**
- Guided Reading, p. 44
- Building Vocabulary, p. 47
- Reteaching Activity, p. 57

**Reading Study Guide** (Spanish and English), pp. 141–142

**Formal Assessment**
- Section Quiz, p. 215

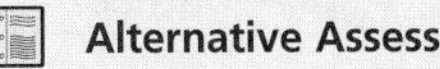

**Alternative Assessment**
- Rubrics, 1.3
- Rubrics, 5.3

**Access for Students Acquiring English/ESL**
- Guided Reading, p. 94

**Technology Resources**

**Humanities Transparency HT27**
- Bird of Washington

**Electronic Teacher Tools with Test Maker**

**ClassZone**
www.mcdougallittell.com

## HISTORY through ART

**Interpreting the Painting** Thomas Cole was the first of the Hudson River painters. He spent weeks at a time walking and sketching in the Catskill Mountains, the White Mountains, and other wilderness areas. Asher Durand traveled with Cole in the Catskills. Before he died, Cole lamented that the wilderness was disappearing: "They are cutting down all the trees in the beautiful valley on which I have looked so often with a loving eye. . . ." Durand's painting was commissioned as a tribute to Cole by a wealthy patron who was inspired by Bryant's eulogy for the painter.

**Possible Responses: its emphasis on nature, emotion, and the individual**

## MORE ABOUT . . .

**Noah Webster**

Noah Webster (1758–1843) recorded uniquely American words such as *skunk, hickory,* and *chowder.* He also advocated revising the spelling of some words, changing, for example, *musik* to *music* and *plough to plow.* It is because of Webster that Americans write *honor* not *honour,* and *theater* and *center* instead of *theatre* and *centre.*

## MORE ABOUT . . .

**American Arts and Artists**

While the Hudson River school focused on the grandeurs of the landscape, other artists in the 1830s and 1840s depicted the daily life of ordinary people. Such paintings of farmers, fur traders, sailors, and storekeepers fit with the spirit of Jacksonian democracy. Engraved copies of these paintings—far less expensive than originals—allowed many Americans to decorate their homes with images of their nation and its people.

**Humanities Transparency HT27**
- Bird of Washington

## HISTORY through ART

Asher Durand was a founder of the Hudson River school of painting. His best-known work, *Kindred Spirits,* was painted in 1849. This romantic work shows two artists inspired by a beautiful landscape. The figures in the painting are Durand's friends, the poet William Cullen Bryant and the painter Thomas Cole.

**What aspects of the painting make it romantic?**

In addition, writers began to use a more American style. A teacher and lawyer named Noah Webster gave guidelines to that style in his *American Dictionary of the English Language.* Webster first published his dictionary in 1828. He later revised it in 1840. The dictionary gave American, not British, spellings and included American slang.

Other writers besides Irving celebrated America's past. Henry Wadsworth Longfellow wrote many poems that retold stories from history. For example, "Paul Revere's Ride" depicted the Revolutionary hero's ride to warn of a British attack. Generations of students memorized lines from the poem, such as, "One if by land, and two if by sea; / And I on the opposite shore will be."

## Creating American Art

Influenced by romanticism, American painters also focused on nature. One group of painters worked in the Hudson River Valley in New York State. **Hudson River school** artists painted peaceful landscapes of mountains, forests, and rivers. Several members of the Hudson River school traveled to find more exciting scenery. For example, Albert Bierstadt took several trips to America's mountainous West. He produced huge paintings that convey the majesty of the American landscape. (See page 310.)



## ACTIVITY OPTIONS

## INDIVIDUAL NEEDS

### LESS PROFICIENT READERS

**Categorizing** To help students understand how the art and literature discussed in the section reflect this period in history, copy the chart on the board before students begin to read. As you read the section with students, discuss each term. Have the students write a definition or description of the term in the first box. Ask students to supply names of writers or artists associated with each word or phrase and add them to the chart under the correct heading. At the end of the section, ask students to quiz each other on the terms.

| Romanticism | Hudson River School | Fireside Poets | Transcendentalism |
|---|---|---|---|
| | | | |
| | | | |
| | | | |
| | | | |

**Background** The National Audubon Society, whose goal is the protection of wildlife today, is named for John James Audubon.

Other artists also went west. John James Audubon came to the United States from France at age 18. Traveling across the continent, Audubon sketched the birds and animals of his adopted country.

Enslaved African Americans also contributed to American art. They made beautiful baskets, quilts, and pottery. Most of these slaves remained anonymous, but one did not. David Drake worked in a South Carolina pottery factory and signed the pottery he created. He was the only factory worker to do so.

## 2 Following One's Conscience

By the 1840s, Americans took new pride in their emerging culture. Ralph Waldo Emerson, a New England writer, encouraged this pride. He urged Americans to cast off European influence and develop their own beliefs. His advice was to learn about life from self-examination and from nature as well as books.

> *"No law can be sacred to me but that of my nature."*
> Ralph Waldo Emerson

Emerson's student, Henry David Thoreau, followed that advice. In 1845, Thoreau moved to a simple cabin he had built by Walden Pond near the town of Concord, Massachusetts. Thoreau furnished it with only a bed, a table, a desk, and three chairs. He wrote about his life in the woods in *Walden.* Thoreau said that people should live by their own individual standards.

***Reading*History**
**A. Making Inferences** What do you think it means to "hear a different drummer"?
A. Possible **Response** to have different opinions or ideas than other people

***A VOICE FROM THE PAST***

If a man does not keep pace with his companions, perhaps it is because he hears a different drummer. Let him step to the music which he hears, however measured or far away.

**Henry David Thoreau,** ***Walden***

Emerson and Thoreau belonged to a group of thinkers with a new philosophy called **transcendentalism.** It taught that the spiritual world is more important than the physical world. It also taught that people can find the truth within themselves—through feeling and intuition.

Because Thoreau believed in the importance of individual conscience, he urged people not to obey laws they considered unjust. Instead of protesting with violence, they should peacefully refuse to obey those laws. This form of protest is called **civil disobedience.** For example, Thoreau did not want to support the U.S. government, which allowed slavery and fought the War with Mexico. Instead of paying taxes that helped to finance the war, Thoreau went to jail.

Another New England transcendentalist, Margaret Fuller, also called for change. In her magazine, *The Dial,* and in her book, *Woman in the Nineteenth Century,* Fuller argued for women's rights.

### Connections TO LITERATURE

**"CIVIL DISOBEDIENCE"**

In his essay "Civil Disobedience," Thoreau wrote that "Under a government which imprisons any unjustly the true place for a just man is also a prison."

Thoreau did land in prison when he refused to pay his taxes. According to legend, Emerson visited Thoreau in jail and asked, "Why are you here?" Thoreau replied, "Why are you not here?"

In the 20th century, Mohandas K. Gandhi of India and Martin Luther King, Jr., of the United States both used civil disobedience to fight injustice.



### INSTRUCT: OBJECTIVE 

**Following One's Conscience**

Key Questions

- How did the fireside poets popularize American poetry?
- How did Ralph Waldo Emerson and Henry David Thoreau put the philosophy of transcendentalism into practice?

### MORE ABOUT . . .

**Ralph Waldo Emerson**

"The only way to have a friend is to be one." "Hitch your wagon to a star." "Nothing great was ever achieved without enthusiasm." "The reward of a thing well done, is to have done it." These lines from Ralph Waldo Emerson's essays became well-known sayings to later generations of Americans. Emerson advocated nonconformity, self-reliance, and independent thought.

### Connections TO LITERATURE

**"Civil Disobedience"**

The unpaid tax that sent Thoreau to jail was a poll tax of $2.00, and he spent one night in jail. Thoreau's nonconformity started early. At Harvard, he flouted the rule requiring students to wear black coats by wearing a green one. In addition to lecturing and writing against slavery, Thoreau also aided African Americans fleeing from slavery along the Underground Railroad.

### ACTIVITY OPTIONS

**INTERDISCIPLINARY LINK: ART**

 BLOCK SCHEDULING

**CREATING POSTERS**

**Class Time** One class period

**Task** Creating posters advertising events and individuals featured at an American culture fair in 1850

**Purpose** To synthesize information about American literature and art in the first half of the 1800s

**Supplies Needed**

- Poster paper or large sheets of plain paper
- Art supplies
- Textbook

**Activity** Have students imagine that they are in charge of publicity for a three-day American Culture Fair in 1850. The fair features presentations by poets, writers of fiction and nonfiction, and artists. Students should create posters advertising the fair. Posters should highlight at least one individual who will present his or her work, including biographical information and descriptions or samples of his or her work. Display completed posters.

**INSTRUCT: OBJECTIVE** 

**Exploring the Human Heart**
Key Questions
- How did poets such as Walt Whitman and Emily Dickinson influence American poetry in the early and mid-1800s?
- Which fiction writers helped shape American literature?

**STRANGE *but* True**

**Gifts on Poe's Grave**
Poe was originally buried in an unmarked grave in 1849. An attempt to mark the grave in 1860 failed when Poe's stone monument was destroyed in a bizarre accident in which a train jumped the tracks and slammed into the yard where the monument had been created. Poe's remains were moved in 1875 to another spot in the cemetery, where family, friends, and admirers erected a new monument. Still, strange rumors have persisted that Poe's remains were never moved in 1875 and still lie somewhere in an unmarked grave nearby. In death, it seems, Poe remains for some a source of mystery.

## ASSESS & RETEACH

**Setting the Stage** Have students fill in the second row on the graphic organizer.

 **Formal Assessment**
- Section Quiz, p. 215

**RETEACHING ACTIVITY**
Have students create flash cards using index cards or 3" x 5" sheets of paper. On each card or paper, students should write the name of one writer, poet, or artist from this section. On the back, students should describe the significance or accomplishment of that individual. When they have completed their set of cards, students can use them to quiz each other about material in the section.

 **In-Depth Resources: Unit 4**
- Reteaching Activity, p. 57

**STRANGE *but* True**

**GIFTS ON POE'S GRAVE**
Every year a mysterious figure dressed in black celebrates Edgar Allan Poe's birthday. He leaves three roses on the author's Baltimore grave at 3:00 A.M.

The puzzling tradition began in 1949, exactly 100 years after Poe's death. In 1993, a new black-coated visitor took over the tradition. The person who began the ritual was ill—and later died in 1999.

Although many witnesses watch the ritual each year, none ask the visitor his name. Poe's fans have always liked mysteries.

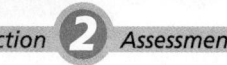

## 3 Exploring the Human Heart

Like Thoreau, other writers broke with tradition. In 1855, poet Walt Whitman published *Leaves of Grass,* a book that changed American poetry. His bold, unrhymed poems praised ordinary people. Emily Dickinson lived in her family's home almost her entire life. She wrote poems on small pieces of paper that she sewed into booklets. Her subjects include God, nature, love, and death. Most of her 1,775 poems were published only after her death. Both Whitman and Dickinson shaped modern poetry by experimenting with language.

Fiction writers of the 1800s also shaped American literature. Edgar Allan Poe wrote terrifying tales that influence today's horror story writers. He also wrote the first detective story, "The Murders in the Rue Morgue."

*Reading***History**
**B. Recognizing Effects** How did Poe influence the fiction that people read today?
**B. Possible Response** by influencing horror stories and inventing the detective story

Nathaniel Hawthorne depicted love, guilt, and revenge during Puritan times in *The Scarlet Letter.* The novel shows that harsh judgment without mercy can lead to tragedy. Hawthorne may have learned that lesson from his family history. One of his ancestors condemned people at the Salem witchcraft trials.

Herman Melville won fame by writing thrilling novels about his experiences as a sailor. In 1851, Melville published his masterpiece, *Moby Dick.* This novel tells about a man's destructive desire to kill a white whale. Although the novel was not popular when it was published, it is widely read now. Several movie versions exist.

These fiction writers portrayed the harmful effects of cruel actions. Other people thought that individuals could alter society for good. Section 3 describes those reformers.

### Section 2 Assessment

**1. Terms & Names**
**Identify:**
- romanticism
- Hudson River school
- transcendentalism
- civil disobedience

**2. Taking Notes**
Use a chart like the one below to list important individual writers and artists. For each one, name or describe one of his or her works.

| Writer or artist | His or her work |
|---|---|
| | |

Which one would you like to learn more about? Why?

**3. Main Ideas**
a. What was romanticism and how did Americans adapt it?
b. What is civil disobedience and what did Thoreau do that is an example of it?
c. How did the writers of the mid-1800s shape modern literature?

**4. Critical Thinking**
**Evaluating** Why do you think the literature and art of the mid-1800s are still valued?
**THINK ABOUT**
- the way they feature U.S. history and culture
- their universal themes—themes that relate to all people in all time periods
- the way they reflect changes happening at that time

**ACTIVITY OPTIONS**
**ART** / **TECHNOLOGY** Choose an American painting, sketch it, and make it into a **jigsaw puzzle;** or make an **audio recording** of a museum guide's description of it.



### Section 2 Assessment

**1. Terms & Names**
**romanticism,** p. 429
**Hudson River school,** p. 430
**transcendentalism,** p. 431
**civil disobedience,** p. 431

**2. Taking Notes**
Washington Irving: "Rip Van Winkle"; James Fenimore Cooper: *The Last of the Mohicans;* Henry David Thoreau: *Walden;* Margaret Fuller: *Woman in the Nineteenth Century;* Emily Dickinson: poems about God, nature, love, and death. Answers will vary. Encourage students to read more by the author they chose.

**3. Main Ideas**
**a.** an art style that stressed the individual, imagination, creativity, and emotion; by celebrating the American wilderness **b.** a peaceful protest in which people refuse to obey laws they consider unjust; he refused to pay taxes **c.** writing that used American dialect; poetry that praised ordinary people; new types of horror

**4. Critical Thinking**
Students may choose the portrayal of historical events or the universal themes of love, God, death, nature, guilt, and revenge.

**ACTIVITY OPTIONS**
 **Alternative Assessment**
- Rubrics for a puzzle, 1.3
- Rubrics for an audio recording, 5.3

# 3 Reforming American Society

**TERMS & NAMES**
revival
Second Great Awakening
temperance movement
labor union
strike
Horace Mann
Dorothea Dix

**MAIN IDEA**

In the mid-1800s, several reform movements worked to improve American education and society.

**WHY IT MATTERS NOW**

Several laws and institutions, such as public schools, date back to this period.

## ONE AMERICAN'S STORY

**Anne Newport Royall was a travel writer. In her 1830 book *Letters from Alabama*, Royall recorded America's growing interest in religion. She also described hearing a preacher at a Tennessee revival, or meeting to reawaken religious faith.**

*A VOICE FROM THE PAST*

His text was, "He that hath ears to hear, let him hear." The people must have been deaf indeed that could not have heard him. . . . He began low but soon bawled to deafening. He spit in his hands, rubbed them against each other, and then would smite them together, till he made the woods ring.

**Anne Newport Royall,** *Letters from Alabama*

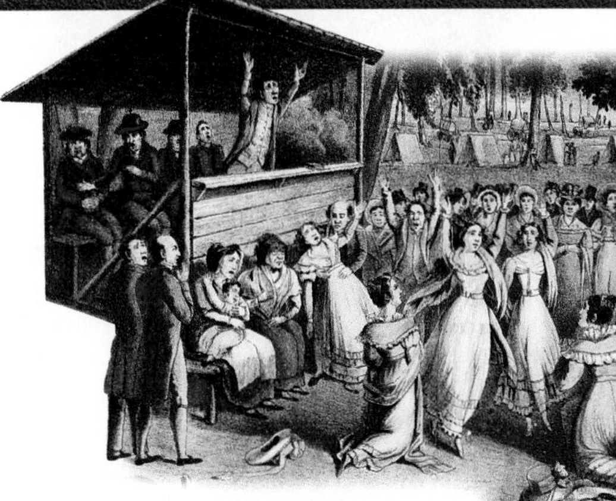
This revival meeting took place during the Second Great Awakening—a rebirth of religious faith named after the Great Awakening of the 1700s.

**Some preachers, like the one Royall saw, were circuit riders. A circuit rider rode from town to town, often holding his meetings in a tent. The preacher gave a sermon urging individuals to give up their sins. This section explains how, in the mid-1800s, many individuals called on Americans to reform, or to improve themselves and their society.**

## 1 A Spirit of Revival

The renewal of religious faith in the 1790s and early 1800s is called the **Second Great Awakening.** Revivalist preachers said that anyone could choose salvation. This appealed to equality-loving Americans. Revivals spread quickly across the frontier. Settlers eagerly awaited the visits of preachers like Peter Cartwright. At the age of 16, Cartwright had given up a life of gambling and joined a Methodist Church. He became a minister and spent more than 60 years preaching on the frontier.

The revival also traveled to Eastern cities. There, former lawyer Charles Grandison Finney held large revival meetings. He preached that "all sin consists in selfishness" and that religious faith led people to help others. Such teaching helped awaken a spirit of reform. Americans began to believe that they could act to make things better.

## SECTION OBJECTIVES

1. To describe the spirit of reform of the early and mid-1800s
2. To evaluate the impact of the early labor movement
3. To describe efforts to improve education and to care for the needy
4. To describe the growth of print media and the utopian movement

**CRITICAL THINKING**

Evaluating, p. 434
Making Inferences, p. 435
Recognizing Effects, pp. 436, 437
Forming and Supporting Opinions, p. 437

## FOCUS & MOTIVATE

### 5-MINUTE WARM-UP

**Making Inferences** The following questions focus on the goals of the temperance movement.

1. Study the poster on page 434. What pledge are readers asked to take?
2. What reward does the poster's picture suggest for temperance?

 **Warm-Up Transparency WT14**

## INSTRUCT

**INSTRUCT: OBJECTIVE 1**

**A Spirit of Revival/Temperance Societies**

Key Questions

- How did the Second Great Awakening foster a spirit of reform?
- Why did many women join the temperance movement?
- How successful was the temperance movement?

**In-Depth Resources: Unit 4**
- Guided Reading, p. 45

**Reading Study Guide** (Spanish and English), pp. 143–144

## RECOMMENDED RESOURCES

**In-Depth Resources: Unit 4**
- Guided Reading, p. 45
- Building Vocabulary, p. 47
- Reteaching Activity, p. 58
- Enrichment Activity, p. 60

**Reading Study Guide** (Spanish and English), pp. 143–144

**Formal Assessment**
- Section Quiz, p. 216

**Alternative Assessment**
- Rubrics, 3.6
- Rubrics, 4.3

**Access for Students Acquiring English/ESL**
- Guided Reading, p. 95

Technology Resources

 **Critical Thinking Trans. CT41**
- Cause and Effect: The Reform Movement

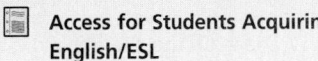

 **Electronic Teacher Tools with Test Maker**

 **ClassZone**
www.mcdougallittell.com

**MORE ABOUT . . .**

**Contemporary Reform Movements**
Various organizations today work for laws designed to prevent drunk driving and to keep alcohol out of the hands of minors. Among those organizations are Mothers Against Drunk Driving (MADD) and Students Against Destructive Decisions (SADD) (formerly Students Against Drunk Driving). SADD asks young adults to sign a Contract for Life, in which the signer pledges to avoid using alcohol and drugs.

**Critical Thinking Transparency CT41**
• Cause and Effect: The Reform Movement

**INSTRUCT: OBJECTIVE 2**
**Fighting for Workers' Rights**
Key Questions
- What were the goals of people who fought for workers' rights?
- How did government and private organizations work for better schools?

**MORE ABOUT . . .**

**Strikes in the New England Mills**
When employers in the 1830s and 1840s cut wages, workers felt that their independence was threatened as well as their pay. Striking workers often compared themselves to the American Patriots during the Revolutionary War, 60 years earlier. They called the factory owners "Tories in disguise" and reprinted the Declaration of Independence. One group of workers began their strike on Washington's birthday. The women of the Lowell mills noted that they were "daughters of freemen" whose ancestors had fought British tyranny.

Temperance pledges often displayed inspiring pictures and mottoes.

## Temperance Societies

Led by churches, some Americans began the **temperance movement,** which is a campaign to stop the drinking of alcohol. Heavy drinking was common in the early 1800s. Some workers spent most of their wages on alcohol—leaving their families without enough money to live on. As a result, many women joined the temperance movement. "There is no reform in which women can act better or more appropriately than temperance," said Mary C. Vaughan.

Temperance workers handed out pamphlets urging people to stop drinking. One pamphlet read, "Drink is the . . . source . . . of nearly all the ills that afflict the human family." Temperance speakers traveled across America asking people to sign a paper pledging to give up alcohol. By 1838, a million people had signed.

**A. Possible Response** It urged people to stop drinking because it cost money that could be better spent on food, clothing, and shelter.

***Reading* History**
**A. Evaluating** How did the temperance movement encourage people to take responsibility for their families?

Temperance also won the support of business owners. Industry needed workers who could keep schedules and run machines. Alcohol made it hard for workers to do either. New England businessman Neal Dow led the fight to make it illegal to sell alcohol. In 1851, Maine banned the sale of liquor. By 1855, 13 other states passed similar laws. But many people opposed these laws, and most were repealed. Still, the movement to ban alcohol remained strong, even into the 20th century.

**Vocabulary**
**repeal:** to cancel

## 2 Fighting for Workers' Rights

As business owners tried to improve workers' habits, workers called for improvements in working conditions. Factory work was noisy, boring, and unsafe. In the 1830s, American workers began to organize.

The young women mill workers in Lowell, Massachusetts, started a labor union. A **labor union** is a group of workers who band together to seek better working conditions. In 1836, the mill owners raised the rent of the company-owned boarding houses where the women lived. About 1,500 women went on **strike,** stopping work to demand better conditions. Eleven-year-old Harriet Hanson helped lead the strikers.

***A VOICE FROM THE PAST***

I . . . started on ahead, saying, . . . "I don't care what you do, I am going to turn out, whether anyone else does or not," and I marched out, and was followed by the others. As I looked back at the long line that followed me, I was more proud than I have ever been since.

**Harriet Hanson,** quoted in *A People's History of the United States*

Other workers called for shorter hours and higher wages. In 1835 and 1836, 140 strikes took place in the eastern United States. Then the Panic



**ACTIVITY OPTIONS**
**INDIVIDUAL NEEDS**

**STUDENTS ACQUIRING ENGLISH/ESL**
**Building Vocabulary** Copy the graphic shown here on the chalkboard. Pronounce the word *reform* and write its definition, "to improve or make better," on the graphic. Then point out the words *Reforming* in the section title and *reformers* on page 436. Discuss the part of speech and meaning of each word. Ask students to add definitions to the graphic. After students have read the section, ask them to give examples of reform that occurred in the early 1800s and to identify reformers who are associated with this movement.

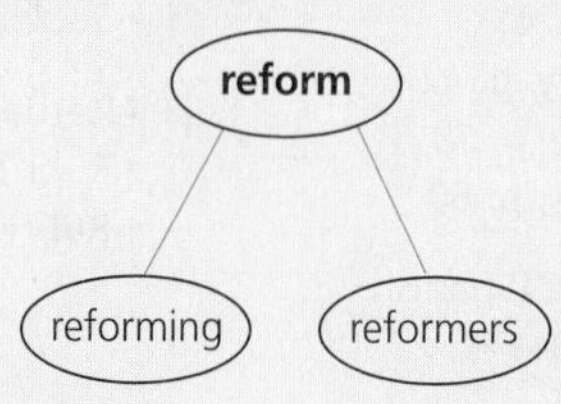

of 1837 brought hard times. Jobs were scarce, and workers were afraid to cause trouble. The young labor movement fell apart. Even so, workers achieved a few goals. For example, in 1840 President Martin Van Buren ordered a ten-hour workday for government workers.

**Background**
President Van Buren's order reduced the workweek from 70 to 60 hours.

## 3 Improving Education

In the 1830s, Americans also began to demand better schools. In 1837, Massachusetts set up the first state board of education in the United States. Its head was **Horace Mann**. Mann called public education "the great equalizer." He also argued that "education creates or develops new treasures—treasures never before possessed or dreamed of by any one." By 1850, many Northern states had opened public elementary schools.

Boston opened the first public high school in 1821. A few other Northern cities followed suit. In addition, churches and other groups founded hundreds of private colleges in the following decades. Many were located in states carved from the Northwest Territory. These included Antioch and Oberlin Colleges in Ohio, the University of Notre Dame in Indiana, and Northwestern University in Illinois.

Women could not attend most colleges. One exception was Oberlin. It was the first college to accept women as well as men. In 1849, English immigrant Elizabeth Blackwell became the first woman to earn a medical degree in the United States. Despite such individual efforts, it was rare for a woman to attend college until the late 1800s.

African Americans also faced obstacles to getting an education. This was especially true in the South. There, teaching an enslaved person to read had been illegal since the Nat Turner Rebellion in 1831. Enslaved African Americans who tried to learn were brutally punished. Even in the North, most public schools barred African-American children.

*Reading* **History**
**B. Making Inferences** Why do you think women and African Americans had a hard time getting an education?
B. Possible Response because of prejudice and discrimination

Few colleges accepted African Americans. Those that did often took only one or two blacks at a time. The first African American to receive a college degree was Alexander Twilight in 1823. John Russwurm received one in 1826 and later began the first African-American newspaper.

Mary Jane Patterson was the first African-American woman to earn a college degree. She graduated from Oberlin in 1862 and went on to work as a teacher.

## Caring for the Needy

As some people promoted education, others tried to improve society's care for its weakest members. In 1841, **Dorothea Dix,** a reformer from Boston, was teaching Sunday school at a women's jail. She discovered some women who were locked in cold, filthy cells



**INSTRUCT: OBJECTIVE 3**
**Improving Education/Caring for the Needy**
Key Questions
- What efforts were made to improve educational opportunities for women?
- What obstacles faced African Americans who wanted an education?
- How did Dorothea Dix improve care for people who were mentally ill?

**MORE ABOUT . . .**
**Oberlin College**
From its founding in 1833, Oberlin announced that it would admit students regardless of race or sex. At first, Oberlin offered women only a short course in literature, but within a few years women were taking the same courses as men. Still, the college administrators believed that their main goal was to prepare women to be better mothers. Women students with different goals—such as Antoinette Brown, who became a minister, and Lucy Stone, later a suffrage leader—often challenged that point of view, even while they relished the education that Oberlin provided.

**ACTIVITY OPTIONS**
**INTERDISCIPLINARY LINK: GOVERNMENT**
 BLOCK SCHEDULING

**WRITING A RESOLUTION**
**Class Time** One class period
**Task** Writing a resolution calling for an educational reform
**Purpose** To formulate ideas for reforming education today and to learn how local governments operate

**Supplies Needed**
- References on education
- Internet access
- Sample resolutions for models

**Activity** As a class, brainstorm a list of desirable improvements in your school, such as enhanced computer access. Divide the class into groups and allow each group to select one reform from the list. Tell the groups to do some research on their reform and then write a resolution for the local school board and/or finance committee of your community asking for the improvement. Present your resolution to the class. You may want to contact a school board member about your resolution.

## AMERICA'S HISTORY MAKERS

**Horace Mann**

Mann considered his advocacy for education as a moral vocation. He once described himself as "circuit rider to the next generation," referring to the circuit riders who rode from town to town to preach at revival meetings. In his effort to improve education, Mann visited schools, gave lectures, started a journal, and lobbied the state legislature. His work made the cause of education reform very popular.

**Dorothea Dix**

Dix traveled around the country to visit places that housed people with mental illnesses. A visit by Dix could cause anxiety for the administrators of these hospitals or asylums. "To have Miss Dix suddenly arrive at your asylum and find anything neglected or amiss, was considerably worse than an earthquake," said one doctor at a mental hospital in Providence, Rhode Island. "Not that she said anything on the spot, but one felt something ominous suspended in the very air."

**Answer: Both overcame poor or unhappy backgrounds, perhaps strengthening their identification with the underdog.**

### INSTRUCT: OBJECTIVE 4

**Spreading Ideas Through Print/ Creating Ideal Communities**

Key Questions

- How did affordable newspapers and new magazines spread ideas through print?
- For what reasons did some Americans attempt to establish utopias? How successful were they?
- How did Shakers organize their communities?

 **In-Depth Resources: Unit 4**
- Enrichment Activity, p. 60

---

## AMERICA'S HISTORY MAKERS

**HORACE MANN**
**1796–1859**

Horace Mann once said in a speech to students, "Be ashamed to die until you have won some victory for humanity." Mann had no reason to be ashamed. As a child, he knew poverty and hardship. He educated himself and later fought for public education for other people.

Toward the end of his life, Mann became president of Antioch College. It committed itself to education for both men and women and equal rights for African Americans.

**DOROTHEA DIX**
**1802–1887**

At the age of 12, Dorothea Dix left an unhappy home to go live with her grandparents in Boston. Just two years later, she began teaching little children.

In 1841, Dix saw the harsh treatment of mentally ill women. Society frowned upon women traveling alone, but Dix defied custom. She went by train to several places where the mentally ill were housed.

Dix wrote a report about her research. (See page 438.) That report changed the care of the mentally ill.

**How might their backgrounds have motivated Dorothea Dix and Horace Mann to become leaders in reform movements?**

simply because they were mentally ill. Visiting other jails, Dix learned that the mentally ill often received no treatment. Instead, they were chained and beaten. Dix pleaded with the Massachusetts Legislature to improve the care of the mentally ill. Later, she traveled all over the United States on behalf of the mentally ill. Her efforts led to the building of 32 new hospitals.

Some reformers worked to improve life for people with other disabilities. Thomas H. Gallaudet started the first American school for deaf children in 1817. Samuel G. Howe founded the Perkins School for the Blind in Boston in the 1830s.

Reformers also tried to improve prisons. In the early 1800s, debtors, lifelong criminals, and child offenders were put in the same cells. Reformers demanded that children go to special jails. They also called for the rehabilitation of adult prisoners. Rehabilitation means preparing people to live useful lives after their release from prison.

*Reading* **History**

**C. Recognizing Effects** How did reformers change the treatment of the mentally ill, the disabled, and prisoners?

**C. Possible Response** The mentally ill were put in hospitals; the deaf and blind had new schools; adult and child prisoners were separated, and reformers tried to rehabilitate prisoners.

### 4 Spreading Ideas Through Print

During this period of reform, Americans began to receive more information about how they should lead their lives. In the 1830s, cheaper newsprint and the invention of the steam-driven press lowered the price of a newspaper to a penny. Average Americans could afford to buy the "penny papers." Penny papers were also popular because, in addition to serious news, they published gripping stories of fires and crimes.

Hundreds of new magazines also appeared. One was the *Ladies' Magazine.* Its editor was Sarah Hale, a widow who used writing to support her family. The magazine advocated education for women. It also



---

**ACTIVITY OPTIONS**

**INTERDISCIPLINARY LINK: LANGUAGE ARTS** — **BLOCK SCHEDULING**

**DICTIONARY OF REFORMERS**

**Class Time** One class period

**Task** Creating biographical dictionaries of 19th-century reformers

**Purpose** To collect and organize information about reformers

**Supplies Needed**
- Art supplies
- Textbook
- Encyclopedias, biographical dictionaries, Internet access

**Activity** Have students make lists of reformers mentioned in this chapter and do research to learn about other reformers from this time period, such as Emma Willard. Have students alphabetize the final list of reformers by last name. Divide the list among the class. For each reformer, students should find birth and death dates and major achievements. Students may write their dictionary entries on separate sheets of paper, make a title page, and staple the pages together to make a book.

suggested that men and women were responsible for different, but equally important, areas of life. The magazine taught that a woman's area was the home and the world of "human ties." A man's area was politics and the business of earning a living for his family. Later, Hale edited *Godey's Lady's Book,* which published poems and stories as well as articles.

## Creating Ideal Communities

While magazines sought to tell people how to live and reform movements tried to change society, some individuals decided to start over. They aimed to build an ideal society, called a utopia.

Two attempts at utopias were New Harmony, Indiana, and Brook Farm, Massachusetts. In both, residents received food and other necessities of life in exchange for work. However, both utopias experienced conflicts and financial difficulties. They ended after only a few years.

*Reading*History
**D. Forming and Supporting Opinions** Why do you think it was hard for utopias to succeed? Give reasons.
**D. Possible Responses** Members might disagree over rules; the people who live in such communities tend to be dreamers and not financially practical; people are often too selfish to live in an "ideal community."

Religious belief led to some utopias. For example, the Shakers followed the beliefs of Ann Lee. She preached that people should lead holy lives in communities that demonstrate God's love to the world. When a person became a Shaker, he or she vowed not to marry or have children. Shakers shared their goods with each other, believed that men and women are equal, and refused to fight for any reason. Shakers set up communities in New York, New England, and on the frontier.

People called them *Shakers* because they shook with emotion during church services. Otherwise, Shaker life was calm. Shakers farmed and built simple furniture in styles that remain popular today. The childless Shakers depended on converts and adopting children to keep their communities going. In the 1840s, the Shakers had 6,000 members—their highest number. In 1999, only seven Shakers remained.

In the 1840s and 1850s, reform found a new direction. Many individuals began to try to win rights for two oppressed groups—women and enslaved persons. Section 4 discusses these efforts.

### MORE ABOUT . . .

**The Shakers**
Shakers were hard workers and their farms prospered. Shakers actively sought new ways to make their labor efficient and easy. They invented many laborsaving devices, including the buzz saw, a revolving oven, and apple corers and parers. They sold products such as garden seeds, herbs and medicines, baskets, boxes, brooms, and woven goods to the public. They were the first to package seeds in the small paper envelopes still used today.

### Section 3 Assessment

**1. Terms & Names**

**Identify:**
- revival
- Second Great Awakening
- temperance movement
- labor union
- strike
- Horace Mann
- Dorothea Dix

**2. Taking Notes**

Create a chart like the one below. Use it to list problems identified by reformers and their solutions to them.

| Problem | Reformer's Solution |
|---|---|
| | |

**3. Main Ideas**

a. How did the Second Great Awakening influence the reform movement?

b. How did labor unions try to force business owners to improve working conditions?

c. What were women's contributions to the reform movement?

**4. Critical Thinking**

**Recognizing Effects** What was the long-term impact of the reform movement that took place in the mid-1800s?

**THINK ABOUT**
- the changes reformers made in education, temperance, prisons, and the care of the disabled
- which of those changes are still in effect today

**ACTIVITY OPTIONS**

**SPEECH**
**CIVICS**

Think of a modern problem that is similar to an issue discussed in this section. Give a **speech** or write a **letter** to a government official suggesting a reform.



### ASSESS & RETEACH

**Setting the Stage** Have students fill in the third row on the graphic organizer.

**Formal Assessment**
- Section Quiz, p. 216

**RETEACHING ACTIVITY**

Have students use a web such as the one below to organize information about the reform movements discussed in this section.

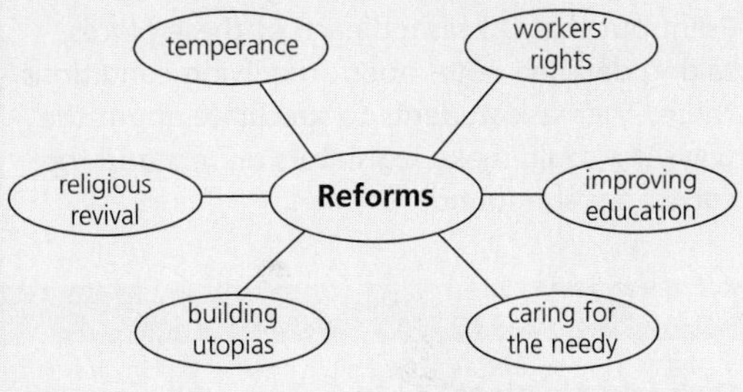

**In-Depth Resources: Unit 4**
- Reteaching Activity, p. 58

### Section 3 Assessment

**1. Terms & Names**

**revival,** p. 433
**Second Great Awakening,** p. 433
**temperance movement,** p. 434
**labor union,** p. 434
**strike,** p. 434
**Horace Mann,** p. 435
**Dorothea Dix,** p. 435

**2. Taking Notes**

poverty caused by drinking—laws that ban alcohol; unsafe work for little pay and long hours—strike; lack of education—public schools and reformed college admittance; mentally ill in jail—hospitals; unorganized prisons—children in special jails and prisoner rehabilitation

**3. Main Ideas**

**a.** It urged people to give up their sins and help others. **b.** They went on strike. **c.** temperance workers; women workers went on strike; tried to improve the care of the mentally ill; published a magazine giving women advice

**4. Critical Thinking**

The creation of public schools, mental hospitals, schools for the deaf and blind, and separate jails for children are all still in existence today.

**ACTIVITY OPTIONS**

**Alternative Assessment**
- Rubrics for a speech, 3.6
- Rubrics for a letter, 4.3

## INTERACTIVE PRIMARY SOURCE

**OBJECTIVE**
The student will be able to describe the living conditions of mentally ill people in jails and poorhouses during the early 1800s and the appeals made by Dorothea Dix on their behalf.

Primary Source Explorer
- *Report to the Massachusetts Legislature*

The Explorer will help students select and produce their own presentations.

Specific information about the document can be found in **A Closer Look.** To learn more about key people and events of the time, students should click on **Life in These Times. What Happened Next** will show the student the impact of the document and tie it to today.

## FOCUS & MOTIVATE

**Evaluating** Tell students that personal research is important in developing an understanding of complicated issues. Ask students to evaluate the extent of Dix's research into the problem of poor housing and care for mentally ill people. To help students evaluate the report by Dix, have students identify the locations Dix highlights for legislators. Point out that Dix visited each of these places, taking detailed notes about the living conditions there. Then ask students to speculate about the ways Dix could make legislators understand the conditions she found.

### MORE ABOUT . . .

**Dix's Investigations**
Dorothea Dix spent 18 months touring places in Massachusetts where mentally ill people were confined. Then she visited Western and Southern states as well as Europe in her efforts to improve care for mentally ill people. In Europe, she met with Pope Pius IX and harshly criticized a local asylum. The pope ordered an investigation and then instituted reforms at the hospital.

INTERACTIVE PRIMARY SOURCE

# Report to the Massachusetts Legislature

**Setting the Stage** After traveling to several places where the mentally ill were kept, Dorothea Dix wrote a report describing the conditions she had discovered. In 1843, she presented her report to lawmakers to alert them to the horrible treatment of the mentally ill. This report has been called the "first piece of social research ever conducted in America." An excerpt from Dorothea Dix's report follows. **See Primary Source Explorer**

### *Report to the Massachusetts Legislature*

Gentlemen: . . . I come to present the strong claims of suffering humanity. I come to place before the Legislature of Massachusetts the condition of the miserable, the desolate, the outcast. I come as the **advocate**[1] of helpless, forgotten, insane, and idiotic men and women; of beings sunk to a condition from which the most unconcerned would start with real horror; of beings wretched in our prisons, and more wretched in our **almshouses.**[2]

I must confine myself to a few examples, but am ready to furnish other and more complete details, if required.

I proceed, gentlemen, briefly to call your attention to the *present* state of insane persons confined within this **Commonwealth,**[3] in *cages, closets, cellars, stalls, pens! Chained, naked, beaten with rods,* and *lashed* into obedience.

I offer the following extracts from my notebook and journal.

*Springfield*: In the jail, one lunatic woman, furiously mad, a state **pauper,**[4] improperly situated, both in regard to the prisoners, the keepers, and herself. It is a case of extreme self-forgetfulness and oblivion to all the decencies of life, to describe which would be to repeat only the grossest scenes. She is much worse since leaving Worcester. In the almshouse of the same town is a woman apparently only needing **judicious**[5] care and some well-chosen employment to make it unnecessary to confine her in solitude in a dreary unfurnished room. Her appeals for employment and companionship are most touching, but the mistress replied "she had no time to attend to her."

*Lincoln:* A woman in a cage. *Medford:* One idiotic subject chained, and one in a close stall for seventeen years. *Pepperell:* One often doubly chained, hand and foot; another violent; several peaceable now. *Brookfield:* One man caged, comfortable. *Granville:* One often closely confined, now losing the use of his

**A CLOSER LOOK**

**ADVOCATE OF THE HELPLESS**

In earlier times, the term *idiotic* did not mean stupid. It was used to describe someone who was mentally retarded.

1. For what groups of people is Dix pleading for help?

**A CLOSER LOOK**

**JUDICIOUS CARE**

Dix describes a woman who needs only some care and a useful task to do.

2. What did the woman's keeper say when Dix pointed that out?

1. **advocate:** a person who pleads another person's cause.
2. **almshouses:** homes for poor people.
3. **Commonwealth:** one of four U.S. states whose constitution uses this term to describe their form of self-government; in this case, Massachusetts.
4. **pauper:** a person who lives on the state's charity.
5. **judicious:** wise and careful.



### TEACHING STRATEGY

**Finding Main Ideas** To help students work through the report, have them copy the graphic shown. In the center circle, write Abuses of People in Asylums. Direct students to put specific examples of abuses in the surrounding circles.

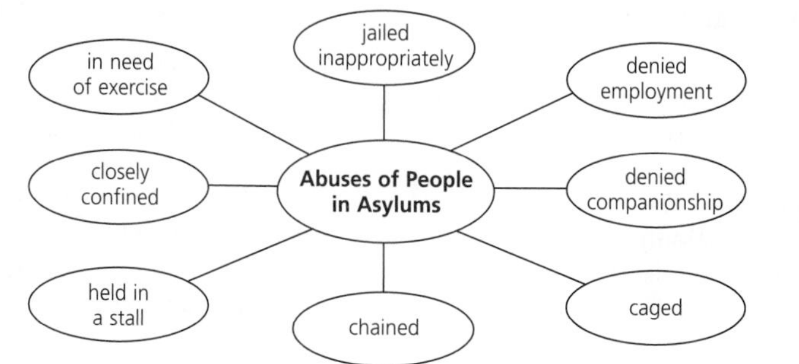

limbs from want of exercise. *Charlemont:* One man caged. *Savoy:* One man caged. *Lenox:* Two in the jail, against whose unfit condition there the jailer protests.

*Dedham:* The insane **disadvantageously**[6] placed in the jail. In the almshouse, two females in stalls, situated in the main building, lie in wooden bunks filled with straw; always shut up. One of these subjects is supposed curable. The overseers of the poor have declined giving her a trial at the hospital, as I was informed, on account of expense.

Besides the above, I have seen many who, part of the year, are chained or caged. The use of cages is all but universal. Hardly a town but can refer to some not distant period of using them; chains are less common; **negligences**[7] frequent; willful abuse less frequent than sufferings proceeding from ignorance, or want of consideration. I encountered during the last three months many poor creatures wandering reckless and unprotected through the country. . . . But I cannot **particularize**.[8] In traversing the state, I have found hundreds of insane persons in every variety of circumstance and condition, many whose situation could not and need not be improved; a less number, but that very large, whose lives are the saddest pictures of human suffering and degradation.

I give a few illustrations; but description fades before reality. . . .

Men of Massachusetts, I beg, I implore, I demand pity and protection for these of my suffering, outraged sex. . . . Become the benefactors of your race, the just guardians of the solemn rights you hold in trust. Raise up the fallen, **succor**[9] the desolate, restore the outcast, defend the helpless, and for your eternal and great reward receive the benediction, "Well done, good and faithful servants, become rulers over many things!"

6. **disadvantageously:** harmfully.
7. **negligences:** careless actions.
8. **particularize:** to name in detail.
9. **succor:** to give help during a time of need.

***A CLOSER LOOK***

**I HAVE SEEN MANY**

**Notice that Dix cites evidence from many different towns.**

**3. Why do you think she includes so many specific details in her report?**

***A CLOSER LOOK***

**MEN OF MASSACHUSETTS**

**When Dix says "Men of Massachusetts," she is still speaking to the members of the state legislature.**

**4. What does Dix want the Massachusetts Legislature to do?**

*Interactive Primary Source Assessment*

**1. Main Ideas**

a. On what evidence did Dorothea Dix base her report about "suffering humanity"?

b. How were the mentally ill treated in Massachusetts?

c. Who did Dorothea Dix ask to help to improve the care of the mentally ill?

**2. Critical Thinking**

**Evaluating** Dix succeeded in convincing the legislature to provide funds for new hospitals. What do you think made her report so persuasive?

**THINK ABOUT**
- the details included in the report
- how Dix got the information to write her report
- the techniques you would use to persuade someone



## INSTRUCT

Key Questions
- What role did Dix see for herself regarding the care of mentally ill people?
- Why does Dix offer so many examples of the way people with mental illnesses or mental handicaps are treated?
- What action does Dix want the legislators to take?
- What kind of reward does Dix suggest for those legislators who act to help mentally ill people?

## MORE ABOUT . . .

**Dix's Career**

Dix also made important contributions to nursing, although she had never received formal training in that profession. During the U.S. Civil War, she served as the Union's Superintendent of Female Nurses. Under her leadership, more than 2,000 women served as Union nurses during the war. At the time, most nurses were volunteers. They took care of their patients in any way necessary—including cleaning, cooking, and doing laundry.

## *Interactive Primary Source Assessment*

**1. Main Ideas**

**a.** on her personal visits to places where mentally ill people were confined and the conditions she witnessed there

**b.** chained; jailed; beaten; kept naked; kept in solitude; put in cages

**c.** the Massachusetts Legislature

**2. Critical Thinking**

**Possible Responses** Dix made a detailed case based on her own research, providing specific examples of the abuse of mentally ill people. She also appealed to the humanity and good will of the legislators, using emotionally charged language.

***A CLOSER LOOK***

1. the mentally ill and the mentally retarded
2. She didn't have time to take care of the woman.
3. to persuade the legislature to do something
4. to protect the mentally ill, especially women; to give them aid and to defend them

## SECTION OBJECTIVES

1. To describe the development of the abolitionist movement
2. To explain the significance of the Underground Railroad
3. To evaluate the results of the women's rights movement
4. To identify important early leaders in the fight for women's rights

**CRITICAL THINKING**

Drawing Conclusions, pp. 441, 445
Comparing, p. 441
Forming and Supporting Opinions, p. 442

**Why It Matters Now**
- Working for Change, pp. 27–28

## FOCUS & MOTIVATE

### 5-MINUTE WARM-UP

**Making Inferences** These questions deal with pressures for reform.

1. Look at the drawing and read the caption on page 445. What does this suggest about the roles of men and women?
2. What do you think the cartoonist's attitude toward women's rights is?

**Warm-Up Transparency WT14**

## INSTRUCT

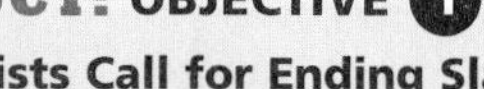
### INSTRUCT: OBJECTIVE 1

**Abolitionists Call for Ending Slavery/ Eyewitnesses to Slavery**

Key Questions
- When did the abolitionist movement begin? What success did it have up to 1807?
- Who were some of the prominent abolitionists?
- What roles did former slaves play in the abolitionist movement?

**In-Depth Resources: Unit 4**
- Guided Reading, p. 46

# 4 Abolition and Women's Rights

**MAIN IDEA**

The spread of democracy led to calls for freedom for slaves and more rights for women.

**WHY IT MATTERS NOW**

The abolitionists and women reformers of this time inspired 20th-century reformers.

**TERMS & NAMES**
abolition
Frederick Douglass
Sojourner Truth
Underground Railroad
Harriet Tubman
Elizabeth Cady Stanton
Seneca Falls Convention
suffrage

### ONE AMERICAN'S STORY

**African-American poet Frances Ellen Watkins Harper was free but grew up in the slave state of Maryland. Harper often wrote about the suffering of enslaved persons. For example, the poem excerpt below describes a woman whose child has been taken from her and sold.**

*A VOICE FROM THE PAST*

They tear him from her circling arms,
Her last and fond embrace.
Oh! never more may her sad eyes
Gaze on his mournful face.

No marvel, then, these bitter shrieks
Disturb the listening air:
She is a mother, and her heart
Is breaking in despair.

**Frances Ellen Watkins Harper,** "The Slave Mother"

**Frances Ellen Watkins Harper impressed audiences with her speaking ability as she called for reform.**

**In the 1850s, Harper lectured against slavery throughout the North. Later in her life, she called for other reforms, such as the right to vote for women. As this section explains, many individuals in the mid-1800s demanded equal rights for African Americans and women.**

## 1 Abolitionists Call for Ending Slavery

**Abolition,** the movement to end slavery, began in the late 1700s. By 1804, most Northern states had outlawed slavery. In 1807, Congress banned the importation of African slaves into the United States. Abolitionists then began to demand a law ending slavery in the South.

David Walker, a free African American in Boston, printed a pamphlet in 1829 urging slaves to revolt. Copies of this pamphlet, *Appeal . . . to the Colored Citizens of the World,* made their way into the South. This angered slaveholders. When Walker heard that his life was in danger, he refused to run away. Shortly afterward, he died mysteriously.

Northern whites also fought slavery. In 1831, William Lloyd Garrison began to publish an abolitionist newspaper, *The Liberator,* in Boston. Of



### RECOMMENDED RESOURCES

**In-Depth Resources: Unit 4**
- Guided Reading, p. 46
- Geography Application, pp. 49–50
- Primary Sources, pp. 51–52
- Literature Selection, pp. 53–55
- Reteaching Activity, p. 59
- History Workshop Resources, p. 61

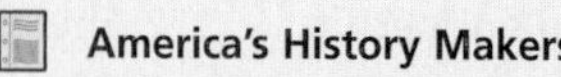
**Reading Study Guide** (Spanish and English), pp. 145–146

**America's History Makers**
- Elizabeth Cady Stanton, pp. 55–56
- Harriet Tubman, pp. 57–58

**Why It Matters Now**
- Working for Change, pp. 27–28

**American History Plays**
- *Lucy Stone, Champion of Women's Rights* by Claire Boyko

**Formal Assessment**
- Section Quiz, p. 217

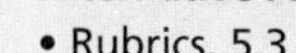
**Alternative Assessment**
- Rubrics, 5.3
- Rubrics, 3.1

**Access for Students Acquiring English/ESL**
- Guided Reading, p. 96
- Geography Application, pp. 98–99

**Technology Resources**

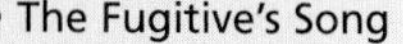
**Humanities Transparency HT28**
- The Fugitive's Song

**Electronic Teacher Tools with Test Maker**

his antislavery stand, he wrote, "I will not retreat a single inch—AND I WILL BE HEARD." Many people hated his views. In 1834, a furious mob in Boston grabbed Garrison and dragged him toward a park to hang him. The mayor stepped in and saved his life.

*Reading*History
**A. Drawing Conclusions** How would the Grimké sisters' background help them as abolitionist speakers?
**A. Possible Response** They could give eyewitness testimony of the horrors of slavery.

Two famous abolitionists were Southerners who had grown up on a plantation. Sisters Sarah and Angelina Grimké believed that slavery was morally wrong. Moving north, they became Quakers and joined the American Anti-Slavery Society. Women were not supposed to lecture in public in the mid-1800s. However, the Grimké sisters spoke out for abolition even though they received criticism for it.

In 1840, abolitionists closely watched the trial of a group of Africans who had rebelled on a slave ship, *Amistad.* Would the rebellious Africans be sent to slavery in Cuba or set free? To win proslavery votes, President Martin Van Buren tried to send them to Cuba. But former president John Quincy Adams helped win their freedom before the Supreme Court in 1841. The Africans returned home in 1842.

## Eyewitnesses to Slavery

Two moving abolitionist speakers, **Frederick Douglass** and **Sojourner Truth,** spoke from their own experience of slavery. In 1842, Douglass announced in a speech that he was a thief: "I stole this head, these limbs, this body from my master, and ran off with them."

Douglass's courage and talent at public speaking won him a career as a lecturer for the Massachusetts Anti-Slavery Society. Poet James Russell Lowell said of him, "The very look and bearing of Douglass are an irresistible logic against the oppression of his race."

People who opposed abolition spread rumors that the brilliant speaker could never have been a slave. To prove them wrong, in 1845 Douglass published an autobiography that vividly narrated his slave experiences. Afterwards, he feared recapture by his owner, so he left America for a two-year speaking tour of Great Britain and Ireland. When Douglass returned, he bought his freedom. He began to publish an antislavery newspaper.

Sojourner Truth also began life enslaved. Originally named Isabella, Sojourner Truth was born in New York State. In 1827, she fled her owners and went to live with Quakers, who set her free. They also helped her win a court battle to recover her young son. He had been sold illegally into slavery in the South.

**B. Possible Responses** Both were former slaves; both were good speakers.
*Reading*History
**B. Comparing** How were Frederick Douglass and Sojourner Truth similar as abolitionists?

A devout Christian, Truth changed her name in 1843 to reflect her life's work: to sojourn (or stay temporarily in a place) and "declare the truth to the people." Speaking for abolition, she drew huge crowds throughout the North.

### AMERICA'S HISTORY MAKERS

**FREDERICK DOUGLASS**
**1817–1895**

Douglass, born Frederick Bailey, was the son of a black mother and a white father. When he was eight, his owner sent him to be a servant for the Auld family. Mrs. Auld defied state law and taught young Frederick to read.

At the age of 16, Douglass returned to the plantation as a field hand. He endured so many whippings he later wrote, "I was seldom free from a sore back."

In 1838, he escaped to the North by hopping a train with a borrowed pass. To avoid recapture, he changed his last name.

**How did Mrs. Auld unknowingly help Douglass become an abolitionist leader? Explain.**



### MORE ABOUT . . .

**Abolition Around the World**

By the end of the Revolution, slavery was still permitted in many European colonies. The British banned the slave trade within their empire in 1807. They abolished slavery altogether in their Caribbean colonies in 1834. Slavery was banned gradually throughout much of Latin America during the 1800s. Slavery in India was abolished by 1861 and in much of Africa by the end of the 1800s. China freed slaves in that country in 1910. Although illegal, slavery nonetheless continues secretly in parts of the world today.

 **In-Depth Resources: Unit 4**
- Primary Source: from the *Liberator,* p. 51

### AMERICA'S HISTORY MAKERS

**Frederick Douglass**

Douglass took his new last name from the hero of *The Lady of the Lake,* a long narrative poem by the Scottish writer Sir Walter Scott. The Douglass in Scott's poem returns home to Scotland years after his entire family has been banished. In 1877, Douglass visited St. Michaels, Maryland, where he had been held as a slave and worked as a field hand. He called on Thomas Auld, his former owner. Auld starved his slaves and gave Douglass many beatings. The elderly Auld apologized for his actions as a slaveholder but also tried to defend them.

**Answer: She taught him to read. This is probably one reason for his great skill as a speaker.**

 **In-Depth Resources: Unit 4**
- Geography Application, pp. 49–50
- Literature Selection: from *Narrative of the Life of Frederick Douglass,* pp. 53–55

 **Humanities Transparency HT28**
- The Fugitive's Song

### ACTIVITY OPTIONS

**INTERDISCIPLINARY LINK: SPEECH** — BLOCK SCHEDULING

**ANALYZING SPEECHES**

**Class Time** One class period

**Task** Analyzing a speech by Frederick Douglass

**Purpose** To evaluate a primary source and to appreciate the eloquence of a great orator

**Supplies Needed**
- Internet access (optional)

**Activity** Present the following quote from an 1852 speech by Frederick Douglass. Tell students that the speech was in honor of the Fourth of July. "This Fourth [of] July is yours, not mine. You may rejoice, I must mourn . . . above your national, tumultuous joy, I hear the mournful wail of millions!" Ask students to write a short paragraph explaining why Douglass says that he cannot celebrate the Fourth of July. The complete speech and others by Douglass may be found by visiting www.mcdougallittell.com

**INSTRUCT: OBJECTIVE 2**

**The Underground Railroad/Harriet Tubman**

Key Questions

- How did the Underground Railroad operate?
- How did Harriet Tubman fight against slavery?

## *Now and* then

**The Underground Railroad**

Some historians estimate that somewhere between 30,000 and 100,000 enslaved Americans traveled the Underground Railroad, beginning in the 1830s and ending at the close of the Civil War. The Underground Railroad Network to Freedom Act, passed by Congress in 1998, instructed the National Park Service to identify and locate important places along the Underground Railroad. By mid-1999, about three dozen sites had been located. Each site has a plaque describing its importance to those seeking freedom.

## MORE ABOUT . . .

**Harriet Tubman**

When Harriet Tubman made her escape from the plantation on Maryland's eastern shore where she was a field hand, she was unable to persuade her brothers and her husband to come with her. When she reached Pennsylvania, she said in a later account, she was free, but she was alone—"a stranger in a strange land." Eventually, Tubman helped to guide six of her brothers, her elderly parents, and a number of other relatives to freedom. During the Civil War, Tubman served as a nurse, scout, and spy for the Union army. She also helped locate and free enslaved African Americans living in the path of advancing Union troops.

**America's History Makers**

- Harriet Tubman, pp. 57–58

## 2 The Underground Railroad

Some abolitionists wanted to do more than campaign for laws ending slavery. Some brave people helped slaves escape to freedom along the Underground Railroad. Neither underground nor a railroad, the **Underground Railroad** was actually an aboveground series of escape routes from the South to the North. On these routes, runaway slaves traveled on foot. They also took wagons, boats, and trains.

Some enslaved persons found more unusual routes to freedom. For example, Henry Brown persuaded a white carpenter named Samuel A. Smith to pack him in a wooden box and ship him to Philadelphia. The box was only two and one half feet deep, two feet wide, and three feet long. It bore the label "This side up with care." Despite the label, Brown spent several miserable hours traveling head down. At the end of about 24 hours, Henry "Box" Brown climbed out of his box a free man in Philadelphia. Brown eventually made his way to Boston and worked on the Underground Railroad.

On the Underground Railroad, the runaways usually traveled by night and hid by day in places called stations. Stables, attics, and cellars all served as stations. At his home in Rochester, New York, Frederick Douglass hid up to 11 runaways at a time.

*Reading*History

**C. Reading a Map** The map on page 447 shows the routes of the Underground Railroad. Notice that most of these routes led to Canada.

### *Now and* then

**THE UNDERGROUND RAILROAD**

In 1996, historian Anthony Cohen took six weeks to travel from Maryland to Canada. Cohen followed the paths runaway slaves had taken 150 years earlier. He is shown below arriving in Canada.

Cohen walked, sometimes as much as 37 miles in a day. He also hitched rides on trains and canal boats.

About those long-ago slaves fleeing toward the hope of freedom, Cohen said, "They had no choice. . . . Nobody would do this if they didn't have to."

## Harriet Tubman

The people who led the runaways to freedom were called conductors. One of the most famous conductors was **Harriet Tubman.** Born into slavery in Maryland, the 13-year-old Tubman once tried to save another slave from punishment. The angry overseer fractured Tubman's skull with a two-pound weight. She suffered fainting spells for the rest of her life but did not let that stop her from working for freedom. In 1849, Tubman learned that her owner was about to sell her. Instead, she escaped. She later described her feelings as she crossed into the free state of Pennsylvania: "I looked at my hands to see if I was the same person now that I was free. There was such a glory over everything."

After her escape, Harriet Tubman made 19 dangerous journeys to free enslaved persons. The tiny woman carried a pistol to frighten off slave hunters and medicine to quiet crying babies. Her enemies offered $40,000 for her capture, but no one caught her. "I never run my train off the track and I never lost a passenger," she proudly declared. Among the people she saved were her parents.

D. Possible Responses They knew how bad slavery was; they felt grateful to the people who helped them and wanted to repay that kindness by helping others.

*Reading*History

**D. Forming and Supporting Opinions** Why do you think escaped slaves such as Brown, Douglass, and Tubman risked their lives to help free others?

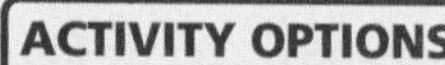

**ACTIVITY OPTIONS**

**INTERDISCIPLINARY LINK: LANGUAGE ARTS** — BLOCK SCHEDULING

**WRITING POEMS**

**Class Time** One class period

**Task** Creating poems for travelers on the Underground Railroad

**Purpose** To create a poem showing an understanding of the difficulty and risks of trying to escape from slavery

**Supplies Needed**

- Words to song "Follow the Drinking Gourd." Visit www.mcdougallitell.com
- Atlases

**Activity** Read the spiritual "Follow the Drinking Gourd" to the class (or play it) and point out some of the symbols it uses to guide escaping slaves to freedom, such as "drinking gourd" for the Big Dipper. Tell students to write their own poem (or song) offering secret advice to runaways on the Underground Railroad to help them reach freedom. Tell students to use an atlas and the map on page 447 for information about the geographic features of the route they will describe.

**Reformers' Hall of Fame**

**William Lloyd Garrison**

Even after being threatened with hanging, Garrison continued to publish his antislavery newspaper, *The Liberator.*

**Sojourner Truth and Harriet Tubman**

Truth spoke out for both abolition and women's rights. Tubman risked her life leading people to freedom on the Underground Railroad.

**Lucretia Mott and Susan B. Anthony**

An abolitionist, Mott also helped lead the movement for women's rights. Anthony fought for women's suffrage into the 20th century.

## 3 Women Reformers Face Barriers

Other women besides the Grimké sisters and Sojourner Truth were abolitionists. Two of these were Lucretia Mott and **Elizabeth Cady Stanton.** Mott and Stanton were part of an American delegation that attended the World Anti-Slavery Convention in London in 1840. These women had much to say about their work. Yet when they tried to enter the convention, they were not allowed to do so. Men angrily claimed that it was not a woman's place to speak in public. Instead, the women had to sit silent behind a heavy curtain.

Vocabulary
**delegation:** a group that represents a larger group

To show his support, William Lloyd Garrison joined them. He said, "After battling so many long years for the liberties of African slaves, I can take no part in a convention that strikes down the most sacred rights of all women."

Stanton applauded Garrison for giving up his chance to speak on abolition, the cause for which he had fought so long. "It was a great act of self-sacrifice that should never be forgotten by women."

However, most people agreed with the men who said that women should stay out of public life. Women in the 1800s enjoyed few legal or political rights. They could not vote, sit on juries, or hold public office. Many laws treated women—especially married women—as children. Single women enjoyed some freedoms, such as being able to manage their own property. But in most states, a husband controlled any property his wife inherited and any wages she might earn.

As the convention ended, Stanton and Mott decided it was time to demand equality for women. They made up their minds to hold a convention for women's rights when they returned home.





### MORE ABOUT . . .

**Lucretia Mott**

Lucretia Coffin Mott and her husband, James Mott, were ardently opposed to slavery. In the early 1800s, they began to boycott all goods produced by slave labor. The Motts did without sugar and molasses. They gave their children special candy made with free labor, although they all agreed it did not taste very good. However, James Mott was in the cotton business and feared that his family would sink into poverty if he gave it up. In 1830, James Mott finally decided he could no longer deal in cotton. He switched his business to wool and after a few months his business was quite successful. Lucretia Mott spoke in Quaker meetings about her refusal to use slave products. She became known as an abolitionist.

### INSTRUCT: OBJECTIVE 3

**Women Reformers Face Barriers/ The Seneca Falls Convention**

Key Questions

- What barriers to equality did women face in the early and mid-1800s?
- How did the abolitionist movement lay the groundwork for the fight for women's rights?
- What did delegates to the Seneca Falls Convention include in their Declaration of Sentiments and Resolutions?

**In-Depth Resources: Unit 4**

- Primary Source: The Seneca Falls Declaration and Resolutions, p. 52

### ACTIVITY OPTIONS

**MULTIPLE LEARNING STYLES: LOGICAL**

BLOCK SCHEDULING

**BOARD GAME**

**Class Time** One class period

**Task** Planning board games about the women's rights movement

**Purpose** To synthesize and analyze information about the women's rights movement

**Supplies Needed**

- Construction paper
- Markers
- Index cards

**Activity** Have student groups plan board games about the women's rights movement. The basic rules should require players to move from start to finish along the game route by correctly answering questions about barriers women faced, the Seneca Falls Convention, and important individuals. Students should divide these tasks: writing questions on the fronts of cards, answering questions on the backs of cards, designing the game board, and writing game rules. You may want to take additional class periods to complete the game. Groups may then exchange and play the board games.

## AMERICA'S HISTORY MAKERS

**Elizabeth Cady Stanton**

Stanton's father was a distinguished New York state lawyer. Many of his clients were women facing poverty because the laws gave all their money—whether from inheritances or earnings—to their husbands. Sometimes husbands drank or gambled away the money. Some widows were dependent on their sons for money to live on, even though the money had been theirs to begin with. In addition, women who divorced usually lost the right to visit their children, without regard to their reasons for leaving their husbands. New York state laws gave a father the exclusive guardianship of his children, even if he was a drunkard or abusive. Later in life, Stanton worked to change legislation involving the rights of women.

**Possible Response:** She was not satisfied with proving that she was as good as men but sought equality for all women.

 **America's History Makers**
- Elizabeth Cady Stanton, pp. 55–56

## INSTRUCT: OBJECTIVE 4

**Continued Calls for Women's Rights**

Key Questions
- How did Maria Mitchell contribute to the women's movement?
- What was Susan B. Anthony's role in the women's movement?
- How successful was the women's movement in the 1800s?

---

**AMERICA'S HISTORY MAKERS**

**ELIZABETH CADY STANTON**
**1815–1902**

Elizabeth Cady Stanton's first memory was the birth of a sister when she was four. So many people said, "What a pity it is she's a girl!" that Stanton felt sorry for the new baby. She later wrote, "I did not understand at that time that girls were considered an inferior order of beings."

When Stanton was 11, her only brother died. Her father said, "Oh, my daughter, I wish you were a boy!" That sealed Stanton's determination to prove that girls were just as important as boys.

**How did Stanton's childhood experiences motivate her to help other people besides herself?**

## The Seneca Falls Convention

Stanton and Mott held the **Seneca Falls Convention** for women's rights in Seneca Falls, New York, on July 19 and 20, 1848. The convention attracted between 100 and 300 women and men, including Frederick Douglass.

Before the meeting opened, a small group of planners debated how to present their complaints. One woman read aloud the Declaration of Independence. This inspired the planners to write a document modeled on it. The women called their document the Declaration of Sentiments and Resolutions. Just as the Declaration of Independence said that "All men are created equal," the Declaration of Sentiments stated that "All men and women are created equal." It went on to list several complaints or resolutions. Then it concluded with a demand for rights.

*A VOICE FROM THE PAST*

Now, in view of this entire disenfranchisement [denying the right to vote] of one-half the people of this country, their social and religious degradation—in view of the unjust laws above mentioned, and because women do feel themselves aggrieved, oppressed, and fraudulently deprived of their most sacred rights, we insist that they have immediate admission to all the rights and privileges which belong to them as citizens of the United States.

Seneca Falls Declaration of Sentiments and Resolutions, 1848

*Reading* **History**

**E. Using Primary Sources** Why did the women at the Seneca Falls Convention believe they deserved rights and privileges?

E. Possible Responses because they make up half the population; because they are citizens of the United States

Every resolution won unanimous approval from the group except **suffrage,** or the right to vote. Some argued that the public would laugh at women if they asked for the vote. But Elizabeth Cady Stanton and Frederick Douglass fought for the resolution. They argued that the right to vote would give women political power that would help them win other rights. The resolution for suffrage won by a slim margin.

The women's rights movement was ridiculed. In 1852, the *New York Herald* poked fun at women who wanted "to vote, and to hustle with the rowdies at the polls" and to be men's equals. The editorial questioned what would happen if a pregnant woman gave birth "on the floor of Congress, in a storm at sea, or in the raging tempest of battle."

## 4 Continued Calls for Women's Rights

In the mid-1800s, three women lent powerful voices to the growing women's movement. Sojourner Truth, Maria Mitchell, and Susan B. Anthony each offered a special talent.

In 1851, Sojourner Truth rose to speak at a convention for women's rights in Ohio. Some participants hissed their disapproval. Because Truth supported the controversial cause of abolition, they feared her



---

**ACTIVITY OPTIONS**

**INDIVIDUAL NEEDS: GIFTED AND TALENTED**

**DEBATING WOMEN'S RIGHTS**

**Class Time** Two class periods

**Task** Debating the issue of women's rights

**Purpose** To research the complaints and resolutions listed in the Declaration of Sentiments and prepare to debate a related question

**Supplies Needed**
- Reference materials on the issue of women's rights
- Internet access for additional resources

**Activity** Have students research some of the issues discussed at the Seneca Falls Convention. Then have them formulate a resolution to debate, such as *Women have equal rights to education,* or *Women should be allowed to own property.* Once students have agreed on a resolution, assign students to argue each side of the issue. Review the rules of debate with the students and set time limits. You might want to have students debate in front of the rest of the class and have the audience vote to determine the winning team.

appearance would make their own cause less popular. But Truth won applause with her speech that urged men to grant women their rights.

*A VOICE FROM THE PAST*

I have heard much about the sexes being equal. I can carry as much as any man, and can eat as much too, if I can get it. I am as strong as any man. . . . If you have woman's rights give it to her and you will feel better. You will have your own rights, and they won't be so much trouble.

**Sojourner Truth,** quoted by Marius Robinson, convention secretary

The scientist Maria Mitchell fought for women's equality by helping to found the Association for the Advancement of Women. Mitchell was an astronomer who discovered a comet in 1847. She became the first woman elected to the American Academy of Arts and Sciences.

**This drawing shows a husband and wife fighting over who will "wear the pants in the family"—that is, who will rule the household.**

Susan B. Anthony was a skilled organizer who worked in the temperance and antislavery movements. She built the women's movement into a national organization. Anthony argued that a woman must "have a purse [money] of her own." To this end, she supported laws that would give married women rights to their own property and wages. Mississippi passed the first such law in 1839. New York passed a property law in 1848 and a wages law in 1860. By 1865, 29 states had similar laws. (Anthony also fought for suffrage. See Chapter 22.)

But women's suffrage stayed out of reach until the 1900s, and the U.S. government did not fully abolish slavery until 1865. As you will read in the next chapter, the issue of slavery began to tear the nation apart in the mid-1800s.

## Section 4 Assessment

**1. Terms & Names**

**Identify:**
- abolition
- Frederick Douglass
- Sojourner Truth
- Underground Railroad
- Harriet Tubman
- Elizabeth Cady Stanton
- Seneca Falls Convention
- suffrage

**2. Taking Notes**

On a time line like the one below, record important events in the historical development of the abolition movement.

1807 ——— 1865

Why does the time line end in 1865?

**3. Main Ideas**

a. Why were freedom of speech and freedom of the press important to the abolitionist movement?

b. What were Frederick Douglass's contributions to the abolitionist movement?

c. What were Elizabeth Cady Stanton's contributions to the women's rights movement?

**4. Critical Thinking**

**Drawing Conclusions** Why do you think that many of the people who fought for abolition also fought for women's rights?

**THINK ABOUT**
- why they opposed slavery
- the social and economic position of women
- what the two causes had in common

**ACTIVITY OPTIONS**

**TECHNOLOGY**
**DRAMA**

With a partner, act out a meeting between a reformer from Section 3 and one from Section 4. **Videotape** their conversation or **perform** it for the class.



## MORE ABOUT . . .

**Maria Mitchell**

Maria Mitchell (1818–1889) was born in the whaling town of Nantucket, Massachusetts. Her father plotted stars for navigation charts, and Maria learned astronomy by working with him. She never attended college because the few colleges open to women had no courses in astronomy.

Mitchell was the first woman elected to the American Academy of Arts and Sciences. She also earned an appointment as a professor of astronomy at Vassar College. In addition to many other accomplishments, Mitchell made important contributions to the study of sun spots.

## ASSESS & RETEACH

**Setting the Stage** Have students fill in the last row on the graphic organizer.

**Formal Assessment**
- Section Quiz, p. 217

**Critical Thinking Transparency CT40**
- Setting the Stage

### RETEACHING ACTIVITY

Write the section objectives on the board and then organize the class into groups of four. Have group members divide the section objectives among themselves, one per member. Each group member should write a short summary of the main ideas for his or her part of the section. Members should then share their summaries with the rest of the group.

**In-Depth Resources: Unit 4**
- Reteaching Activity, p. 59

## Section 4 Assessment

**1. Terms & Names**

**abolition,** p. 440
**Frederick Douglass,** p. 441
**Sojourner Truth,** p. 441
**Underground Railroad,** p. 442
**Harriet Tubman,** p. 442
**Elizabeth Cady Stanton,** p. 443
**Seneca Falls Convention,** p. 444
**suffrage,** p. 444

**2. Taking Notes**

1807—Congress outlaws importation of slaves; 1831—Garrison publishes *The Liberator;* 1841—the slaves of the *Amistad* win their freedom; 1845—Douglass publishes his autobiography; 1849—Tubman escapes and begins working on the Underground Railroad; 1865—the government abolishes slavery; because slavery is abolished

**3. Main Ideas**

**a.** to speak out against slavery; to publish antislavery newspapers
**b.** He spoke against slavery, wrote a book about his life as a slave, and worked on the Underground Railroad. **c.** She helped organize the Seneca Falls Convention.

**4. Critical Thinking**

because both were about gaining freedom and equality for an oppressed group

**ACTIVITY OPTIONS**

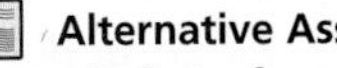
**Alternative Assessment**
- Rubrics for a videotape, 5.3
- Rubrics for an oral performance, 3.1

## GEOGRAPHY *in* HISTORY

**OBJECTIVE**

Students will analyze and interpret information from a map to understand the effects of geographic features on the antislavery effort known as the Underground Railroad.

 **BLOCK SCHEDULING**

### MORE ABOUT . . .

**The Fugitive Slave Act**

After the passage of the Fugitive Slave Act of 1850, movement of slaves to the North and Canada increased dramatically.

The law provided for federal commissioners to help catch runaway slaves and gave big rewards for returning runaways.

In some states, mobs prevented the return of fugitive slaves. Personal liberty laws preventing enforcement of the slave law were passed in other states.

## INSTRUCT

Key Questions

- What kind of personal qualities would a person need to travel on the Underground Railroad?
- Which cities or locations might be the most dangerous for an escaped slave?
- Why might cities in the Northeast be a good destination for fugitive slaves?

**MAP SKILL QUESTIONS**

How can you tell which states are free states and which are slave states?

Which foreign countries were destinations for runaway slaves?

How might weather or time of year affect the movement along the Underground Railroad?

## GEOGRAPHY *in* HISTORY

**PLACE AND MOVEMENT**

# The Underground Railroad

The Underground Railroad was a network of people and places that hid escaping slaves and helped them reach safety in the North or in Canada. One reason slaves often went to Canada is that a U.S. federal law required people to return runaway slaves to their owners. Defying this law, both whites and blacks helped slaves to escape.

The map on page 447 shows the main escape routes. As the map shows, most of the slaves who escaped came from states bordering free states, such as Kentucky and Virginia. Distances from there to the North were relatively short, increasing the chances of reaching freedom. However, the number of slaves who escaped from the Deep South, such as Georgia and South Carolina, was very small, because of the long distances that had to be traveled. While no one knows the exact number, historians estimate that 40,000 to 100,000 people may have used the Underground Railroad on their journey from slavery to freedom.

Among the many people who helped slaves to freedom was former slave Harriet Tubman (far left). She became a well-known guide on the Underground Railroad. She is pictured with her husband (third from left), along with other formerly enslaved people.

### ARTIFACT FILE

**Identity Tag** Enslaved persons were forced to wear tags that identified to whom they belonged.

**Freedom Marker** The "P" on the rock shown here told slaves that they were in Pennsylvania, a free state.



### MUSEUM CONNECTIONS

The Underground Railroad Center will make curricular materials available as well as a genealogy program for tracing African-American heritage.

The National Park Service has published a list of significant Underground Railroad sites and an Underground Railroad Special Resource Study. They can be obtained through the Superintendent of Documents at 202-512-1806.

For more on African-Canadian history and Underground Railroad sites in Canada, visit www.mcdougallittell.com

## On-Line Field Trip

**The National Underground Railroad Freedom Center** is being built in Cincinnati, Ohio. Its collections will include artifacts and primary sources like this poster, which shows that substantial rewards were offered for the recapture of slaves.

STOP THE THIEF!
One Hundred Dollars Reward.
Stolen from the Plantation of Mrs. E. S. FARRAR, on the night of Saturday last, two Negro Girls.
RICHARD T. FARRAR.
September 15, 1862.

Visit www.mcdougallittell.com for more information.

### CONNECT TO GEOGRAPHY

1. **Place** What geographic feature made it more likely that a slave in Missouri would escape to Michigan than to New York?
2. **Movement** In what way did the Underground Railroad differ from other migrations?

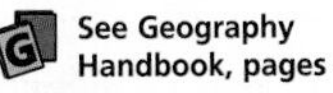
See Geography Handbook, pages 4–5.

### CONNECT TO HISTORY

3. **Drawing Conclusions** How did the Underground Railroad reflect the American people's division over slavery?



### CRITICAL THINKING ACTIVITY

**Recognizing Important Details** Have students make a graphic like the one below. Then have them study the map and list the physical features and geographic elements that would either help or hinder the movement of slaves in the Underground Railroad. Some elements may be on both sides. Students should explain the reasons for their choices.

| Aid the Escape | Hinder |
|---|---|
| | |
| | |
| | |
| | |
| | |

**Class Time** 15 minutes

### MORE ABOUT . . .

**Stations on the Underground Railroad**

Escape routes on the Underground Railroad stretched from Topeka, Kansas, in the West to locations along the United States-Canadian border. Buxton, Amherstburg, Chatham, and Sandwich in southwest Ontario were destinations for hundreds of fugitive slaves. Because of the high number of free blacks living in Baltimore, it was a popular location. It was easy for escaped slaves to blend into the population there. Both Harriet Tubman and Frederick Douglass operated out of the Baltimore area.

### CONNECT TO GEOGRAPHY

1. **Place** the Mississippi River
2. **Movement** Preparations were made in secret, and travelers were in danger of being caught and sent back.

### CONNECT TO HISTORY

1. **Drawing Conclusions** It showed that many Americans opposed slavery and were willing to help slaves escape, despite rewards for their return. It showed that many Northerners opposed slavery and were willing to work against it.

## TERMS & NAMES

1. **immigrant,** p. 423
2. **push-pull factors,** p. 424
3. **civil disobedience,** p. 431
4. **revival,** p. 433
5. **Second Great Awakening,** p. 433
6. **labor union,** p. 434
7. **abolition,** p. 440
8. **Underground Railroad,** p. 442
9. **Seneca Falls Convention,** p. 444
10. **suffrage,** p. 444

## REVIEW QUESTIONS

**Possible Responses**

1. to make a better living for themselves and their families; to escape religious or political discrimination
2. the Christmas tree; gymnasiums; kindergartens; hamburgers; hot dogs
3. It devastated Ireland, prompting 1.5 to 2 million Irish people to leave their homeland.
4. They painted the beauty and majesty of the American landscape.
5. that the spiritual world was more important than the physical world and that people can find truth within themselves through feeling and intuition
6. They depended on a sober workforce.
7. Slave codes made it illegal to teach an enslaved person to read. Few states allowed African-American children to attend public schools, and few colleges accepted African Americans.
8. Frances Ellen Watkins Harper; David Walker; William Lloyd Garrison; Frederick Douglass
9. It was a set of escape routes. Runaway slaves traveled by night and hid by day. "Conductors" helped guide the slaves to freedom.
10. It was a document in which women listed a number of complaints and demanded equal rights.

# Chapter 14 ASSESSMENT

## TERMS & NAMES

Briefly explain the importance of each of the following.

1. immigrant
2. push-pull factors
3. civil disobedience
4. revival
5. Second Great Awakening
6. labor union
7. abolition
8. Underground Railroad
9. Seneca Falls Convention
10. suffrage

## REVIEW QUESTIONS

**The Hopes of Immigrants (pages 423–428)**

1. What factors influenced so many immigrants to come to America in the 1800s?
2. What did Germans contribute to U.S. culture?
3. How did the potato famine affect Irish emigration?

**American Literature and Art (pages 429–432)**

4. How did American artists display the love of nature in their paintings?
5. What did the Transcendentalists believe?

**Reforming American Society (pages 433–439)**

6. Why did many business owners support the temperance movement?
7. Why was it hard for African Americans to receive an education?

**Abolition and Women's Rights (pages 440–447)**

8. Who published antislavery writings?
9. How did the Underground Railroad work?
10. What was the Seneca Falls Declaration of Sentiments and Resolutions?

## CRITICAL THINKING

**1. USING YOUR NOTES**

| | How People Influenced America in the mid-1800s |
|---|---|
| Immigrants | |
| Writers | |
| Reformers | |
| Abolitionists | |
| Women | |

Using your chart, answer the questions below.

a. Who influenced America to make reforms?
b. Compare the goals of abolitionists and women. How are they alike?

**2. ANALYZING LEADERSHIP**

Who is someone from this chapter who exercised leadership by standing up for an unpopular position?

**3. THEME: IMPACT OF THE INDIVIDUAL**

Judging from what you read in this chapter, what methods can individuals use to influence their society?

**4. APPLYING CITIZENSHIP SKILLS**

Who in this chapter displayed good citizenship by taking responsibility for their own behavior or by providing for their families? Give examples.

**5. FORMING AND SUPPORTING OPINIONS**

If someone asked you what was the most important reform of this period, what would you say? Why?

**Interact *with* History**

Think about the laws you proposed before you read the chapter. Has your opinion changed since you read the chapter?

## VISUAL SUMMARY

## A New Spirit of Change

**The Hopes of Immigrants**
Immigrants came to America from many European countries. They strongly influenced American life and culture.

**Reforming American Society**
Inspired by a religious revival, a reform movement swept the country. It aided schools, the workplace, and the disabled.

**American Literature and Art**
American writers and artists of the 1800s produced some of America's greatest works, which are still studied.

**Abolition and Women's Rights**
Whites and blacks united to fight slavery. Women abolitionists expanded their fight to include women's rights as well.



## CRITICAL THINKING

**Possible Responses**

1. **USING YOUR NOTES** **a.** writers; reformers; abolitionists; women **b.** They both sought greater freedom for an oppressed group.
2. **ANALYZING LEADERSHIP** Thoreau disobeyed the law by not paying taxes to support a government he disagreed with. Dix spoke out for the mentally ill even though women were not supposed to speak in public.
3. **THEME: IMPACT OF THE INDIVIDUAL** by creating art; by speaking or writing persuasively for change; by proposing new legislation
4. **APPLYING CITIZENSHIP SKILLS** Immigrants came hoping to provide better lives for their families. People took responsibility for their behavior by signing temperance pledges.
5. **FORMING AND SUPPORTING OPINIONS** labor unions, because they won benefits for workers; public schools, because education is the foundation for progress; laws giving women control of their earnings, because they should be treated the same as men

**Interact *with* History** Student answers will vary but should be supported with evidence from the chapter.

## HISTORY SKILLS

**1. INTERPRETING GRAPHS**

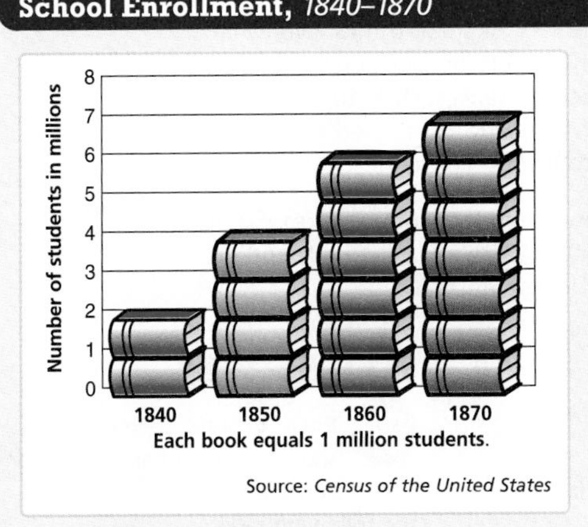


**Basic Graph Elements**

a. On the graph, what does each book stand for?

**Interpreting the Graph**

b. How did school enrollment change during the period from 1840 to 1870?

c. What is the difference in school enrollment between 1840 and 1870?

**2. INTERPRETING PRIMARY SOURCES**

Philip Younger escaped from slavery and eventually went to Canada. He dictated this narrative to Benjamin Drew, who included it in his *A North-Side View of Slavery.*

> I served in slavery fifty-five years, and am now nearly seventy-two years old. . . . I got off by skill. I have children and grandchildren in slavery. I had rather starve to death here, being a free man, than to have plenty in slavery. I cannot be a slave any more—nobody could hold me as a slave now, except in irons. Old as I am, I would rather face the Russian fire, or die at the point of the sword, than go into slavery.
>
> **Philip Younger,** quoted in *A North-Side View of Slavery*

a. What do you think Younger means by saying, "I got off by skill"?

b. How important is his freedom to him?

## ALTERNATIVE ASSESSMENT

**1. INTERDISCIPLINARY ACTIVITY: Literature**

**Reading a Poem Aloud** Choose a poem by Henry Wadsworth Longfellow that includes references to American history. Research the actual event to which the poem refers. Write an introduction that explains whether the poem portrays history accurately. Practice reading the poem until you are comfortable. Then present the poem to the class.

**2. COOPERATIVE LEARNING ACTIVITY**

**Making an Annotated Map** Working in a small group, create an annotated map of the Underground Railroad. Make an enlargement of the map of the Underground Railroad on page 447. Then annotate it, using some of the following suggestions.

- Do research to find the stories of slaves who escaped along the Underground Railroad.
- Put brief, typed summaries of a few stories on the map, with arrows connecting them to the right route.
- Draw illustrations of escape narratives and put them on the map.
- Research to discover appropriate songs and create a recording that can play as people view the map.

**3.**  **PRIMARY SOURCE EXPLORER**

**Preparing a Report** Dorothea Dix did not just stand before the legislature and talk about her own opinions. She gathered evidence and then wrote a persuasive report. Using the CD-ROM, library, and Internet, find out more about her report. Plan your own report that you could present to the student government.

- Choose a problem in your school that you think needs addressing.
- Find evidence of the problem. This may involve interviewing other students or observing events.
- Decide what you want the student government or school board to do about the problem.
- Write your report. Make sure to refer to the evidence that you gathered.

**4. HISTORY PORTFOLIO**

**Option 1** Review your section and chapter assessment activities. Select one that you think is your best work. Then use comments made by your teacher or classmates to improve your work and add it to your portfolio.

**Option 2** Review the questions that you wrote for What Do You Want to Know? on page 422. Write a short report in which you explain the answers to your questions. If any questions were not answered, do research to answer them. Add your report to your portfolio.



## ALTERNATIVE ASSESSMENT

1. INTERDISCIPLINARY ACTIVITY: **Literature**

**Readings should**
- have a clear introduction and conclusion.
- have adequate delivery and establish rapport with the audience.

2. COOPERATIVE LEARNING ACTIVITY

**Maps should**
- be clearly labeled and neatly presented.
- include a legend and title.
- Include either or both physical and political locations.
- have clearly described events and illustrations.

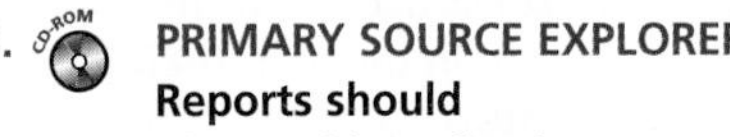
3. PRIMARY SOURCE EXPLORER

**Reports should**
- state the problem clearly.
- present supporting reasons for each position.
- use facts and examples to support major points.
- Use standard grammar, spelling, sentence structure, and punctuation.

4. HISTORY PORTFOLIO

**Option 1 Revised section or chapter assessment activities should**
- address teacher and peer responses to the selected work.
- solve problems present in the first versions of the work.

**Option 2 Short reports should**
- answer questions about the way individuals changed America in the mid-1800s.
- use evidence to develop and support ideas.
- cite sources of information.
- use standard grammar, spelling, sentence structure, and punctuation.

**Critical Thinking Transparency CT42**
- Visual Summary

**Formal Assessment**
- Chapter Test, Forms A and B, pp. 218–225

## HISTORY SKILLS

**Possible Responses**

1. INTERPRETING GRAPHS

**Basic Graph Elements**

**a.** Each book represents 1 million students.

**Interpreting the Graph**

**b.** It increased.

**c.** 5 million students

2. INTERPRETING PRIMARY SOURCES

**a.** He used his wits.

**b.** It is more important than his life.

## HISTORY WORKSHOP

**OBJECTIVE**
Students will create artifacts and make decisions in preparing for the journey to the United States as immigrants.

 **BLOCK SCHEDULING**

## PROCEDURE

Gather the materials listed in the "Toolbox." Divide the class into groups of four or five. Then review the steps for constructing "trunks" and items students will store in them on their journey to the United States.

 **In-Depth Resources: Unit 4**
- History Workshop Resources, p. 61

### MORE ABOUT . . .

**Journey Across the Atlantic**
Even if immigrants could physically carry more possessions, space was limited on ships. Many immigrants traveled to the United States on freight ships, which usually had room for them on return journeys after delivering timber, cotton, tobacco, and other materials to European ports. The cramped steerage quarters where immigrants stayed were poorly ventilated and often unsanitary. Diseases spread rapidly among the passengers.

## HISTORY WORKSHOP

# Pack Your Trunk

For immigrants, packing up to go to a new land required making hard decisions. Wealthy people could ship belongings ahead. Most immigrants, though, carried their belongings in burlap bags, knotted sheets, large baskets, or small trunks. Even children carried small bundles. Only the very basic items or very precious ones could be taken to the United States. Baggage contained practical items such as tools and household items. But some had personal items such as portraits of loved ones. A few people even carried bags of dirt from their home country!

ACTIVITY Pack a trunk with items needed for a new life in the United States. Explain why you chose the items that you have packed. Finally, write a letter to a friend or relative back in Europe about your journey to the United States.

### TOOLBOX

Each group will need:

| | |
|---|---|
| a shoebox | markers or colored pencils |
| assorted magazines (optional) | 3 x 5 note cards |
| craft sticks | masking tape |
| drawing paper or posterboard | styrofoam (optional) |

### STEP BY STEP

**1 Form groups.** Each group should consist of about four or five students. Assign group members the following tasks:
- Do research on what people brought with them when immigrating to the United States.
- Choose ten items that you will need for your new life.
- Present your items in class and give reasons for selecting them.

**2 Research what immigrants brought with them.** In the library or on the Internet (see Researching Your Project on the next page), research what immigrants brought with them to the United States. Make a list of everything you think you'll need for a new life in the United States. Some basic items included
- books
- favorite or special clothing
- toys
- important documents

Real immigrants brought these items to the United States: a mortar and pestle (used to grind spices or medicines), a shoe brush, a coffee grinder, and a paisley shawl.

450

### RECOMMENDED RESOURCES

**BOOKS FOR THE TEACHER**
Ferrie, Joseph P. ***Yankeys Now: Immigrants in the Antebellum United States, 1840–1860.*** New York: Oxford University Press, 1999.
Laxton, Edward. ***The Famine Ships: The Irish Exodus to America.*** New York: Henry Holt, 1998.

**VIDEOS**
***The Irish in America.*** A&E, 1997. Dramatic reenactments, illustrations, letters, and other source material.
***The Golden Door: Our Nation of Immigrants.*** Knowledge Unlimited, revised, 1996. A survey of the country's long history of immigration.

**BOOKS FOR THE STUDENTS**
Freedman, Russell. ***Immigrant Kids.*** New York: Puffin, 1995.
Reimers, David M. ***A Land of Immigrants.*** New York: Chelsea House, 1996.

**3** **Create your items.** From your list, choose ten items that you think will be most important to starting a new life. Then draw pictures of the selected items or cut pictures of them out of a magazine. Attach a craft stick to the back of the picture with masking tape.

**4** **Write reasons.** Think of why you selected each of the ten items. Write the reasons for each item on a separate 3 x 5 note card. Attach each note card to the back of the corresponding picture.

**5** **Decorate the shoebox to look like a trunk.** Using the masking tape, affix your pictures to the rim of the shoebox, or use styrofoam in the bottom of the box to insert the pictures.

**6** **Examine other groups' trunks.** Walk around the room and examine the contents of the other groups' trunks. Compare your trunk with that of your classmates. Share your reasons for selecting certain items.

## WRITE AND SPEAK

**Write a descriptive letter.** Use the point of view of an immigrant. Write a letter to someone in your homeland describing your journey to the United States. Your letter might also describe what you miss most (personal belongings or people, for example) since the move. Read the letters to others in your class.

## HELP DESK

For related information, see pages 423–428 in Chapter 14.

### Researching Your Project

- *They Sought a New World* by William Kurdek and Margaret S. Englehart
- *American Immigration* by Edward G. Hartmann

**Visit www.mcdougallittell.com for more information about the immigrant experience.**

### Did You Know?

Most immigrants traveled in **steerage** or third class. It was the lowest area of the ship, where a steering mechanism was located. A family "berth," or space allotted, in steerage was about six feet square.

Before World War I, fares in steerage to the United States from Europe were never more than $35 and by 1900 were as low as $10.

Shipping companies often fed herring (a kind of fish) to the immigrants. Herring was cheap and nourishing. It was also thought to help prevent seasickness.

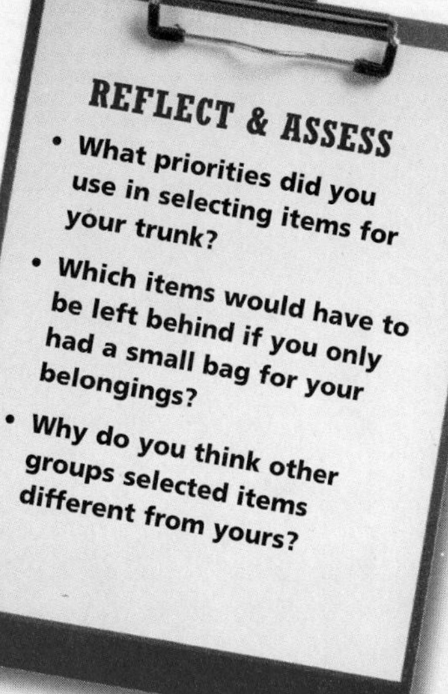

REFLECT & ASSESS
• What priorities did you use in selecting items for your trunk?
• Which items would have to be left behind if you only had a small bag for your belongings?
• Why do you think other groups selected items different from yours?




## MORE ABOUT . . .

**An Immigrant Contribution**

Immigrants brought more than clothing and other personal possessions. In the 1870s, Mennonites, members of a European Protestant church, emigrated from Russia. They brought hardy wheat strains that would grow well in the plains of the United States.

## REFLECT & ASSESS

1. Ask students to consider the usefulness of the items they chose.
2. Students might rank their items by priority, based on what they will need immediately upon arrival in the United States and what items are too personally important to be left behind.
3. Have students interview members of other groups to determine how they set priorities and made their decisions about what items to pack.

**Presentations should**

- provide a clear, concise statement.
- give a workable solution.
- evaluate the effectiveness of the solution.
- explain the originality of the solution.

## MAKING PERSONAL CONNECTIONS

Ask the class to suggest ways they can get involved today to help needy people in their own community. Have students research local organizations that help the needy and report on the kinds of volunteers those organizations need.

## STANDARDS FOR EVALUATION

### HISTORY WORKSHOP

**Trunks should**

- include characteristics of common trunks, such as latches and locks.
- include easily identified items.
- include index cards with written reasons why items were selected.

### WRITE AND SPEAK

**Letters should**

- be written from the point of view of an immigrant.
- describe the journey to the United States.
- provide examples or anecdotes about the journey and about the emotions experienced by the immigrant.

# UNIT 5

## A Nation Divided and Rebuilt 1846–1877



### BEFORE YOU READ

#### Previewing Unit 5

This unit begins as the sectional rivalry between the North and the South is growing deeper. Gradually the question of slavery—its expansion or its abolition—comes to dominate national politics. When Abraham Lincoln wins the presidency with support only from Northern voters, the Southern states decide to leave the Union. The North wins a long, bloody civil war. After the war, slavery is abolished. African Americans briefly hold many new legal rights—until the federal government stops enforcing civil rights laws.

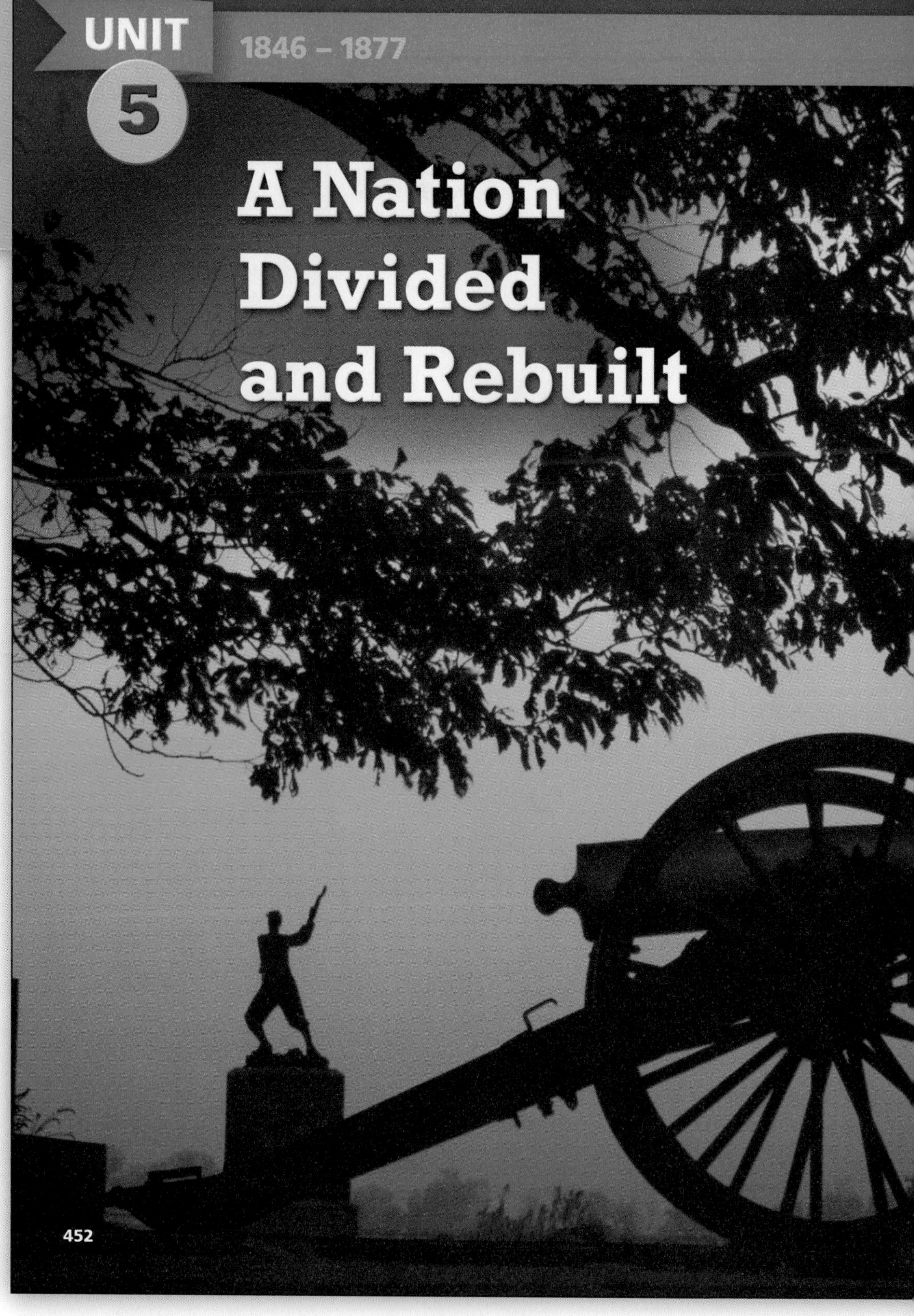

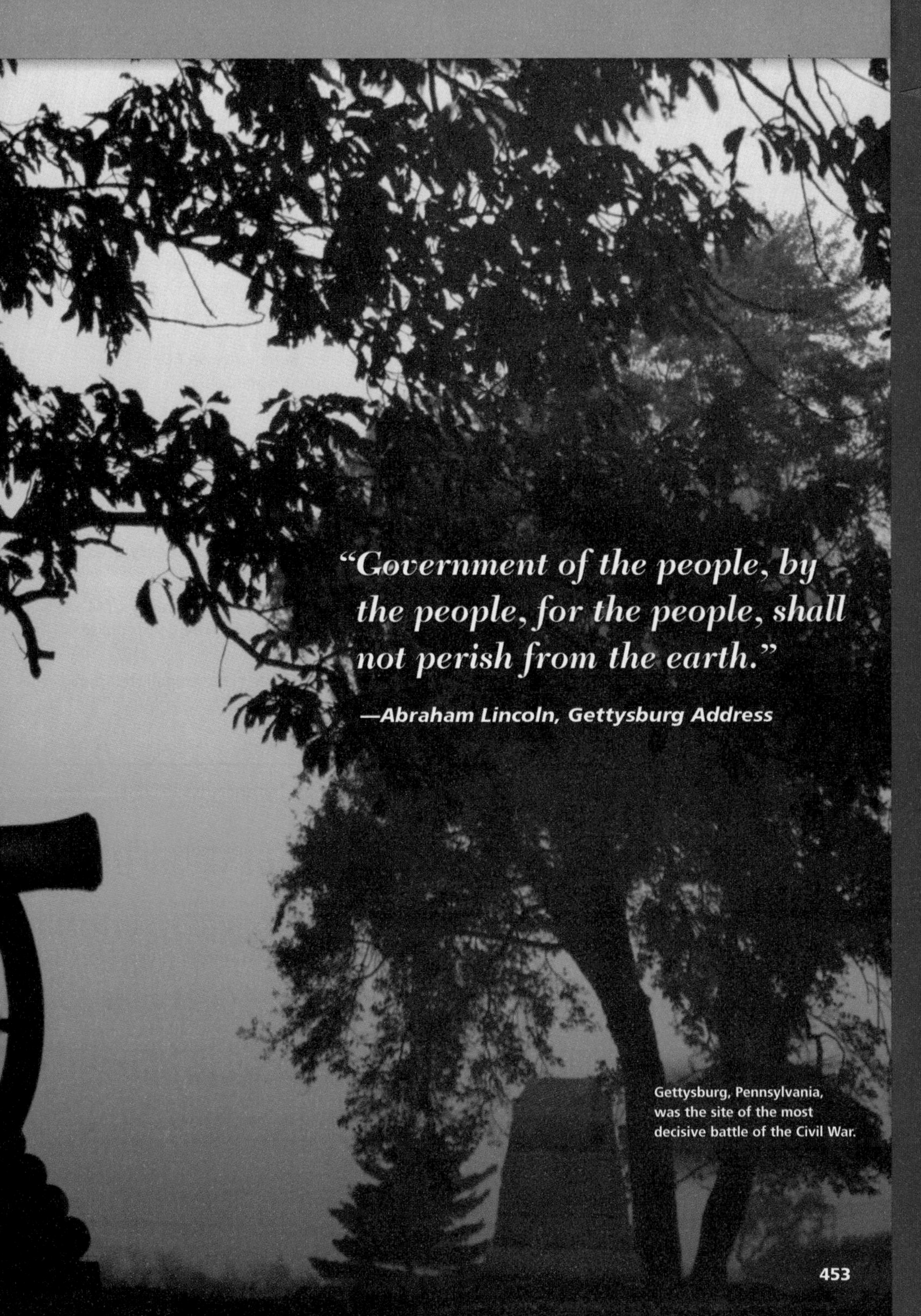

"Government of the people, by the people, for the people, shall not perish from the earth."
—Abraham Lincoln, Gettysburg Address

Gettysburg, Pennsylvania, was the site of the most decisive battle of the Civil War.



## HISTORY FROM VISUALS

**Interpreting the Photograph** The National Military Park at Gettysburg, Pennsylvania, looks peaceful and pleasant in this photograph. Tell students that in 1863, Gettysburg was the site of a three-day battle of the Civil War. More than 50,000 soldiers were killed, wounded, or captured during those three bloody days. Ask students to describe the scene in the photograph using words that appeal to each of the five senses. For example, what sounds might students expect to hear if they were part of the scene photographed? Then ask students to make a second list using words that describe the place during the height of the Battle of Gettysburg.

**Extension** Ask students to use the words from their two lists to write a poem about Gettysburg.

# CHAPTER 15 PLANNING GUIDE
# The Nation Breaking Apart 1846–1861

## CHAPTER RESOURCES

**CHAPTER OVERVIEW**

This chapter describes the growing hostility between the North and the South over slavery, especially its extension to new territories in the West. It also describes how this conflict came to dominate national politics, culminating in the secession of the Southern states after the election of Abraham Lincoln in 1860.

**COPYMASTERS**

**In-Depth Resources: Unit 5**
- Tracing Themes: Diversity and Unity, p. 2
- Building Vocabulary, p. 7

**Interdisciplinary Projects,** pp. 85–90

**TECHNOLOGY**

**Primary Source Explorer**

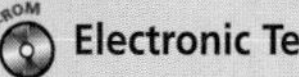
**Electronic Teacher Tools**

**Power Presentations CD-ROM**

**Chapter Summaries on CD** (English and Spanish)

## SECTION 1 Growing Tensions Between North and South pp. 457–461

**KEY IDEAS**

- Tensions grow between the North and the South over slavery.
- Conflict over extending slavery to the new lands taken from Mexico makes slavery a key issue in national politics.
- Congress passes the Compromise of 1850, which settles the problem only temporarily.

**COPYMASTERS**

**In-Depth Resources: Unit 5**
- Setting the Stage, p. 1
- Guided Reading, p. 3
- Reteaching Activity, p. 16

**Economics in History**
- King Cotton, p. 15

**TECHNOLOGY**

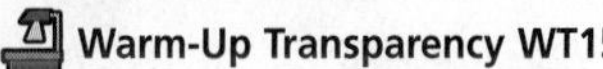
**Warm-Up Transparency WT15**

**Critical Thinking Transparency CT43**
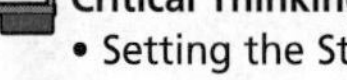
- Setting the Stage

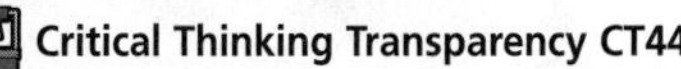
**Critical Thinking Transparency CT44**
- Cause and Effect: The Compromise of 1850

**ClassZone:** www.mcdougallittell.com

## SECTION 2 The Crisis Deepens pp. 462–465

- The Fugitive Slave Act and the controversial novel *Uncle Tom's Cabin* heighten sectional conflict.
- The Kansas-Nebraska Act turns Kansas into a battleground over slavery.
- Violence erupts in Congress when a Southerner attacks Senator Charles Sumner, a leading opponent of slavery.

**COPYMASTERS**

**In-Depth Resources: Unit 5**
- Setting the Stage, p. 1
- Guided Reading, p. 4
- Skillbuilder Practice: Sequencing Events, p. 8
- Literature Selection, pp. 13–15
- Reteaching Activity, p. 17

**America's History Makers**
- Harriet Beecher Stowe, pp. 59–60

**TECHNOLOGY**

**Warm-Up Transparency WT15**

**Humanities Transparency HT29**
- Poster: Eliza on Ice

**Critical Thinking Transparency CT43**
- Setting the Stage

**ClassZone:** www.mcdougallittell.com

## SECTION 3 Slavery Dominates Politics pp. 466–470

- The new Republican Party nominates an antislavery presidential candidate.
- In the *Dred Scott* case, the Supreme Court rules that Congress could not ban slavery in the territories.
- Abraham Lincoln becomes a national figure as a result of his debates with Stephen Douglas over the slavery issue.

**COPYMASTERS**

**In-Depth Resources: Unit 5**
- Setting the Stage, p. 1
- Guided Reading, p. 5
- Primary Sources, pp. 11–12
- Reteaching Activity, p. 18

**America's History Makers**
- Dred Scott, pp. 61–62

**Citizenship Today,** pp. 11–12, 89–90

**TECHNOLOGY**

**Warm-Up Transparency WT15**

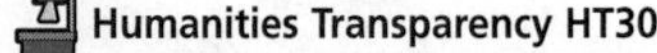
**Humanities Transparency HT30**
- *The Abraham Lincoln Family, 1861* by Francis Carpenter

**Geography Transparency GT15**
- The Slave Population of the South, 1860

**Critical Thinking Transparency CT43**
- Setting the Stage

**ClassZone:** www.mcdougallittell.com

## SECTION 4 Lincoln's Election and Southern Secession pp. 471–477

- The election of 1860 becomes two separate races for president, one in the North and one in the South.
- After Lincoln's election, Southern states secede and form the Confederate States of America.
- Northerners charge that secession is unconstitutional, and compromise fails.

**COPYMASTERS**

**In-Depth Resources: Unit 5**
- Setting the Stage, p. 1
- Guided Reading, p. 6
- Geography Application, pp. 9–10
- Reteaching Activity, p. 19

**American History Plays**
- from *Abe Lincoln in Illinois* by Robert Sherwood

**Why It Matters Now,** pp. 29–30

**Outline Map Activities,** pp. 29–30

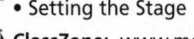

**TECHNOLOGY**

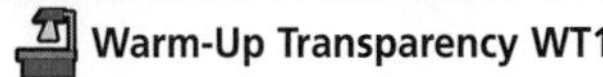
**Warm-Up Transparency WT15**

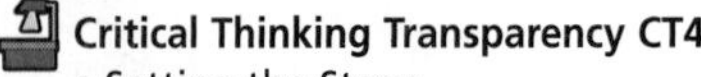
**Critical Thinking Transparency CT43**
- Setting the Stage

**Critical Thinking Transparency CT45**
- Visual Summary

**ClassZone:** www.mcdougallittell.com

 Pupil's Edition
Copymaster
 Overhead Transparency
Audio Library
 CD-ROM
Internet

## ASSESSMENT

**Chapter Assessment,** pp. 476–477

**Formal Assessment**
- Chapter Tests, Forms A and B, pp. 232–239

**Alternative Assessment Book**

**Electronic Teacher Tools with Test Maker**

**Section Assessment,** p. 461

**Formal Assessment**
- Section Quiz, p. 228

**Alternative Assessment Book**
- Rubrics for a documentary, 5.5
- Rubrics for a panel discussion, 3.2

**Electronic Teacher Tools with Test Maker**

**Section Assessment,** p. 465

**Formal Assessment**
- Section Quiz, p. 229

**Alternative Assessment Book**
- Rubrics for a book review, 4.7
- Rubrics for a drawing, 1.3

**Electronic Teacher Tools with Test Maker**

**Section Assessment,** p. 470

**Formal Assessment**
- Section Quiz, p. 230

**Alternative Assessment Book**
- Rubrics for a graph, 2.3
- Rubrics for a map, 2.1

**Electronic Teacher Tools with Test Maker**

**Section Assessment,** p. 475

**Formal Assessment**
- Section Quiz, p. 231

**Alternative Assessment Book**
- Rubrics for a speech, 3.6
- Rubrics for multimedia, 5.4

**Electronic Teacher Tools with Test Maker**

## CUSTOMIZING FOR INDIVIDUAL NEEDS

### Students Acquiring English/ESL

**Reading Study Guide** (English and Spanish), pp. 149–158

**Access for Students Acquiring English/ESL: Spanish Translations,** pp. 100–106

**Chapter Summaries on CD** (English and Spanish)

### Less Proficient Readers

**Reading Study Guide** (English and Spanish), pp. 149–158

**Chapter Summaries on CD** (English and Spanish)

### Gifted and Talented Students

**In-Depth Resources: Unit 1**
- Enrichment Activity, p. 20

**America's History Makers**
- Harriet Beecher Stowe, pp. 59–60
- Dred Scott, pp. 61–62

## CROSS-CURRICULAR CONNECTIONS

### Geography

St. George, Judith. ***Mason & Dixon's Line of Fire.*** New York: Putnam, 1991. Entertaining and original history of the Pennsylvania-Maryland border.

### Civics

Tackach, James. ***The Trial of John Brown.*** San Diego: Lucent, 1998. All the drama of the trial, with background information on Brown's past and his passionate commitment to abolition.

### Humanities: Music

Silverman, Jerry. ***Slave Songs (Traditional Black Music).*** Broomal, PA: Chelsea House Pub., 1993. Background information, guitar chords, and piano accompaniment for each of the 30 songs.

### Interdisciplinary Projects, pp. 85–90

- Math: Analyzing Data
- Science: The Steam Locomotive
- Language Arts: Political Debates
- Home Economics: Cotton Fabrics

### Literature

Rees, Douglas. ***Lightning Time.*** New York: Puffin Books, 1999. Theodore Worth is 14 when he first meets John Brown. Theodore later runs away from his Boston home to follow Brown to Harper's Ferry.

Stowe, Harriet Beecher. ***Uncle Tom's Cabin.*** New York: Modern Library, 1996. The saga of the unforgettable Eliza, Topsy, little Eva, and Uncle Tom. For advanced readers.

### McDougal Littell *The Language of Literature*

- Russell Freedman, from ***Lincoln: A Photobiography*** (biography)

### McDougal Littell Literature Connections

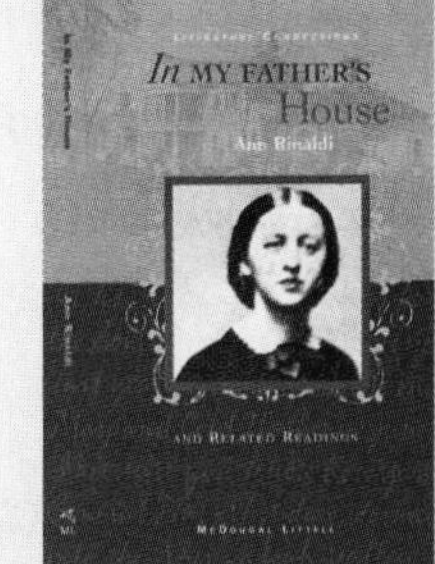


Ann Rinaldi

***In My Father's House***

This historical novel traces the impact of historical events on one Southern family from 1852 through the Civil War.

## ENRICHMENT ACTIVITIES

**Pupil's Edition, pp. 454–477**
**Interact with History,** p. 455
**Economics in History,** p. 458
**Citizenship Today,** p. 469

**In-Depth Resources: Unit 5**
- Geography Application: The South Votes to Secede, pp. 9–10
- Primary Source: African-American Protest Against the *Dred Scott* Decision, p. 11
- Primary Source: John Brown's Raid, p. 12
- Literature Selection: from *Uncle Tom's Cabin,* pp. 13–15

**America's History Makers**
- Harriet Beecher Stowe, pp. 59–60
- Dred Scott, pp. 61–62

**American History Plays**
- from *Abe Lincoln in Illinois* by Robert Sherwood

**Outline Map Activities**
- The Election of 1860, pp. 29–30

**Why It Matters Now**
- Divided Nations, pp. 29–30

**LESSON PLAN OPTIONS (50-MINUTE PERIOD)** (TE) = Teacher's Edition (PE) = Pupil's Edition

| | TEACHER-DIRECTED ACTIVITIES<br>Class Time: 15 minutes | STUDENT-CENTERED ACTIVITIES<br>Class Time: 25 minutes | INDIVIDUAL ACTIVITIES<br>Class Time: 10 minutes |
|---|---|---|---|
| **DAY 1**<br>Introduction<br>pp. 454–456 | **Presentation Options**<br>• Begin with a class discussion of the picture on p. 454 **(PE)**.<br>• Lead a class discussion on the "What Do You Know?" question in Setting the Stage, p. 456. Then introduce the graphic organizer for the chapter **(PE)**. | **Options for Cooperative Learning**<br>• Have student groups discuss the Interact with History questions, p. 455 **(PE)**.<br>• Have student groups respond to the "What Do You Want to Know?" question in Setting the Stage, p. 456 **(PE)**. | **Head Start on Homework Options**<br>• Have students skim Section 1 Main Idea, Why It Matters Now, Terms & Names, and the main headings, p. 457 **(PE)**.<br>• Have students begin Guided Reading activity and Building Vocabulary sheet. |
| **DAY 2**<br>Section 1<br>pp. 457–461 | **Presentation Options**<br>• Begin with the 5-Minute Warm-Up, p. 457 **(TE)**.<br>• Review the Section 1 Main Idea, Why It Matters Now, and Terms & Names, p. 457 **(PE)**.<br>• Lead the students through the Economics in History Feature, p. 458 **(TE)**. | **Options for Cooperative Learning**<br>• Divide students into groups to complete the Economics in History questions, p. 458 **(PE)**.<br>• Have student pairs work together to complete one of the Activity Options in the Section 1 Assessment, p. 461 **(PE)**. | **Head Start on Homework Options**<br>• Have students begin working on Section 1 Assessment, p. 461 **(PE)**.<br>• Have students complete the Geography Skillbuilder questions, p. 464 **(PE)**. |
| **DAY 3**<br>Section 2<br>pp. 462–465 | **Presentation Options**<br>• Begin with the 5-Minute Warm-Up, p. 462 **(TE)**.<br>• Choose 5 key questions for Objectives 1–4 to discuss with the class, pp. 462–465 **(TE)**.<br>• Lead the students through the Skillbuilder Mini-Lesson: Sequencing Events, p. 464 **(TE)**. | **Options for Cooperative Learning**<br>• Divide students into groups and have them complete the Extension Activities for the map, p. 464 **(TE)**.<br>• Have student pairs work together to complete one of the Activity Options in the Section 2 Assessment, p. 465 **(PE)**. | **Head Start on Homework Options**<br>• Have students begin working on Section 2 Assessment, p. 465 **(PE)**.<br>• Have students complete the Reading History questions for Section 3, p. 466–470 **(PE)**. |
| **DAY 4**<br>Section 3<br>pp. 466–470 | **Presentation Options**<br>• Begin with the 5-Minute Warm-Up, p. 466 **(TE)**.<br>• Choose 5 key questions for Objectives 1–4 to discuss with the class, pp. 466–469 **(TE)**. | **Options for Cooperative Learning**<br>• Divide students into groups and have them complete the Citizenship Today questions, p. 469 **(PE)**.<br>• Divide students into groups to have them complete the Interdisciplinary Link, Civics: The *Dred Scott* Case, p. 468 **(TE)**. | **Head Start on Homework Options**<br>• Have students begin working on Section 3 Assessment, p. 470 **(PE)**.<br>• Have students preview Section 4 Main Idea, Why It Matters Now, Terms & Names, and the main headings, p. 471 **(PE)**. |
| **DAY 5**<br>Section 4<br>pp. 471–475 | **Presentation Options**<br>• Begin with the 5-Minute Warm-Up, p. 471 **(TE)**.<br>• Choose 5 key questions for Objectives 1–4 to discuss with the class, pp. 471–474 **(TE)**.<br>• Lead the students through the Critical Thinking Activity, p. 474 **(TE)**. | **Options for Cooperative Learning**<br>• Divide students into groups and have them complete the Interdisciplinary Link, Government: Forming a Government, p. 473 **(TE)**.<br>• Have student pairs work together to complete one of the Activity Options in the Section 4 Assessment, p. 475 **(PE)**. | **Head Start on Homework Options**<br>• Have students complete the Setting the Stage graphic organizer for the chapter, p. 456 **(PE)**.<br>• Have students begin working on the Chapter Assessment, pp. 476–477 **(PE)**.<br>• Prepare for Chapter Test<br>**Formal Assessment,** pp. 232–239 |

**TEACHER-TESTED ACTIVITY** **Barbara Kennedy, Sylvan Middle School, Citrus Heights, California**

## THE ABOLITIONIST CAUSE

**Class Time** 30 minutes

**Task** Creating an advertisement for *Uncle Tom's Cabin*

**Purpose** To identify the antislavery message of *Uncle Tom's Cabin* and the audience at which the novel was aimed

**Supplies Needed**

- Biographical information on Harriet Beecher Stowe and reference material on *Uncle Tom's Cabin*
- Markers, colored pencils
- White art paper

**Activity** After reviewing information on Harriet Beecher Stowe and *Uncle Tom's Cabin,* divide students into groups to design an advertisement for the book. In planning their ads, groups should identify the target audience for the book and think about the message that will appeal to this audience. The ad should suggest the author's position on slavery and how she hopes readers will react to the book. Students might also include quotes from "book reviews" in their ads. When the ads are completed, students can present them to the class.

## BLOCK SCHEDULING — LESSON PLAN OPTIONS (90-MINUTE PERIOD)

### DAY 1

**Interact with History,** p. 455
**Class Time** 20 Minutes

Options for pacing and variety:

- **Peer Teaching** Working in groups of three, students can answer the "What Do You Think?" questions and share their answer to one of the questions with the class.
  **Class Time** 15 minutes

**Setting the Stage,** p. 456
**Class Time** 20 minutes

Options for pacing and variety:

- **Time Saver** Ask students to come to class with a list of "What Do You Want to Know?" questions. **Class Time** 10 minutes

**Section 1,** pp. 457–461
**Class Time** 50 minutes

Options for pacing and variety:

- **Peer Teaching** Have pairs of students create a two column chart comparing the Missouri Compromise and the Compromise of 1850.
  **Class Time** 30 minutes
- **Time Saver** Have students come to class with answers to the Connect to History and Connect to Today questions for the Economics in History feature on page 458. **Class Time** 5 minutes

### DAY 2

**Section 2,** pp. 462–465
**Class Time** 45 minutes

Options for pacing and variety:

- **History on Film** Extend students' knowledge of events leading up to the Civil War with *Causes of the Civil War,* Schlesinger, 1996.
  **Class Time** 35 minutes
- **Time Saver** Use the map on page 464 to summarize the changes taking place in the balance of free states and slave states in the years leading up to war.
  **Class Time** 10 minutes

**Section 3,** pp. 466–470
**Class Time** 45 minutes

Options for pacing and variety:

- **Internet** Extend students' background knowledge of Abraham Lincoln by visiting www.mcdougallittell.com
  **Class Time** 20 minutes
- **Time Saver** Assign the Main Ideas and Critical Thinking questions from the Section Assessment for homework.
  **Class Time** 5 minutes

### DAY 3

**Section 4,** pp. 471–475
**Class Time** 45 minutes

Options for pacing and variety:

- **Peer Evaluation** Have students work in groups to complete the Taking Notes time line on page 475 of the Section Assessment and then discuss the Taking Notes question.
  **Class Time** 15 minutes
- **Time Saver** Ask students to bring to class their answers to the Applying Citizenship Skills question in the Critical Thinking section of the Chapter Assessment.
  **Class Time** 5 minutes

**Chapter 15 Assessment,** pp. 476–477
**Class Time** 40 minutes

Options for pacing and variety:

- **Peer Evaluation** Divide students into small groups. Have each group create a cause-and-effect chart or other graphic organizer to show the road to secession.
  **Class Time** 20 minutes
- **Peer Teaching** Pick eight students and assign each an event on the Visual Summary on page 476. Have students research their events and then make a living time line for the class with each student explaining how his or her event contributed to the dissolution of the Union. **Class Time** 20 minutes

**CHAPTER 15 OBJECTIVE**

The student will understand the conflicts that pulled the North and South apart and the attempts to resolve the issues dividing the country.

## HISTORY FROM VISUALS

**Interpreting the Painting** Tell students that this painting of one of the Lincoln-Douglas debates is an artist's recreation of the event. Ask students to look at the painting carefully and make some inferences about the artist's opinion of Lincoln. Note that Lincoln is in the center of the painting, standing erect. He wears white. Ask students to notice the kinds of men who make up the audience. Then ask how the artist has painted the audience responding to Lincoln. **Possible Response** The audience looks amused, perhaps in response to some clever words that Lincoln might be saying.

**Extension** Point out the campaign posters some of the people in the picture are holding. Ask students to comment on the posters, noting that women were not allowed to vote at this time.

CHAPTER 15

# The Nation Breaking Apart

## 1846–1861

*Section 1* **Growing Tensions Between North and South**
*Section 2* **The Crisis Deepens**
*Section 3* **Slavery Dominates Politics**
*Section 4* **Lincoln's Election and Southern Secession**

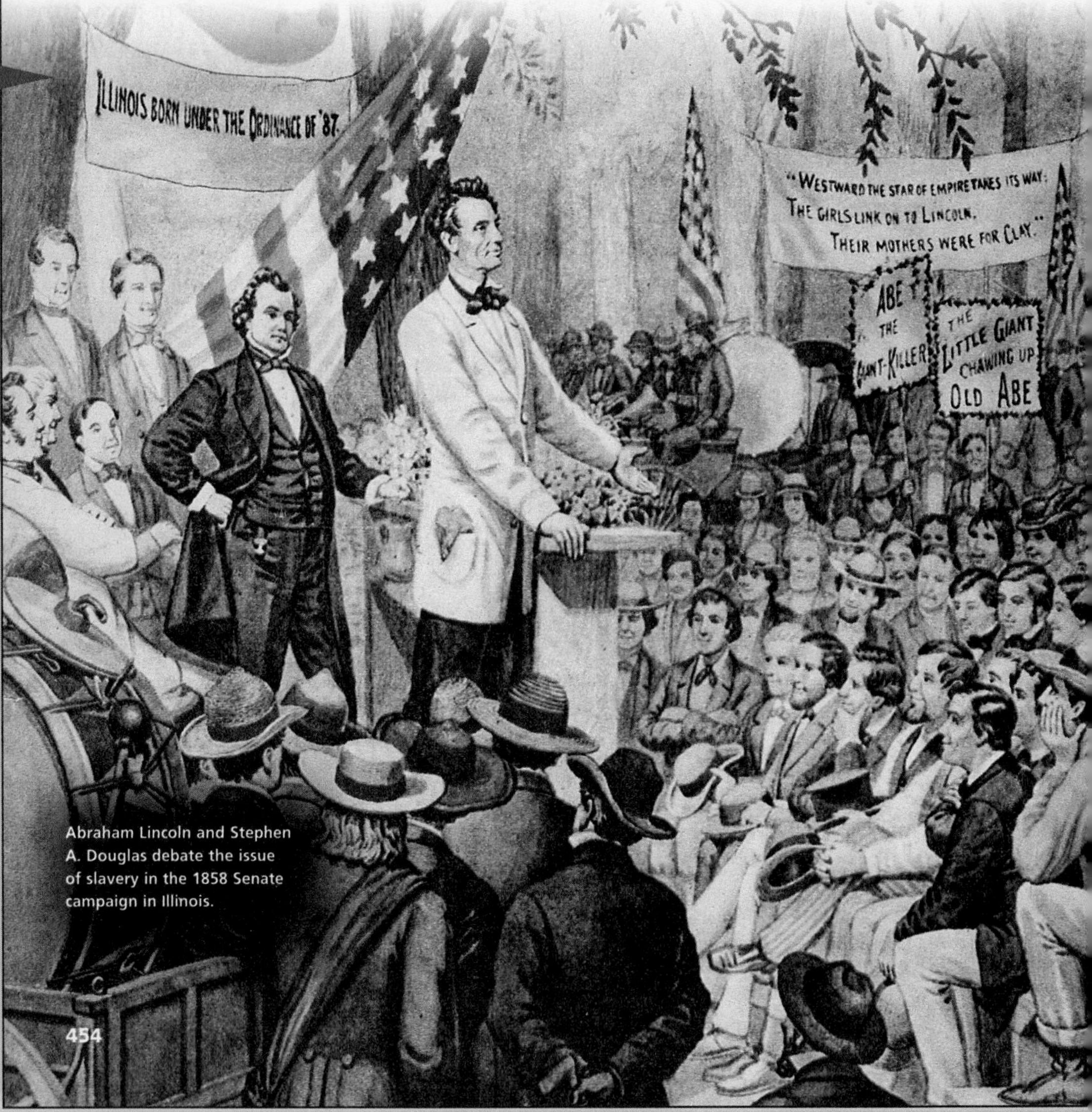

Abraham Lincoln and Stephen A. Douglas debate the issue of slavery in the 1858 Senate campaign in Illinois.

454

## RECOMMENDED RESOURCES

**BOOKS FOR THE TEACHER**

C-Span Staff. ***Traveling Tocqueville's America.*** Baltimore: Johns Hopkins, 1998. Illustrated account of Tocqueville's itinerary.

Kaufman, Kenneth C. ***Dred Scott's Advocate: A Biography of Roswell M. Field.*** Columbia, MO: U. of Missouri Pr., 1996. Unusual look at the famous court case.

Klein, Maury. ***Days of Defiance: Sumner, Secession and the Coming of the Civil War.*** New York: Knopf, 1997. In-depth study of the events that led to that dramatic day at Fort Sumter.

Stowe, Harriet Beecher. ***Dred: A Tale of the Great Dismal Swamp.*** New York: AMS, 1992. A less famous novel by Stowe.

**SOFTWARE**

***African American History: Slavery to Civil War.*** CD-ROM. Queue, 1995.

**VIDEO**

***The Lincoln-Douglas Debates: The House Divides.*** Coronet, The Multimedia Co., 1989. Dramatization of the debates.

**INTERNET**

For more about Abraham Lincoln, visit www.mcdougallittell.com

## Interact *with* History

Disagreements over slavery caused people in the North and the South to lose their tempers. Passions ran so high that fights sometimes broke out between members of Congress.

**You are a representative in Congress in the 1850s. The issue of slavery is causing heated debates. Tensions over slavery have risen so high that respectable men have turned to violence to settle their differences. You worry that soon this violence may affect the entire nation.**

### What Do You Think?

- **Why do you think people feel so strongly about slavery?**
- **Do you think debates, such as those between Lincoln and Douglas, could settle emotional issues without leading to violence?**

# *How would you keep the nation together?*

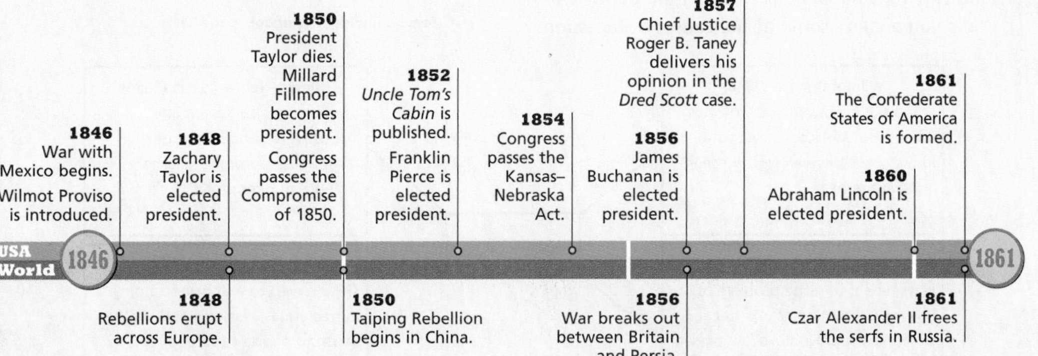

USA
World
1846
1861
1846 War with Mexico begins. Wilmot Proviso is introduced.
1848 Zachary Taylor is elected president.
1850 President Taylor dies. Millard Fillmore becomes president. Congress passes the Compromise of 1850.
1852 *Uncle Tom's Cabin* is published. Franklin Pierce is elected president.
1854 Congress passes the Kansas–Nebraska Act.
1856 James Buchanan is elected president.
1857 Chief Justice Roger B. Taney delivers his opinion in the *Dred Scott* case.
1860 Abraham Lincoln is elected president.
1861 The Confederate States of America is formed.
1848 Rebellions erupt across Europe.
1850 Taiping Rebellion begins in China.
1856 War breaks out between Britain and Persia.
1861 Czar Alexander II frees the serfs in Russia.

## Interact *with* History

**OBJECTIVES**

- To help students grasp the intense feelings aroused by the slavery question
- To help students connect with the people and the events in this chapter

### What Do You Think?

1. Ask students why members of Congress could get angry about a political issue.
2. Ask students, Do you think debates over slavery made the splitting of the nation more likely?

### *How would you keep the nation together?*

Have students think of different ways of settling arguments, including compromising, using arbitration (an outside group or person asked to hear both sides and give a binding judgment), and by thinking of ways to help those adversely affected.

**MAKING PERSONAL CONNECTIONS**

Ask students to think of a time when they had a disagreement with a friend. How were they able to resolve the dispute? Did they need to ask other people (parents, friends, counselors) to help find a solution? Did either side have to change his or her position? make accommodations? compromise?

### TIME LINE DISCUSSION

**Tell students that the issues of slavery and the rights of the states dominated the nation's politics and the attention of the American people during this period.**

- Ask students to identify events on the time line that might show peaceful ways to solve the slavery issue. **Answer** 1850 Compromise; Kansas-Nebraska Act; Dred Scott; Lincoln-Douglas debates
- Have students identify an event that signals a violent end to the slavery debate. **Answer** John Brown's raid
- Ask students if they think Lincoln's election could have been a cause of the formation of the Confederate States.

**Possible Response** Students may already know that Southerners were prepared to secede if Lincoln won the 1860 election.

## BEFORE YOU READ

### Previewing the Theme: Diversity and Unity

Ask students to think of values and ideas about government that the North and South shared or that divided them. **Possible Response** Both the North and the South agreed on the ideals of the American Revolution and the basic freedoms set forth in the Bill of Rights. They differed in their view of slavery and which part of government was most important—state government or national government.

### What Do You Know?

Remind students that the fertile soil and warm climate of the South made it suitable for plantation crops. The system of slavery provided the large labor force that these crops needed. In the North, industry and trade were important factors in the economy. Immigrants provided a source of cheap labor for growing mills and factories.

 **In-Depth Resources: Unit 5**
- Tracing Themes: Diversity and Unity, p. 2

## READ AND TAKE NOTES

### Reading Strategy: Analyzing Causes

Explain to students that the causes of historical events are often more complicated than they seem at first. Analysis involves taking a topic apart to discover different ways of looking at it. To understand historical events, a student must use critical-thinking skills, such as analyzing causes and recognizing effects. By the time students finish the chart, they should be able to describe some of the causes that led to secession.

 **In-Depth Resources: Unit 5**
- Setting the Stage, p. 1

 **Critical Thinking Transparency CT43**
- Setting the Stage

# Chapter 15 SETTING THE STAGE

## BEFORE YOU READ

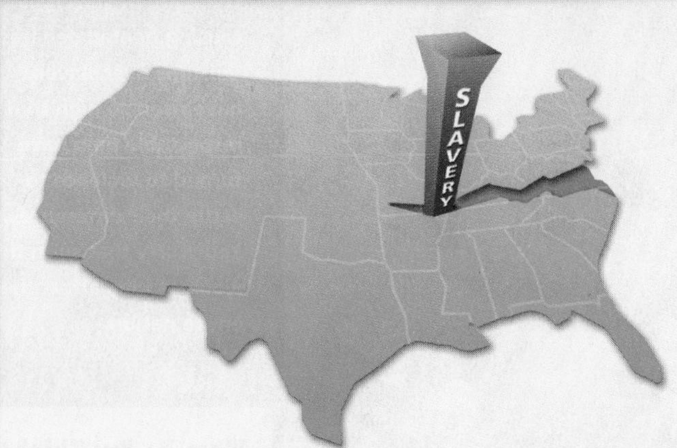


### Previewing the Theme

**Diversity and Unity** As you read in Chapter 14, slavery heightened tensions between Northerners and Southerners. Many people feared that the issue might tear the nation apart. But most Americans hoped that they would be able to solve their problems peacefully. Chapter 15 describes how these tensions led to crisis. It also explains how Americans tried to keep their nation united and how those efforts failed.

### What Do You Know?

What do you think about when you hear the terms *slavery* and *abolition?* Why do you think the issue of slavery caused so much anger and resentment?

**THINK ABOUT**
- what you've learned about differences between the North and the South from books, travel, television, or movies
- reasons people have violent conflicts today

### What Do You Want to Know?

What questions do you have about the sectional crisis that led to the Civil War? Record them in your notebook before you read this chapter.

## READ AND TAKE NOTES

**Reading Strategy: Analyzing Causes** Analyzing causes means looking closely at events and describing why they happened. The diagram below will help you analyze some of the causes of secession.

Use the diagram to take notes on how each issue drove the North and the South farther apart.

 See Skillbuilder Handbook, page R10.

**Wilmot Proviso (1846)**
Bill to outlaw slavery in territories taken from Mexico; caused conflict in Congress between Northerners and Southerners

**Compromise of 1850**
Laws meant to settle problem of slavery; California became free state; new fugitive slave law passed; caused conflict by failing to resolve slavery issue

**SECESSION**

**Kansas–Nebraska Act (1854)**
Law to organize Kansas and Nebraska territories; overturned Missouri Compromise; caused violence in Kansas

**Election of 1860**
Lincoln elected with support only in free states; caused states in Deep South to decide to secede



## TEACHING STRATEGY

### READING THE CHAPTER

This is a chronological chapter focusing on the widening rift between the North and the South. Encourage students to look for causes and effects of events during this time period. Pause after each section to review the events, their causes, and their effects.

### ALTERNATIVE ASSESSMENT

The Chapter Assessment describes three activities for alternative assessment on page 477. You may wish to have students work on these activities during the course of the chapter and then present them at the end.

# 1 Growing Tensions Between North and South

**TERMS & NAMES**
Wilmot Proviso
Free-Soil Party
Henry Clay
Daniel Webster
Stephen A. Douglas
Compromise of 1850

| MAIN IDEA | WHY IT MATTERS NOW |
|---|---|
| Disagreements between the North and the South, especially over the issue of slavery, led to political conflict. | Regional differences can make national problems difficult to resolve. |

## ONE EUROPEAN'S STORY

**Alexis de Tocqueville [TOHK•vihl] was a young French government official from a wealthy family. In 1831, he sailed across the Atlantic Ocean to study American prisons and politics.**

**At one point, Tocqueville traveled in a steamship down the Ohio River. The river was the border between Ohio, a free state, and Kentucky, a slave state. Tocqueville noted what he saw on both sides of the river.**

*A VOICE FROM THE PAST*

The State of Ohio is separated from Kentucky just by one river; on either side of it the soil is equally fertile, and the situation equally favourable, and yet everything is different. Here [on the Ohio side] a population devoured by feverish activity, trying every means to make its fortune. . . . There [on the Kentucky side] are people who make others work for them and show little compassion, a people without energy, mettle or the spirit of enterprise. . . . These differences cannot be attributed to any other cause but slavery. It degrades the black population and enervates [saps the energy of] the white.

**Alexis de Tocqueville,** *Journey to America*

Alexis de Tocqueville

**In this section, you will read about the differences between the North and the South. You will also read about how these differences caused political tensions that threatened to tear the nation apart.**

## 1 North and South Take Different Paths

As you read in Chapter 11, the economies of the North and the South developed differently in the early 1800s. Although both economies were mostly agricultural, the North began to develop more industry and commerce. By contrast, the Southern economy relied on plantation farming.

The growth of industry in the North helped lead to the rapid growth of Northern cities. Much of this population growth came from immigration. In addition, immigrants and Easterners moved west and built farms in the new states formed from the Northwest Territory. Most canals and railroads ran east and west, helping the Eastern and Midwestern states develop strong ties with each other.





## SECTION OBJECTIVES

1. To explain how the abolitionist movement heightened tension between North and South
2. To describe the controversies over slavery in the territories
3. To evaluate how the Wilmot Proviso and potential statehood for California deepened regional divisions
4. To analyze the Compromise of 1850

**CRITICAL THINKING**

Making Generalizations, p. 458
Recognizing Effects, p. 459
Comparing and Contrasting, p. 461

## FOCUS & MOTIVATE

### 5-MINUTE WARM-UP

**Making Inferences** These questions explore differences between the North and the South.

1. Look at the chart on page 458. Which region had a more diversified, or varied, economy?
2. Why do you think the South only produced cotton?

**Warm-Up Transparency WT15**

## INSTRUCT

### INSTRUCT: OBJECTIVE 1

**North and South Take Different Paths**

Key Questions

- How did the economies of the North and the South differ?
- What factors caused the rapid growth of Northern cities?
- Why was there so little investment in industry in the South?

**In-Depth Resources: Unit 5**
- Guided Reading, p. 3

**Reading Study Guide** (Spanish and English), pp. 149–150

## RECOMMENDED RESOURCES

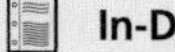

**In-Depth Resources: Unit 5**
- Guided Reading, p. 3
- Building Vocabulary, p. 7
- Reteaching Activity, p. 16

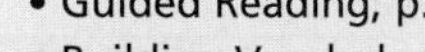

**Reading Study Guide** (Spanish and English), pp. 149–150

**Economics in History**
- King Cotton, p. 15

**Formal Assessment**
- Section Quiz, p. 228

**Alternative Assessment**
- Rubrics, 5.5
- Rubrics, 3.2

**Access for Students Acquiring English/ESL**
- Guided Reading, p. 100

**Technology Resources**

**Critical Thinking Trans. CT44**
- Cause and Effect: The Compromise of 1850

**Electronic Teacher Tools with Test Maker**

**ClassZone**
www.mcdougallittell.com

## Economics *in* History

**OBJECTIVE**
Students will be able to define trade and explain how it works. They will be able to explain how the South and the North benefited from trade with each other.

**Trade and Bartering**
The concept of trade has its roots in the simpler barter system. In a barter, people exchange items or skills that they have for items or skills that they need or want. No money changes hands, nor is any middle person needed.

As societies become more complicated, bartering does not work well. Systems of trade develop in its place. Trade differs from bartering because money is exchanged instead of goods or skills. In addition, goods may change hands many times, and people are involved in these exchanges.

1. **Solving Problems Possible Responses** Trade helps a country get goods that it wants but cannot produce. A country could try to produce these other goods, but it might be too difficult or expensive.
2. **Comparing Possible Responses** Americans sell many different goods, from farm products and machines to technology to television shows and services. Americans buy many of these same products from other countries.

**Economics in History**
- King Cotton, p. 15

**INSTRUCT: OBJECTIVE 2**

**Antislavery and Racism**
Key Questions
- Why did free workers in the North oppose slavery?
- What reasons did Southern slaveholders offer in defense of slavery?

## Economics *in* History

# Trade

Trade is based on a simple idea. If you have something someone else needs or wants, and that person has something you need or want, you exchange, or trade, those two things. After the trade, you should both be better off than before.

The concept of trade works similarly for groups of people. For example, in the early 1800s, the South had few factories. Planters who wanted manufactured goods usually had to buy them from manufacturers in the North or in Europe. To have the cash to buy those goods, Southerners sold other goods, such as cotton, to the North and other countries. Each sold the goods they could produce in order to get money to buy the goods they could not make.

**CONNECT TO HISTORY**
1. **Solving Problems** What problem does trade help a country solve? How else could a country solve this problem?

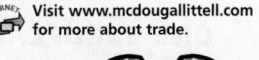

See Skillbuilder Handbook, page R17.

**CONNECT TO TODAY**
2. **Comparing** What goods do Americans sell to other countries today? What goods do Americans buy from other countries?

Visit www.mcdougallittell.com for more about trade.

The South developed differently than the North. A few wealthy planters controlled Southern society. They made great profits from the labor of their slaves. Much of this profit came from trade. Planters relied on exports, especially cotton. Because these plantations were so profitable, planters invested in slaves instead of industry. As a result, the South developed little industry.

Most Southern whites were poor farmers who owned no slaves. Many of these people resented the powerful slaveholders. But poor whites accepted slavery because it kept them off the bottom of society.

*Reading* **History**
**A. Making Generalizations** How did the economies of the North and the South differ?
A. Answer The North was more industrial. The South was more agricultural and used slave labor.

### 2 Antislavery and Racism

The issue of slavery caused tension between the North and the South. In the North, the antislavery movement had slowly been gaining strength since the 1830s. Abolitionists believed that slavery was unjust and should be abolished immediately. Many Northerners who opposed slavery took a less extreme position. Some Northern workers and immigrants opposed slavery because it was an economic threat to them. Because slaves did not work for pay, free workers feared that managers would employ slaves rather than them. Some workers were even afraid that the expansion of slavery might force workers into slavery to find jobs.

Despite their opposition to slavery, most Northerners, even abolitionists, were racist by modern standards. Many whites refused to go to

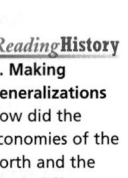

**ACTIVITY OPTIONS**
**INTERDISCIPLINARY LINK: ECONOMICS** — BLOCK SCHEDULING

**VALUE OF COTTON EXPORTS**

**Class Time** 15 minutes

**Task** Analyzing data that shows the value of cotton exports and making a graph illustrating the information

**Purpose** To evaluate the importance of the cotton trade

**Supplies Needed**
- Art supplies (optional)

**Activity** Write the following data on the chalkboard.

| Cotton Exports | | |
|---|---|---|
| 1836–1840 | $321 million | 43% of total U.S. exports |
| 1856–1860 | $744.6 million | 54% of total U.S. exports |

Tell students to make pie graphs illustrating cotton's percentage of total U.S. exports for the two periods given. Ask students to explain why cotton exports were important to the nation as a whole. Ask students what factors may have caused the increase in exports over the 20-year period.

school with, work with, or live near African Americans. In most states, African Americans could not vote.

**Vocabulary**
**racist:** having prejudice based on race

When Northern attacks on slavery increased, slaveholders defended slavery. Most offered the openly racist argument that white people were superior to blacks. Many also claimed that slavery helped slaves by introducing them to Christianity, as well as providing them with food, clothing, and shelter throughout their lives. Slaveholders were determined to defend slavery and their way of life. In this way, the different ideas about slavery brought the North and the South into conflict.

## 3 The Wilmot Proviso

After the Missouri Compromise in 1820, political disagreements over slavery seemed to go away. But new disagreements arose with the outbreak of the War with Mexico in 1846. Many Northerners believed that Southerners wanted to take territory from Mexico in order to extend slavery. To prevent that, Representative David Wilmot of Pennsylvania proposed a bill, known as the **Wilmot Proviso,** to outlaw slavery in any territory the United States might acquire from the War with Mexico.

But slaveholders believed that Congress had no right to prevent them from bringing slaves into any of the territories. They viewed slaves as property. The Constitution, they claimed, gave equal protection to the property rights of all U.S. citizens. The Wilmot Proviso removed the right of slaveholders to take their slaves, which they regarded as property, anywhere in the United States or its territories. Southerners claimed that the bill was unconstitutional.

The Wilmot Proviso divided Congress along regional lines. The bill passed the House of Representatives. But Southerners prevented it from passing the Senate.

Even though the Wilmot Proviso never became law, it had important effects. It led to the creation of the **Free-Soil Party,** a political party dedicated to stopping the expansion of slavery. The party's slogan expressed its ideals—"Free Soil, Free Speech, Free Labor, and Free Men." The Free-Soil Party won more than ten seats in Congress in the election of 1848. More important, the party made slavery a key issue in national politics. Politicians could ignore slavery no longer.

**Connections TO WORLD HISTORY**

**EXPANDING SLAVERY**

William Walker, a Tennessee-born adventurer, wanted to take over land in Central America. In 1855, he joined an army of Nicaraguan rebels and seized power. Walker declared himself president of Nicaragua in 1856. As president, he legalized slavery there.

Troops from nearby countries drove him from power in 1857. The actions of men like Walker helped to convince Northerners that slaveholders were intent on expanding slavery beyond the U.S. South.

***Reading* History**
**B. Recognizing Effects** What were the effects of the Wilmot Proviso?
**B. Possible Response** It divided Congress along regional lines and led to the formation of the Free-Soil Party.

## Controversy over Territories

By 1848, the nation's leaders had begun to debate how to deal with slavery in the lands gained from the War with Mexico. The proposed addition of new states threatened the balance in Congress between North and South. The discovery of gold in California brought thousands of people into that territory. There would soon be enough people in California for it to apply for statehood. Most California residents wanted their state to





### INSTRUCT: OBJECTIVE 3

**The Wilmot Proviso/ Controversy over Territories**

Key Questions

- Why did slaveholders claim that the Wilmot Proviso was unconstitutional?
- Why was the formation of the Free-Soil Party important to national politics?
- What made California's admission as a state controversial?

### Connections TO WORLD HISTORY

**Slavery in the World Today**

Slavery continues to be a threat to poverty-stricken people in some parts of the world. According to a study by the United Nations, about 4 million people are sold into servitude against their will every year. Most are women and girls, although boys and men may also be taken. Many are lured from their homes with false promises of jobs with good pay. Human rights organizations have reported the widespread use of slave labor in China, but the problem is worldwide. In 1998, the U.S. Department of Justice noted that, even in the United States, the problem of enforced servitude is growing worse.

### ACTIVITY OPTIONS

**INDIVIDUAL NEEDS: GIFTED AND TALENTED**

**THE SYSTEM OF SERFDOM IN RUSSIA**

**Class Time** Two class periods

**Task** Preparing a report on serfdom in Russia

**Purpose** To compare the system of serfdom in Russia to the system of slavery in the United States

**Supplies Needed**

- Encyclopedias and/or history books
- Internet access (optional)

**Activity** Have students research the system of serfdom in Russia and write an essay in which they compare the history of serfdom to the history of slavery in the United States. Students should include information about the rights of serfs compared to the rights of slaves; the movement in Russia to end slavery compared to the abolitionist movement; and how the reforms that ended the system of serfdom compared to the way slavery ended in the United States.

be a free state. But this would tip the balance of power clearly in favor of the North. Southerners wanted to divide California in half, making the northern half a free state and the southern half a slave state.

In 1849, President Zachary Taylor proposed that California submit a plan for statehood that year, without going through the territorial stage. By skipping this stage, Taylor's plan gave Southern slaveholders little time to move to California with their slaves.

In March 1850, California applied to be admitted as a free state. With California as a free state, slave states would become a minority in the Senate just as they were in the House. Jefferson Davis, a senator from Mississippi, warned, "For the first time, we are about permanently to destroy the balance of power between the sections."

**Background**
U.S. land gains from the War with Mexico included all or parts of the future states of California, Nevada, Utah, Arizona, New Mexico, and Colorado.

## 4 The Compromise of 1850

California could not gain statehood, however, without the approval of Congress. And Congress was divided over the issue. Behind the scenes, statesmen sought compromise. Taking the lead was Senator **Henry Clay**

This engraving dramatically portrays the Senate debate over the Compromise of 1850.

Henry Clay led the Congress in creating compromises on several important issues during his long career.

John C. Calhoun of South Carolina opposed the Compromise of 1850. He believed the South had no reason to compromise on the issue of slavery.

Daniel Webster spoke eloquently in favor of the compromise.



**INSTRUCT: OBJECTIVE 4**

**The Compromise of 1850**

Key Questions

- Why were Southerners opposed to the admission of California to the Union as a free state?
- What compromise allowed California to join the Union? What were its provisions?
- What roles did Henry Clay, Daniel Webster, and Stephen Douglas play in passing the Compromise of 1850?

**MORE ABOUT . . .**

**The Compromise of 1850 Debates**

Central roles in the debates were played by Henry Clay, Daniel Webster, and John C. Calhoun. All three men were born during the Revolution, all sought to preserve the nation, and all had once entertained presidential ambitions. Furthermore, all three understood that the Compromise of 1850 represented their last opportunity to shape the future of the country.

Webster and Clay were nationalists who worked to hold the Union together. Calhoun was a states'-rights Southerner who believed the discussion was about property rights. He maintained that Southerners had the constitutional right to take slaves to all territories. If these rights were not protected, Calhoun argued, the South might secede.

 **Critical Thinking Transparency CT44**
- Cause and Effect: The Compromise of 1850

**ACTIVITY OPTIONS**

**INDIVIDUAL NEEDS**

**LESS PROFICIENT READERS**

**Finding Main Ideas** Students may have difficulty identifying the provisions of proposed laws and understanding how they affected the growing tension between the North and the South. To help students clarify these provisions, have them create webs for the Wilmot Proviso and the Compromise of 1850. Remind students to think of the term in the center as the main idea and to add important details in the surrounding circles.

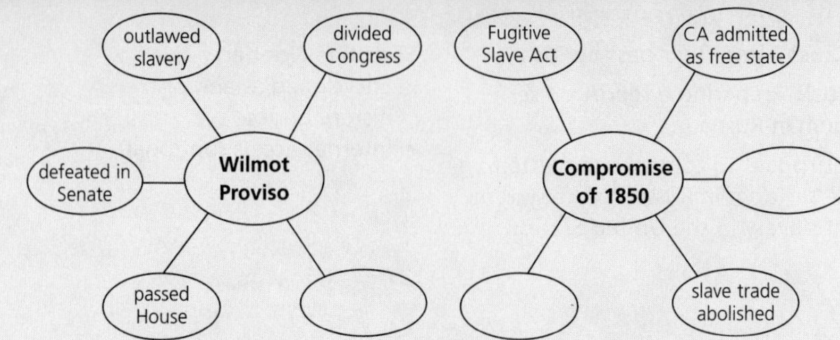

of Kentucky. Clay had helped create the Missouri Compromise in 1820. Now Clay crafted a plan to settle the California problem.

*Reading***History**
**C. Reading a Map** Look at the map on page 464 to see how the Compromise of 1850 affected the territories open to slavery.

1. To please the North, California would be admitted as a free state, and the slave trade would be abolished in Washington, D.C.
2. To please the South, Congress would not pass laws regarding slavery for the rest of the territories won from Mexico, and Congress would pass a stronger law to help slaveholders recapture runaway slaves.

Many people on both sides felt they had to give up too much in this plan. But others were tired of the regional bickering. They wanted to hold the Union together. **Daniel Webster,** senator from Massachusetts, supported the compromise for the sake of the Union.

*A VOICE FROM THE PAST*

I wish to speak today, not as a Massachusetts man, nor as a Northern man, but as an American. . . . I speak today for the preservation of the Union. Hear me for my cause.

**Daniel Webster,** quoted in *The Annals of America*

The job of winning passage of the plan fell to Senator **Stephen A. Douglas** of Illinois. By the end of September, Douglas succeeded, and the plan, now known as the **Compromise of 1850,** became law.

Some people celebrated the compromise, believing that it had saved the Union. But the compromise would not bring peace. In the next section, you will learn how sectional tensions continued to rise.

AMERICA'S HISTORY MAKERS

**STEPHEN A. DOUGLAS**
**1813–1861**

Stephen A. Douglas was one of the most powerful members of Congress in the mid-1800s. In fact, he was called the "Little Giant" because he commanded great respect even though he was only five feet four inches tall.

Perhaps the most important issue that Douglas faced during his career was the expansion of slavery into the territories. Douglas privately hated slavery. But he did not believe a debate on morality would do any good. He suggested that the people of each territory should decide whether or not to allow slavery.

**What groups of Americans agreed with Douglas's position on slavery?**

## Section 1 Assessment

### 1. Terms & Names

**Identify:**
- Wilmot Proviso
- Free-Soil Party
- Henry Clay
- Daniel Webster
- Stephen A. Douglas
- Compromise of 1850

### 2. Taking Notes

Use a chart like the one below to explain the effects of each cause.

| Causes | Effects |
|---|---|
| Abolitionism | |
| Wilmot Proviso | |
| California's application for statehood | |

Which issue do you think most threatened national unity?

### 3. Main Ideas

a. What were two ways that the North and the South differed by the mid-1800s?

b. In what ways was racism common in both the North and the South?

c. How did the War with Mexico lead to conflict between the North and the South?

### 4. Critical Thinking

**Comparing and Contrasting** How was the Compromise of 1850 similar to and different from the Missouri Compromise?

**THINK ABOUT**
- the regional tensions at the time the compromises were proposed
- who proposed each bill
- the provisions of the bills

**ACTIVITY OPTIONS**

**TECHNOLOGY**
**SPEECH**

Imagine you are a television news director. Plan a five-minute **documentary** or organize a **panel discussion** on the Compromise of 1850.





## AMERICA'S HISTORY MAKERS

**Stephen A. Douglas**

Stephen A. Douglas was born in Brandon, Vermont, but migrated to Illinois when he was 20. Douglas became wealthy through land speculation in Illinois. He worked to make Chicago a railroad hub. He believed that great wealth would pour into Illinois when the nation had its first transcontinental railroad. Some historians think that Douglas wanted to settle the issue of slavery in the territories to speed the construction of the railroads.

Douglas died of typhoid fever in 1861. He is buried in Chicago. His tomb bears the words "Tell my children to obey the Laws and uphold the Constitution."

Answer: Southern slaveholders and people who believed each state should make its own laws on slavery

## ASSESS & RETEACH

**Setting the Stage** Have students fill in the boxes for the Wilmot Proviso and the Compromise of 1850 on the graphic organizer.

**Formal Assessment**
- Section Quiz, p. 228

**Critical Thinking Transparency CT43**
- Setting the Stage

**RETEACHING ACTIVITY**

Have one student of a student pair explain the causes and effects of the Wilmot Proviso to his or her partner. Tell the partner to ask questions to clarify the explanation. Then have students switch roles for the Compromise of 1850.

**In-Depth Resources: Unit 5**
- Reteaching Activity, p. 16

## Section 1 Assessment

### 1. Terms & Names

**Wilmot Proviso,** p. 459
**Free-Soil Party,** p. 459
**Henry Clay,** p. 460
**Daniel Webster,** p. 461
**Stephen A. Douglas,** p. 461
**Compromise of 1850,** p. 461

### 2. Taking Notes

Abolitionism—Raised tensions among citizens over the morality of slavery; Wilmot Proviso—Caused political conflict over the legality of slavery in the territories; California's application for statehood—Led to the Compromise of 1850

California, because it would give the free states a majority in both houses of Congress

### 3. Main Ideas

**a.** The North had an industrial economy, while the South had an agricultural one that relied heavily on slave labor. **b.** feelings of white superiority and black inferiority; discrimination **c.** The land won in the war caused conflict over whether slavery would be legal in these new American territories.

### 4. Critical Thinking

Similar: both dealt with the issue of slavery in U.S. territories; Different: the 1850 law upset the balance of number of free and slave states

**ACTIVITY OPTIONS**

**Alternative Assessment**
- Rubrics, 5.5
- Rubrics, 3.2

## SECTION OBJECTIVES

1. To explain how the Fugitive Slave Act and *Uncle Tom's Cabin* affected Northerners
2. To analyze the concept of popular sovereignty
3. To describe the violence in "Bleeding Kansas"
4. To evaluate the attack on Senator Sumner in the Senate

**SKILLBUILDER**
Interpreting Maps: Region p. 464

**CRITICAL THINKING**
Analyzing Points of View, p. 463
Sequencing Events, p. 465
Solving Problems, p. 465

## FOCUS & MOTIVATE

### 5-MINUTE WARM-UP

**Drawing Conclusions** These questions focus on changes in slave and free territory.

1. Look at the maps of the United States on page 464. How many new slave states were added between 1820 and 1854?
2. How much more territory was open to slavery after 1854?

 Warm-Up Transparency WT15

## INSTRUCT

### INSTRUCT: OBJECTIVE 

**The Fugitive Slave Act/*Uncle Tom's Cabin***
Key Questions

- Why did Southerners feel that the Fugitive Slave Act was justified?
- What moral dilemma did the Fugitive Slave Act force Northerners to face?
- Why did white Southerners resent *Uncle Tom's Cabin*?

**In-Depth Resources: Unit 5**
- Guided Reading, p. 4

**America's History Makers**
- Harriet Beecher Stowe, pp. 59–60

**Reading Study Guide** (Spanish and English), pp. 151–152

# 2 The Crisis Deepens

**TERMS & NAMES**
Harriet Beecher Stowe
*Uncle Tom's Cabin*
Fugitive Slave Act
popular sovereignty
Kansas-Nebraska Act
John Brown

| MAIN IDEA | WHY IT MATTERS NOW |
|---|---|
| Turmoil over slavery led to acts of violence. | Violence can make compromise more difficult. |

Harriet Beecher Stowe

### ONE AMERICAN'S STORY

**__Harriet Beecher Stowe__ was outraged when she heard about the part of the Compromise of 1850 that would help slaveholders recapture runaway slaves. She described her feelings about the law.**

*A VOICE FROM THE PAST*

Since the legislative act of 1850, when [I] heard . . . Christian and humane people actually recommending the remanding [returning of] escaped fugitives into slavery, as a duty binding on good citizens, . . . [I] could only think, These men and Christians cannot know what slavery is.

**Harriet Beecher Stowe,** *Uncle Tom's Cabin*

**Stowe's anger motivated her to write *__Uncle Tom's Cabin,__* a novel that portrayed slavery as brutal and immoral. In this section, you will learn how the Compromise of 1850 deepened the division between the North and the South.**

## 1 The Fugitive Slave Act

The 1850 law to help slaveholders recapture runaway slaves was called the **__Fugitive Slave Act__.** People accused of being fugitives under this law could be held without an arrest warrant. In addition, they had no right to a jury trial. Instead, a federal commissioner ruled on each case. The commissioner received five dollars for releasing the defendant and ten dollars for turning the defendant over to a slaveholder.

Southerners felt that the Fugitive Slave Act was justified because they considered slaves to be property. But Northerners resented the Fugitive Slave Act. It required Northerners to help recapture runaway slaves. It placed fines on people who would not cooperate and jail terms on people who helped the fugitives escape. In addition, Southern slave catchers roamed the North, sometimes capturing free African Americans.

The presence of slave catchers throughout the North brought home the issue of slavery to Northerners. They could no longer ignore the fact that, by supporting the Fugitive Slave Act, they played an important role in supporting slavery. They faced a moral choice. Should they



## RECOMMENDED RESOURCES

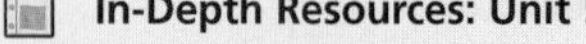

**In-Depth Resources: Unit 5**
- Guided Reading, p. 4
- Building Vocabulary, p. 7
- Skillbuilder Practice, p. 8
- Literature Selection: from *Uncle Tom's Cabin*, pp. 13–15
- Reteaching Activity, p. 17
- Enrichment Activity, p. 20

**Reading Study Guide** (Spanish and English), pp. 151–152

**America's History Makers**
- Harriet Beecher Stowe, pp. 59–60

**Formal Assessment**
- Section Quiz, p. 229

**Alternative Assessment**
- Rubrics, 4.7
- Rubrics, 1.3

**Access for Students Acquiring English/ESL**
- Guided Reading, p. 101
- Skillbuilder Practice, p. 104

**Technology Resources**

 **Humanities Transparency HT29**
- Poster: Eliza on Ice

 **Electronic Teacher Tools with Test Maker**

 **ClassZone**
www.mcdougallittell.com

obey the law and support slavery, or should they break the law and oppose slavery?

## *Uncle Tom's Cabin*

The novel *Uncle Tom's Cabin,* published by Harriet Beecher Stowe in 1852, expressed the moral issues of slavery in a highly dramatic way. The main character of Stowe's novel was Uncle Tom, a respected older slave. The central plot tells of Tom's life under three owners. Two of the owners were kind, but the third—the evil Simon Legree—had Tom beaten. The novel includes dramatic episodes, such as the dangerous journey of an escaped slave named Eliza and her baby across the Ohio River.

*Reading*History
**A. Analyzing Points of View** How does Harriet Beecher Stowe present slavery in *Uncle Tom's Cabin*?
**A. Answer** She presents slavery as a dramatic moral issue. She shows an evil slaveholder abusing his slaves and relates exciting stories of slaves running away to freedom.

*A VOICE FROM THE PAST*

> Eliza made her desperate retreat across the river just in the dusk of twilight. The gray mist of evening, rising slowly from the river, enveloped her as she disappeared up the bank, and the swollen current and floundering masses of ice presented a hopeless barrier between her and her pursuer.
>
> **Harriet Beecher Stowe,** *Uncle Tom's Cabin*

Stowe's book was wildly popular in the North. But white Southerners believed the book falsely criticized the South and slavery.

## 2 The Kansas–Nebraska Act

While the Fugitive Slave Act and *Uncle Tom's Cabin* heightened the conflicts between the North and the South, the issue of slavery in the territories brought bloodshed to the West. In 1854, Senator Stephen A. Douglas of Illinois drafted a bill to organize territorial governments for the Nebraska Territory. He proposed that it be divided into two territories—Nebraska and Kansas.

**Background**
The Nebraska Territory was part of the Louisiana Purchase. It lay north of the 36° 30′ line, so the Missouri Compromise banned slavery there.

To get Southern support for the bill, he suggested that the decision about whether to allow slavery in each of these territories be settled by popular sovereignty. **Popular sovereignty** is a system where the residents vote to decide an issue. If this bill passed, it would result in getting rid of the Missouri Compromise by

In 1854, Bostonians protested the capture of an African American by federal marshals under the Fugitive Slave Act.

463

### MORE ABOUT . . .

***Uncle Tom's Cabin***

Harriet Beecher Stowe drew on some of her own experiences in writing *Uncle Tom's Cabin.* While living in Cincinnati, she watched her family help runaway slaves from across the Ohio River in Kentucky. Stowe's family was remarkable. Her father, Lyman Beecher, was a famous minister. Her brother, Henry Ward Beecher, was also a preacher and a leading abolitionist. Stowe's sister Catharine worked to improve education for women.

 **Humanities Transparency HT29**
- Poster: Eliza on Ice

### INSTRUCT: OBJECTIVE 

**The Kansas-Nebraska Act**

Key Questions
- What is popular sovereignty?
- What groups of people supported the Kansas-Nebraska Act? What groups opposed it?
- How did the Kansas-Nebraska Act change decisions about slavery?

### CRITICAL THINKING ACTIVITY

**Identifying and Solving Problems** Have students complete an outline like this one to analyze the problem faced by many abolitionists with the passage of the Fugitive Slave Law.

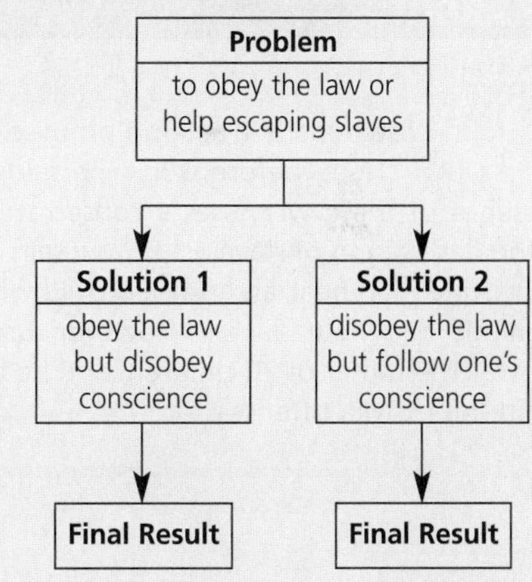


**Class Time** 15 minutes

### ACTIVITY OPTIONS

**MULTIPLE LEARNING STYLES: LINGUISTIC** — BLOCK SCHEDULING

***UNCLE TOM'S CABIN***

**Class Time** 30 minutes

**Task** Reading aloud selected passages from *Uncle Tom's Cabin*

**Purpose** To familiarize students with an important literary work in the nation's history

**Supplies Needed**
- Copies of *Uncle Tom's Cabin*

**Activity** Ask students to practice reading aloud selected sections from *Uncle Tom's Cabin* for presentation to the class. Help students select dramatic scenes, such as Eliza's escape or the death of little Eva. Preview selections for content, language, and dialect appropriate for your class before students begin rehearsing.

 **In-Depth Resources: Unit 5**
- Literature Selection: from *Uncle Tom's Cabin,* pp. 13–15
- Enrichment Activity, p. 20

## HISTORY FROM VISUALS

**Reading the Map** Ask students to point out the differences between the United States at the time of the Missouri Compromise and after the Compromise of 1850. **Possible Responses** Between the Missouri Compromise and the Compromise of 1850, Texas and Florida had become new slave states. Territory in the West, including California, was organized and closed to slavery, while Indian territory and other land in the Southwest were now open to slavery.

**Extension** Have students draw in the Mason-Dixon Line of the Missouri Compromise on a map showing the United States in 1854. Note how many states or parts of states would have changed status.

## INSTRUCT: OBJECTIVE 3

**"Bleeding Kansas"**

Key Questions

- How did proslavery forces ensure that Kansas would elect a proslavery legislature?
- Why did proslavery forces attack Lawrence, Kansas?
- What effects did John Brown's actions have on the situation in Kansas?

## MORE ABOUT . . .

**John Brown**

In 1837, John Brown made a solemn promise in a church in Ohio. "Here, before God," he said, "in the presence of these witnesses, I consecrate my life to the destruction of slavery." Brown said that seeing a white man beat an enslaved child with a shovel made him hate slavery. However, Brown himself was the father of 20 children, and he beat them often for trivial offenses.

### *Free and Slave States and Territories,* 1820–1854

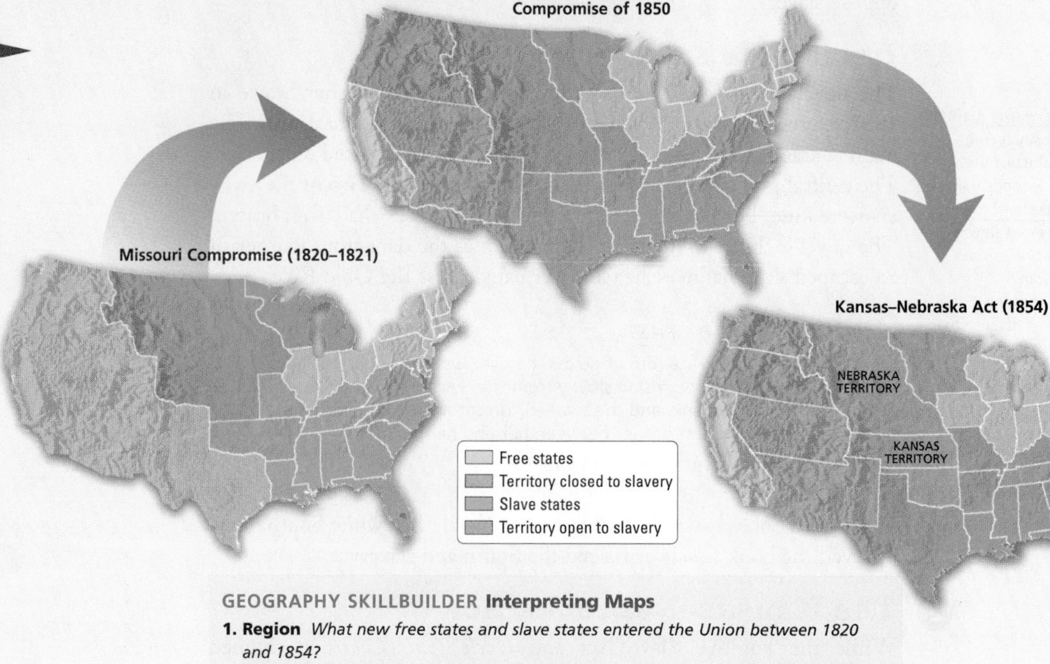


**GEOGRAPHY SKILLBUILDER Interpreting Maps**

1. **Region** *What new free states and slave states entered the Union between 1820 and 1854?*
2. **Region** *How did the Kansas–Nebraska Act change the amount of territory open to slavery?*

Skillbuilder Answers
1. Free states: Michigan, Wisconsin, Iowa, and California. Slave states: Texas, Arkansas, and Florida
2. The Kansas–Nebraska Act opened new territories to slavery.

allowing people to vote for slavery in territories where the Missouri Compromise had banned it.

As Douglas hoped, Southerners applauded the repeal of the Missouri Compromise and supported the bill. Even though the bill angered opponents of slavery, it passed. It became known as the **Kansas–Nebraska Act.** Few people realized that the act would soon turn Kansas into a battleground over slavery.

## 3 "Bleeding Kansas"

Proslavery and antislavery settlers rushed into the Kansas Territory, just west of Missouri, to vote for the territorial legislature. At the time of the election in March 1855, there were more proslavery settlers than antislavery settlers in the territory. But the proslavery forces did not want to risk losing the election. Five thousand Missourians came and voted in the election illegally. As a result, the official Kansas legislature was packed with proslavery representatives.

Vocabulary
**boycott:** refuse to participate in

Antislavery settlers boycotted the official government and formed a government of their own. With political authority in dispute, settlers on both sides armed themselves. In May, a proslavery mob attacked the town of Lawrence, Kansas. The attackers destroyed offices and the



## ACTIVITY OPTIONS

## SKILLBUILDER MINI-LESSON: SEQUENCING EVENTS

BLOCK SCHEDULING

**Explaining the Skill** Students need to understand the order in which things happen—to put them in sequence—to get an accurate sense of the relationship among events.

**Applying the Skill** Write the following events on the board: a) Brown leads the Pottawatomie Massacre. b) Missourians vote in the Kansas election. c) The Kansas-Nebraska Act is passed. d) Anti-slavery forces in Kansas form their own government. e) A proslavery mob attacks Lawrence. Have students put the events in their correct sequence. (1. c 2. b 3. d 4. e 5. a)

After they have finished, discuss the following questions:

1. Why is it important to know that the Kansas-Nebraska Act was passed before Missourians voted in the Kansas election? *(The act said the slavery question would be determined by popular sovereignty. Because the Missourians wanted Kansas to be a slave state, they used numbers to sway the vote.)*
2. Besides numbering events to put them in sequence, how else could you show their chronological order? *(by using a time line)*

**In-Depth Resources: Unit 5**
- Skillbuilder Practice, p. 8

house of the governor of the antislavery government. This attack came to be known as the Sack of Lawrence.

Onto this explosive scene came **John Brown,** an extreme abolitionist. To avenge the Sack of Lawrence, Brown and seven other men went to the cabins of several of his proslavery neighbors and murdered five people. This attack is known as the Pottawatomie Massacre, after the creek near where the victims were found. As news of the violence spread, civil war broke out in Kansas. It continued for three years, and the territory came to be called "Bleeding Kansas."

*Reading* **History**
**B. Sequencing Events** What events in Kansas preceded the Pottawatomie Massacre?
B. Answer Kansas–Nebraska Act (1854); territorial elections (March 1855); Sack of Lawrence (May 1855)

## Violence in Congress 4

While violence was spreading in Kansas in the spring of 1856, blood was also being shed in the nation's capital. In late May, Senator Charles Sumner of Massachusetts delivered a speech attacking the proslavery forces in Kansas. His speech was packed with insults. Sumner even made fun of A. P. Butler, a senator from South Carolina.

Preston Brooks, a relative of Butler, heard about Sumner's speech. To defend Butler and the South, he attacked Sumner, who was sitting at his desk. Brooks hit Sumner over the head with his cane. Sumner tried to defend himself, but his legs were trapped. Brooks hit him 30 times or more, breaking his cane in the assault. (The painting on page 455 shows this event.)

Many Southerners cheered Brooks's defense of the South. But most Northerners were shocked at the violence in the Senate. "Bleeding Kansas" and "Bleeding Sumner" became rallying cries for antislavery Northerners and slogans for a new political party. In the next section, you will learn about the creation of the Republican Party.

**STRANGE *but* True**

**PRESTON BROOKS'S CANE**

Many Americans, Northerners and Southerners alike, were ashamed of the behavior of Sumner and Brooks. But sectional tensions were so high at the time that a large number of Southerners cheered Brooks for his actions.

A number of Brooks's supporters sent him new canes to replace the one he had broken while hitting Sumner on the head. Some of the canes were inscribed with mottoes such as "Hit Him Again."

### Section 2 Assessment

**1. Terms & Names**

**Identify:**
- Harriet Beecher Stowe
- *Uncle Tom's Cabin*
- Fugitive Slave Act
- popular sovereignty
- Kansas–Nebraska Act
- John Brown

**2. Taking Notes**

Use a chart like the one below to compare Northern and Southern views of the issues listed.

| Northern View | Issue | Southern View |
|---|---|---|
| | Fugitive Slave Act | |
| | Kansas–Nebraska Act | |
| | "Bleeding Kansas" | |

**3. Main Ideas**

a. How did the book *Uncle Tom's Cabin* influence national politics?

b. Why was the Kansas–Nebraska Act so controversial?

c. What was the cause of "Bleeding Kansas"?

**4. Critical Thinking**

**Solving Problems** What would you have done to prevent the violence in Kansas?

**THINK ABOUT**
- the repeal of the Missouri Compromise
- popular sovereignty
- the actions of John Brown

**ACTIVITY OPTIONS**

**LITERATURE** / **ART**

Read a chapter of *Uncle Tom's Cabin.* Write a **book review** or make a series of **drawings** illustrating the story.



**INSTRUCT: OBJECTIVE 4**

**Violence in Congress**

Key Questions
- How did Northerners react to the beating of Senator Charles Sumner?
- In what ways did the beating of Senator Sumner represent what was happening in the nation?

**STRANGE *but* True**

**Preston Brooks's Cane**

A House committee investigated the caning affair and recommended Brooks's expulsion. Nevertheless, the House vote followed party and sectional lines and fell short of the needed two-thirds majority. Brooks resigned his seat and his only punishment was a $300 fine. Brooks was embraced as a hero throughout the South, but Northerners turned Sumner into a martyr. Sumner did not return to his Senate seat for two and a half years.

## ASSESS & RETEACH

**Setting the Stage** Have students fill in the box for the Kansas-Nebraska Act on the graphic organizer.

**Formal Assessment**
- Section Quiz, p. 229

**RETEACHING ACTIVITY**

Have students construct a cause-and-effect chain like the one started below to summarize the events surrounding the violence in Kansas.

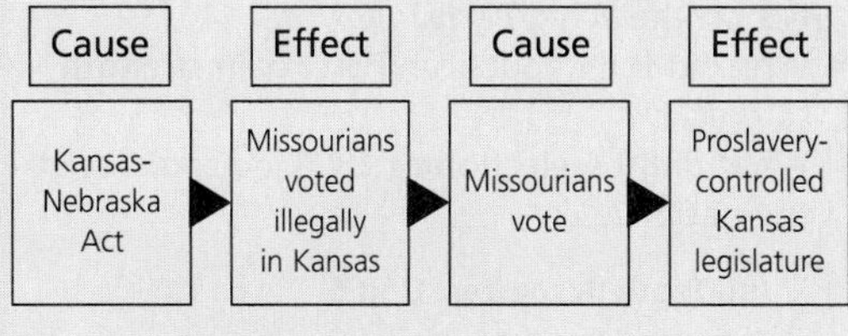


**In-Depth Resources: Unit 5**
- Reteaching Activity, p. 17

### Section 2 Assessment

**1. Terms & Names**

**Harriet Beecher Stowe,** p. 462
***Uncle Tom's Cabin,*** p. 462
**Fugitive Slave Act,** p. 462
**popular sovereignty,** p. 463
**Kansas-Nebraska Act,** p. 464
**John Brown,** p. 465

**2. Taking Notes**

Issue 1: North opposed because it forced them to support slavery; South favored because it upheld slavery; Issue 2: North opposed because it allowed slavery in new areas; South supported because it nullified the Missouri Compromise; Issue 3: North blamed proslavery forces; South blamed abolitionists

**3. Main Ideas**

**a.** It heightened tensions between North and South. **b.** It scrapped the Missouri Compromise, allowing slavery into areas where it was banned. **c.** Antislavery and proslavery forces clashed over contested elections for the territorial legislature in Kansas.

**4. Critical Thinking**

Students might suggest keeping the Missouri Compromise or sending the army to keep order.

**ACTIVITY OPTIONS**

**Alternative Assessment**
- Rubrics for a book review, 4.7
- Rubrics for a drawing, 1.3

## SECTION OBJECTIVES

1. To explain why the Republican Party was formed
2. To summarize the effects of the *Dred Scott* case
3. To analyze the Lincoln-Douglas debates
4. To evaluate the impact of John Brown's raid on Harpers Ferry

**CRITICAL THINKING**

Summarizing, p. 467
Recognizing Effects, p. 468
Making Inferences, p. 469
Identifying Facts and Opinions, p. 470

## FOCUS & MOTIVATE

### 5-MINUTE WARM-UP

**Analyzing Causes and Recognizing Effects**
These questions focus on reasons for the creation of the Republican Party.

1. Read the quotation and look at the medal on page 466. What do they tell you about the reasons for starting the new party?
2. Why do you think people wanted to start a new party?

 **Warm-Up Transparency WT15**

## INSTRUCT

### INSTRUCT: OBJECTIVE 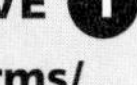

**The Republican Party Forms/ The Election of 1856**

Key Questions

- What was the effect of the Kansas-Nebraska Act on the Whig Party?
- Why did the Republican Party gain strength so quickly?
- What did the election of 1856 indicate about the nation?

**In-Depth Resources: Unit 5**
- Guided Reading, p. 5

**Reading Study Guide** (Spanish and English), pp. 153–154

# 3 Slavery Dominates Politics

**TERMS & NAMES**
Republican Party
John C. Frémont
James Buchanan
*Dred Scott v. Sandford*
Roger B. Taney
Abraham Lincoln
Harpers Ferry

| MAIN IDEA | WHY IT MATTERS NOW |
|---|---|
| Disagreement over slavery led to the formation of the Republican Party and heightened sectional tensions. | The Democrats and the Republicans are the major political parties of today. |

## ONE AMERICAN'S STORY

**Joseph Warren, editor of the Detroit *Tribune,* wanted the antislavery parties of Michigan to join forces. In 1854, his newspaper pushed them to unite.**

*A VOICE FROM THE PAST*

[A convention should be called] irrespective of the old party organizations, for the purpose of agreeing upon some plan of action that shall combine the whole anti-Nebraska, anti-slavery sentiment of the State, upon one ticket [set of candidates endorsed by a political party].

**Detroit *Tribune,*** quoted in *The Origins of the Republican Party*

**This medal shows an early motto of the Republican Party. It also makes clear the Republican connection to the antislavery position of the Free-Soil Party.**

**By July, antislavery politicians from various parties, including the Whigs, Free-Soilers, and some Democrats, had settled their differences. On July 6, they met to form a new party "to concentrate the popular sentiment of this state against the aggression of the slave power." In memory of Thomas Jefferson, they called themselves Republicans. In this section, you will learn why the Republican Party was formed and how it changed American politics in the 1850s.**

## 1 The Republican Party Forms

The creation of the Republican Party grew out of the problems caused by the Kansas–Nebraska Act of 1854. The law immediately caused a political crisis for the Whig Party. Southern Whigs had supported the bill for the same reason that Northern Whigs had opposed it: the bill proposed to open new territories to slavery. There was no room for compromise, so the party split.

The Southern Whigs were destroyed by the split. A few joined the Democratic Party. But most searched for leaders who supported slavery and the Union. The Northern Whigs, however, joined with other opponents of slavery and formed the **Republican Party.**

The Republicans quickly gained strength in the North. "Bleeding Kansas" was the key to the Republican rise. Many people blamed the violence on the Democrats. With the 1856 elections nearing, the



## RECOMMENDED RESOURCES

**In-Depth Resources: Unit 5**
- Guided Reading, p. 5
- Building Vocabulary, p. 7
- Primary Source: African-American Protest Against the *Dred Scott* Decision, p. 11
- Primary Source: John Brown's Raid, p. 12
- Reteaching Activity, p. 18

**Reading Study Guide** (Spanish and English), pp. 153–154

**America's History Makers**
- Dred Scott, pp. 61–62

**Citizenship Today,** pp. 11–12, 89–90

**Formal Assessment**
- Section Quiz, p. 230

**Alternative Assessment**
- Rubrics, 2.3, 2.1

**Access for Students Acquiring English/ESL**
- Guided Reading, p. 102

**Technology Resources**

 **Humanities Transparency HT30**
- *The Abraham Lincoln Family, 1861* by Francis Carpenter

**Geography Transparency GT15**
- The Slave Population of the South, 1860

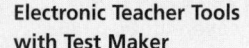

**Electronic Teacher Tools with Test Maker**

 **ClassZone**
www.mcdougallittell.com

Republicans believed that they had an excellent opportunity to gain seats in Congress and win the presidency.

The Republicans needed a strong presidential candidate in 1856 to strengthen their young party. They nominated **John C. Frémont.** Young and handsome, Frémont was a national hero for his explorations in the West, which earned him the nickname the "Pathfinder."

*Reading* **History**
**A. Summarizing** Why did the Republicans nominate Frémont for president in 1856?
A. Answer He was a national hero and opposed slavery in Kansas and California.

Republicans liked Frémont for a couple of reasons. He had spoken in favor of admitting both California and Kansas as free states. Also, he had little political experience and did not have a controversial record to defend. Even so, the Republican position on slavery was so unpopular in the South that Frémont's name did not appear on the ballot there.

## The Election of 1856

The Democrats nominated **James Buchanan** to run for the presidency in 1856. As minister to Great Britain, he had been in England since 1853 and had spoken neither for nor against the Kansas–Nebraska Act.

Buchanan took advantage of his absence from the country. He said little about slavery and claimed that his goal was to maintain the Union. Buchanan appealed to Southerners, to many people in the upper South and the border states, and to Northerners who were afraid that Frémont's election could tear the nation apart.

The American, or Know-Nothing, Party also nominated a presidential candidate in 1856. They chose Millard Fillmore, who had been president, following the death of Zachary Taylor, from 1850 until 1853. But the Know-Nothings were divided over slavery and had little strength.

The 1856 presidential election broke down into two separate races. In the North, it was Buchanan against Frémont. In the South, it was Buchanan against Fillmore. Buchanan won. He carried all the slave states except Maryland, where Fillmore claimed his only victory. Buchanan also won several Northern states.

Although he lost the election, Frémont won 11 Northern states. These results showed two things. First, the Republican Party was a major force in the North. Second, the nation was sharply split over slavery.

## 2 The Case of Dred Scott

The split in the country was made worse by the Supreme Court decision in the case of Dred Scott. Scott had been a slave in Missouri. His owner took him to live in territories where slavery was illegal. Then they returned to Missouri. After his owner's death, Scott sued for his freedom. He argued that he was a free man because he had lived in territories where slavery was illegal. His case, ***Dred Scott v. Sandford,*** reached the Supreme Court in 1856.

**Now and then**

**THIRD-PARTY CANDIDATES**

American politics has usually been dominated by two parties. Most third-party candidates, such as the Republican Frémont in 1856, lose elections. In 1998, Minnesotans broke that pattern when they elected for governor Jesse Ventura of the Reform Party (below).

One reason for Ventura's victory was his celebrity status. He had been a professional wrestler and the host of a popular radio show. His plain speaking appealed to many Minnesotans who felt the major parties were out of touch with the people.

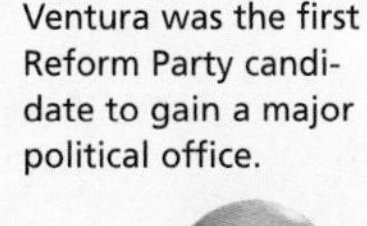

Ventura was the first Reform Party candidate to gain a major political office.

### MORE ABOUT . . .

**John C. Frémont**

Frémont led expeditions to survey and map much of the territory between the Mississippi River and the Pacific Ocean. He joined forces with the famous Kit Carson to complete a survey to the mouth of the Columbia River. His wife, Jessie Benton Frémont, edited her husband's field reports, which were very popular with the public. Frémont was immensely popular in the 1850s and came closer in the election of 1856 than any previous candidate to uniting the antislavery forces.

### *Now and* then

**Third-Party Candidates**

Third-party candidates work against the odds. Political campaigns are very expensive, and it is harder for a candidate from a minor party to raise money than it is for candidates from one of the two major parties. Independent candidates have no party affiliation at all and, as a result, have an even more difficult time raising funds. One successful independent candidate was Lowell P. Weicker, Jr., governor of Connecticut.

### INSTRUCT: OBJECTIVE 2

**The Case of Dred Scott**

Key Questions

- What reason did Scott give to argue that he was a free man?
- How did Judge Taney counter Scott's argument?
- How did the *Dred Scott* decision affect the Missouri Compromise?

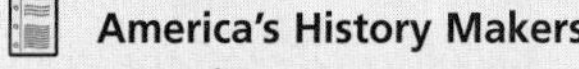

**America's History Makers**
- Dred Scott, pp. 61–62

**In-Depth Resources: Unit 5**
- Primary Source: African-American Protest Against the *Dred Scott* Decision, p. 11

### ACTIVITY OPTIONS

### INDIVIDUAL NEEDS

**LESS PROFICIENT READERS**

**Characterizing Candidates** To help less proficient readers keep track of the candidates in the election of 1856, have them fill in a chart such as the one to the right. Have students circle the name of the winning candidate, Buchanan.

**Candidates for President, 1856**

| | Frémont | Buchanan | Fillmore |
|---|---|---|---|
| Party | | | |
| Region | | | |
| Stand on Slavery | | | |

## MORE ABOUT . . .

**Dred Scott**

By the time the Supreme Court heard Dred Scott's case and ruled against him, Scott was about 65 years old. Manumitted after the decision, he died of tuberculosis after only 16 months of freedom.

Sad as the ruling was for Dred Scott, it was tragic for all African Americans. Not only did Taney's decision allow slavery to spread anywhere in U.S. territory but it also denied the citizenship of free African Americans. Taney wrote that African Americans "had no rights which the white man was bound to respect." Reversing that decision required the Civil War, three constitutional amendments, and a century of activism.

 **Citizenship Today,** pp. 89–90

## INSTRUCT: OBJECTIVE 3

**Lincoln and Douglas Debate**

Key Questions

- How did Lincoln say that the expansion of slavery could be halted?
- How did Douglas's views on the expansion of slavery differ from Lincoln's?
- What effect did the debates have on Lincoln's political career?

## MORE ABOUT . . .

**The Lincoln-Douglas Debates**

Lincoln forced Douglas to explain that his doctrine of popular sovereignty meant that territories could ignore the Supreme Court and keep slavery out. Douglas thus alienated the South. Although he won the Senate seat, he lost his bid to run for president two years later. Lincoln, on the other hand, was invited to speaking engagements throughout the West as a result of the debate. Adding to his fame, 30,000 copies of the transcripts of the debates were sold.

 **Humanities Transparency HT30**
- *The Abraham Lincoln Family, 1861* by Francis Carpenter

Dred Scott (above) first sued for his freedom in 1846. The Supreme Court, led by Chief Justice Roger B. Taney (right), did not rule on the case until 1857. 3

In 1857, the Court ruled against Scott. Chief Justice **Roger B. Taney** [TAW•nee] delivered his opinion in the case. In it, he said that Dred Scott was not a U.S. citizen. As a result, he could not sue in U.S. courts. Taney also ruled that Scott was bound by Missouri's slave code because he lived in Missouri. As a result, Scott's time in free territory did not matter in his case.

In addition, Taney argued that Congress could not ban slavery in the territories. To do so would violate the slaveholders' property rights, protected by the Fifth Amendment. In effect, Taney declared legislation such as the Missouri Compromise unconstitutional.

*Reading* **History**
**B. Recognizing Effects** How did Taney's opinion affect the Missouri Compromise?
**B. Answer** The Missouri Compromise had outlawed slavery in territories north of the Missouri Compromise line. Taney said that Congress could not pass laws to ban slavery in the territories.

Southerners cheered the Court's decision. Many Northerners were outraged and looked to the Republican Party to halt the growing power of Southern slaveholders.

## Lincoln and Douglas Debate

After the *Dred Scott* decision, the Republicans charged that the Democrats wanted to legalize slavery not only in all U.S. territories but also in all the states. They used this charge to attack individual Democrats. Stephen A. Douglas, sponsor of the Kansas–Nebraska Act, was one of their main targets in 1858. That year, Illinois Republicans nominated **Abraham Lincoln** to challenge Douglas for his U.S. Senate seat. In his first campaign speech, Lincoln expressed the Northern fear that Southerners wanted to expand slavery to the entire nation. He set the stage for his argument by using a metaphor from the Bible.

*A VOICE FROM THE PAST*

"A house divided against itself cannot stand." I believe this government cannot endure, permanently half slave and half free. I do not expect the Union to be dissolved—I do not expect the house to fall—but I do expect it will cease to be divided. It will become all one thing, or all the other.

**Abraham Lincoln,** Springfield, Illinois, June 16, 1858

Later in the year, the two men held formal debates across Illinois. The Lincoln–Douglas debates are now seen as models of political debate. At the time, the debates allowed people to compare the short, stocky, well-dressed Douglas with the tall, thin, gawky Lincoln.

The two men squarely addressed the nation's most pressing issue: the expansion of slavery. For Lincoln, slavery was "a moral, a social and a political wrong." But he did not suggest abolishing slavery where it already existed. He argued only that slavery should not be expanded.

Douglas did not share Lincoln's belief that it was the national government's role to prevent the expansion of slavery. Instead, he argued



## ACTIVITY OPTIONS

**INTERDISCIPLINARY LINK: CIVICS** — BLOCK SCHEDULING

**THE *DRED SCOTT* CASE**

**Class Time** Two class periods

**Task** Presenting a mock hearing of the *Dred Scott* case

**Purpose** To understand the complexities of the *Dred Scott* case

**Supplies Needed**
- Encyclopedias and resource material about the *Dred Scott* case

**Activity** Ask students to do research on the *Dred Scott* case, taking notes on cards emphasizing the most important points of the trial. Form groups and have each group divide up the roles of Dred Scott, his lawyer, opposition lawyers, and Chief Justice Taney. Allow each group to present its mock case, including Chief Justice Taney's handing down of the Court's opinion.

## CITIZENSHIP TODAY

# Debating Points of View

Debate has long been an important method of exploring public issues. The Lincoln–Douglas debates drew crowds from all over Illinois to hear Lincoln and Douglas discuss the issues of the day. Debates such as these can help people find out about candidates' views.

Today, the National Forensic League (NFL) sponsors Lincoln–Douglas Debates, competitions for high school students. Many judges, actors, news commentators, and talk show hosts began to develop their debating skills in such competitions.

High school students can benefit from learning to defend their positions in debates. One student explained what she learned from NFL debates. "I learned about how to think really fast and how to respond."

Jessica Bailey of Apple Valley High School in Minnesota won second place in the national Lincoln–Douglas Debates competition in 1998.

### How Do You Debate an Issue?

1. Choose a debate opponent and an issue to debate. (One NFL topic for national competition was whether the federal government should establish an educational policy to increase academic achievement in secondary schools in the United States.)
2. Research the topic you chose.
3. Agree on a format for your debate—how many minutes for presentation, rebuttal, and closing.
4. Debate your opponent in front of the class.
5. Find out how many students in the audience agree with each side, then ask for their reasons.

See Citizenship Handbook, page 248.

Visit www.mcdougallittell.com for more on debates.

that popular sovereignty was the best way to address the issue because it was the most democratic method to do so.

*Reading* **History**
**C. Making Inferences** Why were popular sovereignty and the opinion in the *Dred Scott* case inconsistent?
C. Answer The *Dred Scott* opinion said that territories could not outlaw slavery. Popular sovereignty said that they could.

But popular sovereignty was a problem for Douglas. The Supreme Court decision in the *Dred Scott* case had made popular sovereignty unconstitutional. Why? It said that people could not vote to ban slavery, because doing so would take away slaveholders' property rights. In the debates, Lincoln asked Douglas if he thought people in a territory who were against slavery could legally prohibit it—despite the *Dred Scott* decision.

Douglas replied that it did not matter what the Supreme Court might decide about slavery because "the people have the lawful means to introduce it or exclude it as they please." Douglas won reelection. Lincoln, despite his loss, became a national figure and strengthened his standing in the Republican Party.

## 4 John Brown Attacks Harpers Ferry

**Vocabulary**
**arsenal:** stock of weapons

In 1859, John Brown, who had murdered proslavery Kansans three years before, added to the sectional tensions. Brown had a plan. He wanted to inspire slaves to fight for their freedom. To do this, he planned to capture the weapons in the U.S. arsenal at **Harpers Ferry**, Virginia.

On October 16, 1859, Brown and 18 followers—13 whites and 5 blacks—captured the Harpers Ferry arsenal. They killed four people in the raid. Brown then sent out the word to rally and arm local slaves.





### CITIZENSHIP TODAY

**OBJECTIVE**

Students will be able to explain the importance of debate in exploring public issues in both historic and modern American life.

**The Importance of Debate in American Life**

Some of the speeches given during the debates over the Compromise of 1850 are the most famous in the history of the Congress. Today, members of Congress still debate new bills presented for their votes. Debates have also become an important part of elections. John F. Kennedy and Richard Nixon, the presidential candidates in 1960, engaged in the first televised presidential debates.

**Standards for Evaluation**

**Each speaker should**

- clearly state the problem, position, or topic.
- demonstrate focus and logical organization.
- use appropriate background and research information to defend his or her position.
- conclude with a summarization of the main points and end with an appropriate conclusion.

**Citizenship Today,** pp. 11–12

### INSTRUCT: OBJECTIVE 

**John Brown Attacks Harpers Ferry**

Key Questions

- Why did John Brown attack Harpers Ferry?
- What was the reaction of Northerners to Brown's execution?
- How did Southerners react to the raid?

**Geography Transparency GT15**
- The Slave Population of the South, 1860

**In-Depth Resources: Unit 5**
- Primary Source: John Brown's Raid, p. 12

## ACTIVITY OPTIONS

### INDIVIDUAL NEEDS

**LESS PROFICIENT READERS**

**Charting Comparisons** Ask students to recall the caning of Charles Sumner (page 465). Then ask them to think about John Brown's attack on Harpers Ferry. In a chart, have them show similarities between the two incidents. Instruct students to concentrate on the reasons for the attacks and their effects.

| Similarities Between Charles Sumner and John Brown Incidents | |
|---|---|
| **Brooks's Caning of Sumner** | **Brown's Attack on Harpers Ferry** |
| attack by a Southerner | attack by a Northerner |
| Brooks thought he was avenging his relative and the honor of the South. | Brown thought he was righting wrong done to slaves. |
| Southerners thought he was a hero and martyr. | Northerners thought he was a hero and martyr. |
| incident worsened tensions between North and South | incident worsened tensions between North and South |

## HISTORY through ART

**Interpreting the Painting** John Steuart Curry was born in Kansas in 1897. After living in Europe and Connecticut, Curry returned to Kansas in 1937 and spent five years working on a series of murals in the statehouse in Topeka. He used John Brown as his central symbol of the spirit of Kansas. In the image here, Curry shows Brown as one of nature's forces, with a tornado on one side and a prairie fire on the other. Many Kansans were appalled by Curry's murals and by his choice of Brown as their central figure. In 1941, the Kansas legislators refused to allow Curry to finish the murals. In 1992, the Kansas legislature issued an official apology for its treatment of Curry.

**Extension** Students may wish to view other pictures and paintings of John Brown and compare the portrayals of Brown.

**Possible Response: Curry believes Brown caused the Civil War because he shows Brown standing on soldiers' bodies. Brown looks crazy.**

## ASSESS & RETEACH

**Setting the Stage** Have students complete the box on the election of 1860 on the chapter graphic organizer.

 **Formal Assessment**
- Section Quiz, p. 230

### RETEACHING ACTIVITY

Have students create a time line for the events in this section, beginning with the formation of the Republican Party and ending with John Brown's attack on Harpers Ferry.

 **In-Depth Resources: Unit 5**
- Reteaching Activity, p. 18

### HISTORY through ART

John Steuart Curry painted *The Tragic Prelude* between 1937 and 1942. He shows a wild-eyed John Brown standing on the bodies of Civil War soldiers.

**What do you think Curry's views were on John Brown's role in U.S. history?**

But no slaves joined the fight. The U.S. Marines attacked Brown at Harpers Ferry. Some of his men escaped. But Brown and six others were captured, and ten men were killed.

Brown was then tried for murder and treason. He was convicted and sentenced to hang. On the day he was hanged, abolitionists tolled bells and fired guns in salute. Southerners were enraged by Brown's actions and horrified by Northern reactions to his death.

As the nation headed toward the election of 1860, the issue of slavery had raised sectional tensions to the breaking point. In the next section, you will read about the election of 1860 and its effect on the nation.

### Section 3 Assessment

**1. Terms & Names**

**Identify:**
- Republican Party
- John C. Frémont
- James Buchanan
- *Dred Scott* v. *Sandford*
- Roger B. Taney
- Abraham Lincoln
- Harpers Ferry

**2. Taking Notes**

Use a chart like the one below to take notes on the major events discussed in this section.

| Election of 1856 | |
|---|---|
| *Dred Scott* v. *Sandford* | |
| Lincoln–Douglas debates | |
| Harpers Ferry | |

**3. Main Ideas**

a. What issues led to the creation of the Republican Party?

b. What was Chief Justice Taney's opinion in the *Dred Scott* case?

c. How did John Brown's attack on Harpers Ferry increase tensions between the North and the South?

**4. Critical Thinking**

**Identifying Facts and Opinions** How did Lincoln and Douglas disagree about slavery? Which of their views were facts, and which were opinions?

**THINK ABOUT**
- Lincoln's speech at Springfield in 1858
- Douglas's support of popular sovereignty

**ACTIVITY OPTIONS**

**MATH / GEOGRAPHY** Do research to find election returns from the 1856 presidential election. Make **graphs** or draw a **map** to illustrate the results.

### Section 3 Assessment

**1. Terms & Names**

**Republican Party,** p. 466
**John C. Frémont,** p. 467
**James Buchanan,** p. 467
***Dred Scott* v. *Sandford*,** p. 467
**Roger B. Taney,** p. 468
**Abraham Lincoln,** p. 468
**Harpers Ferry,** p. 469

**2. Taking Notes**

Event 1: Buchanan won, but the election showed the strength of antislavery forces; Event 2: Supreme Court case that undid the Missouri Compromise; Event 3: a series of debates about slavery in the territories; Event 4: John Brown led an assault for weapons on a U.S. arsenal

**3. Main Ideas**

**a.** Slavery in the territories; the Kansas-Nebraska Act; "Bleeding Kansas" **b.** that Scott was not a citizen; he had no right to sue in U.S. courts **c.** It contributed to Southerners' fears that Northerners would stop at nothing to destroy slavery.

**4. Critical Thinking**

Lincoln: Expansion of slavery should be stopped by the national government. Douglas: Popular sovereignty should be used to address slavery. All of their statements were opinions.

### ACTIVITY OPTIONS

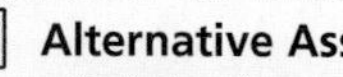 **Alternative Assessment**
- Rubrics for a graph, 2.3
- Rubrics for a map, 2.1

# 4 Lincoln's Election and Southern Secession

**TERMS & NAMES**
platform
secede
Confederate States of America
Jefferson Davis
Crittenden Plan

**MAIN IDEA**

The election of Lincoln led the Southern states to secede from the Union.

**WHY IT MATTERS NOW**

This was the only time in U.S. history that states seceded from the Union.



## SECTION OBJECTIVES

1. To analyze why the Democratic Party split in the election of 1860
2. To identify the issues in the election of 1860
3. To describe the secession of the Southern states from the Union
4. To explain the Union's response to secession

**SKILLBUILDER**
Interpreting Maps: Region, p. 473

**CRITICAL THINKING**
Recognizing Effects, p. 472
Making Inferences, p. 475
Analyzing Points of View, p. 475

 **Why It Matters Now**
- Divided Nations, pp. 29–30

## FOCUS & MOTIVATE

### 5-MINUTE WARM-UP

**Interpreting Maps** These questions focus on the election of 1860.

1. Look at the map on page 473. How many states voted for Lincoln? How many voted for Douglas? for Breckinridge? for Bell?
2. Where did Lincoln have strong support? Where did he have no support?

 **Warm-Up Transparency WT15**

## INSTRUCT

### INSTRUCT: OBJECTIVE 1

**Political Parties Splinter**
Key Questions
- What issue split the Democratic Party?
- What was unusual about the number of candidates for president in 1860?
- What was the aim of the Constitutional Union Party?

 **In-Depth Resources: Unit 5**
- Guided Reading, p. 6

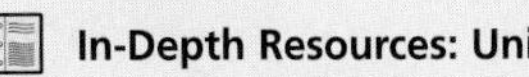 **Reading Study Guide** (Spanish and English), pp. 155–156

## ONE AMERICAN'S STORY

In May 1860, Murat Halstead, a reporter for the Cincinnati *Commercial,* traveled to Chicago to cover the Republican convention. Most people assumed that William Seward of New York would win the party's presidential nomination. But there were other candidates, too.

Throughout the convention, candidates tried to win away Seward's delegates. As the other candidates hoped, Seward failed to win the nomination on the first ballot. Throughout the tense voting, Abraham Lincoln, a lesser-known candidate from Illinois, gained strength. Halstead described the scene as Lincoln received the winning votes.

In 1860, the Republican delegates met in Chicago at a convention hall known as the Wigwam.

*A VOICE FROM THE PAST*

There was a moment's silence. The nerves of the thousands, which through the hours of suspense had been subjected to terrible tension, relaxed, and as deep breaths of relief were taken, there was a noise in the Wigwam [convention hall] like the rush of a great wind [just before] a storm—and in another breath, the storm was there. There were thousands cheering with the energy of insanity.

**Murat Halstead,** *Caucuses of 1860*

Having won the nomination, Lincoln could turn his attention to winning the general election. In this section, you will learn about the election of 1860 and its role in pushing the nation toward civil war.

## 1 Political Parties Splinter

A few weeks before the Republicans nominated Abraham Lincoln, the Democrats held their convention in Charleston, South Carolina. Northern and Southern Democrats disagreed over what to say about slavery in the party's **platform,** or statement of beliefs.

The Southerners wanted the party to defend slavery in the platform.



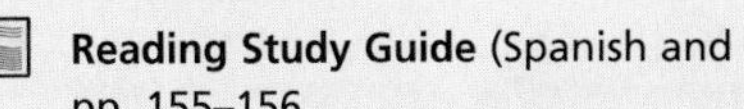

## RECOMMENDED RESOURCES

**In-Depth Resources: Unit 5**
- Guided Reading, p. 6
- Building Vocabulary, p. 7
- Geography Application: The South Votes to Secede, pp. 9–10
- Reteaching Activity, p. 19

**Reading Study Guide** (Spanish and English), pp. 155–156

**Outline Map Activities**
- The Election of 1860, pp. 29–30

**Why It Matters Now**
- Divided Nations, pp. 29–30

**American History Plays**
- from *Abe Lincoln in Illinois* by Robert Sherwood

**Formal Assessment**
- Section Quiz, p. 231

**Alternative Assessment**
- Rubrics, 3.6
- Rubrics, 5.4

**Access for Students Acquiring English/ESL**
- Guided Reading, p. 103
- Geography Application, pp. 105–106

**Technology Resources**

 **Electronic Teacher Tools with Test Maker**

 **ClassZone** www.mcdougallittell.com

**MORE ABOUT . . .**

**The Republican Convention of 1860**

The convention was held in the cattle-filled streets of the young, rowdy town of Chicago in the newly built, first-of-its-kind convention building, the Wigwam. Although the town boasted 57 hotels, so many Republicans came that many slept on pool tables in hotel billiard rooms. The Republicans were a boisterous group that anticipated a win because of the split in the Democratic Party.

**MORE ABOUT . . .**

**John C. Breckinridge**

John Cabell Breckinridge from Kentucky was vice-president of the United States under James Buchanan. When the Civil War began, he joined the Confederacy and served as a general and as Jefferson Davis's secretary of war. At the end of the war, Breckinridge fled abroad where he remained until 1868. Returning to Kentucky, he practiced law and worked for a railroad company.

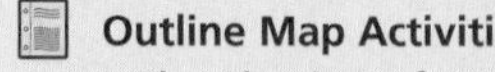

**INSTRUCT: OBJECTIVE 2**

**The Election of 1860**

Key Questions

- How did Breckinridge's stance on the expansion of slavery in the territories differ from Lincoln's?
- Why were Douglas and Bell thought to be moderates?
- What did Southerners fear Lincoln would do after the election?

**Outline Map Activities**

- The Election of 1860, pp. 29–30

But Northerners wanted the platform to support popular sovereignty as a way of deciding whether a territory became a free state or a slave state. The Northerners won the platform vote, causing 50 Southern delegates to walk out of the convention.

The remaining delegates tried to nominate a presidential candidate. Stephen A. Douglas was the leading contender, but the Southerners who stayed refused to back him because of his support for popular sovereignty. Douglas could not win enough votes to gain the nomination.

Finally, the Democrats gave up and decided to meet again six weeks later in Baltimore to choose a candidate. But as the Baltimore convention opened, Northerners and Southerners remained at odds. This time, almost all the Southerners left the meeting.

With the Southerners gone, the Northern Democrats nominated Douglas. Meanwhile, the Southern Democrats decided to nominate their own candidate. They chose John Breckinridge of Kentucky, the current vice-president and a supporter of slavery.

As you read in One American's Story on page 471, the Republicans had already nominated Abraham Lincoln. In addition to Lincoln, Douglas, and Breckinridge, a candidate from a fourth party entered the race. This party was called the Constitutional Union Party, and its members had one aim—to preserve the Union. They nominated John Bell of Tennessee to run for president.

*Reading*History

**A. Recognizing Effects** How did slavery affect U.S. political parties in 1860?

**A. Answer** It split the Democrats in two and led to the formation of the Constitutional Union Party. It also increased the strength of the Republicans.

## 2 The Election of 1860

The election of 1860 turned into two different races for the presidency, one in the North and one in the South. Lincoln and Douglas were the only candidates with much support in the North. Breckinridge and Bell competed for Southern votes.

Lincoln and Breckinridge were considered to have the most extreme views on slavery. Lincoln opposed the expansion of slavery into the territories. Breckinridge insisted that the federal government be required to protect slavery in any territory. Douglas and Bell were considered moderates because neither wanted the federal government to pass new laws on slavery.

This cartoon of the long-legged Abe Lincoln shows him to be the fittest candidate in the 1860 presidential election.

The outcome of the election made it clear that the nation was tired of compromise. Lincoln defeated Douglas in the North. Breckinridge carried most of the South. Douglas and Bell managed to win only in the states between the North and the Deep South. Because the North had more people in it than the South, Lincoln won the election.



**ACTIVITY OPTIONS**

**INDIVIDUAL NEEDS**

**STUDENTS ACQUIRING ENGLISH/ESL**

**Words with Multiple Meanings** Point out the word *splinter* in the heading on page 471. Tell students that *splinter* can be used as a verb and as a noun. As a noun, it means "a tiny piece of wood." In the heading *Political Parties Splinter,* it is used as a verb meaning "to break into pieces." Help students understand how the political parties splintered by asking questions such as:

- What issue caused the Democratic Party to splinter?
- How did its division affect the Democratic Party's performance in the election?

You may wish to have students draw political cartoons illustrating the splintering of the Democratic Party.

## The Election of 1860

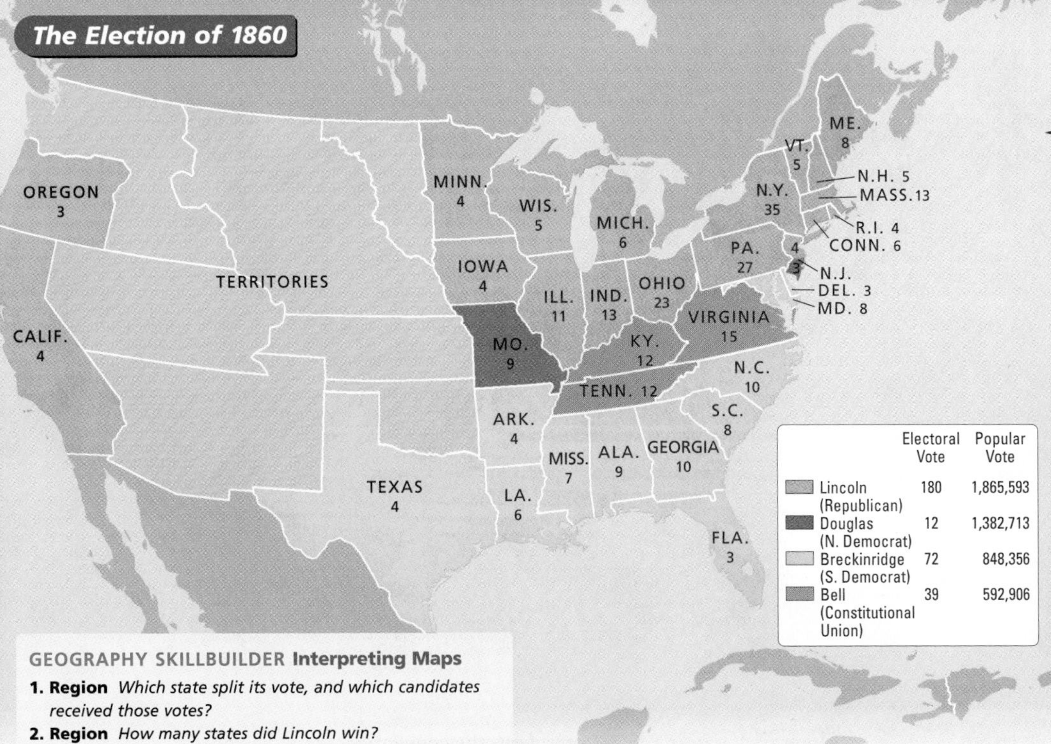


| | Electoral Vote | Popular Vote |
|---|---|---|
| Lincoln (Republican) | 180 | 1,865,593 |
| Douglas (N. Democrat) | 12 | 1,382,713 |
| Breckinridge (S. Democrat) | 72 | 848,356 |
| Bell (Constitutional Union) | 39 | 592,906 |

**GEOGRAPHY SKILLBUILDER Interpreting Maps**

1. **Region** *Which state split its vote, and which candidates received those votes?*
2. **Region** *How many states did Lincoln win?*

Skillbuilder Answers
1. New Jersey; Lincoln 4, Douglas 3
2. 17 and part of New Jersey

Despite Lincoln's statements that he would do nothing to abolish slavery in the South, white Southerners did not trust him. Many were sure that he and the other Republicans would move to ban slavery. As a result, white Southerners saw the Republican victory as a threat to the Southern way of life.

## 3 Southern States Secede

Before the 1860 presidential election, many Southerners had warned that if Lincoln won, the Southern states would **secede,** or withdraw from the Union. Supporters of secession based their arguments on the idea of states' rights. They argued that the states had voluntarily joined the Union. Consequently, they claimed that the states also had the right to leave the Union.

On December 20, 1860, South Carolina became the first state to secede. Other states in the Deep South, where slave labor and cotton production were most common, also considered secession. During the next six weeks, Mississippi, Florida, Alabama, Georgia, Louisiana, and Texas joined South Carolina in secession.

In early February 1861, the states that had seceded met in Montgomery, Alabama. They formed the **Confederate States of America.** The convention named **Jefferson Davis** president of the Confederacy.

**Background**
Before becoming president of the Confederacy, Davis had been a hero during the War with Mexico and a U.S. senator.



### *HISTORY through ART*

**Reading the Map** Ask students if the election might have turned out differently if there had been only one Democratic candidate. Tell them to look at the differences in the popular vote and the electoral vote to formulate their answer. **Possible Responses** 1) Probably not, because, although the Democratic candidate might have won the popular vote, the Republicans would have won the electoral vote. 2) Perhaps yes, because it is possible that a single Democratic candidate might have carried some states that went to Lincoln, giving the Democrats enough electoral votes to win.

**Extension** Have students research the electoral college to understand why Douglas could have won such a large number of popular votes and yet so few electoral votes.

### INSTRUCT: OBJECTIVE 3

**Southern States Secede**
Key Questions
- What argument did some Southerners use to justify secession?
- What were the results of the convention held by the six seceded states?
- How was the Confederate Constitution different from the U.S. Constitution?

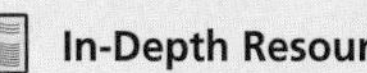
**In-Depth Resources: Unit 5**
- Geography Application, pp. 9–10

### MORE ABOUT . . .

**Jefferson Davis**
The biography of Jefferson Davis contains two small mysteries: his birth date and his middle name. Davis himself was not sure whether he was born in 1807 or 1808. Historians have not been able to verify Davis's middle name, commonly accepted as "Finis." Although records and documents signed by Davis include the middle initial "F," the name is not spelled out on any document. Legend says that Davis's parents named him "Finis," or "the end" because he was their tenth child.

### ACTIVITY OPTIONS

**INTERDISCIPLINARY LINK: GOVERNMENT** — BLOCK SCHEDULING

**FORMING A GOVERNMENT**

**Class Time** 45 minutes

**Task** Forming a new government

**Purpose** To help students understand the complexities of creating the Confederate government

**Supplies Needed**
- History and government books on the United States and on the Confederacy; a copy of the Constitution

**Activity** Challenge students to make some decisions about starting a new government as the secessionists did. Divide the class into groups and ask them to prepare a one-page plan of action for their government that addresses the following questions:
- Brainstorm a list of the first things you will do to start your government.
- What might you follow as a pattern to base your government on? The United States? A different country? What kind of laws will you make and how will you enforce them?

### CRITICAL THINKING ACTIVITY

**Analyzing Points of View** Have students examine Southern justifications of secession and Northern responses by making a spider map. Tell them to write *secession* in the center circle and add information about the two sides on the appropriate lines.

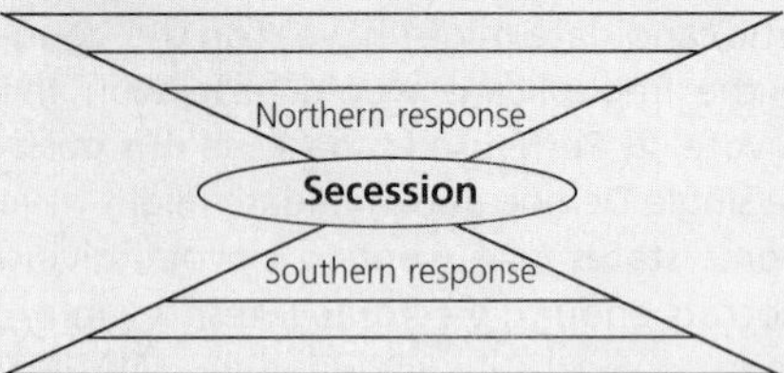


**Class Time** 15 minutes

### MORE ABOUT . . .

**James Russell Lowell**
Lowell was born in Cambridge, Massachusetts, to an established New England family. He was a crusading reformer, working for abolition, women's rights, temperance, and vegetarianism. He became a professor of literature at Harvard and also served as U.S. ambassador to Spain and to England.

## INSTRUCT

### INSTRUCT: OBJECTIVE 4

**The Union Responds to Secession/ Efforts to Compromise Fail**

Key Questions

- How did President Buchanan and other Northerners respond to secession?
- What was the purpose of the Crittenden Plan? Was it successful?
- How did Lincoln try to reassure the South in his First Inaugural Address?

**In his First Inaugural Address, Lincoln argued passionately for the North and the South to preserve the Union.**

Along with naming Davis president, the convention drafted a constitution. The Confederate Constitution was modeled on the U.S. Constitution. But there were a few important differences. For example, the Confederate Constitution supported states' rights. It also protected slavery in the Confederacy, including any territories it might acquire.

Having formed its government, the Confederate states made plans to defend their separation from the Union. Some believed that war between the states could not be avoided. But everyone waited to see what the Union government would do in response.

## 4 The Union Responds to Secession

Northerners considered the secession of the Southern states to be unconstitutional. During his last months in office, President James Buchanan argued against secession. He believed that the states did not have the right to withdraw from the Union because the federal government, not the state governments, was sovereign. If secession were permitted, the Union would become weak, like a "rope of sand." He believed that the U.S. Constitution was framed to prevent such a thing from happening.

Vocabulary
**sovereign:** supreme, self-governing authority

In addition to these issues, secession raised the issue of majority rule. Southerners complained that Northerners intended to use their majority to force the South to abolish slavery. But Northerners responded that Southerners simply did not want to live by the rules of democracy. They complained that Southerners were not willing to live with the election results. As Northern writer James Russell Lowell



### ACTIVITY OPTIONS

### INTERDISCIPLINARY LINK: SPEECH

BLOCK SCHEDULING

**LINCOLN'S FIRST INAUGURAL ADDRESS**

**Class Time** 30 minutes

**Task** Presenting a portion of the First Inaugural Address

**Purpose** To familiarize students with one of the nation's famous speeches and to help them understand the role of oratory in the history of the United States

**Supplies Needed**

- Copies of the First Inaugural Address

**Activity** Have students work alone or in pairs to read and memorize a section of Lincoln's First Inaugural Address. Have students practice their section out loud and then present it to the class. You may allow students who have difficulty memorizing to prepare a reading of their section. After the presentation, discuss how hearing Lincoln present this speech might have affected the listeners.

wrote, "[The Southerners'] quarrel is not with the Republican Party, but with the theory of Democracy."

## Efforts to Compromise Fail

With the states in the lower South forming a new government in Montgomery, Alabama, some people continued to seek compromise. Senator John J. Crittenden of Kentucky developed a compromise plan. The **Crittenden Plan** was presented to Congress in late February 1861, but it did not pass.

*"We must not be enemies."*
**Abraham Lincoln**

With the hopes for compromise fading, Americans waited for Lincoln's inauguration. What would the new president do about the crisis? On March 4, Lincoln took the oath of office and gave his First Inaugural Address. He assured the South that he had no intention of abolishing slavery there. But he spoke forcefully against secession. Then he ended his speech with an appeal to friendship.

*A VOICE FROM THE PAST*

We are not enemies, but friends. We must not be enemies. Though passion may have strained, it must not break our bonds of affection. The mystic chords of memory, stretching from every battle-field and patriot grave, to every living heart and hearthstone, all over this broad land, will yet swell the chorus of the Union, when again touched, as surely they will be, by the better angels of our nature.

**Abraham Lincoln,** *First Inaugural Address*

*Reading* **History**
**B. Making Inferences** What do you think Lincoln meant by "mystic chords of memory"?
B. Possible Response spiritual attachment that he believed Americans had to their nation's history

Lincoln would not press the South. He wanted no invasion. But he would not abandon the government's property there. Several forts in the South, including Fort Sumter in South Carolina, were still in Union hands. These forts would soon need to be resupplied. Throughout March and into April, Northerners and Southerners waited anxiously to see what would happen next. You will find out in the next chapter.

### Section 4 Assessment

**1. Terms & Names**

**Identify:**
- platform
- secede
- Confederate States of America
- Jefferson Davis
- Crittenden Plan

**2. Taking Notes**

Use a time line to fill in the main events that occurred between April 1860 and March 1861.

April 1860 — May 1860 — June 1860 — Nov. 1860 — Feb. 1861 — March 1861

Do you think secession could have been avoided? Why?

**3. Main Ideas**

a. Who were the candidates in the 1860 presidential election, and what policies did each candidate stand for?

b. Which states seceded right after Lincoln's election? How did they justify this action?

c. What attempts did the North and the South make to compromise? What were the results?

**4. Critical Thinking**

**Analyzing Points of View**
Do you think the Southern states seceded to protect slavery or states' rights?

**THINK ABOUT**
- the Southern view of the Fugitive Slave Act
- the Confederate Constitution
- slaveholders' views of the Republican Party

**ACTIVITY OPTIONS**

**SPEECH**
**TECHNOLOGY**

Read Lincoln's First Inaugural Address. Deliver a section of the **speech** before the class or plan an **electronic presentation** about that day and Lincoln's message.





### MORE ABOUT . . .

**The Crittenden Plan**

The Crittenden Plan, or Compromise, as it is sometimes designated, was sponsored by Senator John J. Crittenden of Kentucky. Crittenden proposed that the division established by the Missouri Compromise be extended to the Pacific Ocean. In other words, slavery would be prohibited north of the 36° 30' line set by the Missouri Compromise and protected south of it.

## ASSESS & RETEACH

**Setting the Stage** Have students fill in the box for the Election of 1860 on the graphic organizer on page 456.

**Formal Assessment**
- Section Quiz, p. 231

**Critical Thinking Transparency CT43**
- Setting the Stage

### RETEACHING ACTIVITY

In small groups, have students use the graphic below to discuss the election of 1860.

**In-Depth Resources: Unit 5**
- Reteaching Activity, p. 19

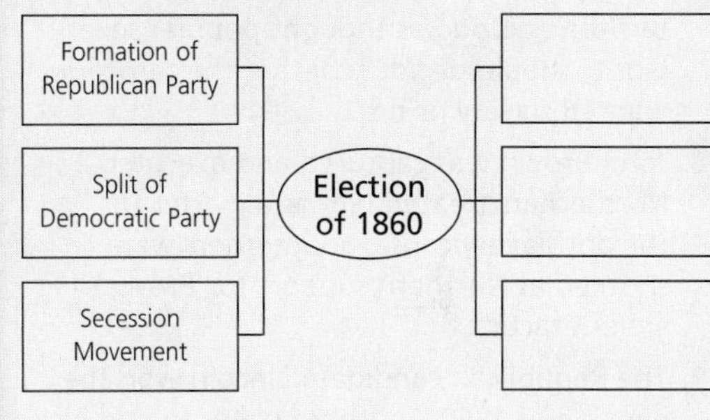


### Section 4 Assessment

**1. Terms & Names**

**platform,** p. 471
**secede,** p. 473
**Confederate States of America,** p. 473
**Jefferson Davis,** p. 473
**Crittenden Plan,** p. 475

**2. Taking Notes**

April 1860: Southern Democrats walk out of the convention; May 1860: Republicans nominate Lincoln; June 1860: Democrats split. November 1860: Lincoln wins election; February 1861: Confederate States of America is formed; March 1861: Lincoln is inaugurated

**3. Main Ideas**

a. Lincoln: opposed the expansion of slavery; Breckinridge: the federal government should protect slavery; Douglas: popular sovereignty; Bell: preserving the Union **b.** SC, MS, FL, AL, GA, LA, and TX; the Union was voluntary **c.** the Crittenden Plan; it was rejected

**4. Critical Thinking**

Students might say that they were defending the rights of states or feared the abolition of slavery.

**ACTIVITY OPTIONS**

**Alternative Assessment**
- Rubrics for a speech, 3.6
- Rubrics for multimedia, 5.4

## TERMS & NAMES

1. **Wilmot Proviso,** p. 459
2. **Compromise of 1850,** p. 461
3. ***Uncle Tom's Cabin,*** p. 462
4. **popular sovereignty,** p. 463
5. **Kansas–Nebraska Act,** p. 464
6. **John Brown,** p. 465
7. **John C. Frémont,** p. 467
8. ***Dred Scott* v. *Sandford,*** p. 467
9. **secede,** p. 473
10. **Confederate States of America,** p. 473

## REVIEW QUESTIONS

**Possible Responses**

1. The North was more industrial while the South remained more agricultural with a heavy reliance on slave labor.
2. They saw it as an attempt to destroy slavery.
3. He worked to get the bill passed by Congress despite regional bickering over the issue.
4. They opposed the law because it forced them to support slavery.
5. The act allowed slavery into territories where it had been banned. Northerners opposed it and Southerners supported it.
6. Democrats took much of the blame for the violence that erupted in Kansas.
7. Lincoln thought that the national government should ban slavery from expanding into new territories. Douglas thought popular sovereignty should decide whether the territories wanted slavery or not.
8. John Brown was captured and executed. Northerners treated him as a martyr for the antislavery cause. Southerners were shocked at Northern support for Brown's violent tactics.
9. The Republican candidate Lincoln won the election of 1860. Southern states feared his motives and seceded from the Union.
10. They argued that they had joined the Union voluntarily and had the right to leave.

# Chapter 15 ASSESSMENT

## VISUAL SUMMARY

### The Nation Breaking Apart

SLAVERY

**1846** Wilmot Proviso

Compromise of **1850**

**1854** Kansas–Nebraska Act

**1855** "Bleeding Kansas"

**1856** Caning of Sumner

**1857** *Dred Scott* v. *Sandford*

**1859** Attack on Harpers Ferry

Election of **1860**

**Secession**

## TERMS & NAMES

Briefly explain the importance of each of the following.

1. Wilmot Proviso
2. Compromise of 1850
3. *Uncle Tom's Cabin*
4. popular sovereignty
5. Kansas–Nebraska Act
6. John Brown
7. John C. Frémont
8. *Dred Scott* v. *Sandford*
9. secede
10. Confederate States of America

## REVIEW QUESTIONS

**Growing Tensions Between North and South (pages 457–461)**

1. How did the North and the South differ in the 1840s?
2. How did Southerners react to the Wilmot Proviso?
3. What was Stephen A. Douglas's role in passing the Compromise of 1850?

**The Crisis Deepens (pages 462–465)**

4. How did Northerners react to the Fugitive Slave Act?
5. Why did most Northerners and Southerners disagree about the Kansas–Nebraska Act?
6. How did "Bleeding Kansas" cause problems for Democrats?

**Slavery Dominates Politics (pages 466–470)**

7. What positions did Lincoln and Douglas take in their debates?
8. What was the result of John Brown's raid on Harpers Ferry?

**Lincoln's Election and Southern Secession (pages 471–475)**

9. What were the results of the election of 1860, and what did these results show?
10. How did Southerners justify secession?

## CRITICAL THINKING

**1. USING YOUR NOTES**

Using your completed diagram, answer the questions below.

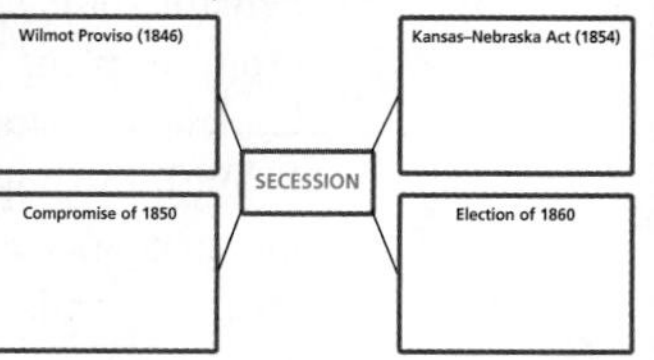


a. What did the Compromise of 1850 and the Kansas–Nebraska Act have in common?

b. Which event do you think caused the most damage to the relationship between the North and the South? Explain.

**2. ANALYZING LEADERSHIP**

Why were the nation's leaders in 1860 unable to compromise like the leaders in 1820 and 1850? Does their failure to compromise in 1860 mean that they were not as capable as earlier leaders?

**3. APPLYING CITIZENSHIP SKILLS**

What alternatives did the states in the lower South have to secession? Which of these alternatives do you think would have been the best choice?

**4. SOLVING PROBLEMS**

How did slavery divide Americans in the 1850s?

**5. THEME: DIVERSITY AND UNITY**

What could have been done in the 1850s to prevent the Southern states from seceding? What did Americans have in common that could have overcome their differences over slavery?

**Interact *with* History**

Now that you have read about the sectional crisis of the 1850s, do you think the solution you came up with at the start of the chapter would have helped keep the Union together? Explain.



## CRITICAL THINKING

**Possible Responses**

1. **USING YOUR NOTES** **a.** Both dealt with the issue of slavery in the territories. **b.** Student responses will vary. Be sure they explain their choice.
2. **ANALYZING LEADERSHIP** In 1860, tensions over slavery were much higher. No, because they faced bigger problems.
3. **APPLYING CITIZENSHIP SKILLS** Student responses will vary. Be sure they give plausible alternatives and explain their choice.
4. **SOLVING PROBLEMS** Many people thought the institution was wrong and inefficient. Others argued that slavery was economically beneficial, that slaves were unfit for freedom, and that it was an important part of Southern culture.
5. **THEME: DIVERSITY AND UNITY** They could have put the issue of slavery to a vote and made a commitment to live with the results. The states had in common a commitment to democracy.

**Interact *with* History** Responses will vary but should be supported by information in the chapter.

476 CHAPTER 15

## HISTORY SKILLS

**1. INTERPRETING MAPS: Region**

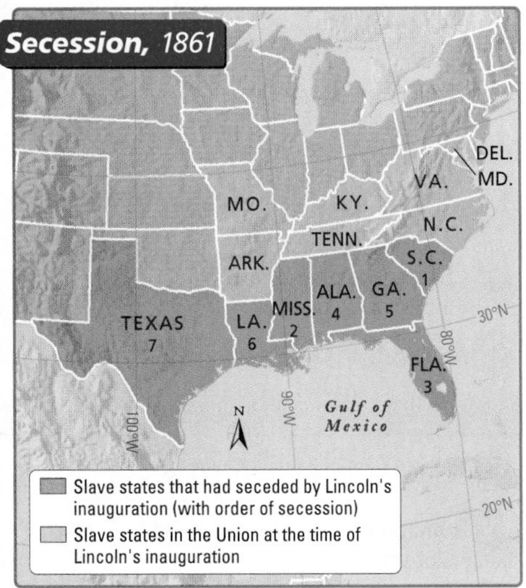


**Basic Map Elements**

a. Which states seceded before Lincoln's inauguration in March, 1861?

**Interpreting the Map**

b. What geographical characteristics did these states have in common?

c. Why do you think these states were the first to secede?

**2. INTERPRETING PRIMARY SOURCES**

A detail of Thomas Hovenden's painting, *The Last Moments of John Brown* (1884), shows Brown being led to the gallows.

a. How does Brown appear in this image?

b. Based on Hovenden's presentation of Brown, what do you think were the artist's views on Brown?

## ALTERNATIVE ASSESSMENT

**1. INTERDISCIPLINARY ACTIVITY: Language Arts**

**Conducting an Interview** Pick one of the important people in this chapter, such as Stephen A. Douglas or Harriet Beecher Stowe. Think about what questions you would ask that person in an interview. Then research that person's biographies, speeches, or writings to see how he or she might answer your questions. Write the interview in question-and-answer format. Use direct quotes as often as possible.

**2. COOPERATIVE LEARNING ACTIVITY**

**Presenting a Mock Trial** The case of Dred Scott went to the Supreme Court. The Court, led by Chief Justice Roger B. Taney, decided against Scott. Did the court reach the right verdict?

Working in a small group, do research on the Dred Scott case. Present a mock trial of the case. Look for information about the roles of Taney, the other justices, Scott, and the other major participants. Have the class render a verdict at the end of the trial. Compare your verdict with the actual historical results.

**3. TECHNOLOGY ACTIVITY**

**Making a Class Presentation** American political parties went through extreme changes in the 1840s and 1850s. Using the Internet or the library, find the election returns of the presidential elections from 1848 to 1860.

 **Visit www.mcdougallittell.com to learn more about presidential elections.**

Use presentation software to teach your class about U.S. presidential elections. Here are some suggestions.

- Use pie charts to show the percentage of votes that went to each party in each election.
- Use bar graphs to show the growth in total popular vote (nationwide) for each party for each election.

**4. HISTORY PORTFOLIO**

**Option 1** Review your section and chapter assessment activities. Select one that you think was your best work. Then use the comments made by your teacher or classmates to improve your work and add it to your portfolio.

**Option 2** Review the questions that you wrote for What Do You Want to Know? on page 456. Then write a short report in which you explain the answers to your questions. If any questions were not answered, do research to answer them. Add your answers to your portfolio.



## ALTERNATIVE ASSESSMENT

1. INTERDISCIPLINARY ACTIVITY: **Language Arts**
**Interviews should**
- reflect the student's understanding of basic concepts relevant to the experiences of the person selected.
- accurately reflect the thoughts and experiences of the subject's life.
- use standard grammar, spelling, sentence structure, and punctuation.

2. COOPERATIVE LEARNING ACTIVITY
**Trials should**
- accurately portray the *Dred Scott* trial.
- have adequate delivery and establish rapport with the audience.
- show evidence of involvement of each person in the group.

3.  TECHNOLOGY ACTIVITY
**Presentations should**
- clearly demonstrate an understanding of the elections of the 1840s and 1850s.
- utilize several sources of information to create charts and graphs.
- show proficiency in the use of technology.

4. HISTORY PORTFOLIO

 **Option 1 Revised section or chapter assessment activities should**
- address teacher and peer responses to the selected work.
- solve problems present in the first versions of the work.

**Option 2 Short reports should**
- answer questions about the sectional differences that led to the Civil War.
- use evidence to develop and support ideas.
- cite sources of information.
- use standard grammar, spelling, sentence structure, and punctuation.

 **Critical Thinking Transparency CT45**
- Visual Summary

 **Formal Assessment**
- Chapter Test, Forms A and B, pp. 232–239

## HISTORY SKILLS

**Possible Responses**

1. INTERPRETING MAPS
**Basic Map Elements**
**a.** Texas, Louisiana, Mississippi, Alabama, Georgia, South Carolina, and Florida
**Interpreting the Map**
**b.** These states were the farthest south.
**c.** They probably felt they had more in common with one another—slavery—than with states that were to the North.

2. INTERPRETING PRIMARY SOURCES
**a.** Brown is shown receiving a kiss from an African-American child. It shows his love for African Americans and his desire to end slavery.
**b.** Based on this image, it is likely Hovenden had a positive view of Brown.

# CHAPTER 16 PLANNING GUIDE

# The Civil War Begins 1861–1862

| | CHAPTER OVERVIEW | COPYMASTERS | TECHNOLOGY |
|---|---|---|---|
| **CHAPTER RESOURCES** | This chapter describes the start of the Civil War and its early battles. It also examines the horrible conditions of warfare, and the increase in casualties resulting from new weapons. | **In-Depth Resources: Unit 5**<br>• Tracing Themes: Citizenship, p. 22<br>• Building Vocabulary, p. 26<br>**Interdisciplinary Projects,** pp. 91–96 | **Primary Source Explorer**<br>**Electronic Teacher Tools**<br>**Power Presentations CD-ROM**<br>**Chapter Summaries on CD** (English and Spanish)<br>**America's Music CD** |
| | **KEY IDEAS** | | |
| **SECTION 1 War Erupts pp. 481–487** | • When Confederates fire on Fort Sumter, Lincoln calls for Union troops.<br>• The border states are of crucial importance and remain in the Union.<br>• The South plans a defensive strategy, while the North takes the offensive, blockading Southern ports. | **In-Depth Resources: Unit 5**<br>• Setting the Stage, p. 21<br>• Guided Reading, p. 23<br>• Skillbuilder Practice, p. 27<br>• Geography Application, pp. 28–29<br>• Primary Source, p. 30<br>• Reteaching Activity, p. 35<br>**America's History Makers,** pp. 63–66<br>**Economics in History,** p. 16<br>**Outline Map Activities,** pp. 31–32 | <br>**Warm-Up Transparency WT16**<br>**Humanities Transparency HT31**<br>• Robert E. Lee<br>**Humanities Transparency HT32**<br>• Union and Confederate Money<br>**Geography Transparency GT16**<br>• Union and Confederate Resources, 1861 |
| **SECTION 2 Life in the Army pp. 488–492** | • Most Civil War soldiers are farmers; many are immigrants; and Union armies eventually accept African-American volunteers.<br>• Army life is filled with hardship and disease.<br>• The development of the rifle and the minié ball increases casualties. | **In-Depth Resources: Unit 5**<br>• Setting the Stage, p. 21<br>• Guided Reading, p. 24<br>• Primary Source, p. 31<br>• Literature Selection, pp. 32–34<br>• Reteaching Activity, p. 36<br>**Why It Matters Now**<br>• Modern Warfare, pp. 31–32 | **Warm-Up Transparency WT16**<br>**Critical Thinking Transparency CT46**<br>• Setting the Stage<br>**Critical Thinking Transparency CT47**<br>• Cause and Effect: Hardships of Civil War Soldiers<br>**ClassZone:** www.mcdougallittell.com |
| **SECTION 3 No End in Sight pp. 493–499** | • Union forces under Ulysses S. Grant win victories in the West but at a high cost in lives.<br>• A Union fleet captures New Orleans.<br>• Confederate troops under Robert E. Lee dominate the war in the East. | **In-Depth Resources: Unit 5**<br>• Setting the Stage, p. 21<br>• Guided Reading, p. 25<br>• Reteaching Activity, p. 37 | **Warm-Up Transparency WT16**<br>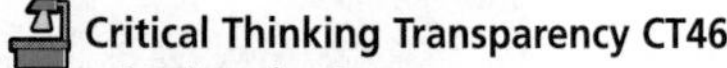<br>**Critical Thinking Transparency CT46**<br>• Setting the Stage<br>**Critical Thinking Transparency CT48**<br>• Visual Summary<br>**ClassZone:** www.mcdougallittell.com |

PE Pupil's Edition
Copymaster
Overhead Transparency
Audio Library
CD-ROM
Internet

## ASSESSMENT

PE **Chapter Assessment,** pp. 498–499

**Formal Assessment**
- Chapter Tests, Forms A and B, pp. 245–252

**Alternative Assessment Book**

**Electronic Teacher Tools with Test Maker**

PE **Section Assessment,** p. 485

**Formal Assessment**
- Section Quiz, p. 242

**Alternative Assessment Book**
- Rubrics for a news article, 4.5
- Rubrics for a Web page, 5.1

**Electronic Teacher Tools with Test Maker**

PE **Section Assessment,** p. 491

**Formal Assessment**
- Section Quiz, p. 243

**Alternative Assessment Book**
- Rubrics for a letter, 4.3
- Rubrics for a map, 2.1

**Electronic Teacher Tools with Test Maker**

PE **Section Assessment,** p. 497

**Formal Assessment**
- Section Quiz, p. 244

**Alternative Assessment Book**
- Rubrics for a map, 2.1
- Rubrics for a diagram, 1.3

**Electronic Teacher Tools with Test Maker**

## CUSTOMIZING FOR INDIVIDUAL NEEDS

### Students Acquiring English/ESL

**Reading Study Guide** (English and Spanish), pp. 159–166

**Access for Students Acquiring English/ESL: Spanish Translations,** pp. 107–112

**Chapter Summaries on CD** (English and Spanish)

### Less Proficient Readers

**Reading Study Guide** (English and Spanish), pp. 159–166

**Chapter Summaries on CD** (English and Spanish)

### Gifted and Talented Students

**In-Depth Resources: Unit 5**
- Enrichment Activity, p. 38

**America's History Makers**
- Abraham Lincoln, pp. 63–64
- Robert E. Lee, pp. 65–66

## CROSS-CURRICULAR CONNECTIONS

### Culture

Van Steenwyk, Elizabeth. ***Mathew Brady: Civil War Photographer.*** New York: Franklin Watts, 1997. Describes the early days of photography and Brady's career. Illustrated with Brady photographs.

### Humanities: Art

McPherson, James M. ***Images of the Civil War: The Paintings of Mort Künstler.*** New York: Gramercy, 1992. A bare-bones text supports 70 color paintings of Civil War scenes by an artist whose work is so accurate and detailed that Civil War buffs comb them for details as if they were photographs.

### Primary Sources

Time-Life Books Editors. ***Soldier Life.*** New York: Time-Life, 1996. Compilation of reminiscences of common soldiers and their families, accompanied by photographs, succeeds in giving a human face to the opposing armies.

### Interdisciplinary Projects, pp. 91–96

- Math: Calculating Income Tax
- Science: Filtering Water
- Language Arts: Journalism: The Inverted Pyramid
- Art: Winslow Homer's Civil War Sketches

### Literature

***The Columbia Book of Civil War Poetry.*** Richard Marius, ed. New York: Columbia U. Press, 1994. Each poem is introduced by a vignette. Contains songs, famous poems, and rare pieces.

Paulsen, Gary. ***A Soldier's Heart.*** New York: Doubleday, 1998. Unsentimental novel that follows 15-year-old Charley as he joins the Minnesota Volunteers, goes through military training, and encounters the excitement, brutality, and fatigue of war.

Rinaldi, Ann. ***Amelia's War.*** New York: Scholastic, 1999. A young Maryland girl tries not to take sides in the war until troops arrive.

### McDougal Littell *The Language of Literature*

- Louisa May Alcott "Civil War Journal" (journal entries)

### McDougal Littell Literature Connections

Irene Hunt

***Across Five Aprils***

This historical novel describes a family with divided loyalties during the Civil War, the sensitive boy left behind to run the farm, and his realization of the horrors of war.

## ENRICHMENT ACTIVITIES

PE **Pupil's Edition, pp. 478–499**
**Interact with History,** p. 479
**Literature Connections,** pp. 486–487
**Technology of the Time,** pp. 492

**In-Depth Resources: Unit 5**
- Geography Application: Fort Sumter Falls, 1861, pp. 28–29
- Primary Source: from *Tad Lincoln's Father,* p. 30
- Primary Source: "Battle Cry of Freedom" and "Bonnie Blue Flag," p. 31
- Literature Selection: "An Episode of War," pp. 32–34

**America's History Makers**
- Abraham Lincoln, pp. 63–64
- Robert E. Lee, pp. 65–66

**America's Music CD**

**Outline Map Activities**
- The Divided Union, 1863 pp. 31–32

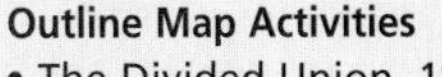

**Why It Matters Now**
- Modern Warfare, pp. 31–32

# CHAPTER 16 PACING GUIDE

**LESSON PLAN OPTIONS (50-MINUTE PERIOD)** **(TE) = Teacher's Edition (PE) = Pupil's Edition**

| | TEACHER-DIRECTED ACTIVITIES<br>Class Time: 15 minutes | STUDENT-CENTERED ACTIVITIES<br>Class Time: 25 minutes | INDIVIDUAL ACTIVITIES<br>Class Time: 10 minutes |
|---|---|---|---|
| **DAY 1**<br>Introduction<br>pp. 478–480 | **Presentation Options**<br>• Begin with a class discussion of the picture on p. 478 **(PE)**.<br>• Lead a class discussion on the "What Do You Know?" question in Setting the Stage, p. 480. Then introduce the graphic organizer for the chapter **(PE)**. | **Options for Cooperative Learning**<br>• Have student groups discuss the Interact with History questions, p. 479 **(PE)**.<br>• Have student groups respond to the "What Do You Want to Know?" question in Setting the Stage, p. 480 **(PE)**. | **Head Start on Homework Options**<br>• Have students skim Section 1 Main Idea, Why It Matters Now, Terms & Names, and the main headings, p. 481 **(PE)**.<br>• Have students begin Guided Reading activity and Building Vocabulary sheet. |
| **DAY 2**<br>Section 1<br>pp. 481–487 | **Presentation Options**<br>• Begin with the 5-Minute Warm-Up, p. 481 **(TE)**.<br>• Review the Section 1 Main Idea, Why It Matters Now, and Terms & Names, p. 481 **(PE)**.<br>• Lead the students through the Skillbuilder Mini-Lesson: Creating a Database, p. 484 **(TE)**. | **Options for Cooperative Learning**<br>• Divide students into groups to work on the Literature Connections questions, pp. 486–487 **(PE)**.<br>• Have student pairs work together to complete one of the Activity Options in the Section 1 Assessment, p. 485 **(PE)**. | **Head Start on Homework Options**<br>• Have students begin working on Section 1 Assessment, p. 485 **(PE)**.<br>• Have students complete the Technology of the Time questions, p. 492 **(PE)**. |
| **DAY 3**<br>Section 2<br>pp. 488–492 | **Presentation Options**<br>• Begin with the 5-Minute Warm-Up, p. 488 **(TE)**.<br>• Choose 5 key questions for Objectives 1–4 to discuss with the class, pp. 488–491 **(TE)**.<br>• Lead students through the Technology of the Time activities, p. 492 **(TE)**. | **Options for Cooperative Learning**<br>• Divide students into groups to work on the Interdisciplinary Link, Music: Civil War Songs, p. 489 **(TE)**.<br>• Have students work in pairs to complete the Reading History questions for the section, pp. 488–491 **(PE)**. | **Head Start on Homework Options**<br>• Have students begin working on Section 2 Assessment, p. 491 **(PE)**.<br>• Have students preview Section 3 Main Idea, Why It Matters Now, Terms & Names, and the main headings, p. 493 **(PE)**. |
| **DAY 4**<br>Section 3<br>pp. 493–497 | **Presentation Options**<br>• Begin with the 5-Minute Warm-Up, p. 493 **(TE)**.<br>• Choose 5 key questions for Objectives 1–4 to discuss with the class, pp. 493–497 **(TE)**.<br>• Lead students through the early battles of the war using the map, pp. 494–495 **(PE)**. | **Options for Cooperative Learning**<br>• Divide students into groups and have them complete the Interdisciplinary Link, Language Arts/Writing: News of War, p. 496 **(TE)**.<br>• Have student pairs work together to complete one of the Activity Options in the Section 3 Assessment, p. 497 **(PE)**. | **Head Start on Homework Options**<br>• Have students complete the Setting the Stage graphic organizer for the chapter, p. 480 **(PE)**.<br>• Have students begin working on the Chapter Assessment, pp. 498–499 **(PE)**.<br>• Prepare for Chapter Test<br>**Formal Assessment,** pp. 245–252 |

TEACHER-TESTED ACTIVITY Nicholas Sysock, Carteret Middle School, Carteret, New Jersey

## TECHNOLOGY OF WAR

**Class Time** One class period

**Task** Reporting on how new technology influenced combat and the outcome of the Civil War

**Purpose** To understand how technology affected the progress and the outcome of the Civil War

**Supplies Needed**

- Reference books and Internet sources on technology of the Civil War
- Markers, colored pencils
- Posterboard

**Activity** Divide students into small groups. Assign each group a specific technological advance of the Civil War. Among the topics students might explore are the development of repeating rifles, ironclads, the telegraph, railroads, or improvements in artillery or ammunition. Have students prepare a report that describes the new technology, how it affected the way the war was fought, and its impact on military strategy or on specific land or sea battles. If appropriate, encourage students to make diagrams that show how the technology they have chosen works.

## BLOCK SCHEDULING — LESSON PLAN OPTIONS (90-MINUTE PERIOD)

### DAY 1

**Interact with History,** p. 479
**Class Time** 20 minutes

Options for pacing and variety:

- Role-Playing Have pairs of students assume the roles of the two federal artillery officers inside Fort Sumter, one from a Southern state and the other from a Northern state. Have the two discuss the "What Do You Think?" questions and share their conclusions with the class. **Class Time** 10 minutes

**Setting the Stage,** p. 480
**Class Time** 20 minutes

Options for pacing and variety:

- Time Saver For a homework assignment, have students make a list of what they already know about the Civil War and a list of three questions they have about the outbreak of the war. **Class Time** 10 minutes

**Section 1,** pp. 481–487
**Class Time** 50 minutes

Options for pacing and variety:

- Time Saver Use the chart on page 484 to summarize the differences in the resources of each side as the Civil War began. **Class Time** 5 minutes
- Internet Extend students' background knowledge of the Civil War by visiting www.mcdougallittell.com **Class Time** 20 minutes

### DAY 2

**Section 2,** pp. 488–492
**Class Time** 45 minutes

Options for pacing and variety:

- Time Saver For a homework assignment, have students complete the Interdisciplinary Activity on page 499 of the Chapter Assessment. Then have them share their letters and reactions to them with the class. **Class Time** 30 minutes
- Peer Evaluation Have student pairs answer the Main Ideas and Critical Thinking questions in the Section Assessment. Then have them exchange papers with another team to evaluate their answers. **Class Time** 15 minutes

**Section 3,** pp. 493–497
**Class Time** 50 minutes

Options for pacing and variety:

- Team Teaching Invite a music teacher to come to the class to discuss and play examples of music from the Civil War. **Class Time** 20 minutes
- History on Film Pick one of the four videos in *The Civil War Legends* series to extend students' knowledge of the roles played by Robert E. Lee, Abraham Lincoln, Stonewall Jackson, or Ulysses S. Grant in the Civil War. Atlas Video. **Class Time** 30 minutes

**Chapter 16 Assessment,** pp. 498–499
**Class Time** 40 minutes

Options for pacing and variety:

- Time Saver For a homework assignment, have students pick two events on the Visual Summary time line and write a paragraph explaining their importance to the war at this point. **Class Time** 5 minutes
- Peer Evaluation Have students work in pairs to answer the Using Your Notes question on page 498. **Class Time** 25 minutes

**CHAPTER 16 OBJECTIVE**

**The student will understand how the Civil War began, its progress during the early years, and its impact on Union and Confederate soldiers.**

CHAPTER 16

# The Civil War Begins 1861–1862

*Section 1* **War Erupts**
*Section 2* **Life in the Army**
*Section 3* **No End in Sight**

## HISTORY FROM VISUALS

**Interpreting the Illustration** Have students study the engraving, read the caption, and explain who the people in the crowd are and what they are doing. **Answer** They are South Carolinians looking from the rooftops of city houses at the bombardment of Fort Sumter. Ask students to describe the onlookers' reactions to the event. **Possible Responses** In general, many of the women look frightened or grief-stricken. Most of the men appear riveted by the action.

**Extension** Have students write a monologue in which one of the people in the illustration tells a grandchild what he or she remembers about standing on the roof on that long-ago day.

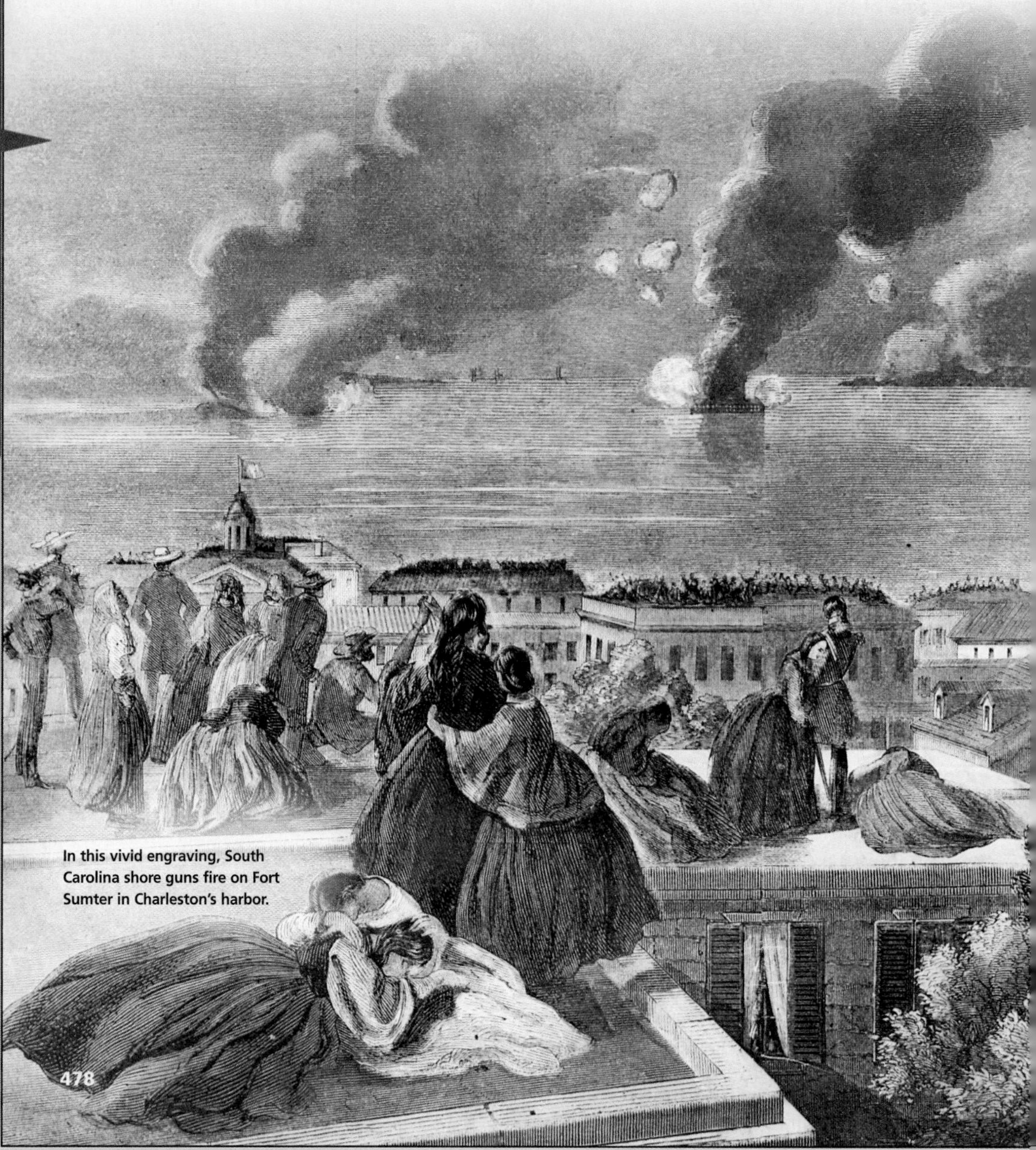

In this vivid engraving, South Carolina shore guns fire on Fort Sumter in Charleston's harbor.

478

## RECOMMENDED RESOURCES

**BOOKS FOR THE TEACHER**

Klein, Maury. ***Days of Defiance: Sumter, Secession, and the Coming of the Civil War.*** New York: Knopf, 1997. A fine account of the last crucial decisions that led to war.

Olsen, Bernard A. ***Upon the Tented Field.*** Red Bank, NJ: Historic Projs., Inc., 1993. Collection of soldiers' letters paints a gripping picture of what the war was really like.

Wakelyn, Jon L., ed. ***Southern Pamphlets on Secession: November 1860–April 1861.*** Chapel Hill: U. of North Carolina Pr., 1996. Compilation of Southern opinions on secession, both pro and con.

**VIDEO**

***The Civil War.*** Episode 1: "The Cause." Ken Burns, dir. PBS, 1989. Opening salvo in the extremely popular nine-cassette epic.

**SOFTWARE**

***American History Inspirer: The Civil War.*** Omaha, NE: Educational Software Institute.

**INTERNET**

For more about the American Civil War, visit www.mcdougallittell.com

## Interact *with* History

This painting shows Fort Sumter from the inside under attack.
damaged fort walls
Federal artillery officers inside Fort Sumter witness bombardment.
stockpile of cannon balls
federal cannon destroyed by Confederate shelling

**The date is April 12, 1861. You and other residents of Charleston, South Carolina, watch the bombardment of Fort Sumter by Confederate forces. This event signals the beginning of the Civil War—a war between factions or regions of the same country.**

### What Do You Think?

- **What sort of physical destruction might take place in a civil war?**
- **What social, political, and economic trouble might be likely to occur in a civil war?**
- **What might happen when a civil war breaks out?**

# *How might a civil war be worse than other wars?*

**USA**

- **March 4, 1861** Abraham Lincoln inaugurated as president.
- **April 12, 1861** Confederate forces fire on Fort Sumter.
- **July 21, 1861** First Battle of Bull Run (Manassas) occurs.
- **March 9, 1862** The warships *Monitor* and *Merrimack* (or *Virginia*) clash.
- **April 6, 1862** Battle of Shiloh takes place.
- **April 25, 1862** New Orleans falls to Union forces.
- **September 17, 1862** Battle of Antietam (Sharpsburg) occurs.

**World**

- **March, 1861** Italy unified under King Victor Emmanuel II.
- **May 13, 1861** Britain declares neutrality in American Civil War.
- **April 13, 1862** France annexes Cochin China (southern Vietnam).
- **May 5, 1862** French troops are defeated at Puebla, Mexico.
- **June 25, 1862** Imperial decree expels foreigners from Japan.
- **September, 1862** Bismarck becomes prime minister of Prussia.

## Interact *with* History

### OBJECTIVES

- To help students describe the bombardment of Fort Sumter
- To help students understand the impact of the outbreak of war

### What Do You Think?

1. Remind students that the goal of armies is to prevent the enemy's ability to move easily, to have food and supplies, and to produce war goods.
2. Students might think about the war's possible disruption of trade, communication, transportation, agriculture, and education, strains on the health care system, and its impact on families.
3. Students might consider that civil wars are always fought in or near the homes of at least one and usually both sides. Civil wars often divide communities and even families.

### *How might a civil war be worse than other wars?*

Encourage students to think about the ways a civil war might disrupt relationships between neighbors and families or disturb economic and trade relationships.

### MAKING PERSONAL CONNECTIONS

Ask students how their lives might be affected if different parts of their town or state went to war. If students could not go to a certain part of town to see friends or relatives, how might they react? How might the economy of their town be affected?

### TIME LINE DISCUSSION

**Remind students that this time line covers a period of just a little over one year. Point out the number of major battles that took place during this year. Also point out that the activities of European nations diverted them from involvement in the United States.**

- Ask how long after Lincoln became president the Civil War began. **Answer** a little over a month
- Ask students which battle of the war shown on this time line was fought at sea. **Answer** March 9, 1862, between the *Monitor* and the *Merrimack*
- Ask students what world event on this time line probably had the greatest impact on the early years of the Civil War. **Answer** Britain's decision to remain neutral

## BEFORE YOU READ

### Previewing the Theme: Citizenship

Have students examine the photographs and notice the differences in the uniforms and flags. Ask them why flags are often an important part of military activities on the battlefield and in preparing soldiers and civilians for war. Ask students what they can learn about the Confederacy and the Union side from studying their flags.

### What Do You Know?

Students might recall some of the devastating civil wars in other parts of the world in the 1990s, such as those in Eastern Europe between Kosovar Albanians and Serbs in Serbia; or among Croats, Serbs, and Muslims in Bosnia. They might also recall the ethnic violence between Hutus and Tutsis that wracked Rwanda in Africa or the massacres in East Timor after that region voted for independence from Indonesia.

**In-Depth Resources: Unit 5**
- Tracing Themes: Citizenship, p. 22

## READ AND TAKE NOTES

### Reading Strategy: Comparing and Contrasting

Tell students that comparing and contrasting involves looking for similarities and differences between two or more things. Before students study the chapter, have them read the categories in the first column of the chart. As they read, ask them to keep those categories in mind as they watch for similarities and differences between the North and the South.

**In-Depth Resources: Unit 5**
- Setting the Stage, p. 21

**Critical Thinking Transparency CT46**
- Setting the Stage

# Chapter 16 SETTING THE STAGE

## BEFORE YOU READ

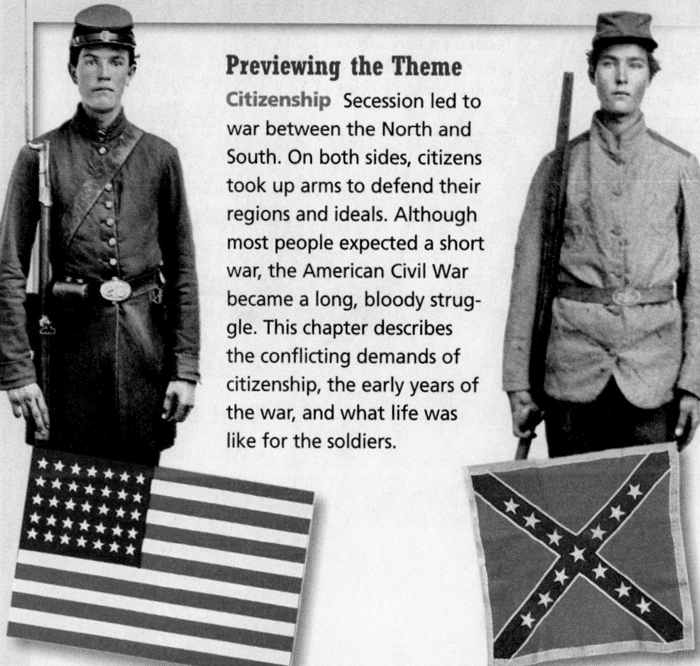

### Previewing the Theme

**Citizenship** Secession led to war between the North and South. On both sides, citizens took up arms to defend their regions and ideals. Although most people expected a short war, the American Civil War became a long, bloody struggle. This chapter describes the conflicting demands of citizenship, the early years of the war, and what life was like for the soldiers.

*Union Soldier*

*Confederate Soldier*

### What Do You Know?

What do you think of when you hear the phrase *civil war?* What would it be like to fight in a war of brother against brother? Where and how did the Civil War begin?

**THINK ABOUT**
- what a civil war is
- what you've learned about the Civil War from movies, television, and books
- reasons that countries threaten to break apart in today's world

### What Do You Want to Know?

What details do you need to help you understand the outbreak of the Civil War? Make a list of those details in your notebook before you read the chapter.

## READ AND TAKE NOTES

**Reading Strategy: Comparing and Contrasting** When you compare, you look for similarities between two or more objects, ideas, events, or people. When you contrast, you look for differences. Comparing and contrasting can be a useful strategy for studying the two sides in a war. Use the chart shown here to compare and contrast the North and the South in the early years of the Civil War.

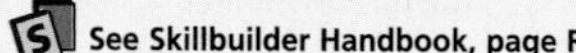

See Skillbuilder Handbook, page R9.

| | North | South |
|---|---|---|
| Reasons for fighting | to preserve Union | to defend homeland |
| Advantages | greater manpower and resources | fighting on their own territory |
| Disadvantages | had to carry battle to enemy | fewer resources and soldiers |
| Military strategy | surrounding and overwhelming the South | holding out until North grew weary |
| Battle victories | Shiloh, Antietam | Bull Run, Seven Days' Battles |



## TEACHING STRATEGY

### READING THE CHAPTER

This is a chronological chapter focusing on the early months of the Civil War. It has a section focusing on life in the military. Encourage students to think about how the events of this chapter would affect the soldiers and sailors of the two sides. Ask them to identify other themes that recur throughout the chapter, such as military strategies, division within families, and hardship in the armies.

### ALTERNATIVE ASSESSMENT

The Chapter Assessment describes three activities for alternative assessment on page 499. You may wish to have students work on these activities during the course of the chapter and then present them at the end.

# 1 War Erupts

**TERMS & NAMES**
Fort Sumter
Robert E. Lee
border state
King Cotton
Anaconda Plan
blockade
First Battle of Bull Run

**MAIN IDEA**

The secession of the Southern states quickly led to armed conflict between the North and the South.

**WHY IT MATTERS NOW**

The nation's identity was in part forged by the Civil War.

## ONE AMERICAN'S STORY

**Two months before the Civil War broke out, 22-year-old Emma Holmes of Charleston began keeping a detailed diary. Like other South Carolinians, Holmes got caught up in the passions that led her state to secede. From a rooftop, she witnessed the event that started the war. She wrote about South Carolina's attack on Fort Sumter, a federal fort in Charleston's harbor, in her diary.**

*A VOICE FROM THE PAST*

[A]t half past four this morning, the heavy booming of cannons woke the city from its slumbers. . . . Every body seems relieved that what has been so long dreaded has come at last and so confident of victory that they seem not to think of the danger of their friends. . . . I had a splendid view of the harbor with the naked eye. We could distinctly see flames amidst the smoke. All the barracks were on fire. . . . With the telescope I saw the shots as they struck the fort and [saw] the masonry crumbling.

**Emma Holmes,** *The Diary of Emma Holmes 1861–1866*

This photograph of Emma Holmes was taken in 1900.

**Many Southerners expected a short war that they would easily win. Northerners expected the same. In this section, you will learn how the war started, how the states divided, and how each side planned to win.**

## 1 First Shots at Fort Sumter

As they seceded from the Union (the states loyal to the United States of America during the Civil War), the Southern states took over most of the federal forts inside their borders. President Abraham Lincoln had to decide what to do about the forts that remained under federal control. Major Robert Anderson and his garrison held on to **Fort Sumter** in the harbor of Charleston, South Carolina, but they were running out of supplies.

If Lincoln supplied the garrison, he risked war. If he ordered the troops to leave the fort, he would be giving in to the rebels. Lincoln informed South Carolina that he was sending supply ships to Fort Sumter. Leaders of the Confederacy (the nation formed by Southern states in 1861) decided to prevent the federal government from holding onto the fort by attacking before the supply ships arrived.





## SECTION OBJECTIVES

1. To describe how fighting began at Fort Sumter
2. To analyze the strengths and weaknesses of each side
3. To explain each side's basic strategy
4. To summarize the results of the First Battle of Bull Run

**SKILLBUILDER**

Interpreting Maps: Location, Region, p. 483
Interpreting Charts, p. 484

**CRITICAL THINKING**

Comparing, pp. 482, 485
Summarizing, p. 483
Supporting Opinions, p. 484

## FOCUS & MOTIVATE

### 5-MINUTE WARM-UP

**Comparing** These questions focus on the resources of each side in the war.

1. Look at the chart on page 484. Which side had more people and more factories?
2. Which of the resources do you think would be most critical to winning a war?

 **Warm-Up Transparency WT16**

## INSTRUCT

### INSTRUCT: OBJECTIVE 1 

**First Shots at Fort Sumter/ Lincoln Calls Out the Militia**

Key Questions

- Why did Lincoln decide to risk war by re-supplying Fort Sumter?
- How did states in the upper South respond to Lincoln's call-up of militia?
- How did Virginia's decision to secede improve the South's chances of winning?

 **In-Depth Resources: Unit 5**
- Guided Reading, p. 23
- Geography Application: Fort Sumter Falls, 1861, pp. 28–29

## RECOMMENDED RESOURCES

**In-Depth Resources: Unit 5**
- Guided Reading, p. 23
- Building Vocabulary, p. 26
- Skillbuilder Practice, p. 27
- Geography Application, pp. 28–29
- Primary Source, p. 30
- Reteaching Activity, p. 35

**Reading Study Guide** (Spanish and English), pp. 159–160

**Economics in History**
- The Value of Border States, p. 16

**Outline Map Activities**
- The Divided Union, 1863, pp. 31–32

**America's History Makers**
- Abraham Lincoln, pp. 63–64
- Robert E. Lee, pp. 65–66

**Formal Assessment**
- Section Quiz, p. 242

**Alternative Assessment**
- Rubrics, 4.5
- Rubrics, 5.1

**Access for Students Acquiring English/ESL**
- Guided Reading, p. 107
- Skillbuilder Practice, p. 110
- Geography Application, pp. 111–112

**Technology Resources**

 **Humanities Transparency HT31**
- Robert E. Lee

 **Humanities Transparency HT32**
- Union and Confederate Money

 **Geography Transparency GT16**
- Union and Confederate Resources, 1861

## AMERICA'S HISTORY MAKERS

**Abraham Lincoln**
Many historians rate Abraham Lincoln as our greatest president. Although his education was limited to a few months in a one-teacher school, he held the country together through its most trying time. As commander in chief, Lincoln showed a surprising gift for military strategy. He never wavered in his commitment to preserving the Union.

**Possible Response: During a war, citizens are often asked to make great sacrifices. A leader who can inspire others is more likely to unite people for a common purpose.**

 **America's History Makers**
- Abraham Lincoln, pp. 63–64

 **In-Depth Resources: Unit 5**
- Primary Source, p. 30

## MORE ABOUT . . .

**Robert E. Lee**
During the Mexican War, Lee served on the staff of General Winfield Scott. General Scott called him the "best soldier I ever saw in the field." Before Lee resigned to lead the Confederate army, President Lincoln offered him a field command of the Union armies. Lee turned the offer down, citing loyalty to Virginia. He was respected and loved by his troops.

 **America's History Makers**
- Robert E. Lee, pp. 65–66

 **Humanities Transparency HT31**
- Robert E. Lee

## INSTRUCT: OBJECTIVE 2

**Choosing Sides/Strengths and Weaknesses**
Key Questions
- Why were the border states important?
- What were the strengths of each side?

 **Economics in History**
- The Value of Border States, p. 16

At 4:30 A.M. on April 12, 1861, shore guns opened fire on the island fort. For 34 hours, the Confederates fired shells into the fort until Anderson was forced to surrender. No one was killed, but the South's attack on Fort Sumter was the beginning of the Civil War.

## Lincoln Calls Out the Militia

Two days after the surrender of Fort Sumter, President Lincoln asked the Union states to provide 75,000 militiamen for 90 days to put down the uprising in the South. Citizens of the North responded with enthusiasm to the call to arms. A New York woman wrote, "It seems as if we never were alive till now; never had a country till now."

**Background**
The state militias were armies of ordinary citizens rather than professional soldiers.

In the upper South, however, state leaders responded with anger. The governor of Kentucky said that the state would "furnish no troops for the wicked purpose of subduing her sister Southern States." In the weeks that followed, Virginia, North Carolina, Tennessee, and Arkansas voted to join the Confederacy.

**AMERICA'S HISTORY MAKERS**

**ABRAHAM LINCOLN**
**1809–1865**
Today, Abraham Lincoln is considered one of the great men of all time. Yet early in his presidency, he was widely criticized and ridiculed. Critics labeled him ignorant, incompetent, and socially crude. As Lincoln grew into his job, however, he gained the respect and affection of many Northerners.

Even as a youth, Lincoln had displayed a gift for public speaking. During the Civil War, through his speeches and writings, Lincoln inspired fellow Americans to "dare to do our duty as we understand it."

**Why would the ability to inspire people be important in a wartime leader?**

As each state seceded, volunteers rushed to enlist, just as citizens did in the North. A young Arkansas enlistee wrote, "So impatient did I become for starting that I felt like ten thousand pins were pricking me in every part of the body, and started off a week in advance of my brothers." Some feared the war would be over before they got the chance to fight.

With Virginia on its side, the Confederacy had a much better chance for victory. Virginia was wealthy and populous, and the Confederacy in May of 1861 moved its capital to Richmond. Virginia also was the home of **Robert E. Lee,** a talented military leader. When Virginia seceded, Lee resigned from the United States Army and joined the Confederacy. Although Lee opposed slavery and secession, he explained, "I cannot raise my hand against my birthplace, my home, my children." He eventually became the commanding general of the Army of Northern Virginia.

*Reading* **History**
**A. Comparing** Why might citizens in both the North and the South have been eager to fight in the Civil War?
**A. Answer** Tensions had been brewing a long time, and on both sides people might have been anxious to see the conflict resolved.

## 2 Choosing Sides

After Virginia seceded, both sides knew that the border states would play a key role in the war's outcome. The **border states**—Delaware, Maryland, Kentucky, and Missouri—were slave states that bordered states in which slavery was illegal. Because of their location and resources, the border states could tip the scales toward one side.

Keeping Maryland in the Union was important for the North. If Maryland seceded, then Washington, D.C., would be cut off from the Union. To hold on to the state, Lincoln considered arresting Maryland lawmakers who backed the South, but he decided against it.



## ACTIVITY OPTIONS

## INDIVIDUAL NEEDS

**STUDENTS ACQUIRING ENGLISH/ESL**

**Figures of Speech** Read aloud the excerpt from Emma Holmes's diary in "A Voice from the Past" on page 481. Explain that writers use figures of speech. A figure of speech is an expression whose meaning goes beyond the dictionary definition of the words being used. Have the students turn to page 484 and look at two of the highlighted words—*King Cotton* and *Anaconda Plan*. Have students find the explanations for these terms. Ask how these are examples of figures of speech.

Then explain that figures of speech also make their writing more interesting. As an example, point out the clause, "the heavy booming of cannons woke the city from its slumbers." Ask students questions such as these: *Do cities actually sleep? What do you think Emma Holmes meant when she wrote that sentence in her diary?*

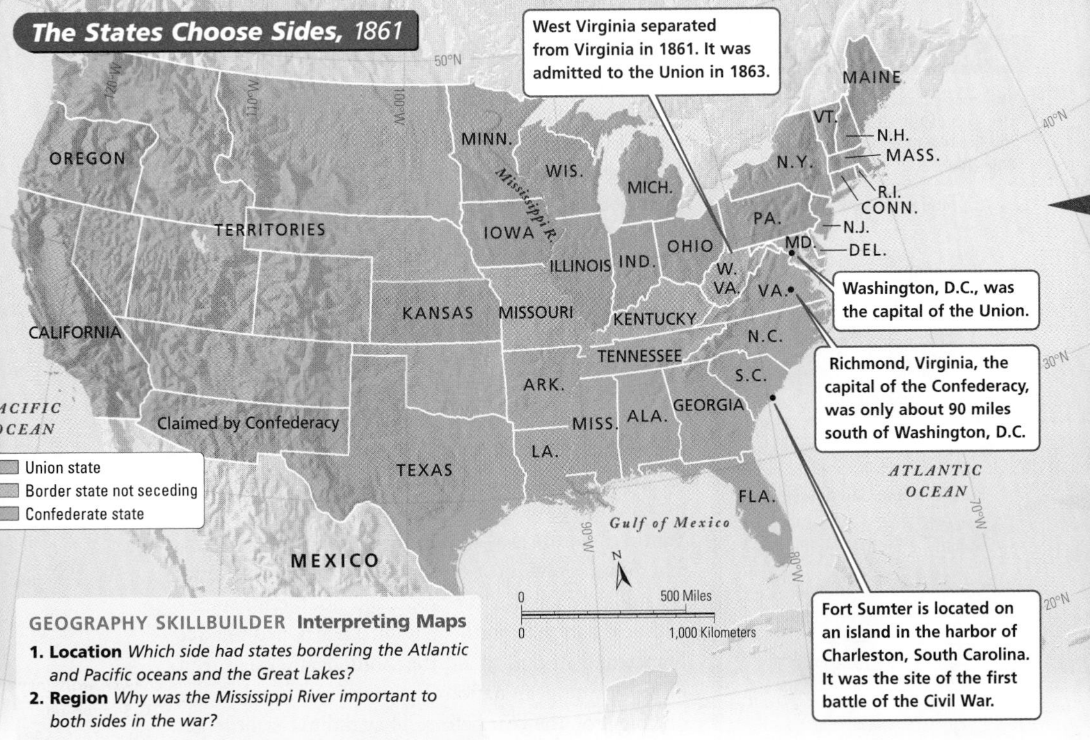


**GEOGRAPHY SKILLBUILDER Interpreting Maps**
1. **Location** *Which side had states bordering the Atlantic and Pacific oceans and the Great Lakes?*
2. **Region** *Why was the Mississippi River important to both sides in the war?*

Skillbuilder Answers
1. Union
2. It provided a means of transportation, communication, trade, and troop movements.

Pro-Union leaders eventually gained control of the Maryland legislature, and the state stayed in the Union.

Kentucky was also important to both sides because of its rivers. For the Union, the rivers could provide an invasion route into the South. For the South, the rivers could provide a barrier. Kentuckians were deeply divided over secession. However, a Confederate invasion in 1861 prompted the state to stay in the Union.

*Reading* **History**
**B. Summarizing** Why were the border states critical to the war's outcome?
**B. Answer** They were critical because of their location and resources.

Both Missouri and Delaware also stayed in the Union. In Virginia, federal troops helped a group of western counties break away. These counties formed the state of West Virginia and returned to the Union. In the end, 24 states made up the Union and 11 joined the Confederacy.

## Strengths and Weaknesses

The Union had huge advantages in manpower and resources. The North had about 22 million people. The Confederacy had roughly 9 million, of whom about 3.5 million were slaves. About 85 percent of the nation's factories were located in the North. The North had more than double the railroad mileage of the South. Almost all the naval power and shipyards belonged to the North.

The Union's greatest asset, however, was President Abraham Lincoln. He developed into a remarkable leader. Lincoln convinced Northerners that democracy depended on preserving the Union.





### HISTORY FROM VISUALS

**Reading the Maps** Ask students to identify the border states. Then have them locate Maryland on the map. Ask why keeping Maryland in the Union was so important to the North. Why might the decision of Missouri and Kentucky to remain in the Union be important? **Possible Responses** Maryland almost surrounded Washington, D.C. Missouri and Kentucky gave Union forces access to the Mississippi River, a key entryway to the South.

**Extension** Have students pick one of the border states that decided not to secede and report on how state leaders made this decision.

**Outline Map Activities**
- The Divided Union, 1863, pp. 31–32

**Geography Transparency GT16**
- Union and Confederate Resources, 1861

### MORE ABOUT . . .

**West Virginia**

Long-standing political and economic differences led Virginia's western counties to form the new state of West Virginia. Few families in the western counties owned slaves, and many opposed slavery. The roads and rivers in this region linked the area's economy more closely with Pennsylvania and Ohio than with the rest of Virginia. However, even though West Virginia joined the Union, people within the new state remained divided in their loyalties. About 25,000 West Virginians joined the Union army, while around 15,000 became Confederate soldiers.

### ACTIVITY OPTIONS

### INTERDISCIPLINARY LINK: MATH

BLOCK SCHEDULING

**RESOURCES OF THE NORTH AND THE SOUTH**

**Class Time** One class period

**Task** Using data to make graphs on the resources of the North and the South during the Civil War

**Purpose** To compare resources of the North and the South

**Supplies Needed**
- Graph paper
- Markers
- Optional: ruler, compass, protractor

**Activity** Have students review the charts on page 484. Then have them make five more graphs using these data that do not include Missouri, Maryland, or Kentucky. **Agriculture:** Millions of bushels of corn: North 396, South 280. Millions of bales of cotton: North .004, South 5. **Livestock:** Millions of horses: North 3.4, South 1.7. Millions of beef cattle: North 5.4, South 7. **Bank Deposits:** Millions of dollars: North 189, South 47. When graphs are complete, have students identify the resources in which the South had the advantage and assess their importance.

**INSTRUCT: OBJECTIVE** 

**The Confederate Strategy/ The Union Strategy**

Key Questions

- What did the Confederacy expect to gain by withholding cotton from the market?
- What was the goal of the Anaconda Plan, and what were its drawbacks?
- How did each side's strategy change as the war continued?

## HISTORY FROM VISUALS

**Reading the Charts** Have students examine the differences in the resources of the Union and Confederacy. In which area did the North have the greatest advantage? **Answer** Industrial workers. How might the population difference between the two sides help the Union? **Possible Response** The North had more people to serve in the army, to work in factories, and to keep the economy going strong while the soldiers were at war.

**Extension** Ask students what factors not shown on these charts might be important to each side.

 **Humanities Transparency HT32**
- Union and Confederate Money

### CRITICAL THINKING ACTIVITY

**Forming and Supporting Opinions** After the class discusses the chart, ask: How might the Confederacy compensate for some of its weaknesses? What advantage might Confederates have in battles that were fought on their own territory?

**Class Time** 10 minutes

**Resources, *1860***

The pie charts show the relative strength of the Union and the Confederacy in population and industry.

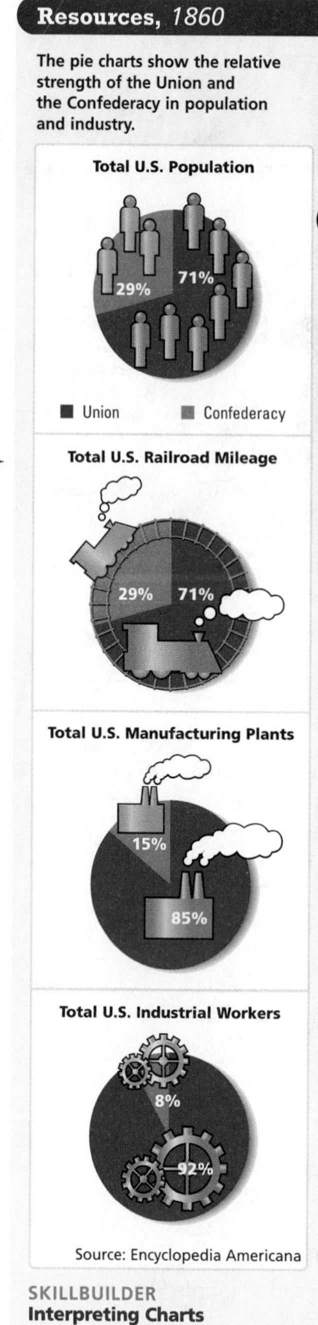


SKILLBUILDER
**Interpreting Charts**
1. *Which side had more resources?*
2. *How might the North's railways and factories have helped its armies?*

The Confederacy had some advantages, too. It began the war with able generals, such as Robert E. Lee. It also had the advantage of fighting a defensive war. This meant Northern supply lines would have to be stretched very far. In addition, soldiers defending their homes have more will to fight than invaders do.

## 3 The Confederate Strategy

At first, the Confederacy took a defensive position. It did not want to conquer the North—it only wanted to be independent. "All we ask is to be let alone," said Confederate President Jefferson Davis. Confederate leaders hoped the North would soon tire of the war and accept Southern independence.

The South also depended on **King Cotton** as a way to win foreign support. Cotton was king because Southern cotton was important in the world market. The South grew most of the cotton for Europe's textile mills. When the war broke out, Southern planters withheld cotton from the market. They hoped to force France and Britain to aid the Confederate cause. But in 1861, European nations had surplus cotton because of a big crop the year before. They did not want to get involved in the American war.

As the war heated up, the South soon moved away from its cautious plans. It began to take the offensive and try for big victories to wreck Northern morale.

## The Union Strategy

The North wanted to bring the Southern states back into the Union. To do this, the North developed an offensive strategy based on General Winfield Scott's **Anaconda Plan.** This plan was designed to smother the South's economy like a giant anaconda snake squeezing its prey.

The plan called for a naval blockade of the South's coastline. In a **blockade,** armed forces prevent the transportation of goods or people into or out of an area. The plan also called for the Union to gain control of the Mississippi River. This would split the Confederacy in two.

One of the drawbacks of Scott's plan was that it would take time to work. But many people, eager for action, were calling for an immediate attack on Richmond, the Confederate capital. Lincoln ordered an invasion of Virginia in the summer of 1861.

*Reading* **History**
**C. Supporting Opinions** At the beginning of the Civil War, which side would you have predicted to win? Why?
**C. Answer** Most students will probably pick the North because it had huge advantages in people and resources. Some students might say the South because Southerners were defending their homes.

**Skillbuilder Answers**
1. the Union
2. The factories produced more supplies that could be delivered by the railways.



## ACTIVITY OPTIONS

### SKILLBUILDER MINI-LESSON: CREATING A DATABASE

BLOCK SCHEDULING

**Explaining the Skill** A database is a collection of related information, such as census figures, charts, graphs, or pictures. A database can be stored and organized to make the information accessible for users. For example, a database on Civil War battles might allow a user to search for information by name of battle, date of battle, state where a battle took place, or military units involved in it. To create a database, decide what information it will contain and how it will be organized. Then gather the information.

**Applying the Skill** Divide students into teams and give each team five note cards. Assign each team a topic related to the war. Have each group do research on the topic. The research may include statistical information, pictures, or other data about the topic. Finally, create a directory of the different ways the data in the database might be accessed by users.

 **In-Depth Resources: Unit 5**
- Skillbuilder Practice, p. 27

## 4 Battle of Bull Run

To take Richmond, the Union army would first have to defeat the Confederate troops stationed at the town of Manassas, Virginia. This was a railway center southwest of Washington, D.C.

**Background**
In the South, the battle was called the First Battle of Manassas. In most cases, the South named a battle after a nearby town. The North used a landmark near the fighting, usually a stream.

On July 21, 1861, Union forces commanded by General Irvin McDowell clashed with Confederate forces headed by General Pierre Beauregard near a little creek called Bull Run north of Manassas. In the North, this battle came to be known as the **First Battle of Bull Run.**

The Confederate Army passes in review before General Pierre Beauregard.

At one point in the battle, a Confederate officer rallied his troops by pointing his sword toward Southern General Thomas J. Jackson. The officer cried, "There is Jackson standing like a stone wall! Rally behind the Virginians!" From this incident, Jackson won the nickname "Stonewall" Jackson. His men held fast against the Union assault.

As fresh troops arrived, the Confederates equaled the Union forces in number and launched a countercharge. Attacking the Union line, they let out a blood-curdling scream. This scream, later called the "rebel yell," caused the Union troops to panic. They broke ranks and scattered.

The Confederate victory in the First Battle of Bull Run thrilled the South and shocked the North. Many in the South thought the war was won. The North realized it had underestimated its opponent. Lincoln sent the 90-day militias home and called for a real army of 500,000 volunteers for three years. In the next section, you will learn what army life was like.

### Section 1 Assessment

**1. Terms & Names**

Identify:
- Fort Sumter
- Robert E. Lee
- border state
- King Cotton
- Anaconda Plan
- blockade
- First Battle of Bull Run

**2. Taking Notes**

Use a Venn diagram to compare and contrast the strengths of the North and the South.

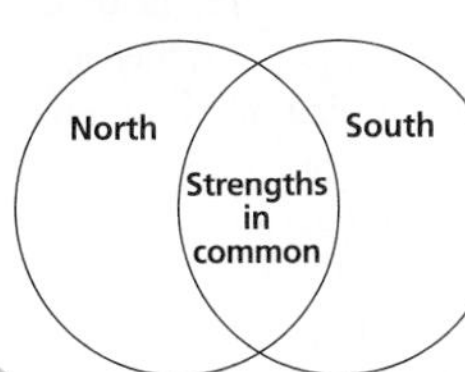


**3. Main Ideas**

a. How did citizens in the North and the South respond to the outbreak of the Civil War?

b. Why were the border states important to both sides in the Civil War?

c. What kind of military strategy did each side develop?

**4. Critical Thinking**

**Comparing** How was the South's situation in the Civil War similar to the situation of the Patriots in the Revolutionary War?

THINK ABOUT
- their reasons for fighting
- their opponents' strengths

**ACTIVITY OPTIONS**

LANGUAGE ARTS / TECHNOLOGY

Read an account of the First Battle of Bull Run. Use the information to write a **news article** or plan the battle's **home page** for the Internet.





### INSTRUCT: OBJECTIVE 4

**Battle of Bull Run**

Key Questions
- What was the Union army's strategic goal in the summer of 1861?
- What conclusions did each side draw from the Northern defeat at Bull Run?

### MORE ABOUT . . .

**First Battle of Bull Run**

Manassas was so close to Washington that many people came out from the city to watch the battle. They came on horseback or in carriages, bringing their picnic baskets, to watch the battle as if it were a pageant. The onlookers included several senators and congressmen. When Union troops began to retreat and Confederate artillery shells came closer, the spectators suddenly realized that war was dangerous. They joined the withdrawing soldiers, adding greatly to the general confusion, as the retreat became a rout.

## ASSESS & RETEACH

**Setting the Stage** Ask students to fill in the graphic organizer on page 480, based on the information in this section.

**Formal Assessment**
- Section Quiz, p. 242

**Critical Thinking Transparency CT46**
- Setting the Stage

### RETEACHING ACTIVITY

Ask students to hypothesize that they are advisers to Lincoln or Davis in 1861. Have them write a report describing the strengths and weaknesses of their own side and of the enemy. The report can conclude with an assessment of their chances of winning the war.

**In-Depth Resources: Unit 5**
- Reteaching Activity, p. 35

### Section 1 Assessment

**1. Terms & Names**

**Fort Sumter,** p. 481
**Robert E. Lee,** p. 482
**border state,** p. 482
**King Cotton,** p. 484
**Anaconda Plan,** p. 484
**blockade,** p. 484
**First Battle of Bull Run,** p. 485

**2. Taking Notes**

North: more manpower; 85 percent of nation's factories; double the railroad mileage; almost all naval power and shipyards; South: first-rate generals; defending the homeland; King Cotton; Both: believed in what they were fighting for; many eager volunteers; public support for the war

**3. Main Ideas**

**a.** excitement; relief; eagerness
**b.** Their location and resources made them pivotal in tipping the scales to one side or the other.
**c.** The South developed a defensive strategy; but it quickly changed to an offensive strategy. The Union developed an offensive strategy.

**4. Critical Thinking**

Both were fighting more powerful opponents, and both believed they were fighting for freedom.

**ACTIVITY OPTIONS**

**Alternative Assessment**
- Rubrics for a news article, 4.5
- Rubrics for a Web page, 5.1

## Literature *Connections*

**OBJECTIVE**
Students analyze a passage from historical fiction that imaginatively depicts the wrenching conflicts within families that the Civil War caused.

 **BLOCK SCHEDULING**

## FOCUS & MOTIVATE

**Making Inferences** To help students picture the events of *Across Five Aprils,* have students examine the photographs and read the caption on page 487. Then ask the following questions.

1. Can you tell from the photographs that the Terrill brothers fought on different sides in the war?
2. Judging by the memorial built after the deaths of the two brothers, how might this tragedy have affected the Terrill family's views on the war?

### MORE ABOUT . . .

***Across Five Aprils***
This volume of historical fiction was a Newbery Award honor book. It is a historically accurate picture of the heartbreaking choices that many families were forced to make during the Civil War. The Creighton family lived in southern Illinois, where the Confederacy had many sympathizers. The novel describes how Jethro Creighton takes on adult responsibilities when his brother goes to war. His father falls ill, and Jethro must manage the family farm during the war.



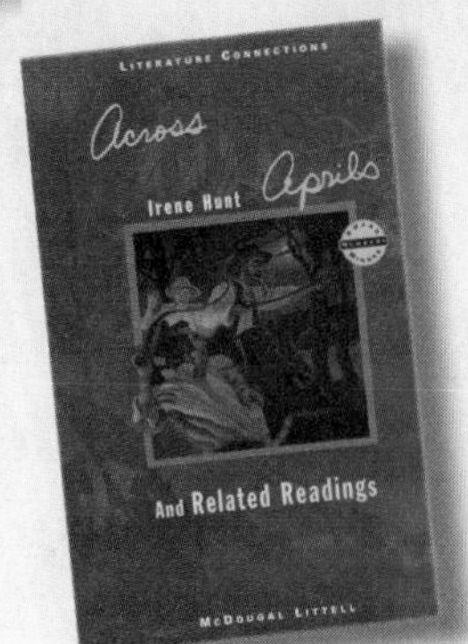


# from *Across* Five *Aprils*

by Irene Hunt

**At the beginning of the Civil War, nine-year-old Jethro Creighton and his family live on a farm in southern Illinois. Although Illinois is a free state that remains in the Union, many people in the area have ties to states where slavery is legal. For example, the Creightons have relatives in "Kaintuck," or Kentucky. When this excerpt begins, Jethro has already seen his brother Tom and his cousin Eb go off to fight for the Union. His other brothers, John and Bill, are trying to decide which side to fight for.**

A line of wild geese flew southward far overhead, and Jethro stood motionless as he watched them disappear from sight. So **engrossed**[1] he was with the flight of the geese that he did not hear Bill's footsteps until his brother was quite near. He caught his breath at sight of Bill's face, which was swollen and beginning to grow discolored from a deep cut and many bruises.

"What's hurt you, Bill?" he asked, his voice barely **audible,**[2] for he was pretty sure he knew.

"We had a fight, Jeth, about an hour ago. We fit like two madmen, I guess."

"You and John?"

Bill's sigh was almost a moan. "Yes, me and John. Me and my brother John."

Jethro could not answer. He stared at the cut above Bill's right eye, from which blood still trickled down his cheek. Somewhere, far off in another field, a man shouted to his horses, and the shout died away in a cry that ran frightened over the brown water of the creek and into the darkening woods.

He had heard cries often that autumn, all through the countryside. They came at night, wakened him, and then lapsed into silence, leaving him in fear and **perplexity**.[3] Sounds once familiar were no longer as they had seemed in other days—his father calling cattle in from the pasture, the sheep dog's bark coming through the fog, the distant creak of the pulley as Ellen drew water for her chickens—all these once familiar sounds had taken on overtones of wailing, and he seemed to hear an echo of that wailing now. He shivered and looked away from his brother's face.

Bill sat down on the ground beside him. "Did ever Ma tell you, Jeth, about when John and me was little and was goin' to school fer the first time? At night I'd git a book and I'd say to Pa, 'What air that word, Pa?' and when he would tell me, I'd turn to John, jest a scant year older, and I'd say, 'Did Pa call it right, Johnny?' Ma and Pa used to laugh at that, but they was pleased to talk about it. They was always set up at John and me bein' so close."

"I know it." Jethro's words came from a tight throat. "What made you fight, Bill?"

"Hard feelin's that have been buildin' up fer weeks, hard feelin's that fin'ly come out in hard words." He held his hand across his eyes for a minute and then spoke quickly. "I'm leavin', Jeth; it ain't that I want to, but it's that I must. The day is comin' when I've got to fight, and I won't fight fer **arrogance**[4] and big money aginst the southern farmer. I won't do it. You tell Pa that. Tell him, too, that I'm takin' my brown mare—she's mine, and I hev the right. Still, it will leave him short, so you tell him that I'm leavin' money I

1. **engrossed:** absorbed; occupied.
2. **audible:** able to be heard.
3. **perplexity:** confusion.
4. **arrogance:** overbearing pride.



### ACTIVITY OPTIONS
### INDIVIDUAL NEEDS

**LESS PROFICIENT READERS**

**Building Language Skills** Match each less proficient reader with a more fluent reader. Duplicate copies of the Literature Connection and give each pair a copy and a highlighter. Have groups go through the reading and underline the dialogue between Jethro and Bill, circling any difficult-to-pronounce or unfamiliar words. Pairs can discuss unfamiliar words and their meanings and pronunciations. Then have one person take the part of Bill and the other of Jethro to practice reading the dialogue aloud.

After the oral reading of the dialogue, have pairs highlight a passage in the reading that is *not* dialogue. Ask them to discuss with each other what this section adds to the reading. Have pairs share the passages they chose and their conclusions with the class.

made at the sawmill and at corn shuckin'; it's inside the cover of his Bible. You tell him to take it and buy another horse."

Jethro was crying unashamedly in the face of his grief. "Don't go, Bill. Don't do it," he begged.

"Jeth . . ."

"I don't want you to go, Bill. I don't think I kin stand it."

"Listen to me, Jeth; you're gittin to be a sizable boy. There's goin' to be a lot of things in the years ahead that you'll have to stand. There'll be things that tear you apart, but you'll have to stand 'em. You can't count on cryin' to make 'em right."

The colors were beginning to fade on Walnut Hill. A light wind bent the dried grass and weeds. Jethro felt choked with grief, but he drew a sleeve across his eyes and tried to look at his brother without further weeping.

"Where will you go, Bill?"

"To Kaintuck. I'll go to Wilse's place first. From there—I don't know."

"Will you fight fer the Rebs?"

Bill hesitated a few seconds. "I've studied this thing, Jeth, and I've hurt over it. My heart ain't in this war; I've told you that. And while I say that the right ain't all on the side of the North, I know jest as well that it ain't all on the side of the South either. But if I hev to fight, I reckon it will be fer the South."

Jethro nodded. There were things you had to endure. After a while he asked, "Air you goin' tonight, Bill?"

"Right away. I've had things packed in that holler tree fer a couple days. I've knowed that this was comin' on, but I couldn't make myself leave. Now I'm goin'. The little mare is saddled and tied down at the molasses press. I'll go as fur as Newton tonight; in the morning I'll take out early."

He got to his feet. "There's lots of things I want to say, but I reckon I best not talk." Without looking at Jethro he laid his hand on the boy's shoulder. "Git all the larnin' you kin—and take keer of yoreself, Jeth," he said and turned abruptly away.

"Take keer of yoreself, Bill," Jethro called after him.

Across the prairies, through the woods, over the brown water of the creek, there was a sound of crying. Jethro ran to a tree and hid his face. He had heard his mother say that if you watch a loved one as he leaves you for a long journey, it's like as not to be the last look at him that you'll ever have.

Like the Creighton brothers, the Terrill brothers had different loyalties. William Rufus Terrill (left) fought for the Union as an artillery officer at Shiloh. His brother, James Terrill (right), was the commanding officer of a Virginia infantry regiment. Both men died in the war. William was killed at Perryville, Kentucky, in 1862; James was killed in battle in 1864. After the war, the family built a memorial to the brothers, which contained the words, "God Alone Knows Which Was Right."

## CONNECT TO HISTORY

1. **Recognizing Effects** How has the Civil War affected the Creighton family? Discuss how the effect reflects what is happening in the country.

**See Skillbuilder Handbook, page R10.**

## CONNECT TO TODAY

2. **Researching** Where have civil wars or internal rebellions taken place in the recent past?

**Visit www.mcdougallittell.com to learn more about other civil wars.**



## INSTRUCT

Key Questions
- How does Jethro react when he learns from Bill that his two brothers have been fighting?
- How has the war changed the relationship between Bill and John?
- What factors seem to have influenced Bill in choosing which side to fight for in the war?
- Why does Bill say he "best not talk"?

### MAKING PERSONAL CONNECTIONS

Ask students if there are political issues today that might divide families the way the Civil War did. Point out that the Vietnam War often caused conflict between parents and children. What issues might students consider worth fighting for today?

### VOCABULARY ACTIVITY

Write the four vocabulary terms on the chalkboard. Have students write four fill-in-the-blank sentences on a sheet of paper with each blank to be completed with one of the vocabulary terms. Be sure students put their answers on their papers. Have students pair up and read their selected sentences aloud, asking their partners to complete the sentences with the correct terms from the list on the board.

## CONNECT TO HISTORY

1. **Recognizing Effects Possible Responses** The war has torn the Creighton family apart, leading two formerly close brothers to fight. Bill decides to leave home because of the tensions between himself and his brother John. The bitter feuds resulting from divided loyalties tore apart many homes as family members differed on the justice of the Confederate or Union cause.

## CONNECT TO TODAY

2. **Researching** Using the *World Almanac,* Internet, or a current encyclopedia, students can find out about recent civil wars or internal rebellions around the world. Civil wars or political unrest have disrupted life in such countries as Sierra Leone, Kenya, Rwanda, Serbia, Indonesia, and Peru. Have students create an annotated map that identifies both the location and causes of recent civil wars or internal unrest.

## SECTION OBJECTIVES

1. To explain who joined the armies
2. To describe military training and supplies of the era
3. To summarize the hardships of army life
4. To identify changes in military technology

### CRITICAL THINKING

Summarizing, p. 489
Making Inferences, p. 490
Drawing Conclusions, p. 491
Forming and Supporting Opinions, p. 491

 **Why It Matters Now**
- Modern Warfare, pp. 31–32

## FOCUS & MOTIVATE

### 5-MINUTE WARM-UP

**Recognizing Effects** These questions focus on the difficulty that new recruits faced in adjusting to army life.

1. Read the quotation on page 488. What reasons does the major give for not wanting his brother to enlist?
2. How do you think the major's 18-year-old brother Jim might have responded to his brother's warning?

 **Warm-Up Transparency WT16**

## INSTRUCT

### INSTRUCT: OBJECTIVE 

**Those Who Fought**
Key Questions
- What were the characteristics and background of a typical soldier?
- What obstacles did African Americans face who wanted to serve?
- Why did so many men volunteer?

 **In-Depth Resources: Unit 5**
- Guided Reading, p. 24
- Primary Source: "Battle Cry of Freedom" and "Bonnie Blue Flag," p. 31

# 2 Life in the Army

**TERMS & NAMES**
hygiene
rifle
minié ball
ironclad

| MAIN IDEA | WHY IT MATTERS NOW |
|---|---|
| Both Union and Confederate soldiers endured many hardships serving in the army during the Civil War. | The hardships endured led to long-lasting bitterness on both sides. |

### ONE AMERICAN'S STORY

**When the Civil War began, Peter Vredenburgh, Jr., the son of a well-known judge, was working as a lawyer in Eatontown, New Jersey. In 1862, he answered President Lincoln's call for an additional 300,000 soldiers. Nearly 26 years old, Vredenburgh became a major in the 14th Regiment New Jersey Volunteer Infantry. Less than two months after joining the regiment, he wrote a letter urging his parents to keep his 18-year-old brother from enlisting.**

Major Peter Vredenburgh, Jr., was an officer in the Union army.

*A VOICE FROM THE PAST*

I am glad that Jim has not joined any Regt. [regiment] and I hope he never will. I would not have him go for all my pay; it would be very improbable that we could both go through this war and come out unharmed. Let him come here and see the thousands with their arms and legs off, or if that won't do, let him go as I did the other day through the Frederick hospitals and see how little account a man's life and limbs are held in by others and what little return he gets in reputation or money for the risk and privations of enlisting and his ideas of the fun of the thing will vanish in thin air.

**Major Peter Vredenburgh, Jr.,** quoted in *Upon the Tented Field*

**On September 19, 1864, Vredenburgh was killed in battle. In this section, you will learn more about other soldiers and what their experiences were like.**

### 1 Those Who Fought

Like Peter Vredenburgh, the majority of soldiers in the Civil War were between 18 and 30 years of age. But both the Confederate and Union armies had younger and older soldiers. Charles Carter Hay was just 11 years old when he joined an Alabama regiment. William Wilkins was 83 when he became one of the Pennsylvania Home Guards.

Farmers made up the largest group among Civil War soldiers. About half the soldiers on both sides came from farms. Having rarely traveled far from their fields, many viewed going off to war as an exciting adventure. Some rode a train for the first time.



## RECOMMENDED RESOURCES

 **In-Depth Resources: Unit 5**
- Guided Reading, p. 24
- Building Vocabulary, p. 26
- Primary Source: "Battle Cry of Freedom" and "Bonnie Blue Flag," p. 31
- Literature Selection, pp. 32–34
- Reteaching Activity, p. 36

**Reading Study Guide** (Spanish and English), pp. 161–162

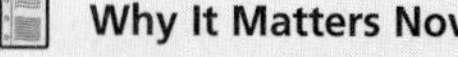

**Why It Matters Now**
- Modern Warfare, pp. 31–32

**Formal Assessment**
- Section Quiz, p. 243

**Alternative Assessment**
- Rubrics, 4.3
- Rubrics, 2.1

**Access for Students Acquiring English/ESL**
- Guided Reading, p. 108

**Technology Resources**

 **Critical Thinking Trans. CT47**
- Cause and Effect: Hardships of Civil War Soldiers

 **America's Music CD**

 **Electronic Teacher Tools with Test Maker**

 **ClassZone**
www.mcdougallittell.com

Although the majority of soldiers in the war were born in the United States, immigrants from other countries also served. German and Irish immigrants made up the largest ethnic groups. One regiment from New York had soldiers who were born in 15 foreign countries. The commanding officer gave orders in seven languages.

At the beginning of the war, African Americans wanted to fight. They saw the war as a way to end slavery. However, neither the North nor the South accepted African Americans into their armies. As the war dragged on, the North finally took African Americans into its ranks. Native Americans served on both sides.

In all, about 2 million American soldiers served the Union, and fewer than 1 million served the Confederacy. The vast majority were volunteers. Why did so many Americans volunteer to fight? Many sought adventure and glory. Some sought an escape from the boredom of farm and factory work. Some signed up because their friends and neighbors were doing it. Others signed up for the recruitment money offered by both sides. Soldiers also fought because they were loyal to their country or state.

*Reading* **History**
**A. Summarizing** How did most men in the North and the South feel about going off to war?
**A. Answer** Most were excited by the idea of adventure and committed to doing their duty for their country.

## Turning Civilians into Soldiers 2

After enlisting, a volunteer was sent to a nearby army camp for training. A typical camp looked like a sea of canvas tents. The tents were grouped by company, and each tent held from two to twenty men. In winter, the soldiers lived in log huts or in heavy tents positioned on a log base. In the Civil War, recruits in training elected their company officers. Both the Union and Confederate armies followed this practice.

A soldier in training followed a set schedule. A bugle or drum awakened the soldier at dawn. After roll call and breakfast, the soldier had the first of several drill sessions. In between drills and meals, soldiers performed guard duty, cut wood for the campfires, dug trenches for latrines (outdoor toilets), and cleaned up the camp.

Shortly after they came to camp, new recruits were given uniforms and equipment. Union soldiers wore blue uniforms, and Confederate soldiers wore gray or

**daily *life***

**DRILL SESSIONS**

"The first thing in the morning is drill. Then drill, then drill again. Then drill, drill, a little more drill. Then drill, and lastly drill." That is the way one soldier described his day in camp.

A soldier in training might have as many as five drill sessions a day, each lasting up to two hours. The soldiers learned to stand straight and march in formation. They also learned to load and fire their guns. Shown drilling below are soldiers of the 22nd New York State Militia near Harpers Ferry, Virginia, in 1862.

**MORE ABOUT . . .**

**Native Americans in the Civil War**

When the Civil War began, the so-called Five Civilized Tribes, who had been forced to move west in the 1830s, had strong ties to the South. These tribes and others lived in Indian Territory (later Oklahoma). The tribes raised several thousand troops for the South, and the Cherokee Stand Watie became a Confederate brigadier general, commanding the First Indian Cavalry Brigade. However, about an equal number of Native Americans fought for the Union side. Indian Territory was devastated, with up to 25 percent of the Creeks, Seminoles, and Cherokees dead. Nearly every building in the territory was destroyed, and most of the people lost everything they owned.

**INSTRUCT: OBJECTIVE 2**

**Turning Civilians into Soldiers**

Key Questions
- What training did soldiers receive?
- Why did both armies have problems providing food, clothing, and shoes for their soldiers?

**daily*life***

**Drill Sessions**

In the 1860s, drilling was a very important part of training because troops were organized into regiments or brigades that were expected to march in formation. To get from a marching formation into a fighting formation required precise, complicated movements. Soldiers who had never worked together as part of a larger unit needed to spend many hours practicing these moves. Otherwise, they risked becoming a mass of confused individuals, rather than a fighting unit, on the battlefield.

**ACTIVITY OPTIONS**

**INTERDISCIPLINARY LINK: MUSIC** — BLOCK SCHEDULING

**CIVIL WAR SONGS**

**Class Time** One class period

**Task** Analyzing primary sources

**Purpose** To gain an understanding of how war songs encouraged patriotism and raised morale

**Supplies Needed**
- Copies of Civil War songs (See *Folk Song USA* by John and Alan Lomax or *The Ballad of America* by John Anthony Scott.)
- Recordings of Civil War songs (e.g., "John Brown's Body," "Tenting Tonight," "Bonnie Blue Flag")

 America's Music CD

**Activity** Play recordings of a Confederate song and a Union song without identifying them. Have students decide which one is which based on careful listening. Then divide the class in half and give each group Confederate or Union lyrics to analyze. Have students identify patriotic or religious themes in each and suggest reasons why soldiers might like the songs. Make a Venn diagram on the chalkboard and hold a class discussion comparing and contrasting the songs that were popular with each army.

**MORE ABOUT . . .**

**Civil War Surgery**

The soft-lead bullets used in Civil War rifles did not chip a bone; they shattered it. As a result, an arm or leg wound often led to the need for amputation. Sometimes, especially in the ill-supplied Confederate army, the doctors had no chloroform to use as an anesthetic for the soldier whose limb they were sawing off. To make matters worse, no one understood why wounds became infected, so doctors saw no need for sterilization or even basic cleanliness. Some did not even wipe off their bone saws as they went from one patient to the next.

**INSTRUCT: OBJECTIVE 3**

**Hardships of Army Life**

Key Questions

- What were the major causes of widespread sickness in army camps?
- How did scientific ignorance contribute to the spread of disease?

 **In-Depth Resources: Unit 5**
- Literature Selection: "An Episode of War" by Stephen Crane, pp. 32–34

 **Critical Thinking Transparency CT47**
- Cause and Effect: Hardships of Civil War Soldiers

**STRANGE *but* True**

**Deadlier than Bullets**

Commenting on the level of care received by wounded or ailing soldiers, the Surgeon General of the Union recalled that the war was fought "at the end of the medical middle ages." In one year of the war, Union officials recorded that virtually every soldier in the Union army came down with diarrhea and dysentery. Many men who survived the war suffered the aftereffects of disease for the rest of their lives.

yellowish-brown uniforms. Getting a uniform of the right size was a problem, however. On both sides, soldiers traded items to get clothing that fit properly.

**Background**
Before uniforms became standardized, soldiers dressed in outfits supplied from home. This caused confusion on the battlefield.

Early in the war, Northern soldiers received clothing of very poor quality. Contractors took advantage of the government's need and supplied shoddy goods. Shoes made of imitation leather, for example, fell apart when they got wet. In the Confederacy, some states had trouble providing uniforms at all, while others had surpluses. Because the states did not always cooperate and share supplies, Confederate soldiers sometimes lacked shoes. Like soldiers in the Revolutionary War, they marched over frozen ground in bare feet. After battles, needy soldiers took coats, boots, and other clothing from the dead.

At the beginning of the war, most soldiers in army camps received plenty of food. Their rations included beef or salt pork, flour, vegetables, and coffee. But when they were in the field, the soldiers' diet became more limited. Some soldiers went hungry because supply trains could not reach them.

**STRANGE *but* True**

**DEADLIER THAN BULLETS**

"Look at our company—21 have died of disease, 18 have become so unhealthy as to be discharged, and only four have been killed in battle." So a Louisiana officer explained the high death rate in the Civil War.

More than twice as many men died of disease as died of battle wounds. Intestinal disorders, including typhoid fever, diarrhea, and dysentery, killed the most. Pneumonia, tuberculosis, and malaria killed many others. Bad water and food, poor diet, exposure to cold and rain, unsanitary conditions, and disease-carrying insects all contributed to the high rate of disease.

## 3 Hardships of Army Life

Civil War soldiers in the field were often wet, muddy, or cold from marching outdoors and living in crude shelters. Many camps were unsanitary and smelled from the odors of garbage and latrines. One Union soldier described a camp near Washington. In the camp, cattle were killed to provide the troops with meat.

*A VOICE FROM THE PAST*

The hides and [waste parts] of the [cattle] for miles upon miles around, under a sweltering sun and sultry showers, would gender such swarms of flies, armies of worms, blasts of stench and oceans of filth as to make life miserable.

**William Keesy,** quoted in *The Civil War Infantryman*

Not only were the camps filthy, but so were the soldiers. They often went weeks without bathing or washing their clothes. Their bodies, clothing, and bedding became infested with lice and fleas.

Poor **hygiene**—conditions and practices that promote health—resulted in widespread sickness. Most soldiers had chronic diarrhea or other intestinal disorders. These disorders were caused by contaminated water or food or by germ-carrying insects. People did not know that germs cause diseases. Doctors failed to wash their hands or their instruments. An observer described how surgeons "armed with long, bloody knives and saws, cut and sawed away with frightful rapidity, throwing the mangled limbs on a pile nearby as soon as removed."

B. Answer attention to hygiene in camps by soldiers and doctors

***Reading*History**
**B. Making Inferences** What changes could have helped lower the spread of disease among soldiers?



**ACTIVITY OPTIONS**

**INDIVIDUAL NEEDS: GIFTED AND TALENTED**

**MEDICINE AND DISEASE IN THE CIVIL WAR**

**Class Time** One class period

**Task** Researching medical aspects of the Civil War

**Purpose** To understand the connection between the state of medical science and the high death rate in the war

**Supplies Needed**
- Reference materials on medical history and on the Civil War

**Activity** Students interested in science or medicine can research one of the diseases that contributed to the high death toll during the Civil War. They might report to the class on how this disease was spread, how it was treated at the time, how it is treated in modern times, or how it is prevented. After each student has made his or her report, the class can discuss how this disease was probably spread on battlefields and in military hospitals and campgrounds during the Civil War.

The naval duel between the Union *Monitor* and the Confederate *Merrimack* (or *Virginia)* took place on March 9, 1862.

## 4 Changes in Military Technology

**Vocabulary**
**casualties:** number of people killed or injured

While camp life remained rough, military technology advanced. Improvements in the weapons of war had far-reaching effects. Battle tactics changed, and casualties soared.

Rifles that used minié balls contributed to the high casualty rate in the Civil War. A **rifle** is a gun with a grooved barrel that causes a bullet to spin through the air. This spin gives the bullet more distance and accuracy. The **minié ball** is a bullet with a hollow base. The bullet expands upon firing to fit the grooves in the barrel. Rifles with minié balls could shoot farther and more accurately than old-fashioned muskets. As a result, mounted charges and infantry assaults did not work as well. Defenders using rifles could shoot more of the attackers before they got close.

C. Answer Rifles with minié balls increased the casualty rate and changed battle tactics.

*Reading*History
**C. Drawing Conclusions** Which changes in military technology had an effect on the average soldier? Why?

**Ironclads,** warships covered with iron, proved to be a vast improvement over wooden ships. In the first ironclad battle, the Confederate *Virginia* (originally named the *Merrimack*) battled the Union *Monitor* off the coast of Virginia in 1862. After hammering away for about four hours, the battle ended in a draw. (See page 492 for more information on ironclads.)

Despite new technology and tactics, neither side gained a decisive victory in the first two years of the war, as you will see in the next section.

### Section 2 Assessment

**1. Terms & Names**
**Identify:**
- hygiene
- rifle
- minié ball
- ironclad

**2. Taking Notes**
Complete the chart below.

| The Typical Civil War Soldier | |
|---|---|
| Age | |
| Occupation | |
| Training | |
| Hardships | |

Which hardship do you think would have been most difficult to endure? Why?

**3. Main Ideas**
a. How were the wartime experiences of Northern and Southern soldiers alike?
b. What factors contributed to the spread of disease among soldiers?
c. How did the use of the rifle and minié ball change combat tactics in the Civil War?

**4. Critical Thinking**
**Forming and Supporting Opinions** What were the motives that led individual soldiers to fight in the Civil War?
**THINK ABOUT**
- the multiple reasons that people had for enlisting
- what you consider valid reasons for fighting

**ACTIVITY OPTIONS**
**LANGUAGE ARTS**
**ART**
Imagine you are a soldier in the Civil War. Write a **letter** home to your parents about your experience or draw an **illustrated map** of your training camp.



### MORE ABOUT . . .

**Civil War Technology**
The Civil War was the first war in which the telegraph and the railroad were vital to a war effort. It was also the first war in which soldiers laid land mines, aimed their rifles with telescopic sites, fired machine guns, and spied on enemy troops from the air—in observation balloons. It was the first war in which soldiers fought from trenches, sometimes using periscopes to peer over the top without making targets of themselves.

### INSTRUCT: OBJECTIVE 4

**Changes in Military Technology**
Key Questions
- What effect did changes in weapons have on the way war was fought?
- What contributed to the high casualty rate in the Civil War?
- Why were ironclads better than wooden warships?

## ASSESS & RETEACH

**Setting the Stage** Tell students to create a diagram like the one on page 480 to compare information about the North and the South for this section.

**Formal Assessment**
- Section Quiz, p. 243

**RETEACHING ACTIVITY**
Have students turn each of the subheads in this section into a question. For example, "Hardships of Army Life" becomes "What were the hardships of army life?" Then have students answer the questions they have created.

**In-Depth Resources: Unit 5**
- Reteaching Activity, p. 36

### Section 2 Assessment

**1. Terms & Names**
**hygiene,** p. 490
**rifle,** p. 491
**minié ball,** p. 491
**ironclad,** p. 491

**2. Taking Notes**
Age: between 18 and 30; Occupation: farmer; Training: many long daily drill sessions; Hardships: inadequate food and clothing, crude shelters, dirty camps that stank, poor personal hygiene, chronic sicknesses, poor medical treatment

**3. Main Ideas**
**a.** Both endured hunger, cold, dirty living conditions, constant sickness, and poor medical treatment.
**b.** contaminated water and food; poor diet; exposure to cold and rain; unsanitary conditions
**c.** Cavalry charges and traditional assaults became outdated.

**4. Critical Thinking**
the desire for adventure; following the example of others; patriotism

**ACTIVITY OPTIONS**

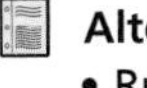

**Alternative Assessment**
- Rubrics for a letter, 4.3
- Rubrics for a map, 2.1

Technology OF THE Time

**OBJECTIVES**

1. To use the diagram of an ironclad to understand why these ships were a significant technological advance
2. To explain how the introduction of ironclads led to a new era in naval warfare

## INSTRUCT

Key Questions

- According to the diagram, what features of the ironclad were geared toward offense? toward defense?
- How do you think the experience of being a sailor on an ironclad would differ from being on another type of ship?
- What aspects of the ironclads reflect the changes in technology that grew out of the Industrial Revolution?
- Judging by the chart, how have warships changed from 1862 to 1972?

### MORE ABOUT . . .

**Ironclads**

The *Merrimack* had been built before the war as a regular 40-gun steam frigate. In April 1861, as Union troops withdrew from the Norfolk Naval Shipyard in Virginia, they sank the *Merrimack* to keep it out of rebel hands. However, Confederate workers repaired the ship, covered it with iron plating, renamed it the *Virginia,* and sent it to sea against the Union blockade. In its first battle, the *Virginia* defeated three Union ships.

Meanwhile, the Union had secretly built its own ironclad, the *Monitor,* which one observer said looked like "a tin can on a shingle." By the end of the war, the U.S. Navy had 626 warships of which 65 were ironclads. Partial ironclads helped Grant in the West in 1862, supporting Union troops on western rivers and the Mississippi.

Technology OF THE Time

# Ironclads

They moved through the water, as one observer put it, "like a huge, half-submerged crocodile." To crew members of traditional wooden ships, the ironclads indeed may have seemed like horrible mechanical monsters.

With a powerful iron hull almost entirely under water and a rotating gun turret, or short tower, an ironclad easily destroyed the older vessels it met. When the *Monitor* and the *Merrimack* (or *Virginia*) clashed during the Civil War in the first battle ever waged between ironclads, a new era of naval warfare had begun. Below is a closer look at the Union's *Monitor*.

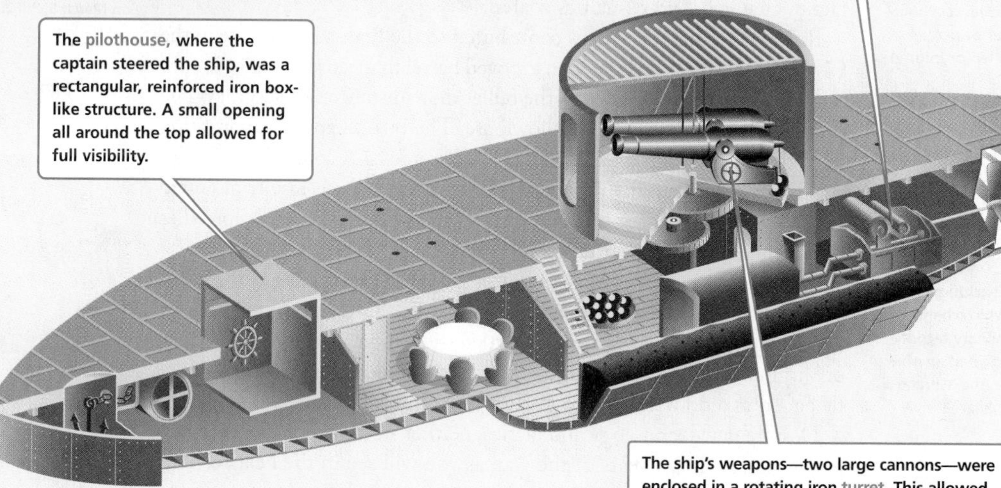

Steam engines powered the ship. They were connected by a propeller shaft to a four-blade propeller. Behind the propeller sat the vessel's rudder. This entire area was heavily protected so the ship could keep moving under heavy fire or ramming.

The pilothouse, where the captain steered the ship, was a rectangular, reinforced iron box-like structure. A small opening all around the top allowed for full visibility.

The ship's weapons—two large cannons—were enclosed in a rotating iron turret. This allowed the guns to fire at an enemy from all directions. Ammunition was passed up to the gunners through a hatch in the floor.

SCALE AND SIZE OF WARSHIPS

| Class, Name, Launch Date | Length | Weight | Number of Crew | Weaponry |
|---|---|---|---|---|
| **Ironclad** (USS *Monitor*) 1862 | 172 ft. | 987 tons | 49 | two 11-inch smoothbore cannons |
| **Battleship** (USS *Maine*) 1889 | 319 ft. | 6,682 tons | 374 | four 10-inch guns, six 6-inch guns, seven rapid-fire 6-pounders, four torpedo tubes |
| **Nuclear Submarine** (USS *Nautilus*) 1954 | 324 ft. | 4,092 tons | 105 | six torpedo tubes |
| **Aircraft Carrier** (USS *Nimitz*) 1972 | 1,092 ft. | 95,000 tons | 6,000 | 24 F-14A Tomcat warplanes, 16 radar guided missiles, six-barrel, 20-millimeter Gatling gun |

**CONNECT TO HISTORY**

1. **Drawing Conclusions** Why would a rotating gun be an advantage in a naval battle?

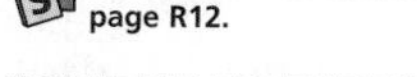
See Skillbuilder Handbook, page R12.

**CONNECT TO TODAY**

2. **Researching** Find out more about modern battleships or aircraft carriers, and write a brief report about their capabilities in battle.

Visit www.mcdougallittell.com for more on military ships.

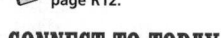

492

**CONNECT TO HISTORY**

1. **Drawing Conclusions Possible Response** As the ship moved during battle, guns could continue to fire at the enemy from any angle. Also the ship could fire at enemy vessels on several sides.

**CONNECT TO TODAY**

2. **Researching** Students can use an encyclopedia or the Internet to learn about modern naval vessels. One standard reference is *Jane's Fighting Ships.* Students who are interested in building models may be able to show the class examples of aircraft carriers, submarines, battleships, or destroyers from recent years. Some students may be interested in researching other changes in technology that occurred during the Civil War, such as the Gatling gun, and so on.

# 3 No End in Sight

TERMS & NAMES
Ulysses S. Grant
Battle of Shiloh
cavalry
Seven Days' Battles
Battle of Antietam

| MAIN IDEA | WHY IT MATTERS NOW |
|---|---|
| In the first two years of the war, neither side gained a decisive victory over the other. | A long war can cause much death and destruction and leave a bitter legacy. |

## ONE AMERICAN'S STORY

**In the summer of 1861, President Lincoln gave George McClellan command of the Union army in the East. The army had recently been defeated at Bull Run. McClellan faced the task of restoring the soldiers' confidence while organizing and training an army that could defeat the Confederates.**

**Within months, McClellan had accomplished the task and won the devotion of his troops. The entire nation expected great things. In November 1861, Lincoln made McClellan general in chief of the entire Union army. But while Lincoln kept urging him to attack Richmond, McClellan kept drilling his troops.**

*A VOICE FROM THE PAST*

[S]oon as I feel that my army is well organized and well disciplined and strong enough, I will advance and force the Rebels to a battle on a field of my own selection. A long time must elapse before I can do that.

**General George McClellan,** quoted in *Civil War Journal: The Leaders*

President Lincoln (right) meets with General McClellan (left) on the Antietam battlefield in 1862.

**Lincoln said McClellan had "the slows." While McClellan was stalling in the East, another general was winning victories in the West.**

## 1 Union Victories in the West

That victorious Union general in the West was **Ulysses S. Grant.** In civilian life, he had failed at many things. But Grant had a simple strategy of war: "Find out where your enemy is, get at him as soon as you can, strike at him as hard as you can, and keep moving on."

In February 1862, Grant made a bold move to take Tennessee. Using ironclad gunboats, Grant's forces captured two Confederate river forts. These were Fort Henry on the Tennessee and Fort Donelson on the nearby Cumberland. (See map on next page.) The seizure of Fort Henry opened up a river highway into the heart of the South. Union gunboats could now travel on the river as far as northern Alabama. When the people of Nashville, Tennessee, heard the forts were lost, they fled the city in panic. A week later, Union troops marched into Nashville.





## SECTION OBJECTIVES

1. To analyze the importance of the Union victories in the West
2. To explain how the fall of New Orleans helped the Union
3. To analyze Lee's victories in the East and his decision to invade the North
4. To describe the outcome of the Battle of Antietam

**SKILLBUILDER**

Interpreting Maps: Location, Region, pp. 494–495

**CRITICAL THINKING**

Contrasting, p. 494
Recognizing Effects, p. 495
Making Inferences, pp. 496, 497

## FOCUS & MOTIVATE

### 5-MINUTE WARM-UP

**Drawing Conclusions** These questions focus on regions where fighting took place.

1. Look at the maps on pages 494–495. In what states did most of the battles in the East take place? in the West?
2. Why might so much of the fighting have taken place in or near border states?

 **Warm-Up Transparency WT16**

## INSTRUCT

**INSTRUCT: OBJECTIVE** 

**Union Victories in the West/ The Battle of Shiloh**

Key Questions

- Why was control of rivers important?
- How did Shiloh signal a change from earlier battles of the war?
- Why did Lincoln refuse to replace Grant?

 **In-Depth Resources: Unit 5**
- Guided Reading, p. 25

 **Reading Study Guide** (Spanish and English), pp. 163–164

## RECOMMENDED RESOURCES

 **In-Depth Resources: Unit 5**
- Guided Reading, p. 25
- Building Vocabulary, p. 26
- Reteaching Activity, p. 37
- Enrichment Activity, p. 38

**Reading Study Guide** (Spanish and English), pp. 163–164

 **Formal Assessment**
- Section Quiz, p. 244

 **Alternative Assessment**
- Rubrics, 2.1
- Rubrics, 1.3

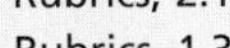

 **Access for Students Acquiring English/ESL**
- Guided Reading, p. 109

Technology Resources

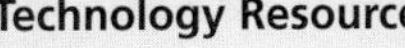

 **Electronic Teacher Tools with Test Maker**

 **ClassZone** www.mcdougallittell.com

## MORE ABOUT . . .

**Shiloh Church**
Ironically, the Battle of Shiloh, the first bloody battle of the war, took its name from a small Methodist church whose name came from the Hebrew word meaning "place of peace."

**In-Depth Resources: Unit 5**
• Enrichment Activity, p. 38

## The Battle of Shiloh

After Grant's river victories, Albert S. Johnston, Confederate commander on the Western front, ordered a retreat to Corinth, Mississippi. Grant followed. By early April, Grant's troops had reached Pittsburg Landing on the Tennessee River. There he waited for more troops from Nashville. Johnston, however, decided to attack before Grant gained reinforcements. Marching his troops north from Corinth on April 6, 1862, Johnston surprised the Union forces near Shiloh Church. The **Battle of Shiloh** in Tennessee turned into the fiercest fighting the Civil War had yet seen.

Commanders on each side rode into the thick of battle to rally their troops. One Union general, William Tecumseh Sherman, had three horses shot out from under him. General Johnston was killed, and the command passed to General Pierre Beauregard. By the end of the day, each side believed that dawn would bring victory.

That night, there was a terrible thunderstorm. Lightning lit up the battlefield, where dead and dying soldiers lay in water and mud. During the night, Union boats ran upriver to ferry fresh troops to Grant's camp. Grant then led an attack at dawn and forced the exhausted Southern troops to retreat.

The cost of the Union victory was staggering. Union casualties at Shiloh numbered over 13,000, about one-fourth of those who had fought. The Confederates lost nearly 11,000 out of 41,000 soldiers. Describing

**A. Answer** Grant was a bold and decisive leader while McClellan was slow and cautious.

*Reading* **History**
**A. Contrasting** How did Grant differ from McClellan as a military leader?

## HISTORY FROM VISUALS

**Reading Maps** Have students identify the places on the larger map that each of the three inset maps depicts in greater detail. Then ask students what river both sides were fighting to control.
**Answer** the Mississippi River. Ask students to suggest why control of the Mississippi would help the Union. **Possible Response** It would provide a way into the South, making the South a battleground of the war, and would cut off Confederate states west of the Mississippi from those to the east of the river.
**Extension** Have students pick one of the battles shown on the map and use encyclopedias and other reference materials to learn more about how geographic features of the area affected the outcome.

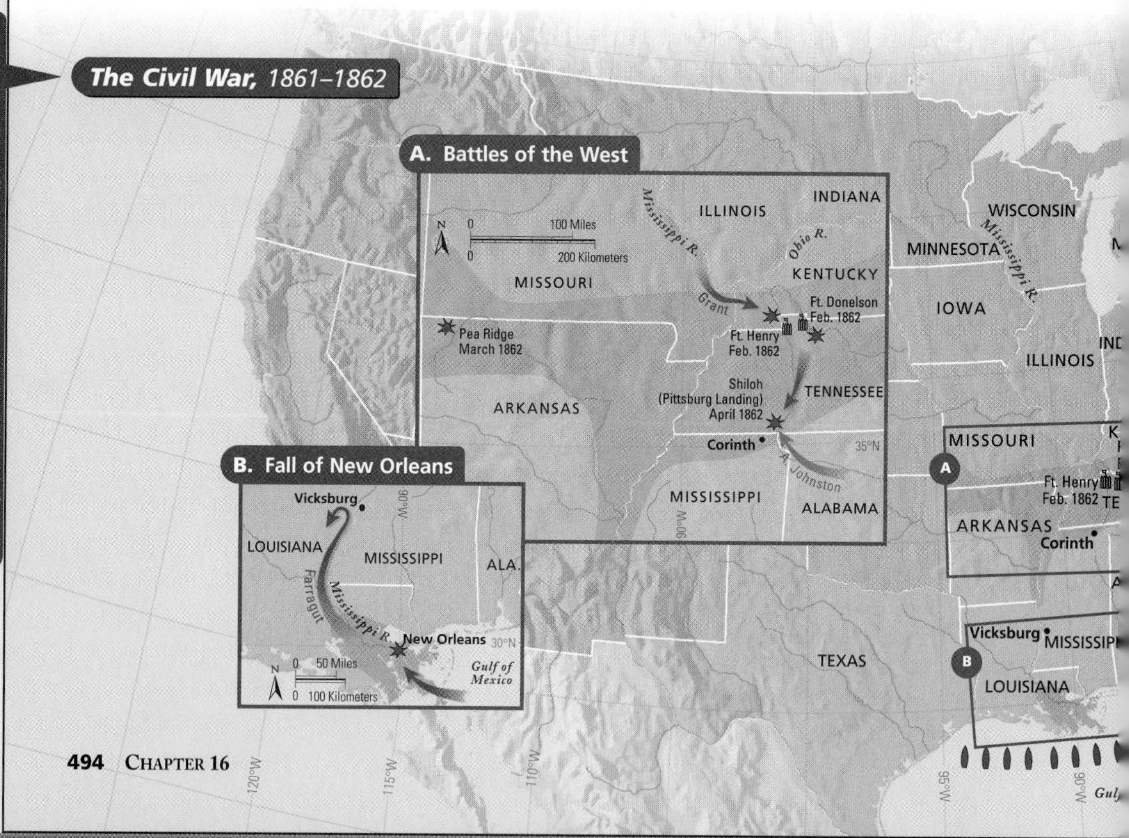

***The Civil War,* 1861–1862**

**A. Battles of the West**

**B. Fall of New Orleans**



## ACTIVITY OPTIONS
## INDIVIDUAL NEEDS

### LESS PROFICIENT READERS

**Sequencing Events** Students may have difficulty sequencing the events that occurred in the first two years of the war. To help them focus on the sequence, list the following major events and battles on the board. Have students find the approximate date for each one and then list them in chronological sequence. When the activity is completed, review the section by discussing the significance of each battle or event.

- Battle of Antietam
- Grant captures Fort Henry and Fort Donelson
- Lee crosses Potomac
- Battle of Shiloh
- Seven Days' Battle at Richmond
- Union army captures New Orleans

the piles of mangled bodies, General Sherman wrote home, "The scenes on this field would have cured anybody of war." Congressmen criticized Grant for the high casualties and urged Lincoln to replace him. But Lincoln replied, "I can't spare this man—he fights."

> ***"I can't spare this man—he fights."***
> **Abraham Lincoln, describing General Grant**

## 2 The Fall of New Orleans

The spring of 1862 brought other bad news for the Confederacy. On April 25, a Union fleet led by David Farragut captured New Orleans, the largest city in the South. Rebel gunboats tried to ram the Union warships and succeeded in sinking one. Farragut's ships had to run through cannon fire and then dodge burning rafts in order to reach the city. Residents stood on the docks and cursed the Yankee invaders, but they were powerless to stop them.

The fall of New Orleans was a heavy blow to the South. Mary Chesnut of South Carolina, the wife of an aide to President Davis, wrote in her diary, "New Orleans gone—and with it the Confederacy. Are we not cut in two?" Indeed, after the victories of General Grant and Admiral Farragut, only a 150-mile stretch of the Mississippi remained in Southern hands. The Union was well on its way to achieving its goal of cutting the Confederacy in two. But guarding the remaining stretch of the river was the heavily armed Confederate fort at Vicksburg, Mississippi.

**B. Answer** It lowered Southern morale. It helped the North cut the South in two.

*Reading***History**
**B. Recognizing Effects** Why was the fall of New Orleans significant?

Skillbuilder Answers
1. Early Union victories took place in the West; early Confederate victories took place in the East.
2. because it was near Union and Confederate capitals

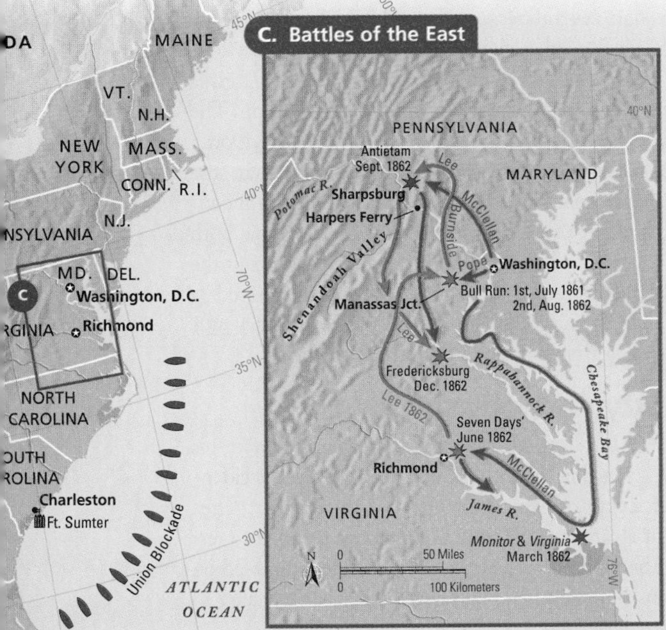


Area controlled by Union
Area won by Union, 1861–1862
Area controlled by Confederacy
Union troop movements
Confederate troop movements
Union victory
Confederate victory
Fort
Capital

0 300 Miles
0 600 Kilometers

**GEOGRAPHY SKILLBUILDER**
1. **Location** *Where did most of the early Union victories take place? Where did early Confederate victories take place?*
2. **Region** *Why did much of the fighting take place in the Virginia-Maryland region?*





**INSTRUCT: OBJECTIVE 2**

**The Fall of New Orleans**

Key Questions
- Why was naval power crucial in capturing New Orleans?
- How did the fall of New Orleans advance Union strategy?

### MORE ABOUT . . .

**The Fall of New Orleans**

The fall of New Orleans not only devastated Southerners like Mary Chesnut but shocked Europeans as well. Henry Adams reported from London, "People here are quite struck aback at . . . news of the capture of New Orleans. It took them three days to make up their minds to believe it. The division of America had become an idea so fixed that they had about shut out . . . any other."

### CRITICAL THINKING ACTIVITY

**Recognizing Effects** Use the cause-and-effect chart below to help students understand the effects of Union victories on the course of the war. How might the outcome of the conflict in the West have been different if the South had been able to hold Fort Henry in Tennessee? What were the effects of the fall of New Orleans? Which battle was most critical to Union success?

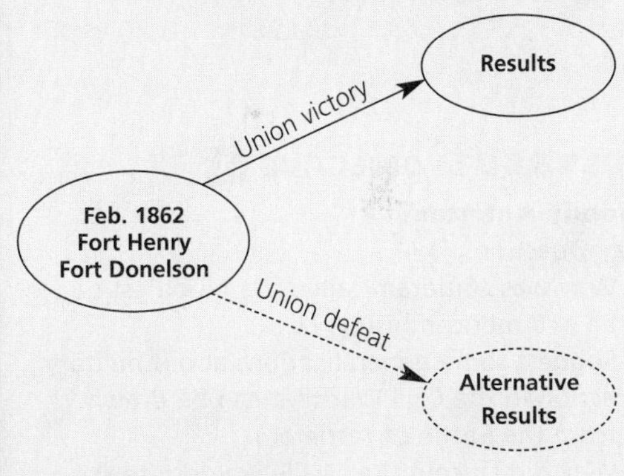


**Class Time** 10 minutes

### ACTIVITY OPTIONS

### MULTIPLE LEARNING STYLES: KINESTHETIC

BLOCK SCHEDULING

**CONDUCT A MILITARY BRIEFING**

**Class Time** One class period

**Task** Conducting a military-style briefing on war strategies and the outcomes of various battles of 1861–1862

**Purpose** To analyze the impact of geography on the Union war effort

**Supplies Needed**
- Reference materials on the battles in 1861–1862
- Wall map of United States
- Pointer

**Activity** Divide students into three groups. Assign each group a major campaign—western battles, eastern battles, or the capture of New Orleans. Within groups assign students different battles. Have them act as military spokespersons preparing and delivering a briefing to the class. Each group's presentations can summarize battle strategy, highlights, outcome, casualties, and significance to the overall campaign. Presenters can also tell how geography influenced strategy or outcome. Encourage students to use a pointer to note the location of the battle on the wall map, trace troop movements, and indicate rivers and other key features.

**INSTRUCT: OBJECTIVE 3**

**Lee Claims Victories in the East/ Lee Invades the North**

Key Questions

- How was Lee able to gain the advantage in the East?
- Why did Lee decide to invade the North?

**AMERICA'S HISTORY MAKERS**

**Jefferson Davis**

Despite his devotion and unswerving commitment to the Southern cause, Davis was not well suited to his position as president of the Confederacy. Haughty and narrow-minded, he was highly sensitive to criticism, quarreled often with most of his generals except Robert E. Lee, and showed poor judgment in choosing friends as members of his administration. He also clearly misread the attitudes of the British, French, and other Europeans toward slavery and the Confederate South.

**Possible Responses: A military leader must be willing to act decisively and independently to achieve objectives, while a politician must be willing to compromise and be flexible to achieve goals.**

**INSTRUCT: OBJECTIVE 4**

**Bloody Antietam**

Key Questions

- Why was Antietam called the bloodiest day in all of American history?
- Suggest some generalizations about military action in the Civil War that can be drawn from the Battle of Antietam.
- Why did Lincoln fire McClellan despite the Union victory at Antietam?

## 3 Lee Claims Victories in the East

Meanwhile, also in the spring of 1862, McClellan finally made his move to try to capture Richmond. He planned to attack the Confederate capital by way of a stretch of land between the York and James rivers. McClellan succeeded in bringing his troops within a few miles of Richmond.

But in June 1862, Robert E. Lee took charge of the Army of Northern Virginia and proceeded to turn the situation around. Lee sent Jeb Stuart and his **cavalry**—soldiers on horseback—to spy on McClellan. With about 1,000 men, Stuart rode around the whole Union army in a few days and reported its size back to Lee. Lee then attacked McClellan's army. The two sides clashed for a week, from June 25 to July 1, 1862, in what became known as the **Seven Days' Battles.** The Army of Northern Virginia suffered heavier losses, but it forced McClellan's army to retreat.

In late August, the Confederates won a second victory at Bull Run, and Union troops withdrew back to Washington. Within just a few months, Lee had ended the Union threat in Virginia.

*Reading*History

**C. Making Inferences** How was Lee's appointment fortunate for the South?

C. Answer It came at a time when the South appeared to be losing; Lee turned the situation around.

**AMERICA'S HISTORY MAKERS**

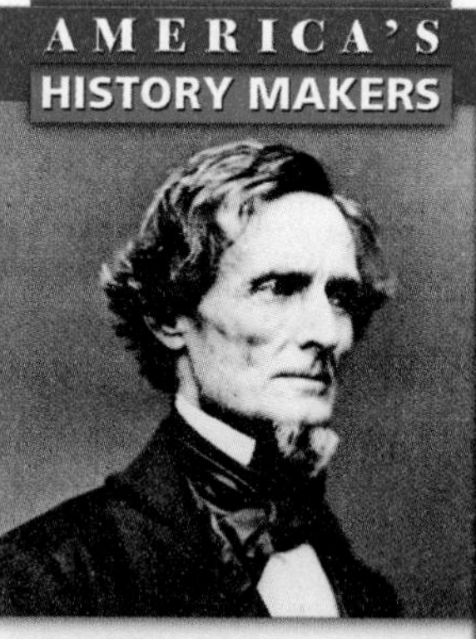

**JEFFERSON DAVIS**
**1808–1889**

Jefferson Davis expected to be given a military command when the Confederacy was formed in 1861. But Davis was chosen President of the Confederacy instead, which stunned and saddened him.

Because of his strong sense of duty and loyalty to the South, Davis accepted the unwelcome post. He had to immediately form a national government and prepare for war at the same time. Davis found it hard to compromise or accept disagreement with his opinions.

**How do the qualities required in a military leader differ from those required in a political leader?**

## Lee Invades the North

Riding a wave of victories, General Lee decided to invade the Union. He wrote to tell President Davis of his plan. Lee thought it was a crucial time, with the North at a low point. Without waiting for Davis's response, Lee crossed the Potomac with his army and invaded Maryland in early September 1862.

Lee had several reasons for taking the war to the North. He hoped a victory in the North might force Lincoln to talk peace. The invasion would give Virginia farmers a rest from war during the harvest season. The Confederates could plunder Northern farms for food.

Lee hoped the invasion would show that the Confederacy could indeed win the war, which might convince Europe to side with the South. By this time, both Britain and France were leaning toward recognizing the Confederacy as a separate nation. They were impressed by Lee's military successes, and their textile industry was now hurting from the lack of Southern cotton.

*Reading*History

**D. Reading a Map** Use the map on page 495 to follow Lee's movements into the North.

## 4 Bloody Antietam

Soon after invading Maryland, Lee drew up a plan for his campaign in the North. A Confederate officer accidentally left a copy of Lee's battle plans wrapped around three cigars at a campsite. When Union troops stopped to rest at the abandoned campsite, a Union soldier stumbled on the plans. The captured plans gave McClellan a chance to stop Lee and his army.



**ACTIVITY OPTIONS**

**INTERDISCIPLINARY LINKS: LANGUAGE ARTS/WRITING** — BLOCK SCHEDULING

**NEWS OF WAR**

**Class Time** One class period

**Task** Writing headlines and news articles on one of the battles or other events discussed in this section

**Purpose** To describe the war effort from differing perspectives

**Supplies Needed**

- Reference materials on the Civil War
- Note cards

**Activity** Divide students into pairs. Have each pair pick one event discussed in the section and write two headlines about this event on a note card. One headline should describe the event as it might have been reported in a Northern paper. The other headline should reflect a Southern perspective. Collect all note cards and redistribute them to different pairs. Have each pair write a two- or three-paragraph article to go along with each headline. Have volunteers read their articles aloud and explain how the language reflects different points of view.

Confederate artillery soldiers lie dead after the Battle of Antietam.

McClellan went on the attack, though he moved slowly as always. On September 17, 1862, at Antietam Creek near Sharpsburg, Maryland, McClellan's army clashed with Lee's. The resulting **Battle of Antietam** was the bloodiest day in all of American history. A Confederate officer later described the battle.

*A VOICE FROM THE PAST*

Again and again . . . by charges and counter-charges, this portion of the field was lost and recovered, until the green corn that grew upon it looked as if it had been struck by a storm of bloody hail. . . . From sheer exhaustion, both sides, like battered and bleeding athletes, seemed willing to rest.

**John B. Gordon,** quoted in *Voices of the Civil War*

After fighting all day, neither side had gained any ground by nightfall. The only difference was that about 25,000 men were dead or wounded. Lee, who lost as much as one-third of his fighting force, withdrew to Virginia. The cautious McClellan did not follow, missing a chance to finish off the crippled Southern army. Lincoln was so fed up that he fired McClellan in November, 1862. In the next chapter, you will learn about the historic action Lincoln took after the Battle of Antietam.

## MORE ABOUT . . .

**George McClellan**

McClellan's military career began well. He graduated second in his class at West Point, and early in the war he took charge of making the Army of the Potomac into a sound fighting force. He saw to it that his soldiers were well supplied with food, clothing, and equipment. And he insisted on good training and strict discipline. The soldiers held him in high respect and affection. However, on the battlefield he was slow to make decisions and reluctant to attack. His habit of overestimating the size of the Confederate forces often kept him from acting decisively.

## *Section 3 Assessment*

**1. Terms & Names**

**Identify:**
- Ulysses S. Grant
- Battle of Shiloh
- cavalry
- Seven Days' Battles
- Battle of Antietam

**2. Taking Notes**

Review the section and find five key events to place on a time line as shown.

1860 — event — event — event — event — event — 1863

Which of these events do you think was most important?

**3. Main Ideas**

a. Why were Union victories in the West and the fall of New Orleans significant to the Union cause?

b. Why did Lee go on the offensive against the North?

c. How did the South's fortunes change after Lee took command of the Army of Northern Virginia?

**4. Critical Thinking**

**Making Inferences** What does Lee's invasion of the North suggest about his qualities as a general and a leader?

**THINK ABOUT**
- Lee's military skills and style
- the North's resources

**ACTIVITY OPTIONS**

**GEOGRAPHY**
**ART**

Develop a new military strategy for either the North or the South. Show your strategy on a **map** or in a **diagram** of troop movements.



## ASSESS & RETEACH

**Setting the Stage** Fill in the categories in the graphic organizer with the appropriate information from this section.

 **Formal Assessment**
- Section Quiz, p. 244

 **Critical Thinking Transparency CT46**
- Setting the Stage

### RETEACHING ACTIVITY

Have students review the battles mentioned in the section. Ask students to pick four battles and write two or three sentences telling how each affected Union and Confederate efforts to win the war.

 **In-Depth Resources: Unit 5**
- Reteaching Activity, p. 37

## *Section 3 Assessment*

**1. Terms & Names**

**Ulysses S. Grant,** p. 493
**Battle of Shiloh,** p. 494
**cavalry,** p. 496
**Seven Days' Battles,** p. 496
**Battle of Antietam,** p. 497

**2. Taking Notes**

Capture of Fort Henry and Fort Donelson, February 1862; Battle of Shiloh, April 6, 1862; Fall of New Orleans, April 25, 1862; Seven Days' Battle, June 25 to July 1, 1862; Battle of Antietam, September 17, 1862

**3. Main Ideas**

**a.** They helped the Union to achieve its goal of cutting the Confederacy in two. **b.** victory might force Lincoln to talk peace; give Virginia farmers a rest during the harvest season; convince Europe to side with the South **c.** end of the Union threat in Virginia; took the offensive against the Union army

**4. Critical Thinking**

Lee was aggressive and willing to take risks. He was a smart leader who planned ahead.

**ACTIVITY OPTIONS**

 **Alternative Assessment**
- Rubrics for a map, 2.1
- Rubrics for a diagram, 1.3

## TERMS & NAMES

1. **Fort Sumter,** p. 481
2. **Robert E. Lee,** p. 482
3. **border state,** p. 482
4. **blockade,** p. 484
5. **hygiene,** p. 490
6. **rifle,** p. 491
7. **ironclad,** p. 491
8. **Ulysses S. Grant,** p. 493
9. **Battle of Shiloh,** p. 494
10. **Battle of Antietam,** p. 497

## REVIEW QUESTIONS

**Possible Responses**

1. April 12, 1861, when the Confederates fired on Fort Sumter
2. more people; 85 percent of the nation's factories; more than double the railroad mileage; almost all the naval power and shipyards, President Lincoln
3. The South planned a defensive war, hoping that the North would give up and King Cotton would cause Europe to aid the Confederacy. The North planned a naval blockade of the South's coastline, a drive to gain control of the Mississippi River, and an attempt to capture the Confederate capital.
4. between 18 and 30 years of age; a farmer; born in the United States; white; patriotic
5. looking for adventure; following what other people were doing; out of a sense of loyalty to their country or state
6. unsanitary living conditions; poor personal hygiene; contaminated water and food; poor diet; exposure to rain, cold, and disease-carrying insects
7. made cavalry charges and traditional assaults outdated
8. cutting the Confederacy in two; by gaining control of forts along the Mississippi
9. McClellan was too cautious.
10. Lee won battles, took the offensive, and turned the war around so that a Confederate victory seemed possible.

# Chapter 16 ASSESSMENT

## TERMS & NAMES

Briefly explain the importance of each of the following.

1. Fort Sumter
2. Robert E. Lee
3. border state
4. blockade
5. hygiene
6. rifle
7. ironclad
8. Ulysses S. Grant
9. Battle of Shiloh
10. Battle of Antietam

## REVIEW QUESTIONS

**War Erupts (pages 481–487)**

1. How and when did the Civil War start?
2. What advantages did the North have at the beginning of the war?
3. What were the war strategies of the two sides?

**Life in the Army (pages 488–492)**

4. What was the typical Civil War soldier like?
5. Why did so many people volunteer to fight in the Civil War?
6. Why was the incidence of disease so high among Civil War soldiers?
7. How did the use of rifles and minié balls change war tactics?

**No End in Sight (pages 493–497)**

8. What goal of the Union strategy did Grant further, and how did he do it?
9. Why did the North have such a hard time capturing Richmond, Virginia?
10. How did Lee's appointment to head the Army of Northern Virginia affect the course of the war?

## CRITICAL THINKING

**1. USING YOUR NOTES**

| | North | South |
|---|---|---|
| Reasons for fighting | | |
| Advantages | | |
| Disadvantages | | |
| Military strategy | | |
| Battle victories | | |

Using your completed chart, answer the questions.

a. Which side seemed likelier to win the war? Why?

b. Which side followed more closely its original strategy in the first two years of the war?

**2. ANALYZING LEADERSHIP**

Think about the leaders discussed in this chapter. Choose one. What character traits helped make him an effective leader?

**3. APPLYING CITIZENSHIP SKILLS**

Which individuals or groups of people demonstrated good and poor citizenship during the war? Explain your choices.

**4. THEME: CITIZENSHIP**

How could people on both sides of the Civil War believe that they were being good citizens by fighting?

**5. MAKING DECISIONS**

In your opinion, was Lincoln correct in deciding to go to war to save the Union? Explain your answer.

**Interact *with* History**

How did the consequences and effects of civil war that you predicted before you read the chapter compare with the actual conditions you read about?

VISUAL SUMMARY
The Civil War, 1861–1862
1861
March 4, 1861 Lincoln inaugurated.
April 12, 1861 Fort Sumter fired upon by rebel forces.
April 15, 1861 Lincoln calls on states to provide 75,000 militiamen.
May 1861 Confederate Congress votes to set up capital in Richmond.
July 21, 1861 First Battle of Bull Run (Manassas)
February 1862 Union forces capture Fort Henry and Fort Donelson.
March 9, 1862 Monitor and Merrimack (Virginia) clash.
April 6, 1862 Battle of Shiloh
April 25, 1862 Fall of New Orleans
June 25 to July 1, 1862 Seven Days' Battles
September 17, 1862 Battle of Antietam (Sharpsburg)
November 1862 Lincoln relieves McClellan of command.
1862

498

## CRITICAL THINKING

**Possible Responses**

1. **USING YOUR NOTES** **a.** Most students would probably favor the North because of its advantages in resources and manpower. **b.** the North
2. **ANALYZING LEADERSHIP** Students might choose Lee, who was brilliant and bold. Or they might choose Grant, who was stubborn and relentless.
3. **APPLYING CITIZENSHIP SKILLS** Students might cite as good the millions of volunteers who fought for their country or the military and civilian leaders who worked to further causes they believed in. They might cite as poor the contractors who sold shoddy military goods to the government.
4. **THEME: CITIZENSHIP** In the North, people believed they were fighting to save the Union and preserve democracy. In the South, people believed they were fighting for the freedom and independence of their state.
5. **MAKING DECISIONS** Students may believe that Lincoln was correct because he succeeded in saving the Union, or Lincoln was wrong because he paid too high a price in human suffering.

**Interact *with* History.** Students might state that the average soldier found army life more difficult than expected.

## HISTORY SKILLS

**1. INTERPRETING MAPS: Movement**

Study the map and answer the questions.

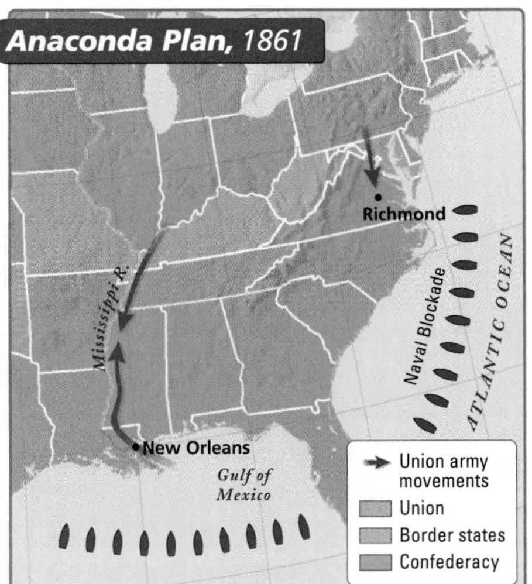


**Basic Map Elements**

a. What is the subject of the map?

b. What do the colors of the states indicate?

**Interpreting the Map**

c. What does the arrow in the East indicate?

d. What two bodies of water did the blockade cover?

**2. INTERPRETING PRIMARY SOURCES**

The following quotation comes from a letter that Robert E. Lee wrote to his sister after Virginia had seceded from the Union and he had resigned from the U.S. Army. Read the quotation and then answer the questions.

> With all my devotion to the Union and the feeling of loyalty and duty of an American citizen, I have not been able to make up my mind to raise my hand against my relatives, my children, my home. I have, therefore, resigned my commission in the Army, and, save in defense of my native state, with the sincere hope that my poor services may never be needed, I hope I may never be called on to draw my sword.
>
> **Robert E. Lee,** quoted in *The Annals of America*

a. What inner conflict does Lee express?

b. What obligation or loyalty does Lee consider greater than his duty to his country?

## ALTERNATIVE ASSESSMENT

**1. INTERDISCIPLINARY ACTIVITY: Literature**

**Reading Letters** Using the library or the Internet, find firsthand accounts of the Civil War and read some letters written by soldiers. Choose one letter to read aloud to the class. Then, pretend you are the person receiving the letter, and describe your reaction to it.

**2. COOPERATIVE LEARNING ACTIVITY**

**Developing a Peace Proposal** The Civil War broke out because the two sides could not reach a compromise. Work in a small group to develop a compromise that would have resolved the conflict between the North and the South. Have one person in the group take the position of a Northerner, another a Southerner, and the third a mediator between the two. Present your proposal to the class for their comments.

**3. TECHNOLOGY ACTIVITY**

**Making a Class Presentation** Life in the army training camps during the Civil War was hard. Information about life in the camps comes from primary sources. Using the library and the Internet, find diaries, letters, photographs, and news articles about daily life.

**Visit www.mcdougallittell.com to learn more about army camps in the Civil War.**

Plan an electronic presentation on army life for your class. Use the list of suggested topics below to begin brainstorming.

- Drawings, maps, and photos that show the design of a typical camp
- Items used for cooking, lodging, sanitation, military drilling, and recreation
- Drills and maneuvers soldiers learned
- Personal belongings of the Yankees and rebels
- Firsthand accounts of camp life from letters and diaries
- Changes in camp life as the war dragged on

**4. HISTORY PORTFOLIO**

**Option 1** Review your section and chapter assessment activities. Select one that you think was your best work. Then use comments made by your teacher or classmates to improve your work and add it to your portfolio.

**Option 2** Review the questions that you wrote for What Do You Want to Know? on page 480. Then write a short report in which you explain the answers to your questions. If any questions were not answered, do research to answer them. Add your answers to your portfolio.



## ALTERNATIVE ASSESSMENT

1. INTERDISCIPLINARY ACTIVITY: **Literature**
   **Letters should**
   - convey information through performance.
   - be read with creativity.
   - reflect an understanding of the letter's contents.

2. COOPERATIVE LEARNING ACTIVITY
   **Proposals should**
   - reflect the use of a problem-solving technique.
   - focus on a compromise that would prevent war.
   - support student positions with evidence or logic.

3.  TECHNOLOGY ACTIVITY
   **Presentations should**
   - clearly demonstrate an understanding of life in army training camps.
   - utilize several primary sources of information to create a variety of information.
   - establish a rapport with the audience.
   - show proficiency in the use of technology.

4. HISTORY PORTFOLIO

 **Option 1 Revised section or chapter assessment activities should**
- address teacher and peer responses to the selected work.
- solve problems present in the first versions of the work.

**Option 2 Short reports should**
- answer questions about the outbreak of the Civil War.
- use evidence to develop and support ideas.
- cite sources of information.
- use standard grammar, spelling, sentence structure, and punctuation.

 **Critical Thinking Transparency CT48**
- Visual Summary

 **Formal Assessment**
- Chapter Test, Forms A and B, pp. 245–252

## HISTORY SKILLS

**Possible Responses**

1. INTERPRETING MAPS
   **Basic Map Elements**
   **a.** the Anaconda Plan of the Union to defeat the Confederacy
   **b.** Union, border, or Confederacy states
   **Interpreting the Map**
   **c.** movement of Union troops toward Confederate capital of Richmond
   **d.** Gulf of Mexico and Atlantic Ocean

2. INTERPRETING PRIMARY SOURCES
   **a.** conflict between loyalty to one's family and home and loyalty to one's country
   **b.** the obligation or loyalty to family and home

# CHAPTER 17 PLANNING GUIDE

# The Tide of War Turns 1863–1865

| | CHAPTER OVERVIEW | COPYMASTERS | TECHNOLOGY |
|---|---|---|---|
| **CHAPTER RESOURCES** | This chapter describes the later stages of the Civil War, with its terrible loss of life and the eventual Union victory. It also describes the war's widespread effects on American society and the assassination of President Lincoln. | **In-Depth Resources: Unit 5**<br>• Tracing Themes: Impact of the Individual, p. 40<br>• Building Vocabulary, p. 45<br>• History Workshop Resources, p. 59<br>**Interdisciplinary Projects,** pp. 97–102 | CD-ROM **Primary Source Explorer**<br>CD-ROM **Electronic Teacher Tools**<br>CD-ROM **Power Presentations CD-ROM**<br>**Chapter Summaries on CD** (English and Spanish)<br>**America's Music CD** |
| | **KEY IDEAS** | | |
| **SECTION 1**<br>**The Emancipation Proclamation**<br>**pp. 503–506** | • Lincoln issues the Emancipation Proclamation.<br>• The public reaction to the proclamation is divided.<br>• The 54th Massachusetts Regiment organizes as one of the first African-American regiments. | **In-Depth Resources: Unit 5**<br>• Setting the Stage, p. 39<br>• Guided Reading, p. 41<br>• Primary Sources, pp. 49–50<br>• Reteaching Activity, p. 54 | **Warm-Up Transparency WT17**<br>**Critical Thinking Transparency CT49**<br>• Setting the Stage<br>INTERNET **ClassZone:** www.mcdougallittell.com |
| **SECTION 2**<br>**War Affects Society**<br>**pp. 507–511** | • As the war drags on, both the North and the South pass draft laws.<br>• The war boosts Northern industry, while the South suffers severe inflation and food shortages.<br>• Women run farms, work in factories, nurse the wounded, and organize relief agencies. | **In-Depth Resources: Unit 5**<br>• Setting the Stage, p. 39<br>• Guided Reading, p. 42<br>• Literature Selection, pp. 51–53<br>• Reteaching Activity, p. 55<br>**America's History Makers**<br>• Clara Barton, pp. 67–68<br>**Economics in History**<br>• Financing the Civil War, p. 17 | **Warm-Up Transparency WT17**<br>**Critical Thinking Transparency CT49**<br>• Setting the Stage<br>INTERNET **ClassZone:** www.mcdougallittell.com |
| **SECTION 3**<br>**The North Wins**<br>**pp. 512–519** | • The Union victory at Gettysburg is a turning point in the war.<br>• Grant wins control of the Mississippi River, while Sherman wages total war across Georgia.<br>• As Grant closes in on Richmond, Lee surrenders at Appomattox Court House, effectively ending the war. | **In-Depth Resources: Unit 5**<br>• Setting the Stage, p. 39<br>• Guided Reading, p. 43<br>• Skillbuilder Practice, p. 46<br>• Reteaching Activity, p. 56<br>**America's History Makers**<br>• Ulysses S. Grant, pp. 69–70<br>**Why It Matters Now**<br>• One Nation, pp. 33–34<br>**Outline Map Activities,** pp. 33–34 | **Warm-Up Transparency WT17**<br>**Humanities Transparency HT33**<br>• Battle of Fredericksburg<br>**Geography Transparency GT17**<br>• Vicksburg Campaign, 1863<br>**Critical Thinking Transparency CT49**<br>• Setting the Stage<br>INTERNET **ClassZone:** www.mcdougallittell.com |
| **SECTION 4**<br>**The Legacy of the War**<br>**pp. 520–525** | • The Civil War leaves 620,000 dead, and President Lincoln is assassinated soon after Lee's surrender.<br>• The Thirteenth Amendment bans slavery in the United States.<br>• The war enlarges federal power and promotes industry in the North but leaves the South devastated. | **In-Depth Resources: Unit 5**<br>• Setting the Stage, p. 39<br>• Guided Reading, p. 44<br>• Geography Application: Booth Assassinates Lincoln, pp. 47–48<br>• Reteaching Activity, p. 57 | **Humanities Transparency HT34**<br>• John Wilkes Booth Poster<br>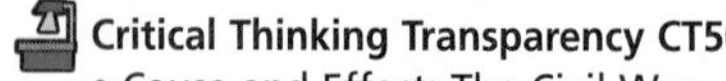 **Critical Thinking Transparency CT50**<br>• Cause and Effect: The Civil War, 1861–1865<br>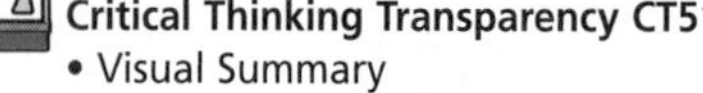 **Critical Thinking Transparency CT51**<br>• Visual Summary<br>CD-ROM **Primary Source Explorer**<br>• *The Gettysburg Address*<br>• *Second Inaugural Address* |

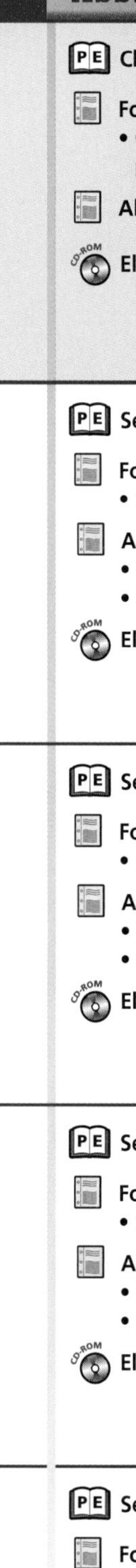

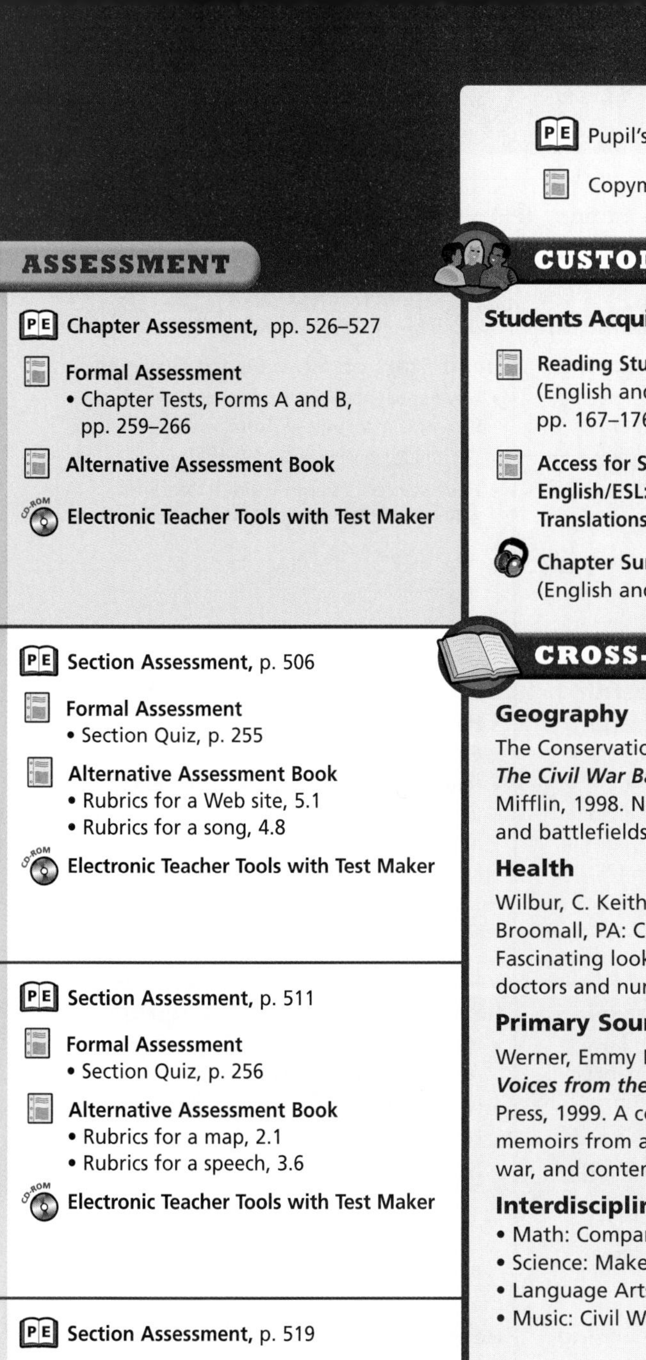
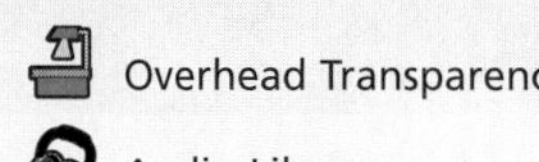

Pupil's Edition
Copymaster
Overhead Transparency
Audio Library
CD-ROM
Internet

## ASSESSMENT

**Chapter Assessment,** pp. 526–527

**Formal Assessment**
- Chapter Tests, Forms A and B, pp. 259–266

**Alternative Assessment Book**

**Electronic Teacher Tools with Test Maker**

**Section Assessment,** p. 506

**Formal Assessment**
- Section Quiz, p. 255

**Alternative Assessment Book**
- Rubrics for a Web site, 5.1
- Rubrics for a song, 4.8

**Electronic Teacher Tools with Test Maker**

**Section Assessment,** p. 511

**Formal Assessment**
- Section Quiz, p. 256

**Alternative Assessment Book**
- Rubrics for a map, 2.1
- Rubrics for a speech, 3.6

**Electronic Teacher Tools with Test Maker**

**Section Assessment,** p. 519

**Formal Assessment**
- Section Quiz, p. 257

**Alternative Assessment Book**
- Rubrics for a map, 2.1
- Rubrics for an article, 4.5

**Electronic Teacher Tools with Test Maker**

**Section Assessment,** p. 523

**Formal Assessment**
- Section Quiz, p. 258

**Alternative Assessment Book**
- Rubrics for a database, 2.6
- Rubrics for a storyboard, 1.6

**Electronic Teacher Tools with Test Maker**

## CUSTOMIZING FOR INDIVIDUAL NEEDS

### Students Acquiring English/ESL

**Reading Study Guide** (English and Spanish), pp. 167–176

**Access for Students Acquiring English/ESL: Spanish Translations,** pp. 113–119

**Chapter Summaries on CD** (English and Spanish)

### Less Proficient Readers

**Reading Study Guide** (English and Spanish), pp. 167–176

**Chapter Summaries on CD** (English and Spanish)

### Gifted and Talented Students

**In-Depth Resources: Unit 5**
- Enrichment Activity, p. 58

**America's History Makers**
- Clara Barton, pp. 67–68
- Ulysses S. Grant, pp. 69–70

## CROSS-CURRICULAR CONNECTIONS

### Geography

The Conservation Fund, Frances H. Kennedy, ed. ***The Civil War Battlefield Guide.*** Boston: Houghton Mifflin, 1998. New edition of a guide to 384 battles and battlefields with 83 maps.

### Health

Wilbur, C. Keith. ***Civil War Medicine, 1861–1865.*** Broomall, PA: Chelsea House Publishing, 1999. Fascinating look at the work and knowledge of doctors and nurses during the war.

### Primary Sources

Werner, Emmy E. ***Reluctant Witnesses: Children's Voices from the Civil War.*** Boulder, CO: Westview Press, 1999. A collection of quotations from children, memoirs from adults who were children during the war, and contemporary newspaper articles.

### Interdisciplinary Projects, pp. 97–102

- Math: Comparing Data on Bar Graphs
- Science: Make a Pinhole Camera
- Language Arts: Civil War Letters
- Music: Civil War Songs

### Literature

Alcott, Louisa May. ***Little Women.*** Boston: Little, Brown, 1968. The much loved classic about a family of girls growing up in New England during the Civil War.

Forrester, Sandra. ***Sound the Jubilee.*** New York: Dutton Lodestar, 1995. Intriguing first novel in which an enslaved family escapes from a plantation to form a community on a Union-held island off the Virginia coast. Based an a historic incident.

Lincoln, Abraham. ***Abraham Lincoln: Speeches and Writings 1859–1865.*** Don E. Fehrenbacher, ed. New York: Literary Classics of United States, 1989. Excellent for browsing or for research.

Morrison, Taylor. ***Civil War Artist.*** Boston: Houghton Mifflin, 1999. Unusual novel about a newspaper artist who follows the Union army at Bull Run.

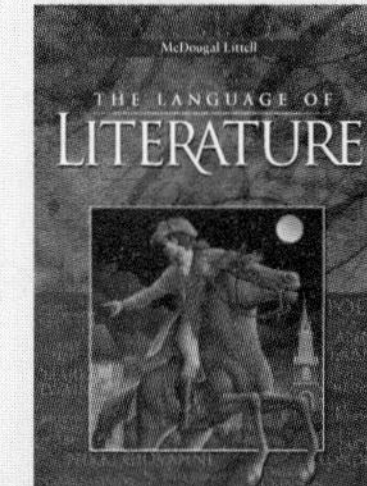


**McDougal Littell**
***The Language of Literature***
Walt Whitman "O Captain! My Captain" (poem)

## ENRICHMENT ACTIVITIES

**Pupil's Edition, pp. 500–529**
**Interact with History,** p. 501
**Geography in History,** pp. 514–515
**Interactive Primary Sources,** pp. 524–525
**History Workshop,** pp. 528–529

**In-Depth Resources: Unit 5**
- Geography Application: Booth Assassinates Lincoln, pp. 47–48
- Primary Source: from "Reply to Emancipation Memorial," p. 49
- Primary Source: A Letter from James Henry Gooding, p. 50
- Literature Selection: from *In My Father's House,* pp. 51–53
- History Workshop Resources, p. 59

**America's History Makers**
- Clara Barton, pp. 67–68
- Ulysses S. Grant, pp. 69–70

**America's Music CD**

**Outline Map Activities**
- The End of the Civil War, 1865, pp. 33–34

**Primary Source Explorer**
- *The Gettysburg Address*
- *Second Inaugural Address*

**Why It Matters Now**
- One Nation, pp. 33–34

# CHAPTER 17 PACING GUIDE

**LESSON PLAN OPTIONS (50-MINUTE PERIOD)** (TE) = Teacher's Edition (PE) = Pupil's Edition

| | TEACHER-DIRECTED ACTIVITIES<br>Class Time: 15 minutes | STUDENT-CENTERED ACTIVITIES<br>Class Time: 25 minutes | INDIVIDUAL ACTIVITIES<br>Class Time: 10 minutes |
|---|---|---|---|
| **DAY 1**<br>Introduction<br>pp. 500–502 | **Presentation Options**<br>• Begin with a class discussion of the picture on p. 500 **(PE).**<br>• Lead a class discussion on the "What Do You Know?" question in Setting the Stage, p. 502. Then introduce the graphic organizer for the chapter **(PE).** | **Options for Cooperative Learning**<br>• Have student groups discuss the Interact with History questions, p. 501 **(PE).**<br>• Have student groups respond to the "What Do You Want to Know?" question in Setting the Stage, p. 502 **(PE).** | **Head Start on Homework Options**<br>• Have students skim Section 1 Main Idea, Why It Matters Now, Terms & Names, and the main headings, p. 503 **(PE).**<br>• Have students begin Guided Reading activity and Building Vocabulary sheet. |
| **DAY 2**<br>Section 1<br>pp. 503–506 | **Presentation Options**<br>• Begin with the 5-Minute Warm-Up, p. 503 **(TE).**<br>• Review the Section 1 Main Idea, Why It Matters Now, and Terms & Names, p. 503 **(PE).**<br>• Lead students in the Critical Thinking Activity, p. 500 **(TE).** | **Options for Cooperative Learning**<br>• Have student pairs work together to complete the Taking Notes chart in the Section 1 Assessment, p. 506 **(PE).**<br>• Have student pairs work together to complete one of the Activity Options in the Section 1 Assessment, p. 506 **(PE).** | **Head Start on Homework Options**<br>• Have students begin working on Section 1 Assessment, p. 506 **(PE).**<br>• Have students preview Section 2 Main Idea, Why It Matters Now, Terms & Names, and the main headings, p. 507 **(PE).** |
| **DAY 3**<br>Section 2<br>pp. 507–511 | **Presentation Options**<br>• Begin with the 5-Minute Warm-Up, p. 507 **(TE).**<br>• Choose 5 key questions for Objectives 1–4 to discuss with the class, pp. 507–510 **(TE).** | **Options for Cooperative Learning**<br>• Divide students into groups and have them complete the Interdisciplinary Link, Math: Calculating Confederate Costs, p. 509 **(TE).**<br>• Have student pairs work together to complete one of the Activity Options in the Section 2 Assessment, p. 511 **(PE).** | **Head Start on Homework Options**<br>• Have students begin working on Section 2 Assessment, p. 511 **(PE).**<br>• Have students complete the Geography in History questions, pp. 514–515 **(PE).** |
| **DAY 4**<br>Section 3<br>pp. 512–519 | **Presentation Options**<br>• Begin with the 5-Minute Warm-Up, p. 512 **(TE).**<br>• Choose 5 key questions for Objectives 1–4 to discuss with the class, pp. 512–518 **(TE).**<br>• Lead the students through the Skillbuilder Mini-Lesson: Making a Time Line, p. 516 **(TE).** | **Options for Cooperative Learning**<br>• Have students complete the History from Visuals Extension Activity, p. 517 **(TE).**<br>• Divide students into groups to have them complete the Interdisciplinary Link, Language Arts: Newspaper Headlines, p. 517 **(TE).** | **Head Start on Homework Options**<br>• Have students begin working on Section 3 Assessment, p. 519 **(PE).**<br>• Have students complete the Reading History questions for Section 4, pp. 520–523 **(PE).** |
| **DAY 5**<br>Section 4<br>pp. 520–525 | **Presentation Options**<br>• Begin with the 5-Minute Warm-Up, p. 520 **(TE).**<br>• Choose 5 key questions for Objectives 1–4 to discuss with the class, pp. 520–522 **(TE).**<br>• Discuss the Cause and Effect chart, p. 523 **(TE).** | **Options for Cooperative Learning**<br>• Divide students into groups and have them complete the Primary Source A Closer Look questions, pp. 524–525 **(PE).**<br>• Have student pairs work together to complete the History Workshop, pp. 528–529 **(PE).** | **Head Start on Homework Options**<br>• Have students complete the Setting the Stage graphic organizer for the chapter, p. 502 **(PE).**<br>• Have students begin working on the Chapter Assessment, pp. 526–527 **(PE).**<br>• Prepare for Chapter Test<br>**Formal Assessment,** pp. 259–266 |

## TEACHER-TESTED ACTIVITY
Ron Campana, Association of Teachers of Social Studies, New York, New York

### ANALYZING A CIVIL WAR FILM

**Class Time** Two or three class periods for viewing films

**Task** Reviewing a movie about the Civil War

**Purpose** To analyze a film about the Civil War for historical accuracy

**Supplies Needed**
- Such films as *Gettysburg, Glory, Gone with the Wind,* or *Red Badge of Courage*
- Videotape player

**Activity** Select three movies about the Civil War for viewing by students. As a class, develop a list of criteria that can be used to evaluate each film for historical accuracy. Divide students into three groups, and assign each group one of the movies. The group can introduce its movie and create a list of questions for class discussion. At the end of the class discussion, the group in charge can also summarize the class's assessment of the movie in terms of its historical accuracy.

## BLOCK SCHEDULING — LESSON PLAN OPTIONS (90-MINUTE PERIOD)

### DAY 1

**Interact with History,** p. 501
**Class Time** 20 Minutes

Options for pacing and variety:
- Role-Playing Divide students into six-member groups. Have three students in each group take the part of Confederate soldiers and the other three the part of Union soldiers. Have each student share with the group how he or she would answer the "What Do You Think?" questions from the perspective of the role assigned. Then have students switch roles and respond to the questions a second time. **Class Time** 15 minutes

**Setting the Stage,** p. 502
**Class Time** 20 minutes

Options for pacing and variety:
- Time Saver For a homework assignment, have students review Chapter 16 and then answer the "What Do You Know?" questions. **Class Time** 5 minutes

**Section 1,** pp. 503–506
**Class Time** 50 minutes

Options for pacing and variety:
- Time Saver For a homework assignment, have students write reaction statements that reflect the views of Northern Democrats, Union Soldiers, abolitionists, white Southerners, and enslaved African Americans on news of the Emancipation Proclamation. **Class Time** 15 minutes
- Peer Teaching Have students work in pairs to create the graphic organizer for the Section Assessment. Students can use their cluster diagram to answer the Taking Notes questions. **Class Time** 15 minutes

### DAY 2

**Section 2,** pp. 507–511
**Class Time** 45 minutes

Options for pacing and variety:
- Peer Teaching Have students work in pairs to create two math word problems using the information in the Daily Life feature on the impact of inflation on page 509. Collect word problems and ask students to answer selected ones. **Class Time** 15 minutes
- Internet Extend students' background knowledge of the Civil War and its aftermath with a look at www.mcdougallittell.com **Class Time** 20 minutes

**Section 3,** pp. 512–519
**Class Time** 45 minutes

Options for pacing and variety:
- Time Saver Use the map on page 517 to summarize the final years of the war and the Union's winning strategies. **Class Time** 15 minutes
- Peer Teaching Have pairs of student take the On-line Field Trip recommended on page 514 in the Geography in History feature and then answer the Connect to Geography and Connect to History questions for this feature. **Class Time** 25 minutes

### DAY 3

**Section 4,** pp. 520–525
**Class Time** 45 minutes

Options for pacing and variety:
- History on Film Extend students' background knowledge of Lincoln's death by viewing *The Lincoln Assassination.* A&E, 1995. **Class Time** 100 minutes
- Peer Teaching Ask a student to summarize the costs of the Civil War for the class using a transparency of the graphs and charts on page 521 as a guide to key points for the presentation. **Class Time** 10 minutes

**Chapter 17 Assessment,** pp. 526–527
**Class Time** 40 minutes

Options for pacing and variety:
- Peer Competition Divide students into four teams. Have each team create a set of ten questions that can be answered with the Terms & Names from all four sections of the chapter. Collect student questions, arrange them by category, and play two rounds of *Jeopardy,* first with two and then with a second set of teams competing against each other. **Class Time** 30 minutes
- Peer Teaching Divide students into an even number of small groups. Have students in each group answer the Critical Thinking questions in the Chapter Assessment and then trade answers with another group to check responses. **Class Time** 15 minutes

**History Workshop,** pp. 528–529
**Class Time** 50 minutes

Options for pacing and variety:
- Time Saver Have students work on steps 1–5 in Create a Medal of Honor. **Class Time** 40 minutes

**CHAPTER 17 OBJECTIVE**
The student will understand the major events of the Civil War from 1863 to 1865 leading to Union victory and the effect of this conflict on the country.

# The Tide of War Turns 1863–1865



## HISTORY FROM VISUALS

**Interpreting the Painting** Ask students to study the painting of a cavalry charge at Yellow Tavern, Virginia, on May 11, 1864. Discuss with them how similar the two sides appear to be. Note the two white horses and the flags. Ask students which side appears to be winning. **Possible Response** The Union forces seem more numerous than their opponents, and the Union forces appear to be on the offensive.

**Extension** Ask students to write a headline for a Confederate and a Union newspaper describing this military action.

Confederate and Union cavalry clash at Yellow Tavern, Virginia, on May 11, 1864.

500

### CRITICAL THINKING ACTIVITY

**Making Inferences** Have students think about the title of this chapter. What do they think it means? Discuss the way the ocean tides change. What factors do students think could cause the war to change?

**Class Time** 10 minutes

## RECOMMENDED RESOURCES

### BOOKS FOR THE TEACHER

Foote, Shelby. ***The Civil War: A Narrative.*** 3 vols. New York: Random, 1986. Careful, balanced, authoritative, and fun to read.

Leonard, Elizabeth D. ***All the Daring of the Soldier.*** New York: Norton, 1999. The remarkable stories of women in the war.

Shaara, Michael. ***The Killer Angels.*** New York: Random, 1993. This superbly researched novel about the Battle of Gettysburg won the Pulitzer Prize and became the basis for a movie.

### VIDEOS

***The Fifty-Fourth Massachusetts.*** A&E Moonbeam, 1996. Documentary history of the black regiment featured in the movie *Glory.*

***The Lincoln Assassination.*** (two cassettes) A&E Moonbeam, 1996. Fascinating minute-by-minute account plus opinions from modern medical and criminal experts.

### SOFTWARE

***Ulysses S. Grant: Unlikely Hero.*** Isis Interactive, 1997. Read from Grant's memoirs.

### INTERNET

For more about the American Civil War, visit www.mcdougallittell.com

## Interact *with* History

Union soldiers, led by General William Tecumseh Sherman, march through Georgia.
Some soldiers fought to save the Union, others to save the Confederacy.
Many soldiers fought to end slavery. Many fought to save it.
Soldiers often fought alongside their friends and wanted to preserve their honor.

**In 1863, you have been a Civil War soldier for two years. The life of a soldier is a hard one. The food is awful. Disease is common. Worst of all is the horrible violence and death. Often you feel the urge to run away and go home.**

### What Do You Think?

- What would you be willing to sacrifice for your country? What if your country fought for something you did not believe in?
- How would the attitudes of fellow soldiers influence your decision?

# *What would inspire you to keep fighting?*

**USA**

**January 1863** Emancipation Proclamation is issued.

**July 1863** Battle of Gettysburg takes place.

Union takes Vicksburg.

**March 1864** Grant is put in charge of all Union armies.

**November 1864** Lincoln is reelected.

**April 1865** Union takes Richmond.

Lee surrenders at Appomattox Court House.

Lincoln is assassinated.

1863 — 1866

**World**

**January 1863** Polish nationalists revolt against Russian rule.

**July 1863** Source of Nile River is found at Lake Victoria in present-day Uganda.

**June 1864** Archduke Maximilian of Austria becomes emperor of Mexico.

**September 1864** First International Workingmen's Association is established, and Karl Marx becomes its leader.

**September 1865** English officials arrest *Fenian* leaders of planned uprising in Ireland.

## Interact *with* History

### OBJECTIVES

- To help students understand the problems facing both Confederate and Union soldiers
- To help students interact with the people and events they will study in the chapter

### What Do You Think?

1. Ask students how they would have responded to soldiers whose attitude about the war differed from theirs.
2. Ask students to discuss the many ways their actions as soldiers might affect the rest of their lives.
3. Have students consider whether refusing to fight for something they don't believe in can be a valid option in wartime.

### *What would inspire you to keep fighting?*

Encourage students to think about the reasons they would continue to fight under difficult conditions.

### MAKING PERSONAL CONNECTIONS

Ask students to think about situations where they have taken a stand for something they believed in, even if their friends or classmates made fun of them. Ask if they ever felt like giving up, just as the Civil War soldiers did during this long, difficult conflict. Why did they continue to stand up for their beliefs?

### TIME LINE DISCUSSION

**Remind students that when the Civil War began, both Northerners and Confederates expected a short war that their side would win easily. Instead, the war dragged on. Many Northerners questioned whether it was worthwhile to fight for a Union that included a slaveholding South.**

- Ask students to find an event on the time line that shows that not all potential soldiers were eager to fight. **Answer** draft riots
- What does the time line tell about Union leadership? **Answer** Grant was put in charge of all Union armies in 1864; Lincoln was reelected in 1864 and assassinated in 1865.
- Which events would lead you to believe the Union is getting closer to victory over the Confederacy? **Answer** victories at Vicksburg and Richmond

## BEFORE YOU READ

### Previewing the Theme: Impact of the Individual

Ask students why it is especially important to have outstanding leaders during wartime. **Possible Response** Without strong leaders to inspire them, people may not make the sacrifices required during a war, or they may lose heart when the war continues longer than expected.

### What Do You Know?

Remind students that the North was better prepared to fight a long war than the Confederacy. The North had a larger population, more industry, better transportation, a stronger navy, and an astute leader in Abraham Lincoln.

**In-Depth Resources: Unit 5**
- Tracing Themes: Impact of the Individual, p. 40

## READ AND TAKE NOTES

### Reading Strategy: Comparing and Contrasting

Explain to students that comparing and contrasting the ways in which the North and the South experienced the war will help them organize the concepts discussed in the chapter. Point out the events listed in the first column of the chart. Encourage students to look for similarities and differences in the ways these events affected the North and the Confederacy and note them on the correct lines.

**In-Depth Resources: Unit 5**
- Setting the Stage, p. 39

**Critical Thinking Transparency CT49**
- Setting the Stage

# Chapter 17 SETTING THE STAGE

## BEFORE YOU READ

### Previewing the Theme

**Impact of the Individual** During the Civil War, thousands of citizens and soldiers acted with great dignity and courage. Leading these men and women were some of the most extraordinary leaders the nation has ever had. You will read more about these citizens and soldiers in Chapter 17.

Robert E. Lee was the military genius at the head of the Confederate armies.

Abraham Lincoln is one of the greatest presidents the United States has ever had.

Jefferson Davis, the Confederate president, had the difficult task of keeping the South united.

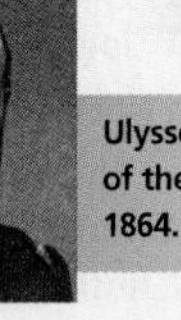

Ulysses S. Grant took charge of the Union armies in March 1864.

### What Do You Know?

What advantages and disadvantages did the North and the South have? Did particular individuals give either side an advantage during the Civil War?

**THINK ABOUT**
- what qualities contribute to the success of military leaders
- the importance of obeying orders for soldiers even if it might mean death

### What Do You Want to Know?

What questions do you have about the later part of the Civil War and how it ended? Make a list of those questions before you read the chapter.

## READ AND TAKE NOTES

**Reading Strategy: Comparing and Contrasting** When you study historical events, it is important to compare and contrast the effects that events had on different individuals and groups. A single event might affect two groups of people in completely different ways. Use the chart below to compare and contrast the impact of events on the Union and the Confederacy in the later years of the Civil War.

See Skillbuilder Handbook, page R9.

| | North | South |
|---|---|---|
| Emancipation Proclamation | Many people are enthusiastic; Democrats are angered | Most whites are enraged; blacks are elated |
| War's Impact | Mild inflation; new possibilities for women | Severe inflation; bread riots; new possibilities for women |
| Northern Victories in Battle | Union confidence rises; Lincoln wins second term | Confederate morale sinks; bid for European recognition is lost |
| Union Wins Civil War | Industrial expansion | Enslaved persons liberated; widespread economic devastation |



## TEACHING STRATEGY

### READING THE CHAPTER

This is a chronological chapter focusing on the turning points and conclusion of the Civil War. Ask students to note the effects of these events and how each led to the end of the war. The chapter also has a focus on the effect of the war on social, economic, and political life. Encourage students to discuss the costs of the war for the North and for the South.

### ALTERNATIVE ASSESSMENT

The Chapter Assessment describes three activities for alternative assessment on page 527. You may wish to have students work on these activities during the course of the chapter and then present them at the end.

# 1 The Emancipation Proclamation

**TERMS & NAMES**
Emancipation Proclamation
54th Massachusetts Regiment

**MAIN IDEA**
In 1863, President Lincoln issued the Emancipation Proclamation, which helped to change the war's course.

**WHY IT MATTERS NOW**
The Emancipation Proclamation was an important step in ending slavery in the United States.

### ONE AMERICAN'S STORY

During the Civil War, abolitionists like Frederick Douglass continued their fight against slavery. Douglass urged President Lincoln to emancipate, or free, enslaved Americans. "Sound policy . . . demands the instant liberation of every slave in the rebel states," he declared.

*A VOICE FROM THE PAST*

To fight against slaveholders, without fighting against slavery, is but a half-hearted business, and paralyzes the hands engaged in it. . . . Fire must be met with water. . . . War for the destruction of liberty [by the South] must be met with war for the destruction of slavery.

**Frederick Douglass,** quoted in *Battle Cry of Freedom*

During the Civil War, Frederick Douglass offered advice to President Lincoln. He urged the president to make the conflict a war against slavery.

Douglass pointed out that the Confederate war effort depended on slave labor. Enslaved Americans worked in Southern mines, fields, and factories. They also built forts and hauled supplies for rebel armies. For both practical and moral reasons, he said, Lincoln should free the slaves. In this section, you will learn how ending slavery became an important goal of the Civil War.

## 1 Calls for Emancipation

Throughout the war, abolitionists such as Frederick Douglass had been urging Lincoln to emancipate enslaved persons. Many criticized the president for being too cautious. Some even charged that Lincoln's lack of action aided the Confederate cause.

Still, Lincoln hesitated. He did not believe he had the power under the Constitution to abolish slavery where it already existed. Nor did he want to anger the four slave states that remained in the Union. He also knew that most Northern Democrats, and many Republicans, opposed emancipation.

Lincoln did not want the issue of slavery to divide the nation further than it already had. Although he disliked slavery, the president's first priority was to preserve the Union. "If I could save the Union without freeing





## SECTION OBJECTIVES

1. To understand the reasons for the call for emancipation
2. To identify the significance of the Emancipation Proclamation
3. To analyze the response to the proclamation
4. To describe the role of African-American soldiers in the war

**CRITICAL THINKING**

Drawing Conclusions, p. 504
Summarizing, p. 505
Identifying Facts, p. 506
Recognizing Effects, p. 506

## FOCUS & MOTIVATE

### 5-MINUTE WARM-UP

**Drawing Conclusions** These questions focus on the impact of Confederate and Union leaders.

1. Look at the brief descriptions of the Union and Confederate leaders on page 502. What qualities do you think are most important in a leader?
2. Do you think a president and an outstanding general will possess the same skills and characteristics? Why or why not?

Warm-Up Transparency WT17

## INSTRUCT

### INSTRUCT: OBJECTIVE 1

**Calls for Emancipation**

Key Questions

- For what reasons did Lincoln hesitate to abolish slavery?
- What was Lincoln's first priority throughout the war?
- Why did Lincoln decide in favor of emancipation?

**In-Depth Resources: Unit 5**
- Guided Reading, p. 41

**Reading Study Guide** (Spanish and English), pp. 167–168

## RECOMMENDED RESOURCES

**In-Depth Resources: Unit 5**
- Guided Reading, p. 41
- Building Vocabulary, p. 45
- Primary Sources, pp. 49–50
- Reteaching Activity, p. 54

**Reading Study Guide** (Spanish and English), pp. 167–168

**Formal Assessment**
- Section Quiz, p. 255

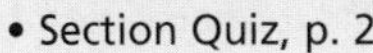

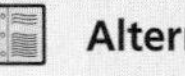
**Alternative Assessment**
- Rubrics, 5.1
- Rubrics, 4.8

**Access for Students Acquiring English/ESL**
- Guided Reading, p. 113

**Technology Resources**

**Electronic Teacher Tools with Test Maker**

**ClassZone**
www.mcdougallittell.com

**INSTRUCT: OBJECTIVE 2**

**The Emancipation Proclamation**

Key Questions

- What did the Emancipation Proclamation accomplish, and why was it important?
- Why did Lincoln free slaves only in the South?

 **In-Depth Resources: Unit 5**

- Primary Source: from "Reply to Emancipation Memorial" by Abraham Lincoln, p. 49

**MORE ABOUT . . .**

**The Emancipation Proclamation**

Secretary of the Treasury Salmon P. Chase said that when Lincoln read the Emancipation Proclamation to the cabinet (see illustration), he said, "I do not wish your advice about the main matter, for that I have determined for myself. . . . I must . . . bear the responsibility of taking the course which I feel I ought to take." Aware of the significance of his action, Lincoln noted that "if my name ever goes into history, it was for this act."

**INSTRUCT: OBJECTIVE 3**

**Response to the Proclamation**

Key Questions

- Why were people living in the North angered by the Emancipation Proclamation?
- Compare the reactions of Union soldiers and white Southerners to the proclamation.

**MORE ABOUT . . .**

**Frederick Douglass**

Frederick Douglass (1817–1895), born a slave in Maryland, eventually escaped to the North. Douglass fled to Great Britain for two years to avoid re-enslavement. There he earned enough money to buy his freedom. He returned to the United States where he founded *The North Star,* a newspaper he published for 17 years. After the war he held several public offices and campaigned for full civil rights for African Americans and women's suffrage.

*any* slave I would do it," he declared. "If I could save it by freeing *all* the slaves I would do it; and if I could save it by freeing some and leaving others alone, I would also do that."

By the summer of 1862, however, Lincoln had decided in favor of emancipation. The war was taking a terrible toll. If freeing the slaves helped weaken the South, then he would do it. Lincoln waited, however, for a moment when he was in a position of strength. After General Lee's forces were stopped at Antietam, Lincoln decided to act.

## 2 The Emancipation Proclamation

On January 1, 1863, Lincoln issued the **Emancipation Proclamation,** which freed all slaves in Confederate territory. The proclamation had a tremendous impact on the public. However, it freed very few slaves. Most of the slaves that Lincoln intended to liberate lived in areas distant from the Union troops that could enforce his proclamation.

**Background** In September 1862, Lincoln issued an early proclamation that gave rebellious states a chance to preserve slavery by rejoining the Union.

Lincoln presents the Emancipation Proclamation to his cabinet.

*A VOICE FROM THE PAST*

On the first day of January, in the year of our Lord one thousand eight hundred and sixty-three, all persons held as slaves within any State or designated part of a State, the people whereof shall then be in rebellion against the United States, shall be then, [thenceforth], and forever free.

**Abraham Lincoln,** from the *Emancipation Proclamation*

Why, critics charged, did Lincoln free slaves only in the South? The answer was in the Constitution. Because freeing Southern slaves weakened the Confederacy, the proclamation could be seen as a military action. As commander-in-chief, Lincoln had this authority. Yet the Constitution did not give the president the power to free slaves within the Union. But Lincoln did ask Congress to abolish slavery gradually throughout the land.

**Reading History** **A. Drawing Conclusions** Why did Lincoln choose to limit his proclamation mostly to rebellious states? **A. Possible Response** He believed that he did not have the authority, under the Constitution, to free slaves elsewhere.

Although the Emancipation Proclamation did not free many enslaved people at the time it was issued, it was important as a symbolic measure. For the North, the Civil War was no longer a limited war whose main goal was to preserve the Union. It was a war of liberation.

## 3 Response to the Proclamation

Abolitionists were thrilled that Lincoln had finally issued the Emancipation Proclamation. "We shout for joy that we live to record this righteous decree," wrote Frederick Douglass. Still, many believed the law should have gone further. They were upset that Lincoln had not freed *all* enslaved persons, including those in the border states.



**ACTIVITY OPTIONS**

**INDIVIDUAL NEEDS**

**STUDENTS ACQUIRING ENGLISH/ESL**

**Understanding Key Terms** Write the words *emancipation* and *proclamation* on the board and under them write the verbs *emancipate* and *proclaim.* Explain to students that emancipate means to liberate or to free and proclaim means to declare or to announce. Ask students what they think the phrase "emancipation proclamation" means. (an announcement of freedom)

To aid students' understanding of the section, ask questions such as the following and have students answer, using complete sentences.

- What historical document did Lincoln think prevented him from emancipating all the slaves in the nation?
- Did the Emancipation Proclamation actually free the Southern slaves? Why or why not?
- How did abolitionists, Northern Democrats, Union soldiers, and white Southerners react to the Emancipation Proclamation?

*Reading* **History**

**B. Summarizing** Why did Northern Democrats oppose the Emancipation Proclamation?

**B. Possible Response** They were against emancipating Southern slaves and thought that it would prolong the war.

Other people in the North, especially Democrats, were angered by the president's decision. Northern Democrats, the majority of whom were against emancipating even Southern slaves, claimed that the proclamation would only make the war longer by continuing to anger the South. A newspaperman in Ohio called Lincoln's proclamation "monstrous, impudent, and heinous . . . insulting to God as to man."

Most Union soldiers, though, welcomed emancipation. One officer noted that, although few soldiers were abolitionists, most were happy "to destroy everything that . . . gives the rebels strength."

White Southerners reacted to the proclamation with rage. Although it had limited impact in areas outside the reach of Northern armies, many slaves began to run away to Union lines. At the same time that these slaves deprived the Confederacy of labor, they also began to provide the Union with soldiers.

## 4 African-American Soldiers

In addition to freeing slaves, the Emancipation Proclamation declared that African-American men willing to fight "will be received into the armed service of the United States."

Frederick Douglass had argued for the recruitment of African-American soldiers since the start of the war. He declared, "Once [you] let the black man get upon his person the brass letters, U.S. . . . there is no power on earth which can deny that he has earned the right to citizenship."

Before the proclamation, the federal government had discouraged the enlistment of African Americans, and only a few regiments were formed. After emancipation, African Americans rushed to join the army. By war's end, about 180,000 black soldiers wore the blue uniform of the Union army.

African-American soldiers were organized in all-black regiments, usually led by white officers. They were often given the worst jobs

Thousands of African Americans, such as these men of the 4th U.S. Colored Troops, fought for the Union during the Civil War.

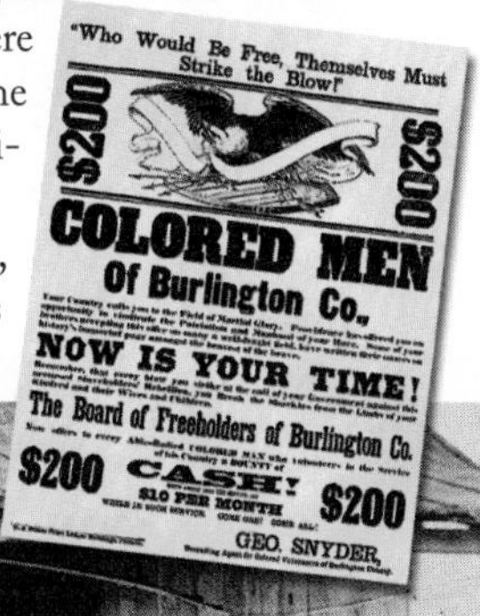


505

## MORE ABOUT . . .

**Europe and the Emancipation Proclamation**

The Emancipation Proclamation was greeted with enthusiasm in Europe and created a strongly pro-Union atmosphere. Workers in Manchester, England, for example, adopted a resolution expressing their praise of Abraham Lincoln for his "firmness in upholding the proclamation of freedom." The proclamation ended any possibility that France and Britain might recognize Confederate independence.

## INSTRUCT: OBJECTIVE 

**African-American Soldiers/ The 54th Massachusetts**

Key Questions

- How did the Emancipation Proclamation affect African-American enlistment in the Union army?
- What obstacles did African-American soldiers face?
- Why did the 54th Massachusetts Regiment become famous?

 **In-Depth Resources: Unit 5**

- Primary Source: A Letter from James Henry Gooding, p. 50

## MORE ABOUT . . .

**African-American Soldiers**

William H. Carney of the 54th Massachusetts Regiment won the Medal of Honor. When the soldier carrying the flag fell wounded at the Battle of Fort Wagner, Carney grabbed the flag and kept it aloft despite having received several bullet wounds. Other African Americans who won the Medal of Honor include Powhatan Beatty and Milton M. Holland. These soldiers both took command of their companies when all their officers were dead or wounded. Decatur Dorsey and Aaron Anderson were given Medals of Honor for bravery in battles in 1865.

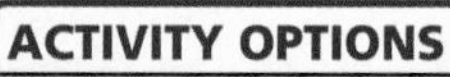

ACTIVITY OPTIONS

## INDIVIDUAL NEEDS

### LESS PROFICIENT READERS

**Previewing** To help students understand how the Civil War affected different aspects of society, have them skim the section, noting the boldfaced headings. Then work with them to turn the headings into questions. Write the questions on the board. Then encourage students to focus their reading in order to answer the questions they have created.

For example, you might want to write the following question for the first heading on the board.

**What were the results of disagreement about the war?**

- Confederate soldiers went on leave or deserted.
- Northern Democrats became Copperheads, opposing the war.

## Now and then

**African Americans in the Military**

Colin Powell once answered a question about the effect of segregation on his own determination to succeed. Powell cited the Confederate general who pleaded with Jefferson Davis not to allow African Americans to serve in the Confederate army. The general wrote, "Don't let this happen. Whatever you do, don't let this happen. Because if blacks can wear a uniform with brass buttons, and a belt with a brass buckle, and if they go and serve and lay down their lives, they are the equal to us. And if that is the case, the whole theory of the Confederacy is a lie."

## ASSESS & RETEACH

**Setting the Stage** Have students fill in the first section on the chapter graphic organizer on page 502.

 **Formal Assessment**
- Section Quiz, p. 255

 **Critical Thinking Transparency CT49**
- Setting the Stage

### RETEACHING ACTIVITY

Divide the class into four groups. Assign each group one of the four objectives in this section. Have each group of students create a poster including the objective, important points about it from the section, and an illustration. Display the posters in class and encourage students to study each one.

 **In-Depth Resources: Unit 5**
- Reteaching Activity, p. 54

### Now and then

**AFRICAN AMERICANS IN THE MILITARY**

During the Civil War, no African-American soldier was promoted above the rank of captain. But times have changed. In 1989, General Colin Powell (shown below) was made a four-star general and named chairman of the Joint Chiefs of Staff—the highest position in the military.

General Powell's appointment was the climax of a long struggle to fully integrate American armed forces. From the Civil War through World War II, African-American soldiers were kept apart from white soldiers and denied equal rights. However, in 1948, President Harry Truman ended segregation in the armed forces. Today the American military is fully integrated.

to do and were paid less than white soldiers. Despite these obstacles, African-American soldiers showed great courage on the battlefield and wore their uniforms with pride. More than one regiment insisted on fighting without pay rather than accepting lower pay than the white soldiers.

*Reading* **History**
**C. Identifying Facts** How did many black soldiers protest when they were offered lower pay than white soldiers?
**C. Possible Response** They insisted on fighting for free rather than take the lower wage.

## The 54th Massachusetts

One unit that insisted on fighting without pay was the **54th Massachusetts Regiment,** one of the first African-American regiments organized in the North. The soldiers of the 54th—among whom were two sons of Frederick Douglass—soon made the regiment the most famous of the Civil War.

The 54th Massachusetts earned its greatest fame in July 1863, when it led a heroic attack on Fort Wagner in South Carolina. The soldiers' bravery at Fort Wagner made the 54th a household name in the North and increased African-American enlistment.

The soldiers of the 54th Massachusetts and other African-American regiments faced grave dangers if captured. Rather than take African Americans as prisoners, Confederate soldiers often shot them or returned them to slavery.

The war demanded great sacrifices, not only from soldiers and prisoners, but also from people back home. In the next section, you will read about the hardships that the Civil War placed on the civilian populations in both the North and the South.

### Section 1 Assessment

**1. Terms & Names**

**Identify:**
- Emancipation Proclamation
- 54th Massachusetts Regiment

**2. Taking Notes**

Use a chart to record responses to the Emancipation Proclamation.

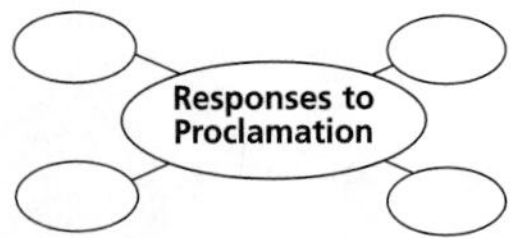


How did the proclamation change Northerners' views of the war?

**3. Main Ideas**

a. What was Lincoln's reason for not emancipating slaves when the war began?

b. Why was the immediate impact of the Emancipation Proclamation limited?

c. Why did black soldiers often face greater hardships than white soldiers?

**4. Critical Thinking**

**Recognizing Effects** How did the Emancipation Proclamation change the role of African Americans in the war?

**THINK ABOUT**
- how the proclamation changed military policy
- the response of many Southern slaves to the proclamation

**ACTIVITY OPTIONS**

**TECHNOLOGY**
**MUSIC**

Do research on the 54th Massachusetts Regiment. Create a **Web site** for the regiment or write a **song** about the soldiers' heroism at Fort Wagner.



### Section 1 Assessment

**1. Terms & Names**

**Emancipation Proclamation,** p. 504
**54th Massachusetts Regiment,** p. 506

**2. Taking Notes**

Abolitionists were glad it was issued but wished that it had gone further; Northern Democrats were worried it would prolong the war; most Union soldiers welcomed it; white Southerners were outraged; It was no longer a war for limited ends; it was a war of liberation.

**3. Main Ideas**

**a.** His first priority was to preserve the Union. **b.** It was effective only in rebellious states and was dependent on the Union army's ability to enforce it. **c.** They were given less pay; when captured they were frequently shot or returned to slavery.

**4. Critical Thinking**

They ran away to the Union line and became soldiers in large numbers.

**ACTIVITY OPTIONS**

 **Alternative Assessment**
- Rubrics for a Web site, 5.1
- Rubrics for a song, 4.8

# 2 War Affects Society

**TERMS & NAMES**
Copperhead
conscription
bounty
income tax
greenback
Clara Barton

**MAIN IDEA**
The Civil War caused social, economic, and political changes in the North and the South.

**WHY IT MATTERS NOW**
Some changes, like the growth of industry, affected Americans long after the end of Civil War.

## ONE AMERICAN'S STORY

**As the Civil War moved into its third year, the constant demand for men and resources began to take its toll back home. Sometimes, the hardships endured by civilians resulted in angry scenes like that witnessed by Agnes, a resident of Richmond, Virginia.**

**On April 3, 1863, Agnes went for her morning walk and soon came upon a group of hungry women and children, who had gathered in front of the capitol. She described the scene as these women and children were joined by other people who were upset by the shortage of food.**

Food became scarce in many places during the Civil War. Here, women demand milk for their hungry families.

*A VOICE FROM THE PAST*

The crowd now rapidly increased, and numbered, I am sure, more than a thousand women and children. It grew and grew until it reached the dignity of a mob—a bread riot.

**Agnes,** quoted in *Reminiscences of Peace and War*

**The mob then went out of control. It broke into shops and stole food, clothing, and other goods. Only the arrival of Confederate president Jefferson Davis and the threat of force ended the riot.**

**In this section, you will read more about hardships that the Civil War caused on the home front. These hardships caused changes in civilian society in both the North and the South.**

## 1 Disagreement About the War

In the spring of 1863, riots like the one in Richmond broke out in a number of Southern towns. Southerners were growing weary of the war and the constant sacrifices it demanded.

Confederate soldiers began to leave the army in increasing numbers. By the end of the year, the Confederate army had lost nearly 40 percent of its men. Some of these men were on leave, but many others were deserters.





## SECTION OBJECTIVES

1. To analyze discontent with the war
2. To explain anger over the draft laws
3. To identify the economic effects of the war and resistance by enslaved Americans
4. To describe how women aided the war effort and to evaluate conditions in Northern and Southern prison camps

**CRITICAL THINKING**

Drawing Conclusions, p. 508
Analyzing Causes, p. 509
Summarizing, p. 510
Making Inferences, p. 511
Making Generalizations, p. 511

## FOCUS & MOTIVATE

### 5-MINUTE WARM-UP

**Making Generalizations** These questions focus on the effect of the Civil War on daily life.

1. Look at the drawing on page 507. Why do you think there wasn't enough milk in Richmond?
2. How would you describe the mood of the people in this illustration?

 **Warm-Up Transparency WT17**

## INSTRUCT

**INSTRUCT: OBJECTIVE 1**

**Disagreement About the War**

Key Questions

- How did discontent with the war affect the Confederate army?
- How did the principle of states' rights affect the Confederate states?
- Who were the Copperheads? How did Lincoln deal with them?

**In-Depth Resources: Unit 5**
- Guided Reading, p. 42
- Building Vocabulary, p. 45

**Reading Study Guide** (Spanish and English), pp. 169–170

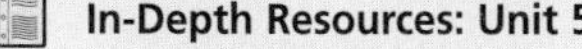

## RECOMMENDED RESOURCES

**In-Depth Resources: Unit 5**
- Guided Reading, p. 42
- Building Vocabulary, p. 45
- Literature Selection: from *In My Father's House*, pp. 51–53
- Reteaching Activity, p. 55

**Reading Study Guide** (Spanish and English), pp. 169–170

**Economics in History**
- Financing the Civil War, p. 17

**America's History Makers**
- Clara Barton, pp. 67–68

**Formal Assessment**
- Section Quiz, p. 256

**Alternative Assessment**
- Rubrics, 2.1
- Rubrics, 3.6

**Access for Students Acquiring English/ESL**
- Guided Reading, p. 114

**Technology Resources**

 **Electronic Teacher Tools with Test Maker**

 **ClassZone** www.mcdougallittell.com

## MORE ABOUT . . .

**Copperheads**

Another source for the name *Copperheads* is the Indian heads cut from copper pennies that antiwar Democrats wore on their coat lapels. Some Copperheads became part of a fifth column directed by Confederates from bases in Canada. Plots were hatched to burn New York City, to capture a warship on the Great Lakes, and to free captured soldiers in Northern prison camps. None of these plots amounted to anything, but their existence was an open secret that hurt the morale of war-weary Northerners.

## INSTRUCT: OBJECTIVE 2

**The Draft Laws**

Key Questions

- Why did poor Southerners complain that the Civil War was "a rich man's war but a poor man's fight"?
- How were Union and Confederate draft laws similar? How were they different?

## MORE ABOUT . . .

**Lincoln and the Writ of Habeas Corpus**

Lincoln claimed that the "great and dangerous insurrection" justified his suspending the right of habeas corpus during the war. For example, he suspended habeas corpus in Maryland in 1861, as delegates traveled to the session of the legislature that would decide whether Maryland would secede. Delegates from southern Maryland, likely to vote for secession, were impounded, and the remaining delegates voted to remain in the Union.

In this political cartoon, the Union defends itself against "Copperheads." This was the name given to Northerners who sympathized with the South.

Faced with the difficulties of waging war, the Confederate states fell into disagreement. The same principle of states' rights that led them to break with the Union kept them from coordinating their war effort. As one Southern governor put it, "I am *still* a rebel . . . no matter who may be in power."

Disagreements over the conduct of the war also arose in the North. Lincoln's main opponents were the **Copperheads,** Northern Democrats who favored peace with the South. (A copperhead is a poisonous snake that strikes without warning.) Lincoln had protesters arrested. He also suspended the writ of habeas corpus, which prevents the government from holding citizens without a trial.

**Vocabulary**
**writ:** a written order issued by a court of law

## 2 The Draft Laws

As the war dragged on, both the North and the South needed more soldiers. As a result, both sides passed laws of **conscription,** also known as the draft. These laws required men to serve in the military.

The Confederates had been drafting soldiers since the spring of 1862. By 1863, all able-bodied white men between the ages of 18 and 45 were required to join the army. However, there were a number of exceptions. Planters who owned 20 or more slaves could avoid military service. In addition, wealthy men could hire substitutes to serve in their place. By 1863, substitutes might cost as much as $6,000. The fact that wealthy men could avoid service caused poor Southerners to complain that it was a "rich man's war but a poor man's fight."

**Reading History**
**A. Drawing Conclusions** Why were many soldiers dissatisfied with the draft laws?
A. Possible Response because it was easier for wealthy men to avoid being conscripted

The Union draft law was passed in March 1863. Like the Confederacy, the Union allowed draftees to hire substitutes. However, the North also offered $300 **bounties,** or cash payments, to men who volunteered to serve. As a result, only a small percentage of men in the North were drafted. Most men volunteered and received the bounty.



## ACTIVITY OPTIONS

### MULTIPLE LEARNING STYLES: SPATIAL

BLOCK SCHEDULING

**A CIVIL WAR RECRUITING POSTER**

**Class Time** One class period

**Task** Creating a recruiting poster for the Civil War

**Purpose** To illustrate reasons for enlisting in either the Union army or the Confederate army

**Supplies Needed**
- Poster paper
- Art supplies

**Activity** Direct students to review the material about the draft laws on this page. Then tell them to create a poster calling for volunteers for either the Union army or the Confederate forces. Posters should be eye-catching and attractive, and should list at least two reasons for signing up. You might suggest that students direct their posters at potential recruits from their own state or city.

Even so, the draft was extremely unpopular. In July 1863, anger over the draft and simmering racial tensions led to the New York City draft riots. For four days, rioters destroyed property and attacked people on the streets. Over 100 people were killed—many of them African Americans.

## 3 Economic Effects of the War

Many people suffered economic hardship during the war. The suffering was severe in the South, where most battles were fought, but the North also experienced difficulties.

Food shortages were very common in the South, partly because so many farmers were fighting in the Confederate army. Moreover, food sometimes could not get to market because trains were now being used to carry war materials. The Confederate army also seized food and other supplies for its own needs.

Another problem, especially in the South, was inflation—an increase in price and decrease in the value of money. The average family food bill in the South increased from $6.65 a month in 1861 to $68 by mid–1863. Over the course of the war, prices rose 9,000 percent in the South.

*Reading* **History**
**B. Analyzing Causes** Why were economic problems particularly bad in the South?
**B. Possible Responses** Most battles were fought there; men left their farms to fight; trains were used to carry war materials instead of food; inflation was more severe.

Inflation in the North was much lower, but prices still rose faster than wages, making life harder for working people. Some people took advantage of wartime demand and sold goods for high prices.

Overall, though, war production boosted Northern industry and fueled the economy. In the short term, this gave the North an economic advantage over the South. In the long term, industry would begin to replace farming as the basis of the national economy.

During the war, the federal government passed two important economic measures. In 1861, it established the first **income tax**—a tax on earnings. The following year, the government issued a new paper currency, known as **greenbacks** because of their color. The new currency helped the Northern economy by ensuring that people had money to spend. It also helped the Union to pay for the war.

Some Southerners in the border states took advantage of the stronger Union economy by selling cotton to Northern traders, in violation of Confederate law. "Yankee gold," wrote one Confederate officer, "is fast accomplishing what Yankee arms could never achieve—the subjugation of our people."

**Vocabulary**
**subjugate:** to bring under control or to conquer

### daily *life*

**INFLATION IN THE SOUTH**

During the Civil War, inflation caused hardship in the North and the South. But inflation was especially severe in the Confederacy, where prices could become outrageously high.

The food prices shown below are from 1864. Consider how many days it took a Confederate soldier to earn enough money to buy each of these foods.

Confederate Soldier's Monthly Pay

## Resistance by Slaves

Another factor that affected the South was the growing resistance from slaves. To hurt the Southern economy, slaves slowed their pace of work or stopped working altogether. Some carried out sabotage, destroying crops and farm equipment to hurt the plantation economy. When white



### MORE ABOUT . . .

**Immigrants and Soldiers**

Many of the antidraft rioters were immigrants. As poor new arrivals, they especially resented being forced into a war while richer men paid to avoid the battle. Nonetheless, immigrants made up a large part of the Union forces. Approximately 200,000 German immigrants fought for the Union with about 150,000 Irish-born soldiers. One regiment from Illinois was composed of German Jews. Irish and German immigrants also fought for the Confederacy, although fewer immigrants lived in the South.

### INSTRUCT: OBJECTIVE 3

**Economic Effects of the War/ Resistance by Slaves**

Key Questions
- In what ways did the war affect the economy of the South?
- What were the short-term and long-term effects of war production in the North?
- How did slaves damage the Southern economy and sabotage the war effort?

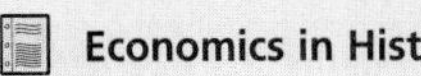

**Economics in History**
- Financing the Civil War, p. 17

**In-Depth Resources: Unit 5**
- Literature Selection: from *In My Father's House* by Ann Rinaldi, pp. 51–53

### daily*life*

**Inflation in the South**

The sharp increase in prices for necessary provisions provoked criticism leveled at farmers and planters. The Atlanta *Southern Confederacy* condemned farmers for their exorbitant prices for produce. Provisions cost 200–400 percent more than before the war, despite the fact that food production costs had not increased and crops were abundant.

### ACTIVITY OPTIONS

**INTERDISCIPLINARY LINK: MATH**

BLOCK SCHEDULING

**CALCULATING CONFEDERATE COSTS**

**Class Time** 20 minutes

**Task** Calculating the cost of a simple breakfast in 1864 in the Confederacy

**Purpose** To use simple math skills to understand the severity of inflation in the South and the hardships it caused for Southerners

**Supplies Needed**
- Calculators (optional)

**Activity** Have students use the information in the chart on this page to calculate the cost of this simple breakfast for four people: scrambled eggs, containing 6 eggs; 1 tablespoon of butter (1/32 of a pound); 1 pot of coffee (about 1/25 of a pound); 1 pitcher of milk (1/2 quart). *(Answer: $8.68)* Then have students figure out how much the same breakfast would cost today to prepare at home.

## MORE ABOUT . . .

**African Americans and Union Forces**

At the start of the war, enslaved African Americans began to escape from their owners and seek safety in Union army camps. However, Union soldiers did not know what to do with the refugees. In the border states, the law required that fleeing slaves be returned to their owners, but few Northern soldiers were willing to take on the role of slave catcher. Eventually Union officers found a loophole that justified the presence of escaped slaves in their camps. They termed the slaves *contraband,* meaning property of war seized from the enemy.

## INSTRUCT: OBJECTIVE 

**Women Aid the War Effort/ Civil War Prison Camps**

Key Questions

- How did the Civil War affect the role of women in society?
- In what ways did women help the war effort?
- How were prisoners of war treated in the North? in the South?

## AMERICA'S HISTORY MAKERS

**Clara Barton**

After the Battle of Bull Run, Clara Barton heard reports of shortages among Union forces. She independently advertised for contributions of foodstuffs and set up an agency to distribute the huge amounts sent in by concerned Northerners. After the war, at President Lincoln's request, she set up a bureau of records to search for soldiers missing in action. Barton threw herself into the creation of the American Red Cross. She was the agency's first president and held that post for 23 years.

Possible Response: by organizing a relief agency to help with the war effort and founding the American Red Cross

 **America's History Makers**
- Clara Barton, pp. 67–68

---

planters fled advancing Union armies, slaves often refused to go along. They stayed behind, waiting for Union soldiers to free them.

Some enslaved people even rose up in rebellion against their overseers. More commonly, though, slaves ran away from plantations to join the Union forces as they pushed farther into Confederate territory. One Union officer described a common sight.

*A VOICE FROM THE PAST*

It was very touching to see the vast numbers of colored [African-American] women following after us with babies in their arms, and little ones like our Anna clinging to their tattered skirts. One poor creature, while nobody was looking, hid two boys, five years old, in a wagon, intending, I suppose that they should see the land of freedom if she couldn't.

**Union officer,** quoted in *The Civil War*

After Lincoln issued the Emancipation Proclamation, the number of slaves fleeing Southern plantations greatly increased. By the end of the war, as many as half a million had fled to Union lines.

**AMERICA'S HISTORY MAKERS**

**CLARA BARTON**
**1821–1912**

Trained as a schoolteacher, Clara Barton was working for the government when the Civil War began. She organized a relief agency to help with the war effort. "While our soldiers stand and fight," she said, "I can stand and feed and nurse them."

She also made food for soldiers in camp and tended to the wounded and dying on the battlefield. At Antietam, she held a doctor's operating table steady as cannon shells burst all around them. The doctor called her "the angel of the battlefield." After the war, Barton founded the American Red Cross.

**How did Clara Barton demonstrate her leadership abilities?**

## 4 Women Aid the War Effort

With so many men away at war, women in both the North and the South assumed increased responsibilities. Women plowed fields and ran farms and plantations. They also took over jobs in offices and factories that had previously been done only by men.

Other social changes came about because of the thousands of women who served on the front lines as volunteer workers and nurses. Susie King Taylor was an African-American woman who wrote an account of her experiences as a volunteer with an African-American regiment. She asked her readers to remember that "many lives were lost,—not men alone but noble women as well."

Relief agencies put women to work washing clothes, gathering supplies, and cooking food for soldiers. Also, nursing became a respectable profession for many women. By the end of the war, around 3,000 nurses had worked under the leadership of Dorothea Dix in Union hospitals. Southern women were also active as nurses and as volunteers on the front.

Women also played a key role as spies in both the North and the South. Harriet Tubman served as a spy for Union forces along the coast of South Carolina. The most famous Confederate spy was Belle Boyd. Although she was arrested six times, she continued her work through much of the war. At one point, she even sent messages from her jail cell by putting them in little rubber balls and tossing them out the window.

*Reading* **History**

**C. Summarizing** How did women participate in the Civil War?

C. Possible Responses They worked on farms and in factories, volunteered on the front lines, and worked as nurses and spies.



---

**ACTIVITY OPTIONS**

**MULTIPLE LEARNING STYLES: INTERPERSONAL**  **BLOCK SCHEDULING**

**A CIVIL WAR DIALOGUE**

**Class Time** Two class periods

**Task** Creating a dialogue about the Civil War from multiple points of view

**Purpose** To understand the effects of the Civil War on people from different regions and of different backgrounds and occupations

**Supplies Needed**
- Books and reference materials on popular history of the Civil War

**Activity** Assign students one of the following roles: drafted Irish immigrant; Confederate deserter; owner of a New England mill; woman managing a farm in Kentucky; nurse on either side; escaped slave with the Union army; soldier in the 54th Massachusetts Regiment; prisoner on either side; spy on either side. Tell students to prepare descriptions of their experiences of the war in their assigned roles. Then allow groups of students to discuss the war from the point of view of their role.

## Civil War Prison Camps

Women caught spying were thrown into jail, but soldiers captured in battle suffered far more. At prison camps in both the North and the South, prisoners of war faced terrible conditions.

One of the worst prison camps in the North was in Elmira, New York. Perhaps the harshest feature of a prisoner's life at the camp was the New York winter. One prisoner called Elmira "an excellent summer prison for southern soldiers, but an excellent place for them to find their graves in the winter." In just one year, more than 24 percent of Elmira's 12,121 prisoners died of sickness and exposure to severe weather.

*Reading***History**
**D. Making Inferences** Why were death rates so high at many Civil War prison camps?
**D. Possible Response** because of poor sanitary conditions and exposure to severe weather

Conditions were also horrible in the South. The camp with the worst reputation was at Andersonville, Georgia. Built to hold 10,000 prisoners, at one point it housed 33,000. Inmates had little shelter from the heat or cold. Most slept in holes scratched in the dirt. Drinking water came from one tiny creek that also served as a sewer. As many as 100 men per day died at Andersonville from starvation, disease, and exposure.

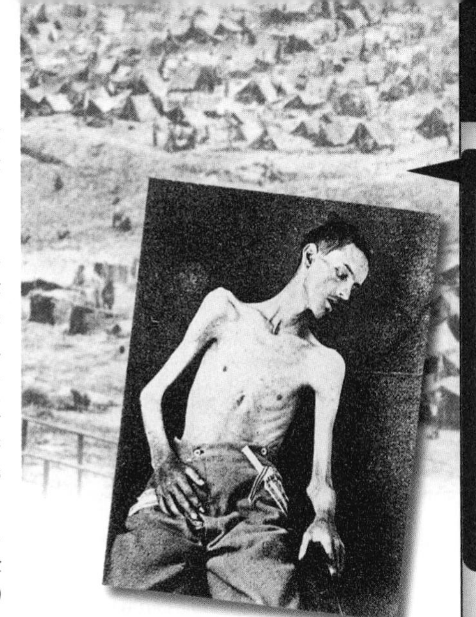

**The terrible conditions at Civil War prison camps caused much suffering and death.**

People who saw the camps were shocked by the condition of the soldiers. The poet Walt Whitman—who served as a Union nurse—described a group of soldiers who returned from a prison camp. He exclaimed, "Can those be *men?* . . . are they not really mummied, dwindled corpses?"

Around 50,000 men died in Civil War prison camps. But this number was dwarfed by the number of dead on the battlefronts and even more from disease in army camps. In the next section, you will read about the bloody battles that led to the end of the Civil War.

### MORE ABOUT . . .

**Treatment of Civil War Prisoners**
The conditions at Andersonville caused the death of 13,000 of the 45,000 men imprisoned there. As reports of the terrible conditions at Andersonville arrived in the North, the Union War Department responded. In 1864, it cut the rations for its prisoners to the same level that the Confederacy said it gave to its prisoners. The ration cut, combined with a huge increase in the number of Confederate prisoners, caused conditions in Northern prisons to decline.

## ASSESS & RETEACH

**Setting the Stage** Have students fill in the second section on the chapter graphic organizer.

 **Formal Assessment**
- Section Quiz, p. 256

### RETEACHING ACTIVITY

Divide students into two groups. Have students in one group complete the graphic organizer below for the Union while students in the other group complete it for the Confederacy.

 **In-Depth Resources: Unit 5**
- Reteaching Activity, p. 55

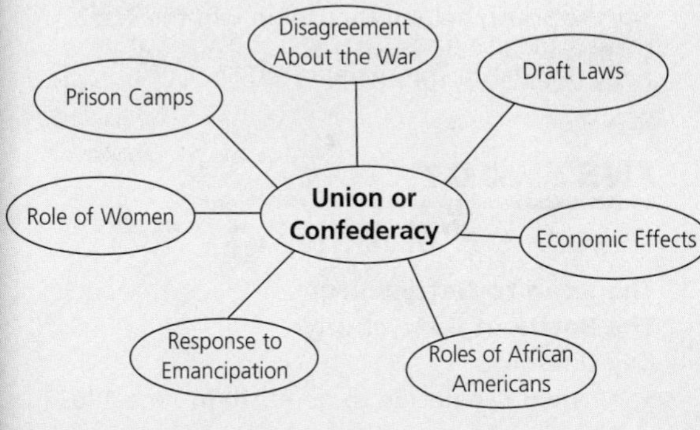


### Section 2 Assessment

**1. Terms & Names**

**Identify:**
- Copperhead
- conscription
- bounty
- income tax
- greenback
- Clara Barton

**2. Taking Notes**

Use a diagram like the one below to compare conditions in the North and South during the later years of war.

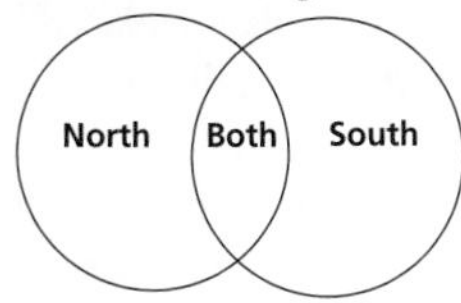


**3. Main Ideas**

a. How did the South's principle of states' rights undermine the Confederate war effort?

b. How did the draft laws in the North and South differ?

c. What conditions at prison camps caused so many to suffer behind enemy lines?

**4. Critical Thinking**

**Making Generalizations** What economic changes took place during the Civil War?

**THINK ABOUT**
- the war's effect on prices
- industry and agriculture
- new economic measures begun by the government

**ACTIVITY OPTIONS**

**GEOGRAPHY** / **SPEECH**

Study Civil War prison camps. Make a **map** showing where they were located or give a **speech** explaining why prisoners should be treated better.



### Section 2 Assessment

**1. Terms & Names**

**Copperhead,** p. 508
**conscription,** p. 508
**bounty,** p. 508
**income tax,** p. 509
**greenback,** p. 509
**Clara Barton,** p. 510

**2. Taking Notes**

North: Copperheads, draft riots, strong industry; South: food shortages, great hardship, slave resistance; Both: dissent over war and draft laws, inflation, women's key role, harsh prison camps

**3. Main Ideas**

**a.** Each state worked in its own interest, preventing the coordination of efforts. **b.** The South required all men between 18 and 45 to enlist, with few exceptions. The North offered a bounty of $300, which led to more volunteers. **c.** exposure to severe weather; poor sanitation

**4. Critical Thinking**

Inflation became a problem, especially in the South; Northern industry grew; the Union initiated an income tax and paper currency.

**ACTIVITY OPTIONS**

**Alternative Assessment**
- Rubrics for a map, 2.1
- Rubrics for a speech, 3.6

## SECTION OBJECTIVES

1. To evaluate the importance of the Battle of Gettysburg
2. To evaluate the importance of the siege of Vicksburg and Sherman's march to the coast
3. To trace the Virginia campaign to Appomattox
4. To describe the surrender at Appomattox

**SKILLBUILDER**

Interpreting Maps: Movement, Location, p. 517

**CRITICAL THINKING**

Making Inferences, p. 513
Drawing Conclusions, p. 517
Contrasting, p. 519

 **Why It Matters Now**
- One Nation, pp. 33–34

## FOCUS & MOTIVATE

### 5-MINUTE WARM-UP

**Making Inferences** These questions compare the strengths of the Union and the Confederacy from 1863 to 1865.

1. Study the map on page 517. How does the size of the area controlled by the Union compare with that controlled by the Confederacy?
2. How do you think Sherman's path through the South helped the Union win the war?

 **Warm-Up Transparency WT17**

## INSTRUCT

### INSTRUCT: OBJECTIVE  1

**The Road to Gettysburg/ The Battle of Gettysburg**

Key Questions
- Why did Lee decide to go north in June 1863?
- Why was Pickett's charge a mistake?
- Why was the Battle of Gettysburg the turning point of the war?

 **In-Depth Resources: Unit 5**
- Guided Reading, p. 43

# 3 The North Wins

**TERMS & NAMES**
Battle of Gettysburg
Pickett's Charge
Ulysses S. Grant
Robert E. Lee
Siege of Vicksburg
William Tecumseh Sherman
Appomattox Court House

| MAIN IDEA | WHY IT MATTERS NOW |
|---|---|
| Thanks to victories, beginning with Gettysburg and ending with Richmond, the Union survived. | If the Union had lost the war, the United States might look very different now. |

### ONE AMERICAN'S STORY

**Joshua Lawrence Chamberlain was a 32-year-old college professor when the war began. Determined to fight for the Union, he left his job and took command of troops from his home state of Maine. Like most soldiers, Chamberlain had to get accustomed to the carnage of the Civil War. His description of the aftermath of one battle shows how soldiers got used to the war's violence.**

*A VOICE FROM THE PAST*

It seemed best to [put] myself between two dead men among the many left there by earlier assaults, and to draw another crosswise for a pillow out of the trampled, blood-soaked sod, pulling the flap of his coat over my face to fend off the chilling winds, and still more chilling, the deep, many voiced moan [of the wounded] that overspread the field.

**Joshua Lawrence Chamberlain,** quoted in *The Civil War*

**During the war, Chamberlain fought in 24 battles. He was wounded six times and had six horses shot out from under him. He is best remembered for his actions at the Battle of Gettysburg, where he courageously held off a fierce rebel attack. In this section, you will read about that battle and others that led to the end of the Civil War.**

In 1862, Joshua Chamberlain was offered a year's travel with pay t study languages in Europe. He ch to fight for the Union instead.

## 1 The Road to Gettysburg

In September 1862, General McClellan stopped General Lee's Northern attack at the Battle of Antietam. But the cautious McClellan failed to finish off Lee's army, which retreated safely to Virginia.

President Lincoln, who was frustrated by McClellan, replaced him with Ambrose Burnside. But Burnside also proved to be a disappointment. At the Battle of Fredericksburg, Virginia, in December 1862, Burnside attacked Confederate troops who had dug trenches. The bloody result was 12,600 Union casualties. This disastrous attack led General Lee to remark, "It is well that war is so terrible—we should grow too fond of it!"

Lincoln replaced Burnside with General Joseph Hooker, who faced Lee the following May at Chancellorsville, Virginia. The result was yet another Union disaster. With half as many men as Hooker, Lee still managed to



## RECOMMENDED RESOURCES

 **In-Depth Resources: Unit 5**
- Guided Reading, p. 43
- Building Vocabulary, p. 45
- Skillbuilder Practice, p. 46
- Reteaching Activity, p. 56

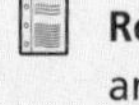 **Reading Study Guide** (Spanish and English), pp. 171–172

**Outline Map Activities**
- The End of the Civil War, 1865, pp. 33–34

 **America's History Makers**
- Ulysses S. Grant, pp. 69–70

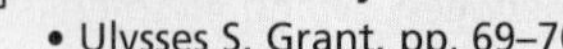

 **Why It Matters Now**
- One Nation, pp. 33–34

**Formal Assessment**
- Section Quiz, p. 257

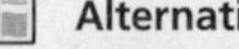 **Alternative Assessment**
- Rubrics, 2.1
- Rubrics, 4.5

**Access for Students Acquiring English/ESL**
- Guided Reading, p. 115
- Skillbuilder Practice, p. 117

**Technology Resources**

 **Humanities Transparency HT33**
- Battle of Fredericksburg

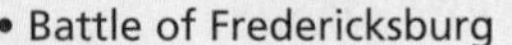

 **Geography Transparency GT17**
- Vicksburg Campaign, 1863

 **Electronic Teacher Tools with Test Maker**

cut the Union forces to pieces. However, the South paid a high price for its victory. As General "Stonewall" Jackson returned from a patrol on May 2, Confederate guards thought he was a Union soldier and shot him in the arm. Shortly after a surgeon amputated the arm, Jackson caught pneumonia. On May 10, Lee's prized general was dead.

In spite of Jackson's tragic death, Lee decided to head North once again. He hoped that a Confederate victory in Union territory would fuel Northern discontent with the war and bring calls for peace. He also hoped a Southern victory would lead European nations to give diplomatic recognition and aid to the Confederacy.

## The Battle of Gettysburg

*Reading* **History**

**A. Reading a Map** Use the map and illustration on pages 514–515 to study Gettysburg's geography.

In late June 1863, Lee crossed into southern Pennsylvania. The Confederates learned of a supply of shoes in the town of Gettysburg and went to investigate. There, on July 1, they ran into Union troops. Both sides called for reinforcements, and the **Battle of Gettysburg** was on.

The fighting raged for three days. On the rocky hills and fields around Gettysburg, 90,000 Union troops, under the command of General George Meade, clashed with 75,000 Confederates.

During the struggle, Union forces tried to hold their ground on Cemetery Ridge, just south of town, while rebel soldiers tried to dislodge them. At times, the air seemed full of bullets. "The balls were whizzing so thick," said one Texan, "that it looked like a man could hold out a hat and catch it full."

The turning point came on July 3, when Lee ordered General George Pickett to mount a direct attack on the middle of the Union line. It was a deadly mistake. Some 13,000 rebel troops charged up the ridge into heavy Union fire. One soldier recalled "bayonet thrusts, sabre strokes, pistol shots . . . men going down on their hands and knees, spinning round like tops . . . ghastly heaps of dead men."

*Reading* **History**

**B. Making Inferences** Why might Lincoln have been disappointed after the Union victory at Gettysburg?

**B. Possible Response** because General Meade did not finish off the army of General Lee

**Pickett's Charge,** as this attack came to be known, was torn to pieces. The Confederates retreated and waited for a Union counterattack. But once again, Lincoln's generals failed to finish off Lee's army. The furious Lincoln wondered when he would find a general who would defeat Lee once and for all.

Even so, the Union rejoiced over the victory at Gettysburg. Lee's hopes for a Confederate victory in the North were crushed. The North had lost 23,000 men, but Southern losses were even greater. Over one-third of Lee's army, 28,000 men, lay dead or wounded. Sick at heart, Lee led his army back to Virginia.

### *America's* HERITAGE

**THE GETTYSBURG ADDRESS**

On November 19, 1863, President Lincoln spoke at the dedication of a cemetery in Gettysburg for the 3,500 soldiers buried there. His speech was short, and few who heard it were impressed. Lincoln himself called it "a flat failure."

Even so, the Gettysburg Address has since been recognized as one of the greatest speeches of all time. In it, Lincoln declared that the nation was founded on "the proposition that all men are created equal." He ended with a plea to continue the fight for democracy so that "government of the people, by the people, for the people shall not perish from the earth."

*See page 524 for the full text of the Gettysburg Address.*

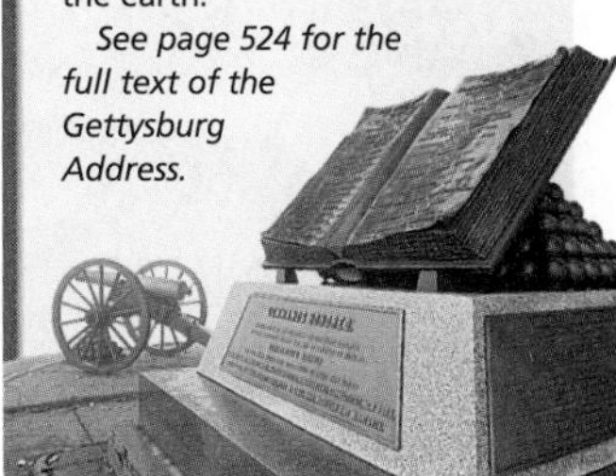



### MORE ABOUT . . .

**The Battle of Chancellorsville**

The Battle of Chancellorsville provides the setting for Stephen Crane's famous Civil War novel *The Red Badge of Courage*. The novel tells the story of a raw recruit named Henry Fleming who runs from combat but later rejoins his regiment. Crane never names the battle in the novel, perhaps in part because soldiers like Henry Fleming often did not know their exact location or the name of the battle they were fighting.

 **Humanities Transparency HT33**
- Battle of Fredericksburg

### *America's* HERITAGE

**The Gettysburg Address**

The featured speaker at the dedication for the cemetery was Edward Everett, the former governor of Massachusetts. His speech lasted almost two hours. While President Lincoln listened, he also edited his own remarks. Although the reporter for the *London Times* said, "The ceremony was rendered ludicrous by . . . the sallies of that poor President Lincoln," Edward Everett disagreed. He wrote the president that "I should be glad if I could flatter myself that I came as near to the central idea of the occasion in two hours as you did in two minutes."

### ACTIVITY OPTIONS

### INDIVIDUAL NEEDS

**LESS PROFICIENT READERS**

**Finding Main Ideas** Students may have difficulty understanding the significance of the key battles that contributed to the Union's victory. To help focus their reading, write the names of the battles on the board and ask students to copy them on a sheet of paper. As you read the section, have students write down the approximate date, significance, and victor in each battle.

Guide students in creating a chart such as the following:

| Battle | Date | Significance | Who Won? |
|---|---|---|---|
| Gettysburg | | | |
| Vicksburg | | | |
| Atlanta | | | |
| Richmond | | | |

## GEOGRAPHY *in* HISTORY

**OBJECTIVE**

Students will analyze and interpret information from a map to understand why Union forces were successful at the Battle of Gettysburg.

 **BLOCK SCHEDULING**

### MORE ABOUT . . .

**The Battle of Gettysburg**

Some military historians hypothesize that Lee chose to invade Pennsylvania in part because his army was in desperate need of supplies. Years of fighting had depleted Virginia, but Pennsylvania offered fresh supplies of food and other necessities. Lee was headed for Harrisburg, a railroad center, when North and South encountered each other in Gettysburg, a town of about 2,400 people. Lee did not have good information about the location of Union troops. His cavalry chief and "eyes and ears," J. E. B. ("Jeb") Stuart, was somewhere between Harrisburg and Gettysburg when the fighting started and did not arrive until the second day.

## INSTRUCT

Key Questions

- Why would moving Confederate troops into Pennsylvania be an advantage for Lee?
- Why did both sides want to control the high ground during the battle?
- How do you think soldiers on both sides were hampered by, and also benefited from, the many trees and small streams on the battlefield?

**MAP SKILL QUESTIONS**

How can you tell which are the Confederate and which are the Union positions?

Which side controlled Seminary Ridge?

Why did Lee want to break the Union control of Cemetery Ridge?

## GEOGRAPHY *in* HISTORY

**PLACE AND HUMAN-ENVIRONMENT INTERACTION**

# Battle of Gettysburg

A monument stands today near a ridge at the Gettysburg battlefield. Labeled the "High Water Mark of the Rebellion," it shows how far Confederate troops advanced against Union lines. There, on July 3, 1863, the South came closest to winning the Civil War.

The fighting began on July 1. When a Confederate force captured Gettysburg, Union defenders took up new positions in the hills south of town. The next day, Confederate troops attacked across a wheat field and peach orchard in an attempt to seize the hill called Little Round Top. But Union forces held their ground.

July 3 was the decisive day. Lee, having failed to crack the side of General Meade's Union line, attacked its center. In an assault that came to be known as Pickett's Charge, some 13,000 men charged uphill across an open field toward the Union lines along Cemetery Ridge. Union soldiers covered the field with rifle and cannon fire. "Pickett's Charge" was a Confederate disaster.

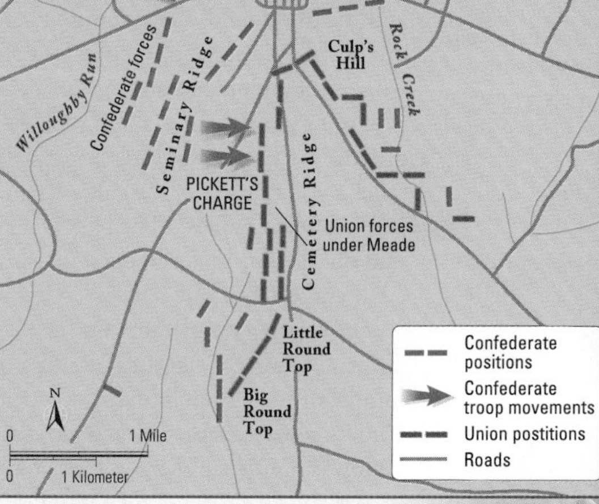

Before beginning the charge named for him, Major General Pickett wrote to his fiancée, "My brave Virginians are to attack in front. Oh, may God in mercy help me."

### ARTIFACT FILE

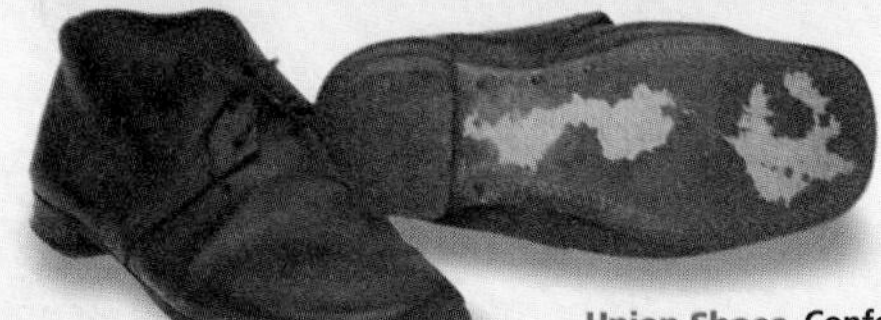

**Union Shoes** Confederate troops first went to Gettysburg after learning of a supply of shoes in the town. The shoes pictured here were cut down by a Union soldier to make them more comfortable.

**Regimental Flag** Flags helped soldiers to identify the different sides during battle. Often, a regiment's flag would show the names of battles it had fought. This flag, which belonged to the 28th North Carolina, was captured at Pickett's Charge.



### MUSEUM CONNECTIONS

The Gettysburg National Military Park Museum was established by federal law in 1895, and at that time it was administered by Civil War veterans. The museum, a memorial to soldiers from both armies, covers 6,000 acres and 26 miles of park roads. The park contains one of the world's largest collections of outdoor sculpture with some 1,400 statues and monuments. The museum's Web site provides a virtual tour of the battlefield and the museum's holdings. To learn more about Gettysburg National Park, visit www.mcdougallittell.com

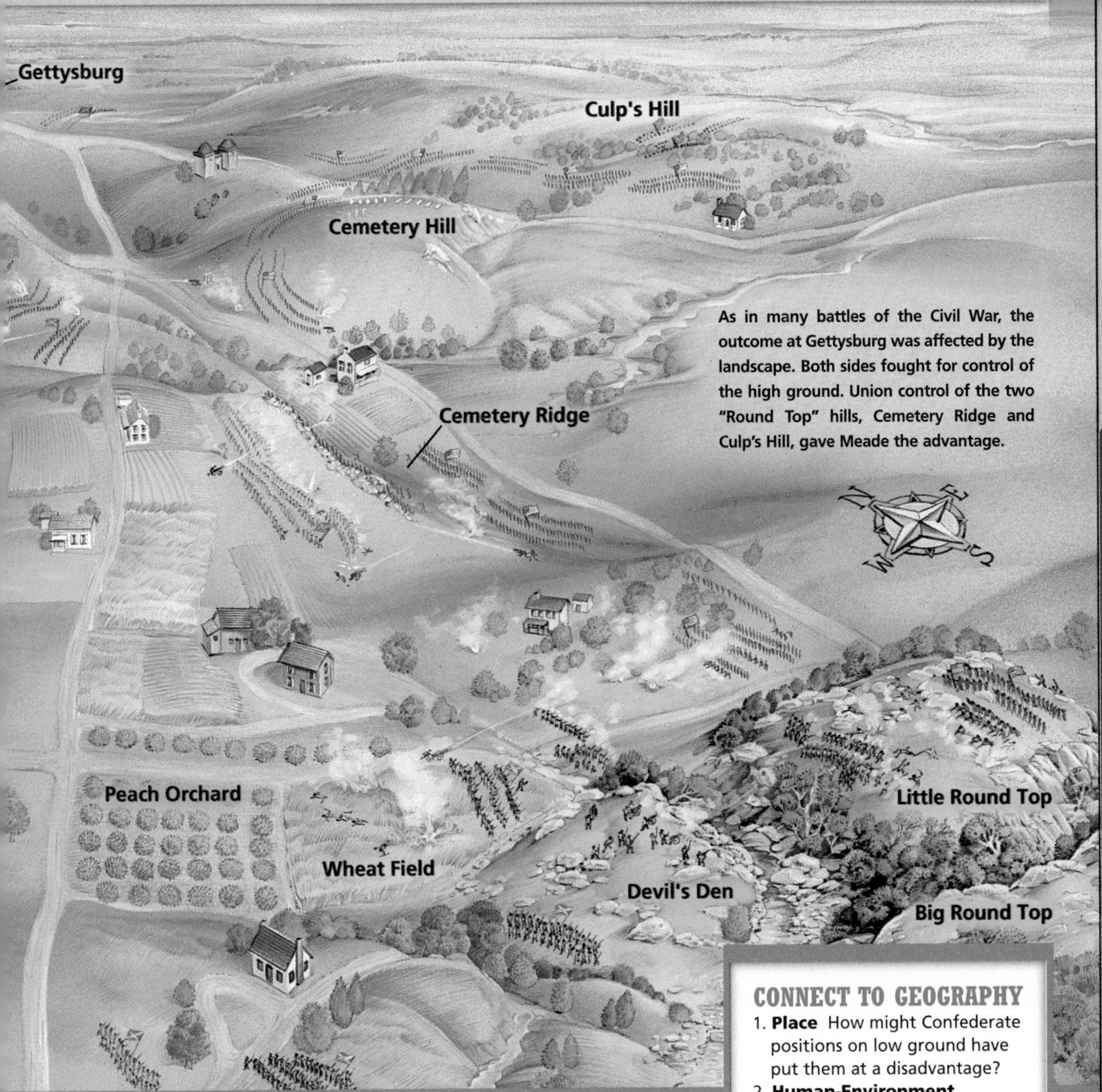

Gettysburg

Culp's Hill

Cemetery Hill

Cemetery Ridge

Peach Orchard

Wheat Field

Devil's Den

Little Round Top

Big Round Top

As in many battles of the Civil War, the outcome at Gettysburg was affected by the landscape. Both sides fought for control of the high ground. Union control of the two "Round Top" hills, Cemetery Ridge and Culp's Hill, gave Meade the advantage.

## On-Line Field Trip

**The Gettysburg National Military Park Museum** contains many objects relating to the Battle of Gettysburg, including this federal bass drum. This heavy drum—two feet in diameter—was harnessed to the neck of a soldier, who beat time with leather-covered wooden mallets.

Visit www.mcdougallittell.com for more information.

### CONNECT TO GEOGRAPHY

1. **Place** How might Confederate positions on low ground have put them at a disadvantage?
2. **Human-Environment Interaction** How might the attitudes of Union soldiers have been affected by fighting in their own territory?

See Geography Handbook, pages 4–5.

### CONNECT TO HISTORY

3. **Making Inferences** Why do you think a Southern victory on Northern soil would have been so significant?



### CRITICAL THINKING ACTIVITY

**Identifying and Solving Problems** Have the students study the map and illustration. Notice there are two ridges, each controlled by one of the sides. Divide the class into two sides, Union and Confederate. Have them devise a different battle plan for Gettysburg. Have each side present their plan. Try to determine which side might have been the winner. Ask how geography played into the battle plan they devised.

**Class Time** 15 minutes

### MORE ABOUT . . .

**Pickett's Charge**

Pickett was 38 years old and engaged to be married. Before the charge, he wrote a note to his fiancée and gave it to General Longstreet to mail. He called to his troops, "Up men, and to your posts! And don't forget that you are from old Virginia." The men followed Pickett cheerfully, one Confederate captain reported. They thought the battle was almost over. A Union officer described their charge: "Right on they move, as with one soul, in perfect order . . . magnificent, grim, irresistible."

### MORE ABOUT . . .

**Troop Movement at Gettysburg**

A Union captain named Frederico Fernández Cavada made aerial sketches of Confederate troop movement from hot-air balloons. Cuban-born Cavada was captured at Gettysburg. He described his prison experiences in a book called *Libby Life.* (Libby Prison, in Richmond, Virginia, was another Confederate war prison, comparable to Andersonville.)

### CONNECT TO GEOGRAPHY

1. **Place** To defeat the Union army, they would have to fight uphill; this is more strenuous and also makes it difficult to find protective cover; the Union soldiers would have found it easy to aim at the Confederates below.
2. **Human-Environment Interaction** Armies usually feel more motivated to defend their own territory than to seize their enemy's territory.

### CONNECT TO HISTORY

3. **Making Inferences** The North would have felt discouraged that a smaller army was able to bring the war to the North and win there; civilians might have begun to call for peace terms that allowed the South to secede.

## AMERICA'S HISTORY MAKERS

**Ulysses S. Grant**

Geoffrey Perrett, author of *Ulysses S. Grant: Soldier and President,* writes of Grant, "Many who met him were left feeling slightly puzzled; some felt more or less cheated. He did not look like a great general, and did not talk like a great general, did not dress like a great general, and did not even appear to consider himself a great general."

 **America's History Makers**
- Ulysses S. Grant, pp. 69–70

**Robert E. Lee**

After the war, Lee spent several months recuperating both physically and mentally; however, he never fully regained his health. At 58 he had no means of support and was concerned about the welfare of his seven children. Lee accepted the presidency of Washington College (later called Washington & Lee University) in Lexington, Virginia. Ironically, "the Rebel General" did not believe in slavery and secession and was deeply attached to the Republic.

**Possible Responses: Grant's determination to go after Lee even if the costs were high helped the Union win. Lee's belief that siding with Virginia was the honorable decision gave the South its greatest general.**

## INSTRUCT: OBJECTIVE 2

**The Siege of Vicksburg**

Key Questions
- How did the citizens of Vicksburg resist Grant's attack?
- What did Grant accomplish for the Union by his victory at Vicksburg?

 **Geography Transparency GT17**
- Vicksburg Campaign, 1863

## INSTRUCT: OBJECTIVE 3

**Sherman's Total War**

Key Questions
- What was Sherman's concept of total war?
- What were the political effects of Sherman's military victories?

## AMERICA'S HISTORY MAKERS

**ULYSSES S. GRANT**
**1822–1885**

**General Ulysses S. Grant** was an unlikely war hero. Although educated at West Point Military Academy, he was a poor student and showed little interest in an army career. With his quiet manner and rumpled uniform, he often failed to impress his fellow officers.

Yet on the battlefield, Grant proved to be a brilliant general. Highly focused and cool under fire, he won the first major Union victories of the war.

Grant was willing to fight Lee—even if the costs were high. He told his generals, "Wherever Lee goes, there you will go also."

**ROBERT E. LEE**
**1807–1870**

**Robert E. Lee** seemed destined for greatness. In his crisp uniform and trim, white beard, Lee was a dashing figure on the battlefield.

Born to a leading Virginia family, Lee was a top student at West Point and won praise for his actions in the Mexican War. General Winfield Scott called him "the very best soldier I have ever seen in the field."

Lee did not want to fight the Union, but he felt he had to stand by Virginia. "I did only what my duty demanded," Lee said. "I could have taken no other course without dishonor."

**How did the tough decisions made by Grant and Lee affect the Civil War?**

## 2 The Siege of Vicksburg

On July 4, 1863, the day after Pickett's Charge, the Union received more good news. In Mississippi, General Ulysses S. Grant had defeated Confederate troops at the **Siege of Vicksburg**.

**Vocabulary**
**siege:** the surrounding of a city, town, or fortress by an army trying to capture it

The previous year, Grant had won important victories in the West that opened up the Mississippi River for travel deep into the South. Vicksburg was the last major Confederate stronghold on the river. Grant had begun his attack on Vicksburg in May 1863. But when his direct attacks failed, he settled in for a long siege. Grant's troops surrounded the city and prevented the delivery of food and supplies. Eventually, the Confederates ran out of food. In desperation, they ate mules, dogs, and even rats. Finally, after nearly a month and a half, they surrendered.

The Union victory fulfilled a major part of the Anaconda Plan. The North had taken New Orleans the previous spring. Now, with complete control over the Mississippi River, the South was split in two.

**Background**
The Anaconda Plan called for blockading Southern ports, taking control of the Mississippi, and capturing Richmond.

With the victories at Vicksburg and Gettysburg, the tide of war turned in favor of the North. Britain gave up all thought of supporting the South. And, in General Grant, President Lincoln found a man who was willing to fight General Lee.

## 3 Sherman's Total War

In March 1864, President Lincoln named General Grant commander of all the Union armies. Grant then developed a plan to defeat the Confederacy. He would pursue Lee's army in Virginia, while Union forces under General **William Tecumseh Sherman** pushed through the Deep South to Atlanta and the Atlantic coast.



**ACTIVITY OPTIONS**

## SKILLBUILDER MINI-LESSON: INTERPRETING TIME LINES

**BLOCK SCHEDULING**

**Explaining the Skill** Time lines depict the chronological order of events. In creating a time line, identify key dates. Then decide on a scale. For example, the time line can be divided into two-, five-, or ten-year intervals. Write key dates below the line and place the events above the line.

**Applying the Skill** Ask students to make a time line of events from 1862 to 1865, including the following battles and events: Antietam, Fredericksburg, Chancellorsville, death of Jackson, Gettysburg, Vicksburg, fall of Atlanta, fall of Savannah.

1. What key events took place between September 1862 and May 10, 1863? *(General McClellan defeated General Lee at Antietam; Battle of Fredericksburg, 1862; Union defeat at Chancellorsville, Va., May 1863; General Jackson died, May 10, 1863)*
2. Why did the tide of war turn against the Confederacy by July 1863? *(victories at Gettysburg and Vicksburg in July 1863)*
3. What are two events in 1864 that were part of Sherman's campaign of total war? *(Atlanta fell in September 1864; Savannah fell in December 1864)*

 **In-Depth Resources: Unit 5**
- Skillbuilder Practice, p. 46

Battling southward from Tennessee, Sherman took Atlanta in September 1864. He then set out on a march to the sea, cutting a path of destruction up to 60 miles wide and 300 miles long through Georgia.

Sherman waged total war: a war not only against enemy troops, but against everything that supports the enemy. His troops tore up rail lines, destroyed crops, and burned and looted towns.

*Reading* **History**

**C. Drawing Conclusions** How might the political situation in the North have been different if Sherman had not taken Atlanta?

**C. Possible Response** McClellan might have won the presidency and changed the course of the war.

Sherman's triumph in Atlanta was important for Lincoln. In 1864, the president was running for reelection, but his prospects were not good. Northerners were tired of war, and Democrats—who had nominated George McClellan—stood a good chance of winning on an antiwar platform.

> **"Let us strive . . . to bind up the nation's wounds."**
>
> **Abraham Lincoln**

Sherman's success changed all that. Suddenly, Northerners could sense victory. Lincoln took 55 percent of the popular vote and won re-election. In his second inaugural speech, Lincoln hoped for a speedy end to the war: "With malice towards none; with charity for all; . . . let us strive on to finish the work we are in; to bind up the nation's wounds; . . . to do all which may achieve and cherish a just, and a lasting peace." (See page 525 for more of Lincoln's Second Inaugural Address.)

In December, Sherman took Savannah, Georgia. He then sent a telegram to Lincoln: "I beg to present you, as a Christmas gift, the city of Savannah, with 150 heavy guns and . . . about 25,000 bales of cotton."

Skillbuilder Answers
1. about 200 miles
2. Petersburg, Virginia

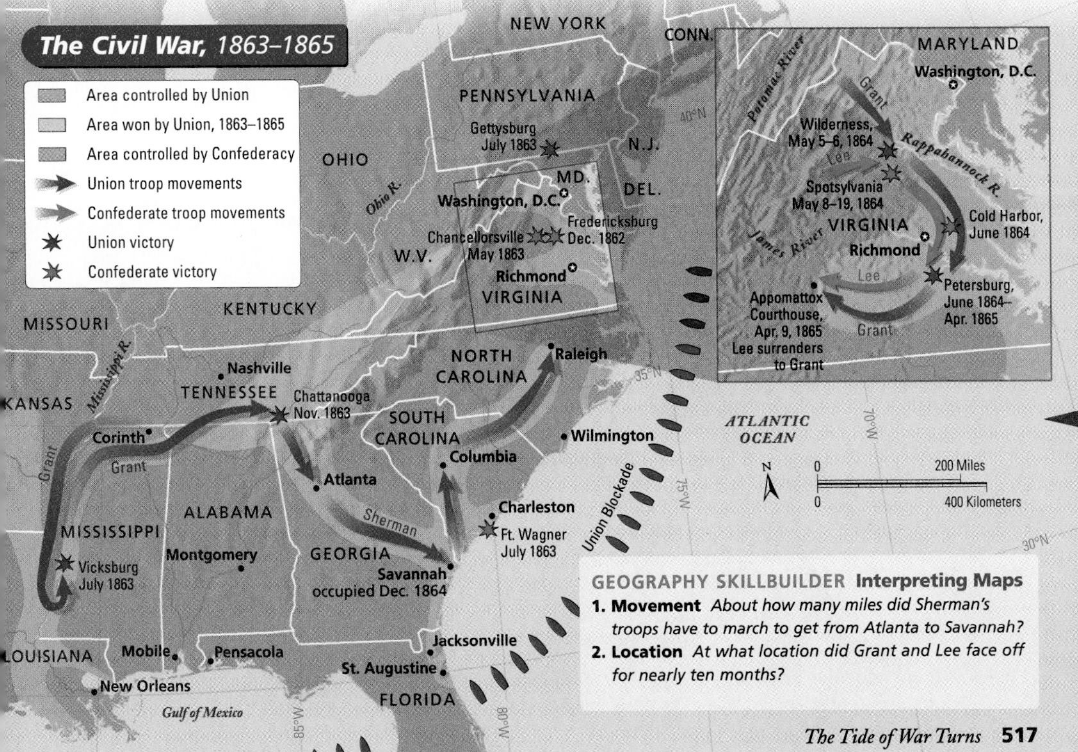


**GEOGRAPHY SKILLBUILDER Interpreting Maps**
1. **Movement** *About how many miles did Sherman's troops have to march to get from Atlanta to Savannah?*
2. **Location** *At what location did Grant and Lee face off for nearly ten months?*



## MORE ABOUT . . .

**The Battle for Atlanta**

Sherman believed "War is cruelty and you cannot refine it." However, he also told Atlanta's mayor, "When peace does come, you may call on me for anything. Then will I share with you the last cracker." After occupying Atlanta, Sherman ordered the civilian population expelled from the city. He believed that Union forces had to undermine the ability of the South to continue the war effort by destroying everything, including the will to resist. His soldiers burned everything of military value in the city before marching out on November 15.

## HISTORY FROM VISUALS

**Reading the Map** The war ended with the fall of Richmond in 1865. What does the map tell you about Union strategy on land? on sea? **Possible Response** The Union army attacked Confederate cities and controlled land within the Confederacy. At the same time, a Union blockade was in place along the Confederate coast.

**Extension** Have students work in pairs to create detailed maps of one section of Sherman's march—for example, from Atlanta to Savannah. Maps should be drawn to scale and include towns and dates.

## ACTIVITY OPTIONS

## INTERDISCIPLINARY LINK: LANGUAGE ARTS

### NEWSPAPER HEADLINES

**Class Time** One class period

**Task** Writing newspaper headlines

**Purpose** To summarize Sherman's progress from Tennessee to Raleigh

**Supplies Needed**
- Reference materials on Sherman's march
- Internet access

**Activity** Ask students to research one of the following stops on Sherman's march to the sea: Chattanooga, Atlanta, Savannah, Columbia, and Raleigh. Tell students to summarize their findings about the campaign in a newspaper headline for the day Sherman's troops took the city. Student papers also should include the date that each city fell to the Union.

**INSTRUCT: OBJECTIVE** 

**Grant's Virginia Campaign/ Surrender at Appomattox**

Key Questions
- Why did Grant want to take Richmond?
- What battles were part of the Virginia campaign?

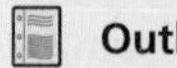 **Outline Map Activities**
- The End of the Civil War, 1865, pp. 33–34

## MORE ABOUT . . .

**Petersburg**

At Petersburg, Union soldiers from the coal-mining region of Pennsylvania dug a 500-foot tunnel under the Confederate lines and filled it with explosives. The tunnel exploded according to plan, creating an enormous crater and forcing a Confederate retreat. Unfortunately, Union strategy collapsed at this point. Northern soldiers poured into the crater—with no way to climb out. Confederate troops rained fire down on the helpless soldiers. The Union lost about 4,000 soldiers as casualties or prisoners. Southern casualties numbered about 1,300.

## HISTORY *through* ART

**Interpreting the Photograph** This photograph, taken in a Union camp, captures the feeling of camp life during the war. Mathew Brady and his staff photographed Civil War battle scenes as well as more mundane scenes of daily military life. Their cameras were slow, so they did not record action shots. Brady's war photographs were widely reproduced; however, after a series of financial problems, he died in poverty.

**Possible Responses: If people were exposed to images of suffering and death caused by war, they might try harder to find peaceful solutions to their problems.**

**In 1861, Congress created the Medal of Honor to reward individual bravery in combat.**

## 4 Grant's Virginia Campaign

*Reading* **History**

**D. Reading a Map** Use the map on page 517 to find the locations of the major battles of Grant's Virginia campaign.

After taking Savannah, Sherman moved north through the Carolinas seeking to meet up with Grant's troops in Virginia. Since May 1864, Grant and his generals had been fighting savage battles against Lee's forces. In battle after battle, Grant would attack, rest, then attack again, all the while moving south toward Richmond.

At the Battle of the Wilderness in May 1864, Union and Confederate forces fought in a tangle of trees and brush so thick that they could barely see each other. Grant lost over 17,000 men, but he pushed on. "Whatever happens," he told Lincoln, "we will not retreat."

At Spotsylvania and Cold Harbor, the fighting continued. Again, the losses were staggering. Grant's attack in June, at Cold Harbor, cost him 7,000 men, most in the first few minutes of battle. Some Union troops were so sure they would die in battle that they pinned their names and addresses to their jackets so their bodies could be identified later.

In June 1864, Grant's armies arrived at Petersburg, just south of Richmond. Unable to break through the Confederate defenses, the Union forces dug trenches and settled in for a long siege. The two sides faced off for ten months.

In the end, though, Lee could not hold out. Grant was drawing a noose around Richmond. So Lee pulled out, leaving the Confederate capital undefended. The Union army marched into Richmond on April 3. One Richmond woman recalled, "Exactly at eight o'clock the Confederate flag that fluttered above the Capitol came

### HISTORY *through* ART

This photograph shows Union officers before the Battle of the Wilderness. Next to the tree on the right is the photographer Mathew Brady. Photography was still a new art when the Civil War began. Brady's Civil War photos represent one of the first examples of photojournalism.

**How might people's attitudes toward war be affected when they can see pictures from the front lines?**

518

## ACTIVITY OPTIONS

**MULTIPLE LEARNING STYLES: BODILY-KINESTHETIC** — BLOCK SCHEDULING

### CIVIL WAR BIOGRAPHIES

**Class Time** Two class periods

**Task** Creating a live biographical exhibit about an important figure from the Civil War

**Purpose** To learn about important leaders in the Civil War

**Supplies Needed**
- Poster paper
- Art supplies
- Reference materials about the Civil War
- Costume materials (optional)

**Activity** Have each student select one important figure from this chapter. Students should do research about the person and then create an exhibit about his or her life. Exhibits may include text, music, and illustrations. On an appointed day, have students set up their exhibits throughout the classroom. Each student should assume the role of the person they have studied. Students may wish to wear appropriate costumes. Allow students to take turns visiting one another's exhibits and interviewing one another in their roles.

down and the Stars and Stripes were run up. . . . We covered our faces and cried aloud."

## Surrender at Appomattox

From Richmond and Petersburg, Lee fled west, while Grant followed in pursuit. Lee wanted to continue fighting, but he knew that his situation was hopeless. He sent a message to General Grant that he was ready to surrender.

On April 9, 1865, Lee and Grant met in the small Virginia town of **Appomattox Court House** to arrange the surrender. Grant later wrote that his joy at that moment was mixed with sadness.

*A VOICE FROM THE PAST*

I felt like anything rather than rejoicing at the downfall of a foe who had fought so long and valiantly, and had suffered so much for a cause, though that cause was, I believe, one of the worst for which a people ever fought, and one for which there was the least excuse. I do not question, however, the sincerity of the great mass of those who were opposed to us.

**Ulysses S. Grant,** *Personal Memoirs*

**STRANGE but True**

**WILMER MCLEAN**

The first major battle of the Civil War was fought on the property of Wilmer McLean. McLean lived in Manassas, Virginia, the site of the Battle of Bull Run. After the battle, McLean decided to move to a more peaceful place. He chose the village of Appomattox Court House (see map on page 517).

When Lee made the decision to surrender in April 1865, he sent Colonel Charles Marshall to find a location for a meeting with Grant. Marshall stopped the first man he saw in the deserted streets of Appomattox Court House. It was Wilmer McLean.

McLean reluctantly offered his home. Thus, the war that began in McLean's back yard ended in his parlor.

Grant offered generous terms of surrender. After laying down their arms, the Confederates could return home in peace, taking their private possessions and horses with them. Grant also gave food to the hungry Confederate soldiers.

After four long years, the Civil War was coming to a close. Its effects would continue, however, changing the country forever. In the next section, you will learn about the long-term consequences of the Civil War.

### Section 3 Assessment

**1. Terms & Names**

**Identify:**
- Battle of Gettysburg
- Pickett's Charge
- Ulysses S. Grant
- Robert E. Lee
- Siege of Vicksburg
- William Tecumseh Sherman
- Appomattox Court House

**2. Taking Notes**

Use a time line like the one below to record key events from Section 3.

1862 — 1866

Which event is considered the turning point of the war?

**3. Main Ideas**

a. Why was the Battle of Gettysburg important?

b. Why was Northern success in the Siege of Vicksburg important?

c. How did Grant treat Confederate soldiers after the surrender at Appomattox Court House?

**4. Critical Thinking**

**Contrasting** How was the Civil War different from wars that Americans had previously fought?

**THINK ABOUT**
- the role of civilians
- Sherman's military strategy

**ACTIVITY OPTIONS**

**GEOGRAPHY** / **LANGUAGE ARTS**: Research the Siege of Vicksburg. Make a **topographic map** of the area or write an **article** describing the soldiers' hardships during the siege.





**STRANGE but True**

**Wilmer McLean**

On the day of the surrender, Lee arrived at McLean's house before Grant. He was dressed in a crisp, gray uniform with an engraved sword by his side. Grant arrived half an hour later. His clothes and sword were spattered with mud. To ease the tension, Grant reminded Lee that they had met during the Mexican War. He later said, "Our conversation grew so pleasant that I almost forgot the object of our meeting."

## ASSESS & RETEACH

**Setting the Stage** Have students fill in the third section of the chart.

 **Formal Assessment**
- Section Quiz, p. 257

**RETEACHING ACTIVITY**

Have students reread the main idea of the section on page 512. Ask them to use the main idea as the topic sentence of a paragraph. The paragraph should identify the significance of the major campaigns that led to Union victory with the fall of Richmond.

 **In-Depth Resources: Unit 5**
- Reteaching Activity, p. 56

### Section 3 Assessment

**1. Terms & Names**

**Battle of Gettysburg,** p. 513
**Pickett's Charge,** p. 513
**Ulysses S. Grant,** p. 516
**Robert E. Lee,** p. 516
**Siege of Vicksburg,** p. 516
**William Tecumseh Sherman,** p. 516
**Appomattox Court House,** p. 519

**2. Taking Notes**

1862: Antietam; Fredericksburg; 1863: Chancellorsville; Gettysburg; Vicksburg; 1864: Grant named head of Union armies; Wilderness; Cold Harbor; Atlanta; Lincoln reelected; Savannah; 1865: Richmond falls; surrender at Appomattox.
Battle of Gettysburg

**3. Main Ideas**

**a.** It ended Lee's hopes for a Confederate victory in the North.
**b.** It would split the South in two and helped propel Grant to the leadership of the Union's armies.
**c.** respectfully; gave them food; allowed them to take their personal possessions home with them

**4. Critical Thinking**

They were fighting one another; the civilian population was more heavily involved; anything that supported troops became a potential target.

**ACTIVITY OPTIONS**

**Alternative Assessment**
- Rubrics for a map, 2.1
- Rubrics for an article, 4.5

## SECTION OBJECTIVES

1. To analyze the economic, physical, and emotional costs of the Civil War
2. To explain the significance of the Thirteenth Amendment
3. To describe the events related to President Lincoln's assassination
4. To summarize the consequences of the Civil War

**SKILLBUILDER**
Interpreting Graphs, p. 521
Interpreting Charts, p. 523

**CRITICAL THINKING**
Contrasting, p. 521
Making Inferences, pp. 521, 523
Summarizing, p. 522

## FOCUS & MOTIVATE

### 5-MINUTE WARM-UP

**Drawing Conclusions** These questions deal with the costs of the Civil War.

1. Look at the graphs on page 521. Which side lost more soldiers? On which side were there more wounded soldiers?
2. How do you think the number of casualties affected the way Northerners and Southerners felt toward each other after the war?

 **Warm-Up Transparency WT17**

## INSTRUCT

### INSTRUCT: OBJECTIVE 

**Costs of the War**
Key Questions

- How did President Lincoln hope to bring the North and South together after the war?
- What were the physical costs of the war?
- What were the economic costs of the war?

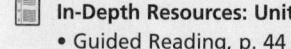

**In-Depth Resources: Unit 5**
- Guided Reading, p. 44

**Reading Study Guide** (Spanish and English), pp. 173–174

# 4 The Legacy of the War

**TERMS & NAMES**
Thirteenth Amendment
John Wilkes Booth

| MAIN IDEA | WHY IT MATTERS NOW |
|---|---|
| The Civil War brought great changes and new challenges to the United States. | The most important change was the liberation of 4 million enslaved persons. |

### ONE AMERICAN'S STORY

**In the spring of 1864, a year before the end of the Civil War, the Union army was running out of cemetery space to bury its war dead. The secretary of war ordered Quartermaster General Montgomery Meigs to find a new site for a cemetery. Without hesitation, Meigs chose Robert E. Lee's plantation in Arlington, Virginia, just across the Potomac River from Washington, D.C. "The grounds about the mansion are admirably adapted to such a use," wrote Meigs in June 1864.**

**Meigs was from Georgia and had served under Lee in the U.S. Army before the war. Unlike Lee, however, Meigs remained loyal to the Union and disagreed strongly with Lee's decision to join the Confederacy. His decision to turn Lee's plantation into a Union cemetery was highly symbolic. The Union soldiers who died fighting Lee's army would be buried in Lee's front yard. That site became Arlington National Cemetery.**

During the Civil War, the government turned Robert E. Lee's Virginia plantation into a graveyard. That graveyard eventually became Arlington National Cemetery.

##  Costs of the War

Many Northerners shared Montgomery Meigs's bitter feelings toward the South. At the same time, many Southerners felt great resentment toward the North. After the war, President Lincoln hoped to heal the nation and bring North and South together again. The generous terms of surrender offered to Lee were part of that effort. Hard feelings remained, however, in part because the costs of the war were so great.

The Civil War was the deadliest war in American history. In four years of fighting, approximately 620,000 soldiers died—360,000 for the Union and 260,000 for the Confederacy. Another 275,000 Union soldiers and 260,000 Confederate soldiers were wounded. Many suffered from their wounds for the rest of their lives.

Altogether, some 3,000,000 men served in the armies of the North and South—around 10 percent of the population. Along with the soldiers, many other Americans had their lives disrupted by the war.



## RECOMMENDED RESOURCES

**In-Depth Resources: Unit 5**
- Guided Reading, p. 44
- Building Vocabulary, p. 45
- Geography Application: Booth Assassinates Lincoln, pp. 47–48
- Reteaching Activity, p. 57
- Enrichment Activity, p. 58
- History Workshop Resources, p. 59

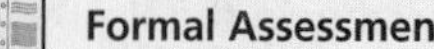

**Reading Study Guide** (Spanish and English), pp. 173–174

**Formal Assessment**
- Section Quiz, p. 258

**Alternative Assessment**
- Rubrics, 2.6
- Rubrics, 1.6

**Access for Students Acquiring English/ESL**
- Guided Reading, p. 116
- Geography Application, pp. 118–119

**Technology Resources**

 **Humanities Transparency HT34**
- John Wilkes Booth Poster

 **Critical Thinking Trans. CT50**
- Cause and Effect: The Civil War, 1861–1865

 **Electronic Teacher Tools with Test Maker**

 **ClassZone**
www.mcdougallittell.com

*Reading* **History**

**A. Contrasting** How did government spending during the Civil War compare to that during previous years?

A. Possible Response The amount spent during the war was five times that spent during the previous 80 years.

The war also had great economic costs. Together, the North and South spent more than five times the amount spent by the government in the previous eight decades. Many years after the fighting was over, the federal government was still paying interest on loans taken out during the war.

2

## The Thirteenth Amendment

One of the greatest effects of the war was the freeing of millions of enslaved persons. As the Union army moved through the South during and after the war, Union soldiers released African Americans from bondage. One of those released was Booker T. Washington, who later became a famous educator and reformer. He recalled the day a Union officer came to his plantation to read the Emancipation Proclamation.

> *A VOICE FROM THE PAST*
>
> After the reading we were told that we were all free, and could go when and where we pleased. My mother, who was standing by my side, leaned over and kissed her children, while tears of joy ran down her cheeks. She explained to us what it all meant, that this was the day for which she had been so long praying, but fearing that she would never live to see.
>
> **Booker T. Washington,** quoted in his autobiography, *Up from Slavery*

*Reading* **History**

**B. Making Inferences** Why was an amendment needed to free enslaved persons even after the Emancipation Proclamation?

B. Possible Responses Many people were still enslaved in the border states. An amendment would be harder to overturn than a law passed by Congress.

The Emancipation Proclamation applied primarily to slaves in the Confederacy, however. Many African Americans in the border states were still enslaved. In 1864, with the war still under way, President Lincoln had approved of a constitutional amendment to end slavery entirely, but it failed to pass Congress.

In January 1865, Lincoln urged Congress to try again to end slavery. This time, the measure—known as the **Thirteenth Amendment**—passed. By year's end, 27 states, including eight in the South, had ratified the amendment. From that point on, slavery was banned in the United States.

*CONNECTIONS TO MATH*

### Costs of the Civil War

**CONFEDERATE CASUALTIES**

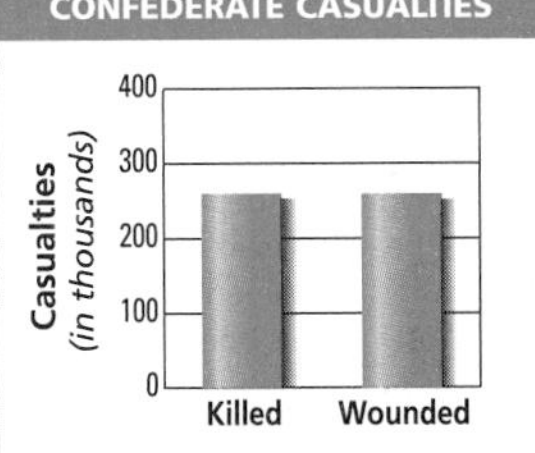


**UNION CASUALTIES**

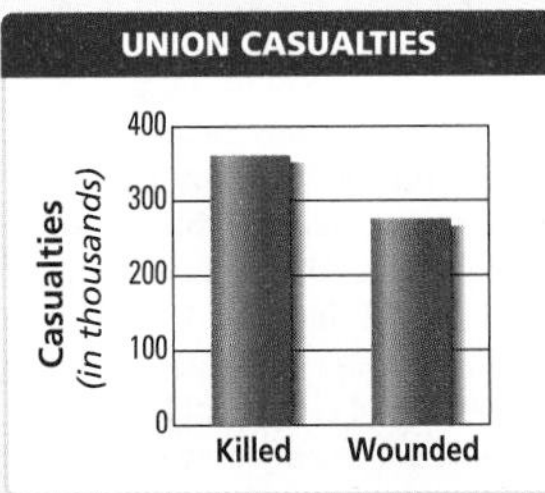


Source: *World Book; Historical Statistics of the United States; The United States Civil War Center*

**ECONOMIC COSTS**

- Federal loans and taxes to finance the war totaled $2.6 billion.
- Federal debt on June 30, 1865, rose to $2.7 billion.
- Confederate debt ran over $700 million.
- Union inflation reached 182% in 1864 and 179% in 1865.
- Confederate inflation rose to 9,000% by the end of the war.

SKILLBUILDER

**Interpreting Graphs**

1. *About how many Confederate soldiers were killed in the Civil War?*
2. *Approximately how many soldiers were wounded in the war?*

Skillbuilder Answers
1. 260,000
2. 500,000

3

## Lincoln's Assassination

Lincoln did not live to see the end of slavery, however. Five days after Lee's surrender at Appomattox, the president and his wife went to see a play at Ford's Theatre in Washington, D.C. During the play, a Confederate supporter, **John Wilkes Booth,** crept into the balcony where the president sat and shot him in the back of the head. Booth then jumped over the railing and landed on the stage. Although he broke his leg in the leap, he managed to escape the theater.





**INSTRUCT: OBJECTIVE 2**

**The Thirteenth Amendment**

Key Questions
- What was required before slavery was abolished throughout the United States?
- When was the Thirteenth Amendment passed?

**HISTORY FROM VISUALS**

**Reading the Graphs** Have students read the title of the entire visual. Then have them explain the relationship between the information in the graphs and the economic costs. **Possible Response** The costs of the war were not only financial but also human.

**Extension** Have the students create a different visual to show the information in these graphs.

**INSTRUCT: OBJECTIVE** 

**Lincoln's Assassination**

Key Questions
- When, where, and by whom was Lincoln assassinated?
- How did Lincoln's death affect the nation?

 **In-Depth Resources: Unit 5**
- Geography Application: Booth Assassinates Lincoln, pp. 47–48

 **Humanities Transparency HT34**
- John Wilkes Booth Poster

**ACTIVITY OPTIONS**

**INDIVIDUAL NEEDS: GIFTED AND TALENTED**

**CIVIL WAR ART AND CIVIL WAR PHOTOGRAPHY**

**Class Time** Two class periods

**Task** Comparing works of art and photographs depicting the Civil War

**Purpose** To analyze works of art depicting historical events

**Supplies Needed**
- Books and reference materials with Civil War art and photographs

**Activity** Have students find both a photograph and a work of art (such as an engraving, drawing, painting, or sculpture) of the same Civil War subject. Then have students do research about the event, the artist, and the photographer. Tell students to prepare an oral presentation in which they discuss both the artwork and the photograph, including an analysis of the purpose of each work, its intended audience, and its medium. Students should also point out any inaccuracies they find in the way the event has been depicted in art.

## Connections TO *LITERATURE*

**Walt Whitman**

Whitman wrote his poem "When Lilacs Last in the Dooryard Bloomed" about the death of Lincoln. Lincoln died in April, and Whitman says in the poem that each year when the lilacs blossom, he will think of the fallen president. Another of Whitman's poems about Lincoln's death is "O Captain! My Captain!"

## MORE ABOUT . . .

**John Wilkes Booth**

Booth was a young, successful actor. Lincoln had seen Booth perform in a play called *The Marble Heart* in November 1863, shortly before the president traveled to Gettysburg where he gave his famous address. In March 1865, Booth and his accomplices tried to kidnap Lincoln at the Soldiers Home outside the city—but Lincoln was not there. Among the people hanged as Booth's accomplices was a woman, Mary Surratt, who ran a boardinghouse in Washington, D.C., where the conspirators, including her son John, sometimes met.

## INSTRUCT: OBJECTIVE 

**Consequences of the War**

Key Questions

- Why did the war change the way people thought about the country?
- How did the war affect the economy in the North and in the South?
- What other challenges did the country face after the war?

 **In-Depth Resources: Unit 5**
- Enrichment Activity, p. 58

## Connections TO *LITERATURE*

**WALT WHITMAN**

**1819–1892**

One of the greatest American poets, Walt Whitman (below) was a large, bearded man whose poetry captured the American spirit. His most famous book of poems, *Leaves of Grass,* praised the values of freedom and democracy.

Whitman was 41 when the Civil War began. Too old for the army, he offered his services as a nurse when his younger brother was wounded at Fredericksburg. He stayed on after that to help at hospitals in Washington, D.C.

Whitman wrote a book of poetry about war. Later editions of the book, which appeared after Lincoln's assassination, included several poems about the president.

That same evening, an accomplice of Booth stabbed Secretary of State William Seward, who later recovered. Another man was supposed to assassinate Vice-President Johnson, but he failed to carry out the attack.

**Vocabulary**
**accomplice:** someone who aids a lawbreaker

Although Booth had managed to escape after shooting the president, Union troops found and killed him several days later. Soldiers also hunted down Booth's accomplices, whom they either hanged or imprisoned.

After Lincoln was shot, he was carried to a house across the street from the theater. The bullet in his brain could not be removed, however. The next morning, April 15, 1865, the president died. He was the first American president to be assassinated.

Lincoln's murder stunned the nation and caused intense grief. In Washington, D.C., people wept in the streets. One man who mourned the nation's loss was the poet Walt Whitman. In one poem, Whitman considered the president's legacy.

***Reading* History**
**C. Summarizing** How did Americans react to the assassination of Lincoln?
**C. Possible Response** People reacted with intense grief and mourning.

***A VOICE FROM THE PAST***

This dust was once the man,
Gentle, plain, just and resolute, under whose cautious hand,
Against the foulest crime in history known in any land or age,
Was saved the Union of these States.

**Walt Whitman,** *This Dust Was Once the Man*

The loss of Lincoln's vast experience and great political skills was a terrible setback for a people faced by the challenge of rebuilding their nation. In both the North and the South, life would never be the same after the Civil War.

## 4 Consequences of the War

In the North, the war changed the way people thought about the country. In fighting to defend the Union, people came to see the United States as a single nation rather than a collection of states. After 1865, people no longer said "the United States *are*" but "the United States *is.*"

The war also caused the national government to expand. Before the war, the government was relatively small and had limited powers. With the demands of war, however, the government grew larger and more powerful. Along with a new paper currency and income tax, the government established a new federal banking system. It also funded railroads, gave western land to settlers, and provided for state colleges. This growth of federal power continued long after the war was over.

**Background**
In the 1850s, an improved way of making steel—the Bessemer process—had been perfected, allowing for the mass production of steel.

The war also changed the Northern economy. New industries such as steel, petroleum, food processing, and manufacturing grew rapidly. By



## ACTIVITY OPTIONS

**INTERDISCIPLINARY LINK: LANGUAGE ARTS**

 BLOCK SCHEDULING

**"O CAPTAIN! MY CAPTAIN!"**

**Class Time** 20 minutes

**Task** Reading a poem by Whitman about Lincoln

**Purpose** To read a contemporary poem about Lincoln and to understand the effect of his death on the American people

**Supplies Needed**
- Copies of "O Captain! My Captain!"

**Activity** Distribute copies of the poem to the class. Have students read it and then ask students to rewrite the first two lines to explain what Whitman means by the ship, the fearful trip, the prize, and the captain. Why does Whitman say that the people should exult and ring bells despite the death of the "captain"?

Then have the students discuss how this poem may reflect the effect of Lincoln's death on the American public. Ask how the poem might have been received by Southerners.

**CAUSE AND EFFECT:** *The Civil War, 1861–1865*

| CAUSES | IMMEDIATE EFFECTS |
|---|---|
| Conflict over slavery in territories | Abolition of slavery |
| Economic differences between North and South | Devastation of South |
| | Reconstruction of South |
| Failure of Congress to compromise | **LONG-TERM EFFECTS** |
| Election of Lincoln as president | Growth of industry |
| Secession of Southern states | Government more powerful |
| Firing on Fort Sumter | Nation reunited |

SKILLBUILDER **Interpreting Charts**

1. *What military event is among the causes of the Civil War?*
2. *What effect did the Civil War have on the federal government?*

Skillbuilder Answers
1. firing on Fort Sumter
2. It made federal authority stronger than that of the states.

the late 1800s, industry had begun to replace farming as the basis of the national economy.

For the South, however, the war brought economic disaster. Farms and plantations were destroyed. About 40 percent of the South's livestock was killed. Fifty percent of its farm machinery was wrecked. Factories were also demolished, and thousands of miles of railroad tracks were torn up. Also gone was the labor system that the South had used—slavery.

Before the war, the South accounted for 30 percent of the nation's wealth. After the war it accounted for only 12 percent. These economic differences between the North and the South would last for decades.

The country faced difficult challenges after the war. How would the South be brought back into the Union, and how would four million former slaves be integrated into national life? You will read more about these challenges in the next chapter.

## Section 4 Assessment

**1. Terms & Names**

**Identify:**
- Thirteenth Amendment
- John Wilkes Booth

**2. Taking Notes**

Use a chart like the one below to record the social, economic, and political legacy of the Civil War.

Legacy of the Civil War

| Society | Economy | Politics |
|---|---|---|
| | | |

Is the legacy of the Civil War still apparent today? How?

**3. Main Ideas**

a. What were some of the human costs of the Civil War?

b. What did the Thirteenth Amendment achieve?

c. What was the state of the Southern economy after the Civil War?

**4. Critical Thinking**

**Making Inferences** How do you think the assassination of President Lincoln affected the nation?

THINK ABOUT
- the reaction of ordinary citizens
- its impact on government

**ACTIVITY OPTIONS**

**MATH** / **TECHNOLOGY**

Read about the postwar economy. Create a **database** on industry in the North or make a **storyboard** for a video on the problems in the South.



## HISTORY FROM VISUALS

**Reading the Chart** Point out the relationship between the two parts of the chart. Ask students to identify the results that were positive for the country as a whole. Then ask which results Southerners would have considered positive.

**Possible Responses** For the country as a whole—the abolition of slavery; reconstruction of the South; a nation reunited; a growth of industry; For the Southerners—the growth of Southern industry

**Extension** Ask students to divide the causes of the Civil War listed on the chart into "Causes Building Over Time" and "Immediate Causes."

**Critical Thinking Transparency CT50**
- Cause and Effect: The Civil War, 1861–1865

## ASSESS & RETEACH

**Setting the Stage** Have students fill in the last section on the chapter graphic organizer.

**Formal Assessment**
- Section Quiz, p. 258

**Critical Thinking Transparency CT49**
- Setting the Stage

### RETEACHING ACTIVITY

Divide the class into four groups. Assign one objective to each student group. Have each group outline the material in the objective using a main idea and supporting detail format. Remind students to title the outlines. Display the completed outlines on a classroom bulletin board.

**In-Depth Resources: Unit 5**
- Reteaching Activity, p. 57

## Section 4 Assessment

**1. Terms & Names**

**Thirteenth Amendment,** p. 521
**John Wilkes Booth,** p. 521

**2. Taking Notes**

Society: death and injury; disruption of lives; freeing of slaves; Economy: cost of war; Northern industrialization; Southern labor system destroyed; Politics: government expansion; Thirteenth Amendment. Answers will vary but students should be able to explain their responses.

**3. Main Ideas**

**a.** Approximately 620,000 casualties, and many lives were disrupted.
**b.** It banned slavery in the United States. **c.** economic disaster; much property was destroyed; the traditional labor system, slavery, was abolished

**4. Critical Thinking**

There was a great sense of tragedy and loss. It would be harder for the nation to confront postwar challenges without his political skills.

### ACTIVITY OPTIONS

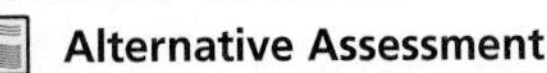
**Alternative Assessment**
- Rubrics for a database, 2.6
- Rubrics for a storyboard, 1.6

## INTERACTIVE PRIMARY SOURCES

**OBJECTIVE**
Students will be able to identify the main points of the Gettysburg Address and Lincoln's Second Inaugural Address, and they will gain appreciation for Lincoln's use of language.

**Primary Source Explorer**
- *The Gettysburg Address*
- *Lincoln's Second Inaugural Address*

The Explorer will help students select and produce their own presentations.

Specific information about the document can be found in **A Closer Look.** To learn more about key people and events of the time, students should click on **Life in These Times. What Happened Next** will show the student the impact of the document, both at home and abroad, and tie the document to today.

## FOCUS & MOTIVATE

**Making Generalizations** Ask students to think about speeches or sermons that they have heard. Tell them to make a list of qualities that they think are important for a speaker to remember. After students have read the Lincoln speeches, ask them to review their lists to find which qualities they contain.

## MORE ABOUT . . .

**The Gettysburg Address**
President Lincoln wrote five different versions of the speech. He also made several changes as he spoke. Probably the most significant change was adding "under God" after the word "nation" in the last sentence. The poetic but simple language of the speech is one reason why it is among the best remembered in American history. The emotional focus of Lincoln's words is on the actions of the soldiers who fought at Gettysburg.

INTERACTIVE PRIMARY SOURCES

# The Gettysburg Address (1863)

**Setting the Stage** On November 19, 1863, officials gathered in Gettysburg, Pennsylvania. They were there to dedicate a national cemetery on the ground where the decisive Battle of Gettysburg had taken place nearly five months earlier. Following the ceremony's main address, which lasted nearly two hours, President Lincoln delivered his Gettysburg Address in just over two minutes. In this famous speech, Lincoln expressed his hopes for the nation. **See Primary Source Explorer**

Four **score**[1] and seven years ago our fathers brought forth on this continent a new nation, conceived in liberty, and dedicated to the proposition that all men are created equal.

Now we are engaged in a great civil war, testing whether that nation or any nation so conceived and so dedicated, can long endure. We are met on a great battlefield of that war. We have come to dedicate a portion of that field, as a final resting place for those who here gave their lives that that nation might live. It is altogether fitting and proper that we should do this.

But, in a larger sense, we cannot dedicate—we can not **consecrate**[2]—we can not hallow—this ground. The brave men, living and dead, who struggled here, have consecrated it, far above our poor power to add or **detract.**[3] The world will little note, nor long remember what we say here, but it can never forget what they did here. It is for us the living, rather, to be dedicated here to the unfinished work which they who fought here have thus far so nobly advanced. It is rather for us to be here dedicated to the great task remaining before us—that from these honored dead we **take increased devotion to**[4] that cause for which they **gave the last full measure of devotion**[5]—that we here highly resolve that these dead shall not have died **in vain**[6]—that this nation, under God, shall have a new birth of freedom—and that government of the people, by the people, for the people, shall not perish from the earth.

**A CLOSER LOOK**
**LINCOLN'S MODESTY**
Lincoln claimed that what he said at Gettysburg would not be long remembered. However, the address soon came to be recognized as one of the best speeches of all time.
1. What features of Lincoln's address make it so memorable?

**A CLOSER LOOK**
**FIGHTING FOR A CAUSE**
Different people fought for different causes during the Civil War. Sometimes, the causes for which people fought changed over the course of the war.
2. What cause is Lincoln referring to in the Gettysburg Address?

1. **score:** a group of 20.
2. **consecrate:** to declare as sacred.
3. **detract:** to take away from.
4. **take increased devotion to:** work harder for.
5. **gave the last full measure of devotion:** sacrificed their lives.
6. **in vain:** for nothing.

524

## TEACHING STRATEGY

**Finding Main Ideas** To help students understand the main idea of the Gettysburg Address, have them copy the chart shown and match the main ideas it presents with the text.

| Main Ideas: The Gettysburg Address |
|---|
| 1. Our colonial leaders created a nation based on equality. |
| 2. We are fighting a war to preserve our country. |
| 3. We are here to dedicate a cemetery on a part of the battlefield. |
| 4. What the soldiers who fought at Gettysburg did is the most important thing, not what the living do to honor them now. |
| 5. The living must dedicate themselves to finishing the work of the soldiers to make sure that freedom will survive and that democracy will endure. |

# Second Inaugural Address (1865)

**Setting the Stage** President Lincoln delivered his Second Inaugural Address just before the end of the Civil War. In this excerpt, he recalled the major cause of the war and vowed to fight for the restoration of peace and unity. **See Primary Source Explorer** 

One-eighth of the whole population were colored slaves. . . . These slaves constituted a peculiar and powerful interest. All knew that this interest was somehow the cause of the war. To strengthen, perpetuate, and extend this interest was the object for which the **insurgents**[1] would rend the Union even by war, while the Government claimed no right to do more than to restrict the territorial enlargement of it. Neither party expected for the war the magnitude or the duration which it has already attained. Neither anticipated that the cause of the conflict might cease with or even before the conflict itself should cease. Each looked for an easier triumph, and a result less fundamental and astounding. Both read the same Bible and pray to the same God, and each invokes His aid against the other. . . . Fondly do we hope, fervently do we pray, that this mighty **scourge**[2] of war may speedily pass away. Yet, if God wills that it continue until all the wealth piled by the **bondsman's**[3] two hundred and fifty years of **unrequited**[4] toil shall be sunk, and until every drop of blood drawn with the lash shall be paid by another drawn with the sword, as was said three thousand years ago, so still it must be said "the judgments of the Lord are true and righteous altogether."

With malice toward none, with charity for all, with firmness in the right as God gives us to see the right, let us strive on to finish the work we are in, to bind up the nation's wounds, to care for him who shall have borne the battle and for his widow and his orphan, to do all which may achieve and cherish a just and lasting peace among ourselves and with all nations.

1. **insurgent:** one that revolts against civil authority.
2. **scourge:** a source of suffering and devastation.
3. **bondsman:** enslaved person.
4. **unrequited:** not paid for.

*A CLOSER LOOK*

**SLAVERY IN TERRITORIES**

Before the Civil War, Northern states wanted to prohibit slavery in territories that would eventually become new states. Southern states fought to expand slavery, fearing the prohibition would threaten slavery where it already existed.

**1. Why did the Southerners fear that prohibiting slavery in new territories might threaten slavery where it already existed?**

*A CLOSER LOOK*

**MALICE TOWARD NONE**

As Northerners became more confident in victory, many looked forward to punishing Southerners, whom they blamed for the war. Lincoln, however, urged citizens to care for one another and work for a just and lasting peace.

**2. Why do you think that Lincoln believed it would be wiser for Americans not to place blame or seek revenge on one another?**

*Interactive Primary Sources Assessment*

**1. Main Ideas**

a. Why might President Lincoln have begun the Gettysburg Address by noting that the country was "dedicated to the proposition that all men are created equal"?

b. According to Lincoln's Second Inaugural Address, why did the Confederacy go to war?

c. To what did Lincoln refer with the phrase "the bondsman's two hundred and fifty years of unrequited toil?"

**2. Critical Thinking**

**Making Inferences** In 1865, if the South had asked to rejoin the Union without ending slavery, do you think Lincoln would have agreed?

**THINK ABOUT**
- what Lincoln identifies as the cause of the war
- what might happen if the war ended but slavery did not



*Interactive Primary Sources Assessment*

**1. Main Ideas**

**a.** because millions of enslaved men and women were still not recognized as equal
**b.** to strengthen, perpetuate, and extend slavery against the wishes of the federal government to restrict its territorial enlargement
**c.** to the work of slaves who had been brought to the United States since the early 1600s

**2. Critical Thinking**

Lincoln would not have accepted the offer. He saw slavery as the cause of the war. Even if the South had returned to the Union, its system of slavery would have caused the same problems and conflicts again.

## INSTRUCT

Key Questions
- What beliefs about the United States does Lincoln express in the Gettysburg Address?
- What is the "unfinished work" that Lincoln believes the living "should dedicate themselves to"?
- In his Second Inaugural Address, what does Lincoln say was the major cause of the war?

### MAKING PERSONAL CONNECTIONS

Ask students to reread the last sentence of the Gettysburg Address and the last sentence of the Second Inaugural Address. Ask students if they think Americans are still working to reach the goals set by Lincoln.

### MORE ABOUT . . .

**The Second Inaugural Address (1865)**

Lincoln's second inauguration was on March 4, 1865. It was a cold and windy day in Washington, D.C. Lincoln stood on the steps of the Capitol Building under its newly completed dome. In the audience stood John Wilkes Booth, an invited guest. Lincoln's tone in the speech is weary and somber. After completing it, Lincoln said, "I am a tired man. Sometimes I think I am the tiredest man on earth."

### *A CLOSER LOOK*

**The Gettysburg Address**

1. Answers will vary, but each answer should include an explanation.
2. The survival of the United States, whose government was dedicated to the proposition that all men are created equal —a government described by Lincoln as "of the people, by the people, and for the people."

**Second Inaugural Address**

1. Slave states would have proportionately less representation in the federal government.
2. Lincoln knew that the task of rebuilding the nation after the war would be less difficult if Americans were able to work together.

## TERMS & NAMES

1. **Emancipation Proclamation,** p. 504
2. **54th Massachusetts Regiment,** p. 506
3. **conscription,** p. 508
4. **Battle of Gettysburg,** p. 513
5. **Ulysses S. Grant,** p. 516
6. **Robert E. Lee,** p. 516
7. **Siege of Vicksburg,** p. 516
8. **William Tecumseh Sherman,** p. 516
9. **Appomattox Court House,** p. 519
10. **Thirteenth Amendment,** p. 521

## REVIEW QUESTIONS

**Possible Responses**

1. because he thought that freeing the slaves would weaken the South and help win the war
2. After the Emancipation Proclamation, they enlisted in large numbers. They fought bravely and made a real contribution.
3. There were food riots in the South, and many men deserted the army. "Copperheads" protested against the war in the North, and draft laws resulted in riots in some places.
4. because it was easier for wealthy people to avoid the draft than poor people
5. by slowing down the pace of their work; carrying out sabotage; by joining the Union army
6. It halted Lee's invasion of the North and helped turn the tide of the war.
7. It devastated the South and raised spirits in the North, helping Lincoln get reelected.
8. He kept attacking Lee's forces in Virginia, pushing Lee back and finally forcing his surrender.
9. It freed slaves throughout the United States, not just in the Confederacy, and outlawed slavery in the whole United States.
10. The war encouraged the growth of industry, which began to replace farming as the basis of the national economy.

# Chapter 17 ASSESSMENT

### TERMS & NAMES

Briefly explain the importance of each of the following.

1. Emancipation Proclamation
2. 54th Massachusetts Regiment
3. conscription
4. Battle of Gettysburg
5. Ulysses S. Grant
6. Robert E. Lee
7. Siege of Vicksburg
8. William Tecumseh Sherman
9. Appomattox Court House
10. Thirteenth Amendment

### REVIEW QUESTIONS

**The Emancipation Proclamation (pages 503–506)**

1. Why did Lincoln issue the Emancipation Proclamation?
2. How did black soldiers aid the war effort?

**War Affects Society (pages 507–511)**

3. How did events on the home front show the toll that war was taking there?
4. Why did some people say the Civil War was a "rich man's war but a poor man's fight"?
5. How did enslaved persons help the Union?

**The North Wins (pages 512–519)**

6. Why was the Battle of Gettysburg so important?
7. How did Sherman's march help the Union?
8. How did Grant defeat Lee?

**The Legacy of the War (pages 520–523)**

9. How was the Thirteenth Amendment different from the Emancipation Proclamation?
10. How did the war change the national economy?

### CRITICAL THINKING

**1. USING YOUR NOTES**

| | North | South |
|---|---|---|
| Emancipation Proclamation | | |
| War's Impact | | |
| Northern Victories in Battle | | |
| Union Wins Civil War | | |

a. How did white and black Southerners react to the Emancipation Proclamation?

b. How did inflation affect the North and the South?

**2. ANALYZING LEADERSHIP**

What qualities made Lincoln an effective leader?

**3. THEME: IMPACT OF THE INDIVIDUAL**

How did General Grant's actions in the war make a crucial difference to the outcome?

**4. FORMING AND SUPPORTING OPINIONS**

One Union relief worker said, "The suffering of men in battle is nothing next to the agony that women feel sending forth their loved ones to war." Do you agree with this statement? Explain why or why not.

**5. APPLYING CITIZENSHIP SKILLS**

How might the behavior of General Grant and President Lincoln toward the Confederacy have helped to begin healing the war-torn nation?

**Interact *with* History**

Having read about the ferocity of battle during the Civil War, do you still believe that you would be inspired to continue the fighting? Why or why not?

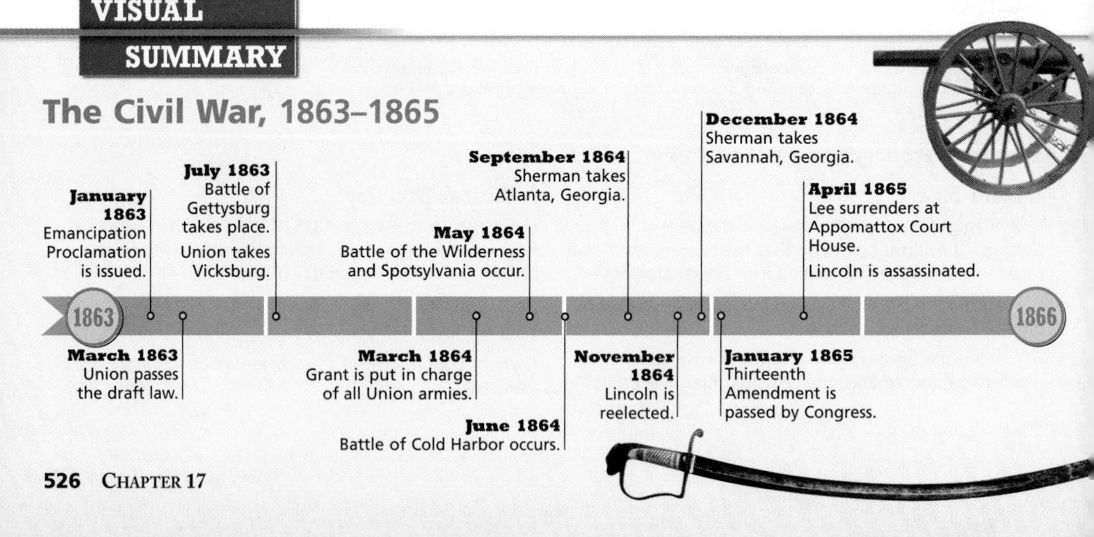
VISUAL SUMMARY
The Civil War, 1863–1865
January 1863 Emancipation Proclamation is issued.
July 1863 Battle of Gettysburg takes place.
Union takes Vicksburg.
May 1864 Battle of the Wilderness and Spotsylvania occur.
September 1864 Sherman takes Atlanta, Georgia.
December 1864 Sherman takes Savannah, Georgia.
April 1865 Lee surrenders at Appomattox Court House.
Lincoln is assassinated.
1863
1866
March 1863 Union passes the draft law.
March 1864 Grant is put in charge of all Union armies.
June 1864 Battle of Cold Harbor occurs.
November 1864 Lincoln is reelected.
January 1865 Thirteenth Amendment is passed by Congress.

## CRITICAL THINKING

**Possible Responses**

1. **USING YOUR NOTES** **a.** White Southerners reacted with rage. Black Southerners fled to Union lines, depriving the South of labor. Many became Union soldiers. **b.** Inflation had an impact on both the North and South, but it was particularly severe in the South.
2. **ANALYZING LEADERSHIP** He seemed to weigh decisions carefully and keep his goals in mind. He had great strength to persevere when conditions were difficult.
3. **THEME: IMPACT OF THE INDIVIDUAL** Grant was determined to win. He took the offensive regardless of the cost. His attitude played a key role in turning the tide of the war.
4. **FORMING AND SUPPORTING OPINIONS** Answers will vary.
5. **APPLYING CITIZENSHIP SKILLS** Their respect and compassion for fellow citizens helped to reduce the hard feelings among the citizens.

**Interact *with* History.** Answers will vary. Some will feel that their principles were still worth fighting for, while others will not.

## HISTORY SKILLS

**1. INTERPRETING MAPS: Location**

Study the map. Answer the questions.

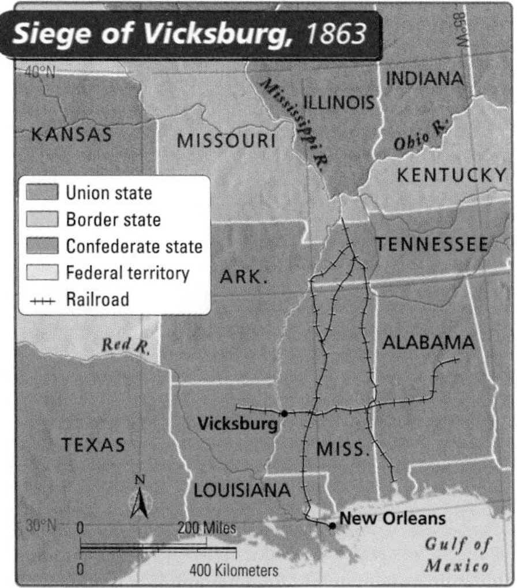


**Basic Map Elements**

a. Which color represents Confederate states?

**Interpreting the Map**

b. Next to what river was Vicksburg built?

c. Why might Vicksburg be important for Southerners supplying the Confederacy from Texas?

**2. INTERPRETING SECONDARY SOURCES**

Historian Bruce Catton describes a brief meeting between two brothers during the Siege of Vicksburg. Read the passage and answer the questions.

> Both boys [were] from Missouri, one of them in Confederate gray and the other in Federal blue. The Confederate had a roll of bills in his hand and gave them to his brother to send to their mother. . . . He couldn't get things out from Vicksburg through the Union lines, Vicksburg being completely surrounded, so he asked his brother to send them to her, and the brother did. There was no shooting while these arrangements were made, then the brothers shook hands and retired to their individual lines, and the shooting started up again.
>
> **Bruce Catton,** from *Reflections on the Civil War*

a. What does this account say about the nature of war?

b. Why might the fact that the brothers came from Missouri pertain to their fighting for different sides?

## ALTERNATIVE ASSESSMENT

**1. INTERDISCIPLINARY ACTIVITY: Science**

**Writing a Report** Do research on the advances in military technology during the Civil War. Write a report that describes the new or improved weapons that were used during the war. Present the report to your class with charts that illustrate the changes and innovations that you describe.

**2. COOPERATIVE LEARNING ACTIVITY**

**Creating a Newspaper** Work with a group of classmates to produce a simple newspaper that covers a specific period of the Civil War. With your group, choose the period you want to cover and decide whether you will take a Northern or Southern viewpoint. Research events and conditions during that period, then select the topics you will cover in your newspaper. Examples include:

- important battles and military strategies
- political news, including government actions and foreign involvement
- social and economic conditions
- profiles of important figures

**3. CD-ROM PRIMARY SOURCE EXPLORER**

Use the Internet, books, and other resources to do research for a multimedia presentation on a Civil War battle. Using presentation software, consider including the following content:

- paintings or written descriptions of the battle
- images of the destruction caused by the conflict
- music from the time period
- statistics on casualties
- diary and journal entries

**4. HISTORY PORTFOLIO**

**Option 1** Review your section and chapter assessment activities. Select one that you think is your best work. Then use comments made by your teacher or classmates to improve your work and add it to your portfolio.

**Option 2** Review the questions that you wrote for What Do You Want to Know? on page 502. Then write a short report in which you explain the answers to your questions. If any questions were not answered, do research to answer them. Add your answers to your portfolio.



## ALTERNATIVE ASSESSMENT

**1. INTERDISCIPLINARY ACTIVITY: Science**
**Reports should**
- have a thesis.
- clearly state facts and examples to support major points.
- include illustrations of Civil War military technology.
- have a bibliography.
- use standard grammar, spelling, sentence structure, and punctuation.

**2. COOPERATIVE LEARNING ACTIVITY**
**Newspapers should**
- use a journalistic style.
- present information in an unbiased way.
- cover the topic adequately.
- have headlines and present and portray the historical events accurately.
- have a clear and attractive layout.
- use standard grammar, spelling, sentence structure, and punctuation.

3.  **PRIMARY SOURCE EXPLORER**
**Presentations should**
- utilize two or more media.
- clearly demonstrate an understanding of the selected Civil War battle.
- show technical proficiency.

**4. HISTORY PORTFOLIO**

**Option 1 Revised section or chapter assessment activities should**
- address teacher and peer responses to the selected work.
- solve problems present in the first versions of the work.

**Option 2 Short reports should**
- answer questions about the later part of the Civil War.
- use evidence to develop and support ideas.
- cite sources of information.
- use standard grammar, spelling, sentence structure, and punctuation.

 **Critical Thinking Transparency CT51**
- Visual Summary

 **Formal Assessment**
- Chapter Test, Forms A and B, pp. 259–266

## HISTORY SKILLS

**Possible Responses**

1. INTERPRETING MAPS
**Basic Map Elements**
**a.** green
**Interpreting the Map**
**b.** Mississippi River
**c.** because Vicksburg controlled important supply routes across the Mississippi

2. INTERPRETING PRIMARY SOURCES
**a.** Students might say that war causes such powerful feelings of right and wrong that even brothers are ready to fight against one another for what they believe is right.
**b.** Missouri was a border state. The state's citizens may have been sympathetic to both sides during the Civil War.

## HISTORY WORKSHOP

**OBJECTIVE**

Students create a cultural artifact, write about a Civil War hero, and role-play activities honoring the hero for his or her actions.

 **BLOCK SCHEDULING**

## PROCEDURE

Gather the materials listed in the "Toolbox." Divide the class into groups of two to three students. Then review the steps for identifying a medal recipient, making a medal of honor, writing the letter, and preparing and delivering the speech.

 **In-Depth Resources: Unit 5**
- History Workshop Resources, p. 59

### MORE ABOUT . . .

**The Medal of Honor**

The Medal of Honor is awarded for deeds of bravery that are "beyond the call of duty." That means that if the hero had not performed the deed, he or she would not have been criticized in any way. Strict criteria govern the awarding of a Medal of Honor, including testimony of heroic action by two eyewitnesses. Several benefits are attached to the nation's highest military honor, including a monthly stipend for life and the right to burial at Arlington National Cemetery.



# Create a Medal of Honor

In 1782, George Washington established the nation's first award to recognize the bravery of American soldiers. It was a purple heart made of cloth and was called the Badge of Military Merit. But the award was not used much after the Revolutionary War. Then, in 1861, Congress created a new award—the Medal of Honor. In the Civil War, 1,520 Union soldiers, including 20 African Americans, received the medal. Today, that medal is the highest United States military award for individual bravery and is commonly referred to as the Congressional Medal of Honor.

ACTIVITY Create a medal of honor for a hero or heroine from either side of the Civil War. Write a letter recommending your hero for the medal. Then read a speech in class as you award your medal to the deserving individual.

### TOOLBOX

Each group will need:

- tops of juice cans or cardboard
- aluminum foil
- pieces of ribbon
- safety pins
- glue
- markers
- scissors
- writing paper

### STEP BY STEP

**1 Form groups.** Each group should consist of three or four students. Each group will:

- identify a Civil War hero or heroine
- create a medal
- write a letter explaining why your group considers that person a hero
- award the medal and read a speech in class

**2 Research a hero.** First, brainstorm characteristics that you think a hero should have. Then, using this chapter, books on the Civil War, or the Internet, select an individual who you think was a hero for either side of the Civil War. Take notes on the actions of the person you selected. The actions should show how that person meets your standards for being a hero.

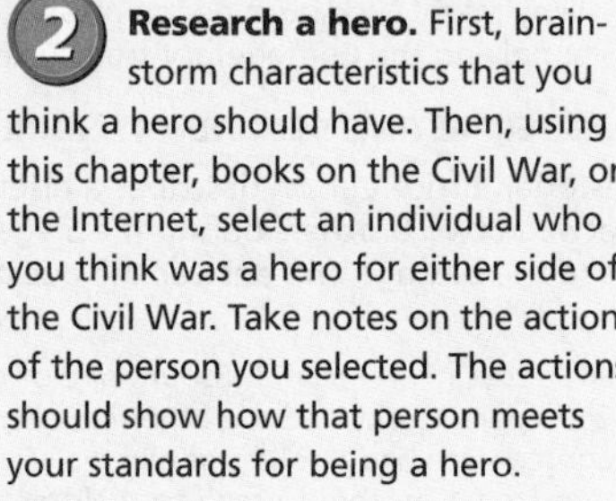

The Congressional Medal of Honor rewards military personnel who risked their lives, "above and beyond the call of duty." In the Civil War, 1,520 Union soldiers, including 20 African Americans, received the Medal of Honor.



### RECOMMENDED RESOURCES

**JOURNALS AND BOOKS FOR THE TEACHER**

***United States of America's Congressional Medal of Honor Recipients and Their Official Citations.*** Highland House II, Inc., 1994.

deLong, Kent. ***War Heroes: True Stories of Honor Recipients.*** Bergin & Garvey, 1993.

Murphy, Edward. ***Vietnam Medal of Honor Heroes.*** New York: Ballantine Books, 1987.

**VIDEOS**

***Decoration Day.*** Republic Pictures Home Video. A Hallmark Hall of Fame presentation about a veteran who refuses the Medal of Honor.

***Glory: The True Story Continues.*** Columbia Tristar. Documentary of the 54th Massachusetts.

**BOOKS FOR THE STUDENTS**

Jacobs, Bruce. ***Heroes of the Army: The Medal of Honor and Its Winners.*** New York: W. W. Norton, 1956.

Doherty, Kiernan. ***Congressional Medal of Honor Recipients.*** Enslow, 1998.

**3 Design your medal.** Think about the shape, images, and words that you will use to make your medal of honor. You may want to look at the example from Chapter 17 and in Civil War books. Sketch a design of your medal in pencil.

**4 Construct your medal.** Using art supplies, construct a medal based on your design. First, construct the medal itself by using a juice can lid or a cardboard pattern. Decorate the medal by using foil and markers. Then add a ribbon and pin.

**5 Write a letter.** The letter should be addressed to the Congress of the United States of America or the Congress of the Confederate States of America. Your letter should give reasons for recommending your hero based on the person's actions. Carefully recopy your letter after you have made any corrections.

**6 Pin up the medal.** Create a Medal of Honor board with other groups in your class. Pin up all the medals you have created. Discuss with other groups the standards your group set for calling a person a hero.

## WRITE AND SPEAK

**Write a Speech** As a Civil War military leader, write a speech praising the courage and bravery of the individual who is receiving the medal. Choose another member of your group to act as the recipient of the award. Read your speech to the class as you award the medal to that person.

## HELP DESK

For related information, see page 518 in Chapter 17.

### Researching Your Project

Visit the library to learn more about the history of military awards or go to your local historical museum to examine actual medals.

**Visit www.mcdougallittell.com to learn more about military awards.**

### Did You Know?

Since the Congressional Medal of Honor was created in 1861, 3,408 persons have received the award. Nineteen persons have received two such awards. Only one woman has received the award.

The Confederate States of America also awarded 43 of its finest men with the Confederate Medal of Honor.

The practice of awarding medals began in Europe during the Middle Ages. Kings realized that giving land to valued knights was too costly, so they gave medals instead.

### REFLECT & ASSESS

- What requirements did you set for awarding a medal of honor?
- What reasons did your letter and speech give for awarding the medal?
- What symbols did you use for your medal? Why did you select them?



### MORE ABOUT . . .

**Congressional Medal of Honor Museums**

The Congressional Medal of Honor Museum is located in Mt. Pleasant, South Carolina, on the hangar deck of the U.S.S. *Yorktown.* It is the centerpiece of the Patriot's Point Naval and Maritime Museum. Another museum honoring Medal of Honor winners, the Hall of Heroes, is planned for construction in Pueblo, Colorado.

### MORE ABOUT . . .

**Dr. Mary Walker (1832–1919)**

Dr. Mary Walker is the only woman to receive the Medal of Honor. A surgeon with the Union army during the Civil War, Walker was captured and held prisoner by the Confederates for four months. She was awarded the Medal of Honor for her medical work on the battlefield and in prison camps. After the war, Dr. Walker campaigned for women's suffrage. She also wrote several books about the role of women in society.

### REFLECT & ASSESS

1. Ask students to defend their reasons for awarding a Medal of Honor.
2. Have students work with a peer editor who makes suggestions to improve the letter and comments on the validity of the reasons.
3. Have students discuss their symbols and defend their choices.

### STANDARDS FOR EVALUATION

**HISTORY WORKSHOP**

**Medals of Honor should**
- appear attractive and realistic.
- include symbols that are appropriate.
- show evidence of research.

**WRITE AND SPEAK**

**Letters and speeches should**
- state opinions clearly.
- include historic details about the hero's actions.
- present convincing reasons for recommending the hero for a medal.

# CHAPTER 18 PLANNING GUIDE
# Reconstruction 1865–1877

| | CHAPTER OVERVIEW | COPYMASTERS | TECHNOLOGY |
|---|---|---|---|
| **CHAPTER RESOURCES** | This chapter focuses on the economic and political effects of Reconstruction in the South, as well as the passage of the 13th, 14th, and 15th Amendments. It also discusses the hardships faced by the newly freed slaves. | **In-Depth Resources: Unit 5**<br>• Tracing Themes: Democratic Ideals, p. 61<br>• Building Vocabulary, p. 65<br>**Interdisciplinary Projects,** pp. 103–108 | CD-ROM **Primary Source Explorer**<br>CD-ROM **Electronic Teacher Tools**<br>CD-ROM **Power Presentations CD-ROM**<br>**Chapter Summaries on CD** (English and Spanish) |
| **SECTION 1**<br>**Rebuilding the Union**<br>**pp. 533–539** | **KEY IDEAS**<br>• Southern states enact black codes to limit the freedom of African Americans.<br>• Congress passes the 14th Amendment stating that all people born in the United States are entitled to equal protection under law.<br>• Congress and the president quarrel over Reconstruction. | **In-Depth Resources: Unit 5**<br>• Setting the Stage, p. 60<br>• Guided Reading, p. 62<br>• Primary Source, p. 69<br>• Reteaching Activity, p. 74<br>**America's History Makers**<br>• Hiram Revels, pp. 71–72<br>**Why It Matters Now**<br>• The New South, pp. 35–36 | **Warm-Up Transparency WT18**<br>**Humanities Transparency HT35**<br>• Political Cartoon: A Carpetbagger Goes South<br>**Geography Transparency GT18**<br>• Southern Military Districts, 1867<br>**Critical Thinking Transparency CT53**<br>• Cause and Effect: Reconstruction |
| **SECTION 2**<br>**Reconstruction and Daily Life**<br>**pp. 540–544** | • Former slaves seek family members and strive for education.<br>• Lacking land, many African-American and poor white farmers become sharecroppers.<br>• White Southerners form the Ku Klux Klan, which uses violence to support white political power. | **In-Depth Resources: Unit 5**<br>• Setting the Stage, p. 60<br>• Guided Reading, p. 63<br>• Geography Application, pp. 67–68<br>• Primary Source, p. 70<br>• Literature Selection, pp. 71–73<br>• Reteaching Activity, p. 75<br>**America's History Makers**<br>• General Oliver O. Howard, pp. 73–74 | **Warm-Up Transparency WT18**<br>**Critical Thinking Transparency CT52**<br>• Setting the Stage<br>INTERNET **ClassZone:** www.mcdougallittell.com |
| **SECTION 3**<br>**End of Reconstruction**<br>**pp. 545–549** | • Congress passes the 15th Amendment, giving African-American men the right to vote.<br>• Political scandals and economic depression weaken Grant's presidency.<br>• Reconstruction ends in 1877, leaving the promise of legal equality for African Americans unfulfilled. | **In-Depth Resources: Unit 5**<br>• Setting the Stage, p. 60<br>• Guided Reading, p. 64<br>• Skillbuilder Practice: Interpreting Charts, p. 66<br>• Reteaching Activity, p. 76<br>**Economics in History**<br>• Understanding the Business Cycle, p. 18<br>**Outline Map Activities**<br>• Election of 1876, pp. 35–36 | **Warm-Up Transparency WT18**<br>**Humanities Transparency HT36**<br>• Parade Celebrating the 15th Amendment<br>**Critical Thinking Transparency CT52**<br>• Setting the Stage<br>**Critical Thinking Transparency CT54**<br>• Visual Summary<br>INTERNET **ClassZone:** www.mcdougallittell.com |

Pupil's Edition | Overhead Transparency | CD-ROM
Copymaster | Audio Library | Internet

## ASSESSMENT

**Chapter Assessment,** pp. 550–551

**Formal Assessment**
- Chapter Tests, Forms A and B, pp. 272–279

**Alternative Assessment Book**

**Electronic Teacher Tools with Test Maker**

**Section Assessment,** p. 537

**Formal Assessment**
- Section Quiz, p. 269

**Alternative Assessment Book**
- Rubrics for a Web page, 5.1
- Rubrics for a speech, 3.6

**Electronic Teacher Tools with Test Maker**

**Section Assessment,** p. 544

**Formal Assessment**
- Section Quiz, p. 270

**Alternative Assessment Book**
- Rubrics for a speech, 3.6
- Rubrics for a mural, 1.11

**Electronic Teacher Tools with Test Maker**

**Section Assessment,** p. 549

**Formal Assessment**
- Section Quiz, p. 271

**Alternative Assessment Book**
- Rubrics for a letter, 4.1
- Rubrics for a law, 4.3

**Electronic Teacher Tools with Test Maker**

## CUSTOMIZING FOR INDIVIDUAL NEEDS

### Students Acquiring English/ESL

**Reading Study Guide** (English and Spanish), pp. 177–184

**Access for Students Acquiring English/ESL: Spanish Translations,** pp. 120–125

**Chapter Summaries on CD** (English and Spanish)

### Less Proficient Readers

**Reading Study Guide** (English and Spanish), pp. 177–184

**Chapter Summaries on CD** (English and Spanish)

### Gifted and Talented Students

**In-Depth Resources: Unit 5**
- Enrichment Activity, p. 77

**America's History Makers**
- Hiram Revels, pp. 71–72
- General Oliver O. Howard, pp. 73–74

## CROSS-CURRICULAR CONNECTIONS

### Culture

Fleischner, Jennifer. ***I Was Born A Slave: The Story of Harriet Jacobs.*** Brookfield, CT: Millbrook, 1997. Based on *Incidents in the Life of a Slave Girl,* this easy-to-read account tells how Jacobs aided former slaves during the Civil War and then became a teacher.

### Geography

Savage, Beth L., ed. ***African American Historic Places.*** Washington, D.C.: Preservation Press, 1994. Beautifully illustrated book with information about over 800 historic sites.

### Popular Culture

Kalman, Bobbie et al. ***19th Century Clothing (Historic Communities).*** New York: Crabtree Publishing, 1993. What Americans wore, how clothing was made, hairstyles, accessories, and grooming.

### Interdisciplinary Projects, pp. 103–108

- Math: Sharecropping Data
- Science: Testing the Soil
- Language Arts: Promoting Literacy
- Art: Reconstruction Era Collage

### Primary Sources

Meltzer, Milton. ***The Black Americans: A History in Their Own Words, 1619–1983.*** New York: HarperTrophy, 1987. Letters, speeches, articles, and other primary sources tell a compelling story.

### Literature

Fast, Howard. Introduction by Eric Foner. ***Freedom Road (American History through Literature).*** Armonk, NY: M.E. Sharpe, 1995. Re-issue of classic story of Gideon Jackson, a former slave who returns from the Union army to Charleston, South Carolina, and makes his way in the new post war society, becoming a member of Congress.

Nixon, Joan Lowry. ***David's Search.*** New York: Delacorte Press, 1998. This volume in Nixon's saga of the Orphan Train Children sees young David Howard, now living with a Texas family, facing a threat by the KKK to his best friend, an African American and former slave.

Robinet, Harriette Gillem. ***Forty Acres and Maybe a Mule.*** New York: S&S, 1998. Young Pascal joins other former slaves as they search for some land to call their own.

## ENRICHMENT ACTIVITIES

**Pupil's Edition, pp. 530–551**
**Interact with History,** p. 531
**Interdisciplinary Challenge,** pp. 538–539

**In-Depth Resources: Unit 5**
- Geography Application: The Economic Effects of the Civil War, 1860–1880, pp. 67–68
- Primary Source: Report on Freedmen's Bureau, p. 69
- Primary Source: A Letter from Jourdan Anderson, p. 70
- Literature Selection: from *Forty Acres and Maybe a Mule,* pp. 71–73

**America's History Makers**
- Hiram Revels, pp. 71–72
- General Oliver O. Howard, pp. 73–74

**Outline Map Activities**
- Election of 1876, pp. 35–36

**Why It Matters Now**
- The New South, pp. 35–36

**LESSON PLAN OPTIONS (50-MINUTE PERIOD)** (TE) = Teacher's Edition (PE) = Pupil's Edition

| | TEACHER-DIRECTED ACTIVITIES<br>Class Time: 15 minutes | STUDENT-CENTERED ACTIVITIES<br>Class Time: 25 minutes | INDIVIDUAL ACTIVITIES<br>Class Time: 10 minutes |
|---|---|---|---|
| **DAY 1**<br>Introduction<br>pp. 530–532 | **Presentation Options**<br>• Begin with a class discussion of the photograph on p. 530 **(PE)**.<br>• Lead a class discussion on the "What Do You Know?" question in Setting the Stage, p. 532. Then introduce the graphic organizer for the chapter **(PE)**. | **Options for Cooperative Learning**<br>• Have student groups discuss the Interact with History questions, p. 531 **(PE)**.<br>• Have student groups respond to the "What Do You Want to Know?" question in Setting the Stage, p. 532 **(PE)**. | **Head Start on Homework Options**<br>• Have students skim Section 1 Main Idea, Why It Matters Now, Terms & Names, and the main headings, p. 533 **(PE)**.<br>• Have students begin Guided Reading activity and Building Vocabulary sheet. |
| **DAY 2**<br>Section 1<br>pp. 533–539 | **Presentation Options**<br>• Begin with the 5-Minute Warm-Up, p. 533 **(TE)**.<br>• Review the Section 1 Main Idea, Why It Matters Now, and Terms & Names, p. 533 **(PE)**.<br>• Choose 5 key questions for Objectives 1–4 to discuss with the class, pp. 533–537 **(TE)**. | **Options for Cooperative Learning**<br>• Divide students into groups to work on the Interdisciplinary Challenge, pp. 538–539 **(PE)**.<br>• Have student pairs work together to complete one of the Activity Options in the Section 1 Assessment, p. 537 **(PE)**. | **Head Start on Homework Options**<br>• Have students begin working on Section 1 Assessment, p. 537 **(PE)**.<br>• Have students preview Section 2 Main Idea, Why It Matters Now, Terms & Names, and the main headings, p. 540 **(PE)**. |
| **DAY 3**<br>Section 2<br>pp. 540–544 | **Presentation Options**<br>• Begin with the 5-Minute Warm-Up, p. 540 **(TE)**.<br>• Choose 5 key questions for Objectives 1–4 to discuss with the class, pp. 540–544 **(TE)**.<br>• Lead the students in a discussion about sharecropping using the diagram on page 543 **(TE)**. | **Options for Cooperative Learning**<br>• Divide students into groups to work on the Interdisciplinary Link, Language Arts: A Dialogue During Reconstruction, p. 542 **(TE)**.<br>• Have student pairs work together to complete the Critical Thinking Activity, p. 543 **(TE)**. | **Head Start on Homework Options**<br>• Have students begin working on Section 2 Assessment, p. 544 **(PE)**.<br>• Have students do the Skillbuilder questions, p. 549 **(PE)**. |
| **DAY 4**<br>Section 3<br>pp. 545–549 | **Presentation Options**<br>• Begin with the 5-Minute Warm-Up, p. 545 **(TE)**.<br>• Choose 5 key questions for Objectives 1–4 to discuss with the class, pp. 545–549 **(TE)**.<br>• Lead the students through the Skillbuilder Mini-Lesson: Interpreting Charts, p. 548 **(TE)**. | **Options for Cooperative Learning**<br>• Divide students into groups and have them complete the Interdisciplinary Link, Civics: Campaign Slogans, p. 546 **(TE)**.<br>• Have student pairs work together to complete the Critical Thinking Activity, p. 547 **(TE)**. | **Head Start on Homework Options**<br>• Have students complete the Setting the Stage graphic organizer for the chapter, p. 532 **(PE)**.<br>• Have students begin working on the Chapter Assessment, pp. 550–551 **(PE)**.<br>• Prepare for Chapter Test<br>**Formal Assessment,** pp. 272–279 |

TEACHER-TESTED ACTIVITY | Lori Leslie, Cedar Bluff Middle School, Knoxville, Tennessee

## DEBATING RECONSTRUCTION

**Class Time** Two class periods, one for preparation and one for presentation

**Task** Holding a debate on Reconstruction

**Purpose** To understand the difficulties the North and the South faced while trying to rebuild the Union

**Supplies Needed**

- Reference books and Internet sources on the Lincoln/Johnson and the Radical Republican plans for Reconstruction

**Activity** Divide the class into two groups: those who oppose Radical Reconstruction and those who support it. Each group should choose a speaker and a writer and then create a list of reasons for its position on Radical Reconstruction. For each reason listed, have students brainstorm possible counterarguments their opponents might make. After 20 minutes of preparation, have each speaker give a short statement of his or her position on Reconstruction and then debate the issue.

## BLOCK SCHEDULING — LESSON PLAN OPTIONS (90-MINUTE PERIOD)

### DAY 1

**Interact with History,** p. 531
**Class Time** 20 minutes

Options for pacing and variety:

- **Role-Playing** Have students imagine they are newly elected African-American members of the House of Representatives representing voters in Southern states during Reconstruction. Have students write short essays describing their thoughts as they watch Congressman Elliott make his speech.
  **Class Time** 10 minutes

**Setting the Stage,** p. 532
**Class Time** 20 minutes

Options for pacing and variety:

- **Time Saver** Assign the "What Do You Know?" and "What Do You Want to Know?" questions for homework. Before students create their "What Do You Want to Know?" questions, have them preview the chapter, looking at headings and illustrations.
  **Class Time** 10 minutes

**Section 1,** pp. 533–539
**Class Time** 50 minutes

Options for pacing and variety:

- **History on Film** Extend students' background knowledge of Reconstruction by having them view *Reconstruction and Segregation,* 1865–1910. Schlessinger Media, 1996.
  **Class Time** 35 minutes
- **Time Saver** For a homework assignment, have students answer the Critical Thinking question in the Section Assessment.
  **Class Time** 15 minutes

### DAY 2

**Interdisciplinary Challenge,** pp. 538–539

Options for pacing and variety:

- **Peer Evaluation** Write the standards for evaluating the Arts Challenges that are included in the Teacher's Edition, p. 538, on the chalkboard. As each group presents its model or written proposal of how it would rebuild Richmond, have the other students evaluate the presentations using these guidelines.
  **Class Time** 30 minutes

**Section 2,** pp. 540–544
**Class Time** 45 minutes

Options for pacing and variety:

- **Time Saver** Use the diagram on page 543 to help students understand the cycle of debt and poverty that sharecroppers faced.
  **Class Time** 10 minutes
- **Internet** Extend students' knowledge of the African-American freedom celebration known as Juneteenth by visiting www.mcdougallittell.com
  **Class Time** 20 minutes

**Section 3,** pp. 545–549
**Class Time** 45 minutes

Options for pacing and variety:

- **Peer Evaluation** Have students work in pairs to answer the four Reading History questions for the section. **Class Time** 15 minutes

**Chapter 18 Assessment,** pp. 550–551
**Class Time** 40 minutes

Options for pacing and variety:

- **Peer Evaluation** Divide the class into three groups to complete the Interdisciplinary Activity on page 551. Ask a third of the class to write a letter about Reconstruction from a member of the old Southern upper class, another third from a newly freed African American, and the remaining third a white Northern carpetbagger. Students should work independently on their letters and then form groups of three to read their letters aloud.
  **Class Time** 30 minutes
- **Peer Teaching** Within small groups, have students share their completed Reading Strategy charts from page 532, explaining the problems and solutions they identified.
  **Class Time** 20 minutes

## CHAPTER 18 OBJECTIVE

The student will describe the political conflict over how to rebuild the South after the Civil War and evaluate the impact of Reconstruction on African Americans and other Southerners.

# Reconstruction

## 1865–1877



### HISTORY FROM VISUALS

**Interpreting the Photograph** Ask students what they think freedom was like for the newly freed slaves in the photograph. What problems did these Americans face when the Civil War ended?
**Possible Responses** Newly freed slaves had to find work, and paid work was scarce in the ruined South. Many newly freed slaves were without the necessities of life—food, clothing, and shelter. Many newly freed slaves wanted to find their families and get an education.

**Extension** Have students write five questions to ask the people in the photograph about their plans and goals for the future.

### CRITICAL THINKING ACTIVITY

**Identifying Problems** Discuss with students the many different ways the Civil War changed life in the South. Ask students to make two lists of tasks required to rebuild the economy of the South and to rebuild the lives of Southerners. One list should contain items that needed immediate attention. The other list should contain items that could have been dealt with over a period of years.

**Class Time** 20 minutes

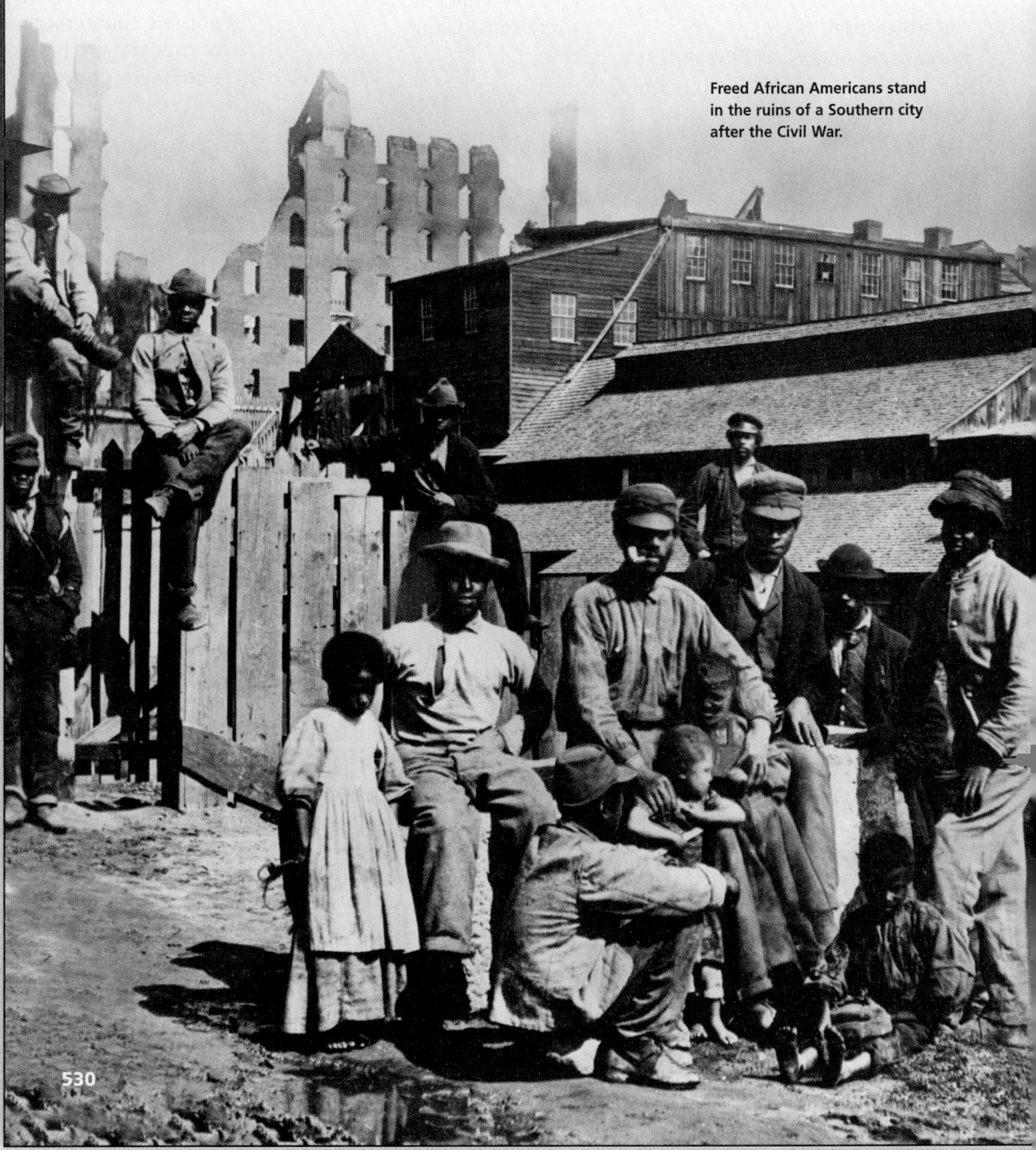

Freed African Americans stand in the ruins of a Southern city after the Civil War.

530

### RECOMMENDED RESOURCES

**BOOKS FOR THE TEACHER**

Campbell, Randolph. ***Grass-Roots Reconstruction in Texas.*** Baton Rouge: Louisiana State U. Pr., 1997. Original research on the economic structures before and after the war.

Foner, Eric. ***Reconstruction: America's Unfinished Revolution, 1863–1877.*** New York: Harper, 1988. Contains new insights into the roles of African Americans in Reconstruction.

Stiles, T. J., compiler and ed. ***In Their Own Words: Robber Barons & Radicals.*** New York: Berkley Pub. Gr., 1997. Varied collection of Reconstruction sources.

**SOFTWARE**

***African-American Experience.*** CD-ROM. Educational Software Institute.

**VIDEOS**

***Richmond: Historic Sights and Haunts.*** Spectre Films, 1992. Battlefields, mansions, monuments, and more.

***Reconstruction and Segregation, 1870–1910.*** Schlessinger Media, 1996. From Lincoln's assassination through the Jim Crow laws.

**INTERNET**

For more about Juneteenth Day, visit www.mcdougallittell.com

## Interact *with* History

In 1874, Congressman Robert B. Elliott of South Carolina made a speech supporting a civil rights bill.
Earlier, former Confederate vice-president Alexander Stephens had spoken against the bill.
Many Southern congressmen ignored Elliott as he spoke.

**The Civil War has just ended, and the Southern states are back in the Union. But the Southern economy is in ruins. Slavery has been abolished. Northerners and Southerners feel deep anger toward one another. As a member of Congress, you must help rebuild the nation.**

### What Do You Think?

- What problems would you face in rebuilding the nation?
- How would you ease tensions between North and South?
- How would you help freed African Americans?

# *How would you rebuild the Union?*

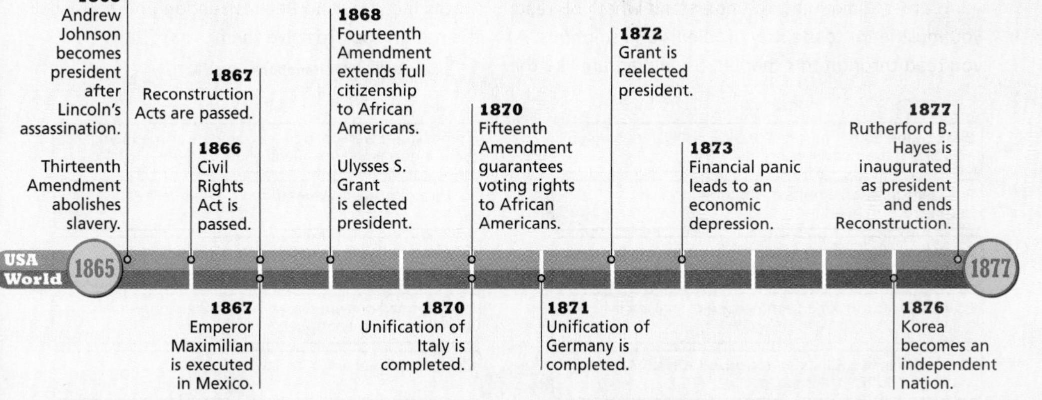

1865 Andrew Johnson becomes president after Lincoln's assassination.
Thirteenth Amendment abolishes slavery.
1867 Reconstruction Acts are passed.
1866 Civil Rights Act is passed.
1868 Fourteenth Amendment extends full citizenship to African Americans.
Ulysses S. Grant is elected president.
1870 Fifteenth Amendment guarantees voting rights to African Americans.
1872 Grant is reelected president.
1873 Financial panic leads to an economic depression.
1877 Rutherford B. Hayes is inaugurated as president and ends Reconstruction.
USA
World
1865
1877
1867 Emperor Maximilian is executed in Mexico.
1870 Unification of Italy is completed.
1871 Unification of Germany is completed.
1876 Korea becomes an independent nation.

## Interact *with* History

### OBJECTIVES

- To help students identify divisions in the country over how to begin Reconstruction and rebuild the nation
- To help students describe possible solutions to the problems involved in rebuilding the nation

### What Do You Think?

1. Have students consider both the physical damage caused by the Civil War and the fundamental changes in society the war brought to the South.
2. Ask students to suggest issues they believe still divided the nation after the war.
3. Ask students to make inferences about attitudes and prejudices that needed to change after the war.

### *How would you rebuild the Union?*

Point out that differences between Northerners and Southerners were so deep that they led to war. Ask students to consider how those differences could complicate proposals for rebuilding the nation. Discuss how such divisions can be healed.

### MAKING PERSONAL CONNECTIONS

Ask students how much they think their opinions about current events and politics are influenced by the region in which they live. Ask them whether they think their opinions might change if they moved to a different region.

### TIME LINE DISCUSSION

**Point out to students that the time line covers the 12 years following the Civil War, known as Reconstruction. Remind them of the bitter feelings among Northerners and Southerners. Remind them, too, that Lincoln has been assassinated. Point out that big changes are taking place in other parts of the world.**

- Ask students to identify the constitutional amendments that resolved the issue of slavery. **Answers** Thirteenth, Fourteenth, and Fifteenth Amendments
- Ask students to identify the year in which federal troops left the South. Then ask students why they think federal troops stayed in the South for ten years. **Answer** 1877; Students may suggest a variety of military or political reasons.
- Ask students to look at the events on the world side of the time line. Ask how the events in Italy and Germany are similar to what has happened in the United States. **Possible Response** Both European nations are now unified, as is the United States.

## BEFORE YOU READ

### Previewing the Theme: Democratic Ideals

Remind students that in his Second Inaugural Address (p. 525), President Lincoln had promised "malice toward none and charity for all" and called for Americans to "bind up the nation's wounds." Ask students whether they think that most Americans would be as forgiving as Lincoln toward those who fought for the other side in the Civil War.

Tell students that the United States still faced difficult problems over rebuilding the devastated South, protecting the rights of African Americans, and overcoming the bitterness between Northerners and white Southerners caused by the Civil War.

### What Do You Know?

Ask students to define the words *reconstruct* and *reconstruction.* Ask students if something that has been broken can be made exactly the same as it was before. Students may want to know if the North and the South ever did overcome their differences.

 **In-Depth Resources: Unit 5**
- Tracing Themes: Democratic Ideals, p. 61

## READ AND TAKE NOTES

### Reading Strategy: Identifying and Solving Problems

Tell students that identifying problems and solutions will help them understand the main issues discussed in the chapter. Ask students to create a diagram similar to the one shown to use as they read the chapter. Encourage them to identify the problems and then look for attempts made by the nation to solve them.

 **In-Depth Resources: Unit 5**
- Setting the Stage, p. 60

 **Critical Thinking Transparency CT52**
- Setting the Stage

# Chapter 18 SETTING THE STAGE

## BEFORE YOU READ

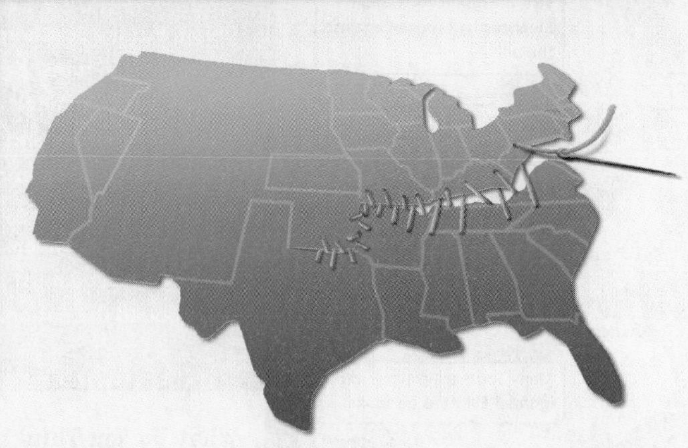

### Previewing the Theme

**Democratic Ideals** After the Union won the war, the nation faced the question of how a democratic government should treat the people who rebelled against it. The Union also faced the question of how to include the millions of freed African Americans in the political process. In this chapter, you will learn how the country struggled to move toward the ideal of equality during Reconstruction.

### What Do You Know?

What do you think it means to reconstruct something? What kinds of things did the U.S. government need to reconstruct after the Civil War? Which of these issues do you think was most important?

**THINK ABOUT**
- what you learned about the Civil War in the last two chapters
- what you've learned about civil rights in the United States from television and movies

### What Do You Want to Know?

What questions do you have about Reconstruction? Record those questions in your notebook before you read this chapter.

## READ AND TAKE NOTES

**Reading Strategy: Identifying and Solving Problems** Sometimes, to understand what you read, you must learn to identify problems and solutions. As you read through this chapter, use a diagram like the one below to take notes on the problems the United States faced during Reconstruction and the actions the nation took to solve them.

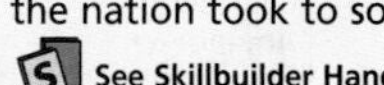
See Skillbuilder Handbook, page R17.

| Problems | Solutions |
|---|---|
| **Black codes** Southern states passed black codes to keep power over former slaves. | Before states were readmitted, Congress made them pass a civil rights amendment and allow black men to vote. |
| **President Johnson** President Johnson blocked Reconstruction measures. | Congress impeached him to remove him from office. |
| **Education** Newly freed African Americans needed an education. | Organizations set up freedmen's schools. |
| **Economy** African Americans needed to make a living. | They farmed on confiscated land, signed work contracts, or sharecropped. |
| **Ku Klux Klan** Ku Klux Klan terrorized African Americans and Republicans. | Congress passed anti-Klan laws. |
| **Voting** Southern states tried to keep African Americans from voting. | Congress passed the Fifteenth Amendment to give them voting rights. |



## TEACHING STRATEGY

### READING THE CHAPTER

This is a thematic chapter focusing on the efforts of the United States to rebuild after the Civil War. Encourage students to note positive and negative changes in attitudes among Americans, political efforts made to improve relations between the North and the South, and attempts to guarantee freedom to African Americans.

### ALTERNATIVE ASSESSMENT

The Chapter Assessment describes three activities for alternative assessment on page 551. You may wish to have students work on these activities during the course of the chapter and then present them at the end.

# 1 Rebuilding the Union

**TERMS & NAMES**
Radical Republicans
Reconstruction
Freedmen's Bureau
Andrew Johnson
black codes
civil rights
Fourteenth Amendment

| MAIN IDEA | WHY IT MATTERS NOW |
|---|---|
| During Reconstruction, the president and Congress fought over how to rebuild the South. | Reconstruction was an important step in the African-American struggle for civil rights. |

## ONE AMERICAN'S STORY

**After the Civil War, Pennsylvania congressman Thaddeus Stevens became a leader of the Radical Republicans. This group of congressmen favored using federal power to create a new order in the South and to promote full citizenship for freed African Americans.**

*A VOICE FROM THE PAST*

The whole fabric of southern society *must* be changed. . . . If the South is ever to be made a safe Republic let her lands be cultivated by the toil of the owners, or the free labor of intelligent citizens.

**Thaddeus Stevens,** quoted in *The Era of Reconstruction* by Kenneth Stampp

**In this section, you will learn how political leaders battled over how to bring the Southern states back into the Union.**

Thaddeus Stevens addresses Congress.

## 1 Reconstruction Begins

After the Civil War ended in 1865, the South faced the challenge of building a new society not based on slavery. The process the federal government used to readmit the Confederate states to the Union is known as **Reconstruction**. Reconstruction lasted from 1865 to 1877.

In his Second Inaugural Address, in March 1865, Lincoln promised to reunify the nation "with malice [harm] toward none, with charity for all." Lincoln's plan included pardoning Confederate officials. It also called for allowing the Confederate states to quickly form new governments and send representatives to Congress.

To assist former slaves, the president established the **Freedmen's Bureau**. This federal agency set up schools and hospitals for African Americans and distributed clothes, food, and fuel throughout the South.

When Lincoln was killed in April 1865, Vice-President **Andrew Johnson** became president. Johnson was a Democrat. The Republicans





## SECTION OBJECTIVES

1. To describe why Reconstruction was needed
2. To analyze the conflict that developed over Reconstruction and identify the goals of Radical Republicans
3. To explain the impact of the Civil Rights Act of 1866 and the Fourteenth Amendment
4. To evaluate the effects of Reconstruction

**CRITICAL THINKING**

Analyzing Causes, p. 534
Making Inferences, p. 535
Finding Main Ideas, p. 536
Drawing Conclusions, p. 537
Evaluating, p. 537

**Why It Matters Now**
- The New South, pp. 35–36

## FOCUS & MOTIVATE

### 5-MINUTE WARM-UP

**Making Inferences** These questions focus on the divisions that remained in the country after the Civil War.

1. Read the quote on page 533. Do you think the speaker is a Southerner? Explain.
2. How do you think most white Southerners would respond to the speaker's plans?

**Warm-Up Transparency WT18**

## INSTRUCT

### INSTRUCT: OBJECTIVE 1

**Reconstruction Begins**

Key Questions
- What challenge did the South face after the Civil War?
- What was Reconstruction?
- What were Johnson's Reconstruction policies?

**In-Depth Resources: Unit 5**
- Guided Reading, p. 62
- Primary Source: Report on the Freedmen's Bureau, p. 69

## RECOMMENDED RESOURCES

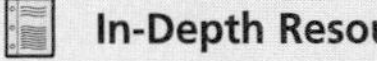

**In-Depth Resources: Unit 5**
- Guided Reading, p. 62
- Building Vocabulary, p. 65
- Primary Source, p. 69
- Reteaching Activity, p. 74

**Reading Study Guide** (Spanish and English), pp. 177–178

**America's History Makers**
- Hiram Revels, pp. 71–72

**Why It Matters Now**
- The New South, pp. 35–36

**Formal Assessment**
- Section Quiz, p. 269

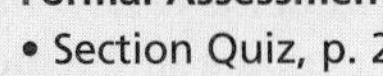

**Alternative Assessment**
- Rubrics, 5.1
- Rubrics, 3.6

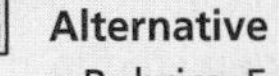

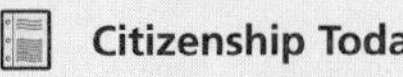

**Citizenship Today**
- Minority Rights, p. 79

**Access for Students Acquiring English/ESL**
- Guided Reading, p. 120

**Technology Resources**

**Critical Thinking Trans. CT53**
- Cause and Effect: Reconstruction

**Humanities Transparency HT35**
- Political Cartoon: A Carpet-bagger Goes South

**Geography Transparency GT18**
- Southern Military Districts, 1867

**Electronic Teacher Tools with Test Maker**

## AMERICA'S HISTORY MAKERS

**Andrew Johnson**

Johnson's first career was as a tailor. His wife taught him how to write and do arithmetic, and he was touchy about his humble beginnings. Johnson was serious and intelligent, but he lacked Lincoln's gift of affability. Many people disliked him strongly. Johnson was elected to the U.S. Senate from Tennessee in 1857. Although he was a Democrat and former slaveholder, he was the only Southern senator to remain loyal to the Union. He was selected as Lincoln's running mate in 1864 to increase the appeal of the Republican ticket to antiwar Democrats.

Possible Response: He may have been sympathetic to Southern slaveholders.

## INSTRUCT: OBJECTIVE 2

**Rebuilding Brings Conflict**

Key Questions

- What policies of new Southern state governments angered Congress?
- How did Congress deal with the Southern states?
- How did the Radical Republicans wish to reorganize the South?

**Geography Transparency GT18**
- Southern Military Districts, 1867

## MORE ABOUT . . .

**Confederate Officials**

Former Confederate president Jefferson Davis spent two years in prison after the Civil War. On his release, he traveled for two years and then worked in various occupations. He died in 1889, never having taken the oath of allegiance to regain his citizenship. However, Congress restored his citizenship in 1978, nearly a century after his death.

Former Confederate vice-president Alexander Stephens won election to Congress in 1866 but was not seated. He later became a journalist and book author and was elected governor of Georgia in 1882. He died in 1883.

**AMERICA'S HISTORY MAKERS**

**ANDREW JOHNSON**
**1808–1875**

Andrew Johnson was a self-educated man whose strong will led to trouble with Congress.

As a former slaveholder from Tennessee, Johnson called for a mild program for bringing the South back into the Union. In particular, he let states decide whether to give voting rights to freed African Americans.

Johnson's policies led to a break with the Radical Republicans in Congress and, finally, to his impeachment trial (see page 537).

**Why might Johnson have chosen not to punish the South?**

had put him on the ticket in 1864 to help win support in the nation's border states. Johnson was a former slaveholder and, unlike Lincoln, a stubborn, unyielding man.

Johnson believed that Reconstruction was the job of the president, not Congress. His policies were based on Lincoln's goals. He insisted that the new state governments ratify the Thirteenth Amendment, which prohibited slavery. He also insisted that they accept the supreme power of the federal government.

Johnson offered amnesty, or official pardon, to most white Southerners. He promised to return their property. In return, they had to pledge loyalty to the United States. At first, the large plantation owners, top military officers, and ex-Confederate leaders were not included in this offer. But they, too, eventually won amnesty.

**Background** Not all Confederate leaders were pardoned. Former Confederate president Jefferson Davis, for example, was imprisoned for treason for two years.

## 2 Rebuilding Brings Conflict

As the Southern states rebuilt, they set up new state governments that seemed very much like the old ones. Some states flatly refused to ratify the Thirteenth Amendment. "This is a white man's government," said the governor of South Carolina, "and intended for white men only."

The Southern states passed laws, known as **black codes,** which limited the freedom of former slaves. In Mississippi, for instance, one law said that African Americans had to have written proof of employment. Anyone without such proof could be put to work on a plantation. African Americans were forbidden to meet in unsupervised groups or carry guns. Because of such laws, many people in the North suspected that white Southerners were trying to bring back the "old South."

**Reading History** **A. Analyzing Causes** What was the main reason Southern states passed black codes?
A. Answer They wanted to return former slaves to their low position in society.

When Congress met in December 1865, its members refused to seat representatives from the South. Many of these Southern representatives had been Confederate leaders only months before.

Under the Constitution, Congress has the right to decide whether its members are qualified to hold office. So instead of admitting the Southerners, Congress set up a committee to study conditions in the South and decide whether the Southern states should be represented. By taking such action, Congress let the president know that it planned to play a role in Reconstruction.

Republicans outnumbered Democrats in both houses of Congress. Most Republicans were moderates who believed that the federal government should stay out of the affairs of individuals and the states.

**Vocabulary** **moderates:** people opposed to extreme views

The Radical Republicans, however, wanted the federal government to play an active role in remaking Southern politics and society. Led by Thaddeus Stevens and Massachusetts senator Charles Sumner, the



**ACTIVITY OPTIONS**

**INTERDISCIPLINARY LINK: CIVICS** — BLOCK SCHEDULING

**POLITICAL CARTOONS**

**Class Time** 45 minutes

**Task** Creating political cartoons about new Southern governments

**Purpose** To illustrate the nature of the Southern governments, the people who ran them, and the laws they passed

**Supplies Needed**
- Art supplies
- Sample political cartoon from a newspaper or magazine

**Activity** Have students create political cartoons about the Southern governments that formed under President Andrew Johnson's Reconstruction policies. Have students review material in the text about the new governments and decide on a single idea to illustrate before beginning their drawings. Remind students to include a descriptive caption with their cartoon. Individuals depicted in the cartoons should be easily identifiable or labeled.

Radical Republicans pose for a formal portrait. Standing (left to right): James F. Wilson, George S. Boutwell, and John A. Logan. Seated: Benjamin F. Butler, Thaddeus Stevens, Thomas Williams, and John A. Bingham.

group also demanded full and equal citizenship for African Americans. Their aim was to destroy the South's old ruling class and turn the region into a place of small farms, free schools, respect for labor, and political equality for all citizens.

## 3 The Civil Rights Act

Urged on by the Radicals, Congress passed a bill promoting **civil rights**—those rights granted to all citizens. The Civil Rights Act of 1866 declared that all persons born in the United States (except Native Americans) were citizens. It also stated that all citizens were entitled to equal rights regardless of their race.

Republicans were shocked when President Johnson vetoed the bill. Johnson argued that federal protection of civil rights would lead "towards centralization" of the national government. He also insisted that making African Americans full citizens would "operate against the white race." Congress voted to override Johnson's veto. That is, two-thirds of the House and two-thirds of the Senate voted for the bill after the president's veto, and the bill became law.

## The Fourteenth Amendment

Republicans were not satisfied with passing laws that ensured equal rights. They wanted equality to be protected by the Constitution itself. To achieve this goal, Congress proposed the **Fourteenth Amendment** in 1866. It stated that all people born in the United States were citizens and had the same rights. All citizens were to be granted "equal protection of the laws." However, the amendment did not establish black suffrage. Instead, it declared that any state that kept African Americans from voting would lose representatives in Congress. This meant that the Southern states would have less power if they did not grant black men the vote.

*Reading History*

**B. Making Inferences** How did the Fourteenth Amendment encourage states to give African Americans the vote?

**B. Answer** It gave the states fewer representatives in Congress if they kept African Americans from voting.

Johnson refused to support the amendment. So did every former Confederate state except Tennessee. This rejection outraged both moderate and Radical Republicans. As a result, the two groups agreed to join forces and passed the Reconstruction Acts of 1867. The passage of these



### MORE ABOUT . . .

**Thaddeus Stevens**

Thaddeus Stevens was a passionate opponent of slavery and supporter of the rights of African Americans. Stevens directed that he be buried among African Americans in a Pennsylvania cemetery after he died. His tombstone carried his own words: "I have chosen this that I might illustrate in my death the principles which I advocated through a long life, Equality of Man before his Creator."

### INSTRUCT: OBJECTIVE 

**The Civil Rights Act/ The Fourteenth Amendment**

Key Questions

- What were the provisions of the Civil Rights Act of 1866 and the Fourteenth Amendment?
- What was the effect of opposition to civil rights legislation?
- What were the provisions of the Reconstruction Act of 1867?

 **Citizenship Today**

- Minority Rights, p. 79

### CRITICAL THINKING ACTIVITY

**Comparing** Copy the chart below on the board. Ask students to complete it, adding details that explain the differences between Johnson's positions and opinions and those of the Radical Republicans.

| | Johnson | Radical Republicans |
|---|---|---|
| Role of government in Reconstruction | | |
| Civil Rights Act of 1866 | | |
| Fourteenth Amendment | | |

**Class Time** 20 minutes

### ACTIVITY OPTIONS

**MULTIPLE LEARNING STYLES: LINGUISTIC** — BLOCK SCHEDULING

**"JEOPARDY" QUESTIONS**

**Class Time** One class period

**Task** Creating questions about Reconstruction immediately after the Civil War

**Purpose** To synthesize information about the early years of Reconstruction

**Supplies Needed**

- Index cards

**Activity** Ask students to write the names of people, events, and concepts on index cards. On the back of each card they should write identifying phrases or definitions for the name or term on the front. Divide the class into teams. Read each definition or phrase. Teams must ask the question for which the phrase or definition is the answer. For example, for "Andrew Johnson," a team might ask, "Who became president after Lincoln?" Students may keep their cards as study aids.

**INSTRUCT: OBJECTIVE** 

**The New Southern Governments/ Johnson Is Impeached**

Key Questions

- What groups controlled the drafting of new state constitutions in the South in 1867?
- What were the effects of the new state constitutions?
- Why was President Johnson impeached? What was the verdict in the impeachment?

 **Humanities Transparency HT35**

- Political Cartoon: A Carpetbagger Goes South

### HISTORY through ART

**Interpreting the Painting** Thomas Waterman Wood (1823–1903) chronicled life in America during a career that spanned the last half of the 1800s. He was fascinated by the growing cultural diversity of the United States, and often included people from a variety of racial and ethnic backgrounds in his paintings. Wood depicted African Americans in a number of his works, as in the one called *To the Polls.* Many of Wood's paintings are exhibited at the T. W. Wood Gallery and Arts Center in Montpelier, Vermont, where he was born.

**Possible Responses: hopeful, joyous, serious, nervous, uncertain**

### MORE ABOUT . . .

**Hiram Revels**

Revels, a minister and educator, filled the unexpired term of Jefferson Davis in the United States Senate. Opponents tried to block his seating in 1870. They argued that since Revels had only become a citizen with the passage of the Fourteenth Amendment in 1866, he did not meet the nine years of citizenship required by the Constitution. Nevertheless, Revels was seated by a Senate vote of 48 to 8.

 **America's History Makers**

- Hiram Revels, pp. 71–72

acts began a period known as Radical Reconstruction. From this point on, Congress controlled Reconstruction.

One of the Reconstruction Acts of 1867 divided the South into five military districts, each run by an army commander. Members of the ruling class before the war lost their voting rights. The law also stated that before the Southern states could reenter the Union, they would have to do two things:

1. They must approve new state constitutions that gave the vote to all adult men, including African Americans.
2. They must ratify the Fourteenth Amendment.

**Background** Attempts to secure voting rights for African Americans applied only to men. Women were not allowed to vote until 1919.

## 4 The New Southern Governments

In 1867, Southern voters chose delegates to draft their new state constitutions. About three-fourths of the delegates were Republicans. About half of the Republicans were poor white farmers. Angry at planters for starting what they called the "rich man's war," these delegates were called scalawags (scoundrels) for going along with Radical Reconstruction.

Another one-fourth of the Republican delegates were known as carpetbaggers—white Northerners who had rushed to the South after the war. Many Southerners accused them, often unfairly, of seeking only to get rich or gain political power.

**Background** Carpetbaggers were said to have headed south carrying only a cheap suitcase, known as a carpetbag.

African Americans made up the rest of the Republican delegates. Of these, half had been free before the war. Most were ministers, teachers, or skilled workers. About 80 percent of them could read.

### HISTORY through ART

*His First Vote,* an 1868 oil painting by Thomas Waterman Wood, shows a new African-American voter.

**How do you think the man felt about voting?**

The new constitutions written by these delegates set up public schools and gave the vote to all adult males. By 1870, voters in all the Southern states had approved their new constitutions. As a result, the former Confederate states were let back into the Union and allowed to send representatives to Congress.

During Reconstruction, more than 600 African Americans served in state legislatures throughout the South, and 14 of the new U.S. congressmen from the South were African Americans. Two African Americans served as U.S. senators during this time. One was Hiram Revels of Mississippi, a minister in the African Methodist Episcopal Church. He had recruited African Americans to fight for the Union during the Civil War.

**C. Answer** Several African Americans were elected to Congress, while hundreds gained seats in state legislatures.

**Reading History**

**C. Finding Main Ideas** What political gains did African Americans make during Reconstruction?

536

### ACTIVITY OPTIONS

### INDIVIDUAL NEEDS: GIFTED AND TALENTED

**DEBATING RECONSTRUCTION**

**Class Time** Two class periods

**Task** Debating the merits of the rival Reconstruction policies

**Purpose** To analyze rival Reconstruction policies

**Supplies Needed**

- Reference materials on Reconstruction
- Internet access
- Two podiums, chairs for debaters, desk for moderator

**Activity** Organize students into two teams, one supporting the Reconstruction policies of President Andrew Johnson and the other supporting the policies of the Radical Republicans. Have students on both teams research specific Reconstruction policies and prepare material for a debate. The teams should debate which policies treated Southern whites and African Americans most fairly and were best for rebuilding the South.

## Johnson Is Impeached

President Johnson fought against many of Congress's reform efforts during Radical Reconstruction. For instance, he chose people friendly to ex-Confederates to serve as military commanders in the South. The conflict between Johnson and Congress soon brought a showdown.

In 1867, Congress passed the Tenure of Office Act, which prohibited the president from firing government officials without the Senate's approval. In February 1868, Johnson fired his secretary of war, Edwin Stanton, over disagreements about Reconstruction. Three days later, the House of Representatives voted to impeach the president. This means that the House formally accused him of improper conduct while in office. By removing Johnson from office, they hoped to strengthen Congress's role in Reconstruction.

This is a ticket to the 1868 impeachment trial of President Johnson.

*Reading* **History**

**D. Drawing Conclusions** Why did Congress decide to impeach President Johnson?

D. Answer Congress believed that Johnson stood in the way of its Reconstruction plans.

The case moved to the Senate for a trial. After several weeks of testimony, the senators prepared to vote. George Julian, a 20-year congressman from Indiana, recalled the tension in the air.

*A VOICE FROM THE PAST*

The galleries were packed, and an indescribable anxiety was written on every face. Some of the members of the House near me grew pale and sick under the burden of suspense. Such stillness prevailed that the breathing in the galleries could be heard at the announcement of each Senator's voice.

**George Julian,** quoted in *Grand Inquests*

**Vocabulary**
**acquitted:** cleared of a charge

In the end, President Johnson was acquitted by a single vote. But much work remained to be done in rebuilding the South. In the next section, you will learn how African Americans in the South worked to improve their lives.

### Section 1 Assessment

**1. Terms & Names**

**Identify:**
- Radical Republicans
- Reconstruction
- Freedmen's Bureau
- Andrew Johnson
- black codes
- civil rights
- Fourteenth Amendment

**2. Taking Notes**

Use a diagram to review the events that led to Johnson's impeachment.

Event 1 → Event 2 → Event 3 → Event 4

Which event seems most important and why?

**3. Main Ideas**

a. What was Lincoln's Reconstruction plan?

b. How did white Southerners plan to restore the "old South"?

c. What impact did the Reconstruction Acts of 1867 have on the South?

**4. Critical Thinking**

**Evaluating** Do you think the House was justified in impeaching President Johnson? Why or why not?

**THINK ABOUT**
- the clash over Reconstruction policies
- Congress's motives for impeaching Johnson

**ACTIVITY OPTIONS**

**TECHNOLOGY**
**SPEECH**

Research an African American who served in Congress during Reconstruction. Design his Internet **home page,** or make a **speech** about his accomplishments.



### MORE ABOUT . . .

**Johnson's Impeachment**

The one vote that acquitted Andrew Johnson was cast by Senator Edmund Ross of Kansas, a Republican. Ross voted against his party, along with six other Republicans, and paid the price. Ross was not reelected, and he died in poverty. John F. Kennedy included Ross in his book *Profiles in Courage* and said that Ross "may well have preserved for ourselves and our posterity constitutional government in the United States."

### MORE ABOUT . . .

**Presidential Impeachment**

Andrew Johnson's impeachment was the first and only impeachment of a president until 1998, when Congress impeached President Bill Clinton on charges that he had committed perjury in his testimony before a grand jury and obstructed justice in an investigation into his relationship with a former White House intern. As with Johnson in 1868, the Senate failed to convict Clinton in 1999.

## ASSESS & RETEACH

**Setting the Stage** Have students fill in the first two rows of the graphic organizer.

**Formal Assessment**
- Section Quiz, p. 269

**Critical Thinking Transparency CT52**
- Setting the Stage

**RETEACHING ACTIVITY**

Have students create annotated time lines for important events discussed in this section. The time lines should include information about the beginning of Reconstruction, the Civil Rights Act, the Fourteenth Amendment, and the important events and debate over the new order in the South and Johnson's impeachment.

**In-Depth Resources: Unit 5**
- Reteaching Activity, p. 74

### Section 1 Assessment

**1. Terms & Names**

**Radical Republicans,** p. 533
**Reconstruction,** p. 533
**Freedmen's Bureau,** p. 533
**Andrew Johnson,** p. 533
**black codes,** p. 534
**civil rights,** p. 535
**Fourteenth Amendment,** p. 535

**2. Taking Notes**

Event 1: Vetoed Civil Rights Act
Event 2: Did not support Fourteenth Amendment
Event 3: Chose pro-Confederate military commanders
Event 4: Fired Secretary Stanton
Ranking of events will vary.

**3. Main Ideas**

**a.** pardoning Confederate officials; allowing Confederate states to form new governments and send officials to Congress **b.** "black codes" or laws to return former slaves to plantation labor **c.** It divided the South into five military districts, and Southern whites lost their voting rights.

**4. Critical Thinking**

Answers will vary. Be sure students support their opinions.

**ACTIVITY OPTIONS**

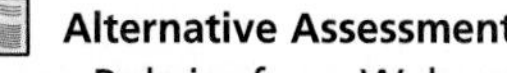

**Alternative Assessment**
- Rubrics for a Web page, 5.1
- Rubrics for a speech, 3.6

*Interdisciplinary* **CHALLENGE**

**OBJECTIVE**
Students will work cooperatively to solve planning and public safety challenges faced by people in Richmond, Virginia, after the Civil War.

 **BLOCK SCHEDULING**

## PROCEDURE

Gather supplies that students might need, such as posterboard and colored markers. For each challenge, have students form groups of three or four. Ask group members to divide the work among themselves. Then have them choose an option for presenting their solution to each challenge.

### ARTS CHALLENGE

**Class Time** 50 minutes

Suggest that students visit the downtown area of their city or town or one nearby. Tell them to sketch a simple block map for one or two blocks and label the buildings and businesses. As an alternative, encourage students to find library books that have pictures of downtown areas in cities.

**POSSIBLE SOLUTIONS**
Student models or proposals might include the following:
- A variety of stores and services drawn from the list on page 539
- A system of streets and bridges

*Interdisciplinary* **CHALLENGE**

# Rebuilding Richmond

You live in Richmond, Virginia, the capital of the Confederacy. It is 1865, and the South faces defeat in the Civil War. On April 2, Confederate officials set fire to supplies in Richmond to prevent the approaching Union army from using them. The fire spreads out of control and destroys downtown Richmond. The next day, Union troops march into the city and take command. You must now help rebuild the city.

COOPERATIVE LEARNING On this page are two challenges you face as a resident of Richmond. Working with a small group, decide how to solve one of these problems. Divide the work among the group members. You will find useful information in the Data File. Be prepared to present your solutions to the class.

This picture shows a street in Richmond before the fire.

### ARTS CHALLENGE

***"We want the burnt district of Richmond to . . . sit proudly again."***

**The smell of charred wood still floats in the breeze. However, spirit and determination fill the air. Warehouses are opening. Newly cleared streets bustle with activity. The rebuilding of Richmond has begun. How would you design one block of Richmond's new downtown business district? Use the Data File for help. Then present your plan using one of these options:**

- Make a model of your new city block.
- Create a written proposal with a rough sketch to illustrate.



## STANDARDS FOR EVALUATION

### ARTS CHALLENGE

**Option 1** Models should
- include a variety of buildings and businesses.
- include labels for buildings.

**Option 2** Proposals should
- describe buildings and businesses on the new block.
- include a rough sketch showing the location of buildings and labels for them.

### CIVICS CHALLENGE

**Option 1** The town meeting should
- clearly establish the problem.
- provide clear, practical solutions.

**Option 2** Emergency laws should
- be practical.
- address specific problems.
- be accompanied by proposals for publicizing them.

### HEALTH CHALLENGE

**Option 1** Letters should
- include requests for specific food items.
- clearly state the request and describe the need.

**Option 2** Flyers should
- state plans clearly.
- be attractive and easy to read.

## DATA FILE

### THE BURNT DISTRICT
- about $30 million damage
- 20 city blocks destroyed, including 900 buildings

**Destroyed Property**
all banks, 20 law offices, 24 grocery stores, 36 merchant shops, 2 carriage factories, 2 paper mills, 7 book and stationery stores, 2 train depots, 3 bridges, a church, a machine shop, a tin shop, a pottery factory, several flour mills and printing offices

**Surviving Property**
capitol and city hall, residential areas, ironworks

### EMERGENCY SERVICES
**Union Army**
- distributes 13,000 food rations
- provides medical help
- guards homes; patrols streets

**American Union Commission**
- hands out food tickets
- distributes 80,000 pounds of flour; feeds soup to 800 people a day
- provides garden seeds and sells shovels at cost to farmers

### REBUILDING
**April 1865**
- rubble is cleared
- markets sell meat, fish, produce
- hotels and bakeries open
- one bridge is rebuilt

**May 1865**
- two banks open
- gas and telegraph service is restored
- river opens to steamboat traffic

**Summer 1865**
- horse-drawn buses operate
- city government is reinstated

**Fall 1865**
- ironworks reopens
- 100 buildings are now under construction

Visit www.mcdougallittell.com to learn more about Reconstruction.

### CIVICS CHALLENGE

*"Open robberies have been perpetrated."*

**Robberies and assaults are commonplace, especially in the burnt area of the downtown. Groups of orphaned children also roam the city, picking pockets to support themselves. Union military police supposedly protect the public. However, soldiers sometimes commit crimes themselves. What would you do to improve public safety? Use the Data File for help. Present your ideas using one of these options:**

- **Hold a town meeting to explore possible solutions.**
- **Create a set of emergency laws, with plans for publicizing them.**

### ACTIVITY WRAP-UP

**Meet as a group to review your responses to rebuilding Richmond. Pick your most creative solution and present it to the class.**

539

### CIVICS CHALLENGE

**Class Time** 50 minutes

Suggest that students make rules for the town meeting and appoint a moderator. Have them copy the decision-making chart in the Citizenship Handbook, page 285, and use it to help them on needed emergency laws. Remind them that Union troops are the most likely enforcers of the new laws.

### POSSIBLE SOLUTIONS

Students' suggestions for town meeting and emergency laws might include the following:
- Appointing city officials
- Curfews to limit the hours people may be on the street
- Supplies of food and clothing for the needy

### ALTERNATIVE ACTIVITY

### HEALTH CHALLENGE

*"there is nothing in the markets but a few small fish"*

**Thousands of war veterans, former slaves, Yankee traders, and newspaper reporters flood Richmond after the South's defeat. However, 80 percent of the city's food supply is lost in the fire. Now, half of Richmond's residents, including many of these newcomers, rely on charity for food. You want to help the rescue effort. Use the Data File for help. Then present your information using one of these options:**

- **Write a letter asking for donations, being specific about the kind of food you need.**
- **Create a flyer describing your plans to distribute food.**

### ACTIVITY WRAP-UP

To help student groups evaluate the creativity of their models, presentations, and proposals, ask them to make a grid with criteria like the one shown. Then have them rate each solution on a scale from 1 to 5.

- Practicality 1 2 3 4 5
- Effectiveness 1 2 3 4 5
- Creativity 1 2 3 4 5

## SECTION OBJECTIVES

1. To describe the responses of African Americans to freedom
2. To trace the establishment of African-American schools
3. To evaluate the impact of land reform, sharecropping, and the contract system
4. To describe the development of the Ku Klux Klan

**CRITICAL THINKING**

Analyzing Causes, pp. 541, 544
Finding Main Ideas, pp. 541, 544
Analyzing Points of View, p. 542
Recognizing Effects, p. 543

## FOCUS & MOTIVATE

### 5-MINUTE WARM-UP

**Making Inferences** These questions focus on changes in the lives of African Americans in the South.

1. Look at the "America's Heritage" feature and photograph on page 541. Why do you think building schools was a priority for newly freed African Americans?
2. What other needs do you think African Americans had after slavery ended?

 **Warm-Up Transparency WT18**

## INSTRUCT

### INSTRUCT: OBJECTIVE 1

**Responding to Freedom**

Key Questions

- Why did many newly freed African Americans leave plantations?
- How did freedom allow African Americans to strengthen family ties?

 **In-Depth Resources: Unit 5**
- Guided Reading, p. 63
- Building Vocabulary, p. 65

 **Reading Study Guide** (Spanish and English), pp. 179–180

# 2 Reconstruction and Daily Life

**TERMS & NAMES**
freedmen's school
sharecropping
Ku Klux Klan
lynch

| MAIN IDEA | WHY IT MATTERS NOW |
|---|---|
| As the South rebuilt, millions of newly freed African Americans worked to improve their lives. | Many important African-American institutions, including colleges, began during Reconstruction. |

### ONE AMERICAN'S STORY

**One day, as the Civil War came to a close, two enslaved women named Mill and Jule saw a fleet of Union gunboats coming up the Mississippi River. Yankee soldiers came ashore and offered them and other slaves passage aboard their boats. On that day, Mill and Jule left the plantation where they had toiled for so long.**

*A VOICE FROM THE PAST*

An' we all got on the boat in a hurry . . . we all give three times three cheers for the gunboat boys, and three times three cheers for big Yankee [soldiers], an' three times three cheers for gov'ment; an' I tell you every one of us, big and little, cheered loud and long and strong, an' made the old river just ring ag'in.

**Mill and Jule,** quoted in *We Are Your Sisters*

Freed people and a federal soldier pose on a South Carolina plantation.

**The Union's victory in the Civil War spelled the end of slavery in America and a new beginning for the nation's millions of newly freed African Americans. In this section, you will learn about the gains and setbacks of former slaves during Reconstruction.**

## 1 Responding to Freedom

African Americans' first reaction to freedom was to leave the plantations. No longer needing passes to travel, they journeyed throughout the region. "Right off colored folks started on the move," recalled one freedman. "They seemed to want to get closer to freedom, so they'd know what it was—like it was a place or a city." Some former slaves returned to the places where they were born. Others went looking for more economic opportunity. Still others traveled just because they could.

African Americans also traveled in search of family members separated from them during slavery. One man walked 600 miles from Georgia to North Carolina to find his family. To locate relatives, people placed advertisements in newspapers. The Freedmen's Bureau helped many families reunite. A Union officer wrote in 1865, "Men are taking



### RECOMMENDED RESOURCES

 **In-Depth Resources: Unit 5**
- Guided Reading, p. 63
- Building Vocabulary, p. 65
- Geography Application: The Economic Effects of the Civil War, 1860–1880, pp. 67–68
- Primary Source, p. 70
- Literature Selection, pp. 71–73
- Reteaching Activity, p. 75

 **Reading Study Guide** (Spanish and English), pp. 179–180

**America's History Makers**
- General Oliver O. Howard, pp. 73–74

**Formal Assessment**
- Section Quiz, p. 270

 **Alternative Assessment**
- Rubrics, 3.6
- Rubrics, 1.11

 **Access for Students Acquiring English/ESL**
- Guided Reading, p. 121
- Geography Application, pp. 124–125

**Technology Resources**

 **Electronic Teacher Tools with Test Maker**

 **ClassZone**
www.mcdougallittell.com

*Reading* **History**

**A. Analyzing Causes** For what reasons did former slaves move?

**A. Answer** They moved to find economic opportunity, to locate family members, and merely to experience the freedom of traveling.

their wives and children, families which had been for a long time broken up are united and oh! such happiness."

Freedom allowed African Americans to strengthen their family ties. Former slaves could marry legally. They could raise families without fearing that their children might be sold. Many families adopted children of dead relatives and friends to keep family ties strong.

## 2 Starting Schools

With freedom, African Americans no longer had to work for an owner's benefit. They could now work to provide for their families. To reach their goal of economic independence, however, most had to learn to read and write. As a result, children and adults flocked to **freedmen's schools** set up to educate newly freed African Americans. Such schools were started by the Freedmen's Bureau, Northern missionary groups, and African-American organizations. Freed people in cities held classes in warehouses, billiard rooms, and former slave markets. In rural areas, classes were held in churches and houses. Children who went to school often taught their parents to read at home.

*Reading* **History**

**B. Finding Main Ideas** Why did freed people desire an education?

**B. Answer** They saw it as a key to economic independence.

In the years after the war, African-American groups raised more than $1 million for education. However, the federal government and private groups in the North paid most of the cost of building schools and hiring teachers. Between 1865 and 1870, the Freedmen's Bureau spent $5 million for this purpose.

**Background**

Most African Americans were illiterate because teaching slaves to read and write had been illegal.

More than 150,000 African-American students were attending 3,000 schools by 1869. About 10 percent of the South's African-American adults could read. A number of them became teachers. Northern teachers, black and white, also went South to teach freed people. Many white Southerners, however, worked against these teachers' efforts. White racists even killed teachers and burned freedmen's schools in some parts of the South. Despite these setbacks, African Americans kept working toward an education.

### *America's* HERITAGE

**BLACK COLLEGES**

Some of today's African-American colleges and universities date back to Reconstruction. The Freedmen's Bureau and other societies raised funds to build many of the schools. Howard University, shown in this photograph, opened in 1867. It was named for General Oliver Otis Howard, head of the Freedmen's Bureau. During Reconstruction, these colleges offered courses ranging from basic reading and writing to medicine and law. They also trained much-needed teachers.

541

### MORE ABOUT . . .

**Responding to Freedom**

Before emancipation, Southern African Americans usually worshiped in separate sections of white churches or held services of their own in secret. Soon after emancipation, African Americans founded their own independent churches, often branches of the Baptist and Methodist churches, throughout the South. Ministers of African-American churches were expected to be community leaders and held great status.

### INSTRUCT: OBJECTIVE 

**Starting Schools**

Key Questions

- Why was education an important goal for African Americans?
- Who aided and who opposed education for African Americans in the South?

### *America's* HERITAGE

**Black Colleges**

The first institution of higher education founded for African Americans was Lincoln University in Chester County, Pennsylvania. The first permanent building for African-American education in the South is Jubilee Hall of Fisk University in Nashville, Tennessee. It was paid for by the profits of the Jubilee Singers, a group of student musicians who introduced the spiritual as an art form to audiences around the world.

 **America's History Makers**
- General Oliver O. Howard, pp. 73–74

### ACTIVITY OPTIONS

**MULTIPLE LEARNING STYLES: INTRAPERSONAL** — BLOCK SCHEDULING

**A LETTER ABOUT FREEDOM**

**Class Time** 30 minutes

**Task** Writing a letter from an African American in the South about life after the Civil War

**Purpose** To apply information about ways the lives of African Americans changed after the war

**Supplies Needed**
- Writing paper

**Activity** Have students write a letter from an African American in one part of the South to a friend or relative in another state. Letters should mention emancipation and one or more of the following topics: efforts to locate family members, freedmen's schools, and plans for the future. Have students either read their letters aloud to the class or post them on the bulletin board.

 **In-Depth Resources: Unit 5**
- Primary Source: A Letter to Colonel P. H. Anderson, p. 70

**INSTRUCT: OBJECTIVE** 

**40 Acres and a Mule/The Contract System/ Sharecropping and Debt**

Key Questions

- Why did many Americans want land reform in the South? What happened to proposals for land reform?
- How did the contract system and sharecropping operate?
- What were the drawbacks of the contract system and sharecropping?
- How did reliance on cotton production contribute to poverty in the Deep South?

 **In-Depth Resources: Unit 5**

- Geography Application: The Economic Effects of the Civil War, 1860–1880, pp. 67–68
- Literature Selection: from *Forty Acres and Maybe a Mule* by Harriette Gillem, p. 71

**MORE ABOUT . . .**

**Land in South Carolina**

The former owners of plantations on the South Carolina sea islands fled during the war, while their slaves stayed behind. After the war, these former slaves hoped to begin farming on small plots of land. However, when federal agents sold the plantations for back taxes, the land was divided into large and expensive tracts more suitable for growing cotton than for family farms. Investors from the North bought 90 percent of the close to 17,000 acres sold. By pooling their money, African Americans managed to purchase about 2,000 acres.

African–American families hoped to own land but were often disappointed.

## 3 40 Acres and a Mule

More than anything else, freed people wanted to own land. As one freedman said, "Give us our own land and we take care of ourselves, but without land, the old masters can hire us or starve us, as they please."

As the Civil War ended, General William T. Sherman suggested that abandoned land in coastal South Carolina be split into 40-acre parcels and given to freedmen. The rumor then spread that all freedmen would get 40 acres and a mule. Most African Americans thought they deserved at least that much. In the end, however, most freedmen never received land. Those who did often had to return it to its former owners after the owners were pardoned by President Johnson. One freedman, Bayley Wyat, protested.

*A VOICE FROM THE PAST*

Our wives, our children, our husbands, [have] been sold over and over again to purchase the lands we now [locate] upon; for that reason we have a divine right to the land. . . . And then didn't we clear the land, and raise the crops of corn, of cotton, of tobacco, of rice, of sugar, of everything.

**Bayley Wyat,** quoted in *Reconstruction: America's Unfinished Revolution*

C. Possible Responses Land would keep them from depending on their former owners; they deserved the land for having worked on it for so long without pay.

Radical Republican leaders Thaddeus Stevens and Charles Sumner pushed to make land reform part of the Reconstruction Acts of 1867. Stevens proposed a plan to Congress that would have taken land from plantation owners and given it to freed people.

Many moderate Republicans and even some Radicals were against the plan. They believed that new civil and voting rights were enough to give African Americans a better life.

*Reading* **History**

**C. Analyzing Points of View** What were some arguments in favor of giving land to freed people?

Supporters of the plan argued that civil rights meant little without economic independence. Land could provide that independence, they claimed. However, Congress did not pass the land-reform plan.

## The Contract System

Without their own property, many African Americans returned to work on plantations. They returned not as slaves but as wage earners. They and the planters both had trouble getting used to this new relationship. "It seems humiliating to be compelled to bargain and haggle with our own servants about wages," wrote the daughter of a Georgia plantation owner. For their part, many freed workers assumed that wages were extra. They thought that the planters still had to house and feed them.

**Background** Civil War deaths and the departure of slaves from plantations created a labor shortage in the South.

After the Civil War, planters desperately needed workers to raise cotton, still the South's main cash crop. African Americans reacted to this demand for labor by choosing the best contract offers. The contract system was far better than slavery. African Americans could decide whom to work for, and planters could not abuse them or split up families.

The contract system still had drawbacks, however. Even the best contracts paid very low wages. Workers often could not leave the plantations



**ACTIVITY OPTIONS**

**INTERDISCIPLINARY LINK: LANGUAGE ARTS**

**A DIALOGUE DURING RECONSTRUCTION**

**Class Time** 30 minutes

**Task** Writing a dialogue

**Purpose** To understand the options available to African Americans in the South after the Civil War

**Supplies Needed**

- Reference materials about Reconstruction

**Activity** Have students work in pairs to write a dialogue between two African Americans after the Civil War. The dialogue should deal with how the two characters will support themselves. It should mention any skills the characters may possess, any money available to them, where they would like to settle, and where they most likely will go. Have the pairs read their dialogues to the class, then make generalizations about the options available to African Americans after the Civil War.

1 Sharecropper is provided land and seed. In exchange, he promises landowner half the crop.

2 Sharecropper buys food and clothing on credit from landowner's store.

3 Sharecropper plants and harvests crop.

4 Sharecropper gives landowner crop to sell. Sharecropper will get half the earnings, minus the cost of his purchases for the year.

5 When settling up, landowner says that sharecropper owes more than he has earned.

6 To pay debt, sharecropper must promise landowner a greater share of next year's crop.

By the time sharecroppers had shared their crops and paid their debts, they rarely had any money left. Often they were uneducated and could not argue with landowners or merchants who cheated them. A sharecropper frequently became tied to one plantation, having no choice but to work until his debts were paid.

without permission. Many owners cheated workers out of wages and other benefits. Worse yet, laws punished workers for breaking their contracts, even if the plantation owners were abusing or cheating them. These drawbacks made many African Americans turn to sharecropping.

## Sharecropping and Debt

Under the **sharecropping** system, a worker rented a plot of land to farm. The landowner provided the tools, seed, and housing. When harvest time came, the sharecropper gave the landowner a share of the crop. This system gave families without land a place to farm and gave landowners cheap labor.

But problems soon arose with the sharecropping system. One cause of these problems was that farmers and landowners had opposite goals. Farmers wanted to grow food to feed their families, but landowners forced them to grow cash crops, such as cotton. As a result, farmers had to buy food from the local store—which was usually owned by the landlord. Most farmers did not have the money to pay for goods. As a result, many were caught in a cycle of debt, as shown in the diagram above. Often farmers had to use one year's harvest to pay the previous year's bills.

*Reading* **History**

**D. Recognizing Effects** What were some problems with the sharecropping system?

D. Possible Responses
Farmers could not feed themselves under it and were caught in a cycle of debt.

White farmers also became sharecroppers. Many had lost their land in the war. Others had lost it to taxes. By 1880, one-third of the white farmers in the Deep South worked someone else's land.

No matter who worked the plantations, much of what they grew was cotton. After the war, the value of cotton dropped. Southern planters responded by trying to produce more of the cash crop—a move that





### HISTORY FROM VISUALS

**Reading the Diagram** Ask students how they think this cycle worked to the advantage of plantation owners. Then ask students to explain what happens in the sharecropper cycle of poverty when the crop yield is very low. **Possible Answers** Owners could rely on farmers who were tied to the plantation. Also, owners could shift the cost of supplies to the sharecroppers. Farmers became even poorer.

**Extension** Ask students to think of ways the sharecroppers might have broken the cycle.

### CRITICAL THINKING ACTIVITY

**Analyzing Causes and Recognizing Effects**
Help students create a cause-and-effect chart on the board to analyze the ways reliance on cotton farming contributed to longtime poverty in the rural South.

**Class Time** 15 minutes

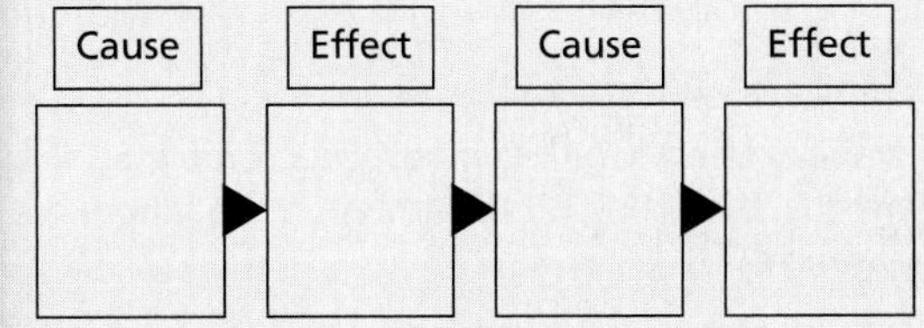


### ACTIVITY OPTIONS

### INDIVIDUAL NEEDS

#### LESS PROFICIENT READERS

**Comparing and Contrasting** To help students understand the differences between the contract system and sharecropping, encourage them to look at the benefits and the drawbacks of each system as they read. You might want to guide students in creating a chart such as the one shown.

| | Contract System | Sharecropping System |
|---|---|---|
| **Benefits** | Earn wages for work<br>Decide who to work for<br>Families stay together | |
| **Drawbacks** | Low wages<br>Can't leave without permission<br>Often cheated, abused by owners | |

**INSTRUCT: OBJECTIVE 4**

**The Ku Klux Klan**

Key Questions
- What were the goals and tactics of the Ku Klux Klan?
- Why was the Klan successful?
- How did the actions of the Klan benefit the Democratic Party?

**MORE ABOUT . . .**

**The Ku Klux Klan**

The Ku Klux Klan was founded at Pulaski, Tennessee, in 1866. Its first leader, called the "Grand Wizard," was Nathan Bedford Forrest, who had been a Confederate general.

Historians believe *klux* is derived from a Greek word—*kyklos*—that means "circle" or "band." The *Ku* and *Klan* apparently were added for the alliteration.

## ASSESS & RETEACH

**Setting the Stage** Have students complete the third, fourth, and fifth rows on the graphic organizer.

**Formal Assessment**
- Section Quiz, p. 270

**RETEACHING ACTIVITY**

Copy the graphic organizer below on the board. Have students complete the web with details from the chapter.

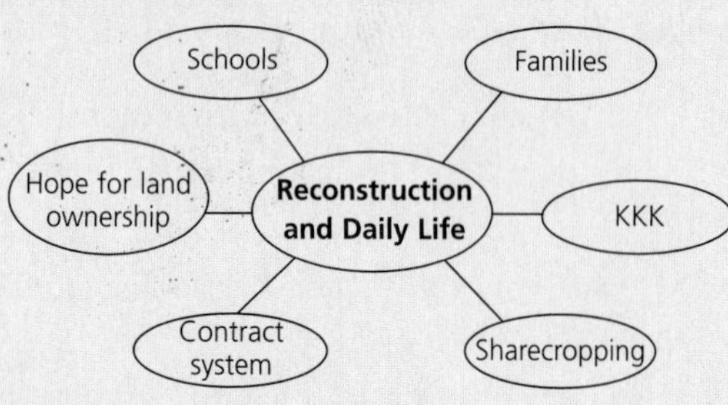


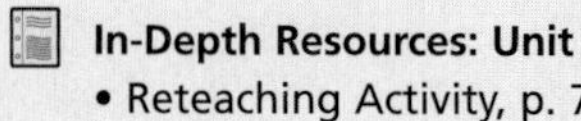

**In-Depth Resources: Unit 5**
- Reteaching Activity, p. 75

drove down prices even further. Growing cotton exhausted the soil and reduced the amount of land available for food crops. As a result, the South had to import half its food. Relying on cotton was one reason the Deep South experienced years of rural poverty.

## 4 The Ku Klux Klan

African Americans in the South faced other problems besides poverty. They also faced violent racism. Many planters and former Confederate soldiers did not want African Americans to have more rights. In 1866, such feelings spurred the rise of a secret group called the **Ku Klux Klan**. The Klan's goals were to restore Democratic control of the South and keep former slaves powerless.

*Reading***History**

**E. Finding Main Ideas** What were the goals of the Ku Klux Klan?

E. Answer Its goals were to restore Democratic control in the South and keep African Americans from gaining power.

These Ku Klux Klan members were arrested after an 1868 riot in Alabama.

The Klan attacked African Americans. Often it targeted those who owned land or had become prosperous. Klansmen rode on horseback and dressed in white robes and hoods. They beat people and burned homes. They even **lynched** some victims, killing them on the spot without a trial as punishment for a supposed crime. The Klan also attacked white Republicans.

Klan victims had little protection. Military authorities in the South often ignored the violence. President Johnson had appointed most of these authorities, and they were against Reconstruction.

The Klan's terrorism served the Democratic Party. As gun-toting Klansmen kept Republicans away from the polls, the Democrats increased their power.

In the next section you will see how planters took back control of the South. You also will learn how they blocked African Americans' attempts to win more rights.

### Section 2 Assessment

**1. Terms & Names**

Identify:
- freedmen's school
- sharecropping
- Ku Klux Klan
- lynch

**2. Taking Notes**

Use a cluster diagram like the one below to review details about sharecropping.

For farmers, what were the advantages and disadvantages of sharecropping?

**3. Main Ideas**

a. How did freedom help strengthen African-American families?

b. How were African Americans educated during Reconstruction?

c. What were the main reasons African Americans wanted their own land?

**4. Critical Thinking**

Analyzing Causes
Despite greater civil rights, why did African Americans still face difficulty in improving their lives?

THINK ABOUT
- the defeat of the land-reform bill
- the Ku Klux Klan's rise
- the attitude of military authorities in the South

**ACTIVITY OPTIONS**

**SPEECH**
**ART**

Make a **speech** to President Johnson or design a **mural** explaining why land should be given to newly freed African Americans.



### Section 2 Assessment

**1. Terms & Names**

**freedmen's school,** p. 541
**sharecropping,** p. 543
**Ku Klux Klan,** p. 544
**lynch,** p. 544

**2. Taking Notes**

family; rent land; tools, seed, housing provided; keep share of crops. Advantages: obtained a plot of land; both the landowner and sharecropper received a share of the crop at harvest time; Disadvantages: forced to grow cash crops, such as cotton; often had to buy their food from a store; got caught in a never-ending cycle of debt

**3. Main Ideas**

**a.** Freedmen could marry legally. They could try to locate lost family members. **b.** in freedmen's schools; classes were held in cities and in rural areas **c.** They believed it was their right to own land and wanted to become economically independent and take care of their families.

**4. Critical Thinking**

because they were unable to own their own land; were afraid to assert their rights for fear of attack by the Ku Klux Klan

**ACTIVITY OPTIONS**

**Alternative Assessment**
- Rubrics for a speech, 3.6
- Rubrics for a mural, 1.11

# 3 End of Reconstruction

**TERMS & NAMES**
Fifteenth Amendment
Panic of 1873
Compromise of 1877

| MAIN IDEA | WHY IT MATTERS NOW |
|---|---|
| As white Southerners regained power, Reconstruction ended, as did black advances toward equality. | Reforms made during Reconstruction made later civil rights gains possible. |

### ONE AMERICAN'S STORY

**Robert B. Elliott was a U.S. congressman from South Carolina during Reconstruction. In 1874, he made a stirring speech supporting a civil rights bill that would outlaw racial discrimination in public services. (See Interact with History, page 531.)**

*A VOICE FROM THE PAST*

The passage of this bill will determine the civil status, not only of the negro but of any other class of citizens who may feel themselves discriminated against. It will form the capstone of that temple of liberty begun on this continent.

**Robert B. Elliott,** quoted in *The Glorious Failure*

Robert B. Elliott lost his political office when Reconstruction ended.

**Elliott was elected South Carolina's attorney general in 1876. He began his term in 1877, just as Reconstruction was ending. That year, federal troops left the South. White Southerners took back control of the region. Quickly, they forced African Americans, including Elliott, out of office.**

**In this section, you will learn about the events that ended Reconstruction. You will also see how Reconstruction's end meant setbacks in the fight for civil rights and equality.**

## 1 The Election of Grant

The Republican Party seemed stronger than ever in 1868. That year, its candidate, General Ulysses S. Grant, won the presidency. During the campaign, the Democrats attacked the Republicans' Reconstruction policies. They blamed the party for granting rights to African Americans.

On Election Day, however, the Republicans won. Grant received 214 electoral votes. His Democratic opponent received only 80. The popular count was much closer. Grant had a majority of only 306,000 votes.

Grant would not have had such a majority without the freedmen's vote. Despite attacks by the Ku Klux Klan, about 500,000 African Americans voted in the South. Most cast their ballots for Grant.





## SECTION OBJECTIVES

1. To evaluate the impact of Grant's election and the passage of the Fifteenth Amendment
2. To analyze Grant's administration
3. To explain events that led to the end of Reconstruction
4. To analyze the legacy of Reconstruction

**SKILLBUILDER**
Interpreting Charts, p. 549

**CRITICAL THINKING**
Comparing, p. 546
Making Inferences, p. 547
Recognizing Effects, pp. 547, 548
Summarizing, p. 548
Drawing Conclusions, p. 549

## FOCUS & MOTIVATE

### 5-MINUTE WARM-UP

**Making Inferences** These questions focus on the end of Reconstruction.

1. Look at the illustrations on pages 546 and 548. How do these images of African-American life differ?
2. What inferences can you make about the end of Reconstruction from these illustrations?

**Warm-Up Transparency WT18**

## INSTRUCT

### INSTRUCT: OBJECTIVE 1

**The Election of Grant/ The Fifteenth Amendment**

Key Questions

- How did Grant's victory in 1868 highlight the role of free African-American voters?
- How did the Fifteenth Amendment protect the rights of African Americans?
- Why did some women protest the passage of the Fifteenth Amendment?

**In-Depth Resources: Unit 5**
- Guided Reading, p. 64

### RECOMMENDED RESOURCES

**In-Depth Resources: Unit 5**
- Guided Reading, p. 64
- Building Vocabulary, p. 65
- Skillbuilder Practice, p. 66
- Reteaching Activity, p. 76

**Reading Study Guide** (Spanish and English), pp. 181–182

**Economics in History**
- Understanding the Business Cycle, p. 18

**Outline Map Activities**
- Election of 1876, pp. 35–36

**Formal Assessment**
- Section Quiz, p. 271

**Alternative Assessment**
- Rubrics, 4.1
- Rubrics, 4.3

**Access for Students Acquiring English/ESL**
- Guided Reading, p. 122
- Skillbuilder Practice, p. 123

Technology Resources

**Humanities Transparency HT36**
- Parade Celebrating the 15th Amendment

**Electronic Teacher Tools with Test Maker**

**ClassZone**
www.mcdougallittell.com

## Now and then

**African Americans in Congress**
The increase in the number of African Americans in Congress has not been steady. Only four African Americans held seats in the House from 1901 to 1955. In 1971, 12 African-American members of the House of Representatives and the House delegate from the District of Columbia formed the Congressional Black Caucus. This group focuses primarily on issues of particular importance to African Americans. It has at times wielded considerable influence in the formation of policies and legislation.

 **Humanities Transparency HT36**
- Parade Celebrating the 15th Amendment

## INSTRUCT: OBJECTIVE 2

**Grant Fights the Klan/ Scandal and Panic Weaken Republicans**
Key Questions
- How did President Grant and Congress challenge the power of the Ku Klux Klan?
- How did scandals weaken Grant's administration and support for the Republican Party?
- How did economic problems hurt the Republican Party?

## MORE ABOUT . . .

**The Klan Today**
Ku Klux Klan movements have swept the country periodically since the 1870s. A Ku Klux Klan movement rose again in the early 1900s. More than 3 million members made the KKK a powerful political force in a number of states in the Midwest and South. The organization faded again beginning in the late 1920s. Another KKK movement emerged in the late 1940s as the civil rights movement gained momentum. The organization still exists, but its membership is very small.

### Now and then

**AFRICAN AMERICANS IN CONGRESS**
Between 1870 and 1877, 16 African Americans served in Congress. Seven are shown in the picture below. Two were senators: Hiram R. Revels and Blanche K. Bruce, both of whom were from Mississippi.

In 1999, there were 38 African Americans in Congress. The longest-serving member was John Conyers, a representative from Michigan elected in 1964. Only two African-American senators were elected in the 20th century. Massachusetts senator Edward W. Brooke served from 1967 to 1979. Illinois senator Carol Moseley-Braun served from 1993 to 1999.

## The Fifteenth Amendment

After Grant's victory, Radical Republicans worried that the Southern states might try to keep African Americans from voting in future elections. To prevent this, Radical leaders proposed a new constitutional amendment.

The **Fifteenth Amendment** stated that citizens could not be stopped from voting "on account of race, color, or previous condition of servitude." (This amendment, like the Fourteenth Amendment, did not apply to Native Americans on tribal lands.) The amendment was ratified in 1870.

*Reading* **History**
**A. Comparing** How was the Fifteenth Amendment a step beyond the Fourteenth Amendment?
**A. Answer** While the Fourteenth Amendment broadly granted equal rights, the Fifteenth Amendment guaranteed voting rights.

The Fifteenth Amendment was not aimed only at the South. African-American men could not vote in 16 states. "We have no moral right to impose an obligation on one part of the land which the rest will not accept," one Radical wrote. With the Fifteenth Amendment, the nation again turned toward democracy.

The Fifteenth Amendment did not apply to women. This made many white women angry. Why couldn't they vote when black men—former slaves—could? Suffragist Elizabeth Cady Stanton protested the idea of uneducated immigrants and freedmen "who never read the Declaration of Independence" making laws for educated white women. Most African-American women were not as angry. To Frances E. W. Harper, a black suffragist and writer, it was important for African Americans to gain voting rights, even if that meant only men at first.

**Vocabulary**
**suffragist:** someone who favors equal voting rights, especially for women

## 2 Grant Fights the Klan

Despite gaining the vote, African Americans in the South continued to be terrorized by the Ku Klux Klan. In 1871, to stop the terror, President Grant asked Congress to pass a tough law against the Klan. Joseph Rainey, a black congressman from South Carolina, had received death threats from the Klan. He urged his fellow lawmakers to support the bill.

*A VOICE FROM THE PAST*

When myself and colleagues shall leave these Halls and turn our footsteps toward our southern home we know not but that the assassin may await our coming. Be it as it may we have resolved to be loyal and firm, and if we perish, we perish! I earnestly hope the bill will pass.

**Joseph Rainey,** quoted in *The Trouble They Seen*

Congress approved the anti-Klan bill. Federal marshals then arrested thousands of Klansmen. Klan attacks on African-American voters declined. As a result, the 1872 presidential election was both fair and peaceful in the South. Grant won a second term.



## ACTIVITY OPTIONS

**INTERDISCIPLINARY LINK: CIVICS** — BLOCK SCHEDULING

**CAMPAIGN SLOGANS**

**Class Time** 45 minutes

**Task** Creating a campaign slogan for the 1872 presidential election

**Purpose** To examine the issues that affected the election

**Supplies Needed**
- Art supplies (optional)
- Poster paper (optional)

**Activity** Have students review the material about the effects of the anti-Klan bill and about the scandals that tarnished the Grant administration. Then have them write a slogan for Grant and the Republican Party directed at voters in either the South or the North. Slogans should be no longer than one phrase or sentence. Students may wish to incorporate their slogan into a campaign poster for Grant. Make a list of all slogans, dividing it into those for the North and those for the South. Then have the class select the slogans they think would be most effective and explain why.

## Scandal and Panic Weaken Republicans

Under the Grant administration, support for the Republicans and Reconstruction weakened. Scandals hurt the administration and caused divisions in the Republican Party. A financial panic further hurt the Republicans and turned the country's attention away from Reconstruction.

President Grant did not choose his advisers well. He put his former army friends and his wife's relatives in government positions. Many of these people were unqualified. Some Grant appointees took bribes. Grant's private secretary, for instance, took money from whiskey distillers who wanted to avoid paying taxes. Grant's secretary of war, General William Belknap, left office after people accused him of taking bribes.

Such scandals deeply outraged many Republicans. In 1872, some Republican officials broke away and formed the new Liberal Republican Party. The Republicans, no longer unified, became less willing to impose tough Reconstruction policies on the South.

*Reading* **History**
**B. Making Inferences** How did Republican scandals hurt Reconstruction?
B. Possible Responses They made the party and its policies seem less moral; they distracted Republican politicians from Reconstruction goals.

In 1873, political corruption and Republican quarreling gave way to a more serious problem. When several powerful Eastern banks ran out of money after making bad loans, a financial panic swept the country. In the **Panic of 1873,** banks across the land closed. The stock market temporarily collapsed. The panic caused an economic depression, a time of low business activity and high unemployment. The railroad industry, which relied on banks for loans, suffered. Within a year, 89 of the country's 364 railroads went broke. Railroad failures left Midwestern farmers with no way to move their crops, and many farmers were ruined.

The depression, which lasted about five years, touched nearly all parts of the economy. By 1875, more than 18,000 companies had folded. Hundreds of workers had lost their jobs. Many Americans blamed the crisis on the Republicans—the party in power. As a result, Democrats won victories in the 1874 congressional and state elections. In the middle of the depression, Americans grew tired of hearing about the South's problems. The nation was losing interest in Reconstruction.

This cartoon from *Puck* magazine shows President Grant weighed down by corruption in his administration.

*Reading* **History**
**C. Recognizing Effects** What resulted from the Panic of 1873?
C. Answer economic depression, bankrupt railroads, ruined farmers, folded companies, lost jobs, and less interest in Reconstruction





### MORE ABOUT . . .

**The Election of 1872**

President Grant easily defeated *New York Tribune* founder and editor Horace Greeley in the 1872 presidential election. Greeley—a vocal, longtime opponent of slavery and a supporter of the Fourteenth and Fifteenth Amendments—favored a general amnesty for Confederates. He even signed the bail bond that released former Confederate president Jefferson Davis from jail. Greeley was nominated by the Liberal Republican Party and, later, by the Democratic National Convention in 1872. He died less than a month after the election.

### MORE ABOUT . . .

**Ulysses S. Grant**

After he left the presidency, Grant suffered personal financial problems similar to the problems that afflicted his administration. Grant had borrowed money to invest in a firm that was set up by a swindler. The firm collapsed. In order to support his family, Grant began writing magazine articles about the Civil War. Then, already suffering from cancer of the throat, he decided to write his memoirs. Grant finished his autobiography only four days before he died.

### CRITICAL THINKING ACTIVITY

**Sequencing Events** Have students make a time line of the events that weakened the Republican Party during Grant's presidency. Tell them to begin the time line with the election of 1868 and end it with the election of 1876.

**Class Time** 30 minutes

**Economics in History**
- Understanding the Business Cycle, p. 18

### ACTIVITY OPTIONS

### INDIVIDUAL NEEDS

#### STUDENTS ACQUIRING ENGLISH/ESL

**Understanding Literal and Figurative Meanings** Ask students to examine the political cartoon on page 547. Point out the caption and read it aloud to students. Ask what students think the phrase *weighed down* means. Elicit or explain that in the literal sense, the phrase means to be burdened with a heavy load. Encourage students to describe objects that weigh people down (heavy backpack, suitcase, uniform, or protective equipment).

Then explain to students that in the figurative sense, the phrase *weighed down* refers to being burdened by issues or problems rather than by objects that you can see or touch. Reread the first three paragraphs in the section "Scandal and Panic Weaken Republicans," and ask students to identify the problems that weighed down President Grant. Then ask students to explain why hiring unqualified people for important jobs and having your employees take bribes would pose problems.

**INSTRUCT: OBJECTIVE** 

**Supreme Court Reversals/ Reconstruction Ends**

Key Questions

- How did Supreme Court decisions affect civil rights for African Americans in the South?
- Why did the presidential election of 1876 lead to the end of Reconstruction?
- What issues were part of the Compromise of 1877?

 **Outline Map Activities**
- Election of 1876, pp. 35–36

**MORE ABOUT . . .**

**The Election of 1876**

The electoral votes of Oregon were also disputed. In total there were 20 disputed electoral votes. The Democrats needed only one vote to win, but the Republicans needed all 20. With the electoral votes from the four disputed states, Hayes would have 185 electoral votes—and would win the election. Tilden, however, had won the popular vote. He polled 4,284,757 votes to Hayes's 4,033,950.

The original commission had seven Republicans, seven Democrats, and one Independent. When the Independent resigned to run for Congress, he was replaced with a Republican. Republicans then controlled the commission, and they voted to give Hayes all 20 contested votes. Hayes became president.

## 3 Supreme Court Reversals

To make matters worse for the Republicans, the Supreme Court began to undo some of the changes that had been made in the South. In an 1876 case, *U.S.* v. *Cruikshank,* the Court ruled that the federal government could not punish individuals who violated the civil rights of African Americans. Only the states had that power, the Court declared. Southern state officials often would not punish those who attacked African Americans. As a result, violence against them increased.

In the 1876 case *U.S.* v. *Reese,* the Court ruled in favor of white Southerners who barred African Americans from voting. The Court stated that the Fifteenth Amendment did not give everyone the right to vote—it merely listed the grounds on which states could not deny the vote. In other words, states could prevent African Americans from voting for other reasons. States later imposed poll taxes and literacy tests to restrict the vote. These Court decisions weakened Reconstruction and blocked African-American efforts to gain full equality.

*Reading*History
**D. Recognizing Effects** How did the Reese and Cruikshank rulings affect African Americans' efforts to gain civil rights?
**D. Answer** One ruling made it easier for attacks against African Americans to go unpunished. The other made it easier to keep them from voting.

## Reconstruction Ends

The final blow to Reconstruction came with the 1876 presidential election. The Democrats nominated Samuel J. Tilden, governor of New York. The Republicans chose Rutherford B. Hayes, governor of Ohio. The race was very close. Victory depended on the electoral votes of South Carolina, Louisiana, and Florida. The votes in those states were so close that both the Democrats and the Republicans claimed victory. A special commission of eight Republicans and seven Democrats made a deal. Under the **Compromise of 1877,** Hayes became president. In return, the Republicans compromised with the Southern Democrats on several issues.

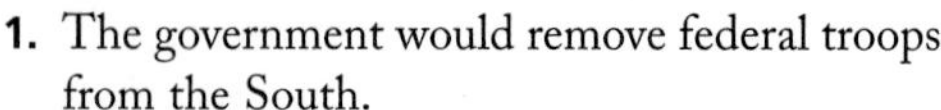

1. The government would remove federal troops from the South.
2. The government would provide land grants and loans for the construction of railroads linking the South to the West Coast.
3. Southern officials would receive federal funds for construction and improvement projects.
4. Hayes would appoint a Democrat to his cabinet.
5. The Democrats promised to respect African Americans' civil and political rights.

This cartoon from *Harper's Weekly* shows a federal soldier as the freedman's only defense against white Southerners.

**E. Answer** scandals that split the Republican Party, the Panic of 1873, the Reese and Cruikshank Supreme Court rulings, and the Compromise of 1877

*Reading*History
**E. Summarizing** What events led to a weakening of support for Reconstruction?

Abolitionist Wendell Phillips was against the compromise. He doubted that the South would respect black rights. "The whole soil of the South is hidden by successive layers of broken promises," he said. "To trust a Southern promise would be fair evidence of insanity."

After the 1876 presidential election, the Reconstruction governments in the South collapsed. The Democrats returned to power, believing that they were the redeemers, or rescuers, of the South.



**ACTIVITY OPTIONS**

**SKILLBUILDER MINI-LESSON: INTERPRETING CHARTS** — BLOCK SCHEDULING

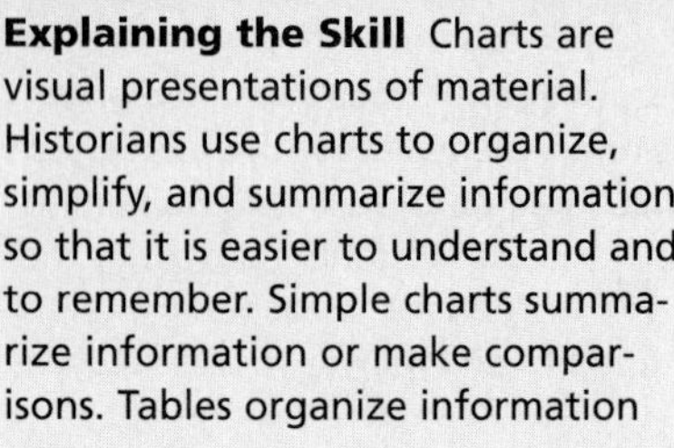

**Explaining the Skill** Charts are visual presentations of material. Historians use charts to organize, simplify, and summarize information so that it is easier to understand and to remember. Simple charts summarize information or make comparisons. Tables organize information into columns and rows. Diagrams provide visual clues to the meaning of information they contain.

**Applying the Skill** Ask students to identify the title of the chart and the kind of information it contains. Then ask the following questions:

1. Which two measures changed the Constitution? *(Fourteenth and Fifteenth Amendments)*
2. Which measures made freed African Americans citizens of the United States? *(Civil Rights Act of 1866 and Fourteenth Amendment)*
3. Which measure was designed to prevent racial discrimination in the courts? Why do you think Congress thought this was important? *(Civil Rights Act of 1875; because it protected African Americans' legal rights)*

 **In-Depth Resources: Unit 5**
- Skillbuilder Practice, p. 66

**Reconstruction: Civil Rights Amendments and Laws**

| | |
|---|---|
| Civil Rights Act of 1866 | • Granted citizenship and equal rights to all persons born in the United States (except Native Americans) |
| Fourteenth Amendment (1868) | • Granted citizenship and equal protection of the laws to all persons born in the United States (except Native Americans) |
| Fifteenth Amendment (1870) | • Protected the voting rights of African Americans |
| Civil Rights Act of 1875 | • Outlawed racial segregation in public services<br>• Ensured the right of African Americans to serve as jurors |

SKILLBUILDER **Interpreting Charts**

1. *Which amendment and law are most similar?*
2. *Which amendment specifically protects voting rights?*

Skillbuilder Answers
1. Civil Rights Act of 1866; Fourteenth Amendment
2. Fifteenth Amendment

## 4 The Legacy of Reconstruction

Historians still argue about the success of Reconstruction. The nation did rebuild and reunite. However, Reconstruction did not achieve equality for African Americans.

After Reconstruction, most African Americans still lived in poverty. Legally, they could vote and hold public office. But few took part in politics. They continued to face widespread violence and prejudice.

During this period, however, African Americans did make lasting gains. Protection of civil rights became part of the U.S. Constitution. The Fourteenth and Fifteenth amendments would provide a legal basis for civil rights laws of the 20th century. Black schools and churches begun during Reconstruction also endured. Reconstruction changed society, putting African Americans on the path toward full equality. In the next unit, you will learn about other changes in American society after the Civil War.

### Section 3 Assessment

**1. Terms & Names**

**Identify:**
- Fifteenth Amendment
- Panic of 1873
- Compromise of 1877

**2. Taking Notes**

Review the chapter and find five key events to place on a time line as shown.

1865 — event — event — 1877
event — event — event

Which event was most important and why?

**3. Main Ideas**

a. What did the Fifteenth Amendment declare?

b. What effect did scandals in the Grant administration have on the Republican Party?

c. What demands did Southern Democrats make in the Compromise of 1877?

**4. Critical Thinking**

**Drawing Conclusions**
Why do you think the Republicans were willing to agree to the Compromise of 1877 and end Reconstruction?

THINK ABOUT
- the election of 1876
- the Panic of 1873
- the Supreme Court rulings

ACTIVITY OPTIONS

**LANGUAGE ARTS**
**CIVICS**

Research Ku Klux Klan activities barring African Americans from voting. Then write a protest **letter to the editor** or propose a **law** to protect voting rights.





### HISTORY FROM VISUALS

**Reading the Chart** Have students note the years each measure was passed. (The four measures were passed over the course of less than ten years.) Ask students why Congress saw the need for further legislation to protect the rights of African Americans after the passage of the Civil Rights Act of 1866 and the Fourteenth Amendment in 1868.
**Possible Responses** Congress saw efforts by white Southerners to ignore the laws and restrict the rights of African Americans. The measures that dealt with voting rights were designed to prevent white Southerners from ending African-American participation and representation in government.

**Extension** Have students research the legal status of Native Americans at the time the Fourteenth Amendment was passed.

### INSTRUCT: OBJECTIVE 4

**The Legacy of Reconstruction**
Key Questions
- What obstacles did African Americans still face after the end of Reconstruction?
- What lasting gains did African Americans make during Reconstruction?

## ASSESS & RETEACH

**Setting the Stage** Have students complete the last row of the graphic organizer.

**Formal Assessment**
- Section Quiz, p. 271

**Critical Thinking Transparency CT52**
- Setting the Stage

**RETEACHING ACTIVITY**
Have students write a summary paragraph that uses the section's Main Idea as the topic sentence. The paragraphs should note the legacy of Reconstruction, efforts to promote the rights and equality of African Americans, and events that led to the end of Reconstruction.

**In-Depth Resources: Unit 5**
- Reteaching Activity, p. 76

### Section 3 Assessment

**1. Terms & Names**

**Fifteenth Amendment,** p. 546
**Panic of 1873,** p. 547
**Compromise of 1877,** p. 548

**2. Taking Notes**

Event 1: Lincoln's death; Event 2: Reconstruction begins; Event 3: Fourteenth Amendment passes; Event 4: Johnson is impeached; Event 5: Grant is elected
Answers will vary as to which event was most important.

**3. Main Ideas**

**a.** The right to vote should not be denied on account of race, color, or previous condition of servitude.
**b.** They helped split the party.
**c.** the removal of federal troops from the South; land grants and loans to build railroads; money for internal improvements; appointment of a Democrat to the cabinet

**4. Critical Thinking**

They wanted to retain their hold on the presidency. The nation was in the midst of a depression and had grown weary of Reconstruction.

**ACTIVITY OPTIONS**

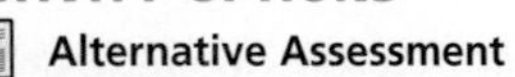

**Alternative Assessment**
- Rubrics for a letter, 4.1
- Rubrics for a law, 4.3

## TERMS & NAMES

1. **Reconstruction,** p. 533
2. **Andrew Johnson,** p. 533
3. **black codes,** p. 534
4. **civil rights,** p. 535
5. **Fourteenth Amendment,** p. 535
6. **sharecropping,** p. 543
7. **lynch,** p. 544
8. **Fifteenth Amendment,** p. 546
9. **Panic of 1873,** p. 547
10. **Compromise of 1877,** p. 548

## REVIEW QUESTIONS

**Possible Responses**

1. a federal agency that assisted former slaves by offering them food and clothing and establishing African-American schools
2. amnesty for most white Southerners; insistence that the new state governments forbid slavery and accept the supreme power of the federal government
3. Scalawags were Southerners who went along with Radical Reconstruction. Carpetbaggers were Northerners who traveled to the South to take part in Reconstruction.
4. He violated the Tenure of Office Act.
5. Congress believed that African Americans' newly gained civil rights were enough to ensure them a better life.
6. the contract system: planters paid former slaves to work their plantations; sharecropping: plantation owners provided farmers with tools and land in exchange for a share of their crops
7. The Klan kept many Republicans away from the polls through violence and intimidation, helping Democrats keep political power.
8. because it gave the right to vote to male immigrants and freedmen but not to women
9. The failure of several powerful banks prompted a financial panic.
10. They took away the federal government's ability to punish civil rights violators, making it easier for whites to deny African Americans the right to vote.

# Chapter 18 ASSESSMENT

## TERMS & NAMES

Briefly explain the importance of each of the following.

1. Reconstruction
2. Andrew Johnson
3. black codes
4. civil rights
5. Fourteenth Amendment
6. sharecropping
7. lynch
8. Fifteenth Amendment
9. Panic of 1873
10. Compromise of 1877

## REVIEW QUESTIONS

**Rebuilding the Union (pages 533–539)**

1. What was the Freedmen's Bureau?
2. What were the main parts of President Johnson's Reconstruction plan?
3. Who were scalawags and carpetbaggers?
4. What reason did the House give for impeaching President Johnson?

**Reconstruction and Daily Life (pages 540–544)**

5. Why did Congress not pass a land-reform plan?
6. What new systems of labor developed in the South after the Civil War?
7. How did the Ku Klux Klan serve the Democratic Party?

**End of Reconstruction (pages 545–549)**

8. Why did the Fifteenth Amendment arouse anger in many women?
9. What caused an economic depression in the 1870s?
10. How did Supreme Court rulings during Reconstruction help weaken African Americans' civil rights?

## CRITICAL THINKING

**1. USING YOUR NOTES**

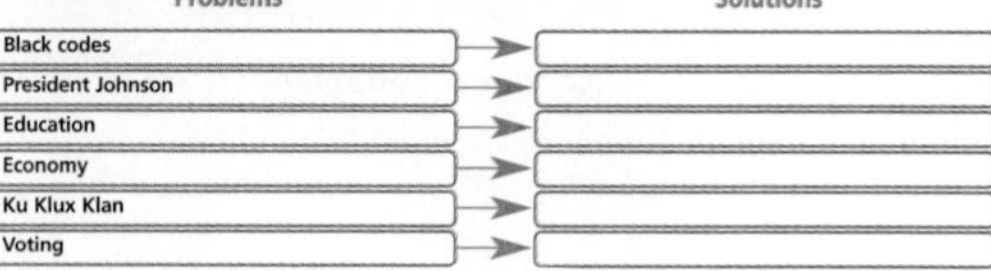


Using your diagram, answer the following questions.

a. What was the solution to the problem of educating African Americans?

b. What was the solution to the problem of Ku Klux Klan violence?

**2. ANALYZING LEADERSHIP**

Why might Reconstruction be considered a time in which the presidency was weak?

**3. THEME: DEMOCRATIC IDEALS**

How did the Fourteenth and Fifteenth amendments promote greater equality for African Americans? How were the amendments limited?

**4. APPLYING CITIZENSHIP SKILLS**

What were the different viewpoints of Elizabeth Cady Stanton and Frances E. W. Harper regarding the Fifteenth Amendment's failure to give women an important right of citizenship—the right to vote?

**5. ANALYZING CAUSES**

What aspect of the Compromise of 1877 likely played the greatest role in ending Reconstruction?

**Interact *with* History**

How did your solutions to rebuilding the nation compare with the actual solutions carried out?

## VISUAL SUMMARY

### Reconstruction

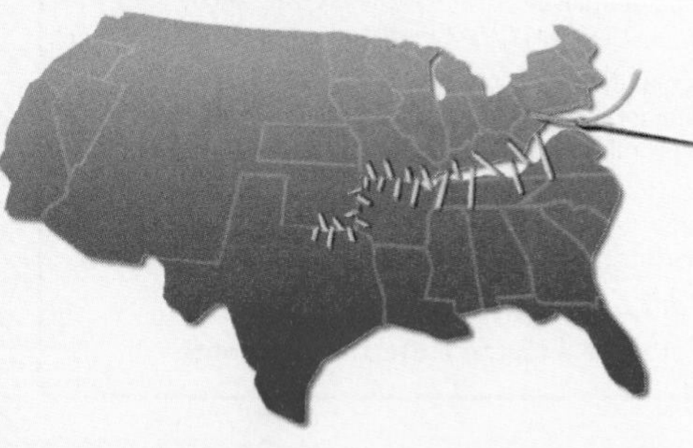

**Rebuilding the Union**

During Reconstruction, Congress decided how the Southern states would be readmitted to the Union and passed laws to improve conditions for freed people.

**Reconstruction and Daily Life**

After slavery ended, freed African Americans reunited their families, attended school, and began working for pay. Racist violence and lack of land slowed their progress.

**End of Reconstruction**

In the 1870s, hostile Supreme Court decisions, the Southern Democrats' return to power, and the withdrawal of federal troops from the South ended Reconstruction.



## CRITICAL THINKING

**Possible Responses**

**1. USING YOUR NOTES a.** Freedmen's schools were established. **b.** anti-Klan laws

**2. ANALYZING LEADERSHIP** because Congress overrode many of Johnson's vetoes, took over Reconstruction, and impeached him; scandals of Grant administration prompted the start of a new Republican Party

**3. THEME: DEMOCRATIC IDEALS** They gained full rights as citizens and won the right to vote. However, the Supreme Court issued rulings that weakened these amendments.

**4. APPLYING CITIZENSHIP SKILLS** Stanton criticized the amendment, believing that it was wrong to continue denying the vote to women, many of whom were better educated than former slaves. Harper believed that granting voting rights to male African Americans was a significant step toward full rights for all.

**5. ANALYZING CAUSES** the removal of federal troops from the South, making it much more difficult for the North to enforce its Reconstruction policies

**Interact *with* History** Students responses will vary but should include elements from the solutions.

## HISTORY SKILLS

**1. INTERPRETING MAPS: Region**

Study the map and then answer the questions.

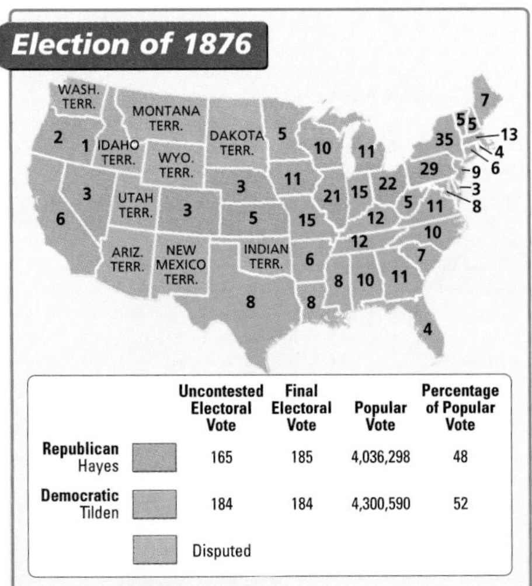


| | Uncontested Electoral Vote | Final Electoral Vote | Popular Vote | Percentage of Popular Vote |
|---|---|---|---|---|
| Republican Hayes | 165 | 185 | 4,036,298 | 48 |
| Democratic Tilden | 184 | 184 | 4,300,590 | 52 |
| Disputed | | | | |

**Basic Map Elements**

a. What is the subject of the map?

**Interpreting the Map**

b. In what region of the country were most of the disputed votes located?

c. What regions voted mostly Republican?

**2. INTERPRETING PRIMARY SOURCES**

This political cartoon shows the effect of the Ku Klux Klan on African-American families in the South. Study the cartoon carefully and then answer the questions.

a. Based on the cartoon, what were the goals of the Ku Klux Klan?

b. What does the cartoon suggest about how the Klan intended to achieve its goals?

## ALTERNATIVE ASSESSMENT

**1. INTERDISCIPLINARY ACTIVITY: Language Arts**

**Writing Letters** Write letters that you imagine the following three people would write about Reconstruction: 1) a member of the old Southern upper class; 2) a newly freed African American; and 3) a white Northern carpetbagger.

**2. COOPERATIVE LEARNING ACTIVITY**

**Conducting an Impeachment Trial** The impeachment trial of Andrew Johnson was a dramatic and colorful event. Many officials pleaded their case either for or against the president.

Working in a small group, research the trial using resources such as diaries, journals, autobiographies, letters, and books. Each group member should choose an official who spoke at the trial and collect some of his quotes. The group should then perform its own trial in front of the class, with each member portraying the official he or she chose. Some possible officials include Thaddeus Stevens, Edmund G. Ross, James W. Grimes, Benjamin Butler, and Chief Justice Samuel Chase.

**3. TECHNOLOGY ACTIVITY**

**Making an Electronic Presentation** Life under the sharecropping system was not easy. Information about sharecropping comes from a variety of sources. Using the library or the Internet, find diaries, memoirs, images, and news articles about life as a sharecropper.

 **Visit www.mcdougallittell.com to learn more about sharecropping.**

Use presentation software to share your information about sharecropping. Consider the suggestions below to get started.

- images or descriptions of a sharecropper's shack
- examples of the crops that were grown by a sharecropper
- facts and quotations about a sharecropper's life

**4. HISTORY PORTFOLIO**

**Option 1** Review your section and chapter assessment activities. Select one that you think is your best work. Then use comments made by your teacher or classmates to improve your work and add it to your portfolio.

**Option 2** Review the questions that you wrote for What Do You Want to Know? on page 532. Then write a short report in which you explain the answers to your questions. If any questions were not answered, do research to answer them. Add your answers to your portfolio.



## ALTERNATIVE ASSESSMENT

1. INTERDISCIPLINARY ACTIVITY: **Language Arts**
**Letters should**
- accurately reflect the thoughts and experiences of the subject's life.
- reflect the student's understanding of basic concepts of Reconstruction.
- use standard grammar, spelling, sentence structure, and punctuation.

2. COOPERATIVE LEARNING ACTIVITY
**Trials should**
- accurately portray the position of the selected official.
- convey information through performance.
- have adequate delivery and establish a rapport with the audience.
- show evidence of involvement of each person in the group.

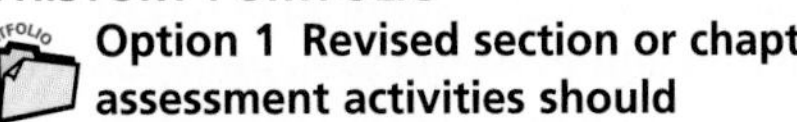
3. TECHNOLOGY ACTIVITY
**Presentations should**
- utilize two or more media.
- clearly demonstrate an understanding of the life of a sharecropper.
- show technical proficiency.

4. HISTORY PORTFOLIO

 **Option 1 Revised section or chapter assessment activities should**
- address teacher and peer responses to the selected work.
- solve problems present in the first versions of the work.

 **Option 2 Short reports should**
- answer questions about Reconstruction.
- use evidence to develop and support ideas.
- cite sources of information.
- use standard grammar, spelling, sentence structure, and punctuation.

 **Critical Thinking Transparency CT54**
- Visual Summary

**Formal Assessment**
- Chapter Test, Forms A and B, pp. 272–279

## HISTORY SKILLS

**Possible Responses**

1. INTERPRETING MAPS
**Basic Map Elements**
**a.** election of 1876
**Interpreting the Map**
**b.** the South
**c.** the North and West

2. INTERPRETING PRIMARY SOURCES
**a.** The Klan's goals were to keep blacks powerless and in fear and to keep whites in power.
**b.** By highlighting weapons, such as knives and guns, the cartoon suggests that the Klan intended to use violence to achieve its goals.

# UNIT 6

## America Transformed

## 1860–1914



### BEFORE YOU READ

#### Previewing Unit 6

Unit 6 describes how the United States changes from a mostly rural, agricultural nation into an urban, industrial one. Farmers, miners, and ranchers settle the West, forcing Native Americans from their lands. Large industries flourish, sparked by the inventions of creative Americans. Millions of immigrants provide the labor for these expanding industries. New ways of communication and marketing begin to shape a mass culture. At the same time, discrimination and cultural differences create deep divisions within American society.

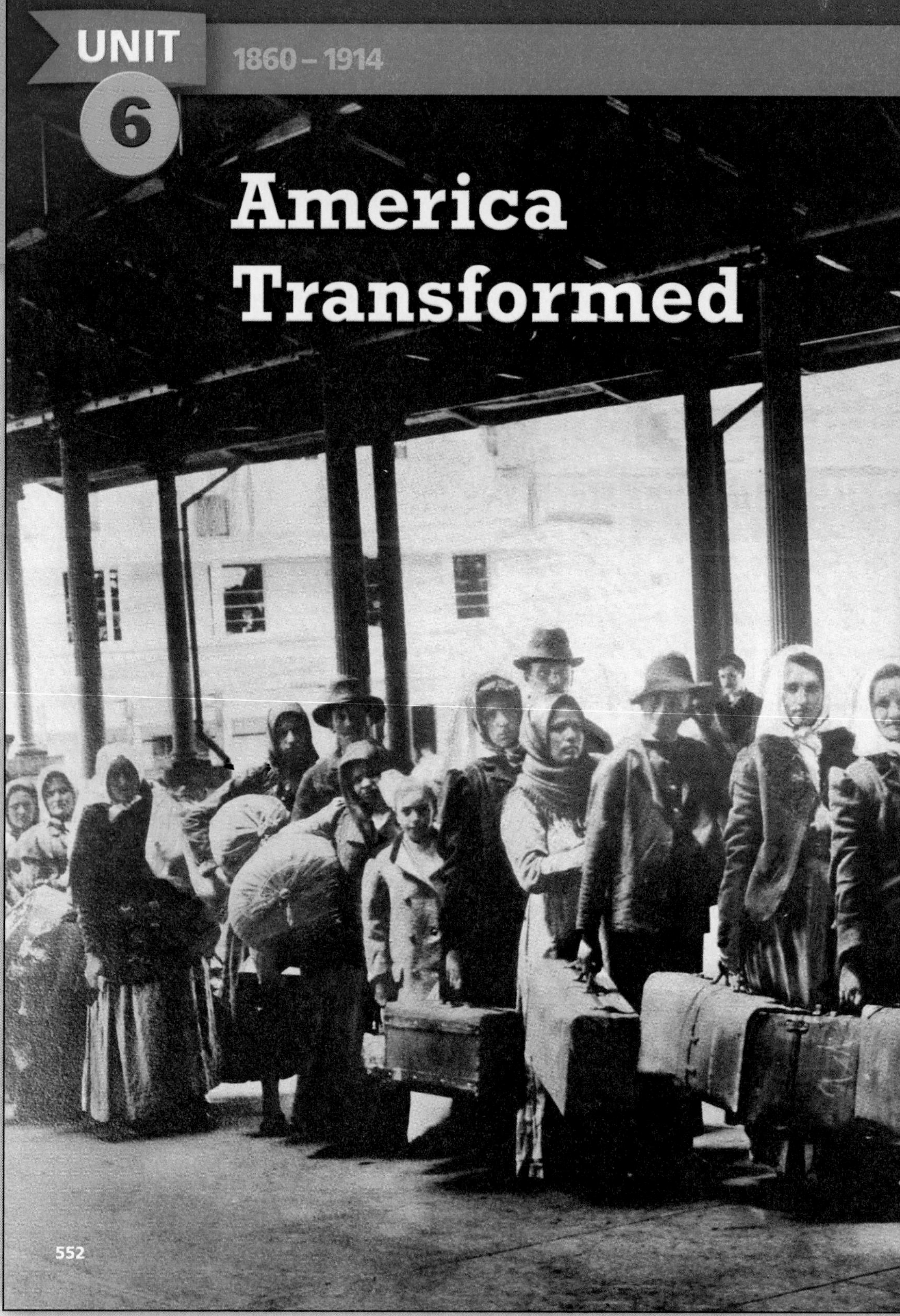

"Give me your tired, your poor,
Your huddled masses, yearning
to breathe free..."
—Emma Lazarus

European immigrants such as those shown in this photograph (taken around 1900) streamed into Ellis Island at the turn of the century.



## HISTORY FROM VISUALS

**Interpreting the Photograph** By the turn of the century, photography was common in the United States. Although color film had not been invented, photographers or studios could hand-tint photographs to provide a color image. Between 1892 and 1954, 12 million immigrants passed through Ellis Island, located a few hundred yards north of the Statue of Liberty. Ask students why this group of immigrants is waiting in line. **Possible Response** They are waiting to be processed through immigration, to have their papers checked, and so on. Discuss with the class the reasons that the United States (or any country) might have for wanting to question or screen newcomers crossing its borders.

**Extension** Have students selecte one of the immigrants included in the photograph. Have students think about the person they have selected, speculate about his or her life, and then write a biography of the person for a museum exhibit about Ellis Island. Biographies should include information about where the person was born, his or her reasons for emigrating, and his or her plans for a new life.

# CHAPTER 19 PLANNING GUIDE

# Growth in the West 1860–1900

## CHAPTER RESOURCES

### CHAPTER OVERVIEW

This chapter discusses the continuing migration of white settlers from the eastern United States to the West, at cost to both Native Americans and people of Mexican heritage. It also describes how Westerners challenged the dominant political parties by forming the Populist Party.

### COPYMASTERS

**In-Depth Resources: Unit 6**
- Tracing Themes: Diversity and Unity, p. 2
- Building Vocabulary, p. 7

**Interdisciplinary Projects,** pp. 109–114

### TECHNOLOGY

**Primary Source Explorer**

**Electronic Teacher Tools**

**Power Presentations CD-ROM**

**Chapter Summaries on CD** (English and Spanish)

**America's Music CD**

## SECTION 1 Miners, Ranchers, and Cowhands pp. 557–561

### KEY IDEAS

- The population of the West increases with the expansion of railroads, mining, and ranching.
- Mining and ranching go through boom times, then weaken in the late 1800s.
- Vigilante groups form to help combat the lawlessness and crime in the West.

### COPYMASTERS

**In-Depth Resources: Unit 6**
- Setting the Stage, p. 1
- Guided Reading, p. 3
- Skillbuilder Practice: Using the Internet, p. 8
- Literature Selection, pp. 13–15
- Reteaching Activity, p. 16

**Outline Map Activities**
- The Population of the West, 1890, pp 37–38

### TECHNOLOGY

**Warm-Up Transparency WT19**

**Geography Transparency GT19**
- Gold and Silver Deposits in the West, 1849–1895

**Critical Thinking Transparency CT55**
- Setting the Stage

**ClassZone:** www.mcdougallittell.com

## SECTION 2 Native Americans Fight to Survive pp. 562–567

### KEY IDEAS

- Conflicts between white settlers and Native Americans culminate at Sand Creek and Little Bighorn.
- Despite treaty promises, Native Americans lose most of their lands.
- The Dawes Act contributes to the destruction of the Native American way of life.

### COPYMASTERS

**In-Depth Resources: Unit 6**
- Setting the Stage, p. 1
- Guided Reading, p. 4
- Geography Application, pp. 9–10
- Primary Source, p. 11
- Reteaching Activity, p. 17

**America's History Makers**
- Sitting Bull, pp. 75–76

**American History Plays**
- *"I Will Fight No More Forever"* by Kathy Wilmore

### TECHNOLOGY

**Warm-Up Transparency WT19**

**Humanities Transparency HT37**
- *Battle of the Little Bighorn* by Kicking Bear

**Critical Thinking Transparency CT55**
- Setting the Stage

**Critical Thinking Transparency CT56**
- Cause and Effect: Native American Wars

**ClassZone:** www.mcdougallittell.com

## SECTION 3 Life in the West pp. 568–573

### KEY IDEAS

- Women have difficult lives in the West but win greater legal rights.
- Cities spring up rapidly at railroad hubs and mining centers.
- Writers and Wild West shows build myths about the West but often ignore the realities.

### COPYMASTERS

**In-Depth Resources: Unit 6**
- Setting the Stage, p. 1
- Guided Reading, p. 5
- Primary Source, p. 12
- Reteaching Activity, p. 18

**America's History Makers**
- Calamity Jane, pp. 77–78

### TECHNOLOGY

**Warm-Up Transparency WT19**

**Humanities Transparency HT38**
- Annie Oakley Poster, 1901

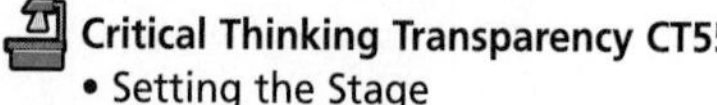

**Critical Thinking Transparency CT55**
- Setting the Stage

**ClassZone:** www.mcdougallittell.com

## SECTION 4 Farming and Populism pp. 574–579

### KEY IDEAS

- The 1862 Homestead Act's offer of free land draws settlers from many countries to the West.
- To combat their economic problems, farmers form the Grange, cooperatives, and the Populist Party.
- The 1890 census shows that the frontier no longer exists.

### COPYMASTERS

**In-Depth Resources: Unit 6**
- Setting the Stage, p. 1
- Guided Reading, p. 6
- Reteaching Activity, p. 19

**Economics in History**
- The Dynamics of Supply and Demand, p. 19

**Why It Matters Now**
- Challenges in the West, pp. 37–38

### TECHNOLOGY

**Warm-Up Transparency WT19**

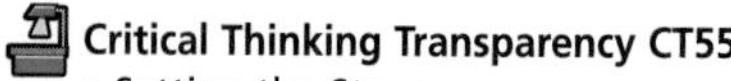

**Critical Thinking Transparency CT55**
- Setting the Stage

**Critical Thinking Transparency CT57**
- Visual Summary

**ClassZone:** www.mcdougallittell.com

Pupil's Edition
Copymaster
Overhead Transparency
Audio Library
CD-ROM
Internet

## ASSESSMENT

**Chapter Assessment,** pp. 580–581

**Formal Assessment**
- Chapter Tests, Forms A and B, pp. 286–293

**Alternative Assessment Book**

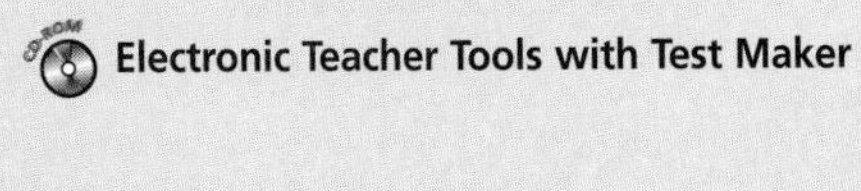

**Electronic Teacher Tools with Test Maker**

---

**Section Assessment,** p. 561

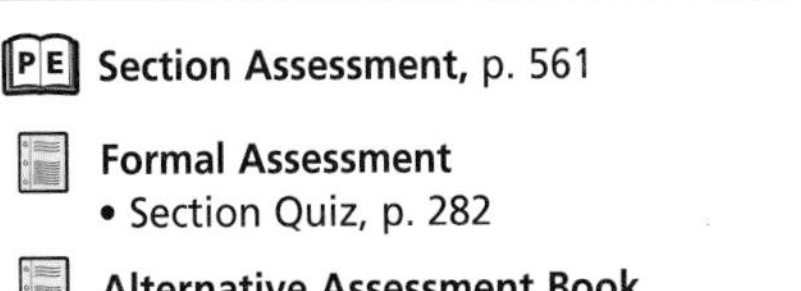

**Formal Assessment**
- Section Quiz, p. 282

**Alternative Assessment Book**
- Rubrics for a biographical sketch, 4.4
- Rubrics for a song, 4.8

**Electronic Teacher Tools with Test Maker**

---

**Section Assessment,** p. 567

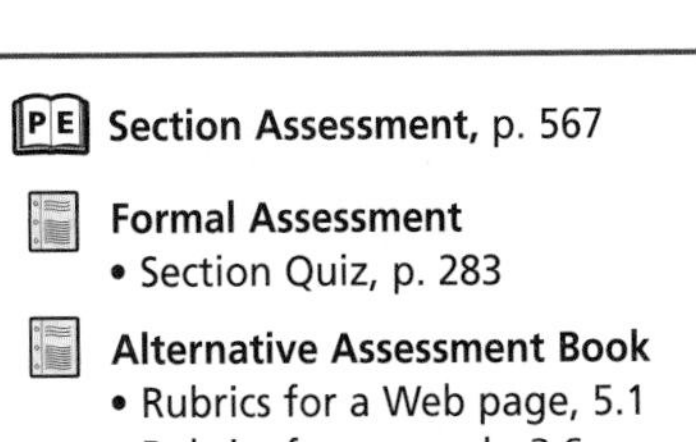

**Formal Assessment**
- Section Quiz, p. 283

**Alternative Assessment Book**
- Rubrics for a Web page, 5.1
- Rubrics for a speech, 3.6

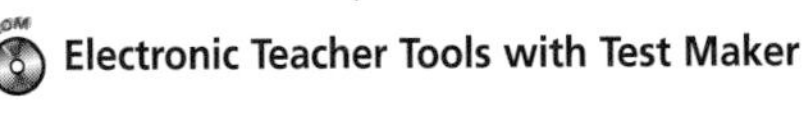

**Electronic Teacher Tools with Test Maker**

---

**Section Assessment,** p. 571

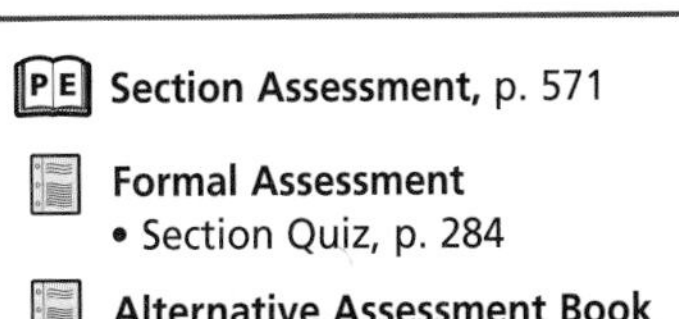

**Formal Assessment**
- Section Quiz, p. 284

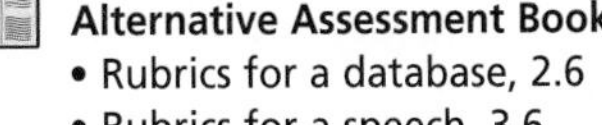

**Alternative Assessment Book**
- Rubrics for a database, 2.6
- Rubrics for a speech, 3.6

**Electronic Teacher Tools with Test Maker**

---

**Section Assessment,** p. 579

**Formal Assessment**
- Section Quiz, p. 285

**Alternative Assessment Book**
- Rubrics for an electronic presentation, 5.4
- Rubrics for a sales pitch, 4.9

**Electronic Teacher Tools with Test Maker**

## CUSTOMIZING FOR INDIVIDUAL NEEDS

### Students Acquiring English/ESL

**Reading Study Guide** (English and Spanish), pp. 185–194

**Access for Students Acquiring English/ESL: Spanish Translations,** pp. 126–132

**Chapter Summaries on CD** (English and Spanish)

### Less Proficient Readers

**Reading Study Guide** (English and Spanish), pp. 185–194

**Chapter Summaries on CD** (English and Spanish)

### Gifted and Talented Students

**In-Depth Resources: Unit 6**
- Enrichment Activity, p. 20

**America's History Makers**
- Sitting Bull, pp. 75–76
- Calamity Jane, pp. 77–78

## CROSS-CURRICULAR CONNECTIONS

### Economics

Brett, Harvey. ***Farmers and Ranchers.*** New York: Holt, 1995. Part of a well-documented series describing how people worked in the West.

### Popular Culture

Wilson, R. L. with Greg Martin. ***Buffalo Bill's Wild West: An American Legend.*** New York: Random House, 1998. Illustrated with photographs and posters.

### Primary Sources

Brown, Dee and Amy Ehrlich. ***Wounded Knee: An Indian History of the American West.*** New York: Holt, 1993. Adapted by Ehrlich from Brown's best-selling *Bury My Heart at Wounded Knee;* a poignant and illuminating collection of original documents.

### Science

Olsen, Sandra L., ed. ***Horses Through Time.*** Boulder, CO: Roberts Rinehart Publishers, 1996. Essays by some of the world's experts on horses. Some of the selections may be difficult to read, but the illustrations are wonderful.

### Interdisciplinary Projects, pp. 109–114

- Math: Sod Houses
- Science: Endangered Species
- Language Arts: Mexican Folk Tales of the Southwest
- Art: Designing Cattle Brands

### Literature

Benchley, Nathaniel. ***Only Earth and Sky Last Forever.*** New York: HarperCollins, 1991. Young Dark Elk leaves the U.S. government agency where he has grown up in order to live free on Indian land.

Erdich, Louise. ***The Birchbark House.*** New York: Hyperion Books, 1999. Acclaimed novel by a well-known writer about an Objibwa band during the period of westward expansion.

Stolz, Mary. ***Cezanne Pinto: A Memoir.*** New York: Knopf, 1994. The memoirs of an African American who escaped from slavery to Canada and later became a cowboy.

### McDougal Littell *The Language of Literature*

- Louis L'Amour, "War Party" (historical fiction)
- Vachel Lindsay, "The Flower-Fed Buffaloes" (poetry)
- Robert Félix Salazar, "The Other Pioneers" (poetry)
- Mark Twain, from ***Roughing It*** (personal narrative)

### McDougal Littell Literature Connections

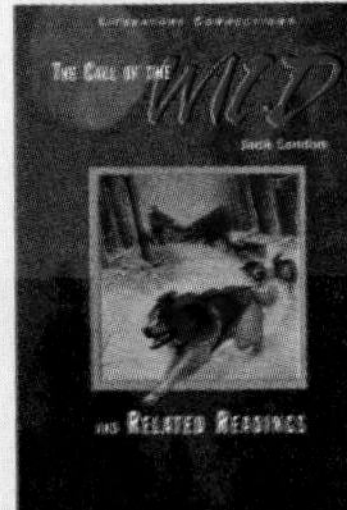


Jack London
***The Call of the Wild***
The story of Buck, a privileged, dignified dog from California who is shipped to Alaska during the 1890s Gold Rush to become a sled dog.

## ENRICHMENT ACTIVITIES

**Pupil's Edition, pp. 554–581**
**Interact with History,** p. 555
**Interdisciplinary Challenge,** pp. 572–573
**Economics in History,** p. 576

**In-Depth Resources: Unit 6**
- Geography Application: Custer's Last Stand, pp. 9–10
- Primary Sources, pp. 11–12
- Literature Selection, pp. 13–15

**America's History Makers**
- Sitting Bull, pp. 75–76
- Calamity Jane, pp. 77–78

**America's Music CD**

**American History Plays**
- *"I Will Fight No More Forever"* by Kathy Wilmore

**Outline Map Activities**
- The Population of the West, 1890, pp 37–38

**Why It Matters Now**
- Challenges in the West, pp. 37–38

# CHAPTER 19 PACING GUIDE

**LESSON PLAN OPTIONS (50-MINUTE PERIOD)** (TE) = Teacher's Edition (PE) = Pupil's Edition

| | TEACHER-DIRECTED ACTIVITIES<br>Class Time: 15 minutes | STUDENT-CENTERED ACTIVITIES<br>Class Time: 25 minutes | INDIVIDUAL ACTIVITIES<br>Class Time: 10 minutes |
|---|---|---|---|
| **DAY 1**<br>Introduction<br>pp. 554–556 | **Presentation Options**<br>• Begin with a class discussion of the picture on p. 554 **(PE).**<br>• Lead a class discussion on the "What Do You know?" question in Setting the Stage, p. 556. Then introduce the graphic organizer for the chapter **(PE).** | **Options for Cooperative Learning**<br>• Have student groups discuss the Interact with History questions, p. 555 **(PE).**<br>• Have student groups respond to the "What Do You Want to Know?" question in Setting the Stage, p. 556 **(PE).** | **Head Start on Homework Options**<br>• Have students skim Section 1 Main Idea, Why It Matters Now, Terms & Names, and the main headings, p. 557 **(PE).**<br>• Have students begin Guided Reading activity and Building Vocabulary sheet. |
| **DAY 2**<br>Section 1<br>pp. 557–561 | **Presentation Options**<br>• Begin with the 5-Minute Warm-Up, p. 557 **(TE).**<br>• Review the Section 1 Main Idea, Why It Matters Now, and Terms & Names, p. 557 **(PE).**<br>• Lead the students through the Skillbuilder Mini-Lesson: Using the Internet, p. 559 **(TE).** | **Options for Cooperative Learning**<br>• Divide students into groups to complete the Critical Thinking Activity, p. 559 **(TE).**<br>• Have student pairs work together to complete one of the Activity Options in the Section 1 Assessment, p. 561 **(PE).** | **Head Start on Homework Options**<br>• Have students begin working on Section 1 Assessment, p. 561 **(PE).**<br>• Have students preview Section 2 Main Idea, Why It Matters Now, Terms & Names, and the main headings, p. 562 **(PE).** |
| **DAY 3**<br>Section 2<br>pp. 562–567 | **Presentation Options**<br>• Begin with the 5-Minute Warm-Up, p. 562 **(TE).**<br>• Choose 5 key questions for Objectives 1–4 to discuss with the class, pp. 562–567 **(TE).**<br>• Lead the students through the Critical Thinking activity, p. 567 **(TE).** | **Options for Cooperative Learning**<br>• Divide students into groups and have them complete the Interdisciplinary Link, Science: The World of the Buffalo, p. 563 **(TE).**<br>• Have student pairs work together to complete one of the Activity Options in the Section 2 Assessment, p. 567 **(PE).** | **Head Start on Homework Options**<br>• Have students begin working on Section 2 Assessment, p. 567 **(PE).**<br>• Have students complete the Reading History questions for Section 2, pp. 562–567 **(PE).** |
| **DAY 4**<br>Section 3<br>pp. 568–573 | **Presentation Options**<br>• Begin with the 5-Minute Warm-Up, p. 568 **(TE).**<br>• Choose 5 key questions for Objectives 1–4 to discuss with the class, pp. 568–571 **(TE).**<br>• Lead the students through the History from Visuals activities, p. 569 **(TE).** | **Options for Cooperative Learning**<br>• Divide students into groups and have them work on the Interdisciplinary Challenge, pp. 572–573 **(PE).**<br>• Have student pairs work together to complete one of the Interdisciplinary Link, Language Arts: Reacting to Farm Problem, p. 577 **(TE).** | **Head Start on Homework Options**<br>• Have students begin working on Section 3 Assessment, p. 571 **(PE).**<br>• Have students complete the Economics in History questions, p. 576 **(PE).** |
| **DAY 5**<br>Section 4<br>pp. 574–579 | **Presentation Options**<br>• Begin with the 5-Minute Warm-Up, p. 574 **(TE).**<br>• Choose 5 key questions for Objectives 1–4 to discuss with the class, pp. 574–579 **(TE).**<br>• Lead the students through the Economics in History feature, p. 576 **(TE).** | **Options for Cooperative Learning**<br>• Divide students into groups and have them complete the Interdisciplinary Link, Language Arts: Reacting to Farm Problems, p. 577 **(TE).**<br>• Have student pairs work together to complete one of the Activity Options in the Section 4 Assessment, p. 579 **(PE).** | **Head Start on Homework Options**<br>• Have students complete the Setting the Stage graphic organizer for the chapter, p. 556 **(PE).**<br>• Have students begin working on the Chapter Assessment, pp. 580–581 **(PE).**<br>• Prepare for Chapter Test<br>**Formal Assessment,** pp. 286–293 |

TEACHER-TESTED ACTIVITY Marci Smith, Hurst-Euless-Bedford ISD, Bedford, Texas

## ANALYZING PHOTOGRAPHS

**Class Time** Two class periods, one for preparation and one for presentation

**Task** Analyzing photographs of the West in the period from 1860 to 1900

**Purpose** To identify and describe images of Western life in the middle to late 1800s

**Supplies Needed**

- Art books and other picture books of life in the West, including paintings by Charles Russell and Frederic Remington
- Overhead projector or computer
- Materials for making transparencies

**Activity** Have each student select one picture from the art books to discuss with the class. Help students make transparencies or slides of their pictures or scan them into a classroom computer. Have students present their pictures to the class using the OSAE method. This technique has students Observe what is happening in the picture, Speculate on why it is happening and who is involved, Analyze the information, and Evaluate what it reveals about the time period. As a concluding activity, each student can write a caption for his or her picture.

## BLOCK SCHEDULING — LESSON PLAN OPTIONS (90-MINUTE PERIOD)

### DAY 1

**Interact with History,** p. 555
**Class Time** 20 minutes

Options for pacing and variety:

- Role-Playing Have students assume the role of a member of this Nebraska sodbuster family. Ask them to imagine that tonight will be their first night in their sod house. Have them write a letter to a friend back East explaining how their life has changed. **Class Time** 20 minutes

**Setting the Stage,** p. 556
**Class Time** 20 minutes

Options for pacing and variety:

- Time Saver Ask students to come to class with a list of words or phrases they associate with the terms *cowboy* and *Wild West.* Have students share their lists with the class and discuss where these associations came from. **Class Time** 10 minutes

**Section 1,** pp. 557–561
**Class Time** 50 minutes

Options for pacing and variety:

- History on Film Extend students' background knowledge of the West by viewing *Boom or Bust: Mining and the Opening of the West.* United Learning. **Class Time** 25 minutes
- Time Saver Have students complete their diagrams of the rise and fall of the cattle industry on page 561 of the Section Assessment at home. **Class Time** 5 minutes

### DAY 2

**Section 2,** pp. 562–567
**Class Time** 45 minutes

Options for pacing and variety:

- Peer Teaching Divide students into small groups. Using the information from the map on page 563, create a different way to present the information to the class. **Class Time** 25 minutes
- Time Saver For a written homework assignment, have students answer the Analyzing Leadership question on page 580 of the Chapter Assessment. **Class Time** 5 minutes

**Section 3,** pp. 568–573
**Class Time** 45 minutes

Options for pacing and variety:

- Peer Teaching Working in pairs, students can list five true-or-false statements about the Old West. Statements can include some common myths about the West. Collect responses and create a true-false quiz for the class. **Class Time** 20 minutes
- Internet Extend students' background knowledge of the American West by visiting www.mcdougallittell.com **Class Time** 20 minutes

### DAY 3

**Interdisciplinary Challenge,** pp. 572–573
**Class Time** 55 minutes

Options for pacing and variety:

- Team Teaching Invite the math teacher to your class to coach student groups as they solve the Math Challenge on page 572. **Class Time** 5 minutes

**Section 4,** pp. 574–579
**Class Time** 45 minutes

Options for pacing and variety:

- Time Saver As a homework assignment, have students complete their Read and Take Notes chart on page 556. **Class Time** 5 minutes
- Peer Teaching Ask three student volunteers to teach the Economics in History feature on page 576 to the class. One can summarize the content, the second can review the supply-and-demand diagram with the class, and the third can ask questions to check student comprehension. **Class Time** 15 minutes

**Chapter 19 Assessment,** pp. 580–581
**Class Time** 40 minutes

Options for pacing and variety:

- Peer Evaluation In four-member groups, have each student answer the review questions for one section of the chapter. When all groups have finished, regroup students so that those who answered questions for the same section can compare and evaluate their answers. **Class Time** 15 minutes
- Peer Teaching Have pairs of students create one Critical Thinking question for the chapter. Then have them exchange questions with another group to evaluate and answer questions. **Class Time** 10 minutes

## CHAPTER 19 OBJECTIVE

The student will understand how miners, ranchers, cowhands, and farmers helped settle the West and how their arrival led to conflict with the Native Americans.

# Growth in the West 1860–1900



## HISTORY FROM VISUALS

**Interpreting the Painting** Have students study the painting by cowboy artist Charles M. Russell. He was one of the most famous painters of the American West, known for works that show action and great detail. Russell worked for some time as a cowboy and trapper himself. Ask students what aspects of their image of the "West" this painting captures. **Possible Responses** Sagebrush, mountains, and cowboys on horseback roping cattle are all images associated with the West of the late 1800s. Ask students what the cowhands might be planning to do with this cow once it is tied up. **Possible Response** They may be preparing to brand it.

**Extension** Have students write a short biographical sketch of one of these cowboys telling where he came from and why he moved west.

Life in the West was hard and dangerous, as this Charles M. Russell painting of cowhands shows.

## RECOMMENDED RESOURCES

**BOOKS FOR THE TEACHER**

Robinson, Charles M., III. ***A Good Year to Die: The Story of the Great Sioux War.*** New York: Random House, 1995. Authentic story of this conflict as seen by the Sioux and the U.S. Cavalry.

Twain, Mark. ***Roughing It.*** New York: Oxford, 1996. Adventures and misadventures of the not-yet-famous writer.

White, Richard. ***"It's Your Misfortune and None of My Own": A New History of the American West.*** Norman, OK: U. of Oklahoma Press, 1993. Groundbreaking account by a leader of the movement for a "new history of the West."

**VIDEO**

***Crazy Horse.*** Time-Life, 1997. Story of the great Oglala Sioux leader.

**INTERNET**

For more about the American West or Exodusters, visit www.mcdougallittell.com

## Interact *with* History

farmland
sod house built into side of hill
horse and wagon

A Nebraska "sodbuster" family takes time away from their chores to pose in front of their sod house.

**It is 1865, and the Civil War has just ended. You are drawn to the West by stories of gold, silver, fertile soil, and free land, and by tales of adventure and new opportunities. Yet you know there would be hardships and unknown dangers. Your life would never be the same.**

### What Do You Think?

- **What might be some of the ways to make a living in the West?**
- **What do you think your daily life would be like in the West?**
- **What would be the biggest difference in your life?**

# *How might your life change in the West?*

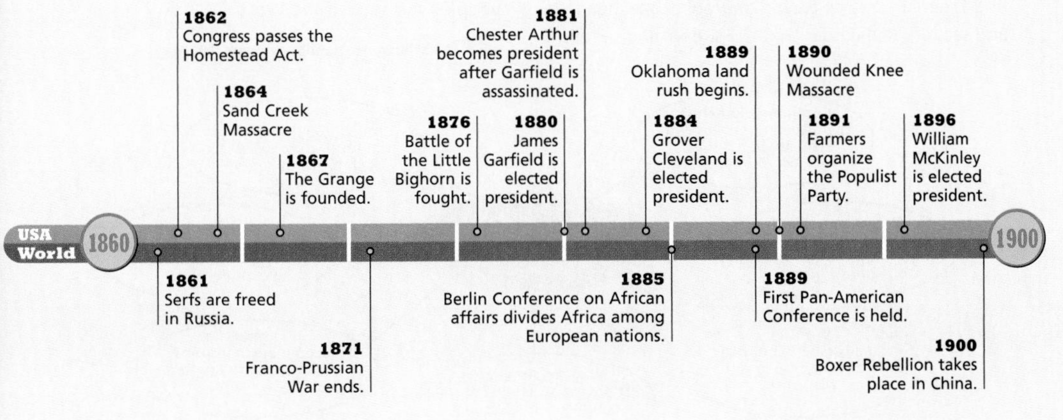
USA
World
1860
1900
1862 Congress passes the Homestead Act.
1864 Sand Creek Massacre
1867 The Grange is founded.
1876 Battle of the Little Bighorn is fought.
1880 James Garfield is elected president.
1881 Chester Arthur becomes president after Garfield is assassinated.
1884 Grover Cleveland is elected president.
1889 Oklahoma land rush begins.
1890 Wounded Knee Massacre
1891 Farmers organize the Populist Party.
1896 William McKinley is elected president.
1861 Serfs are freed in Russia.
1871 Franco-Prussian War ends.
1885 Berlin Conference on African affairs divides Africa among European nations.
1889 First Pan-American Conference is held.
1900 Boxer Rebellion takes place in China.

## Interact *with* History

### OBJECTIVES

- To help students identify some of the challenges and hardships of moving west
- To help students connect with the people and events they will study in this chapter

### What Do You Think?

1. Students might think about the natural resources of the West that Americans knew about at that time—gold, silver, good cattle grazing, and free land.
2. Students might consider how settlers were often isolated from one another and lacked the services typically associated with life in or near a city. They might also consider how families would have to become more self-reliant.
3. Students might consider how moving west might mean breaking ties with friends and family and taking on new responsibilities. It might also mean a more exciting or adventurous life than the one students had back East.

### *How might your life change in the West?*

Encourage students to think about services that are a part of everyday life in settled communities and that would not be available in a sparsely settled area. Students might also consider how the separation from friends and family and the social isolation caused by the great distances between homesteads might affect them.

### MAKING PERSONAL CONNECTIONS

Ask students how they define *adventure.* There are different kinds of adventures. What level of danger are students willing to accept for the sake of adventure?

### TIME LINE DISCUSSION

**Even as North battled South in the Civil War, cowboys, ranchers, miners, and farmers moved westward. The increasing pressure of newcomers caused conflict with Native Americans and, in the end, changed Native American culture forever. Elsewhere in the world, other "empty" areas were also being settled.**

- Ask students what events on the time line suggest that Congress and the federal government were involved in the settlement of the West. **Answer** passing of Homestead Act and conflicts with Native Americans
- Ask students what events on the time line indicate that there was conflict between Native Americans and white settlers. **Answer** Sand Creek Massacre, Battle of the Little Bighorn, Wounded Knee Massacre
- What event indicates that European nations were settling in Africa? **Answer** Berlin Conference

## BEFORE YOU READ

### Previewing the Theme: Diversity and Unity

Have students examine the map and notice the difference in the size of the arrows. Ask students where the largest number of settlers came from.

### What Do You Know?

Students may begin by listing specific movies or television programs about the West that they have seen. Then they may discuss what they have learned about the settling of the West from these and other media. Ask students how their view of the conflicts between Native Americans and ranchers, miners, cowhands, and other white settlers has been influenced by the media.

 **In-Depth Resources: Unit 6**
- Tracing Themes: Diversity and Unity, p. 2

## READ AND TAKE NOTES

### Reading Strategy: Finding Main Ideas

Remind students that main ideas are the most important ideas or topics of paragraphs or sections. Details support and explain the main ideas. Point out the topic in the center of the chart and the main ideas surrounding it. Suggest that students look for details to explain each idea as they read the chapter.

 **In-Depth Resources: Unit 6**
- Setting the Stage, p. 1

 **Critical Thinking Transparency CT55**
- Setting the Stage

# Chapter 19 SETTING THE STAGE

## BEFORE YOU READ

### Preview the Theme

**Diversity and Unity** As Chapter 19 explains, hundreds of thousands of men, women, and children packed up their belongings and went to the West after the Civil War. Most were looking for new opportunities and land of their own; some were seeking freedom or adventure. Their arrival led to conflict with the Native Americans, who were the first occupants of the area.

### What Do You Know?

What do you think about when you hear terms like *cowboy* and *Wild West?* What do you already know about the people, places, and events in the West in the last half of the 19th century?

**THINK ABOUT**
- what you have learned about the West from books, movies, and television
- what happens when different cultures clash

### What Do You Want to Know?

What details do you need to help you understand the settling of the West? Make a list of those details in your notebook before you read the chapter.

## READ AND TAKE NOTES

**Reading Strategy: Finding Main Ideas** To make it easier for you to understand what you read, learn to find the main idea of each paragraph, topic heading, and section. Remember that the supporting details help to explain the main ideas. On the chart below, write down the main ideas about the many diverse people who settled the West.

 See Skillbuilder Handbook, page R5.

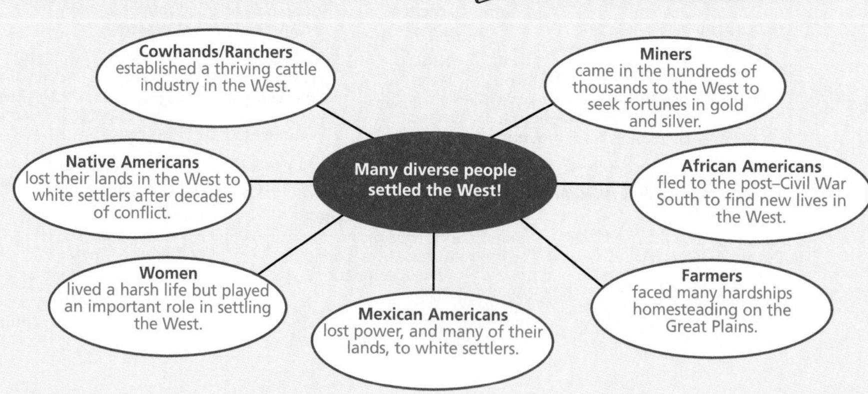

Many diverse people settled the West!
Cowhands/Ranchers established a thriving cattle industry in the West.
Miners came in the hundreds of thousands to the West to seek fortunes in gold and silver.
Native Americans lost their lands in the West to white settlers after decades of conflict.
African Americans fled to the post–Civil War South to find new lives in the West.
Women lived a harsh life but played an important role in settling the West.
Mexican Americans lost power, and many of their lands, to white settlers.
Farmers faced many hardships homesteading on the Great Plains.

556 CHAPTER 19

## TEACHING STRATEGY

### READING THE CHAPTER

This is a thematic chapter focusing on the growth of the West after the Civil War. Encourage students to note the diverse groups of people who settled the West and how life changed for Native Americans as settlement took place.

### ALTERNATIVE ASSESSMENT

The Chapter Assessment describes three activities for alternative assessment on page 581. You may wish to have students work on these activities during the course of the chapter and then present them at the end.

1

# Miners, Ranchers, and Cowhands

**TERMS & NAMES**
frontier
Great Plains
boomtown
long drive
*vaquero*
vigilante

**MAIN IDEA**
Miners, ranchers, and cowhands settled in the West seeking economic opportunities.

**WHY IT MATTERS NOW**
The mining and cattle industries that developed then still contribute to American economic growth.

## ONE AMERICAN'S STORY

**Nat Love was born a slave in Tennessee in 1854. After the Civil War, he was one of thousands of African Americans who left the South and went west. In 1869, Love headed for Dodge City, Kansas. He was 15 and now free.**

**Love's horse taming skills landed him a job as a cowhand. For 20 years, he took part in the cattle drives that brought Texas cattle to Kansas stockyards. He became well known for his expert horsemanship and his rodeo riding and roping. In his 1907 autobiography, Love offered a lively but exaggerated account of his life. He told how he braved hailstorms, fought wild animals, and held off human attackers.**

*A VOICE FROM THE PAST*

I carry the marks of fourteen bullet wounds on different parts of my body, most any one of which would be sufficient to kill an ordinary man. . . . Horses were shot from under me, men killed around me, but always I escaped with a trifling wound at the worst.

**Nat Love,** *The Life and Adventures of Nat Love*

Nat Love was an African-American cowhand who became a rodeo star.

**As you will read in this section, few cowhands led lives as exciting as that described by Nat Love, but they all helped to open a new chapter in the history of the American West.**

### 1 Geography and Population of the West

In the mid-1800s, towns such as St. Joseph and Independence, Missouri, were jumping-off places for settlers going west. They were the last cities and towns before the frontier. The **frontier** was the unsettled or sparsely settled area of the country occupied largely by Native Americans.

Many white settlers thought of the **Great Plains**—the area from the Missouri River to the Rocky Mountains—as empty. (See map on page 558.) Few had been attracted to its rolling plains, dry plateaus, and deserts. However, west of the Rockies, on the Pacific Coast, settlers had followed miners streaming into California after the 1849 gold rush. By 1850, California had gained statehood. Oregon followed in 1859.





## SECTION OBJECTIVES

1. To describe the geography and population of the West
2. To explain how mining in the West led to settlement
3. To describe the cattle industry
4. To analyze how law and order was established in the West

**SKILLBUILDER**
Interpreting Maps: Region, Human-Environment Interaction, p. 558

**CRITICAL THINKING**
Making Inferences, p. 558
Recognizing Effects, p. 559
Analyzing Causes, p. 561
Evaluating, p. 561

## FOCUS & MOTIVATE

### 5-MINUTE WARM-UP

**Comparing** These questions focus on changes in the population of the West from 1850 to 1890.

1. Look at the map on page 558. What was the most densely populated part of the United States in 1850?
2. How had the area along the Missouri River changed by 1890?

 **Warm-Up Transparency WT19**

## INSTRUCT

**INSTRUCT: OBJECTIVE 1**

**Geography and Population of the West**
Key Questions
- Why did few settlers make their homes on the Great Plains?
- What part did railroads play in the settlement of the West?

**In-Depth Resources: Unit 6**
- Guided Reading, p. 3

**Reading Study Guide** (Spanish and English), pp. 185–186

## RECOMMENDED RESOURCES

**In-Depth Resources: Unit 6**
- Guided Reading, p. 3
- Building Vocabulary, p. 7
- Skillbuilder Practice, p. 8
- Literature Selection, pp. 13–15
- Reteaching Activity, p. 16

**Reading Study Guide** (Spanish and English), pp. 185–186

 **Outline Map Activities**
- The Population of the West, 1890, pp. 37–38

**Formal Assessment**
- Section Quiz, p. 282

 **Alternative Assessment**
- Rubrics, 4.4
- Rubrics, 4.8

 **Access for Students Acquiring English/ESL**
- Guided Reading, p. 126
- Skillbuilder Practice, p. 130

**Technology Resources**

 **America's Music CD**

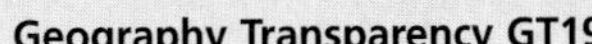

**Geography Transparency GT19**
- Gold and Silver Deposits in the West, 1849–1895

 **Electronic Teacher Tools with Test Maker**

 **ClassZone**
www.mcdougallittell.com

## HISTORY FROM VISUALS

**Reading the Maps** Have students suggest possible reasons why areas in the Rocky Mountains and in present-day Nevada and Montana remained sparsely settled in 1890. **Possible Responses** These were very dry, barren lands with little water for farming, poor soil, or mountainous terrain unsuitable for farming.

**Extension** Have students pick five western states that were sparsely settled in 1890 and use an almanac to find their population density today.

**Outline Map Activities**
- The Population of the West, 1890, pp. 37–38

## INSTRUCT: OBJECTIVE 2

**Mining in the West**

Key Questions
- What developments opened Colorado and Nevada to settlement?
- What effect did gold and silver strikes have on small towns?
- How did the mining process change over time?

**Geography Transparency GT19**
- Gold and Silver Deposits in the West, 1849–1895

## MORE ABOUT . . .

**Virginia City**

The Comstock Lode was known to many as the "Big Bonanza." Bonanza barons, lucky miners who became instant millionaires, built Victorian-style mansions in Virginia City. By 1876, the boomtown had 20 laundries, 54 dry-goods stores, 6 churches, and more than 100 saloons. It also had an opera house and several theaters where actors performed Italian light operas, vaudeville, and even some Shakespeare.

### *The Western Frontier,* 1850–1890

1850

1890

Rocky Mountains

Missouri R.

Great Plains

Mississippi R.

Settled area (2 or more people per square mile)

**GEOGRAPHY SKILLBUILDER**
**Interpreting Maps**
1. **Region** *What change took place in the far western coastal area from 1850 to 1890?*
2. **Human-Environment Interaction** *Which areas of the West generally were unsettled?*

Skillbuilder Answers
1. It was almost totally settled.
2. Possible Response the areas where people find it difficult to live, such as the mountains

The Great Plains had few trees, but its grasslands were home to about 300,000 Native Americans in the mid-1800s. Most followed the buffalo herds that rumbled across the open plains. Despite the presence of these peoples, the United States claimed ownership of the area.

Railroads played a key role in settling the western United States. Trains carried the natural resources of the West—minerals, timber, crops, and cattle—to eastern markets. In turn, trains brought miners, ranchers, and farmers west to develop these resources further. As the railroads opened new areas to white settlement, they also helped to bring an end to the way of life of the West's first settlers—the Native Americans.

**A. Possible Answer** They brought settlers to the West and returned the West's products to the rest of the nation.

*Reading* **History**
**A. Making Inferences** Why were railroads so important to the West?

## 2 Mining in the West

In 1859, gold and silver strikes drew fortune seekers to Colorado and Nevada. As many as 100,000 miners raced to the Rocky Mountains in Colorado after gold was discovered near Pikes Peak. Also in 1859, prospectors hit "pay dirt" at the Comstock Lode in western Nevada. (A lode is a deposit of a valuable mineral buried in layers of rock.) From 1859 to 1880, the Comstock mine produced some $300 million in silver and gold.

**Vocabulary**
**strike:** valuable discovery of a precious mineral

Nearby Virginia City, Nevada, became a **boomtown,** a town that has a sudden burst of economic or population growth. Population jumped from 3,000 in the 1860s to over 20,000 in the 1870s. The writer Samuel Clemens, better known as Mark Twain, captured the excitement of life there.

*A VOICE FROM THE PAST*

The sidewalks swarmed with people. . . . Money was as plenty as dust; [everyone] considered himself wealthy. . . . There were . . . fire companies, brass bands, banks, hotels, theaters . . . gambling palaces . . . street-fights, murders, . . . riots, . . . and a half dozen jails . . . in full operation.

**Mark Twain,** *Roughing It*

Other major strikes took place in the Black Hills of South Dakota in 1874 and at Cripple Creek, Colorado, in 1891. In 1896, gold was discovered in



## ACTIVITY OPTIONS

## INDIVIDUAL NEEDS

**LESS PROFICIENT READERS**

**Sequencing Events** Some students may have difficulty understanding the events and the subsequent effects related to the growth of the mining industry in the West. Reread the section "Mining in the West" with these students and work with them to create a flow chart similar to the one shown.

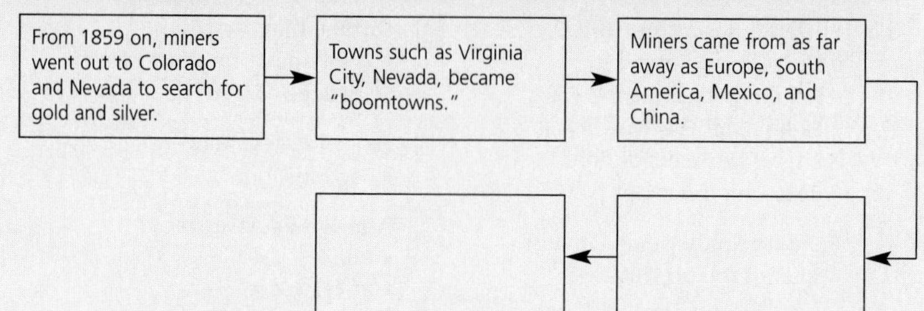

From 1859 on, miners went out to Colorado and Nevada to search for gold and silver.
Towns such as Virginia City, Nevada, became "boomtowns."
Miners came from as far away as Europe, South America, Mexico, and China.

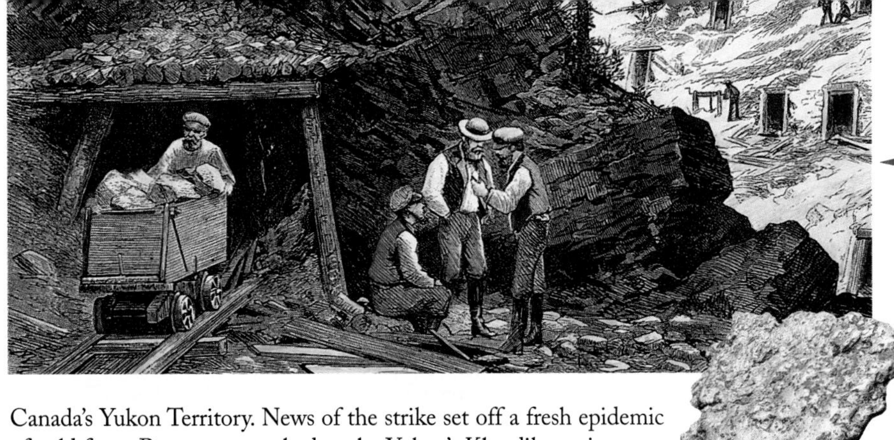

Miners brought ore, like the gold nugget shown, from underground mines that dotted the hillsides.

Canada's Yukon Territory. News of the strike set off a fresh epidemic of gold fever. Prospectors rushed to the Yukon's Klondike region.

The chance to strike it rich drew Americans from both east and west coasts. Gold fever also attracted miners from other parts of the world, including Europe, South America, Mexico, and China. Unfortunately, few prospectors became rich. Most left, disappointed and broke.

Early miners used panning and sluicing to wash sand and gravel from a stream to separate out any bits of precious metal, as you read in Chapter 13. Large mining companies moved in after surface mines no longer yielded gold or silver. Only they could buy the costly, heavy equipment needed to take the precious metals from underground. Water cannons blasted away hillsides to expose gold deposits. In other places, workers sank shafts thousands of feet into the ground to create underground mines. These new methods recovered more precious metals, but in the process stripped hillsides of vegetation and left rivers polluted.

*Reading* **History**
**B. Recognizing Effects** Why did large mining companies replace individual prospectors?
B. Answer Only the companies had the money to buy equipment to mine ore underground.

Paid workers in company mines replaced independent prospectors. The work was hard and dangerous. Dust caused lung problems, and deadly cave-ins could trap miners hundreds of feet below the surface.

By the 1890s, the mining boom was over. Many mines closed because the costs had become too high, and the quality of the ore had dropped. Jobless workers moved elsewhere. Once-thriving communities became ghost towns. Still, the mining boom had lasting effects. Nevada, Colorado, and South Dakota all grew so rapidly that they soon gained statehood.

## 3 The Rise of the Cattle Industry

The cattle trade had existed in the Southwest since the Spanish arrived there in the 1500s. But cattle herds remained small until the Civil War. There were few buyers for western beef because there was no efficient way to get the beef to markets in the more heavily populated cities of the East. The ranchers mostly sold their cattle locally.

The extension of railroad lines from Chicago and St. Louis into Kansas by the 1860s brought changes. An Illinois livestock dealer named Joseph McCoy realized that railroads could bring cattle from Texas ranches to meat-hungry eastern cities. Cowhands had only to drive cattle herds north from Texas to his stockyards in Abilene, Kansas. From there, the beef could be shipped to Chicago and points east by rail car.





### MORE ABOUT . . .

**Miners**

In many ways miners were a diverse group, but most of them were young, single men. In company-owned mines, the top-paying jobs went to native-born Americans and immigrants from western and northern Europe. Immigrants from southern and eastern Europe loaded and pushed carts of ore. Chinese laborers carried ore and rubble out of the mines, made meals, and washed clothes. Hispanics often did exactly the same jobs as other miners but made less money.

### CRITICAL THINKING ACTIVITY

**Comparing** Have students compare the mining methods of early prospectors with the type of mining done later in company mines. What were the risks and rewards of each type of mining?

**Class Time** 10 minutes

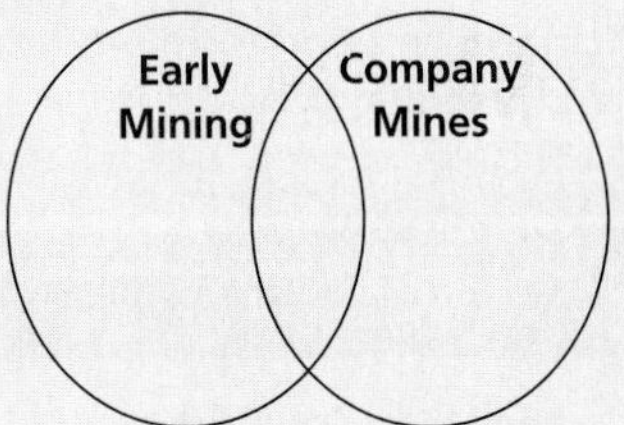


### INSTRUCT: OBJECTIVE 3

**The Rise of the Cattle Industry/ *Vaqueros* and Cowhands**

Key Questions

- What made cattle ranching profitable?
- What was the purpose of the long drive?
- What ranching skills did American cowhands learn from the *vaqueros*?
- What kinds of people became cowhands?

**ACTIVITY OPTIONS**

### SKILLBUILDER MINI-LESSON: USING THE INTERNET

BLOCK SCHEDULING

**Explaining the Skill** The Internet offers a wealth of historical information, providing access to museums, library collections, original government documents, and the opinions of noted scholars. However, in doing Internet research, it is important to evaluate the reliability and usefulness of the sources of information. Reliable sources include universities, libraries, and other educational or government Web sites. Personal Web pages are less reliable.

**Applying the Skill** Have students visit www.mcdougallittell.com to look for two links to the West located on this site. Then have students find a third Web site on the West and write a review of all three sites indicating what types of information each offers, how each is organized, how easy it is to access and find information on each site, and how reliable a source each is.

 **In-Depth Resources: Unit 6**
- Skillbuilder Practice, p. 8

## MORE ABOUT . . .

**The Chisholm Trail**

Although the word *trail* suggests that cattle traveled in a long line on a well-marked path, in fact the cattle on the long drives fanned out across a vast area, coming together mostly at river crossings. Because dozens of herds went north at the same time, cattle spread out to find grass and graze as they went north. A trail boss, ten cowboys, a cook, and a horse wrangler could take 2,500 cattle to the railhead in about three months, averaging 10 to 12 miles a day. In good conditions, longhorn cattle gained weight on the journey north, increasing their value.

## INSTRUCT: OBJECTIVE 

**The "Wild West"/End of the Long Drives**

Key Questions

- What were the main causes of disorder in cow towns?
- How did citizens respond to these threats?
- What ended the long drives?

## daily*life*

**Life of a Cowhand: The Roundup**

After cattle were rounded up, they were branded. Cowhands marked calves with red-hot branding irons to identify them as the property of certain ranches. Branding a calf took about four seconds. On the long drive, many trail bosses carried a small branding book that listed all the ranchers' brands and the ranchers' names and locations. Cattle sometimes wandered hundreds of miles from their ranches. In the West, newspapers printed lists of lost or stray cattle.

 **In-Depth Resources: Unit 6**

- Literature Selection: "Stampede on the Cimarron" by J. Frank Dobie, pp. 13–15

McCoy's plan turned cattle ranching into a very profitable business. Cattle fed on the open range for a year or two and cost the rancher nothing. Ranchers then hired cowhands to round up the cattle and take them to Abilene. There they were sold for as much as ten times their original price. The success of the Abilene stockyards spurred the growth of other Kansas cow towns, including Wichita and Dodge City. The cattle drives to cow towns along the railways were called the **long drives**.

Over time, cowhands followed specific trails across the plains. The first was the Chisholm Trail, which stretched from San Antonio, Texas, to Abilene, Kansas. It was named for Jesse Chisholm, a trader who marked the northern part of the route. From 1867 to 1884, about four million cattle were driven to market on this trail. As cattle raising became more profitable, ranching spread north across the plains from Texas to Montana.

*Reading* **History**

**C. Reading a Map** Use the map on page 581 to locate the Chisholm Trail.

## *Vaqueros* and Cowhands

The first cowhands, or ***vaqueros***, as they were known in Spanish, came from Mexico with the Spaniards in the 1500s. They settled in the Southwest. The *vaqueros* helped Spanish, and later Mexican, ranchers manage their herds. From the *vaquero*, the American cowhand learned to rope and ride. Cowhands also adapted the saddle, spurs, lariat (which they used to rope a calf or steer), and chaps of the *vaqueros*.

About one in three cowhands in the West were either Mexican or African American. Many Mexican cowhands were descendants of the *vaqueros*. Some African-American cowhands were former slaves. They came west at the end of Reconstruction because the enactment of Black Codes in the South put restrictions on their freedom. Also among the cowhands were a large number of former Confederate and Union soldiers.

**Background**

Chaps, from the Spanish word *chaperejos*, were seatless leather pants worn over trousers to protect legs from scrub brush, snakes, and cactus.

## 4 The "Wild West"

At first, the rapidly growing cow towns had no local governments. There were no law officers to handle the fights that broke out as cowhands drank and gambled after a long drive. A more serious threat to law and order came from "con men." These swindlers saw new towns as places to get rich quick by cheating others.

**Vocabulary**

**con man:** a person who cheats victims by first gaining their confidence

**daily *life***

**LIFE OF A COWHAND: THE ROUNDUP**

During some parts of the year, the cowhand's life was downright dull. While cattle grazed on the open range, cowhands sat around the ranch, repairing their gear and doing odd jobs. The pace quickened at roundup time in the spring and fall.

For several weeks, 150 to 250 cowhands from nearby ranches rode hundreds of miles locating cattle. Cowhands from each ranch collected their cattle, removed sick or weak animals, and branded new calves. Then the cowhands were ready for the long drive. A roundup by *vaqueros* is shown in this painting by James Walker.

**ACTIVITY OPTIONS**

**MULTIPLE LEARNING STYLES: MUSICAL** 

**COWBOY STYLES**

**Class Time** One class period

**Task** Analyzing primary sources

**Purpose** To gain an understanding of the daily life of a cowhand

**Supplies Needed**

- Copies of cowboy songs and ballads from such song books as *Cowboy Songs and Other Frontier Ballads* by John and Alan Lomax and *Songs of the Wild West* by Alan Axelrod and Dan Fox

 **America's Music CD**

**Activity** Ask students to prepare a selection of cowboy songs, either live with guitar accompaniment, or from CDs and tapes. Songs may include "Git Along, Little Dogies," "The Old Chisholm Trail," "Night-Herding Song," "The Texas Cowboy," and "The Railroad Corral." These "livestock lullabies" describe both the cowhand's job and his feelings about the work. Have students list five words or phrases that describe the songs and write a paragraph explaining what the songs reveal about cowboy life.

Some Union and Confederate veterans were led to crime by hard feelings left over from the Civil War. Outlaws like John Wesley Hardin, "Billy the Kid," and Jesse and Frank James made crime a way of life. Some women became outlaws, too. Belle Starr, better known as the Bandit Queen, was a legendary horse thief.

For protection, citizens formed vigilante groups. **Vigilantes** were people who took the law into their own hands. They caught suspected criminals and punished them without a trial. Vigilante justice often consisted of hanging suspects from the nearest tree or shooting them on the spot. As towns became more settled, citizens elected a local sheriff or asked the federal government for a marshal. These law officers would arrest lawbreakers and hold them in jail until the time of trial.

**Bandit Queen Belle Starr sits atop a horse she just might have stolen.**

## End of the Long Drives

For about 20 years, the cattle industry boomed. As the railroads extended farther west and south into Texas, the long drives grew shorter. The future looked bright. But by 1886, several developments had brought the cattle boom to an end. First, the price of beef dropped sharply as the supply increased in the early 1880s. It fell from more than $30 a head to $7. Then came the newly invented barbed wire. As more settlers moved to the Great Plains to farm or raise sheep, they fenced in their lands with barbed wire. The open range disappeared, and cattle could no longer pass freely over the trails. Finally, in the harsh winter of 1886–1887, thousands of cattle on the northern Plains froze to death. Many ranchers were put out of business.

Meanwhile, as the mining and cattle industries were developing, the Native Americans of the Great Plains were being pushed off their land, as you will read in the next section.

**D. Answer** arrival of farmers and sheep raisers, use of barbed wire, and harsh weather

*Reading* **History**

**D. Analyzing Causes** What caused the decline of cattle ranching on the open range?

### Section 1 Assessment

**1. Terms & Names**

**Identify:**
- frontier
- Great Plains
- boomtown
- long drive
- *vaquero*
- vigilante

**2. Taking Notes**

Use a diagram to review the rise and fall of the cattle industry.

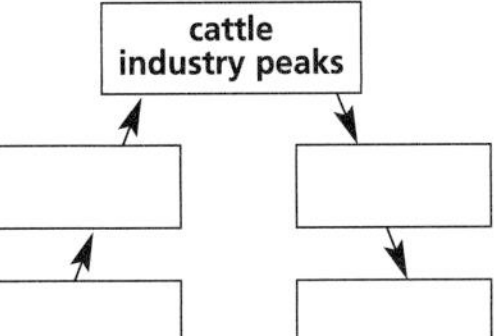


**3. Main Ideas**

a. What economic opportunities drew large numbers of people to the West beginning in the 1860s?

b. How did the transcontinental railroad spur western settlement?

c. What did cowhands learn from the *vaqueros?*

**4. Critical Thinking**

**Evaluating** Could cattle ranchers have stopped the decline of the cattle industry that occurred in the late 1880s?

**THINK ABOUT**
- economic causes
- impact of weather
- changing settlement patterns

**ACTIVITY OPTIONS**

**LANGUAGE ARTS**
**MUSIC**

Do research on a legendary figure of the West such as Wyatt Earp, "Calamity Jane," or Nat Love. Then write a **biographical sketch** or **song** about the person.





### MORE ABOUT . . .

**Belle Starr**

Born Myra Maybelle Shirley, Belle Starr grew up in Missouri, where she spent much time outdoors. Her older brother Bud taught her to ride and shoot. Although legend describes her as the leader of a gang of vicious cattle rustlers, Starr's illegai activities consisted primarily of horse stealing and hiding fugitives from justice. Belle once said of herself, "I regard myself as a woman who has seen much of life." These words are engraved on her tombstone: "Shed not for her the bitter tear / Nor give the heart to vain regret / Tis but the casket that lies here / The gem that filled it sparkles yet."

## ASSESS & RETEACH

**Setting the Stage** Have students fill in the Cowhands/Ranchers, Miners, and African Americans sections on the chapter graphic organizer.

 **Formal Assessment**
- Section Quiz, p. 282

 **Critical Thinking Transparency CT55**
- Setting the Stage

### RETEACHING ACTIVITY

Ask students to write a paragraph each on ranchers, miners, and cowhands. Students should explain why they came west, what they hoped to gain by doing so, and how each group changed the West.

 **In-Depth Resources: Unit 6**
- Reteaching Activity, p. 16

### Section 1 Assessment

**1. Terms & Names**

**frontier,** p. 557
**Great Plains,** p. 557
**boomtown,** p. 558
**long drive,** p. 560
***vaquero,*** p. 560
**vigilante,** p. 561

**2. Taking Notes**

Rises: Railroad lines to Kansas; long drives; Falls: open range fenced in; 1886–1887 blizzards

**3. Main Ideas**

**a.** mining; ranching; farming
**b.** carried natural resources of the West to the East and brought white settlers from the East to the West
**c.** how to rope, ride, and manage their herds

**4. Critical Thinking**

probably not, because they had little control over falling prices, the fencing of the open range, and bad weather

**ACTIVITY OPTIONS**

 **Alternative Assessment**
- Rubrics for a biography, 4.4
- Rubrics for a song, 4.8

## SECTION OBJECTIVES

1. To describe Native American life on the Plains
2. To explain how Plains tribes responded to white attempts to take away their lands
3. To identify the outcome of Native American resistance efforts
4. To evaluate the impact of the Dawes Act on the Plains tribes

**SKILLBUILDER**

Interpreting Maps: Location, Movement, p. 563

**CRITICAL THINKING**

Analyzing Causes, p. 563
Recognizing Effects, pp. 565, 567
Drawing Conclusions, p. 566
Analyzing Points of View, p. 567

## FOCUS & MOTIVATE

### 5-MINUTE WARM-UP

**Recognizing Effects** These questions focus on the effects of white settlement on Native American lands.

1. Look at the map on page 563. During which years was most Native American land west of the Mississippi lost?
2. Where did most Native Americans live after 1890?

 Warm-Up Transparency WT19

## INSTRUCT

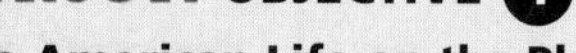

**INSTRUCT: OBJECTIVE 1**

**Native American Life on the Plains**

Key Questions
- How did horses change the way of life of the Plains people?
- Why was the buffalo important to Plains tribes?

 **In-Depth Resources: Unit 6**
- Guided Reading, p. 4

# 2 Native Americans Fight to Survive

**TERMS & NAMES**
reservation
Sand Creek Massacre
Sitting Bull
George A. Custer
Battle of the Little Bighorn
Wounded Knee Massacre
Dawes Act

**MAIN IDEA**

The Native Americans of the Great Plains fought to maintain their way of life as settlers poured onto their lands.

**WHY IT MATTERS NOW**

The taking of their lands led to social and economic problems for Native Americans that continue to this day.

### ONE AMERICAN'S STORY

**Buffalo Bird Woman was a Hidatsa who lived almost 100 years. She was born in 1840. As a child, she and her family made their home along the Missouri River. Later the federal government forced her family onto a reservation. A <u>reservation</u> is land set aside for Native American tribes.**

**The federal government attempted to "Americanize" Native American children, including Buffalo Bird Woman, by sending them away to boarding schools. But Buffalo Bird Woman struggled to hold on to Hidatsa customs. She spoke only her native language and wore traditional dress. As an old woman, she looked back on her early years.**

*A VOICE FROM THE PAST*

Sometimes at evening I sit, looking out on the . . . Missouri [river]. . . . In the shadows I seem . . . to see our Indian village, with smoke curling upward from the earth lodges; and in the river's roar I hear the yells of the warriors, the laughter of . . . children as of old. It is but an old woman's dream. . . . Our Indian life, I know, is gone forever.

**Buffalo Bird Woman,** quoted in *Native American Testimony,* edited by Peter Nabokov

**Buffalo Bird Woman's life spanned the years when Native Americans waged their final fight to keep lands guaranteed to them by treaties. As white settlers claimed Native American hunting grounds, Plains peoples fought a losing battle to save not only their land but their way of life.**

**Buffalo Bird Woman saw the Native American way of life chang[e] forever during he[r] almost 100 years of life.**

## 1 Native American Life on the Plains

Before the arrival of Europeans in the 1500s, most Plains tribes lived in villages along rivers and streams. The women tended crops of beans, corn, and squash. The men hunted deer and elk and in the summer stalked the vast buffalo herds that inhabited the Plains.

In the early 1540s, the Spanish brought the first horses to the Great Plains. The arrival of horses changed the way of life of the Plains people. They quickly became expert riders. By the late 1700s, most Plains tribes kept their own herds of horses. Mounted on horseback, hunters traveled far from their villages seeking buffalo.

## RECOMMENDED RESOURCES

**In-Depth Resources: Unit 6**
- Guided Reading, p. 4
- Building Vocabulary, p. 7
- Geography Application: Custer's Last Stand, pp. 9–10
- Primary Source, p. 11
- Reteaching Activity, p. 17

**Reading Study Guide** (Spanish and English), pp. 187–188

**America's History Makers**
- Sitting Bull, pp. 75–76

**American History Plays**
- *"I Will Fight No More Forever"* by Kathy Wilmore

**Formal Assessment**
- Section Quiz, p. 283

**Alternative Assessment**
- Rubrics, 5.1
- Rubrics, 3.6

**Access for Students Acquiring English/ESL**
- Guided Reading, p. 127
- Geography Application, pp. 131–132

Technology Resources

 **Humanities Transparency HT37**
- *Battle of the Little Bighorn* by Kicking Bear

 **Critical Thinking Trans. CT56**
- Cause and Effect: Native American Wars

 **Electronic Teacher Tools with Test Maker**

 **ClassZone**
www.mcdougallittell.com

The buffalo was central to the life of Plains tribes. Its meat became the chief food in their diet, while its skins served as portable shelters called tepees. Plains women turned buffalo hides into clothing, shoes, and blankets and used buffalo chips (dried manure) as cooking fuel. Bones and horns became tools and bowls. Over time, many Plains tribes developed a nomadic way of life tied to buffalo hunting.

**Vocabulary**
**nomadic:** wandering from place to place **2**

## A Clash of Cultures

When the federal government first forced Native American tribes of the Southeast to move west of the Mississippi in the 1830s, it settled them in Indian Territory. This territory was a huge area that included almost all of the land between the Missouri River and Oregon Territory. Most treaties made by the government with Native Americans promised that this land would remain theirs "as long as Grass grows or water runs."

A. Answer White settlers wanted Native American lands.

**Reading History**
**A. Analyzing Causes** What was the major source of conflict between white settlers and Native Americans?

Unfortunately, these treaty promises would be broken. Government policy was based on the belief that white settlers were not interested in the Plains. The land was considered too dry for farming. However, as wagon trains bound for Oregon and California crossed the Great Plains in the 1850s, some pioneers saw possibilities for farming and ranching on its grasslands. Soon white settlers moved onto the prairies.

These settlers pressured the federal government for more land. They also wanted protection from Native Americans in the area. In 1851, the government responded by calling the Sioux, Cheyenne, Arapaho, and

Skillbuilder Answers
**1. Possible Responses** Great Plains; north-central states and territories; northwest
**2.** Native Americans in the West were forced off their lands and onto reservations.

**INSTRUCT: OBJECTIVE 2**

**A Clash of Cultures**
Key Questions
- Why did the government break its promises not to open Indian Territory to white settlement?
- How did the Sand Creek and Fetterman massacres affect government policy toward Native Americans?

 **Critical Thinking Transparency CT56**
- Cause and Effect: Native American Wars

### Native American Lands in the West, 1850–1890

Land lost by Native Americans
- Before 1850
- 1850–1870
- 1870–1890
- Native American reservations in 1890
- Never formally ceded by treaty

0 — 400 Miles
0 — 800 Kilometers

**MAJOR EVENTS OF THE INDIAN WARS**
1. **Sand Creek Massacre,** 1864
2. **Fetterman Massacre,** 1866
3. **Battle of the Little Bighorn,** 1876
4. **Geronimo surrenders,** 1886
5. **Wounded Knee Massacre,** 1890

**GEOGRAPHY SKILLBUILDER**
**Interpreting Maps**
1. **Location** *In which area of the West did most of the major battles take place?*
2. **Movement** *What was the major change that took place in the West between 1850 and 1890?*

563

### HISTORY FROM VISUALS

**Reading the Maps** Ask students during which time period most Native American groups on the West Coast were forced to give up their land. **Answer** 1850–1870. Ask students to recall what was happening during that time period and how those events impacted Native American lands. **Possible Response** Discovery of gold and silver in the West and the demand for land; settlers wanted lands held by Native Americans. Have students locate the reservations in 1890. Ask them to describe the location of those reservations. **Possible Response** They are in remote locations, in mountainous or dry plains areas.

**Extension** Have students choose one of the Native American groups from the map and research the current status of this group and where its members currently live.

 **Humanities Transparency HT37**
- *Battle of the Little Bighorn*

**ACTIVITY OPTIONS**

**INTERDISCIPLINARY LINK: SCIENCE** — BLOCK SCHEDULING

**THE WORLD OF THE BUFFALO**

**Class Time** One class period

**Task** Preparing an oral report on the history of the buffalo

**Purpose** To understand how the hunting of the buffalo for food and sport affected its survival as a species

**Supplies Needed**
- Encyclopedias and other reference materials on American bison and current endangered species laws
- Poster paper and markers
- Internet access for additional resources

**Activity** Have students prepare illustrated oral reports on the American bison, known to most Americans as the buffalo. Report topics may include how the bison differs from the true buffalo, the bison's range and habitat until the late 1800s, and factors that led to its near extinction. Other possible topics include how scientists worked to ensure the buffalo's survival, the status of the buffalo today, how it is protected, and whether threats to its survival, such as destruction of habitat, exist today.

**INSTRUCT: OBJECTIVE 3**

**Battle of the Little Bighorn/ Resistance in the Northwest and Southwest**

Key Questions

- How did the Battle of the Little Bighorn affect government Indian policy?
- What were the results of efforts by the Nez Perce, Navajo, and Apache to resist removal to reservations?

**In-Depth Resources: Unit 6**

- Geography Application: Custer's Last Stand, pp. 9–10

### HISTORY through ART

**Interpreting the Painting** After graduating from West Point in 1861, Custer joined the Union army. He enjoyed the fighting, writing home that "I would be willing, yes glad, to see a battle every-day during my life." Native Americans had several nicknames for Custer, including "Long Hair," "Son of the Morning Star," and, less poetically, "Hard Backsides." Artist Paxson was born in New York, but moved to Montana where he became a scout and Indian fighter as well as a painter. Paxson completed this painting in 1899.

**Possible Response: The painting shows that the battle was hard fought and that Custer and his troops were hopelessly outnumbered and doomed.**

### MORE ABOUT . . .

**The Battle of the Little Bighorn**

At Sitting Bull's camp in the valley of the Little Bighorn, about 6,000 Indians had gathered. They included Lakota, Cheyenne, Hunkpapa, Oglala, Miniconjou, Sans Arc, Blackfoot Sioux, and Northern Cheyenne. A Cheyenne woman later said, "There were more Indians . . . than I ever saw anywhere together." Custer's scouts were Crow. The scouts tried to warn Custer of the size of the Indian encampment, but Custer replied, "I guess we'll get through them in one day." When Custer finally saw the size of the Indian village, he told his scouts they could leave.

other Plains tribes together near Fort Laramie in present-day Wyoming. Government officials tried to buy back some Native American land and also set boundaries for tribal lands. Many Plains tribes signed the First Treaty of Fort Laramie (1851)—they saw no other choice.

But some Cheyennes and Sioux resisted. They preferred conflict with settlers and soldiers to the restrictions of reservation life. In southeastern Colorado, bands of Cheyenne warriors attacked miners and soldiers. In response, about 1,200 Colorado militia led by Col. John Chivington opened fire on a peaceful Cheyenne village along Sand Creek in 1864. More than 150 Cheyenne men, women, and children were killed in what came to be known as the **Sand Creek Massacre.**

*Reading* **History**

**B. Reading a Map** Locate the site of the Sand Creek Massacre on the map on page 563.

The Plains tribes reacted to such attacks by raiding white settlements. One of the fiercest battles took place in Montana. There the government had begun to build a road called the Bozeman Trail across Sioux hunting grounds. To stop construction, the Sioux attacked construction workers. In 1866, Captain W. J. Fetterman and 80 troopers stumbled into a deadly ambush set by the Sioux. All the soldiers were killed in what was called the Fetterman Massacre.

Such incidents finally forced the government to try to find a way to end the fighting. In 1868, U.S. officials signed the Second Treaty of Fort Laramie with the Sioux, Northern Cheyenne, and Arapaho. The treaty gave these tribes a large reservation in the Black Hills of South Dakota.

## 3 Battle of the Little Bighorn

The Second Treaty of Fort Laramie did not end the trouble between the Sioux and white settlers, though. In 1874, white prospectors discovered gold in the Black Hills. Paying no attention to the Fort Laramie treaty, thousands of miners rushed onto Sioux land. Tribal leaders angrily rejected a government offer to buy back the land. Many Sioux warriors fled the reservation during the

**HISTORY through ART**

Artist Edgar S. Paxson researched the Battle of the Little Bighorn for 20 years to try to accurately re-create the last moments of the fighting. Custer is at the center clutching at a bullet wound in his chest.

**What do you think this painting shows about the fighting at the Little Bighorn?**

ACTIVITY OPTIONS

**INTERDISCIPLINARY LINK: CIVICS** BLOCK SCHEDULING

**CONFLICT ON THE PLAINS**

**Class Time** One class period

**Task** Analyzing the causes and effects of three conflicts that were part of the Indian wars

**Purpose** To use critical-thinking skills to analyze the conflict between Native Americans and whites

**Supplies Needed**

- Reference materials on the Sand Creek Massacre, Fetterman Massacre, and Battle of the Little Bighorn

**Activity** Have students work in groups to research these events: Sand Creek Massacre, Fetterman Massacre, Battle of the Little Bighorn. For each event, have groups determine the causes, the combatants, the effects, and the reactions of Native Americans and white settlers and/or the federal government. Then have each group discuss whether they think these conflicts could have been settled peacefully. Have each group present a proposal for negotiated settlement of a conflict or explain why they think violent conflict was unavoidable.

winter of 1875–1876. They united under the leadership of two Sioux chiefs—**Sitting Bull** and Crazy Horse—to push back the intruders.

The Seventh Cavalry set out to return the Sioux to the reservations. It was commanded by Lieutenant Colonel **George A. Custer,** a hero of the Civil War and of other campaigns against Plains tribes. On June 25, his forces met several thousand Sioux and Cheyennes near the Little Bighorn River in Montana in the **Battle of the Little Bighorn.** In less than two hours, Custer and his men—211 in all—were wiped out.

C. Possible Answer Custer and his men were wiped out, but the military stepped up its actions against Native Americans.

*Reading* **History**

**C. Recognizing Effects** What were the results of the Battle of the Little Bighorn?

News of Custer's defeat shocked the nation. The government responded by stepping up military action. As a result, Little Bighorn was the last major Native American victory. In 1877, Crazy Horse surrendered and Sitting Bull and his followers fled to Canada. In 1881, Sitting Bull's starving band surrendered to U.S. troops and were returned to the reservation.

## Resistance in the Northwest and Southwest

**Background**
Nez Perce means "pierced nose" in French. French-Canadian trappers gave this name to these Native American people because some of them wore jewelry in their noses.

The Nez Perce (nehz PURS) was a Northwest tribe that lived in eastern Oregon and Idaho. Until the 1860s, the Nez Perce lived peacefully on land guaranteed to them by an 1855 treaty. However, as white settlement increased, the government forced them to sell most of their land and move to a narrow strip of territory in Idaho. Most reluctantly agreed, but a group of Nez Perce led by Chief Joseph refused.

In 1877, Chief Joseph and his followers fled north to seek refuge in Canada. For four months, the Nez Perce traveled across 1,000 miles of rugged terrain with army troops in pursuit. About 40 miles from the Canadian border, the army caught up with them. Greatly outnumbered, the Nez Perce surrendered. Chief Joseph spoke for his people when he said, "I will fight no more, forever."

In the Southwest, both the Navajos and Apaches fought against being removed to reservations. U.S. troops ended Navajo resistance in Arizona in 1863 by burning Navajo homes and crops. Most Navajos surrendered. Nearly 8,000 took what they called the "Long Walk," a brutal journey of 300 miles to a reservation in eastern New Mexico. Hundreds died on the way. Their new home was a parched strip of land near the Pecos River. After four years, the government allowed the Navajos to return to Arizona, where many live today.

### Native American Leaders

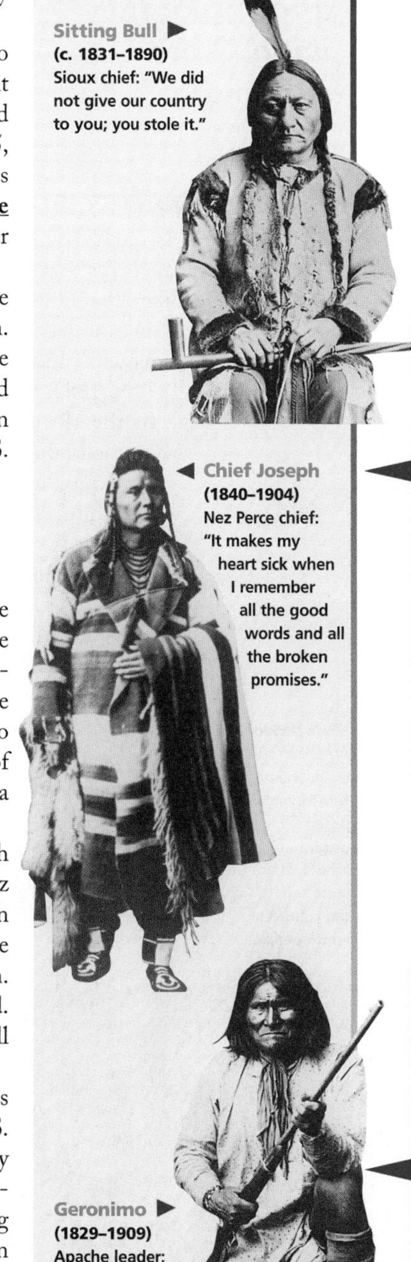

**Sitting Bull** ▶ **(c. 1831–1890)** Sioux chief: "We did not give our country to you; you stole it."

◀ **Chief Joseph (1840–1904)** Nez Perce chief: "It makes my heart sick when I remember all the good words and all the broken promises."

**Geronimo** ▶ **(1829–1909)** Apache leader: "Once I moved about like the wind. Now I surrender."



**America's History Makers**
- Sitting Bull, pp. 75–76

### MORE ABOUT . . .

**Chief Joseph**

During the Nez Perce's long flight from the army, Chief Joseph won the respect of many whites because of his humane treatment of prisoners and his concern for women, children, and the elderly. After the Nez Perce surrendered, Chief Joseph and his followers were sent to a barren stretch of land in Indian Territory, where many in the group died. In 1885, eight years later, Chief Joseph and the other Nez Perce who remained were sent to a reservation in Washington, but not to their original home.

**In-Depth Resources: Unit 6**
- Primary Source: Chief Joseph's Plea for Justice, p. 11

### MORE ABOUT . . .

**Geronimo**

In 1886, in the effort to capture Geronimo, thousands of U.S. soldiers, aided by Native American guides, tracked the Apache leader's small band over 1,600 miles. Although heavily outnumbered, Geronimo and his followers eluded their pursuers for five months. Army troops finally tracked the Apaches to a camp in the Sonora mountains. Geronimo agreed to surrender only after General Nelson Miles promised that the Apache would be allowed to return to Arizona. Instead, Geronimo was eventually sent to the Oklahoma Territory, where he died in 1909.

### ACTIVITY OPTIONS

**INTERDISCIPLINARY LINK: LANGUAGE ARTS** — BLOCK SCHEDULING

**WRITING A BIOGRAPHY**

**Class Time** One class period

**Task** Writing a biography of Sitting Bull, Chief Joseph, or Geronimo

**Purpose** To analyze the treatment of Native American peoples from the perspective of one of their leaders

**Supplies Needed**
- Reference materials on Sitting Bull, Chief Joseph, and Geronimo

**Activity** Have students choose Sitting Bull, Chief Joseph, or Geronimo and research the leader's life, his efforts to resist white settlement or removal to a reservation, and his treatment by the government. Using this information, have students write a short biography of the leader. Students should use the quote from their leader on page 565 in their work. Students may illustrate their biographies with portraits of their subject or copies of other appropriate illustrations. Allow students to read one another's work.

**INSTRUCT: OBJECTIVE 4**

**A Way of Life Ends/The Dawes Act Fails**

Key Questions

- Why did the buffalo almost vanish from the Plains?
- What events led to the Wounded Knee Massacre?
- In what ways did the Dawes Act try to force Native Americans to assimilate?
- What were the effects of the Dawes Act on Native Americans?

**MORE ABOUT . . .**

**The Massacre at Wounded Knee**

Frightened by reports of the Ghost Dancers, the army sent troops to the lands of the Sioux to await developments. Sitting Bull and his people were camped at Standing Rock. Fearful that Sitting Bull was plotting an attack, Lakota police went to arrest him. As the police were taking Sitting Bull into custody, one of his followers shot a policeman. As the policeman fell, he fired and killed Sitting Bull. The Seventh Cavalry followed Sitting Bull's people as they joined another band of Native Americans at Wounded Knee, where the massacre occurred.

*"Once I moved about like the wind. Now I surrender."*
Geronimo

In the early 1870s, the government forced many Apaches to settle on a barren reservation in eastern Arizona. But a group led by Geronimo refused to remain. Escaping the reservation, these Apaches survived by raiding settlers' homes. Geronimo was captured many times but always managed to escape. In 1886, however, he finally surrendered and was sent to prison.

## 4 A Way of Life Ends

As the Native Americans of the Plains battled to remain free, the buffalo herds that they depended upon for survival dwindled. At one time, 30 million buffalo roamed the Plains. However, hired hunters killed the animals to feed crews building railroads. Others shot buffalo as a sport or to supply Eastern factories with leather for robes, shoes, and belts. From 1872 to 1882, hunters killed more than one million buffalo each year.

**Background**
In 1889, fewer than 100 buffalo remained.

By the 1880s, most Plains tribes had been forced onto reservations. With their hunting grounds fast disappearing, some turned in despair to a Paiute prophet named Wovoka. He preached a vision of a new age in which whites would be removed and Native Americans would once again freely hunt the buffalo. To prepare for this time, Wovoka urged Native Americans to perform the chants and movements of the Ghost Dance. Wovoka's hopeful vision quickly spread among the Plains peoples.

Many of Wovoka's followers, especially among the Sioux, fled their reservations and gathered at the Pine Ridge Reservation in South Dakota. White settlers and government officials began to fear that they were preparing for war. The army was sent to track down the Ghost Dancers. They rounded them up, and a temporary camp was made along Wounded Knee Creek in South Dakota, on December 28, 1890. The next day, as the Sioux were giving up their weapons, someone fired a shot. The troopers responded to the gunfire, killing about 300 men, women, and children. The **Wounded Knee Massacre,** as it was called, ended armed resistance in the West.

***Reading* History**
**D. Drawing Conclusions** What was the most important factor in the defeat of the Native Americans?
**D. Possible Answers** Some students may say the overwhelming numbers of white settlers. Others may say government policy or the killing off of the buffalo.

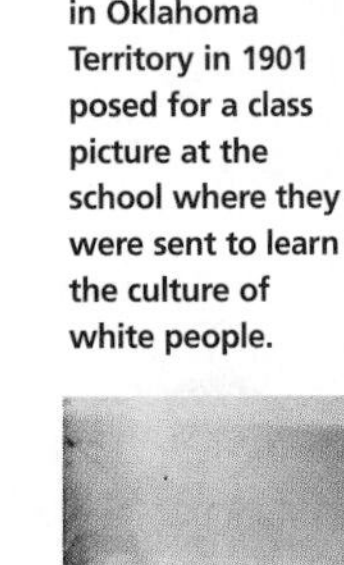

**These Native American students in Oklahoma Territory in 1901 posed for a class picture at the school where they were sent to learn the culture of white people.**

**ACTIVITY OPTIONS**

**INDIVIDUAL NEEDS**

**STUDENTS ACQUIRING ENGLISH/ESL**

**Understanding Figures of Speech** Point out the illustrations and captions on page 565, and ask a volunteer to read aloud the quote by Geronimo. Explain that Geronimo compared himself and his way of life to the wind: "Once I moved about like the wind." Encourage students to explain why Geronimo made that comparison. *(The wind moves freely; it is not stopped by fences or restricted to one place.)*

Ask students to explain how Geronimo's figure of speech describes the plight of Native Americans as described in the section. Have them think of other figures of speech that they can use to describe events or people discussed in the chapter.

## The Dawes Act Fails

Some white Americans had been calling for better treatment of Native Americans for years. In 1881, Helen Hunt Jackson published *A Century of Dishonor,* which listed the failures of the federal government's policies toward Native Americans. About the same time, Sarah Winnemucca, a Paiute reformer, lectured in the East about the injustices of reservation life.

*Reading*History
**E. Analyzing Points of View** Why did reformers support assimilation?
E. Answer Reformers thought that assimilation was the only way for Native Americans to survive.

Many well-meaning reformers felt that assimilation was the only way for Native Americans to survive. Assimilation meant adopting the culture of the people around them. Reformers wanted to make Native Americans like whites—to "Americanize" them.

The **Dawes Act,** passed in 1887, was intended to encourage Native Americans to give up their traditional ways and become farmers. The act divided reservations into individual plots of land for each family. The government sold leftover land to white settlers. The government also sent many Native American children to special boarding schools where they were taught white culture. In "One American's Story," you read about the effort to Americanize Buffalo Bird Woman. But these attempts to Americanize the children still did not make them part of white society.

In the end, the Dawes Act did little to benefit Native Americans. Not all of them wanted to be farmers. Those who did lacked the tools, training, and money to be successful. Over time, many sold their land for a fraction of its real value to white land promoters or settlers.

The situation of Native Americans at the end of the 1800s was tragic. Their lands had been taken and their culture treated with contempt. Not until decades later would the federal government recognize the importance of their way of life. In the next section, you will read about some of the people who settled on Native American lands.

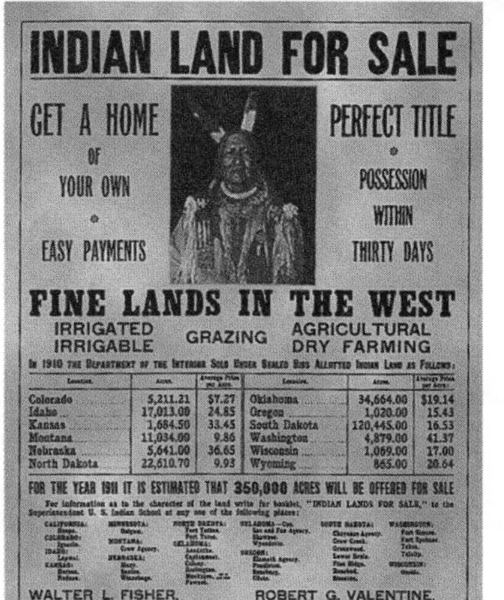


This poster advertised the sale of Native American lands to white settlers.

### Section 2 Assessment

**1. Terms & Names**

**Identify:**
- reservation
- Sand Creek Massacre
- Sitting Bull
- George A. Custer
- Battle of the Little Bighorn
- Wounded Knee Massacre
- Dawes Act

**2. Taking Notes**

Use a chart to compare the life of Plains people before and after the arrival of white settlers.

| | Before | After |
|---|---|---|
| Meeting survival needs | | |
| Customs | | |
| Land use | | |

**3. Main Ideas**

**a.** How did federal government policy toward Native Americans change as white settlers moved to the West?

**b.** How did the destruction of the buffalo affect Plains peoples?

**c.** Why was Wounded Knee a turning point in relations between Native Americans and the government?

**4. Critical Thinking**

**Recognizing Effects** How were the effects of the Dawes Act different from what was intended?

**THINK ABOUT**
- goals of the act
- impact on the land use, culture, and independence of the Plains peoples

**ACTIVITY OPTIONS**

**TECHNOLOGY**
**SPEECH**

Research the life of a Native American leader discussed in this section. Create that person's **Web page** or give a **speech** from this person's perspective.





### CRITICAL THINKING ACTIVITY

**Comparing** A variety of people, from well-meaning reformers in "Friends of the Indian" associations to land speculators and promoters, worked to pass the Dawes Act. What did each group expect the Dawes Act to accomplish? What were the long-term consequences of this act? Use the spider map to help students understand the impact of the Dawes Act.

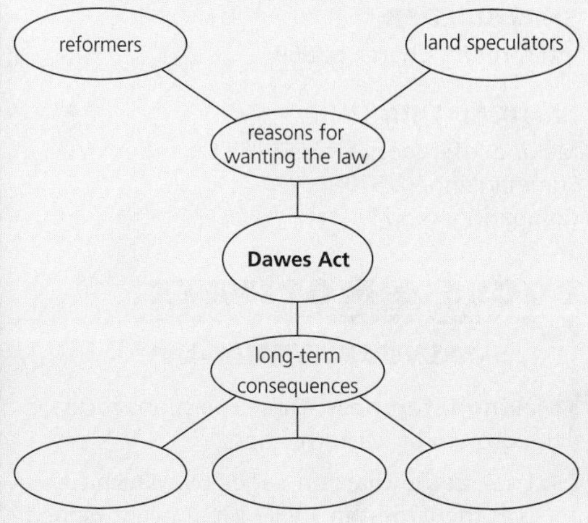


**Class Time** 25 minutes

## ASSESS & RETEACH

**Setting the Stage** Have students fill in the Native Americans section on the graphic organizer.

 **Formal Assessment**
- Section Quiz, p. 283

### RETEACHING ACTIVITY

Have students make a time line of key events in this section, such as the Fetterman Massacre, Battle of the Little Bighorn, Wounded Knee Massacre, and passage of the Dawes Act. For each event listed, have students write a sentence describing its causes and its effects on Native Americans.

 **In-Depth Resources: Unit 6**
- Reteaching Activity, p. 17

### Section 2 Assessment

**1. Terms & Names**

**reservation,** p. 562
**Sand Creek Massacre,** p. 564
**Sitting Bull,** p. 565
**George A. Custer,** p. 565
**Battle of the Little Bighorn,** p. 565
**Wounded Knee Massacre,** p. 566
**Dawes Act,** p. 567

**2. Taking Notes**

Before: hunted buffalo; developed a nomadic way of life; lived in villages; After: buffalo and hunting grounds disappearing and dependent on federal government for food and supplies; nomadic way of life ended; forced onto reservations

**3. Main Ideas**

**a.** Land ceded to Native Americans by treaty was taken from them for white settlement, and they were forced onto reservations. **b.** It took away their primary source of food, clothing, and shelter. **c.** It ended armed resistance by Native Americans in the West.

**4. Critical Thinking**

Goal: better treatment of Native Americans and ensuring their survival; Effect: Native Americans lost their land and culture and were treated with contempt.

**ACTIVITY OPTIONS**

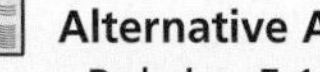 **Alternative Assessment**
- Rubrics, 5.1, 3.6

## SECTION OBJECTIVES

1. To describe the challenges and opportunities for women in the West
2. To analyze the reasons for the growth of western cities
3. To explain how Mexicans were affected by American settlement
4. To identify myths about the West

**SKILLBUILDER**
Interpreting Charts, p. 569

**CRITICAL THINKING**
Making Inferences, pp. 569, 571
Summarizing, p. 570
Comparing, p. 571

## FOCUS & MOTIVATE

### 5-MINUTE WARM-UP

**Making Inferences** These questions focus on the growth of western cities.

1. Look at the chart on page 569. Which city was the largest in 1860? What event helped San Francisco grow in the 1850s?
2. How might each of these economic activities—mining, ranching, and farming—contribute to the growth of these cities?

 **Warm-Up Transparency WT19**

## INSTRUCT

### INSTRUCT: OBJECTIVE 1

**Women in the West**
Key Questions
- What were the challenges of pioneer life for women in the West?
- What legal rights did women in the West gain first?

 **In-Depth Resources: Unit 6**
- Guided Reading, p. 5

 **Reading Study Guide** (Spanish and English), pp. 189–190

# 3 Life in the West

**TERMS & NAMES**
homestead
Mexicano
William "Buffalo Bill" Cody
buffalo soldier

| MAIN IDEA | WHY IT MATTERS NOW |
| --- | --- |
| Diverse groups of people helped to shape both the reality and the myth of the West. | The myth of the West continues to be a part of our culture. |

## ONE AMERICAN'S STORY

**Abigail Scott was born in Illinois in 1834. She was told that her mother remarked at the time, "Poor baby! She'll be a woman some day! . . . A woman's lot is so hard!" At 17, Abigail moved to Oregon by wagon train with her family. Her mother died on the journey. In Oregon, Abigail taught school until she married a farmer named Benjamin Duniway in 1853. When he was disabled in an accident, Abigail assumed the support of her family. She wrote about a day on a pioneer farm with its endless chores.**

*A VOICE FROM THE PAST*

[W]ashing, scrubbing, churning . . . preparing . . . meals in our lean-to kitchen . . . [having] to bake and clean and stew and fry; to be in short, a general pioneer drudge, with never a penny of my own, was not pleasant business.

**Abigail Scott Duniway,** in her autobiography, *Path Breaking*

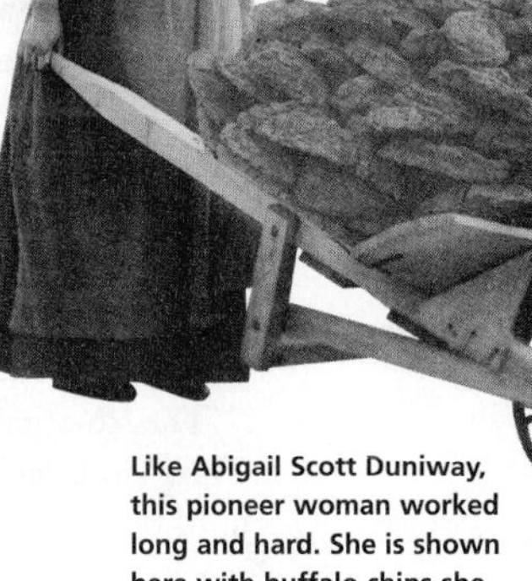

Like Abigail Scott Duniway, this pioneer woman worked long and hard. She is shown here with buffalo chips she has collected on the treeless prairie to use as fuel.

**Later, Duniway grew committed to the cause of women's rights. In 1871, she started a weekly pro-suffrage newspaper. Two years later, she founded the Oregon Equal Suffrage Association.**

**Oregon honored Duniway for her part in the suffrage struggle by registering her as the state's first woman voter. As you will read in this section, women like Duniway helped to shape the West.**

## 1 Women in the West

Women often were not given recognition for their efforts to turn scattered western farms and ranches into settled communities. In their letters and diaries, many women recorded the harshness of pioneer life. Others talked about the loneliness. While men went to town for supplies or did farm chores with other men, women rarely saw their neighbors. Mari Sandoz lived in Nebraska on a **homestead,** a piece of land and the house on it. She wrote that women "had only the wind and the cold and the problems of clothing [and] shelter." Living miles from others, women were their family's doctors—setting broken bones and delivering babies—as well as cooks.



## RECOMMENDED RESOURCES

 **In-Depth Resources: Unit 6**
- Guided Reading, p. 5
- Building Vocabulary, p. 7
- Primary Source, p. 12
- Reteaching Activity, p. 18

**Reading Study Guide** (Spanish and English), pp. 189–190

**America's History Makers**
- Calamity Jane, pp. 77–78

**Formal Assessment**
- Section Quiz, p. 284

**Alternative Assessment**
- Rubrics, 2.6
- Rubrics, 3.6

**Access for Students Acquiring English/ESL**
- Guided Reading, p. 128

**Technology Resources**

 **Humanities Transparency HT38**
- Annie Oakley Poster, 1901

 **Electronic Teacher Tools with Test Maker**

 **ClassZone**
www.mcdougallittell.com

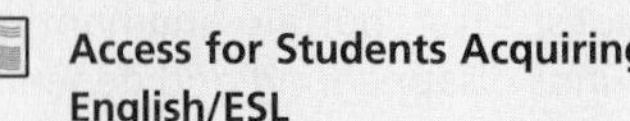

Despite its challenges, western life provided opportunities for women. Most who worked held traditional jobs. They were teachers or servants or gave their families financial support by taking in sewing or laundry. However, a few became sheriffs, gamblers, and even outlaws. In mining camps and cow towns, some even ran dance halls and boarding houses.

Western lawmakers recognized the contributions women made to western settlement by giving them more legal rights than women had in the East. In most territories, women could own property and control their own money. In 1869, Wyoming Territory led the nation in giving women the vote. Esther Morris, who headed the suffrage fight there, convinced lawmakers women would bring law and order to the territory.

When Wyoming sought statehood in 1890, many in Congress demanded that the state repeal its woman suffrage law. But Wyoming lawmakers stood firm. They told Washington, "We may stay out of the Union for 100 years, but we will come in with our women." Congress backed down. By 1900, women had also won the right to vote in Colorado, Utah, and Idaho.

*Reading* **History**
**A. Making Inferences** Why were women in the West the first to win the right to vote?
A. Possible Answer Lawmakers recognized that women played an important role in the settlement and life of the West.

## 2 The Rise of Western Cities

Cities seemed to grow overnight in the West. Gold and silver strikes made instant cities of places like Denver in Colorado Territory and brought new life to sleepy towns like San Francisco in California. These cities prospered, while much of the area around them remained barely settled. San Francisco grew from a small town to a city of about 25,000 in just one year after the 1849 gold rush.

Miners who flocked to the "Pikes Peak" gold rush of 1859 stopped first in Denver to buy supplies. Not even a town in 1857, Denver was the capital of Colorado Territory by 1867. A decade later, it became the state capital when Colorado was admitted into the Union. The decision by Denver citizens to build a railroad to link their city with the transcontinental railroad sent population soaring. In 1870, it had about 4,800 residents. In 1890, it had nearly 107,000.

The railroads also brought rapid growth to other towns in the West. Omaha, Nebraska, flourished as a meatprocessing center for cattle ranches in the area. Portland, Oregon, became a regional

**Population of Western Cities**

| CITY | 1860 | 1890 |
|---|---|---|
| Denver | 2,603* | 106,713 |
| Omaha | 1,883 | 140,452 |
| Portland | 2,874 | 46,385 |
| San Francisco | 56,802 | 298,997 |

SKILLBUILDER **Interpreting Charts**
*Which city had the largest increase in numbers of people, 1860–1890?*

*1861 Territorial Census
Sources: *Population Abstract of the United States; Colorado Republic*

Skillbuilder Answers
San Francisco—142,195 people

San Francisco, 1847

San Francisco, 1850

569



### MORE ABOUT . . .

**Women's Rights in Wyoming**
Wyoming women were not only the first women in the nation to win the vote but also the first women to serve on juries. In 1870, Wyoming became the first territory or state to allow women to serve on juries.

### INSTRUCT: OBJECTIVE 2

**The Rise of Western Cities**
Key Questions
- What factors led to the rapid growth of western cities?
- How did the railroads affect the population of western cities?

### HISTORY FROM VISUALS

**Reading the Chart** Ask students which cities had fewer than 25,000 people in 1860. **Answer** Denver, Omaha, Portland. Ask students which city grew most slowly between 1860 and 1890. **Answer** Portland. While mining was important to the growth of San Francisco, what evidence suggests that its economic base had become more diversified by 1890? **Possible Response** Its population soared even after the mining boom ended, suggesting that other economic activities continued to provide jobs and draw people there.

**Extension** Have students locate each city on a U.S. map and write a sentence about how its location contributed to its growth.

### ACTIVITY OPTIONS

### INTERDISCIPLINARY LINK: MATH

BLOCK SCHEDULING

**PROFILES OF WESTERN CITIES**

**Class Time** One class period

**Task** Making a bar graph showing the growth of western cities between 1860 and 1890

**Purpose** To analyze and compare growth patterns of western cities

**Supplies Needed**
- Graph paper
- Colored markers

**Activity** Have students make their own population bar graphs by using the information in the pupil edition on page 569 and the information below.

| | 1860 | 1890 | | 1860 | 1890 |
|---|---|---|---|---|---|
| Des Moines | 3,965 | 50,093 | Kansas City | 4,418 | 132,716 |
| Los Angeles | 4,385 | 50,395 | San Antonio | 8,235 | 37,673 |

Then ask: Which cities here have similar rates of growth? *(Des Moines, Los Angeles, and Portland)* Which city grew most rapidly? *(Omaha)*

**INSTRUCT: OBJECTIVE 3**

**Mexicanos in the Southwest**

Key Questions

- What attracted English-speaking settlers to the Southwest?
- How did Anglo-American settlement affect Mexicans and people of Spanish descent living in the Southwest?

**MORE ABOUT . . .**

**Wyatt Earp**

Earp first gained fame as a sharpshooter when he worked as a buffalo hunter. After working as a lawman in Kansas, he moved to Tombstone, Arizona, where he served as deputy sheriff and then marshall. One of Earp's most famous exploits was a gunfight near the O.K. Corral in Tombstone. Wyatt, his brothers Virgil and Morgan, and his friend Doc Holliday faced off against the Clanton clan. Rancher Ike Clanton and his sons had long engaged in cattle rustling and other illegal activities.

**INSTRUCT: OBJECTIVE 4**

**The Myth of the Old West/The Real West**

Key Questions

- What were some myths about the American West?
- How were these myths spread?
- How was the real West different from the mythical West?

**In-Depth Resources: Unit 6**

- Primary Source: from *An Autobiography of Buffalo Bill*, p. 12

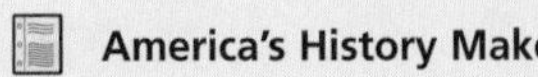

**America's History Makers**

- Calamity Jane, pp. 77–78

**Humanities Transparency HT38**

- Annie Oakley Poster, 1901

***Legends of the Old West***

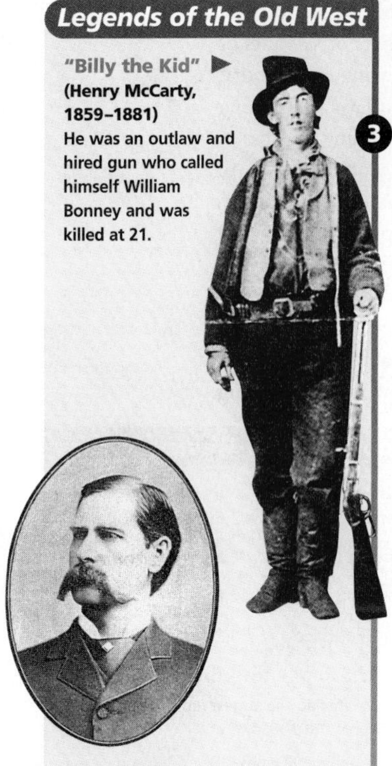

**"Billy the Kid" ▶ (Henry McCarty, 1859–1881)** He was an outlaw and hired gun who called himself William Bonney and was killed at 21.

**▲ Wyatt Earp (1848–1929)** He was a frontier peace officer, gunfighter, and gambler in towns such as Dodge City, Kansas, and Tombstone, Arizona.

**◀ "Calamity Jane" (Martha Jane Canary, c. 1852–1903)** She had a legendary career as a wagon driver, scout, and Wild West Show performer.

market for fish, grain, and lumber. While these cities were growing on the Great Plains and Pacific coast, the Southwest was also developing.

## 3 Mexicanos in the Southwest

The Southwest included what are now New Mexico, Texas, Arizona, and California. For centuries, it had been home to people of Spanish descent whose ancestors had come from Mexico. These Spanish-speaking southwesterners called themselves **Mexicanos.**

*Reading* **History**
**B. Summarizing** Who were the Mexicanos?
**B. Answer** They were Spanish-speaking inhabitants of the Southwest whose ancestors were originally from Mexico.

In the 1840s, the annexation of Texas and Mexico's defeat in the Mexican War brought much of the Southwest under the control of the United States. Soon after, English-speaking white settlers—called Anglos by the Mexicanos—began arriving. These pioneers were attracted to the Southwest by opportunities in ranching, farming, and mining. Their numbers grew in the 1880s and 1890s, as railroads connected the region with the rest of the country.

As American settlers crowded into the Southwest, the Mexicanos lost economic and political power. Many also lost land. They claimed their land through grants from Spain and Mexico. But American courts did not usually recognize these grants. One Mexicano remarked that "the North Americans . . . consider us unworthy to form with them one nation and one society." Only in New Mexico Territory did Hispanic society survive despite Anglo-American settlement.

## 4 The Myth of the Old West

America's love affair with the West began just as the cowboy way of life was vanishing in the late 1800s. To most Americans, the West had become a larger-than-life place where brave men and women tested themselves against hazards of all kinds and won. Easterners eagerly bought "dime novels" filled with tales of daring adventures. Sometimes the hero was a real person like Wyatt Earp or "Calamity Jane." But the plots were fiction or exaggerated accounts of real-life incidents.

Also adding to the myth were more serious works of fiction, like Owen Wister's bestselling novel about Wyoming cowhands, *The Virginian* (1902). Such works showed little of the drabness of daily life in the West. White settlers—miners, ranchers, farmers, cowhands, and law officers—played heroic roles not only in novels but also in plays and, later, in movies.



**ACTIVITY OPTIONS**

**INDIVIDUAL NEEDS**

**LESS PROFICIENT READERS**

**Finding Supporting Details** To help students efficiently read the section, write several main ideas from the section on the board. Read the main ideas aloud with students and ask them to look for supporting details for each as they read. When students have finished, work with them as a group to review the details they found. You might want to list the following main ideas.

- Despite its challenges, western life provided opportunities for women.
- Cities seemed to grow overnight in the West.
- White settlers in the Southwest caused changes in the lives of Mexicans.
- The real West was different from the myths of the West.

C. Answer In the myth, brave white settlers tamed the frontier through their own efforts. In reality, settlers got much help from the government, and Native Americans and Mexicanos lost their land.

**Background** From 1866 to 1898, some 12,500 African Americans served in the West in the 9th and 10th Cavalry and the 24th and 25th Infantry regiments.

Native Americans generally appeared as villains. African Americans were not even mentioned.

**William "Buffalo Bill" Cody,** a buffalo hunter turned showman, brought the West to the rest of the world through his Wild West show. Cody recognized people's fascination with the West. His show, with its reenactments of frontier life, played before enthusiastic audiences across the country and in Europe.

## The Real West

The myth of the Old West overlooked the contributions of many peoples. The first cowhands, as you read earlier, were the Mexican *vaqueros*. Native Americans and African Americans played a role in cattle ranching, too. Many African Americans also served in the U.S. Army in the West, where Native Americans nicknamed them **"buffalo soldiers."** And the railroads would not have been built without the labor of Chinese immigrants.

Western legends often highlighted the attacks by Native Americans on soldiers or settlers. But the misunderstandings and broken treaties that led to the conflicts were usually overlooked.

Historians also say that the image of the self-reliant westerner who tames the wild frontier ignores the important role played by the government in western settlement. Settlers needed the help of the army to remove Native Americans. The government also aided in the building of the railroads and gave the free land that drew homesteaders to the West. You will read about these homesteaders and the problems that they faced in the next section.

*Reading* **History**
**C. Comparing** How does the real West compare to the myth of the West?

### Now and then

**THE WEST IN POPULAR CULTURE**

The distorted picture of life in the West that had been part of popular culture for decades eventually changed. Starting in the late 1970s, the view became more realistic, especially in motion pictures.

For example, the hardships of the cattle drives were shown in *Lonesome Dove* (1989). The sufferings of Native Americans were portrayed in *Dances With Wolves* (1990). The role of women in the West was dramatized in *Sarah, Plain and Tall* (1991). And the contributions of African Americans were noted in *Buffalo Soldiers* (1997), pictured below.

### Section 3 Assessment

**1. Terms & Names**

**Identify**
- homestead
- Mexicano
- William "Buffalo Bill" Cody
- buffalo soldier

**2. Taking Notes**

Use a chart to compare Wild West myths with the realities of western life.

| Myth | Real life |
|---|---|
| | |

What do you think is the most well-known myth about the West?

**3. Main Ideas**

a. How were women's contributions to the West recognized by western lawmakers?

b. Which factors led to the growth of such western cities as Denver, Omaha, and San Francisco?

c. How did the arrival of Anglo-Americans change life for Spanish-speaking residents of the Southwest?

**4. Critical Thinking**

**Making Inferences** What changed the attitudes of western lawmakers about giving women voting rights?

**THINK ABOUT**
- new roles for women
- need for stability in western communities
- part played by women in settlement

**ACTIVITY OPTIONS**

**MATH** / **SPEECH**: Pick a western city mentioned in this section. Create a **database** of information about the city or give a **short speech** describing its growth.





### *Now and* then

**The West in Popular Culture**

The portrayal of Native Americans in movies and television has changed as filmmakers have paid more attention to Native American culture. Today, for example, many filmmakers use Native American consultants to ensure that costumes accurately reflect the clothing of the tribal group represented. In most older Westerns, white actors played the roles of Native Americans. Today, such roles are almost always played by Native Americans.

### MORE ABOUT . . .

**Buffalo Soldiers**

By 1869, the U.S. Army had 35 permanent regiments. Of that number, 4 regiments—the 9th and 10th Cavalry and the 24th and 25th Infantry—consisted entirely of African Americans. The major task of these units on the western frontier was to protect settlers. Their nickname, "buffalo soldiers," is believed to be a term of honor given to them by Native Americans who compared their strength, persistence, and fighting spirit to that of the buffalo.

## ASSESS & RETEACH

**Setting the Stage** Have students fill in the sections on women and Mexican Americans on the chapter graphic organizer.

 **Formal Assessment**
- Section Quiz, p. 284

**RETEACHING ACTIVITY**

Have each student write a paragraph summarizing Section 3. Tell students to leave blanks for key terms and the names of people or places. After they have completed their summaries, have pairs of students exchange papers and fill in the blanks on the summary they receive.

 **In-Depth Resources: Unit 6**
- Reteaching Activity, p. 18

### Section 3 Assessment

**1. Terms & Names**

**homestead,** p. 568
**Mexicano,** p. 570
**William "Buffalo Bill" Cody,** p. 571
**buffalo soldier,** p. 571

**2. Taking Notes**

Myths: larger-than-life place with brave men and women who were rugged individuals, often attacked by Native Americans; Real life: cowhand's life often dull; Native Americans had genuine grievances that led to hostilities.
Answers will vary.

**3. Main Ideas**

**a.** They gained property, voting rights, and control over their money. **b.** gold and silver strikes; railroad links; growth of meat-processing centers and regional markets **c.** Mexicanos lost economic and political power.

**4. Critical Thinking**

the realization that women were helping to settle the West and to turn farms and ranches into safe, stable communities

**ACTIVITY OPTIONS**

 **Alternative Assessment**
- Rubrics for a database, 2.6
- Rubrics for a speech, 3.6

## Interdisciplinary CHALLENGE

**OBJECTIVE**

Students work cooperatively to solve math, language arts, and art challenges faced by a manager of a Wild West show.

 **BLOCK SCHEDULING**

## PROCEDURE

Gather supplies that students might need, such as posterboard, colored markers, and graph paper. For each challenge, have students form groups of three or four. Ask group members to divide the work among themselves. Then have them choose an option for presenting their solution.

### MATH CHALLENGE

**Class Time** 50 minutes

Suggest that students bring in pie charts and financial tables from newspapers and magazines to use as models.

- The pie chart should contain six categories of expenses plus a category for profit. The expense categories are Salaries, Rents, Advertising, Printing, Groceries/Ammunition, and Miscellaneous Expenses. Specific costs in each category are found in the Data File.
- Make sure students know how to calculate profit. Students might discuss the fact that less than 1 percent (.69 percent) of total income is profit.
- Make sure students understand that 100 percent of revenue equals $287,000. The percentage of revenue spent on each type of expense is calculated by dividing the cost of each expense by total revenue. For example, rents: $58,000 divided by $287,000 = 20.2%. Thus around 20 percent of the total income was spent on rents.

## Interdisciplinary CHALLENGE

# Stage a Wild West Show!

You are the manager of Buffalo Bill's Wild West, the biggest and most famous of the 50 outdoor circuses and shows performing in the United States in the 1880s. Your job is to keep the show running smoothly. You oversee publicity and keep performers and livestock housed, fed, and supplied with the gear they need. You also manage finances.

COOPERATIVE LEARNING On this page are three challenges you face as the manager of Buffalo Bill's Wild West show. Working with a small group, decide how to deal with each challenge. Choose an option, assign a task to each group member, and do the activity. You will find useful information in the Data File.

### MATH CHALLENGE

*"over $280,000"*

**What a season you had from May to September of 1886! The show took in more than $280,000. But you had big expenses, too. You want to compare income and expenses so you can make changes to increase profits. Use the Data File for more statistics. Then present your summary using one of these options:**

- **Make a line graph comparing income and expenses.**
- **Make a pie chart showing how you spent the income—that is, what your expenses were. Include one sector for profit (the difference between total income and total expenses). Label each sector with the percentage.**

### LANGUAGE ARTS CHALLENGE

*"the thunder of hoofs"*

**Over the last three days, attendance at the show has slacked off. To meet expenses and generate a profit, you need to fill 15,000 seats. You decide to stir up interest using the local newspaper. Use the Data File for information. Then promote the show.**

- **Write an article dramatizing the Wild West show.**
- **Write a script to be used by the master of ceremonies.**

572

## STANDARDS FOR EVALUATION

### MATH CHALLENGE

**Option 1** Graph should
- be clearly labeled.
- present accurate figures.

**Option 2** Pie chart should
- have clearly labeled sectors.
- accurately reflect calculated percentages.

### LANGUAGE ARTS CHALLENGE

**Option 1** Article should
- make the show sound exciting and inviting.
- describe at least two show acts.

**Option 2** Script should
- introduce at least three events in a dramatic style.
- engage the listener.

### ART CHALLENGE

**Option 1** Large poster should
- indicate times and fees.
- reflect the content of at least one major show act.

**Option 2** Action posters should
- dramatize the show.
- give show times and fees.

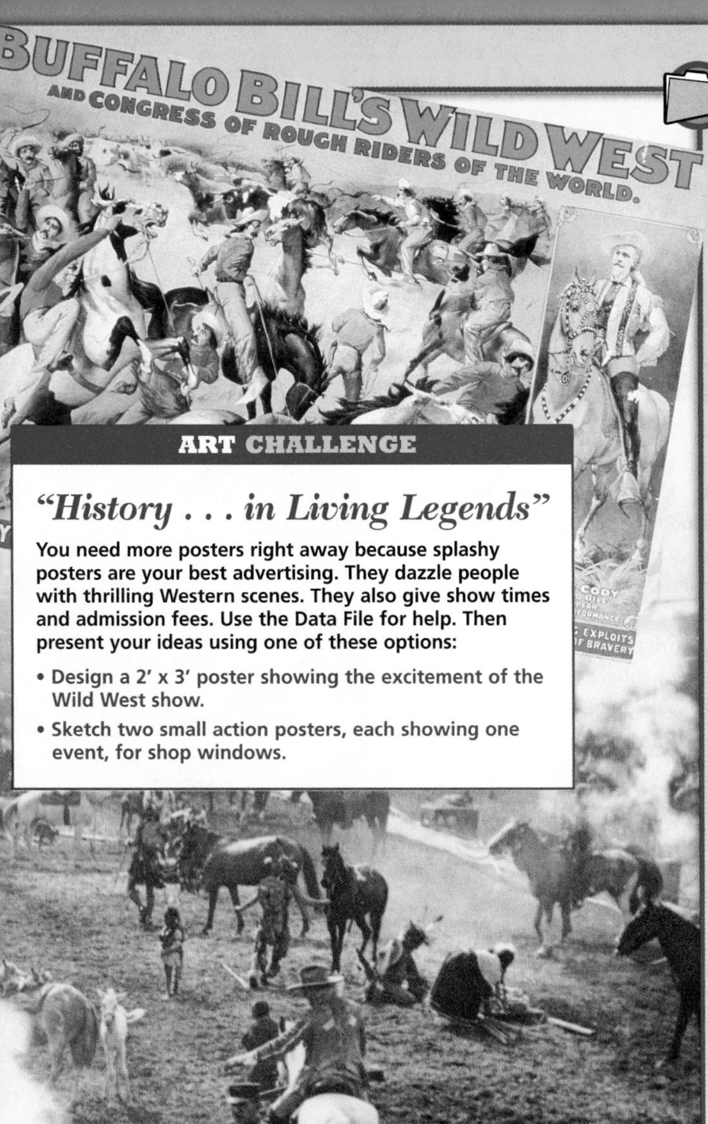

BUFFALO BILL'S WILD WEST
AND CONGRESS OF ROUGH RIDERS OF THE WORLD.


## ART CHALLENGE

### "History . . . in Living Legends"

**You need more posters right away because splashy posters are your best advertising. They dazzle people with thrilling Western scenes. They also give show times and admission fees. Use the Data File for help. Then present your ideas using one of these options:**

- **Design a 2' x 3' poster showing the excitement of the Wild West show.**
- **Sketch two small action posters, each showing one event, for shop windows.**

## ACTIVITY WRAP-UP

Present to the class **Meet as a group to review your methods of promoting and charting the success of your Wild West show. Evaluate which of your solutions is the best for each challenge. Once you have chosen one solution for each, make a class presentation. Each group member should take part.**

## DATA FILE

### WILD WEST SHOW

- 3-hour show; admission, 50¢

**Major Show Acts**

- "Star-Spangled Banner" Overture
- Grand Review of Buffalo Bill Cody and cast on horseback
- Annie Oakley shoots card targets, apple off her poodle's head
- Reenactments of covered wagons crossing the prairie; a Native American buffalo hunt; outlaws attacking a mail coach; a battle between army and Native Americans
- Sharpshooting by Buffalo Bill

**Show Crew and Gear**

- crew of 700—including Buffalo Bill, Annie Oakley, Sitting Bull, cowhands, Native Americans, 36-piece band, cooks, blacksmiths, teams to set up grandstand and tents
- animals—including 500 horses, 10 mules, 5 steers, 18 buffalo
- gear—including covered wagons and tepees, guns and ammunition, living and dressing room tents, dining tents, booths selling popcorn, souvenirs, and canvas scenery backdrops, 26-car train for transport

**INCOME AND EXPENSES**

May 9–September 25, 1886

**Total income:** $287,000 (from attendance)

**Total expenses:** $285,000

Owners', managers', key performers' salaries: $55,000

Rents: $58,000

Advertising: $17,000

Printing: $4,000

Groceries/ammunition: $7,000

Miscellaneous expenses: $144,000 (other wages, livestock feed, electricity, medical, security, etc.)

**Visit www.mcdougallittell.com to learn more about the Old West.**



## LANGUAGE ARTS CHALLENGE

**Class Time** 50 minutes

To help students write their newspaper articles, suggest that they review the Data File on the Wild West show. Articles dramatizing the show can vividly describe exciting or interesting aspects of two or three major show acts. The scripts can use statistics and information on show crew and gear as well as information on the acts to provide entertaining commentary on the Wild West show.

**POSSIBLE SOLUTIONS**

Articles may focus on

- celebrities such as Sitting Bull or Annie Oakley.
- exciting acts such as sharpshooting.

## ART CHALLENGE

**Class Time** 50 minutes

Have groups brainstorm ideas for posters and then select one idea for the large format poster or two ideas for action posters. Direct students to the Data File for subject ideas.

**POSSIBLE SOLUTIONS**

The posters for Cody's shows were some of the best of their time. Between 6,000 to 8,000 posters were put up to advertise a show. They were all posted on the same day. When Cody took his Wild West show to France, some posters showed Cody's face superimposed on a running buffalo with the phrase "Je Viens," which means "I am coming." Other posters for the show included images of Custer's Last Stand and cowboys and Indians doing trick riding.

## ACTIVITY WRAP-UP

To help students evaluate which of their options is the most successful solution to each challenge, have them evaluate their newspaper articles and posters in terms of creativity, originality, and persuasive appeal. Have them examine their charts and graphs in terms of how clearly each reflects the financial status of the show.

## SECTION OBJECTIVES

1. To explain how the U.S. government encouraged western settlement
2. To describe farming life on the Great Plains
3. To analyze the rise of the Populist Party
4. To evaluate the significance of the frontier in American life

**CRITICAL THINKING**

Analyzing Causes, p. 575
Summarizing, p. 577
Analyzing Points of View, p. 578
Drawing Conclusions, p. 579

**Why It Matters Now**
- Challenges in the West, pp. 37–38

## FOCUS & MOTIVATE

### 5-MINUTE WARM-UP

**Making Inferences** These questions focus on farmers' opinions about the railroads.

1. Look at the cartoon on page 577. What is happening in the drawing? What is the farmer trying to do?
2. What is the artist's opinion of the railroads?

**Warm-Up Transparency WT19**

## INSTRUCT

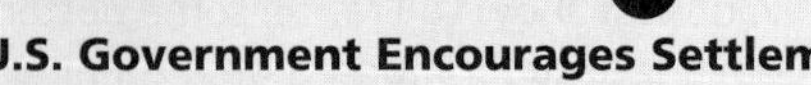

### INSTRUCT: OBJECTIVE 1

**U.S. Government Encourages Settlement**

Key Questions
- How did the federal government encourage western settlement?
- What attracted African Americans and European immigrants to the West?

**In-Depth Resources: Unit 6**
- Guided Reading, p. 6

**Reading Study Guide** (Spanish and English), pp. 191–192

# 4 Farming and Populism

**TERMS & NAMES**
Homestead Act
Exoduster
sodbuster
Grange
cooperative
Populist Party
gold standard
William Jennings Bryan

**MAIN IDEA**

A wave of farmers moved to the Plains in the 1800s and faced many economic problems.

**WHY IT MATTERS NOW**

Farmers are facing similar economic problems today.

Railroad posters advertise lands in the West.

### ONE AMERICAN'S STORY

**From 1865 to 1900, about 800,000 Swedes left their homeland in northern Europe. Sweden's population was soaring, and good farmland was becoming scarce. Most Swedes were farmers. They were drawn to the United States by the promise of more and better land.**

**For Olaf Olsson, the acres of free land offered to settlers by the U.S. government was an unbelievable opportunity. Shortly after he arrived in 1869, Olsson wrote home to tell friends and family what awaited them in America.**

*A VOICE FROM THE PAST*

We do not dig gold with pocket knives, we do not expect to become . . . rich in a few days or in a few years, but what we aim at is to own our own homes. . . . The advantage which America offers is not to make everyone rich at once, without toil or trouble, but . . . that the poor . . . [can] secure a large piece of good land almost without cost, that they can work up little by little.

**Olaf Olsson,** quoted in *The Swedish Americans,* by Allyson McGill

**As you will read in this section, many Americans as well as immigrants from all parts of Europe shared Olsson's optimism. They uprooted their families to start a new life on the Plains.**

## 1 U.S. Government Encourages Settlement

For years, people had been calling on the federal government to sell western land at low prices. Before the Civil War, Southern states fought such a policy. They feared that a big westward migration would result in more nonslave states. Once the South left the Union, however, the way was clear for a new land policy. To interest both American and immigrant families like the Olssons in going west, the federal government passed the **Homestead Act** in 1862. This law offered 160 acres of land free to anyone who agreed to live on and improve the land for five years.

After Reconstruction ended in 1877, African Americans in the South faced harsh new forms of discrimination. (See Chapter 18.) By 1879,



## RECOMMENDED RESOURCES

**In-Depth Resources: Unit 6**
- Guided Reading, p. 6
- Building Vocabulary, p. 7
- Reteaching Activity, p. 19
- Enrichment Activity, p. 20

**Reading Study Guide** (Spanish and English), pp. 191–192

**Economics in History**
- The Dynamics of Supply and Demand, p. 19

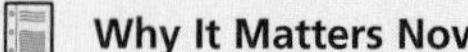

**Why It Matters Now**
- Challenges in the West, pp. 37–38

**Formal Assessment**
- Section Quiz, p. 285

**Alternative Assessment**
- Rubrics, 5.2
- Rubrics, 4.9

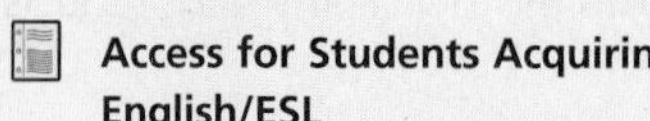

**Access for Students Acquiring English/ESL**
- Guided Reading, p. 129

**Technology Resources**

**Electronic Teacher Tools with Test Maker**

**ClassZone**
www.mcdougallittell.com

leaders like Benjamin "Pap" Singleton of Tennessee had convinced thousands to migrate to new homes in Kansas. They compared themselves to the biblical Hebrews led out of slavery in Egypt and called themselves **Exodusters.** One of them, John Solomon Lewis, remarked, "When I landed on the soil of Kansas, I looked on the ground and I says this is free ground." In all, some 50,000 African Americans settled in Kansas, Missouri, Indiana, and Illinois.

Thousands of European immigrants also sought a new start in the West. Swedes, like Olaf Olsson, joined Germans, Norwegians, Ukrainians, and Russians on the Great Plains. They often first learned about the West from land agents for American railroad companies. These salesmen traveled throughout Europe with pamphlets proclaiming "Land for the Landless! Homes for the Homeless."

From 1850 to 1870, the government gave millions of acres of public land to the railroads to promote railroad expansion. The railroads resold much of the land to settlers. This not only made the railroad companies rich, but it also supplied new customers for railroad services. The railroads' sales pitch worked. In the 1860s, so many Swedes and Norwegians settled in Minnesota that a local editor wrote, "It seems as if the Scandinavian Kingdoms were being emptied into this state."

*Reading* **History**

**A. Analyzing Causes** How did the railroads help to settle the West?

## Life on the Farming Frontier

A. Possible Answer The railroads promoted their lands in the West to the people of Europe and attracted hundreds of thousands of Europeans to America.

Once pioneers reached their new homes on the plains, they faced many challenges never mentioned by the land agents. The plains were nearly treeless. So farmers were forced to build their first homes from blocks of sod. Sod is the top layer of prairie soil that is thickly matted with grass roots.

For fuel, the **sodbusters,** as the farmers were called, burned corn cobs or "cow chips" (dried manure). In many places, sodbusters had to dig wells more than 280 feet deep to reach the only water. Blizzards, prairie fires, hailstorms, tornadoes, grasshoppers, and drought added to the misery of life on the plains. Many settlers, such as Katherine Kirk of South Dakota, wondered whether they had the courage "to stick it out."

**Connections TO *SCIENCE***

**SOD HOUSES**

To build their dwellings, Plains farmers, or sodbusters, like the Nebraska family pictured here, cut the tough buffalo grass of the prairie into two-or three-foot strips. Then they laid chunks of sod into two rows as walls. The walls were often 36 inches thick.

Prairie grass was thick. Its roots grew outward under the soil, often connecting with one another. This held the sod together. The roots also provided a layer of insulation. So sod houses, or soddies, stayed warm in the winter and cool in the summer. But their roofs leaked rain and dirt, and the walls housed mice, snakes, and insects.

575



**MORE ABOUT . . .**

**The Exodusters**

To reach Kansas, many former slaves took riverboats as far as St. Louis, but others walked the entire way to Kansas. In 1877, former slaves from Kentucky started a settlement in southwest Kansas that they named Nicodemus. To survive their first winter before they could harvest a crop, some of the new Kansans worked for the Kansas Pacific Railroad, and others earned money by selling buffalo bones. By 1887, Nicodemus was a thriving town with churches, a store, and two newspapers.

**INSTRUCT: OBJECTIVE** 

**Life on the Farming Frontier/ The Problems of Farmers**

Key Questions

- How did new inventions help farmers meet the challenges of the Plains?
- What financial problems did farmers in the West and South face in the 1870s?
- How did state and local government respond to farmers' demands for help?

 **In-Depth Resources: Unit 6**

- Enrichment Activity, p. 20

**Connections TO *SCIENCE***

**Sod Houses**

Prairie families made the roofs of their sod houses out of willow poles topped by grass, a layer of clay from the nearest stream bank, and blocks of sod, grass-side up. During heavy spring rains, the roofs leaked. One sodbuster recalled that the "water would drip on the stove while I was cooking and I would have to keep tight lids on the skillets to prevent mud from falling into the food." Even in dry weather bits of dirt and dust came down from the ceiling. To solve this problem, sodbusters tacked cheesecloth to the ceiling or plastered the inside walls with a lime-and-sand mixture.

**ACTIVITY OPTIONS**

**INTERDISCIPLINARY LINK: ART**

**BLOCK SCHEDULING**

**ATTRACTING SETTLERS TO THE PLAINS**

**Class Time** One class period

**Task** Creating a poster

**Purpose** To identify ways the U.S. government encouraged settlement of the Plains

**Supplies Needed**

- Reference materials on the Homestead Act, the Exodusters, and European immigration to the Great Plains
- Posterboard
- Art supplies

**Activity** Tell students that they are executives at the Pioneer Advertising Agency. Their job is to create posters and slogans that can be used to attract immigrants or Americans from the East to the Great Plains. Working in pairs, have students select a target audience for their campaign, such as Swedes, Russians, or African Americans in the South. Have students create advertisements that focus on the economic opportunities, the richness of the soil, or other potential rewards of settlement.

MORE ABOUT . . .

**Barbed Wire**

The inventor of the first patented and successful barbed wire was Joseph Glidden of DeKalb, Illinois. Glidden's success inspired others, who patented more than 530 different kinds of barbed wire.

New inventions helped farmers to meet some of these challenges. A steel plow invented by John Deere in 1838 and improved upon by James Oliver in 1868 sliced through the tough sod. Windmills adapted to the plains pumped water from deep wells to the surface. Barbed wire allowed farmers to fence in land and livestock. Reapers made the harvesting of crops much easier, and threshers helped farmers to separate grain or seed from straw. These inventions also made farm work more efficient. From 1860 to 1890, farmers doubled their production of wheat.

## The Problems of Farmers

As farmers became more efficient, they grew more and more food. The result was that farmers in the West and South watched with alarm as prices for farm crops began to drop lower and lower in the 1870s.

Economics *in* History

**OBJECTIVE**

Students will be able to explain how supply and demand influence production, consumption, and the cost of goods.

**Understanding Supply and Demand**

By the 1870s, several factors increased the supply of farm products and lowered prices, creating hard times for farmers. During the 1870s, new lands came under cultivation in Canada, Australia, New Zealand, and Argentina, making more food available on world markets. In the United States as well, the number of acres of land devoted to farming more than doubled between 1870 and 1900. Not only was more land farmed but the output per U.S. farm worker also increased as a result of mechanization and improved farming methods. Oversupply pushed prices of crops down to well below the average cost of producing them.

**Economics in History**
- The Dynamics of Supply and Demand, p. 19

Economics *in* History

## Supply and Demand

Farmers in the West were having economic problems in the 1880s. The supply of food was increasing rapidly, but consumer demand was growing slowly. To attract more consumers, farmers had to drop the prices of their products.

The farmers were experiencing the **law of supply and demand.** The amount of economic goods available for sale is the **supply.** The willingness and ability of consumers to spend money for goods and services is **demand.** The price of goods is set by the supply of that good and the demand for that good.

At a lower price, businesses produce less of a good because they will make less money. As the price rises, they produce more. Consumer demand works in the opposite way. Consumers want to buy more of the good when the price is lower—after all, it costs them less. They buy less when the price is higher. The actual price of a good results from a compromise—how much consumers are willing to pay and how little businesses are willing to take for the good.

1 Prices are high.
2 Producers want to increase supply.
3 More goods push price down.
4 Demand increases.
5 Producer increases supply.
6 Price decreases again.
7 Producer supplies less.
8 Prices increase and demand falls
$$$
$$
$

**CONNECT TO HISTORY**

1. **Recognizing Effects** Suppose farmers found a new market for their wheat—the people in another country, for instance. What effect would that have on price? Why?

See Skillbuilder Handbook, page R10.

**CONNECT TO TODAY**

2. **Comparing** How does the price of blue jeans show the law of supply and demand?

Visit www.mcdougallittell.com to learn more about supply and demand.

576 CHAPTER 19

**CONNECT TO HISTORY**

1. **Recognizing Effects** A new market for wheat means increased demand for this commodity. As demand increases, the price of wheat is likely to rise. As its price goes up, more farmers will decide to grow wheat. Eventually the wheat supply will increase, pushing its price down.

**CONNECT TO TODAY**

2. **Comparing** Students may discuss the price of designer jeans, with distinctive labels and trademarks, compared to the price of ordinary jeans. Students may note that designers deliberately set a high price for their jeans to make them a status item.

(See "Economics in History" on page 576.) Wheat that sold for $1.45 a bushel after the Civil War was 49 cents 30 years later. One reason for lower prices was overproduction. Farmers were growing more food because additional farmland had been opened up and farming methods and machines had improved.

"The Grange Awakening the Sleepers" (1873) shows a farmer trying to warn the country about the menace of the railroads.

Receiving less money for their crops was bad enough. But at the same time farmers had to spend more to run a farm. New farm machinery and railroad rates were especially costly. Railroads charged the farmers high fees to carry their crops to market. The railroads also usually owned the grain elevators where crops were stored until shipment. Farmers had no choice but to pay the high costs of storage that railroads charged.

Farmers were angry. They began to work together to seek solutions to their problems. In 1867, farmers had formed the **Grange,** officially known as the Patrons of Husbandry. The group's main purpose at first had been to meet the social needs of farm families who lived great distances from one another. However, as economic conditions got worse, Grange members took action. They formed **cooperatives.** These are organizations owned and run by their members. The cooperatives bought grain elevators and sold crops directly to merchants. This allowed farmers to keep more of their profits.

Farmers also began to demand action from the government to change their circumstances. For example, Grangers asked states to regulate railroad freight rates and storage charges. Illinois, Minnesota, Wisconsin, and Iowa did so. In 1877, the Supreme Court backed the farmers in their fight against the railroads. In *Munn* v. *Illinois,* the Court ruled that states and the federal government could regulate the railroads because they were businesses that served the public interest.

B. Possible Answer They formed the Grange, demanded action from the government, and organized the Populist Party.

**B. Summarizing** What steps did farmers take to seek solutions to their problems?

## 3 The Rise of Populism

In 1890, several farm groups joined together to try to gain political power. They formed the **Populist Party,** or People's Party. The Populists wanted the government to adopt a free silver policy, that is, the unlimited coining of silver. Since silver was plentiful, more money would be put in circulation. They believed that increasing the money supply would cause inflation. Inflation, in turn, would result in rising prices. Higher prices for crops would help farmers pay back the money that they had borrowed to improve their farms.

Opponents of free silver wanted to keep the gold standard. Under the **gold standard,** the government backs every dollar with a certain amount





### MORE ABOUT . . .

**New Farm Machinery**

Even before the Civil War, farm experts had begun urging farmers to increase productivity by purchasing mechanized farm equipment. An 1857 *Scientific American* editorial advised that "Every farmer who has a hundred acres of land should have at least the following: a combined reaper and mower, a horse rake, a seed planter and mower, . . . a thresher and grain cleaner, a portable grist mill, a corn sheller, . . . three harrows, a roller, two cultivators, and three plows."

### MORE ABOUT . . .

***Munn* v. *Illinois***

In this case, grain elevator operators sued Illinois over an 1871 state law that fixed the maximum prices operators could charge farmers for grain storage. The Supreme Court ruled that when a business's property serves an important public purpose, the public's interest in the property overrides certain rights of the owner. During the 1930s, this case was often cited as a precedent in support of New Deal efforts to regulate private businesses.

### INSTRUCT: OBJECTIVE 3

**The Rise of Populism/The Election of 1896**

Key Questions
- Why did Populists favor a free silver policy?
- What were the arguments for and against free silver?
- Who were the candidates in the election of 1896? What were the campaign positions of each candidate?

### ACTIVITY OPTIONS

**INTERDISCIPLINARY LINK: LANGUAGE ARTS**

BLOCK SCHEDULING

**REACTING TO FARM PROBLEMS**

**Class Time** One class period

**Task** Writing a letter to a newspaper commenting on the problems of farmers in the 1870s

**Purpose** To identify the problems facing farmers in the West and the South and their responses to these problems

**Supplies Needed**
- Reference materials on the Grange, *Munn* v. *Illinois*, and farm problems in the 1860s and 1870s

**Activity** Have students assume the roles of farmers, railroad owners, bankers, or industrialists and write letters to the newspaper commenting on one of these statements: 1) The railroads are unfair to farmers; 2) The federal government has a responsibility to help farmers; 3) Falling prices are the fault of farmers; 4) The Supreme Court ruled wisely in *Munn* v. *Illinois*; 5) The government has no right to regulate the railroads.

## AMERICA'S HISTORY MAKERS

**William Jennings Bryan**

Although Bryan failed in his drive to become president, he continued in the national spotlight long after his defeat. In 1913, President Woodrow Wilson named him secretary of state, a position he held until 1915. Committed to neutrality during World War I, he resigned at that time to protest Wilson's policies toward Germany. Bryan gained public attention again in 1925 in the famous Scopes trial. A firm believer in a literal reading of the Bible, Bryan helped prosecute a Tennessee schoolteacher accused of teaching students the theory of evolution.

**Possible Response: Bryan influenced reform by keeping his ideas before the public and by speaking and campaigning.**

## INSTRUCT: OBJECTIVE 4

**The Closing of the Frontier**

Key Questions

- What events symbolized the closing of the frontier?
- Why do historians today question Turner's opinions about the importance of the frontier to American life?

## MORE ABOUT . . .

**The Oklahoma Land Rush**

The eager settlers who lined up on April 22, 1889, to take part in the land rush were called "Boomers." They traveled on foot, horse, and even bicycle. However, as they made their way through the territory, Boomers were shocked to find "Sooners" already defending claims in the former Indian Territory. Sooners were settlers who had illegally crossed army lines to get a head start on their claims.

AMERICA'S HISTORY MAKERS

**WILLIAM JENNINGS BRYAN**
**1860–1925**

William Jennings Bryan was known as the "silver-tongued orator from Nebraska." His powerful voice and his strong belief in the "common people" won him two terms in Congress and a presidential nomination at age 36. He made and lost two more bids for president in 1900 and 1908.

Although he never again held elective office, Bryan remained influential in the Democratic Party. Many reforms that he fought for, such as an eight-hour workday and woman suffrage, later became law.

**How do you think Bryan was able to influence reform without being elected president?**

of gold. Since the gold supply is limited, fewer dollars are in circulation. Inflation is less likely. This protects the value of money by keeping prices down.

In 1892, the Populist Party platform called for free silver to expand the money supply, government ownership of railroads, shorter working hours, and other political reforms. The Populist presidential candidate, James B. Weaver, lost to Grover Cleveland. But he won more than a million votes—a good showing for a third-party candidate.

## The Election of 1896

By the next presidential campaign, money issues mattered much more to voters. The nation had suffered through a serious depression, the Panic of 1893. The Republican candidate, William McKinley, favored the gold standard. He warned that "free silver" would mean higher prices for food and other goods.

The Populists joined the Democratic Party in supporting **William Jennings Bryan** of Nebraska. Bryan urged the Democratic convention to support free silver in his stirring "Cross of Gold" speech.

*A VOICE FROM THE PAST*

Burn down your cities and leave our farms, and your cities will spring up again as if by magic; but destroy our farms and the grass will grow in the street of every city in the country. . . . [We] . . . answer . . . their demand for a gold standard by saying . . . : You shall not press down upon the brow of labor this crown of thorns. You shall not crucify mankind upon a cross of gold.

**William Jennings Bryan,** Democratic Convention speech, July 8, 1896

*Reading* **History**

**C. Analyzing Points of View** What point was William Jennings Bryan making about the importance of farms?

C. Possible Response Bryan was saying that farms are more important than cities and that without them the country could not survive.

Farmers in the South and the West voted overwhelmingly for Bryan. But McKinley, who was backed by industrialists, bankers, and other business leaders, won the East and the election by about half a million votes. This election was the beginning of the end for the Populist Party.

## 4 The Closing of the Frontier

By the late 1880s, fenced-in fields had replaced open plains. The last remaining open land was in Indian Territory. The Oklahoma land rush of 1889 symbolized the closing of the frontier. At the blast of the starting gun on April 22, thousands of white settlers rushed to claim two million acres of land that had once belonged to Native Americans. In May 1890, this part of Indian Territory officially became Oklahoma Territory. In 1890, 17 million people lived between the Mississippi and the Pacific. That year the Census Bureau declared that the country no longer had a continuous frontier line—the frontier no longer existed.



ACTIVITY OPTIONS

## INDIVIDUAL NEEDS: GIFTED AND TALENTED

**TURNER: RIGHT OR WRONG?**

**Class Time** One class period

**Task** Evaluating Frederick Jackson Turner's ideas about the significance of closing the frontier

**Purpose** To analyze Turner's ideas on the importance of the frontier

**Supplies Needed**

- Reference materials on Frederick Jackson Turner and his ideas

**Activity** Have students review Turner's beliefs about the frontier and review the concept of manifest destiny in Chapter 13. Then use these questions to have a roundtable discussion: Was the advance of western settlement a positive development? Was it inevitable? How can Turner's beliefs be linked to the idea of manifest destiny? What evidence suggests that opportunities for Americans did not end with the closing of the frontier?

Thousands of settlers rushed into Oklahoma Territory in 1889 to claim the last open land on the frontier.

D. Possible Answer Turner believed that America's history and character were shaped by the fact that there was always a frontier with free land available for settlement.

*Reading* **History**

**D. Using Secondary Sources** What did Frederick Jackson Turner believe about the frontier?

To many, the frontier was what had made America unique. In 1893, historian Frederick Jackson Turner wrote an influential essay on the frontier. Turner said that the frontier was a promise to all Americans, no matter how poor, that they could advance as far as their abilities allowed. To Turner the frontier meant opportunity, and its closing marked the end of an era.

*A VOICE FROM THE PAST*

Up to our own day American history has been in a large degree the history of the colonization of the Great West. The existence of an area of free land, its continuous recession, and the advance of American settlement westward, explain American development.

**Frederick Jackson Turner,** "The Significance of the American Frontier"

Today many historians question Turner's view. They think he gave too much importance to the frontier in the nation's development and in shaping a special American character. These historians point out that the United States remains a land of opportunity long after the frontier's closing.

In the next chapter, you will learn how an industrial society developed in the East during the same period that the West was settled.

## Section 4 Assessment

### 1. Terms & Names

**Identify:**
- Homestead Act
- Exoduster
- sodbuster
- Grange
- cooperative
- Populist Party
- gold standard
- William Jennings Bryan

### 2. Taking Notes

Review the chapter and find five key events to place on a time line as shown.

1860 — event — event — 1890
event — event — event

What do you think was the most important event?

### 3. Main Ideas

a. How did the federal government encourage and support settlement of the Plains?

b. Which groups of people moved onto the Plains in the late 1800s? Why did they come?

c. Which problems in the 1890s led farmers to take political action?

### 4. Critical Thinking

**Drawing Conclusions**
Why did the Grange favor government regulation of the railroads?

**THINK ABOUT**
- powers of monopolies
- importance of railroads to farmers
- railroad freight and storage rates

**ACTIVITY OPTIONS**

**TECHNOLOGY**
**SPEECH**

Pick one invention that helped farmers on the Plains. Plan an **electronic presentation** on the invention or deliver a **sales pitch** to potential buyers.



## MORE ABOUT . . .

**Frederick Jackson Turner**

Turner believed that European immigrants had been changed for the better in the process of settling North America. He held that frontier life promoted "rugged individualism" and helped produce the democratic political institutions that made the United States unique. Historians today point out that Turner's thesis ignores the brutal treatment of Native Americans and the key role of women, African Americans, Asians, and Mexican Americans in western settlement.

## ASSESS & RETEACH

**Setting the Stage** Have students fill in the section on farmers on the chapter graphic organizer.

**Formal Assessment**
- Section Quiz, p. 285

**Critical Thinking Transparency CT55**
- Setting the Stage

### RETEACHING ACTIVITY

Ask students to write the following key terms and names on a note card: Grange, cooperative, Populist Party, gold standard, William Jennings Bryan. Then have them write a definition or description on the reverse side. Have students explain how the terms relate to the main idea of the section.

**In-Depth Resources: Unit 6**
- Reteaching Activity, p. 19

## Section 4 Assessment

### 1. Terms & Names

**Homestead Act,** p. 574
**Exoduster,** p. 575
**sodbuster,** p. 575
**Grange,** p. 577
**cooperative,** p. 577
**Populist Party,** p. 577
**gold standard,** p. 577
**William Jennings Bryan,** p. 578

### 2. Taking Notes

Event 1: Homestead Act of 1862;
Event 2: formation of Grange, 1867;
Event 3: *Munn* v. *Illinois,* 1877;
Event 4: formation of Populist Party, 1890;
Event 5: closing of frontier, 1890

Answers will vary.

### 3. Main Ideas

**a.** by passing the Homestead Act and by giving public land to the railroads to promote expansion **b.** African Americans from the South, migrants from the East, and European immigrants all sought economic opportunities. **c.** falling prices for crops; high freight rates and fees for grain elevators

### 4. Critical Thinking

to reduce the power of the railroad monopoly; to guarantee more fair rates for farmers

### ACTIVITY OPTIONS

**Alternative Assessment**
- Rubrics for a presentation, 5.2
- Rubrics for a speech, 4.9

## TERMS & NAMES

1. **frontier,** p. 557
2. **long drive,** p. 560
3. **reservation,** p. 562
4. **Battle of the Little Bighorn,** p. 565
5. **Dawes Act,** p. 567
6. **homestead,** p. 568
7. **Mexicano,** p. 570
8. **Homestead Act,** p. 574
9. **sodbuster,** p. 575
10. **Populist Party,** p. 577

## REVIEW QUESTIONS

**Possible Responses**

1. They came in large numbers, built towns, and helped territories to become states.
2. Cowhands drove cattle from Texas ranches to railroad stops in Kansas where the cattle were sold for many times their original price before being sent by rail to the East.
3. the dropping price of beef as the supply increased; the open range being fenced in by barbed wire; harsh winter of 1886–1887 that killed off cattle
4. White settlers wanted the land that had been ceded to Native Americans by treaty, and the Native Americans resisted when the government tried to buy back the land or take it by force.
5. They fought battles with white settlers and army troops.
6. Women gained the right to own property, control their own money, and vote.
7. The role of Native Americans, African Americans, and the government in settling the West is now stressed, as well as the origins of the conflict between Native Americans and white settlers.
8. by passing the Homestead Act, which gave free land to prospective settlers and gave public land to the railroads to promote expansion
9. to meet the social needs of farmers and to improve their economic condition by forming cooperatives
10. when there was no more open land for settlement

# Chapter 19 ASSESSMENT

## VISUAL SUMMARY

### Growth of the West

The West

### Miners

Miners were attracted to the West by gold and silver strikes. Mining contributed to the population growth of many western territories.

### Cowhands & Ranchers

Ranchers and cowhands established a thriving cattle industry. New settlement, barbed wire, and bad weather ended the cattle boom.

### Native Americans

Government policies, wars, and the destruction of the buffalo led to the defeat of the Plains peoples and to their placement on reservations.

### Homesteaders

Hundreds of thousands of homesteaders settled on the Plains. Their life was hard, but they used new technologies to increase their output.

## TERMS & NAMES

Briefly explain the importance of each of the following.

1. frontier
2. long drive
3. reservation
4. Battle of the Little Bighorn
5. Dawes Act
6. homestead
7. Mexicano
8. Homestead Act
9. sodbuster
10. Populist Party

## REVIEW QUESTIONS

**Miners, Ranchers, and Cowhands (pages 557–561)**

1. What role did miners play in the settlement of the West?
2. What made cattle ranching so profitable in the late 1800s?
3. What ended the boom in the cattle business?

**Native Americans Fight to Survive (pages 562–567)**

4. What caused conflict between Native Americans and white settlers on the Great Plains?
5. How did Native Americans resist white settlement?

**Life in the West (pages 568–573)**

6. What rights did women in the West gain before women in Eastern states?
7. How has the myth of the "Wild West" been revised?

**Farming and Populism (pages 574–579)**

8. How did the federal government encourage people to settle on the Great Plains?
9. What were the goals of the Grange?
10. What marked the closing of the frontier?

## CRITICAL THINKING

**1. USING YOUR NOTES**

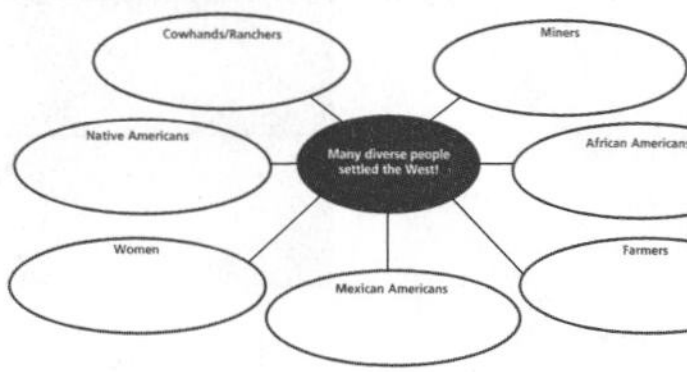


Using your completed chart, answer the questions below.

a. What were the main reasons that drew people to the West?

b. Which groups do you think benefited from being in the West and which groups did not? Explain.

**2. APPLYING CITIZENSHIP SKILLS**

What are the dangers of vigilante justice?

**3. THEME: DIVERSITY AND UNITY**

Why might the contributions of women and Native Americans, African Americans, and other ethnic groups have been overlooked in early books and films on the West?

**4. ANALYZING LEADERSHIP**

Why did the Nez Perce Chief Joseph decide to surrender? What other choices might he have made?

**5. CONTRASTING**

How did ranchers and sodbusters differ over land use? Why did these differences lead to conflict?

**6. FORMING AND SUPPORTING OPINIONS**

What do you think would be the most difficult challenge in starting a new life on the Great Plains? Give reasons for your answer.

**Interact *with* History**

Now that you have read the chapter, would you still make the same statements about how your life would change in the West? Explain.

## CRITICAL THINKING

**Possible Responses**

1. **USING YOUR NOTES** **a.** economic opportunity; less discrimination **b.** Benefited: women, miners, farmers, cowhands, and ranchers. Did not benefit: Native Americans, Mexican Americans, African Americans.
2. **APPLYING CITIZENSHIP SKILLS** It denies the accused basic legal rights.
3. **THEME: DIVERSITY AND UNITY** Prejudice and racism played a part. Many books and films were created by whites.
4. **ANALYZING LEADERSHIP** He surrendered because his people were starving. They could have fought to the death.
5. **CONTRASTING** Ranchers saw the land as free for their use in grazing their cattle. Sodbusters fenced in their land with barbed wire.
6. **FORMING AND SUPPORTING OPINIONS** Opinions will vary. Some may say leaving friends and family, making a living, or working long hours.

**Interact *with* History** Answers will vary. In their responses, students should show understanding of the events in the chapter.

## HISTORY SKILLS

**1. INTERPRETING MAPS: Movement**

Study the map. Answer the questions.

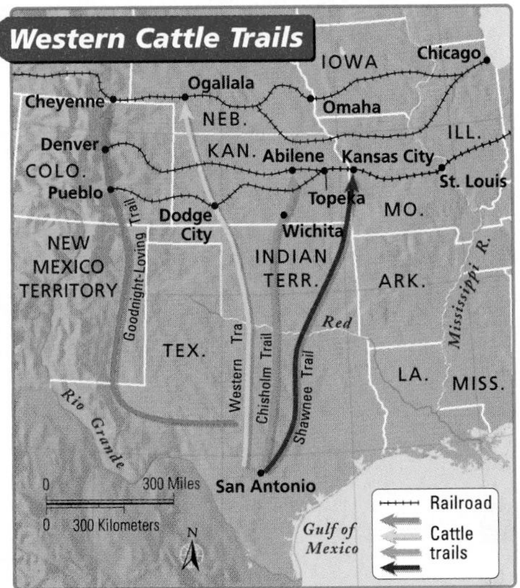


**Basic Map Elements**

a. What is the subject of the map?

b. What do the arrows indicate?

**Interpreting the Map**

c. What is the longest cattle trail?

d. How many miles did it cover?

**2. INTERPRETING PRIMARY SOURCES**

This quotation by Charles Goodnight, a Texas rancher and founder of the Goodnight-Loving Trail (see above map), appeared in *The West* by Geoffrey Ward.

> All in all, my years on the trail were the happiest I ever lived. There were many hardships and dangers, of course, that called on all a man had of endurance and bravery; but when all went well there was no other life so pleasant. Most of the time we were solitary adventurers in a great land as fresh and new as a spring morning, and we were free and full of the zest of darers.

a. What does Goodnight think about life on a cattle trail?

b. How does Goodnight describe the West?

## ALTERNATIVE ASSESSMENT

**1. INTERDISCIPLINARY ACTIVITIES: Art**

**Analyzing Visual Images of the West** Look through magazines and books to find images that portray the West today. Create a display of pictures with captions that explains whether each picture portrays the real or legendary Wild West.

**2. COOPERATIVE LEARNING ACTIVITY**

**Performing Dramatic Readings** Drawing on the many journals, diaries, and other primary sources left by sodbusters, create a Voices of the Plains play. Working in small groups, have students research such topics as "the journey west," "first impressions," "dugouts and soddies," "farming the plains," "women's work and worries." Within groups, members can create presentations using these suggestions.

- Choose and research a topic.
- Select quotations related to the topic.
- Pick writers to compose lines to introduce and make transitions between quotations, and choose readers to perform readings.

**3. TECHNOLOGY ACTIVITY**

**Designing a "Legends of the West" Web Site** The "Wild West" of the late 1800s was a land of myth and legend. It was peopled by a cast of memorable characters whose exploits, real and imagined, have been portrayed in books, motion pictures, and television. Use the library or search the Internet for information on the "Wild West."

**Visit www.mcdougallittell.com to learn more about the West.**

Design a "Wild West" Web site following the suggestions below.

- Select the legendary personalities to be featured.
- Include words and images that capture the flavor of the West.
- Choose musical selections to add background.
- Find Web sites that would be good links for visitors to your page.

**4. PORTFOLIO ACTIVITY**

**Option 1** Review your section and chapter assessment activities. Select one that you think was your best work. Use comments made by your teacher or classmates to improve your work. Add this activity to your history portfolio

**Option 2** Review the list of details that you wanted to know about the West on page 556. Then write a short report in which you explain the details you have learned. Add this report to your portfolio.



## ALTERNATIVE ASSESSMENT

**1. INTERDISCIPLINARY ACTIVITIES: Art**

**Each student's display should**

- be neatly presented and creative.
- be clearly captioned.
- present information in a style that will aid the viewer in comparing the real and legendary Wild West.

**2. COOPERATIVE LEARNING ACTIVITY**

**Dramatic reading should**

- have a clear focus and be well organized.
- include quotes related to the topic.
- highlight interesting details of life on the Plains.

**3. TECHNOLOGY ACTIVITY**

**The Web site should**

- clearly state the purpose of the Web site.
- identify sources of materials used.
- provide ample background information on the legendary personalities featured.
- contain at least three links.

**4. HISTORY PORTFOLIO**

**Option 1 Revised section or chapter assessment activities should**

- address teacher and peer responses to the selected work.
- solve problems present in the first versions of the work.

**Option 2 Short reports should**

- describe the details that students learned about the West.
- cite sources of information.
- use standard grammar, spelling, sentence structure, and punctuation.

**Critical Thinking Transparency CT57**

- Visual Summary

**Formal Assessment**

- Chapter Test, Forms A and B, pp. 286–287

## HISTORY SKILLS

**Possible Responses**

1. INTERPRETING MAPS

**Basic Map Elements**

**a.** western cattle trails

**b.** four different cattle trails

**Interpreting the Map**

**c.** Goodnight-Loving Trail

**d.** about 1,000 miles

2. INTERPRETING PRIMARY SOURCES

**a.** Goodnight said that there was no other life as pleasant, even though there were many hardships and dangers.

**b.** He said that it was a fresh and new land.

CHAPTER 20 PLANNING GUIDE

# An Industrial Society 1860–1914

| | CHAPTER OVERVIEW | COPYMASTERS | TECHNOLOGY |
|---|---|---|---|
| **CHAPTER RESOURCES** | This chapter discusses the growth of industry, the expansion of the railroads, and the rise of big business in the late 1800s. It also describes workers' efforts to organize unions and demand better wages and shorter hours. | **In-Depth Resources: Unit 6**<br>• Tracing Themes: Economics in History, p. 22<br>• Building Vocabulary, p. 27<br>**Interdisciplinary Projects**, pp. 115–120 | Primary Source Explorer<br>Electronic Teacher Tools<br>Power Presentations CD-ROM<br>Chapter Summaries on CD (English and Spanish) |
| | **KEY IDEAS** | | |
| **SECTION 1**<br>**The Growth of Industry**<br>**pp. 585–589** | • Many factors contribute to American industrial growth: natural resources, immigration, inventions, capital.<br>• The business cycle alternates periods of growth with times of hardship.<br>• New inventions and technology revolutionize American industry. | **In-Depth Resources: Unit 6**<br>• Setting the Stage, p. 21<br>• Guided Reading, p. 23<br>• Reteaching Activity, p. 36<br>**America's History Makers**<br>• Thomas Edison, pp. 79–80<br>• Granville T. Woods, pp. 81–82 | Warm-Up Transparency WT20<br>Critical Thinking Transparency CT58<br>• Setting the Stage<br>Critical Thinking Transparency CT59<br>• Cause and Effect: Industrial Growth<br>ClassZone: www.mcdougallittell.com |
| **SECTION 2**<br>**Railroads Transform the Nation**<br>**pp. 590–593** | • The transcontinental railroad links the east and west coasts.<br>• Railroad companies set up standard time zones to make train schedules accurate.<br>• Railroads unite the country and open new areas to settlement. | **In-Depth Resources: Unit 6**<br>• Setting the Stage, p. 21<br>• Guided Reading, p. 24<br>• Primary Source, p. 31<br>• Literature Selections, pp. 33–35<br>• Reteaching Activity, p. 37<br>**Outline Map Activities**<br>• Railroads in 1900, pp. 39–40 | Warm-Up Transparency WT20<br>Humanities Transparency HT39<br>• Railroad Advertisement<br>Critical Thinking Transparency CT58<br>• Setting the Stage<br>ClassZone: www.mcdougallittell.com |
| **SECTION 3**<br>**The Rise of Big Business**<br>**pp. 594–599** | • Corporations offer a new way of organizing larger businesses.<br>• Tycoons such as John D. Rockefeller and Andrew Carnegie dominate their industries by creating monopolies and trusts.<br>• The South continues to depend on cotton farming. | **In-Depth Resources: Unit 6**<br>• Setting the Stage, p. 21<br>• Guided Reading, p. 25<br>• Skillbuilder Practice: Using an Electronic Card Catalog, p. 28<br>• Geography Application: Natural Resources and the Oil and Steel Industries, pp. 29–30<br>• Reteaching Activity, p. 38 | Warm-Up Transparency WT20<br>Geography Transparency GT20<br>• Mining and Industry, 1860–1890<br>Critical Thinking Transparency CT58<br>• Setting the Stage<br>ClassZone: www.mcdougallittell.com |
| **SECTION 4**<br>**Workers Organize**<br>**pp. 600–603** | • Workers form unions to combat low wages and dangerous working conditions.<br>• Business owners and the government join forces against unions, using troops to end strikes.<br>• Samuel Gompers founds the American Federation of Labor (AFL). | **In-Depth Resources: Unit 6**<br>• Setting the Stage, p. 21<br>• Guided Reading, p. 26<br>• Primary Source, p. 32<br>• Reteaching Activity, p. 39<br>**Economics in History**<br>• The Union Struggle, p. 20<br>**Why It Matters Now**<br>• The Changing Economy, pp. 39–40 | Warm-Up Transparency WT20<br>Humanities Transparency HT40<br>• Homestead Strike<br>Critical Thinking Transparency CT58<br>• Setting the Stage<br>Critical Thinking Transparency CT60<br>• Visual Summary<br>ClassZone: www.mcdougallittell.com |

Pupil's Edition · Copymaster · Overhead Transparency · Audio Library · CD-ROM · Internet

## ASSESSMENT

**Chapter Assessment,** pp. 604–605

**Formal Assessment**
- Chapter Tests, Forms A and B, pp. 300–307

**Alternative Assessment Book**

**Electronic Teacher Tools with Test Maker**

**Section Assessment,** p. 589

**Formal Assessment**
- Section Quiz, p. 296

**Alternative Assessment Book**
- Rubrics for a display, 1.10
- Rubrics for a Web page, 5.1

**Electronic Teacher Tools with Test Maker**

**Section Assessment,** p. 593

**Formal Assessment**
- Section Quiz, p. 297

**Alternative Assessment Book**
- Rubrics for a memorial, 1.3
- Rubrics for multimedia, 5.4

**Electronic Teacher Tools with Test Maker**

**Section Assessment,** p. 597

**Formal Assessment**
- Section Quiz, p. 298

**Alternative Assessment Book**
- Rubrics for a graph, 2.3
- Rubrics for an oral report, 3.6

**Electronic Teacher Tools with Test Maker**

**Section Assessment,** p. 603

**Formal Assessment**
- Section Quiz, p. 299

**Alternative Assessment Book**
- Rubrics for an editorial, 4.1
- Rubrics for a poster, 1.1

**Electronic Teacher Tools with Test Maker**

## CUSTOMIZING FOR INDIVIDUAL NEEDS

### Students Acquiring English/ESL

**Reading Study Guide** (English and Spanish), pp. 195–204

**Access for Students Acquiring English/ESL: Spanish Translations,** pp. 133–139

**Chapter Summaries on CD** (English and Spanish)

### Less Proficient Readers

**Reading Study Guide** (English and Spanish), pp. 195–204

**Chapter Summaries on CD** (English and Spanish)

### Gifted and Talented Students

**In-Depth Resources: Unit 6**
- Enrichment Activity, p. 40

**America's History Makers**
- Thomas Edison, pp. 79–80
- Granville T. Woods, pp. 81–82

## CROSS-CURRICULAR CONNECTIONS

### Economics

Gourley, Catherine. ***Good Girl Work: Factories, Sweatshops, and How Women Changed Their Role in the American Workforce.*** Brookfield, CT: Millbrook Press, 1999. The detailed personal histories of girls and women who labored long hours for little money and of the women who ultimately protested against these conditions.

### Geography

Murphy, Jim. ***Across America on an Emigrant Train.*** New York: Clarion, 1993. In 1879, writer Robert Louis Stevenson traveled to California by train. His journal vividly describes his adventure and forms the basis for the author's account of the development of the transcontinental railroads.

### Science

Amram, Fred M. et al. ***African-American Inventors: Lonnie Johnson, Frederick McKinley Jones, Marjorie Steward Joyner, Elijah McCoy, Garrett Augustus Morgan.*** Mankato, MN: Capstone Press, 1996. Short, easy-to-read information about creative inventors.

### Interdisciplinary Projects, pp. 115–120

- Math: Reading Railroad Schedules
- Science: Transmitting Sound
- Language Arts: Horatio Alger Stories
- Music: Railroad Songs

### Literature

Gross, Virginia T. ***The Day It Rained Forever: A Story of the Johnstown Flood.*** New York: Puffin Books, 1993. A novel set during the 1889 flood that destroyed a mill town.

Rappaport, Doreen. ***Trouble at the Mines.*** New York: Crowell, 1987. Rosie Wilson's family is deeply involved in the 1898 strike in the coal mining town of Arno, Pennsylvania.

Yee, Paul. ***Tales from Gold Mountain: Stories of the Chinese in the New World.*** Groundwood Books, 1999. Eight stories drawn from the experiences of Chinese immigrants.

### McDougal Littell *The Language of Literature*

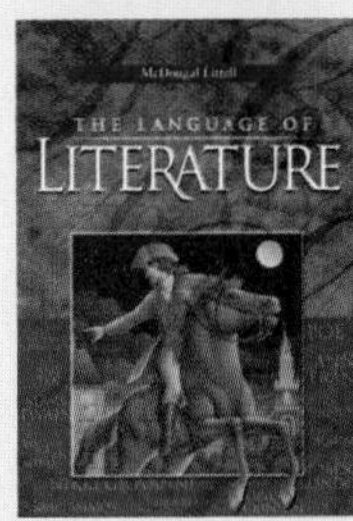


- Traditional, *John Henry*

## ENRICHMENT ACTIVITIES

**Pupil's Edition, pp. 582–605**
**Interact with History,** p. 583
**Geography in History,** pp. 598–599

**In-Depth Resources: Unit 6**
- Geography Application: Natural Resources and the Oil and Steel Industries, pp. 29–30
- Primary Source: A Letter from the Chinese Six Companies, p. 31
- Primary Source: An Interview with Pauline Cuoio Pepe, p. 32
- Literature Selections, pp. 33–35

**America's History Makers**
- Thomas Edison, pp. 79–80
- Granville T. Woods, pp. 81–82

**Outline Map Activities**
- Railroads in 1900, pp. 39–40

**Why It Matters Now**
- The Changing Economy, pp. 39–40

**LESSON PLAN OPTIONS (50-MINUTE PERIOD)** (TE) = Teacher's Edition (PE) = Pupil's Edition

| | TEACHER-DIRECTED ACTIVITIES<br>Class Time: 15 minutes | STUDENT-CENTERED ACTIVITIES<br>Class Time: 25 minutes | INDIVIDUAL ACTIVITIES<br>Class Time: 10 minutes |
|---|---|---|---|
| **DAY 1**<br>Introduction<br>pp. 582–584 | **Presentation Options**<br>• Begin with a class discussion of the picture on p. 582 **(PE)**.<br>• Lead a class discussion on the "What Do You Know?" question in Setting the Stage, p. 584. Then introduce the graphic organizer for the chapter **(PE)**. | **Options for Cooperative Learning**<br>• Have student groups discuss the Interact with History questions, p. 583 **(PE)**.<br>• Have student groups respond to the "What Do You Want to Know?" question in Setting the Stage, p. 584 **(PE)**. | **Head Start on Homework Options**<br>• Have students skim Section 1 Main Idea, Why It Matters Now, Terms & Names, and the main headings, p. 585 **(PE)**.<br>• Have students begin Guided Reading activity and Building Vocabulary sheet. |
| **DAY 2**<br>Section 1<br>pp. 585–589 | **Presentation Options**<br>• Begin with the 5-Minute Warm-Up, p. 585 **(TE)**.<br>• Review the Section 1 Main Idea, Why It Matters Now, and Terms & Names, p. 585 **(PE)**.<br>• Discuss the business cycle, using the History from Visuals, p. 586 **(TE)**. | **Options for Cooperative Learning**<br>• Working in pairs or small groups, have students begin the Multiple Learning Styles: Visual, Creating Your Own Invention, p. 588 **(TE)**.<br>• Have student pairs work together to complete one of the Activity Options in the Section 1 Assessment, p. 589 **(PE)**. | **Head Start on Homework Options**<br>• Have students begin working on Section 1 Assessment, p. 589 **(PE)**.<br>• Have students preview Section 2 Main Idea, Why It Matters Now, Terms & Names, and the main headings, p. 590 **(PE)**. |
| **DAY 3**<br>Section 2<br>pp. 590–593 | **Presentation Options**<br>• Begin with the 5-Minute Warm-Up, p. 590 **(TE)**.<br>• Choose 5 key questions for Objectives 1–4 to discuss with the class, pp. 590–593 **(TE)**.<br>• Lead the students through the History from Visuals, p. 592 **(TE)**. | **Options for Cooperative Learning**<br>• Divide students into groups and have them complete the Geography Skillbuilder, p. 593 **(PE)**.<br>• Have student pairs work together to complete one of the Activity Options in the Section 2 Assessment, p. 593 **(PE)**. | **Head Start on Homework Options**<br>• Have students begin working on Section 2 Assessment, p. 593 **(PE)**.<br>• Have students answer the questions for History Through Art, p. 596 **(PE)**. |
| **DAY 4**<br>Section 3<br>pp. 594–599 | **Presentation Options**<br>• Begin with the 5-Minute Warm-Up, p. 594 **(TE)**.<br>• Choose 5 key questions for Objectives 1–4 to discuss with the class, pp. 594–597 **(TE)**.<br>• Lead students through the Skillbuilder Mini-Lesson: Using an Electronic Card Catalog, p. 596 **(TE)**. | **Options for Cooperative Learning**<br>• Divide students into groups and have them complete the Geography in History questions, pp. 598–599 **(PE)**.<br>• Have student pairs work together to complete one of the Activity Options in the Section 3 Assessment, p. 597 **(PE)**. | **Head Start on Homework Options**<br>• Have students begin working on Section 3 Assessment, p. 597 **(PE)**.<br>• Have students complete the Reading History questions for Section 3, pp. 594–597 **(PE)**. |
| **DAY 5**<br>Section 4<br>pp. 600–603 | **Presentation Options**<br>• Begin with the 5-Minute Warm-Up, p. 600 **(TE)**.<br>• Choose 5 key questions for Objectives 1–4 to discuss with the class, pp. 600–603 **(TE)**.<br>• Lead students through the Critical Thinking Activity, p. 602 **(TE)**. | **Options for Cooperative Learning**<br>• Divide students into groups and have them work on the Critical Thinking activity, p. 602 **(TE)**.<br>• Have student pairs work together to complete one of the Activity Options in the Section 4 Assessment, p. 603 **(PE)**. | **Head Start on Homework Options**<br>• Have students complete the Setting the Stage graphic organizer for the chapter, p. 584 **(PE)**.<br>• Have students begin working on the Chapter Assessment, pp. 604–605 **(PE)**.<br>• Prepare for Chapter Test<br>**Formal Assessment,** pp. 300–307 |

TEACHER-TESTED ACTIVITY Philip Rodriguez, McNair Middle School, San Antonio, Texas

## EVALUATING NEW INDUSTRIES

**Class Time** 20 minutes

**Task** Evaluating new industries of the late 1800s and early 1900s

**Purpose** To assess the importance of new industries to the way of life in the period 1860–1914

**Supplies Needed**
- Notepads and pens

**Activity** After completing Section 2, write the following question on the chalkboard: Which industry had the greatest impact on society in the late 1800s—steel, electricity, telephone, or railroads? Identify one corner of the classroom for each of the four choices. Ask students to vote for their choice by moving silently to the appropriate corner of the room. Within groups in each corner, have students briefly explain why they made this particular choice. Let each group pick a spokesperson to summarize the group's opinions and present them to the class.

## BLOCK SCHEDULING — LESSON PLAN OPTIONS (90-MINUTE PERIOD)

### DAY 1

**Interact with History,** p. 583
**Class Time** 20 Minutes

Options for pacing and variety:
- Role-Playing Have each student assume the role of a worker at a factory where workers are on strike. Ask for a show of hands of those who would and would not join the strike. Match non-strikers with strikers and have each student explain to the other why he or she decided as such. **Class Time** 15 minutes

**Setting the Stage,** p. 584
**Class Time** 20 minutes

Options for pacing and variety:
- Time Saver For a homework assignment, ask students to study the cartoon of John D. Rockefeller and explain why they think this cartoon was chosen for Previewing the Theme and why they think the cartoonist depicts Rockefeller as a king. **Class Time** 10 minutes

**Section 1,** pp. 585–589
**Class Time** 50 minutes

Options for pacing and variety:
- Peer Teaching Working in pairs, students can create a cause-and-effect chart showing the reasons for the quickening pace of U.S. industrialization after the Civil War. **Class Time** 10 minutes
- Time Saver Use the chart on page 586 to summarize the business cycle for students. **Class Time** 5 minutes

### DAY 2

**Section 2,** pp. 590–593
**Class Time** 45 minutes

Options for pacing and variety:
- History on Film Extend students' knowledge of the railroads and other aspects of the Industrial Revolution in the United States by viewing *The American Industrial Revolution.* United Learning, 1997. **Class Time** 35 minutes
- Team Teaching Invite the music teacher to share with the class folksongs about Casey Jones, John Henry, and other railroad workers who have become American folk heroes celebrated in song. **Class Time** 25 minutes

**Section 3,** pp. 594–599
**Class Time** 45 minutes

Options for pacing and variety:
- Internet Extend students' background knowledge of Andrew Carnegie by visiting www.mcdougallittell.com **Class Time** 25 minutes
- Peer Teaching Divide students into groups of four to debate the Critical Thinking question in the Section Assessment, "Do wealthy people have a duty to become philanthropists?" Have each group share the outcome of its debate with the class. **Class Time** 15 minutes

### DAY 3

**Section 4,** pp. 600–603
**Class Time** 45 minutes

Options for pacing and variety:
- Time Saver For a homework assignment, have students create a summary of the section using the Terms & Names on page 600. **Class Time** 5 minutes
- Peer Teaching Have groups of students complete the Cooperative Learning activity for the Chapter Assessment using labor leaders like Samuel Gompers or Eugene V. Debs or activists like Mother Jones for the monologue. **Class Time** 40 minutes

**Chapter 20 Assessment,** pp. 604–605
**Class Time** 40 minutes

Options for pacing and variety:
- Peer Competition Divide into teams to play a game of "Who Am I?" using the many inventors, business leaders, and labor leaders discussed in the chapter. Give each team the names of two historical figures and have team members write five clues to their identity. Clues should become progressively easier. Teams win points according to how quickly they guess the identity of each person. **Class Time** 35 minutes

**CHAPTER 20 OBJECTIVE**

The student will understand how the growth of industry and big business changed the nation.

# An Industrial Society 1860–1914



## HISTORY FROM VISUALS

**Interpreting the Painting** John Ferguson Weir titled this painting *Forging the Shaft.* Weir tried to capture in his paintings the excitement and dignity of work in heavy industry. Tell students to look closely at the painting. Ask them to make some inferences about the workers who are depicted in the painting and about the kind of work they are doing. **Possible Responses** The work looks like it would be hot, strenuous, and dangerous. Laborers probably were not highly paid, but their work required skill as well as strength.

**Extension** Have students speculate about what the workers in the picture are doing. Ask students questions such as, What do you think the fire is doing to the metal? Why is the man in the foreground sitting down? What might his job entail? What might the finished object be used for?

These laborers are working in a foundry, a place where metal is cast.

582

## RECOMMENDED RESOURCES

**BOOKS FOR THE TEACHER**

Gordon, Sarah H. ***Passage to Union: How the Railroads Transformed American Life, 1829–1929.*** Chicago: Ivan Dee, 1997. Includes anecdotes, train lore, and contemporary comment.

Jones, Mary Harris, and Charles H. Kerr. ***The Autobiography of Mother Jones: Pittston Strike Commemorative Edition.*** Chicago: C. H. Kerr Pub., 1996. She was a tiny, white-haired widow who led a crusade for workers' rights.

**SOFTWARE**

***History of Railroads,*** Version 2.0. Multieducator, Inc., 1997. Dramatic story of the "Iron Horse" in photos, video clips, and multimedia presentations.

**VIDEO**

***The Masses and the Millionaires: The Homestead Strike.*** Learning Corporation of America. Short (26-minute) look at a bitter event.

**INTERNET**

For more about Andrew Carnegie, visit www.mcdougallittell.com

## Interact *with* History

**The year is 1894. You work in a factory that is unheated and badly lit. The machine that you operate is dangerous. The economy is doing poorly, so the factory has cut your wages. Some of your coworkers have gone out on strike. They want better pay and working conditions.**

### What Do You Think?

- What are some risks you would be taking if you join the strike?
- What might you gain if you take part in the strike?
- What other methods might you use to persuade your employer to meet your demands?

# *Would you join the strike? Why or why not?*

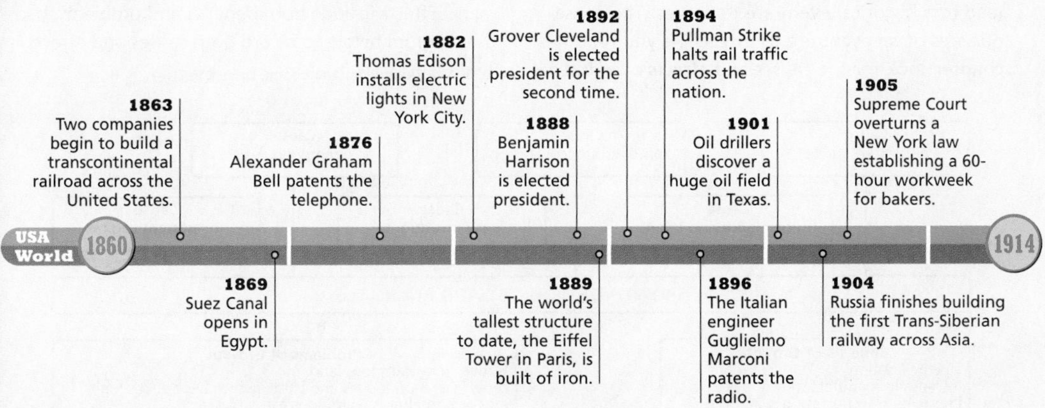

USA
World
1860
1863 Two companies begin to build a transcontinental railroad across the United States.
1869 Suez Canal opens in Egypt.
1876 Alexander Graham Bell patents the telephone.
1882 Thomas Edison installs electric lights in New York City.
1888 Benjamin Harrison is elected president.
1889 The world's tallest structure to date, the Eiffel Tower in Paris, is built of iron.
1892 Grover Cleveland is elected president for the second time.
1894 Pullman Strike halts rail traffic across the nation.
1896 The Italian engineer Guglielmo Marconi patents the radio.
1901 Oil drillers discover a huge oil field in Texas.
1904 Russia finishes building the first Trans-Siberian railway across Asia.
1905 Supreme Court overturns a New York law establishing a 60-hour workweek for bakers.
1914

## Interact *with* History

### OBJECTIVES

- To help students understand the difficulties of workers' lives before unions were formed and appropriate labor laws were passed
- To help students connect with the people and the events in this chapter

### What Do You Think?

1. Have students look at the illustration before answering. Encourage them to picture themselves as a member of a working-class family during this time period.
2. Tell students to think about the working conditions that their employers might be able to change and those that they cannot.
3. Suggest that students think of methods they have used in solving problems—compromise, arbitration (using an outside person or group), and debating the issues.

### *Would you join the strike? Why or why not?*

Suggest to students that they weigh the possible gains of going on strike against the potential losses. Point out that workers could not know whether the strike would be successful. Encourage students to try to make their decision based on the knowledge people had at that time, not with the advantage of historical hindsight.

### MAKING PERSONAL CONNECTIONS

Ask students to think about various jobs that they have done for pay. Did students think they were treated and paid fairly? If they thought they were not paid enough for the work, did they try to change the situation? How?

### TIME LINE DISCUSSION

**During the years following the Civil War, daily life for most Americans changed dramatically. New inventions led to new industries and new means of travel and communication in the United States and in other parts of the world. While big business grew, workers tried to work together for fair wages and working conditions.**

- Ask students to name the inventions listed on the time line. **Answers** telephone, electric lights, radio
- Ask students which events have to do with workers' rights. **Answers** Pullman strike, 1905 Supreme Court decision
- Ask students what the opening of the Suez Canal and the completion of the Trans-Siberian railroad indicate about transportation. **Answer** Transportation was improving in many parts of the world.

## BEFORE YOU READ

### Previewing the Theme: Economics in History

Ask students why a new industry might suddenly boom. Suggest that they think of reasons why natural resources might become accessible and lead to the development of new industries. Ask students how a new invention might lead to a new industry.

The late 1800s was a period of great progress in many areas in American life. However, the contrast between the life of the privileged and the life of the poor was marked. Many workers endured deplorable conditions. Employers seemed to have little sympathy for the workers.

### What Do You Know?

Suggest that students think of new businesses—for example, "e-businesses" that operate on the Internet. Ask students for examples of new companies that operate on the Internet. Ask them why they think such businesses grow quickly. Discuss invention, supply and demand, and the importance of investment to new Internet start-ups.

**In-Depth Resources: Unit 6**
- Tracing Themes: Economics in History, p. 22

## READ AND TAKE NOTES

### Reading Strategy: Analyzing Causes and Recognizing Effects

Review the concepts of cause and effect with students. Point out that the diagram shows multiple causes for the growth of industry and railroads in the United States, as well as multiple effects resulting from this growth. Suggest that students use the diagram to help them organize the information in the chapter.

**In-Depth Resources: Unit 6**
- Setting the Stage, p. 21

**Critical Thinking Transparency CT58**
- Setting the Stage

# Chapter 20 SETTING THE STAGE

## BEFORE YOU READ

Business leader John D. Rockefeller is shown as a wealthy king. Notice which industries are the "jewels in his crown."

### Previewing the Theme

**Economics in History** As Chapter 20 explains, natural resources and new inventions caused industry to boom in the late 1800s. Some businesses grew very large and made great profits by wiping out competitors and paying low wages. Workers banded together to demand higher pay and better working conditions.

### What Do You Know?

Do you know of any businesses that started back in the 1800s? How do businesses grow?

**THINK ABOUT**
- businesses that you see in your community
- businesses that are advertised on television, in magazines or newspapers, or on the Internet

### What Do You Want to Know?

What facts and details would help you understand how a nation of small businesses became a nation of giant corporations? In your notebook, list the facts and details you hope to learn from this chapter.

## READ AND TAKE NOTES

**Reading Strategy: Analyzing Causes and Recognizing Effects** The conditions or actions that lead to a historical event are its causes. The consequences of an event are its effects. As you read the chapter, look for the causes and effects of industrial and railroad growth. Causes include geographical factors and actions by individuals and the government. Effects include both benefits and problems. Use the diagram below to record both causes and effects.

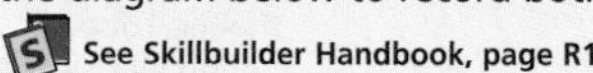
See Skillbuilder Handbook, page R10.

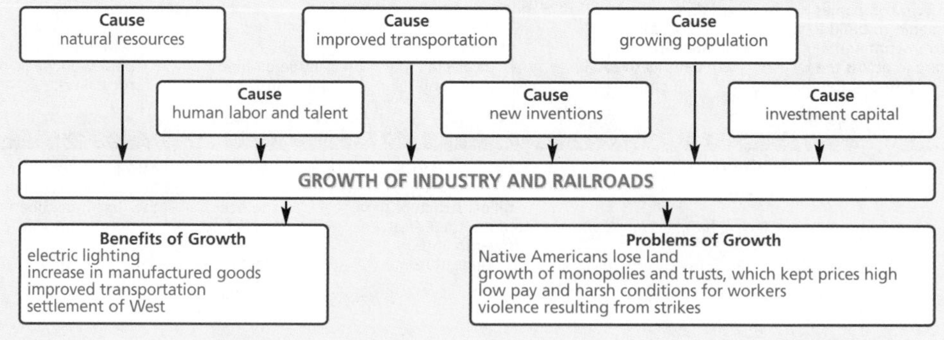




## TEACHING STRATEGY

### READING THE CHAPTER

This is a thematic chapter focusing on the effects of the growth of industry and railroads on the nation. Encourage students to note how inventions changed American life. Direct students to note the effects of industrialization on different groups of Americans, such as business leaders, workers, and immigrants.

### ALTERNATIVE ASSESSMENT

The Chapter Assessment describes three activities for alternative assessment on page 605. You may wish to have students work on these activities during the course of the chapter and then present them at the end.

# 1 The Growth of Industry

**TERMS & NAMES**
petroleum
patent
business cycle
Bessemer steel process
generator
Thomas Edison
Alexander Graham Bell
Centennial Exhibition

**MAIN IDEA**
The growth of industry during the years 1860 to 1914 transformed life in America.

**WHY IT MATTERS NOW**
Modern businesses rely on many of the inventions and products developed during that time.

## ONE AMERICAN'S STORY

**In the 1850s, most Americans lit their homes with oil lamps. They could have used kerosene, an oil made from coal, but it was expensive. Then, in 1855, a chemist released a report saying that kerosene could be made more cheaply from an oily flammable liquid called petroleum.**

**However, people didn't know how to obtain petroleum from its source deep in the earth. They just gathered the petroleum that had seeped to the surface, which was a time-consuming process. So several men decided to try drilling for oil. One of these men was Edwin Drake, who in 1857 visited a site in Pennsylvania where petroleum oozed to the surface.**

*A VOICE FROM THE PAST*

Within ten minutes after my arrival . . . I had made up my mind that [petroleum] could be obtained in large quantities by Boreing as for Salt Water.

**Edwin Drake,** quoted in *The Americans: The Democratic Experience*

**Drake began drilling through bedrock in 1859. In August, he struck oil, an event that launched the oil industry. It was one of many new industries that developed after the mid-1800s, as this section explains.**

The wooden structure is Drake's first oil well.

## 1 The Industrial Revolution Continues

In the late 1700s, the establishment of textile mills in New England was an early sign of industrialization, or the growth of industry, in the United States. By the mid-1800s, the use of factories had spread to other industries and other regions. The pace of industrialization became more rapid after the Civil War. Several factors helped U.S. industries grow.

1. **Plentiful natural resources.** America had immense forests and large supplies of water. It also had vast mineral wealth, including coal, iron, copper, silver, and gold. Industry used these resources to manufacture a variety of goods.



## SECTION OBJECTIVES

1. To identify factors that nurtured the Industrial Revolution
2. To explain how business cycles reflected rapid economic growth
3. To describe the growth of the steel and electric-power industries
4. To analyze how inventions changed American life

**SKILLBUILDER**
Interpreting Charts, p. 586
Interpreting Graphs, p. 589

**CRITICAL THINKING**
Recognizing Effects, pp. 586, 589
Drawing Conclusions, p. 587
Finding Main Ideas, p. 587
Analyzing Points of View, p. 588

## FOCUS & MOTIVATE

### 5-MINUTE WARM-UP

**Drawing Conclusions** These questions focus on inventions that changed American life.

1. Look at the illustrations on pages 588 and 589. Which inventors are discussed in the graphic? Which inventions mentioned do you use?
2. Why do you think these inventors created new products?

 **Warm-Up Transparency WT20**

## INSTRUCT

**INSTRUCT: OBJECTIVE** 

**The Industrial Revolution Continues**
Key Questions
- How did immigration affect industry?
- What factors helped U.S. industries grow?
- What role did banks and wealthy individuals play in the growth of the economy?

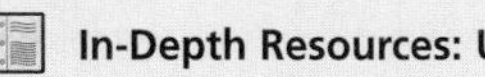
**In-Depth Resources: Unit 6**
- Guided Reading, p. 23

 **Critical Thinking Transparency CT59**
- Cause and Effect: Industrial Growth

## RECOMMENDED RESOURCES

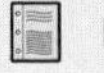 **In-Depth Resources: Unit 6**
- Guided Reading, p. 23
- Building Vocabulary, p. 27
- Reteaching Activity, p. 36
- Enrichment Activity, p. 40

 **Reading Study Guide** (Spanish and English), pp. 195–196

**America's History Makers**
- Thomas Edison, pp. 79–80
- Granville T. Woods, pp. 81–82

 **Formal Assessment**
- Section Quiz, p. 296

 **Alternative Assessment**
- Rubrics, 1.1
- Rubrics, 5.1

 **Access for Students Acquiring English/ESL**
- Guided Reading, p. 133

**Technology Resources**

 **Critical Thinking Trans. CT59**
- Cause and Effect: Industrial Growth

 **Electronic Teacher Tools with Test Maker**

 **ClassZone**
www.mcdougallittell.com

## MORE ABOUT . . .

**Patents and Inventions**

In the late 1800s, the number of new patents skyrocketed as inventions multiplied. Before the Civil War, the Patent Office issued an average of 500 patents a year. In 1897, however, it issued 22,000 patents. Even the head of the Patent Office, Charles H. Duell, did not believe that such a trend could continue. "Everything that can be invented has been invented," Duell stated in 1899, and he recommended closing the office.

## INSTRUCT: OBJECTIVE 2

**The Business Cycle**

Key Questions

- Why does the economy grow during a boom?
- How are economic booms and busts related?
- How did the panics of 1873 and 1893 affect industry and workers?

## HISTORY FROM VISUALS

**Reading the Chart** Ask students what factors they think contribute to expansion and thus to a high peak. Then tell them that a contraction follows the high point. Finally, ask why they think a period of expansion begins after growth hits the trough? **Possible Responses** Expansion: Jobs are plentiful and the economy is good, so people buy more and invest more. Contraction: Prices are high due to earlier demand; people start to buy less, making supplies greater than demand; less is produced, and people are laid off. Trough: Prices get very low during the trough, so people think it's a good time to buy and invest.

**Extension** Ask students in what phase they think today's economy is. Have them give ways to find the answer.

2. **Improved transportation.** In the early 1800s, steamboats, canals, and railroads made it possible to ship items long distances. Railroad building boomed after the Civil War. As shipping raw materials and finished goods to markets became even easier, industry grew.
3. **Growing population.** From 1860 to 1900, the U.S. population grew from 31.5 million to 76 million. This led to a growing need for goods. The demand for goods spurred the growth of industry.
4. **High immigration.** Between 1860 and 1900, about 14 million people immigrated to the United States. Many of them knew specialized trades, such as metalworking. Such knowledge was valuable to industries. In addition, unskilled immigrants supplied the labor that growing industry needed.
5. **New inventions.** New machines and improved processes helped industry produce goods more efficiently. Inventors applied for patents for the machines or processes they invented. A **patent** is a government document giving an inventor the exclusive right to make and sell his or her invention for a specific number of years.
6. **Investment capital.** When the economy was thriving, many businesses made large profits. Hoping to share in those profits, banks and wealthy people lent businesses money. The businesses used this capital to build factories and buy equipment.

**Background** Some of these canals were built because of Henry Clay's American System. (See Chapter 11.)

**Vocabulary** **capital:** money and property used in a business

**Skillbuilder Answers**
1. It is much greater.
2. No. Some have higher rates of production than others.

## 2 The Business Cycle

American industry did not grow at a steady pace; it experienced ups and downs. This pattern of good and bad times is called the **business cycle.** During good times, called booms, people buy more, and some invest in business. As a result, industries and businesses grow. During bad times, called busts, spending and investing decrease. Industries lay off workers and make fewer goods. Businesses may shrink—or even close. Such a period of low economic activity is a depression.

America experienced depressions in 1837 and 1857. Both were eventually followed by periods of strong economic growth. In the late 1800s, there were two harsh depressions, also called panics. The depression of 1873 lasted five years. At its height, three million people were out of work. During the depression that began in 1893, thousands of businesses failed, including more than 300 railroads.

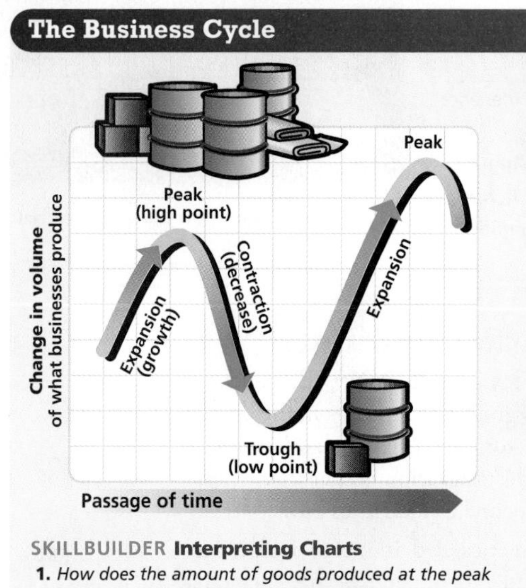


**SKILLBUILDER Interpreting Charts**
1. *How does the amount of goods produced at the peak compare to the amount at the trough?*
2. *Are all peaks equally prosperous? Explain.*

**A. Possible Response** They lose their jobs and have trouble making ends meet.

***Reading* History**
**A. Recognizing Effects** How do you think depressions affect ordinary people?



## ACTIVITY OPTIONS

### INTERDISCIPLINARY LINK: ECONOMICS

BLOCK SCHEDULING

**THE BUSINESS CYCLE GAME**

**Class Time** Two class periods

**Task** Creating a board game based on the phases of the business cycle

**Purpose** To understand the causes and effects of the business cycle

**Supplies Needed**
- Art supplies
- Posterboard

**Activity** Divide the class into small groups, then tell each group to create a board game in which a business tries to survive a complete business cycle. Students may base their game board on the chart on this page or design another. Games should use these variables: production costs rise; raw materials become unavailable; prices rise; customers buy less; inventories build up; you lay off workers; pessimism clouds nation; you make cutbacks; you close factory; prices decline; customers increase orders; new inventions spur sales; optimistic feelings prevail; prices rise.

Even with these economic highs and lows, industries in the United States grew tremendously between 1860 and 1900. Overall, the amount of manufactured goods increased six times during these years.

## 3 Steel: The Backbone of Industry

The steel industry contributed to America's industrial growth. Before the mid-1800s, steel was very expensive to manufacture because the steel-making process used huge amounts of coal. In the 1850s, William Kelly in the United States and Henry Bessemer in England independently developed a new process for making steel. It used less than one-seventh of the coal that the older process used. This new manufacturing technique was called the **Bessemer steel process.**

Because the Bessemer process cut the cost of steel, the nation's steel output increased 500 times between 1867 and 1900. Industry began to make many products out of steel instead of iron. These products included plows, barbed wire, nails, and beams for buildings. But the main use of steel throughout the late 1800s was for rails for the expanding railroads. (See Section 2.)

*Reading*History
**B. Drawing Conclusions** Which industries benefited from the steel products mentioned here?
B. Answer agriculture, construction, railroads

## Edison and Electricity

Another industry that grew during the late 1800s was the electric-power industry. By the 1870s, inventors had designed efficient generators. A **generator** is a machine that produces electric current. As a result, people grew eager to tap the power of electricity.

The inventor who found the most ways to use electricity was **Thomas Edison.** In 1876, he opened a laboratory in Menlo Park, New Jersey. He employed many assistants, whom he organized into teams to do research. Edison's laboratory invented so many things that Edison received more than 1,000 U.S. patents, more than any other individual inventor.

Edison would start with an idea for a possible invention. Then he would work hard to make that idea a reality—even if problems arose.

C. Possible Response No. Although the idea comes in a burst of intuition, perfecting the idea takes hard work.

*Reading*History
**C. Finding Main Ideas** According to Edison, is inventing easy?

### A VOICE FROM THE PAST

It has been just so in all my inventions. The first step is an intuition—and comes with a burst, *then* difficulties arise. . . . "Bugs"—as such little faults and difficulties are called—show themselves and months of anxious watching, study and labor are requisite [needed] before commercial success—or failure—is certainly reached.

**Thomas Edison,** quoted in *Edison* by Matthew Josephson

Edison's most famous invention was practical electric lighting. Other inventors had already created electric lights, but they were too bright and

### Connections TO SCIENCE

**IRON VS. STEEL**

Why is the comic book hero Superman also called the man of steel? People often use the word *steel* as a synonym for strength.

Steel is an iron alloy—a blend of iron and other materials such as carbon. But steel is stronger and more durable than iron. That is why steel replaced iron in many industries in the late 1800s. A giant ladle (bucket) used to pour melted steel is pictured below.

Stainless steel, invented in the early 1900s, has an additional benefit: it doesn't rust. Stainless steel is used in tools, machines, and many household items, such as pots, pans, and utensils.





**INSTRUCT: OBJECTIVE** 

**Steel: The Backbone of Industry/ Edison and Electricity**

Key Questions

- How did the development of the Bessemer steel process change the steel industry?
- How did Edison describe the process of inventing?
- How did Edison change the way of life in America?

 **America's History Makers**
- Thomas Edison, pp. 79–80

### Connections TO SCIENCE

**Iron vs. Steel**

The combination of iron with various alloys gives steel its special characteristics. Carbon steel, which accounts for 90 percent of the world's steel production, contains no more than 2 percent carbon. If more carbon is added, the result is cast iron—familiar material for skillets. Low-alloy steel (made from less than 5 percent of metals such as nickel or chromium) is exceptionally strong; it is used for machine parts, structural parts of buildings, bridges, and aircraft. High-alloy steel usually contains 5 to 30 percent alloys and is used when appearance and resistance to oxidation are important.

### MORE ABOUT . . .

**The Wizard of Menlo Park**

In many ways, Edison's laboratories in Menlo Park were the first technological "think tank." Edison was involved in the invention or improvement of dozens of devices—the electric light, the phonograph, the stock ticker, the microphone, the dictating machine, the electric generator, motion pictures, and more. Although Edison was a self-taught tinkerer, he employed dozens of college-educated scientists. Menlo Park became the model for later industrial research-and-development organizations.

## ACTIVITY OPTIONS

### INDIVIDUAL NEEDS

**LESS PROFICIENT READERS**

**Setting a Purpose for Reading** To help students set a purpose and focus their reading, write on the board the names of the inventors discussed in the section, listed to the right. Ask if students have heard of any of them, and if so, ask them to share what they know. Then suggest that as students read the section, they look for information provided about each inventor. Have students add to the list by including inventions and other important facts about the inventors.

| Inventors | |
|---|---|
| William Kelly | Elias Howe |
| Henry Bessemer | Jan Matzeliger |
| Thomas Edison | Isaac Singer |
| Alexander Graham Bell | Granville T. Woods |
| Christopher Latham Sholes | Margaret Knight |

## MORE ABOUT . . .

**Thomas A. Edison**

When he was 15, Edison pulled a child from the path of a train. To show his gratitude, the child's father, a telegraph operator, gave Edison telegraph lessons. At a young age, Edison began to lose his hearing. He became skillful at guessing the parts of people's speech that he could not hear. This skill served him well as a telegraph operator because he often needed to fill in incomplete messages. Edison often received news reports by telegraph. As a result, he became interested in business and politics. Some of his first inventions were improvements on the telegraph.

## INSTRUCT: OBJECTIVE 4

**Bell and the Telephone/ Inventions Change Industry**

Key Questions

- Why was the telephone "the greatest marvel ever achieved in electrical science"?
- How did other inventions of the 19th century change the way of life in America?

**In-Depth Resources: Unit 6**
- Enrichment Activity, p. 40

## MORE ABOUT . . .

**Alexander Graham Bell**

Bell was influenced greatly by his father, Alexander Melville Bell, who taught deaf-mutes how to speak. Alexander Graham and his two brothers helped their father demonstrate his method of teaching people to speak. After moving to the United States, Alexander Graham Bell opened a school in Boston for teachers of the deaf. Helen Keller was his prodigy. Bell was only 29 when he developed the first working telephone.

CONNECTIONS TO SCIENCE

**American Inventors, 1870–1900**

**Thomas A. Edison**

Imagine life without being able to burn lights 24 hours a day. Or without movies and recorded music. Edison invented not only the light bulb but also the phonograph and a moving-picture viewer.

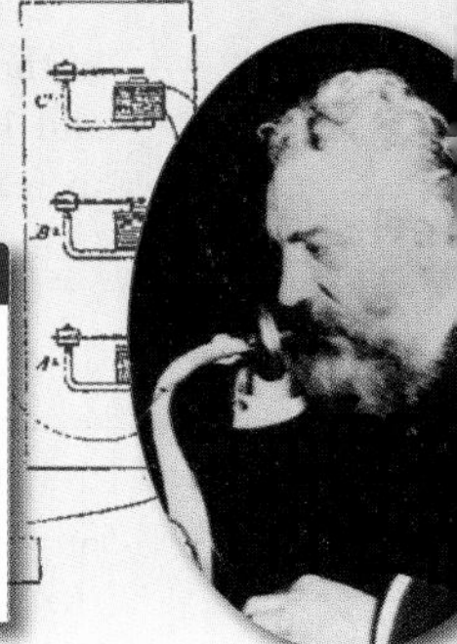


**Alexander Graham Bell**

As a teacher of the deaf, Bell experimented to learn how vowel sounds are produced. This led to his interest in the electrical transmission of speech.

flickery for home use. Edison figured out how to make a safe, steady light bulb. He also invented a system to deliver electricity to buildings.

By 1882, he had installed electric lighting in a half-mile-square area of New York City. Electric lighting quickly replaced gaslights. By the late 1880s, Edison's factory produced about a million light bulbs a year.

## 4 Bell and the Telephone

Electricity played a role in communications devices invented during the 1800s. In 1835, Samuel Morse developed the telegraph. It allowed people to use electrical impulses to send messages over long distances.

The next step in communications was the telephone, invented by **Alexander Graham Bell.** He was a Scottish immigrant who taught deaf students in Boston. At night, Bell and his assistant, Thomas Watson, tried to invent a device to transmit human speech using electricity.

After years of experiments, Bell succeeded. One day in March 1876, he was adjusting the transmitter in the laboratory in his apartment. Watson was in another room with the receiver. The two doors between the rooms were shut. According to Watson's memoirs, Bell accidentally spilled acid on himself and said, "Mr. Watson, come here. I want you." Watson rushed down the hall. He burst into the laboratory, exclaiming that he had heard and understood Bell's words through the receiver.

Bell showed his telephone at the **Centennial Exhibition** in June 1876. That was an exhibition in Philadelphia to celebrate America's 100th birthday. There, several of the world's leading scientists and the emperor of Brazil saw his demonstration. Afterward, they declared, "Here is the greatest marvel ever achieved in electrical science."

*Reading* **History**

**D. Analyzing Points of View** Why do you think the scientists said this about the telephone?

**D. Possible Response** They were excited that it would improve communication.

## Inventions Change Industry

The telephone industry grew rapidly. By 1880, more than 50,000 telephones had been sold. The invention of the switchboard allowed more and more people to connect into a telephone network. Women commonly worked in the new job of switchboard operator.

The typewriter also opened jobs for women. Christopher Latham Sholes helped invent the first practical typewriter in 1867. He also



## ACTIVITY OPTIONS

**MULTIPLE LEARNING STYLES: SPATIAL (VISUAL)**

BLOCK SCHEDULING

**CREATING YOUR OWN INVENTION**

**Class Time** One to two class periods

**Task** Inventing a new product

**Purpose** To understand the process of invention

**Supplies Needed**
- Graph or drafting paper
- Art supplies

**Activity** Students may work alone, in pairs, or in small groups for this activity. Challenge students to think like inventors such as Bell and Edison. Tell them to brainstorm a list of new products that will solve problems shared by many people. Then have students choose one of their ideas, draw a picture of their product, list the materials it would require, and write a description of it. Allow students to share their inventions with the class.

J. E. MATZELIGER.
LASTING MACHINE.
Patented Mar. 20, 1883.


**Jan Matzeliger**

An immigrant from Dutch Guiana, Matzeliger worked in a shoe factory. To reduce the time needed to fasten shoe leather to the sole by hand, he invented a machine to do the job. It increased production by 1,400 percent!

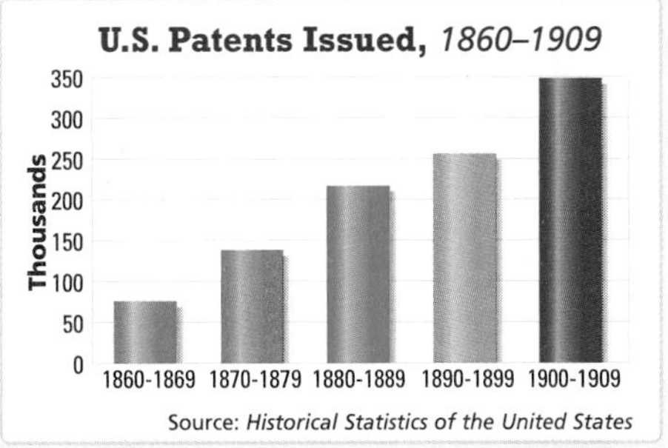


Source: *Historical Statistics of the United States*

SKILLBUILDER **Interpreting Graphs**

1. *How many more patents were issued from 1900 to 1909 than from 1860 to 1869?*
2. *Was this a time of increasing or decreasing inventiveness?*

improved the machine and sold his rights to it to a manufacturer who began to make typewriters in the 1870s.

The sewing machine also changed American life. Elias Howe first patented it in 1846. In the next few years, the sewing machine received many design improvements. Isaac Singer patented a sewing machine in 1851 and continued to improve it. It became a bestseller and led to a new industry. In factories, people produced ready-made clothes. Instead of being fitted to each buyer, clothes came in standard sizes and popular styles. Increasingly, people bought clothes instead of making their own.

Other inventors helped industry advance. African-American inventor Granville T. Woods patented devices to improve telephone and telegraph systems. Margaret Knight invented machines for the packaging and shoemaking industries and also improved motors and engines.

Of all the up-and-coming industries of the middle 1800s, one would have a larger impact on American life than any other. That was the railroad industry. You will read about railroads in Section 2.

Skillbuilder Answers
1. approximately 275,000
2. increasing inventiveness

## Section 1 Assessment

**1. Terms & Names**

**Identify:**
- petroleum
- patent
- business cycle
- Bessemer steel process
- generator
- Thomas Edison
- Alexander Graham Bell
- Centennial Exhibition

**2. Taking Notes**

Use a cluster diagram like the one below to list some of the inventions of the late 1800s.

How has one of these inventions recently been improved?

**3. Main Ideas**

a. What factors contributed to industrial growth in the United States?

b. What is the business cycle?

c. What caused the steel-making industry to boom and why?

**4. Critical Thinking**

**Recognizing Effects** How did the inventions of the late 1800s make it easier to do business?

THINK ABOUT
- electric generators and light bulbs
- the telephone
- the typewriter

ACTIVITY OPTIONS

SCIENCE | TECHNOLOGY

Choose an invention and learn more about it. Create a **display** explaining how it works or design a **Web page** linking to sites with more information.





### HISTORY FROM VISUALS

**Reading the Graph** Have students note the span of years on the graph. Ask them to write one sentence that describes the change in the number of patents issued from the period 1860–1869 to the period 1900–1909. **Possible Response** Between 1900 and 1909, 275,000 more patents were issued than in the decade 1860–1869.

**Extension** Have students work in pairs to find information about other inventors of the period and their inventions.

**America's History Makers**
- Granville T. Woods, pp. 81–82

### ASSESS & RETEACH

**Setting the Stage** Have students fill in the appropriate boxes about natural resources and inventions in the Cause section and the Benefits of Growth box in the effects section on the graphic organizer.

**Critical Thinking Transparency CT58**
- Setting the Stage

**Formal Assessment**
- Section Quiz, p. 296

### RETEACHING ACTIVITY

Have the class play "Industry Baseball." Appoint four students to act as pitcher (to ask questions), umpires, and scorekeeper. Have them make up questions based on the section or present them with questions of your own. Divide the rest of the class into two teams of batters—batting is answering questions. Batters advance to bases depending on whether they answer the question correctly (advance one base) or answer incorrectly (strike out). After one out, the other team is at bat. The team with the most students to cross home plate is the winner.

**In-Depth Resources: Unit 6**
- Reteaching Activity, p. 36

## Section 1 Assessment

**1. Terms & Names**

**petroleum,** p. 585
**patent,** p. 586
**business cycle,** p. 586
**Bessemer steel process,** p. 587
**generator,** p. 587
**Thomas Edison,** p. 587
**Alexander Graham Bell,** p. 588
**Centennial Exhibition,** p. 588

**2. Taking Notes**

Inventions: oil well; generator; light bulb; telephone; typewriter; sewing machine. Answers will vary. Students may choose electric typewriter, cordless and cell telephones.

**3. Main Ideas**

**a.** plentiful natural resources; improved transportation; growing population **b.** a pattern of good and bad times in business **c.** the development of the Bessemer steel process, because it substantially cut the cost of making steel

**4. Critical Thinking**

Answers will vary but should include references to the electric generator and light bulbs, telephones, and typewriters.

ACTIVITY OPTIONS

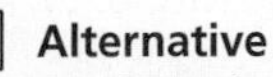

**Alternative Assessment**
- Rubrics for a display, 1.1
- Rubrics for a Web page, 5.1

## SECTION OBJECTIVES

1. To analyze the funding for the first transcontinental railroad
2. To identify the groups that worked on the first transcontinental railroad
3. To describe the linking together of the two railroads
4. To evaluate the changes brought about by the railroads

**SKILLBUILDER**
Interpreting Maps: Region, Place, p. 592

**CRITICAL THINKING**
Drawing Conclusions, p. 591
Evaluating, p. 593
Recognizing Effects, p. 593

## FOCUS & MOTIVATE

### 5-MINUTE WARM-UP

**Making Inferences** These questions focus on the growth of the railroads.

1. Look at the map of the railroads on page 592. In what ways did railroads change the entire nation?
2. Why do you think time zones were created?

 **Warm-Up Transparency WT20**

## INSTRUCT

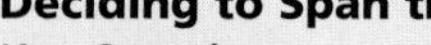

### INSTRUCT: OBJECTIVE 1

**Deciding to Span the Continent**
Key Questions
- Why did Americans want to build a transcontinental railroad?
- How was the transcontinental railroad financed?

 **In-Depth Resources: Unit 6**
- Guided Reading, p. 24
- Building Vocabulary, p. 27

 **Reading Study Guide** (Spanish and English), pp. 197–198

# 2 Railroads Transform the Nation

**TERMS & NAMES**
transcontinental railroad
standard time

| MAIN IDEA | WHY IT MATTERS NOW |
|---|---|
| The railroads tied the nation together, speeded industrial growth, and changed U.S. life. | The railroad first made possible our modern system of shipping goods across the country. |

### ONE AMERICAN'S STORY

**Ah Goong was one of thousands of Chinese workers on the Western railroads in the late 1800s. Building a railroad across steep mountains was dangerous. In some places, the workers had to blast rock from a cliff wall to build bridges and tunnels. The lightest Chinese climbed into wicker baskets at the top of the cliff. Others lowered the baskets hundreds of feet to the blasting site. Years later, Ah Goong's granddaughter described her grandfather's job.**

*A VOICE FROM THE PAST*

Swinging near the cliff, Ah Goong . . . dug holes, then inserted gunpowder and fuses. He worked neither too fast nor too slow, keeping even with the others. The basketmen signaled one another to light the fuses. He struck match after match and dropped the burnt matches over the sides. At last his fuse caught; he waved, and the men above pulled hand over hand hauling him up, pulleys creaking.

**Maxine Hong Kingston,** *China Men*

Chinese immigrants—like the one at the lower left—helped build several railroads in the West.

**Irishmen and Americans also worked on the railroads. This section discusses the building of the railroads and how they changed America.**

## 1 Deciding to Span the Continent

Americans had talked about building a **transcontinental railroad**—one that spanned the entire continent—for years. Such a railroad would encourage people to settle the West and develop its economy. In 1862, Congress passed a bill that called for two companies to build a transcontinental railroad across the center of the United States.

The Central Pacific was to start in Sacramento, California, and build east. The Union Pacific was to start in Omaha, Nebraska, and build west. To build the railroad, these two companies had to raise large sums of money. The government lent them millions of dollars. It also gave them 20 square miles of public land for every mile of track they laid. The railroad companies could then sell the land to raise money.

With the guarantees of loans and land, the railroads attracted many investors. The Central Pacific began to lay its first track in 1863. The



## RECOMMENDED RESOURCES

 **In-Depth Resources: Unit 6**
- Guided Reading, p. 24
- Building Vocabulary, p. 27
- Primary Source, p. 31
- Literature Selections, pp. 33–35
- Reteaching Activity, p. 37

**Reading Study Guide** (Spanish and English), pp. 197–198

**Outline Map Activities**
- Railroads in 1900, pp. 39–40

**Formal Assessment**
- Section Quiz, p. 297

**Alternative Assessment**
- Rubrics, 1.4
- Rubrics, 5.4

**Access for Students Acquiring English/ESL**
- Guided Reading, p. 134

**Technology Resources**

 **Humanities Transparency HT39**
- Railroad Advertisement

 **Electronic Teacher Tools with Test Maker**

 **ClassZone**
www.mcdougallittell.com

Union Pacific laid its first rail in July 1865 (after the Civil War had ended).

## 2 Building the Railroad

The Central Pacific faced a labor shortage because most men preferred to try to strike it rich as miners. Desperate for workers, the Central Pacific's managers overcame the widespread prejudice against the Chinese and hired several dozen of them. The Chinese were small and weighed, on average, no more than 110 pounds. But they were efficient, fearless, and hard working.

They also followed their own customs, which led to an unexpected benefit for the railroad company. The Chinese drank tea instead of unboiled water, so they were sick less often than other workers. Pleased with the Chinese workers, the company brought more men over from China. At the peak of construction, more than 10,000 Chinese worked on the Central Pacific.

**Background**
Boiling water kills germs.

The Union Pacific hired workers from a variety of backgrounds. After the Civil War ended in 1865, former soldiers from both North and South flocked to work on the railroad. Freed slaves came, too. But one of the largest groups of Union Pacific workers was immigrants, many from Ireland.

*Reading*History
**A. Drawing Conclusions** Why did the Union Pacific have a larger supply of workers?
A. Possible Response because its starting point was closer to the East, the most populated part of the country

Both railroads occasionally hired Native Americans. Washos, Shoshones, and Paiutes all assisted the race of the rails across the deserts of Nevada and Utah.

**daily life**

**RAILROAD CAMPS**

Union Pacific workers often worked 12-hour days. Graders had the job of leveling the roadbed. After a day of hard labor, they slept in small dirt shanties like the one below.

Track layers lived together in groups of 100 to 135, in railroad cars with three layers of bunk beds. The cars were parked at the end of the just-finished track. Workers ate in a dining car with their plates nailed to the table. They gobbled a quick meal of beef, beans, and bread. As soon as one group of 125 workers was done, the next group filed in.

## 3 Railroads Tie the Nation Together

Only short, undergrown trees dotted the vast open space. To the south shimmered the Great Salt Lake. In the east rose the bluish shapes of the Rocky Mountains. Across that space, from opposite directions, the workers of the Central Pacific and the Union Pacific toiled. By May 10, 1869, Central Pacific workers had laid 690 miles of track. Union Pacific workers had laid 1,086 miles. Only one span of track separated the two lines at their meeting point at Promontory, Utah.

*Reading*History
**B. Reading a Map** Using the map on page 592, find the Union Pacific and Central Pacific Railroads. Notice how they connect Omaha to Sacramento.

Hundreds of railroad workers, managers, spectators, and journalists gathered on that cool, windy day to see the transcontinental railroad completed. Millions of Americans waited to hear the news by telegraph. A band played as a Chinese crew and an Irish crew laid the last rails. The last spike, a golden one, was set in place. First, the president of the Central Pacific raised a hammer to drive in the spike. After he swung the hammer down, the crowd roared with laughter. He had missed. The vice-president of the Union Pacific took a turn and also missed. But the telegraph operator couldn't see and had already sent the message: "done." People across the nation celebrated.

This golden spike united the Central Pacific and Union Pacific Railroads.





**INSTRUCT: OBJECTIVE 2**

**Building the Railroad**

Key Questions

- What problems did the Central Pacific face when hiring workers?
- How did Chinese workers benefit the Central Pacific?
- Where did the Union Pacific get workers?

 **Humanities Transparency HT39**
- Railroad Advertisement

 **In-Depth Resources: Unit 6**
- Primary Source: A Letter from the Chinese Six Companies, p. 31
- Literature Selections, pp. 33–35

**daily life**

**Railroad Camps**

The Central Pacific workers faced many problems. Because of high temperatures in the California desert, flatcars with large tanks of water were needed. Because there were no trees in the desert for railroad ties and firewood, wood had to be brought in by train. Workers suffered through 44 blizzards during one winter in the Sierras; one storm lasted 13 days. Avalanches fell onto camps and tracks.

**INSTRUCT: OBJECTIVE 3**

**Railroads Tie the Nation Together**

Key Questions

- How did the Union Pacific and Central Pacific companies celebrate the completion of the transcontinental railroad?
- What happened in the railroad industry after the transcontinental railroad was built?

 **Outline Map Activities**
- Railroads in 1900, pp. 39–40

**ACTIVITY OPTIONS**

**INDIVIDUAL NEEDS**

**LESS PROFICIENT READERS**

**Identifying Facts** In order to help focus students' attention on the facts provided about the creation of the transcontinental railroad, create a chart such as the one shown on the board. As students read, have them look for the facts to answer the questions *why, where, who,* and *when* about the creation of the railroad.

| | |
|---|---|
| **WHAT?** | the transcontinental railroad |
| **WHY?** | to build a transcontinental railroad that would go across the center of the United States |
| **WHO?** | Central Pacific and Union Pacific railroads |
| **WHERE?** | Union Pacific: from Sacramento, California, to Promontory Point, Utah<br>Central Pacific: from Omaha, Nebraska, to Promontory Point, Utah |
| **WHEN?** | 1863–1869 |

**INSTRUCT: OBJECTIVE 4**

**Railroad Time/Economic and Social Changes**
Key Questions
- Why did the country need a standard time?
- How did the railroads benefit the economy?

**MORE ABOUT . . .**

**Railroad Time**
Railroad engineers were very flexible about their schedules. An engineer on the Old Colony Railroad in Massachusetts stopped to collect eggs from an elderly woman every day. Once she persuaded him to wait until her hen laid an egg to make a full dozen! The Delaware, Lackawanna, and Western Railroad (the D.L. & W.) was nicknamed the "Delay, Linger, and Wait"; the Newburgh, Dutchess, and Connecticut (the N.D. & C.) became the "Never Did and Couldn't."

**HISTORY FROM VISUALS**

**Reading the Map** Ask students if any states have no railroads. Then ask if more railroad tracks run north to south or east to west. Have students speculate why this might be so. **Possible Responses** Railroad tracks are shown in all states; more run east to west; it was more important in the industrialized North to connect to neighboring states for commerce; because the South was agricultural, it had less need to ship to neighboring states and built fewer railroads.

**Extension** Have students trace a route by rail from Savannah, Georgia, to Salt Lake City, Utah; and from Seattle, Washington, to Fort Worth, Texas.

The Union Pacific-Central Pacific line was the first transcontinental railroad. By 1895, four more U.S. lines had been built across the continent. Between 1869 and 1890, the amount of money railroads earned carrying freight grew from $300 million to $734 million per year.

**Background**
Canada had also built a transcontinental railroad, so there were six altogether.

## 4 Railroad Time

The railroads changed America in a surprising way: they altered time. Before the railroads, each community determined its own time, based on calculations about the sun's travels. This system was called "solar time." Solar time caused problems for people who scheduled trains crossing several time zones and for travelers.

*A VOICE FROM THE PAST*

I have been annoyed and perplexed by the changes in the time schedules of connecting railroads. My watch could give me no information as to the arrival and departure of trains, nor of the time for meals.

**John Rodgers,** quoted in *Passage to Union*

Skillbuilder Answers
1. Eastern
2. Eastern and Central—position in country; Mountain—Rocky Mountains and other ranges; Pacific—the nearby ocean

To solve this problem, the railroad companies set up **standard time.** It was a system that divided the United States into four time zones. Although the plan went into effect on November 18, 1883, Congress did not adopt standard time until 1918. By then, most Americans saw its benefit because following schedules had become part of daily life.

***Railroads of the Transcontinental Era,* 1865–1900**

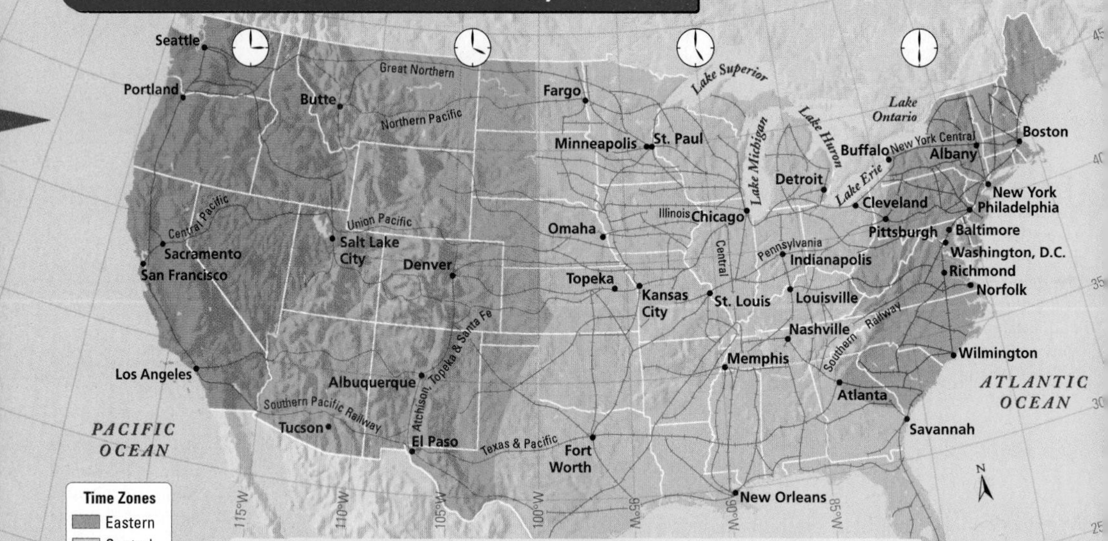

**GEOGRAPHY SKILLBUILDER Interpreting Maps**
1. **Region** *Were there more railroads in the Eastern or Western half of the country?*
2. **Place** *What do you think each of the four time zones was named for?*

592

**ACTIVITY OPTIONS**
**MULTIPLE LEARNING STYLES: MUSICAL** — BLOCK SCHEDULING

**A RAILROAD SONG**

**Class Time** 30 minutes

**Task** Learning a railroad song

**Purpose** To appreciate the effects of the railroads on American culture

**Supplies Needed**
- Song books such as *Folk Song USA* by John and Alan Lomax, *Fireside Book of Folk Songs* by Margaret Bradford Boni, or *A Treasury of American Song* by Olin Downes and Elie Siegmeister
- Tapes and CDs
- A guitar (optional)

**Activity** Ask for a volunteer to practice the guitar or piano accompaniment for one of the songs mentioned in the "Connections to Art & Music" on page 593. If no student volunteers, play a recording of one of the songs. If students seem not to know the words, repeat the song two or three times until they are ready to sing along. Encourage students to harmonize as they sing. As a concluding activity, ask students why railroad songs have remained popular even though railroads have less impact on American life today.

## Economic and Social Changes

The railroads changed people's lives in many other important ways. They helped create modern America.

1. **Linked the economies of the West and East.** From the West, the railroads carried eastward raw materials such as lumber, livestock, and grain. Materials like these were processed in Midwestern cities such as Chicago and Cleveland. (See Geography in History on pages 598–599.) From Eastern cities, in turn, came manufactured goods, which were sold to Westerners.
2. **Helped people settle the West.** Railroads were lifelines for settlers. Trains brought them lumber, farm equipment, food, and other necessities and hauled their crops to market.
3. **Weakened the Native American hold on the West.** As Chapter 19 explained, the railroads carried hunters who killed off the herds of buffalo. They also brought settlers and miners who laid claim to Native American land.
4. **Gave people more control of the environment.** Before railroads, people lived mainly where there were waterways, such as rivers. Roads were primitive. Railroads made possible cities such as Denver, Colorado, which had no usable waterways.

Just as railroads changed life for many Americans in the late 1800s, so did big business. You will read about big business in Section 3.

C. Possible Response
Positive—linking the economies, settling the West, and controlling the environment. Negative—weakening Native American hold on the West.

*Reading* **History**
**C. Evaluating** Which of these four changes do you think were positive, and which were negative?

### Connections TO ART & MUSIC

**RAILROAD HEROES**

Several American songs celebrate railroad heroes. One tells of Casey Jones, an engineer who saved lives. He slammed on the brakes as his train rounded a bend and plowed into a stalled freight train. He died but slowed the train enough to save his passengers.

Another song tells of a mythical worker named John Henry, shown below. This ballad celebrates an African American's strength in a track-laying race against a steam-driven machine.

### Connections TO *ART & MUSIC*

**Railroad Heroes**

Trains figure prominently in other famous American folk songs. Carl Sandburg's *American Songbag,* a collection of folk songs published in 1927, contains more than 20 railroad songs, including two versions of "Casey Jones." Sandburg includes "Railroad Bill," a song about "a mighty bad man." Another famous railroad song is "Poor Paddy Works on the Railway," a tune about Irish railroad workers.

## ASSESS & RETEACH

**Setting the Stage** Have students fill in the boxes for the causes, benefits, and problems pertaining to the railroads.

**Formal Assessment**
- Section Quiz, p. 297

### RETEACHING ACTIVITY

Have students copy the graphic below and fill it in with information from the section.

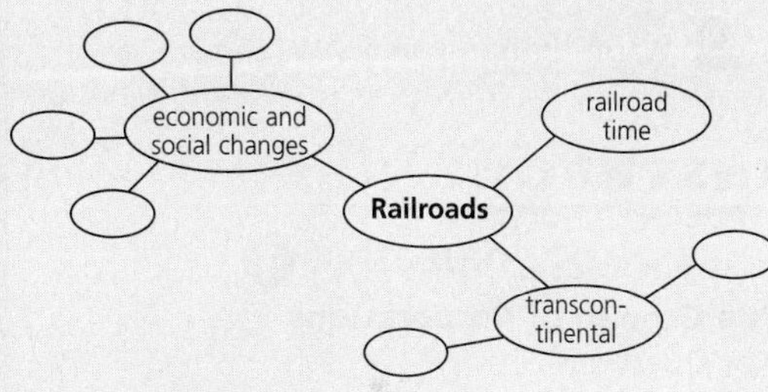


**In-Depth Resources: Unit 6**
- Reteaching Activity, p. 37

## Section 2 Assessment

**1. Terms & Names**

**Identify:**
- transcontinental railroad
- standard time

**2. Taking Notes**

Using a chart like the one below, record which groups of people helped build the transcontinental railroad.

| Central Pacific | Union Pacific |
|---|---|
| | |

Which group worked on both railroads?

**3. Main Ideas**

a. Why did the federal government want a transcontinental railroad built?

b. How did the government encourage the building of the railroad?

c. Why was standard time created?

**4. Critical Thinking**

**Recognizing Effects** Which of the trends started by railroads are still part of the modern business world?

**THINK ABOUT**
- railroads' effect on time
- the way they linked the economy
- the way they changed where people settled

**ACTIVITY OPTIONS**

**ART** / **TECHNOLOGY**

You have been asked to honor those who built the transcontinental railroad. Design a **memorial** or create the opening screen of a **multimedia presentation.**



## Section 2 Assessment

**1. Terms & Names**

**transcontinental railroad,** p. 590
**standard time,** p. 592

**2. Taking Notes**

Central Pacific: Chinese, Native Americans; Union Pacific: Civil War veterans, freed slaves, Irish immigrants, Native Americans. Native Americans worked on both railroads.

**3. Main Ideas**

**a.** to encourage people to settle the West and help develop its economy **b.** It gave the railroad companies 20 miles of land for every mile of track built. **c.** It was too hard to make train schedules when every community went by its own time.

**4. Critical Thinking**

strict schedules; doing business with faraway places; building in places where water transportation was not available

**ACTIVITY OPTIONS**

**Alternative Assessment**
- Rubrics for a memorial, 1.4
- Rubrics for multimedia, 5.4

## SECTION OBJECTIVES

1. To analyze the growth of corporations
2. To describe monopolies and trusts and evaluate their effects
3. To summarize the positive and negative aspects of the Gilded Age
4. To evaluate the development of the economy of the South

**CRITICAL THINKING**

Analyzing Points of View, p. 595
Contrasting, p. 596
Making Inferences, p. 597
Forming and Supporting Opinions, p. 597

## FOCUS & MOTIVATE

### 5-MINUTE WARM-UP

**Making Inferences** These questions focus on the rise of business and the Gilded Age.

1. Look at the cartoon on page 594. What opinion does the cartoonist express of Jay Gould, the person illustrated?
2. Why do you think the cartoonist may have had that opinion?

 **Warm-Up Transparency WT20**

## INSTRUCT

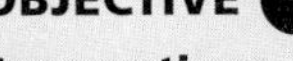

### INSTRUCT: OBJECTIVE 1

**The Growth of Corporations**

Key Questions

- How did businesses change in the late 1800s?
- What advantages do corporations have that smaller businesses do not have?

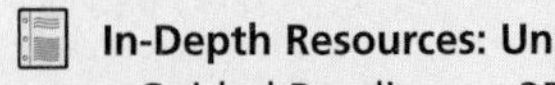

**In-Depth Resources: Unit 6**
- Guided Reading, p. 25

**Reading Study Guide** (Spanish and English), pp. 199–200

# 3 The Rise of Big Business

**TERMS & NAMES**
robber baron
corporation
John D. Rockefeller
Andrew Carnegie
monopoly
trust
philanthropist
Gilded Age

| MAIN IDEA | WHY IT MATTERS NOW |
|---|---|
| Business leaders guided industrial expansion and created new ways of doing business. | These leaders developed the modern corporation, which dominates business today. |

### ONE AMERICAN'S STORY

**In 1853, when Jay Gould was 17, he visited New York. Big-city wealth impressed Gould. After returning to his small hometown, he told a friend, "Crosby, I'm going to be rich. I've seen enough to realize what can be accomplished by means of riches, and I tell you I'm going to be rich."**

**"What's your plan?" his friend asked.**

**"I have no immediate plan," Gould replied. "I only see the goal. Plans must be formed along the way."**

**Gould achieved his goal. By the time he died in 1892, he was worth $77 million. He made a lot of his money using methods that are illegal today—such as bribing officials and selling fake stock. Most of his deals involved railroads, including the Union Pacific.**

**Jay Gould was a robber baron. A robber baron was a business leader who became wealthy through dishonest methods. This section discusses other business leaders and their companies.**

Jay Gould used methods such as trickery and false reports to "bowl over" his competition.

## 1 The Growth of Corporations

Until the late 1800s, most businesses were owned directly by one person or by a few partners. Then advances in technology made many business owners want to buy new equipment. One way to raise money to do so was to turn their businesses into corporations. A **corporation** is a business owned by investors who buy part of the company through shares of stock. A corporation has advantages over a privately owned business:

1. By selling stock, a corporation can raise large amounts of money.
2. A corporation has a special legal status and continues to exist after its founders die. Banks are more likely to lend a corporation money.
3. A corporation limits the risks to its investors, who do not have to pay off the corporation's debts.

In the late 1800s, few laws regulated corporations. This led to the growth of a few giant corporations that dominated American industry. The oil and steel industries are examples of this process.



## RECOMMENDED RESOURCES

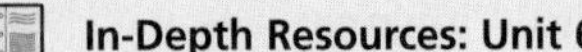

**In-Depth Resources: Unit 6**
- Guided Reading, p. 25
- Building Vocabulary, p. 27
- Skillbuilder Practice, p. 28
- Geography Application, pp. 29–30
- Reteaching Activity, p. 38

**Reading Study Guide** (Spanish and English), pp. 199–200

**Formal Assessment**
- Section Quiz, p. 298

**Alternative Assessment**
- Rubrics, 2.3
- Rubrics, 3.6

**Access for Students Acquiring English/ESL**
- Guided Reading, p. 135
- Skillbuilder Practice, p. 137
- Geography Application, pp. 138–139

**Technology Resources**

 **Geography Transparency GT20**
- Mining and Industry, 1860–1890

**Electronic Teacher Tools with Test Maker**

 **ClassZone**
www.mcdougallittell.com

## ❷ The Oil and Steel Industries

As Section 1 explained, the oil and steel industries began to grow in the late 1800s. Two men dominated these industries. **John D. Rockefeller** led the oil industry, and **Andrew Carnegie** controlled the steel industry.

**Vocabulary**
**refinery:** a plant that purifies oil

John D. Rockefeller built his first refinery in 1863. He decided that the best way to make money was to put his competitors out of business. A company that wipes out its competitors and controls an industry is a **monopoly**. Rockefeller bought other refineries. He made secret deals with railroads to carry his oil at a lower rate than his competitors' oil. He also built and purchased his own pipelines to carry oil.

Rockefeller's most famous move to end competition was to develop the trust in 1882. A **trust** is a legal body created to hold stock in many companies, often in the same industry. Rockefeller persuaded other oil companies to join his Standard Oil Trust. By 1880, the trust controlled 95 percent of all oil refining in the United States—and was able to set a high price for oil. The public had to pay that price because they couldn't buy oil from anyone else. As head of Standard Oil, Rockefeller earned millions of dollars. He also gained a reputation as a ruthless robber baron.

*Reading* **History**
**A. Analyzing Points of View** Why do you think people thought monopolies were unfair?
A. Possible Response They didn't like the way monopolies kept prices high.

Businessmen in other industries began to follow Rockefeller's example. Trusts were formed in the sugar, cottonseed oil, and lead-mining industries. Many people felt that these monopolies were unfair and hurt the economy. But the government was slow to regulate them.

Rockefeller tried to control all the companies in his industry. By contrast, Andrew Carnegie tried to beat his competition in the steel industry

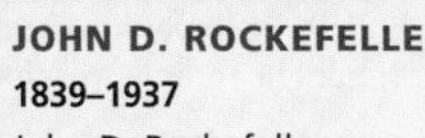


**JOHN D. ROCKEFELLER**
**1839–1937**

John D. Rockefeller was born to a poor family in upstate New York. From his mother, he learned the habit of frugality—he avoided unnecessary spending. "Willful waste makes woeful want" was a saying that Rockefeller's mother passed down to him.

By 1897, he had made millions and millions of dollars. Instead of keeping all that vast fortune for himself and his family, he spent the rest of his life donating money to several worthy causes.

**ANDREW CARNEGIE**
**1835–1919**

When Andrew Carnegie was 12, he and his family moved from Scotland to Pennsylvania. Carnegie's first job was in a cotton mill.

Later he worked in a telegraph office. There he was noticed by a railroad superintendent, who hired Carnegie as his assistant. Carnegie learned not only about running a big business but also about investing money. Eventually, he quit to start his own business.

Despite his fortune, Carnegie once wrote that none of his earnings gave him as much happiness as his first week's pay.

**Compare the characters of Rockefeller and Carnegie. What do you think made each of them successful?**



### INSTRUCT: OBJECTIVE 

**The Oil and Steel Industries**

Key Questions

- What methods did Rockefeller use to gain control of the oil industry?
- How did Carnegie's methods of gaining control of the steel industry differ from Rockefeller's?

 **Geography Transparency GT20**
- Mining and Industry, 1860–1890

 **In-Depth Resources: Unit 6**
- Geography Application: Natural Resources and the Oil and Steel Industries, pp. 29–30

### AMERICA'S HISTORY MAKERS

**John D. Rockefeller**

Rockefeller's mother started her son on his first business enterprise when he was just seven years old: raising turkeys. Later he hoed potatoes for 37 cents a day. He lent his savings back to the farmer and quickly found that, by earning interest, he could "let . . . money be my slave [rather] than be the slave of money." His philanthropic donations include the land for the United Nations building, the Lincoln Performing Arts Center in New York City, and the restoration of colonial Williamsburg.

**Andrew Carnegie**

Carnegie learned how to invest money from his boss, the superintendent of the Pennsylvania Railroad. At the age of 24, Carnegie took over the job of superintendent. In a famous essay, Carnegie spelled out his beliefs about money, the doctrine that came to be called the Gospel of Wealth. Carnegie said that riches brought the responsibility of helping others. Carnegie said, ". . . a man who dies rich dies disgraced."

Answer: They both had known poverty and were hard workers. Rockefeller was frugal. Carnegie was a quick learner.

### ACTIVITY OPTIONS

### INDIVIDUAL NEEDS

**STUDENTS ACQUIRING ENGLISH/ESL**

**Understanding Idiomatic Expressions** Point out the political cartoon on page 594, and read the caption aloud to students. Ask students what they think the expression *bowl over* means. Elicit or explain that the phrase means "to overwhelm or overpower." Look at the cartoon with students and discuss the tactics Jay Gould used to overpower anyone who might become competition for him.

Then point out the expression *wipes out* in the second paragraph on page 595. Elicit or explain that the phrase means "to eliminate." Ask students why John D. Rockefeller wanted to "wipe out" his competitors.

Finally, ask students to identify characteristics of Jay Gould, John D. Rockefeller, and other robber barons, based on what they read in this section. Then have them think of expressions that would describe the robber barons.

**INSTRUCT: OBJECTIVE** 

**The Gilded Age**

Key Questions

- What were some of the characteristics of the "Gilded Age"?
- Why is its name appropriate for the era?

**MORE ABOUT . . .**

**Horatio Alger**

Alger contributed several stories to magazines, but it was his serialization of *Ragged Dick; or, Street Life in New York with the Bootblacks* that made him an overnight success. He wrote over a hundred books in the next 30 years. In all of them, the protagonist is a poor, honest boy who becomes rich by cheerful hard work, perseverance, and a stroke of luck. Although Alger's books were formulaic, they sold over 20 million copies.

***HISTORY through ART***

**Interpreting the Painting and the Photograph** Draw students' attention to the lovely furniture, the figurines, and the fancy chandelier. Point out the formal dress worn by the Vanderbilts and note that the room is one of many in their mansion.

Have students compare the parlor to the tenement room. Tell them to count the people in this family. Explain that there might be a small kitchen that isn't in the picture, and that this family would have shared a bathroom with several other families.

**Possible Response: The rich had spacious homes with elaborate decor, fancy clothes, and luxury items. The poor had cramped, rundown housing, simple clothes, and no luxury items.**

by making the best and cheapest product. To do so, he sought to control all the processes related to the manufacture of steel. He bought the mines that supplied his iron ore, and the ships and railroads that carried that ore to his mills. Carnegie's company dominated the U.S. steel industry from 1889 to 1901, when he sold it.

Rockefeller and Carnegie were multimillionaires. They also were both **philanthropists,** people who give large sums of money to charities. Rockefeller donated money to the University of Chicago and Rockefeller University in New York. Carnegie also gave money to universities, and he built hundreds of public libraries. During his life, Rockefeller gave away more than $500 million. Carnegie gave away more than $350 million.

*Reading***History**

**B. Contrasting** How did the methods that Carnegie and Rockefeller used to eliminate competition differ?

B. Possible Response Rockefeller actually took over his competitors; Carnegie took over all the processes related to steel so that he could beat his competitors with a better, cheaper product.

## 3 The Gilded Age

The rags-to-riches stories of people such as Rockefeller and Carnegie inspired many Americans to believe that they too could grow rich. Stories like theirs also inspired writer Horatio Alger. He wrote popular stories about poor boys who worked hard and became quite successful.

Inspiring as these stories were, they hid an important truth. Most people who made millions of dollars had not been raised in poverty. Many belonged to the upper classes and had attended college. Most began their careers with the advantage of money or family connections.

For the rich, the late 1800s was a time of fabulous wealth. Writers Mark Twain and Charles Warner named the era the **Gilded Age.** To

***HISTORY through ART***

Artist Seymour Guy painted this portrait of the Vanderbilts, one of the wealthiest families in America. It shows them in their New York mansion. Notice the gilded picture frames and the expensive furnishings.

Photographer Jessie Tarbox Beals shot this photograph of a poor family in a tenement. A tenement is an apartment house that is usually rundown and very overcrowded. This family probably had only this tiny space.

**What do these two images tell you about the differences between the way rich and poor people lived during the Gilded Age?**

**ACTIVITY OPTIONS**

**SKILLBUILDER MINI-LESSON: USING AN ELECTRONIC CARD CATALOG**

**Explaining the Skill** The electronic card catalog is user-friendly. The user controls the search for a book by pressing keys marked "backup," "next," and "previous." The user can find the title, author, facts of publication, call number, and availability of any book in the catalog. The user may search the catalog by author, title, or subject.

**Applying the Skill** Explain to students how to use the electronic card catalog. Then direct them to the school or public library to look up books about the Gilded Age. After they return, ask these questions:

1. What three categories can you use to search in the card catalog? *(author, title, or subject)*
2. What information does the on-line catalog give you about a book? *(the title, author, facts of publication, other connected subjects, call number, and availability of book)*

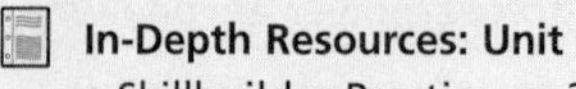

**In-Depth Resources: Unit 6**
- Skillbuilder Practice, p. 28

Vocabulary
**gold leaf:** gold that has been pounded into thin sheets

gild is to coat an object with gold leaf. Gilded decorations were popular during the era. But the name has a deeper meaning. Just as gold leaf can disguise an object of lesser value, so did the wealth of a few people mask society's problems, including corrupt politics and widespread poverty.

## 4 The South Remains Agricultural

One region that knew great poverty was the South. The Civil War had left the South in ruins. Industry did grow in some Southern areas, such as Birmingham, Alabama. Founded in 1871, Birmingham developed as an iron- and steel-producing town. In addition, cotton mills opened from southern Virginia to Alabama. Compared with the Northern economy, however, the Southern economy grew very slowly after the war.

Most of the South remained agricultural. As you have read, many Southern landowners rented their land to sharecroppers who paid a large portion of their crops as rent. Often sharecroppers had to buy their seed and tools on credit. The price of cotton, the South's main crop, was very low. Sharecroppers made little money from selling cotton and had difficulty paying what they owed. And because most sharecroppers had little education, merchants cheated them, increasing their debt.

*Reading*History
**C. Making Inferences** What is Fortune implying about the storekeeper?
C. Possible Response that the man deliberately cheated his father

*A VOICE FROM THE PAST*

My father once kept an account . . . of the things he "took up" at the store as well as the storekeeper. When the accounts were footed [added] up at the end of the year the thing became serious. The storekeeper had $150 more against my father than appeared on the latter's book. . . . It is by this means that [sharecroppers] are swindled and kept forever in debt.

**T. Thomas Fortune,** testimony to a Senate committee, 1883

At the same time that sharecroppers struggled to break free of debt, workers in the industrial North also faced injustices. In the next section, you will learn how labor unions tried to fight back.

### Section 3 Assessment

**1. Terms & Names**

**Identify:**
- robber baron
- corporation
- John D. Rockefeller
- Andrew Carnegie
- monopoly
- trust
- philanthropist
- Gilded Age

**2. Taking Notes**

Use a Venn diagram like the one shown to compare and contrast Rockefeller and Carnegie.

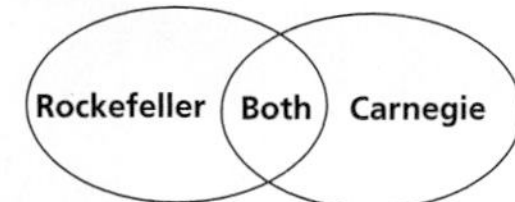


Whose business methods do you agree with more?

**3. Main Ideas**

a. Why did the number of corporations grow in the late 1800s?

b. Who is an example of a robber baron? Why?

c. Why was the South so much less industrial than the North?

**4. Critical Thinking**

**Forming and Supporting Opinions** Do you think that wealthy people have a duty to become philanthropists? Explain your opinion.

**THINK ABOUT**
- Carnegie and Rockefeller
- how most wealthy people gain their money
- the differences between the rich and the poor

**ACTIVITY OPTIONS**

**MATH**
**SPEECH**

In your local or school library, look up the business cycle. Create a **graph** of the cycle for the last century or prepare an **oral report** to Congress on the trends.





**INSTRUCT: OBJECTIVE 4**

**The South Remains Agricultural**

Key Questions
- Why did the economy of the South grow slowly?
- How did the sharecropping system affect workers?

**MORE ABOUT . . .**

**Birmingham**

Now the largest city in Alabama, Birmingham was founded in 1871 after the Civil War by a land company backed by railroad officials. The site of the city was a small village, selected for its location at the junction of both east-west and north-south railroads. It was named after Birmingham, England, one of Great Britain's great industrial centers. Birmingham lived up to its name, becoming the South's center of iron production and later its center of steel production.

## ASSESS & RETEACH

**Setting the Stage** Have students fill in the boxes with the causes, benefits, and problems of the rise of big business.

 **Formal Assessment**
- Section Quiz, p. 298

**RETEACHING ACTIVITY**

Have student pairs create brief quizzes (10–15 questions) about the material in this section. Then have students exchange quizzes and discuss the answers.

 **In-Depth Resources: Unit 6**
- Reteaching Activity, p. 38

### Section 3 Assessment

**1. Terms & Names**

**robber baron,** p. 594
**corporation,** p. 594
**John D. Rockefeller,** p. 595
**Andrew Carnegie,** p. 595
**monopoly,** p. 595
**trust,** p. 595
**philanthropist,** p. 596
**Gilded Age,** p. 596

**2. Taking Notes**

Rockefeller: oil industry; created trusts; Both: started simply; became multimillionaires and philanthropists; Carnegie: steel industry; tried to make best and cheapest product

Answers will vary as to whom students agree with more.

**3. Main Ideas**

**a.** They could raise money more easily than other businesses, they limited risks to investors, and they were not heavily regulated. **b.** Gould; because he bribed officials and sold fake stock; Rockefeller; because he created a trust **c.** The Civil War had left the South in ruins, and much of the land was given over to sharecropping.

**4. Critical Thinking**

Responses will vary. Students should think about where the wealthy get their money and how the economy creates a wealthy class.

**ACTIVITY OPTIONS**

 **Alternative Assessment**
- Rubrics for a graph, 2.3
- Rubrics for an oral report, 3.6

## GEOGRAPHY *in* HISTORY

**OBJECTIVE**
Students will analyze and interpret information from a map to understand the effects of geographic features and resources on the development of the Midwest.

 **BLOCK SCHEDULING**

## MORE ABOUT . . .

**The Canned Food Industry**
In 1817, the first canning factories appeared in America. Union soldiers in the Civil War carried canned meat, oysters, and vegetables. After the war, cans were machine-cut. Giant canning factories sprouted up, especially in Chicago, which used assembly lines to mass-produce its food products. The canning industry inspired other inventions, such as a mechanical pea-gathering and shelling machine and a machine to fillet fish.

## INSTRUCT

Key Questions
- Why was the Erie Canal important to the growth of the Midwest?
- What caused the boom in industry and manufacturing in the Midwest?
- How did the Midwest's natural resources affect its development?

**MAP SKILLS QUESTIONS**

In the late 1800s, what form of transportation would you have used to ship factory parts from Buffalo to Chicago?

Where are most of the sawmill centers located? Why do you think they were located there?

Which areas in the Midwest had meatpacking?

In what ways was Chicago connected to other parts of the nation?

## GEOGRAPHY *in* HISTORY

**REGION AND HUMAN-ENVIRONMENT INTERACTION**

# Industry in the Midwest

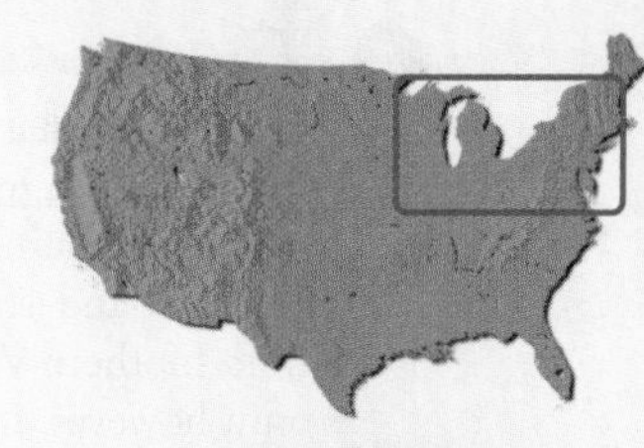

The Midwest is the region around the Great Lakes and the Upper Mississippi Valley. The region saw explosive growth during the 1800s. The first wave came after 1825, when the Erie Canal linked the East with the Great Lakes region. The second wave, caused by investments in products related to the Civil War (1861–1865), saw a boom in mining, farming, forestry, and meat-packing. By 1890, 29 percent of the country's manufacturing employment was in the Midwest, and the next big wave of growth was just beginning. New industries included steel and steel products, such as train rails and skyscraper beams.

Transportation and resources spurred the region's growth. Coal, oil, iron ore, limestone, and lumber were abundant, and the land was fertile. Trains, rivers, and lakes connected the Midwest to markets in the East and South and brought in raw materials from the West. The map on page 599 shows the resources of the lower Great Lakes and how transportation by rail and water joined regions.

The industries of the Midwest used raw materials that came both from their own region and from other regions of the country. For example, the cattle in this photograph of the Chicago stockyards came by rail from the ranches of the West. In contrast, the logs being floated down the river came from the pine forests of Michigan and Wisconsin.

### ARTIFACT FILE

**A Quick Dinner** Midwestern meat-packing companies advertised canned meats as a way to save time feeding a hungry family.

**Affordable Housing** People began to build with wooden siding over a frame of wooden two-by-fours. These homes were cheap and quick to construct.



## MUSEUM CONNECTIONS

The museum of the Chicago Historical Society is dedicated to the multicultural heritage of Chicago and of Illinois. In addition to its extensive collection of research materials about Chicago history, the Society also houses a large collection of material relating to Abraham Lincoln and an outstanding costume collection, as well as paintings, sculpture, and photographs. The Society estimates its collection at about 20 million items.

Iron ore from the Lake Superior region and coal from southern Illinois were used to manufacture steel.

## On-Line Field Trip

**The Chicago Historical Society** in Chicago, Illinois, contains photographs, documents, and artifacts such as this Western Electric typewriter, made in 1900. Typewriters enabled office workers to produce neat, clean documents quickly.

Visit www.mcdougallittell.com for more information.

### CONNECT TO GEOGRAPHY

1. **Region** What advantages did the Midwest have that helped it become highly industrialized?
2. **Human-Environment Interaction** How did the development of railroads add to the region's advantages?

See Geography Handbook, pages 4–5.

### CONNECT TO HISTORY

3. **Analyzing Causes** Chicago was a big meatpacking center. Why do you think that industry chose to locate there?





### CRITICAL THINKING ACTIVITY

**Recognizing Important Details** Ask students to copy the web below and add resources and details about each category from the feature.

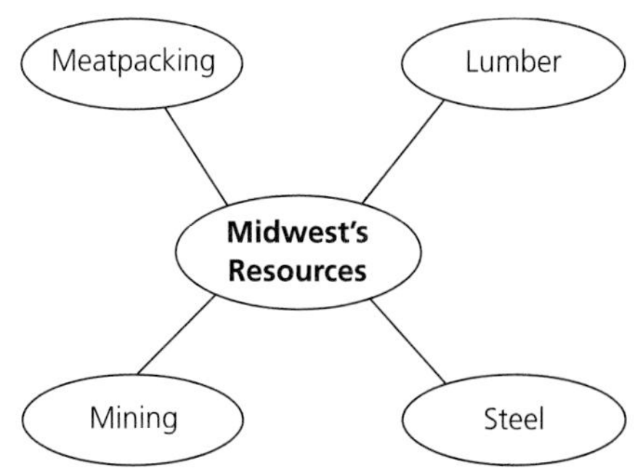


**Class Time** 20 minutes

### MORE ABOUT . . .

**Chicago**

On October 8, 1871, a fire broke out in the barn behind the O'Leary house in Chicago. One of the family's cows is usually blamed for starting the fire by kicking over a lantern. The fire spread quickly, destroying about 3 square miles of the city and about $200 million in property. After the fire, boosters claimed that Chicago would come back stronger than ever. Investors, recognizing the city's potential for growth, helped the city rebuild. By the end of the 19th century, Chicago had become the nation's second-largest city.

### CONNECT TO GEOGRAPHY

1. **Region** The Midwest had abundant natural resources, such as timber, minerals, and oil, as well as rivers and lakes for shipping. The land was fertile for agricultural purposes.
2. **Human-Environment Interaction** The railroads made it easier to ship goods to places where there were no waterways, natural or man-made. Railroads were also able to connect to waterways, so shippers often used both methods.

### CONNECT TO HISTORY

3. **Analyzing Causes** Many railroad lines could connect easily with Chicago, which would have made it much easier to bring cattle to market. It also was linked to shipping on the Great Lakes and to the Mississippi River by a canal.

## SECTION OBJECTIVES

1. To describe working conditions in the late 1800s
2. To trace the beginnings of the labor movement
3. To evaluate union setbacks and significant strikes
4. To describe the founding of the American Federation of Labor

**CRITICAL THINKING**

Analyzing Causes, pp. 601, 602
Recognizing Effects, p. 602
Identifying Problems, p. 603
Drawing Conclusions, p. 603

 **Why It Matters Now**
- The Changing Economy, pp. 39–40

## FOCUS & MOTIVATE

### 5-MINUTE WARM-UP

**Making Inferences** These questions focus on working conditions in the late 1800s.

1. Look at the picture on page 601. What can you infer from the photograph about working conditions in the late 1800s?
2. Why do you think families sent their children to work?

 **Warm-Up Transparency WT20**

## INSTRUCT

### INSTRUCT: OBJECTIVE 

**Workers Face Hardships**
Key Questions
- Why were workers discontented with working conditions in the late 1800s?
- How did workers try to improve working conditions?

 **In-Depth Resources: Unit 6**
- Guided Reading, p. 26

 **Reading Study Guide** (Spanish and English), pp. 201–202

# 4 Workers Organize

**TERMS & NAMES**
sweatshop
Knights of Labor
socialism
Haymarket affair
Pullman Strike
Eugene V. Debs
Samuel Gompers
American Federation of Labor (AFL)

| MAIN IDEA | WHY IT MATTERS NOW |
|---|---|
| To increase their ability to bargain with management, workers formed labor unions. | Many of the modern benefits that workers take for granted were won by early unions. |

### ONE AMERICAN'S STORY

**In 1867, Mary Harris Jones lost her husband and four children during a yellow fever epidemic in Memphis. For the rest of her life, she dressed in black as a sign of mourning. Moving from Memphis to Chicago, Jones started a dressmaking business. But the great Chicago fire of 1871 destroyed everything she owned. Instead of giving up in despair, Jones found a cause to fight for.**

*A VOICE FROM THE PAST*

From the time of the Chicago fire I became more and more engrossed [interested] in the labor struggle and I decided to take an active part in the efforts of the working people to better the conditions under which they worked and lived.

**Mary Harris Jones,** *Autobiography of Mother Jones*

**Jones became an effective labor leader who organized meetings, gave speeches, and helped strikers. Workers loved her so much that they called her Mother Jones. In this section, you will learn why workers went on strike in the late 1800s and the results of those strikes.**

Mother Jones won the love of working people by fighting for their rights.

## 1 Workers Face Hardships

Business owners of the late 1800s wanted to keep their profits high, so they ran their factories as cheaply as possible. Some cut costs by requiring workers to buy their own tools or to bring coal to heat the factories. Others refused to buy safety equipment. For example, railroads would not buy air brakes or automatic train-car couplers. Because of this, 30,000 railroad workers were injured and 2,000 killed every year.

If a factory became too crowded, the owner rarely built a larger one. Instead, the owner sent part of the work to be done by smaller businesses that critics called sweatshops. **Sweatshops** were places where workers labored long hours under poor conditions for low wages. Often both children and adults worked there.

Factory and sweatshop workers did the same jobs, such as sewing collars or making buttonholes, all day long. They grew bored and did not



### RECOMMENDED RESOURCES

 **In-Depth Resources: Unit 6**
- Guided Reading, p. 26
- Building Vocabulary, p. 27
- Primary Source, p. 32
- Reteaching Activity, p. 39

**Reading Study Guide** (Spanish and English), pp. 201–202

**Economics in History**
- The Union Struggle, p. 20

**Why It Matters Now**
- The Changing Economy, pp. 39–40

 **Formal Assessment**
- Section Quiz, p. 299

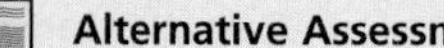 **Alternative Assessment**
- Rubrics, 4.1
- Rubrics, 1.1

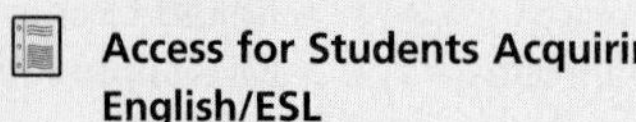 **Access for Students Acquiring English/ESL**
- Guided Reading, p. 136

**Technology Resources**

 **Humanities Transparency HT40**
- Homestead Strike

 **Electronic Teacher Tools with Test Maker**

 **ClassZone**
www.mcdougallittell.com

experience the satisfaction that came from making an entire product themselves. Further, both factory and sweatshop owners kept wages low. In the 1880s, the average weekly wage was less than $10. This barely paid a family's expenses. If a worker missed work due to illness or had any unexpected bills, the family went into debt. Workers began to feel that only other working people could understand their troubles.

Child labor was common in the late 1800s, and as this boy's bare feet demonstrate, safety practices were rare.

*A VOICE FROM THE PAST*

They know what it is to bring up a family on ninety cents a day, to live on beans and corn meal week in and week out, to run in debt at the stores until you cannot get trusted [credit] any longer, to see the wife breaking down . . . , and the children growing sharp and fierce like wolves day after day because they don't get enough to eat.

**A railroad worker,** quoted in the *Philadelphia Inquirer,* July 23, 1877

**Vocabulary**
**negotiate:** to discuss something in order to reach an agreement

So discontented workers joined together to try to improve their lives. They formed labor unions—groups of workers that negotiated with business owners to obtain better wages and working conditions.

## 2 Early Unions

As you read in Chapter 14, the first labor unions began in the mid-1800s but were unable to win many improvements for workers. After the Civil War, some unions started to form national organizations. One of these was the **Knights of Labor.** This was a loose federation of workers from all different trades. Unlike many labor organizations, the Knights allowed women and, after 1878, African-American workers to join their union. They inspired many people to support their cause.

Then, beginning in 1873, the United States fell into a serious economic depression. Over the next four years, millions of workers took pay cuts, and about one-fifth lost their jobs. In July 1877, the Baltimore and Ohio (B & O) Railroad declared a wage cut of 10 percent. The day the pay cut was to go into effect, B & O workers in Martinsburg, West Virginia, refused to run the trains. No labor union had called the strike. The workers themselves had stopped working on their own.

> *"[Working people] know what it is to bring up a family on ninety cents a day."*
> A railroad worker, 1877

A. Possible Response because the strike was damaging the economy

**ReadingHistory**
**A. Analyzing Causes** Why do you think the president acted to stop the strike?

This work stoppage was the Railroad Strike of 1877. As the news spread, workers in many cities and in other industries joined in. This threw the country into turmoil. In several cities, state militias battled angry mobs. President Rutherford B. Hayes called out federal troops. Before the two-week strike ended, dozens of people were killed.

The strike did not prevent the railroad pay cut, but it showed how angry American workers had become. In 1884–1885, railroaders again went out on strike. This time they went on strike against the Union



### MORE ABOUT . . .

**Women and Children at Work**

The number of women and children in the work force doubled between 1870 and 1890 to 4 million women workers and 1.5 million child workers (ages 10–15). The death rate for female workers was twice that of other workers. Women were paid less than men, were the first to be laid off, and often endured abuse from male coworkers and bosses. Children often earned only pennies, but at best they received about half the pay of a male adult worker.

### INSTRUCT: OBJECTIVE 2

**Early Unions**

Key Questions

- How did the Knights of Labor differ from other unions?
- What were the effects of the depression of 1873 for workers?
- What events helped strengthen the Knights of Labor from the late 1870s to the mid-1880s?

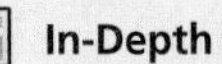

**In-Depth Resources: Unit 6**
- Primary Source: An Interview with Pauline Cuoio Pepe, p. 32

### MORE ABOUT . . .

**The Knights of Labor**

The Noble Order of the Knights of Labor began as a secret society of tailors. It was vertically organized, including all workers in a given industry, regardless of skill or trade. Although it accepted African Americans, the organization supported the Chinese Exclusion Act of 1882 because its members feared competition from Chinese workers. When Terence Powderly took office in 1879, the Knights flourished, growing to 700,000. Powderly worked for better working conditions—an eight-hour day, the abolition of child labor, equal pay for equal work, and the graduated income tax.

### ACTIVITY OPTIONS

**INDIVIDUAL NEEDS: GIFTED AND TALENTED**

**WORKING CONDITIONS**

**Class Time** Two class periods

**Task** Finding primary source material about working conditions in the late 1800s

**Purpose** To practice research skills and to understand how difficult the lives of working-class people were

**Supplies Needed**
- Reference materials
- Internet access

**Activity** Have students research working conditions in the late 1800s using books and Internet sites. Direct students to find at least three quotations from workers in different industries describing some aspect of their workdays. Students should copy the quotes, not to exceed one or two paragraphs, and document their sources with the title, author, and date of the book or the full Web site address and its supporting organization. Allow students to read their quotations to the class.

### INSTRUCT: OBJECTIVE 3

**Union Setbacks/**
**The Homestead and Pullman Strikes**

Key Questions
- Why did business and government leaders fear unions?
- What were the causes and effects of the Haymarket affair?
- Why did the Homestead and Pullman Strikes fail?

 **Economics in History**
- The Union Struggle, p. 20

 **Humanities Transparency HT40**
- Homestead Strike

#### CRITICAL THINKING ACTIVITY

**Evaluating** Discuss with students the dilemma faced by workers who wanted better pay and working conditions. If they went out on strike, they might lose their jobs. Most workers at this time had little money saved. A long strike could mean ruin and hunger for their families. Use the problem/solution outline to help students understand the conflict workers faced between their desire and need for better pay and conditions and their fear of the consequences of striking.

**Class Time** 25 minutes

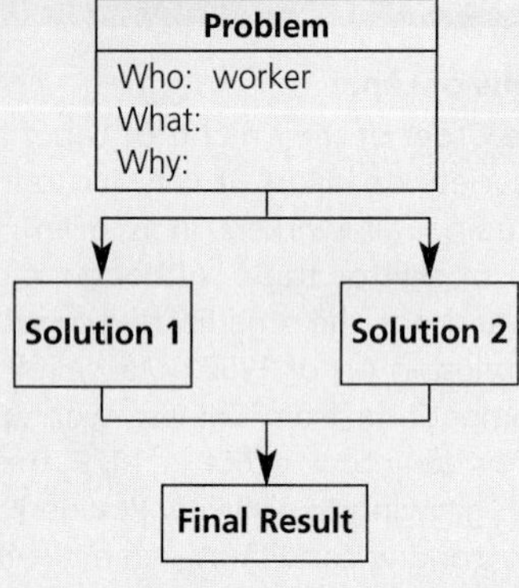


Pacific and two other railroads. The strikers, who were members of the Knights of Labor, gained nationwide attention when they won their strike. Hundreds of thousands of new workers joined the union.

## 3 Union Setbacks

The growth of labor unions scared many business leaders. They blamed the labor movement on socialists and anarchists. Socialists believe in **socialism.** In that economic system, all members of a society are equal owners of all businesses—they share the work and the profits. Anarchists are far more extreme. They want to abolish all governments.

Business and government leaders feared that unions might spread such ideas, so they tried to break union power. In Chicago in 1886, the McCormick Harvester Company locked out striking union members and hired strikebreakers to replace them. On May 3, union members, strikebreakers, and police clashed. One union member was killed.

The next day, union leaders called a protest meeting at Haymarket Square. Held on a rainy evening, the rally was small. As police moved in to end the meeting, an unknown person threw a bomb. It killed 7 police and wounded about 60. The police then opened fire on the crowd, killing several people and wounding about a hundred. This conflict was called the **Haymarket affair.**

*Reading* **History**
**B. Recognizing Effects** Did the action of the bomber make it seem more or less likely that anarchists were behind union activity? Explain.
**B. Possible Response** More—throwing a bomb at policemen fit with the anarchist theory of abolishing government.

Afterward, the Chicago police arrested hundreds of union leaders, socialists, and anarchists. Opposition to unions increased. The membership in the Knights of Labor dropped rapidly—even though that wasn't the union that had called the meeting at Haymarket Square.

## The Homestead and Pullman Strikes

Labor conflicts grew more bitter. In 1892, Andrew Carnegie reduced wages at his steel mills in Homestead, Pennsylvania, but the union refused to accept the cut. The company responded by locking out union workers from the mills and announcing that it would hire nonunion labor. The company also hired 300 armed guards. In response, the locked-out workers gathered weapons. The guards arrived on July 6, and a battle broke out that left ten people dead. The Pennsylvania state militia began to escort the nonunion workers to the mills. After four months, the strike collapsed, breaking the union.

**One night during the Pullman Strike, some 600 freight cars were burned.**

Workers lost another dispute in 1894. In that depression year, many railroad companies went bankrupt. To stay in business, the Pullman Palace Car Company, which made railroad cars,

*Reading* **History**
**C. Analyzing Causes** Why was it so difficult for early unions to win against big business?
**C. Possible Response** because big business had so much money and could hire nonunion laborers and armed guards



**ACTIVITY OPTIONS**

**MULTIPLE LEARNING STYLES: LINGUISTIC** — **BLOCK SCHEDULING**

#### FORMING A UNION

**Class Time** One to two class periods

**Task** Researching a union in the student's community

**Purpose** To give students a greater understanding of the role unions play

**Supplies Needed**
- Reference materials about unions
- Internet access

**Activity** Have groups of students research a union or unions found in their community. Each group should create a document containing the purpose and goals of the selected union, the type of work the union members do, and the role of the union in their community.

cut workers' pay 25 percent. But Pullman did not lower the rent it charged workers to live in company housing. After their rent was deducted from the lower pay, many Pullman workers took home almost nothing.

The Pullman workers began the **Pullman Strike,** a strike which spread throughout the rail industry in 1894. When the Pullman Company refused to negotiate, American Railway Union president **Eugene V. Debs** called on all U.S. railroad workers to refuse to handle Pullman cars. Rail traffic in much of the country came to a halt. President Grover Cleveland called out federal troops, which ended the strike. Debs was put in jail.

**Now and then**

**MODERN BENEFITS WON BY UNIONS**

Many people today begin work at 9:00 A.M. and end at 5:00 P.M. Contrast this 8-hour workday with the 10- to 12-hour day of most 19th-century workers. The 8-hour day was one benefit won by labor unions. Others include workers' compensation (insurance that pays for injuries received on the job), pensions, laws against child labor, two-day weekends, sick pay, and vacation pay. By winning these benefits, unions improved the work lives of many Americans.

## 4 Gompers Founds the AFL

Not all companies treated workers as harshly as Carnegie and Pullman did. For instance, in the 1880s, the soap company Procter & Gamble began to give its employees an extra half day off a week. It also began a profit-sharing plan, in which a company gives part of its profits to workers.

D. Possible Response long hours and low pay

*Reading*History

**D. Identifying Problems** What problems did the AFL try to solve?

However, workers at most companies received low wages and few benefits. So in spite of the opposition to unions, the labor movement did not die. In 1886, labor leader **Samuel Gompers** helped found a new national organization of unions called the **American Federation of Labor (AFL).** Gompers served as AFL president for 37 years.

The AFL focused on improving working conditions. By using strikes, boycotts, and negotiation, the AFL won shorter working hours and better pay for workers. By 1904, it had about 1.7 million members.

In the next few decades, labor unions helped change the way all Americans worked. At the same time, city growth and immigration transformed America. You will read about that in Chapter 21.

### Section 4 Assessment

**1. Terms & Names**

**Identify:**
- sweatshop
- Knights of Labor
- socialism
- Haymarket affair
- Pullman Strike
- Eugene V. Debs
- Samuel Gompers
- American Federation of Labor (AFL)

**2. Taking Notes**

Review this section and find five key events to place on a time line like the one below.

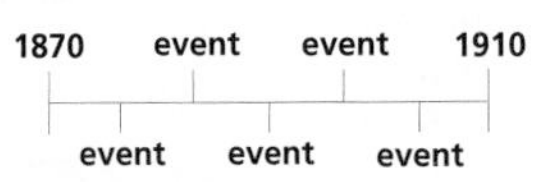


**3. Main Ideas**

a. What hardships did workers face in the late 1800s?

b. What happened to unions after the protest at Haymarket Square?

c. How did Carnegie's company break the union at the Homestead mills?

**4. Critical Thinking**

**Drawing Conclusions** In your opinion, was the government more supportive of unions or business in the late 1800s? Explain.

THINK ABOUT
- the Railroad Strike of 1877
- the Homestead Strike
- the Pullman Strike

**ACTIVITY OPTIONS**

**LANGUAGE ARTS**
**ART**

Decide whether unions should be encouraged. Write an **editorial** or create a **public message poster** expressing your opinion.



### Now and then

**Modern Benefits Won by Unions**

During the New Deal and World War II, union membership grew steadily. By 1955, fully one-third of the nonfarm workers in the United States belonged to a union. During the 1960s and 1970s, however, union membership began to decline. By the mid-1970s, only one-fourth of American workers were union members; and by the mid-1980s, that share was down to one-sixth. One reason for the decline was that fewer people worked in manufacturing. Some had moved from blue-collar wage work to white-collar jobs at higher salaries. But others had lost the security of full-time employment for part-time jobs or temporary work.

### INSTRUCT: OBJECTIVE 4

**Gompers Founds the AFL**

Key Questions
- How did the AFL differ from other unions?
- How did the AFL improve working conditions for its members?

### ASSESS & RETEACH

**Setting the Stage** Have students fill in the appropriate boxes about organized labor in the Problems of Growth section on the graphic organizer.

**Critical Thinking Transparency CT58**

**Formal Assessment**
- Section Quiz, p. 299

**RETEACHING ACTIVITY**

Have students pair up. Then have one student from each pair pick one of the main topics in this section and summarize it for his or her partner. The partner will do the same for another section, and so on until each section has been summarized. Tell the listening partner to make any additions or corrections to the summary.

**In-Depth Resources: Unit 6**
- Reteaching Activity, p. 39

### Section 4 Assessment

**1. Terms & Names**

**sweatshop,** p. 600
**Knights of Labor,** p. 601
**socialism,** p. 602
**Haymarket affair,** p. 602
**Pullman Strike,** p. 603
**Eugene V. Debs,** p. 603
**Samuel Gompers,** p. 603
**American Federation of Labor (AFL),** p. 603

**2. Taking Notes**

Event 1: 1877, Railroad Strike of 1877; Event 2: 1886, Haymarket Square protest and founding of AFL; Event 3: 1892, Homestead Strike; Event 4: 1894, Pullman Strike; Event 5: 1904, AFL membership at 1.7 million

**3. Main Ideas**

**a.** low wages; long hours; unsafe conditions **b.** Unions were blamed for the violence, many labor leaders were arrested, and union membership declined. **c.** It locked out union members, hired strikebreakers and armed guards, and used the militia to escort nonunion workers to work.

**4. Critical Thinking**

Opinions will vary, but most students will say that the government was more supportive of business.

**ACTIVITY OPTIONS**

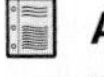
**Alternative Assessment**
- Rubrics for an editorial, 4.1
- Rubrics for a poster, 1.1

## TERMS & NAMES

1. **patent,** p. 586
2. **business cycle,** p. 586
3. **transcontinental railroad,** p. 590
4. **standard time,** p. 592
5. **corporation,** p. 594
6. **John D. Rockefeller,** p. 595
7. **Andrew Carnegie,** p. 595
8. **Haymarket affair,** p. 602
9. **Pullman Strike,** p. 603
10. **American Federation of Labor (AFL),** p. 603

## REVIEW QUESTIONS

**Possible Responses**

1. They take out patents—government documents giving them the exclusive right to make or sell their inventions.
2. Edison invented the first practical light bulb and a safe way to deliver electricity to buildings. Bell invented the telephone.
3. the western mountain ranges
4. The Central Pacific president and the Union Pacific vice-president tried to hammer in a ceremonial spike. A telegraph operator signaled the country that the railroads were joined.
5. a business that wipes out its competitors and controls an industry
6. A trust is a legal body created to hold stock in many industries. People thought they were unfair because they were monopolies that kept prices high.
7. Some people grew fabulously wealthy, and gilded decorations were popular among the rich. However, gilded also implies that the top layer of wealth hid something less valuable, such as society's problems.
8. socialism and anarchism
9. It began when the Pullman Company lowered wages but not rents, so workers went on strike. It ended when President Cleveland called out federal troops.
10. Debs led the American Railway Union, and Gompers led the AFL.

**VISUAL SUMMARY**

## An Industrial Society

**Long-Term Causes**
- plentiful natural resources
- building of canals and railroads in early 1800s

**Immediate Causes**
- continued building of railroads in late 1800s
- growing population and high immigration
- new inventions and industrial processes
- investment capital and development of corporations

**GROWTH of INDUSTRY**

STRIKE

**Immediate Effects**
- increased amount of manufactured goods
- growth of large corporations, monopolies, and trusts
- poor conditions for workers in factories and sweatshops
- labor unions and strikes

**Long-Term Effects**
- economies of East and West linked together
- labor movement wins permanent changes, such as reduced working hours

604

# Chapter 20 ASSESSMENT

## TERMS & NAMES

Briefly explain the importance of each of the following.

1. patent
2. business cycle
3. transcontinental railroad
4. standard time
5. corporation
6. John D. Rockefeller
7. Andrew Carnegie
8. Haymarket affair
9. Pullman Strike
10. American Federation of Labor (AFL)

## REVIEW QUESTIONS

**The Growth of Industry (pages 585–589)**

1. How do inventors protect their rights to what they invent?
2. What did Thomas Edison and Alexander Graham Bell invent?

**Railroads Transform the Nation (pages 590–593)**

3. What geographic feature made building the Central Pacific difficult?
4. What took place when workers connected the Central Pacific and the Union Pacific?

**The Rise of Big Business (pages 594–599)**

5. What is a monopoly?
6. What are trusts, and why did some people think they were bad for the country?
7. Why did writers Mark Twain and Charles Warner name the late 1800s the Gilded Age?

**Workers Organize (pages 600–603)**

8. What ideas did business leaders fear that unions would spread?
9. How did the Pullman Strike begin and end?
10. Which unions were led by Eugene V. Debs and Samuel Gompers?

## CRITICAL THINKING

**1. USING YOUR NOTES**

Using your completed chart, answer the questions below.

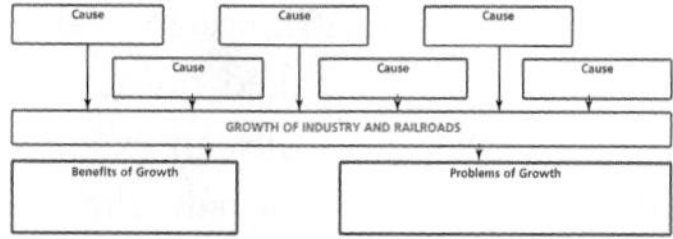


a. How did the growth of railroads act as a cause of industrial growth?

b. Who do you think benefited most from the growth of industry? Explain.

**2. THEME: ECONOMICS IN HISTORY**

Who is someone from this chapter that might view the United States as a land of economic opportunity? Explain your answer.

**3. ANALYZING LEADERSHIP**

What characteristics of a good leader did Mother Jones possess?

**4. APPLYING CITIZENSHIP SKILLS**

Were John D. Rockefeller and Andrew Carnegie good citizens? Support your answer with details from this chapter.

**5. COMPARING**

How were the problems of sharecroppers, described on page 597, similar to those of Pullman workers, described on pages 602–603?

**6. DRAWING CONCLUSIONS**

Why do you think unions were more successful at attracting members in the late 1800s than in the early 1800s?

**Interact *with* History**

Now that you have read the chapter, would you change your mind about joining the strike? Explain.

## CRITICAL THINKING

**Possible Responses**

1. **USING YOUR NOTES** **a.** Railroad building was part of improved transportation that led to industrial growth. **b.** business leaders, because they grew very wealthy
2. **THEME: ECONOMICS IN HISTORY** Carnegie or Rockefeller, because they went from poverty to riches; the immigrants who came to the United States and found jobs
3. **ANALYZING LEADERSHIP** She was organized, bold, helpful, and caring.
4. **APPLYING CITIZENSHIP SKILLS** yes, because they gave away millions to charity; no, because they used ruthless means to acquire their wealth
5. **COMPARING** Both were at the mercy of a system that kept their earnings low and their expenses high.
6. **DRAWING CONCLUSIONS** More people worked in industry, and conditions grew even worse.

**Interact *with* History** Student answers will vary, but they should explain what details from the chapter influenced them.

## HISTORY SKILLS

### 1. INTERPRETING GRAPHS

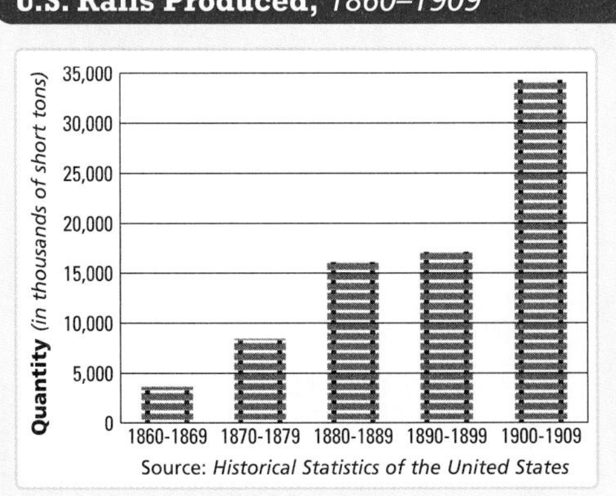


**Basic Graph Elements**

a. What period of time does this graph cover?

b. What was the general trend in rail production?

**Interpreting the Graph**

c. Which decade saw the biggest change in rail production?

d. What does this graph indicate about what was happening in the railroad industry?

### 2. INTERPRETING PRIMARY SOURCES

This memoir was written by James Davis, who was secretary of labor during the 1920s. In 1886, when he was 12, he worked in a mill making wrought iron.

> In this mill there is a constant din by day and night. Patches of white heat glare from the opened furnace doors like the teeth of some great, dark dingy devil grinning across the smoky vapors of the Pit. Half-naked, soot-smeared fellows fight the furnace hearths with hooks, rabbles, and paddles. Their scowling faces are lit with fire like sailors manning their guns in a night fight when a blazing fire ship is bearing down upon them. The sweat runs down their backs and arms and glistens in the changing lights. Brilliant blues and rays of green and bronze come from the coruscating [sparkling] metal, molten yet crystallizing into white-hot frost within the furnace puddle.
>
> **James Davis,** *The Iron Puddler*

a. What were working conditions like in the mill where Davis worked?

b. Do you think Davis liked his work? Use details from the passage to support your answer.

## ALTERNATIVE ASSESSMENT

### 1. INTERDISCIPLINARY ACTIVITY: Science

**Diagramming a Process** Do research to find out how iron is converted to steel in the Bessemer process. Make a diagram that shows the process. Use terms from science to describe what happens to different elements during the heating process. Share your diagram with the class.

### 2. COOPERATIVE LEARNING ACTIVITY

**Performing a Monologue** Working in a small group, research the life of a business or labor leader from this chapter. Write and perform a monologue in which the leader discusses his or her life. After the presentation, ask the class to discuss what they learned from your monologue. Assign group members one or more of the following tasks:

a. researching the person's life

b. writing the monologue

c. editing the monologue

d. finding costumes and props

e. creating sound effects (if necessary)

f. directing the rehearsals

g. acting out the monologue

### 3. TECHNOLOGY ACTIVITY

**Creating a Database** Using the Internet, reference materials such as *Historical Statistics of the United States,* or other printed material, compile statistics that could be used to create a database of information about industrialization in the United States. Consider researching the following topics:

- production figures for various goods
- number of strikes or work stoppages
- income of various industries
- value of the plants and machinery owned by various industries

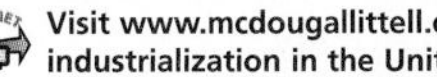

Visit www.mcdougallittell.com to learn more about industrialization in the United States.


### 4. HISTORY PORTFOLIO

**Option 1** Review your section and chapter assessment activities. Select one that you think is your best work. Then use comments made by your teacher or classmates to improve your work and add it to your portfolio.

**Option 2** Review the questions that you wrote for What Do You Want to Know? on page 584. Then write a short report in which you explain the answers to your questions. If any questions were not answered, do research to answer them. Add your report to your portfolio.



## ALTERNATIVE ASSESSMENT

1. INTERDISCIPLINARY ACTIVITY: Science
   Diagrams should
   - present the concept of the Bessemer process in a manner clear to the viewers.
   - use correct scientific terms to describe the process.
   - exhibit creativity.
   - demonstrate grade-level artistic skill.

2. COOPERATIVE LEARNING ACTIVITY
   Monologues should
   - present information that reflects the student's understanding of basic concepts relevant to the experiences of the person selected.
   - accurately reflect the thoughts and experiences of the subject's life.
   - show evidence of involvement of each person in the group.

3.  TECHNOLOGY ACTIVITY
   Databases should
   - present a variety of information from several sources.
   - present information accurately.
   - clearly identify sources of information.

4. HISTORY PORTFOLIO

    **Option 1 Revised section or chapter assessment activities should**
   - address teacher and peer responses to the selected work.
   - solve problems present in the first versions of the work.

   **Option 2 Short reports should**
   - answer questions about how America changed to an industrial society.
   - use evidence to develop and support ideas.
   - cite sources of information.
   - use standard grammar, spelling, sentence structure, and punctuation.

 **Critical Thinking Transparency CT60**
- Visual Summary

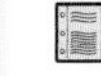 **Formal Assessment**
- Chapter Test, Forms A and B, pp. 300–307

## HISTORY SKILLS

**Possible Responses**

1. INTERPRETING GRAPHS
   **Basic Map Elements**
   **a.** 1860 to 1909
   **b.** It increased.
   **Interpreting the Graph**
   **c.** 1900 to 1909
   **d.** It must have been booming because the companies kept needing more rails.

2. INTERPRETING PRIMARY SOURCES
   **a.** loud, hot, dirty, lit by fire
   **b.** Yes—he uses lively, interesting descriptions and comparisons, such as a night battle at sea. No—he makes the reader feel how hot and dirty it was.

CHAPTER 21 PLANNING GUIDE

# Changes in American Life, 1880–1914

| | CHAPTER OVERVIEW | COPYMASTERS | TECHNOLOGY |
|---|---|---|---|
| **CHAPTER RESOURCES** | This chapter discusses urbanization, changing trends in immigration, racial segregation in the South, and violence against African Americans and other ethnic minorities. It also describes the formation of mass culture through education, entertainment, and consumerism. | **In-Depth Resources: Unit 6**<br>• Tracing Themes: Diversity and Unity, p. 42<br>• Building Vocabulary, p. 47<br>• History Workshop Resources, p. 61<br>**Interdisciplinary Projects,** pp. 121–126 | **Primary Source Explorer**<br>**Electronic Teacher Tools**<br>**Power Presentations CD-ROM**<br>**Chapter Summaries on CD** (English and Spanish)<br>**America's Music CD** |
| | **KEY IDEAS** | | |
| **SECTION 1 Cities Grow and Change pp. 609–613** | • Skyscrapers, elevators, and streetcars encourage urbanization.<br>• Reformers try to solve the problems of urban poverty and slums.<br>• Political machines are often corrupt but also help city dwellers. | **In-Depth Resources: Unit 6**<br>• Setting the Stage, p. 41<br>• Guided Reading, p. 43<br>• Primary Source, p. 51<br>• Reteaching Activity, p. 56<br>**America's History Makers**<br>• Jane Addams, pp. 83–84<br>**Citizenship Today,** pp. 13–14<br>**Outline Map Activities,** pp. 41–42 | **Warm-Up Transparency WT21**<br>**Geography Transparency GT21**<br>• Growth of Cities, 1860–1900<br>**Critical Thinking Transparency CT61**<br>• Setting the Stage<br>**Critical Thinking Transparency CT62**<br>• Cause and Effect: Urban Growth<br>**ClassZone:** www.mcdougallittell.com |
| **SECTION 2 The New Immigrants pp. 614–619** | • New immigrants arrive from southern and eastern Europe and from Asia.<br>• Many immigrants work in sweatshops and live in ethnic neighborhoods.<br>• Nativist feelings lead to restrictions on immigration. | **In-Depth Resources: Unit 6**<br>• Setting the Stage, p. 41<br>• Guided Reading, p. 44<br>• Skillbuilder Practice: Taking Notes, p. 48<br>• Geography Application: Immigration, 1907, pp. 49–50<br>• Literature Selections, pp. 53–55<br>• Reteaching Activity, p. 57 | **Warm-Up Transparency WT21**<br>**Critical Thinking Transparency CT61**<br>• Setting the Stage<br>**ClassZone:** www.mcdougallittell.com |
| **SECTION 3 Segregation and Discrimination pp. 620–625** | • Jim Crow laws enforce segregation in the South.<br>• African Americans organize to combat racism, segregation, and lynchings.<br>• Chinese and Mexican immigrants face racism in the West. | **In-Depth Resources: Unit 6**<br>• Setting the Stage, p. 41<br>• Guided Reading, p. 45<br>• Primary Source, p. 52<br>• Reteaching Activity, p. 58<br>**America's History Makers,** pp. 85–86<br>**Citizenship Today,** pp. 91–92<br>**American History Plays**<br>• *Daniel Hale Williams, Pioneer Surgeon* by Mary Satchell | **Warm-Up Transparency WT21**<br>**Critical Thinking Transparency CT61**<br>• Setting the Stage<br>**Primary Source Explorer**<br>• from *Crusade for Justice*<br>• *Like Country Pretty Much*<br>**ClassZone:** www.mcdougallittell.com |
| **SECTION 4 Society and Mass Culture pp. 626–629** | • Public education expands, and newspapers increase readership.<br>• Advertising, department stores, and catalogs promote new products.<br>• World's Fairs, spectator sports, and entertainment shape mass culture. | **In-Depth Resources: Unit 6**<br>• Setting the Stage, p. 41<br>• Guided Reading, p. 46<br>• Reteaching Activity, p. 59<br>**Economics in History**<br>• The Rise of Department Stores, p. 21<br>**Why It Matters Now**<br>• The Modern Mass Culture, pp. 41–42 | **Warm-Up Transparency WT21**<br>**Humanities Transparency HT41**<br>• Edison Concert Phonograph<br>**Humanities Transparency HT42**<br>• Football Game<br>**Critical Thinking Transparency CT63**<br>• Visual Summary<br>**ClassZone:** www.mcdougallittell.com |

Pupil's Edition | Overhead Transparency | CD-ROM
Copymaster | Audio Library | Internet

## ASSESSMENT

**Chapter Assessment,** pp. 630–631

**Formal Assessment**
- Chapter Tests, Forms A and B, pp. 314–321

**Alternative Assessment Book**

**Electronic Teacher Tools with Test Maker**

---

**Section Assessment,** p. 613

**Formal Assessment**
- Section Quiz, p. 310

**Alternative Assessment Book**
- Rubrics for a letter, 4.3
- Rubrics for a picture, 1.3

**Electronic Teacher Tools with Test Maker**

---

**Section Assessment,** p. 617

**Formal Assessment**
- Section Quiz, p. 311

**Alternative Assessment Book**
- Rubrics for a spreadsheet, 5.6
- Rubrics for a map, 2.1

**Electronic Teacher Tools with Test Maker**

---

**Section Assessment,** p. 623

**Formal Assessment**
- Section Quiz, p. 312

**Alternative Assessment Book**
- Rubrics for a biography, 4.4
- Rubrics for a Web Site, 5.1

**Electronic Teacher Tools with Test Maker**

---

**Section Assessment,** p. 629

**Formal Assessment**
- Section Quiz, p. 313

**Alternative Assessment Book**
- Rubrics for a poster, 1.1
- Rubrics for an advertisement, 4.9

**Electronic Teacher Tools with Test Maker**

## CUSTOMIZING FOR INDIVIDUAL NEEDS

### Students Acquiring English/ESL

**Reading Study Guide** (English and Spanish), pp. 205–214

**Access for Students Acquiring English/ESL: Spanish Translations,** pp. 140–146

**Chapter Summaries on CD** (English and Spanish)

### Less Proficient Readers

**Reading Study Guide** (English and Spanish), pp. 205–214

**Chapter Summaries on CD** (English and Spanish)

### Gifted and Talented Students

**In-Depth Resources: Unit 6**
- Enrichment Activity, p. 60

**America's History Makers**
- Jane Addams, pp. 83–84
- W. E. B. Du Bois, pp. 85–86

## CROSS-CURRICULAR CONNECTIONS

### Culture

Hoobler, Dorothy and Thomas Hoobler. ***The Chinese American Family Album.*** New York: Oxford University Press, 1998. The immigrant experience through intimate portraits. Features vintage photographs and an introduction by Bette Bao Lord.

### Economics

Bundles, A'Leilia Perry. ***Madam C. J. Walker (Black Americans of Achievement).*** Broomall, PA: Chelsea House Pub., 1991. A biography of the entrepreneur, millionaire, and philanthropist by her great-great-great granddaughter.

### Geography

Samuelson, Tim et al. ***Above Chicago: A New Collection of Original Aerial Photographs of Chicago.*** San Francisco: Cameron & Co., 1992. The layout of the great city through aerial photographs.

### Popular Culture

Alter, Judy. ***Vaudeville: The Birth of Show Business.*** New York: Franklin Watts, 1998. Short account of the new theater form.

### Interdisciplinary Projects, pp. 121–126

- Math: Catalog Sales
- Science: Making Nut Butter
- Language Arts: Anecdotes About the Immigrant Experience
- Music: Scott Joplin

### Literature

Armstrong, William H. ***Sounder.*** New York: HarperCollins, 1989. Story of poverty and injustice as they affect a Southern black sharecropper's family.

Gregory, Kristiana. ***Earthquake at Dawn.*** New York: HBJ/Gulliver, 1992. Daisy Valentine is caught up in the terror and heroism of the San Francisco earthquake. Includes Irvine's actual photographs.

Schur, Maxine Rose. ***The Circlemaker.*** New York: Puffin Books, 1996. Mendel flees forcible induction into the czar's army and hopes to make his way to New York.

### McDougal Littell *The Language of Literature*

- Jack London, "The Story of an Eyewitness" (informative nonfiction)
- Immigrant Voices, "I Was Dreaming to Come to America" (memoir)
- Laurence Yep, "The Great Rat Hunt" (memoir)

### McDougal Littell Literature Connections

Laurence Yep

***Dragonwings***

A young Chinese immigrant comes to San Francisco at the turn of the century to join his father. They meet dangerous people and new friends and pursue long-held dreams.

## ENRICHMENT ACTIVITIES

**Pupil's Edition, pp. 606–633**
**Interact with History,** p. 607
**Citizenship Today,** p. 612
**Literature Connections,** pp. 618–619
**Interactive Primary Sources,** pp. 624–625
**History Workshop,** pp. 632–633

**In-Depth Resources: Unit 6**
- Geography Application, pp. 49–50
- Primary Sources, pp. 51–52
- Literature Selections, pp. 53–55
- History Workshop Resources, p. 61

**America's History Makers**
- Jane Addams, pp. 83–84
- W. E. B. Du Bois, pp. 85–86

**America's Music CD**

**American History Plays**
- *Daniel Hale Williams, Pioneer Surgeon* by Mary Satchell

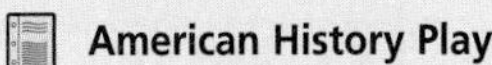

**Outline Map Activities,** pp. 41–42

**Primary Source Explorer**
- from *Crusade for Justice*
- *Like Country Pretty Much*

**Why It Matters Now,** pp. 41–42

# CHAPTER 21 PACING GUIDE

**LESSON PLAN OPTIONS (50-MINUTE PERIOD)** **(TE) = Teacher's Edition (PE) = Pupil's Edition**

| | TEACHER-DIRECTED ACTIVITIES<br>Class Time: 15 minutes | STUDENT-CENTERED ACTIVITIES<br>Class Time: 25 minutes | INDIVIDUAL ACTIVITIES<br>Class Time: 10 minutes |
|---|---|---|---|
| **DAY 1**<br>Introduction<br>pp. 606–608 | **Presentation Options**<br>• Begin with a class discussion of the picture on p. 606 **(PE)**.<br>• Lead a class discussion on the "What Do You Know?" question in Setting the Stage, p. 608. Then introduce the graphic organizer for the chapter **(PE)**. | **Options for Cooperative Learning**<br>• Have student groups discuss the Interact with History questions, p. 607 **(PE)**.<br>• Have student groups respond to the "What Do You Want to Know?" question in Setting the Stage, p. 608 **(PE)**. | **Head Start on Homework Options**<br>• Have students skim Section 1 Main Idea, Why It Matters Now, Terms & Names, and the main headings, p. 609 **(PE)**.<br>• Have students begin Guided Reading activity and Building Vocabulary sheet. |
| **DAY 2**<br>Section 1<br>pp. 609–613 | **Presentation Options**<br>• Begin with the 5-Minute Warm-Up, p. 609 **(TE)**.<br>• Review the Section 1 Main Idea, Why It Matters Now, and Terms & Names, p. 609 **(PE)**.<br>• Lead the students through Citizenship Today, p. 612 **(TE)**. | **Options for Cooperative Learning**<br>• Divide students into groups to complete the Citizenship Today questions, p. 612 **(PE)**.<br>• Have student pairs work together to complete one of the Activity Options in the Section 1 Assessment, p. 613 **(PE)**. | **Head Start on Homework Options**<br>• Have students begin working on Section 1 Assessment, p. 613 **(PE)**.<br>• Have students begin reading the Literature Connections, pp. 618–619 **(PE)**. |
| **DAY 3**<br>Section 2<br>pp. 614–619 | **Presentation Options**<br>• Begin with the 5-Minute Warm-Up, p. 614 **(TE)**.<br>• Choose 5 key questions for Objectives 1–4 to discuss with the class, pp. 614–617 **(TE)**.<br>• Lead students through the Skillbuilder Mini-Lesson: Taking Notes, p. 615 **(TE)**. | **Options for Cooperative Learning**<br>• Divide students into groups and have them work on the Literature Connections, pp. 618–619 **(PE)**.<br>• Have student pairs work together to complete one of the Activity Options in the Section 2 Assessment, p. 617 **(PE)**. | **Head Start on Homework Options**<br>• Have students begin working on Section 2 Assessment, p. 617 **(PE)**.<br>• Have students preview Section 3 Main Idea, Why It Matters Now, Terms & Names, and the main headings, p. 620 **(PE)**. |
| **DAY 4**<br>Section 3<br>pp. 620–625 | **Presentation Options**<br>• Begin with the 5-Minute Warm-Up, p. 620 **(TE)**.<br>• Choose 5 key questions for Objectives 1–4 to discuss with the class, pp. 620–623 **(TE)**.<br>• Lead the students through the Interactive Primary Sources, pp. 624–625 **(TE)**. | **Options for Cooperative Learning**<br>• Divide students into groups and have them complete the Primary Source A Closer Look questions, pp. 624–625 **(PE)**.<br>• Have student pairs work together to complete one of the Activity Options in the Section 3 Assessment, p. 623 **(PE)**. | **Head Start on Homework Options**<br>• Have students begin working on Section 3 Assessment, p. 623 **(PE)**.<br>• Have students begin working on the Taking Notes question in the Section 4 Assessment, p. 629 **(PE)**. |
| **DAY 5**<br>Section 4<br>pp. 626–629 | **Presentation Options**<br>• Begin with the 5-Minute Warm-Up, p. 626 **(TE)**.<br>• Choose 5 key questions for Objectives 1–4 to discuss with the class, pp. 626–629 **(TE)**. | **Options for Cooperative Learning**<br>• Divide students into groups to complete the History Workshop, pp. 632–633 **(PE)**.<br>• Have student pairs work together to complete one of the Activity Options in the Section 4 Assessment, p. 629 **(PE)**. | **Head Start on Homework Options**<br>• Have students complete the Setting the Stage graphic organizer for the chapter, p. 608 **(PE)**.<br>• Have students begin working on the Chapter Assessment, pp. 630–631 **(PE)**.<br>• Prepare for Chapter Test<br>**Formal Assessment,** pp. 314–321 |

**TEACHER-TESTED ACTIVITY** **Ron Campana, Association of Teachers of Social Studies, New York, New York**

## A LOOK BACK IN TIME

**Class Time** Four class periods

**Task** Building a diorama depicting some aspect of American life at the turn of the century

**Purpose** To better understand events in American life between 1880 and 1914 by accurately re-creating a scene in miniature

**Supplies Needed**

- Reference materials about life in the late 1800s or early 1900s in the United States
- Large cardboard boxes; sheets of cardboard for making houses and other buildings; miniature figures of people, animals, and furniture or modeling clay to make figures
- Paints and brushes, tree branches, plastic plants from hobby or pet shops

**Activity** Working in groups, students should decide what to depict in their dioramas. Possibilities include a street scene in a town or city, immigrants arriving in America, settlers in the West, an amusement park or World's Fair, a baseball game, the Wright brothers' first flight, and so on. Each group should research its scene and create an initial layout on paper. Dioramas can be constructed in large boxes. Modeling clay can be used to build up the ground surface with buildings glued to the groundwork and plants and figures added. Allow each group to present and explain its diorama.

## BLOCK SCHEDULING — LESSON PLAN OPTIONS (90-MINUTE PERIOD)

### DAY 1

**Interact with History,** p. 607
**Class Time** 20 Minutes

Options for pacing and variety:

- **Role-Playing** Have students assume the roles of immigrants arriving at Ellis Island in the 1890s. Have students decide what country they came from and use the "What Do You Think?" questions as prompts to create a written monologue. **Class Time** 20 minutes

**Setting the Stage,** p. 608
**Class Time** 20 minutes

Options for pacing and variety:

- **Time Saver** For a homework assignment, have students think about people they may have met who were immigrants and the challenges the newcomers faced. Then have them answer the "What Do You Know?" questions. **Class Time** 5 minutes

**Section 1,** pp. 609–613
**Class Time** 50 minutes

Options for pacing and variety:

- **History on Film** Extend students' background knowledge of immigration by viewing *Immigration and Cultural Change.* Schlessinger Media, 1996. **Class Time** 30 minutes
- **Peer Teaching** Divide students into small groups. Have each group create eight fill-in-the-blank statements about the content of this section that can be completed with the Terms & Names for the section. Have groups exchange statements and complete the ones given to them. **Class Time** 20 minutes

### DAY 2

**Section 2,** pp. 614–619
**Class Time** 45 minutes

Options for pacing and variety:

- **Internet** Extend students' background knowledge of the immigrant experience by visiting www.mcdougallittell.com **Class Time** 20 minutes
- **Time Saver** To compare and contrast the immigrant experience between 1841 and 1860 with that of immigrants between 1881 and 1990, use the chart on page 615. **Class Time** 5 minutes

**Section 3,** pp. 620–625
**Class Time** 45 minutes

Options for pacing and variety:

- **Time Saver** For a homework assignment, have students complete the Activity Option on page 623 of the Section Assessment. **Class Time** 5 minutes
- **Peer Teaching** Have pairs of students answer the Analyzing Leadership question on page 630 of the Chapter Assessment. Have groups share their answers with the class. **Class Time** 10 minutes

### DAY 3

**Section 4,** pp. 626–629
**Class Time** 45 minutes

Options for pacing and variety:

- **Peer Evaluation** Divide students into five groups. Have each group teach the class one of the subsections of Section 4. Lessons should include one or two questions for class discussion. **Class Time** 20 minutes
- **Time Saver** Assign the Taking Notes and Critical Thinking activities from the Section Assessment on page 629 for homework. **Class Time** 10 minutes

**History Workshop,** pp. 632–633
**Class Time** 50 minutes

Options for pacing and variety:

- **Time Saver** Have students answer the Reflect and Assess questions on page 633 independently at home and then share their answers within groups in class. **Class Time** 10 minutes

**Chapter 21 Assessment,** pp. 630–631
**Class Time** 40 minutes

Options for pacing and variety:

- **Peer Evaluation** Have students work in small groups to prepare a summary of the chapter. Have them refer to the information that they wrote for the Using Your Notes graphic organizers to help recall chapter content. **Class Time** 10 minutes
- **Peer Teaching** Have pairs of students write two supporting statements for each of the four main ideas in the Chapter Assessment Visual Summary. **Class Time** 10 minutes

**CHAPTER 21 OBJECTIVE**
The student will understand the social, economic, and cultural changes in American life from the late 19th century to the beginning of World War I.

## HISTORY FROM VISUALS

**Interpreting the Photograph** Ask students to study the photograph of people walking along Mulberry Street on New York's Lower East Side around 1900. Have them make inferences about how people lived in this section of New York City at the turn of the century. **Possible Responses** The area looks crowded and busy. People bought produce and other goods at outdoor stalls. Most buildings are four or five stories tall, with shops on the ground floors. The upper floors may be apartments. People travel on foot, and goods move by horse-drawn wagons.

**Extension** Have students write the headings for five advertising posters that might have been found on Mulberry Street when this photograph was taken.

# CHAPTER 21 Changes in American Life

## 1880–1914

*Section 1* **Cities Grow and Change**
*Section 2* **The New Immigrants**
*Section 3* **Segregation and Discrimination**
*Section 4* **Society and Mass Culture**

Crowds of people walk, work, and shop on Mulberry Street in New York's Lower East Side.

606

## RECOMMENDED RESOURCES

**BOOKS FOR THE TEACHER**

Lukas, J. Anthony. ***Big Trouble.*** NY: Simon & Schuster, 1997. Murder, labor troubles, and skullduggery in Idaho at the turn of the century.

Theobald, Paul. ***Call School: Rural Education in the Midwest to 1918.*** Carbondale, IL: S. Illinois U. Pr., 1995. The little red schoolhouse—an American institution.

Wells, Ida B. ***Southern Horrors & Other Writings: The Anti-Lynching Campaign of Ida B. Wells, 1892–1900.*** Ed. J. J. Royster. NY: St. Martin's, 1996. Powerful and disturbing, with a useful introduction.

**SOFTWARE**

***The Golden Door: The Italian Immigrant Experience in the United States.*** Social Studies School Service, 1997. Experience Ellis Island and immigrant life in New York around 1900.

**VIDEO**

***The Brooklyn Bridge.*** PBS Video, 1982. The dangers and challenges of building the famous bridge.

**INTERNET**

For more about the Statue of Liberty and Ellis Island, visit www.mcdougallittell.com

## Interact *with* History

Ellis Island in New York Harbor was the port of entry for most European immigrants. It opened in 1892.
Many immigrants looked for friends who had already come to America.
Most immigrants came to America with just a few dollars and a small number of treasured personal possessions.

**It is 1900, and you have decided to leave your native country. After a long and difficult voyage, you arrive in the United States. Now you need to find a new home and a job. You have to create a new life in a strange land.**

### What Do You Think?

- What caused you to leave your native country?
- What problems did you face on your voyage?
- What do you hope to find in the United States?

# *How will you make a home in your new country?*

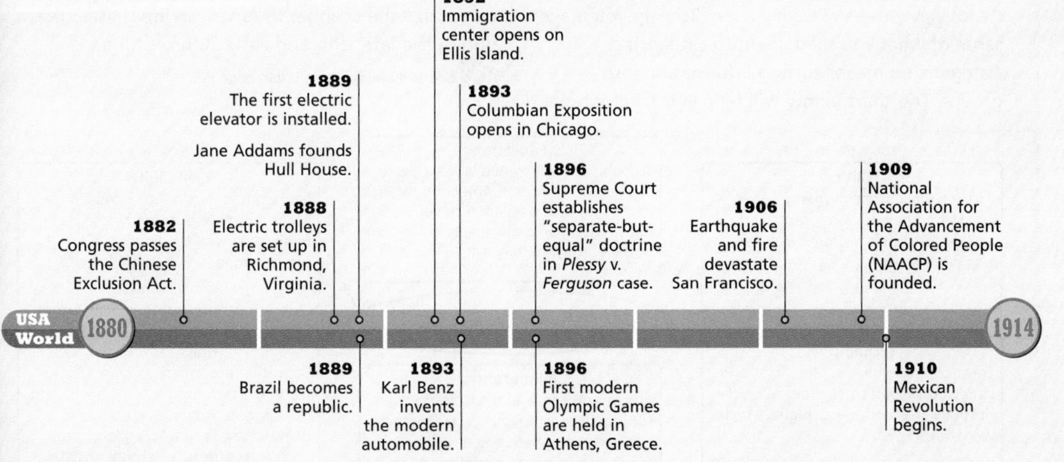




## Interact *with* History

### OBJECTIVES

- To help students understand how life in America changed during the late 19th and early 20th centuries
- To help students identify with the people, events, and situations they will learn about in this chapter

### What Do You Think?

1. Ask students why the immigrants might have left their original countries to move to the United States.
2. Ask students to think about a long ocean voyage in primitive conditions in a boat full of strangers.
3. Have students speculate about how immigrants learned about the United States.

### *How will you make a home in your new country?*

Encourage students to think about the journey that these immigrants had just completed, the unfamiliar city that confronted them, and the need to communicate with strangers in a new language. Encourage students to be as concrete as possible in considering the immigrants' experience.

### MAKING PERSONAL CONNECTIONS

Ask students to think about any major changes they have made in their own lives, such as moving to a new home, a new city, or a new country. Have them compare and contrast the changes they have experienced with those of these early-20th-century immigrants.

### TIME LINE DISCUSSION

**Point out to students that in the period covered in the time line, a new group of immigrants began arriving in the United States, mostly from southern and eastern Europe. When they arrived, they found an industrialized country in which technology and social conditions were both changing rapidly.**

- Ask students to identify events that indicate technological change in the United States and elsewhere. **Answer** invention of the electric trolley, the electric elevator, and the automobile
- Follow up by asking them to make inferences about how these technological achievements would have affected life. **Possible Responses** They would have improved transportation, allowed the construction of taller buildings, and accelerated urban growth.
- Ask students to make inferences about the significance of the name and date of the exposition in Chicago. **Possible Response** It might commemorate Columbus's 1492 voyage 400 years earlier.
- Encourage the class to discuss why it might seem particularly appropriate to celebrate Columbus's voyage in an era of new immigration. **Possible Response** His voyage marked the beginning of European immigration to the Americas.

## BEFORE YOU READ

### Previewing the Theme: Diversity and Unity

Ask students to think of reasons why the social and economic changes during this period might have resulted in tensions, including racial and ethnic discrimination.

Ask why native-born Americans at the time might have been concerned about the arrival of immigrants. **Possible Responses** They might have feared that a larger work force would lead to lower wages. They might also have been concerned about the languages, customs, and religions of the newcomers.

### What Do You Know?

Ask students what motives for immigration to the Americas they have discussed in earlier chapters. **Possible Responses** the desire for religious freedom (Pilgrims, Puritans, Quakers, Catholics); the desire for a new economic start (debtors and indentured servants); escape from famine (Irish in the 1840s and 1850s).

 **In-Depth Resources: Unit 6**
- Tracing Themes: Diversity and Unity, p. 42

## READ AND TAKE NOTES

### Reading Strategy: Categorizing

Tell students that categorizing information means sorting information into groups. Arranging information may help the student with such critical-thinking skills as comparing and contrasting or identifying causes and effects. When the chart is finished, students should be able to identify reasons for some of the changes in American life in the late 19th and early 20th centuries.

 **In-Depth Resources: Unit 6**
- Setting the Stage, p. 41

 **Critical Thinking Transparency CT61**
- Setting the Stage

# Chapter 21 SETTING THE STAGE

## BEFORE YOU READ

### Previewing the Theme

**Diversity and Unity** Chapter 21 discusses how American society went through deep changes at the end of the 19th century. The economy became more industrial. Millions of immigrants came to the United States. Cities grew rapidly. These changes caused tensions in the nation. Immigrants and racial minorities faced discrimination.

### What Do You Know?

What do you think about when you hear the term *immigration?* Why do people move to different countries? What kinds of challenges might immigrants face in their new country?

**THINK ABOUT**
- what you know about immigration from your own experience or the experience of your family
- what would make you want to move away from your home

### What Do You Want to Know?

What questions do you have about American life around 1900? Write them in your notebook before you read the chapter.

## READ AND TAKE NOTES

**Reading Strategy: Categorizing** To help you make sense of what you read, learn to categorize. Categorizing means sorting information into groups. The chart below will help you take notes and categorize the changes in American life that occurred during the late 19th and early 20th centuries.

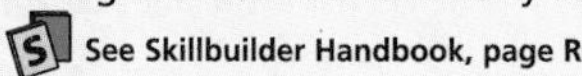
See Skillbuilder Handbook, page R6.

**Changes in American Life**

**Politics**
Political machines emerged in cities. They often helped immigrants and built many public facilities. But they also were corrupt.

**Education**
Schools were segregated in many parts of the country. African Americans set up schools for their own advancement. Public education grew greatly at the turn of the century. Literacy rates increased.

**Civil Rights**
Segregation expanded, mostly in the South. Nonwhites faced discrimination in all regions of the country. NAACP was founded.

**Technology**
Elevators, steel beams, electricity, and streetcars helped cities grow. Wright brothers invented the airplane. Movies were developed.

**Immigration**
Immigrants came to the United States for jobs. New immigrants came, especially from southern and eastern Europe. Immigrants contributed to the growth of political machines.

**Mass Culture**
Education expanded. Increased literacy led to greater popularity of books and newspapers. Advertising increased demand for goods. Parks, fairs, sports, and movies provided leisure activities.



## TEACHING STRATEGY

### READING THE CHAPTER

This is a thematic chapter focusing on changes in American life at the turn of the 20th century. Tell students, as they read, to identify section titles and headings that could be used as categories in the chart above. Discuss the details that pertain to each category. Pause after each section to discuss the changes that students identified for inclusion in the chart.

### ALTERNATIVE ASSESSMENT

The Chapter Assessment describes three activities for alternative assessment on page 631. You may wish to have students work on these activities during the course of the chapter and then present them at the end.

# 1 Cities Grow and Change

**TERMS & NAMES**
urbanization
tenement
slum
social gospel
Jane Addams
Hull House
political machine
Tammany Hall

**MAIN IDEA**
Industrialization and immigration caused American cities to grow rapidly.

**WHY IT MATTERS NOW**
Modern American city life first emerged during this period.

## ONE AMERICAN'S STORY

**Carl Jensen came to the United States from Denmark in 1906. Like most of the millions of immigrants who came to America around the turn of the century, he immediately began to look for work. He described the crush of people, including himself, who were searching for jobs in New York.**

*A VOICE FROM THE PAST*

Along thirty miles of water front I wandered in search of work . . . waiting through rain and sleet and snow with gangs of longshoremen [dockworkers] to reach the boss before he finished picking the men he wanted. . . . Strong men crushed each other to the ground in their passion for work.

**Carl Jensen,** quoted in *A Sunday between Wars*

Shipyards in growing cities provided jobs for many Americans.

**Jensen eventually found work in New York's garment, or clothing, district. At the turn of the century, the promise of work drew millions of people like Carl Jensen from around the world to American cities. In this section, you will read about the rapid growth of American cities.**

## 1 Industrialization Expands Cities

The Industrial Revolution, which had been changing how people worked, also changed *where* people worked. Since colonial days, most Americans had lived and worked in rural areas. But in the late 1800s, that began to change as more and more people moved to cities to find jobs.

Industries were drawn to cities because cities offered good transportation and plentiful workers. Increasing numbers of factory jobs appeared in America's cities, followed by more workers to fill those jobs. The growth of cities that resulted from these changes is called **urbanization.**

Many of the people who moved to American cities were immigrants like Carl Jensen. People also migrated from America's farms to the cities. Once there, even workers with few skills could usually find steady work.





## SECTION OBJECTIVES

1. To explain how industrialization changed city life
2. To understand how technology and the streetcar altered city life
3. To describe urban living conditions and how reformers tried to improve them
4. To analyze how political machines influenced city governments

### CRITICAL THINKING

Recognizing Effects, p. 610
Summarizing, p. 611
Making Inferences, p. 612
Comparing and Contrasting, p. 613
Evaluating, p. 613

## FOCUS & MOTIVATE

### 5-MINUTE WARM-UP

**Drawing Conclusions** These questions focus on city life.

1. Look at the photograph on page 611. What urban problems does this picture suggest?
2. Why do you think many immigrants who arrived in New York lived in tenements?

**Warm-Up Transparency WT21**

## INSTRUCT

### INSTRUCT: OBJECTIVE 1

**Industrialization Expands Cities**

Key Questions

- How did the Industrial Revolution change where Americans worked?
- Why did urban population increase in the late 1800s?

**In-Depth Resources: Unit 6**
- Guided Reading, p. 43

**Reading Study Guide** (Spanish and English), pp. 205–206

## RECOMMENDED RESOURCES

**In-Depth Resources: Unit 6**
- Guided Reading, p. 43
- Building Vocabulary, p. 47
- Primary Source, p. 51
- Reteaching Activity, p. 56

**Reading Study Guide** (Spanish and English), pp. 205–206

**Outline Map Activities**
- Growth of Cities in the Great Lakes Region, pp. 41–42

**America's History Makers**
- Jane Addams, pp. 83–84

**Citizenship Today,** pp. 13–14

**Formal Assessment**
- Section Quiz, p. 310

**Alternative Assessment**
- Rubrics, 4.3
- Rubrics, 1.3

**Access for Students Acquiring English/ESL**
- Guided Reading, p. 140

Technology Resources

**Critical Thinking Transparency CT62**
- Cause and Effect: Urban Growth

**Geography Transparency GT21**
- Growth of Cities, 1860–1900

**Electronic Teacher Tools with Test Maker**

**ClassZone**
www.mcdougallittell.com

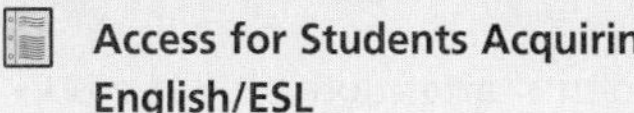

**MORE ABOUT . . .**

**Building a Skyscraper**
Louis Henri Sullivan (1856–1924) was one of America's greatest architects. A leader of the Chicago school of architecture, he was an early developer of the skyscraper. He designed the Wainwright Building in St. Louis (1891), which was one of the first examples of the vertical line of the skyscraper. Sullivan believed that practicality was more important than beauty. He popularized the expression "Form follows function."

**INSTRUCT: OBJECTIVE** 

**Technology Changes City Life/ The Streetcar City**
Key Questions
- How did new technologies change urban architecture and transportation?
- How was life in the streetcar city different from life in the walking city?
- Why might people living in suburbs want to become part of the city?

 **Outline Map Activities**
- Growth of Cities in the Great Lakes Region, pp. 41–42

**MORE ABOUT . . .**

**Transportation and Urban Growth**
Innovations in urban transportation radically changed the lives of city dwellers and the landscape of their cities. By 1895, there were 10,000 miles of streetcar tracks in American cities. San Francisco introduced the now-familiar cable car, driven by moving underground cables, in 1873. In Boston, electric subways began running beneath the city's streets in 1897.

 **Critical Thinking Transparency CT62**
- Cause and Effect: Urban Growth

 **Geography Transparency GT21**
- Growth of Cities, 1860–1900

CONNECTIONS TO SCIENCE
**Building a Skyscraper**

Modern cities depend on skyscrapers to increase the space for people to live and work. Steel, electricity, and elevators make skyscrapers possible.

1 **STEEL FRAMES** Steel beams can carry much more weight than brick or stone walls. The strength of the steel allows architects to design extremely tall buildings.

2 **WINDOWS** In skyscrapers, the outer walls do not support the weight of the building; the steel beams do. As a result, many skyscrapers have outer walls made of glass to allow sunlight inside.

3 **ELEVATOR** Tall buildings would be useless if people could not reach all of the floors. Elevators powered by electricity make such tall buildings practical.

## 2 Technology Changes City Life

New technologies helped cities absorb the millions of people who flocked there. For example, new technologies made possible the construction of skyscrapers, buildings that looked tall enough to scrape the sky. Skyscrapers helped cities grow and made modern city life possible.

The elevator was a key invention for constructing tall buildings that could hold greater numbers of people. Before the 1860s, buildings rarely rose higher than four stories because it was hard for people to climb to the top. In 1889, the Otis Elevator Company installed the first electric elevator. Now buildings could be more than a few stories tall because people no longer had to walk up to the higher floors. As a result, buildings could hold more people.

The use of steel also helped to increase the height of buildings. In 1885, the Home Insurance Building in Chicago boasted an iron and steel skeleton that could hold the immense weight of the skyscraper's floors and walls. The building climbed to ten stories. Skyscrapers changed city skylines forever.

A. Answer Industries that required new workers sprang up in cities. Industrialization attracted more people to the cities. New technologies helped cities support growing urban populations.

*Reading*History
**A. Recognizing Effects** How did industry and technology help cities grow?

## The Streetcar City

As electricity helped change the way people traveled inside buildings, it also changed how people traveled around cities. Before industrialization, people walked or used horse-drawn vehicles to travel over land. But by 1900, electric streetcars in American cities were carrying more than 5 billion passengers a year. Streetcars and trains changed the walking city into the streetcar city.

**Background** Streetcars are also called trolleys.



**ACTIVITY OPTIONS**

**INDIVIDUAL NEEDS**

**LESS PROFICIENT READERS**

**Finding Main Ideas** As a way to focus students' attention and set a purpose for reading, write the headings from this section on the board and identify them as Main Ideas (MI). As you read the section together, have students identify the important details (D) that support each main idea. Write them in an outline format.

MI: Industrialization Expands Cities
- D: Industries were drawn to cities.
- D: Cities offered jobs.
- D: Cities offered transportation.
- D: Unskilled workers could find jobs.

In 1888, Richmond, Virginia, became the first American city to have a transportation system powered by electricity. Other cities soon installed their own electric streetcars. The streetcars could quickly carry people to work and play all over the city. Some cities, such as Chicago, moved their electric streetcars above the street level, creating elevated, or "el," lines. Other cities, like New York, placed their city rail lines in underground tunnels, making subways.

The streetcar city spread outward from the city's center in ways the walking city never could. The ability to live farther away from work helped new suburbs to develop around cities. Some people in the suburbs wanted to become part of the city they bordered. That way they also could be served by the city's transportation system. Largely due to public transportation, cities expanded. For example, in 1889, Chicago annexed several suburbs and more than doubled its population as well as its area.

**Vocabulary**
**annex:** to add

## 3 Urban Disasters and Slums

The concentration of people in cities increased the danger of disasters because people and buildings were packed closely together. For example, in 1906, a powerful earthquake rocked San Francisco. The tremors caused large fires to tear through the city. The central business district was destroyed. About 700 people died, and nearly $400 million in property was damaged. But natural disasters were not the only source of danger for the people of the cities. Poverty and disease also threatened their lives.

As people flocked to cities, overcrowding became a serious problem. It was especially serious for families who could not afford to buy a house. Such families usually lived in rented apartments or tenements. A **tenement** is an apartment house that is usually run-down and overcrowded.

Old buildings, landlord neglect, poor design, and little government control led to dangerous conditions in many tenements. Poor families who could not afford to rent a place of their own often needed to move in with other families. This resulted in severely overcrowded tenements. Inadequate garbage pick-up also caused problems. Tenants sometimes dumped their garbage into the narrow air shafts between tenements. There was little fresh air, and the smell was awful.

Many tenements had no running water. Residents had to collect water

**B. Possible Response** It was unpleasant. Tenements were overcrowded, smelly, and noisy. There was poor ventilation and little sanitation.

***Reading* History**
**B. Summarizing** What was it like to live in a turn-of-the-century tenement?

**HISTORY through ART**

This photograph by Lewis Hine shows a family of Italian immigrants in their cramped, decaying tenement in New York City in 1912. Often photographers, such as Hine, had their subjects pose for their pictures to create the strongest effect.

**What effect do you think Hine wanted this photograph to have?**

**INSTRUCT: OBJECTIVE 3**

**Urban Disasters and Slums/ Reformers Attack Urban Problems**

Key Questions

- What were some of the causes of housing problems in tenements in the late 19th century?
- How did the social gospel movement try to help the poor?
- What was the role of settlement houses in the cities?

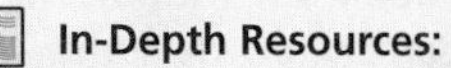

**In-Depth Resources: Unit 6**
- Primary Source: from *How the Other Half Lives* by Jacob Riis, p. 51

**HISTORY *through* ART**

**Interpreting the Photograph** Photographer Lewis Hine thought that photography was a powerful tool for reform. He documented the experiences of new immigrants, capturing on film their arrival at the docks, their homes in tenements, and their work in sweatshops. Between 1908 and 1912, Hine took hundreds of photographs of child workers for the National Child Labor Committee.

**Possible Response: Hine hoped that people who saw the photograph would want to help families like this one escape poverty.**

**ACTIVITY OPTIONS**

**MULTIPLE LEARNING STYLES: SPATIAL**

**BLOCK SCHEDULING**

**CITY PLANNING**

**Class Time** One class period

**Task** Designing a plan for a neighborhood of working-class families

**Purpose** To gain an understanding of the problems faced by 19th-century slum dwellers

**Supplies Needed**
- Drawing paper, pens, colored pencils
- Reference materials about 19th-century cities

**Activity** Suggest that students research living conditions in 19th-century tenements, paying special attention to primary-source photographs of these neighborhoods. Brainstorm the elements in a neighborhood that provide for its citizens' needs. Divide the class into small groups. Each group should draw a street plan for a 19th-century neighborhood of working-class people. Students could also include drawings of the kinds of multifamily or single-family homes they would include in their plan. Display the completed plans in class and discuss them.

## MORE ABOUT . . .

**Tenement Dwellings**

To improve slum conditions, officials in New York City passed a law in 1879 that established minimum standards for plumbing and electricity. The law also required that every bedroom have a window. Landlords began building dumbbell tenements, which were five- or six-story buildings with a floor plan shaped like a barbell. This shape allowed for a narrow air shaft between buildings and a window for each room. But windows on a dark air shaft provided scarcely any daylight. And the "fresh air" that came in from the air shaft usually stank of the garbage that people dumped into the shaft.

from a faucet on the street. The water could be heated for bathing. But it was often unsafe for drinking. Sewage flowed in open gutters and threatened to spread disease among tenement dwellers.

A neighborhood with such overcrowded, dangerous housing was called a **slum.** The most famous example was New York City's Lower East Side. But every city had slums. After visiting Chicago's slums, the British writer Rudyard Kipling wrote in disgust, "Having seen it [Chicago], I urgently desire never to see it again."

## Reformers Attack Urban Problems

Many Americans were also disgusted by poverty and slums. Some people fought to reform, or create changes, that would solve these problems. They were known as urban reformers.

The social gospel movement provided one basis for these beliefs. The **social gospel** movement aimed to improve the lives of the poor. Led by Protestant ministers, the ideas of the movement were based on Christian values. The most important concerns of the social gospel movement were labor reforms, such as abolishing child labor. Some reformers inspired by the movement opened settlement houses. They helped the poor and immigrants improve their lives. Settlement houses offered services such as daycare, education, and health care to needy people in slum neighborhoods.

C. Answer Christian values inspired many reformers to help the poor.

*Reading* **History**

**C. Making Inferences** How did Christian values support the social gospel movement?

## CITIZENSHIP TODAY

**OBJECTIVE**

Students will identify a local community problem and create a plan to solve it.

**David Levitt**

In addition to collecting food from school cafeterias, Levitt has convinced restaurants to donate food to his project, Food for Thought. Levitt also asked manufacturers to donate containers to store the food he collected. Levitt also worked with a member of the Florida State Legislature on a bill requiring that all Florida public schools donate lunchroom leftovers to food pantries or homeless shelters. The legislation became law in the summer of 1999.

**Citizenship Today,** pp. 13–14

## CITIZENSHIP TODAY

## Community Service

Since the United States began, citizens have shared concerns about their communities. Many citizens, such as Jane Addams in 1889, have identified problems and proposed solutions to them.

In 1993, sixth-grader David Levitt asked his principal if the leftover food from the school cafeteria could be sent to a program to feed needy people. David was told that many restrictions prevented giving away the food.

Determined to get food to people who needed it, David talked to the school board, the state health department, and private companies to convince them to back his program. Today, more than 500,000 pounds of food from schools has been given to hungry people in the Seminole, Florida, area.

David Levitt carries supplies for his food pantry program.

### How Do You Participate in Your Community?

1. In a small group, think about problems within your community. Make a list of those problems.
2. Choose one problem to work on.
3. Gather information about the problem. Keep a log of your sources to use again.
4. After you gather information, brainstorm solutions to the problem. Create a plan to carry out one solution.
5. Present the problem and your plan to the class.

See the Citizenship Handbook, page 286.

Visit www.mcdougallittell.com to learn more about community service.



## STANDARDS FOR EVALUATION: CITIZENSHIP TODAY

**Each plan should**

- focus on a community problem.
- be well researched and well organized.
- clearly explain the group's perception of the problem.
- propose a course of action.
- identify the steps the group would take to carry out its solutions.
- use language effectively.

Many settlement house founders were educated middle-class women. **Jane Addams** founded Chicago's **Hull House** in 1889 with Ellen Gates Starr. Hull House soon became a model for other settlement houses, including New York's Henry Street Settlement House, which Lillian D. Wald established in 1889.

## 4 Political Machines Run Cities

Political machines were another type of organization that addressed the problems of the city. A **political machine** is an organization that influences enough votes to control a local government.

Political machines gained support by trading favors for votes. For example, machine bosses gave jobs or food to supporters. In return, supporters worked and voted for the machine. Political machines also did many illegal things. They broke rules to win elections. They accepted bribes to affect government actions.

The most famous political machine was **Tammany Hall** in New York City. It was led by William Marcy Tweed. Along with his greedy friends, "Boss" Tweed stole enormous amounts of money from the city.

Despite such corruption, political machines did a number of good things for cities. They built parks, sewers, schools, roads, and orphanages in many cities. In addition, machine politicians often helped immigrants get settled in the United States by helping them find jobs or homes. Many immigrants gratefully supported the political machine after this kind of help. In the next section, you will learn more about immigration.

**D. Answer** They were similar in that they tried to solve urban problems and help immigrants. They were different in that the political machines were corrupt.

*Reading* **History**

**D. Comparing and Contrasting** How were settlement houses and political machines similar? How were they different?

### AMERICA'S HISTORY MAKERS

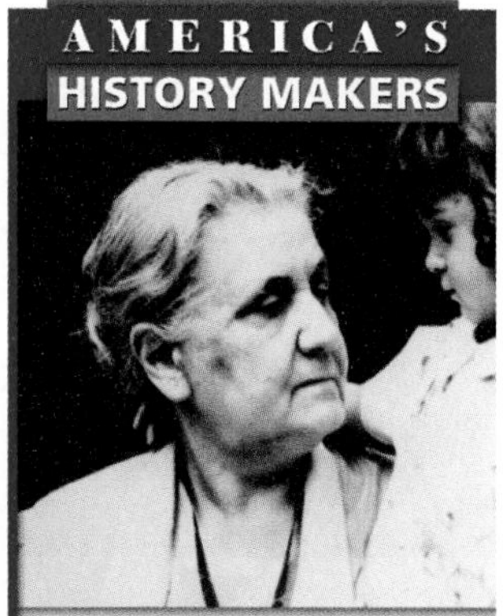

**JANE ADDAMS**
**1860–1935**

Jane Addams founded Hull House as an "effort to aid in the solution of the social and industrial problems which are [caused] by the modern conditions of life in a great city."

In addition to Hull House, Addams was active in many other areas. She fought for the passage of laws to protect women workers and outlaw child labor. She also worked to improve housing and public health. In 1931, she was awarded a share of the Nobel Peace Prize for her efforts.

**Why did Jane Addams found Hull House?**

### Section 1 Assessment

**1. Terms & Names**

**Identify:**
- urbanization
- tenement
- slum
- social gospel
- Jane Addams
- Hull House
- political machine
- Tammany Hall

**2. Taking Notes**

Use a chart like the one below to show the causes and effects of urban growth.

| Cause | Effect |
|---|---|
| Steel | |
| Elevators | |
| Streetcars | |
| Immigration | |

**3. Main Ideas**

a. Why did immigrants and farmers settle in big cities at the end of the 19th century?

b. What are two inventions that made modern city life possible?

c. What urban problems did reformers try to solve?

**4. Critical Thinking**

**Evaluating** What were some of the advantages and disadvantages of machine politics?

**THINK ABOUT**
- the problems faced by immigrants and cities
- Tammany Hall and "Boss" Tweed

**ACTIVITY OPTIONS**

**LANGUAGE ARTS**
**ART**

It is 1900, and you have just moved to an American city. Write a **letter** to friends back home or draw a **picture** that describes your new home.



### AMERICA'S HISTORY MAKERS

**Jane Addams**

Jane Addams was born in Cedarville, Illinois, to Quaker parents. She traveled to Europe, where she was impressed by a settlement house, Toynbee Hall, in a poor section of London. Addams decided to create a settlement house in Chicago. She also worked for the establishment of juvenile courts, housing codes, factory safety inspections, and workers' compensation. A pacifist, Addams was president of the Women's International League for Peace and Freedom from 1915 to 1919.

**Answer: to help solve problems caused by industrialization and modern urban life**

**America's History Makers**
- Jane Addams, pp. 83–84

### INSTRUCT: OBJECTIVE 4

**Political Machines Run Cities**

Key Questions
- How did political machines affect city life in the late 19th century?
- What problems could result when a political machine controlled a local government?

## ASSESS & RETEACH

**Setting the Stage** Have students use the main ideas from this section to fill in the first block on the graphic organizer.

**Formal Assessment**
- Section Quiz, p. 310

**Critical Thinking Transparency CT61**
- Setting the Stage

**RETEACHING ACTIVITY**

Divide the class into four groups. Assign one section objective to each group. Have the group identify the key concepts in each objective on a graphic organizer, such as a word web, chart, or spider map on a large piece of drawing paper.

**In-Depth Resources: Unit 6**
- Reteaching Activity, p. 56

### Section 1 Assessment

**1. Terms & Names**

**urbanization,** p. 609
**tenement,** p. 611
**slum,** p. 612
**social gospel,** p. 612
**Jane Addams,** p. 613
**Hull House,** p. 613
**political machine,** p. 613
**Tammany Hall,** p. 613

**2. Taking Notes**

Steel: provided materials to build skyscrapers; Elevators: allowed people to get to the top floors of skyscrapers; Streetcars: allowed people to move around cities; Immigration: increased city population and led to some overcrowding

**3. Main Ideas**

**a.** to find work **b.** electricity; elevators; public transportation; skyscrapers **c.** poverty; crime; sanitation; disease

**4. Critical Thinking**

Advantages: Machine politicians helped people get jobs and food. Disadvantages: They broke the law to stay in power.

**ACTIVITY OPTIONS**

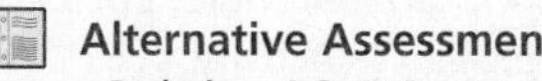
**Alternative Assessment**
- Rubrics, 4.3, 1.3

## SECTION OBJECTIVES

1. To describe changes in immigration patterns in the late 1800s
2. To understand where and how immigrants settled and the jobs they took
3. To explain the process of assimilation and efforts to restrict immigration

**SKILLBUILDER**
Interpreting Graphs, p. 615

**CRITICAL THINKING**
Identifying Problems, p. 615
Making Inferences, p. 616
Making Generalizations, p. 617

## FOCUS & MOTIVATE

### 5-MINUTE WARM-UP

**Drawing Conclusions** These questions focus on the union movement.

1. Look at the photograph on page 616. What is an issue that the workers are concerned about?
2. How can you tell that the labor movement includes different immigrant groups?

 Warm-Up Transparency WT21

## INSTRUCT

### INSTRUCT: OBJECTIVE 

**The New Immigrants**
Key Questions

- Compare the experiences of immigrants entering the United States in New York, in California, and in Texas.
- How did patterns of immigration change at the end of the 19th century?

 **In-Depth Resources: Unit 6**

- Guided Reading, p. 44
- Building Vocabulary, p. 47
- Geography Application: Immigration, 1907, pp. 49–50
- Literature Selection: "The New Colossus" by Emma Lazarus, p. 53

# 2 The New Immigrants

**TERMS & NAMES**
new immigrants
Ellis Island
Angel Island
melting pot
assimilation
Chinese Exclusion Act

| MAIN IDEA | WHY IT MATTERS NOW |
|---|---|
| Millions of immigrants—mostly from southern and eastern Europe—moved to the United States. | The new immigrants had an important role in shaping American culture in the 20th century. |

### ONE AMERICAN'S STORY

**In 1907, 10-year-old Edward Corsi left Italy to come to America. After two weeks at sea, he caught his first sight of the Statue of Liberty. He described the reaction of the people on the ship.**

*A VOICE FROM THE PAST*

This symbol of America . . . inspired awe in the hopeful immigrants. Many older persons among us, burdened with a thousand memories of what they were leaving behind, had been openly weeping. . . . Now somehow steadied, I suppose, by the concreteness of the symbol of America's freedom, they dried their tears.

**Edward Corsi,** *In the Shadow of Liberty*

**Every day, thousands of immigrants like Corsi streamed through Ellis Island, the nation's immigration station. In this section, you will learn about the immigrants who came to the United States around 1900 and how they affected the nation.**

The Statue of Liberty and Ellis Island were two of the first things many immigrants saw of the United States.

### 1 The New Immigrants

Until the 1890s, most immigrants to the United States had come from northern and western Europe. But after 1900, fewer northern Europeans immigrated, and more southern and eastern Europeans did. This later group of immigrants came to be known as the **new immigrants.** Southern Italy sent large numbers of immigrants. Many Jews from eastern Europe and Slavic peoples, such as Poles and Russians, also immigrated.

**Ellis Island** was the first stop for most immigrants from Europe. There, they were processed before they could enter the United States. First, they had to pass a physical examination. Those with serious health problems or diseases were sent home. Next, they were asked a series of questions: Name? Occupation? How much money do you have?

Louis Adamic came to America from Slovenia, in southeastern Europe, in 1913. Adamic described the night he spent on Ellis Island. He and many other immigrants slept on bunk beds in a huge hall. Lacking a warm blanket, the young man "shivered, sleepless, all night, listening to snores" and dreams "in perhaps a dozen different languages."



## RECOMMENDED RESOURCES

**In-Depth Resources: Unit 6**

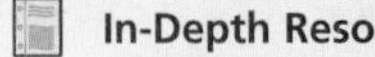

- Guided Reading, p. 44
- Building Vocabulary, p. 47
- Skillbuilder Practice, p. 48
- Geography Application: Immigration, 1907, pp. 49–50
- Literature Selections, pp. 53–55
- Reteaching Activity, p. 57
- Enrichment Activity, p. 60

**Reading Study Guide** (Spanish and English), pp. 207–208

**Formal Assessment**

- Section Quiz, p. 311

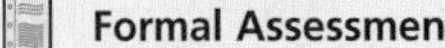

**Alternative Assessment**

- Rubrics, 5.6
- Rubrics, 2.1

**Access for Students Acquiring English/ESL**

- Guided Reading, p. 141
- Skillbuilder Practice, p. 144
- Geography Application, pp. 145–146

**Technology Resources**

 **Electronic Teacher Tools with Test Maker**

 **ClassZone**
www.mcdougallittell.com

CONNECTIONS TO MATH

## U.S. Immigration, *1841–1900*

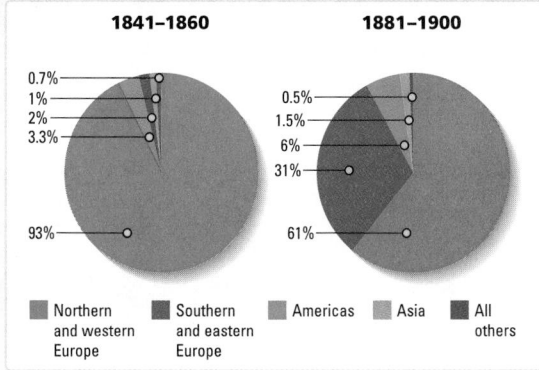

**1841–1860**

0.7% · 1% · 2% · 3.3% · 93%

**1881–1900**

0.5% · 1.5% · 6% · 31% · 61%

Northern and western Europe · Southern and eastern Europe · Americas · Asia · All others

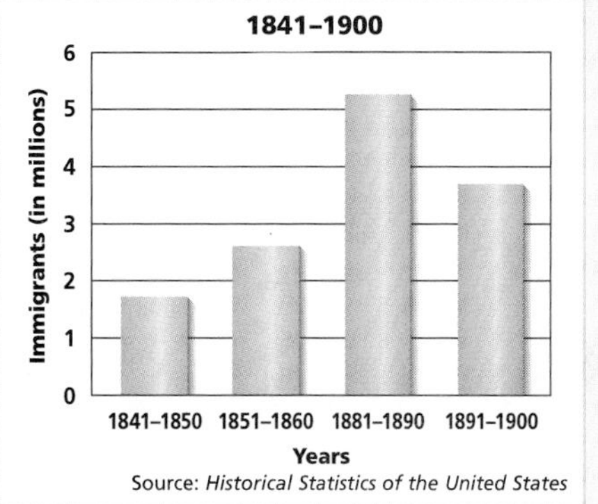


SKILLBUILDER **Interpreting Graphs**

1. *About how many immigrants came to the United States from 1841 to 1860?*
2. *About how many southern and eastern European immigrants came to the United States from 1881 to 1900?*

Skillbuilder Answers
1. about 4.3 million
2. about 2.8 million

While European immigrants passed through Ellis Island on the East Coast, Asians landed at **Angel Island** in San Francisco Bay. In Angel Island's filthy buildings, most Chinese immigrants were held for several weeks. One unhappy prisoner carved in the wall, "For what reason must I sit in jail? It is only because my country is weak and my family poor."

Many Mexican immigrants entered the United States through Texas. Jesús [heh•SOOS] Garza recalled how simple his journey was. "I paid my $8, passed my examination, then changed my Mexican coins for American money and went to San Antonio, Texas."

## 2 Settling in America

Immigrants settled where they could find jobs. Many found work in American factories. The immigrants contributed to the growth of cities such as New York, Boston, Philadelphia, Pittsburgh, and Chicago. About half of the new immigrants settled in four industrial states: Massachusetts, New York, Pennsylvania, and Illinois.

Once in America, newer immigrants looked for people from the same village in the old country to help them find jobs and housing. People with similar ethnic backgrounds often moved to the same neighborhoods. As a result, ethnic neighborhoods with names like "Little Italy" and "Chinatown" became common in American cities.

The immigrants living in these communities pooled money to build places of worship for their neighborhoods. They published newspapers in their native languages. They commonly supported political machines, often led by politicians who had also come from their country of origin. Such politicians could speak the native language and help new arrivals feel comfortable. Most importantly, politicians could help immigrants find jobs.

**A. Answer** They pooled resources to build places of worship in their neighborhoods, published newspapers in their native languages, and joined political machines.

*Reading*History
**A. Identifying Problems** How did immigrants show creativity in solving problems?

***"I paid my $8, passed my examination, . . . and went to San Antonio."***
Jesús Garza



### HISTORY FROM VISUALS

**Interpreting the Graphs** Point out the different kinds of information presented on the three graphs. Have students discuss how the origins of immigrants changed between 1841–1860 and 1881–1900. Ask: Which two groups show the greatest increase from the first time period to the second? **Answer** southern and eastern Europe and the Americas. Ask students to summarize the overall changes in immigration that the whole set of graphs depicts. **Possible Responses** Immigration increased tremendously between the 1840s and the 1880s; most immigrants were still coming from Europe, but they came from different regions of Europe.

**Extension** Using the pie graphs and the bar graph, have students estimate approximately how many millions of immigrants came from northern and western Europe and southern and eastern Europe from 1841 to 1860 and from 1881 to 1900. Ask them to present their answers on a bar graph.

### INSTRUCT: OBJECTIVE 2

**Settling in America/ Immigrants Take Tough Jobs**

Key Questions
- What were the most important influences on where immigrants settled in the United States?
- In what ways did immigrant communities help new arrivals adjust to life in the United States?
- How did the types of work that immigrants could find vary from one part of the country to another?

**In-Depth Resources: Unit 6**
- Literature Selection: from *In the Shadow of Liberty* by Edward Corsi, pp. 54–55

### ACTIVITY OPTIONS

### SKILLBUILDER MINI-LESSON: TAKING NOTES

BLOCK SCHEDULING

**Explaining the Skill** Well-organized notes summarize the main ideas and important details in a reading assignment or a lecture. When taking notes from a book, students should first look at headings and key words. Remind them that maps, graphs, and photos may also include significant information.

**Applying the Skill** Ask students to take notes on the material on pages 614–615. They can use the headings in the text as the major headings in their notes. Remind them to be alert to the boldfaced terms and to the pictures and graphs. Notes need not be complete sentences. Then ask these questions:

1. What is the main idea in "The New Immigrants"? *(Before 1890, most immigrants came from northern and western Europe; after 1900, more southern and eastern Europeans came to the United States.)*
2. What general information can you gather from the keywords—Ellis Island and Angel Island—and from the graphs and pictures? *(Immigrants entered the country at two places; most came from Europe between 1841 and 1900.)*

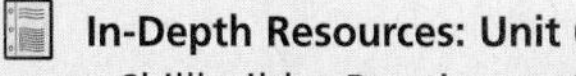

**In-Depth Resources: Unit 6**
- Skillbuilder Practice, p. 48

## MORE ABOUT . . .

**Sweatshops**

Sweatshops were makeshift factories set up in dimly lit, poorly ventilated buildings. Most sweatshops had only a half-dozen to a dozen workers, often women and children. They received low wages and worked long hours at top speed on a piecework basis. For example, a reformer reported in the 1880s that a typical young woman, Kate Crowley, sewed from 6 A.M. to 9 P.M. to earn 20 cents a day. Industries that relied on the sweatshop system included cigar making, bookbinding, and most of the garment trades.

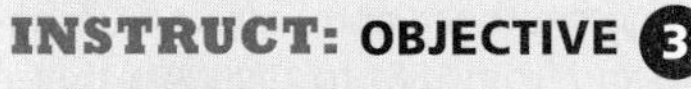

## INSTRUCT: OBJECTIVE 3

**Becoming Americans/ Restrictions on Immigration**

Key Questions

- What did the process of assimilation mean for the new immigrants?
- How did native-born Americans respond to the new immigrants?
- Why did the United States begin to restrict immigration in the 1880s?

**In-Depth Resources: Unit 6**
- Enrichment Activity, p. 60

### CRITICAL THINKING ACTIVITY

**Recognizing Effects** Have students examine how immigrants' places of origin affected where they settled in the United States. Use the following chart to help students organize the information.

| Place of Origin | Where They Settled |
|---|---|
| | |

**Class Time** 10 minutes

## ACTIVITY OPTIONS

## INDIVIDUAL NEEDS

### LESS PROFICIENT READERS

**Using the Narrative** After students read the section, explain that some of the information about the new immigrants is presented in the form of quotations. These quotations describe first-person experiences. As students read, have them look specifically for six quotes. Have volunteers identify the speaker in each case and his or her country of origin. Locate the country of origin on a world map. Then have students discuss how each quotation supports information in the section.

Labor unions helped immigrants fit into American life. The various languages on the signs at this rally show the ethnic diversity in the labor movement.

## Immigrants Take Tough Jobs

Immigrants took whatever jobs they could get. Many immigrants worked in Northern factories. As you read in Chapter 20, most factories offered low wages, long hours, and unsafe conditions. Many European immigrants who had settled in the East found jobs in sweatshops for about $10 a week. One observer of textile sweatshops noted, "The faces, hands, and arms to the elbows of everyone in the room are black with the color of the cloth on which they are working."

While European immigrants settled mostly in the East and Midwest, Asian immigrants settled mostly in the West. Many Chinese immigrants worked on the railroad. Others settled in Western cities where they set up businesses such as restaurants and stores. Large numbers of Japanese immigrants first came to Hawaii in 1885 to work on sugar plantations. Others settled on the mainland, where they fished, farmed, and worked in mines.

Immigrants from Mexico came to the Southwest. Mexican immigration increased after 1910 when revolution in that country forced people to flee. Growers and ranchers in California and Texas used the cheap labor Mexican immigrants offered. Owners of copper mines in Arizona hired Mexicans as well.

*Reading* **History**

**B. Making Inferences** What did all the immigrants seem to have in common?

**B. Answer** They settled near where they first entered the United States, and they took whatever kind of work needed cheap laborers.

## 3 Becoming Americans

Some Americans have described the United States as a **melting pot,** or a place where cultures blend. The new immigrants blended into American society as earlier immigrants had. This process of blending into society is called **assimilation.** Most new immigrants were eager to assimilate. To do so, they studied English and how to be American citizens.

Many workers began to assimilate at work. Employers and labor unions both tried to "Americanize" immigrant workers by offering classes in citizenship and English. A Lithuanian worker explained that his labor union helped him learn to "read and speak and enjoy life like an American." He then became an interpreter for the union to help other Lithuanians become Americans.

At the same time the immigrants were learning about America, they were also *changing* America. Immigrants did not give up their cultures right away. Bits and pieces of immigrant languages, foods, and music worked their way into the rest of American culture.

Despite their efforts to assimilate, immigrants faced prejudice from native-born Americans. Many Protestants feared the arrival of Catholics and Jews. Other native-born Americans thought immigrants would not fit into democratic society because they would be controlled by political machines. Such prejudices led some native-born Americans to push for restrictions to reduce the numbers of new immigrants coming to America.

**Now and then**

**LATE 20TH-CENTURY IMMIGRATION**

Historians refer to the people who came to the United States around 1900 as the "new immigrants." But an even newer wave of immigrants has been coming to the United States since the 1980s.

From 1981 to 1996, nearly 13.5 million people immigrated to the United States. About 6.5 million came from other nations in the Western Hemisphere. In the same period, 4.8 million people came from Asia.

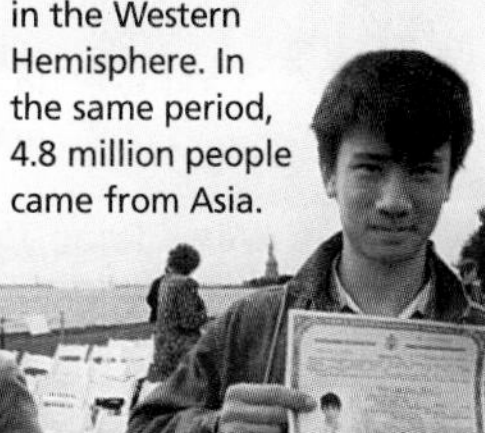

## Restrictions on Immigration

Many native-born Americans also feared they would have to compete with immigrants for jobs. Immigrants were desperate for jobs and would often take work for lower wages in worse conditions than other Americans. Some Americans worried that there would not be enough jobs for everyone.

In 1882, Congress began to pass laws to restrict immigration. They placed taxes on new immigrants and banned specific groups, such as beggars and people with diseases. Nonwhites faced deeper prejudice than European immigrants, and Asians faced some of the worst. In 1882, Congress passed the **Chinese Exclusion Act**. It banned Chinese immigration for ten years.

**Background** The Chinese Exclusion Act was renewed in 1892. In 1902, the ban was made permanent. It was not repealed until 1943.

The Chinese Exclusion Act was not the only example of prejudice in America around 1900. As you will read in the next section, racial discrimination was common throughout the United States.

### Section 2 Assessment

**1. Terms & Names**

**Identify:**
- new immigrants
- Ellis Island
- Angel Island
- melting pot
- assimilation
- Chinese Exclusion Act

**2. Taking Notes**

Use a chart to take notes on immigrant experiences in the United States.

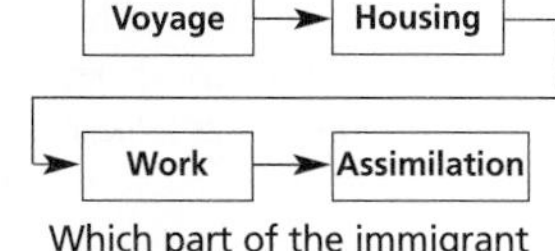


Which part of the immigrant experience was the most difficult?

**3. Main Ideas**

a. How were the new immigrants different from earlier immigrants?

b. How did immigrants support one another?

c. Why did nonwhite immigrants have a harder time assimilating than European immigrants did?

**4. Critical Thinking**

**Making Generalizations** How well does the idea of the melting pot reflect U.S. immigration around 1900?

**THINK ABOUT**
- assimilation
- immigrant languages and cultures
- ethnic neighborhoods

**ACTIVITY OPTIONS**

**MATH**
**GEOGRAPHY**

Research immigration to your city or state. Create a **spreadsheet** of this information or draw a **map** showing immigration routes.





### Now and then

**Late 20th-Century Immigration**

In 1965, the United States eliminated racial and ethnic criteria from its immigration laws. In 1990, the Immigration Reform and Control Act gave amnesty to millions of undocumented residents. It increased the number of immigrants allowed each year and reaffirmed preferences for relatives of U.S. citizens and resident aliens. Recent grounds for excluding some immigrants include communicable diseases, physical or mental disorders, being a danger to others, drug addiction or drug trafficking, and illiteracy.

## ASSESS & RETEACH

**Setting the Stage** Have students fill in the second block on the chapter graphic organizer with information from this section.

 **Formal Assessment**
- Section Quiz, p. 311

**RETEACHING ACTIVITY**

Divide the class into three groups. Ask the students in each group to outline the material for one of the three objectives in the section. Create a master outline on the board, incorporating the main points from each subsection.

 **In-Depth Resources: Unit 6**
- Reteaching Activity, p. 57

### Section 2 Assessment

**1. Terms & Names**

**new immigrants,** p. 614
**Ellis Island,** p. 614
**Angel Island,** p. 615
**melting pot,** p. 616
**assimilation,** p. 616
**Chinese Exclusion Act,** p. 617

**2. Taking Notes**

Voyage: long trip; forced to wait in immigration center; Housing: ethnic neighborhoods; Work: took jobs in any industry that was hiring; low wages; Assimilation: learned U.S. politics, culture, and language Students might say the voyage because it was hard, or assimilation because it lasted for years.

**3. Main Ideas**

**a.** They came from southern and eastern Europe versus the earlier ones who came from northern and western Europe. **b.** They helped each other find housing and work and settled together in neighborhoods. **c.** because they were easier to target with discrimination

**4. Critical Thinking**

accurate because many aspects of immigrant cultures were accepted, or inaccurate because ethnic neighborhoods persisted

**ACTIVITY OPTIONS**

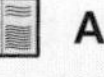 **Alternative Assessment**
- Rubrics, 5.6, 2.1

## Literature Connections

**OBJECTIVE**

Students analyze a passage from historical fiction depicting the situations and events that took place during the San Francisco earthquake and their impact on the city's inhabitants.

 **BLOCK SCHEDULING**

## FOCUS & MOTIVATE

**Drawing Conclusions** To help students picture the events in *Dragonwings,* have them study the photograph on page 619 and answer the following questions:

1. What evidence of destruction do you see in the photograph?
2. What effect do you think this event might have on people throughout San Francisco?

### MORE ABOUT . . .

***Dragonwings***

In this historical novel, a young Chinese immigrant comes to San Francisco at the turn of the century to join his father, Windrider. As they pursue long-held dreams, the father and son meet both dangerous people and new friends. One of the historical events described in the novel is the San Francisco earthquake of 1906.

### MORE ABOUT . . .

**The San Francisco Earthquake**

The earthquake struck San Francisco at 5:13 A.M. on April 18, 1906. Fires broke out across the city when gas lines ruptured and gas lamps overturned, setting the escaping gas alight. Because the water mains were also damaged, there was no way to fight the fires. The city burned for three days.



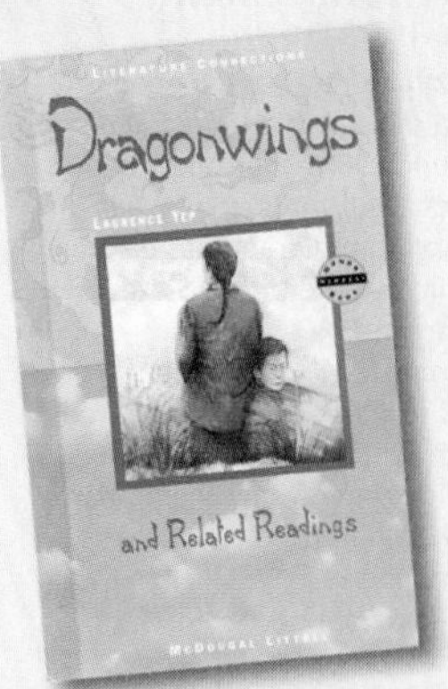

# from Dragonwings

### by Laurence Yep

**In 1903, eight-year-old Moon Shadow makes the long journey from China to join his father in San Francisco. After living for a time in Chinatown, the two move into a white neighborhood where Moon Shadow's father takes a job as a handyman working for Miss Whitlaw, who runs a boarding house for elderly people. Moon Shadow makes friends with Miss Whitlaw's niece Robin. In April of 1906, their world is turned upside down. As Moon Shadow goes outside to fetch water from the pump, an earthquake hits San Francisco, endangering rich and poor, young and old, American and immigrant alike.**

The morning was filled with that soft, gentle twilight of spring, when everything is filled with soft, dreamy colors and shapes; so when the earthquake hit, I did not believe it at first. It seemed like a nightmare where everything you take to be the rock-hard, solid basis for reality becomes unreal.

Wood and stone and brick and the very earth became fluidlike. The pail beneath the pump jumped and rattled like a spider dancing on a hot stove. The ground deliberately seemed to slide right out from under me. I landed on my back hard enough to drive the wind from my lungs. The whole world had become unglued. Our stable and Miss Whitlaw's house and the tenements to either side heaved and bobbed up and down, riding the ground like ships on a heavy sea. Down the alley mouth, I could see the cobblestone street **undulate**[1] and twist like a red-backed snake.

From inside our stable, I could hear the cups and plates begin to rattle on their shelves, and the equipment on Father's work table clattered and rumbled **ominously.**[2]

Suddenly the door banged open and Father stumbled out with his clothes all in a bundle. "It's an earthquake, I think," he shouted. He had washed his hair the night before and had not had time to twist it into a **queue,**[3] so it hung down his back long and black.

He looked around in the back yard. It was such a wide, open space that we were fairly safe there. Certainly more safe than in the frame doorway of our stable. He got into his pants and shirt and then his socks and boots.

"Do you think one of the mean dragons is doing all this?" I asked him.

"Maybe. Maybe not." Father had sat down to stuff his feet into his boots. "Time to wonder about that later. Now you wait here."

He started to get to his feet when the second tremor shook and he fell forward flat on his face. I heard the city bells ringing. They were rung by no human hand—the earthquake had just shaken them in their steeples. The second tremor was worse than the first. From all over came an immense wall of noise: of metal tearing, of bricks crashing, of wood breaking free from wood nails, and all. Everywhere, what man had built came undone. I was looking at a tenement house to our right and it just seemed to shudder and then collapse. One moment there were solid wooden walls and the next moment it had fallen with the cracking of wood and the tinkling of glass and the screams of people inside.

1. **undulate:** to move like a wave.
2. **ominously:** threateningly.
3. **queue:** a long braid of hair hanging down the back.



### ACTIVITY OPTIONS

### INDIVIDUAL NEEDS

**LESS PROFICIENT READERS**

**Building Language Skills** This passage makes extensive use of descriptive words (adjectives) and similes. Explain to students that a simile is a comparison. Encourage them to find the similes in the first column—"like a nightmare"; "like a spider"; "like ships on a heavy sea"; "like a red-backed snake." Discuss why the author uses such comparisons. How do they make it easier to imagine what Moon Shadow was experiencing? Encourage students to invent some similes of their own for the experience of being in an earthquake or other violent natural event.

The author uses another device—italics—to highlight words that would have been spoken in English. Ask students what language they think Moon Shadow and his father would have used when speaking to each other. *(Chinese)* Ask what language the father and Miss Whitlaw would have used. *(English)* Ask them to find the statements in italics and to explain why they would have been in English.

Mercifully, for a moment, it was lost to view in the cloud of dust that rose up. The debris surged against Miss Whitlaw's fence and toppled it over with a creak and a groan and a crash. I saw an arm sticking up from the mound of rubble and the hand was twisted at an impossible angle from the wrist. Coughing, Father pulled at my arm. "Stay here now," he ordered and started for Miss Whitlaw's.

I turned. Her house was still standing, but the tenement house to the left had partially collapsed; the wall on our side and part of the front and back had just fallen down, revealing the apartments within: the laundry hanging from lines, the old brass beds, and a few lucky if astonished people just looking out dazedly on what had once been walls. I could see Jack sitting up in bed with his two brothers. His mother and father were standing by the bed holding on to Maisie. Their whole family crowded into a tiny two-room apartment. Then they were gone, disappearing in a cloud of dust and debris as the walls and floor collapsed. Father held me as I cried.

Miss Whitlaw came out onto her porch in her nightdress and a shawl. She pulled the shawl tighter about her shoulders. *"Are you all right?"*

*"Yes,"* Father said, patting me on the back. "Aren't we, Moon Shadow?"

"Yes." I wiped my eyes on my sleeves.

*"Is everyone okay inside?"* Father asked Miss Whitlaw.

She nodded. We joined her on the porch and walked with her into her house. Robin was sitting on the stairs that led up to the second floor. She huddled up, looking no longer like the noisy, **boisterous**[4] girl I knew. The front door was open before her. She must have gone outside to look. *"Just about the whole street's gone."*

From up the stairs we could hear the **querulous**[5] old voices of the boarders demanding to know what had happened. Miss Whitlaw shouted up the stairs, "Everything's all right."

*"Are you sure?"* Father asked quietly.

Miss Whitlaw laughed. *"From top to bottom. Papa always built well. He said he wanted a house that could hold a herd of thundering elephants—that was what he always called Mama's folks. He never liked them much."*

*"It's gone,"* Robin repeated. *"Just about the whole street's gone."*

*"Oh, really now."* Miss Whitlaw walked past Robin. We followed her out the front door to the front porch. Robin was right.

4. **boisterous:** loud, noisy.

5. **querulous:** complaining.

San Franciscans watch the destruction caused by the 1906 earthquake and the resulting fire.

**CONNECT TO HISTORY**

1. **Finding Main Ideas** How does the earthquake affect the neighborhood that Moon Shadow lives in?

See Skillbuilder Handbook, page R5.

**CONNECT TO TODAY**

2. **Researching** What happened in San Francisco after the quake? Did it affect the immigrants differently than others?

Visit www.mcdougallittell.com to learn more about the San Francisco earthquake.

619

## INSTRUCT

Key Questions

- Why do you think Moon Shadow asks his father if "one of the mean dragons is doing all this"?
- Why was Miss Whitlaw's boarding house undamaged while the surrounding tenements collapsed?
- What do you think will happen next to the characters in this story?

### MAKING PERSONAL CONNECTIONS

Ask students to think about how people in their communities prepare for a natural disaster such as the one described in this selection. How can they find information about disaster relief centers in their cities and communities? What can they do to make that information available to people in their neighborhoods?

### VOCABULARY ACTIVITY

Ask students to identify some of the vivid words that the author uses to describe Moon Shadow's experience. Ask them to list five details that make the earthquake seem real to the reader.

### HISTORY FROM VISUALS

**Interpreting the Photograph** Have students identify details in the photograph that reflect this fictional account of the San Francisco earthquake. **Possible Responses** Buildings are destroyed; smoke or clouds of dust loom in the background; people are in the streets staring at the rubble.

### CONNECT TO HISTORY

1. **Finding Main Ideas** **Possible Response** It destroys the tenements that are less well built than Miss Whitlaw's boarding house. Many people inside are killed when their buildings collapse.

### CONNECT TO TODAY

2. **Researching** Students should use the Internet and books in the school library to find out what happened to San Francisco after the earthquake. (One excellent eyewitness account was written by Jack London.) Answers can focus on how the city was rebuilt, including such dangerous errors as pushing the rubble into San Francisco Bay and building new structures on it. Despite the disaster, the city revived its plan to hold the World's Fair in 1915.

## SECTION OBJECTIVES

1. To understand how racism caused discrimination and the spread of segregation
2. To describe the impact of *Plessy* v. *Ferguson* and explain why African Americans organized
3. To understand the effects of violence and racism throughout the country

**CRITICAL THINKING**

Recognizing Effects, p. 621
Identifying Problems, p. 621
Making Inferences, p. 622
Solving Problems, p. 623

## FOCUS & MOTIVATE

### 5-MINUTE WARM-UP

**Making Inferences** These questions focus on segregation in schools.

1. Look at the photograph on page 621. What can you infer from the photograph about conditions in this school?
2. What factors might explain why this school had few books and little furniture?

 **Warm-Up Transparency WT21**

## INSTRUCT

### INSTRUCT: OBJECTIVE 1

**Racism Causes Discrimination/ Segregation Expands in the South**

Key Questions

- How did inaccurate science contribute to racism?
- How did Southern states begin to restrict African Americans' rights after the end of Reconstruction?
- What were the effects of Jim Crow laws and segregation in the South?

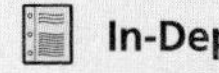 **In-Depth Resources: Unit 6**
- Guided Reading, p. 45

**Reading Study Guide** (Spanish and English), pp. 209–210

# 3 Segregation and Discrimination

**TERMS & NAMES**
racial discrimination
Jim Crow
segregation
*Plessy* v. *Ferguson*
Booker T. Washington
W. E. B. Du Bois
NAACP
Ida B. Wells

| MAIN IDEA | WHY IT MATTERS NOW |
|---|---|
| Racial discrimination ran through American society in the late 19th and early 20th centuries. | Modern American society continues to face the problems caused by racism and discrimination. |

### ONE AMERICAN'S STORY

**African-American sisters Bessie and Sadie Delany grew up in Raleigh, North Carolina, at the turn of the century. Almost 100 years later, they still remembered their first taste of racial discrimination, different treatment on the basis of race.**

*A VOICE FROM THE PAST*

We were about five and seven years old at the time. Mama and Papa used to take us to Pullen Park in Raleigh for picnics, and that particular day, the trolley driver told us to go to the back. We children objected loudly, because we always liked to sit in the front, where the breeze would blow your hair. That had been part of the fun for us. But Mama and Papa just gently told us to hush and took us to the back without making a fuss.

**Sarah L. Delany and A. Elizabeth Delany,** *Having Our Say*

Bessie (left) and Sadie Delany

**Millions of Americans were familiar with the racial discrimination described by the Delanys. As you will read in this section, it was common throughout the United States.**

## 1 Racism Causes Discrimination

As you read in earlier chapters, racist attitudes had been developing in America since the introduction of slavery. The low social rank held by slaves led many whites to believe that whites were superior to blacks. Whites held similar attitudes towards Asians, Native Americans, and Latin Americans. Even most scientists of the day believed that whites were superior to nonwhites. However, no scientists believe this today.

Such attitudes led whites to discriminate against nonwhites across the country. The most obvious example of racial discrimination was in the South. Southern blacks had their first taste of political power during Reconstruction. (See Chapter 18.) But when Reconstruction ended in 1877, Southern states began to restrict African Americans' rights.



### RECOMMENDED RESOURCES

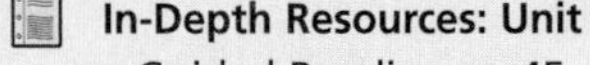

**In-Depth Resources: Unit 6**
- Guided Reading, p. 45
- Building Vocabulary, p. 47
- Primary Source, p. 52
- Reteaching Activity, p. 58

**Reading Study Guide** (Spanish and English), pp. 209–210

**America's History Makers**
- W. E. B. Du Bois, pp. 85–86

**American History Plays**
- *Daniel Hale Williams, Pioneer Surgeon* by Mary Satchell

**Citizenship Today,** pp. 91–92

**Formal Assessment**
- Section Quiz, p. 312

**Alternative Assessment**
- Rubrics, 4.4
- Rubrics, 5.1

**Access for Students Acquiring English/ESL**
- Guided Reading, p. 142

**Technology Resources**

 **Electronic Teacher Tools with Test Maker**

 **ClassZone**
www.mcdougallittell.com

## Segregation Expands in the South

One way for whites to weaken African-American political power was to restrict their voting rights. For example, Southern states passed laws that set up literacy, or reading, tests and poll taxes to prevent African Americans from voting. White officials made sure that blacks failed literacy tests by giving unfair exams. For example, white officials sometimes gave blacks tests written in Latin. Poll taxes kept many blacks from voting because they didn't have enough cash to pay the tax.

Such laws threatened to prevent poor whites from voting, too. To keep them from losing the vote, several Southern states added grandfather clauses to their constitutions. Grandfather clauses stated that a man could vote if he or an ancestor, such as a grandfather, had been eligible to vote before 1867. Before that date, most African Americans, free or enslaved, did not have the right to vote. Whites could use the grandfather clause to protect their voting rights. Blacks could not.

*Reading* **History**

**A. Recognizing Effects** What was the purpose behind literacy tests, poll taxes, and grandfather clauses?

A. Answer to prevent African Americans from voting without preventing poor whites from voting

In addition to voting restrictions, African Americans faced Jim Crow laws. **Jim Crow** laws were meant to enforce **segregation,** or separation, of white and black people in public places. As a result, separate schools, trolley seats, and restrooms were common throughout the South.

## 2 *Plessy* v. *Ferguson*

African Americans resisted segregation, but they had little power to stop it. In 1892, Homer Plessy, an African American, sued a railroad company, arguing that segregated seating violated his Fourteenth Amendment right to "equal protection of the laws."

In 1896, the case of ***Plessy* v. *Ferguson*** reached the Supreme Court. The Court ruled against Plessy. It argued that "separate but equal" facilities did not violate the Fourteenth Amendment. This decision allowed Southern states to maintain segregated institutions.

*Reading* **History**

**B. Identifying Problems** Why was a policy of "separate but equal" unfair?

B. Answer Separate facilities were almost never equal, with black facilities typically being inferior.

But the separate facilities were not equal. White-controlled governments and companies allowed the facilities for African Americans to decay. African Americans would have to organize to fight for equality.

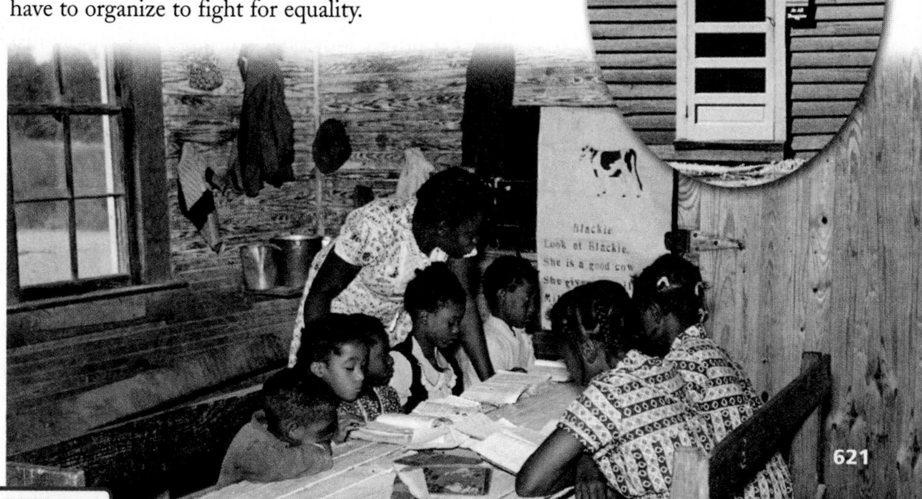


Segregation forced African Americans to use separate entrances from whites and to attend separate, usually inferior, schools like the one shown below.

621

### MORE ABOUT . . .

**Jim Crow Laws**

"Jim Crow" was a character in a minstrel show who did a song-and-dance routine with the chorus "Jump, Jim Crow!" The name eventually came to be a denigrating term for "African American" and was used as a label for the new segregation laws.

### INSTRUCT: OBJECTIVE 

***Plessy* v. *Ferguson*/ African Americans Organize**

Key Questions

- What were the social and political effects of *Plessy* v. *Ferguson* on African-American life?
- How did Booker T. Washington and W. E. B. Du Bois differ in their approaches to achieving equality for African Americans?

 **In-Depth Resources: Unit 6**

- Primary Source, p. 52

### MORE ABOUT . . .

**Homer Plessy**

In 1890, Louisiana passed a law requiring separate compartments in railway cars for whites and African Americans. Homer Plessy, a shoemaker, joined a committee of African Americans who planned to test the constitutionality of the law. Plessy, who claimed to be one-eighth African American, sat in the "white" car for a train trip from New Orleans to Covington, Louisiana, and refused to move. He was arrested and then proceeded to take his case through the Louisiana courts and finally to the Supreme Court.

 **Citizenship Today,** pp. 91–92

### ACTIVITY OPTIONS

### INDIVIDUAL NEEDS: GIFTED AND TALENTED

**THE SUPREME COURT AND SEGREGATION**

**Class Time** Two class periods

**Task** Analyzing the effect of Supreme Court rulings on segregation

**Purpose** To familiarize students with two landmark Supreme Court rulings on segregation in the United States

**Supplies Needed**

- Reference materials on *Plessy* v. *Ferguson* (1896) and *Brown* v. *Board of Education of Topeka* (1954)
- Internet access for additional resources
- Writing materials

**Activity** Have students begin by doing additional research on *Plessy* v. *Ferguson* and on the key 1954 Supreme Court decision that reversed *Plessy*'s principle of "separate but equal," *Brown* v. *Board of Education of Topeka.* Students might also research the effects of the 1954 decision on school systems in their own communities. Finally, students should write "legal briefs" summarizing the two Court opinions.

## MORE ABOUT . . .

**Booker T. Washington**

Booker T. Washington (1856–1915) believed that economic progress, not civil and political rights, was the key to improving the lives of African Americans. Unlike Du Bois, Washington believed that African Americans could benefit more from practical, vocational training than from a liberal arts education. Washington's approach won support from influential white leaders—from John D. Rockefeller to Theodore Roosevelt, who invited him to the White House in 1901, causing an uproar among segregationists.

## AMERICA'S HISTORY MAKERS

**W. E. B. Du Bois**

W. E. B. Du Bois was born in Great Barrington, Massachusetts, and graduated from Fisk University. In 1895, he earned a Ph.D. from Harvard University, the first African American to do so. In his 1903 book *The Souls of Black Folk,* Du Bois argued that the greatest force for human progress was "the power of the ballot." Committed to political action, Du Bois criticized Booker T. Washington's approach as a materialistic "gospel of work and money."

**Possible Response: Students might suggest that the Talented Tenth would be successful in disproving white stereotypes of most African Americans.**

 **America's History Makers**
- W. E. B. Du Bois, pp. 85–86

## INSTRUCT: OBJECTIVE 

**Violence in the South and North/ Racism in the West**

Key Questions
- What was the purpose of the violence aimed at African Americans in the South?
- What were similarities and differences between racism in the North and in the South?
- How did racism affect immigrants and citizens of Asian and Mexican ancestry?

## African Americans Organize

**Booker T. Washington** was an early leader in the effort to achieve equality. He had been born into slavery. But after the Civil War, he became a teacher. In 1881, he founded the Tuskegee Institute in Alabama to help African Americans learn trades and gain economic strength. Washington hired talented teachers and scholars, such as George Washington Carver.

**Background** Carver made important discoveries to improve farming.

To gain white support for Tuskegee, Washington did not openly challenge segregation. As he said in an 1895 speech in Atlanta, in "purely social matters" whites and blacks "can be as separate as the fingers, yet one as the hand in all things essential to mutual progress."

However, some blacks disagreed with Washington's views. **W. E. B. Du Bois** (doo•BOYS) encouraged African Americans to reject segregation.

*A VOICE FROM THE PAST*

Is it possible . . . that nine millions of men can make effective progress in economic lines if they are deprived of political rights? . . . If history and reason give any distinct answer to these questions, it is an emphatic *No.*

**W. E. B. Du Bois,** *The Souls of Black Folk*

***Reading*History** **C. Making Inferences** In what way did Washington and Du Bois disagree about how to achieve African-American progress?

C. Possible Response Washington emphasized economic growth over social equality. Du Bois thought it was more important to end segregation immediately.

**AMERICA'S HISTORY MAKERS**

**W. E. B. DU BOIS**
**1868–1963**

W. E. B. Du Bois grew up in a middle-class home. He went to college and earned his doctorate at Harvard. Du Bois became one of the most distinguished scholars of the 20th century.

Du Bois fought against segregation. He believed that the best way to end it would be to have educated African Americans lead the fight. He referred to this group of educated African Americans as the "Talented Tenth"—the most educated 10 percent of African Americans.

**Why do you think Du Bois believed the Talented Tenth should lead the fight against segregation?**

In 1909, Du Bois and other reformers founded the National Association for the Advancement of Colored People, or the **NAACP**. The NAACP played a major role in ending segregation in the 20th century.

## 3 Violence in the South and North

Besides discrimination, African Americans in the South also faced violence. The Ku Klux Klan, which first appeared during Reconstruction, used violence to keep blacks from challenging segregation. More than 2,500 African Americans were lynched between 1885 and 1900.

**Ida B. Wells,** an African-American journalist from Memphis, led the fight against lynching. After three of her friends were lynched in 1892, she mounted an anti-lynching campaign in her newspaper. When whites called for Wells herself to be lynched, she moved to Chicago. But she continued her work against lynching. (See Interactive Primary Sources, page 624.)

Like Wells, many blacks moved north to escape discrimination. Public facilities there were not segregated by law. But Northern whites still discriminated against blacks. Blacks could not get housing in white neighborhoods and usually were denied good jobs. Anti-black feelings among whites sometimes led to violence. In 1908, whites in Springfield, Illinois, attacked blacks who had moved there. The whites lynched two blacks within a half mile of Abraham Lincoln's home.



**ACTIVITY OPTIONS**

**INTERDISCIPLINARY LINK: GOVERNMENT/CIVICS** — **BLOCK SCHEDULING**

### A TASK FORCE FOR PROGRESS

**Class Time** One class period

**Task** Working as a task force to set priorities for a goal

**Purpose** To analyze the relative importance of three approaches to social change at the turn of the century

**Supplies Needed**
- Reference material about racial discrimination toward African Americans at the turn of the century
- Information about Booker T. Washington, W. E. B. Du Bois, and Ida B. Wells

**Activity** Divide the class into three groups. Explain that three leading black activists each gave priority to a different aspect of the struggle for equal rights—economic improvement (Booker T. Washington), political and intellectual activism (W. E. B. Du Bois), and a campaign against violence (Ida B. Wells). Assign each group one of these leaders and tell the group to work as a task force to advocate for that leader's approach. Let each group present its position to the class.

## Racism in the West

Chinese immigrants who came to the West in the 1800s also faced severe discrimination. Chinese laborers received lower wages than whites for the same work. Sometimes, Chinese workers faced violence. In 1885, white workers in Rock Springs, Wyoming, refused to work in the same mine as Chinese workers. The whites stormed through the Chinese part of town, shooting Chinese people and burning buildings. During the attack, 28 Chinese people were killed and 15 were wounded.

At the same time, Mexicans and African Americans who came to the American Southwest were forced into peonage (PEE•uh•nihj). In this system of labor, people are forced to work until they have paid off debts. Congress outlawed peonage in 1867, but some workers were still forced to work to repay debts. In 1911, the U.S. Supreme Court declared such labor to be the same as peonage. As a result, the Court struck down such forms of labor as a violation of the Thirteenth Amendment.

Despite the problems caused by racism, many Americans had new opportunities to enjoy their lives at the turn of the century. In the next section, you will learn about changes in people's daily lives.

**The Workingmen's Party of California produced this anti-Chinese poster during the 1880s.**

**Background**
The Thirteenth Amendment banned "involuntary servitude"—another term for slavery.

### Section 3 Assessment

**1. Terms & Names**

**Identify:**
- racial discrimination
- Jim Crow
- segregation
- *Plessy* v. *Ferguson*
- Booker T. Washington
- W. E. B. Du Bois
- NAACP
- Ida B. Wells

**2. Taking Notes**

Use a chart to identify people and events related to racial discrimination at the turn of the century.

| People | |
|---|---|
| Events | |

Which person do you think did the most to end racial discrimination?

**3. Main Ideas**

a. What were Jim Crow laws?

b. How did discrimination against African Americans in the North differ from discrimination in the South?

c. What did Chinese immigrants and Mexican immigrants have in common?

**4. Critical Thinking**

**Solving Problems** What could have been done to end racial discrimination against nonwhites in the United States at the turn of the century?

**THINK ABOUT**
- attitudes of whites about nonwhites
- the efforts of nonwhites to find jobs and security
- competition for jobs

**ACTIVITY OPTIONS**

**LANGUAGE ARTS**
**TECHNOLOGY**

Research a civil rights leader from the turn of the century. Write a short **biography** of that person or design a **Web site** devoted to the work of that person.



### MORE ABOUT . . .

**Chinese in America**

The Chinese immigrant population in the United States grew from 7,520 in 1850 to more than 100,000 by 1880. Chinese workers formed a major part of the labor force in the West. In addition to working on the transcontinental railroad, Chinese workers were indispensable to important industries in California. For example, about one-third of all woolen mill operators and more than one-half of all shoemakers were Chinese. Yet in 1882, Congress declared all these immigrants "aliens ineligible for citizenship" because they were not white. Japanese immigrants were later declared ineligible as well.

## ASSESS & RETEACH

**Setting the Stage** Have students fill in the section on the graphic organizer that applies to this section.

 **Formal Assessment**
- Section Quiz, p. 312

### RETEACHING ACTIVITY

Have students create an annotated time line of the major events discussed in this section, beginning with the end of Reconstruction in 1877 and ending with the 1911 Supreme Court decision that struck down labor performed to repay debts as peonage. Display the time line in class and encourage students to make up questions that can be answered by annotations on the time line.

 **In-Depth Resources: Unit 6**
- Reteaching Activity, p. 58

### Section 3 Assessment

**1. Terms & Names**

**racial discrimination,** p. 620
**Jim Crow,** p. 621
**segregation,** p. 621
***Plessy* v. *Ferguson*,** p. 621
**Booker T. Washington,** p. 622
**W. E. B. Du Bois,** p. 622
**NAACP,** p. 622
**Ida B. Wells,** p. 622

**2. Taking Notes**

People: Homer Plessy; Ida B. Wells; Booker T. Washington; W. E. B. Du Bois; Events: *Plessy* v. *Ferguson* (1896); Springfield, Illinois, race riot (1908); founding of NAACP (1909); Rock Springs massacre (1885).

Student responses will vary.

**3. Main Ideas**

**a.** laws, mostly in the South, that segregated whites and blacks in public places **b.** no segregation laws, but informal segregation created segregated neighborhoods **c.** Both settled mostly in the American West, took low-paying jobs, and faced racial discrimination.

**4. Critical Thinking**

Nonwhites needed to work together to fight against discrimination. Wages for all people needed to be equal to control job competition.

**ACTIVITY OPTIONS**

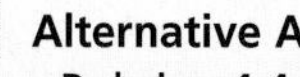 **Alternative Assessment**
- Rubrics, 4.4, 5.1

## INTERACTIVE PRIMARY SOURCES

**OBJECTIVE**
Students will be able to analyze the account of the lynchings and explain Wells's viewpoint.

Primary Source Explorer
- *Crusade for Justice* by Ida B. Wells
- *Like Country Pretty Much* by Kee Low

The Explorer will help students select and produce their own presentations.

Specific information about the document can be found in **A Closer Look.** To learn more about key people and events of the time, students should click on **Life in These Times. What Happened Next** will show the student the impact of the document and tie it to today.

## FOCUS & MOTIVATE

**Drawing Conclusions** Ask students to read the title of the selection and "Setting the Stage." Ask them to define *autobiography.* Discuss how an autobiography might differ from some of the primary sources they have used before.

### MORE ABOUT . . .

**The Great Migration**
An African American from Mississippi who moved to Chicago wrote home to a friend, "I just begin to feel like a man. It's a great pleasure knowing that you have got some privilege. My children are going to the same school with whites and I don't have to [h]umble to no one. I have registered—Will vote in the next election."

## INSTRUCT

Key Questions
- Why were the black storeowners "made to feel that they were not welcome"?
- What was the main idea of the lead article in Wells's newspaper?
- Why did the lynching change "the whole course" of Ida B. Wells's life?

---

INTERACTIVE PRIMARY SOURCES

# from *Crusade for Justice*

**Setting the Stage** Ida B. Wells was the editor of the *Free Speech and Headlight,* a small Baptist newspaper in Memphis, Tennessee. She used the paper to attack the evils of Jim Crow, especially lynching. In her autobiography, *Crusade for Justice,* she described the events that led to the lynching of three of her friends. **See Primary Source Explorer**

While I was thus carrying on the work of my newspaper . . . there came the lynching in Memphis which changed the whole course of my life. . . .

Thomas Moss, Calvin McDowell, and Henry Stewart owned and operated a grocery store. . . . There was already a grocery owned and operated by a white man who **hitherto**[1] had had a **monopoly**[2] on the trade of this thickly populated colored suburb. Thomas's grocery changed all that, and he and his **associates**[3] were made to feel that they were not welcome by the white grocer. . . .

About ten o'clock that [one Saturday] night, . . . shots rang out in the back room of the store. The men stationed there had seen several white men stealing through the rear door and fired on them without a moment's pause. Three of these men were wounded, and others fled and gave the alarm.

Sunday morning's paper came out with **lurid**[4] headlines telling how officers of the law had been wounded while in the **discharge**[5] of their duties. . . . The same newspaper told of the arrest and jailing of the **proprietor**[6] of the store and many of the colored people. . . .

On Tuesday following, . . . a body of picked [white] men was admitted to the jail. . . . This mob took out of their cells Thomas Moss, Calvin McDowell, and Henry Stewart. . . . They were loaded on a switch engine of the railroad which ran back of the jail, carried a mile north of the city limits, and horribly shot to death.

Although stunned by the events of that hectic week, the *Free Speech* [Wells's newspaper] felt that it must carry on. Its [lead article] for that week said:

> The city of Memphis has demonstrated that neither character nor standing **avails**[7] the Negro if he dares to protect himself against the white man or become his rival. There is nothing we can do about the lynching now, as we are out-numbered and without arms. The white mob could help itself to ammunition without pay, but the order was rigidly enforced against the selling of guns to Negroes. There is therefore only one thing left that we can do; save our money and leave a town which will neither protect our lives and property, nor give us a fair trial in the courts, but takes us out and murders us in cold blood when accused by white persons.

**A CLOSER LOOK**
**ECONOMIC COMPETITION**
**Moss, McDowell, and Stewart were African Americans who opened a grocery store near a white-owned store in a black neighborhood.**
**1. Why might the opening of the black-owned grocery store lead to problems?**

**A CLOSER LOOK**
**LYNCHINGS**
**There was a sharp increase in the number of lynchings in the United States in the 1890s. From 1891 to 1900, more than 1,100 African Americans were lynched.**
**2. Why do you think the number of lynchings increased in this period?**

**A CLOSER LOOK**
**THE GREAT MIGRATION**
**Between 1890 and 1920, hundreds of thousands of African Americans left the South to escape racism. This movement is called the Great Migration.**
**3. Why does Wells's newspaper advise African Americans to move away in the wake of the lynching?**

1. **hitherto:** until this time.
2. **monopoly:** exclusive control by one person or group.
3. **associates:** friends or partners.
4. **lurid:** causing shock or horror.
5. **discharge:** performance of duty.
6. **proprietor:** owner.
7. **avails:** helps.



---

### TEACHING STRATEGY

**Sequencing Events** To help students understand the sequence of events described in this excerpt, have them copy the graphic organizer on the right and use the information in Wells's account to complete it.

**Event 1:** Three black men start a grocery store that competes with a store owned by a white grocer. → **Event 2:** Several white men enter the back of the store at night. → **Event 3:** The storeowners shoot at the men. Three are wounded. → **Event 4:** The storeowners are arrested. → **Event 5:** A mob takes the three black men from the jail and kills them.

# Like Country Pretty Much

**Setting the Stage** Kee Low was a Chinese immigrant. He had come to the United States in 1876. He was interviewed in 1924 as part of a project by scholars to create a "Survey of Race Relations." This is an excerpt from that interview. In it, Kee Low tells his story. Despite the racism, he still "like country pretty much." **See Primary Source Explorer** CD-ROM

I arrived in San Francisco in 1876, 49 years ago. Come to San Francisco when country one hundred years old. People treat Chinese rotten then. Don't blame people much at that time. Chinese and European not educated as much then as today. More civilized today. People drive Chinese out of country. . . .

I was living on the waterfront, and they told me to get out one day. Sunday morning, they come together and drive Chinese out. . . . They want to get us out to San Francisco, to go on steamer, and we stayed on the **wharf**[1] all night, and they bring us little black coffee and little bread in morning. We pretty hungry. The last day, some of the citizens, Judge Greene, Judge Hanford, United States Attorney, nice fellow want to help us. . . . Judge Greene told the Chinese that those who wanted to stay and make good citizens could stay, and those who wanted to go could go. One half wanted to go, and one half wanted to stay. . . .

There were so many around the streets that they had to have somebody to protect these people. Some of the **hobos**[2] tried to make them go back to the wharf, but volunteers tried to keep these fellows away. They **commenced**[3] shooting and kill one of them. So Chinese people get excited when gun begin to sound, so they throw shoes, blankets and everything and run. I was uptown myself. I didn't intend to go. I ran outside to see what happened because I was so excited. . . . Call up one or two friends of mine and tell them get killed, and we better get out of the way. We run out in woods. Build fire. Pretty cold. I told friends, we got to protect ourselves. We got to get out of here.

1. **wharf:** landing place for ships.
2. **hobos:** homeless people.
3. **commenced:** began.

**A CLOSER LOOK**

**RACIST ATTITUDES**

Some people believe that racism is caused by ignorance.

**4. Why does Kee Low believe that discrimination against the Chinese was worse in the 1870s than in the 1920s?**

**A CLOSER LOOK**

**REASONS TO STAY**

Despite the violence that they faced for having Asian ancestry, half of the Chinese with Kee Low wanted to stay in the United States.

**5. Why do you think Asian-Americans stayed in the United States despite discrimination?**

*Interactive Primary Sources Assessment*

**1. Main Ideas**

a. What do the accounts of Wells and Low have in common?

b. How did the officers of the law behave differently in the report by Low than in the one by Wells?

c. What conclusions do Wells and Low come to about how someone should respond to discrimination?

**2. Critical Thinking**

**Forming and Supporting Opinions** Do you think Wells and Low were right to flee racism? Why?

**THINK ABOUT**

- the causes of racism
- the threat of violence to Wells and Low





## INSTRUCT

Key Questions

- Why would Kee Low's recollections have been useful to scholars creating a "Survey of Race Relations"?
- Why did half the Chinese immigrants decide to leave San Francisco?
- What does the excerpt show about race relations between Chinese immigrants and native-born Americans during this period?

### MAKING PERSONAL CONNECTIONS

To help students understand the situation that Kee Low faced, ask students to review what they read in Section 3 about the experiences of Chinese immigrants in America during this period. Write students' contributions on the board. After reading the excerpt, discuss the connections between the historical context and Kee Low's experience.

### A CLOSER LOOK

1. Economic competition often led to violence. The black-owned store competed directly with the white-owned store.
2. More blacks were beginning to make economic progress, and many racist whites wanted to stop them.
3. The paper suggests that African Americans are denied the ability to defend themselves and therefore must leave.
4. He believes that Chinese and Europeans were less educated in the 1870s, but they are more civilized today. That's what made racism worse in the 1870s.
5. Despite the discrimination, many Asians had already made new lives for themselves and did not want to go back to Asia.

## Interactive Primary Sources Assessment

**1. Main Ideas**

**a.** Both tell of violence against nonwhites caused by racism.

**b.** Wells tells of officers of the court acting against the African-American grocers. Low tells of judges giving Chinese immigrants an opportunity to stay in the United States.

**c.** Wells and Low both advise people to flee to a place where they won't be subject to racial violence.

**2. Critical Thinking**

Some students may say they were right to flee because they could not overcome racism on their own, and their lives were in danger. Other students might say that Wells and Low should have stayed and fought for their rights.

## SECTION OBJECTIVES

1. To understand how education and publishing grew during this period
2. To identify the impact of modern advertising and new products on people's lives
3. To trace the growth of leisure time activities
4. To describe popular leisure activities

**CRITICAL THINKING**

Summarizing, p. 627
Comparing and Contrasting, p. 628
Making Inferences, p. 629

**Why It Matters Now**
- The Modern Mass Culture, pp. 41–42

## FOCUS & MOTIVATE

### 5-MINUTE WARM-UP

**Making Inferences** These questions focus on leisure at the turn of the century.

1. Look at Leisure Activities shown on page 628. What does the development of leisure-time activities indicate about the economy?
2. Which of the activities illustrated are still popular today?

**Warm-Up Transparency WT21**

## INSTRUCT

### INSTRUCT: OBJECTIVE 1

**Education and Publishing Grow**

Key Questions
- What was the relationship between immigration and public education?
- How did the increase in public schools affect society?
- How did reading more newspapers affect people's lives?

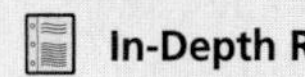

**In-Depth Resources: Unit 6**
- Guided Reading, p. 46

**Reading Study Guide** (Spanish and English), pp. 211–212

# 4 Society and Mass Culture

**TERMS & NAMES**
- mass culture
- Joseph Pulitzer
- William Randolph Hearst
- department store
- mail-order catalog
- leisure
- vaudeville
- ragtime

**MAIN IDEA**

Industrialization and new technologies created a mass culture in the United States.

**WHY IT MATTERS NOW**

Modern American mass culture had its beginnings during this period.

### ONE AMERICAN'S STORY

**Mary Ellen Chase dreaded her first day of teaching at a new school. Many of the boys were larger than she and were known to be troublemakers. But she would do her best to control the class.**

*A VOICE FROM THE PAST*

I stormed up and down. . . . This pathetic pretense of courage, aided by the mad flourishing of my razor strop, brought forth . . . the expression of respectful fear on the faces of the young giants.

**Mary Ellen Chase,** quoted in *The Good Old Days—They Were Terrible!*

**Students work on their lessons in this New York City classroom in 1906.**

**Discipline was a key goal of education in the 1800s. Education also helped create a common culture for the millions of Americans who went to school. In this section, you will learn how education helped create an American mass culture—a common culture experienced by large numbers of people.**

## 1 Education and Publishing Grow

Immigration caused enormous growth in American schools. To teach citizenship and English to immigrants, new city and state laws required children to attend school. Between 1880 and 1920, the number of children attending school more than doubled. To serve the growing number of students, the number of public high schools increased from 2,526 in 1890 to 14,326 in 1920.

The growth of education increased American literacy. Reading became more popular. Americans read large numbers of novels. Dime novels were especially popular. They sold for ten cents each and told exciting tales of romance and adventure, often set in the West or on the high seas.

Americans also read more newspapers. Tough competition pushed newspaper publishers to try all sorts of gimmicks to outsell their rivals. For example, **Joseph Pulitzer,** owner of the *New York World,* and



## RECOMMENDED RESOURCES

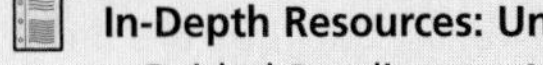

**In-Depth Resources: Unit 6**
- Guided Reading, p. 46
- Reteaching Activity, p. 59
- History Workshop Resources, p. 61

**Reading Study Guide** (Spanish and English), pp. 211–212

**Economics in History**
- The Rise of Department Stores, p. 21

**Why It Matters Now**
- The Modern Mass Culture, pp. 41–42

**Formal Assessment**
- Section Quiz, p. 313

**Alternative Assessment**
- Rubrics, 1.1
- Rubrics, 4.9

**Access for Students Acquiring English/ESL**
- Guided Reading, p. 143

**Technology Resources**

**Humanities Trans. HT41, HT42**
- Edison Concert Phonograph
- Football Game

**America's Music CD**

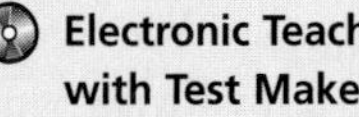

**Electronic Teacher Tools with Test Maker**

**ClassZone**
www.mcdougallittell.com

Background
By 1898, each of these newspapers sold more than a million copies a day.

**William Randolph Hearst,** owner of the *New York Morning Journal,* were fierce competitors. They filled the pages of their papers with spectacular stories. They also added special features, such as comics and sports.

## 2 Modern Advertising and New Products

Newspapers had a wide influence on American life, including the rise of modern advertising. Advertisers used images of celebrities in newspapers and magazines to tempt people to buy products. They advertised everything from cereal to jewelry to soap. Some ads played on people's fears. For example, advertisers might scare a young woman concerned about her appearance into buying a particular brand of face cream. Advertising was effective in turning brand names into household words.

Advertisements also helped people learn about new products. At the turn of the century, new inventions, such as the electric washing machine, promised to help people do their household chores more easily. Because women did most of these chores as well as most of the shopping, manufacturers marketed these new devices to women.

One of the places people could buy these—and many other—goods was in department stores. **Department stores** sold everything from clothing to furniture to hardware. The Chicago businessman Marshall Field discovered as a sales clerk that he could increase his sales by paying close attention to each woman customer. Field opened his own department store in downtown Chicago with the motto, "Give the lady what she wants."

People who did not live near a department store could order goods through the mail. Companies like Montgomery Ward and Sears Roebuck sent catalogs to customers. These **mail-order catalogs** included pictures and descriptions of merchandise. People could place their orders by mail, and the company would deliver the product. Richard Sears claimed that he sold 10,000 items a minute.

In 1896, the post office made it easier for people to receive goods through the mail by establishing a new delivery system. Rural free delivery brought packages directly to homes in rural areas. Now people in these areas could get the same goods as people in the cities.

A. Answers Department stores and mail-order catalogs supplied a variety of consumer desires; rural free delivery brought goods to remote places; and advertising convinced people to want new products.

*Reading* **History**
**A. Summarizing** What developments changed American methods of selling at the turn of the century?

**STRANGE *but* True**

**BICYCLES TO AIRPLANES**

At the turn of the century, two bicycle mechanics invented a machine that would help advertisers and businessmen reach new customers. In 1892, Orville and Wilbur Wright opened a bicycle shop in Ohio. They used the profits to fund experiments in aeronautics, the construction of aircraft.

In 1903, the Wright brothers took a gasoline-powered airplane that they had designed to a sandy hill outside Kitty Hawk, North Carolina. On December 17 of that year, Orville made the first successful flight of a powered aircraft in history. By 1918, the U.S. Postal Service began airmail service that made it faster and easier for people to get goods.

## 3 Urban Parks and World's Fairs

Advertising and shopping were not the only daily activities changing at this time. **Leisure,** or free time, activities also changed. In cities, new parks provided people with entertainment. The increasing number of people working in factories and offices liked going to parks to get some sunshine and fresh air. Parks helped bring grass and trees back into city landscapes.

627



**INSTRUCT: OBJECTIVE 2**

**Modern Advertising and New Products**
Key Questions
- How did advertisers seek to influence people?
- What new ways of merchandising developed?
- What do these developments suggest about life in America during this period?

**Economics in History**
- The Rise of Department Stores, p. 21

**STRANGE *but* True**

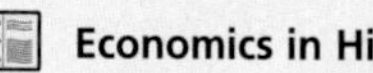

**Bicycles to Airplanes**

The Wright brothers knew that they needed strong and steady winds to fly their airplane. They obtained a list of windy places in the United States from the U.S. Weather Bureau. They selected Kitty Hawk from that list. When Orville Wright flew at Kitty Hawk for the first time, the wind was blowing at a speed of 20–27 miles per hour. In later flights, the Wright brothers showed that planes could fly without powerful winds.

**INSTRUCT: OBJECTIVE 3**

**Urban Parks and World's Fairs**
Key Questions
- How did new ways of working lead to a demand for new types of leisure activities?
- What new forms of leisure activities developed in this era?
- How did world's fairs affect the way Americans thought about themselves?

**ACTIVITY OPTIONS**

**INDIVIDUAL NEEDS**

**STUDENTS ACQUIRING ENGLISH/ESL**

**Finding Main Ideas** Point out to students the phrase *mass culture* in the section title on page 626. Tell them that mass culture is the set of experiences and ideas shared by many Americans across the whole country. Ask them to identify factors in this section that promoted the development of such a shared culture in the early 1900s. Students may recognize the influence of widespread public education, nationwide mail-order catalogs, and shared interest in spectator sports, among other examples. Then ask the class to consider what factors influence American mass culture today. They may suggest such examples as television, nationally known brand names and store chains, malls, and movies, as well as some of the same factors that shaped life a century ago, such as sports.

## MORE ABOUT . . .

### Amusement Parks

Trolley companies supported the development of amusement parks at the end of their lines, often by a lake, to encourage people to ride the trolleys on the weekends. These parks usually had picnic tables, dance halls, games, and a few rides. The parks were a huge success. In 1894, Captain Paul Boynton opened the first modern amusement park, Paul Boynton's Water Chutes in Chicago. The Water Chutes charged an entrance fee. It was so successful that Boynton opened another amusement park at Coney Island, on Long Island, in 1895.

## INSTRUCT: OBJECTIVE 4

### Spectator Sports/Going to the Show

Key Questions
- Why might spectator sports and other new forms of entertainment develop in urban rather than rural areas?
- What did the existence of the Negro baseball leagues indicate about American society?
- How did these new forms of entertainment contribute to the growth of mass culture?

**Humanities Transparency HT41, HT42**
- Edison Concert Phonograph
- Football Game

### Leisure Activities

▼ **Coney Island** Visitors to New York's Coney Island cool off in the Steeple-chase Pool.

▼ **World's Fair** Visitors to the 1893 world's fair in Chicago saw exotic sights, such as elephants.

▼ **Football** Excited fans watch the 1881 Harvard–Yale football game at the Polo Grounds in New York.

Central Park in New York City is the nation's best-known urban park. Opened in 1876, Central Park looked like the country. Trees and shrubs dotted its gently rolling landscape. Winding walkways let city dwellers imagine they were strolling in the woods. People could also ride bicycles and play sports in the park.

In addition to urban parks, amusement parks provided a place people could go for fun. The most famous amusement park was Coney Island in New York City. Completed in 1904, Coney Island had shops, food vendors, and exciting rides like roller coasters. One immigrant woman said Coney Island "is just like what I see when I dream of heaven!"

World's fairs provided another wildly popular form of entertainment for Americans. Between 1876 and 1916, several U.S. cities, including Philadelphia, Chicago, St. Louis, and San Francisco, hosted world's fairs. The fairs were designed to show off American technology. The 1876 fair in Philadelphia displayed Alexander Graham Bell's newly invented telephone. Millions of people attended these fairs. Nearly 10 million attended the Philadelphia fair alone. Visitors were drawn to foods, shows, and amusements. The historian Thomas Schlereth described the giant wheel built by George Ferris at the 1893 Chicago fair.

*Reading***History**
**B. Comparing and Contrasting** What did urban parks and world's fairs have in common?
**B. Answer** Both provided outdoor leisure activities for large numbers of people.

*A VOICE FROM THE PAST*

Chicago's answer to Paris's 1889 Eiffel Tower, Ferris's 264-foot bicycle wheel in the sky dominated the landscape. With thirty-six cars, each larger than a Pullman coach and capable of holding 60 people, the wheel, when fully loaded, rotated 2,160 people in the air.

**Thomas Schlereth,** *Victorian America*

## 4 Spectator Sports

During this time, spectator sports also became popular entertainment. Baseball, football, boxing, and many other sports drew thousands of people to fields and gyms around the country.

Baseball was the most popular sport. Summer games drew crowds of enthusiastic fans. By the 1890s, baseball had standardized rules and a published schedule of games. Racial discrimination kept African-American baseball players out of baseball's American and National Leagues. In order to compete, African Americans formed their own teams in



## ACTIVITY OPTIONS

### MULTIPLE LEARNING STYLES: MUSICAL

BLOCK SCHEDULING

#### RAGTIME

**Class Time** One class period

**Task** Comparing musical genres from different eras

**Purpose** To gain an understanding of ragtime music and its influence on later musical styles

**Supplies Needed**
- Recordings of ragtime, jazz, and rap music
- Books about ragtime

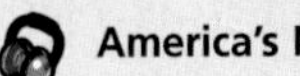

**Activity** Suggest that students research ragtime music by listening to cassettes and CDs in the library listening room or in class. They may want to consult with a music teacher. To understand the influence of ragtime on other forms of American music, students should also listen to examples of other musical styles, such as jazz, rock 'n' roll, rap, or hip-hop. Students should explain how they think ragtime might have influenced a more recent musical style. They should use recordings to demonstrate the influence.

the Negro American League and the Negro National League. (See Geography in History, pages 722–723.)

## Going to the Show

In addition to sports, other forms of live entertainment attracted large audiences. **Vaudeville,** for example, featured a mixture of song, dance, and comedy. A show would have a series of acts leading up to an exciting end, which advertisers billed as the "wow finish."

New types of music also began to be heard. **Ragtime,** a blend of African-American songs and European musical forms, was an important new musical form. African-American composer Scott Joplin heard ragtime while he traveled through black communities from New Orleans to Chicago. Joplin's "Maple Leaf Rag," published in 1899, became a hit in the first decade of the 20th century.

Early in the 20th century, movies began to compete with live entertainment. The first movies were silent and were added as the final feature of a vaudeville show. Soon storefront theaters appeared that showed only movies. After 1905, these movie theaters were called nickelodeons because they charged just a nickel for admission.

Movies, music, sports, and advertising contributed to shaping modern American mass culture. People across the nation experienced many of these things. In the next chapter, you will learn about different nationwide changes—the reform movements of the Progressive era.

C. Answer Unlike live performances, the same movies could be shown all over the country at the same time.

*Reading* **History**

**C. Making Inferences** How do you think movies contributed to mass culture?

### America's HERITAGE

**RAGTIME**

Tired of slow waltz music, young people eagerly embraced ragtime at the turn of the century. The name probably came from a description of the rhythm of black dance music as "ragged time." Ragtime's exciting beat inspired the names of such songs as "Irresistible Fox Trot Rag," "That Fascinating Rag," and "That Nifty Rag."

Ragtime had an enormous influence on American music. Throughout the 20th century, American musical styles such as jazz, blues, rock-and-roll, rap, and rhythm-and-blues built on the style of ragtime.

Scott Joplin

## Section 4 Assessment

### 1. Terms & Names

**Identify:**
- mass culture
- Joseph Pulitzer
- William Randolph Hearst
- department store
- mail-order catalog
- leisure
- vaudeville
- ragtime

### 2. Taking Notes

Use a diagram like the one below to note the changes that created a mass culture at the turn of the century.

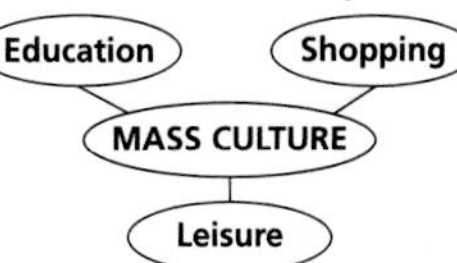


### 3. Main Ideas

a. What did dime novels and newspapers have in common?

b. How did mail-order catalogs affect the way people shopped?

c. What did visitors see at world's fairs?

### 4. Critical Thinking

**Making Inferences** Why did mass culture emerge during this period?

THINK ABOUT
- the impact of newspapers
- advertising and catalogs
- the development of leisure time

**ACTIVITY OPTIONS**

**ART** / **LANGUAGE ARTS** Research a world's fair from the turn of the century. Then make a **poster** or write a **newspaper advertisement** that will attract people to the fair.





### America's HERITAGE

**Ragtime**

This type of rhythmic music, which was popular in the United States from 1895 to 1915, probably developed from military music and music that accompanied minstrel-show dances. Ragtime compositions, which were called "rags," were played on the piano or by small bands with various combinations of instruments. Besides Scott Joplin, who was known as the "King of Ragtime," other important composers were Joseph F. Lamb and James Scott.

 **America's Music CD**

## ASSESS & RETEACH

**Setting the Stage** Have students fill in the fourth part on the graphic organizer for this chapter.

 **Formal Assessment**
- Section Quiz, p. 313

 **Critical Thinking Transparency CT61**
- Setting the Stage

**RETEACHING ACTIVITY**

Divide the class into four teams and assign one of the objectives in the section to each team. Ask each group to make up a series of headlines for newspapers of the period that identifies key events in each objective. Post the headlines on a classroom bulletin board.

 **In-Depth Resources: Unit 6**
- Reteaching Activity, p. 59

## Section 4 Assessment

### 1. Terms & Names

**mass culture,** p. 626
**Joseph Pulitzer,** p. 626
**William Randolph Hearst,** p. 627
**department store,** p. 627
**mail-order catalog,** p. 627
**leisure,** p. 627
**vaudeville,** p. 629
**ragtime,** p. 629

### 2. Taking Notes

Education: school enrollments; literacy increased; Shopping: department stores; mail-order catalogs; national advertising; Leisure: amusement parks; world's fairs; sports; vaudeville shows; ragtime; movies

### 3. Main Ideas

**a.** Both reached wider audiences because more people were literate.
**b.** They allowed people in rural areas to buy the same products through the mail that city dwellers could get directly from stores.
**c.** technology exhibits (telephone) and new amusements (Ferris wheel)

### 4. Critical Thinking

More people were exposed to advertising and information about sports, leisure, and culture.

**ACTIVITY OPTIONS**

 **Alternative Assessment**
- Rubrics, 1.1, 4.9

## TERMS & NAMES

1. **urbanization,** p. 609
2. **Jane Addams,** p. 613
3. **political machine,** p. 613
4. **Ellis Island,** p. 614
5. **assimilation,** p. 616
6. **Jim Crow,** p. 621
7. ***Plessy* v. *Ferguson*,** p. 621
8. **W. E. B. Du Bois,** p. 622
9. **Joseph Pulitzer,** p. 626
10. **leisure,** p. 627

## REVIEW QUESTIONS

**Possible Responses**

1. Streetcar lines changed the walking city into the streetcar city. People began to move away from the city center to suburbs reached by streetcar lines.
2. disease, fire, crime
3. They offered services to voters and businesses, who in turn provided votes and financial support.
4. southern and eastern Europe
5. Most Europeans came through Ellis Island. Many Asians came through Angel Island. Many Mexicans came through Texas.
6. They believe that cultures brought by people from around the world melt together in the United States.
7. It held that segregation was not unconstitutional and introduced the doctrine of "separate but equal."
8. spoke out against lynching; established schools and training programs; fought for civil rights; founded the NAACP
9. a common culture experienced by large numbers of people
10. People could get away from the pollution and overcrowding of the city to appreciate greenery and space for recreation.

# Chapter 21 ASSESSMENT

## TERMS & NAMES

Briefly explain the importance of each of the following.

1. urbanization
2. Jane Addams
3. political machine
4. Ellis Island
5. assimilation
6. Jim Crow
7. *Plessy* v. *Ferguson*
8. W. E. B. Du Bois
9. Joseph Pulitzer
10. leisure

## REVIEW QUESTIONS

**Cities Grow and Change (pages 609–613)**

1. How did public transportation change city life?
2. What dangers did urban overcrowding pose to tenement dwellers?
3. How did big-city political machines keep their power?

**The New Immigrants (pages 614–619)**

4. Where did most American immigrants come from around 1900?
5. How did immigrants enter the United States?
6. Why have some people described the United States as a melting pot?

**Segregation and Discrimination (pages 620–625)**

7. Why was *Plessy* v. *Ferguson* an important Supreme Court decision?
8. What did African-American leaders do to fight discrimination?

**Society and Mass Culture (pages 626–629)**

9. What is mass culture?
10. How did city parks improve city life?

## CRITICAL THINKING

**1. USING YOUR NOTES**

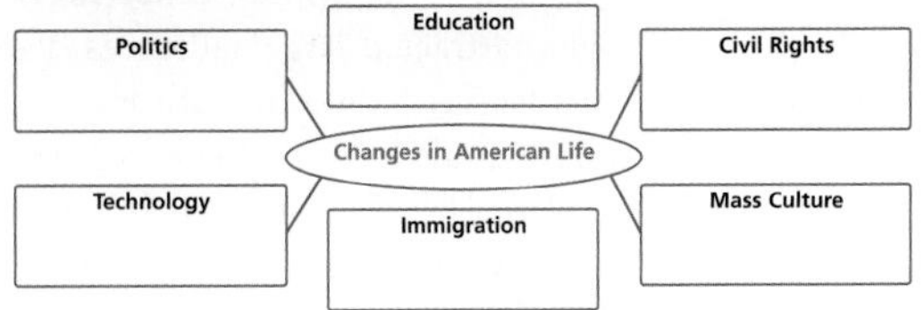


Using your completed chart, answer the questions below:

a. What changes did increased immigration cause?
b. How did the growing popularity of spectator sports and movies help bring about mass culture?
c. Which changes helped immigrants assimilate into American life?

**2. ANALYZING LEADERSHIP**

Think about the actions of Booker T. Washington and W. E. B. Du Bois. What approach did each take against discrimination? Whose approach do you think was the most likely to be effective?

**3. THEME: DIVERSITY AND UNITY**

How do you think the emergence of mass culture around 1900 affected immigrants and nonwhites?

**4. APPLYING CITIZENSHIP SKILLS**

What kinds of things prevented African Americans and immigrants from having full citizenship? How did they attempt to participate in American politics?

### Interact *with* History

Have your ideas about how you'll make a home in the United States changed after reading the chapter? Explain.

## VISUAL SUMMARY

### Changes in American Life

**Cities Grow and Change**
Industrialization caused American cities to grow.

**The New Immigrants**
Large numbers of immigrants, especially from southern and eastern Europe, came to the United States.

**American Life Around 1900**

**Segregation and Discrimination**
Racial and ethnic minorities faced discrimination across the country.

**Society and Mass Culture**
New leisure activities and mass culture emerged at this time.

## CRITICAL THINKING

**Possible Responses**

1. USING YOUR NOTES **a.** urbanization; reform movements; discrimination; immigration restriction; machine politics **b.** They allowed large numbers of people to share similar experiences. **c.** improved schooling; advertising; mail-order catalogs; movies; amusement parks; sports
2. ANALYZING LEADERSHIP Washington believed that African Americans should concentrate on education and work before striving for full political or social integration. Du Bois believed that segregation should end immediately. Student answers will vary.
3. THEME: DIVERSITY AND UNITY In some ways, it helped both groups participate in new aspects of American society that were widely available.
4. APPLYING CITIZENSHIP SKILLS Jim Crow laws, not being able to vote; The NAACP and political machines were ways they used politics to try to get the government to meet their needs.

**Interact *with* History.** Some students may say they discovered immigrating to the United States was more difficult than they believed. Others might mention specific things they would do, such as visit a political boss or look for friends from home.

## HISTORY SKILLS

### 1. INTERPRETING GRAPHS

Study the graph and answer the questions.

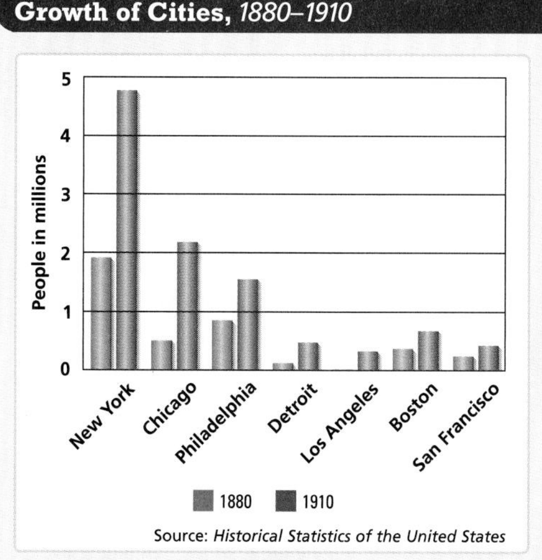

Source: *Historical Statistics of the United States*

**Basic Graph Elements**

a. What cities are shown on the graph?

b. What were the three largest U.S. cities in 1910?

**Interpreting the Graph**

c. Which city's population increased by the greatest amount between 1880 and 1910?

d. Which city's population increased by the greatest percentage between 1880 and 1910?

### 2. INTERPRETING PRIMARY SOURCES

Advertisements urged Americans to buy all sorts of goods, such as bicycles. Study the ad carefully. Answer the questions.

a. How does the picture portray the activity of cycling?

b. How do you think this advertisement might convince people to buy bicycles?

## ALTERNATIVE ASSESSMENT

### 1. INTERDISCIPLINARY ACTIVITY: Math

**Making a Graph** Do research to determine the number of immigrants who came from various countries between 1880 and 1914. Find out where immigrants come from today. Make a graph that displays your findings. Explain your graph to the class.

### 2. COOPERATIVE LEARNING ACTIVITY

**Designing a Park** Cities across the United States built parks at the turn of the century. They wanted to provide city dwellers with places to enjoy grass, trees, and fresh air as well as all sorts of leisure activities. What kinds of things would you want to be able to do in a park?

Working in small groups, research city parks built in the late 1800s. Design a park that could please as many urban residents as possible. Make sure to take into account the following.

a. sports fields

b. areas for rest and relaxation

c. places for nature and wildlife

d. buildings for food and restrooms

### 3. CD-ROM PRIMARY SOURCE EXPLORER

**Creating a Museum Exhibit** Racial discrimination has been a sad feature of American history. There is a large amount of information about racism and the ways that racial and ethnic minorities have tried to overcome it. Using the CD-ROM or your local library, collect information on discrimination and civil rights.

Create a museum exhibit about discrimination and civil rights in your hometown using the ideas below.

- Include information on groups that faced discrimination.
- Find biographies about any important civil rights leaders in your town.
- Collect primary sources, such as newspaper articles or autobiographies, that discuss important events.
- Draw a diagram that shows a floor plan for your exhibit.

### 4. HISTORY PORTFOLIO

**Option 1** Review your section and chapter assessment activities. Select one that you think was your best work. Then use comments made by your teacher or classmates to improve your work, and add it to your portfolio.

**Option 2** Review the questions that you wrote for What Do You Want to Know? on page 608. Then write a short report in which you explain the answers to your questions. If any questions were not answered, do research to answer them. Add your answers to your history portfolio.



## ALTERNATIVE ASSESSMENT

1. INTERDISCIPLINARY ACTIVITY: **Math**
   **Graphs should**
   - present information accurately.
   - use bar, line, or pie styles.
   - present the information in a style that will aid the viewer in understanding the information.
   - be presented neatly.

2. COOPERATIVE LEARNING ACTIVITY
   **Designs should**
   - be presented in a manner clear to the viewers.
   - include areas for sports, recreation, nature and wildlife, and service buildings.
   - exhibit creativity.
   - be presented neatly.

3. CD-ROM PRIMARY SOURCE EXPLORER
   **Exhibits should**
   - have a complete introductory overview.
   - contain accurate and well-described textual information, including primary sources.
   - use a variety of media.
   - have a floor plan.
   - be accompanied by well-informed and lively student presenters.

4. HISTORY PORTFOLIO

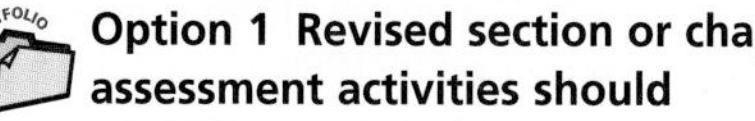

**Option 1 Revised section or chapter assessment activities should**
- address teacher and peer responses to the selected work.
- solve problems present in the first versions of the work.

**Option 2 Short reports should**
- answer questions about American life around 1900.
- use evidence to develop and support ideas.
- cite sources of information.
- use standard grammar, spelling, sentence structure, and punctuation.

**Critical Thinking Transparency CT63**
- Visual Summary

**Formal Assessment**
- Chapter Test, Forms A and B, pp. 314–321

## HISTORY SKILLS

**Possible Responses**

1. INTERPRETING GRAPHS
   **Basic Graph Elements**
   **a.** Boston, Chicago, Detroit, Los Angeles, New York, Philadelphia, and San Francisco
   **b.** New York, Chicago, Philadelphia
   **Interpreting the Graph**
   **c.** New York's
   **d.** Los Angeles's

2. INTERPRETING PRIMARY SOURCES
   **a.** It shows middle-class people enjoying a ride through the countryside.
   **b.** The riders appear to be having a good time. Also, they are attractive and appear to be middle class. The ad might persuade people that cycling is a good activity for middle-class people.

## HISTORY WORKSHOP

**OBJECTIVE**

Students will create cultural artifacts, role-play activities, and present issues relating to the technological advances in America at the end of the 19th century.

 **BLOCK SCHEDULING**

## PROCEDURE

Gather the materials listed in the "Toolbox." Then divide the class into groups of three to four students. Review the steps for researching and creating an exhibit for a classroom fair and for preparing a speech.

 **In-Depth Resources: Unit 6**
- History Workshop Resources, p. 61

### MORE ABOUT . . .

**Early Automobiles**

Henry Ford (1863–1947) began experimenting in the early 1890s with the new internal combustion engine and produced his first car in 1896. The Ford Motor Company was established in 1903 with $28,000 in capital. Its success was assured with the introduction of the Model N (1906–1907). The famous Model T appeared in 1908.

Another important contributor to the design and manufacture of cars at the turn of the century was Ransom E. Olds, whose one-cylinder, three-horsepower Oldsmobile (1901–1906) was really a motorized buggy. However, at $650, the Oldsmobile was more affordable than most other early cars.

### HISTORY FROM VISUALS

**Interpreting the Photograph** Have students identify details in the photograph that illustrate how technology was changing the lives of many Americans. **Possible Response** The people are driving to and from the fair in automobiles; in the distance stands a huge Ferris wheel.

## HISTORY WORKSHOP

# Create an Exhibit

In 1904 the Louisiana Purchase Exposition, better known as the St. Louis World's Fair, opened to great fanfare. The event celebrated the 100th anniversary of the U.S. purchase of the Louisiana Territory from France in 1803. Taking five years to plan and opening a year late, the fair focused on education and American technology. The automobile was among the most notable attractions at the fair. People from 63 countries and 43 states gathered in St. Louis.

People stroll down The Great Pike at the St. Louis World's Fair.

ACTIVITY Create an exhibit that reflects some aspect of technology at the end of the 19th century. Then make a classroom fair. Write an article about it and give a speech describing your favorite exhibit.

### TOOLBOX

Each group will need:

- bifold (type of poster board that folds open)
- poster board
- drawing paper
- markers
- scissors
- pencils
- glue
- cardboard

### STEP BY STEP

**1 Form groups.** Each group should consist of three or four students. During the workshop, each group will be expected to:

- research technology and inventions just prior to 1904
- design and create an exhibit for a classroom fair
- write a news report about the fair
- give a speech in praise of a favorite exhibit at the fair

**2 Research the fair.** Using this chapter, books on the St. Louis fair, or the Internet, find out what kinds of exhibits were displayed. Also research the technology and inventions of the time. Some themes of the fair's massive exhibit halls are listed below. Pick one theme on which to focus. Then brainstorm ideas for your exhibit and choose the best one.

| World's Fair Themes | |
|---|---|
| transportation | education |
| technology | the arts |

The New York-to-St. Louis Automobile Parade arrives at the St. Louis World's Fair.

632

### RECOMMENDED RESOURCES

**BOOKS FOR THE TEACHER**

Heller, Alfred. ***World's Fairs and the End of Progress: An Insider's View.*** Corte Madera, CA: World's Fair, Inc., 1999.

Mattie, Erik. ***World's Fairs.*** New York: Princeton Architectural Press, 1998.

**VIDEOS**

***Come to the Fairs.*** Episode 6 of ***A Walk Through the 20th Century with Bill Moyers.*** 55 minutes. PBS Video, 1988.

***Exits and Entrances: Showbiz in a Lively Era.*** 19 minutes, b/w. Re-released from The March of Time, Forum Edition Series by Time, Inc.

**BOOKS FOR THE STUDENTS**

Alter, Judy. ***Meet Me at the Fair.*** New York: Franklin Watts, 1997.

Hilton, Suzanne. ***Here Today, Gone Tomorrow: The Story of World's Fairs and Expositions.*** Philadelphia: Westminster Press, 1978.

**3 Design your exhibit.** Think about what your group wants to create. Using drawing paper, sketch a design of the exhibit in pencil. Next to your sketch, list all the items you'll need for the exhibit. Assign each person in your group certain items to bring for the next class period.

**4 Lay out your display.** Use the images and text you found to visually organize the three-panel display. Vary the size of the images, type-size of the text, and include color to make your layout clear and interesting. Remember to create a title.

A Machine for the New Century

**5 Create a mini St. Louis fair.** Along with the other groups, arrange the exhibits around the classroom. Walk around the room and look at the other groups' exhibits. Discuss with other groups how you created your exhibit.

## WRITE AND SPEAK

**Write a newspaper article.** Cover the fair as a journalist from another city. Write an article about the classroom fair, describing the atmosphere as well as the exhibits. Then give a speech in praise of the outstanding exhibit of the fair.

### HELP DESK

For related information, see pages 627–628 in Chapter 21.

**Researching Your Project**

- *The Song of the Molimo* by Jane Cutler

INTERNET Visit www.mcdougallittell.com for links to sites about world's fairs.

**Did You Know?**

One vender at the fair had difficulty selling tea in the hot St. Louis summer. As a result, he began putting ice cubes in the tea, and sales of his "iced tea" soared.

Though there has been some controversy over who invented the ice-cream cone, the St. Louis World's Fair was the place it became popular. One story states that a vendor at the fair rolled a waffle into a cone-shaped holder when another vendor ran out of dishes. However, Italo Marchiony of New York City claimed to have been selling ice-cream cones since 1896.

### REFLECT & ASSESS

- How did your group come up with its idea?
- How does your design fit into the theme of the St. Louis fair?
- What criteria did you use when judging the exhibits?





### MORE ABOUT . . .

**The St. Louis World's Fair**

St. Louis pulled out all the stops to make its 1904 World's Fair spectacular. Construction workers changed the course of a river, reshaped a lake, and covered 1,275 acres with magnificent buildings, gardens, and pavilions. Nighttime visitors were awed by the electric lights that sparkled everywhere; some lights even illuminated artificial waterfalls with changing colors. Each of the eight huge exhibition halls covered several acres. These gleaming white palaces looked as if they were carved from solid marble—but in fact they were made from "staff," a mixture of manila fibers and plaster of paris, which would last only a few years.

### REFLECT & ASSESS

1. Ask students to support their ideas for the exhibits in the classroom fair by referring to their notes on technology and inventions prior to 1904.
2. Have students work with peer editors to assess how well their designs fit the theme of the St. Louis World's Fair.
3. Have students write postcards from the viewpoint of visitors to the fair. Discuss what features would have seemed most striking about it.

## STANDARDS FOR EVALUATION

### HISTORY WORKSHOP

**Exhibits should**

- appear well constructed and imaginative.
- include a news report that describes the exhibits accurately.
- show evidence of planning, research, and organization.

### WRITE AND SPEAK

**Newspaper articles should**

- describe events clearly.
- include historical details about the fair.
- include details about the fair that would be of interest to readers in another city.

# UNIT 7

## Modern America Emerges
1880–1920



**BEFORE YOU READ**

### Previewing Unit 7

Unit 7 describes how the modern United States begins to take shape in the late 1800s and early 1900s. Many Americans become part of the Progressive movement, hoping to solve the problems resulting from urbanization and industrialization. Progressivism leads to greater government involvement in many aspects of life. Starting with the move to gain colonies overseas and ending with efforts to make peace after World War I, the United States also begins to play a greater role in world affairs.

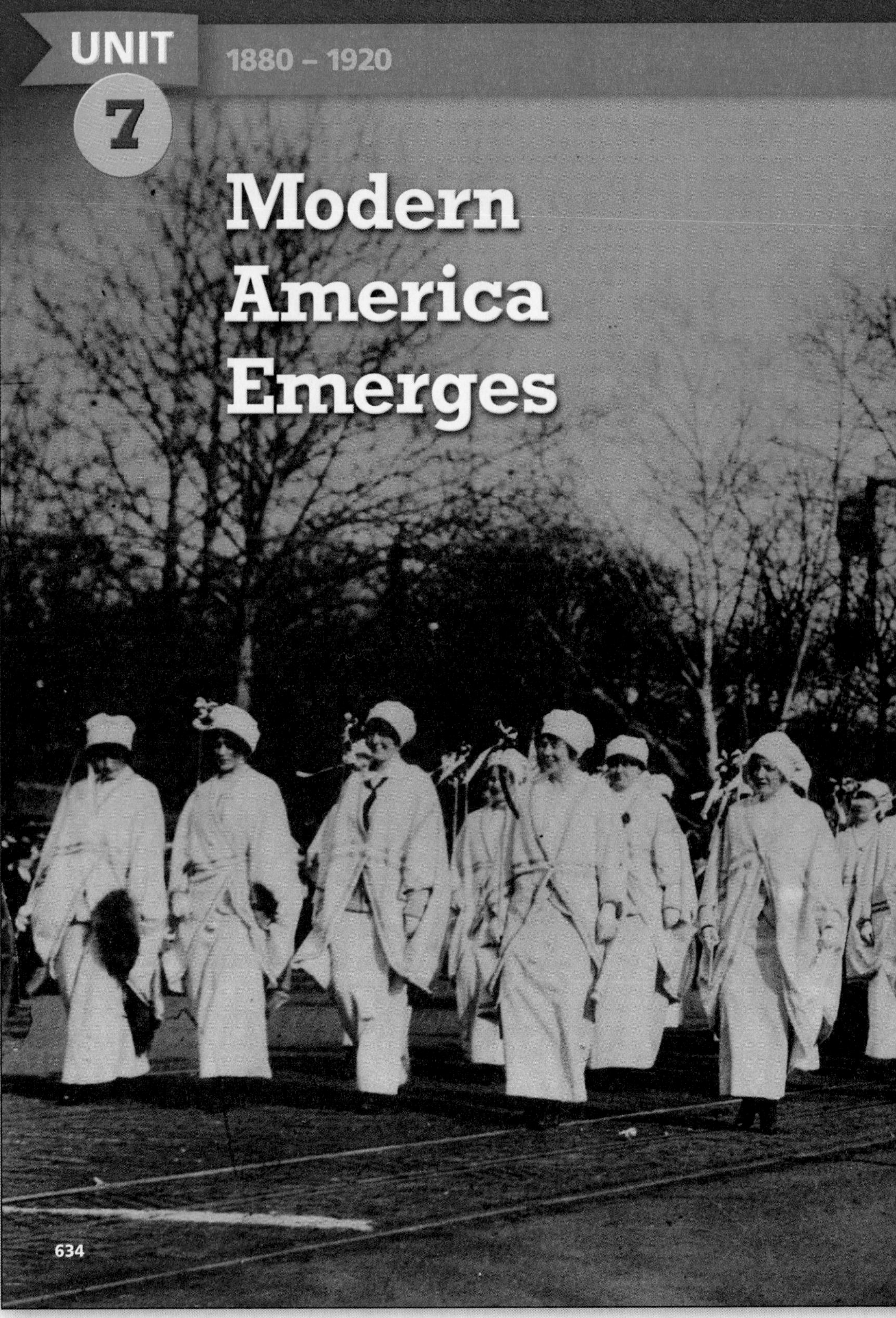

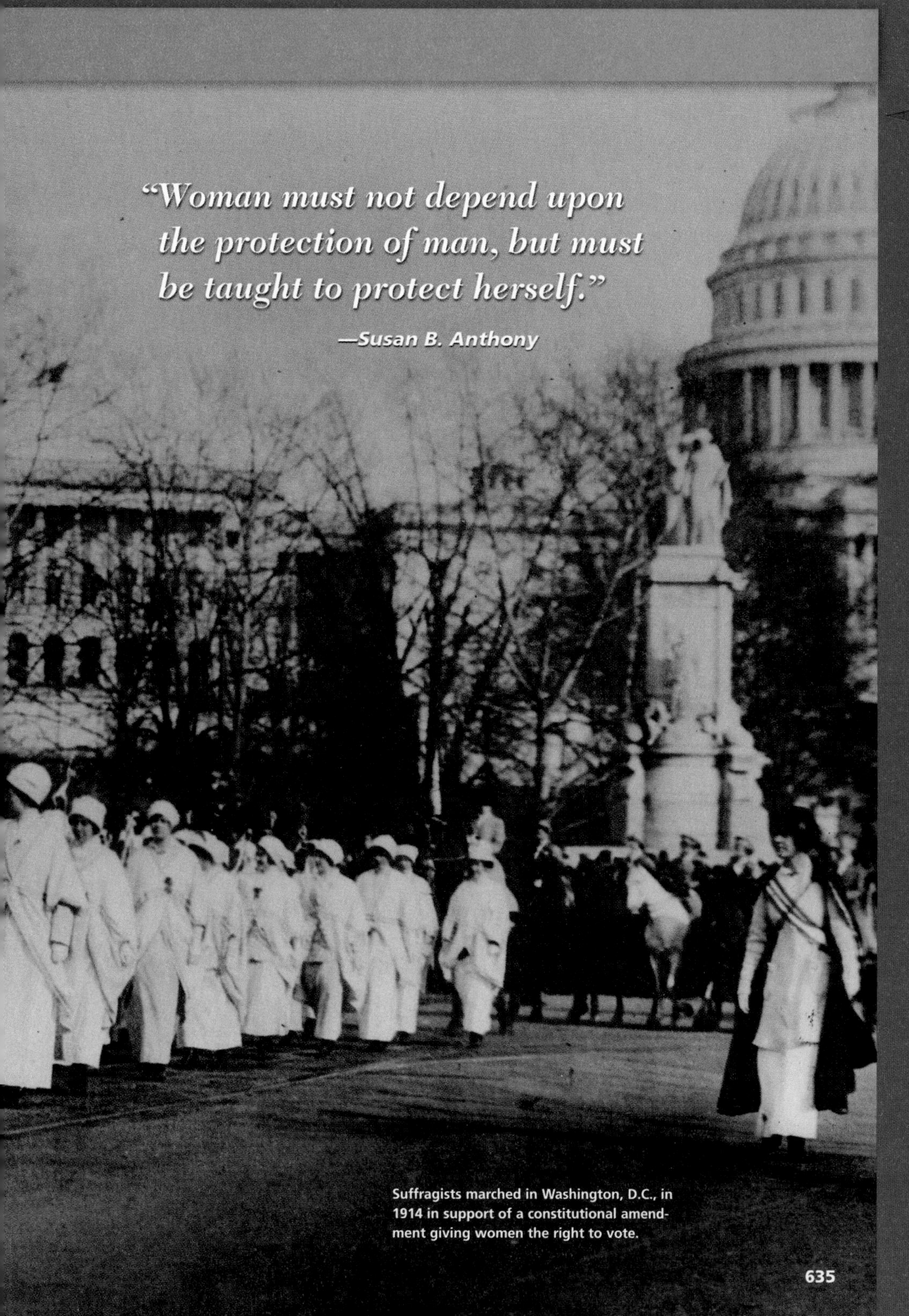

"Woman must not depend upon the protection of man, but must be taught to protect herself."
—Susan B. Anthony

Suffragists marched in Washington, D.C., in 1914 in support of a constitutional amendment giving women the right to vote.



## HISTORY FROM VISUALS

**Interpreting the Photograph** By 1914, when this photograph was taken, newspapers routinely included photographs as part of their coverage of events. Point out the striking effect made by the women dressed all in white. Tell students that suffragists often wore white for their marches. White symbolizes purity, and suffragists argued that women's votes would combat corruption in government. Note with students the women's dress—long skirts, hats, and gloves. The first suffrage parade was held in 1910. Ask students why a march such as this one would have been newsworthy. **Possible Response** Women often did not participate in politics or public demonstrations.

**Extension** Ask students to write slogans for banners for this parade.

CHAPTER 22 PLANNING GUIDE

# The Progressive Era 1890–1920

## CHAPTER RESOURCES

**CHAPTER OVERVIEW**

This chapter discusses the social, economic, and political reforms of the Progressive Era, including the presidencies of Theodore Roosevelt, William Howard Taft, and Woodrow Wilson. It also describes women's struggle to win the vote.

**COPYMASTERS**

**In-Depth Resources: Unit 7**
- Tracing Themes: Impact of the Individual, p. 2
- Building Vocabulary, p. 6

**Interdisciplinary Projects,** pp. 127–132

**TECHNOLOGY**

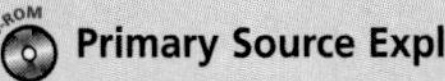

**Primary Source Explorer**

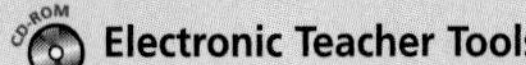

**Electronic Teacher Tools**

**Power Presentations CD-ROM**

**Chapter Summaries on CD** (English and Spanish)

## SECTION 1 Roosevelt and Progressivism pp. 639–645

**KEY IDEAS**

- Progressives expand democracy by promoting the direct primary, initiative, referendum, and recall.
- Roosevelt supports a Square Deal by breaking up business trusts.
- Roosevelt also signs the Pure Food and Drug Act and creates national parks.

**COPYMASTERS**

**In-Depth Resources: Unit 7**
- Setting the Stage, p. 1
- Guided Reading, p. 3
- Skillbuilder Practice, p. 7
- Primary Source, p. 10
- Literature Selection, pp. 12–14
- Reteaching Activity, p. 15

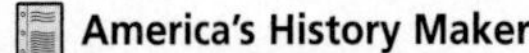

**America's History Makers**
- Theodore Roosevelt, pp. 87–88

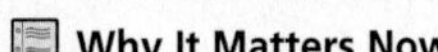

**Why It Matters Now**
- Environmentalism, pp. 43–44

**TECHNOLOGY**

**Humanities Transparency HT43**
- Meat Cutters

**Humanities Transparency HT44**
- Political Cartoon: The Trust Giant's Point of View by Horace Taylor

**Geography Transparency GT22**
- Progressive Reforms, 1915

**Critical Thinking Transparency CT65**
- Cause and Effect: The Progressive Movement

## SECTION 2 Taft and Wilson as Progressives pp. 646–649

**KEY IDEAS**

- Constitutional amendments create the income tax, allow direct election of senators, and establish Prohibition.
- Woodrow Wilson wins the presidency in a three-way election in 1912.
- Wilson strengthens antitrust laws and reforms the banking and monetary systems.

**COPYMASTERS**

**In-Depth Resources: Unit 7**
- Setting the Stage, p. 1
- Guided Reading, p. 4
- Geography Application: Election of 1912, pp. 8–9
- Reteaching Activity, p. 16

**Economics in History**
- Tariffs and Taxes, p. 22

**TECHNOLOGY**

**Warm-Up Transparency WT22**

**Critical Thinking Transparency CT64**
- Setting the Stage

**ClassZone:** www.mcdougallittell.com

## SECTION 3 Women Win New Rights pp. 650–653

**KEY IDEAS**

- Women take on new roles outside the home.
- Many women Progressives work in settlement houses, helping the urban poor.
- After more than 70 years of struggle, women win the right to vote with the 19th Amendment.

**COPYMASTERS**

**In-Depth Resources: Unit 7**
- Setting the Stage, p. 1
- Guided Reading, p. 5
- Primary Source, p. 11
- Reteaching Activity, p. 17

**America's History Makers**
- Susan B. Anthony, pp. 89–90

**Outline Map Activities**
- Politics and Reform, 1919, pp. 43–44

**TECHNOLOGY**

**Warm-Up Transparency WT22**

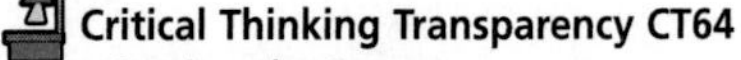

**Critical Thinking Transparency CT64**
- Setting the Stage

**Critical Thinking Transparency CT66**
- Visual Summary

**ClassZone:** www.mcdougallittell.com

PE Pupil's Edition

Copymaster

Overhead Transparency

Audio Library

CD-ROM

Internet

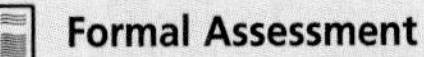

## ASSESSMENT

PE **Chapter Assessment,** pp. 654–655

**Formal Assessment**
- Chapter Tests, Forms A and B, pp. 327–334

**Alternative Assessment Book**

**Electronic Teacher Tools with Test Maker**

---

PE **Section Assessment,** p. 643

**Formal Assessment**
- Section Quiz, p. 324

**Alternative Assessment Book**
- Rubrics for a brochure, 1.13
- Rubrics for a map, 2.1

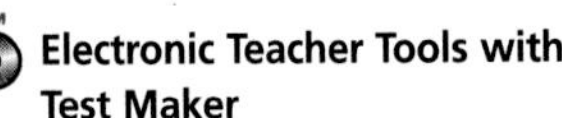
**Electronic Teacher Tools with Test Maker**

---

PE **Section Assessment,** p. 649

**Formal Assessment**
- Section Quiz, p. 325

**Alternative Assessment Book**
- Rubrics for a script, 3.1
- Rubrics for a Web page, 5.1

**Electronic Teacher Tools with Test Maker**

---

PE **Section Assessment,** p. 653

**Formal Assessment**
- Section Quiz, p. 326

**Alternative Assessment Book**
- Rubrics for a script, 3.1
- Rubrics for a Web page, 5.1

**Electronic Teacher Tools with Test Maker**

## CUSTOMIZING FOR INDIVIDUAL NEEDS

### Students Acquiring English/ESL

**Reading Study Guide** (English and Spanish), pp. 215–222

**Access for Students Acquiring English/ESL: Spanish Translations,** pp. 147–152

**Chapter Summaries on CD** (English and Spanish)

### Less Proficient Readers

**Reading Study Guide** (English and Spanish), pp. 215–222

**Chapter Summaries on CD** (English and Spanish)

### Gifted and Talented Students

**In-Depth Resources: Unit 7**
- Enrichment Activity, p. 18

**America's History Makers**
- Theodore Roosevelt, pp. 87–88
- Susan B. Anthony, pp. 89–90

## CROSS-CURRICULAR CONNECTIONS

### Civics

Sullivan, George. ***The Day the Women Got the Vote: A Photo History of the Women's Right Movement.*** New York: Scholastic, 1994. A photographic record of the fight for the vote.

### Culture

Freedman, Russell, Lewis Hine (photographer). ***Kids at Work: Lewis Hine and the Crusade Against Child Labor.*** New York: Clarion Books, 1998. Moving photographs by the great reformer with informative, well-written text.

### Geography

Pyne, Stephen J. ***How the Canyon Became Grand: A Short History.*** New York: Viking, 1998. The author knows the canyon from the point of view of a rafter and a hiker, as well as a historian.

### Language Arts

Ritchie, Donald A. ***American Journalists: Getting the Story.*** New York: Oxford U. Press, 1998. The personal and professional lives of 60 American journalists from 1700 to the present.

### Interdisciplinary Projects, pp. 127–132

- Math: Women in the Workplace
- Science: Classifying Rocks
- Language Arts: Journalism: The Muckrakers
- Physical Education: Theodore Roosevelt and Physical Fitness

### World History

Holmes, Burton et al. ***London (World 100 Years Ago).*** Chelsea House Publishers, 1998. A pictorial description of one of Europe's great cities in the 1890s.

### Literature

Alger, Horatio. ***Jed, the Poorhouse Boy.*** Mattituck, NY: Amereon, 1976. One of Alger's typical boy heroes rises from famine to fortune by means of good moral character, combined with pluck and luck.

O. Henry. ***41 Stories by O. Henry.*** New York: New American Library, 1991. Stories are arranged geographically in this anthology of works by the master of the surprise ending. Many stories present interesting views of city life in the Progressive Era.

Roosevelt, Theodore. ***A Bully Father: Theodore Roosevelt's Letters to His Children.*** New York: Random House, 1995. An intimate glimpse into the life of a very active family.

Taylor, Mildred D. ***The Well.*** New York: Viking Penguin, 1998. In 1910, the African-American Logan family of Mississippi share water with their neighbors—white and black alike—despite the possibility of racial violence. A good look at life before World War I.

## ENRICHMENT ACTIVITIES

PE **Pupil's Edition, pp. 636–655**
**Interact with History,** p. 637
**Geography in History,** pp. 644–645
**Economics in History,** p. 647

**In-Depth Resources: Unit 7**
- Geography Application: Election of 1912, pp. 8–9
- Primary Source: from "Philadelphia: Corrupt and Contented," p. 10
- Primary Source: Debating New Roles for Women, p. 11
- Literature Selection: from *The Jungle*, pp. 12–14

**America's History Makers**
- Theodore Roosevelt, pp. 87–88
- Susan B. Anthony, pp. 89–90

**Outline Map Activities**
- Politics and Reform, 1919, pp. 43–44

**Why It Matters Now**
- Environmentalism, pp. 43–44

## LESSON PLAN OPTIONS (50-MINUTE PERIOD) (TE) = Teacher's Edition (PE) = Pupil's Edition

| | TEACHER-DIRECTED ACTIVITIES<br>Class Time: 15 minutes | STUDENT-CENTERED ACTIVITIES<br>Class Time: 25 minutes | INDIVIDUAL ACTIVITIES<br>Class Time: 10 minutes |
|---|---|---|---|
| **DAY 1**<br>Introduction<br>pp. 636–638 | **Presentation Options**<br>• Begin with a class discussion of the photographs on p. 636 **(PE)**.<br>• Lead a class discussion on the "What Do You Know?" question in Setting the Stage, p. 638. Then introduce the graphic organizer for the chapter **(PE)**. | **Options for Cooperative Learning**<br>• Have student groups discuss the Interact with History questions, p. 637 **(PE)**.<br>• Have student groups respond to the "What Do You Want to Know?" question in Setting the Stage, p. 638 **(PE)**. | **Head Start on Homework Options**<br>• Have students skim Section 1 Main Idea, Why It Matters Now, Terms & Names, and the main headings, p. 639 **(PE)**.<br>• Have students begin Guided Reading activity and Building Vocabulary sheet. |
| **DAY 2**<br>Section 1<br>pp. 639–645 | **Presentation Options**<br>• Begin with the 5-Minute Warm-Up, p. 639 **(TE)**.<br>• Review the Section 1 Main Idea, Why It Matters Now, and Terms & Names, p. 639 **(PE)**.<br>• Lead the students through the Skillbuilder Mini-Lesson: Identifying and Solving Problems, p. 642 **(TE)**. | **Options for Cooperative Learning**<br>• Divide students into groups to work on the Geography in History questions, p. 645 **(PE)**.<br>• Have student pairs work together to complete one of the Activity Options in the Section 1 Assessment, p. 643 **(PE)**. | **Head Start on Homework Options**<br>• Have students begin working on Section 1 Assessment, p. 643 **(PE)**.<br>• Have students complete the answers to the Reading History questions in Section 2, pp. 639–643 **(PE)**. |
| **DAY 3**<br>Section 2<br>pp. 646–649 | **Presentation Options**<br>• Begin with the 5-Minute Warm-Up, p. 646 **(TE)**.<br>• Choose 5 key questions for Objectives 1–4 to discuss with the class, pp. 646–649 **(TE)**.<br>• Lead the students through the Economics in History feature, p. 647 **(TE)**. | **Options for Cooperative Learning**<br>• Divide students into groups to work on the Economics in History questions, p. 647 **(PE)**.<br>• Have student pairs work together to complete one of the Activity Options in the Section 2 Assessment, p. 649 **(PE)**. | **Head Start on Homework Options**<br>• Have students begin working on Section 2 Assessment, p. 649 **(PE)**.<br>• Have students preview Section 3 Main Idea, Why It Matters Now, Terms & Names, and the main headings, p. 650 **(PE)**. |
| **DAY 4**<br>Section 3<br>pp. 650–653 | **Presentation Options**<br>• Begin with the 5-Minute Warm-Up, p. 650 **(TE)**.<br>• Choose 5 key questions for Objectives 1–4 to discuss with the class, pp. 650–653 **(TE)**.<br>• Lead a discussion on the amendments to the Constitution using the History from Visuals, p. 653 **(TE)**. | **Options for Cooperative Learning**<br>• Divide students into groups and have them complete the Interdisciplinary Link, Language Arts: A Suffrage Speech, p. 652 **(TE)**.<br>• Have student pairs work together to complete one of the Activity Options in the Section 3 Assessment, p. 653 **(PE)**. | **Head Start on Homework Options**<br>• Have students complete the Setting the Stage graphic organizer for the chapter, p. 638 **(PE)**.<br>• Have students begin working on the Chapter Assessment, pp. 654–655 **(PE)**.<br>• Prepare for Chapter Test<br>**Formal Assessment,** pp. 327–334 |

TEACHER-TESTED ACTIVITY Suzanne Hidalgo, Serrano Middle School, Highland, California

## BIOGRAPHY IN A BAG

**Class Time** Two class periods, one for preparation and one for presentation

**Task** Creating an artifact bag on a prominent historical figure of the Progressive Era

**Purpose** To understand the roles played by various historical figures in the period from 1890 to 1920

**Supplies Needed**

- Encyclopedias, reference books, and other sources of biographical information
- Drawing paper and rulers
- Markers and colored pencils
- Brown bags and scissors

**Activity** Divide the class into pairs. Assign each pair a historical figure of the era such as Teddy Roosevelt, Jane Addams, Ida Tarbell, or Susan B. Anthony. Tell students that they will be creating artifacts about their historical figure to place inside their bags. For example, among the artifacts in Ida Tarbell's bag might be a newspaper and in Susan B. Anthony's, a ballot. After creating their artifacts, each pair can give a short presentation introducing the person and explaining how each artifact is connected with the person's life or place in the history of the period.

## BLOCK SCHEDULING — LESSON PLAN OPTIONS (90-MINUTE PERIOD)

### DAY 1

#### Interact with History, p. 637
**Class Time** 20 minutes

Options for pacing and variety:

- Peer Teaching Have students work in small groups to make a two-column chart showing the four major social problems of the Progressive Era and possible causes of these problems. Then have each group discuss the qualities that would help a leader tackle these problems. **Class Time** 20 minutes

#### Setting the Stage, p. 638
**Class Time** 20 minutes

Options for pacing and variety:

- Time Saver For a homework assignment, have students review the chapters in the unit on industrialization and immigration and provide written answers to the "What Do You Know?" and "What Do You Want to Know?" questions. **Class Time** 5 minutes

#### Section 1, pp. 639–645
**Class Time** 50 minutes

Options for pacing and variety:

- Internet Extend students' background knowledge of the Progressive Era by visiting www.mcdougallittell.com **Class Time** 20 minutes
- Time Saver For a homework assignment, ask students to use the information from Section 1 to begin filling in their Problem-Solution charts from Read and Take Notes on page 638. **Class Time** 5 minutes

### DAY 2

#### Section 2, pp. 646–649
**Class Time** 45 minutes

Options for pacing and variety:

- Peer Teaching Working in groups, students can analyze the chart on taxes in the Economics in History feature on page 647. Then have them answer the Connect to History and Connect to Today questions. **Class Time** 10 minutes
- History on Film Extend students' background knowledge of Roosevelt, Taft, and Wilson by showing them selected segments of *1900–1909* and *1910–1919* in the *History of the 20th Century* video series. ABC Video. **Class Time** 30 minutes

#### Section 3, pp. 650–653
**Class Time** 45 minutes

Options for pacing and variety:

- Time Saver Assign the Critical Thinking question in the Section Assessment on page 653 for homework. **Class Time** 5 minutes
- Role-Playing Have two students role-play a conversation between a woman reformer of this period such as Jane Addams, Susan B. Anthony, or Carrie Chapman Catt and a talk-show host. The two can discuss the reformer's achievements, disappointments, and hopes for the future. **Class Time** 10 minutes

#### Chapter 22 Assessment, pp. 654–655
**Class Time** 40 minutes

Options for pacing and variety:

- Peer Competition Divide students into groups. Have each group pick three famous people from this period and create a statement that reflects the views of this person on an issue of the Progressive Era. Have each group read its statement aloud as others try to guess the identity of the speaker. **Class Time** 20 minutes
- Peer Teaching Within groups, have students share information from their Chapter Assessment, Using Your Notes chart on page 654 to make a group chart. Working together, group members can then answer the Using Your Notes questions. **Class Time** 20 minutes

**CHAPTER 22 OBJECTIVE**
The student will examine the nation's social and political problems at the turn of the 20th century and the ways people worked to solve them.

# The Progressive Era 1890–1920

*Section 1* **Roosevelt and Progressivism**
*Section 2* **Taft and Wilson as Progressives**
*Section 3* **Women Win New Rights**

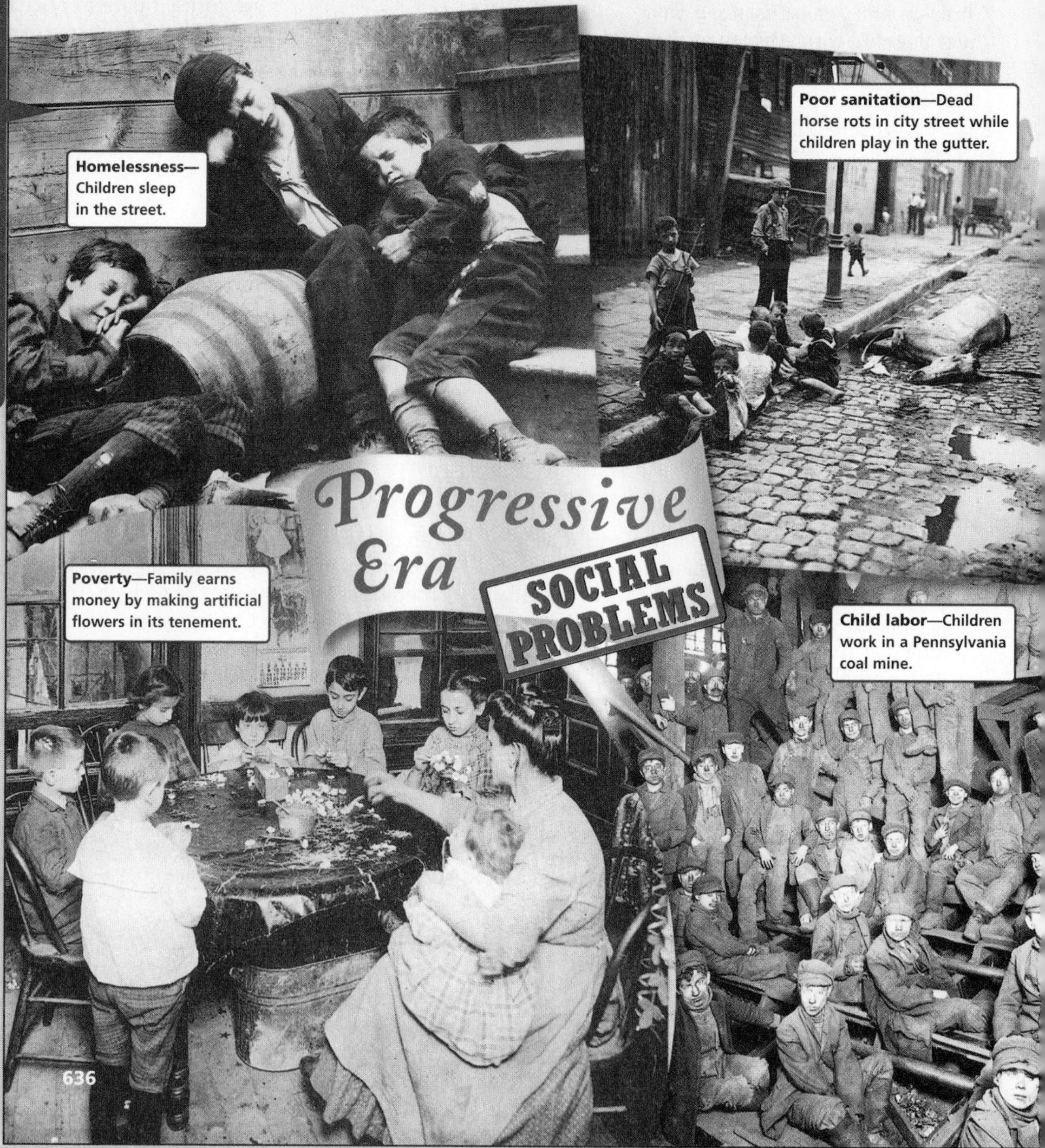

## HISTORY FROM VISUALS

**Interpreting the Photographs** Ask students to study each photograph and read the inset caption. Then encourage them to use visual clues to discuss the lives of the people in the photos. Suggest that they think about how the poverty shown in the photos might affect people's health. **Possible Responses** Students should recognize that the conditions in the photographs might lead to the spread of disease, short lives, and feelings of hopelessness.

**Extension** Ask students to list three reasons why all Americans should have been concerned about the conditions in the photographs.

**CRITICAL THINKING ACTIVITY**

**Making Inferences** Ask students to infer what kind of people took the photographs on this page, what their goals might have been in taking the photos, and how successfully they met those goals.

**Class Time** 10 minutes

Progressive Era
SOCIAL PROBLEMS

**Homelessness**—Children sleep in the street.

**Poor sanitation**—Dead horse rots in city street while children play in the gutter.

**Poverty**—Family earns money by making artificial flowers in its tenement.

**Child labor**—Children work in a Pennsylvania coal mine.

636

## RECOMMENDED RESOURCES

**BOOKS FOR THE TEACHER**

Davis, Allen Freeman. ***American Heroine: The Life and Legend of Jane Addams.*** New York: Oxford, 1973. Covers Addams's life and changing public image.

Flexnor, Eleanor and Ellen Fitzpatrick. ***Century of Struggle: The Woman's Rights Movement in the United States.*** Cambridge, MA: Belknap Press, 1996.

Morris, Edmund. ***The Rise of Theodore Roosevelt.*** New York: Ballantine Books, 1979. Winner of the Pulitzer Prize and the American Book Award.

Muir, John. ***John Muir: His Life and Letters and Other Writings.*** Ed. by Terry Gifford. Seattle, WA: Mountaineers Books, 1996. A collection including parts of Muir's autobiography and other less famous selections of his vivid writing.

**VIDEO**

***The Complete Yellowstone.*** Finley-Holiday, 1992. An outstanding four-season tour of the park that Roosevelt preserved for the people.

**INTERNET**

For more about the United States in the Progressive Era, visit www.mcdougallittell.com

## Interact *with* History

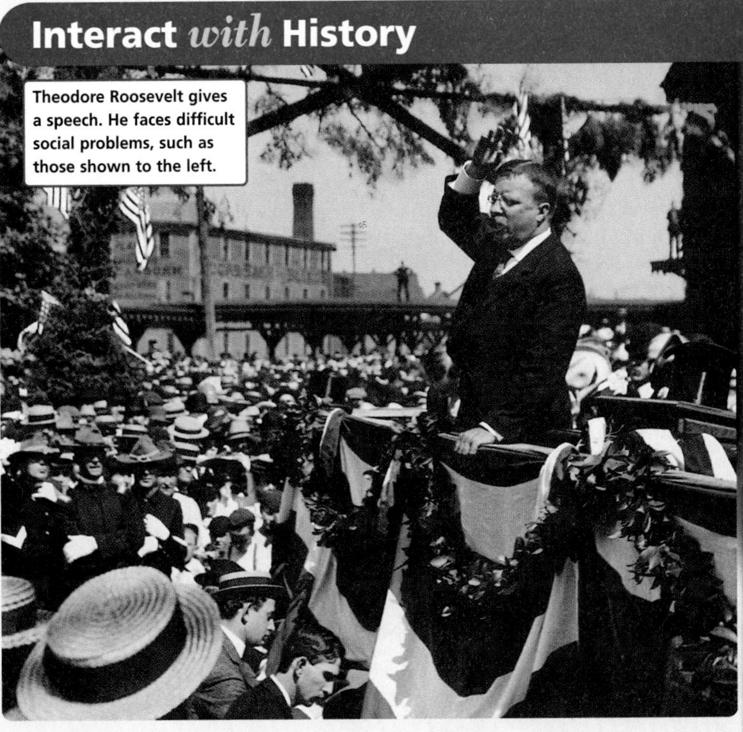

Theodore Roosevelt gives a speech. He faces difficult social problems, such as those shown to the left.

**It is 1901, and Theodore Roosevelt has suddenly become president. You and all Americans are counting on him to help end child labor, poverty, business abuses, and political corruption. You're anxious to see what actions the new president will take to solve these problems.**

### What Do You Think?

- **What different problems do the photographs show?**
- **What qualities would a leader need to tackle such problems?**
- **What might be the cause of these different problems?**

# *How would you solve one of these problems?*

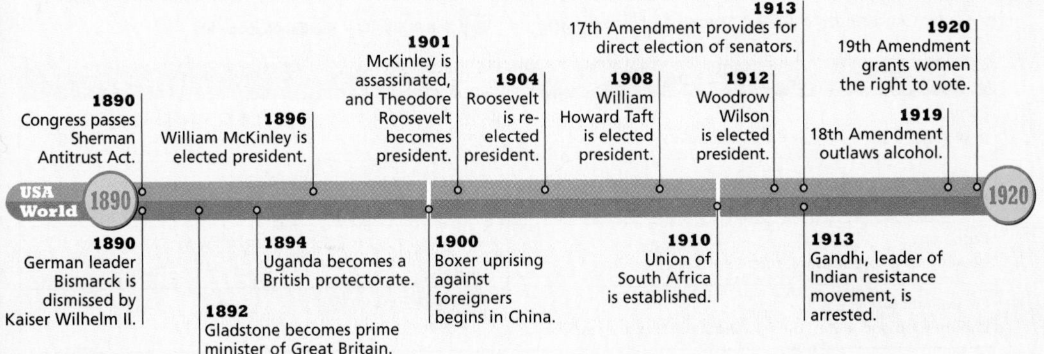
USA
World
1890
1920
1890 Congress passes Sherman Antitrust Act.
1896 William McKinley is elected president.
1901 McKinley is assassinated, and Theodore Roosevelt becomes president.
1904 Roosevelt is re-elected president.
1908 William Howard Taft is elected president.
1912 Woodrow Wilson is elected president.
1913 17th Amendment provides for direct election of senators.
1919 18th Amendment outlaws alcohol.
1920 19th Amendment grants women the right to vote.
1890 German leader Bismarck is dismissed by Kaiser Wilhelm II.
1892 Gladstone becomes prime minister of Great Britain.
1894 Uganda becomes a British protectorate.
1900 Boxer uprising against foreigners begins in China.
1910 Union of South Africa is established.
1913 Gandhi, leader of Indian resistance movement, is arrested.

## Interact *with* History

### OBJECTIVES

- To help students describe social problems facing the nation
- To help students identify problem solving used by individuals to improve social conditions

### What Do You Think?

1. Encourage students to see more than one problem in each picture.
2. Ask students to remember the qualities of the leaders they have studied and the problems they faced.
3. Ask students what groups are most likely to be the victims of these problems.

### *How would you solve one of these problems?*

Why do you think the problems haven't been solved? Why do you think the main question asks you to solve just one problem instead of all four? Ask students to consider immediate short-term solutions as well as long-term solutions. Remind students of the problem-solving techniques found in the Citizenship Handbook (page 285).

### MAKING PERSONAL CONNECTIONS

Ask students to think about which problems pictured still exist in U.S. cities today. What are some of today's social problems that are not shown in the photographs? Do you think social problems are worse today than a century ago? Why?

### TIME LINE DISCUSSION

**The Progressive Era was a time of great energy. Middle-class reformers worked hard to correct social problems. Politicians campaigned hard, promising that the government would respond to voters' needs. Still others worked to bring economic reform.**

- Ask students to identify the laws passed during the era that gave more power to U.S. citizens.
  **Answer** the Seventeenth and Nineteenth Amendments, passed at the end of the Progressive Era
- How does the Eighteenth Amendment reflect attempts at social reform?
  **Answer** It outlawed alcohol, which was seen as a social problem.
- What events showed unrest in other parts of the world?
  **Answers** Boxer uprising, arrest of Gandhi

## BEFORE YOU READ

### Previewing the Theme: Impact of the Individual

Ask students how strong, popular leaders can be instrumental in solving difficult social problems. **Possible Response** A strong, popular leader is able to motivate citizens to work together, to vote, and to put pressure on politicians to make changes.

### What Do You Know?

Ask students if they can name one contemporary person or group that is well known for working to correct a social problem. Be sure students also name the cause being supported. Then ask them if they think one person or group can make a difference in solving social problems. Have them explain their reasoning.

 **In-Depth Resources: Unit 7**
- Tracing Themes: Impact of the Individual, p. 2

## READ AND TAKE NOTES

### Reading Strategy: Identifying and Solving Problems

Tell students that identifying problems and working toward solutions is a process that takes place over time. Before they read, have students look at the problems identified in the first column of the chart. As they read, have them look for the corresponding solutions.

 **In-Depth Resources: Unit 7**
- Setting the Stage, p. 1

 **Critical Thinking Transparency CT64**
- Setting the Stage

# Chapter 22 SETTING THE STAGE

## BEFORE YOU READ

### Previewing the Theme

**Impact of the Individual** The problems caused by the growth of industries and cities sparked a variety of reform movements. This chapter shows that individual reformers and reform groups shared a strong desire to solve problems in American society.

A social worker pays a visit to a poor family.

### What Do You Know?

What do you know about life in American cities in the early 1900s? What problems plagued the cities? How have people living in cities overcome obstacles?

**THINK ABOUT**
- what you've learned in previous chapters
- what you know about urban problems today

### What Do You Want to Know?

What questions do you have about the reform movements of the early 1900s? Record your questions in your notebook before you read the chapter.

## READ AND TAKE NOTES

**Reading Strategy: Identifying and Solving Problems** This chapter focuses on the problems that Americans faced at the turn of the century and how they worked to solve those problems. A graphic organizer can help you keep track of problems and solutions. Major problems faced by the nation at the turn of the century are listed in the first column of the chart below. As you read, record solutions for these problems in the second column of the chart.

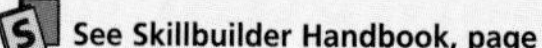

See Skillbuilder Handbook, page R17.

| PROBLEM | SOLUTION |
|---|---|
| **Political:** patronage; limited suffrage and democracy | Pendleton Civil Service Act; direct primary; initiative; referendum; recall; 17th and 19th amendments |
| **Social:** poverty; alcohol abuse | settlement houses; 18th Amendment |
| **Economic:** power of big corporations; unemployment | Clayton Antitrust Act; campaign for minimum wage laws; socialism |
| **Environmental:** impure food and water; diminishing natural resources | Pure Food and Drug Act national parks |



## TEACHING STRATEGY

### READING THE CHAPTER

This is a thematic chapter focusing on the goals of various reform movements. Set a purpose for reading by telling students to identify individual reformers or reform groups and their goals as they read. Pause after each section to review their findings.

### ALTERNATIVE ASSESSMENT

The Chapter Assessment describes three activities for alternative assessment on page 655. You may wish to have students work on these activities during the course of the chapter and then present them at the end.

# 1 Roosevelt and Progressivism

**TERMS & NAMES**
progressivism
muckrakers
direct primary
initiative
referendum
recall
Sherman Antitrust Act
Theodore Roosevelt

**MAIN IDEA**

Reformers tried to solve the problems of the cities. They gained a champion in Theodore Roosevelt.

**WHY IT MATTERS NOW**

Many of the reforms of the Progressive Era have had an effect on life in America today.

### ONE AMERICAN'S STORY

**Newspaper journalist Nellie Bly worked for *The New York World.* In 1887, Bly wanted to investigate the Women's Lunatic Asylum in New York City. An asylum is a place where people with mental illness can get help. She faked mental illness and fooled doctors so that she could become a patient there. After spending ten days in the asylum, Bly wrote a newspaper article about what she had witnessed. She described being forced to take ice cold baths.**

*A VOICE FROM THE PAST*

My teeth chattered and my limbs were goose-fleshed and blue with cold. Suddenly I got, one after the other, three buckets of water over my head—ice-cold water, too—into my eyes, my ears, my nose and my mouth.

**Nellie Bly,** quoted in *Nellie Bly: Daredevil, Reporter, Feminist*

**She reported that nurses choked and beat patients. Shortly after Bly's stories appeared, conditions at the asylum improved.**

**Bly also wrote about poor conditions in slums, factories, prisons, and nursing homes. Like other reformers, she wanted to correct the wrongs in American society. All of these reformers made up the Progressive movement around the turn of the century.**

Nellie Bly

## 1 The Rise of Progressivism

As you saw in Chapter 21, the rapid growth of cities and industries in the United States at the turn of the century brought many problems. Among them were poverty, the spread of slums, and poor conditions in factories. A depression in the 1890s made problems worse. In addition, corrupt political machines had won control of many city and state governments. Big corporations had gained power over the economy and government.

To attack these problems, individuals organized a number of reform movements. These reformers believed in the basic goodness of people. They also believed in democracy. The reformers were mostly native born and middle-class. They could be found in either political party. Their reform movements came to be grouped under the label **progressivism**.





## SECTION OBJECTIVES

1. To identify the goals of the Progressive movement
2. To analyze Theodore Roosevelt's "Square Deal"
3. To evaluate Roosevelt's qualities as an activist president
4. To summarize Roosevelt's conservation policies

**CRITICAL THINKING**

Finding Main Ideas, pp. 640, 643
Summarizing, p. 641
Making Inferences, p. 642
Recognizing Effects, p. 643

**Why It Matters Now**
- Environmentalism, pp. 43–44

## FOCUS & MOTIVATE

### 5-MINUTE WARM-UP

**Analyzing Causes** These questions focus on progressive goals for the country.

1. Read "A Voice from the Past" on page 641. What does Roosevelt mean by a "square deal"?
2. What might prevent a person from receiving a "square deal"?

**Warm-Up Transparency WT22**

## INSTRUCT

**INSTRUCT: OBJECTIVE 1**

**The Rise of Progressivism**

Key Questions
- In which three basic areas did reformers seek change?
- What qualities did most progressives share?
- Who were the muckrakers, and how did they contribute to the Progressive movement?

**In-Depth Resources: Unit 7**
- Guided Reading, p. 3

**Reading Study Guide** (Spanish and English), pp. 215–216

### RECOMMENDED RESOURCES

**In-Depth Resources: Unit 7**
- Guided Reading, p. 3
- Building Vocabulary, p. 6
- Skillbuilder Practice, p. 7
- Primary Source, p. 10
- Literature Selection, pp. 12–14
- Reteaching Activity, p. 15

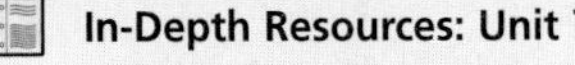

**Reading Study Guide** (Spanish and English), pp. 215–216

**America's History Makers**
- Theodore Roosevelt, pp. 87–88

**Why It Matters Now**
- Environmentalism, pp. 43–44

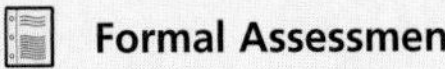

**Formal Assessment**
- Section Quiz, p. 324

**Alternative Assessment**
- Rubrics, 1.13
- Rubrics, 2.1

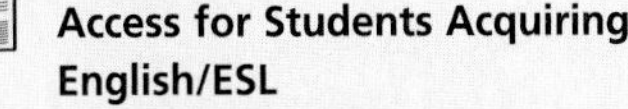

**Access for Students Acquiring English/ESL**
- Guided Reading, p. 147
- Skillbuilder Practice, p. 150

Technology Resources

**Humanities Trans. HT43, HT44**
- Meat Cutters
- Political Cartoon: The Trust Giant's Point of View

**Critical Thinking Trans. CT65**
- Cause and Effect: The Progressive Movement

## *Now and* then

**Big Business and Competition**

The United States District Court for the District of Columbia filed its suit against Microsoft Corporation in May 1998. The court based its case on sections 1 and 2 of the Sherman Act, charging Microsoft with "anticompetitive" behavior and with monopolizing the software industry. Microsoft denied that it had a monopoly and claimed that all its actions were legitimate efforts to compete in a fast-moving industry. Commentators noted that the computer industry moves so quickly that by the time the lengthy court battle was over, the industry would already have changed enough to make the court's decision moot.

### INSTRUCT: OBJECTIVE 

**Reforming Government and Expanding Democracy/Promoting Social Welfare/Creating Economic Reform**

Key Questions

- How did the Civil Service Act improve government?
- What reforms in government expanded democracy?
- In which areas were social reformers most active?
- How did the Sherman Antitrust Act change business practices?

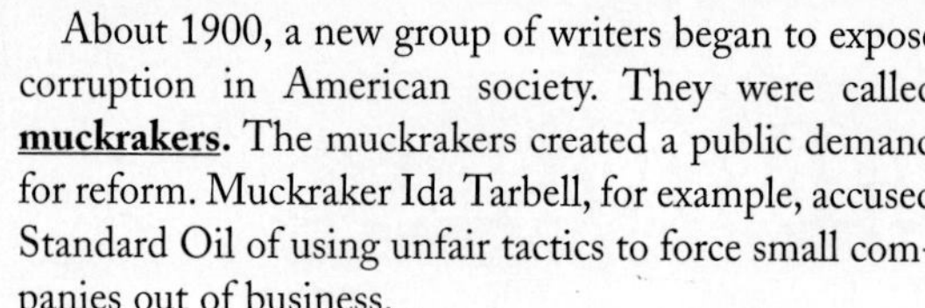

**BIG BUSINESS AND COMPETITION**

In the late 1800s, John D. Rockefeller made a fortune as he gained control of most of the nation's oil refineries, oil fields, and pipelines. In 1906, the government filed an antitrust suit against Rockefeller's Standard Oil. This resulted in its breakup in 1911. The cartoon below shows Standard Oil as an octopus.

In the 1990s, Bill Gates became the richest man in the world as he built Seattle-based Microsoft into a computer software giant. In 1998, the government filed an antitrust suit against Microsoft. It charged the company with using illegal tactics to gain a monopoly with its computer operating system and Web browser.

About 1900, a new group of writers began to expose corruption in American society. They were called **muckrakers.** The muckrakers created a public demand for reform. Muckraker Ida Tarbell, for example, accused Standard Oil of using unfair tactics to force small companies out of business.

The progressive reformers shared at least one of three basic goals: first, to reform government and expand democracy; second, to promote social welfare; third, to create economic reform.

## 2 Reforming Government and Expanding Democracy

In the 1870s and 1880s, elected officials often handed out government jobs and contracts. In return, they won political support. This practice was called patronage. It became a hot political issue during the presidencies of Rutherford B. Hayes, James Garfield, and Chester Arthur. Finally, Congress passed the Pendleton Civil Service Act in 1883. This law required people to take civil service exams for certain government jobs. It also prevented elected officials from firing civil service workers for political reasons.

In the 1890s and early 1900s, progressive leaders in a number of states sought to expand democracy. They wanted to give voters more control over their government. In 1903, under progressive governor Robert M. La Follette, Wisconsin became the first state to establish a direct primary. In a **direct primary,** voters, rather than party conventions, choose candidates to run for public office.

*Reading* **History**

**A. Finding Main Ideas** What was the main goal behind the progressive reforms of government?

A. Answer They aimed to give voters a larger voice in the government.

In Oregon, newspaper editor William S. U'Ren promoted three reforms besides the direct primary.

1. **Initiative**—This reform allowed voters to propose a law directly.
2. **Referendum**—In this reform, a proposed law was submitted to the vote of the people.
3. **Recall**—This reform allowed people to vote an official out of office.

In the years that followed, many other states adopted one or more of these progressive reforms.

## Promoting Social Welfare

This goal addressed such problems as poverty, unemployment, and poor working conditions. You read about the social gospel and settlement house movements in Chapter 21. Leaders in these movements promoted many social-welfare reforms. For example, Jane Addams provided social services



### ACTIVITY OPTIONS

**INDIVIDUAL NEEDS: GIFTED AND TALENTED**

**THE MUCKRAKERS**

**Class Time** Two class periods

**Task** Researching the work of one muckraking writer and preparing an oral report

**Purpose** To help students understand the work of the muckrakers and their role in exposing corruption

**Supplies Needed**

- Reference materials about muckrakers and copies of their books
- Internet access

**Activity** Divide the students into three groups. Tell students to choose one of the prominent muckrakers, such as Ida M. Tarbell, Lincoln Steffens, or Upton Sinclair. Students should research the life and work of the writer they select and read selections from the writer's work. In an oral report, each group should summarize its findings and evaluate the success of its writer in exposing social problems and helping to correct them. Students should submit a bibliography of sources consulted for their report.

 **In-Depth Resources: Unit 7**

- Primary Source, p. 10

to the poor at Hull House. She also worked to help the unemployed. Florence Kelley, also from Hull House, pushed for minimum wage laws and limits on women's working hours.

Another group of reformers who wanted to improve social welfare were the prohibitionists. They worked to prevent alcohol from ruining people's lives. The prohibitionists built on the temperance movement of the 1800s.

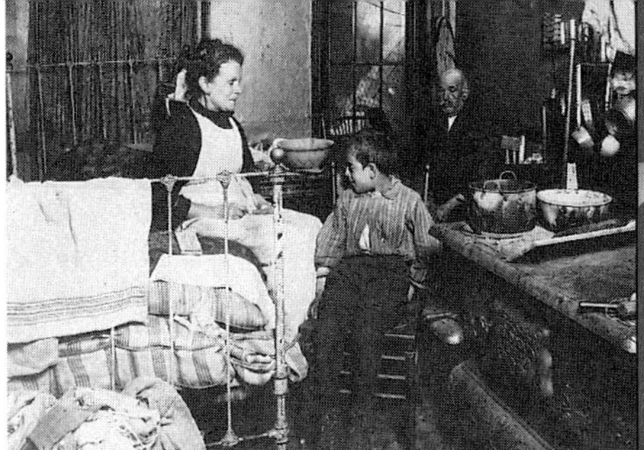

This photograph shows an immigrant family in a crowded tenement at the turn of the century.

## Creating Economic Reform

The third progressive goal was to create economic reform. This meant limiting the power of big business and regulating its activities. By the late 1800s, business leaders in some major industries had formed trusts. These were combinations of businesses. The business firms in a trust worked together to cut prices and squeeze out competitors. Then the trust would raise prices and make larger profits.

The **Sherman Antitrust Act** of 1890 made it illegal for corporations to gain control of industries by forming trusts. However, the government did not enforce the law at first. Enforcement required a strong president.

*Reading* **History**
**B. Summarizing** How did progressives pursue their three basic goals?
B. Answer Progressives established direct primary, initiative, referendum, and recall. They provided services to poor and campaigned for aid to unemployed, minimum wage laws, limits on women's working hours, and prohibition. They broke up trusts and regulated industries.

## 3 Roosevelt and the Square Deal

**Theodore Roosevelt**—the first progressive president—provided this strength and leadership. He came to the presidency by accident, however. In 1898, Roosevelt won fame fighting in the Spanish-American War in Cuba. He returned from Cuba a war hero and was elected governor of New York. In 1900, Roosevelt ran on the Republican ticket as President McKinley's vice president.

Then an assassin shot McKinley, just six months after his inauguration. Roosevelt became president when McKinley died on September 14, 1901. At age 42, Roosevelt was the youngest person ever to become president. He brought his boundless energy to the office. The president often joined his six children in playing in the White House. Americans admired Roosevelt's zest for living. He gained the public's support for reform.

> *"I believe in a square deal."*
> Theodore Roosevelt

Roosevelt began his reforms with an effort to break up the corporate trusts. He thought industries should be regulated for the public interest.

> *A VOICE FROM THE PAST*
>
> When I say I believe in a square deal I do not mean, and nobody who speaks the truth can mean, that he believes it possible to give every man the best hand. If the cards do not come to any man, or if they do come, and he has not got the power to play them, that is his affair. All I mean is that there shall not be any crookedness in the dealing.
>
> **Theodore Roosevelt,** speech on April 5, 1905

Roosevelt saw government as an umpire. Its purpose was to ensure fairness, or a "square deal," for workers, consumers, and big business.



### MORE ABOUT . . .

**Hull House**
Hull House eventually included 13 buildings and a playground, as well as a camp near Lake Geneva, Wisconsin. The facilities included a day nursery, a gym, a community kitchen, and a boarding house for working girls. Hull House offered college-level courses in different subjects as well as training in art, music, and crafts such as bookbinding. It also sponsored the Hull House Players, a theater group. In addition, the facility provided the opportunity for young social workers to acquire training. Many prominent social workers and reformers lived there at one time or another.

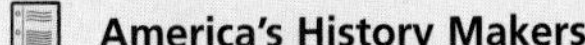

### INSTRUCT: OBJECTIVE 3

**Roosevelt and the Square Deal/ Roosevelt Leads Progressive Reforms**
Key Questions
- How did Roosevelt view the role of government in reform?
- How did Roosevelt's "square deal" affect trusts?
- What progressive reforms did President Roosevelt help launch?
- What steps did Roosevelt take to regulate the meat-packing industry?

**America's History Makers**
- Theodore Roosevelt, pp. 87–88

**Critical Thinking Transparency CT65**
- Cause and Effect: The Progressive Movement

### ACTIVITY OPTIONS
### INDIVIDUAL NEEDS

**STUDENTS ACQUIRING ENGLISH/ESL**

**Social Studies Vocabulary** To help students understand the many specialized vocabulary words in this section, have students add the following list to their personal dictionaries: *journalist, progressive, civil service, muckraker, regulate, investigation, banned, crusader, outdoorsman, preserved, refuge, monuments.*

Next have students look up the words in a dictionary. Help them understand each word by discussing its meaning, use, and other forms in which it may appear. Then have students write a definition of each word in their own words. Have the students find each word in the text. (They are listed in the order in which they appear.) Ask students to read the text sentence aloud and explain what it means. Finally, have students write original sentences including the new terms.

## MORE ABOUT . . .

**Roosevelt and the Trusts**

Theodore Roosevelt was known as a "trust buster." One of Roosevelt's targets as a "bad" trust was the Northern Securities Company, a huge railroad conglomerate headed by J. P. Morgan. When the case against Northern Securities began, J. P. Morgan was reported to have approached Roosevelt as he might have approached a business crony. Morgan allegedly said to Roosevelt, "If we have done anything wrong, send your man to my man and they can fix it up."

 **Humanities Transparency HT44**
- Political Cartoon: The Trust Giant's Point of View

## MORE ABOUT . . .

***The Jungle***

Sinclair's novel describes the disgusting conditions in a meat-packing plant in great detail. For example, Sinclair describes thousands of rats scampering over piles of meat in a packing plant. The meat-packers put out poisoned bread for rats and then threw the dead rats and any uneaten bread into the sausage hoppers with the meat. American meat sales fell dramatically immediately after the book's publication.

 **Humanities Transparency HT43**
- Meat Cutters

 **In-Depth Resources: Unit 7**
- Literature Selection: from *The Jungle* by Upton Sinclair, pp. 12–14

To root out "crookedness," Roosevelt used the Sherman Antitrust Act. Since its passage in 1890, many corporations had ignored the law, which was intended to regulate the trusts. No one had enforced it—no one, that is, until Roosevelt became president in 1901.

At the end of 1901, the nation's railroads were run by a handful of companies. The power of railroads continued to grow. It was not surprising, therefore, that one of Roosevelt's first targets was the railroads. He used the Sherman Antitrust Act to bust up a railroad trust.

Roosevelt was not against big business as such. However, he opposed any trust he thought worked against the national interest. In addition to the railroad trust, Roosevelt broke up the Standard Oil Company and a tobacco trust. In all, the government filed suit against 44 corporations during Roosevelt's presidency.

*Reading* **History**

**C. Making Inferences** How do you think big business leaders regarded President Roosevelt? Why?

C. Answer They probably disliked him because he filed suits against so many trusts.

## Roosevelt Leads Progressive Reforms

As president, Roosevelt had a great deal of power to push progressive ideas. To make such ideas into law, however, he needed help. Roosevelt got it as voters began pressuring their senators and representatives. As a result, Congress passed laws that helped change American society.

Roosevelt acted to regulate the meat-packing industry after reading Upton Sinclair's *The Jungle*. The novel describes a packing plant in which dead rats end up in the sausage. Sinclair focused attention on the poor sanitary conditions under which the meat-packers worked. "I aimed at the public's heart, and by accident I hit it in the stomach," he noted.

Roosevelt launched an investigation of the meat-packing industry. In 1906, he signed the Meat Inspection Act. This act created a government meat inspection program. Roosevelt also signed the Pure Food and Drug Act. This law banned the sale of impure foods and medicines.

While Roosevelt tried to win a square deal for most Americans, he did not push for civil rights for African Americans. He believed that discrimination was morally wrong. However, he did not take the political risk of leading a fight for civil rights.

**Shown at the left is the cover of Upton Sinclair's novel, *The Jungle*. The photograph shows immigrant workers stuffing sausages in a Chicago meat-packing house.**

642

## ACTIVITY OPTIONS

### SKILLBUILDER MINI-LESSON: IDENTIFYING AND SOLVING PROBLEMS

BLOCK SCHEDULING

**Explaining the Skill** Identifying solutions to problems will help you understand historical events. *Problems* may be defined as obstacles that stop people from reaching their goals. Historical problems may have affected many people or only a few.

**Applying the Skill** Tell students that solving problems requires identifying problems, understanding what causes the problems, thinking of ways to solve the problems, and implementing the best solution. Draw the flow chart on the board. Tell students to copy it and complete it with information about one of the following problems: patronage, limited voter control of government, control of businesses by trusts, impure food, loss of natural resources. You may want to review the problem-solving steps found on page 285.

 **In-Depth Resources: Unit 7**
- Skillbuilder Practice, p. 7

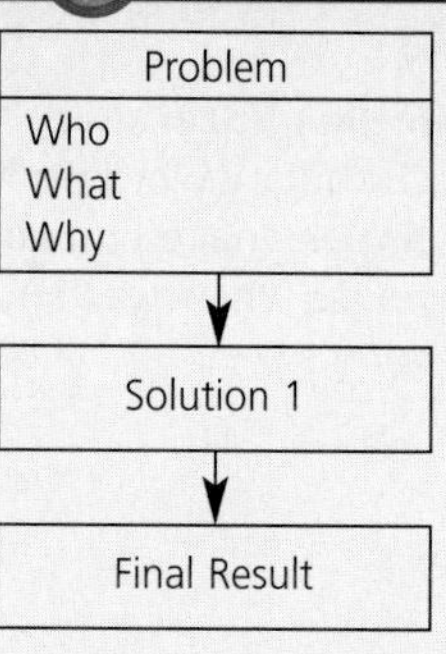

## 4 Conservation

Roosevelt was a strong crusader for conservation—controlling how America's natural resources were used. As an outdoorsman and hunter, he had observed the gradual loss of natural resources. He camped with naturalist John Muir for four days in Yosemite, California. Because he loved the Yosemite Valley so much, he set out to preserve Yosemite and other areas for people's "children and their children's children."

Roosevelt preserved more than 200 million acres of public lands. He established the nation's first wildlife refuge at Pelican Island, Florida. He doubled the number of national parks in the United States. At one point, Congress refused to establish any more national parks. Roosevelt used the Antiquities Act to create national monuments instead. In this way, he preserved the Grand Canyon and the Petrified Forest in Arizona. Roosevelt spoke of the glories of the Grand Canyon while visiting the site in 1903.

**D. Answer** He did so in order to create national parks and monuments despite Congress's objections.

*Reading* **History**
**D. Finding Main Ideas** Why did President Roosevelt bypass Congress?

*A VOICE FROM THE PAST*

Leave it as it is. You cannot improve on it. The ages have been at work on it, and man can only mar it.

**Theodore Roosevelt**, quoted in *Yellowstone*

Both the Grand Canyon and the Petrified Forest have since become national parks. America's next president, William Howard Taft, was not as interested in conservation. However, he did continue Roosevelt's progressive reforms, as you will read in the next section.

### AMERICA'S HISTORY MAKERS

**THEODORE ROOSEVELT**
**1858–1919**

From his youth on, Theodore Roosevelt lived what he called the "strenuous life." He rode horses, hiked, boxed, wrestled, and played tennis. In winter, he swam in the icy Potomac River. He hunted rhinoceros in Africa, harpooned devilfish in Florida, and boated down the Amazon.

Americans loved reading of his exploits and affectionately referred to him as "Teddy" or "T.R." Once, on a hunting trip, he refused to shoot a bear cub. News of the event resulted in a new toy—the teddy bear.

**How did Roosevelt's active style of living carry over into his presidency?**

### Section 1 Assessment

**1. Terms & Names**

**Identify:**
- progressivism
- muckrakers
- direct primary
- initiative
- referendum
- recall
- Sherman Antitrust Act
- Theodore Roosevelt

**2. Taking Notes**

Use a chart to list examples of progressive reforms.

| Goals | Reforms |
|---|---|
| To expand democracy | |
| To protect social welfare | |
| To create economic reform | |

Which reform was most important? Explain.

**3. Main Ideas**

**a.** What kinds of problems did progressives attempt to solve?

**b.** What did President Roosevelt mean by a "square deal," and how did he try to achieve it?

**c.** What were Roosevelt's achievements in the field of conservation?

**4. Critical Thinking**

**Recognizing Effects** In what ways do the reforms that President Roosevelt promoted affect your life today?

**THINK ABOUT**
- the quality of the food you eat
- natural resources that have been preserved

**ACTIVITY OPTIONS**

**ART**
**GEOGRAPHY**

Do research on one of the natural areas that President Roosevelt preserved. Create a **travel brochure** or an illustrated **map** of the area.





### AMERICA'S HISTORY MAKERS

**Theodore Roosevelt**

The outspokenness that endeared Roosevelt to the American public appalled many conservative Republicans. When Roosevelt was nominated for vice-president, Ohio Senator Mark Hanna asked his fellow Republicans, "Don't any of you realize that there's only one life between that madman and the presidency?" When Hanna learned that McKinley had died, he fumed, "Now look! That d-----d cowboy is president of the United States!"

Possible Response: Roosevelt was an activist president who promoted reforms and used the power of the government to bring about change.

### INSTRUCT: OBJECTIVE 

**Conservation**

Key Questions
- Why did Roosevelt think it was important to preserve public land?
- How did Roosevelt bypass Congress to preserve the Grand Canyon and the Petrified Forest?

### ASSESS & RETEACH

**Setting the Stage** Have students place information in the appropriate boxes on the graphic organizer.

**Formal Assessment**
- Section Quiz, p. 324

**Critical Thinking Transparency CT64**
- Setting the Stage

**RETEACHING ACTIVITY**

Divide students into four groups, and assign one area of American life—government, social welfare, economy, and environment—to each group. Have each group identify reforms, with dates, that affected its area of life. Have students use their lists to create a class time line.

**In-Depth Resources: Unit 7**
- Reteaching Activity, p. 15

### Section 1 Assessment

**1. Terms & Names**

**progressivism,** p. 639
**muckrakers,** p. 640
**direct primary,** p. 640
**initiative,** p. 640
**referendum,** p. 640
**recall,** p. 640
**Sherman Antitrust Act,** p. 641
**Theodore Roosevelt,** p. 641

**2. Taking Notes**

To expand democracy: direct primary; initiative; referendum; recall. To protect social welfare: aid to the unemployed; minimum wage laws; limits on women's working hours; prohibition. To create economic reform: break up trusts; regulate industry

Answers will vary.

**3. Main Ideas**

**a.** poverty; the spread of slums; poor working conditions in factories; the power of big corporations
**b.** a fair situation for everyone; by breaking up trusts and regulating industries **c.** He added to the forest reserves, doubled the national parks, created the first wildlife refuge, and preserved natural wonders.

**4. Critical Thinking**

Students consume safer foods and medicines and can enjoy many natural resources.

**ACTIVITY OPTIONS**

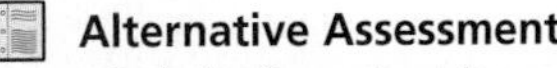

**Alternative Assessment**
- Rubrics for a brochure, 1.13
- Rubrics for a map, 2.1

## GEOGRAPHY *in* HISTORY

**OBJECTIVE**

Students will analyze maps and interpret information to learn about early efforts to protect America's wilderness areas and about the National Park System.

 **BLOCK SCHEDULING**

## MORE ABOUT . . .

**John Muir**

John Muir was the unofficial leader of the early American preservationists. He was born in Scotland but spent much of his childhood on a homestead in Wisconsin. Throughout his youth, Muir was irresistibly drawn to the world of nature. After an accident nearly cost him his sight in 1867, he began a walking trip that ended in Florida. Then he headed for California, where he first saw the Yosemite Valley while working as a sheepherder. Muir spent much of the rest of his life in the Sierra Nevadas and the Yosemite Valley.

## INSTRUCT

Key Questions

- How did Theodore Roosevelt help preserve the American wilderness?
- What problems led to the formation of the National Park Service?
- Why are most of the national parks located in the West?

**MAP SKILL QUESTIONS**

Which state has the most national parks?

Which national park is located in the Northeast?

In which two national parks would you expect to visit caves?

GEOGRAPHY *in* HISTORY

REGION AND HUMAN-ENVIRONMENT INTERACTION

# The National Parks Movement

As the United States expanded westward, two things became evident. First, this was a land of astonishing beauty. Second, this unspoiled beauty would not last if it wasn't protected.

President Theodore Roosevelt may have given the conservation movement its most significant boost. An outdoorsman, naturalist, and visionary, he established the U.S. Forest Service and set aside more than 200 million acres of public lands as national parks, forests, monuments, and wildlife refuges.

Creating parks was just the first step in protecting these lands. Problems arose that had not been foreseen. These problems included a lack of funds and growing numbers of tourists and researchers. In 1916, the National Park Service was established with the goal of saving the parks for future generations.

In 1903, Teddy Roosevelt (left) joined conservationist John Muir (right) for a camping trip. Their trip took them from the "big trees" of the Sequoia forest to the wonders of the Yosemite Valley. This photo of Roosevelt and Muir was taken at Glacier Point in Yosemite. Both men wanted to protect the magnificent beauty of America's most spectacular regions.

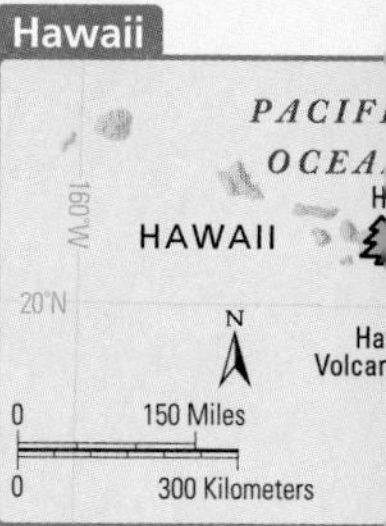


## ARTIFACT FILE

**Sequoia National Park** is a land of giants. In a forest where many trees are more than 250 feet high, it is difficult to get a sense of scale when looking at the biggest of these giants. The General Sherman Tree, shown here, is the largest tree by volume in the world. A number of trees in Sequoia National Park are named for Civil War generals.

**Everglades National Park** in Florida is part of the approximately 1,500,000-acre Everglades region. This wetland habitat is home to birds, especially waders such as herons, egrets, and ibis, and is famous for its alligators.

644

## MUSEUM CONNECTIONS

The National Park Service (NPS) operates museums in over 300 parks. The NPS Web site allows users to explore each park's collection by subject area. In addition, visitors can view the "treasures" of the museums in a selected region of the country. For example, "treasures" of the Pacific West include Native American artifacts, historic photographs of the logging industry, and fossils. For the Internet location of the "Treasures of the Nation" virtual exhibit, visit www.mcdougallittell.com

National parks are identified on the map above. The National Park System includes many areas, all of which are under the management of the National Park Service (NPS).

## On-Line Field Trip

**Yellowstone National Park** was designated the world's first national park in 1872. Covering about 2,200,000 acres, Yellowstone is still the largest national park in the United States. There are many geysers in Yellowstone, including Old Faithful (at right).

Visit www.mcdougallittell.com for more information.

### CONNECT TO GEOGRAPHY

1. **Region** What might be two reasons the national parks are concentrated where they are?
2. **Human-Environment Interaction** What effects might visits from many tourists have on a national park?

See Geography Handbook, page 17.

### CONNECT TO HISTORY

3. **Analyzing Causes** What general mood of the era made the late 1800s a likely time for successfully starting a national park?



### CONNECT TO GEOGRAPHY

1. **Region** There are more open spaces in the West, and there are also fewer people.
2. **Human-Environment Interaction** Too many visits might begin to have a negative impact on the environment. Too many cars and too much litter and pollution could spoil the beauty of the park.

### CONNECT TO HISTORY

3. **Analyzing Causes** The reform spirit of the late 1800s probably made the national parks movement more feasible.

### CRITICAL THINKING ACTIVITY

**Evaluating** Most Americans accept the idea of setting aside wilderness lands to preserve them for future generations. However, some people think that the nation would be better served if private businesses were allowed to use the resources found in the many acres of land belonging to the National Park Service. Have students make a graphic like the one below and brainstorm some of the reasons in favor of preservation and some of the reasons in favor of using the resources found in protected areas.

| Reasons For | Reasons Against |
|---|---|
| | |
| | |
| | |
| | |

**Class Time** 20 minutes

### MORE ABOUT . . .

**Yellowstone**

Congress established Yellowstone as a "public park" in 1872. However, no one was exactly sure what "park" meant. Some people came to Yellowstone to hunt buffalo, and ranchers brought their cattle in to graze. While large groups with as many as 300 horses rode in the park, bandits waited to take the riders' wallets. One person even opened a saloon in the park. Eventually, legislation and funding allowed the National Park Service to set and enforce rules for the use of park land.

## SECTION OBJECTIVES

1. To evaluate Taft's progressive policies
2. To identify the progressive qualities of the Sixteenth and Seventeenth Amendments
3. To summarize Wilson's record as a progressive president
4. To analyze reasons for the passage of the Eighteenth Amendment

**CRITICAL THINKING**
Drawing Conclusions, p. 648
Summarizing, p. 649
Making Inferences, p. 649

## FOCUS & MOTIVATE

### 5-MINUTE WARM-UP

**Making Inferences** These questions focus on the progressive reforms of Taft and Wilson.

1. Read the headings on pages 646–649. What evidence indicates that progressive policies continued after Roosevelt left the White House?
2. Who were the two presidents after Roosevelt?

**Warm-Up Transparency WT22**

## INSTRUCT

### INSTRUCT: OBJECTIVE 1

**Taft and Progressivism**
Key Questions
- How did Taft continue Roosevelt's progressive policies?
- What other progressive reforms did Taft promote?
- Why did Taft disappoint some progressives?

**In-Depth Resources: Unit 7**
- Guided Reading, p. 4
- Building Vocabulary, p. 6

**Reading Study Guide** (Spanish and English), pp. 217–218

# 2 Taft and Wilson as Progressives

**TERMS & NAMES**
William Howard Taft
Sixteenth Amendment
Seventeenth Amendment
Clayton Antitrust Act
Federal Reserve Act

| MAIN IDEA | WHY IT MATTERS NOW |
|---|---|
| Progressive reforms continued under William Howard Taft and Woodrow Wilson. | Constitutional amendments passed during this time affect Americans today. |

### ONE AMERICAN'S STORY

**During the Progressive Era, many Americans became disturbed by the problems caused by capitalism. Some even turned to socialism. This is a system in which business and industry are totally controlled by the state. Labor leader Eugene V. Debs became a socialist while serving time in prison for his role in a labor strike. In 1894, as head of the American Railway Union, Debs supported a strike by the workers who made railroad cars. When the federal government broke up the strike, Debs defied the courts. He was sent to prison for six months.**

**In the 1908 presidential election, Debs ran as the Socialist Party candidate. In his campaign, he urged American workers to consider what competition was like in a capitalist system.**

*A VOICE FROM THE PAST*

Competition was natural enough at one time, but do you think you are competing today? . . . Against whom? Against Rockefeller? About as I would if I had a wheelbarrow and competed with the Santa Fe [railroad] from here to Kansas City.

**Eugene V. Debs,** quoted in *The Annals of America*

The forceful speeches of Eugene V. Debs attracted large audiences.

**Debs made a decent showing in the election, winning more than 420,000 votes. However, the Republican candidate Taft did better and was elected.**

## Taft and Progressivism

In the 1908 election, Debs ran against Republican **William Howard Taft** and Democrat William Jennings Bryan. Neither Debs nor Bryan stood much of a chance against Taft. He was Roosevelt's handpicked successor. Roosevelt's popularity swayed many people to vote for Taft, who promised to follow Roosevelt's progressive policies.

Taft continued Roosevelt's attack on trusts. During his four years in office, Taft pursued almost twice as many antitrust suits as Roosevelt had in nearly eight years in office. But Taft received less credit for his progressivism because he became allied with conservative Republicans rather



## RECOMMENDED RESOURCES

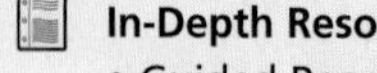
**In-Depth Resources: Unit 7**
- Guided Reading, p. 4
- Building Vocabulary, p. 6
- Geography Application: Election of 1912, pp. 8–9
- Reteaching Activity, p. 16

**Reading Study Guide** (Spanish and English), pp. 217–218

**Economics in History**
- Tariffs and Taxes, p. 22

**Formal Assessment**
- Section Quiz, p. 325

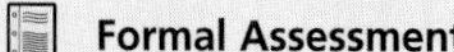
**Alternative Assessment**
- Rubrics, 4.4
- Rubrics, 5.1

**Access for Students Acquiring English/ESL**
- Guided Reading, p. 148
- Geography Application, pp. 151–152

**Technology Resources**

**Geography Transparency GT22**
- Progressive Reforms, 1915

**Electronic Teacher Tools with Test Maker**

**ClassZone**
www.mcdougallittell.com

than Roosevelt's progressive Republicans. Nevertheless, Taft did move forward with progressive reforms. His reforms addressed the progressive goals of democracy, social welfare, and economic reform. Two of the major progressive achievements under President Taft were constitutional amendments.

##  Two Progressive Amendments

The **Sixteenth Amendment** was passed in 1909 and ratified in 1913. It gave Congress the power to create income taxes. The Constitution previously did not allow direct taxes on an individual's income. This amendment was intended to provide a means of spreading the cost of running the government among more people. The income tax soon became the main source of federal revenue.

### Economics *in* History

# Types of Taxes

The Sixteenth Amendment, ratified in 1913, made it constitutional for the federal government to have an income tax. Congress quickly passed an income tax law the same year. The income tax provides revenue to the federal government by taxing profits and earnings. In a graduated income tax, larger incomes are taxed at higher rates than smaller incomes. The income tax is only one of several taxes that governments use to raise money.

**INCOME TAXES**

1. **Individual:** You pay a percentage of what you earn at work or from investments. Under the payroll deduction plan, income taxes are deducted (taken out) from your wages or salary before you get your paycheck.
2. **Corporate:** Corporations pay a percentage of their profits in income tax.

**PROPERTY TAXES**

People pay taxes on property they own, such as land or a house. Property taxes are often used to support public services such as schools.

**TYPES OF TAXES**

**SALES TAXES**

Sales tax is imposed on the retail price of merchandise and collected by the retailer. For example, when you buy a pair of jeans, you pay sales tax, which will be listed on your receipt.

**ESTATE TAXES**

This tax is charged against the value of the property of a person who has died. It is also called the "death tax" because it is collected from the dead person's estate before the estate is passed on to the heirs.

**CONNECT TO HISTORY**

1. **Making Inferences** How might a corporate income tax fit the goals of the Progressive Era?

See Skillbuilder Handbook, page R11.

**CONNECT TO TODAY**

2. **Drawing Conclusions** Some states that have a sales tax do not charge that tax on the purchase of goods like food or clothing. Why do you think they make an exception for these purchases?

Visit www.mcdougallittell.com to learn more about taxes.





**INSTRUCT: OBJECTIVE 2**

**Two Progressive Amendments**

Key Questions

- What power did Congress gain from the passage of the Sixteenth Amendment?
- How did the Seventeenth Amendment expand democracy?
- In what way did the Sixteenth and Seventeenth Amendments support progressive goals?

### Economics *in* History

**OBJECTIVE**

Students will be able to identify different types of taxes and to explain how income taxes provide income to the federal government.

**The Federal Government and Taxes**

The issue of taxes had been a problem for Americans since the Revolution. The inability of the Continental Congress to raise money through taxes nearly caused the Patriots to lose the war. Congress passed legislation authorizing an income tax in the mid-1890s, but the Supreme Court declared that the income tax was unconstitutional. The Sixteenth Amendment changed the Constitution to give Congress the power to tax income.

Economics in History
- Tariffs and Taxes, p. 22

**CONNECT TO HISTORY**

1. **Making Inferences** The reform goals of the Progressive Era would probably suggest that corporations have a responsibility to pay their share of taxes to support social goals.

**CONNECT TO TODAY**

2. **Drawing Conclusions** Items such as food or clothing are often regarded as necessities and are therefore sometimes exempted from taxes.

**STRANGE *but* True**

**From President to Chief Justice**
Taft truly disliked political life. He described his presidential campaign as "one of the most uncomfortable four months of my life." After his term as president, Taft taught law at Yale University until his appointment to the Supreme Court. He remained in that post until 1930. Of his time as the country's leader, he wrote, "I don't remember that I ever was president."

**INSTRUCT: OBJECTIVE 3**

**The Election of 1912/The Wilson Presidency**
Key Questions
- What problem within the Republican Party helped Woodrow Wilson win the 1912 election?
- How did the Clayton Antitrust Act uphold Wilson's beliefs about big business and workers?
- How did the Federal Reserve Act improve the nation's banking system?

 **In-Depth Resources: Unit 7**
- Geography Application: Election of 1912, pp. 8–9

**CRITICAL THINKING ACTIVITY**
**Making Inferences** Read with the class the first full paragraph on page 649 and discuss what happens when the Federal Reserve Board lowers interest rates. Ask students to explain what happens when the Fed raises interest rates.
**Class Time** 10 minutes

**STRANGE *but* True**

**FROM PRESIDENT TO CHIEF JUSTICE**
William Howard Taft was the only man in American history to serve first as president and then as chief justice of the U.S. Supreme Court. He had always wanted to be a Supreme Court justice. Even his mother said, "I do not want my son to be President. His is a judicial mind and he loves the law."

Taft was unhappy as president. When he left office, he said: "I'm glad to be going. This is the lonesomest place in the world." Eight years later, in 1921, President Warren G. Harding appointed Taft to the Supreme Court.

Taft is shown here in his judicial robes.

The **Seventeenth Amendment** was ratified in 1913. It provided for the direct election of U.S. senators by voters in each state. Formerly, state legislatures had chosen U.S. senators. Under this system, many senators obtained their positions through corrupt bargains. Because of this, the Senate was called the "Millionaires' Club." The Seventeenth Amendment gave people a more direct voice in the government.

*Reading*History
**A. Drawing Conclusions** Why are the Sixteenth and Seventeenth amendments considered progressive?
A. Answer
The Sixteenth Amendment was intended as a way to spread out the cost of running the government fairly. The Seventeenth Amendment addresses the progressive goal of expanding democracy.

## 3 The Election of 1912

Taft achieved a number of progressive reforms. However, a deep split developed between him and progressive leaders in the Republican Party. Still, with the support of conservative Republicans, Taft won the party's nomination as its presidential candidate in 1912.

However, many progressive Republicans supported Theodore Roosevelt. He had entered the race and formed the Progressive Party, also known as the Bull Moose Party.

The Democrats chose Governor Woodrow Wilson of New Jersey as their presidential candidate. Eugene Debs again entered the race as the Socialist candidate. With the Republicans deeply divided, Wilson won the election.

## The Wilson Presidency

As president, Wilson established a progressive record. Wilson believed that "bigness" itself was dangerous. He wanted the government to use its powers to break up monopolies—groups that sought complete control over an industry. He also wanted the government to help workers in their struggles against business owners.

At Wilson's urging, Congress passed the **Clayton Antitrust Act** of 1914. The new law laid down rules forbidding business practices that lessened competition. A business, for example, could no longer buy the stock of a competitor. The Clayton Act gave the government more power to regulate trusts. In addition, the Clayton Act was also prolabor:

1. It said labor unions and farm organizations could merge and expand.
2. It limited the ability of the courts to force workers to end strikes.
3. It legalized such labor tactics as strikes, picketing, and boycotts.

Vocabulary
**boycott:** an attempt to pressure a business by refusing to buy a product or use a service

During Wilson's two terms, reforms to the nation's financial system occurred. In 1913, the **Federal Reserve Act** was passed. This improved the nation's monetary and banking system. The law created the modern banking system, which resembles a pyramid. At the top is the Federal Reserve Board, which is appointed by the president. Next are 12 Federal Reserve Banks for different regions of the country. These are "bankers'



**ACTIVITY OPTIONS**

**MULTIPLE LEARNING STYLES: SPATIAL**

**BLOCK SCHEDULING**

**CREATING A GRAPHIC ORGANIZER**
**Class Time** 30 minutes
**Task** Creating a graphic that shows the organization of the Federal Reserve system
**Purpose** To understand how the nation's banking system operates

**Supplies Needed**
- Paper
- Art supplies

**Activity** Tell students to review the paragraphs on pages 648–649 about the Federal Reserve system. Then tell students to create a graphic organizer that illustrates the material, showing the Federal Reserve Board, the Federal Reserve Banks, and member banks. The organizer should indicate that members of the board are appointed by the president. When organizers are complete, allow students to compare their work and change their organizers if they wish.

banks." They serve the bottom level—the member banks.

The Federal Reserve Act created a more flexible currency system by allowing banks to control the money supply. To raise money, for example, the Federal Reserve Board, or "Fed," lowers the interest rate that it charges member banks. These banks then borrow more from the Fed and thus have more money to lend to people and businesses.

President Wilson throws out a baseball at the opening game of the 1916 season.

*Reading* **History**
**B. Summarizing** What were some of Wilson's achievements as a progressive president?
B. Answer His achievements included the Clayton Antitrust Act and the Federal Reserve Act.

Wilson did no more to advance civil rights for African Americans than Roosevelt did. In fact, Wilson approved the segregation, or separation, of African-American and white employees in the federal government. Throughout the Progressive Era, presidents Roosevelt, Taft, and Wilson did not actively promote civil rights for African Americans.

## 4 The Eighteenth Amendment

Another amendment passed during the Progressive Era was the Eighteenth Amendment. This is also called the Prohibition Amendment. During Wilson's administration, supporters of prohibition gained strength. Reformers thought an alcohol ban would reduce poverty. They argued that liquor added to unemployment and violence. Business leaders saw that alcohol made workers less efficient. Finally, in 1917, Congress passed a constitutional amendment. The Eighteenth Amendment prohibited the manufacture and sale of alcoholic beverages. The states ratified the amendment in 1919.

In the next section, you will read about the most important amendment of the era—the Nineteenth Amendment, which gave women the vote.

### Section 2 Assessment

**1. Terms & Names**

**Identify:**
- William Howard Taft
- Sixteenth Amendment
- Seventeenth Amendment
- Clayton Antitrust Act
- Federal Reserve Act

**2. Taking Notes**

Complete the chart to review some of the major reforms of both the Taft and Wilson administrations.

| Law | Description |
|---|---|
| Sixteenth Amendment | |
| Clayton Antitrust Act | |
| Federal Reserve Act | |

**3. Main Ideas**

a. What caused the Republican Party to split in 1912?

b. What were the major progressive accomplishments of Wilson's presidency?

c. What did the Federal Reserve Act do?

**4. Critical Thinking**

**Making Inferences** Why did progressive presidents do little to advance civil rights for African Americans?

THINK ABOUT
- the goals of progressivism
- the groups of people that progressivism aimed to help

**ACTIVITY OPTIONS**

**LANGUAGE ARTS**
**TECHNOLOGY**

Research one of the people mentioned in this section. Then write the **script** for the first 10 minutes of his documentary or design his **Web page**.



### INSTRUCT: OBJECTIVE 4

**The Eighteenth Amendment**

Key Questions
- Why did many progressive reformers support prohibition?
- What were the major provisions of the Eighteenth Amendment?

**Geography Transparency GT22**
- Progressive Reforms, 1915

### MORE ABOUT . . .

**Prohibition**

The Women's Christian Temperance Union (WCTU) led the campaign for prohibition laws. Many women joined the WCTU because they wanted to stop the abuse of women and children by men under the influence of alcohol. In addition to its crusade against alcohol, the WCTU worked to help women and children in other ways. For example, the organization provided shelters for the homeless and day nurseries for children.

### ASSESS & RETEACH

**Setting the Stage** Have students place information in the appropriate boxes on the graphic organizer.

**Formal Assessment**
- Section Quiz, p. 325

**RETEACHING ACTIVITY**

Have students create graphics like the one below to show how progressive reforms solved problems during the Taft and Wilson administrations.

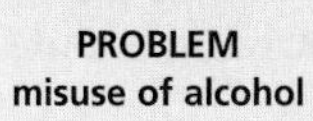

| PROBLEM | → | SOLUTION |
|---|---|---|
| misuse of alcohol | | prohibition |

**In-Depth Resources: Unit 7**
- Reteaching Activity, p. 16

### Section 2 Assessment

**1. Terms & Names**

**William Howard Taft,** p. 646
**Sixteenth Amendment,** p. 647
**Seventeenth Amendment,** p. 648
**Clayton Antitrust Act,** p. 648
**Federal Reserve Act,** p. 648

**2. Taking Notes**

Sixteenth Amendment: gave Congress the power to create income taxes; Clayton Antitrust Act: forbade any business practice that "substantially" lessened competition; legalized certain labor tactics; Federal Reserve Act: created the Federal Reserve system, consisting of 12 Federal Reserve Banks, supervised by the Federal Reserve Board

**3. Main Ideas**

**a.** Some Republicans wanted to nominate Taft for president, others Roosevelt. They split so each could run their own candidate. **b.** the Clayton Antitrust Act, the Federal Reserve Act, and the Prohibition Amendment **c.** It established the Federal Reserve Board and improved the nation's banking system.

**4. Critical Thinking**

They were promoting equal opportunity and justice for the white poor and working class.

**ACTIVITY OPTIONS**

**Alternative Assessment**
- Rubrics, 4.4, 5.1

## SECTION OBJECTIVES

1. To identify changes in the lives of women during the Progressive Era
2. To describe the contributions of women progressives
3. To describe early actions in the movement for woman suffrage
4. To analyze events that led to passage of the Nineteenth Amendment

**SKILLBUILDER**

Interpreting Maps: Region, Human-Environment Interaction, p. 652
Interpreting Charts, p. 653

**CRITICAL THINKING**

Finding Main Ideas, p. 651
Recognizing Effects, p. 653
Comparing and Contrasting, p. 653

## FOCUS & MOTIVATE

### 5-MINUTE WARM-UP

**Drawing Conclusions** These questions focus on woman suffrage.

1. Look at the photo and map on page 652. What important reform does the map illustrate?
2. In which states could women not vote in 1919?

 **Warm-Up Transparency WT22**

## INSTRUCT

### INSTRUCT: OBJECTIVE 1

**New Roles for Women**

Key Questions

- How had industry and technology changed women's work by the turn of the century?
- What kind of jobs outside the home were available to women at the turn of the century?

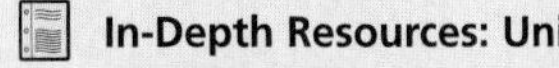 **In-Depth Resources: Unit 7**
- Guided Reading, p. 5
- Primary Source, p. 11

**Reading Study Guide** (Spanish and English), pp. 219–220

# 3 Women Win New Rights

**TERMS & NAMES**
Susan B. Anthony
Carrie Chapman Catt
Nineteenth Amendment

| MAIN IDEA | WHY IT MATTERS NOW |
| --- | --- |
| Women became leaders in social reform movements and won the right to vote during the Progressive Era. | Today, American women enjoy the right to vote because of women reformers in the Progressive Era. |

## ONE AMERICAN'S STORY

**After graduating from nursing school in 1891, Lillian Wald briefly studied medicine. Then a friend asked her to teach a home nursing class at a school for immigrants in New York City. One day a child asked Wald to help her sick mother, who was absent from the class. Following the child home, Wald was shocked by what she saw.**

*A VOICE FROM THE PAST*

Over broken asphalt, over dirty mattresses and heaps of refuse we went. The tall houses reeked with rubbish. . . . There were two rooms and a family of seven not only lived here but shared their quarters with boarders.

**Lillian Wald,** quoted in *Always a Sister*

**The experience gave Wald a new mission. Inspired to help such poor immigrants, she founded the Nurses' Settlement. This was later called the Henry Street Settlement. It was the first visiting nurse program in the country not run by a religious group. The program mainly helped poor women and children.**

**In this section, you will read about others like Wald who worked to make life better for all women.**

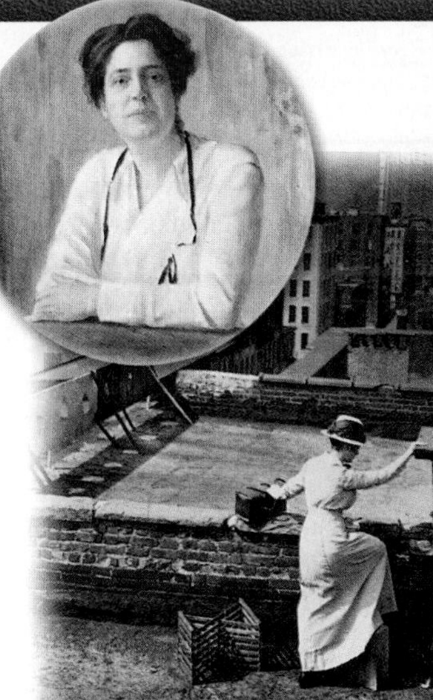

(Above left) Lillian Wald. (Above) A visiting nurse takes a shortcut between two tenements.

## 1 New Roles for Women

The social reform movements of the Progressive Era were led by educated, middle-class women. At the turn of the century, women like Wald were looking for new roles outside the home. The growth of industry had changed many urban, middle-class homes. These homes now had indoor running water and electric power for lamps and vacuum cleaners.

In addition, factories produced the products that women once made in the home, such as soap, clothing, and canned goods. Such technological advances reduced some of the unpleasant work of homemaking. At the same time, families were becoming smaller as women had fewer children.



## RECOMMENDED RESOURCES

 **In-Depth Resources: Unit 7**
- Guided Reading, p. 5
- Building Vocabulary, p. 6
- Primary Source, p. 11
- Reteaching Activity, p. 17
- Enrichment Activity, p. 18

**Reading Study Guide** (Spanish and English), pp. 219–220

**Outline Map Activities**
- Politics and Reform, 1919, pp. 43–44

**America's History Makers**
- Susan B. Anthony, pp. 89–90

**Citizenship Today,** p. 78

**Formal Assessment**
- Section Quiz, p. 326

**Alternative Assessment**
- Rubrics, 4.4
- Rubrics, 5.1

**Access for Students Acquiring English/ESL**
- Guided Reading, p. 149

**Technology Resources**

 **Electronic Teacher Tools with Test Maker**

 **ClassZone**
www.mcdougallittell.com

As a result, the homemaker's role began to change. High schools, colleges, and women's clubs offered courses in home economics and domestic science. In these courses, women were encouraged to apply the latest methods to running their homes.

Other women responded to changes in the home by taking jobs in factories, offices, and stores. Women worked as telephone operators, store clerks, and typists. Those who gained a college education could pursue a profession. The choices were limited to such fields as teaching and nursing. Women who could afford to were expected to quit their jobs when they married. In 1890, approximately 30 percent of women between the ages of 20 and 24 worked outside the home. However, only about 15 percent between the ages of 25 and 44 did so.

*Reading* **History**

**A. Finding Main Ideas** How and why did women's roles begin to change around the turn of the century?

A. Answer Women began taking jobs outside the home because housework took less of their time and because many middle-class, educated women sought a meaningful way to participate in society.

## 2 Women Progressives

The social reform movements that many middle-class, college-educated women took part in were focused on helping people. These included the settlement house and prohibition movements. A settlement house is a community center providing assistance to residents—particularly immigrants—in a slum neighborhood.

Jane Addams was a good example of the progressive female leader. After graduating from college, Addams sought a meaningful way to participate in society. She was financially independent. A visit to a settlement house in a London slum inspired her to start a similar program in Chicago. She was helped by her friend Ellen Starr.

With donations from wealthy Chicagoans, Addams and Starr rented an old mansion. Hull House was located in a poor, immigrant neighborhood. Within just a few years, they organized a full program of services, classes, and clubs. These were run by a group of young women residents and over 90 volunteers. Hull House served as an information bureau for new immigrants. It also helped the unemployed find jobs. It offered a kindergarten, a day nursery, after-school youth clubs, nutrition classes, and a concert program. Workers also pressured politicians for improved city services for the neighborhood.

*A VOICE FROM THE PAST*

One function of the settlement to its neighborhood somewhat resembled that of the big brother whose mere presence in the playground protected the little ones from bullies.

**Jane Addams,** quoted in *Women and the American Experience*

The young women residents of Hull House received no salary and had to pay for their room and board. This meant that they had to be financially

**Connections TO LITERATURE**

**WOMEN OUTSIDE THE HOME**

Charlotte Perkins Gilman (shown below) was an influential writer on women's rights. She wanted to free women from housework to pursue careers. In *Women and Economics* (1898), Gilman argued that a wife's dependency on her husband limited her personal development.

In *Concerning Children* (1900) and *The Home* (1903), she proposed that families live in large apartments. These would have centralized nurseries and a staff devoted to cooking, cleaning, and child-care. This support would free women to work outside the home.



### Connections TO *LITERATURE*

**Women Outside the Home**

In addition to her works of nonfiction, Gilman was an accomplished fiction writer. Her 1890 short story "The Yellow Wallpaper" is the story of a depressed woman who is oppressed by society's constraints and by her husband's kind, but total, control over her life. Gilman wrote the story in part to expose the futility of "rest cures" prescribed for women.

### INSTRUCT: OBJECTIVE 

**Women Progressives**

Key Questions

- What qualities did many women progressive reformers share?
- What were the goals of settlement houses?
- For what reforms did Jane Addams, Florence Kelley, and Carry Nation work?

### MORE ABOUT . . .

**Reformers at Hull House**

Some of the most outstanding young people of their time were attracted to work at Hull House. The noteworthy reformers who came to live at Hull House include Alice Hamilton. Hamilton studied medicine at Johns Hopkins Medical School and then taught pathology at the Women's Medical School of Northwestern University of Chicago. She lived at Hull House and contributed to its programs. Julia Lathrop also worked at Hull House. Her main goals were to improve the health of children and to set up special courts for juveniles.

### ACTIVITY OPTIONS

### INDIVIDUAL NEEDS

**LESS PROFICIENT READERS**

**Focusing on Important Details** Help students set a purpose for reading and focus on important details. Copy the graphic at right on the board. Point out the section title to students. Tell them that they will be reading about women leaders in social reform. Read the list of names with students. Then ask students to look for these names as they read and take notes regarding their contributions. Following this procedure may prepare less proficient readers to complete the chart in the assessment section.

| Name of Reformer | Contributions |
|---|---|
| Charlotte Perkins Gilman | |
| Jane Addams | |
| Florence Kelley | |
| Carry Nation | |
| Susan B. Anthony | |
| Carrie Chapman Catt | |

## MORE ABOUT . . .

**Carry Nation**

Carry Moore married at the age of 19, but she soon learned that her husband was an alcoholic. She left him shortly after the birth of her daughter. Carry and her second husband, David Nation, moved to a frontier town in Texas. When they moved to a small town in Kansas, Carry Nation began her campaign against alcohol and the frontier-town fixture—the saloon. As her fame grew, people in many towns begged Nation to help them close down the bars. To help fund her work, Nation sold pewter hatchet pins.

## INSTRUCT: OBJECTIVE 

**Suffrage for Women**

Key Questions
- What was the goal of the woman suffrage movement?
- Why did NAWSA campaign in the states to win the vote for women?
- How did women throughout the country obtain the right to vote?

 **America's History Makers**
- Susan B. Anthony, pp. 89–90

 **In-Depth Resources: Unit 7**
- Enrichment Activity, p. 18

## HISTORY FROM VISUALS

**Reading the Map** Have students study the map, identifying each section of the country and its position on woman suffrage prior to the Nineteenth Amendment. Have students locate their own state and identify its suffrage stance.

**Extension** Ask students to use an encyclopedia to find out when women won the right to vote in the territory of Alaska.

 **Outline Map Activities**
- Politics and Reform, 1919, pp. 43–44

independent. For some, Hull House provided training for other public service. Florence Kelley, for example, worked at Hull House from 1891 to 1898. She later became secretary of the National Consumers' League. This group promoted better working conditions in factories and stores.

Another prominent but controversial progressive leader was Carry Nation. She campaigned for prohibition. Nation had once been married to an alcoholic. Tall and strong, she adopted dramatic methods in her opposition to alcoholic beverages. In the 1890s, she smashed saloons with a hatchet. This caused law enforcement officials to arrest her for disturbing the peace. Although some people criticized Nation, her efforts helped bring about passage of the Eighteenth Amendment in 1919.

## 3 Suffrage for Women

Many women progressives were active in the struggle for woman suffrage, or the right to vote. American women fought longer for the right to vote than they did for any other reform. Some leaders in the fight died before realizing their goal.

In 1890, two separate woman suffrage groups merged to form the National American Woman Suffrage Association (NAWSA). Elizabeth Cady Stanton served as its first president. Two years later, in 1892, **Susan B. Anthony** became president. She held the position until 1900. Expressing their frustration over the difficulty of gaining suffrage, Elizabeth Cady Stanton and Susan B. Anthony wrote, "Words can not describe the indignation, the humiliation a proud woman feels for her sex in disfranchisement [being deprived of the right to vote]."

**Background** Because she helped organize the woman suffrage movement, Susan B. Anthony became the first woman to be pictured on a U.S. coin.

NAWSA at first focused on state campaigns to win the right to vote, since earlier efforts at passing a federal amendment had failed. But by 1896, only four states allowed women to vote. These were Wyoming, Utah, Idaho, and Colorado. Between 1896 and 1910, women did not gain the right to vote in a single state. Then, between 1910 and 1914, seven more Western states approved full suffrage for women.

**Skillbuilder Answers**
1. in the East and Southeast
2. There was probably greater equality in the West and less reliance on traditional roles for women.

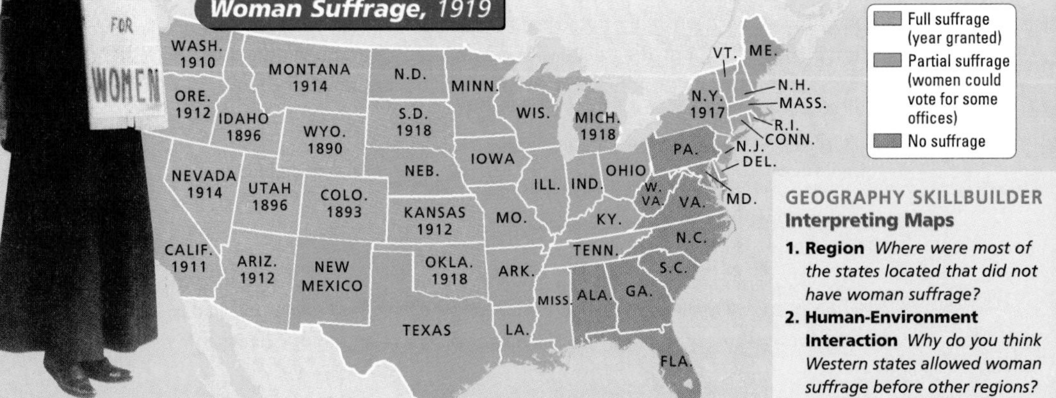


**GEOGRAPHY SKILLBUILDER**
**Interpreting Maps**
1. **Region** *Where were most of the states located that did not have woman suffrage?*
2. **Human-Environment Interaction** *Why do you think Western states allowed woman suffrage before other regions?*

652

## ACTIVITY OPTIONS

**INTERDISCIPLINARY LINK: LANGUAGE ARTS** — BLOCK SCHEDULING

### A SUFFRAGE SPEECH

**Class Time** One class period

**Task** Writing and presenting a speech in favor of woman suffrage

**Purpose** To help students understand the long campaign for the right of American women to vote

**Supplies Needed**
- Reference materials on the suffrage movement
- Podium (optional)
- Pencils, paper

**Activity** After students have read the material on suffrage for women, discuss with them the reasons women wanted to vote. Give students 15 minutes to make notes for a three-minute extemporaneous speech in favor of woman suffrage. Choose students at random to deliver their speeches. Ask class members to rate speakers on a five-point scale for content, delivery, posture, gestures, and rapport with the audience.

| The Progressive Amendments, *1909–1920* | | | |
|---|---|---|---|
| **Number** | **Description** | **Passed by Congress** | **Ratified by States** |
| 16th | Federal income tax | 1909 | 1913 |
| 17th | Senators elected by people rather than state legislatures | 1912 | 1913 |
| 18th | Manufacture, sale, or transport of alcohol prohibited | 1917 | 1919 |
| 19th | Woman suffrage (VOTE 4 WOMEN) | 1919 | 1920 |

SKILLBUILDER **Interpreting Charts**

1. *For which amendment was there the longest gap between passage by Congress and ratification by states?*
2. *What do the dates 1909 and 1920 represent in this chart?*

Skillbuilder Answers
1. 16th Amendment
2. the passage of the first and the ratification of the last of the Progressive amendments

## 4 The Nineteenth Amendment

The Western successes turned the tide in favor of woman suffrage. The United States' entry into World War I in 1917 made the final difference. During the war, membership in NAWSA reached 2 million. **Carrie Chapman Catt,** president of NAWSA, argued that the nation could no longer deny the right to vote to women, who were supporting the war effort by selling war bonds and organizing benefits. President Wilson urged the Senate to pass a women's suffrage amendment. He called passage "vital to the winning of the war."

In 1918, the House passed the **Nineteenth Amendment,** which gave women full voting rights. The Senate approved the amendment in 1919. In 1920, the states ratified it. In the final state campaigns, women staged marches, parades, and rallies around the country. Charlotte Woodard had attended the first women's rights convention in 1848 at Seneca Falls as a teenager. In 1920, the 91-year-old Woodard voted in a presidential election for the first time.

B. Answer the string of successes in Western states granting full suffrage to women, the growth in NAWSA membership, and women's contribution to the war effort during World War I

*Reading* **History**

**B. Recognizing Effects** What factors helped women gain the right to vote?

### Section 3 Assessment

**1. Terms & Names**

Identify:
- Susan B. Anthony
- Carrie Chapman Catt
- Nineteenth Amendment

**2. Taking Notes**

Use a chart to record the achievements of some women leaders of the era.

| Progressive Achievements | |
|---|---|
| Lillian Wald | |
| Jane Addams | |
| Florence Kelley | |

Which achievement seems greatest and why?

**3. Main Ideas**

a. How did women's roles expand near the turn of the century?

b. What was the background of many women who became leaders in social reform movements?

c. How did World War I influence the passage of the Nineteenth Amendment?

**4. Critical Thinking**

**Comparing and Contrasting** In what ways was the struggle for woman suffrage similar to and different from African Americans' struggle for equal rights?

THINK ABOUT
- the restrictions that both groups faced
- how long they struggled for basic rights

ACTIVITY OPTIONS

LANGUAGE ARTS / TECHNOLOGY — Research one of the women reformers discussed in this chapter. Then write the **script** for the first 10 minutes of her documentary or design her **Web page.**





### HISTORY FROM VISUALS

**Reading the Chart** Remind students that the amendments shown represent progressive solutions to political or social problems. Ask students to summarize the problems progressives tried to solve with the passage of each of the amendments.

**Extension** Have students draw a political cartoon about the passage of one of the amendments shown in the chart.

### INSTRUCT: OBJECTIVE 4

**The Nineteenth Amendment**

Key Questions
- How did World War I affect the campaign for woman suffrage?
- How did women work for the required state ratification of the Nineteenth Amendment?

 **Citizenship Today,** p. 76

### ASSESS & RETEACH

**Setting the Stage** Have students complete the appropriate boxes on the graphic organizer.

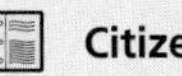 **Formal Assessment**
- Section Quiz, p. 326

**Critical Thinking Transparency CT64**
- Setting the Stage

### RETEACHING ACTIVITY

Divide the class into pairs and assign a paragraph of the section to each pair. Have pairs work together to summarize the paragraph in one or two sentences. Allow students to share their summary statements.

 **In-Depth Resources: Unit 7**
- Reteaching Activity, p. 17

### Section 3 Assessment

**1. Terms & Names**

**Susan B. Anthony,** p. 652
**Carrie Chapman Catt,** p. 653
**Nineteenth Amendment,** p. 653

**2. Taking Notes**

Lillian Wald: began the first nonreligious visiting nurse program in the country; Jane Addams: began Hull House; Florence Kelley: head of the National Consumers' League, which promoted fair working conditions in factories and stores Answers will vary.

**3. Main Ideas**

**a.** They gained an education, took jobs outside the home, or worked for social reform. **b.** Mostly educated, middle-class women led the social reform movement. **c.** Women argued that they should be given the right to vote since they were working to support the war effort.

**4. Critical Thinking**

Both groups had limited rights and were restricted in their job choices. Both groups struggled for centuries to gain basic rights.

ACTIVITY OPTIONS

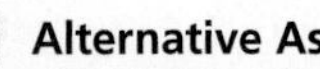 **Alternative Assessment**
- Rubrics for a script, 4.4
- Rubrics for a Web page, 5.1

## TERMS & NAMES

1. **progressivism,** p. 639
2. **muckrakers,** p. 640
3. **referendum,** p. 640
4. **Theodore Roosevelt,** p. 641
5. **William Howard Taft,** p. 646
6. **Sixteenth Amendment,** p. 647
7. **Seventeenth Amendment,** p. 648
8. **Susan B. Anthony,** p. 652
9. **Carrie Chapman Catt,** p. 653
10. **Nineteenth Amendment,** p. 653

## REVIEW QUESTIONS

**Possible Responses**

1. the problem of corruption in government; poverty; unemployment; overcrowding; poor working conditions; alcohol abuse; limiting the power of big business
2. by passing such reforms as the direct primary, initiative, referendum, and recall
3. a fair and honest opportunity for all—workers, consumers, and big business
4. He preserved about 150 million acres of forests, doubled the national parks, and established the first wildlife refuge.
5. Taft broke up many more trusts than Roosevelt did.
6. The Sixteenth Amendment expanded democracy by creating an equitable taxation system. The Seventeenth Amendment expanded democracy by allowing for the direct election of U.S. senators.
7. Wilson thought "bigness" in itself was dangerous, whereas Roosevelt believed big business just needed to be regulated.
8. Technological advances had decreased the burden of housework, families were becoming smaller, and many women took jobs outside the home.
9. Most women progressives were middle class and college educated.
10. the increase in the number of Western states that gave women the right to vote; the growth in the membership of NAWSA; the U.S. entry into World War I and women's work in the war effort

# Chapter 22 ASSESSMENT

## TERMS & NAMES

Briefly explain the importance of each of the following.

1. progressivism
2. muckrakers
3. referendum
4. Theodore Roosevelt
5. William Howard Taft
6. Sixteenth Amendment
7. Seventeenth Amendment
8. Susan B. Anthony
9. Carrie Chapman Catt
10. Nineteenth Amendment

## REVIEW QUESTIONS

**Roosevelt and Progressivism (pages 639–645)**

1. What problems did progressivism address?
2. How did progressive reformers expand democracy in the states?
3. What was Roosevelt's "square deal"?
4. What were Roosevelt's achievements in the area of conservation?

**Taft and Wilson as Progressives (pages 646–649)**

5. In what area did Taft achieve a more impressive progressive record than Roosevelt?
6. What progressive goals did the Sixteenth and Seventeenth amendments address?
7. How did Wilson's position on big business differ from Roosevelt's?

**Women Win New Rights (pages 650–653)**

8. How did women's lives change around 1900?
9. What was the background of many women progressives?
10. What helped further the passage of the Nineteenth Amendment in 1918?

## CRITICAL THINKING

**1. USING YOUR NOTES**

| PROBLEM | SOLUTION |
|---|---|
| Political: patronage; limited suffrage and democracy | |
| Social: poverty; alcohol abuse | |
| Economic: power of big corporations; unemployment | |
| Environmental: impure food and water; diminishing natural resources | |

Use your completed chart from the beginning of this chapter to answer these questions.

a. Which solution to a problem do you think was most effective? Why?

`b. Which solution was least effective and why?

c. To which problem on the chart might you offer a different solution, and what is your solution?

**2. ANALYZING LEADERSHIP**

Based on their domestic record, which president—Roosevelt, Taft, or Wilson—was most effective? Why?

**3. APPLYING CITIZENSHIP SKILLS**

Why might women at the turn of the century consider the right to vote important enough to devote their lives to fighting for it?

**4. THEME: IMPACT OF THE INDIVIDUAL**

In what ways did individuals affect the political, social, and economic life of the country during the Progressive Era?

**Interact *with* History**

How did your solution to one of the social problems of the Progressive Era compare to the solutions proposed by reformers?

## VISUAL SUMMARY

### The Progressive Era

Corruption plagues the government.

Congress passes the Pendleton Civil Service Act (1883).

Theodore Roosevelt becomes president.

Roosevelt breaks up trusts, establishes "square deal," and advocates national parks.

Abuses in industry, politics, business, and labor are widespread.

Congress passes the Pure Food and Drug Act (1906), progressive amendments, Federal Reserve Act (1913), and the Clayton Antitrust Act (1914).

Women lack social justice and equality.

Vote for WOMEN

Women work to establish settlement houses, fight for woman suffrage, and gain 19th Amendment (1920).

## CRITICAL THINKING

**Possible Responses**

1. USING YOUR NOTES **a.** the Nineteenth Amendment, since it gave half the population the right to vote **b.** the Prohibition Amendment, since it was repealed in less than 15 years **c.** Treatment programs could be suggested as an alternative solution to the problem of alcohol abuse.
2. ANALYZING LEADERSHIP Responses will vary but should include references to each president's achievements and the effects of their programs on the nation.
3. APPLYING CITIZENSHIP SKILLS Many women had gained an education and were seeking full equality as citizens, which began with the right to vote.
4. THEME: IMPACT OF THE INDIVIDUAL Social reformers like Jane Addams, Carry Nation, and Susan B. Anthony aided the poor and working class, pressed for prohibition, and struggled for woman suffrage. Presidents Roosevelt, Taft, and Wilson made progressivism a national policy by breaking up trusts and regulating business.

**Interact *with* History** Responses will vary, but students should use the information in the chapter to compare with their predictions.

## HISTORY SKILLS

### 1. INTERPRETING GRAPHS

Study the graph below. Then answer the questions that follow.

**Election of 1912**

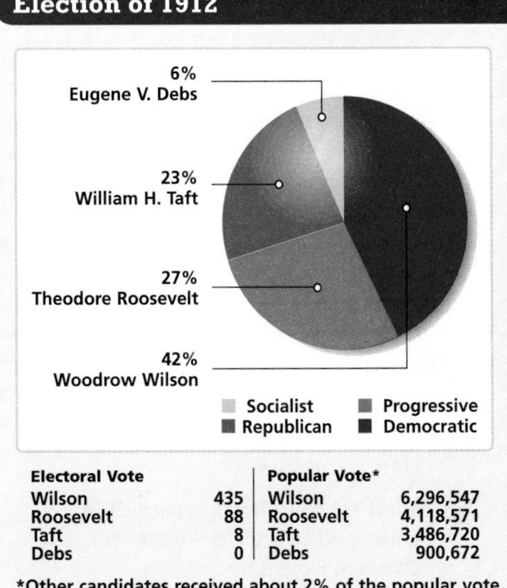


| Electoral Vote | | Popular Vote* | |
|---|---|---|---|
| Wilson | 435 | Wilson | 6,296,547 |
| Roosevelt | 88 | Roosevelt | 4,118,571 |
| Taft | 8 | Taft | 3,486,720 |
| Debs | 0 | Debs | 900,672 |

***Other candidates received about 2% of the popular vote.**

a. What percentage of the popular vote did Eugene V. Debs win?

b. How many electoral votes did Woodrow Wilson win?

c. Who won the second greatest total of popular votes?

### 2. INTERPRETING PRIMARY SOURCES

Following is an excerpt from Woodrow Wilson's first inaugural address, delivered on March 4, 1913. Read the excerpt and then answer the questions that follow.

> There can be no equality of opportunity . . . if men and women and children be not shielded in their lives . . . from the consequences of great industrial and social processes which they cannot alter, control, or singly cope with. . . . Sanitary laws, pure-food laws, and laws determining conditions of labor which individuals are powerless to determine for themselves are intimate parts of the very business of justice and legal efficiency.
>
> **Woodrow Wilson,** First Inaugural Address, March 4, 1913

a. What is Wilson promoting in this passage?

b. What values are reflected in this passage?

## ALTERNATIVE ASSESSMENT

### 1. INTERDISCIPLINARY ACTIVITY: Geography

**Creating a Map** Investigate women's suffrage in other parts of the world. Create a world map on which you show the date that women gained the right to vote in selected countries throughout the world. What conclusions can you draw from your map?

### 2. COOPERATIVE LEARNING ACTIVITY

**Performing a Play** Working in a small group, research the problems that African Americans faced in the United States during the Progressive Era, and investigate President Wilson's attitudes toward civil rights. Imagine a small group of African-American leaders visiting President Wilson to confront him about his record. Write a script for the meeting, and assign roles to each group member. Then practice and stage a performance for the class.

### 3. TECHNOLOGY ACTIVITY

**Making an Electronic Presentation** America's national parks offer a variety of educational and recreational experiences. Information about the parks is available from many different sources. Using the library and the Internet, find information about national parks that interest you. Which park or parks would you most like to visit? If you were designing a national park, which features would you most like to include?

**Visit www.mcdougallittell.com to learn more about national parks.**

Create a class presentation about the national parks using presentation software and the suggestions below.

- A map of a national park, showing the location of various features and attractions.
- Lodging for a national park that you would like to use. Incorporate features from hotels and lodgings in national parks that you have researched.
- Your description of the most important features of a national park that you would like to visit.
- A database of facts about the national parks.

### 4. HISTORY PORTFOLIO

**Option 1** Review your section and chapter assessment activities. Select one that you think was your best work. Then use comments made by your teacher or classmates to improve your work, and add it to your portfolio.

**Option 2** Review the questions that you wrote for What Do You Want to Know? on page 638. Then write a short report in which you explain the answers to your questions. If any questions were not answered, do research to answer them. Add your answers to your portfolio.



## ALTERNATIVE ASSESSMENT

1. INTERDISCIPLINARY ACTIVITY: **Geography**
**Maps should**
- show a sampling of countries from around the world.
- provide dates from around the world.
- include clear, informative labels.

2. COOPERATIVE LEARNING ACTIVITY
**Plays should**
- include stage directions that describe the setting, cast of characters, and props.
- contain authentic-sounding dialogue.
- dramatize moments from the meeting between Wilson and African-American leaders.

3. TECHNOLOGY ACTIVITY
**Class presentations should**
- create oral, visual, or written explanations of social studies materials about the national parks.
- reflect the use of a variety of sources to acquire information.
- show technical proficiency.

4. HISTORY PORTFOLIO

**Option 1 Revised section or chapter assessment activities should**
- address teacher and peer responses to the selected work.
- solve problems present in the first versions of the work.

**Option 2 Short reports should**
- answer questions about the Progressive movement and the problems of cities.
- use evidence to develop and support ideas.
- cite sources of information.
- use standard grammar, spelling, sentence structure, and punctuation.

**Critical Thinking Transparency CT66**
- Visual Summary

**Formal Assessment**
- Chapter Test, Forms A and B, pp. 327–334

## HISTORY SKILLS

**Possible Responses**

1. INTERPRETING GRAPHS
   **a.** 6 percent
   **b.** 435
   **c.** Roosevelt

2. INTERPRETING PRIMARY SOURCES
   **a.** He is promoting laws that regulate sanitary and working conditions in industry.
   **b.** the value of equal opportunity for all, justice for all, and worth of the individual

CHAPTER 23 PLANNING GUIDE

# Becoming a World Power 1880–1917

| | CHAPTER OVERVIEW | COPYMASTERS | TECHNOLOGY |
|---|---|---|---|
| **CHAPTER RESOURCES** | This chapter describes how the United States acquires new territories, goes to war with Spain, and becomes involved with countries in Asia and Latin America. | **In-Depth Resources: Unit 7**<br>• Tracing Themes: Expansion, p. 20<br>• Building Vocabulary, p. 24<br>**Interdisciplinary Projects,** pp. 133–138 | **Primary Source Explorer**<br>**Electronic Teacher Tools**<br>**Power Presentations CD-ROM**<br>**Chapter Summaries on CD** (English and Spanish) |
| **SECTION 1 The United States Continues to Expand pp. 659–661** | **KEY IDEAS**<br>• Economic and military interests, along with a feeling of cultural superiority, fuel U.S. imperialist policies.<br>• William Seward acquires Alaska.<br>• The United States annexes Hawaii after American planters overthrow the islands' queen. | **In-Depth Resources: Unit 7**<br>• Setting the Stage, p. 19<br>• Guided Reading, p. 21<br>• Primary Source, p. 28<br>• Reteaching Activity, p. 32<br>**America's History Makers**<br>• Queen Liliuokalani, pp. 91–92<br>**Economics in History**<br>• The Economic Causes of Imperialism, p. 23 | **Warm-Up Transparency WT23**<br>**Critical Thinking Transparency CT67**<br>• Setting the Stage<br>**Critical Thinking Transparency CT68**<br>• Cause and Effect: U.S. Policies for Overseas Expansion<br>**ClassZone:** www.mcdougallittell.com |
| **SECTION 2 The Spanish-American War pp. 662–667** | • Influenced by economic interests and support for Cuban rebels, the United States goes to war with Spain.<br>• U.S. forces win victories in the Philippines and in Cuba.<br>• The United States retains control of new territories after the war, despite anti-imperialist opposition. | **In-Depth Resources: Unit 7**<br>• Setting the Stage, p. 19<br>• Guided Reading, p. 22<br>• Skillbuilder Practice: Identifying Facts and Opinions, p. 25<br>• Literature Selection, pp. 30–31<br>• Reteaching Activity, p. 33<br>**America's History Makers**<br>• José Marti, pp. 93–94<br>**Citizenship Today,** pp. 15–16 | **Warm-Up Transparency WT23**<br>**Critical Thinking Transparency CT67**<br>• Setting the Stage<br>**ClassZone:** www.mcdougallittell.com |
| **SECTION 3 U.S. Involvement Overseas pp. 668–673** | • The United States seeks economic and political influence in Japan, China, and the Pacific region.<br>• The United States builds the Panama Canal, a shortcut between the Atlantic and Pacific Oceans.<br>• The United States becomes increasingly involved in Latin America. | **In-Depth Resources: Unit 7**<br>• Setting the Stage, p. 19<br>• Guided Reading, p. 23<br>• Geography Application, pp. 26–27<br>• Primary Source, p. 29<br>• Reteaching Activity, p. 34<br>**Why It Matters Now**<br>• Modern U.S. Territories, pp. 45–46<br>**Outline Map Activities**<br>• U.S. Territorial Influence, 1867–1917, pp. 45–46 | **Warm-Up Transparency WT23**<br>**Humanities Transparency HT45**<br>• Political Cartoon: The Boxer Rebellion<br>**Humanities Transparency HT46**<br>• Panama Canal Stamp<br>**Geography Transparency GT23**<br>• The Panama Canal Shortcut, 1914<br>**Critical Thinking Transparency CT69**<br>• Visual Summary |

PE Pupil's Edition
Copymaster
Overhead Transparency
Audio Library
CD-ROM
Internet

## ASSESSMENT

**PE Chapter Assessment,** pp. 674–675

**Formal Assessment**
- Chapter Tests, Forms A and B, pp. 340–347

**Alternative Assessment Book**

**Electronic Teacher Tools with Test Maker**

**PE Section Assessment,** p. 661

**Formal Assessment**
- Section Quiz, p. 337

**Alternative Assessment Book**
- Rubrics for a video, 5.3
- Rubrics for a mural, 1.11

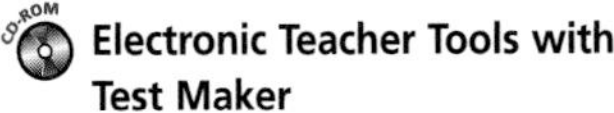

**Electronic Teacher Tools with Test Maker**

**PE Section Assessment,** p. 667

**Formal Assessment**
- Section Quiz, p. 338

**Alternative Assessment Book**
- Rubrics for a news script, 4.5
- Rubrics for a database, 5.6

**Electronic Teacher Tools with Test Maker**

**PE Section Assessment,** p. 673

**Formal Assessment**
- Section Quiz, p. 339

**Alternative Assessment Book**
- Rubrics for a model, 1.10
- Rubrics for a graph, 2.3

**Electronic Teacher Tools with Test Maker**

## CUSTOMIZING FOR INDIVIDUAL NEEDS

### Students Acquiring English/ESL

**Reading Study Guide** (English and Spanish), pp. 223–230

**Access for Students Acquiring English/ESL: Spanish Translations,** pp. 153–158

**Chapter Summaries on CD** (English and Spanish)

### Less Proficient Readers

**Reading Study Guide** (English and Spanish), pp. 223–230

**Chapter Summaries on CD** (English and Spanish)

### Gifted and Talented Students

**In-Depth Resources: Unit 7**
- Enrichment Activity, p. 35

**America's History Makers**
- Queen Liliuokalani, pp. 91–92
- José Marti, pp. 93–94

## CROSS-CURRICULAR CONNECTIONS

### Culture

Blumberg, Rhoda. ***Commodore Perry in the Land of the Shogun.*** New York: Lothrop, 1985. The story of Perry's remarkable voyage to Japan, addressing both economic and cultural issues.

### Government

Abodaher, David J. ***Puerto Rico: America's 51st State?*** New York: Watts, 1993. A history of the island, with a lengthy section on the leadership of the Munoz family (Luis Munoz Rivera and his son Luis Munoz Marin).

### Popular Culture

Fleming, Thomas. ***Behind the Headlines.*** New York: Walker, 1989. The story of American newspapers.

### Humanities: Art

Finley, Carol. ***Art of the Far North: Inuit Sculpture, Drawing, and Painting.*** Minneapolis: Lerner, 1998. Gorgeous photographs of art works by, and a short history of, the Inuit people of Alaska and elsewhere.

### Interdisciplinary Projects, pp. 133–138

- Math: Data on Territorial Expansion
- Science: Camouflage
- Language Arts: Yellow Journalism
- Art: Comic Strips

### Literature

Head, Judith. ***Culebra Cut (Adventures in Time).*** Minneapolis: Carolrhoda Books, 1995. William disobeys his doctor father and sneaks out to explore the most difficult stretch in the construction of the Panama Canal.

Krakauer, John. ***Into the Wild.*** New York: Random, 1996. For advanced readers, the gripping true story of young Chris McCandless's idealistic but inadequately prepared retreat to the Alaskan wilderness.

Schorr, Mark. ***Bully!*** New York: St. Martin's, 1985. Fictional adventure in which the president goes undercover to break up a threatening secret society.

### McDougal Littell Literature Connections

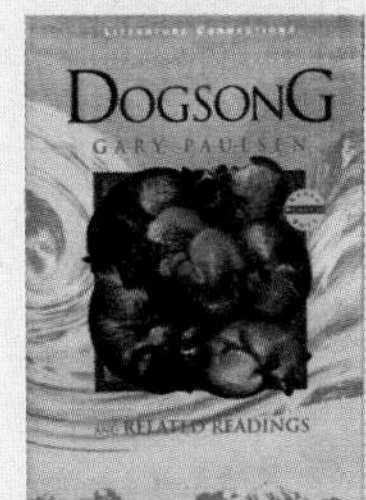


Gary Paulsen
***Dogsong***
A 14-year-old Eskimo youth prepares to leave the modern world to embrace the old ways.

## ENRICHMENT ACTIVITIES

**PE Pupil's Edition, pp. 656–675**
**Interact with History,** p. 657
**Citizenship Today,** p. 664
**Technology of the Time,** p. 671

**In-Depth Resources: Unit 7**
- Geography Application: Pancho Villa Raids New Mexico, pp. 26–27
- Primary Source: from *Hawaii Story by Hawaii's Queen,* p. 28
- Primary Source: The Roosevelt Corollary, p. 29
- Literature Selection: from *Simple Verses* by Jose Marti, pp. 30–31

**America's History Makers**
- Queen Liliuokalani, pp. 91–92
- José Marti, pp. 93–94

**Outline Map Activities**
- U.S. Territorial Influence, 1867–1917, pp. 45–46

**Why It Matters Now**
- Modern U.S. Territories, pp. 45–46

**LESSON PLAN OPTIONS (50-MINUTE PERIOD)** (TE) = Teacher's Edition (PE) = Pupil's Edition

| | TEACHER-DIRECTED ACTIVITIES<br>Class Time: 15 minutes | STUDENT-CENTERED ACTIVITIES<br>Class Time: 25 minutes | INDIVIDUAL ACTIVITIES<br>Class Time: 10 minutes |
|---|---|---|---|
| **DAY 1**<br>Introduction<br>pp. 656–658 | **Presentation Options**<br>• Begin with a class discussion of the picture on p. 656 **(PE)**.<br>• Lead a class discussion on the "What Do You Know?" question in Setting the Stage, p. 658. Then introduce the graphic organizer for the chapter **(PE)**. | **Options for Cooperative Learning**<br>• Have student groups discuss the Interact with History questions, p. 657 **(PE)**.<br>• Have student groups respond to the "What Do You Want to Know?" question in Setting the Stage, p. 658 **(PE)**. | **Head Start on Homework Options**<br>• Have students skim Section 1 Main Idea, Why It Matters Now, Terms & Names, and the main headings, p. 659 **(PE)**.<br>• Have students begin Guided Reading activity and Building Vocabulary sheet. |
| **DAY 2**<br>Section 1<br>pp. 659–661 | **Presentation Options**<br>• Begin with the 5-Minute Warm-Up, p. 659 **(TE)**.<br>• Review the Section 1 Main Idea, Why It Matters Now, and Terms & Names, p. 659 **(PE)**. | **Options for Cooperative Learning**<br>• Divide students into groups to work on the Taking Notes question in the Section 1 Assessment, p. 661 **(PE)**.<br>• Have student pairs work together to complete one of the Activity Options in the Section 1 Assessment, p. 661 **(PE)**. | **Head Start on Homework Options**<br>• Have students begin working on Section 1 Assessment, p. 661 **(PE)**.<br>• Have students complete the Geography Skillbuilder questions for the maps on pp. 699, 670, 672 **(PE)**. |
| **DAY 3**<br>Section 2<br>pp. 662–667 | **Presentation Options**<br>• Begin with the 5-Minute Warm-Up, p. 662 **(TE)**.<br>• Choose 5 key questions for Objectives 1–4 to discuss with the class, pp. 662–667 **(TE)**.<br>• Lead the students through the Skillbuilder Mini-Lesson: Identifying and Solving Problems, p. 664 **(TE)**. | **Options for Cooperative Learning**<br>• Divide students into groups to work on the Citizenship Today activity, p. 664 **(PE)**.<br>• Have student pairs work together to complete one of the Activity Options in the Section 2 Assessment, p. 667 **(PE)**. | **Head Start on Homework Options**<br>• Have students begin working on Section 2 Assessment, p. 667 **(PE)**.<br>• Have students preview Section 3 Main Idea, Why It Matters Now, Terms & Names, and the main headings, p. 668 **(PE)**. |
| **DAY 4**<br>Section 3<br>pp. 668–673 | **Presentation Options**<br>• Begin with the 5-Minute Warm-Up, p. 668 **(TE)**.<br>• Choose 5 key questions for Objectives 1–4 to discuss with the class, pp. 668–673 **(TE)**.<br>• Lead students through the Technology of the Time, p. 671 **(TE)**. | **Options for Cooperative Learning**<br>• Divide students into groups and have them complete the Technology of the Time questions, p. 671 **(PE)**.<br>• Have student pairs work together to complete one of the Activity Options in the Section 3 Assessment, p. 673 **(PE)**. | **Head Start on Homework Options**<br>• Have students complete the Setting the Stage graphic organizer for the chapter, p. 658 **(PE)**.<br>• Have students begin working on the Chapter Assessment, pp. 674–675 **(PE)**.<br>• Prepare for Chapter Test<br>**Formal Assessment,** pp. 340–347 |

TEACHER-TESTED ACTIVITY **Brian McKenzie, Dr. Charles Drew Science Magnet School, Buffalo, New York**

## THE PANAMA CANAL

**Class Time** Two class periods

**Task** Creating a map and a journal record of a trip through the Panama Canal

**Purpose** To identify the location and importance of the Panama Canal to the United States

**Supplies Needed**

- Outline maps of the world
- Markers or colored pencils
- Globe

**Activity** Divide the class into four or five groups. Assign each group a journey through the Panama Canal, for example (a) a U.S. naval vessel traveling from Hawaii to Cuba, (b) a U.S. merchant ship traveling from Boston, Massachusetts, to China, or (c) a U.S. passenger vessel traveling from New York to San Francisco. Assign each group member a role such as captain, crew member, or passenger. Passengers can be business leaders, prospectors, politicians, and so on. Each group should map its journey and write three journal entries about the trip, including a description of the passage through the canal.

## BLOCK SCHEDULING — LESSON PLAN OPTIONS (90-MINUTE PERIOD)

### DAY 1

**Interact with History,** p. 657
**Class Time** 20 minutes

Options for pacing and variety:

- Peer Teaching Divide students into groups of three. Have them list the reasons that a plantation owner from the U.S. mainland living in Hawaii might have for wanting Hawaii to be part of the United States. Then have them list the reasons why native Hawaiians might resist becoming an American state. Once the lists are complete, have students imagine they are the U.S. president in 1893 and answer the "What Do You Think?" questions. **Class Time** 20 minutes

**Setting the Stage,** p. 658
**Class Time** 20 minutes

Options for pacing and variety:

- Time Saver For a homework assignment, have students write a paragraph explaining how Manifest Destiny, the Louisiana Purchase, and the War with Mexico are related to the theme of expansion in American history. **Class Time** 5 minutes

**Section 1,** pp. 659–661
**Class Time** 50 minutes

Options for pacing and variety:

- Internet Extend students' background knowledge of imperialism by visiting www.mcdougallittell.com **Class Time** 20 minutes
- Time Saver Assign the Taking Notes and Main Idea questions in the Section Assessment as homework. **Class Time** 5 minutes

### DAY 2

**Section 2,** pp. 662–667
**Class Time** 45 minutes

Options for pacing and variety:

- History on Film Extend students' background knowledge of the Spanish-American War and U.S. intervention in Latin America by viewing *The United States and the World.* Schlessinger Media, 1996. **Class Time** 35 minutes
- Peer Teaching After students read Citizenship Today on page 664, divide the class into small groups to complete the feature activity. Students can find many national and regional newspapers online. Have each group report its answer to the question "Can you find bias in the media?" **Class Time** 40 minutes

**Section 3,** pp. 668–673
**Class Time** 45 minutes

Options for pacing and variety:

- Team Teaching Invite a science teacher to explain how locks help ships move through a canal. **Class Time** 10 minutes
- Time Saver Use the map on page 672 to summarize U.S. involvement in Latin America from 1898 to 1917. **Class Time** 10 minutes

**Chapter 23 Assessment,** pp. 674–675
**Class Time** 40 minutes

Options for pacing and variety:

- Peer Teaching Have students review the chapter and make a list of the foreign countries in which the United States was involved. For each place listed, have students identify the economic and military reasons for involvement and the role Americans' belief in their cultural superiority may have played in this action. **Class Time** 15 minutes
- Peer Evaluation Have students review the Interact with History question on page 674, consider their earlier responses, and share their current responses with the class. **Class Time** 10 minutes

**CHAPTER 23 OBJECTIVE**

The student will understand the growing expansionism that shaped United States foreign policy and led to the acquisition of new territories during the late 1800s and early 1900s.

CHAPTER 23

# Becoming a World Power

## 1880–1917

*Section 1* **The United States Continues to Expand**
*Section 2* **The Spanish-American War**
*Section 3* **U.S. Involvement Overseas**

### HISTORY FROM VISUALS

**Interpreting the Painting** Explain that on December 16, 1906, the fleet, which included 16 sparkling new battleships, steamed out of Virginia, across the Atlantic Ocean, and continued from there on a journey around the globe. Ask students what feelings the fleet inspired in the painter. Ask them why the United States might have sent the ships on such a journey. **Possible Responses** The painter felt proud to be an American; the United States wanted to show its power to the world.

**Extension** Have students use a globe to trace the route that the fleet took around the world: from Hampton Roads, Virginia, to Trinidad, Brazil, Chile, Peru, Mexico, San Francisco, Honolulu, New Zealand, Australia, Philippine Islands, Japan, China, Ceylon, Suez, Gibraltar, and back to Hampton Roads. Point out that the fleet used the new Suez Canal. Suggest that students speculate about the countries the United States might have wanted to impress with the fleet.

The United States "Great White Fleet" symbolized the nation's presence as a global power at the beginning of the 20th century.



### CRITICAL THINKING ACTIVITY

**Drawing Conclusions** Tell students that during the late 1890s, many Americans wanted the United States to expand overseas. Other Americans opposed such expansion. Have students make a two-column chart listing possible reasons in favor of expansion and possible reasons against it. Tell students to save their charts to revise as they read the chapter.

**Class Time** 15 minutes

### RECOMMENDED RESOURCES

**BOOKS FOR THE TEACHER**

Dougherty, Michael. ***To Steal a Kingdom: Probing Hawaiian History.*** Waimanalo, HI: Island Style Pr., 1992. Distinctly pro-Hawaiian account of the islands' colorful history.

McPhee, John. ***Coming into the Country.*** New York: Farrar, 1977. The acclaimed journalist on Alaska.

Rodriguez-Luis, Julio. ***Re-Reading José Martí (1853–1895): One Hundred Years Later.*** Albany: State U. of New York Pr., 1999. A thoughtful reassessment of both Martí's literary and political contributions.

**SOFTWARE**

***Who Built America? From Centennial Celebration of 1876 to the Great War of 1914.*** CD-ROM. Voyager, 1993. By the American School History Project. Video, audio, images, and documents.

**VIDEO**

***A Man, a Plan, a Canal: Panama.*** PBS/Nova, 1987. The dreams, disasters, and triumphs of this great engineering feat, with author David McCullough.

**INTERNET**

For more about the Age of Imperialism, visit www.mcdougallittell.com

## Interact *with* History

Foreign sugar growers, including many Americans, developed large plantations in the kingdom of Hawaii.

Workers loaded sugar cane on wagons for shipment to processing plants.

Planters used cheap immigrant labor, especially from Asia.

Wealthy planters dominated Hawaii's economy.

**In 1893, American sugar planters in the kingdom of Hawaii think that they could make more money if Hawaii were an American state. So they stage a revolt and take control of the government. Now they want you, the U.S. president, to take control of Hawaii.**

### What Do You Think?

- **What interests does the United States have in other countries?**
- **How important is protecting those interests?**
- **How important are the opinions of another country's citizens?**

# *When should you get involved in the affairs of another country?*

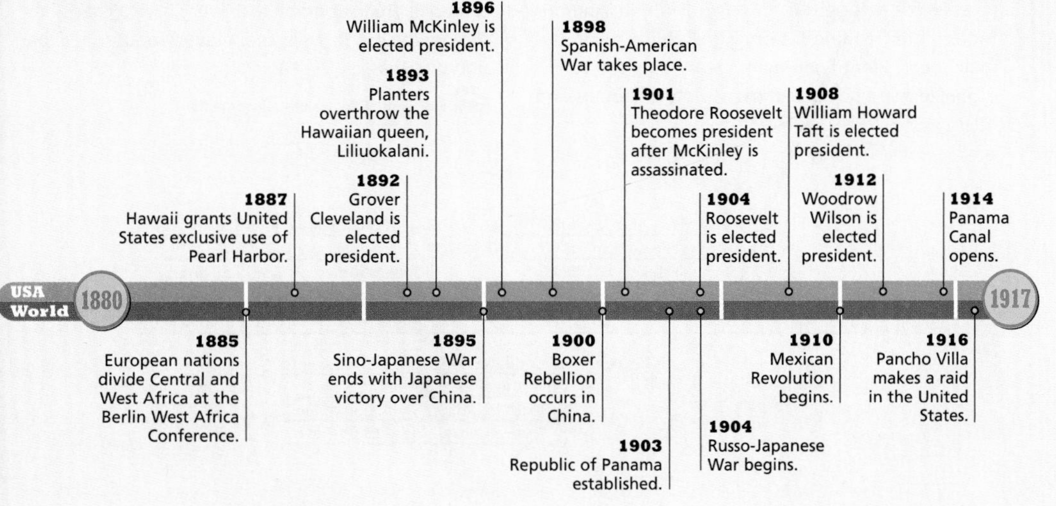

USA
World
1880
1917
1887 Hawaii grants United States exclusive use of Pearl Harbor.
1892 Grover Cleveland is elected president.
1893 Planters overthrow the Hawaiian queen, Liliuokalani.
1896 William McKinley is elected president.
1898 Spanish-American War takes place.
1901 Theodore Roosevelt becomes president after McKinley is assassinated.
1904 Roosevelt is elected president.
1908 William Howard Taft is elected president.
1912 Woodrow Wilson is elected president.
1914 Panama Canal opens.
1885 European nations divide Central and West Africa at the Berlin West Africa Conference.
1895 Sino-Japanese War ends with Japanese victory over China.
1900 Boxer Rebellion occurs in China.
1903 Republic of Panama established.
1904 Russo-Japanese War begins.
1910 Mexican Revolution begins.
1916 Pancho Villa makes a raid in the United States.




## Interact *with* History

### OBJECTIVES

- To help students understand some of the complex issues involved in the acquisition of new territories
- To help students connect with the people and the events in this chapter

### What Do You Think?

1. Have students consider questions such as why the planters were in Hawaii, how they treated local people, and who benefited from their activities.
2. Which other nations might be in competition with you for the resources of a location like Hawaii?
3. What potential problems might result from involvement in other countries' affairs?

### *When should you get involved in the affairs of another country?*

Suggest that students think of incidents in recent history in which the United States has sent troops or diplomats to other countries. Ask them what reasons the United States gave for becoming involved in these countries. Then ask how these reasons differ from or are similar to the reasons the United States might have become involved in Hawaii.

### MAKING PERSONAL CONNECTIONS

Ask students if they have ever become involved in the personal affairs of a friend or acquaintance. What consequences did their involvement have for them personally or for the friend?

### TIME LINE DISCUSSION

**In the late 19th century, few Americans were interested in national expansion overseas. However, they were eager to find overseas markets for their agricultural and industrial products. Soon the United States became linked to other countries by ties that went beyond basic economics.**

- Ask students to identify two events that suggest American involvement in the affairs of other nations for trade purposes. **Possible Answer** Hawaii grants use of Pearl Harbor; Planters overthrow Queen Liliuokalani; Panama Canal opens
- Ask students to find the war in which the United States was involved. Then ask them to speculate on who won the war and why the war was so short. **Possible Answer** Spanish-American War. The United States won because it was more powerful.
- Ask students what events on the time line indicate worldwide unrest and conflict. **Answer** African division; overthrow of Queen Liliuokalani; Sino-Japanese War; Boxer Rebellion; Spanish-American War; Russo-Japanese War; Mexican Revolution; raid by Pancho Villa

## BEFORE YOU READ

### Previewing the Theme: Expansion

Ask students to think of reasons many Americans would want to expand their territory and their interests to other parts of the world. Then ask them to think of reasons other Americans would not want the country to expand.

Many Americans saw other countries expand by colonizing other countries as their own. They wanted the United States to take colonies of its own. Other Americans opposed colonization of weaker countries by stronger ones. They thought such actions were contrary to the principles of the American Revolution.

### What Do You Know?

Review with students the expansion of the United States from 13 small states huddled along the Atlantic Coast to a nation spanning an entire continent. Remind them that the frontier was officially closed, and the continent was considered "settled." Some Americans wanted to find new frontiers overseas.

 **In-Depth Resources: Unit 7**
- Tracing Themes: Expansion, p. 20

## READ AND TAKE NOTES

**Reading Strategy: Finding Main Ideas**
Tell students that many historical events are complicated. They are the result of a combination of many different forces, opinions, and actions. Being able to identify main ideas will help students understand the combinations that result in a specific event. Point out that recording main ideas on a chart will make complex information more accessible.

 **In-Depth Resources: Unit 7**
- Setting the Stage, p. 19

 **Critical Thinking Transparency CT67**
- Setting the Stage

# Chapter 23 SETTING THE STAGE

## BEFORE YOU READ

### Previewing the Theme

**Expansion** By the end of the 1800s, the United States had become a world power. The nation used its economic and military strength to expand its influence in both Latin America—the part of the Americas south of the United States—and Asia. Some Americans worried that U.S. expansion overseas might weaken the nation's democratic principles. These are the issues and events explored in Chapter 23.

USA
PANAMA
PHILIPPINES

**The American eagle spreads its wings over Asia and Latin America in this political cartoon from 1904.**

### What Do You Know?

Was expansion something new, or was it a force that you have seen before in the history of the United States?

**THINK ABOUT**
- the idea of Manifest Destiny
- the Louisiana Purchase
- the War with Mexico

### What Do You Want to Know?

What do you think might have caused the United States to expand overseas at the end of the 1800s? Make a list of the possible reasons before you read the chapter.

## READ AND TAKE NOTES

**Reading Strategy: Finding Main Ideas** An important skill for reading history is the ability to find main ideas. Identifying main ideas helps you to organize and understand the variety of details and examples that support those ideas. Use a chart like the one below to write main ideas about U.S. expansion overseas.

 **See Skillbuilder Handbook, page R5.**

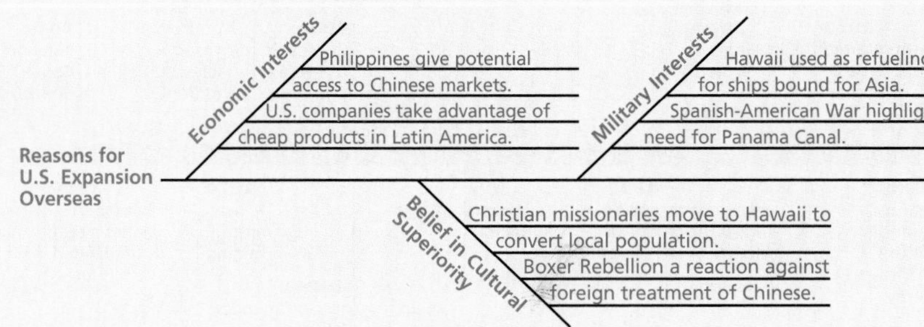
Reasons for U.S. Expansion Overseas
Economic Interests
Philippines give potential access to Chinese markets.
U.S. companies take advantage of cheap products in Latin America.
Military Interests
Hawaii used as refueling stop for ships bound for Asia.
Spanish-American War highlights need for Panama Canal.
Belief in Cultural Superiority
Christian missionaries move to Hawaii to convert local population.
Boxer Rebellion a reaction against foreign treatment of Chinese.

658 CHAPTER 23

## TEACHING STRATEGY

### READING THE CHAPTER

This is a chronological chapter focusing on U.S. expanding interests and influence in Latin America and Asia. Encourage students to think about what was happening around the world that encouraged this expansion. Pause after each section to review the main ideas and supporting facts that are presented.

### ALTERNATIVE ASSESSMENT

The Chapter Assessment describes three activities for alternative assessment on page 675. You may wish to have students work on these activities during the course of the chapter and then present them at the end.

# 1 The United States Continues to Expand

**TERMS & NAMES**
imperialism
William Seward
Queen Liliuokalani

| MAIN IDEA | WHY IT MATTERS NOW |
|---|---|
| The United States expanded its interest in world affairs and acquired new territories. | During this period, the United States acquired Alaska and Hawaii as territories. |

Naval historian Alfred Thayer Mahan at the turn of the century

## ONE AMERICAN'S STORY

**Alfred T. Mahan joined the U.S. Navy in the 1850s and served for nearly 40 years. In the 1890s, Mahan made use of his decades of experience to write several books on the historical importance of sea power. In one passage, he discussed the economic importance of trading stations and colonies.**

*A VOICE FROM THE PAST*

The trading-station . . . [was] the same as the . . . colony. In both cases the mother-country had won a foothold in a foreign land, seeking a new outlet for what it had to sell, a new sphere for its shipping, more employment for its people, and more comfort and wealth for itself.

**A. T. Mahan,** *The Influence of Sea Power upon History, 1660–1805*

**Mahan encouraged government officials to build up American naval forces so that the United States could compete with other powerful nations. In this section you will learn how the United States began to extend its influence beyond the national boundaries.**

## 1 Reasons for U.S. Expansion

Americans had always sought to expand the size of their nation. Throughout the 19th century, they extended their control toward the Pacific Coast. By the 1880s, however, many leaders became convinced that the United States should join the imperialist powers of Europe and establish colonies overseas. **Imperialism**—the policy by which stronger nations extend their economic, political, or military control over weaker territories—was a trend around the world.

European nations had been establishing colonies for centuries. In the late 19th century, Africa became a major area of European expansion. By the early 20th century, only two countries in Africa—Ethiopia and Liberia—remained independent.

Imperialist countries also competed for territory in Asia, especially in China. There, European nations had to compete with Japan, which had also become a world power by the end of the 1800s.





## SECTION OBJECTIVES

1. To identify the factors that led to American imperialism
2. To explain the role of William Seward in American expansion
3. To describe the annexation of Hawaii

**SKILLBUILDER**
Interpreting Maps: Location, p. 660

**CRITICAL THINKING**
Making Inferences, pp. 660, 661

## FOCUS & MOTIVATE

### 5-MINUTE WARM-UP

**Making Inferences** These questions focus on the annexation of Hawaii.

1. Look at the map on page 660. What two new territories had the United States acquired by 1898?
2. How did the location of these territories differ from previous areas of expansion by the United States?

 Warm-Up Transparency WT23

## INSTRUCT

**INSTRUCT: OBJECTIVE 1**

**Reasons for U.S. Expansion**
Key Questions
- What is imperialism?
- Where were imperialist powers establishing colonies?
- What factors led to American imperialism?

 **In-Depth Resources: Unit 7**
- Guided Reading, p. 21

 **Reading Study Guide** (Spanish and English), pp. 223–224

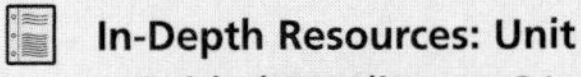

## RECOMMENDED RESOURCES

**In-Depth Resources: Unit 7**
- Guided Reading, p. 21
- Building Vocabulary, p. 24
- Primary Source, p. 28
- Reteaching Activity, p. 32

**Reading Study Guide** (Spanish and English), pp. 223–224

**Economics in History**
- The Economic Causes of Imperialism, p. 23

**America's History Makers**
- Queen Liliuokalani, pp. 91–92

**Formal Assessment**
- Section Quiz, p. 337

**Alternative Assessment**
- Rubrics, 5.3
- Rubrics, 1.11

**Access for Students Acquiring English/ESL**
- Guided Reading, p. 153

**Technology Resources**

 **Critical Thinking Trans. CT68**
- Cause and Effect: U.S. Policies for Overseas Expansion

 **Electronic Teacher Tools with Test Maker**

**ClassZone**
www.mcdougallittell.com

## MORE ABOUT . . .

**American Attitudes Toward Imperialism**

In the late 1800s, few average Americans paid attention to foreign policy. The nation's relations with other countries were the province of the "thoughtful men of the country," such as Theodore Roosevelt and Grover Cleveland. If the United States had secure foreign markets for its farm products and manufactured goods, these leaders thought, the nation could avoid economic depression and labor agitation.

 **Economics in History**
- The Economic Causes of Imperialism, p. 23

 **Critical Thinking Transparency CT68**
- Cause and Effect: U.S. Policies for Overseas Expansion

## INSTRUCT: OBJECTIVE 

**Seward and Alaska**

Key Questions
- What contributions did William Seward make to American expansionism?
- How did the United States acquire Alaska?
- How did many Americans view the acquisition of Alaska?

## HISTORY FROM VISUALS

**Reading the Map** Remind students that the inset showing Hawaii is not drawn to the scale of the large map. The small box showing Hawaii is in scale. Ask students how far the Hawaiian Islands are from the southwest coast of the United States. **Answer** about 2,500 miles away

**Extension** Have students research the current populations of Alaska and Hawaii.

Most Americans gradually came to approve of the idea of expansion overseas. Three factors helped to fuel the development of American imperialism.

1. **Economic Interests.** Economic leaders argued that expansion would increase U.S. financial prosperity. Industry had greatly expanded after the Civil War. Many industrialists saw new colonies as a potential source of cheap raw materials. Agriculture had also expanded. Farmers pointed out that colonies would mean new markets for their products.
2. **Military Interests.** In his books, Alfred T. Mahan had argued that economic interests went hand-in-hand with military interests. Foreign policy experts agreed. They urged U.S. leaders to follow the European example and establish a military presence overseas.
3. **Belief in Cultural Superiority.** Many Americans believed that their government, religion, and even race were superior to those of other societies. Some people hoped to spread democratic ideas overseas. Others saw a chance to advance Christianity. Racist ideas about the inferiority of the nonwhite populations in many foreign countries were also used to justify American imperialism.

*Reading* **History**
**A. Making Inferences** Why might economic and military interests go hand in hand?
**A. Possible Response** If a country's economic interests were threatened, the military would be needed to protect them.

Each of these developments—economic interests, military interests, and a belief in cultural superiority—led the United States to a larger role on the world stage.

Skillbuilder Answers
1. Russia
2. Oahu

**Alaska, 1867 & Hawaii, 1898**

RUSSIA
Arctic Circle
Alaska, 1867
United States and its possessions
180°
160°W
140°W
120°W
100°W
60°N
40°N
20°N
PACIFIC OCEAN
NORTH AMERICA
UNITED STATES
Hawaiian Islands, 1898
Kauai
Oahu
Molokai
Pearl Harbor
Maui
Hawaii
Tropic of Cancer
N
0 2,000 Miles
0 4,000 Kilometers

GEOGRAPHY SKILLBUILDER
**Interpreting Maps**
1. **Location** *What country lies to the west of Alaska?*
2. **Location** *On which Hawaiian island is Pearl Harbor?*

660

## 2 Seward and Alaska

A strong backer of expansion was **William Seward,** Secretary of State under presidents Abraham Lincoln and Andrew Johnson. Seward made his biggest move in 1867, when he arranged the purchase of Alaska from Russia.

Not everyone was pleased by Seward's move, though. At the time, the $7.2-million deal was widely criticized. Newspapers called Alaska a "Polar Bear Garden" and "Seward's Icebox." Even so, the purchase of the resource-rich territory turned out to be a great bargain for the United States.

**Background**
In the late 1800s, large gold fields were discovered in Alaska. The territory was also rich in fur-bearing animals, timber, copper, coal, and oil.

Throughout his career, Seward continued to pursue new territory. Before he retired in 1869, he considered acquiring the Hawaiian Islands, a group of volcanic and coral islands in the central Pacific Ocean. That would not happen, however, for almost 30 more years.

## ACTIVITY OPTIONS

### INDIVIDUAL NEEDS

**LESS PROFICIENT READERS**

**Finding Main Ideas** The following questions are designed to help students focus on the main ideas of the section. Write the questions on the board. Have students read the questions, then read the section to find the answers. Use the questions and answers to review the section.

- What were three reasons in favor of U.S. expansion overseas?
- Why did William Seward want to purchase Alaska?
- Why did planters in Hawaii want the United States to annex Hawaii?

## 3 The Annexation of Hawaii

*Reading* **History**
**B. Reading a Map** Locate the Hawaiian Islands on the map on page 660.

In the early 1800s, Christian missionaries from the United States had moved to the Kingdom of Hawaii to convert the local population. Some of the missionaries' descendants started sugar plantations. By the late 1800s, wealthy planters dominated Hawaii's economy.

In 1891, **Queen Liliuokalani** (lee•LEE•oo•oh•kah•LAH•nee) became the leader of Hawaii. Believing that planters had too much influence, she wanted to limit their power. Around the same time, U.S. trade laws changed to favor sugar grown exclusively in American states.

American planters in Hawaii were upset by these threats to their political and economic interests. In January 1893, they staged a revolt. With the help of U.S. Marines, they overthrew the queen and set up their own government. They then asked to be annexed by the United States.

**Vocabulary**
**annex:** to add

U.S. leaders already understood the value of the islands. In 1887, they had pressured Hawaii to allow a U.S. naval base at Pearl Harbor, the kingdom's best port. The base became an important refueling station for American merchant and military ships bound for Asia.

Thus, when President Benjamin Harrison received the planters' request in 1893, he gave his approval and sent a treaty to the Senate. But before the Senate could act, Grover Cleveland became president. He did not approve of the planters' actions and withdrew the treaty. Hawaii would not be annexed until 1898, during the Spanish-American War. In the next section, you will read about the events that led to that war.

### AMERICA'S HISTORY MAKERS

**QUEEN LILIUOKALANI**
**1838–1917**

As a young princess, Liliuokalani received a western education and toured the world. Although she learned about many cultures, she remained committed to Hawaii. An excellent musician, she wrote the famous Hawaiian song "Aloha Oe [Farewell to Thee]."

She was the first queen of Hawaii and proved to be a good leader. She resisted the foreign takeover of Hawaii and inspired a revolt against the planters. Only in 1895, when the safety of her supporters was threatened, did she agree to give up her throne.

**How did Queen Liliuokalani protect her followers after planters seized power?**

### Section 1 Assessment

**1. Terms & Names**

**Identify:**
- imperialism
- William Seward
- Queen Liliuokalani

**2. Taking Notes**

Use a chart like the one shown to record causes of U.S. expansion overseas in the late 1800s.

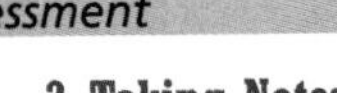

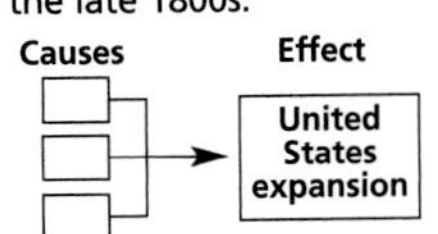


Which was the most important cause?

**3. Main Ideas**

a. Where was the focus of U.S. expansion before the late 1800s?

b. How did William Seward contribute to U.S. expansion?

c. Why did the American planters' request for the annexation of Hawaii fail in the early 1890s?

**4. Critical Thinking**

**Making Inferences** What benefits were American planters looking for when they staged a revolt in 1893?

**THINK ABOUT**
- the new policies of Queen Liliuokalani
- changes in U.S. trade laws

**ACTIVITY OPTIONS**

**TECHNOLOGY**
**ART**

Read more about Hawaii's Queen Liliuokalani. Outline a **video presentation** on the overthrow of the queen or plan a **mural** that depicts the event.





### INSTRUCT: OBJECTIVE 3

**The Annexation of Hawaii**
Key Questions
- Why did Queen Liliuokalani want to limit the planters' power?
- Why did American planters in Hawaii feel that their interests were being threatened?

### AMERICA'S HISTORY MAKERS

**Queen Liliuokalani**
When Liliuokalani became queen, she refused to renew a treaty granting commercial concessions and a naval base to the United States. Her stand alienated her from foreign businessmen in Hawaii. Led by Sanford B. Dole, the pineapple magnate, they deposed her. Liliuokalani appealed to President Cleveland, who ordered her reinstatement. Dole ignored the order. The planters set up a republic, with Dole as president.

**Answer: She abdicated so that her supporters would not be harmed.**

**America's History Makers**
- Queen Liliuokalani, pp. 91–92

**In-Depth Resources: Unit 7**
- Primary Source, p. 28

### ASSESS & RETEACH

**Setting the Stage** Have students write information about Hawaii and Alaska on the appropriate lines on the graphic organizer.

**Formal Assessment**
- Section Quiz, p. 337

**Critical Thinking Transparency CT67**
- Setting the Stage

**RETEACHING ACTIVITY**
In groups of three, have students discuss the three main headings of this chapter. Ask each student to talk about one of the three sections. The two listeners should listen to clarify or add information.

**In-Depth Resources: Unit 7**
- Reteaching Activity, p. 32

### Section 1 Assessment

**1. Terms & Names**

**imperialism,** p. 659
**William Seward,** p. 660
**Queen Liliuokalani,** p. 661

**2. Taking Notes**

Causes: Americans sought markets and raw materials; they wanted to establish a military presence overseas; belief in the superiority of American culture also fueled expansion. Answers will vary, but students should be able to explain their response.

**3. Main Ideas**

**a.** The focus was only on the North American continent. **b.** He negotiated the purchase of Alaska from Russia for $7.2 million. **c.** The newly elected president, Grover Cleveland, disapproved of their actions.

**4. Critical Thinking**

to prevent the queen from reducing their political influence; to increase the value of their sugar if Hawaii became an American territory

**ACTIVITY OPTIONS**

**Alternative Assessment**
- Rubrics for a video, 5.3
- Rubrics for a mural, 1.11

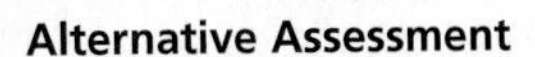

## SECTION OBJECTIVES

1. To identify the reasons for the Spanish-American War
2. To trace the progress of the Spanish-American War in the Philippines and in the Caribbean
3. To analyze the results of the war
4. To explain the goals of the Anti-Imperialist League

**SKILLBUILDER**

Interpreting Maps: Movement, Location, p. 665

**CRITICAL THINKING**

Forming Opinions, pp. 663, 667
Making Inferences, pp. 664, 666
Finding Main Ideas, p. 667

 **Why It Matters Now**
- Modern U.S. Territories, pp. 45–46

## FOCUS & MOTIVATE

### 5-MINUTE WARM-UP

**Drawing Conclusions** These questions focus on the Spanish-American War.

1. Look at the map on page 665. Where did the Spanish-American War take place?
2. Why do you think no route for Spanish troops or ships is shown on the map of the Philippines?

 **Warm-Up Transparency WT23**

## INSTRUCT

### INSTRUCT: OBJECTIVE 

**Rebellion Against Spain/ The United States Goes to War**

Key Questions
- Why did Cuba rebel against Spain?
- How did Americans respond to the Cuban revolution?
- What factors influenced the United States to declare war against Spain?

 **In-Depth Resources: Unit 7**
- Guided Reading, p. 22
- Building Vocabulary, p. 24
- Literature Selection, pp. 30–32

**America's History Makers,** pp. 93–94

# 2 The Spanish-American War

**MAIN IDEA**

Independence movements in Spanish colonies led to the Spanish-American War in 1898.

**WHY IT MATTERS NOW**

U.S. involvement in Latin America and Asia expanded greatly after the Spanish-American War.

**TERMS & NAMES**

yellow journalism
U.S.S. *Maine*
Spanish-American War
Rough Riders
Platt Amendment
Anti-Imperialist League
Luis Muñoz Rivera

### ONE AMERICAN'S STORY

**José Martí was forced to leave Cuba in the 1870s, when he was still a teenager. In those years, the Caribbean island was a Spanish colony, and he had spoken out for independence. Martí later described the terrible conditions that existed under Spanish rule.**

*A VOICE FROM THE PAST*

Cuba's children . . . suffer in indescribable bitterness as they see their fertile nation enchained and also their human dignity stifled . . . all for the necessities and vices of the [Spanish] monarchy.

**José Martí,** quoted in *José Martí, Mentor of the Cuban Nation*

José Martí dedicated his life to the Cuban struggle for independence from Spain.

**After being forced out of Cuba, Martí spent much of his life in the United States. In 1892, he was elected to lead the Cuban Revolutionary Party. At the Party's headquarters in New York City, Martí began to plan a revolt against Spain that began in 1895.**

**Martí's lifelong struggle for Cuban independence made him a symbol of liberty throughout Latin America. In this section, you will read how U.S. disapproval of Spain's treatment of Cubans led to the Spanish-American War.**

### 1 Rebellion Against Spain

The Spanish empire was crumbling at the end of the 19th century. Spain had once controlled most of the Americas, including land that became part of the United States. By the 1890s, however, it owned only a few colonies. Among them were the Philippine Islands in the Pacific and the Caribbean islands of Cuba and Puerto Rico. (See the maps on page 665.) Many of the inhabitants of these colonies had begun to demand independence.

Cubans had revolted against Spain several times in the second half of the nineteenth century. Each time, Spanish soldiers defeated the rebels. In 1895, an ongoing economic depression had increased Cubans' anger over Spanish rule, and they rebelled again. José Martí, who had helped to organize the rebellion from New York, returned to Cuba. He was killed in a skirmish with Spanish troops shortly after, but the revolt continued.



### RECOMMENDED RESOURCES

 **In-Depth Resources: Unit 7**
- Guided Reading, p. 22
- Building Vocabulary, p. 24
- Skillbuilder Practice, p. 25
- Literature Selection: from *Simple Verses,* pp. 30–31
- Reteaching Activity, p. 33
- Enrichment Activity, p. 35

**Reading Study Guide** (Spanish and English), pp. 225–226

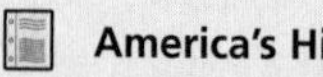 **America's History Makers**
- José Martí, pp. 93–94

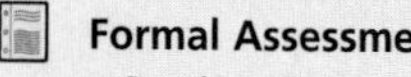 **Citizenship Today,** pp. 15–16

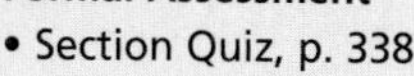 **Formal Assessment**
- Section Quiz, p. 338

**Alternative Assessment**
- Rubrics, 4.5
- Rubrics, 5.6

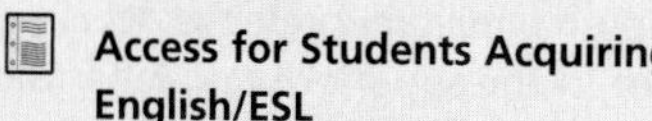 **Access for Students Acquiring English/ESL**
- Guided Reading, p. 154
- Skillbuilder Practice, p. 156

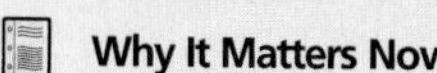 **Why It Matters Now**
- Modern U.S. Territories, pp. 45–46

**Technology Resources**

 **Electronic Teacher Tools with Test Maker**

 **ClassZone**
www.mcdougallittell.com

Spain sent General Valeriano "the Butcher" Weyler to crush the rebels. Weyler's methods were harsh. He forced many Cubans from their homes and placed them in camps guarded by Spanish troops. Thousands died of starvation and disease in the camps.

The revolt in Cuba caused alarm in the United States. Business leaders were concerned because the fighting disrupted U.S. trade with Cuba. Most Americans, however, became outraged when the press began to describe the brutality of Spanish officials. Two New York City newspapers, in particular, stirred up people's emotions.

The *World,* owned by Joseph Pulitzer, and the *New York Journal,* owned by William Randolph Hearst, were battling for customers. Both owners were able to attract readers by printing stories that described—and often exaggerated—news about Spanish cruelty. This sensational style of writing was known as **yellow journalism.** It was named after "The Yellow Kid," a popular comic strip that ran in the two New York papers.

*Reading* **History**
**A. Forming Opinions** How can newspapers affect public opinion?
A. Possible Response Students may point out that thousands of people read the same newspaper.

## The United States Goes to War

William McKinley, the U.S. president in 1898, did not want war. "I have been through [the Civil War]," he told a friend. "I have seen the dead piled up, and I do not want to see another."

Even so, public opinion—stirred up by sensational newspaper reports—forced McKinley to take action. He demanded that Spain halt its harsh treatment of Cubans. Spain did bring General Weyler home, but conditions remained severe.

In January 1898, McKinley sent the **U.S.S. *Maine*** to Cuba. Riots had broken out in the capital, Havana, and the battleship was dispatched to protect U.S. citizens. Then, the following month, the *Maine* exploded and sank in Havana's harbor, killing 260 sailors.

No one knows what caused the explosion. Most historians today believe that it was an accident. For example, a spark might have set off an explosion in the ship's coal bunker. Even so, Americans blamed Spain.

**The explosion of the *Maine* and accounts of the event by yellow journalists led many Americans to favor war against Spain.**

663



## MORE ABOUT . . .

**William Randolph Hearst and the Spanish-American War**

Hearst was confident of his power to shape events. In 1898, anticipating the outbreak of war between Spain and Cuba, he sent artist Frederic Remington to Cuba to cover the event. Remington cabled Hearst, "Everything is quiet. There is no trouble here. I wish to return." Hearst reportedly wired back, "Please remain. You furnish the pictures. I'll furnish the war."

### CRITICAL THINKING ACTIVITY

**Drawing Conclusions** Draw a two-column chart on the board like the one below. Ask students to write reasons for declaring war against Spain in one column and reasons against declaring war in the other. Then discuss with students the role of propaganda in instigating the war.

| Reasons Against War | Reasons for War |
|---|---|
| | |

**Class Time** 10 minutes

## MORE ABOUT . . .

**The *Maine***

The U.S.S. *Maine* arrived in Havana Harbor on January 25, 1898. Spanish officials came aboard the vessel with the customary welcome. The vessel exploded on February 15 at 9:40 P.M. President McKinley was awakened with the news around 2:00 A.M. About an hour later, the Pulitzer paper the *World* had an issue on the streets with a four-column headline trumpeting the news.

**In-Depth Resources: Unit 7**
• Enrichment Activity, p. 36

## ACTIVITY OPTIONS

### INDIVIDUAL NEEDS: GIFTED AND TALENTED

**COMMENTARY ON THE WAR**

**Class Time** Two class periods

**Task** Comparing responses to the Spanish-American War by American writers

**Purpose** To read and compare writing by Mark Twain, Stephen Crane, and Walt Whitman

**Supplies Needed**
• Internet access

**Activity** Direct students to the Library of Congress Web site on the Spanish-American War. See www.mcdougallittell.com for the address. Divide the class into three groups and assign each group one of the three writers whose response to the war is discussed and quoted: Twain, Crane, or Whitman. Students should read the material on the writer, summarize it, and select one short representative quotation to read to the class.

**CITIZENSHIP TODAY**

**OBJECTIVE**
Students will understand the importance of detecting bias in the media in order to avoid mistaking opinion for fact.

**The Legacy of Yellow Journalism**
Although the era of yellow journalism instigated by the Hearst-Pulitzer rivalry ended after the turn of the century, many of its trappings linger on. Banner headlines, color comics, political cartoons, and copious illustrations have become widespread in the newspaper industry. Yellow journalism's spiritual descendants, the tabloids, still depend on sensationalism.

**Standards for Evaluation**
**Each report should**
- clearly state its purpose and provide supporting examples from news stories.
- educate the reader on detecting bias in news stories.
- follow the rules of spelling, grammar, and punctuation.

**Citizenship Today,** pp. 15–16

**CITIZENSHIP TODAY**

# Detecting Bias in the Media

Professional journalists try to report the news without bias—that is, without letting their personal opinions or those of their employer influence what they write. Unbiased reporting allows citizens to weigh the facts, come to their own understanding of issues and events, and act accordingly.

As you have read, journalists and their employers do not always avoid bias. Before the United States declared war on Spain in 1898, "yellow journalists" deliberately exaggerated stories to help sell newspapers. These stories helped to turn public opinion in favor of the Spanish-American War. They reflected a bias—that the United States should declare war on Spain.

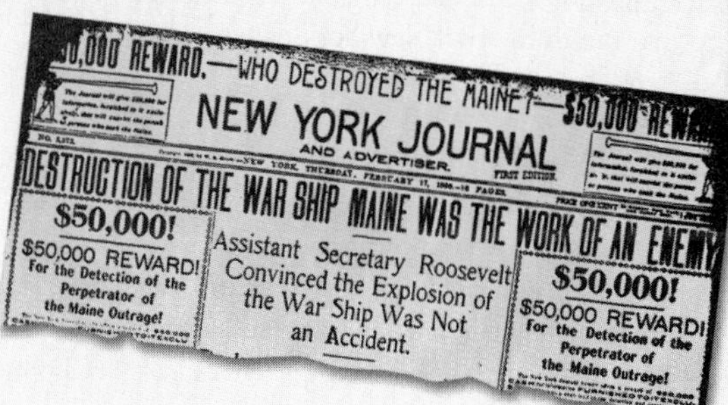
$50,000 REWARD.—WHO DESTROYED THE MAINE?—$50,000 REWARD.

NEW YORK JOURNAL
AND ADVERTISER.

DESTRUCTION OF THE WAR SHIP MAINE WAS THE WORK OF AN ENEMY

$50,000!
$50,000 REWARD! For the Detection of the Perpetrator of the Maine Outrage!

Assistant Secretary Roosevelt Convinced the Explosion of the War Ship Was Not an Accident.

$50,000!
$50,000 REWARD! For the Detection of the Perpetrator of the Maine Outrage!

William Randolph Hearst ran this headline in his *New York Journal* before authorities had a chance to determine the cause of the *Maine's* explosion.

### Can You Find Bias in the Media?

1. With a small group, collect news stories from different sources that cover the same issue or event.
2. Record any differences in the way a specific issue or event is covered by the sources you have selected.
3. Review the differences and decide whether any of the sources showed bias in their coverage.
4. Write a report that describes any bias you might detect. Explain why the biased source might have reported the story the way it did.

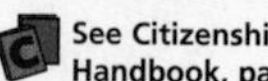
See Citizenship Handbook, page 284.

Visit www.mcdougallittell.com to learn more about the news media.

"Remember the Maine!" became a call to arms. On April 20, 1898, President McKinley signed a congressional resolution that called for Cuba's independence and demanded a withdrawal of Spanish forces. He gave Spain three days to respond. Spain refused, and the **Spanish-American War** began.

## 2 The War in the Philippines

The United States went to war to fight for Cuban freedom. But the first major battle of the Spanish-American War took place in a Spanish colony on the other side of the world—the Philippine Islands. Many Filipinos, as the inhabitants of the islands were called, had also revolted against Spanish rule in the 1890s.

Before the war began, the Filipino independence movement had attracted the attention of Theodore Roosevelt. At that time, Roosevelt was assistant secretary of the navy. He put a fleet of American ships in Hong Kong on alert. Their leader, Commodore George Dewey, prepared his forces and made contact with the head of the Filipino rebel forces, Emilio Aguinaldo (eh•MEE•lyoh AH•gee•NAHL•doh).

When the war began, Dewey set out for Manila, the Philippine capital, where part of the Spanish fleet was located. The battle in Manila Bay began early on the morning of May 1, 1898. By a little past noon,

**B. Possible Response** He recognized the importance of the Philippines to U.S. interests.

*Reading* **History**
**B. Making Inferences** Why did Theodore Roosevelt put the U.S. fleet in Hong Kong on alert?



**INSTRUCT: OBJECTIVE 2**

**The War in the Philippines/ The War in the Caribbean**
Key Questions
- How did Theodore Roosevelt's actions affect the outcome of the war?
- Why did Americans regard Commodore Dewey as a hero?
- How did the American forces defeat the Spanish in Cuba?

**ACTIVITY OPTIONS**

**SKILLBUILDER MINI-LESSON: IDENTIFYING FACTS AND OPINIONS** — BLOCK SCHEDULING

**Explaining the Skill** It is important to distinguish fact from opinion when you read history. Facts can be checked for accuracy. Facts include dates, statistics, and statements that can be proved. Opinions are the beliefs of the writer or speaker. Opinions may be assertions, claims, hypotheses, or judgments.

**Applying the Skill** Have students read the clipping on page 664 and the text under the heading "The United States Goes to War" on page 663. Ask them to make a chart that summarizes the facts and lists the opinions from both sources. Then ask the following questions:

1. How does the language differ in the two pieces of writing? *(newspaper: emotional; text: factual, nonemotional)*
2. What opinion is expressed in the newspaper clipping? *(The* Maine *was deliberately destroyed by the Spanish.)*
3. How could the facts in the text paragraph be proved? *(Facts could be verified in primary sources or histories of the time.)*
4. Why would the newspaper state opinion as if it were fact? *(to sell newspapers; to influence the public to go to war)*

**In-Depth Resources: Unit 7**
- Skillbuilder Practice, p. 25

Dewey's forces had destroyed the Spanish fleet. About 380 Spanish sailors were dead or wounded. No Americans died. U.S. troops, aided by Filipino rebels, took control of Manila in August.

Dewey became an instant hero in the United States. Thousands of babies born at the time of the victory in Manila Bay were named for him, and a chewing gum called "Dewey's Chewies" became popular.

## The War in the Caribbean

When the Spanish-American War began, the U.S. Army had only 28,000 men. Within four months, over 200,000 more joined up. Among the new recruits was Theodore Roosevelt, who had resigned from the Navy Department to volunteer.

Roosevelt helped to organize the First United States Volunteer Cavalry. This unit was nicknamed the **Rough Riders**. Its recruits included cowboys, miners, college students, New York policemen, athletes, and Native Americans.

In June, the Rough Riders and about 16,000 other soldiers—nearly a quarter of them African American—gathered in Tampa, Florida. They then set out for Santiago, a Spanish stronghold in southern Cuba. When the Rough Riders arrived, their dark-blue wool uniforms were too hot for the Cuban climate. Also, many of the soldiers came down with tropical diseases. Even so, they fought their way toward Santiago.

In order to gain control of Santiago's port, American troops had to capture San Juan Hill. They attacked the Spanish on July 1.

Skillbuilder Answers
1. in the port of Hong Kong on the Chinese mainland
2. about 150 miles

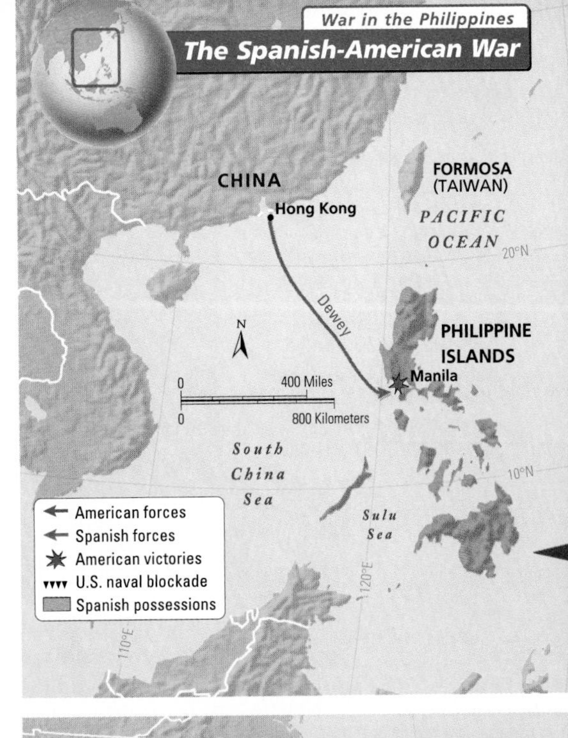


War in the Caribbean
The Spanish-American War

UNITED STATES
ATLANTIC OCEAN
Gulf of Mexico
Tampa
FLORIDA
Santiago
Santiago Harbor
San Juan Hill July 1, 1898
Spanish fleet destroyed July 3, 1898
BAHAMAS (Br.)
U.S.S. Maine sunk, Feb. 1898
Havana
CUBA
Tropic of Cancer
Santiago
HAITI
PUERTO RICO
DOMINICAN REPUBLIC
JAMAICA (Br.)
Caribbean Sea
400 Miles
800 Kilometers

**GEOGRAPHY SKILLBUILDER Interpreting Maps**
1. **Movement** *Where was Dewey's fleet before it steamed toward the Philippines?*
2. **Location** *About how far is Havana from the tip of southern Florida?*

665

## MORE ABOUT . . .

**Commodore Dewey**

Dewey requested an assignment in the Pacific because he thought there might be a war in the area. He researched and learned about the Philippines and prepared his fleet for battle. After the war, some people speculated that Dewey might run for president. Instead, promoted to admiral, he served as president of the general board of the navy.

## HISTORY FROM VISUALS

**Reading the Map** Ask students to study the map key. Then have them locate the U.S. naval blockade and U.S. victories. Ask why destroying the Spanish fleet at Santiago was important. Finally, have them trace the movements of U.S. and Spanish forces in the Caribbean. **Possible Responses** The blockade was outside Santiago Harbor; victories occurred at Manila Harbor, Santiago, and outside the harbor at Santiago. The defeat at Santiago prevented the Spanish from victory in the Caribbean. U.S. forces went southeast from Florida.

**Extension** Have students use a map of the world to determine how far Cuba is from the Philippine Islands.

## MORE ABOUT . . .

**The Rough Riders**

The Rough Riders were an odd assortment of men, united by their skills and ability with horses. Only 1 in 20 applicants was accepted. Unless dressed in their uniforms, the Rough Riders wore a motley assortment of gear. Many of the New York socialites and students from Ivy League colleges wore expensive shirts by exclusive tailors, while the polo players wore custom-fitted English breeches and beautiful boots. The cowboys wore sombreros, and they carried their own guns.

## ACTIVITY OPTIONS

**INTERDISCIPLINARY LINK: WORLD HISTORY**

BLOCK SCHEDULING

### HISTORY OF THE PHILIPPINES

**Class Time** One class period

**Task** Creating a short history of the Philippines

**Purpose** To provide background for learning about U.S. involvement in the Philippines

**Supplies Needed**
- Encyclopedias and reference books about the Philippines
- Internet access

**Activity** Divide students into small groups. Tell each group to create a brief history of the Philippine Islands to 1920. The group should divide topics among its members, and each member should be responsible for one topic and provide a list of sources he or she consulted. Groups should assemble the topics, make a cover, and staple their histories. Encourage students to use their histories as background material.

## HISTORY through ART

**Interpreting the Painting** Point out that the painting is romanticized and full of action. Not only are the soldiers represented inaccurately on horseback, but Roosevelt is brandishing his sword heroically; the soldiers look determined and are urging their nose-flaring horses on; at least one flag and one hat are flying; and a grenade has been thrown in the right foreground.

**Possible Response: They were the Rough Riders, so the artist showed them on horseback. The artist romanticized the charge.**

## INSTRUCT: OBJECTIVE 3

**Results of the War**

Key Questions

- What demands did the United States make of Spain after the war?
- How did Filipinos respond to U.S. colonization of their country?
- What restrictions did the Platt Amendment impose upon Cuba?

## CRITICAL THINKING ACTIVITY

**Analyzing Causes and Recognizing Effects**

Dictate this statement to students: "The United States emerged as a world power as a result of the Spanish-American War." Ask students to write a brief paragraph supporting this statement. Before they write their paragraphs, have them make a chart like the one below that lists the causes and the results of the war.

| Causes of the Spanish-American War | Results of the Spanish-American War |
|---|---|
| Spanish atrocities in Cuba | Territories gained—Guam, Puerto Rico, the Philippines |

**Class Time** 15 minutes

## HISTORY through ART

On July 1, 1898, U.S. troops, including the Rough Riders, attacked San Juan Hill outside of Santiago, Cuba. This painting shows Theodore Roosevelt leading a cavalry charge up the hill—even though the regiment's horses had been left behind in Florida.

**Why did the artist show the Rough Riders on horses when they made their charge on foot?**

African-American soldiers from the Tenth Cavalry began to drive the Spanish back. Roosevelt and the Rough Riders joined them as they rushed forward and captured the hill.

Two days later, American ships destroyed Spain's fleet as it tried to escape Santiago Harbor. On July 17, the city surrendered. A week later, U.S. forces took Puerto Rico. Finally, on August 12, 1898, Spain signed a truce. To U.S. Secretary of State John Hay, it had been "a splendid little war." For Spain, four centuries of glory had come to an end.

## 3 Results of the War

Although the war had been fought over Cuba, U.S. leaders demanded that Spain give up other colonies after the war—including Puerto Rico, the island of Guam, and the Philippines. Spain had no choice but to agree. The final peace treaty was signed in Paris in December 1898.

One of the most difficult questions for U.S. leaders after the war was what to do with the Philippines. Filipinos had fought alongside Americans during the war and believed that Spain's defeat would bring them independence. But President McKinley eventually decided that the Philippines should become an American colony.

Filipinos were bitterly disappointed. Led by Emilio Aguinaldo, they began to fight against their new colonial rulers. American troops sent to put down the resistance were not able to restore order until 1902.

The United States was also reluctant to grant Cuba complete independence. First, Cuba had to add the **Platt Amendment** to its constitution. This gave the United States the right to intervene in Cuban affairs anytime there was a threat to "life, property, and individual liberty." Cuba also had to allow a U.S. naval base at Guantánamo Bay.

Puerto Rico became an American territory. The United States set up a government and appointed the top officials. Puerto Ricans had little to

*Reading* **History**

**C. Making Inferences** Why did the United States demand that Spain give up territories in addition to Cuba?

**C. Possible Response** U.S. leaders might have thought the territories would be economically or militarily useful.



**ACTIVITY OPTIONS**

**INTERDISCIPLINARY LINK: SCIENCE**

**BLOCK SCHEDULING**

**ERADICATING YELLOW FEVER**

**Class Time** One class period

**Task** Researching and reporting on the elimination of yellow fever in Cuba

**Purpose** To learn about a medical advance of the period and to practice research skills

**Supplies Needed**

- Encyclopedias and other reference material on Cuba and yellow fever
- Internet access

**Activity** Tell students that yellow fever is a dangerous disease. In the late 1800s, Dr. Carlos Finlay of Cuba hypothesized that the disease was transmitted by mosquitoes. Tell students to use reference materials to find the following facts: how army researchers tested Finlay's hypothesis; the name of the American physician who led the campaign to rid Cuba of yellow fever; the year in which Cuba was clear of yellow fever.

say in their own affairs. Only in 1917 would the United States agree to make Puerto Rico a self-governing territory and grant U.S. citizenship to all Puerto Ricans.

## 4 The Anti-Imperialist League

U.S. treatment of Spain's former colonies after the Spanish-American War disappointed many people in the United States.

Several well-known Americans, including businessman Andrew Carnegie, reformer Jane Addams, and writer Mark Twain, joined with others to form the **Anti-Imperialist League.** Members of the League believed that Americans should not deny other people the right to govern themselves.

*Reading* **History**

**C. Finding Main Ideas** Why did the Anti-Imperialist League oppose U.S. efforts to collect colonies?

C. The League believed people should govern themselves and that "imperialism is hostile to liberty."

*A VOICE FROM THE PAST*

> We hold that the policy known as imperialism is hostile to liberty. . . . We regret that it has become necessary in the land of Washington and Lincoln to reaffirm that all men, of whatever race or color, are entitled to life, liberty, and the pursuit of happiness.
>
> From the *Platform of the American Anti-Imperialist League*

The voice of the Anti-Imperialist League was lost, however, in the roar of popular approval of the Spanish-American War.

Many Americans hoped that their nation would surpass the glory of the old Spanish empire. In the next section, you will read more about how the United States continued its involvement overseas.

**AMERICA'S HISTORY MAKERS**

**LUIS MUÑOZ RIVERA**
**1859–1916**

**Luis Muñoz Rivera** devoted his life to obtaining self-government for Puerto Rico—first from Spain and then from the United States.

After Spain granted Puerto Rico self-rule in 1897, Muñoz Rivera joined the government. He resigned and renewed his struggle when Puerto Rico became a U.S. territory.

Muñoz Rivera died just before the United States granted Puerto Ricans U.S. citizenship and a large measure of self-government.

**In what ways did Muñoz Rivera use his leadership skills to help his country?**

### Section 2 Assessment

**1. Terms & Names**

Identify:
- yellow journalism
- U.S.S. *Maine*
- Spanish-American War
- Rough Riders
- Platt Amendment
- Anti-Imperialist League
- Luis Muñoz Rivera

**2. Taking Notes**

Use a time line to record the major events of the Spanish-American War.

Spanish-American War, 1898

About how long did the Spanish-American War last?

**3. Main Ideas**

a. What led to the Cuban rebellion against Spain in 1895?

b. What was the first major military event of the Spanish-American War?

c. What happened in the Philippines after the war?

**4. Critical Thinking**

**Forming Opinions** Did the United States betray its democratic principles when it made the Philippines a colony?

THINK ABOUT
- the public's response to yellow journalists and U.S. military victories
- the work of the Anti-Imperialist League

**ACTIVITY OPTIONS**

**LANGUAGE ARTS**
**MATH**

Research the Spanish-American War. Write a **television news script** covering a major battle or create a **database** of wartime casualties.





### AMERICA'S HISTORY MAKERS

**Luis Muñoz Rivera**

Muñoz Rivera headed the first Puerto Rican cabinet under U.S. occupation. In that position, he argued for free trade between the U.S. and Puerto Rico, opposed military governorship, and pleaded for greater self-government. Muñoz Rivera moved to New York City, where he published the bilingual *Puerto Rican Herald,* which dealt with the island's problems. As resident commissioner of Puerto Rico in Washington, D.C. (1910–1916), he helped Puerto Ricans obtain U.S. citizenship.

Possible Response: Muñoz Rivera served his country by working in the government. He always lobbied for self-rule for Puerto Rico.

### INSTRUCT: OBJECTIVE 4

**The Anti-Imperialist League**

Key Questions
- Why did Americans set up the Anti-Imperialist League?
- How did most Americans feel about the results of the war?

### ASSESS & RETEACH

**Setting the Stage** Have students write information about the Spanish-American War on the appropriate lines on the graphic organizer.

**Formal Assessment**
- Section Quiz, p. 338

**RETEACHING ACTIVITY**

In groups of five, have students assume the roles of William Randolph Hearst, President McKinley, Theodore Roosevelt, Mark Twain, and Luis Muñoz Rivera. Have students take turns speaking as if they were that individual, explaining their views of the Spanish-American War and its results.

**In-Depth Resources: Unit 7**
- Reteaching Activity, p. 33

### Section 2 Assessment

**1. Terms & Names**

**yellow journalism,** p. 663
**U.S.S. *Maine*,** p. 663
**Spanish-American War,** p. 664
**Rough Riders,** p. 665
**Platt Amendment,** p. 666
**Anti-Imperialist League,** p. 667
**Luis Muñoz Rivera,** p. 667

**2. Taking Notes**

April: the explosion of the *Maine* results in a declaration of war; May: Dewey destroys Spanish fleet in Manila Bay; July: attack on San Juan Hill occurs and Puerto Rico is taken by the United States; August: Spain signs a truce; December: final peace treaty signed in Paris
approximately five months

**3. Main Ideas**

**a.** resentment of Spanish rule aggravated by an ongoing economic depression **b.** Dewey's destruction of the Spanish fleet in Manila Bay **c.** After the United States took the country as a colony, U.S. troops had to fight to defeat the Filipino resistance to American rule.

**4. Critical Thinking**

Answers will vary but should be supported by evidence in the chapter.

**ACTIVITY OPTIONS**

**Alternative Assessment**
- Rubrics for a news script, 4.5
- Rubrics for a database, 5.6

## SECTION OBJECTIVES

1. To explain how the United States became a world power
2. To describe the development of the Panama Canal
3. To analyze U.S. involvement in Latin America
4. To evaluate the use of "big stick diplomacy"

**SKILLBUILDER**
Interpreting Maps: Place, Region, p. 669
Interpreting Maps: Location, Movement, p. 670
Interpreting Maps: Location, Place, p. 672

**CRITICAL THINKING**
Recognizing Causes, p. 669
Summarizing, p. 670
Making Inferences, p. 672
Drawing Conclusions, p. 673

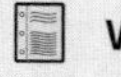
**Why It Matters Now**
- Modern U.S. Territories, pp. 45–46

## FOCUS & MOTIVATE

### 5-MINUTE WARM-UP

**Making Inferences** These questions focus on U.S. involvement in Asia and Latin America.

1. Look at the map on page 669. Why might the United States want influence in Asia?
2. Look at the map on page 672. How was the United States involved in Latin America?

**Warm-Up Transparency WT23**

## INSTRUCT

### INSTRUCT: OBJECTIVE 1

**A Power in the Pacific/ The United States in China**
Key Questions
- How did the United States become a power in the Pacific?
- How did Perry's voyages affect Japan?
- Why was the Open Door Policy important to the United States?

**In-Depth Resources: Unit 7**
- Guided Reading, p. 23

**Reading Study Guide** (Spanish and English), pp. 227–228

# 3 U.S. Involvement Overseas

**TERMS & NAMES**
sphere of influence
Open Door Policy
Boxer Rebellion
Panama Canal
Roosevelt Corollary

**MAIN IDEA**
In the early 1900s, the United States expanded its involvement in Asia and Latin America.

**WHY IT MATTERS NOW**
The United States still trades extensively with Asian and Latin American countries.

### ONE AMERICAN'S STORY

**In 1852, President Millard Fillmore sent Commodore Matthew Perry on a mission to open Japan to U.S. trade. For over two centuries, Japan's rulers had kept the country closed to most foreigners. Perry wanted to break Japan's traditional policy with a demonstration of American power.**

*A VOICE FROM THE PAST*

[I was determined] to adopt an entirely contrary plan of proceedings from that of all others who had . . . visited Japan on the same errand [to open up trade]: to demand as a right and not to [ask] as a favor those acts of courtesy which are due from one civilized nation to another.

**Commodore Matthew Perry,** *Personal Journal*

**Perry arrived in Japan in July 1853 but was not able to win a trade agreement. He departed but returned the next year with more warships. Under the threat of force, the Japanese gave in. In March 1854, Japan signed a treaty giving American ships access to its ports. In this section, you will read more about U.S. involvement in Asia, as well as in Latin America.**

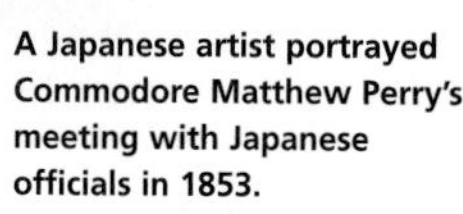
A Japanese artist portrayed Commodore Matthew Perry's meeting with Japanese officials in 1853.

### 1 A Power in the Pacific

Throughout the 1800s, the United States continued to expand its involvement in Asia. Toward the end of the century, the United States acquired a chain of islands—including Hawaii and Guam—that stretched across the Pacific Ocean to Asia.

During the Spanish-American War, Americans fought in the Philippine Islands, a Spanish colony in eastern Asia. After the war, the United States annexed the islands and put down the Filipino independence movement.

Some Americans objected to the annexation of the Philippines. However, supporters of imperialism, such as Indiana senator Albert Beveridge, applauded U.S. actions. Beveridge boasted, "The Philippines



## RECOMMENDED RESOURCES

**In-Depth Resources: Unit 7**
- Guided Reading, p. 23
- Building Vocabulary, p. 24
- Geography Application, pp. 26–27
- Primary Source, p. 29
- Reteaching Activity, p. 34

**Reading Study Guide** (Spanish and English), pp. 227–228

**Outline Map Activities**
- U.S. Territorial Influence, 1867–1917, pp. 45–46

**Why It Matters Now**
- Modern U.S. Territories, pp. 45–46

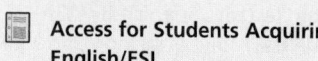

**Formal Assessment**
- Section Quiz, p. 339

**Alternative Assessment**
- Rubrics, 1.10
- Rubrics, 2.3

**Access for Students Acquiring English/ESL**
- Guided Reading, p. 155
- Geography Application, pp. 157–158

**Technology Resources**

**Humanities Trans. HT45, HT46**
- Political Cartoon: The Boxer Rebellion
- Panama Canal Stamp

**Geography Transparency GT23**
- The Panama Canal Shortcut, 1914

**Electronic Teacher Tools with Test Maker**

are ours forever. And just beyond the Philippines are China's [unlimited] markets. We will not retreat from either. . . . The power that rules the Pacific is the power that rules the world."

Many Americans looked forward to the profits promised by Asian markets and resources. Others saw a chance to extend U.S. democracy and culture in the region. The Philippines would provide a base for these activities.

> ***"The power that rules the Pacific . . . rules the world."***
> **Albert Beveridge**

## The United States in China

As Senator Beveridge noted, control of the Philippines gave Americans greater access to China. However, by the time the United States acquired the islands, other imperialist nations, including Japan, were already deeply involved in China.

When Commodore Perry opened Japan to U.S. trade in the 1850s, he also opened the nation to western ideas. After Perry's voyages, Japan began to modernize and soon emerged as a world power. In the 1890s, Japan demonstrated its strength in a successful war against China.

After the war, both Japan and the major European powers expanded their **spheres of influence** in China. These were areas where foreign nations claimed special rights and economic privileges. By the late 1890s, France, Germany, Britain, Japan, and Russia had established prosperous settlements along the coast of China. They also claimed exclusive rights to railroad construction and mining development in the nation's interior.

The competition for spheres of influence worried U.S. leaders who wanted access to China's markets and resources. In 1899, Secretary of State John Hay asked nations involved in the region to follow an **Open Door Policy**. This meant that no single country should have a monopoly on trade with China. Eventually, most of the nations accepted Hay's proposal.

Many Chinese people were not pleased by the presence of foreigners. One group, called the "Boxers," was angered by the privileges given to foreigners and the disrespect they showed toward Chinese traditions. In 1900, Chinese resentment toward foreigners' attitude of cultural superiority led to a violent uprising known as the **Boxer Rebellion**. Many foreigners were killed before the uprising was put down by an international force.

*Reading* **History**
**A. Recognizing Causes** Why did John Hay propose the Open Door Policy?
**A. Possible Response** He worried that other nations in China would prevent U.S. access to the country's markets.

Skillbuilder Answers
1. Portugal
2. Britain

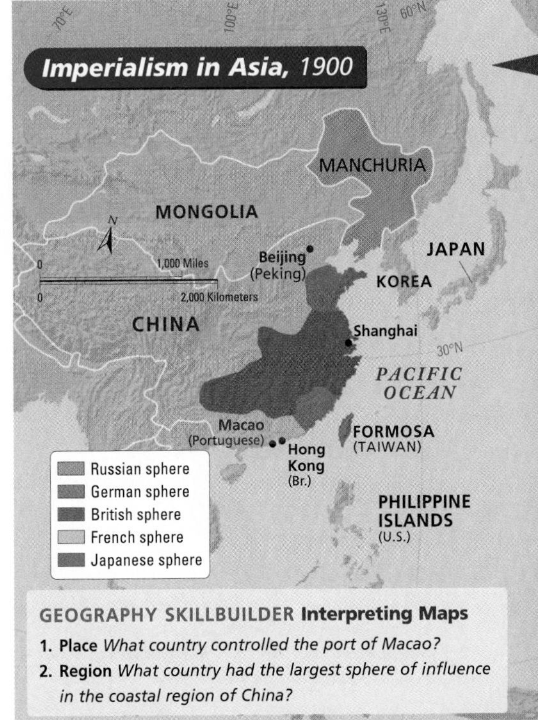


**GEOGRAPHY SKILLBUILDER Interpreting Maps**
1. **Place** *What country controlled the port of Macao?*
2. **Region** *What country had the largest sphere of influence in the coastal region of China?*

669

### MORE ABOUT . . .

**The United States and Japan**
President Roosevelt believed it was vital to have an American presence in Asia. He worried about Japan's growing power in the Pacific. After war broke out between Russia and Japan in 1904, Roosevelt agreed to serve as a peacemaker, hoping to keep Japan from winning a complete victory. The Japanese were not happy with the resulting treaty, but Roosevelt won the Nobel Peace Prize for his efforts.

### HISTORY FROM VISUALS

**Interpreting the Map** Ask students to name the countries in Asia where the United States had a sphere of influence in 1900. Then ask them to name the countries that had spheres of influence in China. Finally, ask students how these facts relate to the Open Door Policy. **Possible Responses** the Philippines; Russia, Germany, Great Britain, France, and Japan; the United States had no influence in China but did not want other countries to monopolize its trade with China

**Extension** Have students look in an almanac to find out the status of Manchuria, Macao, Hong Kong, and Shanghai today.

### MORE ABOUT . . .

**The Boxer Rebellion**
In growing resentment against foreign influence, some Chinese joined secret societies dedicated to ridding the country of "foreign devils." The most famous of these societies was called the Society of the Righteous and Harmonious Fists, or the Boxers. In 1900, the Boxers rebelled against Western influence and besieged the European section of Beijing. Troops from Europe, Japan, and the United States defeated the Boxers.

 **Humanities Transparency HT45**
- Political Cartoon: The Boxer Rebellion

### ACTIVITY OPTIONS
### INDIVIDUAL NEEDS

**STUDENTS ACQUIRING ENGLISH/ESL**

**Expanding Vocabulary** Write the word *imperial* on the board and define it as "relating to an empire." Tell students that *imperial* also means "ruling over extensive territories." Begin a word pyramid with *imperial* at the top. Ask students to skim the chapter looking for words that have *imperial* as a base. Write them below *imperial* to form a pyramid. *(imperialism, imperialist, anti-imperialist)* Define each word and ask students to use it in a sentence.

| | imperialism | |
|---|---|---|
| imperialism | imperialist | anti-imperialist |

**INSTRUCT: OBJECTIVE** 

**The Panama Canal/Building the Canal**

Key Questions

- Why did the United States want a canal to connect the Atlantic and Pacific Oceans?
- How did the United States obtain the land for the Panama Canal?
- What were some of the costs of building the Panama Canal?

 **Humanities Transparency HT46**
- Panama Canal Stamp

## MORE ABOUT . . .

**Rebellion in Panama**

When the Colombian Senate turned down a treaty giving up land for the canal, a group of people with financial interests in a canal through Panama sent agents to stir up rebellion. Philippe Bunau-Varilla was able to coordinate an uprising in Panama with the arrival of the U.S. gunboat *Nashville.* It seems unlikely that the navy was aware of the impending revolt, which was carried out quietly. On November 6, 1903, the United States recognized the new nation. The first minister to the United States from Panama was none other than Bunau-Varilla.

## HISTORY FROM VISUALS

**Reading the Map** Ask students to use the map to identify the geographical difficulties in building the canal (mountains, rivers). Ask students to use the scale to measure approximately how many miles a ship would cover, sailing from the Pacific to the Atlantic Ocean. **Answer** about 40 miles

**Extension** Ask students to do research on the work of Dr. William Gorgas in eliminating yellow fever from Panama.

 **Geography Transparency GT23**
- The Panama Canal Shortcut, 1914

## 2 The Panama Canal

As American interests in the Pacific expanded, easy access to the region became vital. For that reason, U.S. leaders proposed a canal to connect the Atlantic and Pacific oceans. A canal would mean that U.S. ships would not have to travel around South America. The Spanish-American War, fought in both oceans, also made clear the need for such a shortcut.

The South American nation of Colombia controlled the best spot for the canal—the Isthmus of Panama. But Colombia was unwilling to give up this land. Ignoring Colombia's right to control its territory, President Roosevelt sent the U.S. Navy to support a revolution on the isthmus. Out of this revolution, the new nation of Panama was created in 1903.

**Vocabulary**
**isthmus:** a narrow strip of land connecting two larger masses of land

The new Panamanian leaders gave the U.S. government rights to a ten-mile-wide strip of land called the Canal Zone. There, the United States would build the **Panama Canal,** the shortcut that would connect the Atlantic and Pacific oceans.

Some people in Latin America and the United States opposed Roosevelt's actions. They believed that he had interfered in Colombia's affairs in order to cheat it out of land. In 1921, the United States finally paid Colombia $25 million for the loss of Panama.

***Reading*History**
**B. Summarizing** What political difficulty faced U.S. leaders who wanted to build the Panama Canal?
B. Possible Response Colombia did not want to sell the land needed for the construction of the canal.

## Building the Canal

Building the canal was extremely difficult. The land was swampy and full of mosquitoes that carried the organism that causes malaria. In spite of the difficulties, the project moved forward. When Roosevelt visited Panama in 1906, he wrote a letter describing the work.

Skillbuilder Answers
1. Miraflores Locks
2. Southeast

**Panama Canal**

ATLANTIC OCEAN
N
Canal route
Canal Zone
Colón
Cristóbal
Chagres R.
Gatún Locks
Gatún Dam
Gatún Lake
Madden Lake
Madden Dam
Chagres R.
Gaillard (Culebra) Cut
Pedro Miguel Locks
Miraflores Locks
Miraflores Lake
Panama City
Balboa
0 10 Miles
0 10 Kilometers
PACIFIC OCEAN

**GEOGRAPHY SKILLBUILDER Interpreting Maps**
1. **Location** *Which locks are closest to Panama City?*
2. **Movement** *In which direction do ships move through the canal from the Atlantic Ocean to the Pacific Ocean?*

**A VOICE FROM THE PAST**

Steam shovels are hard at it; scooping huge masses of rock and gravel and dirt previously loosened by the drillers and dynamite blasters, loading it on trains which take it away. . . . They are eating steadily into the mountain cutting it down and down. . . . It is an epic feat.

**Theodore Roosevelt,** from a letter sent to his son

More than 45,000 workers, including many black West Indians, labored for years on the canal. They did not finish the work until 1914. The canal cost $352 million, the most expensive project up to that time. It was expensive in human terms, too. More than 5,000 workers died from diseases or accidents.

**Background**
In 1977, the United States signed a treaty that transfers ownership of the canal to Panama on December 31, 1999.

670

## ACTIVITY OPTIONS

**MULTIPLE LEARNING STYLES: SPATIAL** — BLOCK SCHEDULING

**BUILDING A LOCK**

**Class Time** One class period

**Task** Building a lock

**Purpose** To understand how locks work and why they are necessary for canal travel

**Supplies Needed**
- Reference material on locks
- Waterproof material for the canal, such as a length of plastic rain guttering or several plastic soda bottles cut in half lengthwise
- Pieces of Styrofoam or other waterproof material for the gates
- Large plastic dishpan
- Dirt, water, toy boat

**Activity** Have students build their own single lock in a box or crate. Help students cut the plastic material for the canal and have them fit two gates so they keep out the water. Have students arrange dirt around the "canal" to make it look more realistic. When they have finished, have them demonstrate how the lock works, filling the lock chamber slowly with water so the toy boat is lifted up. Then have students explain how a system of locks can raise and lower a ship.

# How the Panama Canal Works

Engineers faced a problem in building the Panama Canal. Because of the region's different landscape elevations, no waterway would remain level. They solved this dilemma by building three sets of *locks*—water-filled chambers that raise or lower ships to match a canal's different water levels.

1. The lock gates open on one end to allow the ship to enter.
2. The gates close, and water is pumped in or out depending on whether the ship is moving up or down.
3. Once the water in the chamber and the canal ahead is level, the second gate opens and the ship moves on.

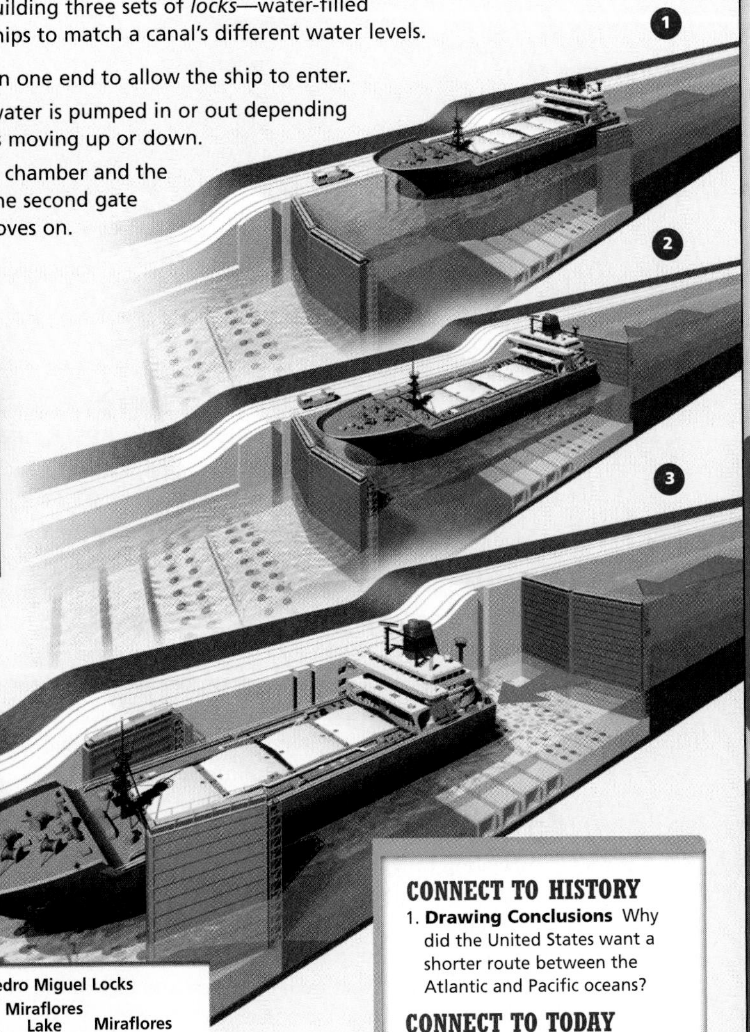

The locks, whose steel gates rise six stories high, can hold as much as 26 million gallons of water—enough to supply a major U.S. city for one day.

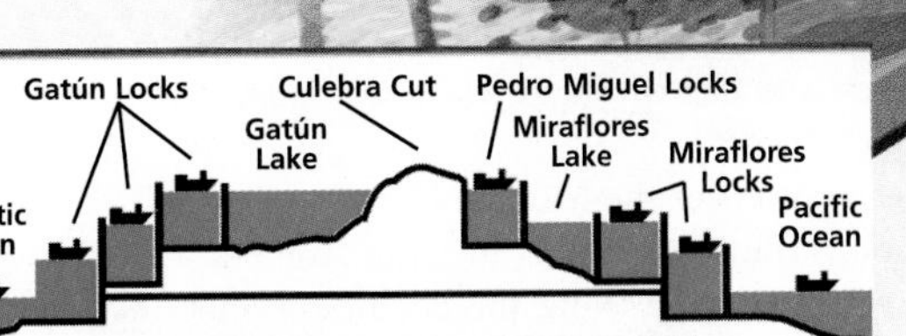


This cross-section shows the different elevations and locks that a ship moves through on the 8–9 hour trip through the canal. Before the canal was built, a trip around South America could take two months.

### CONNECT TO HISTORY

1. **Drawing Conclusions** Why did the United States want a shorter route between the Atlantic and Pacific oceans?

### CONNECT TO TODAY

2. **Researching** What is the economic and political status of the Panama Canal today?

Visit www.mcdougallittell.com to learn more about the Panama Canal.

671

## Technology OF THE Time

### OBJECTIVES

1. To explain the need for a system of locks on the Panama Canal
2. To explain the technology used to build the lock system of the Panama Canal

**BLOCK SCHEDULING**

### INSTRUCT

Key Questions

- What problems did builders of the canal face?
- Look at the first picture. Is the ship going to be moved to a higher or a lower elevation?
- How many different elevations do you see in the diagram?

### MORE ABOUT . . .

**The History of Locks**

In 1373, the Dutch developed the pound (chamber) lock to lift vessels to different elevations, the most significant innovation in canal construction. Leonardo da Vinci is said to have invented a kind of canal gate, designed to withstand more water pressure than previous gates.

### MORE ABOUT . . .

**Building the Panama Canal**

Building the Panama Canal was an enormous feat. When it was completed, the Panama Canal included the world's largest earth dam, the largest system of locks built to that time, and the largest swinging gates ever completed. The most difficult part of the canal to build was the Culebra Cut. One problem in this cut was moving out the dirt and rock that workers loosened. More than 4,000 wagons hauled by 160 locomotives were used to haul out the debris. As the cut deepened, the danger of landslides grew.

### CONNECT TO HISTORY

1. **Drawing Conclusions** U.S. interests in Asia demanded easier access to the Pacific; in order to move its naval forces around the world more quickly; to improve trade by providing a shorter route for goods to travel

### CONNECT TO TODAY

2. **Researching** Students can use up-to-date encyclopedias or the Internet to learn about the current economic and political status of the canal. Have them write a brief report on their findings.

## HISTORY FROM VISUALS

**Reading the Map** Ask students to use the map to find a reason for U.S. concern about the stability of Latin American nations. **Possible Responses** The countries of Latin America are close to the United States; access to the Panama Canal is through the Caribbean.

**Extension** Have students select one Latin American country to which the United States sent troops between 1898 and 1917. Have them research its current government and economy.

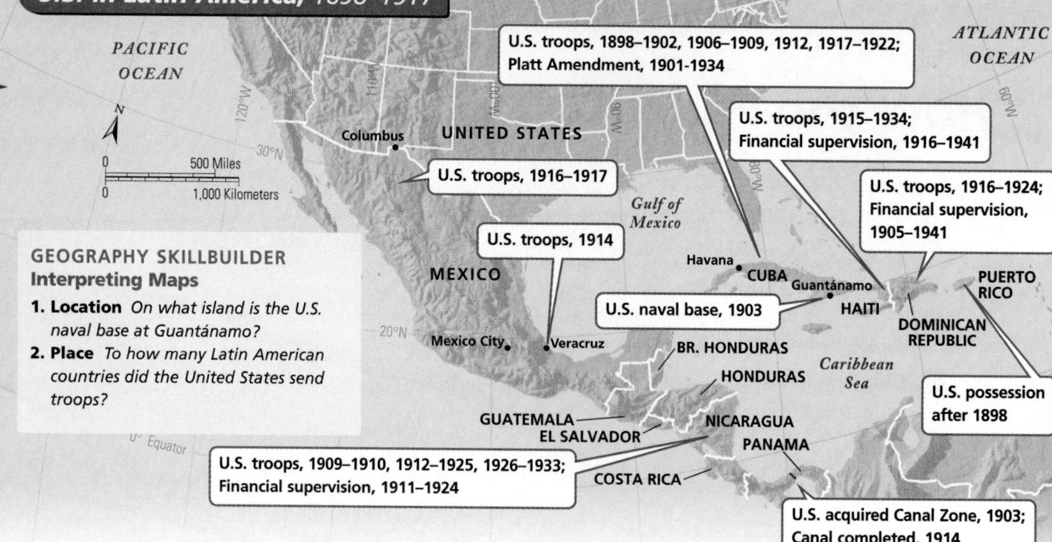


**GEOGRAPHY SKILLBUILDER**
**Interpreting Maps**
1. **Location** *On what island is the U.S. naval base at Guantánamo?*
2. **Place** *To how many Latin American countries did the United States send troops?*

Skillbuilder Ans
1. Cuba
2. Five—Mexico, Nicaragua, Cuba, Haiti, and the Dominican Republic

## 3 U.S. Involvement in Latin America

The Panama Canal was only one sign of U.S. involvement in Latin America. As the U.S. economy continued to grow, so did Americans' interest in the resources of their southern neighbors.

Businesses in the United States found that they could cheaply buy food and raw materials—for example, bananas, coffee, and copper—from Latin America. They shipped these goods to the United States and sold them for higher prices. U.S. companies also bought large amounts of land in the region for farming and mining.

As economic interests drew the United States deeper into Latin American affairs, U.S. leaders became concerned about political stability in the region. They were especially worried that instability might tempt European nations to intervene in the region.

*Reading* **History**
**C. Making Inferences** Why was the United States interested in the political stability of Latin America?
**C. Possible Response** It wanted to make sure that its economic interests in the region were not threatened.

## 4 Policing the Hemisphere

During his presidency, Theodore Roosevelt made it clear that the United States would remain the dominant power in the Western Hemisphere. He summed up his foreign policy toward the region with an African saying: "Speak softly, but carry a big stick." Roosevelt, however, rarely spoke softly. He made sure that everyone knew the United States would use military force if its interests were threatened.

Roosevelt reminded European powers of the Monroe Doctrine—the policy that prevented other nations from intervening in Latin America. In 1904, he added the **Roosevelt Corollary**. Now, the doctrine would not only prevent European intervention in Latin America; it also authorized the United States to act as a "policeman" in the region. That is, U.S. leaders would now intervene in Latin America's domestic affairs

**Vocabulary**
**corollary:** a statement that follows logically from an earlier statement



## INSTRUCT: OBJECTIVE 3

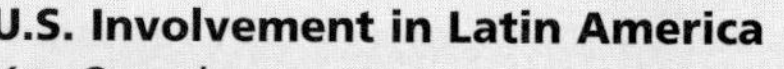

**U.S. Involvement in Latin America**

Key Questions
- How did economic interests influence the relations between the United States and Latin American nations?
- Why were U.S. leaders concerned about Latin America's political stability?

## INSTRUCT: OBJECTIVE 4

**Policing the Hemisphere**

Key Questions
- Why did Roosevelt add the Roosevelt Corollary to the Monroe Doctrine?
- How did other U.S. presidents use the Roosevelt Corollary and "big stick diplomacy"?
- How did the American and the Latin American views of U.S. policing policies differ?

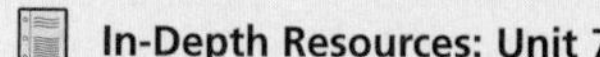

**In-Depth Resources: Unit 7**
- Geography Application: Pancho Villa Raids New Mexico, pp. 26–27
- Primary Source: The Roosevelt Corollary to the Monroe Doctrine, p. 29

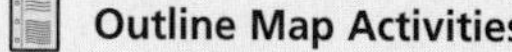

**Outline Map Activities**
- U.S. Territorial Influence, 1867–1917, pp. 45–46

## ACTIVITY OPTIONS

**INTERDISCIPLINARY LINK: GOVERNMENT/CIVICS**

**BLOCK SCHEDULING**

### INTERVENTION ABROAD

**Class Time** One class period

**Task** Describing U.S. intervention and its effects

**Purpose** To understand the intended goal and the effects of U.S. intervention in Latin America

**Supplies Needed**
- Reference books
- Encyclopedias
- Internet access

**Activity** Ask students to choose one of the following countries: the Dominican Republic, Cuba, Nicaragua, Mexico. Tell students to research the reasons for U.S. intervention in their chosen country, the form of the intervention, and its effects. Students may present their findings in a written or oral report. They may also summarize their findings in a graphic organizer. Students may work alone or in groups.

when they believed that such action was necessary to maintain stability.

In 1905, the United States used the Roosevelt Corollary to take control of the Dominican Republic's finances after the country failed to pay its foreign debts. A year later, when a revolt threatened Cuba's government, the policy was used to send troops there.

Later presidents expanded on Roosevelt's "big stick diplomacy." William Howard Taft urged American businesses to invest in Latin America, promising military action if anything threatened these investments. He kept his word. In 1912, Taft sent marines to Nicaragua to restore order.

**Background**
Taft's policy was known as "dollar diplomacy."

President Taft's successor, Woodrow Wilson, also intervened in Latin America. When a revolution in Mexico began to threaten U.S. interests, Wilson took action. In 1914, he sent a fleet to Veracruz after U.S. sailors were arrested. Two years later, he sent troops into Mexico after a Mexican revolutionary named Pancho Villa (PAHN•choh VEE•yah) raided New Mexico and killed 19 Americans in the town of Columbus.

Americans rarely questioned U.S. actions in Latin America. They saw their nation as a good police officer, maintaining peace and preventing disorder. But many Latin Americans saw the United States as an imperial power that cared only about its own interests. This mistrust continues to trouble U.S. relations with its neighbors. In the next chapter, you will read about U.S. involvement in another part of the world—Europe.

## Now and then

**GLOBO COP?**

In the early 1900s, the United States used its "police powers" in the Western Hemisphere. Today, U.S. forces participate in police actions all over the globe. This fact has led some journalists to call the United States the "Globo Cop."

In the 1990s, U.S. forces helped lead international police actions in Somalia (see photo below), Yugoslavia, and other areas in crisis. The United States also led the Gulf War forces that liberated Kuwait after it was seized by Iraq.

The United States continues to patrol its own hemisphere, too. In 1989, U.S. troops invaded Panama to overthrow dictator Manuel Noriega.

## Section 3 Assessment

### 1. Terms & Names

**Identify:**
- sphere of influence
- Open Door Policy
- Boxer Rebellion
- Panama Canal
- Roosevelt Corollary

### 2. Taking Notes

Use a chart like the one below to record details about U.S. involvement in Asia and Latin America.

| Asia | Latin America |
|---|---|
| | |

How was U.S. involvement in Asia different from that in Latin America?

### 3. Main Ideas

a. Why was the United States interested in the Philippines?

b. Why was the nation of Panama created in 1903?

c. How did the Roosevelt Corollary change U.S. foreign policy?

### 4. Critical Thinking

**Drawing Conclusions**
Why did the United States become so heavily involved in Asia and Latin America?

**THINK ABOUT**
- U.S. economic growth
- American military interests

**ACTIVITY OPTIONS**

**SCIENCE** / **MATH**

Research the Panama Canal. Build a simple **model** of the canal or create a **graph** that shows how many ships use the canal each year.





## Now and then

**Globo Cop?**
In 1977, the United States and the Republic of Panama signed two treaties transferring control of the canal to Panama on December 31, 1999. The United States retained the right to defend the neutrality of the canal. In 1990, U.S. troops entered Panama to oust Noriega, an accused drug trafficker. Noriega stood trial in the United States, and in 1992, he was convicted on several charges and sentenced to 40 years in prison. Relations with Panama suffered as a result of the intervention, which many Panamanians call an invasion.

## ASSESS & RETEACH

**Setting the Stage** Have students write information about Latin America and China on the appropriate lines on the graphic organizer.

**Formal Assessment**
- Section Quiz, p. 339

**Critical Thinking Transparency CT67**
- Setting the Stage

**RETEACHING ACTIVITY**

Have students make a list of the countries discussed in this section, then write one fact or event having to do with each country's association with the United States.

**In-Depth Resources: Unit 7**
- Reteaching Activity, p. 34

## Section 3 Assessment

### 1. Terms & Names

**sphere of influence,** p. 669
**Open Door Policy,** p. 669
**Boxer Rebellion,** p. 669
**Panama Canal,** p. 670
**Roosevelt Corollary,** p. 672

### 2. Taking Notes

Asia: Filipino independence defeated; U.S. economic interests in China; Open Door Policy; Latin America: Panama Canal; economic interests; Roosevelt Corollary
Students may say that the United States faced less competition in Latin America.

### 3. Main Ideas

**a.** because it gave the United States access to Asian markets **b.** Colombia was reluctant to sell land in Panama to the United States for the canal. **c.** It authorized U.S. intervention into Latin America's domestic affairs.

### 4. Critical Thinking

Business leaders were looking for new markets and for raw materials.

**ACTIVITY OPTIONS**

**Alternative Assessment**
- Rubrics for a model, 1.10
- Rubrics for a graph, 2.3

## TERMS & NAMES

1. **imperialism,** p. 659
2. **Queen Liliuokalani,** p. 661
3. **yellow journalism,** p. 663
4. **Spanish-American War,** p. 664
5. **Rough Riders,** p. 665
6. **Anti-Imperialist League,** p. 667
7. **Open Door Policy,** p. 669
8. **Boxer Rebellion,** p. 669
9. **Panama Canal,** p. 670
10. **Roosevelt Corollary,** p. 672

## REVIEW QUESTIONS

**Possible Responses**

1. other world powers were taking overseas colonies; economic and military interests; a belief in cultural superiority
2. The public criticized him. Alaska was called "a polar bear garden" and "Seward's icebox."
3. Its location in the central Pacific Ocean made it ideal as a refueling station for U.S. military and merchant ships on their way to Asia. Also, there were many American sugar planters there.
4. He believed that the planters had acted improperly and illegally.
5. A revolt broke out in Cuba in 1895. Reports of Spanish cruelty toward Cubans in the U.S. press united public opinion behind the Cubans. The explosion of the *Maine* also put enormous pressure on the president to act.
6. Dewey's destruction of the Spanish fleet in Manila Bay and the Battle of San Juan Hill near Santiago, Cuba
7. Cuba, Puerto Rico, the Philippines, and Guam
8. By taking control of the Philippines, they had gained an important foothold in the region.
9. The Spanish-American War showed the importance of being able to move warships between the two oceans rapidly. Also, a canal would dramatically reduce the length of trading voyages.
10. All three presidents intervened in Latin America to maintain peace and stability there and to protect U.S. economic interests in the region.

# Chapter 23 ASSESSMENT

## VISUAL SUMMARY

### Becoming a World Power

#### The United States Continues to Expand

In the late 1800s, the United States began to expand overseas.

- Alaska was purchased from Russia.
- Planters took over Hawaii's government.

#### The Spanish-American War

Events in Cuba, a Spanish colony in the Caribbean, led to the Spanish-American War.

- U.S. forces won victories in the Caribbean and in Asia.
- Spain gave up its colonies in Cuba, Puerto Rico, the Philippines, and Guam.

#### U.S. Involvement Overseas

In both Asia and Latin America, the United States began to play a larger role.

- U.S. leaders insisted on an Open Door Policy in China.
- The United States built the Panama Canal.

## TERMS & NAMES

1. imperialism
2. Queen Liliuokalani
3. yellow journalism
4. Spanish-American War
5. Rough Riders
6. Anti-Imperialist League
7. Open Door Policy
8. Boxer Rebellion
9. Panama Canal
10. Roosevelt Corollary

## REVIEW QUESTIONS

**The United States Continues to Expand (pages 659–661)**

1. Why did Americans become interested in overseas expansion in the late 1800s?
2. How did the public react when William Seward negotiated the purchase of Alaska in 1867?
3. Why did the United States take an interest in Hawaii?
4. Why might President Cleveland have wanted to restore Liliuokalani to the Hawaiian throne?

**The Spanish-American War (pages 662–667)**

5. How did the Spanish-American War begin?
6. What were the most important battles of the war?
7. What territory did the United States take control of as a result of its victory over the Spanish?

**U.S. Involvement Overseas (pages 668–673)**

8. Why did U.S. leaders want access to China's markets after the Spanish-American War?
9. Why was there an interest in building a canal across Latin America?
10. How were the Latin American policies of Roosevelt, Taft, and Wilson similar?

## CRITICAL THINKING

**1. USING YOUR NOTES**

Using your completed chart, answer the questions below.

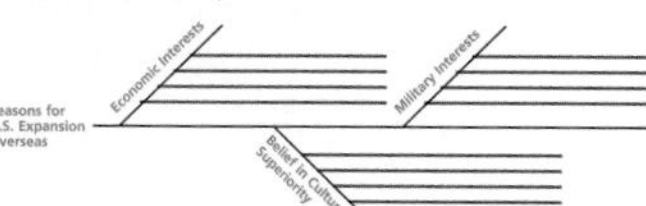

a. How did U.S. economic interests in Latin America influence the foreign policy of the United States?

b. In what ways was the Boxer Rebellion a reaction to the attitude of foreigners in China?

**2. ANALYZING LEADERSHIP**

What qualities made Theodore Roosevelt an effective leader?

**3. THEME: EXPANSION**

How did U.S. expansion at the end of the 19th century compare with expansion that occurred earlier? Discuss both similarities and differences.

**4. APPLYING CITIZENSHIP SKILLS**

How might the activities of the Anti-Imperialist League have helped to remind citizens of their democratic responsibilities?

**5. FORMING OPINIONS**

The "yellow journalism" of major newspapers influenced U.S. foreign policy at the turn of the century. How does modern media, such as television, shape public opinion today?

**Interact *with* History**

How has your study of U.S. involvement overseas at the turn of the century influenced your opinion about getting involved in the affairs of another country?

## CRITICAL THINKING

**Possible Responses**

1. **USING YOUR NOTES** **a.** As American economic interests in Latin America grew, U.S. foreign policy toward the region was changed to protect those interests. **b.** Boxers resented the privileges given to foreigners living in China and the disrespect they showed to Chinese traditions.
2. **ANALYZING LEADERSHIP** Students might mention his foresight in ordering Dewey to prepare for war, or his aggressive foreign policy.
3. **THEME: EXPANSION** Students might mention that it was similar because difficult questions were raised about the treatment of people who lived in the areas of expansion, or that it was different because Americans were now expanding onto other continents.
4. **APPLYING CITIZENSHIP SKILLS** They attempted to show citizens and leaders that some of the nation's policies toward Spain's former colonies betrayed the democratic principles of the United States.
5. **FORMING OPINIONS** Answers will vary but students should be able to explain their responses.

**Interact *with* History** Student responses will vary but should include information from this chapter and other chapters.

## HISTORY SKILLS

### 1. INTERPRETING GRAPHS

Study the graph and then answer the questions.

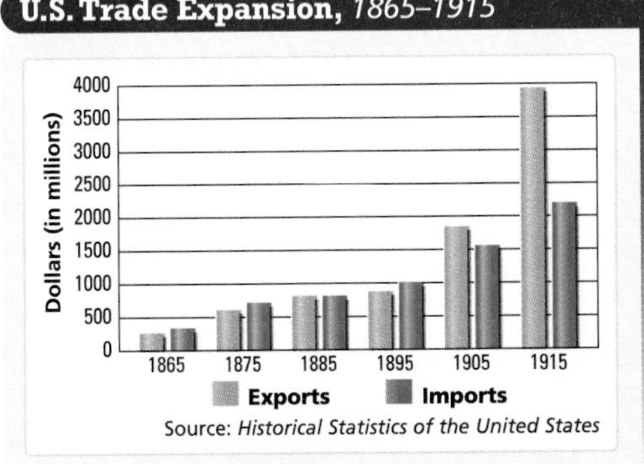


**Basic Graph Elements**

a. What does this graph represent?

**Interpreting the Graph**

b. What were the values of U.S. exports in 1865 and 1915?

c. What were the values of U.S. imports in 1865 and 1915?

### 2. INTERPRETING PRIMARY SOURCES

W. A. Rogers's political cartoon from 1904 shows Theodore Roosevelt tugging the U.S. Navy around the Caribbean.

a. What do you think this cartoon is about?

b. Why did the cartoonist portray Roosevelt with a big stick?

## ALTERNATIVE ASSESSMENT

### 1. INTERDISCIPLINARY ACTIVITY: Geography

**Making a Map** During the 19th century, the United States acquired several islands in the Pacific Ocean. Do more research on U.S. possessions in the Pacific and make a map that shows the islands' locations.

### 2. COOPERATIVE LEARNING ACTIVITY

**Creating a News Story** Imagine that you are a journalist in the late 1800s. The publisher of the *New York Journal,* William Randolph Hearst, has asked you to put together a team of reporters and artists. With your team, plan and write an illustrated news story for the *Journal* that features an important event from the Spanish-American War.

### 3. TECHNOLOGY ACTIVITY

**Creating a Multimedia Presentation** When the United States annexed the Philippines after the Spanish-American War, Filipinos rose in rebellion. Use the Internet, books, and other resources for a multimedia presentation on the Philippine-American war that resulted from the rebellion.

**Visit www.mcdougallittell.com to learn more about U.S. expansion overseas.**

Using presentation software, consider including the following content:

- descriptions or images of battles
- the views of Filipino and American soldiers, including African-American troops
- public opinion in the two countries
- statistics of casualties suffered by both sides during the conflict

### 4. HISTORY PORTFOLIO

**Option 1** Review your section and chapter assessment activities. Select one that you think is your best work. Then use comments made by your teacher or classmates to improve your work and add it to your portfolio.

**Option 2** Review the questions that you wrote for What Do You Want to Know? on page 658. Then write a short report in which you explain the answers to your questions. If any questions were not answered, do research to answer them. Add your answers to your portfolio.



## ALTERNATIVE ASSESSMENT

1. INTERDISCIPLINARY ACTIVITY: **Geography**

**Maps should**
- identify both physical and political locations.
- be clearly labeled and neatly presented.
- include a legend and title.

2. COOPERATIVE LEARNING ACTIVITY

**News stories should**
- use a journalistic style.
- present information about the event in an unbiased way.
- cover the topic adequately.
- be neatly presented.
- use standard grammar, spelling, sentence structure, and punctuation.

3. TECHNOLOGY ACTIVITY

**Presentations should**
- utilize two or more media.
- clearly demonstrate an understanding of the Philippine-American war.
- show technical proficiency.

4. HISTORY PORTFOLIO

**Option 1 Revised section or chapter assessment activities should**
- address teacher and peer responses to the selected work.
- solve problems present in the first versions of the work.

**Option 2 Short reports should**
- answer questions about U.S expansion in the late 1800s.
- use evidence to develop and support ideas.
- cite sources of information.
- use standard grammar, spelling, sentence structure, and punctuation.

**Critical Thinking Transparency CT69**
- Visual Summary

**Formal Assessment**
- Chapter Test, Forms A and B, pp. 340–347

## HISTORY SKILLS

**Possible Responses**

1. INTERPRETING MAPS

**Basic Graph Elements**

**a.** the growth of U.S. trade between 1865 and 1915

**Interpreting the Graph**

**b.** about 300 million and 3.9 billion dollars

**c.** about 350 million and 2.2 billion dollars

2. INTERPRETING PRIMARY SOURCES

**a.** U.S. policy toward Latin America; the Monroe Doctrine and the Roosevelt Corollary

**b.** Roosevelt was fond of quoting an African saying: "Speak softly, but carry a big stick."

# CHAPTER 24 PLANNING GUIDE

# World War I 1914–1920

| | CHAPTER OVERVIEW | COPYMASTERS | TECHNOLOGY |
|---|---|---|---|
| **CHAPTER RESOURCES** | This chapter describes the underlying causes of World War I, the outbreak of war in Europe, and the issues that lead the United States to intervene on the side of the Allies. It also discusses the effects of the war on the home front and the long-term results of the war. | **In-Depth Resources: Unit 7**<br>• Tracing Themes: America in the World, p. 37<br>• Building Vocabulary, p. 42<br>• History Workshop Resources, p. 57<br>**Interdisciplinary Projects,** pp. 139–144 | 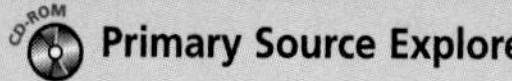<br>**Primary Source Explorer**<br>**Electronic Teacher Tools**<br>**Power Presentations CD-ROM**<br>**Chapter Summaries on CD** (English and Spanish)<br>**America's Music CD** |
| | **KEY IDEAS** | | |
| **SECTION 1**<br>**War Breaks Out in Europe**<br>**pp. 679–685** | • The underlying causes of war in Europe include imperialism, nationalism, militarism, and entangling alliances.<br>• New technology raises the death tolls.<br>• At first the United States remains neutral, but in 1917 Americans join the Allies. | **In-Depth Resources: Unit 7**<br>• Setting the Stage, p. 36<br>• Guided Reading, p. 38<br>• Skillbuilder Practice, p. 43<br>• Reteaching Activity, p. 52<br>**America's History Makers**<br>• Jeannette Rankin, pp. 95–96<br>**Economics in History**<br>• Russian Communism, p. 24<br>**Outline Map Activities,** pp. 47–48 | **Warm-Up Transparency WT24**<br>**Critical Thinking Transparency CT70**<br>• Setting the Stage<br>**ClassZone:** www.mcdougallittell.com |
| **SECTION 2**<br>**America Joins the Fight**<br>**pp. 686–690** | • To build an army quickly, the United States enacts a military draft.<br>• American destroyers form convoys to protect Allied ships.<br>• American troops take part in the fighting in France twice until the truce on November 11, 1918. | **In-Depth Resources: Unit 7**<br>• Setting the Stage, p. 36<br>• Guided Reading, p. 39<br>• Geography Application: Meuse-Argonne Offensive, pp. 44–45<br>• Literature Selection, pp. 48–51<br>• Reteaching Activity, p. 53 | **Warm-Up Transparency WT24**<br>**Critical Thinking Transparency CT70**<br>• Setting the Stage<br>**Critical Thinking Transparency CT71**<br>• Cause and Effect: Effects of World War I on Europe<br>**ClassZone:** www.mcdougallittell.com |
| **SECTION 3**<br>**Life on the Home Front**<br>**pp. 691–694** | • On the home front, Americans buy war bonds and conserve food.<br>• Wartime propaganda and fear of dissent lead to laws that seriously undercut freedom of speech.<br>• In the Great Migration, many African Americans leave the South for industrial jobs in Northern cities. | **In-Depth Resources: Unit 7**<br>• Setting the Stage, p. 36<br>• Guided Reading, p. 40<br>• Primary Source, p. 46<br>• Reteaching Activity, p. 54 | **Warm-Up Transparency WT24**<br>**Humanities Transparency HT47**<br>• Political Cartoon: The Red Scare<br>**Humanities Transparency HT48**<br>• *The Migrants Arrived in Great Numbers* by Jacob Lawrence<br>**ClassZone:** www.mcdougallittell.com |
| **SECTION 4**<br>**The Legacy of World War I**<br>**pp. 695–699** | • Wilson sets an idealistic plan for peace in the Fourteen Points.<br>• The U.S. Senate rejects the Treaty of Versailles and the League of Nations.<br>• The postwar period is marked by industrial strikes, the Red Scare, and race riots. | **In-Depth Resources: Unit 7**<br>• Setting the Stage, p. 36<br>• Guided Reading, p. 41<br>• Primary Source, p. 47<br>• Reteaching Activity, p. 55<br>**America's History Makers**<br>• Woodrow Wilson, pp. 97–98<br>**Why It Matters Now**<br>• The Fourteen Points Today, pp. 47–48 | **Warm-Up Transparency WT24**<br>**Geography Transparency GT24**<br>• The League of Nations, 1919<br>**Critical Thinking Transparency CT72**<br>• Visual Summary<br>**Primary Source Explorer**<br>• *The Fourteen Points*<br>**ClassZone:** www.mcdougallittell.com |

Pupil's Edition | Overhead Transparency | CD-ROM
Copymaster | Audio Library | Internet

## ASSESSMENT

**Chapter Assessment,** pp. 700–701

**Formal Assessment**
- Chapter Tests, Forms A and B, pp. 354–361

**Alternative Assessment Book**

**Electronic Teacher Tools with Test Maker**

**Section Assessment,** p. 683

**Formal Assessment**
- Section Quiz, p. 350

**Alternative Assessment Book**
- Rubrics for a model, 1.10
- Rubrics for a diagram, 1.3

**Electronic Teacher Tools with Test Maker**

**Section Assessment,** p. 690

**Formal Assessment**
- Section Quiz, p. 351

**Alternative Assessment Book**
- Rubrics for an audiotape, 5.3
- Rubrics for a letter, 4.3

**Electronic Teacher Tools with Test Maker**

**Section Assessment,** p. 694

**Formal Assessment**
- Section Quiz, p. 352

**Alternative Assessment Book**
- Rubrics for a broadcast, 5.3
- Rubrics for a calculation, 2.2

**Electronic Teacher Tools with Test Maker**

**Section Assessment,** p. 698

**Formal Assessment**
- Section Quiz, p. 353

**Alternative Assessment Book**
- Rubrics for an editorial, 4.1
- Rubrics for a cartoon, 1.2

**Electronic Teacher Tools with Test Maker**

## CUSTOMIZING FOR INDIVIDUAL NEEDS

### Students Acquiring English/ESL

**Reading Study Guide** (English and Spanish), pp. 231–240

**Access for Students Acquiring English/ESL: Spanish Translations,** pp. 159–165

**Chapter Summaries on CD** (English and Spanish)

### Less Proficient Readers

**Reading Study Guide** (English and Spanish), pp. 231–240

**Chapter Summaries on CD** (English and Spanish)

### Gifted and Talented Students

**In-Depth Resources: Unit 7**
- Enrichment Activity, p. 56

**America's History Makers**
- Jeannette Rankin, pp. 95–96
- Woodrow Wilson, pp. 97–98

## CROSS-CURRICULAR CONNECTIONS

### Geography

Griess, Thomas, ed. ***Atlas for the Great War.*** Garden City Park, NY: Avery Pub. Group, 1986. Spiral-bound book of maps.

### Humanities: Art

Sharpe, Mike et al. ***Aviation Art.*** Holt, MN: Thunder Bay Press,1998. Reproductions of artwork featuring airplanes; includes brief descriptions of events depicted.

### Primary Sources

Brown, Gene. ***Conflict in Europe and the Great Depression: World War I (1914–1940).*** Brookfield, CT: Twenty-First Century, 1995. Brief account includes many primary sources; well illustrated and attractive.

### Science

Bowen, Ezra. ***Knights of the Air.*** New York: Time-Life 1980. Lavishly illustrated history of the planes and men of World War I.

### Interdisciplinary Projects, pp. 139–144

- Math: Counting the Troops: Problem Solving
- Science: Buoyancy
- Language Arts: Poetry of World War I
- Health: The Flu Epidemic of 1918

### Literature

Martinello, Marian L. ***Cedar Fever.*** San Antonio: Corona, 1992. In Texas during World War I, a girl must face the mixed reactions of neighbors to the fact that she is of German descent.

North, Sterling. ***Rascal.*** New York: Puffin Books, 1963. Wonderful story of a boy and his pet raccoon in the Midwest set against the background of the war.

Rostkowski, Margaret I. ***After the Dancing Days.*** New York: HarperCollins, 1986. Thirteen-year-old Annie Metcalf forms a friendship with a hideously scarred young soldier. A touching and thought-provoking coming-of-age story.

Voight, Cynthia. ***Tree by Leaf.*** New York: S&S, 1988. Clothilde faces changes in her life after her father defies her grandfather and enlists to fight in the war, then returns home badly wounded.

## ENRICHMENT ACTIVITIES

**Pupil's Edition, pp. 676–703**
**Interact with History,** p. 677
**Interdisciplinary Challenge,** pp. 684–685
**Interactive Primary Source,** p. 699
**History Workshop,** pp. 702–703

**In-Depth Resources: Unit 7**
- Geography Application: Meuse-Argonne Offensive, pp. 44–45
- Primary Source: "Over There," p. 46
- Primary Source: An Appeal for Support of the League of Nations, p. 47
- Literature Selection: "In Another Country," pp. 48–51
- History Workshop Resources, p. 57

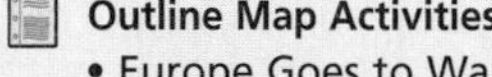
**America's History Makers**
- Jeannette Rankin, pp. 95–96
- Woodrow Wilson, pp. 97–98

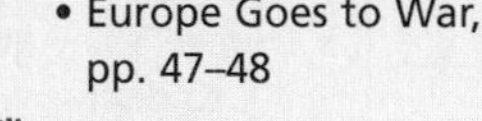
**Outline Map Activities**
- Europe Goes to War, pp. 47–48

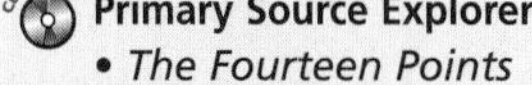
**Primary Source Explorer**
- *The Fourteen Points*

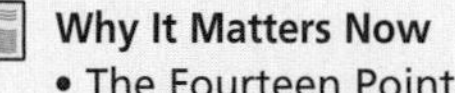
**Why It Matters Now**
- The Fourteen Points Today, pp. 47–48

# CHAPTER 24 PACING GUIDE

**LESSON PLAN OPTIONS (50-MINUTE PERIOD)** (TE) = Teacher's Edition (PE) = Pupil's Edition

| | TEACHER-DIRECTED ACTIVITIES<br>Class Time: 15 minutes | STUDENT-CENTERED ACTIVITIES<br>Class Time: 25 minutes | INDIVIDUAL ACTIVITIES<br>Class Time: 10 minutes |
|---|---|---|---|
| **DAY 1**<br>Introduction<br>pp. 676–678 | **Presentation Options**<br>• Begin with a class discussion of the picture on p. 676 **(PE)**.<br>• Lead a class discussion on the "What Do You Know?" question in Setting the Stage, p. 678. Then introduce the graphic organizer for the chapter **(PE)**. | **Options for Cooperative Learning**<br>• Have student groups discuss the Interact with History questions, p. 677 **(PE)**.<br>• Have student groups respond to the "What Do You Want to Know?" question in Setting the Stage, p. 678 **(PE)**. | **Head Start on Homework Options**<br>• Have students skim Section 1 Main Idea, Why It Matters Now, Terms & Names, and the main headings, p. 679 **(PE)**.<br>• Have students begin Guided Reading activity and Building Vocabulary sheet. |
| **DAY 2**<br>Section 1<br>pp. 679–685 | **Presentation Options**<br>• Begin with the 5-Minute Warm-Up, p. 679 **(TE)**.<br>• Review the Section 1 Main Idea, Why It Matters Now, and Terms & Names, p. 679 **(PE)**.<br>• Lead the students through the Skillbuilder Mini-Lesson: Recognizing Effects, p. 682 **(TE)**. | **Options for Cooperative Learning**<br>• Divide students into groups to work on the Critical Thinking Activity, p. 682 **(TE)**.<br>• Have student pairs work together to complete one of the Activity Options in the Section 1 Assessment, p. 683 **(PE)**. | **Head Start on Homework Options**<br>• Have students begin working on Section 1 Assessment, p. 683 **(PE)**.<br>• Have students preview Section 2 Main Idea, Why It Matters Now, Terms & Names, and the main headings, p. 686 **(PE)**. |
| **DAY 3**<br>Section 2<br>pp. 686–690 | **Presentation Options**<br>• Begin with the 5-Minute Warm-Up, p. 686 **(TE)**.<br>• Choose 5 key questions for Objectives 1–4 to discuss with the class, pp. 686–690 **(TE)**.<br>• Lead the students through the History from Visuals, p. 688 **(TE)**. | **Options for Cooperative Learning**<br>• Divide students into groups and have them work on the Interdisciplinary Challenge, pp. 684–685 **(PE)**.<br>• Have student pairs work together to complete one of the Activity Options in the Section 2 Assessment, p. 690 **(PE)**. | **Head Start on Homework Options**<br>• Have students begin working on Section 2 Assessment, p. 690 **(PE)**.<br>• Have students complete the answers to the Main Idea question in the Section 3 Assessment, p. 694 **(PE)**. |
| **DAY 4**<br>Section 3<br>pp. 691–694 | **Presentation Options**<br>• Begin with the 5-Minute Warm-Up, p. 691 **(TE)**.<br>• Choose 5 key questions for Objectives 1–4 to discuss with the class, pp. 691–694 **(TE)**.<br>• Discuss with students the Critical Thinking Activity, p. 692 **(TE)**. | **Options for Cooperative Learning**<br>• Divide students into groups and have them complete the Interdisciplinary Activity, Civics: Hold a Debate, p. 692 **(TE)**.<br>• Have student pairs work together to complete one of the Activity Options in the Section 3 Assessment, p. 694 **(PE)**. | **Head Start on Homework Options**<br>• Have students begin working on Section 3 Assessment, p. 694 **(PE)**.<br>• Have students preview Section 4 Main Idea, Why It Matters Now, Terms & Names, and the main headings, p. 695 **(PE)**. |
| **DAY 5**<br>Section 4<br>pp. 695–699 | **Presentation Options**<br>• Begin with the 5-Minute Warm-Up, p. 695 **(TE)**.<br>• Choose 5 key questions for Objectives 1–4 to discuss with the class, pp. 695–698 **(TE)**.<br>• Lead the students through the Interactive Primary Source, p. 699 **(TE)**. | **Options for Cooperative Learning**<br>• Have student pairs work together to complete the Primary Source A Closer Look questions, p. 699 **(PE)**.<br>• Divide students into groups to complete the History Workshop, pp. 702–703 **(PE)**. | **Head Start on Homework Options**<br>• Have students complete the Setting the Stage graphic organizer for the chapter, p. 678 **(PE)**.<br>• Have students begin working on the Chapter Assessment, pp. 700–701 **(PE)**.<br>• Prepare for Chapter Test<br>**Formal Assessment, pp. 354–361** |

**TEACHER-TESTED ACTIVITY** **Suzanne Hidalgo, Serrano Middle School, Highland, California**

## SECRET CODED MESSAGE

**Class Time** Two class periods

**Task** Creating a picture code to relay a message to classmates

**Purpose** To understand the complexity of the Allied efforts to win the war

**Supplies Needed**
- White drawing paper
- Markers

**Activity** Divide the class into groups of four. Have each group create a code using symbols, numbers, or pictures to represent each letter of the alphabet. Have students write coded messages on their drawing paper about an important battle. Post the messages around the room and have groups rotate from message to message, trying to decipher the codes of other groups. Then ask students why codes are used in wartime. Have the class create its own guidelines for deciding which communications must be sent in code.

## BLOCK SCHEDULING — LESSON PLAN OPTIONS (90-MINUTE PERIOD)

### DAY 1

**Interact with History,** p. 677
**Class Time** 20 minutes

Options for pacing and variety:
- Peer Teaching In small groups, have students discuss how a family of five—made up of a grandparent, mother, father, and two teenagers—might support the war effort. Have students use the "What Do You Think?" questions to structure their discussion. **Class Time** 10 minutes

**Setting the Stage,** p. 678
**Class Time** 20 minutes

Options for pacing and variety:
- Time Saver For a homework assignment, ask students to write a paragraph describing how they think a "world war" is different from a civil war. **Class Time** 10 minutes

**Section 1,** pp. 679–685
**Class Time** 50 minutes

Options for pacing and variety:
- Internet Extend students' background knowledge of trench warfare by visiting www.mcdougallittell.com **Class Time** 20 minutes
- Time Saver Use the map on page 680 to help students understand how the network of competing alliances helped cause World War I. **Class Time** 5 minutes

### DAY 2

**Interdisciplinary Challenge,** pp. 684–685
**Class Time** 55 minutes

Options for pacing and variety:
- Team Teaching Invite the physical education teacher to coach student groups as they solve the Physical Education challenge. **Class Time** 30 minutes
- Peer Teaching Share with each group the Standards for Evaluation for each challenge on page 684 of the Teacher's Edition. Have each group decide which of its solutions to a challenge comes closest to meeting these criteria. **Class Time** 10 minutes

**Section 2,** pp. 686–690
**Class Time** 45 minutes

**Section 3,** pp. 691–694
**Class Time** 45 minutes

Options for pacing and variety:
- Team Teaching Invite a music teacher to the class to help students with the Interdisciplinary Activity on page 701 of the Chapter Assessment. **Class Time** 25 minutes
- Time Saver Have students answer the Reading History questions for the section as a homework assignment. **Class Time** 25 minutes

### DAY 3

**Section 4,** pp. 695–699
**Class Time** 45 minutes

Options for pacing and variety:
- Peer Teaching Divide students into seven groups to participate in the Cooperative Learning Activity on page 701 of the Chapter Assessment. **Class Time** 40 minutes
- History on Film Extend students' knowledge of World War I and Wilson's fight for the League of Nations with *World War I: A Documentary on the Role of the USA.* Encyclopaedia Britannica. **Class Time** 30 minutes

**Chapter 24 Assessment,** pp. 700–701
**Class Time** 40 minutes

Options for pacing and variety:
- Peer Teaching Divide students into groups of four. Have each student in a group answer the Review Questions for one of the four sections. Have students share answers within groups. **Class Time** 20 minutes
- Peer Evaluation Have student pairs complete the History Skills questions on page 700 and share their responses with another group. **Class Time** 15 minutes

**History Workshop,** pp. 702–703
Options for pacing and variety
- Time Saver Have students work on steps 1–4 in Campaign for Liberty Bonds as homework. **Class Time** 5 minutes

**CHAPTER 24 OBJECTIVE**

The student will understand how the United States became involved in World War I, how Americans mobilized for war, and how President Wilson attempted to shape the peace.

# World War I

## 1914–1920



### HISTORY FROM VISUALS

**Interpreting the Photograph** Have students study the photograph on page 676 and read the caption. Explain to the students that this photograph illustrates what was called "going over the top." The smoke is caused by artillery fire from the enemy. Ask students to describe ways this battle scene differs from the paintings that they saw earlier from the American Revolution and the Civil War. **Possible Responses** Students might mention the absence of many elements featured in earlier paintings: colorful flags, officers on horseback, swords, or even a visible enemy. The most striking features in this picture are the trenches and the war-torn earth. Trenches served as a place to live, a staging area for assaults, and protection against enemy fire.

**Extension** Have the students write a paragraph describing one soldier's thoughts as he climbed up the ladder and prepared to advance across the field.

This photograph shows a battlefield view of trench warfare during World War I.

676

### RECOMMENDED RESOURCES

**BOOKS FOR THE TEACHER**

Bishop, Alan and Mark Bostridge, eds. ***Letters from a Lost Generation: First World War Letters of Vera Brittain and Four Friends.*** Boston: Northeastern U. Pr., 1999. Military, civilian, and medical viewpoints are poignantly represented.

Iezzoni, Lynette. ***Influenza, 1918: The Worst Epidemic in American History.*** Foreword by David McCullough. New York: TV Books, 1999. It killed 30 million people worldwide—550,000 in the United States—and it could happen again.

**VIDEO**

***Last Voyage of the* Lusitania.** National Geographic, 1996. History of the disaster combined with a great undersea detective story.

**INTERNET**

For more about World War I, visit www.mcdougallittell.com

## Interact *with* History

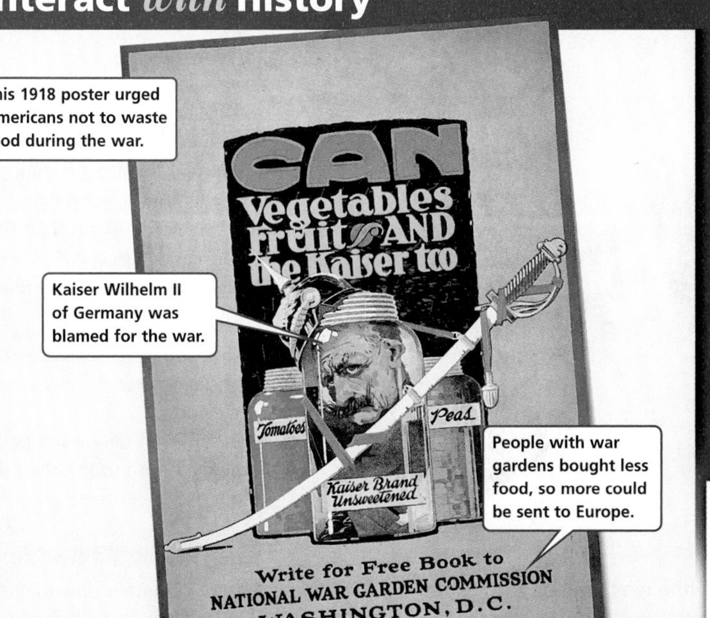

CAN
Vegetables
Fruit AND
the Kaiser too
Tomatoes
Peas
Kaiser Brand
Unsweetened
Write for Free Book to
NATIONAL WAR GARDEN COMMISSION
WASHINGTON, D.C.
Charles Lathrop Pack, President
P.S. Ridsdale, Secretary


This 1918 poster urged Americans not to waste food during the war.

Kaiser Wilhelm II of Germany was blamed for the war.

People with war gardens bought less food, so more could be sent to Europe.

**The year is 1918, and the United States has been drawn into World War I. Each citizen is called upon to help the war effort. Some will join the American armed forces and go to fight in Europe. Others will work in factories at home, producing weapons and supplies. Even children will do their part.**

### What Do You Think?

- How can Americans at home help win the war?
- What might U.S. soldiers experience in Europe?
- How might being at war affect the country?

# *How will you support the war effort?*

**USA / World**

**1914**

**August 15, 1914** U.S.-built Panama Canal officially opens.

**June 28, 1914** Austria-Hungary's Archduke Franz Ferdinand is assassinated, starting World War I.

**May 7, 1915** Many Americans die as German U-boat sinks *Lusitania.*

**February–December, 1915** Allies and Central Powers clash at Gallipoli in the Ottoman Empire.

**November 7, 1916** Woodrow Wilson is reelected president.

**July–November, 1916** French, British, and Germans suffer huge losses at the Battle of the Somme.

**April 2, 1917** Wilson asks Congress to declare war on Germany.

**January 8, 1918** President Wilson proposes League of Nations.

**March 3, 1918** Russia withdraws from the war.

**November 11, 1918** The Allies defeat the Central Powers, ending World War I.

**June 28, 1919** The Allies and Germany sign the Treaty of Versailles.

**November 2, 1920** Warren G. Harding is elected president.

**1920**



## Interact *with* History

### OBJECTIVES

- To help students identify ways Americans on the home front contributed to the war effort
- To help students connect with the people and events they will study in this chapter

### What Do You Think?

1. Remind students that much of the wartime effort takes place off the battlefield. They should think about production of military supplies and food, and transporting them to the troops.
2. Tell students that many soldiers had not been far from their homes in the United States, let alone been in Europe. Remind them that most had no military experience.
3. Ask students to think about how the government would find the money for supporting a war.

### *How will you support the war effort?*

Encourage students to think about various ways a family might contribute money, time, or food and other essential materials to the war effort. Ask students why conservation and recycling might be important at this time.

### MAKING PERSONAL CONNECTIONS

Point out that although the United States is not at war, many Americans today contribute food, clothing, or money to aid victims of conflicts in other countries. Have students describe some of the ways Americans today show support for U.S. soldiers serving overseas or help victims of war in other parts of the world.

### TIME LINE DISCUSSION

**Remind students that the opening question for Chapter 23 was "When should you get involved in the affairs of another country?" Tell them that this question remains a major issue in the years covered by this chapter.**

- Ask students how long Europeans were involved in the war before the United States became involved. **Answer** almost three years
- Ask students what event shown on the time line might have contributed to the U.S. decision to enter the war. **Possible Response** sinking of the *Lusitania*
- Which event or events suggest the war might be winding down? **Possible Responses** Wilson proposes League of Nations; Russia withdraws from war
- About how long after the defeat of the Central Powers did it take before a peace treaty was signed? **Answer** about eight months

## BEFORE YOU READ

### Previewing the Theme:
**America in the World**

Ask students what the magnet is doing. Have them discuss why Americans might be reluctant to become involved in a war in Europe. Remind students of U.S. activities in Chapter 23. Ask how becoming a world power would affect a decision to enter a war.

### What Do You Know?

Students' discussion about the phrase "world war" will probably include impressions of World War II as well as World War I. Tell students that both Americans and Europeans at the time first called the 1914–1918 conflict "The Great War." Ask them to consider how the name change—from the Great War to the World War to World War I—reflects later historical developments. Students might also discuss what they think the term *trench warfare* means and who they think the major combatants were.

 **In-Depth Resources: Unit 7**
- Tracing Themes: America in the World, p. 37

## READ AND TAKE NOTES

**Reading Strategy: Recognizing Effects**

Remind students that one cause may lead to multiple effects. Point out the cause noted on the chart ("World War I") and the rays pointing to many effects. Encourage students to look for the effects of the war on the nation as they read.

 **In-Depth Resources: Unit 7**
- Setting the Stage, p. 36

 **Critical Thinking Transparency CT70**
- Setting the Stage

# Chapter 24 SETTING THE STAGE

## BEFORE YOU READ

### Previewing the Theme

**America in the World** Although the United States was reluctant to join World War I, American involvement helped the Allies win the war. The war also brought about permanent changes in American society. Chapter 24 explains how the United States became involved in the war, how it mobilized for war, and how it tried to establish a lasting peace.

### What Do You Know?

What do you think of when you hear the phrase "world war"? How many countries might have participated in the war? Where did most of the fighting take place?

**THINK ABOUT**
- what you've learned about World War I from movies or television
- reasons that millions of people might choose to risk their lives in a global conflict

### What Do You Want to Know?

What details do you need to help you understand what is involved in waging a world war? Make a list of these details in your notebook before you read the chapter.

## READ AND TAKE NOTES

**Reading Strategy: Recognizing Effects** To help you make sense of what you read, learn to analyze the effects of important historical events. The chart below will help you analyze some of the effects of World War I, both on the world and on the United States. In each box, fill in a different effect. Add more boxes if you need to.

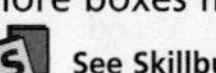 See Skillbuilder Handbook, page R10.

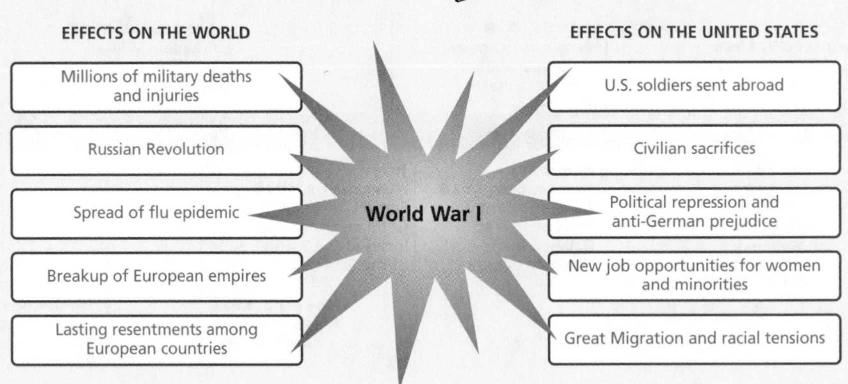




## TEACHING STRATEGY

### READING THE CHAPTER

This is a chronological chapter focusing on the events that led up to American participation in World War I, as well as the events of the war and its legacy. Remind students that war not only affects the soldiers but also those on the home front. Encourage students to note how American lives were changed by the war.

### ALTERNATIVE ASSESSMENT

The Chapter Assessment describes three activities for alternative assessment on page 701. You may wish to have students work on these activities during the course of the chapter and then present them at the end.

# 1 War Breaks Out in Europe

**MAIN IDEA**

After World War I broke out, the United States eventually joined the Allied side.

**WHY IT MATTERS NOW**

This was the first time that the United States was involved in a European conflict.

**TERMS & NAMES**

militarism
Central Powers
Allies
trench warfare
U-boat
Woodrow Wilson
neutrality
Zimmermann telegram

## ONE AMERICAN'S STORY

**While the United States was forming its own empire, European nations were competing to expand their empires. Rivalry poisoned relationships among these nations. In the spring of 1914, tensions were running high in Europe. President Woodrow Wilson sent Colonel Edward M. House, his trusted advisor, to study the situation.**

**House gave the president a troubling report. He compared Europe to an open keg of gunpowder. "It only requires a spark," he said, "to set the whole thing off." Soon the spark ignited. On June 28, 1914, a young Serbian man shot and killed Archduke Franz Ferdinand. The archduke was the heir to the throne of Austria-Hungary. One month later, Austria declared war on Serbia. One by one, the nations of Europe chose sides and the Great War, later called World War I, began.**

Archduke Franz Ferdinand and his wife are murdered at Sarajevo on June 28, 1914.

## 1 Causes of World War I

A single action, the assassination of the archduke, started World War I. But the conflict had many underlying causes.

1. **Imperialism.** Britain, France, Germany, and Italy competed for colonies in Africa and Asia. Because it had fewer colonies than Britain and France, Germany felt it deserved more colonies to provide it with resources and buy its goods.
2. **Nationalism.** Europeans were very nationalistic, meaning that they had strong feelings of pride, loyalty, and protectiveness toward their own countries. They wanted to prove their nations were the best. They placed their countries' interests above all other concerns. In addition, some ethnic groups hoped to form their own separate nations and were willing to fight for such a cause.
3. **Militarism.** The belief that a nation needs a large military force is **militarism**. In the decades before the war, the major powers built up their armies and navies.



## SECTION OBJECTIVES

1. To identify the causes of World War I
2. To describe the stalemate in the trenches and the new technology used in the conflict
3. To explain why the United States decided to join the Allies
4. To describe how the Russian Revolution affected the war effort

**SKILLBUILDER**

Interpreting Maps: Location, Region, p. 680

**CRITICAL THINKING**

Making Inferences, p. 682
Analyzing Causes, p. 683

## FOCUS & MOTIVATE

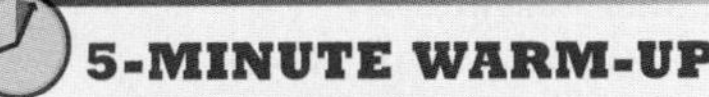

### 5-MINUTE WARM-UP

**Recognizing Effects** These questions focus on events leading to World War I.

1. Look at the chart and map on page 680. In what part of Europe did the early events take place?
2. Using the chart, list the allies of Serbia, Russia, and Austria-Hungary.

 **Warm-Up Transparency WT24**

## INSTRUCT

### INSTRUCT: OBJECTIVE 1

**Causes of World War I**

Key Questions

- What were the underlying causes of World War I?
- How did the network of alliances make a small event dangerous?
- What nations belonged to the Central Powers? to the Allies?

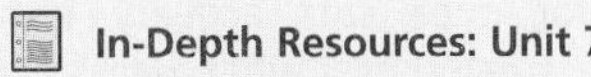

**In-Depth Resources: Unit 7**
- Guided Reading, p. 38

## RECOMMENDED RESOURCES

**In-Depth Resources: Unit 7**
- Guided Reading, p. 38
- Building Vocabulary, p. 42
- Skillbuilder Practice, p. 43
- Reteaching Activity, p. 52
- Enrichment Activity, p. 56

**Reading Study Guide** (Spanish and English), pp. 231–232

**Economics in History**
- Russian Communism, p. 24

**Outline Map Activities**
- Europe Goes to War, pp. 47–48

**America's History Makers**
- Jeanette Rankin, pp. 95–96

**Formal Assessment**
- Section Quiz, p. 350

**Alternative Assessment**
- Rubrics, 1.10
- Rubrics, 1.3

**Access for Students Acquiring English/ESL**
- Guided Reading, p. 159
- Skillbuilder Practice, p. 163

**Technology Resources**

 **Electronic Teacher Tools with Test Maker**

 **ClassZone**
www.mcdougallittell.com

## HISTORY FROM VISUALS

**Reading the Map and the Chart** Which of the Allied nations border Germany? **Answer** France, Belgium, Russia. Why was Germany at a military disadvantage in a war against France and Russia? **Possible Response** Germany could be attacked from both the east and the west simultaneously. How does that situation explain why Germany declared war as soon as Russia began to mobilize? **Possible Response** Germany feared that it would soon face war on two fronts and therefore must strike quickly.

**Extension** Serbia has appeared and disappeared from the map of Europe several times. Have students research the changes that have taken place in Serbian sovereignty since 1914.

 **Outline Map Activities**
- Europe Goes to War, pp. 47–48

## INSTRUCT: OBJECTIVE 

**Stalemate in the Trenches/ A War of New Technology**

Key Questions
- What mistaken assumptions about the war did people make in its early days?
- How did trench warfare differ from earlier forms of warfare?
- What new technology was used in World War I, and how did it affect the way war was fought?

## MORE ABOUT . . .

**Trench Warfare**

Otto Dix, a German soldier, described the miseries of trench warfare this way: "Lice, rats, barbed wire, fleas, shells, bombs, underground caves, corpses, blood, liquor, mice, cats, artillery, filth, bullets, mortars, fire, steel: that is what war is."

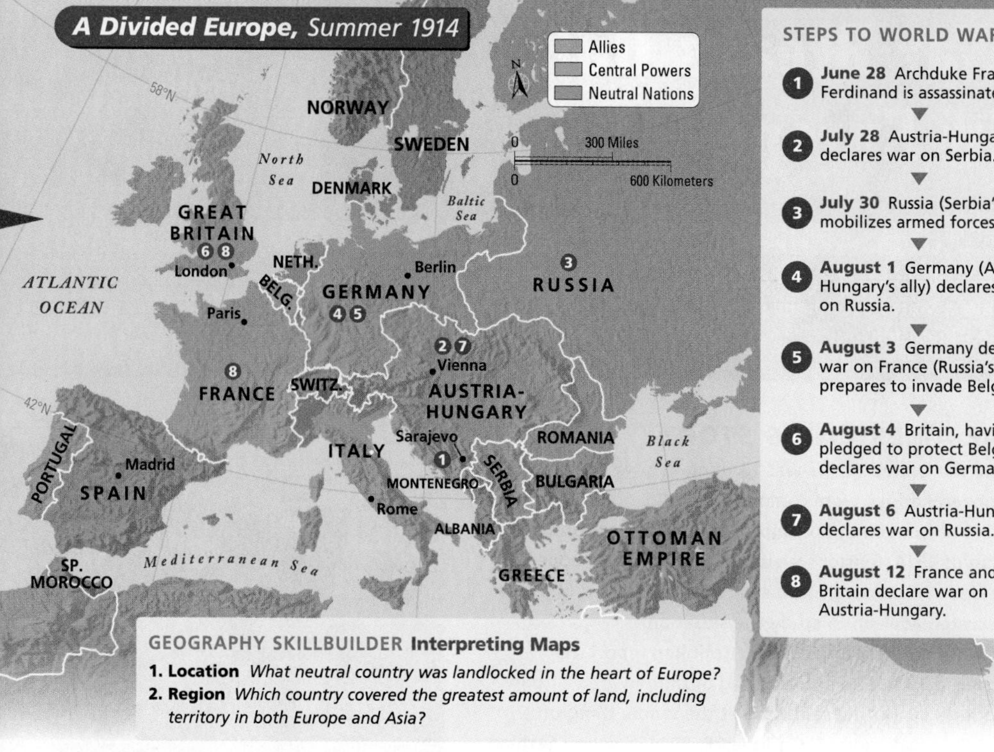


**STEPS TO WORLD WAR I**

1. **June 28** Archduke Franz Ferdinand is assassinated.
2. **July 28** Austria-Hungary declares war on Serbia.
3. **July 30** Russia (Serbia's ally) mobilizes armed forces.
4. **August 1** Germany (Austria-Hungary's ally) declares war on Russia.
5. **August 3** Germany declares war on France (Russia's ally); prepares to invade Belgium.
6. **August 4** Britain, having pledged to protect Belgium, declares war on Germany.
7. **August 6** Austria-Hungary declares war on Russia.
8. **August 12** France and Britain declare war on Austria-Hungary.

**GEOGRAPHY SKILLBUILDER Interpreting Maps**
1. **Location** *What neutral country was landlocked in the heart of Europe?*
2. **Region** *Which country covered the greatest amount of land, including territory in both Europe and Asia?*

Skillbuilder Answers
1. Switzerland
2. Russia

4. **Alliances** In 1914, a tangled network of competing alliances bound European nations together. An attack on one nation forced all its allies to come to its aid. Any small conflict could become a larger war.

European nations had divided into two opposing alliances. The **Central Powers** were made up of Austria-Hungary, Germany, the Ottoman Empire, and Bulgaria. They faced the Allied Powers, or **Allies,** consisting of Serbia, Russia, France, Great Britain, Italy, and seven other countries.

**Background** The Ottoman Empire included modern-day Turkey and Syria.

## 2 Stalemate in the Trenches

When the war began in August, most people on both sides assumed it would be over within a few months. With France as its goal, the German army invaded Belgium on August 4, 1914. Despite stiff resistance, the Germans fought their way west into France. They reached the Marne River about 40 miles from Paris. There the French, supported by the British, rallied and prepared to fight back. The First Battle of the Marne, in September 1914, stopped the German advance.

*Reading* **History** **A. Reading a Map** On the map on page 688, find the site of the first Battle of the Marne.

Instead of one side quickly defeating the other, the two sides stayed stuck in the mud for more than three years. The soldiers were fighting a new kind of battle, **trench warfare.** Troops huddled at the bottom of rat-infested trenches. They fired artillery and machine guns at each other. Lines of trenches stretched across France from the English Channel to the border with Switzerland. (See pages 684–685 for an

**Vocabulary** **trench:** a long, deep ditch dug for protection



## ACTIVITY OPTIONS
## INDIVIDUAL NEEDS

**STUDENTS ACQUIRING ENGLISH/ESL**

**Understanding Key Terms** Write the heading "Stalemate in the Trenches" on the board. Explain to students that a stalemate is a contest, or challenge, in which neither side is a clear winner. Ask students to brainstorm situations that might end in a stalemate, or a tie. Students might suggest sporting events or an election.

Read the section "Stalemate in the Trenches" with students. Then ask them to point out the statements in the text that support the heading.
- "Neither side could win a clear victory."
- ". . . often without gaining an inch for either side."
- "Neither side could claim victory."

illustration of the trenches.) For more than three years, the battle lines remained almost unchanged. Neither side could win a clear victory.

In the trenches, soldiers faced the constant threat of sniper fire. Artillery shelling turned the area between the two opposing armies into a "no man's land" too dangerous to occupy. When soldiers left their trenches to attack enemy lines, they rushed into a hail of bullets and clouds of poison gas.

When battles did take place, they cost many thousands of lives, often without gaining an inch for either side. The Battle of the Somme (SAHM), between July and November 1916, resulted in more than 1.2 million casualties. British dead or wounded numbered over 400,000. German losses totaled over 600,000, and French nearly 200,000. Despite this, the Allies gained only about seven miles.

*Reading*History
**B. Reading a Map** Find the site of the Battle of the Somme on the map on page 688.

## A War of New Technology

New technology raised the death toll. The tank, a British invention, smashed through barbed wire, crossed trenches, and cleared paths through no man's land. Soldiers also had machine guns that fired 600 bullets a minute. Poison gas, used by both sides, burned and blinded soldiers.

World War I was the first major conflict in which airplanes were used in combat. By 1917, fighter planes fought each other far above the clouds. Manfred von Richthofen, known as the Red Baron, was Germany's top ace. An ace was an aviator who had downed five or more enemy aircraft. Von Richthofen shot down over 80 enemy planes.

At sea, the Germans used submarines, which they called **U-boats,** to block trade. They were equipped with both guns and torpedoes. German U-boats sank over 11 million tons of Allied shipping.

**Background**
U-boat was short for "undersea boat."

**New Technology of War**

First used effectively during World War I, these new weapons caused high casualties.



681

### MORE ABOUT . . .

**Poison Gas**

The Germans were the first to use poison gas, releasing chlorine against the Russians in January 1915. Four months later, the Germans opened 6,000 cylinders of chlorine gas along an eight-mile line on the Western Front during the Second Battle of Ypres. Soon the Allies were using gas as well. Eventually, chlorine was replaced by phosgene, which in turn gave way to even more deadly mustard gas. The effects of gas were so terrible—and it was so likely to blow back onto the very troops that released it—that after the war it was outlawed by international agreement.

### MORE ABOUT . . .

**Airplanes in World War I**

Although the airplane was first used in World War I, it had little effect on the conflict's outcome. Bombers were too clumsy and their bombs too small to do much damage. Few bombers hit their targets with any precision. One exception was a German air strike in which a single bomb destroyed 9,000 tons of high explosives on July 20, 1916. Airplanes did prove to be very useful for aerial photography.

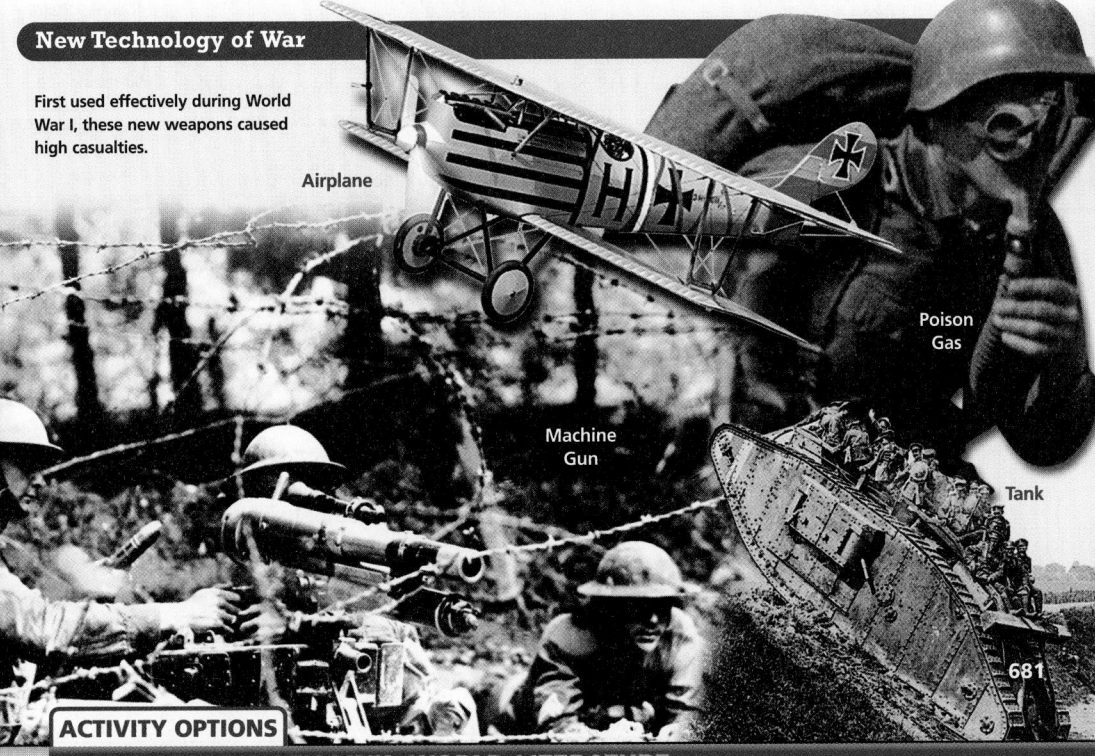
**In-Depth Resources: Unit 7**
- Enrichment Activity, p. 56

### ACTIVITY OPTIONS

**INTERDISCIPLINARY LINK: WORLD LITERATURE** — BLOCK SCHEDULING

**ANALYZING WAR POETRY**

**Class Time** One class period

**Task** Reading and analyzing a poem by one of the British war poets of World War I

**Purpose** To analyze views of the war as expressed in poetry

**Supplies Needed**
- Biographies of Rupert Brooke, Wilfred Owen, and Siegfried Sassoon
- Copies of "The Soldier" by Brooke, "Anthem for Doomed Youth" by Owen, and "The General" by Sassoon

**Activity** Have three volunteers give oral reports on Rupert Brooke, Wilfred Owen, or Siegfried Sassoon. Then divide students into small groups and distribute the three poems. "The Soldier" is a patriotic poem typical of the first war years, when many Britons still associated battle with glorious charges. The other poems, written later, capture the bitterness or horror of this new kind of warfare. Have students compare and contrast the views of war in the poems and share their observations with the class.

**INSTRUCT: OBJECTIVE 3**

**America's Path to War**

Key Questions

- What factors suggest that Americans hoped not to be drawn into the war?
- How did the sinking of the *Lusitania* affect U.S. public opinion?
- What events led President Wilson to ask for a declaration of war in April 1917?

 **America's History Makers**

- Jeanette Rankin, pp. 95–96

**MORE ABOUT . . .**

**The Sinking of the *Lusitania***

The rules of naval warfare required warships to warn merchant ships before attacking and to try to save the lives of passengers and crew. But submarines depended on surprise. Their thinly armored hulls and limited fire power made them easy targets when they surfaced. Nor did they have space to take survivors aboard. Moreover, the *Lusitania* was carrying a large cargo of ammunition to Britain, and Germany had publicly warned Americans not to travel on the ship.

**CRITICAL THINKING ACTIVITY**

**Drawing Conclusions** Have students review the quote from Wilson's message to Congress on page 683. According to Wilson, what was his reason for declaring war? In what ways might his reasons for going to war differ from those of Allied powers already involved in the conflict? Why was it important for Wilson to have the support of the American people before asking Congress for a declaration of war?

**Class Time** 10 minutes

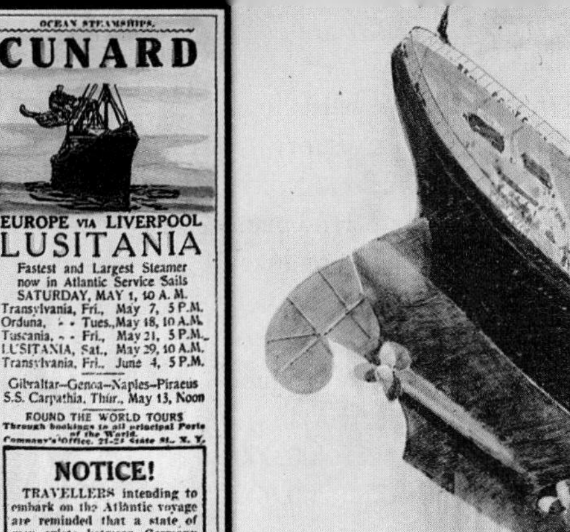

OCEAN STEAMSHIPS.

CUNARD

EUROPE VIA LIVERPOOL

LUSITANIA

Fastest and Largest Steamer now in Atlantic Service Sails SATURDAY, MAY 1, 10 A. M.

Transylvania, Fri., May 7, 5 P.M.
Orduna, - - Tues., May 18, 10 A.M.
Tuscania, - - Fri., May 21, 5 P.M.
LUSITANIA, Sat., May 29, 10 A.M.
Transylvania, Fri., June 4, 5 P.M.

Gibraltar–Genoa–Naples–Piraeus
S.S. Carpathia, Thur., May 13, Noon

ROUND THE WORLD TOURS
Through bookings to all principal Ports of the World.
Company's Office, 21-24 State St., N. Y.

NOTICE!

TRAVELLERS intending to embark on the Atlantic voyage are reminded that a state of war exists between Germany and her allies and Great Britain and her allies; that the zone of war includes the waters adjacent to the British Isles; that, in accordance with formal notice given by the Imperial German Government, vessels flying the flag of Great Britain, or of any of her allies, are liable to destruction in those waters and that travellers sailing in the war zone on ships of Great Britain or her allies do so at their own risk.

IMPERIAL GERMAN EMBASSY

WASHINGTON, D. C., APRIL 22, 1915.

The British liner *Lusitania* is sunk off the Irish coast by a German submarine on May 7, 1915.

## 3 America's Path to War

When the war started in 1914, President **Woodrow Wilson** announced a policy of **neutrality**, refusing to take sides in the war. A popular song, "I Didn't Raise My Boy to Be a Soldier," expressed the antiwar sentiment of many Americans.

Over time, however, German attacks shifted public opinion to the Allied cause. In the fall of 1914, Britain set up a naval blockade of German ports, seizing all goods bound for Germany. In response, German submarines sank all Allied merchant ships they found off the British coast. In May 1915, a German U-boat torpedoed the British passenger ship *Lusitania*, killing 1,198 people, including 128 Americans. The sinking turned many Americans against Germany.

But President Wilson kept the United States neutral. He demanded that the German government halt unrestricted submarine warfare, and it agreed. In the election of 1916, the Democratic party's campaign slogan, "He kept us out of war," appealed to voters. Wilson won reelection.

Desperate to defeat Britain, Germany resumed unrestricted submarine warfare at the end of January 1917. Its military leaders knew this action would bring the United States into the war. However, they hoped to win the war before the Americans arrived.

The next month, another blow to German-American relations came from the **Zimmermann telegram.** The telegram was discovered by the British, who passed it on to the Americans. In it, Arthur Zimmermann, the German foreign minister, told the German ambassador in Mexico to propose that Mexico join the Germans. In exchange, Germany would help Mexico get back its "lost" territories of Texas, New Mexico, and Arizona. Americans were furious.

***Reading* History**

**C. Making Inferences** Why did the sinking of the *Lusitania* turn Americans against Germany?

**C. Possible Responses** because Americans died in the attack; because it was cruel to attack an unarmed passenger ship



**ACTIVITY OPTIONS**

**SKILLBUILDER MINI-LESSON: RECOGNIZING EFFECTS** — BLOCK SCHEDULING

**Explaining the Skill** Identifying causes and effects helps historians see how events are related and why they occurred. Most events have both multiple causes and multiple effects. Sometimes clue words such as *brought about, led to, as a result of, consequently,* and *thus* are used to indicate effects.

**Applying the Skill** Ask students to read the text under the heading "America's Path to War." Have them identify three cause-and-effect events that led to the final effect—declaring war. Use a cause-and-effect diagram to trace the events. Then ask these questions:

1. How did the Germans' attack on ships lead to American involvement in the war? *(The sinking of the* Lusitania *turned Americans against Germany; the sinking of three American ships was the final cause.)*
2. What effect did the Zimmermann telegram have on Americans' attitudes about Germany? *(It made them furious.)*

 **In-Depth Resources: Unit 7**

- Skillbuilder Practice, p. 43

In March, German submarines sank three American ships. President Wilson asked for a declaration of war.

> *A VOICE FROM THE PAST*
>
> The world must be made safe for democracy. . . . We desire no conquest. . . . We are but one of the champions of the rights of mankind. We shall be satisfied when those rights have been made . . . secure.
>
> **Woodrow Wilson,** message to Congress, April 2, 1917

***"The world must be made safe for democracy."***
Woodrow Wilson

Six senators and 50 representatives, including the first woman in Congress, Jeanette Rankin of Montana, voted against going to war. But the majority shared the president's commitment to join the Allies.

## 4 Revolution in Russia

Events in Russia made U.S. entry into the war more urgent for the Allies. By early 1915, the huge Russian army had been outfought by a smaller German army led by better-trained officers. In August 1915, Czar Nicholas II insisted on taking control of the troops himself. His poor leadership was blamed for more deaths. By 1917, food shortages led to riots, and soaring inflation led to strikes by angry workers in Russia.

In March 1917, Czar Nicholas II was forced to step down. A temporary government continued the unpopular war until November. In that month the Bolsheviks, a communist group led by Vladimir Ilich Lenin, took power. Communism is a political system in which the government owns key parts of the economy, and there is no private property.

Because the war had devastated Russia, Lenin at once began peace talks with Germany. In March 1918, Russia withdrew from the war by signing the Treaty of Brest-Litovsk. German troops could now turn from Russia to the Western front. The Allies urged American troops to come quickly, as you will read in the next section.

**D. Answer** Its army was losing, its economy was ruined, the war was unpopular, and a revolution brought a new government.

*Reading*History
**D. Analyzing Causes** What led Russia to pull out of the war?

### Section 1 Assessment

**1. Terms & Names**

**Identify:**
- militarism
- Central Powers
- Allies
- trench warfare
- U-boat
- Woodrow Wilson
- neutrality
- Zimmermann telegram

**2. Taking Notes**

Write at least four events that brought the United States into World War I.

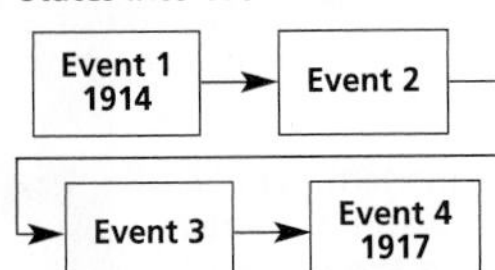


Which of these events was most important? Why?

**3. Main Ideas**

a. What were the long-term causes of World War I?

b. Why were Americans divided over the issue of remaining neutral?

c. Why was Russia's withdrawal from the war in 1917 a blow to Allies?

**4. Critical Thinking**

**Analyzing Causes** How did imperialism, nationalism, and militarism work to reinforce each other?

THINK ABOUT
- the goals of each
- how nationalism might encourage military buildup
- how nationalism contributed to the race for colonies

**ACTIVITY OPTIONS**

**SCIENCE** / **ART**

Research one of the new weapons of World War I. Explain how it works using a **model,** or draw an illustrated **diagram** of a defense against the weapon.

**INSTRUCT: OBJECTIVE 4**

**Revolution in Russia**

Key Questions
- What events in Russia forced Czar Nicholas II to give up his throne?
- Why did Russia withdraw from the war?
- How did Russia's withdrawal affect the Allied war effort?

**Economics in History**
- Russian Communism, p. 24

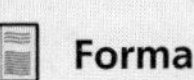

## ASSESS & RETEACH

**Setting the Stage** Have students fill in at least two boxes on the chapter graphic organizer based on the information in this section.

**Formal Assessment**
- Section Quiz, p. 350

**Critical Thinking Transparency CT70**
- Setting the Stage

**RETEACHING ACTIVITY**

Ask students to use the following terms and names in a short essay explaining how the United States became a participant in World War I: *Allies, Central Powers, U-boat, neutrality, Woodrow Wilson,* Lusitania, *unrestricted submarine warfare.*

**In-Depth Resources: Unit 7**
- Reteaching Activity, p. 52

### Section 1 Assessment

**1. Terms & Names**

**militarism,** p. 679
**Central Powers,** p. 680
**Allies,** p. 680
**trench warfare,** p. 680
**U-boat,** p. 681
**Woodrow Wilson,** p. 682
**neutrality,** p. 682
**Zimmermann telegram,** p. 682

**2. Taking Notes**

**Event 1.** Germany invades Belgium; **Event 2.** U-boat sinks *Lusitania;* **Event 3.** Germany resumes unrestricted submarine warfare; **Event 4.** Zimmermann telegram discovered. Students may say the resumption of unrestricted submarine warfare or the Zimmermann telegram; reasons will vary.

**3. Main Ideas**

a. imperialism, nationalism, militarism, and alliances **b.** They did not want to go to war, but they were angry about German attacks on merchant ships and the Zimmermann telegram's threat. **c.** because it freed German troops to concentrate on the Western Front

**4. Critical Thinking**

Nationalism led to imperialism. Protecting an empire and competing for more territory required militarism.

**ACTIVITY OPTIONS**

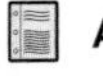

**Alternative Assessment**
- Rubrics for a model, 1.10
- Rubrics for a diagram, 1.3

*Interdisciplinary* **CHALLENGE**

**OBJECTIVE**

Students work cooperatively to solve physical education, health, and science challenges faced by a platoon leader assigned to the Western Front in World War I.

 **BLOCK SCHEDULING**

## PROCEDURE

Gather supplies that students might need, such as paper for booklets. For each challenge, have students form groups of three or four. Ask group members to divide the work among themselves. Then have groups choose an option for presenting their solution.

**PHYSICAL EDUCATION CHALLENGE**

**Class Time** 50 minutes

Students can focus on ways to improve physical fitness. From playing sports, taking physical education classes in school, or seeing exercise programs on television, some students may know exercise routines to improve fitness.

**POSSIBLE SOLUTIONS**

Student strategies for improving fitness might include

- adapted exercises for use in a narrow, restricted space.
- exercises for improving strength using available equipment.

*Interdisciplinary* **CHALLENGE**

# Survive Trench Warfare

You are a platoon leader assigned to a section of the front in central France. You have 60 men under your command. Day and night, through constant rain, earthen trenches full of sticky mud serve as your only protection. Sometimes, you think, the cold, rain, mud, rats, and fatigue are tougher to endure than a German bombardment.

COOPERATIVE LEARNING On this page are two challenges you face as a soldier during World War I. Working with a small group, decide how to deal with each challenge. Choose an option, assign a task to each group member, and do the activity. You will find useful information in the Data File. Be prepared to present your solutions to the class.

**PHYSICAL EDUCATION CHALLENGE**

*"They must have 20 or 30 pounds of mud on them."*

**Until now, no one thought the trenches would be a permanent part of this war. So you, like the other soldiers along the front, weren't trained to cope with heavy, thick mud, 70-pound backpacks, and the other demands of living and fighting in these conditions. You learned on the job. Now you've been ordered to contribute ideas for a training program that will prepare recruits for the trenches. Look at the Data File for help. Then present your ideas using one of these options:**

- **Design an exercise regimen to strengthen troops for the trenches.**
- **Write a booklet of survival tips based on your platoon's experiences.**



**STANDARDS FOR EVALUATION**

**PHYSICAL EDUCATION CHALLENGE**

**Option 1** Exercises should

- be simple and require little equipment.
- be designed to improve strength.

**Option 2** Booklets should

- use simple, straightforward language.
- explain how each tip aids in survival.
- list any materials or equipment needed.

**HEALTH CHALLENGE**

**Option 1** Strategies for keeping feet dry should

- be easy to apply.
- include materials or supplies soldiers were likely to be able to obtain.

**Option 2** Role-plays should

- convey information about trench-foot prevention.
- use informal, conversational dialogue.
- be engaging as well as informative.

**NUTRITION CHALLENGE**

**Option 1** Suggestions for improving the soldiers' diet should

- note the absence of fruits and vegetables.
- propose ways of obtaining the missing elements, such as bartering or foraging.
- show awareness of basic nutritional needs.

**Option 2** Suggestions for supplementing soldiers' daily diet might include

- buying or bartering for them.
- foraging for these foods.

## HEALTH CHALLENGE

*"Your feet swell to two or three times . . . normal size."*

**You're worried about your men getting trench foot. You've heard horror stories about men whose feet swelled so much they couldn't pull off their boots. Some of these men developed gangrene and had their feet amputated. The key to preventing trench foot is staying dry. What will you do? Use the Data File for help. Then present your solution using one of these options:**

- Come up with a way to keep the men's feet dry.
- Role-play a conversation with veteran soldiers about preventing trench foot.

## ACTIVITY WRAP-UP

Present to the Class **As a group, review your methods of surviving the trenches. Pick the most creative solution for each challenge, and present these solutions to the class.**

## DATA FILE

### THE TRENCHES

- Trenches covered about 450 miles between the North Sea and the Swiss border.
- In France, ten-foot-deep trenches were dug into the ground and topped with sandbag parapets.
- Inside was a fire step, a ledge two or three feet up from bottom of the trench, used by sentries or troops firing.
- The sides were held up by sandbags and timber.

### A SOLDIER'S GEAR

60–75 pounds of gear, including blankets, waterproof ground-sheet, extra boots and occasionally waterproof gum boots, quilted coat, shovel for digging trenches, helmet, wire clippers, pail for rations, 2 quarts of water, 4 days' food, 200 cartridges, 6 hand grenades, gas mask, 3 pairs of socks, soap, toothbrush, bottle of whale oil, towel, rifle, bayonet

### TRENCH FOOD

beef stew, corned beef, bread, hard biscuits, pork and beans, tins of jam, butter, sugar, tea

### PROBLEMS

- **trench foot:** condition caused by feet staying wet 24 hours a day; feet swell, turn numb and blue; if not treated, gangrene sets in and feet must be amputated; helped by rubbing whale oil on feet, changing to dry socks three times daily
- **mud:** mud traps the wounded until some drown, clogs rifles and gear, weighs men down, causes trench walls to fall in
- **rats:** huge rats, big as rabbits, infest the trenches

**Visit www.mcdougallittell.com for more on trench warfare.**

*World War I* **685**

## ACTIVITY WRAP-UP

Booklets, role-plays, and presentations should

- provide a clear, concise statement of the problem.
- give a workable solution.
- evaluate the effectiveness of the solution.
- assess the creativity of the solution.

## HEALTH CHALLENGE

**Class Time** 50 minutes

Suggest that students review the Data File information on the causes of trench foot. Students might also find reference material on the topic. Within groups, students can discuss simple ways of keeping feet dry, waterproofing boots, and reducing mud and standing water in the trenches. Effects of trench foot were somewhat similar to those of frostbite, with which students may be more familiar.

### POSSIBLE SOLUTIONS

Trench foot, also called immersion foot, is caused by overexposure to cold, damp conditions. The best way to treat trench foot is by warming the foot. This treatment was not available in the unheated trenches, but since soldiers were regularly rotated out of the trenches, the problem could be treated in army hospitals away from the battlefield.

### ALTERNATIVE ACTIVITY

## NUTRITION CHALLENGE

*". . . the first meal we've had in three days . . ."*

**You are concerned about rations for your soldiers. When your unit is under fire, you may not get a hot meal for hours or even days. You know that adequate nutrition is important for good health.**

- Study the information on army rations. Then list the basic food groups that are well represented and those that are not.
- Suggest ways to supplement the daily rations with the food groups that are lacking, so that your platoon stays healthy.

## SECTION OBJECTIVES

1. To describe how the United States developed and deployed its armed forces
2. To summarize the effects of American entry into the war
3. To explain how U.S. troops helped the Allies push back the Germans
4. To describe how the war ended

**SKILLBUILDER**

Interpreting Maps: Location, Movement, p. 688
Interpreting Graphs, p. 690

**CRITICAL THINKING**

Finding Main Ideas, p. 687
Recognizing Effects, pp. 689, 690
Evaluating, p. 689

## FOCUS & MOTIVATE

### 5-MINUTE WARM-UP

**Recognizing Effects** These questions help students understand aspects of the Western Front.

1. Look at the map on page 688. In what country were most battles of the war on the Western Front fought?
2. About how far were the Germans pushed back by the time of the armistice? How long did that take?

 Warm-Up Transparency WT24

## INSTRUCT

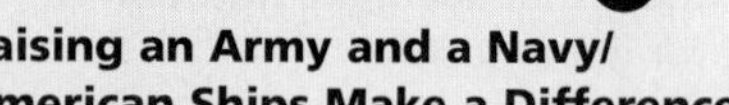

**INSTRUCT: OBJECTIVE 1**

**Raising an Army and a Navy/ American Ships Make a Difference**

Key Questions

- How did Americans prepare for war?
- What part did women and African Americans play in military operations?
- How did the Allies respond to German submarine attacks?

 **In-Depth Resources: Unit 7**
- Guided Reading, p. 39

# 2 America Joins the Fight

**TERMS & NAMES**
John J. Pershing
American Expeditionary Force
convoy system
Second Battle of the Marne
Alvin York
armistice

**MAIN IDEA**
U.S. forces helped the Allies win World War I.

**WHY IT MATTERS NOW**
For the first time, the United States asserted itself as a world power.

### ONE AMERICAN'S STORY

**Eddie Rickenbacker was America's most famous flying ace. He was one of the first Americans to get a look at the trenches from the cockpit of an airplane. The date was March 6, 1918. It was, recalled Rickenbacker, the first flyover of the battlefield by a "made-in-America Squadron." What Rickenbacker saw shocked him.**

*A VOICE FROM THE PAST*

[T]here appeared to be nothing below but these old battered ditches . . . and billions of shell holes. . . . [N]ot a tree, a fence . . . nothing but . . . ruin and desolation. The whole scene was appalling.

**Eddie Rickenbacker,** *Fighting the Flying Circus*

**Rickenbacker went on to distinguished service as a wartime aviator. As you will read in this section, he and other U.S. soldiers helped the Allies win the war.**

**An American gun crew advances against German positions in 1918. The ruin that Rickenbacker described is apparent.**

## 1 Raising an Army and a Navy

The U.S. Army was not ready for war. American fighting forces consisted of fewer than 200,000 soldiers, many of them recent recruits. To meet its need for troops, the government began a draft. This system of choosing people for forced military service was first used during the Civil War. In May 1917, Congress passed the Selective Service Act. This act required all males between the ages of 21 and 30 to sign up for military service. By the end of 1918, nearly 3 million men had been drafted.

About 2 million American soldiers went to France. They served under General **John J. Pershing** as the **American Expeditionary Force,** or AEF. British commanders asked the U.S. government to have AEF troops join existing French and British combat units. Wilson refused. He believed that having "distinct and separate" American combat units would guarantee the United States a major role in the peace talks at war's end. Most U.S. troops fought separately, but some fought under Allied command.



### RECOMMENDED RESOURCES

 **In-Depth Resources: Unit 7**
- Guided Reading, p. 39
- Building Vocabulary, p. 42
- Geography Application: Meuse-Argonne Offensive, pp. 44–45
- Literature Selection: "In Another Country," pp. 48–51
- Reteaching Activity, p. 53

**Reading Study Guide** (Spanish and English), pp. 233–234

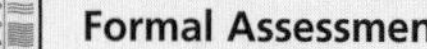 **Formal Assessment**
- Section Quiz, p. 351

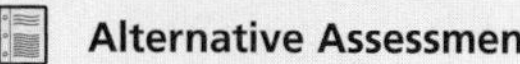 **Alternative Assessment**
- Rubrics, 5.3
- Rubrics, 4.3

**Access for Students Acquiring English/ESL**
- Guided Reading, p. 160
- Geography Application, pp. 164–165

**Technology Resources**

 **Critical Thinking Trans. CT71**
- Cause and Effect: Effects of World War I on Europe

 **Electronic Teacher Tools with Test Maker**

 **ClassZone**
www.mcdougallittell.com

Close to 50,000 American women also served in World War I. Some volunteered for overseas duty with the American Red Cross. However, for the first time in American history, women also served in the military. The Navy, desperate for clerical workers, took about 12,000 female volunteers. The Marine Corps accepted 305 female recruits, known as Marinettes. Over 1,000 women went overseas for the Army. Nurses made up the largest group of females in the armed forces. However, women also acted as interpreters, operated switchboards, entertained troops, and drove ambulances for the AEF.

**Reading History**
**A. Finding Main Ideas** How did women serve in the U.S. armed forces?
A. Answer as clerical workers, nurses, interpreters, switchboard operators, entertainers, and ambulance drivers

Around 400,000 African Americans served in the armed forces. More than half of them served in France. As they had at home, African-American troops overseas faced discrimination. However, it came from white American soldiers rather than from their European allies. At first, the Army refused to take black draftees. However, responding to pressure from African-American groups, the military eventually created two African-American combat divisions.

## American Ships Make a Difference

In the first years of the war, German U-boat attacks on supply ships were a serious threat to the Allied war effort. American Rear Admiral William S. Sims convinced the Allies to adopt a system of protection. In a **convoy system,** a heavy guard of destroyers escorted merchant ships across the Atlantic in groups. Begun in May 1917, this strategy quickly reduced the loss rate.

Another American tactic gave the Allies added protection from the U-boat menace. Beginning in June 1918, the Allies laid a barrier of 70,000 mines in the North Sea. The 180-mile-long minefield made U-boat access to the North Atlantic almost impossible. Admiral Sims called the North Sea minefield "one of the wonders of the war."

**Vocabulary**
**mines:** hidden explosive devices

### MORE ABOUT . . .

**African Americans in World War I**

More than 370,000 African Americans served in the armed forces during World War I. Of those, the great majority were barred from combat, despite their training. They were limited to manual labor and service positions. But about 100,000 African-American troops did see action, often under French command. In France, the black soldiers faced less discrimination than they did under the Jim Crow laws in the United States. Some chose to stay in France for that reason, but others returned to the United States determined to make their native country live up to its democratic promise.

### MORE ABOUT . . .

**Mines and Minefields**

During the war, navies on both sides laid two kinds of mines on the ocean floor. Contact mines exploded when a ship's hull hit one of the detonator "horns" that extended from the mine casing. Controlled mines were fired from the shore to protect harbors. Early in the war, the Germans were far ahead of the British in the development of mines, in part because the British had ethical objections to using such devices. By 1918, however, the British not only used mines but had developed a new type—a magnetic mine, detonated by the magnetic field of a ship passing over the mine.

**Convoy System**

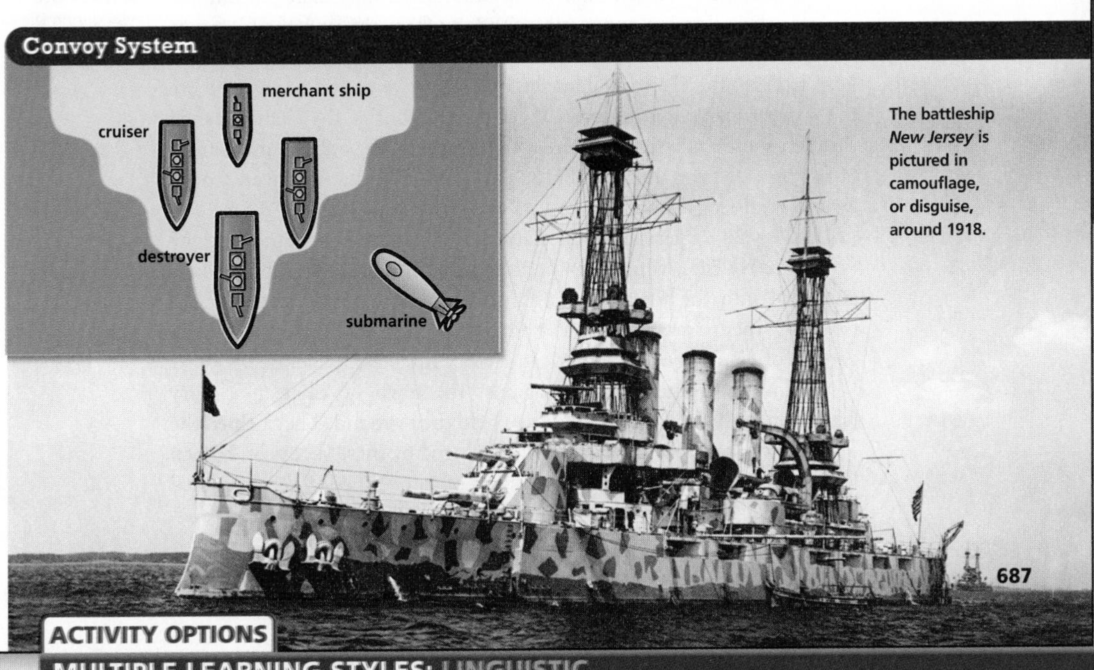


The battleship *New Jersey* is pictured in camouflage, or disguise, around 1918.



### ACTIVITY OPTIONS

**MULTIPLE LEARNING STYLES: LINGUISTIC** — BLOCK SCHEDULING

**SIGNING UP THE TROOPS**

**Class Time** One class period

**Task** Writing a dialogue between an army or navy recruiter and a prospective recruit

**Purpose** To gain an understanding of the motives that led Americans to join the war effort

**Supplies Needed**
- Reference materials on the pay, benefits, and duties of the armed forces and the American Red Cross in World War I
- Strips of blank paper and a container

**Activity** On strips of paper, write the following: *Red Cross worker; sailor in a convoy; combat soldier; military clerical worker; nurse; ambulance driver; entertainer.* Put the strips in a container and divide students into pairs. Have each pair draw a slip and create a dialogue between a prospective recruit and a recruiter looking for someone to fill the position on the slip. The dialogue should include questions and answers about why the recruit should join; what the dangers, duties, and benefits of service are; and what military training or life at the front might be like.

## The Western Front, 1914–1918

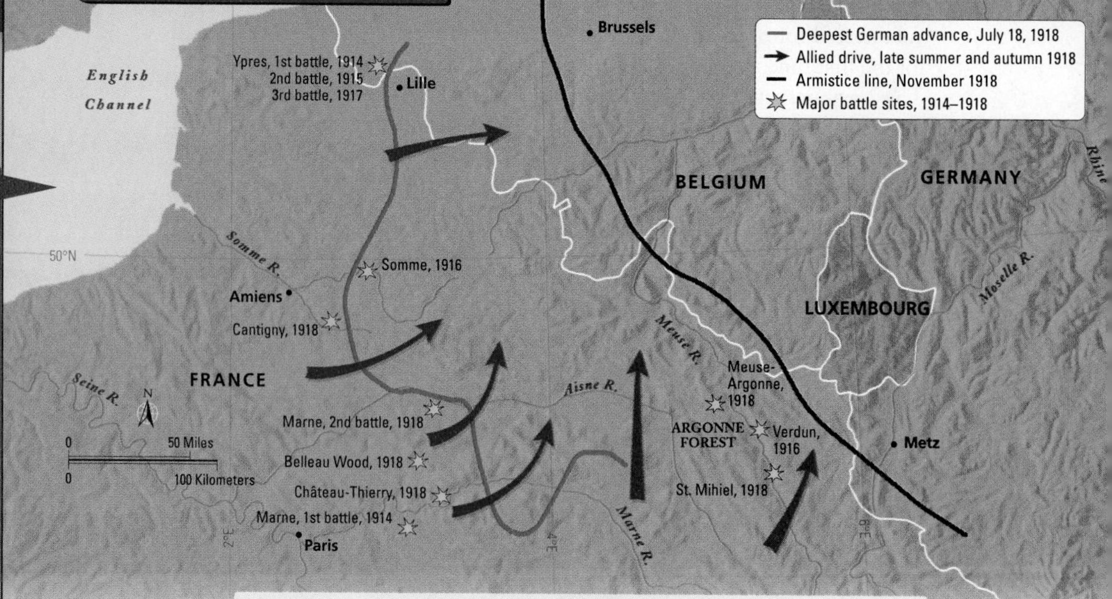

**GEOGRAPHY SKILLBUILDER Interpreting Maps**

1. **Location** *What three battles occurred closest to the Armistice line?*
2. **Movement** *In what two directions did the Allied drives move?*

Skillbuilder Answers
1. Meuse-Argonne, Verdun, St. Mihiel
2. east and north

## HISTORY FROM VISUALS

**Reading the Map** Discuss the following questions with the class: How do the dates on the map prove that most of the battles accomplished little? **Possible Response** There was little movement from year to year; for example, there were battles at Ypres in 1914, 1915, and 1917. Why was there no fighting in Germany? **Answer** The armistice was signed before German troops retreated that far.

**Extension** Have students pick one of the battles on the Western Front and create a map of the battle showing battle lines and troop movements.

## ❷ American Troops Enter the War

By the time the first American troops arrived in France in June 1917, the Allies had been at war for almost three years. The small force of 14,000 Yanks boosted the morale of the battle-weary Allies. However, almost a year would pass before the bulk of the American troops landed in Europe.

**Background**
American soldiers were also called *doughboys*. This term was used even during the Civil War.

After their Russian opponents withdrew from the war, the Germans and the other Central Powers prepared to finish the fight in France. In March 1918, the Germans launched an offensive to end the war before the Americans arrived in force. Within two months, they had smashed through the French lines, reaching the Marne River only 50 miles from Paris. Just in time, in May 1918, one million fresh American troops arrived ready for action.

On May 28, American soldiers attacked the French town of Cantigny (kahn•tee•NYEE), which was occupied by the Germans. The soldiers advanced into the town, blasting enemy soldiers out of trenches and dragging them from cellars. Within two hours, the Yanks had taken control of Cantigny. The American victory lifted Allied morale.

When the Germans moved against the town of Château-Thierry (shah•toh•tyeh•REE), the Americans held their ground. They helped the French stop the German advance. Encouraged by these successes, French General Ferdinand Foch, commander of the Allied forces, ordered General Pershing's American forces to retake Belleau (beh•LOH) Wood.



## INSTRUCT: OBJECTIVE ❷

**American Troops Enter the War**

Key Questions
- How did the arrival of American troops in Europe affect the Allies?
- What role did American troops play in countering the German offensive in 1918?

## MORE ABOUT . . .

**Belleau Wood**

Belleau Wood was one of the first major American battles against the Germans. American forces launched six successive assaults against German soldiers dug into the mile-square wood. It took U.S. troops about three weeks of heavy fighting to clear the wood. The cost in human lives was high—1,800 Americans killed and about 7,000 wounded. J. E. Redinell of the American Marine Brigade made these notes in his diary: "Not a house left standing. Ammunition dump . . . blown to pieces. . . . Dead horses & cows lying out in the fields. So this was the price of war."

## ACTIVITY OPTIONS

### INTERDISCIPLINARY LINK: GEOGRAPHY

BLOCK SCHEDULING

**WAR CORRESPONDENTS, 1918**

**Class Time** One class period

**Task** Preparing an oral report on a battle that occurred in 1918

**Purpose** To analyze the impact of the battle on the war effort

**Supplies Needed**
- Reference materials on major battles
- Posterboard and markers, or overhead projector and transparency of Western Front

**Activity** Divide students into groups and assign each a 1918 battle to cover as war correspondents. Have the groups prepare oral reports on when and where each battle was fought, its objective, the effects of geographic factors such as terrain, and the battle's impact on the Allied advance. Presentations can include a map of the battle site, or presenters can locate the battlefield on a transparency of the Western Front. Have groups deliver their reports in the order in which the fighting took place.

This was a forest near the Marne River well defended by German troops. American soldiers succeeded, but at a fearful cost. One unit lost 380 of its 400 men. However, the Americans had proved themselves in combat.

## 3 Pushing the Germans Back

The **Second Battle of the Marne** in the summer of 1918 was the turning point of the war. It began with a German drive against the French line. During three days of heavy fighting, about 85,000 Americans helped the Allies halt the German advance. The Allies then took the initiative. They cut the enemy off from its supply lines and forced the Germans back.

For the rest of the war, the Allies advanced steadily. By early September, the Germans had lost all the territory they had gained since the spring. September 26, 1918, marked the beginning of the final Meuse-Argonne (myooz•ahr•GAHN) offensive. Around 1.2 million U.S. soldiers took part in a massive drive to push back the German line between the Argonne Forest and the Meuse River. The war's final battle left 26,000 Americans dead. But by November, the Germans were retreating.

*Reading*History
**B. Recognizing Effects** What was the effect of the Meuse-Argonne offensive?
B. Answer
It made the Germans retreat.

The Meuse-Argonne offensive made a hero of American soldier **Alvin York**. At first, Tennessee-born Sergeant York seemed an unlikely candidate for military fame. Because of his religious beliefs, he tried unsuccessfully to avoid the draft. He refused to bear arms on religious grounds. An army captain convinced him to change his mind. In October 1918, in the Argonne Forest, York attacked German machine gunners, killing 25 of them. Other German soldiers surrendered, and York returned to the American lines with 132 captives.

*Reading*History
**C. Evaluating** What was heroic about Sergeant York?
C. Possible Answer He killed 25 German machine gunners; he captured 132 Germans; he put aside his personal beliefs to serve in the military.

Another American hero was pilot Eddie Rickenbacker. He won fame as the U.S. "ace of aces" for shooting down a total of 26 enemy planes. Just before the Meuse-Argonne offensive, he attacked seven German planes, sending two of them crashing to the ground. This action won him the Medal of Honor.

Four African-American combat units also received recognition for their battlefield valor. Fighting under French commanders, the 369th, 371st, and 372nd regiments (and part of the 370th) were awarded France's highest honor, the Croix de Guerre. The 369th spent more continuous time on the front lines than any other American unit. Although under intense fire for 191 days, it never lost a foot of ground.

**Connections TO LITERATURE**

**LITERATURE OF WORLD WAR I**

Several notable American writers served in World War I. They included Ernest Hemingway, the poet E. E. Cummings, and John Dos Passos. Hemingway drove an ambulance for the Italian army. He put this experience into his war novel *A Farewell to Arms*. Cummings wrote of his time in France in *The Enormous Room*.

Dos Passos, who also worked as an ambulance driver, once explained what attracted him to the battlefront: "What was war like, we wanted to see with our own eyes. I wanted to see the show."

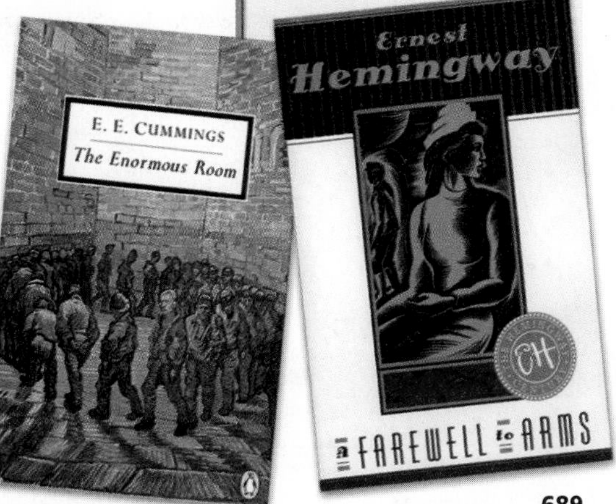


689

### INSTRUCT: OBJECTIVE 

**Pushing the Germans Back**

Key Questions

- Why was the Second Battle of the Marne a turning point in the war?
- How did American soldiers demonstrate qualities of courage and heroism in the war?

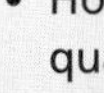 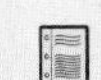  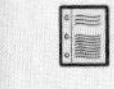 **In-Depth Resources: Unit 7**
- Geography Application: Meuse-Argonne Offensive, pp. 45–46

### Connections TO *LITERATURE*

**Literature of World War I**

Working as an ambulance driver for the American Red Cross, E. E. Cummings had his most difficult encounters with the French government. After a French censor read some of the letters Cummings wrote home in 1917, Cummings was taken prisoner and held in a French prison on suspicion of treasonous correspondence. He remained there until he was located by the American embassy. He described his war experiences in *The Enormous Room.*

 **In-Depth Resources: Unit 7**
- Literature Selection: "In Another Country" by Ernest Hemingway, pp. 48–51

### MORE ABOUT . . .

**Eddie Rickenbacker**

Eddie Rickenbacker was well known as a race car driver before the war began. He first went to France as General Pershing's driver but soon transferred to the aviation division as an engineering instructor. He learned to fly on his own time and in March 1918 joined the 94th Aero Squadron of the U.S. Army Air Service. After the war, he became a successful businessman and in 1930 received the Congressional Medal of Honor for his wartime services.

### ACTIVITY OPTIONS

### INDIVIDUAL NEEDS: GIFTED AND TALENTED

**HEROISM THEN AND NOW**

**Class Time** One class period

**Task** Comparing and contrasting heroes of World War I with heroes of today

**Purpose** To create a definition of heroism and compare heroes in different decades

**Supplies Needed**
- Biographies, encyclopedias, and other reference materials on Alvin York and Eddie Rickenbacker
- Internet access for additional resources

**Activity** As a class, list people who are American heroes today. Have students explain why they admire and respect these people. Ask students to review the biographical information on York and Rickenbacker and identify the traits that made them heroes. Compare and contrast these characteristics with those of current heroes. Ask students what traits wartime and peacetime heroes have in common and how they differ.

## INSTRUCT: OBJECTIVE 4

**Germany Stops Fighting**

Key Questions
- What events made Germany's surrender likely?
- What were the costs of the war?

**Critical Thinking Transparency CT71**
- Cause and Effect: Effects of World War I on Europe

### HISTORY FROM VISUALS

**Reading the Graph** Ask students why the United States suffered far fewer casualties than the other combatants. **Answer** The United States entered the war much later than the others. Which side suffered more casualties altogether? **Answer** the Allies

**Extension** Have students find out how American military deaths in World War I compare with American military deaths in World War II, the Korean War, or the Vietnam War.

## ASSESS & RETEACH

**Setting the Stage** Have students fill in the fourth box on the chapter graphic organizer.

**Formal Assessment**
- Section Quiz, p. 351

### RETEACHING ACTIVITY

Have each student create headlines for events described in this section, from "First U.S. Forces Land in France" to "Armistice Declared." Ask students to trade headlines and write a short article to accompany each headline.

**In-Depth Resources: Unit 7**
- Reteaching Activity, p. 53

---

Americans were proud of the contribution their troops made to the war effort. They helped shift the balance in favor of the Allies.

Skillbuilder Answers
1. Germany, Russia
2. approximately 5.25%

## 4 Germany Stops Fighting

After the defeat of the Meuse-Argonne, General Erich Ludendorff advised the German government to seek peace. In early November, Germany's navy mutinied and its allies dropped out. On November 9, the Kaiser stepped down. Two days later Germany agreed to an **armistice**, an end to fighting. On November 11, 1918, at 11:00 A.M.—the 11th hour of the 11th day of the 11th month—all fighting ceased.

**Background** For many years after the war, Americans celebrated Armistice Day as a national holiday.

About 8.5 million soldiers died in the war, and about 21 million were wounded. Before he was killed in battle, one British soldier summed up the war's tragic costs.

CONNECTIONS TO MATH

**Military Deaths in World War I***

Lives lost (in thousands): 0, 250, 500, 750, 1000, 1250, 1500, 1750, 2000

France, Britain, Russia, Germany, Austria-Hungary, U.S.

*Not all countries are listed.
Source: *Over There*, by Byron Farwell

SKILLBUILDER
**Interpreting Charts**
1. *Which two nations on the chart suffered the most deaths?*
2. *U.S. deaths were about what percentage of combined French and British deaths?*

*A VOICE FROM THE PAST*

The sufferings of the men at the Front, of the wounded whose flesh and bodies are torn in a way you cannot conceive; the sorrow of those at home. . . . What a cruel and mad diversion of human activity!

**William John Mason,** quoted in *The Lost Generation of 1914*

Millions of civilians in Europe, Asia, and Africa also died in the war—from starvation and disease. In the next section, you will learn how the war affected U.S. civilians.

### Section 2 Assessment

**1. Terms & Names**

Identify:
- John J. Pershing
- American Expeditionary Force
- convoy system
- Second Battle of the Marne
- Alvin York
- armistice

**2. Taking Notes**

Create a web to show how American groups or individuals helped fight the war.

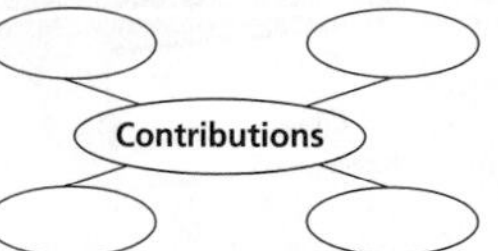


Whose contribution was most surprising?

**3. Main Ideas**

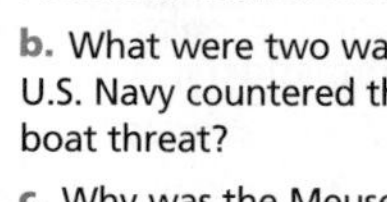

a. Why did Wilson want U.S. forces to fight as a separate American combat unit?

b. What were two ways the U.S. Navy countered the U-boat threat?

c. Why was the Meuse-Argonne offensive a turning point in the war?

**4. Critical Thinking**

**Recognizing Effects** How important was America's entry into the war to the Allied cause?

THINK ABOUT
- the morale of Allied troops
- troop strength
- performance in battle

**ACTIVITY OPTIONS**

MUSIC / LANGUAGE ARTS

Make an **audiotape** of music or sounds that suggest the stages of the war, or write a **letter** in the voice of a soldier in the war.



---

### Section 2 Assessment

**1. Terms & Names**

**John J. Pershing,** p. 686
**American Expeditionary Force,** p. 686
**convoy system,** p. 687
**Second Battle of the Marne,** p. 689
**Alvin York,** p. 689
**armistice,** p. 690

**2. Taking Notes**

AEF ground troops helped push back the German line; women served as nurses, clerical workers, ambulance drivers; U.S. naval forces escorted merchant ships and mined the North Sea; Sergeant York killed 25 enemy machine gunners and took 132 prisoners. Answers will vary.

**3. Main Ideas**

a. He thought it would guarantee the United States a major role in the peace talks after the war. **b.** They guarded merchant ships and laid mines to keep U-boats out of the North Atlantic. **c.** It forced the Germans into retreat.

**4. Critical Thinking**

very important because U.S. troops were fresh and had higher morale than the Allied troops who had been fighting for three years

### ACTIVITY OPTIONS

**Alternative Assessment**
- Rubrics for an audiotape, 5.3
- Rubrics for a letter, 4.3

690 CHAPTER 24

# 3 Life on the Home Front

**TERMS & NAMES**
- war bonds
- propaganda
- Espionage Act
- Sedition Act
- Oliver Wendell Holmes
- Great Migration

| MAIN IDEA | WHY IT MATTERS NOW |
|---|---|
| The war required sacrifice for Americans at home and changed life in other ways. | Some wartime changes were permanent, such as black migration to Northern cities. |

### ONE AMERICAN'S STORY

**On the home front, the war opened up new jobs for women. Most of the women who took these jobs were already in the work force. Carrie Fearing worked for the Railroad Administration. When the war ended, female workers were laid off. Fearing wrote to the railroad director, hoping to keep her job.**

*A VOICE FROM THE PAST*

> We never took a soldier's place, a soldier would not do the work we did . . . such as sweeping, picking up waste and paper and hauling steel shavings. . . . We . . . were liked and respected by all who knew us. . . . We like our job very much and I hope you will . . . place us back at the shop.
>
> **Carrie Fearing,** quoted in *Women, War, and Work*

In May 1918, these women worked in the Union Pacific Railroad freight yard in Cheyenne, Wyoming.

**Like Fearing, most women who helped the country get ready for war were pleased to have wartime jobs. They were proud of the part they had played in getting the country ready for war.**

## 1 Mobilizing for War

To prepare for war, the government needed money. World War I cost the United States $35.5 billion. Americans helped pay almost two-thirds of that amount by buying government war bonds. **War bonds** were low-interest loans by civilians to the government, meant to be repaid in a number of years. To sell the bonds, officials held Liberty Loan drives. Posters urged citizens to "Come Across or the Kaiser Will." Hollywood actors like Charlie Chaplin toured the country selling bonds to starstruck audiences.

Schoolchildren rolled bandages and collected tin cans, paper, toothpaste tubes, and apricot pits. The pits were burned and made into charcoal for gas mask filters. Some Boy Scout troops even sold war bonds. So that more food could be sent to soldiers, people planted "victory gardens" in backyards and vacant lots. Women's groups came together in homes and churches to knit socks and sweaters and sew hospital gowns.



## SECTION OBJECTIVES

1. To describe how Americans mobilized for war
2. To analyze the effects of wartime propaganda in the United States
3. To explain the causes of the Great Migration
4. To summarize the impact of the 1918 flu epidemic

### CRITICAL THINKING

Finding Main Ideas, p. 692
Recognizing Effects, pp. 692, 694
Analyzing Points of View, p. 693
Making Inferences, p. 694

## FOCUS & MOTIVATE

### 5-MINUTE WARM-UP

**Drawing Conclusions** These questions help students understand the role of women in the war effort on the home front.

1. In what way does the picture on page 691 illustrate a change in women's roles in society?
2. Look at the poster on page 692. In what way does it reflect the traditional roles of women?

**Warm-Up Transparency WT24**

## INSTRUCT

### INSTRUCT: OBJECTIVE 1

**Mobilizing for War**

Key Questions
- How did American civilians contribute to the effort to win the war?
- How did the war lead to greater government control of the economy?
- Why did the government need to create the Committee on Public Information?

**In-Depth Resources: Unit 7**
- Guided Reading, p. 40
- Primary Source, p. 46

**Reading Study Guide** (Spanish and English), pp. 235–236

## RECOMMENDED RESOURCES

**In-Depth Resources: Unit 7**
- Guided Reading, p. 40
- Building Vocabulary, p. 42
- Primary Source: "Over There" by George M. Cohan, p. 46
- Reteaching Activity, p. 54

**Reading Study Guide** (Spanish and English), pp. 235–236

**Formal Assessment**
- Section Quiz, p. 352

**Alternative Assessment**
- Rubrics, 5.3
- Rubrics, 2.2

**Access for Students Acquiring English/ESL**
- Guided Reading, p. 161

Technology Resources

**Humanities Transparency HT47**
- Political Cartoon: The Red Scare

**Humanities Transparency HT48**
- *The Migrants Arrived in Great Numbers* by Jacob Lawrence

**Electronic Teacher Tools with Test Maker**

**ClassZone**
www.mcdougallittell.com

**MORE ABOUT . . .**

**Helping on the Home Front**
One wag left this cheery poem about home-front conservation.

Our Mondays are meat-less,
Our Tuesdays are sweet-less,
We are getting more eat-less each day.
Our bread, it is wheat-less,
Our beds, they are sheet-less,
They've gone to the YMCA.

**CRITICAL THINKING ACTIVITY**

**Recognizing Effects** Explore with students the impact of propaganda on Americans at home. How did propaganda support the war effort? What was an intended consequence of the propaganda? What was an unintended consequence?

**Class Time** 10 minutes

**INSTRUCT: OBJECTIVE 2**

**Intolerance and Suspicion**
Key Questions

- How did war propaganda contribute to anti-German prejudice?
- Why did some Americans criticize the Espionage Act and the Sedition Act?
- How did the Supreme Court justify the constitutionality of those acts?

 **Humanities Transparency HT47**
- Political Cartoon: The Red Scare

To persuade women to buy war bonds, this poster appealed to their love of family.

Patriotic citizens also saved food by observing wheatless Mondays and Wednesdays, when they ate no bread, and meatless Tuesdays. To save gas, they stopped their Sunday pleasure drives. The government limited civilian use of steel and other metals. Women donated their corsets with metal stays to scrap drives. Manufacturers stopped making tin toys for children and removed metal from caskets.

*Reading* **History**
**A. Finding Main Ideas** What were civilians asked to do for the war effort?
A. Possible Answers
to buy war bonds; to conserve food, gas, and metal; to make items needed by soldiers

The war brought more government control of the economy. To produce needed war supplies, in 1917 President Wilson set up the War Industries Board. The board had great power. It managed the buying and distributing of war materials. It also set production goals and ordered construction of new factories. With the president's approval, the board also set prices. Another government agency, the National War Labor Board, settled conflicts between workers and factory owners.

To rally citizen support, Wilson created the Committee on Public Information. The committee's writers, artists, photographers, and filmmakers produced **propaganda,** opinions expressed for the purpose of influencing the actions of others. They sold the war through posters, pamphlets, and movies. One popular pamphlet, "How the War Came to America," came out in Polish, German, Swedish, Bohemian, and Spanish. In movie houses, audiences watched such patriotic films as *Under Four Flags* and *Pershing's Crusaders.*

## 2 Intolerance and Suspicion

Patriotic propaganda did much to win support for the war. But its anti-German, anti-foreign focus also fueled prejudice. Suddenly people distrusted anything German. A number of towns with German names changed their names. Berlin, Maryland, became Brunswick. People called sauerkraut "liberty cabbage," and hamburger became "Salisbury steak." Owners of German shepherds took to calling their pets "police dogs."

*Reading* **History**
**B. Recognizing Effects** How did war propaganda fuel prejudice?
B. Answer
It made people distrust all things German.

On June 15, 1917, Congress passed the **Espionage Act.** The **Sedition Act** followed in May 1918. These laws set heavy fines and long prison terms for such anti-war activities as encouraging draft resisters. The laws made it illegal to criticize the war. U.S. courts tried more than 1,500 pacifists, socialists, and other war critics. Hundreds went to jail. Socialist party leader Eugene Debs gave a speech arguing that the war was fought by poor workingmen for the profit of wealthy business owners. For this talk, a judge sentenced him to ten years in prison.

The government ignored complaints that the rights of Americans were being trampled. In the 1919 decision in *Schenck* v. *United States,* the Supreme Court upheld the Espionage Act. Schenck, convicted of



**ACTIVITY OPTIONS**

**INTERDISCIPLINARY LINK: CIVICS** BLOCK SCHEDULING

**HOLD A DEBATE**

**Class Time** One class period

**Task** Debating the constitutionality of limiting freedom of speech

**Purpose** To evaluate whether freedom of speech should be curtailed during wartime

**Supplies Needed**
- Reference materials on the Espionage and Sedition Acts
- Holmes's opinions in *Schenck* v. *United States* and *Abrams* v. *United States* (optional)
- Copies of the First Amendment

**Activity** Organize a debate on this topic: *Resolved: The government should have the right to limit freedom of speech during wartime.* To prepare for the debate, divide students into three groups. Ask one group to prepare arguments in favor of the resolution, while the second group prepares arguments against the resolution. The third group will act as judges in the debate and can prepare for the debate by developing the format, length, rules, and criteria for determining the winner.

distributing pamphlets against the draft, had argued that the Espionage Act violated his right to free speech. Justice **Oliver Wendell Holmes** wrote the court's opinion.

*A VOICE FROM THE PAST*

The most stringent [strict] protection of free speech would not protect a man in falsely shouting fire in a theater and causing a panic. . . . The question in every case is whether the words used . . . are of such a nature as to create a clear and present danger that they will bring about . . . evils that Congress has a right to prevent.

**Oliver Wendell Holmes,** *Schenck* v. *United States, 1919*

*Reading* **History**
**C. Analyzing Points of View** Why did Justice Holmes believe that free speech could be limited?
C. Answer because he thought that some words could harm the nation

Justice Holmes argued that free speech, guaranteed by the First Amendment, could be limited, especially in wartime.

## 3 New Jobs and the Great Migration

As soldiers went off to battle, the United States faced a labor shortage. Northern factories gearing up for war were suddenly willing to hire workers they had once rejected. Throughout the South, African Americans heeded the call. Between 1910 and 1920, about 500,000 African Americans moved north to such cities as New York, Chicago, Detroit, Cleveland, and St. Louis. This movement became known as the **Great Migration.** African Americans left to escape the bigotry, poverty, and racial violence of the South. They hoped for a better life in the North.

**HISTORY through ART**

*The Migration of the Negro,* Panel No. 1 (1940–41), by Jacob Lawrence, shows three of the most common destinations for African Americans leaving the South.

**What does the painting suggest about the departure of African Americans from the South?**

**INSTRUCT: OBJECTIVE 3**

**New Jobs and the Great Migration**

Key Questions
- Why did African Americans leave the South and come to Northern cities during the Great Migration?
- What factors led Mexicans to come to the United States after 1910?
- How did work opportunities for women change during the war?

### *HISTORY through ART*

**Interpreting the Painting** Jacob Lawrence was born while the United States was at war in 1917. As a teenager in the 1930s, he took classes at the Harlem Art Workshop, where he met many of the writers and thinkers who had taken part in the Harlem Renaissance of the 1920s. Lawrence often used the bright colors of folk art to portray grim urban realities.

**Possible Response: The painting suggests that great numbers of African Americans made the trip and that they went to large cities such as Chicago, New York, and St. Louis. The lattices suggest departure gates at a railroad or bus station.**

**Humanities Transparency HT48**
- *The Migrants Arrived in Great Numbers* by Jacob Lawrence

### MORE ABOUT . . .

**The Great Migration**

In the South, white farm owners tried hard to stop the migration. They needed farm laborers to plant and harvest crops, and many feared that wages would rise as the labor supply decreased. State and local governments passed laws to stop labor recruiters from looking for workers. Plantation managers used violence or threats of violence to try to keep African Americans from going North. Despite harassment, the migration continued.

### ACTIVITY OPTIONS

### INDIVIDUAL NEEDS

**LESS PROFICIENT READERS**

**Creating a Study Guide** You may want to prepare a study guide to help students read and take notes efficiently. A guide will also help them get a better picture of what life on the home front was really like. Prepare a set of questions about the most important topics from the section. As students read, ask them to use the questions as a guide and to look for facts and details to answer them.

A study guide might include such questions as the following:
- How did Americans mobilize, or assemble and make ready, for the war?
- How did the war create an atmosphere of intolerance and suspicion?
- What new jobs did the war effort create? Who filled these jobs?
- What was the Great Migration? What motivated those who migrated?
- What were the short-term effects of the flu epidemic?

**INSTRUCT: OBJECTIVE** 

**The Flu Epidemic of 1918**

Key Questions

- How was the flu epidemic made worse by the war?
- How did Americans try to protect themselves from the epidemic?
- What was the effect of the epidemic worldwide?

**Now and then**

**The Flu Epidemic**

To stop contagion, San Francisco officials passed laws requiring residents to wear surgical masks. In Chicago, theater owners refused to let in coughing patrons. Some Americans suspected the Germans of introducing germ warfare. Rumors circulated that German U-boats had brought the flu across the Atlantic. However, such rumors stopped after thousands of Germans also fell sick.

## ASSESS & RETEACH

**Setting the Stage** Have students fill in the fifth and sixth boxes on the chapter graphic organizer.

 **Formal Assessment**

- Section Quiz, p. 352

**RETEACHING ACTIVITY**

Ask students to write a paragraph that explains and supports the main idea stated at the beginning of this section.

 **In-Depth Resources: Unit 7**

- Reteaching Activity, p. 54

New jobs were opening up in the American Southwest. These jobs were fueled by the growth of railroads and irrigated farming. A revolution was under way in Mexico, and the chaos led many Mexicans to flee across the border after 1910. Many immigrants settled in Texas, Arizona, Colorado, and California. Most became farm workers. During the war years, some went to Northern cities to take better-paying factory jobs.

The wartime labor shortage also meant new job choices for women. Women replaced male workers in steel mills, ammunition factories, and assembly lines. Women served as streetcar conductors and elevator operators. The war created few permanent openings for women, but their presence in these jobs gave the public a wider view of their abilities. Women's contributions during the war helped them win the vote.

*Reading* **History**

**D. Recognizing Effects** What groups gained new jobs as a result of the war?

D. Answer African Americans, Mexican Americans, and women

**Now and then**

**THE FLU EPIDEMIC**

In 1918, flu victims often came down with pneumonia and died within a week. Today, bacterial infections such as pneumonia resulting from the flu can be controlled with antibiotics.

The 1998 discovery of the frozen remains of a 1918 flu victim in an Alaskan cemetery may one day lead to a better understanding of the virus. Scientists have found a genetic link between the 1918 flu virus and swine flu, a virus first found in pigs. The Alaskan find may help scientists develop vaccines to protect against future flu outbreaks.

## 4 The Flu Epidemic of 1918

Another result of the war was a deadly flu epidemic that swept the globe in 1918. It killed more than 20 million people on six continents by the time it disappeared in 1919. It had no known cure. Spread around the world by soldiers, the virus took some 500,000 American lives. People tried desperately to protect themselves. Everywhere, schools and other public places shut down to limit the flu's spread.

In the army, more than a quarter of the soldiers caught the disease. In some AEF units, one-third of the troops died. Germans fell victim in even larger numbers than the Allies. World War I brought death and disease to millions. It would also have longer-term effects, as you will read in Section 4.

### Section 3 Assessment

**1. Terms & Names**

**Identify:**

- war bonds
- propaganda
- Espionage Act
- Sedition Act
- Oliver Wendell Holmes
- Great Migration

**2. Taking Notes**

Make a chart like the one below to show reasons for wartime shifts in population.

| | Shift | Reason(s) |
|---|---|---|
| African Americans | | |
| Mexicans | | |

How similar were the two groups' reasons for moving?

**3. Main Ideas**

**a.** What were three ways American families could contribute to the war effort?

**b.** What was the purpose of the Espionage and Sedition Acts? What groups were most affected by them?

**c.** What kinds of new job opportunities did the war create for women and minorities?

**4. Critical Thinking**

**Making Inferences** What were the positive and the negative consequences of American wartime propaganda?

**THINK ABOUT**

- contributions to war effort
- effect on opponents of war and on German-Americans

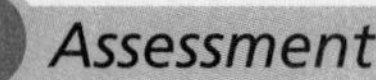

**ACTIVITY OPTIONS**

**SPEECH**

**MATH**

Deliver a **radio broadcast** on the importance of conserving food, or make a **calculation** of the amount of food your class wastes monthly.



### Section 3 Assessment

**1. Terms & Names**

**war bonds,** p. 691
**propaganda,** p. 692
**Espionage Act,** p. 692
**Sedition Act,** p. 692
**Oliver Wendell Holmes,** p. 693
**Great Migration,** p. 693

**2. Taking Notes**

African Americans: Shift: moved from the South to Northern cities; Reason: to gain employment and to escape the bigotry, poverty, and racial violence of the South; Mexicans: Shift: moved to the American Southwest and Northern cities; Reason: to gain jobs and to escape the chaos and violence of the Mexican Revolution.

**3. Main Ideas**

**a.** buy war bonds; plant victory gardens; sew clothes for soldiers **b.** to keep people from undermining the war effort; pacifists, socialists, and other war critics **c.** jobs in factories that made war materials and in jobs previously held by men

**4. Critical Thinking**

Positive: it caused people to support the war; encouraged patriotism; Negative: led to hatred of Germans, foreigners, and war critics.

**ACTIVITY OPTIONS**

 **Alternative Assessment**

- Rubrics for a broadcast, 5.3
- Rubrics for a calculation, 2.2

# The Legacy of World War I

**TERMS & NAMES**
League of Nations
Fourteen Points
Treaty of Versailles
reparations
Red Scare
Palmer raids

**MAIN IDEA**

After the war, Americans were divided over foreign policy and domestic issues.

**WHY IT MATTERS NOW**

The war affected the role the United States played in the world during the rest of the century.

## ONE AMERICAN'S STORY

**Massachusetts Senator Henry Cabot Lodge had favored U.S. entry into the war. However, he opposed President Wilson's idea that the United States join an international organization. The League of Nations was such an organization set up to settle conflicts through negotiation. Lodge warned against joining an alliance that would require the United States to guarantee the freedom of other nations.**

*A VOICE FROM THE PAST*

If we guarantee any country . . . its independence . . . we must [keep] at any cost . . . our word. . . . I wish [the American people] carefully to consider . . . whether they are willing to have the youth of America ordered to war by other nations.

**Henry Cabot Lodge,** speech to the Senate, February 28, 1919

**Speeches like Lodge's helped turn the public against the League and gave President Wilson the most crushing defeat of his political career. In this section, you will learn how the United States and Europe adjusted to the end of the war.**

Senator Henry Cabot Lodge (1850–1924) opposed U.S. entry into the League of Nations.

## 1 Wilson's Fourteen Points

In January 1918, President Wilson spoke to Congress about his goals for peace. This was ten months before the end of the war. His statement became known as the **Fourteen Points** (see page 699). The speech called for smaller military forces, an end to secret treaties, freedom of the seas, and free trade. It also called for changes in national boundaries. Most of these changes gave independence to peoples formerly ruled by Austria-Hungary or the Ottoman Empire.

For Wilson, the fourteenth point mattered most. He called for an association of nations to peacefully settle disputes. This association was to become the League of Nations, which Republicans like Lodge opposed. Wilson firmly believed that acceptance of his Fourteen Points by the warring parties would bring about what he called a "peace without victory."





## SECTION OBJECTIVES

1. To summarize Wilson's Fourteen Points
2. To describe the Treaty of Versailles
3. To identify the reasons for the Red Scare
4. To explain why racial tensions increased in the postwar period

**SKILLBUILDER**

Interpreting Maps: Region, p. 697

**CRITICAL THINKING**

Recognizing Effects, pp. 696, 697
Analyzing Causes, pp. 696, 698
Analyzing Points of View, p. 698

 **Why It Matters Now**
- The Fourteen Points Today, pp. 47–48

## FOCUS & MOTIVATE

### 5-MINUTE WARM-UP

**Recognizing Effects** These questions will help students analyze the effects of World War I.

1. Look at the map on page 697. How many new nations were created?
2. What kinds of problems do you think these new nations will face?

 **Warm-Up Transparency WT24**

## INSTRUCT

### INSTRUCT: OBJECTIVE 1

**Wilson's Fourteen Points**

Key Questions
- What were President Wilson's goals for peace?
- Why was formation of the League of Nations especially important to Wilson?

 **In-Depth Resources: Unit 7**
- Guided Reading, p. 41

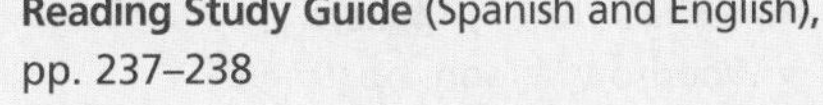

**Reading Study Guide** (Spanish and English), pp. 237–238

 **Geography Transparency GT24**
- The League of Nations, 1919

## RECOMMENDED RESOURCES

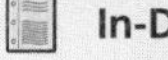

**In-Depth Resources: Unit 7**
- Guided Reading, p. 41
- Building Vocabulary, p. 42
- Primary Source, p. 47
- Reteaching Activity, p. 55
- History Workshop Resources, p. 57

**Reading Study Guide** (Spanish and English), pp. 237–238

**America's History Makers**
- Woodrow Wilson, pp. 97–98

**Why It Matters Now**
- The Fourteen Points Today, pp. 47–48

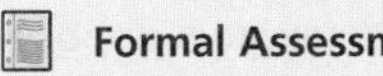

**Formal Assessment**
- Section Quiz, p. 353

**Alternative Assessment**
- Rubrics, 4.1
- Rubrics, 1.2

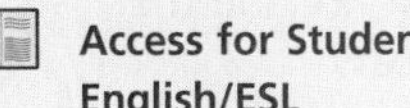

**Access for Students Acquiring English/ESL**
- Guided Reading, p. 162

**Technology Resources**

 **Geography Transparency GT24**
- The League of Nations, 1919

 **Electronic Teacher Tools with Test Maker**

 **ClassZone**
www.mcdougallittell.com

**INSTRUCT: OBJECTIVE 2**

**Treaty of Versailles**

Key Questions

- How were Wilson's goals for peace different from the aims of Britain, France, and Italy?
- What were the key terms of the Treaty of Versailles?
- Why was the treaty controversial?

**In-Depth Resources: Unit 7**
- Primary Source, p. 47

**MORE ABOUT . . .**

**The Treaty of Versailles**

In its final form, the Treaty of Versailles included only about four of Wilson's Fourteen Points. Idealists who had supported Wilson's goals were disappointed, and many of them now denounced the treaty. Others charged that the treaty was too pro-British, or too soft on Germany, or too likely to involve the United States in foreign conflicts. Yet the majority of Americans favored the treaty.

**AMERICA'S HISTORY MAKERS**

**Woodrow Wilson**

Woodrow Wilson, born in Virginia, was the first Southerner to become president since the Civil War. Before entering politics, he was a professor of political science and a university president. Wilson was committed to progressive measures such as banking reform and antitrust regulation. But he refused to support woman suffrage, and he allowed the return of racial segregation in federal agencies. For his efforts at the Paris peace conference, Wilson was awarded the Nobel Peace Prize for 1919.

**Possible Response: If Wilson had been less stiff and unbending, he might have been able to work out a compromise with Lodge and the Republican senators, and the treaty might have been ratified.**

**America's History Makers**
- Woodrow Wilson, pp. 97–98

## 2 Treaty of Versailles

Wilson led the U.S. delegation to the peace conference in France. Though many Europeans considered him a hero, conference leaders did not. The leaders of Britain, France, and Italy did not share Wilson's vision of "peace without victory." They wanted Germany to pay heavily for its part in the war.

The **Treaty of Versailles** (vuhr•SY) forced Germany to accept full blame for the war. Germany was stripped of its colonies and most of its armed forces. It was also burdened with $33 billion in **reparations**—money that a defeated nation pays for the destruction caused by a war. The treaty divided up the empires of Austria-Hungary and the Ottomans. It created Yugoslavia and Czechoslovakia and recognized Poland's independence.

*Reading***History**

**A. Recognizing Effects** How were the Central Powers punished by the Treaty of Versailles?

A. Answer Germany lost its colonies and army. It had to admit war guilt and pay reparations. The Austro-Hungarian and Ottoman Empires were broken up.

Wilson managed to include the League of Nations in the treaty. He firmly believed the League would help to keep the peace. He returned home to seek Senate approval for the treaty. But the Republican-run Senate was dead set against it. Senator Henry Cabot Lodge kept delaying a vote on the treaty.

**AMERICA'S HISTORY MAKERS**

**WOODROW WILSON**

**1856–1924**

A gifted speaker, Woodrow Wilson had a strong sense of duty, and he inspired great loyalty. Yet he could be a harsh judge of others, stiff and unbending in his relations with people. Sculptor Jo Davidson remarked that "He invoked fear and respect . . . but not affection." Though not America's best-loved president, he still commands respect. When historians list the nation's best presidents, Wilson often ranks in the top ten.

**How might Wilson's character have worked against approval of the Treaty of Versailles?**

After weeks of delay, Wilson decided to make his case to the public. In September of 1919, he began a cross-country speaking trip to build support for the League. In about 21 days, he traveled almost 10,000 miles and gave over 30 speeches.

*A VOICE FROM THE PAST*

In the covenant [agreement] of the League of Nations, the moral forces of the world are mobilized . . . . They consent . . . to submit every matter of difference between them to the judgment of mankind, and just so certainly as they do that, . . . war will be pushed out of the foreground of terror in which it has kept the world.

**Woodrow Wilson,** speech in Pueblo, Colorado, on September 25, 1919

Shortly after giving this speech, Wilson collapsed from strain. Later, he suffered a stroke from which he never fully recovered.

Negotiations to get the treaty through Congress continued, but Americans were not eager for more foreign commitments. Lodge and his supporters offered to accept the treaty if major changes were made in the League. Wilson refused to compromise. As a result, the United States did not ratify the treaty. The League of Nations was formed without the United States.

B. Answer Americans did not want more foreign commitments, and Wilson would not compromise on the League of Nations to get the treaty passed.

*Reading***History**

**B. Analyzing Causes** Why didn't the United States ratify the Treaty of Versailles?

The war and the Treaty of Versailles failed to make Europe "safe for democracy." In the next decades, Germany's resentment of the treaty grew. The treaty planted the seeds of World War II, an even more deadly conflict to come.



**ACTIVITY OPTIONS**

**INTERDISCIPLINARY LINK: GOVERNMENT**

**BLOCK SCHEDULING**

**CREATE A CARTOON**

**Class Time** One class period

**Task** Creating a political cartoon about the Treaty of Versailles

**Purpose** To contrast the perspectives of various nations on the outcome of the Paris peace conference

**Supplies Needed**
- Reference material on the Paris peace conference and the Versailles Treaty
- Markers and posterboard

**Activity** Divide students into eight groups, six of which represent Britain, France, Germany, Italy, Poland, and Yugoslavia, and two that represent the United States. Have each group prepare a cartoon expressing the opinion of people within that country on the final treaty. One U.S. group should create a cartoon favoring ratification of the treaty, while the other group uses the cartoon to express opposition to it.

## Postwar Europe, 1919

New nations

GEOGRAPHY SKILLBUILDER **Interpreting Maps**
1. **Region** *What new nations were created after the war?*
2. **Region** *In what part of Europe were most of the new nations located?*

### EFFECTS OF WORLD WAR I ON EUROPE

| IMMEDIATE EFFECTS | LONG-TERM EFFECTS |
|---|---|
| Revolution in Russia | Breakup of empires |
| Allied victory | Formation of League of Nations |
| Destruction in Europe | Resentments leading to World War II |

## 3 Strikes and the Red Scare

The Treaty of Versailles was not the only issue that divided Americans after the war. Shortly after the war ended, the United States experienced a number of labor strikes. For example, in Seattle, Washington, in February 1919, more than 55,000 workers took part in a peaceful general strike. The shutdown paralyzed the city.

Some Americans saw efforts to organize labor unions as the work of radicals, people who favor extreme measures to bring about change. The strikes sparked fears of a communist revolution like the one that toppled the Russian czar. In 1919–1920, this fear created a wave of panic called the **Red Scare** (communists were called *reds*). Public fear was heightened by the discovery of mail bombs sent to government officials. Many believed the bombs were the work of anarchists. Anarchists are radicals who do not believe in any form of government.

In January 1920, Attorney General A. Mitchell Palmer took action. He ordered federal agents and local police to raid the homes and headquarters of suspected radicals. His agents arrested at least 6,000 people in the **Palmer raids.** Without search warrants, agents burst into homes and offices and dragged citizens off to jail.

The Red Scare was not only antiradical but also antiforeign. During the Red Scare, two Italian-born anarchists, Nicola Sacco and Bartolomeo Vanzetti, were arrested for killing two men in an armed robbery in

**Background**
In 1919, police, steelworkers, and coal miners also went on strike.

C. Answer
It resulted in thousands of raids and arrests of suspected radicals.

*Reading* **History**
**C. Recognizing Effects** What resulted from the Red Scare?

Skillbuilder Answers
1. Finland, Estonia, Latvia, Lithuania, Poland, Czechoslovakia, Yugoslavia
2. Eastern Europe



### HISTORY FROM VISUALS

**Reading the Map** Have students compare this map to the one of Europe in 1914 on page 680. Which countries have lost the most territory compared to their 1914 borders? **Answer** Austria-Hungary, Germany, and Russia. What kind of problems might this new structure create in the future? **Possible Response** Countries that lost territory might be resentful and hope to recover it in a future war.

**Extension** Some students could make overhead transparencies of the political boundaries within Europe showing changes between the beginning and end of the 20th century—1914; 1919; 1950; 2000. Let them show these transparencies as overlays in a presentation to the class.

### INSTRUCT: OBJECTIVE 

**Strikes and the Red Scare**
Key Questions
- What were the causes of the Red Scare?
- What groups were most affected by the Red Scare?

### MORE ABOUT . . .

**The Palmer Raids**
The Palmer raids particularly targeted the Socialist Party and the Industrial Workers of the World (IWW), a union for unskilled workers. Both groups had also been attacked under the Espionage and Sedition Acts for opposing the war. The government denied socialist newspapers' mailing permits and canceled the party's public rallies. Government agents raided IWW headquarters and jailed union leaders. Vigilantes who beat or even killed IWW organizers went unpunished. The Palmer raids are considered one of the worst assaults on civil liberties in American history.

### ACTIVITY OPTIONS

### INDIVIDUAL NEEDS

**LESS PROFICIENT READERS**

**Creating a Concept Web** As students have read in the text, the Treaty of Versailles marked the end of World War I and planted the seeds for World War II. Write *Treaty of Versailles* on the board. As they read, ask students to look for important details about the treaty to add to a web. Write their ideas around the central concept.

Treaty of Versailles
- forced Germany to accept blame for the war
- Germany to pay $33 billion in reparations
- created new countries
- not ratified by the United States

**INSTRUCT: OBJECTIVE 4**

**Racial Tensions Increase/ Longing for "Normalcy"**

Key Questions

- What social changes caused racial tensions to increase in the postwar years?
- Why might African-American soldiers have expected less prejudice and discrimination at home after the war?
- Why did Harding's promise of "normalcy" appeal to voters?

## ASSESS & RETEACH

**Setting the Stage** Have students fill in the final sections on the chapter graphic organizer.

 **Formal Assessment**
- Section Quiz, p. 353

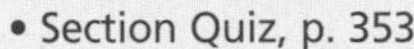

 **Critical Thinking Transparency CT70**
- Setting the Stage

**RETEACHING ACTIVITY**

Have students find at least one cause and one effect for each of these events: signing of Versailles Treaty; Wilson's cross-country speaking trip; the Senate fight over treaty ratification; the Red Scare; the race riots of 1919.

 **In-Depth Resources: Unit 7**
- Reteaching Activity, p. 55

Massachusetts. They claimed they were innocent, but both were found guilty and executed. Their trial attracted worldwide attention.

## 4 Racial Tensions Increase

Americans also saw a rise in racial tensions after the war. Between 1910 and 1920, the Great Migration brought a half million African Americans to northern cities. In the cities where African Americans had settled in large numbers, whites and blacks competed for factory jobs and housing.

On July 2, 1917, tensions erupted into a race riot in East St. Louis, Illinois. The trouble began when blacks were brought in to take the jobs of white union members who had gone on strike. A shooting incident touched off a full-scale riot.

Two years later, African-American soldiers returning from the war found their social plight unchanged. They had fought to make the world "safe for democracy." At home, though, they were still second-class citizens.

Simmering resentments over housing, job competition, and segregation exploded during the summer of 1919. In 25 cities around the country, race riots flared. In Chicago, a black man swimming in Lake Michigan drifted into the white section of a beach. Whites stoned him until he drowned. Thirteen days of rioting followed. Before it ended, 38 people were dead.

*Reading* **History**

**D. Analyzing Causes** How did the war contribute to racial tensions?

**D. Answer** African Americans moved to cities and were resented when they competed with whites for wartime jobs and housing. African-American soldiers had fought for democracy but did not find it at home.

## Longing for "Normalcy"

By the time campaigning began for the 1920 election, Americans felt drained. Labor strikes, race riots, the Red Scare, and the fight over the Versailles Treaty and the League of Nations had worn them out. Voters were ready for a break. Republican candidate Warren G. Harding of Ohio offered them one. His promise to "return to normalcy" appealed to voters. Harding won a landslide victory. In the next chapter, you will learn about American life after his election.

### Section 4 Assessment

**1. Terms & Names**

**Identify:**
- League of Nations
- Fourteen Points
- Treaty of Versailles
- reparations
- Red Scare
- Palmer raids

**2. Taking Notes**

Create a diagram to examine the war's effects on Europe and America.

| Effects of World War I | |
|---|---|
| Europe | United States |
| | |

Which effects were positive and which were negative?

**3. Main Ideas**

a. Why did Germany resent the Treaty of Versailles?

b. Why did Lodge and other Republicans oppose joining the League of Nations?

c. What caused the Red Scare? Who was most affected by it?

**4. Critical Thinking**

**Analyzing Points of View** Why was Wilson unable to get other powers to accept his goals for the peace conference?

**THINK ABOUT**
- conflicting goals
- practicality of Wilson's aims
- attitudes of other nations towards U.S. contributions during the war

**ACTIVITY OPTIONS**

**LANGUAGE ARTS**
**ART**

Imagine that you work for a newspaper. Write an **editorial** about the Palmer raids, or draw a political **cartoon** about the raids.

### Section 4 Assessment

**1. Terms & Names**

**League of Nations,** p. 695
**Fourteen Points,** p. 695
**Treaty of Versailles,** p. 696
**reparations,** p. 696
**Red Scare,** p. 697
**Palmer raids,** p. 697

**2. Taking Notes**

Europe: destruction and millions of deaths; Russian revolution; breakup of German, Austro-Hungarian, and Ottoman empires; creation of new nations; United States: political division; strikes; Red Scare and Palmer raids; job opportunities for African Americans, Mexicans, and women. Answers will vary.

**3. Main Ideas**

a. because it forced Germany to accept blame for the war, and demanded that it pay reparations **b.** because they thought joining the League could force the United States to go to war **c.** fears that strikes and mail bombs were signs of a coming Communist revolution; foreigners and radicals

**4. Critical Thinking**

After all they had endured and lost, "peace without victory" probably seemed too generous and possibly dangerous to the other powers.

**ACTIVITY OPTIONS**

 **Alternative Assessment**
- Rubrics for an editorial, 4.1
- Rubrics for a cartoon, 1.2

# The Fourteen Points

**Setting the Stage** Nine months after the United States entered World War I, President Wilson delivered to Congress a statement of war aims. This statement became known as the "Fourteen Points." In the speech, President Wilson set forth 14 proposals for reducing the risk of war in the future. Numbers have been inserted to help identify the main points, as well as those omitted. **See Primary Source Explorer** 

All the peoples of the world are in effect partners . . . , and for our own part we see very clearly that unless justice be done to others it will not be done to us. The program of the world's peace, therefore, is our program; and that program, . . . as we see it, is this:

[1] Open **covenants**[1] of peace, openly arrived at, after which there shall be no private international understandings of any kind but diplomacy shall proceed always frankly and in the public view.

[2] Absolute freedom of navigation upon the seas . . . in peace and in war. . . .

[3] The removal, so far as possible, of all economic barriers and the establishment of an equality of trade conditions among all the nations. . . .

[4] Adequate guarantees given and taken that national **armaments**[2] will be reduced. . . .

[5] A free, open-minded, and absolutely impartial adjustment of all colonial claims, based upon . . . the principle that . . . the interests of the populations concerned must have equal weight with the . . . claims of the government whose title is to be determined.

[6–13: These eight points deal with specific boundary changes.]

[14] A general association of nations must be formed under specific covenants for the purpose of affording mutual guarantees of political independence and territorial **integrity**[3] to great and small states alike.

*—Woodrow Wilson*

1. **covenants:** binding agreements.
2. **armaments:** weapons and supplies of war.
3. **integrity:** the condition of being whole or undivided; completeness.

*A CLOSER LOOK*

**THE VALUE OF OPENNESS**

The first of Wilson's points attempts to solve one of the problems that caused the outbreak of World War I—agreements between nations arrived at in secret.

**1. How might agreements arrived at in public prevent another world war?**

*A CLOSER LOOK*

**BALANCING CLAIMS**

Wilson frequently appeals to fairness, balance, and impartiality in settling competing claims.

**2. What might be unusual about a leader such as Wilson calling for an impartial adjustment of colonial claims?**

*A CLOSER LOOK*

**LEAGUE OF NATIONS**

Wilson proposes that nations join a formal organization to protect one another.

**3. Why did Wilson believe that such an organization would benefit the world?**

*Interactive Primary Source Assessment*

**1. Main Ideas**

a. Why should diplomacy avoid private dealings and proceed in public view?

b. How might equality of trade be important to keeping the peace?

c. What must nations join together to guarantee?

**2. Critical Thinking**

**Evaluating** The first five points address issues that Wilson believed had caused the war. How successful do you think Wilson's ideas have been in the rest of the 20th century?

**THINK ABOUT**

- other conflicts since World War I
- peacekeeping efforts around the world





## INTERACTIVE PRIMARY SOURCE

**OBJECTIVE**

Students will be able to identify and explain the key points from President Wilson's "Fourteen Points" address to Congress.

 Primary Source Explorer
- *The Fourteen Points*

The Explorer will help students select and produce their own presentations.

Specific information about the document can be found in **A Closer Look.** To learn more about key people and events of the time, students should click on **Life in These Times. What Happened Next** will show the student the impact of the document and tie it to today.

## FOCUS & MOTIVATE

**Analyzing Points of View** Have the students read the opening paragraph of the document. What view does Wilson have of other nations? What role does he see for the United States?

## INSTRUCT

Key Questions
- What point reflects concern about secret alliances? about militarism? about imperialism? about nationalism?
- How is the proposal about a League of Nations related to the above concerns?

*Interactive Primary Source Assessment*

**1. Main Ideas**

a. Diplomacy should proceed in public view so that nations will be aware of the consequences of their actions.

b. If nations trade under equal terms, they are less likely to have economic disputes, which could turn into military disputes.

c. Nations must join together to guarantee that they can remain politically independent and not have their territory taken.

**2. Critical Thinking**

Students may say that Wilson's ideas have not been very successful because after World War I, nations continued to engage in secret dealings, military buildups, and repression of other nations. Other students might say that Wilson's ideas gained more success later with the United Nations and its peacekeeping efforts, arms reduction treaties, and successful movements for national independence.

*A CLOSER LOOK*

1. The alliance system before World War I pulled one country after another into the war. Not every country knew all the conditions of various treaties, which made the situation more unstable.
2. Usually leaders of powerful nations argue for their country's narrow interests. Wilson seems willing to consider the claims of others—specifically the colonial populations.
3. He might have thought that nations would be less likely to go to war if they knew that other nations would intervene to keep peace.

## TERMS & NAMES

1. **militarism,** p. 679
2. **Allies,** p. 680
3. **trench warfare,** p. 680
4. **Zimmermann telegram,** p. 682
5. **American Expeditionary Force,** p. 686
6. **convoy system,** p. 687
7. **propaganda,** p. 692
8. **Great Migration,** p. 693
9. **Treaty of Versailles,** p. 696
10. **Red Scare,** p. 697

## REVIEW QUESTIONS

**Possible Responses**

1. imperialism, nationalism, militarism, and alliances
2. The United States did not want to send soldiers abroad to fight the war.
3. Germany's sinking of the unarmed ship *Lusitania* and the resulting American deaths; Germany's resumption of unrestricted submarine warfare in 1917; the discovery of the Zimmermann telegram
4. They set up the convoy system to escort merchant ships, and they mined the North Sea.
5. It boosted Allied morale and helped Allied forces beat back German advances.
6. Its forces were defeated in the Meuse-Argonne offensive; its navy mutinied; its other allies dropped out; and its Kaiser stepped down.
7. They bought war bonds, conserved food and war materials, made clothing for soldiers, and took jobs in war industries.
8. It passed the Espionage and Sedition Acts, which outlawed antiwar actions and speech, sending hundreds of people to jail.
9. Wilson wanted "peace without victory" and measures to settle international disputes peacefully. His European allies wanted harsh punishment for Germany.
10. The Senate was afraid that if it accepted the treaty and the League of Nations, other countries could force the United States to go to war to settle international disputes.

# Chapter 24 ASSESSMENT

## TERMS & NAMES

Briefly explain the importance of each of the following.

1. militarism
2. Allies
3. trench warfare
4. Zimmermann telegram
5. American Expeditionary Force
6. convoy system
7. propaganda
8. Great Migration
9. Treaty of Versailles
10. Red Scare

## REVIEW QUESTIONS

**War Breaks Out in Europe (pages 679–685)**

1. What were the sources of tension between the European powers that led to war?
2. Why did the United States at first remain neutral in the war between the Allies and the Central Powers?
3. What brought the United States into the war on the Allied side?

**America Joins the Fight (pages 686–690)**

4. How did the Allies fight the German U-boat threat?
5. How did U.S. entry into the war affect the Allies?
6. What led Germany to agree to an armistice?

**Life on the Home Front (pages 691–694)**

7. How did U.S. civilians aid the war effort?
8. How did Congress contribute to increased prejudice and intolerance on the home front?

**The Legacy of World War I (pages 695–699)**

9. How did Wilson's goals for the peace conference differ from those of his European allies?
10. Why did the Senate reject the Treaty of Versailles?

## CRITICAL THINKING

**1. USING YOUR NOTES**

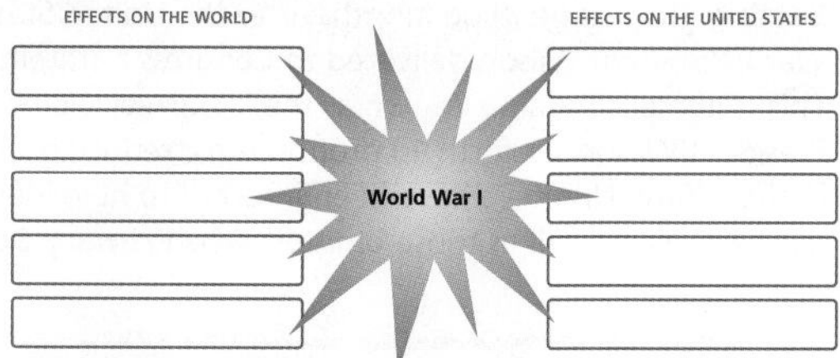


Using your chart, answer the questions below.

a. Were the effects of the war greater in Europe or the United States?
b. What political effects did the war have on the United States?
c. How did the war affect African-American civilians?

**2. APPLYING CITIZENSHIP SKILLS**

Are limitations on freedom of speech justified by war? Explain your opinion.

**3. THEME: AMERICA IN THE WORLD**

How did Wilson's view of the role the United States should play in world affairs compare with Theodore Roosevelt's view of America's role?

**4. ANALYZING LEADERSHIP**

Do you think Wilson's refusal to compromise to get the Treaty of Versailles through Congress was a good decision? Why?

**Interact *with* History**

How accurately did you predict the ways in which American citizens might support the war effort?

## VISUAL SUMMARY

### World War I

**War Breaks Out in Europe**

When the Allies and the Central Powers went to war in Europe, the United States reluctantly joined the Allies.

**America Joins the Fight**

Millions of U.S. soldiers and civilian volunteers went abroad and helped the Allies win the war.

**Life on the Home Front**

The war required Americans to sacrifice many things, even political freedoms. The war also brought new jobs.

**The Legacy of World War I**

The war broke up European empires and left lasting social changes in the United States.

## CRITICAL THINKING

**Possible Responses**

1. **USING YOUR NOTES** **a.** in Europe **b.** The United States became more politically repressive, tolerating racial and ethnic violence and limiting freedom of speech. **c.** The war encouraged African Americans to move North for jobs, despite discrimination.
2. **APPLYING CITIZENSHIP SKILLS** Students may say that limitations are necessary during wartime so as not to endanger the country or its soldiers, or that wartime limitations are dangerous because they keep people from expressing valid opinions about government policies.
3. **THEME: AMERICA IN THE WORLD** Wilson viewed the United States as a peacemaker that would fight only for ideals. Roosevelt wanted the United States to act more forcefully.
4. **ANALYZING LEADERSHIP** Students might say that it was a sign of weakness because the Treaty of Versailles did not pass, or that it showed strength of character because he did not compromise.

**Interact *with* History** Answers will vary. Be sure students include the predictions made at the beginning of the chapter.

700 CHAPTER 24

## HISTORY SKILLS

### 1. INTERPRETING MAPS: Movement

Study the map. Answer the questions.

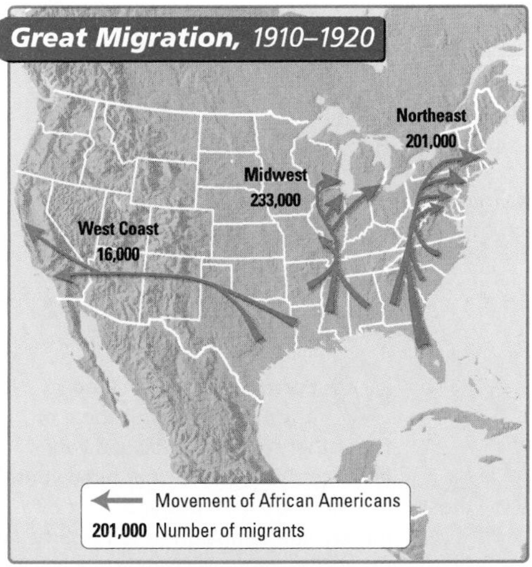


Source: *Historical Statistics of the United States*

**Basic Map Elements**

a. What is the subject of the map?

b. What do the arrows indicate?

**Interpreting the Map**

c. In what general directions did migration take place?

d. Of these directions, in which direction did the fewest African Americans move?

### 2. INTERPRETING PRIMARY SOURCES

This famous World War I poster shows Uncle Sam, a national symbol. Study the poster and answer the questions.

a. How does Uncle Sam's clothing show that he stands for the United States?

b. What was the purpose of this propaganda poster?

I WANT YOU
FOR U.S. ARMY
NEAREST RECRUITING STATION


## ALTERNATIVE ASSESSMENT

### 1. INTERDISCIPLINARY ACTIVITY: Music

**Analyzing Music of the War Years** During World War I, songs such as "Johnny I Hardly Knew You" protested the war, while "Over There" and "Pack Up Your Troubles" cheered the troops. Analyze the lyrics of a wartime song, examining its attitude toward the war.

### 2. COOPERATIVE LEARNING ACTIVITY

**Negotiating a Treaty** Working in seven groups, do research on the Paris peace conference that created the Treaty of Versailles. Have each group represent one of these nations: Germany, France, Britain, the United States, Italy, Japan, Poland. Hold a mock conference in which delegates present their goals and debate resolutions to be included in the treaty. Compare your treaty with the actual historical results.

- Identify the national interests of your country for the postwar settlement.
- Make a list of goals and issues you want discussed at the conference.
- Choose a chief spokesperson for your group.

### 3.  PRIMARY SOURCE EXPLORER

**Planning Peace** Shortly after America's entry into World War I, President Wilson was planning for peace. He wanted to reduce the risk of war in the future. For this purpose, he came up with his Fourteen Points. Using the CD-ROM, the library, and the Internet, find out more about the Fourteen Points.

Create your own plan for peace using the suggestions below.

- Draw up a plan for peace that might apply to your classroom or community.
- Adapt ideas from the Fourteen Points that you think will work for your classroom or community.
- Decide how peace can be enforced in the classroom and in wider communities.
- Discuss whether working to establish peace might involve setting restrictions on personal liberty.

### 4. HISTORY PORTFOLIO

**Option 1** Review your section and chapter assessment activities. Select one that you think is your best work. Then use comments made by your teacher or classmates to improve your work and add it to your portfolio.

**Option 2** Review the details that you listed for What Do You Want to Know? on page 678. Then write a short report in which you explain the detailed information that you acquired. Add your answers to your portfolio.



## ALTERNATIVE ASSESSMENT

1. INTERDISCIPLINARY ACTIVITY: Music
**Analyses should**
- begin with an introduction and have a thesis.
- specifically highlight song lyrics.
- present supporting reasons for the analysis.
- clearly draw a conclusion that supports the thesis.
- use standard grammar, spelling, and punctuation.

2. COOPERATIVE LEARNING ACTIVITY
**Treaties should**
- reflect the use of a problem-solving technique.
- focus on a compromise that would ensure peace.
- identify the positions of each of the nations in the conference.
- support positions with evidence or logic.

3.  PRIMARY SOURCE EXPLORER
**Peace plans should**
- reflect the use of a problem-solving technique.
- adapt ideas from the Fourteen Points.
- reflect an understanding of the community and the problems it faces.

4. HISTORY PORTFOLIO

 **Option 1 Revised section or chapter assessment activities should**
- address teacher and peer responses to the selected work.
- solve problems present in the first versions of the work.

**Option 2 Short reports should**
- answer questions about waging "world war."
- use evidence to develop and support ideas.
- cite sources of information.
- use standard grammar, spelling, and punctuation.

 **Critical Thinking Transparency CT72**
- Visual Summary

 **Formal Assessment**
- Chapter Test, Forms A and B, pp. 354–361

## HISTORY SKILLS

**Possible Responses**

1. INTERPRETING MAPS
**Basic Map Elements**
**a.** the Great Migration
**b.** the movement of African Americans
**Interpreting the Map**
**c.** to the Northeast, Midwest, and West Coast
**d.** to the West Coast

2. INTERPRETING PRIMARY SOURCES
**a.** He is dressed in red, white, and blue—the colors of the U.S. flag. On his hat is a white star on a blue background, like the stars on the flag.
**b.** Its purpose was to encourage young men to join the army by making them feel it was their duty.

## HISTORY WORKSHOP

**OBJECTIVE**

Students make a Liberty Bonds poster and write a patriotic speech to understand how the Committee on Public Information worked to build support for the war effort.

 **BLOCK SCHEDULING**

## PROCEDURE

Gather the materials listed in the "Toolbox." Divide the class into groups of four or five. Then review the steps for making the Liberty Bond poster and for preparing a persuasive speech.

 **In-Depth Resources: Unit 7**
- History Workshop Resources, p. 57

### HISTORY FROM VISUALS

**Interpreting the Poster** Have students point out the ways the poster conveys a positive and patriotic message through both words and images. **Possible Responses** Words suggest that buying war bonds will "help America's sons," or soldiers, and lead the nation to victory. The image shows a calm, motherly person reaching out to viewers in a welcoming and encouraging way.



# Campaign for Liberty Bonds

To rally Americans to support World War I, the government set up the Committee on Public Information (CPI). This agency called on creative individuals to join "the world's greatest adventure in advertising." Speakers gave patriotic speeches in theaters, hotels, and restaurants. Artists designed posters persuading Americans to buy Liberty Bonds. These loans to the government helped fund the war effort. Liberty Bonds were actually sold through four Liberty Loan drives in 1917 and 1918.

ACTIVITY Create a poster to help the government raise money for World War I. In addition, write and present a patriotic speech that wins public support of the war.

**TOOLBOX**

Each group will need:

| | |
|---|---|
| poster board | drawing paper |
| colored markers | glue |
| pencils | scissors |

Posters such as this one appealed to patriotism and love of family to sell Liberty Bonds.

### STEP BY STEP

**1** **Form an imaginary ad agency.** Meet with three or four other students to discuss your latest contract: The CPI has hired your agency to create a poster as part of a nationwide campaign to sell Liberty Bonds and promote World War I. Your group will:
- do research on Liberty Bonds
- design and create a poster advertising Liberty Bonds
- write and deliver a "pep talk" persuading people to buy Liberty Bonds

**2** **Research Liberty Bonds.** Look on the Internet, in this chapter, or in books about World War I to find out more about Liberty Bonds and to see actual posters. As you look over the posters, think about the feelings the posters bring out. What images and words seem most powerful or persuasive?



### RECOMMENDED RESOURCES

**BOOKS FOR THE TEACHER**

Farwell, Byron. ***Over There.*** New York: W.W. Norton, 1999.

***Our American Century: End of Innocence, 1910–1920***. Alexandria, VA: Time-Life, 1998.

**VIDEOS**

***Woodrow Wilson: The Fight for a League of Nations.*** Educational Video Network, 1991. Uses newsreel footage to trace Wilson's fight for the League of Nations.

***World War I.*** CBS News, 1994. A 9-hour, 11-part series tracing the war from beginning to end.

**BOOKS FOR THE STUDENTS**

Clare, John D., ed. ***First World War.*** Orlando, FL: Gulliver/Harcourt Brace, 1995.

Dolan, Edward F. ***America in World War I.*** Brookfield, CT: Millbrook, 1996.

Jantzen, Steven. ***Hooray for Peace, Hurrah for War.*** New York: Facts on File, 1991.

**3** **Choose a theme for your poster.** Persuading people to buy Liberty Bonds means that you need to show that winning World War I is important. One way is to appeal to people's emotions. For example, the poster can appeal to their sense of fear, pride, or love of family.

**4** **Sketch out your idea.** Write out a slogan and choose images based on the theme of your poster. Make sure your words and pictures communicate the same feeling and message. Draw an outline of the images and the letters. Then cut both the letters and images out. Be sure that they're large enough to be seen from several yards away.

**5** **Create the poster.** Decide where the art and writing will appear. Experiment with the arrangement of the art and the writing. Move them around. Do not overwhelm your viewers with too many images or too many words. Use vivid, patriotic colors for your poster.

**6** **Create a bulletin board display.** Pin or tape your poster on the wall, along with the posters of the other groups. As you examine the other posters, compare and contrast your poster with the others.

## WRITE AND SPEAK

**Write a patriotic speech.** As a group, write a two-minute "pep talk" persuading people to buy Liberty Bonds and to support the soldiers fighting overseas. Include reasons why the war is worth fighting. Each group member should be prepared to deliver the speech, using the poster you made as a visual aid.

## HELP DESK

For related information, see pages 691–692 in Chapter 24.

### Researching Your Project

- *World War I* by Gail Stewart
- *Causes and Consequences of World War I* by Stewart Ross

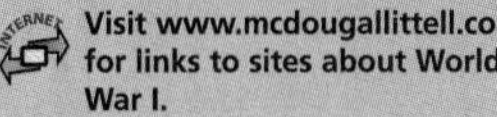

**Visit www.mcdougallittell.com for links to sites about World War I.**

### Did You Know?

The CPI used about 75,000 lecturers. They gave around 755,190 speeches to about 300 million people in 5,000 towns.

Even children were moved by advertising slogans to help fund the war: "Lick a stamp and lick the kaiser." Children filled books with war stamps, each worth 25 cents. These stamps were then converted into government bonds.

Even President Wilson helped to raise money for the war effort. He sold wool from sheep raised on the White House lawn.

### REFLECT & ASSESS

- **What aspects of your poster do you think will inspire people to buy Liberty Bonds?**
- **How well does your speech inspire patriotic feeling about the war?**
- **Which do you think is a more powerful means of persuasion—your poster or your speech?**



## MORE ABOUT . . .

**Liberty Bonds**

During the Liberty Loan Campaigns, composer John Philip Sousa wrote "Liberty Bond March." Movie stars Douglas Fairbanks and Mary Pickford toured the country raising millions of dollars for Liberty Bonds. Americans all over the United States attended bond rallies. One noon-hour rally on the steps of the New York Public Library featured a musical-comedy star whose English fiancé had just been killed on the Western Front. The crowd at this rally bought $85,000 worth of Liberty Bonds.

## MORE ABOUT . . .

**Government Bonds**

Today, Americans continue to invest in their government by buying bonds. Many Americans buy savings bonds and other kinds of bonds from the federal government. Some bonds provide money to banks to lend to home buyers for mortgages or are used to support such public works as the construction of dams or power plants. Local governments also sell bonds to raise money for building schools and other public projects.

## REFLECT & ASSESS

1. Student posters may have symbols or words that inspire patriotism, remind viewers of the reasons that bonds are needed, or suggest the dangers American soldiers face fighting the war.
2. Students may want to examine their speeches for phrases that remind the listener of the reasons Americans are fighting in this war, of their grievances against Germany, and of their feelings of loyalty and love toward the United States.
3. Have students identify the strengths and limitations of each form of communication.

## STANDARDS FOR EVALUATION

### HISTORY WORKSHOP

**Posters should**

- appeal to people's emotions.
- state clearly what people should do to help.
- communicate a single message in both words and pictures.

### WRITE AND SPEAK

**Speeches should**

- have a clear and simple message.
- give reasons why buying bonds is important and necessary.
- elicit patriotic feelings.
- tell the audience what action the speaker wants them to take.

# UNIT 8

## Depression, War, and Recovery
## 1919–1960



### BEFORE YOU READ

#### Previewing Unit 8

Unit 8 describes great changes that occur as the United States moves from economic boom to depression, from an uneasy peace to a second world war. The nation prospers during the "Roaring Twenties." But the prosperity of the 1920s does not last, and the Great Depression challenges American resources. New Deal legislation changes the role of government in American life. The United States joins World War II after Japan bombs Pearl Harbor, and Americans make great sacrifices to win the war. During the 1950s, the United States enjoys prosperity once more but is embroiled in a cold war with the Soviet Union and lives under the threat of nuclear destruction.

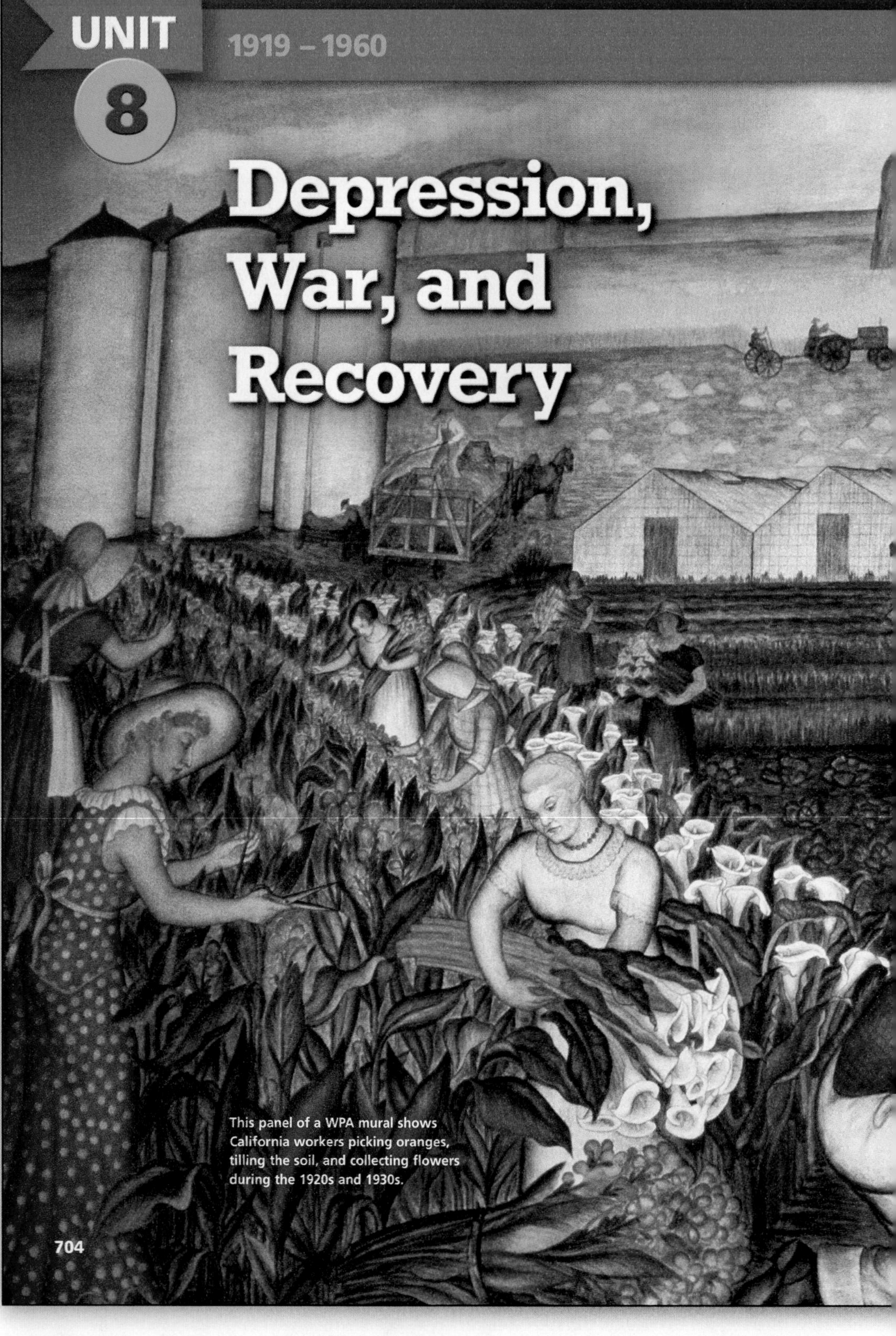


This panel of a WPA mural shows California workers picking oranges, tilling the soil, and collecting flowers during the 1920s and 1930s.

"The test of our progress . . . is whether we provide enough for those who have too little."
—Franklin Delano Roosevelt
CALIFORNIA ORANGES
CALIFORNIA ORANGES
CALIFORNIA
CALIFORNIA ORANGES
NRA


705

## HISTORY FROM VISUALS

**Interpreting the Painting** Tell students that the painting shown here is a 1934 fresco by California artist Maxine Albro. She painted the fresco, called *California,* in the Coit Tower in San Francisco as part of a WPA project. Twenty-six artists and 19 assistants worked to create more than 3,000 square feet of murals in the tower. Albro was assigned the subject "agriculture." Albro remembers visiting greenhouses near San Francisco and the the vineyards of Sonoma County as part of her research. The figures in her mural include some of the other artists working on the Coit Tower project.

Ask students what impression of California the mural creates. Why might this impression have been important during the time of economic hardship when the painting was created? **Possible Response** The painting portrays California as a land of plenty. This vision may have given people hope during hard times.

**Extension** To find reproductions of Coit Tower murals, students can visit www.mcdougallittell.com

## CHAPTER 25 PLANNING GUIDE

# The Roaring Twenties 1919–1929

| | CHAPTER OVERVIEW | COPYMASTERS | TECHNOLOGY |
|---|---|---|---|
| **CHAPTER RESOURCES** | The chapter discusses the decade of the 1920s, which began as a "return to normalcy" but in fact saw substantial changes in American business, technology, consumerism, and roles for women and African Americans. It also describes the Harlem Renaissance, the Lost Generation, and the emergence of mass culture. | **In-Depth Resources: Unit 8**<br>• Tracing Themes: Science and Technology, p. 2<br>• Building Vocabulary, p. 6<br>**Interdisciplinary Projects,** pp. 145–150 | **Primary Source Explorer**<br>**Electronic Teacher Tools**<br>**Power Presentations CD-ROM**<br>**Chapter Summaries on CD** (English and Spanish)<br>**America's Music CD** |
| **SECTION 1 The Business of America pp. 709–712** | **KEY IDEAS**<br>• Warren G. Harding's administration is marred by scandal.<br>• As president, Calvin Coolidge supports laissez-faire economics and isolationism.<br>• The assembly line revolutionizes manufacturing, and installment buying encourages consumerism. | **In-Depth Resources: Unit 8**<br>• Setting the Stage, p. 1<br>• Guided Reading, p. 3<br>• Skillbuilder Practice, p. 7<br>• Reteaching Activity, p. 15<br>**Economics in History**<br>• Understanding the Stock Market, p. 25<br>**Outline Map Activities**<br>• Routes of Air Mail Delivery, 1929, pp. 49–50 | **Warm-Up Transparency WT25**<br>**Humanities Transparency HT49**<br>• Political Cartoon: Coolidge Plays the Saxophone<br>**Critical Thinking Transparency CT73**<br>• Setting the Stage<br>**ClassZone:** www.mcdougallittell.com |
| **SECTION 2 Changes in Society pp. 713–716** | • Fads and dances reflect the youth culture of the Roaring Twenties, and new job opportunities open for women.<br>• Prohibition bans the sale of alcohol, but bootleg liquor is sold in speakeasies.<br>• American society faces deep economic and social divisions. | **In-Depth Resources: Unit 8**<br>• Setting the Stage, p. 1<br>• Guided Reading, p. 4<br>• Reteaching Activity, p. 16<br>**America's History Makers**<br>• Edna St. Vincent Millay, pp. 99–100 | **Warm-Up Transparency WT25**<br>**Critical Thinking Transparency CT73**<br>• Setting the Stage<br>**Critical Thinking Transparency CT74**<br>• Cause and Effect: Social Changes in the 1920s<br>**ClassZone:** www.mcdougallittell.com |
| **SECTION 3 The Jazz Age and the Harlem Renaissance pp. 717–723** | • Americans use their increasing leisure time to enjoy radio, movies, and spectator sports.<br>• The Harlem Renaissance is a flowering of African-American culture.<br>• Disillusioned by war and materialism, some writers become known as the Lost Generation. | **In-Depth Resources: Unit 8**<br>• Setting the Stage, p. 1<br>• Guided Reading, p. 5<br>• Geography Application, pp. 8–9<br>• Primary Sources, pp. 10–11<br>• Literature Selection, pp. 12–14<br>• Reteaching Activity, p. 17<br>**America's History Makers**<br>• Duke Ellington, pp. 101–102<br>**Why It Matters Now,** pp. 49–50 | **Warm-Up Transparency WT25**<br>**Humanities Transparency HT50**<br>• *Aspiration* by Aaron Douglas<br>**Geography Transparency GT25**<br>• America's Increase in Leisure Time, 1890–1920<br>**Critical Thinking Transparency CT75**<br>• Visual Summary |

Pupil's Edition | Copymaster | Overhead Transparency | Audio Library | CD-ROM | Internet

## ASSESSMENT

Chapter Assessment, pp. 724–725

**Formal Assessment**
- Chapter Tests, Forms A and B, pp. 367–374

**Alternative Assessment Book**

**Electronic Teacher Tools with Test Maker**

**Section Assessment,** p. 712

**Formal Assessment**
- Section Quiz, p. 364

**Alternative Assessment Book**
- Rubrics for a diagram, 1.3
- Rubrics for an advertisement, 4.9

**Electronic Teacher Tools with Test Maker**

**Section Assessment,** p. 716

**Formal Assessment**
- Section Quiz, p. 365

**Alternative Assessment Book**
- Rubrics for a poster, 1.1
- Rubrics for a song, 4.8

**Electronic Teacher Tools with Test Maker**

**Section Assessment,** p. 721

**Formal Assessment**
- Section Quiz, p. 366

**Alternative Assessment Book**
- Rubrics for a trading card, 1.7
- Rubrics for a home page, 5.1

**Electronic Teacher Tools with Test Maker**

## CUSTOMIZING FOR INDIVIDUAL NEEDS

### Students Acquiring English/ESL

**Reading Study Guide** (English and Spanish), pp. 241–248

**Access for Students Acquiring English/ESL: Spanish Translations,** pp. 166–171

**Chapter Summaries on CD** (English and Spanish)

### Less Proficient Readers

**Reading Study Guide** (English and Spanish), pp. 241–248

**Chapter Summaries on CD** (English and Spanish)

### Gifted and Talented Students

**In-Depth Resources: Unit 8**
- Enrichment Activity, p. 18

**America's History Makers**
- Edna St. Vincent Millay, pp. 99–100
- Duke Ellington, pp. 101–102

## CROSS-CURRICULAR CONNECTIONS

### Culture

Bloom, Harold (designer). ***Black American Poets and Dramatists of the Harlem Renaissance.*** Chelsea House, 1994. Anthology with biographical information about some of the great writers of the United States.

### Humanities: Music

Awmiller, Craig. ***This House on Fire: The Story of the Blues.*** New York: Watts, 1996. The musician-author portrays the blues and the great blues artists from the early 1900s to the 1960s.

### Popular Culture

McKissack, Patricia. ***Black Diamond: The Story of the Negro Baseball Leagues.*** Madison, WI: Demco, 1995. Richly detailed, enjoyable history of the players, the teams, and their game.

### Science

Szabo, Corinne. ***Sky Pioneer: A Photobiography of Ameila Earhart.*** Washington: National Geographic, 1997. Brief, heavily illustrated biography of the famous flier.

### Interdisciplinary Projects, pp. 145–150

- Math: Analyzing Statistics
- Science: How Airplanes Fly
- Language Arts: Advertising in the 1920s
- Music: Jazz

### Literature

Levine, Gail Carson. ***Dave at Night.*** New York: HarperCollins, 1999. When young Dave runs away from the Hebrew Home for Boys, he becomes a part of the world of the Harlem Renaissance.

Lindbergh, Charles. ***The Spirit of St. Louis.*** New York: Scribner, 1998. Pulitzer-Prize winning memoir written in 1953.

Lindbergh, Reeve. ***Under a Wing: A Memoir.*** New York: Simon & Schuster, 1998. A funny, lyrical, and observant memoir by the youngest daughter of Charles and Anne Morrow Lindbergh.

### McDougal Littell *The Language of Literature*

- Gwendolyn Brooks. "Speech to the Young" (poetry)
- Langston Hughes. "Mother to Son" (poetry)
- James Weldon Johnson. "Lift Every Voice and Sing" (song)
- Anne Morrow Lindbergh. "Diary Entry" (memoir)

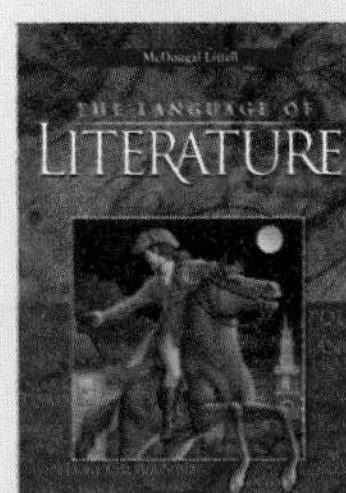


- Reeve Lindbergh. "Flying" (memoir)
- Edna St. Vincent Millay. "Ballad of the Harp Weaver" (poetry)
- Dorothy Parker. "The Choice" (poetry)
- Carl Sandburg. "Jazz Fantasia" (poetry)

## ENRICHMENT ACTIVITIES

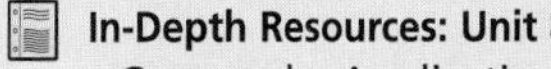

**Pupil's Edition, pp. 706–725**
**Interact with History,** p. 707
**Geography in History,** pp. 722–723

**In-Depth Resources: Unit 8**
- Geography Application: The Historic Flight of "Lucky Lindy," pp. 8–9
- Primary Source, p. 10
- Primary Source, p. 11
- Literature Selection: Poetry by Langston Hughes, pp. 12–14

**America's History Makers**
- Edna St. Vincent Millay, pp. 99–100
- Duke Ellington, pp. 101–102

**America's Music CD**

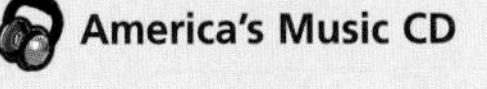
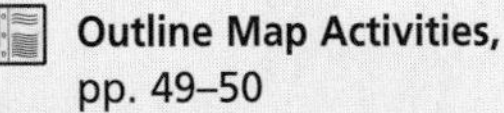

**Outline Map Activities,** pp. 49–50

**Why It Matters Now,** pp. 49–50

**LESSON PLAN OPTIONS (50-MINUTE PERIOD)** (TE) = Teacher's Edition (PE) = Pupil's Edition

| | TEACHER-DIRECTED ACTIVITIES<br>Class Time: 15 minutes | STUDENT-CENTERED ACTIVITIES<br>Class Time: 25 minutes | INDIVIDUAL ACTIVITIES<br>Class Time: 10 minutes |
|---|---|---|---|
| **DAY 1**<br>Introduction<br>pp. 706–708 | **Presentation Options**<br>• Begin with a class discussion of the picture on p. 706 **(PE)**.<br>• Lead a class discussion on the "What Do You Know?" question in Setting the Stage, p. 708. Then introduce the graphic organizer for the chapter **(PE)**. | **Options for Cooperative Learning**<br>• Have student groups discuss the Interact with History questions, p. 707 **(PE)**.<br>• Have student groups respond to the "What Do You Want to Know?" question in Setting the Stage, p. 708 **(PE)**. | **Head Start on Homework Options**<br>• Have students skim Section 1 Main Idea, Why It Matters Now, Terms & Names, and the main headings, p. 709 **(PE)**.<br>• Have students begin Guided Reading activity and Building Vocabulary sheet. |
| **DAY 2**<br>Section 1<br>pp. 709–712 | **Presentation Options**<br>• Begin with the 5-Minute Warm-Up, p. 709 **(TE)**.<br>• Review the Section 1 Main Idea, Why It Matters Now, and Terms & Names, p. 709 **(PE)**.<br>• Lead the students through the Skillbuilder Mini-Lesson: Making Generalizations, p. 710 **(TE)**. | **Options for Cooperative Learning**<br>• Divide students into groups to work on the Interdisciplinary Link, Popular Culture: Americans and Their Automobiles, p. 711 **(TE)**.<br>• Have student pairs work together to complete one of the Activity Options in the Section 1 Assessment, p. 712 **(PE)**. | **Head Start on Homework Options**<br>• Have students begin working on Section 1 Assessment, p. 712 **(PE)**.<br>• Have students begin working on the Taking Notes question for Section 2 Assessment, p. 716 **(PE)**. |
| **DAY 3**<br>Section 2<br>pp. 713–716 | **Presentation Options**<br>• Begin with the 5-Minute Warm-Up, p. 713 **(TE)**.<br>• Choose 5 key questions for Objectives 1–4 to discuss with the class, pp. 713–716 **(TE)**. | **Options for Cooperative Learning**<br>• Divide students into groups to work on the Critical Thinking Activity, p. 715 **(TE)**.<br>• Have student pairs work together to complete one of the Activity Options in the Section 2 Assessment, p. 716 **(PE)**. | **Head Start on Homework Options**<br>• Have students begin working on Section 2 Assessment, p. 716 **(PE)**.<br>• Have students complete the Reading History questions for Section 2, pp. 713–716 **(PE)**. |
| **DAY 4**<br>Section 3<br>pp. 717–723 | **Presentation Options**<br>• Begin with the 5-Minute Warm-Up, p. 717 **(TE)**.<br>• Choose 5 key questions for Objectives 1–4 to discuss with the class, pp. 717–720 **(TE)**.<br>• Lead the students through the Geography in History feature, pp. 722–723 **(TE)**. | **Options for Cooperative Learning**<br>• Divide students into groups and have them complete the Geography in History questions, pp. 722–723 **(PE)**.<br>• Have student pairs work together to complete one of the Activity Options in the Section 3 Assessment, p. 721 **(PE)**. | **Head Start on Homework Options**<br>• Have students complete the Setting the Stage graphic organizer for the chapter, p. 708 **(PE)**.<br>• Have students begin working on the Chapter Assessment, pp. 724–725 **(PE)**.<br>• Prepare for Chapter Test<br>**Formal Assessment,** pp. 367–374 |

TEACHER-TESTED ACTIVITY James Sorenson, Chippewa Middle School, Des Plaines, Illinois

## TALKING ABOUT THE TWENTIES

**Class Time** One class period

**Task** Expressing opinions about the 1920s

**Purpose** To express and support statements of opinion about people and events of the 1920s

**Supplies Needed**

- Writing paper and pencils
- Pink, yellow, and green index cards or construction paper

**Activity** Based on the information in the chapter, ask students to write strong statements of opinion such as these: (1) Harding was a great president; (2) Andrew Mellon was right; Congress should lower taxes; (3) The president is to blame for corruption in government. Give each student three index cards of different colors. On the pink card, have students write, "I disagree," on the yellow card, "I am not sure," and on the green card, "I agree." Have students raise the appropriate card as you read their statements. After reading each statement, have two or three students explain and defend their opinions to the class.

## BLOCK SCHEDULING — LESSON PLAN OPTIONS (90-MINUTE PERIOD)

### DAY 1

**Interact with History,** p. 707
**Class Time** 20 minutes

Options for pacing and variety:

- Role-Playing Have students imagine they are living in the early 1920s. Divide the class into groups of three. Let each student in a group pick one of the inventions in the Interact with History illustration and explain to others in the group how this invention might affect daily life. **Class Time** 15 minutes

**Setting the Stage,** p. 708
**Class Time** 20 minutes

Options for pacing and variety:

- Time Saver For a homework assignment, have students write two or three sentences explaining why they think the decade was called the Roaring Twenties. Have them record their responses along with "What Do You Want to Know?" questions in their notebooks. **Class Time** 5 minutes

**Section 1,** pp. 709–712
**Class Time** 50 minutes

Options for pacing and variety:

- History on Film Extend students' knowledge of Charles Lindbergh by viewing *Lindbergh's Great Race.* Churchill, 1996. **Class Time** 45 minutes
- Time Saver Assign the Main Ideas questions in the Section Assessment as a homework assignment. **Class Time** 5 minutes

### DAY 2

**Section 2,** pp. 713–716
**Class Time** 45 minutes

Options for pacing and variety

- Time Saver Have students prepare the Geography in History feature on pages 722–723 as a homework assignment. Have students bring in written responses to the Connect to Geography and Connect to History questions. **Class Time** 5 minutes
- Internet Extend students' background knowledge of the Roaring Twenties by visiting www.mcdougallittell.com **Class Time** 20 minutes

**Section 3,** pp. 717–723
**Class Time** 50 minutes

Options for pacing and variety

- Peer Teaching Have student pairs read aloud the poem by Langston Hughes in Interpreting Primary Sources on page 725. Have them share their reactions to the poem with each other and the class. **Class Time** 15 minutes
- Time Saver Have students complete their Read and Take Notes charts for the chapter as a homework assignment. **Class Time** 15 minutes

**Chapter 25 Assessment,** pp. 724–725
**Class Time** 40 minutes

Options for pacing and variety:

- Peer Evaluation Have student pairs answer the Critical Thinking questions from the Chapter Assessment. Then have them make up one additional Critical Thinking question to pose to the class. **Class Time** 20 minutes
- Peer Teaching As an alternative assessment, have groups of students complete the Technology Activity on page 725. **Class Time** 40 minutes

## CHAPTER 25 OBJECTIVE

The student will identify advances in American technology during the 1920s and evaluate the far-reaching effects of those technological advances on American business and culture.

# The Roaring Twenties 1919–1929

Section 1 **The Business of America**
Section 2 **Changes in Society**
Section 3 **The Jazz Age and the Harlem Renaissance**

### HISTORY FROM VISUALS

**Interpreting the Illustration** Ask students to look at the illustration and point out specific ways in which the clothing, hairstyles, and activity of the people illustrated differ from those of people in illustrations from previous time periods. **Possible Responses** The young woman's hair and dress are much shorter and much less restrictive; she and the band are engaged in a lively dance that is very different from anything seen in previous chapters.

**Extension** Ask students to find out when *Life* magazine began publishing. Then discuss how a national magazine such as *Life* helped to spread new ideas, fashions, and trends. Ask students how they learn about new fads.

The carefree spirit of the Roaring Twenties is captured on this magazine cover from 1926.

706

### CRITICAL THINKING ACTIVITY

**Making Inferences** Ask students what they can infer about the life of the young people in the illustration. For example, are they poor, rich, or middle class? In what sort of place might they be dancing? Ask students what evidence in the picture they might use to back up their inferences.

**Class Time** 10 minutes

### RECOMMENDED RESOURCES

**BOOKS FOR THE TEACHER**

Dumenil, Lynn. ***The Modern Temper: American Culture and Society in the 1920s.*** New York: Hill & Wang, 1995. The author argues cogently that issues arising in the 1920s are still important.

Giovanni, Nikki, ed. ***Shimmy Shimmy Shimmy Like My Sister Kate: Looking at the Harlem Renaissance through Poems.*** New York: Holt, 1996. Poems by 23 writers with commentary by Giovanni.

Pegram, Thomas R. ***Battling Demon Rum: The Struggle for a Dry America, 1800–1933.*** Chicago: Ivan R. Dee, 1998. A thorough and engrossing history of American attitudes toward alcohol.

**SOFTWARE**

***Women's Rights . . . The Story So Far.*** New Multimedia. CD-ROM. Includes 650 articles, 350 photographs, 21 biographies.

**VIDEO**

***Progressives, Populists, and Reform in America (1890–1917).*** Guidance Associates. Compares historical and present-day reformers.

**INTERNET**

For more about the Roaring Twenties, visit www.mcdougallittell.com

## Interact *with* History

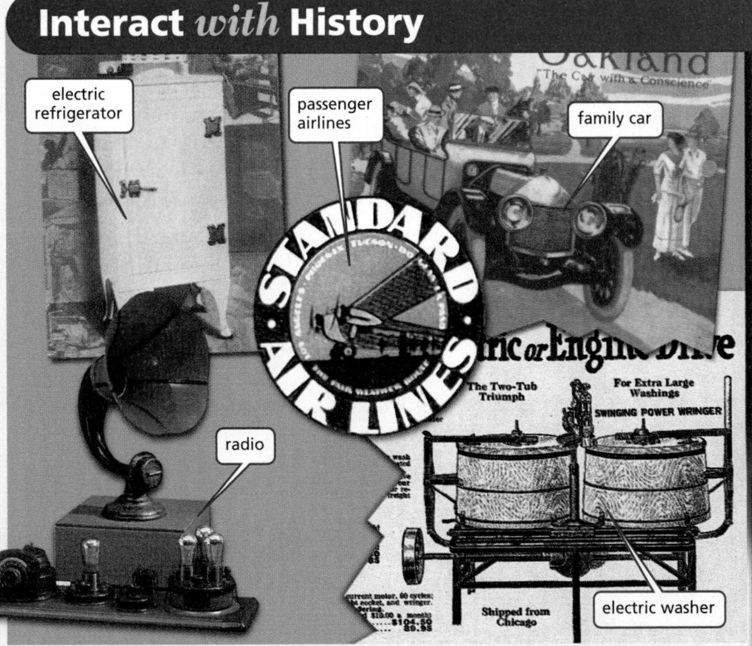
electric refrigerator
passenger airlines
family car
radio
electric washer
Oakland
"The Car with a Conscience"
STANDARD AIR LINES
Electric or Engine Drive
The Two-Tub Triumph
For Extra Large Washings
SWINGING POWER WRINGER
Shipped from Chicago

**World War I is over, and a new decade has begun. There is peace in the world and prosperity at home. It is a time of exciting social, cultural, economic, and technological change. You see new products and new ideas coming into your life.**

### What Do You Think?

- **How will these new ideas and products change your life?**
- **Will these changes make life better and easier? How?**
- **Which class of people will be affected most by these changes?**

# *Which changes in culture or technology will affect your life the most?*

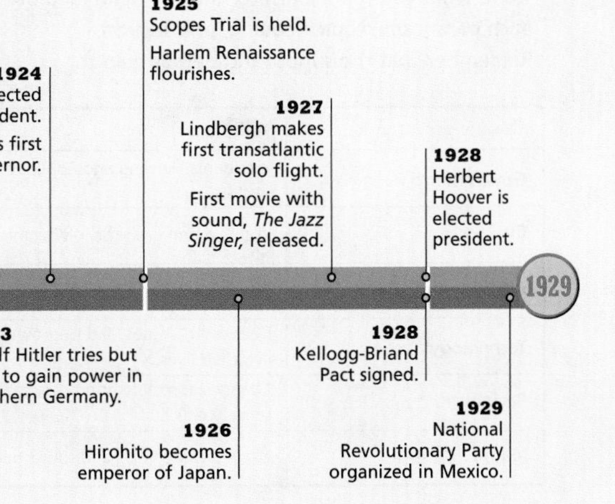
USA
World
1919
1920 Warren G. Harding is elected president.
1923 Calvin Coolidge becomes president.
1924 Coolidge is elected president.
Nellie Tayloe Ross is first woman elected governor.
1925 Scopes Trial is held.
Harlem Renaissance flourishes.
1927 Lindbergh makes first transatlantic solo flight.
First movie with sound, *The Jazz Singer,* released.
1928 Herbert Hoover is elected president.
1929
1921 Chinese Communist Party is founded.
1922 Benito Mussolini is named Italy's prime minister.
1923 Adolf Hitler tries but fails to gain power in southern Germany.
1926 Hirohito becomes emperor of Japan.
1928 Kellogg-Briand Pact signed.
1929 National Revolutionary Party organized in Mexico.

## Interact *with* History

### OBJECTIVES

- To analyze the scope of technological advances in the 1920s
- To evaluate the ways in which new technologies change daily life

### What Do You Think?

1. Ask students which item they would try out first.
2. Have students think about the changes that travel by car and airplane may bring to society.
3. Remind students that in the 1920s the middle class was not as large as today.

### *What changes in culture or technology will affect your life the most?*

Suggest that students consider both positive and negative effects of changes.

### MAKING PERSONAL CONNECTIONS

Ask students to discuss new technologies that they think will be commonplace by the time they graduate from high school. For example, do students think most computers will operate by vocal commands rather than from a keyboard?

### TIME LINE DISCUSSION

**Tell students that after World War I, Americans were shocked and disillusioned. They wanted to distance themselves from the troubles in Europe and in other parts of the world. Some Americans tried to "forget" the horrors of war by pursuing the fun and freedom new technologies provided.**

- Ask students to identify events on the time line that relate to new technologies. **Answers** Lindbergh's transatlantic solo flight; first movie with sound
- Ask students to identify an event on the USA side that signals a change in society. **Answer** Nellie Ross elected first woman governor.
- How does this event show change? **Possible Answer** Women are becoming more active and accepted in politics.
- Ask students to identify events that signal changes in nations around the world. **Answer** Chinese Communist Party founded, Mussolini named prime minister, Hitler fails, Hirohito becomes emperor, National Revolutionary Party organized in Mexico

## BEFORE YOU READ

### Previewing the Theme: Science and Technology

Ask students to speculate about the ways in which science and technology brought changes to American life in the 1920s.

The "Roaring Twenties" were a raucous time in more ways than one. Factories, machines, appliances, automobiles, and airplanes filled the air with new industrial-age noise. Radio and moving pictures—with sound—added to the din. The sound of jazz, a truly American style of music, spread throughout the country.

### What Do You Know?

Ask students to list short phrases, names, and events that they associate with the Roaring Twenties. Then ask them to look at the chapter illustrations and captions for additional items to add to their lists.

 **In-Depth Resources: Unit 8**
- Tracing Themes: Science and Technology, p. 2

## READ AND TAKE NOTES

### Reading Strategy: Finding Main Ideas

Tell students that finding main ideas as they read will help them focus on the most important information in a chapter or section. Point out the categories in the chart that list major areas in American life that changed dramatically during the 1920s. Tell students to look for the main ideas about each category as they read the chapter.

 **In-Depth Resources: Unit 8**
- Setting the Stage, p. 1

 **Critical Thinking Transparency CT73**
- Setting the Stage

# Chapter 25 SETTING THE STAGE

## BEFORE YOU READ

### Previewing the Theme

**Science and Technology** As Chapter 25 explains, the 1920s were a time of peace and economic prosperity for many Americans. Consumer buying, the growth of the automobile industry, and the development of new technologies helped business to expand and changed the way people lived. The Roaring Twenties also brought new ideas, new attitudes, and new forms of entertainment.

More cars meant traffic jams—like this one in St. Louis in 1920.

### What Do You Know?

What do you already know about the Roaring Twenties? What were the issues and who were the personalities that made this decade "roar"?

**THINK ABOUT**
- how the 1920s have been portrayed in movies, television, and historical fiction
- what happens to a country when rapid changes take place

### What Do You Want to Know?

What additional information do you want about the issues and personalities of the 1920s? Record questions you may have in your notebook before you read the chapter.

## READ AND TAKE NOTES

**Reading Strategy: Finding Main Ideas** To understand what you read, learn to find the main idea of each paragraph, topic heading, and section. Remember that the supporting details help to explain the main idea. On the chart below, write down the main idea in this chapter for each category of American life.

 See Skillbuilder Handbook, page R5.

| Categories | Main Ideas |
|---|---|
| Government | Presidents Harding and Coolidge support business to promote America's economic well-being. |
| Business | Business booms in the 1920s, and the standard of living rises for many Americans. |
| Agriculture | Farmers are hit hard as the value of farm products falls. |
| Technology | New technologies lead to growth in business and changes in the way Americans live their lives. |
| Society | Changes in society bring new attitudes and new lifestyles to the nation, but some changes cause conflict. |
| Popular Culture | Movies, radio, jazz, and sports become popular entertainment. |



## TEACHING STRATEGY

### READING THE CHAPTER

This is a thematic chapter focusing on the changes that occurred during the 1920s in government, business, agriculture, technology, society, and popular culture. Encourage students to pause after reading each section and identify the main ideas for the categories listed in the chart. Have the students identify changes that are occurring in society as a result of science and technology.

### ALTERNATIVE ASSESSMENT

The Chapter Assessment describes three activities for alternative assessment on page 725. You may wish to have students work on these activities during the course of the chapter and then present them at the end.

# 1 The Business of America

**TERMS & NAMES**
Warren G. Harding
Teapot Dome Scandal
Calvin Coolidge
laissez faire
isolationist
Kellogg-Briand Pact
assembly line
installment buying

**MAIN IDEA**

The government supported business and kept a hands-off policy in other matters.

**WHY IT MATTERS NOW**

How involved the government should be in the economy remains an issue today.

## ONE AMERICAN'S STORY

**Warren G. Harding** was a pleasant man of whom it was said he "looked like a president." He was happiest relaxing or playing cards with his closest friends. But urged on by his wealthy and ambitious wife, Florence Kling Harding, he rose from small-town newspaper publisher, to U.S. senator from Ohio, to Republican presidential candidate.

The advice from Republican Party leaders in 1920 was "Keep Warren at home. Don't let him make any speeches." So Harding spent most of the 1920 election race campaigning from his front porch in Marion, Ohio. But Harding was what the voters wanted. He promised them prosperity at home and peace abroad, and they elected him president. Mrs. Harding supposedly said, "Well, Warren Harding, I have got you the Presidency; what are you going to do with it?"

In this section, you will read about Presidents Warren G. Harding and Calvin Coolidge, the booming economy of the Roaring Twenties, and the new technologies that helped businesses to grow.

Warren G. Harding and his wife, Florence Kling Harding, at their home in Marion, Ohio.

## 1 Harding and the "Return to Normalcy"

After some 20 years of reform and war, Americans were ready for the "normalcy" promised by Harding in the election and at his inauguration.

*A VOICE FROM THE PAST*

Our supreme task is the resumption of our onward, normal way. Reconstruction, readjustment, restoration all these must follow. I would like to hasten them.

**Warren G. Harding,** Inaugural Address, March 4, 1921

As president, Harding wanted to lift the burden of taxes and regulations from the shoulders of Americans. To do this, he proposed lower taxes and "less government in business and more business in government." He also sought higher tariffs on foreign goods to help American companies.

Harding chose a pro-business cabinet. The secretary of the treasury was Andrew W. Mellon, one of the wealthiest men in the United States.





## SECTION OBJECTIVES

1. To summarize events of the Harding presidency
2. To analyze economic policies of the Coolidge administration
3. To describe U.S. foreign policy during the 1920s
4. To examine the changes resulting from technological advances

**CRITICAL THINKING**

Drawing Conclusions, pp. 710, 712
Recognizing Effects, p. 711
Summarizing, p. 712

## FOCUS & MOTIVATE

### 5-MINUTE WARM-UP

**Making Inferences** These questions focus on government support of business.

1. Read the Calvin Coolidge quote on page 710. What did Coolidge mean by his statement about business?
2. Do you think Coolidge would try to restrict or encourage the growth of large businesses?

Warm-Up Transparency WT25

## INSTRUCT

### INSTRUCT: OBJECTIVE 1

**Harding and the "Return to Normalcy"**

Key Questions

- How did Harding attempt to meet his goals for his administration?
- What was the "Ohio Gang," and what part did it play in Harding's presidency?

**In-Depth Resources: Unit 8**
- Guided Reading, p. 3

**Reading Study Guide** (Spanish and English), pp. 241–242

## RECOMMENDED RESOURCES

**In-Depth Resources: Unit 8**
- Guided Reading, p. 3
- Building Vocabulary, p. 6
- Skillbuilder Practice, p. 7
- Reteaching Activity, p. 15

**Reading Study Guide** (Spanish and English), pp. 241–242

**Economics in History**
- Understanding the Stock Market, p. 25

**Outline Map Activities**
- Routes of Air Mail Delivery, 1929, pp. 49–50

**Formal Assessment**
- Section Quiz, p. 364

**Alternative Assessment**
- Rubrics, 1.3
- Rubrics, 4.9

**Access for Students Acquiring English/ESL**
- Guided Reading, p. 166
- Skillbuilder Practice, p. 169

Technology Resources

**Humanities Transparency HT49**
- Political Cartoon: Coolidge Plays the Saxophone

**Electronic Teacher Tools with Test Maker**

**ClassZone**
www.mcdougallittell.com

## STRANGE *but* True

**President Sworn in by Father**

Coolidge's father, John, administered the presidential oath of office by the light of a kerosene lamp, while Calvin placed his right hand on the family Bible. When they finished, both men promptly went back to bed!

## MORE ABOUT . . .

**Harding as President**

Both his supporters and his critics acknowledged Harding's honesty and loyalty. "What's a fellow to do," Harding was overheard saying, "when his own friends double-cross him?" Even when he discovered that his loyalty had been misplaced, Harding could not accuse his friends. Most historians agree that his conflicting feelings about his friends' behavior caused Harding's death.

## INSTRUCT: OBJECTIVE 2

**Coolidge Takes Over**

Key Questions

- How did Coolidge's attitude toward hard work and prosperity affect the relationship between the federal government and the business community?
- What is the economic theory of laissez faire?
- Which groups faced economic hardship during the Coolidge presidency? Why?

**Economics in History**
- Understanding the Stock Market, p. 25

**Humanities Transparency HT49**
- Political Cartoon: Coolidge Plays the Saxophone

### STRANGE but True

**PRESIDENT SWORN IN BY FATHER**

On August 2, 1923, Vice-President Calvin Coolidge went to bed early at his family home in Plymouth Notch, Vermont. During the night, Coolidge's father received news by telegram that Harding had died. He then woke his son. The U.S. attorney general urged Coolidge to take the oath of office as soon as possible. At 2:47 A.M. on August 3, 1923, John Coolidge, a justice of the peace, administered the oath to his son.

The New York Times. EXTRA

PRESIDENT HARDING DIES SUDDENLY; STROKE OF APOPLEXY AT 7:30 P. M.; CALVIN COOLIDGE IS PRESIDENT

Mellon persuaded Congress to lower taxes and balance the budget. Herbert Hoover, an engineer who organized aid to Europe in World War I, was secretary of commerce. He worked to cut federal government waste.

While some of Harding's cabinet choices, like Mellon and Hoover, were excellent, a number were unqualified, and even corrupt. These men had been Harding's friends back in Ohio and were known as the "Ohio Gang." They used their government positions to make money illegally. Their actions helped to wreck the Harding presidency. The worst scandal involved Secretary of the Interior Albert Fall. It was called the **Teapot Dome Scandal.** Fall took bribes and made illegal deals with oil executives to drill on oil-rich government land in Teapot Dome, Wyoming.

*Reading* **History**

**A. Drawing Conclusions** How did members of the Ohio Gang take advantage of their friendship with Harding?

**A. Possible Answer** They used their positions in government to make money illegally.

Rumors of corruption in the Harding administration began to be heard in 1923. Harding, who was politically and personally honest, was alarmed. He had once said, "I knew that this job would be too much for me." Tired and depressed, Harding went on a speaking tour in the summer of 1923. It was then that he learned the full extent of the corruption. He died suddenly while on the trip, on August 2, 1923. The American people mourned his death, but they were shocked when the scandals became public.

## 2 Coolidge Takes Over

Vice-President **Calvin Coolidge** became president when Harding died. He moved quickly to try to clean up the scandals. His efforts limited the political damage to the Republican Party, and Coolidge was elected president in his own right in 1924. He defeated Democrat John W. Davis and Robert M. La Follette, the Progressive Party nominee.

Coolidge and those who voted for him felt that prosperity would be the reward of those who worked hard. As a friend of business, Coolidge agreed with the economic theory of **laissez faire.** It stated that business, if left unregulated by the government, would act in a way that would benefit the nation. In 1925, Coolidge stated his belief that "the chief business of the American people is business." He said that Americans were concerned with "prospering in the world." Under the Coolidge administration, business prospered and so did many Americans.

**Vocabulary**

**laissez faire:** to allow to do (French)

*"The chief business of the American people is business."*

Calvin Coolidge

Coolidge also believed that it was not the government's job to help people with social and economic problems. Farmers were one group that Coolidge refused to help. Because new machinery had been introduced, farmers were producing more food than the nation needed. So food prices were dropping.



## ACTIVITY OPTIONS

### SKILLBUILDER MINI-LESSON: MAKING GENERALIZATIONS

BLOCK SCHEDULING

**Explaining the Skill** A generalization is a broad judgment about a trend or development based on facts and/or statistics. Making generalizations allows students to simplify information to make it easier to work with. Students must learn to make generalizations without oversimplifying.

**Applying the Skill** Tell students to reread pages 709–710, and then ask them to make one generalization about Harding as president. To help students formulate a generalization, ask questions such as the following:

1. What were President Harding's positive achievements? *(lowering taxes, balancing the budget, eliminating waste)*
2. What were the problems in Harding's administration? *(corruption, misuse of federal funds and lands)*
3. What generalization can you make about Harding's problems with the presidency? *(Possible Response: Harding was an honest person but unable to control his friends.)*

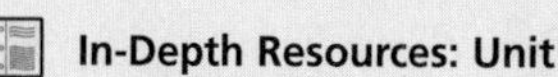

**In-Depth Resources: Unit 8**
- Skillbuilder Practice, p. 7

Congress passed a bill that required the government to buy the extra food. This would have raised prices. But Coolidge vetoed the bill.

Like Harding, Coolidge was an **isolationist.** Both believed that the United States should stay out of other nations' affairs except in matters of self-defense. Both supported efforts to avoid war.

Coolidge's major peace effort was the **Kellogg-Briand Pact** of 1928. This pact, or treaty, was signed by 15 nations who pledged not to make war against one another except in self-defense. Most Americans supported the treaty. They hoped that if war were outlawed, it would disappear. Then they could concentrate on their own lives.

## 3 Technology Changes American Life

The economy was booming in the 1920s. Both Harding and Coolidge kept government regulation to a minimum, and business flourished. Part of the "roar" in the Roaring Twenties was the growth in the nation's wealth. The average annual income per person rose more than 35 percent during the period—from $522 to $716. This increase in income gave Americans more money to buy goods and to spend on leisure activities.

Automobiles had the greatest impact on life during the 1920s. Henry Ford, who built his first successful automobile in 1896, was determined to make a car that most people could afford. At the Ford Motor Company in Detroit, his dream came true with a car called the Model T. In 1920, Ford produced more than a million automobiles, at a rate of one per minute. Each car cost the consumer $335.

To speed up production and lower costs and prices, Ford used an **assembly line.** In an assembly line, the product moves along a conveyor belt across the factory. Workers at various stations add parts as the belt moves past them. By the mid-1920s, a Model T came off a Ford assembly line every ten seconds.

B. Possible Answer The assembly line reduced the costs of automobiles because the manufacturer was able to lower prices by producing more cars at a faster rate.

*Reading* **History**

**B. Recognizing Effects** What effect did the assembly line have on the price of cars?

1923 Model T Ford

### How an Automobile Assembly Line Works

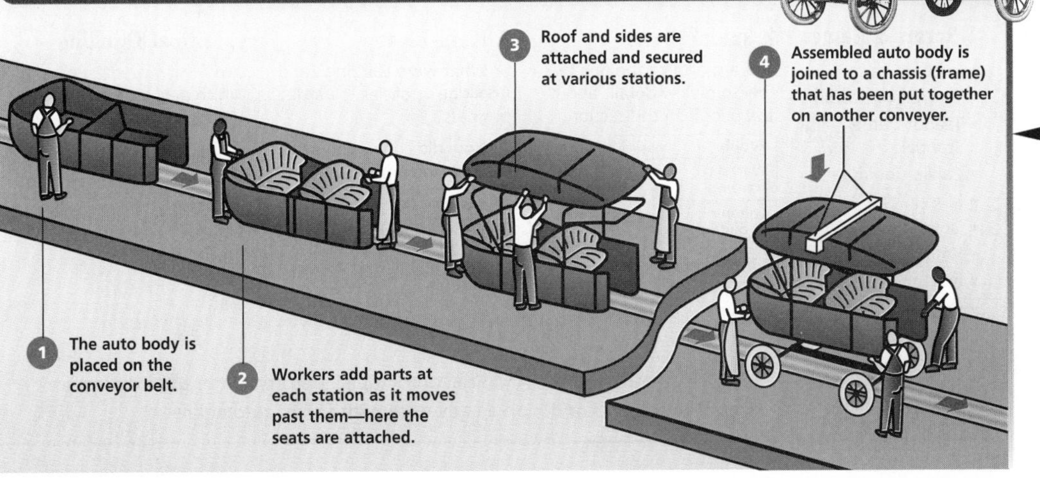

1 The auto body is placed on the conveyor belt.
2 Workers add parts at each station as it moves past them—here the seats are attached.
3 Roof and sides are attached and secured at various stations.
4 Assembled auto body is joined to a chassis (frame) that has been put together on another conveyer.

711

### MORE ABOUT . . .

**Isolationist Policy**

The Harding-Coolidge isolationist policy exactly suited most Americans after World War I. Many Americans felt that the sacrifices they made during the war were worthless because world peace had not materialized. Americans were also tired of the responsibilities brought on by progressive reform crusades.

### INSTRUCT: OBJECTIVE 3

**Technology Changes American Life**

Key Questions

- Why did the standard of living rise in the 1920s?
- How did the use of the assembly line affect factory work?
- How did new technologies change American life?
- How did installment buying and advertising change the American economy?

**Outline Map Activities**

- Routes of Air Mail Delivery, 1929, pp. 49–50

### MORE ABOUT . . .

**Henry Ford and the Assembly Line**

Assembly-line work was boring and exhausting, and turnover was high at Ford plants. In 1914, Ford cut the workday from ten to nine hours at his factories. In addition, he raised workers' pay to $5.00 a day. Besides guaranteeing plenty of workers for his plants, Ford's action had another result. By raising workers' wages, Ford was creating new customers for his products because workers could afford to buy Ford cars.

### ACTIVITY OPTIONS

**INTERDISCIPLINARY LINK: POPULAR CULTURE**

 BLOCK SCHEDULING

**AMERICANS AND THEIR AUTOMOBILES**

**Class Time** 30 minutes

**Task** Identifying ways the popularity of the automobile changed American life

**Purpose** To understand the scope of social change caused by the automobile

**Supplies Needed**

- Reference materials about the automobile and about the 1920s
- Internet access

**Activity** Have students brainstorm ways in which the automobile changed American life. Divide students into small groups and assign each group a category: travel services, young people, new industries, cities, advertising, and leisure activities. Groups should spend ten minutes brainstorming a list of changes related to their category that were sparked by use of the automobile. Ask a member of each group to write its list on the board. Then ask students to make generalizations based on the lists.

**INSTRUCT: OBJECTIVE 4**

**The Air Age Begins**

Key Questions

- When did the air age begin in the United States?
- How did commercial air travel affect Americans?

## ASSESS & RETEACH

**Setting the Stage** Have students fill in the first four rows on the graphic organizer.

 **Formal Assessment**
- Section Quiz, p. 364

 **Critical Thinking Transparency CT73**
- Setting the Stage

**RETEACHING ACTIVITY**

Copy the graphic below onto the board. Then divide students into five groups. Assign one section subhead to each group. Have each group add details to the graphic.

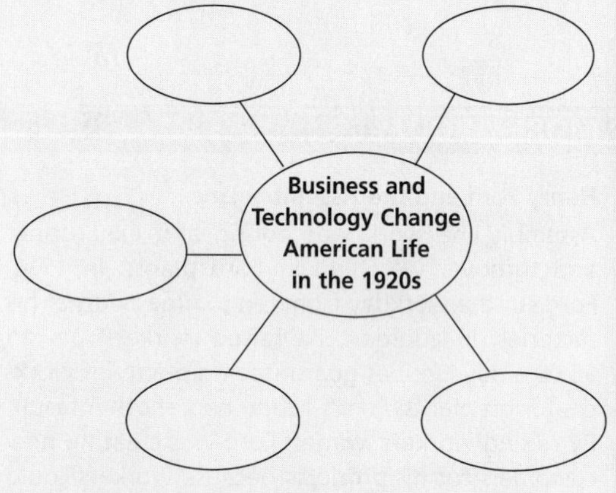

 **In-Depth Resources: Unit 8**
- Reteaching Activity, p. 15

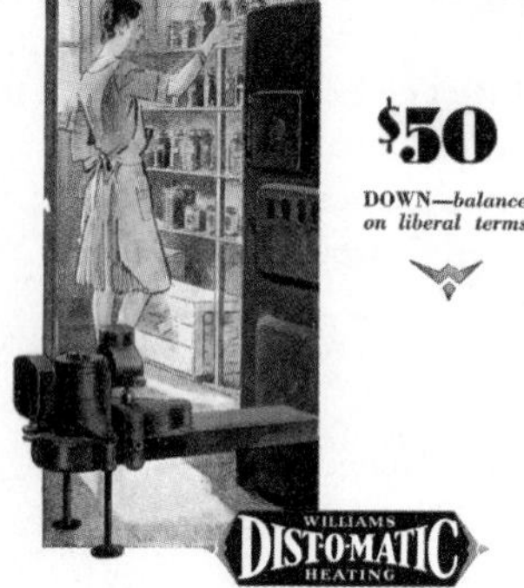


Credit allowed consumers to buy the latest products—$50 down and small monthly payments bought this new oil heater.

Other advances in technology improved life. New machines turned out products faster and cheaper. Once-costly items were now available to many consumers. Some consumers used credit and paid for their purchases through **installment buying.** This allowed repaying the amount borrowed in small monthly payments. National advertising also got its start at this time, as a way of helping to promote new products.

Cheap fuel powered the new prosperity. Petroleum and electricity became widely available. These power sources made possible new inventions and advances in technology that made life easier, such as electric vacuum cleaners, washers, sewing machines, toasters, and fans. However, it was mostly only the white middle class that could afford these new products.

*Reading* **History**
**C. Summarizing** How did advances in technology change the lives of Americans?
C. Possible Answer Cheaper products meant people could afford to buy the many new products available to them—this made life easier and gave Americans more leisure time.

## 4 The Air Age Begins

The 1920s also marked the beginning of the air age. After World War I, many former military pilots bought old war planes and worked as crop-dusters, stunt fliers, and flight instructors. In 1918, the Post Office Department began air mail service. Airplanes had found new uses.

Transatlantic flights by Charles A. Lindbergh in 1927 and Amelia Earhart in 1928 and 1932 helped to promote the idea of commercial air transportation. Pan American Airways, founded in 1927, became the nation's first passenger airline. By the end of the decade, its operations were drawing distant cities closer together both in North and South America.

In the next section, you will read about more changes in life in the United States and the conflicts these changes caused.

### Section 1 Assessment

**1. Terms & Names**

**Identify:**
- Warren G. Harding
- Teapot Dome Scandal
- Calvin Coolidge
- laissez faire
- isolationist
- Kellogg-Briand Pact
- assembly line
- installment buying

**2. Taking Notes**

Use a chart like the one below to review details about the people in this section.

| People | Details |
|---|---|
| Warren G. Harding | |
| Calvin Coolidge | |
| Henry Ford | |

**3. Main Ideas**

a. What were Harding's and Coolidge's policies toward business?

b. How did corruption affect the Harding administration?

c. How did new technology help business to grow during the 1920s?

**4. Critical Thinking**

**Drawing Conclusions** Which developments in the 1920s added to prosperity?

THINK ABOUT
- government's role in the economy
- advances made in technology

**ACTIVITY OPTIONS**

**TECHNOLOGY**
**ART**

Research an aspect of the American automobile industry. Either draw a **diagram** of how a car works or design an **advertisement** for an automobile.



### Section 1 Assessment

**1. Terms & Names**

**Warren G. Harding,** p. 709
**Teapot Dome Scandal,** p. 710
**Calvin Coolidge,** p. 710
**laissez faire,** p. 710
**isolationist,** p. 711
**Kellogg-Briand Pact,** p. 711
**assembly line,** p. 711
**installment buying,** p. 712

**2. Taking Notes**

Harding: president whose administration was marked by scandal; Coolidge: president who promoted business; Ford: producer of the inexpensive Model T automobile and developer of the assembly line

**3. Main Ideas**

**a.** higher tariffs, lower taxes, and little government interference **b.** It wrecked Harding's administration. **c.** Technological advances made goods cheaper and faster. Consumers bought more goods and this helped business grow.

**4. Critical Thinking**

technological developments; cheap power sources; government's hands-off approach to business; new products for consumers; credit buying

**ACTIVITY OPTIONS**

 **Alternative Assessment**
- Rubrics for a diagram, 1.3
- Rubrics for an advertisement, 4.9

# 2 Changes in Society

**TERMS & NAMES**
flapper
Prohibition
Al Capone
NAACP
Marcus Garvey
fundamentalism
Ku Klux Klan

**MAIN IDEA**

Changes in society in the 1920s brought new attitudes and lifestyles but also caused divisions and conflict.

**WHY IT MATTERS NOW**

Many of the social issues of the 1920s continue to challenge American society today.

## ONE AMERICAN'S STORY

**Poet Edna St. Vincent Millay was one of many young people who rebelled against traditional values in the 1920s. She had left her home in Maine to study poetry at Vassar College in New York. She graduated in 1917 as World War I neared its end. Then she moved to the Greenwich Village section of New York City. There Millay lived among artists and writers whose ideas were different from those traditionally held by society. She wrote poems about love and the carefree lifestyle of the 1920s.**

*A VOICE FROM THE PAST*

My candle burns at both ends;
It will not last the night;
But ah, my foes, and oh, my friends—
It gives a lovely light!

**Edna St. Vincent Millay,** "First Fig," from *A Few Figs from Thistles*

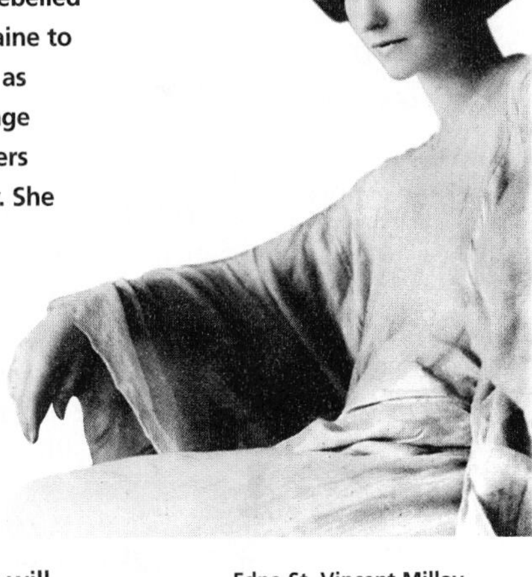

Edna St. Vincent Millay became a bestselling poet and a symbol of her time.

**Millay was a symbol of the 1920s woman. In this section, you will read about the changing roles of young people and women, problems facing African Americans, and conflicts that came to divide society.**

## 1 Youth in the Roaring Twenties

The 1920s were called the Roaring Twenties. According to author F. Scott Fitzgerald, "The uncertainties of 1919 were over. America was going on the greatest, gaudiest spree in history." During the decade, youth and its culture were celebrated. For the first time, young people as a group rebelled against the values of the past and the authority of their elders. The under-25 generation wanted fun and freedom. Many of them experimented with new fashions, attitudes, and ways of behavior.

Young people stayed in school longer, and more went to college. School became a place for socializing as well as learning. Young people expressed their new freedom in daring new clothes, lively songs and dances, and silly fads. Men wore extra-wide floppy pants and sported hair slicked down close to the head. Women wore a shorter hairstyle called a *bob* to match the shorter dresses of the period.





## SECTION OBJECTIVES

1. To identify changes in the roles of young people and women
2. To analyze how Prohibition led to lawlessness
3. To examine changes in the lifestyles of African Americans
4. To explain how the changes of the 1920s caused conflict in society

**CRITICAL THINKING**

Recognizing Effects, pp. 714, 716
Analyzing Points of View, p. 715
Analyzing Causes, p. 716

## FOCUS & MOTIVATE

### 5-MINUTE WARM-UP

**Making Inferences** These questions focus on the effects of changes in the 1920s.

1. Read the poem on page 713. What will happen to a candle that is burning at each end? How does the contemporary expression "burn out" relate to the poem?
2. Why are people likely to burn out during a time of great change?

 **Warm-Up Transparency WT25**

## INSTRUCT

### INSTRUCT: OBJECTIVE 1 

**Youth in the Roaring Twenties/ New Roles for Women**

Key Questions

- In what ways did the lives of young Americans change during the 1920s?
- How did increased personal freedom change women's lives?
- What political gains did women make in the 1920s?

**In-Depth Resources: Unit 8**
- Guided Reading, p. 4
- Building Vocabulary, p. 6

**America's History Makers**
- Edna St. Vincent Millay, pp. 99–100

## RECOMMENDED RESOURCES

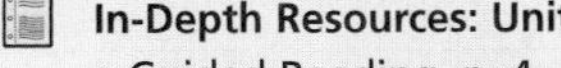

**In-Depth Resources: Unit 8**
- Guided Reading, p. 4
- Building Vocabulary, p. 6
- Reteaching Activity, p. 16
- Enrichment Activity, p. 18

**Reading Study Guide** (Spanish and English), pp. 243–244

**America's History Makers**
- Edna St. Vincent Millay, pp. 99–100

**Formal Assessment**
- Section Quiz, p. 365

**Alternative Assessment**
- Rubrics, 1.1
- Rubrics, 4.8

**Access for Students Acquiring English/ESL**
- Guided Reading, p. 167

**Technology Resources**

 **Critical Thinking Trans. CT74**
- Cause and Effect: Social Changes in the 1920s

 **Electronic Teacher Tools with Test Maker**

 **ClassZone**
www.mcdougallittell.com

## MORE ABOUT . . .

**John Held, Jr., and the Flapper**

The term *flapper* is said to come from the fad of wearing unbuckled galoshes that "flapped." Along with the cartoonist Held, writer F. Scott Fitzgerald is also given credit for creating the image of the flapper. Held drew covers for two of Fitzgerald's books, *The Vegetable* and *Tales of the Jazz Age.* As young women read Fitzgerald's description of racy, rebellious girls and looked at Held's caricatures, they tried to dress and act like a perfect "flapper."

**In-Depth Resources: Unit 8**
- Enrichment Activity, p. 18

## MORE ABOUT . . .

**Women's Work**

Although women were working outside the home in greater numbers, most women considered their jobs temporary. They worked before marriage or to help out in a family crisis. Even if they worked for most of their lives, most women remained at entry-level positions. Although women worked as teachers, they seldom held jobs as principals or administrators. In retail stores or offices, women worked as clerks and typists but they rarely were promoted to managers.

**Critical Thinking Transparency CT74**
- Cause and Effect: Social Changes in the 1920s

**The flapper appeared on many magazine covers during the 1920s.**

The Charleston was a favorite dance. It involved wild, flailing movements of the arms and legs. Dance marathons became the rage. In these contests, couples would dance nonstop for days. Songs also captured the high spirits of the decade. Among the most popular tunes were "Runnin' Wild" and "Ain't We Got Fun." Many young people imitated the behavior of favorite stars from Hollywood movies. Other fads included crossword puzzles, mah-jongg, and flagpole sitting (sitting on a platform on top of a flagpole for days).

**Background**
Mah-jongg was a game from China played with small painted tiles.

The spirited behavior of young women during the decade was just one way women's lives changed.

## New Roles for Women

The symbol of the 1920s American woman was the **flapper**. The flapper was the creation of John Held, Jr., a magazine illustrator. Flappers often wore bobbed hair, makeup, and dresses that fell to just below the knee. They were always eager to try something new, whether it was a new fashion, behavior, dance, or fad.

During the 1920s, women took more active roles in their life than ever before. They had more personal freedom. They drove cars, played sports, went to college, and took jobs. Margaret Sanger, a reformer who focused on women's health issues, described these women.

*A VOICE FROM THE PAST*

Today women are on the whole much more individual. They possess as strong likes and dislikes as men. They live more and more on the plane of social equality with men . . . [and] there is more enjoyable companionship and real friendship between men and women.

**Margaret Sanger,** quoted in *A More Perfect Union*

A. Answer
Women drove cars, went to college, got jobs, and gained the right to vote.

The prosperity of the 1920s opened new job opportunities for women in business offices, retail stores, factories, and various professions. College graduates most often became teachers and nurses, but also librarians, social workers, and bankers. Women with less education worked in factories or in offices as typists and secretaries or in stores as clerks and cashiers. Attitudes toward marriage also changed. Men and women came to view marriage as more of an equal partnership. Women still had the responsibility of housework and child rearing. But labor-saving appliances and timesaving convenience foods made life easier.

***Reading* History**
**A. Recognizing Effects** What were some of the effects of women's greater opportunities?

Because of the 19th Amendment, women were able to vote for the first time in 1920. Some even ran for political office. In 1924, two were elected governor—Nellie Tayloe Ross in Wyoming and Miriam "Ma" Ferguson in Texas. But political gains for women were slow. By 1928, only 145 women held seats in state legislatures across the country.



## ACTIVITY OPTIONS
## INDIVIDUAL NEEDS

**LESS PROFICIENT READERS**

**Identifying Important Details** Some students may have difficulty identifying details that support the main ideas of this section. To help these students organize the information, draw the following chart on the board. As they read, have them identify important details and record them in the chart. The completed chart can be used to review the section.

**Changes in Society**

| Group | Changes |
| --- | --- |
| Youth | rebelled against values of the past<br>wanted fun and freedom<br>stayed in school longer |
| Women | |
| African Americans | |

## ❷ Prohibition and Lawlessness

Another change in American society came on January 16, 1920. That was the date when the 18th Amendment went into effect. The amendment was commonly called **Prohibition,** the ban on the manufacture and sale of alcohol. Many people saw Prohibition as a victory of small-town, Protestant Americans over city dwellers. Supporters felt that Prohibition would promote morality and good health. To enforce the ban, Congress had passed the Volstead Act in 1919.

Saloons were forced to close their doors. But many Americans did not consider drinking harmful or sinful. They resented government interference. People who wanted alcohol found endless ways to get it. For instance, illegal nightclubs known as speakeasies sold liquor. People called bootleggers made their living by transporting and selling liquor illegally. Others simply brewed their own homemade liquor.

**Background**
*Bootlegger* came from the old smugglers' practice of carrying liquor in the legs of boots.

One unfortunate result of Prohibition was the growth of organized crime. In nearly every major city, criminal gangs battled for control of bootlegging operations. The most ruthless crime boss of the era was **Al Capone** in Chicago. With a private army of 700 criminals, he violently seized control of the city's 10,000 speakeasies. By the late 1920s, most Americans had come to see Prohibition as a failure. It was repealed by the 21st Amendment in 1933. Prohibition ended, but organized crime did not end with it.

## ❸ Changes for African Americans

*Reading* **History**
**B. Reading a Map** Locate cities with significant African-American populations on the map on page 723.

The 1920s also brought major changes to the lives of many African Americans. To find better jobs, African Americans had begun moving north in the early 1900s. As you read in Chapter 24, this movement was called the Great Migration. The jobs that they held in industries during World War I raised their expectations for a better life.

In the North, African Americans gained some economic and political power. But they still faced discrimination in jobs and housing. Rising tensions between African Americans and whites in Northern cities led to over 25 race riots in 1919 alone. The movement of an additional 1.5 million African Americans to these cities during the 1920s increased tensions even more.

The National Association for the Advancement of Colored People **(NAACP)** tried to protect the constitutional rights of African Americans. The NAACP worked to make people aware of crimes against African Americans. But it was unable to get Congress to pass legislation to help African Americans fight against discrimination.

C. Possible Answer moving to Africa

*Reading* **History**
**C. Analyzing Points of View** What action did Marcus Garvey believe would improve the lives of African Americans?

Daily threats and discrimination made some African Americans lose faith in America. **Marcus Garvey,** the founder of the Universal Negro Improvement Association, called for a return to Africa and the formation of a separate nation there. He said, "If Europe is for the Europeans, then Africa shall be for the black peoples of the world." Few African Americans migrated to Africa. But Garvey set an example for future black political movements.

Marcus Garvey led a Back-to-Africa movement in the 1920s.

715

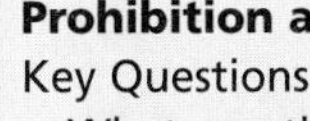

### INSTRUCT: OBJECTIVE ❷

**Prohibition and Lawlessness**
Key Questions
- What was the intended effect of Prohibition?
- What was Prohibition's initial effect? What were its later effects?
- Why was the 18th Amendment repealed?

### MORE ABOUT . . .

**Prohibition and Lawlessness**
Prohibition proved almost impossible to enforce. Drinkers carried and smuggled liquor in every conceivable container. A German tourist observed in 1927, "I learned that not everything in America was what it seemed to be. I discovered, for instance, that a spare tire could be filled with substances other than air, that one must not look too deeply into certain binoculars, and that teddy bears, which suddenly acquired tremendous popularity among the ladies, very often had hollow stomachs."

### CRITICAL THINKING ACTIVITY

**Cause and Effect** Ask students to complete the chart showing the intended effects of Prohibition and the actual effects.
**Class Time** 15 minutes

| Prohibition | |
|---|---|
| **Intended Effects** | **Actual Effects** |
| | |
| | |

### INSTRUCT: OBJECTIVE ❸

**Changes for African Americans**
Key Questions
- What were the major causes of tension between whites and African Americans in Northern cities?
- Why was the NAACP unsuccessful in protecting the rights of African Americans?
- What were the goals of Marcus Garvey's UNIA?

### ACTIVITY OPTIONS

**INDIVIDUAL NEEDS: GIFTED AND TALENTED**

**COMPARING HISTORIANS' TREATMENT OF PROHIBITION**

**Class Time** One class period

**Task** Comparing the presentation of Prohibition by different historians

**Purpose** To evaluate different viewpoints of a historical period

**Supplies Needed**
- Copies of popular histories of the United States, such as *What Every American Should Know About American History, Don't Know Much About History, Our Glorious Century, Only Yesterday*

**Activity** Tell each student to use a different popular history and locate the material in it dealing with Prohibition. Tell students to read the material and take notes in two columns, listing facts presented in one column and the author's opinions and generalizations about the period in the second column. Have students share their findings, compare presentations, and then decide which book is the most objective in its treatment of Prohibition.

**INSTRUCT: OBJECTIVE 4**

**A Divided Society**

Key Questions

- Why did changes in society lead to conflict?
- What conflict arose during the 1920s between religion and science and technology?
- What changes in the 1920s led to a rebirth of the Ku Klux Klan?

**MORE ABOUT . . .**

**The Scopes Trial**

Among the many lawyers involved in the Scopes trial, two dominated the headlines. William Jennings Bryan argued for the prosecution. Bryan was the candidate who had riveted the Democratic convention in 1896 with his "Cross of Gold" speech. Clarence Darrow, the nation's most famous trial lawyer, served on the defense team. When the court refused Darrow permission to summon scientists as expert witnesses, he put Bryan on the stand as an expert on the Bible. This trial was the first to be broadcast live—on radio—to the American public.

## ASSESS & RETEACH

**Setting the Stage** Have students fill in row five on the graphic organizer.

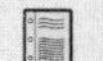 **Formal Assessment**
- Section Quiz, p. 365

**RETEACHING ACTIVITY**

Have students work as a group to compose five generalizations for the section, using the section headings as the beginnings of their sentences. The five finished generalizations should be as complete and valid as possible. Students should discuss supporting details as they work on the generalizations.

 **In-Depth Resources: Unit 8**
- Reteaching Activity, p. 16

More than 40,000 Ku Klux Klan members march in Washington, D.C., in 1925, to show their growing political power.

## 4 A Divided Society

Some groups felt threatened by the changes in society in the 1920s. Conflicts developed over ideas and values. Divisions between groups resulted—between African Americans and whites, the native-born and immigrants, and the urban and rural communities. Science and religion also were in conflict.

In religion, a movement called **fundamentalism** gained both recognition and political power. Fundamentalists believed in a literal, or word-for-word, interpretation of the Bible. They did not want the theory of evolution taught in public schools because it opposed their belief in the biblical story of creation. Evolution is the scientific theory that living things developed over millions of years from earlier and simpler forms of life.

Fundamentalists succeeded in banning the teaching of evolution in Tennessee and 12 other states. In 1925, in Dayton, Tennessee, biology teacher John Scopes broke this law. He took this action to test whether the law could be enforced. Scopes's trial attracted national attention. The jury found Scopes guilty, but the Tennessee Supreme Court reversed the decision. Controversy over the teaching of evolution continues today.

*Reading History*

**D. Analyzing Causes** What action taken by fundamentalists caused John Scopes to break the law in Tennessee?

D. Answer Fundamentalists succeeded in banning the teaching of evolution in public schools.

Another reaction to changes in society was the rebirth of the **Ku Klux Klan.** The Klan called for a "racially and morally pure" America. It became strong in several states, including some outside the South. By 1924, the Klan claimed as many as five million members. It tried to influence national, state, and local politics by using violence against African Americans and other groups. Its power began to decrease by the end of the decade because of personal and financial scandals in the organization.

In this section, you read about divisions in society. In the next, you will learn how mass media and popular culture brought Americans together.

### Section 2 Assessment

**1. Terms & Names**
- flapper
- Prohibition
- Al Capone
- NAACP
- Marcus Garvey
- fundamentalism
- Ku Klux Klan

**2. Taking Notes**

Use a cluster diagram to review the fads of the Roaring Twenties.

Which fads of the 1920s had lasting influence?

**3. Main Ideas**

a. How did the Roaring Twenties change the lives of young people?

b. What factors were responsible for the changes in women's lives?

c. What were the conflicts that divided society?

**4. Critical Thinking**

**Recognizing Effects** How was American society transformed in the 1920s?

THINK ABOUT
- roles of young people and women
- migration of African Americans
- conflicts between groups

**ACTIVITY OPTIONS**

ART / MUSIC — Draw a **poster** with an image that represents the Roaring Twenties or write a **song** capturing the spirit of the times.



### Section 2 Assessment

**1. Terms & Names**

**flapper,** p. 714
**Prohibition,** p. 715
**Al Capone,** p. 715
**NAACP,** p. 715
**Marcus Garvey,** p. 715
**fundamentalism,** p. 716
**Ku Klux Klan,** p. 716

**2. Taking Notes**

shorter hemlines, flagpole sitting, bobbed hairstyles, dance marathons, silly songs

Answers will vary.

**3. Main Ideas**

a. They rebelled against past values and experimented with new values and behavior. **b.** prosperity; labor-saving appliances and convenience foods; the 19th Amendment
c. between African Americans and whites; the native-born and immigrants; urban and rural communities; science and religion

**4. Critical Thinking**

Young people and women had greater freedom, large numbers of African Americans had moved to the North, and society was divided over ideas and values.

**ACTIVITY OPTIONS**

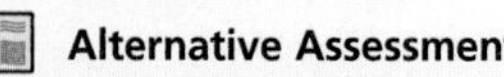 **Alternative Assessment**
- Rubrics, 1.1, 4.8

# 3 The Jazz Age and the Harlem Renaissance

**TERMS & NAMES**
jazz
mass media
popular culture
Harlem Renaissance
Lost Generation
expatriate

**MAIN IDEA**

Popular culture was influenced by the mass media, sports, and the contributions of African Americans.

**WHY IT MATTERS NOW**

Much of today's popular culture had its origins in this period.

## ONE AMERICAN'S STORY

**The decade known as the Roaring Twenties was also called the Jazz Age, because the lively, loose beat of jazz captured the carefree spirit of the times. Jazz was developed by African-American musicians in New Orleans. That city was the home of Louis Armstrong, who became one of the world's great jazz musicians.**

**As a child, Armstrong often listened to jazz played at funeral processions and dance halls. He was raised by a poor, single mother and started working at age seven. His job was collecting junk in a horse-drawn wagon. While in the wagon, Armstrong often played a small tin horn.**

*A VOICE FROM THE PAST*

I had a little tin horn, the kind the people celebrate with. I would blow this long tin horn without the top on it. Just hold my fingers close together. Blow it as a call for old rags, bones, bottles or anything that people had to sell. . . . The kids loved the sounds of my tin horn!

**Louis Armstrong,** quoted in *Louis Armstrong* by Sandford Brown

Louis Armstrong brought New Orleans jazz to the North in the 1920s.

**Later, Armstrong learned to play the trumpet. With other jazz musicians, he spread this new music to other parts of the country—from Chicago to New York's Harlem—and then to Europe.**

**In this section, you will read more about the spread of popular culture, the Harlem Renaissance, and the artists of the Lost Generation.**

## 1 More Leisure Time for Americans

Laborsaving appliances and shorter working hours gave Americans more leisure time. Higher wages also gave them money to spend on leisure activities. People wanted more fun, and they were willing to spend money to have it. Americans paid 25 cents or more to see a movie—an increase of at least 5 times the price in the previous decade. By the end of the 1920s, there were more than 100 million weekly moviegoers.

In addition to attending movies, some Americans went to museums and public libraries. Others bought books and magazines. Sales rose by





## SECTION OBJECTIVES

1. To analyze characteristics of the popular culture of the 1920s
2. To explain how sports figures became popular heroes
3. To identify the achievements of the Harlem Renaissance
4. To identify writers of the Lost Generation

**CRITICAL THINKING**

Recognizing Effects, pp. 718, 720
Summarizing, p. 719
Analyzing Causes, p. 721
Evaluating, p. 721

**Why It Matters Now**
- A Diverse and Vibrant Culture, pp. 49–50

## FOCUS & MOTIVATE

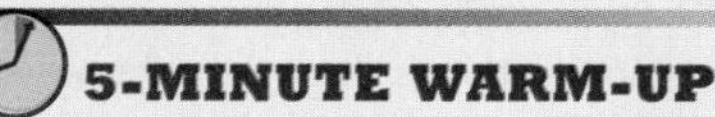

**5-MINUTE WARM-UP**

**Drawing Conclusions** These questions focus on the popular culture of the 1920s.

1. Look at the photographs and read the captions on pages 717–718. What kinds of people and pastimes became popular during the 1920s?
2. Which of the pastimes do you think attracted the greatest following? Why?

 **Warm-Up Transparency WT25**

## INSTRUCT

**INSTRUCT: OBJECTIVE** 

**More Leisure Time for Americans/ Mass Media and Popular Culture**

Key Questions
- Why did some Americans have more leisure time in the 1920s?
- How did mass media change American society in the 1920s?

**In-Depth Resources: Unit 8**
- Guided Reading, p. 5

 **Geography Transparency GT25**
- America's Increase in Leisure Time, 1890–1920

**RECOMMENDED RESOURCES**

**In-Depth Resources: Unit 8**
- Guided Reading, p. 5
- Building Vocabulary, p. 6
- Geography Application, pp. 8–9
- Primary Sources, pp. 10–11
- Literature Selection, pp. 12–14
- Reteaching Activity, p. 17

**Reading Study Guide** (Spanish and English), pp. 245–246

**America's History Makers**
- Duke Ellington, pp. 101–102

**Why It Matters Now**
- A Diverse and Vibrant Culture, pp. 49–50

**Formal Assessment**
- Section Quiz, p. 366

**Alternative Assessment**
- Rubrics, 1.7
- Rubrics, 5.1

**Access for Students Acquiring English/ESL**
- Guided Reading, p. 168

Technology Resources

 **Humanities Transparency HT50**
- *Aspiration* by Aaron Douglas

 **Geography Transparency GT25**
- America's Increase in Leisure Time, 1890–1920

 **America's Music CD**

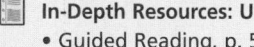

**MORE ABOUT . . .**

**Mass Media**

Radio quickly became a big business in the 1920s. The first radio stations were owned by radio equipment companies or by institutions such as universities and churches. For example, in 1926, KFUO in St. Louis was operated by Concordia Lutheran Seminary. WTAM of Cleveland, Ohio, was operated by Willard Storage Battery Company. Nielson Radio Supply of Phoenix broadcast station KFCB. Soon, however, advertisers began buying "air time." Sponsors and shows were sometimes closely linked, as in the *Everready Hour.*

**MORE ABOUT . . .**

**Helen Wills**

Helen Wills was a doctor's daughter from San Francisco. She joined a tennis club when she was 14 and she played every day, but she said that she learned how to play well mostly by watching better players: "Children are great imitators. I watched the seniors play, and the visiting Australian champions." Wills went on to win the Wimbledon singles championship eight times. She won a total of 31 major tennis titles, including 7 U.S. championships, 4 French championships, and an Olympic gold medal. Her professional name was Helen Wills Moody after she married in 1929.

 **America's History Makers**
- Duke Ellington, pp. 101–102

 **In-Depth Resources: Unit 8**
- Primary Source: from "The Age of Play" by Robert Duffus, p. 10

**Celebrities of the 1920s**

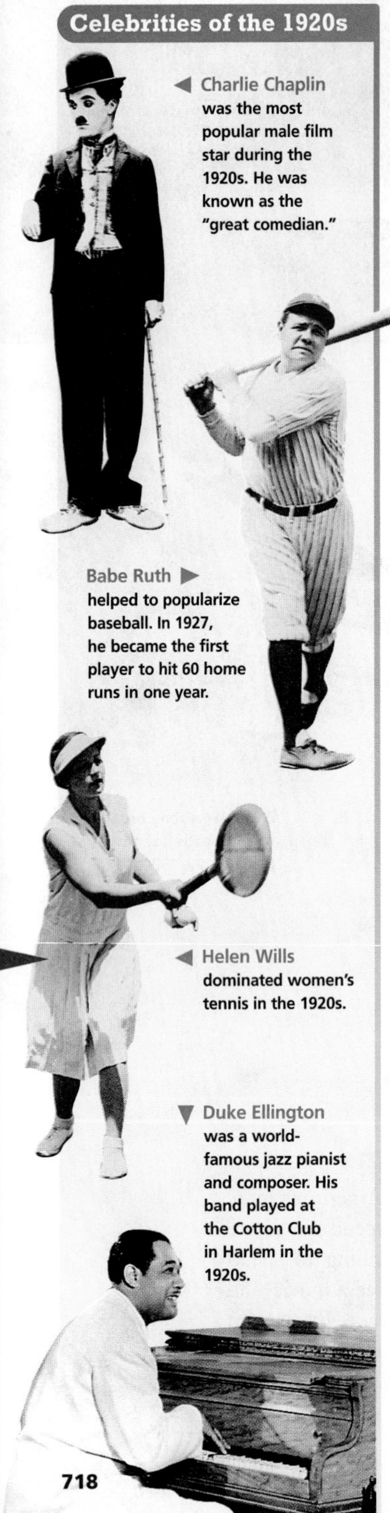

◀ **Charlie Chaplin** was the most popular male film star during the 1920s. He was known as the "great comedian."

**Babe Ruth** ▶ helped to popularize baseball. In 1927, he became the first player to hit 60 home runs in one year.

◀ **Helen Wills** dominated women's tennis in the 1920s.

▼ **Duke Ellington** was a world-famous jazz pianist and composer. His band played at the Cotton Club in Harlem in the 1920s.

50 percent. Americans also spent time listening to the radio, talking on the telephone, playing games, and driving their cars. In 1929, Americans spent about $4 billion on entertainment—a 100 percent jump in a decade.

But not all Americans were able to take part equally in leisure-time activities or in the consumer culture of the 1920s. Some, like African Americans and Hispanic Americans, had their time and choices limited by factors such as income and race.

*Reading***History**
**A. Recognizing Effects** What was the main effect that laborsaving devices and reduced working hours had on Americans' lives?
**A. Answer** more time to spend on leisure activities

## Mass Media and Popular Culture

New types of **mass media**—communications that reach a large audience—began to take hold in the 1920s. Radio and movies provided entertainment and spread the latest ideas about fashions and lifestyles.

The first commercial radio broadcast took place in Pittsburgh at station KDKA in 1920. Other radio stations soon emerged. The number of households with radios jumped from about 60,000 in 1922 to 10 million in 1929. Radio stations broadcast news, sports, music, comedy, and commercials. Not only were Americans better informed than before, but listening to the same radio programs united the nation.

Of all the powerful new influences of the 1920s, none shaped the ideas and dreams of Americans more than motion pictures. The moviemaking industry was centered in Hollywood, California.

Movies gave people an escape into worlds of glamour and excitement they could never enter. Audiences flocked to movie theaters to see their favorite actors and actresses. These included Charlie Chaplin, Mary Pickford, Douglas Fairbanks, Clara Bow, and Rudolph Valentino. Movies also spread American popular culture to Europe. **Popular culture** included songs, dances, fashions, and even slang expressions like scram (leave in a hurry) and ritzy (elegant).

Moviemakers like Samuel Goldwyn, the Warner brothers, and Louis B. Mayer made fortunes overnight. For most of the 1920s, films were silent. In 1927, *The Jazz Singer* introduced sound. Another *talkie* caused a sensation in 1928—Walt Disney's cartoon *Steamboat Willie,* featuring Mickey Mouse. Within a few years, all movies were talkies.



**ACTIVITY OPTIONS**

**INDIVIDUAL NEEDS**

**STUDENTS ACQUIRING ENGLISH/ESL**

**Specialized Vocabulary** Write the following terms on the board:
- *leisure time*
- *mass media*
- *popular culture*
- *heroes*

Review each term and help students arrive at its meaning. Ask students to explain how each term relates to culture in the United States during the 1920s. Then discuss how each term relates to today's culture. You may want to prompt a discussion by asking questions such as these:
- How do most Americans spend their *leisure time* today?
- What influence does *mass media* have on you?
- What songs represent today's *popular culture*?
- Who do you think is a modern *hero*? Why?

## ❷ A Search for Heroes

Another leisure activity was watching sporting events and listening to them on the radio. Sporting events of all types—baseball, football, hockey, boxing, golf, and tennis—enjoyed rising attendance. Boxing became very popular. Fans who could not attend the fights listened to matches on the radio or saw them on newsreels shown at movie theaters. The Jack Dempsey–Gene Tunney boxing match of 1926 drew 120,000 fans.

*Reading* **History**

**B. Summarizing** What were some of the changes that came about in popular entertainment in the 1920s?

**B. Possible Answer** Movies and sports became popular. Americans had more free time and the mass media helped to bring them these forms of entertainment.

In the 1920s, professional baseball gained many new fans because games were broadcast on radio. As a result, fans flocked to major league ballparks. In New York City, fans went to Yankee Stadium, which opened in 1923, to watch the "Bronx Bombers"—the nickname for the New York Yankees. Even college football and basketball attracted huge crowds.

Sports figures captured the imagination of the American public. They became heroes because they restored Americans' belief in the power of the individual to improve his or her life. Babe Ruth of the Yankees was baseball's top home-run hitter. Someone once asked Ruth why his $80,000 salary was higher than the president's. Ruth supposedly replied, "Well, I had a better year."

Baseball players weren't the only sports heroes. Golfers idolized Bobby Jones. People cheered Helen Wills and Bill Tilden on the tennis courts. In 1926, New York City threw a huge homecoming parade for Gertrude Ederle, the first woman to swim the English Channel. Americans also made national heroes of two daring young fliers—Charles A. Lindbergh and Amelia Earhart.

### AMERICA'S HISTORY MAKERS

**CHARLES A. LINDBERGH**
**1902–1974**

Charles A. Lindbergh took flying lessons in 1922 and bought his first airplane in 1923. Four years later, in May 1927, he became the first person to fly nonstop alone across the Atlantic Ocean.

Lindbergh had heard about an offer of $25,000 to anyone who could fly nonstop from New York to Paris. Piloting his single engine monoplane, the *Spirit of St. Louis,* without radio or parachute, Lindbergh flew some 3,600 miles in 33½ hours. "Lucky Lindy" became an instant hero.

**AMELIA EARHART**
**1897–1937**

Amelia Earhart was often called "Lady Lindy" because of both her physical resemblance to Charles Lindbergh and her similar accomplishments as a pilot.

Earhart took flying lessons in 1921 and bought her first plane in 1922. Noted for her courage and independence, she flew where no women had gone before. She was the first woman to cross the Atlantic in a plane (as a passenger) in 1928 and the first to fly solo across the Atlantic in 1932. She disappeared on a round-the-world flight in 1937. What happened remains a mystery to this day.

**Why do you think Lindbergh and Earhart became American heroes?**





**INSTRUCT: OBJECTIVE ❷**

**A Search for Heroes**

Key Questions

- Why did sports events grow in popularity during the 1920s?
- Why did the American public view many sports figures as heroes?
- Who were some sports heroes of the 1920s?

**MORE ABOUT . . .**

**Sports Heroes**

In 1926, Gertrude C. Ederle became the first woman to swim across the English Channel. The record-breaking young swimmer had won one gold and two bronze medals in the 1924 Olympics in Paris. Ederle swam the 35 miles from Cape Griz-Nez, France, to Dover, England, in 14 hours and 31 minutes, beating the previous record by 1 hour and 52 minutes.

**AMERICA'S HISTORY MAKERS**

**Charles A. Lindbergh**

After his transatlantic flight, Lindbergh promoted flying and worked for several airlines. In 1929, he married Anne Morrow, whom he met while visiting South America as a goodwill ambassador. She learned to fly, and the couple made many flights together, charting new airline routes. Anne Morrow Lindbergh was known for her writing.

**Amelia Earhart**

At the time of her disappearance, Earhart was trying to fly around the world at the equator. A 16-day search by the Navy with 4,000 men in 10 ships and 65 airplanes found nothing. No trace of Earhart has ever been found, and her disappearance remains one of contemporary history's unsolved mysteries.

**Possible Response:** because they were young and daring, and their achievements made people believe again in the power of the individual

 **In-Depth Resources: Unit 8**

- Geography Application: The Historic Flight of "Lucky Lindy," pp. 8–9

**ACTIVITY OPTIONS**

**INTERDISCIPLINARY LINK: GEOGRAPHY** — BLOCK SCHEDULING

**AN AVIATOR'S ROUTE**

**Class Time** One class period

**Task** Creating a map of Lindbergh's route across the Atlantic Ocean

**Purpose** To use mapping skills to trace a specific route

**Supplies Needed**

- Reference materials about Lindbergh's flight
- Copies of *We* and *The Spirit of St. Louis* (optional)
- Internet access

**Activity** Have students research Lindbergh's flight and find descriptions of his route. Then have them use an outline map (or draw a map of North America and Europe) to show Lindbergh's starting point (near New York City) and route over the following points: Cape Cod; St. John's, Newfoundland; the southwest coast of Ireland; the southwest tip of England; the English Channel; Cherbourg; Paris. Tell students to title their maps and include a key. Routes drawn correctly should trace an arc of a circle.

**INSTRUCT: OBJECTIVE** 

**The Harlem Renaissance**

Key Questions

- What did the term *Harlem Renaissance* symbolize?
- Why did African-American artists and writers congregate in Harlem?
- What is jazz?

 **In-Depth Resources: Unit 8**

- Primary Source: from "Negro Literature for Negro Students" by Alice Dunbar-Nelson, p. 11
- Literature Selection, pp. 12–14

### HISTORY through ART

**Interpreting the Painting** Lois Mailou Jones was raised in Boston and spent her summers on Martha's Vineyard, where she began painting in watercolors. Like many expatriate African Americans, Jones studied art and painted in Paris for a number of years. In 1930, she helped establish the art department at Howard University. Jones married the Haitian artist Louis Vergniaud Pierre-Noel in 1953. The influence of her time in Haiti and Africa is apparent in Jones's work. Her paintings are noteworthy for their use of color and sense of structure and design.

**Possible Responses: The painting includes elements of Egyptian culture and also elements of American culture, such as skyscrapers.**

 **Humanities Transparency HT50**

- *Aspiration* by Aaron Douglas

**INSTRUCT: OBJECTIVE 4**

**The Lost Generation**

Key Questions

- What ideas and emotions characterized the Lost Generation?
- Why did some American artists go to Paris? What is an expatriate?
- What were some themes of the expatriate writers of the 1920s?

### HISTORY *through* ART

Artists of the Harlem Renaissance celebrated the cultural traditions and the life experiences of African Americans. This painting by Lois Mailou Jones is entitled *The Ascent of Ethiopia.*

**How does the artist show the link between African and American culture?**

## 3 The Harlem Renaissance

Wartime military service and work in war industries had given African Americans a new sense of freedom. They migrated to many cities across the country, but it was New York City that turned into the unofficial capital of black America. In the 1920s, Harlem, a neighborhood on New York's West Side, was the world's largest black urban community.

The migrants from the South brought with them new ideas and a new kind of music called jazz. Soon Harlem produced a burst of African-American cultural activity known as the **Harlem Renaissance,** which began in the 1920s and lasted into the 1930s. It was called a renaissance because it symbolized a rebirth of hope for African Americans.

**Vocabulary**
**renaissance:** rebirth (French)

Harlem became home to writers, musicians, singers, painters, sculptors, and scholars. There they were able to exchange ideas and develop their creativity. Among Harlem's residents were poets Langston Hughes, James Weldon Johnson, and Countee Cullen and novelists Claude McKay and Zora Neale Hurston. Hughes was perhaps Harlem's most famous writer. He wrote about the difficult conditions under which African Americans lived.

Jazz became widely popular in the 1920s. It was a form of music that combined African rhythms, blues, and ragtime to produce a unique sound. Jazz spread from its birthplace in New Orleans to other parts of the country and made its way into the nightclubs of Harlem. These nightclubs featured popular jazz musicians such as Louis Armstrong and Duke Ellington, and singers such as the jazz and blues great, Bessie Smith. Harlem's most famous nightclub was the Cotton Club. It made stars of many African-American performers, but only white customers were allowed in the club.

*Reading* **History**

**C. Recognizing Effects** What changes to popular culture resulted from African Americans migrating to the North?

**C. Possible Answer** African Americans who migrated to the North introduced jazz music and ideas from their life experiences.

## 4 The Lost Generation

For some artists and writers, the decade after the war was not a time of celebration but a time of deep despair. They had seen the ideas of the Progressives end in a senseless war. They were filled with resentment and they saw little hope for the future. They were called the **Lost Generation.**



**ACTIVITY OPTIONS**

**MULTIPLE LEARNING STYLES: MUSICAL** — **BLOCK SCHEDULING**

**ALL THAT JAZZ**

**Class Time** One class period

**Task** Defining jazz music

**Purpose** To listen to and identify characteristics of an American musical form

**Supplies Needed**

- Recordings of a variety of early jazz musicians, such as Louis Armstrong, Duke Ellington, Ella Fitzgerald, and Bessie Smith

 **America's Music CD**

**Activity** Encourage students to bring early jazz recordings to class. Remind them that jazz is a distinctively American form of music, combining blues, ragtime, and African rhythms. Play an example of each of these types of music so students can listen for these elements in the jazz music played. Play cuts by as many different musicians as time permits. Ask students to make notes about the characteristics of the music they hear. Compile their ideas and create a class definition of jazz.

For many of them, only one place offered freedom and tolerance. That was Paris. The French capital became a gathering place for American **expatriates,** people who choose to live in a country other than their own. Among the American expatriates living in Paris was the young novelist Ernest Hemingway. As an ambulance driver in Europe during World War I, he had seen the war's worst. His early novels, *The Sun Also Rises* and *A Farewell to Arms,* reflected the mood of despair that followed the war.

*Reading*History
**D. Analyzing Causes** Why did many American writers become expatriates and live in Paris?
D. Possible Answer They rejected the values and lifestyles of 1920s America and felt that Paris offered them the freedom to express their ideas.

Novelists F. Scott Fitzgerald and Sinclair Lewis were two other members of the Lost Generation. Fitzgerald and his wife, Zelda, lived the whirlwind life of the Jazz Age—fast cars, nightclubs, wild parties, and trips to Paris. His masterpiece, *The Great Gatsby,* is a tragic story of wealthy New Yorkers whose lives spin out of control. The novel is a portrait of the dark side of the Roaring Twenties.

Lewis wrote *Babbitt,* a novel that satirized, or made fun of, the American middle class and its concern for material possessions.

F. Scott Fitzgerald is pictured here in France with his wife, Zelda. He published his masterpiece, *The Great Gatsby,* while living there.

*A VOICE FROM THE PAST*

It's the fellow with four to ten thousand a year . . . and an automobile and a nice little family in a bungalow . . . that makes the wheels of progress go round! . . . That's the type of fellow that's ruling America today; in fact, it's the ideal type to which the entire world must tend, if there's to be a decent, well-balanced . . . future for this little old planet!

**Sinclair Lewis, *Babbitt***

The social values and materialistic lifestyles criticized by Lewis soon came to an end. As you will read in the next chapter, the soaring economy that brought prosperity in the 1920s came to a crashing halt. It was followed by a worldwide economic depression in the 1930s.

## Section 3 Assessment

**1. Terms & Names**

**Identify**
- jazz
- mass media
- popular culture
- Harlem Renaissance
- Lost Generation
- expatriate

**2. Taking Notes**

Use the chart to review facts about mass media.

| Radio | Movies |
|---|---|
| | |

How did mass media change the lives of Americans?

**3. Main Ideas**

a. Which two factors gave Americans more leisure time?

b. What effect did radio have on sports?

c. Why was Harlem called the unofficial capital of black America?

**4. Critical Thinking**

**Evaluating** What contributions to popular culture occurred in the 1920s?

THINK ABOUT
- the impact of World War I
- the power of mass media
- new social values

**ACTIVITY OPTIONS**

**ART**
**TECHNOLOGY**

Find an image and important facts about a noted person in this section. Draw a **trading card** or plan that person's **home page** for the Internet.



### MORE ABOUT . . .

**Expatriate Writers**

Ernest Hemingway is considered by many critics to be the most "American" of writers, creating characters who exemplify the traits of individualism, strength, and courage. Hemingway's prose style was unique: simple, direct, and spare.

During the 1920s, Sinclair Lewis published, in addition to *Babbitt, Main Street, Arrowsmith,* and *Elmer Gantry.* Like *Babbitt, Arrowsmith* also targeted self-satisfied, middle-class puritanical Americans, while *Elmer Gantry* aimed at religious hypocrisy. In 1930, Lewis became the first American writer to win the Nobel Prize for literature.

## ASSESS & RETEACH

**Setting the Stage** Have students fill in the last row on the graphic organizer.

 **Formal Assessment**
- Section Quiz, p. 366

 **Critical Thinking Transparency CT73**
- Setting the Stage

### RETEACHING ACTIVITY

Divide the class into four groups. Assign each group one of the topics below. Each group should write a paragraph on the influence of its topic on popular culture. Each group should read its paragraph to the class.

 **In-Depth Resources: Unit 8**
- Reteaching Activity, p. 17

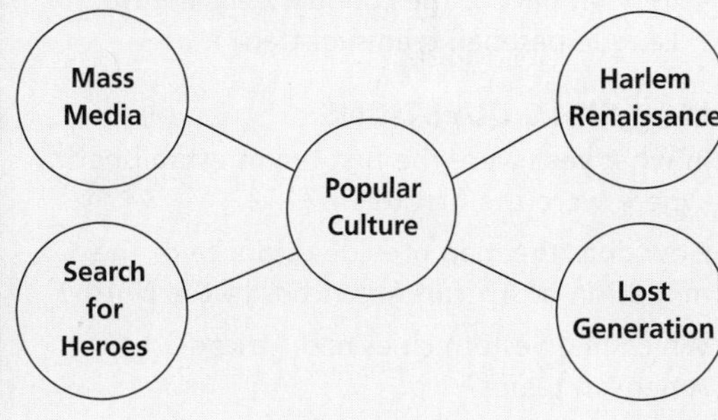

## Section 3 Assessment

**1. Terms & Names**

**jazz,** p. 717
**mass media,** p. 718
**popular culture,** p. 718
**Harlem Renaissance,** p. 720
**Lost Generation,** p. 720
**expatriate,** p. 721

**2. Taking Notes**

Radio: sales of radio sets; stations broadcast news, sports, music, comedies, and commercials; brought nation closer together; Movies: spread popular culture; moviemaking centered in Hollywood; gave people an escape

They spent their leisure time listening to the radio or watching movies. Mass media spread popular culture.

**3. Main Ideas**

**a.** laborsaving devices and reduced working hours **b.** Radio popularized different sports and athletes like Babe Ruth. **c.** because Harlem became a place where African-American writers, musicians, singers, painters, and sculptors lived and worked

**4. Critical Thinking**

The new mass media—radio and movies—contributed to the spread of popular culture and materialistic consumerism of the decade.

**ACTIVITY OPTIONS**

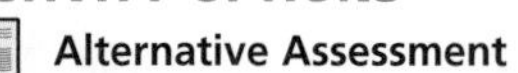 **Alternative Assessment**
- Rubrics for a trading card, 1.7
- Rubrics for a home page, 5.1

## GEOGRAPHY *in* HISTORY

**OBJECTIVE**
Students will analyze a map and interpret information to learn about African-American baseball leagues and their impact.

 **BLOCK SCHEDULING**

## MORE ABOUT . . .

**Raising Expense Money**
Negro leagues played shorter seasons than the white professional teams. The short season allowed teams time to "barnstorm"—tour and play exhibition teams, which raised more money than league play. Some teams supported themselves all year by barnstorming. For example, the Kansas City Monarchs barnstormed for five seasons when they had no league affiliation (1931–1936). The Monarchs equipped themselves with a portable park-lighting system that allowed them to play at night. That innovation wasn't introduced in the professional white leagues until the late 1930s.

## INSTRUCT

Key Questions
- How did migration of African Americans from the South to the North contribute to the rise of black baseball teams?
- How did the African-American teams support themselves?
- In what part of the country were the Negro League baseball teams located?

**MAP SKILL QUESTIONS**
In what year were the first teams established? Where were the first teams?

How does the map provide evidence of the migration of African Americans to the North?

Which midwestern cities had African-American teams?

GEOGRAPHY *in* HISTORY

LOCATION AND REGION

# African-American Baseball Leagues

More than a million African Americans left the South from 1917 to 1929. They were lured to large cities by the offer of higher wages and the increased demand for labor. It was during this period of growing urbanization that the Negro baseball leagues were formed. The map on the next page shows cities with notable teams in the 1920s and 1930s. Each city had an African-American population large enough and wealthy enough to support a team.

Most teams were owned by African Americans. To raise money for expenses, teams needed to play as many games as possible. Thus, they traveled constantly. Stopping in big cities and small towns, they played other African-American teams or white amateur and professional teams. Eventually, teams of African-American all-stars played exhibitions against professional white all-stars.

In 1920, Andrew "Rube" Foster persuaded owners of seven other teams to join him in forming the first Negro baseball league—the Negro National League. Foster (pictured in suit at right) was a former player and then owner of the Chicago American Giants. The Negro American League got started in 1937. After major league baseball was integrated by Jackie Robinson in 1947, the Negro leagues began to decline.

## ARTIFACT FILE

**Memorabilia**
The baseball jersey and shoes pictured here are part of the uniform worn by a player from one of the traveling teams of the period.

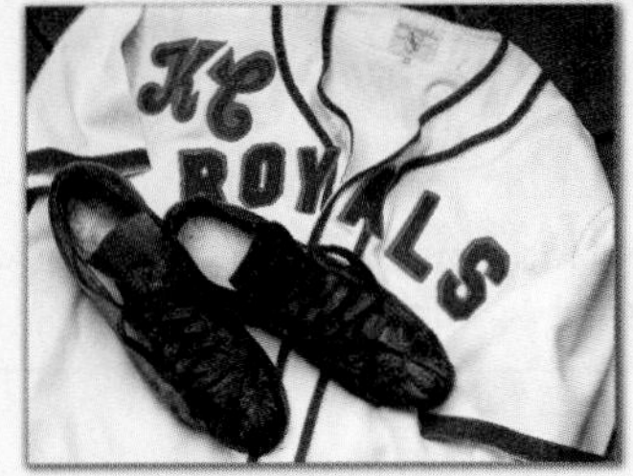


**Pittsburgh Crawfords**
The Pittsburgh Crawfords, shown here with the team's bus, was one of the best teams in the Negro leagues in the 1930s. The success of traveling teams helped to boost revenues of African-American-owned hotels and restaurants in every city that they played.

722

## MUSEUM CONNECTIONS

The National Baseball Hall of Fame and Museum opened in 1939. Players elected to the Hall of Fame are honored with plaques, and artifacts of current Hall-of-Famers are displayed. Permanent exhibits include *The Records Room, No-Hitters,* and *Baseball Around the World. Pride and Passion: The African-American Baseball Experience* is a new exhibit. Another display tells the story of women in baseball.

The Negro Leagues Baseball Museum features a multimedia exhibit arranged in a time line of African-American and baseball history from the 1860s to the 1950s. The exhibit includes bronze cast sculptures of the most important players in the Negro Leagues.

For more about the Negro Leagues and the Baseball Hall of Fame, visit www.mcdougallittell.com

## Cities with Notable African-American Baseball Teams, 1920s–1930s

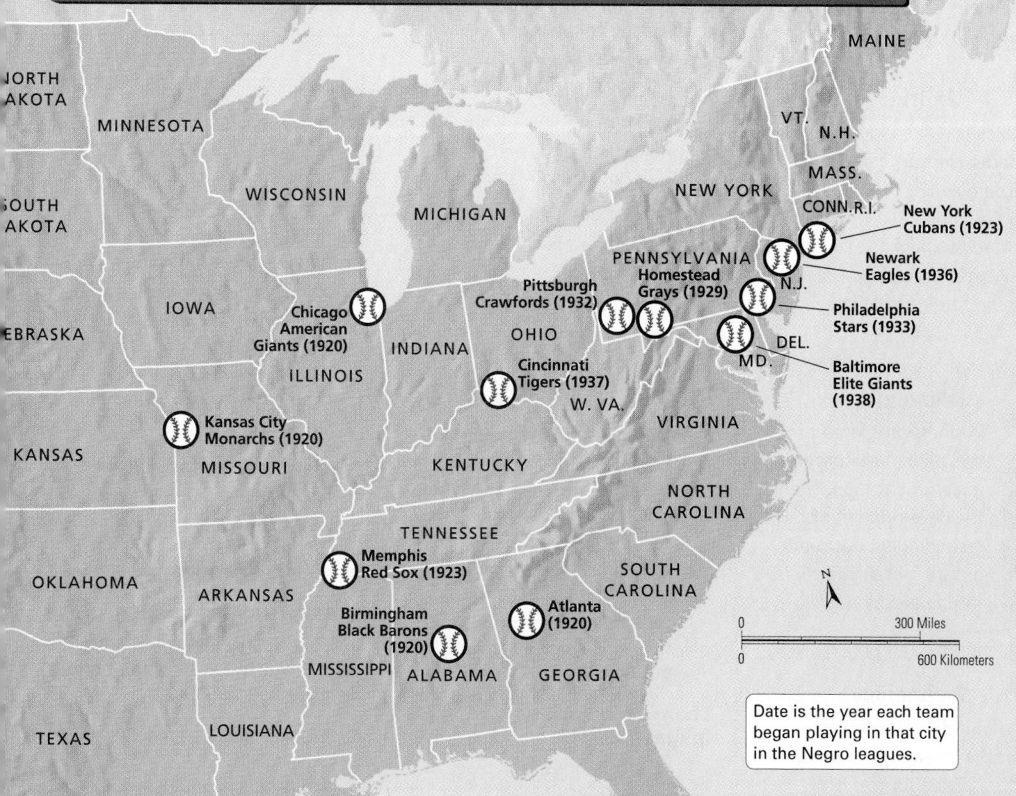


## On-Line Field Trip

**National Baseball Hall of Fame and Museum**

The Negro leagues have been widely honored. This poster is from the National Baseball Hall of Fame and Museum in Cooperstown, New York. In Kansas City, Missouri, the Negro Leagues Baseball Museum also keeps the memory of these teams alive.

Visit www.mcdougallittell.com for more information.

### CONNECT TO GEOGRAPHY

1. **Location** Which cities had notable teams in the 1920s and 1930s?
2. **Region** Why do you think that African-American teams were located mainly in cities in the East?

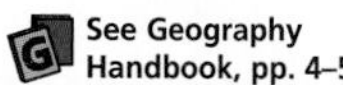
See Geography Handbook, pp. 4–5.

### CONNECT TO HISTORY

3. **Evaluating** How did the migration of African Americans from the South to Northern cities lead to the rise of Negro baseball leagues?



### CRITICAL THINKING ACTIVITY

**Making Inferences** Draw a graphic organizer such as the one below on the board. Ask students to fill in the web with as many businesses and industries as they can think of that might have been affected by Negro League games in their community.

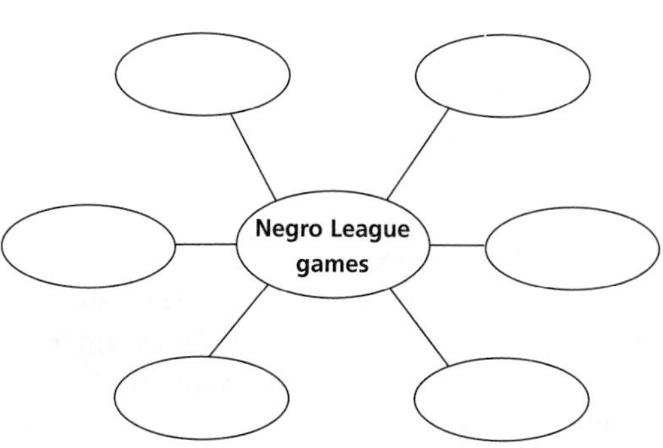


**Class Time** 20 minutes

### MORE ABOUT . . .

**The Negro Leagues**

The Negro American League was not the only game in town for all-black baseball teams. Other important leagues include the Texas Negro League and the Negro Southern League. During their official seasons, most Negro League teams played between 40 and 60 games. However, teams might play as many as 150 additional games against weaker, non-league teams.

The Negro leagues began to decline after major league baseball was integrated in 1947. That year, shortstop Jackie Robinson joined the Brooklyn Dodgers; soon other African-American players followed him into the majors.

### CONNECT TO GEOGRAPHY

1. **Location** New York City, New York; Newark, New Jersey; Philadelphia, Pennsylvania; Homestead, Pennsylvania; Pittsburgh, Pennsylvania; Baltimore, Maryland; Cincinnati, Ohio; Chicago, Illinois; Kansas City, Missouri; Memphis, Tennessee; Birmingham, Alabama; Atlanta, Georgia
2. **Region** because these cities were in the region most easily reached by migrating African Americans, and because there were large black populations in these cities to support the teams

### CONNECT TO HISTORY

3. **Evaluating** African Americans migrated to Northern cities in large enough numbers to support the formation of baseball teams.

## TERMS & NAMES

1. **Warren G. Harding,** p. 709
2. **Calvin Coolidge,** p. 710
3. **isolationist,** p. 711
4. **Kellogg-Briand Pact,** p. 711
5. **NAACP,** p. 715
6. **Marcus Garvey,** p. 715
7. **fundamentalism,** p. 716
8. **mass media,** p. 718
9. **Harlem Renaissance,** p. 720
10. **Lost Generation,** p. 720

## REVIEW QUESTIONS

**Possible Responses**

1. Both believed that the United States should stay out of other nations' affairs except in matters of self-defense and supported efforts to avoid war.
2. Business, if left unregulated by the government, would act in a way that would benefit the nation.
3. government support, technological advances, and cheap fuel
4. Young people experimented with new fashions, attitudes, and ways of behavior.
5. The flapper was a young woman who wore bobbed hair, makeup, and short dresses and who was always eager to try something new.
6. Because of the 19th Amendment, women were able to vote and to run for public office.
7. between African Americans and whites; the native-born and immigrants; urban and rural communities; science and religion
8. songs, dances, and fashions
9. There was more leisure time to listen to sports being broadcast on radio and more money to attend sporting events.
10. The lively, loose beat of jazz captured the spirit of the times.

**VISUAL SUMMARY**

## The Roaring Twenties

### Politics

Republican presidents Warren G. Harding and Calvin Coolidge supported business in the United States and isolationism in foreign relations.

### Economics

Business prospered in the 1920s, helped by government support and the development of new technologies. But some groups, notably farmers, faced hardships.

### Technology

Technological developments, such as the assembly line, and cheap, available sources of power, such as electricity and petroleum, powered the new prosperity.

### Society and Culture

Changes in society brought new attitudes and lifestyles, especially for young people and women. Movies, radio, jazz, and sports became popular forms of entertainment.

724

# Chapter 25 ASSESSMENT

## TERMS & NAMES

Briefly explain the importance of each of the following.

1. Warren G. Harding
2. Calvin Coolidge
3. isolationist
4. Kellogg-Briand Pact
5. NAACP
6. Marcus Garvey
7. fundamentalism
8. mass media
9. Harlem Renaissance
10. Lost Generation

## REVIEW QUESTIONS

**The Business of America (pages 709–712)**

1. How was the foreign policy of Harding and Coolidge isolationist?
2. What was the economic theory of laissez faire?
3. Which factors contributed to the nation's growing wealth during the 1920s?

**Changes in Society (pages 713–716)**

4. What changes took place in the behavior and values of young people during the 1920s?
5. What was the image of the *flapper?*
6. How did the 19th Amendment change women's lives?
7. What were some of the divisions in society in the 1920s?

**The Jazz Age and the Harlem Renaissance (pages 717–723)**

8. What were three examples of American popular culture?
9. Which factors contributed to the popularity of sports?
10. Why are the 1920s also called the Jazz Age?

## CRITICAL THINKING

**1. USING YOUR NOTES**

| Categories | Main Ideas |
|---|---|
| Government | |
| Business | |
| Agriculture | |
| Technology | |
| Society | |
| Popular Culture | |

Using your completed chart, answer the questions below.

a. What role did government choose to play in the economy?

b. How did technology affect life during the 1920s?

c. How did popular culture change the habits of society?

**2. ANALYZING LEADERSHIP**

Think about the political leaders discussed in this chapter. Which of their characteristics made them good or poor leaders?

**3. APPLYING CITIZENSHIP SKILLS**

In what other ways could people have protested Prohibition besides disregarding the law?

**4. THEME: SCIENCE AND TECHNOLOGY**

How did advances in technology contribute to the prosperity of the United States during the 1920s?

**5. DRAWING CONCLUSIONS**

Explain how the African-American migration to the North and the spread of jazz contributed to the cultural diversity of the United States.

**Interact *with* History**

In your opinion, which changes in American life discussed in this chapter would have affected you the most?

## CRITICAL THINKING

**Possible Responses**

**1. USING YOUR NOTES** **a.** Government supported business to promote prosperity. **b.** New technologies changed the way Americans lived. **c.** Movies, radio, jazz, and sports became popular entertainment.

**2. ANALYZING LEADERSHIP** Harding and Coolidge both promoted government policies that aided business. Harding, however, let friendship interfere with his cabinet choices, and this wrecked his presidency.

**3. APPLYING CITIZENSHIP SKILLS** Students may say that people could have held demonstrations to show their disapproval or written to Congress.

**4. THEME: SCIENCE AND TECHNOLOGY** Advances made once-costly items available to the middle class. Products that were made more efficiently resulted in lower prices for consumers.

**5. DRAWING CONCLUSIONS** African Americans brought their jazz music as well as new ideas with them as they moved to Northern cities. A burst of African-American cultural activity resulted from this migration.

**Interact *with* History** Answers will vary.

## HISTORY SKILLS

**1. INTERPRETING GRAPHS**

Study the graph and then answer the questions.

**Urbanization of America, *1910–1930***

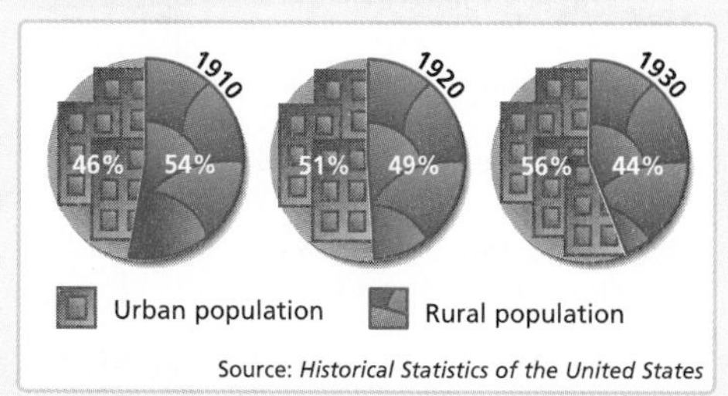


Source: *Historical Statistics of the United States*

a. What was the total percentage increase in the urban population from 1910 to 1930?

b. During which 10-year period did the United States become more urban than rural?

**2. INTERPRETING PRIMARY SOURCES**

Read the poem below, which was written by Langston Hughes, an African American. Then answer the questions that follow.

> I, too, sing America.
>
> I am the darker brother.
> They send me to eat in the kitchen
> When company comes,
> But I laugh,
> And eat well,
> And grow strong.
>
> Tomorrow,
> I'll be at the table
> When company comes.
> Nobody'll dare
> Say to me,
> "Eat in the kitchen,"
> Then.
>
> Besides,
> They'll see how beautiful I am
> And be ashamed—
>
> I, too, am America.
>
> **Langston Hughes**, "I, Too"

a. What is the subject of the poem?

b. What change does Hughes see taking place?

## ALTERNATIVE ASSESSMENT

**1. INTERDISCIPLINARY ACTIVITY: Language Arts**

**Writing a Report** Do research to learn how cars are made on an assembly line today. Describe the procedure for manufacturing a car from start to finish. Include the method of production, materials used, and the time it takes to make a car. Share your report with the class.

**2. COOPERATIVE LEARNING ACTIVITY**

**Writing or Drawing an Advertisement** National advertising became an important way to promote new products to the public during the 1920s. Working in a small group, write a radio ad or draw a magazine ad for a product that made life easier during the 1920s, such as a car, refrigerator, toaster, vacuum cleaner, sewing machine, fan, or washer. Make sure your advertisement covers the following ideas:

a. Do research on the product. Describe the product in the 1920s.

b. How will the product improve life for Americans?

c. How much does the product cost?

**3. TECHNOLOGY ACTIVITY**

**Planning a Web Page on the Roaring Twenties** The 1920s were years of great creativity. American popular culture was being spread throughout the nation and abroad by radio and movies. Use the library or search the Internet for information about the music, fashions, fads, and celebrities of the period.

**Visit www.mcdougallittell.com to learn more about the Roaring Twenties.**

Create a Roaring Twenties Web page by following the suggestions below.

- Select appropriate images of personalities, fashions, and fads.
- Include biographical information and quotations.
- Choose music that captures the spirit of the era.
- Decide which Web sites would be good links for visitors to your page.

**4. PORTFOLIO ACTIVITY**

**Option 1** Review your section and chapter assessment activities. Select one that you think was your best work. Use comments made by your teacher or classmates to improve your work, and then add it to your portfolio.

**Option 2** Review the questions that you wrote for "What Do You Want to Know?" on page 708. Then write a brief report explaining the answers to your questions. Add your work to your history portfolio.



## ALTERNATIVE ASSESSMENT

1. INTERDISCIPLINARY ACTIVITY: Language Arts
**Reports should**
   - clearly describe the process of an assembly line.
   - include facts and examples to support the description.
   - cite sources of information.
   - use standard grammar, spelling, sentence structure, and punctuation.

2. COOPERATIVE LEARNING ACTIVITY
**Advertisements should**
   - clearly present persuasive reasons for purchasing the product.
   - use persuasive language in slogans or memorable sentences.
   - utilize colorful language and verbal images.
   - use standard grammar in the script or print materials.

3.  TECHNOLOGY ACTIVITY
**Web pages should**
   - make effective use of pictures, icons, and music of the 1920s.
   - contain at least three links.
   - contain written summaries that will encourage browsers to visit other Web sites.
   - show technical proficiency.

4. HISTORY PORTFOLIO

**Option 1 Revised section or chapter assessment activities should**
- address teacher and peer responses to the selected work.
- solve problems present in the first versions of the work.

**Option 2 Short reports should**
- answer questions about the 1920s.
- use evidence to develop and support ideas.
- cite sources of information.
- use standard grammar, spelling, sentence structure, and punctuation.

**Critical Thinking Transparency CT75**
- Visual Summary

**Formal Assessment**
- Chapter Test, Forms A and B, pp. 367–374

## HISTORY SKILLS

**Possible Responses**

1. INTERPRETING GRAPHS
   **a.** 10 percent
   **b.** became 51 percent urban during 1910–1920

2. INTERPRETING PRIMARY SOURCES
   **a.** the position of African Americans in the United States
   **b.** Hughes sees African Americans gaining power and white people realizing how poorly they have treated them.

CHAPTER 26 PLANNING GUIDE

# The Great Depression and New Deal 1929–1940

| | CHAPTER OVERVIEW | COPYMASTERS | TECHNOLOGY |
|---|---|---|---|
| **CHAPTER RESOURCES** | The chapter discusses the stock market crash of 1929 and the Depression that followed, along with the New Deal policies of Franklin Roosevelt. The chapter also describes the effects of the Depression and the Dust Bowl on ordinary Americans. | **In-Depth Resources: Unit 8**<br>• Tracing Themes: Economics in History, p. 20<br>• Building Vocabulary, p. 25<br>• History Workshop Resources, p. 39<br>**Interdisciplinary Projects,** pp. 151–156 | **Primary Source Explorer**<br>**Electronic Teacher Tools**<br>**Power Presentations CD-ROM**<br>**Chapter Summaries on CD** (English and Spanish)<br>**America's Music CD** |
| | **KEY IDEAS** | | |
| **SECTION 1**<br>**Hoover and the Crash**<br>**pp. 729–733** | • During the 1920s, speculation in the stock market paves the way for the Crash of 1929.<br>• President Hoover relies on volunteer efforts to combat the Depression.<br>• Franklin Delano Roosevelt wins the 1932 election. | **In-Depth Resources: Unit 8**<br>• Setting the Stage, p. 19<br>• Guided Reading, p. 21<br>• Primary Source, p. 29<br>• Reteaching Activity, p. 34<br>**Economics in History**<br>• The Great Depression, p. 26 | **Warm-Up Transparency WT26**<br>**Critical Thinking Transparency CT76**<br>• Setting the Stage<br>**ClassZone:** www.mcdougallittell.com |
| **SECTION 2**<br>**Roosevelt and the New Deal**<br>**pp. 734–738** | • FDR's program of legislation, called the New Deal, includes measures for relief, recovery, and reform.<br>• In 1935, FDR and the Congress pass the Social Security Act and numerous other measures known as the Second New Deal.<br>• The New Deal slows in the late 1930s. | **In-Depth Resources: Unit 8**<br>• Setting the Stage, p. 19<br>• Guided Reading, p. 22<br>• Skillbuilder Practice: Making Public Speeches, p. 26<br>• Reteaching Activity, p. 35<br>**America's History Makers**<br>• Franklin D. Roosevelt, pp. 103–104<br>**Why It Matters Now**<br>• Government Youth Programs, pp. 51–52 | **Warm-Up Transparency WT26**<br>**Critical Thinking Transparency CT76**<br>• Setting the Stage<br>**Critical Thinking Transparency CT77**<br>• Cause and Effect: The Great Depression<br>**ClassZone:** www.mcdougallittell.com |
| **SECTION 3**<br>**Life During the Depression**<br>**pp. 739–745** | • Drought and erosion create the Dust Bowl, which devastates the Great Plains.<br>• Writers, artists, and moviemakers portray the hunger, hardship, and homelessness of the Depression.<br>• FDR includes more women and minorities in government, and New Deal laws help labor unions. | **In-Depth Resources: Unit 8**<br>• Setting the Stage, p. 19<br>• Guided Reading, p. 23<br>• Primary Source, p. 30<br>• Literature Selection, pp. 31–33<br>• Reteaching Activity, p. 36<br>**America's History Makers,** pp. 105–106<br>**American History Plays**<br>• *Mary McLeod Bethune, Dream Maker* by Mary Satchell<br>**Outline Map Activities,** pp. 51–52 | **Warm-Up Transparency WT26**<br>**Humanities Transparency HT51**<br>• Child in the South by Walker Evans<br>**Geography Transparency GT26**<br>• Unemployment, 1930–1931<br>**ClassZone:** www.mcdougallittell.com |
| **SECTION 4**<br>**The Effects of the New Deal**<br>**pp. 746–749** | • New Deal programs lead to a larger role for the federal government.<br>• Several key programs of the New Deal are still in effect.<br>• The New Deal sets the terms for political debate between liberal and conservative in the following decades. | **In-Depth Resources: Unit 8**<br>• Setting the Stage, p. 19<br>• Guided Reading, p. 24<br>• Geography Application: Presidential Elections, 1932–1940, pp. 27–28<br>• Reteaching Activity, p. 37<br>**Citizenship Today,** p. 78 | **Warm-Up Transparency WT26**<br>**Humanities Transparency HT52**<br>• *WPA Sunday* by Ben Shahn<br>**Critical Thinking Transparency CT76**<br>• Setting the Stage<br>**Critical Thinking Transparency CT78**<br>• Visual Summary<br>**ClassZone:** www.mcdougallittell.com |

PE Pupil's Edition
Copymaster
Overhead Transparency
Audio Library
CD-ROM
Internet

## ASSESSMENT

PE **Chapter Assessment,** pp. 750–751

**Formal Assessment**
- Chapter Tests, Forms A and B, pp. 381–388

**Alternative Assessment Book**

**Electronic Teacher Tools with Test Maker**

PE **Section Assessment,** p. 733

**Formal Assessment**
- Section Quiz, p. 377

**Alternative Assessment Book**
- Rubrics for a graph, 2.3
- Rubrics for a news bulletin, 4.5

**Electronic Teacher Tools with Test Maker**

PE **Section Assessment,** p. 738

**Formal Assessment**
- Section Quiz, p. 378

**Alternative Assessment Book**
- Rubrics for a political cartoon, 1.2
- Rubrics for a Web page, 5.1

**Electronic Teacher Tools with Test Maker**

PE **Section Assessment,** p. 743

**Formal Assessment**
- Section Quiz, p. 379

**Alternative Assessment Book**
- Rubrics for a monologue, 3.1
- Rubrics for a comic strip, 1.3

**Electronic Teacher Tools with Test Maker**

PE **Section Assessment,** p. 749

**Formal Assessment**
- Section Quiz, p. 380

**Alternative Assessment Book**
- Rubrics for an interview, 3.3
- Rubrics for an audio recording, 5.3

**Electronic Teacher Tools with Test Maker**

## CUSTOMIZING FOR INDIVIDUAL NEEDS

### Students Acquiring English/ESL

**Reading Study Guide** (English and Spanish), pp. 249–258

**Access for Students Acquiring English/ESL: Spanish Translations,** pp. 172–178

**Chapter Summaries on CD** (English and Spanish)

### Less Proficient Readers

**Reading Study Guide** (English and Spanish), pp. 249–258

**Chapter Summaries on CD** (English and Spanish)

### Gifted and Talented Students

**In-Depth Resources: Unit 8**
- Enrichment Activity, p. 38

**America's History Makers**
- Franklin D. Roosevelt, pp. 103–104
- Eleanor Roosevelt, pp. 105–106

## CROSS-CURRICULAR CONNECTIONS

### Culture

Uys, Errol Lincoln. ***Riding the Rails: Teenagers on the Move During the Great Depression.*** New York: TV Books, 1999. Fascinating information about the lives, adventures, and misadventures of the more than 250,000 young people who rode freight trains across the nation.

### Economics

Morris, Scott Edward (ed.), Harm J. De Blij (designer). ***The Economy of the World (Understanding and Using Maps).*** Broomall, PA: Chelsea House Pub., 1995. Information about economics presented visually.

### Government

Freedman, Russell. ***Franklin Delano Roosevelt.*** New York: Clarion, 1990. A photobiography showing the many sides of a remarkable man.

### Humanities: Art

Partridge, Elizabeth. ***Restless Spirit: The Life and Work of Dorothea Lange.*** New York: Viking, 1998. Illustrated with more than 60 images by the famous chronicler of the Depression.

### Interdisciplinary Projects, pp. 151–156

- Math: Analyzing and Graphing Data
- Science: Soil Erosion
- Language Arts: Oral History
- Art: Social History Scrapbook

### Literature

Curtis, Christopher Paul. ***Bud, Not Buddy.*** New York: Delacorte, 1999. A funny, far-fetched tale set in Michigan during the Depression tells how Bud takes off from his foster home to find his father.

De Young, C. Coco. ***A Letter to Mrs. Roosevelt.*** New York: Delacorte, 1999. When her family is about to lose their home, Margo Bandini writes to Eleanor Roosevelt asking for help. Based on true family story.

Hesse, Karen. ***Out of the Dust.*** New York: Scholastic, 1997. Unforgettable, original poems about life on a dried-up Oklahoma wheat farm by a 15-year-old girl named Billie Jo.

### McDougal Littell *The Language of Literature*

- Woody Guthrie. "This Land Is Your Land" (song)

### McDougall Littell Literature Connections

Wilson Rawls

***Where the Red Fern Grows***

Set in the Depression on a farm in the Ozarks, this story tells of dreams, hard work, and the love of a boy for his hunting dogs.

## ENRICHMENT ACTIVITIES

PE **Pupil's Edition, pp. 726–753**
**Interact with History,** p. 727
**Economics in History,** p. 732
**Literature Connections,** pp. 744–745
**History Workshop,** pp. 752–753

**In-Depth Resources: Unit 8**
- Geography Application, pp. 27–28
- Primary Sources, pp. 29–30
- Literature Selection, pp. 31–33
- History Workshop Resources, p. 39

**America's History Makers**
- Franklin D. Roosevelt, pp. 103–104
- Eleanor Roosevelt, pp. 105–106

**America's Music CD**

**American History Plays**
- *Mary Mcleod Bethune, Dream Maker* by Mary Satchell

**Outline Map Activities,** pp. 51–52

**Why It Matters Now,** pp. 51–52

# CHAPTER 26 PACING GUIDE

**LESSON PLAN OPTIONS (50-MINUTE PERIOD)** (TE) = Teacher's Edition (PE) = Pupil's Edition

| | TEACHER-DIRECTED ACTIVITIES<br>Class Time: 15 minutes | STUDENT-CENTERED ACTIVITIES<br>Class Time: 25 minutes | INDIVIDUAL ACTIVITIES<br>Class Time: 10 minutes |
|---|---|---|---|
| **DAY 1**<br>Introduction<br>pp. 726–728 | **Presentation Options**<br>• Begin with a class discussion of the photograph on p. 726 **(PE)**.<br>• Lead a class discussion on the "What Do You know?" question in Setting the Stage, p. 728. Then introduce the graphic organizer for the chapter **(PE)**. | **Options for Cooperative Learning**<br>• Have student groups discuss the Interact with History questions, p. 727 **(PE)**.<br>• Have student groups respond to the "What Do You Want to Know?" question in Setting the Stage, p. 728 **(PE)**. | **Head Start on Homework Options**<br>• Have students skim Section 1 Main Idea, Why It Matters Now, Terms & Names, and the main headings, p. 729 **(PE)**.<br>• Have students begin Guided Reading activity and Building Vocabulary sheet. |
| **DAY 2**<br>Section 1<br>pp. 729–733 | **Presentation Options**<br>• Begin with the 5-Minute Warm-Up, p. 729 **(TE)**.<br>• Review the Section 1 Main Idea, Why It Matters Now, and Terms & Names, p. 729 **(PE)**.<br>• Lead the students through the Economics in History feature, p. 732 **(TE)**. | **Options for Cooperative Learning**<br>• Divide students into groups to work on the Economics in History questions, p. 732 **(PE)**.<br>• Have student pairs work together to complete one of the Activity Options in the Section 1 Assessment, p. 733 **(PE)**. | **Head Start on Homework Options**<br>• Have students begin working on Section 1 Assessment, p. 733 **(PE)**.<br>• Have students complete the Skillbuilder questions on, p. 737 **(PE)**. |
| **DAY 3**<br>Section 2<br>pp. 734–738 | **Presentation Options**<br>• Begin with the 5-Minute Warm-Up, p. 734 **(TE)**.<br>• Choose 5 key questions for Objectives 1–4 to discuss with the class, pp. 734–737 **(TE)**.<br>• Lead the students through the Skillbuilder Mini-Lesson: Making Public Speeches, p. 737 **(TE)**. | **Options for Cooperative Learning**<br>• Divide students into groups and have them work on the Interdisciplinary Link, Geography: Geography of the TVA, p. 736 **(TE)**.<br>• Have student pairs work together to complete one of the Activity Options in the Section 2 Assessment, p. 738 **(PE)**. | **Head Start on Homework Options**<br>• Have students begin working on Section 2 Assessment, p. 738 **(PE)**.<br>• Have students preview Section 3 Main Idea, Why It Matters Now, Terms & Names, and the main headings, p. 739 **(PE)**. |
| **DAY 4**<br>Section 3<br>pp. 739–745 | **Presentation Options**<br>• Begin with the 5-Minute Warm-Up, p. 739 **(TE)**.<br>• Choose 5 key questions for Objectives 1–4 to discuss with the class, pp. 739–743 **(TE)**.<br>• Lead a discussion on the Dust Bowl migrants using the History from Visuals, p. 740 **(TE)**. | **Options for Cooperative Learning**<br>• Divide students into groups and have them complete the Multiple Learning Styles: Linguistic activity , p. 742 **(TE)**.<br>• Have student pairs work together to complete one of the Activity Options in the Section 3 Assessment, p. 743 **(PE)**. | **Head Start on Homework Options**<br>• Have students begin working on Section 3 Assessment, p. 743 **(PE)**.<br>• Have students complete the Literature Connections questions, pp. 744–745 **(PE)**. |
| **DAY 5**<br>Section 4<br>pp. 746–749 | **Presentation Options**<br>• Begin with the 5-Minute Warm-Up, p. 746 **(TE)**.<br>• Choose 5 key questions for Objectives 1–4 to discuss with the class, pp. 746–749 **(TE)**.<br>• Lead a discussion on the effects of the New Deal using the History from Visuals, p. 747 **(TE)**. | **Options for Cooperative Learning**<br>• Divide student into groups to complete the History Workshop, pp. 752–753 **(PE)**.<br>• Have student pairs work together to complete one of the Activity Options in the Section 4 Assessment, p. 749 **(PE)**. | **Head Start on Homework Options**<br>• Have students complete the Setting the Stage graphic organizer for the chapter, p. 728 **(PE)**.<br>• Have students begin working on the Chapter Assessment, pp. 750–751 **(PE)**.<br>• Prepare for Chapter Test<br>**Formal Assessment,** pp. 381–388 |

TEACHER-TESTED ACTIVITY Patricia B. Carlson, Swanson Middle School, Arlington, Virginia

## NEW DEAL POSTER CAMPAIGN

**Class Time** One class period for preparation and one for presentation

**Task** Creating posters to explain FDR's New Deal programs

**Purpose** To understand how the New Deal helped citizens, industries, and the economy

**Supplies Needed**
- Reference materials and Internet resources on New Deal programs
- Posterboard and construction paper
- Markers, scissors, and glue

**Activity** Divide the class into small groups. Have each group define FDR's major goals during the first Hundred Days and categorize his programs according to the "three R's"—relief, recovery, and reform. Groups can pick one of the three R's and design a poster campaign promoting its specific New Deal programs. Posters should persuade the public that these programs will provide relief for the poor, recovery for agriculture and industry, or reforms of the economy. Display posters in the classroom. As a follow-up activity, have students choose one program and write a paragraph evaluating its effect on the nation.

## BLOCK SCHEDULING — LESSON PLAN OPTIONS (90-MINUTE PERIOD)

### DAY 1

**Interact with History,** p. 727
**Class Time** 20 minutes

Options for pacing and variety:
- **Role-Playing** In small groups have students enact a radio interview of the recipients of food at this soup kitchen. The interviewers should prepare questions about which 1932 presidential candidate each recipient is likely to vote for and why. **Class Time** 20 minutes

**Setting the Stage,** p. 728
**Class Time** 20 minutes

Options for pacing and variety:
- **Time Saver** For a homework assignment, have students create the Read and Take Notes graphic organizer. Remind students to complete the organizer as they read the chapter. **Class Time** 5 minutes

**Section 1,** pp. 729–733
**Class Time** 50 minutes

Options for pacing and variety:
- **Time Saver** Use the graphs on page 730 to introduce students to the economic problems of the Great Depression. **Class Time** 10 minutes
- **Peer Teaching** Ask a pair of students to review the Economics in History lesson on page 732 as well as the information at www.mcdougallittell.com on recession and depression. Have them create their own diagram or transparency to teach the class the differences between these two troughs in the business cycle. **Class Time** 15 minutes

### DAY 2

**Section 2,** pp. 734–738
**Class Time** 45 minutes

Options for pacing and variety:
- **Role-Playing** Assign small groups of students the roles suggested in the Cooperative Learning Activity on page 751 of the Chapter Assessment. Have students debate the question posed in the activity from the perspectives of the leaders whose role each student plays. **Class Time** 40 minutes
- **Internet** Extend students' background knowledge of Franklin D. Roosevelt by visiting www.mcdougallittell.com **Class Time** 20 minutes

**Section 3,** pp. 739–745
**Class Time** 45 minutes

Options for pacing and variety:
- **Time Saver** For a homework assignment after the completion of this section, have students create the speech or art Activity Option in the Section Assessment. **Class Time** 5 minutes
- **History on Film** Extend students' background knowledge of the Great Depression by showing students the first half of *Two Great Crusades.* The second half discusses World War II and can be used with Chapter 27. Mastervision. **Class Time** 30 minutes

### DAY 3

**Section 4,** pp. 746-–749
**Class Time** 45 minutes

Options for pacing and variety:
- **Time Saver** Use the charts on page 747 to introduce the section and summarize the effects of the New Deal. **Class Time** 10 minutes
- **Peer Evaluation** Have student pairs create a report card that shows their personal assessment of Roosevelt's response to the Depression. **Class Time** 10 minutes

**History Workshop,** pp. 752–753

Options for pacing and variety:
- **Team Teaching** Invite an art teacher to the class to talk to students about the artworks of the Federal Art Project and about some of the famous muralists and artists of the Depression. **Class Time** 20 minutes

**Chapter 26 Assessment,** pp. 750–751
**Class Time** 40 minutes

Options for pacing and variety:
- **Peer Teaching** Have pairs of students use the Visual Summary on page 750 as an outline to write a speech on the causes and the effects of the Great Depression and New Deal. Pick several pairs to deliver their speeches to the class. **Class Time** 20 minutes
- **Peer Teaching** Ask one student to assume the role of a supporter of Roosevelt and the other a critic. Match critics and supporters and have each explain his or her viewpoint to the other. **Class Time** 15 minutes
- **Peer Evaluation** Working in groups of four, students can use their completed Using Your Notes charts to write a short paper assessing and comparing the leadership skills of Hoover and FDR. **Class Time** 15 minutes

**CHAPTER 26 OBJECTIVE**

The student will understand the causes and effects of the Great Depression and how President Franklin Roosevelt ended the economic downturn and permanently changed the role of government in the United States.

CHAPTER 26

# The Great Depression and New Deal 1929–1940



## HISTORY FROM VISUALS

**Interpreting the Photograph** Have students study the photograph and caption and discuss how this picture compares with photographs of homeless people today. Where might the framed pictures on the walls of the shack have come from? **Answer** They may have come from the man's former home or from garbage cans or trash dumps. Ask students what the men's dress might indicate about their homelessness. **Possible Response** Their clothes are not torn or mismatched. Students might infer that they are newly poor.

**Extension** Have the students write a paragraph describing the expression on the face of the man in the center of the picture.

Homeless people used scrap materials to build shacks in a New York City alley during the Great Depression.

726

## RECOMMENDED RESOURCES

### BOOKS FOR THE TEACHER

Galbraith, John K. ***The Great Crash 1929.*** Boston: Houghton Mifflin, 1997. A pivotal work by one of the nation's most noted economists.

McElvaine, Robert S. ***The Great Depression: America, 1929–1941.*** New York: Times Books. Balanced account of the great crisis.

Watkins, Tom H. ***The Great Depression: America in the 1930s.*** Critics called this companion to the PBS TV series of the same name "riveting" and "dramatic."

### SOFTWARE

***Voices of the 30s.*** CD-ROM for Mac. Contains primary sources, photographs, art, selections from literature, and more. Sunburst, 1994.

### VIDEO

***The Great Depression.*** Four videocassettes, narrated by Mario Cuomo. Contains newsreel footage, interviews, and commentary by historians. The History Channel, 1998.

### INTERNET

For more about Franklin D. Roosevelt, visit www.mcdougallittel.com

# Interact *with* History

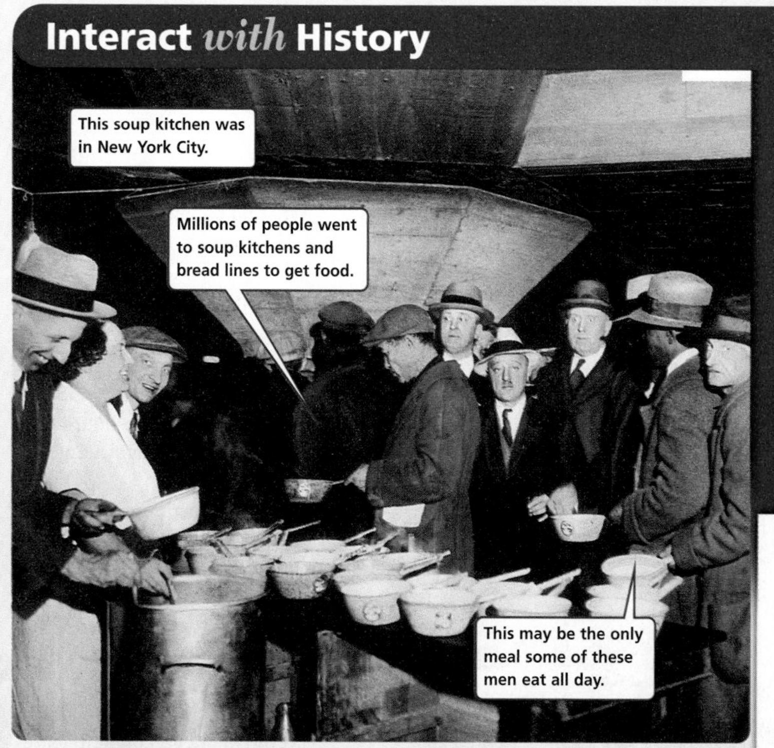

This soup kitchen was in New York City.
Millions of people went to soup kitchens and bread lines to get food.
This may be the only meal some of these men eat all day.

**It's 1932. The economy is bad, and millions of people are out of work. Some are starving.**

**Two men are running for president. One says the government should give money to the poor. The other says this will make people stop looking for jobs. He wants charity groups to help people in need.**

### What Do You Think?

- **Is the government responsible for everyone's well-being?**
- **What responsibility do individuals have to help others?**
- **What is the best way to help people out of poverty?**

## *Who do you think should help the poor?*

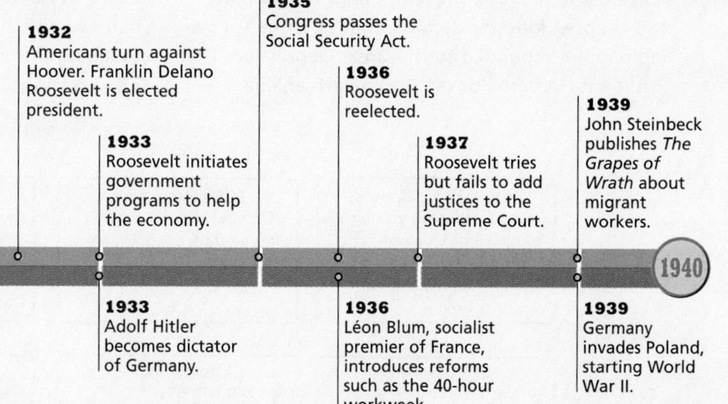

### OBJECTIVES

- To help students analyze different points of view about helping the needy
- To help students connect with the people and events they will study in this chapter

### What Do You Think?

1. What happens to a society in which some people are very wealthy and many people are very poor?
2. How much can private individuals help people in need? Should an average citizen try to find homeless people places to live? Are ordinary citizens responsible for helping others to find food, child care, or medicine?
3. What kinds of programs really help people in need?

### *Who do you think should help the poor?*

Encourage students to examine their beliefs about the role of government. Students might compare the benefits and the costs of private agencies or individuals helping the poor with government-supported poverty programs. Ask students which types of programs they think are likely to be more effective.

### MAKING PERSONAL CONNECTIONS

Have students identify some of the public and private agencies in their own community that work to help people move out of poverty. If possible, have students describe the services they offer, the people they serve, and how the public and private programs are alike and different.

### TIME LINE DISCUSSION

**In the 1930s, the courage and spirit of Americans were tested. As Americans plunged from prosperity into poverty, the government seemed unable to help them. The election of Franklin Roosevelt and the New Deal restored American belief in the future. Laws passed during this time changed the role of government.**

- Ask students what event marked the start of the Great Depression. **Answer** the stock market crash
- Ask students to name the two men who served as president during the Great Depression. **Answer** Hoover and Roosevelt
- Ask students how Hoover's and Roosevelt's approach to the problems of the Depression differ. **Possible Response** Roosevelt acts to involve government in solving the problems. Hoover believes the country does not need government help.
- What effect does the Depression have in other parts of the world? **Possible Responses** In Asia, Japan attacks Manchuria. The French establish a 40-hour work week.

## BEFORE YOU READ

### Previewing the Theme: Economics in History

Ask students what aspects of American life each of the pictures suggests. How did the creator of this needle-book cover feel about the New Deal, Roosevelt's program to help the economy? In what sense is this illustration a form of New Deal propaganda?

### What Do You Know?

Students might recall what they already know about the hardships Americans experienced during the Great Depression or about the actions Franklin Roosevelt took to help those in need. Students may have seen pictures of bread lines, soup kitchens, shantytowns, or the dust storms in the Dust Bowl.

 **In-Depth Resources: Unit 8**
- Tracing Themes: Economics in History, p. 20

## READ AND TAKE NOTES

**Reading Strategy: Evaluating**

Explain to students that evaluating involves making a judgment based on information. Before they read, have students study the chart and read the three headings: "Hoover's Responses," "FDR's Responses," and "Citizens' Responses." As they read, have them take notes regarding how each individual or group responded to the Great Depression. When students complete the chart, they can use the details they have identified to evaluate the three responses.

 **In-Depth Resources: Unit 8**
- Setting the Stage, p. 19

 **Critical Thinking Transparency CT76**
- Setting the Stage

# Chapter 26 SETTING THE STAGE

## BEFORE YOU READ

### Previewing the Theme

**Economics in History** Chapter 26 explains how the prosperity of the 1920s ended suddenly. The years of unemployment and hard times that followed are known as the Great Depression. To improve economic conditions, President Roosevelt and Congress enacted programs that permanently changed the U.S. government.

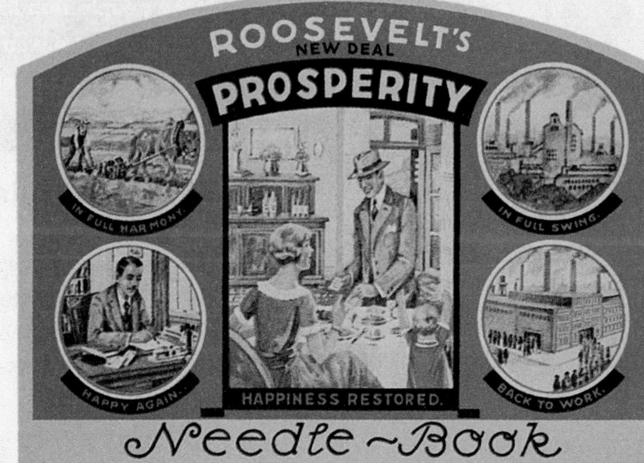


### What Do You Know?

What do people do to get by when they are unable to find work? Where can they turn for help besides the government?

**THINK ABOUT**
- stories you may have heard about the Great Depression
- movies and books about people with economic struggles

### What Do You Want to Know?

What questions do you have you want to know about how the Great Depression affected Americans? What facts and details would you like to learn about government actions during that period? In your notebook, list the things you hope to learn from this chapter.

## READ AND TAKE NOTES

**Reading Strategy: Evaluating** To evaluate is to make a judgment about something. As you read this chapter, look for details about how the following people responded to the Great Depression: President Herbert Hoover, President Franklin Delano Roosevelt, and ordinary citizens (civilians). Record those details in a chart like the one below. Then evaluate how effective those responses were at making the situation better.

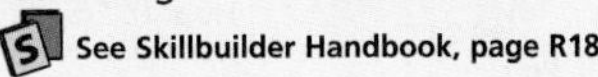
See Skillbuilder Handbook, page R18.

GREAT DEPRESSION

| Hoover's Responses | FDR's Responses | Citizens' Responses |
|---|---|---|
| Didn't interfere in economy<br>Rugged individualism<br>Encouraged charity<br>Limited, late relief efforts | Tried new ideas<br>Fireside chats<br>New Deal<br>Second New Deal | Rejected Hoover and supported FDR<br>Turned to bread lines<br>Recorded hard times in art<br>Developed fear of the future |
| **Effectiveness**<br>Answers will vary. | **Effectiveness**<br>Answers will vary. | **Effectiveness**<br>Answers will vary. |



## TEACHING STRATEGY

### READING THE CHAPTER

This is a thematic chapter focusing on the effects of the Great Depression and the New Deal. Encourage students to use their completed charts to evaluate whether responses were effective. For example, ask students whether Hoover's decision to not interfere with the economy was a wise one. Why or why not? Take time to point out how the changes in the role of government in the lives of people are reflected in today's society.

### ALTERNATIVE ASSESSMENT

The Chapter Assessment describes three activities for alternative assessment on page 751. You may wish to have students work on these activities during the course of the chapter and then present them at the end.

# 1 Hoover and the Crash

**TERMS & NAMES**
Herbert Hoover
speculation
buying on margin
Black Tuesday
Crash of 1929
Great Depression
public works projects
Bonus Army

**MAIN IDEA**
After the stock market crash of 1929, the U.S. economy sank into the worst depression in its history.

**WHY IT MATTERS NOW**
Today the government regulates banking and the stock exchange to prevent such severe depressions.

## ONE AMERICAN'S STORY

**Not everyone prospered in the 1920s. For example, many farmers suffered poverty because farm prices stayed low. Republican senator George Norris from Nebraska joined a group of lawmakers called the farm bloc, who sought to pass new laws to aid farmers. Norris also criticized bankers for not caring about farmers' problems.**

*A VOICE FROM THE PAST*

When the great leaders of banking and industry can see no further than the artificial prosperity that comes to Big Business while those who toil on farms are getting no return for their labor, then indeed we have a right to question the wisdom of our financial leaders.

**George Norris,** "The Farmers' Situation, a National Danger"

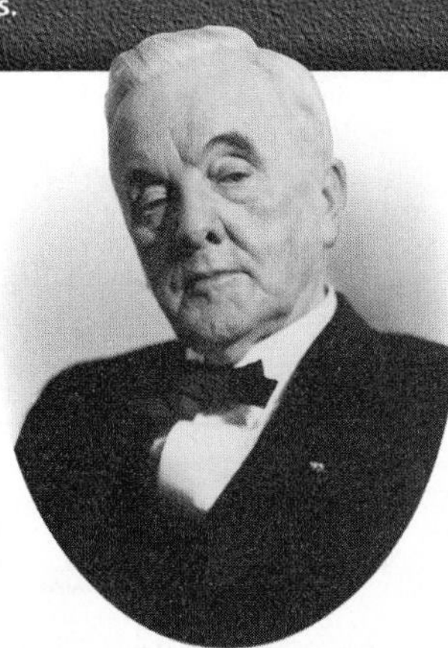

Instead of holding to pure Republican ideas, Norris said he "would rather be right than regular."

**Norris also urged the building of government-owned power plants in rural areas. He was unusual because most Republicans believed that government should not interfere in the economy. Section 1 explains how Republican policies came under attack when the economy failed.**

## 1 Problems in the Economy

Secretary of Commerce **Herbert Hoover** became the Republican candidate for president in 1928. In a speech, he stated, "We shall soon . . . be in sight of the day when poverty will be banished from this nation." But the overall prosperity of the 1920s hid the fact that some industries were in trouble. These included agriculture, railroads, textile mills, and mines.

The growing wealth of the richest Americans also hid the struggle of the majority. By 1929, 71 percent of American families earned less than \$2,500 per year, the minimum needed to live decently. Some people had no jobs. African Americans in particular had high jobless rates.

During the 1920s, industries had improved efficiency and begun to produce more goods. But the income of middle-class and poor people didn't rise enough for them to purchase the extra goods. Products piled up in warehouses, causing a problem. Unless businesses sold their products, they couldn't pay for materials, salaries, equipment, or shipping.





## SECTION OBJECTIVES

1. To identify the problems of the U.S. economy in the 1920s
2. To summarize the causes of the stock market crash and the Great Depression
3. To analyze how President Hoover responded to the Great Depression
4. To explain why Hoover lost the 1932 election to Roosevelt

**SKILLBUILDER**
Interpreting Graphs, p. 730

**CRITICAL THINKING**
Analyzing Causes, p. 731
Solving Problems, p. 732
Making Inferences, p. 733
Contrasting, p. 733

## FOCUS & MOTIVATE

### 5-MINUTE WARM-UP

**Recognizing Effects** These questions focus on economic problems of the 1920s.

1. Look at the graph on Short-Term Consumer Debt on page 730. Why did consumers use borrowed money to buy goods?
2. Why is it dangerous to the economy to have high consumer debt?

 **Warm-Up Transparency WT26**

## INSTRUCT

### INSTRUCT: OBJECTIVE 

**Problems in the Economy**
Key Questions
- What economic problems were hidden by the general prosperity of the nation in the 1920s?
- Why did prosperity depend on the sale of more goods?
- What were the risks of buying goods on credit and buying stocks on margin?

 **In-Depth Resources: Unit 8**
- Guided Reading, p. 21

## RECOMMENDED RESOURCES

 **In-Depth Resources: Unit 8**
- Guided Reading, p. 21
- Building Vocabulary, p. 25
- Primary Source: Testimony before the House Committee on Labor by Oscar Ameringer, p. 29
- Reteaching Activity, p. 34
- Enrichment Activity, p. 38

**Reading Study Guide** (Spanish and English), pp. 249–250

**Economics in History**
- The Great Depression, p. 26

**Formal Assessment**
- Section Quiz, p. 377

**Alternative Assessment**
- Rubrics, 2.3
- Rubrics, 3.1

**Access for Students Acquiring English/ESL**
- Guided Reading, p. 172

**Technology Resources**

 **Electronic Teacher Tools with Test Maker**

 **ClassZone**
www.mcdougallittell.com

## HISTORY FROM VISUALS

**Reading the Graphs** Tell students that a line graph is a way to display data that changes over time. Read aloud the title of each graph and ask students to identify the information it contains. Ask for volunteers to read aloud the caption for each graph. Ask students to find the income of the average farm in 1923. **Answer** $800.00

**Extension** Have students make a line graph showing the following data:

**Wholesale Prices of Selected Commodities**
**Annual Averages to the Nearest Half-Cent**

| | 1925 | 1929 | 1930 | 1931 |
|---|---|---|---|---|
| Wheat, bushel | $1.435 | $1.035 | $0.67 | $0.40 |
| Corn, bushel | 0.70 | 0.80 | 0.60 | 0.32 |
| Raw cotton, pound | 0.235 | 0.19 | 0.135 | 0.085 |
| Wool, pound | 1.40 | 0.985 | 0.765 | 0.62 |
| Tobacco, pound | 0.17 | 0.185 | 0.13 | 0.08 |

## MORE ABOUT . . .

**Stock Market Speculation**

Many factors contributed to stock market speculation. The Hoover administration kept interest rates low, which made it possible for speculators to borrow money to buy stocks. As the federal government paid off its World War I bonds, large amounts of money entered the economy. By 1929, many stocks were greatly overvalued. Prices of stocks were rising much more rapidly than the real economy.



## Economic Problems, *1920–1929*

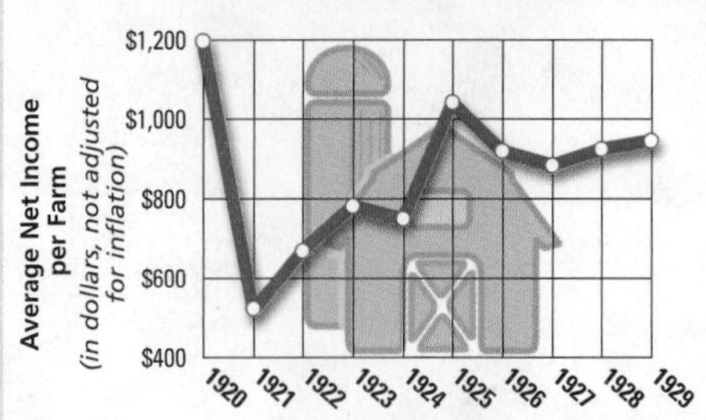


**Average Net Income per Farm** Notice the big drop in average farm income between 1920 and 1921. Although farm income generally rose during the decade, it did not reach the 1920 level.

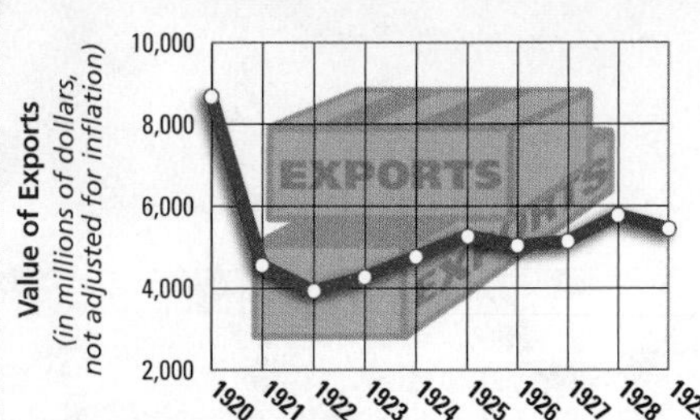


**Value of Exports** Notice the drop between 1920 and 1921. For the next eight years, exports remained generally the same. U.S. businesses barely increased the amount they sold overseas.

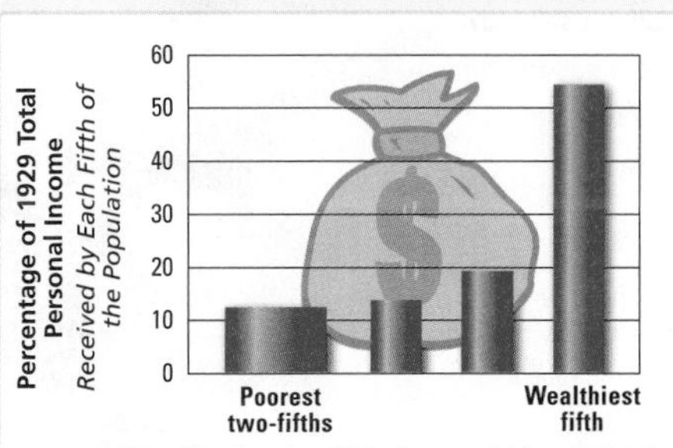


**Income Distribution** In 1929, the wealthiest fifth of the population had more income than the other four-fifths combined. Poor and middle-class people could not afford to buy many consumer goods. This hurt business.

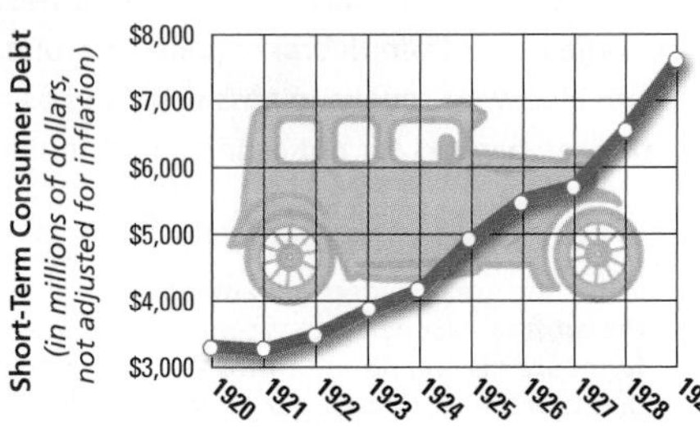


**Short-Term Consumer Debt** If people do not earn enough to buy what they want, they may take out loans or buy on credit. Short-term consumer debt skyrocketed from 1920 to 1929.

Sources: *Historical Statistics of the United States; A Study of Saving in the United States*

**SKILLBUILDER Interpreting Graphs**

1. *Which of these problems affected individuals, and which affected businesses?*
2. *By how much did short-term consumer debt rise from 1920 to 1929?*

Skillbuilder Answers
1. individuals—farm income, income distribution, consumer debt; businesses—value of exports, income distribution, consumer debt
2. about $4½ billion

Some consumers bought goods anyway—on credit. But when their debt grew higher than they could repay, they stopped buying new items. Unsold goods piled up even more.

Yet stock market prices kept climbing. Americans who could afford it rushed to buy stocks. Increasingly, investors bought on **speculation,** buying and selling stocks in the hope of making a quick profit.

Investors also began **buying on margin**—they paid a small part of a stock's price as a down payment and borrowed the rest. When they sold the stock, they repaid the loan and kept the profit. The system worked as long as prices rose. But if prices fell, borrowers couldn't repay their loans because they had to sell the stock for less than they paid for it.

Despite these problems, people believed Hoover when he predicted growing prosperity. In 1928, he won the presidency by a landslide.

**Vocabulary**
**credit:** an agreement to pay over time, instead of all at once



## ACTIVITY OPTIONS

## INTERDISCIPLINARY LINK: MATHEMATICS

BLOCK SCHEDULING

### COMPARING GRAPHS

**Class Time** One class period

**Task** Making a line graph of consumer debt in the 1990s

**Purpose** To compare trends in consumer debt in the 1920s and the 1990s

**Supplies Needed**
- Graph paper
- Markers

**Activity** Have students review the graphs on Economic Problems on page 730. Then have them make a line graph of consumer debt for the period 1990–1997 using these data. All figures are in billions of dollars:

| 1990 | 1991 | 1992 | 1993 | 1994 | 1995 | 1996 | 1997 |
|---|---|---|---|---|---|---|---|
| $813.0 | $799.9 | $804.6 | $863.9 | $988.8 | $1,131.9 | $1,214.9 | $1,264.1 |

After completing their graphs, have them compare the Consumer Debt graph on page 730 with their own for the 1990s. Ask students in which period consumer debt rose more rapidly.

## ❷ The Crash and the Great Depression

On September 3, 1929, the value of stocks on the New York Stock Exchange reached a high point. Then prices drifted downward. On October 23, prices dropped sharply. The next morning, people tried to sell thousands of shares before their value dropped further. Many of those who had bought on margin were forced to sell stocks to pay off their loans.

This heavy selling drove prices even lower. Because more people wanted to sell stocks than to buy them, prices had to go down to attract purchasers. But the quickly falling prices scared off buyers. Meanwhile, sellers hurried to unload their shares at the best price they could get.

On October 24, a record 12.9 million shares were traded. But the worst was yet to come. On October 29, **Black Tuesday,** investors sold 16.4 million shares of stocks at prices much lower than they had been selling for a month earlier. The plunge in stock market prices, called the **Crash of 1929,** was the first event of a terrible economic depression.

After the stock market crash, banks began to demand that people pay back the money they had borrowed to buy stocks. When people could not repay these loans, banks ran short of money. This frightening news sent people running to the banks to withdraw their savings. But banks typically do not keep enough cash on hand to pay all of their depositors at once. Unable to pay their depositors, many banks simply closed. By March 1933, about 9,000 banks had gone out of business.

**Background**
This pattern of selling stocks and withdrawing deposits because of fear is the reason the depressions of the 1800s are also called panics.

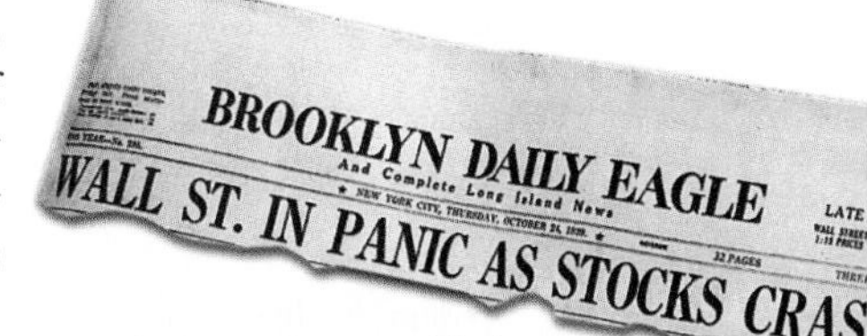
BROOKLYN DAILY EAGLE
WALL ST. IN PANIC AS STOCKS CRASH

Businesses felt the impact next. Many already had warehouses filled with more goods than they could sell. Because the economy's problems scared people, they stopped buying new goods. As a result, businesses sold less and less. Tens of thousands of businesses went bankrupt.

To survive, many businesses fired workers. Unemployment grew to 25 percent by 1933. As more people lost jobs, they bought fewer products—and companies laid off even more workers. Unable to pay their bills, thousands of people lost their homes, and millions went hungry.

The United States had experienced economic depressions before. But no depression caused as much suffering or lasted as long as this one—from 1929 to World War II. Therefore, it is called the **Great Depression.**

The Great Depression also affected millions of people around the world. For example, many European countries had borrowed money from U.S. banks to rebuild after World War I. When the American economy failed, so did Europe's. Hard times spread around the globe.

A. Possible Response
Because he was president, they assumed he had the power to fix the economy.

*Reading* **History**
**A. Analyzing Causes** Why do you think people expected Hoover to end the Depression?

## ❸ Hoover Acts Conservatively

Americans looked to the president to end the hard times. Along with most Republicans, Hoover feared that government interference might hurt the economy even more. Even so, he did try to fight the Depression, but his actions often backfired. For example, he tried to balance the





### INSTRUCT: OBJECTIVE ❷

**The Crash and the Great Depression**
Key Questions
- What part did buying on margin and panic selling play in the crash of 1929?
- How was the Great Depression different from earlier economic depressions?

### MORE ABOUT . . .

**The Crash of 1929**
Most of the early losers on Wall Street were speculators, not ordinary citizens. By October, an average stock had lost almost one-fourth of its value. By mid-November, industrial stocks had lost half their value. Although the market seemed to stabilize by mid-1931, stock prices kept falling into the summer of 1932. From October 1929 until June 1932, General Motors fell from 73 points to 8, U.S. Steel from 262 points to 21, Montgomery Ward from 138 to 4, and RCA from 101 to 2.5.

 **In-Depth Resources: Unit 8**
- Enrichment Activity, p. 38

### INSTRUCT: OBJECTIVE ❸

**Hoover Acts Conservatively**
Key Questions
- Why was Hoover reluctant to involve the government in solving the nation's economic problems?
- Why did many Americans blame Hoover for their suffering?
- Why did Hoover's public works projects fail to boost the economy?

 **In-Depth Resources: Unit 8**
- Primary Source, p. 29

**ACTIVITY OPTIONS**

**INDIVIDUAL NEEDS**

**LESS PROFICIENT READERS**

**Analyzing Causes and Recognizing Effects** Some students may have difficulty understanding the economic problems of the 1920s. On the board, write the following causes and effects in a chart like the one shown here. Read each entry in the chart and ask students to supply the corresponding cause or effect.

| Cause | Effect |
|---|---|
| **Stock prices dropped on October 23.** | <Investors sold their stocks.> |
| <People could not repay loans to banks.> | **Banks ran short of money.** |
| **Business sold fewer products.** | <Businesses fired workers.> |

## Economics *in* History

**OBJECTIVE**
Students will be able to describe a business cycle and distinguish between a recession and a depression.

**Understanding the Business Cycle**
The business cycle has been described as lengthy periods of gradual business growth interspersed with sharp and usually shorter periods of contraction and decline. At the peak of an expansion in the business cycle, factories operate at full or near full capacity, wages are high, and unemployment is low. Because the periods of expansion are usually longer and more frequent than the contractions, the U.S. economy has grown over time. Before the Great Depression that began in 1929, the United States had severe depressions in 1837, 1873, 1893, and 1907.

1. **Evaluating Possible Response** They lasted for years, not months, and the economy not only stopped growing but actually lost value.
2. **Making Inferences Possible Response** It would be more severe and affect more countries because the United States is a bigger player in foreign trade.

**Economics in History**
- The Great Depression, p. 26

## MORE ABOUT . . .

**Effects of the Depression**
The Depression touched almost every aspect of American life. In 1932, half the workers in some industrial cities had no jobs. In Toledo, Ohio, 80 percent of workers were unemployed. Historians estimate that from 1 to 2 million unemployed men roamed the country. The marriage rate and the birth rate dropped. Over 750 Chicago teachers lost their homes by mid-1932. Even Babe Ruth was affected by the Depression. The Yankees cut his salary by $10,000 in 1932.

## Economics *in* History

# Recession and Depression

Many people hoped the economy would fix itself because they believed depressions were a natural part of the business cycle (shown below). Economies go through ups and downs. The period when an economy is at its worst is a trough. There are two kinds of troughs—recessions and depressions. A depression is more severe.

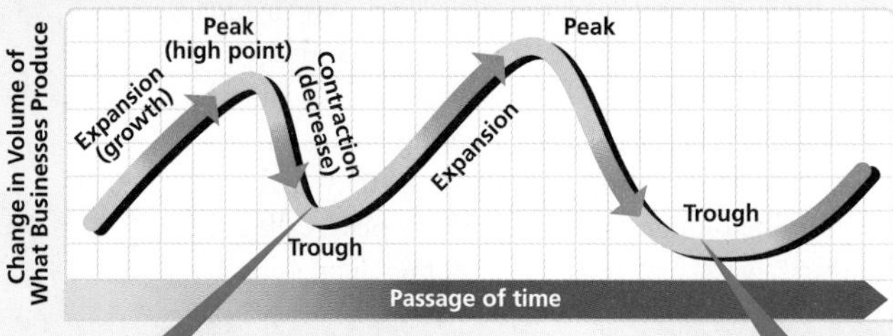


**Recession**
- The production of a nation's goods and services goes down each month for six months.
- Business owners produce less and invest less in new equipment and facilities. They also lay off workers.
- Consumers buy fewer goods.

**Depression**
- The production of goods and services drops lower than in a recession.
- The period of no economic growth is longer than in a recession. Unemployment is higher.
- The slowdown may spread to other countries; international trade declines dramatically.

**CONNECT TO HISTORY**
1. **Evaluating** Why were the hard times of the 1930s a depression, not a recession?

See Skillbuilder Handbook, page R18.

**CONNECT TO TODAY**
2. **Making Inferences** How would today's world be affected differently by a depression in the United States than by one in Holland? Explain.

Visit www.mcdougallittell.com to learn more about economics.

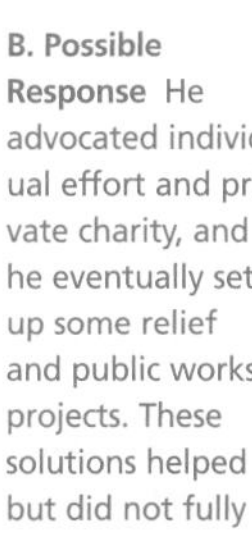

federal budget by cutting government spending and raising taxes. This pulled money out of the economy, which made the slump worse.

Some of Hoover's actions made him very unpopular. For example, he believed that federal relief—aid to the poor—would make people too dependent on government. So he would not support giving relief. In his view, one answer to the hard times was a quality he called "rugged individualism." In 1931, Hoover said, "We cannot legislate ourselves out of a world economic depression. We can and will work ourselves out."

Hoover also stressed the value of volunteer efforts. He encouraged churches and private charities such as the Salvation Army and the Red Cross to help needy Americans. In 1932, private giving did reach a record level—but it still wasn't enough to help everyone in need.

As unemployment, hunger, and homelessness grew, people became bitter toward the president. They blamed him for their suffering. They called empty pockets turned inside out "Hoover flags." And they called villages of wretched huts that housed homeless people "Hoovervilles."

Finally, Hoover softened his stand against government relief. States received some federal money to give to the needy. And in 1932, Hoover set up an agency to lend money to states, cities, and towns. This money would be used for **public works projects**—government-funded projects to build public resources such as roads and dams. These projects would create jobs. But Hoover's actions proved to be too little and too late.

B. Possible Response He advocated individual effort and private charity, and he eventually set up some relief and public works projects. These solutions helped but did not fully succeed.

*Reading* **History**
**B. Solving Problems** What were Hoover's solutions to the problems caused by the Depression, and did they succeed?



**ACTIVITY OPTIONS**
**INTERDISCIPLINARY LINK: ECONOMICS** — BLOCK SCHEDULING

**PLAYING THE MARKET IN THE 1920s**

**Class Time** One or two class periods

**Task** Simulating investment in the stock market

**Purpose** To understand how speculation and buying on margin can inflate stock prices and lead to a crash

**Supplies Needed**
- Play money
- Calculators
- Signs with stock names and prices from the 1920s
- Ledger paper for recordkeeping

**Activity** Divide the class into teams of four to six students. Give each team $1,000 in play money to invest in stocks. During each investment round, teams can buy and sell stocks at 1920s prices, either by paying full price or buying on margin. Explain what buying on margin means. Allow several rounds of investing in which teams can make a profit. Then pick an arbitrary point at which the market "crashes." Afterwards, have students write a paragraph summarizing the experience.

# 4 Hoover Loses to Roosevelt

In the summer of 1932, a dramatic event made Hoover even more unpopular. Congress had promised World War I veterans a bonus for wartime service. The bonuses were not due to be paid until the 1940s. But many of the ex-soldiers were jobless and wanted early payment. Some decided to march to Washington, D.C., to ask Congress to pass such a law. Through May and June, the **Bonus Army** of 12,000 to 15,000 veterans poured into Washington and set up camps around the city. Some of them were accompanied by their families.

U.S. troops used tanks and grenades to force the Bonus Army from their camps.

The Senate, backed by Hoover, voted down a bill that called for a bonus payment. Most veterans gave up and returned home, but a few thousand remained to protest.

At the end of July, General Douglas MacArthur decided on his own to drive the Bonus Army from Washington. MacArthur's troops threw tear gas and prodded the veterans and their children with bayonets. One veteran was shot to death. The American public reacted angrily.

*Reading* **History**

**C. Making Inferences** Why do you think Evalyn McLean became so angry?

C. Possible Response because she was upset at seeing the U.S. Army turn against U.S. citizens

*A VOICE FROM THE PAST*

I saw in a news reel the tanks, the cavalry, and the gas-bomb throwers running those wretched Americans out of our capital. I was so raging mad I could have torn the theater down.

**Evalyn Walsh McLean,** *Father Struck It Rich*

Because of the attack, Americans turned against Hoover more than ever. In the 1932 presidential election, Democratic candidate Franklin Delano Roosevelt carried all but six states. Section 2 explains how Roosevelt tried to end the Depression with new federal programs.

## Section 1 Assessment

**1. Terms & Names**

**Identify:**
- Herbert Hoover
- speculation
- buying on margin
- Black Tuesday
- Crash of 1929
- Great Depression
- public works projects
- Bonus Army

**2. Taking Notes**

Use a diagram like the one below to show the sequence of events that led from the stock market crash to massive unemployment.

**3. Main Ideas**

a. What weaknesses existed in the economy during the 1920s?

b. What is buying on margin, and how was it a problem?

c. Why did Hoover become unpopular with many Americans?

**4. Critical Thinking**

**Contrasting** How did Hoover's view of the federal government and that of most Americans differ?

**THINK ABOUT**
- Hoover's attitude about federal relief
- why Americans blamed Hoover for their suffering
- what Americans might have expected from Hoover

**ACTIVITY OPTIONS**

**MATH**
**SPEECH**

Research the changes in stock market value from September through October 1929. Create a **graph** or give a series of **radio news bulletins** about the changes.





**INSTRUCT: OBJECTIVE 4**

**Hoover Loses to Roosevelt**

Key Questions
- Why did World War I veterans gather in Washington, D.C., in 1932?
- Who removed the veterans?
- How did the treatment of Bonus Army protesters affect the 1932 election?

**CRITICAL THINKING ACTIVITY**

**Identifying and Solving Problems** Ask students why they think Americans were angry about the treatment of the Bonus Army protesters. What are some other ways Hoover might have resolved the conflict? Have students use the graphic organizer to consider this issue.

**Class Time** 10 minutes

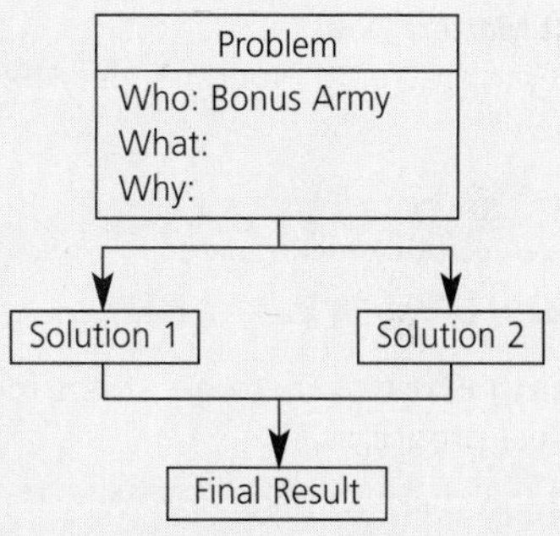



## ASSESS & RETEACH

**Setting the Stage** Have students fill in the first section on the graphic organizer.

**Formal Assessment**
- Section Quiz, p. 377

**Critical Thinking Transparency CT76**
- Setting the Stage

**RETEACHING ACTIVITY**

Ask students to write a summary of Section 1 in which they leave key terms and names of people blank. Have pairs of students exchange papers and complete each other's summaries.

**In-Depth Resources: Unit 8**
- Reteaching Activity, p. 34

## Section 1 Assessment

**1. Terms & Names**

**Herbert Hoover,** p. 729
**speculation,** p. 730
**buying on margin,** p. 730
**Black Tuesday,** p. 731
**Crash of 1929,** p. 731
**Great Depression,** p. 731
**public works projects,** p. 732
**Bonus Army,** p. 733

**2. Taking Notes**

stock market crash→banks failed→businesses sold less and laid off workers→massive unemployment

**3. Main Ideas**

**a.** industries were struggling; wages were low; income and foreign trade decreased; debt rose **b.** paying part of a stock's price as a down payment and borrowing the rest; when prices dropped, people had to repay their loans **c.** He opposed federal relief and attacked the Bonus Army.

**4. Critical Thinking**

Hoover thought the government should not interfere in the economy or hand out charity; Americans disagreed.

**ACTIVITY OPTIONS**

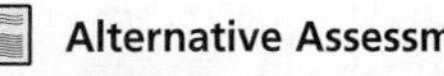

**Alternative Assessment**
- Rubrics for a graph, 2.3
- Rubrics for a bulletin, 3.1

## SECTION OBJECTIVES

1. To describe Roosevelt's immediate attempts to improve conditions for Americans
2. To evaluate criticisms of the New Deal
3. To identify the Social Security Act and other programs of the Second New Deal
4. To explain Roosevelt's efforts to change the Supreme Court

**SKILLBUILDER**

Interpreting Charts, p. 737

**CRITICAL THINKING**

Drawing Conclusions, p. 735
Analyzing Causes, p. 737
Recognizing Effects, p. 738
Analyzing Points of View, p. 738

 **Why It Matters Now**
- Government Youth Programs, pp. 51–52

## FOCUS & MOTIVATE

### 5-MINUTE WARM-UP

**Recognizing Effects** These questions focus on New Deal programs.

1. Look at the chart on page 737. Which programs involved creation of jobs?
2. How does this chart illustrate the broad scope of the programs of the New Deal?

 **Warm-Up Transparency WT26**

## INSTRUCT

### INSTRUCT: OBJECTIVE 

**Roosevelt Takes Charge/The Hundred Days**

Key Questions
- How did FDR differ from Hoover in his approach to the nation's problems?
- How did FDR restore confidence in banks?
- What were three major goals of the programs passed during the Hundred Days?

 **In-Depth Resources: Unit 8**
- Guided Reading, p. 22
- Building Vocabulary, p. 25

# 2 Roosevelt and the New Deal

**TERMS & NAMES**
Franklin Delano Roosevelt
fireside chat
New Deal
Hundred Days
Social Security Act
Second New Deal
deficit spending

**MAIN IDEA**

After becoming president, Franklin D. Roosevelt took many actions to fight the Great Depression.

**WHY IT MATTERS NOW**

Roosevelt increased government's role in helping needy Americans and regulating the financial industry.

### ONE AMERICAN'S STORY

**Dynamite Garland's father had worked for the railroad. But when the Depression struck, Dynamite's father lost his job, and her family had to move into a garage that a landlord let them have rent-free.**

*A VOICE FROM THE PAST*

We had a coal stove, and we had to each take turns, the three of us kids, to warm our legs. It was awfully cold when you opened those garage doors. . . . In the morning, we'd get out and get some snow and put it on the stove and melt it and wash around our faces. Never the neck or anything. Put on our two pairs of socks on each hand and two pairs of socks on our feet, and long underwear and lace it up with Goodwill shoes. Off we'd walk, three, four miles to school.

**Dynamite Garland,** quoted in *Hard Times*

**Children such as Dynamite Garland and the girls in this photograph suffered greatly from hunger and poverty during the Depression.**

**Starting in 1933, Franklin Delano Roosevelt, the new Democratic president, created a number of programs to help the economy and people like Dynamite. This section describes those programs.**

## 1 Roosevelt Takes Charge

Millions of people lacked food and shelter. Yet the country had to endure a frustrating four-month wait from the November election to Roosevelt's inauguration. The Twentieth Amendment, which moved the inauguration date to January, was not ratified until 1933. President Roosevelt, nicknamed FDR, was finally inaugurated on March 4, 1933.

Roosevelt differed from Hoover in two important ways. First, he gave Americans hope, beginning with his inaugural address: "Let me assert my firm belief that the only thing we have to fear is fear itself." Second, he was willing to try new ideas and change the way government worked. Though he had no fixed plan to end the Depression, he set up a "brain trust" of advisers, including college professors and economists.

Roosevelt took three immediate steps that boosted public confidence. First, he declared a "bank holiday"—a temporary shutdown of all banks.



## RECOMMENDED RESOURCES

 **In-Depth Resources: Unit 8**
- Guided Reading, p. 22
- Building Vocabulary, p. 25
- Skillbuilder Practice, p. 26
- Reteaching Activity, p. 35

**Reading Study Guide** (Spanish and English), pp. 251–252

**America's History Makers**
- Franklin D. Roosevelt, pp. 103–104

 **Why It Matters Now**
- Government Youth Programs, pp. 51–52

**Formal Assessment**
- Section Quiz, p. 378

**Alternative Assessment**
- Rubrics, 1.2
- Rubrics, 5.1

**Access for Students Acquiring English/ESL**
- Guided Reading, p. 173
- Skillbuilder Practice, p. 176

**Technology Resources**

 **Critical Thinking Trans. CT77**
- Cause and Effect: The Great Depression

 **Electronic Teacher Tools with Test Maker**

 **ClassZone**
www.mcdougallittell.com

*Reading*History

**A. Drawing Conclusions** Did Roosevelt's first fireside chat affect the public the way he wanted? Explain.
A. Possible Response Yes. People demonstrated their faith in the banks by re-depositing their money.

Second, he promised that only the banks that were in good shape would be allowed to reopen.

Third, the day before the banks reopened, FDR gave the first of many **fireside chats.** In these radio talks, he explained his policies in a warm, friendly style. He said it was safer to "keep your money in a reopened bank than under the mattress." The next day, people deposited more money into the banks than they withdrew.

## The Hundred Days

During the campaign, FDR had pledged a "new deal" for Americans. This snappy phrase, the **New Deal,** came to stand for FDR's programs to fight the Depression.

In the session of Congress lasting from March 9 to mid-June 1933, Roosevelt sent Congress a pile of new bills. Many of them passed with little debate in this famous session of Congress, called the **Hundred Days.**

The laws passed during the Hundred Days had three major goals, known as the "three Rs."

1. **relief** for the hungry and jobless
2. **recovery** for agriculture and industry
3. **reforms** to change the way the economy worked

FDR wanted not only to ease suffering but also to try to prevent such a severe depression from happening again. The major programs passed during the Hundred Days included relief, recovery, and reform plans that related to jobs, banking, wages, and agriculture. The chart on page 737 lists several major programs and explains what those programs accomplished.

## 2 Responses to the New Deal

**Vocabulary**
**socialism:** an economic system in which businesses are owned by the government, not individuals

Some conservatives thought the New Deal went too far. They opposed the growth of the federal government and questioned how it would pay for all the new programs. They also feared that the New Deal was moving the country toward socialism.

Yet, other critics charged that the New Deal didn't go far enough. Louisiana senator Huey Long declared, "Unless we provide for redistribution of wealth in this country, the country is doomed." But Long's motives were far from noble. For years, he had ruled his state like a dictator. Attacking FDR was a way to increase his own power.

Father Charles Coughlin, a priest with a popular radio program, also argued for changing the economy to help the poor. He eventually began to blame Jews for the nation's problems. In the 1940s, the Catholic Church stopped his broadcasts. Another critic, Francis Townshend, proposed giving $200 a month to every American over age 60. He said a sales tax would pay for the pension, but economists disputed his figures.

### AMERICA'S HISTORY MAKERS

**FRANKLIN DELANO ROOSEVELT**
**1882–1945**

A distant cousin of Theodore Roosevelt, Franklin D. Roosevelt became a New York state senator when he was 29. Later, he served as assistant secretary of the Navy.

At the age of 39, FDR caught polio. For the rest of his life, he walked with braces or rode in a wheelchair. Despite this, he continued in politics and was elected governor of New York in 1928.

The public rarely saw photos revealing FDR's disability. Even so, many Americans sensed that he was a man who understood trouble. This quality helped him as a leader during the Depression.

**How would an understanding of trouble help Roosevelt to lead?**

### AMERICA'S HISTORY MAKERS

**Franklin Delano Roosevelt**
FDR refused to be an invalid. He began a vigorous exercise program for his upper body. He once said proudly of the results, "Maybe my legs aren't so good, but look at those shoulders." Many people were so captivated by his vigor and confidence that they remained largely unaware of the extent of his dependence on braces and crutches.

**Possible Response: Because he had suffered and overcome great difficulties himself, FDR was sensitive to the suffering of others and believed he could help them.**

**America's History Makers**
• Franklin D. Roosevelt, pp. 103–104

### MORE ABOUT . . .

**Huey Long**
Known as the "Kingfish," Huey Long gained national attention first as governor of Louisiana and then as a U.S. senator. Long became an outspoken critic of FDR in 1933, calling the president too conservative and proposing to redistribute the nation's wealth through a tax-the-rich scheme he called "Share Our Wealth." Long was considering running for president when he was assassinated in 1935.

### INSTRUCT: OBJECTIVE 2

**Responses to the New Deal**
Key Questions
- Why did many conservatives oppose the New Deal?
- Why did Father Coughlin, Huey Long, and Francis Townshend criticize the New Deal?
- How did voters show their support for the New Deal?

### ACTIVITY OPTIONS
### INDIVIDUAL NEEDS

**LESS PROFICIENT READERS**
**Identifying Details** To help students focus their reading, draw a Main Idea and Details chart on the board. Before students read, point out the four main ideas in Section 2. Tell students to look for details about each main idea as they read. Record the details as students identify them.

| Main Idea | Details |
|---|---|
| New Deal | FDR's program to fight the Depression<br>relief for the hungry<br>recovery for agriculture and industry<br>reforms to improve the economy |
| Response to the New Deal | |
| Second New Deal | |
| Slowdown of the New Deal | |

## Connections TO *SCIENCE*

**The Tennessee Valley Authority**

The TVA uses the power of water to generate electricity. Dams built throughout the Tennessee River Valley stop the flow of water, which builds up behind the dam, forming a lake. The force of the water creates great pressure. When water is released from the dam into an electricity-generating system, it spins large turbines that drive the electric generators, producing electric current.

CONNECTIONS TO SCIENCE

### The Tennessee Valley Authority

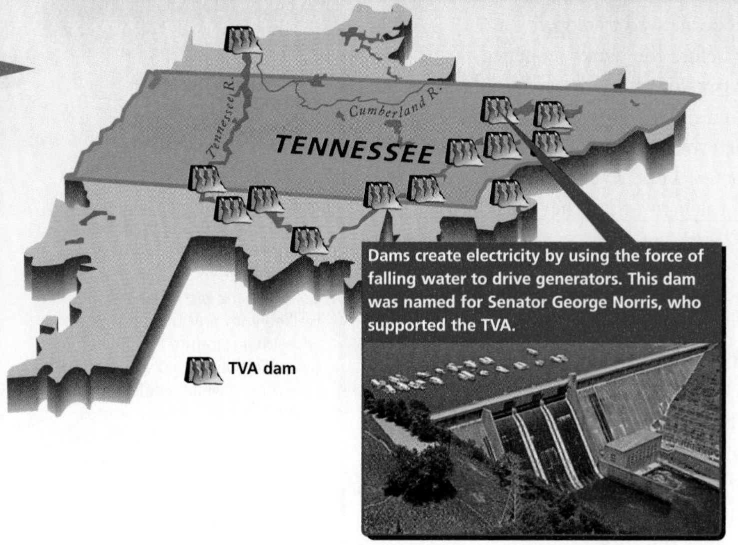


Dams create electricity by using the force of falling water to drive generators. This dam was named for Senator George Norris, who supported the TVA.

**FACTS ABOUT THE TVA**

- The TVA supplies power to an area of about 80,000 square miles, shown in dark and light green to the left. The region uses more than 100 billion kilowatt-hours of electricity. This is 65 times as much as in 1933.
- There are more than 40 TVA dams.
- Users of TVA power pay about a third less for their electricity than other Americans.
- The TVA dams also help control flooding on the Tennessee River.

In the 1934 congressional elections, voters had a chance to react to these criticisms. The party in power usually loses seats in a nonpresidential election. But, indicating their support for Roosevelt, voters in this election sent even more Democrats to Congress.

## 3 The Second New Deal

Although he rejected Townshend's plan, FDR did want to help the elderly. Bank failures and the stock market crash had stolen the savings of many old people. Some had lost their homes or had to beg for food.

In August 1935, Congress passed one of the most important bills of the century. Under the **Social Security Act,** workers and employers made payments into a special fund, from which they would draw a pension after they retired. The act also gave help to laid-off workers, disabled workers, and needy families with dependent children.

**Background**
Townshend's plan had been very popular with the public. FDR knew his own popularity would increase if he proposed a pension.

*A VOICE FROM THE PAST*

We have tried to frame a law which will give some measure of protection to the average citizen and to his family against the loss of a job and against poverty-ridden old age.

**Franklin D. Roosevelt,** quoted in *Promises to Keep*

Social Security was part of a set of programs passed in 1935. These became known as the **Second New Deal.** Other programs of the Second New Deal are listed in the chart on the next page.

In 1936, the Democrats nominated Roosevelt for a second term. Business leaders opposed his reelection because they feared higher taxes. They also thought he was increasing government power at their expense. But a widespread alliance of working-class Americans supported FDR.



**INSTRUCT: OBJECTIVE 3**

**The Second New Deal**

Key Questions
- Who benefited from passage of the Social Security Act?
- Why were the FDR programs passed in 1935 called the Second New Deal?

**CRITICAL THINKING ACTIVITY**

**Drawing Conclusions** Have students make a two-column chart of the various services government provides today. Beside each service, have students identify groups that benefit from these services. After the chart is completed, have them discuss which of these services they consider to be essential.

**Class Time** 20 minutes

**ACTIVITY OPTIONS**

**INTERDISCIPLINARY LINK: GEOGRAPHY** — BLOCK SCHEDULING

**GEOGRAPHY OF THE TVA**

**Class Time** 30 minutes

**Task** Making a map of the rivers and states affected by the TVA

**Purpose** To identify the area affected by the TVA and to appreciate the size of the project

**Supplies Needed**
- Encyclopedias and other research materials on the TVA
- Internet access
- Atlas maps
- Outline map of the United States (optional)
- Art supplies

**Activity** Have students use encyclopedias, the Internet, and other reference materials to find out which states and rivers were affected by the TVA. Have them work in groups to fill in an outline map or a map they sketch with the states involved in the TVA, major rivers affected, and major dams and power plants. Then have groups write at least two generalizations about the way geography affected the TVA and the way the TVA affected the environment.

## Major Programs of the New Deal

| | PROGRAMS | ACCOMPLISHMENTS |
|---|---|---|
| Hundred Days, 1933 | **FERA** (Federal Emergency Relief Administration) | Provided federal money for relief projects to the roughly 13 million unemployed |
| | **PWA** (Public Works Administration) | Created jobs by having people build highways, bridges, and other public works |
| | **AAA** (Agricultural Adjustment Administration) | Regulated farm production and promoted soil conservation |
| | **TVA** (Tennessee Valley Authority) | Planned development of the Tennessee Valley region |
| | **CCC** (Civilian Conservation Corps) | Hired young men to plant trees, build dams, and work on other conservation projects |
| | **FDIC** (Federal Deposit Insurance Corporation) | Protected the money of depositors in insured banks |
| | **NRA** (National Recovery Administration) | Regulated industry and raised wages and prices |
| Second New Deal, 1935 | **WPA** (Works Progress Administration) | Established large-scale national works programs to create jobs |
| | **REA** (Rural Electrification Administration) | Brought electricity to rural areas |
| | **NYA** (National Youth Administration) | Set up job programs for young people and helped them continue their education |
| | **Wagner Act** | Protected labor's right to form unions and set up a board to hear labor disputes |
| | **Social Security Act** | Provided workers with unemployment insurance and retirement benefits |

SKILLBUILDER **Interpreting Charts**

1. *How did the PWA and the CCC help both those who were hired and the nation as a whole?*
2. *How did the Second New Deal help both young and old workers?*

### HISTORY FROM VISUALS

**Interpreting the Charts** Ask students to identify a New Deal program that provided short-term relief. **Answer** FERA. What problem did the FDIC seek to correct? **Answer** Bank failures. How might the presence of the FDIC make bank failures less likely? **Answer** Depositors would be less likely to panic and withdraw their money because they would know their money was protected. Which programs are still in use today? **Possible Answers** Social Security, FDIC, TVA, and REA

**Extension** Have students research one of the New Deal programs to find out why it was started, how it was administered, and what it achieved.

*Reading* **History**

**B. Analyzing Causes** Why did many African Americans switch to the Democratic Party?

**B. Possible Response** They appreciated FDR's programs to help the poor.

Skillbuilder Answers
1. They provided jobs for individuals; they built public works and planted trees to benefit the nation.
2. The NYA helped provide jobs and education for the young; Social Security offered pensions to the old.

They included African Americans, who until then had remained loyal to the Republican Party—the party of Lincoln, who had issued the Emancipation Proclamation during the Civil War. However, FDR's programs to help the poor convinced many African Americans to vote Democrat. On Election Day, FDR won every state except Maine and Vermont.

## 4 Roosevelt Fights the Supreme Court

From the high point of his 1936 victory, Roosevelt's presidency took a downward turn. Most of the nine justices of the Supreme Court didn't support FDR's programs. Using the power of judicial review (see Chapter 10), in 1935 the Court struck down laws that it believed gave the federal government too much power. These actions threatened to destroy the New Deal.

In 1937, FDR asked Congress to pass a bill allowing him to add up to six justices to the Supreme Court. He planned to appoint justices who shared his ideas about government. This would give him the majority he



### INSTRUCT: OBJECTIVE 

**Roosevelt Fights the Supreme Court/ The New Deal Slows Down**

Key Questions
- Why did FDR want to add more justices to the Supreme Court?
- How did his attempt to pack the Court hurt FDR?
- Why did criticism of FDR increase after 1937?

ACTIVITY OPTIONS

### SKILLBUILDER MINI-LESSON: MAKING PUBLIC SPEECHES

BLOCK SCHEDULING

**Explaining the Skill** Advance preparation is a key aspect of successful public speaking. Before preparing a speech, research and take notes on your topic. Consider your audience and the goals you want to accomplish. Skillful speakers tailor their remarks to their audience. Practice presenting your speech to a friend to gain confidence and familiarity with the content. Speak slowly and make eye contact with the audience.

**Applying the Skill** Tell students to imagine that they have been asked to write and deliver a fireside chat, telling the radio audience about the "three R's" of the New Deal.

As a class discuss the following questions:
1. Who is the audience for this speech?
2. What are the goals for this speech?
3. What are five key points I want to make on this topic?

Pair students and have each student practice delivering his or her speech to the partner. Conclude by having volunteers give their speeches to the class.

 **In-Depth Resources: Unit 8**
- Skillbuilder Practice, p. 26

MORE ABOUT . . .

**FDR's Court Packing**

By 1937, the Supreme Court had ruled against the Roosevelt Administration in 11 out of 16 cases. Calling the justices "nine old men," FDR proposed a major reorganization of the Supreme Court. The number of justices had been fixed at nine since 1869, and FDR's attempt at court packing outraged some of his staunchest supporters. The Senate defeated the proposal 70 to 22. However, the justices also realized that they could not continue to overturn programs that had broad support. After the court narrowly accepted the next New Deal program, one humorist commented, "A switch in time saves nine."

## ASSESS & RETEACH

**Setting the Stage** Have students fill in the section on the graphic organizer titled "FDR's Responses."

 **Formal Assessment**
- Section Quiz, p. 378

**RETEACHING ACTIVITY**

Have each student write a paragraph identifying the three major goals of the New Deal and describing one program that attempted to carry out each goal.

 **In-Depth Resources: Unit 8**
- Reteaching Activity, p. 35

**"Dr. Roosevelt" reassures the Constitution that the New Deal won't harm it. Instead, FDR blames "Nurse Supreme Court" for any problems.**

needed to save his programs from being overturned. Both Republicans and Democrats harshly criticized FDR's "court-packing" bill. They said it interfered with the system of checks and balances that were set up by the U.S. Constitution. Congress agreed and voted it down.

In the end, Roosevelt did achieve his goal of a more sympathetic Court. Within the next two and a half years, retirements and deaths allowed Roosevelt to name five liberal justices to the bench. But the president may have lost more than he won. His clumsy attempt to pack the Court with allies damaged his image and gave ammunition to his critics.

*Reading* **History**

**C. Recognizing Effects** What was the outcome of Roosevelt's attempt to pack the Court?

**C. Possible Response** His bill failed to pass, and more people began to criticize him.

## The New Deal Slows Down

Opposition to Roosevelt grew after the "court-packing" attempt. Then in late 1937, the economy worsened again. The amount of goods produced by industry fell, and unemployment rose. Many blamed FDR for the downturn.

Critics also attacked Roosevelt's use of **deficit spending**, or using borrowed money to fund government programs. Roosevelt himself had doubts about it. Even though some economists said that huge amounts of deficit spending were needed to boost the economy, FDR hesitated to take that course. He proposed few new programs in his second term. Meanwhile, as Section 3 explains, Americans continued to suffer from harsh economic conditions.

### Section 2 Assessment

**1. Terms & Names**

**Identify:**
- Franklin Delano Roosevelt
- fireside chat
- New Deal
- Hundred Days
- Social Security Act
- Second New Deal
- deficit spending

**2. Taking Notes**

Use a chart like the one below to list FDR's major programs and whether you think each program's goal was relief, recovery, or reform (or a combination of these).

| Program | Goal |
|---|---|
| | |

Which programs created jobs?

**3. Main Ideas**

**a.** How did Roosevelt give Americans hope?

**b.** What happened during the period known as the Hundred Days?

**c.** What were the consequences of FDR's attempt to increase the size of the Supreme Court?

**4. Critical Thinking**

**Analyzing Points of View** What were some of the different reasons that people criticized FDR?

**THINK ABOUT**
- the conservatives
- Huey Long, Father Coughlin, and Francis Townshend
- those who opposed the "court-packing" bill

**ACTIVITY OPTIONS**

**ART**
**TECHNOLOGY**

Choose one aspect of the New Deal that you have an opinion about. Create a **political cartoon** or design a **Web page** expressing your opinion.



### Section 2 Assessment

**1. Terms & Names**

**Franklin Delano Roosevelt,** p. 734
**fireside chat,** p. 735
**New Deal,** p. 735
**Hundred Days,** p. 735
**Social Security Act,** p. 736
**Second New Deal,** p. 736
**deficit spending,** p. 738

**2. Taking Notes**

FERA: relief; PWA: relief; AAA: recovery; TVA: recovery; CCC: relief and reform; FDIC: reform; NRA: recovery and reform; WPA: relief; REA: recovery; NYA: relief; Wagner Act: reform; Social Security: relief and reform

PWA, CCC, WPA, and NYA

**3. Main Ideas**

**a.** He gave inspiring speeches, and took immediate action. **b.** FDR proposed legislation for relief, recovery, and reform, and Congress passed most of it with little debate. **c.** The bill failed, and his reputation suffered because people thought he was interfering with the system of checks and balances.

**4. Critical Thinking**

for increasing the size of the government; the cost of new programs; and his activist federal policies

**ACTIVITY OPTIONS**

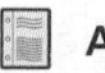 **Alternative Assessment**
- Rubrics for a cartoon, 1.2
- Rubrics for a Web page, 5.1

# 3 Life During the Depression

**TERMS & NAMES**
Dust Bowl
Eleanor Roosevelt
Congress of Industrial Organizations (CIO)
sit-down strike

**MAIN IDEA**

During the Depression, most Americans knew great hardship.

**WHY IT MATTERS NOW**

Because of this, a generation was scarred by suffering in ways that later generations were not.

## ONE AMERICAN'S STORY

**Born to former slaves, Mary McLeod Bethune refused to accept the racial stereotype that all she could be was a servant. She gained an education and went on to found Bethune-Cookman College. In 1936, FDR named her director of the Division of Negro Affairs at the National Youth Administration. Bethune ran training programs for 600,000 African-American young people. She also supervised her college from afar. Because of her health, her doctor told her to stop working so hard.**

*A VOICE FROM THE PAST*

I promise to reform, but in an hour the promise is forgotten. For I am my mother's daughter, and the drums of Africa still beat in my heart. They will not let me rest while there is a single Negro boy or girl without a chance to prove his worth.

**Mary McLeod Bethune,** "Faith That Moved a Dump Heap"

A friend of Mrs. Roosevelt, Mary McLeod Bethune became the first African-American woman to head a federal agency.

**Section 3 discusses the difficulty of living during the Depression—and the efforts of people like Bethune to make the hard times easier.**

### 1 The Dust Bowl Destroys Lives

In the early 1930s, a drought hit the Great Plains and lasted for several years. Even before then, the overgrazing of livestock and the overplowing of fields had damaged the land by destroying the natural grasses whose roots anchored the soil. A journalist wrote, "You could hear the fields crack and dry, and the only movement in the down-driving heat was the dead withering of the dry blighted leaves on the twigs."

Winds picked up dirt from the dry, exposed fields. During dust storms, noon turned into night as walls of dust filled the air and hid the sun. Dust damaged farms across a 150,000-square-mile region called the **Dust Bowl,** which covered parts of Kansas, Oklahoma, Texas, Colorado, and New Mexico. Dust storms ripped through the plains for years until rain and improved farming methods finally brought relief.

With their crops buried under layers of dirt, ruined farmers loaded their belongings onto trucks and set off with their families to find work.





## SECTION OBJECTIVES

1. To analyze the effects of the Dust Bowl
2. To describe life during the Depression and the efforts of artists to portray that era
3. To explain how women and minorities were affected by the Depression and the New Deal
4. To summarize the gains made by unions during the Depression

**SKILLBUILDER**
Interpreting Maps: Place, Movement, p. 740

**CRITICAL THINKING**
Summarizing, p. 741
Making Inferences, p. 742
Contrasting, p. 742
Recognizing Effects, p. 743

## FOCUS & MOTIVATE

### 5-MINUTE WARM-UP

**Drawing Conclusions** These questions focus on the Dust Bowl migration.

1. Look at the map on page 740. Where were farmers especially hard hit by dust storms?
2. Where did many people living in the Dust Bowl go?

**Warm-Up Transparency WT26**

## INSTRUCT

**INSTRUCT: OBJECTIVE 1**

**The Dust Bowl Destroys Lives**

Key Questions
- What farming practices made the 1930s drought worse?
- What forced the mass migration of farmers from the Dust Bowl?
- Why did many migrants go to California?

**In-Depth Resources: Unit 8**
- Guided Reading, p. 23

**Reading Study Guide** (Spanish and English), pp. 253–254

## RECOMMENDED RESOURCES

**In-Depth Resources: Unit 8**
- Guided Reading, p. 23
- Building Vocabulary, p. 25
- Primary Source, p. 30
- Literature Selection, pp. 31–33
- Reteaching Activity, p. 36

**Reading Study Guide** (Spanish and English), pp. 253–254

**Outline Map Activities**
- The Great Depression, pp. 51–52

**America's History Makers**
- Eleanor Roosevelt, pp. 105–106

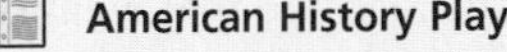

**American History Plays**
- *Mary Mcleod Bethune, Dream-maker* by Mary Satchell

**Formal Assessment**
- Section Quiz, p. 379

**Alternative Assessment**
- Rubrics, 3.1
- Rubrics, 1.3

**Access for Students Acquiring English/ESL**
- Guided Reading, p. 174

**Technology Resources**

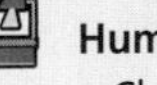

**Humanities Transparency HT51**
- Child in the South

**Geography Transparency GT26**
- Unemployment, 1930–1931

**America's Music CD**

**Electronic Teacher Tools with Test Maker**

## HISTORY FROM VISUALS

**Reading the Map** Ask students in which geographic region most of the dust storms occurred. **Answer** Great Plains. What natural feature forms part of the eastern boundary of the Dust Bowl? **Answer** Missouri River. When Dust Bowl refugees could not find work in California, where did they go? **Answer** Oregon and Washington

**Extension** Although Highway 66 has been largely replaced by interstate highways, efforts have been made to save many of the buildings along its route. Have students report to the class on why this highway has become a part of American folklore.

**Outline Map Activities**
- The Great Depression, pp. 51–52

## MORE ABOUT . . .

**Dust Storms**
Dust storms sometimes lasted several days. Driven by high winds, they could produce clouds of dirt as high as 8,000 feet and might bring thunder and lightning with them. A March 1935 storm destroyed Nebraska's entire wheat crop and swept away twice as much dirt as workers dug up to construct the Panama Canal. A few children trapped outside in a sudden dust storm suffocated.

## INSTRUCT: OBJECTIVE 

**Living Through Hard Times/ Artists Portray the Struggle**
Key Questions
- How were women, children, and families affected by the Depression?
- How did writers and photographers try to capture the hardships of the Depression?

**In-Depth Resources: Unit 8**
- Primary Source, p. 30
- Literature Selection, pp. 31–33

**Geography Transparency GT26**
- Unemployment, 1930–1931

### Dust Bowl Migration, 1930–1940

This photograph demonstrates why the dust storms were often called "black blizzards."

**GEOGRAPHY SKILLBUILDER Interpreting Maps**
1. **Place** *Which states suffered the most damage from the dust storms?*
2. **Movement** *What were the main highways that people took to leave the Dust Bowl, and where did they lead?*

Skillbuilder Answers
1. Kansas, Colorado, New Mexico, Texas, Oklahoma
2. Highway 30 led to Oregon; Highway 66 led to California.

Many drove west on Route 66, the main highway to California. They had heard that California's farms needed workers.

But as the newcomers poured in, California farm towns quickly became overcrowded. Families lived in tiny shacks. By 1940, about 2.5 million people fleeing the Dust Bowl had made their way to California and other Pacific coast states. Because many had come from Oklahoma, they were sometimes called "Okies."

*Reading* **History**
**A. Reading a Map** Look at the map above. Notice the three states that most Dust Bowl migrants went to.

## 2 Living Through Hard Times

Not just in the Dust Bowl, but all over the country, families suffered. Even after the recovery measures of the New Deal, unemployment remained high. In 1936, for example, 9 million people had no jobs.

Without work, families couldn't afford to buy food. Bread lines offering food to the hungry appeared across the country. In January 1931, New York's 82 bread lines served an average of 85,000 small meals a day: bread and soup or bread and stew. Men, women, and children waited in these lines for their daily food. Some fainted from hunger while they waited.

Many people also lost their homes. Thousands of homeless people sought shelter under bridges and overpasses. One woman remembered "people living in old, rusted out car bodies. . . . There were people living in shacks made of orange crates. One family with a whole lot of kids were living in a piano box."



## ACTIVITY OPTIONS

**INTERDISCIPLINARY LINK: SCIENCE**

**ANALYZING THE DUST BOWL DISASTER**

**Class Time** One class period

**Task** Preparing a diagram that illustrates environmental problems related to the Dust Bowl

**Purpose** To analyze causes of the Dust Bowl and to identify the steps taken to prevent its reoccurrence

**Supplies Needed**
- Reference materials on the Dust Bowl, the prevention of soil erosion, shelter belts, and the Soil Conservation Service
- Internet access
- Posterboard
- Art supplies

**Activity** Have students research how soil erosion, overgrazing, and plowing up of grasslands contributed to the Dust Bowl disaster. Have students find out how shelter belts, contour plowing, and other land management practices are used today on the Great Plains to prevent soil erosion. Then have students create an illustration or diagram of one cause of the Dust Bowl and one measure that helps correct the problem.

Children had to grow up fast during the Depression. To add to their family's income, boys worked after school or even dropped out of school. Often girls had to stay home to look after younger children. Sometimes teenagers who failed to find jobs ran away from home to avoid burdening their families. By late 1932, perhaps a quarter million teens roamed the country. They sneaked onto freight trains, begged for food, and lived in squatter camps along the railroad tracks.

Family life suffered as many unemployed men felt a loss of status. They sometimes became irritable and quarreled with their families. Working women came under pressure to give up their jobs to jobless men. In fact, some New Deal projects would hire a woman only if her husband had a job. Even so, poverty forced many women to work as servants or at other low-paying jobs that men didn't want.

**B. Possible Responses** lack of food, loss of home, some children leaving school or leaving home, men losing jobs and status in family, quarrels

***Reading* History**

**B. Summarizing** What were the various hardships suffered by families during the Depression?

## Artists Portray the Struggle

Many books of the period described the hard times. *Let Us Now Praise Famous Men* (1941) by James Agee and Walker Evans reported on the harsh lives of tenant farmers. John Steinbeck's novel *The Grapes of Wrath* (1939) told of Okies who had been evicted from their farms.

**Vocabulary**
**evicted:** forced to leave property

*A VOICE FROM THE PAST*

Carloads, caravans, homeless and hungry; twenty thousand and fifty thousand and a hundred thousand and two hundred thousand. They streamed over the mountains, hungry and restless—restless as ants, scurrying to find work to do—to lift, to push, to pull, to pick, to cut—anything, any burden to bear, for food. The kids are hungry. We got no place to live. Like ants scurrying for work, for food, and most of all for land.

**John Steinbeck,** *The Grapes of Wrath*

The African-American writer Richard Wright was one of many writers who were hired by the Works Progress Administration. Freed from his economic worries, he also wrote creatively in his spare time and produced the novel *Native Son* (1940). It depicts one African American's anger about society's racism.

### daily*life*

**HAVING FUN DURING HARD TIMES**

To forget life's troubles, people went to the movies. At first, the Depression caused attendance to decline. But audiences soon grew as hard times made people eager for entertainment.

Viewers flocked to escapist movies such as *The Wizard of Oz.* People also saw realistic movies about the times, such as *The Grapes of Wrath,* based on John Steinbeck's novel.

Reading comic books about superheroes also was a popular pastime. Comic books were first published in 1933. *Superman* was introduced in 1938.

▼ *The Grapes of Wrath*

▼ *Gone with the Wind*

◀ *The Wizard of Oz*

741



**MORE ABOUT . . .**

**The Struggle for Jobs**

As unemployment rates rose during the Depression, Americans began to quarrel over who "deserved" a job. According to public opinion polls, many people thought working women were taking jobs away from men. (The truth was that men and women rarely competed for the same kinds of work.) As a result, many married women lost their jobs, even if they were the sole support of their families. Adults also feared job competition from teenagers. In fact, historians have argued that the idea of the "teenager" was invented in the 1930s to keep young people in school longer and out of the work force.

**Humanities Transparency HT51**
- Child in the South

**daily*life***

**Having Fun During Hard Times**

During the 1930s, more Americans than ever before went to the movies. Viewers were excited by the new talkies that came on the screen after 1927. Some saved their hard-earned coins to see the comedies of the Marx Brothers, W. C. Fields, and Mae West. The films of all three made fun of the manners and pretensions of the rich.

People also found relief from their troubles by singing or listening to folk music. Oklahoma-born Woody Guthrie, a folksinger and songwriter, traveled across the United States, singing and strumming his guitar and writing more than a thousand songs. Many of them remain popular today. One of his best-loved songs is "This Land Is Your Land."

**ACTIVITY OPTIONS**

**INDIVIDUAL NEEDS**

**STUDENTS ACQUIRING ENGLISH/ESL**

**Understanding Literary Techniques** Read aloud the excerpt from John Steinbeck's *The Grapes of Wrath* on page 741. Discuss the comparison Steinbeck draws between tenant farmers and ants. Ask questions such as:

- What word does Steinbeck use to describe how the ants and the farmers move? *(scurry)*
- In what ways are the tenant farmers and the ants alike? *(Both are restless; they both scurry to find work to do; some of the scurrying of ants and farmers seems ineffective.)*

Read the quotation a second time. Ask students to listen to the rhythm of the words. Help students to hear the short, jabbing phrases that capture the quick, jabbing movement of ants.

Then ask students to tell how the excerpt and the comparison support the information under the heading "Living Through Hard Times."

## AMERICA'S HISTORY MAKERS

**Eleanor Roosevelt**

Historians consistently rank Eleanor Roosevelt as the most influential American woman of the century. She was an active supporter of racial justice during her husband's administration and after his death. In 1945, she became a delegate to the United Nations. She chaired the UN Commission on Human Rights and helped in the writing and passage of the Universal Declaration of Human Rights.

Possible Response: The satisfaction and sense of achievement she felt in helping others encouraged her to overcome her shyness and become an activist and social reformer.

 **America's History Makers**
- Eleanor Roosevelt, pp. 105–106

### INSTRUCT: OBJECTIVE 

**Women in the New Deal/ Minorities and the Depression**

Key Questions
- What role did women and African Americans play in the Roosevelt administration?
- How did FDR justify his failure to support passage of antilynching laws by Congress?
- How did the Depression and the New Deal affect Mexican Americans and Native Americans?

## MORE ABOUT . . .

**Women in the New Deal**

The New Deal brought many middle-class, professional women back into politics. Many became advisers or directors of New Deal social welfare programs. Eleanor Roosevelt, who prodded her husband to bring women into government, gave this advice to women reformers: "Get into the game and stay in it. Throwing mud from the outside won't help. Building up from the inside will."

### AMERICA'S HISTORY MAKERS

**ELEANOR ROOSEVELT**
**1884–1962**

Eleanor Roosevelt had an unhappy childhood. Her parents died when she was young, and the grandmother who raised her criticized Eleanor frequently.

In 1905, she married her distant cousin Franklin. When FDR entered politics, she was shy and disliked attending public events.

During World War I, Eleanor did volunteer work and discovered the joy of helping others. This gave her confidence. By the time FDR became governor of New York, Eleanor was actively working for social reform. She continued to do so as first lady.

**How did Eleanor Roosevelt change from an insecure person to a leader for social reform?**

Photographers also captured Depression-era suffering. Dorothea Lange was one of several photographers whom the government hired to document the times. Her pictures show the hard lives of poor people during the Depression. (See pages 745 and 751.)

## 3 Women in the New Deal

The first lady, **Eleanor Roosevelt,** worked to help poor Americans. Because her husband had a disability, Mrs. Roosevelt acted as his "eyes and ears." She toured the country, visiting coal mines, work camps, and hospitals to find out how programs were working. Then she told the president what she learned and made suggestions.

In March 1933, Eleanor Roosevelt began to hold regular press conferences for women reporters. At these, the first lady introduced the women who ran New Deal programs. During Roosevelt's presidency, more women held positions with the government than ever before.

In 1933, the president named Frances Perkins secretary of labor, which made her the first female cabinet officer. Years earlier, Perkins had assisted Jane Addams at Chicago's Hull House. As secretary of labor, she supported laws granting a minimum wage, a limit on child employment, and unemployment compensation.

*Reading History*
**C. Making Inferences** Why do you think Eleanor Roosevelt publicized the women who worked in government?
C. Possible Response She wanted to promote women's rights and thought publicity about their accomplishments would help.

## Minorities and the Depression

Mary McLeod Bethune was one of several African Americans who played a role in the government. They were called FDR's "Black Cabinet." This group included William Hastie and Robert C. Weaver. Hastie was a brilliant young lawyer who worked in the Department of the Interior. Weaver, an economist who had graduated from Harvard, became the president's adviser on racial issues.

Though he included more African Americans in government, FDR failed to back civil rights laws. For example, he did not support an antilynching bill. FDR opposed lynching but feared upsetting Southern white congressmen. Roosevelt said, "If I come out for the antilynching bill now, [the Southerners] will block every bill I ask Congress to pass to keep America from collapsing." In spite of this, African Americans remained loyal to the president because of his efforts to help the poor.

The Depression also greatly affected Mexican Americans. Many lived in rural areas, especially in the Southwest. Increasingly, migrants from other areas competed with them for jobs. Mexican Americans living in cities also had difficulty finding scarce jobs. While many Mexican Americans did benefit from New Deal programs, in general they received less aid than other groups.

D. Answer Mexican Americans received fewer benefits.

*Reading History*
**D. Contrasting** How did African Americans and Mexican Americans benefit differently from the New Deal?



**ACTIVITY OPTIONS**

**MULTIPLE LEARNING STYLES: LINGUISTIC** 

**CREATING A SOUND COLLAGE**

**Class Time** One class period

**Task** Creating a sound collage of people who lived through the Depression

**Purpose** To gain an understanding of the hardships of daily life during the Depression

**Supplies Needed**
- First-person accounts of life during the Depression, such as Studs Terkel's *Hard Times* and Milton Meltzer's *Brother, Can You Spare a Dime?*
- Tape recorder and audiotapes

 America's Music CD

**Activity** Working in groups, have students skim collections of first-person accounts of life during the Depression. Tell students to select four or five passages to use in a "Voices of the Depression" sound collage. Students may select passages about similar topics, for example, riding the rails. Have groups decide in what order to record the pieces and prepare short introductions for each selection. Have each group record its selections for class presentations. Groups may add music and sound effects to their recordings.

During the 1930s, immigration from Mexico declined. In addition, many immigrants returned to Mexico. Some left on their own; the federal government deported others. Some of those who were forced to leave were U.S. citizens whose rights were ignored. Because they feared deportation, many Mexican Americans stopped applying for aid.

Life improved somewhat for Native Americans. In 1934, Congress passed the Indian Reorganization Act, which restored some reservation lands to Indian ownership. It also created the Indian Arts and Crafts Board to promote native arts.

In early 1939, a women's group refused to rent a hall for opera star Marian Anderson's performance because of her race. So Mrs. Roosevelt asked her to sing at the Lincoln Memorial.

## 4 Unions Gain Strength

Some minorities joined a new labor organization. The country's largest labor organization was the American Federation of Labor (AFL). It was open only to skilled workers, such as plumbers and electricians. Labor leader John L. Lewis wanted industrywide unions that included both skilled and unskilled workers. He and other leaders founded the **Congress of Industrial Organizations (CIO),** which broke from the AFL in 1938. It was more open to women and minorities than the AFL.

**Background**
John L. Lewis had been president of the United Mine Workers of America since 1920.

In the 1930s, the labor movement used an effective bargaining tactic called the **sit-down strike.** Instead of walking off their jobs, striking workers remained idle inside the plant. As a result, factory owners could not hire strikebreakers to do the work.

The Wagner Act, passed in 1935, gave unions the ability to negotiate better working conditions. Union membership jumped from 2.7 million in 1933 to 7.0 million in 1937. The growing strength of labor unions was just one legacy of the New Deal. Section 4 discusses other legacies of the Great Depression and the New Deal.

### Section 3 Assessment

**1. Terms & Names**

**Identify:**
- Dust Bowl
- Eleanor Roosevelt
- Congress of Industrial Organizations (CIO)
- sit-down strike

**2. Taking Notes**

Use a cluster diagram like the one below to record details about life during the Depression.

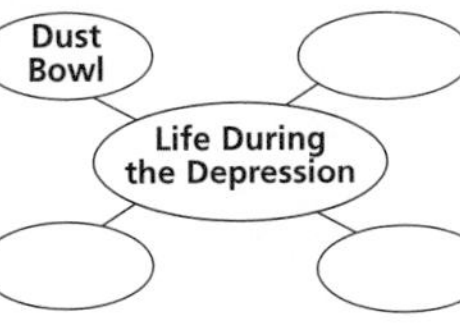


**3. Main Ideas**

a. How did storms in the Dust Bowl contribute to economic problems?

b. What effect did the Depression have on families?

c. How did Eleanor Roosevelt help her husband, the president?

**4. Critical Thinking**

**Recognizing Effects** What were some positive and negative results of the government's policies toward minorities during the Depression?

**THINK ABOUT**
- African Americans
- Mexican Americans
- Native Americans

**ACTIVITY OPTIONS**

**SPEECH**
**ART**

You have been asked to teach young children about life during the Depression. Write and perform a **monologue** or create a **comic strip** about it.





### MORE ABOUT . . .

**The Indian Reorganization Act**

The Indian Reorganization Act, sometimes called "A New Deal for Indians," improved relations between the government and Native Americans. The act reversed much of the Dawes Act, which had divided up tribal land and stripped tribes of their sovereignty. Over 7 million acres of land were returned to Native American control.

### INSTRUCT: OBJECTIVE 

**Unions Gain Strength**

Key Questions
- How did the CIO differ from the AFL?
- How did the New Deal strengthen unions?

### ASSESS & RETEACH

**Setting the Stage** Have students fill in the section on the graphic organizer titled "Citizens' Responses."

 **Formal Assessment**
- Section Quiz, p. 379

**RETEACHING ACTIVITY**

Have students copy the chart below and add details showing how each group was affected by the New Deal.

| Group | Effects of the New Deal |
|---|---|
| women | |
| African Americans | |
| Mexican Americans | |
| Native Americans | |
| unions | |

**In-Depth Resources: Unit 8**
- Reteaching Activity, p. 36

### Section 3 Assessment

**1. Terms & Names**

**Dust Bowl,** p. 739
**Eleanor Roosevelt,** p. 742
**Congress of Industrial Organizations (CIO),** p. 743
**sit-down strike,** p. 743

**2. Taking Notes**

Dust Bowl: dust storms, ruined farms, migrants, lack of jobs; family life: unemployment, hunger, breadlines, homelessness; art: portrayed hard times, escapist art, movies for recreation; labor unions: CIO, growing strength of labor, sit-down strike

**3. Main Ideas**

**a.** Storms blew the soil away and ruined crops; many lost farms and could not find work. **b.** unemployment, hunger; homelessness; children left home to work **c.** She traveled the country to see how people and programs were doing and reported to him.

**4. Critical Thinking**

Positive: some benefits from FDR's programs to help the poor; Negative: no support for civil rights or anti-lynching laws; discrimination; deportation

**ACTIVITY OPTIONS**

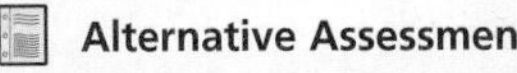
**Alternative Assessment**
- Rubrics, 3.1, 1.3

## Literature Connections

**OBJECTIVE**

Students analyze a passage from historical fiction that imaginatively depicts the lives of an African-American family in Mississippi during the Depression.

 **BLOCK SCHEDULING**

## FOCUS & MOTIVATE

**Making Inferences** To help the students picture the events of *Roll of Thunder, Hear My Cry,* have them study the image on page 745 and answer the following questions.

1. How are sharecroppers different from owners of the land?
2. In which part of the United States would you expect to find sharecroppers?

### MORE ABOUT . . .

*Roll of Thunder, Hear My Cry*

Mildred Taylor was awarded a Newbery Medal for this work of historical fiction set in the rural South during the Great Depression. In this novel, the Logan family struggles to hold on to its land as it fights bigotry and racism. The closeness of family members helps them withstand discrimination. A critic for the *New York Times Book Review* has said that the author writes "not with rancor or bitterness of indignities, but with pride, strength, and respect for humanity."

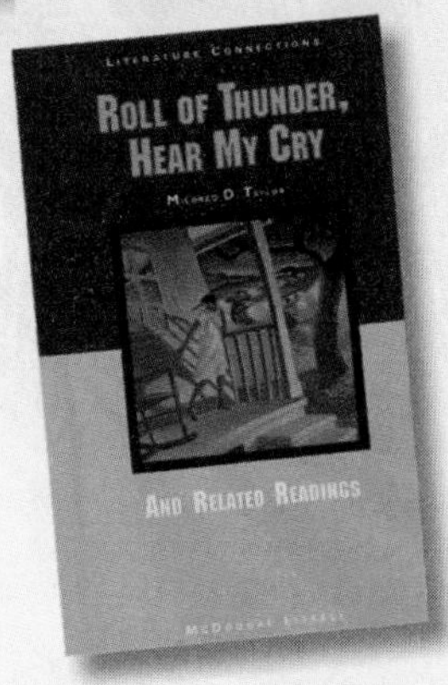

from

# ROLL OF THUNDER, HEAR MY CRY

by Mildred D. Taylor

**Even before the Depression, many African Americans struggled with poverty. When the Depression began, hard times made it more difficult for them to get ahead—or to keep what they had. Because the Logan family owns land in Mississippi, they are better off than their sharecropper neighbors. But they also have more to lose.**

"Little Man, would you come on? You keep it up and you're gonna make us late."

My youngest brother paid no attention to me. Grasping more firmly his newspaper-wrapped notebook and his tin-can lunch of cornbread and oil sausages, he continued to concentrate on the dusty road. He lagged several feet behind my other brothers, Stacey and Christopher-John, and me, attempting to keep the rusty Mississippi dust from swelling with each step and drifting back upon his shiny black shoes and the cuffs of his corduroy pants by lifting each foot high before setting it gently down again. Always meticulously neat, six-year-old Little Man never allowed dirt or tears or stains to mar anything he owned. Today was no exception.

"You keep it up and make us late for school, Mama's gonna wear you out," I threatened, pulling with exasperation at the high collar of the Sunday dress Mama had made me wear for the first day of school—as if that event were something special. It seemed to me that showing up at school at all on a bright August-like October morning made for running the cool forest trails and wading barefoot in the forest pond was concession enough; Sunday clothing was asking too much. Christopher-John and Stacey were not too pleased about the clothing or school either. Only Little Man, just beginning his school career, found the prospects of both intriguing.

"Y'all go ahead and get dirty if y'all wanna," he replied without even looking up from his studied steps. "Me, I'm gonna stay clean."

"I betcha Mama's gonna 'clean' you, you keep it up," I grumbled.

"Ah, Cassie, leave him be," Stacey admonished, frowning and kicking testily at the road.

"I ain't said nothing but—"

Stacey cut me a wicked look and I grew silent. His disposition had been irritatingly sour lately. If I hadn't known the cause of it, I could have forgotten very easily that he was, at twelve, bigger than I, and that I had promised Mama to arrive at school looking clean and ladylike. "Shoot," I mumbled finally, unable to restrain myself from further comment, "it ain't my fault you gotta be in Mama's class this year."

Stacey's frown deepened and he jammed his fists into his pockets, but said nothing.

Christopher-John, walking between Stacey and me, glanced uneasily at both of us but did not interfere. A short, round boy of seven, he took little interest in troublesome things, preferring to remain on good terms with everyone. Yet he was always sensitive to others and now, shifting the handle of his lunch can from his right hand to his right wrist and his smudged notebook from his left hand to his left armpit, he stuffed his free hands into his pockets and attempted to make his face as moody as Stacey's and as cranky as mine. But after a few moments he seemed to forget that he was supposed to be grouchy and began whistling cheerfully. There was little that could make Christopher-John unhappy for very long, not even the thought of school.

I tugged again at my collar and dragged my feet in the dust, allowing it to sift back onto my socks and shoes like gritty red snow. I hated the dress. And the shoes. There was little I could do in a dress, and as for shoes, they imprisoned freedom-loving feet accustomed to the feel of the warm earth.



### ACTIVITY OPTIONS

### INDIVIDUAL NEEDS

**LESS PROFICIENT READERS**

**Building Language Skills** Pair less proficient readers with more able readers. Have each pair complete a chart like the one shown, adding details about the appearance, personality, and actions of each character listed. Have pairs pick out the words, phrases, and specific details the author uses to make each family member come alive for the reader.

| Character | Details |
|---|---|
| Little Man | |
| Stacey | |
| Christopher-John | |
| Cassie | |
| Papa | |

"Cassie, stop that," Stacey snapped as the dust billowed in swirling clouds around my feet. I looked up sharply, ready to protest. Christopher-John's whistling increased to a raucous, nervous shrill, and grudgingly I let the matter drop and trudged along in moody silence, my brothers growing as pensively quiet as I.

Before us the narrow, sun-splotched road wound like a lazy red serpent dividing the high forest bank of quiet, old trees on the left from the cotton field, forested by giant green-and-purple stalks, on the right. A barbed-wire fence ran the length of the deep field, stretching eastward for over a quarter of a mile until it met the sloping green pasture that signaled the end of our family's four hundred acres. An ancient oak tree on the slope, visible even now, was the official dividing mark between Logan land and the beginning of a dense forest. Beyond the protective fencing of the forest, vast farming fields, worked by a multitude of sharecropping families, covered two thirds of a ten-square-mile plantation. That was Harlan Granger land.

Once our land had been Granger land too, but the Grangers had sold it during Reconstruction to a Yankee for tax money. In 1887, when the land was up for sell again, Grandpa had bought two hundred acres of it, and in 1918, after the first two hundred acres had been paid off, he had bought another two hundred. It was good rich land, much of it still virgin forest, and there was no debt on half of it. But there was a **mortgage**[1] on the two hundred acres bought in 1918 and there were taxes on the full four hundred, and for the past three years there had not been enough money from the cotton to pay both and live on too.

That was why Papa had gone to work on the railroad.

In 1930 the price of cotton dropped. And so, in the spring of 1931, Papa set out looking for work, going as far north as Memphis and as far south as the Delta country. He had gone west too, into Louisiana. It was there he found work laying track for the railroad. He worked the remainder of the year away from us, not returning until the deep winter when the ground was cold and barren. The following spring after the planting was finished, he did the same. Now it was 1933, and Papa was again in Louisiana laying track.

I asked him once why he had to go away, why the land was so important. He took my hand and said in his quiet way: "Look out there, Cassie girl. All that belongs to you. You ain't never had to live on nobody's place but your own and long as I live and the family survives, you'll never have to. That's important. You may not understand that now, but one day you will. Then you'll see."

I looked at Papa strangely when he said that, for I knew that all the land did not belong to me. Some of it belonged to Stacey, Christopher-John, and Little Man, not to mention the part that belonged to Big Ma, Mama, and Uncle Hammer, Paper's older brother who lived in Chicago. But Papa never divided the land in his mind; it was simply Logan land. For it he would work the long, hot summer pounding steel; Mama would teach and run the farm; Big Ma, in her sixties, would work like a woman of twenty in the fields and keep the house; and the boys and I would wear threadbare clothing washed to dishwater color; but always, the taxes and the mortgage would be paid.

1. **mortgage:** the transfer of a deed to property, usually in exchange for a loan.

**This Dorothea Lange photograph shows sharecroppers like the Logans' neighbors.**

### CONNECT TO HISTORY

1. **Analyzing Causes** Which of the economic problems shown in the graphs on page 730 has been making life hard for the Logan family?

**See Skillbuilder Handbook, page R10.**

### CONNECT TO TODAY

2. **Researching** What are current interest rates on mortgages?

**Visit www.mcdougallittell.com to learn more about the Great Depression.**

745

## INSTRUCT

Key Questions

- What can you learn from this selection about the way Mama has raised the Logan family?
- Why is the family in danger of losing its land?
- How does the author show the importance of land ownership to the family?
- What has the family had to sacrifice to hold on to its land?

### MAKING PERSONAL CONNECTIONS

Ask students to think about something that they worked very hard for, such as a good grade in a difficult subject or money to buy an item of clothing or sports equipment. What kinds of sacrifices did it take to accomplish their goal?

### VOCABULARY ACTIVITY

Have students make a list of the phrases that help them understand how poor the Logans were.

### HISTORY FROM VISUALS

**Interpreting the Photograph** Have students explain what a sharecropper is. Ask students how a sharecropper's attitude toward the land he or she farms might be different from the Logans' feeling about their land.

### CONNECT TO HISTORY

1. **Analyzing Causes** The drop in farm income has made life hard for the Logans.

### CONNECT TO TODAY

2. **Researching** Answers will vary but can be verified in the newspaper or on the Internet.

## SECTION OBJECTIVES

1. To summarize the lasting effects of the Depression
2. To explain the expansion of government in social and economic life
3. To evaluate New Deal programs that are still important today
4. To describe current political debates arising from the New Deal

**SKILLBUILDER**
Interpreting Graphs, p. 747

**CRITICAL THINKING**
Recognizing Effects, p. 747
Analyzing Causes, p. 748
Analyzing Points of View, p. 749
Drawing Conclusions, p. 749

## FOCUS & MOTIVATE

### 5-MINUTE WARM-UP

**Recognizing Effects** These questions focus on the three areas of the economy affected by the New Deal.

1. Look at the graphs on page 747. In what year was one-fourth of the labor force unemployed?
2. Can you think of reasons why unemployment and business failures increased in 1938?

 Warm-Up Transparency WT26

## INSTRUCT

### INSTRUCT: OBJECTIVE 

**Lasting Effects of the Depression**
Key Questions
- How did the Depression change the ways people thought about the future?
- What started the economy growing again?

 **In-Depth Resources: Unit 8**
- Guided Reading, p. 24
- Geography Application: Presidential Elections, 1932–1940, pp. 27–28

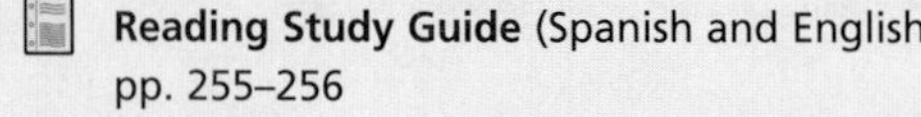 **Reading Study Guide** (Spanish and English), pp. 255–256

# 4 The Effects of the New Deal

**TERMS & NAMES**
Securities and Exchange Commission
liberal
conservative

**MAIN IDEA**
The Depression and the New Deal had many long-term effects on U.S. government and society.

**WHY IT MATTERS NOW**
Politicians still debate how large a role government should play in American life.

### ONE AMERICAN'S STORY

**Until 1935, Ward James worked as a writer for a New York publisher. Then he lost his job. His wife and son went to Ohio to live with her parents. James moved in with a friend and applied for government relief. Even after he got a steady writing job with the WPA, Ward James continued to worry about what would happen next.**

*A VOICE FROM THE PAST*

Everyone was emotionally affected. We developed a fear of the future which was very difficult to overcome. Even though I eventually went into some fairly good jobs, there was still this constant dread: everything would be cut out from under you and you wouldn't know what to do. It would be even harder, because you were older.

**Ward James,** quoted in *Hard Times*

The fear and despair described by Ward James was felt by many unemployed people during the Depression.

**Years after the Depression, James still had "a little fear . . . that it might happen again." As this section explains, both the Depression and the New Deal had lasting effects on Americans and their government.**

## 1 Lasting Effects of the Depression

Americans like Ward James who lived through the Depression often saw themselves as the survivors of a terrible battle. For the rest of their lives, many feared losing their money and property again. One elderly government worker bought land whenever she could afford it so that if the Depression returned, she would "have something to live off."

Virginia Durr, who had worked for the federal government under FDR, said that the Depression affected people in two ways. "The great majority reacted by thinking money is the most important thing in the world. . . . And there was a small number of people who felt the whole system was lousy. You have to change it."

The New Deal did not end the Depression. Even with all the new programs, the government still wasn't spending enough money to jump-start a stalled economy. Then, in the 1940s, World War II changed the situation. To fight in that war, the government had to purchase guns,



## RECOMMENDED RESOURCES

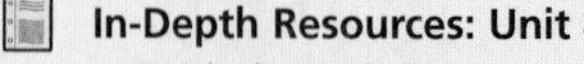 **In-Depth Resources: Unit 8**
- Guided Reading, p. 24
- Building Vocabulary, p. 25
- Geography Application: Presidential Elections, 1932–1940, pp. 27–28
- Reteaching Activity, p. 37
- History Workshop Resources, p. 39

**Reading Study Guide** (Spanish and English), pp. 255–256

**Citizenship Today,** p. 83

**Formal Assessment**
- Section Quiz, p. 380

**Alternative Assessment**
- Rubrics, 4.5
- Rubrics, 5.3

**Access for Students Acquiring English/ESL**
- Guided Reading, p. 175
- Geography Application, pp. 177–178

**Technology Resources**

 **Humanities Transparency HT52**
- *WPA Sunday*

 **Electronic Teacher Tools with Test Maker**

 **ClassZone**
www.mcdougallittell.com

tanks, ships, airplanes, and other military equipment. The defense industry hired many people, who then had more money to spend. The U.S. economy started growing again.

Although the New Deal didn't end the Depression, it forever changed the U.S. government. As Supreme Court justice John Clarke told FDR, "You have put a new face upon the social and political life of our country."

> *"We developed a fear of the future."*
>
> Ward James

## A Larger Role for Government

President Roosevelt increased the president's power. Under FDR, the White House became the center of government. More than other early-20th-century presidents, Roosevelt proposed bills and programs for Congress to consider instead of waiting for Congress to act.

Other nations also saw the rise of strong leaders. But at the same time, those nations saw a loss of freedom. For example, during the Depression, Germany elected Adolf Hitler, who became a dictator. The United States did have some leaders who abused power—such as Huey Long—but they never became president. FDR's leadership and his concern for the poor helped Americans keep their faith in democracy.

As well as increasing the president's power, Roosevelt also expanded the federal government. Because of the New Deal, the federal government became directly responsible for people's well-being in a way it had not

*Reading*Hist 2

**A. Recognizing Effects** How did FDR increase the president's power?

**A. Possible Response** He took on the role of initiating laws, which had mostly belonged to Congress.

Skillbuilder Answers

1. Yes. The unemployment rate and the numbers of bank and business failures all declined.
2. Bank closings. They dropped to almost nothing.

CONNECTIONS TO MATH

### Effects of the New Deal, *1929–1941*

**Although Franklin Roosevelt's New Deal programs did not end the Depression, they did make some economic conditions better. Use these graphs to determine how the New Deal—begun in 1933—affected the unemployment rate, the number of bank closings, and the number of business failures.**

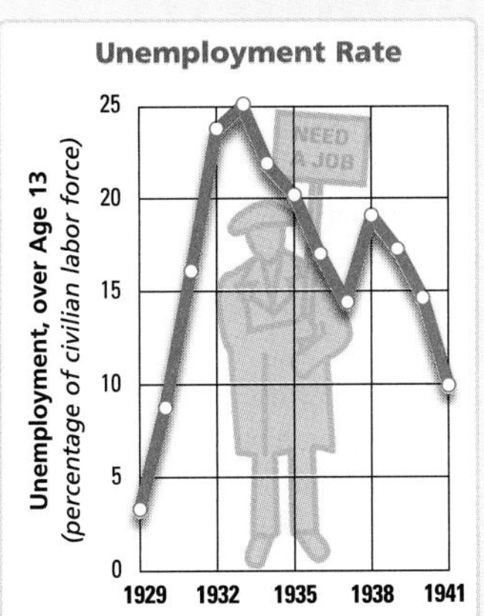


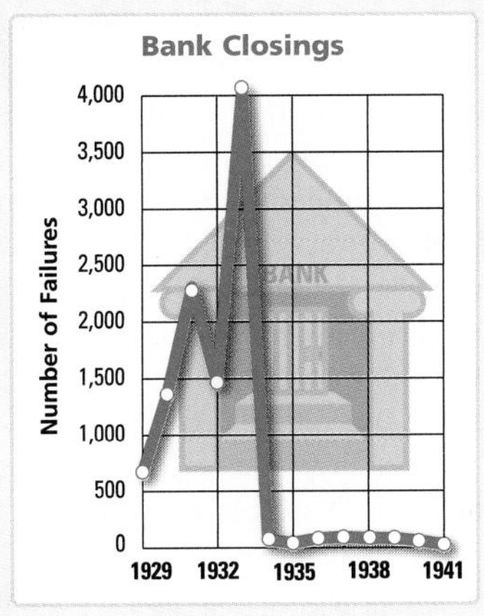


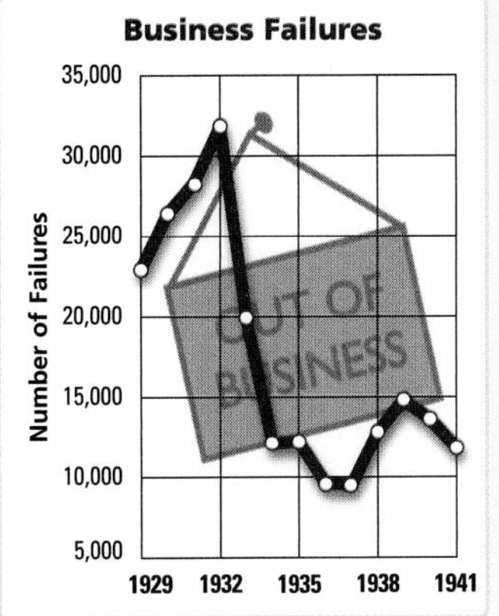


Sources: *Historical Statistics of the United States*

SKILLBUILDER **Interpreting Graphs**

1. *Judging from these graphs, did the Depression's negative effects on business improve after FDR took office in 1933? Explain.*
2. *In which area was there the biggest change for the better?*



**INSTRUCT: OBJECTIVE 2**

**A Larger Role for Government**

Key Questions

- How did FDR's leadership promote democracy?
- What kind of leadership did many other nations choose at this time?
- How did the New Deal change the way Americans viewed the federal government?

 **Citizenship Today,** p. 83

**MORE ABOUT . . .**

**Rise of Dictatorships in Europe**

In Europe, the enormous hardship and uncertainty caused by the Great Depression led many nations to accept authoritarian leaders. In Italy, fascist dictator Benito Mussolini rose to power in the early 1920s. In Germany, the Depression followed by soaring inflation contributed to the growth of the extremist, virulently anti-Semitic Nazi party and to Adolf Hitler's takeover of the government in 1933.

**HISTORY FROM VISUALS**

**Reading the Graphs** Ask students to describe the relationship between the unemployment rate and business failures. **Possible Response** If there are more business failures, there is likely to be higher unemployment. Conversely, as business failures decrease, unemployment is likely to decrease. Ask which graph shows that public confidence in the economy increased after FDR took office. **Answer** bank closings

**Extension** Have students do research to find the statistics for these three categories for their community.

**ACTIVITY OPTIONS**

**INDIVIDUAL NEEDS: GIFTED AND TALENTED**

**EVALUATING THE PRESIDENT**

**Class Time** One class period

**Task** Developing criteria and writing an assessment of FDR's leadership during the Great Depression

**Purpose** To evaluate President Roosevelt's response to the Great Depression

**Supplies Needed**

- Reference materials on FDR and the New Deal
- Historians' assessments of FDR

**Activity** Have students work as a group to create a list of general criteria to evaluate a president's performance in office. For example, students might consider such qualities as leadership, judgment, effectiveness in managing the economy, communication skills, and so on. Have each student write a short evaluation of FDR's first two terms as president using the list of criteria. Students should cite the work of at least two historians in their papers and provide a bibliography.

## HISTORY through ART

**Interpreting the Painting** William Gropper was a leading artist of the 1930s. His works often reflected his concerns about social responsibilities and class inequalities. The WPA Federal Arts Project provided work for artists such as Gropper. Writers were employed through the Federal Writers Project, while actors appeared on stages around the country in plays about current social issues through the Federal Theater Project.

**Possible Responses: Positive: they are clearly hard at work, working cooperatively. The building materials imply that it is a large construction project that may be for the public's use.**

 **Humanities Transparency HT52**
- *WPA Sunday*

## INSTRUCT: OBJECTIVE 

**New Deal Programs Today**

Key Questions
- What impact do former New Deal programs have on labor unions?
- What current programs guard against a future economic collapse like the Crash of 1929?
- What protects bank customers from bank failures today?

## MORE ABOUT . . .

**Securities and Exchange Commission**

Congress created the Securities and Exchange Commission in 1934 after an investigation into the operations of the New York Stock Exchange. The committee uncovered misleading sales practices and stock maneuvers that contributed to the 1929 crash. Congress decided that a regulatory agency was needed to restore investor confidence. Among the changes instituted by the SEC were rules that prevented unfair use of nonpublic or insider information in stock trading.

### HISTORY through ART

The Works Progress Administration (WPA) created many jobs. One of the WPA's most enduring legacies is the art that it commissioned. Much WPA art was used to decorate public places, such as post offices and government buildings. This mural by William Gropper shows the building of a dam.

**What attitude did Gropper want to convey about laborers?**

been before. It now made relief payments, served school lunches, and ran a program providing pensions. People came to see the federal government, not their state or local governments, as the protector of their welfare.

The federal government went into debt to provide this aid. FDR used deficit spending both to fund the New Deal and to pay for the war. Since then, deficit spending has often been part of the federal budget.

## 3 New Deal Programs Today

Several of FDR's New Deal programs continue to help Americans today. Some of the more important programs that still exist offer the following benefits and protections.

1. **A National Pension System.** The Social Security system pays out old-age pensions (and has been expanded to include aid to other groups). It is funded through taxes on employers and employees.
2. **Oversight of Labor Practices.** Created by the Wagner Act, the National Labor Relations Board (NLRB) oversees labor unions. It also investigates disputes between management and labor.
3. **Agricultural Price Supports.** This program pays farmers to raise crops for domestic use rather than export. To receive payments, farmers must agree to limit the space they devote to certain crops.
4. **Protection for Savings.** After the bank holiday of 1933, the Federal Deposit Insurance Corporation (FDIC) was created. The FDIC insures bank deposits up to $100,000. It replaces the deposits of individuals if banks close.
5. **Regulation of the Stock Market.** A federal agency called the **Securities and Exchange Commission** watches the stock market. It makes sure companies follow fair practices for trading stocks.

B. Possible Response because the stock market crash was the first event of the Depression and created a great deal of fear

*Reading* **History**

**B. Analyzing Causes** Why do you think FDR wanted to create an agency to oversee the stock market?



## ACTIVITY OPTIONS

### INTERDISCIPLINARY LINK: GOVERNMENT/CIVICS

BLOCK SCHEDULING

**LIBERALS AND CONSERVATIVES**

**Class Time** One class period

**Task** Comparing the positions of liberals and conservatives on several issues

**Purpose** To compare the two major political philosophies of the United States

**Supplies Needed**
- Reference material on current political debates, such as newspaper and magazine articles
- Internet access

**Activity** Clearly define the difference between a liberal and a conservative. Next have students scan newspapers and news magazines and identify several current political issues, such as health care. Choose one or two issues. Write a summary of each issue on the board. Have students work in pairs to identify the broad liberal and conservative approaches to each issue. Then have pairs make a graphic organizer or a political cartoon illustrating the difference in the stances of each philosophy.

## 4 An Ongoing Political Debate

The issues that came out of the New Deal continue to shape American politics. For example, Democrats and Republicans still argue about whether federal or local government should be responsible for various programs. In addition, Democrats are more likely to be liberal and Republicans are more likely to be conservative in their political beliefs. A **liberal** in politics favors government action to bring about social and economic reform. A **conservative** favors fewer government controls and more individual freedom in economic matters.

Despite these lingering disagreements, some New Deal programs are still so popular that everyone supports them. For example, neither party wants to end Social Security, even though the system is in trouble. The amounts that people pay in through payroll taxes today do not completely pay for pensions. The system may run out of money sometime in the future.

In early 1999, President Bill Clinton announced a plan to save Social Security by using extra money from the federal budget. The Republicans accepted his plan. They knew that saving Social Security is a priority for Americans and that voters might grow angry if they made a political fight of the issue.

FDR probably would have approved. "The great public," Roosevelt said, "is interested more in government than in politics." Roosevelt felt that party labels mattered little as long as politicians "did the big job that their times demanded to be done."

In the 1940s, President Roosevelt would face another big job. He had to lead the country in fighting a world war. Chapter 27 discusses World War II and America's role in it.

**Now and then**

**SOCIAL SECURITY**

Today, many young people worry that the Social Security trust fund won't have enough money for their pensions. For one thing, people live longer now than they did in the 1930s. Also, the percentage of people receiving benefits keeps increasing compared to the number paying into the system. Last, Social Security benefits have been expanded since the 1930s.

SOCIAL SECURITY USA ADMINISTRATION

**C. Possible Response** It shouldn't be run according to political theories, but rather it should do what needs to be done for the people.

*Reading*History
**C. Analyzing Points of View** How would you summarize FDR's view of government's role?

### Section 4 Assessment

**1. Terms & Names**

**Identify:**
- Securities and Exchange Commission
- liberal
- conservative

**2. Taking Notes**

Use a bulleted list like the one shown below to list the legacy of the Depression and New Deal.

**Legacy of the Depression and New Deal**
- __________
- __________
- __________
- __________

What part of the legacy affects politics today?

**3. Main Ideas**

a. What psychological impact did the Depression have on many Americans?

b. What finally pulled the United States out of its economic depression?

c. How do today's political differences date back to the Depression?

**4. Critical Thinking**

**Drawing Conclusions** Of the following New Deal programs, which one do you think affects your life the most? Explain.

**THINK ABOUT**
- Social Security
- Federal Deposit Insurance Corporation
- Securities and Exchange Commission

**ACTIVITY OPTIONS**

**LANGUAGE ARTS / TECHNOLOGY** Ask your grandparents or other older relatives what they think the legacy of the Depression and New Deal is. Prepare a **written interview** or an **audio recording**.



### Now and then

**Social Security**

Both the rise in life expectancy and the decline in birth rates are contributing to demographic changes that will affect Social Security. At the time today's workers retire they will be supported by those still working. Social Security taxes paid by workers today are used to provide current retirees with Social Security benefits. In 1950, there were 16 workers for every person receiving Social Security benefits. By 2030, only two workers will be paying taxes for each recipient.

**INSTRUCT: OBJECTIVE 4**

**An Ongoing Political Debate**

Key Questions
- How do the political beliefs of liberals and conservatives on the role of government tend to differ?
- Why are both major political parties concerned about Social Security today?

### ASSESS & RETEACH

**Setting the Stage** Have students examine their completed chart and evaluate how effective the responses of Hoover, FDR, and citizens were to the Great Depression.

**Formal Assessment**
- Section Quiz, p. 380

**Critical Thinking Transparency CT76**
- Setting the Stage

**RETEACHING ACTIVITY**

Organize students into groups of four. Assign one section subhead to each student in a group. Have students summarize the material in their subsection. Members should then share their summaries with the rest of the group.

**In-Depth Resources: Unit 8**
- Reteaching Activity, p. 37

### Section 4 Assessment

**1. Terms & Names**

**Securities and Exchange Commission,** p. 748
**liberal,** p. 749
**conservative,** p. 749

**2. Taking Notes**
- a national pension system
- agricultural price supports
- protection for savings
- regulation of the stock market

Politics today is affected by the liberal-conservative split and by concern over the future of Social Security.

**3. Main Ideas**

**a.** Many Americans never recovered from their fear of losing their jobs and property. **b.** high government spending to pay the expenses associated with World War II
**c.** Political parties still disagree about who should be responsible for certain programs.

**4. Critical Thinking**

Answers will vary. Be sure students support their opinions with information from the chapter and their own experiences.

**ACTIVITY OPTIONS**

**Alternative Assessment**
- Rubrics for an interview, 4.5
- Rubrics for an audio recording, 5.3

## TERMS & NAMES

1. **Herbert Hoover,** p. 729
2. **Crash of 1929,** p. 731
3. **Great Depression,** p. 731
4. **Franklin Delano Roosevelt,** p. 734
5. **New Deal,** p. 735
6. **deficit spending,** p. 738
7. **Dust Bowl,** p. 739
8. **Eleanor Roosevelt,** p. 742
9. **liberal,** p. 749
10. **conservative,** p. 749

## REVIEW QUESTIONS

**Possible Responses**

1. Once prices began to fall, people rushed to sell stocks before their value fell too low to pay off loans; falling prices scared off buyers; with more sellers than buyers, prices continued to fall.
2. private charities
3. People blamed Hoover, who grew even more unpopular and lost the election.
4. a group of college professors and economists who advised FDR on how to end the Depression
5. radio talks in which Roosevelt explained his policies to the nation in a warm, friendly style that calmed fears
6. He was afraid to commit to as much deficit spending as some economists advised, and he had also been receiving a lot of criticism.
7. Some portrayed people's struggle to survive, and some created escapist works.
8. the sit-down strike, in which striking workers did not walk off their jobs but rather occupied the factory; it was highly successful
9. The federal government became directly responsible for people's well-being in a way it had not been before.
10. Social Security



## VISUAL SUMMARY

### The Great Depression and New Deal

**CAUSES**

- problems in agriculture and some industries
- unequal income distribution
- too much inventory
- too much debt
- stock market speculation

BROOKLYN DAILY EAGLE

WALL ST. IN PANIC AS STOCKS CRASH

**DEPRESSION**

- stock market crash
- bank and business failures
- high unemployment
- hunger and homelessness

**NEW DEAL**

- relief for the hungry and jobless
- recovery for agriculture and industry
- reforms to change the way the economy worked

**LONG-TERM EFFECTS**

- fear of future
- more influence by federal government
- more presidential power
- long-term government programs
- debate between conservatives and liberals



## TERMS & NAMES

Briefly explain the importance of each of the following.

1. Herbert Hoover
2. Crash of 1929
3. Great Depression
4. Franklin Delano Roosevelt
5. New Deal
6. deficit spending
7. Dust Bowl
8. Eleanor Roosevelt
9. liberal
10. conservative

## REVIEW QUESTIONS

**Hoover and the Crash (pages 729–733)**

1. Why did stock prices fall so quickly during the stock market crash?
2. Who did President Hoover think should help the needy?
3. How did MacArthur's attack on the Bonus Army affect the 1932 election?

**Roosevelt and the New Deal (pages 734–738)**

4. What was the "brain trust"?
5. What were fireside chats, and how did they affect the country?
6. Why didn't Roosevelt propose many new programs during his second term?

**Life During the Depression (pages 739–745)**

7. How did writers and filmmakers respond to the hard times?
8. What new bargaining tactic did labor unions use, and how did it work?

**The Effects of the New Deal (pages 746–749)**

9. How did the New Deal change the role of the federal government in American life?
10. What New Deal program remains popular even though it is in financial trouble?

## CRITICAL THINKING

**1. USING YOUR NOTES**

Using your completed chart, answer the questions below.

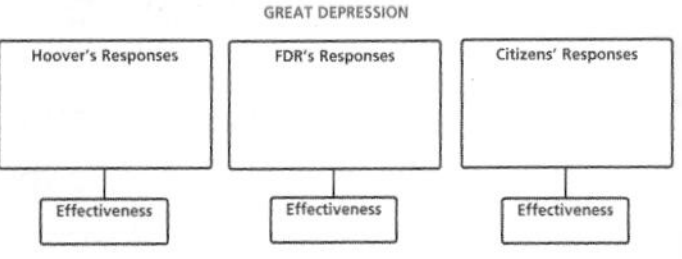


a. What do you think was Hoover's most successful response to the Depression?

b. Judging from his responses to the Depression, do you think that FDR was one of our greatest presidents? Explain.

**2. ANALYZING LEADERSHIP**

During the Depression, many countries turned to strong leaders. How did the Depression-era leadership of Germany differ from that of the United States?

**3. ANALYZING CAUSES**

Review the economic problems that led to the Depression. What similar problems exist in the economy today?

**4. THEME: ECONOMICS IN HISTORY**

What reforms did FDR make to ensure that the United States would never again experience such a severe depression?

**5. APPLYING CITIZENSHIP SKILLS**

How were each of the following citizenship skills important during the Depression: voting, staying informed about issues, and community service?

**Interact *with* History**

Now that you have read the chapter, would you give the same answer to the question, "Who do you think should help the poor?" Explain why or why not.

## CRITICAL THINKING

**Possible Responses**

1. **USING YOUR NOTES a.** his finally agreeing to fund public works projects **b.** Answers will vary. Be sure students support their opinions.
2. **ANALYZING LEADERSHIP** Both Hitler and FDR were strong leaders, but Hitler became a dictator, while FDR helped preserve Americans' faith in democracy.
3. **ANALYZING CAUSES** Answers will vary but might include a volatile stock market, a large gap in income between rich and poor, a large trade deficit, or problems in certain industries.
4. **THEME: ECONOMICS IN HISTORY** regulation of the stock market, federal insurance to protect savings accounts, conservation to prevent erosion
5. **APPLYING CITIZENSHIP SKILLS** voting: because Americans had to choose between leaders with very different ideas; staying informed: because there was much disagreement on combating the Depression; community service: to provide charity to the poor

**Interact *with* History** Answers will vary, but many students will say that a combination of private charity and government intervention is needed.

## HISTORY SKILLS

**1. INTERPRETING CHARTS**

Study the chart. Then answer the questions.

**Roosevelt's Presidential Elections**

| ELECTION YEAR | TOTAL VOTES | VOTES FOR FDR |
|---|---|---|
| 1932 | 39,749,382 | 22,825,016 |
| 1936 | 45,642,303 | 27,747,636 |
| 1940 | 49,840,443 | 27,263,448 |
| 1944 | 47,974,819 | 25,611,936 |

Source: *New York Times Almanac*

**Basic Chart Elements**

a. What presidential elections does this chart cover?

b. Who won each of the elections?

**Interpreting the Chart**

c. What percentage of the vote did FDR win in each election?

d. Most of FDR's programs were proposed in 1933 and 1935. Based on the election numbers, did his programs make him more or less popular?

**2. INTERPRETING PRIMARY SOURCES**

This photograph, taken by Dorothea Lange, is one of the most famous images of the Great Depression. It shows a mother and her children in a camp for migrant workers in 1936.

a. How would you describe this woman's expression?

b. Why do you think this photograph is often used to illustrate the effects of the Depression on individuals?

## ALTERNATIVE ASSESSMENT

**1. INTERDISCIPLINARY ACTIVITY: Science**

**Diagramming a Dam** Find out how hydroelectric dams, such as those built by the TVA, turn the energy of flowing water into electricity. Draw a diagram or illustration explaining this process.

**2. COOPERATIVE LEARNING ACTIVITY**

**Debating Government Policy** Working in a small group, have each group member take on the role of a Depression-era leader and hold a panel discussion in which you debate the following question: Should the government go into debt to help the poor? Before holding the discussion, do further research on your leader's beliefs. Possible leaders to choose include the following.

- Herbert Hoover
- Franklin Delano Roosevelt
- Eleanor Roosevelt
- Huey Long
- Father Coughlin
- Francis Townshend
- a conservative Republican

**3. TECHNOLOGY ACTIVITY**

**Preparing a Multimedia Presentation** Choose an aspect of the Great Depression that you would like to learn more about. Using books, the Internet, and software, research your topic. Then prepare a multimedia presentation. Consider including oral histories, quotations from FDR's speeches, Depression-era photographs and art, excerpts from literature, and videotaped interviews with older relatives.

**Visit www.mcdougallittell.com to learn more about the Great Depression.**

**4. HISTORY PORTFOLIO**

**Option 1** Review your section and chapter assessment activities. Select one that you think is your best work. Then use comments made by your teacher or classmates to improve your work and add it to your portfolio.

**Option 2** Review the questions that you wrote for What Do You Want to Know? on page 728. Then write a short report in which you explain the answers to your questions. If any questions were not answered, do research to answer them. Add your answers to your portfolio.



## ALTERNATIVE ASSESSMENT

**1. INTERDISCIPLINARY ACTIVITY: Science**
**Diagrams should**

- represent the concept of power from a hydroelectric dam in a manner clear to the viewers.
- exhibit creativity.
- demonstrate grade-level artistic skill.

**2. COOPERATIVE LEARNING ACTIVITY**
**Discussions should**

- focus on the central question.
- reflect the student's understanding of the experiences of the person he or she selected to represent.
- support each student's position with evidence or logic.
- demonstrate that students can appropriately respond to each other's statements.

**3.**  **TECHNOLOGY ACTIVITY**
**Presentations should**

- utilize two or more media about the Depression.
- clearly demonstrate an understanding of the concepts presented.
- show technical proficiency.

**4. HISTORY PORTFOLIO**

**Option 1 Revised section or chapter assessment activities should**

- address teacher and peer responses to the selected work.
- solve problems present in the first versions of the work.

**Option 2 Short reports should**

- answer questions about the Great Depression.
- use evidence to develop and support ideas.
- cite sources of information.
- use standard grammar, spelling, sentence structure, and punctuation.

**Critical Thinking Transparency CT78**

- Visual Summary

**Formal Assessment**

- Chapter Test, Forms A and B, pp. 381–388

## HISTORY SKILLS

**Possible Responses**

**1. INTERPRETING CHARTS**

**Basic Chart Elements**

**a.** 1932, 1936, 1940, 1944

**b.** FDR

**Interpreting the Chart**

**c.** 57, 61, 55, 53

**d.** The programs seemed to make him more popular.

**2. INTERPRETING PRIMARY SOURCES**

**a.** sad, exhausted, hopeless, full of pain

**b.** The woman's worn face and ragged clothes, and the refusal of her children to look at the camera, show how much suffering they have endured.

## HISTORY WORKSHOP

**OBJECTIVE**
Students paint a WPA mural, write an exhibit note explaining how the mural reflects the type of work people did during the Great Depression, and give a speech dedicating the mural.

 **BLOCK SCHEDULING**

## PROCEDURE

Gather the materials listed in the "Toolbox." Divide the class into groups of four or five. Then review the steps for making the WPA mural.

 **In-Depth Resources: Unit 8**
- History Workshop Resources, p. 39

### HISTORY FROM VISUALS

**Interpreting the Mural** Point out to students the different types of work being done in this Warren Hunter mural. Ask students to think about the skills needed for each kind of work. Discuss with students the painter's regard for the dignity of work and workers. Have students suggest reasons why a post office was chosen as the site for the mural. **Possible Responses** The murals mainly appeared in public buildings, and many people could see and enjoy the mural if it was in a post office.

## HISTORY WORKSHOP

# Paint a WPA Mural

Franklin Roosevelt once remarked that "the very soundness of our democratic institutions depends on the determination of our government to give employment to idle [people]." Indeed, one of Roosevelt's New Deal programs, the Works Progress Administration's (WPA) Federal Art Project (FAP), provided creative work for artists during the Great Depression. These artists created more than 2,500 murals and 100,000 paintings. Many of the works celebrate American workers. The paintings mainly appeared in schools, post offices, and other public buildings.

A man shoes a horse in part of the mural shown above.

ACTIVITY Create your own WPA mural, as artists did during the Great Depression. Then write an exhibit note that tells viewers about your mural. Finally, give a speech dedicating your mural to your school.

### TOOLBOX

Each group will need:

- pencils
- drawing paper
- newspapers to protect desks and floor
- yardstick
- poster-sized/oversized sheets of art paper
- water-based paints
- paintbrushes

Warren Hunter painted this mural in 1939 on the wall of the post office in Alice, Texas.

### STEP BY STEP

**1 Form artist groups.** Meet with three or four other students to discuss your new art project. Imagine that you have all signed a work contract with the WPA. Your job is to create a mural to show Americans at work during the Great Depression.

**2 Research the WPA and the FAP.** Use the Internet, encyclopedias, or books about the Great Depression to brainstorm ideas for your mural. Jot down the types of work people were doing, the structures they were building, and the machinery they were using. With your group, discuss these ideas and answer these questions to help plan your mural:
- Who should be in the mural?
- What should they look like?
- What should they be doing?
- What colors would best represent the subject of your mural?

**3 Sketch your mural.** Using a pencil, accurately sketch your mural on drawing paper. This drawing should be a much smaller version of the mural you will paint later.

752

### RECOMMENDED RESOURCES

**JOURNALS AND BOOKS FOR THE TEACHER**

Bustard, Bruce I. ***A New Deal for the Arts.*** Seattle, WA: University of Washington Press, 1997.

Harris, Jonathan. ***Federal Art and National Culture.*** New York: Cambridge University Press, 1995.

Leuchtenburg, William. ***The FDR Years.*** New York: Columbia University Press, 1995.

**VIDEOS**

***The Helping Hand.*** Corporation for Entertainment and Learning, Inc., 1984. Explores the work of New Deal programs.

***The New Deal.*** New York Times Educational Media, 1995. Uses archival footage to explore many aspects of the New Deal through three videos and teacher's guides.

**BOOKS FOR THE STUDENTS**

Freedman, Russell. ***Franklin Delano Roosevelt.*** New York: Clarion Books, 1990.

**4** **Draw a grid over the sketch.** A grid consists of lines drawn across and down a drawing to form squares. Like individual puzzle pieces, each square contains a part of the picture. Use a yardstick to make your grid lines straight.

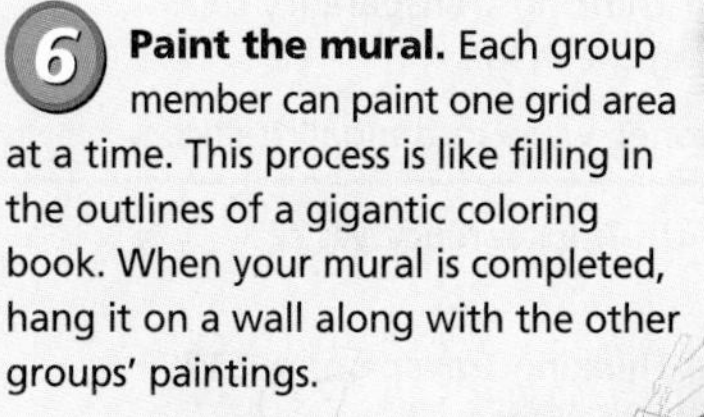

**5** **Transfer the design to larger paper.** Draw another grid on oversized paper that has the same number of squares as the scale drawing. This time, though, the grid should be much larger—as large as the oversized paper. Make sure the grid lines are faint. Now copy the original drawing one square at a time.

**6** **Paint the mural.** Each group member can paint one grid area at a time. This process is like filling in the outlines of a gigantic coloring book. When your mural is completed, hang it on a wall along with the other groups' paintings.

## WRITE AND SPEAK

Write an exhibit note about how the mural reflects the type of work people did during the Great Depression. Attach the explanation to the back of the mural. Then, in a classroom dedication ceremony, deliver a speech dedicating your mural to your school.

## HELP DESK

For related information, see page 748 in Chapter 26.

### Researching Your Project

- *Life During the Great Depression* by Dennis Nishi
- *The New Deal* by Gail Stewart

**Visit www.mcdougallittell.com to learn more about the Great Depression.**

### Did You Know?

Between 1935 and 1943, the WPA employed 8.5 million people and spent $11 billion. The average wage was $55 a month. The government poverty level at the time was $100 a month.

The agency built
- 651,087 miles of roads
- 125,110 public buildings
- 8,192 parks
- 853 airports

Among these projects were New York City's famed Lincoln Tunnel and the Fort Knox gold depository, located in Kentucky.

### REFLECT & ASSESS

- **Compare and contrast your image with those of the other groups.**
- **Why did you choose the particular image in your mural?**
- **How well does your mural represent the history, social issues, and culture of the time?**



### MORE ABOUT . . .

**Federal Arts Project**

The FAP was the New Deal jobs program for artists. In addition to creating murals and decorating public buildings, FAP workers collected and catalogued folk arts and crafts, preserving them for future generations.

Many murals created by FAP artists were painted in a style known as "social realism" because it focused on the roles of ordinary working people in the life of the nation. By using public funds to help artists continue their work, the FAP changed the public's perception of the arts. Many Americans recognized for the first time that artists contributed to society just as factory workers and business executives did.

### REFLECT & ASSESS

1. Students can compare and contrast the colors, shapes, and types of images chosen; the way the earlier time period is suggested; and the ways the individual images fit together to form a mural.
2. Students can explain the reasons for their choices by showing how each image in the mural reflects the theme.
3. Have students identify details in their mural that show the history, social issues, or culture of the 1930s. Students might ask themselves how viewers can tell that their mural reflects an earlier period in American history.

### STANDARDS FOR EVALUATION

**HISTORY WORKSHOP**

**Murals should**
- be colorful and creative.
- show people at work during the Great Depression.
- include the work of all group members.
- be historically accurate.

**WRITE AND SPEAK**

**Speeches should**
- explain why the images in the mural were chosen.
- give reasons for dedicating the mural to the school.

CHAPTER 27 PLANNING GUIDE

# The Rise of Dictators and World War II 1931–1945

| | CHAPTER OVERVIEW | COPYMASTERS | TECHNOLOGY |
|---|---|---|---|
| **CHAPTER RESOURCES** | The chapter discusses the events that led to World War II and the course of the war in Europe, Africa, and the Pacific. It also describes the effects of the war on the home front and the long-term results of the war. | **In-Depth Resources: Unit 8**<br>• Tracing Themes: America in the World, p. 41<br>• Building Vocabulary, p. 47<br>**Interdisciplinary Projects,** pp. 157–162 | CD-ROM **Primary Source Explorer**<br>CD-ROM **Electronic Teacher Tools**<br>CD-ROM **Power Presentations CD-ROM**<br>**Chapter Summaries on CD** (English and Spanish) |
| **SECTION 1 Steps to War pp. 757–762** | **KEY IDEAS**<br>• Dictators come to power in Europe.<br>• Germany overruns much of western Europe and attacks the USSR.<br>• The United States enters the war after Japan attacks Pearl Harbor. | **In-Depth Resources: Unit 8**<br>• Setting the Stage, p. 40<br>• Guided Reading, p. 42<br>• Primary Source, p. 51<br>• Reteaching Activity, p. 56<br>**Outline Map Activities,** pp. 53–54 | **Warm-Up Transparency WT27**<br>**Geography Transparency GT27**<br>• The Japanese Attack on Pearl Harbor, 1941<br>**Critical Thinking Transparency CT79**<br>• Setting the Stage<br>INTERNET **ClassZone:** www.mcdougallittell.com |
| **SECTION 2 War in Africa and Europe pp. 763–769** | • American men and women join the armed forces, fighting around the world.<br>• The Allies turn the tide of war against Germany in 1943 and 1944.<br>• Allied troops find the concentration camps where Nazis murdered 6 million Jews. | **In-Depth Resources: Unit 8**<br>• Setting the Stage, p. 40<br>• Guided Reading, p. 43<br>• Geography Application, pp. 49–50<br>• Reteaching Activity, p. 57<br>**America's History Makers,** pp. 107–108<br>**American History Plays**<br>• *Rescued from the Holocaust* by Sean Price | **Warm-Up Transparency WT27**<br>**Critical Thinking Transparency CT79**<br>• Setting the Stage<br>**Primary Source Explorer**<br>• *A Voice from the Holocaust*<br>INTERNET **ClassZone:** www.mcdougallittell.com |
| **SECTION 3 War in the Pacific pp. 770–773** | • Japan wins early battles in the Pacific, but the U.S. Navy is victorious at Midway.<br>• The Allies fight from island to island toward Japan.<br>• The United States drops two atomic bombs. | **In-Depth Resources: Unit 8**<br>• Setting the Stage, p. 40<br>• Guided Reading, p. 44<br>• Skillbuilder Practice: Making Decisions, p. 48<br>• Reteaching Activity, p. 58 | **Warm-Up Transparency WT27**<br>**Humanities Transparency HT53**<br>• Navajo Code Talkers<br>**Critical Thinking Transparency CT79**<br>• Setting the Stage<br>INTERNET **ClassZone:** www.mcdougallittell.com |
| **SECTION 4 The Home Front pp. 774–779** | • U.S. factories gear up for wartime.<br>• Women fill many new factory jobs, and FDR bans racial discrimination in defense industries.<br>• Japanese Americans are forced into internment camps. | **In-Depth Resources: Unit 8**<br>• Guided Reading, p. 45<br>• Primary Source, p. 52<br>• Literature Selection, pp. 53–55<br>• Reteaching Activity, p. 59<br>**America's History Makers,** pp. 109–110<br>**Citizenship Today,** pp. 17–18<br>**Economics in History,** p. 27 | **Warm-Up Transparency WT27**<br>**Humanities Transparency HT54**<br>• Americans Will Always Fight for Liberty<br>**Critical Thinking Transparency CT79**<br>• Setting the Stage<br>INTERNET **ClassZone:** www.mcdougallittell.com |
| **SECTION 5 The Legacy of the War pp. 780–783** | • The United States helps war-torn Europe and Japan rebuild.<br>• The G.I. Bill of Rights offers returning soldiers new opportunities.<br>• The United Nations is established to try to prevent future wars. | **In-Depth Resources: Unit 8**<br>• Setting the Stage, p. 40<br>• Guided Reading, p. 46<br>• Reteaching Activity, p. 60<br>**Why It Matters Now**<br>• The War's Continuing Impact, pp. 53–54 | **Warm-Up Transparency WT27**<br>**Critical Thinking Transparency CT80**<br>• Cause and Effect: World War II<br>**Critical Thinking Transparency CT81**<br>• Visual Summary<br>INTERNET **ClassZone:** www.mcdougallittell.com |

Pupil's Edition · Copymaster · Overhead Transparency · Audio Library · CD-ROM · Internet

## ASSESSMENT

**Chapter Assessment,** pp. 784–785

**Formal Assessment**
- Chapter Tests, Forms A and B, pp. 396–403

**Alternative Assessment Book**

**Electronic Teacher Tools with Test Maker**

---

**Section Assessment,** p. 762

**Formal Assessment**
- Section Quiz, p. 391

**Alternative Assessment Book**
- Rubrics for a journal entry, 4.3
- Rubrics for a map, 2.1

**Electronic Teacher Tools with Test Maker**

---

**Section Assessment,** p. 768

**Formal Assessment**
- Section Quiz, p. 392

**Alternative Assessment Book**
- Rubrics for a map, 2.1
- Rubrics for a database, 2.6

**Electronic Teacher Tools with Test Maker**

---

**Section Assessment,** p. 773

**Formal Assessment**
- Section Quiz, p. 393

**Alternative Assessment Book**
- Rubrics for a biography, 4.4
- Rubrics for a diagram, 1.3

**Electronic Teacher Tools with Test Maker**

---

**Section Assessment,** p. 777

**Formal Assessment**
- Section Quiz, p. 394

**Alternative Assessment Book**
- Rubrics for a report, 2.5
- Rubrics for a mural, 1.11

**Electronic Teacher Tools with Test Maker**

---

**Section Assessment,** p. 783

**Formal Assessment**
- Section Quiz, p. 395

**Alternative Assessment Book**
- Rubrics for a news article, 4.5
- Rubrics for a speech, 3.6

**Electronic Teacher Tools with Test Maker**

## CUSTOMIZING FOR INDIVIDUAL NEEDS

### Students Acquiring English/ESL

**Reading Study Guide** (English and Spanish), pp. 259–270

**Access for Students Acquiring English/ESL: Spanish Translations,** pp. 179–186

**Chapter Summaries on CD** (English and Spanish)

### Less Proficient Readers

**Reading Study Guide** (English and Spanish), pp. 259–270

**Chapter Summaries on CD** (English and Spanish)

### Gifted and Talented Students

**In-Depth Resources: Unit 8**
- Enrichment Activity, p. 61

**America's History Makers**
- Dwight D. Eisenhower, pp. 107–108
- Daniel K. Inouye, pp. 109–110

## CROSS-CURRICULAR CONNECTIONS

### Culture

Aaseng, Nathan. ***Navajo Code Talkers.*** New York: Walker, 1992. Fascinating story, not only of the science behind code making but of Navajo life on the reservations and in the military.

### Economics

Colman, Penny. Shakti Gawain, contr. ***Rosie the Riveter: Women Working on the Home Front in World War II.*** New York: Knopf, 1995. A broad overview of women war workers, with period photos and quotes.

### Science

Cohen, Daniel. ***The Manhattan Project.*** Brookfield, CT: Twenty-First Century Books, 1999. Explains the science of the bomb and the history of its development.

### World History

Stalcup, Ann. ***On the Home Front: Growing Up in Wartime England.*** Hamden, CT: Shoe String Press, 1998. A factual account that includes the author's memories and historical information.

### Interdisciplinary Projects, pp. 157–162

- Math: Rationing with Fractions
- Science: Blood Banking
- Language Arts: Reporting World War II
- Art: World War II Photography

### Literature

Houston, Jeanne Wakatsuki. ***Farewell to Manzanar: A True Story of Japanese American Experience During and After the World War II Internment.*** New York: Bantam Books, 1983. Modern classic tells about life in an internment camp. For advanced readers.

### McDougal Littell *The Language of Literature*

- Goodrich and Hackett. "Diary of Anne Frank" (drama)
- Willy Lindwer. from ***The Last Seven Months of Anne Frank*** (interview)

### McDougal Littell Literature Connections

Frances Goodrich and Albert Hacket

***The Diary of Anne Frank***

A play based on the famous diary of the Jewish girl who hid with her family from the Nazis.

Theodore Taylor

***The Cay***

Shipwrecked and blinded during World War II, a young boy must rely on Timothy, an old black man, for survival. The prejudiced boy learns to respect and love Timothy.

## ENRICHMENT ACTIVITIES

**Pupil's Edition, pp. 754–785**
**Interact with History,** p. 755
**Interactive Primary Source,** p. 769
**Citizenship Today,** p. 776
**Interdisciplinary Challenge,** pp. 778–779

**In-Depth Resources: Unit 8**
- Geography Application, pp. 49–50
- Primary Source, p. 51
- Primary Source, p. 52
- Literature Selection, pp. 53–55

**America's History Makers**
- Dwight D. Eisenhower, pp. 107–108
- Daniel K. Inouye, pp. 109–110

**America's Music CD**

**American History Plays**
- *Rescued from the Holocaust* by Sean Price

**Outline Map Activities,** pp. 53–54

**Why It Matters Now,** pp. 53–54

# CHAPTER 27 PACING GUIDE

**LESSON PLAN OPTIONS (50-MINUTE PERIOD)** (TE) = Teacher's Edition (PE) = Pupil's Edition

| | TEACHER-DIRECTED ACTIVITIES<br>Class Time: 15 minutes | STUDENT-CENTERED ACTIVITIES<br>Class Time: 25 minutes | INDIVIDUAL ACTIVITIES<br>Class Time: 10 minutes |
|---|---|---|---|
| **DAY 1**<br>Introduction<br>pp. 754–756 | **Presentation Options**<br>• Begin with a class discussion of the picture on p. 754 **(PE)**.<br>• Lead a class discussion on the "What Do You Know?" question in Setting the Stage, p. 756. Then introduce the graphic organizer for the chapter **(PE)**. | **Options for Cooperative Learning**<br>• Have student groups discuss the Interact with History questions, p. 755 **(PE)**.<br>• Have student groups respond to the "What Do You Want to Know?" question in Setting the Stage, p. 756 **(PE)**. | **Head Start on Homework Options**<br>• Have students skim Section 1 Main Idea, Why It Matters Now, Terms & Names, and the main headings, p. 757 **(PE)**.<br>• Have students begin Guided Reading activity and Building Vocabulary sheet. |
| **DAY 2**<br>Section 1<br>pp. 757–762 | **Presentation Options**<br>• Begin with the 5-Minute Warm-Up, p. 757 **(TE)**.<br>• Review the Section 1 Main Idea, Why It Matters Now, and Terms & Names, p. 757 **(PE)**. | **Options for Cooperative Learning**<br>• Divide students into groups to complete the Interdisciplinary Link, Humanities: Debate, p. 759 **(TE)**.<br>• Have student pairs work together to complete one of the Activity Options in the Section 1 Assessment, p. 762 **(PE)**. | **Head Start on Homework Options**<br>• Have students begin working on Section 1 Assessment, p. 762 **(PE)**.<br>• Have students complete the Interactive Primary Source A Closer Look questions, p. 769 **(PE)**. |
| **DAY 3**<br>Section 2<br>pp. 763–769 | **Presentation Options**<br>• Begin with the 5-Minute Warm-Up, p. 763 **(TE)**.<br>• Lead students through the Interactive Primary Source, p. 769 **(TE)**. | **Options for Cooperative Learning**<br>• Divide students into groups and have them complete the History form Visuals Extension activity, p. 764 **(PE)**.<br>• Have student pairs work together to complete one of the Activity Options in the Section 2 Assessment, p. 768 **(PE)**. | **Head Start on Homework Options**<br>• Have students begin working on Section 2 Assessment, p. 768 **(PE)**.<br>• Have students complete the Critical Thinking Activity, p. 767 **(TE)**. |
| **DAY 4**<br>Section 3<br>pp. 770–773 | **Presentation Options**<br>• Begin with the 5-Minute Warm-Up, p. 770 **(TE)**.<br>• Lead the students through the Skillbuilder Mini-Lesson: Making Decisions, p. 772 **(TE)**. | **Options for Cooperative Learning**<br>• Divide students into groups and have them complete the Geography Skillbuilder and the History from Visuals, p. 771 **(PE, TE)**.<br>• Have student pairs work together to complete one of the Activity Options in the Section 3 Assessment, p. 773 **(PE)**. | **Head Start on Homework Options**<br>• Have students begin working on Section 3 Assessment, p. 773 **(PE)**.<br>• Have students complete the Reading History questions for Section 4, pp. 774–777 **(PE)**. |
| **DAY 5**<br>Section 4<br>pp.774–779 | **Presentation Options**<br>• Begin with the 5-Minute Warm-Up, p. 774 **(TE)**.<br>• Choose 5 key questions for Objectives 1–4 to discuss with the class, pp. 774–777 **(TE)**. | **Options for Cooperative Learning**<br>• Divide students into groups and have them complete the Citizenship Today questions, p. 776 **(PE)**.<br>• Divide students into groups and have them complete the Interdisciplinary Challenge, pp. 778–779 **(PE)**. | **Head Start on Homework Options**<br>• Have students begin working on Section 4 Assessment, p. 777 **(PE)**.<br>• Have students preview Section 5 Main Idea, Why It matters Now, Terms & Names, and the main headings, p. 780 **(PE)**. |
| **DAY 6**<br>Section 5<br>pp. 780–783 | **Presentation Options**<br>• Begin with the 5-Minute Warm-Up, p. 780 **(TE)**.<br>• Lead students through Critical Thinking Activity, p. 783 **(TE)**. | **Options for Cooperative Learning**<br>• Divide students into small groups and begin work on the Interdisciplinary Link, Civics: War Memorials, p. 781 **(TE)**.<br>• Have student pairs work together to complete one of the Activity Options in the Section 5 Assessment, p. 783 **(PE)**. | **Head Start on Homework Options**<br>• Have students complete the Setting the Stage graphic organizer for the chapter, p. 756 **(PE)**.<br>• Have students begin working on the Chapter Assessment, pp. 784–785 **(PE)**.<br>• Prepare for Chapter Test<br>**Formal Assessment,** pp. 369–403 |

**TEACHER-TESTED ACTIVITY** Meg Robbins, Wilbraham Middle School, Wilbraham, Massachusetts

## TO WAR OR NOT?

**Class Time** One class period

**Task** Holding a debate on whether or not the United States should enter World War II

**Purpose** To understand conflicting views on American entry into World War II prior to the Japanese attack on Pearl Harbor

**Supplies Needed**

- Reference materials and Internet resources on American attitudes about joining the Allied war effort before December 1941

**Activity** Divide the class into four-member groups. Assign half the groups to research and develop arguments in favor of entering the war before the Japanese attack on Pearl Harbor. Tell the other groups to research and argue that the United States should remain neutral. Each group should prepare a two-minute statement of position on the question, "Should we help our European allies?" After all groups have presented their position statements, each group will give another two-minute statement in rebuttal of its opponents' arguments.

## BLOCK SCHEDULING — LESSON PLAN OPTIONS (90-MINUTE PERIOD)

### DAY 1

**Interact with History,** p. 755
**Class Time** 20 minutes

Options for pacing and variety:

- Role-Playing Working in pairs, students can assume the roles of draft-age young Americans who have just learned about the attack on Pearl Harbor. Have students create a written dialogue between the two that includes their answers to the Interact with History questions. Have student pairs read their dialogues to the class. **Class Time** 20 minutes

**Setting the Stage,** p. 756
**Class Time** 20 minutes

Options for pacing and variety:

- Time Saver For a homework assignment, have students preview the section, looking at subsection heads and illustrations, and then make a list of "What Do You Want to Know?" questions for the section. **Class Time** 5 minutes

**Section 1,** pp. 757–762
**Class Time** 50 minutes

Options for pacing and variety:

- History on Film Extend students' background knowledge of the rise of dictators by viewing *Hitler* or *Mussolini* in the *Heroes and Tyrants of the Twentieth Century* series. Granada. **Class Time** 60 minutes
- Time Saver Assign the Analyzing Leadership question in the Chapter Assessment for homework. **Class Time** 5 minutes

### DAY 2

**Section 2,** pp. 763–769
**Class Time** 45 minutes

Options for pacing and variety:

- Internet Extend students' background knowledge of D-Day by visiting www.mcdougallittell.com **Class Time** 20 minutes
- Peer Evaluation Have student pairs complete the Primary Source Explorer Activity on page 785 of the Chapter Assessment and make class presentations on the Holocaust. For links to a Web site on the Holocaust, visit www.mcdougallittell.com **Class Time** 40 minutes

**Section 3,** pp. 770–773
**Class Time** 45 minutes

Options for pacing and variety:

- Time Saver Use the map on page 771 to help students visualize the strategy of island hopping. **Class Time** 10 minutes
- Peer Evaluation Have small groups of students work together to complete the Taking Notes and Main Ideas questions in the Section Assessment. **Class Time** 20 minutes

### DAY 3

**Section 4,** pp. 774–779
**Class Time** 45 minutes

**Interdisciplinary Challenge,** pp. 778–779
**Class Time** 45 minutes

Options for pacing and variety:

- Team Teaching Invite a Home Economics teacher to visit the class to assist student groups in solving the Home Economics Challenge. **Class Time** 30 minutes

**Section 5,** pp. 780–783
**Class Time** 45 minutes

Options for pacing and variety:

- Time Saver Use the chart on page 781 to sum up the war's cost in human terms. **Class Time** 5 minutes
- Peer Evaluation Have pairs of students identify a Main Idea for each of the subsections of Section 5 and write two or three sentences of supporting details for each main idea. **Class Time** 15 minutes

**Chapter 27 Assessment,** pp. 784–785
**Class Time** 40 minutes

Options for pacing and variety:

- Peer Teaching Have student pairs identify events from the Visual Summary that they consider to be turning points in the war and write a paragraph explaining their choices. **Class Time** 10 minutes
- Peer Teaching Divide the class into groups of five. Have each student in a group answer the Review Questions for one of the five sections. Have students share answers within groups. **Class Time** 20 minutes

## CHAPTER 27 OBJECTIVE

The student will understand the causes, major battles, and consequences of World War II.

### HISTORY FROM VISUALS

**Interpreting the Photograph** Ask the students to study the photograph of the battleship U.S.S. *West Virginia* burning after the Japanese attack on Pearl Harbor. Ask them to draw conclusions about the amount of damage the aerial attack had on the U.S. fleet. **Possible Response** The attack was devastating, causing many deaths and extensive damage to the U.S. fleet.

**Extension** Have the students write newspaper headlines or prepare radio announcements about the attack on Pearl Harbor.

# The Rise of Dictators and World War II

## 1931–1945

*Section 1* **Steps to War**
*Section 2* **War in Africa and Europe**
*Section 3* **War in the Pacific**
*Section 4* **The Home Front**
*Section 5* **The Legacy of the War**

The battleship U.S.S. *West Virginia* burns in Pearl Harbor in Hawaii after the Japanese attack on December 7, 1941.

754

### RECOMMENDED RESOURCES

**BOOKS FOR THE TEACHER**

Buderi, Robert. ***The Invention that Changed the World: How a Small Group of Radar Pioneers Won the Second World War and Launched a Technological Revolution.*** New York: S&S, 1996. Well-told story of secret scientific collaboration between the U.S. and Britain.

Terkel, Studs. ***"The Good War": An Oral History of World War Two.*** The war seen through many eyes.

Wiesel, Elie. ***All Rivers Run to the Sea: Memoirs.*** New York: Knopf, 1995. Long-awaited narrative by Nobel Prize winner and Holocaust survivor.

**SOFTWARE**

***Executive Order 9066: The Incarceration of Japanese Americans During World War II.*** CD-ROM. Grolier, 1998. Includes primary sources and a guide.

***World War II: Sources and Analysis.*** CD-ROM. Granada Learning, 1995. Reference source concentrating on the war's effects on individuals.

**VIDEO**

***Victory at Sea.*** Columbia/Tristar. 6 vols. Episode 1, "Design for War." First of many episodes released in 1952, with score by Richard Rodgers.

**INTERNET**

For more about D-Day, visit www.mcdougallittell.com

## Interact *with* History

Adolf Hitler, leader of Nazi Germany, is shown carving up the world for the dictators to devour.

Benito Mussolini, Italy's leader, takes his slice of the world.

General Tojo, the prime minister of Japan, awaits his portion.

**The year is 1941, and the American naval base at Pearl Harbor has been bombed. Now the United States has joined the Allies in World War II. The Allies face dangerous opponents in leaders such as Hitler, Mussolini, and Tojo. You must do your part to help defeat them.**

### What Do You Think?

- **What threat do dictators pose to the world?**
- **What would you be willing to sacrifice to defeat dictators?**

# *Would you risk your life to fight against dictators?*

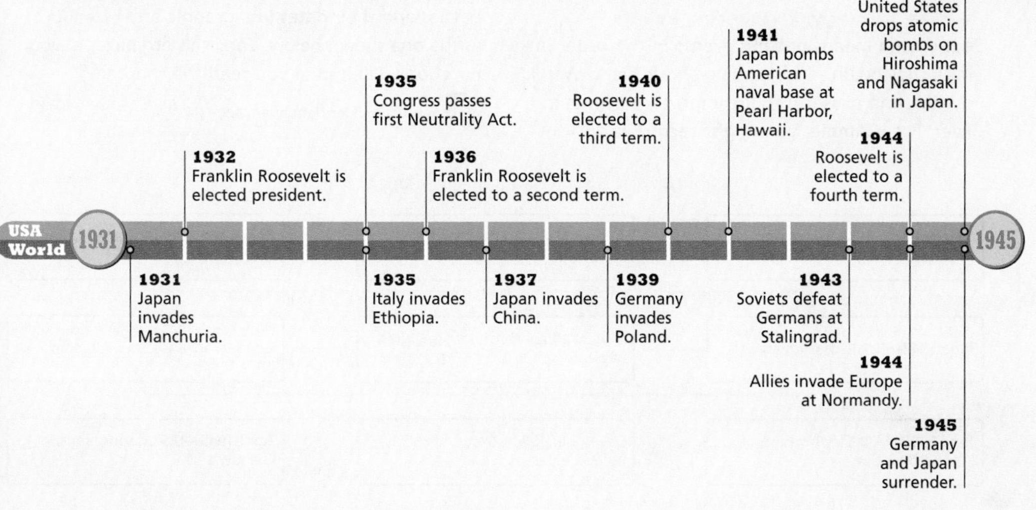
USA
World
1931
1945
1932 Franklin Roosevelt is elected president.
1935 Congress passes first Neutrality Act.
1936 Franklin Roosevelt is elected to a second term.
1940 Roosevelt is elected to a third term.
1941 Japan bombs American naval base at Pearl Harbor, Hawaii.
1944 Roosevelt is elected to a fourth term.
1945 United States drops atomic bombs on Hiroshima and Nagasaki in Japan.
1931 Japan invades Manchuria.
1935 Italy invades Ethiopia.
1937 Japan invades China.
1939 Germany invades Poland.
1943 Soviets defeat Germans at Stalingrad.
1944 Allies invade Europe at Normandy.
1945 Germany and Japan surrender.

## Interact *with* History

### OBJECTIVES

- To help students understand the struggle against the rule of dictators in World War II
- To help students connect with the people and events they will study in this chapter

### What Do You Think?

1. Ask students to think about how freedoms such as speech, press, and assembly are treated in a dictatorship.
2. How should citizens of a democracy respond to the actions of a dictator?

### *Would you risk your life to fight against dictators?*

Have students identify what dangers would be involved in fighting a dictator and what might happen if no one fights against a dictator.

### MAKING PERSONAL CONNECTIONS

Ask students to recall how they have dealt with neighborhood or school bullies. Do ways of dealing with bullies, such as appeasement or fighting back, resemble the way democratic nations dealt with dictators in the 1930s and 1940s?

### TIME LINE DISCUSSION

**During the late 1930s, the shadows of war loomed over Europe and Asia. Americans hoped to stay out of the conflict, although when war began in Europe, many Americans wanted to help Great Britain battle Germany and Italy. However, when Japan bombed Pearl Harbor, the U.S. declared war and devoted all its resources to winning the war.**

- Ask students to identify events that indicate major trouble was brewing in the world. **Possible Answer** Japan invades Manchuria, Italy invades Ethiopia, Japan invades China, and Germany invades Poland.
- Ask which continents were involved in war-related events shown on the time line. **Answer** Europe, Africa, Asia
- Why would the Japanese choose to bomb Pearl Harbor? **Possible Answer** to prevent American ships from moving toward Japan
- How many terms as president did Roosevelt serve? **Answer** four
- Why do you think Roosevelt was reelected so many times? **Possible Answer** He was a good president, and wartime made people reluctant to change leaders.

## BEFORE YOU READ

### Previewing the Theme: America in the World

Ask the students to explain why the people of the United States tried to stay out of World War II. **Possible Responses** Many Americans were bitter that the tremendous loss of life during World War I had not brought lasting peace. In addition, the economic problems that the country faced during the 1930s made Americans wary of conflicts with other countries.

### What Do You Know?

Ask students what associations they have with the words *Nazi, blitzkrieg, concentration camps, Luftwaffe, D-Day, rationing.* Allow students to share comments about World War II films. Discuss student ideas about the causes of the war.

 **In-Depth Resources: Unit 8**
- Tracing Themes: America in the World, p. 41

## READ AND TAKE NOTES

**Reading Strategy: Sequencing Events**
Explain to students that to sequence events means to list them in chronological order, the order in which they occurred. Explain that the arrows on the chart indicate the order of events. Tell students that using the chart will help them remember the important events in the chapter and what may have happened as a result of each.

 **In-Depth Resources: Unit 8**
- Setting the Stage, p. 40

 **Critical Thinking Transparency CT79**
- Setting the Stage

# Chapter 27 SETTING THE STAGE

## BEFORE YOU READ

War in Europe and Africa
War in the Pacific

### Previewing the Theme

**America in the World** The United States tried to stay out of World War II. But after the attack on Pearl Harbor, the United States entered the war. Chapter 27 describes U.S. participation in the war. It also explains how the war changed the role of the United States in the world.

### What Do You Know?

What do you think of when you hear the word *dictator* and the phrase *World War II*? Where did the fighting take place in this war?

**THINK ABOUT**
- what you've heard about dictators from the news
- what you have learned about World War II from books, movies, or television

### What Do You Want to Know?

What questions do you have about World War II? Record these questions in your notebook before you read the chapter.

## READ AND TAKE NOTES

**Reading Strategy: Sequencing Events**
Sequencing means putting events in the order in which they occurred. In learning about World War II, you will find it useful to list important events in order. For example, you might record important battles and their dates in a graphic organizer such as the one shown below. Copy this organizer in your notebook. Fill it in as you read the chapter.

 See Skillbuilder Handbook, page R4.

IMPORTANT BATTLES IN EUROPE, AFRICA, AND THE PACIFIC
September 1, 1939—Germany invades Poland
August 1940—Battle of Britain intensifies
December 7, 1941—Japan bombs Pearl Harbor
June 1942—Battle of Midway
August 1942—Battle of Stalingrad begins
November 1942—Allies stop German advance at El Alamein inNorth Africa
June 6, 1944—D-Day invasion of Europe by Allies
December 1944—Battle of the Bulge begins
April 1945—U.S. Marines invade Okinawa

## TEACHING STRATEGY

### READING THE CHAPTER

This is a chronological chapter focusing on the events leading up to World War II and on America's involvement in the war—on the battlefield and at home. Encourage students to look for reasons why the United States became involved and how the war affected the lives of Americans.

### ALTERNATIVE ASSESSMENT

The Chapter Assessment describes three activities for alternative assessment on page 785. You may wish to have students work on these activities during the course of the chapter and then present them at the end.

# 1 Steps to War

**TERMS & NAMES**
fascism
Adolf Hitler
Nazi Party
Joseph Stalin
Axis
appeasement
Lend-Lease Act
Pearl Harbor

**MAIN IDEA**
The rise of dictators in Europe and Asia led to World War II.

**WHY IT MATTERS NOW**
Aggressive rulers still threaten peace today.

## ONE AMERICAN'S STORY

**One of George Messersmith's duties as a U.S. diplomat in Austria in the 1930s was to watch events in Central Europe closely. What he saw happening in Germany worried him. Although Germany had been devastated after its defeat in World War I, it was again on the rise. In March 1936, Messersmith described what he saw.**

Adolf Hitler greets a crowd of more than one million people at a Harvest Festival in 1937.

*A VOICE FROM THE PAST*

The National Socialist [Nazi] regime in Germany is based on a program of ruthless force, which program has for its aim, first, the enslavement of the German population to a National Socialist social and political program, and then to use the force of these 67 million people for the extension of German political and economic sovereignty over South-Eastern Europe—thus putting it into a position to dominate Europe completely.

**George Messersmith,** quoted in *The Making of the Second World War*

**Messersmith's predictions would soon prove true. In the coming years, Germany and its allies threw the world into war, as you will read in this section.**

## 1 The Rise of Dictators

By the mid-1930s, dictators, or absolute rulers, had seized control in several countries—Italy, Germany, Japan, and the Soviet Union. Their rise to power was due to economic and political factors that dated back to the end of World War I.

The treaties that ended the war had left many nations feeling betrayed. Japan and Italy, for example, had helped to win the war. However, both were dissatisfied by the peace treaties. Italy gained less territory than it wanted. Japan felt ignored by the European powers. Of the losing countries, Germany was treated the most severely. The winners stripped Germany of more than 10 percent of its territory and all of its overseas colonies. The winners also forced Germany to disarm. And they made Germany pay for war damages and accept responsibility for the war.





## SECTION OBJECTIVES

1. To understand the rise of dictators before World War II
2. To identify how dictators expanded their territories
3. To describe how Germany began World War II
4. To explain how the United States helped the Allies and why it entered the war

**SKILLBUILDER**
Interpreting Maps: Movement, Place, p. 760

**CRITICAL THINKING**
Finding Main Ideas, p. 758
Analyzing Points of View, p. 759
Making Inferences, pp. 760, 761
Analyzing Causes, p. 762

## FOCUS & MOTIVATE

### 5-MINUTE WARM-UP

**Drawing Conclusions** These questions focus on the war in Europe before 1941.

1. Look at the map on page 760. Where did Germany attack in 1939?
2. Which side controlled most of Europe and northern Africa by 1941?

**Warm-Up Transparency WT27**

## INSTRUCT

**INSTRUCT: OBJECTIVE 1**

**The Rise of Dictators/ Mussolini, Hitler, and Stalin**
Key Questions
- Why were dictators able to gain control in Italy, Germany, Japan, and the Soviet Union?
- What were the goals of Hitler, Mussolini, and Stalin?

**In-Depth Resources: Unit 8**
- Guided Reading, p. 42

**Reading Study Guide** (Spanish and English), pp. 259–260

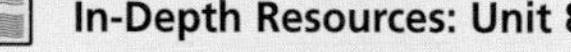

**RECOMMENDED RESOURCES**

**In-Depth Resources: Unit 8**
- Guided Reading, p. 42
- Building Vocabulary, p. 47
- Primary Source: from *Journey to Washington* by Daniel Inouye, p. 51
- Reteaching Activity, p. 56

**Reading Study Guide** (Spanish and English), pp. 259–260

**Outline Map Activities**
- The Axis Powers at Their Peak of Control in Europe, 1942, pp. 53–54

**Formal Assessment**
- Section Quiz, p. 391

**Alternative Assessment**
- Rubrics, 4.3
- Rubrics, 2.1

**Access for Students Acquiring English/ESL**
- Guided Reading, p. 179

Technology Resources

**Geography Transparency GT27**
- The Japanese Attack on Pearl Harbor, 1941

**Electronic Teacher Tools with Test Maker**

**ClassZone**
www.mcdougallittell.com

## Connections TO *SCIENCE*

**German Scientists**
As a child, Albert Einstein was slow to learn language and at nine was still not fluent in German. However, he was so brilliant that his name is used as a synonym for *genius.* Einstein formulated the theories of relativity and also worked with radiation physics and thermodynamics. He came to the United States in 1933 to work at the Institute for Advanced Studies in Princeton, New Jersey, where he stayed until his death in 1955.

### CRITICAL THINKING ACTIVITY

**Comparing** Have students examine in what ways Mussolini, Hitler, and Stalin were alike and different. Use the chart below to help students organize the information.

| | Nation | Political Movement | Action |
|---|---|---|---|
| Mussolini | | | |
| Hitler | | | |
| Stalin | | | |

**Class Time** 15 minutes

### INSTRUCT: OBJECTIVE 2

**Dictators Seek to Expand Territory/ Appeasement at Munich**
Key Questions
- How did Italy, Germany, and Japan each expand their territories in the 1930s?
- What was the Axis?
- What did Winston Churchill mean in his statement about the Munich Agreement?

## Connections TO SCIENCE

**GERMAN SCIENTISTS**
Many scientists left Germany or gave up their German citizenship after the Nazis took power. The most famous German scientist to do so was the physicist Albert Einstein (below).

Einstein, a German Jew, was visiting the United States when Hitler took control of Germany in 1933. Einstein announced he would not return home. "I shall live only in a country where civil liberty, tolerance, and equality of all citizens before the law prevail," he said. Einstein played a key role in convincing President Roosevelt to support research that would lead to the development of nuclear weapons.

Meanwhile, World War I had left the economies of Europe in ruins. Both sides emerged from the war heavily in debt. There was some economic growth in the 1920s. But the world economic situation collapsed with the Great Depression of the 1930s. Mass unemployment caused widespread unrest. Many Europeans turned to new leaders to solve these problems.

*Reading* **History**
**A. Finding Main Ideas** What factors led to the rise of dictators after World War I?
A. Possible Responses Unfavorable terms in the Treaty of Versailles upset the people of some nations. The Great Depression also made people turn to dictators who promised relief.

## Mussolini, Hitler, and Stalin

One new leader was Benito Mussolini of Italy. Shortly after World War I, Mussolini began a political movement known as **fascism** (FASH•IZ•uhm). Fascists preached an extreme form of patriotism and nationalism that was often linked to racism. They oppressed people who did not share their views. In 1922, Mussolini became prime minister of Italy. In 1925, he established a dictatorship and took the title *Il Duce* (eel DOO•chay), or "the Leader."

In Germany, **Adolf Hitler** led the fascist National Socialist German Workers' Party, or **Nazi Party.** Throughout the early 1930s, the Nazis gained power by preaching German racial superiority. They also promised to avenge the nation's defeat in World War I. In 1933, the Nazis won control of the government. Hitler then overthrew the constitution. He called himself *der Führer* (duhr FYUR•uhr), or "the Leader."

**Vocabulary**
**avenge:** to get revenge

In the Soviet Union, the Communists tightened their grip on power during the 1920s and 1930s. V.I. Lenin, who led the Communist takeover of Russia in 1917, died in 1924. His successor was **Joseph Stalin.** Under Stalin, the government tried to control every aspect of life in the nation. It crushed any form of opposition.

**Background**
In theory, Communists and fascists have opposing ideas about government and society. Despite these differences, Stalin and Hitler were both brutal dictators.

## 2 Dictators Seek to Expand Territory

While dictators were gaining power in Europe, the military was gaining increasing power in Japan. By 1931, the Japanese military pushed the island nation to grab more land and resources. That year, the Japanese attacked Manchuria, a province in northern China rich in natural resources. They conquered the region within months.

Both Italy and Germany also sought new territory. In 1935, Italy attacked Ethiopia, one of the few independent African nations. Italian troops roared in with machine guns, tanks, and airplanes. By the spring of 1936, *Il Duce* had his first conquest.

That same year, Hitler moved troops into the Rhineland, a region of Germany along the French border. Under the Treaty of Versailles, the Rhineland was to remain free of German forces. The French government was outraged by the treaty violation. However, it took no action. Nor did the League of Nations.



### ACTIVITY OPTIONS
### INDIVIDUAL NEEDS

**LESS PROFICIENT READERS**

**Sequencing Events** To help students focus their reading on the sequence of events leading up to World War II, list important dates from 1925 to 1941 on the board. Ask students to copy the list in their notebooks and then, as they read, write down a significant event or events for each date, creating a vertical time line. This process may also help students complete the sequence chart in the "Critical Thinking" section of the Chapter 27 Assessment on page 784.

| Date | Event |
|---|---|
| 1925 | Mussolini establishes a dictatorship in Italy. |
| 1933 | Nazis and Hitler control Germany. |
| 1936 | Mussolini conquers Ethiopia.<br>Hitler and Mussolini form the Rome-Berlin Axis. |
| 1938 | Hitler invades Austria. |
| 1939 | Hitler conquers Czechoslovakia. |

**HISTORY through ART**

Spanish artist Pablo Picasso expresses the horrors of war in his painting *Guernica* (GUAHR•nih•keh), shown above. Picasso created this work after German planes destroyed much of the Spanish town of Guernica in April 1937, during the Spanish Civil War. Through Picasso's painting, the town became a symbol of the destructiveness of air warfare.

**What characteristics of war does the painting bring out?**

In 1936, Hitler and Mussolini formed an alliance known as the Rome-Berlin Axis. After this treaty, Germany, Italy, and their allies became known as the **Axis**. That year, a civil war erupted in Spain. The conflict pitted Spain's fascist-style military against the country's elected government. Hitler and Mussolini supplied the fascist forces with troops, weapons, and aircraft. In April 1939, Spain's army declared victory over the government and established a dictatorship.

**Background**
Some Americans went to Spain to fight against the fascists. They were known as the Abraham Lincoln Battalion.

In 1938, Hitler invaded Austria, home to mostly German-speaking peoples. He insisted that the Austrians wanted to be part of Germany. Many residents of Austria and Germany welcomed the unification.

## Appeasement at Munich

After taking over Austria, Hitler set his sights on the Sudetenland. This was a region of Czechoslovakia where many people of German descent lived. Czechoslovakia, though, did not want to give up the region.

France and Russia pledged their support to Czechoslovakia if Germany attacked. Suddenly, Europe teetered on the brink of another war. Britain's prime minister, Neville Chamberlain, stepped in. He met with Hitler in an attempt to calm the situation. But their talks made little progress.

On September 29, 1938, Hitler and Chamberlain met in Munich, Germany. By the next day, the two sides had made a breakthrough and signed an agreement. Germany gained control of the Sudetenland. In return, Hitler promised to stop seeking any more territory.

The Munich Agreement was an example of the British and French policy known as **appeasement**. Under this policy, they met Germany's demands in order to avoid war. Chamberlain returned home from Munich and triumphantly announced that he had achieved "peace in our time."

Others, however, disagreed with appeasement. Winston Churchill reportedly wrote of the agreement: "[Britain and France] had to choose between war and shame. They chose shame. They will get war, too."

**B. Possible Response** The British and French leaders supported appeasement because they wanted to avoid war. Churchill opposed this policy because he believe war was inevitable.

***Reading*History**
**B. Analyzing Points of View** What were the different points of view about the policy of appeasement?



### HISTORY through ART

**Interpreting the Painting** Picasso uses images from Spanish folk culture in his painting *Guernica*. The figure of the bull, for example, may symbolize the forces of fascism, while the dying horse may represent the plight of the Spanish people. The town's destruction is shown through glimpses of walls, tiled roofs, and flames shooting from a burning house at the right. Heads and arms emerge from the wreckage. Critics regard this as one of the 20th century's greatest works of social protest.

**Possible Response: the terrible destructiveness of war and its effects on the innocent; violence, pain, and confusion; people screaming and dying; things being destroyed**

### MORE ABOUT . . .

**The Abraham Lincoln Brigade**
About 2,800 American volunteers fought on the Republican side in the Spanish Civil War from January 1937 until November 1938. Many were Communists, most were students, and few had any military experience. About 900 were killed in action.

### ACTIVITY OPTIONS

**INTERDISCIPLINARY LINK: HUMANITIES** — BLOCK SCHEDULING

**DEBATE**

**Class Time** One class period

**Task** Creating an art piece on the destructiveness of war

**Purpose** To create a representation of social protest art

**Supplies Needed**
- Copies of Picasso's *Guernica*
- Art supplies

**Activity** Explain to students that Picasso's *Guernica* is considered one of the 20th century's greatest pieces of social protest art. Remind them this work was created before the destructiveness of the atomic bomb was known. Have them think about the destructiveness of war and ways to portray that destructiveness in a two- or three-dimensional style. Then have them create a piece of art. You may want to have a "mini" art show to display the works.

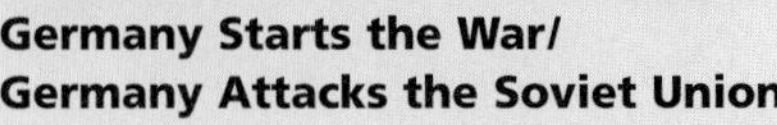

INSTRUCT: OBJECTIVE 3

**Germany Starts the War/ Germany Attacks the Soviet Union**

Key Questions

- What was the result of the nonaggression pact between Germany and the Soviet Union?
- What caused Great Britain and France to declare war on Germany?
- In what ways did Hitler's strategy in Russia backfire?

## HISTORY FROM VISUALS

**Reading the Map** Point out the areas of the map that correspond to the map legend. Have the students compare the size of the landmass controlled in 1941 by the Allies, the Axis, and the neutral nations. **Possible Response** The Axis powers controlled much more land in Europe and Africa in 1941 than the Allies or the neutral nations.

**Extension** Ask students to research the effects of the Axis advance through Europe on Great Britain.

**Outline Map Activities**

- The Axis Powers at Their Peak of Control in Europe, 1942, pp. 53–54

## CRITICAL THINKING ACTIVITY

**Interpreting Maps** Students can use the map to understand how Germany fought a war on two fronts. Ask them to list the countries that Germany took over or attacked in each of the following years:

| Year | Country Taken Over or Attacked |
|---|---|
| 1938 | |
| 1939 | |
| 1940 | |
| 1941 | |

Ask students to suggest why Germany might have followed this sequence. **Possible Response** Germany took over its weakest neighbors, then attacked progressively stronger countries—Poland, France, USSR.

**Class Time** 15 minutes

## 3 Germany Starts the War

Hitler soon broke the promise he had made in Munich. In March 1939, his troops moved in and conquered the rest of Czechoslovakia. The *Führer* then declared his intent to seize territory from Poland. Britain and France warned that an attack on Poland would mean war.

Britain and France assumed they had an ally in Stalin. After all, the Soviet Union and Germany were bitter enemies. However, in August 1939, Germany and the Soviet Union signed a nonaggression pact. In it, they agreed not to declare war on each other. On September 1, 1939, Germany invaded Poland. Great Britain and France declared war on Germany two days after the invasion of Poland. World War II had begun.

The Germans introduced a new method of warfare known as *blitzkrieg* ("lightning war"). It stressed speed and surprise in the use of tanks, troops, and planes. German forces drove deep into Poland. As Germany conquered western Poland, the Soviet Union invaded from the east. In less than a month, Poland fell to the invading armies.

In April 1940, Hitler conquered Denmark and overran Norway. A month later, Germany launched a *blitzkrieg* against Belgium, Luxembourg, and the Netherlands. British and French troops could do little to stop the advancing Germans.

*Reading* **History**

**C. Making Inferences** Why do you think Stalin signed a nonaggression pact with Hitler?

C. Possible Response Some might say he feared the Germans would defeat the Soviets.

**Skillbuilder Answers** 1. 1940 west; 1941 east 2. Portugal, Spain, Ireland, Switzerland, and Sweden

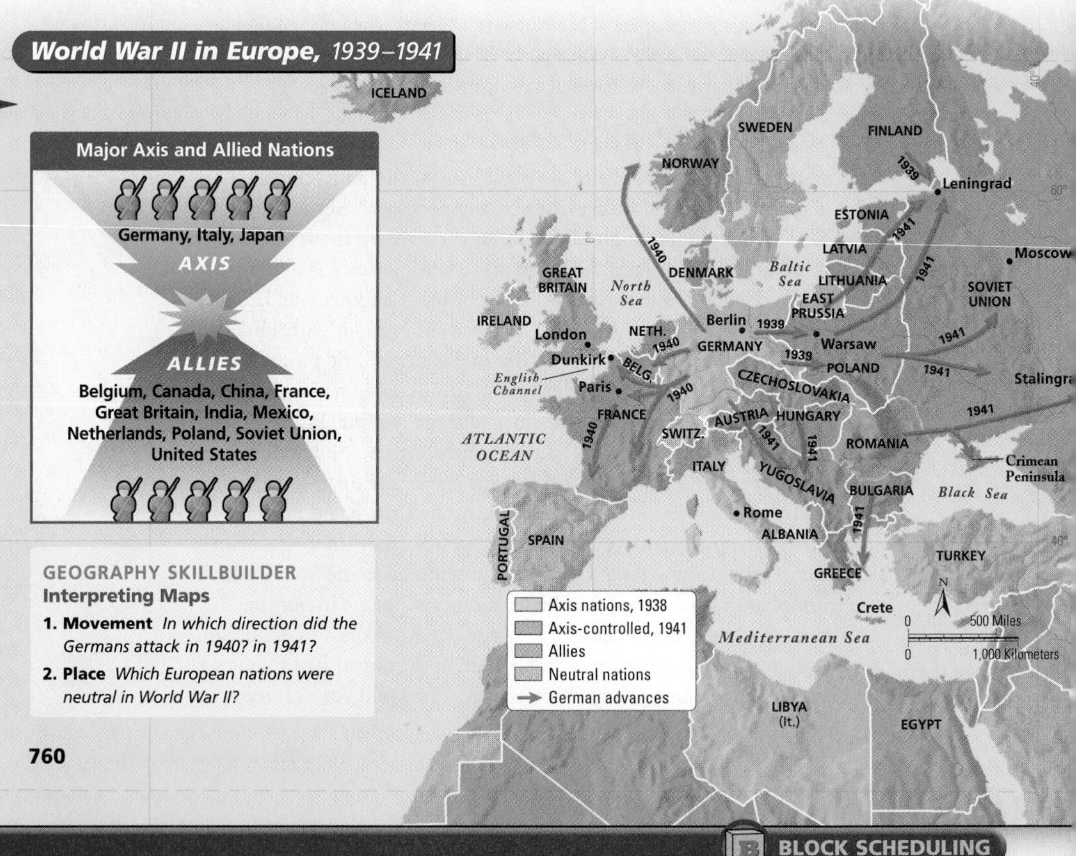


**GEOGRAPHY SKILLBUILDER**
**Interpreting Maps**

1. **Movement** *In which direction did the Germans attack in 1940? in 1941?*
2. **Place** *Which European nations were neutral in World War II?*

760

## ACTIVITY OPTIONS

**MULTIPLE LEARNING STYLES: LINGUISTIC**

**BLOCK SCHEDULING**

### LIVE REPORTING

**Class Time** 30 minutes

**Task** Reporting current events

**Purpose** To gain an understanding of key World War II events

**Supplies Needed**

- Library resources on key events and battles of World War II

**Activity** Tell students to research the evacuation at Dunkirk or the Battle of Britain. Tell students to prepare a one-minute radio news broadcast, including the "five w's" of journalism—who, what, when, where, and why. In their broadcasts, students may interview military personnel and civilians, as played by other students. Students may tape-record their broadcasts or present them live.

As each nation surrendered, British soldiers retreated to the French seaport of Dunkirk on the English Channel. Under heavy German bombardment, British vessels evacuated nearly 340,000 British, French, and Belgian troops.

In June 1940, the Germans launched a major offensive against France. In less than two weeks, they reached Paris. Days later, France surrendered. Hitler believed that Great Britain would seek peace after France fell.

Even though France had fallen, the British had no intention of quitting. Churchill, the new British prime minister, declared, "We shall defend every village, every town, and every city." Hitler soon made plans to invade Britain. To do so, however, he needed to destroy Britain's Royal Air Force, often called the RAF. In the summer of 1940, the German air force, or Luftwaffe (LUFT•VAHF•eh), and the RAF fought in the skies over Britain.

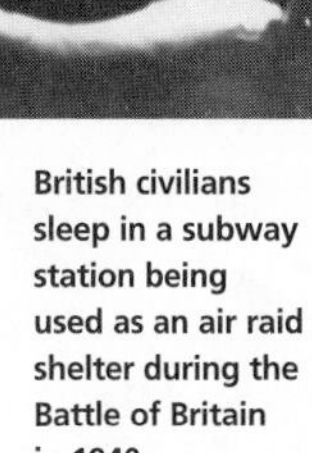

British civilians sleep in a subway station being used as an air raid shelter during the Battle of Britain in 1940.

German planes also unleashed massive bombing attacks on London and other civilian targets. By September, however, the Battle of Britain had left Hitler frustrated. The RAF was holding off the Luftwaffe. And despite constant bombing, the British people did not surrender.

**D. Possible Responses** Some students might say that Hitler wanted to surprise them. Others might say that he waited to attack until after he had defeated France. He didn't want to fight both at the same time.

## Germany Attacks the Soviet Union

While Hitler's forces conquered Western Europe, Stalin's troops invaded Finland in November 1939. The Soviets then seized the countries of Estonia, Latvia, and Lithuania along the Baltic Sea. Despite their partnership, Hitler and Stalin distrusted each other. Hitler feared Soviet ambitions in Europe. He also wanted Soviet wheat and oil fields.

*Reading*History

**D. Making Inferences** Why did Hitler attack the Soviet Union just months after signing the nonaggression pact?

As a result, Hitler invaded the Soviet Union in June 1941. German forces moved easily through the giant country. They inflicted heavy casualties on Soviet troops. Then Hitler made a major mistake. He decided not to concentrate all his forces against Moscow. Instead, he reinforced his armies heading north toward Leningrad and south toward the Crimean Peninsula. The Germans tried to capture Leningrad from September 1941 to January 1944. About one million citizens died, many from starvation. But the city never fell to the Germans.

As German troops approached Moscow in December 1941, they ran into the harshest Russian winter in decades. Many German soldiers suffered frostbite. German tanks and weapons broke down in the cold. The Nazi advance had ground to a halt, and Soviet forces drove the Germans back.





### MORE ABOUT . . .

**Winston Churchill**

Winston Churchill was the prime minister of Great Britain from 1940 to 1945 and 1951 to 1955. During the Battle of Britain, Churchill was the heart and soul of the British people, visiting scenes of devastation after air bombings and broadcasting radio reports to the nation. In 1940, he commended the Royal Air Force, saying "Never in the field of human conflict was so much owed by so many to so few."

When the German invasion of Britain appeared imminent, Churchill expressed Britain's determination to stand fast: "We shall go on to the end. We shall defend our island, whatever the cost may be. We shall fight on the beaches, we shall fight on the landing grounds, we shall fight in the fields and in the streets, we shall fight in the hills. We shall never surrender."

### MORE ABOUT . . .

**The Siege of Leningrad**

German armies surrounded Leningrad in autumn 1941, just as the brutal Russian winter closed in. Hitler said the city would soon "fall like a leaf." But the Leningraders refused to surrender. During the winter of 1941–42, people in the city lived on a few ounces of bread a day. They ate cats, dogs, rats, and sparrows. People collapsed of hunger and died in the city streets, their bodies lying frozen under the snows until spring. For 890 days, German armies besieged the city. Then Soviet troops drove them back. The siege ended in January 1944.

### ACTIVITY OPTIONS

**INTERDISCIPLINARY LINK: SPEECH** — BLOCK SCHEDULING

**SPEECHES**

**Class Time** One class period

**Task** Evaluating public speeches

**Purpose** To evaluate the effectiveness of World War II speeches

**Supplies Needed**
- CDs or cassettes of speeches by FDR, Churchill, or famous broadcasters, such as Edward R. Murrow
- Three or more CD or tape players

**Activity** Locate cassettes or CDs of World War II speeches or broadcasts. Divide students into three groups. Set up a different recording for each group. Appoint a group recorder. Ask students to collectively summarize each speech and evaluate the speaker's delivery and the speech's effectiveness. Ask groups to share their findings in a class discussion, including quoting a particularly memorable phrase from the speech.

**INSTRUCT: OBJECTIVE** 

**The United States Aids the Allies/ Japan Attacks Pearl Harbor**

Key Questions
- How did the United States help the Allies?
- What were the immediate effects of the attack on Pearl Harbor?

 **In-Depth Resources: Unit 8**
- Primary Source, p. 51

 **Geography Transparency GT27**
- The Japanese Attack on Pearl Harbor, 1941

### *America's* HERITAGE

**U.S.S. *Arizona* Memorial**

The *Arizona* was launched in June 1915. The ship served with the Atlantic Fleet during World War I and sailed as part of the honor fleet accompanying President Wilson to France for the Paris Peace Conference in 1918. The *Arizona* was in dry dock at Pearl Harbor for repairs when the Japanese attacked on December 7, 1941. The night before the attack, *Arizona's* band had come in second in a contest. The band members, still asleep when the attack came, all perished. The *Arizona* became a symbol for Americans at war, especially for those in the navy.

## ASSESS & RETEACH

**Setting the Stage** Have students fill in the first row on the chapter graphic organizer.

 **Formal Assessment**
- Section Quiz, p. 391

 **Critical Thinking Transparency CT79**
- Setting the Stage

**RETEACHING ACTIVITY**

Have students create an annotated time line of 12 events leading to the U.S. entry into World War II in December 1941.

 **In-Depth Resources: Unit 8**
- Reteaching Activity, p. 56

## 4 The United States Aids the Allies

While the Nazis advanced, President Roosevelt tried to help the Allies by supplying them with arms and other materials. "We must be the great arsenal of democracy," he declared. He proposed the **Lend-Lease Act** to address this issue. This measure allowed the United States to lend or lease raw materials, equipment, and weapons to the Allied nations. Congress approved the act in 1941. Under Lend-Lease, the United States sent about $50 billion worth of war goods to the Allies.

### *America's* HERITAGE

**U.S.S. *ARIZONA* MEMORIAL**

The U.S.S. *Arizona* suffered extensive damage during the attack on Pearl Harbor. The ship sank, and 1,177 of its crew died. The nation chose not to raise the ship. Instead, officials created a memorial (shown below) that sits above the sunken hull.

The names of all the crewmen who perished aboard the ship are carved on the memorial. To commemorate the 50th anniversary of the attack, President George Bush visited the site and dropped flowers in the water above the ship.

## Japan Attacks Pearl Harbor

In 1940, Japan joined the alliance with Germany and Italy. In 1941, an even more warlike government came to power in Japan. Its leader was Hideki Tojo (HEE•deh•kee TOH•JOH), an army general. The Tojo government made plans to invade the Dutch East Indies—a source of oil—and Asian territories.

In the eyes of Japan's rulers, only one thing stood in their way—the United States Navy. On December 7, 1941, Japanese warplanes bombed the huge American naval base at **Pearl Harbor** in Hawaii. Before the day was over, about 2,400 Americans—both servicemen and civilians—died. Many of the American warplanes and ships were destroyed or damaged.

President Roosevelt asked Congress to declare war on Japan. He called December 7, 1941, "a date which will live in infamy." The nation quickly united behind him. On December 11, Germany and Italy declared war on the United States. In the next section, you will read about U.S. participation in the war in Europe.

E. Possible Response access to raw materials, such as oil

*Reading*History

**E. Analyzing Causes** What was the main source of conflict between Japan and the United States?

### Section 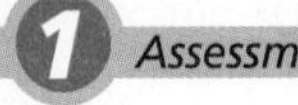 Assessment

**1. Terms & Names**

**Identify:**
- fascism
- Adolf Hitler
- Nazi Party
- Joseph Stalin
- Axis
- appeasement
- Lend-Lease Act
- Pearl Harbor

**2. Taking Notes**

Use a diagram to review events that led to American participation in World War II.

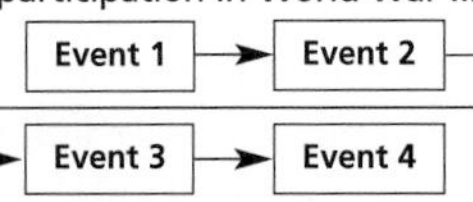


Which of these events do you think was the most important? Why?

**3. Main Ideas**

a. Who were the main Axis powers? Who were the main Allied powers?

b. Why was Hitler unable to conquer Great Britain?

c. What event prompted U.S. entry into the war?

**4. Critical Thinking**

**Analyzing Causes** Why do you think dictators such as Hitler and Mussolini were able to gain such power in the years before World War II?

**THINK ABOUT**
- the peace treaties of World War I
- the worldwide depression

**ACTIVITY OPTIONS**

**LANGUAGE ARTS**
**GEOGRAPHY**

Imagine that you are a citizen of one of the countries invaded by Germany. Write a **journal entry** describing the invasion or draw a **map** of the invasion route.



### Section  Assessment

**1. Terms & Names**

**fascism,** p. 758
**Adolf Hitler,** p. 758
**Nazi Party,** p. 758
**Joseph Stalin,** p. 758
**Axis,** p. 759
**appeasement,** p. 759
**Lend-Lease Act,** p. 762
**Pearl Harbor,** p. 762

**2. Taking Notes**

Event 1: Japan invades Manchuria (1931); Event 2: Munich Conference (1938); Event 3: Germany invades Poland (1939); Event 4: Japan attacks Pearl Harbor (1941)

German invasion of Poland because it started the war

**3. Main Ideas**

**a.** Axis: Germany, Italy, Japan; Allies: United States, Great Britain, France **b.** Germany was never able to control the skies over Britain, and the British never surrendered. **c.** the attack on Pearl Harbor

**4. Critical Thinking**

Feelings of betrayal by the World War I peace treaties and economic depression caused people to turn to strong leaders who would restore their nations' prosperity and power.

**ACTIVITY OPTIONS**

**Alternative Assessment**
- Rubrics for a journal, 4.3
- Rubrics for a map, 2.1

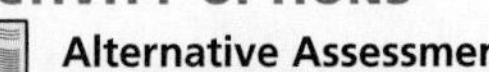

# 2 War in Africa and Europe

**TERMS & NAMES**
Dwight D. Eisenhower
D-Day
Battle of the Bulge
Yalta Conference
Holocaust

**MAIN IDEA**
The Allies defeated the Axis powers in Europe and Africa.

**WHY IT MATTERS NOW**
During World War II, the United States assumed a leading role in world affairs that continues today.

### ONE AMERICAN'S STORY

**Private First Class Richard Courtney could hardly believe it. Rumors had been circulating for weeks that his 26th Infantry Division was heading overseas to fight the Nazis in Europe. Now it was finally happening. His ship pulled out of New York harbor on a late summer morning in 1944. As the ship started down the river and headed out to sea, Courtney, a 19-year-old native of Altoona, Pennsylvania, described his feelings.**

*A VOICE FROM THE PAST*

I was eager to see all the ships in the harbor and to look up at the *Statue of Liberty,* which I had seen two years before on a trip to New York with my father. . . . For a moment I considered missing Mass and staying on deck with the others to see the statue. Then my better sense took over, and I headed down the stairs to Mass. As soon as Mass ended, I hurried up the stairs and rushed out on deck to see water, nothing but water. Well, Old Girl [Statue of Liberty], I will just have to wait for the return trip to see you again.

**Richard Courtney,** *Normandy to the Bulge*

U.S. troops stand beside their train as they wait to travel overseas for duty in World War II.

**Courtney was just one of millions of soldiers who left American shores to fight around the world. In this section, you will learn how American troops, along with those of its allies, defeated Germany and Italy and freed Europe.**

## 1 Mobilizing for War

The Japanese attack on Pearl Harbor pulled the United States into World War II. Now, there was little time to waste. The nation quickly had to build up its armed forces. Millions of Americans volunteered for duty. Millions more were drafted, or selected for military service. Under the Selective Service Act, all men between the ages of 18 and 38 had to register for military service.

Those who served represented many of the nation's ethnic and racial groups. For example, more than 300,000 Mexican Americans fought in Europe as well as Asia. Nearly one million African Americans served in





## SECTION OBJECTIVES

1. To explain how the United States mobilized for war
2. To identify major battles in Africa and Italy
3. To trace the course of the war in Europe
4. To describe the horrors of the Holocaust

**SKILLBUILDER**
Interpreting Maps: Movement, Place, p. 764

**CRITICAL THINKING**
Making Decisions, p. 764
Summarizing, p. 765
Finding Main Ideas, p. 767
Supporting Opinions, p. 768

## FOCUS & MOTIVATE

### 5-MINUTE WARM-UP

**Comparing** These questions focus on the theatres of war in Africa and Europe.

1. Look at the map on page 764. Which side appears to be winning the war? What evidence can you use to defend your answer?
2. From which directions did the Allies attack Germany in 1945?

 **Warm-Up Transparency WT27**

## INSTRUCT

### INSTRUCT: OBJECTIVE 1

**Mobilizing for War**
Key Questions
- How did the United States build up its armed forces quickly?
- How did the armed forces represent U.S. diversity?

**In-Depth Resources: Unit 8**
- Guided Reading, p. 43
- Building Vocabulary, p. 47

**Reading Study Guide** (Spanish and English), pp. 261–262

## RECOMMENDED RESOURCES

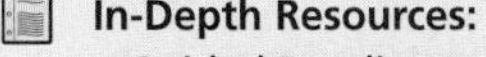

**In-Depth Resources: Unit 8**
- Guided Reading, p. 43
- Building Vocabulary, p. 47
- Geography Application: The North Africa Campaign, 1942–1943, pp. 49–50
- Reteaching Activity, p. 57

**Reading Study Guide** (Spanish and English), pp. 261–262

**America's History Makers**
- Dwight D. Eisenhower, pp. 107–108

**American History Plays**
- *Rescued from the Holocaust* by Sean Price

**Formal Assessment**
- Section Quiz, p. 392

**Alternative Assessment**
- Rubrics, 2.1, 2.6

**Access for Students Acquiring English/ESL**
- Guided Reading, p. 180
- Geography Application, pp. 185–186

**Technology Resources**

**Electronic Teacher Tools with Test Maker**

**ClassZone**
www.mcdougallittell.com

## MORE ABOUT . . .

**African-American Soldiers**
The 92nd Infantry Division was the one black division involved in infantry combat in Europe during World War II. The unit began fighting in Italy in 1944, only after the government reversed its official policy to restrict African-American soldiers to noncombatant assignments. The division fought heroically, receiving more than 12,000 decorations and citations for bravery.

## INSTRUCT: OBJECTIVE 

**Battles in Africa and Italy**
Key Questions
- Why was gaining control of Egypt important for the Axis powers?
- What led to the surrender of Italy's government?

 **In-Depth Resources: Unit 8**
- Geography Application: The North Africa Campaign, 1942–1943, pp. 49–50

## HISTORY FROM VISUALS

**Reading the Map** Point out the different bodies of water on the map. Have the students discuss the importance of the Mediterranean Sea to the strategy of the Allies. **Possible Responses** The Mediterranean gave the Allies access to the Italian mainland through Sicily. They also used the Mediterranean to reach northern Africa and Greece.

**Extension** Have students research one of the following battles or campaigns in detail: Stalingrad, North African campaign, Anzio, the Battle of the Bulge.

the armed forces. Native Americans and Asian Americans also took part in the struggle. African-American and some Japanese-American soldiers fought in segregated, or separate, units. For example, the 99th Fighter Squadron, known as the Tuskegee Airmen, consisted of African-American pilots. They served in North Africa and Italy.

More than 300,000 women also served in the U.S. armed forces. Many worked for the Women's Army Corps (WAC) as mechanics, drivers, and clerks. Others joined the Army and Navy Nurse Corps. Thousands of women also joined the U.S. Navy and Coast Guard, where they performed important noncombat duties.

**A. Answer** Churchill convinced the Americans that it would be better to push the Nazis out of Africa and invade Europe through Italy.

## 2 Battles in Africa and Italy

The Allies began making plans to invade Europe. The Americans wanted to land in France as soon as possible. Stalin agreed. But Churchill believed the Allies were not prepared for such an invasion. He convinced the Americans that the Allies should first drive the Germans out of North Africa. This action would help the Allies gain control of the Mediterranean and open the way to invade Europe through Italy.

***Reading* History**
**A. Making Decisions** Why did the Allies decide to attack the Nazis in North Africa before invading France?

Since the summer of 1940, Britain had been battling Axis forces for control of northern Africa—especially Egypt. Without Egypt, the British would lose access to the Suez Canal. The canal was the shortest sea route to Asia and the Middle Eastern oil fields.

**Skillbuilder Answers**
1. the Soviet Union
2. Tunisia

### *World War II in Europe and Africa, 1942–1945*

The Tuskegee Airmen were an all-black unit of pilots that fought in North Africa and Italy.

Axis nations, 1938
Axis-controlled, 1941
Allies
Neutral nations
Allied advances

**GEOGRAPHY SKILLBUILDER**
**Interpreting Maps**
1. **Movement** *Which Allied power captured Berlin?*
2. **Place** *What was the last territory in North Africa held by the Axis?*

764

## ACTIVITY OPTIONS

### INTERDISCIPLINARY LINK: GEOGRAPHY

**BLOCK SCHEDULING**

**MAKING A MAP**

**Class Time** One class period

**Task** Creating a map of World War II battles in North Africa

**Purpose** To trace the course of the war in North Africa in some detail and to gain understanding of the effect of geographical features on military campaigns

**Supplies Needed**
- Atlases
- Reference materials about World War II campaigns in North Africa
- Internet access
- Outline maps of North Africa (optional)

**Activity** Have students work in groups to create a detailed map of the major military campaigns of World War II in North Africa. Each group member should be responsible for certain information on the map: geographical features, political boundaries and major cities, German advances, Allied advances, major battles. Students should combine their information on a clearly drawn map, including a title and map key.

British troops in northern Africa faced a tough opponent in Germany's General Erwin Rommel. Rommel's skills had earned him the nickname "The Desert Fox." He commanded Germany's Afrika Korps, including two powerful tank divisions. In June 1942, Rommel's tanks pushed the British lines to the Egyptian town of El Alamein. The Desert Fox was just 200 miles from the Suez Canal.

He would go no further, however. The British stopped the German advance at El Alamein and then forced them to retreat. A wave of Allied troops, led by American General **Dwight D. Eisenhower,** landed in northern Africa in November 1942. They advanced toward Rommel's army in Tunisia. In February 1943, the two sides clashed. The inexperienced Americans fell to Rommel's forces. However, the Allies regrouped and continued attacking. In May, the Axis powers in northern Africa surrendered. The Allies now could establish bases from which to attack southern Europe.

The invasion of Italy got under way with an attack on the island of Sicily in July 1943. Allied and German forces engaged in a month of bitter fighting. American nurse June Wandrey recalled trying to help the wounded.

**A VOICE FROM THE PAST**

Many wounded soldiers' faces still haunt my memory. I recall one eighteen year old who had just been brought in from the ambulance to the shock ward. I went to him immediately. He looked up at me trustingly, sighed and asked, "How am I doing, Nurse?" . . . I put my hands around his face, kissed his forehead and said, "You are doing just fine, soldier." He smiled sweetly and said, "I was just checking up." Then he died. Many of us shed tears in private.

**June Wandrey,** quoted in *We're in This War, Too*

AMERICA'S HISTORY MAKERS

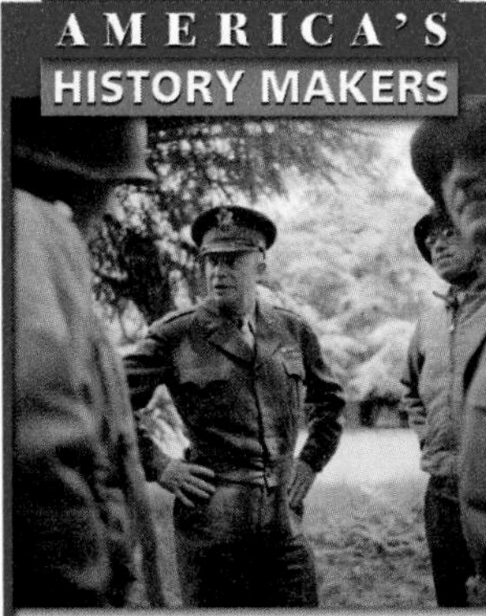

**DWIGHT D. EISENHOWER**
**1890–1969**

If ever there was a general who cared about his troops, it was General Dwight Eisenhower. As Allied forces battled in Italy, Eisenhower learned that he and another general were scheduled to stay in two large villas. He was not happy. He exploded.

> That's *not* my villa! And that's not General Spaatz' villa! None of those will belong to any general as long as I'm Boss around here. This is supposed to be a rest center—for combat men—not a playground for the Brass!

**How might Eisenhower's concern for the common soldier have affected his standing with the troops?**

## AMERICA'S HISTORY MAKERS

**Dwight D. Eisenhower**

Dwight D. Eisenhower was born in Texas and graduated from West Point in 1915. In World War II, he commanded U.S. forces in Great Britain and led the invasion of North Africa and Italy. Later he was appointed supreme commander of Allied Forces in Western Europe and planned the D-Day invasion. In 1945, he became army chief of staff. After serving briefly as president of Columbia University, "Ike" became supreme commander of NATO (North Atlantic Treaty Organization) in 1951. He was elected president in 1952 and served two terms.

**Possible Responses: Soldiers would have appreciated Eisenhower's concern for them and felt that he understood their problems. They probably felt great respect for and loyalty to him.**

**America's History Makers**
- Dwight D. Eisenhower, pp. 107–108

The Allies forced the Germans out of Sicily and then swept into Italy. By this time, the Italians had turned on Mussolini. Officials had imprisoned their leader. However, he escaped. The new Italian government surrendered to the Allies in September 1943.

**B. Answer** The harsh winter weakened the German army, and the Soviets fiercely defended Stalingrad, forcing the Germans to give up.

## 3 The Allied Advance and D-Day

Meanwhile, Germany's difficulties in the Soviet Union had grown worse. In September 1942, German forces attacked the Russian city of Stalingrad, an important industrial center. A brutal battle took place. The Soviet army fiercely defended the city. As winter approached, the German commander begged Hitler to let him retreat. The *Führer* refused.

*Reading* **History**
**B. Summarizing** What prevented the Germans from conquering the Soviet Union?

Fighting continued through the winter. The trapped Germans had no food or supplies. Many thousands of Nazi soldiers froze or starved to death. In February 1943, the remaining German troops surrendered.

**INSTRUCT: OBJECTIVE 3**

**The Allied Advance and D-Day**

Key Questions
- What problems did German forces face in the Soviet Union?
- Why was D-Day important?
- Where did the Germans launch their final assault in Europe?



**ACTIVITY OPTIONS**

**INTERDISCIPLINARY LINK: LANGUAGE ARTS** — BLOCK SCHEDULING

**DIARY ENTRIES**

**Class Time** 30 minutes

**Task** Writing diary entries

**Purpose** To understand how soldiers reacted to their experiences in battle

**Supplies Needed**
- Reference material about D-Day and the Battle of the Bulge

**Activity** Have students read accounts of the invasion at Normandy or the Battle of the Bulge. Have each student write a diary entry from the point of view of an Allied soldier after one of these battles. Entries should include factual materials such as the names of commanding officers, dates, and geographic locations.

## HISTORY FROM VISUALS

**Reading the Map** Point out the directional lines that indicate where the Allied troops landed in Normandy. Have students discuss the significance of the invasion on the war effort. Why did the Allies use a seaborne invasion instead of an aerial one? **Possible Response:** The Germans had superior air power.

**Extension** Have students create a map showing a close-up of the Normandy coast and the attack points of the Allied forces.

## MORE ABOUT . . .

**D-Day**

The Allies worked successfully to convince the Germans that the Allied attack on Europe would come at Calais. A fleet of unseaworthy landing craft was sent to British ports across the English Channel from Calais. On the day of the invasion, navy launches towed special balloons toward Calais and Boulogne. The balloons created radar patterns like those of large ships. Bombers dropped streamers of tinfoil to further confuse German radar operators. Planes even dropped dummies in parachutes at Calais and other locations.

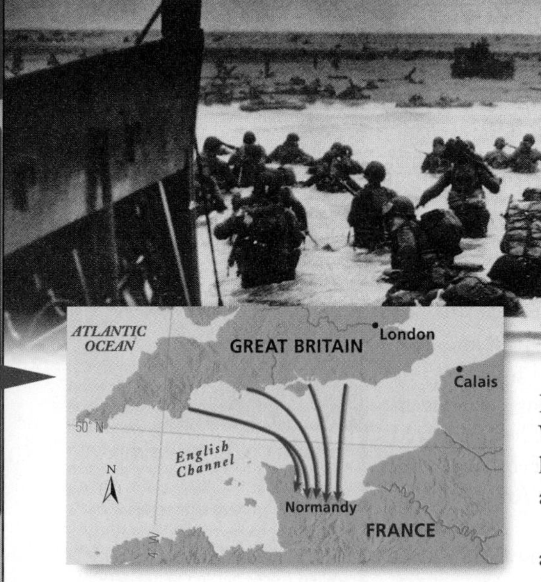


American troops storm Omaha Beach in Normandy in northern France on June 6, 1944.

Each side had suffered staggering losses. With Germany's defeat at Stalingrad, its hopes of conquering the Soviet Union appeared gone.

Hitler soon had other things to worry about in the West. In June 1944, the Allies' plan to invade France got under way. On the morning of June 6, more than 5,000 ships and landing craft carried more than 130,000 soldiers across the English Channel to a region in northern France called Normandy. The attackers included American, British, and Canadian forces. The day of this historic assault became known as **D-Day.** It was the largest seaborne invasion in history.

The attack surprised the German forces positioned along the beach. Nonetheless, they defended the region fiercely. As Allied troops hit the shore, they endured a hail of gun and mortar fire. More than 10,000 Allied soldiers were killed or wounded as they attempted to move inland. By the end of the day, however, the Allies had secured the beaches.

**Background** The Germans were surprised by the attack at Normandy because many, including Hitler, thought it would occur at Calais—150 miles away—where the English Channel is narrowest.

By the end of June 1944, 850,000 Allied troops had poured into France. They moved inland toward Paris, battling German troops along the way. On August 25, Allied forces liberated, or freed, the French capital. As they continued fighting to recapture the rest of France from the Germans, numerous American heroes emerged. One of them was Audie Murphy, the most decorated U.S. soldier of World War II. In January 1945, German troops attacked Murphy's unit in France. The 20-year-old Murphy climbed on a burning tank destroyer and used its machine gun to kill about 50 enemy troops. The U.S. government awarded him the Medal of Honor, the nation's highest military award.

As Allied forces advanced through Europe from the west, Soviet troops were beating back Hitler's army in the East. In December 1944, the German leader launched one final assault. In what became known as the **Battle of the Bulge,** German troops attacked Allied forces in the Ardennes region in Belgium and Luxembourg. The Nazi troops overwhelmed the Allies and pushed them back. U.S. forces regrouped and defeated the Germans. The Battle of the Bulge was costly. German casualties totalled 120,000. Meanwhile, nearly 80,000 Americans were killed, captured, or wounded.



## ACTIVITY OPTIONS

## INDIVIDUAL NEEDS

### LESS PROFICIENT READERS

**Setting a Purpose** To help students understand the significance of the events discussed in this section, provide them with purpose-setting questions to answer as they read. You might want to provide questions such as the following related to D-Day, the Battle of the Bulge, the Yalta Conference, and the Holocaust.

- Where and when did the D-Day invasion take place? What was the result of this invasion?
- Where and when did the Battle of the Bulge take place? What was the outcome of this battle?
- Who attended the Yalta Conference? What plans did they make?
- Who were the victims of the Holocaust? Why did Hitler order the events of the Holocaust?

## ❹ Victory in Europe

By February 1945, the Germans were retreating everywhere. That month, Allied leaders met in the Soviet resort of Yalta. Attending the **Yalta Conference** were the "Big Three" as they were called—Roosevelt, Churchill, and Stalin. During the conference, these leaders made plans for the end of the war and the future of Europe.

*Reading* **History**
**C. Finding Main Ideas** What was the purpose and outcome of the Yalta Conference?
C. Answer Churchill, Stalin, and Roosevelt made plans for the Soviet Union to declare war on Japan after Germany surrendered. They agreed to form an international peacekeeping organization.

Stalin promised to declare war on Japan after Germany surrendered. The three leaders also agreed to establish a postwar international peacekeeping organization. In addition, they discussed the type of governments that would be set up in Eastern Europe after the war.

Churchill, Roosevelt, and Stalin meet during the Yalta Conference in 1945.

By the time of the Yalta Conference, President Roosevelt was in poor health. In April 1945, just months after being sworn in for a fourth term, the president died. Roosevelt's vice-president, Harry S. Truman, succeeded him. As the nation mourned Roosevelt's death, the new president continued the war effort.

In late April 1945, the Russians reached Berlin. Deep inside his air-raid bunker, Adolf Hitler sensed the end was near. On April 30, the man who had conquered much of Europe committed suicide.

On May 2, the Soviet Army captured Berlin. Five days later, German leaders officially signed an unconditional surrender at General Eisenhower's headquarters in France. The Allies declared the next day, May 8, as V-E Day, or Victory in Europe Day. The war in Europe was finally over.

## The Horrors of the Holocaust

**Vocabulary**
**concentration camp:** place where Germans held persecuted groups during World War II

As the Allies fought toward Berlin, they made a shocking discovery. Scattered throughout German-occupied Europe were concentration camps where Jews and people of other persecuted groups had been murdered. The world would soon learn of the horrifying events that took place behind German lines during the war. In what has become known as the **Holocaust,** the Nazis killed about 6 million Jewish men, women, and children—more than two-thirds of the Jews in Europe. The Nazis also killed millions of people of other ethnic groups, including Gypsies, Russians, and Poles. An estimated 11 million people were killed in all.

The roots of the Holocaust lay in Adolf Hitler's intense racism. He preached that other groups, particularly the Jews, were inferior to Germans. As he rose to power in the 1930s, Hitler blamed the Jews for many of Germany's troubles. After becoming leader of Germany, Hitler enforced anti-Semitism, prejudice against Jews, in numerous ways. He denied Jews many of their rights and possessions.





**INSTRUCT: OBJECTIVE** 

**Victory in Europe/ The Horrors of the Holocaust**

Key Questions

- What was the purpose of the Yalta Conference? Who attended it?
- When did the war in Europe end?
- What was the Holocaust? What were its results?

**CRITICAL THINKING ACTIVITY**

**Analyzing Causes** Have students analyze the causes that led to V-E Day by considering the military and political events affecting the war in Europe. Use a spider map such as the one below to help students organize the information in their responses.

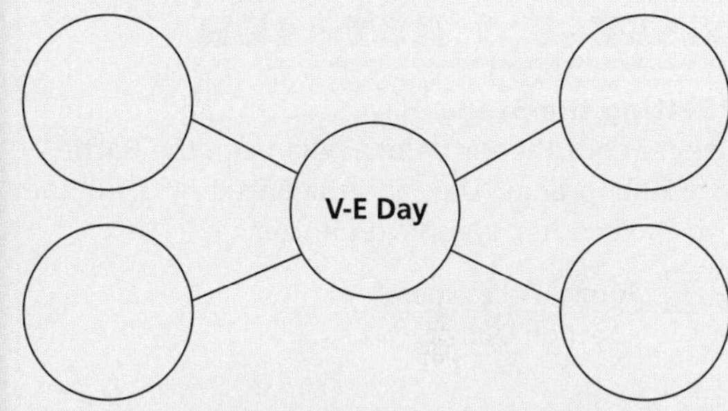


**Class Time** 15 minutes

**MORE ABOUT . . .**

**Gypsies in the Holocaust**

Although the great majority of those who were murdered in Nazi death camps were Jews, they were not the only victims of Hitler's persecution. Like Jews, the Gypsies (or Romani) were targeted on racial grounds. In 1938, Nazis began to deport Gypsies to camps. At Buchenwald in 1940, Nazis killed 250 Roma children in a terrible test of the chemical later used in the gas chambers. There is no accurate record of the number of Gypsies who died under Nazi rule, but estimates range from 500,000 to 1.5 million. The Gypsies call these years the *Porrajmos* (the Devouring).

**ACTIVITY OPTIONS**

**MULTIPLE LEARNING STYLES: INTERPERSONAL** — BLOCK SCHEDULING

**A YALTA DIALOGUE**

**Class Time** One class period

**Task** Creating a short dialogue among FDR, Churchill, and Stalin at Yalta

**Purpose** To understand the significance of the decisions made by the leaders at Yalta

**Supplies Needed**

- Reference materials about the Yalta Conference and about FDR, Churchill, and Stalin

**Activity** Have students research the personalities of the three leaders who met at Yalta and the major decisions they reached at the conference. Then have students work in groups of three to create original dialogues portraying the "Big Three" making one important decision at the meeting. Allow groups to present their dialogues to the rest of the class. Then ask the class to research the actual decisions reached at Yalta.

## MORE ABOUT . . .

### The Holocaust

One of the most famous victims of the Holocaust is Anne Frank (1929–1945). She was a Jewish girl living in Amsterdam during World War II. Anne and her family spent four years hiding in secret rooms in a warehouse to escape the Nazis. They were captured in 1944, and the entire family died in concentration camps except for Anne's father. The insightful diary that Anne kept during her years in hiding was published in English as *The Diary of a Young Girl.* The book has been translated into more than 30 languages and has been dramatized on stage and screen.

## ASSESS & RETEACH

**Setting the Stage** Have students add information about the Battle of El Alamein, the Battle of Stalingrad, D-Day, and the Battle of the Bulge to the chapter graphic organizer.

**Formal Assessment**
- Section Quiz, p. 392

### RETEACHING ACTIVITY

Divide the class into four groups. Assign one objective to each group. Have students write a 60-second news report that includes the main ideas in the assigned objective. Have one or two group members present the report to the rest of the class. Ask students from other groups to take turns asking one key question about the material in the report.

**In-Depth Resources: Unit 8**
- Reteaching Activity, p. 57

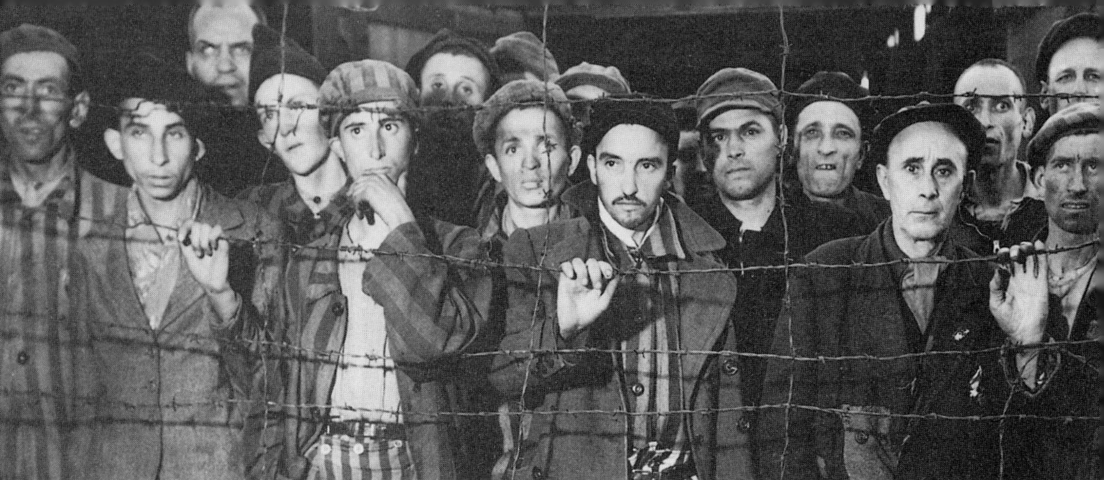

Survivors of the concentration camp at Buchenwald in central Germany stand behind a fence in April 1945.

Soon after war broke out, Germany's anti-Semitic policies took an even darker turn. In a policy decision labeled "The Final Solution," Nazi leaders set out to murder every Jew under German rule. To accomplish this evil scheme, the Germans built huge facilities known as concentration camps. Officials crammed Jews into railroad boxcars and sent them to these camps. They forced able-bodied people to work. All others were slaughtered. The Germans carried out their killings with terrible efficiency. For example, they killed hundreds of people at a time in gas chambers disguised as showers. They then burned the bodies in large ovens or open pits. The largest concentration camp was Auschwitz in Poland. More than 1 million people are thought to have been murdered there.

On reaching the camps, the advancing Allies were outraged by what they saw. The Allies would battle this type of hate and bias by bringing German leaders to trial for what they had done. First, however, they had to defeat the Japanese. In the next section, you will read about the war in the Pacific.

## Section  Assessment

### 1. Terms & Names

**Identify:**
- Dwight D. Eisenhower
- D-Day
- Battle of the Bulge
- Yalta Conference
- Holocaust

### 2. Taking Notes

Use a cluster diagram like the one shown below to identify the key battles and events that led to the Allies' victory in Europe.

### 3. Main Ideas

**a.** How did the United States build an army for the war?

**b.** Why did the Allies try to conquer North Africa before attacking southern Europe?

**c.** Why was the Battle of Stalingrad considered the turning point of the war in the east?

### 4. Critical Thinking

**Supporting Opinions** How might the war have been different if Hitler had decided to fight alongside the Soviet Union instead of against it?

**THINK ABOUT**
- the difficulties of fighting a two-front war
- the resources of Germany and the Soviet Union

**ACTIVITY OPTIONS**

**GEOGRAPHY**
**TECHNOLOGY**

Research the El Alamein battle. Draw a **map** of the battle or make a **database** showing the resources, such as the weapons and troops, of each side.



## Section 2 Assessment

### 1. Terms & Names

**Dwight D. Eisenhower,** p. 765
**D-Day,** p. 766
**Battle of the Bulge,** p. 766
**Yalta Conference,** p. 767
**Holocaust,** p. 767

### 2. Taking Notes

Battle of El Alamein: Allies begin to push Nazis out of Africa; Battle of Stalingrad: Soviets turn the tide against the Nazis; Invasion of Sicily: Allies begin drive toward Germany in central Europe; D-Day: Allies make major invasion of Europe

### 3. Main Ideas

**a.** through a government draft and volunteers **b.** They needed to establish bases along the Mediterranean from which to launch their attacks. **c.** In losing the battle, the Germans lost all hope of conquering the Soviet Union.

### 4. Critical Thinking

Germany might have won because it could have focused only on Western Europe instead of having to fight a war on two fronts.

### ACTIVITY OPTIONS

**Alternative Assessment**
- Rubrics for a map, 2.1
- Rubrics for a database, 2.6

# A Voice from the Holocaust

**Setting the Stage** Elie Wiesel (EHL•ee vee•ZEHL) was a Jewish boy from Romania. In 1944, when Wiesel was just 15, the Nazis sent the Jews of his town to Auschwitz in Poland. Wiesel's mother and one of his sisters died there. Wiesel and his father were sent to the Buchenwald concentration camp, where Wiesel's father died just a few months before the camp was liberated. In this excerpt from *Night,* Wiesel describes the terror he experienced on his way to Auschwitz. **See Primary Source Explorer**

The train stopped at Kaschau, a little town on the **Czechoslovak frontier.**[1] We realized then that we were not going to stay in Hungary. Our eyes were opened, but too late.

The door of the car slid open. A German officer, accompanied by a Hungarian lieutenant-interpreter, came up and introduced himself.

"From this moment, you come under the authority of the German army. Those of you who still have gold, silver, or watches in your possession must give them up now. Anyone who is later found to have kept anything will be shot on the spot. Secondly, anyone who feels ill may go to the hospital car. That's all."

The Hungarian lieutenant went among us with a basket and collected the last possessions from those who no longer wished to taste the bitterness of terror. "There are eighty of you in this wagon," added the German officer. "If anyone is missing, you'll all be shot, like dogs. . . ."

They disappeared. The doors were closed. We were caught in a trap, right up to our necks. The doors were nailed up; the way back was finally cut off. The world was a cattle wagon **hermetically**[2] sealed.

*—Elie Wiesel*

1. **Czechoslovak frontier:** the border of Czechoslovakia, a former European country occupied by Germany during World War II.
2. **hermetically:** thoroughly.

***A CLOSER LOOK***

**A REIGN OF TERROR**

**The Germans attempt to rule their captives with a combination of brutality and terror.**

1. What does the narrator mean when he describes "those who no longer wished to taste the bitterness of terror"?

***A CLOSER LOOK***

**A CLOSED WORLD**

**The Jews as well as others were transported to the death camps in railway wagons.**

2. What might be the effect of sealing people up in railway cars?

*Interactive Primary Source Assessment*

**1. Main Ideas**

a. What does the narrator mean when he says, "Our eyes were opened, but too late"?

b. What would be the effect on people of uprooting them from their homes?

c. This excerpt is from a book called *Night.* What might be the meaning of the title?

**2. Critical Thinking**

**Analyzing Causes** The horrors of the Holocaust followed from viewing and treating other people as less than human. What elements in this excerpt show the Germans treating the Jews this way?

**THINK ABOUT**

- the words and images used, both by the narrator and those he quotes
- the relations between those with power and those without



## INTERACTIVE PRIMARY SOURCE

**OBJECTIVE**

Students will understand the brutality of the Nazi regime and the horror of the Holocaust.

**Primary Source Explorer**
- *A Voice from the Holocaust*

## FOCUS & MOTIVATE

**Making Inferences** Have students read the title and Setting the Stage. Then ask students to explain why Wiesel named his book *Night* and what the subject of the excerpt might be. Write student answers on the chalkboard. Have students review their answers after they have read the excerpt.

## INSTRUCT

Key Questions
- Why are Wiesel and the other 79 passengers in the train cattle car?
- What is the meaning of the last sentence?

## MORE ABOUT . . .

**Elie Wiesel**

After Elie Wiesel left Buchenwald concentration camp in 1945, he studied philosophy at the University of Paris and became a journalist, writing for French and Israeli newspapers. Later, he moved to the United States, where he became a professor at Boston University in 1976. Wiesel, a prolific author, was awarded the Nobel Peace Prize in 1986. Wiesel has said that every human has the duty to "speak truth against power." He has also said that indifference to evil is worse than evil itself.

*Interactive Primary Source Assessment*

**1. Main Ideas**

**a.** They realized they were being taken to a concentration camp.
**b.** It would make them sad and weak, unable to fight back. It would also allow the Nazis to control their land more easily.
**c.** It might refer to the dark times faced by Wiesel and other victims of the Holocaust.

**2. Critical Thinking**

The Nazis took away the people's possessions and threatened them with death, to shoot them "like dogs."

***A CLOSER LOOK***

1. Those who have kept back any of their possessions will be shot, so it is better to give up the possessions immediately rather than risk death if they are later discovered.
2. People would be likely to feel cut off from any hope of aid or assistance from the outside world.

## SECTION OBJECTIVES

1. To explain how Japan expanded its empire before 1942
2. To identify Midway as the turning point of the war in the Pacific
3. To understand the strategy of island hopping and the purpose of invading Iwo Jima and Okinawa
4. To describe how the use of atomic weapons ended the war

**SKILLBUILDER**
Interpreting Maps: Location, p. 771

**CRITICAL THINKING**
Evaluating, p. 771
Finding Main Ideas, p. 772
Summarizing, p. 772
Forming Opinions, p. 773

## FOCUS & MOTIVATE

### 5-MINUTE WARM-UP

**Making Generalizations** These questions focus on the war in the Pacific.

1. Look at the map on page 771. Where were the major Pacific battles in relation to the Japanese mainland?
2. What do the arrows show about the Allied strategy in the Pacific?

 **Warm-Up Transparency WT27**

## INSTRUCT

### INSTRUCT: OBJECTIVE 

**Japan Expands Its Empire**
Key Questions

- What was the extent of Japanese conquests by 1942?
- Why did General MacArthur say, "I shall return"?

 **In-Depth Resources: Unit 8**
- Guided Reading, p. 44

 **Reading Study Guide** (Spanish and English), pp. 263–264

# 3 War in the Pacific

**TERMS & NAMES**
Bataan Death March
Battle of Midway
island hopping
Manhattan Project
Hiroshima

| MAIN IDEA | WHY IT MATTERS NOW |
|---|---|
| After early losses, the Allies defeated the Japanese in the Pacific. | Since the war, the United States has continued to play a major role in Asia. |

### ONE AMERICAN'S STORY

**In April 1942, more than 70,000 Filipino and American troops surrendered to the Japanese on the Bataan Peninsula in the Philippines. From there, the Japanese marched the starving, exhausted soldiers about 60 miles to a prison camp. Along the way, about 10,000 prisoners lost their lives to shootings, beatings, and starvation. Sergeant Sidney Stewart was an American soldier in the Bataan Death March.**

Thousands of American prisoners endure the Bataan Death March.

*A VOICE FROM THE PAST*

The sun beat down on my throbbing head. I thought only of bringing my feet up, putting them down, bringing them up. Along the road the jungle was a misty green haze, swimming before my sweat-filled eyes.

The hours dragged by, and a great many of the prisoners reached the end of their endurance. The drop-outs became more numerous. They fell by the hundreds in the road. . . .

There was a crack of a pistol and the shot rang out across the jungle. There was another shot, and more shots, and I knew that, straggling along behind us, was a clean-up squad of Japanese, killing their helpless victims on the white dusty road. . . . The shots continued, goading us on. I gritted my teeth. "Oh, God, I've got to keep going. I can't stop. I can't die like that."

**Sidney Stewart,** *Give Us This Day*

**Allied and Japanese forces fought for more than three years in the Pacific. As you will read in this section, the fighting was brutal before the Allies emerged victorious.**

## 1 Japan Expands Its Empire

At the same time as the attack on Pearl Harbor, Japanese forces launched attacks throughout the Pacific. By Christmas, Japan controlled Hong Kong, Thailand, and the U.S. islands of Guam and Wake.

The Japanese also pushed further into Southeast Asia, attacking Malaya and Burma. Great Britain, which ruled these lands and Hong Kong, fought back. But British forces proved to be no match for the Japanese invaders. Japan conquered the region within a few months.



## RECOMMENDED RESOURCES

**In-Depth Resources: Unit 8**
- Guided Reading, p. 44
- Building Vocabulary, p. 47
- Skillbuilder Practice, p. 48
- Reteaching Activity, p. 58
- Enrichment Activity, p. 61

**Reading Study Guide** (Spanish and English), pp. 263–264

**Formal Assessment**
- Section Quiz, p. 393

**Alternative Assessment**
- Rubrics, 4.4
- Rubrics, 1.3

**Access for Students Acquiring English/ESL**
- Guided Reading, p. 181
- Skillbuilder Practice, p. 184

**Technology Resources**

 **Humanities Transparency HT53**
- Navajo Code Talkers

 **Electronic Teacher Tools with Test Maker**

 **ClassZone**
www.mcdougallittell.com

But it took Japan longer to conquer the Philippines. They invaded the islands in December 1941 and pushed the Allied forces from the capital city of Manila onto the Bataan Peninsula. American and Filipino troops, led by U.S. General Douglas MacArthur, then fought the Japanese to a standstill for several months.

As fighting raged in the Philippines, the Allies feared that the Japanese might invade Australia. President Roosevelt ordered MacArthur to withdraw to Australia in March 1942. But MacArthur promised, on reaching Australia, "I shall return." Shortly after MacArthur left, the Japanese mounted an offensive. The U.S. troops on Bataan surrendered and endured the brutal Bataan Death March. The situation looked bleak for the Allies. But the momentum would soon turn.

> ***"I shall return."***
> **Gen. Douglas MacArthur**

## MORE ABOUT . . .

**Bataan**

After MacArthur left the Philippines for Australia, Major General Wainwright took command of the debilitated Allied forces. The Japanese quickly broke through American lines. MacArthur had ordered Wainwright not to surrender; however, his commander, Major-General Edward King, ignored MacArthur's order and surrendered on April 9 to avoid a bloodbath. Already exhausted and starving, the 76,000 Filipino and American prisoners of war were then forced to march 60 miles without food or water. Thousands died. About 2,000 Allied soldiers managed to escape to Corregidor.

## 2 The Allies Turn the Tide at Midway

In the spring of 1942, the Allies began to turn the tide against the Japanese. The push began in April, with a daring air raid on Japanese cities, including Tokyo. Lieutenant Colonel James Doolittle led 16 bombers in the attack. Doolittle's raid caused little damage. But it shocked Japan's leaders and boosted the Allies' morale.

In May, the U.S. Navy clashed with Japanese forces in the Coral Sea off Australia. For the first time in naval history, enemy ships fought a battle without seeing each other. Instead, war planes launched from aircraft carriers fought the battle. Neither side won a clear victory in the Battle of the Coral Sea. However, the Americans had successfully blocked Japan's push toward Australia.

The opposing navies clashed again in June off the island of Midway in the central Pacific. The U.S. Navy destroyed four Japanese carriers and at least 250 planes. America lost one carrier and about 150 planes. The **Battle of Midway**, in June 1942, was a turning point in the war.

A. Answer It stopped the Japanese advance in the Pacific and was the first naval battle when the enemy ships did not see each other.

***Reading* History**

**A. Evaluating** What was the significance of the Battle of the Coral Sea?

Skillbuilder Answers
1. Okinawa
2. about 4,000

## INSTRUCT: OBJECTIVE 2

**The Allies Turn the Tide at Midway**

Key Questions
- How did the Allies turn the tide of war against the Japanese?
- Why was the Battle of the Coral Sea unique?

**World War II in the Pacific, 1941–1945**

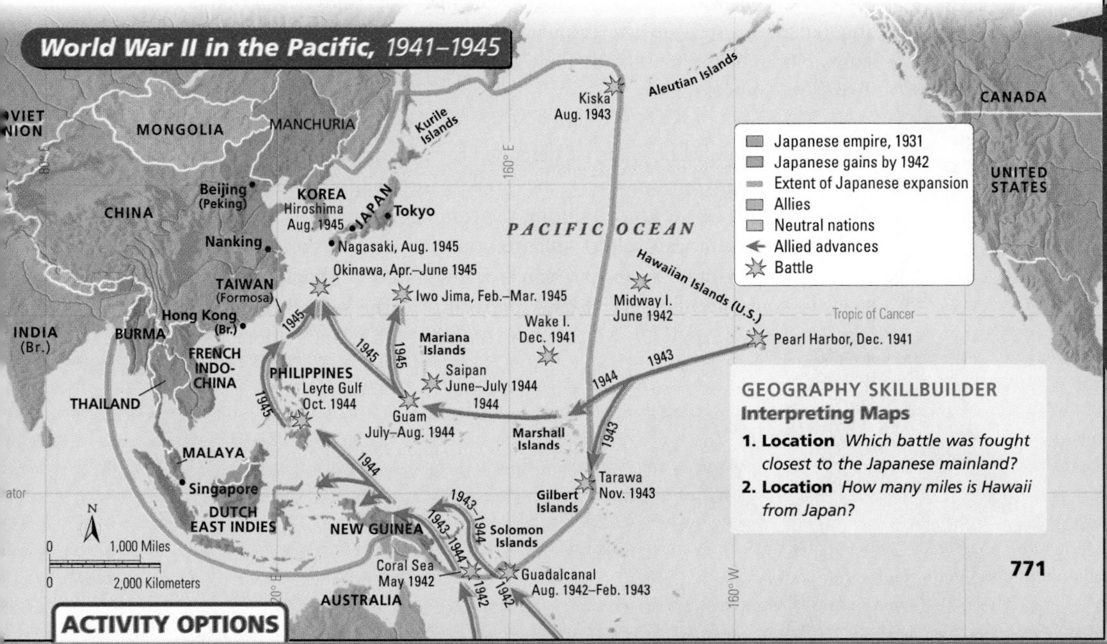

Japanese empire, 1931
Japanese gains by 1942
Extent of Japanese expansion
Allies
Neutral nations
Allied advances
Battle

Kiska Aug. 1943
Aleutian Islands
Kurile Islands
Hiroshima Aug. 1945
Tokyo
Nagasaki, Aug. 1945
Okinawa, Apr.–June 1945
Iwo Jima, Feb.–Mar. 1945
Midway I. June 1942
Wake I. Dec. 1941
Pearl Harbor, Dec. 1941
Saipan June–July 1944
Guam July–Aug. 1944
Leyte Gulf Oct. 1944
Tarawa Nov. 1943
Coral Sea May 1942
Guadalcanal Aug. 1942–Feb. 1943
PACIFIC OCEAN

**GEOGRAPHY SKILLBUILDER**
**Interpreting Maps**

1. **Location** *Which battle was fought closest to the Japanese mainland?*
2. **Location** *How many miles is Hawaii from Japan?*

771

## HISTORY FROM VISUALS

**Reading the Map** Point out the relative size of the Japanese empire in 1931 and 1942. Ask students to discuss the importance of Japan's gains in the Pacific. **Possible Response** Japan had become a strong military force in the area and controlled an empire made up, in part, of many islands.

**Extension** Ask students to use the map to identify problems faced by Japan in defending its empire against Allied attack.

## ACTIVITY OPTIONS

## INDIVIDUAL NEEDS

### STUDENTS ACQUIRING ENGLISH/ESL

**Understanding Expressions** Write the heading "The Allies Turn the Tide at Midway" on the board. Explain to students that the expression "turn the tide" refers to daily variations in the ocean. It means to change the course or direction of events. The tide of the war in the Pacific began with steady Japanese victories. Ask students to predict what will happen in the war if the Allies "turn the tide." *(The Allies will take control and eventually defeat the Japanese.)* Then have students read to find out if and how this happened. Ask them to find examples in the text to support their predictions.

**INSTRUCT: OBJECTIVE** 

**The Allies Advance/ Iwo Jima and Okinawa**

Key Questions

- How did the Allied strategy of island hopping help them gain control of the Pacific?
- What was the military significance of the Allied invasion of Iwo Jima?

**MORE ABOUT . . .**

**Code Talkers**

The Navajo language was used for codes because only about 25 non-Navajo people in the world could speak it. The Navajos made up words for war terms that did not exist in their language. For example, they used the names of birds for airplanes and used the word for eggs for bombs. They spelled out the names of people and places, using Navajo words for letters of the alphabet.

 **Humanities Transparency HT53**
- Navajo Code Talkers

**MORE ABOUT . . .**

***Kamikaze* Attacks**

The word *kamikaze* means "divine wind" in Japanese. It refers to the strong winds that drove off the Mongol fleets threatening Japan in 1274 and 1281. Organized *kamikaze* attacks began in 1944. However, wounded Japanese pilots or those with damaged planes had often deliberately crashed into American ships. Admiral William F. Halsey said that the only war weapon he feared was the Japanese suicide air attacks.

## 3 The Allies Advance

After the Battle of Midway, the Allies went on the attack to liberate the lands Japan had conquered. Rather than attempt to retake every Japanese-held island, the Allies decided to invade islands that were not heavily defended by the Japanese. The Allies could then use the captured islands to stage further attacks. This strategy was known as **island hopping.**

The two sides fought an important battle on the island of Guadalcanal. U.S. Marines marched ashore in August 1942. Six months of bitter fighting followed. In February 1943, the Allies finally won. They had gained their first major land victory against the Japanese.

Playing a role in this victory—and many others throughout the Pacific—was a group of Navajo Indians. To keep Japanese intelligence from breaking its codes, the U.S. military had begun using the Navajo language to transmit important messages. The marines recruited about 400 Navajos to serve as Code Talkers. They accompanied troops into battle and helped them communicate safely.

In October 1944, Allied forces invaded the Philippines. The effort included a massive naval battle off the Philippine island Leyte (LAY•tee). About 280 ships participated. The Allies won the three-day battle. Japan's navy was so badly damaged that it was no longer a threat. Allied forces came ashore. They liberated Manila in March 1945. General MacArthur, three years after leaving the Philippines, had returned.

Although they lost the fight in the Philippines, the Japanese increased their use of a new weapon—the *kamikaze* (KAH•mih• KAH•zee), or suicide pilot. *Kamikazes* filled their planes with explosives and crashed them into Allied warships. Japanese pilots volunteered for these suicide missions. But they couldn't stop Allied advances.

*Reading History*

**B. Finding Main Ideas** What was the Allies' strategy in the Pacific?

**B. Answer** They planned to island hop towards Japan. They attacked islands that the Japanese defended weakly, in order to move within striking distance of Japan.

U.S. Marines raise a flag atop Mount Suribachi on Iwo Jima.

## Iwo Jima and Okinawa

By early 1945, with Japan's defenses weakened, the Allies began bombing Japan. To step up the campaign, however, they had to establish bases closer to the mainland. They chose the Japanese-held islands of Iwo Jima and Okinawa.

In February 1945, U.S. marines invaded Iwo Jima. In April, they invaded Okinawa. The Japanese defended the islands fiercely. The Allies had to fight hard for every inch they took. More than 23,000 U.S. soldiers were killed or wounded during the campaign for Iwo Jima. In late February, American soldiers planted the U.S. flag at the top of the island's Mount Suribachi, signaling their victory, though fighting continued for several days afterward. In the several months it took the U.S. Marines to conquer both islands, more than 18,000 U.S. men died. Japanese deaths exceeded 120,000.

**C. Answer** The Allies met strong resistance. The Allies took the islands. More than 18,000 Americans and 120,000 Japanese died in these battles.

*Reading History*

**C. Summarizing** What happened during the battles for Iwo Jima and Okinawa?

**ACTIVITY OPTIONS**

**SKILLBUILDER MINI-LESSON: MAKING DECISIONS**

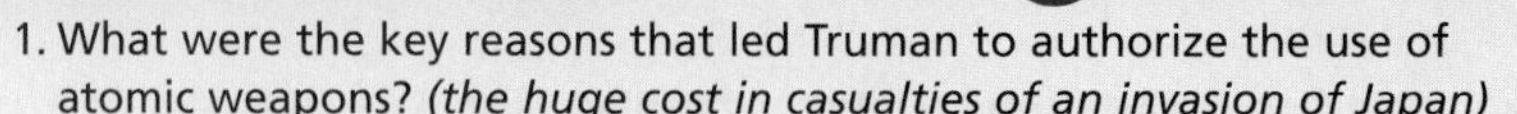

**Explaining the Skill** Making decisions requires a person to identify possible courses of action, to predict and to evaluate the likely results of each choice, and then to decide on one of the options.

**Applying the Skill** In 1945, President Truman made the difficult decision to use the atomic bomb against Japan. Discuss some of the possibilities that Truman considered, such as invading Japan or staging a demonstration of the bomb. Then ask students the following questions:

1. What were the key reasons that led Truman to authorize the use of atomic weapons? *(the huge cost in casualties of an invasion of Japan)*
2. What were the costs and benefits of the decision? *(costs: deaths of about 140,000 Japanese; illnesses and deaths from radiation poisoning; unleashing of atomic weapons; benefits: ending of war without invading Japan)*
3. Do you think Truman made the right decision? Defend your answer. *(Answers will vary, but students should cite evidence.)*

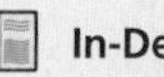 **In-Depth Resources: Unit 8**
- Skillbuilder Practice, p. 48

## 4 Atomic Weapons End the War

In the summer of 1945, Japan continued to fight. The Allies planned to invade Japan in November 1945. American military leaders feared that an invasion of mainland Japan might cost 200,000 American casualties. Therefore, American officials considered the use of an atomic bomb.

Shortly after entering the war, the United States set up the **Manhattan Project** in 1942. This was a top-secret program to build an atomic bomb. Led by American scientist J. Robert Oppenheimer, the project team worked for three years to construct the weapon.

Soon after officials successfully tested the bomb, Truman told Japan that if it did not surrender, it faced destruction. The Japanese refused to give in. On August 6, 1945, the B-29 bomber *Enola Gay* dropped an atomic bomb on the city of **Hiroshima.** The explosion killed more than 70,000 people and turned five square miles into a wasteland. Still, the Japanese refused to surrender. On August 9, the United States dropped a second atomic bomb on Nagasaki, killing another 40,000. On August 14, Japan surrendered.

**Background**
By the end of 1945, another 70,000 people had died due to injuries and radiation caused by the atomic bomb dropped on Hiroshima.

The Japanese city of Hiroshima was leveled by the atomic bomb.

On September 2, 1945, Japanese and Allied leaders met aboard the U.S. battleship *Missouri* in Tokyo Bay. There, Japanese officials signed an official letter of surrender.

The war changed forever the lives of the soldiers who fought in it. In the next section, you will learn about how the war affected Americans back home.

### Section 3 Assessment

**1. Terms & Names**

**Identify:**
- Bataan Death March
- Battle of Midway
- island hopping
- Manhattan Project
- Hiroshima

**2. Taking Notes**

Use a diagram like the one shown to list events that led to the defeat of Japan.

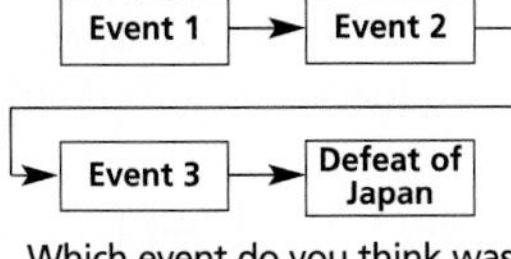


Which event do you think was most important, and why?

**3. Main Ideas**

a. Why was the Battle of Midway considered such an important victory for the Allies?

b. Why did the Allies want to conquer the islands of Iwo Jima and Okinawa?

c. What event finally prompted Japan to surrender?

**4. Critical Thinking**

**Forming Opinions** What might be the arguments for and against using the atomic bomb on Japan?

**THINK ABOUT**
- the consequences of invading Japan
- the bomb's destructive power

**ACTIVITY OPTIONS**

**LANGUAGE ARTS**
**SCIENCE**

Research the Manhattan Project. Write a **biography** of one of the scientists on the project or draw a **diagram** explaining how the atomic bomb worked.





**INSTRUCT: OBJECTIVE** 

**Atomic Weapons End the War**
Key Questions
- What was the purpose of the Manhattan Project?
- What prompted American officials to use the atomic bomb?

**In-Depth Resources: Unit 8**
- Enrichment Activity, p. 61

**MORE ABOUT . . .**

**Building the Bomb**
The atomic bomb was developed at a secret location at Los Alamos, New Mexico. Los Alamos was chosen because it was far from any city and difficult to reach. Hundreds of scientists, technicians, and army support staff lived at Los Alamos. They used a post office address in Santa Fe for their mail. Outgoing mail was censored, and journeys away from Los Alamos required special permission from security officers.

### ASSESS & RETEACH

**Setting the Stage** Have students add information about the Battle of Midway and the Battle of Okinawa to the chapter graphic organizer.

 **Formal Assessment**
- Section Quiz, p. 393

**RETEACHING ACTIVITY**
Divide the class into three groups and assign each group one of the three section objectives. Ask each group to make a sentence outline of the material in the objective, using main topics and subtopics. Display the completed outlines on a classroom bulletin board.

 **In-Depth Resources: Unit 8**
- Reteaching Activity, p. 58

### Section 3 Assessment

**1. Terms & Names**

**Bataan Death March,** p. 770
**Battle of Midway,** p. 771
**island hopping,** p. 772
**Manhattan Project,** p. 773
**Hiroshima,** p. 773

**2. Taking Notes**

Event 1: Battle of Midway (June 1942); Event 2: Invasion of the Philippines (October 1944); Event 3: Atomic bomb dropped on Hiroshima (August 1945)

Answers will vary but should include the significance of the event in the war effort.

**3. Main Ideas**

**a.** It dealt a crippling blow to the Japanese naval fleet. **b.** so they could establish air bases close to Japan **c.** the dropping of the second atomic bomb on Nagasaki

**4. Critical Thinking**

For: It would prevent the losses that would occur in an invasion of the Japanese mainland. Against: It is too powerful and would kill many civilians.

**ACTIVITY OPTIONS**

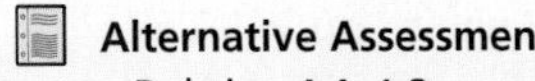 **Alternative Assessment**
- Rubrics, 4.4, 1.3

## SECTION OBJECTIVES

1. To explain the wartime economy of the United States
2. To identify opportunities for women and minorities during the war
3. To describe the internment of Japanese Americans during World War II

**CRITICAL THINKING**

Recognizing Effects, p. 775
Comparing and Contrasting, pp. 776, 777

## FOCUS & MOTIVATE

**Drawing Conclusions** These questions focus on the changing role of women in the U.S. economy during the war.

1. Look at the photograph on page 774. How did women help win the war?
2. Why did the demand for women workers increase during the war?

 **Warm-Up Transparency WT27**

## INSTRUCT

### INSTRUCT: OBJECTIVE 1

**Wartime Production**

Key Questions

- How did the war affect the nation's economy?
- Why were certain goods scarce during World War II?
- How did the government raise money to pay for the war?

**In-Depth Resources: Unit 8**
- Guided Reading, p. 45

**Reading Study Guide** (Spanish and English), pp. 265–266

**Economics in History**
- The Growing Economic Role of Government, p. 27

# 4 The Home Front

**TERMS & NAMES**
War Production Board
rationing
Rosie the Riveter
A. Philip Randolph
*bracero* program
Japanese-American internment

| MAIN IDEA | WHY IT MATTERS NOW |
|---|---|
| Americans at home made great contributions to the Allied victory. | World War II caused lasting changes in the lives of civilians. |

### ONE AMERICAN'S STORY

**Margaret "Peggy" Hooper of San Pedro, California, was 17 years old when the United States entered the war. Her father went off to fight. Eventually, Hooper took a job as an "incoming inspector" at an aircraft plant. Her duties included keeping time sheets and inspecting materials. She often described her work in her letters to a friend serving with the Pacific fleet.**

*A VOICE FROM THE PAST*

Gosh, we have been working hard at work lately. Just rushed to death and never getting through. Our production schedule has been doubled and still we work harder and put out more all the time. . . .

You had better be careful how you talk to me 'cause I have developed a big muscle in my right arm and a good strong one in my left arm, so take it easy, kid.

**Margaret Hooper,** quoted in *Since You Went Away*

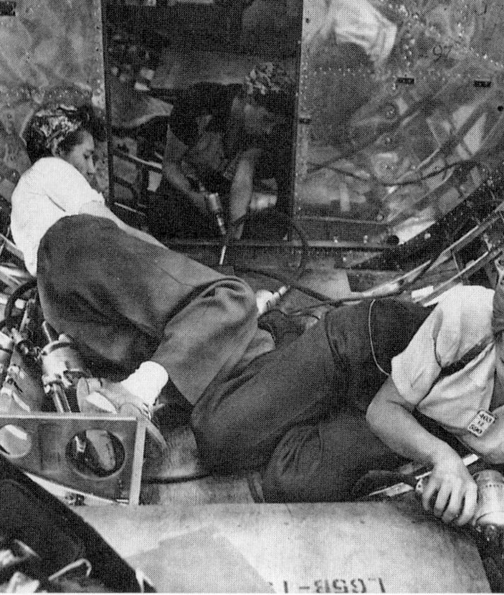

Women factory workers rivet the interior of an airplane during World War II.

**World War II created jobs for thousands of citizens such as Peggy Hooper. Americans on the home front worked together to help achieve an Allied victory, as you will read in this section.**

## 1 Wartime Production

The effort to defeat the Axis powers took more than just soldiers. American forces needed planes, tanks, weapons, parachutes, and other supplies. Under the guidance of the **War Production Board** (WPB), factories churned out materials around the clock. By 1945, the country had built about 300,000 aircraft and 75,000 ships. The United States was producing 60 percent of all Allied ammunition.

With so many factories in need of workers, jobs became easy to find. In effect, the war ended the Great Depression. Shortly after the war began, the nation's unemployment rate fell. The country's yearly gross national product (GNP) rose to new heights during the war. The GNP is the total value of all the goods and services produced by a nation



## RECOMMENDED RESOURCES

**In-Depth Resources: Unit 8**
- Guided Reading, p. 45
- Building Vocabulary, p. 47
- Primary Source, p. 52
- Literature Selection, pp. 53–55
- Reteaching Activity, p. 59

**Reading Study Guide** (Spanish and English), pp. 265–266

**Economics in History**
- The Growing Economic Role of Government, p. 27

**America's History Makers**
- Daniel K. Inouye, pp. 109–110

**Citizenship Today,** pp. 17–18

**Formal Assessment**
- Section Quiz, p. 394

**Alternative Assessment**
- Rubrics, 4.2
- Rubrics, 1.11

**Access for Students Acquiring English/ESL**
- Guided Reading, p. 182

**Technology Resources**

 **Humanities Transparency HT54**
- Americans Will Always Fight for Liberty

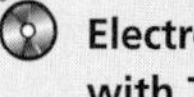 **Electronic Teacher Tools with Test Maker**

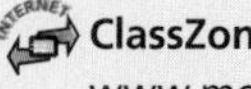 **ClassZone**
www.mcdougallittell.com

during a year. Between 1939 and 1945, the U.S. GNP soared from $90.5 billion to nearly $212 billion.

Because the armed forces needed so many materials, some of the items Americans took for granted became scarce. For example, American auto makers did not produce any cars between 1942 and 1945. Instead, they built tanks, jeeps, and airplanes. Items such as gasoline, tires, shoes, meat, and sugar were also in short supply. To divide these scarce goods among its citizens, the government established a system of **rationing.** Under this system, families received a fixed amount of a certain item.

*Reading* **History**
**A. Recognizing Effects** How did World War II affect the U.S. economy?
A. Answer It ended the Great Depression by providing jobs to millions of Americans. But it also caused shortages and rationing of many goods.

The war was expensive. To help pay the cost, the government raised income taxes and sold war bonds. These bonds were loans that the government promised to repay with interest. Movie stars urged people to buy war bonds. Americans bought billions of dollars worth of bonds.

## 2 Opportunities for Women and Minorities

With so many men fighting overseas, the demand for women workers rose sharply. In 1940, about 14 million women worked—about 25 percent of the nation's labor force. By 1945, that number had climbed to more than 19 million—roughly 30 percent of the work force. Women worked in munitions factories, shipyards, and offices.

Much of the nation welcomed the growing numbers of women into the workplace. The country promoted **"Rosie the Riveter"**—an image of a strong woman hard at work at an arms factory—as its cherished symbol for its new group of wage earners.

The war also created new job opportunities for minorities. More than 1 million African Americans worked in the defense industry during the war years. Many of these jobs were along the West Coast and in the North. As a result, more than 1 million African Americans migrated from the South during the war. Many traveled to California and such Northern cities as Detroit and Chicago. The inflow of African Americans often inflamed racial tensions. In 1943, a terrible race riot broke out in Detroit. Federal troops had to restore order after 34 people were killed.

On paper, at least, African Americans enjoyed equal rights in some workplaces. **A. Philip Randolph,** an African-American labor leader, had helped achieve these rights in 1941. Randolph had threatened to lead an African-American protest march for better jobs through Washington, D.C. President Roosevelt sought to avoid such a march. As a result, he issued Executive Order 8802. It outlawed job discrimination in defense industries working for the federal government.

**Background**
A. Philip Randolph was the leader of the Brotherhood of Sleeping Car Porters, a powerful African-American labor union.

A. Philip Randolph and Eleanor Roosevelt chat at a labor rally in 1946.

Other minorities lent their hand to the home-front effort. Some 46,000 Native Americans left their reservations to work in the nation's



### MORE ABOUT . . .

**Rationing**

To compensate for war-related shortages, Americans simply changed their habits. To save gasoline, they drove more slowly, shared rides with neighbors, or used railroads for long-distance transportation. The government banned pleasure driving and imposed a nationwide speed limit of 35 miles per hour. Factories stopped making household appliances, so some neighbors shared washing machines and irons. Fuel rationing, which began in the cold winter of 1942–1943, posed more serious problems. Each home's ration was barely enough to heat homes to 65 degrees.

### INSTRUCT: OBJECTIVE 2

**Opportunities for Women and Minorities**

Key Questions

- How did the war provide opportunities for American women and members of minority groups?
- How did wartime conditions affect U.S. race relations?

**In-Depth Resources: Unit 8**
- Primary Source: An Interview with Peggy Terry, p. 52

### MORE ABOUT . . .

**A. Philip Randolph**

Civil rights leader A. Philip Randolph (1889–1979) began his work for African Americans as a labor activist. In 1925, he organized the Brotherhood of Sleeping Car Porters, a labor union for the men who worked on the overnight railroad cars. In 1927, he started *The Messenger,* a monthly news magazine for black workers. In 1948, he helped to persuade President Harry Truman to integrate the armed forces. And in 1963, he was a director of the March on Washington for Jobs and Freedom, at which Martin Luther King, Jr., gave his "I Have a Dream" speech. In a statement on his 80th birthday, Randolph said, "Freedom is never granted; it is won."

### ACTIVITY OPTIONS

**MULTIPLE LEARNING STYLES: INTERPERSONAL** — BLOCK SCHEDULING

**PERSUASIVE POSTERS**

**Class Time** One class period

**Task** Creating a poster to persuade the public to buy war bonds, conserve gasoline, or work in war industries

**Purpose** To appreciate the importance of civilian efforts in winning the war

**Supplies Needed**
- Reference materials on war-bond drives, gasoline rationing, war work, and government efforts to build support for its programs
- Internet access

**Activity** Have students research government efforts to win civilian support for its policies. Encourage students to find examples of posters about bond drives, rationing, and women at work in war industries. Tell students to make their own posters in a similar style. On the back of each poster, students should explain the purpose of the poster and how its message would help win the war.

**Humanities Transparency HT54**
- Americans Will Always Fight for Liberty

**INSTRUCT: OBJECTIVE** 

**The Internment of Japanese Americans**

Key Questions

- How did other Americans' fear and suspicion affect Japanese Americans during World War II?
- What were internment camps?

 **America's History Makers**
- Daniel K. Inouye, pp. 109–110

 **In-Depth Resources: Unit 8**
- Literature Selection, pp. 53–55

war industries. Tens of thousands of Hispanics—people with ancestors from Spanish-speaking lands—also joined the ranks of the country's war-related laborers. Included in this group were thousands of Mexicans who migrated to the United States at the government's request. During the war years, the nation faced a serious shortage of farm workers. The government responded by hiring Mexicans to perform the much-needed labor. This policy was known as the ***bracero* program**. By mid-1945, more than 120,000 *braceros* worked on farms throughout the country.

Meanwhile, Mexican Americans struggled against prejudice and sometimes violence. In Los Angeles, for example, U.S. sailors often fought with "zoot suiters." These were young Mexican-American men who wore zoot suits—an outfit consisting of a broad-brimmed hat, a knee-length jacket, and baggy-legged pants. In what became known as the zoot-suit riots, groups of American servicemen attacked Mexican Americans. Beginning the night of June 3, 1943, the violence lasted 10 days before it was brought under control by police.

**B. Answer** Both groups enjoyed new job opportunities but continued to face racial discrimination. Both groups faced race riots with whites.

*Reading* **History**

**B. Comparing and Contrasting** What did the African-American and Hispanic-American experiences during World War II have in common?

## 3 The Internment of Japanese Americans

In the aftermath of Pearl Harbor, a growing number of Americans began to direct their anger toward people of Japanese ancestry. Many Americans saw Asian immigrants as a threat to their jobs. Many also believed that Asians could never fit into American society. As a result,

**CITIZENSHIP TODAY**

**OBJECTIVE**

Students will be able to understand the importance of writing a letter to government representatives about a civic issue that concerns them.

**History of Civil Liberties Act of 1988**

Representative Norman Minetta of California and Senator Daniel Inouye of Hawaii sponsored a bill in 1980 that established the Commission on Wartime Relocation and Internment of Civilians. The commission recommended a cash payment to internees and urged the president to offer a national apology to Japanese Americans for their treatment during the war. These recommendations were incorporated into the Civil Liberties Act. As a result, a payment of $20,000 was made to each of the surviving 60,000 internees.

**Citizenship Today**, pp. 17–18

**CITIZENSHIP TODAY**

# Writing to Government Officials

In the late 1970s, Japanese Americans asked the government to redress, or make up for, the injustice of the World War II internment. A letter-writing campaign by Japanese Americans helped secure passage of the Civil Liberties Act of 1988. This act included a formal apology and authorized payments of $20,000 each to Japanese Americans who were interned. The act also established a public-education program to prevent such discrimination in the future.

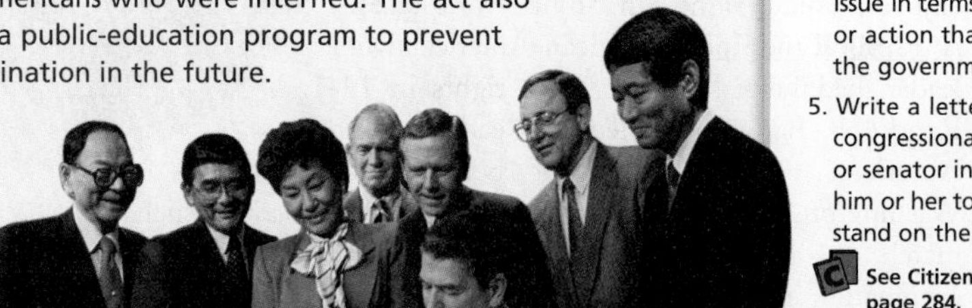

**President Ronald Reagan signs the Civil Liberties Act of 1988.**

### How Do You Write to Government Officials?

1. Think about public issues that are important to you.
2. Choose one issue about which you would like the government to adopt a certain policy or take a certain action.
3. Gather information about the issue.
4. Refine your position on the issue in terms of a specific policy or action that you would like the government to follow.
5. Write a letter to your congressional representative or senator in which you urge him or her to take a particular stand on the issue.

 **See Citizenship Handbook, page 284.**

**Visit www.mcdougallittell.com for more information on contacting elected officials.**

776

**STANDARDS FOR EVALUATION: CITIZENSHIP TODAY**

**Each letter should**

- focus on an issue of concern to students.
- clearly explain the student's position on the issue.
- support the position with facts and opinions.
- use language and tone effectively and correctly.
- urge the legislator to take a course of action.

Congress banned practically all immigrants from Asia in 1924.

In the days and weeks after Pearl Harbor, several newspapers declared Japanese Americans to be a security threat. President Roosevelt eventually responded to the growing anti-Japanese hysteria. In February 1942, he signed an order that allowed for the removal of Japanese and Japanese Americans from the Pacific Coast. This action came to be known as the **Japanese-American internment.** More than 110,000 men, women, and children were rounded up. They had to sell their homes and possessions and leave their jobs.

Soldiers stand by as Japanese Americans in San Francisco board a bus to take them to an internment camp.

These citizens were placed in internment camps, areas where they were kept under guard. In these camps, families lived in single rooms with little privacy. About two-thirds of the people interned were *Nisei* (NEE•say), Japanese Americans born in the United States.

The nation's fear of disloyalty from Japanese Americans was unfounded. Many of the camp internees raised the American flag each morning. In addition, thousands of young men in the camps volunteered to fight for the United States. The all-*Nisei* units, the 442nd Infantry and the 100th Infantry, fought in Europe. They were among the most highly decorated units in the war. One member, Daniel Inouye, showed extreme courage. After being severely wounded, he continued to lead his platoon in an attack in Italy. He lost his right arm, but earned the Distinguished Service Cross. In the next section, you will learn about other effects that World War II had on the both the United States and the world.

**Background**
Daniel Inouye later became a U.S. senator from the state of Hawaii.

## Section 4 Assessment

**1. Terms & Names**

**Identify:**
- War Production Board
- rationing
- Rosie the Riveter
- A. Philip Randolph
- *bracero* program
- Japanese-American internment

**2. Taking Notes**

Use a cluster diagram like the one shown to review the ways in which Americans at home contributed to the war effort.

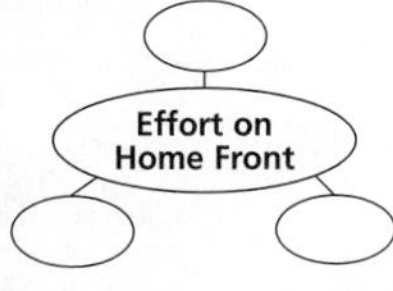


**3. Main Ideas**

a. How did the war lift the nation out of the Great Depression?

b. How did the war spur an African-American migration at home?

c. What action did the U.S. government take against many Japanese Americans during the war?

**4. Critical Thinking**

**Comparing and Contrasting** How were the war years a time of both opportunity and struggle for American women and minorities?

**THINK ABOUT**
- Rosie the Riveter
- African-American migrants
- zoot-suit riots

**ACTIVITY OPTIONS**

**LANGUAGE ARTS**
**ART**

Research the wartime life of one of the groups mentioned in this section. Write a **report** or design a **mural** about its members' experiences during the war.



### CRITICAL THINKING ACTIVITY

**Evaluating** Have students summarize arguments for and against Japanese internment. Then discuss with students why internment was unconstitutional.

**Class Time** 15 minutes

### MORE ABOUT . . .

**Wartime Policies on Japanese Americans**

Even before the United States declared war on Japan, President Roosevelt asked Chicago businessman Curtis Munson to find out if Japanese Americans were a security threat to the country. Munson's report stated that Japanese Americans would not be spies or saboteurs. Other government officials agreed with his conclusions.

However, Lt. General John DeWitt, head of the Western Defense Command, disagreed. Believing the Japanese Americans to be a security threat to the United States, DeWitt wanted to keep them out of restricted areas.

## ASSESS & RETEACH

**Setting the Stage** Have students review their completed graphic organizers and add dates and events from this section.

**Formal Assessment**
- Section Quiz, p. 394

### RETEACHING ACTIVITY

Divide the class into small groups. Assign one of the three section objectives to each group. Ask the students to create a series of headlines for newspaper articles about important historical events and trends described in each objective in the section. Display the headlines in class.

**In-Depth Resources: Unit 8**
- Reteaching Activity, p. 59

## Section 4 Assessment

**1. Terms & Names**

**War Production Board,** p. 774
**rationing,** p. 775
**Rosie the Riveter,** p. 775
**A. Philip Randolph,** p. 775
***bracero* program,** p. 776
**Japanese-American internment,** p. 777

**2. Taking Notes**

rationing; paying higher taxes; buying war bonds

**3. Main Ideas**

**a.** It prompted a surge in production, raising the country's gross national product and lowering unemployment. **b.** Large numbers of African Americans left the South to find war-related jobs. **c.** It placed them in internment camps.

**4. Critical Thinking**

The war created economic opportunities for women and minorities; however, both groups continued to struggle against racism and discrimination.

**ACTIVITY OPTIONS**

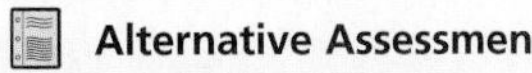
**Alternative Assessment**
- Rubrics, 4.2, 1.11

## *Interdisciplinary* CHALLENGE

**OBJECTIVE**
Students work cooperatively to meet some of the challenges faced by Americans on the home front during World War II.

 **BLOCK SCHEDULING**

## PROCEDURE

Gather supplies that students might need, such as pens, paper, colored pencils, crayons, tape recorders and blank audiocassettes, CDs or cassette recordings of songs popular during World War II. For each challenge, have students form groups of three or four. Ask group members to divide the work among themselves. Then have them choose an option for presenting their solutions.

### MUSIC CHALLENGE

**Class Time** 50 minutes

To help students create songs, suggest that they listen to popular music from the 1940s. They might consider referencing the following morale-boosting events from the war:
- ways people worked together
- military victories

**POSSIBLE SOLUTIONS**
Use the following suggestions to help students create their songs.
- Compose a cheerful melody and add words.
- Write new lyrics referring to the World War II era for a current song.
- Write the lyrics for a song and then compose music for it.

*Interdisciplinary* CHALLENGE

# Build Morale on the Home Front

You are an American helping to fight the war from the home front. You have friends and family stationed in Europe and the Pacific. You worry about them every day. To help them and the rest of your family and friends through the war, you do everything you can to keep morale high.

COOPERATIVE LEARNING On this page are three challenges you face as an American on the home front during World War II. Working with a small group, decide how to meet each challenge. Choose an option, assign a task to each group member, and do the activity. You will find useful information in the Data File. Be prepared to present your solutions to the class.

### MUSIC CHALLENGE

## *"Jukebox Saturday Night"*

**Everybody loves the Andrews Sisters and Glenn Miller's big band sound. People whistle tunes like "Jukebox Saturday Night," a favorite of jitterbugging bobbysoxers. You want to write a snappy song with catchy lyrics to brighten people's moods in these tough times. Present your song using one of these options:**
- Sing your song in an audition for the bandleader.
- Tape record your song to send to the bandleader.

### HOME ECONOMICS CHALLENGE

## *"Make it do, or do without"*

**It's up to you to help with the war effort. How will you do it? You know that factories need certain materials to manufacture supplies for the war effort. And the troops need food. What can you do to help the troops fighting overseas? Use the Data File for help. Then present your ideas using one of these options:**
- Create a list of activities that you and your friends can participate in to help the war effort, both by collecting materials and saving food.
- Write a letter to a relative serving in the armed forces explaining how the activities of you and your friends have helped him and his fellow soldiers.

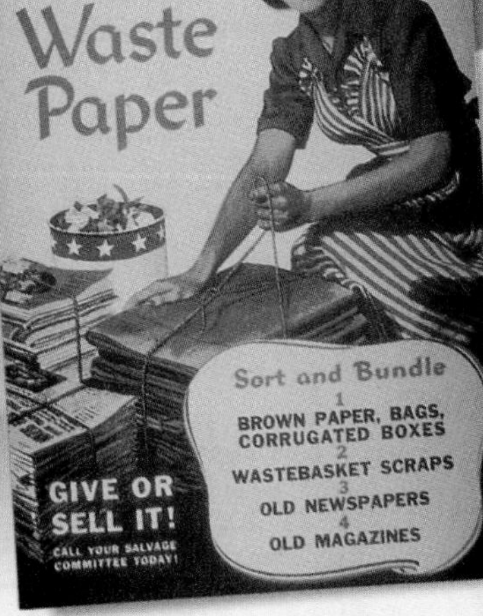
Save Waste Paper
Sort and Bundle
1 BROWN PAPER, BAGS, CORRUGATED BOXES
2 WASTEBASKET SCRAPS
3 OLD NEWSPAPERS
4 OLD MAGAZINES
GIVE OR SELL IT!
CALL YOUR SALVAGE COMMITTEE TODAY!

## STANDARDS FOR EVALUATION

### MUSIC CHALLENGE

**Option 1** Song auditions should
- include a brief introduction to the song.
- be well rehearsed.

**Option 2** Tape recordings should
- include the performers' names.
- be carefully recorded.

### HOME ECONOMICS CHALLENGE

**Option 1** Lists of activities should
- include a variety of materials and foods.
- describe activities.

**Option 2** Letters to relatives should
- clearly describe activities.
- explain the motives for the activities.

### ART CHALLENGE

**Option 1** Comic books should
- include dialogue and drawings.
- include a fully developed story with a beginning, middle, and end.

**Option 2** Cover illustrations should
- include an exciting scene from the story.
- include a title and captions that capture the reader's attention.

## ART CHALLENGE

### "POW!". . . "OW!!"

**These days, battle stories crackle over the radio and fill the daily papers, bringing worry into every waking hour. The comic book adventures of Captain America help you cope with all the frightening news. This bold superpatriot and his pal Bucky find and defeat Nazis working in American factories, radio stations, and transportation systems. A recent Captain America tale gave you the idea for a super-spy character who helps the troops fighting overseas. You decide to send your idea to Joe Simon and Jack Kirby, creators of Captain America. Present your idea using one of these options:**

- **Create a short comic book of your hero's exploits.**
- **Design a cover illustrating your comic superhero.**

## ACTIVITY WRAP-UP

**Present to the class** **As a group, review your methods of boosting wartime morale. Evaluate which of your solutions is the best.**

**Present your solutions to the class.**

## DATA FILE

### Life on the Home Front

- People collect tinfoil, old tools, scrap metal, lard, and bacon grease for making arms and ammunition.
- Rationed gas and tires force workers to rise early and take buses, trolleys, and trains to work. People stay home at night.
- People share housing to cut costs and provide child care for working mothers. Neighbors use each other's appliances.
- Bobby pins, can openers, flash-light batteries, boxed candy, lawn mowers, alarm clocks, and other everyday items are scarce.
- People save fuel by keeping houses at 65 degrees.

### Victory Gardens

- Americans plant gardens on rooftops, in backyards, and on vacant lots, producing beans, radishes, carrots, squash, corn, and tomatoes.
- Housewives preserve corn relish, stewed tomatoes, and fruit jams.

### Popular Music

**Big Bands** The Glenn Miller Orchestra is one of the most popular bands. It creates a special sound, mixing a clarinet and saxophones. The band's hits include "Don't Sit Under the Apple Tree (With Anyone Else But Me)," "When Johnny Comes Marching Home," "My Prayer," "Moonlight Serenade," and "A String of Pearls."

**Andrews Sisters** These three sisters harmonize on songs, including "I'll Be With You in Apple Blossom Time" and "Boogie Woogie Bugle Boy of Company B."

**Visit www.mcdougallittell.com to learn more about the home front.**





## HOME ECONOMICS CHALLENGE

**Class Time** 50 minutes

Suggest that students brainstorm the kinds of materials that they can collect in their homes and neighborhoods. Ask them to brainstorm ways to collect and store items, such as cooking fat.

**POSSIBLE SOLUTIONS**

Here are ways people collected needed items during World War II:

- There were official stations for collecting cooking fat, and there were drives to collect newspapers, scrap metal, aluminum, and rubber. Some people used wheelbarrows to bring items to collection centers.
- People adapted recipes to use available food. Many people ate game, such as rabbit. Others baked cakes with no sugar or eggs.

## ART CHALLENGE

**Class Time** 50 minutes

To present their ideas visually, students might use these kinds of visuals in their comic books or covers:

- symbols—images that represent concepts or issues
- caricatures—drawings that exaggerate or distort character to convey a message

**POSSIBLE SOLUTIONS**

Here are ways cartoonists work to produce comic strips:

- Brainstorm the characters and plot or the name and costume of their superhero.
- Use newspaper comic strips as models for placing dialogue boxes and narrative.

## ACTIVITY WRAP-UP

To help student groups evaluate the creativity of their challenge solutions, ask them to make a grid with criteria like the one shown. Then have them rate each solution on a scale from 1 to 5.

| | | | | | |
|---|---|---|---|---|---|
| Originality | 1 | 2 | 3 | 4 | 5 |
| Presentation | 1 | 2 | 3 | 4 | 5 |
| Audience Impact | 1 | 2 | 3 | 4 | 5 |
| Overall Effectiveness | 1 | 2 | 3 | 4 | 5 |

## SECTION OBJECTIVES

1. To evaluate the costs of the war
2. To identify ways in which the war changed American society
3. To describe the purpose and outcome of the Nuremberg Trials
4. To describe the goals of the United Nations and to identify postwar international tensions

**SKILLBUILDER**
Interpreting Charts, p. 781

**CRITICAL THINKING**
Finding Main Ideas, p. 781
Solving Problems, p. 782
Analyzing Causes, p. 783

**Why It Matters Now**
- The War's Continuing Impact, pp. 53–54

## FOCUS & MOTIVATE

### 5-MINUTE WARM-UP

**Drawing Conclusions** These questions focus on international relations after World War II.

1. Look at the cartoon on page 783. Who do the figures in the cartoon symbolize?
2. What is the cartoonist's view of the UN?

**Warm-Up Transparency WT27**

## INSTRUCT

### INSTRUCT: OBJECTIVE 1

**The War's Human Cost/ Economic Winners and Losers**
Key Questions
- What were the human costs of World War II?
- How did the war affect the world's economies?

**In-Depth Resources: Unit 8**
- Guided Reading, p. 46

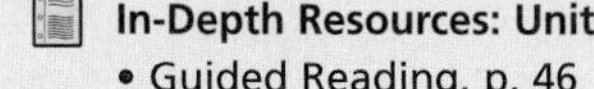

**Reading Study Guide** (Spanish and English), pp. 267–268

**Critical Thinking Transparency CT80**
- Cause and Effect: World War II

# 5 The Legacy of the War

**TERMS & NAMES**
Marshall Plan
G.I. Bill of Rights
Nuremberg trials
United Nations

| MAIN IDEA | WHY IT MATTERS NOW |
|---|---|
| World War II had deep and lasting effects on the United States and the world. | As a result of World War II, the United States became the dominant power in the world. |

## ONE AMERICAN'S STORY

**When the end of the war came, Elliot Johnson was excited. He was finally going home. At an army dismissal parade, however, one of his captains told the troops that it might not be so easy to put the war behind them.**

*A VOICE FROM THE PAST*

When it was over, we all threw our hats in the air and screamed and yelled and cheered. . . . I recall very well one of the captains standing and looking at us without cheering. "You guys are anxious to get home and put this all behind you," he said. "But you don't understand how big a part of your life this has been. "You'll put it all behind you for about ten years, and then someday you'll hear a marching band. You'll pick up the beat and it will all come back to you and you'll be right back here on the parade ground marching again." And he was right.

**Elliot Johnson,** quoted in *The Homefront*

Soldiers celebrate being discharged from the service on May 12, 1945, at Fort Dix, New Jersey.

**From the soldiers who survived it to the families who lost a loved one, World War II affected millions of Americans. The great struggle also touched the United States and the world in many other ways, as you will read in this section.**

## 1 The War's Human Cost

No war has claimed so many lives or caused so much destruction as World War II. The human cost on both sides was immense. About 20 million soldiers were killed, and millions more were wounded. The Soviet Union suffered the greatest losses, with at least 7.5 million military deaths and another 5 million people wounded. More than 400,000 American soldiers died and more than 600,000 were wounded.

Civilian casualties also numbered in the millions. Both the Allied and Axis powers had fought a war without boundaries. They bombed cities, destroyed villages, and brought destruction to civilian life. Again, the Soviet Union experienced the worst losses. All told, about 20 million



## RECOMMENDED RESOURCES

**In-Depth Resources: Unit 8**
- Guided Reading, p. 46
- Building Vocabulary, p. 47
- Reteaching Activity, p. 60

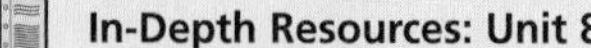

**Reading Study Guide** (Spanish and English), pp. 267–268

**Why It Matters Now**
- The War's Continuing Impact, pp. 53–54

**Formal Assessment**
- Section Quiz, p. 395

**Alternative Assessment**
- Rubrics, 4.5
- Rubrics, 3.6

**Access for Students Acquiring English/ESL**
- Guided Reading, p. 183

Technology Resources

**Critical Thinking Trans. CT80**
- Cause and Effect: World War II

**Electronic Teacher Tools with Test Maker**

**ClassZone**
www.mcdougallittell.com

Soviet citizens died in the struggle. China, which also endured years of attack from Japan in the 1930s, lost about 10 million civilians.

The war also created an enormous wave of refugees. They included orphans, prisoners of war, survivors of Nazi concentration camps, and those who fled advancing armies. After the war, 21 million refugees, most starving and homeless, tried to put their lives back together amid the ruins of Europe and Asia.

**World War II Military Casualties, *1939–1945***

| NATION | DEAD | WOUNDED |
|---|---|---|
| Soviet Union | 7,500,000 | 5,000,000 |
| Germany | 3,500,000 | 7,250,000 |
| China | 2,200,000 | 1,762,000 |
| Japan | 1,219,000 | 295,247 |
| United States | 405,399 | 671,278 |
| Great Britain | 329,208 | 348,403 |
| France | 210,671 | 390,000 |
| Italy | 77,494 | 120,000 |

Source: *World Book*

SKILLBUILDER **Interpreting Charts**

1. *Which two nations suffered the most casualties in World War II?*
2. *Which of the major combatants suffered the fewest casualties?*

Skillbuilder Answers
1. Soviet Union and Germany
2. Italy

## Economic Winners and Losers

*Reading*History
**A. Finding Main Ideas** Why did the United States emerge from World War II so strong?
A. Answer No battles were fought on American territory so the nation suffered no destruction, and the war ended the Great Depression.

The war left many of the world's economies in ruins. Bombing campaigns had destroyed factories, transportation centers, and other important buildings. Only the United States—where no major battles were fought (except for Pearl Harbor)—came out of the war with a strong economy. The boom in industry during the war had pulled the nation out of the Great Depression. After the war, the U.S. economy continued to grow.

With the world's strongest economy, the United States set out to help rebuild the shattered economies of Europe and Japan. U.S. forces occupied Japan for several years after the war. During that time, they introduced programs that put Japan on the road to recovery. In 1948, Congress approved the **Marshall Plan** to help boost the economies of Europe. The plan was named after the man who came up with it, Secretary of State George C. Marshall. Under the plan, the United States gave more than $13 billion to help the nations of Europe get back on their feet.

## 2 Changes in American Society

The nation faced important social changes in the years following the war. For one thing, the country had to deal with the return of millions of soldiers. With so many servicemen suddenly back home, the competition for jobs and education was great. The government responded by passing a law that is commonly known as the **G.I. Bill of Rights** or G.I. Bill. This measure provided educational and economic help to veterans. The government paid for returning soldiers' schooling and provided them with a living allowance. More than 7.8 million World War II veterans attended school under the G.I. Bill.

The return of so many fighting men also created a great demand for housing. The Truman administration took steps to address the country's housing shortage. However, many Americans had to live in crowded urban slums or in country shacks.





### HISTORY FROM VISUALS

**Reading the Chart** Have students read aloud the title and column headings of the chart. Ask students to calculate the total dead and wounded for the Allied nations and for the countries of the Axis. How do the totals compare? **Possible Response** The Allies had 10.6 million war dead and approximately 8,200,000 wounded. The Axis powers suffered approximately 4.8 million dead and almost 7.7 million wounded.

**Extension** Ask students to find out the total number of deaths caused by the war throughout the world.

### INSTRUCT: OBJECTIVE 2

**Changes in American Society**
Key Questions
- How did the return of service people from the war affect American life?
- How did American society change during the war?

### MORE ABOUT . . .

**The G.I. Bill of Rights**
The effects of this legislation were significant. Many African-American soldiers used the opportunity to go to college. In addition, many Americans who might not have owned businesses or received a college education were able to advance economically and professionally. The financial aid had a positive effect on the economy by accelerating the demand for goods and services in the postwar era.

### ACTIVITY OPTIONS

**INTERDISCIPLINARY LINK: CIVICS**

BLOCK SCHEDULING

**WAR MEMORIALS**

**Class Time** 45 minutes

**Task** Planning a monument commemorating some aspect of World War II

**Purpose** To appreciate the tremendous costs of the war in human life and effort

**Supplies Needed**
- Reference materials about World War II
- Reference materials on various World War II memorials
- Internet access
- Art supplies

**Activity** Have students decide on one aspect of World War II to commemorate in a memorial. Possibilities include the Holocaust, women's work in war industries, or the sacrifices of members of the armed forces. Students should decide what kind of memorial would be appropriate, such as a statue, a library, or a museum. Students should plan the memorial, including both written descriptions and sketches. Students may work alone or in groups.

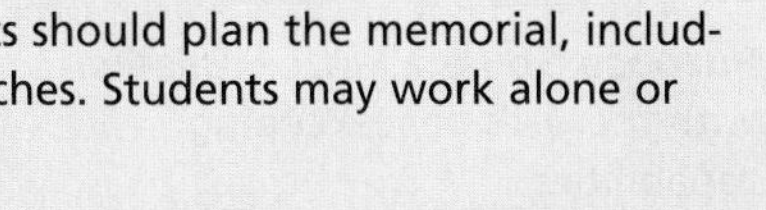

**INSTRUCT: OBJECTIVE 3**

**The Nuremberg Trials**

Key Questions

- What was the purpose of the Nuremberg trials?
- What important ideal was upheld by the Nuremberg trials?

**Now and then**

**War Crimes**

In November 1994, the United Nations Security Council set up the International Criminal Tribunal for Rwanda. The tribunal was established to prosecute people responsible for the massacres that took place in Rwanda in 1994. Like the civil wars in the former Yugoslavia, the conflict in Rwanda involved members of different ethnic groups. Between 500,000 to 1 million members of the minority Tutsi people were killed by rival Hutu people, who controlled the government. Hutus who opposed the massacres were also killed.

**INSTRUCT: OBJECTIVE 4**

**Creation of the United Nations/ International Tensions**

Key Questions

- What is the major purpose of the United Nations?
- What caused postwar tension between the United States and the Soviet Union?

The U.S. soldiers who returned home found an America that had changed. During the war, millions of Americans had moved to find war-related jobs in California and in the cities. Included in this group was a large number of African Americans. By war's end, hundreds of thousands of African Americans had moved from the South to various Northern cities and California. There, they lived in overcrowded ghettos and experienced prejudice. However, many also found economic opportunity.

**Now and then**

**WAR CRIMES**

More than 40 years after the Nuremberg trials (shown below), the world community once again brought army officials to trial for war crimes. These crimes were committed during brutal civil wars in the former Yugoslavia from 1991 to 1999. An international tribunal met in The Hague in 1996 to begin trying persons for their role in the conflicts.

These civil wars pitted Serbs, Croats, Bosnians, and Albanians against each other. Many people, especially Serbs, were accused of undertaking a policy of "ethnic cleansing"—the systematic attempt to rid a region of people from certain ethnic groups, often by killing them.

## 3 The Nuremberg Trials

As the United States dealt with important matters at home, the nation also joined the world in dealing with war crimes. The international community put together a court to try Nazi leaders for their role in World War II.

The trial opened in November 1945 in Nuremberg, Germany. The original 24 defendants included some of Hitler's top officials. The charges against them included crimes against humanity. These crimes referred to the Nazis' murder of millions of Jews and others. In his opening argument, the U.S. chief counsel at Nuremberg spelled out why a trial was necessary.

*A VOICE FROM THE PAST*

What makes this inquest significant is that these prisoners represent sinister influences that will lurk in the world long after their bodies have returned to dust. They are living symbols of racial hatreds, of terrorism and violence, and of the arrogance and cruelty of power.

**Robert H. Jackson,** *The Nürnberg Case*

After nearly a year-long trial, 19 of the defendants were found guilty. Twelve were sentenced to death. About 185 other Nazi leaders were found guilty in later trials. The **Nuremberg trials** upheld an important idea: People are responsible for their actions, even in wartime.

## 4 Creation of the United Nations

The war helped to establish another principle—nations must work together in order to secure world peace. The outbreak of World War II demonstrated the weakness of the League of Nations, the international peacekeeping body created after the First World War. The League was weak in large part because the United States had refused to join out of a strong desire to stay out of foreign affairs. Toward the end of World War II, President Roosevelt urged his fellow Americans not to turn their backs on the world again.

The country listened. In April 1945, delegates from 50 nations—including the United States—met in San Francisco to discuss creating a new international peace organization. In June, all 50 nations approved

**B. Answer** Lack of U.S. participation made the League of Nations too weak to be effective. He wanted the UN to succeed.

*Reading* **History**

**B. Solving Problems** Why did President Roosevelt support U.S. participation in the United Nations?



**ACTIVITY OPTIONS**

**INDIVIDUAL NEEDS: GIFTED AND TALENTED**

**THE UNITED NATIONS**

**Class Time** One class period

**Task** Creating a five-minute news report about a recent peacekeeping activity

**Purpose** To familiarize students with the UN's peacekeeping capabilities

**Supplies Needed**

- Reference materials about the UN
- Current information about UN peacekeeping activities
- Internet access
- Audio/video equipment

**Activity** Working in small groups, students should research recent UN peacekeeping missions. Groups should write a script for a five-minute television or radio news report about the mission. The reports should explain when and why the conflict began, identify the combatants, and tell when the UN became involved. Reports should also include information about the countries supplying troops for the mission. Students can either tape their presentation or present it to the class.

the charter creating the new peacekeeping body known as the **United Nations**, or UN.

## International Tensions

The horrors of World War II had caused many countries to work together toward lasting peace. However, tensions still arose among nations in the wake of the war. For example, in 1948 the United Nations helped found the nation of Israel to create a homeland for the Jews in Palestine. Fighting immediately broke out as neighboring Arab nations attacked Israel. In addition, colonies around the world began fighting for their independence.

*Reading* **History**
**C. Reading a Map** Look at the map on page R33 to find out where Israel is.

The United States, however, was more concerned with the rise of the Soviet Union. Despite suffering so much damage and loss of life, the Soviet Union emerged from World War II as a great power. It had conquered much of Eastern Europe.

During the war, the United States and the Soviet Union had been uneasy partners. After the war, Stalin angered the United States by breaking a wartime promise to promote democracy in the nations he had occupied in Eastern Europe. Instead, Stalin forced the countries to live under Communist regimes. The Soviet Union wanted to spread communism. The United States wanted to halt it. This led to future conflict.

**Background**
An important reason for U.S. leaders to drop the atomic bombs on Japan was to make the Soviets fear U.S. power.

Finally, the end of the war marked the beginning of the atomic age. The atomic bombs dropped on Japan showed the world a powerful new weapon. In the next chapter, you will learn how atomic weapons increased tensions between the United States and the Soviet Union.

**D.R. Fitzpatrick drew this cartoon, entitled ". . . Shall Not Have Died in Vain." He hoped the memory of U.S. losses would push Americans to support the UN and preserve peace.**

### Section 5 Assessment

**1. Terms & Names**
**Identify:**
- Marshall Plan
- G.I. Bill of Rights
- Nuremberg trials
- United Nations

**2. Taking Notes**
Use a cluster diagram like the one shown to review the effects of World War II.

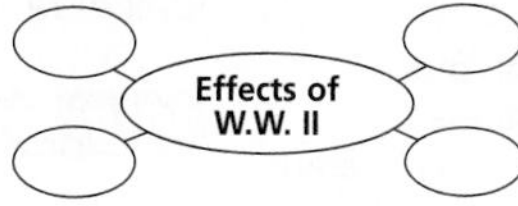


Which effect seems the most important to you?

**3. Main Ideas**
**a.** What was the Marshall Plan?
**b.** How did the G.I. Bill of Rights help World War II veterans?
**c.** What principles did the Nuremberg trials establish?

**4. Critical Thinking**
**Analyzing Causes** Why did the United States emerge from the war so much better off than other nations?

**THINK ABOUT**
- the geographic location of the United States
- the role of American industry

**ACTIVITY OPTIONS**
**LANGUAGE ARTS**
**SPEECH**
As a reporter, research and write a **news article** on a defendant at the Nuremberg trials or, as a lawyer, deliver a closing **speech** against a defendant.





### CRITICAL THINKING ACTIVITY

**Analyzing Causes** Have students examine the causes that led to growing tensions between the United States and the Soviet Union after World War II. Have students use a diagram like the one below to organize their information.

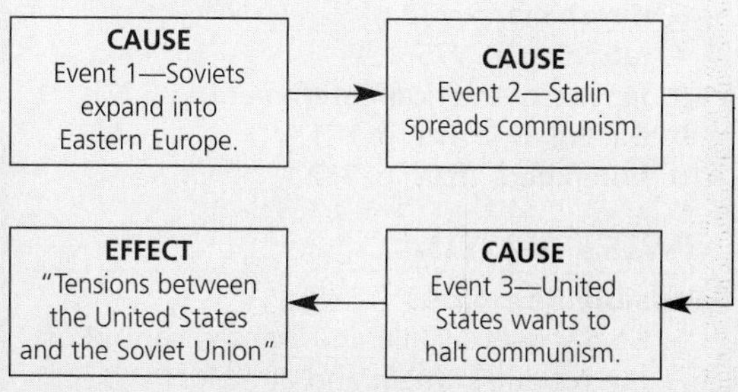


**Class Time** 15 minutes

## ASSESS & RETEACH

**Setting the Stage** Have students review the information on the chapter graphic organizer.

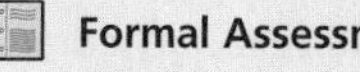

**Formal Assessment**
- Section Quiz, p. 395

**Critical Thinking Transparency CT79**
- Setting the Stage

### RETEACHING ACTIVITY

Have each student write a five-item test about this chapter section. Students should write the answers to their test on a separate sheet of paper. Have students exchange tests with a partner and complete their partner's test. Pairs should work together to correct both tests.

**In-Depth Resources: Unit 8**
- Reteaching Activity, p. 60

### Section 5 Assessment

**1. Terms & Names**
**Marshall Plan,** p. 781
**G.I. Bill of Rights,** p. 781
**Nuremberg trials,** p. 782
**United Nations,** p. 783

**2. Taking Notes**
large numbers of casualties; defeat of fascism; weakening of national economies; Nuremberg trials; formation of the UN; and use of nuclear weapons

Most will choose defeat of fascism as the most important effect.

**3. Main Ideas**
**a.** The United States donated money to the nations of Europe to help them rebuild their economies. **b.** It provided them with tuition for college and other economic assistance. **c.** that people are responsible for their actions, even in wartime; that following orders was no excuse for taking part in genocide

**4. Critical Thinking**
The war pulled the U.S. economy out of depression; also, no battles were fought on American soil, leaving the United States with almost no physical damage.

**ACTIVITY OPTIONS**

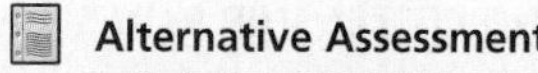

**Alternative Assessment**
- Rubrics, 4.5, 3.6

## TERMS & NAMES

1. **Adolf Hitler,** p. 758
2. **Pearl Harbor,** p. 762
3. **D-Day,** p. 766
4. **Holocaust,** 767
5. **Battle of Midway,** p. 771
6. **Hiroshima,** p. 773
7. **rationing,** p. 775
8. **Japanese-American internment,** p. 777
9. **G.I. Bill of Rights,** p. 781
10. **Nuremberg trials,** p. 782

## REVIEW QUESTIONS

**Possible Responses**

1. He distrusted Stalin and wanted control of the country's wheat and oil fields.
2. a program in which the United States lent raw materials, equipment, and weapons to the Allied nations
3. They served as nurses, mechanics, drivers, clerks, and also performed duties with the U.S. Navy and Coast Guard.
4. the name of the day the Allies launched a massive invasion of France; because it marked the beginning of the Allies' drive to regain Western Europe
5. the Allies' plan to attack only weakly defended Japanese-held islands instead of trying to liberate all of them
6. the top-secret U.S. plan to build the atomic bomb
7. producing the enormous amount of war-related materials; cutting back on everyday goods and donating household items needed in the war
8. decades-old prejudices against Japanese Americans, coupled with the belief that they were disloyal to the American war effort and posed a security risk
9. the Soviet Union
10. tensions between colonies and their ruling nations and between the United States and the Soviet Union

## VISUAL SUMMARY

### The Rise of Dictators and World War II

■ Asia and the Pacific ■ Europe and Africa

#### 1931–1941

- 1931 Japan invades Manchuria.
- 1933 Hitler comes to power in Germany.
- 1936 Germany and Italy form Axis.
- 1938 Germany takes over Austria.
- 1939 Germany invades Poland. World War II begins.
- 1940 Germany invades France. Battle of Britain fought.
- 1941 Japanese attack Pearl Harbor.

#### 1942

- Japanese stopped at Battle of Coral Sea.
- Japanese defeated at Battle of Midway.

#### 1943

- Soviets defeat Germans at Stalingrad.
- Allies stop Axis advance in North Africa.
- Allies invade Italy. Italy surrenders.

#### 1944

- Allies invade Europe at Normandy.
- Allies invade the Philippines.

#### 1945

- Allies invade Iwo Jima and Okinawa.
- Germany surrenders.
- United States drops atomic bombs on Hiroshima and Nagasaki.
- Japan surrenders.





## TERMS & NAMES

Briefly explain the importance of each of the following.

1. Adolf Hitler
2. Pearl Harbor
3. D-Day
4. Holocaust
5. Battle of Midway
6. Hiroshima
7. rationing
8. Japanese-American internment
9. G.I. Bill of Rights
10. Nuremberg trials

## REVIEW QUESTIONS

**Steps to War (pages 757–762)**

1. Why did Hitler attack the Soviet Union?
2. What was the Lend-Lease program?

**War in Africa and Europe (pages 763–769)**

3. What role did women play in the war?
4. What was D-Day and why was it significant?

**War in the Pacific (pages 770–773)**

5. What was the strategy of island hopping?
6. What was the Manhattan Project?

**The Home Front (pages 774–779)**

7. In what ways did Americans at home contribute to the war effort?
8. Why did the nation put thousands of Japanese Americans in internment camps during the war?

**The Legacy of the War (pages 780–783)**

9. Which nation lost the most soldiers and civilians in the war?
10. What international tensions arose after World War II?

## CRITICAL THINKING

**1. USING YOUR NOTES**

IMPORTANT BATTLES IN EUROPE, AFRICA, AND THE PAC

September 1, 1939—Germany invades Poland

April 1945—U.S. Mar Okinawa

Use your chart to answer these questions.

a. Which battle that you listed occurred first?

b. Which battle was the most important?

**2. ANALYZING LEADERSHIP**

Do you agree or disagree with Neville Chamberlain's policy of appeasement? Explain.

**3. APPLYING CITIZENSHIP SKILLS**

Imagine you are a Japanese American in an internment camp. If you were to write a letter of protest to the government, what violations of your rights would you describe in the letter?

**4. THEME: AMERICA IN THE WORLD**

Why do think the United States joined the United Nations after World War II, when it had refused to join the League of Nations after World War I?

**5. COMPARING AND CONTRASTING**

What role did racism play in the Holocaust and the internment of Japanese Americans? How was the level of racism different?

**Interact *with* History**

After reading the chapter, would you make the same choice about whether to risk your life to fight against dictators that you made at the beginning of the chapter? Explain.

## CRITICAL THINKING

**Possible Responses**

1. **USING YOUR NOTES** **a.** Battle of Britain **b.** the Battle of Stalingrad because it broke the advance of the Nazis
2. **ANALYZING LEADERSHIP** Answers will vary. Students who agree might reason that Europe had just finished a bloody world war, and Chamberlain did not want to subject people to more suffering. Those who disagree might reason that men such as Hitler respond only to the threat of force.
3. **APPLYING CITIZENSHIP SKILLS** Responses will vary but should include right to be free, violated citizens' rights, and other civil liberties.
4. **THEME: AMERICA IN THE WORLD** America now recognized that it had to participate in any new international peacekeeping organization.
5. **COMPARING AND CONTRASTING** The Germans saw the Jews and other groups as despicable and inferior, while the Americans viewed Japanese Americans as untrustworthy. Each nation was practicing racism. Germany, however, carried its racism to the extent of genocide.

**Interact *with* History** Answers will vary. Encourage students to consider the additional information they have now that they have read the chapter.

## HISTORY SKILLS

**1. INTERPRETING MAPS: Movement**

Study the map and answer the questions.

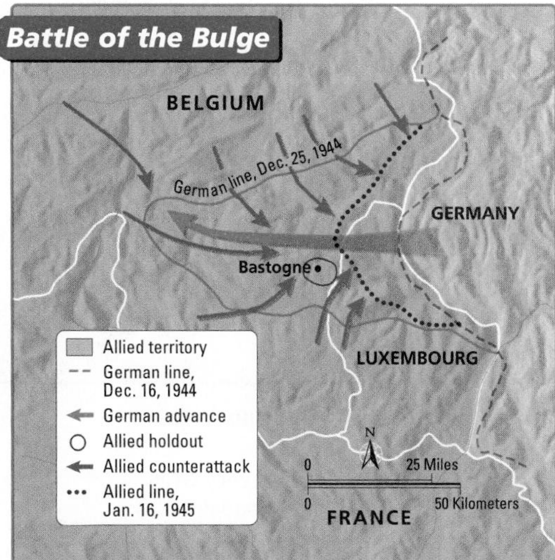


**Basic Map Elements**

a. In what countries was the Battle of the Bulge fought?

b. During what time period was the battle fought?

**Interpreting the Map**

c. About how many miles westward had the Germans advanced by Christmas 1944?

d. Why was this battle called the Battle of the Bulge?

**2. INTERPRETING PRIMARY SOURCES**

This poster shows a woman factory worker during World War II.

a. What does this poster reveal about women's roles in the war?

b. What does this image suggest about the abilities of women?

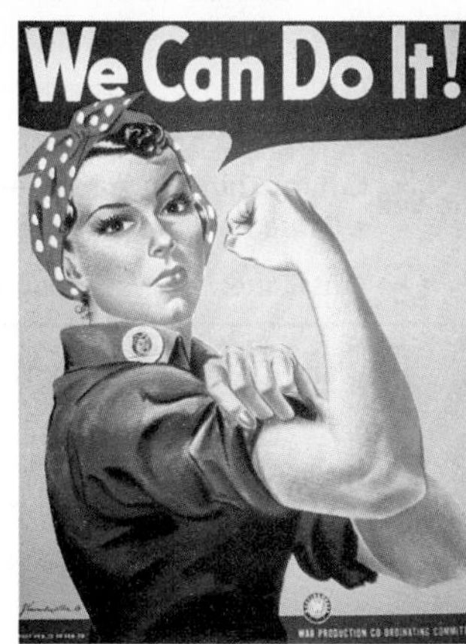


## ALTERNATIVE ASSESSMENT

**1. INTERDISCIPLINARY ACTIVITY: Language Arts**

**Writing a Diary** Imagine you are a woman who has found a job as a welder in a shipyard during the war. Write a diary entry describing the changes the war has brought to your life.

**2. COOPERATIVE LEARNING ACTIVITY**

**Creating a News Broadcast** With a group of three to five students, create a news show about the experiences of Americans at home or abroad during World War II. Choose a specific year between 1941 and 1945 and a specific location, such as a hospital, factory, or battle front.

- Take on the roles of anchor, reporter, or interviewees.
- Write a script for your role.
- Conduct your "broadcast" in front of the class.

**3. CD-ROM PRIMARY SOURCE EXPLORER**

**Making a Class Presentation** Using the Internet, library, and the CD-ROM, do further research on the Holocaust and present your findings to the class. Some suggested topic ideas are given below.

- Examine in more depth one of the Nazi camps in Europe.
- Research individual experiences of the Holocaust, such as those of Elie Wiesel, Anne Frank, or Gerda Weissman Klein.
- Build a Holocaust collage, using photographs and other visuals along with corresponding captions.
- Create a map depicting the location of all of the Nazi concentration camps in Europe.
- Examine U.S. response to the Holocaust from 1942 to 1945.

**4. HISTORY PORTFOLIO**

**Option 1** Review your section and chapter assessment activities. Select one that you think is your best work. Then use comments made by your teacher or classmates to improve your work and add it to your portfolio.

**Option 2** Review the questions that you wrote for What Do You Want to Know? on page 756. Then write a short report in which you explain the answers to your questions. Add your answers to your portfolio.



## ALTERNATIVE ASSESSMENT

**1. INTERDISCIPLINARY ACTIVITY: Language Arts**

**Diaries should**

- accurately reflect the thoughts and experiences of the subject's life.
- reflect the student's understanding of basic concepts.
- be relevant to the experiences of the subject.
- use standard grammar, spelling, sentence structure, and punctuation.

**2. COOPERATIVE LEARNING ACTIVITY**

**News broadcasts should**

- portray the experiences accurately and in a dramatic style.
- use standard interview techniques.
- clearly demonstrate an understanding of the concepts presented.
- use correct grammar in script.

**3.**  **PRIMARY SOURCE EXPLORER**

**Presentations should**

- clearly demonstrate an undertanding of the Holocaust.
- utilize several sources of information.
- have adequate delivery and establish rapport with the audience.
- show proficiency in the use of technology.

**4. HISTORY PORTFOLIO**

 **Option 1 Revised section or chapter assessment activities should**

- address teacher and peer responses to the selected work.
- solve problems present in the first versions of the work.

**Option 2 Short reports should**

- answer questions about Word War II.
- use evidence to develop and support ideas.
- cite sources of information.
- use standard grammar, spelling, sentence structure, and punctuation.

 **Critical Thinking Transparency CT81**

- Visual Summary

 **Formal Assessment**

- Chapter Test, Forms A and B, pp. 396–403

## HISTORY SKILLS

**Possible Responses**

1. INTERPRETING MAPS

**Basic Map Elements**

**a.** Belgium and Luxembourg

**b.** December 16, 1944, to January 16, 1945

**Interpreting the Map**

**c.** about 50 miles

**d.** because the German attack created a bulge in the Allied lines

2. INTERPRETING PRIMARY SOURCES

**a.** Women workers were important for the War Production Coordinating Committee.

**b.** It suggests that women are strong and can do any important job that needs to be done.

# The Cold War and the American Dream 1945–1960

| | CHAPTER OVERVIEW | COPYMASTERS | TECHNOLOGY |
|---|---|---|---|
| **CHAPTER RESOURCES** | The chapter discusses the postwar period, including the development of the Marshall Plan, the origins of the Cold War, the fear of communism within the United States and abroad, and the armed intervention in Korea. It also describes the social and cultural changes of the Fifties. | **In-Depth Resources: Unit 8**<br>• Tracing Themes: Economics in History, p. 63<br>• Building Vocabulary, p. 67<br>**Interdisciplinary Projects,** pp. 163–168 | CD-ROM **Primary Source Explorer**<br>CD-ROM **Electronic Teacher Tools**<br>CD-ROM **Power Presentations CD-ROM**<br>**Chapter Summaries on CD** (English and Spanish)<br>**America's Music CD** |
| **SECTION 1 Peacetime Adjustments and the Cold War pp. 789–794** | **KEY IDEAS**<br>• Demand for consumer goods and new housing creates an economic boom.<br>• Labor unrest and political divisions trouble Truman's presidency.<br>• The United States and the Soviet Union go from allies to rivals in the Cold War. | **In-Depth Resources: Unit 8**<br>• Skillbuilder Practice, p. 68<br>• Geography Application, pp. 69–70<br>• Literature Selection, pp. 73–75<br>**America's History Makers,** pp. 111–114<br>**Economics in History,** p. 28<br>**Why It Matters Now,** pp. 55–56<br>**Outline Map Activities,** pp. 55–56 | **Warm-Up Transparency WT28**<br>**Geography Transparency GT28**<br>• Berlin Airlift, 1948–1949<br>**Critical Thinking Transparency CT82**<br>• Setting the Stage<br>INTERNET **ClassZone:** www.mcdougallittell.com |
| **SECTION 2 The Korean War and McCarthyism pp. 795–799** | • The United States goes to war in Korea to stop the spread of communism.<br>• The Korean War ends in a stalemate.<br>• The Cold War produces McCarthyism and an arms race. | **In-Depth Resources: Unit 8**<br>• Setting the Stage, p. 62<br>• Guided Reading, p. 65<br>• Primary Source: A Speech by Margaret Chase Smith, p. 71<br>• Reteaching Activity, p. 77 | **Warm-Up Transparency WT28**<br>**Humanities Transparency HT55**<br>• Political Cartoon: "I can't do this to me" by Herblock<br>**Critical Thinking Transparency CT82**<br>• Setting the Stage<br>**Critical Thinking Transparency CT83**<br>• Cause and Effect: The Cold War<br>INTERNET **ClassZone:** www.mcdougallittell.com |
| **SECTION 3 The Fifties pp. 800–805** | • During the baby boom, many Americans move to the suburbs.<br>• Television and rock 'n' roll dominate pop culture.<br>• In 1960, John F. Kennedy becomes the first Catholic to be elected president. | **In-Depth Resources: Unit 8**<br>• Setting the Stage, p. 62<br>• Guided Reading, p. 66<br>• Primary Source: from *The Other America,* p. 72<br>• Reteaching Activity, p. 78 | **Warm-Up Transparency WT28**<br>**Humanities Transparency HT56**<br>• *After the Prom* by Norman Rockwell<br>**Critical Thinking Transparency CT82**<br>• Setting the Stage<br>**Critical Thinking Transparency CT84**<br>• Visual Summary<br>INTERNET **ClassZone:** www.mcdougallittell.com |

Pupil's Edition | Overhead Transparency | CD-ROM
Copymaster | Audio Library | Internet

## ASSESSMENT

**Chapter Assessment,** pp. 806–807

**Formal Assessment**
- Chapter Tests, Forms A and B, pp. 409–416

**Alternative Assessment Book**

**Electronic Teacher Tools with Test Maker**

**Section Assessment,** p. 794

**Formal Assessment**
- Section Quiz, p. 406

**Alternative Assessment Book**
- Rubrics for a letter, 4.3
- Rubrics for a picture, 1.3

**Electronic Teacher Tools with Test Maker**

**Section Assessment,** p. 799

**Formal Assessment**
- Section Quiz, p. 407

**Alternative Assessment Book**
- Rubrics for a report, 2.5
- Rubrics for a design, 1.3

**Electronic Teacher Tools with Test Maker**

**Section Assessment,** p. 803

**Formal Assessment**
- Section Quiz, p. 408

**Alternative Assessment Book**
- Rubrics for a Web page, 5.1
- Rubrics for a song, 4.8

**Electronic Teacher Tools with Test Maker**

## CUSTOMIZING FOR INDIVIDUAL NEEDS

### Students Acquiring English/ESL

**Reading Study Guide** (English and Spanish), pp. 271–278

**Access for Students Acquiring English/ESL: Spanish Translations,** pp. 187–192

**Chapter Summaries on CD** (English and Spanish)

### Less Proficient Readers

**Reading Study Guide** (English and Spanish), pp. 271–278

**Chapter Summaries on CD** (English and Spanish)

### Gifted and Talented Students

**In-Depth Resources: Unit 8**
- Enrichment Activity, p. 79

**America's History Makers**
- Harry S. Truman, pp. 111–112
- George C. Marshall, pp. 113–114

## CROSS-CURRICULAR CONNECTIONS

### Civics

Cohen, Daniel. ***Joseph McCarthy: The Misuse of Political Power.*** Brookfield, CT: Millbrook, 1996. A fair, well-told biography of the most-feared man of his era.

### Humanities: Art

Phillips, Lisa. ***The American Century: Art and Culture, 1950–2000.*** New York: Norton, 1999. This catalog for an exhibit at the Whitney Museum of Art provides an overview of American art in the second half of the century. Contains short sidebars on topics such as Hollywood, modern dance, and music. For advanced readers.

### Humanities: Music

Shirley, David. ***The History of Rock and Roll.*** New York: Watts, 1997. From Elvis to Nirvana, this book provides an overview of the singers and groups that led the rock 'n' roll revolution.

### Science

Stwertka, Albert. ***The World of Atoms and Quarks (Scientific American Sourcebook Series).*** New York: Twenty-First Century, 1995. A short, understandable overview of the world of protons, electrons, and atomic energy.

### Interdisciplinary Projects, pp. 163–168

- Math: Solving Algebraic Expressions
- Science: Physics of Frisbees
- Language Arts: 1950s TV Comedy
- Physical Education: 1950s Dance Party

### Literature

Choi, Sook Nyul. ***Year of Impossible Goodbyes.*** Boston: Houghton, 1991. Story of a North Korean woman, Sookan, as her homeland is first occupied by the Japanese, then dominated by Russian Communists. Her only option then becomes a dangerous escape to South Korea.

Conrad, Pam. ***Our House: The Stories of Levittown.*** New York: Scholastic, 1994. A series of stories set in Levittown trace changes in the community.

Salter, James. ***The Hunters.*** Washington: Counterpoint, 1997. What was it really like to be a young fighter pilot in the Korean War? Story based on the author's personal experiences.

### McDougal Littell *The Language of Literature*

- Doris Kearns Goodwin. "Wait Til Next Year" (memoir)

### McDougal Littell Literature Connections

Literature Connections
So Far from the Bamboo Grove
and Related Readings
McDougal Littell

Yoko Kawashimav Watkins

***So Far from the Bamboo Grove***

The odyssey of a Japanese family from Korea to Japan at the end of World War II. Young Yoko, her sister, and her mother become refugees but have the strength to prevail.

## ENRICHMENT ACTIVITIES

**Pupil's Edition, pp. 786–807**
**Interact with History,** p. 787
**Geography in History,** pp. 804–805

**In-Depth Resources: Unit 8**
- Geography Application, pp. 69–70
- Primary Source, p. 71
- Primary Source, p. 72
- Literature Selection: The Threat of Nuclear War, pp. 73–75

**America's History Makers**
- Harry S. Truman, pp. 111–112
- George C. Marshall, pp. 113–114

**Outline Map Activities,** pp. 55–56

**Why It Matters Now,** pp. 55–56

# CHAPTER 28 PACING GUIDE

**LESSON PLAN OPTIONS (50-MINUTE PERIOD)** **(TE) = Teacher's Edition (PE) = Pupil's Edition**

| | TEACHER-DIRECTED ACTIVITIES | STUDENT-CENTERED ACTIVITIES | INDIVIDUAL ACTIVITIES |
|---|---|---|---|
| | Class Time: 15 minutes | Class Time: 25 minutes | Class Time: 10 minutes |
| **DAY 1**<br>Introduction<br>pp. 786–788 | **Presentation Options**<br>• Begin with a class discussion of the picture on p. 786 **(PE)**.<br>• Lead a class discussion on the "What Do You Know?" question in Setting the Stage, p. 788. Then introduce the graphic organizer for the chapter **(PE)**. | **Options for Cooperative Learning**<br>• Have student groups discuss the Interact with History questions, p. 787 **(PE)**.<br>• Have student groups respond to the "What Do You Want to Know?" question in Setting the Stage, p. 788 **(PE)**. | **Head Start on Homework Options**<br>• Have students skim Section 1 Main Idea, Why It Matters Now, Terms & Names, and the main headings, p. 789 **(PE)**.<br>• Have students begin Guided Reading activity and Building Vocabulary sheet. |
| **DAY 2**<br>Section 1<br>pp. 789–794 | **Presentation Options**<br>• Begin with the 5-Minute Warm-Up, p. 789 **(TE)**.<br>• Review the Section 1 Main Idea, Why It Matters Now, and Terms & Names, p. 789 **(PE)**.<br>• Lead the students through the Skillbuilder Mini-Lesson: Summarizing, p. 790 **(TE)**. | **Options for Cooperative Learning**<br>• Divide students into groups to work on the Interdisciplinary Link, Mathematics: Analyzing Election Returns, p. 791 **(TE)**.<br>• Have student pairs work together to complete one of the Activity Options in the Section 1 Assessment, p. 794 **(PE)**. | **Head Start on Homework Options**<br>• Have students begin working on Section 1 Assessment, p. 794 **(PE)**.<br>• Have students complete the History from Visuals Extension activity, p. 792 **(TE)**. |
| **DAY 3**<br>Section 2<br>pp. 795–799 | **Presentation Options**<br>• Begin with the 5-Minute Warm-Up, p. 795 **(TE)**.<br>• Choose 5 key questions for Objectives 1–4 to discuss with the class, pp. 795–798 **(TE)**.<br>• Lead the students in a discussion of the Korean War using the History from Visuals feature, p. 796 **(TE)**. | **Options for Cooperative Learning**<br>• Divide students into groups to work on the Interdisciplinary Link, Science: The Space Race, p. 798 **(TE)**.<br>• Have student pairs work together to complete one of the Activity Options in the Section 2 Assessment, p. 799 **(PE)**. | **Head Start on Homework Options**<br>• Have students begin working on Section 2 Assessment, p. 799 **(PE)**.<br>• Have students complete the Critical Thinking Activity, p. 799 **(TE)**. |
| **DAY 4**<br>Section 3<br>pp. 800–805 | **Presentation Options**<br>• Begin with the 5-Minute Warm-Up, p. 800 **(TE)**.<br>• Choose 5 key questions for Objectives 1–4 to discuss with the class, pp. 800–803 **(TE)**.<br>• Lead students through the Geography in History feature, pp. 804–805 **(TE)**. | **Options for Cooperative Learning**<br>• Divide students into groups and have them complete the Geography in History questions, pp. 804–805 **(PE)**.<br>• Have student pairs work together to complete one of the Activity Options in the Section 3 Assessment, p. 803 **(PE)**. | **Head Start on Homework Options**<br>• Have students complete the Setting the Stage graphic organizer for the chapter, p. 788 **(PE)**.<br>• Have students begin working on the Chapter Assessment, pp. 806–807 **(PE)**.<br>• Prepare for Chapter Test<br>**Formal Assessment,** pp. 409–416 |

TEACHER-TESTED ACTIVITY — Pam Kniffin and Tammy Leiber, Navasota Junior High School, Navasota, Texas

## COMPARING TV LIFE IN THE FIFTIES WITH TODAY

**Class Time** Two class periods

**Task** Comparing the way television sitcoms portrayed family life in the 1950s with the media's portrayal of family life today

**Purpose** To help students compare and contrast images of American life in the 1950s and today

**Supplies Needed**

- Videotapes of such 1950s TV programs as *The Dick Van Dyke Show, I Love Lucy, Ozzie and Harriet, Father Knows Best,* or *Leave It to Beaver*
- Videotapes of current sitcoms about American families

**Activity** Show a 15–20 minute clip from one of the 1950s TV shows. After viewing the clip, have the class develop a list of at least five positive and five negative aspects of life in the 1950s based on this show. Then show a clip of similar length from a current TV show and repeat the process. After the students watch the more recent program, have students discuss the extent to which family life has changed. Remind them to consider the differences between families in real life and those portrayed on TV in both eras.

## BLOCK SCHEDULING — LESSON PLAN OPTIONS (90-MINUTE PERIOD)

### DAY 1

**Interact with History,** p. 787
**Class Time** 20 minutes

Options for pacing and variety:

- **Time Saver** For a homework assignment, have each student write a paragraph describing his or her American Dream. Then in class assign students to small groups to discuss their conceptions of the American Dream using the "What Do You Think?" questions. **Class Time** 15 minutes

**Setting the Stage,** p. 788
**Class Time** 20 minutes

Options for pacing and variety:

- **Time Saver** Ask students to come to class with two lists. One list should describe what they already know about the Cold War. The second should include questions they have about this topic. **Class Time** 5 minutes

**Section 1,** pp. 789–794
**Class Time** 50 minutes

Options for pacing and variety:

- **Time Saver** To provide students with an overview of the postwar economy, use the chart on page 790. **Class Time** 10 minutes
- **Internet** Students can extend their background knowledge of Levittown by visiting www.mcdougallittell.com **Class Time** 20 minutes

### DAY 2

**Section 2,** pp. 795–799
**Class Time** 45 minutes

Options for pacing and variety:

- **History on Film** Extend students' knowledge of the McCarthy era by viewing *The Red Scare: Ordinary Americans,* a thoughtful look at how McCarthyism affected the lives of eight average Americans. Close Up Foundation, 1999. **Class Time** 35 minutes
- **Peer Teaching** Divide students into small groups to debate the Applying Citizenship Skills, Critical Thinking question on page 806. Have groups share their conclusions with the class. **Class Time** 20 minutes

**Section 3,** pp. 800–805
**Class Time** 45 minutes

Options for pacing and variety:

- **Peer Teaching** Appoint a panel of student "experts" to research and report to the class on music, Hollywood movies, TV, dance, fashion, and other aspects of popular culture in the 1950s. **Class Time** 20 minutes
- **Peer Evaluation** Have student pairs compare their Taking Notes webs and discuss their answers to the Critical Thinking question in the Section Assessment. **Class Time** 10 minutes

**Chapter 28 Assessment,** pp. 806–807
**Class Time** 40 minutes

Options for pacing and variety:

- **Peer Evaluation** Working in groups, students can review their completed Using Your Notes chart on page 806 and explain why topics such as labor unions, strikes, and communism became major issues in Truman's or Eisenhower's presidency. Students can also discuss whether they agree with the actions each leader took in response to these issues. **Class Time** 20 minutes

**CHAPTER 28 OBJECTIVE**

The student will understand how conflict developed between the democratic, capitalist United States and the authoritarian, Communist Soviet Union and how Americans reacted to the economic prosperity and rapid change of the postwar period.

**HISTORY FROM VISUALS**

**Interpreting the Photograph** Have students study the photograph and read the caption and the writing on the showroom window. Ask students if they know in what decades rock 'n' roll music became popular. Ask if anyone knows what *Sputnik* was. Why might the car dealer have put these words on the showroom window? **Possible Responses** to spark curiosity or interest in the cars sold inside, to draw attention to the showroom

To what groups might the Edsel ad appeal? **Possible Response** The ad might appeal to people who want to be in style by owning the latest color and model of car. Have students compare the Edsel with today's cars, noting differences in size and style.

**Extension** Have students research the short history of the Edsel, one of Detroit's most famous failures.

CHAPTER 28

# The Cold War and the American Dream 1945–1960



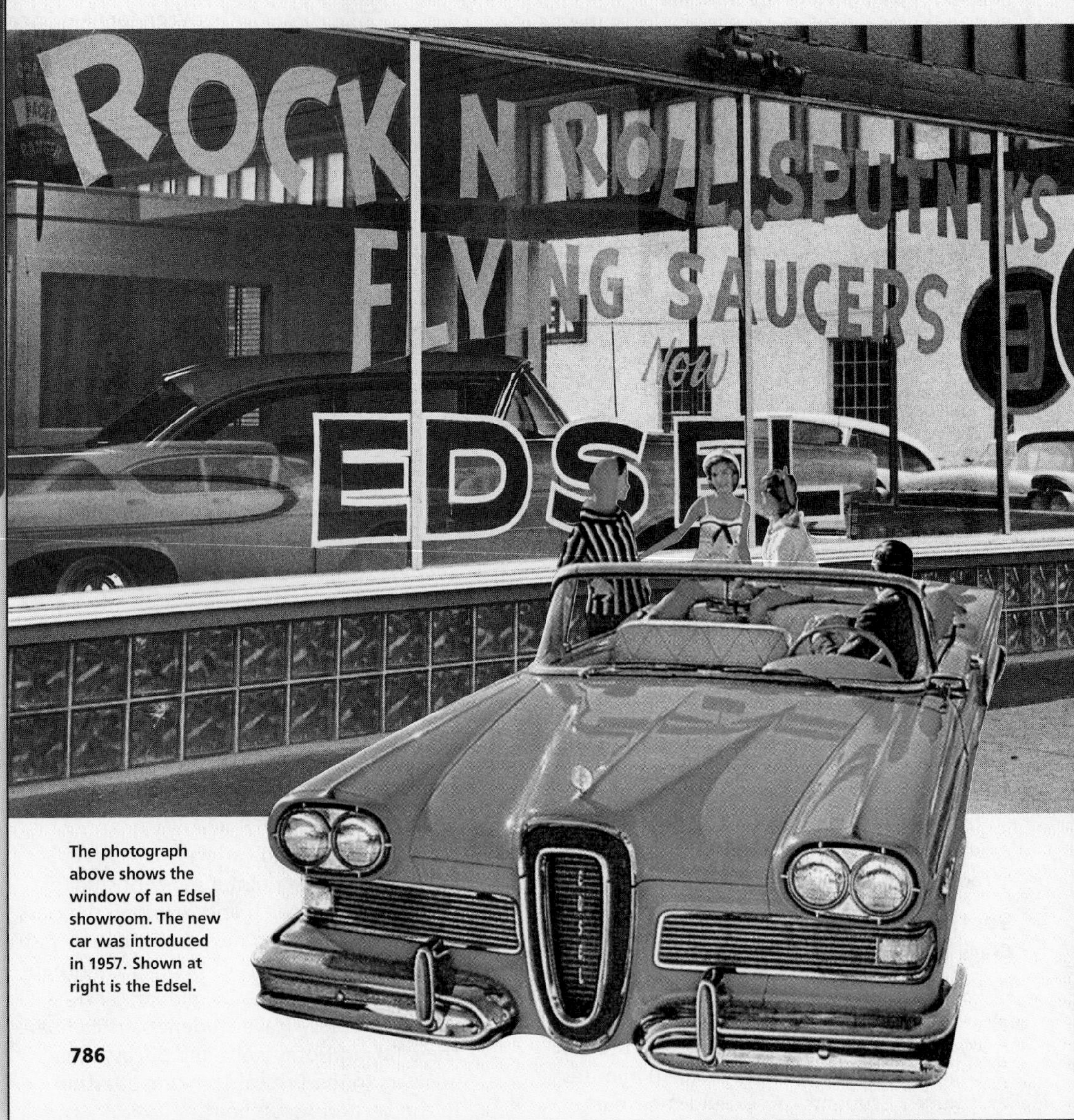


The photograph above shows the window of an Edsel showroom. The new car was introduced in 1957. Shown at right is the Edsel.



**RECOMMENDED RESOURCES**

**BOOKS FOR THE TEACHER**

Coontz, Stephanie. ***The Way We Never Were: American Families and the Nostalgia Trap.*** New York: Basic Books, 1992. A fascinating look at the "good old days."

Fried, Richard M. ***Nightmare in Red: The McCarthy Era in Perspective.*** New York: Oxford, 1990. Gripping history of troubled times.

Halberstam, David. ***The Fifties.*** New York: Fawcett, 1994. Acclaimed, superbly written account of the decade.

**SOFTWARE**

***The Cold War: Decisions, Decisions.*** CD-ROM. Tom Snyder, 1997. Focuses on foreign policy decisions in the nuclear age.

**VIDEO**

***Picture This.*** Focuses on Hollywood in the Cold War. Part of *The Century,* a 12-part series by ABC News, narrated by Peter Jennings. 1-800-225-5222.

**INTERNET**

For more about Levittown, Pennsylvania, visit www.mcdougallittell.com

## Interact *with* History

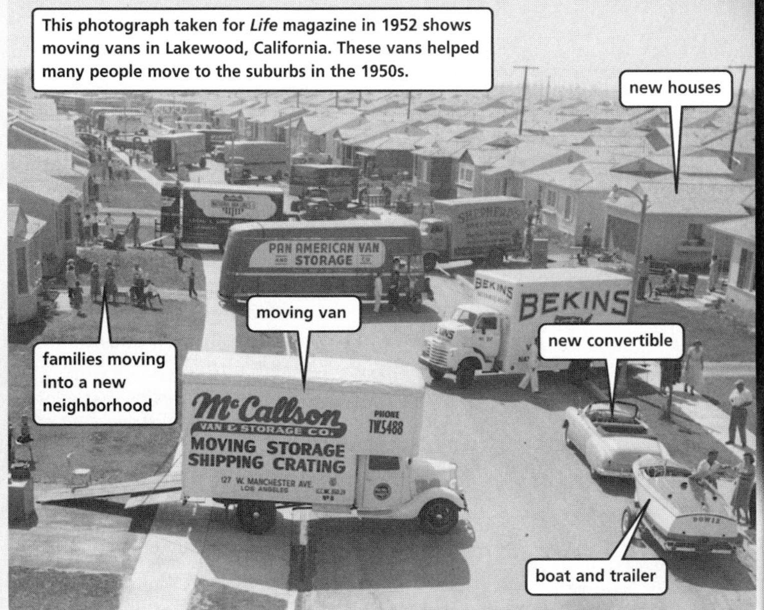
new houses
moving van
families moving into a new neighborhood
new convertible
boat and trailer
PAN AMERICAN VAN AND STORAGE
BEKINS
McCallson
VAN & STORAGE CO.
MOVING STORAGE
SHIPPING CRATING

This photograph taken for *Life* magazine in 1952 shows moving vans in Lakewood, California. These vans helped many people move to the suburbs in the 1950s.

**In the 1950s, American technology produced a flood of consumer goods. These included cars and houses in suburbs springing up across the country. You and your family have moved to a new house in a growing suburb—which some people think of as the American Dream.**

### What Do You Think?

- How might the American Dream be connected to prosperity?
- How might the American Dream involve helping others?
- How might the American Dream be connected to democracy, equality, and justice?

# *What is the American Dream to you?*

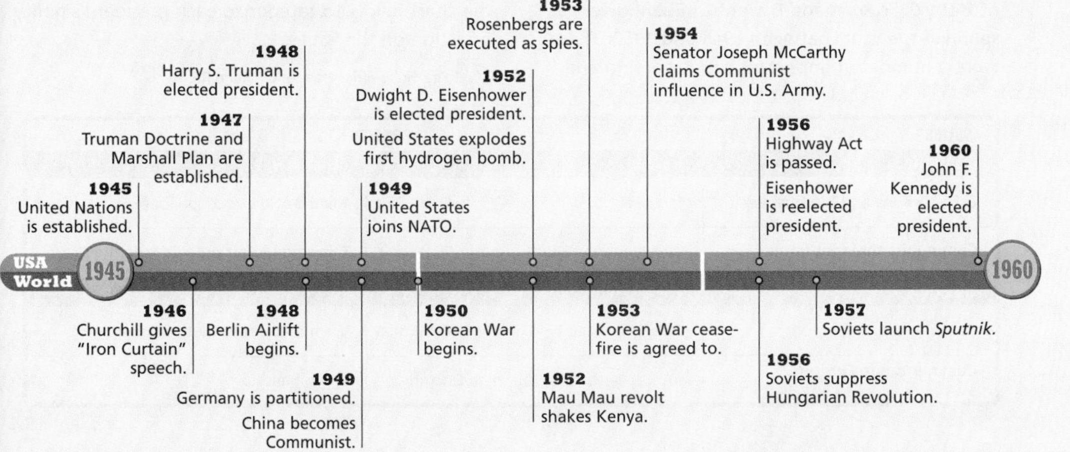
USA
World
1945
1960
1945 United Nations is established.
1947 Truman Doctrine and Marshall Plan are established.
1948 Harry S. Truman is elected president.
1949 United States joins NATO.
1952 Dwight D. Eisenhower is elected president. United States explodes first hydrogen bomb.
1953 Rosenbergs are executed as spies.
1954 Senator Joseph McCarthy claims Communist influence in U.S. Army.
1956 Highway Act is passed. Eisenhower is reelected president.
1960 John F. Kennedy is elected president.
1946 Churchill gives "Iron Curtain" speech.
1948 Berlin Airlift begins.
1949 Germany is partitioned. China becomes Communist.
1950 Korean War begins.
1952 Mau Mau revolt shakes Kenya.
1953 Korean War cease-fire is agreed to.
1956 Soviets suppress Hungarian Revolution.
1957 Soviets launch *Sputnik*.

## Interact *with* History

### OBJECTIVES

- To identify what Americans in the 1950s believed to be the American Dream
- To help students connect with the people and events they will study in this chapter

### What Do You Think?

1. Have students list what the American Dream meant to Americans of previous eras, such as immigrants of the 1840s, African Americans in the South after the Civil War, homesteaders of the 1870s, or industrialists of the 1890s.
2. Ask students to describe a society in which all citizens have achieved the American Dream.
3. Have students discuss why, when the U.S. Constitution says that all Americans are equal under the law, Americans are not equal in wealth, education, or access to health care.

### *What is the American Dream to you?*

Point out that for many people the American Dream includes hopes for the future. Encourage students to think about what they would like their lives to be like 10, 15, or 30 years from now. Students' American Dreams might consist of a vision for their future and their family's future and might include the community or the nation as well.

### MAKING PERSONAL CONNECTIONS

Have students discuss how their visions of the American Dream differ from those of their parents' or grandparents' generations. Ask students what events in their lifetime have affected their ideas about the American Dream and their hopes for the future.

### TIME LINE DISCUSSION

**After World War II, Americans wanted to get on with their lives. Business boomed and so did the birthrate. However, a new kind of war—a "Cold War"—brought fears of the spread of communism throughout the world and of nuclear destruction.**

- Which U.S. events suggest the United States was worried about national security? **Possible Responses** United States explodes hydrogen bomb, Rosenbergs are executed, McCarthy claims Communist influence in U.S. Army
- Which events suggest security was a worldwide worry? **Possible Response** Korean War, Mau Mau revolt, Soviets suppress Hungarian Revolution
- Can you identify organizations shown on the time line that were focused on making the world safe? **Possible Response** United Nations, NATO

## BEFORE YOU READ

### Previewing the Theme:
**Economics in History**

Ask students why the items in the picture indicate prosperity. Students might mention the sports car. Point out that even up to 1960, one family car or none was a common occurrence. Also point out that eating out after years of wartime rationing was a change in lifestyle.

### What Do You Know?

Students might recall what they already know about the two sides in the Cold War. Many students may have learned about the 1950s through an interest in rock 'n' roll, through movies and TV shows such as *Grease* and *Happy Days,* or through books and movies about spies during the Cold War.

 **In-Depth Resources: Unit 8**
- Tracing Themes: Economics in History, p. 63

## READ AND TAKE NOTES

**Reading Strategy: Categorizing**

Remind students that to categorize means to organize ideas or events into groups. The items in each group have something in common. For example, historical events in a group might have happened during a certain time or in a certain area of the world. Review the terms *foreign* and *domestic* with students. Discuss the organization of the chart and suggest that students use a similar chart to organize the ideas and events they read about in the chapter.

 **In-Depth Resources: Unit 8**
- Setting the Stage, p. 62

 **Critical Thinking Transparency CT82**
- Setting the Stage

# Chapter 28 SETTING THE STAGE

## BEFORE YOU READ

### Previewing the Theme

**Economics in History** After more than 15 years of depression and war, the United States entered a time of economic prosperity and rapid change. This chapter explains how the United States came into conflict with the Soviet Union.

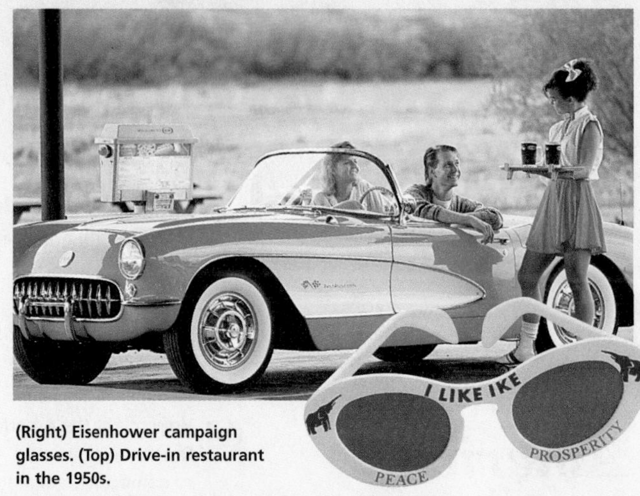


(Right) Eisenhower campaign glasses. (Top) Drive-in restaurant in the 1950s.

### What Do You Know?

What do you think of when you hear the phrase *the American Dream*? What sorts of dreams might a people and a nation have?

**THINK ABOUT**
- what you have learned about the 1950s from television and movies
- hopes and dreams that might be achieved both through and outside of politics

### What Do You Want to Know?

What additional information do you want to know about the Cold War and the American Dream? Record the sort of information you want in your notebook before you read the chapter.

## READ AND TAKE NOTES

**Reading Strategy: Categorizing** The presidencies of Harry S. Truman and Dwight D. Eisenhower spanned the years between 1945 and 1960. There were a number of important issues, foreign and domestic, that both presidents had to deal with. Use the chart below to categorize each president's policy or action on the issues.

 See Skillbuilder Handbook, page R6.

| ISSUES | PRESIDENTS | |
|---|---|---|
| **Domestic** | **Truman** | **Eisenhower** |
| **Labor unions and big business** | Fair Deal | Middle-of-the-road policies |
| **Communist threat at home** | Loyalty Review Board | Opposed McCarthy's attack on the Army |
| **Foreign** | | |
| **Korea** | Called on UN to help defend South Korea | Went to Korea; armistice signed |
| **Communism in Europe** | NATO; Marshall Plan; Truman Doctrine | Brinksmanship |



## TEACHING STRATEGY

### READING THE CHAPTER

This is a thematic chapter focusing on the political and social changes in the nation in the postwar decade. Encourage students to look for the economic and social changes affecting the nation. Also look for the impact of fears about the spread of communism on foreign and domestic activity.

### ALTERNATIVE ASSESSMENT

The Chapter Assessment describes three activities for alternative assessment on page 807. You may wish to have students work on these activities during the course of the chapter and then present them at the end.

# 1 Peacetime Adjustments and the Cold War

**TERMS & NAMES**
Harry S. Truman
Fair Deal
Cold War
containment
Truman Doctrine
NATO
Marshall Plan

**MAIN IDEA**

Americans looked for prosperity after World War II. They also fought communism in the Cold War.

**WHY IT MATTERS NOW**

The U.S. economy grew rapidly, and the nation's role in the world expanded after World War II.

## ONE AMERICAN'S STORY

**Harold Russell was a soldier, not an actor. Even so, in 1946 he won an Academy Award for best supporting actor in the Hollywood film *The Best Years of Our Lives.* Russell played an amputee struggling to adjust to civilian life after World War II. It was a role he knew well. As a paratrooper, Sergeant Russell had lost both hands in a grenade explosion. He was then fitted with hooks. Russell had to teach himself and others to accept his disability.**

*A VOICE FROM THE PAST*

I was all right. My problem was to make the people I met feel at ease. I just acted myself and didn't sulk in corners hiding the hooks. When my neighborhood friends saw I was okay and laughing they said to themselves, "Why should we feel sorry for him? He's getting along better than we are."

**Harold Russell,** quoted in *Life,* December 16, 1946

Sergeant Harold Russell demonstrates to other disabled veterans how to drink a cup of coffee.

**Russell won a second special Academy Award for "bringing hope and courage to his fellow veterans." As you will read in this section, millions of returning soldiers like Russell were preparing to restart their lives at the end of World War II.**

### 1 Adjusting to Peace

The United States had spent the years 1941–1945 fighting World War II. Now, the country was at peace. The aircraft industry and other defense plants were changing over to making goods for peacetime. As part of this process, most industries reduced their work force. Factories shut down, and more than 10 million returning war veterans were looking for work.

Returning servicemen flooded the job market. Veterans won out over female workers in the competition for jobs in the first years after the war. In the aircraft industry, more than 800,000 workers—mostly women—were laid off. Several years after the war ended, as the economy boomed, employment rates for women began to return to wartime peaks. However, often these jobs were in traditional women's fields, such as office work and teaching.





## SECTION OBJECTIVES

1. To describe how the economy changed after World War II
2. To evaluate Truman's response to labor unrest and civil rights issues
3. To analyze the origins of the Cold War and containment policies
4. To explain how fear of communism affected international relations and domestic politics

**SKILLBUILDER**
Interpreting Charts, p. 790
Interpreting Maps: Location, Region, p. 792

**CRITICAL THINKING**
Making Inferences, p. 790
Comparing and Contrasting, p. 792
Forming Opinions, p. 794

**Why It Matters Now**
- The United States and Russia Today, pp. 55–56

## FOCUS & MOTIVATE

### 5-MINUTE WARM-UP

**Drawing Conclusions** These questions focus on the postwar economy.

1. Look at the charts on page 790. Did the American economy strengthen, stay the same, or weaken in the 1950s?
2. Why is home ownership a good indicator of change in the U.S. economy?

**Warm-Up Transparency WT28**

## INSTRUCT

### INSTRUCT: OBJECTIVE 

**Adjusting to Peace/The Postwar Economy**
Key Questions
- Why did the nation's economy boom in the postwar period?
- How did prosperity lead to inflation?
- Why did demand for housing increase?

**In-Depth Resources: Unit 8**
- Guided Reading, p. 64

## RECOMMENDED RESOURCES

**In-Depth Resources: Unit 8**
- Guided Reading, p. 64
- Building Vocabulary, p. 67
- Skillbuilder Practice, p. 68
- Geography Application, pp. 69–70
- Literature Selection, pp. 73–75
- Reteaching Activity, p. 76

**Reading Study Guide** (Spanish and English), pp. 271–272

**Economics in History,** p. 28

**Outline Map Activities,** pp. 55–56

**America's History Makers**
- Harry S. Truman, pp. 111–112
- George C. Marshall, pp. 113–114

**Why It Matters Now,** pp. 55–56

**Formal Assessment**
- Section Quiz, p. 406

**Alternative Assessment**
- Rubrics, 4.3
- Rubrics, 1.3

**Access for Students Acquiring English/ESL**
- Guided Reading, p. 187
- Skillbuilder Practice, p. 190
- Geography Application, pp. 191–192

**Technology Resources**

**Geography Transparency GT28**
- Berlin Airlift, 1948–1949

**Electronic Teacher Tools with Test Maker**

## HISTORY FROM VISUALS

**Interpreting Charts** Ask students what the median family income was for a family in 1949. **Answer** about $4,200. During what two-year period in the 1950s did median family income change the least? **Answer** 1953–1955. What might this suggest about the economy? **Possible Response** It may suggest that the economy was beginning to slow down or expand less rapidly.

**Extension** Have students make a graphic organizer showing how rising home ownership affects other industries.

 **Economics in History**
- Measuring the Postwar Boom, p. 28

## MORE ABOUT . . .

**William Levitt and Levittown**

William Levitt broke the home-building process down into 27 steps. Carpenters, tilers, and roofers each had tasks. One worker's only job was to go from house to house installing washing machines. Levitt first learned mass production techniques for building houses during the war, when he and his brother Alfred were hired by the federal government to build more than 2,300 housing units for defense workers in Norfolk, Virginia.

## INSTRUCT: OBJECTIVE 2

**Labor Unrest and Civil Rights/ The Fair Deal**

Key Questions
- Why did labor unrest increase after the war?
- What were the results of Truman's efforts to improve civil rights for African Americans?
- Which of the goals of the Fair Deal were achieved?

CONNECTIONS TO MATH

**A Changing Economy**

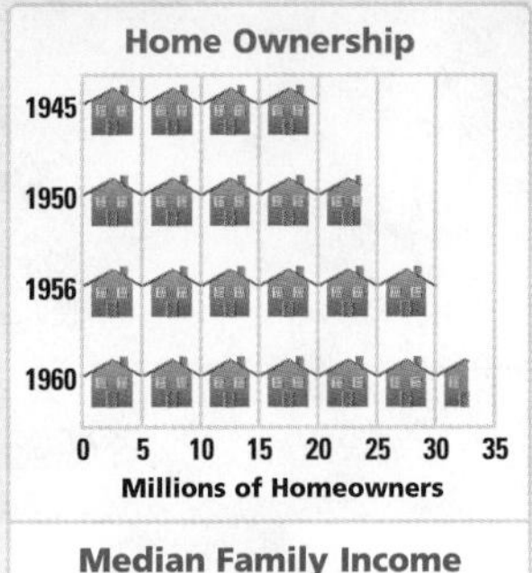

Source: *Historical Statistics of the United States*

SKILLBUILDER
**Interpreting Charts**
1. *What period showed the biggest increase in home ownership?*
2. *About how much did family income increase in the years 1947 to 1959?*

Skillbuilder Answers
1. 1950–1956
2. about $1,700

## The Postwar Economy

Instead of slowing down, as many had feared, the nation's economy boomed. During the war years, few consumer goods had been produced. After the war, people were starting families and buying new homes. They wanted cars, washing machines, toasters, and all the other goods they had put off buying during wartime. American factories were fitted out with new machinery and tools to make different products.

The spending spree led to inflation, or a rise in prices. During the war, the government had put controls on prices and wages. After the war, in 1946, the controls on prices were lifted. Consumer goods were still in short supply. People had plenty of money to spend, but few goods to buy. As a result, the demand for goods increased, and prices skyrocketed.

After the war, the number of marriages increased. At first, a housing shortage forced many newlyweds to move in with relatives. Government-guaranteed housing loans for veterans under the G.I. Bill spurred the demand for new houses. Businessman William Levitt saw a way to meet this demand. He applied assembly-line techniques to home building. His mass-produced houses were so cheap that many people could afford them. He built Levittown in 1947 on Long Island, New York. Three years later, 17,500 homes had turned the farmland into an instant suburb. However, not everyone benefited from the postwar boom.

*Reading*History
**A. Making Inferences** Why did Levitt's houses become so popular?
A. Answer because the houses were affordable and people wanted to have more independence

## 2 Labor Unrest and Civil Rights

During the war, unions had agreed to give up pay raises. When the government put controls on wages, the unions agreed not to strike. But with the war over, workers faced with rising prices demanded better pay. In 1946, the United States entered one of the most strike-torn years in its history. More than one million workers joined strikes in the automobile, steel, meatpacking, and electrical industries.

Later that year, both miners and railway workers also went out on strike. Although President **Harry S. Truman** was a friend of labor, he feared these strikes would cripple the nation. During the railroad strike, he threatened to draft all railroad workers into the army. He said he would have the army run the trains. But the strike was settled before Truman could carry out his threat.

African Americans were still excluded from prosperity and full equality in the postwar world. World War II had raised the hopes of African Americans for greater equality. Many African-American veterans expected their wartime service to be recognized. Particularly in the



ACTIVITY OPTIONS

## SKILLBUILDER MINI-LESSON: SUMMARIZING

BLOCK SCHEDULING

**Explaining the Skill** Summarizing is a way of condensing information. It is important to write summaries in your own words. To create a summary, begin by identifying topic sentences that state the main ideas of a paragraph or reading. Find statements of fact, numbers, dates, or other information that supports each idea. Use these main ideas and supporting details to prepare the summary.

**Applying the Skill** Direct students' attention to the subsection "Labor Unrest and Civil Rights." Have students write a summary of the subsection. They can begin by taking notes, identifying the main ideas in each of the four paragraphs of the subsection. After recording these main ideas, have students find supporting details for each idea and combine main ideas and supporting details to create their summaries. Remind students to paraphrase the information or put it into their own words.

 **In-Depth Resources: Unit 8**
- Skillbuilder Practice, p. 68

South, however, little had changed. In many Southern states, African Americans who attempted to vote were threatened, fired from their jobs, and even murdered.

To deal with these problems, President Truman created a commission on civil rights. He issued an executive order in July 1948 ending racial segregation and discrimination in the armed forces. Truman also asked Congress for an anti-lynching law and an end to the poll tax as a requirement for voting. However, when southern Democrats in Congress balked at the proposals, Truman backed off. Nonetheless, he was the first president to make equal rights a national issue. The action he took began the federal government's effort to deal with racial issues.

**Background**
In some southern states a poll tax had to be paid in order to vote.

## The Fair Deal

In 1946, fears about the economy hurt the Democrats. Voters sent a Republican majority to Congress. The new Congress wanted to block Truman's programs. Congress turned down his plans to provide federal funds for housing, education, and health care. Congress also limited the power of unions by passing the 1947 Taft-Hartley Act. This act outlawed the closed shop, a workplace that hired only union members. The act also gave the president the power to require an 80-day cooling-off period before a strike.

As the 1948 presidential election campaign opened, few political experts believed President Truman would keep his job. Polls showed the Republican candidate, New York Governor Thomas E. Dewey, to be the clear favorite. Even within his own party, few of Truman's supporters thought that he could win.

Ignoring politicians and pollsters, Truman took his campaign to the people. Hiring a special train, he made a tour through hundreds of cities and small towns. Wherever his train stopped, Truman blasted the "do-nothing" Republican Congress because it passed little legislation. His strategy worked. When the votes were counted, he had won an upset victory over Dewey. The Democrats had also regained control of Congress.

After his victory, Truman presented Congress with a package of reforms he called the Fair Deal. He hoped to extend the social programs begun with FDR's New Deal. The **Fair Deal** called for new projects to create jobs, build public housing, and end racial discrimination in hiring. Many Republicans and southern Democrats worked together to block his plans. Congress passed few of his proposals. Only his low-cost public housing measure became law. In addition to problems at home, Truman faced major problems abroad.

### AMERICA'S HISTORY MAKERS

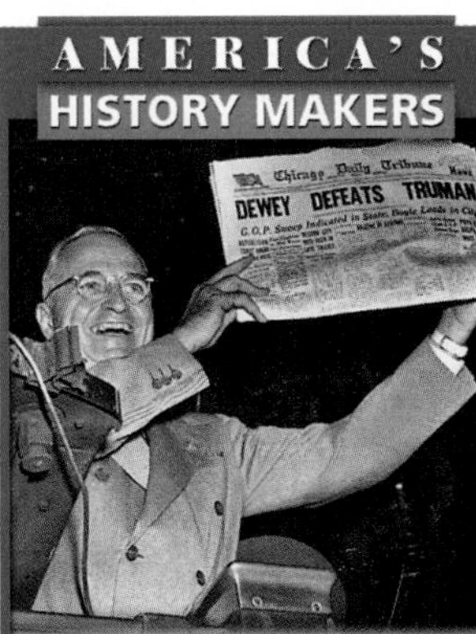


**HARRY S. TRUMAN**
**1884–1972**

During Harry Truman's 1948 whistle-stop campaign, he traveled many thousands of miles in eight weeks. He was often accompanied by his daughter and wife.

Audiences enjoyed his straightforward manner and his spirited attacks on the Republicans. He blamed the Republicans for the nation's problems. When the votes were counted, Truman won an upset victory over his opponent, Thomas Dewey. A Chicago newspaper (above) mistakenly declared Dewey the winner in the close contest.

**What might Truman's whistle-stop campaign suggest about his character?**





### MORE ABOUT . . .

**The Election of 1948**

One reason few political experts thought Truman would win was that he faced strong opposition, even within his own party. In 1948, two wings of the Democratic Party refused to support the Truman ticket. Many liberal New Dealers left the party to support the Progressive candidate for president, Henry Wallace. At the Democratic convention, four Southern states left the convention when delegates put a strong civil rights plank in the party platform. These states formed a States Rights' party (Dixiecrats) with South Carolina's Strom Thurmond as its presidential candidate.

### AMERICA'S HISTORY MAKERS

**Harry S. Truman**

On his whistle-stop tour, Truman made more than 550 speeches as he crisscrossed the nation. Truman's colorful campaign style was in sharp contrast to Thomas E. Dewey's bland, stodgy image. One reporter said of Dewey's campaign appearances that he "doesn't seem to walk, he coasts out like a man who has been mounted on casters and given a tremendous shove from behind." In his speeches, Dewey worked hard to avoid discussing issues, and he even took time off from electioneering to plan his inauguration.

**Possible Response: The campaign suggested that he was a fighter. Persistent and hardworking, he was not easily discouraged.**

 **America's History Makers**
- Harry S. Truman, pp. 111–112

### ACTIVITY OPTIONS

**INTERDISCIPLINARY LINK: MATHEMATICS** — BLOCK SCHEDULING

**ANALYZING ELECTION RETURNS**

**Class Time** 30 minutes

**Task** Solving mathematical problems about the 1948 election

**Purpose** To analyze Truman's victory in the election of 1948

**Supplies Needed**
- Calculators

**Activity** Give students these data on the 1948 election:

| *Candidate* | *Popular Vote* | *Electoral Vote* |
|---|---|---|
| Truman | 24,105,812 | 303 |
| Dewey | 21,970,065 | 189 |
| Thurmond | 1,169,021 | 39 |
| Wallace | 1,157,172 | 0 |

What percentage of the popular and electoral vote might Truman have won if neither third-party candidate had run and these voters had supported Truman? *(popular 54.6%, electoral 64.4%)*

**INSTRUCT: OBJECTIVE** 

**Origins of the Cold War/ Containing Communism Abroad**

Key Questions

- What issue divided the Western democracies and the Soviet Union immediately after the war?
- How was the issue resolved?
- What steps did Truman take to stop the spread of communism?

 **In-Depth Resources: Unit 8**

- Geography Application: Communist Governments After World War II, pp. 69–70

## MORE ABOUT . . .

**Truman and Stalin**

President Truman believed the best way to deal with Stalin was to be friendly but firm. Aside from the political future of Eastern Europe, another major point of conflict between the United States and the Soviets was the U.S. monopoly on atomic power. After negotiations failed between the Soviets and the Americans over international control of atomic energy, Soviet fear and mistrust increased.

## HISTORY FROM VISUALS

**Reading the Map** Point out the location of Berlin and the inset map showing the division of Berlin into sectors. Have students name the country in which Berlin is located. **Answer** East Germany. What three countries controlled West Berlin? **Answer** United States, France, Britain. What Warsaw Pact nation stood between East Germany and the Soviet Union? **Answer** Poland

**Extension** Have students make a chart listing the nations that belong to NATO today and the year in which each became a member.

 **Outline Map Activities**

- Europe After World War II, pp. 55–56

## 3 Origins of the Cold War

After World War II, the capitalist Western democracies came into increasing conflict with the communist Soviet Union. Their differing economic and political systems resulted in misunderstandings. During the war, the Western democracies were allied with the Soviet Union. They were united in the struggle to defeat Nazi Germany. However, as victory grew nearer, the West and the Soviet Union distrusted each other.

The most difficult issue was the political future of Eastern Europe. In the final battles of the war, the Soviets freed Eastern European states from Nazi rule. Then Soviet forces occupied those states, including the eastern sector of Germany. The Soviet leader Joseph Stalin promised free elections to the nations of Eastern Europe. However, when the war ended, Stalin installed pro-Soviet governments throughout Eastern Europe.

Stalin feared that free elections in Eastern Europe might result in the election of anti-Soviet governments on its borders. The Western democracies saw Stalin's occupation of Eastern Europe differently. President Truman believed that Stalin intended to spread communism worldwide.

Truman was determined to protect Western Europe from the threat of Soviet expansion. As the gap between the Soviet Union and the Western democracies widened, tensions developed. The resulting **Cold War** was a conflict that pitted the United States against the Soviet Union. The two nations never directly confronted each other on the battlefield. However, the threat of deadly conflict lasted for decades.

**B. Answer** Stalin saw Eastern Europe as a buffer against invasion from the West. The Western democracies believed Stalin was spreading communism in Europe.

*Reading*History

**B. Comparing and Contrasting** How did the Soviet Union and the West view Eastern Europe?

**Skillbuilder Answers**
1. Portugal
2. West Germany, Greece, Turkey

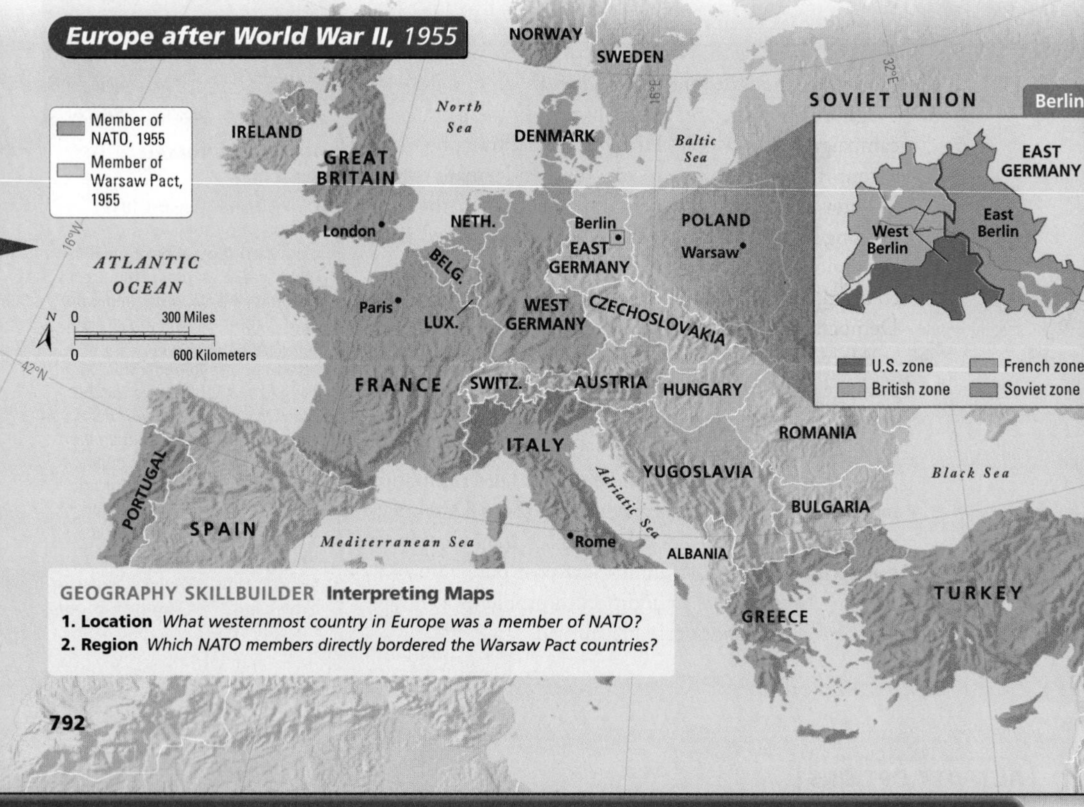


**GEOGRAPHY SKILLBUILDER Interpreting Maps**
1. **Location** *What westernmost country in Europe was a member of NATO?*
2. **Region** *Which NATO members directly bordered the Warsaw Pact countries?*

792

## ACTIVITY OPTIONS

## INDIVIDUAL NEEDS

### STUDENTS ACQUIRING ENGLISH/ESL

**Understanding a Metaphor** Direct students to the quotation by Winston Churchill on page 793. Read the quotation aloud and explain that "iron curtain" is a metaphor for the policy of isolation developed by the Soviet Union. Through this policy, the Soviet Union cut itself and Eastern Europe off from the noncommunist countries of the world. Trade, travel, and communication were strictly limited. As a result, the countries on either side of the "curtain" had little contact. Explain or elicit from students why Churchill's phrase *iron curtain* came to represent this political situation. As students read the chapter, have them note the different ways in which the countries on opposite sides of the iron curtain developed.

## Containing Communism Abroad

As tensions between the United States and the Soviet Union were increasing, Britain's Winston Churchill visited the United States in 1946. He warned the world of Soviet aims.

*A VOICE FROM THE PAST*

From Stettin in the Baltic to Trieste in the Adriatic, an iron curtain has descended across the continent. Behind that line lie all the . . . states of Central and Eastern Europe. . . . All these . . . populations . . . lie in the Soviet sphere and all are subject . . . not only to Soviet influence but to . . . increasing . . . control from Moscow.

**Winston Churchill,** "Iron Curtain" speech, Fulton, Missouri

*"An iron curtain has descended across the continent."*
Winston Churchill

**Background**
Truman's containment policy was first announced in 1947 in response to Soviet pressure on Greece and Turkey.

The Truman Administration's main strategy in the Cold War was its containment policy. The goal of **containment** was to stop the spread of communism. This meant that the United States would work in military and nonmilitary ways to contain communism. Next, Truman announced the **Truman Doctrine,** which promised aid to people struggling to resist threats to democratic freedom.

In 1948, there was alarm over communist control of Eastern Europe. This led to formation of the North Atlantic Treaty Organization (NATO). The **NATO** alliance included the United States, Canada, and ten Western European nations. In response, the Soviet Union and Eastern European nations formed the Warsaw Pact (see map on page 792).

### MORE ABOUT . . .

**The Truman Doctrine**

The immediate cause for the Truman Doctrine was a civil war in Greece in which Communist-backed rebels fought the conservative government. Truman believed that the Soviets were supporting the Greek rebels. He declared, "If Greece should fall under the control of an armed minority . . . confusion and disorder might well spread throughout the entire Middle East."

## 4 Marshall Plan and Berlin Airlift

Hoping to prevent the spread of communism, the United States came up with a plan to revive the war-torn economies of Europe. The plan was named for Truman's Secretary of State, George C. Marshall. The **Marshall Plan** offered $13 billion in aid to western and southern Europe. The plan helped the nations of Europe rebuild.

**Reading History**
**C. Reading a Map** Use the map on page 792 to see how Berlin was divided among the four nations.

The European nation in which the Cold War almost turned hot was Germany. In June of 1945, the Allies had agreed to a temporary division of Germany into four zones. These were controlled by the Soviet Union, France, Great Britain, and the United States. The Western powers merged their zones and made plans to unite them as West Germany. Stalin feared a united Germany might threaten the Soviet Union.

Berlin, Germany's former capital, lay within the eastern zone, still held by the Soviet Union. Like Germany, it too had been divided into East and West Berlin. In 1948, Stalin hoped to force the Western powers to abandon the city. His forces blocked access to Berlin.

Truman responded by approving a huge airlift of food, fuel, and equipment into the city. For nearly a year,

An American plane brings supplies to Berlin during the airlift.

793

### INSTRUCT: OBJECTIVE 

**Marshall Plan and Berlin Airlift/ Fear of Communism at Home**

Key Questions
- What was the goal of the Marshall Plan?
- How did Truman respond to the Soviet blockade of Berlin, and did his initiative succeed?
- How was fear of communism expressed in the United States during the early 1950s?

 **America's History Makers**
- George C. Marshall, pp. 113–114

### MORE ABOUT . . .

**Berlin Blockade and Airlift**

The Berlin blockade failed to have the effect the Soviets had hoped for. Instead of slowing the unification of the French, British, and American zones, it spurred the Western powers to integrate their zones more rapidly. In 1949, a constitution was drafted for a West German government, and the Federal Republic of Germany came into being in May 1949. During the 11 months of the Berlin airlift, U.S. and British planes delivered 2.3 million tons of food, fuel, machinery, and other supplies to West Berlin at a cost of $224 million.

 **Geography Transparency GT28**
- Berlin Airlift, 1948–1949

### ACTIVITY OPTIONS

**INTERDISCIPLINARY LINK: LANGUAGE ARTS**

 BLOCK SCHEDULING

**COLD WAR DECISION MAKING**

**Class Time** One class period

**Task** Writing an essay on a Cold War policy decision

**Purpose** To analyze foreign policy decisions of the Truman administration

**Supplies Needed**
- Reference materials on the Truman Doctrine, NATO, Marshall Plan, and Berlin blockade and airlift
- Internet access

**Activity** Divide students into four groups and tell them that they are foreign policy advisers to President Truman. Assign each group one of these questions: (a) Should the United States issue the Truman Doctrine? (b) join NATO? (c) aid war-torn Europe? (d) break the Berlin blockade? Have each group brainstorm the positive and negative consequences of different responses to their question. Then have each group prepare a position paper for Truman outlining alternatives, risks, and recommendations for action.

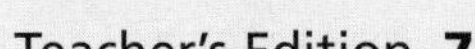

## MORE ABOUT . . .

**The Rosenbergs**
Julius and Ethel Rosenberg were the first U.S. civilians to be put to death for espionage. They were convicted of attempting to pass data on nuclear weapons to the Soviets. The secret information was given to the Rosenbergs by Ethel's brother, David Greenglass, who worked as a machinist at the atomic bomb project at Los Alamos, New Mexico. Ethel's brother received 15 years in prison after he agreed to become the government's chief witness against his sister and her husband.

**In-Depth Resources: Unit 8**
- Literature Selection: The Threat of Nuclear War, pp. 73–75

## ASSESS & RETEACH

**Setting the Stage** Have students fill in information about domestic and foreign issues under President Truman on the chapter graphic organizer.

**Formal Assessment**
- Section Quiz, p. 406

**Critical Thinking Transparency CT82**
- Setting the Stage

### RETEACHING ACTIVITY

Working in pairs, have students create outlines of the section and use their outlines to write a summary of Section 1.

**In-Depth Resources: Unit 8**
- Reteaching Activity, p. 76

Ethel and Julius Rosenberg were executed despite numerous pleas to spare their lives.

U.S. and British cargo planes made 275,000 flights into Berlin. They carried supplies to the city's residents. In 1949, Stalin called off the blockade. By May 1949, Germany had been divided into communist East Germany and democratic West Germany.

## Fear of Communism at Home

After World War II, a growing number of Americans feared that communism would gain strength within the United States. In part this was a response to the Soviet occupation of Eastern Europe. At first, attention focused on Americans who belonged to the U.S. Communist party who, it was feared, might spy for Russia.

Two famous spy trials made such fears believable. Alger Hiss was a former State Department official. He was accused of passing military information to the Soviet Union. Tried for lying under oath, he was sentenced to five years in prison in 1950. Ethel and Julius Rosenberg were members of the American Communist party. In 1951, they were convicted of passing atomic secrets to the Russians. They were executed in 1953.

Truman fought Republican charges that his administration was soft on communism. He issued an executive order requiring 3 million government workers to undergo loyalty checks. Federal workers who objected to signing loyalty oaths lost their jobs. Between 1947 and 1951, loyalty boards forced over 3,000 government workers to resign.

The anticommunist crusade gave new life to the House Un-American Activities Committee (HUAC). In 1947, HUAC began targeting actors, directors, and writers in the movie industry for suspected communist ties. Within the entertainment industry, lists of names circulated among the Hollywood movie studios. These were blacklists—unofficial lists of people thought to be communists. The careers of the people on these lists were ruined. As you will read in the next section, fear of communism dominated American life in the early 1950s.

### Section 1 Assessment

**1. Terms & Names**
**Identify:**
- Harry S. Truman
- Fair Deal
- Cold War
- containment
- Truman Doctrine
- NATO
- Marshall Plan

**2. Taking Notes**
In a chart, explain the goals of these Cold War programs.

| Program | Goal |
|---|---|
| Containment policy | |
| Truman Doctrine | |
| Marshall Plan | |
| NATO | |

**3. Main Ideas**
a. Why was inflation a concern in the early postwar period?
b. What were the causes of the Cold War?
c. Why did the United States experience fear of communism after the war?

**4. Critical Thinking**
**Forming Opinions** Do you think an exaggerated fear of communism could occur again? Explain.
**THINK ABOUT**
- relations between the United States and Russia today
- American attitudes toward opposing views
- beliefs about communism

**ACTIVITY OPTIONS**
**LANGUAGE ARTS / ART**
Imagine that you were a child in Berlin during the airlift. Write a **letter** to a pen pal in the United States, or draw a **picture** describing your experiences.



### Section 1 Assessment

**1. Terms & Names**
**Harry S. Truman,** p. 790
**Fair Deal,** p. 791
**Cold War,** p. 792
**containment,** p. 793
**Truman Doctrine,** p. 793
**NATO,** p. 793
**Marshall Plan,** p. 793

**2. Taking Notes**
Containment policy: stop spread of communism; Truman Doctrine: help people fight for democracy; Marshall Plan: help Western Europe rebuild; NATO: form military alliance to defend Western Europe

**3. Main Ideas**
**a.** Prices skyrocketed because too much money was chasing too few goods. **b.** various rivalries between the Soviet Union and the United States **c.** because of Soviet occupation of Eastern Europe and a concern that members of the Communist Party would spy for Russia

**4. Critical Thinking**
Answers will vary. Some students may say yes because people are still intolerant of the unknown, others may say no because we have learned from history.

**ACTIVITY OPTIONS**

**Alternative Assessment**
- Rubrics for a letter, 4.3
- Rubrics for a picture, 1.3

# 2 The Korean War and McCarthyism

**TERMS & NAMES**
Mao Zedong
38th parallel
Korean War
Joseph McCarthy
brinksmanship
arms race
H-bomb
space race

**MAIN IDEA**

The Cold War and the Korean War produced a far-reaching form of anticommunism.

**WHY IT MATTERS NOW**

Reckless charges damaged personal lives and set up a climate of suspicion that affected Americans for years.

## ONE AMERICAN'S STORY

**John Stewart Service was one of thousands of Americans whose lives were turned upside down by the anticommunism of the postwar era. Service was born in China of missionary parents. He spent his childhood and teenage years there before coming to the United States for college. His firsthand knowledge of China made him a respected member of the Foreign Service. As a China expert, he warned the State Department of the weakness of China's anticommunist Nationalist party.**

**In 1949, the Communists took control of China. Angry Americans wanted someone to blame. Service's good advice was forgotten. He became one of the first State Department officials blamed for the loss of China to the Communists. Although a loyalty board cleared him of charges of disloyalty, he lost his job. The Supreme Court later ruled that he had been unfairly dismissed. As you will read in this section, many innocent Americans suffered a similar fate.**

John Stewart Service defends himself before the Senate Foreign Relations Committee against charges that he worked with Communists.

## 1 Origins of the Korean War

In September 1949, the Communists defeated the anticommunist Nationalists in a civil war in China. The Nationalists were supported by the United States. **Mao Zedong** became head of the new Communist state. The Nationalist government, headed by Chiang Kai-shek, fled to the island of Taiwan, formerly Formosa, off the coast of the Chinese mainland. Many Americans were shocked by the fall of the Nationalist government. They viewed the takeover as part of a Communist plot to rule the world. They blamed the State Department for failing to stop the Communist revolution. American fear of communism grew. Events in Korea contributed to this fear.

Korea had been a Japanese colony for half a century when Japan surrendered to the Allies at the end of World War II. In 1945, Soviet troops occupied Korea north of the **38th parallel,** or line of latitude. American forces took control south of this line. Aided by the Soviets, a Communist government came to power in North Korea. In South Korea, a noncommunist leader supported by the United States governed.





## SECTION OBJECTIVES

1. To explain how the Korean War began
2. To trace the course of the Korean War through the cease-fire
3. To evaluate the anticommunist campaign of Joseph McCarthy
4. To describe the Cold War policies of President Eisenhower

**SKILLBUILDER**
Interpreting Maps: Movement, Region, p. 796

**CRITICAL THINKING**
Making Inferences, p. 797
Summarizing, p. 798
Drawing Conclusions, p. 799

## FOCUS & MOTIVATE

### 5-MINUTE WARM-UP

**Recognizing Effects** These questions focus on the Korean War.

1. Look at the map on page 796. Where is the prewar boundary between North and South Korea?
2. Where is the armistice line? How much territory changed hands?

 **Warm-Up Transparency WT28**

## INSTRUCT

### INSTRUCT: OBJECTIVE 1

**Origins of the Korean War/ Fighting Breaks Out in Korea**

Key Questions
- Why did U.S. fear of communism increase after Mao Zedong came to power?
- How did the Korean War begin?
- What role did the United Nations play?

 **In-Depth Resources: Unit 8**
- Guided Reading, p. 65
- Building Vocabulary, p. 67

 **Reading Study Guide** (Spanish and English), pp. 273–274

## RECOMMENDED RESOURCES

 **In-Depth Resources: Unit 8**
- Guided Reading, p. 65
- Building Vocabulary, p. 67
- Primary Source: A Speech by Margaret Chase Smith, p. 71
- Reteaching Activity, p. 77

 **Reading Study Guide** (Spanish and English), pp. 273–274

**Formal Assessment**
- Section Quiz, p. 407

**Alternative Assessment**
- Rubrics, 4.2
- Rubrics, 1.10

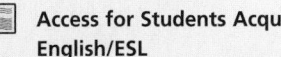

 **Access for Students Acquiring English/ESL**
- Guided Reading, p. 188

Technology Resources

 **Humanities Transparency HT55**
- Political Cartoon: "I can't do this to me"

 **Critical Thinking Transparency CT83**
- Cause and Effect: The Cold War

 **Electronic Teacher Tools with Test Maker**

 **ClassZone**
www.mcdougallittell.com

## MORE ABOUT . . .

**The Inchon Landing**

At first, the Joint Chiefs of Staff refused MacArthur's request for a landing at Inchon, but he persisted. He said, "Inchon will succeed. And it will save 100,000 lives." Six days later he got the go-ahead. The landing surprised the North Koreans and enabled the UN forces to cut enemy supply lines. UN forces attacked the North Korean army from both north and south, taking more than 125,000 prisoners.

## Fighting Breaks Out in Korea

In June 1950, North Korean forces crossed the 38th parallel into South Korea. The conflict that followed became known as the **Korean War.** President Truman viewed Korea as a test case for his containment policy. He responded promptly. The United States appealed to the United Nations (UN) to stop the Communist move into South Korea. Sixteen nations provided soldiers for a UN force. However, U.S. troops made up most of the force and did most of the fighting. General Douglas MacArthur, former World War II hero in the Pacific, served as commander of all UN forces.

In early fighting, the North Koreans pushed the South Koreans back almost to Pusan. This city was on the southeastern tip of the Korean peninsula. MacArthur reversed the situation by landing his troops at Inchon. This was a port city behind the North Korean lines. It was a daring, dangerous plan, but it worked.

Squeezed between enemy troops coming at them from the north and south, the North Koreans soon retreated across the 38th parallel. General MacArthur requested permission of his superiors to pursue the enemy into North Korea. The UN and President Truman agreed. The president hoped the invasion might lead to a reunion of the two Koreas. The UN forces pushed northward beyond the 38th parallel (latitude) toward the Yalu

Skillbuilder Answers
1. Communist forces
2. South Korea

## HISTORY FROM VISUALS

**Reading the Maps** Point out the title of the map series and the titles of each individual map. Ask students what natural feature forms the border between China and North Korea. **Answer** Yalu River. How many times did Seoul change hands during the war? **Answer** four. What evidence can you find that the war ended in a stalemate? **Possible Response** The armistice line is very close to the prewar boundary.

**Extension** Have students research one battle of the Korean War and report to the class on where and when it was fought and its outcome.

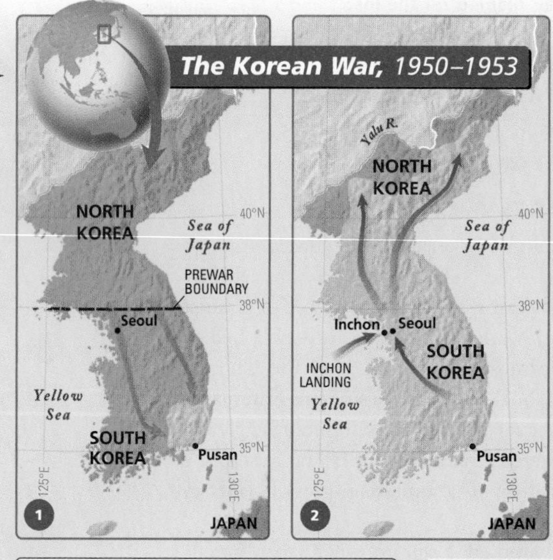


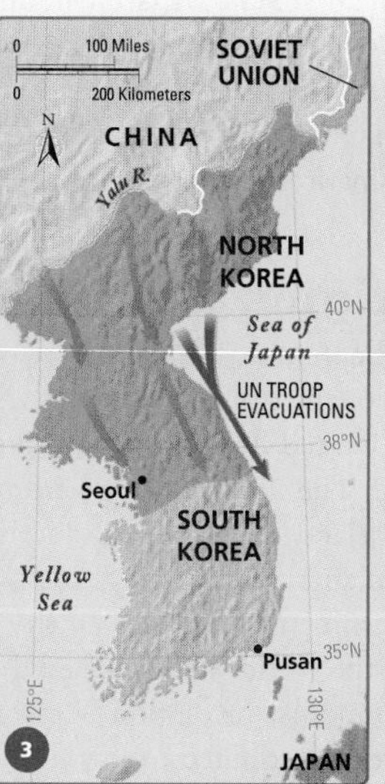

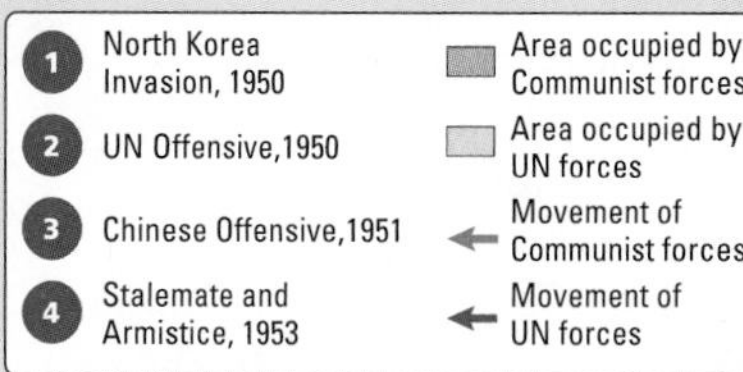


**GEOGRAPHY SKILLBUILDER Interpreting Maps**

1. **Movement** *In map 1, which forces moved south almost to Pusan?*
2. **Region** *Compare the prewar boundary in map 1 with the armistice line in map 4. Which side gained slightly more territory?*

796

## ACTIVITY OPTIONS

## INDIVIDUAL NEEDS

### LESS PROFICIENT READERS

**Finding Main Ideas** To help students understand material on the course of the Korean War, copy the chart at the right onto the board. Read aloud the main ideas as you preview the section and have students copy the chart. Then ask them to write details under each main idea as they read the chart.

| The Origins of the Korean War | Fighting the War | China's Role in the War | The Frustrating End of the War |
|---|---|---|---|
| | | | |

River, the boundary separating China from North Korea. The Chinese warned them to stop.

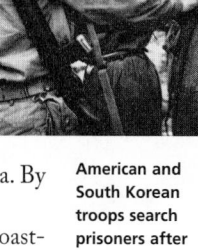

American and South Korean troops search prisoners after the Inchon landing.

## 2 China Enters the Conflict

Communist China saw the movement of UN forces into North Korea as a threat to China's security. Chinese leaders warned that a further advance would force them to enter the war. Ignoring this warning, UN forces pushed on toward the Yalu River. On November 25, 1950, hundreds of thousands of Chinese Communist troops attacked in human waves across the Yalu River into North Korea. They drove UN troops back to South Korea. By early 1951, the two sides were deadlocked along the 38th parallel.

*Reading*History
**A. Reading a Map** Find the 38th parallel on the maps on page 796. Notice the movement of communist and UN forces back and forth across this parallel.

General MacArthur requested permission to blockade China's coastline and bomb China. Truman refused. The president feared that such action would draw the Soviet Union in and make the conflict a world war. The general went over the president's head to win support for his war aims. He spoke and wrote to newspaper and magazine publishers. He also wrote to Republican leaders.

As president, Truman was commander-in-chief of the armed forces. He viewed MacArthur's public criticism of his orders as undermining civilian control of the military. As a result, Truman fired MacArthur and ordered him home. When MacArthur returned to the United States, his admirers treated him as a hero. His farewell speech to Congress won the sympathy of many. "I now close my military career and just fade away—an old soldier who tried to do his duty as God gave him the light to see that duty. Good-bye." Despite support for MacArthur, Truman refused to back down. Most Americans came to agree with the president's actions.

*Reading*History
**B. Making Inferences** What effect might MacArthur's actions have had on the idea of civilian control of the military?
**B. Answer** Most students will probably think that MacArthur's actions were likely to undermine civilian control.

## War Ends in Stalemate

As the war dragged on, it became more unpopular. In July 1951, Truman accepted a Soviet suggestion that truce talks begin. The talks dragged on for two years. They continued through the 1952 presidential campaign. When Truman decided not to run again, the Democrats chose Illinois governor Adlai Stevenson as their candidate. The Republicans picked World War II hero General Dwight D. Eisenhower. Ike, as voters liked to call him, criticized the unpopular war. He promised to go to Korea to seek a speedy end to the conflict.

Eisenhower made good on his promise when he won a landslide victory. During talks with the North Koreans and Chinese, he agreed to compromise to end the war. But he also warned privately that he was ready to use nuclear weapons and carry the war into China. A cease-fire ended the fighting in July 1953. The two Koreas were left more or less where they had been in 1950 with a border near the 38th parallel. Communism had been contained in Korea. However, Americans felt frustrated by the indecisive war. Some politicians selfishly made use of this frustration.



**INSTRUCT: OBJECTIVE 2**

**China Enters the Conflict/ War Ends in Stalemate**

Key Questions
- When and why did China enter the Korean War?
- Why did Truman fire MacArthur?
- What were the terms of the 1953 cease-fire?

**MORE ABOUT . . .**

**Douglas MacArthur**

MacArthur was self-centered and dramatic. One historian has written, "His favorite pronoun was the first person." Truman had little use for MacArthur. Before the Korean War began, Truman had written in a memo, "And what to do with Mr. Prima Donna, Brass Hat, Five Star MacArthur." After Truman fired him, conservative Republicans tried in three subsequent elections to make MacArthur the Republican candidate for president. In 1952, MacArthur became chairman of the board for the Remington Rand Corporation.

**ACTIVITY OPTIONS**

**MULTIPLE LEARNING STYLES: VISUAL**

 **BLOCK SCHEDULING**

**POLITICAL CARTOONS**

**Class Time** One class period

**Task** Creating a series of cartoons showing changes in American public opinion on the Korean War

**Purpose** To analyze how American attitudes toward the war in Korea changed over time

**Supplies Needed**
- Reference materials on the Korean War and Truman's firing of MacArthur
- Posterboard
- Art supplies

**Activity** Have students draw cartoons showing American attitudes toward the war at different time periods. Some students might draw cartoons about the war in 1950, during the North Korean invasion and the UN landing at Inchon; in 1951, after the Chinese offensive or Truman's firing of MacArthur; or in 1952–1953, after the stalemate, armistice, or Ike's election. Select cartoons for display and discuss how each cartoonist views the war and how he or she makes that point of view known in the cartoon.

### INSTRUCT: OBJECTIVE 

**McCarthy and Communism**

Key Questions

- How did Joseph McCarthy exploit Americans' fears of communism?
- How were Americans affected by McCarthyism?
- What events led to McCarthy's loss of influence?

 **In-Depth Resources: Unit 8**

- Primary Source: A Speech by Margaret Chase Smith, p. 71

### MORE ABOUT . . .

**Joseph McCarthy**

McCarthy was a little-known senator until he charged the State Department with harboring Communists. Although he failed to name even one "card-carrying Communist" working for the federal government, he gained supporters among Americans discouraged by Communist expansion in Eastern Europe and China. During the 36-day Army-McCarthy hearings, many Americans saw McCarthy on television. His brutal questioning of witnesses led to public disgust. He was condemned by the Senate for conduct "contrary to Senate traditions."

 **Humanities Transparency HT55**

- Political Cartoon: "I can't do this to me"

### INSTRUCT: OBJECTIVE 

**Eisenhower and the Cold War**

Key Questions

- In what ways was John Foster Dulles's approach to the Cold War different from Truman's?
- What started the arms race? the space race?
- How did the May 1960 U-2 incident affect U.S.-Soviet relations?

 **Critical Thinking Transparency CT83**

- Cause and Effect: The Cold War

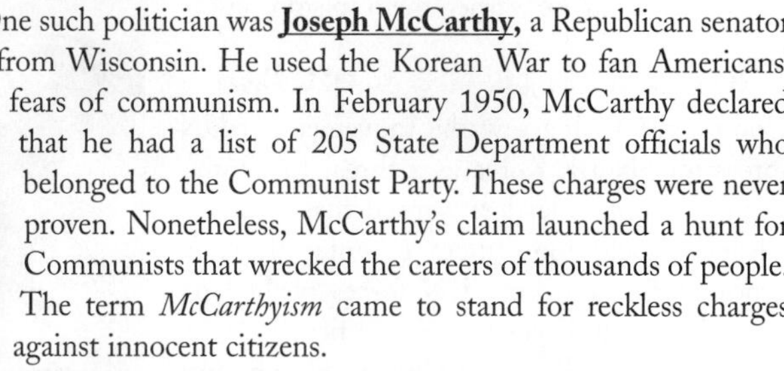

Senator Joseph McCarthy during the 1954 Army-McCarthy hearings

## 3 McCarthy and Communism

One such politician was **Joseph McCarthy**, a Republican senator from Wisconsin. He used the Korean War to fan Americans' fears of communism. In February 1950, McCarthy declared that he had a list of 205 State Department officials who belonged to the Communist Party. These charges were never proven. Nonetheless, McCarthy's claim launched a hunt for Communists that wrecked the careers of thousands of people. The term *McCarthyism* came to stand for reckless charges against innocent citizens.

In the spring of 1954, the Senate held hearings. During these nationally televised Army-McCarthy hearings, McCarthy accused the U.S. Army of "coddling Communists." Army spokesmen then charged McCarthy's staff with improper conduct. McCarthy responded with unsupported charges against a young lawyer helping to represent the Army. Joseph Welch, the Army counsel, spoke out against McCarthy.

*A VOICE FROM THE PAST*

Until this moment, Senator, I think I never really gauged your cruelty or your recklessness. . . . Senator. You have done enough. Have you no sense of decency, sir, at long last? Have you left no sense of decency?

**Joseph Welch,** Army-McCarthy hearings, April 22, 1954

Americans watching the exchange between McCarthy and Welch were shocked by McCarthy's conduct. After the Senate issued a statement censuring, or criticizing, his conduct, he faded from public view.

*Reading* **History**

**C. Summarizing** What were some of McCarthy's charges?

**C. Possible Answer** State Department officials were Communists; U.S. Army coddled Communists; accused individuals of being Communists

## 4 Eisenhower and the Cold War

Like Truman, President Eisenhower waged the Cold War. Eisenhower's Secretary of State was John Foster Dulles. Dulles rejected Truman's containment policy. He favored a more aggressive stand. He urged the overthrow of Communist governments. In 1956, Dulles announced that the United States would go to the brink of war to combat communism. This approach was known as **brinksmanship.**

In August 1949, Americans learned that the Soviet Union had produced an atomic bomb, in part by using information stolen by Soviet spies. The two superpowers were soon locked in an **arms race**, developing weapons with more destructive power. In 1952, the United States built a hydrogen bomb, or **H-bomb.** Three years later the Soviets tested their H-bomb. Fear led both sides to build up huge nuclear stockpiles.

In the 1950s, both the United States and the Soviet Union helped allies and weakened enemies around the world. In 1953 in Iran, the U.S. government's Central Intelligence Agency (CIA) helped topple a leader whom they thought might seek Soviet aid. In 1954, the CIA trained an army that succeeded in overthrowing Guatemala's President Jacobo Arbenz Guzmán. The United States believed he favored communism.



### ACTIVITY OPTIONS

**INTERDISCIPLINARY LINK: SCIENCE**

 BLOCK SCHEDULING

**THE SPACE RACE**

**Class Time** One class period

**Task** Creating an illustrated time line showing scientific advances in space exploration between 1957 and the present

**Purpose** To identify milestones in the exploration of space

**Supplies Needed**

- Reference materials on space exploration
- Internet access for additional resources
- Oversized sheets of art paper, paints, pencils, and markers

**Activity** Divide students into five groups. Assign each group a ten-year period from 1957 to the present. Using encyclopedias and other reference materials, have groups make illustrated time lines showing key achievements in space research during their decade. For each event, have groups prepare a drawing and caption that describes the achievement and the country or countries with which it was associated. Attach completed time lines in chronological order for classroom display. Then discuss how competition encouraged scientific breakthroughs and how more recent cooperation has affected space exploration.

During Eisenhower's presidency, the Suez Canal in Egypt, which connected the Mediterranean Sea and the Red Sea, was at the center of another Cold War conflict. In 1955, Egypt's ties with the Soviet Union angered Britain and the United States. The two Western powers withdrew aid to Egypt. Gamal Abdel Nasser, Egypt's leader, reacted by seizing the canal, which was owned by France and Britain. France, Britain, and Israel jointly attacked Egypt. The Soviet Union threatened to support Egypt. The United States, along with the Soviets and the rest of the UN, pressured France, Britain, and Israel to withdraw from Egypt. The UN imposed a cease-fire.

In 1957, the superpowers began a **space race.** The Soviet Union stunned the world by launching the world's first space satellite. They sent *Sputnik* into orbit around the earth. This meant that the Soviet Union had a missile powerful enough to reach the United States. American scientists raced to launch a satellite. Congress set aside billions of dollars for space research.

Eisenhower suggested easing tensions through face-to-face talks. A setback to such efforts occurred in May 1960. The president was to meet in Paris with Soviet Premier Nikita Khrushchev. Two weeks before the meeting, the Soviets shot down an American U-2 plane. The spy plane had been flying over the Soviet Union. Eisenhower denied the aircraft was a spy plane until the pilot was captured. Khrushchev demanded an apology. When the president refused, the talks collapsed. Meanwhile, America was changing at home, as you will read in the next section.

## Connections TO SCIENCE

**SPUTNIK**

The 184-pound *Sputnik 1* (shown below), whose name means "traveling companion," was the first man-made object to orbit the Earth. Circling every 96 minutes, it remained in orbit until early 1958. *Sputnik 2* carried a dog into space.

In 1961, the Soviet Union sent Yuri Gagarin into space to orbit the earth. The Americans lagged behind because the rockets that carried U.S. satellites were smaller and less powerful. The early Soviet lead disappeared, however, as American scientists and engineers found ways to improve rocket design, construction, and testing.

## Section 2 Assessment

**1. Terms & Names**

Identify:
- Mao Zedong
- 38th parallel
- Korean War
- Joseph McCarthy
- brinksmanship
- arms race
- H-bomb
- space race

**2. Taking Notes**

Create a time line of up to five events that played a part in the Korean War from its beginning to end.

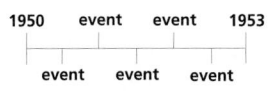

1950 — event — event — 1953
event — event — event

Which event do you think was most important? Why?

**3. Main Ideas**

a. Why did war break out in Korea? How did it end?

b. Why was McCarthy able to wield so much power during the 1950s?

c. How did Eisenhower's approach to the Cold War differ from Truman's?

**4. Critical Thinking**

Drawing Conclusions

How was U.S. involvement in Korea an example of the Truman Doctrine in action?

THINK ABOUT
- U.S. concerns about North Korean leadership
- U.S. goals for ending conflict
- the conflict's outcome

**ACTIVITY OPTIONS**

SCIENCE
ART

Research the problems of putting a satellite in orbit. Prepare a **report** explaining how these problems were solved, or draw a **design** of a rocket.





### CRITICAL THINKING ACTIVITY

**Comparing and Contrasting** Have students compare and contrast Truman's and Eisenhower's views on the Cold War. In what ways were Truman's containment policy and Dulles's brinksmanship approach different? How were they alike? Have students use a Venn diagram to compare the policies.

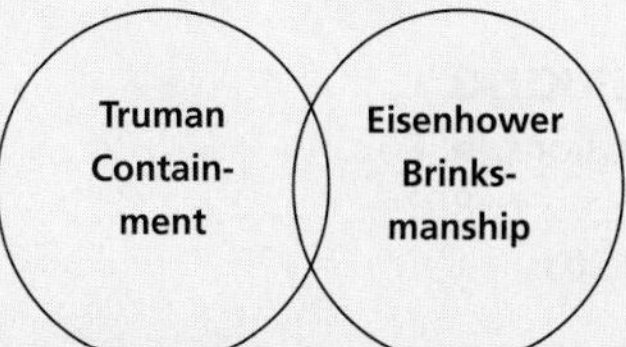


**Class Time** 10 minutes

### Connections TO *SCIENCE*

***Sputnik***

When *Sputnik 2* rocketed a dog named Laika into orbit, it became the first living creature to travel in space. Laika's safe return to Earth proved that animals could survive the effects of microgravity, or near weightlessness. Later *Sputnik* missions used animal passengers to test life-support systems.

## ASSESS & RETEACH

**Setting the Stage** Have students add information on the Korean War, McCarthyism, and Eisenhower and the Cold War to the chapter graphic organizer.

**Formal Assessment**
- Section Quiz, p. 407

### RETEACHING ACTIVITY

Have each student make a chart showing the causes and effects of the Korean War. Have them pick one cause and describe how it led to the conflict.

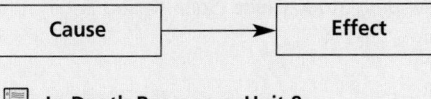

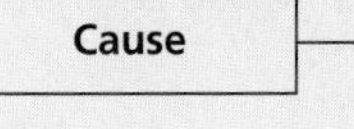

**In-Depth Resources: Unit 8**
- Reteaching Activity, p. 77

## Section 2 Assessment

**1. Terms & Names**

**Mao Zedong,** p. 795
**38th parallel,** p. 795
**Korean War,** p. 796
**Joseph McCarthy,** p. 798
**brinksmanship,** p. 798
**arms race,** p. 798
**H-bomb,** p. 798
**space race,** p. 799

**2. Taking Notes**

June 1950: North Korean troops cross 38th parallel; November 1950: Chinese troops enter war; early in 1951: two sides deadlocked; July 1951: truce talks begin; July 1953: cease-fire

Answers will vary.

**3. Main Ideas**

**a.** North Koreans crossed the 38th parallel; the war ended in stalemate and cease-fire. **b.** He played on fears of communism. **c.** Eisenhower allowed his secretary of state to pursue a more aggressive policy toward the Soviet Union called brinksmanship.

**4. Critical Thinking**

The North Korean invasion of South Korea exemplified the Truman Doctrine principle of aid to people struggling to resist threats to their democratic freedoms.

### ACTIVITY OPTIONS

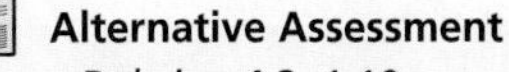

**Alternative Assessment**
- Rubrics, 4.2, 1.10

# 3 The Fifties

**TERMS & NAMES**
suburb
baby boom
sunbelt
rock 'n' roll

| MAIN IDEA | WHY IT MATTERS NOW |
|---|---|
| While the United States was locked in a Cold War, social and economic changes took place in American life. | The American economy and popular culture continue to spread their influence around the globe. |

## SECTION OBJECTIVES

1. To identify the groups that were left out of the prosperity of the 1950s
2. To summarize changes in American life during the 1950s
3. To analyze the American Dream and how pop culture and rock 'n' roll affected society
4. To describe the outcome of the 1960 election

**CRITICAL THINKING**
Drawing Conclusions, p. 802
Making Inferences, p. 803
Contrasting, p. 803

## FOCUS & MOTIVATE

### 5-MINUTE WARM-UP

**Making Inferences** These questions focus on the popular culture of the 1950s.

1. Look at the "Faces of the Fifties" on page 802. How were the careers of these famous people alike?
2. Are today's "famous faces" athletes and entertainers? Explain.

 **Warm-Up Transparency WT28**

## INSTRUCT

### INSTRUCT: OBJECTIVE 1

**The Domestic Scene in the Fifties**
Key Questions
- Where did many poor Americans live in the 1950s?
- Why did emigration from Mexico increase?
- What were some of the Eisenhower administration's domestic programs?

 **In-Depth Resources: Unit 8**
- Guided Reading, p. 66
- Primary Source: from *The Other America* by Michael Harrington, p. 72

 **Reading Study Guide** (Spanish and English), pp. 275–276

## ONE AMERICAN'S STORY

**LaVern Baker was one of many talented African-American artists to play a part in the popular music of the 1950s. Among her best known songs are "Tweedlee Dee," "Jim Dandy," and "See See Rider." As was the case with many other black rhythm-and-blues musicians, her records at first sold mostly to African-American teenagers. White singers covered, or copied, her songs. These remakes became hits. Disk jockeys played them over and over for their white radio audiences. Baker was annoyed that remakes of her songs by white singers outsold her originals. She made the following comment about one such singer.**

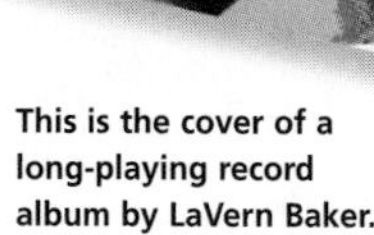

This is the cover of a long-playing record album by LaVern Baker.

*A VOICE FROM THE PAST*

When I went to Australia with Bill Haley, Big Joe Turner, the Platters, and Freddy Bell and the Bellboys, I left her my [flight] insurance policy. I sent it to her with a letter, "Since I'll be away and you won't have anything new to copy, you might as well take this."

**LaVern Baker,** quoted in *USA Today,* March 12, 1997

**In 1990, Baker's importance as a recording artist was confirmed. The Rock and Roll Hall of Fame honored Baker by making her a member. The following section describes social, political, and cultural changes during the 1950s.**

## 1 The Domestic Scene in the Fifties

Not everyone prospered in the 1950s. In 1957, nearly one out of every five Americans lived in poverty. Many of the nation's poorest were in cities. In his book *The Other America* (1962), Michael Harrington called attention to the forgotten poor. They were the people left behind as more well-to-do Americans headed for the **suburbs**—residential areas surrounding a city. Shops and businesses moved to suburbia as well.

Fewer people remained in the city to pay taxes for such services as garbage collection, firefighting, and road repair. Often those most affected by urban decay were African Americans and Latinos. Many could not afford homes in the suburbs.



## RECOMMENDED RESOURCES

 **In-Depth Resources: Unit 8**
- Guided Reading, p. 66
- Building Vocabulary, p. 67
- Primary Source: from *The Other America* by Michael Harrington, p. 72
- Reteaching Activity, p. 78
- Enrichment Activity, p. 79

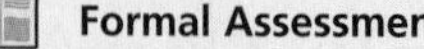

**Reading Study Guide** (Spanish and English), pp. 275–276

**Formal Assessment**
- Section Quiz, p. 408

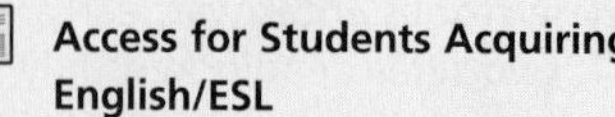

**Alternative Assessment**
- Rubrics, 5.1
- Rubrics, 4.8

**Access for Students Acquiring English/ESL**
- Guided Reading, p. 189

**Technology Resources**

 **Humanities Transparency HT56**
- *After the Prom* by Norman Rockwell

 **Electronic Teacher Tools with Test Maker**

 **ClassZone**
www.mcdougallittell.com

In the 1950s, immigration from Mexico increased greatly. Many people crossed the border illegally. Others came through the government-sponsored *bracero,* or temporary worker, program. The *braceros* found jobs on farms in the Southwest and Midwest. There they often earned low wages and endured difficult living and working conditions.

Vocabulary
***bracero:*** laborer, from the Spanish word *brazo,* which means "arm"

Despite this, when the program ended, many stayed on illegally. Employers took advantage of them. Fearful of being sent back to Mexico, workers were forced to work longer hours for lower pay.

When Eisenhower ran for president, he promised to steer a middle course. Once elected, Eisenhower pleased business leaders and conservatives without upsetting moderates and liberals. Although he disliked big government spending programs, Eisenhower kept most New Deal programs. He agreed to expand Social Security. He increased the minimum wage for workers. He also created the Department of Health, Education, and Welfare. He even backed some new spending. For example, Congress passed the Highway Act of 1956. This act provided $32 billion to build 41,000 miles of highway.

## 2 Changes Sweep America

In the postwar period, Americans began to feel more prosperous. The Depression and World War II had led many couples to put off marrying and starting a family. Now with the economy booming, Americans were getting married and having children. During the 1950s, the United States grew by almost 30 million people. This increase was mostly because of the **baby boom,** a sharp increase in the U.S. birthrate following World War II (from about 1946 through 1961). The number of families with three or four children increased dramatically.

The baby boom also spurred the growth of suburbs. Growing families left crowded city apartments for a house in the suburbs. Irving, Texas, a suburb of Dallas, was typical. In 1950, it had around 2,600 residents. Ten years later, 45,000 people lived there. To serve the suburbs, shopping centers, movie theaters, and restaurants sprouted up on what was once farmland. As suburbs grew, car sales exploded. In the suburbs, owning a car was a necessity. Few buses or other forms of public transportation existed.

In the 1950s, Americans not only moved from city to suburb. They also moved from the north and east to the south and west. The movement of people to the **sunbelt** increased the population of the warmer states of the South and Southwest. In the 1960s, California surpassed New York as the nation's most populous state.

### STRANGE but True

**FROM AUTOBAHN TO INTERSTATE**

In the 1930s, Germany began to build a vast network of limited access, four-lane highways called *autobahns.* Germans believed these roads would have great military value.

During World War II, General Eisenhower saw the German road system firsthand. He was impressed by the way these highways enabled Germans to quickly move troops and supplies. President Eisenhower remembered Germany's *autobahns* when he called on Congress to pass the Highway Act of 1956. This act created the nation's first interstate highway system. A cloverleaf interchange is shown below.

### MORE ABOUT . . .

**Baby Boom**

During the early postwar period, the birthrate went up dramatically. In the Depression years, the birthrate had been as low as 19 births per 1,000 people. By 1950, the rate was 24 births per 1,000 people, an increase of 25 percent. The birthrate remained high throughout the 1950s. However, since the 1960s, the birthrate in the United States has been declining. By 1997, there were 14.6 births per 1,000, a considerable drop from the 1950s baby boom.

### INSTRUCT: OBJECTIVE 

**Changes Sweep America**

Key Questions

- How did the baby boom contribute to the growth of the suburbs?
- How did suburbanization change American transportation?
- What other population shift occurred in the 1950s?

### STRANGE *but* True

**From Autobahn to Interstate**

The interstate system led to critical changes in transportation even before it was finished. Trucks replaced trains as the major cargo carriers. Workers, especially those living in the suburbs, commuted most frequently by car instead of by public transportation. In the 1950s and 1960s, around three-fourths of federal transportation funds were allocated for highway construction. Only 1 percent went to urban mass transit.

### ACTIVITY OPTIONS

**INDIVIDUAL NEEDS: GIFTED AND TALENTED**

**ANALYZING CAUSES AND RECOGNIZING EFFECTS**

**Class Time** One class period

**Task** Making a graphic organizer that shows the effects of major social changes of the 1950s

**Purpose** To analyze the impact of the social changes that took place during the 1950s

**Supplies Needed**

- Reference materials on migration to the suburbs, the sunbelt, and the impact of television on life in the 1950s

**Activity** On the board, list the following social changes of the 1950s: (1) Americans move to the suburbs; (2) Americans move to the sunbelt; (3) The United States experiences a baby boom; (4) TV viewing becomes widespread. Have students make a chart showing the long-term and short-term effects of each change. Then have students pick one change and write a report describing how their lives might be different if this change had not taken place.

 **In-Depth Resources: Unit 8**

- Enrichment Activity, p. 79

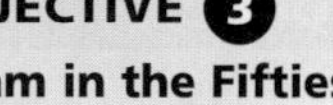

**INSTRUCT: OBJECTIVE 3**

**The American Dream in the Fifties/ Pop Culture and Rock 'n' Roll**

Key Questions
- What was the American Dream for many people in the 1950s?
- Why did some people criticize suburban life?
- How did television and rock 'n' roll change the way people spent their leisure time?
- What characterized the beatniks?

**MORE ABOUT . . .**

**Elvis Presley**

Elvis was driving a truck in Memphis, Tennessee, making $40 a week, when he became a teenage idol. When Presley appeared on *The Ed Sullivan Show,* Sullivan insisted that the TV cameras show Elvis only from the waist up, lest viewers object to his swiveling hips. Presley was well aware of the reasons for his appeal. "My voice," he said, "is just an ordinary voice. What people come to see is how I use it. If I stand still while I'm singing, I'm a dead man. I might as well go back to drivin' a truck."

**MORE ABOUT . . .**

**Lucy and Desi**

In 1952, when *I Love Lucy* was hugely popular, Lucy got pregnant in real life. Although the producers and writers of the show wanted to write the pregnancy into the show, the advertisers took a little convincing. They finally agreed but decided that the word *pregnant* could not be said on the air. So, until she delivered Desi Arnaz, Jr., on January 19, 1953, Lucy was said to be *expecting.* Some 44 million people watched the show about the character Ricky's birth.

***Faces of the Fifties***

◀ **Willie Mays,** the great center fielder, is shown at bat for the San Francisco Giants.

**Elvis Presley** ▶ dressed in a gold suit for the cover of his album ***50,000,000 Elvis Fans Can't Be Wrong*** (RCA).

◀ **Marilyn Monroe** was a popular film star in the 1950s.

**Lucille Ball and Desi Arnaz** starred in the popular television show ***I Love Lucy.*** ▼

## 3 The American Dream in the Fifties

For millions of mainly white Americans, life in the suburbs was the American dream. They were happy to live in affordable, single-family houses. People welcomed the chance to send their children to good schools. Americans shopped in malls where parking was free and easy to find. They didn't care if their houses looked alike. Parents wanted a safe place in which to raise their children.

Many critics worried that Americans were being forced to fit into suburban life. Some argued that in business offices and suburbs, people felt pressured to conform—that is, to agree with the beliefs and ideas of the majority. Yet most Americans seemed willing to conform for the rewards of a comfortable life.

*Reading* **History**

**A. Drawing Conclusions** What might be some of the advantages and disadvantages of fitting in?

A. Answer Advantages might include a sense of belonging to a community and having a comfortable life. Disadvantages might include conformity and materialism.

In the 1950s, popular magazines, films, and television programs praised women for their roles as homemakers. *Time* magazine called women the "keeper[s] of the suburban dream." But not all women felt fulfilled in this role. Some felt bored or isolated. Those working outside the home had limited job choices. Openings were largely in nursing, teaching, and office work.

By the mid-1950s, American industry was churning out goods for consumers to buy. The economy was booming. Americans filled their houses with dishwashers, washing machines, clothes dryers, and vacuum cleaners. The suburban living room or den showed off the family's television, tape recorder, and high-fidelity record player. The garage held a lawn mower. Barbecue equipment and patio furniture filled the backyard. Owning the latest car or appliance came to be a symbol of social standing and success. The advertising industry encouraged consumers to join the spending spree. Television helped advertisers lure buyers to stores and car showrooms.

## Pop Culture and Rock 'n' Roll

In the 1950s, Hollywood cranked out westerns, musicals, and romances. However, movie attendance plummeted as more and more people stayed home to watch TV. By 1960, nine out of ten households owned a set. One of the most popular shows of the decade was the situation comedy (sitcom) *I Love Lucy.* It starred Lucille Ball as the zany wife of bandleader Desi Arnaz. In *Father Knows Best* and many other Fifties sitcoms,



**ACTIVITY OPTIONS**

**INTERDISCIPLINARY LINK: POPULAR CULTURE**

**BLOCK SCHEDULING**

**COMPARING AMERICAN DREAMS**

**Class Time** One class period

**Task** Writing journal entries to describe how a teenager in the 1950s spent leisure time

**Purpose** To analyze how the youth culture has changed since the 1950s

**Supplies Needed**
- Reference materials on popular culture in the 1950s
- Internet access

**Activity** Have student groups research the activities and interests of teenagers in the 1950s. Students can research music, clothing styles, movies, television shows, slang, sports, and fads. Have each group use its information to create a "Week in the Life" journal of a 1950s teenager. After students have shared their journal entries with the class, discuss how the lives of teenagers today are similar to and different from those of teenagers in the 1950s.

*Reading*History

**B. Making Inferences** Do you think such television shows reflected life in the average American family? Why?

B. Answer
Students will probably understand that such shows did not reflect reality but rather presented an ideal.

cheerful moms kept the house spotless. The dads worked to support the family. On *Father Knows Best,* Mr. Anderson exercised kindly but firm control over his children, who seldom rebelled.

Young children watched *Lassie, The Lone Ranger, The Howdy Doody Show,* and the *Mickey Mouse Club.* Their teenage sisters and brothers had fallen head over heels for another form of entertainment—**rock 'n' roll** music. In 1955, Bill Haley and His Comets hit it big with "Rock Around the Clock." By the mid-1950s, Chuck Berry, Little Richard, Fats Domino, and other black musicians held the spotlight with white rockers like Jerry Lee Lewis. But the largest fan club belonged to Elvis Presley. With such songs as "Heartbreak Hotel" and "Don't Be Cruel," he became the king of rock 'n' roll. His onstage bumps and shakes delighted teenagers.

In the mid-1950s, Allen Ginsberg and Jack Kerouac led a group of poets and writers. They protested what they saw as the shallowness and conformity of American society. Known as "beatniks," their followers filled coffeehouses to hear their heated attacks on "square" society. A Democratic presidential candidate, John F. Kennedy, also wanted to shake up the dullness of the Eisenhower years.

## 4 The Election of 1960

The 1960 presidential election was one of the closest in U.S. history. John Fitzgerald Kennedy, Democratic senator from Massachusetts, defeated Richard M. Nixon, Eisenhower's vice president. At age 43, Kennedy was the nation's youngest elected president. He was also the first Catholic president. Kennedy had campaigned to "get this country moving again" after the Eisenhower years. Kennedy and Nixon staged the first televised presidential debates. Kennedy's youthful energy and confidence helped him to win. In the next chapter, you will read about Kennedy's role in setting domestic policy, including civil rights.

### Section 3 Assessment

**1. Terms & Names**

**Identify:**
- suburb
- baby boom
- sunbelt
- rock 'n' roll

**2. Taking Notes**

Create a web like the one below to examine the way life was changing the United States in the 1950s.

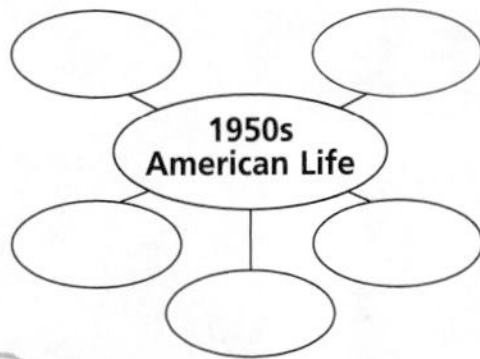


**3. Main Ideas**

a. How did the movement to the suburbs affect the urban poor?

b. What caused the 1950s baby boom? How did the baby boom contribute to suburban growth?

c. How did television affect American life in the 1950s?

**4. Critical Thinking**

**Contrasting** Do you think the American Dream for most Americans today would be the same as it was in the 1950s? Why?

THINK ABOUT
- expectations about suburban/urban living
- changes in transportation and workplace

**ACTIVITY OPTIONS**

**TECHNOLOGY / MUSIC** Research one aspect of music in the 1950s, and either plan a **Web page** to share your information, or write your own **song** that fits this time period.





**MORE ABOUT . . .**

**Rock 'n' Roll**

Many of the first rock 'n' roll musicians were African-American migrants from the rural South who came North during and after World War II. In 1941, blues singer Muddy Waters came to Chicago from rural Mississippi. His band used the electric guitar for traditional country blues. Along with Ray Charles and Chuck Berry, Waters helped create the new musical style known as rhythm and blues, the predecessor of rock 'n' roll.

 **Humanities Transparency HT56**
- *After the Prom* by Norman Rockwell

**INSTRUCT: OBJECTIVE** 

**The Election of 1960**

Key Questions
- What attracted voters to John F. Kennedy in the 1960 election?
- In what ways was Kennedy's election unique?

## ASSESS & RETEACH

**Setting the Stage** Have students complete the chapter graphic organizer.

 **Formal Assessment**
- Section Quiz, p. 408

 **Critical Thinking Transparency CT82**
- Setting the Stage

**RETEACHING ACTIVITY**

Have students write a paragraph describing at least four ways American life changed during the 1950s. Have students pick the change they think has had the greatest impact on American life and explain why.

 **In-Depth Resources: Unit 8**
- Reteaching Activity, p. 78

### Section 3 Assessment

**1. Terms & Names**

**suburb,** p. 800
**baby boom,** p. 801
**sunbelt,** p. 801
**rock 'n' roll,** p. 803

**2. Taking Notes**

suburban living; population shifts; entertainment; economic changes; The Other America

**3. Main Ideas**

**a.** Many urban poor were left behind in decaying neighborhoods.
**b.** returning servicemen eager to start families and the booming U.S. economy; Many of these young families wanted a home of their own.
**c.** Movie attendance declined, and TV shows shaped ideas about family life and acceptable behavior.

**4. Critical Thinking**

Some students might answer that the American Dream is still based on ideas of prosperity and comfort; others may feel that material prosperity isn't enough.

**ACTIVITY OPTIONS**

 **Alternative Assessment**
- Rubrics, 5.1, 4.8

## GEOGRAPHY *in* HISTORY

**OBJECTIVE**
Students will analyze and interpret information from a map to understand the effects of Route 66 on the roadside culture.

 **BLOCK SCHEDULING**

### MORE ABOUT . . .

**Route 66**
Besides "America's Main Street," Route 66 has also been called the "Mother Road" and "The Will Rogers Highway." Unlike almost all other highways of its day, which went east-west or north-south, Route 66 takes a diagonal course. Early on, it was a particularly popular route for truckers because it avoided the harsh winters of Northern highways. In the 1960s, the television series *Route 66,* starring George Maharis, made the highway familiar to millions of Americans.

## INSTRUCT

Key Questions
- Where did Route 66 start and end?
- What was a primary use for Route 66 during the Depression? in the 1940s?
- How did Route 66 change during the 1950s?
- Why is Route 66 largely unused today?

**MAP SKILL QUESTIONS**
What town marked the halfway point on Route 66?

What bodies of water are at either end of the route?

In what states might travelers be most concerned about blizzards and snowstorms blocking the highway?

In what states might travelers be concerned about dust storms and very hot weather?

Why was Route 66 a good all-weather route for travelers?

## GEOGRAPHY *in* HISTORY

**MOVEMENT AND HUMAN-ENVIRONMENT INTERACTION**

# Route 66

America was changing, and few things contributed more to that change than U.S. Highway Route 66. Completed in the summer of 1926, this road connected small towns from Chicago to Los Angeles. Its course across the Heartland enabled farmers to move grain and produce to the big cities.

In the 1930s, farmers escaping the Great Plains' Dust Bowl fled westward along this highway. The first service stations—full-service gas stations—were built along Route 66. In the 1940s, it became an important route for the movement of troops and supplies. By the 1950s, a culture had developed along the highway. This roadside culture included the motor hotel (or motel), roadside diners, and tourist traps.

So many people were on the road that bigger, faster, wider highways were needed. These highways didn't go through the small towns connected by Route 66. With the new superhighways bypassing them, many of the well-known sights along Route 66 vanished.

### ARTIFACT FILE



**America's Main Street**
Many of the towns, tourist traps, and beauty spots along Route 66 became popular destinations. Route 66 was often called "America's Main Street" because it ran through the centers of the small towns it connected.

**Roadside Drive-In**
Roadside food stands such as this one in Seligman, Arizona, were found all along Route 66.

804

### MUSEUM CONNECTIONS

The National Route 66 Museum in Elk City, Oklahoma, has road signs, materials, and memorabilia about people who lived and worked along the road.

Eight Route 66 states—Illinois, Missouri, Kansas, Oklahoma, Texas, New Mexico, Arizona, and California—have nonprofit organizations dedicated to preserving and promoting this historic route. The California Historic Route 66 Association publishes a newsletter and a guide to the route in California. Most of these associations have Internet Web sites.

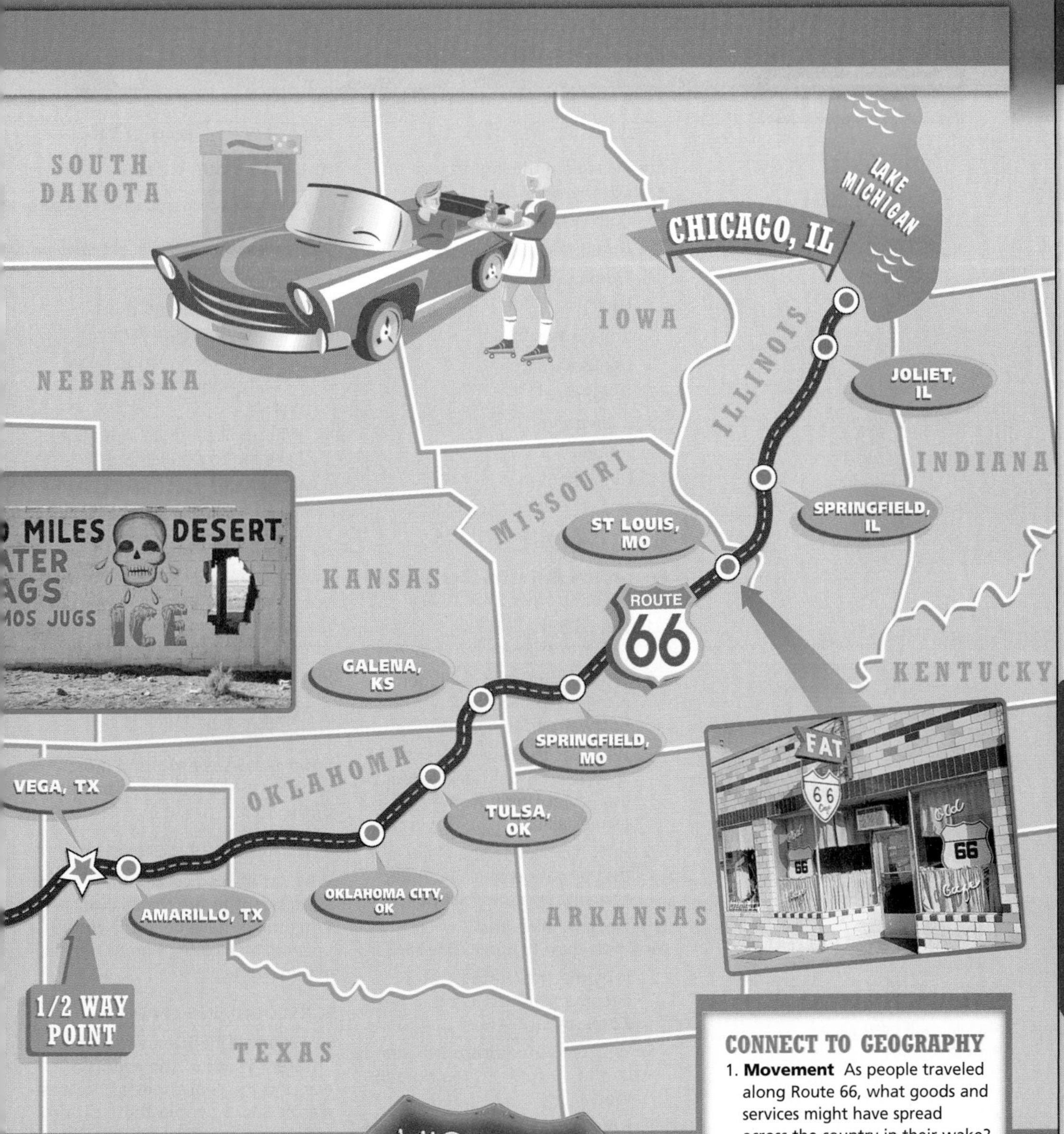

## On-Line Field Trip

**The National Route 66 Museum** is in Elk City, Oklahoma. Many such organizations preserve historic landmarks along Route 66. Each of the states along the road has its own Route 66 Association. There is also a National Historic Route 66 Federation.

Visit www.mcdougallittell.com for more information.

### CONNECT TO GEOGRAPHY

1. **Movement** As people traveled along Route 66, what goods and services might have spread across the country in their wake?
2. **Human-Environment Interaction** In what ways did the movement of Americans over this highway change the environment?

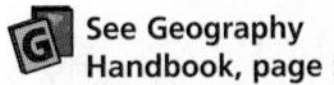
See Geography Handbook, page 5.

### CONNECT TO HISTORY

3. **Drawing Conclusions** In what ways did Route 66 contribute to the American Dream?

805

### CRITICAL THINKING ACTIVITY

**Recognizing Important Details** Have students make a graphic like the one below. In the first column are five geographic features crossed by Route 66. Have students compare this map with a physical map of the United States and list a Route 66 state in which each geographic feature can be found.

| Geographic Features | Route 66 State |
|---|---|
| Mississippi River | |
| Great Plains | |
| Rio Grande | |
| Grand Canyon | |
| Mojave Desert | |

**Class Time** 15 minutes

### MORE ABOUT . . .

**Route 66**

Beginning in 1933, in the middle of the Great Depression, thousands of jobless young men worked on road gangs paving the final stretches of Route 66. The road was finally designated as "continuously paved" in 1938. In the late 1940s and 1950s, Route 66 became an important migratory route for Northerners leaving Chicago, New York City, and other Eastern cities for the sunbelt.

### CONNECT TO GEOGRAPHY

1. **Movement** Truckers carried farm crops from rural communities to markets along with automobile supplies and other goods. Business owners provided food, lodging, and other services along the route.
2. **Human-Environment Interaction** Motels, stores, and gas stations replaced the countryside and helped small towns grow and expand. Pollutants from car exhausts affected air quality, and traffic created noise pollution. Litter along the highway also affected the environment.

### CONNECT TO HISTORY

3. **Drawing Conclusions** Students might consider how Route 66 contributed to the mobility of Americans and gave them access to places, people, and experiences they might not otherwise have been able to afford.

## TERMS & NAMES

1. **Cold War,** p. 792
2. **containment,** p. 793
3. **Truman Doctrine,** p. 793
4. **NATO,** p. 793
5. **Korean War,** p. 796
6. **brinksmanship,** p. 798
7. **space race,** p. 799
8. **baby boom,** p. 801
9. **sunbelt,** p. 801
10. **rock 'n' roll,** p. 803

## REVIEW QUESTIONS

**Possible Responses**

1. guaranteed housing loans for veterans under the G.I. Bill
2. After the war, price controls were lifted, and prices soared because too much money was chasing too few goods.
3. The Western allies saw Eastern Europe as a zone of Soviet occupation; the Soviets saw Eastern Europe as an invasion route into their homeland.
4. NATO was a military alliance against Communist expansion into Europe, and the Marshall Plan aided the economies of Western Europe. Thus, both this military arm and economic arm were means of containing the Soviet threat.
5. The United States did not want South Korea's democratic government to fall to North Korea's Communist government.
6. because it ended with a cease-fire and a stalemate rather than a clear victory
7. He played on people's fear of Communist expansion abroad and Communist spies at home.
8. minorities such as African Americans and Latinos
9. The baby boom fueled the growth of suburbs as soldiers returning from World War II and Korea sought to start families in homes of their own away from the city.
10. They had more money to spend, and television commercials and other advertisements urged consumers to spend.

**VISUAL SUMMARY**

## The Cold War and the American Dream

### At Home

**1940s:**
- Truman faces labor unrest.
- Fear of communism spreads.
- Fair Deal is proposed.
- Equal rights for all remains a problem.

**1950s:**
- The economy booms under Eisenhower.
- McCarthy gains and loses power.
- Billions are spent on space research.
- Rock 'n' roll transforms popular culture.

### Abroad

**1940s:**
- Truman Doctrine is announced.
- Marshall Plan offers aid to Europe.
- Berlin airlift takes place.
- NATO is formed.

**1950s:**
- Korean War ends in stalemate.
- Dulles practices brinksmanship.
- *Sputnik* is launched.
- Arms race takes place between superpowers.

806

# Chapter 28 ASSESSMENT

## TERMS & NAMES

Briefly explain the importance of each of the following.

1. Cold War
2. containment
3. Truman Doctrine
4. NATO
5. Korean War
6. brinksmanship
7. space race
8. baby boom
9. sunbelt
10. rock 'n' roll

## REVIEW QUESTIONS

**Peacetime Adjustments and the Cold War (pages 789–794)**

1. How did the federal government help veterans?
2. Why was inflation a bigger problem than recession in the postwar period?
3. Why was the fate of Eastern Europe an issue that divided the Soviet Union from its former allies?
4. How did the Marshall Plan and the formation of NATO reflect Truman's containment policy?

**The Korean War and McCarthyism (pages 795–799)**

5. Why did the United States become involved in the Korean War?
6. Why were Americans frustrated by the outcome of the Korean War?
7. How was McCarthy able to gain such a powerful hold on the government and the American public?

**The Fifties (pages 800–805)**

8. What groups were left out of postwar prosperity?
9. What factors boosted the growth of suburbs?
10. Why did Americans become bigger consumers in the 1950s?

## CRITICAL THINKING

**1. USING YOUR NOTES**

| ISSUES | PRESIDENTS | |
|---|---|---|
| Domestic | Truman | Eisenhower |
| Labor unions and big business | | |
| Communist threat at home | | |
| Foreign | | |
| Korea | | |
| Communism in Europe | | |

Using your completed chart, answer the questions below.

a. Which policy or action might have increased the chances of war?

b. What policies or actions might have led to a stalemate?

c. In your opinion, could anything have been done to end the Korean War sooner?

**2. APPLYING CITIZENSHIP SKILLS**

Was McCarthyism or communism a greater threat to the American way of life? Explain (or support) your opinion.

**3. THEME: ECONOMICS IN HISTORY**

What factors contributed most strongly to the economic prosperity of the 1950s?

**4. ANALYZING LEADERSHIP**

Why did Truman consider it his duty as president to fire MacArthur? What might have been the consequences of allowing him to remain in Korea?

**5. RECOGNIZING EFFECTS**

Soviet and American leaders had different views of the events of war and the challenges of the postwar period. How did these different views contribute to the mistrust and fear of the Cold-War era?

**Interact *with* History**

How did the American Dream you discussed before you read the chapter compare with the dreams that people actually pursued?

## CRITICAL THINKING

**Possible Responses**

1. **USING YOUR NOTES** **a.** brinksmanship, the Truman Doctrine, and NATO **b.** brinksmanship, the Truman Doctrine, NATO, and the Marshall Plan **c.** earlier peace talks or earlier threat of nuclear weapons
2. **APPLYING CITIZENSHIP SKILLS** Students may argue for either position, although both were threats to democratic values.
3. **THEME: ECONOMICS IN HISTORY** consumer demand, increase in marriages
4. **ANALYZING LEADERSHIP** He thought he had to assert civilian control of the military. If MacArthur had remained in Korea, he might have started a world war with China.
5. **RECOGNIZING EFFECTS** American leaders feared the spread of communism throughout the world. Soviet leaders feared another invasion of their country from the west and so wanted to establish pro-Soviet governments on their borders.

**Interact *with* History** Have students compare their dream to one in which material possessions play a big part.

## HISTORY SKILLS

### 1. INTERPRETING GRAPHS

Gross National Product (GNP) means the total value of all goods and services produced by a nation. Study the graph and then answer the questions.

**Gross National Product,** *1945–1959*

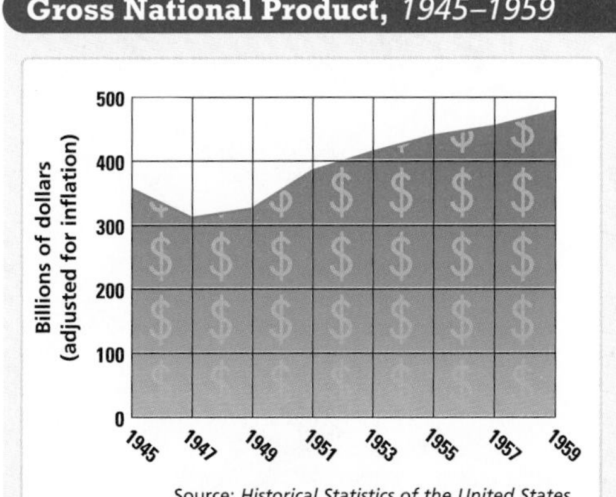


Source: *Historical Statistics of the United States*

a. In dollars, approximately how much did the GNP increase between 1945 and 1951?

b. About how much did the GNP increase between 1951 and 1959?

### 2. INTERPRETING PRIMARY SOURCES

The following cartoon shows a buyer or perhaps salesman discussing cars with Uncle Sam. Study the cartoon and then answer the questions that follow.

*So Russia Launched a Satellite, but Has It Made a Car With Fins Yet?*

a. Which is more important for a country's security—consumer goods or space technology?

b. In the opinion of the cartoonist, how might the American Dream be rooted in technology?

## ALTERNATIVE ASSESSMENT

### 1. INTERDISCIPLINARY ACTIVITY: Speech

**Debating NATO's Role** Since the collapse of the Soviet Union, many former Warsaw Pact nations have wanted to become NATO members. Research and debate the question: What are some of the advantages and disadvantages of expanding NATO?

### 2. COOPERATIVE LEARNING ACTIVITY

**Examining Images of the 1950s** Examine images of the American family and family life in the media of the 1950s. Working in groups, look at advertisements in magazines and books of the era, and if possible view TV reruns of 1950s sitcoms. Present your findings as a short TV show about a 1950s family. Groups can prepare for the presentations using these suggestions.

- Make a list of media images you want to present.
- Assign group members roles as writers, actors, directors, and narrator.
- Identify any props or costumes needed.

### 3. TECHNOLOGY ACTIVITY

**Making a Class Presentation** Popular culture in the 1950s included music, television, and movies. Using the library and the Internet, find articles and pictures about popular shows, music, and celebrities of the period.

**Visit www.mcdougallittell.com to learn more about the Fifties.**

Prepare an electronic presentation about one aspect of popular culture of the Fifties. Use these suggestions or a topic of your own.

- Music: lyrics, bands, performers, record companies
- Movies: stars, popular films, drive-ins
- Fashion: clothing, dress, hairstyles, teen life
- Television: stars, shows, viewing habits

### 4. HISTORY PORTFOLIO

**Option 1** Review your section and chapter assessment activities. Select one that you think was your best work. Then use comments made by your teacher or classmates to improve your work, and add it to your portfolio.

**Option 2** Review the information that you hoped to acquire for What Do You Want to Know? on page 788. Then write a short report in which you explain the information. If any information seems incomplete, do research to expand it. Add your report to your portfolio.



## ALTERNATIVE ASSESSMENT

**1. INTERDISCIPLINARY ACTIVITY: Speech**
**Debates should**

- have two sides with clearly stated positions on the debate topic.
- support positions and refute the opponent's position with evidence.
- have appropriate responses to each other's statements.

**2. COOPERATIVE LEARNING ACTIVITY**
**TV shows should**

- portray the 1950s accurately and in a dramatic style.
- clearly demonstrate an understanding of family life and the media of the 1950s.
- show evidence of involvement of each person in the group.
- show technical proficiency.

**3.**  **TECHNOLOGY ACTIVITY**
**Presentations should**

- utilize two or more media.
- clearly demonstrate an understanding of the popular culture in the 1950s.
- show technical proficiency.

**4. HISTORY PORTFOLIO**

**Option 1 Revised section or chapter assessment activities should**

- address teacher and peer responses to the selected work.
- solve problems present in the first versions of the work.

**Option 2 Short reports should**

- answer questions about the Cold War and the American Dream.
- use evidence to develop and support ideas.
- cite sources of information.
- use standard grammar, spelling, sentence structure, and punctuation.

**Critical Thinking Transparency CT84**

- Visual Summary

**Formal Assessment**

- Chapter Test, Forms A and B, pp. 409–416

## HISTORY SKILLS

**Possible Responses**

**1. INTERPRETING GRAPHS**

**a.** approximately $30 billion

**b.** approximately $90 billion

**2. INTERPRETING PRIMARY SOURCES**

**a.** Both are probably important—consumer goods contribute to the satisfaction of the population with their government and way of life; space technology is important in terms of developing new and important scientific breakthroughs.

**b.** Many material possessions that make up the American Dream are developed by science and technology.

# UNIT 9

## Tensions at Home and Abroad

### 1954 to Present



**BEFORE YOU READ**

### Previewing Unit 9

Soon after World War II, African Americans launch a powerful movement that achieves greater civil rights and inspires Hispanics, women, and Native Americans to begin their own crusades for equal rights. At the same time, growing U.S. military involvement in Vietnam deeply divides the country. The turbulent presidency of Richard Nixon tests the faith of Americans in the Constitution. In the 1990s, the debate over the country's direction becomes heated, while vast societal changes reshape Americans' lives.

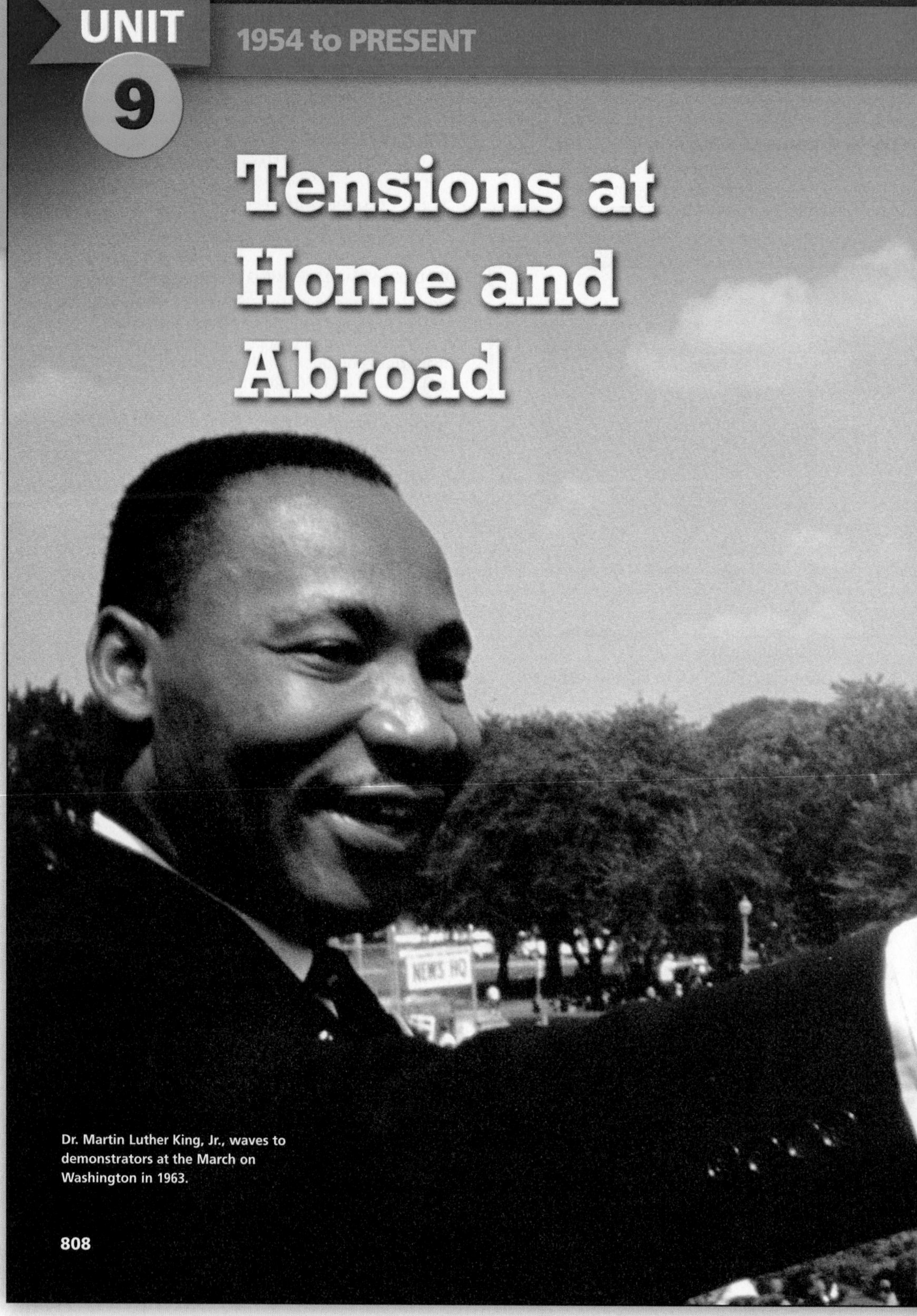


Dr. Martin Luther King, Jr., waves to demonstrators at the March on Washington in 1963.

"I have a dream that my four little children . . . will not be judged by the color of their skin, but by the content of their character."
—Dr. Martin Luther King, Jr.
809


## HISTORY FROM VISUALS

**Interpreting the Photograph** Tell students that in the 1950s, African Americans began a new stage in their struggle to win civil rights. At the 1963 March on Washington, all the nation's major civil rights leaders worked together. Of all those leaders, none commanded more respect and affection than Dr. Martin Luther King, Jr. The photographer captures King's delight in the size of the crowd. Ask students what they know of this movement from earlier history courses or from television documentaries. Ask students to describe King's audience. **Possible Responses** The audience includes whites and African Americans, and people of many different ages.

**Extension** Ask students to trace the movement that made the birthday of Dr. Martin Luther King, Jr., a national holiday.

CHAPTER 29 PLANNING GUIDE

# The Civil Rights Era 1954–1975

| | CHAPTER OVERVIEW | COPYMASTERS | TECHNOLOGY |
|---|---|---|---|
| **CHAPTER RESOURCES** | This chapter discusses the civil rights movement, focusing on the Supreme Court decision that overturned school segregation, the Montgomery bus boycott, and African Americans' struggle for voting rights. It describes the expansion of the struggle as women, Hispanics, and Native Americans also sought new rights. | **In-Depth Resources: Unit 9**<br>• Tracing Themes: Democratic Ideals, p. 2<br>• Building Vocabulary, p. 6<br>**Interdisciplinary Projects,** pp. 169–174 | **Primary Source Explorer**<br>**Electronic Teacher Tools**<br>**Power Presentations CD-ROM**<br>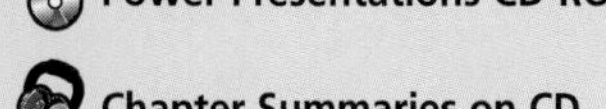 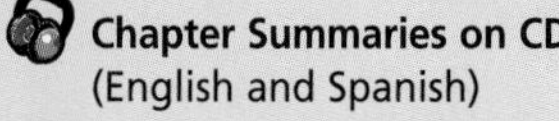 **Chapter Summaries on CD** (English and Spanish)<br>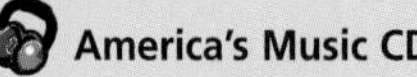 **America's Music CD** |
| | **KEY IDEAS** | | |
| **SECTION 1**<br>**Origins of the Civil Rights Movement**<br>**pp. 813–817** | • The Supreme Court outlaws school segregation in *Brown* v. *Board of Education* in 1954.<br>• Martin Luther King, Jr., leads the Montgomery bus boycott.<br>• Despite threats and violence, African Americans integrate schools and hold sit-ins. | **In-Depth Resources: Unit 9**<br>• Setting the Stage, p. 1<br>• Guided Reading, p. 3<br>• Geography Application: School Integration, 1954–1960, pp. 8–9<br>• Primary Source, p. 10<br>• Reteaching Activity, p. 15<br>**America's History Makers**<br>• Martin Luther King, Jr., pp. 115–116<br>**Citizenship Today,** pp. 93–94 | **Warm-Up Transparency WT29**<br>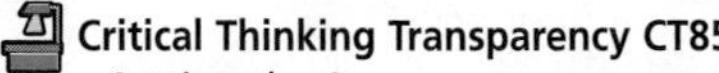 **Critical Thinking Transparency CT85**<br>• Setting the Stage<br> **ClassZone:** www.mcdougallittell.com |
| **SECTION 2**<br>**Kennedy, Johnson, and Civil Rights**<br>**pp. 818–823** | • Civil rights leaders use marches to generate support.<br>• In the mid-1960s, landmark legislation marks civil rights victories.<br>• Divisions emerge in the civil rights movement in the late 1960s. | **In-Depth Resources: Unit 9**<br>• Setting the Stage, p. 1<br>• Guided Reading, p. 4<br>• Literature Selection, pp. 12–14<br>• Reteaching Activity, p. 16<br>**American History Plays**<br>• *I Have a Dream* by Aileen Fisher<br>**Economics in History**<br>• Poverty Amidst Plenty, p. 29<br>**Outline Map Activities,** pp. 57–58 | **Warm-Up Transparency WT29**<br>**Humanities Transparency HT57**<br>• Civil Rights March<br>**Critical Thinking Transparency CT85**<br>• Setting the Stage<br> **ClassZone:** www.mcdougallittell.com |
| **SECTION 3**<br>**The Equal Rights Struggle Expands**<br>**pp. 824–829** | • Mexican Americans form *La Raza Unida* for better jobs and education.<br>• Native Americans seek greater self-determination.<br>• Women work to end discrimination in jobs, pay, and legal rights. | **In-Depth Resources: Unit 9**<br>• Setting the Stage, p. 1<br>• Guided Reading, p. 5<br>• Skillbuilder Practice: Categorizing, p. 7<br>• Primary Source, p. 11<br>• Reteaching Activity, p. 17<br>**America's History Makers**<br>• Cesar Chavez, pp. 117–118<br>**Why It Matters Now**<br>• Equality in Education, pp. 57–58 | **Humanities Transparency HT58**<br>• Cesar Chavez<br>**Geography Transparency GT29**<br>**Critical Thinking Transparency CT86**<br>• Cause and Effect: The Civil Rights Movement<br>**Critical Thinking Transparency CT87**<br>• Visual Summary<br>**Primary Source Explorer**<br>• *I Have a Dream*<br>• *An Open Letter* |

Pupil's Edition
Copymaster
Overhead Transparency
Audio Library
CD-ROM
Internet

## ASSESSMENT

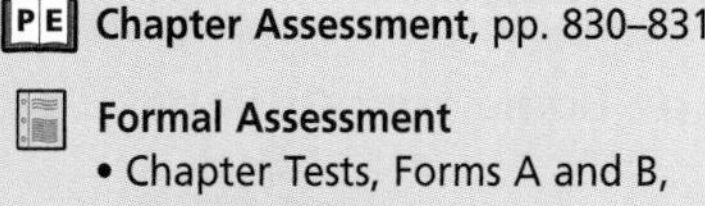

**Chapter Assessment,** pp. 830–831

**Formal Assessment**
- Chapter Tests, Forms A and B, pp. 422–429

**Alternative Assessment Book**

**Electronic Teacher Tools with Test Maker**

**Section Assessment,** p. 817

**Formal Assessment**
- Section Quiz, p. 419

**Alternative Assessment Book**
- Rubrics for a wall of fame, 1.4
- Rubrics for a Web page, 5.1

**Electronic Teacher Tools with Test Maker**

**Section Assessment,** p. 823

**Formal Assessment**
- Section Quiz, p. 420

**Alternative Assessment Book**
- Rubrics for a poster, 1.1
- Rubrics for a speech, 3.6

**Electronic Teacher Tools with Test Maker**

**Section Assessment,** p. 827

**Formal Assessment**
- Section Quiz, p. 421

**Alternative Assessment Book**
- Rubrics for multimedia, 5.4
- Rubrics for a pamphlet, 1.13

**Electronic Teacher Tools with Test Maker**

## CUSTOMIZING FOR INDIVIDUAL NEEDS

### Students Acquiring English/ESL

**Reading Study Guide** (English and Spanish), pp. 279–286

**Access for Students Acquiring English/ESL: Spanish Translations,** pp. 193–198

**Chapter Summaries on CD** (English and Spanish)

### Less Proficient Readers

**Reading Study Guide** (English and Spanish), pp. 279–286

**Chapter Summaries on CD** (English and Spanish)

### Gifted and Talented Students

**In-Depth Resources: Unit 9**
- Enrichment Activity, p. 18

**America's History Makers**
- Martin Luther King, Jr., pp. 115–116
- Cesar Chavez, pp. 117–118

## CROSS-CURRICULAR CONNECTIONS

### Civics

Fireside, Harvey and Sarah Betsy Fuller. ***Brown v. Board of Education: Equal Schooling for All.*** Hillside, NJ: Enslow Publishers, 1994. Describes the historical context of the landmark Court decision and provides many quotes from the people involved.

### Culture

Haskins, James. ***The March on Washington.*** New York: HarperCollins, 1993. The inside story of what it took to organize and bring off the famous 1963 March on Washington.

### Primary Sources

Levine, Ellen. ***Freedom's Children: Young Civil Rights Activists Tell Their Own Stories.*** New York: Putnam, 1993. First-person accounts by 30 African-American kids who worked for civil rights.

### Humanities: Music

Ferris, Jerri. ***What I Had Was Singing: The Story of Marian Anderson.*** Minneapolis: Lerner, 1994. Brief, well-researched biography of the African-American opera singer, whose career was intertwined with the civil rights movement. Excellent photographs.

### Interdisciplinary Projects, pp. 169–174

- Math: Using a Bar Graph to Compare Data
- Science: Jet Power
- Language Arts: Civil Rights Speech
- Art: Latino Art

### Literature

Beals, Melba Pattilo and Anne Greenberg (ed.). ***Warriors Don't Cry: A Searing Memoir of the Battle to Integrate Little Rock's Central High.*** New York: Pocket Books, 1994. Abridged account by one of the African-American students who desegregated Central High.

Carlson, Lori M. ***Cool Salsa: Bilingual Poems on Growing Up Latino in the United States.*** New York: Holt, 1994. Contains 37 poems in English and in Spanish by Latino and Latina writers.

Curtis, Paul. ***The Watsons Go to Birmingham—1963.*** New York: Delacorte, 1995. A family journeys from Michigan to Alabama where they witness the horror of a church bombing.

### McDougal Littell *The Language of Literature*

- Rudolfo Anaya. "One Million Volumes" (speech)

### McDougal Littell Literature Connections

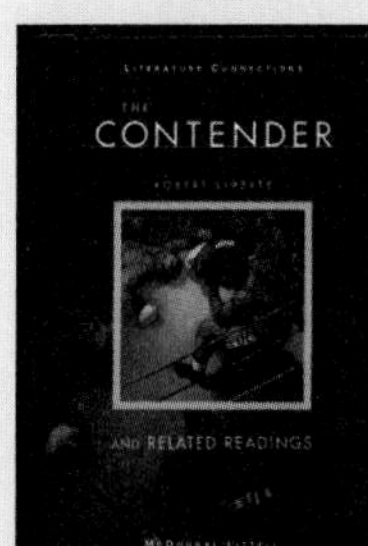


Robert Lipsyte
*The Contender*
Living in Harlem during the 1960s civil rights movement, a high school dropout puts himself through the rigor and discipline of boxing training and wonders whether he has the heart of a contender.

## ENRICHMENT ACTIVITIES

**Pupil's Edition, pp. 810–831**
**Interact with History,** p. 811
**Interactive Primary Sources,** pp. 828–829

**In-Depth Resources: Unit 9**
- Geography Application: School Integration, 1954–1960, pp. 8–9
- Primary Source, p. 10
- Primary Source, p. 11
- Literature Selection, pp. 12–14

**America's History Makers**
- Martin Luther King, Jr., pp. 115–116
- Cesar Chavez, pp. 117–118

**America's Music CD**

**American History Plays,**
- *I Have a Dream* by Aileen Fisher

**Outline Map Activities,** pp. 57–58

**Why It Matters Now,** pp. 57–58

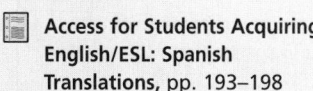

# CHAPTER 29 PACING GUIDE

**LESSON PLAN OPTIONS (50-MINUTE PERIOD)** **(TE) = Teacher's Edition (PE) = Pupil's Edition**

| | TEACHER-DIRECTED ACTIVITIES<br>Class Time: 15 minutes | STUDENT-CENTERED ACTIVITIES<br>Class Time: 25 minutes | INDIVIDUAL ACTIVITIES<br>Class Time: 10 minutes |
|---|---|---|---|
| **DAY 1**<br>Introduction<br>pp. 810–812 | **Presentation Options**<br>• Begin with a class discussion of the photograph on p. 810 **(PE)**.<br>• Lead a class discussion on the "What Do You Know?" question in Setting the Stage, p. 812. Then introduce the graphic organizer for the chapter **(PE)**. | **Options for Cooperative Learning**<br>• Have student groups discuss the Interact with History questions, p. 811 **(PE)**.<br>• Have student groups respond to the "What Do You Want to Know?" question in Setting the Stage, p. 812 **(PE)**. | **Head Start on Homework Options**<br>• Have students skim Section 1 Main Idea, Why It Matters Now, Terms & Names, and the main headings, p. 813 **(PE)**.<br>• Have students begin Guided Reading activity and Building Vocabulary sheet. |
| **DAY 2**<br>Section 1<br>pp. 813–817 | **Presentation Options**<br>• Begin with the 5-Minute Warm-Up, p. 813 **(TE)**.<br>• Review the Section 1 Main Idea, Why It Matters Now, and Terms & Names, p. 813 **(PE)**.<br>• Choose 5 key questions for Objectives 1–4 to discuss with the class, pp. 813–817 **(TE)**. | **Options for Cooperative Learning**<br>• Divide students into groups to work on the Interdisciplinary Link, Civics: Local History, p. 816 **(TE)**.<br>• Have student pairs work together to complete one of the Activity Options in the Section 1 Assessment, p. 817 **(PE)**. | **Head Start on Homework Options**<br>• Have students begin working on Section 1 Assessment, p. 817 **(PE)**.<br>• Have students preview Section 2 Main Idea, Why It Matters Now, Terms & Names, and the main headings, p. 818 **(PE)**. |
| **DAY 3**<br>Section 2<br>pp. 818–823 | **Presentation Options**<br>• Begin with the 5-Minute Warm-Up, p. 818 **(TE)**.<br>• Choose 5 key questions for Objectives 1–4 to discuss with the class, pp. 818–822 **(TE)**.<br>• Lead the class through the Critical Thinking Activity, p. 819 **(TE)**. | **Options for Cooperative Learning**<br>• Divide students into groups to work on the Interdisciplinary Link, World History: The Influence of Gandhi, p. 819 **(TE)**.<br>• Have student pairs work together to complete one of the Activity Options in the Section 2 Assessment, p. 823 **(PE)**. | **Head Start on Homework Options**<br>• Have students begin working on Section 2 Assessment, p. 823 **(PE)**.<br>• Have students complete the Primary Source A Closer Look questions, pp. 828–829 **(PE)**. |
| **DAY 4**<br>Section 3<br>pp. 824–829 | **Presentation Options**<br>• Begin with the 5-Minute Warm-Up, p. 824 **(TE)**.<br>• Choose 5 key questions for Objectives 1–4 to discuss with the class, pp. 824–826 **(TE)**.<br>• Lead the students through the Skillbuilder Mini-Lesson: Categorizing, p. 825 **(TE)**. | **Options for Cooperative Learning**<br>• Divide students into groups and have them complete the Critical Thinking Activity, p. 825 **(TE)**.<br>• Have student pairs work together to complete one of the Activity Options in the Section 3 Assessment, p. 827 **(PE)**. | **Head Start on Homework Options**<br>• Have students complete the Setting the Stage graphic organizer for the chapter, p. 812 **(PE)**.<br>• Have students begin working on the Chapter Assessment, pp. 830–831 **(PE)**.<br>• Prepare for Chapter Test<br>**Formal Assessment,** pp. 422–429 |

TEACHER-TESTED ACTIVITY **Marci Smith, Hurst-Euless-Bedford ISD, Bedford, Texas**

## HAVE WE REACHED THE DREAM?

**Class Time** One class period

**Task** Analyzing and expressing an opinion on changes in race relations

**Purpose** To evaluate changes in relations among groups within American society since the civil rights movement of the 1960s

**Supplies Needed**

- Copies of Dr. Martin Luther King, Jr.'s, "I Have a Dream" speech or the excerpt on text page 828
- Audio- or videotaped version of King's "I Have a Dream" speech
- Two large posterboard signs, one saying "Yes, Completely" and the other saying "No, Not at All"

**Activity** Write the following question on the chalkboard: *Have we as a nation reached the point where people are judged not by the color of their skin, but by the content of their character?* As the class listens to a recording of King's speech, encourage students to think about the question on the chalkboard. Then place the "Yes, Completely" sign at one end of the room and the "No, Not at All" sign at the other. Tell students to move quietly to the point along the line between the two signs where their opinion lies. Allow each person to make a brief statement in support of his or her opinion. Allow time for rebuttal.

## BLOCK SCHEDULING — LESSON PLAN OPTIONS (90-MINUTE PERIOD)

### DAY 1

**Interact with History,** p. 811
**Class Time** 20 minutes

Options for pacing and variety:

- Role-Playing Ask students to suppose they are among the college students at the lunch counter in Greensboro, North Carolina, in 1960, staging the first civil rights sit-in. Ask students to write a statement explaining why they joined the sit-in, what they hope to accomplish, what risks they are taking, whether they are afraid, and why they are willing to take these risks. **Class Time** 15 minutes

**Setting the Stage,** p. 812
**Class Time** 20 minutes

Options for pacing and variety:

- Time Saver Ask students to come to class with their own definitions of "civil rights" and an explanation of why civil rights are important in a democratic society.
  **Class Time** 10 minutes

**Section 1,** pp. 813–817
**Class Time** 50 minutes

Options for pacing and variety:

- Peer Teaching Divide students into four groups. Assign each group one of these headlines: *Brown* Overturns *Plessy;* Montgomery Bus Boycott; Showdown in Little Rock; Sit-ins Spread. Have each group write a newspaper article to go with its headline.
  **Class Time** 15 minutes
- Internet Extend students' background knowledge of the American civil rights movement by visiting www.mcdougallittell.com
  **Class Time** 20 minutes

### DAY 2

**Section 2,** pp. 818–823
**Class Time** 45 minutes

Options for pacing and variety:

- History on Film Extend students' knowledge of the civil rights movement by viewing portions of the seven videos in the award-winning *Eyes on the Prize* series. PBS.
  **Class Time** 50 minutes
- Time Saver Use the map on page 821 to reinforce students' understanding of the impact of civil rights protests and the Voting Rights Act on African-American voter registration. **Class Time** 10 minutes

**Section 3,** pp. 824–829
**Class Time** 45 minutes

Options for pacing and variety:

- Peer Evaluation Have student pairs answer the Main Idea and Critical Thinking questions in the Section Assessment. **Class Time** 5 minutes
- Time Saver Have students find partners and compare their Read and Take Notes charts from page 812, checking each other's charts for completeness and accuracy.
  **Class Time** 5 minutes

**Chapter 29 Assessment,** pp. 830–831
**Class Time** 40 minutes

Options for pacing and variety:

- Peer Teaching Have students in groups of three work together to add a third column to their completed Cause and Events chart on page 830. For each event listed, have students list one effect. Have groups exchange charts and compare responses.
  **Class Time** 25 minutes
- Peer Evaluation Working in groups, have students pick three events from the Visual Summary time line and write a paragraph explaining how each event affected the struggle for civil rights from 1954 to 1968.
  **Class Time** 10 minutes

**CHAPTER 29 OBJECTIVE**

**The student will identify the origins of the civil rights movement, its major leaders, their methods, and the achievements of the movement through 1975.**

# The Civil Rights Era 1954–1975

*Section 1* **Origins of the Civil Rights Movement**
*Section 2* **Kennedy, Johnson, and Civil Rights**
*Section 3* **The Equal Rights Struggle Expands**

## HISTORY FROM VISUALS

**Interpreting the Photograph** Ask students to look closely at the photograph of the March on Washington and classify the people in the picture by race, gender, age, and other relevant factors. Then ask students what this photograph of participants in the March on Washington tells them about the early days of the civil rights movement.

**Possible Responses** The crowd includes African Americans and whites; men and women; old, young, and middle-aged people; men in suits and ties, men in overalls, women in cotton dresses. The photograph shows that the civil rights movement attracted all sorts of Americans.

**Extension** Ask students to explain the following quote about the March on Washington: "An extraordinary demonstration of interracial unity, the March on Washington stood as the high-water mark in the struggle for civil rights."

Civil rights marchers sing at the March on Washington in 1963.



### CRITICAL THINKING ACTIVITY

**Making Inferences** Ask students to speculate about why civil rights leaders chose to hold their mass march in Washington, D.C.

**Class Time** 10 minutes

## RECOMMENDED RESOURCES

**BOOKS FOR THE TEACHER**

Branch, Taylor. ***Parting the Waters: America in the King Years, 1954–63.*** New York: Simon and Schuster, 1989. Pulitzer Prize–winning account of a turbulent era.

Hampton, Henry and Steve Fayer. ***Voices of Freedom: An Oral History of the Civil Rights Movement from the 1950s Through the 1980s.*** Drawing on almost 1,000 interviews, presents the civil rights movement through the words of the people who lived it.

**SOFTWARE**

***Decisions, Decisions: Prejudice.*** Tom Snyder Productions, 1997. Presents compelling situations for students to resolve.

**VIDEOS**

***Eyes on the Prize.*** PBS, 1991. Award-winning series on seven videocassettes.

***Four Little Girls.*** 40 Acres & a Mule Film Works, 1998. Spike Lee's remarkable documentary on the fatal bombing of the black church in Alabama that killed four children in 1964.

**INTERNET**

For more about the American civil rights movement, visit www.mcdougallittell.com

## Interact *with* History

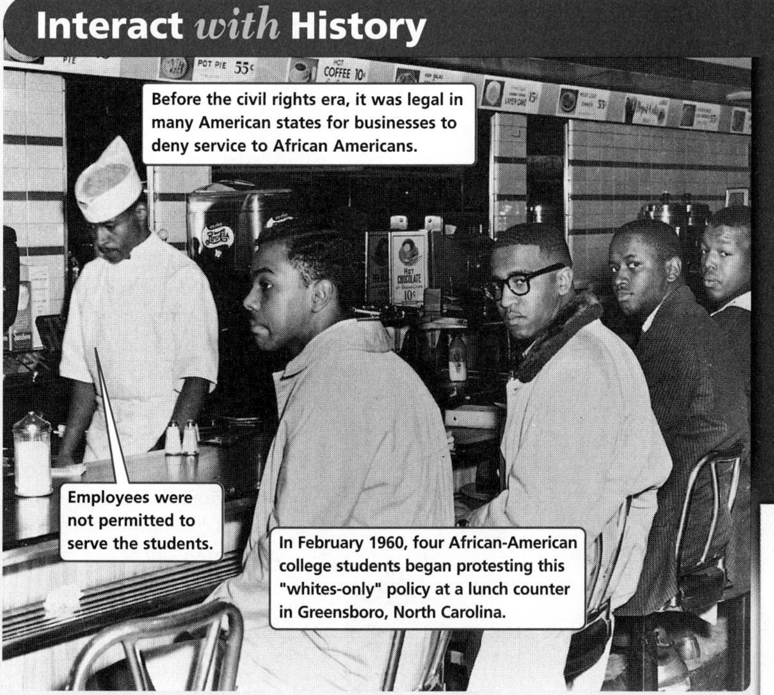

Before the civil rights era, it was legal in many American states for businesses to deny service to African Americans.
Employees were not permitted to serve the students.
In February 1960, four African-American college students began protesting this "whites-only" policy at a lunch counter in Greensboro, North Carolina.

**It is 1960, and you live in a Southern city. For decades, African Americans in the South have endured racial segregation. Now they are protesting against it—in spite of the risk of being attacked. You must decide whether or not you will participate in the protests and in what way.**

### What Do You Think?

- What policy do the students in the picture hope to change?
- How far would you be willing to go to help the protesters?
- In what ways, besides protesting, could you help to end segregation?

# *How would you stop injustice in society?*

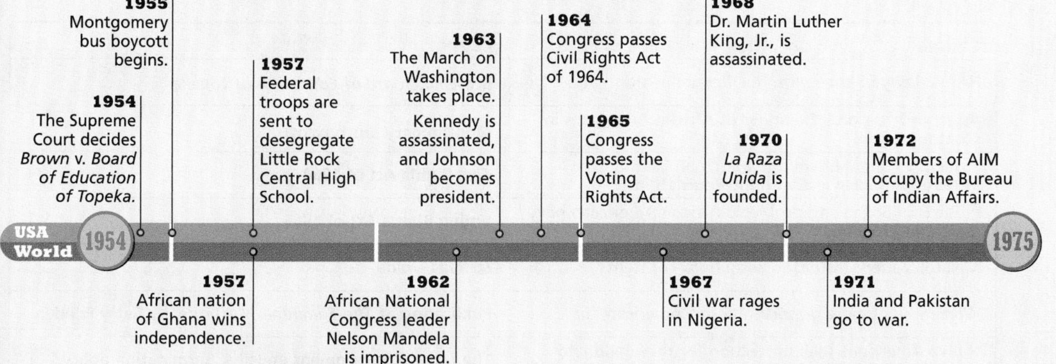




## Interact *with* History

### OBJECTIVES

- To understand the reasons for civil rights protests and the dangers faced by protesters
- To help students connect with the people and the events in this chapter

### What Do You Think?

1. What are some of the historical roots of segregation?
2. What might be the consequences of participating in civil rights demonstrations?
3. What methods, other than protests and demonstrations, have Americans used to correct wrongs and improve society?

### *How would you stop injustice in society?*

Suggest that students weigh the needs for change with the dangers of protest. Ask students to think about the risks taken by civil rights protesters. Ask: Would you endure shouted taunts? spitting? snubs from your family, friends, and neighbors? threatening phone calls? attacks by dogs and fire hoses? threats to your family? arrest? bombings? shootings?

### MAKING PERSONAL CONNECTIONS

Ask students to give examples of people they know or know about who have worked to correct an injustice. Have students describe the injustice and the methods the people used to change it.

### TIME LINE DISCUSSION

**The experiences of African Americans during World War II laid the groundwork for the civil rights movement of the 1950s, 1960s, and 1970s. African Americans were determined to achieve full political and social equality. Brilliant leadership, media coverage, and sympathetic presidents helped in the struggle.**

- Ask students to determine which areas of American life were affected by the civil rights movement. **Possible Responses** education, transportation, voting
- Ask students what types of tactics were used by the civil rights movement to gain equality. **Possible Responses** Supreme Court cases, boycotts, marches
- Which groups other than African Americans also worked for equality? **Possible Responses** Native Americans, Spanish-speaking Americans

# Chapter 29 SETTING THE STAGE

## BEFORE YOU READ

### Previewing the Theme: Democratic Ideals

Segregation and discrimination were flagrant violations of the American ideals of fairness and equality. The civil rights movement forced Americans to face their failures and take action to make changes.

### What Do You Know?

Review with students events following the Civil War that led to the institutionalization of segregation and discrimination, especially *Plessy* v. *Ferguson.* Remind students of the contributions of African Americans during World War II and the determination of returning African-American veterans to eliminate segregation.

 **In-Depth Resources: Unit 9**
- Tracing Themes: Democratic Ideals, p. 2

## BEFORE YOU READ

### Previewing the Theme

**Democratic Ideals** For a century after the Civil War, the United States refused to provide equal rights for African Americans. Chapter 29 tells about the African-American struggle for equality. It also explains how African-American protests for equal rights spread to other groups, including Hispanics, Native Americans, and women.

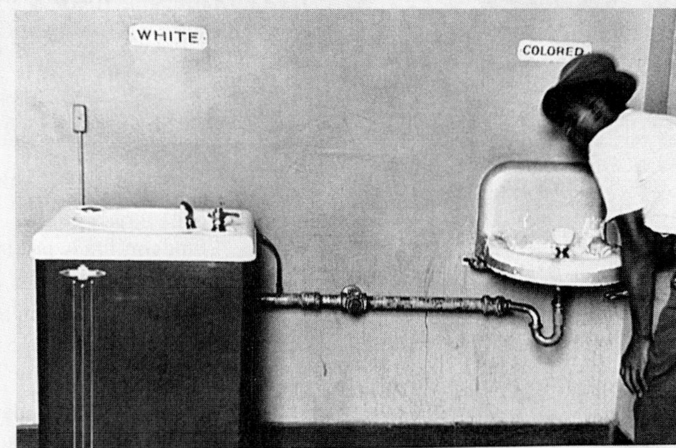


### What Do You Know?

What do you think of when people talk about civil rights? Why have some people in the United States been denied their civil rights? Why are civil rights important in a democratic society?

**THINK ABOUT**
- what you have learned about racism, segregation, and discrimination in earlier chapters
- what you have learned about famous civil rights leaders from your parents or teachers

### What Do You Want to Know?

What questions do you have about civil rights? Write those questions in your notebook before you read the chapter.

## READ AND TAKE NOTES

**Reading Strategy: Analyzing Causes**

Explain to students that the chart on page 812 lists several important events of the civil rights movement and of other rights movements. Remind students that by analyzing the causes of events, they will understand why they happened. Remind students that causes and their effects may make chains, with the effect of one cause becoming the cause of another effect and so on.

 **In-Depth Resources: Unit 9**
- Setting the Stage, p. 1

 **Critical Thinking Transparency CT85**
- Setting the Stage

## READ AND TAKE NOTES

**Reading Strategy: Analyzing Causes** Copy the chart below in your notebook. Use it to take notes on the cause of each event listed in the chart.

See Skillbuilder Handbook, page R10.

| Causes | Events |
|---|---|
| NAACP lawyers challenge the *Plessy* decision. | ***Brown* v. *Board of Education of Topeka*** |
| Arrest of Parks and the anger of African Americans in Montgomery | **Montgomery bus boycott** |
| Protests in Birmingham and March on Washington increase pressure for civil rights legislation. | **Civil Rights Act of 1964** |
| Protests in Selma and problems African Americans have registering to vote | **Voting Rights Act of 1965** |
| Mexican Americans organize to fight for rights. | ***La Raza Unida*** |
| Women want more opportunities in American life. | **Publication of *The Feminine Mystique*, by Betty Friedan** |
| Native Americans seek protection for their land and their traditional cultures. | **The federal government ends its "termination policy."** |



## TEACHING STRATEGY

### READING THE CHAPTER

This is a chronological chapter focusing on African Americans' struggle for civil rights and other rights movements. Ask students to note how African Americans' protests served as models for the protests by other groups, including Hispanics, Native Americans, and women.

### ALTERNATIVE ASSESSMENT

The Chapter Assessment describes three activities for alternative assessment on page 831. You may wish to have students work on these activities during the course of the chapter and then present them at the end.

# 1 Origins of the Civil Rights Movement

**MAIN IDEA**

Changes after World War II helped African Americans make progress in their struggle for equality.

**WHY IT MATTERS NOW**

The African-American struggle for equality became a model for modern protest movements.

**TERMS & NAMES**

- Thurgood Marshall
- *Brown* v. *Board of Education of Topeka*
- Montgomery bus boycott
- Dr. Martin Luther King, Jr.
- SCLC
- sit-in
- SNCC

## ONE AMERICAN'S STORY

**On December 1, 1955, Rosa Parks, an African-American woman from Montgomery, Alabama, boarded a bus to go home after work. Along the way, a group of white people climbed aboard. The bus driver told Parks and a few other African Americans to give up their seats for the whites and move to the back of the bus. All of them except Parks got up to move. She described what happened next.**

*A VOICE FROM THE PAST*

The driver of the bus saw me still sitting there, and he asked was I going to stand up. I said, "No." He said, "Well, I'm going to have you arrested." Then I said, "You may do that."

**Rosa Parks,** *Rosa Parks: My Story*

Rosa Parks rides a bus in Montgomery, Alabama, in 1956.

**The bus driver called the police, who arrested Parks. The arrest angered Montgomery's African-American community. They respected Parks for her long history of fighting for civil rights. She had been an officer in the local chapter of the NAACP. She had also been put off buses in the past for defying segregation. As Section 1 explains, her arrest would spark a movement that began to tear down segregation in America.**

## 1 Postwar Changes Strengthen Protests

Since the Civil War, African Americans had fought for equality. Their goals included full political rights, better job opportunities, and an end to segregation. But before World War II, they had had little success. Several changes made their efforts more successful after the war.

First, more Americans began to see racism as evil. Racist attitudes had supported the discrimination that oppressed African Americans. Many white Americans saw that racist beliefs had contributed to the rise of Adolf Hitler and the Holocaust. As a result, they began to recognize that racism had no place in the United States.

In addition, the war made African Americans more determined than ever to win equality at home. Having fought for freedom in Europe, African Americans wanted a share of it in the United States, too.



## SECTION OBJECTIVES

1. To identify factors that contributed to the civil rights movement
2. To explain the significance of *Brown* v. *Board of Education of Topeka*
3. To analyze the effects of civil rights victories
4. To describe the process of school desegregation in Little Rock and the numerous sit-ins throughout the South

**CRITICAL THINKING**

Making Inferences, p. 814
Recognizing Effects, p. 815
Solving Problems, p. 817
Contrasting, p. 817

## FOCUS & MOTIVATE

### 5-MINUTE WARM-UP

**Making Inferences** These questions focus on desegregation in Little Rock.

1. Look at the photograph on page 816. How would you describe the crowd surrounding Elizabeth Eckford?
2. Why did school desegregation make these people angry?

 **Warm-Up Transparency WT29**

## INSTRUCT

**INSTRUCT: OBJECTIVE 1**

**Postwar Changes Strengthen Protests**

Key Questions

- How did World War II change attitudes about segregation?
- What effect did the movement of African Americans to cities have on the civil rights movement?

 **In-Depth Resources: Unit 9**
- Guided Reading, p. 3

**Reading Study Guide** (Spanish and English), pp. 279–280

## RECOMMENDED RESOURCES

 **In-Depth Resources: Unit 9**
- Guided Reading, p. 3
- Building Vocabulary, p. 6
- Geography Application: School Integration, 1954–1960, pp. 8–9
- Primary Source: Elizabeth Eckford's Long Walk to School, p. 10
- Reteaching Activity, p. 15

**Reading Study Guide** (Spanish and English), pp. 279–280

**America's History Makers**
- Martin Luther King, Jr., pp. 115–116

**Citizenship Today**
- *Brown* v. *Board of Education,* pp. 93–94

**Formal Assessment**
- Section Quiz, p. 419

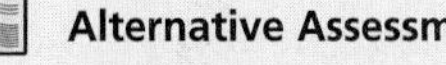

**Alternative Assessment**
- Rubrics, 1.4, 5.1

**Access for Students Acquiring English/ESL**
- Guided Reading, p. 193
- Geography Application, pp. 197–198

Technology Resources

 **Critical Thinking Trans. CT86**
- Cause and Effect: The Civil Rights Movement

 **Electronic Teacher Tools with Test Maker**

 **ClassZone**
www.mcdougallittell.com

## INSTRUCT: OBJECTIVE 

***Brown* Overturns *Plessy***

Key Questions

- How did the *Plessy* decision affect segregation?
- What was the Supreme Court's decision in the *Brown* case?

 **In-Depth Resources: Unit 9**

- Geography Application: School Integration, 1954–1960, pp. 8–9

 **Critical Thinking Transparency CT86**

- Cause and Effect: The Civil Rights Movement

### MORE ABOUT . . .

***Brown* v. *Board of Education***

The name given to the 1954 desegregation case is the name of Oliver Brown, a welder from Kansas City. Brown sued to overturn a Kansas state law allowing school systems to operate segregated schools. Under that law, his eight-year-old daughter, Linda, was forced to travel by bus and walk through a railroad switchyard to reach an all-black school, although the Browns lived only a few blocks from a white school.

 **Citizenship Today,** pp. 93–94

### MORE ABOUT . . .

**Rosa Parks**

Rosa Parks, a seamstress earning $23.00 a week at a local department store, supported herself and her invalid husband. She claims that on that fateful December day, she didn't refuse to give up her seat because she was tired, but rather because she ". . . was tired of giving in." In the summer before her arrest, Mrs. Parks had attended the Highlander Folk School in Monteagle, Tennessee, an experiment in interracial living designed to break down barriers between the races. Mrs. Parks's experience there convinced her that the barriers of racial discrimination could and must be broken.

African Americans also gained important resources to help them fight segregation. More blacks had moved into cities to work. They made more money and formed more contacts with one another at work, on the street, and in churches. These changes helped to make the civil rights protests successful.

**Background** Churches played a key role in the movement. They offered spiritual and moral support, buildings for meetings, and ministers as leaders.

## 2 *Brown* Overturns *Plessy*

The NAACP, the oldest civil rights organization in the United States, benefited from these changes. Before the war, it had established a fund to pay for legal challenges to segregation. Even so, the "separate but equal" doctrine remained in effect well into the 1950s. This doctrine had been established by *Plessy* v. *Ferguson* in 1896.

In the early 1950s, African Americans in several states sued to end segregation in, or integrate, public schools. Up to this point, white-controlled school boards had provided white children with better schoolhouses and newer books and equipment than they provided to black children. **Thurgood Marshall,** the NAACP counsel, led the attorneys who challenged the segregation laws in the courts.

**Vocabulary** **integrate:** to open to people of all races or ethnic groups; to desegregate

In 1954, Thurgood Marshall persuaded the Supreme Court that racial segregation in public schools was not constitutional.

In the early 1950s, the Supreme Court heard these cases under the name ***Brown* v. *Board of Education of Topeka*.** On May 17, 1954, Chief Justice Earl Warren delivered the Court's historic opinion on these cases.

> *A VOICE FROM THE PAST*
>
> We conclude that in the field of public education the doctrine of "separate but equal" has no place. Separate educational facilities are inherently unequal.
>
> **Chief Justice Earl Warren,** *Brown* v. *Board of Education of Topeka*

The *Brown* decision was limited to public schools. But many people hoped that it would eventually end segregation in other public facilities. In the meantime, civil rights supporters hoped that black children would receive the same educational opportunities as white children. But the Supreme Court did not say how desegregation was to occur until a year later.

**Reading History** **A. Making Inferences** Why might the *Brown* decision lead to the end of segregation in other public facilities? A. Possible Response If educational facilities segregated by race could not be equal, the same was true of other public facilities.

At that time, the Court ordered public schools to desegregate "with all deliberate speed." This ruling, which was known as *Brown II,* actually gave segregated school districts *more* time to desegregate. A few places, such as Washington, D.C., desegregated quickly. But in most places, white-controlled schools resisted desegregation.

## 3 Montgomery Bus Boycott

In 1955, about six months after the *Brown II* decision, Rosa Parks was arrested, as you read in One American's Story on page 813. News of her arrest quickly reached



### ACTIVITY OPTIONS

### INDIVIDUAL NEEDS

**STUDENTS ACQUIRING ENGLISH/ESL**

**Understanding Key Terms** Before students begin to read this section, review the terms *segregation, desegregation, integration,* and *boycott* with students. Explain that *segregation* is the enforced separation or isolation of a certain group, such as a race. As they read the section, ask students to give examples of how and where African Americans were segregated in the United States.

Explain that both *desegregation* and *integration* refer to the end of enforced separation. Point out that *integrate* means to bring together or unite.

Finally, discuss the term *boycott* as an organized, mass refusal to use a service or buy a product. Ask students if they think that a boycott would be successful in bringing about a change in society today.

the other members of her church. The church members issued a notice to other African-American churches and local groups. It said, "If Negroes did not ride the buses, they [the buses] could not operate. We are, therefore, asking every Negro to stay off the buses Monday in protest of the arrest and trial." This protest, called the **Montgomery bus boycott,** began that day.

**Background** African Americans made up 70 percent of the riders on Montgomery's buses.

That evening, local NAACP leaders held a meeting to decide whether to continue the boycott. A 26-year-old Baptist minister from Atlanta, Georgia, named **Dr. Martin Luther King, Jr.,** spoke to the group.

*A VOICE FROM THE PAST*

> There comes a time that people get tired. We are here this evening to say to those who have mistreated us so long that we are tired—tired of being segregated and humiliated; tired of being kicked about by the brutal feet of oppression.
>
> **Martin Luther King, Jr.,** quoted in *Stride Toward Freedom*

The church members vowed to continue the boycott. It went on for 13 months. Boycotters, including some whites, organized car pools, rode bikes, or walked to their jobs and schools. King and other leaders endured death threats, bombings, and jailings. The violent reactions of whites to the nonviolent boycott gained the attention of the national media.

Meanwhile, the Montgomery bus segregation law had been challenged in court. On November 13, 1956, the Supreme Court ruled that the law was unconstitutional. African Americans once again boarded the buses in Montgomery. This time they sat wherever they pleased.

*Reading*History **B. Recognizing Effects** What were the most important results of the Montgomery bus boycott?
**B. Possible Responses** It ended segregation on Montgomery's buses, led to the founding of SCLC, and made Dr. King a recognized civil rights leader.

The boycott had several important results. First, it ended segregation on Montgomery buses. Second, it led to the founding of the Southern Christian Leadership Conference (**SCLC**). SCLC coordinated civil rights protests across the South. Third, the boycott made Dr. King one of the best-known civil rights leaders in the nation.

**AMERICA'S HISTORY MAKERS**

**MARTIN LUTHER KING, JR.**
**1929–1968**

Fresh out of school, King had been in Montgomery about a year when he became leader of the bus boycott. But his courage and brilliant speaking abilities made him the ideal leader for the civil rights movement.

King learned about nonviolence by studying writers and thinkers such as Mohandas Gandhi. He came to believe that only love could convert people to the side of justice. He described the power of nonviolent resisters: "We will wear you down by our capacity to suffer. And in winning our freedom . . . we will win you in the process."

**Why do you think King was well-suited to lead a nonviolent protest?**

## Massive Resistance

Civil rights victories upset many Southern whites. Polls showed that more than 80 percent opposed school desegregation. Segregationists fought back against African Americans and civil rights organizations. The Ku Klux Klan used beatings, arson, and murder to threaten African Americans who pursued their civil rights.

Many whites, especially among the middle class, organized groups known as White Citizens Councils to prevent desegregation. The opposition of whites to desegregation became known as massive resistance. It was very effective in delaying desegregation.





**INSTRUCT: OBJECTIVE 3**

**Montgomery Bus Boycott/ Massive Resistance**

Key Questions

- What was the goal of the Montgomery bus boycott?
- What were the results of the boycott?
- What was the reaction of Southern whites to civil rights victories for blacks?

**AMERICA'S HISTORY MAKERS**

**Martin Luther King, Jr.**

When activists formed the Montgomery Improvement Association to spearhead the Montgomery bus boycott, King became head primarily because no one else wanted the job. In King's first speech at an MIA meeting, he said, "We come here tonight to be saved from that patience that makes us patient with anything less than freedom and justice." King clung to his philosophy of love and nonviolence despite threats, bombings, jailings, and scorn from whites and from blacks who thought he moved too slowly. When he was assassinated, King was on his way to lead a Poor People's March in Washington.

Possible Response: He believed deeply that love, not violence, would convert people to the side of justice.

**America's History Makers**
- Martin Luther King, Jr., pp. 115–116

**MORE ABOUT . . .**

**SCLC**

Although membership in SCLC is open to all, most of its members are African-American Protestant ministers. Besides King, the first activists of SCLC included Ralph Abernathy, Andrew Young, and Jesse Jackson. In the late 1960s, SCLC focused on problems of poverty and urban violence. After King was assassinated, Abernathy became president of SCLC.

**ACTIVITY OPTIONS**

**MULTIPLE LEARNING STYLES: LINGUISTIC** — BLOCK SCHEDULING

**READERS' THEATER**

**Class Time** Two class periods

**Task** Creating a readers' theater presentation about either the Montgomery bus boycott or about Martin Luther King, Jr.

**Purpose** To understand the importance of the bus boycott or achievements of Martin Luther King, Jr.

**Supplies Needed**
- Reference materials about the bus boycott and the life of Martin Luther King, Jr.
- Internet access
- Stools (optional)

**Activity** Divide students into groups of six or eight. Tell them that in readers' theater, presenters sit in a semicircle and read their parts from their scripts. A presenter may read more than one part. Students should gather quotes and memoirs of the bus boycott or of King's life and form them into a dramatic script. Then students should divide the material and highlight their parts on a copy of the script. Groups should practice reading through their presentations before performing them.

**INSTRUCT: OBJECTIVE** 

**Showdown in Little Rock/ Sit-Ins Energize the Movement**

Key Questions
- How did the Arkansas state government try to block school desegregation?
- What did President Eisenhower do to end the standoff with Governor Faubus?
- How did sit-ins advance blacks' civil rights?

**MORE ABOUT . . .**

**The Little Rock Nine**

The nine students who walked through the shouting, spitting crowd at Central High in 1957 became high achievers. Ernest Green served as Assistant Secretary of Housing and Urban Affairs under President Carter. Minnijean Brown Trickey is a writer and social worker, and Eckford also is a social worker. Jefferson Thomas works for the Department of Defense. Dr. Terence Roberts is a clinical psychologist, while Carlotta Walls Lanier works in real estate. Gloria Ray Karlmark was a writer and publisher before she retired. Thelma Mothershed-Wair was a teacher and now volunteers in a program for abused women.

***HISTORY through ART***

**Interpreting the Photograph** Will Counts took this photograph for the Associated Press. Tell students that in 1997, the Little Rock Nine gathered at Central High School to mark the 40th anniversary of their attempt to desegregate the school. Elizabeth Eckford and Hazel Bryan Massey embraced one another. Massey is the person directly behind Eckford in the photograph. Massey has apologized for her behavior. Ask students to contrast Elizabeth Eckford's demeanor and actions with those around her.

**Possible Responses: It shows angry, out-of-control people screaming at a young woman trying to walk to school.**

**In-Depth Resources: Unit 9**
- Primary Source, p. 10

## 4 Showdown in Little Rock

Massive resistance threatened the desegregation of schools in Little Rock, Arkansas, in 1957. Following the *Brown* case, the Little Rock school board made plans to integrate. It called for nine African-American students to enroll at Central High School in September 1957.

**Background**
The nine African-American students chosen to integrate Central High School became known as the Little Rock Nine.

As the start of the school year neared, segregationists tried to block the integration of the school. Arkansas governor Orval Faubus sided with the segregationists. On September 3, he ordered National Guard troops to prevent the African-American students from entering the school the next morning.

Eight of the students had received phone calls saying someone would drive them to the high school for their safety. When they arrived, the National Guard troops turned them away. The family of the ninth student, Elizabeth Eckford, had no telephone. She took a bus to school alone that morning. When she arrived, a mob of angry whites followed her toward the school's doors.

She saw a guard let some white students pass, so she went up to him. But he did not move out of the way. Later Eckford wrote, "When I tried to squeeze past him, he raised his bayonet. . . . Somebody started yelling, 'Lynch her! Lynch her!'" Finally, a white woman guided Eckford away from the mob and took her home.

**Vocabulary**
**lynch:** to execute illegally, especially by hanging

For three weeks, Faubus refused to allow the African-American students into the school—even after meeting with President Dwight Eisenhower. The president did not want to force the governor to obey the law, but he eventually realized that it was his only choice.

***HISTORY through ART***

Elizabeth Eckford faced an angry mob as she walked to Little Rock Central High School on September 4, 1957. She had made her black-and-white dress especially for her first day of school at Central High.

**How does the photograph show the emotions stirred by desegregation?**

816

**ACTIVITY OPTIONS**

**INTERDISCIPLINARY LINK: CIVICS**

**BLOCK SCHEDULING**

**LOCAL HISTORY**

**Class Time** One class period

**Task** Researching the process of desegregation in your state or community

**Purpose** To help students understand the history of states and communities in the 1950s

**Supplies Needed**
- Reference materials on desegregation, and state and local history
- Internet access

**Activity** Have students research the history of the integration of public schools in your state, city, or community. If your community has always been integrated, choose a city near you. Remember that desegregation could also apply to Hispanic Americans, Asian Americans, and Native Americans. Allow students to choose one of the following methods of presenting their findings: an annotated time line, interviews with school officials, an illustrated report, or an oral report.

On September 24, Eisenhower ordered the 101st Airborne Division into Little Rock. The Little Rock Nine rode to school, escorted by jeeps armed with machine guns. Paratroopers lined the streets and protected the students as they entered Central High.

## Sit-Ins Energize the Movement

Victories like the one in Little Rock encouraged civil rights supporters to continue their fight. In February 1960, four African-American college students began a sit-in to desegregate a lunch counter at a store in Greensboro, North Carolina. A **sit-in** is a protest in which people sit in a place and refuse to move until their demands are met. The students sat down at the lunch counter and ordered coffee. The waitress refused to serve them because they were African Americans.

> ***"The doctrine of 'separate but equal' has no place."***
>
> **From *Brown* v. *Board of Education***

C. Possible Response They staged nonviolent sit-ins to demonstrate publicly their disapproval of discrimination.

*Reading***History**
C. Solving Problems How did African Americans end discrimination at many lunch counters?

That first day, the students stayed for 45 minutes. They came back each day that week with more protesters. By Thursday, there were more than 100 protesters, including some whites. Over the following weeks, thousands of protesters took part in sit-ins across the South.

As the sit-ins spread, segregationists began to abuse the protesters. They covered the protesters with ammonia and itching powder. They yelled at them, beat them, and burned them with cigarettes. Some protesters went to jail. But other protesters replaced them at the counters. The sit-ins were an effective protest tactic. They forced many stores with lunch counters to serve African Americans.

Many civil rights leaders saw the success of the sit-ins and supported an organization for young people. Out of this movement, the Student Nonviolent Coordinating Committee (**SNCC**) was formed. Through SNCC, SCLC, and other groups, the civil rights movement increased the pressure for change in the 1960s, as you will read in the next section.

### Section 1 Assessment

**1. Terms & Names**

Identify:
- Thurgood Marshall
- *Brown* v. *Board of Education of Topeka*
- Montgomery bus boycott
- Dr. Martin Luther King, Jr.
- SCLC
- sit-in
- SNCC

**2. Taking Notes**

Use a cluster diagram to record details about the early civil rights movement.

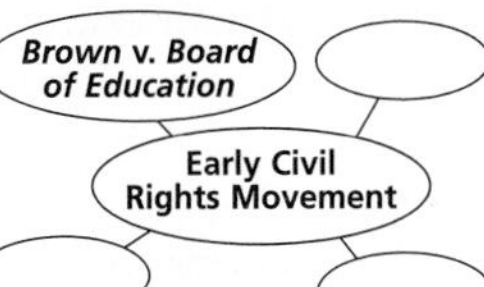


**3. Main Ideas**

a. How did World War II help lead to the civil rights movement?

b. What role did Thurgood Marshall play in challenging segregation?

c. How did Martin Luther King, Jr., become a well-known civil rights leader?

**4. Critical Thinking**

**Contrasting** How did the tactics used by civil rights protesters differ from the response of many Southern whites?

THINK ABOUT
- the Montgomery bus boycott
- the events in Little Rock
- the nature of sit-ins

ACTIVITY OPTIONS

ART / TECHNOLOGY

You have been asked to honor people in the civil rights movement. Create a **wall of fame,** or plan a **Web page** that pays tribute to several of them.



### MORE ABOUT . . .

**President Eisenhower Calls in the Troops**

Eisenhower had not supported the *Brown* decision. However, once the decision was rendered, he quickly abolished segregation in the Washington, D.C., schools. He also signed the 1957 Civil Rights Act, a weak attempt to give federal protection to black voter registration in the South. Eisenhower tried talking Faubus out of intervening in desegregation. He believed strongly in not interfering with local governments but felt Faubus left him no choice. His dispatch of the popular "Screaming Eagles" made it clear that, as commander-in-chief of all U.S. forces, he, not Faubus, was in command.

## ASSESS & RETEACH

**Setting the Stage** Have students fill in the causes for *Brown* v. *Board of Education of Topeka* and the Montgomery bus boycott on the chapter graphic organizer.

 **Formal Assessment**
- Section Quiz, p. 419

 **Critical Thinking Transparency CT85**
- Setting the Stage

### RETEACHING ACTIVITY

In groups of three, have students take roles of Rosa Parks, Elizabeth Eckford, and one of the four Greensboro, North Carolina, freshman protesters. Have students explain what the person whose role they have taken did to further the civil rights movement.

 **In-Depth Resources: Unit 9**
- Reteaching Activity, p. 15

### Section 1 Assessment

**1. Terms & Names**

**Thurgood Marshall,** p. 814
***Brown* v. *Board of Education of Topeka*,** p. 814
**Montgomery bus boycott,** p. 815
**Dr. Martin Luther King, Jr.,** p. 815
**SCLC,** p. 815
**sit-in,** p. 817
**SNCC,** p. 817

**2. Taking Notes**

*Brown* v. *Board of Education:* challenged school segregation; Montgomery bus boycott: Supreme Court rules bus segregation unconstitutional; Little Rock: governor sends troops to prevent integration, Eisenhower sends troops to enforce integration; Sit-Ins: college students try to desegregate lunch counters

**3. Main Ideas**

**a.** African-American soldiers who had fought for freedom in Europe wanted it at home. **b.** He was the lawyer for the NAACP, and he tried *Brown* v. *Board of Education.* **c.** His eloquence helped convince others to extend the Montgomery bus boycott, and he displayed courage when his life was threatened.

**4. Critical Thinking**

Many Southern whites turned to hate and violence, unlike the civil rights protesters, who used peaceful and legal methods to challenge segregation.

ACTIVITY OPTIONS

 **Alternative Assessment**
- Rubrics 1.4, 5.1

## SECTION OBJECTIVES

1. To evaluate the effects of the 1960 election and the Birmingham protests
2. To analyze the events that led to passage of the Civil Rights Act of 1964
3. To describe President Johnson's role in the civil rights movement
4. To explain divisions in the civil rights movement

**SKILLBUILDER**
Interpreting Maps: Place, p. 821
Interpreting Charts, p. 822

**CRITICAL THINKING**
Drawing Conclusions, pp. 819, 821
Making Inferences, pp. 820, 823
Forming Opinions, p. 823

## FOCUS & MOTIVATE

### 5-MINUTE WARM-UP

**Making Inferences** These questions focus on the impact of the campaign for voter rights.

1. Look at the map on page 821. Why do you think more African Americans were not registered voters in 1960?
2. What reasons might there be for the increases in voter registration?

 **Warm-Up Transparency WT29**

## INSTRUCT

### INSTRUCT: OBJECTIVE 

**Kennedy and Civil Rights/ Protests in Birmingham**
Key Questions
- What action increased African-American support for Kennedy in the 1960 election?
- What was the purpose of the Freedom Rides?
- Why did civil rights leaders choose Birmingham as a location for protests?

**In-Depth Resources: Unit 9**
- Guided Reading, p. 4
- Building Vocabulary, p. 6

**Reading Study Guide** (Spanish and English), pp. 281–282

# 2 Kennedy, Johnson, and Civil Rights

**MAIN IDEA**
The civil rights movement led to the end of legal segregation.

**WHY IT MATTERS NOW**
African Americans still face discrimination but now have more opportunities than before.

**TERMS & NAMES**
Freedom Ride
CORE
March on Washington
Civil Rights Act of 1964
Freedom Summer
Voting Rights Act
Great Society
Malcolm X

### ONE AMERICAN'S STORY

**Jim Zwerg, a white student from Wisconsin, joined a Freedom Ride in May 1961. <u>Freedom Rides</u> were protests against segregation on interstate busing in the South. During the rides, whites would sit in the back of a bus. African Americans would sit in the front and refuse to move. At bus terminals along the route, black riders would try to use "whites only" facilities.**

**Zwerg and the other freedom riders expected trouble from segregationists on the journey. In Montgomery, Alabama, segregationists savagely attacked the freedom riders.**

**Zwerg was beaten unconscious. But he was not the only victim. Black or white, man or woman, few freedom riders were spared. In this section, you will read how the Freedom Rides and other protests helped African Americans win support for civil rights.**

John Lewis (left) and Jim Zwerg of SNCC are covered with blood after being beaten in Montgomery.

## 1 Kennedy and Civil Rights

In 1960, Americans elected a new president. Although civil rights was not the main issue in the campaign, it played an important role. The Democrats nominated John F. Kennedy, a senator from Massachusetts. The Republicans nominated Vice-President Richard Nixon. During the campaign, the candidates had similar positions on most issues. But many Americans thought that Kennedy was more dynamic.

Late in the campaign, police arrested Martin Luther King, Jr., in Georgia. Kennedy called King's wife, and Robert Kennedy, the candidate's brother, arranged for King's release. That one act dramatically increased African-American support for Kennedy. The election was one of the closest in U.S. history, and Kennedy won.

As president, Kennedy had to work with a Congress that was reluctant to act on civil rights issues. In the early 1960s, Southern Democrats supported segregation. Kennedy did not want to anger Southern Democrats because they could weaken his presidency.

Even so, activists continued to pressure the federal government. In May 1961, the Congress of Racial Equality (<u>CORE</u>) planned Freedom Rides to desegregate interstate buses, or buses that travel between states.



### RECOMMENDED RESOURCES

**In-Depth Resources: Unit 9**
- Guided Reading, p. 4
- Building Vocabulary, p. 6
- Literature Selection: Two Songs About Birmingham, pp. 12–14
- Reteaching Activity, p. 16

**Reading Study Guide** (Spanish and English), pp. 281–282

**Economics in History**
- Poverty Amidst Plenty, p. 29

**Outline Map Activities**
- Civil Rights Hot Spots, 1954–1968, pp. 57–58

**American History Plays**
- *I Have a Dream* by Aileen Fisher

**Formal Assessment**
- Section Quiz, p. 420

**Alternative Assessment**
- Rubrics, 1.1
- Rubrics, 3.6

**Access for Students Acquiring English/ESL**
- Guided Reading, p. 194

Technology Resources

**Humanities Transparency HT57**
- Civil Rights March

 **America's Music CD**

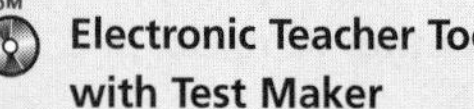
**Electronic Teacher Tools with Test Maker**

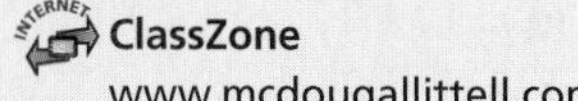
**ClassZone**
www.mcdougallittell.com

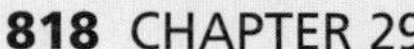

Despite attacks on the freedom riders by segregationists along the route, the riders would not give up. Kennedy had to do something. Finally, he sent a group of federal marshals to protect the riders. Four months later, the federal government issued an order integrating interstate bus facilities. The riders had achieved their goal.

A. Possible Response because they would gain sympathy and support when the public heard about or saw the violence

## Protests in Birmingham

In the early 1960s, the civil rights movement gained strength across the South. African Americans in Birmingham, Alabama, wanted to integrate public facilities and gain better job and housing opportunities. Local civil rights leaders invited King and SCLC to join the protests.

*Reading* **History**

**A. Drawing Conclusions** Why did civil rights leaders choose to protest in cities where they were likely to face violence?

Birmingham was a great opportunity for protesters to expose the evils of segregation. They knew that Eugene "Bull" Connor, the city's Public Safety commissioner, was likely to use violence to stop the protests. They also knew that the sight of segregationists attacking nonviolent protesters would increase the pressure for change.

The protests began in April 1963. After about a week, the police arrested King, who had traveled to Birmingham for the protests. From jail, King wrote an eloquent defense of the protests.

*A VOICE FROM THE PAST*

I guess it is easy for those who have never felt the stinging darts of segregation to say, "Wait." . . . [But] there comes a time when the cup of endurance runs over, and men are no longer willing to be plunged into an abyss [a bottomless pit] of injustice.

**Martin Luther King, Jr.,** "Letter from Birmingham Jail"

SCLC recruited children for the Birmingham marches. The police used dogs and firehoses on the marchers. People across the nation saw this on television and were horrified. Soon, Birmingham's white leaders agreed to

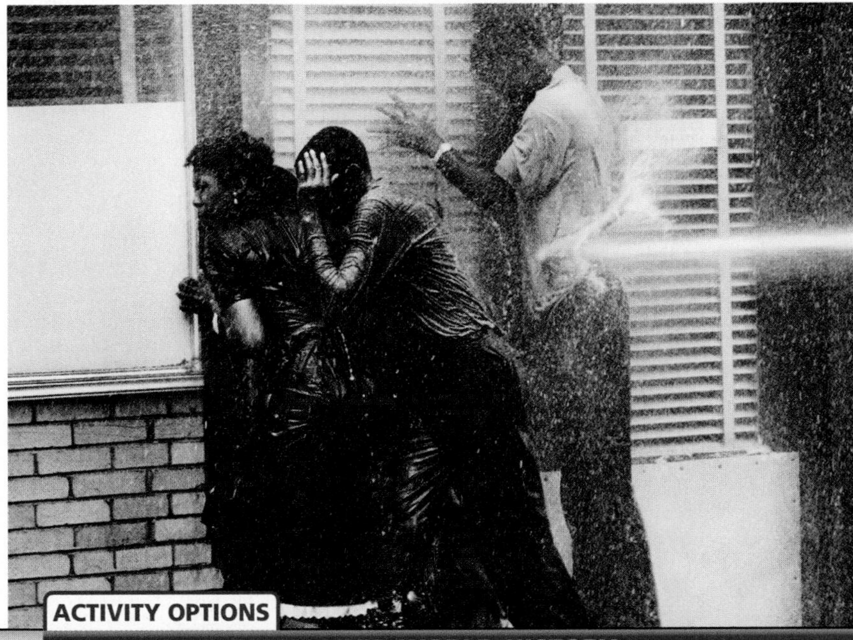

**The firehoses used on Birmingham protesters had enough force to tear people's clothes and send small children skidding down the street.**





### CRITICAL THINKING ACTIVITY

**Recognizing Effects** The Birmingham marches had effects that ranged far beyond the city limits. Have students copy the graphic organizer below and summarize the major immediate and long-range effects of the protest.

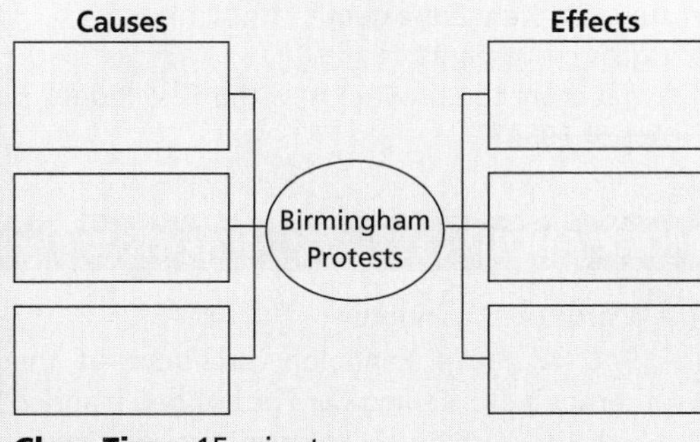


**Class Time** 15 minutes

### MORE ABOUT . . .

**The Birmingham Children's March**

Civil rights leaders planned to embarrass Birmingham city officials by filling Birmingham's jails with children, especially teenagers. However, they did not anticipate the level of violence directed at the children. They were attacked by dogs, sprayed with high-pressure torrents from firehoses, and beaten by billy-club-wielding policemen. Over 900 children were jailed during the first day of the march. The next day, more children marched down the streets of Birmingham.

 **In-Depth Resources: Unit 9**

- Literature Selection: Two Songs About Birmingham, pp. 12–14

ACTIVITY OPTIONS

### INTERDISCIPLINARY LINK: WORLD HISTORY

BLOCK SCHEDULING

**THE INFLUENCE OF GANDHI**

**Class Time** One class period

**Task** Researching the life and teachings of Mohandas Gandhi

**Purpose** To learn about the influence of Gandhi on the civil rights movement

**Supplies Needed**
- Reference materials about Gandhi's influence on Martin Luther King, Jr., and other civil rights leaders
- Books of quotations, including quotes from Gandhi
- Internet access
- Posterboard, art supplies

**Activity** Students should research the life of Mohandas Gandhi and his influence on Martin Luther King, Jr., and other civil rights leaders. Then students should select one short quotation from Gandhi. Tell students to make a poster including this quotation and its link to the American civil rights movement. They may use any style they prefer, such as collage. Students should be prepared to discuss their quote in terms of Gandhi's life and his influence on the civil rights movement.

**INSTRUCT: OBJECTIVE 2**

**The March on Washington/ New Civil Rights Laws**

Key Questions

- What were some of the effects of the March on Washington?
- How did Kennedy's death affect the civil rights movement?
- What were the provisions of the Civil Rights Act of 1964?

**MORE ABOUT . . .**

**The March on Washington**

In 1941, A. Philip Randolph, president of the Brotherhood of Sleeping Car Porters, had planned a march on Washington to dramatize discrimination against African Americans in war-related industries. President Roosevelt had worked hard to stave off the march. He created a national Fair Employment Practices Committee, and Randolph called off the march. However, 20 years later, Randolph, now 73, planned a new march "for jobs and freedom." Bayard Rustin, another civil rights leader who had worked on the 1941 march, also helped plan the March on Washington.

**MORE ABOUT . . .**

**Kennedy's Assassination**

The news of Kennedy's assassination went out over the news wires at 1:34 P.M. Many Americans remember exactly where they were when they heard the terrible news that the young president had been shot. Millions stayed by their televisions for four days watching as Kennedy's coffin was displayed at the Rotunda of the Capitol and then taken to Arlington National Cemetery for burial.

desegregate lunch counters, remove segregation signs, and employ more African Americans in downtown stores.

## 2 The March on Washington

The events in Birmingham caused many Americans to support passage of new laws to protect the civil rights of all people. Civil rights organizations planned a huge demonstration in Washington, D.C., to build support for civil rights legislation.

On August 28, 1963, about 250,000 people took part in the **March on Washington,** as the demonstration became known. The march ended at the Lincoln Memorial. The high point of the march came when King delivered his "I Have a Dream" speech. (For a section from King's speech, see page 828.) During this speech, King spoke these famous words.

*Reading History*

**B. Making Inferences** Why might marchers have chosen the Lincoln Memorial as the place to end their march?

**B. Possible Response** because of Lincoln's role in freeing enslaved persons and advancing the civil rights of African Americans

> *A VOICE FROM THE PAST*
>
> I have a dream that my four little children will one day live in a nation where they will not be judged by the color of their skin, but by the content of their character.
>
> **Martin Luther King, Jr.**, from "I Have a Dream"

The March on Washington united many groups that called for passage of civil rights laws. President Kennedy promised support.

## New Civil Rights Laws

Tragically, though, President Kennedy did not live long enough to fulfill this promise. On November 22, 1963, Kennedy and Vice-President Lyndon Baines Johnson went to Texas to campaign. As the presidential motorcade passed through Dallas, thousands of people greeted the president. Suddenly, shots rang out. Kennedy slumped forward; he'd been hit. The president died within an hour.

**Background**

The man accused of shooting Kennedy, Lee Harvey Oswald, was killed two days later by another assassin.

The tragedy deeply saddened the nation. Schools, factories, and businesses closed as citizens mourned their slain leader. The assassination of President Kennedy would remain a central event in the memories of many Americans in the decades to come.

Lyndon Johnson became president after Kennedy's death. He promised to continue Kennedy's policies. Johnson moved quickly on civil rights. He argued that "no memorial oration or eulogy could more eloquently honor President Kennedy's memory than the earliest possible passage of the civil rights bill." The nation's grief led to broad support for the bill.

**Kennedy's flag-draped casket is drawn through the streets of Washington, D.C., during the slain leader's funeral procession.**



In July, the **Civil Rights Act of 1964** was signed into law. The law banned segregation in public places, such as hotels, restaurants, and theaters. It also created the Equal Employment Opportunity Commission to prevent job discrimination. At long last, segregation was officially illegal throughout the United States.

**ACTIVITY OPTIONS**

**MULTIPLE LEARNING STYLES: MUSICAL**

**BLOCK SCHEDULING**

**CIVIL RIGHTS SONGS**

**Class Time** One class period

**Task** Learning songs of the civil rights movement and identifying some of the artists who popularized these songs

**Purpose** To appreciate a significant part of our musical heritage

**Supplies Needed**

- Reference materials about the music of the civil rights protests
- CDs or cassettes of civil rights songs such as "Go Tell It on the Mountain," "We Shall Overcome," "Oh, Freedom," "I'm on My Way" by performers such as Odetta, Joan Baez, and Peter, Paul, and Mary

**Activity** Divide the class into groups, including one strong singer in each group. Have student groups do research to learn what songs protesters sang during the Freedom Rides and at the March on Washington. Each group should choose one civil rights song and learn it well enough to lead the class in a sing-along. Encourage students to accompany themselves on guitar or piano.

 **America's Music CD**

## 3 Fighting for Voting Rights

White Southerners had long used literacy tests, poll taxes, and violence to keep African Americans from voting. The Civil Rights Act of 1964 barred states from using different voting standards for blacks and whites. In the same year, the states ratified the Twenty-Fourth Amendment. It outlawed poll taxes. Even so, African Americans in the South still found it difficult to vote. As a result, they lobbied Congress to pass a strong voting rights law.

In 1964, SNCC organized a voter-registration drive for Southern blacks. The program was called **Freedom Summer.** It brought Northern college students into Mississippi to work with SNCC organizers. The young volunteers endured bombings, beatings, arrests, and murder while performing their work. Even so, they managed to add about 1,200 African Americans to voter registration rolls.

C. Possible Response By showing a national audience the terrible effects of discrimination, television helped to win support for the movement.

*Reading* **History**
**C. Drawing Conclusions** How did television help to advance the civil rights movement?

Early in 1965, King and SCLC organized voter-registration drives in Selma, Alabama, including a protest march to Montgomery. On March 7, as the marchers crossed a bridge at the edge of Selma, state troopers on horseback attacked them. Americans watched as the violence was broadcast on national television. Pressure for federal action rose.

President Johnson told Alabama Governor George Wallace that he would not tolerate any more violence. When the march to Montgomery resumed, the president sent troops to protect it. He also used the public's anger at the incident to push for action on voting rights.

*Reading* **History**
**D. Reading a Map** Use the map below to see how the registration of African-American voters increased throughout the South.

Johnson used the considerable political skills he had acquired when he was a senator to push a voting rights bill through Congress. On August 6, 1965, he signed the **Voting Rights Act** into law. It banned literacy tests and other laws that kept blacks from registering to vote. It also sent federal officials to register voters. Within weeks, the percentage of African Americans in Selma who registered to vote increased from 10 percent to 60 percent.

Skillbuilder Answer Mississippi

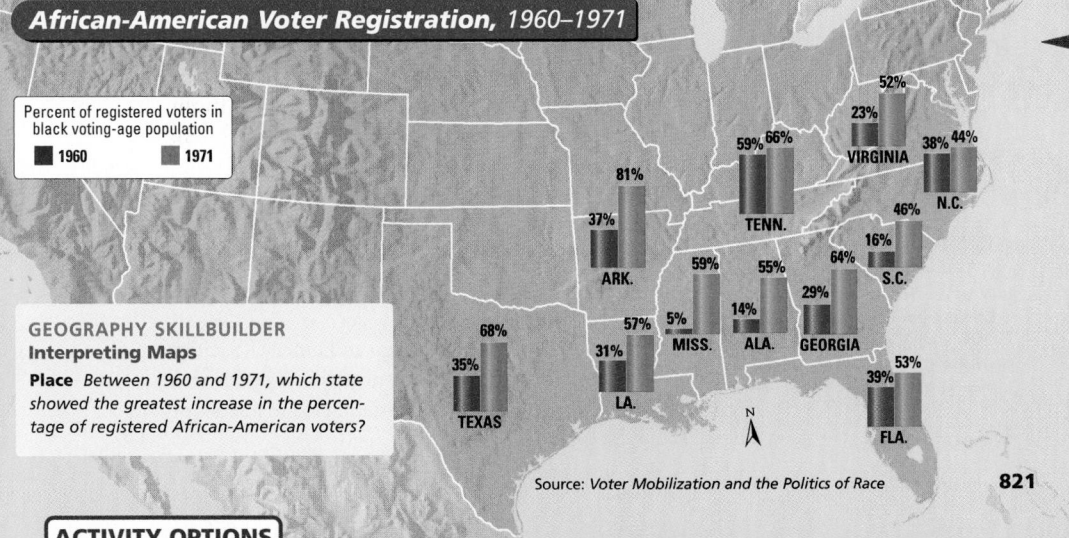

### *African-American Voter Registration, 1960–1971*

Percent of registered voters in black voting-age population
1960 | 1971

| | 1960 | 1971 |
|---|---|---|
| VIRGINIA | 23% | 52% |
| N.C. | 38% | 44% |
| TENN. | 59% | 66% |
| ARK. | 37% | 81% |
| S.C. | 16% | 46% |
| MISS. | 5% | 59% |
| ALA. | 14% | 55% |
| GEORGIA | 29% | 64% |
| LA. | 31% | 57% |
| TEXAS | 35% | 68% |
| FLA. | 39% | 53% |

Source: *Voter Mobilization and the Politics of Race*

GEOGRAPHY SKILLBUILDER
**Interpreting Maps**
**Place** *Between 1960 and 1971, which state showed the greatest increase in the percentage of registered African-American voters?*

821



**INSTRUCT: OBJECTIVE** 

**Fighting for Voting Rights/ Johnson and the Great Society**

Key Questions
- What was the purpose of Freedom Summer?
- What were the effects of the Voting Rights Act of 1965?
- How did the Great Society help the poor, disenfranchised, and elderly?

**Humanities Transparency HT57**
- Civil Rights March

### MORE ABOUT . . .

**Mississippi in the 1960s**
Mississippi was chosen for Freedom Summer because, in the 1960s, 86 percent of its nonwhite families lived below the national poverty line. Although 45 percent of the population was black, only 5 percent of the black population was registered to vote. Those attempting to register to vote had to pass a literacy test that involved "reading and interpreting" a section of the state constitution. White registrars decided who passed the test. African Americans with doctoral degrees failed it, but most whites, even those with little education, passed.

### HISTORY FROM VISUALS

**Reading the Map** Ask students which Southern state had the lowest percentage of African-American registered voters in 1960 and which had the lowest in 1971. Then ask which Southern state had the highest percentage of African-American registered voters in 1960 and which had the highest in 1971. **Responses** lowest 1960: Mississippi; lowest 1971: North Carolina; highest 1960: Tennessee; highest 1971: Arkansas

**Extension** Ask students to find current voter registration statistics for the states shown on the map.

### ACTIVITY OPTIONS

**INTERDISCIPLINARY LINK: MATHEMATICS** — BLOCK SCHEDULING

**USING MATH TO MAKE A GENERALIZATION**

**Class Time** 20 minutes

**Task** Using math to make a generalization about the increase in voter registration

**Purpose** To help students use statistics to make a generalization

**Supplies Needed**
- Reference materials about Freedom Summer and the voter registration drive

**Activity** Have students look at the map on this page. Ask students to use mental math or calculators to determine the percentage by which African-American voter registration increased in each of the states shown in the South from 1961 to 1971. Finally, ask students to write a one-sentence generalization using their answer.

**INSTRUCT: OBJECTIVE** 

**Divisions in the Civil Rights Movement**

Key Questions

- Why were efforts to improve life for blacks in Northern cities frustrated?
- What were the goals of the Nation of Islam?
- How did the civil rights movement change after King's assassination?

 **Economics in History**
- Poverty Amidst Plenty, p. 29

 **Outline Map Activities**
- Civil Rights Hot Spots, 1954–1968, pp. 57–58

## MORE ABOUT . . .

**The Great Society**

President Johnson dreamed of a nation with no hunger, no poverty, and no discrimination. He gave memorable speeches describing that dream. Great Society legislation that he signed included bills about seat belt standards, mass transportation, national parks, food stamps, land and water conservation, arts funding, drug abuse, housing and urban development, higher education, fair packaging and labeling, child abuse, and age discrimination.

## HISTORY FROM VISUALS

**Reading the Chart** Ask students to describe the part of the American population most affected by each of the pieces of legislation described in the chart. **Possible Responses** Civil Rights Act—African Americans and members of other minority groups; Voting Rights Act—African Americans; Medical Care Act—senior citizens, the poor; Elementary and Secondary School Act—students and teachers

**Extension** Have students find out what other legislation was passed as part of the Great Society.

President Johnson signs the Medicare bill into law on July 30, 1965.

# Johnson and the Great Society

The Civil Rights Act and the Voting Rights Act were important parts of the reform plan supported by President Johnson. Shortly after taking office, Johnson asked Americans to seek a "great society [that] demands an end to poverty and racial injustice." His program was called the **Great Society**. It provided a series of programs to help the disenfranchised, the poor, the elderly, and women. It also included legislation to promote education, end discrimination, and protect the environment.

**Vocabulary**
**disenfranchised:** people deprived of the rights of citizenship, especially the right to vote

Many of the programs were passed and still exist today, such as Medicare and Medicaid. Medicare provides health insurance for senior citizens, while Medicaid provides medical care for the poor.

In addition, Congress passed the Elementary and Secondary School Act, which provided new federal funds for education. Laws were also passed to protect the environment. Congress strengthened the 1960 Clean Water and 1963 Clean Air acts. And it passed legislation to protect endangered species and to preserve millions of acres of wilderness.

### The Great Society

**Civil Rights Act (1964)**
Outlawed discrimination in public places, created the Equal Employment Opportunity Commission, and barred states from using different standards for voter registration for whites and blacks

**Voting Rights Act (1965)**
Banned literacy tests and used federal registrars to register voters

**Medical Care Act (1965)**
Established Medicare and Medicaid programs to assist the aged and the poor with medical care

**Elementary and Secondary School Act (1965)**
Provided federal aid to education

SKILLBUILDER
**Interpreting Charts**
1. *What act created the Equal Employment Opportunity Commission?*
2. *What acts helped to increase the number of African-American voters?*

Skillbuilder Answers
1. Civil Rights Act (1964)
2. Civil Rights Act (1964) and Voting Rights Act (1965)

# Divisions in the Civil Rights Movement

In the late 1960s, with the civil rights laws of Johnson's Great Society already passed, civil rights leaders disagreed about what steps to take next. The SCLC and other organizations wanted to expand the nonviolent struggle. But some groups wanted the movement to become more aggressive.

In 1966, King and the SCLC joined protests in Chicago. In the North, there were no laws that denied African Americans their civil rights—white people simply discriminated against them. Whites would not sell property in certain areas to African Americans, and some white employers refused to hire black workers.

In spite of the protests, white Chicagoans were no more interested in desegregation than Southern whites had been. Chicago Mayor Richard J. Daley made only a few minor changes before SCLC abandoned its campaign.

African Americans in Chicago and other U.S. cities were frustrated with their lack of political power and economic opportunity. This frustration led to a series of



## ACTIVITY OPTIONS

## INDIVIDUAL NEEDS

**LESS PROFICIENT READERS**

**Finding Main Ideas** Help students identify the main ideas about the divisions in the civil rights movement. Copy the graphic organizer shown onto the chalkboard. Help students add information to the graphic as they read the section.

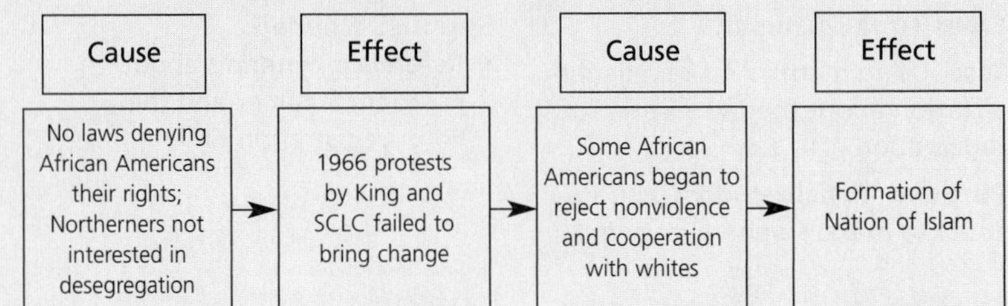

riots in the late 1960s. Nationwide, 164 riots broke out in the first 9 months of 1967. Then, on April 4, 1968, Martin Luther King, Jr., was assassinated in Memphis, Tennessee. As the nation mourned the slain civil rights leader, African-American neighborhoods across the country exploded in anger. Over 45 people died in the rioting.

*Reading*History
**E. Forming Opinions** Why did race riots take place in Northern cities?
E. Possible Response because discrimination existed in the North, even though it was not written into law

Some African Americans had begun to reject nonviolence and cooperation with whites. In 1966, SNCC's black members forced white members out of the organization. Stokely Carmichael, the new leader of SNCC, began to call for "black power." Carmichael and others wanted blacks to create their own organizations under their own control to fight white racism.

Malcolm X speaks at a rally in Harlem in 1963.

The Nation of Islam, a branch of Islam founded in the United States, also urged African Americans to separate from whites. In the 1960s, the Nation was led by Elijah Muhammad, but the group's most popular personality was **Malcolm X**.

By the mid-1960s, Malcolm X rejected the separatist ideas of the Nation of Islam and left the group. During a trip to Mecca, in Saudi Arabia, he had met Muslims of all races. He began to picture a world where all races could live together in peace. But he had little time to spread his new message. In 1965, he was gunned down by members of the Nation of Islam.

**Background**
Mecca is the holiest city for Muslims.

From the late 1960s on, civil rights progress came slowly for African Americans. But the African-American struggle for equality encouraged civil rights movements among other oppressed groups, as you will read in the next section.

## Section 2 Assessment

**1. Terms & Names**

**Identify:**
- Freedom Ride
- CORE
- March on Washington
- Civil Rights Act of 1964
- Freedom Summer
- Voting Rights Act
- Great Society
- Malcolm X

**2. Taking Notes**

Use a time line like the one shown to record important events of the civil rights movement.

1960 — event — event — 1968
event — event — event

In what year was the voter registration drive in Selma?

**3. Main Ideas**

a. Why did civil rights workers believe that Birmingham was a good place to protest?

b. How did civil rights workers fight to improve African-American voting rights?

c. Why did the movement begin to break apart?

**4. Critical Thinking**

**Making Inferences** Why do you think African Americans placed so much importance on the right to vote?

THINK ABOUT
- who and what they might want to vote for
- what they were willing to endure to win voting rights
- how Southern whites kept them from voting

**ACTIVITY OPTIONS**

**ART** / **SPEECH**

Imagine that you are taking part in the March on Washington. Design a **poster** you could carry, or deliver a **speech** in favor of civil rights.





## MORE ABOUT . . .

### Malcolm X

Malcolm X was named Malcolm Little when he was born in Omaha, Nebraska, in 1925. He grew up in Lansing, Michigan, where his father was an outspoken minister and a follower of Marcus Garvey. The KKK burned down the Littles' house and two years later, Malcolm's father was murdered. Young Malcolm spent time in detention homes. He moved to Boston, where he was arrested for burglary. While in jail, Malcolm became a member of the Black Muslim faith, or the Nation of Islam. He changed his last name to X, a custom of many members of the Nation of Islam.

## ASSESS & RETEACH

**Setting the Stage** Have students fill in the causes for the Montgomery bus boycott, the Civil Rights Act of 1964, and the Voting Rights Act of 1965 on the chapter graphic organizer.

**Formal Assessment**
- Section Quiz, p. 420

### RETEACHING ACTIVITY

Divide students into groups of six so that each student can be in charge of one heading in this section. Have each student review his or her section and make up three or four questions about it to ask the other group members. The student asking questions should coach the members of the group if they are not certain of the answers.

**In-Depth Resources: Unit 9**
- Reteaching Activity, p. 16

## Section 2 Assessment

**1. Terms & Names**

**Freedom Ride,** p. 818
**CORE,** p. 818
**March on Washington,** p. 820
**Civil Rights Act of 1964,** p. 820
**Freedom Summer,** p. 821
**Voting Rights Act,** p. 821
**Great Society,** p. 822
**Malcolm X,** p. 823

**2. Taking Notes**

1960: Kennedy elected president; 1961: CORE starts Freedom Rides; 1963: March on Washington; 1964: Civil Rights Act, Freedom Summer; 1965: voter registration drive in Selma, Voting Rights Act; 1966: SCLC protests in Chicago; 1968: King assassinated

1965

**3. Main Ideas**

**a.** They knew "Bull" Connor would probably respond violently, and that would gain them publicity. **b.** They took part in Freedom Summer, and they led protests in Selma, Alabama. **c.** Some African Americans abandoned nonviolence; the Nation of Islam called for blacks to separate from whites.

**4. Critical Thinking**

because they could use the vote to elect African Americans to office and to vote for candidates who favored civil rights legislation

### ACTIVITY OPTIONS

**Alternative Assessment**
- Rubrics for a poster, 1.1
- Rubrics for a speech, 3.6

## SECTION OBJECTIVES

1. To describe how Mexican Americans organized to promote reforms
2. To compare the political differences among Hispanic Americans
3. To describe the goals and successes of Native American protests for rights and recognition
4. To evaluate reasons for the women's movement and to describe its efforts to win rights for women

### CRITICAL THINKING

Summarizing, p. 825
Comparing, p. 826
Analyzing Causes, p. 827
Analyzing Points of View, p. 827

 **Why It Matters Now**
- Equality in Education, pp. 57–58

## FOCUS & MOTIVATE

### 5-MINUTE WARM-UP

**Drawing Conclusions** These questions focus on the equal rights movement.

1. Look at the photographs on pages 824, 826, and 827. How do they demonstrate the expansion of the struggle for equal rights?
2. How do you think the successes of the African-American civil rights movement affected other groups in America?

 **Warm-Up Transparency WT29**

## INSTRUCT

### INSTRUCT: OBJECTIVE 

**Mexican Americans Organize**

Key Questions
- What were the goals of *La Raza?*
- What demands did Mexican-American students make in Los Angeles?

 **In-Depth Resources: Unit 9**
- Guided Reading, p. 5
- Primary Source, p. 11

 **America's History Makers**
- Cesar Chavez, pp. 117–118

# 3 The Equal Rights Struggle Expands

**MAIN IDEA**

The African-American struggle for equality inspired other groups to fight for equality.

**WHY IT MATTERS NOW**

Nonwhites and women continue to fight for equality today.

**TERMS & NAMES**

Cesar Chavez
National Congress of American Indians
Betty Friedan
NOW
ERA

### ONE AMERICAN'S STORY

**Cesar Chavez** was born in Yuma, Arizona, in 1927. In the 1940s, he and his family worked as migrant laborers in the California fields. (Migrant workers travel from place to place in search of work.) One time, they found work picking peas. The whole family, parents and six children, worked. Chavez described the poor pay for such hard work.

*A VOICE FROM THE PAST*

They [the managers] would take only the peas they thought were good, and they only paid you for those. The pay was twenty cents a hamper, which had to weigh in at twenty-five pounds. So in about three hours, the whole family made only twenty cents.

**Cesar Chavez,** *Cesar Chavez: Autobiography of* La Causa

Cesar Chavez, head of the National Farm Workers Association, marches with striking grape pickers in the 1960s. (*Huelga* is the Spanish word for strike.)

In 1962, Chavez decided to start a union for farm workers. But the owners refused to recognize the union. Chavez used the example set by Martin Luther King, Jr., to change their minds.

Responding to Chavez's call, workers went on strike. Then Chavez asked people not to buy produce harvested by nonunion workers. The tactics worked. In 1970, 26 major California growers signed a contract with the union. It gave the workers higher wages and new benefits. The victory of Chavez and his union showed how the fight for equal rights spread beyond African Americans, as you will read in this section.

## 1 Mexican Americans Organize

The farm workers' struggle inspired other Mexican Americans. By the 1960s, most Mexican Americans lived in cities in the Southwest and California. In 1970, Mexican Americans formed *La Raza Unida* (lah RAH•sah oo•NEE•dah)—"the united people." *La Raza* fought for better jobs, pay, education, and housing. It also worked to elect Mexican Americans to public office.

Mexican-American students also began to organize. They wanted reform in the school system. The students demanded such changes as



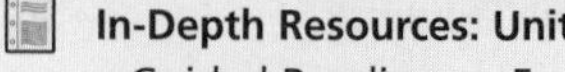

## RECOMMENDED RESOURCES

**In-Depth Resources: Unit 9**
- Guided Reading, p. 5
- Building Vocabulary, p. 6
- Skillbuilder Practice, p. 7
- Primary Source, p. 11
- Reteaching Activity, p. 17
- Enrichment Activity, p. 18

**Reading Study Guide** (Spanish and English), pp. 283–284

**America's History Makers**
- Cesar Chavez, pp. 117–118

**Why It Matters Now**
- Equality in Education, pp. 57–58

**Formal Assessment**
- Section Quiz, p. 421

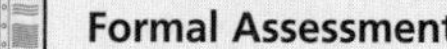

**Alternative Assessment**
- Rubrics, 5.4
- Rubrics, 1.13

**Access for Students Acquiring English/ESL**
- Guided Reading, p. 195
- Skillbuilder Practice, p. 196

**Technology Resources**

 **Humanities Transparency HT58**
- Cesar Chavez

 **Geography Transparency GT29**
- States Reject the Equal Rights Amendment, 1972–1982

**Background**
Many Mexican Americans prefer to be called Chicanos, or Chicanas if they are female.

better facilities, more courses on the Mexican-American experience, and more Mexican-American teachers.

In 1968, students in Los Angeles walked out of classes to press their demands. At first, school authorities reacted harshly to the walkouts and arrested many of the protesters. Even so, they eventually admitted to the poor conditions of many schools and met with protesters to discuss solutions. By the early 1970s, many of the reforms that the students demanded had been made.

## 2 Hispanic Diversity

Hispanics, including Mexican Americans, trace their roots to Spanish-speaking countries and cultures. Because these countries are commonly known as Latin America, some people from these areas refer to themselves as Latinos.

Because Hispanic Americans come from many different countries, they sometimes have little in common. For example, among Mexican Americans, immigration and citizenship are important issues. Puerto Ricans, however, are already U.S. citizens and are not troubled by such issues.

Similarly, many Cubans came to the United States as political refugees after Communists took power in Cuba. They tend to be more politically conservative than other Hispanics. Such differences make it difficult for Hispanic Americans to achieve political unity.

A. Possible Responses Most Hispanics have a language in common—Spanish. Even so, they come from many different countries and backgrounds.

**Reading History**
**A. Summarizing** What are the factors that unite and separate Hispanics?

**America's HERITAGE**

**CINCO DE MAYO**

During the civil rights era, many Americans learned to appreciate the variety of cultural traditions that make their nation unique.

For example, many Americans now join in the celebration of the Mexican holiday Cinco de Mayo (5th of May). This holiday commemorates the 1862 victory of Mexican troops over the French Army in Puebla, Mexico.

The holiday reflects the national pride of Mexicans over the defeat of a superior fighting power. But the holiday has also taken on a broader meaning for all Americans as a celebration of the right of all people to self-determination. A Cinco de Mayo gathering is shown below.

## 3 Native Americans Unite

Native Americans, like Hispanics, often had difficulty uniting to address common problems. But in the 1950s, that began to change. In 1953, the federal government began a "termination policy" that ended federal protection of land and other assets held by Native American tribes. One result of this policy was the decline of traditional Native American cultures.

Native Americans protested against these policies. The **National Congress of American Indians** (NCAI)—founded in 1944 to promote the "common welfare" of Native Americans—led the protests. Under pressure, the federal government changed the policy in 1958.

The success of these protests inspired a new generation of Native American activists to fight for their rights. In 1961, more than 400 Native Americans from dozens of tribes met in Chicago. They issued a statement they titled the Declaration of Indian Purpose. In it, they demanded the "right to choose our own way of life" and the "responsibility of preserving precious heritage."

In 1968, a group of Native Americans founded the American Indian Movement (AIM). AIM was more aggressive than other organizations in demanding rights for people on reservations and greater recognition of





### CRITICAL THINKING ACTIVITY

**Comparing** Have students create a chart showing the different concerns of various Hispanic groups. If possible, have students do research to learn what other issues are important to Hispanics.

**Class Time** 15–60 minutes

### INSTRUCT: OBJECTIVE 2

**Hispanic Diversity**
Key Questions
- What is meant by the terms *Hispanic* and *Latino?*
- What are some of the issues facing Hispanic groups in the United States?
- How might the differences among various Hispanic groups affect their ability to win reforms?

### America's HERITAGE

**A Mexican Celebration**
From October 31 to November 2, many Mexican-American families celebrate the Day of the Dead. Families decorate the graves of their loved ones and enjoy special foods. Day of the Dead celebrations are becoming very popular in many U.S. cities. For example, the Modern Art Museum of Fort Worth, Texas, holds an annual Day of the Dead exhibition and celebration.

### INSTRUCT: OBJECTIVE 3

**Native Americans Unite**
Key Questions
- How did Native Americans begin to unite for reform?
- In what ways did the NCAI and AIM differ?
- What was the result of Native American protests and court cases in the 1970s?

**ACTIVITY OPTIONS**

### SKILLBUILDER MINI-LESSON: CATEGORIZING

BLOCK SCHEDULING

**Explaining the Skill** Facts can be understood and retained more easily if they are organized into categories. By grouping similar events into the same category, one can see the relationships among them. It also becomes easier to compare and contrast events within categories.

**Applying the Skill** Ask students to think of the various struggles against discrimination described in this chapter. Then have them answer the following questions.

1. Into what categories might you divide the events of this chapter? *(nonviolent protests/violent protests; ethnic discrimination/gender-based discrimination; African-American civil rights/Hispanic civil rights/Native American civil rights/women's rights)*
2. Choose one of the categories from your answer to the first question above. How does grouping the items in that category help you understand more about each one? *(Categorizing highlights similarities and differences; if you are in sympathy with one group, recognizing the similarities of other groups may make you more sympathetic to them.)*

 **In-Depth Resources: Unit 9**
- Skillbuilder Practice, p. 7

## MORE ABOUT . . .

**Native Americans in the 1960s**

In the 1960s, Native Americans were less prosperous and less healthy than any other minority group in the United States. Their unemployment rate was ten times the national average; their annual income was $1,000 less than that of African Americans. Life expectancy of Native Americans was 20 years less than the national average. Suicide was 100 times more frequent among Native American youths than among whites.

## INSTRUCT: OBJECTIVE 4

**The Women's Movement**

Key Questions

- What kinds of discrimination did women face in the 1960s?
- What were NOW's goals?
- Why did the Equal Rights Amendment die without being ratified?

 **Geography Transparency GT29**

- States Reject the Equal Rights Amendment, 1972–1982

## MORE ABOUT . . .

**Betty Friedan**

In the late 1950s, Betty Friedan was a wife, mother, and suburban housewife. She was also a journalist and a graduate of Smith College. She began a survey of her college classmates and found that many of them experienced "a strange stirring, a sense of dissatisfaction, a yearning . . ." Friedan called these feelings of dissatisfaction "the problem that has no name." Her survey eventually led to Friedan's seminal book *The Feminine Mystique*. In her book, Friedan said that women needed meaningful work outside their homes.

Native Americans petition for the return of tribal artifacts at the state capital in Albany, New York, in 1970.

tribal laws. In 1972, members of AIM occupied the Bureau of Indian Affairs in Washington, D.C., for seven days. Russell Means, one of the group's leaders, declared, "We don't want civil rights in the white man's society—we want our own sovereign rights."

In the early 1970s, Native Americans protested to force the government to provide them with more federal aid. In addition, the Indian Self-Determination Act of 1975 gave tribal governments more control over social programs, law enforcement, and education. Other victories came through winning court cases. Native Americans won back some of their lands. They have also gone to court over rights to water, hunting, and fishing.

*Reading* **History**

**B. Comparing** Did any African-American organizations during the civil rights era have goals similar to AIM?
**B. Possible Response** The Nation of Islam also advocated separation from white society.

## 4 The Women's Movement

In the 1960s, women also demanded equal rights. Early in the decade, women were kept out of many jobs. They faced discrimination in many male-dominated businesses. For example, there were few female police officers. The military also limited the jobs open to women.

Women also had limited legal rights. Married women, for example, faced problems in signing contracts, selling property, and getting credit. A woman could lose her job if she became pregnant. In addition, society pressured women to quit their jobs when they married. Women who wanted to work at jobs outside their homes were seen as "unnatural." **Betty Friedan** described the problems women faced in her 1963 book, *The Feminine Mystique.*

*A VOICE FROM THE PAST*

We can no longer ignore that voice within women that says: "I want something more than my husband and my children and my home."

**Betty Friedan,** *The Feminine Mystique*

Friedan's words helped give direction to a movement for women's liberation. In 1966, Friedan helped to found the National Organization for Women (**NOW**). Some of NOW's major goals were to help women get good jobs and equal pay for their work.

In response to women's groups, Congress passed the Equal Rights Amendment (**ERA**) in 1972 and sent it to the states for ratification. The proposed amendment stated, "Equality of rights under the law shall not be denied or abridged by the United States or any State on account of sex." For the amendment to be added to the Constitution, 38 of the 50 states had to ratify it.

**Background**
An Equal Rights Amendment was initially proposed in 1923, after women gained the right to vote.

The amendment faced strong opposition, even from some women. Phyllis Schlafly, ERA's most famous opponent, argued that it would



## ACTIVITY OPTIONS

### INDIVIDUAL NEEDS: GIFTED AND TALENTED

**COMPARING THE HISTORY OF MINORITY GROUPS**

**Class Time** Two class periods
**Task** Creating a comparative report
**Purpose** To compare two different American minority groups

**Supplies Needed**
- Internet access
- Library resources on American minority groups

**Activity** Have students work alone or in small groups to compare one aspect of the history of two American minority groups. Tell students to limit their topic to make it manageable. For example, students might compare the protests of Mexican Americans in the 1970s to the protests of African Americans in the early 1960s. Have students present the results of their research in an essay or in an oral presentation.

 **In-Depth Resources: Unit 9**
- Enrichment Activity, p. 18

## Women's Rights Leaders, *1972*

In July 1972, women's rights leaders met in Washington, D.C., to demand that women play a larger role in the upcoming presidential conventions.

1 **Bella Abzug** was a U.S. representative from New York.

2 **Gloria Steinem** was the founding editor of *Ms.* magazine.

3 **Shirley Chisholm** was a U.S. representative from New York and ran for president in 1972.

4 **Betty Friedan** wrote *The Feminine Mystique* and was the cofounder and first president of NOW.

C. Possible Response It was not ratified by enough states (38).

*Reading* **History**

**C. Analyzing Causes** Why wasn't the ERA added to the Constitution even though it was passed in 1972?

destroy American families and that the problems of feminists were not the government's business. She wrote, "It would be a tragic mistake for our nation to succumb to the tirades and demands of a few women who are seeking a constitutional cure for their personal problems."

In 1982, the extended deadline for ratification passed. The amendment died because it fell three states short of ratification. Other reforms, however, reduced the inequality between women and men. Sections of the Civil Rights Act of 1964 and the Higher Education Act of 1972 outlawed discrimination against women. These two laws helped to expand opportunities for women in education, sports, and the workplace.

The civil rights movements that followed World War II greatly changed life in the United States. As you will read in the next chapter, the war in Vietnam also changed the nation.

## Section 3 Assessment

### 1. Terms & Names

**Identify:**
- Cesar Chavez
- National Congress of American Indians
- Betty Friedan
- NOW
- ERA

### 2. Taking Notes

Use a chart like the one shown to record important details about the struggle for equal rights.

| Mexican Americans | Native Americans | Women |
|---|---|---|
| | | |

How do the positions women hold today reflect changes won in the civil rights era?

### 3. Main Ideas

**a.** What was *La Raza Unida,* and what did it do?

**b.** What was the Declaration of Indian Purpose?

**c.** How did Betty Friedan help to launch the women's liberation movement?

### 4. Critical Thinking

**Analyzing Points of View** What were the different opinions about the ERA?

**THINK ABOUT**
- what NOW and other women's groups would have thought of it
- what Phyllis Schlafly thought of it

**ACTIVITY OPTIONS**

**TECHNOLOGY**
**LANGUAGE ARTS**

Plan part of a **multimedia presentation** focusing on one of the groups mentioned in this section, or write a **pamphlet** explaining that group's goals.





### MORE ABOUT . . .

**Women's Rights Advances**

Legislative advances for women include the passage of Title IX of the Higher Education Act in 1972, which prevents discrimination against women in educational programs or federal financial assistance; an Equal Opportunity Act that strengthens the enforcement of the original Equal Employment Opportunity Commission; and a tax break for working parents.

## ASSESS & RETEACH

**Setting the Stage** Have students fill in the causes for *La Raza Unida, The Feminine Mystique,* and the end of the termination policy on the chapter graphic organizer.

**Formal Assessment**
- Section Quiz, p. 421

**Critical Thinking Transparency CT85**
- Setting the Stage

### RETEACHING ACTIVITY

Create a chart like the one below outlining the issues faced by Hispanics, Native Americans, and women in achieving full equality. Have the students fill in the boxes.

| | Hispanics | Native Americans | Women |
|---|---|---|---|
| Issues | | | |
| Unique Problems | | | |
| Successes | | | |

**In-Depth Resources: Unit 9**
- Reteaching Activity, p. 17

## Section 3 Assessment

### 1. Terms & Names

**Cesar Chavez,** p. 824
**National Congress of American Indians,** p. 825
**Betty Friedan,** p. 826
**NOW,** p. 826
**ERA,** p. 826

### 2. Taking Notes

Mexican Americans: *La Raza Unida* fought to elect Chicanos; Native Americans: issued Declaration of Indian Purpose, Self-Determination Act of 1975; Women: publication of *The Feminine Mystique,* founded NOW. Equal-rights laws opened new political and economic opportunities for women.

### 3. Main Ideas

**a.** a Mexican-American organization that fought for better conditions and for Mexican Americans in government **b.** a statement in which Native Americans demanded the rights and responsibilities to preserve their way of life **c.** She wrote *The Feminine Mystique,* and she helped to found NOW.

### 4. Critical Thinking

NOW supported the ERA and campaigned actively for it; conservatives like Phyllis Schlafly opposed it and tried to persuade people that it would harm the nation.

**ACTIVITY OPTIONS**

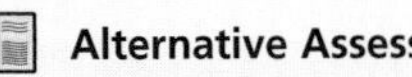

**Alternative Assessment**
- Rubrics, 5.4, 1.13

## INTERACTIVE PRIMARY SOURCES

**OBJECTIVE**

Students will appreciate the oratory of Martin Luther King, Jr.'s, "I Have a Dream" speech and analyze a letter from Cesar Chavez describing the nature of the farm workers' protests.

Primary Source Explorer
- *I Have a Dream*
- *An Open Letter*

The Explorer will help students select and produce their own presentations.

Specific information about the document can be found in **A Closer Look.** To learn more about key people and events of the time, students should click on **Life in These Times. What Happened Next** will show the student the impact of the document both at home and abroad and tie the document to today.

## FOCUS & MOTIVATE

**Comparing** Have students read the first sentence of Martin Luther King, Jr.'s, speech and the last sentence of Cesar Chavez's letter. Ask them to describe the similarities between the topics of the two sentences. Then ask students to speculate about the contents of the two documents based on the two sentences they have read.

### MORE ABOUT . . .

**King's Speaking Style**

While he was studying to become a minister, Martin Luther King, Jr., worked hard at learning how to preach from the pulpit. He took nine courses related to preaching while he was in the seminary, and he was a gifted preacher even as a student. King did not shout in his sermons, as Taylor Branch has said, "But he preached like someone who wanted to shout and this gave him an electrifying hold over the congregation." King learned as a student to win in turn the minds, the imaginations, and the hearts of his listeners.

INTERACTIVE PRIMARY SOURCES

# I Have a Dream

**Setting the Stage** On August 28, 1963, Martin Luther King, Jr., gave his most famous speech at the March on Washington. In it, he shared his dream of equality for all. **See Primary Source Explorer** 

**A CLOSER LOOK**

**ABRAHAM LINCOLN**

**In his speech, King made references to Abraham Lincoln. He specifically referred to the Emancipation Proclamation and used the phrase "Five score years ago" to remind his listeners of the opening of the Gettysburg Address.**

**1. Why do you think King would refer to Lincoln's speeches?**

**A CLOSER LOOK**

**THE AMERICAN DREAM**

**The American dream can mean different things to different people. Usually, however, it refers to the freedom and opportunity for Americans to lead their own lives.**

**2. How do civil rights fit into the American dream?**

**A CLOSER LOOK**

**GOING TO JAIL**

**Dr. King—who was arrested 30 times for civil rights activities—said that, with the faith that some day all men will be treated as equals, people will be ready to go to jail together.**

**3. Why do you think civil rights workers were willing to go to jail?**

I am happy to join with you today in what will go down in history as the greatest demonstration for freedom in the history of our nation.

Five score years ago, a great American, in whose symbolic shadow we stand today, signed the Emancipation Proclamation. . . . But one hundred years later, the Negro still is not free. One hundred years later, the life of the Negro is still sadly crippled by the **manacle**[1] of segregation and the chains of discrimination.

So we've come here today to dramatize a shameful condition. . . .

I say to you today, my friends, that even though we face the difficulties of today and tomorrow, I still have a dream. It is a dream deeply rooted in the American dream.

I have a dream that one day this nation will rise up and live out the true meaning of its **creed**[2] —we hold these truths to be self-evident that all men are created equal.

I have a dream that my four little children will one day live in a nation where they will not be judged by the color of their skin but by the content of their character.

I have a dream today!

This is our hope. This is the faith that I will go back to the South with. . . . With this faith we will be able to work together, to pray together, to struggle together, to go to jail together, to stand up for freedom together, knowing that we will be free one day. This will be the day, this will be the day when all of God's children will be able to sing with new meaning "My country 'tis of thee, sweet land of liberty, of thee I sing. Land where my fathers died, land of the Pilgrim's pride, from every mountainside, let freedom ring!" And if America is to be a great nation, this must become true.

And when this happens, when we allow freedom to ring, when we let it ring from every tenement and every hamlet, from every state and every city, we will be able to speed up that day when all of God's children, black men and white men, Jews and **Gentiles**,[3] Protestants and Catholics, will be able to join hands and sing in the words of the old Negro spiritual, "Free at last, free at last. Thank God Almighty, we are free at last."

*Martin Luther King, Jr.*

1. **manacle:** handcuff.
2. **creed:** statement of belief.
3. **Gentile:** Non-Jewish person.

828

### TEACHING STRATEGY

**Comparing and Contrasting** Ask students to create a Venn diagram that compares and contrasts the "I Have a Dream" speech with "An Open Letter." To stimulate student thinking, have them consider the following questions: 1) How is the impact of a speech different from that of a letter? 2) What audience is each document aimed at? 3) What appeals to the emotions does each document make? 4) How is the structure of the documents similar? How is it different?

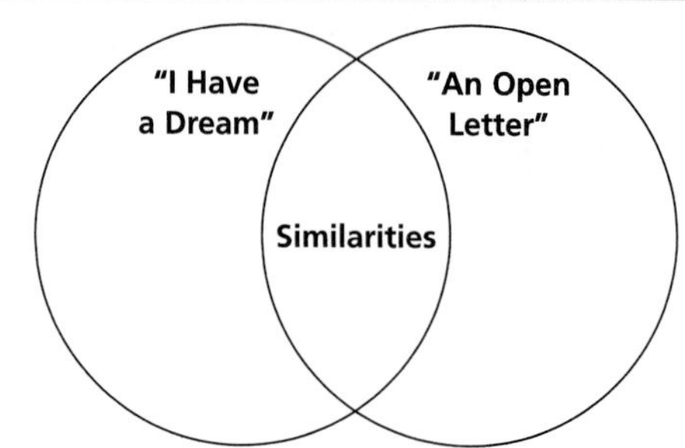

# An Open Letter

**Setting the Stage** In 1969, Cesar Chavez wrote a letter in which he denied accusations that he had used violence to win decent wages and better benefits for farm workers. **See Primary Source Explorer**

Today . . . we remember the life and sacrifice of Martin Luther King, Jr., who gave himself totally to the nonviolent struggle for peace and justice. In his letter from Birmingham Jail, Dr. King describes better than I could our hopes for the strike and boycott: "Injustice must be exposed, with all the tension its exposure creates, to the light of human conscience and the air of national opinion before it can be cured." For our part, I admit that we have seized upon every tactic and strategy consistent with the morality of our cause to expose that injustice and thus to heighten the sensitivity of the American conscience so that farmworkers will have without bloodshed their own union and the dignity of bargaining with their **agribusiness**[1] employers. . . .

Our strikers here in **Delano**[2] and those who represent us throughout the world are well trained for this struggle. . . . They have been taught not to lie down and die or to flee in shame, but to resist with every ounce of human endurance and spirit. To resist not with retaliation in kind but to overcome with love and compassion, with **ingenuity**[3] and creativity, with hard work and longer hours, with stamina and patient **tenacity**[4], with truth and public appeal, with friends and allies, with mobility and discipline, with politics and law, and with prayer and fasting. They were not trained in a month or even a year; after all, this new harvest season will mark our fourth full year of strike and even now we continue to plan and prepare for the years to come. . . .

We shall overcome and change it not by retaliation or bloodshed but by a determined nonviolent struggle carried on by those masses of farmworkers who intend to be free and human.

*Cesar E. Chavez*

1. **agribusiness:** farming as a large-scale business operation.
2. **Delano:** a farming city in California.
3. **ingenuity:** imagination or cleverness.
4. **tenacity:** persistence.

**A CLOSER LOOK**

**AGRIBUSINESS**

**Farm workers were excluded from the National Labor Relations Act of 1935—the law that gives most Americans the right to organize a union. By 1975, pressure from Chavez had convinced lawmakers in California to allow farm workers in the state to organize unions.**

**1. Why do you think farm workers wanted to organize a union?**

**A CLOSER LOOK**

**TRAINING FOR PROTESTS**

**During the civil rights era, protesters often received extensive training before participating in marches, demonstrations, and sit-ins. Chavez explains that farm workers were also trained for the struggle.**

**2. Why do you think that training for nonviolent protest might be necessary?**

*Interactive Primary Sources Assessment*

**1. Main Ideas**

a. Why does King declare that the United States is not living up to its creed?

b. What does King say must happen before America can be considered a truly great nation?

c. Why do you think Cesar Chavez refers to King in his speech?

**2. Critical Thinking**

**Comparing and Contrasting** In what ways were the problems that King and Chavez wrote about similar and different?

THINK ABOUT
- the kinds of discrimination they faced
- their hopes for the future

829

## INSTRUCT

Key Questions
- Why did Martin Luther King, Jr., begin the second paragraph of his speech with the words "Five score years ago . . ."?
- What is the effect of King's repetition of the phrase "I have a dream"?
- Why are Chavez's followers trained before participating in protests?
- Why does Chavez use the phrase "We shall overcome . . ." at the beginning of the last paragraph?

**MAKING PERSONAL CONNECTIONS**

After students have read and analyzed the "I Have a Dream" speech, ask them to think about their own dreams for the future of the United States. Ask them to write a statement or draw a picture explaining one of their dreams.

**MORE ABOUT . . .**

**Cesar Chavez**

Chavez was greatly influenced by the nonviolent philosophy of Gandhi and Martin Luther King, Jr. In a Gandhi-like gesture, Chavez fasted for 36 days to point out the continued injustices to farm workers, including child labor, sexual harassment of female workers, and the ongoing exposure of farm workers to pesticides. Chavez received the Medal of Freedom posthumously in 1994.

*Interactive Primary Sources Assessment*

**1. Main Ideas**

**a.** Although the Declaration of Independence stated that "all men are created equal," many Americans still faced discrimination and inequality because of the color of their skin.
**b.** All Americans, including African Americans, must enjoy the same freedoms.
**c.** Chavez wants to point out that the farm workers also followed nonviolence like King.

**2. Critical Thinking**

Chavez was primarily trying to solve economic problems, while King's focus was on political and legal problems. Both leaders expressed their hopes that all people would be free.

***A CLOSER LOOK***

**I Have A Dream**

1. King wants to convince people that the civil rights movement is a continuation of the work done by Lincoln.
2. People can only live the American dream if they have civil rights.
3. to show their respect for the law while standing up for what they believed

**An Open Letter**

1. Without a union, farm workers would have a hard time bargaining with the large businesses that employed them.
2. Protesters need to learn how to avoid the urge to fight back, to avoid injury, and how to help those who might be injured during protests.

## TERMS & NAMES

1. ***Brown* v. *Board of Education of Topeka,*** p. 814
2. **Montgomery bus boycott,** p. 815
3. **Dr. Martin Luther King, Jr.,** p. 815
4. **March on Washington,** p. 820
5. **Civil Rights Act of 1964,** p. 820
6. **Voting Rights Act,** p. 821
7. **Great Society,** p. 822
8. **Cesar Chavez,** p. 824
9. **National Congress of American Indians,** p. 825
10. **ERA,** p. 826

## REVIEW QUESTIONS

**Possible Responses**

1. After African Americans fought against racism abroad during World War II, they were prepared to fight harder against it back home; many African Americans had moved to cities, where greater resources and closer contacts increased the movement's strength.
2. Immediate: ended segregation in public schools; Long-term: ended segregation in all public facilities
3. Some whites joined the movement, but most were upset and angered by the changes and violently resisted.
4. Southern Democrats supported segregation, and he needed their support to avoid weakening his presidency.
5. The demands of civil rights leaders and their followers eventually gained widespread support among the American public, forcing politicians to take action.
6. It aided the disenfranchised, the poor, the elderly, and women. The programs also promoted education, fought discrimination, and protected the environment.
7. by struggling to form a union in California
8. The diversity of the Hispanic population made it challenging to organize a unified movement.
9. They believed the federal government's policies were causing the decline of traditional Native American cultures.
10. legal and job discrimination

# Chapter 29 ASSESSMENT

## VISUAL SUMMARY

### The Civil Rights Era

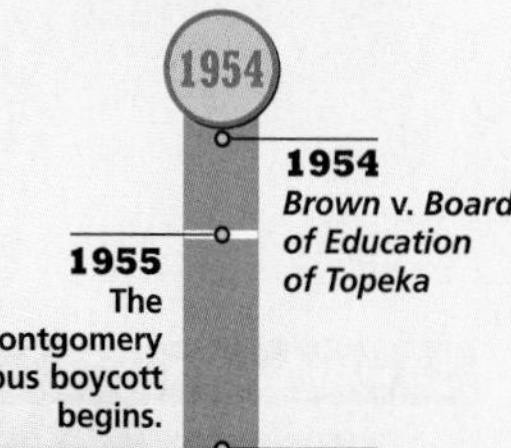

1954

**1954** *Brown* v. *Board of Education of Topeka*

**1955** The Montgomery bus boycott begins.

**1957** Federal troops are sent to desegregate Little Rock Central High School.

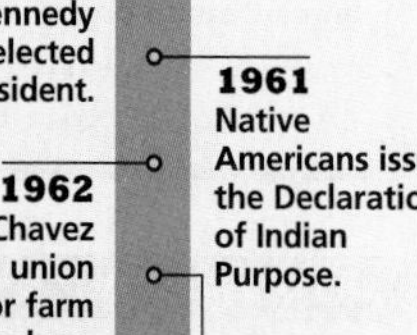

**1960** John F. Kennedy is elected president.

**1961** Native Americans issue the Declaration of Indian Purpose.

**1962** Cesar Chavez starts a union for farm workers.

**1963** March on Washington

Kennedy is assassinated, and Johnson becomes president.

**1964** Civil Rights Act

**1965** Voting Rights Act

Malcolm X is assassinated.

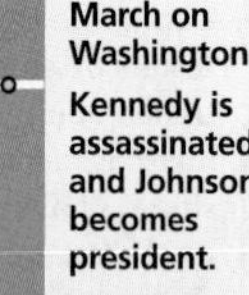

**1968** Martin Luther King, Jr., is assassinated.

**1970** *La Raza Unida* is founded.

**1972** Congress passes the Equal Rights Amendment, but it is never ratified by the states.

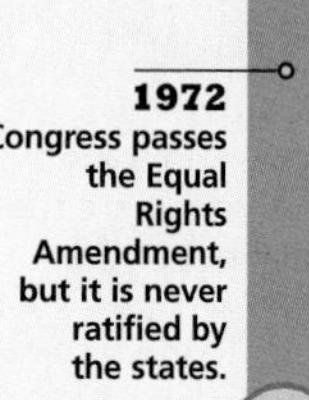

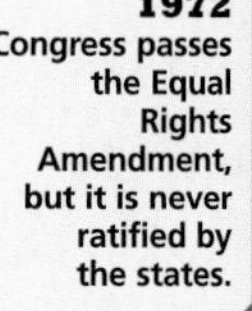

1975



## TERMS & NAMES

Briefly explain the importance of each of the following.

1. *Brown* v. *Board of Education of Topeka*
2. Montgomery bus boycott
3. Martin Luther King, Jr.
4. March on Washington
5. Civil Rights Act of 1964
6. Voting Rights Act
7. Great Society
8. Cesar Chavez
9. National Congress of American Indians
10. ERA

## REVIEW QUESTIONS

**Origins of the Civil Rights Movement (pages 813–817)**

1. What factors helped to give strength to the demands of the civil rights movement?
2. What were the immediate and long-term effects of *Brown* v. *Board of Education of Topeka?*
3. How did white people react to civil rights protests?

**Kennedy, Johnson, and Civil Rights (pages 818–823)**

4. What factors made it difficult for Kennedy to act on civil rights?
5. Why did Congress eventually pass civil rights legislation?
6. What effects did Johnson's Great Society legislation have?

**The Equal Rights Struggle Expands (pages 824–829)**

7. How did farm workers participate in the equal rights movement?
8. What challenges did Hispanics face in their civil rights struggle?
9. Why did Native Americans protest U.S. government policy?
10. What kinds of discrimination did women challenge during the civil rights era?

## CRITICAL THINKING

**1. USING YOUR NOTES**

Using your completed chart, answer the questions below.

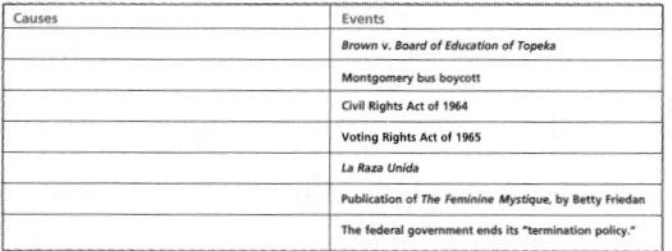

| Causes | Events |
|---|---|
| | *Brown* v. *Board of Education of Topeka* |
| | Montgomery bus boycott |
| | Civil Rights Act of 1964 |
| | Voting Rights Act of 1965 |
| | *La Raza Unida* |
| | Publication of *The Feminine Mystique,* by Betty Friedan |
| | The federal government ends its "termination policy." |

a. What causes resulted in the Supreme Court decision *Brown* v. *Board of Education of Topeka?*

b. What forces led Betty Friedan to write *The Feminine Mystique?*

**2. ANALYZING LEADERSHIP**

What qualities do you think made Martin Luther King, Jr., an effective leader?

**3. THEME: DEMOCRATIC IDEALS**

How did participants in the civil rights movement advance the democratic ideals of the United States?

**4. APPLYING CITIZENSHIP SKILLS**

How did the nonviolent methods used by protesters during the civil rights movement demonstrate good citizenship?

**5. MAKING GENERALIZATIONS**

In what ways do you think the lives of Americans today might differ from the lives of Americans who lived before the civil rights movement?

**Interact *with* History**

How has your study of the civil rights era influenced your decision about the ways in which you would act to change injustices in society?

## CRITICAL THINKING

**Possible Responses**

1. **USING YOUR NOTES** **a.** the legal challenges by the NAACP to the "separate but equal" doctrine established by *Plessy* v. *Ferguson* **b.** the legal and economic discrimination faced by women in the United States
2. **ANALYZING LEADERSHIP** He was well educated, a brilliant speaker, and passionate about seeking justice for all Americans.
3. **THEME: DEMOCRATIC IDEALS** The actions of these citizens compelled the nation's leaders to act to safeguard their civil rights.
4. **APPLYING CITIZENSHIP SKILLS** Protesters showed their respect for the law by acting nonviolently and being willing to suffer the consequences.
5. **MAKING GENERALIZATIONS** The establishment of legal protections has helped to improve the quality of life for minority populations.

**Interact *with* History** Students may say that they would become more active participants. They may also note the effective challenges to discrimination in the legal system and decide to become lawyers.

## HISTORY SKILLS

### 1. INTERPRETING GRAPHS

Study the graph. Answer the questions.

**Poverty in America,** *1962–1974*

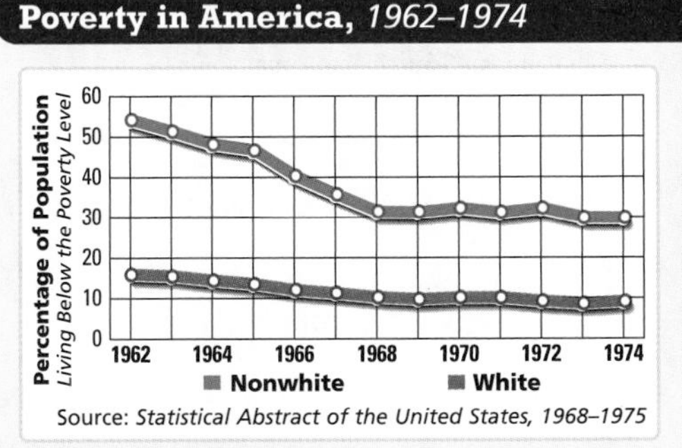

Source: *Statistical Abstract of the United States, 1968–1975*

**Basic Graph Elements**

a. What does the graph show?

**Interpreting the Graph**

b. Which group of people does the chart show as having a lower rate of poverty?

c. What was the difference between the poverty rates of whites and nonwhites in 1974?

### 2. INTERPRETING PRIMARY SOURCES

In 1976, Anthony Gauthier painted *Freedom*. Examine the painting and answer the questions.

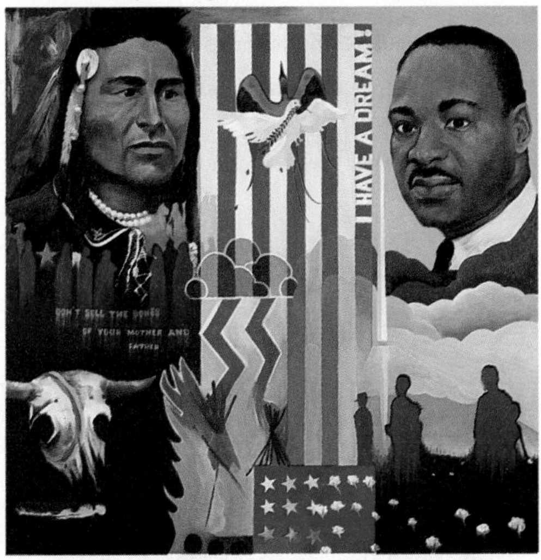


a. Why do you think the artist showed a Native American with Martin Luther King, Jr.?

b. How did the artist change the U.S. flag to make a statement?

## ALTERNATIVE ASSESSMENT

### 1. INTERDISCIPLINARY ACTIVITY: Language Arts

**Writing Your Representative** The House of Representatives is considering the Voting Rights Act. Your representative is against the act because it will reduce his or her chances for reelection. Write a letter trying to persuade your representative to support the bill.

### 2. COOPERATIVE LEARNING ACTIVITY

**Organizing a March** With a small group, think of a way in which you could make your community a better place for everyone to live. Then organize a march that will raise awareness of the group's plan. Remember to consider the following:

- How will you recruit and organize marchers?
- What would be the best route for the march?
- Is permission from local officials required to march?
- Will you need to consider food and sanitation?

### 3. PRIMARY SOURCE EXPLORER

**Creating a Radio Special** Many people say that the civil rights movement reached its climax on August 28, 1963. On that day, about 250,000 people arrived in Washington, D.C., to peacefully protest racial discrimination and show support for civil rights legislation. Use the CD-ROM, Internet, books, and other resources to create a special radio broadcast on the March on Washington. Consider including the following content:

- descriptions of and sound bytes from marchers
- the recollections of participants in the march
- recordings of speeches made at the gathering
- different newspaper accounts of the march

### 4. HISTORY PORTFOLIO

**Option 1** Review your section and chapter assessment activities. Select one that you think is your best work. Then use comments made by your teacher or classmates to improve your work, and add it to your portfolio.

**Option 2** Review the questions that you wrote for What Do You Want to Know? on page 812. Then write a short report in which you explain the answers to your questions. If any questions were not answered, do research to answer them. Add your answers to your portfolio.



## ALTERNATIVE ASSESSMENT

**1. INTERDISCIPLINARY ACTIVITY: Language Arts**
**Letters should**
- clearly state a position about the issue.
- present supporting reasons for the chosen position.
- clearly rebut other viewpoints.
- use standard grammar, spelling, sentence structure, and punctuation.

**2. COOPERATIVE LEARNING ACTIVITY**
**Plans for a march should**
- outline a goal to be achieved.
- have a planned set of activities for the kickoff and for the final destination of the march.
- have a publicity or media plan.
- include a planned route and contingencies for the march.

**3. PRIMARY SOURCE EXPLORER**
**Radio specials should**
- portray the historical event accurately and in a dramatic style.
- clearly demonstrate an understanding of the March on Washington.
- include information from the event participants
- show technical proficiency.

**4. HISTORY PORTFOLIO**

**Option 1 Revised section or chapter assessment activities should**
- address teacher and peer responses to the selected work.
- solve problems present in the first versions of the work.

**Option 2 Short reports should**
- answer questions about civil rights.
- use evidence to develop and support ideas.
- cite sources of information.
- use standard grammar, spelling, sentence structure, and punctuation.

**Critical Thinking Transparency CT87**
- Visual Summary

**Formal Assessment**
- Chapter Test, Forms A and B, pp. 422–429

## HISTORY SKILLS

**Possible Responses**

**1. INTERPRETING GRAPHS**

**Basic Graph Elements**

**a.** the percentage of the white and nonwhite population living below the poverty line

**Interpreting the Graph**

**b.** whites

**c.** The poverty rate for whites is about 9 percent, while the poverty rate for nonwhites is about 30 percent.

**2. INTERPRETING PRIMARY SOURCES**

**a.** He believed that as minorities, they faced common challenges and problems in the United States.

**b.** He replaces stars with cotton plants to emphasize the contribution of enslaved persons to the United States. He makes some stripes run zigzag, so they look like a Native American design.

CHAPTER 30 PLANNING GUIDE

# The Vietnam War Years 1954–1975

| | CHAPTER OVERVIEW | COPYMASTERS | TECHNOLOGY |
|---|---|---|---|
| **CHAPTER RESOURCES** | This chapter discusses the developments that lead to U.S. involvement in Vietnam, from the decision to aid the French forces there in the early 1950s to the decision to send American combat troops in the mid-1960s. It also describes the growing opposition to the war, and the deep divisions developing within American society. | **In-Depth Resources: Unit 9**<br>• Tracing Themes: America in the World, p. 20<br>• Building Vocabulary, p. 24<br>**Interdisciplinary Projects,** pp. 175–180 | **Primary Source Explorer**<br>**Electronic Teacher Tools**<br>**Power Presentations CD-ROM**<br>**Chapter Summaries on CD** (English and Spanish) |
| **SECTION 1 Cold War Roots of the Conflict pp. 835–839** | **KEY IDEAS**<br>• The United States aids France, which is trying to retain control of Vietnam.<br>• Communist North Vietnamese forces invade South Vietnam.<br>• Trying to contain communism, the United States aids South Vietnam and challenges the USSR over missiles in Cuba. | **In-Depth Resources: Unit 9**<br>• Setting the Stage, p. 19<br>• Guided Reading, p. 21<br>• Primary Source, p. 28<br>• Reteaching Activity, p. 33<br>**America's History Makers**<br>• John F. Kennedy, pp. 119–120<br>**Economics in History**<br>• The Space Race Pays Off, p. 30<br>**Outline Map Activities**<br>• The Vietnam War, 1954–1975, pp. 59–60 | **Warm-Up Transparency WT30**<br>**Humanities Transparency HT59**<br>• Soviet Missiles in Cuba<br>**Critical Thinking Transparency CT88**<br>• Setting the Stage<br>**ClassZone:** www.mcdougallittell.com |
| **SECTION 2 War Expands in Vietnam pp. 840–845** | • As the war escalates, the number of American troops in Vietnam grows.<br>• Despite superior technology, U.S. forces cannot win decisive victories.<br>• As the war drags on, American morale sinks. | **In-Depth Resources: Unit 9**<br>• Setting the Stage, p. 19<br>• Guided Reading, p. 22<br>• Geography Application: The Fall of a South Vietnamese Village, 1965, pp. 26–27<br>• Primary Source, p. 29<br>• Literature Selection, pp. 30–32<br>• Reteaching Activity, p. 34<br>**America's History Makers**<br>• Lyndon B. Johnson, pp. 121–122 | **Warm-Up Transparency WT30**<br>**Critical Thinking Transparency CT88**<br>• Setting the Stage<br>**ClassZone:** www.mcdougallittell.com |
| **SECTION 3 The Vietnam War Ends pp. 846–849** | • The antiwar movement challenges both the war and the draft.<br>• Richard Nixon first escalates the war and then withdraws U.S. troops.<br>• The Vietnam War leaves a legacy of distrust and division. | **In-Depth Resources: Unit 9**<br>• Setting the Stage, p. 19<br>• Guided Reading, p. 23<br>• Skillbuilder Practice: Forming and Supporting Opinions, p. 25<br>• Reteaching Activity, p. 35<br>**Citizenship Today,** p. 80<br>**Why It Matters Now**<br>• The Impact of Vietnam, pp. 59–60 | **Humanities Transparency HT60**<br>• Antiwar Poster<br>**Geography Transparency GT30**<br>• U.S. Troops Around the World, 1975<br>**Critical Thinking Transparency CT89**<br>• Cause and Effect: The War in Vietnam<br>**Critical Thinking Transparency CT90**<br>• Visual Summary |

PE Pupil's Edition | Copymaster | Overhead Transparency | Audio Library | CD-ROM | Internet

## ASSESSMENT

**Chapter Assessment,** pp. 850–851

**Formal Assessment**
- Chapter Tests, Forms A and B, pp. 435–442

**Alternative Assessment Book**

**Electronic Teacher Tools with Test Maker**

**Section Assessment,** p. 839

**Formal Assessment**
- Section Quiz, p. 432

**Alternative Assessment Book**
- Rubrics for an interview, 3.3
- Rubrics for a sign, 1.1

**Electronic Teacher Tools with Test Maker**

**Section Assessment,** p. 845

**Formal Assessment**
- Section Quiz, p. 433

**Alternative Assessment Book**
- Rubrics for an exhibit, 1.5
- Rubrics for a label, 4.9

**Electronic Teacher Tools with Test Maker**

**Section Assessment,** p. 849

**Formal Assessment**
- Section Quiz, p. 434

**Alternative Assessment Book**
- Rubrics for an essay, 4.2
- Rubrics for statistics, 2.7

**Electronic Teacher Tools with Test Maker**

## CUSTOMIZING FOR INDIVIDUAL NEEDS

### Students Acquiring English/ESL

**Reading Study Guide** (English and Spanish), pp. 287–294

**Access for Students Acquiring English/ESL: Spanish Translations,** pp. 199–204

**Chapter Summaries on CD** (English and Spanish)

### Less Proficient Readers

**Reading Study Guide** (English and Spanish), pp. 287–294

**Chapter Summaries on CD** (English and Spanish)

### Gifted and Talented Students

**In-Depth Resources: Unit 9**
- Enrichment Activity, p. 36

**America's History Makers**
- John F. Kennedy, pp. 119–120
- Lyndon B. Johnson, pp. 121–122

## CROSS-CURRICULAR CONNECTIONS

### Civics

Brown, Gene. ***The Nation in Turmoil: Civil Rights and the Vietnam War, (1960–1973).*** New York: Twenty-First Century Books, 1995. Presents primary source material outlining major events of the 1960s.

### Government

Finkelstein, Norman. ***Thirteen Days/Ninety Miles: The Cuban Missile Crisis.*** New York: Messner, 1994. Using information not available at the time, the author depicts the Cold War crisis as it was seen by both sides.

### Primary Sources

Denenberg, Barry. ***Voices from Vietnam.*** New York: Scholastic, 1995. A compilation of quotes from soldiers, officers, politicians, celebrities, and reporters, showing the struggle to understand the Vietnam War.

### Humanities: Art

Ashabranner, Brent. ***Their Names to Live: What the Vietnam Memorial Means to Americans.*** Photography by Jennifer Ashabranner. New York: Twenty-First Century, 1998. Photographs show the powerful reactions of visitors to the Wall.

### Interdisciplinary Projects, pp. 175–180

- Math: Estimating Weight
- Science: Acid Rain
- Language Arts: Slang of the Vietnam War
- Health: Agent Orange

### Literature

Myers, Walter Dean. ***Fallen Angels.*** New York: Scholastic, 1991. A teenager named Perry goes from Harlem to Vietnam, where he meets both courage and cowardice, idealism and manipulation. Powerful and gritty. For mature readers.

Nelson, Theresa. ***And One for All.*** New York: Orchard, 1989. When they were very young, the three kids swore to be friends forever. Now seniors in high school, Geraldine's brother Wing wants to go fight while their best friend Sam plans to protest the war . . . and Geraldine is torn between conflicting loyalties.

Whelan, Gloria. ***Goodbye, Vietnam.*** New York: Random House, 1993. Mai and her family must leave Vietnam, and they make the dangerous journey along the Mekong Delta to the sea and then by boat to Hong Kong.

### McDougal Littell Literature Connections

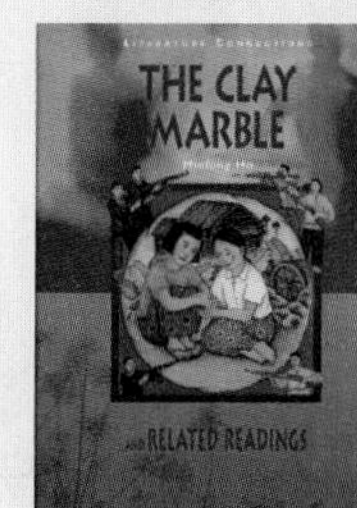


Minfong Ho

***The Clay Marble***

Set in a Cambodian refugee camp in the early 1980s, this novel describes how a young girl copes, helped by stories and a special marble.

## ENRICHMENT ACTIVITIES

**Pupil's Edition, pp. 832–851**
**Interact with History,** p. 833

**In-Depth Resources: Unit 9**
- Geography Application: The Fall of a South Vietnamese Village, 1965, pp. 26–27
- Primary Source, p. 28
- Primary Source, p. 29
- Literature Selection, pp. 30–32

**America's History Makers**
- John F. Kennedy, pp. 119–120
- Lyndon B. Johnson, pp. 121–122

**Outline Map Activities**
- The Vietnam War, 1954–1975, pp. 59–60

**Why It Matters Now,** pp. 59–60

**LESSON PLAN OPTIONS (50-MINUTE PERIOD)** **(TE) = Teacher's Edition (PE) = Pupil's Edition**

| | TEACHER-DIRECTED ACTIVITIES<br>Class Time: 15 minutes | STUDENT-CENTERED ACTIVITIES<br>Class Time: 25 minutes | INDIVIDUAL ACTIVITIES<br>Class Time: 10 minutes |
|---|---|---|---|
| **DAY 1**<br>Introduction<br>pp. 832–834 | **Presentation Options**<br>• Begin with a class discussion of the photograph on p. 832 **(PE).**<br>• Lead a class discussion on the "What Do You Know?" question in Setting the Stage, p. 834. Then introduce the graphic organizer for the chapter **(PE).** | **Options for Cooperative Learning**<br>• Have student groups discuss the Interact with History questions, p. 833 **(PE).**<br>• Have student groups respond to the "What Do You Want to Know?" question in Setting the Stage, p. 834 **(PE).** | **Head Start on Homework Options**<br>• Have students skim Section 1 Main Idea, Why It Matters Now, Terms & Names, and the main headings, p. 835 **(PE).**<br>• Have students begin Guided Reading activity and Building Vocabulary sheet. |
| **DAY 2**<br>Section 1<br>pp. 835–839 | **Presentation Options**<br>• Begin with the 5-Minute Warm-Up, p. 835 **(TE).**<br>• Review the Section 1 Main Idea, Why It Matters Now, and Terms & Names, p. 835 **(PE).**<br>• Choose 5 key questions for Objectives 1–4 to discuss with the class, pp. 835–839 **(TE).** | **Options for Cooperative Learning**<br>• Divide students into groups to work on the Interdisciplinary Link, World Culture: Exploring Vietnamese Culture, p. 836 **(TE).**<br>• Have student pairs work together to complete one of the Activity Options in the Section 1 Assessment, p. 839 **(PE).** | **Head Start on Homework Options**<br>• Have students begin working on Section 1 Assessment, p. 839 **(PE).**<br>• Have students study the photographs in Section 2 and write a description of the war based on the photographs, pp. 840–845 **(PE).** |
| **DAY 3**<br>Section 2<br>pp. 840–845 | **Presentation Options**<br>• Begin with the 5-Minute Warm-Up, p. 840 **(TE).**<br>• Choose 5 key questions for Objectives 1–4 to discuss with the class, pp. 840–844 **(TE).**<br>• Lead the students through the Critical Thinking Activity, p. 842 **(TE).** | **Options for Cooperative Learning**<br>• Divide students into groups to work on Multiple Learning Styles, Interpersonal: Preparing a Newscast, p. 844 **(TE).**<br>• Have student pairs work together to complete one of the Activity Options in the Section 2 Assessment, p. 845 **(PE).** | **Head Start on Homework Options**<br>• Have students begin working on Section 2 Assessment, p. 845 **(PE).**<br>• Have students preview Section 3 Main Idea, Why It Matters Now, Terms & Names, and the main headings, p. 845 **(PE).** |
| **DAY 4**<br>Section 3<br>pp. 846–849 | **Presentation Options**<br>• Begin with the 5-Minute Warm-Up, p. 846 **(TE).**<br>• Choose 5 key questions for Objectives 1–4 to discuss with the class, pp. 846–848 **(TE).**<br>• Lead the students through the Skillbuilder Mini-Lesson: Forming and Supporting Opinions, p. 847 **(TE).** | **Options for Cooperative Learning**<br>• Divide students into groups and have them complete the Critical Thinking Activity, p. 849 **(TE).**<br>• Have student pairs work together to complete one of the Activity Options in the Section 3 Assessment, p. 849 **(PE).** | **Head Start on Homework Options**<br>• Have students complete the Setting the Stage graphic organizer for the chapter, p. 834 **(PE).**<br>• Have students begin working on the Chapter Assessment, pp. 850–851 **(PE).**<br>• Prepare for Chapter Test<br>**Formal Assessment,** pp. 435–442 |

TEACHER-TESTED ACTIVITY James Sorenson, Chippewa Middle School, Des Plaines, Illinois

## DIALOGUE AT THE WALL

**Class Time** One class period

**Task** Writing a dialogue between two people attending the dedication of the Vietnam Veterans Memorial in Washington, D.C.

**Purpose** To explore differing perspectives on the Vietnam War

**Supplies Needed**

- Articles and other reference materials and Internet sources on the Vietnam Veterans Memorial
- Photographs of the memorial

**Activity** Display photographs of the Vietnam Veterans Memorial as you read from one or two articles about the Vietnam Wall. Tell students to consider what it would have been like to be present at the dedication of the memorial on November 13, 1982. Assign roles by having students draw slips of paper from a box, or allow students to choose one of the following roles: Vietnam veteran, antiwar protester, Vietnamese immigrant, religious leader, government official, or parent who lost a child in the war. Ask students to write a dialogue their character might have had with a friend as they stood at the Wall.

## BLOCK SCHEDULING — LESSON PLAN OPTIONS (90-MINUTE PERIOD)

### DAY 1

**Interact with History,** p. 833
**Class Time** 20 minutes

Options for pacing and variety:

- Role-Playing Divide students into pairs, with one student representing an antiwar demonstrator and the other a supporter of the Vietnam War. Have them discuss the "What Do You Think?" questions with each answering from his or her differing perspective. At the conclusion of their discussion, have them make a list of three statements on which they can both agree and three statements about which they disagree. **Class Time** 10 minutes

**Setting the Stage,** p. 834
**Class Time** 20 minutes

Options for pacing and variety:

- Time Saver For a homework assignment, have students make a three-column chart headed *What I Know, What I Want to Know,* and *What I Learned.* Have students complete columns 1 and 2 before reading the chapter. Column 3 can be completed as part of the Chapter Assessment. **Class Time** 10 minutes

**Section 1,** pp. 835–839
**Class Time** 50 minutes

Options for pacing and variety:

- Peer Teaching Working in groups, students can begin the Cooperative Activity in the Chapter Assessment on page 851. In this section, have students work on a script for an introductory section of the documentary, focusing on the origins of the war. **Class Time** 30 minutes
- Time Saver As a homework assignment, have students begin filling in their Read and Take Notes chart on page 834 with reasons for and against involvement in Vietnam.
**Class Time** 5 minutes

### DAY 2

**Section 2,** pp. 840–845
**Class Time** 45 minutes

Options for pacing and variety:

- Time Saver Use the chart on page 840 to summarize the escalation of U.S. involvement in Vietnam. Class Time 10 minutes
- History on Film Extend students' background knowledge of the debate over the Vietnam War by having students view *Choosing Sides: I Remember Vietnam/The War at Home.* A&E, 1997–98. **Class Time** 1 hour, 40 minutes

**Section 3,** pp. 846–849
**Class Time** 45 minutes

Options for pacing and variety:

- Peer Teaching Have student pairs discuss and then report to the class their response to the Critical Thinking question in the Section Assessment. **Class Time** 10 minutes
- Internet Extend students' background knowledge of the Vietnam Veterans Memorial with a visit to www.mcdougallittell.com
**Class Time** 20 minutes

**Chapter 30 Assessment,** pp. 850–851
**Class Time** 40 minutes

Options for pacing and variety:

- Peer Teaching Have student pairs exchange their homework answers to the Chapter Review questions. They should compare answers and correct any incorrect answers.
**Class Time** 10 minutes
- Peer Evaluation Divide the class into five-member groups, and have each student in the group answer a different Critical Thinking question in the Chapter Assessment on page 850. Each student can share his or her response with the group. Have each group pick its response to one of the questions to share with the class.
**Class Time** 20 minutes

**CHAPTER 30 OBJECTIVE**

The student will analyze the roots of the Vietnam War, American participation in the war, and the divisions that the war created in the United States.

## HISTORY FROM VISUALS

**Interpreting the Photograph** The photograph shows a man holding a child up to kiss a name engraved onto the Vietnam Veterans Memorial in Washington, D.C. Tell students that the memorial, also called The Wall, includes the names of Americans who died in Vietnam during the war. Ask students why they think the child is kissing one of the names. Then ask why they think the memorial evokes strong emotions in visitors. **Possible Responses** The boy may be kissing the name of a relative who died in Vietnam. Many people leave flowers and mementos honoring those who fought in Vietnam. The memorial prompts complex memories connected to the war.

**Extension** Have students research the Vietnam Women's Memorial, honoring the military women who served in the war.

### CRITICAL THINKING ACTIVITY

**Forming and Supporting Opinions** Ask students to suggest reasons that would justify U.S. involvement in an overseas war today. Record students' opinions on a web map on the board. After the discussion, point out to students how their opinions vary. Tell them that Americans were also divided in the 1960s over whether the United States should be involved in the Vietnam War.

**Class Time** 15 minutes

# CHAPTER 30 The Vietnam War Years 1954–1975

*Section 1* **Cold War Roots of the Conflict**
*Section 2* **War Expands in Vietnam**
*Section 3* **The Vietnam War Ends**

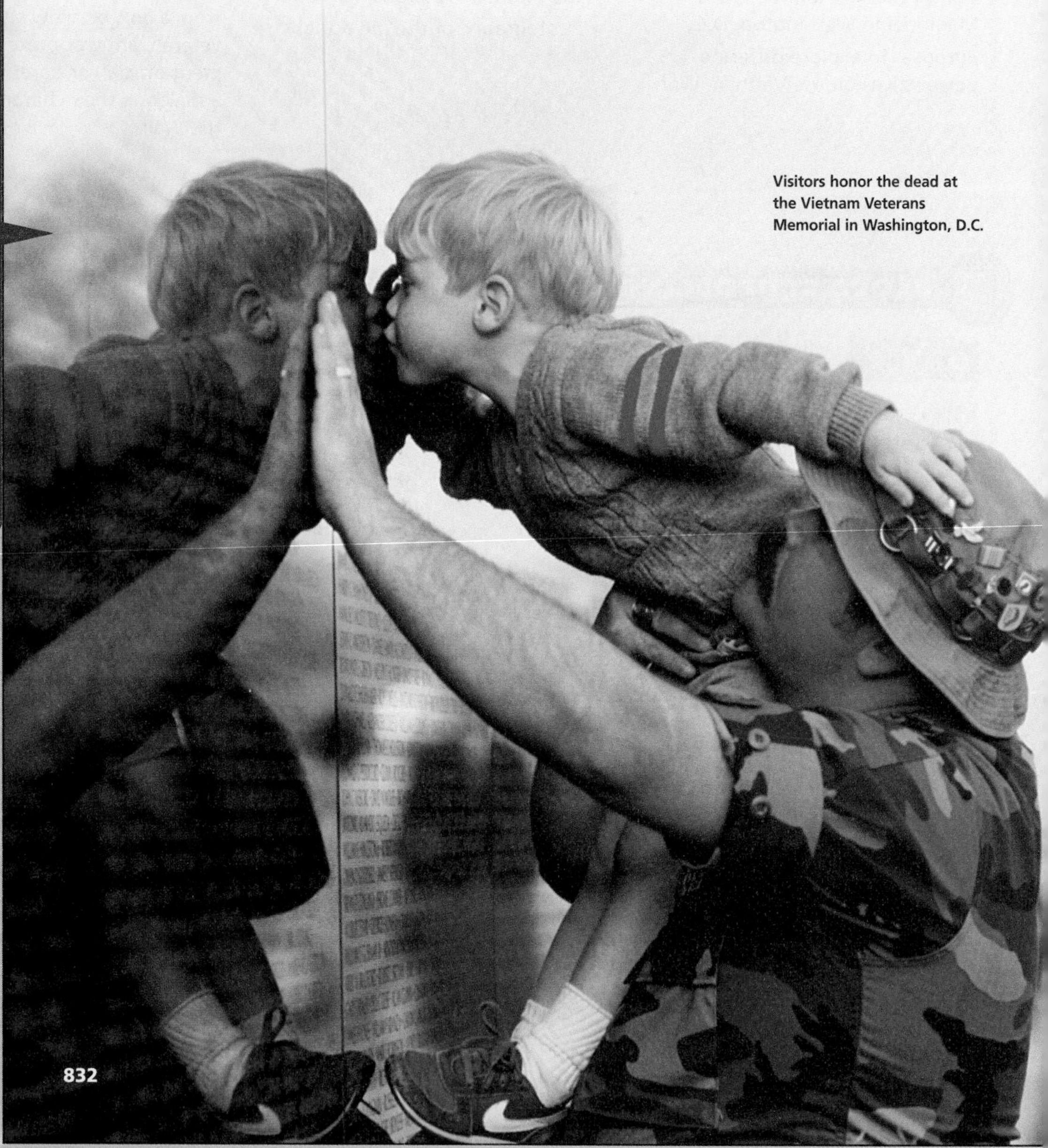

Visitors honor the dead at the Vietnam Veterans Memorial in Washington, D.C.

832

## RECOMMENDED RESOURCES

**BOOKS FOR THE TEACHER**

Herr, Michael. ***Dispatches.*** New York: Vintage Books, 1991. The hardships and strain of war as experienced by one of the nation's finest reporters.

Small, Melvin. ***Give Peace a Chance: Exploring the Vietnam Antiwar Movement.*** Syracuse, NY: Syracuse U. Pr., 1992. With a foreword by George McGovern, these essays explore the movement's strategies, tactics, and membership.

Terry, Wallace (ed.) ***Bloods: An Oral History of the Vietnam War by Black Veterans.*** New York: Random House, 1984. A biting, raw, and still riveting oral history.

**SOFTWARE**

***The Sixties: America 1960–1970.*** Multieducator. Uses many media to explore a tumultuous decade.

**VIDEO**

***No Man's Land.*** *Part 2: The Fall,* from *The Century* series. ABC Video, 1999. Focuses on the last months of the Vietnam War.

**INTERNET**

For more about the Vietnam Veterans Memorial, visit www.mcdougallittell.com

## Interact *with* History

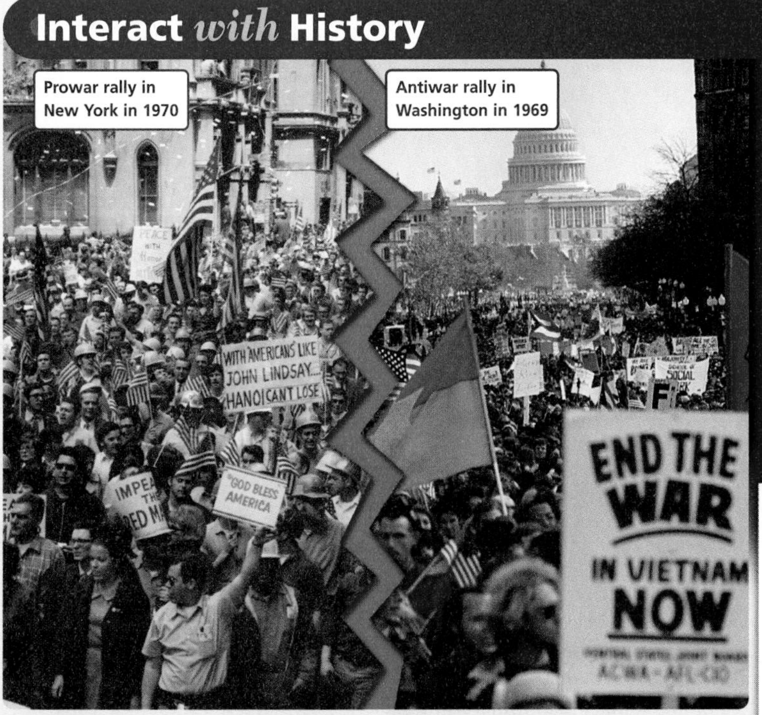

WITH AMERICANS LIKE
JOHN LINDSAY...
HANOI CAN'T LOSE
GOD BLESS
AMERICA
END THE
WAR
IN VIETNAM
NOW
ACWA - AFL-CIO


Prowar rally in New York in 1970

Antiwar rally in Washington in 1969

**You are a young person in 1969. Your country is at war to stop Communists from taking over South Vietnam. College students have organized huge protests against the war and the draft. Many people think such protests are unpatriotic and an insult to the soldiers who are fighting.**

### What Do You Think?

- **Should the United States try to stop the spread of communism in Vietnam?**
- **Why are so many people against the war?**
- **Is it unpatriotic to criticize the government? To refuse army service?**

# *Would you support the war?*

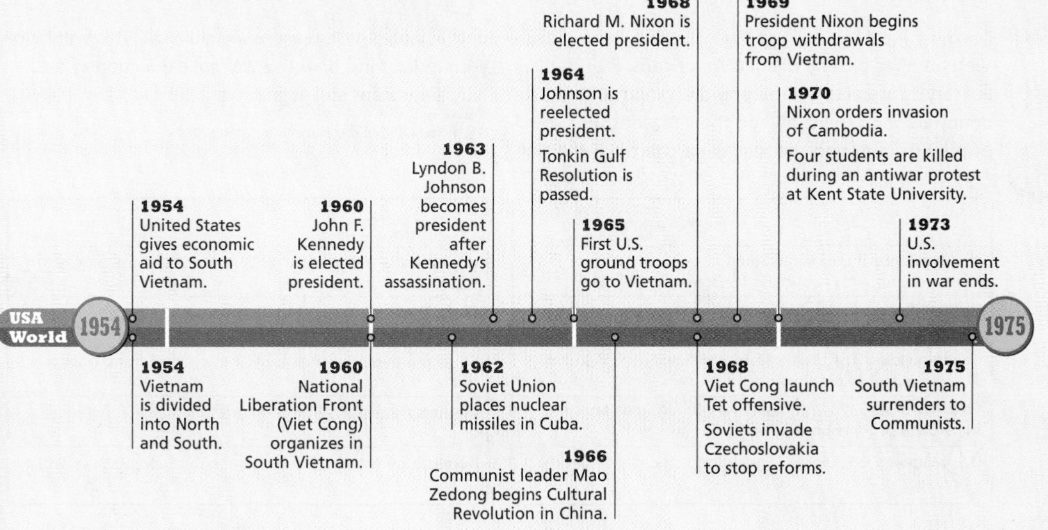




## Interact *with* History

**OBJECTIVES**

- To form and support opinions about the Vietnam War
- To evaluate the actions of antiwar protesters and prowar supporters

### What Do You Think?

1. Ask students which groups of Americans they would expect to support the war.
2. In what way would Americans show opposition to the war?
3. Have students consider whether there should be limits on the freedom to criticize the government and its actions.

### *Would you support the war?*

Remind students that public opinion changed as the war continued. Suggest that students consider what the average American knew about Vietnam at the beginning of the war.

**MAKING PERSONAL CONNECTIONS**

Ask students whether they know anybody who served in the Vietnam War. Ask if they know anyone who worked to end the war. Have these people's views about the war changed over time?

## TIME LINE DISCUSSION

**United States involvement in Vietnam began as part of the Cold War effort to contain communism. The role of the United States in Southeast Asia became a matter of intense dispute and heated emotions.**

- Ask students to make an inference about the United States choosing to support South Vietnam in 1954. **Possible Response** South Vietnam was viewed as more democratic than North Vietnam.
- Ask why troops might have been sent to Vietnam in 1965. **Possible Response** to protect the South Vietnamese government
- Ask students in what ways Richard Nixon changed the course of the war. **Possible Response** He began troop withdrawals and invaded Cambodia.
- Ask students to identify other events that were aspects of the Cold War. **Possible Response** The Soviet Union placed missiles in Cuba; Soviets invaded Czechoslovakia to stop reforms.

## BEFORE YOU READ

### Previewing the Theme: America in the World

Ask students whether they think the United States had a responsibility to stop the spread of communism. Then have them consider what sacrifices were made in that effort.

The U.S. government feared the dangers to this country if friendly countries became Communist. Many feared that the loss of Vietnam would lead to the loss of other Southeast Asian countries and would encourage Communists to try to take over countries elsewhere.

### What Do You Know?

Explain to students that the Vietnam War was recorded in detail on film and on television. As a result, many Americans at home witnessed the war in a totally new, vivid, and sometimes horrifying way. Some observers referred to Vietnam as the war "fought in American living rooms."

 **In-Depth Resources: Unit 9**
- Tracing Themes: America in the World, p. 20

## READ AND TAKE NOTES

### Reading Strategy: Analyzing Points of View

A person's point of view is based on his or her knowledge, experience, and personal background. Explain to students that understanding another's point of view requires them to try to understand how that person thinks. Encourage students to think about the points of view of those who took a stand on U.S. involvement in the Vietnam War. Suggest that students list the points of view they read about in a chart. Point out the pros and cons of involvement in the war listed on the chart.

 **In-Depth Resources: Unit 9**
- Setting the Stage, p. 19

 **Critical Thinking Transparency CT88**
- Setting the Stage

# Chapter 30 SETTING THE STAGE

## BEFORE YOU READ

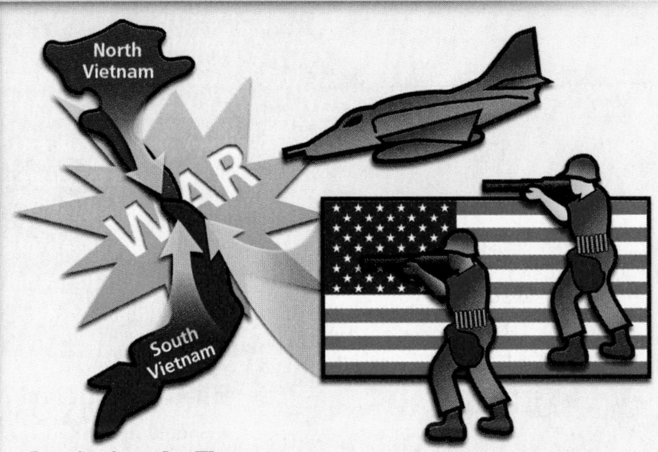


### Previewing the Theme

**America in the World** The United States became involved in the Vietnam War to stop the spread of communism in Asia. As more U.S. troops were sent there, doubts grew about whether they could achieve their mission. Eventually, the United States withdrew its soldiers and became more cautious about fighting foreign wars. Chapter 30 explains the history and legacy of the war in Vietnam.

### What Do You Know?

What images spring to mind when you hear the word *Vietnam?* What have you learned about the Vietnam War from movies, books, or relatives' stories? Have you seen the Vietnam Veterans Memorial or any other Vietnam memorials?

**THINK ABOUT**
- whether Americans seem proud of or ashamed of the war
- how this war differed from World War II or other wars you know about

### What Do You Want to Know?

In your notebook, write down any questions you have about the war. Later, note the answers if you learn them in this chapter.

## READ AND TAKE NOTES

**Reading Strategy: Analyzing Points of View** The Vietnam War bitterly divided Americans. Presidents, military strategists, ordinary soldiers, and college students, among others, all had their reasons for supporting or opposing the war. On a chart like the one below, note these reasons as you read. This will help you understand how the war split the country and why Americans still argue over it today.

 **See Skillbuilder Handbook, page R8.**

| Reasons for Involvement in Vietnam |
|---|
| **French alliance** If the United States does not aid France, France may not aid in opposing the Soviets in Europe. |
| **Domino theory** If South Vietnam falls to communism, other Asian countries may fall as well. |
| **Nation-building** The United States can help South Vietnam establish a democratic government. |
| **Cold War crises** Cold War crises make the United States fear the growth of communist power. |
| **U.S. weaponry** Superior U.S. weaponry can easily defeat the Viet Cong. |

| Reasons Against Involvement in Vietnam |
|---|
| **U.S. interests** The war is a civil war that does not directly threaten the United States. |
| **Draft** The draft to select soldiers is unfair. |
| **Social programs** The war takes money away from social programs. |
| **Vietnamese civilians** The war harms Vietnamese civilians. |
| **Domestic unrest** The war causes too much domestic unrest. |



## TEACHING STRATEGY

This is a chronological chapter describing how the United States became involved in Vietnam, the increasing controversy over its involvement, and its decision to withdraw its troops. Encourage students to understand the reasoning behind Americans' decisions to support or oppose the war. Ask them also to consider how events in the war may have changed people's minds about their stance on the war.

**ALTERNATIVE ASSESSMENT**

The Chapter Assessment describes three activities for alternative assessment on page 851. You may wish to have students work on these activities during the course of the chapter and then present them at the end.

# 1 Cold War Roots of the Conflict

**TERMS & NAMES**
Ngo Dinh Diem
French Indochina
Ho Chi Minh
domino theory
Viet Cong
Ho Chi Minh Trail
Cuban missile crisis

**MAIN IDEA**

The United States entered the Vietnam War to stop the spread of communism.

**WHY IT MATTERS NOW**

The United States still becomes involved in foreign struggles for political reasons.

Edward Lansdale was one of the earliest U.S. military advisers sent to Vietnam.

## ONE AMERICAN'S STORY

**Edward Lansdale, a U.S. military officer, went to South Vietnam in June 1954. His mission: to stop the spread of communism in Vietnam. He would try to do this by helping the non-Communist government of South Vietnam resist being taken over by Communist North Vietnam. Lansdale believed that the United States could defeat communism by "exporting the American way" and "winning the hearts and minds of the people" with generous economic and military aid.**

**Lansdale became a trusted adviser to Ngo Dinh Diem (uhng•oh dihn zih•ehm), the leader of South Vietnam. At Lansdale's urging, the United States helped support Diem's unpopular government. Within a year, Lansdale reported, "The Free Vietnamese are now becoming unified and learning how to cope with the Communist enemy."**

**Lansdale was too optimistic. U.S. involvement in Vietnam grew into the longest war the United States ever fought—and one in which it failed. The war would deeply divide not only the Vietnamese but also Americans. In this section, you will learn how the United States first became involved in Vietnam.**

## 1 Vietnam After World War II

From the late 1800s until World War II, France ruled Vietnam as part of its colony of **French Indochina.** The colony also included neighboring Laos (LAH•ohs) and Cambodia. (See the map on page 837.) During this colonial period, France increased its wealth by exporting rice and rubber from Vietnam. But Vietnamese peasants lost their land and grew poor.

The Vietnamese never accepted French rule. Various groups of nationalists, who wanted Vietnam to become an independent nation, staged revolts against the French. In 1930, a revolutionary leader named **Ho Chi Minh** (hoh chee mihn) united three Communist groups to form the Indochinese Communist Party (ICP). This new party called for an independent Vietnam controlled by peasants and other workers.





## SECTION OBJECTIVES

1. To analyze the roots of the war
2. To describe the domino theory and the division of Vietnam
3. To identify the Viet Cong and their goals
4. To describe U.S. responses to Communist threats around the world

**SKILLBUILDER**

Interpreting Maps: Location, p. 837

**CRITICAL THINKING**

Analyzing Causes, pp. 836, 839
Analyzing Points of View, p. 837
Making Inferences, p. 838
Evaluating, p. 839

## FOCUS & MOTIVATE

### 5-MINUTE WARM-UP

**Making Inferences** These questions focus on the Vietnam War.

1. Look at the map and photograph on page 837. What Asian countries were directly affected by the Vietnam War?
2. Using the photograph as evidence, what can you infer about the technology available to the Communists?

 **Warm-Up Transparency WT30**

## INSTRUCT

**INSTRUCT: OBJECTIVE 1**

**Vietnam After World War II**

Key Questions

- How did World War II affect efforts for Vietnamese independence?
- Who was the revolutionary leader of the Vietnamese Communists?

 **In-Depth Resources: Unit 9**
- Guided Reading, p. 21

 **Reading Study Guide** (Spanish and English), pp. 287–288

## RECOMMENDED RESOURCES

 **In-Depth Resources: Unit 9**
- Guided Reading, p. 21
- Building Vocabulary, p. 24
- Primary Source: from *Thirteen Days,* p. 28
- Reteaching Activity, p. 33

 **Reading Study Guide** (Spanish and English), pp. 287–288

**Economics in History**
- The Space Race Pays Off, p. 30

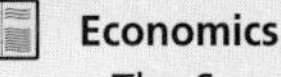 **Outline Map Activities**
- The Vietnam War, 1954–1975, pp. 59–60

**America's History Makers**
- John F. Kennedy, pp. 119–120

**Formal Assessment**
- Section Quiz, p. 432

**Alternative Assessment**
- Rubrics, 3.3
- Rubrics, 1.1

**Access for Students Acquiring English/ESL**
- Guided Reading, p. 199

**Technology Resources**

 **Humanities Transparency HT59**
- Soviet Missiles in Cuba

 **Electronic Teacher Tools with Test Maker**

 **ClassZone**
www.mcdougallittell.com

**MORE ABOUT . . .**

**Ho Chi Minh**

Ho Chi Minh was born in 1890 in a small village in central Vietnam. His name at the time was Nguyen That Thanh. He lived for a while in Paris, where he changed his name to Nguyen Ai Quoc (Nguyen the Patriot) and joined the French Communist Party. He chose the name Ho Chi Minh ("He Who Enlightens") in 1945. He hoped this name would appeal to moderate Vietnamese who might otherwise be reluctant to follow a radical revolutionary. He died in 1969.

**INSTRUCT: OBJECTIVE 2**

**Truman and Eisenhower Aid the French/ Dividing North and South**

Key Questions

- Why did the United States agree to help France fight the Viet Minh?
- How did the Geneva Accords end the war between the Viet Minh and the French?
- Why were the elections required by the Geneva Accords never held?

**Outline Map Activities**

- The Vietnam War, 1954–1975, pp. 59–60

**MORE ABOUT . . .**

**The First U.S. Casualty in Vietnam**

The United States sent several officers to Vietnam immediately after World War II to look for Allied prisoners of war and missing Americans and to gather information about the situation there. One of them, Lieutenant Colonel A. Peter Dewey, was on his way to the Saigon airport in September 1945, when he was shot and killed, presumably by Viet Minh members who thought he was French. Dewey was the first American serviceman killed in Vietnam.

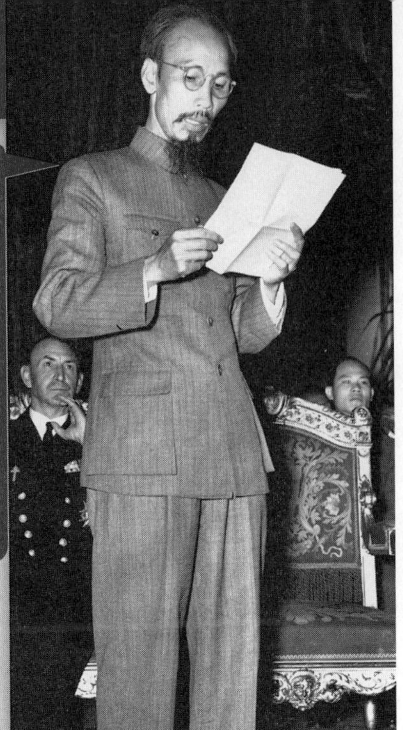

Ho Chi Minh speaks to a French audience in 1946.

The Indochinese Communist Party organized protests by peasants against the French government. The French responded by arresting suspected Communists and executing a number of leaders. Ho Chi Minh, who was living in China, was sentenced to death without being present.

In 1940, during World War II, Japan took over Indochina. The next year, Ho Chi Minh secretly returned to Vietnam and hid in a jungle camp. Under his direction, the ICP joined with other nationalists to form an organization called the Viet Minh. The Viet Minh trained soldiers to fight to make Vietnam independent of all foreign rulers. Because Japan was an enemy of the United States in World War II, the U.S. government aided Ho Chi Minh and the Viet Minh in their fight against the Japanese.

After the Japanese surrendered to the Allies in August 1945, Ho Chi Minh declared Vietnam's independence before a cheering crowd in Hanoi. But France soon tried to regain control of Vietnam. Ho Chi Minh sought a peaceful solution to the conflict with France.

**A. Answer** The Vietnamese wanted independence from French colonial rule.

***Reading*History**

**A. Analyzing Causes** What was the original source of the conflict in Vietnam?

***A VOICE FROM THE PAST***

If they force us into war, we will fight. The struggle will be atrocious [terrible], but the Vietnamese people will suffer anything rather than renounce [give up] their freedom.

**Ho Chi Minh,** quoted in *Vietnam: A History* by Stanley Karnow

***Reading*History**

**B. Reading a Map** Use the map on page 837 to find Haiphong and Hanoi.

In 1946, war broke out between the Viet Minh and France. The French bombed Haiphong, and the Viet Minh attacked Hanoi.

## 2 Truman and Eisenhower Aid the French

As France fought to hold on to power in Vietnam, the United States struggled against the Soviet Union in the Cold War. President Truman followed a policy of containment, working to prevent the spread of communism in Western Europe.

In the fall of 1949, Communists gained control of China. This event made American leaders worry about the spread of communism in Asia. When France asked the United States for aid to help them fight the Viet Minh, the United States agreed. One reason was that U.S. leaders needed French support in opposing the Soviets in Europe. Another reason was that the United States did not want Vietnam to become Communist.

The United States entered the conflict in Vietnam in 1950, when President Truman offered $10 million in military aid to the French. After Dwight D. Eisenhower became president in 1953, he continued aiding the French war effort in Vietnam.



**ACTIVITY OPTIONS**

**INTERDISCIPLINARY LINK: WORLD CULTURE** — BLOCK SCHEDULING

**EXPLORING VIETNAMESE CULTURE**

**Class Time** Two class periods

**Task** Creating a product to illustrate an aspect of Vietnamese culture

**Purpose** To explore the complex culture of Vietnam

**Supplies Needed**

- Encyclopedias and research materials about Vietnam
- Internet access
- Cooking supplies and utensils (optional)
- Posterboard
- Art supplies

**Activity** Divide the class into groups and assign each group one aspect of Vietnamese culture. Aspects may include Chinese influence, languages, ethnic groups, cuisine, religion, architecture, and music. Groups should research their assigned cultural aspect and then decide how to present their findings to the class. Products may include Vietnamese dishes for the class to share or musical tapes with several short selections and an explanation of each. Groups may also make posters or present skits or dialogues.

*Reading***History**

**C. Analyzing Points of View** Why did Truman and Eisenhower support the French in Vietnam?

C. Answer They wanted French support against the Soviets in Europe, and they did not want Vietnam to have a Communist government.

Both Truman and Eisenhower used the **domino theory** to explain the need to support anti-Communists in Vietnam. According to this theory, if a country fell to communism, nearby countries would also topple, like a row of dominoes standing on end. U.S. leaders feared that if Vietnam became Communist, the rest of Southeast Asia would follow.

## Dividing North and South

Even with limited U.S. support, France could not defeat the Viet Minh. In 1954, the Viet Minh overran French forces at Dien Bien Phu, in northwestern Vietnam. In May 1954, France met with the Viet Minh for peace talks in Geneva, Switzerland. The two sides reached an agreement called the Geneva Accords. This agreement divided Vietnam into North and South along the 17th parallel, or at 17°N latitude. Surrounding this line was a demilitarized zone, or DMZ. The split was meant to be temporary, however. The two sides agreed to hold elections in 1956 for a single government that would reunify the country.

Until then, the Geneva Accords allowed for separate governments in the North and the South. Ho Chi Minh and the Communists controlled North Vietnam. Ngo Dinh Diem, an anti-Communist, became prime minister and, later, president of South Vietnam. Thousands of anti-Communists from the North fled to the South. The United States provided ships for their transportation.

Skillbuilder Answers
1. China
2. Hanoi, Haiphong, and Dien Bien Phu are in North Vietnam. Hue, Da Nang, and Saigon are in South Vietnam.

### MORE ABOUT . . .

**The Battle of Dien Bien Phu**

The Vietnamese prepared for the battle at Dien Bien Phu for months ahead. They built simple roads and bridges. Then they dragged heavy howitzers and antiaircraft guns into position above the village, using only muscle power. With these weapons, the Vietnamese were able to prevent French airplanes from bringing in supplies or reinforcements.

North Vietnamese Communists carry supplies to South Vietnamese Communist rebels.

**GEOGRAPHY SKILLBUILDER Interpreting Maps**
1. **Location** *What country lies along the northern border of North Vietnam?*
2. **Location** *What cities on the map are in North Vietnam? In South Vietnam?*

837

### HISTORY FROM VISUALS

**Interpreting the Map** The Ho Chi Minh Trail became a major supply route for Communist forces in South Vietnam. Ask students why the Communists moved supplies and soldiers through neighboring countries instead of directly across the border between North and South Vietnam. **Possible Responses** The Ho Chi Minh Trail provided access to many parts of North and South Vietnam. In addition, the narrow demilitarized zone between North and South Vietnam was easily blocked. It was impossible to stop the flow of supplies along the Ho Chi Minh Trail.

**Extension** Have students research the countries through which the Ho Chi Minh Trail passed. How did their governments respond to the trail?

### ACTIVITY OPTIONS

**INTERDISCIPLINARY LINK: GEOGRAPHY** — BLOCK SCHEDULING

#### WRITING A DOCUMENTARY SCRIPT

**Class Time** Two class periods

**Task** Preparing a script for a television program on the geography of Vietnam

**Purpose** To learn about the geography of North and South Vietnam

**Supplies Needed**
- Encyclopedias and reference materials about the geography of Vietnam
- Internet access

**Activity** Divide students into several groups. Have each group research one of the following aspects of the geography of Vietnam: size, climate, physical features, Mekong Delta, major cities, ecology. When all have completed their research, each group should write one portion of a script for a television documentary about the country. Then groups should work together to assemble the final script for their documentary.

**INSTRUCT: OBJECTIVE 3**

**The Viet Cong Oppose Diem**

Key Questions
- Why did the Diem government fail to win the support of the people?
- Who were the Viet Cong?
- How did the Viet Cong use the Ho Chi Minh Trail?

**MORE ABOUT . . .**

**Opposition to Diem**

Diem was Roman Catholic, while the majority of the population of South Vietnam was Buddhist. The Diem government discriminated against Buddhists in a number of ways, and, in one shocking case, troops opened fire on a crowd gathered to hear a speech by a Buddhist leader. In protest, several Buddhist monks burned themselves to death on the streets of Saigon. American and Vietnamese officials worried that Diem's growing unpopularity would help the Communists win the war.

**INSTRUCT: OBJECTIVE 4**

**Kennedy Faces Communist Threats/ The Diem Government Falls**

Key Questions
- What Cold War crises helped persuade President Kennedy to aid South Vietnam?
- What caused the fall of the Diem government in South Vietnam?

**Economics in History**
- The Space Race Pays Off, p. 30

**In-Depth Resources: Unit 9**
- Primary Source, p. 28

Ho Chi Minh enjoyed great popularity in North Vietnam, while Diem had little support from the people of South Vietnam. As a result, Diem refused to hold national elections in 1956. President Eisenhower supported him, later saying, "If the elections had been held in 1956, Ho Chi Minh would have won 80% of the vote."

Instead, Eisenhower sent more aid and advisers to South Vietnam to help the Diem government. U.S. advisers described their mission as "nation-building."

## 3 The Viet Cong Oppose Diem

In spite of U.S. aid, Diem did not establish a democratic government in South Vietnam. Instead, his government was corrupt. In the countryside, for example, he let landlords take back land given to peasants. In addition, he jailed, tortured, and killed opponents.

Diem's opponents included South Vietnamese Communists. In 1960, they joined with other dissatisfied South Vietnamese to form the National Liberation Front. Diem ridiculed the group by calling them the **Viet Cong**, for Vietnamese Communists. This name became the commonly used term for the group.

The Viet Cong fought to overthrow the Diem government and reunite the country under Communist rule. North Vietnam supported the Viet Cong, sending soldiers and supplies along a network of paths called the **Ho Chi Minh Trail**. This supply line wove through the jungles and mountains of neighboring Laos and Cambodia. By 1963, when John F. Kennedy was in the White House, the Viet Cong were close to victory.

*Reading History*
**D. Making Inferences** Why was the Diem government unpopular?
**D. Answer** Diem let landlords take back peasants' land, and he jailed, tortured, and killed his opponents.

*Reading History*
**E. Reading a Map** Find the Ho Chi Minh Trail on the map on page 837.

## 4 Kennedy Faces Communist Threats

President Kennedy continued to send military advisers and equipment to South Vietnam. By late 1963, the United States had more than 16,000 military personnel there. Kennedy faced a number of Cold War crises that influenced him to keep supporting the fight against communism in Vietnam.

The first was the Bay of Pigs invasion in April 1961. An army of Cuban exiles, trained by the United States, invaded Cuba. They planned to overthrow the country's Communist leader, Fidel Castro. Cuban troops easily crushed the invasion, humiliating the United States.

Then in June 1961, the Soviet Union threatened to close off Western access to West Berlin because so many East Germans were fleeing there to escape communism. Tensions rose when Kennedy insisted on West Berlin's independence. The Soviets and East Germans then built the Berlin Wall, a heavily guarded barrier dividing West Berlin from Communist East Berlin and East Germany. The wall, which made it harder for East Germans to flee, became a symbol of Communist oppression.

A woman in West Berlin talks across the Berlin Wall to her mother in East Berlin.



**ACTIVITY OPTIONS**

**INDIVIDUAL NEEDS**

**STUDENTS ACQUIRING ENGLISH/ESL**

**Understanding Expressions** Point out the statement on page 839, "In a frightening showdown between the two superpowers, the Soviets agreed to remove the missiles, and the United States promised not to invade Cuba." Ask students to think of other words with the prefix *super-*. They may suggest *superman, supermarket, superhero, superstar, superhighway.*

Ask students to use context to determine what the word superpower means. *(a state with enough military and economic power to give it influence over a bloc of countries)* Tell students that after World War II, there were two superpowers, the United States and the Soviet Union. Both countries had great economic and military power, including nuclear weapons. Both influenced other countries with which they maintained alliances. With the breakup of the Soviet Union in 1991, the United States remains the world's only superpower.

The **Cuban missile crisis** in October 1962 was Kennedy's most serious confrontation with the Soviets. Fidel Castro, believing the United States planned another attack on Cuba, had asked for more Soviet military aid. The United States learned that the Soviets had put nuclear missiles in Cuba. These missiles could reach U.S. cities within minutes. Kennedy weighed his choices. "The greatest danger of all," he told the country, "would be to do nothing." In a frightening showdown between the two superpowers, the Soviets agreed to remove the missiles, and the United States promised not to invade Cuba.

*Reading* **History**
**F. Analyzing Causes** What Cold War crises made Kennedy increase his commitment to fight communism in Asia?
F. Answer
The Bay of Pigs invasion, the Berlin Wall, and the Cuban missile crisis made Kennedy fear Communist power.

These Cold War crises fed American fears that the Soviet Union might become the strongest world power. In this climate of fear and suspicion, the United States made a greater effort to contain communism in Asia by sending more money and military advisers to South Vietnam.

## The Diem Government Falls

As U.S. aid increased, so did South Vietnamese opposition to Diem. American officials told Diem to make political, economic, and military reforms. But he refused.

**Vocabulary**
**coup (koo):** a sudden takeover by a small group

The Kennedy administration lost faith in Diem. With U.S. support, a military coup overthrew Diem on November 1, 1963. Against Kennedy's wishes, the coup's leaders killed Diem. In a terrible and unrelated turn of events, President Kennedy was assassinated three weeks later. Vice-President Lyndon Johnson became president. He deepened U.S. involvement in the Vietnam War, as you will see in the next section.

### AMERICA'S HISTORY MAKERS

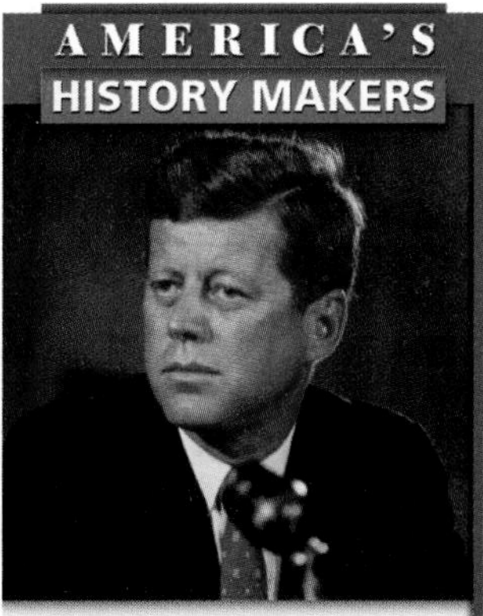

**JOHN F. KENNEDY**
**1917–1963**

In 1960, at age 43, John F. Kennedy became the youngest U.S. president ever elected. Handsome and energetic, he inspired belief in the country's capabilities.

Many Americans regard the Cuban missile crisis as Kennedy's finest moment of leadership. This conflict brought the United States to the brink of nuclear war. Kennedy considered bombing the Soviet missile sites in Cuba and invading the country before deciding it was safer to blockade Cuba and keep bargaining with Soviet leader Nikita Khrushchev.

**How did the missile crisis show Kennedy's leadership?**

### Section 1 Assessment

**1. Terms & Names**

**Identify:**
- Ngo Dinh Diem
- French Indochina
- Ho Chi Minh
- domino theory
- Viet Cong
- Ho Chi Minh Trail
- Cuban missile crisis

**2. Taking Notes**

Review the section and identify a key event for each year on the time line.

1930, 1940, 1945, 1946, 1950, 1954, 1960, 1963

What event brought the United States into the Vietnam conflict?

**3. Main Ideas**

a. What were Ho Chi Minh's goals for Vietnam?

b. How did the Cold War affect American decisions regarding Vietnam?

c. What level of involvement did the Truman, Eisenhower, and Kennedy administrations have in Vietnam?

**4. Critical Thinking**

**Evaluating** How did U.S. support of the Diem government involve a conflict of values?

THINK ABOUT
- American beliefs in democracy and individual rights
- the actions of the Diem government

**ACTIVITY OPTIONS**

**SPEECH**
**ART**

Record imaginary **radio interviews** with Ho Chi Minh and Ngo Dinh Diem about Vietnam, or construct **signs** that their supporters might carry in a demonstration.



### MORE ABOUT . . .

**The Cuban Missile Crisis**

President Kennedy revealed the presence of Soviet missiles in Cuba in a televised address on October 22, 1962. Kennedy ordered American ships into position to block Soviet ships headed to Cuba. For six days, the world waited for something to happen. Finally, the Soviet Union ordered 25 ships off their course to Cuba. The Soviets agreed to remove their missiles in return for an American promise not to invade Cuba, as well as a secret promise to remove U.S. nuclear missiles from Turkey.

**Humanities Transparency HT59**
- Soviet Missiles in Cuba

### AMERICA'S HISTORY MAKERS

**John F. Kennedy**

In 1940, just after graduating from college, Kennedy wrote a book called *Why England Slept.* It discussed the attempts by Britain and France to appease Hitler. Kennedy was determined not to repeat such a mistake with the Soviet Union.

Answer: He acted decisively and kept the peace while bargaining with Khrushchev to end the crisis.

**America's History Makers**
- John F. Kennedy, pp. 119–120

## ASSESS & RETEACH

**Setting the Stage** Have students complete the first three boxes in the column "Reasons for Involvement in Vietnam" on the graphic organizer.

**Formal Assessment**
- Section Quiz, p. 432

**Critical Thinking Transparency CT88**
- Setting the Stage

**RETEACHING ACTIVITY**

Have students create annotated time lines for important events discussed in this section.

**In-Depth Resources: Unit 9**
- Reteaching Activity, p. 33

### Section 1 Assessment

**1. Terms & Names**

**Ngo Dinh Diem,** p. 835
**French Indochina,** p. 835
**Ho Chi Minh,** p. 835
**domino theory,** p. 837
**Viet Cong,** p. 838
**Ho Chi Minh Trail,** p. 838
**Cuban missile crisis,** p. 839

**2. Taking Notes**

1930: Indochinese Communist Party forms; 1940: Japan takes over Indochina; 1945: Vietnam declares independence; 1946: Viet Minh and France at war; 1950: U.S. offers military aid to France; 1954: France surrenders; Vietnam divides; 1960: Viet Cong organizes; 1963: Diem overthrown

the offering of aid to France

**3. Main Ideas**

a. He wanted Vietnam to be independent of foreign rule. **b.** It made the United States determined to fight communism all over the world. **c.** Each succeeding president sent more military aid and advisers.

**4. Critical Thinking**

American beliefs in democracy and individual rights conflicted with American support of Diem's corrupt, oppressive, and unpopular government.

**ACTIVITY OPTIONS**

**Alternative Assessment**
- Rubrics, 3.3, 1.1

## SECTION OBJECTIVES

1. To describe events that led the United States to send combat troops to Vietnam
2. To analyze the kind of war U.S. troops faced
3. To explain U.S. military tactics
4. To describe the Tet offensive and sinking U.S. morale

**SKILLBUILDER**
Interpreting Maps: Location, p. 844

**CRITICAL THINKING**
Finding Main Ideas, p. 841
Analyzing Causes, p. 842
Drawing Conclusions, pp. 843, 844
Analyzing Points of View, p. 845

## FOCUS & MOTIVATE

### 5-MINUTE WARM-UP

**Making Inferences** To help students understand how some Americans saw the expanding Vietnam War, have them answer the following questions.

1. Look at the political cartoon on page 845. How are the people of South Vietnam represented?
2. What is the cartoonist's opinion of the war?

 **Warm-Up Transparency WT30**

## INSTRUCT

### INSTRUCT: OBJECTIVE 

**Johnson Sends Combat Troops**
Key Questions
- What power did the Gulf of Tonkin resolution give the president?
- How did U.S. involvement in South Vietnam escalate after 1964?

 **In-Depth Resources: Unit 9**
- Guided Reading, p. 22
- Building Vocabulary, p. 24

 **Reading Study Guide** (Spanish and English), pp. 289–290

# 2 War Expands in Vietnam

**TERMS & NAMES**
Gulf of Tonkin Resolution
escalation
William Westmoreland
guerrilla warfare
napalm
Agent Orange
Tet offensive

| MAIN IDEA | WHY IT MATTERS NOW |
|---|---|
| America sent ground troops to Vietnam expecting victory, but soldiers soon grew frustrated. | The Vietnam War taught Americans that superior military strength does not always ensure victory. |

## ONE AMERICAN'S STORY

**Reginald Edwards landed in Vietnam in 1965, the first year American combat troops were sent there. Despite two years of training, he was unprepared for the experience. It was nothing like his dream of "landing on this beach like they did in World War II." On night patrols through the dark countryside, Edwards and his fellow marines shot at whatever moved. Their first large-scale attack on the enemy proved disastrous.**

*A VOICE FROM THE PAST*

We had received fire. All of a sudden we could see people in front of us. Instead of waiting for air [support], we returned the fire, and you could see people fall. . . . Come to find out it was Bravo Company. What the VC [Viet Cong] had done was [lure] Bravo Company in front of us. . . . It was our own people. That's the bodies we saw falling. . . . I think we shot up maybe 40 guys in Bravo Company.

**Private Reginald "Malik" Edwards,** quoted in *Bloods: An Oral History of the Vietnam War by Black Veterans*

**American soldiers take aim in the Vietnamese jungle.**

**In this section, you will learn why the Vietnam War created such confusion and why people questioned how the war was conducted.**

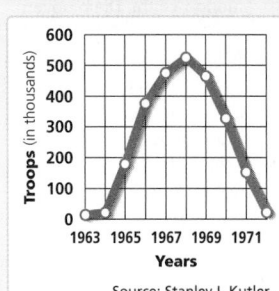

**U.S. Troops in Vietnam**

Troops (in thousands): 0, 100, 200, 300, 400, 500, 600
Years: 1963, 1965, 1967, 1969, 1971

Source: Stanley I. Kutler, *Encyclopedia of the Vietnam War*

## 1 Johnson Sends Combat Troops

The assassination of President Diem in 1963 brought chaos to South Vietnam. One ineffective leader after another headed the government. Meanwhile, the North Vietnamese kept shipping more aid to the Viet Cong. By late 1964, combined Viet Cong and North Vietnamese forces controlled much of the South Vietnamese countryside.

Like earlier presidents, Lyndon Johnson did not want to lose Vietnam to communism. As a result, he increased U.S. efforts in Vietnam.

In the summer of 1964, Johnson's military advisers made plans to bomb North Vietnam. They wanted to



## RECOMMENDED RESOURCES

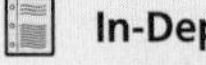 **In-Depth Resources: Unit 9**
- Guided Reading, p. 22
- Building Vocabulary, p. 24
- Geography Application: The Fall of a South Vietnamese Village, 1965, pp. 26–27
- Literature Selection: from *Fallen Angels,* pp. 30–32
- Reteaching Activity, p. 34

**Reading Study Guide** (Spanish and English), pp. 289–290

**America's History Makers**
- Lyndon B. Johnson, pp. 121–122

**Formal Assessment**
- Section Quiz, p. 433

**Alternative Assessment**
- Rubrics, 1.5
- Rubrics, 4.9

**Access for Students Acquiring English/ESL**
- Guided Reading, p. 200
- Geography Application, pp. 203–204

**Technology Resources**

 **Electronic Teacher Tools with Test Maker**

 **ClassZone**
www.mcdougallittell.com

pressure Ho Chi Minh to stop supporting the Viet Cong. But no bombing could start unless Congress approved the plan. A shooting incident off the coast of North Vietnam spurred Congress to give its approval.

The U.S. destroyer *Maddox* had been patrolling in the Gulf of Tonkin when North Vietnamese torpedo boats fired on it. Two days later, on August 4, the *Maddox* and another destroyer reported a second attack. However, no one could confirm this attack. There had been thunderstorms that night, and the weather could have affected the radar screens. U.S. jet pilots flying overhead said they had seen no North Vietnamese boats.

*Reading* **History**

**A. Finding Main Ideas** What did the Gulf of Tonkin Resolution do?
A. Answer It gave the president the power to use military force in Vietnam.

Despite doubts about the second attack, Johnson asked Congress to pass the **Gulf of Tonkin Resolution.** This gave the president the power to use military force in Vietnam. All but two senators voted for the resolution. The "yes" vote in the House was unanimous.

In March 1965, Johnson began bombing North Vietnam. At about the same time, he sent the first combat ground troops to Vietnam. Their numbers grew from 75,000 in the middle of 1965 to 184,000 by the end of 1965.

This policy of **escalation,** or increasing military involvement in Vietnam, continued over the next few years. General **William Westmoreland,** the commander of U.S. forces in South Vietnam, asked for more and more troops. By the end of 1968, there were more than 536,000 American military personnel in South Vietnam.

AMERICA'S HISTORY MAKERS

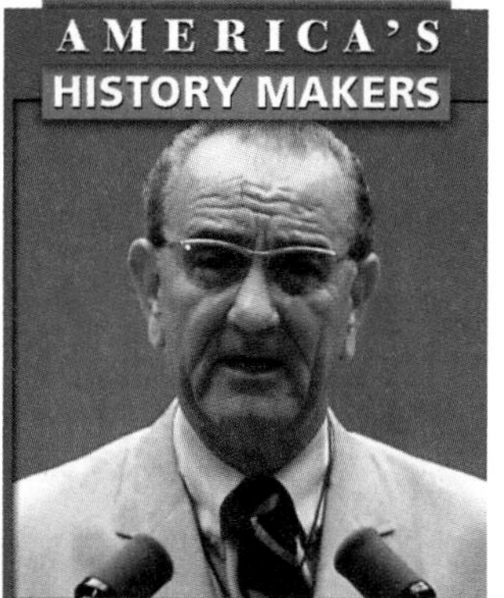

**LYNDON JOHNSON**
**1908–1973**

Lyndon Johnson wanted people to remember him as a social reformer. The Great Society was the name for his wide-ranging domestic programs, which included reforms in education, medical care for the elderly, aid to cities, and support for civil rights.

The Vietnam War overshadowed Johnson's achievements. He was tormented by the deaths and the social divisions the war brought. His goals for the country were blocked by the war, which still had not ended when he died.

**How would you describe Johnson's presidency?**

## 2 A Frustrating War

Many Americans thought that, with their superior weapons, U.S. ground forces would quickly defeat the Viet Cong and drive them out of the villages. Many conditions frustrated American soldiers, however. First of all, they could wage only a limited war, partly because the government feared drawing China into the conflict.

**Background**
The average World War II soldier was 26 and served for three years. Many soldiers in Vietnam had fathers who had fought in World War II.

Also, most U.S. soldiers in Vietnam were young and inexperienced. The average soldier was 19 and served a one-year tour of duty. Officers served even shorter tours, on average six months. The short tours meant that by the time soldiers and officers had gained enough experience, their tours of duty were over.

The Vietnam War differed from World War II in that there was no frontline. The Viet Cong mixed with the general population and operated everywhere, attacking U.S. troops in the countryside and in the cities. Even a shoeshine boy on a city street corner might toss a grenade into an army bus carrying American soldiers. Marine captain E. J. Banks described his frustration: "You never knew who was the enemy and who was the friend. . . . The enemy was all around you."





### AMERICA'S HISTORY MAKERS

**Lyndon Johnson**
President Johnson became intensely involved in the day-to-day operations in Vietnam. He made nightly visits, often in a dressing gown, to the White House situation room in search of up-to-date information on the war. He made military appointments, approved promotions, decided where troops should be deployed, and even selected bombing targets.

Possible Responses: tragic, disappointing, well-intentioned, misguided

 **America's History Makers**
- Lyndon B. Johnson, pp. 121–122

### INSTRUCT: OBJECTIVE 2

**A Frustrating War**
Key Questions
- What conditions frustrated American soldiers in South Vietnam?
- How did the Vietnam War differ from World War II?
- How were Vietnam's land and climate hard on American troops?
- How difficult an enemy were the Viet Cong?

 **In-Depth Resources: Unit 9**
- Literature Selection: from *Fallen Angels,* pp. 30–32

### HISTORY FROM VISUALS

**Reading the Graph** Direct students to the line graph on page 840. Point out that the number of U.S. troops in Vietnam peaked in 1968. In the presidential election of 1968, Richard Nixon defeated Vice-President Hubert Humphrey, who was supported by President Johnson. Ask students how important they think the growing number of U.S. troops in Vietnam was as an election issue. **Possible Response** With so many American soldiers serving in Vietnam, the war was among the most important issues.

**Extension** Have students research other issues that were important in the 1968 election.

### ACTIVITY OPTIONS
### INDIVIDUAL NEEDS

**LESS PROFICIENT READERS**

**Setting a Purpose** To focus students' attention on the key events discussed in this section, provide them with purpose-setting questions, such as the ones below, to answer as they read. Have them read the question, the heading, and the text under the headings. Then go back to the question and give an answer using the headings as part of the answer.
- How did Johnson step up the war effort? *(Johnson sends combat troops.)*
- Describe the conditions that American soldiers faced. *(a frustrating war)*
- List some of the war tactics used by American troops. Why were these tactics controversial? *(stripping the jungle, search-and-destroy missions)*
- What was the Tet offensive? When did it take place? What was the result of the Tet offensive for the Viet Cong? What was its effect on the Americans? *(the surprise Tet offensive, U.S. morale sinks)*

## MORE ABOUT . . .

**Booby Traps**
Americans called the Viet Cong's covered pits with sharpened bamboo stakes "punji pits." Other booby traps included artillery shells buried under the floors of huts or hanging from tree branches. Booby traps accounted for more than 10 percent of American casualties during the war.

### CRITICAL THINKING ACTIVITY

**Comparing and Contrasting** Have students use a chart to compare and contrast the Vietnam War and World War II for American troops. You might want to create the chart on the board or have students work with partners to create their own charts. Students should keep their charts for use as study aids.

| Categories | World War II | Vietnam War |
|---|---|---|
| U.S. Allies | | |
| U.S. Opponents | | |
| U.S. Weapons | | |
| Enemy's Weapons | | |
| Type of Warfare | | |

**Class Time** 20 minutes

### INSTRUCT: OBJECTIVE 3

**Stripping the Jungle/ Search-and-Destroy Missions**
Key Questions
- How and why did American troops destroy the Vietnamese landscape?
- What was the purpose of American search-and-destroy missions?
- What were the effects of search-and-destroy tactics?

 **In-Depth Resources: Unit 9**
- Geography Application: The Fall of a South Vietnamese Village, 1965, pp. 26–27

**Vietnam Warfare**

Booby Traps
**The Viet Cong hid deadly booby traps made of sharpened sticks.**

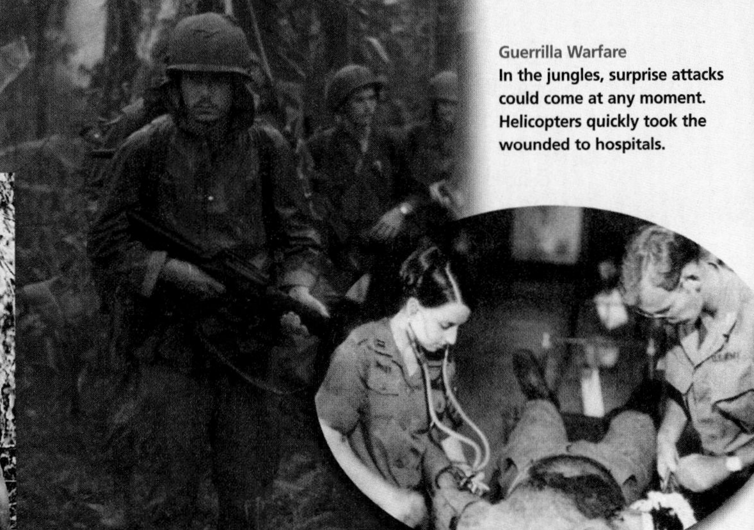

Guerrilla Warfare
**In the jungles, surprise attacks could come at any moment. Helicopters quickly took the wounded to hospitals.**

The style of fighting in Vietnam also differed from that in World War II. Because they could not match American firepower, the Viet Cong relied on **guerrilla warfare,** surprise attacks by small bands of fighters. Viet Cong guerrillas would suddenly emerge from networks of underground tunnels to fight. Then they would disappear back into the tunnels. They riddled the countryside and jungles with land mines and booby traps, such as bamboo stakes hidden in covered pits. They hung grenades from trees and hid them in bushes. Every day, U.S. Army and Navy nurses treated young soldiers with gruesome wounds.

**Background**
Nearly 7,500 women served in Vietnam as nurses.

Even the land and climate of Vietnam proved difficult. The heat was suffocating and the rain almost constant. Soldiers sweated through tangled jungles. After wading through flooded rice paddies, they had to pick leeches off their feet and legs. American soldier Warren Wooten said, "It seemed like the whole country was an enemy. The animals, the reptiles, the insects, the plants. And the people."

Finally, the Viet Cong were a very dedicated enemy. They took heavy losses, built up their ranks again, and kept on fighting year after year because they believed in their cause. An American who interviewed Viet Cong prisoners noted, "They see the war entirely as one of defense of their country against the invading Americans, who, in turn, are seen merely as successors to the French."

***Reading*History**
**B. Analyzing Causes** Why was the war so hard for the United States to win?
B. Possible Response U.S. troops could wage only a limited war; the enemy relied on guerrilla warfare and was very dedicated.

## 3 Stripping the Jungle

One of the strengths of the Viet Cong was their ability to hide in the jungle and in underground tunnels. To reveal and destroy Viet Cong hideouts, American troops used chemicals that ruined the landscape.



**ACTIVITY OPTIONS**
**INTERDISCIPLINARY LINK: LANGUAGE ARTS** — BLOCK SCHEDULING

### WRITING FROM DIFFERENT POINTS OF VIEW

**Class Time** One class period

**Task** Writing descriptions of the Vietnam War

**Purpose** To understand the fighting in Vietnam from the viewpoint of a Viet Cong fighter, an American soldier, or a Vietnamese civilian

**Supplies Needed**
- Reference materials about the Vietnam War
- Internet access

**Activity** Have the students choose either a Vietnamese civilian, a Viet Cong fighter, or an American soldier. Then review the material in the section and in references. Ask the students to write a description of the war from the perspective of the person they selected. Have students share their viewpoint with someone in the class whose viewpoint is different.

Search-and-Destroy Missions
U.S. soldiers destroyed villages suspected of hiding Viet Cong.

Napalm
U.S. planes dropped fiery napalm bombs to wipe out Viet Cong bases. Napalm is jellied gasoline.

Over wide areas, U.S. planes dropped bombs of **napalm,** jellied gasoline that burns violently. Planes also sprayed **Agent Orange,** a chemical that kills plants, over the jungles.

Such chemicals helped destroy the hideouts and food supplies of the Viet Cong. But in the process, they also harmed innocent Vietnamese villagers. This undermined the villagers' support for the United States. Later, people learned that Agent Orange harmed U.S. soldiers as well. Veterans exposed to it have suffered from skin diseases and cancers.

## Search-and-Destroy Missions

Search-and-destroy missions were another American war tactic that terrorized Vietnamese villagers. In such missions, soldiers hunted Viet Cong and burned or bombed villages thought to be sheltering them. Marine sergeant William Ehrhart described how search-and-destroy missions affected South Vietnamese peasants.

C. Answer Their war tactics destroyed the land and terrorized villagers.

*Reading* **History**

**C. Drawing Conclusions** Why did Americans fail to "win the minds and hearts of the people" in Vietnam?

*A VOICE FROM THE PAST*

Their homes had been wrecked, their chickens killed, their rice confiscated [taken away]—and if they weren't pro-Vietcong before we got there, they sure . . . were by the time we left.

**William Ehrhart,** quoted in *Vietnam: A History* by Stanley Karnow

These destructive methods defeated the purpose of "winning the hearts and minds" of the villagers and turning them against communism. Furthermore, even if the tactics did clear a village of Viet Cong temporarily, the Viet Cong usually returned later.





### MORE ABOUT . . .

**Fighting in Vietnam**

American military leaders had difficulty measuring the success of operations in Vietnam. Because there was no "front line," gaining or losing territory had little meaning. Americans used "body counts," the number of enemy troops killed, to judge their performance. Body counts were often unreliable for two reasons. First, it was difficult to make an accurate count of enemy dead; many of the dead were noncombatants. Second, some officers inflated the count to make it appear that their operations had been more successful than they really were.

### MORE ABOUT . . .

**Allies in Vietnam**

About 69,000 troops from allied nations fought alongside U.S. and South Vietnamese troops during the war. Australia, New Zealand, the Philippines, South Korea, and Thailand, all members of SEATO (Southeast Asia Treaty Organization) initially supported efforts to control Communist expansion in Southeast Asia. Despite intense pressure from the United States, however, these nations did not increase their limited involvement in Vietnam.

### ACTIVITY OPTIONS

**INTERDISCIPLINARY LINK: HEALTH**  BLOCK SCHEDULING

#### HEALTH RISKS IN VIETNAM

**Class Time** 45 minutes

**Task** Reporting on health problems caused by the war

**Purpose** To analyze the health problems caused by the war

**Supplies Needed**
- Reference materials on the Vietnam War
- Internet access

**Activity** Have students research one or more of the health problems affecting Americans and Vietnamese during and after the Vietnam War. Problems may include injuries from bullets, bombs, and booby traps; tropical diseases; contamination with herbicides and other chemicals; and problems caused by psychological trauma during the war. Students should present their findings in written or oral reports.

**INSTRUCT: OBJECTIVE** 

**The Surprise Tet Offensive/ U.S. Morale Sinks**

Key Questions

- What was the Tet offensive?
- What effect did the Tet offensive have on the attitudes of Americans toward the war?
- How did the My Lai episode illustrate a breakdown in morale and discipline among U.S. troops?

**MORE ABOUT . . .**

**Doubts About the War**

Among the problems faced by U.S. officials in the Vietnam War was what came to be known as the *credibility gap.* This term referred to doubts about the reliability of information provided by military and government officials. The credibility gap widened with the Tet offensive in 1968, which cast into doubt official U.S. claims that the Viet Cong were too weak to launch such a fierce attack.

**HISTORY FROM VISUALS**

**Reading the Map** Remind students that, unlike World War II, the Vietnam War had no "front lines." The Viet Cong attacked cities throughout South Vietnam during the Tet offensive. Ask students how supplies from North Vietnam reached Viet Cong forces scattered throughout the country. **Answer** by way of the Ho Chi Minh Trail

**Extension** Explain that many U.S. and South Vietnamese troops expected little fighting on the Tet holiday. Have students research Tet and report back to the class on traditional activities that mark the holiday in Vietnam.

## 4 The Surprise Tet Offensive

By the end of 1967, the war had caused great destruction, but neither side was close to victory. Still, U.S. military officials claimed that they would soon win. Then, on January 30 and 31, 1968, the Communists launched the **Tet offensive.** This was a surprise attack on U.S. military bases and more than 100 cities and towns in South Vietnam. It came during Tet, the Vietnamese celebration of the lunar New Year.

In preparation for the Tet offensive, the Viet Cong hid weapons in vegetable trucks, food trucks, peddlers' carts, and even coffins. They smuggled these weapons into South Vietnamese cities. Soldiers dressed in civilian clothes entered the cities on buses, on motorcycles, and on foot. No one could tell them apart from the war refugees who streamed into the cities from the countryside or from visitors coming for the holiday.

The Viet Cong fought to take over the cities during the offensive. They killed not only enemy soldiers but also government officials, schoolteachers, doctors, and priests.

**Background** In the Tet offensive, enemy forces invaded the U.S. embassy compound in Saigon, killing five Americans.

The Tet offensive was a military defeat for the Communists. They gained no cities and lost 45,000 soldiers, while the South Vietnamese lost 2,300 soldiers and the United States 1,100.

But the attack stunned Americans. General Westmoreland had recently declared, "We have turned the corner," suggesting that victory was in sight. The Tet offensive raised doubts that this was true. Many government and business leaders began to think that the United States could not win the war, except at too high a price.

Skillbuilder Answers
1. South Vietnam
2. The country was not very secure.

**Tet Offensive, Jan. 30–Feb. 24, 1968**



**GEOGRAPHY SKILLBUILDER Interpreting Maps**
1. **Location** *In what country were the major battles?*
2. **Location** *What did the number and location of attacks suggest about the country's security?*

The Tet offensive also made many Americans ask whether the U.S. mission in Vietnam was wise. To retake some cities, troops had to almost level them with bombing and shelling. Speaking of the city of Ben Tre, a U.S. major said, "It became necessary to destroy the town in order to save it." The quote became an example of what many considered the senselessness of the war.

Because of the doubts it raised, the Tet offensive became a turning point in the war. Afterward, President Johnson changed his war policy. When General Westmoreland asked for 206,000 more troops, to take advantage of the enemy's weakness, President Johnson said no. Then, on March 31, 1968, Johnson said that he would stop bombing most of North Vietnam and would seek to

**D. Answer** It was a failure because the Viet Cong gained no cities and lost many soldiers. It was a success because it made Americans doubt that they could win the war easily.

***Reading* History**

**D. Drawing Conclusions** How was the Tet offensive both a failure and a success for the Viet Cong?

844

**ACTIVITY OPTIONS**

**MULTIPLE LEARNING STYLES: INTERPERSONAL** — BLOCK SCHEDULING

**PREPARING A NEWSCAST**

**Class Time** 45 minutes

**Task** Simulating television interviews

**Purpose** To gain insight into important events in the Vietnam War

**Supplies Needed**
- Reference materials about the Vietnam War
- Internet access

**Activity** Divide students into pairs. Partners should choose the role of television news reporter or soldier. Reporters should prepare at least three questions to elicit the soldier's opinion on the course of the war, the Tet offensive, and the My Lai massacre. Students in the role of soldier should answer questions based on their reading in the text and additional research. Have students prepare a videotape or a written account of the interview.

bargain for peace. In the same speech, he announced that he would not run for another term as president.

### U.S. Morale Sinks

As the Vietnam War went on, it wore down American soldiers. They fought hard and bravely, but many were losing faith that the United States could win the war. The South Vietnamese government did not have the loyalty of the people. In addition, the South Vietnamese army often avoided fighting. American soldiers asked why they were fighting a war the Vietnamese did not want to fight themselves.

The low morale of American forces in Vietnam became clear when news of the My Lai (mee ly) massacre broke in 1969. The incident happened on March 16, 1968. A U.S. platoon led by Lieutenant William Calley, Jr., rounded up and shot between 175 and 500 unarmed civilians, mostly women, children, and old men. A U.S. helicopter pilot rescued some civilians by threatening to fire on the soldiers. To Americans, My Lai represented a horrifying breakdown in morality and discipline in the armed forces. In 1971, a colonel warned that U.S. forces were "in a state approaching collapse."

**Background**
Calley was jailed briefly, but many saw him as a scapegoat because charges were dropped against higher-ranking officers.

In the next section, you'll learn how the United States withdrew from the Vietnam War.

"I DON'T KNOW IF EITHER SIDE IS WINNING, BUT I KNOW WHO'S LOSING."

This 1968 cartoon by Herblock comments on the war's cost to civilians.

## Section 2 Assessment

### 1. Terms & Names

**Identify:**

- Gulf of Tonkin Resolution
- escalation
- William Westmoreland
- guerrilla warfare
- napalm
- Agent Orange
- Tet offensive

### 2. Taking Notes

On a chart like the one below, note the war's effects on Vietnamese villagers and on U.S. soldiers.

Effects of War

| Villagers | U.S. Soldiers |
|---|---|
| | |
| | |
| | |
| | |

### 3. Main Ideas

a. How did President Johnson escalate U.S. involvement in the Vietnam War?

b. What made fighting the war so frustrating for American soldiers?

c. How was the Tet offensive a turning point in the war?

### 4. Critical Thinking

**Analyzing Points of View** Were the Viet Cong right to see the Americans "merely as successors to the French"?

**THINK ABOUT**

- the goals of the French in Vietnam
- the goals of the Americans in Vietnam
- the actions of the French and the Americans

**ACTIVITY OPTIONS**

**SCIENCE** / **HEALTH**

Investigate the health effects of Agent Orange reported by Vietnam veterans. Design a science **exhibit** or create a **warning label** to share your findings.





**MORE ABOUT . . .**

**Johnson's Decision Not to Seek Another Term**
President Johnson's announcement that he would not seek reelection stunned the country. In the New Hampshire Democratic primary held earlier in March, Eugene McCarthy—an outspoken antiwar senator from Minnesota—won 42 percent of the vote compared to Johnson's 48 percent. The surprisingly close vote was a political setback for Johnson.

**MORE ABOUT . . .**

**Calley's Court Martial**
After news of the My Lai incident broke, a number of soldiers, veterans, and officers were accused of murder and of covering up the incident. Only five were court-martialed, and only one was convicted. Lieutenant Calley was found guilty of the premeditated murder of at least 22 Vietnamese civilians. He was sentenced to life imprisonment. In 1974, a federal district court overturned his conviction and he was released.

## ASSESS & RETEACH

**Setting the Stage** Have students complete the fifth box in the column "Reasons for Involvement in Vietnam" on the chapter graphic organizer.

 **Formal Assessment**
- Section Quiz, p. 433

**RETEACHING ACTIVITY**
Have partners develop outlines of the section. Students should use the section's main idea as the topic sentence. Partners should use the subheadings throughout the section for the Roman numeral headings in their outlines.

 **In-Depth Resources: Unit 9**
- Reteaching Activity, p. 34

## Section 2 Assessment

### 1. Terms & Names

**Gulf of Tonkin Resolution,** p. 841
**escalation,** p. 841
**William Westmoreland,** p. 841
**guerrilla warfare,** p. 842
**napalm,** p. 843
**Agent Orange,** p. 843
**Tet offensive,** p. 844

### 2. Taking Notes

Villagers: harmed by chemicals that destroyed landscape and food supplies; terrorized; left homeless; killed; U.S. soldiers: frustrated; vulnerable to surprise attack and booby traps; demoralized by difficult physical conditions

### 3. Main Ideas

**a.** He ordered the bombing of North Vietnam and sent combat troops to South Vietnam. **b.** They could only wage a limited war, guerrilla warfare meant unexpected attacks, and the land and climate were difficult.
**c.** Americans realized that they would not easily win the war; many doubted the wisdom of continuing.

### 4. Critical Thinking

Some students may say no because Americans had no economic interest in Vietnam. Others may agree because both countries fought to keep Vietnam from communism.

**ACTIVITY OPTIONS**

 **Alternative Assessment**
- Rubrics, 1.5, 4.9

## SECTION OBJECTIVES

1. To analyze the growing antiwar movement in the United States
2. To describe the events that made 1968 a turning point of the war
3. To explain Nixon's Vietnam strategy and the U.S. withdrawal from Vietnam
4. To analyze the legacy of the Vietnam War

**CRITICAL THINKING**

Analyzing Points of View, p. 847
Making Inferences, pp. 848, 849
Forming and Supporting Opinions, p. 849

 **Why It Matters Now**
- The Impact of Vietnam, pp. 59–60

## FOCUS & MOTIVATE

### 5-MINUTE WARM-UP

**Making Inferences** These questions focus on the killings at Kent State.

1. Read "One American's Story" on page 846 and look at the photograph. What is happening in the photo?
2. How do you think this photograph might have affected the attitudes of Americans toward the war and toward antiwar protesters?

 **Warm-Up Transparency WT30**

## INSTRUCT

**INSTRUCT: OBJECTIVE** 

**A Growing Antiwar Movement**

Key Questions
- Why did some Americans protest against the Vietnam War?
- How did the draft system increase opposition to the war and link the antiwar movement to the civil rights movement?

 **In-Depth Resources: Unit 9**
- Guided Reading, p. 23

**Reading Study Guide** (Spanish and English), pp. 291–292

# 3 The Vietnam War Ends

**TERMS & NAMES**
- doves
- hawks
- Richard Nixon
- Vietnamization
- Cambodia
- Twenty-sixth Amendment
- War Powers Act

| MAIN IDEA | WHY IT MATTERS NOW |
|---|---|
| The Vietnam War divided Americans and had lasting effects in the United States and Southeast Asia. | Lessons of the Vietnam War still influence the United States whenever it gets involved in a foreign conflict. |

### ONE AMERICAN'S STORY

**Mary Ann Vecchio was just 14 years old when she suddenly became a symbol of the anguish that the Vietnam War caused Americans. A student journalist snapped Vecchio's picture as she knelt over a dead student at Kent State University in Ohio. The youth was Jeffrey Glenn Miller, one of four students killed by the National Guard during an antiwar demonstration on May 4, 1970. Looking back 25 years later, Vecchio described her feelings of disbelief.**

*A VOICE FROM THE PAST*

I couldn't believe that people would kill people over what they thought, just because he demonstrated against the Vietnam War—that they would shoot you over it. I couldn't believe . . . . There was nothing I could do for Jeffrey or any of the other students. And that's part of history and that'll remain with me for the rest of my life.

**Mary Ann Vecchio Gillum,** conference at Emerson College, April 23, 1995

**Mary Ann Vecchio cries out in horror after the Kent State shootings in May 1970.**

**In this section, you will learn how growing opposition to the war eventually led the United States to pull its troops out of Vietnam.**

##  A Growing Antiwar Movement

As the war escalated in the mid-1960s, antiwar feeling grew among Americans at home. Religious leaders, civil rights leaders, teachers, students, journalists, and others protested the war for a variety of reasons. Some believed that the United States had no business involving itself in another country's civil war. Others believed that the methods of fighting the war were immoral. Still others thought that the costs to American society were too high.

College students formed a large and vocal group of protesters. They particularly opposed the draft, which required young men to serve in the military. In demonstrations around the country, young men burned their



### RECOMMENDED RESOURCES

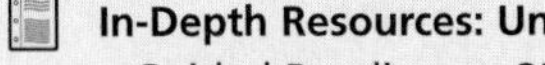

**In-Depth Resources: Unit 9**
- Guided Reading, p. 23
- Building Vocabulary, p. 24
- Skillbuilder Practice, p. 25
- Reteaching Activity, p. 35
- Enrichment Activity, p. 36

**Reading Study Guide** (Spanish and English), pp. 291–292

**America's History Makers**
- Maya Lin, pp. 123–124

**Why It Matters Now,** pp. 59–60

**Citizenship Today,** p. 80

**Formal Assessment**
- Section Quiz, p. 434

**Alternative Assessment**
- Rubrics, 4.2
- Rubrics, 2.7

**Access for Students Acquiring English/ESL**
- Guided Reading, p. 201
- Skillbuilder Practice, p. 202

**Technology Resources**

 **Humanities Transparency HT60**
- Antiwar Poster

 **Critical Thinking Trans. CT89**
- Cause and Effect: The War in Vietnam

 **Geography Transparency GT30**
- U.S. Troops Around the World, 1975

draft cards. About 50,000 people staged such a protest in front of the Pentagon on October 21, 1967.

Opponents of the draft pointed out its unfairness. Most draftees were poor. Middle- and upper-class youths could delay being drafted by enrolling in college. They also sought advice from draft counselors, doctors, and lawyers to help them avoid service. Certain medical conditions or religious beliefs, for example, could keep them out of the military.

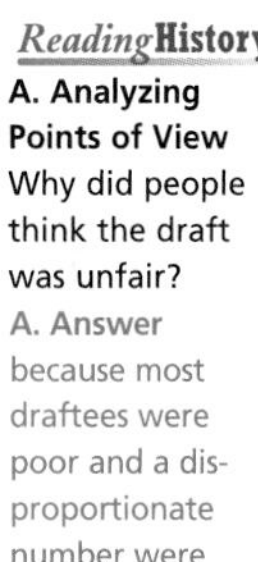

*Reading* **History**
**A. Analyzing Points of View** Why did people think the draft was unfair?
A. Answer because most draftees were poor and a disproportionate number were African American

Another unfair aspect of the draft was the high number of African Americans called to serve. African Americans made up about 20 percent of combat troops in Vietnam. In 1965, they accounted for 24 percent of U.S. Army combat deaths. Yet they were only 11 percent of the male population in the United States.

For this and other reasons, the antiwar movement became linked with the civil rights movement. In 1967, civil rights leader Martin Luther King, Jr., spoke out against the Vietnam War. Noting that the war took money away from antipoverty programs, he declared, "I was increasingly compelled to see the war as an enemy of the poor."

By 1967, it was clear that the Vietnam War was dividing Americans into two camps. Even within families, people took opposite sides. Those who opposed the war were called **doves**. Those who supported it were known as **hawks**. Supporters of the war staged marches of their own. Believing that antiwar protesters were unpatriotic, they popularized such slogans as "America—love it or leave it."

## 2 1968—A Turning Point

As you learned in Section 2, the Tet offensive in January 1968 made Americans doubt that they could win the war. Walter Cronkite, a respected TV news anchorman, visited Vietnam in February. After returning, he ended a special report with his own opinion of the war. He concluded that the United States was not winning but was in a deadlock.

*A VOICE FROM THE PAST*

[T]he only rational way out, then, will be to negotiate, not as victors, but as an honorable people who lived up to their pledge to defend democracy, and did the best they could.

**Walter Cronkite,** *A Reporter's Life*

President Johnson took Cronkite's words to heart. "If I've lost Cronkite, I've lost middle America," he reportedly said.

That summer, the Democratic National Convention in Chicago reflected the country's turmoil. Democrats chose Hubert Humphrey, Johnson's vice-president, as their nominee. Outside the convention hall, TV

**daily *life***

**THE "TELEVISION WAR"**

The Vietnam War was the first "television war," broadcast each night on the evening news. Reports rarely showed actual battles, partly because much of the fighting occurred off and on and at night, between small units.

Networks also tried to avoid gruesome scenes because they did not want to offend viewers. In addition, the networks agreed not to show any American dead or wounded so that their families would not see them on the screen. Still, the images of war shocked TV audiences.

847



**MORE ABOUT . . .**

**Antiwar Demonstrations**

Antiwar protests grew larger as the war dragged on. Some early protests included "teach-ins" in 1965. During those teach-ins, college and university faculty members discussed the nature of the Vietnam War. About 3,500 students attended one of the first teach-ins at the University of Michigan in 1965. Just two years later, in April 1967, about 130,000 people in New York marched against the war.

 **Humanities Transparency HT60**
- Antiwar Poster

**INSTRUCT: OBJECTIVE 2**

**1968—A Turning Point**

Key Questions
- Why was Walter Cronkite's opinion of the war important?
- How did the Democratic National Convention in 1968 reflect the turmoil of the nation?
- What campaign promise did Richard Nixon make about the Vietnam War?

**daily*life***

**The "Television War"**

Television coverage of the Vietnam War became more critical of U.S. conduct in the war after a report by Morley Safer of CBS News in August 1965. Safer's broadcast showed U.S. Marines burning the homes of civilians. After the war, General Westmoreland charged that television and other media coverage had hurt U.S. efforts in Vietnam. For example, he complained that intense and graphic media coverage had made the Tet offensive into a psychological victory for the Viet Cong.

**ACTIVITY OPTIONS**

**SKILLBUILDER MINI-LESSON: FORMING AND SUPPORTING OPINIONS** 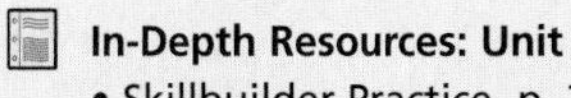 **BLOCK SCHEDULING**

**Explaining the Skill** Historians do more than reconstruct facts about the past. They form opinions as they interpret the past and judge the importance of historical events and people. Historians also support their opinions with logic, facts, examples, quotes, and references to events.

**Applying the Skill** Write the following questions on the chalkboard. Tell students to use material in the chapter to complete their responses.

1. Should the United States have become involved in Vietnam? *(Student responses will vary.)*
2. What evidence supports a need for U.S. involvement? *(Communist efforts to take over South Vietnam; the domino theory; quotations from presidents)*
3. What evidence supports the argument that the United States should not have become involved? *(lack of Vietnamese support for the Saigon government; South Vietnam's refusal to hold elections in 1956; inability to win the war; the destruction caused by the war)*

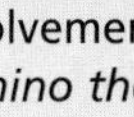 **In-Depth Resources: Unit 9**
- Skillbuilder Practice, p. 25

**INSTRUCT: OBJECTIVE** 

**Nixon's Vietnam Strategy/ Withdrawal from Vietnam**

Key Questions

- What were Nixon's strategies for ending the war?
- How did the revelations of previously secret U.S. policies in Vietnam affect the American public?
- How did the Vietnam War end?

 **Citizenship Today,** p. 79

**MORE ABOUT . . .**

**The Pentagon Papers**

The 7,000-page, 47-volume Pentagon Papers detailed the Vietnam policies of the United States from 1945 to 1968. The Nixon administration turned to the courts in an attempt to stop publication of the papers. However, the Supreme Court ruled that the *New York Times* and other newspapers had a First Amendment right to publish them.

**INSTRUCT: OBJECTIVE** 

**Legacy of the Vietnam War**

Key questions

- What effects did the war have in Vietnam?
- How many U.S. soldiers were killed or wounded in the war?
- How was passage of the Twenty-sixth Amendment connected to the war?
- Why did Congress pass the War Powers Act?

 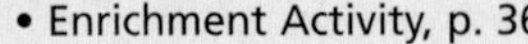

**In-Depth Resources: Unit 9**
- Enrichment Activity, p. 36

 **Geography Transparency GT30**
- U.S. Troops Around the World, 1975

 **Critical Thinking Transparency CT89**
- Cause and Effect: The War in Vietnam

cameras showed police clubbing antiwar demonstrators and bystanders. The chaos helped Republican candidate **Richard Nixon** win the presidency in 1968. In his campaign, Nixon promised to "bring an honorable end to the war in Vietnam."

## 3 Nixon's Vietnam Strategy

In July 1969, Nixon announced his strategy of **Vietnamization.** It called for gradually withdrawing U.S. forces and turning the ground fighting over to the South Vietnamese. Nixon promised to withdraw 25,000 of the 543,000 U.S. ground troops in Vietnam by the end of the year. However, Nixon had already begun secret bombing raids of **Cambodia,** a country bordering Vietnam. This bombing was meant to stop North Vietnamese troops and supplies from moving along the Ho Chi Minh Trail. Many people grew angry when they learned that the government had widened the war and hidden its actions.

**Background** In 1970, a U.S. invasion of Cambodia sparked protests at Kent State and many other colleges.

Public anger and distrust of the government grew after Daniel Ellsberg released the Pentagon Papers to the *New York Times* in 1971. Ellsberg had helped research and write these secret Defense Department papers. They showed that the four previous presidential administrations had not been honest with the public about U.S. involvement and goals in Vietnam.

## Withdrawal from Vietnam

Promising that peace was at hand, Nixon was reelected by a landslide in 1972. On January 27, 1973, the United States and South Vietnam signed a peace agreement with North Vietnam and the Viet Cong. The United States agreed to withdraw all its troops, and North Vietnam agreed not to invade South Vietnam. On March 29, the last U.S. troops left Vietnam. For the United States, the war was over.

Thousands try to escape during the fall of Saigon.

But for the Vietnamese, the war continued. In 1975, North Vietnam launched a massive invasion of South Vietnam. On April 30 of that year, Communist forces captured Saigon, which they renamed Ho Chi Minh City. The war then ended.

*Reading* **History**

**B. Making Inferences** Why did fighting begin again after the peace agreement?

**B. Possible Responses** North Vietnam had not achieved its goal of reunifying the country, and the United States was unlikely to step in.

## 4 Legacy of the Vietnam War

The Vietnam War caused terrible destruction and suffering in Southeast Asia. More than 1.2 million North and South Vietnamese died in the conflict. American bombing and chemical spraying caused lasting damage to farmland and forests. The war ruined Vietnam's economy, leaving many in poverty. After the North Vietnamese set up Communist rule in the

848

**ACTIVITY OPTIONS**

**INDIVIDUAL NEEDS: GIFTED AND TALENTED**

**VIETNAM'S EFFECTS ON FOREIGN POLICY**

**Class Time** One class period

**Task** Analyzing the effects of the Vietnam War on future U.S. foreign policy

**Purpose** To explore the consequences of the Vietnam War

**Supplies Needed**
- Reference materials on the Vietnam War and War Powers Act
- Internet access

**Activity** Have students research the effects of the Vietnam War and the War Powers Act on U.S. action in Grenada (1983), Panama (1989), the Persian Gulf (1991), or Kosovo (1999). Students should research how Presidents Reagan, Bush, or Clinton complied with the War Powers Act. Students should write a two-paragraph summary of their findings and include a list of the articles they used for research.

reunited country, many Vietnamese fled. By 1980, almost 173,000 had come to the United States.

The Vietnam War also took a heavy toll on American soldiers. About 58,000 died, and more than 300,000 were wounded. Many suffered permanent, disabling injuries. Returning soldiers often had recurring nightmares and other stress-related problems. To make things worse, they came home to a public that treated them coldly.

The Vietnam War had far-reaching political effects in the United States. The **Twenty-sixth Amendment,** passed in 1971, lowered the voting age from 21 to 18. Its supporters argued persuasively that anyone old enough to be drafted should be allowed to vote. The government ended the draft in 1973 because so many people opposed it. The nation now relies on an all-volunteer military.

**Background**
Although there is no draft now, 18-year-old men must still register with the Selective Service in case Congress orders a draft in the future.

Another legacy of Vietnam is that Americans have been less willing to get involved in overseas wars. In 1973, Congress passed the **War Powers Act,** which limits the president's war-making powers. The president must report to Congress within 48 hours if troops have been sent into a hostile situation without a declaration of war. They can remain for no more than 90 days unless Congress permits them to.

***Reading* History**
**C. Making Inferences** Why did the Vietnam War influence Congress to pass the War Powers Act?
C. Answer President Johnson was able to expand U.S. involvement in Vietnam without a formal declaration of war by Congress.

Finally, the war made many Americans distrust government leaders, who sometimes misled the public about actions in Vietnam. In Chapter 31, you will read about the Watergate scandal, which further shook confidence in government and brought down Nixon's presidency.

## *America's* HERITAGE

**VIETNAM VETERANS MEMORIAL**

The public finally honored those who served in Vietnam with the Vietnam Veterans Memorial, designed by Maya Lin and unveiled in Washington, D.C., on November 13, 1982. Etched into this V-shaped black granite wall are the names of all Americans killed in the war.

At the Wall, as it is known, visitors leave letters, flowers, and mementos. Many believe that the monument has helped heal the divisions created by the war. As the father of a veteran noted, "It doesn't say whether the war was right or wrong. . . . It just says, 'Here is the price we paid.'"

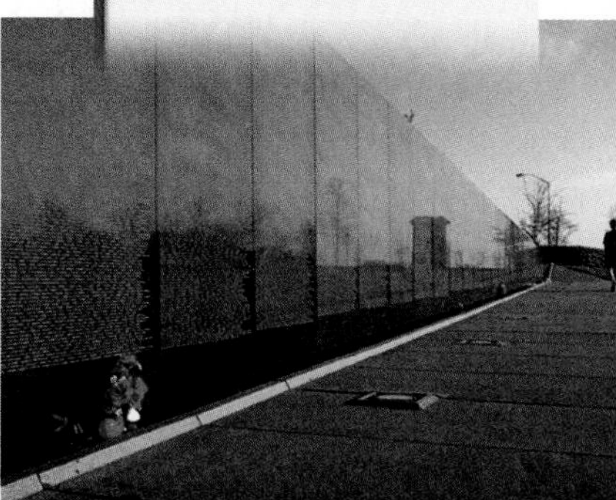

## Section 3 Assessment

**1. Terms & Names**

**Identify:**
- doves
- hawks
- Richard Nixon
- Vietnamization
- Cambodia
- Twenty-sixth Amendment
- War Powers Act

**2. Taking Notes**

Use a chart like this one to review information about the antiwar movement.

Groups — Antiwar movement — Reasons for opposition — Events

**3. Main Ideas**

a. Why did more and more Americans oppose the war after 1968?

b. How did the Vietnam War end?

c. In what major ways did the war affect Southeast Asia and the United States?

**4. Critical Thinking**

**Forming and Supporting Opinions** What is your opinion of the way the United States ended its involvement in the Vietnam War?

THINK ABOUT
- what happened to South Vietnam
- what options the United States had

**ACTIVITY OPTIONS**

**LITERATURE** / **MATH** — Compare the Vietnam War to World War II by writing an **essay** on two pieces of war literature or by presenting comparable **statistics.**





## *America's* HERITAGE

**Vietnam Veterans Memorial**

The original memorial included the black granite wall and a statue of American soldiers. A nearby bronze statue of three women nurses aiding a wounded soldier was unveiled in 1993. The statue honors the thousands of women who served in the Vietnam War.

 **America's History Makers**
- Maya Lin, pp. 123–124

### CRITICAL THINKING ACTIVITY

**Recognizing Effects** On the board, write the following headings: Vietnamese people; soldiers who fought in Vietnam; U.S. foreign policy; attitudes of Americans toward government. Tell students to make a chart showing the effect of the war in each category.

**Class Time** 20 minutes

## ASSESS & RETEACH

**Setting the Stage** Tell students to complete the five rows in the right-hand column on the chapter graphic organizer.

 **Formal Assessment**
- Section Quiz, p. 434

 **Critical Thinking Transparency CT88**
- Setting the Stage

### RETEACHING ACTIVITY

Have students write at least one question about the material in each of the section subheads. Students should write the answers to the questions on a separate sheet of paper. Have students switch papers with a partner and complete their partner's test. Pairs of students should correct their tests together.

 **In-Depth Resources: Unit 9**
- Reteaching Activity, p. 35

## Section 3 Assessment

**1. Terms & Names**

**doves,** p. 847
**hawks,** p. 847
**Richard Nixon,** p. 848
**Vietnamization,** p. 848
**Cambodia,** p. 848
**Twenty-sixth Amendment,** p. 849
**War Powers Act,** p. 849

**2. Taking Notes**

Groups: religious leaders, civil rights leaders, teachers, college students, journalists; Reasons: it was a civil war; it was immoral; the costs were too high; it took money away from social programs; Events: demonstrations; draft card burnings; protests; publications

**3. Main Ideas**

**a.** They began to question motivations behind the war. **b.** The United States withdrew in 1973, and North Vietnamese took over South Vietnam in 1975. **c.** Students might arrange answers in two columns, one for the United States and one for Southeast Asia.

**4. Critical Thinking**

Some students may think that it was right to withdraw troops, while others will disagree.

### ACTIVITY OPTIONS

 **Alternative Assessment**
- Rubrics for essay, 4.2
- Rubrics for statistics, 2.7

## TERMS & NAMES

1. **Ho Chi Minh,** p. 835
2. **domino theory,** p. 837
3. **Viet Cong,** p. 838
4. **Ho Chi Minh Trail,** p. 838
5. **guerrilla warfare,** p. 842
6. **Agent Orange,** p. 843
7. **Tet offensive,** p. 844
8. **Richard Nixon,** p. 848
9. **Vietnamization,** p. 848
10. **Twenty-sixth Amendment,** p. 849

## REVIEW QUESTIONS

**Possible Responses**

1. It needed France's support against the Soviets in Europe, and it did not want Vietnam to have a Communist government.
2. Vietnam was divided into Communist North and non-Communist South, and elections were to be held in 1956.
3. the failed Bay of Pigs invasion in Cuba, the Berlin Wall, and the Cuban missile crisis
4. He went beyond Kennedy by starting a heavy bombing campaign and sending large numbers of combat troops to Vietnam.
5. the need to limit the war to avoid China's entry; soldiers' youth and inexperience; guerrilla warfare; difficult terrain and climate
6. Chemicals destroyed the landscape and food supplies, while search-and-destroy missions terrorized villagers and left them homeless.
7. The Communists gained no cities and lost many soldiers; it made the United States doubt its ability to win the war.
8. People believed the United States should not get involved in another country's civil war; the methods of fighting were immoral; the draft was unfair.
9. Vietnamization; secret bombings of Cambodia to destroy Communist supply lines; a peace agreement in 1973
10. the war killed or wounded thousands of soldiers; led to the end of the draft and the passage of the 26th Amendment; led Americans to distrust government; increased isolationism

## VISUAL SUMMARY

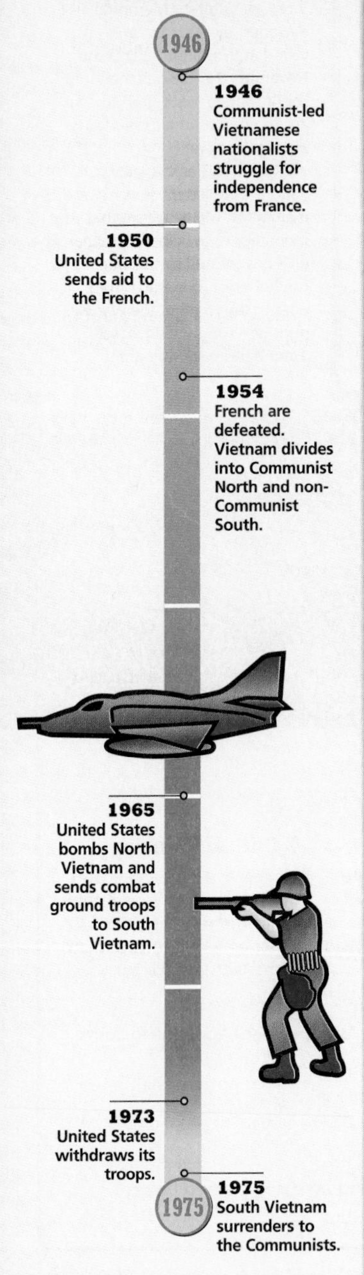

The Vietnam War Years
1946
1946 Communist-led Vietnamese nationalists struggle for independence from France.
1950 United States sends aid to the French.
1954 French are defeated. Vietnam divides into Communist North and non-Communist South.
1965 United States bombs North Vietnam and sends combat ground troops to South Vietnam.
1973 United States withdraws its troops.
1975 South Vietnam surrenders to the Communists.
1975

## TERMS & NAMES

Briefly explain the importance of each of the following.

1. Ho Chi Minh
2. domino theory
3. Viet Cong
4. Ho Chi Minh Trail
5. guerrilla warfare
6. Agent Orange
7. Tet offensive
8. Richard Nixon
9. Vietnamization
10. Twenty-sixth Amendment

## REVIEW QUESTIONS

**Cold War Roots of the Conflict (pages 835–839)**

1. Why did the United States decide to support France in its fight against the Viet Minh?
2. What decisions about Vietnam were laid out in the 1954 Geneva Accords?
3. What Cold War crises made President Kennedy continue to aid Ngo Dinh Diem's government in South Vietnam?

**War Expands in Vietnam (pages 840–845)**

4. How was President Johnson's Vietnam policy different from President Kennedy's?
5. What kept U.S. troops from defeating the Viet Cong quickly?
6. How did American war tactics affect Vietnamese villagers?
7. How was the Tet offensive both a defeat and a victory for the Communists?

**The Vietnam War Ends (pages 846–849)**

8. Why did many Americans protest against the war?
9. What policies did President Nixon pursue in Vietnam?
10. What long-term political effects did the Vietnam War have on the United States?

## CRITICAL THINKING

**1. USING YOUR NOTES**

| Reasons for involvement in Vietnam |
| --- |
| French alliance |
| Domino theory |
| Nation building |
| Cold War crises |
| U.S. weaponry |

| Reasons against involvement in Vietnam |
| --- |
| U.S. interests |
| Draft |
| Social programs |
| Vietnamese civilians |
| Domestic unrest |

Using your completed chart from the beginning of this chapter, answer the questions.

a. Which do you consider the strongest reason in support of American involvement in the Vietnam War?

b. Which do you consider the strongest reason against American involvement in the Vietnam War?

c. Which side do you think is more persuasive? Why?

**2. ANALYZING LEADERSHIP**

How would you evaluate President Johnson's leadership during the Vietnam War and his decision not to seek a second term as president?

**3. APPLYING CITIZENSHIP SKILLS**

During the Vietnam War, many Americans had to choose between obeying laws and following their consciences. In your opinion, what is the right thing to do in such a situation?

**4.THEME: AMERICA IN THE WORLD**

How do you think involvement in the Vietnam War affected the reputation of the United States among other nations? Why?

**5. DRAWING CONCLUSIONS**

Would the United States have become involved in the Vietnam War if the Cold War had not been going on? Explain your opinion.

**Interact *with* History**

If you had lived during the Vietnam War, what would have determined whether you supported or opposed the war?

## CRITICAL THINKING

**Possible Responses**

1. **USING YOUR NOTES** **a.** Students' answers will vary. **b.** Students' answers will vary. **c.** Accept any response that students can support.
2. **ANALYZING LEADERSHIP** Students may say that Johnson was a poor leader for letting the war overshadow his domestic programs, or that not seeking reelection was an example of good leadership.
3. **APPLYING CITIZENSHIP SKILLS** Students might say that morality is higher than law; or the good of the whole nation supersedes personal beliefs.
4. **THEME: AMERICA IN THE WORLD** Students might say that it was damaged because America supported an oppressive, unpopular government in South Vietnam, or that it was enhanced because America proved that it would fight against Communist expansion.
5. **DRAWING CONCLUSIONS** Most students will say no because its main reason was to stop the spread of communism.

**Interact *with* History** Answers will vary, but should be supported by information in the chapter.

## HISTORY SKILLS

### 1. INTERPRETING CHARTS

Read the chart and then answer the questions.

**U.S. Deaths in Four Wars**

| WAR | BATTLE DEATHS | OTHER DEATHS* |
|---|---|---|
| World War I | 53,513 | 63,195 |
| World War II | 292,131 | 115,185 |
| Korean War | 33,629 | 20,617 |
| Vietnam War | 47,244 | 10,446 |

*accidents, diseases, etc.

Source: Harry G. Summers, Jr., *Vietnam War Almanac*

**Basic Chart Elements**

a. What is the subject of the chart?

b. What is the difference between the second and third columns?

**Interpreting the Chart**

c. Which war or wars caused more battle deaths than the Vietnam War?

d. Which war had the lowest ratio of nonbattle deaths to battle deaths?

### 2. INTERPRETING PRIMARY SOURCES

Read this passage by a Vietnamese woman, addressed to an American veteran of the Vietnam War. Then answer the questions.

> You came to Vietnam, willingly or not, because your country demanded it. Most of you did not know, or fully understand, the different wars my people were fighting when you got here. For you, it was a simple thing: democracy against communism. For us, that was not our fight at all. How could it be? We knew little of democracy and even less about communism. For most of us it was a fight for independence—like the American Revolution.
>
> **Le Ly Hayslip,** *When Heaven and Earth Changed Places*

a. What did American soldiers misunderstand, according to Hayslip?

b. What seems to be Hayslip's attitude toward Americans?

## ALTERNATIVE ASSESSMENT

### 1. INTERDISCIPLINARY ACTIVITY: Music

**Analyzing Antiwar Songs** Research antiwar songs of the late 1960s and early 1970s. Choose one song, play it for the class, and talk about the meaning of its lyrics. Explain what the song adds to your understanding of the Vietnam era.

### 2. COOPERATIVE ACTIVITY

**Making a Video Documentary** Work in a group to create and present a video documentary about the Vietnam War and its impact on the country or your town. As part of your research, talk to adults who lived through the Vietnam era and who have different perspectives on the war. You might try to locate a soldier or nurse who served, someone who faced the draft but was not called to serve, an antiwar demonstrator, or someone who lost a loved one in the war.

### 3. TECHNOLOGY ACTIVITY

**Planning a Web Site** Most Americans still know little about the country of Vietnam. Plan a Web site that will give future classes geographical, historical, and cultural background on Vietnam before they study the war. Use the library and the Internet, or contact colleges, museums, or Vietnamese organizations to get started.

**Visit www.mcdougallittell.com for more information on Vietnam.**

Your site might include the following things.

- Detailed maps of Vietnam and its major cities
- Photographs of people, landscapes, and art objects
- A listing of products grown or made in Vietnam
- Biographies of important people in Vietnamese history
- Excerpts from stories, poetry, or memoirs by Vietnamese writers
- Internet links to other sites

### 4. HISTORY PORTFOLIO

**Option 1** Review your section and chapter assessment activities. Select one that you think is your best work. Use comments made by your teacher or classmates to improve your work, then add it to your portfolio.

**Option 2** Review the questions that you wrote for What Do You Want to Know? on page 834. Then write a short report in which you explain the answers to your questions. If any questions were not answered, do research to answer them.



## ALTERNATIVE ASSESSMENT

1. INTERDISCIPLINARY ACTIVITY: **Music**

**Song analyses should**

- show an understanding of the protest against the Vietnam War.
- identify elements of the lyrics such as images, symbols, rhythm, and rhyme that are associated with the meaning of the song.
- relate the lyrics to the historical events occurring when the song was written and performed.

2. COOPERATIVE LEARNING ACTIVITY

**Video documentaries should**

- portray the experiences of the interviewees accurately and in a dramatic style, possibly using artifacts and images.
- use standard interview techniques.
- clearly demonstrate an understanding of the Vietnam Era.
- use correct grammar in the script.

3.  TECHNOLOGY ACTIVITY

**Web sites should**

- contain at least three links.
- make effective use of pictures and icons.
- contain written summaries that will encourage browsers to visit other Web sites
- show technical proficiency.

4. HISTORY PORTFOLIO

**Option 1 Revised section or chapter assessment activities should**

- address teacher and peer responses to the selected work.
- solve problems present in the first versions of the work.

**Option 2 Short reports should**

- answer questions about the Vietnam War.
- use evidence to develop and support ideas.
- cite sources of information.
- use standard grammar, spelling, sentence structure, and punctuation.

**Critical Thinking Transparency CT90**

- Visual Summary

**Formal Assessment**

- Chapter Test, Forms A and B, pp. 435–442

## HISTORY SKILLS

**Possible Responses**

1. INTERPRETING CHARTS

**Basic Chart Elements**

**a.** U.S. deaths in four wars

**b.** The second column lists battle deaths; the third column lists deaths from other causes.

**Interpreting the Chart**

**c.** World War I and World War II

**d.** the Vietnam War

2. INTERPRETING PRIMARY SOURCES

**a.** Americans thought that the conflict in Vietnam was a simple struggle between democracy and communism, but it was actually a fight for national independence.

**b.** Hayslip seems to show understanding and sympathy for Americans.

# Years of Doubt 1969–1981

| | CHAPTER OVERVIEW | COPYMASTERS | TECHNOLOGY |
|---|---|---|---|
| **CHAPTER RESOURCES** | The chapter traces the Nixon presidency from its peak of foreign successes through the gradual revelation of the extent of the Watergate scandal. It describes the administrations of Presidents Ford and Carter and the Reagan victory in 1981. | **In-Depth Resources: Unit 9**<br>• Tracing Themes: Citizenship, p. 38<br>• Building Vocabulary, p. 42<br>**Interdisciplinary Projects,** pp. 181–186 | 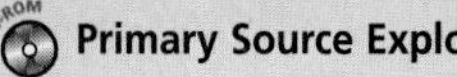 **Primary Source Explorer**<br>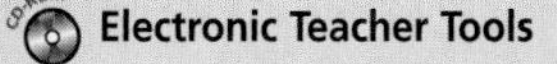 **Electronic Teacher Tools**<br>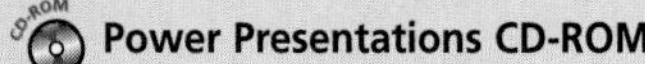 **Power Presentations CD-ROM**<br>**Chapter Summaries on CD** (English and Spanish) |
| **SECTION 1 Nixon Confronts Problems pp. 855–858** | **KEY IDEAS**<br>• Nixon has difficulty with Congress.<br>• The nation's economy stalls.<br>• Nixon has success in foreign relations, particularly with China and the Soviet Union. | **In-Depth Resources: Unit 9**<br>• Setting the Stage, p. 37<br>• Guided Reading, p. 39<br>• Reteaching Activity, p. 51<br>**America's History Makers**<br>• Henry Kissinger, pp. 125–126<br>**Economics in History**<br>• Inflation Eats Away at the Dollar, p. 31 |  **Warm-Up Transparency WT31**<br>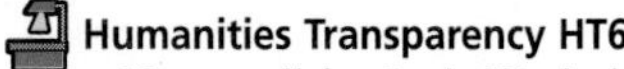 **Humanities Transparency HT61**<br>• *Moonwalk* by Andy Warhol<br>**Geography Transparency GT31**<br>• The United States Receives OPEC Oil, 1970s<br> **Critical Thinking Transparency CT91**<br>• Setting the Stage<br>**ClassZone:** www.mcdougallittell.com |
|  **SECTION 2 Watergate Brings Down Nixon pp. 859–861** | • Republicans burgle the Democratic campaign headquarters.<br>• Nixon denies involvement.<br>• As investigations reveal wrongdoing, Nixon resigns rather than face impeachment. | **In-Depth Resources: Unit 9**<br>• Setting the Stage, p. 37<br>• Guided Reading, p. 40<br>• Geography Application: The Geography of the Watergate Scandal, pp. 44–45<br>• Primary Source, p. 46<br>• Reteaching Activity, p. 52<br>**America's History Makers**<br>• Barbara Jordan, pp. 127–128 | **Warm-Up Transparency WT31**<br>**Humanities Transparency HT62**<br>• White House Cartoon<br>**Critical Thinking Transparency CT91**<br>• Setting the Stage<br>**Critical Thinking Transparency CT92**<br>• Cause and Effect: The Watergate Scandal<br>**ClassZone:** www.mcdougallittell.com |
| **SECTION 3 Issues of the Seventies pp. 862–867** | • Vice-President Gerald Ford becomes president in 1974.<br>• President Carter has difficulty with Congress.<br>• The Iran hostage crisis contributes to Reagan's victory in 1980. | **In-Depth Resources: Unit 9**<br>• Setting the Stage, p. 37<br>• Guided Reading, p. 41<br>• Skillbuilder Practice, p. 43<br>• Primary Source, p. 47<br>• Literature Selection, pp. 48–50<br>• Reteaching Activity, p. 53<br>**Why It Matters Now**<br>• Overcoming Challenges, pp. 61–62<br>**Outline Map Activities**<br>• The Middle East: Resolution and Crisis, 1979, pp. 61–62 |  **Warm-Up Transparency WT31**<br>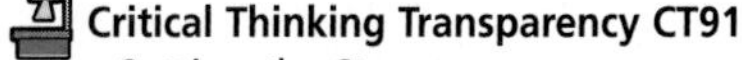 **Critical Thinking Transparency CT91**<br>• Setting the Stage<br>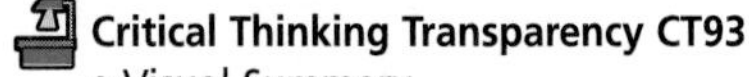 **Critical Thinking Transparency CT93**<br>• Visual Summary<br>**ClassZone:** www.mcdougallittell.com |

PE Pupil's Edition
Copymaster
Overhead Transparency
Audio Library
CD-ROM
Internet

## ASSESSMENT

PE **Chapter Assessment,** pp. 868–869

**Formal Assessment**
- Chapter Tests, Forms A and B, pp. 448–455

**Alternative Assessment Book**

**Electronic Teacher Tools with Test Maker**

PE **Section Assessment,** p. 858

**Formal Assessment**
- Section Quiz, p. 445

**Alternative Assessment Book**
- Rubrics for a cartoon, 1.2
- Rubrics for a press release, 4.5

**Electronic Teacher Tools with Test Maker**

PE **Section Assessment,** p. 861

**Formal Assessment**
- Section Quiz, p. 446

**Alternative Assessment Book**
- Rubrics for a broadcast, 5.3
- Rubrics for a magazine feature, 4.5

**Electronic Teacher Tools with Test Maker**

PE **Section Assessment,** p. 865

**Formal Assessment**
- Section Quiz, p. 447

**Alternative Assessment Book**
- Rubrics for a graph, 2.3
- Rubrics for a cartoon, 1.2

**Electronic Teacher Tools with Test Maker**

## CUSTOMIZING FOR INDIVIDUAL NEEDS

### Students Acquiring English/ESL

**Reading Study Guide** (English and Spanish), pp. 295–302

**Access for Students Acquiring English/ESL: Spanish Translations,** pp. 205–210

**Chapter Summaries on CD** (English and Spanish)

### Less Proficient Readers

**Reading Study Guide** (English and Spanish), pp. 295–302

**Chapter Summaries on CD** (English and Spanish)

### Gifted and Talented Students

**In-Depth Resources: Unit 9**
- Enrichment Activity, p. 54

**America's History Makers**
- Henry Kissinger, pp. 125–126
- Barbara Jordan, pp. 127–128

## CROSS-CURRICULAR CONNECTIONS

### Culture

Stewart, Gail, ed. ***The 1970s (Cultural History of the United States Through the Decades).*** San Diego: Lucent Books, 1999. An overview of the people, places, trends, and events of the decade.

### Economics

Brown, Paul. ***Energy and Resources.*** New York: Franklin Watts, 1998. Discusses the aims of the 1992 Earth Summit and its plan for attaining sustainable development.

### Government

Cohen, Daniel. ***Watergate: Deception in the White House.*** Brookfield, CT: Millbrook, 1998. Discusses the Watergate break-in and the events of the scandal.

### Science

Archer, Jules. ***To Save the Earth: The American Environmental Movement.*** New York: Viking, 1998. Detailed, highly illuminating biographies of four environmental pioneers: John Muir, David McTaggart, Rachel Carson, and David Foreman.

### Interdisciplinary Projects, pp. 181–186

- Math: Analyzing Poll and Survey Data
- Science: Alternative Methods for Waste Disposal
- Language Arts: Investigative Reporting
- Art: Recycled Art

### Literature

Hopkins, Lee Bennett, ed. ***Hand in Hand: An American History Through Poetry.*** New York: S&S, 1994. Poetry in nine chronological sections with brief historical notes make up this wide-ranging, diverse, and browsable anthology.

Klass, David. ***California Blue.*** New York: Scholastic, 1994. Seventeen-year-old John Rodgers loves his local redwood forest. John's discovery of a rare butterfly in the forest creates conflicts with his logger-father's job. Powerfully written.

White, Ellen Emerson. ***The President's Daughter.*** Scholastic, 1994. When her mother is elected president, a teenage girl must deal with the pressure of living in the spotlight.

### McDougal Littell Literature Connections

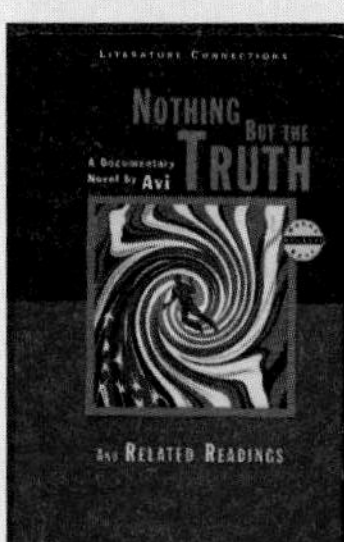


Avi

***Nothing But the Truth***

Philip, a high school goof-off, hums along when the National Anthem is played over the school intercom. This instigates a battle involving patriotism, school policy, the national media . . . and a struggle for justice.

## ENRICHMENT ACTIVITIES

PE **Pupil's Edition, pp. 852–869**
**Interact with History,** p. 853
**Economics in History,** p. 857
**Interdisciplinary Challenge,** pp. 866–867

**In-Depth Resources: Unit 9**
- Geography Application: The Geography of the Watergate Scandal, pp. 44–45
- Primary Source, p. 46
- Primary Source, p. 47
- Literature Selection, pp. 48–50

**America's History Makers**
- Henry Kissinger, pp. 125–126
- Barbara Jordan, pp. 127–128

**Outline Map Activities**
- The Middle East: Resolution and Crisis, 1979, pp. 61–62

**Why It Matters Now**
- Overcoming Challenges, pp. 61–62

# CHAPTER 31 PACING GUIDE

**LESSON PLAN OPTIONS (50-MINUTE PERIOD)** (TE) = Teacher's Edition (PE) = Pupil's Edition

| | TEACHER-DIRECTED ACTIVITIES<br>Class Time: 15 minutes | STUDENT-CENTERED ACTIVITIES<br>Class Time: 25 minutes | INDIVIDUAL ACTIVITIES<br>Class Time: 10 minutes |
|---|---|---|---|
| **DAY 1**<br>Introduction<br>pp. 852–854 | **Presentation Options**<br>• Begin with a class discussion of the picture on p. 852 **(PE)**.<br>• Lead a class discussion on the "What Do You Know?" question in Setting the Stage, p. 854. Then introduce the graphic organizer for the chapter **(PE)**. | **Options for Cooperative Learning**<br>• Have student groups discuss the Interact with History questions, p. 853 **(PE)**.<br>• Have student groups respond to the "What Do You Want to Know?" question in Setting the Stage, p. 854 **(PE)**. | **Head Start on Homework Options**<br>• Have students skim Section 1 Main Idea, Why It Matters Now, Terms & Names, and the main headings, p. 855 **(PE)**.<br>• Have students begin Guided Reading activity and Building Vocabulary sheet. |
| **DAY 2**<br>Section 1<br>pp. 855–858 | **Presentation Options**<br>• Begin with the 5-Minute Warm-Up, p. 855 **(TE)**.<br>• Review the Section 1 Main Idea, Why It Matters Now, and Terms & Names, p. 855 **(PE)**.<br>• Choose 5 key questions for Objectives 1–4 to discuss with the class, pp. 855–858 **(TE)**. | **Options for Cooperative Learning**<br>• Divide students into groups to work on the Economics in History questions, p. 857 **(PE)**.<br>• Have student pairs work together to complete one of the Activity Options in the Section 1 Assessment, p. 858 **(PE)**. | **Head Start on Homework Options**<br>• Have students begin working on Section 1 Assessment, p. 858 **(PE)**.<br>• Have students complete the Critical Thinking Activity, p. 857 **(TE)**. |
| **DAY 3**<br>Section 2<br>pp. 859–861 | **Presentation Options**<br>• Begin with the 5-Minute Warm-Up, p. 859 **(TE)**.<br>• Choose 5 key questions for Objectives 1–4 to discuss with the class, pp. 859–861 **(TE)**.<br>• Lead the students through the Critical Thinking Activity, p. 861 **(TE)**. | **Options for Cooperative Learning**<br>• Divide students into pairs to answer the History through Art question, p. 860 **(PE)**.<br>• Have student pairs work together to complete one of the Activity Options in the Section 2 Assessment, p. 861 **(PE)**. | **Head Start on Homework Options**<br>• Have students begin working on Section 2 Assessment, p. 861 **(PE)**.<br>• Have students choose one of the Interdisciplinary Challenges to complete, pp. 866–867 **(PE)**. |
| **DAY 4**<br>Section 3<br>pp. 862–867 | **Presentation Options**<br>• Begin with the 5-Minute Warm-Up, p. 862 **(TE)**.<br>• Choose 5 key questions for Objectives 1–4 to discuss with the class, pp. 862–865 **(TE)**.<br>• Lead the students through the Skillbuilder Mini-Lesson: Drawing Conclusions, p. 864 **(TE)**. | **Options for Cooperative Learning**<br>• Divide students into groups and have them complete the Interdisciplinary Challenge, pp. 866–867 **(PE)**.<br>• Have student pairs work together to complete one of the Activity Options in the Section 3 Assessment, p. 865 **(PE)**. | **Head Start on Homework Options**<br>• Have students complete the Setting the Stage graphic organizer for the chapter, p. 854 **(PE)**.<br>• Have students begin working on the Chapter Assessment, pp. 868–869 **(PE)**.<br>• Prepare for Chapter Test<br>**Formal Assessment**, pp. 448–445 |

**TEACHER-TESTED ACTIVITY** Patricia Baron Carlson, Swanson Middle School, Arlington, Virginia

## ENERGY PANEL CRISIS

**Class Time** Two class periods for preparation and one for presentation

**Task** Investigating alternative energy sources and recommending fuel sources that the United States should develop in the future

**Purpose** To understand America's dependence on oil for fuel and to evaluate possibilities for alternative energy sources

**Supplies Needed**

- Reference books and Internet addresses for alternative energy sources
- Accounts of the OPEC oil embargo and the energy crises of the 1970s

**Activity** Have students brainstorm a list of energy sources now used in the United States. Review the energy crisis and OPEC oil embargo to illustrate the reasons for concern about dependence on foreign oil. Divide the class into six groups. Have five groups research various alternative energy sources such as solar, nuclear, wind, hydroelectric, or synthetic fuel. Ask the sixth group to develop questions about these sources, focusing on their cost, practicality, safety, and environmental effects. Have the five energy groups present their findings to the sixth group and answer its questions.

## BLOCK SCHEDULING — LESSON PLAN OPTIONS (90-MINUTE PERIOD)

### DAY 1

**Interact with History,** p. 853
**Class Time** 20 minutes

Options for pacing and variety:

- Peer Teaching Have small groups of students discuss why Nixon's resignation caused a crisis and how this crisis was different from others that the United States had faced in its history. **Class Time** 10 minutes

**Setting the Stage,** p. 854
**Class Time** 20 minutes

Options for pacing and variety:

- Time Saver Assign the two questions in the "What Do You Know?" section for homework. Then discuss students' responses to "What Do You Want to Know?" in class, making a list of questions on the chalkboard. **Class Time** 10 minutes

**Section 1,** pp. 855–858
**Class Time** 50 minutes

Options for pacing and variety:

- Peer Teaching Assign a group of four students to teach the class the Economics in History feature on page 857. The team should define inflation, explain the graph to the class, answer the Connect to History and Connect to Today questions with the class, and make up three questions to ask the class to check students' comprehension. **Class Time** 30 minutes
- Time Saver Have students work in pairs to complete the Taking Notes chart and Main Ideas questions in the Section Assessment. **Class Time** 10 minutes

### DAY 2

**Section 2,** pp. 859–861
**Class Time** 45 minutes

Options for pacing and variety:

- Internet Extend students' background knowledge of the Watergate scandal by visiting www.mcdougallittell.com **Class Time** 20 minutes

**Section 3,** pp. 862–867
**Class Time** 45 minutes

Options for pacing and variety:

- Peer Teaching Have students work in pairs to complete the Analyzing Leadership question on page 868. **Class Time** 10 minutes
- History on Film Extend students' background knowledge of the 1970s by viewing one of the ten videos in the *Sensational 70s* series. ABC News. **Class Time** 60 minutes

**Interdisciplinary Challenge,** pp. 866–867
**Class Time** 45 minutes

Options for pacing and variety:

- Team Teaching Invite a science teacher to coach student groups as they solve the Science Challenge on page 867. **Class Time** 30 minutes
- Peer Evaluation Write the Standards for Evaluation for the Language Arts Challenge found on page 866 of the Teacher's Edition on the chalkboard. Have students use these criteria to evaluate one another's editorials or speeches. **Class Time** 25 minutes

**Chapter 31 Assessment,** pp. 868–869
**Class Time** 40 minutes

Options for pacing and variety:

- Peer Teaching Divide students into small groups to create a written summary of the chapter using the information in the Visual Summary as a guide. **Class Time** 15 minutes
- Peer Evaluation As an alternative assessment for the chapter, have students create a Bicentennial Web site following the instructions outlined in the Technology Activity on page 869. **Class Time** 45 minutes

## CHAPTER 31 OBJECTIVE

**The student will evaluate the presidency of Richard Nixon, the Watergate scandal, and the efforts of presidents Ford and Carter to solve the problems facing the nation in the 1970s.**

# CHAPTER 31 Years of Doubt

## 1969–1981

NUCLEAR ACCIDENT AT THREE MILE ISLAND
IRANIANS TAKE AMERICANS HOSTAGE
NATION SUFFERS ENERGY CRISIS
SORRY NO GAS
Save our Water
WATERGATE BREAK-IN LEADS TO PRESIDENTIAL SCANDAL
852

### HISTORY FROM VISUALS

**Interpreting the Photographs** The collage of photographs shows images that illustrate some of the problems of the 1970s. Ask students to study the photographs and read the captions that accompany them. Ask students to make a generalization about the 1970s based on the images. **Possible Responses** Energy issues, a presidential scandal, and the taking of American hostages in Iran troubled Americans during the 1970s.

**Extension** Separate students into four groups, and assign one image to each group. Ask each group to locate additional images illustrating the same issue. Ask the groups to display their images when the class discusses that issue.

### CRITICAL THINKING ACTIVITY

**Identifying and Solving Problems** Ask students to think about the problems illustrated on page 852. Which of these problems still concern Americans today? How have Americans worked to solve these problems? How successful have they been?

**Class Time** 10 minutes

### RECOMMENDED RESOURCES

**BOOKS FOR THE TEACHER**

Adelman, M. A. ***The Genie Out of the Bottle: World Oil Since 1970.*** Cambridge, MA: MIT Pr., 1995. A leading economist writes a readable history of the OPEC oil monopoly.

Schell, Jonathan. ***The Time of Illusion.*** New York: Random House, 1976. A thoughtful chronicle that discusses Watergate in the larger context of world affairs.

**VIDEOS**

***NASA: The 25th Year.*** Video Comm., Inc., 1987. Chronicles the first quarter-century of the U.S. space program, with its tragedies, glitches, and glories.

***We the People: The Presidency and the Constitution.*** Close-Up Foundation, 1992. Nixon, Ford, Carter, and Reagan discuss the office of the chief executive.

**SOFTWARE**

***Watergate: Computer Version.*** Thomas W. Henderson. Instructive activities that promote understanding of the Watergate scandal.

**INTERNET**

For more about Watergate, visit www.mcdougallittell.com

## Interact *with* History

**It is the evening of August 8, 1974. You are watching television when your favorite program is interrupted by a speech from President Richard M. Nixon. Looking grim and tired, Nixon says that he will resign the next day. You wonder how the country will cope with the crisis.**

### What Do You Think?

- **What happens when a president resigns from office? Has a president resigned before?**
- **How has the government functioned when a president has died?**
- **What other crises has the country faced?**

# *How is America able to survive a crisis and move on?*

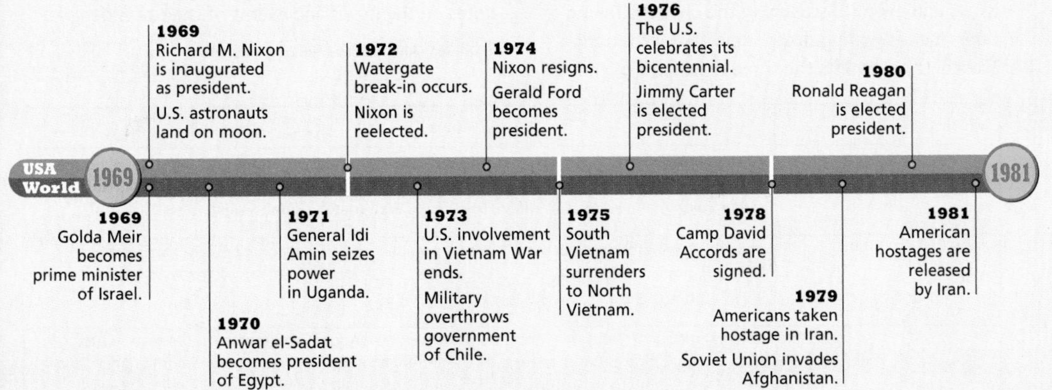

USA
World
1969
1981
1969 Richard M. Nixon is inaugurated as president. U.S. astronauts land on moon.
1972 Watergate break-in occurs. Nixon is reelected.
1974 Nixon resigns. Gerald Ford becomes president.
1976 The U.S. celebrates its bicentennial. Jimmy Carter is elected president.
1980 Ronald Reagan is elected president.
1969 Golda Meir becomes prime minister of Israel.
1970 Anwar el-Sadat becomes president of Egypt.
1971 General Idi Amin seizes power in Uganda.
1973 U.S. involvement in Vietnam War ends. Military overthrows government of Chile.
1975 South Vietnam surrenders to North Vietnam.
1978 Camp David Accords are signed.
1979 Americans taken hostage in Iran. Soviet Union invades Afghanistan.
1981 American hostages are released by Iran.




## Interact *with* History

### OBJECTIVES

- To identify some of the governmental issues of Watergate
- To pose and answer questions about how the nation operates during a crisis such as Watergate

### What Do You Think?

1. Ask students to recall other ways the presidency has been vacated.
2. Ask students to recall constitutional provisions for the transfer of power when a president cannot complete his term.
3. Ask students what effects a presidential scandal would have on the nation's foreign relations, economy, and politics.

### *How is America able to survive a crisis and move on?*

Encourage students to think about the confidence that Americans have in their government's ability to handle a crisis and how leadership changes affect Americans' attitudes and actions.

### MAKING PERSONAL CONNECTIONS

Ask students to think about a crisis that has occurred in their lives. It could be a personal event, a weather-related event, or other community event. Was government intervention needed? Did people look to the government for help? Explain responses.

### TIME LINE DISCUSSION

**In the 1970s, world attention focused on the Middle East, where enormous reserves of oil belonged to Arab nations with which the United States had very limited relationships. Inflation, the high price of oil, the Watergate scandal, and the Iran hostage crisis made the 1970s a tense and sometimes grim period in American history.**

- How do changes in leadership in the 12 years represented on the time line support the chapter title "Years of Doubt"? **Possible Response** By electing a different president every four years, Americans indicated that they had little confidence in each president.
- Ask students to identify other countries that changed leaders in the 1970s. **Answers** Egypt, Uganda, Chile
- In what ways do the changes in the identified countries differ from those in the United States? **Possible Response** Power was seized in Uganda and Chile. Americans elected their presidents.
- How might the hostage crisis in Iran in 1979 have affected the 1980 election? **Possible Response** American voters may have been unhappy that the Carter administration could not solve the crisis, and they turned to Reagan.

## BEFORE YOU READ

### Previewing the Theme: Citizenship

Ask students to think of the expectations Americans hold for their government. During turbulent times like the 1970s, Americans may seek to change their leadership and make changes in the way government works.

### What Do You Know?

Point out to students that the faith of many Americans in their government had been shaken by some of the revelations about covert government operations during the Vietnam War.

 **In-Depth Resources: Unit 9**
- Tracing Themes: Citizenship, p. 38

## READ AND TAKE NOTES

**Reading Strategy: Taking Notes**

Before they read, have students find the names of the three presidents in the first column of the chart. As they read, have them takes notes about the major issues and events of each administration.

 **In-Depth Resources: Unit 9**
- Setting the Stage, p. 37

 **Critical Thinking Transparency CT91**
- Setting the Stage

# Chapter 31 SETTING THE STAGE

## BEFORE YOU READ

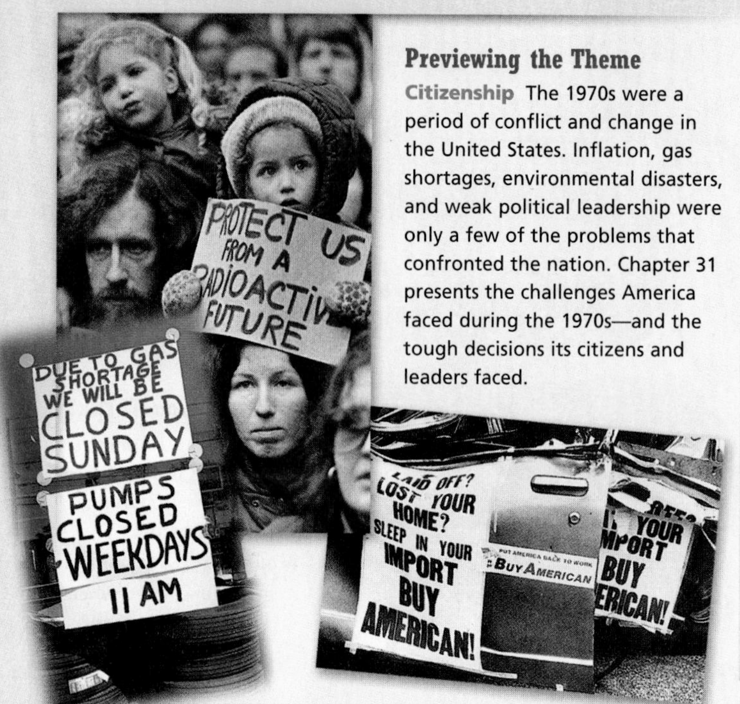


### Previewing the Theme

**Citizenship** The 1970s were a period of conflict and change in the United States. Inflation, gas shortages, environmental disasters, and weak political leadership were only a few of the problems that confronted the nation. Chapter 31 presents the challenges America faced during the 1970s—and the tough decisions its citizens and leaders faced.

### What Do You Know?

What do you already know about the problems of the 1970s, such as inflation and the energy crisis? Were they different from problems the country faced at other times in its history?

**THINK ABOUT**
- what you have learned about the 1970s from books, movies, television, and popular music
- how the nation has reacted to economic, political, and social problems in the past

### What Do You Want to Know?

What would you like to know about Watergate and other crises of the 1970s? In your notebook, record what you hope to learn from this chapter.

## READ AND TAKE NOTES

**Reading Strategy: Taking Notes** To help you remember what you read, take notes about the major issues and events discussed in this chapter. Taking notes means writing down important information. The chart below lists the three presidents of the 1970s—Richard Nixon, Gerald Ford, and Jimmy Carter. As you read, use a chart like the one below to take notes on the issues and events of their presidencies.

 See Skillbuilder Handbook, page R3.

| President | Issues and Events |
|---|---|
| Nixon | elected with conservative support; cuts Great Society programs; supports revenue sharing; promises end to social unrest; fights inflation, unemployment, recession, and energy crisis; eases Cold War tension with China and Soviet Union; involved in Watergate scandal; resigns |
| Ford | appointed vice-president; succeeds Nixon as president; pardons Nixon; popularity drops; tries to fight inflation with voluntary WIN program; negotiates Helsinki Accords; defeated by Jimmy Carter |
| Carter | defeats Ford in 1976 election; promises honesty in government and support for human rights; clashes with Congress; faces energy crisis, inflation, and unemployment; negotiates Panama Canal Treaties and Camp David Accords; supports environmental movement; Iran hostage crisis partly responsible for his defeat in 1980 by Ronald Reagan |



## TEACHING STRATEGY

### READING THE CHAPTER

This is a chronological chapter focusing on the administrations of Nixon, Ford, and Carter. When students have completed the chart, have them use the data they recorded to identify similarities and differences among the administrations. You might want to begin by asking questions such as: During which two administrations was the environment a major issue?

### ALTERNATIVE ASSESSMENT

The Chapter Assessment describes three activities for alternative assessment on page 869. You may wish to have students work on these activities during the course of the chapter and then present them at the end.

# 1 Nixon Confronts Problems

**TERMS & NAMES**
Richard M. Nixon
Henry Kissinger
revenue sharing
détente
SALT

**MAIN IDEA**
President Richard M. Nixon faced the challenge of governing a deeply divided America.

**WHY IT MATTERS NOW**
Social, economic, and political divisions are still part of American life.



## SECTION OBJECTIVES

1. To identify domestic problems facing the nation in 1968
2. To evaluate Nixon's actions to restore law and order
3. To summarize American economic conditions in the early 1970s
4. To describe how President Nixon pursued his foreign policy goals

**CRITICAL THINKING**
Recognizing Effects, p. 856
Analyzing Causes, p. 856
Making Inferences, p. 858

## FOCUS & MOTIVATE

### 5-MINUTE WARM-UP

**Finding Main Ideas** These questions focus on problems facing America in the 1970s.

1. Read the "Main Idea," "Why It Matters Now," and the section headings on pages 855–857. What problems did Richard Nixon face as president?
2. Which of the problems of the 1970s have been solved? Which have lessened? Which have disappeared?

 **Warm-Up Transparency WT31**

## INSTRUCT

**INSTRUCT: OBJECTIVE 1**

**A Divided America**
Key Questions
- What major problems did society face when President Nixon took office?
- How successful was Nixon in cutting spending and reforming the welfare system?
- What was the purpose of revenue sharing?

 **In-Depth Resources: Unit 9**
- Guided Reading, p. 39

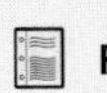 **Reading Study Guide** (Spanish and English), pp. 295–296

## ONE AMERICAN'S STORY

Shortly after his election as president in November 1968, **Richard M. Nixon** began selecting his cabinet and closest advisers. Most of his choices were wealthy business executives or lawyers. But one who did not fit this description was **Henry Kissinger**. Kissinger was a professor at Harvard University and a Jewish refugee from Nazi Germany. He had become a well-known foreign-policy expert.

Nixon picked Kissinger to be his national security adviser because he felt that Kissinger had great intelligence, insight, and experience. Nixon also found that he and Kissinger had very similar ideas about politics. Both men were practical politicians who did not let their ideologies, or beliefs, get in the way of their actions.

*A VOICE FROM THE PAST*

The statesman manipulates [shrewdly manages] reality; his first goal is survival. . . . He is conscious of many great hopes which have failed, of many good intentions that could not be realized.

**Henry A. Kissinger,** *American Foreign Policy*

President Richard Nixon (left) walks with Henry Kissinger, his national security adviser.

That statement might just as easily have been written by President Nixon. In this section, you will learn how Nixon used a practical approach to try to solve problems at home and, with Kissinger's help, abroad.

## 1 A Divided America

As president, Richard M. Nixon would have liked to focus on foreign policy and leave domestic issues to his cabinet. But he became president at a time when America was being torn apart by inflation, racial problems, and conflict over the war in Vietnam. Also, he had won the presidency in 1968 by only a narrow margin. His major support came from conservatives. They wanted him to shrink the federal government and end Lyndon Johnson's Great Society programs.

Nixon hoped to cut the cost of running the federal government and turn some of its activities over to the states. But both houses of Congress were controlled by the Democrats. As a result, he took a more moderate



## RECOMMENDED RESOURCES

 **In-Depth Resources: Unit 9**
- Guided Reading, p. 39
- Building Vocabulary, p. 42
- Reteaching Activity, p. 51

 **Reading Study Guide** (Spanish and English), pp. 295–296

 **Economics in History**
- Inflation Eats Away at the Dollar, p. 31

 **America's History Makers**
- Henry Kissinger, pp. 125–126

 **Formal Assessment**
- Section Quiz, p. 445

 **Alternative Assessment**
- Rubrics, 1.2
- Rubrics, 4.5

 **Access for Students Acquiring English/ESL**
- Guided Reading, p. 205

**Technology Resources**

 **Humanities Transparency HT61**
- *Moonwalk* by Andy Warhol

 **Geography Transparency GT31**
- The United States Receives OPEC Oil, 1970s

 **Electronic Teacher Tools with Test Maker**

## Now *and* then

**Destination Moon**

Since the first moonwalk, NASA has explored the solar system with other manned flights and unmanned satellites and planetary space probes. As part of the space shuttle program, astronauts conduct scientific experiments while orbiting around the earth. Future plans for the U.S. space program include completion of the space station *Freedom,* landing an astronaut on Mars, and developing a permanent lunar base.

 **Humanities Transparency HT61**
- *Moonwalk* by Andy Warhol

### INSTRUCT: OBJECTIVE 2

**Law-and-Order Politics**

Key Questions
- Why did President Nixon appoint conservative judges to the Supreme Court?
- What steps did Nixon take to end crime and protests?

### INSTRUCT: OBJECTIVE 3

**A Troubled Economy**

Key Questions
- What serious economic problems did the nation face in the 1970s?
- Why were Nixon's efforts to raise employment unsuccessful?
- How did OPEC's cut in oil shipments affect the U.S. economy?

 **In-Depth Resources: Unit 9**
- Enrichment Activity, p. 54

 **Geography Transparency GT31**
- The United States Receives OPEC Oil, 1970s

---

**Now *and* then**

**DESTINATION MOON**

On July 20, 1969, with 600 million people viewing on television, Apollo 11 astronaut Neil Armstrong stepped onto the moon and said, "That's one small step for a man, one giant leap for mankind." Edwin Aldrin (shown below) soon joined him. The excitement of the first moon landing gave Americans a sense of unity during a troubled time.

On July 31, 1999, an American space probe was sent crashing into the moon's surface. Its purpose was to see whether there was water on the moon. This flight took place almost 30 years to the day after the historic first landing.

approach at first. But he did veto many spending bills passed by the Democratic Congress. Included were cuts in funds for education and low-income housing—Great Society programs.

In 1969, President Nixon attempted to change the existing welfare system, which had been criticized by conservatives. But he could not get congressional agreement. He was more successful in starting **revenue sharing.** Under revenue sharing, the federal government gave back some tax money it collected to state and local governments. These governments could spend the money on any number of different programs. The plan was supported by both parties and passed Congress in 1972.

*Reading* **History**

**A. Recognizing Effects** How did Nixon try to shrink the size of the federal government?

**A. Possible Answer** Nixon cut funds for Great Society programs and returned some federal tax money to the states.

## 2 Law-and-Order Politics

During the presidential campaign, Nixon had said that he would restore law and order. He promised an end to the social unrest and rioting of the late 1960s. Nixon also promised a return to traditional values.

One way to his goal, Nixon thought, was to appoint more conservative justices to the Supreme Court. He believed that these justices would rule against loose interpretations of the law. Such interpretations, Nixon and his supporters felt, were partly to blame for rising crime. During his first term, he appointed four new justices.

Nixon also used all the powers of the federal government to "crack down" on crime and protest. He directed the Central Intelligence Agency and the Federal Bureau of Investigation to investigate some of his political enemies. Nixon would later excuse any illegal acts by claiming they were needed for the nation's security.

## 3 A Troubled Economy

Civil unrest and crime were not the only problems President Nixon had to face. He inherited serious economic troubles. Under the Johnson administration, the government began spending huge amounts of money on programs to aid the poor *and* on fighting the Vietnam War. But taxes were not raised to cover these expenses. As a result, the government spent more money than it collected in taxes. This practice is called deficit spending.

Deficit spending put a great deal of money into circulation in the late 1960s. At the same time, the economy began to slow down. By 1970, the economy had gone into a recession. With the recession, fewer goods were produced. The increase in the money supply and the decrease in products to buy caused inflation. (See Economics in History on the next page.)

Inflation caused problems for all Americans, but especially the poor. One mother said, "I used to be able to go to the store with $50 and come back with six or seven bags of groceries. Now I'm lucky if I come back

*Reading* **History**

**B. Analyzing Causes** What were causes of the nation's troubled economy?

**B. Possible Answer** The Johnson administration spent money on programs for the poor and on the Vietnam War, but it did not raise taxes to cover these expenses.



---

**ACTIVITY OPTIONS**

**INDIVIDUAL NEEDS**

**LESS PROFICIENT READERS**

**Sequencing Events** Some students may not understand the sequence of events that caused economic problems during Nixon's presidency. To help them, draw the graphic organizer shown here on the board. Next to it, write these terms: *deficit, recession, inflation,* and *unemployment.* As students read, have them write the terms in the correct spaces. Have students use the completed graphic to explain how the problems are related.

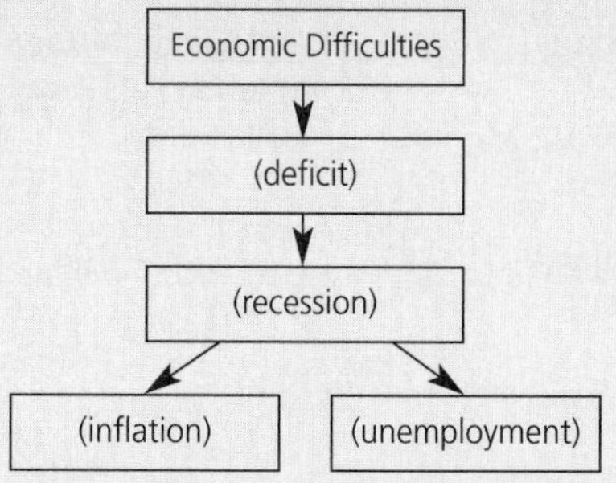

with three." When Nixon took office in 1969, the inflation rate was about 5 percent. That was twice the rate it had been earlier in the decade. Increasing unemployment was another problem. It doubled from about 3 percent in 1969 to 6 percent in 1971.

Nixon tried different ways to help the economy. He cut spending. He also placed a temporary freeze on wage and price increases. Inflation dropped but only temporarily. Then, in 1973, the economy was jolted by the actions of the Organization of Petroleum Exporting Countries (OPEC).

OPEC raised its prices and cut its shipments of oil to the United States. OPEC, which was made up mainly of Arab nations, took these actions in part to protest America's support of Israel in the Yom Kippur War of 1973. That war was fought between Israel and its Arab neighbors. In a few months, gas prices quadrupled. Inflation and unemployment soared to new heights.

Vocabulary
**quadrupled:** multiplied by four

Besides these serious economic problems at home, Nixon also faced tough challenges in foreign policy.

## Economics *in* History

# Inflation

Inflation is a rise in prices across the economy. When the price of milk goes up, that's a price increase. When the prices of gasoline, clothing, food, housing, and health care all go up, that's inflation.

Sometimes prices rise because there's more demand for goods than there are goods available to buy. This happened after World War II. During the war years, factories had produced weapons and supplies for the war effort. After the war, it took a while for factories to produce enough peacetime goods to meet consumer demand.

Sometimes prices rise because businesses increase their prices to cover their rising costs. This was the case in the 1970s, when the rising price of oil sent up the prices of many different goods and services.

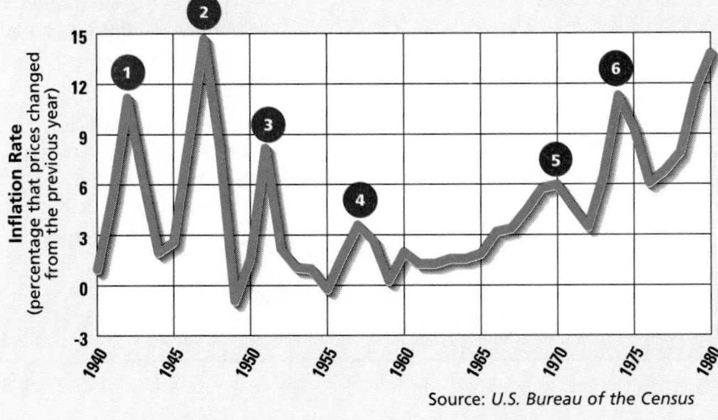


Source: *U.S. Bureau of the Census*

1 World War II
2 Postwar boom
3 Korean War
4 Suez crisis
5 Vietnam War
6 Arab oil embargo—oil prices increase

### CONNECT TO HISTORY

1. **Making Inferences** Why do you think oil price increases had such a widespread effect on the economy?

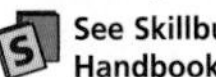
See Skillbuilder Handbook, page R11.

### CONNECT TO TODAY

2. **Researching** Find out what the rate of inflation has been in the most recent two years. How does today's inflation rate compare with that when Nixon came to office and when he left?

Visit www.mcdougallittell.com to learn more about inflation.



### CRITICAL THINKING ACTIVITY

**Analyzing Causes and Recognizing Effects**

Construct a cause-and-effect chain that explains the state of America's economy in the early 1970s. What caused deficit spending? What was the effect of deficit spending? What caused the 1970 recession? What were the effects of the recession? What caused inflation and unemployment?

**Class Time** 10 minutes

## Economics *in* History

### OBJECTIVE

Students will be able to explain inflation and identify the factors that contribute to a high rate of inflation.

**Inflation**

The oil embargo raised the price of a barrel of oil by 400 percent. American oil companies raised their prices accordingly, and so did other businesses that used petroleum products. The petroleum shortage caused Americans to buy fuel-efficient cars from Germany and Japan. With declining sales, U.S. automakers cut production and laid off workers. Cuts soon spread to other industries. By 1975, the economy had fallen into the worst slump since the Great Depression.

**Economics in History**
- Inflation Eats Away at the Dollar, p. 31

### CONNECT TO HISTORY

1. **Making Inferences** **Possible Response** because transportation is an important part of the economy and because petroleum is needed in the manufacture of many products

### CONNECT TO TODAY

2. **Researching** Direct students to the Web site of the Bureau of the Census. For the address, visit www.mcdougallittell.com

**INSTRUCT: OBJECTIVE** 

**Nixon Eases the Cold War**

Key Questions
- Why were Nixon's dealings with China a triumph?
- How did Nixon's trip to China affect relations with the Soviet Union?
- What was the purpose of the SALT?

 **America's History Makers**
- Henry Kissinger, pp. 125–126

## AMERICA'S HISTORY MAKERS

**Richard M. Nixon**

In the election of 1968, Nixon claimed to represent the "silent majority," the Americans who paid taxes and voted but would not protest or picket. His successes with China and the Soviet Union surprised both his critics and his supporters. Nixon said of his visit to China that he had bridged "16,000 miles and twenty-two years of hostility."

**Possible Responses: Nixon was a bright, determined person who was not easily discouraged.**

## ASSESS & RETEACH

**Setting the Stage** Have students add information about Nixon's first term to the chapter graphic organizer.

 **Formal Assessment**
- Section Quiz, p. 445

 **Critical Thinking Transparency CT91**
- Setting the Stage

**RETEACHING ACTIVITY**

Divide the class into small groups and assign each group a section topic: government spending, civil disorder, inflation and unemployment, foreign relations. Each group should identify Nixon's goals, actions, and results in the assigned area. Groups can share their findings.

 **In-Depth Resources: Unit 9**
- Reteaching Activity, p. 51

AMERICA'S HISTORY MAKERS

**RICHARD M. NIXON**
**1913–1994**

Richard Nixon entered politics in 1946 when he ran as a Republican for Congress. He was bright and ambitious. Some opponents, though, said that he would do anything to gain political power. Within seven years, he was vice-president of the United States.

In 1960, Nixon lost the presidential election to John Kennedy. In 1962, he was defeated for governor of California. Most thought his career over. But he battled back and was elected president in 1968. He is shown here in China in 1972 with his wife, Pat.

**What characteristics did Nixon show as a leader?**

## 4 Nixon Eases the Cold War

Nixon's main foreign-policy goal was world stability. During his 1968 presidential campaign, Nixon pledged to end the Vietnam War quickly and honorably. As you learned in Chapter 30, it took four years to negotiate a cease-fire with the North Vietnamese.

Nixon's most important triumph came in dealings with the People's Republic of China. He had long opposed the Communists, who took power in China in 1949. But Nixon believed a nation of a billion people could not be ignored. He asked Henry Kissinger to find a way to improve relations with China, even though they knew many Americans would be opposed. Kissinger arranged for Nixon to visit China in February 1972. This trip led to the opening of diplomacy and trade with the Chinese.

Nixon's China trip affected American relations with the Soviet Union, which was having conflicts with China. The Soviets feared closer relations between the United States and China. So they invited Nixon to Moscow in May 1972. As a result, Soviet-American relations improved. This easing of tensions between rivals is called **détente**—a French word. The policy of détente led the two nations to sign the Strategic Arms Limitation Treaty of 1972 (**SALT**). This pact limited the number of each country's nuclear weapons, easing fears of nuclear war.

Nixon's triumphs in foreign policy helped make him look like a sure winner for reelection in 1972. But, as you will read in the next section, events that occurred in that campaign eventually destroyed his presidency.

**C. Possible Answer** Because the Soviet Union was worried about the United States becoming closer to China, with whom they were having conflicts, they improved relations with the United States.

*Reading***History**

**C. Making Inferences** What effect did improved American-Chinese relations have on Soviet-American relations?

### Section 1 Assessment

**1. Terms & Names**

**Identify:**
- Richard M. Nixon
- Henry Kissinger
- revenue sharing
- détente
- SALT

**2. Taking Notes**

Use a spider diagram to describe problems Nixon faced in his first term.

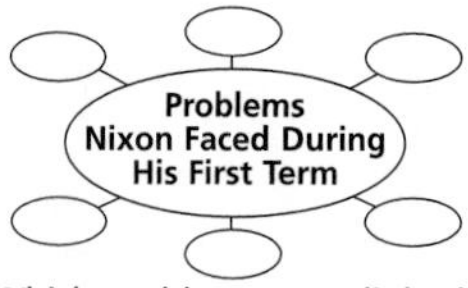



Which problems were linked?

**3. Main Ideas**

a. How did Nixon try to show support for law-and-order politics?

b. What economic problems developed during Nixon's first term as president?

c. How did Nixon change the country's relationship with China? with Russia?

**4. Critical Thinking**

**Making Inferences** Nixon often surprised Americans in the policies that he supported. Which do you think was most surprising? Why?

**THINK ABOUT**
- his economic policies, such as deficit spending
- his appointment of conservative justices
- the policy of détente

**ACTIVITY OPTIONS**

**ART**
**LANGUAGE ARTS**

Draw a **political cartoon** or write a **press release** describing one of Nixon's policies or achievements from his first term as president.



### Section 1 Assessment

**1. Terms & Names**

**Richard M. Nixon,** p. 855
**Henry Kissinger,** p. 855
**revenue sharing,** p. 856
**détente,** p. 858
**SALT,** p. 858

**2. Taking Notes**

Problems: inflation, racial problems, protests over the Vietnam War, recession, unemployment, crime, Cold War tensions

Answers will vary. Some students may say inflation, recession, and unemployment are linked.

**3. Main Ideas**

**a.** He appointed more conservative Supreme Court justices and encouraged a crackdown on crime and protests. **b.** inflation, recession, unemployment, energy crisis
**c.** Nixon opened diplomatic relations and trade with China and eased tensions with the USSR.

**4. Critical Thinking**

Nixon's policy of détente was the most surprising because of his long opposition to the Communists.

**ACTIVITY OPTIONS**

 **Alternative Assessment**
- Rubrics for a cartoon, 1.2
- Rubrics for a press release, 4.5

# 2 Watergate Brings Down Nixon

**TERMS & NAMES**
Committee to Reelect the President
Watergate scandal

**MAIN IDEA**
Nixon's involvement in the Watergate scandal caused a political crisis that forced him to resign.

**WHY IT MATTERS NOW**
Watergate led many Americans to have less confidence in government and politicians.

## ONE AMERICAN'S STORY

**Barbara Jordan grew up in a poor home in Houston, Texas, in the 1940s. Early on, she realized that her voice was one of her greatest assets. She had a strong, deep, beautiful voice and a gift for reciting dramatic poetry. Jordan was also highly intelligent. After graduating from Boston University Law School in 1959, she became interested in politics. She began her career as a volunteer worker for John Kennedy in his 1960 presidential campaign against Richard Nixon.**

**Jordan went on to become the first African-American woman from the South elected to the U.S. Congress. The 1972 election that sent her to the House of Representatives also saw Nixon's reelection as president. Two years later, at impeachment hearings in the House Judiciary Committee, Jordan warned that Nixon's actions during that campaign and his presidency were threats to the Constitution.**

*A VOICE FROM THE PAST*

My faith in the Constitution is whole, it is complete, it is total, and I am not going to sit here and be an idle spectator to the diminution [lessening], the subversion [undermining], the destruction of the Constitution.

**Barbara Jordan,** speech in House Judiciary Committee, July 25, 1974

**As a member of the House Judiciary Committee, Representative Barbara Jordan of Texas recommended the impeachment of President Nixon.**

**In this section, you will read about the events that led Nixon, Jordan, and the nation into the political nightmare that ended his presidency.**

## 1 The 1972 Presidential Election

The 1972 presidential campaign did not appear to be much of a race for President Nixon. His diplomatic successes in China and the Soviet Union and Kissinger's negotiations to end the Vietnam War were triumphs for the president. The Republicans nominated him overwhelmingly for reelection.

Nixon's Democratic opponent was George McGovern. McGovern was a liberal senator from South Dakota who spoke out against the Vietnam War. McGovern had strong support from young people, African Americans, and members of the women's movement. But Nixon won with the largest victory of any Republican candidate to that time.





## SECTION OBJECTIVES

1. To analyze the 1972 presidential election
2. To trace events leading to the Watergate scandal
3. To describe the Watergate investigation and Nixon's resignation
4. To evaluate the effects of the Watergate scandal

**CRITICAL THINKING**
Making Inferences, p. 860
Recognizing Effects, p. 861
Forming and Supporting Opinions, p. 861

## FOCUS & MOTIVATE

### 5-MINUTE WARM-UP

**Recognizing Effects** These questions explore the misuse of presidential power.

1. Read Barbara Jordan's quote on page 859. What does she think is happening to the Constitution?
2. Read the caption under Jordan's picture. What action did she take to protect the Constitution?

 **Warm-Up Transparency WT31**

## INSTRUCT

**INSTRUCT: OBJECTIVE** 

**The 1972 Presidential Election**
Key Questions
- Why did Nixon's reelection seem assured?
- Who was the Democratic candidate in 1972?
- Why was President Nixon's victory notable?

**In-Depth Resources: Unit 9**
- Guided Reading, p. 40
- Building Vocabulary, p. 42

**Reading Study Guide** (Spanish and English), pp. 297–298

## RECOMMENDED RESOURCES

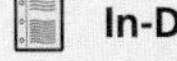 **In-Depth Resources: Unit 9**
- Guided Reading, p. 40
- Building Vocabulary, p. 42
- Geography Application: The Geography of the Watergate Scandal, pp. 44–45
- Primary Source, p. 46
- Reteaching Activity, p. 52

**Reading Study Guide** (Spanish and English), pp. 297–298

**America's History Makers**
- Barbara Jordan, pp. 127–128

**Formal Assessment**
- Section Quiz, p. 446

**Alternative Assessment**
- Rubrics, 5.3
- Rubrics, 4.5

**Access for Students Acquiring English/ESL**
- Guided Reading, p. 206
- Geography Application, pp. 209–210

Technology Resources

 **Humanities Transparency HT62**
- White House Cartoon

 **Critical Thinking Trans. CT92**
- Cause and Effect: The Watergate Scandal

 **Electronic Teacher Tools with Test Maker**

**INSTRUCT: OBJECTIVE** 

**The Watergate Scandal**

Key Questions

- What event was at the heart of the Watergate scandal?
- How did President Nixon try to cover up the Watergate break-in?

 **In-Depth Resources: Unit 9**

- Geography Application: The Geography of the Watergate Scandal, pp. 44–45
- Primary Source, p. 46

 **Humanities Transparency HT62**

- White House Cartoon

 **Critical Thinking Transparency CT92**

- Cause and Effect: The Watergate Scandal

**HISTORY *through* ART**

**Interpreting the Cartoon** Political cartoons usually appear on the editorial pages of newspapers, because—like editorials—these cartoons express an opinion. Cartoonist Paul Conrad has won the Pulitzer Prize three times for his work. Conrad and other cartoonists of the era found Nixon an easy subject to draw. His sharp nose, heavy brows, and dark beard were instantly recognizable even when, as here, little of his face is visible.

**Possible Response: By showing Nixon himself tapping into the Democratic Party's phones, the cartoonist is suggesting that the president was directly involved in Watergate and he is lying.**

**INSTRUCT: OBJECTIVE** 

**Nixon Resigns**

Key Questions

- Why did John Dean decide to testify against President Nixon?
- What evidence against the president emerged during the Senate investigation?
- Why did Nixon decide to resign?
- How did Americans react to Watergate?

 **America's History Makers**

- Barbara Jordan, pp. 127–128

**HISTORY *through* ART**

The Watergate scandal was the subject of thousands of political cartoons. Here, cartoonist Paul Conrad shows Nixon attempting to tap the telephones at the Democratic Party headquarters in the Watergate building.

**What do you think the cartoon suggests about Nixon's involvement in the Watergate scandal?**

"HE SAYS HE'S FROM THE PHONE COMPANY..."

## 2 The Watergate Scandal

An almost certain victory in the 1972 presidential election had not been enough for Nixon. He had wanted to win big. By doing so, he would help Republicans take control of Congress, and he would gain more power. To ensure this landslide victory, many people working for him engaged in various illegal activities.

*Reading* **History**

**A. Making Inferences** Why did Nixon want a big win in the 1972 presidential election?

**A. Possible Answer** Nixon wanted to help the Republican party take control of Congress and gain more power for himself.

These activities started coming to light on June 17, 1972. Five men were caught breaking into Democratic Party headquarters in the Watergate office-apartment complex in Washington, D.C. The burglars had cameras and listening devices for the telephones. They were linked to Nixon's reelection campaign staff, called the **Committee to Reelect the President.** Nixon may not have known in advance about the break-in. But in less than a week, he was talking to his aides about covering up any White House connection to the Watergate burglary to avoid a scandal.

The cover-up involved lies told by President Nixon and his aides. It involved payments to the Watergate burglars and others to lie. It involved using the CIA to halt an FBI investigation of Watergate. These illegal actions by Nixon and his aides to cover up Watergate and other related crimes came to be called the **Watergate scandal.**

The Watergate break-in stayed on the back pages of most newspapers in the 1972 campaign. But some reporters kept investigating. They found more evidence tying Nixon to Watergate. In February 1973, the Senate began an investigation. The threat to Nixon's presidency was building.

## 3 Nixon Resigns

The Senate Watergate investigation began with the questioning of members of the reelection committee and the White House staff. Within six weeks, the investigation was closing in on the president's closest advisers—H. R. Haldeman, John Ehrlichman, former Attorney-General John Mitchell, and John Dean. On March 21, 1973, Dean, one of the president's attorneys, spoke to Nixon about the worsening situation.

**Background**

Eventually, 25 members of the Nixon administration were convicted and served prison terms for crimes connected to Watergate.

*A VOICE FROM THE PAST*

I think that there is no doubt about the seriousness of the problem we've got. We have a cancer within, close to the Presidency, that is growing. It is growing daily.

**John Dean,** quoted in *The White House Transcripts*

Dean was warning about money needed to keep the burglars quiet. Nixon agreed to pay the "hush money." He now clearly had committed a crime.

As more Watergate information was being uncovered, Dean decided to tell all to the Senate. He said that the president had been involved in the



**ACTIVITY OPTIONS**

**INDIVIDUAL NEEDS: GIFTED AND TALENTED**

**WATERGATE AND THE CONSTITUTION**

**Class Time** One class period

**Task** Creating a diagram illustrating how the system of checks and balances operated during Watergate

**Purpose** To gain an understanding of how the Constitution protected the United States from a misuse of presidential power

**Supplies Needed**

- Reference materials on the constitutional system of checks and balances, the Watergate investigation, and executive privilege

**Activity** Have students review the material on the system of checks and balances on page 246 and on page 261. Have them illustrate this system in a rough diagram. Then have students research the Watergate investigation, adding details of actions by the executive, judicial, and legislative branches of government to the diagram. Then students should prepare a final version of their diagram.

cover-up for months. But Nixon denied any knowledge. It was Dean's word against Nixon's until mid-July. Then a White House aide revealed that Nixon had been taping conversations in his office. A long battle over the tapes began in the courts.

Meanwhile, more bad news came for Nixon. It was revealed that Vice-President Spiro Agnew had accepted bribes as governor of Maryland and continued taking them as vice-president. Not wanting to face impeachment, Agnew resigned in October 1973. Nixon then nominated Congressman Gerald Ford of Michigan as the new vice-president.

President Nixon put on an upbeat face as he left Washington after resigning on August 9, 1974.

Evidence of the president's role in the cover-up continued to grow, but he told the country that he had done nothing wrong. He said, "I am not a crook." Then, in January 1974, the House Judiciary Committee began an impeachment investigation. It reviewed court testimony, Senate transcripts, and documents from special prosecutors. Nixon did not give them his tapes but released edited transcripts. The committee felt it had a strong case even without the tapes. In July, both Democrats and Republicans on the committee approved impeachment charges.

On August 5, Nixon was forced by a court order to release full transcripts of the tapes. The evidence that he had been involved in the cover-up from the beginning—what investigators called "a smoking gun"—had been recorded on the tapes. On August 9, 1974, Richard Nixon resigned. Vice-President Gerald Ford was then sworn in as the next president.

Watergate was one of the worst political scandals in the nation's history. Many Americans lost faith in the government and its leaders. This lack of confidence weakened the government, especially the president. As you will read in the following section, the next two presidents—Gerald Ford and Jimmy Carter—worked hard to try to restore the presidency.

B. Possible Answer Many Americans lost faith in the government and their leaders.

*Reading* **History**

**B. Recognizing Effects** How did the Watergate scandal change many Americans' view of their government?

## Section 2 Assessment

**1. Terms & Names**

**Identify:**
- Committee to Reelect the President
- Watergate scandal

**2. Taking Notes**

Use a time line like the one below to trace the events of the Watergate scandal.

June 1972 — event — event — event — event — August 1974

Which event made Nixon's downfall almost certain?

**3. Main Ideas**

a. Why did Nixon want a big win in the 1972 election?

b. What kinds of illegal activities was Nixon involved with in the Watergate scandal?

c. What was the outcome of the Watergate scandal?

**4. Critical Thinking**

**Forming and Supporting Opinions** What do you think would have happened if President Nixon had apologized for Watergate rather than trying to cover it up?

THINK ABOUT
- when the break-in occurred
- how the nation reacted to past scandals

**ACTIVITY OPTIONS**

**TECHNOLOGY** / **LANGUAGE ARTS**: Interview someone who remembers Watergate. Either create a **radio broadcast** of the interview or write it as a **question-and-answer magazine feature.**





### CRITICAL THINKING ACTIVITY

**Forming and Supporting Opinions** Executive privilege is the right of the president to keep secret any information that he believes will threaten national security or hinder the federal executive branch from doing its work. Nixon invoked executive privilege in refusing to turn over the Oval Office tapes. Ask students what kind of information they think should be protected by executive privilege.

**Class Time** 10 minutes

### MORE ABOUT . . .

**Outcome of the Watergate Investigation**

The Watergate investigation produced evidence for "high crimes and misdemeanors" in five categories: (1) breaking and entering/assault; (2) illegal campaign contributions; (3) illegal campaign tactics, such as forged letters and telegrams; (4) cover-up/obstruction of justice; (5) miscellaneous offenses, such as tax evasion and misappropriation of federal funds for personal use.

## ASSESS & RETEACH

**Setting the Stage** Have students add information about Nixon's second term to the chapter graphic organizer.

**Formal Assessment**
- Section Quiz, p. 446

### RETEACHING ACTIVITY

Have students work as a group to create a cause-effect chain of events from President Nixon's reelection in 1972 to his resignation in 1974.

**In-Depth Resources: Unit 9**
- Reteaching Activity, p. 52

## Section 2 Assessment

**1. Terms & Names**

**Committee to Reelect the President,** p. 860
**Watergate scandal,** p. 860

**2. Taking Notes**

June 1972: Watergate break-in; February 1973: Senate investigates; March 1973: John Dean testifies before Senate; January 1974: House Judiciary Committee begins impeachment hearings; July 1974: Judiciary Committee votes to impeach Nixon; August 1974: President Nixon resigns

Answers will vary.

**3. Main Ideas**

**a.** so the Republicans could gain control of Congress, giving him more power **b.** He lied about his involvement in the cover-up, he agreed to pay the Watergate burglars, and he used the CIA to halt an FBI investigation. **c.** The president was forced to resign, and many Americans lost faith in the government and its leaders.

**4. Critical Thinking**

Some students may say he might not have been forced to resign or face impeachment. Others may say that nothing he could have done would have allowed him to stay in office.

**ACTIVITY OPTIONS**

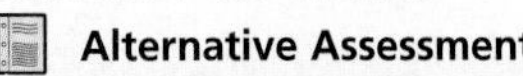

**Alternative Assessment**
- Rubrics, 5.3, 4.5

## SECTION OBJECTIVES

1. To summarize events of the Ford presidency
2. To evaluate the Carter presidency
3. To describe the environmental movement
4. To analyze the 1980 presidential race

**CRITICAL THINKING**

Drawing Conclusions, p. 863
Making Inferences, p. 863
Finding Main Ideas, p. 864
Comparing, p. 865

 **Why It Matters Now**
- Overcoming Challenges, pp. 61–62

## FOCUS & MOTIVATE

### 5-MINUTE WARM-UP

**Summarizing** These questions focus on the nation after the Watergate scandal.

1. Read President Ford's quote on page 862. What does he say about the role of people in the American democracy?
2. What does President Ford suggest people do to get over the Watergate scandal?

 **Warm-Up Transparency WT31**

## INSTRUCT

### INSTRUCT: OBJECTIVE 

**Ford Takes Over**

Key Questions
- How did President Ford try to restore confidence in the presidency?
- What steps did Ford take to improve the economy?
- What were Ford's successes and failures in foreign affairs?

 **In-Depth Resources: Unit 9**
- Guided Reading, p. 41

**Reading Study Guide** (Spanish and English), pp. 299–300

# 3 Issues of the Seventies

**TERMS & NAMES**
- Gerald Ford
- Jimmy Carter
- Camp David Accords
- environmentalism
- Rachel Carson
- Iran hostage crisis

| MAIN IDEA | WHY IT MATTERS NOW |
|---|---|
| Presidents Ford and Carter had a difficult time solving the nation's problems after Watergate. | These problems helped lead to a conservative mood in the United States. |

### ONE AMERICAN'S STORY

**On August 9, 1974, Vice-President Gerald Ford became president after Richard Nixon resigned. A year earlier, Nixon had chosen Ford as his vice-president. He replaced Spiro Agnew, who had resigned in disgrace. During 25 years as a congressman from Michigan, Ford had gained a reputation for integrity and openness.**

**As president, Ford inherited a nation that had suffered through the years of Vietnam and Watergate. He tried to reassure Americans that the turmoil of the Nixon years was behind them in his first speech.**

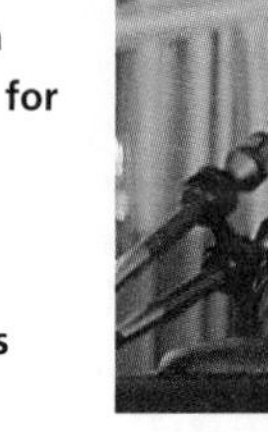

President Gerald Ford speaks to the nation from the White House.

*A VOICE FROM THE PAST*

My fellow Americans, our long national nightmare is over. Our Constitution works; our great Republic is a Government of laws and not of men. Here the people rule. . . . As we bind up the internal wounds of Watergate, more painful and more poisonous than those of foreign wars, let us restore the golden rule to our political process, and let brotherly love purge our hearts of suspicion and of hate.

**Gerald Ford,** speech on August 9, 1974

**As part of the healing process, Ford decided to pardon former President Nixon. Ford's pardon of Nixon brought him much criticism and added to the divisions in the country.**

**In this section, you will learn more about the difficulties Presidents Ford and Jimmy Carter faced as they tried to govern in the 1970s.**

## 1 Ford Takes Over

In his first weeks in office, Ford set out to restore confidence in the presidency. He soothed the nation with his plain speaking, openness, and willingness to talk to the press and to work with Congress.

However, within a month, Ford lost the support of many Americans when he pardoned Richard Nixon for any crimes he might have committed during the Watergate scandal. It had been Ford's hope to spare the country the spectacle of a former president being brought to trial. But



### RECOMMENDED RESOURCES

 **In-Depth Resources: Unit 9**
- Guided Reading, p. 41
- Building Vocabulary, p. 42
- Skillbuilder Practice, p. 43
- Primary Source, p. 47
- Literature Selection: "Saying Things," pp. 48–50
- Reteaching Activity, p. 53
- Enrichment Activity, p. 54

**Reading Study Guide** (Spanish and English), pp. 299–300

**Outline Map Activities**
- The Middle East: Resolution and Crisis, 1979, pp. 61–62

**Why It Matters Now**
- Overcoming Challenges, pp. 61–62

**Formal Assessment**
- Section Quiz, p. 447

**Alternative Assessment**
- Rubrics, 2.3
- Rubrics, 1.2

**Access for Students Acquiring English/ESL**
- Guided Reading, p. 207
- Skillbuilder Practice, p. 208

**Technology Resources**

 **Electronic Teacher Tools with Test Maker**

 **ClassZone**
www.mcdougallittell.com

**ReadingHistory**

**A. Drawing Conclusions** Why were many Americans upset with President Ford over Nixon's pardon?

A. Answer Many Americans thought that Nixon should be charged with crimes for his role in Watergate.

**Vocabulary**

**human rights:** basic rights and freedoms to which all human beings are entitled, such as freedom of speech

many people felt strongly that Nixon should be charged with crimes because of the Watergate cover-up. Ford's popularity dropped sharply.

Making life even tougher for Ford was the fact that the economy was not in good shape. Inflation was spiraling higher while a recession was throwing more people out of work. Many Americans were having a hard time making ends meet. Ford proposed a voluntary campaign to "Whip Inflation Now." He asked Americans to cut spending and energy use. The WIN plan received much publicity but failed to help the economy.

In foreign affairs, Ford had mixed success. He asked Congress to help South Vietnam when the cease-fire in the Vietnam War broke down in 1974. But Congress refused. In 1975, he negotiated a treaty with European nations and Canada called the Helsinki Accords. This pact spelled out basic human rights for the citizens of the signer nations.

Ford's pardon of Nixon and his difficulty in improving the economy caused him problems in the 1976 presidential campaign. He only narrowly won his party's nomination over California governor Ronald Reagan.Then he lost the presidency in a close election to Democrat **Jimmy Carter.**

Carter was a former peanut farmer and governor of Georgia. He had run for president as a Washington outsider and one who would "never lie" to the American people. He promised honesty in government and support for human rights throughout the world.

**ReadingHistory** 2

**B. Making Inferences** How did Jimmy Carter benefit from the Watergate scandal?

B. Possible Answer Because people were suspicious of their government, they elected Carter, a Washington outsider.

## Carter as President

Many Americans were still suspicious of their government as Carter took office in 1977. Since Carter had never served in Washington, Americans hoped that he would bring fresh ideas to the presidency.

Carter immediately tried to show that he was one of the people. On inauguration day, he and his family walked from the Capitol to the White House rather than take the traditional limousine. However, being a Washington outsider would make political life difficult for Carter.

Carter and Congress often clashed. One point of conflict was the energy crisis. Early in 1977, shortages of oil and natural gas forced many schools and businesses to close. In response, Carter asked Americans to conserve energy. He also sent a national energy program to Congress. It would cut oil imports, increase production of oil and natural gas at home, and promote alternative energy sources like coal and nuclear and solar energy.

After months of debate, Congress passed some of the measures. But they were of little help when OPEC again sharply raised oil prices. Inflation surged beyond 10 percent. Unemployment rose. Like Nixon and Ford, Carter could not solve the nation's economic problems.

**America's HERITAGE**

**THE BICENTENNIAL**

On July 4, 1976, the United States celebrated the 200th anniversary of the Declaration of Independence. The Bicentennial, as it was called, was a year-long birthday party. People in every corner of the nation celebrated with special events.

Americans also used the time to reflect on the nation's progress. Women, African Americans, Hispanic Americans, Native Americans, and others still faced discrimination. Yet Americans were proud of what had been achieved, and the celebration helped the nation move beyond the turmoil of the early 1970s.

**America's HERITAGE**

**The Bicentennial**

One highlight of the Bicentennial year included the world's largest birthday cake in Philadelphia. In Chicago, 1,776 immigrants from many nations were sworn in as American citizens. "Tall ships" (sailing ships named for their high masts) sailed to New York City from around the world. Across the country, fireworks lit the sky—33 tons were exploded in Washington, D.C.

**INSTRUCT: OBJECTIVE 2**

**Carter as President**

Key Questions

- Why did Carter's inexperience in national politics appeal to Americans?
- How successful was Carter in getting legislation passed in Congress?
- What were Carter's successes in foreign relations?

**MORE ABOUT . . .**

**Jimmy Carter**

Carter continued his "common touch" immediately upon arrival in the White House. He reduced White House staff, sold the presidential yacht, and ordered his subordinates to drive their own cars. He began civil service reforms and introduced a strict code of government ethics.

**ACTIVITY OPTIONS**

**INDIVIDUAL NEEDS**

**STUDENTS ACQUIRING ENGLISH/ESL**

**Using Metaphors** Explain to the students that a metaphor is a figure of speech. A word that usually has one meaning is used in a new way, often as a symbol. In the quotation from Gerald Ford on page 862, there are many metaphors. Ask students to find some of these metaphors. You may want to prompt the discussion by asking such questions as these:

- Why does Ford call Watergate a "long national nightmare"?
- What does he mean when he speaks of the "wounds of Watergate," calling them "painful" and "poisonous"?
- How is the phrase "the golden rule" a metaphor?
- What does "a Government of laws and not of men" mean? Is it a metaphor?

## Connections TO WORLD HISTORY

**Middle East Peace Process**

Carter had little knowledge of the complex issues of the Middle East before he became president. When peace talks between Prime Minister Begin and President Sadat stalled, Carter invited the two leaders for a three-day session at Camp David, the presidential retreat in Maryland. The session lasted nearly two weeks and resulted in the Camp David Accords. Their diplomacy won Begin and Sadat the Nobel Peace Prize.

Connections TO WORLD HISTORY

**MIDDLE EAST PEACE PROCESS**

The signing of the Camp David Accords in 1978 by (left to right) Prime Minister Menachem Begin of Israel, President Carter, and President Anwar el-Sadat of Egypt was the first important step in the attempt to bring peace to the Middle East.

In 1998, another step was taken when President Bill Clinton brought Palestinian leader Yasir Arafat and Israeli Prime Minister Benjamin Netanyahu together to sign a peace agreement called the Wye River Accords.

Carter had more success in accomplishing his foreign-policy goals. He wanted to end the long-standing conflict with Panama over the Panama Canal. As you read in Chapter 23, the Panama Canal was built and controlled by the United States. Most Americans wanted it to stay that way. But Carter thought winning the good will of Latin America was worth losing control of the canal. Under treaties signed in 1977, the United States agreed to give the canal to Panama in 2000.

Carter also tried to reduce tensions in the Middle East. In 1978, he helped to negotiate the **Camp David Accords.** Under these agreements, Egypt and Israel signed the first peace treaty between Israel and an Arab nation, thus ending 30 years of conflict.

## INSTRUCT: OBJECTIVE 

**The Environmental Movement Begins**

Key Questions

- What problems did Rachel Carson address in *Silent Spring?*
- What environmental laws were passed during the 1970s?
- How successful were the regulations in preventing environmental crises?

 **In-Depth Resources: Unit 9**

- Primary Source: "Pollution" by Tom Lehrer, p. 47
- Literature Selection: "Saying Things" by Gary Soto, pp. 48–50

## 3 The Environmental Movement Begins

Protection of the environment was also a goal of Carter's. He supported a movement to save the environment that had gained momentum in the 1970s. Actually, the first laws to protect the nation's natural environment had been passed in the late 1800s. But **environmentalism,** or work toward protecting the environment, only began to attract wide public attention in the 1960s. In 1962, biologist **Rachel Carson** wrote of the dangers of heavy pesticide use in her bestseller, *Silent Spring.* She warned that some of these chemicals could kill animals, cause disease, and destroy the environment unless their use was limited or stopped.

*Reading* **History**

**C. Finding Main Ideas** What role did Rachel Carson play in the environmental movement?

C. Possible Answer Rachel Carson helped attract attention to environmental problems with her book *Silent Spring.*

In 1969, a huge oil spill near Santa Barbara, California, polluted miles of beaches and killed many marine animals. The cry for tougher laws to protect the environment grew. In the 1970s, Nixon, Ford, and Carter all proposed laws to restrict pesticide use, to regulate the cleanup of oil spills, and to curb air and water pollution. With these laws in effect, many polluted lakes began to recover, and high levels of some air pollutants began to drop. But environmental disasters continued to occur.

In 1979, an accident occurred at the Three Mile Island nuclear power plant in Pennsylvania. Radioactive water leaked out of the plant, causing

## MORE ABOUT . . .

**The Three Mile Island Incident**

The Nuclear Regulatory Commission found that the amount of radioactivity released at Three Mile Island was not large enough to cause a serious health risk. However, the Three Mile Island meltdown was significant because it was a major challenge to 20th-century Americans' uncritical acceptance of advanced technology.



ACTIVITY OPTIONS

## SKILLBUILDER MINI-LESSON: DRAWING CONCLUSIONS

 BLOCK SCHEDULING

**Explaining the Skill** Drawing a conclusion means analyzing the implications of what you have read and forming a judgment about its meaning and consequences. To draw conclusions, students must think about information they read in light of their own knowledge and experience.

**Applying the Skill** Ask the students to read "Connections to World History" on page 864 and the second paragraph under the photo. Then ask the following:

1. What conclusion can you draw about U.S. involvement in the Middle East peace process? *(U.S. leaders view peace in the Middle East as vital to U.S. security, and they continue to work to promote peace.)*
2. Where can you find information to check the conclusion you have drawn? *(newsmagazines, encyclopedia articles, and yearbooks)*

 **In-Depth Resources: Unit 9**

- Skillbuilder Practice, p. 43

fears that the nuclear reactor might explode. Within a week, the reactor was shut down. Disaster was averted. To assure people it was safe, Carter visited Three Mile Island. But not long after, he faced another disaster—a political one—in Iran.

## 4 Reagan and the Conservatives Win

*Reading*History
**D. Reading a Map** Locate Tehran, the capital of Iran, in the map on this page.

For decades, the United States had supported the Shah (king) of Iran. In 1979, Muslim leaders overthrew his government. When Carter allowed the Shah to come to the United States for medical treatment, Iranians struck back at the United States. On November 4, 1979, they overran the American embassy in Iran's capital of Tehran and took 52 Americans hostage. The **Iran hostage crisis** had begun.

Carter tried negotiating to get Iran's leaders to release the hostages but without success. He approved a secret military mission, but it failed. The continuing crisis affected the election in 1980. Americans blamed Carter for the plight of the hostages, for the nation's economic ills, and for making America look weak to the world.

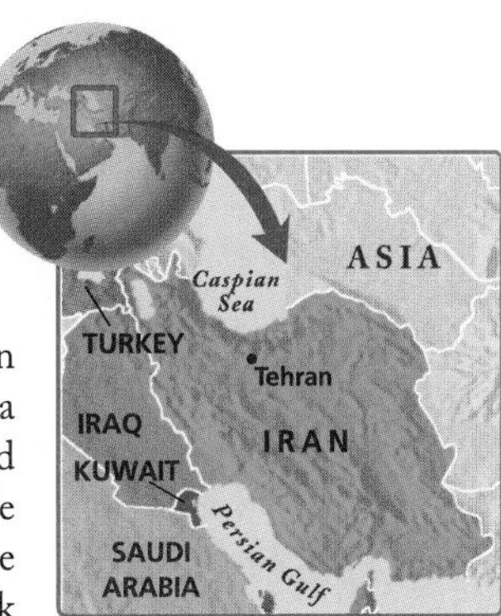


Meanwhile, support for conservative ideas had been growing for more than a decade. The Republicans chose a conservative—Ronald Reagan, a former actor and California governor—to be their candidate in 1980. He vowed that, if elected president, he would not allow the United States to be pushed around. Reagan's get-tough talk appealed to many voters.

Carter eventually won release of the hostages. But the majority of voters had already decided that it was time for a change and elected Reagan president. The hostages left Iran on January 20, 1981, the day Reagan was inaugurated. In the next chapter, you will read how Ronald Reagan took the nation in a more conservative direction.

### Section 3 Assessment

**1. Terms & Names**

**Identify:**
- Gerald Ford
- Jimmy Carter
- Camp David Accords
- environmentalism
- Rachel Carson
- Iran hostage crisis

**2. Taking Notes**

Use a chart to list the high and low points of both the Ford and Carter presidencies.

| Presidency | High points | Low points |
|---|---|---|
| Gerald Ford | | |
| Jimmy Carter | | |

Which do you think was the highest point of each? Why?

**3. Main Ideas**

**a.** Why did Carter win the 1976 election over Ford?

**b.** What were some problems related to energy use that occurred during Carter's term?

**c.** What progress did the environmental movement make during the 1960s and the 1970s?

**4. Critical Thinking**

**Comparing** How would you compare the strengths and weaknesses of Ford and Carter? Use events from their presidencies to support your answer.

**THINK ABOUT**
- actions each took to draw Americans together
- response to economic and foreign-policy issues

**ACTIVITY OPTIONS**

**MATH**
**ART**

Research inflation in the 1970s. Make a **graph** to show the annual rate change or create a **political cartoon** about inflation's effect on people's lives.



### INSTRUCT: OBJECTIVE 4

**Reagan and the Conservatives Win**
Key Questions
- What were some causes of the 1979 Iran hostage crisis?
- How did Carter react to the crisis? What effects did his actions have?
- What factors contributed to the conservative win in the 1980 election?

**Outline Map Activities**
- The Middle East: Resolution and Crisis, 1979, pp. 61–62

### ASSESS & RETEACH

**Setting the Stage** Have students add information about Ford and Carter to the chapter graphic organizer.

**Formal Assessment**
- Section Quiz, p. 447

**Critical Thinking Transparency CT91**
- Setting the Stage

**RETEACHING ACTIVITY**

Have students use a graphic organizer such as the one below to summarize the issues of the 1970s as well as presidential actions taken to meet the issues.

| Issue | President | Action |
|---|---|---|
| | | |
| | | |
| | | |
| | | |
| | | |

**In-Depth Resources: Unit 9**
- Reteaching Activity, p. 53

### Section 3 Assessment

**1. Terms & Names**

**Gerald Ford,** p. 862
**Jimmy Carter,** p. 863
**Camp David Accords,** p. 864
**environmentalism,** p. 864
**Rachel Carson,** p. 864
**Iran hostage crisis,** p. 865

**2. Taking Notes**

Ford—High point: negotiation of Helsinki Accords. Low points: pardon of Nixon; failure of WIN program; loss in 1976; Carter—High points: negotiation of Panama Canal Treaties and Camp David Accords. Low points: clashes with Congress; Iran hostage crisis; loss in 1980

Answers will vary.

**3. Main Ideas**

**a.** Ford lost support because of his pardon of Nixon and because the economy was weak, while Carter was viewed as someone who had fresh ideas. **b.** OPEC raised prices; inflation and unemployment grew. **c.** People became more aware of the need to protect the environment, leading to environmental legislation.

**4. Critical Thinking**

Answers will vary but should include failure of economic policies, success of foreign affairs, and loss of a second-term election.

**ACTIVITY OPTIONS**

**Alternative Assessment**
- Rubrics for a graph, 2.3
- Rubrics for a cartoon, 1.2

## *Interdisciplinary* CHALLENGE

**OBJECTIVE**
Students will work cooperatively to meet some of the social, political, and scientific challenges to American citizens posed in the 1970s by environmental damage.

 **BLOCK SCHEDULING**

## PROCEDURE

Gather supplies that students might need, such as posterboard, colored markers, pencils, and paper. For each challenge, have students form groups of three or four. Ask group members to divide the work among themselves. Then have them choose an option for presenting their solution.

### LANGUAGE ARTS CHALLENGE

**Class Time** 50 minutes

To help students present their ideas verbally, suggest that they choose one area of environmental danger from the "Environmental Problems" list on page 867. Encourage students to scan magazine and newspaper articles for strong, vivid verbs and adjectives.

**POSSIBLE SOLUTIONS**
Here are some of the ways environmentalists moved people in the 1970s:
- They presented graphic images of what the world would be like unless environmental problems were corrected.
- They suggested a variety of actions to help solve the problems of pollution.

## *Interdisciplinary* CHALLENGE

# Save the Environment!

You are a citizen of the 1970s who has joined the fight against pollution, waste, and the destruction of the Earth's natural resources. Each year on Earth Day, you help out with community clean-ups. You are interested in finding ways to rally public opinion and help save the planet.

COOPERATIVE LEARNING On this page are three challenges you face as an American concerned about the environment. Working with a small group, decide how to deal with each challenge. Select an option, assign a task to each group member, and do the activity. You will find useful information in the Data File. Present your solutions to the class.

### LANGUAGE ARTS CHALLENGE

## *"the community of living things"*

**You are worried that lack of concern about the environment may result in a permanently damaged world. The destruction of natural resources by individuals and industry continues. You decide to promote a campaign to save the environment. Present your ideas using one of these options:**

- **Write an editorial describing environmental dangers and promoting conservation.**
- **Make a speech to rally people in support of conservation.**

866

## STANDARDS FOR EVALUATION

### LANGUAGE ARTS CHALLENGE

**Option 1** Editorials should
- clearly identify environmental problems, their consequences, and possible solutions.
- present supporting facts as evidence.

**Option 2** Speeches should include
- the consequences of continued environmental damage.
- the benefits of conservation measures.

### ART CHALLENGE

**Option 1** Advertisements should
- use illustrations and words to present information clearly.
- describe the harm of pollution in a clear and objective style.

**Option 2** Cartoons should
- portray the harm done by air pollutants.
- present the benefits of public transportation for the environment and for travelers.

### SCIENCE CHALLENGE

**Option 1** Diagrams should
- explain the way oil pollution harms the environment, through visual devices.
- contain a brief, clear caption that summarizes the main idea.

**Option 2** Role-plays of explanations should
- explain the harm done by oil pollution.
- present information to support a viewpoint.
- summarize main points and recommend action.

**ART CHALLENGE**

### *"the air we breathe for life"*

**Ozone alert! TV announcers warn families to keep small children at home. The elderly, especially those with lung and heart problems, must stay inside. You wish that people understood the terrible effects of air pollution better so they might start demanding cleaner air. You decide to take action. Present your ideas using one of these options:**

- Design a public service ad for magazines explaining how air pollutants harm the body.
- Draw a cartoon asking people to use public transportation.

**SCIENCE CHALLENGE**

### *"the lakes and rivers and oceans"*

News of an oil spill off California's shores has sparked your concern for the environment. You are sickened by pictures of oil-soaked beaches and thousands of injured and dead animals. You want to help rid the oceans of this menace. Use the Data File for information. Then present your ideas, using one of these options:

- Create a labeled diagram for your local paper showing why oil pollution harms most sea life.
- Role-play a community meeting in which you explain how offshore oil pollution damages sea life.

Prevent Pollution

**ACTIVITY WRAP-UP**

Present to the class **Meet with the group to review your methods of helping to save the environment. Select a solution that best meets each challenge and then present them to the class.**

## DATA FILE

**ENVIRONMENTAL PROBLEMS**

Air and water pollution, acid rain, destruction of the ozone layer, toxic chemical disposal, extinction of wildlife, oil spills, destruction of forests, overpopulation

**OCEAN LIFE ZONES**

- Shorelines support crabs, oysters, shore birds, and other marine life.
- Open ocean over the continental shelf supports the largest amount of sea life, including algae, lobsters, thousands of fish species, turtles, seals, sharks, and whales.
- Deep ocean supports a smaller variety.

**SOURCES OF OCEAN OIL POLLUTION**

Offshore oil production, vessel accidents, natural seepage, nontanker and tanker shipping operations, waste car oil

**AIR POLLUTANTS**

- sources—fossil fuels, cars, power plants, industry, ozone
- effects—smog; eye irritation; impaired judgment; chest pains; lung, nerve, and kidney damage; cancer; birth defects

**WAYS TO CLEAN WATER**

- Install oil pollution prevention equipment on ships.
- Car owners, cities, and industry recycle used oil.

**REDUCE AIR POLLUTION**

- Burn fewer fossil fuels.
- Take public transportation.
- Improve car efficiency.
- Use sun and wind power.

**Visit www.mcdougallittell.com to learn more about the environment.**

867

**ART CHALLENGE**

**Class Time** 50 minutes

Suggest that students look at current magazines, television, or billboards to find examples of public service advertisements and cartoons. Students may make a display of the best examples they find.

**POSSIBLE SOLUTIONS**

Students' ads and cartoons might feature pictures of

- people boarding a city bus.
- workers carpooling.
- people walking or bicycling to work.

**SCIENCE CHALLENGE**

**Class Time** 50 minutes

Suggest that students research the topic of oil pollution to find diagrams to use as models. Suggest that they also look for statistics or other numerical information that makes the destruction of sea life or coastline habitat more meaningful.

**POSSIBLE SOLUTIONS**

Students' diagrams and role-plays might include the following points:

- Oil does the most damage in coral reefs and intertidal zones.
- Marine mammals and diving birds lose insulation from cold water when oil covers their feathers and fur. Animals swallow oil when they try to clean themselves.
- Fish exposed to oil may develop diseases and reproductive problems.

**ACTIVITY WRAP-UP**

To help student groups evaluate the creativity of their challenge solutions, ask them to make a grid with criteria like the one shown. Then have them rate each solution on a scale from 1 to 5.

| | | | | | |
|---|---|---|---|---|---|
| Originality | 1 | 2 | 3 | 4 | 5 |
| Persuasive appeal | 1 | 2 | 3 | 4 | 5 |
| Audience impact | 1 | 2 | 3 | 4 | 5 |
| Overall effectiveness | 1 | 2 | 3 | 4 | 5 |

## TERMS & NAMES

1. **Richard M. Nixon,** p. 855
2. **Henry Kissinger,** p. 855
3. **revenue sharing,** p. 856
4. **détente,** p. 858
5. **Watergate scandal,** p. 860
6. **Gerald Ford,** p. 862
7. **Jimmy Carter,** p. 863
8. **Camp David Accords,** p. 864
9. **environmentalism,** p. 864
10. **Iran hostage crisis,** p. 865

## REVIEW QUESTIONS

**Possible Responses**

1. He wanted to shrink the size of the federal government and cut Great Society programs.
2. He appointed conservative justices to the Supreme Court and used all the powers of the federal government to crack down on crime and protest.
3. inflation, unemployment, recession, and an energy crisis
4. He recognized China's government and opened diplomatic and trade relations.
5. Nixon wanted a big win in the 1972 election, and many people working for him engaged in illegal activities to ensure this landslide victory.
6. They found evidence tying Nixon to the scandal.
7. The House Judiciary Committee voted articles of impeachment, and Nixon resigned rather than be impeached.
8. People voted against Ford because he pardoned Nixon and because he was not able to improve economic conditions.
9. Carter negotiated the Panama Canal Treaties and the Camp David Accords, but he could not solve America's economic crisis.
10. Voters liked Reagan's "get-tough" talk and his belief in the ideas of patriotism, optimism, and self-sufficiency.

# Chapter 31 ASSESSMENT

## TERMS & NAMES

Briefly explain the importance of each of the following.

1. Richard M. Nixon
2. Henry Kissinger
3. revenue sharing
4. détente
5. Watergate scandal
6. Gerald Ford
7. Jimmy Carter
8. Camp David Accords
9. environmentalism
10. Iran hostage crisis

## REVIEW QUESTIONS

**Nixon Confronts Problems (pages 855–858)**

1. What kinds of government programs did Nixon propose to deal with America's social problems?
2. How did Nixon try to promote "law and order"?
3. What were the economic problems Nixon faced?
4. How was Nixon's foreign policy toward China different from that of previous presidents?

**Watergate Brings Down Nixon (pages 859–861)**

5. What were the chief causes of the Watergate scandal?
6. What did reporters and others find when they looked more deeply into the Watergate burglary?
7. What were the events that caused Nixon to resign?

**Issues of the Seventies (pages 862–867)**

8. What were the main reasons people did not vote for Gerald Ford in the 1976 election?
9. What successes did Carter have with foreign policy and what problems did he have at home?
10. What appealed to voters about Ronald Reagan in the 1980 election?

## CRITICAL THINKING

**1. USING YOUR NOTES**

| President | Issues and Events |
|---|---|
| Nixon | |
| Ford | |
| Carter | |

Use your completed chart to answer these questions.

a. What issues did all three presidents have to deal with during their terms? Which were the most frequently occurring issues of their presidencies?

b. Which of the presidents do you think faced the most difficult issues? Explain.

**2. ANALYZING LEADERSHIP**

What characteristics did Nixon, Ford, and Carter have that made them good leaders? Poor leaders?

**3. THEME: CITIZENSHIP**

What could Americans do to help their country during the 1970s?

**4. FORMING AND SUPPORTING OPINIONS**

Do you think Nixon's actions showed that his main goal was to survive during the events of Watergate? Explain your answer.

**5. EVALUATING**

Do you think that Ford made a good decision in pardoning Nixon? Explain why or why not.

**Interact *with* History**

Did your ideas about how the nation survives a crisis agree or disagree with what you read?

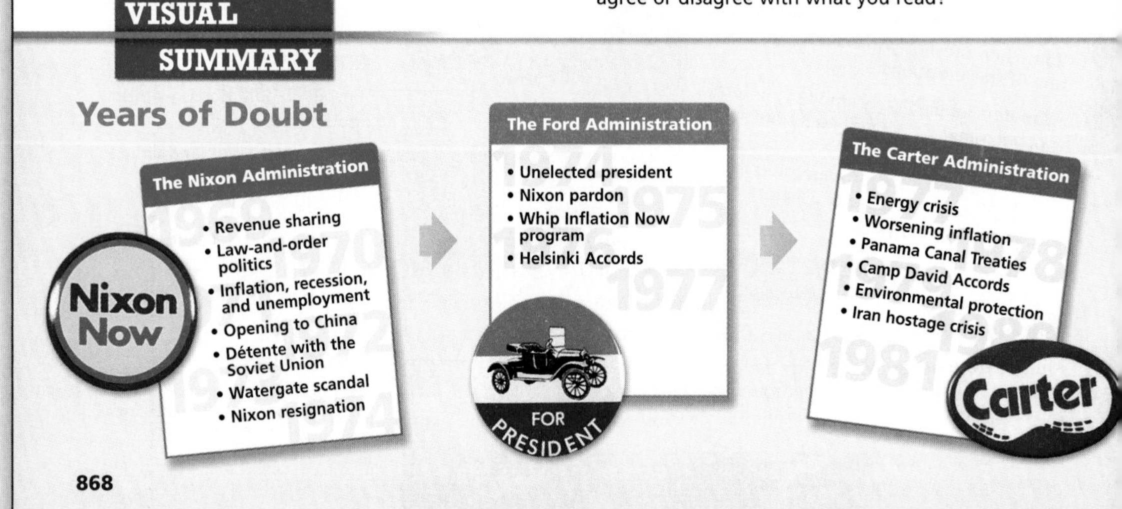

VISUAL SUMMARY
Years of Doubt
The Nixon Administration
• Revenue sharing
• Law-and-order politics
• Inflation, recession, and unemployment
• Opening to China
• Détente with the Soviet Union
• Watergate scandal
• Nixon resignation
Nixon Now
The Ford Administration
• Unelected president
• Nixon pardon
• Whip Inflation Now program
• Helsinki Accords
FOR PRESIDENT
The Carter Administration
• Energy crisis
• Worsening inflation
• Panama Canal Treaties
• Camp David Accords
• Environmental protection
• Iran hostage crisis
Carter




## CRITICAL THINKING

**Possible Responses**

1. **USING YOUR NOTES** **a.** economic problems; inflation, unemployment, and the energy crisis **b.** Most students will probably say Nixon, because of the Watergate scandal that led to his resignation.
2. **ANALYZING LEADERSHIP** All three tried to solve the nation's problems, and all tried to promote world stability. But Nixon used illegal means to stay in office, Ford did not see the severity of the nation's economic problems, and Carter was unable to work well with Congress.
3. **THEME: CITIZENSHIP** save energy and protect the environment
4. **FORMING AND SUPPORTING OPINIONS** Yes, he lied, he ordered money to be given to the burglars to lie, and he used all of the president's powers in the cover-up.
5. **EVALUATING** Students may say that the pardon was a good idea because the country did not need to go through a trial and because Nixon had suffered enough by losing the presidency, or that the pardon was not good because Nixon never had to admit guilt in court.

**Interact *with* History** Students' answers will vary based on their original answer.

## HISTORY SKILLS

**1. INTERPRETING GRAPHS**

Study the graph and then answer the questions.

**Major Energy Sources, *1850–1980***

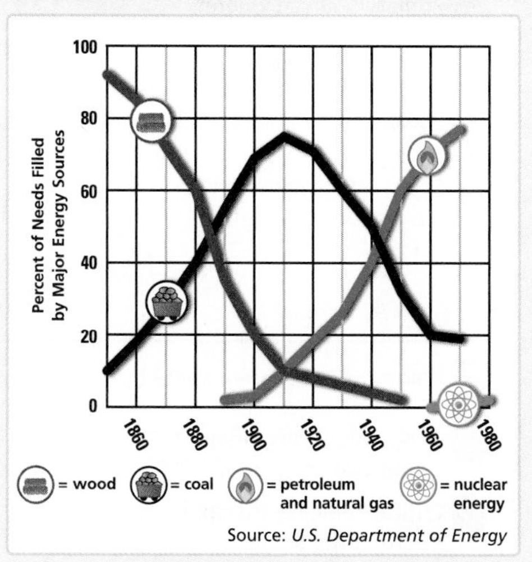


Source: *U.S. Department of Energy*

a. What fuel supplied most of the nation's energy between 1850 and 1880?

b. When did petroleum and natural gas begin being used as fuel?

c. What was the percentage increase in the use of coal from 1850 to 1910?

**2. INTERPRETING PRIMARY SOURCES**

The following excerpt was written by a citizens' group after a 1970 oil spill off the coast of Santa Barbara, California. Read the excerpt and then answer the questions.

> Centuries of careless neglect of the environment have brought [hu]mankind to a final crossroads. The quality of our lives is eroded and our very existence threatened by our abuse of the natural world. . . . We, therefore, resolve to act. We propose a revolution in conduct toward an environment which is rising in revolt against us. Granted that ideas and institutions long established are not easily changed; yet today is the first day of the rest of our life on this planet. We will begin anew.
>
> Santa Barbara Declaration of Environmental Rights, 1970

a. What kinds of problems does this excerpt from the *Santa Barbara Declaration* discuss?

b. What is the general solution that it proposes?

## ALTERNATIVE ASSESSMENT

**1. INTERDISCIPLINARY ACTIVITY: Geography**

**Making a Map** Research the territory that was the subject of the negotiations at Camp David in 1979. Make a three-dimensional map that shows the land, including its location relative to Egypt, Israel, and the other countries of the Middle East. Use your map to identify the resources of the territory.

**2. COOPERATIVE LEARNING ACTIVITY**

**Performing a Play** The fall of President Richard Nixon was one of the most dramatic events of modern American history. Working in a small group, research Nixon's last two years in office. Pick one event from this time and write a one-act play about the incident. Use primary sources, such as diaries or tape transcripts, to create your dialogue. Present your play and ask for comments from your classmates.

**3. TECHNOLOGY ACTIVITY**

**Designing a Bicentennial Web Site** The 200th anniversary of independence was a cause for celebration for Americans everywhere. President Ford told the nation to "break out the flag, strike up the band, light up the sky." It was a time to reflect on how the nation began, where it was then, and what might happen next. Use the library and the Internet to find information about the celebration. Also make use of what you have learned about the nation's history from your textbook.

**Visit www.mcdougallittell.com to learn more about the United States Bicentennial celebration.**

Design a Bicentennial Web site. Use the suggestions below to get started.

- Locate images showing Bicentennial highlights.
- Choose music that captures the spirit of the celebration.
- Highlight important events in the nation's history.
- Include the words and images of historic figures.
- Select Web sites that would be good links for visitors to your site.

**4. PORTFOLIO ACTIVITY**

**Option 1** Review your section and chapter assessment activities. Select one that you think is your best work. Then use comments made by your teacher or classmates to improve your work and add it to your portfolio.

**Option 2** Review the questions that you wrote in your notebook for What Do You Want to Know? on page 854. Then write a short report explaining your answers. Add your work to your history portfolio.



## ALTERNATIVE ASSESSMENT

1. INTERDISCIPLINARY ACTIVITY: **Geography**
   **Maps should**
   - include both physical and political locations in a three-dimensional presentation.
   - identify the resources of the region.
   - be clearly labeled and neatly presented.
   - include a legend and title.

2. COOPERATIVE LEARNING ACTIVITY
   **Plays should**
   - accurately portray the event selected.
   - convey information through visuals, primary sources, and performance.
   - exhibit creativity in creating the scene.
   - show evidence of involvement of each person in the group.

3. TECHNOLOGY ACTIVITY
   **Bicentennial Web sites should**
   - make effective use of text, pictures, icons, and music.
   - contain at least three links.
   - have written summaries that encourage browsers to visit other Web sites.
   - show technical proficiency.

4. HISTORY PORTFOLIO

**Option 1 Revised section or chapter assessment activities should**
- address teacher and peer responses to the selected work.
- solve problems present in the first versions of the work.

**Option 2 Short reports should**
- answer questions about Watergate or other crises of the 1970s.
- use evidence to develop and support ideas.
- cite sources of information.
- use standard grammar, spelling, sentence structure, and punctuation.

**Critical Thinking Transparency CT93**
- Visual Summary

**Formal Assessment**
- Chapter Test, Forms A and B, pp. 448–455

## HISTORY SKILLS

**Possible Responses**

1. INTERPRETING GRAPHS
   **a.** wood
   **b.** in the late 1880s and early 1890s
   **c.** It increased from almost 20 percent to about 75 percent.

2. INTERPRETING PRIMARY SOURCES
   **a.** neglect of the environment and abuse of the natural world
   **b.** a revolution in conduct toward the environment

CHAPTER 32 PLANNING GUIDE

# Entering a New Millennium 1981–present

| | CHAPTER OVERVIEW | COPYMASTERS | TECHNOLOGY |
|---|---|---|---|
| **CHAPTER RESOURCES** | This chapter traces the many changes in American life in recent times. It discusses the conservative administrations of Reagan and Bush and describes Clinton's difficulty in accomplishing his goals. It describes America's newest residents. | **In-Depth Resources: Unit 9**<br>• Tracing Themes: Diversity and Unity, p. 56<br>• Building Vocabulary, p. 60<br>• History Workshop Resources, p. 73<br>**Interdisciplinary Projects,** pp. 187–192 | **Primary Source Explorer**<br>**Electronic Teacher Tools**<br>**Power Presentations CD-ROM**<br>**Chapter Summaries on CD** (English and Spanish) |
| **SECTION 1**<br>**Conservatives Reshape Politics**<br>**pp. 873–877** | **KEY IDEAS**<br>• Reagan's administration deals with the Iran-Contra affair.<br>• War erupts in the Persian Gulf and Kosovo.<br>• Clinton is impeached but acquitted. | **In-Depth Resources: Unit 9**<br>• Setting the Stage, p. 55<br>• Guided Reading, p. 57<br>• Skillbuilder Practice, p. 61<br>• Reteaching Activity, p. 69<br>**America's History Makers,** pp. 129–132<br>**Economics in History,** p. 32<br>**Outline Map Activities,** pp. 63–64 | **Warm-Up Transparency WT32**<br>**Geography Transparency GT32**<br>• Cold War Ends, 1989–1990<br>**Critical Thinking Transparency CT94**<br>• Setting the Stage<br>**Critical Thinking Transparency CT95**<br>• Cause and Effect: Changing American Life<br>**ClassZone:** www.mcdougallittell.com |
| **SECTION 2**<br>**Technological and Economic Changes**<br>**pp. 878–882** | • Computers and technology transform American life.<br>• Changes in the economy have positive and negative effects.<br>• A global economy and scientific breakthroughs bring change. | **In-Depth Resources: Unit 9**<br>• Setting the Stage, p. 55<br>• Guided Reading, p. 58<br>• Geography Application: U.S. Trade, 1995, pp. 62–63<br>• Primary Source, p. 64<br>• Reteaching Activity, p. 70<br>**Citizenship Today,** p. 82<br>**Why It Matters Now**<br>• Changes in Modern America, pp. 63–64 | **Warm-Up Transparency WT32**<br>**Humanities Transparency HT63**<br>• Visualization of Internet Traffic<br>**Critical Thinking Transparency CT94**<br>• Setting the Stage<br>**ClassZone:** www.mcdougallittell.com |
| **SECTION 3**<br>**The New Americans**<br>**pp. 883–885** | • New immigrants increase diversity.<br>• Some Americans think that immigrants take jobs and that too many enter illegally.<br>• Recent immigrants make many contributions. | **In-Depth Resources: Unit 9**<br>• Setting the Stage, p. 55<br>• Guided Reading, p. 59<br>• Primary Source, p. 65<br>• Literature Selection, pp. 66–68<br>• Reteaching Activity, p. 71 | **Warm-Up Transparency WT32**<br>**Humanities Transparency HT64**<br>• Pot Luck Quilt<br>**Critical Thinking Transparency CT94**<br>• Setting the Stage<br>**Critical Thinking Transparency CT96**<br>• Visual Summary<br>**ClassZone:** www.mcdougallittell.com |

PE Pupil's Edition
Copymaster
Overhead Transparency
Audio Library
CD-ROM
Internet

## ASSESSMENT

PE **Chapter Assessment,** pp. 886–887

**Formal Assessment**
- Chapter Tests, Forms A and B, pp. 461–468

**Alternative Assessment Book**

**Electronic Teacher Tools with Test Maker**

PE **Section Assessment,** p. 877

**Formal Assessment**
- Section Quiz, p. 458

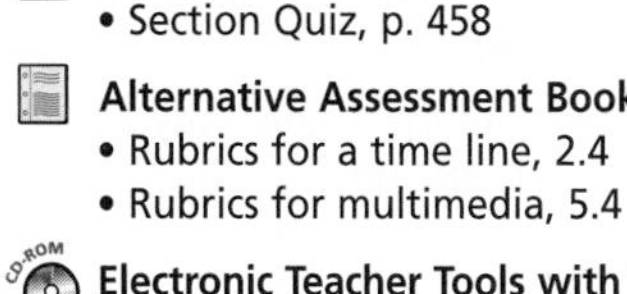

**Alternative Assessment Book**
- Rubrics for a time line, 2.4
- Rubrics for multimedia, 5.4

**Electronic Teacher Tools with Test Maker**

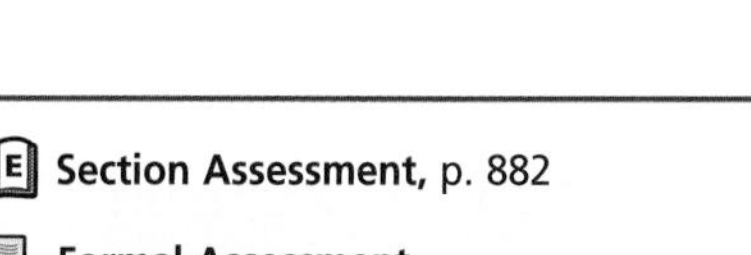

PE **Section Assessment,** p. 882

**Formal Assessment**
- Section Quiz, p. 459

**Alternative Assessment Book**
- Rubrics for a Web page, 5.1
- Rubrics for a skit, 3.1

**Electronic Teacher Tools with Test Maker**

PE **Section Assessment,** p. 885

**Formal Assessment**
- Section Quiz, p. 460

**Alternative Assessment Book**
- Rubrics for a table, 2.2
- Rubrics for a speech, 3.6

**Electronic Teacher Tools with Test Maker**

## CUSTOMIZING FOR INDIVIDUAL NEEDS

### Students Acquiring English/ESL

**Reading Study Guide** (English and Spanish), pp. 303–310

**Access for Students Acquiring English/ESL: Spanish Translations,** pp. 211–216

**Chapter Summaries on CD** (English and Spanish)

### Less Proficient Readers

**Reading Study Guide** (English and Spanish), pp. 303–310

**Chapter Summaries on CD** (English and Spanish)

### Gifted and Talented Students

**In-Depth Resources: Unit 9**
- Enrichment Activity, p. 72

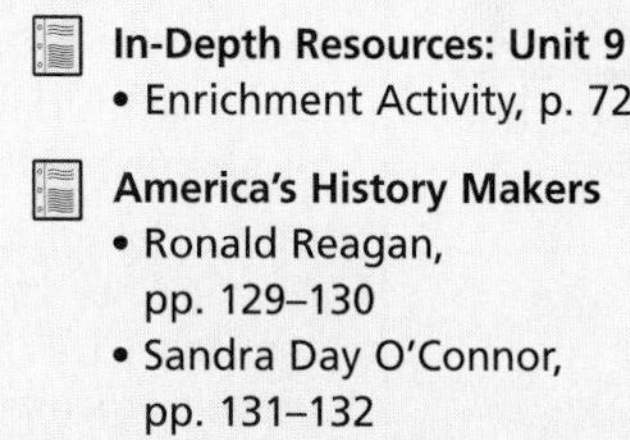

**America's History Makers**
- Ronald Reagan, pp. 129–130
- Sandra Day O'Connor, pp. 131–132

## CROSS-CURRICULAR CONNECTIONS

### Culture

Fernandez-Shaw, Carlos M. ***The Hispanic Presence in North America from 1492 to Today.*** Trans. by Alfonso Bertodano Stourton and others. New York: Facts on File, 1991. A valuable reference tool includes a general historical overview and a state-by-state study.

### Economics

O'Toole, Thomas. ***Global Economics.*** Minneapolis: Lerner, 1991. Emphasizes the contrasts between overdeveloped and underdeveloped countries.

### Science

Wunch, Susi Trautmann. ***The Adventures of Soujourner: The Mission to Mars That Thrilled the World.*** New York: Mikaya Press, 1998. Wonderful story of the voyage and the breathtaking photos it supplied.

### World History

Andryszewki, Tricia. ***Kosovo: The Splintering of Yugoslavia.*** Brookfield, CT: Millbook Press, 1999. Reviews the history of the area and reports on the success and failure of mediations.

### Interdisciplinary Projects, pp. 187–192

- Math: Computers and Binary Language
- Science: Robots
- Language Arts: Metaphors for a Muticultural Society
- Art: Computer Art

### Literature

Allison, Anthony. ***Hear These Voices: Youth at the Edge of the Millennium.*** New York: Dutton, 1999. Mesmerizing testimonies from teenagers from around the world who have endured addiction, AIDS, neglect, and abuse. The book also contains interviews with adults who have intervened to help. For mature students.

Filipovic, Zlata. ***Zlata's Diary: A Child's Life in Sarajevo.*** New York: Penguin Books, 1995. The famous wartime diary of a girl records both ordinary events and the horrors of war.

Lutzeier, Elizabeth. ***The Wall.*** New York: Holiday House, 1992. Two teenage girls come together as friends in East Germany and become involved in the turbulent events just before the fall of the Berlin Wall.

### McDougal Littell Literature Connections

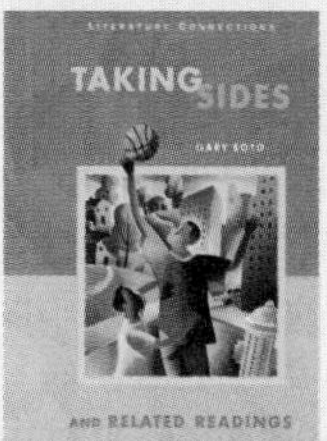


Gary Soto

***Taking Sides***

A Mexican-American youth has trouble adjusting after he moves from the inner city to the suburbs.

## ENRICHMENT ACTIVITIES

PE **Pupil's Edition, pp. 870–889**
**Interact with History,** p. 871
**Technology of the Time,** p. 880
**History Workshop,** pp. 888–889

**In-Depth Resources: Unit 9**
- Geography Application: U.S. Trade, 1995, pp. 62–63
- Primary Source: from *The Road Ahead,* p. 64
- Primary Source: "A Rainbow Century" by Clarence Page, p. 65
- Literature Selection, pp. 66–68
- History Workshop Resources, p. 73

**America's History Makers**
- Ronald Reagan, pp. 129–130
- Sandra Day O'Connor, pp. 131–132

**Outline Map Activities**
- The Former Yugoslavia, 1999, pp. 63–64

**Why It Matters Now**
- Changes in Modern America, pp. 63–64

# CHAPTER 32 PACING GUIDE

**LESSON PLAN OPTIONS (50-MINUTE PERIOD)** **(TE) = Teacher's Edition (PE) = Pupil's Edition**

| | TEACHER-DIRECTED ACTIVITIES<br>Class Time: 15 minutes | STUDENT-CENTERED ACTIVITIES<br>Class Time: 25 minutes | INDIVIDUAL ACTIVITIES<br>Class Time: 10 minutes |
|---|---|---|---|
| **DAY 1**<br>Introduction<br>pp. 870–872 | **Presentation Options**<br>• Begin with a class discussion of the picture on p. 870 **(PE)**.<br>• Lead a class discussion on the "What Do You Know?" question in Setting the Stage, p. 872. Then introduce the graphic organizer for the chapter **(PE)**. | **Options for Cooperative Learning**<br>• Have student groups discuss the Interact with history questions, p. 871 **(PE)**.<br>• Have student groups respond to the "What Do You Want to Know?" question in Setting the Stage, p. 872 **(PE)**. | **Head Start on Homework Options**<br>• Have students skim Section 1 Main Idea, Why It Matters Now, Terms & Names, and the main headings, p. 873 **(PE)**.<br>• Have students begin Guided Reading activity and Building Vocabulary sheet. |
| **DAY 2**<br>Section 1<br>pp. 873–877 | **Presentation Options**<br>• Begin with the 5-Minute Warm-Up, p. 873 **(TE)**.<br>• Review the Section 1 Main Idea, Why It Matters Now, and Terms & Names, p. 873 **(PE)**.<br>• Lead the students through the Skillbuilder Mini-Lesson: Evaluating, p. 875 **(TE)**. | **Options for Cooperative Learning**<br>• Divide students into groups to complete the Interdisciplinary Link, Mathematics: Defense Spending and the National Debt, p. 874 **(TE)**.<br>• Have student pairs work together to complete one of the Activity Options in the Section 1 Assessment, p. 877 **(PE)**. | **Head Start on Homework Options**<br>• Have students begin working on Section 1 Assessment, p. 877 **(PE)**.<br>• Have students complete the Technology of the Time questions, p. 880 **(PE)**. |
| **DAY 3**<br>Section 2<br>pp. 878–882 | **Presentation Options**<br>• Begin with the 5-Minute Warm-Up, p. 878 **(TE)**.<br>• Choose 5 key questions for Objectives 1–4 to discuss with the class, pp. 878–881 **(TE)**.<br>• Discuss the computer revolution using the Technology of the Time feature, p. 880 **(TE)**. | **Options for Cooperative Learning**<br>• Divide students into groups to complete the Interdisciplinary Link, Science: Medical Miracles, p. 881 **(TE)**.<br>• Have student pairs work together to complete one of the Activity Options in the Section 2 Assessment, p. 882 **(PE)**. | **Head Start on Homework Options**<br>• Have students begin working on Section 2 Assessment, p. 882 **(PE)**.<br>• Have students complete the Skillbuilder and the History from Visuals Extension activities, p. 884 **(PE, TE)**. |
| **DAY 4**<br>Section 3<br>pp. 883–885 | **Presentation Options**<br>• Begin with the 5-Minute Warm-Up, p. 883 **(TE)**.<br>• Choose 5 key questions for Objectives 1–4 to discuss with the class, pp. 883–885 **(TE)**.<br>• Lead the class through the Critical Thinking Activity, p. 885 **(TE)**. | **Options for Cooperative Learning**<br>• Divide students into groups and have them complete the History Workshop, pp. 888–889 **(PE)**.<br>• Have student pairs work together to complete one of the Activity Options in the Section 3 Assessment, p. 885 **(PE)**. | **Head Start on Homework Options**<br>• Have students complete the Setting the Stage graphic organizer for the chapter, p. 872 **(PE)**.<br>• Have students begin working on the Chapter Assessment, pp. 886–887 **(PE)**.<br>• Prepare for Chapter Test<br>**Formal Assessment,** pp. 461–468 |

**TEACHER-TESTED ACTIVITY** Pam Kniffin and Tammy Leiber, Navasota Junior High School, Navasota, Texas

## GREAT AMERICANS POSTAGE STAMP COLLECTION

**Class Time** Two class periods

**Task** Choosing a contemporary American to honor on a postage stamp

**Purpose** To identify people who have had a significant, positive impact on American society from 1980 to the present

**Supplies Needed**

- News articles and other reference and biographical materials on contemporary Americans in various fields—science, education, business, politics, and the arts
- Colored pencils or markers and drawing paper

**Activity** Ask each student to design a postage stamp in honor of a person he or she feels should be recognized for bettering American life. Students should present drawings of their stamps with statements explaining their choices to a panel of student judges. The design of the stamp should indicate the nature of its subject's achievements. In the statement, each student should try to persuade the judges that the person he or she has chosen is worthy of this honor.

## BLOCK SCHEDULING — LESSON PLAN OPTIONS (90-MINUTE PERIOD)

### DAY 1

**Interact with History,** p. 871
**Class Time** 20 minutes

Options for pacing and variety:
- Time Saver Assign the "What Do You Think?" questions to students as a homework assignment. Have students share their answers to the question "What do you think the United States and the world need most from your generation?" with the class. **Class Time** 15 minutes

**Setting the Stage,** p. 872
**Class Time** 20 minutes

Options for pacing and variety:
- Time Saver For a homework assignment, have students make a list of what they think are current trends in one of these areas: technology, politics, economics, immigration. **Class Time** 10 minutes

**Section 1,** pp. 873–877
**Class Time** 50 minutes

Options for pacing and variety:
- Peer Evaluation Have student pairs work together to complete the Taking Notes chart in the Section Assessment and prepare a written response to the Taking Notes question. **Class Time** 15 minutes
- Internet Extend students' background knowledge of the fall of the Berlin Wall by visiting www.mcdougallittell.com **Class Time** 20 minutes

### DAY 2

**Section 2,** pp. 878–882
**Class Time** 45 minutes

Options for pacing and variety:
- Team Teaching Invite a science teacher to the class to discuss with students some of the recent advances taking place in medical science or technology. **Class Time** 20 minutes
- Time Saver Have students read the Technology of the Time feature on page 880 as a homework assignment and complete the Connect to History and Connect to Today questions. **Class Time** 5 minutes

**Section 3,** pp. 883–885
**Class Time** 45 minutes

Options for pacing and variety:
- Peer Teaching Have students turn each of the subsection headings for Section 3 into questions and prepare answers to these questions. Ask students to exchange questions with a partner and prepare answers to the questions received. **Class Time** 20 minutes
- History on Film Extend students' background knowledge of current trends in immigration by viewing *The Golden Door: Our Nation of Immigrants.* Knowledge Unlimited, 1996. **Class Time** 25 minutes

**Chapter 32 Assessment,** pp. 886–887
**Class Time** 40 minutes

Options for pacing and variety:
- Peer Teaching Working in groups of three have students add one event to the Millennium time line in the Visual Summary on page 886 for each year since 1999. **Class Time** 20 minutes
- Peer Evaluation Have student pairs answer the Interpreting Maps question in the Chapter Assessment. Have each pair make up one additional question about the map. **Class Time** 10 minutes

## CHAPTER 32 OBJECTIVE

The student will describe how conservatives changed domestic policy and how world events affected U.S. foreign policy. The student will analyze how technology changed daily life and how immigrants helped create a more diverse society.

# Entering a New Millennium

## 1981–present



### HISTORY FROM VISUALS

**Interpreting the Photograph** Have students study the photograph and read the caption. Ask how viewing a picture on a Web site is different from looking at one in a museum or an art gallery. How do this painter's tools and goals differ from those of a traditional artist? **Possible Responses** The lighting and position of a painting in a museum are the same for each visitor; viewers may be almost anywhere when they see computer art. Traditional artists use paints and canvas to create work to last for centuries. This artist uses computer technology to create art that lasts only a short time.

**Extension** Have the students do research to find definitions of *computer art* and *cyber art.*

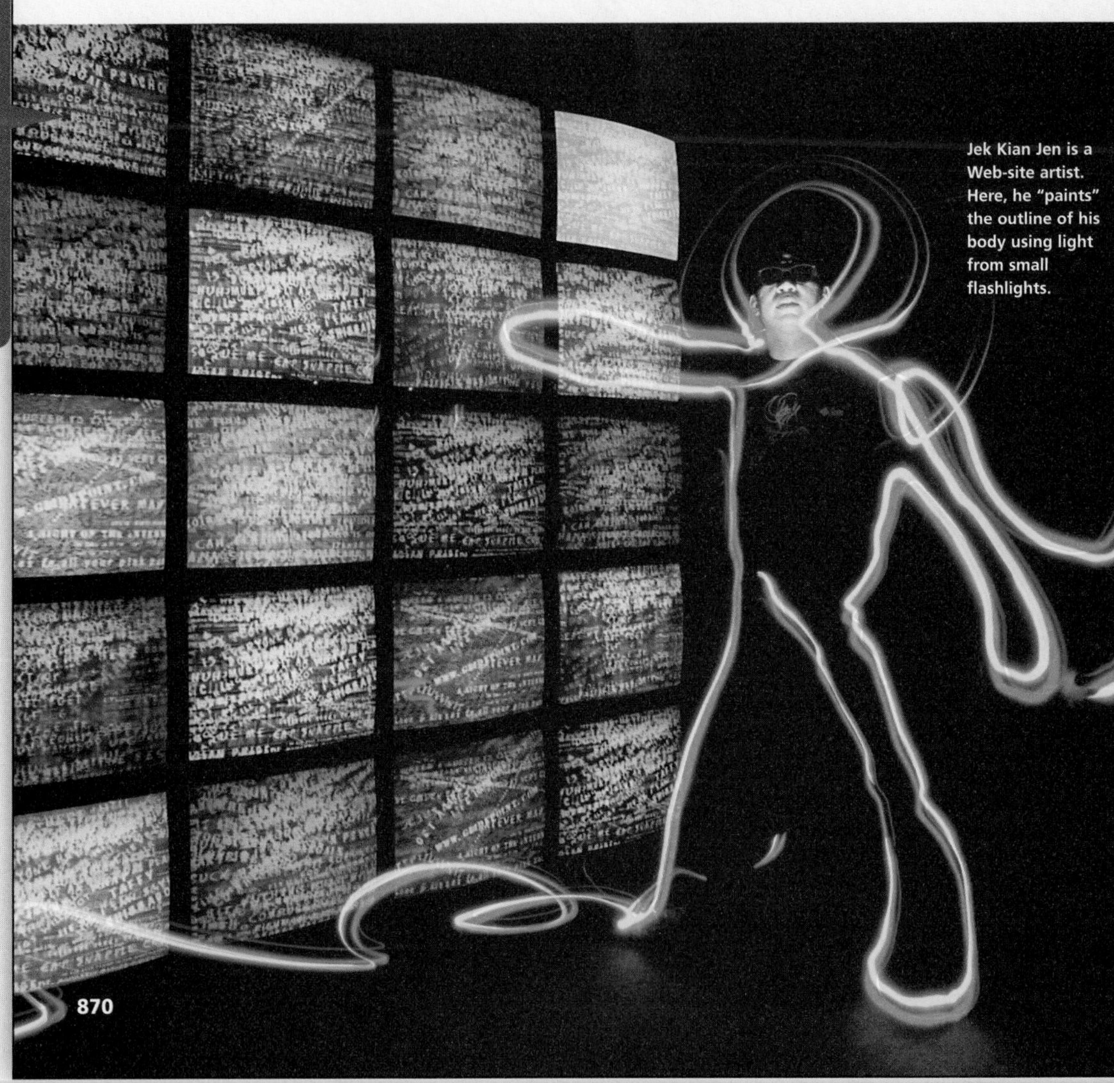

Jek Kian Jen is a Web-site artist. Here, he "paints" the outline of his body using light from small flashlights.



### RECOMMENDED RESOURCES

**BOOKS FOR THE TEACHER**

Countryman, Edward. ***Americans: A Collision of Histories.*** New York: Hill and Wang, 1996. Bancroft Prize winner describes the interactions of ethnic groups in our history.

Evans, Harold. ***The American Century.*** New York: Knopf, 1998. Large-format, magnificently designed and illustrated, this prize-winning look at the 20th century is epic in scope and in conception.

LaFeber, Walter. ***Michael Jordan and the New Global Capitalism.*** New York: Norton, 1999. A prominent historian combines economics, biography, and social history to trace the effects of the partnership among basketball, Nike, and high-tech telecommunications.

**SOFTWARE**

***SkyTrip America.*** Discovery Channel Multimedia, 1996. Soar through time and space and keep a journal as you travel.

**VIDEO**

***Desert Triumph.*** CBS, 1991. Compiled from news reports on the Gulf War.

**INTERNET**

For more about the Berlin Wall, visit www.mcdougallittell.com

## Interact *with* History

Sixteen-year-old Andre McGregor is already a high-tech businessman.

Shown holding a computer board, he designs Web pages. He also tutors adults in how to use technology.

**The time is four years from now, and you're about to finish high school. Your friends ask about your plans for the future. At graduation, the speaker urges your class not just to focus on earning money but also to care about making the world a better place. How can you do that?**

### What Do You Think?

- What are your talents, and how could you use them to benefit both yourself and society?
- What things do you really enjoy doing?
- What do you think the United States and the world need most from your generation?

# *What can you contribute to the future?*

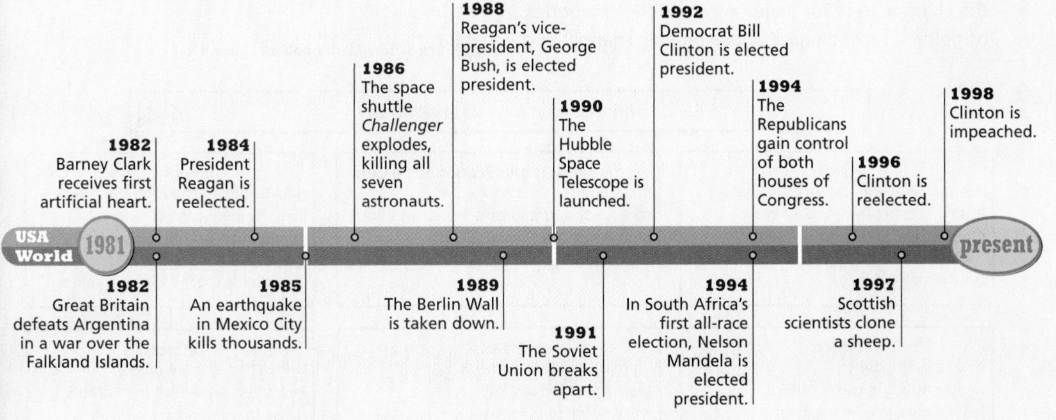

USA
World
1981
present
1982 Barney Clark receives first artificial heart.
1984 President Reagan is reelected.
1986 The space shuttle *Challenger* explodes, killing all seven astronauts.
1988 Reagan's vice-president, George Bush, is elected president.
1990 The Hubble Space Telescope is launched.
1992 Democrat Bill Clinton is elected president.
1994 The Republicans gain control of both houses of Congress.
1996 Clinton is reelected.
1998 Clinton is impeached.
1982 Great Britain defeats Argentina in a war over the Falkland Islands.
1985 An earthquake in Mexico City kills thousands.
1989 The Berlin Wall is taken down.
1991 The Soviet Union breaks apart.
1994 In South Africa's first all-race election, Nelson Mandela is elected president.
1997 Scottish scientists clone a sheep.

## Interact *with* History

### OBJECTIVES

- To help students identify some ways in which their generation is likely to help the world
- To help students connect with the people and events they will study in this chapter

### What Do You Think?

1. Students might define talents broadly as the activities they enjoy. Their talents can be their special interests, such as singing, dancing, or computer programming.
2. Students might think about courses they like in school; hobbies; sports they enjoy playing; clubs they belong to; and in-school or after-school activities they take part in.
3. Students might discuss the types of national and international problems the United States and the world are likely to face when they are adults. Examine the different ways adults today participate in their local communities and in state and national government decision making to solve problems at each level.

### *What can you contribute to the future?*

Encourage students to focus on their strengths and to consider role models among people in their community. They may also consider organizations that are involved in social, political, and environmental causes. Remind them that working with others is often essential to being effective.

### MAKING PERSONAL CONNECTIONS

Have students describe some of the ways people their age are already working to make the world a better place. They might note examples of teenage entrepreneurs such as Andre McGregor, teenagers involved in volunteer activities, or young stars in the entertainment world.

### TIME LINE DISCUSSION

**World politics changed dramatically in the last two decades of the millennium. In U.S. politics, the conservative trend reached its peak with the elections of Reagan and Bush. Technological advances also produced changes in the lives of many.**

- Which events listed show the influence of technology in our lives? **Possible Responses** artificial heart, space shuttle, Hubble space telescope, cloning of sheep
- Which events illustrate the expansion of democracy? **Possible Responses** the Berlin Wall taken down; South Africa's first all-race election
- Ask students what connection might exist between the fall of the Berlin Wall and the breakup of the Soviet Union. **Possible Response** The collapse of the Wall suggests the weakening of Soviet power.

## BEFORE YOU READ

### Previewing the Theme: Diversity and Unity

Ask students how they think this composite photograph of a possible American of the future would differ from a composite drawing of an American in 1776. Have students name the countries of origin of the first colonists and generalize about the countries of origin of many of today's immigrants.

### What Do You Know?

Have students suggest reasons why immigrants have come to the United States in recent decades. They might think about events in Asia and Latin America, such as wars and economic downturns. Students may also describe ways increasing diversity in the United States has influenced dress styles, music, and eating habits.

 **In-Depth Resources: Unit 9**
- Tracing Themes: Diversity and Unity, p. 56

## READ AND TAKE NOTES

### Reading Strategy: Recognizing Effects

Tell students that recognizing effects involves understanding the relationship between policies and events and their corresponding consequences. Point out the three categories listed on the chart under the title "Influences on America, 1981–Today." As students read, have them take notes about the effects of each major event.

 **In-Depth Resources: Unit 9**
- Setting the Stage, p. 55

 **Critical Thinking Transparency CT94**
- Setting the Stage

# Chapter 32 SETTING THE STAGE

## BEFORE YOU READ

SPECIAL ISSUE
TIME
Take a good look at this woman. She was created by a computer from a mix of several races. What you see is a remarkable preview of . . .
THE NEW FACE OF AMERICA
How Immigrants Are Shaping the World's First Multicultural Society


**This magazine cover is symbolic of U.S. diversity. To create it, *Time* used a computer to blend the features of people of many different races.**

### Previewing the Theme

**Diversity and Unity** As this chapter explains, during the 1980s and 1990s, Republicans and Democrats fought for control of the national government. World events also affected U.S. politics. At the same time, technology changed daily life, and U.S. society became more diverse as immigrants from around the world continued to come to America.

### What Do You Know?

How closely do you follow current events? What do you think are the major trends in the United States today?

**THINK ABOUT**
- political events in the news
- the latest changes in technology
- how immigration is affecting the United States

### What Do You Want to Know?

What would you like to know about our most recent presidents? What questions do you have about technology? What do you want to learn about recent patterns of immigration? Record your questions in your notebook before you read this chapter.

## READ AND TAKE NOTES

**Reading Strategy: Recognizing Effects** The consequences of an event are its effects. As you read the chapter, look for major events in the categories of politics, technological and economic change, and immigration. Notice how these events affected U.S. society. Record your information on a chart like the one below.

 See Skillbuilder Handbook, page R10.

**Influences on America, 1981–Today**

| Politics | Technological and Economic Change | Immigration |
|---|---|---|
| Reagan's election, conservative goals<br>Bush's election, Persian Gulf War<br>Clinton's election, struggles with Congress, and impeachment<br>conflict in Kosovo | growing use of technology<br>service economy, information revolution<br>global economy, downsizing<br>scientific breakthroughs | non-European immigration<br>illegal immigration<br>immigrants contribute to arts, sports, business<br>immigrants share American values |
| **Effects** | **Effects** | **Effects** |
| disgust with politics<br>people afraid to run for office<br>fear of involvement in world | more connected to world<br>fears about job security<br>workers learning new skills | United States more diverse<br>mixed feelings about immigrants<br>richer culture and arts |



## TEACHING STRATEGY

### READING THE CHAPTER

This is a thematic chapter focusing on the effects of major events in America from 1980 to the present. When they complete the chart, encourage students to review the information. Ask them whether they believe that one policy or event had a more profound effect on the United States than the others. If so, ask them to support their opinion with data.

### ALTERNATIVE ASSESSMENT

The Chapter Assessment describes three activities for alternative assessment on page 887. You may wish to have students work on these activities during the course of the chapter and then present them at the end.

# 1 Conservatives Reshape Politics

**TERMS & NAMES**
Ronald Reagan
supply-side economics
Iran-Contra affair
George Bush
Persian Gulf War
Bill Clinton
NAFTA

**MAIN IDEA**

The country became more conservative, leading to Republican political victories.

**WHY IT MATTERS NOW**

In response, the Democratic Party became less liberal and even adopted some conservative ideas.



## SECTION OBJECTIVES

1. To identify Reagan's conservative goals and his beliefs about communism
2. To evaluate the Bush presidency
3. To analyze Clinton's conflicts with Congress
4. To explain the causes of the war in Kosovo

**CRITICAL THINKING**

Analyzing Causes, pp. 874, 876
Summarizing, p. 875
Recognizing Effects, p. 877
Drawing Conclusions, p. 877

## FOCUS & MOTIVATE

### 5-MINUTE WARM-UP

**Recognizing Effects** These questions focus on differences between Democrats and Republicans in the 1980s.

1. Look at the campaign button on page 873. Who are the two men shown on the button? What office are they running for?
2. Why are televised debates an important part of modern political campaigns?

 **Warm-Up Transparency WT32**

## INSTRUCT

**INSTRUCT: OBJECTIVE 1**

**Reagan's Conservative Goals/ A Tough Anti-Communist Stand**

Key Questions
- What were Reagan's goals for his presidency?
- What steps did Reagan and Gorbachev take to improve U.S.-Soviet relations?
- What was the Iran-Contra affair?

 **In-Depth Resources: Unit 9**
- Guided Reading, p. 57

 **America's History Makers**
- Sandra Day O'Connor, pp. 131–132

 **Critical Thinking Transparency CT95**
- Cause and Effect: Changing American Life

## ONE AMERICAN'S STORY

**As the owner of a popular restaurant, Mike Savic knew the mood in his working-class Chicago neighborhood. In the fall of 1980, most of his customers were frightened. Unemployment and inflation were rising. President Jimmy Carter seemed to have no answers. Yet, Carter was asking the American people to reelect him. Most of Savic's neighbors had supported Carter in 1976, but now they turned to Carter's Republican opponent, former California governor Ronald Reagan.**

This campaign button is from the 1980 debate between Jimmy Carter and Ronald Reagan.

*A VOICE FROM THE PAST*

People have been talking. . . . Some of them in this neighborhood have been laid off four, six months. Or their neighbor is out of work. People don't like to see their neighbors out of work. And they've been scared. . . . The ones who'd been talking that they were for Carter, well, they changed. They were talking different. They were going for Reagan.

**Mike Savic,** quoted in the *Chicago Tribune,* November 6, 1980

**In 1980, millions of Democrats voted for Reagan in the hope that he could fix the economy. With their help, Reagan won the election. This section covers the presidencies of Reagan and his two successors.**

## 1 Reagan's Conservative Goals

President Reagan was a conservative. In his 1981 inaugural address, he declared, "Government is not the answer to the problem; government is the problem." Reagan pursued the following conservative goals.

1. **Lower Taxes.** Reagan preached **supply-side economics**. This theory held that if people paid fewer taxes, they would save more money. Banks could loan that money to businesses, who could invest in ways to improve productivity. The supply of goods would increase, driving down prices. At Reagan's urging, Congress lowered income taxes by 25 percent over three years.
2. **Deregulation.** The president deregulated, or eased restrictions on, many industries. Reagan believed that business would grow more rapidly if government interfered with it less.



## RECOMMENDED RESOURCES

 **In-Depth Resources: Unit 9**
- Guided Reading, p. 57
- Building Vocabulary, p. 60
- Skillbuilder Practice, p. 61
- Reteaching Activity, p. 69

**Reading Study Guide** (Spanish and English), pp. 303–304

 **Economics in History**
- Reaganomics, p. 32

 **Outline Map Activities**
- The Former Yugoslavia, 1999, pp. 63–64

 **America's History Makers**
- Ronald Reagan, pp. 129–130
- Sandra Day O'Connor, pp. 131–132

 **Formal Assessment**
- Section Quiz, p. 458

 **Alternative Assessment**
- Rubrics, 2.4
- Rubrics, 5.4

 **Access for Students Acquiring English/ESL**
- Guided Reading, p. 211
- Skillbuilder Practice, p. 214

Technology Resources

 **Critical Thinking Trans. CT95**
- Cause and Effect: Changing American Life

 **Geography Transparency GT32**
- Cold War Ends, 1989–1990

 **Electronic Teacher Tools with Test Maker**

## AMERICA'S HISTORY MAKERS

**Ronald Reagan**

Historians agree that Reagan was a skillful campaigner and a gifted public speaker. Before entering politics, he had been an actor for nearly 30 years and had appeared in more than 50 movies. In his speeches, Reagan repeatedly stressed traditional values and focused on such simple, easy-to-understand themes as the value of work, the family, patriotism, and self-reliance.

**Possible Response: It helps people feel more confident about the future.**

 **America's History Makers**
- Ronald Reagan, pp. 129–130

 **Economics in History**
- Reaganomics, p. 32

## MORE ABOUT . . .

**Iran-Contra Affair**

In 1985, Reagan officials arranged for the CIA to buy arms from the Department of Defense and sell them to private individuals who in turn sold them to Iran in exchange for promises of help in getting hostages released. In November 1987, a joint report of congressional committees held Reagan accountable for the "secrecy, deception, and disdain for the law" that marked the affair.

## INSTRUCT: OBJECTIVE 2

**Bush and a Changing World**

Key Questions
- How did Gorbachev and Yeltsin differ in their attitudes toward communism?
- What led to the breakup of the Soviet Union?
- What were the causes and the outcome of the Persian Gulf War?
- Why did Bush face problems in his 1992 reelection bid?

 **Geography Transparency GT32**
- Cold War Ends, 1989–1990

### AMERICA'S HISTORY MAKERS

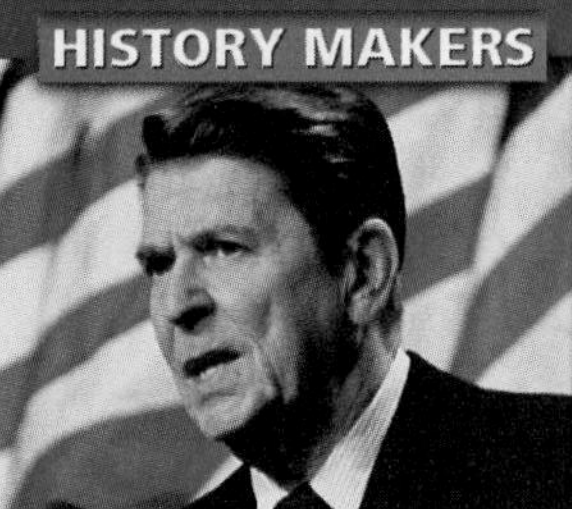

**RONALD REAGAN**
**1911–**

One reason for Ronald Reagan's popularity was his unfailing optimism at a time when many Americans felt uncertain. Not even an assassination attempt could dampen his spirits.

In 1981, a gunman shot the president. When Reagan's wife, Nancy, arrived at the hospital, Reagan told her, "Honey, I forgot to duck."

In addition, he remarked to the doctors who were about to operate on him, "Please tell me you're Republicans."

**Why might it be important for a leader to convey a sense of optimism and high spirits?**

3. **Fewer Government Programs.** Reagan fought to end or weaken many government programs, from affirmative action to environmental regulations.
4. **A Conservative Supreme Court.** Reagan named three conservative judges to the Supreme Court. One of them, Sandra Day O'Connor, was the first woman to sit on the nation's highest court.

At first, inflation rose, and unemployment stayed high. But by 1983, inflation decreased, and more people found jobs. Business boomed. Even so, Reagan's policies created a problem. Because of the tax cut, the federal government took in less money and had to resort to deficit spending. As a result, the national debt doubled from 1981 to 1986.

Vocabulary
**deficit spending:** using borrowed money to fund government programs

## A Tough Anti-Communist Stand

Reagan opposed communism. To compete militarily with the Soviet Union, he began the most expensive arms buildup in history. It cost more than $2 trillion.

In 1985, Mikhail Gorbachev became the new leader of the Soviet Union. He and Reagan met four times to discuss improving U.S.-Soviet relations and easing the threat of nuclear war. They signed the Intermediate-Range Nuclear Force (INF) Treaty in 1987. Under that treaty, the two countries agreed to destroy all of their medium-range missiles.

The Reagan administration also decided to support the anti-Communist side in several conflicts, including two Central American civil wars. In El Salvador, the United States backed the government against Communist-led rebels. In Nicaragua, America provided aid to anti-Communist rebels known as Contras.

This aid resulted in a scandal, known as the **Iran-Contra affair.** In 1986, Americans learned that the U.S. government had sold weapons to Iran in return for help in freeing American hostages in the Middle East. The money from these sales went to the Contras. This action violated a law that barred the U.S. government from funding the rebels. President Reagan claimed he never knew about the deal. But investigators concluded that he should have kept track of what his administration was doing.

*Reading* **History**
**A. Analyzing Causes** Why did investigators hold Reagan responsible for the Iran-Contra affair?
**A. Answer** He was the head of the administration and should have kept track of what his staff was doing.

## 2 Bush and a Changing World

Despite the scandal, Reagan and his administration remained popular. In 1988, Reagan's vice-president, **George Bush,** ran for president and won. During his presidency, dramatic foreign events took place.

In 1989, several Eastern European countries ended Communist rule. This angered old-time Communists in the Soviet Union. In August 1991, a group of them tried to take over the Soviet government. Boris Yeltsin, a Russian reform leader, fought the takeover attempt and won.



### ACTIVITY OPTIONS

**INTERDISCIPLINARY LINK: MATHEMATICS** — BLOCK SCHEDULING

**DEFENSE SPENDING AND THE NATIONAL DEBT**

**Class Time** One class period

**Task** Making a graph showing the national debt and defense spending, 1981–1986

**Purpose** To compare increases in defense spending and in the national debt during the Reagan administration

**Supplies Needed**
- Calculator
- Graph paper
- Colored pencils

**Activity** Tell students that at the same time that Reagan cut taxes, he also began the largest peacetime military buildup in U.S. history. Give students these data on the national debt and on defense spending. Have them make a line graph comparing the data. All numbers are in billions of dollars. Then have them write a two-sentence generalization about the data.

| | 1981 | 1982 | 1983 | 1984 | 1985 | 1986 |
|---|---|---|---|---|---|---|
| Debt | 997.9 | 1,142.0 | 1,377.2 | 1,572.3 | 1,823.1 | 2,125.3 |
| Defense | 180.5 | 209.3 | 234.7 | 253.0 | 279.0 | 299.7 |

Unlike Gorbachev, who wanted to reform communism, Yeltsin and others wanted to get rid of it. One by one, the republics that made up the Soviet Union declared their independence from it. In December 1991, Yeltsin and the leaders of these nations joined in a loose alliance called the Commonwealth of Independent States (CIS). The Soviet Union, once a superpower, was gone. Its breakup marked the end of the Cold War.

A crisis also erupted in the Middle East. In August 1990, Iraq invaded its neighbor Kuwait—a major supplier of oil. The United States, led by Bush, and the United Nations (UN) organized a group of 39 nations to free Kuwait by fighting the **Persian Gulf War.** In mid-January 1991, they began bombing Iraqi military targets. A month later, ground forces moved into Kuwait and drove the Iraqis out of that country.

*Reading History*
**B. Summarizing** What were two major world events that happened during George Bush's presidency?
**B. Answer** the end of the Cold War and the Persian Gulf War

The war's success boosted George Bush's popularity, and he seemed certain to win reelection in 1992. Then the economy stalled. By the spring of 1992, the U.S. unemployment rate had climbed to around 7 percent—a six-year high. Americans began to think that Bush was good at foreign policy but ineffective with problems at home. In November, they elected his Democratic opponent, Arkansas governor **Bill Clinton.**

**Connections TO WORLD HISTORY**

**THE BERLIN WALL FALLS**

Communists built the Berlin Wall in 1961 to separate Communist East Berlin from West Berlin. In November 1989, as communism began to fall, East Germans tore down the wall. The photograph below shows Germans celebrating the opening of the wall. Andreas Ramos witnessed the event.

*The final slab was moved away. A stream of East Germans began to pour through. . . . Looking around, I saw an indescribable joy in people's faces. It was the end of the government telling people what not to do, it was the end of the Wall, the war, the East, the West.*

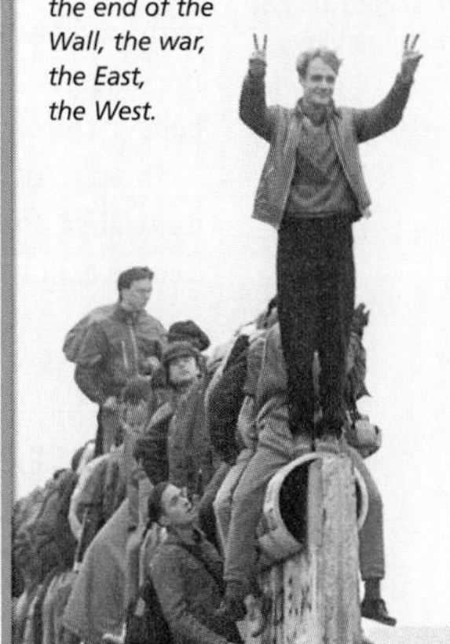

## 3 Clinton's Fights with Congress

One of President Clinton's first acts was to try to reform the health-care system. Millions of Americans had no insurance, and health-care costs were rising sharply. Clinton asked his wife, Hillary Rodham Clinton, to design a health-care plan—which she presented to Congress in 1993. Opponents criticized the plan as costing too much, and Congress chose not to vote on it. But it did pass a law allowing workers to keep their medical insurance when they change jobs.

**Background** Most developed countries have nationalized health insurance, a government program that pays for the health care of most citizens. The United States does not.

Clinton did win passage of the North American Free Trade Agreement **(NAFTA)** in 1993. NAFTA would eventually eliminate tariffs in an effort to increase trade among Mexico, Canada, and the United States.

In the 1994 elections, Republicans took control of both houses of Congress. Clinton and the new Congress could not agree on a budget for 1995. Because funding was uncertain, government agencies shut down twice in late 1995. The American public grew angry with both sides. Finally, they reached a budget agreement.

The two sides did work together to pass welfare reform, a long-time conservative goal. In August 1996, Clinton signed a bill ending the federal government's guaranteed aid to needy families. The law gave states grants of money to spend on welfare. It also cut the length of time people could receive benefits.





### Connections TO WORLD HISTORY

**The Berlin Wall Falls**
During the 1950s, Germans could travel fairly freely from one part of Berlin to the other. As dissatisfaction with communism grew, East Germans fled to West Germany in increasing numbers. By 1961, more than 1,000 East Germans were escaping to West Berlin every day. East Germany built the concrete and barbed wire Berlin Wall in August 1961 to prevent East Germans from leaving. The Wall became a symbol for rigid and, at times, deadly state control.

### MORE ABOUT . . .

**Persian Gulf War**
The Persian Gulf region sustained extensive environmental damage during the war. The Iraqis set hundreds of Kuwaiti oil wells on fire. The smoke from these fires caused serious air pollution in Iran, Iraq, Kuwait, and parts of west and southwest Asia. During the war, Iraqi soldiers also dumped about 465 million gallons of crude oil into the Persian Gulf, killing wildlife and causing long-term damage to the waters of the gulf.

### INSTRUCT: OBJECTIVE 3

**Clinton's Fights with Congress**
Key Questions
- How successful was President Clinton in working with Congress?
- What was the goal of NAFTA?
- What was the outcome of Clinton's impeachment hearing in the House?

### ACTIVITY OPTIONS

### SKILLBUILDER MINI-LESSON: EVALUATING

BLOCK SCHEDULING

**Explaining the Skill** Historians evaluate everything from the weaknesses of presidents to the reasons for the fall of nations. An important part of making good evaluations is forming standards to evaluate actions or events. One way to evaluate is to look at the positives and negatives of an historical action.

**Applying the Skill** Have students read the second paragraph on this page. Then ask what Bush was trying to accomplish in the Middle East. Next look for statements or negative results of his actions. Then make an overall judgment. Use a diagram to help evaluate the actions.

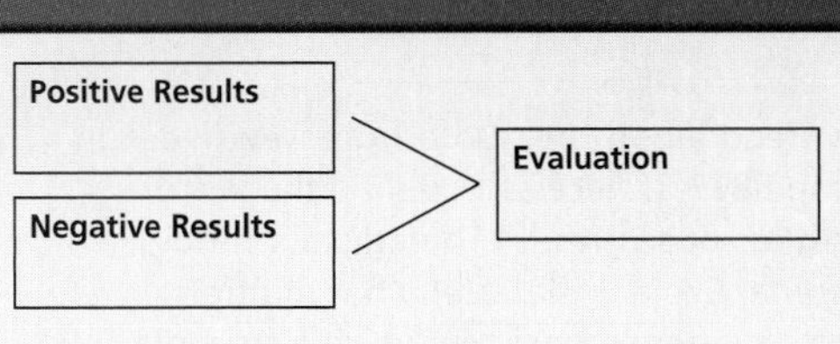


**In-Depth Resources: Unit 9**
- Skillbuilder Practice, p. 61

**MORE ABOUT . . .**

**Impeachment**
Bill Clinton was only the second president in U.S. history to be impeached. The first was Andrew Johnson, who in 1868 was impeached and acquitted by a margin of one vote. In 1974, the Judiciary Committee of the House of Representatives voted three articles of impeachment against Richard Nixon, but he resigned before hearings began. In Clinton's Senate trial, senators acquitted Clinton by a vote of 55 not guilty to 45 guilty on one charge, and 50 to 50 on the other. For conviction, 67 guilty votes were needed.

**INSTRUCT: OBJECTIVE 4**

**War in Kosovo/Ongoing Issues**
Key Questions
- What led to war in Kosovo?
- What was the outcome of the fighting?
- What impact do some people fear the Clinton scandal will have on American attitudes toward politics?

**CRITICAL THINKING ACTIVITY**

**Evaluating** Have students review the quote from Jonathan Alter on page 877. Ask students why intense media coverage might discourage qualified citizens from running for public office. What kinds of questions should newspaper reporters ask politicians? Are there any subjects that should be off limits? Why or why not?

**Class Time** 10 minutes

Weather
Today: Variably cloudy, showers. High 53. Low 44.
Monday: Variably cloudy, warmer. High 62. Low 45.
Details, Page B2.

The Washington Post

Sunday, December 20, 1998

Inside: Book World, TV Week, The Post Magazine, Comics
$1.50

# Clinton Impeached

## House Approves Articles Charging Perjury, Obstruction

Although the House impeached President Clinton, the Senate did not find him guilty.

In 1996, Clinton was reelected. But his second term in office was marked by scandal. Independent Prosecutor Kenneth Starr was assigned to investigate a land deal that Clinton took part in during the 1970s. During that investigation, Starr learned damaging information. The president had had an improper relationship with a young White House intern. And he allegedly had lied under oath about it.

When the charges became public in January 1998, Clinton denied them. Later, he admitted to the relationship but insisted that he hadn't lied under oath. In December 1998, the House of Representatives voted to impeach him. The House approved two articles of impeachment, charging Clinton with perjury and obstruction of justice. In general, Republicans voted for impeachment while Democrats voted against it. This led many people to believe that the prosecution of Clinton was part of a political attack.

**Background**
Clinton was the second president to be impeached, or formally charged with wrongdoing. The first was Andrew Johnson. (See Chapter 18.)

In spite of the charges, Clinton remained popular. The Senate opened its trial of President Clinton in January 1999. Nearly a month later, the Senate acquitted him on both charges. Bill Clinton remained in office.

## War in Kosovo

Despite his troubles at home, the president still had to act as a world leader. In 1999, Clinton helped to lead a group of nations dealing with a crisis in Europe. The Eastern European country of Yugoslavia had been created after World War I. It had six republics, the largest of which was Serbia. Many ethnic and religious groups lived in Yugoslavia. Some of them distrusted the other groups because of ancient grudges.

**Vocabulary**
**ethnic:** cultural

In the early 1990s, four Yugoslav republics declared independence. The Serbs tried to stop them, leading to a bloody war. In time, the UN negotiated peace in the region. The four republics remained independent—leaving only Serbia and Montenegro within Yugoslavia.

Serbia has a region called Kosovo (KAW•suh•VOH), inhabited mostly by people of Albanian descent. The Albanians speak a different language and practice a different religion from the Serbs. Serbia tried to wipe out Albanian culture in Kosovo, so Kosovo sought independence. In the late 1990s, a group called the Kosovo Liberation Army (KLA) began to carry out violent attacks against Serbian officials. The Serbian government bombed villages and fought the KLA. It also began trying to drive the Albanians out of their homes in Serbia by using violence and murder.

**C. Possible Response** The Serbian government used violence and murder in Kosovo; the KLA carried out violent attacks against officials.

*Reading* **History**
**C. Analyzing Causes** How did both sides contribute to the Kosovo conflict?

In 1999, the North Atlantic Treaty Organization (NATO) took action against Serbia. The United States took a lead role in this effort. In March, NATO began to drop bombs on Serbia. Several months of bombing and international negotiations followed. In June 1999, the Serbian leader agreed to withdraw his troops from Kosovo. After the troops pulled out,



**ACTIVITY OPTIONS**

**INDIVIDUAL NEEDS**

**STUDENTS ACQUIRING ENGLISH/ESL**

**Understanding an Opinion** Read aloud the quote from *Newsweek* in "A Voice from the Past" on page 877. If necessary, define the word *contemptuous* as being "worthless or scornful." Then discuss Teddy Roosevelt's use of the word *arena.* Explain that *arena* has multiple meanings. One meaning refers to a general area in which a struggle takes place. For example, the jungle can be an arena for a battle. Encourage students to explain what they think Roosevelt had in mind when he used the phrase *the arena.* Ask students why they think Jonathan Alter believes that it will be difficult to get good people to enter this arena.

officials discovered horrifying evidence of torture and massacres carried out by Serbian forces.

## Ongoing Issues

The conflict in Kosovo left many Americans feeling concerned about U.S. intervention overseas. Even after the Serbian troops withdrew, people wondered how a permanent peace could come to a region that had known such bitter conflicts.

The impeachment of Clinton also caused anxiety. Some people feared that the scandal would fuel the public's growing disgust with politics. Others wondered if the intense media coverage of politicians would discourage citizens from running for public office. Journalist Jonathan Alter saw both happening.

**The Former Yugoslavia, 1999**



D. Answer People will look down on politics, and it will be hard to get good candidates.

*Reading* **History**

**D. Recognizing Effects** What effect does Alter believe the impeachment will have on politics?

> *A VOICE FROM THE PAST*
>
> The country will grow even more contemptuous [scornful] of those who serve in what Teddy Roosevelt called "the arena." Getting good people to run for office will be hard in this meaner political culture.
>
> **Jonathan Alter,** *Newsweek,* October 19, 1998

Despite these worries, many Americans felt excited about the future because of advances in technology. Section 2 discusses those changes.

### *Section 1 Assessment*

**1. Terms & Names**

**Identify:**
- Ronald Reagan
- supply-side economics
- Iran-Contra affair
- George Bush
- Persian Gulf War
- Bill Clinton
- NAFTA

**2. Taking Notes**

Use a chart like the one shown to record important details about the terms of three presidents.

| Reagan | |
|---|---|
| Bush | |
| Clinton | |

What do you think was the greatest achievement by any of these presidents?

**3. Main Ideas**

a. What were the positive and negative effects of Reagan's economic policies?

b. Why was Bush defeated when he ran for reelection?

c. Why did Clinton and other NATO leaders decide to bomb Serbia?

**4. Critical Thinking**

**Drawing Conclusions**
What do you think was the strongest force shaping U.S. politics from 1981 to 2000—economics or foreign affairs?

**THINK ABOUT**
- Reagan's goals and actions
- the events of Bush's presidency
- the events of Clinton's presidency

**ACTIVITY OPTIONS**

**ART**
**TECHNOLOGY**

You have been asked to summarize the politics of the years 1981–2000. Create an **illustrated time line,** or plan part of a **multimedia presentation.**





### HISTORY FROM VISUALS

**Reading the Map** Using a historical atlas, ask students to name the countries shown on the map that were a part of Yugoslavia from the post-World War I period until the early 1990s. **Answer** Slovenia, Croatia, Macedonia, Bosnia-Herzegovina. What was the political status of these four places in 1999? **Answer** They were independent nations.

**Extension** Have students use a world almanac to prepare a chart comparing the current population, ethnic makeup, resources, and GNP of Yugoslavia and the four nations that were once part of it.

**Outline Map Activities**
- The Former Yugoslavia, 1999, pp. 63–64

## ASSESS & RETEACH

**Setting the Stage** Have students fill in the boxes on the chart on politics and its effects.

**Formal Assessment**
- Section Quiz, p. 458

**Critical Thinking Transparency CT94**
- Setting the Stage

### RETEACHING ACTIVITY

Have students make a chart with four columns labeled President, Achievements, Domestic Problems, and Foreign Crises. In the first column, have students list Reagan, Bush, and Clinton. Have students complete the chart with the highlights of each president's term.

| President | Achievements | Domestic Problems | Foreign Crises |
|---|---|---|---|
| Reagan | | | |
| Bush | | | |
| Clinton | | | |

**In-Depth Resources: Unit 9**
- Reteaching Activity, p. 69

### *Section 1 Assessment*

**1. Terms & Names**

**Ronald Reagan,** p. 873
**supply-side economics,** p. 873
**Iran-Contra affair,** p. 874
**George Bush,** p. 874
**Persian Gulf War,** p. 875
**Bill Clinton,** p. 875
**NAFTA,** p. 875

**2. Taking Notes**

Reagan: cut taxes, increased deficit, backed anticommunists in Central America, Iran-Contra affair; Bush: end of Cold War, Persian Gulf War, lost reelection; Clinton: NAFTA, welfare reform, scandal, conflict in Kosovo

Answers will vary.

**3. Main Ideas**

**a.** Positive: inflation and unemployment decreased; Negative: the deficit ballooned **b.** The economy had taken a downturn, and people felt that he was not solving domestic problems. **c.** Serbian attacks on the ethnic Albanian population

**4. Critical Thinking**

Responses will vary, but students should cite evidence to support their opinions.

**ACTIVITY OPTIONS**

**Alternative Assessment**
- Rubrics for a time line, 2.4
- Rubrics for multimedia, 5.4

## SECTION OBJECTIVES

1. To analyze the impact of new technology on daily life and the economy
2. To explain how economic change affected workers in the 1990s
3. To describe the global economy
4. To identify recent scientific breakthroughs

**CRITICAL THINKING**

Drawing Conclusions, p. 879
Analyzing Points of View, p. 881
Identifying Facts and Opinions, p. 882
Forming and Supporting Opinions, p. 882

 **Why It Matters Now**
- Changes in Modern America, pp. 63–64

## FOCUS & MOTIVATE

### 5-MINUTE WARM-UP

**Recognizing Effects** These questions focus on computer technology since the 1940s.

1. Look at the photograph and caption on page 880, top right. In what ways have computers changed since the ENIAC?
2. In what ways have computers changed the lives of all people?

 **Warm-Up Transparency WT32**

## INSTRUCT

### INSTRUCT: OBJECTIVE 

**Technology and Daily Life**

Key Questions
- How have computers and the Internet changed communications and research?
- How do cellular phones differ from conventional telephones?

 **In-Depth Resources: Unit 9**
- Guided Reading, p. 58
- Building Vocabulary, p. 60

 **Reading Study Guide** (Spanish and English), pp. 305–306

# 2 Technological and Economic Changes

**TERMS & NAMES**
Internet
e-commerce
service economy
information revolution
downsizing

| MAIN IDEA | WHY IT MATTERS NOW |
|---|---|
| Advances in science and technology have improved daily life and created a global economy. | Technology continues to change American homes, leisure activities, and workplaces. |

## ONE AMERICAN'S STORY

**In the late 1990s, technology transformed business. One reason was the <u>Internet</u>, a worldwide computer network. Some enterprising people developed <u>e-commerce</u>, business that is conducted over the Internet.**

**Jeff Bezos was a pioneer of e-commerce. In 1994, he decided to open a bookstore on-line. The idea caught on quickly. From 1997 to 1999, the number of customers using his bookstore grew from 2 million to 11 million. Bezos doesn't define his job as selling books but as giving buyers more choice.**

*A VOICE FROM THE PAST*

Our business is helping customers make purchasing decisions. . . . It all has to do with the balance of power shifting away from companies and toward consumers.

**Jeff Bezos,** quoted in "Companies Wired for the Bottom Line," *Newsweek,* September 20, 1999

Jeff Bezos revolutionized the bookselling industry by putting it on-line.

**Although 1999 passed without his company's making a profit, Bezos wasn't worried. He was investing his earnings to make the business grow for the future. Other businesspeople seemed to agree with Bezos's optimism about e-commerce. The number of Internet businesses exploded as the year 2000 approached. Section 2 explains other ways that the Internet and technology changed American life.**

## 1 Technology and Daily Life

As the 20th century drew to a close, thousands of institutions from hospitals to airports to banks relied on computers to perform essential tasks. Computer use also grew in homes and schools. By 1997, about 35 percent of all U.S. households had a personal computer. And from 1985 to 1998, the number of computers in classrooms leaped from 630,000 to more than 8 million.

Computers and the Internet revolutionized both communication and research. Using the Internet, a person can track down information on nearly any subject. Internet users can also send and receive electronic messages called e-mail. In addition, they can shop at on-line stores.

## RECOMMENDED RESOURCES

 **In-Depth Resources: Unit 9**
- Guided Reading, p. 58
- Building Vocabulary, p. 60
- Geography Application: U.S. Trade, 1995, pp. 62–63
- Primary Source, p. 64
- Reteaching Activity, p. 70
- Enrichment Activity, p. 72

**Reading Study Guide** (Spanish and English), pp. 305–306

 **Why It Matters Now**
- Changes in Modern America, pp. 63–64

 **Citizenship Today,** p. 80

 **Formal Assessment**
- Section Quiz, p. 459

 **Alternative Assessment**
- Rubrics, 5.1
- Rubrics, 3.1

 **Access for Students Acquiring English/ESL**
- Guided Reading, p. 212
- Geography Application, pp. 215–216

**Technology Resources**

 **Humanities Transparency HT63**
- Visualization of Internet Traffic

 **Electronic Teacher Tools with Test Maker**

 **ClassZone**
www.mcdougallittell.com

Other forms of new technology have transformed American life. One popular example is the battery-powered cellular telephone. People can carry these phones with them anywhere. Between 1990 and 1997, the number of cellular phone subscribers in the United States grew dramatically from 5.3 million to 55.3 million.

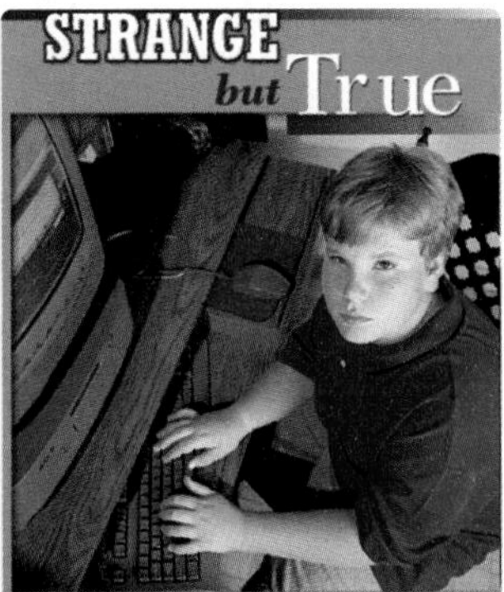


INTERNET 911

In April 1997, 12-year-old Sean Redden was using the Internet at his home in Texas when he saw a startling message: "Help me. I'm having trouble breathing."

The message was from 20-year-old Tarja Laitinen of Finland. While using the Internet, she'd had a severe attack of asthma.

Sean's mother called 911. This led to a series of phone calls that ended up with Tarja's being rushed to a Finnish hospital. Sean, with the help of the Internet, had saved Tarja's life!

## 2 A Changing Economy

For much of the 20th century, manufacturing made up a major share of the U.S. economy. By the year 2000, that had changed drastically. The computer age fueled the growth of the service economy. In a **service economy,** most jobs provide services instead of producing goods. By 1996, about 71 percent of all workers had jobs in the service industry. Many of these jobs—such as lawyers, teachers, engineers, and Web-site designers—focused on providing knowledge and information.

Some experts said the United States was going through an **information revolution.** This meant that technology had radically changed the way information was delivered—and gave people access to far more information than ever before. This improved the productivity of many industries.

*Reading* **History**
**A. Drawing Conclusions** Why is the Internet an important part of the information revolution?
A. Possible Response because it improved communication and research

Computers changed not just industries, but also the lives of most individual workers. For example, engineers began to use computers to test new car designs. In large companies, workers from many departments were able to share information through computer networks. Filmmakers used computers to create animated characters that would react on-screen with live actors.

## Economic Change Affects Workers

The dramatic changes in the economy were both good news and bad news for U.S. workers. During the 1990s, high-tech industries created many new, high-paying jobs for skilled workers.

Yet other workers faced hard times. The decline of manufacturing meant the loss of factory jobs. The newly unemployed workers faced an uncertain future. They had earned good wages in the factory, although many of them were not highly skilled or educated. Most new jobs required specialized skills. As a result, job seekers had to obtain education and training. Or they had to settle for lower-paying jobs.

**Background**
Downsizing most often occurs during hard times but also can take place when the economy is strong.

Highly skilled workers also lost jobs. Many corporations engaged in **downsizing**—reducing the number of workers to increase company profits. During the 1990s, companies let go of hundreds of thousands of workers. In addition, many mergers—in which two companies join—took place. When two companies merge, it creates a situation in which people hold duplicate jobs, so mergers usually lead to layoffs.



### STRANGE *but* True

**Internet 911**

The Internet is a worldwide computer network linking tens of millions of government, education, business, and personal computers. When the Internet was first introduced, it was used largely for e-mail, bulletin boards, and newsgroups. In the 1990s, the World Wide Web, the Internet information retrieval service, made it possible for ordinary users to move quickly and easily from one Internet site to another.

 **Humanities Transparency HT63**
- Visualization of Internet Traffic

### INSTRUCT: OBJECTIVE 

**A Changing Economy/ Economic Change Affects Workers**

Key Questions
- How have computers fueled the growth of the service economy?
- What have been some costs and benefits of the recent advances in technology?

 **Citizenship Today,** p. 82

### MORE ABOUT . . .

**Technology Demand**

It took 20 years to sell the first 1 million TV sets, but only 4 1/2 years to sell 1 million cellular telephones. Today, Americans seem quite willing to use all kinds of high-tech products, such as fax machines and CD players. The microwave oven gained rapid acceptance. Almost unknown in the 1970s, microwaves could be found in three out of four American homes by the late 1980s.

### ACTIVITY OPTIONS
### INDIVIDUAL NEEDS

**LESS PROFICIENT READERS**

**Categorizing** Read aloud this sentence: "Section 2 explains other ways that the Internet and technology changed American life." As you read the section with the class, ask students to cite examples of these changes. Record their findings in a list. When the list is completed, help students sort and classify the information so they can complete the cluster diagram in the Section Assessment.

## Technology OF THE Time

**OBJECTIVES**

1. To use photographs of computers and computer parts to learn about the computer revolution
2. To describe the changes taking place in the development of the computer

## INSTRUCT

Key Questions

- In what ways have computers changed since the 1950s?
- What advances in computers did the computer chip make possible?
- What are some uses for virtual reality and for personal computers in the 1990s?

### MORE ABOUT . . .

**Virtual Reality**

To experience virtual reality, a user puts on a headset containing a pair of miniature television screens, one for each eye. The headset is connected by wire to a computer with special software. The computer generates sounds and three-dimensional images that give the wearer a feeling of being part of a very lifelike world. A tracking device built into the headset senses where the user is looking and adjusts the computer images as the user's head moves.

**In-Depth Resources: Unit 9**
- Primary Source: from *The Road Ahead* by Bill Gates, p. 64
- Enrichment Activity, p. 72

Technology OF THE Time

# The Computer Revolution

Would you be impressed if a scientist came to you and said, "I can take a machine, reduce it to one-thousandth of its present size, and yet increase its power"? That is exactly what happened with computers during the last half of the 20th century. Today, personal computers can perform more operations more quickly than the first giant computers did. In addition, the first computers were very expensive and difficult to maintain. The development of inexpensive personal computers made it possible for small businesses and ordinary families to use the latest technology.

**1940s**

**ENIAC** One of the first general-purpose electronic computers, the ENIAC used 18,000 vacuum tubes (which looked a bit like light bulbs). ENIAC took up 1,500 square feet, about one-third of a basketball court. It was used for mathematical calculations and could do 5,000 additions a second.

**1970s**

**Commodore PET** Computer chips made the personal computer possible. The Commodore PET was the first personal computer designed to be sold to the public. It cost only $595—but had just 12K of memory.

**Computer Chip** Vacuum tubes were replaced first by transistors and later by tiny computer chips. By the 1970s, all of a computer's operations were contained on a small number of chips, wired to a control board.

**1990s**

**Virtual Reality** The personal computers of the 1990s grew increasingly powerful and were able to perform sophisticated jobs. Here, an interior designer uses a virtual-environment program to recreate a room. Computers were also used in engineering and film animation.

FUTURE

**CONNECT TO HISTORY**

1. **Recognizing Effects** Do you think the development of the personal computer had a positive or negative effect on the economy? Explain.

See Skillbuilder Handbook, page R10.

**CONNECT TO TODAY**

2. **Identifying Problems** What problem might the computer industry try to solve next?

Visit www.mcdougallittell.com to learn more about computers.

880

**CONNECT TO HISTORY**

1. **Recognizing Effects** **Possible Responses** Positive: Students might argue that sales of PCs created jobs for people making and selling computers and software and created a variety of new jobs in high-tech fields, such as systems analyst and consultant. It also may have made many workers more productive. Negative: Students might point out that computers cost some workers their jobs.

**CONNECT TO TODAY**

2. **Identifying Problems** **Possible Responses** They may try to make computers more user-friendly through voice recognition and activation. They will find ways to make them smaller, faster, and more powerful.

Eventually, most laid-off workers did find other jobs. But in an effort to cut costs, many companies began to hire people as part-time or temporary workers. Part-time and temporary jobs generally offered less pay and fewer benefits than full-time jobs.

*Reading*History
**B. Analyzing Points of View** Why do you think Golly believes working for a corporation is unstable?
B. Possible Response because she lost her job three times

Because of these trends, more people began to work for themselves. For example, Jeanne Golly grew frustrated after losing three different jobs with corporations. In 1995, she started her own consulting firm. "Anything has to be more stable than corporate life," she said. By 1997, the number of self-employed persons had risen to more than 10 million.

Although layoffs made headlines, more jobs were created than lost during the 1990s. The advances in technology helped to create a strong economy in which both unemployment and inflation were low.

## 3 A More Global Economy

Technology helped to build a more global economy—in which countries around the world are linked through business. Through the Internet, companies on different continents could do business as if they were in the same city. Trade and investment among nations expanded.

Corporations also built factories and offices in other countries. By 1995, for example, more than 3 million Japanese cars were made at U.S. plants. And businesses in different countries merged to form multinational corporations. For example, in May 1998, the German company Daimler-Benz AG bought the Chrysler Corporation. This created a worldwide auto giant, Daimler Chrysler.

President Clinton saw the growth of world trade as a chance for America to sell more goods and create more jobs. This was why he urged Congress to pass NAFTA.

**Background**
NAFTA is the North American Free Trade Agreement. See Section 1.

The global economy caused problems for some U.S. workers. To cut costs, some businesses moved their operations from the United States to countries where wages were lower. In the mid-1990s, for example, a large U.S. clothing maker moved many of its sewing operations to Mexico, the Caribbean, and Central America. Thousands of U.S. workers lost their jobs.

Because of global trade, the economies of various countries had become more closely linked. Nations were more likely to suffer from each other's financial woes. For example, in October 1997, Hong Kong's stock market fell, which caused stock markets from Europe to North America to drop. In the summer of 1998, Russia temporarily experienced an economic collapse, which also caused markets to fall.

**Now *and* then**

**PREPARING FOR TOMORROW'S JOBS**

In the past, many workers spent their entire careers at one company. By the 1990s, workers were changing jobs often to gain more pay or more challenging assignments.

Workers today also have more chances to work overseas. For example, 27-year-old Anne Larlarb has already worked in England and Thailand. In the photo above, she uses e-mail to keep in touch with friends.

If these trends continue, future workers will need to be flexible, quick learners, and open to other cultures.

## 4 Scientific Breakthroughs

In the last decades of the 20th century, the world of medicine saw many breakthroughs. Engineers developed smaller, more precise surgical





**INSTRUCT: OBJECTIVE 3**

**A More Global Economy**
Key Questions
- What changes led to the growth of world trade in the 1990s?
- What problems did the global economy cause for U.S. workers?

**In-Depth Resources: Unit 9**
- Geography Application: U.S. Trade, 1995, pp. 62–63

### *Now and* then

**Preparing for Tomorrow's Jobs**
By 2006, just 12 percent of the labor force may hold jobs in manufacturing. Many of the new jobs for 21st-century graduates will be in the service sector, in such areas as software development and computer consulting. For tomorrow's blue-collar workers, there are likely to be more and more jobs laying cables and repairing the chips that connect today's computer networks.

**INSTRUCT: OBJECTIVE 4**

**Scientific Breakthroughs**
Key Questions
- What new technologies are helping to make surgery and diagnosis of diseases more effective?
- How has the treatment of AIDS changed?
- What breakthroughs have occurred in space exploration?

**ACTIVITY OPTIONS**

**INTERDISCIPLINARY LINK: SCIENCE**  BLOCK SCHEDULING

**MEDICAL MIRACLES**

**Class Time** One class period

**Task** Preparing an oral report on changes taking place in an area of medical research

**Purpose** To identify changes taking place in medicine

**Supplies Needed**
- Medical encyclopedias and reference materials on current breakthroughs in medicine
- Internet access

**Activity** Divide students into groups. Assign each group one of these topics: heart disease, birth defects, diabetes, cancer, memory loss, gene mapping, organ transplants, obesity. Have each group prepare an illustrated report on its topic. Reports on diseases should describe current treatments and recent advances. Reports on new procedures should focus on how the procedure is done and why advances in this procedure may result in new breakthroughs.

## MORE ABOUT . . .

**Cloning Dolly**
When embryologist Dr. Ian Wilmut at the Roslin Institute in Edinburgh, Scotland, cloned the sheep known as Dolly, he replaced the genetic material in a sheep's egg with the DNA from udder or mammary cells of an adult donor sheep. After the DNA was implanted, the embryo that developed was transplanted into the sheep that gave birth to Dolly, a lamb identical to the donor sheep that provided the DNA.

## ASSESS & RETEACH

**Setting the Stage** Have students complete the boxes on Technological and Economic Change and its effects on the chapter chart.

 **Formal Assessment**
- Section Quiz, p. 459

### RETEACHING ACTIVITY

Have students work in pairs to create outlines of the section. Have them use their outlines to write a section summary.

 **In-Depth Resources: Unit 9**
- Reteaching Activity, p. 70

This firefighter has received an artificial arm with the ability to sense heat.

instruments. These and new technologies such as lasers allowed doctors to perform surgery through tiny incisions in the body, which heal more quickly than large cuts. New tests helped doctors to make better diagnoses.

Scientists developed new drugs that offer greater hope for a cure for cancer. New drugs and treatments also slowed the rate at which AIDS (acquired immune deficiency syndrome) kills infected people.

In 1997, Scottish scientists cloned the first mammal—a sheep. This set off a furious debate. Many feared that cloning human beings could be next. Some insisted that cloning would help to improve the human species. Others argued that the process is unethical.

**Vocabulary**
**clone:** to make a genetic duplicate of a living being

*Reading* **History**
**C. Identifying Facts and Opinions** Is Representative Ehlers expressing a fact or an opinion? Explain.
**C. Possible Response** It is an opinion because it is based on his values, not facts.

*A VOICE FROM THE PAST*

Creating life in the laboratory is totally inappropriate and so far removed from the process of marriage and parenting that . . . we must rebel against the very concept of human cloning. It is simply wrong to experiment with the creation of human life in this way.

**U.S. Representative Vernon Ehlers,** statement to U.S. Congress

In nonmedical science, the United States and other nations began to build an international space station. The station was scheduled to be finished in the early 2000s. Nations will use it to research the stars, planets, and galaxies.

While technology and science shape the years to come, so too will people. Section 3 discusses the nation's diverse population and how these many groups are shaping American society.

## Section 2 Assessment

**1. Terms & Names**
**Identify:**
- Internet
- e-commerce
- service economy
- information revolution
- downsizing

**2. Taking Notes**
Use a cluster diagram like the one shown to list changes in technology, the economy, and science.

Technology — Economy — CHANGES — Science

**3. Main Ideas**
a. How did the information revolution change jobs?
b. Why did the rise of the global economy cause some workers to worry?
c. What advances did scientists make in the field of medicine?

**4. Critical Thinking**
**Forming and Supporting Opinions** What job skills do you think you will need for the future? Why?
**THINK ABOUT**
- the changes in technology and science
- the changes in the economy

**ACTIVITY OPTIONS**
**TECHNOLOGY / DRAMA**
What technological marvel would you like to see invented? Design a **Web page** advertising the new technology, or perform a **skit** showing someone using it.



## Section 2 Assessment

**1. Terms & Names**
**Internet,** p. 878
**e-commerce,** p. 878
**service economy,** p. 879
**information revolution,** p. 879
**downsizing,** p. 879

**2. Taking Notes**
Technology: personal computers, Internet, cellular phones, DVDs; Economy: high-tech industries, loss of industrial jobs, downsizing, mergers, more self- and part-time employment; Science: medical advances, cloning, international space station

**3. Main Ideas**
**a.** Industrial jobs declined; more and more jobs involved the delivery of knowledge and information.
**b.** Some workers feared their companies would move to another country and leave them without jobs. **c.** New instruments improved surgery; new drugs improved treatment of cancer and AIDS patients.

**4. Critical Thinking**
Responses will vary. Students may say that they should study computers, math, and science because of the technological revolution.

**ACTIVITY OPTIONS**
**Alternative Assessment**
- Rubrics for a Web page, 5.1
- Rubrics for a skit, 3.1

# 3 The New Americans

**TERMS & NAMES**
Immigration Reform and Control Act of 1986



**MAIN IDEA**
Due to immigration, the United States grew more diverse.

**WHY IT MATTERS NOW**
Americans of all backgrounds share common goals: the desire for equal rights and economic opportunity.

## ONE AMERICAN'S STORY

**Born in the Dominican Republic, Junot Díaz came to the United States with his family when he was seven. He started writing when he was just 13. In 1996, at the age of 28, he published his first book of stories. Díaz writes about being Dominican but believes his stories are universal; that is, they have meaning for everyone.**

*A VOICE FROM THE PAST*

I am Dominican and that for me is important, but I also know that there is this whole idea that if you are a Dominican that's not universal, that's not American. But, I argue that [my stories] are universal and American.

**Junot Díaz,** quoted in *Frontera*

**Junot Díaz won praise for his stories about being Dominican.**

**Díaz and millions of other recent immigrants have made important contributions to the nation's growth. This section discusses how these new Americans are making the United States a more diverse nation.**

## 1 Immigrants Affect American Society

From 1981 to 1996, nearly 13.5 million people came to the United States. These new immigrants increased U.S. diversity. Most of the immigrants who arrived in America during earlier periods had come from Europe. Nearly 85 percent of the arrivals since 1981 came from either Latin America or Asia. The Census Bureau predicts that the U.S. Hispanic population will increase from 11 percent to 16 percent by 2020. The Asian population will climb from 3 percent to nearly 6 percent by then.

One cause of the recent surge in immigration is the Immigration and Nationality Act of 1965. It allowed people from a greater variety of countries to enter the United States. The lure of America also plays a role. As earlier immigrants did, many of the newcomers came to the United States seeking economic opportunity and, in some cases, political freedom.

U.S. citizens have mixed feelings about immigration. Some argue that immigrants take jobs from citizens. Many Americans also worry about the number of immigrants who enter the United States illegally. Officials



## SECTION OBJECTIVES

1. To analyze the attitudes of Americans toward recent immigration
2. To identify the contributions of immigrants to American society
3. To describe some of the beliefs and values Americans share

**SKILLBUILDER**
Interpreting Charts, p. 884

**CRITICAL THINKING**
Drawing Conclusions, p. 884
Making Inferences, p. 885
Comparing and Contrasting, p. 885

## FOCUS & MOTIVATE

### 5-MINUTE WARM-UP

**Drawing Conclusions** These questions focus on changes in immigration patterns.

1. Look at the chart on page 884. Compare the two lists. How are they different?
2. From what country does the largest number of recent immigrants come?

**Warm-Up Transparency WT32**

## INSTRUCT

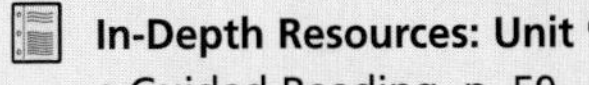

### INSTRUCT: OBJECTIVE 1

**Immigrants Affect American Society**
Key Questions
- How have U.S. immigration patterns changed since 1981?
- What has led to the recent surge in immigration?
- Why do some Americans oppose immigration?

**In-Depth Resources: Unit 9**
- Guided Reading, p. 59

**Reading Study Guide** (Spanish and English), pp. 307–308

## RECOMMENDED RESOURCES

**In-Depth Resources: Unit 9**
- Guided Reading, p. 59
- Building Vocabulary, p. 60
- Primary Source, p. 65
- Literature Selection: from *The Woman Warrior,* pp. 66–68
- Reteaching Activity, p. 71
- History Workshop Resources, p. 73

**Reading Study Guide** (Spanish and English), pp. 307–308

**Formal Assessment**
- Section Quiz, p. 460

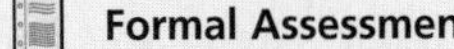

**Alternative Assessment**
- Rubrics, 2.2
- Rubrics, 3.6

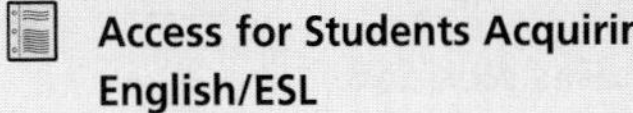

**Access for Students Acquiring English/ESL**
- Guided Reading, p. 213

**Technology Resources**

**Humanities Transparency HT64**
- Pot Luck Quilt

**Electronic Teacher Tools with Test Maker**

**ClassZone**
www.mcdougallittell.com

## HISTORY FROM VISUALS

**Interpreting Charts** For each chart, have students put the countries listed into categories based on the continent where the country is located. Ask: How are the two lists different and why do you think they differ? **Possible Responses** The countries on the 1990 list are predominantly European. The 1981–1996 list is Asian and Latin American. Like the earlier migration of Europeans seeking opportunity, later immigrants come from nations where opportunities are limited.

**Extension** Have students pick one of the countries listed under Origins of Immigrants, 1981–1996, and research the reasons for emigration from this country to the United States in recent years. Have students present their findings in an oral report.

## MORE ABOUT . . .

**The Changing Face of Immigration**

The Immigration and Nationality Act of 1965 opened the door to Asians and Latin Americans, giving priority to the reunification of families by allowing U.S. citizens to bring over close relatives. The act also gave priority to refugees, making it possible for Vietnamese, Cubans, and newcomers from war-torn countries in Central America to enter the United States as never before. By 1997, nearly one in ten U.S. residents was foreign-born, the highest level since 1930.

**In-Depth Resources: Unit 9**
- Primary Source, p. 65
- Literature Selection: from *The Woman Warrior* by Maxine Hong Kingston, pp. 66–68

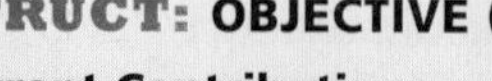

## INSTRUCT: OBJECTIVE 2

**Immigrant Contributions**

Key Questions
- How have immigrants contributed to the nation's economic growth?
- How have immigrants contributed to sports and the arts?

### The American People

| Ancestry of Americans, 1990 | (descendants, in thousands) |
|---|---|
| 1. German | 58,000 |
| 2. Irish | 39,000 |
| 3. English | 33,000 |
| 4. African | 24,000 |
| 5. Italian | 15,000 |
| 6. Mexican | 12,000 |
| 7. French | 10,000 |
| 8. Native American | 9,000 |
| 9. Polish | 9,000 |
| 10. Dutch | 6,000 |

| Origins of Immigrants, 1981–1996 | (immigrants, in thousands) |
|---|---|
| 1. Mexico | 3,300 |
| 2. Philippines | 840 |
| 3. China* | 730 |
| 4. Vietnam | 720 |
| 5. Dominican Republic | 510 |
| 6. India | 500 |
| 7. Korea | 450 |
| 8. Soviet Union† | 420 |
| 9. El Salvador | 360 |
| 10. Jamaica | 320 |

* China includes Taiwan.
† The Soviet Union broke apart in 1991. This figure includes the former Soviet republics.

Source: *U.S. Bureau of the Census*

**SKILLBUILDER Interpreting Charts**
1. *Compare the origins of recent immigrants to the ancestry of Americans overall. Are any the same?*
2. *How might the list of top ten ancestry groups change in the future?*

**Skillbuilder Answers**
**Possible Responses**
1. Only Mexico
2. Mexican might move to a higher position; eventually, Dutch might drop off the list and a new ancestry, perhaps Asian in origin, might appear.

estimate that in 1996, about 5 million illegal immigrants lived in the United States. Roughly 2.7 million were thought to be from Mexico.

Because illegal immigrants are here secretly, they do not pay income taxes. Yet they receive government services, such as police protection. As a result, some people feel that they are a drain on the U.S. economy. Congress passed the **Immigration Reform and Control Act of 1986** to strengthen immigration laws and enforcement measures. But illegal immigrants continued to cross America's borders.

**Background**
An illegal immigrant is someone who enters the United States secretly and without filling out the appropriate government forms.

## 2 Immigrant Contributions

Recent immigrants have brought, and continue to bring, many talents to the United States. The National Science Foundation estimates that 23 percent of all U.S. residents with doctorate degrees in engineering and science are foreign-born. High-tech industries, such as those located in Silicon Valley, California, have benefited from their skills.

In addition, immigrants are an important source of labor. Some studies indicate that without immigrants, the workforce might actually begin to shrink by 2015. In other words, U.S. businesses wouldn't be able to hire enough people to maintain their productivity.

**Reading History**
**A. Drawing Conclusions** What have immigrants contributed to the economy?
A. Answer specialized knowledge and skills; labor

Immigrants also make sports much more exciting. In 1998 and 1999, Dominican-born Sammy Sosa thrilled baseball fans by battling Mark McGwire for the home run record. Immigrants have also starred in other sports such as basketball, football, soccer, and golf.

Many immigrants enrich American arts and culture. Latin music, for example, has become very popular. Chinese-born author Bette Bao Lord has written popular books for children and adults. In addition,



## ACTIVITY OPTIONS

### INDIVIDUAL NEEDS: GIFTED AND TALENTED

**DEBATING IMMIGRATION**

**Class Time** One class period

**Task** Debating the issue of immigration

**Purpose** To form and express opinions about the issue of immigration

**Supplies Needed**
- Library references, including newsmagazine articles on immigration
- Internet access

**Activity** Pick one of these statements for a class debate: 1) Immigration should be restricted. 2) Wealth should not be the basis for admission of immigrants. Divide students into two groups to research the statement chosen. Groups should research arguments for and against the statement. Have each group select a student to serve as their debater. Establish rules before the debate and tell debaters what side of the statement they will argue.

immigrants, and their sons and daughters, are acting in a greater number of movies. "When immigrants come to America they bring their culture, and that culture becomes part of a new country," noted Cuban-born singer Gloria Estefan. "It makes everyone stronger."

## 3 What Americans Have In Common

While immigrants bring their culture to America, many of them also have embraced American ways. They wear American clothes, adopt American customs, and learn English.

They also share the American belief in certain ideals. The ideas of democracy and freedom that motivated people in 1776 still inspire Americans today. Ken Burns, a documentary filmmaker, explained that these beliefs make America unique in the world.

*Reading* **History**

**B. Making Inferences** Judging from this quotation, how does Ken Burns view the future of the United States?

**B. Possible Responses** He is optimistic. He believes that Americans have shared values and will continue to try to improve themselves and their country.

***A VOICE FROM THE PAST***

There is no other country on Earth that is configured like ours. Every other nation is there because of race, religion, language, ethnicity, or geography. We are here only because we agreed to subscribe to the words on four pieces of paper—the U.S. Constitution. Unlike every other country, which sees itself as an end unto itself, we see ourselves as evolving. We're not satisfied. We're not willing to rest on our laurels. We think we can get better. We think we've got someplace to go.

**Ken Burns,** quoted in *America West*

Today the United States is a very different nation from the one founded in 1776. Democratic rights have expanded to include more and more people. As the United States moves into the future, it will no doubt continue to change. Tolerance and cooperation will be essential.

Citizens of all colors and backgrounds will play a vital role in shaping what America will be. So will today's students. You have a part to play in helping the United States embrace people from every culture and land. You are the generation that will create the America of the future.

### Section 3 Assessment

**1. Terms & Names**

**Identify:**

- Immigration Reform and Control Act of 1986

**2. Taking Notes**

Use a diagram like the one shown to record the effects of recent immigration on the United States.

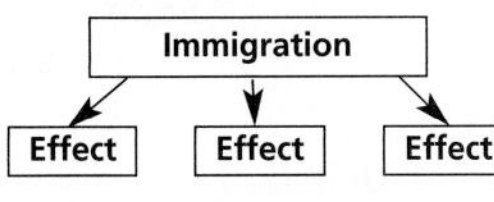


How has immigration affected your life?

**3. Main Ideas**

a. How did the Immigration and Nationality Act of 1965 help create a more diverse population?

b. In what areas of American society have immigrants made contributions?

c. What ideals do both immigrant and native-born Americans believe in?

**4. Critical Thinking**

**Comparing and Contrasting** How was the immigration that occurred in the years 1981–2000 similar to and different from earlier waves of immigration?

**THINK ABOUT**

- the immigration you read about in Chapter 14
- the immigration you read about in Chapter 21

**ACTIVITY OPTIONS**

**MATH**

**SPEECH**

Survey ten people outside your class to learn their ethnic background. Present your findings as a **table** like the one on page 884 or in a **speech.**

### INSTRUCT: OBJECTIVE 3

**What Americans Have in Common**

Key Questions

- What traditions and ideals do immigrants share with native-born Americans?
- How has the nation become more democratic since its founding in 1776?
- Why are tolerance and cooperation essential to the nation's future success?

**Humanities Transparency HT64**
- Pot Luck Quilt

### CRITICAL THINKING ACTIVITY

**Forming and Supporting Opinions** Read the quote from Ken Burns on page 885. Ask students: What does Burns think is unique about the way the United States was founded? How does Burns think Americans differ from other people in their attitude toward their own achievements and the future? Do you think it is easier or harder than it was in 1776 for Americans to find common ground? Give reasons for your opinions.

**Class Time** 10 minutes

## ASSESS & RETEACH

**Setting the Stage** Have students complete the chart by filling in the boxes on immigration and its effects.

**Formal Assessment**
- Section Quiz, p. 460

**Critical Thinking Transparency CT94**
- Setting the Stage

### RETEACHING ACTIVITY

Ask students to write two or more sentences providing supporting details for each of these statements: 1) Recent immigration has increased diversity. 2) U.S. citizens have mixed feelings about immigration. 3) Immigrants have made major contributions to American life.

**In-Depth Resources: Unit 9**
- Reteaching Activity, p. 71

### Section 3 Assessment

**1. Terms & Names**

**Immigration Reform and Control Act of 1986,** p. 884

**2. Taking Notes**

Effects: a more diverse population, resentment by native-born Americans, enrichment of American culture and arts

Answers will vary.

**3. Main Ideas**

**a.** It allowed people from a greater variety of countries than before to enter the United States. **b.** business, the arts, sports, culture **c.** democracy, freedom, the values of the U.S. Constitution

**4. Critical Thinking**

Different: 1981–2000 immigrants came from a wider variety of countries. Similar: reasons for immigrating, such as desire for economic opportunity and for freedom and democracy

**ACTIVITY OPTIONS**

**Alternative Assessment**
- Rubrics, 2.2, 3.6

## TERMS & NAMES

1. **Ronald Reagan,** p. 873
2. **supply-side economics,** p. 873
3. **Iran-Contra affair,** p. 874
4. **George Bush,** p. 874
5. **Persian Gulf War,** p. 875
6. **Bill Clinton,** p. 875
7. **Internet,** p. 878
8. **service economy,** p. 879
9. **information revolution,** p. 879
10. **Immigration Reform and Control Act of 1986,** p. 884

## REVIEW QUESTIONS

**Possible Responses**

1. He cut taxes and tried to deregulate business.
2. The U.S. government sold weapons to Iran in exchange for help in freeing American hostages, then sent the money from the weapon sales to help the Contras in Nicaragua.
3. It was a leader in the UN coalition that fought Iraq.
4. The House passed two articles of impeachment—perjury and obstruction of justice. At the trial, the Senate did not find him guilty.
5. research, send and receive e-mail, and shop
6. Often after a merger, many workers lost jobs.
7. Some people thought that scientists would move on to human cloning, which would help improve the human species; others found cloning a violation of natural processes.
8. for economic opportunity and, at times, political freedom
9. labor and specialized skills
10. because the majority of immigrants in recent times come from Asia or Latin America

# Chapter 32 ASSESSMENT

**VISUAL SUMMARY**

## Entering a New Millennium

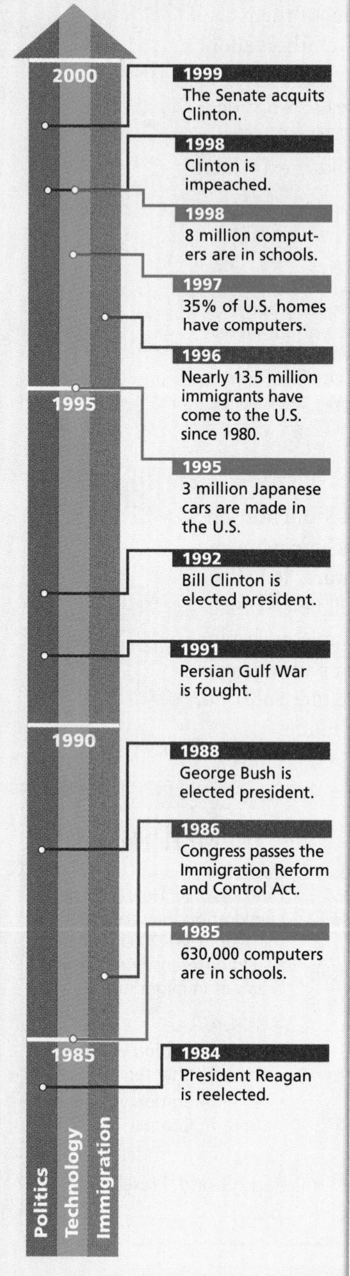
2000
1999
The Senate acquits Clinton.
1998
Clinton is impeached.
1998
8 million computers are in schools.
1997
35% of U.S. homes have computers.
1996
Nearly 13.5 million immigrants have come to the U.S. since 1980.
1995
1995
3 million Japanese cars are made in the U.S.
1992
Bill Clinton is elected president.
1991
Persian Gulf War is fought.
1990
1988
George Bush is elected president.
1986
Congress passes the Immigration Reform and Control Act.
1985
630,000 computers are in schools.
1985
1984
President Reagan is reelected.
Politics
Technology
Immigration

886

## TERMS & NAMES

Briefly explain the importance of each of the following.

1. Ronald Reagan
2. supply-side economics
3. Iran-Contra affair
4. George Bush
5. Persian Gulf War
6. Bill Clinton
7. Internet
8. service economy
9. information revolution
10. Immigration Reform and Control Act of 1986

## REVIEW QUESTIONS

**Conservatives Reshape Politics (pages 873–877)**

1. How did Reagan try to improve the economy?
2. What happened in the Iran-Contra affair?
3. What role did the United States play during the Persian Gulf War?
4. What happened during Clinton's impeachment and trial?

**Technological and Economic Changes (pages 878–882)**

5. What did the Internet allow its users to do?
6. How did corporate mergers affect individuals?
7. What were the different reactions to cloning?

**The New Americans (pages 883–885)**

8. Why did the recent wave of immigrants come to the United States?
9. What do immigrants contribute to the economy?
10. Why do experts think the United States will become more diverse?

## CRITICAL THINKING

**1. USING YOUR NOTES**

Using your completed chart, answer the questions below.

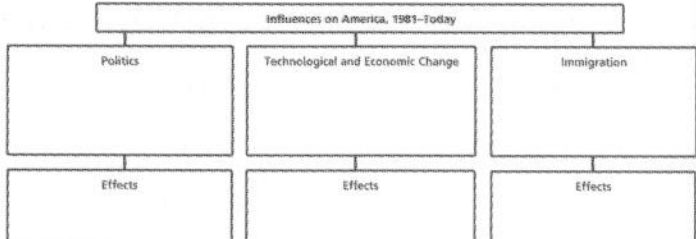
Influences on America, 1981–Today
Politics
Technological and Economic Change
Immigration
Effects
Effects
Effects

a. What were the effects of recent political events?

b. What were the main technological and economic changes?

**2. ANALYZING LEADERSHIP**

Judging from what you read in this chapter, what issues will a U.S. president face in the 21st century?

**3. APPLYING CITIZENSHIP SKILLS**

In what ways have recent immigrants demonstrated good citizenship here in the United States?

**4. THEME: DIVERSITY AND UNITY**

What ideas and goals help to unify Americans of different racial and ethnic backgrounds?

**5. MAKING INFERENCES**

Are U.S. citizens likely to be more or less welcoming to immigrants in good economic times? Explain.

**Interact *with* History**

Now that you have read about recent changes in the United States, what new ideas do you have about how you can contribute to the future?

## CRITICAL THINKING

**Possible Responses**

1. USING YOUR NOTES a. People have less respect for politicians, and fewer people are willing to run for office. b. wider use of computers and the Internet, transition to service economy, global economy, downsizing, advances in medicine and science
2. ANALYZING LEADERSHIP Answers might include political disillusionment, various world conflicts, ethical questions related to technology, and building unity in an increasingly diverse nation.
3. APPLYING CITIZENSHIP SKILLS They are contributing to the economy and culture of their new nation.
4. THEME: DIVERSITY AND UNITY the belief in democracy and the desire for economic opportunity and freedom
5. MAKING INFERENCES probably more, because they won't be perceived as a threat to scarce jobs

**Interact *with* History** Answers will vary.

## HISTORY SKILLS

**1. INTERPRETING MAPS: Movement**

Study the map. Then answer the questions.

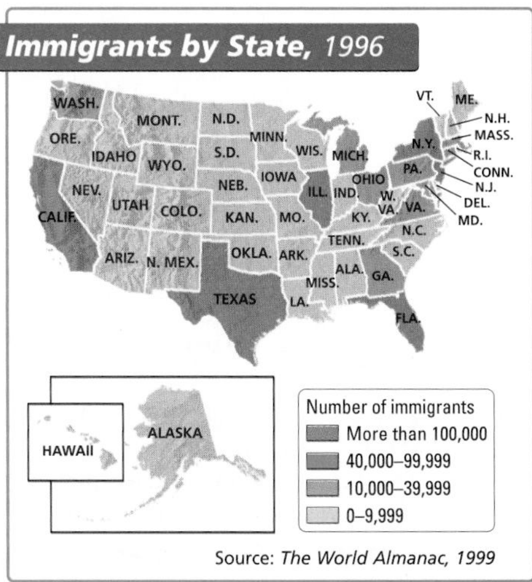


Source: *The World Almanac, 1999*

**Basic Map Elements**

a. What year's statistics does this map show?

b. What do the various colors of the states indicate?

**Interpreting the Map**

c. Which states have the highest numbers of immigrants?

d. How would you describe what those states have in common?

**2. INTERPRETING PRIMARY SOURCES**

This photograph shows a robot that was designed to play a keyboard instrument.

a. What are some of the separate skills that humans need to play keyboard instruments? Think of both physical and mental skills.

b. If a robot can play a keyboard instrument, what else might it be able to do? Consider how else it might use the separate skills involved in the task.

## ALTERNATIVE ASSESSMENT

**1. INTERDISCIPLINARY ACTIVITY: Science**

**Explaining a Medical Advance** Research a recent advance in medical science, such as a new medicine, treatment, or diagnostic test. Give a brief speech explaining the advance to the class.

**2. COOPERATIVE LEARNING ACTIVITY**

**Creating a Front Page** With three other students, create a newspaper front page that reports on the major events of the late 20th century. Three of the students will each write an article. The fourth student will be responsible for finding images for each story. Possible story topics are

- the arrival of a new device, the computer
- the number of recent immigrants to America reaches 13 million
- the most recent presidential election

Type and print out the stories and arrange them with their images on a large piece of paper. Show the front page to the class and have each student read his or her story aloud.

**3. TECHNOLOGY ACTIVITY**

**Designing a Web Page** What do you think the United States will be like in ten years? Design a Web page that presents your vision. Your Web page may include pictures and descriptions that portray your ideas. It should also include links to other sites that discuss technology, politics, or social issues. Draw a design of what the page will look like. Also provide written descriptions and addresses of other Web sites that are linked to yours.

 **Visit www.mcdougallittell.com to see sample Web pages.**

**4. HISTORY PORTFOLIO**

**Option 1** Review your section and chapter assessment activities. Select one that you think is your best work. Then use comments by your teacher or classmates to improve your work, and add it to your portfolio.

**Option 2** Review the questions that you wrote for What Do you Want to Know? on page 872. Then write a short report in which you explain the answers to your questions. If any questions were not answered, do research to answer them. Add your answers to your portfolio.



## ALTERNATIVE ASSESSMENT

1. INTERDISCIPLINARY ACTIVITY: **Science**

**Speeches should**
- present information that reflects the student's understanding of basic concepts or ideas about the medical advance.
- have a clear introduction and conclusion.
- have adequate delivery and establish rapport with the audience.

2. COOPERATIVE LEARNING ACTIVITY

**Front pages should**
- use a journalistic style.
- present information in an unbiased way.
- have a headline and images for each article, and present the events accurately.
- have a neatly presented layout.

3.  TECHNOLOGY ACTIVITY

**Web pages should**
- contain at least three links and include Web site addresses in print.
- make effective use of pictures and icons.
- contain written summaries that will encourage browsers to visit other Web sites.
- show technical proficiency.

4. HISTORY PORTFOLIO

 **Option 1 Revised section or chapter assessment activities should**
- address teacher and peer responses to the selected work.
- solve problems present in the first versions of the work.

**Option 2 Short reports should**
- answer questions about presidents, technology, or patterns of immigration.
- use evidence to develop and support ideas.
- cite sources of information.
- use standard grammar, spelling, sentence structure, and punctuation.

 **Critical Thinking Transparency CT96**
- Visual Summary

 **Formal Assessment**
- Chapter Test, Forms A and B, pp. 461–468

## HISTORY SKILLS

**Possible Responses**

1. INTERPRETING MAPS

**Basic Map Elements**

**a.** 1996

**b.** the number of their residents who are foreign-born

**Interpreting the Map**

**c.** New York and California

**d.** They are on the coast, contain a major city, and have a history of high immigration. They are traditional ports of entry for immigrants.

2. INTERPRETING PRIMARY SOURCES

**a.** to read music, to lift fingers individually and strike keys with them, to have each hand performing a different function, to count time

**b.** Answers will vary but might include typing, running a calculator, or operating machinery that has push buttons.

## *HISTORY* WORKSHOP

**OBJECTIVE**
Students make a time capsule for the 1950s, 1960s, 1970s, 1980s, or 1990s, and record a message describing the contents to be placed inside.

 **BLOCK SCHEDULING**

## PROCEDURE

Gather the materials listed in the "Toolbox." Divide the class into groups of four or five. Then review the steps for making the time capsule.

 **In-Depth Resources: Unit 9**
- History Workshop Resources, p. 73

### MORE ABOUT . . .

**Time Capsules**
World's fairs have often been occasions for making time capsules. Besides the capsule from the 1939–1940 World's Fair due to be opened in 6939, another time capsule was built for the 1964–1965 World's Fair, also in New York. During the celebration of the nation's Bicentennial in 1976, many American communities and organizations made time capsules. Planning began in the late 1990s for millennium time capsules.

### HISTORY FROM VISUALS

**Interpreting the Photographs** Have students point out the differences in the hairstyles and the clothing in the pictures from the 1950s, 1960s, and 1970s. How is the makeup of the 1960s family in the photo different from that of the traditional 1950s family? **Possible Response** The 1950s family has two parents and three children, while the 1960s family has multiple couples living together.



# Make a Time Capsule

A time capsule is a sealed container that preserves records and artifacts from the present for people in the future. Ancient Babylonians and Egyptians began this custom by carving messages inside their temples. These records give people today an idea of what life was like thousands of years ago. One of the first modern time capsules is in Oglethorpe, Georgia. Sealed in 1940, it is not due to be opened until 8113. It contains such things as a Donald Duck doll and 640,000 pages on microfilm.

ACTIVITY With a group, construct a time capsule. Write an explanation of the contents and your predictions or dreams for the future. Then record this explanation on a cassette tape.

A family from the 1960s poses in front of their house.

### TOOLBOX

Each group will need:

| | |
|---|---|
| posterboard | stapler |
| aluminum foil | markers |
| cellophane | 3 x 5 notecards |
| scissors | blank cassette tape |
| duct or masking tape | cassette recorder |

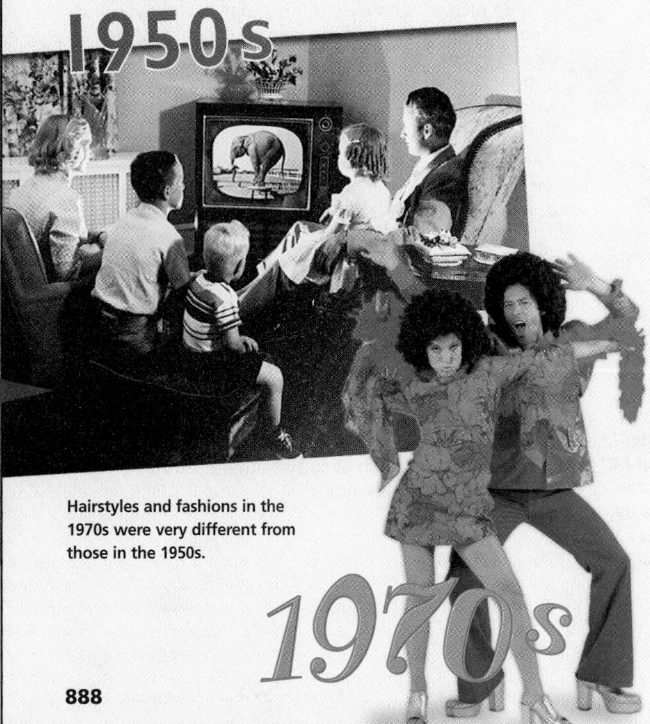

Hairstyles and fashions in the 1970s were very different from those in the 1950s.

### STEP BY STEP

**1** **Form groups.** Meet with three to four students to create a time capsule. To complete this project, groups will be expected to
- do research on a particular decade
- identify artifacts from that decade to place in a time capsule
- construct a time capsule
- write an explanation of the contents, and record it on an audio cassette

**2** **Choose the 1950s, 1960s, 1970s, 1980s, or 1990s.** Use the Internet, encyclopedias, or books about that decade to brainstorm ideas for the contents of your time capsule. Each person should jot down items on a piece of paper. A sample is shown below. With your group, discuss these items and decide which ones you'd like to use. Be sure to include enough items so that people opening the capsule many years from now will have a complete picture of your decade.

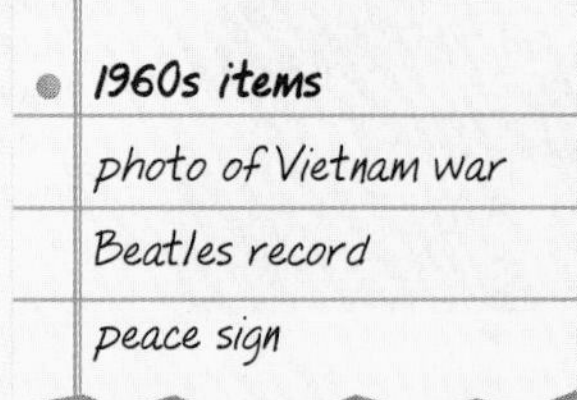




### RECOMMENDED RESOURCES

**BOOKS FOR THE TEACHER**

Editors of Reader's Digest. ***Our Glorious Century.*** Pleasantville, NY: Reader's Digest, 1994.

Editors of Time-Life Books. ***Time of Transition: The 70s. (Our American Century, Vol. 7)*** Alexandria, VA: Time-Life Books, 1998.

Jennings, Peter and Todd Brewster. ***The Century.*** New York: Doubleday, 1998.

**VIDEOS**

***History of the 20th Century.*** ABC Video, 1982. Set of nine videocassettes, one dealing with each decade of the century from 1900 to 1979.

***The Sixties: The Decade That Changed America.*** Scholastic/NBC News, 1994. Uses historical footage from NBC News Archives to give an overview of the 1960s.

***History of the 80s.*** MPI Media Group, 1991. Draws on the resources of ABC News to capture the political, social, and cultural highlights of the 1980s.

**BOOKS FOR THE STUDENTS**

Caney, Steven. ***Make Your Own Time Capsule.*** New York: Workman Publishing, Inc.

Javna, John and Gordon. ***60s! A Catalog of Memories and Artifacts.*** New York: St. Martin's, 1988.

**3 Build the time capsule.** First, cut a small square out of the middle of the posterboard to make a window. Using tape or a stapler, place the cellophane over the hole. Then roll the posterboard so that it forms a large cylinder. Tape or staple the ends of the posterboard together. Place aluminum foil over one end of your time capsule—using tape to secure it.

**4 Decorate the time capsule.** Use markers to decorate the outside of the time capsule. These decorations should reflect your decade. Also, include a message that is connected with your decade. Be sure to explain when the capsule should be opened.

**5 Select your items.** Use the actual item, or a picture. On each 3 x 5 card, write an explanation of the items you've selected and explain their purpose. Attach a card to each picture or item. Be sure to include the year the item was first used.

**6 Present the contents to the class.** Using your notecards, explain to the class why you chose these items. Place the notecards inside the time capsule. Wait until you make your audio cassette to seal the time capsule—and be sure to include it.

## WRITE AND SPEAK

Write a paragraph describing your time capsule. Include your predictions and dreams for future generations. Then record your message on an audio cassette and place it inside the time capsule. After sealing the time capsule, put it on display with the other time capsules.

## HELP DESK

For related information, see Chapters 29, 30, 31, and 32.

### Researching Your Project

"Time Immemorial," *Popular Mechanics*, February 1999.

**Visit www.mcdougallittell.com for links to sites about time capsules.**

### Did You Know?

Westinghouse Electric Company coined the term *time capsule.* The company built one for the New York World's Fair of 1939–1940. The capsule is due to be opened in 6939. To preserve the capsule's contents, the company formed a new metal alloy called Cupaloy. It combined the durability of steel with the ability of copper to prevent corrosion.

The designers figured people living in the 70th century may not know the time capsule exists. So they created *The Book of Record.* It gives the time capsule's location and was placed in libraries all over the world.

### REFLECT & ASSESS

- **Why did you choose the particular artifacts in your time capsule?**
- **How do you think future generations might react to the articles in your time capsule?**
- **How well do your items represent the history, social issues, and culture of your decade?**



## MORE ABOUT . . .

**Contents of Time Capsules**

In Grand Island, Nebraska, residents decided to fill a millennium time capsule as part of their Year 2000 celebration. Among the ideas for items to be included were likenesses of "heroes of youth," including Jack Armstrong, Davy Crockett, Roy Rogers, the Lone Ranger, Li'l Orphan Annie, Captain Midnight, Superman, G.I. Joe, Teenage Mutant Ninja Turtles, and the Power Rangers. The owner of a local coin shop suggested including a series of quarters because this coin has changed its look several times over the past 100 years.

## REFLECT & ASSESS

1. Students can discuss whether the item chosen makes a fashion statement about the decade; reflects social values, political beliefs, or leisure-time activities; or describes some aspect of popular culture, such as a favorite movie, song, TV show, or dance of the decade.
2. Students might examine each object to see if its use is clear from looking at it. They can discuss whether they think people will still use this item in 50, 100, or 200 years.
3. Although some items will probably belong in several groups, have students divide their items into three groups: historical, social, and cultural artifacts. Students should make sure they have several items in each category.

## STANDARDS FOR EVALUATION

### HISTORY WORKSHOP

**Time capsules should**
- be neatly presented and creative.
- reflect the time period chosen.
- have a variety of artifacts.
- be historically accurate.

### WRITE AND SPEAK

**Taped messages should**
- explain why each item was chosen.
- explain how each item was used.
- be clear and well organized.

# Creating America

## A History of the United States




890

# Table of Contents





**R1**

# 1.1 Summarizing

## Defining the Skill

When you **summarize,** you restate a paragraph, passage, or chapter in fewer words. You include only the main ideas and most important details. It is important to use your own words when summarizing.

## Applying the Skill

The passage below tells about Harriet Tubman, a prominent member of the Underground Railroad. She helped runaway slaves to freedom. Use the strategies listed below to help you summarize the passage.

### How to Summarize

**Strategy ①** Look for topic sentences stating the main idea. These are often at the beginning of a section or paragraph. Briefly restate each main idea—in your own words.

**Strategy ②** Include key facts and any numbers, dates, amounts, or percentages from the text.

**Strategy ③** After writing your summary, review it to see that you have included only the most important details.

**HARRIET TUBMAN**

① One of the most famous conductors on the Underground Railroad was Harriet Tubman. ② Born into slavery in Maryland, the 13-year-old Tubman once tried to save another slave from punishment. The angry overseer fractured Tubman's skull with a two-pound weight. She suffered fainting spells for the rest of her life but did not let that stop her from working for freedom. When she was 25, Tubman learned that her owner was about to sell her. Instead, ② she escaped.

After her escape, ② Harriet Tubman made 19 dangerous journeys to free enslaved persons. The tiny woman carried a pistol to frighten off slave hunters and medicine to quiet crying babies. Her enemies offered $40,000 for her capture, but ② no one caught her. "I never run my train off the track and I never lost a passenger," she proudly declared. Among the people she saved were her parents.

### Write a Summary

You can write your summary in a paragraph. The paragraph at right summarizes the passage you just read.

③ *Harriet Tubman was one of the most famous conductors on the Underground Railroad. She had been a slave, but she escaped. She later made 19 dangerous journeys to free other slaves. She was never captured.*

## Practicing the Skill

Turn to Chapter 6, Section 2, "Colonial Resistance Grows." Read "The Boston Tea Party" and write a paragraph summarizing the passage.

# 1.2 Taking Notes

## Defining the Skill

When you **take notes,** you write down the important ideas and details of a paragraph, passage, or chapter. A chart or an outline can help you organize your notes to use in the future.

## Applying the Skill

The following passage describes President Washington's cabinet. Use the strategies listed below to help you take notes on the passage.

### How to Take and Organize Notes

**Strategy 1** Look at the title to find the main topic of the passage.

**Strategy 2** Identify the main ideas and details of the passage. Then summarize the main idea and details in your notes.

**Strategy 3** Identify key terms and define them. The term *cabinet* is shown in boldface type and underlined; both techniques signal that it is a key term.

**Strategy 4** In your notes, use abbreviations to save time and space. You can abbreviate words such as *department (dept.), secretary (sec.), United States (U.S.),* and *president (pres.)* to save time and space.

1 WASHINGTON'S CABINET

2 The Constitution gave Congress the task of creating departments to help the president lead the nation. The 2 president had the power to appoint the heads of these departments, which became his 3 **cabinet.**

Congress created three departments. Washington chose talented people to run them. 2 For secretary of war, he picked Henry Knox, a trusted general during the Revolution. 2 For secretary of state, Washington chose Thomas Jefferson. He had been serving as ambassador to France. The State Department oversaw U.S. foreign relations. For secretary of the treasury, Washington turned to the brilliant 2 Alexander Hamilton.

### Make a Chart

Making a chart can help you take notes on a passage. The chart below contains notes from the passage you just read.

| 2 Item | Notes |
|---|---|
| I. 3 cabinet | heads of 4 depts.; 4 pres. appoints heads |
| a. War Dept. | Henry Knox; 4 sec. of war; former Revolutionary War general |
| b. State Dept. | Thomas Jefferson; sec. of state; oversees relations between 4 U.S. and other countries |
| c. Treasury Dept. | Alexander Hamilton; sec. of the treasury |

## Practicing the Skill

Turn to Chapter 3, Section 3, "Founding the Middle and Southern Colonies." Read "Maryland and the Carolinas" and use a chart to take notes on the passage.

# 1.3 Sequencing Events

## Defining the Skill

**Sequence** is the order in which events follow one another. By being able to follow the sequence of events through history, you can get an accurate sense of the relationship among events.

## Applying the Skill

The following passage describes the sequence of events involved in Britain's plan to capture the Hudson River Valley during the American Revolution. Use the strategies listed below to help you follow the sequence of events.

### How to Find the Sequence of Events

**Strategy ❶** Look for specific dates provided in the text. If several months within a year are included, the year is usually not repeated.

**Strategy ❷** Look for clues about time that allow you to order events according to sequence. Words such as *day, week, month,* or *year* may help to sequence the events.

**BRITAIN'S STRATEGY**

Burgoyne captured Fort Ticonderoga in ❶ July 1777. From there, it was 25 miles to the Hudson River, which ran to Albany. ❷ Burgoyne took three weeks to reach the Hudson. On ❶ August 3, Burgoyne received a message from Howe. He would not be coming north, Howe wrote, because he had decided to invade Pennsylvania to try to capture Philadelphia and General Washington. "Success be ever with you," Howe's message said. But General Burgoyne needed Howe's soldiers, not his good wishes. Howe did invade Pennsylvania. In ❶ September 1777, he defeated—but did not capture—Washington at the Battle of Brandywine.

### Make a Time Line

Making a time line can help you sequence events. The time line below shows the sequence of events in the passage you just read.

July 1777: Burgoyne captures Fort Ticonderoga.
Three weeks after the capture of Fort Ticonderoga: Burgoyne reaches the Hudson.
August 3, 1777: Howe writes that he will not join Burgoyne.
September 1777: Howe defeats Washington at Brandywine.

## Practicing the Skill

Turn to Chapter 2, Section 1, "Spain Claims an Empire." Read "Europeans Explore Foreign Lands" and make a time line showing the sequence of events in that passage.

R4

# 1.4 Finding Main Ideas

## Defining the Skill

The **main idea** is a statement that summarizes the main point of a speech, an article, a section of a book, or a paragraph. Main ideas can be stated or unstated. The main idea of a paragraph is often stated in the first or last sentence. If it is the first sentence, it is followed by sentences that support that main idea. If it is the last sentence, the details build up to the main idea. To find an unstated idea, you must use the details of the paragraph as clues.

## Applying the Skill

The following paragraph describes the role of women in the American Revolution. Use the strategies listed below to help you identify the main idea.

### How to Find the Main Idea

**Strategy ①** Identify what you think may be the stated main idea. Check the first and last sentences of the paragraph to see if either could be the stated main idea.

**Strategy ②** Identify details that support that idea. Some details explain the main idea. Others give examples of what is stated in the main idea.

**WOMEN IN THE REVOLUTION**

① Many women tried to help the army. Martha Washington and other wives followed their husbands to army camps. ② The wives cooked, did laundry, and nursed sick or wounded soldiers. ② A few women even helped to fight. ② Mary Hays earned the nickname "Molly Pitcher" by carrying water to tired soldiers during a battle. ② Deborah Sampson dressed as a man, enlisted, and fought in several engagements.

### Make a Chart

Making a chart can help you identify the main idea and details in a passage or paragraph. The chart below identifies the main idea and details in the paragraph you just read.

**Main Idea:** *Women helped the army during the Revolution.*

**Detail:** *They cooked and did laundry.*
**Detail:** *They nursed the wounded and sick soldiers.*
**Detail:** *They helped to fight.*
**Detail:** *One woman, Molly Pitcher, carried water to soldiers during battles.*

## Practicing the Skill

Turn to Chapter 5, Section 1, "Early American Culture." Read "Women and the Economy" and create a chart that identifies the main idea and the supporting details.



R5

# 1.5 Categorizing

## Defining the Skill

To **categorize** is to sort people, objects, ideas, or other information into groups, called categories. Historians categorize information to help them identify and understand patterns in historical events.

## Applying the Skill

The following passage contains information about the reasons people went west during the mid-1800s. Use the strategies listed below to help you categorize information.

### How to Categorize

**Strategy 1** First, decide what kind of information needs to be categorized. Decide what the passage is about and how that information can be sorted into categories.

For example, find the different motives people had for moving west.

**Strategy 2** Then find out what the categories will be. To find why many different groups of people moved west, look for clue words such as *some, other,* and *another.*

**Strategy 3** Once you have chosen the categories, sort information into them. Of the people who went west, which ones had which motives?

**THE LURE OF THE WEST**

1 People had many different motives for going west. 2 One motive was to make money. 2 *Some* people called speculators bought huge areas of land and made great profits by selling it to thousands of settlers. 2 *Other* settlers included farmers who dreamed of owning their own farms in the West because land was difficult to acquire in the East. 2 *Another* group to move west was merchants. They hoped to earn money by selling items that farmers needed. Finally, 2 *some* people went west for religious reasons. These people included 2 missionaries, who wanted to convert the Native Americans to Christianity, and Mormons, who wanted a place where they could practice their faith without interference.

### Make a Chart

Making a chart can help you categorize information. You should have as many columns as you have categories. The chart below shows how the information from the passage you just read can be categorized.

3

| Motives | Money | Land | Religion |
|---|---|---|---|
| Groups | • speculators<br>• merchants | • farmers | • missionaries<br>• Mormons |

## Practicing the Skill

Turn to Chapter 14, Section 3, "Reforming American Society." Read "Improving Education" and make a chart in which you categorize the changes happening in elementary, high school, and college education.

# 1.6 Making Public Speeches

## Defining the Skill

A speech is a talk given in public to an audience. Some speeches are given to persuade the audience to think or act in a certain way, or to support a cause. You can learn how to **make public speeches** effectively by analyzing great speeches in history.

## Applying the Skill

The following is an excerpt from the "I Have a Dream" speech delivered by Martin Luther King, Jr., in 1963 in Washington, D.C. Use the strategies listed below to help you analyze King's speech and prepare a speech of your own.

### How to Analyze and Prepare a Speech

**Strategy 1** Choose one central idea or theme and organize your speech to support it. King organized his speech around his dream of equality.

**Strategy 2** Use words or images that will win over your audience. King referred to the Declaration of Independence when he used the words "all men are created equal."

**Strategy 3** Repeat words or images to drive home your main point—as if it is the "hook" of a pop song. King repeats the phrase "I have a dream."

**I HAVE A DREAM**

1 I have a dream that one day this nation will rise up and live out the true meaning of its creed—we hold these truths to be 2 self-evident that all men are created equal.

3 I have a dream that one day on the red hills of Georgia the sons of former slaves and the sons of former slave owners will be able to sit down together at the table of brotherhood.

3 I have a dream that my four little children will one day live in a nation where they will not be judged by the color of their skin but by the content of their character.

3 I have a dream today!

### Make an Outline

Making an outline like the one to the right will help you make an effective public speech.

**Title:** I Have a Dream

**I. Introduce Theme:** I have a dream
- A. This nation will live up to its creed
- B. Quote from the Declaration of Independence: that all men are created equal

**II. Repeat theme:** I have a dream
- A. Sons of former slaves and slave owners will sit together in brotherhood
- B. My four children will be judged by their character, not by their skin color

**III. Conclude:** I have a dream

## Practicing the Skill

Turn to Chapter 12, Section 2, "Jackson's Policy Toward Native Americans." Read the section and choose a topic for a speech. First, make an outline like the one to the right to organize your ideas. Then write your speech. Next, practice giving your speech. Make it a three-minute speech.



R7

# 2.1 Analyzing Points of View

## Defining the Skill

**Analyzing points of view** means looking closely at a person's arguments to understand the reasons behind that person's beliefs. The goal of analyzing a point of view is to understand a historical figure's thoughts and opinions about a topic.

## Applying the Skill

The following passage describes the Panic of 1837 and two politicians' points of view about it. Use the strategies listed below to help you analyze their points of view.

### How to Analyze Points of View

**Strategy 1** Look for statements that show you a person's view on an issue. For example, Van Buren said he believed the economy would improve if he took no action. Clay thought the government should do something to help the people.

**Strategy 2** Think about why people might take the positions they took. Clay was in a different political party than Van Buren. Why do you think he would disagree with Van Buren's argument?

**Strategy 3** Write a summary that explains why different people took different positions on the issue.

**THE PANIC OF 1837**

The Panic of 1837 caused severe hardship. People had little money, so manufacturers had few customers for their goods. Almost 90 percent of factories in the East closed. Jobless workers could not afford food or rent. Many people went hungry.

1 Whig senator Henry Clay wanted the government to do something to help the people. 1 President Van Buren, a Democrat, disagreed. He believed that the economy would improve if left alone. He argued that "the less government interferes with private pursuits the better for the general prosperity." Many Americans blamed Van Buren for the Panic, though he had taken office only weeks before it started. The continuing depression made it difficult for him to win reelection in 1840.

### Make a Diagram

Using a diagram can help you analyze points of view. The diagram below analyzes the views of Clay and Van Buren in the passage you just read.

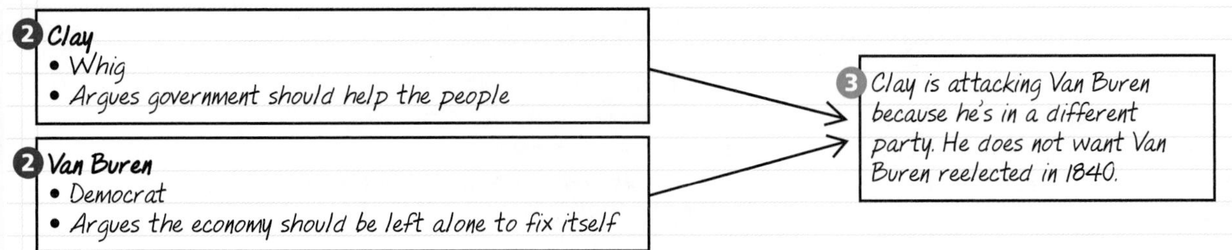

2 Clay
• Whig
• Argues government should help the people
2 Van Buren
• Democrat
• Argues the economy should be left alone to fix itself
3 Clay is attacking Van Buren because he's in a different party. He does not want Van Buren reelected in 1840.


## Practicing the Skill

Turn to the Interactive Primary Sources on pages 238 and 239. Read the selections by James Madison and George Mason. Make a chart to analyze their opposing points of view on the Constitution.

# 2.2 Comparing and Contrasting

## Defining the Skill

**Comparing** means looking at the similarities and differences between two or more things. **Contrasting** means examining only the differences between them. Historians compare and contrast events, personalities, behaviors, beliefs, and situations in order to understand them.

## Applying the Skill

The following paragraph describes the American and British troops during the Revolutionary War. Use the strategies listed below to help you compare and contrast these two armies.

### How to Compare and Contrast

**Strategy 1** Look for two aspects of the subject that may be compared and contrasted. This passage compares the British and American troops to show why the Americans won the war.

**Strategy 2** To contrast, look for clue words that show how two things differ. Clue words include *by contrast, however, except,* and *yet.*

**Strategy 3** To find similarities, look for clue words indicating that two things are alike. Clue words include *both, like, as,* and *similarly.*

**WHY THE AMERICANS WON**

1 By their persistence, the Americans defeated the British even though they faced many obstacles. The Americans lacked training and experience. They were often short of supplies and weapons. 2 *By contrast,* the British forces ranked among the best trained in the world. They were experienced and well-supplied professional soldiers. 2 *Yet,* the Americans also had advantages that enabled them to win. These advantages over the British were better leadership, foreign aid, a knowledge of the land, and motivation. Although 3 *both* the British and the Americans were fighting for their lives, 2 the Americans were also fighting for their property and their dream of liberty.

### Make a Venn Diagram

Making a Venn diagram will help you identify similarities and differences between two things. In the overlapping area, list characteristics shared by both subjects. Then, in the separate ovals, list the characteristics of each subject not shared by the other. This Venn diagram compares and contrasts the British and American soldiers.

American Soldiers:
• lacked experience and training
• short of supplies and weapons
• had better leadership
• received foreign aid
• had knowledge of the land
• fought for liberty and property
Both:
fought for their lives
British Soldiers:
• best trained in the world
• experienced
• well-supplied

## Practicing the Skill

Turn to Chapter 5, Section 1, "Early American Culture." Read "Young People at Work" and make a Venn diagram showing the similarities and differences between the roles of boys and girls in colonial America.

R9

# 2.3 Analyzing Causes; Recognizing Effects

## Defining the Skill

A **cause** is an action in history that makes something happen. An **effect** is the historical event that is the result of the cause. A single event may have several causes. It is also possible for one cause to result in several effects. Historians identify cause-and-effect relationships to help them understand why historical events took place.

## Applying the Skill

The following paragraph describes events that caused changes in Puritan New England. Use the strategies listed below to help you identify the cause-and-effect relationships.

### How to Analyze Causes and Recognize Effects

**Strategy 1** Ask why an action took place. Ask yourself a question about the title and topic sentence, such as, "What caused changes in Puritan society?"

**Strategy 2** Look for effects. Ask yourself, "What happened?" (the effect). Then ask, "Why did it happen?" (the cause). For example, What caused the decline of Puritan religion in New England?

**Strategy 3** Look for clue words that signal causes, such as *cause* and *led to.*

**1 CHANGES IN PURITAN SOCIETY**

1 The early 1700s saw many changes in New England society. 2 One of the most important changes was the gradual decline of the Puritan religion in New England. There were a number of reasons for that decline.

3 One *cause* of this decline was the increasing competition from other religious groups. Baptists and Anglicans established churches in Massachusetts and Connecticut, where Puritans had once been the most powerful group. 3 Political changes also *led to* a weakening of the Puritan community. In 1691, a new royal charter for Massachusetts granted the vote based on property ownership instead of church membership.

### Make a Diagram

Using a diagram can help you understand causes and effects. The diagram below shows two causes and an effect for the passage you just read.

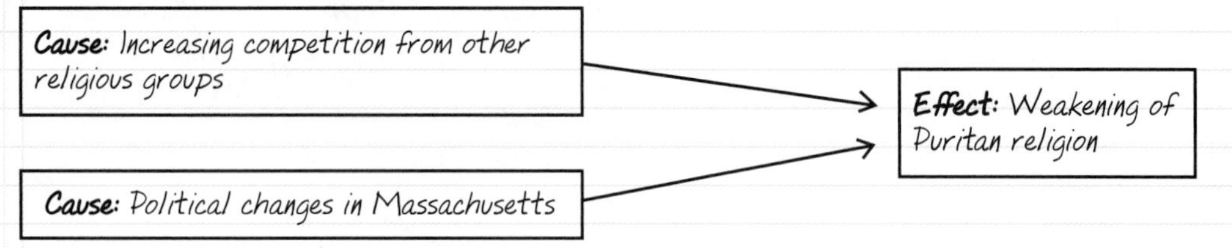


## Practicing the Skill

Turn to Chapter 2, Section 1, "Spain Claims an Empire." Read "Reasons for Spanish Victories" and make a diagram about the causes and effects of the Spanish conquest of the Americas.

# 2.4 Making Inferences

## Defining the Skill

Inferences are ideas that the author has not directly stated. **Making inferences** involves reading between the lines to interpret the information you read. You can make inferences by studying what is stated and using your common sense and previous knowledge.

## Applying the Skill

The passage below describes the strengths and weaknesses of the North and the South as the Civil War began. Use the strategies listed below to help you make inferences from the passage.

### How to Make Inferences

**Strategy 1** Read to find statements of facts and ideas. Knowing the facts will give you a good basis for making inferences.

**Strategy 2** Use your knowledge, logic, and common sense to make inferences that are based on facts. Ask yourself, "What does the author want me to understand?" For example, from the facts about population, you can make the inference that the North would have a larger army than the South. See other inferences in the chart below.

**ADVANTAGES OF THE NORTH AND THE SOUTH**

The North had more people and resources than the South. 1 The North had about 22 million people. 1 The South had roughly 9 million, of whom about 3.5 million were slaves. In addition, 1 the North had more than 80 percent of the nation's factories and almost all of the shipyards and naval power. The South had some advantages, too. 1 It had able generals, such as Robert E. Lee. 1 It also had the advantage of fighting a defensive war. Soldiers defending their homes have more will to fight than invaders do.

### Make a Chart

Making a chart will help you organize information and make logical inferences. The chart below organizes information from the passage you just read.

| 1 Stated Facts and Ideas | 2 Inferences |
|---|---|
| The North had about 22 million people.<br>The Confederacy had about 9 million, less the 3.5 million slaves. | The North would have a larger army than the South. |
| The North had more factories, naval power, and shipyards. | The North could provide more weapons, ammunition, and ships for the war. |
| The Confederacy had excellent generals. | The Confederacy had better generals, which would help it overcome other disadvantages. |
| The Confederacy was fighting a defensive war. | Confederate soldiers would fight harder because they were defending their homes and families. |

## Practicing the Skill

Turn to Chapter 11, Section 1, "Early Industry and Inventions." Read "The Industrial Revolution Begins" and use a chart like the one above to make inferences about early industry.



R11

# 2.5 Drawing Conclusions

## Defining the Skill

**Drawing conclusions** means analyzing what you have read and forming an opinion about its meaning. To draw conclusions, look at the facts and then use your own common sense and experience to decide what the facts mean.

## Applying the Skill

The following passage presents information about the Intolerable Acts and the colonists' reactions to them. Use the strategies listed below to help you draw conclusions about those acts.

### How to Draw Conclusions

**Strategy ❶** Read carefully to identify and understand all the facts, or statements, that can be proven true.

**Strategy ❷** List the facts in a diagram and review them. Use your own experiences and common sense to understand how the facts relate to each other.

**Strategy ❸** After reviewing the facts, write down the conclusion you have drawn about them.

**THE INTOLERABLE ACTS**

❶ In 1774, Parliament passed a series of laws to punish the Massachusetts colony and serve as a warning to other colonies. ❶ These laws were so harsh that colonists called them the **Intolerable Acts**. One of the acts closed the port of Boston. Others banned committees of correspondence and allowed Britain to house troops wherever necessary.

In 1773, Sam Adams had written, "I wish we could arouse the continent." ❶ The Intolerable Acts answered his wish. Other colonies immediately offered Massachusetts their support.

### Make a Diagram

Making a diagram can help you draw conclusions. The diagram below shows how to organize facts and inferences to draw a conclusion about the passage you just read.

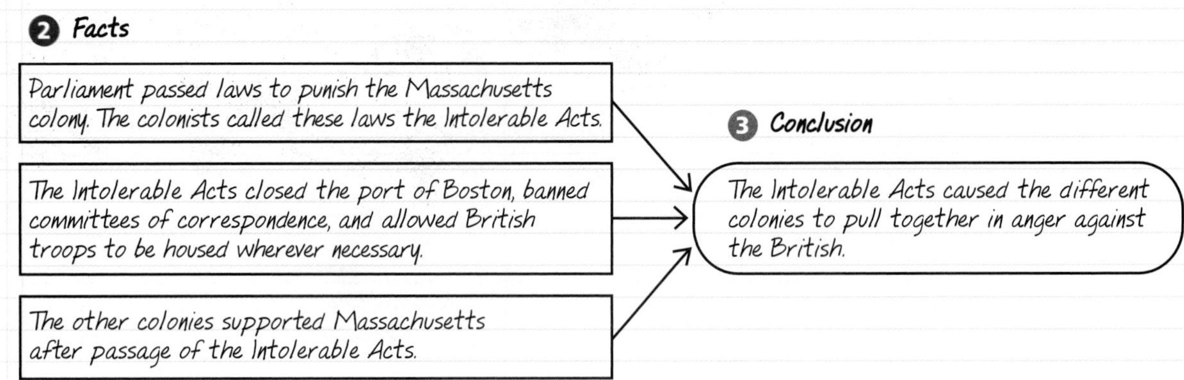

❷ Facts
Parliament passed laws to punish the Massachusetts colony. The colonists called these laws the Intolerable Acts.
The Intolerable Acts closed the port of Boston, banned committees of correspondence, and allowed British troops to be housed wherever necessary.
The other colonies supported Massachusetts after passage of the Intolerable Acts.
❸ Conclusion
The Intolerable Acts caused the different colonies to pull together in anger against the British.


## Practicing the Skill

Turn to Chapter 3, Section 2, "New England Colonies." Read "The Salem Witchcraft Trials" and use the diagram above as a model to draw conclusions about the trials.

# 2.6 Making Decisions

## Defining the Skill

**Making decisions** involves choosing between two or more options, or courses of action. In most cases, decisions have consequences, or results. Sometimes decisions may lead to new problems. By understanding how historical figures made decisions, you can learn how to improve your decision-making skills.

## Applying the Skill

The following passage describes Lincoln's decisions regarding federal forts after the Southern states seceded. Use the strategies listed below to help you analyze his decisions.

### How to Make Decisions

**Strategy 1** Identify a decision that needs to be made. Think about what factors make the decision difficult.

**Strategy 2** Identify possible consequences of the decision. Remember that there can be more than one consequence to a decision.

**Strategy 3** Identify the decision that was made.

**Strategy 4** Identify actual consequences that resulted from the decision.

**FIRST SHOTS AT FORT SUMTER**

1 Lincoln had to decide what to do about the forts in the South that remained under federal control. A Union garrison still held **Fort Sumter**, but they were running out of supplies. 2 If Lincoln supplied the garrison, he risked war. 2 If he withdrew the garrison, he would be giving in to the rebels. 3 Lincoln informed South Carolina that he was sending supply ships to Fort Sumter. 4 Confederate leaders decided to prevent the federal government from holding on to the fort by attacking before the supply ships arrived. No one was killed, but 4 the South's attack on Fort Sumter signaled the beginning of the Civil War.

### Make a Flow Chart

A flow chart can help you identify the process of making a decision. The flow chart below shows the decision-making process in the passage you just read.

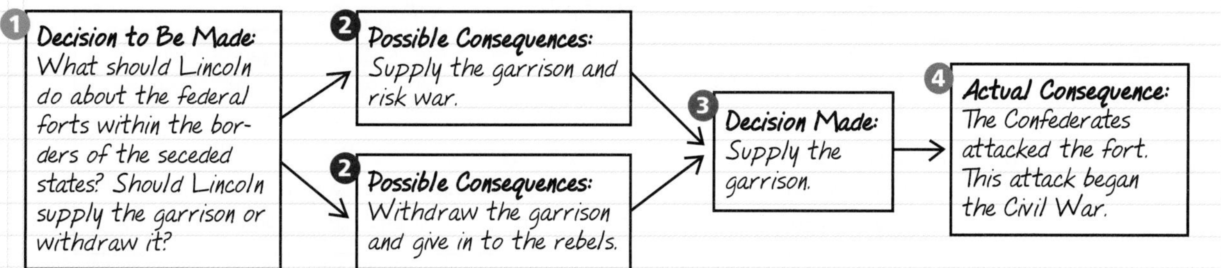


## Practicing the Skill

Turn to Chapter 6, Section 1, "Tighter British Control." Read "The Colonies Protest the Stamp Act" and make a flow chart to identify a decision and its consequences described in that section.

# 2.7 Recognizing Propaganda

## Defining the Skill

**Propaganda** is communication that aims to influence people's opinions, emotions, or actions. Propaganda is not always factual. Rather, it uses one-sided language or striking symbols to sway people's emotions. Modern advertising often uses propaganda. By thinking critically, you will avoid being swayed by propaganda.

## Applying the Skill

The following political cartoon shows Andrew Jackson dressed as a king. Use the strategies listed below to help you understand how it works as propaganda.

### How to Recognize Propaganda

**Strategy ❶** Identify the aim, or purpose, of the cartoon. Point out the subject and explain the point of view.

**Strategy ❷** Identify those images on the cartoon that viewers might respond to emotionally and identify the emotions.

**Strategy ❸** Think critically about the cartoon. What facts has the cartoon ignored?

BORN TO COMMAND.
OF VETO MEMORY.
HAD I BEEN CONSULTED.
KING ANDREW THE FIRST.

### Make a Chart

Making a chart will help you think critically about a piece of propaganda. The chart below summarizes the information from the anti-Jackson cartoon.

| | |
|---|---|
| ❶ *Identify Purpose* | *The cartoon portrays Jackson negatively by showing him as a king.* |
| ❷ *Identify Emotions* | *The cartoonist knows that Americans like democracy. So he portrays Jackson as a king because kings are not usually supporters of democracy. He also shows Jackson standing on a torn U.S. Constitution—another thing that Americans love.* |
| ❸ *Think Critically* | *The cartoon shows Jackson vetoing laws. But it ignores the fact that those actions were not against the Constitution. The president has the power to veto legislation. In this case, Jackson was exercising the power of the presidency, not acting like a king.* |

## Practicing the Skill

Turn to Chapter 6, Section 2, "Colonial Resistance Grows," and look at the engraving *The Bloody Massacre* on page 165. Use a chart like the one above to think critically about the engraving as an example of propaganda.

# 2.8 Identifying Facts and Opinions

## Defining the Skill

**Facts** are events, dates, statistics, or statements that can be proved to be true. **Opinions** are the judgments, beliefs, and feelings of a writer or speaker. By identifying facts and opinions, you will be able to think critically when a person is trying to influence your own opinion.

## Applying the Skill

The following passage tells about the Virginia Plan for legislative representation offered at the Constitutional Convention of 1787. Use the strategies listed below to help you distinguish facts from opinions.

### How to Recognize Facts and Opinions

**Strategy ①** Look for specific information that can be proved or checked for accuracy.

**Strategy ②** Look for assertions, claims, and judgments that express opinions. In this case, one speaker's opinion is expressed in a direct quote.

**Strategy ③** Think about whether statements can be checked for accuracy. Then, identify the facts and opinions in a chart.

**ANTIFEDERALIST VIEWS**

① Antifederalists published their views about the Constitution in newspapers and pamphlets. ① They thought the Constitution took too much power away from the states and did not protect the rights of the people. They charged that the Constitution would destroy American liberties. As one Antifederalist wrote, ② "it is truly astonishing that a set of men among ourselves should have had the [nerve] to attempt the destruction of our liberties."

### Make a Chart

The chart below analyzes the facts and opinions from the passage above.

| *Statement* | ③ *Can It Be Proved?* | ③ *Fact or Opinion* |
|---|---|---|
| *Antifederalists published their views in newspapers and pamphlets.* | *Yes. Check newspapers and other historical documents.* | *Fact* |
| *They thought the Constitution took too much power away from the states.* | *Yes. Check newspapers and other historical documents.* | *Fact* |
| *It is astonishing that some Americans would try to destroy American liberties.* | *No. This cannot be proved. It is what one speaker believes.* | *Opinion* |

## Practicing the Skill

Turn to Chapter 11, Section 3, and read the section entitled "The Missouri Compromise." Make a chart in which you analyze key statements to determine whether they are facts or opinions.



R15

# 2.9 Forming and Supporting Opinions

## Defining the Skill

When you **form opinions,** you interpret and judge the importance of events and people in history. You should always **support your opinions** with facts, examples, and quotes.

## Applying the Skill

The following passage describes events that followed the gold rush. Use the strategies listed below to form and support your opinions about the events.

### How to Form and Support Opinions

**Strategy (1)** Look for important information about the events. Information can include facts, quotations, and examples.

**Strategy (2)** Form an opinion about the event by asking yourself questions about the information. For example, How important was the event? What were its effects?

**Strategy (3)** Support your opinions with facts, quotations, and examples. If the facts do not support the opinion, then rewrite your opinion so it is supported by the facts.

**THE IMPACT OF THE GOLD RUSH**

By 1852, the gold rush was over. (1) While it lasted, about 250,000 people flooded into California. (1) This huge migration caused economic growth that changed California. (1) The port city San Francisco grew to become a center of banking, manufacturing, shipping, and trade. (1) However, the gold rush ruined many *Californios. Californios* are the Hispanic people of California. The newcomers did not respect *Californios,* their customs, or their legal rights. (1) In many cases, Americans seized their property.

Native Americans suffered even more. (1) Thousands died from diseases brought by the newcomers. (1) Miners hunted down and killed thousands more. (1) By 1870, California's Native American population had fallen from 150,000 to only about 30,000.

### Make a Chart

Making a chart can help you organize your opinions and supporting facts. The following chart summarizes one possible opinion about the impact of the gold rush.

| | |
|---|---|
| (2) *Opinion* | *The effects of the gold rush were more negative than positive.* |
| (3) *Facts* | *Californios were not respected, and their land was stolen.* |
| | *Many Native Americans died from diseases, and others were killed by miners. Their population dropped from 150,000 to about 30,000.* |

## Practicing the Skill

Turn to Chapter 11, Section 3, "Nationalism and Sectionalism." Read "The Missouri Compromise" and form your own opinion about the compromise and its impact. Make a chart like the one above to summarize your opinion and the supporting facts and examples.

# 2.10 Identifying and Solving Problems

## Defining the Skill

**Identifying problems** means finding and understanding the difficulties faced by a particular group of people during a certain time. **Solving problems** means understanding how people tried to remedy those problems. By studying how people solved problems in the past, you can learn ways to solve problems today.

## Applying the Skill

The following paragraph describes problems that the Constitutional Convention faced on the issues of taxation, representation, and slavery. Use the strategies listed below to help you see how the Founders tried to solve these problems.

### How to Identify Problems and Solutions

**Strategy ①** Look for the difficulties, or problems, people faced.

**Strategy ②** Consider how the problem affected people with different points of view. For example, the main problem described here was how to count the population of each state.

**Strategy ③** Look for solutions people tried to deal with each problem. Think about whether the solution was a good one for people with differing points of view.

**SLAVERY AND THE CONSTITUTION**

Because the House of Representatives would have members according to the population of each state, ① the delegates had to decide who would be counted in the population of each state. The Southern states had many more slaves than the Northern states had. ② Southerners wanted the slaves to be counted as part of the general population for representation but not for taxation. ② Northerners argued that slaves were not citizens and should not be counted for representation, but that slaves should be counted for taxation. ③ The delegates decided that three-fifths of the slave population would be counted in the population to determine both representation and taxes.

### Make a Chart

Making a chart will help you identify and organize information about problems and solutions. The chart below shows problems and solutions included in the passage you just read.

| ① Problem | ② Differing Points of View | ③ Solution |
|---|---|---|
| Northerners and Southerners couldn't agree on how to count population because of slavery in the South. | Southerners wanted slaves counted for representation but not for taxation. Northerners wanted slaves counted for taxation but not for representation. | Delegates decided that three-fifths of the slave population should be counted. |

## Practicing the Skill

Turn to Chapter 8, Section 2, "Creating the Constitution." Read "The Convention Assembles" and "The Virginia Plan." Then make a chart that summarizes the problems faced by the delegates at the Constitutional Convention and the solutions they agreed on.

# 2.11 Evaluating

## Defining the Skill

To **evaluate** is to make a judgment about something. Historians evaluate the actions of people in history. One way to do this is to examine both the positives and negatives of a historical action, then decide which is stronger—the positive or the negative.

## Applying the Skill

The following passage describes Susan B. Anthony's fight for women's rights. Use the strategies listed below to evaluate how successful she was.

### How to Evaluate

**Strategy ❶** Before you evaluate a person's actions, first determine what that person was trying to do. In this case, think about what Anthony wanted to accomplish.

**Strategy ❷** Look for statements that show the positive, or successful, results of her actions. For example, Did she achieve her goals?

**Strategy ❸** Also look for statements that show the negative, or unsuccessful, results of her actions. Did she fail to achieve something she tried to do?

**Strategy ❹** Write an overall evaluation of the person's actions.

**SUSAN B. ANTHONY**

❶ Susan B. Anthony was a skilled organizer who fought for women's rights. ❷ She successfully built the women's movement into a national organization. Anthony believed that a woman must have money of her own. To this end, she supported laws that would give married women rights to control their own property and wages. ❷ Mississippi passed the first such law in 1839. New York passed a property law in 1848 and a wages law in 1860. ❸ Anthony also wanted to win the vote for women but failed to convince lawmakers to pass this reform in her lifetime. This reform did go through in 1920, 14 years after her death.

### Make a Diagram for Evaluating

Using a diagram can help you evaluate. List the positives and negatives of the historical person's actions and decisions. Then make an overall judgment. The diagram below shows how the information from the passage you just read can be diagrammed.

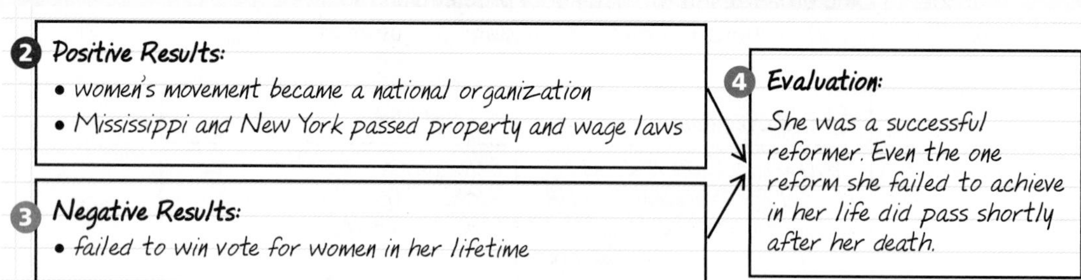

❷ Positive Results:
• women's movement became a national organization
• Mississippi and New York passed property and wage laws
❸ Negative Results:
• failed to win vote for women in her lifetime
❹ Evaluation:
She was a successful reformer. Even the one reform she failed to achieve in her life did pass shortly after her death.


## Practicing the Skill

Turn to Chapter 2, Section 3, "The Spanish and Native Americans." Read "The Columbian Exchange" and make a diagram in which you evaluate whether the Columbian Exchange had mainly a positive or negative impact on the world.

# 2.12 Making Generalizations

## Defining the Skill

To **make generalizations** means to make broad judgments based on information. When you make generalizations, you should gather information from several sources.

## Applying the Skill

The following three passages contain different views on George Washington. Use the strategies listed below to make a generalization about these views.

### How to Make Generalizations

**Strategy** ❶ Look for information that the sources have in common. These three sources all discuss George Washington's ability as a military leader.

**Strategy** ❷ Form a generalization that describes Washington in a way that all three sources would agree with. State your generalization in a sentence.

**WASHINGTON'S LEADERSHIP**

❶ Washington learned from his mistakes. After early defeats, he developed the strategy of dragging out the war to wear down the British. ❶ Despite difficulties, he never gave up.

—*Creating America*

❶ [Washington] was no military genius. . . . But he was a great war leader. Creating an army out of unpromising material, he kept it in being against great odds.

—*The Limits of Liberty*

❶ [Washington] certainly deserves some merit as a general, that he . . . can keep General Howe dancing from one town to another for two years together, with such an army as he has.

—*The Journal of Nicholas Cresswell, July 13, 1777*

### Make a Chart

Using a chart can help you make generalizations. The chart below shows how the information you just read can be used to generalize about people's views of Washington.

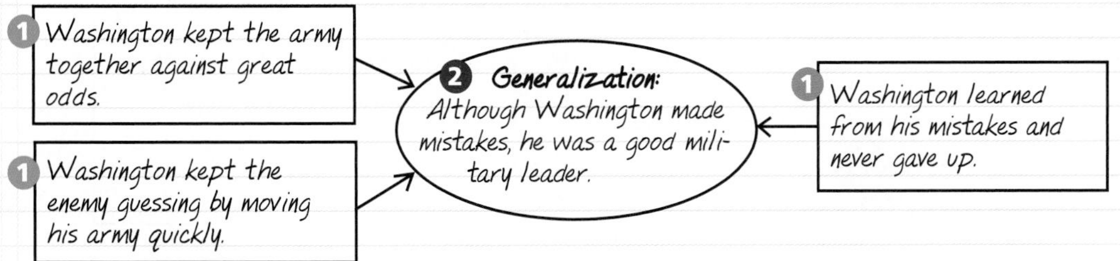


## Practicing the Skill

Turn to Chapter 16, Section 1, "War Erupts." Read "Choosing Sides." Also read the excerpt from *Across Five Aprils* on pages 486–487. Then use a chart like the one above to make a generalization about how the outbreak of the Civil War affected Americans.

# 3.1 Using Primary and Secondary Sources

## Defining the Skill

**Primary sources** are materials written or made by people who lived during historical events and witnessed them. Primary sources can be letters, journal entries, speeches, autobiographies, or artwork. Other kinds of primary sources are government documents, census surveys, and financial records. **Secondary sources** are materials written by people who did not participate in an event. History books are secondary sources.

## Applying the Skill

The following passage contains both a primary source and a secondary source. Use the strategies listed below to help you read them.

### How to Read Primary and Secondary Sources

**Strategy 1** Distinguish secondary sources from primary sources. The first paragraph is a secondary source. The Declaration of Independence is a primary source. The secondary source explains something about the primary source.

**Strategy 2** Analyze the primary source and consider why the author produced it. Consider what the document was supposed to achieve and who would read it.

**Strategy 3** Identify the author of the primary source and note when and where it was written.

1 The core idea of the Declaration is based on the philosophy of John Locke. This idea is that people have unalienable rights, or rights that government cannot take away. Jefferson stated this belief in what was to become the Declaration's best-known passage.

> 2 We hold these truths to be self-evident, that all men are created equal, that they are endowed by their Creator with certain unalienable Rights, that among these are Life, Liberty and the pursuit of Happiness.
>
> 3 —Thomas Jefferson, *The Declaration of Independence,* 1776

### Make a Chart

Making a chart will help you summarize information from primary sources and secondary sources. The chart below summarizes the information from the passage you just read.

| | |
|---|---|
| *Author* | *Thomas Jefferson* |
| *Document* | *The Declaration of Independence* |
| *Notes on Primary Source* | *The Declaration says that "all men are created equal." It also says that people have "unalienable rights." These rights include the right to life and the right to liberty, as well as a right to pursue happiness.* |
| *Notes on Secondary Source* | *Jefferson based his ideas on those of John Locke. Locke had written about rights that governments could not take away from the people.* |

## Practicing the Skill

Turn to Chapter 6, Section 3, "The Road to Lexington and Concord." Read "Between War and Peace" and make a chart like the one above to summarize the information in the primary source and the secondary source.

# 3.2 Interpreting Graphs

## Defining the Skill

**Graphs** use pictures and symbols, instead of words, to show information. There are many different kinds of graphs. Bar graphs, line graphs, and pie graphs are the most common. Bar graphs compare numbers or sets of numbers. The length of each bar shows a quantity. It is easy to see how different categories compare on a bar graph.

## Applying the Skill

The bar graph below shows numbers of immigrants coming to the United States between 1821 and 1860. Use the strategies listed below to help you interpret the graph.

### How to Interpret a Graph

**Strategy 1** Read the title to identify the main idea of the graph.

**Strategy 2** Read the vertical axis (the one that goes up and down) on the left side of the graph. This one shows the number of immigrants in thousands. Each bar represents the number of immigrants during a particular decade.

**Strategy 3** Read the horizontal axis (the one that runs across the bottom of the graph). This one shows the four decades from 1821 to 1860.

**Strategy 4** Summarize the information shown in each part of the graph. Use the title to help you focus on what information the graph is presenting.

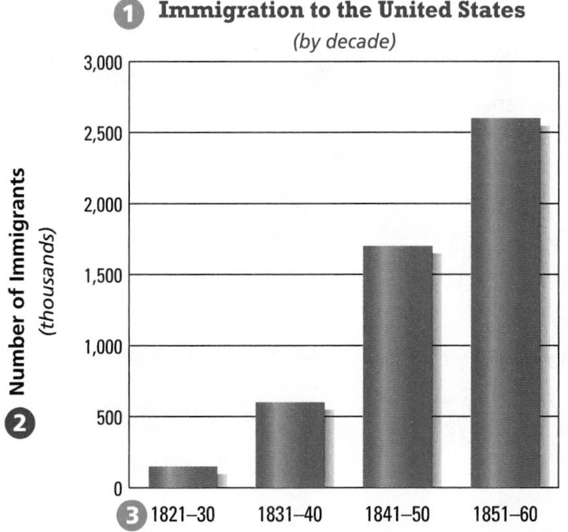


### Write a Summary

Writing a summary will help you understand the information in the graph. The paragraph to the right summarizes the information from the bar graph.

4 *Immigration to the United States increased between 1821 and 1860. Between 1821 and 1830, fewer than 200,000 immigrants arrived. In the next decade, more than 500,000 immigrants came. During the 1840s, more than 1.5 million immigrants arrived, and that number increased to more than 2.5 million in the 1850s.*

## Practicing the Skill

Turn to Chapter 2, Section 4, "Beginnings of Slavery in the Americas." Look at the graph entitled "Slaves Imported to the Americas, 1493–1810" and write a paragraph in which you summarize what you learned from it.



R21

# 3.3 Interpreting Charts

## Defining the Skill

**Charts** present information in a visual form. They organize, simplify, and summarize information in a way that makes that information easy to read and understand. Tables and diagrams are examples of commonly used charts.

## Applying the Skill

The chart below shows the number of slaves who were imported to the Americas between 1601 and 1810. Use the strategies listed below to help you interpret the information in the chart.

### How to Interpret a Chart

**Strategy 1** Read the title. It will tell you what the chart is about.

**Strategy 2** Read the labels to see how the information in the chart is organized. In this chart, it is organized by region and years.

**Strategy 3** Study the data in the chart to understand the facts that the chart intends to show.

**Strategy 4** Summarize the information shown in each part of the chart. Use the title to help you focus on what information the chart is presenting.

*1601–1810*

**1 Slaves Imported to the Americas** *(in thousands)*

| 2 *REGION/COUNTRY* | *1601–1700* | *1701–1810* |
|---|---|---|
| 3 British N. America | * | 348 |
| British Caribbean | 263.7 | 1,401.3 |
| French Caribbean | 155.8 | 1,348.4 |
| Spanish America | 292.5 | 578.6 |
| Dutch Caribbean | 40 | 460 |
| Danish Caribbean | 4 | 24 |
| Brazil (Portugal) | 560 | 1,891.4 |

*= less than 1,000

Source: Philip D. Curtin, *The Atlantic Slave Trade*

### Write a Summary

Writing a summary can help you understand the information given in a chart. The paragraph to the right summarizes the information in the chart "Slaves Imported to the Americas, 1601–1810."

4 *The chart shows how many slaves were imported to the Americas between 1601 and 1810. It divides the Americas into seven regions. It also divides the time period into two parts: 1601–1700 and 1701–1810. The number of slaves imported increased greatly from the 1600s to the 1700s. More slaves were imported to Brazil than to any other region.*

## Practicing the Skill

Turn to Chapter 27, Section 5, and look at the chart entitled "World War II Military Casualties, 1939–1945." Study the chart and write a paragraph in which you summarize what you learned from it.

# 3.4 Interpreting Time Lines

## Defining the Skill

A **time line** is a visual list of events and dates shown in the order in which they occurred. Time lines can be horizontal or vertical. On horizontal time lines, the earliest date is on the left. On vertical time lines, the earliest date is often at the top.

## Applying the Skill

The time line below lists dates and events during the presidencies of John Adams, Andrew Jackson, and Martin Van Buren. Use the strategies listed below to help you interpret the information.

### How to Read a Time Line

**Strategy 1** Read the dates at the beginning and end of the time line. These will show the period of history that is covered. The time line below is a dual time line. It includes items related to two topics. The labels show that the information covers U.S. events and world events.

**Strategy 2** Read the dates and events in sequential order, beginning with the earliest one. Pay particular attention to how the entries relate to each other. Think about which events caused later events.

**Strategy 3** Summarize the focus, or main idea, of the time line. Try to write a main idea sentence that describes the time line.

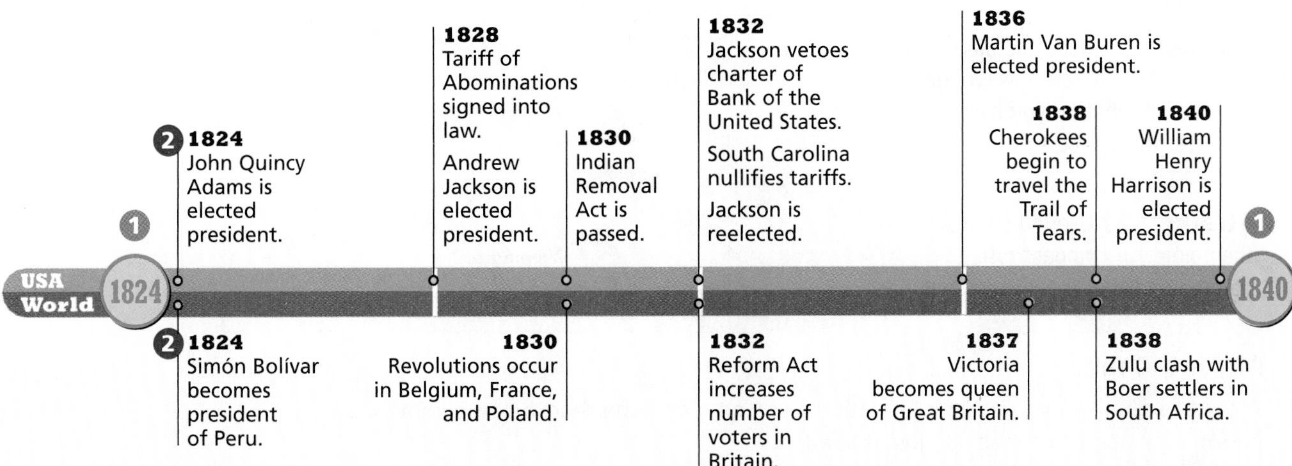

USA
World
1824
1840
1
1
2 1824 John Quincy Adams is elected president.
1828 Tariff of Abominations signed into law.
Andrew Jackson is elected president.
1830 Indian Removal Act is passed.
1832 Jackson vetoes charter of Bank of the United States.
South Carolina nullifies tariffs.
Jackson is reelected.
1836 Martin Van Buren is elected president.
1838 Cherokees begin to travel the Trail of Tears.
1840 William Henry Harrison is elected president.
2 1824 Simón Bolívar becomes president of Peru.
1830 Revolutions occur in Belgium, France, and Poland.
1832 Reform Act increases number of voters in Britain.
1837 Victoria becomes queen of Great Britain.
1838 Zulu clash with Boer settlers in South Africa.

### Write a Summary

Writing a summary can help you understand information shown on a time line. The summary to the right states the main idea of the time line and tells how the events are related.

3 *The time line covers the period between 1824, when John Quincy Adams was elected president, and 1840, when William Henry Harrison was elected president. During that period of time, Andrew Jackson and Martin Van Buren also served as president. The time line shows that the important issues in the United States were tariffs, banking, and relations with Native Americans.*

## Practicing the Skill

Turn to Chapter 15, page 455, and write a summary of the information shown on the time line.

R23

# 3.5 Reading a Map

## Defining the Skill

**Maps** are representations of features on the earth's surface. Some maps show political features, such as national borders. Other maps show physical features, such as mountains and bodies of water. You can understand maps better once you know how to recognize these elements.

## Applying the Skill

The following map shows the Battle of Yorktown during the Revolution. Use the strategies listed below to help you identify the elements common to most maps.

### How to Read a Map

**Strategy 1** Read the title. This identifies the main idea of the map.

**Strategy 2** Look for the grid of lines that form a pattern of squares over the map. These numbered lines are the lines of latitude (horizontal) and longitude (vertical). They indicate the location of the area on the earth.

**Strategy 3** Read the map key. It is usually in a box. This will give you the information you need to interpret the symbols or colors on the map.

**Strategy 4** Use the scale and the pointer, or compass rose, to determine distance and direction.

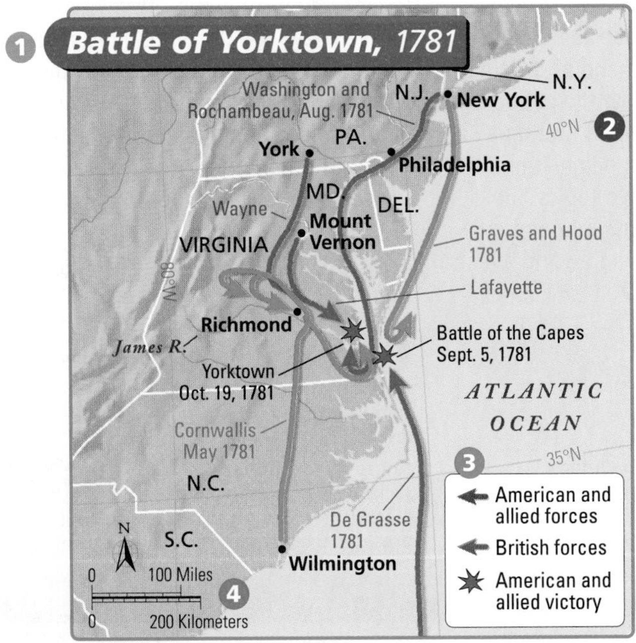


### Make a Chart

A chart can help you organize information given on maps. The chart below summarizes information about the map you just studied.

| Title | Battle of Yorktown, 1781 |
|---|---|
| Location | between latitude 40° N and 35° N, just east of longitude 80° W |
| Map Key Information | blue = American and allied forces, red = British forces |
| Scale | 7/16 in. = 100 miles, 9/16 in. = 200 km |
| Summary | British commanders Graves and Hood sailed south from New York. They were defeated by De Grasse at the Battle of the Capes. British commander Cornwallis marched north from Wilmington, North Carolina, to Virginia, where he was defeated by American forces. |

## Practicing the Skill

Turn to Chapter 1, Section 5, "Early European Explorers." Read the map entitled "Exploration Leads to New Sea Routes" and make a chart to identify information on the map.

# 3.6 Reading a Special-Purpose Map

## Defining the Skill

**Special-purpose maps** help people focus on a particular aspect of a region, such as economic development in the South. These kinds of maps often use symbols to indicate information.

## Applying the Skill

The following special-purpose map indicates the products of the Southern colonies. Use the strategies listed below to help you identify the information shown on the map.

### How to Read a Special-Purpose Map

**Strategy 1** Read the title. It tells you what the map is intended to show.

**Strategy 2** Read the legend. This tells you what each symbol stands for. This legend shows the crops that were grown in various Southern colonies.

**Strategy 3** Look for the places on the map where the symbol appears. These tell you the places where each crop was grown.

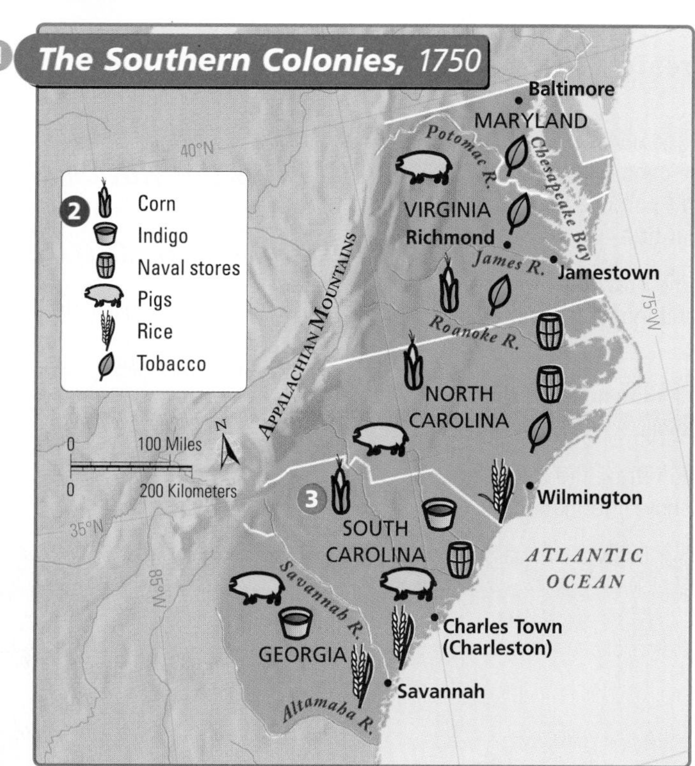


### Make a Chart

A chart can help you understand special-purpose maps. The chart below shows information about the special-purpose map you just studied.

| | Corn | Indigo | Naval stores | Pigs | Rice | Tobacco |
|---|---|---|---|---|---|---|
| Maryland | | | | | | x |
| Virginia | x | | | x | | x |
| North Carolina | x | | x | x | x | x |
| South Carolina | x | x | x | x | x | |
| Georgia | | x | | x | x | |

## Practicing the Skill

Turn to Chapter 4, Section 1, "New England: Land and Sea." Look at the special-purpose map entitled "The New England Colonies" and make a chart that shows information about products from New England.





R25

# 3.7 Creating a Map

## Defining the Skill

**Creating a map** involves representing geographical information. When you draw a map, it is easiest to use an existing map as a guide. On the map you draw, you can show geographical information. You can also show other kinds of information, such as data on climates, population trends, resources, or routes. Often, this data comes from a graph or a chart.

## Applying the Skill

Below is a map that a student created to show information about the number of slaves in 1750. Read the strategies listed below to see how the map was created.

### How to Create a Map

**Strategy 1** Select a title that identifies the geographical area and the map's purpose. Include a date in your title.

**Strategy 2** Draw the lines of latitude and longitude using short dashes.

**Strategy 3** Create a key that shows the colors.

**Strategy 4** Draw the colors on the map to show information.

**Strategy 5** Draw a compass rose and scale.

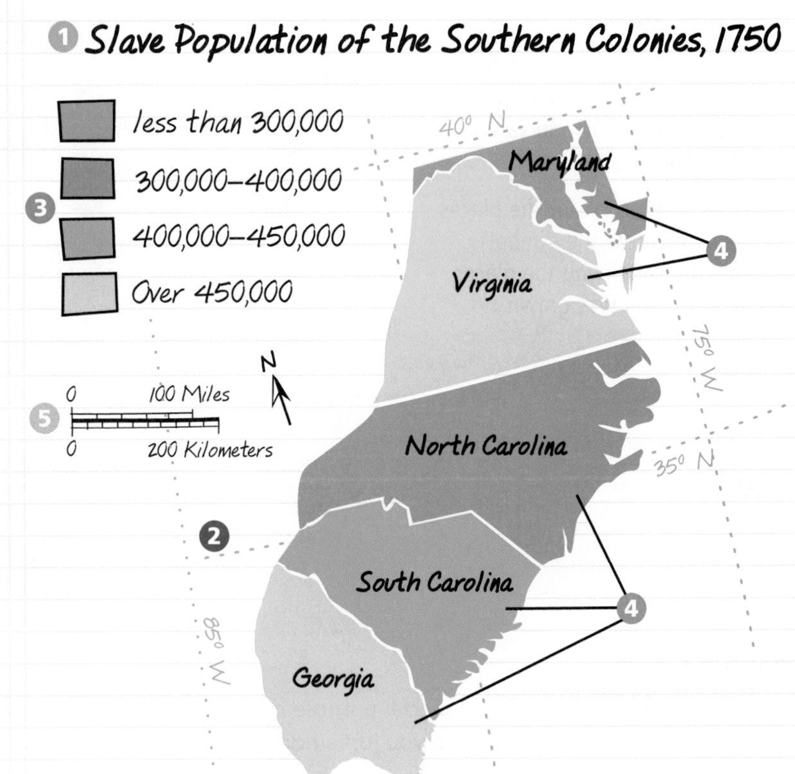


## Practicing the Skill

Make your own map. Turn to page 104 in Chapter 3 and study the graph entitled "The 13 Colonies." Use the strategies described above to create a map that shows the 13 colonies and the dates that they were founded. You can use the map on page 102 of that chapter as a guide.

# 3.8 Interpreting Political Cartoons

## Defining the Skill

**Political cartoons** are cartoons that use humor to make a serious point. Political cartoons often express a point of view on an issue better than words do. Understanding signs and symbols will help you to interpret political cartoons.

## Applying the Skill

The cartoon below shows Abraham Lincoln and the other candidates running for the presidency in 1860. Use the strategies listed below to help you understand the cartoon.

### How to Interpret a Political Cartoon

**Strategy 1** Identify the subject by reading the title of the cartoon and looking at the cartoon as a whole.

**Strategy 2** Identify important symbols and details. The cartoonist uses the image of a running race to discuss a political campaign. The White House is the finish line.

**Strategy 3** Interpret the message. Why is Lincoln drawn so much taller than the other candidates? How does that make him the fittest candidate?

### Make a Chart

Making a chart will help you summarize information from a political cartoon. The chart below summarizes the information from the cartoon above.

| | |
|---|---|
| *Subject* | *"A Political Race" (The Election of 1860)* |
| *Symbols and Details* | *Running is a symbol for a political campaign. Lincoln is the tallest and fastest candidate.* |
| *Message* | *3 Lincoln is pulling ahead of the other candidates in the campaign for the presidency.* |

## Practicing the Skill

Turn to Chapter 18, Section 3, "End of Reconstruction." Look at the political cartoon on page 547. It shows a cartoonist's view of corruption in President Grant's administration. Use a chart like the one above and the strategies outlined to interpret the cartoon.





R27

# 4.1 Using an Electronic Card Catalog

## Defining the Skill

An **electronic card catalog** is a library's computerized search program that will help you find information about the books and other materials in the library. You can search the catalog by entering a book title, an author's name, or a subject of interest to you. The electronic card catalog will give you information about the materials in the library. This information is called bibliographic information. You can use an electronic card catalog to create a bibliography (a list of books) on any topic you are interested in.

## Applying the Skill

The screen shown below is from an electronic search for information about Thomas Jefferson. Use the strategies listed below to help you use the information on the screen.

### How to Use an Electronic Card Catalog

**Strategy 1** Begin searching by choosing either subject, title, or author, depending on the topic of your search. For this search, the user chose "Subject" and typed in the words "Jefferson, Thomas."

**Strategy 2** Once you have selected a book from the results of your search, identify the author, title, city, publisher, and date of publication.

**Strategy 3** Look for any special features in the book. This book is illustrated, and it includes bibliographical references and an index.

**Strategy 4** Locate the call number for the book. The call number indicates the section in the library where you will find the book. You can also find out if the book is available in the library you are using. If not, it may be in another library in the network.

```
Search Request:
(1) Subject        Title        Author

Find  Options  Locations  Backup  Startover  Help

(2) Miller, Douglas T. Thomas Jefferson and the
creation of America. New York: Facts on File,
1997.
          AUTHOR: Miller, Douglas T.
      (2)  TITLE: Thomas Jefferson and the
                  creation of America/Douglas T.
                  Miller.
   (2) PUBLISHED: New York: Facts on File, ©1997.
          PAGING: vi, 122p. : ill ; 24 cm.
          SERIES: Makers of America.
       (3) NOTES: Includes bibliographical
                  references (p. 117-118) and index.
(4) CALL NUMBER:  1. 973.46 N61T 1997–Book Available–
```

## Practicing the Skill

Turn to Chapter 10, "The Jefferson Era," and find a topic that interests you, such as the Federalists, the Louisiana Purchase, the Lewis and Clark expedition, or the War of 1812. Use the SUBJECT search on an electronic card catalog to find information about your topic. Make a bibliography of books about the subject. Be sure to include the author, title, city, publisher, and date of publication for all the books included.

# 4.2 Creating a Database

## Defining the Skill

A **database** is a collection of data, or information, that is organized so that you can find and retrieve information on a specific topic quickly and easily. Once a computerized database is set up, you can search it to find specific information without going through the entire database. The database will provide a list of all information in the database related to your topic. Learning how to use a database will help you learn how to create one.

## Applying the Skill

The chart below is a database for the significant battles of the Civil War. Use the strategies listed below to help you understand and use the database.

### How to Create a Database

**Strategy ①** Identify the topic of the database. The keywords, or most important words, in this title are "Civil War" and "Battles." These words were used to begin the research for this database.

**Strategy ②** Identify the kind of data you need to enter in your database. These will be the column headings of your database. The key words "Battle," "Date," "Location," and "Significance" were chosen to focus the research.

**Strategy ③** Identify the entries included under each heading.

**Strategy ④** Use the database to help you find information quickly. For example, in this database you could search for "Union victories" to find a list of significant battles won by the North.

① SIGNIFICANT CIVIL WAR BATTLES

| ② BATTLE | DATE | LOCATION | SIGNIFICANCE |
|---|---|---|---|
| ③ Fort Sumter | April 12, 1861 | Charleston, SC | Beginning of the Civil War |
| First Battle of Bull Run (Manassas) | July 21, 1861 | Virginia | Confederate victory |
| Shiloh | April 6–7, 1862 | Tennessee (near Shiloh Church) | ④ Union victory |
| Antietam | September 17, 1862 | Sharpsburg, MD | No clear victory; considered bloodiest battle of war |
| Gettysburg | July 1–3, 1863 | Gettysburg, PA | Retreat of Confederacy |
| Vicksburg | Three-month siege ending July 3, 1863 | Vicksburg, MS | Union gained control of Mississippi River |
| Chattanooga | November 23–25, 1863 | Chattanooga, TN | ④ Union victory |
| Atlanta | September 2, 1864 | Atlanta, GA | ④ Union victory; helped convince Confederacy of defeat |

## Practicing the Skill

Create a database for U.S. presidents through the Civil War that shows each president's home state, political party, and years served as president. Use the informaton in "Presidents of the United States" on pages R40–R42 to provide the data. Use a format like the one above for your database.



R29

# 4.3 Using the Internet

## Defining the Skill

The Internet is a computer network that connects to universities, libraries, news organizations, government agencies, businesses, and private individuals throughout the world. Each location on the Internet has a home page with its own address, or URL (universal resource locator). With a computer connected to the Internet, you can reach the home pages of many organizations and services. The international collection of home pages, known as the World Wide Web, is a good source of up-to-date information about current events as well as research on subjects in history.

## Applying the Skill

The Web page below shows the links for Chapter 6 of *Creating America.* Use the strategies listed below to help you understand how to use the Web page.

### How to Use the Internet

**Strategy 1** Go directly to a Web page. For example, type http://www.mcdougallittell.com in the box at the top of the screen and press ENTER (or RETURN). The Web page will appear on your screen. Then click on ClassZone and find the link to *Creating America.*

**Strategy 2** Explore the *Creating America* links. Click on any one of the links to find out more about a specific subject. These links take you to other pages at this Web site. Some pages include links to related information that can be found at other places on the Internet.

**Strategy 3** When using the Internet for research, you should confirm the information you find. Web sites set up by universities, government agencies, and reputable news sources are more reliable than other sources. You can often find information about the creator of a site by looking for copyright information.

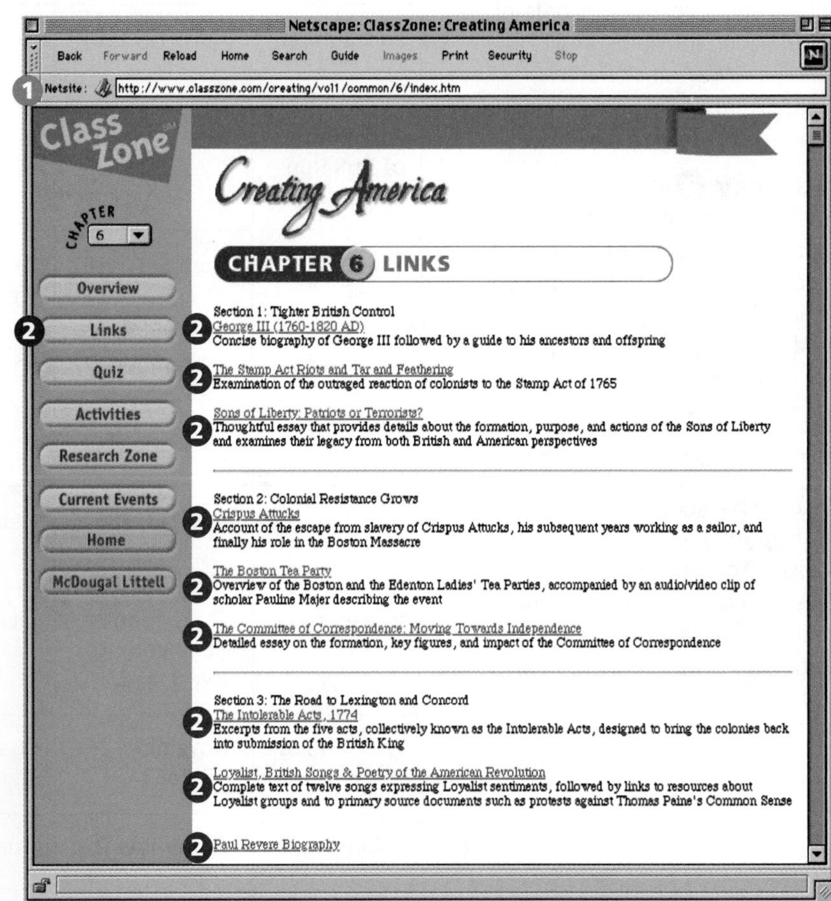


## Practicing the Skill

Turn to Chapter 14, Section 2, "American Literature and Art." Read the section and make a list of topics you would like to research. If you have Internet access, go to the McDougal Littell home page at http://www.mcdougallittell.com and click on ClassZone. There you will find links that provide more information about the topics in the section.

# 4.4 Creating a Multimedia Presentation

## Defining the Skill

Movies, CD-ROMs, television, and computer software are different kinds of media. To **create a multimedia presentation,** you need to collect information in different media and organize them into one presentation.

## Applying the Skill

The scene below shows students using computers to create a multimedia presentation. Use the strategies listed below to help you create your own multimedia presentation.

### How to Create a Multimedia Presentation

**Strategy 1** Identify the topic of your presentation and decide which media are best for an effective presentation. For example, you may want to use slides or posters to show visual images of your topic. Or, you may want to use CDs or audiotapes to provide music or spoken words.

**Strategy 2** Research the topic in a variety of sources. Images, text, props, and background music should reflect the historical period of the event you choose.

**Strategy 3** Write the script for the presentation. You could use a narrator and characters' voices to tell the story. Primary sources are an excellent source for script material.

**Strategy 4** Videotape the presentation. Videotaping the presentation will preserve it for future viewing and allow you to show it to different groups of people.

## Practicing the Skill

Turn to Chapter 24, "World War I." Choose a topic from the chapter and use the strategies listed above to create a multimedia presentation about it.





R31

# World Political

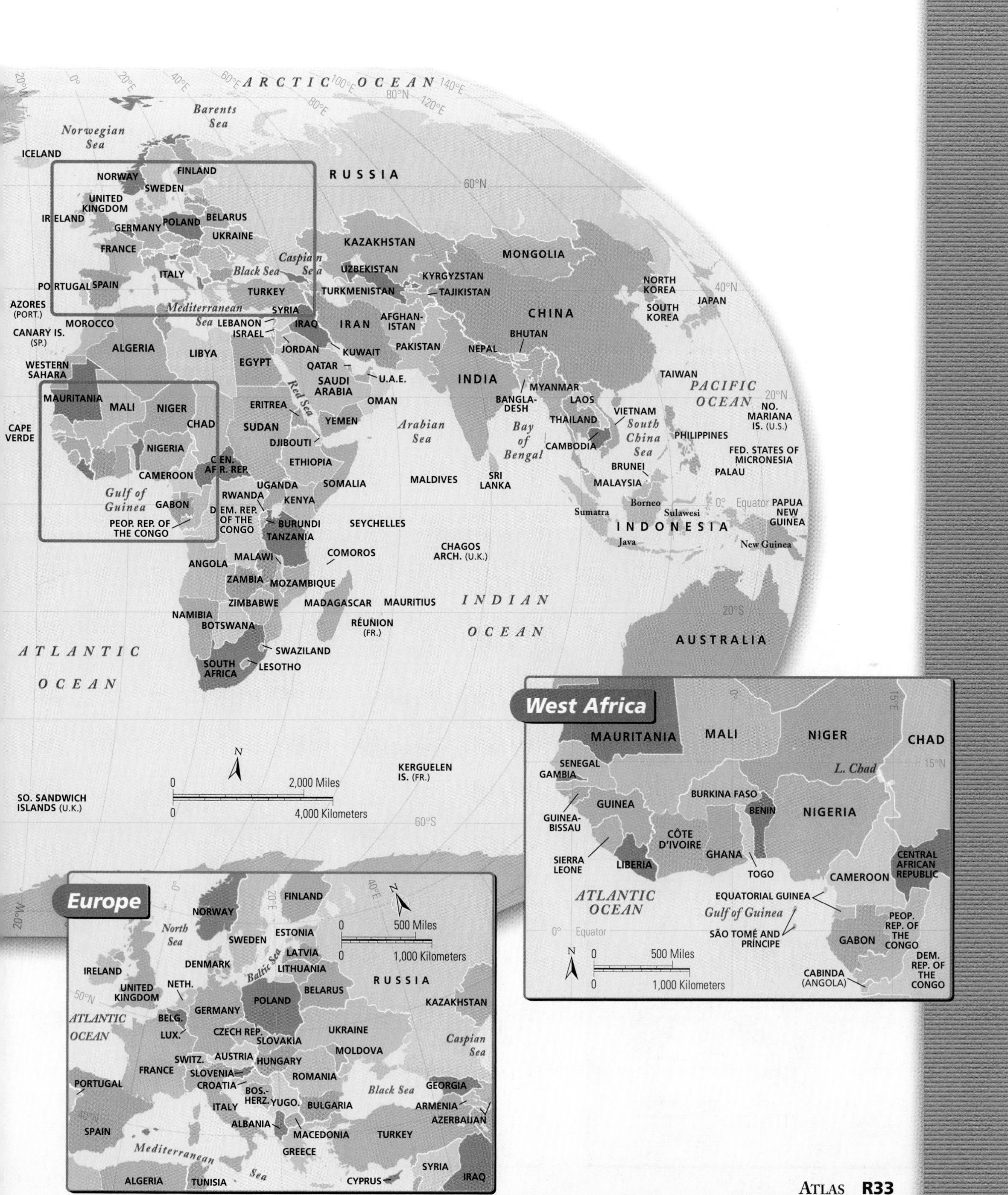
ARCTIC OCEAN
Barents Sea
Norwegian Sea
ICELAND
NORWAY
FINLAND
SWEDEN
RUSSIA
UNITED KINGDOM
IRELAND
GERMANY
POLAND
BELARUS
UKRAINE
FRANCE
KAZAKHSTAN
MONGOLIA
ITALY
Black Sea
Caspian Sea
UZBEKISTAN
KYRGYZSTAN
PORTUGAL
SPAIN
TURKEY
TURKMENISTAN
TAJIKISTAN
NORTH KOREA
SOUTH KOREA
JAPAN
AZORES (PORT.)
Mediterranean Sea
SYRIA
LEBANON
ISRAEL
IRAQ
IRAN
AFGHANISTAN
CHINA
MOROCCO
CANARY IS. (SP.)
ALGERIA
LIBYA
EGYPT
JORDAN
KUWAIT
PAKISTAN
NEPAL
BHUTAN
WESTERN SAHARA
QATAR
SAUDI ARABIA
U.A.E.
INDIA
TAIWAN
PACIFIC OCEAN
MAURITANIA
MALI
NIGER
ERITREA
Red Sea
OMAN
BANGLADESH
MYANMAR
LAOS
CAPE VERDE
CHAD
SUDAN
YEMEN
Arabian Sea
Bay of Bengal
THAILAND
VIETNAM
South China Sea
NO. MARIANA IS. (U.S.)
NIGERIA
DJIBOUTI
CAMBODIA
PHILIPPINES
FED. STATES OF MICRONESIA
CEN. AFR. REP.
ETHIOPIA
BRUNEI
PALAU
CAMEROON
UGANDA
SOMALIA
MALDIVES
SRI LANKA
MALAYSIA
Gulf of Guinea
GABON
RWANDA
KENYA
Borneo
Equator
PAPUA NEW GUINEA
DEM. REP. OF THE CONGO
BURUNDI
SEYCHELLES
Sumatra
Sulawesi
INDONESIA
PEOP. REP. OF THE CONGO
TANZANIA
Java
New Guinea
CHAGOS ARCH. (U.K.)
MALAWI
COMOROS
ANGOLA
ZAMBIA
MOZAMBIQUE
ZIMBABWE
MADAGASCAR
MAURITIUS
INDIAN OCEAN
NAMIBIA
BOTSWANA
RÉUNION (FR.)
ATLANTIC OCEAN
SWAZILAND
AUSTRALIA
SOUTH AFRICA
LESOTHO
KERGUELEN IS. (FR.)
0 2,000 Miles
0 4,000 Kilometers
SO. SANDWICH ISLANDS (U.K.)
West Africa
MAURITANIA
MALI
NIGER
CHAD
SENEGAL
GAMBIA
L. Chad
BURKINA FASO
GUINEA
BENIN
NIGERIA
GUINEA-BISSAU
CÔTE D'IVOIRE
SIERRA LEONE
LIBERIA
GHANA
TOGO
CENTRAL AFRICAN REPUBLIC
CAMEROON
ATLANTIC OCEAN
EQUATORIAL GUINEA
Gulf of Guinea
SÃO TOMÉ AND PRÍNCIPE
GABON
PEOP. REP. OF THE CONGO
0 500 Miles
0 1,000 Kilometers
CABINDA (ANGOLA)
DEM. REP. OF THE CONGO
Europe
NORWAY
FINLAND
North Sea
SWEDEN
ESTONIA
0 500 Miles
0 1,000 Kilometers
LATVIA
DENMARK
LITHUANIA
IRELAND
Baltic Sea
RUSSIA
UNITED KINGDOM
NETH.
BELARUS
POLAND
KAZAKHSTAN
GERMANY
ATLANTIC OCEAN
BELG.
LUX.
CZECH REP.
SLOVAKIA
UKRAINE
Caspian Sea
SWITZ.
AUSTRIA
HUNGARY
MOLDOVA
FRANCE
SLOVENIA
ROMANIA
CROATIA
PORTUGAL
BOS.-HERZ.
YUGO.
BULGARIA
Black Sea
GEORGIA
ARMENIA
ITALY
AZERBAIJAN
ALBANIA
SPAIN
MACEDONIA
TURKEY
Mediterranean Sea
GREECE
SYRIA
ALGERIA
TUNISIA
CYPRUS
IRAQ

# United States Political

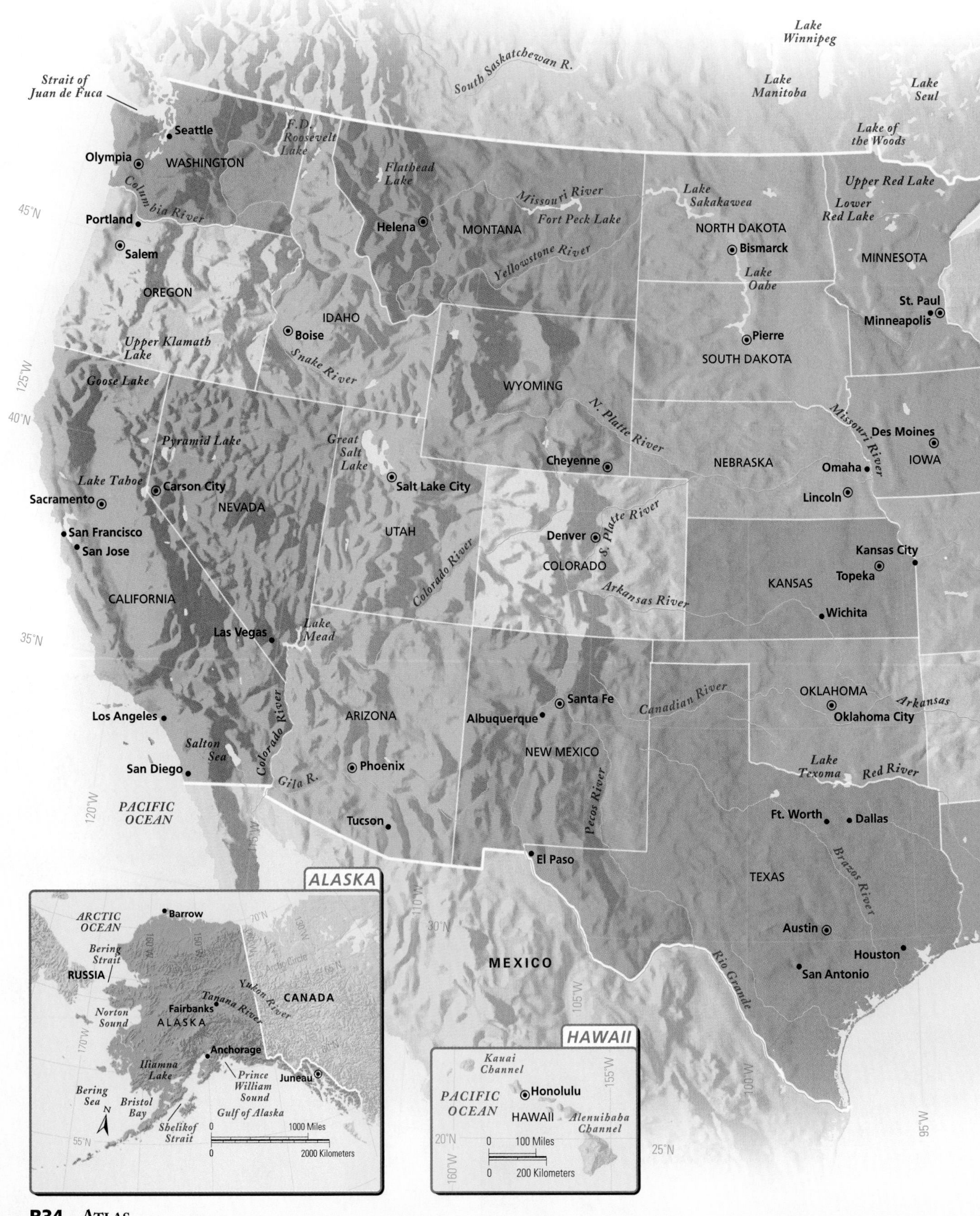

Strait of Juan de Fuca
Seattle
Olympia
WASHINGTON
F.D. Roosevelt Lake
Columbia River
Portland
Salem
OREGON
Upper Klamath Lake
Goose Lake
Flathead Lake
Helena
MONTANA
Missouri River
Fort Peck Lake
Yellowstone River
South Saskatchewan R.
Lake Winnipeg
Lake Manitoba
Lake Seul
Lake of the Woods
Upper Red Lake
Lower Red Lake
Lake Sakakawea
NORTH DAKOTA
Bismarck
Lake Oahe
MINNESOTA
St. Paul
Minneapolis
Pierre
SOUTH DAKOTA
IDAHO
Boise
Snake River
WYOMING
N. Platte River
Missouri River
Des Moines
IOWA
Omaha
NEBRASKA
Lincoln
Cheyenne
Pyramid Lake
Great Salt Lake
Salt Lake City
Lake Tahoe
Carson City
Sacramento
NEVADA
UTAH
San Francisco
San Jose
Denver
S. Platte River
COLORADO
Colorado River
Arkansas River
Kansas City
Topeka
KANSAS
Wichita
CALIFORNIA
Las Vegas
Lake Mead
Los Angeles
Salton Sea
San Diego
Colorado River
Gila R.
ARIZONA
Phoenix
Tucson
Santa Fe
Albuquerque
NEW MEXICO
Pecos River
Canadian River
OKLAHOMA
Oklahoma City
Arkansas
Lake Texoma
Red River
Ft. Worth
Dallas
El Paso
TEXAS
Brazos River
Austin
Houston
San Antonio
Rio Grande
MEXICO
PACIFIC OCEAN
45°N
40°N
35°N
30°N
25°N
125°W
120°W
115°W
110°W
105°W
100°W
95°W
ALASKA
ARCTIC OCEAN
Barrow
Bering Strait
RUSSIA
CANADA
Yukon River
Tanana River
Fairbanks
ALASKA
Norton Sound
Anchorage
Juneau
Iliamna Lake
Prince William Sound
Bering Sea
Bristol Bay
Shelikof Strait
Gulf of Alaska
Arctic Circle
70°N
65°N
60°N
55°N
170°W
160°W
150°W
140°W
130°W
0
1000 Miles
2000 Kilometers
HAWAII
Kauai Channel
PACIFIC OCEAN
Honolulu
HAWAII
Alenuihaha Channel
20°N
160°W
155°W
0
100 Miles
200 Kilometers

CANADA
Lake Nipigon
Lake Superior
Gouin Reservoir
Lake St. John
Cabonga Reservoir
St. Lawrence R.
Ottawa R.
Lake Nipissing
Georgian Bay
Lake Simcoe
Lake Huron
Lake Ontario
Lake St. Clair
Lake Erie
Lake Michigan
Lake Winnebago
Lake Champlain
Bay of Fundy
MAINE
Augusta
Montpelier
VERMONT
NEW HAMPSHIRE
Concord
Connecticut R.
Hudson R.
Albany
Boston
MASSACHUSETTS
NEW YORK
Providence
RHODE ISLAND
Hartford
CONNECTICUT
Long Island
New York
NEW JERSEY
Trenton
Philadelphia
Dover
Delaware Bay
DELAWARE
Baltimore
Washington, D.C.
Annapolis
MARYLAND
Chesapeake Bay
WISCONSIN
Madison
Milwaukee
MICHIGAN
Lansing
Detroit
Buffalo
Toledo
Cleveland
PENNSYLVANIA
Harrisburg
Susquehanna R.
Pittsburgh
Chicago
Mississippi River
OHIO
Columbus
ILLINOIS
INDIANA
Indianapolis
Springfield
Cincinnati
WEST VIRGINIA
Charleston
Richmond
VIRGINIA
Jefferson City
St. Louis
Ohio River
Frankfort
KENTUCKY
MISSOURI
Raleigh
Pamlico Sound
Winston-Salem
NORTH CAROLINA
Knoxville
Cumberland River
Nashville
TENNESSEE
ARKANSAS
Memphis
Tennessee River
SOUTH CAROLINA
Columbia
Savannah River
ATLANTIC OCEAN
River
Little Rock
Atlanta
Birmingham
ALABAMA
GEORGIA
MISSISSIPPI
Montgomery
LOUISIANA
Jackson
Alabama R.
Jacksonville
Tallahassee
Baton Rouge
New Orleans
Lake Pontchartrain
Breton Sound
FLORIDA
Tampa
St. Petersburg
Lake Okeechobee
Gulf of Mexico
BAHAMAS
Miami
Straits of Florida
National capital
State capital
N
0
500 Miles
0
1000 Kilometers
45°N
40°N
35°N
30°N
25°N
70°W
75°W
80°W
85°W
90°W
PUERTO RICO
ATLANTIC OCEAN
San Juan
PUERTO RICO
Caguas
Ponce
18°N
66°W
0
100 Miles
0
100 Kilometers
Caribbean Sea



R35

# United States Physical

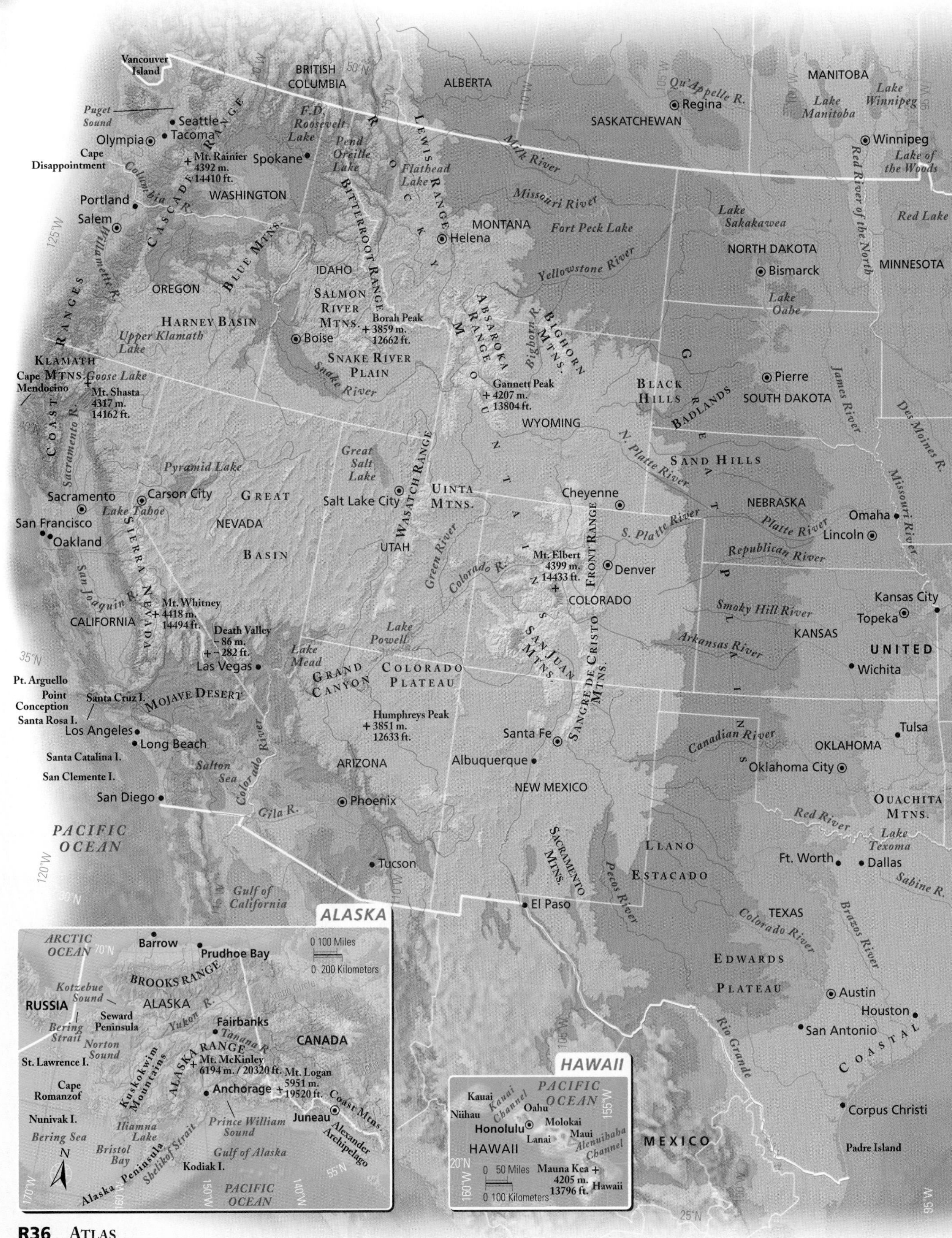

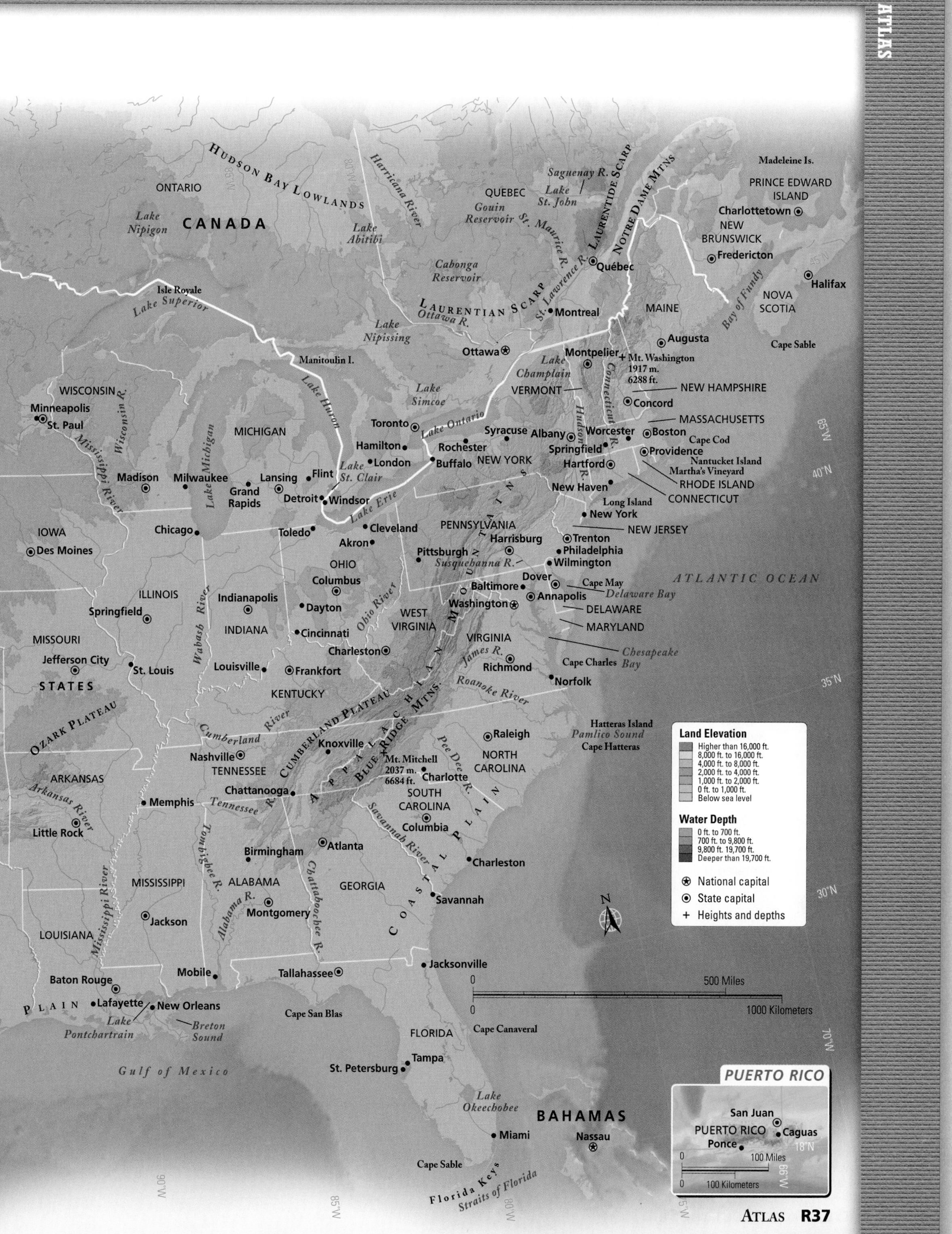
CANADA
ONTARIO
QUEBEC
HUDSON BAY LOWLANDS
Lake Nipigon
Lake Abitibi
Harricana River
Gouin Reservoir
Saguenay R.
Lake St. John
St. Maurice R.
LAURENTIDE SCARP
NOTRE DAME MTNS
Madeleine Is.
PRINCE EDWARD ISLAND
Charlottetown
NEW BRUNSWICK
Fredericton
Halifax
NOVA SCOTIA
Bay of Fundy
Cape Sable
Québec
St. Lawrence R.
Cabonga Reservoir
LAURENTIAN SCARP
Ottawa R.
Montreal
Ottawa
Isle Royale
Lake Superior
Lake Nipissing
Manitoulin I.
Lake Huron
Lake Simcoe
Lake Ontario
Toronto
Hamilton
London
Lake St. Clair
Buffalo
Rochester
Syracuse
Albany
MAINE
Augusta
Montpelier
Mt. Washington 1917 m. 6288 ft.
Lake Champlain
VERMONT
NEW HAMPSHIRE
Concord
Connecticut R.
Hudson R.
MASSACHUSETTS
Worcester
Boston
Cape Cod
Springfield
Providence
Hartford
Nantucket Island
Martha's Vineyard
RHODE ISLAND
New Haven
CONNECTICUT
Long Island
New York
NEW YORK
NEW JERSEY
Trenton
Philadelphia
Wilmington
Dover
Cape May
Delaware Bay
DELAWARE
MARYLAND
Baltimore
Annapolis
Washington
ATLANTIC OCEAN
Chesapeake Bay
Cape Charles
Norfolk
Richmond
James R.
VIRGINIA
Roanoke River
WISCONSIN
Wisconsin R.
Minneapolis
St. Paul
Mississippi River
MICHIGAN
Lake Michigan
Madison
Milwaukee
Lansing
Flint
Grand Rapids
Detroit
Windsor
Lake Erie
Chicago
Toledo
Cleveland
Akron
IOWA
Des Moines
PENNSYLVANIA
Harrisburg
Pittsburgh
Susquehanna R.
OHIO
Columbus
Dayton
Cincinnati
Ohio River
ILLINOIS
Springfield
Indianapolis
INDIANA
Wabash River
WEST VIRGINIA
Charleston
MISSOURI
Jefferson City
St. Louis
Louisville
Frankfort
KENTUCKY
STATES
OZARK PLATEAU
CUMBERLAND PLATEAU
BLUE RIDGE MTNS.
APPALACHIAN MOUNTAINS
Cumberland River
Knoxville
Nashville
TENNESSEE
Mt. Mitchell 2037 m. 6684 ft.
Charlotte
NORTH CAROLINA
Raleigh
Hatteras Island
Pamlico Sound
Cape Hatteras
Pee Dee R.
ARKANSAS
Arkansas River
Memphis
Tennessee R.
Chattanooga
SOUTH CAROLINA
Columbia
Little Rock
Savannah River
COASTAL PLAIN
Birmingham
Atlanta
Charleston
MISSISSIPPI
ALABAMA
GEORGIA
Tombigbee R.
Chattahoochee R.
Alabama R.
Savannah
Montgomery
Jackson
LOUISIANA
Mississippi River
Mobile
Tallahassee
Jacksonville
Baton Rouge
PLAIN
Lafayette
New Orleans
Lake Pontchartrain
Breton Sound
Cape San Blas
FLORIDA
Cape Canaveral
Gulf of Mexico
Tampa
St. Petersburg
Lake Okeechobee
Miami
BAHAMAS
Nassau
Cape Sable
Florida Keys
Straits of Florida
Land Elevation
Higher than 16,000 ft.
8,000 ft. to 16,000 ft.
4,000 ft. to 8,000 ft.
2,000 ft. to 4,000 ft.
1,000 ft. to 2,000 ft.
0 ft. to 1,000 ft.
Below sea level
Water Depth
0 ft. to 700 ft.
700 ft. to 9,800 ft.
9,800 ft. 19,700 ft.
Deeper than 19,700 ft.
National capital
State capital
Heights and depths
N
0
500 Miles
0
1000 Kilometers
PUERTO RICO
San Juan
PUERTO RICO
Caguas
Ponce
18°N
66°W
0
100 Miles
0
100 Kilometers
40°N
35°N
30°N
65°W
70°W
75°W
80°W
85°W
90°W

# FACTS About the STATES

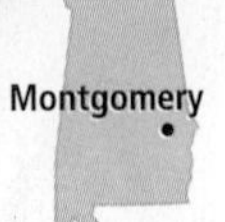


**Alabama**
4,352,000 people
52,237 sq. mi.
Rank in area: 30
Entered Union in 1819

**Alaska**
614,000 people
615,230 sq. mi.
Rank in area: 1
Entered Union in 1959

**Arizona**
4,669,000 people
114,006 sq. mi.
Rank in area: 6
Entered Union in 1912

**Arkansas**
2,538,000 people
53,182 sq. mi.
Rank in area: 28
Entered Union in 1836

**California**
32,667,000 people
158,869 sq. mi.
Rank in area: 3
Entered Union in 1850

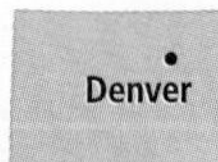


**Colorado**
3,971,000 people
104,100 sq. mi.
Rank in area: 8
Entered Union in 1876

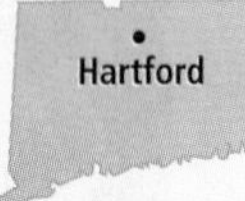


**Connecticut**
3,274,000 people
5,544 sq. mi.
Rank in area: 48
Entered Union in 1788

**Delaware**
744,000 people
2,397 sq. mi.
Rank in area: 49
Entered Union in 1787

**District of Columbia**
523,000 people
68 sq. mi.

**Florida**
14,916,000 people
59,928 sq. mi.
Rank in area: 23
Entered Union in 1845

**Georgia**
7,642,000 people
58,977 sq. mi.
Rank in area: 24
Entered Union in 1788

**Hawaii**
1,193,000 people
6,459 sq. mi.
Rank in area: 47
Entered Union in 1959

**Idaho**
1,229,000 people
83,574 sq. mi.
Rank in area: 14
Entered Union in 1890

**Illinois**
12,045,000 people
57,918 sq. mi.
Rank in area: 25
Entered Union in 1818

**Indiana**
5,899,000 people
36,420 sq. mi.
Rank in area: 38
Entered Union in 1816

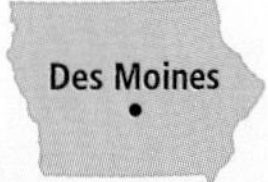


**Iowa**
2,862,000 people
56,276 sq. mi.
Rank in area: 26
Entered Union in 1846

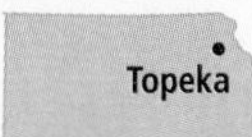


**Kansas**
2,629,000 people
82,282 sq. mi.
Rank in area: 15
Entered Union in 1861

**Kentucky**
3,936,000 people
40,411 sq. mi.
Rank in area: 37
Entered Union in 1792

**Louisiana**
4,369,000 people
49,650 sq. mi.
Rank in area: 31
Entered Union in 1812

**Maine**
1,244,000 people
33,741 sq. mi.
Rank in area: 39
Entered Union in 1820

**Maryland**
5,135,000 people
12,297 sq. mi.
Rank in area: 42
Entered Union in 1788

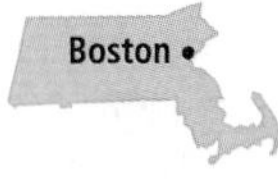


**Massachusetts**
6,147,000 people
9,241 sq. mi.
Rank in area: 45
Entered Union in 1788

**Michigan**
9,817,000 people
96,705 sq. mi.
Rank in area: 11
Entered Union in 1837

**Minnesota**
4,725,000 people
86,943 sq. mi.
Rank in area: 12
Entered Union in 1858

**Mississippi**
2,752,000 people
48,286 sq. mi.
Rank in area: 32
Entered Union in 1817

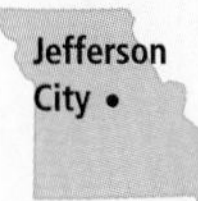


**Missouri**
5,439,000 people
69,709 sq. mi.
Rank in area: 21
Entered Union in 1821

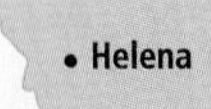


**Montana**
880,000 people
147,046 sq. mi.
Rank in area: 4
Entered Union in 1889

Sources: U.S. Bureau of the Census, 1998 population estimates.
*World Almanac and Book of Facts,* 1999
*Statistical Abstract of the United States,* 1998

**Nebraska**
1,663,000 people
77,359 sq. mi.
Rank in area: 16
Entered Union in 1867

**Nevada**
1,747,000 people
110,567 sq. mi.
Rank in area: 7
Entered Union in 1864

**New Hampshire**
1,185,000 people
9,283 sq. mi.
Rank in area: 44
Entered Union in 1788

**New Jersey**
8,115,000 people
8,215 sq. mi.
Rank in area: 46
Entered Union in 1787

**New Mexico**
1,737,000 people
121,598 sq. mi.
Rank in area: 5
Entered Union in 1912

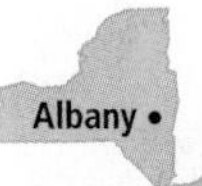


**New York**
18,175,000 people
53,989 sq. mi.
Rank in area: 27
Entered Union in 1788

**North Carolina**
7,546,000 people
52,672 sq. mi.
Rank in area: 29
Entered Union in 1789

**North Dakota**
638,000 people
70,704 sq. mi.
Rank in area: 18
Entered Union in 1889

**Ohio**
11,209,000 people
44,828 sq. mi.
Rank in area: 34
Entered Union in 1803

**Oklahoma**
3,347,000 people
69,903 sq. mi.
Rank in area: 20
Entered Union in 1907

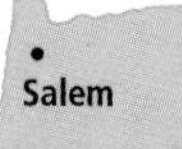


**Oregon**
3,282,000 people
97,132 sq. mi.
Rank in area: 10
Entered Union in 1859

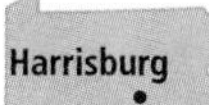


**Pennsylvania**
12,001,000 people
46,058 sq. mi.
Rank in area: 33
Entered Union in 1787

**Rhode Island**
988,000 people
1,231 sq. mi.
Rank in area: 50
Entered Union in 1790

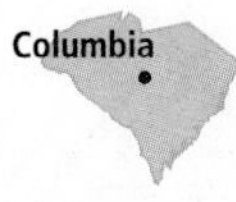


**South Carolina**
3,836,000 people
31,189 sq. mi.
Rank in area: 40
Entered Union in 1788

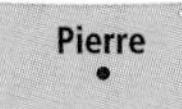


**South Dakota**
738,000 people
77,121 sq. mi.
Rank in area: 17
Entered Union in 1889

**Tennessee**
5,431,000 people
42,145 sq. mi.
Rank in area: 36
Entered Union in 1796

**Texas**
19,760,000 people
267,277 sq. mi.
Rank in area: 2
Entered Union in 1845

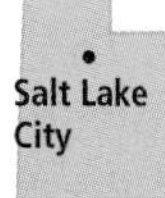


**Utah**
2,100,000 people
84,904 sq. mi.
Rank in area: 13
Entered Union in 1896

**Vermont**
591,000 people
9,615 sq. mi.
Rank in area: 43
Entered Union in 1791

**Virginia**
6,791,000 people
42,326 sq. mi.
Rank in area: 35
Entered Union in 1788

**Washington**
5,689,000 people
70,637 sq. mi.
Rank in area: 19
Entered Union in 1889

**West Virginia**
1,811,000 people
24,232 sq. mi.
Rank in area: 41
Entered Union in 1863

**Wisconsin**
5,224,000 people
65,500 sq. mi.
Rank in area: 22
Entered Union in 1848

**Wyoming**
481,000 people
97,819 sq. mi.
Rank in area: 9
Entered Union in 1890

## ***United States:*** *Major Dependencies*

- American Samoa—63,786 people; 90 sq. mi.
- Guam—151,716 people; 217 sq. mi.
- Commonwealth of Puerto Rico—3,887,652 people; 3,508 sq. mi.
- Virgin Islands of the United States—119,827 people; 171 sq. mi.
- Midway Islands—no indigenous inhabitants; 2 sq. mi.
- Wake Atoll—no indigenous inhabitants; 3 sq. mi.

# PRESIDENTS of the UNITED STATES

Here are some little-known facts about the presidents of the United States:

- Only former president to serve in Congress: John Quincy Adams
- First president born in the new United States: Martin Van Buren (eighth president)
- Only president who was a bachelor: James Buchanan
- First left-handed president: James A. Garfield
- Largest president: William H. Taft (6 feet 2 inches, 326 pounds)
- Youngest president: Theodore Roosevelt (42 years old)
- Oldest president: Ronald Reagan (77 years old when he left office in 1989)
- First president born west of the Mississippi River: Herbert Hoover (born in West Branch, Iowa)
- First president born in the 20th century: John F. Kennedy (born May 29, 1917)

1 **George Washington**
**1789–1797**
No Political Party
Birthplace: Virginia
Born: February 22, 1732
Died: December 14, 1799

2 **John Adams**
**1797–1801**
Federalist
Birthplace: Massachusetts
Born: October 30, 1735
Died: July 4, 1826

3 **Thomas Jefferson**
**1801–1809**
Democratic Republican
Birthplace: Virginia
Born: April 13, 1743
Died: July 4, 1826

4 **James Madison**
**1809–1817**
Democratic Republican
Birthplace: Virginia
Born: March 16, 1751
Died: June 28, 1836

5 **James Monroe**
**1817–1825**
Democratic Republican
Birthplace: Virginia
Born: April 28, 1758
Died: July 4, 1831

6 **John Quincy Adams**
**1825–1829**
Democratic Republican
Birthplace: Massachusetts
Born: July 11, 1767
Died: February 23, 1848

7 **Andrew Jackson**
**1829–1837**
Democrat
Birthplace: South Carolina
Born: March 15, 1767
Died: June 8, 1845

8 **Martin Van Buren**
**1837–1841**
Democrat
Birthplace: New York
Born: December 5, 1782
Died: July 24, 1862

9 **William H. Harrison**
**1841**
Whig
Birthplace: Virginia
Born: February 9, 1773
Died: April 4, 1841

10 **John Tyler**
**1841–1845**
Whig
Birthplace: Virginia
Born: March 29, 1790
Died: January 18, 1862

11 **James K. Polk**
**1845–1849**
Democrat
Birthplace: North Carolina
Born: November 2, 1795
Died: June 15, 1849

12 **Zachary Taylor**
**1849–1850**
Whig
Birthplace: Virginia
Born: November 24, 1784
Died: July 9, 1850

**13 Millard Fillmore**
**1850–1853**
Whig
Birthplace: New York
Born: January 7, 1800
Died: March 8, 1874

**14 Franklin Pierce**
**1853–1857**
Democrat
Birthplace: New Hampshire
Born: November 23, 1804
Died: October 8, 1869

**15 James Buchanan**
**1857–1861**
Democrat
Birthplace: Pennsylvania
Born: April 23, 1791
Died: June 1, 1868

**16 Abraham Lincoln**
**1861–1865**
Republican
Birthplace: Kentucky
Born: February 12, 1809
Died: April 15, 1865

**17 Andrew Johnson**
**1865–1869**
National Union
Birthplace: North Carolina
Born: December 29, 1808
Died: July 31, 1875

**18 Ulysses S. Grant**
**1869–1877**
Republican
Birthplace: Ohio
Born: April 27, 1822
Died: July 23, 1885

**19 Rutherford B. Hayes**
**1877–1881**
Republican
Birthplace: Ohio
Born: October 4, 1822
Died: January 17, 1893

**20 James A. Garfield**
**1881**
Republican
Birthplace: Ohio
Born: November 19, 1831
Died: September 19, 1881

**21 Chester A. Arthur**
**1881–1885**
Republican
Birthplace: Vermont
Born: October 5, 1829
Died: November 18, 1886

**22 24 Grover Cleveland**
**1885–1889, 1893–1897**
Democrat
Birthplace: New Jersey
Born: March 18, 1837
Died: June 24, 1908

**23 Benjamin Harrison**
**1889–1893**
Republican
Birthplace: Ohio
Born: August 20, 1833
Died: March 13, 1901

**25 William McKinley**
**1897–1901**
Republican
Birthplace: Ohio
Born: January 29, 1843
Died: September 14, 1901

**26 Theodore Roosevelt**
**1901–1909**
Republican
Birthplace: New York
Born: October 27, 1858
Died: January 6, 1919

**27 William H. Taft**
**1909–1913**
Republican
Birthplace: Ohio
Born: September 15, 1857
Died: March 8, 1930

**28 Woodrow Wilson**
**1913–1921**
Democrat
Birthplace: Virginia
Born: December 28, 1856
Died: February 3, 1924

**29 Warren G. Harding**
**1921–1923**
Republican
Birthplace: Ohio
Born: November 2, 1865
Died: August 2, 1923


R41

# PRESIDENTS of the UNITED STATES

30 **Calvin Coolidge**
**1923–1929**
Republican
Birthplace: Vermont
Born: July 4, 1872
Died: January 5, 1933

31 **Herbert C. Hoover**
**1929–1933**
Republican
Birthplace: Iowa
Born: August 10, 1874
Died: October 20, 1964

32 **Franklin D. Roosevelt**
**1933–1945**
Democrat
Birthplace: New York
Born: January 30, 1882
Died: April 12, 1945

33 **Harry S. Truman**
**1945–1953**
Democrat
Birthplace: Missouri
Born: May 8, 1884
Died: December 26, 1972

34 **Dwight D. Eisenhower**
**1953–1961**
Republican
Birthplace: Texas
Born: October 14, 1890
Died: March 28, 1969

35 **John F. Kennedy**
**1961–1963**
Democrat
Birthplace: Massachusetts
Born: May 29, 1917
Died: November 22, 1963

36 **Lyndon B. Johnson**
**1963–1969**
Democrat
Birthplace: Texas
Born: August 27, 1908
Died: January 22, 1973

37 **Richard M. Nixon**
**1969–1974**
Republican
Birthplace: California
Born: January 9, 1913
Died: April 22, 1994

38 **Gerald R. Ford**
**1974–1977**
Republican
Birthplace: Nebraska
Born: July 14, 1913

39 **James E. Carter, Jr.**
**1977–1981**
Democrat
Birthplace: Georgia
Born: October 1, 1924

40 **Ronald W. Reagan**
**1981–1989**
Republican
Birthplace: Illinois
Born: February 6, 1911

41 **George H. W. Bush**
**1989–1993**
Republican
Birthplace: Massachusetts
Born: June 12, 1924

42 **William J. Clinton**
**1993–**
Democrat
Birthplace: Arkansas
Born: August 19, 1946

# GAZETTEER

The Gazetteer identifies important places and geographical features in this book. Entries include a short description, often followed by two page numbers. The first number refers to a text page on which the entry is discussed, and the second, in italics, refers to a map where the place appears. (The reference *Atlas* is to the section of U.S. and world maps on pages R32–R37.) In addition, some entries include rounded-off geographical coordinates. There are entries for all U.S. states (with capital cities).

**Africa** world's second largest continent. *Atlas*

**Alabama** 22nd state. Capital: Montgomery. *Atlas*

**Alamo** Texas mission in San Antonio captured by Mexico in 1836. (29°N 98°W), 402, *m405*

**Alaska** 49th state. Capital: Juneau. *Atlas*

**Antarctica** continent at the South Pole. *Atlas*

**Antietam** Maryland creek; site of bloodiest day's fighting in the Civil War. (39°N 77°W), 497, *m495*

**Appalachian Mountains** mountain range running from Alabama into Canada. 126, *m127*

**Appomattox Court House** town near Appomattox, Virginia, where Lee surrendered to Grant on April 9, 1865. (37°N 79°W), 519, *m517*

**Arizona** 48th state. Capital: Phoenix. *Atlas*

**Arkansas** 25th state. Capital: Little Rock. *Atlas*

**Asia** world's largest continent. *Atlas*

**Atlantic Ocean** ocean forming east boundary of the United States. *Atlas*

**Australia** island country between Indian and Pacific oceans; also the world's smallest continent. *Atlas*

**Austria-Hungary** one of the Central Powers in World War I; after the war, divided into smaller countries. 680, *m680*

**Aztec Empire** former region of Mexico once under Aztec control. 63, *m63*

**Backcountry** identification for former undeveloped region beginning in the Appalachian Mountains and extending west. 126, *m127*

**Baltimore** Maryland city on Chesapeake Bay. (39°N 77°W), 332, *m331*

**Bay of Pigs** (Bahía de Cochinos) inlet on south coast of Cuba; site of 1961 ill-fated, U.S.-backed Cuban invasion attempt. (22°N 81°W), 838

**Beringia** former land bridge connecting Asia with North America and now under waters of Bering Strait. (66°N 169°W), 27, *m28*

**Berlin** capital of Germany; divided into East and West Berlin, 1948–1989. (53°N 13°E), 793, *m792*

**Boston** capital of Massachusetts; site of early colonial unrest and conflict. (42°N 71°W), 165, *m172*

**Bull Run** stream 30 miles southwest of Washington, D.C.; site of first land battle of Civil War. (39°N 78°W), 485, *m495*

**Bunker Hill** hill now part of Boston; its name misidentifies Revolutionary War battle fought at nearby Breed's Hill. (42°N 71°W), 177

**Cahokia** Illinois Mound Builders site; village taken from British by Clark in 1778. (39°N 90°W), 31, *m203*

**California** 31st state. Capital: Sacramento. *Atlas*

**Canada** nation sharing northern U.S. border. *Atlas*

**Caribbean Sea** expanse of the Atlantic Ocean between the Gulf of Mexico and South America. *Atlas*

**Central America** area of North America between Mexico and South America. *m72, Atlas*

**Charleston** as Charles Town, largest Southern colonial city; South Carolina site of first Civil War shots, at offshore Fort Sumter. (33°N 80°W), 481, *m483*

**Charlestown** former town, now part of Boston; site of both Bunker and Breed's hills. (42°N 71°W ), 177, *m172*

**Chicago** large Illinois city on Lake Michigan. (42°N 88°W), 602, *Atlas*

**China** large nation in Asia. *Atlas*

**Colorado** 38th state. Capital: Denver. *Atlas*

**Concord** Massachusetts city and site of second battle of the Revolutionary War. (42°N 71°W), 172, *m172*

**Confederate States of America** nation formed by 11 Southern states during the Civil War. Capital: Richmond, Virginia. 473 and 482, *m483*

**Connecticut** 5th state. Capital: Hartford. *Atlas*

**Cuba** Caribbean island south of Florida. 662, *m665*

**Delaware** 1st state. Capital: Dover. *Atlas*



R43

**District of Columbia (D.C.)** self-governing federal district between Virginia and Maryland, made up entirely of the city of Washington, the U.S. capital. (39°N 77°W), 305, *Atlas*

**Dominican Republic** nation sharing the island of Hispaniola with Haiti. 673, *m672*

**England** southern part of Great Britain. *Atlas*

**English Channel** narrow waterway separating Great Britain from France. 69, *m764*

**Erie Canal** all-water channel dug out to connect the Hudson River with Lake Erie. 355, *m355*

**Europe** second smallest continent, actually a peninsula of the Eurasian landmass. *Atlas*

**Florida** 27th state. Capital: Tallahassee. *Atlas*

**Fort McHenry** fort in Baltimore harbor where 1814 British attack inspired U.S. national anthem. (39°N 77°N), 332, *m331*

**Fort Sumter** fort in Charleston, South Carolina, harbor where 1861 attack by Confederates began the Civil War. (33°N 80°W), 481, *m483*

**France** nation in western Europe; it aided America in the Revolutionary War. *Atlas*

**Gadsden Purchase** last territory (from Mexico, 1853) added to continental United States. 411, *m410*

**Georgia** 4th state. Capital: Atlanta. *Atlas*

**Germany** nation in central Europe; once divided into West and East Germany, 1949–1990. *Atlas*

**Gettysburg** Pennsylvania town and site of 1863 Civil War victory for the North that is considered war's turning point. (40°N 77°W), 513, *m514*

**Ghana** first powerful West African trading empire. 40, *m40*

**Great Britain** European island nation across from France; it consists of England, Scotland, and Wales. *Atlas*

**Great Lakes** five connected lakes—Ontario, Erie, Huron, Michigan, and Superior—on the U.S. border with Canada. 355, *m355*

**Great Plains** vast grassland region in the central United States. 393, *m395*

**Gulf of Mexico** body of water forming southern U.S. boundary from east Texas to west Florida. *Atlas*

**Haiti** nation sharing the island of Hispaniola with Dominican Republic. *Atlas*

**Harpers Ferry** village today in extreme eastern West Virginia where John Brown raided stored U.S. weapons in 1859. (39°N 78°W), 469, *m495*

**Hawaii** 50th state. Capital: Honolulu. *Atlas*

**Hiroshima** Japanese city destroyed by U.S. atomic bomb dropped to end World War II. (34°N 132°E), 771, *m771*

**Hispaniola** West Indies island (shared today by Dominican Republic and Haiti) that Columbus mistook for Asia. 52, *m51*

**Hudson River** large river in eastern New York. 100, *m95*

**Idaho** 43rd state. Capital: Boise. *Atlas*

**Illinois** 21st state. Capital: Springfield. *Atlas*

**Indiana** 19th state. Capital: Indianapolis. *Atlas*

**Indian Territory** area, mainly of present-day Oklahoma, that in the 1800s became land for relocated Native Americans. 376, *m376*

**Iowa** 29th state. Capital: Des Moines. *Atlas*

**Iran** Middle East nation. 865, *m865*

**Iraq** Middle East nation whose 1990 invasion of Kuwait led to the Persian Gulf War. 875, *m865*

**Ireland** island country west of England whose mid-1800s famine caused more than one million people to emigrate to America. 426, *Atlas*

**Israel** Jewish nation in the Middle East. 864, *Atlas*

**Italy** nation in southern Europe. *Atlas*

**Jamestown** community in Virginia that was the first permanent English settlement in North America. 87, *m87*

**Japan** island nation in east Asia. *Atlas*

**Kansas** 34th state. Capital: Topeka. *Atlas*

**Kentucky** 15th state. Capital: Frankfort. *Atlas*

**Kosovo** province of the Yugoslavian republic of Serbia. 876, *m877*

**Kuwait** tiny, oil-rich Middle East nation. 875, *m865*

**Latin America** region made up of Mexico, Caribbean Islands, and Central and South America, where Latin-based languages of Spanish, French, or Portuguese are spoken. 359, *m672*

**Lexington** Massachusetts city and site of first Revolutionary War battle in 1775. (42°N 71°W), 173, *m172*

**Little Bighorn River** Montana site of Sioux and Cheyenne victory over Custer. (46°N 108°W), 565, *m563*

**Little Rock** capital of Arkansas and site of 1957 school-desegregation conflict. 816, *Atlas*

**Los Angeles** 2nd largest U.S. city, on California's coast. 824, *m804*

**Louisiana** 18th state. Capital: Baton Rouge. *Atlas*

**Louisiana Purchase** land west of the Mississippi River purchased from France in 1803. 319, *m320*

**Lowell** Massachusetts city built in early 1800s as planned factory town. (43°N 71°W), 342

**Maine** 23rd state. Capital: Augusta. *Atlas*

**Mali** early West African trading empire succeeding Ghana empire. 41, *m40*

**Maryland** 7th state. Capital: Annapolis. *Atlas*

**Massachusetts** 6th state. Capital: Boston. *Atlas*

**Mexico** nation sharing U.S. southern border. *Atlas*

**Michigan** 26th state. Capital: Lansing. *Atlas*

**Middle East** eastern Mediterranean region that includes countries such as Iran, Iraq, Syria, Kuwait, Jordan, Saudi Arabia, Israel, and Egypt. 864, *m764, m865*

**Minnesota** 32nd state. Capital: St. Paul. *Atlas*

**Mississippi** 20th state. Capital: Jackson. *Atlas*

**Mississippi River** second longest U.S. river, south from Minnesota to the Gulf of Mexico. 146, *m153*

**Missouri** 24th state. Capital: Jefferson City. *Atlas*

**Missouri River** longest U.S. river, east from the Rockies to the Mississippi River. 303, *m302*

**Montana** 41st state. Capital: Helena. *Atlas*

**Montgomery** Alabama capital and site of 1955 African-American bus boycott. (32°N 86°W), 813, *m350*

**Nagasaki** Japanese port city, one-third of which was destroyed by U.S. atomic bomb dropped to end World War II. (33°N 130°E), 773, *m771*

**Nebraska** 37th state. Capital: Lincoln. *Atlas*

**Nevada** 36th state. Capital: Carson City. *Atlas*

**New England** northeast U.S. region made up of Maine, New Hampshire, Vermont, Massachusetts, Rhode Island, and Connecticut. 109, *m110*

**New France** first permanent French colony in North America. 70, *m148*

**New Hampshire** 9th state. Capital: Concord. *Atlas*

**New Jersey** 3rd state. Capital: Trenton. *Atlas*

**New Mexico** 47th state. Capital: Santa Fe. *Atlas*

**New Netherland** early Dutch colony that became New York in 1664. 70

**New Orleans** Louisiana port city at mouth of the Mississippi River. *Atlas*

**New Spain** former North American province of the Spanish Empire, made up mostly of present-day Mexico and the southwest United States. 71, *m72*

**New York** 11th state. Capital: Albany. *Atlas*

**New York City** largest U.S. city, at the mouth of the Hudson River; temporary U.S. capital, 1785–1790. *Atlas*

**Normandy** region of northern France where Allied invasion in 1944 turned tide of World War II. 766, *m766*

**North America** continent of Western Hemisphere north of Panama-Colombia border. *Atlas*

**North Carolina** 12th state. Capital: Raleigh. *Atlas*

**North Dakota** 39th state. Capital: Bismarck. *Atlas*

**North Korea** Communist country in Asia, bordering eastern China. 795, *m796*

**North Vietnam** northern region of Vietnam, established in 1954; reunified with South Vietnam in 1975 after Vietnam War. 837, *m837*

**Northwest Territory** U.S. land north of the Ohio River to the Great Lakes and west to the Mississippi River; acquired in 1783. 223, *m226*

**Ohio** 17th state. Capital: Columbus. *Atlas*

**Ohio River** river that flows from western Pennsylvania to the Mississippi River. *Atlas*

**Oklahoma** 46th state. Capital: Oklahoma City. *Atlas*

**Oregon** 33rd state. Capital: Salem. *Atlas*

**Oregon Country** former region of northwest North America claimed jointly by Britain and the United States until 1846. 318, *m320*

**Oregon Trail** pioneer wagon route from Missouri to the Oregon Territory in the 1840s and 1850s. 394, *m393*

**Pacific Ocean** world's largest ocean, on the west coast of the United States. *Atlas*

**Panama Canal** ship passageway cut through Panama in Central America, linking Atlantic and Pacific oceans. (8°N 80°W), 670, *m670*

**Pearl Harbor** naval base in Hawaii; site of surprise Japanese aerial attack in 1941. (21°N 158°W), 661 *m660*

**Pennsylvania** 2nd state. Capital: Harrisburg. *Atlas*

**Persian Gulf** waterway between Saudi Arabia and Iran, leading to Kuwait and Iraq. 875, *m865*

**Philadelphia** large port city in Pennsylvania; U.S. capital, 1790–1800. (40°N 76°W), 229, *Atlas*

**Philippine Islands** Pacific island country off the southeast coast of China. 662, *m665*

**Plymouth** town on Massachusetts coast and site of Pilgrim landing and colony. (42°N 71°W), 93, *m95*

**Portugal** nation in southwestern Europe; leader in early oceanic explorations. 49, *m51*

**Potomac River** historic river separating Virginia from Maryland and Washington, D.C. 496, *m495*

**Puerto Rico** Caribbean island that has been U.S. territory since 1898. 667, *m665*

**Quebec** major early Canadian city; also a province of eastern Canada. 146, *m148*

**Rhode Island** 13th state. Capital: Providence. *Atlas*

**Richmond** Virginia capital that was also the capital of the Confederacy. (38°N 77°W), 482, *m483*

**Rio Grande** river that forms part of the border between the United States and Mexico. *Atlas*

**Roanoke Island** island off the coast of North Carolina; 1585 site of the first English colony in the Americas. (36°N 76°W), 85, *m87*

**Rocky Mountains** mountain range in the western United States and Canada. *Atlas*

**Russia** large Eurasian country, the major republic of the former Soviet Union (1922–1991). 680, *m680*

**St. Augustine** oldest permanent European settlement (1565) in the United States, on Florida's northeast coast. (30°N 81°W), 68, *m63*

**St. Lawrence River** Atlantic-to-Great Lakes waterway used by early explorers of mid-North America. 146, *m148*

**St. Louis** Missouri city at the junction of the Missouri and Mississippi rivers. (39°N 90°W), 320, *Atlas*

**San Antonio** Texas city and site of the Alamo. (29°N 99°W), 402, *m405*

**San Francisco** major port city in northern California. (38°N 123°W), 416, *m592*

**San Salvador** West Indies island near the Bahamas where Columbus first landed in the Americas. (24°N 74°W), 52, *m51*

**Santa Fe Trail** old wagon route from Missouri to Santa Fe in Mexican province of New Mexico. 395, *m395*

**Songhai** early West African trading empire succeeding Mali empire. 42, *m40*

**South America** continent of Western Hemisphere south of Panama-Colombia border. *Atlas*

**South Carolina** 8th state. Capital: Columbia. *Atlas*

**South Dakota** 40th state. Capital: Pierre. *Atlas*

**South Korea** East Asian country bordering North Korea. 795, *m796*

**South Vietnam** southern region of Vietnam, established in 1954; reunified with North Vietnam in 1975 after Vietnam War. 837, *m837*

**Soviet Union** country created in 1922 by joining Russia and other republics; in 1991, broken into independent states. 757, *m760*

**Spain** nation in southwestern Europe; early empire builder in the Americas. 50, *m51*

**Tennessee** 16th state. Capital: Nashville. *Atlas*

**Tenochtitlán** Aztec Empire capital; now site of Mexico City. 64, *m63*

**Texas** 28th state. Capital: Austin. *Atlas*

**Utah** 45th state. Capital: Salt Lake City. *Atlas*

**Valley Forge** village in southeast Pennsylvania and site of Washington's army camp during winter of 1777–1778. (40°N 75°W), 202, *m209*

**Vermont** 14th state. Capital: Montpelier. *Atlas*

**Vicksburg** Mississippi River site of major Union victory (1863) in Civil War. (32°N 91°W), 516, *m517*

**Vietnam** country in Southeast Asia; divided into two regions (1954–1975), North and South, until end of Vietnam War. 835, *m837*

**Virginia** 10th state. Capital: Richmond. *Atlas*

**Washington** 42nd state. Capital: Olympia. *Atlas*

**Washington, D.C.** capital of the United States since 1800; makes up whole of District of Columbia (D.C.). (39°N 77°W), 305, *Atlas*

**West Africa** region from which most Africans were brought to the Americas. 39, *m40*

**Western Hemisphere** the half of the world that includes the Americas. 75, *m74*

**West Indies** numerous islands in the Caribbean Sea, between Florida and South America. 111, *m111*

**West Virginia** 35th state. Capital: Charleston. *Atlas*

**Wisconsin** 30th state. Capital: Madison. *Atlas*

**Wounded Knee** South Dakota site that was scene of 1890 massacre of Sioux. (43°N 102°W), 566, *m563*

**Wyoming** 44th state. Capital: Cheyenne. *Atlas*

**Yorktown** Virginia village and site of American victory that sealed British defeat in Revolutionary War. (37°N 77°W), 209, *m209*

# GLOSSARY

## A

**abolition** (AB uh LIHSH uhn) *n.* the movement to end slavery. (p. 440)

**abridge** (uh BRIHJ) *v.* to reduce. (p. 266)

**AEF** *n.* the American Expeditionary Force, U.S. forces during World War I. (p. 686)

**affirmation** (AF uhr MAY shuhn) *n.* a statement declaring that something is true. (p. 257)

**African Diaspora** (AF rih kuhn dy AS puhr uh) *n.* the forced removal of Africans from their homelands to serve as slave labor in the Americas. (p. 78)

**Agent Orange** *n.* a chemical that kills plants. (p. 843)

**Albany Plan of Union** *n.* the first formal proposal to unite the American colonies, put forth by Benjamin Franklin. (p. 149)

**Alien and Sedition** (si DISH uhn) **Acts** *n.* a series of four laws enacted in 1798 to reduce the political power of recent immigrants to the United States. (p. 306)

**allies** (AL yz) *n.* an alliance of Serbia, Russia, France, Great Britain, Italy, and seven other countries during World War I. (p. 680)

**ally** (AL eye) *n.* a country that agrees to help another country achieve a common goal. (p. 200)

**American Federation of Labor (AFL)** *n.* a national organization of labor unions founded in 1886. (p. 603)

**American System** *n.* a plan introduced in 1815 to make the United States economically self-sufficient. (p. 354)

**Anaconda** (AN uh KAH duh) **Plan** *n.* a strategy by which the Union proposed to defeat the Confederacy in the Civil War. (p. 484)

**Angel Island** *n.* the first stop in the United States for most immigrants coming from Asia. (p. 615)

**Antifederalist** (AN tee FED uhr uh list) *n.* a person who opposed the ratification of the U.S. Constitution. (p. 234)

**Anti-Imperialist** (AN tee im PEER y uh LIZT) **League** *n.* a group of well-known Americans that believed the United States should not deny other people the right to govern themselves. (p. 667)

**Appalachian** (AP uh LAY chee uhn) **Mountains** *n.* a mountain range that stretches from eastern Canada south to Alabama. (p. 126)

**appeasement** (uh PEEZ muhnt) *n.* the granting of concessions to a hostile power in order to keep the peace. (p. 757)

**appellate** (uh PEL it) *adj.* having power to review court decisions. (p. 260)

**Appomattox** (AP uh MAT uhks) **Court House** *n.* the Virginia town where Robert E. Lee surrendered to Ulysses S. Grant in 1865, ending the Civil War. (p. 519)

**apprentice** (uh PREN tis) *n.* a beginner who learns a trade or a craft from an experienced master. (p. 137)

**appropriation** (uh PROH pree AY shuhn) *n.* public funds set aside for a specific purpose. (p. 253)

**archaeologist** (AHR kee AHL uh jist) *n.* a scientist who studies the human past by examining the things people left behind. (p. 27)

**armistice** (AHR mi stis) *n.* an end to fighting. (p. 690)

**arms race** *n.* from the late 1940s to the late 1980s, the United States and the Soviet Union tried to top each other by developing weapons with great destructive power. (p. 798)

**Articles of Confederation** *n.* a document, adopted by the Continental Congress in 1777 and finally approved by the states in 1781, that outlined the form of government of the new United States. (p. 222)

**artifact** (AHR tuh FAKT) *n.* a tool or other object made by humans. (p. 27)

**artillery** (ahr TIL uhr ee) *n.* a cannon or large gun. (p. 177)

**artisan** (AHR ti zuhn) *n.* a skilled worker, such as a weaver or a potter, who makes goods by hand; a craftsperson. (p. 117)

**assimilation** (uh SIM uh LAY shuhn) *n.* the process of blending into society. (p. 616)

**Axis** (AK sis) *n.* Germany, Italy, and their allies during World War II. (p. 757)

## B

**baby boom** *n.* the term for the generation born between 1946 and 1961, when the U.S. birthrate sharply increased following World War II. (p. 801)

**Backcountry** *n.* a colonial region that ran along the Appalachian Mountains through the far western part of the New England, Middle, and Southern colonies. (p. 109)

**Bacon's Rebellion** *n.* a revolt against powerful colonial authority in Jamestown by Nathaniel Bacon and a group of landless frontier settlers that resulted in the burning of Jamestown in 1676. (p. 89)

**bail** (bayl) *n.* money paid as security by arrested persons to guarantee they will return for trial. (p. 268)

**Bataan** (buh TAN) **Death March** *n.* in 1942, the Japanese marched 70,000 Filipino and American soldiers 60 miles to a prison camp. (p. 768)

**Battle of Antietam** (an TEE tuhm) *n.* a Civil War battle in 1862 in which 25,000 men were killed or wounded. (p. 497)

**Battle of Fallen Timbers** *n.* in 1794, an American army defeated 2,000 Native Americans in a clash over control of the Northwest Territory. (p. 299)

**Battle of Gettysburg** (GET eez BURG) *n.* an 1863 battle in the Civil War in which the Union defeated the Confederacy, ending hopes for a Confederate victory in the North. (p. 513)

**Battle of Midway** *n.* a victory for the United States over the Japanese in a 1942 naval battle that was a turning point of World War II. (p. 770)

**Battle of Quebec** (kwi BEK) *n.* a battle won by the British over the French, and the turning point in the French and Indian War. (p. 150)

**Battle of Shiloh** (SHY loh) *n.* an 1862 battle in which the Union forced the Confederacy to retreat in some of the fiercest fighting in the Civil War. (p. 494)

**Battle of Yorktown** *n.* the last major battle of the Revolutionary War, which resulted in the surrender of British forces in 1781. (p. 210)

**Battle of the Alamo** (AL uh MOH) *n.* in 1836, Texans defended a church called the Alamo against the Mexican army; all but five Texans were killed. (p. 403)

**Battle of the Bulge** *n.* a month-long battle of World War II in which the Allies turned back the last major German offensive of the war. (p. 764)

**Battle of the Little Bighorn** *n.* an 1876 battle in which the Sioux and the Cheyenne wiped out an entire force of U.S. troops. (p. 565)

**Battle of the Thames** (temz) *n.* an American victory over the British in the War of 1812, which ended the British threat to the Northwest Territory. (p. 332)

**Battles of Saratoga** (SAR uh TOH guh) *n.* a series of conflicts between British soldiers and the Continental Army in 1777 that proved to be a turning point in the Revolutionary War. (p. 199)

**bayonet** (BAY uh net) *n.* a long steel knife attached to the end of a gun. (p. 202)

**Bear Flag Revolt** *n.* the 1846 rebellion by Americans against Mexican rule in California. (p. 409)

**Benin** (buh NIN) *n.* a West African kingdom that arose near the Niger River delta in the 1300s. (p. 43)

**Bessemer** (BES uh muhr) **steel process** *n.* a new way of making steel that was developed in the 1850s and caused steel production to soar. (p. 587)

**bill of attainder** (uh TAYN duhr) *n.* a law that condemns a person without a trial in court. (p. 255)

**Bill of Rights** *n.* the first ten amendments to the U.S. Constitution, added in 1791, and consisting of a formal list of citizens' rights and freedoms. (p. 237)

**black code** *n. a* law passed by Southern states that limited the freedom of former slaves. (p. 534)

**Black Tuesday** *n.* a name given to October 29, 1929, when stock prices fell sharply. (p. 731)

**blockade** *n.* when armed forces prevent the transportation of goods or people into or out of an area. (p. 484)

**Bonus Army** *n.* in 1932, thousands of veterans streamed into Washington demanding bonuses that they never received. (p. 733)

**boomtown** *n.* a town that has a sudden burst of economic or population growth. (p. 558)

**border state** *n.* a slave state that bordered states in which slavery was illegal. (p. 482)

**Boston Massacre** (MAS uh kuhr) *n.* a clash between British soldiers and Boston colonists in 1770, in which five of the colonists, including Crispus Attucks, were killed. (p. 165)

**Boston Tea Party** *n.* the dumping of 342 chests of tea into Boston Harbor by colonists in 1773 to protest the Tea Act. (p. 167)

**bounty** (BOWN tee) *n.* a reward or cash payment given by a government. (pp. 271, 508)

**Boxer Rebellion** *n.* in 1900, Chinese resentment toward foreigners' attitude of cultural superiority resulted in this violent uprising. (p. 669)

**boycott** (BOI KOT) *n.* a refusal to buy certain goods. (p. 161)

***bracero*** (bruh SAIR oh) **program** *n.* the hiring of Mexicans to perform much-needed labor during World War II. (p. 774)

**brinksmanship** (BRINGKS muhn SHIP) *n.* in international politics, the act of pushing a dangerous situation to the limits; for example, the United States going to the brink of war to stop Communism. (p. 798)

***Brown* v. *Board of Education of Topeka, Kansas*** *n.* a 1954 case in which the Supreme Court ruled that "separate but equal" education for black and white students was unconstitutional. (p. 814)

**buck** *n.* a buckskin from an adult male deer was a unit of money for settlers. (p. 127)

**buffalo soldier** *n.* a name given by Native Americans to African Americans serving in the U.S. army in the West. (p. 571)

**business cycle** *n.* the pattern of good times and bad times in the economy. (p. 586)

**buy on margin** *v.* to pay a small part of a stock's price and then borrow money to pay for the rest. (p. 730)

## C

**cabinet** *n.* a group of department heads who serve as the president's chief advisers. (p. 294)

**California gold rush** *n.* in 1849, large numbers of people moved to California because gold had been discovered there. (p. 413)

**Cambodia** (kam BOW dee uh) *n.* a country bordering Vietnam. (p. 848)

**Camp David Accords** *n.* in 1979, under these agreements, Egypt and Israel signed a peace treaty that ended 30 years of conflict. (p. 864)

**caravel** (KAR uh VEL) *n.* a ship with triangular sails that allowed it to sail into the wind and with square sails that carried it forward when the wind was at its back. (p. 49)

**cash crop** *n.* a crop grown by a farmer to be sold for money rather than for personal use. (p. 115)

**cavalry** *n.* soldiers on horseback. (p. 496)

**Centennial** (sen TEN ee uhl) **Exhibition** *n.* an exhibition in Philadelphia in 1876 that celebrated America's 100th birthday. (p. 588)

**Central Powers** *n.* an alliance of Austria-Hungary, Germany, the Ottoman Empire, and Bulgaria during World War I. (p. 680)

**charter** *n.* a written contract issued by a government giving the holder the right to establish a colony. (p. 87)

**checks and balances** *n.* the ability of each branch of government to exercise checks, or controls, over the other branches. (p. 246)

**Chinese Exclusion Act** *n.* enacted in 1882, this law banned Chinese immigration for ten years. (p. 617)

**civil disobedience** (DIS uh BEE dee uhns) *n.* peacefully refusing to obey laws one considers unjust. (p. 431)

**civilization** (SIV uh li ZAY shuhn) *n.* a form of culture characterized by city trade centers, specialized workers, organized forms of government and religion, systems of record keeping, and advanced tools. (p. 29)

**civil rights** *n.* rights granted to all citizens. (p. 535)

**Civil Rights Act of 1964** *n.* this act banned segregation in public places and created the Equal Employment Opportunity Commission. (p. 820)

**clan** *n.* a large group of families that claim a common ancestor. (p. 127)

**Clayton Antitrust Act** *n.* a law passed in 1914 that laid down rules forbidding business practices that lessened competition; it gave the government more power to regulate trusts. (p. 648)

**Cold War** *n.* the state of hostility, without direct military conflict, that developed between the United States and the Soviet Union after World War II. (p. 792)

**Columbian** (kuh LUM bee uhn) **Exchange** *n.* the transfer of plants, animals, and diseases between the Western and the Eastern hemispheres. (p. 74)

**committee of correspondence** *n.* a group of people in the colonies who exchanged letters on colonial affairs. (p. 166)

**Committee to Reelect the President** *n.* an organization linked to the break-in at the Democratic National Committee headquarters that set off the Watergate scandal. (p. 860)

**common law** *n.* a system of law developed in England, based on customs and previous court decisions. (p. 268)

**Compromise of 1850** *n.* a series of Congressional laws intended to settle the major disagreements between free states and slave states. (p. 461)

**Compromise of 1877** *n.* the agreement that resolved an 1876 election dispute: Rutherford B. Hayes became president and then removed the last federal troops from the South. (p. 548)

**compulsory process** *n.* a required procedure. (p. 267)

**Conestoga** (KON i STOW guh) **wagon** *n.* a vehicle with wide wheels, a curved bed, and a canvas cover used by American pioneers traveling west. (p. 117)

**Confederate States of America** *n.* the confederation formed in 1861 by the Southern states after their secession from the Union. (p. 473)

**Congress of Industrial Organizations (CIO)** *n.* a labor organization that broke away from the American Federation of Labor in 1938. (p. 743)

***conquistador*** (kon KWIS tuh DAWR) *n.* a Spaniard who traveled to the Americas as an explorer and a conqueror in the 16th century. (p. 63)

**conscription** (kuhn SKRIP shuhn) *n.* a law that required men to serve in the military or be drafted. (p. 508)

**conservative** *n.* a person who favors fewer government controls and more individual freedom in economic matters. (p. 749)

**Constitutional Convention** *n.* a meeting held in 1787 to consider changes to the Articles of Confederation; resulted in the drafting of the Constitution. (p. 229)

**containment** (kuhn TAYN muhnt) *n.* the blocking by one nation of another nation's attempts to spread influence—especially the efforts of the United States to block the spread of Soviet Communism during the late 1940s and early 1950s. (p. 793)

**Continental Army** *n.* a colonial force authorized by the Second Continental Congress in 1775, with George Washington as its commanding general. (p. 177)

**convene** (kuhn VEEN) *v.* to call together. (p. 259)

**convoy system** *n.* a heavy guard of destroyers that escorts merchant ships during wartime. (p. 687)

**cooperative** (koh OP uhr uh tiv) *n.* an organization owned and run by its members. (p. 577)

**Copperheads** *n.* Abraham Lincoln's main political opponents; they favored peace with the South. (p. 508)

**CORE** *n.* the Congress of Racial Equality, a group that planned Freedom Rides to desegregate interstate buses. (p. 818)

**corporation** *n.* a business owned by investors who buy part of the company through shares of stock. (p. 594)

**cotton gin** *n.* a machine invented in 1793 that cleaned cotton much faster and far more efficiently than human workers. (p. 348)

**counsel** (KOWN suhl) *n.* a lawyer. (p. 267)

**Crash of 1929** *n.* the plunge in stock market prices. (p. 731)

**Crittenden** (KRIT uhn duhn) **Plan** *n.* a compromise introduced in 1861 that might have prevented secession. (p. 475)

**Crusades** (kroo SAYDZ) *n.* a series of wars to capture the Holy Land, launched in 1096 by European Christians. (p. 45)

**Cuban Missile Crisis** *n.* in 1962, the United States and the Soviet Union almost went to war because the Soviets had placed nuclear missiles in Cuba. (p. 839)

**culture** (KUL chuhr) *n.* a way of life shared by people with similar arts, beliefs, and customs. (p. 28)

## D

**Dawes** (dawz) **Act** *n.* a law, enacted in 1887, that distributed reservation land to individual owners. (p. 567)

**D-Day** *n.* June 6, 1944, the day the Allies invaded France during World War II. (p. 764)

**Declaration of Independence** *n.* the document, written in 1776, in which the colonies declared independence from Britain. (p. 180)

**deficit** (DEF i sit) **spend** *v.* to use borrowed money to fund government programs. (p. 738)

**department store** *n.* a store that sells everything from clothing to furniture to hardware. (p. 627)

**depression** *n.* a severe economic slump. (p. 386)

**desert** (di ZURT) *v.* to leave military duty without intending to return. (p. 203)





R49

**détente** (day TAHNT) *n.* an easing of tensions between the United States and the Soviet Union during the Cold War. (p. 858)

**direct primary** *n.* voters, rather than party conventions, choose candidates to run for public office. (p. 640)

**diversity** (di VUR si tee) *n.* a variety of people. (p. 117)

**doctrine of nullification** (NUL uh fi KAY shuhn) *n.* a right of a state to reject a federal law that it considers unconstitutional. (p. 381)

**domestication** (doh MES ti KAY shuhn) *n.* the practice of breeding plants or taming animals to meet human needs. (p. 28)

**domino** (DOM uh NOH) **theory** *n.* a theory stating that if a country fell to communism, nearby countries would also fall to communism. (p. 837)

**dove** *n.* a person opposed to war. (p. 847)

**downsize** *v.* to reduce the number of workers in order to increase company profits. (p. 879)

***Dred Scott* v. *Sandford*** *n.* an 1856 Supreme Court case in which a slave, Dred Scott, sued for his freedom because he had been taken to live in territories where slavery was illegal; the Court ruled against Scott. (p. 467)

**due process of law** *n.* fair treatment under the law. (p. 267)

**dust bowl** *n.* the area of dust-damaged farms across a 150,000-square-mile region during the early 1930s. (p. 739)

## E

**elector** *n.* a voter. (p. 249)

**Ellis Island** *n.* the first stop in the United States for most immigrants coming from Europe. (p. 614)

**Emancipation** (i MAN suh PAY shuhn) **Proclamation** *n.* an executive order issued by Abraham Lincoln on January 1, 1863, freeing the slaves in all regions in rebellion against the Union. (p. 504)

**Embargo** (em BAHR goh) **Act of 1807** *n.* an act that stated that American ships were no longer allowed to sail to foreign ports, and it also closed American ports to British ships. (p. 328)

**emigrant** (EM i gruhnt) *n.* a person who leaves a country. (p. 423)

***encomienda*** (en koh mee YEN duh) *n.* a grant of Native American labor. (p. 72)

**English Bill of Rights** *n.* an agreement signed by William and Mary to respect the rights of English citizens and of Parliament, including the right to free elections. (p. 144)

**enlightenment** (en LYT n muhnt) *n.* an 18th-century movement that emphasized the use of reason and the scientific method to obtain knowledge. (p. 140)

**enumeration** (i NOO muh RAY shuhn) *n.* an official count, such as a census. (p. 249)

**environmentalism** (en VY ruhn MEN tl IZ uhm) *n.* work toward protecting the environment. (p. 864)

**equity** (EK wi tee) *n.* a system of justice not covered under common law. (p. 269)

**ERA** *n.* the Equal Rights Amendment, a proposed amendment that would give equality of rights regardless of sex; the amendment died in 1982. (p. 826)

**Erie** (EER ee) **Canal** *n.* completed in 1825, this waterway connected New York City and Buffalo, New York. (p. 355)

**escalation** (ES kuh LAY shuhn) *n.* the policy of increasing military involvement, as in Vietnam. (p. 841)

**Espionage** (ES pee uh NAHZH) **Act** *n.* passed in 1917, this law set heavy fines and long prison terms for antiwar activities and for encouraging draft resisters. (p. 692)

**European Middle Ages** *n.* a period from the late 400s to about the 1300s, during which Europeans turned to feudalism and the manor system. (p. 44)

**exoduster** (EKS suh duhs tuhr) *n.* an African American who left the South for the West and compared himself or herself to Biblical Hebrews who left slavery in Egypt. (p. 575)

**expatriate** (ek SPAY tree it) *n.* a citizen of one country who takes up residence in another country. (p. 721)

**ex post facto** (EKS pohst FAK toh) **law** *n.* a law that would make an act a criminal offense after it was committed. (p. 255)

## F

**factory system** *n.* a method of production that brought many workers and machines together into one building. (p. 341)

**Fair Deal** *n.* a program under Harry Truman that called for new projects to create jobs, new public housing, and an end to racial discrimination in hiring. (p. 791)

**fall line** *n.* the point at which a waterfall prevents large boats from moving farther upriver. (p. 126)

**famine** (FAM in) *n.* a severe food shortage. (p. 426)

**fascism** (FASH iz uhm) *n.* a political philosophy that advocates a strong, centralized, nationalistic government headed by a powerful dictator. (p. 756)

**federalism** *n.* a system of government where power is shared among the central (or federal) government and the states. (pp. 234, 245)

**Federalists** *n.* supporters of the Constitution. (p. 234)

***Federalist Papers*** *n.* a series of essays defending and explaining the Constitution. (p. 235)

**Federal Judiciary** (joo DISH ee ER ee) **Act** *n.* it helped create a court system and gave the Supreme Court six members. (p. 294)

**Federal Reserve Act** *n.* a law passed in 1913 that "created" the nation's banking system and instituted a flexible currency system. (p. 648)

**felony** (FEL uh nee) *n.* a serious crime. (p. 253)

**feudalism** (FYOOD l IZ uhm) *n.* a political system in which the king allows nobles the use of his land in exchange for their military service and their protection of people living on the land. (p. 44)

**Fifteenth Amendment** *n.* passed in 1870, this amendment to the U.S. Constitution stated that citizens could not be stopped from voting "on account of race, color, or previous condition of servitude." (p. 546)

**54th Massachusetts Regiment** *n.* one of the first African-American regiments organized to fight for the Union in the Civil War. (p. 506)

**fireside chat** *n.* the name of Franklin Roosevelt's radio broadcasts in which he explained his policies. (p. 735)

**First Battle of Bull Run** *n.* an 1861 battle of the Civil War in which the South shocked the North with a victory. (p. 485)

**flapper** *n.* a young woman who embraced the fashions and urban attitudes of the 1920s. (p. 714)

**foreign** (FAWR in) **policy** *n.* relations with the governments of other countries. (p. 304)

**Fort Sumter** *n.* a federal fort located in the harbor of Charleston, South Carolina; the Southern attack on Fort Sumter marked the beginning of the Civil War. (p. 481)

**forty-niner** *n.* a person who went to California to find gold, starting in 1849. (p. 412)

**Fourteen Points** *n.* President Woodrow Wilson's goals for peace after World War I. (p. 695)

**Fourteenth Amendment** *n.* an amendment to the U.S. Constitution, passed in 1868, that made all persons born or naturalized in the United States—including former slaves—citizens of the country. (p. 535)

**First Continental Congress** *n.* a meeting of delegates in 1774 from all the colonies except Georgia to uphold colonial rights. (p. 171)

**Freedmen's Bureau** *n.* a federal agency set up to help former slaves after the Civil War. (p. 533)

**freedmen's school** *n.* a school set up to educate newly freed African Americans. (p. 541)

**Freedom Ride** *n.* a protest against segregation on interstate busing in the South. (p. 818)

**Freedom Summer** *n.* in 1964, the SNCC organized a voter-registration drive. (p. 821)

**Free Soil Party** *n.* a political party dedicated to stopping the expansion of slavery. (p. 459)

**French and Indian War** *n.* a conflict in North America from 1754 to 1763 that was part of a worldwide struggle between France and Britain; Britain defeated France and gained French Canada. (p. 147)

**French Indochina** (IN doh CHY nuh) *n.* a French colony that included present-day Vietnam, Laos, and Cambodia. (p. 835)

**frontier** (frun TEER) *n.* unsettled or sparsely settled area occupied largely by Native Americans. (p. 557)

**Fugitive Slave Act** *n.* an 1850 law to help slaveholders recapture runaway slaves. (p. 462)

**French Revolution** *n.* in 1789, the French launched a movement for liberty and equality. (p. 301)

**fundamentalist** *n.* a person who believes in a literal, or word-for-word, interpretation of the bible. (p. 716)

**Fundamental Orders of Connecticut** *n.* a set of laws that were established in 1639 by a Puritan congregation who had settled in the Connecticut Valley and that expanded the idea of representative government. (p. 95)

## G

**generator** *n.* a machine that produces electric current. (p. 587)

**Ghana** (GAH nuh) *n.* a West African empire in the 8th–11th centuries A.D. (p. 39)

**G.I. Bill of Rights** *n.* passed in 1944, this bill provided educational and economic help to veterans. (p. 779)

**Gilded** (gil did) **Age** *n.* an era during the late 1800s of fabulous wealth. (p. 596)

**"Glorious Revolution"** *n.* the overthrow of English King James II in 1688 and his replacement by William and Mary. (p. 144)

**gold standard** *n.* a policy under which the government backs every dollar with a certain amount of gold. (p. 577)

**Grange** (graynj) *n.* formed in 1867, the Patrons of Husbandry tried to meet the social needs of farm families. (p. 577)

**Great Awakening** *n.* a revival of religious feeling in the American colonies during the 1730s and 1740s. (p. 139)

**Great Compromise** *n.* the Constitutional Convention's agreement to establish a two-house national legislature, with all states having equal representation in one house and each state having representation based on its population in the other house. (p. 232)

**Great Depression** *n.* a period, lasting from 1929 to 1941, in which the U.S. economy was in severe decline and millions of Americans were unemployed. (p. 731)

**Great Migration** *n.* the movement of Puritans from England to establish settlements around the world, including 20,000 who sailed for America (p. 94); the movement of African Americans between 1910 and 1920 to northern cities from the South. (p. 693)

**Great Plains** *n.* the area from the Missouri River to the Rocky Mountains. (p. 557)

**Great Society** *n.* a program started by President Lyndon Johnson that provided help to the poor, the elderly, and women, and also promoted education and outlawed discrimination. (p. 822)

**greenback** *n.* paper currency issued by the federal government during the Civil War. (p. 509)

**gristmill** (GRIST MIL) *n.* a mill in which grain is ground to produce flour or meal. (p. 115)

**guerrilla** (guh RIL uh) *n.* a soldier who weakens the enemy with surprise raids and hit-and-run attacks. (p. 207)

**guerrilla warfare** *n.* surprise attacks by small bands of fighters. (p. 842)

**Gulf of Tonkin Resolution** *n.* congressional resolution that gave the president power to use military force in Vietnam. (p. 841)

## H

***hacienda*** (HAH see EN duh) *n.* a large farm or estate. (p. 72)

**Harlem Renaissance** *n.* a flowering of African-American artistic creativity during the 1920s, centered in the Harlem community of New York City. (p. 720)





R51

**Harpers Ferry** *n.* a federal arsenal in Virginia that was captured in 1859 during a slave revolt. (p. 469)

**Hausa** (HOW suh) *n.* a West African people who lived in what is now northern Nigeria after A.D. 1000. (p. 42)

**hawk** *n.* a person who supports war. (p. 847)

**Haymarket affair** *n.* in 1886, a union protest resulted in about 100 dead after an unknown person threw a bomb, and police opened fire on the crowd. (p. 602)

**H-bomb** *n.* a hydrogen bomb. (p. 798)

**Hiroshima** (HEER uh SHEE muh) *n.* the first city in Japan that was hit by an atomic bomb on August 6, 1945. (p. 771)

**Ho Chi Minh** (HOH CHEE MIN) **Trail** *n.* a network of paths that the Viet Cong used to move soldiers and supplies during the Vietnam War. (p. 838)

**Holocaust** ( HOL uh KAWST) *n.* the systematic killing by Germany during World War II of about six million Jews as well as millions from other ethnic groups. (p. 765)

**homestead** *n.* land to settle on and farm. (p. 568)

**Homestead Act** *n.* passed in 1862, this law offered 160 acres of land free to anyone who agreed to live on and improve the land for five years. (p. 574)

**House of Burgesses** *n.* created in 1619, the first representative assembly in the American colonies. (p. 88)

**Hudson River school** *n.* a group of artists living in the Hudson River Valley in New York. (p. 430)

**Hull House** *n.* founded in 1889, a model for other settlement houses of the time. (p. 613)

**Hundred Days** *n.* in his first hundred days, from March 9 to mid-June 1933, Franklin Roosevelt sent Congress many new bills. (p. 735)

**hygiene** (HY JEEN) *n.* conditions and practices that promote health. (p. 490)

## I

**immigrant** *n.* a person who settles in a new country. (p. 423)

**Immigration Reform and Control Act of 1986** *n.* a law that is designed to strengthen immigration laws and enforcement measures. (p. 884)

**immunity** *n.* legal protection. (p. 262)

**impeachment** *n.* the process of accusing a public official of wrongdoing. (p. 249)

**imperialism** *n.* the policy by which stronger nations extend their economic, political, or military control over weaker nations or territories. (p. 659)

**impressment** *n.* the act of seizing by force. (p. 327)

**inaugurate** (in AW gyuh RAYT) *v.* to swear in or induct into office in a formal ceremony. (p. 293)

**income tax** *n.* a tax on earnings. (p. 509)

**indentured servant** *n.* a person who sold his or her labor in exchange for passage to America. (p. 88)

**Indian Removal Act** *n.* this 1830 act called for the government to negotiate treaties that would require Native Americans to relocate west. (p. 376)

**Indian Territory** *n.* present-day Oklahoma and parts of Kansas and Nebraska to which Native Americans were moved under the Indian Removal Act of 1830. (p. 376)

**indictment** (in DYT muhnt) *n.* a written statement issued by a grand jury charging a person with a crime. (p. 250)

**indigo** *n.* a plant grown in the Southern colonies that yields a deep blue dye. (p. 121)

**individual right** *n.* a personal liberty and privilege guaranteed to U.S. citizens by the Bill of Rights. (p. 247)

**Industrial Revolution** *n.* in late 18th-century Britain, factory machines began replacing hand tools and manufacturing replaced farming as the main form of work. (p. 341)

**inferior court** *n.* a court with less authority than the Supreme Court. (p. 260)

**inflation** *n.* an increase in the price of goods and services and a decrease in the value of money. (p. 386)

**information revolution** *n.* a time when technology has radically changed how much information and the way information is delivered. (p. 879)

**initiative** (i NISH uh tiv) *n.* the procedure that allows voters to propose a law directly. (p. 640)

**inoperative** *adj.* no longer in force. (p. 274)

**installment buy** *v.* to buy something by making small monthly payments. (p. 712)

**insurrection** (IN suh REK shuhn) *n.* open revolt against a government. (p. 271)

**interchangeable part** *n.* a part that is exactly like another part. (p. 343)

**Internet** *n.* a worldwide computer network. (p. 878)

**Intolerable Acts** *n.* a series of laws enacted by Parliament in 1774 to punish Massachusetts colonists for the Boston Tea Party. (p. 170)

**Iran-Contra affair** *n.* in 1986, the U.S. government sold weapons to Iran for help in freeing American hostages in the Middle East, and the money from the sale went to the Contra rebels in El Salvador. (p. 874)

**Iran hostage crisis** *n.* on November 4, 1979, a group of Iranians overran the American embassy in Iran's capital of Tehran and took 52 Americans hostage. (p. 865)

**ironclad** *n.* a warship covered with iron. (p. 491)

**Iroquois** (IR uh KWOH) **League** *n.* a 16th-century alliance of the Cayuga, Mohawk, Oneida, Onondaga, and Seneca Native American groups living in the eastern Great Lakes region. (p. 37)

**irrigation** *n.* the practice of bringing water to crops. (p. 29)

**Islam** (is LAHM) *n.* a religion founded by the prophet Muhammad in the 600s, which teaches that there is one God, named Allah. (p. 41)

**island hopping** *n.* a World War II strategy in which the Allies invaded islands that the Japanese weakly defended in order to stage further attacks. (p. 770)

**isolationist** *n.* a person who believed that the United States should stay out of other nations' affairs except in self-defense. (p. 711)

## J

**Jacksonian Democracy** *n.* the idea of spreading political power to all the people, thereby ensuring majority rule. (p. 370)

**Jamestown** *n.* the first permanent English settlement in North America. (p. 87)

**Jay's Treaty** *n.* the agreement that ended dispute over American shipping during the French Revolution. (p. 302)

**jazz** *n.* a new kind of music in the 1920s that captured the carefree spirit of the times. (p. 717)

**Jim Crow** *n.* laws meant to enforce separation of white and black people in public places in the South. (p. 621)

**joint-stock company** *n.* a business in which investors pool their wealth in order to turn a profit. (p. 86)

**judicial** (joo DISH uhl) **review** *n.* the principle that the Supreme Court has the final say in interpreting the Constitution. (p. 317)

**Judiciary** (joo DISH ee ER ee) **Act of 1801** *n.* a law that increased the number of federal judges, allowing President John Adams to fill most of the new spots with Federalists. (p. 316)

## K

**Kansas-Nebraska Act** *n.* an 1854 law that established the territories of Kansas and Nebraska and gave their residents the right to decide whether to allow slavery. (p. 464)

**kayak** (KY AK) *n.* a small boat made of animal skins. (p. 33)

**Kellogg-Briand Pact** *n.* in 1928, this pact was signed by many nations who pledged not to make war against each other except in self-defense. (p. 711)

**King Cotton** *n.* cotton was called king because cotton was important to the world market, and the South grew most of the cotton for Europe's mills. (p. 484)

**King Philip's War** *n.* a war between the Puritan colonies and Native Americans in 1675–1676. (p. 96)

**Knights of Labor** *n.* an organization of workers from all different trades formed after the Civil War. (p. 601)

**Korean War** *n.* a conflict between North Korea and South Korea, lasting from 1950 to 1953; the United States, along with other UN countries, fought on the side of the South Koreans, and China fought on the side of the North Koreans. (p. 796)

**Ku Klux Klan** *n.* a group formed in 1866 that wanted to restore Democratic control of the South and to keep former slaves powerless; the group called for a "racially and morally pure" America. (pp. 544, 716)

## L

**labor union** *n.* a group of workers who band together to seek better working conditions. (p. 434)

**laissez faire** (LES ay FAIR) *n.* a theory that stated that business, if unregulated, would act in a way that would benefit the nation. (p. 710)

**Land Ordinance of 1785** *n.* a law that established a plan for surveying and selling the federally owned lands west of the Appalachian Mountains. (p. 223)

**land speculator** *n.* a person who buys huge areas of land for a low price and then sells off small sections of it at high prices. (p. 394)

**League of Nations** *n.* an organization set up after World War I to settle international conflicts. (p. 695)

**leisure** (LEE zhuhr) *n.* free time. (p. 627)

**Lend-Lease** *n.* a 1941 law that allowed the United States to ship arms and supplies, without immediate payment, to nations fighting the Axis powers. (p. 760)

**Lewis and Clark expedition** *n.* a group led by Meriwether Lewis and William Clark who explored the lands of the Louisiana Purchase beginning in 1803. (p. 320)

**Lexington and Concord** *n.* sites in Massachusetts of the first battles of the American Revolution. (p. 173)

**liberal** *n.* a person who favors government action to bring about social and economic reform. (p. 749)

**limited government** *n.* the principle that requires all U.S. citizens, including government leaders, to obey the law. (p. 247)

**lode** *n.* a deposit of mineral buried in rock. (p. 558)

**Lone Star Republic** *n.* the nickname of the republic of Texas, given in 1836. (p. 405)

**long drive** *n.* taking cattle by foot to a railway. (p. 560)

**Lost Generation** *n.* the generation of the 1920s after World War I, when men and women saw little hope for the future. (p. 720)

**Louisiana** (loo EE zee AN uh) **Purchase** *n.* the 1803 purchase of the Louisiana Territory from France. (p. 319)

**Lowell mills** *n.* textile mills located in the factory town of Lowell, Massachusetts, founded in 1826. (p. 342)

**Loyalist** *n.* an American colonist who supported the British in the American Revolution. (p. 173)

## M

**mail-order catalog** *n.* a publication that contains pictures and descriptions of items so that people can order by mail. (p. 627)

**Magna Carta** *n.* "Great Charter;" a document guaranteeing basic political rights in England, approved by King John in 1215. (p. 141)

**Mali** (MAH lee) *n.* a West African empire from the 13th–15th centuries that grew rich from trade. (p. 41)

**Manhattan Project** *n.* the top-secret program set up in 1942 to build an atomic bomb. (p. 771)

**manifest destiny** *n.* the belief that the United States was destined to stretch across the continent from the Atlantic Ocean to the Pacific Ocean. (p. 407)

**manor system** *n.* a system in which lords divided their lands into estates, which were farmed mostly by serfs who received protection from the lord in return. (p. 45)

***Marbury* v. *Madison*** *n.* an 1803 case in which the Supreme Court ruled that it had the power to abolish laws by declaring them unconstitutional. (p. 317)

**March on Washington** *n.* a huge civil rights demonstration in Washington, D.C., in 1963. (p. 820)



**R53**

**Marshall Plan** *n.* approved in 1948, the United States gave more than $13 billion to help the nations of Europe after World War II. (p. 779)

**mass culture** *n.* a common culture experienced by large numbers of people. (p. 626)

**mass media** *n.* communications that reach a large audience. (p. 718)

**matrilineal** (MAT ruh LIN ee uhl) *adj.* a society in which ancestry is traced through the mother. (p. 36)

**Mayflower Compact** *n.* an agreement established by the men who sailed to America on the *Mayflower,* which called for laws for the good of the colony and set forth the idea of self-government. (p. 93)

**melting pot** *n.* a place where cultures blend. (p. 616)

**mercantilism** (MUHR kuhn tee LIZ uhm) *n.* an economic system in which nations increase their wealth and power by obtaining gold and silver and by establishing a favorable balance of trade. (p. 61)

**mercenary** (MUR suh NER ee) *n.* a professional soldier hired to fight for a foreign country. (p. 195)

**Mexican Cession** (sesh uhn) *n.* a vast region given up by Mexico after the War with Mexico; it included the present-day states of California, Nevada, Utah, most of Arizona, and parts of New Mexico, Colorado, and Wyoming. (p. 411)

***Mexicano*** (may hi KAH noh) *n.* a person of Spanish descent whose ancestors had come from Mexico and settled in the Southwest. (p. 570)

**Middle Passage** *n.* the middle leg of the triangular trade route—the voyage from Africa to the Americas—that brought captured Africans into slavery. (p. 78)

**migrate** *v.* to move from one location to another. (p. 27)

**militarism** *n.* the belief that a nation needs a large military force. (p. 679)

**militia** (muh LISH uh) *n.* a force of armed civilians pledged to defend their community during the American Revolution. (p. 170); an emergency military force that is not part of the regular army. (p. 254)

**minié** (MIN ee) **ball** *n.* a bullet with a hollow base. (p. 491)

**Minuteman** *n.* a member of the colonial militia who was trained to respond "at a minute's warning." (p. 170)

**misdemeanor** (mis di MEE nuhr) *n.* a violation of the law. (p. 259)

**mission** *n.* a settlement created by the Church in order to convert Native Americans to Christianity. (p. 72)

**missionary** *n.* a person sent by the Church to preach, teach, and convert native peoples to Christianity. (p. 61)

**Missouri Compromise** *n.* a series of laws enacted in 1820 to maintain the balance of power between slave states and free states. (p. 358)

**monopoly** *n.* a company that eliminates its competitors and controls an industry. (p. 595)

**Monroe Doctrine** *n.* a policy of U.S. opposition to any European interference in the Western Hemisphere, announced by President Monroe in 1823. (p. 359)

**Montgomery bus boycott** *n.* in 1955, African Americans boycotted the public buses in Montgomery, Alabama, in response to the arrest of Rosa Parks, who refused to give up her seat to a white person. (p. 815)

**Mormon** *n.* a member of a church founded by Joseph Smith in 1830. (p. 397)

**Mound Builder** *n.* an early Native American who built large earthen structures. (p. 31)

**mountain man** *n.* a fur trapper or explorer who opened up the West by finding the best trails through the Rocky Mountains. (p. 393)

**muckraker** *n.* around 1900, the term for a journalist who exposed corruption in American society. (p. 640)

**Muslim** (MUZ luhm) *n.* a follower of Islam. (p. 41)

## N

**NAACP** *n.* formed in 1909, the National Association for the Advancement of Colored People. (pp. 622, 715)

**NAFTA** *n.* passed in 1993, the North American Free Trade Agreement created a free trade block among the United States, Mexico, and Canada. (p. 875)

**napalm** (NAY PAHM) *n.* a jellied gasoline that burns violently. (p. 843)

**nationalism** *n.* a feeling of pride, loyalty, and protectiveness toward one's country. (p. 354)

**nativist** *n.* a native-born American who wanted to eliminate foreign influence. (p. 428)

**NATO** *n.* the North Atlantic Treaty Organization is a military alliance formed in 1949 by ten Western European countries, the United States, and Canada. (p. 793)

**natural-born citizen** *n.* a citizen born in the United States or a commonwealth of the United States or to parents who are U.S. citizens living outside the country. (p. 257)

**naturalization** *n.* a way to give full citizenship to a person born in another country. (pp. 253, 270)

**Navigation Acts** *n.* a series of laws passed by Parliament, beginning in 1651, to ensure that England made money from its colonies' trade. (p. 112)

**navigator** *n.* a person who plans the course of a ship while at sea. (p. 49)

**Nazi** (NAHT see) **Party** *n.* the National Socialist German Workers' Party; came to power under Adolf Hitler in the 1930s. (p. 756)

**NCAI** *n.* the National Congress of American Indians was founded in 1944 and aimed to promote the "common welfare" of Native Americans. (p. 825)

**neutral** (NOO truhl) *adj.* not siding with one country or the other. (p. 302)

**neutrality** (noo TRAL i tee) *n.* refusing to take sides in a war. (p. 682)

**New Deal** *n.* President Franklin Roosevelt's programs to fight the Great Depression. (p. 735)

**New France** *n.* a fur-trading post established in 1608 that became the first permanent French settlement in North America. (p. 70)

**new immigrant** *n.* a person from southern or eastern Europe who entered the United States after 1900. (p. 614)

**New Jersey Plan** *n.* a plan of government proposed at the Constitutional Convention in 1787 that called for a one-house legislature in which each state would have one vote. (p. 231)

**Nineteenth Amendment** *n.* an amendment to the U.S. Constitution, ratified in 1920, which gave women full voting rights. (p. 653)

***Nisei*** (NEE say) *n.* a Japanese American born in the United States. (p. 775)

**Northwest Ordinance** *n.* it described how the Northwest Territory was to be governed and set conditions for settlement and settlers' rights. (p. 223)

**Northwest Territory** *n.* territory covered by the Land Ordinance of 1785, which included land that formed the states of Ohio, Indiana, Michigan, Illinois, Wisconsin, and part of Minnesota. (p. 223)

**NOW** *n.* founded in 1966, the National Organization for Women pushed to get women good jobs at equal pay. (p. 826)

**Nuremberg** (NOOR uhm BURG) **Trials** *n.* the court proceedings held in Nuremberg, Germany, after World War II, in which Nazi leaders were tried for war crimes. (p. 780)

## O

**Open Door Policy** *n.* in 1899, the United States asked nations involved in Asia to follow a policy in which no one country controlled trade with China. (p. 669)

**Oregon Trail** *n.* a trail that ran westward from Independence, Missouri, to the Oregon Territory. (p. 396)

**overseer** *n.* a worker hired by a planter to watch over and direct the work of slaves. (p. 122)

## P

**pacifist** (PAS uh fist) *n.* a person morally opposed to war. (p. 209)

**Palmer raids** *n.* in 1920, federal agents and police raided the homes of suspected radicals. (p. 697)

**Panama** (PAN uh MAH) **Canal** *n.* a shortcut through Panama that connects the Atlantic and the Pacific oceans. (p. 670)

**Panic of 1837** *n.* a financial crisis in which banks closed and the credit system collapsed. (p. 386)

**Panic of 1873** *n.* a financial crisis in which banks closed and the stock market collapsed. (p. 547)

**Parliament** (PAHR luh muhnt) *n.* England's chief lawmaking body. (p. 142)

**patent** *n.* a government document giving an inventor the exclusive right to make or sell his or her invention for a specific number of years. (p. 586)

**Patriot** *n.* an American colonist who sided with the rebels in the American Revolution. (p. 173)

**patroon** (puh TROON) *n.* a person who brought 50 settlers to New Netherland and in return received a large land grant and other special privileges. (p. 101)

**Pearl Harbor** *n.* a naval base in Hawaii that was hit in a surprise attack by Japan on December 7, 1941. (p. 760)

**Persian** (PUR zhen) **Gulf War** *n.* in 1990–1991, the United States and the UN drove Iraq out of Kuwait, a country the Iraqis had invaded in 1990. (p. 875)

**petroleum** *n.* an oily, flammable liquid. (p. 585)

**philanthropist** (fil LAN thruh pist) *n.* a person who gives large sums of money to charities. (p. 596)

**Pickett's Charge** *n.* General George Pickett led a direct attack on Union troops during the 1863 Civil War battle at Gettysburg; the attack failed. (p. 513)

**piedmont** *n.* a broad plateau that leads to the foot of a mountain range. (p. 126)

**Pilgrim** *n.* a member of the group that rejected the Church of England, sailed to America, and founded the Plymouth Colony in 1620. (p. 92)

**Pinckney's** (PINGK neez) **Treaty** *n.* a 1795 treaty with Spain that allowed Americans to use the Mississippi River and to store goods in New Orleans; made the 31st parallel the southern U.S. border. (p. 302)

**plantation** *n.* a large farm that raises cash crops. (p. 73)

**platform** *n.* a statement of beliefs. (p. 471)

**Platt Amendment** *n.* a result of the Spanish-American War, which gave the United States the right to intervene in Cuban affairs when there was a threat to "life, property, and individual liberty." (p. 666)

***Plessy* v. *Ferguson*** *n.* an 1896 case in which the Supreme Court ruled that separation of the races in public accommodations was legal. (p. 621)

**political machine** *n.* an organization that influences enough votes to control a local government. (p. 613)

**political party** *n.* a group of people that tries to promote its ideas and influence government, and also backs candidates for office. (p. 304)

**Pontiac's** (PON tee AKS) **Rebellion** *n.* a revolt against British forts and American settlers in 1763, led in part by Ottawa war leader Pontiac, in response to settlers' claims of Native American lands and to harsh treatment by British soldiers. (p. 151)

**popular culture** *n.* items such as music, fashion, and movies that are popular among a large number of people. (p. 718)

**popular sovereignty** (SOV uhr in tee) *n.* a government in which the people rule (p. 244); a system in which the residents vote to decide an issue. (p. 463)

**Populist Party** *n.* also known as the People's Party and formed in the 1890s, this group wanted a policy that would raise crop prices. (p. 577)

**prejudice** (PREJ uh dis) *n.* a negative opinion that is not based on facts. (p. 427)

**printing press** *n.* a machine invented about 1455 by Johannes Gutenberg. (p. 47)

**privateer** (PRY vuh TEER) *n.* a privately owned ship that has government permission during wartime to attack an enemy's merchant ships. (p. 204)

**Proclamation** (PRAHK luh MAY shuhn) **of 1763** *n.* an order in which Britain prohibited its American colonists from settling west of the Appalachian Mountains. (p. 151)



R55

**profit** *n.* money a business makes, after subtracting the costs of doing business from the income. (p. 48)

**progressivism** (pruh GREHS ih VIHZ uhm) *n.* an early 20th-century reform movement seeking to return control of the government to the people, to restore economic opportunities, and to correct injustices in American life. (p. 639)

**prohibition** (PROH uh BIHSH uhn) *n.* the banning of the manufacture, sale, and possession of alcoholic beverages. (p. 715)

**propaganda** (PRAHP uh GAN duh) *n.* an opinion expressed for the purpose of influencing the actions of others. (p. 692)

**proprietary** (pruh PRY ih TEHR ee) **colony** *n.* a colony with a single owner. (p. 101)

***pro tempore*** (proh TEHM puh ree) *adv.* Latin phrase meaning "for the time being." (p. 250)

**public works project** *n.* a government-funded project to build public resources such as roads and dams. (p. 732)

**Pullman Strike** *n.* a nationwide railway strike that spread throughout the rail industry in 1894. (p. 603)

**Puritan** *n.* a member of a group from England that settled the Massachusetts Bay Colony in 1630 and sought to reform the practices of the Church of England. (p. 94)

**push-pull factor** *n.* a factor that pushes people out of their native lands and pulls them toward a new place. (p. 424)

## Q

**Quaker** (KWAY kuhr) *n.* a person who believed all people should live in peace and harmony; accepted different religions and ethnic groups. (p. 101)

**quarter** *v.* to give a place to stay. (p. 267)

**Quartering Act** *n.* a law passed by Parliament in 1765 that required the colonies to house and supply British soldiers. (p. 160)

**quorum** (KWAWR uhm) *n.* the minimum number of members that must be present for official business to take place. (p. 251)

## R

**racial** (RAY shuhl) **discrimination** (dih SKRIHM uh NAY shuhn) *n.* different treatment based on a person's race. (p. 620)

**racism** (RAY SIHZ uhm) *n.* the belief that some people are inferior because of their race. (p. 79)

**radical** (RAD ih kuhl) *n.* a person who takes extreme political positions. (p. 313)

**Radical Republican** (rih PUHB lih kuhn) *n.* a congressman who, after the Civil War, favored using the government to create a new order in the South and to give African Americans full citizenship and the right to vote. (p. 533)

**ragtime** *n.* a blend of African-American songs and European musical forms. (p. 629)

**ratification** (RAT uh fih KAY shuhn) *n.* official approval. (p. 264)

**ration** (RASH uhn) *v.* to distribute a fixed amount of a certain item. (p. 773)

**recall** *v.* to vote an official out of office. (p. 640)

**Reconstruction** *n.* the process the U.S. government used to readmit the Confederate states to the Union after the Civil War. (p. 533)

**Red Scare** *n.* in 1919–1920, a wave of panic from fear of a Communist revolution. (p. 697)

**referendum** (REHF uh REHN duhm) *n.* when a proposed law is submitted to a vote of the people. (p. 640)

**Reformation** *n.* a 16th-century religious movement to correct problems in the Roman Catholic Church. (p. 47)

**Renaissance** (REHN ih SAHNS) *n.* a period of European history, lasting from the 1300s to 1600, that brought increased interest in art and learning. (p. 46)

**rendezvous** (RAHN day VOO) *n.* a meeting. (p. 197)

**reprieve** (rih PREEV) *n.* a delay or cancellation of punishment. (p. 259)

**republic** (rih PUHB lihk) *n.* a government in which people elect representatives to govern for them. (p. 222)

**republicanism** (rih PUHB lih keh NIHZ uhm) *n.* the belief that government should be based on the consent of the people; people exercise their power by voting for political representatives. (pp. 214, 245)

**Republican Party** *n.* the political party formed in 1854 by opponents of slavery in the territories. (p. 466)

**reservation** *n.* land set aside by the U.S. government for Native American tribes. (p. 562)

**revenue** (REHV uh noo) *n.* income a government collects to cover expenses. (pp. 160, 252)

**revenue sharing** *n.* the distribution of federal money to state and local governments with few or no restrictions on how it is spent. (p. 856)

**revival** (rih VY vuhl) *n.* a meeting designed to reawaken religious faith. (p. 433)

**rifle** *n.* a gun with a grooved barrel that causes a bullet to spin through the air. (p. 491)

**robber baron** *n.* a business leader who became wealthy through dishonest methods. (p. 594)

**rock 'n' roll** *n.* a form of popular music, characterized by heavy rhythms and simple melodies, that developed from rhythm and blues in the 1950s. (p. 803)

**romanticism** (roh MAN tih SIHZ uhm) *n.* a European artistic movement that stressed the individual, imagination, creativity, and emotion. (p. 429)

**Roosevelt Corollary** (KAWR uh lehr ee) *n.* a 1904 addition to the Monroe Doctrine allowing the United States to be the "policeman" in Latin America. (p. 672)

**Rosie the Riveter** (RIHV iht uhr) *n.* an image of a strong woman hard at work at an arms factory during World War II. (p. 773)

**Rough Rider** *n.* a member of the First United States Volunteer Cavalry, organized by Theodore Roosevelt during the Spanish-American War. (p. 665)

**royal colony** *n.* a colony ruled by governors appointed by a king. (p. 103)

**salutary** (SAL yuh TEHR ee) **neglect** *n.* a hands-off policy of England toward its American colonies during the first half of the 1700s. (p. 144)

**SALT** *n.* the Strategic Arms Limitation Treaty, a treaty signed in 1972 between the United States and the Soviet Union; it limited nuclear weapons. (p. 858)

**Sand Creek Massacre** (MAS uh kuhr) *n.* an 1864 attack in which more than 150 Cheyenne men, women, and children were killed by the Colorado militia. (p. 564)

**Santa Fe** (SAN tuh FAY) **Trail** *n.* a trail that began in Missouri and ended in Santa Fe, New Mexico. (p. 395)

**SCLC** *n.* the Southern Christian Leadership Conference, a group that coordinated civil rights protests across the South. (p. 815)

**secede** (sih SEED) *v.* to withdraw. (p. 473)

**secession** (sih SEHSH uhn) *n.* withdrawal. (p. 383)

**Second Battle of the Marne** (mahrn) *n.* a 1918 battle during World War I that marked the turning point in the war; allied troops along with Americans halted the German advance into France. (p. 689)

**Second Continental Congress** *n.* a governing body whose delegates agreed, in May 1775, to form the Continental Army and to approve the Declaration of Independence. (p. 177)

**Second Great Awakening** *n.* the renewal of religious faith in the 1790s and early 1800s. (p. 433)

**Second New Deal** *n.* a set of programs passed in 1935 to fight the Great Depression. (p. 736)

**sectionalism** (SEHK shuh nuh LIHZ uhm) *n.* the placing of the interests of one's own region ahead of the interests of the nation as a whole. (p. 357)

**Securities and Exchange Commission** *n.* an agency that watches the stock market and makes sure companies follow fair practices for trading stocks. (p. 748)

**Sedition** (sih DIHSH uhn) **Act** *n.* a 1918 law that made it illegal to criticize the war; it set heavy fines and long prison terms for those who engaged in antiwar activities. (p. 692)

**segregation** (SEHG rih GAY shuhn) *n.* separation, especially of races. (p. 621)

**Seneca** (SEHN ih kuh) **Falls Convention** *n.* a women's rights convention held in Seneca Falls, New York, in 1848. (p. 444)

**separation of powers** *n.* the division of basic government roles into branches. (p. 246)

**service economy** *n.* an economy in which most jobs provide services instead of producing goods. (p. 879)

**servitude** (SUR vih TOOD) *n.* a state of belonging to an owner or master. (p. 270)

**Seven Days' Battles** *n.* an 1862 Civil War battle in which the Confederacy forced the Union to retreat before it could capture the Southern capital of Richmond. (p. 496)

**Seventeenth Amendment** *n.* an amendment to the U.S. Constitution, ratified in 1913, that provided for the direct election of U.S. senators. (p. 648)

**sharecropping** *n.* a system in which landowners gave farm workers land, seed, and tools in return for a part of the crops they raised. (p. 543)

**Shays's** (SHAY zuhz) **Rebellion** *n.* an uprising of debt-ridden Massachusetts farmers in 1787. (p. 225)

**Sherman Antitrust Act** *n.* a law passed in 1890 that made it illegal for corporations to gain control of industries by forming trusts. (p. 641)

**Siege** (seej) **of Vicksburg** *n.* an 1863 Union victory in the Civil War that enabled the Union to control the entire Mississippi River. (p. 516)

**sit-down strike** *n.* a strike in which workers remain idle inside the plant or factory. (p. 743)

**Sixteenth Amendment** *n.* an amendment to the U.S. Constitution, ratified in 1913, that gave Congress the power to create income taxes. (p. 647)

**slash-and-burn agriculture** (ag rih kuhl chuhr) *n.* a farming method in which people clear fields by cutting and burning trees and grasses, the ashes of which fertilize the soil. (p. 37)

**slave code** *n.* a law passed to regulate the treatment of slaves. (p. 79)

**slavery** *n.* the practice of holding a person in bondage for labor. (p. 76)

**slum** *n.* a neighborhood with overcrowded and dangerous housing. (p. 612)

**smuggle** *v.* to illegally import or export goods. (p. 112)

**SNCC** *n.* formed in 1960, the Student Nonviolent Coordinating Committee was created to give young people a larger role in the civil rights movement. (p. 817)

**social gospel** (GAHS puhl) *n.* a movement aimed at improving the lives of the poor. (p. 612)

**socialism** *n.* an economic system in which all members of a society are equal owners of all businesses; members share the work and the profits. (p. 602)

**Social Security Act** *n.* a law, passed in 1935, that requires workers and employers to make payments into a fund, from which they draw a pension after they retired. (p. 736)

**sodbuster** *n.* a farmer on the frontier. (p. 575)

**Songhai** (SAWNG HY) *n.* a West African empire that succeeded Mali and controlled trade from the 1400s to 1591. (p. 42)

**Sons of Liberty** *n.* a group of colonists who formed a secret society to oppose British policies at the time of the American Revolution. (p. 161)

**space race** *n.* a competition, beginning in 1957, between the Soviet Union and the United States in the exploration of space. (p. 799)

**Spanish-American War** *n.* a war in 1898 that began when the United States demanded Cuba's independence from Spain. (p. 664)

**Spanish Armada** (ahr MAH duh) *n.* a fleet of ships sent in 1588 by Philip II, the Spanish king, to invade England and restore Roman Catholicism. (p. 69)

**speculation** (SPEHK yuh LAY shuhn) *n.* buying and selling of a stock in the hope of making a quick profit. (p. 730)

**sphere of influence** *n.* an area where foreign nations claim special rights and economic privileges. (p. 669)

**spiritual** *n.* a religious folk song. (p. 351)

**spoils system** *n.* the practice of winning candidates giving government jobs to political backers or supporters. (p. 373)

**Stamp Act** *n.* a 1765 law passed by Parliament that required all legal and commercial documents to carry an official stamp showing a tax had been paid. (p. 160)

**standard time** *n.* a system adopted in 1918 that divided the United States into four time zones. (p. 592)

**states' rights** *n.* theory that said that states had the right to judge when the federal government had passed an unconstitutional law. (p. 307)

**steerage** *n.* the cheapest deck or place on a ship. (p. 423)

**Stono** (STOH noh) **Rebellion** *n.* a 1739 uprising of slaves in South Carolina, leading to the tightening of already harsh slave laws. (p. 123)

**strategy** *n.* an overall plan of action. (p. 196)

**strike** *v.* to stop work to demand better working conditions. (p. 434)

**subsistence farm** *n.* a farm that produces enough food for the family with a small additional amount for trade. (p. 110)

**suburb** *n.* a residential area that surrounds a city. (p. 800)

**suffrage** *n.* the right to vote. (pp. 262, 444)

**Sugar Act** *n.* a law passed by Parliament in 1764 that placed a tax on sugar, molasses, and other products shipped to the colonies; also called for harsh punishment of smugglers. (p. 160)

**sunbelt** *n.* the warmer states of the South and Southwest. (p. 801)

**supply-side economics** *n.* the idea that lowering taxes will lead to increases in jobs, savings, investments, and so lead to an increase in government revenue. (p. 873)

**sweatshop** *n.* a place where workers labored long hours under poor conditions for low wages. (p. 600)

## T

**Tammany** (TAM uh nee) **Hall** *n.* a famous political machine, located in New York City in the late 19th century. (p. 613)

**tariff** *n.* a tax on imported goods. (p. 296)

**Tariff of Abominations** *n.* an 1828 law that raised the tariffs on raw materials and manufactured goods; it upset Southerners who felt that economic interests of the Northeast were determining national economic policy. (p. 381)

**Teapot Dome Scandal** *n.* episode caused by Secretary of the Interior Albert B. Fall's leasing of oil-rich public land to private companies for money and land. (p. 710)

**technology** *n.* the use of tools and knowledge to meet human needs. (p. 32)

***Tejano*** (tuh HAH noh) *n.* a person of Spanish heritage who considered Texas to be home. (p. 400)

**temperance movement** *n.* a campaign to stop the drinking of alcohol. (p. 434)

**tender** *n.* money. (p. 255)

**tenement** *n.* an apartment building that is usually run-down and overcrowded. (p. 611)

**Tet** (tet) **offensive** *n.* in 1968, a surprise attack by the Viet Cong on U.S. military bases and more than 100 cities and towns in South Vietnam during Tet, the Vietnamese celebration of the lunar New Year. (p. 844)

**Thirteenth Amendment** *n.* an amendment to the U.S. Constitution, adopted in 1865, banning slavery and involuntary servitude in the United States. (p. 521)

**38th parallel** *n.* the area north of this latitude in Korea occupied by Soviet troops in 1945. (p. 795)

**Three-Fifths Compromise** *n.* the Constitutional Convention's agreement to count three-fifths of a state's slaves as population for purposes of representation and taxation. (p. 232)

**Townshend** (TOWN zuhnd) **Acts** *n.* a series of laws passed by Parliament in 1767 that suspended New York's assembly and established taxes on goods brought into the British colonies. (p. 163)

**Trail of Tears** *n.* the tragic journey of the Cherokee people from their homeland to Indian Territory between 1838 and 1839; thousands of Cherokee died. (p. 377)

**transcendentalism** (TRAN sen DEN tl IZ uhm) *n.* a 19th-century philosophy that taught the spiritual world is more important than the physical world and that people can find truth within themselves through feeling and intuition. (p. 431)

**transcontinental** (TRANS kon tuh NEN tl) **railroad** *n.* a railroad that spanned the entire continent. (p. 590)

**Treaty of Ghent** (gent) *n.* treaty, signed in 1814, which ended the War of 1812; no territory exchanged hands and trade disputes were not resolved. (p. 333)

**Treaty of Greenville** *n.* a 1795 agreement in which 12 Native American tribes surrendered much of present-day Ohio and Indiana to the U.S. government. (p. 300)

**Treaty of Guadalupe Hidalgo** (GWAHD loop hi DAH goh) *n.* the 1848 treaty ending the U.S. war with Mexico; Mexico ceded nearly one-half of its land to the United States. (p. 410)

**Treaty of Paris** *n.* the 1763 treaty that ended the French and Indian War; Britain gave up all of North America east of the Mississippi River. (p. 150)

**Treaty of Paris of 1783** *n.* the treaty that ended the Revolutionary War, confirming the independence of the United States and setting the boundaries of the new nation. (p. 212)

**Treaty of Tordesillas** (TAWR duh SEE uhs) *n.* the 1494 treaty in which Spain and Portugal agreed to divide the lands of the Western Hemisphere between them and moved the Line of Demarcation to the west. (p. 61)

**Treaty of Versailles** (vuhr SY) *n.* the 1919 treaty that ended World War I. (p. 696)

**trench warfare** *n.* a kind of warfare during World War I in which troops huddled at the bottom of trenches and fired artillery and machine guns at each other. (p. 680)

**triangular trade** *n.* the transatlantic system of trade in which goods, including slaves, were exchanged between Africa, England, Europe, the West Indies, and the colonies in North America. (p. 111)

**tribunal** (try BYOO nuhl) *n.* a court. (p. 253)

**Truman Doctrine** *n.* a policy that promised aid to people struggling to resist threats to democratic freedom. (p. 793)

**trust** *n.* a legal body created to hold stock in many companies, often in the same industry. (p. 595)

**tundra** (TUN druh) *n.* a treeless plain that remains frozen under its top layer of soil. (p. 33)

**Twenty-sixth Amendment** *n.* an amendment to the U.S. Constitution, adopted in 1971 and lowering the voting age from 21 to 18. (p. 849)

## U

**unanimous** (yoo NAN uh muhs) **consent** *n.* complete agreement. (p. 264)

***Uncle Tom's Cabin*** *n.* a novel published by Harriet Beecher Stowe in 1852 that portrayed slavery as brutal and immoral. (p. 462)

**unconstitutional** *n.* something that contradicts the law of the Constitution. (p. 317)

**Underground Railroad** *n.* a series of escape routes used by slaves escaping the South. (p. 442)

**United Nations** *n.* an international peacekeeping organization to which most nations in the world belong, founded in 1945 to promote world peace, security, and economic development. (p. 781)

**urbanization** *n.* growth of cities resulting from industrialization. (p. 609)

**U.S.S. *Maine*** *n.* a U.S. warship that mysteriously exploded and sank in the harbor of Havana, Cuba, on February 15, 1898. (p. 663)

## V

***vaquero*** (vah KAIR oh) *n.* a cowhand that came from Mexico with the Spaniards in the 1500s. (p. 560)

**vaudeville** (VAWD vil) *n.* a form of live stage entertainment with a mixture of songs, dance, and comedy. (p. 629)

**viceroyalty** (VYS ROI uhl tee) *n.* a province ruled by a viceroy, who ruled in the king's name. (p. 71)

**Viet Cong** *n.* a Vietnamese Communist. (p. 838)

**Vietnamization** (vee ET nuh mi ZAY shuhn) *n.* a strategy of gradually withdrawing U.S. forces and turning the ground fighting over to the South Vietnamese during the Vietnam War. (p. 848)

**vigilante** (vij uh LAN tee) *n.* a person willing to take the law into his or her own hands. (p. 561)

**Virginia Plan** *n.* a plan proposed by Edmund Randolph, a delegate to the Constitutional Convention in 1787, that proposed a government with three branches and a two-house legislature in which representation would be based on a state's population or wealth. (p. 231)

**Voting Rights Act of 1965** *n.* this law banned literacy tests and other laws that kept African Americans from registering to vote. (p. 821)

## W

**war bond** *n.* a low-interest loan by civilians to the government, meant to be repaid in a number of years. (p. 691)

**War Hawk** *n.* a westerner who supported the War of 1812. (p. 329)

**War Powers Act** *n.* passed in 1973, this limits the president's war-making powers without consulting Congress. (p. 849)

**War Production Board** *n.* an agency established during World War II to coordinate the production of military supplies by U.S. industries. (p. 772)

**Watergate scandal** *n.* a scandal resulting from the Nixon administration's attempt to cover up its involvement in the 1972 break-in at the Democratic National Committee headquarters in the Watergate apartment complex in Washington, D.C. (p. 860)

**Webster-Hayne debate** *n.* an 1830 debate between Daniel Webster and Robert Hayne over the doctrine of nullification. (p. 382)

**Whig** (hwig) **Party** *n.* a political party organized in 1834 to oppose the policies of Andrew Jackson. (p. 387)

**Whiskey Rebellion** *n.* a 1794 protest against the government's tax on whiskey, which was valuable to the livelihood of backcountry farmers. (p. 301)

**Wilderness Road** *n.* the trail into Kentucky that woodsman Daniel Boone helped to build. (p. 221)

**Wilmot** (WIL muht) **Proviso** (pruh VY zoh) *n.* an 1846 proposal that outlawed slavery in any territory gained from the War with Mexico. (p. 459)

**Wounded Knee Massacre** *n.* the massacre by U.S. soldiers of 300 unarmed Native Americans at Wounded Knee Creek, South Dakota, in 1890. (p. 566)

**writ** (rit) **of assistance** *n.* a search warrant that allowed British officers to enter colonial homes or businesses to search for smuggled goods. (p. 164)

## X

**XYZ Affair** *n.* a 1797 incident in which French officials demanded a bribe from U.S. diplomats. (p. 306)

## Y

**Y2K** *n.* a computer problem caused by computer programs using only the last two digits of a year and complicated by the arrival of the year 2000. (p. 878)

**Yalta** (YAWL tuh) **Conference** *n.* in 1945, Franklin Roosevelt, Winston Churchill, and Joseph Stalin discussed plans for the end of World War II and the future of Europe. (p. 765)

**yellow journalism** *n.* a style of journalism that exaggerates and sensationalizes the news. (p. 663)

**Yoruba** (YOH roo bah) *n.* a West African people who formed several states southwest of the Niger River. (p. 42)

## Z

**Zimmermann telegram** *n.* a message sent in 1917 by the German foreign minister to the German ambassador in Mexico, proposing a German-Mexican alliance and promising to help Mexico regain Texas, New Mexico, and Arizona if the United States entered World War I. (p. 682)

# SPANISH GLOSSARY

## A

**abolition** [abolición] *s.* movimiento para eliminar la esclavitud. (p. 440)

**abridge** [abreviar] *v.* reducir. (p. 266)

**AEF** *s.* Fuerza Expedicionaria Estadounidense, fuerzas de EE. UU. durante la primera guerra mundial. (p. 686)

**affirmation** [afirmación] *s.* declaración de que algo es cierto. (p. 257)

**African Diaspora** [diáspora africana] *s.* traslado forzado de los africanos, desde su patria a las Américas para trabajar allí como esclavos. (p. 78)

**Agent Orange** [agente naranja] *s.* herbicida que mata las plantas. (p. 843)

**Albany Plan of Union** [Plan de la Unión de Albany] *s.* primera propuesta formal para unir las colonias norteamericanas, presentado por Benjamín Franklin. (p. 149)

**Alien and Sedition Acts** [leyes de Extranjeros y Sedición] *s.* serie de cuatro leyes promulgadas en 1798 para reducir el poder político de inmigrantes recién llegados a Estados Unidos. (p. 306)

**allies** [aliados] *s.* alianza de Serbia, Rusia, Francia, Gran Bretaña, Italia y otros siete países durante la primera guerra mundial. (p. 680)

**ally** [aliado] *s.* país que acuerda ayudar a otro país a alcanzar un objetivo común. (p. 200)

**American Federation of Labor (AFL)** [Federación Norteamericana del Trabajo] *s.* organización nacional de sindicatos obreros fundada en 1886. (p. 603)

**American System** [Sistema Americano] *s.* plan presentado en 1815 para hacer autosuficiente a Estados Unidos. (p. 354)

**Anaconda Plan** [Plan Anaconda] *s.* estrategia de tres pasos mediante la cual la Unión se proponía derrotar a la Confederación durante la guerra civil estadounidense. (p. 484)

**Angel Island** [isla del Ángel] *s.* primera parada en Estados Unidos para la mayoría de los inmigrantes que venían de Asia. (p. 615)

**Antifederalist** [antifederalista] *s.* persona que se oponía a la ratificación de la Constitución de los Estados Unidos. (p. 234)

**Anti-Imperialist League** [Liga Antiimperialista] *s.* grupo de estadounidenses importantes que creían que Estados Unidos no debía negarle a otras personas el derecho de gobernarse a sí mismas. (p. 667)

**Appalachian Mountains** [montes Apalaches] *s.* cadena de montañas que se extiende desde el este de Canadá hacia el sur, hasta Alabama. (p. 126)

**appeasement** [apaciguamiento] *s.* otorgamiento de concesiones a una potencia hostil con el fin de mantener la paz. (p. 757)

**appellate** [de apelación] *adj.* que tiene el poder de reexaminar decisiones de las cortes. (p. 260)

**Appomattox Court House** [Appomattox] *s.* pueblo de Virginia donde Robert E. Lee se rindió a Ulysses s. Grant en 1865, finalizando así la guerra civil. (p. 519)

**apprentice** [aprendiz] *s.* joven que aprende un oficio o una artesanía de un maestro experto. (p. 137)

**appropiation** [apropiación] *s.* fondos públicos que se reservan para un propósito específico. (p. 253)

**archaeologist** [arqueólogo] *s.* científico que estudia el pasado humano examinando artículos que dejó la gente. (p. 27)

**armistice** [armisticio] *s.* suspención de la lucha en una guerra. (p. 690)

**arms race** [carrera de armamento] *s.* desde fines de los años cuarenta hasta fines de los años ochenta, Estados Unidos y la Unión Soviética trataron de superarse una a la otra desarrollando armas de mayor poder destructivo. (p. 798)

**Articles of Confederation** [Artículos de Confederación] *s.* documento, adoptado por el Congreso Continental en 1777 y finalmente aprobado por los estados en 1781, que delineaba la forma de gobierno de los nuevos Estados Unidos. (p. 222)

**artifact** [artefacto] *s.* herramienta u otro artículo hecho por seres humanos. (p. 27)

**artillery** [artillería] *s.* cañon o arma grande. (p. 177)

**artisan** [artesano] *s.* obrero especializado, como un tejedor a telar o un alfarero, que hace artículos a mano; artífice. (p. 117)

**assimilation** [asimilación] *s.* proceso de integrarse a una sociedad. (p. 616)

**Axis** [Eje] *s.* Alemania, Italia y sus aliados durante la segunda guerra mundial. (p. 757)

## B

**baby boom** *s.* término para la generación que nació en Estados Unidos entre 1946 y 1961, cuando el índice de natalidad aumentó marcadamente después de la segunda guerra mundial. (p. 801)

**Backcountry** [tierras fronterizas] *s.* región colonial que se extendía a lo largo de los montes Apalaches a través de la sección oeste de Nueva Inglaterra y las colonias del centro y del sur. (p. 109)

**Bacon´s Rebellion** [Rebelión de Bacon] *s.* levantamiento contra la poderosa autoridad colonial de Jamestown por Nathaniel Bacon y un grupo de habitantes de la frontera que resultó en la quema de Jamestown en 1676. (p. 89)

**bail** [fianza] *s.* dinero que pagan como fianza las personas arrestadas para garantizar que van a regresar para el juicio. (p. 268)

**Bataan Death March** [Marcha de la Muerte de Bataan] *s.* en 1942 los japoneses forzaron a 70,000 soldados filipinos y estadounidenses a marchar 60 millas a un campo de prisioneros. (p. 768)

**Battle of Antietam** [batalla de Antietam] *s.* batalla de la guerra civil, en 1862, en que murieron o resultaron heridos 25,000 hombres. (p. 497)

**Battle of Fallen Timbers** *s.* en 1794 el ejército estadounidense derrotó a 2,000 amerindios en un enfrentamiento por el control del territorio del Noroeste. (p. 299)

**Battle of Gettysburg** [batalla de Gettysburg) *s.* batalla de 1863 de la guerra civil en que la Unión derrotó a la Confederación, poniendo fin a la esperanza de una victoria confederada en el Norte. (p. 513)

**Battle of Midway** *s.* victoria de Estados Unidos sobre los japoneses en una batalla naval de 1942 que señaló un cambio decisivo en la segunda guerra mundial. (p. 770)

**Battle of Quebec** [batalla de Quebec] *s.* batalla en la que los británicos derrotaron a los franceses y cambio decisivo en la guerra Francesa y Amerindia. (p. 150)

**Battle of Shiloh** [batalla de Shiloh] *s.* batalla de 1862 en que la Unión obligó a la Confederación a retroceder; fue una de las batallas más encarnizadas de la guerra civil. (p. 494)



R60

**Battle of Yorktown** [batalla de Yorktown] *s.* última batalla importante de la guerra Revolucionaria que resultó en la capitulación de las fuerzas británicas en 1781. (p. 210)

**Battle of the Alamo** [batalla de El Álamo] *s.* en 1836 los texanos defendieron contra el ejército mexicano una misión llamada El Álamo; sobrevivieron sólo cinco texanos (p. 403)

**Battle of the Bulge** [batalla del Bolsón] *s.* batalla de la segunda guerra mundial de un mes de duración en que los aliados lograron rechazar la última gran ofensiva alemana de la guerra. (p. 764)

**Battle of the Little Bighorn** [batalla del Little Bighorn] *s.* batalla de 1876 en que los sioux y los cheyennes aniquilaron toda una partida militar estadounidense. (p. 565)

**Battle of the Thames** [batalla de Thames] *s.* victoria estadounidense sobre los británicos en la guerra de 1812 que puso fin a la amenaza británica en el Territorio del Noroeste. (p. 332)

**Battles of Saratoga** [batallas de Saratoga] *s.* serie de conflictos en 1777, entre soldados británicos y el Ejército Continental que resultó en un cambio decisivo en la guerra Revolucionaria. (p. 199)

**bayonet** [bayoneta] *s.* largo cuchillo de acero colocado en el extremo de un arma de fuego. (p. 202)

**Bear Flag Revolt** [revuelta de la Bandera del Oso] *s.* rebelión de 1846 por los estadounidenses contra el dominio mexicano en California. (p. 409)

**Benin** [Benín] *s.* reino de África Occidental que se estableció cerca del delta del río Níger en el siglo XIV y se transformó en un estado importante en el siglo XV. (p. 43)

**Bessemer steel process** [proceso siderúrgico Bessemer] *s.* manera nueva de producir acero desarrollada hacia 1850 que causó un gran incremento en la producción siderúrgica. (p. 587)

**bill of attainder** [decreto de proscripción] *s.* ley que condena a una persona sin juicio ante un tribunal. (p. 255)

**Bill of Rights** [Carta de Derechos] *s.* diez primeras enmiendas a la Constitución de Estados Unidos, adoptadas en 1791, que consisten en una lista formal de los derechos y libertades de los ciudadanos. (p. 237)

**black code** [código negro] *s.* ley pasada por los estados sureños que limitaba la libertad de los antiguos esclavos. (p. 534)

**Black Tuesday** [martes negro] *s.* nombre que se le da al 29 de octubre de 1929, cuando se desplomó el precio de las acciones. (p. 731)

**blockade** [bloqueo] *s.* acción de las fuerzas armadas que impide la entrada o salida de mercaderías o personas. (p. 484)

**Bonus Army** [Ejército de la Prima] *s.* en 1932 miles de veteranos marcharon a Washington demandando el pago de una prima que nunca habían recibido. (p. 733)

**boomtown** [pueblo en auge] *s.* pueblo que tiene una explosión repentina de crecimiento económico o demográfico. (p. 558)

**border state** [estado fronterizo] *s.* estados esclavistas fronterizos a estados en que la esclavitud era ilegal. (p. 482)

**Boston Massacre** [Matanza de Boston] *s.* choque en 1770 entre soldados británicos y colonos de Boston en que perecieron cinco de los colonistas, incluso Crispus Attucks. (p. 165)

**Boston Tea Party** [Motín del Té de Boston] *s.* como protesta contra el Acta del té, en 1773 los colonos arrojaron al puerto de Boston 342 cajones de té. (p. 167)

**bounty** [gratificación] *s.* recompensa o pago en dinero que da un gobierno. (pp. 271, 508)

**Boxer Rebellion** [Rebelión bóxer] *s.* en 1900 el resentimiento chino contra la actitud de superioridad cultural de los extranjeros resultó en este violento levantamiento. (p. 669)

**boycott** [boicot] *v.* negarse a comprar ciertos productos. (p. 161)

***bracero* program** [programa bracero] *s.* uso de trabajadores mexicanos en la época de escasez de labriegos durante la segunda guerra mundial. (p. 774)

**brinksmanship** *s.* política internacional, el acto de empujar al límite una situación peligrosa; por ejemplo: los Estados Unidos yendo al borde de la guerra para parar el comunismo. (p. 798)

***Brown* v. *Board of Education of Topeka, Kansas*** [Brown contra el Consejo de Educación de Topeka, Kansas] *s.* caso de 1954 en que la Corte Suprema declaró que la doctrina educativa de "iguales pero separados" para los blancos y los afroamericanos no era constitucional. (p. 814)

**buck** [ciervo] gamuza obtenida de la piel de un ciervo adulto, o unidad de dinero de los colonos. (p. 127)

**buffalo soldier** [soldado búfalo] *s.* apodo que los amerindios les dieron a los afroamericanos que servían en el ejército estadounidense del oeste. (p. 571)

**business cycle** [ciclo económico] *s.* serie de períodos de la economía buenos y malos. (p. 586)

**buy on margin** [comprar valores a crédito] *s.* pagar una pequeña parte del precio de una acción y pagar el resto con un préstamo. (p. 730)

## C

**cabinet** [gabinete ministerial] *s.* grupo de ministros que actúan como los asesores princpales del presidente. (p. 294)

**California gold rush** [fiebre del oro de California] *s.* en 1849 gran cantidad de gente se fue a California porque allí se había descubierto oro. (p. 413)

**Cambodia** [Camboya] *s.* país fronterizo de Vietnam. (p. 848)

**Camp David Accords** [acuerdos de Camp David] *s.* en 1979, basados en estos acuerdos, Egipto e Israel firmaron un tratado de paz que puso fin a 30 años de conflicto. (p. 864)

**caravel** [carabela] *s.* barco con velas triangulares que le permitían navegar hacia el viento y con velas cuadradas que lo llevaban hacia delante cuando soplaba viento en popa. (p. 49)

**cash crop** [cultivo comercial] *s.* cultivo que produce un agricultor para venderlo por dinero y no para su uso personal. (p. 115)

**cavalry** [caballería] *s.* soldados montados a caballo. (p. 496)

**Centennial Exhibition** [Exposición del Centenario] *s.* exposición de 1876 en Filadelfia que celebró el centésimo cumpleaños de Estados Unidos. (p. 588)

**Central Powers** [Potencias Centrales] *s.* alianza de Austria-Hungría, Alemania, el Imperio otomano y Bulgaria durante la primera guerra mundial. (p. 680)

**charter** [cédula] *s.* contrato escrito que concede un gobierno otorgando al que lo recibe el derecho a establecer una colonia. (p. 87)

**checks and balances** [frenos y cortapisas] *s.* capacidad de cada rama del gobierno de usar frenos o controles sobre las otras ramas. (p. 246)

**Chinese Exclusion Act** [ley de Exclusión para chinos] *s.* aprobada en 1882, esta ley prohibía la inmigración china por diez años. (p. 617)

**civil disobedience** [desobediencia civil] *s.* negarse pacíficamente a obedecer leyes que uno considera injustas. (p. 431)

**civilization** [civilización] *s.* forma de cultura caracterizada por ciudades con centros de comercio, trabajadores especializados, formas de gobierno y religión organizadas, sistemas de mantener registros, y herramientas avanzadas. (p. 29)

**civil rights** [derechos civiles] *s.* derecho otorgado a todos los ciudadanos. (p. 535)

**Civil Rights Act of 1964** [ley de Derechos Civiles de 1964] *s.* esta ley prohibía la segregación racial en los lugares públicos y creó la Comisión para la Igualdad de Oportunidades de Empleo. (p. 820)

**clan** [clan] *s.* grupo grande de familias procedentes de un antepasado común. (p. 127)

**Clayton Antitrust Act** [ley Anti-trust Clayton] *s.* ley aprobada en 1914 que establecía reglas que prohibían prácticas comerciales que disminuyeran la competencia y le daba al gobierno más poder para reglamentar los trusts. (p. 648)

**Cold War** [guerra fría] *s.* estado de hostilidad, sin conflicto militar directo, que se desarrolló entre Estados Unidos y la Unión Soviética después de la segunda guerra mundial. (p. 792)

**Columbian Exchange** [transferencia colombina] *s.* transferencia de plantas, animales y enfermedades entre el hemisferio occidental y el oriental. (p. 74)

**committee of correspondence** [comité de correspondencia] *s.* grupo de personas de las colonias que se intercambiaban cartas sobre asuntos coloniales. (p. 166)

**Committee to Reelect the President** [Comité de Reelección del Presidente] *s.* organización cuya conexión con el allanamiento de la Sede Central del Partido Demócrata hizo estallar el escándalo Watergate. (p. 860)

**common law** [derecho consuetudinario] *s.* sistema de leyes desarrollado en Inglaterra, basado en costumbres y decisiones jurídicas anteriores. (p. 268)

**Compromise of 1850** [Acuerdo de 1850] *s.* serie de medidas del Congreso para resolver los desacuerdos principales entre los estados libres y los esclavistas. (p. 461)

**Compromise of 1877** [Acuerdo de 1877] *s.* acuerdo que resolvió la disputa sobre las elecciones de 1876: se declaró presidente a Rutherford B. Hayes, quien entonces retiró las tropas federales que quedaban en el Sur. (p. 548)

**compulsory process** [proceso obligatorio] *s.* procedimiento requerido. (p. 267)

**Conestoga wagon** [carreta conestoga] *s.* vehículo que tenía ruedas anchas, caja de carro curvada y capota de lona y se usaba para transportar gente y artículos. (p. 117)

**Confederate States of America** [Estados Confederados de América] *s.* confederación constituida en 1861 por los estados sureños después de separarse de la Unión. (p. 473)

**Congress of Industrial Organizations (CIO)** [Congreso de Organizaciones Industriales] *s.* organización sindical que en 1938 se separó de la Federación Norteamericana del Trabajo. (p. 743)

***conquistador*** [conquistador] *s.* español que en el siglo XVI viajó a las Américas para explorar y conquistar. (p. 63)

**conscription** [conscripción] *s.* ley que requería que los hombres sirvieran en las fuerzas armadas o que fueran reclutados. (p. 508)

**conservative** [conservador] *s.* persona que está a favor de menos controles gubernamentales y más libertad individual en cuestiones de la economía. (p. 749)

**Constitutional Convention** [Convención Constitucional] *s.* reunión realizada en 1787 para considerar cambios a los Artículos de Confederación, que resultó en la redacción de la Constitución. (p. 229)

**containment** [contención] *s.* bloqueo de una nación en la expansión de la influencia de otras naciones, especialmente los esfuerzos de Estados Unidos por bloquear la expansión de la influencia soviética hacia fines de los años cuarenta y comienzos de los cincuenta. (p. 793)

**Continental Army** [Ejército Continental] *s.* fuerzas coloniales autorizadas en 1775 por el segundo Congreso Continental, con George Washington como su comandante en jefe. (p. 177)

**convene** [convocar] *v.* llamar a reunión. (p. 259)

**convoy system** [sistema de convoyes] *s.* fuerte flotilla de destructores que escolta a los barcos mercantes durante épocas de guerra. (p. 687)

**cooperative** [cooperativa] *s.* organización propiedad de los asociados que la dirigen. (p. 577)

**Copperheads** [víboras cobrizas] *s.* los principales adversarios políticos de Abraham Lincoln; abogaban por la paz con el Sur. (p. 508)

**CORE** [Congreso para la Igualdad Racial] *s.* grupo que planeó freedom rides o viajes en autobús por todo el Sur para eliminar la segregación racial en los autobuses interestatales. (p. 818)

**corporation** [corporación] *s.* empresa propiedad de inversionistas que compran parte de la compañía mediante acciones. (p. 594)

**cotton gin** [desmontadora de algodón] *s.* máquina inventada en 1793 que limpiaba el algodón con mucha más rapidez y eficiencia que los obreros humanos. (p. 348)

**Crash of 1929** [Crack de 1929] *s.* el desplome de los precios de las acciones. (p. 731)

**Crittenden Plan** [Plan de Crittenden] *s.* acuerdo presentado en 1861 que podría haber evitado la secesión. (p. 475)

**Crusades** [cruzadas] *s.* serie de guerras para capturar la Tierra Santa, iniciada en 1096 por cristianos europeos. (p. 45)

**Cuban Missile Crisis** [crisis de los misiles cubanos] *s.* en 1962 casi estalló la guerra entre Estados Unidos y la Unión Soviética porque ésta había instalado misiles nucleares en Cuba. (p. 839)

**culture** [cultura] *s.* manera de vida compartida por gente que tiene artes, creencias y costumbres semejantes. (p. 28)

## D

**Dawes Act** [ley Dawes] *s.* ley, aprobada en 1887, que distribuía la tierra de las reservas amerindias a dueños individuales. (p. 567)

**D-Day** [día D] *s.* 6 de junio de 1944, día en que los aliados invadieron a Francia durante la segunda guerra mundial. (p. 764)

**Declaration of Independence** [Declaración de Independencia] *s.* documento, escrito en 1776, en que las colonias declararon su independendia de Gran Bretaña. (p. 180)

**deficit** [déficit] spend *v.* usar dinero prestado para financiar programas del gobierno. (p. 738)

**department store** [almacén departamental] *s.* tienda que vende de todo, desde ropa a muebles a artículos de ferretería. (p. 627)

**depression** [depresión] *s.* aguda crisis económica. (p. 386)

**desert** [desertar] *v.* abandonar el servicio militar sin intenciones de regresar. (p. 203)

**détente** [distensión] *s.* disminución de las tensiones entre EE. UU. y la Unión Soviética durante la guerra fría. (p. 858)

**direct primary** [elecciones primarias directas] *s.* el electorado, y no las convenciones de partido, eligen a los candidatos para los cargos públicos. (p. 640)

**diversity** [diversidad] *s.* variedad de gente. (p. 117)

**doctrine of nullification** [doctrina de la invalidación] *s.* derecho de un estado a rechazar una ley federal que considerase inconstitucional. (p. 381)

**domestication** [domesticación] *s.* práctica de criar plantas o amansar animales para satisfacer las necesidades humanas. (p. 28)

**domino theory** [teoría del dominó] *s.* teoría que sostenía que si un país caía en la órbita comunista, los países vecinos también caerían en el comunismo. (p. 837)

**dove** [paloma] *s.* persona opuesta a la guerra. (p. 847)

**downsize** [reducir el tamaño] *v.* disminuir una empresa el número de sus empleados para incrementar las ganancias. (p. 879)

***Dred Scott* v. *Sandford*** [Dred Scott contra Sandford] *s.* caso de 1865 de la Corte Suprema en que un esclavo, Dred Scott, entabló juicio por su libertad porque su amo lo había llevado a vivir en territorios donde la esclavitud era ilegal; la Corte dictaminó contra Scott. (p. 467)

**due process of law** [proceso legal debido] *s.* tratamiento justo bajo la ley. (p. 267)

**dust bowl** [cuenca de polvo] *s.* fincas arruinadas por el polvo a comienzos de los años treinta, en una región de unas 150,000 millas cuadradas. (p. 739)

## E

**elector** [elector] *s.* votante. (p. 249)

**Ellis Island** [isla Ellis] *s.* para la mayoría de los inmigrantes que vienen de Europa, la primera parada en Estados Unidos. (p. 614)

**Emancipation Proclamation** [Proclama de Emancipación] *s.* orden ejecutiva dictada por Abraham Lincoln el 1.° de enero de 1863, que liberaba a los esclavos de todas las regiones insurgentes contra la Unión. (p. 504)

**Embargo Act of 1807** [ley de Embargo de 1807] *s.* ley que dictaminaba que los barcos estadounidenses ya no estaban autorizados para ir a puertos extranjeros y que también cerraba los puertos de Estados Unidos a los barcos británicos. (p. 328)

**emigrant** [emigrante] *s.* persona que abandona un país. (p. 423)

***encomienda*** [encomienda] *s.* concesión del trabajo de los amerindios. (p. 72)

**English Bill of Rights** [Carta de Derechos Ingleses] *s.* acuerdo firmado por Guillermo y María por el que prometían respetar los derechos del Parlamento y los ciudadanos ingleses, incluso el derecho a elecciones libres. (p. 144)

**enlightenment** [Ilustración] *s.* movimiento del siglo XVIII que enfatizaba el uso de la razón y el método científico para obtener conocimiento. (p. 140)

**enumeration** [enumeración] *s.* recuento oficial, como un censo. (p. 249)

**environmentalism** [ecologismo] *s.* trabajo dedicado a proteger el medio ambiente. (p. 864)

**equity** [equidad] *s.* sistema de justicia no cubierto bajo la ley común. (p. 269)

**ERA** *s.* Enmienda para la Igualdad de Derechos, enmienda constitucional propuesta para dar igualdad de derechos sin consideración de sexo; la propuesta murió en 1982. (p. 826)

**Erie Canal** [canal de Erie] *s.* completado en 1825, esta vía navegable conectaba a la ciudad de Nueva York con Buffalo, New York. (p. 355)

**escalation** [escalada] *s.* política de aumentar la intervención militar en Vietnam. (p. 841)

**Espionage Act** [ley sobre el Espionaje] *s.* aprobada en 1917, esta ley establecía multas severas y muchos años de prisión para quienes participaran en actividades contra la guerra o alentaran a los que resistían la conscripción. (p. 692)

**European Middle Ages** [Edad Media europea] *s.* período desde fines del siglo V hasta aproximadamente el siglo XIV, durante el cual los europeos adoptaron el feudalismo y el sistema señorial. (p. 44)

**exodusters** *s.* afroamericanos que abandonaron el Sur para irse al Oeste y se comparaban a los hebreos bíblicos que habían escapado la esclavitud de Egipto. (p. 575)

**expatriate** [expatriado] *s.* ciudadano de un país que establece su residencia en otro país. (p. 721)

**ex post facto law** [ley ex post facto] *s.* ley que hace que un acto sea una ofensa criminal aprobada después de cometido el acto. (p. 255)

## F

**factory system** [sistema fabril] *s.* un método de producción que juntó a obreros y máquinas en el mismo edificio. (p. 341)

**Fair Deal** [Trato Justo] *s.* programa presentado por Harry Truman que proponía proyectos nuevos para crear trabajos, construir viviendas públicas y acabar con la discriminación racial en el empleo. (p. 791)

**fall line** *s.* punto a partir del cual una catarata impide que los barcos grandes continúen río arriba. (p. 126)

**famine** [hambruna] *s.* severa escasez de alimentos. (p. 426)

**fascism** [fascismo] *s.* filosofía política que propugna un fuerte gobierno nacionalista centralizado, con un dictador poderoso a la cabeza. (p. 756)

**federalism** [federalismo] *s.* sistema de gobierno en que el poder está dividido entre el gobierno central (o federal) y los estados. (pp. 234, 245)

**Federalists** [federalistas] *s.* partidarios de la Constitución. (p. 234)

***Federalist Papers*** [*El federalista*] *s.* serie de ensayos que defienden y explican la Constitución, escritos por Alexander Hamilton, James Madison y John Jay. (p. 235)

**Federal Judiciary Act** [ley de la Judicatura Federal] *s.* ayudó a establecer un sistema de tribunales; le dio al Tribunal Supremo seis miembros. (p. 294)

**Federal Reserve Act** [ley de la Reserva Federal] *s.* ley aprobada en 1913 que creó el sistema bancario de la nación e instituyó un sistema monetario flexible. (p. 648)

**felony** [felonía] *s.* delito grave. (p. 253)

**feudalism** [feudalismo] *s.* sistema político en que el rey concedía a sus nobles el uso de sus tierras a cambio de su prestación militar y la protección de la gente que vivía en esas tierras. (p. 44)

**Fifteenth Amendment** [Enmienda Decimoquinta] *s.* aprobada en 1870, esta enmienda a la Constitución de Estados Unidos declaraba que a los ciudadanos no se les podía impedir que votaran "por motivo de raza, color ni condición anterior de esclavitud". (p. 546)

**54th Massachusetts Regiment** [54.° Regimiento de Massachusetts] *s.* regimientos afroamericano organizado para luchar por la Unión en la guerra civil. (p. 506)

**fireside chats** [charlas al calor de la lumbre] *s.* nombre dado a las radioemisiones de Franklin Roosevelt en las que explicaba sus medidas. (p. 735)

**First Battle of Bull Run** [primera batalla de Bull Run] *s.* una batalla de la guerra civil, de 1861, en que el Sur horrorizó al Norte con una victoria. (p. 485)





R63

**flapper** *s.* jovencita librepensadora que abrazaba las modas y actitudes urbanas nuevas de los años veinte. (p. 714)

**foreign policy** [política exterior] *s.* relaciones con los gobiernos de otros países. (p. 304)

**Fort Sumter** [fuerte Sumter] *s.* fuerte federal ubicado en el puerto de Charleston, Carolina del Sur; el ataque sureño al fuerte Sumter marcó el comienzo de la guerra civil. (p. 481)

**forty-niner** [buscador de ventura del 49] *s.* persona que fue a California en búsqueda de oro, empezando en 1849. (p. 412)

**Fourteen Points** [Catorce puntos] *s.* los objetivos del presidente Woodrow Wilson para la paz que siguió a la primera guerra mundial. (p. 695)

**Fourteenth Amendment** [Enmienda Decimocuarta] *s.* enmienda a la Constitución de Estados Unidos, aprobada en 1868, que hizo ciudadanos del país a todas las personas nacidas en Estados Unidos o naturalizadas, incluso a los antiguos esclavos. (p. 535)

**First Continental Congress** [primer Congreso Continental] *s.* reunión en 1774 de delegados de todas las colonias, excepto Georgia, para defender los derechos coloniales. (p. 171)

**Freedmen's Bureau** [Agencia de Manumisos] *s.* agencia federal establecida para ayudar a los antiguos esclavos después de la guerra civil. (p. 533)

**freedmen's school** [escuela para los manumisos] *s.* escuela establecida por la Agencia de Manumisos para educar a los recientes libertos afroamericanos. (p. 541)

**Freedom Ride** [Viaje por la Libertad] *s.* protesta contra la segregación racial en los autobuses interestatales del Sur. (p. 818)

**Freedom Summer** [Verano de la Libertad] *s.* en 1964 el Comité de Estudiantes no Violentos organizó una campaña de registro de votantes. (p. 821)

**Free Soil Party** [Partido del Suelo Libre] *s.* partido político dedicado a parar la expansión de la esclavitud. (p. 459)

**French and Indian War** [guerra Francesa y Amerindia] *s.* conflicto en Norteamérica, entre 1754 y 1763, que fue parte de una lucha mundial entre Francia y Gran Bretaña y que terminó con la derrota de Francia y el traspaso del Canadá francés a Gran Bretaña. (p. 147)

**French Indochina** [Indochina Francesa] *s.* colonia francesa que incluía lo que es hoy Vietnam, Laos y Camboya. (p. 835)

**frontier** [frontera] *s.* región sin o con muy pocos asentamientos ocupada mayormente por amerindios. (p. 557)

**Fugitive Slave Act** [ley de los Esclavos Fugitivos] *s.* ley de 1850 para ayudar a los dueños de esclavos a recapturar los esclavos fugados. (p. 462)

**French Revolution** [Revolución francesa] *s.* en 1789 los franceses iniciaron un movimiento por la libertad y la igualdad. (p. 301)

**fundamentalist** [fundamentalista] *s.* persona que cree en la interpretación textual, o palabra por palabra, de la Biblia. (p. 716)

**Fundamental Orders of Connecticut** [Órdenes Fundamentales de Connecticut] *s.* conjunto de leyes establecidas en 1639 por una congregación puritana que se había asentado en el valle del río Connecticut y que ampliaban la idea de un gobierno representativo. (p. 95)

## G

**generator** [generador] *s.* máquina que produce corriente eléctrica. (p. 587)

**Ghana** [Ghana] *s.* imperio del África Occidental entre los siglos VIII y XI d.de C. (p. 39)

**G.I. Bill of Rights** [Carta de Derechos del Soldado] *s.* aprobada en 1944, esta ley ofrecía ayuda educacional y económica a los veteranos. (p. 779)

**Gilded Age** [Edad Dorada] *s.* época de fines del siglo XIX de fabulosa riqueza. (p. 596)

**"Glorious Revolution"** [Revolución gloriosa] *s.* derrocamiento, en 1688, del rey inglés Jacobo II y su substitución por Guillermo y María. (p. 144)

**gold standard** [patrón oro] *s.* sistema en que el gobierno garantiza cada dólar con una cierta cantidad de oro. (p. 577)

**Grange** [La Quinta] *s.* creada en 1867 por un grupo de agricultores para tratar de satisfacer las necesidades sociales de las familias granjeras. (p. 577)

**Great Awakening** [Gran Despertar] *s.* renovación del sentimiento religioso en las colonias norteamericanas durante las décadas de 1730 a 1750. (p. 139)

**Great Compromise** [Gran Compromiso] *s.* acuerdo en la Convención Constitucional que estableció una legislatura nacional de dos cámaras; en una de estas cámaras, todos los estados tendrían representación igual, en la otra, cada estado tendría representación basada en su población. (p. 232)

**Great Depression** [gran depresión] *s.* período que duró desde 1929 hasta 1941, en que la economía de Estados Unidos declinó severamente y millones de estadounidenses estaban sin empleo. (p. 731)

**Great Migration** [Gran Emigración] *s.* movimiento de puritanos que salieron de Inglaterra para establecer asentamientos por todo el mundo, incluyendo a 20,000 que partieron para América (p. 94); el movimiento de afroamericanos entre 1910 y 1920 del Sur hacia las ciudades del Norte. (p. 693)

**Great Plains** [Grandes Llanuras] *s.* región desde el río Missouri hasta las montañas Rocosas. (p. 557)

**Great Society** [gran sociedad] *s.* programa iniciado por Lyndon Johnson para ayudan a los pobres, los ancianos y las mujeres y también promovía la educación, prohibía la discriminación racial y protegía el medio ambiente. (p. 822)

**greenback** [billete verde] *s.* papel moneda emitido por el gobierno federal durante la guerra civil. (p. 509)

**gristmill** [molino harinero] *s.* molino en que el grano se muele para producir cualquier tipo de harina. (p. 115)

**guerrilla** [guerrillero] *s.* soldado que debilita al enemigo con asaltos inesperados y ataques relámpagos. (p. 207)

**guerrilla warfare** [guerra de guerrillas] *s.* ataques inesperados por bandas pequeñas de guerrilleros. (p. 842)

**Gulf of Tonkin Resolution** [Resolución del golfo de Tonkín] *s.* resolución del Congreso que dio al presidente el poder de usar fuerza militar en Vietnam. (p. 841)

## H

***hacienda*** [hacienda] *s.* granja grande o finca. (p. 72)

**Harlem Renaissance** [renacimiento de Harlem] *s.* florecimiento de la creatividad artística afroamericana durante los años veinte, centrada en la comunidad de Harlem de la ciudad de Nueva York. (p. 720)

**Harpers Ferry** *s.* arsenal federal en Virginia, capturado en 1859 durante un levantamiento de esclavos. (p. 469)

**Hausa** [hausa] *s.* gente de África Occidental que después del año 1000 d.C. vivió en lo que ahora es la región norte de Nigeria. (p. 42)

**hawk** [halcón] *s.* persona que apoya la guerra. (p. 847)

**Haymarket affair** [asunto Haymarket] *s.* mitín de protesta sindicalista que resultó aproximadamente en un centenar de muertes después de que un desconocido tiró una bomba y la policía abrió fuego contra la multitud. (p. 602)

**H-bomb** [bomba H] *s.* bomba de hidrógeno. (p. 798)

**Hiroshima** [Hiroshima] *s.* primera ciudad del Japón contra la cual se lanzó la bomba atómica el 6 de agosto de 1945 durante la segunda guerra mundial. (p. 771)

**Ho Chi Minh Trail** [ruta de Ho Chi Minh] *s.* red de sendas que usó el Vietcong para mover soldados y provisiones durante la guerra de Vietnam. (p. 838)

**Holocaust** [Holocausto] *s.* matanza sistemática en Alemania, durante la segunda guerra mundial, de unos seis millones de judíos así como millones de otros grupos étnicos. (p. 765)

**homestead** [residencia] *s.* tierra para asentarse y construir una casa. (p. 568)

**Homestead Act** [ley de Residencia] *s.* aprobada en 1862, esta ley ofrecía 160 acres de tierra gratis a cualquiera que acordara ocuparla y trabajarla por cinco años. (p. 574)

**House of Burgesses** [Cámara de los Burgueses] *s.* creada en 1619, la primera asamblea representativa de las colonias norteamericanas. (p. 88)

**Hudson River School** [Escuela del río Hudson] *s.* grupo de artistas que vivían en el valle del río Hudson del estado de New York. (p. 430)

**Hull House** [Casa Hull] *s.* fundada en 1889, fue modelo para otras casas de acogida de la época. (p. 613)

**Hundred Days** [Cien Días] *s.* durante sus cien primeros días, del 9 de marzo a mediados de junio de 1933, Franklin Roosevelt mandó al Congreso muchos proyectos de ley nuevos. (p. 735)

**hygiene** [higiene] *s.* condiciones y prácticas que fomentan la buena salud. (p. 490)

## I

**immigrant** [inmigrante] *s.* persona que se establece en un país nuevo. (p. 423)

**Immigration Reform and Control Act of 1986** [ley de Reforma y Control de la Inmigración] *s.* ley pasada para reforzar las leyes de inmigración y las medidas para su cumplimiento. (p. 884)

**immunity** [inmunidad] *s.* protección legal. (p. 262)

**impeachment** [imputación] *s.* proceso de acusar a un funcionario público de un delito en el desempeño de sus funciones. (p. 249)

**imperialism** [imperialismo] *s.* política por la cual las naciones más poderosas extienden su control económico, político o militar sobre territorios o naciones más débiles. (p. 659)

**impressment** [secuestro] *s.* el acto de capturar personas a la fuerza. (p. 327)

**inaugurate** [investir] *v.* conferir un cargo oficial en una ceremonia formal. (p. 293)

**income tax** [impuesto sobre la renta] *s.* impuesto sobre los ingresos. (p. 509)

**indentured servant** [siervo escriturado] *s.* persona que vendía su trabajo a cambio de pasaje a Norteamérica. (p. 88)

**Indian Removal Act** [ley del Traslado de los Indígenas] *s.* esta ley de 1830 requería que el gobierno negociara tratados para el traslado de los amerindios al oeste. (p. 376)

**Indian Territory** [territorio Indio] *s.* lo que hoy son Oklahoma y partes de Kansas y Nebraska a la cual se trasladó a los amerindios bajo la ley del Traslado de los Indígenas de 1830. (p. 376)

**indictment** [acusación] *s.* declaración escrita dictada por un jurado de acusación que inculpa a una persona de un delito. (p. 250)

**indigo** [añil] *s.* planta que cultivaban las colonias sureñas de la cual se obtiene un colorante azul oscuro. (p. 121)

**individual right** [derecho individual] *s.* libertad y privilegio personal que garantiza a los ciudadanos estadounidenses la Carta de Derechos. (p. 247)

**Industrial Revolution** [revolución industrial] *s.* en la Inglaterra de fines del siglo XVIII, las maquinarias de fábrica empezaron a reemplazar las herramientas manuales, y la producción de bienes manufacturados reemplazó la agricultura como el principal modo de trabajo. (p. 341)

**inferior court** [tribunal inferior] *s.* corte con autoridad menor que la del Tribunal Supremo. (p. 260)

**inflation** [inflación] *s.* subida en el precio de los productos y los servicios y disminución del valor del dinero. (p. 386)

**information revolution** [revolución de la información] *s.* proceso tecnológico que ha cambiado radicalmente el volumen y el modo de transmitir información. (p. 879)

**initiative** [iniciativa] *s.* el procedimiento que permite a los votantes proponer una ley directamente. (p. 640)

**inoperative** [inoperante] *adj.* que no está vigente. (p. 274)

**installment buy** [comprar a cuotas] *v.* comprar algo haciendo pequeños pagos mensuales. (p. 712)

**insurrection** [insurrección] *s.* levantamiento abierto contra un gobierno. (p. 271)

**interchangeable part** [parte intercambiable] *s.* parte que es exactamente igual a otra parte. (p. 343)

**Internet** [Internet] *s.* interconexión mundial de redes informáticas. (p. 878)

**Intolerable Acts** [leyes Intolerables] *s.* serie de leyes aprobadas en 1774 por el Parlamento para castigar a Massachusetts por el Motín del Té de Boston. (p. 170)

**Iran-Contra affair** [asunto Irán-Contra] *s.* en 1986 el gobierno de Estados Unidos vendió armas a Irán a cambio de ayuda para liberar a los rehenes estadounidenses en el Oriente Medio y el dinero de la venta fue a los rebeldes Contra de El Salvador. (p. 874)

**Iran hostage crisis** [crisis de los rehenes de Irán] *s.* el 4 de noviembre de 1979 un grupo de iraníes invadieron la embajada de Estados Unidos en Teherán, capital de Irán, y tomaron de rehenes a 52 estadounidenses. (p. 865)

**ironclad** [acorazado] *s.* buque de guerra cubierto de hierro. (p. 491)

**Iroquois League** [Liga Iroquesa] *s.* alianza del siglo XVI entre los pueblos amerindios cayuga, mohawk, oneida, onondaga y seneca, que vivían en la región oriental de los Grandes lagos. (p. 37)

**irrigation** [irrigación] *s.* práctica de llevar agua a los cultivos. (p. 29)

**Islam** [islam] *s.* religión fundada por el profeta Mahoma en el siglo VII, que enseña que hay un solo Dios: Alá. (p. 41)

**island hopping** [brincar de isla a isla] *v.* estrategia usada durante la segunda guerra mundial según la cual los aliados invadían islas débilmente defendidas por los japoneses para así lanzar nuevos ataques. (p. 770)

**isolationist** [aislacionista] *s.* persona que creía que Estados Unidos debía mantenerse apartado de los asuntos de las otras naciones, excepto en defensa propia. (p. 711)

## J

**Jacksonian Democracy** [democracia jacksoniana] *s.* idea de extender el poder político a toda la gente asegurando de ese modo el gobierno de la mayoría. (p. 370)

**Jamestown.** *s.* primer asentamiento inglés permanente en Norteamérica. (p. 87)

**Jay's Treaty** [Tratado de Jay] *s.* el acuerdo que puso fin a la disputa sobre los derechos marítimos estadounidenses durante la Revolución francesa. (p. 302)

**jazz** [jazz] *s.* tipo nuevo de música en los años veinte que capturó el despreocupado espíritu de la época. (p. 717)

**Jim Crow** [ley Jim Crow] *s.* ley que imponía la separación entre la gente blanca y la de piel negra en los lugares públicos del Sur. (p. 621)

**joint-stock company** [sociedad por acciones] *s.* empresa en que los inversionistas colocan su dinero en un fondo común con la intención de sacar ganancias. (p. 86)

**judicial review** [revisión judicial] *s.* principio de que el Tribunal Supremo tiene la última palabra en la interpretación de la Constitución. (p. 317)

**Judiciary Act of 1801** [ley Judicial de 1801] *s.* ley que aumentó el número de jueces federales, permitiéndole al presidente John Adams cubrir la mayoría de los puestos nuevos con federalistas. (p. 316)

## K

**Kansas-Nebraska Act** [ley de Kansas-Nebraska] *s.* ley de 1854 que estableció los territorios de Kansas y Nebraska y otorgó a sus habitantes el derecho a decidir si querían o no permitir la esclavitud. (p. 464)

**kayak** [kayak] *s.* embarcación pequeña hecha de piel de animales. (p. 33)

**Kellogg-Briand Pact** [Pacto Kellogg-Briand] *s.* en 1928 firmaron este pacto muchas naciones que prometieron no declararse en guerra entre ellas excepto en defensa propia. (p. 711)

**King Cotton** [rey Algodón] *s.* al algodón se lo llamaba rey porque era importante en el mercado mundial y el Sur cultivaba la mayor parte del algodón que usaban las fábricas textiles de Europa. (p. 484)

**King Philip's War** [guerra del rey Felipe] *s.* guerra entre las colonias puritanas y los amerindios que se libró entre 1675 y 1676. (p. 96)

**Knights of Labor** [Caballeros del Trabajo] *s.* organización de obreros de oficios diferentes formada después de la guerra civil. (p. 601)

**Korean War** [guerra de Corea] *s.* conflicto entre Corea del Norte y Corea del Sur que duró desde 1950 a 1953; Estados Unidos, junto con otros países de las Naciones Unidas, luchó del lado de los coreanos del Sur y China luchó del lado de los coreanos del Norte. (p. 796)

**Ku Klux Klan** *s.* grupo constituido en 1866 que quería restaurar el control del Sur a los demócratas y mantener sumisos a los antiguos esclavos. (p. 544)

## L

**labor union** [sindicato laboral] *s.* obreros que se unen para tratar de conseguir mejores condiciones de trabajo. (p. 434)

**laissez faire** [dejad hacer] *s.* teoría que declaraba que el comercio no sujeto a regulaciones actuaría de manera beneficiosa a la nación. (p. 710)

**Land Ordinance of 1785** [Ordenanza de Tierras de 1785] *s.* ley que establecía un plan para la agrimensura y venta de las tierras públicas al oeste de los montes Apalaches. (p. 223)

**land speculator** [especulador en tierras] *s.* persona que compra grandes extensiones de terreno a precio bajo y luego vende secciones pequeñas a precios altos. (p. 394)

**League of Nations** [Sociedad de Naciones] *s.* organización establecida después de la primera guerra mundial para resolver conflictos internacionales. (p. 695)

**leisure** *s.* tiempo libre. (p. 627)

**Lend-Lease** [ley de Préstamo y Arriendo] *s.* ley que le permitió a Estados Unidos mandar a las naciones que luchaban contra el Eje armas y suministros sin requerir pago inmediato. (p. 760)

**Lewis and Clark expedition** [expedición de Lewis y Clark] *s.* grupo dirigido por Meriwether Lewis y William Clark que exploró las tierras de la Compra de Luisiana empezando en 1803. (p. 320)

**Lexington and Concord** *s.* escenarios, en Massachusetts, de las primeras batallas de la Revolución norteamericana. (p. 173)

**liberal** [liberal] *s.* persona que favorece acción por parte del gobierno para lograr la reforma social y económica. (p. 749)

**limited government** [gobierno limitado] *s.* principio que requiere que todos los ciudadanos estadounidenses, incluso los líderes gubernamentales, obedezcan la ley. (p. 247)

**lode** [veta] *s.* mineral enterrado entre capas de roca. (p. 558)

**Lone Star Republic** [República de la Estrella Solitaria] *s.* apodo de la República de Texas, que se le dio en 1836. (p. 405)

**long drive** [largo arreo] *s.* arreo de ganado al ferrocarril. (p. 560)

**Lost Generation** [generación perdida] *s.* la generación de los años veinte, después de la primera guerra mundial cuando hombres y mujeres veían pocas esperanzas para el futuro. (p. 720)

**Louisiana Purchase** [Compra de Luisiana] *s.* en 1803, la compra a Francia del Territorio de Luisiana. (p. 319)

**Lowell mills** [fábricas de Lowell] *s.* fábricas textiles ubicadas en el pueblo manufacturero de Lowell, Massachusetts, fundado en 1826. (p. 342)

**Loyalist** [realista]. *s.* colono norteamericano que apoyaba a los británicos durante la Revolución norteamericana. (p. 173)

## M

**mail-order catalog** [catálogo de venta por correo] *s.* publicación que contenía fotografías y la descripción de los artículos para que la gente encargara por correo. (p. 627)

**Magna Carta** [Carta Magna] *s.* "Gran Cédula Real"; documento que garantizaba los derechos políticos básicos en Inglaterra, aprobada por el rey Juan en el año 1215. (p. 141)

**Mali** [Malí] *s.* imperio del África Occidental desde el siglo XIII hasta el siglo XVI y que se enriqueció gracias al comercio. (p. 41)

**Manhattan Project** [Proyecto Manhattan] *s.* programa ultrasecreto establecido en 1942 para construir una bomba atómica. (p. 771)

**manifest destiny** [destino manifiesto] *s.* creencia de que era el destino de Estados Unidos extenderse por todo el continente, desde al océano Atlántico al océano Pacífico. (p. 407)

**manor system** [sistema señorial] *s.* sistema en que los nobles dividían sus tierras en propiedades, cultivadas mayormente por los siervos, quienes recibían la protección del noble. (p. 45)

***Marbury v. Madison*** [Marbury contra Madison] *s.* caso de 1803 en que el Tribunal Supremo dictaminó que tenía el poder de invalidar leyes declarándolas inconstitucionales. (p. 317)

**March on Washington** [Marcha a Washington] *s.* enorme manifestación por los derechos civiles en Washington, D.C. en 1963. (p. 820)

**Marshall Plan** [Plan Marshall] *s.* aprobado en 1948, autorizó a Estados Unidos a dar más de trece mil millones de dólares para ayudar a la recuperación de las naciones de Europa después de la segunda guerra mundial. (p. 779)

**mass culture** [cultura de masas] *s.* cultura común compartida por grandes números de personas. (p. 626)

**mass media** [medios de comunicación de masas] *s.* comunicaciones que alcanzan a un público muy grande. (p. 718)

**matrilineal** [por línea materna] *adj.* sociedad en que la ascendencia se determina mediante la madre. (p. 36)

**Mayflower Compact** [Pacto del Mayflower] *s.* acuerdo firmado por los hombres que viajaron a América en el Mayflower, que requería leyes para el bien de la colonia y establecía el concepto de autogobierno. (p. 93)

**melting pot** [crisol de culturas] *s.* lugar donde las culturas se amalgaman. (p. 616)

**mercantilism** [mercantilismo] *s.* sistema económico en que las naciones tratan de aumentar su riqueza y poder obteniendo oro y plata y estableciendo una balanza comercial favorable. (p. 61)

**mercenary** [mercenario] *s.* soldado profesional contratado para luchar por un país extranjero. (p. 195)

**Mexican Cession** [Cesión mexicana] *s.* extensa región cedida por México después de la guerra con México; incluía los actuales estados de California, Nevada, Utah, la mayor parte de Arizona y partes de Nuevo México, Colorado y Wyoming. (p. 411)

***Mexicano*** [mexicano] *s.* persona de ascendencia española cuyos antepasados habían venido de México y se habían establecido en el sudoeste. (p. 570)

**middle passage** [travesía intermedia] *s.* parte intermedia de la ruta del comercio triangular (el viaje de África a las Américas) que traía africanos capturados a la esclavitud. (p. 78)

**migrate** [migrar] *v.* mudarse de un lugar a otro. (p. 27)

**militarism** [militarismo] *s.* creencia de que una nación necesita una fuerza militar grande. (p. 679)

**militia** [milicia] *s.* fuerza de civiles armados comprometidos a defender su comunidad durante la Revolución norteamericana. (p. 170); fuerza militar de emergencia, que no es parte del ejército profesional. (p. 254)

**minié ball** [bala minié] *s.* bala con base hueca. (p. 491)

**Minuteman** [minutero] *s.* miembro de la milicia colonial entrenado para responder "con un minuto de aviso". (p. 170)

**misdemeanor** [fechoría] *s.* violación de la ley. (p. 259)

**mission** [misión] *s.* asentamiento creado por la Iglesia con el propósito de convertir a los amerindios al cristianismo. (p. 72)

**missionary** [misionero] *s.* persona enviada por la Iglesia para predicar, enseñar y convertir a los indígenas al cristianismo. (p. 61)

**Missouri Compromise** [Acuerdo de Missouri] *s.* serie de leyes aprobadas en 1820 para mantener el equilibrio del poder político entre los estados esclavistas y los libres. (p. 358)

**monopoly** [monopolio] *s.* compañía que elimina a sus competidores y controla una industria. (p. 595)

**Monroe Doctrine** [Doctrina Monroe] *s.* política de oposición estadounidense a cualquier interferencia europea en el hemisferio occidental, proclamada por el presidente Monroe en 1823. (p. 359)

**Montgomery bus boycott** [Boicoteo al transporte público de Montgomery] *s.* en 1955 los afroamericanos boicotearon el transporte público de Montgomery, Alabama, en respuesta al arresto de Rosa Parks, quien se había negado a dejar su asiento a una persona blanca. (p. 815)

**Mormon** [mormón] *s.* miembro de una iglesia fundada por Joseph Smith en 1830. (p. 397)

**Mound Builder** [constructor de túmulos] *s.* amerindio primitivo que construía grandes estructuras de tierra. (p. 31)

**mountain man** [hombre de las montañas] *s.* trampero o explorador que abrió el oeste hallando sendas a través de las montañas Rocosas. (p. 393)

**muckraker** [revuelve estiércol] *s.* hacia comienzos del siglo XX, periodista que exponía la corrupción dentro de la sociedad estadounidense. (p. 640)

**Muslim** [musulmán] *s.* adherente del islam. (p. 41)

## N

**NAACP** *s.* constituida en 1909, la Asociación Nacional para el Progreso de la Gente de Color. (pp. 622, 715)

**NAFTA** [Tratado Norteamericano de Libre Comercio] *s.* aprobado en 1993, el Tratado Norteamericano de Libre Comercio o zona de libre comercio entre Estados Unidos, México y Canadá. (p. 875)

**napalm** [napalm] *s.* gasolina gelatinosa que arde violentamente. (p. 843)

**nationalism** [nacionalismo] *s.* sentido de orgullo, lealtad y protección hacia el país de uno. (p. 354)

**nativist** [nativista] *s.* estadounidense nativo que quería eliminar toda influencia extranjera. (p. 428)

**NATO** [OTAN] *s.* la Organización del Tratado del Atlántico Norte es una alianza militar constituida en 1949 por diez países de la Europa occidental, Estados Unidos y Canadá. (p. 793)

**natural-born citizen** [ciudadano nato] *s.* ciudadano nacido en Estados Unidos o en un estado asociado o dependencia de Estados Unidos, o a padres que son ciudadanos estadounidenses que viven fuera del país. (p. 257)

**naturalization** [naturalización] *s.* manera de darle ciudadanía completa a una persona nacida en otro país. (pp. 253, 270)

**Navigation Acts** [Actas de Navegación] *s.* serie de leyes aprobadas por el Parlamento, empezando en 1651, para asegurarse Inglaterra de que el comercio de sus colonias le rindiera ganancias económicas. (p. 112)

**navigator** [oficial de derrota] *s.* persona que planea el rumbo de un barco mientras está en el mar. (p. 49)

**Nazi Party** [Partido Nazi] *s.* partido Alemán Nacionalsocialista de los Trabajadores, llegó al poder bajo Adolfo Hitler en 1930. (p. 756)

**NCAI** *s.* Congreso Nacional de Amerindios, fundado en 1944 para promover el "bienestar común" de los amerindios. (p. 825)

**neutral** [neutral] *adj.* que no apoya ni a un país ni al otro. (p. 302)

**neutrality** [neutralidad] *s.* rechazo de la idea de apoyar a un país u otro durante una guerra. (p. 682)

**New Deal** [Nuevo Trato] *s.* programas de Franklin Roosevelt para luchar contra la depresión. (p. 735)

**New France** [Nueva Francia] *s.* puesto para el comercio de las pieles establecido en 1608 que se convirtió en el primer asentamiento francés permanente en Norteamérica. (p. 70)

**new immigrant** [inmigrante nuevo] *s.* persona del sur y el este de Europa que entró a Estados Unidos después de 1900. (p. 614)

**New Jersey Plan** [Plan de Nueva Jersey] *s.* plan de gobierno propuesto en 1787 en la Convención Constitucional que proponía una cámara legislativa única en que cada estado tendría un solo voto. (p. 231)

**Nineteenth Amendment** [Enmienda Decimonovena] *s.* enmienda a la Constitución de Estados Unidos ratificada en 1920 que dio a las mujeres el derecho absoluto a votar. (p. 653)





R67

***Nisei*** [nisei] *s.* estadounidense japonés nacido en Estados Unidos. (p. 775)

**Northwest Ordinance** [Ordenanza del Noroeste] *s.* describe cómo se iba a gobernar el territorio del Noroeste y establecía las condiciones para el asentamiento, así como los derechos de los colonos. (p. 223)

**Northwest Territory** [territorio del Noroeste] *s.* territorio organizado por la Ordenanza de Tierras de 1785, que incluía tierras que formaron los estados de Ohio, Indiana, Michigan, Illinois, Wisconsin y parte de Minnesota. (p. 223)

**NOW** *s.* fundada en 1966, la Organización Nacional de la Mujer adelantó una campaña para que las mujeres consiguieran empleos con paga igual a la de los hombres. (p. 826)

**Nuremberg Trials** [Juicios de Nuremberg] *s.* procesos judiciales que tuvieron lugar en Nuremberg, Alemania, después de la segunda guerra mundial, en que se enjuició a líderes nazis por sus crímenes de guerra. (p. 780)

## O

**Open Door Policy** [política de puertas abiertas] *s.* en 1899 Estados Unidos instó a las naciones que tenían intereses en China a que siguieran una política según la cual ningún país controlaría el comercio con China. (p. 669)

**Oregon Trail** [Camino de Oregón] *s.* camino hacia el oeste que iba de Independence, Missouri, al territorio de Oregón. (p. 396)

**overseer** [capataz] *s.* persona contratada por el dueño de una plantación para vigilar a los esclavos y dirigir su trabajo. (p. 122)

## P

**pacifist** [pacifista] *s.* persona moralmente opuesta a la guerra. (p. 209)

**Palmer raids** [allanamientos de Palmer] *s.* en 1920 agentes federales y la policía allanaron los hogares de personas que se sospechaba que eran radicales. (p. 697)

**Panama Canal** [canal de Panamá] *s.* atajo a través de Panamá que conecta los océanos Atlántico y Pacífico. (p. 670)

**Panic of 1837** [pánico de 1837] *s.* crisis financiera con clausura de bancos y colapso del sistema crediticio, que resultó en muchas quiebras y serio desempleo. (p. 386)

**Panic of 1873** [pánico de 1873) *s.* crisis financiera en que los bancos se clausuraron y la bolsa de comercio se derrumbó. (p. 547)

**Parliament** [Parlamento] *s.* el cuerpo legislativo principal de Inglaterra. (p. 142)

**patent** [patente] *s.* documento del gobierno que otorga a un inventor el derecho exclusivo a hacer o vender su invención durante un determinado número de años. (p. 586)

**Patriot** [patriota] *s.* colono norteamericano que durante la Revolución norteamericana estaba a favor de los rebeldes. (p. 173)

**patroon** [patrono] *s.* persona que traía 50 colonos a Nueva Holanda y a cambio recibía una gran concesión de tierras y otros privilegios especiales. (p. 101)

**Pearl Harbor** *s.* base naval en Hawai atacada de sorpresa por Japón el 7 de diciembre de 1941. (p. 760)

**Persian Gulf War** [guerra del Golfo Pérsico] *s.* en 1991 Estados Unidos y las Naciones Unidas echaron a Iraq de Kuwait, país que los iraquíes habían invadido en 1990. (p. 875)

**petroleum** [petróleo] *s.* líquido aceitoso e inflamable. (p. 585)

**philanthropist** [filántropo] *s.* persona que da grandes sumas de dinero a las organizaciones benéficas. (p. 596)

**Pickett's Charge** [carga de Pickett] *s.* en 1863 el general George Pickett dirigió una carga frontal contra las fuerzas de la Unión durante la batalla de la guerra civil en Gettysburg; el ataque fracasó. (p. 513)

**piedmont** [tierras bajas] *s.* ancha extensión de tierra llana al pie de una cadena de montañas. (p. 126)

**Pilgrim** [peregrino] *s.* miembros del grupo que rechazó la Iglesia de Inglaterra, viajó a América y fundó la colonia de Plymouth en 1620. (p. 92)

**Pinckney's Treaty** [Tratado de Pinckney] *s.* tratado de 1795 con España que otorgaba a Estados Unidos el uso del río Mississippi y el derecho a depositar bienes en Nueva Orleans; creó el paralelo 31 como el límite sur de Estados Unidos. (p. 302)

**plantation** [plantación] *s.* finca grande para cultivos comerciales. (p. 73)

**platform** [plataforma] *s.* declaración de creencias. (p. 471)

**Platt Amendment** [Enmienda Platt] *s.* resultado de la guerra entre Estados Unidos y España, dio a Estados Unidos el derecho a intervenir en los asuntos de Cuba cuando existiera amenaza a la "vida, propiedad y libertad individual". (p. 666)

***Plessy* v. *Ferguson*** [Plessy contra Ferguson] *s.* caso de 1896 en que el Tribunal Supremo dictaminó que la separación de las razas en las instalaciones públicas era legal. (p. 621)

**political machine** [maquinaria política] *s.* organización que logra votos suficientes para controlar un gobierno local. (p. 613)

**political party** [partido político] *s.* grupo de personas que trata de promover sus ideas y ejercer su influencia sobre el gobierno, y que también apoya a candidatos a los cargos públicos. (p. 304)

**Pontiac's Rebellion** [rebelión de Pontiac] *s.* rebelión de 1763 contra los fuertes británicos y los colonos norteamericanos, dirigida en parte por el líder ottawa Pontiac, en reacción a los colonos que demandaban las tierras de los amerindios, así como a la severidad con que trataban a éstos los soldados británicos. (p. 151)

**popular culture** [cultura popular] *s.* cosas como la música, la moda y las películas que son populares dentro de una cantidad grande de personas. (p. 718)

**popular sovereignty** [soberanía popular] *s.* gobierno en que gobierna la gente (p. 244); sistema en que los ciudadanos votan para decidir un asunto. (p. 463)

**Populist Party** [Partido Populista] *s.* también conocido como el Partido del Pueblo y constituido en 1890, este grupo quería una política que aumentara el precio de lo que cultivaban los granjeros. (p. 577)

**prejudice** [prejuicio] *s.* opinión negativa no basada en los hechos. (p. 427)

**printing press** [imprenta] *s.* máquina inventada por Johannes Gutenberg alrededor de 1455. (p. 47)

**privateer** [corsario] *s.* barco de propiedad particular autorizado por un gobierno que está en guerra a atacar los barcos de la marina mercante enemiga. (p. 204)

**Proclamation of 1763** [Proclama de 1763] *s.* orden por la cual Gran Bretaña les prohibía a los colonos norteamericanos establecer asentamientos al oeste de los montes Apalaches. (p. 151)

**profit** [ganancia] *s.* cantidad de dinero que saca una empresa depués de descontar a las entradas los gastos empresariales. (p. 48)



R68

**progressivism** [progresismo] *s.* movimiento reformista de principios del siglo XX que buscaba devolver el control del gobierno al pueblo, restablecer oportunidades económicas y corregir las injusticias de la vida estadounidense. (p. 639)

**prohibition** [prohibición] *s.* proscripción de la fábrica, venta y posesión de bebidas alcohólicas. (p. 715)

**propaganda** [propaganda] *s.* opinión expresada con el propósito de influir en las acciones de otras personas. (p. 692)

**proprietary colony** [colonia de proprietario] *s.* colonia de un único dueño. (p. 101)

***pro tempore*** *adv.* latín para "por el momento". (p. 250)

**public works project** [proyecto de obras públicas] *s.* proyecto patrocinado por el gobierno para construir recursos públicos, como caminos y diques. (p. 732)

**Pullman Strike** [huelga de Pullman] *s.* huelga nacional de ferrocarriles que se extendió por toda la industria ferroviaria en 1894. (p. 603)

**Puritan** [puritano] *s.* miembro de un grupo de Inglaterra que se asentó en la Colonia de la bahía de Massachusetts en 1630 y trató de reformar las prácticas de la Iglesia de Inglaterra. (p. 94)

**push-pull factor** *s.* factor que empuja a la gente a irse de su tierra natal y las atrae a un lugar nuevo. (p. 424)

## Q

**Quaker** [cuáquero] *s.* persona que creía que todas las personas debieran vivir en paz y armonía; aceptaba a religiones y grupos étnicos diferentes. (p. 101)

**quarter** [acuartelar] *v.* dar alojamiento. (p. 267)

**Quartering Act** [ley de Acuartelamiento] *s.* ley aprobada por el Parlamento en 1765 que requería que las colonias alojaran a los soldados británicos y los aprovisionaran. (p. 160)

**quorum** [quórum] *s.* número mínimo de miembros que deben estar presentes para que pueda empezar a deliberar oficialmente una asamblea. (p. 251)

## R

**racial discrimination** [discriminación racial] *s.* tratamiento diferente por motivos de raza. (p. 620)

**racism** [racismo] *s.* creencia de que alguna gente es inferior a causa de su raza. (p. 79)

**radical** [radical] *s.* persona que adopta posiciones políticas extremas. (p. 313)

**Radical Republican** [republicano radical] *s.* diputado que después de la guerra civil estaba a favor de usar el gobierno para crear un nuevo orden en el Sur y dar la ciudadanía total y derecho al voto a los afroamericanos. (p. 533)

**ragtime** *s.* mezcla de canciones afroamericanas y formas musicales europeas. (p. 629)

**ratification** [ratificación] *s.* aprobación oficial. (p. 264)

**ration** [racionar] *v.* distribuir una cantidad fija de cierto artículo. (p. 773)

**recall** [destituir] *v.* votar para sacar a un funcionario de su cargo. (p. 640)

**Reconstruction** [Reconstrucción] *s.* proceso que usó el gobierno de Estados Unidos para readmitir a los estados confederados a la Unión después de la guerra civil. (p. 533)

**Red Scare** [Terror Rojo] *s.* entre 1919 y 1920, ola de pánico sobre una posible revolución comunista. (p. 697)

**referendum** [referéndum] *s.* cuando una ley que se ha propuesto se somete al voto del pueblo. (p. 640)

**Reformation** [Reforma] *s.* movimiento religioso del siglo XVI para corregir los problemas de la Iglesia Católica Romana. (p. 47)

**Renaissance** [Renacimiento] *s.* período de la historia europea que duró desde el siglo XIV hasta comienzos del XVII y que acrecentó el interés por el arte y el saber. (p. 46)

**rendezvous** [encuentro] *s.* reunión. (p. 197)

**reprieve** [indultar] *n.* cancelación de un castigo. (p. 259)

**republic** [república] *s.* gobierno en que el pueblo elige representantes para que lo gobiernen. (p. 222)

**republicanism** [republicanismo] *s.* creencia de que el gobierno se debe basar en el consentimiento del pueblo; el pueblo ejercita su poder votando por representantes políticos. (pp. 214, 245)

**Republican Party** [Partido Republicano] *s.* el partido político constituído en 1854 por los que se oponían a la esclavitud en los territorios. (p. 466)

**reservation** [reserva] *s.* tierras destinadas por el gobierno de Estados Unidos para las tribus amerindias. (p. 562)

**revenue** [rentas públicas] *s.* entradas que recibe un gobierno para cubrir sus gastos. (pp. 160, 252)

**revenue sharing** [reparto de las rentas públicas] *s.* la distribución de dinero federal a los estados y gobiernos locales con pocas o no restricciones en la manera cómo se gasta. (p. 856)

**revival** [renacimiento religioso] *s.* reunión diseñada para revivir la fe religiosa. (p. 433)

**rifle** [rifle] *s.* arma de barril estriado que hace que la bala vaya girando por el aire. (p. 491)

**robber baron** [capitalista inescrupuloso] *s.* líder industrial que se hizo acaudalado usando medios deshonestos. (p. 594)

**rock 'n' roll** *s.* tipo de música popular caracterizada por ritmos pesados y melodías simples que se desarrolló del rhythm and blues en los años cincuenta. (p. 803)

**romanticism** [romanticismo] *s.* movimiento artístico europeo que acentuaba al individuo, la imaginación, la creatividad y la emoción. (p. 429)

**Roosevelt Corollary** [Corolario de Roosevelt] *s.* la adición en 1904 a la Doctrina Monroe permitiendo a los Estados Unidos a actuar de "policía" en Latinoamérica. (p. 672)

**Rosie the Riveter** [Rosita la Remachadora] *s.* imagen de una mujer fuerte trabajando duro en una fábrica de armas durante la segunda guerra mundial. (p. 773)

**Rough Rider** *s.* miembro del Primer Regimiento Estadounidense de Voluntarios de Caballería que organizó Theodore Roosevelt y que luchó en la guerra entre España y Estados Unidos. (p. 665)

**royal colony** [colonia real] *s.* colonia regida por gobernadores nombrados por un rey. (p. 103)

## S

**salutary neglect** [indiferencia beneficiosa] *s.* política de no interferir Inglaterra en los asuntos de sus colonias norteamericanas durante la primera mitad del siglo XVIII. (p. 144)

**SALT** *s.* Tratado sobre Limitación de Armas Estratégicas firmado en 1972 entre Estados Unidos y la Unión Soviética; limitaba las armas nucleares. (p. 858)

**Sand Creek Massacre** [masacre de Sand Creek] *s.* un ataque en 1864, en el que más de 150 hombres, mujeres y niños del pueblo cheyene murieron a manos de la milicia de Colorado. (p. 564)

**Santa Fe Trail** [Camino de Santa Fe] *s.* camino hacia el oeste que iba de Missouri a Santa Fe, New Mexico. (p. 395)

**SCLC** *s.* Conferencia de Líderes Cristianos del Sur, grupo que coordinó por todo el sur las protestas para promover los derechos civiles. (p. 815)

**secede** [separarse] *v.* retirarse. (p. 473)

**secession** [secesión] *s.* separarse como parte de Estados Unidos. (p. 383)

**Second Battle of the Marne** [segunda batalla del Marne] *s.* en 1918 esta batalla de la primera guerra mundial marcó el cambio decisivo en el curso de la guerra; las tropas aliadas junto con las estadounidenses detuvieron el avance alemán hacia el interior de Francia. (p. 689)

**Second Continental Congress** [segundo Congreso Continental] *s.* organismo de gobierno cuyos delegados acordaron en mayo de 1775 organizar el Ejército Continental y aprobar la Declaración de Independencia. (p. 177)

**Second Great Awakening** [segundo Gran Despertar] *s.* renovación de la fe religiosa durante fines del siglo XVIII y comienzos del XIX. (p. 433)

**Second New Deal** [segundo Nuevo Trato] *s.* conjunto de programas que se pasaron en 1935 para luchar contra la depresión. (p. 736)

**sectionalism** [seccionalismo] *s.* colocar los intereses de la región propia por encima de los de la nación como unidad. (p. 357)

**Securities and Exchange Commission** *s.* [Comisión de Valores y Bolsa] *s.* agencia que vigila la bolsa de valores y hace que las empresas sigan procedimientos honestos en la venta de acciones. (p. 748)

**Sedition Act** [ley de Sedición] *s.* ley aprobada en 1918 que hacía ilegal la crítica de la guerra. Imponía fuertes multas y largos períodos de encarcelamiento para los que participaran en actividades contra la guerra. (p. 692)

**segregation** [segregación] *s.* separación. (p. 621)

**Seneca Falls Convention** [convención de Seneca Falls] *s.* convención sobre los derechos de la mujer llevada a cabo en Seneca Falls, New York, en 1848. (p. 444)

**separation of powers** [separación de poderes] *s.* división de las funciones básicas del gobierno en tres ramas. (p. 246)

**service economy** [economía de servicios] *s.* economía en que la mayoría de los empleos suministran servicios en lugar de producir mercancías. (p. 879)

**servitude** [servitud] *s.* práctica de pertenecer a un dueño o amo. (p. 270)

**Seven Days' Battles** [batallas de los Siete Días] *s.* batalla de 1862 de la guerra civil en que la Confederación forzó a la Unión a retroceder después de un intento fracasado de capturar la capital sureña de Richmond. (p. 496)

**Seventeenth Amendment** [Enmienda Decimoséptima] *s.* enmienda a la Constitución estadounidense, ratificada en 1913, que autorizaba la elección directa de los senadores estadounidenses por el electorado de cada estado. (p. 648)

**sharecropping** [aparcería] *s.* sistema en que los terratenientes daban a los agricultores tierra, semilla y herramientas a cambio de parte de la cosecha. (p. 543)

**Shays's Rebellion** [revuelta de Shay] *s.* sublevación de granjeros adeudados de Massachusetts en 1787. (p. 225)

**Sherman Antitrust Act** [ley Antitrust Sherman] *s.* ley aprobada en 1890 que declaró ilegal que las corporaciones obtuvieran control de las industrias formandos trusts. (p. 641)

**Siege of Vicksburg** [sitio de Vicksburg] *s.* victoria unionista de 1863, durante la guerra civil que le permitió a la Unión controlar todo el río Misisipí. (p. 516)

**sit-down strike** *s.* [huelga de brazos caídos] huelga en que los obreros permanecen dentro de la fábrica pero se niegan a trabajar. (p. 743)

**Sixteenth Amendment** [Enmienda Decimosexta] *s.* enmienda a la Constitución de Estados Unidos, ratificada en 1913, que dio al Congreso el poder de crear impuestos a las rentas. (p. 647)

**slash-and-burn agriculture** [agricultura de corte y quema] *s.* método agrícola en que la gente preparaba los campos cortando y quemando árboles y pastos, cuyas cenizas fertilizaban la tierra. (p. 37)

**slave code** [código de los esclavos] *s.* ley pasada para reglamentar el tratamiento de los esclavos. (p. 79)

**slavery** [esclavitud] *s.* sistema de servidumbre humana involuntaria. (p. 76)

**slum** [barrio bajo] *s.* barrio de casas abarrotadas de gente y peligrosas. (p. 612)

**smuggle** [contrabandear] *v.* importar o exportar mercancías ilegalmente. (p. 112)

**SNCC** *s.* organizado en 1960, el Comité Coordinador No Violento de Estudiantes se creó para dar a los jóvenes un papel más importante en el movimiento por los derechos civiles. (p. 817)

**social gospel** [evangelio social] *s.* movimiento cuyo objetivo era mejorar la vida de los pobres. (p. 612)

**socialism** [socialismo] *s.* sistema económico en que todos los miembros de una sociedad son propietarios por igual de todas las empresas; los miembros comparten el trabajo y las ganancias (p. 602)

**Social Security Act** [ley de Seguridad Social] *s.* según esta ley aprobada en 1935, los empleados y los empresarios hacían pagos a un fondo especial, del cual podían recibir una jubilación después de retirarse. (p. 736)

**sodbuster** *s.* granjero de la frontera. (p. 575)

**Songhai** *s.* imperio de África Occidental que sucedió a Malí y controló el comercio desde el siglo XV hasta fines del XVI. (p. 42)

**Sons of Liberty** [Hijos de la Libertad] *s.* grupo de colonos que formaron una sociedad secreta para oponerse a las políticas británicas en los tiempos de la revolución norteamericana. (p. 161)

**space race** [carrera para conquistar el espacio] *s.* empezando en 1957, la Unión Soviética y Estados Unidos comenzaron a competir en la exploración del espacio. (p. 799)

**Spanish-American War** *s.* guerra de 1898 que comenzó cuando Estados Unidos demandó que España le concediera la independencia a Cuba. (p. 664)

**Spanish Armada** [Armada española] *s.* flota de buques enviada en 1588 por el rey español Felipe Segundo para invadir a Inglaterra y restaurar allí el catolicismo romano. (p. 69)

**speculation** [especulación] *s.* comprar y vender acciones con la esperanza de obtener una ganancia rápida. (p. 730)

**sphere of influence** [esfera de influencia] *s.* región donde las naciones extranjeras demandan derechos especiales y privilegios económicos. (p. 669)

**spiritual** [canción espiritual] *s.* canción folklórica religiosa. (p. 351)

**spoils system** [sistema de prebendas] *s.* práctica de otorgar los candidatos elegidos empleos gubernamentales a los simpatizantes políticos. (p. 373)

**Stamp Act** [ley del Timbre] *s.* ley aprobada por el Parlamento en 1765 que requería que todos los documentos comerciales y legales llevaran un timbre oficial que indicaba que se había pagado un impuesto. (p. 160)

**standard time** [hora oficial] *s.* sistema adoptado en 1918 que dividió a Estados Unidos en cuatro zonas horarias. (p. 592)

**states' rights** [derechos estatales] *s.* teoría que sostenía que los estados tenían el derecho a decidir cuándo el gobierno federal había pasado una ley inconstitucional. (p. 307)

**steerage** [tercera clase] *s.* nivel o lugar más barato de un barco. (p. 423)

**Stono Rebellion** [Rebelión de Stono] *s.* sublevación de esclavos de 1739, en Carolina del Sur, que resultó en que se hicieran aún más estrictas las leyes que controlaban a los esclavos. (p. 123)

**strategy** [estrategia] *s.* plan general de acción. (p. 196)

**strike** [declararse en huelga] *v.* suspender los obreros el trabajo para tratar de conseguir condiciones de trabajo mejores. (p. 434)

**subsistence farm** *v.* una granja que produce bastante alimento para la familia con sólo una pequeña cantidad para vender. (p. 110)

**suburb** [barrio residencial] *s.* área residencial que rodea a una ciudad. (p. 800)

**suffrage** [sufragio] *s.* derecho a votar. (pp. 262, 444)

**Sugar Act** [ley del Azúcar] *s.* ley aprobada por el Parlamento en 1764 que impuso impuestos al azúcar, la melaza y otros productos que llegaban a las colonias; también establecía severos castigos para los contrabandistas. (p. 160)

**sunbelt** *s.* estados más cálidos del sur y el suroeste. (p. 801)

**supply-side economics** [economía de la oferta] *s.* idea de que si se reducen los impuestos aumenta el número de empleos así como los ahorros y las inversiones, todo lo cual hace que aumenten las entradas del gobierno. (p. 873)

**sweatshop** *s.* lugar donde los obreros trabajaban largas horas en condiciones muy malas por salarios muy bajos. (p. 600)

## T

**Tammany Hall** *s.* famosa maquinaria política de la ciudad de Nueva York de fines del siglo XIX. (p. 613)

**tariff** [arance aduanero] *s.* impuesto a las mercancías importadas. (p. 296)

**Tariff of Abominations** [arancel de las Abominaciones] *s.* ley de 1828 que subió los aranceles de las materias primas y las manufacturas; alteró a los sureños, quienes sentían que la política económica nacional la estaban determinando los intereses económicos del noreste. (p. 381)

**Teapot Dome Scandal** [escándalo de Teapot Dome] *s.* episodio causado por el ministro del Interior Albert B. Fall quien arrendó ricas reservas públicas de petróleo a compañías privadas a cambio de dinero y tierras. (p. 710)

**technology** [tecnología] *s.* uso de herramientas y conocimiento para satisfacer las necesidades humanas. (p. 32)

***Tejano*** [tejano] *s.* persona de ascendencia española que consideraba a Texas su hogar. (p. 400)

**temperance movement** [movimiento de la templanza] *s.* campaña para acabar con el consumo de las bebidas alcohólicas. (p. 434)

**tender** *s.* dinero (p. 255)

**tenement** [casa de vecindad] *s.* edificio de apartamentos generalmente en muy malas condiciones y atestado. (p. 611)

**Tet offensive** [ofensiva del Tet] *s.* en 1968, ataque sorpresa por las tropas del Vietcong contra las bases militares estadounidenses y más de 100 ciudades y pueblos de Vietnam del Sur durante el Tet, la celebración del año nuevo lunar vietnamita. (p. 844)

**Thirteenth Amendment** [Enmienda Decimotercera] *s.* enmienda a la Constitución de Estados Unidos adoptada en 1865 que abolía la esclavitud y la servidumbre involuntaria en Estados Unidos. (p. 521)

**38th parallel** *s.* la región al norte de esta latitud ocupada por las tropas soviéticas en 1945. (p. 795)

**Three-Fifths Compromise** [Acuerdo de los Tres Quintos] *s.* acuerdo de la Convención Constitucional que establecía que, para efectos de la representación y del cobro de impuestos, se contarían como parte de la población tres quintos de los esclavos de un estado. (p. 232)

**Townshend Acts** [leyes de Townshend] *s.* serie de leyes aprobadas por el Parlamento en 1767 que suspendieron la Asamblea de Nueva York y establecieron impuestos a las mercancías importadas a las colonias británicas. (p. 163)

**Trail of Tears** [Sendero de las Lágrimas] *s.* trágica marcha del pueblo cherokee desde sus tierras hasta el Territorio Indio, entre 1838 y 1839; miles de cherokees murieron. (p. 377)

**transcendentalism** [trascendentalismo] *s.* filosofía del siglo XIX que enseñaba que el mundo espiritual es más importante que el mundo físico y que las personas pueden hallar la verdad dentro de sí mismas mediante los sentimientos y la intuición. (p. 431)

**transcontinental railroad** [ferrocarril transcontinental] *s.* ferrocarril que se extendía por todo el continente. (p. 590)

**Treaty of Ghent** [Tratado de Gante] *s.* tratado firmado en 1814 que puso fin a la guerra de 1812; no cambió de dueño ningún territorio ni se resolvieron los conflictos comerciales. (p. 333)

**Treaty of Greenville** [Tratado de Greenville] *s.* acuerdo de 1795 por el cual 12 tribus amerindias cedieron al gobierno de Estados Unidos gran parte de lo que hoy son los estados de Ohio e Indiana. (p. 300)

**Treaty of Guadalupe Hidalgo** [Tratado de Guadalupe Hidalgo] *s.* tratado de 1848 que puso fin a la guerra estadounidense con México; México cedió California y Nuevo México a los Estados Unidos. (p. 410)

**Treaty of Paris** [Tratado de París] *s.* tratado de 1763 que puso fin a la guerra Francesa y Amerindia; Inglaterra entregó toda norteamérica del este del río Mississippi. (p. 150)

**Treaty of Paris of 1783** [Tratado de París de 1783] *s.* tratado que puso fin a la guerra Revolucionaria, confirmó la independencia de Estados Unidos y estableció los límites de la nueva nación. (p. 212)

**Treaty of Tordesillas** [Tratado de Tordesillas] *s.* tratado de 1494 por el cual España y Portugal acordaron repartirse las tierras del hemisferio occidental y movieron la línea de demarcación hacia el oeste. (p. 61)

**Treaty of Versailles** [Tratado de Versailles] *s.* tratado de 1919 que puso fin a la primera guerra mundial. (p. 696)

**trench warfare** [guerra de trincheras] *s.* clase de guerra durante la primera guerra mundial en que los combatientes se apiñaban en zanjas fortificadas y se disparaban artillería y fuego de ametralladora. (p. 680)

**triangular trade** [comercio triangular] *s.* sistema de comercio transatlántico en que se intercambiaban mercancías, incluso esclavos, entre África, Inglaterra, Europa, las Antillas y las colonias de Norte América. (p. 111)

**tribunal** [tribunal] *s.* corte. (p. 253)

**Truman Doctrine** [Doctrina Truman] *s.* política que prometía ayuda a la gente que luchaba por resistir las amenazas a la libertad democrática. (p. 793)

**trust** *s.* cuerpo legal creado para tener una cartera de acciones de varias empresas, con frecuencia en la misma industria. (p. 595)

**tundra** [tundra] *s.* pradera sin árboles que está permanentemente helada debajo de su capa de superior de tierra. (p. 33)

**Twenty-sixth Amendment** [Enmienda Vigésima Sexta] *s.* enmienda a la Constitución de Estados Unidos, adoptada en 1971, redujo la edad del derecho a votar de los 21 a los 18 años. (p. 849)

## U

**unanimous consent** [consentimiento unánime] *s.* acuerdo completo. (p. 264)

***Uncle Tom's Cabin*** [*La cabaña del tío Tom*] *s.* novela publicada por Harriet Beecher Stowe en 1852, que mostraba la esclavitud como brutal e inmoral. (p. 462)

**unconstitutional** [inconstitucional] *adj.* que contradice la ley de la constitución. (p. 317)

**Underground Railroad** [ferrocarril clandestino] *s.* serie de rutas de escape que usaban los esclavos para escaparse del Sur. (p. 442)

**United Nations** [Naciones Unidas] *s.* organización internacional para mantener la paz a la que pertenecen la mayoría de las naciones del mundo, creada en 1945 para promover la paz, seguridad y desarrollo económico del mundo. (p. 781)

**urbanization** [urbanización] *s.* crecimiento de las ciudades como resultado de la industrialización. (p. 609)

**U.S.S. *Maine*** *s.* barco de guerra estadounidense que explotó misteriosamente y se hundió en el puerto de La Habana, Cuba, el 15 de febrero de 1898. (p. 663)

## V

***vaquero*** [vaquero] *s.* peón de ganado que vino de México con los españoles en el siglo XVI. (p. 560)

**vaudeville** [vodevil] *s.* tipo de espectáculo teatral en vivo con mezcla de canciones, baile y comedia. (p. 629)

**viceroyalty** [virreinato] *s.* provincia regida por un virrey, que gobernaba en nombre del rey. (p. 71)

**Viet Cong** *s.* comunista vietnamita. (p. 838)

**Vietnamization** [vietnamización] *s.* estrategia de la guerra de Vietnam de retirar las fuerzas estadounidenses gradualmente y dejar la lucha terrestre en manos de los vietnamitas del Sur. (p. 848)

**vigilante** [vigilante] *s.* persona dispuesta a tomar la ley en sus propias manos. (p. 561)

**Virginia Plan** *s.* plan presentado por Edmund Randolph, delegado a la Convención Constitucional de 1787, que proponía un gobierno de tres ramas y una legislatura bicameral en la que la representación se basaría en la población o la riqueza de un estado. (p. 231)

**Voting Rights Act of 1965** [ley de los Derechos al Voto] *s.* esta ley prohibía las pruebas de lectura y escritura y otras leyes que impedían que los afroamericanos se anotaran para votar. (p. 821)

## W

**war bond** [bono de guerra] *s.* préstamo de interés bajo de la población civil al gobierno, que se pagaría dentro de un número de años. (p. 691)

**War Hawk** *s.* habitante de las regiones del oeste que apoyaba la guerra de 1812. (p. 329)

**War Powers Act** [ley de Poderes de Guerra] *s.* aprobada en 1973, esta ley limita los poderes del presidente para declarar la guerra sin consultar el Congreso. (p. 849)

**War Production Board** [Junta de Producción Bélica] *s.* agencia establecida durante la segunda guerra mundial para coordinar la producción de suministros militares por las empresas estadounidenses. (p. 772)

**Watergate scandal** [escándalo de Watergate] *s.* escándalo que resultó de los esfuerzos del gobierno de Nixon por encubrir su participación en el allanamiento de la Sede Central del Partido Demócrata en el edificio de apartamentos Watergate. (p. 860)

**Webster-Hayne debate** [debate Webster-Hayne] *s.* debate de 1830 entre Daniel Webster y Robert Hayne sobre la doctrina de la invalidación. (p. 382)

**Whig Party** [Partido Whig] *s.* partido político organizado en 1834 en oposición a las políticas de Andrew Jackson. (p. 387)

**Whiskey Rebellion** [rebelión del Whisky] *s.* protesta de 1794 contra el impuesto que impuso el gobierno al whisky, valioso medio económico de los granjeros de la frontera. (p. 301)

**Wilderness Road** [Camino al Desierto] *s.* sendero a Kentucky que ayudó a construir el pionero Daniel Boone. (p. 221)

**Wilmot Proviso** [Claúsula de Wilmot] *s.* propuesta de 1846 que excluía la esclavitud de cualquier territorio adquirido como resultado de la guerra con México. (p. 459)

**Wounded Knee Massacre** [masacre de Wounded Knee] *s.* masacre de 1890 por soldados estadounidenses de 300 amerindios desarmados, en Wounded Knee Creek, Dakota del Sur. (p. 566)

**writ of assistance** [mandato judicial de transferencia] *s.* orden de registro que permitía a los oficiales británicos entrar en los hogares o comercios coloniales en busca de contrabando. (p. 164)

## X

**XYZ Affair** [asunto XYZ] *s.* incidente de 1797 en que funcionarios franceses demandaron que los diplomáticos estadounidenses les pagaran un soborno. (p. 306)

## Y

**Y2K** [año 2000] *s.* problema de computadora causado por programas de computadoras que usan sólo los dos últimos dígitos de un año; complicado por la llegada del año 2000. (p. 878)

**Yalta Conference** [Conferencia de Yalta] *s.* en 1945 Franklin Roosevelt, Winston Churchill y Joseph Stalin discutieron planes para el fin de la segunda guerra mundial y el futuro de Europa. (p. 765)

**yellow journalism** [periodismo amarillo] *s.* estilo de periodismo que usa la exageración y el sensacionalismo para presentar las noticias. (p. 663)

**Yoruba** [Yoruba] *s.* gente de África Occidental que constituyó varios estados al sudoeste del río Níger. (p. 42)

## Z

**Zimmermann telegram** [telegrama de Zimmerman] *s.* mensaje enviado en 1917 por el ministro de Relaciones Exteriores alemán al embajador alemán en México proponiendo una alianza entre México y Alemania y prometiendo ayudar a México a recuperar Texas, New Mexico y Arizona si Estados Unidos entraba en la guerra. (p. 682)

An *i* preceding a page reference in italics indicates that there is an illustration, and usually text information as well, on that page. An *m* or a *c* preceding an italic page reference indicates a map or a chart, as well as text information on that page.

## A





R73

## B

## C





R75

## D





R77

## E

# F





R79

## G

## H





R81

# I

## J



## K





R83

R85

## N





R86

R87

# O



# P

# Q





R89

# R

S





**R91**

## T





R93

## U



## V

R95

## X



## Y



## Z

# ACKNOWLEDGMENTS

## TEXT ACKNOWLEDGMENTS

**Chapter 1,** page 28: map, "New Paths to the Americas," *U.S. News & World Report,* October 12, 1998, page 62. Copyright © October 12, 1998, U.S. News and World Report. Visit us at our Web site at www.usnews.com for additional information. Adapted by permission of U.S. News & World Report.

page 33: Excerpt from "Navajo Blessing Way," from *Language and Art in the Navajo Universe* by Gary Witherspoon, page 26 (Ann Arbor: The University of Michigan Press, 1977). Reprinted by permission of The University of Michigan Press.

**Chapter 6,** pages 174–175: Excerpt from *Johnny Tremain* by Esther Forbes. Copyright © 1943 by Esther Forbes Hoskins, copyright renewed by Linwood M. Erskine, Jr., executor of the Estate of Esther Forbes Hoskins. Reprinted by permission of Houghton Mifflin Company. All rights reserved.

**Chapter 9,** page 300: "Obeying Rules and Laws," from *Government in America* by Richard J. Hardy. Copyright © 1995 by Houghton Mifflin Company. All rights reserved. Reprinted by permission.

**Chapter 16,** pages 486–487: Excerpt from *Across Five Aprils* by Irene Hunt. Copyright © 1964 by Irene Hunt. All rights reserved. Reprinted by permission of Shirley Beem on behalf of the author.

**Chapter 17,** pages 508, 509, 510, 512, 513, 516, 518, 519: Excerpts from *The Civil War* by Kenneth Burns, Ric Burns, and Geoffrey Ward. Copyright © 1990 by American Documentaries, Inc. Reprinted by permission of Alfred A. Knopf, a division of Random House, Inc.

**Chapter 19,** page 562: Excerpt from "Wahenee: An Indian Girl's Story Told by Herself to Gilbert L. Wilson," *North Dakota History,* Vol. 38, Nos. 1 & 2. Copyright © 1971 State Historical Society of North Dakota. Used by permission.

**Chapter 21,** pages 618–619: Excerpt from *Dragonwings* by Laurence Yep. Copyright © 1975 by Laurence Yep. Used by permission of HarperCollins Publishers.

pages 624–625: Excerpt from *Crusade for Justice: The Autobiography of Ida B. Wells,* edited by Alfreda M. Duster. Copyright © 1970 by The University of Chicago. All rights reserved. Reprinted by permission of The University of Chicago Press.

**Chapter 25,** page 713: "First Fig" by Edna St. Vincent Millay, from *Collected Poems,* HarperCollins Publishers. Copyright 1922, 1950 by Edna St. Vincent Millay. All rights reserved. Reprinted by permission of Elizabeth Barnett, literary executor.

page 725: "I, Too," from *Collected Poems* by Langston Hughes. Copyright © 1994 by the Estate of Langston Hughes. Reprinted by permission of Alfred A. Knopf, a division of Random House, Inc.

**Chapter 26,** page 744–745: Excerpt from *Roll of Thunder, Hear My Cry* by Mildred D. Taylor. Copyright © 1976 by Mildred D. Taylor. Used by permission of Dial Books for Young Readers, a division of Penguin Putnam Inc.

**Chapter 27,** page 767: Excerpt from *Night* by Elie Wiesel, translated by Stella Rodway. Copyright © 1960 by MacGibbon & Kee. Copyright renewed 1988 by The Collins Publishing Group. Reprinted by permission of Hill and Wang, a division of Farrar, Straus & Giroux, Inc.

**Chapter 28,** page 800: Excerpt from "Remembering LaVern Baker, a strong-willed R&B original" by Steve Jones, *USA Today,* March 12, 1997. Copyright © 1997 USA Today. Reprinted with permission.

**Chapter 29,** page 815: Excerpt from *Stride Toward Freedom: The Montgomery Story* by Martin Luther King, Jr. Copyright © 1958 by Martin Luther King, Jr., copyright renewed 1986 by Coretta Scott King. Reprinted by arrangement with The Heirs to the Estate of Martin Luther King, Jr., c/o Writers House, Inc., as agent for the proprietor.

page 819: Excerpt from "Letter from the Birmingham Jail" by Martin Luther King, Jr. Copyright © 1963 by Martin Luther King, Jr., copyright renewed 1991 by Coretta Scott King. Reprinted by arrangement with The Heirs to the Estate of Martin Luther King, Jr., c/o Writers House, Inc., as agent for the proprietor.

pages 820, 828: Excerpts from "I Have a Dream" by Martin Luther King, Jr. Copyright © 1963 by Martin Luther King, Jr., copyright renewed 1991 by Coretta Scott King. Reprinted by arrangement with The Heirs to the Estate of Martin Luther King, Jr., c/o Writers House, Inc., as agent for the proprietor.

Copyright © César E. Chávez Foundation. Reprinted by permission of the César E. Chávez Foundation.

**Chapter 32,** page 873: Excerpt from "Election no surprise to ordinary folk" by Anne Keegan, *Chicago Tribune,* November 6, 1980. Copyright © 1980 by the Chicago Tribune Company. All rights reserved. Used with permission.

page 883: Excerpt from "Dominican Dominion" by Maximo Zeledon, *Frontera Magazine,* Issue 5. Reprinted by permission of Frontera Magazine.

McDougal Littell Inc. has made every effort to locate the copyright holders for selections used in this book and to make full acknowledgment for their use. Omissions brought to our attention will be corrected in a subsequent edition.

## ART CREDITS

### Cover and Frontispiece

*cover background* Copyright © Bob Gelberg/SharpShooters.
*frontispiece background* The Granger Collection, New York.
**Amelia Earhart:** Copyright © Albert L. Bresnik.
**Maya Lin:** Copyright © 1999 Richard Howard/Black Star.
**Juan Seguín:** Detail of *Juan Seguin* (1838), Jefferson Wright. Texas State Library and Archives Commission.
**Harry S. Truman:** White House Collection. Copyright © White House Historical Association. Courtesy of the Harry S. Truman Library.
**Ida Bell Wells:** The Granger Collection, New York.
**Abigail Adams:** *Portrait traditionally said to be Abigail Adams* (about 1795), artist unknown. Oil on canvas, 30 1/4" x 26 1/2", N-150.55. Photo by Richard Walker. Copyright © New York State Historical Association, Cooperstown, New York.
**Zitkala-Să:** Negative no. Mss 299, William F. Hansen Collection, Photographic Archives, Harold B. Lee Library, Brigham Young University, Provo, Utah.
**Benjamin Franklin:** Copyright © Joseph-Siffrede Duplessis/Wood River Gallery/PNI.
**Abraham Lincoln:** The Library of Congress.
**Martin Luther King, Jr:** Photo by Howard Sochrer/Life Magazine, copyright © Time Inc.

### Table of Contents

**viii–xvii** *background* The Granger Collection, New York; **viii** *top* Benin *Horn-Blower* (about 1550–1680) unknown African artist. Nigeria, Court of Benin, Bini Tribe. Bronze, 24 7/8" x 11 5/8" x 6 3/4" (63 cm x 29.4 cm x 17.2 cm). The Metropolitan Museum of Art, The Michael C. Rockefeller Memorial Collection, gift of Nelson A. Rockefeller, 1972 (1978.412.310). Photograph copyright © 1983 The Metropolitan Museum of Art; *bottom* The Granger Collection, New York; **ix** *top* Copyright © Michael Gadomski/Photo Researchers, Inc.; *center* The Granger Collection, New York; *bottom* Library of Congress; **x** *top* Copyright © R. Kord/H. Armstrong Roberts; *center* Detail of *George Washington in the Uniform of a British Colonial Colonel* (1772), Charles Willson Peale. Washington-Custis-Lee Collection. Washington and Lee University, Lexington, Virginia; *bottom* Corbis; **xi** *top* Copyright © 1998 North Wind Pictures; *center* National Museum of American History, Smithsonian Institution; *bottom* Illustration by Patrick Whelan; **xii** *top* From the collections of the Minnesota Historical Society; *bottom left* The Granger Collection, New York; *bottom right* Copyright © 1998 Louis Psihoyos/Matrix; **xiii** *top* Copyright © George Peter Alexandre Healy/Wood River Gallery/PNI; *center* Courtesy of Stamatelos Brothers Collection. Photo by Larry Sherer. Copyright © 1991 Time-Life Books Inc.; *bottom* The Granger Collection, New York; **xiv** *top, Northern Pacific Railroad. The Pioneer Route to Fargo Moorhead Town Bismark Dakota and Montana and the Famous Valley of the Yellowstone* (about 1885), Creator–Poole Brothers, Printers. Broadside. Chicago Historical Society; *bottom* The Granger Collection, New York; **xv** *top* Doubleday, Page and Company, New York, 1906, second issue; *center, Portrait of Queen Liliuokalani,* date and artist unknown. Bishop Museum; *bottom left* The Granger Collection, New York; *bottom right* Culver Pictures; **xvi** *top* Copyright © Stock Montage; *center* The Granger Collection, New York; *bottom* Copyright © Rob Boudreau/Tony Stone Images; **xvii** *top* Corbis-Bettmann; *center* NASA; *bottom* Copyright © Charles Feil/Stock Boston/PNI.

### Geography Handbook

**2** *top right* Copyright © H. Abernathy/H. Armstrong Roberts; *center left* Copyright © Warren Morgan/H. Armstrong Roberts; *bottom* Copyright © 1996 Denver A. Bryan; **3** *top* Copyright © Nathan Benn/Stock Boston; *bottom right* Copyright © Andy Sacks/Tony Stone Images; **4–5** The Granger Collection, New York;

**4** *top* Copyright © 1997 David Noble/FPG International; **5** *top* Copyright © John Coletti/Stock Boston; *center* Copyright © Bill Horsman/Stock Boston; **6** *top* Copyright © George Mobley/NGS Image Collection; *center* Copyright © Lowell Georgia/NGS Image Collection; *bottom left* The Granger Collection, New York; **10** *top* Copyright © T. Algire/H. Armstrong Roberts; *bottom* Copyright © Ken Graham/Tony Stone Images; **11** *top* Copyright © SuperStock; *bottom* Copyright © Tom Dietrich/Tony Stone Images; **12** *top* Copyright © Zane Williams/Tony Stone Images; *bottom* Copyright © Eastcott/Momatiuk/Tony Stone Images; **13** *top* Copyright © SuperStock; *bottom* Copyright © F. Sieb/H. Armstrong Roberts; **14–15** Illustration by Ken Goldammer; **16** *top* Copyright © M. Schneiders/H. Armstrong Roberts; *bottom* Copyright © D. Frazier/H. Armstrong Roberts; **17** *top left* Copyright © Ron Levy/Liaison Agency; *top right, center right, bottom right* Copyright © Steve Adams/NGS Image Collection; *bottom left* Copyright © Cathlyn Melloan/Tony Stone Images; **18** *bottom* Copyright © J. Marshall/The Image Works; **19** *left* Culver Pictures; *right* Copyright © Santi Visalli/The Image Bank.

## Unit 1

**22–23** Copyright © R. Kord/H. Armstrong Roberts.

**Chapter 1, 24, 25** The Granger Collection, New York; **26** *top* Werner Forman/Art Resource, New York; *center* Copyright © Aldona Sabalis/Photo Researchers, Inc.; *bottom* Copyright © Stuart Dee/The Image Bank; **27** Courtesy of Rock Art Foundation, San Antonio, Texas; **28** *center left* Courtesy Arizona State Museum, University of Arizona, Tucson, Arizona. Photo copyright © 1996 Jerry Jacka; **29** Copyright © Francois Gohier/Photo Researchers, Inc.; **30** Copyright © SuperStock; **32** *background* Photo of Bill Reid by R. Bettner. Collection Canadian Museum of Civilization, #K96-215 [or K96-216]. Reprinted with permission of Ms. Martine Reid; *foreground* Bear sculpture (1962), Bill Reid. 248 cm x 136 cm x 126 cm, U.B.C. Gift of Dr. Walter Koerner. Courtesy U.B.C. Museum of Anthropology, Vancouver, Canada; **34** National Museum of Anthropology, Mexico City, Mexico/Werner Forman Archive/Art Resource, New York; **35** Smithsonian Institution, Washington, D.C.; **36** *background* Copyright © Richard Saker/AllSport; *bottom left* Copyright © Salamander Picture Library; **39** Copyright © Thomas D. W. Friedmann/Photo Researchers, Inc.; **40** *left* Copyright © Aldona Sabalis/Photo Researchers, Inc.; **41** The Granger Collection, New York; **42** PNI; **43** The Metropolitan Museum of Art, The Michael C. Rockefeller Memorial Collection, gift of Nelson A. Rockefeller, 1972 (1978.412.310). Photograph copyright © 1983 The Metropolitan Museum of Art; **44** Copyright © Stock Montage; **45** Illustration by Alexander Verbitsky; **47** *The School of Athens* (1508), Raphael (Raffaello Santi). Stanza della Segnatura, Vatican City, Vatican. Photo copyright © Erich Lessing/Art Resource, New York; **49** Detail of *St. Vincent Polyptych* (date unknown), Nuno Gonçalves. Museu Nacional de Arte Antiga, Lisbon, Portugal. Copyright © Scala/Art Resource, New York; **50** *Portrait of a Man, Called Christopher Columbus* (1519), Sebastiano del Piombo. Oil on canvas, 42" x 34 3/4". The Metropolitan Museum of Art, gift of J. Pierpont Morgan, 1900; **52** Archivio Fotografico del Museo Preistorico Etnografico L. Pigorini, Rome. Photo by Lorenzo de Masi; **53** By courtesy of the Bibliothèque Nationale, Paris; **55** *bottom* Courtesy of John Goss; **56** Copyright © Francois Gohier/Photo Researchers, Inc.; **57** Photos by Sharon Hoogstraten.

**Chapter 2, 58, 59** The Granger Collection, New York; **61** Detail of *Pope Alexander VI Borgia Kneeling in Prayer* (date unknown), Bernardino Pinturicchio. Sala die Misteri della Fede, Appartamento Borgia, Vatican Palace, Vatican State/Scala/Art Resource, New York; **64** Corbis; **65** Aztec mask (early 16th century), artist unknown. Turquoise, pearl shell. Werner Forman Archive/British Museum, London/Art Resource, New York; **66** The Granger Collection, New York; **67** *top, The Last Voyage of Henry Hudson* (1881), John Collier. Tate Gallery, London/Art Resource, New York; **68** PNI; **69** *Sea Battle between the Spanish Armada and English Naval Forces* (about 1600), Hendrik Corneliez Vroom. Oil on canvas, 91 cm x 153 cm. Landesmuseum Ferdinandeum, Innsbruck, Austria. Photo copyright © Erich Lessing/Art Resource, New York; **71** The Granger Collection, New York; **73** The British Library; **75** PNI; **76** Copyright © The Fotomas Index; **77** Corbis; **78** *left* The Newberry Library, Chicago; *right, Slaves Below Deck of Albanez* (date unknown), Francis Meynell. Copyright © National Maritime Museum Picture Library, London.

**Chapter 3, 82** The Granger Collection, New York; **83** Colonial Williamsburg Foundation; **85** British Museum; **87** AP/Wide World Photos; **88** *Pocahontas* (1616), Simon van de Passe. Engraving, 6 7/8" x 4 3/4" (17.5 cm x 12 cm). Published in the *Baziliologia*, London, 1618. National Portrait Gallery, Smithsonian Institution/Art Resource, New York; **89** The Granger Collection, New York; **90–91** Illustration by Ivan Lapper. Copyright © The Reader's Digest Association; **92** The Granger Collection, New York; **93** *The Mayflower in Plymouth Harbor* (1882), William Halsall. Courtesy of the Pilgrim Society, Plymouth, Massachusetts; **94** *top* Copyright © SuperStock; *bottom* Copyright © Andrew J. Martinez/Photo Researchers, Inc.; **95** *bottom* The Granger Collection, New York; **96** *left* Courtesy of American Antiquarian Society; *right* The New York Public Library; **97** *Trial of George Jacobs for Witchcraft, 1692* (1855), T. H. Matteson. Oil on canvas, acc. #1246. Peabody Essex Museum, Salem, Massachusetts. Photo by Mark Sexton; **100** Detail of *Peter Stuyvesant and the Trumpeter (The Wrath of Peter Stuyvesant)* (1835), Asher B. Durand. Oil on canvas, 24 1/4" x 30 1/4", accession no. 1858.28. Copyright © Collection of The New-York Historical Society; **101** Copyright © Tom Dietrich/Tony Stone Images; **103** Brown Brothers; **105** Colonial Williamsburg Foundation.

**Chapter 4, 106, 107** The Granger Collection, New York; **109** *Sperm Whaling: No. 2, The Capture* (1862), A. Van Best and R. S. Gifford. Lithograph by Endicott and Company, corrected by Benjamin Russell, 16 3/4 x 25 3/4" (43 cm x 65 cm). N.M.A.H., Harry Peters "America on Stone" Lithography Collection; **110** *right* Copyright © Thomas Neill; **112** North Carolina Collection, University of North Carolina Library at Chapel Hill; **114** Detail of *Quaker Meeting* (date unknown), Egbert Van Heemskerk. The Quaker Collection, Haverford (Pennsylvania) College Library; **115** *right* Reprinted with permission of Philipsburg Manor, Tarrytown, New York; **116** The Granger Collection, New York; **118** Library of Congress; **119** Detail of *George Mason* (1811), Dominic W. Boudet. Oil on canvas, 30" x 25" (76.2 cm x 63.5 cm). Virginia Museum of Fine Arts, Richmond. Gift of David K. E. Bruce. Photo by Ron Jennings. Copyright © Virginia Museum of Fine Arts; **120** *right* Copyright © Chip Henderson/Tony Stone Images; **121** Virginia Historical Society, Richmond, Virginia; **122** The Granger Collection, New York; **124** *bottom left* Smithsonian Institution, Washington, D.C.; *bottom right background* Photo copyright © Dorothy Miller; *bottom right foreground* Copyright © The New York Botanical Garden; **125** *bottom center* Copyright © Old Dartmouth Historical Society, New Bedford (Massachusetts) Whaling Museum; **126** The Granger Collection, New York; **127** *right* Copyright © Michael P. Gadomski/Photo Researchers, Inc.; **128** Copyright © Mark McGehearty/AllSport; **129** *Catching the Wild Horse* (date unknown), George Catlin. Oil on canvas, 12 1/4" x 16 1/4". The Thomas Gilcrease Institute of American History and Art, Tulsa, Oklahoma.

**Chapter 5, 132** Virginia Historical Society, Richmond, Virginia; **133** Library of Congress; **137, 139** The Granger Collection, New York; **140** Corbis; **141** Detail of *Increase Mather* (1688), John Vander Spriett. Courtesy of the Massachusetts Historical Society; **142** Courtesy of Knox County, Illinois Teen Court; **143** The Granger Collection, New York; **145** *left* Corbis; *right* The Newberry Library, Chicago; **146** Detail of *Braddock's Defeat* (1903), Edward Deming. State Historical Society of Wisconsin Museum Collection; **147** Library of Congress; **149, 151** The Granger Collection, New York.

## Unit 2

**154–155** Copyright © William Johnson/Stock Boston.

**Chapter 6, 156, 157** The Granger Collection, New York; **158** *top* Colonial Williamsburg Foundation; *center* Detail of *The Battle of Princeton* (date unknown), William Mercer. The Historical Society of Pennsylvania; *bottom* The Granger Collection, New York; **159** *James Otis Arguing Against the Writs of Assistance in the Old Towne House* (1901), Robert Reid. Courtesy Commonwealth of Massachusetts Art Commission; **160** *top* Rare Books Division, The New York Public Library. Astor, Lenox, and Tilden Foundations; *bottom* Emmet Collection, Manuscripts and Archives Division, The New York Public Library. Astor, Lenox, and Tilden Foundations; **161, 162** The Granger Collection, New York; **163** Copyright © Stock Montage; **164** Copyright © Collection of The New-York Historical Society; **165** The Granger Collection, New York; **166** *left* The Granger Collection, New York; *right, John Adams* (date unknown), John Trumbull. National Portrait Gallery, Smithsonian Institution/Art Resource, New York; **167** The Granger Collection, New York; **168–169** Copyright © McDougal Littell Inc.; **170** Copyright © Paul Mozell/Stock Boston; **173** Copyright © Charles Winters/Stock Boston; **174** Copyright © McDougal Littell Inc.; **175** The Granger Collection, New York; **176** *Portrait traditionally said to be*

*Abigail Adams* (about 1795), artist unknown. Oil on canvas, 30 1/4" x 26 1/2", N-150.55. Photo by Richard Walker. Copyright © New York State Historical Association, Cooperstown, New York; **177** Detail of *The Death of General Warren at the Battle of Bunker's Hill, 17 June 1775* (date unknown), John Trumbull. Oil on canvas. Yale University Art Gallery, Trumbull Collection; **178** Library of Congress; **179** *top* The Granger Collection, New York; *bottom* Library of Congress; **180** *top* Detail of *The Declaration of Independence, 4 July 1776* (date unknown), John Trumbull. Oil on canvas. Yale University Art Gallery, Trumbull Collection; *bottom* Copyright © R. Kord/H. Armstrong Roberts; **181, 182** The Granger Collection, New York; **187** *bottom* Clement Library, University of Michigan; **88** The Granger Collection, New York; **189** Photos by Sharon Hoogstraten.

**Chapter 7, 190** *March to Valley Forge* (1883), William B. T. Trego. Courtesy of Stacey Swigart, The Valley Forge Historical Society; **191, 192** The Granger Collection, New York; **193** Haym Salomon Home for Nursing and Rehabilitation, Brooklyn, New York. Courtesy of American Jewish Historical Society, Waltham, Massachusetts, and New York, New York; **194** *George Washington in the Uniform of a British Colonial Colonel* (1772), Charles Willson Peale. Washington-Custis-Lee Collection. Washington and Lee University, Lexington, Virginia; **195** *top* From *American Story: The Revolutionaries.* Courtesy of the Jamestown-Yorktown Educational Trust. Photo by Katherine Wetzel. Copyright © 1996 Time-Life Books Inc.; **196** *Washington Crossing the Delaware* (1851), Emanuel Gottlieb Leutze. Oil on canvas, 149" x 255". The Metropolitan Museum of Art, gift of John S. Kennedy, 1897; **197** *bottom* The Granger Collection, New York; **198** Copyright © Michael Newman/PhotoEdit/PNI; **199** *Two American Flags Flown by John Paul Jones in 1779* (date unknown), unknown Dutch artist. Watercolor. Chicago Historical Society; **200, 201** The Granger Collection, New York; **202** From *American Story: The Revolutionaries.* Courtesy of the Jamestown-Yorktown Educational Trust. Photo by Katherine Wetzel. Copyright © 1996 Time-Life Books Inc.; **205** The Granger Collection, New York; **206** Library of Congress; **208** Illustration by Bill Cigliano; **210** *Surrender of Lord Cornwallis at Yorktown* (date unknown), John Trumbull. Yale University Art Gallery, Trumbull Collection; **211** Private collection; **212** The Granger Collection, New York; **215** Courtesy of the Massachusetts Historical Society; **216** Private collection.

**Chapter 8, 218** The Granger Collection, New York; **219** *The Signing of the Constitution* (date unknown), H. C. Chandler. Art Resource, New York; **221** Detail of *Daniel Boone Escorting Settlers Through the Cumberland Gap* (1851–1852), George Caleb Bingham. Oil on canvas, 36 1/2" x 50 1/4". Washington University Gallery of Art, St. Louis (Missouri). Gift of Nathaniel Phillips, 1890; **222, 225** *top* The Granger Collection, New York; **225** *bottom* Copyright © Thad Samuels Abell II/NGS Image Collection; **226** *bottom left* Copyright © John E. Fletcher & Arlan R. Wiler/NGS Image Collection; *bottom right* William L. Clements Library, Map Division, University of Michigan; **227** *top* The Granger Collection, New York; *bottom* Courtesy of the Shelby County (Ohio) Historical Society; **228** Corbis; *inset* Library of Congress; **229** Copyright © Joseph Nettis/Tony Stone Images; **230** The Granger Collection, New York; **231** PNI; **234** The Granger Collection, New York; **235** *left, Portrait of John Jay* (c. 1783, 1804–1808), Gilbert Stuart, believed to have been begun by and finished by John Trumbull. National Portrait Gallery, Smithsonian Institution/Art Resource, New York; **235** *right,* **236** The Granger Collection, New York.

### Constitution Handbook

**242** *left* The Granger Collection, New York; *right* Copyright © Ivan Massar/Black Star; **243** *top* Copyright © Bob Daemmrich/The Image Works; *center* Copyright © Topham/The Image Works; *bottom* Courtesy of The New York Times; **244** *bottom* Copyright © J. L. Atlan/Sygma; **245** *top* Copyright © Robert E. Daemmrich/Tony Stone Images; **247** *top* Copyright © Engelhardt/St. Louis Post-Dispatch; *bottom* Copyright © Patrick Forden/Sygma; **248** *background* The Granger Collection, New York; **248** *inset,* **257** AP/Wide World Photos; **258** *top right* Copyright © Archive Photos; *top left* Culver Pictures; *center right* Copyright © 1972 Magnum Photos, Inc.; *center left* AP/Wide World Photos; *bottom right* Courtesy Ronald Reagan Library; **264** AP/Wide World Photos; **265** Copyright © Collection of The New-York Historical Society; **267** Copyright © Baron Wolman/Tony Stone Images; **268** *left* Copyright © Jean-Marc Giboux/Liaison Agency; *right* Copyright © Bob Dremmrich/Sygma; **270** Copyright © 1993 Ron Rovtar/FPG International; **272** The Granger Collection, New York; **273** *left* Copyright © 1998 FPG International; *right* Copyright © Cynthia Johnson/Liaison Agency; **274** Franklin D. Roosevelt Library; **277** Copyright © Rock the Vote Inc.

### Citizenship Handbook

**280** AP/Wide World Photos; **281** *background* Copyright © Bob Daemmrich; *foreground* Copyright © 1994 Mark Harmel/FPG International; **284** Copyright © Bob Daemmrich/The Image Works; **285** Copyright © David Young-Wolff/Tony Stone Images; **286** AP/Wide World Photos.

### Unit 3

**288–289** Copyright © Marvin E. Newman/The Image Bank.

**Chapter 9, 290** The Granger Collection, New York; **291** *Washington's First Cabinet* (date unknown), Alonzo Chappel. Courtesy of CNA; **292** Washington inaugural buttons, 1789. National Museum of American History, Smithsonian Institution; **294** AP/Wide World Photos; **295** *Portrait of Alexander Hamilton* (about 1796), James Sharples (the Elder). National Portrait Gallery, Smithsonian Institution/Art Resource, New York; **297** Copyright © Larry Stevens/Nawrocki Stock Photo Inc.; **298** Chicago Historical Society; **299** *right* Ohio Historical Society; **301** *Execution of Louis XVI* (18th century), anonymous. Colored engraving. Musée de la Ville de Paris, Musée Carnavalet, Paris; **303** Mount Vernon Ladies Association; **305** *top* The Granger Collection, New York; *center right* Maryland Historical Society; **306** The Granger Collection, New York.

**Chapter 10, 310** *The Rocky Mountains, Lander's Peak* (1863), Albert Bierstadt (1830–1902). Oil on canvas, 73 1/2" x 120 3/4". The Metropolitan Museum of Art, Rogers Fund, 1907 (07.123). Photograph copyright © 1979 The Metropolitan Museum of Art; **311** *Chasing Off Grizzlies.* Tab. 36 of atlas accompanying the English edition of Prince Maximilian of Wied's *Travels in the Interior of North America.* By Lucas Webber after Carl Bodmer, published by Ackermann and Company, London, December 1, 1842. Colored engraving, 12" x 17 1/2"; plate size, 15 1/2" x 21 1/4"; on trimmed stock, 17" x 23 1/2"; **313** *left, Thomas Jefferson* (date unknown), Rembrandt Peale. Copyright © Collection of the New-York Historical Society; *right* Boston Athenaeum; **314** The Granger Collection, New York; **315** *center right* Kirby Collection of Historical Paintings, Lafayette College; *bottom background* Monticello/Thomas Jefferson Memorial Foundation, Inc.; *bottom center* Polygraph, 1806. John Isaac Hawkins, Charles Willson Peale. University of Virginia. Photo courtesy of Monticello/Thomas Jefferson Memorial Foundation, Inc.; **316** Boston Athenaeum; **317** Copyright © James Blair/NGS Image Collection; **318, 319** The Granger Collection, New York; **320** *inset* Copyright © Addison Geary/Stock Boston/PNI; **321** *Lewis and Clark at Three Forks* (date unknown), E. S. Paxson. Mural in the Montana State Capitol. Courtesy of the Montana Historical Society. Photo by John Reddy; **322** Copyright © 1998 North Wind Pictures; **323** National Museum of American History, Smithsonian Institution; **324** *center left* Copyright © Stock Montage; *center right, The Surrounder, Chief of the Tribe* (1833), George Catlin. Oto tribe. National Museum of American Art, Smithsonian Institution/Art Resource, New York; *bottom center, bottom right* Peabody Museum, Harvard University. Copyright © President and Fellows of Harvard College. Photo by Hillel Burger; **325** *center left, Mink, a Pretty Girl* (1832), George Catlin. National Museum of American Art, Smithsonian Institution/Art Resource, New York; *center right, Steep Wing, a Brave of the Bad Arrow Points Band* (1832), George Catlin. Teton Dakota (Western Sioux). National Museum of American Art, Smithsonian Institution/Art Resource, New York; *bottom* Whaling Chief's Hat, Makah or Nootka. Cedar bark, bear grass, unidentified mammal hair, remnant feathers, leather thong. H 22 cm, D 27 cm. PM# 99-12-10/53080. Peabody Museum, Harvard University. Copyright © President and Fellows of Harvard College. Photo by Hillel Burger; **326** Detail of *Decatur Boarding the Tripolitan Gunboat* (date unknown), Dennis Malone Carter. Oil on canvas. Courtesy of the Naval Historical Foundation; **327** Library of Congress; **328** The Granger Collection, New York; **330** *left* White House Collection. Copyright © White House Historical Association; *right* The Granger Collection, New York; **332** National Museum of American History, Smithsonian Institution; **334** *top, Thomas Jefferson* (date unknown), Rembrandt Peale. Copyright © Collection of the New-York Historical Society; *bottom* National Museum of American History, Smithsonian Institution; **335** *Ograbme, or, The American Snapping Turtle* (1807), D. Longworth. Negative no. 7278. Copyright © Collection of The New-York Historical Society; **336** *top left* Elk skin bound journal (1805), William Clark. Ink on paper. Missouri Historical Society;

*right, bottom* Copyright © 1998 North Wind Pictures; **337** Photos by Sharon Hoogstraten.

**Chapter 11, 338, 339, 341** Corbis-Bettmann; **342** The Granger Collection, New York; **343** Illustration by Patrick Whelan; **344** Corbis-Bettmann; **345** Copyright © Stock Montage; **346–347** Illustrations by Randal Birkey; **348** The Granger Collection, New York; **349** Illustration by Patrick Whelan; **351** Detail of *Plantation Burial* (1860), John Antrobus. Williams Research Center, The Historic New Orleans Collection. Photo copyright © Jan White Brantley; **352** Corbis-Bettmann; **353** The Granger Collection, New York; **354** Corbis-Bettmann; **355** *right inset* The Granger Collection, New York; **356, 357** *right inset* Corbis-Bettmann.

## Unit 4

**364–365** Layne Kennedy/Corbis.

**Chapter 12, 366** The Granger Collection, New York; **367** Chicago Historical Society; **368** Copyright © Collection of the New-York Historical Society; **369** Redwood Library and Athenaeum, Newport, Rhode Island; **370** *left, John Quincy Adams* (1858), George Healy. Oil on canvas, 62" x 47". White House Collection. Copyright © White House Historical Association; *right, Andrew Jackson* (1845), Thomas Sully. Oil on canvas, 20 3/8" x 17 1/4". Copyright © 1996 Board of Trustees, National Gallery of Art, Washington, D.C. Andrew W. Mellon Collection; **371** The Hermitage: Home of President Andrew Jackson, Nashville, Tennessee. Photo of ribbon by Sharon Hoogstraten; **372** Copyright © The News-Sentinel, Fort Wayne, Indiana; **373** *left* The Granger Collection, New York; *right* Culver Pictures; **374** *Sequoyah, Indian Statesman* (date unknown), anonymous, after Charles Bird King. Hand-colored lithograph, J. T. Bowen lithography company. National Portrait Gallery, Smithsonian Institution/Art Resource, New York; **375** Copyright © J. Pat Carter/Liaison Agency; **377** *The Trail of Tears* (date unknown), Robert Lindneux. Woolaroc Museum, Bartlesville, Oklahoma; **378** The Granger Collection, New York; **379** *top, John Caldwell Calhoun* (about 1818–1825), attributed to Charles Bird Kind. Oil on canvas, 76.2 cm x 63.5 cm. National Portrait Gallery, Smithsonian Institution/Art Resource, New York; **379** *bottom,* **381** *top* The Granger Collection, New York; **381** *bottom* The Museum of the Confederacy, Richmond, Virginia. Photo by Katherine Wetzel; **382** Detail of *Webster's Reply to Hayne* (date unknown), George Healy. Courtesy Boston Art Commission; **384** *top* The Granger Collection, New York; *bottom inset, Nicholas Biddle* (1839), Henry Inman. Oil on canvas [1978.2]. The Historical Society of Pennsylvania; **385** The Granger Collection, New York; **386** Copyright © Collection of The New-York Historical Society; **389** Library of Congress.

**Chapter 13, 390** Denver Public Library, Western History Department; **391** National Archives; **393** *Jedediah Smith in the Badlands* (date unknown), Harvey Dunn. The South Dakota Art Museum Collection; **394** Copyright © United States Postal Service; **395** *inset* Copyright © Ric Ergenbright; **396** Skillet, negative no. OrHi 97119. Oregon Historical Society; **400** The Granger Collection, New York; **401** *top* Broadsides Collection, The Center for American History, The University of Texas at Austin; **402** Copyright © Bob Daemmrich/Stock Boston/PNI; **403** *The Battle of the Alamo* (about 1913), Frederick C. Yohn. Courtesy Continental Insurance; **404** *left* Texas State Library and Archives Commission; **404** *right,* **406** The Granger Collection, New York; **408** *inset,* **412** Courtesy of the California History Room, California State Library, Sacramento, California; **413** Copyright © Collection of The New-York Historical Society; **414** Courtesy of Levi Strauss Company; **415, 417** Courtesy of the California History Room, California State Library, Sacramento, California; **419** *bottom* From the collections of the Minnesota Historical Society.

**Chapter 14, 420** Courtesy Meserve-Kunhardt Collection, Mount Kisco, New York; **421** The Granger Collection, New York; **422** The New York Public Library; **423** *background* From the collections of the Minnesota Historical Society; *foreground* Copyright © Collection of The New-York Historical Society; **424** *center* The Granger Collection, New York; **427** Michael S. Yamashita/Corbis; **428** The Granger Collection, New York; **429** From *The Headless Horseman* by Natalie Standiford, illustrated by Donald Cook. Illustration copyright © 1992 Donald Cook. Reprinted by permission of Random House, Inc.; **430** The Granger Collection, New York; **432** *background* Photo by Simon Marsden/The Marsden Archive; **433** The Granger Collection, New York; **434** Copyright © Archive Photos; **435** Department of Archives, Oberlin (Ohio) College; **436, 440** The Granger Collection, New York; **441** Chester County Historical Society, West Chester, Pennsylvania; **442** Copyright © 1996 Wayne Sorce; **443** *from left to right* The Granger Collection, New York; The Granger Collection, New York; The Granger Collection, New York; The Granger Collection, New York; Corbis-Bettmann; **444** The Granger Collection, New York; **445** *The Discord* (1885), F. Heppenheimer. Color lithograph, negative no. 51038. Copyright © Collection of The New-York Historical Society; **446** *center* Library of Congress; *bottom right, bottom left* Copyright © 1998 Louis Psihoyos/Matrix; **447** *bottom* From the Collections of the National Underground Railroad Freedom Center, Cincinnati, Ohio; **450** *paisley shawl* Photo by Sharon Hoogstraten; *all other items* From the collections of the Minnesota Historical Society; **451** Photos by Sharon Hoogstraten.

## Unit 5

**452–453** Corbis.

**Chapter 15, 454, 455, 457, 460** The Granger Collection, New York; **461** Corbis; **462** Hulton-Deutsch Collection/Corbis; **463** *left* The Granger Collection, New York; *right* Corbis-Bettmann; **466** From the Collection of David J. and Janice L. Frent; **467** AFP/Corbis; **468, 471** The Granger Collection, New York; **472** Lloyd Ostendorf Collection; **474** *background* Hulton-Deutsch Collection/Corbis; *inset* Copyright © George Peter Alexandre Healy/Wood River Gallery/PNI; **477** *The Last Moments of John Brown* (1884), Thomas Hovenden. Oil on canvas, 77 3/8" x 63 1/4". The Metropolitan Museum of Art, gift of Mr. and Mrs. Carl Stoeckel, 1897. Photograph copyright © 1982 The Metropolitan Museum of Art.

**Chapter 16, 478, 479** The Granger Collection, New York; **480** *top left, top right* Library of Congress; *bottom left, bottom right* The Granger Collection, New York; **482** The Lincoln Museum, Fort Wayne, Indiana. #0-43; **485** Copyright © H. Armstrong Roberts; **486** Copyright © McDougal Littell Inc.; **487** *left* Courtesy of Brian C. Pohanka; *right* Massachusetts Commandery Military Order of the Loyal Legion and the U.S. Army Military History Institute; **488** Bureau of Archives and History, New Jersey State Library; **489** Corbis-Bettmann; **490** Culver Pictures; **491** The Granger Collection, New York; **492** Illustration by Alexander Verbitsky; **493** Library of Congress; **496** U.S. Signal Corps photo no. 111-B-4146 (Brady Collection) in the National Archives; **497** Chicago Historical Society; **498** *left, center* Photos by Larry Sherer. Copyright © Time-Life Books Inc.; *bottom right* Fort Sumter National Park.

**Chapter 17, 500** *Cavalry Charge at Yellow Tavern, Virginia, May 11, 1864* (1871), H. W. Chaloner. Oil on canvas, 31" x 47 7/8". Garbisch no. 61.1, purchased from Kenneth E. Snow by Garbisches (1961). Presented by the Estate of Edgar William and Bernice Chrysler Garbisch. Photo by West Point Museum Collections, United States Military Academy; **501** Corbis-Bettmann; **502** *top left, top right, bottom left* Library of Congress; *bottom right* The Granger Collection, New York; **503** Corbis; **504** The Granger Collection, New York; **505** *top* Copyright © Archive Photos; *bottom* Library of Congress; **507** Culver Pictures; **508** The Granger Collection, New York; **510** American Red Cross; **511** *background* Corbis; *foreground* Massachusetts Commandery Military Order of the Loyal Legion and the U.S. Army Military History Institute; **512** The Pejepscot Historical Society; **513** Copyright © 1994 Kunio Owaki/The Stock Market; **514–515** *background* Illustration by Ken Goldammer; **514** *center* Library of Congress; *bottom left* From *Echoes of Glory: Arms & Equipment of The Union.* Photo by Larry Sherer. Copyright © 1991 Time-Life Books Inc.; *bottom right* The Museum of the Confederacy, Richmond, Virginia. Photo by Katherine Wetzel; **515** *bottom* From *Echoes of Glory: Arms & Equipment of The Union.* Photo by Larry Sherer. Copyright © 1991 Time-Life Books Inc.; **516** Library of Congress; **518** *top left* Courtesy of Stamatelos Brothers Collection. Photo by Larry Sherer. Copyright © 1991 Time-Life Books Inc.; *bottom* Courtesy Meserve-Kunhardt Collection, Mount Kisco, New York; **520** Copyright © Robert M. Anderson/Uniphoto, Inc.; **522** National Archives; **526** *top right* Manassas National Battlefield Park, National Park Service. Photo by Larry Sherer; *bottom right* Collection of Old Capitol Museum of Mississippi History; **528** *center left, center* High Impact Photography/Copyright © Time-Life Books Inc.; *center right* Courtesy of Stamatelos Brothers Collection. Photo by Larry Sherer. Copyright © 1991 Time-Life Books Inc.; **529** Photos by Sharon Hoogstraten.

**Chapter 18, 530** Corbis-Bettmann; **531** *The Shackle Broken—by the Genius of Freedom.* Color lithograph. Pub. by E. Sachs & Co., Baltimore, 1874. Chicago Historical Society; **533, 534** The Granger Collection, New York; **535** Corbis; **536** *His First Vote*